ENDEAVOUR SURVEYORS LTD

Chrissie Davis, Principle Su
www.endeavoursurveyors.
Chrissie@endeavoursurveyor
Tel: 07723 026269   07545 597112

WITHDRAWN

Yacht and Small Craft Surveyor specialising in GRP and Wooden Yachts,

Survey Reports available:-

Pre purchase Condition Report

Pre Purchase Structural Report

Insurance Surveys

Damage and Repair Reports

Valuations

Free Quotations,

I travel to all areas,

Full colour reports with pictures, sent out as a bound hard copy and free CD version, fast and efficient service

Marval Marine

Make a winning decision

Your choice of marine electronics is one of the most important decisions you will have to make as a boat owner, next to choosing the boat itself of course.

When you buy Raymarine equipment, you are buying into world-class performance, top-notch integration, and the latest proven design technologies. Years of research and development, and customer feedback have resulted in the 'simple-on-the-outside, sophisticated-on-the-inside' design philosophy that is behind all our intuitive easy-to-use equipment.

Worldwide support and warranty

That's why Raymarine has a worldwide network of product-trained distributors and service dealers and offers a comprehensive warranty to handle the unexpected… wherever you decide to go.

For product information, visit your local stockist or go to **www.raymarine.co.uk**

2010/MA26/e

Raymarine®
…world leaders in marine electronics.

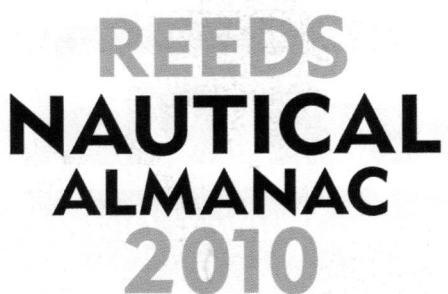

REEDS NAUTICAL ALMANAC 2010

ADLARD COLES NAUTICAL

EDITORS **Andy Du Port and Rob Buttress**

Free updates are available at www.reedsalmanac.co.uk

Published by Adlard Coles Nautical 2009

Copyright © Nautical Data Ltd 1980-2003

Copyright © Adlard Coles Nautical 2004-2009

IMPORTANT SAFETY NOTE AND LEGAL DISCLAIMER

This Almanac is intended as an aid to navigation only and to assist with basic planning for your passage. The information, charts, maps and diagrams in this Almanac should not be relied on for navigational purposes and should always be used in conjunction with current official hydrographic data. Whilst every care has been taken in its compilation, this Almanac may contain inaccuracies and is no substitute for the relevant official hydrographic charts and data, which should always be consulted in advance of, and whilst, navigating in the relevant area. Before setting out you should also check local conditions with the harbourmaster or other appropriate office responsible for your intended area of navigation.

Before using any waypoint or coordinate listed in this Almanac it must first be plotted on an appropriate official hydrographic chart to check its usefulness, accuracy and appropriateness for the prevailing weather and tidal conditions.

To the extent that the editors or publishers become aware that corrections are required, these will be published on the website www.reedsalmanac.co.uk. Readers should therefore regularly check the website for any such corrections. Data in this Almanac is corrected up to Weekly Edition 26/2009 of Admiralty Notices to Mariners.

The publishers, editors and their agents accept no responsibility for any errors or omissions, or for any accident, loss or damage (including without limitation any indirect, consequential, special or exemplary damages) arising from the use or misuse of, or reliance upon, the information contained in this Almanac.

The decision to use and rely on any of the data in this Almanac is entirely at the discretion of, and is the sole responsibility of, the Skipper or other individual in control of the vessel in connection with which it is being used or relied upon.

Adlard Coles Nautical
36 Soho Square
London, W1D 3QY
Tel: +44 (0)207 758 0200
Fax: +44 (0)207 758 0222/0333
Email: info@reedsalmanac.co.uk
www.reedsalmanac.co.uk

Almanac manager
Chris Stevens

Cartography
Chris Stevens, Garold West

Cover photograph
Bembridge Harbour
www.bembridgeharbour.co.uk

**ISBN 978 1 4081 1340 0 - Reeds Nautical
Almanac 2010**

**ISBN 978 1 4081 1370 7 - Reeds Looseleaf
Almanac 2010**

**ISBN 978 1 4081 1371 4 - Reeds Looseleaf
Update Pack 2010**

A CIP catalogue record for this book is available from the British Library.

Printed in the UK.

ADVERTISEMENT SALES

Enquiries about advertising space should be addressed to: MS Publications, 2nd Floor, Ewer House, 44-46 Crouch Street, Colchester, Essex, CO3 3HH.
Tel: +44 (0)1206 506223
Fax: +44 (0)1206 500228

Chapter Contents

Navigational Contents

5 ANCHOR STATUS
AWARDED BY THE TYHA
⚓ ⚓ ⚓ ⚓ ⚓

Jersey Marinas

Jersey Harbours

For further information contact
our Marine Leisure Centre on
+44 (0) 1534 447730 or visit:
www.jersey-harbours.com

Jersey

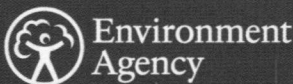

next time you visit Rye,
why not bring your boat...

Visitor's berths are available from £14 per night including power, water, shower and toilet facilities.
Permanent moorings are also available.
The yearly charge for a 9 metre boat is just £1,005.71.
Contact the Harbour Office for more details.

Rye Harbour Office, New Lydd Road, Camber, Rye, East Sussex TN31 7QS. Tel: 01797 225225.

Email: rye.harbour@environment-agency.gov.uk
Website: www.environment-agency.gov.uk/harbourofrye

2010/MA18/e

Introduction

0.1 INTRODUCTION

0.1.1 Editorial

Adlard Coles Nautical is delighted to publish the 2010 Reeds Nautical Almanac, and we welcome Rob Buttress to the Almanac team, taking over from Neville Featherstone as Co-Editor. Neville retired after a great number of years' dedicated service to the Almanac, and many readers will know him either through his long connection with Reeds or may have met him in his Westerly Fulmar *JUNO*. He still cruises far and wide, and we wish him continued safe and happy sailing. Rob is an experienced yachtsman who, after a career marketing marine navigation products, spent several years as a professional skipper in large sailing yachts, mainly in the Caribbean and Mediterranean. He has written two books: *Using PCs on Board* (ACN) and the *West Aegean Cruising Companion* (Wiley).

Once again, we have striven to produce a thoroughly up to date Almanac which contains all the data needed to plan your boating activities, whether they be coastal sailing or long distance cruising. At sea, a comprehensive and reliable Almanac, in conjunction with fully corrected official charts, provides the skipper/navigator with a source of information which is independent of electronics. While chartplotters, GPS, radar, AIS, laptops and the rest are invaluable aids to safe navigation, they do all depend on a power source which, in even the best maintained yachts, is capable of failure at some time. When that happens, it is a case of 'back to basics': paper charts, a 2B pencil, a good Almanac and the knowledge to go with them!

Some of the many improvements to this year's Almanac are shown below. However, the bulk of the work involves processing literally thousands of relatively minor amendments and corrections – many of which are collected by our loyal team of Harbour Agents – which enable us to produce 'The Yachtsman's Bible'.

We wish you a very safe and enjoyable sailing season.

0.1.2 Improvements in the 2010 Almanac

Chapter 3 (Navigation) Most of the navigational warnings section has been transferred to Chapter 5 (Communications), a more logical home for this material.

Chapter 5 (Communications) This chapter has been expanded to include a section on navigational warnings, gunfacts/subfacts information and contact details for SAR authorities.

Chapter 6 (Weather) A new map is included to assist with selecting VHF channels for receipt of MSI broadcasts by HM Coastguard.

Chapter 7 (Safety) See Chapter 5 above for details of material which has been transferred from this chapter.

Chapter 8 (First Aid) Now contains expanded advice on recognising a stroke and what to do.

Chapter 9 (Harbours, coasts and tides) Tide Tables for 11 new Standard Ports (Chichester, Margate, Harwich, River Tees, Rosyth, Invergordon, Tarbert Island, River Foyle, Zeebrugge, Boulogne and La Coruña) have been included, and the differences for the relevant Secondary Ports amended as necessary. Airports and ferryports which may be of significance to cruising yachts are now shown on the maps at the start of each geographical Area.

Area 1 (SW England) The chartlet of the River Exe has been redrawn to show the extensive changes in the approaches. The Portland chartlet has been enlarged and revised to show the Weymouth and Portland National Sailing Academy – in preparation for the 2012 Olympics – and the new marina.

Area 3 (SE England) The Dover Strait map (9.3.14) has been revised to show many changes to buoys; it now also includes the northern limits of the Inshore Traffic Zones.

Area 4 (E England) The map of the Thames Estuary (9.4.7) has been redrawn to bring it fully up to date and also to help with orientation in this very busy area. The chartlet of Lowestoft has again been redrawn to enable the whole of the harbour to be included. This means the scale is rather smaller, but all the essential details are still shown.

Area 15 (Germany) Changes to buoyage in the Terschelling-German Bight TSS, German Bight Western Approaches TSS and Jade Approach TSS.

Area 16 (Netherlands and Belgium) Major works at Hoek van Holland; a new chartlet depicts many buoyage changes and the small craft route across the Maasgeul.

Area 17 (N France) Important light changes at Ouistreham.

Area 18 (Central N France) Heavy silting in Portbail (also published in the April 2009 online update).

Area 24 (Portugal & Azores) Chartlet shows the new marina at Ponta Delgada, Azores.

0.2 A FAMILY OF ALMANACS

0.2.1 Reeds Nautical Almanac

This Almanac (RNA) contains in one volume all the nautical information needed to navigate around the British Isles and from West Denmark to Gibraltar, backed up, of course, by fully corrected official charts. For updates see section 0.6.2.

0.2.2 Reeds Looseleaf Nautical Almanac is an identical looseleaf version of RNA in a stout binder. Annual update packs allow data to be varied to suit individual needs.

0.2.3 Three Regional Almanacs in wire-bound softback format provide geographic coverage as below:

> **Reeds Channel Almanac:** The Isles of Scilly to Dover and Dunkerque to the Chenal du Four.
> **Reeds Western Almanac:** The western UK and the coasts of Ireland.
> **Reeds Eastern Almanac:** The eastern UK and the Dutch and Belgian coasts.

0.2.4 Reeds Marina Guide is an extremely useful free booklet which accompanies all the above Almanacs. It contains a classified directory of nautical services, with details and plans of marinas in the UK, Ireland and Channel Islands.

0.2.5 Reeds PBO Small Craft Almanac is compiled and published by Adlard Coles Nautical in association with *Practical Boat Owner* magazine. It contains all the data needed for passage planning around the British Isles and from Denmark to Gibraltar, including the Azores.

0.2.6 Reeds Western Mediterranean Almanac, published by Bloc Marine, contains detailed chartlets, navigation and harbour information in both English and French. It covers S and E Spain, the Balearics, the S of France, Corsica, Sardinia, N Italy, Sicily, Malta and Tunisia.

0.2.7 Reeds Spain and Portugal Almanac, published by Bloc Marine, is in both English and Spanish. It covers N, S and E Spain, the Balearics, Portugal, Canary Islands, Tunisia and Morocco.

0.2.8 Reeds Italy and Croatia Almanac, published by Bloc Marine, is in both English and Italian. It covers the entire Italian coast, N Croatia, Corsica, Sardinia, Sicily, Malta, Tunisia

and Morocco, and comes in two versions – one with a DVD containing extra pilotage content and navigation software.

0.3   OTHER REEDS TITLES

Related to the family of Reeds Almanacs and published under the Reeds brand are:

- *Reeds Astro Navigation Tables 2010*. Concise, light and able to lie flat on the chart table, this annual publication contains all the information an ocean-going sailor needs in order to navigate by the sun, moon, planets and stars.
- *Reeds Yacht Buyer's Guide* is a complete reference to new and second-hand yachts in the 6–12m (20–40ft) size range. It is ideal for prospective buyers.
- *Reeds Skipper's Handbook,* 5th edition, is a handy aide memoire which quickly answers most nautical queries.
- *Reeds Maritime Flag Handbook* is a handy pocket-size guide to national maritime flags, special ensigns, yacht club burgees and signal flags, plus flag usage and etiquette.

Visit www.acblack.com for details of other titles.

0.4   USING THE ALMANAC

0.4.1   Numbering system

The nine chapters contain numbered sections. In Chapter 7, for example, sections are numbered 7.1 to 7.14. Within section 7.1 the key paragraphs are numbered 7.1.1 and 7.1.2.

Diagrams are numbered: Fig 7(1) to Fig 7(5).

Tables are similarly numbered: Table 7(1).

Each main harbour entry is shown with the chapter number (9), the Area number and a sequential number within that Area. Thus Plymouth is shown as 9.1.15.

0.4.2   Contents and Index

Main subject headings and page numbers are listed on the contents page at the start of each chapter and geographic Area. A General Index and Gazetteer are at the back of each Almanac.

0.5   HELP IMPROVE THE ALMANACS

0.5.1   Improvements and corrections

Suggestions, however minor, for improving or correcting the Almanacs are always welcome, especially if based on personal knowledge. Not every suggestion can be implemented, but all are carefully considered. Please send your comments by email, if possible, to updates@reedsalmanac.co.uk or direct to the relevant Editor (see below). Otherwise, a note to Adlard Coles Nautical (see page v) will be forwarded as necessary.

Andy Du Port (aduport@reedsalmanacs.co.uk) is responsible for the Introduction, Chapters 3, 4, 7, 8 and the introduction to Chapter 9 as well as Areas 1 to 13 (the whole of the UK and Ireland). Rob Buttress (rob@reedsalmanacs.co.uk) is responsible for all the other Chapters and Areas (the Continent from Denmark to Gibraltar including the Azores).

0.5.2   Harbour Agents

Our Harbour Agents provide the Editors with invaluable local information which is not always available from official sources. Vacancies are advertised below and on our website www.reedsalmanac.co.uk. If you would like to earn a free copy of the Almanac every year, please apply to the relevant editor with a brief summary of your nautical qualifications. Our Agents either live in or close to the relevant port or are regular visitors. An easy rapport with the Harbourmaster and/or the local Marina Manager is essential.

0.5.3   Agents wanted

Currently there are vacancies at the following harbours:

UK: River Tyne/N Shields, River Tay, Aberdeen, Peterhead, Kinlochbervie, Loch Sunart, Tobermory, Rathlin Island.
Republic of Ireland: Wexford, Kilmore Quay, Waterford, Fenit Hbr, Kilrush.
West Denmark: Most harbours.
Germany: Nord-Ostsee Kanal, East Frisian Islands.
Netherlands: Delfzijl, Lauwersoog, Den Helder, Harlingen, Rotterdam and Terneuzen.
France: St Valéry-en-Caux, Paris, Port-en-Bessin, River Rance, Port Blanc, Trébeurden, Primel-Trégastel, Loctudy, Iles de Glénan, Port-Tudy, Port Haliguen, St Gilles-Croix-de-Vie, Les Sables d'Olonne, Royan, Port-Médoc, Arcachon, Capbreton, Anglet/Bayonne and St Jean de Luz.
N/NW Spain: Most hbrs, *except* Bilbao, Santander, Gijon, La Coruña, Rias de Ares, Betanzos and Camariñas.
Portugal: The Azores.
SW Spain: Mazagon, Chipiona, Sevilla, Cadiz, Sancti Petri, Barbate, Tarifa, Algeciras, Tangier and Ceuta.

0.6   CORRECTIONS

0.6.1   Sources of corrections

This Almanac is corrected to Weekly edition No 26/2009 of Admiralty Notices to Mariners. Corrections to UKHO charts and publications are downloadable at www.ukho.gov.uk/ProductsandServices/MartimeSafety/Pages/NMPublic.aspx or available from Admiralty Chart Agents (ACA) and certain Port Authorities.

It is important that this Almanac, charts and other navigational publications are kept fully corrected. Data changes frequently and may well affect safety of life at sea. *See* NP 294 'How to correct your charts the Admiralty way' for further guidance.

0.6.2   Updates

Free monthly updates to the Almanacs from January to June are downloadable at www.reedsalmanac.co.uk/updates.asp When completed, you may wish to tick them off in the table below. Please register online if you wish to be notified by email of when the updates are available to download.

0.6.3 Record of corrections

2009 Admiralty Weekly Notices to Mariners

25 ☐	26 ☐	27 ☐	28 ☐	29 ☐	30 ☐
31 ☐	32 ☐	33 ☐	34 ☐	35 ☐	36 ☐
37 ☐	38 ☐	39 ☐	40 ☐	41 ☐	42 ☐
43 ☐	44 ☐	45 ☐	46 ☐	47 ☐	48 ☐
49 ☐	50 ☐	51 ☐	52 ☐		

2010 Admiralty Weekly Notices to Mariners

1 ☐	2 ☐	3 ☐	4 ☐	5 ☐	6 ☐
7 ☐	8 ☐	9 ☐	10 ☐	11 ☐	12 ☐
13 ☐	14 ☐	15 ☐	16 ☐	17 ☐	18 ☐
19 ☐	20 ☐	21 ☐	22 ☐	23 ☐	24 ☐
25 ☐	26 ☐	27 ☐	28 ☐	29 ☐	30 ☐
31 ☐	32 ☐	33 ☐	34 ☐	35 ☐	36 ☐
37 ☐	38 ☐	39 ☐	40 ☐	41 ☐	42 ☐
43 ☐	44 ☐	45 ☐	46 ☐	47 ☐	48 ☐
49 ☐	50 ☐	51 ☐	52 ☐		

2010 Reeds monthly online updates

Jan ☐	Feb ☐	Mar ☐	Apr ☐	May ☐	Jun ☐

0.7 ACKNOWLEDGEMENTS & PERMISSIONS

The Editors thank the many authorities which have kindly provided information essential to the preparation of this Almanac.

This product has been derived in part from material obtained with the permission of the UK Hydrographic Office, HM Stationery Office and the following authorities: Trinity House, the Northern Lighthouse Board, HM Nautical Almanac Office, HM Revenue and Customs, the Meteorological Office, the Maritime and Coastguard Agency, the BBC, IBA, RNLI, PLA and ABP.

Important contributions have also been made by the following authorities in the Republic of Ireland and continental Europe: The Commissioners of Irish Lights, Deutsche Gesellschaft zur Rettung Schiffbrüchiger (DgzRS), Koninklijke Nederlandse Redding Maatschappij (KNRM).

In particular we thank Harbourmasters, Marina Managers, our Harbour Agents and numerous individual yachtsmen who have contributed new ideas and suggestions based on their invaluable local knowledge.

0.7.1 Permissions

Information from Admiralty charts, the Admiralty List of Lights, Admiralty Tide Tables, Admiralty Sailing Directions and the Admiralty List of Radio Signals is reproduced with the permission of the UK Hydrographic Office (Licence No GB DQ – 001 – Adlard Coles) and the Controller of HMSO.

Extracts from the following are published by permission of the Controller of HM Stationery Office:

International Code of Signals, 1969; Meteorological Office Weather Services for Shipping. Phases of the Moon and Sun/ Moon rising and setting times are included by permission of HM Nautical Almanac Office.

UK and Foreign tidal predictions and curves are supplied by the UK Hydrographic Office, with the permission (and Authorisation Numbers) of the following authorities to use the Standard Port predictions stated:

- Danish Safety Administration, Farvandsvæsnet: Esbjerg.
- SHOM, France: Dunkerque, Boulogne, Dieppe, Le Havre, Cherbourg, St Malo, Brest, Pointe de Grave; and Brest tidal coefficients (207/2009).
- Rijkswaterstaat, The Netherlands: Vlissingen and Hoek van Holland.
- Vlaamse Hydrografie, Belgium: Zeebrugge.
- BSH, Germany: Helgoland, Wilhelmshaven and Cuxhaven (11123/2008-07).
- Marinho Instituto Hidrográfico, Portugal: Lisboa (19/2009).
- Instituto Hidrográfico de la Marina, Spain: La Coruña (03/09).

Tidal stream diagrams are reproduced from Admiralty charts and tidal stream atlases by permission of the UKHO and the Controller of HMSO.

Tidal stream diagrams in 9.1.5, and the tidal stream arrows in 9.12.3 and 9.13.3, are printed by kind permission of the Royal Cruising Club and the Irish Cruising Club respectively.

0.7.2 Disclaimer

Neither the UK Hydrographic Office nor any other National HO has verified the information in this product and none accepts liability for the accuracy of reproduction or any modifications made thereafter. No National HO warrants that this product satisfies national or international regulations regarding the use of the appropriate products for navigation.

1

Reference Data

Fig 1(1) Admiralty chart symbols

Symbol	Description	Symbol	Description	Symbol	Description
	Power transmission line with pylons and safe overhead clearance as defined by the responsible authority		Church, chapel		Drying contour LW line, Chart Datum
			Radio mast, television mast		Blue ribbon or differing blue tints may be shown
	Vertical clearance above HAT		Monument (including column, pillar, obelisk, statue)		Anchoring prohibited
			Chimney		
	Submarine cable		Flare stack (on land)		Marine Farm
	Buried pipeline		Tanks		Wreck, depth unknown, danger to navigation
	Overfalls, tide rips and races		Crane		Wreck, depth unknown, no danger to navigation
3 kn	Flood stream Mean spring rate		Bird sanctuary	Wk	Wreck, depth obtained by sounding
3 Kn	Ebb stream Mean spring rate	CG	Coastguard Station	Wk	Wreck, swept by wire to the depth shown
D	Designated position of tabulated tidal streams		Woods in general		Wreck showing any part at level of chart datum
(a) (b)	Examples: (a) fixed beacon; (b) buoy		Withy - starboard hand		Rock which covers and uncovers, height above chart datum
	Limit of safety zone around offshore installation		Withy - port hand		Rock awash at level of chart datum
	Major light		Floodlit		Dangerous underwater rock of unknown depth
	Port hand lt bcn (PHM)		Marsh		Dangerous underwater rock of known depth
	Fishing harbour		Kelp		Recommended anchorage
	Fishing prohibited		Fog signal		Rescue station, lifeboat station, rocket station
V	Visitors' berth		Yacht berths, no facilities		Yacht harbour, Marina
	Fuel station (Petrol, Diesel)	V	Visitor's buoy		Harbourmaster's Office
	Public slipway		Mooring buoy		Customs office
	Water tap		Laundrette		Hospital
	Public landing, steps, ladder		Yacht Club, Sailing Club		Post office

1.1 ABBREVIATIONS AND SYMBOLS

The following more common abbreviations and symbols feature in Reeds Almanacs and in some Admiralty charts and publications. See also Fig 1(1). Admiralty chart 5011 (a booklet) is the authority for Abbreviations and Symbols.

@	Internet café/access
AB	Alongside berth
ABP	Associated British Ports
AC, ⌂	Shore power (electrical)
AC, ACA	Admiralty Chart, AC Agent
ACN	Adlard Coles Nautical (Publisher)
Aff Mar	Affaires Maritimes
AIS	Automatic Identification System
aka	Also known as
ALL	Admiralty List of Lights
ALRS	Admiralty List of Radio Signals
Al	Alternating light
ANWB	Association of road & waterway users (Dutch)
ATM	Automatic telling machine, cashpoint
ATT	Admiralty Tide Tables
ATT	Atterisage (landfall/SWM) buoy
Auto	Météo Répondeur Automatique
B.	Bay, Black
Bank (money)	ⓑ. See also ATM
Bar, ⌂	Licensed bar, Public house, Inn
BH	Boat Hoist (+ tons)
Bk	Broken (nature of seabed)
Bkwtr	Breakwater
BMF	British Marine Federation
BMS	Bulletin Météorologique Spécial (Strong wind/Gale warning)
Bn, bcn(s)	Beacon, beacon(s)
BSH	German Hydrographic Office/chart(s)
BST	British Summer Time (= DST)
Bu	Blue
BWB	British Waterways Board
By(s)	Buoy, buoys
BY, ⌂	Boatyard
C.	Cape, Cabo, Cap
C	Crane (+ tons)
c	Coarse (sand; nature of seabed)
ca	Cable (approx 185m long)
Cas	Castle
CD	Chart datum (tidal)
CEVNI	Code Européen de Voies de la Navigation Intérieure (inland waterway signs etc)
cf ⌂	Compare, cross-refer to
CG	Coastguard
CH, ⌂	Chandlery
chan	Channel (navigational)
Ch	Channel (VHF)
Ch, ⌂	Church
Chy	Chimney
Col	Column, pillar, obelisk
CPA	Closest Point of Approach
CROSS	Centre Régional Opérationnel de Surveillance et Sauvetage (= MRCC)
CRS	Coast Radio Station
C/S	COSPAS/SARSAT (satellite)
Cy	Clay (nature of seabed)
D	Diesel (supply by hose)
Dec	Declination (of the Sun)
dest	Destroyed
DF, D/F	Radio Direction Finding
DG	De-gaussing (range)
DGPS	Differential GPS
Dia	Diaphone (fog signal)
Dir Lt	Directional light

discont	Discontinued
DLR	Dockland Light Railway
Dn(s)	Dolphin(s)
DR	Dead Reckoning
DSC	Digital Selective Calling
DST	Daylight Saving Time
DW	Deep Water (route)
DYC	Dutch Yacht Chart(s)
DZ	Danger Zone (buoy)
E	East
ECM	East cardinal mark (buoy/beacon)
ED	Existence doubtful. European Datum
EEA	European Economic Area
EI	Electrical repairs
Ⓔ	Electronic repairs
Elev	Elevation
Ent	Entrance, entry, enter
EP, △	Estimated position
ETA	Estimated Time of Arrival
ETD	Estimated Time of Departure
F	Fixed light
f	Fine (eg sand; nature of seabed)
F&A	Fore and aft (berth/mooring)
FFL	Fixed and Flashing light
Fl	Flashing light
FM	Frequency Modulation
Foc	Free of charge
Fog Det lt	Fog Detector light
Freq, Fx	Frequency
FS	Flagstaff, Flagpole
ft	Foot, feet
Ft,	Fort
FV	Fishing vessel
FW	Fresh water supply
G	Gravel (nature of seabed), Green
Gas, Gaz	Calor Gas, Camping Gaz
GC	Great Circle
GDOP	Geometric Dilution of Precision (GPS)
GHA	Greenwich Hour Angle
GLA	General Lighthouse Authority
GMDSS	Global Maritime Distress & Safety System
grt	Gross Registered Tonnage
Gy	Grey
H, h, Hrs	Hour(s)
H−, H+	Minutes before, after the whole hour
H24	Continuous
HAT	Highest Astronomical Tide
HF	High Frequency
HFP	High Focal Plane (buoy)
HIE	Highlands & Islands Enterprise
HJ	Day service only, sunrise to sunset
HM	Harbour Master
HMRC	HM Revenue & Customs
HMSO	Her Majesty's Stationery Office
HN	Night service only, sunset to sunrise
HO	Office hours, Hydrographic Office
(hor)	Horizontally disposed (lights)
hPa	Hectopascal (= 1millibar)
HT	High Tension (overhead electricity line)
HW	High Water
HX	No fixed hours
IALA	International Association of Lighthouse Authorities
iaw	In accordance with
IDM	Isolated Danger Mark (buoy/beacon)
IHO	International Hydrographic Organisation
IMO	International Maritime Organisation
INMARSAT	International Maritime Satellite Organisation

intens	Intensified (light sector)
IPTS	International Port Traffic Signals
IQ	Interrupted quick flashing light
IRPCS	International Regulations for the Prevention of Collisions at Sea
Is, I	Island, Islet
ISAF	International Sailing Federation
Iso	Isophase light
ITU	International Telecommunications Union
ITZ	Inshore Traffic Zone (TSS)
IUQ	Interrupted ultra quick flashing light
IVQ	Interrupted very quick flashing light
kn	Knot(s)
Kos	Kosangas
kW	Kilowatts
L	Lake, Loch, Lough, Landing place
Lat	Latitude
LAT	Lowest Astronomical Tide
Lanby, ⌐	Large automatic navigational buoy
LB, ♦	Lifeboat, inshore lifeboat
Ldg	Leading (light)
LF	Low frequency
L Fl	Long flash
LH	Left hand
LNG	Liquefied Natural Gas
LNTM	Local Notice To Mariners
LOA	Length overall
Long	Longitude
LPG	Liquefied Petroleum Gas
LT	Local time
Lt(s), ☆ ✫	Light(s)
⬥	Light float, minor
Lt V, ⌐	Light vessel; Lt float, major; Lanby
M	Moorings. Nautical (sea) mile(s). Mud
m	Metre(s)
Mag	Magnetic. Magnitude (of star)
Mb, mb	Millibar (= 1 hectopascal, hPa)
MCA	Maritime and Coastguard Agency
ME	Marine engineering repairs
Met/Météo	Meteorology/Météorologie (weather)
MHWN	Mean High Water Neaps
MHWS	Mean High Water Springs
MHz	Megahertz
ML	Mean Level (tidal)
MLWN	Mean Low Water Neaps
MLWS	Mean Low Water Springs
MMSI	Maritime Mobile Service Identity
Mo	Morse
Mon	Monument. Monday
MRCC	Maritime Rescue Co-ordination Centre
MRSC	Maritime Rescue Sub-Centre (not in the UK)
MSI	Maritime Safety Information
N	North
Navi	Navicarte (French charts)
NB	Nota Bene. Notice Board
NCI, ©	National Coastwatch Institution
NCM	North Cardinal Mark (buoy/beacon)
NGS	Naval Gunfire Support (buoy)
NM	Notice(s) to Mariners
np	Neap tides
NP	Naval Publication (plus number)
NRT	Net registered tonnage
NT	National Trust (land/property)
Obscd	Obscured
Obstn	Obstruction
Oc	Occulting light
ODAS	Ocean Data Acquisition System (buoy)
Or	Orange (see also Y)
OT	Other times
P	Petrol (supply by hose). Pebbles
(P)	Preliminary (NM)
PA	Position approximate
Pax	Passenger(s)
PC	Portuguese chart
PD	Position doubtful
PHM	Port-hand Mark (buoy/beacon)
PLA	Port of London Authority
PO, ✉	Post Office
Pos	Position
Prog	Prognosis (weather charts)
prom	Prominent
PSSA	Particularly Sensitive Sea Area
Pt(e).	Point(e)
⛽	Pumpout facility
Pta	Punta (point)
Q	Quick flashing light
QHM	Queen's Harbour Master
qv	Refer to (quod vide)
R	Red. Restaurant ✕. River.
Racon	Radar transponder beacon
Ramark	Radar beacon
RCD	Recreational Craft Directive
RDF	Radio Direction Finding
RG	Emergency RDF station
RH	Right hand
Rk, Rky	Rock, Rocky (nature of seabed)
RNLI	Royal National Lifeboat Institution
ROI	Republic of Ireland
R/T	Radiotelephony
Ru	Ruins
RYA	Royal Yachting Association
S	South, Sand (nature of seabed)
S, St, Ste	Saint(s)
SAMU	Service d'Aide Médicale Urgente (ambulance)
SAR	Search and Rescue
SBM	Single buoy mooring
SC	Sailing Club. Spanish chart
SCM	South Cardinal Mark (buoy/beacon)
SD	Sailing Directions. Semi-diameter (of sun)
SD	Sounding of doubtful depth
sf	Stiff (nature of seabed)
Sh	Shells (nature of seabed). Shoal
SHM	Simplified Harmonic Method (tides); Starboard-hand Mark (buoy/beacon)
SHOM	Service Hydrographique et Océanographique de la Marine (FrenchHO/Chart)
Si	Silt (nature of seabed)
SIGNI	Signalisation de la Navigation Intérieure
SM	Sailmaker
✕	Shipwright (esp wooden hulls)
SMS	Short Message Service (mobile texting)
SNSM	Société Nationale de Sauvetage en Mer
so	Soft (eg mud; nature of seabed)
SOLAS	Safety of Life at Sea (IMO Convention)
Sp	Spire
sp	Spring tides
SPM	Special Mark (buoy/beacon)
SR	Sunrise
SRR	Search and Rescue Region
SS	Sunset. Signal Station
SSB	Single Sideband (radio)
St	Stones (nature of seabed)
Stbd	Starboard
subm	Submerged
SWM	Safe Water Mark (buoy/beacon)
sy	Sticky (eg mud; nature of seabed)

(T), (Temp)	Temporary
tbc	To be confirmed
tbn	To be notified
TD	Temporarily Discontinued (fog signal)
TE	Temporarily Extinguished (light)
tfn	Till further notice
Tr, twr	Tower
T/R	Traffic Report (route notification)
TSS	Traffic Separation Scheme
≠	In transit with, ie ldg marks/lts
uncov	Uncovers
UQ	Ultra Quick flashing light
UT	Universal Time (= approx GMT)
Var	Variation (magnetic)
(vert)	Vertically disposed (lights)
Vi	Violet
vis	Visibility, visible
VLCC	Very large crude carrier (Oil tanker)

VNF	Voie Navigable de France (canals)
VQ	Very Quick flashing light
VTS	Vessel Traffic Service
W	West. White
WCM	West Cardinal Mark (buoy/beacon)
Wd	Weed (nature of seabed)
I	Wind turbine
wef	With effect from
WGS	World Geodetic System (GPS datum)
Wi-Fi	Wireless Fidelity (internet access)
WIP	Work in progress
Wk, ⌁ ⊕	Wreck (see also Fig 1(1))
WMO	World Meteorological Organisation
WPT, ⊕	Waypoint
Wx	Weather
WZ	Code for UK coastal navigation warning
Y	Yellow, Amber, Orange
YC, Γ	Yacht Club

1.2 POSTAL AND E-MAIL ADDRESSES WITH WEBSITES

Note: Only yacht clubs which provide Sailing directions or Pilot books on a regular basis are included.

Adlard Coles Nautical (Imprint of A & C Black)
36 Soho Square, London W1D 3QY. adlardcoles@acblack.com www.reedsalmanac.co.uk ☎ 0207 775 0200. ✆ 0207 775 0222.

Amateur Yacht Research Society
BCM AYRS, London WC1N 3XX. ☎ 01727 862268.
✆ 08700 526657 office@ayrs.org www.ayrs.org

Association of Brokers and Yacht Agents: see Yacht designers and Surveyors Association.

BBC Radio
Broadcasting House, London W1A 1AA. ☎ 020 7580 4468. www.bbc.co.uk

Bristol Channel Yachting Association
Hill House, 14 Victoria Place, Newport, Gwent NP20 4TZ.
☎ 01934 633798/07720 579144. www.bristolchannel.co.uk secretary@bristolchannel.co.uk.

British Marine Federation (BMF)
Marine House, Thorpe Lea Road, Egham, Surrey TW20 8BF.
☎ 01784 473377. ✆ 01784 439678. www.britishmarine.co.uk info@britishmarine.co.uk

British Sub-Aqua Club
Telford's Quay, S Pier Road, Ellesmere Port, Cheshire CH65 4FL.
☎ 0151 350 6200/✆ 6215. www.bsac.com postmaster@bsac.com

British Waterways
64 Clarendon Rd, Watford, Herts WD17 1DA. ☎ 01923 201120; 0800 47 999 47 (SOS). ✆ 201400. www.britishwaterways.co.uk

British Waterways (Caledonian Canal)
Canal Office, Seaport marina, Muirtown Wharf, Highlands & Islands IV3 5LS. ☎ 01463 72550. www.waterscape.com

British Waterways (Crinan Canal)
Canal Office, Pier Square, Ardrishaig, Highlands & Islands PA30 8DZ. ☎ 01546 603210. ✆ 01603941. www.waterscape.com

British Waterways (Scotland)
Canal House, Applecross St, Glasgow G4 9SP. ☎ 0141 332 6936. ✆ 0141 331 1688. www.britishwaterways.co.uk/scotland enquiries.scotland@britishwaterways.co.uk

Clyde Cruising Club
Suite 101, The Pentagon Centre, 36 Washington Street, Glasgow G3 8AZ. ☎ 0141 221 2774. ✆ 0141 221 2775. hazel@clyde.org www.clyde.org

Coastguard, HM See Maritime & Coastguard Agency.

Conference of Yacht Cruising Clubs
www.cycc.org.uk hon.sec@cycc.org.uk

Cowes Combined Clubs
18 Bath Rd, Cowes, Isle of Wight PO31 7QN. ☎ 01983 295744. ✆ 01983 295329. www.cowesweek.co.uk admin@cowesweek.co.uk

Cruising Association (CA)
CA House, 1 Northey St, Limehouse Basin, London E14 8BT. ☎ 020 7537 2828. ✆ 020 7537 2266 www.cruising.org.uk office @cruising.org.uk

Cutty Sark Trust
2 Greenwich Church St, London SE10 9BG. ☎ 020 8858 2698;
✆ 6976. www.cuttysark.org.uk enquiries@cuttysark.org.uk

ECMWF (European Centre for Medium-range Weather Forecasts) The Director, ECMWF, Shinfield Park, Reading RG2 9AX, UK. Telefax +44 118 986 9450. www.ecmwf.int

Flag Institute, The
38 Hill St, London W1J 5NS. Secretary ☎ 01932 240820. www.flaginstitute.org/ info@flaginstitute.org

Forth Yacht Clubs Association
www.fyca.org.uk info@fyca.org.uk

Guernsey Tourist Board
PO Box 459, Longue Rue, St Martin's, Guernsey GY1 6AF. ☎ 01481 723552; ✆ 714951. www.visitguernsey.com

HM Revenue and Customs (HMRC)
Helpline ☎ 0845 010 9000; or enquiries.estn@hmrc.gsi.gov.uk www.hmrc.gov.uk

Hydrographic Office, The United Kingdom
Admiralty Way, Taunton, Somerset TA1 2DN.
☎ 01823 337900. ✆ 01823 284077. www.ukho.gov.uk helpdesk@ukho.gov.uk

Imray, Laurie, Norie & Wilson Ltd
Wych House, The Broadway, St Ives, Cambs PE27 5BT.
☎ 01480 462114. ✆ 01480 496109. www.imray.com enquiries@imray.com

Inland Waterways Association
PO Box 114, Rickmansworth, Herts WD3 1ZY. ☎ 01923 711114. ✆ 897000. iwa@waterways.org.uk www.waterways.org.uk

Institute of Marine Engineers
80 Coleman St, London EC2R 5BJ. ☎ 020 7382 2600;
✆ 020 7382 2670. www.imarest.org info@imarest.org

International Institute of Marine Surveyors
3 Stone Lane, Gosport, Hants PO12 1SS. ☎ 023 9258 8000;
✆ 023 9258 8002. www.iims.org.uk iims@compuserve.com

International Maritime Organisation (IMO)
4 Albert Embankment, London SE1 7SR. ☎ 020 7735 7611.
🕾 020 7587 3210. www.imo.org info@imo.org

International Maritime Satellite Org. (Inmarsat)
99 City Rd, London EC1Y 1AX. ☎ 020 7728 1777.
🕾 020 7728 1142. www.inmarsat.com customer_care@inmarsat.com

International Sailing Federation (ISAF)
Ariadne House, Town Quay, Southampton SO14 2AQ.
☎ 02380 635111. 🕾 02380 635789. www.sailing.org
secretariat@isaf.co.uk

Jersey Tourist Office
Liberation Place, St Helier, Jersey JE1 1BB. ☎ 01534 448800.
🕾 01534 448898. www.jersey.com info@jersey.com

Junior Offshore Group
28 Nodes Road, Cowes, Isle of Wight PO31 8AB.
☎/🕾 01983 291192. www.jog.org.uk secretary@jog.org.uk

Kelvin Hughes Ltd
Kilgraston House, Southampton St, Southampton SO15 2ED.
☎ 023 8063 4911. 🕾 023 8033 0014. www.bookharbour.com
southampton@kelvinhughes.co.uk

Little Ship Club
Bell Wharf Lane, Upper Thames St, London EC4R 3TB.
☎ 020 7236 7729. 🕾 020 7236 9100. www.little-ship-club.co.uk

Lloyd's
One Lime Street, London EC3M 7HA. ☎ 020 73271000;
🕾 020 7327 6827. www.lloyds.com helpdesk@lloyds.com

Lloyd's Register
(Passenger Ship and Special Service Craft Group), 71 Fenchurch St, London EC3M 4BS. ☎ 020 7423 2325;
🕾 020 7423 2016. marine@lr.org www.lr.org

Manx Sailing and Cruising Club
The Lookout, Queen's Promenade, Ramsey, Isle of Man IM8 1BG.
☎ 01624 813494. 🕾 01624 822825. contact@msandcc.org
www.msandcc.org

Marine Accident Investigation Branch (MAIB)
Carlton House, Carlton Place, Southampton SO15 2DZ.
☎ 023 8039 5500. 🕾 023 8023 2459. maib@dft.gsi.gov.uk
www.maib.gov.uk

Marine Leisure Association
24 Peterscroft Ave, Ashurst, Southampton SO40 7AB.
☎ 023 8029 3822. 🕾 023 8029 3888.
info@marineleisure.co.uk www.marineleisure.co.uk

Maritime and Coastguard Agency (MCA)
Spring Place, 105 Commercial Rd, Southampton SO15 1EG.
☎ 023 8032 9100; Info 0870 6006 505. 🕾 023 8032 9105.
www.mcga.gov.uk infoline@mcga.gov.uk

Maritime Trust (see Cutty Sark Trust, LH column)

Meteorological Office
FitzRoy Road, Exeter EX1 3PB. ☎ 0870 900 0100. 🕾 0870 900 5050. ☎ +44 (0)1392 885680. 🕾 +44 (0)1392 885681. www.metoffice.gov.uk enquiries@metoffice.gov.uk

Motor Boat and Yachting
IPC Media, The Blue Fin Building, 110 Southwark St, London
SE1 0SU. ☎ 020 3148 4651. 🕾 020 3148 8128. www.mby.com
mby@ipcmedia.com

National Coastwatch Institution (NCI)
www.nci.org.uk Contact: Mr Nick Heath, ☎/🕾 01548 580615.
n.heath279@btinternet.com

National Federation of Sea Schools (see Marine Leisure Ass)

National Imports Relief Unit (NIRU)
Killyhevlin Industrial Estate, Enniskillen, Co. Fermanagh BT74
4EJ. ☎ 02866 321225. 🕾 02866 324018. customs.hmrc.gov.uk
enquiries.niru.rbs@hmrc.gsi.gov.uk

Nautical Data Limited
Book Barn, Westbourne, Hants PO10 8RS. ☎ 01243 389352.
🕾 01243 379136. www.nauticaldata.com

Nautical Institute, The
202 Lambeth Road, London SE1 7LQ. ☎ 020 7928 1351;
🕾 020 7401 2817. sec@nautinst.org www.nautinst.org

Northern Lighthouse Board
84 George St, Edinburgh EH2 3DA. ☎ 0131 4733100.
🕾 0131 220 2093. www.nlb.org.uk enquiries@nlb.org.uk

North West Venturers Yacht Club
Gallows Point, Beaumaris, Anglesey LL58 8YL. ☎ 01248
810023. www.nwvyc.org.uk webmaster@nwvyc.org.uk

Ocean Cruising Club
☎ 020 7099 2678 secretary@oceancruisingclub.org
www.oceancruisingclub.org

Ofcom (Office of communications)
Riverside House, 2a Southwark Bridge Road, London SE1
9HA. ☎ 020 7981 3000; 🕾 020 7981 3333. www.ofcom.org.
uk licensingcentre@ofcom.org.uk

Port of London Authority (PLA)
London River House, Royal Pier Rd, Gravesend DA12 2BG.
☎ 01474 562200. 🕾 01474 562281 www.pla.co.uk.

Practical Boat Owner
Westover House, West Quay Road, Poole, Dorset BH15 1JG.
☎ 01202 440820. 🕾 440860.
www.pbo.co.uk pbo@ipcmedia.com

Registry of Shipping and Seamen (RSS)
UK Ship Register, Anchor Court, Keen Rd, Cardiff CF24 5JW;
☎ 02920 448 800; 🕾 029 20 448 820. www.ukshipregister.
co.uk Part I (Pleasure vessels) ☎ 02920 448 866.
Part III (SSR) ☎ 02920 448 813.

Royal Cruising Club (RCC)
www.rcc.org.uk sue@lennane.co.uk See Royal Thames YC.

Royal Institute of Naval Architects
10 Upper Belgrave St, London SW1X 8BQ. ☎ 020 7235 4622;
🕾 020 7259 5912. hq@rina.org.uk www.rina.org.uk

Royal Institute of Navigation (RIN)
1 Kensington Gore, London SW7 2AT. ☎ 020 7591 3130.
🕾 020 7591 3131. www.rin.org.uk info@rin.org.uk

Royal National Lifeboat Institution (RNLI)
West Quay Road, Poole, Dorset BH15 1HZ. ☎ 01202 663000.
🕾 01202 663167. info@rnli.org www.rnli.org.uk

Royal Naval Sailing Association (RNSA)
10 Haslar Marina, Haslar Rd, Gosport, Hants PO12 1NU.
☎ 023 9252 1100. 🕾 023 9252 1122. www.rnsa.net
gensecrnsa@btconnect.com

Royal Northumberland Yacht Club
South Harbour, Blyth, Northumberland NE24 3PB.
☎ 01670 353636. www.rnyc.org.uk hon.sec@rnyc.org.uk

Royal Ocean Racing Club (RORC)
20 St James's Place, London SW1A 1NN. ☎ 020 7493 2248.
🕾 020 7493 5252. www.rorc.org info@rorc.org.uk
RORC Rating Office, Seahorse Building, Bath Rd, Lymington,
Hants SO41 3SE. ☎ 01590 677030; 🕾 01590 679478

Royal Thames Yacht Club (RTYC)
60 Knightsbridge, London SW1X 7LF. ☎ 0207 235 2121
🕾 0207 245 9470. www.royalthames.com club@royalthames.com

Royal Yachting Association (RYA)
RYA House, Ensign Way, Hamble, SO31 4YA. ☎ 023 8060
4100. 🕾 023 8060 4299. www.rya.org.uk admin@rya.org.uk

Royal Yachting Association (Scotland)
Caledonia House, South Gyle, Edinburgh EH12 9DQ.
☎ 0131 317 7388. 🕾 0131 317 8566. www.ryascotland.org.uk
admin@ryascotland.co.uk

Royal Yacht Squadron
The Castle, Cowes, Isle of Wight PO31 7QT
☎ 01983 292191. 📠 01983 200253.
www.rys.org.uk   mail@rys.org.uk

Sailing Today
Swanwick Marina, Hamble, Southampton SO31 1ZL.
☎ 01489 585225. 📠 01489 565054.
www.sailingtoday.co.uk editor@sailingtoday.co.uk

Small Ships Register See Registry of Shipping and Seamen.

Society of Consulting Marine Engineers and Ships Surveyors,
202 Lambeth Rd, London SE1 7JW; ☎ 020 7261 0869;
📠 020 7261 0871. sec@scmshq.org www.scmshq.org

Solent Cruising and Racing Association
Regatta House, Bath Road, Cowes, Isle of Wight PO31 7QN.
☎ 01983 295744. 📠 01983 295329. www.scra.org.uk

Sport England
3rd floor, Victoria House, Bloomsbury Sq, London WC1B 4SE.
☎ 0845 8508 508. 📠 020 7383 5740. info@sportengland.org
www.sportengland.org

Stanfords Charts
See Imray, Laurie, Norie & Wilson Ltd. ☎ 01480 462114.
📠 01480 496109.   www.imray.com/stanfordscharts/

Stanfords Ltd (Covent Garden)
12-14 Long Acre, London WC2E 9LP. ☎ 0207 8361321.
📠 0207 8360189. sales@stanfords.co.uk www.stanfords.co.uk

Stationery Office, The
St Crispin's, Duke St, Norwich NR3 1PD. ☎ 01603 622211.
Also: TSO, 123 Kingsway, London WC2B 6PQ, ☎ 020 7242 6393.
📠 020 7242 6394. www.tsoshop.co.uk
customer.services@tso.co.uk

Trinity House, Corporation of
Tower Hill, London EC3N 4DH. ☎ 020 7481 6900.
📠 020 7480 7662. www.trinityhouse.co.uk enquiries@thls.org

Yacht Charter Association Ltd: see Marine Leisure Association

Yacht Designers and Surveyors Association (inc Assoc'n
of Brokers & Yacht Agents) The Glass Works, Penns Rd,
Petersfield GU32 2EW. info@ybdsa.co.uk www.ybdsa.co.uk
☎ 01730 710425. 📠 01730 710423.

Yacht Harbour Association Ltd
Evegate Park Barn, Station Rd, Smeeth, Ashford TN25 6SX.
☎ 01303 814434. 📠 01303 814364. www.berthsearch.com

Yachting Journalists' Association
36 Church Lane, Lymington SO41 3RB. ☎ 01590 673894.
www.yja.co.uk sec@yja.co.uk

Yachting Monthly
IPC Media, The Blue Fin Building, 110 Southwark Street,
London SE1 0SU. ☎ 0203 148 4872. 📠 0203 148 8128.
yachting_monthly@ipcmedia.com www.yachtingmonthly.com

Yachting World
IPC Media, The Blue Fin Building, 110 Southwark Street,
London SE1 0SU. ☎ 0203 148 4846. 📠 0203 148 8127.
yachting_world@ipcmedia.com www.yachtingworld.co.uk

BELGIUM
Belgian Tourist Information Centre
Grasmarkt 63, B-1000 Brussels. ☎ +32 2 504 0390
📠 +32 2 504 0270. www.visitbelgium.com

British Embassy
85 Aarlenstraat, 1040 Brussels. ☎ +32 2 2876 211
📠 +32 2 287 62 70 (Consular).

Royal Belgian Sailing Club
Zeebrugge ☎ +32 50 544 903.

Royal Meteorological Institute of Belgium
Ringlaan 3, B-31180 Brussels. ☎ +32 2 373 0508.
📠 +32 2 373 0528. rmiinfo@oma.be

Royal Yacht Club van Belgie, Antwerpen ☎ +32 3 219 2784.

Vlaamse Hydrografie
Administratief Centrum, Vrijhavenstraat 3, B-8400 Oostende.
☎ +32 3 222 0811. 📠 +32 3 231 2062
www.vlaamsehydrografie.be kust@vlaanderen.be.

DENMARK
British Embassy
Kastelsvej 36-40, DK-2100 København Ø.
☎ +45 35 44 52 42. 📠 +45 35 44 52 53 (Consular). info@britishembassy.dk

Danish Hydrographic Office
Kort-og Matrikelstyrelsen, Rentemestervej 8, DK-2400
København. ☎ +45 35 87 50 50. 📠 +45 35 87 50 57. kms@kms.dk

Danmarks Meteorologiske Institut (DMI)
Lyngbyvej 100, DK-2100 København Ø. ☎ +45 39 15 75 00.
📠 +45 39 27 10 80. www.dmi.dk

Dansk Sejlunion
(Danish sailing association) Stadion 20, 2605 Brøndby.
☎ +45 43 26 26 26. 📠 +45 43 26 21 91.

DMU Danske Fritidssejlere
(Motorboats) Tjørnelund 32, 2635 Ishøj. ☎ +45 43 53 66 67.

Søfartsstyrelsen (Danish Maritime Authority)
Søsportens Sikkerhedsråd (Safety for yachts)
Vermundsgade 38C, DK-2100 København Ø.
☎ +45 39 27 15 15. 📠 +45 39 17 44 01
www.dma.dk dma@dma.dk

FRANCE
British Embassy
35 rue du Faubourg St Honoré, 75383 Paris, Cedex 08,
☎ +33 1 44 51 31 00. 📠 +33 1 44 51 31 27 (Consular).

Comité d'Etudes et des Services des Assureurs Maritimes
20 rue Vivienne, 75082 Paris. ☎ 1 42 96 12 13. 📠 1 42 96 34 59.

CROSS Corsen
Pte de Corsen, 29810 Plouarzel. ☎ +33 2 98 89 3131.
📠 +33 2 98 89 65 75. corsen@mrccfr.eu

CROSS Étel
Av. Bougo, Chateau de la Garenne, 56410 Etel. ☎ +33 2 97 55 35 35. 📠 +33 2 97 55 49 34. etel@mrccfr.eu

CROSS Gris Nez
62179 Audinghen. ☎ +33 3 21 87 21 87. 📠 +33 3 21 87 78 55.
gris_nez@mrccfr.eu

CROSS Jobourg
Route d'Auderville, 50440 Jobourg. ☎ +33 2 33 52 72 13.
📠 +33 2 33 52 71 72. jobourg@mrccfr.eu

Douanes - Bureau d'Information
23 bis, rue de l'Université, 75700 Paris. ☎ +33 1 44 74 47 03.
📠 +33 1 44 74 49 37.

International Hydrographic Organisation
4 Quai Antoine 1er, BP 445, MC 98011 Monaco Cedex. ☎ +37 7 93 10 81 00; 📠 +37 7 93 10 8140. www.iho.int info@ihb.mc

Météo-France
1 Quai Branly, 75340 Paris Cedex 07. www.meteo.fr marine@meteo.fr ☎ +33 1 45 56 74 36. 📠 +33 1 45 56 71 70.

Service Hydrographique et Océanographique de la Marine
13 rue du Chatellier, CS 92803, 29228 Brest Cedex 2.
☎ +33 2 98 03 09 17. 📠 +33 2 98 47 11 42. www.shom.fr

Société Nationale de Sauvetage en Mer (SNSM)
9 rue de Chaillot, 75116 Paris. ☎ +33 1 56 89 30 00. 🖷 +33 1 56 89 30 01.

Yacht Club de France
41 ave Foch, 75116 Paris. ☎ +33 1 47 04 10 00. 🖷 1 47 04 10 01.

GERMANY
British Embassy
Wilhelmstrasse 70, 10117 Berlin. ☎ +49 30 2045 7-0. 🖷 +49 30 2045 7594. www.ukingermany.fco.gov.uk inforequests@fco.gov.de

Bundesamt für Seeschiffahrt und Hydrographie (BSH). (German HO) Bernhard-Nocht-Str 78, 20359 Hamburg. ☎ +49 40 3190-0. 🖷 +49 40 3190 50 00. www.bsh.de

Deutscher Gesellschaft zur Rettung Schiffbrüchiger (DGzRS = Rescue service). PO Box 10 63 40, 28063 Bremen. ☎ +49 421 53707-0. 🖷 +49 421 53707-690. www.dgzrs.de info@dgzrs.de

Deutscher Segler-Verbrand
(Yachting association) Gründgensstr 18, 22309 Hamburg. ☎ 00 49 40 632 0090. 🖷 00 49 40 6320 0928. www.dsv.org

Deutscher Wetterdienst (DWD)
Frankfurter Str 135, 63067 Offenbach. ☎ +49 69 80 620. 🖷 +49 69 8062 4484. www.dwd.de seeschifffahrt@dwd.de

National Tourist Board
Beethovenstrasse 69, D-60325 Frankfurt/Main. ☎ +49 0 6997 4640. 🖷 +49 0 6975 1903. info@d-z-t.com www.germany-tourism.de

Seefunk - DP07 (Coast radio company)
Estedeich 84, D-21129 Hamburg. ☎ +49 40 2385 5782. 🖷 +49 40 7413 4242. info@dp07.com www.dp07.com

IRELAND, REPUBLIC OF
British Embassy
29 Merrion Road, Ballsbridge, Dublin 4. ☎ +353 1 205 3700. www.britishembassy.ie consular.dubli@fco.gov.uk

Irish Coastguard (IRCG)
Department of Transport, Kildare Street, Dublin 2, RoI. ☎ +353 1 670 7444. www.transport.ie info@transport.ie

Irish Cruising Club
www.irishcruisingclub.com contact@irishcruisingclub.com

Irish Lights, Commissioners of
Harbour Road, Dun Laoghaire, Co Dublin, RoI. ☎ +353 1 2715400; 🖷 +353 1 2715564. www.cil.ie info@cil.ie

Irish Sailing Association
3 Park Rd, Dun Laoghaire, Co Dublin. ☎ +353 1 280 0239. 🖷 +353 1 280 7558. www.sailing.ie

Irish Tourist Board
150 New Bond St, London W1S 2AQ. ☎ 0207 518 0800. 🖷 0207 493 9065. info@irishtouristboard.co.uk www.ireland.travel.co.uk

Met Eireann (Irish Met Service)
HQ, Glasnevin Hill, Dublin 9. ☎ +353 1 806 4200; 🖷 +353 1 806 4247. www.met.ie met.eireann@met.ie

NETHERLANDS
ANWB Hoofdkantoor
PO Box 93200, 2509 BA Den Haag. ☎ +31 70 314 7147. 🖷 +31 70 314 6966.

British Embassy
Lange Voorhout 10, 2514 ED Den Haag. ☎ +31 70 427 0427. 🖷 +31 70 427 0345 www.ukinnl.fco.gov.uk ukinnl@fco.gov.uk

Dienst der Hydrografie
Van der Burchlaan 31, PO Box 90701, 2509 LS Den Haag. ☎ +31 70 316 2800. 🖷 +31 70 316 2843. info@hydro.nl www.hydro.nl

Koninklijke Nederlands Meteorologisch Instituut
Postbus 210, Wilhelminalaan 10, 3730 AE De Bilt. ☎ +30 220 6911. 🖷 +30 221 0407. www.knmi.nl

Koninklijke Nederlands Watersport Verbond
PO Box 85393, 3508 AJ Utrecht. ☎ +31 30 656 6550. 🖷 +31 30 656 4783.

Koninklijke Nederlandse Motorboot Club
Zoorstede 7, 3431 HK Nieuwegein. ☎ 00 31 30 603 9935. 🖷 00 31 30 605 3834.

Stichting Classificatie Waterrecreatiebedrijven
PO Box 93345, 2509 AH Den Haag. ☎ +31 70 328 3807.

PORTUGAL
British Embassy
Rua de São Bernardo 33, 1249-082 Lisboa. ☎ +351 21 3924 000. 🖷 +351 21 3914 185. chancery@lisbon.mail.fco.gov.uk

Hydrographic Office
Instituto Hidrografico, Rua das Trinas 49, 1296 Lisboa. ☎ +351 21 3914 000. 🖷 +351 21 3914 199. www.hidrografico.pt mail@hidrografico.pt

Instituto de Meteorologia
Rua C, Aeroporto, 1749-077 Lisboa. ☎ +351 21 8447010. 🖷 +351 21 844 74333. www.meteo.pt informacoes@meteo.pt

SPAIN
British Embassy
Calle de Fernando el Santo 16, 28010 Madrid. ☎ +34 91 700 82 00. 🖷 +34 91 700 83 09.

Instituto Hidrografico de la Marina
Plaza de San Severiano No 3, 11007 CADIZ. ☎ +34 956 599 414. 🖷 +34 956 275 358. www.armada.mde.es/ihm orpflota@fn.mde.es

Instituto Nacional de Meteorologa
C/Leonardo Prieto Castro, 8 (Ciudad Universitaria), 28071 Madrid. ☎ +34 91 581 9810. 🖷 +34 91 581 9811. www.inm.es infomet@inm.es

Spanish Tourist Office
2nd floor, 79 New Cavendish St, London W1W 6XB; ☎020 7486 8077, 🖷 020 7186 8034. www.spain.info www.tourspain.uk londres@tourspain.es

---

1.3 2010 CALENDAR AND EPHEMERIS
1.3.1 UK public holidays 2010
Jan 1
Jan 4 (Scotland only)
Mar 17 (N Ireland only)
Apr 2 (Good Friday)
Apr 5, Easter Monday, Not Scotland
May 3
May 31
Jul 12 (N Ireland only)
Aug 2 (Scotland only)
Aug 30 (Not Scotland)
Dec 25/27 – 25th is a Saturday
Dec 26/28 – 26th is a Sunday

1.3.2 Eclipses visible from the British Isles & Europe
- Total eclipse of the Moon, Dec 21 2010 between 0632 and 1002UT. Totality lasts from 0740 to 0854. Not a vintage year.

1.4   CONVERSION TABLES

1.4.1   Conversion factors

To convert	Multiply by	To convert	Multiply by
Area			
sq in to sq mm	645·16	sq mm to sq in	0·00155
sq ft to sq m	0·0929	sq m to sq ft	10·76
Length (See 1.4.2 for Feet to metres, and vice versa)			
in to mm	25·4	mm to in	0·0394
yds to m	0·914	m to yds	1·094
fathoms to m	1·8288	m to fathoms	0·5468
nautical miles (M) to kilometres	1·852	kilometres to nautical miles	·0·539957
nautical miles to statute miles	1·1515	statute miles to nautical miles	0·8684
(1 cable equals 0·1 M, approx 185m)			
Velocity (See also 6.1.1 Beaufort scale)			
ft/sec to m/sec	0·3048	m/sec to ft/sec	3·281
ft/sec to miles/hr	0·682	miles/hr to ft/sec	1·467
ft/sec to knots	0·592	knots to ft/sec	1·689
ft/min to m/sec	0·0051	m/sec to ft/min	196·8
knots to miles/hr	1·1515	miles/hr to knots	0·868
knots to km/hr	1·852	km/hr to knots	0·54
knots to m/sec	0·5144	m/sec to knots	1·944
Mass			
oz to grams	28·35	grams to oz	0·0353
lb to kg	0·4536	kg to lb	2·205
tons to tonnes (1000 kg)	1·016	tonnes to tons (2240 lb)	0·9842
Pressure			
inches of mercury to millibars	33·86	millibars to inches of mercury	0·0295
lb/sq in to kg/sq cm	0·0703	kg/sq cm to lb/sq in	14·22
lb/sq in to atmospheres	0·068	atmospheres to lb/sq in	14·7
Volume			
cu in to cu cm (cc or ml)	16·387	cu cm (cc or ml) to cu in	0·061
cu ft to cu metres	0·0283	cu metres to cu ft	35·31
cu ft to galls	6·25	galls to cu ft	0·16
cu ft to litres	28·33	litres to cu ft	0·035
Capacity			
pints to litres	0·568	litres to pints	1·76
Imp galls to litres	4·546	litres to Imp galls	0·22
Imp galls to US galls	1·2	US galls to Imp galls	0·833
Torque			
lbf ft to Nm	1·3558	Nm to lbf ft	0·7376
kgf m to Nm	9·8066	Nm to kgf m	0·102
lbf ft to kgf m	0·1383	kgf m to lbf ft	7·233

1.4.2   Feet to metres, metres to feet

Explanation: The central columns of figures in bold type can be referred to the left to convert metres into feet, or to the right to convert feet into metres, e.g. five lines down: 5 metres = 16·40 feet, or 5 feet = 1·52 metres. Alternatively multiply feet by 0·3048 for metres, or multiply metres by 3·2808 for feet.

Feet		Metres	Feet		Metres	Feet		Metres	Feet		Metres
3·28	**1**	0·30	45·93	**14**	4·27	88·58	**27**	8·23	131·23	**40**	12·19
6·56	**2**	0·61	49·21	**15**	4·57	91·86	**28**	8·53	134·51	**41**	12·50
9·84	**3**	0·91	52·49	**16**	4·88	95·14	**29**	8·84	137·80	**42**	12·80
13·12	**4**	1·22	55·77	**17**	5·18	98·43	**30**	9·14	141·08	**43**	13·11
16·40	**5**	1·52	59·06	**18**	5·49	101·71	**31**	9·45	144·36	**44**	13·41
19·69	**6**	1·83	62·34	**19**	5·79	104·99	**32**	9·75	147·64	**45**	13·72
22·97	**7**	2·13	65·62	**20**	6·10	108·27	**33**	10·06	150·92	**46**	14·02
26·25	**8**	2·44	68·90	**21**	6·40	111·55	**34**	10·36	154·20	**47**	14·33
29·53	**9**	2·74	72·18	**22**	6·71	114·83	**35**	10·67	157·48	**48**	14·63
32·81	**10**	3·05	75·46	**23**	7·01	118·11	**36**	10·97	160·76	**49**	14·94
36·09	**11**	3·35	78·74	**24**	7·32	121·39	**37**	11·28	164·04	**50**	15·24
39·37	**12**	3·66	82·02	**25**	7·62	124·67	**38**	11·58	167·32	**51**	15·54
42·65	**13**	3·96	85·30	**26**	7·92	127·95	**39**	11·89	170·60	**52**	15·84

1.5   TIME

Zone Time For timekeeping purposes the world is divided into 24 Time Zones, each 15° of Longitude wide (like orange segments). Zone 0 (7½°E to 7½°W) straddles 0° longitude (the Greenwich Meridian). Zones east of it and ahead of it in time are labelled Zone –1, –2 and so on to –11. Zones to the west (later in time) are +1, +2 etc to +11.

1.5.1   Universal Time (UT) is just that; a benchmark for the planet to which broadcast times, times of sunrise/set, scientific data etc are often referred. UT is the Standard time kept in Zone 0, at least in theory; in practice there are deviations for geographic reasons.

UT is replacing GMT in common parlance (except in the BBC World Service); they are virtually identical.

1.5.2   Standard time, also called legal time, is that kept in different countries but modified by DST in the summer.

> **UT** is the Standard Time in the UK, including the Channel Islands and Northern Ireland, the Irish Republic, Iceland, Faeroes, Portugal and Morocco.
>
> **UT –1** is the Standard Time in Denmark, Germany, The Netherlands, Belgium, France, Spain and Gibraltar. Standard Time is 1 hour earlier than UT (ie –0100). 1 hour should therefore be subtracted from Standard Time to give UT, or added to UT to give Standard Time.
>
> **UT +1** is the Standard Time in the Azores. Standard Time is one hour later than UT (ie +0100). 1 hour should therefore be subracted from UT to give Standard Time, or added to Standard Time in order to give UT.

Standard Time for each country is also included in Chapter 9 within the Special Notes for that country.

1.5.3   Daylight Saving Time (DST), or BST in the UK, is an artificial adjustment of 1 hour ahead of Standard Time made during the summer months in most European and many other countries.

In EU countries DST is kept from the last Sunday in March until the Saturday before the last Sunday in October (but in Denmark DST ends on the last Sunday in October). Thus in the UK DST is kept from 0100 UT Sunday Mar 28 2010 until 0100 UT Sunday October 31 2010.

1.5.4   Tide Tables Zone Time is quoted at the top left corner of each page of tide tables. In countries whose Zone Time is called –0100 (merely a 4 digit connotation meaning –1 hour), subtract 1 hour from the printed tide times to give UT. If this confuses, remember that the times with a tinted background are Standard Times. In the summer (no tinted background) add 1 hour to the printed times to obtain DST.

RADIO TIME SIGNALS

1.5.5   BBC Radio time signals in the UK
Broadcasts given 1 hr earlier when DST in force.

BBC Radio 1
Mainland 97·6 – 99·8 MHz. Channel Islands 97·1 MHz
Mon-Thu, 0630, 0900, 1000.
Fri, 0630, 0900, 1000, 1900.
Sat & Sun, no information.

BBC Radio 2
Mainland 88 – 90·2 MHz. Channel Islands 89·6 MHz
Mon-Fri, 0700, 0800, 1700.
Sat & Sun, no information.

BBC Radio 3
Mainland 90·2 – 92·4 MHz. Channel Islands 91·1 MHz
Mon-Sat, 0700, 0800. **Sun,** 0700.

BBC Radio 4
LW 198 kHz

FM England: 92·4 – 94·6 MHz
Scotland, parts of Wales & N Ireland, 94·7 – 96·1 MHz, 103·5 – 104·9 MHz.
Channel Islands: 94·8 MHz

MW Plymouth 774 kHz; Redruth 756 kHz; London and Northern Ireland 720 kHz; Tyneside 603 kHz; Aberdeen 1449 kHz; Carlisle 1495 kHz.
Every hour of every day except 1800, 2200, 0000.

1.5.6   The BBC World Service provides time signals on the following frequencies kHz at the times shown below:

A:	198	G:	7230	M:	12095
B:	648	H:	7325	N:	15070
C:	1296	I:	9410	O:	15340
D:	3955	J:	9750	P:	17640
E:	6195	K:	9760	Q:	17705
F:	7150	L:	9915		

Time	A	B	C	D	E	F	G	H	I	J	K	L	M	N	O	P	Q
0000	♦	♦						♦				♦	♦	♦			
0200	♦	♦	♦		♦			♦	♦			♦	♦				
0300	♦	♦	♦		♦	♦	♦	♦				♦	♦				
0400	♦			♦	♦		♦	♦				♦					
0500	♦			♦	♦			♦				♦	♦				
0600		♦	♦					♦				♦	♦				
0700		♦				♦	♦		♦		♦	♦		♦			
0800		♦					♦		♦	♦	♦		♦			♦	♦
0900		♦						♦	♦	♦	♦	♦		♦		♦	♦
1100		♦						♦	♦		♦	♦		♦		♦	♦
1200		♦						♦			♦	♦		♦		♦	♦
1300		♦							♦		♦	♦		♦		♦	♦
1500		♦							♦		♦	♦		♦		♦	♦
1600		♦		♦					♦			♦		♦			♦
1700		♦			♦				♦				♦	♦			
1800									♦				♦	♦			
1900		♦							♦			♦	♦				
2000		♦		♦				♦	♦			♦	♦				
2200	♦	♦		♦				♦	♦			♦	♦	♦		♦	
2300	♦	♦						♦	♦			♦	♦	♦	♦		♦

1.5.7   Worldwide time signals
Anthorn (54°54'N 03°16'W), UK (MSF) broadcasts UT signals continuously on 60 kHz. Signal strength is adequate in the UK and can be received widely in N and W Europe.

Fort Collins, Colorado (WWV) and Kekaha, Hawaii (WWVH) broadcast UT signals continuously on frequencies 2·5, 5, 10, 15 and 20 (not Kekaha) MHz. The station is identified by voice (English) at every H and H+30. The hour is signalled by a 1500 Hz tone and minutes and seconds by 1200 Hz tones. WWV broadcasts Atlantic weather in two parts at H+08 and H+09 and weather in the Eastern N. Pacific at H+10.

1.6   VOCABULARIES

English, German, Dutch, French, Spanish and Portuguese vocabularies of useful words are listed, for easy reference, under broad subject headings on the eight following pages.

English	Deutsch	Nederlands	Français	Español	Português
ON ARRIVAL	**BEI ANKUNFT**	**BIJ AANKOMST**	**À L'ARRIVÉE**	**AL LLEGAR**	**CHEGADA**
Beam	Schiffsbreite	Breedte	Largeur	Manga	Boca
Certificate of competence	Befähigungszeugnis	Getuigschrift	Permis bateau	Título	Certificado de competência
Crew list	Besatzungsliste	Bemanningslijst	Liste d'équipage	Lista de tripulación	Lista da tripulação
Customs	Zoll	Douane	Douanes	Aduana	Alfândega
Draught	Tiefgang	Diepgang	Tirant d'eau	Calado	Calado
Insurance certificate	Versicherungspolice	Verzekeringsbewijs	Attestation d'assurance	Certificado de seguro	Certificado de seguro
Length over all (LOA)	Länge über Alles (LüA)	Lengte over alles (LOA)	Longeur hors-tout	Eslora total	Comprimento fora a fora
Passport	Reisepaß	Paspoort	Passeport	Pasaporte	Passaporte
Port of registry	Heimathafen	Thuishaven	Quartier maritime	Puerto de matricula	Porto de registo
Port police	Polizei	Haven politie	Police du port	Policia de puerto	Policia maritima
Pratique	Frei Verkehrserlaubnis	Inklaren	Libre-pratique	Libre prática	Livre prática
Registration certificate	Registrierungszertifikat	Zeebrief	Acte de francisation	Certificado de Registro	Certificado de Registro
Ship's logbook	Logbuch	Logboek	Livre de bord	Cuaderno de bitácora	Diário de bordo
Ship's papers	Schiffspapiere	Scheepspapieren	Papiers de bord	Documentación del barco	Documentação do barco
Surveyor	Gutachter	Opzichter, expert	Expert maritime	Inspector	Inspector
VAT certificate	Mehrwertsteuerbescheinigung	BTW-dokument	Attestation de TVA	Certificado IVA	Certificado de IVA
ASHORE	**AN LAND**	**AAN LAND**	**À TERRE**	**A TIERRA**	**A TERRA**
Airport	Flughafen	Vliegveld	Aéroport	Aeropuerto	Aeroporto
Bakery	Bäckerei	Bakkerij	Boulangerie, patisserie	Panaderia	Padaria, Pastelaria
Bank	Bank	Bank	Banque	Banco	Banco
Bus station	Busbahnhof	Busstation	Gare routière	Estación de autobuses	Estação do autocarro
Butcher	Fleischerei	Slagerij	Boucherie	Carniceria	Açougue
Chandlery	Yachtausrüster	Scheepswinkel	Shipchandler	Efectos navales	Aprestos
Chemist	Apotheke	Apotheek	Pharmacie	Farmacia	Farmácia
Dentist	Zahnarzt	Tandarts	Dentiste	Dentista	Dentista
Engineer	Motorenservice	Monteur	Mécanicien	Mecánico	Engenheiro
Exchange (money)	Wechselstelle	Geldwisselkantoor	Bureau de change	Cambio	Cambio
Garage	Autowerkstatt	Garage	Garage	Garage	Oficina mecânica
Hospital	Krankenhaus	Ziekenhuis	Hôpital	Hospital	Hospital
Ironmongery	Eisenwarenhandlung	IJzerhandelaar	Quincaillerie	Quincalleria	Loja de ferragens
Launderette	Waschsalon	Wasserette	Laverie	Lavanderia	Lavanderia
Market	Markt	Markt	Marché	Mercado	Mercado
Post office	Postamt	Postkantoor	Bureau de poste, PTT	Correos	Correio, CTT
Railway station	Bahnhof	Station	Gare de chemin de fer	Estación de ferrocanil	Estação de comboios
Sailmaker	Segelmacher	Zeilmaker	Voilier	Velero, veleria	Veleiro
Shops	Geschäfte	Winkels	Boutiques	Tiendas	Lojas
Stamps, postal	Marken	Postzegels	Timbres	Sellos	Selos
Supermarket	Supermarkt	Supermarkt	Supermarché	Supermercado	Supermercado
HARBOUR	**HAFEN**	**HAVEN**	**PORT**	**PUERTO**	**PORTO**
Anchoring, anchorage	Ankern, Ankerplatz	Ankeren, ankerplaats	Mouiller l'ancre	Fondeadero	Fundeadouro
Boathoist	Bootskran	Botenlift	Travelift	Travelift	Portico elevador
Boatyard	Bootswerft	Jachtwerf	Chantier naval	Astilleros	Estaleiro
Breakwater, mole	Außenmole	Pier	Brise-lame	Escollera	Quebra-mar, molhe
Bridge, pedestrian	Schlengel	Loopbrug	Passerelle	Pasarela	Ponte movediça
Bridge, swing	Drehbrücke	Draaibrug	Pont tournant	Puente giratorio	Ponte giratória
Cable (electrical)	Kabel	Kabel	Câble	Cable	Cabo (electrico)
Commercial port	Handelshafen	Commerciële haven	Port de commerce	Puerto comercial	Porto comercial
Crane	Kran	Kraan	Grue	Grua	Grua
Drying port	Trockenfallender Hafen	Droogvallende haven	Port d'échouage	Puerto seco	Porto secar
Dues, berthing tariff	Hafengebühren	Havengeld	Tarifs portuaire	derechos de puerto	Taxas
Ferry	Fähre	Veerboot	Ferry, bac, transbordeur	Ferry	ferry
Fishing harbour	Fischereihafen	Vissershaven	Port de pêche	Puerto de pesca	Porto de pesca

English	Deutsch	Nederlands	Français	Español	Português
Fuel berth	Tankstelle	Bunkerplaats	Ponton à carburants	Surtidor	Estação de serviço
Harbour entrance	Hafeneinfahrt	Haveningang	Entrée du port	Entrada de puerto	Entrada
Harbour guide	Hafenhandbuch	Haven gids	Guide du port	Guia del puerto	Guia de Porto
Harbour master	Hafenmeister	Havenmeester	Capitaine du port	Capitán del puerto	Capitão marítimo
Height, headroom	Höhe	Hoogte	Hauteur	Alturas	Altura
Jetty	Steg	Steiger	Jetée	Malecón	Molhe
Landing place	Anlegeplatz	Plaats om aan land te gaan	Débarcadère	Desembarcadero	Desembarcadouro
Lock	Schleuse	Sluis	Ecluse	Esclusa	Eclusa
Marina, yacht harbour,	Yachthafen	Jachthaven	Port de plaisance	Puerto deportivo	Doca de recreio
Mast crane	Mastenkran	Mastenkraan	Grue	Grúa	Guindaste (mastro
Mooring (buoy)	Anlegen	Meerplaats	Coffre d'amarrage	Fondeadero	Bóia de atracação
Permitted	Erlaubt	Toegestaan	Autorisé	Permitido	Autorizado
Pier	Pier, Mole	Pier	Appontement/quai	Muelle	Molhe
Prohibited	Verboten	Verboden	Interdit	Prohibido	Proibido
Slip, slipway	Slip, Slipbahn	Helling	Cale	Varadero	Rampa
Water, fresh	Süßwasser	Zoet water	Eau douce	Agua dulce	Água doce
Yacht club	Yachtclub	Jachtclub	Club nautique	Club náutico	Clube nautico
NAVIGATION	**NAVIGATION**	**NAVIGATIE**	**NAVIGATION**	**NAVIGACION**	**NAVEGAÇÃO**
Abeam	Querab	Dwarsscheeps	Par le travers	Por el través	Por de través
Ahead	Voraus	Voor	Par l'avant	Avante	À proa
Astern	Achteraus	Achter	Par l'arrière	Atrás	À popa
Buoy	Tonne	Boei/ton	Bouée	Boya	Bóia
Binoculars	Fernglas	Verrekijker	Jumelles	Prismáticos	Binóculos
Channel (navigational)	Kanal	Kanaal/geul	Chenal	Canal	Canal
Chart	Seekarte	Zeekaart	Carte	Carta náutica	Carta hidrográfica
Compass	**Kompaß**	**Kompas**	**Compas**	**Compás**	**Agulha**
Bearing	Peilung	Peiling	Relèvement	Marcación	Azimute
Compass course	Kompaßkurs	Kompaskoers	Cap du compas	Rumbo de aguja	Rumo do agulha
Course True	Wahrer Kurs	Ware Koers	Cap vrai	Rumbo verdadero	Rumo verdadeiro
Deviation	Missweisung	Deviatie	Déviation	Desvio	Desvios
East	Ost	Oost	Est	Este	Este
Handbearing compass	Handpeilkompass	Handpeil kompas	Compas de relèvement	Compás de marcaciones	Agulha portátil
North	Nord	Noord	Nord	Norte	Norte
South	Süd	Zuid	Sud	Sur	Sul
Variation	Variation	Variatie	Déclinaison magnétique	Variación	Variação
West	West	West	Ouest	Oeste	Oeste
Current	Strömung	Stroom	Courant	Corriente	Corrente
Dead reckoning	Koppelnavigation	Gegist bestek	Navigation à l'estime	Estima	Navegação estimada
Degree	Grad	Graad	Degré	Grado	Grau
Depth	Wassertiefe	Diepte	Profondeur	Profundidad	Profundidade
Distance	Entfernung	Afstand, verheid	Distance	Distancia	Distância
Downstream	Flußabwärts	Stroomafwaarts	En aval	Río abajo	Jusante
Dredged (channel)	Baggerrinne	Gebaggerd (geul)	Dragué	Dragado	Dragado
Echosounder	Echolot	Dieptemeter	Sondeur	Sonda	Sondador acústica
Estimated position	Gegißte Position	Gegiste positie	Point estimé	Posición estimada	Posição estimada
Firing range	Schießgebiet	Schietoefeningen	Zone de tir	Zona de tiro	Zone de tiro
Hazard	Hindernis	Gevaar	Danger	Peligro	Perigo
Latitude	Geographische Breite	Breedte	Latitude	Latitud	Latitude
Leeway	Abdrift	Drift	Dérive	Sotavento	Abatimento
Lights list	**Leuchtfeuerverzeichnis**	**Lichtenlijst**	**Liste des feux**	**Libro de faros**	**Lista de faróis**
Leading lights	Richtfeuer	Geleidelichten	Feux d'alignement	Luz de enfilación	Farol de enfiamento
Lighthouse	Leuchtturm	Vuurtoren	Phare	Faro	Farol
Lightship	Feuerschiff	Lichtschip	Bâteau-feu	Buque faro	Barco-farol

English	Deutsch	Nederlands	Français	Español	Português
Log	Log	Log	Loch	Corredera	Odómetro
Longitude	Geographische Länge	Lengte	Longitude	Longitud	Longitude
Nautical mile	Seemeile	Zeemijl	Mille nautique	Milla marina	Milha marítima
Numbers	**Nummern**	**Nummers**	**Nombres**	**Numeros**	**Números**
One	Ein	Een	Un	Uno	Um
Two	Zwei	Twee	Deux	Dos	Dois
Three	Drei	Drie	Trois	Tres	Três
Four	Vier	Vier	Quatre	Cuatro	Quatro
Five	Fünf	Vijf	Cinq	Cinco	Cinco
Six	Sechs	Zes	Six	Seis	Seis
Seven	Sieben	Zeven	Sept	Siete	Sete
Eight	Acht	Acht	Huit	Ocho	Oito
Nine	Neun	Negen	Neuf	Nueve	Nove
Ten	Zehn	Tien	Dix	Diez	Dez
Pilot (guide)	Lotse	Loods, Gids	Pilote	Práctico	Roteiro da costa, Pilôto
Port (side)	Backbord	Bakboord	Bâbord	Babor	Bombordo
Prohibited area	Sperrgebiet	Verboden gebied	Zone interdite	Zona de prohibida	Zonaproibida
River mouth	Flußmündung	Riviermond	Embouchure	Desembocadura	Foz
Starboard	Steuerbord	Stuurboord	Tribord	Estribor	Estibordo
Tide	**Tide, Gezeiten**	**Getijde**	**Marée**	**Marea**	**Maré**
Chart datum	Kartennull	Reductievlak	Zero des cartes	Datum	Zero hidrográfico
Covers	Deckt	Onderlopend	Couvre	Cubierto	Cobre
Dries	Trockenfallend	Droogvallend	Découvre	Descubierto	Fica em sêco
Ebb	Ebbe	Eb	Jusant	Marea menguante	Corrente evasante
Flood	Flut	Vloed	Flot	Flujo de marea	Corrente de enchente
High water	Hochwasser	Hoogwater	Pleine mer	Pleamar	Praia mar
Low water	Niedrigwasser	Laagwater	Basse mer	Bajamar	Baixa-mar
Neaps	Nipptide	Doodtij	Morte-eau	Marea muerta	Mares mortas
Springs	Springtide	Springtij, springvloed	Vive-eau	Marea viva	Mares vivas
Tidal streams	Gezeitenströme	Getijstromen	Courants de marée	Corrientes de marea	Correntes de maré
Tide tables	Tidenkalender	Getijdetafel	Annuaire des marées	Anuario de mareas	Tabela de marés
Underwater	Unterwasser	Onderwater	Immergé	Debajo del agua	Submerso
Upstream	Flußaufwärts	Stroomopwaarts	En amont	Aguasarriba	Montante
Waypoint	Wegepunkt	Waypoint/Route punt	Point de destination	Waypoint	Ponto de chegada
Wreck	Wrack	Wrak	Epave	Naufragio	Naufrágio
METEOROLOGY	**METEOROLOGIE**	**METEOROLOGIE**	**METEO**	**METEOROLOGÍA**	**METEOROLOGIA**
Area	Gebiet	Gebied	Zone	Zona	Área
Clouds, cloudy	Wolken	Wolken	Nuages, nuageux	Nublado	Nublado
Cold	Kalt	Koud	Froid	Frio	Frio
Direction	Richtung	Richting	Direction	Dirección	Indicação
Forecast	Vorhersage	Vooruitzicht	Prévision	Previsión	Previsão
Fresh, cool, chilly	Frisch	Fris	Frais	Fresco	Fresco, frio
Local	Örtlich	Plaatselijk	Local	Local	Local
Outlook	Aussichten	Vooruitzicht	Evolution probable	Evolución probable ulterior	Prospecto
Precipitation	**Niederschlag**	**Neerslag**	**Précipitation**	**Precipitación**	**Precipitação**
Drizzle	Niesel	Motregen	Bruine	Llovizna	Chuvisco
Frequent	Häufig	Veelvuldig	Fréquent	Frecuente	Freqüente
Hail	Hagel	Hagel	Grêle	Granizo	Saraiva
Heavy	Schwer	Zwaar	Abondant	Abundante	Forte
Isolated	Vereinzelt	Geïsoleerd	Isolé	Aislado	Isolado
Lightning	Blitze	Bliksem	Eclair de foudre	Relampago	Relâmpago
Rain	Regen	Regen	Pluie	lluvia	Chuva
Scattered	Vereinzelt	Verspreid	Esparses	Difuso	Esporádico

English	Deutsch	Nederlands	Français	Español	Português
Shower	Schauer	Bui	Averse	Chubasco	Aguaceiro
Sleet	Schneeregen	Natte sneeuw	Neige fondue	Aguanieve	Geada miúda
Snow	Schnee	Sneeuw	Neige	Nieve	Neve
Thunder	Donner	Donder	Tonnerre	Trueno	Trovão
Thunderstorm	Gewitter	Onweer	Orage	Tormenta	Trovoada
Pressure systems	**Luftdrucksysteme**	**Druk**	**Pression**	**Presión**	**Pressão**
Air mass	Luftmasse	Luchtmassa	Masse d'air	Masa de aire	Massa de ar
Cold front	Kaltfront	Koufront	Front froid	Frente frío	Frente fria
Decrease	Abnahme	Afnemen	Affaiblissement	Disminuir	Enfraquecer
Deep	Tief	Diep	Profond	Profundo	Profundo
Deepening	Vertiefend	Verdiepend	Se creusant	Ahondamiento	Agravar-se
Disturbance	Störung	Storing	Perturbation	Perturbación	Perturbação
Extending	Ausdehnung	Uitstrekkend	S'étendant	Extendiendose	Alastrando
Falling	Fallend	Dalend	Baissant	Bajando	Descendo
Filling	Auffüllend	Vullend	Se comblant	Rellenandose	Encher-se
Front	Front	Front	Front	Frente	Frente
Gradient	Druckgefälle	Gradiënt	Gradient	Gradiente	Gradiente
High (anticyclone)	Hoch	Hoog, Hogedrukgebied	Anticyclone	Alta presión, Anticiclón	Anticiclone
Isobar	Isobare	Isobaar	Isobare	Isobaro	Isóbaro
Low (depression)	Tief, Sturmtief	Laag, Depressie	Dépression	Baja presión, Depresión	Depressão
Moving	Bewegend	Bewegend	Se déplacant	Movimiento, moviendose	Afastar-se
Occlusion, occluded	Okklusion	Occlusie	Occlus	Oclusión	Oclusão
Quickly	Schnell	Snel	Rapidement	Rápidamente	Rápidamente
Ridge	Hochdruckbrücke	Rug	Dorsale, crête	Cresta	Crista
Rising	Ansteigend	Stijgend	Montant	Subiendo	Subindo
Slowly	Langsam	Langzaam	Lentement	Lentamente	Lentamente
Steady	Gleichbleibend	Vast	Stable	Fijo	Constante
Trough	Trog, Tiefausläufer	Trog	Thalweg	Seno	Linha de baixa pressão
Warm front	Warmfront	Warmtefront	Front chaud	Frente calido	Frente quente
Sea/sea state	**See/Seegang**	**Zee**	**Mer**	**Mar**	**Mar**
Breakers	Brecher	Brekende zee	Lames déferlantes	Rompientes	Arrebentação
Calm	Flaute	Kalmte	Calme	Calma	Calma
Choppy	Kabbelig	Kort en steil	Croisée, hachée, clapot	Picada	Mareta
Overfalls (tide race)	Stromkabbelung	Stromkabbeling	Clapot, brisants	Escarceos, remolino	Bailadeiras
Rough	Rauh	Ruw	Forte	Fuerte marejada	Agitado
Seaway	Seegang	Zeegang	Haute mer	Alta mar	Mare alta
Short, steep	Kurz, steil	Kort, steil	Vagues courtes, creuse	Mar corta, gruesa	Mar curta, cavado
Slight	Leicht	Licht	Légère, peu agitée	Marejadilla	Ligeiramente
Swell	Schwell	Deining	Houle	Mar de fondo	Ondulação
Sun	Sonne	Zon	Soleil	Sol	Sol
Sunrise	Sonnenaufgang	Zonsopgang	Lever du soleil	Orto	Nascer do sol
Sunset	Sonnenuntergang	Zonsondergang	Coucher du soleil	Ocaso	Pôr do sol
Synoptic situation	Wetterlage	Synoptische toestand	Situation générale	Situación sinóptica	Situação sinóptica
Visibility	**Sichtweite**	**Zicht**	**Visibilité**	**Visibilidad**	**Visibilidade**
Dispersing	Auflösend	Oplossend	Se dispersant	Disipación	Limpando
Extensive	Ausgedehnt	Uitgebreid	Etendu	Extenso	Extenso
Fog	Nebel	Mist	Brouillard	Niebla	Nevoeiro
Fog bank	Nebelbank	Mistbank	Banc de brume	Banco de niebla	Banco do nevoeiro
Good	Gut	Goed	Bon	Bueno	BOM
Haze	Diesig	Nevelig	Brume	Calina	Cerração
Mist	Dunst	Nevel	Brume légere	Neblina	Neblina
Moderate	Mäßig	Matig	Médiocre, reduite	Moderado	Moderada
Poor	Schlecht	Slecht	Mauvais	Malo	Fraca má
Weather	Wetter	Weerraport	Temps	Tiempo	Boletim meteorológico

English — Wind/Beaufort/direction

English	Deutsch	Nederlands	Français	Español	Português
Wind/Beaufort/direction	**Wind**	**Wind**	**Vent**	**Viento**	**Vento**
F0, Calm	Windstille	Stil	Calme	Calma	Calma
F1, Light airs	Leiser Zug	Flauw en stil	Très légère brise	Ventolina	Aragem
F2, Light breeze	Leichte Brise	Flauwe koelte	légère brise	Flojito	Fraco
F3, Gentle breeze	Schwache Brise	Lichte koelte	Petite brise	Flojo	Bonançoso
F4, Moderate breeze	Mäßige Brise	Matige koelte	Jolie brise	Bonancible	Moderado
F5, Fresh breeze	Frische Brise	Frisse bries	Bonne brise	Fresquito	Frêsco
F6, Strong breeze	Starker Wind	Stijve bries	Vent frais	Fresco	Muito frêsco
F7, Near gale	Steifer Wind	Harde wind	Grand frais	Freschacón	Forte
F8, Gale	Stürmischer Wind	Stormachtig	Coup de vent	Duro	Muito forte
F9, Strong gale	Sturm	Storm	Fort coup de vent	Muy duro	Tempestuoso
F10, Storm	Schwerer Sturm	Zware storm	Tempête	Temporal	Temporal
Backing	Rückdrehender Wind	Krimpende wind	Vent revenant	Rolar el viento	Sentido retrógrado
Gale warning	Sturmwarnung	Stormwaarschuwing	Avis de coup de vent	Aviso de viento duro	Aviso de vento muito forte
Gust	Windstoß	Windvlaag	Rafale	Ráfaga, racha	Rajada
Increasing	Zunehmend	Toenemend	Augmentant	Aumentar	Aumentando
Land breeze	Landbrise	Landbries	Brise de terre	Brisa de tierra	Brisa da terra
Moderating	Abnehmend	Afnemend	Décroissant	Disminuyendo	Decrescendo
Sea breeze	Seebrise	Zeebries	Brise de mer	Brisa de mar	Brisa do mar
Squall	Bö	Windbui	Grain	Turbonada	Borrasca
Variable	Umlaufend	Veranderlijk	Variable	Variable	Variável
Veering	Rechtdrehend	Ruimende wind	Virant	Cambiar	Sentido horário

SAFETY/EMERGENCY	SICHERHEIT/NOTFALL	VEILIGHEID/NOODGEVAL	SECURITE/URGENCE	SEGURIDAD/EMERGENCIAS	SEGURANÇA/EMERGÊNCIAS
Aground	Aufgelaufen	Vastgelopen	Echoué	Encallado	Encalhar
Capsize	Kentern	Omslaan	Sancir, chavirer	Volcó	Virar-se
Coastguard	Küstenwache	Kustwacht	Gendarmerie maritime	Guarda costas	Policia marítima
Collision	Kollision	Aanvaring	Abordage	Colisión, abordaje	Colisão abalroamento
Dismasted	Mastbruch	Mastbreuk	Démâté	Desarbolar	Partir o mastro
Distress	Seenot	Nood	Détresse	Socorro	Distress
Distress flares	Signalraketen	Noodvuurwerk	Fusées de détresse	Bengalas	Fachos de socorro
Dragging anchor	Schlierender Anker	Krabbend anker	Chasser sur l'ancre	Ancla garreando	Ancora agarrar
EPIRB	Seenotfunkboje	EPIRB	Balise de détresse	Baliza	EPIRB
Fire extinguisher	Feuerlöscher	Brandblusser	Extincteur	Extintor	Extintor
Harness, safety	Sicherheitsgurt	Harnas	Harnais	Arnés de seguridad	Cinto de segurança
Help!	Hilfe!	Help!	Au secours!	¡Socorro!	Socorro!
Lifeboat	Rettungsboot	Reddingsboot	Canot de sauvetage	Lancha de salvamento	Barco salva-vidas
Lifejacket	Schwimmweste	Reddingsvest	Gilet de sauvetage	Chaleco salvavidas	Colete de salvação
Liferaft	Rettungsinsel	Reddingsvlot	Radeau de sauvetage	Balsa salvavidas	Jangada de salvação
Man overboard	Mann über Bord	Man over boord	Homme à la mer	Hombre al agua	Homem ao mar
Seacock	Seeventil	Afsluiter	Vanne	Grifos de fondo	Torneira de segurança
Seaworthy	Seetüchtig	Zeewaardig	Marin	Marinero	Condição de navegar
Sinking	Sinken	Zinkend	En train de couler	Hundiendose	Afundate
Tow line	Schleppleine	Sleeplijn	Filin de remorque	Cabo remolque	Cabo de rebocador

MEDICAL	MEDIZINISCHES	MEDISCHE	MEDICALE	MEDICO	MÉDICAS
Antibiotic	Antibiotika	Antibiotica	Antibiotique	Antibiotico	Antibiótico
Bandage	Verband	Verband	Pansement	Vendas	Ligadura
Bleeding	Blutend	Bloeden	Saignement	Sangrando	Sangrar
Burns	Verbrennung	Brandwonden	Brûlures	Quemadura	Queimadura
Concussion	Gehirnerschütterung	Hersenschudding	Traumatisme crânien	Conmoción	Traumatismo
Dehydration	Austrocknung	Uitdroging	Déshydratation	Deshidratación	Desidratação
Dentist	Zahnarzt	Tandarts	Dentiste	Dentista	Dentista
Doctor	Doktor	Dokter/arts	Médecin	Médico	Médico
Drown(ing)	Ertrinken	Verdrinken, (verdrinking)	Noyade, (se noyant)	Ahogarse	Afogar-se

English	Deutsch	Nederlands	Français	Español	Português
Exhaustion	Erschöpfung	Uitputting	Epuisement	Agotamiento	Exausto
Fever	Fieber	Koorts	Fièvre	Fiebre	Febre
First aid	Erste Hilfe	Eerste hulp	Premier secours	Primeros auxillos	Primeiros socorros
Fracture	Fraktur	Breuk	Fracture	Fractura	Fractura
Headache	Kopfschmerz	Hoofdpijn	Mal à la tête	Dolor de cabeza	Dor de cabeça
Heart attack	Herzanfall	Hartaanval	Crise cardiaque	Ataque corazón	Ataque cardíaco
Hospital	Krankenhaus	Ziekenhuis	Hôpital	Hospital	Hospital
Hypothermia	Unterkühlung	Onderkoeling	Hypothermie	Hipotermia	Hipotermia
Illness	Krankheit	Ziekte	Maladie	Enfermo	Doença
Injury	Verletzung	Verwonding	Blessure	Lesión	Lesão
Pain	Schmerz	Pijn	Douleur	Dolor	Dôr
Painkiller(s)	Schmerztabletten	Pijnstillers	Analgésique	analgesico	Analgésico
Poisoning	Vergiftung	Vergiftiging	Empoisonnement	Envenenamiento	Envenenamento
Pulse	Puls	Hartslag	Pouls	Pulso	Pulso
Rest	Ruhen	Rust	Repos	Reposo	Descanso
Seasickness	Seekrankheit	Zeeziekte	Mal de mer	Mareo	Enjoar
Shock	Schock	Shock	Choc	Choque	Choque
Splint	Schiene	Spalk	Attelle	Tablilla	Colocar em talas
Sticking plaster	Heftpflaster	Pleister	Pansement adhésif	Esparadrapo	Adesivo
Stomach upset	Bauchbeschwerden	Maag van streek	Indigestion	Mal de estómago	Cólicas
Stretcher	Trage	Draagbaar	Brancard	Camilla	Maca
Sunburn	Sonnenbrand	Zonnebrand	Coup de soleil	Quemadura del sol	Queimadura de sol
Swelling	Schwellung	Zwelling	Enflure	Hinchazón	Inchaço
Toothache	Zahnschmerzen	Tandpijn	Rage de dents	Dolor de muelas	Dôr dos dentes
Unconscious	Bewußtlos	Bewusteloos	Inconscient	Inconsciente	Inconsciente
Wound	Wunde	Wond	Blessure	Herida	Ferida

THE BOAT	DAS BOOT	DE BOOT	LE BATEAU	EL BARCO	DO BARCO
Rigging and Sails	Rigg und Segel	Tuigage en Zeilen	Gréement et Voiles	Jarcias y Velas	Massame e Velas
Babystay	Babystay	Baby stag	Bas-étai	Babystay	Babystay
Backstay	Achterstag	Achterstag	Pataras	Estay de popa	Brandal fixo da pôpa
Batten	Segellatte	Zeillat	Latte	Sables	Régua
Beating	Kreuzen	Kruisen	Au prés	Ciñendo	Bolinar
Boom	Baum	Giek	Bôme	Botavara	Retranca
Clevis pin	Schäkelbolzen	Borstbout	Axe à anneau brisé	Pasador de seguridad	Perno com troço de argola
Foresail	Vorsegel	Voorzeil	Voile avant/foc	Foque	Pana de proa
Forestay	Vorstag	Voorstag	Etai	Estay de proa	Estai real
Genoa	Genua	Genua	Génois	Génova	Genoa
Halyard	Fall	Val	Drisse	Driza	Adriça
Jib	Fock	Fok	Foc	Foque	Fiocco
Mainsail	Großegel	Grootzeil	Grand' voile	Mayor	Vela grande
Mast	Mast	Mast	Mât	Mast	Mastro
Mast track	Mastschiene	Mastrail	Rail	Carril	Calha do mastro
Mizzen	Besan	Bezaan	Artimon	Mesana	Mezena
Reaching	Raumschots	Ruime wind	Au portant	Viento a través	A um largo
Rod kicker	Rod kicker	Giekophouder	Hale-bas rigide	Contra rigido	Rod kicker
Roller reefing foresail	Rollfock	Rolfock	Génois à enrouleur	Enrollador de génova	Genoa de enrolar
Running	Vorm Wind	Voor de wind	Vent arrière	Viento à favor	Vento à pôpa
Sheet	Schot	Schoot	Ecoute	Escota	Escota
Shrouds	Wanten	Wanten	Haubans	Obenques	Enxarcia
Spinnaker	Spinnaker	Spinnaker	Spi	Spi	Spinnaker
Spinnaker boom	Spinnakerbaum	Spinnaker boom	Tangon de spi	Tangon	Pau de spinnaker
Spreader, crosstree	Saling	Zaling	Barre de flèche	Crucetas	Vaus
Staysail	Stagsegel	Stagzeil	Trinquette	Trinqueta	Estai

English	Deutsch	Nederlands	Français	Español	Português
Storm jib	Sturmfok	Stormfok	Tourmentin	Tormentin	Estai de tempo
Topping lift	Dirk (for the boom)	Kraanlijn, Dirk	Balancine	Amantillo	Amantilho
Trysail	Trysegel	Stormzeil, Trysail	Voile de cape	Vela de capa	Cachapana
Upwind	Am Wind	Aan de wind/te loevert	Au vent	Vienta en contra	Bolinando
Whipping twine	Takelgarn	Takelgaren	Fil à surlier	Piolilla	Cordão de pequeña bitola
Working jib	Arbeitsfock	Werkfok	Foc de route	Foque	Estai
On deck	**An Deck**	**Aan dek**	**Sur le pont**	**En cubierta**	**No convés**
Aft	Achtern, achteraus	Achter, achteruit	En arrière	Atrás	À ré
Ahead	Voraus	Vooruit	Par l'avant	Avante	À proa
Anchor	Anker	Anker	Ancre	Ancla	Ferro
Anchor chain	Ankerkette	Ankerketting	Chaîne d'ancre	Cadena	Amarra
Anchor warp	Ankerleine	Ankerlijn	Orin	Cabo de fondeo	Espia do ferro
Astern	achtern	Achteruit, slaan	Par l'arrière	Hacia atrás	À popa
Block	Block	Blok	Poulie	Motón	Moitão
Bow	Bug	Boeg	Etrave	Proa	Proa
Bridgedeck	Brückendeck	Brugdek	Bridgedeck	Cubierta de puente	Pavimento da ponte
Cockpit	Cockpit	Cockpit	Cockpit	Bañera	Cockpit
Deck	Deck	Dek	Pont	Cubierta	Convés
Dinghy, Tender	Jolle, Beiboot	Bijboot	Annexe	Chinchorro, Bote	Escaler, Côco
Fender	Fender	Stootwil	Défense	Defensa	Defensa
Inflatable (dinghy)	Schlauchboot	Opblaasbare boot	Gonflable	Bote hinchable	Inflável
Ladder	Leiter	Ladder, Trap	Echelle	Escala	Escada
Pulpit	Bugkorb	Preekstoel	Balcon avant	Púlpito	Guarda proeiro
Pushpit	Heckkorb	Hekrailing	Balcon arrière	Balcón de popa	Varandim
Railing	Reling	Railing	Filières	Guardamencebos	
Rope	Tauwerk	Touw	Cordage	Cabo, Cuerda, Cabulleria	Cabo, Corda
Rudder	Ruder	Roer	Safran, Gouvernail	Pala de Timón	Leme
Shackle	Schäkel	Sluiting	Manille	Grillete	Manilha
Ship	Schiff	Schip	Navire	Buque	Navio
Stanchion	Seerelingsstütze	Scepter	Chandelier	Candelero	Balaústre
Stern	Heck	Spiegel/hek	Arrière	Popa	Popa
Superstructure	Aufbau	Opbouw	Superstructure	Superestructura	Super-estrutura
Tiller	Pinne	Helmstok	Barre franche	Caña	Cana de leme
Toe rail	Fußleiste	Voetrail	Rail de fargue	Regala	Amurada inferior
Topsides	Rumpfseiten	Bovenwaterschip	Oeuvres mortes	Obra muerta	Costada
Wheel, steering	Steuerrad	Stuurwiel	Barre à roue	Rueda	Roda do leme
Winch	Winsch	Lier	Winch	Winche	Molinete
Windlass, capstan	Ankerwinsch	Ankerlier, Kaapstander	Guindeau	Molinete	Molinete do ferro
Yacht, sailing	Segelyacht	Zeilboot	Voilier	Velero	Veleiro
Below deck	**Unter Deck**	**Onderdeks**	**Sous le pont**	**Bajo cubierta**	**Abaixo do convés**
Bilge	Bilge	Bilge	Galbord	Sentina	Esgôto
Bilge keel	Kimmkiel	Kimkiel	Bi-quilles	Quillas	Quilha dupla
Bilge pump	Bilgepumpe	Bilge pomp	Pompe de cale	Bomba de achique	Bomba de esgoto
Cabin	Kajüte	Kajuit	Cabine	Cabina	Cabine
Calorifier	Wärmespender	Verwarming	Echangeur de chaleur	Calentador	Calorifico
Companionway	Niedergang	Opgang	Descente	Entrada cámera	Escotilha de passagem
Deckhead	Kajütdach	Kajuitdak	Tête de pont	Techo de cabina	Cabeço do convés
Fin keel	Kurzkiel	Vinkiel	Quille courte	Quilla de aleta	Patilhão
Fresh water tank	Frischwassertank	Drinkwatertank	Réservoir d'eau douce	Tanque de agua dulce	Tanque de aguada
Galley	pantry/Kombüse	Kombuis	Cuisine	Cocina	Cozinha
Gas alarm	Gasmelder	Gasalarm	Alarme anti-gaz	Alarma de gas	Alarme de gás
Holding tank	Schmutzwassertank	Vuilwatertank	Réservoir à eaux usées	Tanque aguas negras	Deposito de esgotos
Hull	Rumpf	Romp	Coque	Carena	Casco

English	Deutsch	Nederlands	Français	Español	Português
Keel	Kiel	Kiel	Quille	Quilla	Quilha
Long keel	Langkiel	Langkieler	Quille longue	Quilla corrida	Quilha corrida
Oven	Backofen	Oven	Four	Horno	Forno
Skeg	Skeg	Scheg	Talon	Skeg	Skeg
Underwater hull	Unterwasserschiff	Onderwaterschip	Oeuvres vives	Obra viva	Obras vivas
ELECTRICS	**ELEKTROTECHNIK**	**ELECTRICITEIT**	**ELECTRIQUES**	**ELECTRICOS**	**ELECTRICO**
Alternator	Wechselstromgenerator	Generator	Alternateur	Alternador	Alternador
Battery	Batterie	Accu, batterij	Batterie/accumulateur	Batería	Bateria
Battery charger	Batterieladegerät	Acculader	Chargeur de batterie	Cargador debatería	Carregador debateria
Bulb	Glühbirne	Lamp	Ampoule	Bombilla	Lâmpada
Circuit breaker	Ausschalter	Automaat	Disjoncteur	Disyuntor	Interruptor
Coil	Spule	Spoel	Bobine	Bobina	Bobine
Dynamo	Lichtmaschine	Dynamo	Dynamo	Dinamo	Dinâmo
Electrical wiring	Elektrik	Elektrische bedrading	Réseau électrique	Circuito eléctrico	Circuito electrico
Fuse	Sicherung	(Hoofd)Zekering	Fusible	Fusible	Fusivel
Invertor	Wechselrichter	Inverter	Convertisseur	Inverter	Inversor
Regulator (voltage)	Spannungsregler	Spanningsregelaar	Régulateur de tension	Regulador	Regulador
Shore power	Landanschluß	Walstroom	Courant de secteur	Corriente de tierra	Corrente alterna
Solar panel	Solarzellen	Zonnepaneel	Paneau solaire	Placa solar	Painel solar
Soldering iron	Lötkolben	Soldeerbout	fer à souder	Soldador eléctrico	ferro de soldar
Switch	Schalter	Schakelaar	Interrupteur	Interruptor	Interruptor
THE ENGINE	**DER MOTOR**	**DE MOTOR**	**LE MOTEUR**	**EL MOTOR**	**DO MOTOR**
Air filter	Luftfilter	Luchtfilter	Filtre à air	Filtro a aire	Filtro de ar
Carburettor	Vergaser	Carburateur	Carburateur	Carburador	Carburador
Cooling water	Kühlwasser	Koelwater	Eau de refroidissement	Agua refrigerado	Agua fresca
Diesel	Diesel	Dieselolie	Gazole	Gas-oil	Gasóleo
Drive belt	Treibriemen	Aandrijfriem	Courroie d'entrainement	Correa de transmisión	Correia
Engine mount	Motorfundament	Motorsteun	Support moteur	Bancada del motor	Fixe do motor
Engine oil	Motoröl	Motorolie	Huile de moteur	Aceite de motor	Óleo do motor
Exhaust pipe	Auspuff	Uitlaat	Tuyau d'échappement	Tubo de escape	Tubo de escape
Fuel filter	Kraftstoffilter	Brandstoffilter	Filtre de carburant	Filtro de combustible	Filtro de gasóleo
Fuel tank	Tank, Brennstofftank	Brandstof tank	Réservoir à carburant	Tanque de combustible	Tanque de combustivel
Gasket	Dichtung	Pakking	Joint	Empaquetadura junta	Junta
Gearbox	Getriebekasten	Keerkoppeling	Boîte de vitesses	Caja de cambio	Caixa de velocidades
Grease	Fett	Vet	Graisse	Grasa	Massa
Head gasket	Zylinderkopfdichtung	Koppakking	Joint de culasse	Junta de culata	Junta do cabeça
Injector	Einspritzdüse	Injector, Verstuiver	Injecteur	Inyector	Injector
Jubilee clip	Schlauchklemme	Slangklem	Collier de serrage	Abrazadera	Abraçadeira ajustàavel
Methylated spirits	Brennspiritus	Spiritus/Methylalcohol	Alcool à brûler	Alcohol desnaturalizada	Alcool metilico
Oil filter	Ölfilter	Oliefilter	Filtre à huile	Filtro de aceite	Filtro de óleo
Outboard motor	Außenbordmotor	Buitenboordmotor	Moteur hors-bord	Motor fuerabordas	Motor fora de borda
Paraffin	petroleum	Petroleum, Kerosine	Kérosène, Pétrole	Petróleo, Keroseno	Petróleo
P-bracket	Wellenlagerbock	Schroefas uithouder	Support d'hélice	Casquillo	Polée em P
Petrol	Benzin	Benzine	Essence	Gasolina	Gasolina
Propeller	Propeller, Schraube	Schroef	Hélice	Hélice	Hélice
Propeller shaft	Schraubenwelle	Schroefas	Arbre d'hélice	Eje de la hélice	Veio do hélice
Spark plug	Zündkerze	Bougie	Bougie	Bujía	Vela
Starter	Anlasser	Startmotor	Démarreur	Motor de arranque	Motor de arranque
Stern gland	Stopfbuchse	Schroefasdoorvoer	Presse étoupe	Bocina	Bucim
Throttle	Gas	Gashendel	Accélérateur	Acelerador	Acelerador
Two-stroke	Zweitakt	Tweetakt	A deux temps	Dos tiempos	De dois tempos
Water pump	Wasserpumpe	Waterpomp	Pompe à eau	Bomba de agua	Bomba de água

2

Regulations

2.1 CRUISING FORMALITIES

Before your annual cruise check that Yacht and Personal documents are in-date. It saves time, especially abroad, if all documents are in transparent files for easy inspection.

Yacht documents
Registration certificate (2.1.1). Marine insurance valid for the intended cruising area, including adequate third-party cover (2.1.2). Proof of VAT status (2.4). Ship's radio licence (5.4.3). Ship's Log, itinerary and a crew list.

Personal documents
Valid passports and European health insurance card (8.2). Radio Operator's certificate of competence (5.4.3).

International Certificate of Competence
An International Certificate of Competence (ICC) (Pleasure Craft), valid for 5 years, is required in most European countries, especially those whose inland waterways are to be cruised. It can be endorsed for power or sail, inland or coastal waters, or all four.

The inland waterways endorsement requires a short, written test on CEVNI (ColRegs and buoyage in European inland waterways), but this does not apply to UK inland waterways. If evidence of Competence (eg Day Skipper or above) is not held, a practical test must be passed before the ICC is issued. E-mail certification@rya.org.uk or call ☎ 0845 345 0376.

Health regulations
Comply with health regulations (eg report any infectious disease); check if vaccination certificates are needed.

2.1.1 Registration
The Merchant Shipping Act 1995 and related Merchant Shipping (Registration of Ships) Regulations govern the registration of British ships in the UK.

The Register of British Ships is in 4 parts, covering:

Part I   Merchant ships and pleasure vessels.
Part II   Fishing vessels.
Part III   Small ships (Small Ships Register).
Part IV   Bareboat charter ships.

- Registration under Part I is a relatively complex and expensive business (£124), since a yacht has to be surveyed and follows the same procedure as a large merchant vessel. It costs £49 to renew for 5 years. The certificate establishes the ship's nationality and tonnage. Details of registered ownership and mortgages can be obtained from the RSS at Cardiff.

- Part III, *The Small Ships Register (SSR)*, is for owners who want a simple registration, to prove the yacht's nationality and meet registration requirement for a privileged ensign, but it registers neither 'Title' nor mortgages. A small ship is defined as < 24m LOA. The cost is £25 for five years, and measurement only requires taking the boat's LOA.

Application forms and the online SSR registration service are at www.ukshipregister.co.uk. For further details contact the UK Ship Register-RSS, Anchor Court, Keen Road, Cardiff CF24 5JW. ☎ 029 2044 8800; 🖷 029 2044 8820. rss@mcga.gov.uk

2.1.2 Insurance
Every cruising boat should be adequately insured against loss or damage. The insured value should be the cost of replacing the boat and all equipment. Third-party cover for up to £3,000,000 is also needed. The cruising area must be adjusted and paid for if cruising beyond the usual limits. Failure to disclose all relevant facts may invalidate a policy.

2.2 HM REVENUE & CUSTOMS (HMR&C)

2.2.1 The European Union (EU)
EU yachtsmen can move freely within the EU, provided Customs duty, VAT, or any other Customs charges, have been paid in an EU country. Most nations make random checks on yachts and you may be asked for evidence that VAT, or its equivalent, has been paid on your vessel. See 2.3 for notes on using UK-bought red diesel overseas. See also 2.3.1.

EU members are listed in Notice No 8. The Channel Islands and the Canary Islands do not operate a VAT system under EU rules, and are therefore treated as outside the EU.

2.2.2 Customs Notice No 8 (Dec 2002)
This Notice *'Sailing your pleasure craft to and from the UK'* (with Update 2 of April 2004) is the UK's interpretation of what the law says about pleasure craft and compliance with HM Revenue & Customs requirements, as summarised below; it is a good idea to have a copy aboard.

This Notice and further information may be obtained from the National Advice Service, ☎ 0845 010 9000 or +44 208 929 0152, which is open M-F, 0800-2000. Or visit HM Revenue & Customs website at: **www.hmrc.gov.uk**

Yachtsmen are warned that a boat may be searched at any time. Penalties are severe for non-declaration of prohibited or restricted goods, and the carriage and non-declaration of prohibited drugs and firearms. If goods are smuggled the vessel may be seized and the persons concerned may be liable to prosecution, a heavy fine and/or prison sentence.

2.2.3 Duty-free stores
Duty-free stores may be allowed on vessels going south of Brest or north of the N bank of the R. Eider (Denmark), by prior application to a Customs office. Duty-free stores cannot be taken to the Republic of Ireland nor to the Channel Islands. Contact the National Advice Service for details of how to embark stores and of the conditions to be satisfied. For more information read Notice 69A *Duty free ship's stores*.

2.2.4 C1331 Pleasure craft departing the UK
- To another EU country: No report is needed, unless a Customs Officer asks for one.
- To a country which is outside the EU:

You must notify HM Customs of your departure on Form C1331, Part 1 *'Leaving the UK'*, available from most YCs, marinas, Customs offices, the National Advice Service or via the HMR&C website. Before you expect to leave the UK, return the completed Part 1 to a Customs Officer, put it in a Customs post box or take/post it to a Customs office. C1331 is valid for 48 hrs from the stated time of departure. If departure is not notified, delay, inconvenience and possible prosecution may result on return. Keep Part 2 *'Arriving in the UK'* on board for use on your return. If your voyage is abandoned, Part 2, marked 'Voyage abandoned', should be returned to where the original form was sent.

2.2.5 Arrival from an EU country
If arriving directly from another EU country there is no need to fly flag 'Q', complete any paperwork, or contact Customs. You must, however, contact the Customs 'Yachtline' on 0845 723 1110 if you have goods to declare, or have non-EU nationals on board. You must also declare animals or birds; prohibited or restricted goods, eg controlled drugs, firearms, radio transmitters not accepted in the UK; counterfeit goods; duty-free stores; or the boat itself if duty and VAT are owed on it. Further details are in *Notice No 1*.

2.2.6 Arrival from a non-EU country

If arriving directly from a non-EU country (including the Channel Islands), yachts are subject to Customs control. When inside the 12-mile limit, ie UK Territorial Waters, fly flag 'Q' where most easily seen (lowering it when formalities are complete); and fill in Part 2 of Form C1331.

On arrival, call the Customs 'Yachtline' 0845 723 1110 and inform them if: VAT has not been paid on the vessel; goods in excess of your allowances as detailed in Notice 1, or duty-free stores are on board; you have prohibited or restricted goods; a crew has a notifiable illness or needs immigration clearance; repairs or modifications (not running repairs) have been made since leaving the EU.

Comply with any instructions from the Customs Officer; failure to do so may incur a penalty. Do not land anybody or goods or transfer them to another vessel until a Customs Officer says you may.

2.2.7 Immigration

In most yachting centres the Customs Officer also acts as the Immigration Officer. The skipper is responsible for ensuring that any non-EU national aboard gets an Immigration Officer's permission to enter the UK from any country except the Isle of Man, the Channel Islands or ROI.

2.2.8 Customs telephone numbers

The National Yachtline (☎ 0845 723 1110) must only be used by yachtsmen wishing to clear Customs on return to the UK from a non-EU country (2.2.6). Use the National Advice Service (☎ 0845 010 9000) for all other Customs queries and requests for forms and notices.

2.2.9 Drug smuggling

The prevention of drug smuggling is a key role for HMR&C. Public support is very important. If you see a suspicious incident or know of suspicious activity, call 0800 595000. This is a 24 hours, 7/7 free and anonymous hotline. There may be a reward.

2.3 FOREIGN CUSTOMS

Other EU countries should apply the regulations outlined in 2.2.1 to 2.2.6 above, and any Customs formalities are likely to be minimal. If boarded by Customs, stay polite and helpful at all times. Before departure, skippers are recommended to check the procedures in force in their destination country.

Diesel: Keep receipts for red diesel bought in the UK and stored in main fuel tank (marked 'duty paid' if possible); also log engine hours.

2.3.1 The Schengen Treaty

In 1985 France, Germany, Luxembourg, Netherlands and Belgium signed a Convention which abolished internal border controls, establishing a single external border, around what is sometimes called 'Schengen-land'. Today all 25 EU members, except the UK and Eire, are signatories to Schengen and the decisions taken since 1985 are now part of EU law.

Those travelling from the UK to a Schengen country, or vice versa, are crossing the external border and may be subject to additional checks. Thus, Belgium and the Netherlands require a vessel to report on arrival *even if coming from another EU country*. The RYA national forms available for download from their website (www.rya.org.uk/boatingabroad/Pages/customsformalities.aspx), which are simply a crew list (DoB, place of birth, passport No, nationality) and brief itinerary (last/next ports, dates etc).

In practice these forms are not always requested, but if you have them aboard you may avoid fines which can legally be imposed for not observing Schengen/EU law. On arrival check with the HM whether any Customs or Immigration forms need to be completed.

2.4 VAT AND THE SINGLE MARKET

An EU resident can move a yacht between member states without restriction, providing VAT has been paid. Documentary evidence supporting a vessel's VAT status should be carried at all times.

A leaflet *UK guide for Yachts,* available on the Customs website, gives further advice; see also *Notice 8*, section 6.

2.4.1 Temporary Importation (TI)

TI is a complex process likely to affect few yachtsmen. The maximum stay in the EU is 18 months. See *Notice 8*, Section 5 and *Notice 308*, available on the Customs website or from the National Advice Service. On arrival in the UK fill in Form C108 as well as the usual Form C1331.

2.5 INTERNATIONAL REGULATIONS FOR PREVENTING COLLISIONS AT SEA

The 1972 International Regulations for Preventing Collisions at Sea (IRPCS) are also referred to as the Colregs or Rule of the Road. They should be read as an entity, with the explanatory notes and associated diagrams below. See also *Learning the Rule of the Road* (Basil Mosenthal/ACN), the RYA booklet G2 and *The Mariner's Handbook* NP 100.

Because the exact wording of certain Rules is very important, Rules 2, 3 (in part), 5–10, 12–19 and 25 are quoted verbatim in *blue italics* and then briefly discussed – especially those of specific interest to yachtsmen. This does not imply that this chapter should be consulted in the heat of the moment – since all mariners must have a sound working knowledge of the Rules – but an aide-memoire is sometimes handy.

2.5.1 Part A: General

Rule 1 (Application) is mainly introductory and therefore not quoted verbatim, but note that many harbours have their own local rules – which must be obeyed.

Rule 2 (Responsibility).

(a) Nothing in these Rules shall exonerate any vessel, or the owner, master or crew thereof, from the consequences of any neglect to comply with these Rules or of the neglect of any precaution which may be required by the ordinary practice of seamen, or by the special circumstances of the case.

(b) In construing and applying these Rules due regard shall be had to all dangers of navigation and collision and to all special circumstances, including the limitations of the vessels involved, which may make a departure from these Rules necessary to avoid immediate danger.

The Rules must be interpreted in a seamanlike way. No vessel has a 'right of way' over another regardless of special circumstances – eg other vessels under way or at anchor, shallow water, poor visibility, TSS, fishing fleets, etc – or the handling characteristics of the vessels concerned in the prevailing conditions. Sometimes vessels may need to depart from the Rules to avoid immediate danger (2b).

Rule 3 (Definitions). The following are selected extracts:

(c) 'Sailing vessel' means any vessel under sail provided that propelling machinery, if fitted, is not being used.

(f) *'Vessel not under command' means one which through some exceptional circumstance is unable to manoeuvre as required by these Rules and is therefore unable to keep out of the way of another vessel.*

(g) *'Vessel restricted in her ability to manoeuvre' means one which from the nature of her work is thus restricted ... (6 examples are given)*

(h) *'Vessel constrained by her draught' means a power-driven vessel which, because of her draught in relation to the available depth and width of navigable water is severely restricted in her ability to deviate from the course she is following.*

(i) *'Underway' means that a vessel is not at anchor, or made fast to the shore, or aground. (Note: 'Making way' means progressing through the water, rather than drifting.)*

(l) *'Restricted visibility' means any condition in which visibility is restricted by fog, mist, falling snow, heavy rainstorms, sandstorms or any other similar causes.*

(m) *A 'Wing-in-Ground (WIG) craft' means a multimodal craft which, in its main operational mode, flies in close proximity to the surface by utilising surface-effect action.*

2.5.2 Part B: Steering and Sailing Rules
Section I – In any condition of visibility

Rule 4 (Application) is self-explanatory. In complying with Rules 4–18 ask yourself, and answer, the following three questions and take action if so required:

> - Is there a risk of collision?
> - If there is, am I the give-way vessel?
> - If I am, what action must I take?

This is not part of the IRPCS, but it concentrates the mind.

Rule 5 (Look-out).

Every vessel shall at all times maintain a proper look-out by sight and hearing as well as by all available means appropriate in the prevailing circumstances and conditions so as to make a full appraisal of the situation and of the risk of collision.

Look-out means not only by eyes and ears, but also by radar and VHF, especially at night or in low visibility. Do not neglect blind arcs, eg look below the genoa and directly to windward. Rule 5 is arguably the most important Rule of all.

Rule 6 (Safe speed).

Every vessel shall at all times proceed at a safe speed so that she can take proper and effective action to avoid collision and be stopped within a distance appropriate to the prevailing circumstances and conditions so as to make a full appraisal of the situation and of the risk of collision. In determining a safe speed the following factors are among those taken into account:

(a) *By all vessels:*
   (i) *the state of visibility;*
   (ii) *the traffic density including concentrations of fishing vessels or any other vessels;*
   (iii) *the manoeuvrability of the vessel with special reference to stopping distance and turning ability in the prevailing conditions;*
   (iv) *at night the presence of background light such as from shore lights or from back scatter of her own lights;*
   (v) *the state of wind, sea and current, and the proximity of navigational hazards;*
   (vi) *the draught in relation to the available depth of water;*

(b) *Additionally, by vessels with operational radar:*
   (i) *the characteristics, efficiency and limitations of the radar equipment;*
   (ii) *any constraints imposed by the radar range scale in use;*
   (iii) *the effect on radar detection of the sea state, weather and other sources of interference;*
   (iv) *the possibility that small vessels, ice and other floating objects may not be detected by radar at an adequate range;*
   (v) *the number, location and movement of vessels detected by radar;*
   (vi) *the more exact assessment of the visibility that may be possible when radar is used to determine the range of vessels or other objects in the vicinity.*

The conditions which determine what is a safe speed are clearly listed. Excessive speed gives less time to assess the situation and take avoiding action, and produces a worse collision if such action fails. Even 4 knots may be too fast in a crowded river.

Rule 7 (Risk of collision).

(a) *Every vessel shall use all available means appropriate to the prevailing circumstances and conditions to determine if risk of collision exists. If there is any doubt such risk shall be deemed to exist.*

(b) *Proper use shall be made of radar equipment if fitted and operational, including long-range scanning to obtain early warning of risk of collision and radar plotting or equivalent systematic observation of detected objects.*

(c) *Assumptions shall not be made on the basis of scanty information, especially scanty radar information.*

(d) *In determining if risk of collision exists the following considerations shall be among those taken into account:*
   (i) *such risk shall be deemed to exist if the compass bearing of an approaching vessel does not appreciably change;*
   (ii) *such risk may sometimes exist even when an appreciable bearing change is evident, particularly*

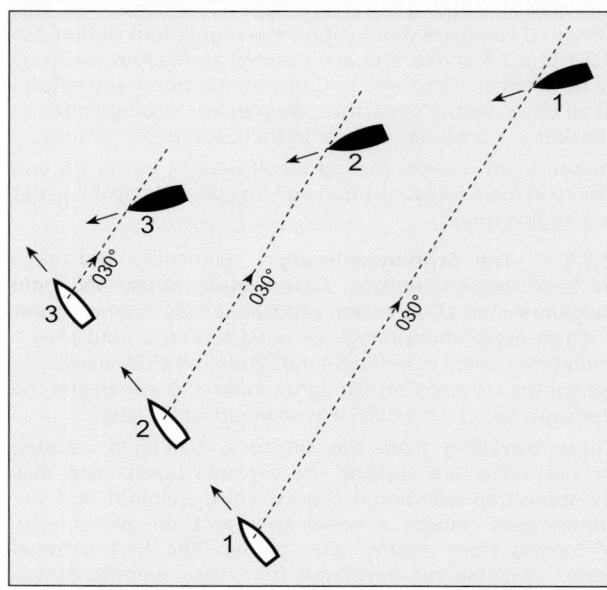

Fig 2(1) Rule 7. The bearing of black from white is steady on 030°. Well before reaching position 2, white should have altered to starboard by at least 45° to pass astern of black.

when approaching a very large vessel or a tow or when approaching a vessel at close range.

A yacht should take a series of compass bearings on a closing ship. Unless the bearings change appreciably, a risk of collision exists; see Fig 2(1). If in doubt, assume that there is a risk. Radar, properly used, offers early warning of risk of collision, but careful systematic plotting of contacts is needed to obtain maximum collision-avoidance data.

Rule 8 (Action to avoid collision).

(a) *Any action taken to avoid collision shall be taken in accordance with the Rules of this Part and shall, if the circumstances of the case admit, be positive, made in ample time and with due regard to the observance of good seamanship.*

(b) *Any alteration of course and/or speed to avoid collision shall, if the circumstances of the case admit, be large enough to be readily apparent to another vessel observing visually or by radar; a succession of small alterations of course and/or speed should be avoided.*

(c) *If there is sufficient sea room, alteration of course alone may be the most effective action to avoid a close-quarters situation provided that it is made in good time, is substantial and does not result in another close-quarters situation.*

(d) *Action taken to avoid collision with another vessel shall be such as to result in passing at a safe distance. The effectiveness of the action shall be carefully checked until the other vessel is finally past and clear.*

(e) *If necessary to avoid collision or allow more time to assess the situation, a vessel shall slacken her speed or take all way off by stopping or reversing her means of propulsion.*

(f) (i) *A vessel which by any of these Rules is required not to impede the passage or safe passage of another vessel shall, when required by the circumstances of the case, take early action to allow sufficient sea room for the safe passage of the other vessel.*

   (ii) *A vessel required not to impede the passage or safe passage of another vessel is not relieved of this obligation if approaching the other vessel so as to involve risk of collision and shall, when taking action, have full regard to the action which may be required by the Rules of this Part.*

   (iii) *A vessel the passage of which is not to be impeded remains fully obliged to comply with the Rules of this Part when the two vessels are approaching one another so as to involve risk of collision.*

Any such actions must be positive, seamanlike and taken early. Large alterations of course and/or speed are more obvious to the other vessel, especially at night or on radar. Turn away (even through 180°), slow down, stop (or go astern). In avoiding one vessel, watch out for others.

Rule 9 (Narrow channels).

(a) *A vessel proceeding along the course of a narrow channel or fairway shall keep as near to the outer limit of the channel or fairway which lies on her starboard side as is safe and practicable.*

(b) *A vessel of less than 20 metres in length or a sailing vessel shall not impede the passage of a vessel which can safely navigate only within a narrow channel or fairway.*

(c) *A vessel engaged in fishing shall not impede the passage of any other vessel navigating within a narrow channel or fairway.*

(d) *A vessel shall not cross a narrow channel or fairway if such crossing impedes the passage of a vessel which can safely navigate only within such channel or fairway. The latter vessel may use the sound signal prescribed in Rule 34 (d) if in doubt as to the intention of the crossing vessel.*

(e) (i) *In a narrow channel or fairway when overtaking can take place only if the vessel to be overtaken has to take action to permit safe passing, the vessel intending to overtake shall indicate her intention by sounding the appropriate signal prescribed in Rule 34 (c) (i). The vessel to be overtaken shall, if in agreement, sound the appropriate signal prescribed in Rule 34 (c) (ii) and take steps to permit safe passing. If in doubt she may sound the signals prescribed in Rule 34 (d).*

   (ii) *This Rule does not relieve the overtaking vessel of her obligation under Rule 13.*

(f) *A vessel nearing a bend or an area of a narrow channel or fairway where other vessels may be obscured by an intervening obstruction shall navigate with particular alertness and caution and shall sound the appropriate signal prescribed in Rule 34 (e).*

(g) *Any vessel shall, if the circumstances of the case admit, avoid anchoring in a narrow channel.*

Rule 9 (a) requires a vessel … to keep as near to the starboard side of a narrow channel as is safe and practicable. Yachts and other small craft can often keep outside the channel altogether, thus ensuring even greater safety.

Rule 10 (Traffic Separation Schemes).

(a) *This Rule applies to traffic separation schemes adopted by the Organization (IMO) and does not relieve any vessel of her obligation under any other Rule.*

(b) *A vessel using a traffic separation scheme shall:*
   (i) *proceed in the appropriate traffic lane in the general direction of traffic flow for that lane;*
   (ii) *so far as practicable keep clear of a traffic separation line or separation zone;*
   (iii) *normally join or leave a traffic lane at the termination of the lane, but when joining or leaving from either side shall do so at as small an angle to the general direction of traffic flow as practicable.*

(c) *A vessel shall so far as practicable avoid crossing traffic lanes, but if obliged to do so shall cross on a heading as nearly as practicable at right angles to the general direction of traffic flow.*

(d) (i) *A vessel shall not use an inshore traffic zone when she can safely use the appropriate traffic lane within the adjacent traffic separation scheme. However, vessels of less than 20 metres in length, sailing vessels and vessels engaged in fishing may use the inshore traffic zone.*

   (ii) *Notwithstanding sub-paragraph (d) (i) a vessel may use an inshore traffic zone when en route to or from a port, offshore installation or structure, pilot station or any other place situated within the traffic zone, or to avoid immediate danger.*

(e) *A vessel other than a crossing vessel or a vessel joining or leaving a lane shall not normally enter a separation zone or cross a separation line except:*
   (i) *in cases of emergency to avoid immediate danger;*
   (ii) *to engage in fishing within a separation zone.*

(f) A vessel navigating in areas near the terminations of traffic separation schemes shall do so with particular caution.

(g) A vessel shall so far as practicable avoid anchoring in a traffic separation scheme or in areas near its terminations.

(h) A vessel not using a traffic separation scheme shall avoid it by as wide a margin as is practicable.

(i) A vessel engaged in fishing shall not impede the passage of any vessel following a traffic lane.

(j) A vessel of less than 20 metres in length or a sailing vessel shall not impede the safe passage of a power-driven vessel following a traffic lane.

(k) A vessel restricted in her ability to manoeuvre when engaged in an operation for the maintenance of safety of navigation in a traffic separation scheme is exempted from complying with this Rule to the extent necessary to carry out the operation.

(l) A vessel restricted in her ability to manoeuvre when engaged in an operation for the laying, servicing or picking up of a submarine cable, within a traffic separation scheme, is exempted from complying with this Rule to the extent necessary to carry out the operation.

TSS are essential to the safety of larger vessels and are shown in Chapter 9 and on most charts. Whilst inconvenient for yachtsmen, TSS shall be avoided where possible, or accepted as another element of passage planning. All vessels, including yachts, must comply with Rule 10.

Fig 2(2) illustrates how to cross a TSS (10c). Note well that craft <20m LOA, and any sailing yacht, shall not impede a power vessel using a traffic lane (10j). However, when two vessels meet or converge in a TSS with a risk of collision, Rule 10 does not modify any other provisions of the IRPCS.

Fig 2(2) Rule 10c. A yacht crossing a TSS lane shall head at right angles to the lane axis, as in (a), regardless of the course made good as a result of wind or tidal streams. Yacht (b) is not heading at right angles and is therefore contravening Rule 10(c).

Yachts should use inshore traffic zones (ITZ). It is unusual and certainly undesirable for yachts to use TSS lanes, due to the substantial speed difference between yachts and large vessels. Yachts using TSS lanes may be told by the monitoring radar station (eg Dover CG, CROSS Corsen) to leave asap.

2.5.3 Section II – Vessels in sight of one another
Rule 11 (Application) is self explanatory.

Rule 12 (Sailing vessels).
(a) When two sailing vessels are approaching one another,

so as to involve risk of collision, one of them shall keep out of the way of the other as follows:

(i) when each has the wind on a different side, the vessel which has the wind on the port side shall keep out of the way of the other;

(ii) when both have the wind on the same side, the vessel which is to windward shall keep out of the way of the vessel which is to leeward;

(iii) if a vessel with the wind on the port side sees a vessel to windward and cannot determine with certainty whether the other vessel has the wind on the port or on the starboard side, she shall keep out of the way of the other.

(b) For the purposes of this Rule the windward side shall be deemed to be the side opposite to that on which the mainsail is carried or, in the case of a square-rigged vessel, the side opposite to that on which the largest fore-and-aft sail is carried.

Rule 12 does not apply if either yacht is motor sailing. When two yachts under sail are at risk of collision, (a) (i) and (ii) are clear.

(a) (iii) applies where it is unclear which tack a windward yacht is on. Fig 2(3) illustrates the practical application of Rule 12 in these three cases.

Fig 2(3) Rule 12. A port tack yacht keeps clear. If both yachts are on the same tack the windward boat keeps clear. If in doubt, port tack always keeps clear.

Rule 12 (a) (iii) might also cause doubt in 2 other practical situations:

• The windward side is deemed, Rule 12 (b), to be the side opposite to that on which the mainsail is set or would be set, if sailing under a headsail alone. When sailing under spinnaker alone, windward would be the side on which its boom is set.

- When hove-to, windward is determined by the side on which the mainsail is set, or would be set if not hoisted.

Rule 13 (Overtaking).

(a) *Notwithstanding anything contained in the Rules of Part B, Sections I & II any vessel overtaking any other shall keep out of the way of the vessel being overtaken.*

(b) *A vessel shall be deemed to be overtaking when coming up with another vessel from a direction more than 22½° abaft her beam, that is, in such a position with reference to the vessel she is overtaking, that at night she would be able to see only the sternlight of that vessel but neither of her sidelights.*

(c) *When a vessel is in any doubt as to whether she is overtaking another, she shall assume that this is the case and act accordingly.*

(d) *Any subsequent alteration of the bearing between the two vessels shall not make the overtaking vessel a crossing vessel within the meaning of these Rules or relieve her of the duty of keeping clear of the overtaken vessel until she is finally past and clear.*

An overtaking vessel, whether power or sail, shall keep clear of the vessel being overtaken. It is courteous, but not in the IRPCS, for an overtaking yacht under sail to pass to leeward of the yacht being overtaken.

Rule 14 (Head-on situation).

(a) *When two power-driven vessels are meeting on reciprocal or nearly reciprocal courses so as to involve risk of collision each shall alter her course to starboard so that each shall pass on the port side of the other.*

(b) *Such a situation shall be deemed to exist when a vessel sees the other ahead or nearly ahead and by night she could see the masthead lights of the other in a line or nearly in a line and/or both sidelights and by day she observes the corresponding aspect of the other vessel.*

(c) *When a vessel is in any doubt as to whether such a situation exists she shall assume that it does exist and act accordingly.*

When two power-driven vessels approach head-on, or nearly so, with risk of collision, each must alter course to starboard, to pass port to port. The alteration should be large enough as to be obvious to the other vessel, sounding one short blast, if in audible range, to make intentions clear.

Rule 15 (Crossing situation).

When two power-driven vessels are crossing so as to involve risk of collision, the vessel which has the other on her own starboard side shall keep out of the way and shall, if the circumstances of the case admit, avoid crossing ahead of the other vessel.

The give-way vessel would normally alter to starboard to pass astern of the other. A yacht with limited power and speed should, if possible, avoid crossing ahead of the other. Exceptionally, an alteration to port may be justified (eg shoal water to starboard), in which case a large alteration may be needed to avoid crossing ahead of the other.

Rule 16 (Action by give-way vessel).

Every vessel which is directed to keep out of the way of another vessel shall, so far as possible, take early and substantial action to keep well clear.

'*Early ... substantial ... well clear*' are the key words, ie don't dither, nibble or get into a close-quarters situation.

Rule 17 (Action by stand-on vessel).

(a) (i) *Where one of two vessels is to keep out of the way, the other shall keep her course and speed.*

   (ii) *The latter vessel may however take action to avoid collision by her manoeuvre alone, as soon as it becomes apparent to her that the vessel required to keep out of the way is not taking appropriate action in compliance with these Rules.*

(b) *When, from any cause, the vessel required to keep her course and speed finds herself so close that collision cannot be avoided by the action of the give-way vessel alone, she shall take such action as will best aid to avoid collision.*

(c) *A power-driven vessel which takes action in a crossing situation in accordance with sub-paragraph (a) (ii) of this Rule to avoid collision with another power-driven vessel shall, if the circumstances of the case admit, not alter course to port for a vessel on her own port side.*

(d) *This Rule does not relieve the give-way vessel of her obligation to keep out of the way.*

This Rule describes a deteriorating sequence of events (1–3 below) and the actions that a stand-on vessel may or shall (ie must) take if it appears that the give-way vessel is failing to keep clear.

1. At least in the initial stages, the stand-on vessel should maintain her course/speed (17a.i) for fear of inducing a collision by needless avoiding action of her own.

2. The stand-on vessel may manoeuvre to avoid collision (17a. ii) if it appears that the give-way vessel is failing to keep clear. In so manoeuvring a power-driven vessel shall, if possible, not alter course to port for a vessel on her own port side (17c). Usually she would alter substantially to starboard, to reduce the risk of both vessels turning towards each other.

3. When the stand-on vessel finds herself so close that collision cannot be avoided by the action of the give-way vessel alone, the stand-on vessel *shall* take such action (17b), as will best aid to avoid collision. This is likely to be drastic, eg Full astern and/or helm hard over.

Rule 18 (Responsibilities between vessels).

Except where Rules 9, 10 and 13 otherwise require:

(a) *A power-driven vessel underway shall keep out of the way of:*
   (i) *a vessel not under command;*
   (ii) *a vessel restricted in her ability to manoeuvre;*
   (iii) *a vessel engaged in fishing;*
   (iv) *a sailing vessel.*

(b) *A sailing vessel underway shall keep out of the way of:*
   (i) *a vessel not under command;*
   (ii) *a vessel restricted in her ability to manoeuvre;*
   (iii) *a vessel engaged in fishing.*

(c) *A vessel engaged in fishing when underway shall, so far as possible, keep out of the way of:*
   (i) *a vessel not under command;*
   (ii) *a vessel restricted in her ability to manoeuvre.*

(d) (i) *Any vessel other than a vessel not under command or a vessel restricted in her ability to manoeuvre shall, if the circumstances of the case admit, avoid impeding the safe passage of a vessel constrained by her draught, exhibiting the signals in Rule 28.*

(ii) *A vessel constrained by her draught shall navigate with particular caution having full regard to her special condition.*

(e) *A seaplane on the water shall, in general, keep well clear of all vessels and avoid impeding their navigation. In circumstances, however, where risk of collision exists, she shall comply with the Rules of this Part.*

(f) (i) *A WIG craft shall, when taking off, landing and in flight near the surface, keep well clear of all other vessels and avoid impeding their navigation.*

    (ii) *A WIG craft operating on the water surface shall comply with the Rules of this Part as a power-driven vessel.*

Rule 18 lays down priorities according to manoeuvrability. The hierarchy is clear and logical: (b) applies to yachts. New para (f) includes WIG craft, defined in Rule 3 (m). It flies on an air-cushion created by its own very fast forward speed; it is more an aircraft than a vessel.

2.5.4 Section III – Vessels in restricted visibility
Rule 19 (Restricted visibility).

(a) *This Rule applies to vessels not in sight of one another when navigating in or near an area of restricted visibility.*

(b) *Every vessel shall proceed at a safe speed adapted to the prevailing circumstances and conditions of restricted visibility. A power-driven vessel shall have her engines ready for immediate manoeuvre.*

(c) *Every vessel shall have due regard to the prevailing circumstances and conditions of restricted visibility when complying with the Rules of Section 1 of this Part.*

(d) *A vessel which detects by radar alone the presence of another vessel shall determine if a close-quarters situation is developing and/or risk of collision exists. If so, she shall take avoiding action in ample time, provided that when such action consists of an alteration of course, so far as possible the following shall be avoided:*

    (i) *an alteration of course to port for a vessel forward of the beam, other than for a vessel being overtaken;*

    (ii) *an alteration of course towards a vessel abeam or abaft the beam.*

(e) *Except where it has been determined that a risk of collision does not exist, every vessel which hears apparently forward of her beam the fog signal of another vessel, or which cannot avoid a close-quarters situation with another vessel forward of her beam, shall reduce her speed to the minimum at which she can be kept on her course. She shall if necessary take all her way off and in any event navigate with extreme caution until danger of collision is over.*

This rule can cause difficulty due to misunderstanding and/ or the negative nature of para (d). Stand-on and give-way vessels, as in Section II of the Rules, no longer exist in fog. Every vessel is simply trying to avoid other unseen vessels whose presence, ie fog signal, is only heard or detected by radar. Safe speed (b) is commonsense, but is sometimes ignored by commercial ships. Slowing down to maintain steerage way for a fog signal forward of the beam (e) has limited application to an already slow-moving yacht.

Radar can save your life, but only if it is efficiently used and correctly interpreted by an experienced operator. Rule 7c warns against making assumptions based on scanty information, especially radar information. AIS, if

fitted and switched on in both vessels, may resolve such assumptions.

If a vessel is detected by radar alone (d), decide whether a collision risk exists and/or a close-quarters situation is developing. If so, take early action to avoid collision.

(d) (i) and (ii) tell you what you should *avoid* doing. Try to envisage the situations which these two clauses address. It may help to transpose their words into more positive terms:

> • Turn to starboard in all cases except for a vessel on or abaft your starboard beam, or for a vessel being overtaken.

Safety dictates that you should: sound the appropriate fog signal, keep a good look-out, deploy an efficient radar reflector and use radar if fitted. Consider also using the engine to assist manoeuvrability, especially in light winds. In thick fog it is best to anchor in shallow water; not easy if you are crossing a TSS in mid-Channel. Heaving to in the central separation zone to await better visibility might be an option, but see Rule 10 (b) and (e).

2.5.5 Part C: Lights and shapes
Many of the Rules (20–31) in Part C are semi-technical, not relevant to yachts or can be studied in slow time. The verbatim text is therefore only included for Rule 25 (Lights and shapes for sailing vessels underway).

Rule 20 (Application).
Part C Rules must be complied with in all weathers. All lights and shapes must comply with Annex I. The required lights must be shown from sunset to sunrise, and by day in low visibility. The required shapes must be displayed by day.

Rule 21 (Definitions).
Six types of navigation lights are defined, see Fig 2(4). A vessel <20m LOA may combine her side lights into 1 lantern on the fore and aft centreline, Rule 21 (b). A masthead lt, aka steaming lt, is rarely at the masthead; see Annex 1, para 2.

Rule 22 (Visibility of lights).
This Rule gives the *minimum* visibility range of lights shown by vessels of different LOAs. If <12m: masthead, stern and all-round 2M; side 1M. 12-50m: masthead 5M (but 3M if <20m); stern, side and all-round 2M. See Fig 2(4).

Rule 23 (Power-driven vessels underway).
(a) specifies a masthead light forward and a second, higher light aft if >50m LOA; plus sidelights and sternlight.
(b) refers to the all-round Fl Y light on an air-cushion vessel.
(c) a WIG craft must show a high-intensity all-round Fl R light.
(d) (i) A power-driven vessel <12m LOA may combine her masthead and stern lights into one all-round Ⓦ light.

Rule 24 (Towing and pushing).
This Rule is lengthy and detailed and need not concern yacht owners. However all mariners should know the lights shown by tugs and their tows; see Fig 2(5).

Rule 25 (Sailing vessels underway and vessels under oars).
(a) *A sailing vessel underway shall exhibit:*
    (i) *sidelights; (ii) a sternlight.*
(b) *In a sailing vessel <20m LOA, the lights prescribed in para (a) of this Rule may be combined in one lantern at or near the top of the mast where it can best be seen.*
(c) *A sailing vessel underway may, in addition to the lights prescribed at (a) of this Rule, exhibit at or near the top of the mast where they can best be seen two all-round*

lights, in a vertical line, the upper being red and the lower green, but these lights shall not be exhibited in conjunction with the combined lantern permitted by paragraph (b) of this Rule.

(d) (i) A sailing vessel <7m LOA shall, if practicable, exhibit the lights prescribed in paragraphs (a) or (b) of this Rule, but if she does not, she shall have ready at hand an electric torch or lighted lantern showing a white light which shall be exhibited in sufficient time to prevent collision.

   (i) A vessel under oars may exhibit the lights prescribed in this Rule for sailing vessels, but if she does not, she shall have ready at hand an electric torch or lighted lantern showing a white light which shall be exhibited in sufficient time to prevent collision.

(e) A vessel proceeding under sail when also being propelled by machinery shall exhibit forward where it can best be seen a conical shape, apex downwards.

The tricolour light at (b) shall not be switched on at the same time as the normal side and stern lights, and must never be used when under power. It gives max brilliance for minimum battery drain, but note that LED lights easily out-perform conventional lights in power consumption and brilliance, but cost much more. In congested waters or where there are shore lights in the background, the normal side and stern lights are deemed much easier to see from the bridge of a large ship than a masthead tricolour.

Rule 26 (Fishing vessels). All mariners should know the lights shown by fishing vessels; see Fig 2(5).

Rule 27 (Vessels not under command, or restricted in their ability to manoeuvre).
All mariners should know the lights shown by such vessels. They do not apply to vessels <12m LOA. If engaged in diving operations exhibit a rigid replica of flag 'A' at least 1m high.

Rule 28 (Vessels constrained by their draught).
All mariners should know the lights shown by such vessels; see Fig 2(5).

Rule 29 (Pilot vessels).
All mariners should know the lights shown by such vessels; see Fig 2(5).

Rule 30 (Vessels anchored or aground).
Yachts at ⚓, like other vessels, *shall* show an ⚓ light or ball; see Fig 2(5). This stipulation warns other mariners and has safety and insurance implications. Abroad, especially in the Netherlands and Germany, the ball requirement is often strictly enforced. Rules 30e and 30f grant 2 minor exemptions for yachts <7m LOA and <12m LOA.

Rule 31 (Seaplanes).
This Rule applies to WIG craft as well as seaplanes.

2.5.6 Part D: Sound and light signals
Rule 32 (Definitions).

A whistle in a yacht effectively means a foghorn.
· A short blast on a foghorn lasts about 1 second.
— A prolonged blast lasts four to six seconds.

Rule 33 (Equipment for sound signals).
Vessels >12m LOA must have a whistle; plus a bell if >20m. A boat <12m LOA may make an efficient sound signal by other means, judged by audibility within the enclosed bridge of a large ship and against conflicting background noises.

Rule 34 (Manoeuvring and warning signals).
Power-driven vessels in sight of each other:
The following sound signals (short or long blasts on a foghorn) may also be supplemented by light flashes:

·	I am altering course to starboard.
··	I am altering course to port.
···	I am operating astern propulsion.
·····	I do not understand your intentions/actions or I doubt if sufficient action is being taken to avoid collision.

In a narrow channel:

——·	I intend to overtake on your starboard side.
——··	I intend to overtake you on your port side.
—·—·	I agree with your overtaking signal.
—	Warning by vessel nearing a bend where other vessels may not be visible.

Rule 35 (Sound signals in restricted visibility).

—	Power-driven vessel making way.
——	Power-driven vessel underway, but stopped and not making way.
—··	Vessel not under command; restricted in her ability to manoeuvre; constrained by her draught; or engaged in fishing, towing or pushing; **or a sailing vessel**.
—···	Vessel being towed, or if more than one vessel is towed, the last vessel in the tow.
····	Pilot vessel engaged on pilotage duties.

The maximum interval between sound signals for vessels underway in restricted visibility is two minutes, but more frequently if other craft are near.

For flag and sound signals which have a special meaning under IRPCS, see the asterisked items in Fig 5(1).

Bell rung rapidly for about 5 seconds, every minute.
= Vessel at anchor.

After the above signal, gong rung rapidly for about 5 seconds every minute; the bell being sounded in the fore part of the vessel and the gong aft
= Vessel of 100m or more in length at anchor.
·—· Vessel at anchor (optional extra sound signal).

Bell rung rapidly for about 5 seconds, with three separate and distinct strokes of the bell before and after the rapid ringing
= Vessel aground.

Rule 36 (Signals to attract attention).
These signals, whether sound or light, must be such as not to be mistaken for other signals in these Rules or an aid to navigation. Avoid using high intensity strobe lights.

Rule 37 (Distress signals).
See Annex IV and Chapter 7, Fig 7(1).

2.5.7 Annexes I to IV
Annex I: vertical/horizontal positioning and technical details of lights and shapes in various vessels.

Annex II: lights which may be shown by fishing vessels working close together.

Annex III: technical details of frequencies, audibility and directional properties of sound signals.

Annex IV: distress signals; see also Chapter 7, Fig 7(1).

Fig 2(4) Navigation lights

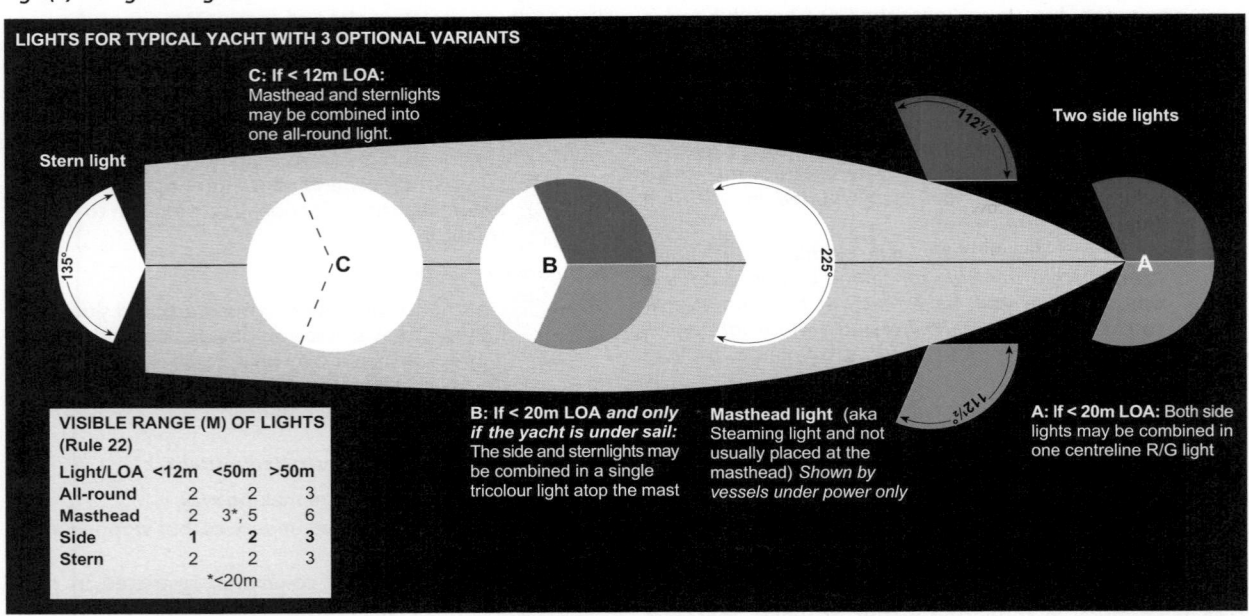

LIGHTS FOR TYPICAL YACHT WITH 3 OPTIONAL VARIANTS

C: If < 12m LOA:
Masthead and sternlights may be combined into one all-round light.

Two side lights

Stern light

135°

C

B

225°

112½°

112½°

A

VISIBLE RANGE (M) OF LIGHTS (Rule 22)			
Light/LOA	**<12m**	**<50m**	**>50m**
All-round	2	2	3
Masthead	2	3*, 5	6
Side	1	2	3
Stern	2	2	3
		*<20m	

B: If < 20m LOA and only if the yacht is under sail: The side and sternlights may be combined in a single tricolour light atop the mast

Masthead light (aka Steaming light and not usually placed at the masthead) *Shown by vessels under power only*

A: If < 20m LOA: Both side lights may be combined in one centreline R/G light

PLAN VIEWS OF LIGHTS FOR SAILING VESSELS UNDERWAY AND UNDER SAIL ONLY
Note: If motor-sailing, the lights appropriate for a power-driven vessel must be shown, as below

Sailing vessel <7m shows, if practicable, side and sternlights; if not, a white light to prevent collision. Rule 25 d i

Sailing vessel <20m may show:

Either tricolour light atop the mast. Rule 25 b

Or combined centreline side lights plus stern light. Rule 25 a

Sailing vessel >20m Separate sidelights and sternlight. Rule 25 a

Sailing vessel under sail may show (in addition to other lights) two all-round lights, red over green, near the top of the mast, **but never** at the same time as a tricolour light atop the mast. Rule 25 c

PLAN VIEWS OF LIGHTS FOR POWER-DRIVEN VESSELS UNDERWAY AND SAILING CRAFT UNDER POWER

<7m and <7 knots (all-round light and, if practicable, side lights). Rule 23 d ii

<12m (combined masthead & sternlight). Rule 23 d i

<20m (sidelights combined in one centreline light). Rule 21 b

>20m showing masthead, stern and separate sidelights. Rule 21 a, b, c

>50m with two masthead lights, the aft one higher. Rule 23 a i & ii

Fig 2(5) Principal navigation lights and shapes. (Note: All vessels seen from starboard side)

Vessels being towed and towing

Vessel towed shows sidelights (forward) and sternlight

Tug shows two masthead lights, sidelights, sternlight, yellow towing light

Towing by day — Length of tow more than 200m

Towing vessel and tow display diamond shapes. By night, the towing vessel shows three masthead lights instead of two as for shorter tows

Motor sailing

Cone point down, forward. At night the lights of a power-driven vessel underway

Vessel fishing

All-round red light over all-round white, plus sidelights and sternlight when making way

Fishing/Trawling

A shape consisting of two cones point to point in a vertical line one above the other

Vessel trawling

All-round green light over all-round white, plus sidelights and sternlight when making way

Vessel restricted in her ability to manoeuvre

All-round red, white, red lights vertically, plus normal steaming lights when making way

Three shapes in a vertical line: ball, diamond, ball

Not under command

Two all-round red lights, plus sidelights and sternlight when making way

Two balls vertically

Dredger

All round red, white, red lights vertically, plus two all-round red lights (or two balls) on foul side, and two all-round green (or two diamonds) on clear side

Divers down

Letter 'A' International Code

Constrained by draught

Three all-round red lights in a vertical line, plus normal steaming lights. By day — a cylinder

Pilot boat

All-round white light over all-round red, plus sidelights and sternlight when underway, or anchor light

Vessel at anchor

All-round white light; if over 50m, a second light aft and lower

Ball forward

Vessel aground

Anchor light(s), plus two all-round red lights in a vertical line

Three balls in a vertical line

2.5.8 Learning the Collision Regulations

Most of this chapter deals with the vitally important Rules of the Collision Regulations (ColRegs). To many people learning these is a chore; something to be swotted up, often parrot-fashion, so as to pass an exam – and then be forgotten. This is not learning, it is simply a memory test without understanding of the subject.

Remember the ColRegs are written by seamen for seamen, unambiguously and in language which leaves little room for misunderstandings. Every word or sentence reflects a real life situation which has occurred at sea. They are steeped in practicality and hard won experience. Above all they exist to prevent collisions and hence save lives.

If we can adopt a better way of learning then what seemed like a chore may turn out to be a pleasure. Start from the Known and move with growing interest towards the Unknown. Grasp the big picture, in this case a site map below, showing how the ColRegs consist of five Parts (A-E), sub-divided, as required, into Sections; thence into the 38 individual Rules; finally 4 Annexes with technical minutiae.

Now for the details: As you study each Rule envisage the scenario which is being described. Ask yourself 'Do I fully understand this Rule?' 'What would I do in this situation?' This is the best way of gaining a sound working knowledge of the Rules – and disposing of that parrot.

PARTS	SECTIONS		RULES	ANNEXES
A: GENERAL	None		1–3	N/A
B: STEERING & SAILING	I	In any visibility	4–10	N/A
	II	In sight of one another	11–18	N/A
	III	In restricted visibility	19	N/A
C: LIGHTS & SHAPES	None		20–31	Annex I
				Annex II
D: SOUND & LIGHT SIGNALS	None		32–37	Annexes III and IV
E: EXEMPTIONS	None		38	N/A

3

Navigation

Navigation

Fig 3(1)   Passage planning form

DATE .... FROM ....ETD .... VIA .... TO .... ETA ....

TIMES OF SUNRISE .... SUNSET .... MOON RISE .... MOONSET .... WATCH SYSTEM ☐

CHARTS ☐   DOCUMENTS ☐   CUSTOMS ☐   PAY DUES ☐   CG (T/R) ☐   FUEL ☐   WATER ☐   FOOD ☐

WEATHER FORECAST   ....

DEPARTURE PORT VHF .... HM ☎ ....

BRIDGE TIMES ....

LOCK/GATE TIMES...

BAR CROSSING TIMES ....

DEPARTURE WINDOW ....

DEPARTURE PROCEDURE ....

....

....

VTS DETAILS ....

....

....

STANDARD PORT, TIDES (SP/NP, HW/LW TIMES & HEIGHTS)

....

....

....

DEPARTURE PORT TIDES (HW/LW TIMES & HEIGHTS) ....

....

....

TIDAL STREAMS ON DEPARTURE ....

....

....

EN ROUTE

TIDAL STREAM ANALYSIS ....

....

....

....

....

TIDAL GATES (TIMES) ....

....

TIDE RACES ....

....

TRAFFIC SEPARATION SCHEMES....................

....

PROHIBITED AREAS/DANGERS ....

PRINCIPAL LIGHTS/MARKS ....

....

....

LEG DETAILS

FROM	TO	WPT	TRK°M	DIST	TIME	REMARKS

DESTINATION PORT VHF .... HM ☎ ....

ARRIVAL PROCEDURE ....

....

BAR CROSSING TIMES ....

LOCK/GATE/SILL TIMES ....

BRIDGE TIMES ....

ACCESS WINDOW ....

ALTERNATE PORT VHF .... HM ☎ ....

ARRIVAL PROCEDURE ....

....

BAR CROSSING TIMES ....

LOCK/GATE/SILL TIMES ....

BRIDGE TIMES ....

ACCESS WINDOW ....

3.1 PASSAGE PLANNING AND SOLAS V

Before you start to navigate you need to plan: where you are going, how to get there and what factors may influence the plan. To most people this is commonsense; it is also the law. Regulation 34 in Chapter V of the International Convention for Safety of Life at Sea (SOLAS), **Safe Navigation and avoidance of dangerous situations,** is quite short but extra guidance is given to small craft skippers in the MCA's Pleasure Craft Information Pack at www.mcga.gov.uk/c4mca/mcga-safety_information.htm.

All voyages/passages by any vessel that goes to sea must be pre-planned. 'Going to sea' is defined as proceeding beyond sheltered waters. Even in very familiar waters every passage, however short, should be pre-planned, but for small craft the degree of planning may be less than for big ships.

Although the passage plan need not be recorded on paper, in the event of legal action a written plan is clear proof that planning has been done. It can also be referred to during the passage. A suggested passage planning form is at Fig 3(1) opposite. When completed this would constitute a reasonable passage plan. The blank form may be photocopied and modified to suit individual needs.

Spot checks on small craft are very unlikely but, following any accident or incident, the MCA would have clear authority to take action under the Merchant Shipping Act if it could be proved that the skipper did not carry out any form of passage planning.

3.1.1 SOLAS V, Regulation 34 (paraphrased)
All passage plans should at least consider the following:

- **Limitations of the vessel:** Is your craft suitable for the intended passage? Is proper safety equipment and enough fuel, water and stores onboard?
- **Crew:** Is the crew sufficiently experienced and physically capable? How will they cope with cold, fatigue or seasickness?
- **Navigational dangers:** Are you aware of navigational dangers which may affect the passage? Check up-to-date charts, pilot books and the current Reeds Almanac.
- **Tides:** Do you know the times and heights of HW & LW at departure, destination and alternative ports? Are you aware of tidal streams and races expected on passage? Does your passage plan make best use of all tidal data?
- **Weather:** Is the forecast suitable for the likely duration of the passage? Whilst at sea what updates can be obtained?
- **Contingency plan:** Have you an alternative plan to cope with deteriorating weather, gear failure, accident or injury? Which ports of refuge or bolt-holes are available?
- **GPS**: Do not become over-reliant on GPS or chart-plotters. They *can* fail, usually at the most awkward moment. Can you navigate safely without them?
- **Information ashore:** Does someone ashore know your plans and what to do should they become concerned? Have you completed and returned a CG66, the Voluntary Identification Scheme? (See 7.14.2)

3.1.2 Passage planning form
The following notes amplify some of the items on the form:

- Tidal streams may prevent sensible progress – off headlands or in narrow passages, for example.

Record the times (or 'gates') when they will be favourable.
- Note which harbours and marinas have bars, sills or locks. These may affect times of entry and departure.
- Prepare a detailed pilotage plan for entry/exit to any unfamiliar harbour; a sketch always helps.
- Look up and record relevant VHF channels for ports of departure and arrival, and for possible weather forecasts while on passage.

Time spent planning is never wasted.

3.2 ESSENTIAL NAVIGATION

Yacht navigation has been revolutionised by GPS, freeing us of much work and worry but also tempting us to become navigationally lazy. This is manifested by skippers who do not ensure that a Dead Reckoning (DR) plot is kept in parallel with GPS navigation. This may just be acceptable provided:

- Position, heading and distance by log are recorded hourly (or at some other appropriate interval) in the logbook; *and*
- A DR plot is started as soon as there is any doubt about the reliability of the vessel's electrical systems, GPS or other electronic aids.

3.2.1 Dead reckoning navigation
A properly adjusted compass, an accurate timepiece and a log to measure distance run are the essential tools of DR navigation. Tidal stream atlases and charts of oceanic currents (if applicable) come a close second.

A DR plot starts from your last known position, plotted on the chart with the time alongside. An hour or so later, depending on circumstances, the time, log reading, distance run and course steered are recorded in the logbook. These are then plotted on the chart to obtain an updated DR position.

This DR position will be more accurate if an estimate of the boat's leeway is first applied to the course steered. For example, a yacht steering 090° with a N'ly wind might make 5° of leeway. 095° would therefore be plotted instead of 090°.

To refine this DR position still further, plot the tidal stream vector, direction and rate, experienced over the past hour; this data is obtained from a tidal stream atlas or tidal diamonds on the chart. It results in an Estimated Position (EP). The EP is the most accurate position obtainable in the absence of a visual, electronic or other fix.

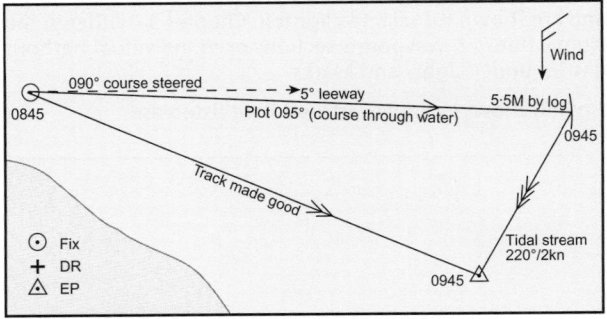

Fig 3(2) A DR/EP plot

By using conventional symbols on the chart (Fig 3(2)), others can immediately appreciate what they see and check the accuracy of the navigator's work. A good navigator always welcomes a second opinion.

3.2.2   Navigational wrinkles
Distance, speed and time equations are:

Distance (M)	=	Speed (kn) x time (hours)
Speed	=	Distance ÷ Time
Time	=	Distance ÷ Speed

Table 3(2) tabulates distance, speed and time values.

Pilotage may be defined as 'Navigation when there is no time for plotting'. Meticulous pre-planning, especially in very narrow waters, is needed. See 3.9 for use of chart-plotters.

Blind pilotage. In 6 minutes (1/10 hour) you will cover 1/10 of your speed in miles. So at 4 knots you will cover 0·4 miles (or 4 cables); at 5·5 knots you will cover 5·5 cables. In 3 minutes you will cover half that distance; in 12 minutes, twice the distance. This 'wrinkle' can be invaluable when calculating your ETA at the next buoy when buoy-hopping in low visibility.

A Dutchman's log can be used when the ship's log has failed. Time how long it takes for an object dropped at the bows to pass the stern. Speed (kn) = (0·592 x LOA (ft)) ÷ T (seconds). Thus for an LOA of 34ft and a time of 5 seconds, the speed will be 34 x 0·592 ÷ 5 = 4 knots.

References: *The Adlard Coles Book of Navigation* (ACN) covers coastal navigation in depth. *Reeds Skipper's Handbook* (ACN) gives similar information in a more concise format.

'It is not the ship so much as the skilled sailing that assures the prosperous voyage.' (George William Curtis 1817–62)

3.3   LIGHTS

3.3.1   Light characteristics
Abbreviations and characteristics of marine lights are shown in Fig 3(5) and in AC 5011 (Symbols and Abbreviations used on Admiralty Charts).

3.3.2   Light sectors, arcs of visibility
Coloured sector lights are used to indicate dangerous areas (usually red) or to guide a vessel through a narrow passage (usually white). A white sector is often flanked by red and green sectors: red is seen if too far to port; green to starboard. The limits of light sectors, arcs of visibility and the alignment of directional and leading lights, are listed **as seen from seaward**. All bearings are True, given clockwise from north, and are shown for selected lights in Chapter 9 – either in the Lights, buoys & waypoints sections or in individual harbour entries under Lights and Marks.

Fig 3(3) shows a simple sectored light listed as:

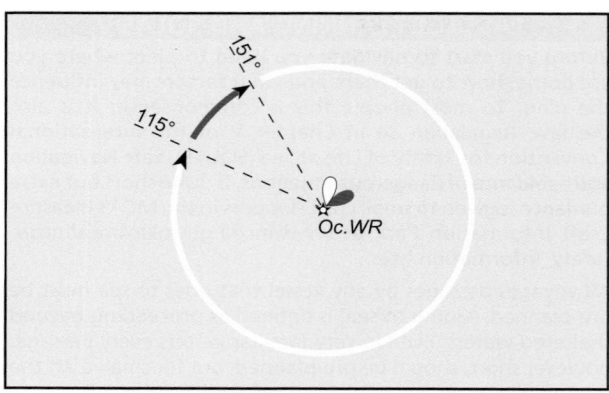

Fig 3(3) A simple sectored light

*Oc WR 4s 37m **W17M**, R13M; 151°-W-115°-R-151°.* The light, showing white and red sectors, occults every 4s, is 37 metres above the level of MHWS, its white sector has a nominal range of 17 miles (ranges greater than 15 miles are in **bold**) and the red light's range is 13 miles. The white sector is visible when it bears 151° clockwise to 115°, an arc of 324°; the red sector is visible when it bears 115° to 151°, an arc of 36°.

In Fig 3(4) is a slightly more complex sectored light listed as:

Q WRG 9m 10M; 015°-G-058°-W-065°-R-103°-G-143·5°-W-146·5°-R-015°.

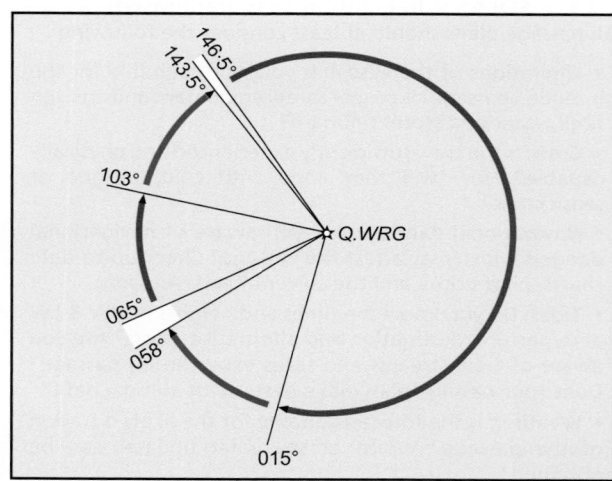

Fig 3(4) A more complex sectored light

This quick flashing light has white, red and green sectors, is 9m above MHWS and has a nominal range of 10M. By inspection there are two sets of WRG sectors providing directional guidance to vessels approaching from SW and NW. In each case a narrow (7° and 3°) white sector is flanked by a red sector to port and a green sector to starboard.

Fig 3(5) Light characteristics

CLASS OF LIGHT	International abbreviations	National abbreviations	Illustration — Period shown
FIXED	F		
OCCULTING (duration of light longer than dark)			
Single-occulting	Oc	Occ	
Group-occulting	eg Oc(2)	Oc(2)	
Composite group-occulting	eg Oc(2+3)	Gp Occ(2+3)	
ISOPHASE (light and dark equal duration)	Iso		
FLASHING (duration of light shorter than dark)			
Single-flashing	Fl		
Long-flashing (flash 2s or longer)		L Fl	
Group-flashing	eg Fl(3)	Gp Fl(3)	
Composite group-flashing	eg Fl(2+1)	Gp Fl(2+1)	
QUICK (50 to 79 flashes per minute, usually 50 or 60)			
Continuous quick	Q	Qk Fl	
Group quick	eg Q(3)	Qk Fl(3)	
Interrupted quick	IQ	Int Qk Fl	
VERY QUICK (80 to 159 flashes per minute, usually 100 or 120)			
Continuous very quick	VQ	V Qk Fl	
Group very quick	eg VQ(3)	V Qk Fl(3)	
Interrupted very quick	IVQ	Int V Qk Fl	
ULTRA QUICK (160 or more flashes per minute, usually 240 to 300)			
Continuous ultra quick	UQ		
Interrupted ultra quick	IUQ		
MORSE CODE	eg Mo (K)		
FIXED AND FLASHING	F Fl		
ALTERNATING	eg Al. WR	Alt. WR	

COLOUR	International abbreviations	NOMINAL RANGE in miles		International abbreviations
White	W (may be omitted)	Light with single range	eg	15M
Red	R	Light with two different ranges	eg	15/10M
Green	G	Light with three or more ranges	eg	15-7M
Blue	Bu	PERIOD is given in seconds	eg	90s
Violet	Vi	DISPOSITION Horizontally disposed		(hor)
Yellow	Y	Vertically disposed		(vert)
Orange	Y			
Amber	Y	ELEVATION is given in metres (m) above the level of MHWS		

3.4   IALA BUOYAGE (REGION A)

IALA buoyage system – Regions

Region A, shown here, includes Europe; Region B covers the Americas and the Pacific.

Note that different rules (the CEVNI Code) apply on Inland Waterways in Europe.

3.4.1 Cardinal marks (buoys and beacons) indicate where the best navigable water lies relative to a danger or hazard and, specifically, that:

- The deepest water is on the named side of the mark
- The named side is the safe side on which to pass

They may also be used to emphasise a bend or fork in a channel, or to mark the end of a shoal.

Cardinal marks are referenced to the points of the compass and named after the quadrant in which they are placed relative to the danger or hazard they mark. The four quadrants (N, E, S and W) are defined by the True bearings NW-NE, NE-SE, SE-SW and SW-NW from the danger or hazard. It follows that you should normally pass north of a NCM, east of an ECM and so on.

Topmarks: 2 black cones in various unique combinations. Colour: yellow & black bands (black always relates to the points of the cones), as shown in the diagram. Lights: always white, Q or VQ, as defined in Fig 3(5). The number of flashes relates to the 'clock code': a NCM at 12

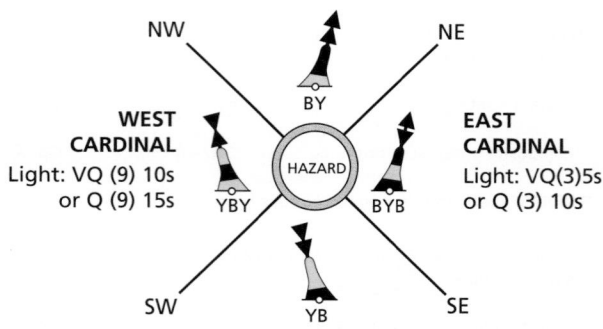

NORTH CARDINAL
Light: VQ or Q

WEST CARDINAL
Light: VQ (9) 10s or Q (9) 15s

HAZARD

EAST CARDINAL
Light: VQ(3)5s or Q (3) 10s

SOUTH CARDINAL
Light: VQ (6) + L Fl 10s or Q (6) + L Fl 15s

o'clock flashes continuously; an ECM at 3 o'clock flashes groups of 3; a SCM flashes groups of 6 + a long flash (at least 2 secs duration); and a WCM flashes groups of 9.

3.4.2 Lateral marks indicate the sides of a well-defined channel according to the direction of buoyage (3.4.8). If PHM or SHM marks do not rely on shape for identification, they carry the appropriate topmarks where practicable. In Region A:

- PHM marks are red. Shape: can, spar or pillar. Topmark, if fitted: red can. Even numbering. Light: red; any rhythm except (2+1).

- SHM marks are green (exceptionally, black). Shape: conical, spar or pillar. Topmark, if fitted: green cone, point up. Odd numbering. Light: green; any rhythm except (2+1).

Port hand marks (PHM)

Navigable channel

Direction of buoyage

Starboard hand marks (SHM)

3.4.3 Preferred channel marks At a channel junction the preferred channel may be shown by a lateral mark with red or green bands. The alternate channel (to the same destination) lies on the other side of this mark. Topmarks are those of a PHM or SHM. Think of a PCP (see below) as a SHM modified by a R band, and the PCS as a PHM modified by a G band.

Preferred channel to port (PCP)
SHM mark, green with red band. Light (if fitted): Fl (2+1) G.

Preferred channel to starboard (PCS)
PHM mark, red with green band. Light (if fitted): Fl (2+1) R.

Preferred channel   GRG   *Alternate channel*   GRG

Alternate channel   RGR   *Preferred channel*   RGR

3.4.4 Isolated danger marks (IDM) are placed on or above an isolated danger of limited extent, eg a rock or a wreck, which has navigable water all around it.

Colour: black with red band(s). Topmark: 2 black balls (vert). Light, if any, is a group of two white flashes, Fl (2).

3.4.5 Safe water marks (SWM) indicate that there is navigable water all round the mark. They are used as centreline, mid-channel or landfall marks.

Shape: spherical, pillar or spar. Colour: red & white vertical stripes. Topmark: 1 R ball, but only on pillar or spar buoys. Light, if any, is white, occulting, isophase, L Fl 10s or Morse code 'A' (· —).

3.4.6 Special marks are not of navigational significance but indicate a special area usually depicted on the chart, eg spoil grounds, naval exercise areas, water-ski and bathing areas. Other features include yacht racing marks, cables or pipelines, outfalls, ODAS buoys and TSS marks (where conventional channel marks might cause confusion).

Colour: yellow. Shape: optional, but not conflicting with lateral or safe water marks. If can or conical buoys are used they indicate the side on which to pass. Topmark if fitted: yellow X. Light if fitted: yellow, any rhythm not used for Cardinal, IDM and SWM marks.

3.4.7 New dangers Emergency wreck-marking buoys are used before other marks can be deployed. They are pillar or spar shaped with blue & yellow vert stripes; WRECK is painted vert in black on yellow; optional topmark yellow +; light Al Bu/Y 3s 4M; Racon 'D' (—··) and/or AIS are optional.

YBu 🛆 🛆 YBu

Newly discovered hazards – wrecks, obstructions, rocks or shoals – are marked by IALA cardinal or lateral buoys, often 4 or more where the risk to other vessels is high. For emphasis one of the marks may be duplicated until the hazard has been adequately publicised. A Racon coded 'D' (—··) and/or an AIS transducer may also be fitted.

3.4.8 Conventional direction of buoyage
This is defined as either: the **Local** direction when entering estuaries and large waterways from seaward.
Or elsewhere as the **General** direction of buoyage which in principle is clockwise around continents.
Around the UK the general direction is N up the W coast and the Irish Sea, E up the English Channel, thence N up the North Sea (necessitated by the clockwise direction around mainland Europe).
If there is doubt, the direction is marked on charts by a broad arrowhead as shown in 3.4.2. Off Orfordness, Suffolk, for example, the local direction into the Thames Estuary is SW but the general direction is N.

3.5 SATELLITE NAVIGATION
3.5.1 GPS
The NAVSTAR Global Positioning System (GPS) is a military navigation system, owned and operated by the United States Department of Defense (DoD). It provides world-wide, 24 hours a day, precise position, velocity and time information to anyone with a suitable receiver. The system consists of at least 24 operational satellites, orbiting 10,900M (20,200km) above the earth, in 6 orbital planes inclined at 55° to the equator. Positional accuracy is available to 33m for 95% of the time; for the remaining 5% of the time errors of up to 100m are theoretically possible. Signal propagation delays in the ionosphere and troposphere can cause errors of up to 5m; other system errors are up to 2·5m.

Before May 2000 the accuracy of GPS was degraded by Selective Availability (SA) for non-military use. Since then SA has been discontinued because increasingly accessible correction techniques rendered it superfluous.

The accuracy of GPS can be enhanced by Differential GPS (DGPS) and by various overlay systems such as the European Geostationary Navigation Overlay Service (EGNOS) (see 3.5.2). However, the accuracy obtainable from the Standard Positioning Service (as opposed to the Precise Positioning Service for military use) is generally quite adequate for yachting purposes. Bear in mind that GPS may be more accurate than some older charts. Also, many charts are not yet referred to the WGS84 datum, and corrections must be made before plotting positions obtained from GPS (see 3.5.5).

When choosing one of the many GPS receivers available, consider size (handheld, portable or fixed installation); check that it has multi-channels (12+ is the norm) and that it can receive EGNOS. Compatibility with Galileo (see 3.5.4) may also influence your choice. Much depends on where it is to be used, the degree of accuracy required and cost.

3.5.2 EGNOS
EGNOS is a Wide Area Augmentation System (WAAS) which began operating in 2005. The 'Wide Area' is bounded approximately by Iceland, Murmansk, Greece and Marrakesh. Many receivers now display a 'WAAS operating' indication. Measured performance (99% accuracy of 1–2m) far exceeds expectations. EGNOS is due to cease operating in about 2013 after Galileo is fully established.

EGNOS utilises 3 geostationary satellites and a network of 34 ground stations for ranging and integrity monitoring, plus 4 master control centres and 6 up-link stations. Graphic displays indicate system accuracy and reliability.

Most new GPS receivers are EGNOS-enabled. Check that your existing receiver is enabled so as to get the benefits of this system. For the latest info visit: www.esa.int/esaNA/egnos.html.

3.5.3 GPS integrity monitoring
Urgent information is given in MSI broadcasts by HM CG on VHF or MF, and by Navtex message category J; see Chapter 6, Weather.
The US CG issues daily status information which may be found on www.navcen.uscg.gov. The US Government states that, although GPS is primarily for military use, it is committed to provide the best possible service to civil and commercial users worldwide – both in times of peace and conflict.

3.5.4 Other satellite-based systems

The *Global Navigation Satellite System* (GLONASS) is operated by the Russian Federation and is similar to GPS. Currently (2009) 20 out of the intended 24 satellites are in orbit, of which 19 are operational.

Galileo, an independent European satellite system, compatible with GPS but promising even greater accuracy, is not expected to be fully operational until about 2013.

For a detailed description of the theory and use of GPS and other satellite-based systems see *The Adlard Coles Book of Electronic Navigation* by Tim Bartlett (ACN). For a more technical description refer to *Admiralty List of Radio Signals Vol 2, NP282*.

3.5.5 Horizontal datums

Horizontal datums are models for specifying position on the Earth's surface. GPS uses the World Geodetic System 84 datum (WGS84).

With the exception of much of the coast of Ireland and the west coast of Scotland, Admiralty charts of UK waters have now been converted from OSGB36 to WGS84 or the compatible ETRS 89 datum. Most charts of NW Europe are referenced to WGS84, depending on the originating nations. Many charts of Iberia are still to ED 50 but progress is being made. All harbour chartlets in this edition of RNA are referenced to WGS84.

GPS fixes can be plotted directly onto charts which are referenced to WGS84 but not onto charts which are still referenced to another datum. Before plotting, the WGS84 coordinates read from the GPS receiver must be converted to the datum of the chart in use.

The datum used is always printed on the chart, normally under 'SATELLITE-DERIVED POSITIONS'. This gives the Lat/Long corrections to be applied to satellite positions before plotting them on the chart. The difference between WGS 84 and other horizontal datums varies randomly with location and can amount to several hundred metres, up to a maximum of 7 miles in the Pacific.

Most receivers contain many datums. The user has 2 options:

- Set the receiver to the datum of the chart in use. The datum corrections will automatically be applied by the receiver's software. This method is convenient, but not the most accurate, due to the random nature of the differences and software limitations.

- Set the receiver to WGS84. Before plotting positions, manually apply the corrections given on the chart.

The second option is advised by UKHO. Until the conversion to WGS84 is 100% complete, always check the datum of your chart. Do not assume that an adjacent chart will use the same datum. See ALRS Vol 2 for further information.

3.6 LORAN-C, NELS AND eLORAN

Loran-C is a terrestrial navaid, originated in WWII, using hyperbolic techniques based on Master and Secondary stations which form a chain. 26 such chains (in USA, Canada, Saudi Arabia, India, China, Russia and the Pacific) still operate. Loran-C uses LF groundwave signals to achieve ranges up to 1500M. Groundwave accuracy is about 100m, decreasing with range.

3.6.1 NELS (NW European Loran-C System) covers a land/sea area broadly defined by Biscay, Denmark, North Cape,

Svalbard, Jan Mayen Island, Iceland and Ireland. Operational stations include: 4 in Norway (Værlandet, Bø, Barlevåg, Jan Mayen Is), 1 in Faeroe Islands (Ejde, Danish), 1 in the UK (Anthorn), 2 in France (Lessay, Soustons) and 1 in Germany (Sylt). The four chains and their unique group repetition intervals (GRI) are: Ejde (9007), Bø (7001), Sylt (7499) and Lessay (6731).

3.6.2 eLORAN (enhanced-Loran) is modernised Loran-C.

The main difference is the inclusion of a digital data channel (loran Data Channel) on the Loran signal itself. Using this channel, differential-Loran corrections (similar to those used in DGPS) and integrity information can be transmitted to users. Accuracy is between 8m and 20m. eLoran is being actively promoted by the UK government, Trinity House, Northern Lights and Irish Lights as an independent ,terrestrial back-up and complement to GPS and Galileo.

3.7 ELECTRONIC CHARTS

Electronic charts are many and varied. They fall into two main types, raster and vector, produced as a cartridge-type chip for use in electronic chart plotters, and as CDs for PCs, or a combination of both. Coverage is virtually worldwide with the emphasis on the British Isles, NW Europe, S Europe, the Mediterranean and Caribbean. When buying electronic charts it is essential to ascertain what updating/chart correction service is provided; it may be a simple part-exchange of old for new for a reasonable fee. Electronic charts are excellent value for money when compared with Admiralty paper charts or a set of Leisure Folios. ARCS (Admiralty Raster Chart Service) has a licence system with update discs supplied weekly, quarterly or annually. See *The Electronic Yachtmaster* (DVD) by Tom Cunliffe, www.tomcunliffe.com

3.7.1 Raster charts

Raster charts are produced by scanning the paper version of the chart. To many users they look reassuringly familiar as they are selective but exact electronic copies of originals. ARCS charts are Admiralty raster charts; Maptech is the US equivalent.

Adjacent charts can be automatically linked (known as quilting) to prevent 'sailing off the edge' of the previous one.

Users should be aware that zooming in on a raster chart does not necessarily produce more detail, it simply enlarges the image. Detailed larger scale charts of the area are included in the folio for this purpose. Some raster charts enjoy the benefits listed under vector charts, below.

3.7.2 Vector charts

Vector charts are produced by re-digitising paper charts. They are used in most dedicated chart plotters and build the information up in layers such as seabed detail, depth contours, buoyage, and topographic features. Specific layers can be de-selected to increase the clarity of the plotter display.

The data is seamless, which usually enables the user to buy one chart (as a cartridge) covering a specific area such as the Central English Channel rather than a folio of charts. The chart provides total cartographic coverage right down to harbour details. Zooming in provides large scale coverage with more detail, rather than a simple enlargement of the chart image. Zooming out provides a smaller scale overview of the area.

Vector charts are 'intelligent' and interact with their host systems which allows the user to interrogate chart symbols or be warned of impending dangers. Blue Charts, C-Map, and Navionics are examples of vector charts.

3.8   WAYPOINTS

3.8.1   Waypoint navigation

- A waypoint (WPT or ⊕) is, quite simply, any geographical position, normally expressed as a Latitude and Longitude, and usually associated with electronic navigation. It may be a departure, destination or alternate port, an en route turning point, a position at a safe distance off a headland, hazard, lighthouse, buoy, navigational mark, or any chosen position in the open sea.

- In Chapter 9 the waypoint for each harbour under the NAVIGATION sub-heading is a safe position from which to begin the approach. The WPT below the title is the harbour entrance – a good final waypoint.

- In 'Lights, buoys & waypoints' (section 4 of each Area) are the positions of selected lights and buoys which may be used as waypoints, but see 3.8.2 below. The Lat/Long, taken from a large scale chart, is usually stated to 0'·01 of a minute.

- Discrepancies in position may result from different horizontal datums, incomplete data or survey data deemed inadequate by modern standards. Charts may also contain very small integral errors.

- 'Track' means track over the ground (not heading). For example, if required to approach a harbour (or waypoint) on a track of 090°, keep the waypoint on a constant bearing of 090°. Any significant deviation from that track could stand you into danger.

3.8.2   Loading waypoints

The following measures will help to prevent errors being made when working with waypoints:

- Be painstakingly accurate. Work without interruption.

- While planning your route, plot intended waypoints on the chart(s) before loading them into electronic memories. This ensures that the track(s) between waypoints will not lead into danger, across shoals, rocks or even over dry land.

- Published waypoints should *never* be loaded without first plotting their positions on the chart. It helps to label each waypoint with a number or name.

- Undetected errors in Lat/Long values can cause major navigational problems, usually at the most awkward moment.

- Verify that positions have been accurately extracted from the paper chart.

- Use the correct format for entering data into a specific receiver.

- Measure tracks/distances on the chart and record the results in a simplified passage plan.

- Check that tracks/distances between waypoints, as computed by the receiver, agree with those measured directly off the paper chart.

- Check longitude for the correct E or W hemisphere, especially when near the Greenwich Meridian.

- Ask another crew member to double-check your work.

3.9   CHART PLOTTERS

Chart plotters, all linked to GPS receivers, fall into three main categories: handheld/portable, fixed and PC-based. Their greatest benefit is that they continuously display the boat's track and position on a moving electronic chart; many also give full tidal data. Their downside is that they may make navigators lazy, to the extent that a total GPS failure could leave some navigators unable to navigate safely; see the second bullet point below and section 3.2.

Advanced plotters can be interfaced with an autopilot, engine data, instrument data and video/live-cam coverage of remote onboard areas. Some display depth sounder, fish finder and radar overlays on the same screen as the chart. A wide selection is available and choice depends on what the buyer requires and can afford. Be aware that:

- Although a chart plotter greatly assists the navigator, it does not replace the need to navigate. It is excellent for pilotage in narrow waters where the necessary fixes cannot be plotted quickly enough. Safe navigation is the watchkeeper's prime responsibility, not least if an autopilot is coupled to a GPS.

- GPS may on rare occasions be interrupted or even fail completely. It therefore remains essential to log the boat's position, course and speed as an independent record. This will form the basis from which to derive and maintain a DR/EP plot; see 3.2.

3.9.1   Handheld and portable chart plotters

Modern handheld plotters offer electronic chart displays with all the usual GPS features. Although they are capable of chart overview, they should not be used as the primary navigation system due to their very limited screen size. They are ideal for those seeking the benefits of GPS but wishing to use paper charts; or as an independent back-up to the boat's primary GPS receiver and plotter.

Portable plotters have a screen at least 3" x 4" (75 x 103mm), about the smallest practical size to avoid excessive zooming; it provides the features of a larger fixed plotter and allows full use of vector chart layers. They are ideal as the primary system in smaller craft or as a cockpit display and back-up in larger craft. They can be removed in harbour for security and also used ashore for passage planning.

3.9.2   Fixed plotters

Fixed plotters are permanently mounted, usually at the chart table, with optional repeaters elsewhere. The larger displays are suitable for the primary navigation system with appropriate back-ups. Advanced plotters have split or multiple screens and, with professional installation, allow much onboard data to be displayed as described above.

3.9.3   PC based plotters

PCs, laptops and PDAs (personal digital assistants) are increasingly used at sea. A PC with navigational software, electronic charts and linked to a GPS receiver provides real-time navigation with, in effect, a chart plotter display. Software add-ons include tidal stream data, forecasts, communication links, autopilot controls and, for the racing yachtsman, tactical features such as tacking and gybing angles, instrument displays, countdown timing and startline overview. Laptops require linking to a GPS unit using an NMEA input. Configuration and a reliable power supply may pose problems. The advantages are that PCs can be taken ashore for security and passage planning.

3.10 RADAR AND AIS

3.10.1 Radar

Radar (**Ra**dio **D**irection **a**nd **R**ange) is used for both collision avoidance and navigation. To realise its full potential a sound understanding of its operation and limitations is required. The manufacturer's instruction book should be read carefully; time spent practising with the set to obtain optimum performance in different conditions will build confidence. Many controls have automatic default settings, but sometimes the best results can be obtained by manual tuning. Correct interpretation of the displayed information is fundamental to success.

Small craft radars transmit very short concentrated pulses of microwaves at a frequency of about 9500 MHz (X-band) and 3cm wavelength. Each pulse lasts less than a microsecond (pulse length) and the number of pulses transmitted per second (pulse repetition frequency or PRF) is normally between 800 and 3000. The reflected pulses are displayed on a screen.

Typical small craft radars can be interfaced with a flux gate compass to give three heading modes:

- **North-up:** North is at the top of the display, same as the chart. Recommended as it helps general orientation.
- **Head-up:** Ship's current heading at the top of the display. As the heading changes, the picture rotates; all bearings of radar returns are relative to the ship's head.
- **Course-up:** The selected course is at the top of the display. If a new course is selected, the picture rotates. As heading alters the heading marker moves in unison.

The ship is usually at the centre of the display, apparently stationary (*relative motion* mode), but can be offset so that a larger area of the screen is ahead, astern or abeam of the vessel. On most sets it is possible to select *true motion* where the vessel moves across the screen and the land stays still. This may seem ideal but there are disadvantages: contacts closing on a steady bearing are not obvious; precise speed input is essential; the image has to be reset whenever you get near the edge of the screen. Advanced radars can have split screens for simultaneous displays of radar picture, chart plotter and/or echosounder data.

For detailed references see *Using Radar* by Robert Avis (ACN) or *The Adlard Coles Book of Radar* by Borje Wallin (ACN).

3.10.2 Radar for collision avoidance

Having mastered the controls of your radar, you will need to be able to track individual contacts, assessing their course, speed, closest point of approach (CPA) and risk of collision. Practice makes perfect; you should be able to track and assess up to 3 contacts simultaneously.

In relative motion mode another vessel's course and speed are not obvious from the radar display; it needs to be worked out by resolving the relative velocity triangle.

- A vessel moving in the same direction and at the same speed as you is stationary relative to your boat; its echo should be bold and well defined.
- Collision will occur if another contact is on a steady bearing with its range decreasing, and no avoiding action is taken by either vessel.
- To decide the correct action to take, plot the contact at regular intervals to determine its course, speed, CPA and time to CPA. If the bearing changes, assess whether the vessel will cross ahead or astern of you.

- Plotting intervals depend on the contact's rate of closure. Keep plotting until all risk of collision is over.
- Some commercial vessels greatly exceed the safe speed stipulated by Rules 6 and 19b. Small craft skippers should be aware of this when deciding what avoiding action to take in restricted visibility.

When navigating in poor visibility a thorough working knowledge of Rule 19 of the ColRegs (IRPCS) is absolutely essential. Rule 19 is unusual in that:

- It differs markedly from Rules 11–18 (*Conduct of vessels in sight of one another*) which clearly distinguish between stand-on and give-way vessels. Rule 19 contains no such distinction; every vessel is responsible for keeping clear of others.
- It states what avoiding actions should **not** be taken, leaving the mariner to infer what positive options are open to him. These boil down to:
- Alter to starboard for a vessel forward of the beam (unless you are overtaking) and alter away from a vessel abeam or abaft the beam.
- In practice this means that you should always alter your course to starboard **except** for a vessel on your own starboard quarter – or if you are overtaking.

GRP yachts produce a poor radar return, so a good reflector is essential.

3.10.3 Radar as an aid to navigation

When used properly radar is a very useful aid to navigation, but it does have limitations:

- Radar cannot see behind other objects or around corners; it may not pick up small objects, or differentiate between two targets that are close together. Objects with flat surfaces, such as buildings or cliffs, reflect better than those with curved or sloping surfaces. A low coastline which is below the radar horizon will not be detected but returns from more distant high ground may be received, giving a false impression of the range of the nearest land. Approach with caution.
- Radar beams do not discriminate so well in bearing as they do in range, so 3 ranges will give a better fix than 3 radar bearings.
- The distance of the radar horizon is slightly greater than that of the visible horizon under average atmospheric conditions. It is given by $R = 2 \cdot 2 \times \sqrt{H^s}$ where R = Range (M) and H^s scanner height (m). Most small craft radars have a max range of 16 to 24M depending upon power output and scanner and target heights.

3.10.4 AIS

Automatic Identification System (AIS) was originated to monitor SOLAS traffic in key areas (in the Minches, for example, to safeguard the marine environment), and in choke points (for example, the Dover Strait). It is also widely used to assist in collision avoidance by automatically and continuously identifying, tracking and displaying other vessels' movements.

Each ship's course and speed vector is shown by a tadpole-like symbol on an AIS screen or overlaid on radar, chart plotter or PC. This data may also appear in a text box as heading, COG & SOG, range, CPA (in some sets); Lat/Long, ship's name (derived from its MMSI), and her status – under power or sail, anchored, constrained by draught, restricted in her ability to manoeuvre, not under command, fishing, etc. Range scales are usually 1, 2, 4, 8, 16 and 32M.

AIS must be fitted in passenger ships and all commercial vessels >300 GRT.

Caveats: Some ships do not switch on their AIS; some only display 3 lines of text, not a plot; in busy areas only the strongest signals may be shown; AIS may distract a bridge watchkeeper from his radar watch (yachts may therefore not be detected); unlike eyes and radar, AIS does not yet feature in IRPCS; GPS/electronic failures invalidate AIS.

AIS is not mandatory for leisure craft, but it is worth considering. Accurate and continuous display of other ships' courses and speeds (over the ground) removes any doubts when these parameters are derived solely from basic radar information. AIS sets suitable for small craft are available from about £200 (receive only) to over £600. Note: AIS is to some extent dependent on user inputs, and it is *not* a radar despite what some advertisements may imply!

3.11 RACONS (RADAR BEACONS)

A Racon is a transponder beacon often fitted to major light vessels, lighthouses and important buoys. It appears on charts as a magenta circle marked *Racon*. When triggered by a vessel's radar transmission it emits a distinctive coded return, much more easily recognised than a normal radar return.

Fig 3(6) Radar beacon responses

A Racon's return or 'flash' appears on the radar display as a line or narrow sector radiating outwards from a point slightly beyond the Racon's actual position. Thus a vessel's distance from the Racon, measured from where the flash begins, is slightly more than the actual distance. This is due to the slight response delay in the Racon apparatus. The coded identification flash is usually a Morse Code letter whose dashes/dots form a bold tail; see Fig 3(6). Racons fitted to temporary 'new danger' buoys are coded 'D', have a 10M range and are 'frequency agile'.

A Racon's maximum range is typically 10M, but may be greater. In practice, range depends on the power and elevation of both the Racon and vessel's radar. Thus a radar with 2–3kW power and scanner height 5m might not receive a buoy-mounted Racon, height also 5m, until only 6M from it.

Abnormal radio propagation may cause a spurious flash to be seen far beyond the quoted range, appearing along the correct bearing but at random ranges. A flash can only be relied upon if it seems to be stable and is within its quoted range. At short ranges a Racon can cause unwanted interference on the radar which may be reduced by adjusting the rain clutter control on the radar receiver.

3.11.1 Racon details
Racons are shown under 'Lights, buoys and waypoints' for each Area in Chapter 9 of this Almanac. Details given are:

- The Morse identification signal.
- Approximate maximum reception range (M).
- The angular sector within which the Racon signal can be received, if other than 360°.

Most Racons respond through 360° and scan the 3cm (X-band) frequency range. Frequency agile Racons respond automatically to both 3cm and 10cm (S-band) emissions. But the agile response is switched off for a few seconds every minute, so that the Racon response does not obscure any radar echoes which are needed.

3.11.2 Ramarks
Ramarks are similar to Racons except that they transmit continuously; they are not triggered by a ship's radar. The transmission forms a line of Morse characters which radiates from the centre of the radar display to its edge, and cannot therefore give any distance-off. They are shown on the chart by a magenta circle labelled *Ramark*.

3.12 NAVIGATIONAL WARNINGS

Navigational warnings are promulgated for 16 NavAreas (I–XVI) worldwide. An Area co-ordinator oversees each NavArea and handles inputs from national and other authorities. The 3 types of navigational warnings are:

NavArea warnings which deal with Oceanic matters and are transmitted by SafetyNet and Navtex at scheduled times in English and other languages.

Coastal warnings, up to 250M offshore, are issued by a national authority and broadcast in English or the local language by Navtex, SafetyNet or VHF Coast radio stations. These warnings cover navaids, lights, buoys, rocks, wrecks, naval exercises, SAR operations, cable laying, piracy, etc.

Local warnings supplement the above for inshore waters and within port limits. They are issued by port, pilotage or CG authorities in English and/or the local language.

Full details for all the Areas covered by this Almanac, including broadcast times, are in Chapter 5.

3.13 HAZARDS

3.13.1 Submarines
Fishing vessels, and occasionally yachts, have been snagged or hit by submarines operating just below the surface. The risk is greatest in the western English Channel, Irish Sea, Firth of Clyde, North Channel and West Scotland, especially at night. Submarine exercise areas are shown by name and/or number in 9.8.22 and 9.9.16.

If possible avoid submarine exercise areas shown on the charts, but when in an exercise area the best advice is:

- Listen to and take heed of Subfacts (See Chapter 5).
- Keep clear of any vessel flying Code flags 'NE2' to indicate that submarines are in the vicinity.
- Run the engine (even when under sail) and operate the echo sounder.
- At night show navigation lights on pulpit and stern; they are more likely to be seen by a submarine at periscope depth than a tricolour at the masthead.

3.13.2 Gunfacts
Gunfacts are warnings of intended naval gunnery and missile practice firings, and underwater explosions. They do not restrict the passage of any vessel, and the onus for safety is on the firing warship. For further details see Chapter 5.

3.13.3 Mines

In the unlikely event of coming across a mine at sea:

- Do not prod it with a boathook, and do not shoot at it – a bullet may pierce the mine but not detonate it. It could then wash ashore in a dangerous state.

- Do not try to tow it to port. Financial rewards for such action have been discontinued.

- Keep a copy of NP100 (The Mariner's Handbook) by your bunk. It is a mine of information. For example, if a mine approaches you whilst at anchor, deflect it from your vessel by creating an off-boat current around it with a fire hose.

- Do tell the Coastguard on Ch 16; it may be the only Sécurité call you ever make.

3.14 OFFSHORE ENERGY INSTALLATIONS

Gas and oil fields have featured in the North Sea since the 1960s. With careful passage planning and a detailed study of AC 2182A, B, C and D they can usually be avoided at a safe distance without undue detours. Most are protected by Safety zones, usually 500m radius, in which it is a criminal offence for unauthorised vessels to enter, anchor or fish. The simple message to small craft navigators is *stay well clear of all such installations at all times*.

3.14.1 Wind farms

Wind farms (groups of wind turbines) are proliferating, mostly in the shallow waters over coastal banks. These are areas which small craft would not normally cross, especially in bad weather. The wind turbines give early visual warning of where the intervening navigable channels lie. Thus they may assist rather than hinder the navigator.

A typical example is the large (80 turbines) wind farm in depths of 5–12m off the W coast of Denmark within the notorious Horns Rev (reef) 9M WSW of Blåvandshuk; see Area 14, Fig 14(1). All turbines have FR lights and the 10M perimeter is marked by 12 Fl Y lts and 2 Racons. The adjacent Slugen Channel through Horns Rev is unaffected.

By 2010 numbers and generating capacity of wind turbines worldwide are forecast to rise steeply. Wind farms will tend to move into deeper waters (20–25m) and further offshore, 23M (42km).

More information is in the relevant Areas of this Almanac and at: www. mcga.gov.uk, www.bwea.com/offshore (British Wind Energy Association) and www.thecrown estate.co.uk.

3.14.2 Effects on navaids

Trials show that wind farms have no adverse effects on GPS, magnetic compasses and VHF. Predictably, small craft radar performance is degraded by blind or shadow areas, and by large or spurious echoes. Mariners should report to the MCA or RYA any unusual effects found in or near a wind farm.

3.14.3 Navigating within a wind farm

The best advice is **stay well clear of all wind farms at all times**. There is rarely any good reason to enter a wind farm. Any emergencies whilst in a wind farm will probably require outside assistance: a PAN PAN or MAYDAY call.

Whilst navigation within a wind farm is not prohibited, the MCA advise that it should only be undertaken after a 'reasoned judgement of the risks involved'.

Consider also the following:

- Bad weather, poor visibility and darkness exacerbate the risks.

- Sea state, height of tide, depths and tidal streams may cause turbulence around the pylons.

- Wind turbulence and fickle conditions caused by the turbines may make sailing difficult.

- A 50m radius safety zone exists around each pylon with 700m spacing between pylons.

- No anchoring is possible due to submarine cables.

3.15 NAVIGATIONAL TABLES

Brief explanations and notes, where necessary, are given below on how to use the tables on the following pages.

Table 3 (1) – Distance of horizon

Enter with height (m/ft) of eye, and extract the theoretical distance (M) of horizon. Actual distance could be reduced by abnormal refraction. Maximum height of eye is desirable; climbing onto the boom may double your height of eye.

TABLE 3(1) DISTANCE OF HORIZON					
Height of eye		Horizon distance	Height of eye		Horizon distance
metres	feet	M	metres	feet	M
1	3·3	2·1	21	68·9	9·5
2	6·6	2·9	22	72·2	9·8
3	9·8	3·6	23	75·5	10·0
4	13·1	4·1	24	78·7	10·2
5	16·4	4·7	25	82·0	10·4
6	19·7	5·1	26	85·3	10·6
7	23·0	5·5	27	88·6	10·8
8	26·2	5·9	28	91·9	11·0
9	29·6	6·2	29	95·1	11·2
10	32·8	6·6	30	98·4	11·4
11	36·1	6·9	31	101·7	11·6
12	39·4	7·2	32	105·0	11·8
13	42·7	7·5	33	108·3	12·0
14	45·9	7·8	34	111·6	12·1
15	49·2	8·1	35	114·8	12·3
16	52·5	8·3	36	118·1	12·5
17	55·8	8·6	37	121·4	12·7
18	59·1	8·8	38	124·7	12·8
19	62·3	9·1	39	128·0	13·0
20	65·6	9·3	40	131·2	13·2

Table 3(2) – Distance, speed and time

Enter with time (minutes or decimals of an hour, if using a calculator) and speed (kn) to determine distance run (M). Or extract speed or time as a function of the other two variables; for example speed over a measured mile. For speeds >20kn, use multiples of lesser speeds.

TABLE 3(2) DISTANCE, SPEED AND TIME

TIME Decimal of hr	Mins	3.0	4.0	5.0	6.0	7.0	8.0	9.0	10.0	11.0	12.0	13.0	14.0	15.0	16.0	17.0	18.0	19.0	20.0	Mins	TIME Decimal of hr
.0167	1		0.1	0.1	0.1	0.1	0.1	0.2	0.2	0.2	0.2	0.2	0.2	0.3	0.3	0.3	0.3	0.3	0.3	1	.0167
.0333	2	0.1	0.1	0.2	0.2	0.2	0.3	0.3	0.3	0.4	0.4	0.4	0.5	0.5	0.5	0.6	0.6	0.6	0.7	2	.0333
.0500	3	0.1	0.2	0.2	0.3	0.3	0.4	0.4	0.5	0.5	0.6	0.6	0.7	0.7	0.8	0.8	0.8	0.9	1.0	3	.0500
.0667	4	0.2	0.3	0.3	0.4	0.5	0.5	0.6	0.7	0.7	0.8	0.9	0.9	1.0	1.1	1.1	1.2	1.3	1.3	4	.0667
.0833	5	0.2	0.3	0.4	0.5	0.6	0.7	0.7	0.8	0.9	1.0	1.1	1.2	1.2	1.3	1.4	1.5	1.6	1.7	5	.0833
.1000	6	0.3	0.4	0.5	0.6	0.7	0.8	0.9	1.0	1.1	1.2	1.3	1.4	1.5	1.6	1.7	1.8	1.9	2.0	6	.1000
.1167	7	0.4	0.5	0.6	0.7	0.8	0.9	1.1	1.2	1.3	1.4	1.5	1.6	1.8	1.9	2.0	2.1	2.2	2.3	7	.1167
.1333	8	0.4	0.5	0.7	0.8	0.9	1.1	1.2	1.3	1.5	1.6	1.7	1.9	2.0	2.1	2.3	2.4	2.5	2.7	8	.1333
.1500	9	0.4	0.6	0.7	0.9	1.0	1.2	1.3	1.5	1.6	1.8	1.9	2.1	2.2	2.4	2.5	2.7	2.8	3.0	9	.1500
.1667	10	0.5	0.7	0.8	1.0	1.2	1.3	1.5	1.7	1.8	2.0	2.2	2.3	2.5	2.7	2.8	3.0	3.2	3.3	10	.1667
.1833	11	0.5	0.7	0.9	1.1	1.3	1.5	1.6	1.8	2.0	2.2	2.4	2.6	2.7	2.9	3.1	3.3	3.5	3.7	11	.1833
.2000	12	0.6	0.8	1.0	1.2	1.4	1.6	1.8	2.0	2.2	2.4	2.6	2.8	3.0	3.2	3.4	3.6	3.8	4.0	12	.2000
.2167	13	0.6	0.9	1.1	1.3	1.5	1.7	2.0	2.2	2.4	2.6	2.8	3.0	3.2	3.5	3.7	3.9	4.1	4.3	13	.2167
.2333	14	0.7	0.9	1.2	1.4	1.6	1.9	2.1	2.3	2.6	2.8	3.0	3.3	3.5	3.7	4.0	4.2	4.4	4.7	14	.2333
.2500	15	0.7	1.0	1.2	1.5	1.8	2.0	2.2	2.5	2.7	3.0	3.2	3.5	3.7	4.0	4.2	4.5	4.7	5.0	15	.2500
.2667	16	0.8	1.1	1.3	1.6	1.9	2.1	2.4	2.7	2.9	3.2	3.5	3.7	4.0	4.3	4.5	4.8	5.1	5.3	16	.2667
.2833	17	0.8	1.1	1.4	1.7	2.0	2.3	2.5	2.8	3.1	3.4	3.7	4.0	4.2	4.5	4.8	5.1	5.4	5.7	17	.2833
.3000	18	0.9	1.2	1.5	1.8	2.1	2.4	2.7	3.0	3.3	3.6	3.9	4.2	4.5	4.8	5.1	5.4	5.7	6.0	18	.3000
.3167	19	1.0	1.3	1.6	1.9	2.1	2.5	2.9	3.2	3.5	3.8	4.1	4.4	4.8	5.1	5.4	5.7	6.0	6.3	19	.3167
.3333	20	1.0	1.3	1.7	2.0	2.3	2.7	3.0	3.3	3.7	4.0	4.3	4.7	5.0	5.3	5.7	6.0	6.3	6.7	20	.3333
.3500	21	1.0	1.4	1.7	2.1	2.4	2.8	3.1	3.5	3.8	4.2	4.5	4.9	5.2	5.6	5.9	6.3	6.6	7.0	21	.3500
.3667	22	1.1	1.5	1.8	2.2	2.6	2.9	3.3	3.7	4.0	4.4	4.8	5.1	5.5	5.9	6.2	6.6	7.0	7.3	22	.3667
.3833	23	1.1	1.5	1.9	2.3	2.7	3.1	3.4	3.8	4.2	4.6	5.0	5.4	5.7	6.1	6.5	6.9	7.3	7.7	23	.3833
.4000	24	1.2	1.6	2.0	2.4	2.8	3.2	3.6	4.0	4.4	4.8	5.2	5.6	6.0	6.4	6.8	7.2	7.6	8.0	24	.4000
.4167	25	1.3	1.7	2.1	2.5	2.9	3.3	3.8	4.2	4.6	5.0	5.4	5.8	6.3	6.7	7.1	7.5	7.9	8.3	25	.4167
.4333	26	1.3	1.7	2.2	2.6	3.0	3.5	3.9	4.3	4.8	5.2	5.6	6.1	6.5	6.9	7.4	7.8	8.2	8.7	26	.4333
.4500	27	1.3	1.8	2.2	2.7	3.1	3.6	4.0	4.5	4.9	5.4	5.8	6.3	6.7	7.2	7.6	8.1	8.5	9.0	27	.4500
.4667	28	1.4	1.9	2.3	2.8	3.3	3.7	4.2	4.7	5.1	5.6	6.1	6.5	7.0	7.5	7.9	8.4	8.9	9.3	28	.4667
.4833	29	1.5	1.9	2.4	2.9	3.4	3.9	4.3	4.8	5.3	5.8	6.3	6.8	7.2	7.7	8.2	8.7	9.2	9.7	29	.4833
.5000	30	1.5	2.0	2.5	3.0	3.5	4.0	4.5	5.0	5.5	6.0	6.5	7.0	7.5	8.0	8.5	9.0	9.5	10.0	30	.5000
.5167	31	1.6	2.1	2.6	3.1	3.6	4.1	4.7	5.2	5.7	6.2	6.7	7.2	7.8	8.3	8.8	9.3	9.8	10.3	31	.5167
.5333	32	1.6	2.1	2.7	3.2	3.7	4.3	4.8	5.3	5.9	6.4	6.9	7.5	8.0	8.5	9.1	9.6	10.1	10.7	32	.5333
.5500	33	1.6	2.2	2.7	3.3	3.8	4.4	4.9	5.5	6.0	6.6	7.1	7.7	8.2	8.8	9.3	9.9	10.4	11.0	33	.5500
.5667	34	1.7	2.3	2.8	3.4	4.0	4.5	5.1	5.7	6.2	6.8	7.4	7.9	8.5	9.1	9.6	10.2	10.8	11.3	34	.5667
.5833	35	1.7	2.3	2.9	3.5	4.1	4.7	5.2	5.8	6.4	7.0	7.6	8.2	8.7	9.3	9.9	10.5	11.1	11.7	35	.5833
.6000	36	1.8	2.4	3.0	3.6	4.2	4.8	5.4	6.0	6.6	7.2	7.8	8.4	9.0	9.6	10.2	10.8	11.4	12.0	36	.6000
.6117	37	1.8	2.4	3.1	3.7	4.3	4.9	5.5	6.1	6.7	7.3	8.0	8.6	9.2	9.8	10.4	11.0	11.6	12.2	37	.6117
.6333	38	1.9	2.5	3.2	3.8	4.4	5.1	5.7	6.3	7.0	7.6	8.2	8.9	9.5	10.1	10.8	11.4	12.0	12.7	38	.6333
.6500	39	1.9	2.6	3.2	3.9	4.5	5.2	5.8	6.5	7.1	7.8	8.4	9.1	9.7	10.4	11.0	11.7	12.3	13.0	39	.6500
.6667	40	2.0	2.7	3.3	4.0	4.7	5.3	6.0	6.7	7.3	8.0	8.7	9.3	10.0	10.7	11.3	12.0	12.7	13.3	40	.6667
.6833	41	2.0	2.7	3.4	4.1	4.8	5.5	6.1	6.8	7.5	8.2	8.9	9.6	10.2	10.9	11.6	12.3	13.0	13.7	41	.6833
.7000	42	2.1	2.8	3.5	4.2	4.9	5.6	6.3	7.0	7.7	8.4	9.1	9.8	10.5	11.2	11.9	12.6	13.3	14.0	42	.7000
.7167	43	2.2	2.9	3.6	4.3	5.0	5.7	6.5	7.2	7.9	8.6	9.3	10.0	10.8	11.5	12.2	12.9	13.6	14.3	43	.7167
.7333	44	2.2	2.9	3.7	4.4	5.1	5.9	6.6	7.3	8.1	8.8	9.5	10.3	11.0	11.7	12.5	13.2	13.9	14.7	44	.7333
.7500	45	2.2	3.0	3.7	4.5	5.2	6.0	6.7	7.5	8.2	9.0	9.7	10.5	11.2	12.0	12.7	13.5	14.2	15.0	45	.7500
.7667	46	2.3	3.1	3.8	4.6	5.4	6.1	6.9	7.7	8.4	9.2	10.0	10.7	11.5	12.3	13.0	13.8	14.6	15.3	46	.7667
.7833	47	2.3	3.1	3.9	4.7	5.5	6.3	7.0	7.8	8.6	9.4	10.2	11.0	11.7	12.5	13.3	14.1	14.9	15.7	47	.7833
.8000	48	2.4	3.2	4.0	4.8	5.6	6.4	7.2	8.0	8.8	9.6	10.4	11.2	12.0	12.8	13.6	14.4	15.2	16.0	48	.8000
.8167	49	2.5	3.3	4.1	4.9	5.7	6.5	7.4	8.2	9.0	9.8	10.6	11.4	12.2	13.1	13.9	14.7	15.5	16.3	49	.8167
.8333	50	2.5	3.3	4.2	5.0	5.8	6.7	7.5	8.3	9.2	10.0	10.8	11.7	12.5	13.3	14.2	15.0	15.8	16.7	50	.8333
.8500	51	2.5	3.4	4.2	5.1	5.9	6.8	7.6	8.5	9.3	10.2	11.0	11.9	12.7	13.6	14.4	15.3	16.1	17.0	51	.8500
.8667	52	2.6	3.5	4.3	5.2	6.1	6.9	7.8	8.7	9.5	10.4	11.3	12.1	13.0	13.9	14.7	15.6	16.5	17.3	52	.8667
.8833	53	2.6	3.5	4.4	5.3	6.2	7.1	7.9	8.8	9.7	10.6	11.5	12.4	13.2	14.1	15.0	15.9	16.8	17.7	53	.8833
.9000	54	2.7	3.6	4.5	5.4	6.3	7.2	8.1	9.0	9.9	10.8	11.7	12.6	13.5	14.4	15.3	16.2	17.1	18.0	54	.9000
.9167	55	2.8	3.7	4.6	5.5	6.4	7.3	8.3	9.2	10.1	11.0	11.9	12.8	13.8	14.7	15.6	16.5	17.4	18.3	55	.9167
.9333	56	2.8	3.7	4.7	5.6	6.5	7.5	8.4	9.3	10.3	11.2	12.1	13.1	14.0	14.9	15.9	16.8	17.7	18.7	56	.9333
.9500	57	2.8	3.8	4.7	5.7	6.6	7.6	8.5	9.5	10.4	11.4	12.3	13.3	14.2	15.2	16.1	17.1	18.0	19.0	57	.9500
.9667	58	2.9	3.9	4.8	5.8	6.8	7.7	8.7	9.7	10.6	11.6	12.6	13.5	14.5	15.5	16.4	17.4	18.4	19.3	58	.9667
.9833	59	2.9	3.9	4.9	5.9	6.9	7.9	8.8	9.8	10.8	11.8	12.8	13.8	14.7	15.7	16.7	17.7	18.7	19.7	59	.9833
1.0000	60	3.0	4.0	5.0	6.0	7.0	8.0	9.0	10.0	11.0	12.0	13.0	14.0	15.0	16.0	17.0	18.0	19.0	20.0	60	1.0000

Table 3(3) – Distance off by vertical sextant angle (VSA)
From height (m/ft) of the object read across to the VSA obtained (corrected for index error). At the top of the table read off the distance (M) of the object.

If the base of, say, a lighthouse is below the horizon, the VSA will over-read the distance. For very precise ranges, add the amount by which sea level is below MHWS to the height of the object (above MHWS) – before entering the table.

TABLE 3(3)	DISTANCE OFF BY VERTICAL SEXTANT ANGLE															
HEIGHT OF OBJECT		DISTANCE OF OBJECT (NAUTICAL MILES)														
ft	m	0·2	0·4	0·6	0·8	1·0	1·2	1·4	1·6	1·8	2·0	2·4	2·8	3·2	3·6	4·0	5·0
		° ′	° ′	° ′	° ′	° ′	° ′	° ′	° ′	° ′	° ′	° ′	° ′	° ′	° ′	° ′	° ′
33	10	1 33	0 46	0 31	0 23	0 19	0 15	0 13	0 12	0 10							
39	12	1 51	0 56	0 37	0 28	0 22	0 19	0 16	0 14	0 12	0 11	0 10					
46	14	2 10	1 05	0 43	0 32	0 26	0 22	0 19	0 16	0 14	0 13	0 11					
53	16	2 28	1 14	0 49	0 37	0 30	0 25	0 21	0 19	0 16	0 15	0 12	0 11				
59	18	2 47	1 24	0 56	0 42	0 33	0 28	0 24	0 21	0 19	0 17	0 14	0 12	0 10			
66	20	3 05	1 33	1 02	0 46	0 37	0 31	0 27	0 23	0 21	0 19	0 15	0 13	0 12	0 10		
72	22	3 24	1 42	1 08	0 51	0 41	0 34	0 29	0 26	0 23	0 20	0 17	0 15	0 13	0 11	0 10	
79	24	3 42	1 51	1 14	0 56	0 45	0 37	0 32	0 28	0 25	0 22	0 19	0 16	0 14	0 12	0 11	
85	26	4 01	2 01	1 20	1 00	0 48	0 40	0 34	0 30	0 27	0 24	0 20	0 17	0 15	0 13	0 12	
92	28	4 19	2 10	1 27	1 05	0 52	0 43	0 37	0 32	0 29	0 26	0 22	0 19	0 16	0 14	0 13	0 10
98	30	4 38	2 19	1 33	1 10	0 56	0 46	0 40	0 35	0 31	0 28	0 23	0 20	0 17	0 15	0 14	0 11
105	32	4 56	2 28	1 39	1 14	0 59	0 49	0 42	0 37	0 33	0 30	0 25	0 21	0 19	0 16	0 15	0 12
112	34	5 15	2 38	1 45	1 19	1 03	0 53	0 45	0 39	0 35	0 31	0 26	0 23	0 20	0 17	0 16	0 13
118	36	5 33	2 47	1 51	1 24	1 07	0 56	0 48	0 42	0 37	0 33	0 28	0 24	0 21	0 19	0 17	0 13
125	38	5 41	2 56	1 58	1 28	1 11	0 59	0 50	0 44	0 39	0 35	0 29	0 25	0 22	0 20	0 18	0 14
131	40	6 10	3 05	2 04	1 33	1 14	1 02	0 53	0 46	0 41	0 37	0 31	0 27	0 23	0 21	0 19	0 15
138	42	6 28	3 15	2 10	1 37	1 18	1 05	0 56	0 49	0 43	0 40	0 32	0 28	0 24	0 22	0 19	0 16
144	44	6 46	3 24	2 16	1 42	1 22	1 08	0 58	0 51	0 45	0 41	0 34	0 29	0 25	0 23	0 20	0 16
151	46	7 05	3 33	2 22	1 47	1 25	1 11	1 01	0 53	0 47	0 43	0 36	0 30	0 27	0 24	0 21	0 17
157	48	7 23	3 42	2 28	1 51	1 29	1 14	1 04	0 56	0 49	0 45	0 37	0 32	0 28	0 25	0 22	0 18
164	50	7 41	3 52	2 35	1 56	1 33	1 17	1 06	0 58	0 52	0 46	0 39	0 33	0 29	0 26	0 23	0 19
171	52	7 59	4 01	2 41	2 01	1 36	1 20	1 09	1 00	0 54	0 48	0 40	0 34	0 30	0 27	0 24	0 19
177	54	8 18	4 10	2 47	2 05	1 40	1 23	1 12	1 03	0 56	0 50	0 42	0 36	0 31	0 28	0 25	0 20
184	56	8 36	4 19	2 53	2 10	1 44	1 27	1 14	1 05	0 58	0 52	0 43	0 37	0 32	0 29	0 26	0 21
190	58	8 54	4 29	2 59	2 15	1 48	1 30	1 17	1 07	1 00	0 54	0 45	0 38	0 34	0 30	0 27	0 21
197	60	9 12	4 38	3 05	2 19	1 51	1 33	1 20	1 10	1 02	0 56	0 46	0 40	0 35	0 31	0 28	0 22
203	62	9 30	4 47	3 12	2 24	1 55	1 36	1 22	1 12	1 04	0 58	0 48	0 41	0 36	0 32	0 29	0 23
210	64	9 48	4 56	3 18	2 28	1 59	1 39	1 25	1 14	1 06	0 59	0 49	0 42	0 37	0 33	0 30	0 24
217	66	10 06	5 05	3 24	2 33	2 02	1 42	1 27	1 17	1 08	1 01	0 51	0 44	0 38	0 34	0 31	0 25
223	68	10 24	5 15	3 30	2 38	2 06	1 45	1 30	1 19	1 10	1 03	0 53	0 45	0 39	0 35	0 32	0 25
230	70	10 42	5 24	3 36	2 42	2 09	1 48	1 33	1 21	1 12	1 05	0 54	0 46	0 41	0 36	0 32	0 26
236	72	11 00	5 33	3 42	2 47	2 14	1 51	1 35	1 24	1 14	1 07	0 56	0 48	0 42	0 37	0 33	0 27
246	75	11 27	5 47	3 52	2 54	2 19	1 56	1 39	1 27	1 17	1 10	0 58	0 50	0 44	0 39	0 35	0 28
256	78	11 54	6 01	4 01	3 01	2 24	2 01	1 43	1 30	1 20	1 12	1 00	0 52	0 45	0 40	0 36	0 29
266	81	12 20	6 14	4 10	3 08	2 30	2 05	1 47	1 34	1 23	1 15	1 03	0 54	0 47	0 42	0 38	0 30
276	84	12 47	6 28	4 19	3 15	2 36	2 10	1 51	1 37	1 27	1 18	1 05	0 56	0 49	0 43	0 39	0 31
289	88	13 22	6 46	4 32	3 24	2 43	2 16	1 57	1 42	1 31	1 22	1 08	0 58	0 51	0 45	0 41	0 33
302	92	13 57	7 05	4 44	3 33	2 51	2 22	2 02	1 47	1 35	1 25	1 11	1 01	0 53	0 47	0 43	0 34
315	96	14 32	7 23	4 56	3 42	2 58	2 28	2 07	1 51	1 39	1 29	1 14	1 04	0 56	0 49	0 45	0 36
328	100	15 07	7 41	5 09	3 52	3 05	2 35	2 13	1 56	1 43	1 33	1 17	1 06	0 58	0 52	0 46	0 37
341	104	15 41	7 59	5 21	4 01	3 13	2 41	2 18	2 01	1 47	1 36	1 20	1 09	1 00	0 54	0 48	0 39
358	109	16 24	8 22	5 36	4 12	3 22	2 48	2 24	2 06	1 52	1 41	1 24	1 12	1 03	0 56	0 51	0 40
374	114	17 06	8 45	5 51	4 24	3 31	2 56	2 31	2 12	1 58	1 46	1 28	1 16	1 06	0 59	0 53	0 42
394	120	17 57	9 12	6 10	4 38	3 42	3 05	2 39	2 19	2 04	1 51	1 33	1 20	1 10	1 02	0 56	0 45
427	130	19 20	9 57	6 40	5 01	4 01	3 21	2 52	2 31	2 14	2 01	1 41	1 26	1 15	1 07	1 00	0 48
459	140	20 42	10 42	7 11	5 24	4 19	3 36	3 05	2 42	2 24	2 10	1 48	1 33	1 21	1 12	1 05	0 52
492	150	22 03	11 27	7 41	5 47	4 38	3 52	3 19	2 54	2 35	2 19	1 56	1 39	1 27	1 17	1 10	0 56
574	175	25 17	13 17	8 57	6 44	5 24	4 30	3 52	3 23	3 00	2 42	2 15	1 56	1 41	1 30	1 21	1 05
656	200	28 22	15 07	10 12	7 41	6 10	5 09	4 25	3 52	3 26	3 05	2 35	2 13	1 56	1 43	1 33	1 14
738	225		16 54	11 27	8 38	6 56	5 47	4 58	4 21	3 52	3 29	2 54	2 29	2 10	1 56	1 44	1 24
820	250		18 39	12 41	9 35	7 41	6 25	5 30	4 49	4 17	3 52	3 13	2 46	2 25	2 09	1 56	1 33
902	275		20 22	13 54	10 31	8 27	7 03	6 03	5 18	4 43	4 15	3 32	3 02	2 39	2 22	2 08	1 42
984	300		22 03	15 07	11 27	9 12	7 41	6 36	5 47	5 09	4 38	3 52	3 19	2 54	2 35	2 19	1 51
1148	350			17 29	13 17	10 42	8 57	7 41	6 44	6 00	5 24	4 30	3 52	3 23	3 00	2 42	2 10
1312	400			19 48	15 07	12 11	10 12	8 46	7 41	6 51	6 10	5 09	4 25	3 52	3 26	3 05	2 28

Tables 3(4) & 3(5) – Checking a compass for accuracy

The accuracy of a boat's magnetic compass can be checked against the true bearing of the sun at sunrise or sunset. The sun's declination and the boat's approximate latitude are all that are needed; no sextant or sight reduction tables.

Since bearings probably cannot be taken with the steering compass, steer the boat directly towards or away from the rising or setting sun, aligning it with the mast.

Due to refraction, which is about 34' when observing bodies on the horizon, the sun's bearing should be taken when its lower limb is just over half a diameter above the horizon.

Table 3(4) – Sun's declination

Enter with the appropriate date band and read across to the centre column.

Extract and record declination (bold type), noting whether it is North or South.

Table 3(5) – True bearing of sun at sunrise and sunset

Enter with the approximate latitude and declination, obtained from Table 3(4). Extract the tabulated bearing.

The True bearing is measured from North if declination is North, or from South if declination is South; towards the East if rising or towards the West if setting.

For example on 26 Aug, declination 10°N and latitude 45°N: the tabulated bearing is 75·8°, say 76°. If the sun is rising the True bearing will be N76°E, ie 076°T.

Apply local magnetic variation to 076°T and compare the result with the compass reading to determine deviation on the course steered.

3 examples of different Dec N/S and whether rising/setting:

Lat	Dec	SR/SS	Tab brg	True bearing	
45°	10°N	Setting	76°	N76°W	= 284°
45°	10°S	Rising	76°	S76°E	= 104°
45°	10°S	Setting	76°	S76°W	= 256°

Table 3(4) Sun's declination for 2010

SOUTH		DECLINATION	NORTH	
	Dec 06 - Jan 05	23°		Jun 04 - Jul 07
Jan 06 - Jan 12	Nov 29 - Dec 05	22°	May 28 - Jun 03	Jul 08 - Jul 14
Jan 13 - Jan 17	Nov 24 - Nov 28	21°	May 22 - May 27	Jul 15 - Jul 20
Jan 18 - Jan 22	Nov 19 - Nov 23	20°	May 18 - May 21	Jul 21 - Jul 25
Jan 23 - Jan 26	Nov 15 - Nov 18	19°	May 13 - May 17	Jul 26 - Jul 29
Jan 27 - Jan 29	Nov 11 - Nov 14	18°	May 09 - May 12	Jul 30 - Aug 02
Jan 30 - Feb 02	Nov 08 - Nov 10	17°	May 06 - May 08	Aug 03 - Aug 06
Feb 03 - Feb 05	Nov 04 - Nov 07	16°	May 02 - May 05	Aug 07 - Aug 09
Feb 06 - Feb 08	Nov 01 - Nov 03	15°	Apr 29 - May 01	Aug 10 - Aug 12
Feb 09 - Feb 11	Oct 29 - Oct 31	14°	Apr 26 - Apr 28	Aug 13 - Aug 16
Feb 12 - Feb 14	Oct 26 - Oct 28	13°	Apr 23 - Apr 25	Aug 17 - Aug 19
Feb 15 - Feb 17	Oct 23 - Oct 25	12°	Apr 20 - Apr 22	Aug 20 - Aug 22
Feb 18 - Feb 20	Oct 20 - Oct 22	11°	Apr 17 - Apr 19	Aug 23 - Aug 25
Feb 21 - Feb 23	Oct 18 - Oct 19	10°	Apr 14 - Apr 16	Aug 26 - Aug 27
Feb 24 - Feb 25	Oct 15 - Oct 17	9°	Apr 11 - Apr 13	Aug 28 - Aug 30
Feb 26 - Feb 28	Oct 12 - Oct 14	8°	Apr 09 - Apr 10	Aug 31 - Sep 02
Mar 01 - Mar 03	Oct 09 - Oct 11	7°	Apr 06 - Apr 08	Sep 03 - Sep 05
Mar 04 - Mar 05	Oct 07 - Oct 08	6°	Apr 03 - Apr 05	Sep 06 - Sep 07
Mar 06 - Mar 08	Oct 04 - Oct 06	5°	Apr 01 - Apr 02	Sep 08 - Sep 10
Mar 09 - Mar 10	Oct 02 - Oct 03	4°	Mar 29 - Mar 31	Sep 11 - Sep 13
Mar 11 - Mar 13	Sep 29 - Oct 01	3°	Mar 27 - Mar 28	Sep 14 - Sep 15
Mar 14 - Mar 15	Sep 26 - Sep 28	2°	Mar 24 - Mar 26	Sep 16 - Sep 18
Mar 16 - Mar 18	Sep 24 - Sep 25	1°	Mar 21 - Mar 23	Sep 19 - Sep 20
Mar 19 - Mar 20	Sep 21 - Sep 23	0°	Mar 19 - Mar 20	Sep 21 - Sep 23

TABLE 3(5) TRUE BEARING OF SUN AT SUNRISE AND SUNSET

DECLINATION

LAT	0°	1°	2°	3°	4°	5°	6°	7°	8°	9°	10°	11°	LAT
30°	90	88.8	87.7	86.5	85.4	84.2	83.1	81.9	80.7	79.6	78.4	77.3	30°
31°	90	88.8	87.7	86.5	85.3	84.2	83.0	81.9	80.6	79.5	78.3	77.1	31°
32°	90	88.8	87.6	86.5	85.3	84.1	82.9	81.7	80.5	79.4	78.2	77.0	32°
33°	90	88.8	87.6	86.4	85.2	84.0	82.8	81.6	80.4	79.2	78.0	76.8	33°
34°	90	88.8	87.6	86.4	85.2	84.0	82.7	81.5	80.3	79.1	77.9	76.7	34°
35°	90	88.8	87.5	86.3	85.1	83.9	82.7	81.4	80.2	79.0	77.8	76.5	35°
36°	90	88.8	87.5	86.3	85.0	83.8	82.6	81.3	80.1	78.8	77.6	76.3	36°
37°	90	88.7	87.5	86.2	85.0	83.7	82.5	81.2	80.0	78.7	77.4	76.2	37°
38°	90	88.7	87.5	86.2	84.9	83.6	82.4	81.1	79.8	78.5	77.3	76.0	38°
39°	90	88.7	87.4	86.1	84.8	83.6	82.3	81.0	79.7	78.4	77.1	75.8	39°
40°	90	88.7	87.4	86.1	84.8	83.5	82.1	80.8	79.5	78.2	76.9	75.6	40°
41°	90	88.7	87.3	86.0	84.7	83.4	82.0	80.7	79.4	78.0	76.7	75.3	41°
42°	90	88.6	87.3	86.0	84.6	83.3	81.9	80.6	79.2	77.8	76.5	75.1	42°
43°	90	88.6	87.3	85.9	84.5	83.1	81.8	80.4	79.0	77.6	76.3	74.9	43°
44°	90	88.6	87.2	85.8	84.4	83.0	81.6	80.2	78.8	77.4	76.0	74.6	44°
45°	90	88.6	87.2	85.7	84.3	82.9	81.5	80.1	78.6	77.2	75.8	74.3	45°
46°	90	88.6	87.1	85.7	84.2	82.8	81.3	79.9	78.4	77.0	75.5	74.0	46°
47°	90	88.5	87.1	85.6	84.1	82.6	81.2	79.7	78.2	76.7	75.2	73.7	47°
48°	90	88.5	87.0	85.5	84.0	82.5	81.0	79.5	78.0	76.5	75.0	73.4	48°
49°	90	88.5	86.9	85.4	83.9	82.4	80.8	79.3	77.7	76.2	74.6	73.1	49°
50°	90	88.4	86.9	85.3	83.8	82.2	80.6	79.1	77.5	75.9	74.3	72.7	50°
51°	90	88.4	86.8	85.2	83.6	82.0	80.4	78.8	77.2	75.6	74.0	72.4	51°
52°	90	88.4	86.7	85.1	83.5	81.9	80.2	78.6	76.9	75.3	73.6	71.9	52°
53°	90	88.3	86.7	85.0	83.3	81.7	80.0	78.3	76.6	74.9	73.2	71.5	53°
54°	90	88.3	86.6	84.9	83.2	81.5	79.8	78.0	76.3	74.6	72.8	71.1	54°
55°	90	88.2	86.5	84.8	83.0	81.3	79.5	77.7	76.0	74.2	72.4	70.6	55°
56°	90	88.2	86.4	84.6	82.8	81.0	79.2	77.4	75.6	73.8	71.9	70.0	56°
57°	90	88.2	86.3	84.5	82.6	80.8	78.9	77.0	75.2	73.3	71.4	69.5	57°
58°	90	88.1	86.2	84.3	82.4	80.5	78.6	76.7	74.8	72.8	70.9	68.9	58°
59°	90	88.1	86.1	84.2	82.2	80.3	78.3	76.3	74.3	72.3	70.3	68.3	59°
60°	90	88.0	86.0	84.0	82.0	80.0	77.9	75.9	73.8	71.8	69.7	67.6	60°

DECLINATION

LAT	12°	13°	14°	15°	16°	17°	18°	19°	20°	21°	22°	23°	LAT
30°	76.1	74.9	73.8	72.6	71.4	70.3	69.1	67.9	66.7	65.5	64.4	63.2	30°
31°	76.0	74.8	73.6	72.4	71.2	70.0	68.9	67.7	66.5	65.3	64.1	62.9	31°
32°	75.8	74.6	73.4	72.2	71.0	69.8	68.6	67.4	66.2	65.0	63.8	62.6	32°
33°	75.6	74.4	73.2	72.1	70.8	69.6	68.4	67.1	65.9	64.7	63.5	62.2	33°
34°	75.5	74.2	73.0	71.8	70.6	69.3	68.1	66.9	65.6	64.4	63.1	61.9	34°
35°	75.3	74.1	72.8	71.6	70.3	69.1	67.8	66.6	65.3	64.1	62.8	61.5	35°
36°	75.1	73.8	72.6	71.3	70.1	68.8	67.5	66.3	65.0	63.7	62.4	61.1	36°
37°	74.9	73.6	72.4	71.1	69.8	68.5	67.2	65.9	64.6	63.3	62.0	60.7	37°
38°	74.7	73.4	72.0	70.8	69.5	68.2	66.9	65.6	64.3	62.9	61.6	60.3	38°
39°	74.5	73.2	71.9	70.5	69.2	67.9	66.6	65.2	63.9	62.5	61.2	59.8	39°
40°	74.2	72.9	71.6	70.2	68.9	67.6	66.2	64.8	63.5	62.1	60.7	59.3	40°
41°	74.0	72.7	71.3	69.9	68.6	67.2	65.8	64.4	63.0	61.6	60.2	58.8	41°
42°	73.7	72.4	71.0	69.6	68.2	66.8	65.4	64.0	62.6	61.2	59.7	58.3	42°
43°	73.5	72.1	70.7	69.3	67.9	66.4	65.0	63.6	62.1	60.7	59.2	57.7	43°
44°	73.2	71.8	70.3	68.9	67.5	66.0	64.6	63.1	61.6	60.1	58.6	57.1	44°
45°	72.9	71.4	70.0	68.5	67.0	65.6	64.1	62.6	61.1	59.5	58.0	56.4	45°
46°	72.6	71.1	69.6	68.1	66.6	65.1	63.6	62.0	60.5	58.9	57.4	55.8	46°
47°	72.2	70.7	69.2	67.7	66.2	64.6	63.1	61.5	59.9	58.3	56.7	55.0	47°
48°	71.9	70.3	68.8	67.2	65.7	64.1	62.5	60.9	59.3	57.6	55.9	54.3	48°
49°	71.5	69.9	68.4	66.8	65.1	63.5	61.9	60.2	58.6	56.9	55.2	53.4	49°
50°	71.1	69.5	67.9	66.2	64.6	62.9	61.3	59.6	57.8	56.1	54.3	52.6	50°
51°	70.7	69.1	67.4	65.7	64.0	62.3	60.6	58.8	57.1	55.3	53.5	51.6	51°
52°	70.3	68.6	66.9	65.1	63.4	61.6	59.9	58.1	56.3	54.4	52.5	50.6	52°
53°	69.8	68.1	66.3	64.5	62.7	60.9	59.1	57.3	55.4	53.5	51.5	49.5	53°
54°	69.3	67.5	65.7	63.9	62.0	60.2	58.3	56.4	54.4	52.4	50.4	48.3	54°
55°	68.7	66.9	65.1	63.2	61.3	59.4	57.4	55.4	53.4	51.3	49.2	47.1	55°
56°	68.2	66.3	64.4	62.4	60.5	58.5	56.5	54.4	52.3	50.1	47.9	45.7	56°
57°	67.6	65.6	63.6	61.6	59.6	57.5	55.4	53.3	51.1	48.9	46.5	44.2	57°
58°	66.9	64.9	62.8	60.8	58.7	56.5	54.3	52.1	49.8	47.4	45.0	42.5	58°
59°	66.2	64.1	62.0	59.8	57.6	55.4	53.1	50.8	48.4	45.9	43.3	40.7	59°
60°	65.4	63.3	61.1	58.8	56.5	54.2	51.8	49.4	46.8	44.2	41.5	38.6	60°

Table 3(6) – Distance off lights when rising or dipping
Enter with height of eye and height of light to extract the range (M) of a light when it first rises above, or finally dips below, the horizon. This range, with a bearing, gives a fix.

TABLE 3(6) LIGHTS – DISTANCE OFF (M) WHEN RISING OR DIPPING											
HEIGHT OF LIGHT						**HEIGHT OF EYE**					
		metres	1	2	3	4	5	6	7	8	9	10
metres	feet	feet	3	7	10	13	16	20	23	26	30	33
10	33		8·7	9·5	10·2	10·8	11·3	11·7	12·1	12·5	12·8	13·2
12	39		9·3	10·1	10·8	11·4	11·9	12·3	12·7	13·1	13·4	13·8
14	46		9·9	10·7	11·4	12·0	12·5	12·9	13·3	13·7	14·0	14·4
16	53		10·4	11·2	11·9	12·5	13·0	13·4	13·8	14·2	14·5	14·9
18	59		10·9	11·7	12·4	13·0	13·5	13·9	14·3	14·7	15·0	15·4
20	66		11·4	12·2	12·9	13·5	14·0	14·4	14·8	15·2	15·5	15·9
22	72		11·9	12·7	13·4	14·0	14·5	14·9	15·3	15·7	16·0	16·4
24	79		12·3	13·1	13·8	14·4	14·9	15·3	15·7	16·1	16·4	17·0
26	85		12·7	13·5	14·2	14·8	15·3	15·7	16·1	16·5	16·8	17·2
28	92		13·1	13·9	14·6	15·2	15·7	16·1	16·5	16·9	17·2	17·6
30	98		13·5	14·3	15·0	15·6	16·1	16·5	16·9	17·3	17·6	18·0
32	105		13·9	14·7	15·4	16·0	16·5	16·9	17·3	17·7	18·0	18·4
34	112		14·2	15·0	15·7	16·3	16·8	17·2	17·6	18·0	18·3	18·7
36	118		14·6	15·4	16·1	16·7	17·2	17·6	18·0	18·4	18·7	19·1
38	125		14·9	15·7	16·4	17·0	17·5	17·9	18·3	18·7	19·0	19·4
40	131		15·3	16·1	16·8	17·4	17·9	18·3	18·7	19·1	19·4	19·8
42	138		15·6	16·4	17·1	17·7	18·2	18·6	19·0	19·4	19·7	20·1
44	144		15·9	16·7	17·4	18·0	18·5	18·9	19·3	19·7	20·0	20·4
46	151		16·2	17·0	17·7	18·3	18·8	19·2	19·6	20·0	20·3	20·7
48	157		16·5	17·3	18·0	18·6	19·1	19·5	19·9	20·3	20·6	21·0
50	164		16·8	17·6	18·3	18·9	19·4	19·8	20·2	20·6	20·9	21·3
55	180		17·5	18·3	19·0	19·6	20·1	20·5	20·9	21·3	21·6	22·0
60	197		18·2	19·0	19·7	20·3	20·8	21·2	21·6	22·0	22·3	22·7
65	213		18·9	19·7	20·4	21·0	21·5	21·9	22·3	22·7	23·0	23·4
70	230		19·5	20·3	21·0	21·6	22·1	22·5	22·9	23·2	23·6	24·0
80	262		20·7	21·5	22·2	22·8	23·3	23·7	24·1	24·5	24·8	25·2

3.16   SUNRISE/SET TIMES 2010

Showing times of Sunrise (SR) and Sunset (SS) for every 4th day, the table below is much simpler than in earlier editions.

This does not imply any lack of accuracy since the times of Sunrise and Sunset never change by more than 8 minutes (and often by only 1–3 minutes) between the given dates.

The tables are based on Longitude 0°, so longitude corrections are required: add 4 minutes of time for every degree West of Greenwich; subtract if East.

Latitudes 56°N, 48°N and 40°N are chosen so as to split into 3 equal bands the 24° span of latitude from Shetland 60°N to Gibraltar 36°N. Be sure to enter the correct table.

Times are in UT – add 1 hour in non-shaded months to convert to BST

LATITUDE 56°N

	Rise	Set	Rise	Set	Rise	Set	Rise	Set	Rise	Set	Rise	Set
	JANUARY		FEBRUARY		MARCH		APRIL		MAY		JUNE	
1	08 31	15 36	07 55	16 33	06 52	17 34	05 31	18 38	04 17	19 39	03 22	20 34
4	08 30	15 40	07 49	16 39	06 44	17 40	05 23	18 44	04 10	19 45	03 19	20 38
7	08 29	15 44	07 43	16 46	06 37	17 47	05 15	18 50	04 03	19 51	03 17	20 42
10	08 26	15 49	07 37	16 53	06 29	17 53	05 08	18 56	03 57	19 57	03 15	20 44
13	08 24	15 54	07 30	16 59	06 21	17 59	05 00	19 02	03 51	20 03	03 14	20 47
16	08 20	16 00	07 23	17 06	06 13	18 05	04 52	19 09	03 46	20 08	03 13	20 49
19	08 16	16 06	07 16	17 12	06 05	18 11	04 45	19 15	03 40	20 14	03 13	20 50
22	08 12	16 12	07 09	17 19	05 57	18 18	04 38	19 21	03 36	20 19	03 13	20 51
25	08 07	16 18	07 02	17 25	05 50	18 24	04 30	19 27	03 31	20 24	03 14	20 51
28	08 02	16 24	06 54	17 32	05 42	18 30	04 23	19 33	03 27	20 29	03 16	20 50
31	07 57	16 31			05 34	18 36			03 23	20 33		

	JULY		AUGUST		SEPTEMBER		OCTOBER		NOVEMBER		DECEMBER	
1	03 18	20 49	04 04	20 08	05 04	18 55	06 03	17 36	07 07	16 20	08 07	15 31
4	03 21	20 47	04 09	20 02	05 10	18 47	06 09	17 28	07 13	16 13	08 11	15 29
7	03 24	20 45	04 15	19 55	05 16	18 39	06 15	17 20	07 19	16 07	08 16	15 27
10	03 28	20 42	04 21	19 49	05 21	18 31	06 21	17 12	07 26	16 01	08 20	15 26
13	03 32	20 39	04 27	19 42	05 27	18 23	06 27	17 05	07 32	15 56	08 23	15 25
16	03 36	20 35	04 33	19 35	05 33	18 15	06 33	16 57	07 38	15 51	08 26	15 25
19	03 41	20 31	04 38	19 28	05 39	18 07	06 39	16 50	07 44	15 46	08 28	15 26
22	03 46	20 26	04 44	19 20	05 45	18 00	06 45	16 43	07 50	15 41	08 30	15 27
25	03 51	20 21	04 50	19 13	05 51	17 52	06 52	16 36	07 56	15 37	08 31	15 29
28	03 56	20 16	04 56	19 05	05 57	17 44	06 58	16 29	08 01	15 34	08 32	15 31
31	04 02	20 10	05 02	18 57			07 04	16 22			08 31	15 35

Times are in UT – add 1 hour in non-shaded months to convert to BST

LATITUDE 48°N

	Rise JANUARY	Set	Rise FEBRUARY	Set	Rise MARCH	Set	Rise APRIL	Set	Rise MAY	Set	Rise JUNE	Set
1	07 50	16 17	07 28	17 00	06 41	17 44	05 39	18 30	04 42	19 13	04 05	19 51
4	07 50	16 20	07 24	17 05	06 36	17 49	05 33	18 34	04 37	19 17	04 03	19 54
7	07 49	16 24	07 20	17 09	06 30	17 53	05 27	18 38	04 33	19 21	04 02	19 56
10	07 48	16 27	07 15	17 14	06 24	17 58	05 21	18 43	04 28	19 25	04 01	19 58
13	07 46	16 31	07 10	17 19	06 18	18 02	05 15	18 47	04 24	19 29	04 00	20 00
16	07 44	16 35	07 05	17 24	06 12	18 07	05 09	18 51	04 20	19 33	04 00	20 02
19	07 42	16 40	07 00	17 29	06 05	18 11	05 03	18 56	04 17	19 37	04 00	20 03
22	07 39	16 44	06 55	17 33	05 59	18 15	04 58	19 00	04 13	19 41	04 01	20 03
25	07 36	16 49	06 49	17 38	05 53	18 20	04 53	19 04	04 10	19 44	04 01	20 04
28	07 33	16 53	06 43	17 43	05 47	18 24	04 47	19 09	04 08	19 47	04 03	20 04
31	07 29	16 58			05 41	18 28			04 06	19 50		

	Rise JULY	Set	Rise AUGUST	Set	Rise SEPTEMBER	Set	Rise OCTOBER	Set	Rise NOVEMBER	Set	Rise DECEMBER	Set
1	04 04	20 03	04 36	19 36	05 18	18 41	05 59	17 40	06 45	16 42	07 28	16 09
4	04 06	20 02	04 40	19 32	05 22	18 35	06 03	17 34	06 49	16 37	07 32	16 08
7	04 09	20 01	04 44	19 27	05 26	18 29	06 07	17 28	06 54	16 33	07 35	16 07
10	04 11	19 59	04 48	19 22	05 30	18 23	06 12	17 22	06 58	16 29	07 39	16 07
13	04 14	19 57	04 52	19 17	05 34	18 17	06 16	17 16	07 03	16 25	07 41	16 07
16	04 17	19 55	04 56	19 12	05 38	18 11	06 20	17 10	07 08	16 22	07 44	16 07
19	04 20	19 52	05 00	19 06	05 42	18 05	06 25	17 04	07 12	16 18	07 46	16 08
22	04 24	19 49	05 04	19 01	05 46	17 58	06 29	16 59	07 16	16 15	07 47	16 10
25	04 27	19 45	05 08	18 55	05 50	17 52	06 34	16 54	07 21	16 13	07 49	16 11
28	04 31	19 41	05 12	18 49	05 55	17 46	06 38	16 48	07 25	16 11	07 49	16 14
31	04 35	19 37	05 16	18 43			06 43	16 44			07 50	16 16

LATITUDE 40°N

	Rise JANUARY	Set	Rise FEBRUARY	Set	Rise MARCH	Set	Rise APRIL	Set	Rise MAY	Set	Rise JUNE	Set
1	07 22	16 45	07 09	17 19	06 34	17 52	05 44	18 24	05 00	18 54	04 33	19 23
4	07 22	16 48	07 06	17 23	06 29	17 55	05 40	18 27	04 57	18 58	04 32	19 25
7	07 22	16 51	07 03	17 26	06 25	17 58	05 35	18 30	04 53	19 00	04 31	19 27
10	07 22	16 54	06 59	17 30	06 20	18 01	05 30	18 33	04 50	19 03	04 31	19 28
13	07 21	16 57	06 56	17 33	06 15	18 05	05 26	18 36	04 47	19 06	04 31	19 30
16	07 20	17 00	06 52	17 37	06 10	18 08	05 21	18 39	04 44	19 09	04 31	19 31
19	07 18	17 04	06 48	17 40	06 05	18 11	05 17	18 42	04 42	19 12	04 31	19 32
22	07 17	17 07	06 44	17 44	06 01	18 14	05 12	18 45	04 39	19 15	04 32	19 32
25	07 15	17 11	06 40	17 47	05 56	18 17	05 08	18 48	04 37	19 17	04 32	19 33
28	07 12	17 14	06 35	17 50	05 51	18 20	05 04	18 51	04 35	19 20	04 33	19 33
31	07 10	17 18			05 46	18 23			04 34	19 22		

	Rise JULY	Set	Rise AUGUST	Set	Rise SEPTEMBER	Set	Rise OCTOBER	Set	Rise NOVEMBER	Set	Rise DECEMBER	Set
1	04 35	19 33	04 58	19 14	05 28	18 32	05 56	17 43	06 29	16 58	07 02	16 35
4	04 36	19 32	05 01	19 11	05 30	18 27	05 59	17 38	06 32	16 54	07 05	16 35
7	04 38	19 32	05 04	19 07	05 33	18 22	06 02	17 33	06 36	16 51	07 08	16 35
10	04 40	19 30	05 07	19 04	05 36	18 17	06 05	17 28	06 39	16 48	07 11	16 35
13	04 42	19 29	05 09	19 00	05 39	18 12	06 08	17 24	06 43	16 46	07 13	16 35
16	04 44	19 27	05 12	18 56	05 42	18 07	06 11	17 19	06 46	16 43	07 15	16 36
19	04 47	19 25	05 15	18 51	05 45	18 03	06 14	17 15	06 49	16 41	07 17	16 37
22	04 49	19 23	05 18	18 47	05 47	17 58	06 18	17 11	06 53	16 39	07 19	16 38
25	04 52	19 21	05 21	18 43	05 50	17 53	06 21	17 07	06 56	16 38	07 20	16 40
28	04 55	19 18	05 24	18 38	05 53	17 48	06 24	17 03	06 59	16 36	07 21	16 42
31	04 57	19 15	05 27	18 33			06 28	16 59			07 22	16 44

3.17 MOONRISE/SET TIMES 2010

The table below is much simpler than that in earlier editions. It gives the times of Moonrise (MR) and Moonset (MS) for every 4th day; interpolation is necessary for other days. The aim is simply to indicate whether the night in question will be brightly moonlit, partially moonlit or pitch black – depending, of course, on cloud cover.

The table is based on Longitude 0°. To correct for longitude, add

4 minutes of time for every degree West; subtract if East.

Latitudes 56°N, 48°N and 40°N are chosen so as to split into 3 equal bands the 24° span of latitude from Shetland 60°N to Gibraltar 36°N. Be sure to enter the correct table.

** Indicates that the phenomenon does not occur.

The phase of the Moon, ie New Moon, 1st Quarter, Full Moon and Last Quarter, are shown on Tide tables and in detail on the penultimate page of Chapter 4 (Tides).

Times are in UT – add 1 hour in non-shaded months to convert to BST

LATITUDE 56°N

	Rise	Set	Rise	Set	Rise	Set	Rise	Set	Rise	Set	Rise	Set
	JANUARY		**FEBRUARY**		**MARCH**		**APRIL**		**MAY**		**JUNE**	
1	16 39	09 07	20 27	08 20	19 22	06 37	22 51	05 41	23 53	05 20	23 42	07 36
4	21 27	10 02	** **	08 56	23 56	07 18	01 15	07 30	01 02	08 39	00 05	11 18
7	00 24	10 35	03 37	10 06	02 31	08 46	03 01	10 56	01 48	12 22	00 35	15 00
10	04 34	11 31	06 09	12 53	04 37	11 55	03 42	14 38	02 17	16 04	01 25	19 02
13	07 34	13 53	07 05	16 37	05 24	15 38	04 10	18 23	03 00	20 05	03 52	21 57
16	08 44	17 34	07 33	20 18	05 52	19 21	04 57	22 24	04 59	23 22	08 19	23 03
19	09 14	21 16	08 04	** **	06 29	23 18	07 07	00 39	09 05	00 23	12 47	23 41
22	09 42	** **	09 20	02 50	08 08	01 47	11 18	02 18	13 32	01 08	17 05	00 12
25	10 43	03 51	12 56	05 27	12 03	03 54	15 49	03 01	17 56	01 48	20 25	01 54
28	13 57	06 59	17 47	06 25	16 45	04 43	20 20	03 43	21 42	03 12	21 48	05 18
31	18 53	08 07			21 23	05 22			23 25	06 20		

	Rise	Set	Rise	Set	Rise	Set	Rise	Set	Rise	Set	Rise	Set
	JULY		**AUGUST**		**SEPTEMBER**		**OCTOBER**		**NOVEMBER**		**DECEMBER**	
1	22 23	09 02	21 14	11 40	21 04	14 25	22 18	14 47	00 25	14 11	02 34	13 00
4	22 53	12 41	22 24	15 31	** **	16 49	01 16	15 52	04 56	14 55	06 57	14 12
7	23 52	16 36	00 18	18 21	03 49	17 48	05 56	16 35	09 23	16 19	09 59	17 04
10	01 29	19 51	04 51	19 29	08 34	18 31	10 32	17 46	12 03	19 26	11 08	20 53
13	05 52	21 09	09 35	20 10	12 59	19 50	13 35	20 32	13 03	23 11	11 43	** **
16	10 30	21 49	14 00	21 13	15 38	22 44	14 44	** **	13 36	01 35	12 20	02 55
19	14 53	22 41	17 04	23 43	16 38	01 12	15 19	02 38	14 16	05 15	13 40	06 41
22	18 22	** **	18 17	02 08	17 11	04 50	15 54	06 17	15 48	08 59	16 58	09 20
25	19 54	03 04	18 52	05 49	17 47	08 30	17 07	10 03	19 18	11 20	21 25	10 26
28	20 32	06 48	19 23	09 27	19 05	12 14	20 06	12 46	23 39	12 18	00 20	11 08
31	21 02	10 25	20 25	13 14			** **	13 56			04 40	12 12

LATITUDE 48°N

	Rise	Set	Rise	Set	Rise	Set	Rise	Set	Rise	Set	Rise	Set
	JANUARY		**FEBRUARY**		**MARCH**		**APRIL**		**MAY**		**JUNE**	
1	17 19	08 25	20 27	08 15	19 17	06 37	22 08	06 15	23 01	06 12	23 16	08 09
4	21 33	09 52	** **	09 21	23 18	07 47	00 21	08 24	00 22	09 17	** **	11 25
7	00 09	10 54	02 47	10 57	01 37	09 40	02 24	11 31	01 33	12 34	00 48	14 42
10	03 49	12 17	05 20	13 41	03 54	12 36	03 29	14 47	02 26	15 50	02 04	18 15
13	06 41	14 46	06 42	16 57	05 06	15 53	04 22	18 06	03 35	19 24	04 42	21 13
16	08 15	18 01	07 34	20 13	05 58	19 10	05 35	21 39	05 51	22 33	08 40	22 49
19	09 10	21 16	08 30	23 37	07 01	22 39	07 58	** **	09 34	** **	12 37	23 54
22	10 02	** **	10 12	01 59	09 01	00 54	11 44	01 50	13 30	01 06	16 26	00 44
25	11 31	03 04	13 36	04 45	12 37	03 18	15 44	03 01	17 23	02 13	19 33	02 47
28	14 44	06 12	17 53	06 14	16 46	04 37	19 43	04 13	20 49	04 03	21 18	05 55
31	19 04	07 52			20 51	05 46			22 50	07 02		

	Rise	Set	Rise	Set	Rise	Set	Rise	Set	Rise	Set	Rise	Set
	JULY		**AUGUST**		**SEPTEMBER**		**OCTOBER**		**NOVEMBER**		**DECEMBER**	
1	22 18	09 12	21 37	11 19	21 54	13 36	22 58	14 05	00 38	14 04	02 21	13 17
4	23 11	12 26	23 12	14 44	** **	16 10	01 36	15 38	04 39	15 16	06 14	14 56
7	00 01	15 54	01 07	17 37	04 04	17 39	05 45	16 51	08 37	17 06	09 13	17 48
10	02 21	19 03	05 12	19 16	08 17	18 52	09 49	18 31	11 21	20 07	10 47	21 11
13	06 17	20 51	09 23	20 26	12 12	20 38	12 48	21 17	12 45	23 27	11 45	** **
16	10 24	21 59	13 17	21 57	14 53	23 28	14 21	** **	13 41	01 34	12 45	02 33
19	14 16	23 19	16 14	** **	16 17	01 39	15 18	02 42	14 44	04 50	14 27	05 55
22	17 29	00 43	17 51	02 41	17 13	04 52	16 17	05 57	16 36	08 12	17 37	08 39
25	19 22	03 43	18 48	05 56	18 12	08 07	17 53	09 19	19 53	10 42	21 34	10 13
28	20 24	07 01	19 43	09 09	19 52	11 27	20 48	12 03	23 45	12 08	00 10	11 22
31	21 16	10 14	21 09	12 31			** **	13 40			04 00	12 53

Times are in UT – add 1 hour in non-shaded months to convert to BST

LATITUDE 40°N

	Rise	Set	Rise	Set	Rise	Set	Rise	Set	Rise	Set	Rise	Set
	JANUARY		FEBRUARY		MARCH		APRIL		MAY		JUNE	
1	17 46	07 56	20 27	08 11	19 14	06 37	21 40	06 39	22 27	06 46	22 57	08 31
4	21 37	09 45	** **	09 38	22 53	08 08	** **	08 58	** **	09 43	** **	11 30
7	** **	11 07	02 14	11 31	01 03	10 15	01 58	11 55	01 22	12 42	00 57	14 28
10	03 19	12 49	04 48	14 12	03 25	13 04	03 20	14 53	02 32	15 41	02 31	17 45
13	06 06	15 19	06 25	17 12	04 54	16 03	04 30	17 54	03 58	18 56	05 15	20 43
16	07 54	18 19	07 35	20 09	06 03	19 02	06 01	21 09	06 24	22 01	08 55	22 38
19	09 07	21 16	08 49	23 15	07 24	22 12	08 32	** **	09 54	** **	12 31	** **
22	10 17	** **	10 46	01 26	09 36	00 20	12 02	01 29	13 28	01 04	15 59	01 07
25	12 03	02 33	14 04	04 16	13 00	02 53	15 40	03 01	17 00	02 32	19 00	03 21
28	15 14	05 40	17 57	06 07	16 46	04 33	19 17	04 33	20 15	04 36	20 57	06 19
31	19 11	07 41			20 29	06 04			22 26	07 30		

	Rise	Set	Rise	Set	Rise	Set	Rise	Set	Rise	Set	Rise	Set
	JULY		AUGUST		SEPTEMBER		OCTOBER		NOVEMBER		DECEMBER	
1	22 14	09 19	21 53	11 05	22 27	13 03	23 25	13 37	00 48	13 58	02 11	13 29
4	23 24	12 15	23 43	14 14	00 29	15 43	01 50	15 28	04 27	15 30	05 46	15 26
7	00 25	15 25	01 40	17 08	04 15	17 33	05 36	17 02	08 06	17 38	08 43	18 18
10	02 55	18 31	05 26	19 06	08 05	19 07	09 20	19 00	10 53	20 35	10 31	21 25
13	06 36	20 37	09 14	20 38	11 41	21 09	12 17	21 47	12 32	23 38	11 46	** **
16	10 20	22 07	12 49	22 27	14 23	23 57	14 04	** **	13 44	01 34	13 02	02 18
19	13 51	23 46	15 42	00 06	16 02	01 58	15 18	02 46	15 04	04 32	14 58	05 25
22	16 55	01 16	17 32	03 04	17 14	04 53	16 33	05 43	17 08	07 40	18 04	08 11
25	18 59	04 10	18 46	06 02	18 30	07 51	18 23	08 49	20 17	10 16	21 40	10 03
28	20 18	07 10	19 58	08 57	20 24	10 56	21 17	11 34	23 49	12 00	00 02	11 32
31	21 27	10 05	21 39	12 02			** **	13 28			03 33	13 21

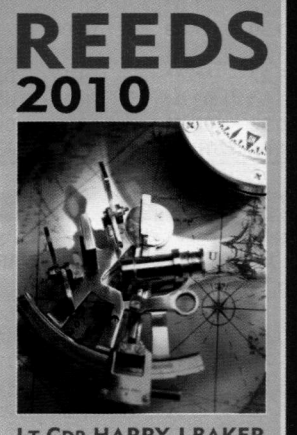

4

Tides

Tides

4.1 INTRODUCTION

This chapter provides background information on the use of the tidal data in Chapter 9, where the times and heights of HW and LW are given for Standard Ports, and time and height differences for their Secondary Ports. Tides are predicted for average meteorological conditions. See 4.8 for meteorological effects.

4.1.2   Admiralty Tide Tables (ATT) are the source for all tidal data in this Almanac; they are published in 4 volumes:

- Vol 1 (NP 201) UK and Ireland (including Channel ports from Hoek van Holland to Brest);
- Vol 2 (NP 202) Europe (excluding UK, Ireland and Channel ports), Mediterranean and the Atlantic;
- Vol 3 (NP 203) Indian Ocean and South China Sea;
- Vol 4 (NP 204) Pacific Ocean.

4.1.3   Spanish Secondary Ports referenced to Lisboa
In Areas 23 and 25, some Spanish secondary ports have Lisboa as Standard Port. Time differences for these ports, when applied to the printed times of HW and LW for Lisboa (UT), automatically give HW and LW times in the Zone Time for Spain (ie UT –1), *not* Portugal (UT). No other corrections are required, except for DST when applicable.

4.2 DEFINITIONS

Chart Datum (CD)
CD is the reference level from which heights of tide are predicted and charted depths are measured. In the UK it normally approximates to LAT, and the tide will not frequently fall below it. The actual depth of water in any particular position is the charted depth plus the height of tide.

Lowest Astronomical Tide (LAT)
LAT is the lowest level which can be predicted under average meteorological, and any combination of astronomical, conditions. This level will not be reached every year. Storm surges can cause even lower levels to be reached.

Highest Astronomical Tide (HAT)
HAT is the highest level which can be predicted to occur under average meteorological conditions and under any combination of astronomical conditions, except storm surges. It is the level above which vertical clearances under bridges and power lines are measured; see 4.5.

Ordnance Datum (Newlyn)
Ordnance Datum (Newlyn) is the datum of the land levelling system on mainland England, Scotland and Wales, and to which all features on UK land maps are referred. The difference between Ordnance Datum (Newlyn) and CD is shown at the foot of each page of tide tables in this Almanac. Differences between CD and foreign land levelling datums are similarly quoted.

Charted depth
Charted depths are printed on charts in metres and decimetres (0·1m) and show the depth of water below CD. (Not to be confused with a sounding which is the actual depth of water (charted depth + height of tide) in a particular position.)

Drying height
A drying height is the height above CD of any feature which at times is covered by water. The figures, in metres and decimetres, are underlined on the chart. The depth of water over a drying feature is the height of tide minus the drying height. If the result is negative, then the feature is uncovered at that time.

Vertical clearances under bridges and power lines
These are measured above HAT. Some older charts may still show clearances above MHWS; see 4.5.

Elevation of lights
The charted height of a light (its elevation) is measured above MHWS.

Height of tide
The height of the tide is the vertical distance of the sea level above (or very occasionally below) CD. Predicted heights are given in metres and decimetres.

Rise/Fall of tide
The Rise of the tide is the amount the tide has risen since the earlier Low Water. The Fall of a tide is the amount the tide has fallen since the last High Water.

Duration
Duration is the time between LW and the next HW, normally slightly more than six hours. It can be used to calculate the approximate time of LW when only the time of HW is known.

Interval
The interval is a period of time quoted in hours and minutes before (–) or after (+) HW. Intervals are printed in hourly increments (–6hrs to +6hrs) along the bottom of each tidal curve diagram in Chapter 9.

Spring tides
Spring tides occur roughly every 16 days, near to Full ○ and New ● Moon, when the tide-raising forces of Sun and Moon are at a maximum. See 4.9 for phases of the Moon.

Neap tides
Neaps occur roughly every 16 days, near the Moon's first ◑ and last ◐ quarters, when the tide-raising forces of Sun and Moon are at a minimum. See 4.9 for phases of the Moon.

Mean High Water and Low Water Springs/Neaps
MHWS and MHWN are the means of predicted HW heights of Sp or Np tides over a period of 18·6 years. Similarly, MLWS and MLWN are the means of LW heights for Sp and Np tides respectively. Mean tide level (MTL) is the mean of the above values.

Mean Sea Level (MSL or ML)
This is the average level of the sea's surface over a long period, preferably 18·6 years.

Range
The range of a tide is the difference between the heights of successive HWs and LWs. Spring range is the difference between MHWS and MLWS, and Neap range is the difference between MHWN and MLWN.

Tidal Coefficients, as used in France, indicate the range of a tide. Daily values are listed and explained in 9.20.26; they are valid for all Areas in this Almanac.

Standard Ports have tidal characteristics observed over a long period and are suitable as a reference for secondary ports on the adjacent coasts.

Secondary Ports have similar tidal characteristics to those of their Standard Port. Time and height differences are applied to the Standard Port predictions. 'Secondary' does not imply lesser importance.

Fig 4(1) Tidal definitions

4.3 CALCULATING TIMES AND HEIGHTS OF HIGH AND LOW WATER

4.3.1 Standard Ports

The 59 Standard Ports, for which daily predictions are given in Chapter 9, are listed below by their geographic Areas:

1 Falmouth, Plymouth, Dartmouth, Portland.
2 Poole, Southampton, Portsmouth, Chichester.
3 Shoreham, Dover.
4 Margate, Sheerness, London Bridge, Walton-on-the-Naze, Harwich, Lowestoft.
5 Immingham, R Tees, Tyne (North Shields).
6 Rosyth, Leith, Aberdeen.
7 Invergordon, Wick, Lerwick.
8 Stornoway, Ullapool, Oban.
9 Greenock.
10 Liverpool, Holyhead.
11 Milford Haven, Avonmouth.
12 Dublin, Cobh, Tarbert Island.
13 Belfast, Lough Foyle, Galway.
14 Esbjerg.
15 Helgoland, Cuxhaven and Wilhelmshaven.
16 Hoek van Holland, Vlissingen, Zeebrugge.
17 Dunkerque, Boulogne-sue-Mer, Dieppe, Le Havre, Cherbourg.
18 St Malo.
19 St Peter Port, St Helier.
20 Brest (See 9.20.26 for coefficients).
22 Pointe de Grave.
23 La Coruña.
24 Lisboa.
25 Gibraltar.

Predicted times and heights of HW and LW are tabulated for each Standard Port. Note that these are only predictions and take no account of the effects of wind and barometric pressure (see 4.8). See 1.5 for Zone times and Daylight Saving Time (DST).

4.3.2 Secondary Ports – times of HW and LW

Each Secondary Port listed in Chapter 9 has a data block for calculating times of HW and LW. The following example is for Braye (Alderney):

TIDES −0400 Dover; ML 3·5; Duration 0545
Standard Port ST HELIER (⟶)

Times				Height (metres)			
High Water		Low Water		MHWS	MHWN	MLWN	MLWS
0300	0900	0200	0900	11·0	8·1	4·0	1·4
1500	2100	1400	2100				
Differences BRAYE							
+0050	+0040	+0025	+0105	−4·8	−3·4	−1·5	−0·5

In this example −0400 Dover means that, on average, HW Braye is 4 hours 00 minutes before HW Dover (the Range and times of HW Dover are in Area 3 and on the bookmark).

ML (or MSL) is defined in 4.2.

Duration 0545 means that LW Braye occurs 5 hours and 45 minutes before the next HW.

The arrow (⟶) after the Standard Port's name points to where the tide tables are in the book.

The most accurate method of prediction uses Standard Port times and Secondary Port time differences as in the block. When HW at St Helier occurs at 0300 and 1500, the difference is +0050, and thus HW at Braye occurs at 0350 and 1550. When HW at St Helier occurs at 0900 and 2100, the difference is +0040, and HW at Braye occurs at 0940 and 2140.

If, as will usually be the case, HW St Helier occurs at some other time, then the difference for Braye must be found by interpolation, either by eye, by the graphical method or by calculator.

So when HW St Helier occurs at 1200 (midway between 0900 and 1500), the difference is +0045 (midway between +0040 and +0050), and therefore HW Braye is 1245.

The same method is used for calculating the times of LW. Times thus obtained are in the Secondary Port's Zone Time. For calculating heights of HW and LW see 4.3.3.

4.3.3 Secondary Ports – heights of HW and LW

The Secondary Port data block also contains height differences which are applied to the heights of HW and LW at the Standard Port. When the height of HW at St Helier is 11·0m (MHWS), the difference is –4·8m, so the height of HW Braye is 6·2m (MHWS). When the height of HW St Helier is 8·1m (MHWN), the difference is –3·4m, and the height of HW at Braye is 4·7m (MHWN).

If, as is likely, the height of tide at the Standard Port differs from the Mean Spring or Neap level, then the height difference must also be interpolated: by eye, by graph or by calculator. Thus if the height of HW St Helier is 9·55m (halfway between MHWS and MHWN), the difference is –4·1m, and the height of HW Braye is 5·45m (9·55–4·1m).

4.3.4 Graphical method for interpolating time and height differences

Any suitable squared paper can be used, having chosen convenient scales; see Figs 4(2) and 4(3).
Example: using the data for Braye in 4.3.2, find the time and height differences for HW at Braye if HW St Helier occurs at 1126, height 8·9m.

Time difference
On the horizontal axis of Fig 4(2) select a scale for the time at St Helier covering 0900 to 1500 (for which the relevant time differences for Braye are known). On the vertical axis the scale must cover +0040 to +0050, the time differences given for 0900 and 1500.

Plot point A, the time difference (+0040) for HW St Helier at 0900; and point B, the time difference (+0050) for HW St Helier at 1500. Join AB. Enter the graph at time 1126 (HW St Helier); intersect AB at C then go horizontally to read +0044 on the vertical axis. On that morning HW Braye is 44 minutes after HW St Helier, ie 1210.

Height difference
In Fig 4(3) the horizontal axis covers the height of HW at St Helier (ie 8·1 to 11·0m) and the vertical axis shows the relevant height differences (–3·4 to –4·8m).

Plot point D, the height difference (–3·4m) at Neaps when the height of HW St Helier is 8·1m; and E, the height difference (–4·8m) at Springs when the height of HW St Helier is 11·0m. Join DE.

Enter the graph at 8·9m (the height of HW St Helier that morning) and mark F where that height meets DE. From F follow the horizontal line to read off the corresponding height difference: –3·8m. So that morning the height of HW Braye is 5·1m.

Fig 4(2)

4.4 CALCULATING INTERMEDIATE TIMES AND HEIGHTS OF TIDE

4.4.1 Standard Ports

Intermediate heights and times are best calculated from the Mean Spring and Neap Curves for Standard Ports in Chapter 9. Examples below are for Leith, on a day when the predictions are:

	UT	Ht (m)
22	0202	5·3
	0752	1·0
TU	1417	5·4
	2025	0·5

Example 1: Find the height of tide at Leith at 1200.

• On the Leith tidal curve diagram, Fig 4(4), plot the heights of HW and LW before and after the required time. Join them by a diagonal line.

Fig 4(3)

• Enter the HW time and other times as necessary in the boxes below the curves.

• From the required time, go vertically to the curves. The Spring curve is red, and the Neap curve (where it differs) is blue. Interpolate between the curves by comparing the actual range, in this example 4·4m, with the Mean Ranges printed beside the curves. Never extrapolate. Here the Spring curve applies.

• Go horizontally to the diagonal line first plotted, thence vertically to the height scale, to extract 4·2m.

Example 2: Find the time in the afternoon when the height of tide has fallen to 3·7m.

• On Fig 4(5) plot the heights of HW and LW above and below the required height of tide. Join them by a sloping line.

• In the boxes below the curves enter HW time and other hourly times to cover the required timescale.

• From the required height, drop vertically to the diagonal line and thence horizontally to the curves. Interpolate between them as in Example 1; do not extrapolate. In this example the actual range is 4·9m, so the Spring curve applies.

• Drop vertically to the time scale, and read off the time required: 1637.

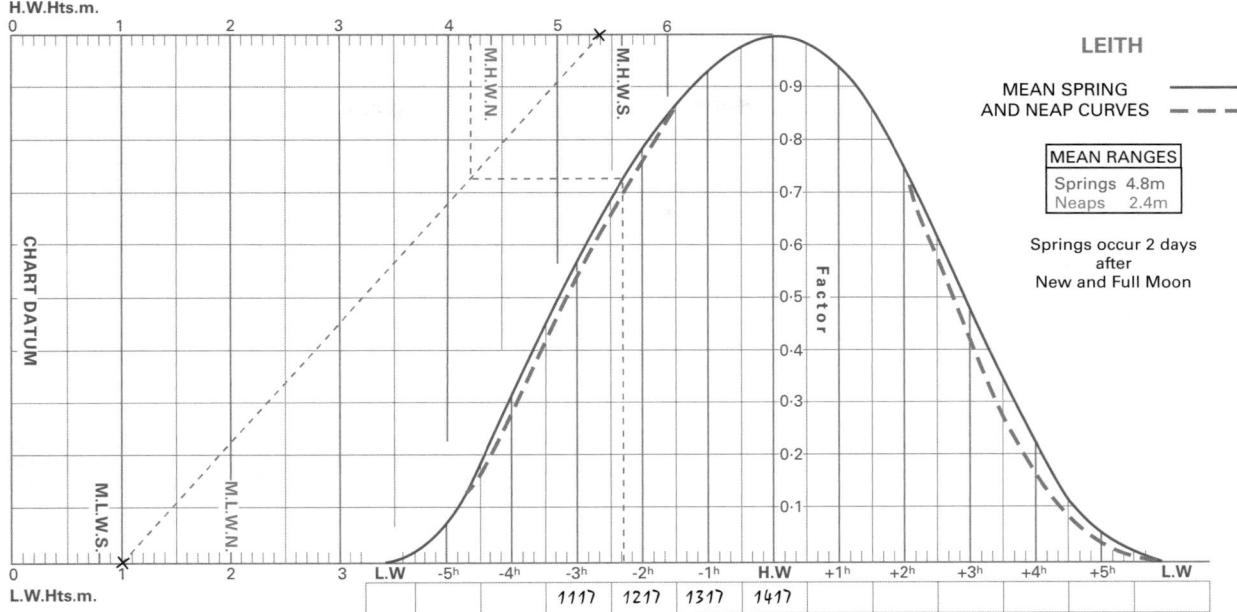

Fig 4(4) Curve for example 1

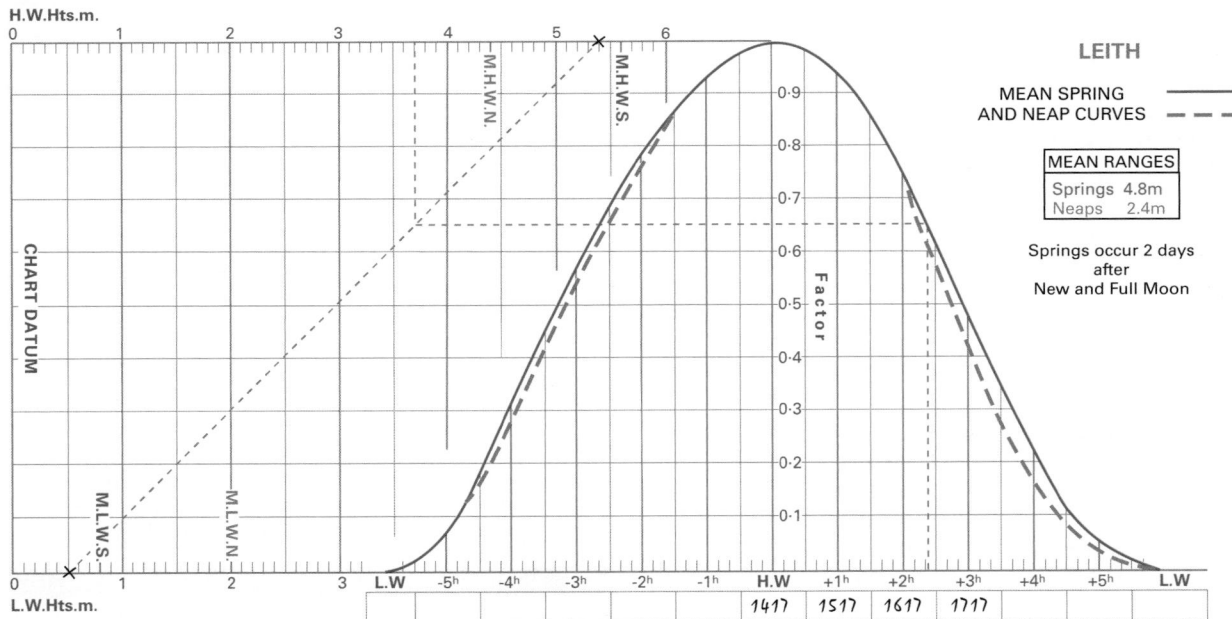

Fig 4(5) Curve for example 2

4.4.2 Secondary Ports

On coasts where the tidal curves for adjacent Standard Ports change little in shape, and where the duration of rise or fall at the Secondary Port is similar to its relevant Standard Port (ie where HW and LW time differences are nearly the same), intermediate times and heights are calculated from the tidal curves for the Standard Port in a similar manner to 4.4.1. The curves are entered with the times and heights of HW and LW at the Secondary Port, calculated as in 4.3.2 and 4.3.3.

Interpolate by eye between the curves, using the range at the Standard Port as argument. Do not extrapolate – use the Spring curve for ranges greater than Springs, and the Neap curve for ranges less than Neaps. With a large change in duration between Springs and Neaps the results may have a slight error, greater near LW.

For places between Christchurch and Selsey Bill (where the tidal regime is complex) special curves are given in 9.2.9.

4.4.3 The use of factors

Factors (in green on tidal curves) are another method of tidal calculation, but the Admiralty tidal prediction form (see 9.2.9) no longer contains the relevant fields. A factor of 1 = HW, and 0 = LW. Tidal curve diagrams show the factor of the range attained at times before and after HW. Thus the factor represents the percentage of the mean range (for the day in question) which has been reached at any particular time. Simple equations used are:

	Range x Factor = Rise
or	Factor = Rise ÷ Range

In determining or using the factor it may be necessary to interpolate between the Spring and Neap curves as described in 4.4.2.

Factors are particularly useful when calculating hourly height predictions for ports with special tidal problems (9.2.9).

4.4.4 The Rule of Twelfths

The Rule of Twelfths estimates by mental arithmetic the height of the tide between HW and LW. It assumes that the duration of rise or fall is 6 hours, the curve is symmetrical and approximates to a sine curve. *Thus the rule is invalid in the Solent, for example, where these conditions do not apply, nor should it be used if accuracy is critical.*

The rule states that from one LW to the next HW, and vice versa, the tide rises or falls by:

1/12th of its range in the 1st hour
2/12ths of its range in the 2nd hour
3/12ths of its range in the 3rd hour
3/12ths of its range in the 4th hour
2/12ths of its range in the 5th hour
1/12th of its range in the 6th hour

4.4.5 Co-Tidal and Co-Range charts

These charts are used to predict tidal times and heights for an offshore position, as distinct from port or coastal locations which are covered by tide tables. There are Admiralty charts for the following offshore areas of NW Europe:

5057	Dungeness to Hoek van Holland
5058	British Isles and adjacent waters
5059	Southern North Sea

They depict Co-Range and Co-Tidal lines, as defined below, with detailed instructions for use.

A Co-Range line joins points of equal Mean Sp (or Np) Range which are simply the difference in level between MHWS and MLWS (or MHWN and MLWN).

A Co-Tidal line joins points of equal Mean HW (or LW) Time Interval. This is defined as the mean time interval between the passage of the Moon over the Greenwich Meridian and the time of the next HW (or LW) at the place concerned.

To find times and heights of tide at an offshore location, say in the Thames Estuary, needs some pre-planning especially if intending to navigate through a shallow gap. The *Tidal Stream Atlas for the Thames Estuary* (NP 249) also contains Co-Tidal and Co-Range charts. These are more clearly arranged and described than charts 5057–5059, but prior study is still necessary. The calculations require predictions for Sheerness, Walton-on-the-Naze or Margate, as relevant to the vessel's position.

4.5 CALCULATING CLEARANCES BELOW OVERHEAD OBJECTS

A diagram often helps when calculating vertical clearances below bridges, power cables etc. Fig 4(6) shows the relationship to CD. The height of such objects as shown on the chart is usually measured above HAT, so the actual clearance will almost always be more. The height of HAT above CD is given at the foot of each page of the tide tables. Most Admiralty charts now show clearances above HAT, but check the **Heights** block below the chart Title.

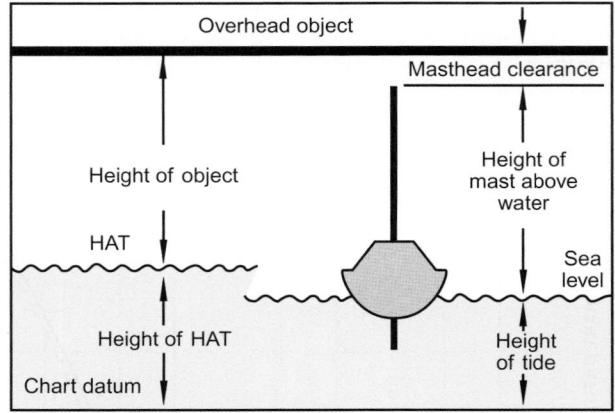

Fig 4(6) Calculating masthead clearance

Insert the dimensions into the following formula, carefully observing the conventions for brackets:

Masthead clearance = (Height of object above HAT + height of HAT above CD) minus (height of tide at the time + height of the masthead above waterline)

4.6 TIDAL PREDICTION BY COMPUTER

Tidal prediction by computer is simple, fast and accurate, and is therefore arguably better than by manual means. The UKHO offers three tidal prediction programmes.

4.6.1 EasyTide

EasyTide is a free, on-line tidal prediction service for the leisure sailor. It provides tidal predictions for the current day, and the next 6 consecutive days. Times and heights of HW and LW for the required port are presented in both tabular and graphical formats. Over 6,000 standard and secondary ports are available worldwide. To open EasyTide visit www.ukho.gov.uk/easytide.

4.6.2   DP 560 SHM for Windows

DP (Digital Product) 560 SHM for Windows, the Simplified Harmonic Method of tidal prediction, is a simple programme supplied on CD. It is accurate, fast and user-friendly. It costs about £35 and has no date limit; any number of ports can be stored.

The user inputs Harmonic Constants which can be found either in Part III of Admiralty Tide Tables (NP201-204; £25 per volume) or in Tidal Harmonic Constants for European Waters (NP 160; £10.35). ATT are updated annually, NP 160 approx 5 yearly, so it is important to use the latest version.

Predictions are displayed as a printable graph of height v time for up to 24 hours and 7 consecutive days.

4.6.3   TotalTide

TotalTide (DP 550) is claimed to be the world's most comprehensive tidal prediction system. It is aimed primarily at commercial shipping and satisfies SOLAS Regulations and the UK Merchant Shipping Safety of Navigation Regulations 2002. It may thus be carried in lieu of paper tide tables.

TotalTide gives fast and accurate tidal predictions for over 7,000 ports and tidal stream data for more than 3,000 locations worldwide. The CD contains a free calculation programme. There are 10 Area Data Sets (ADS), with world-wide coverage costing about £500. However, each ADS can be bought for about £73. Areas 1-4 (see below) are in one ADS.

Access is via a permit system. Annual updates are available, and are essential to satisfy safety regulations, although TotalTide will still run without them but less accurately.

The ten ADS cover:

1–4.	Europe, Mediterranean and northern waters
5.	Indian Ocean and Red Sea to Singapore
6.	Singapore to Japan
7.	Australia, Borneo and Philippines
8.	Pacific Ocean, including New Zealand
9.	North America (east coast) and Caribbean
10.	South Atlantic and Indian Ocean (southern part)

TotalTide displays 7 days of times and heights of HW and LW in both tabular and graphical formats. Other useful facilities include: a display of heights at specified times and time intervals; a continuous plot of height against time; indications of periods of daylight and twilight, moon phases, springs/neaps; the option to insert the yacht's draft; calculations of under-keel and overhead clearances.

TotalTide will run on most versions of Microsoft Windows with Internet Explorer v 4.01 or greater, but check your system is compatible before buying.

4.6.4   Commercial software

Various commercial firms sell tidal prediction software for use on computers or calculators. Such software is mostly based on NP 159 and can often predict many years ahead. It remains essential to install annual updates.

4.7   TIDAL STREAMS

Tidal streams are the horizontal movement of water caused by the vertical rise and fall of the tide; see Fig 4(8). They normally change direction about every six hours. They are quite different from ocean currents, such as the Gulf Stream, which run indefinitely in the same direction.

The direction (set) of a tidal stream is always that towards which it is running. The speed (rate) of tidal streams is important to yachtsmen: about 2kn is common, 6–8kn is not unusual in some areas at Springs; 16kn has been recorded in the Pentland Firth!

4.7.1   Tidal stream atlases

Admiralty Tidal Stream Atlases, listed below, show the rate and set of tidal streams in the more important areas around the UK and NW Europe.

The set is shown by arrows graded in weight and, where possible, in length to indicate the rate. Thus $\longrightarrow$ is a weak stream and $\longrightarrow$ a strong stream. The figures against the arrows give the mean Np and Sp rates in tenths of a knot; thus 19,34 indicates a mean Np rate of 1·9kn and a mean Sp rate of 3·4kn. The comma between 19 and 34 is roughly where the observations were made. Inshore eddies are rarely shown in detail due to limitations of scale.

Tidal stream chartlets in this Almanac are derived from the following Admiralty Tidal Stream Atlases.

NP	Ed'n	Year	Title
209	4th	1986	Orkney and Shetland Islands
218	5th	1995	N coast of Ireland, W coast of Scotland
219	2nd	1991	Portsmouth Hbr and approaches
220	2nd	1991	Rosyth Hbr and approaches
221	2nd	1991	Plymouth Hbr and approaches
222	1st	1992	Firth of Clyde and approaches
233	3rd	1995	Dover Strait
249	2nd	1985	Thames Estuary, with co-tidal charts
250	4th	1992	English Channel
251	4th	2005	North Sea, S part
252	4th	2005	North Sea, NW part
253	2nd	2004	North Sea, E part
254	1st	2003	Falmouth to Teignmouth
255	1st	2004	Falmouth to Padstow, inc Scilly
256	4th	1992	Irish Sea and Bristol Channel
257	3rd	1973	Approaches to Portland
258	1st	2006	Bristol Channel, Lundy–Avonmouth
259	1st	2006	Irish Sea, E part
263	1st	2003	Lyme Bay
264	5th	1993	Channel Islands and adjacent France
265	2nd	2005	France, west coast
337	4th	1993	The Solent and adjacent waters

Useful information is also given in Admiralty Pilots: times of slack water, when the tide turns, overfalls and/or races etc.

Along open coasts the tidal stream does not necessarily turn at HW and LW; it often occurs at about half tide. The tidal stream usually turns earlier inshore than offshore. In larger bays the tide often sets inshore towards the coast.

The Yachtsman's Manual of Tides by Michael Reeve-Fowkes (ACN) covers all theoretical and practical aspects of tides. It includes four regional **Tidal Atlases**: *Western Channel; Central Channel and the Solent; Southern North Sea and Eastern Channel; Channel ports and approaches*. These are also available separately. The atlases are referenced to HW Cherbourg and include annual Cherbourg tide tables (which are downloadable free from www.adlardcoles.com).

Tidal streams referred to HW Aberdeen

Hours		◇	Geographical Position			Ⓐ		59°13'·0N 2°43'·0W	Ⓑ		59°12'·0N 2°52'·1W
Before High Water	6	Direction of streams (degrees)		Rates at spring tides (knots)	Rates at neap tides (knots)	–6	204	5·0	2·0	148	2·5	1·0
	5					–5	205	5·2	2·1	149	4·7	1·9
	4					–4	207	4·0	1·5	137	3·7	1·5
	3					–3	205	2·5	1·0	129	2·2	0·9
	2					–2		0·0	0·0	118	1·1	0·5
	1					–1	026	2·9	1·1	065	0·6	0·2
High Water						0	023	4·1	1·6	347	1·1	0·5
After High Water	1					+1	024	4·5	1·8	330	2·4	1·0
	2					+2	025	4·0	1·6	320	4·2	1·7
	3					+3	026	3·0	1·2	310	4·0	1·6
	4					+4	034	1·2	0·5	309	2·4	1·0
	5					+5	209	1·7	0·7	328	1·3	0·5
	6					+6	204	4·8	2·0	145	1·2	0·5

Fig 4(7) Tidal stream diamonds

4.7.2   Tidal stream diamonds

Lettered diamonds (◇) on many medium scale charts refer to tables on the chart giving the most accurate tidal stream set and rate (for springs and neaps) at hourly intervals before and after HW at a convenient Standard Port. See Fig 4(7).

The tidal stream diamonds above are extracted from the table on AC 2250 which covers the eastern part of the Orkney Islands. The streams are referred to HW Aberdeen.

Diamond 'A' is located in the 1M wide Sound of Eday (between the islands of Eday and Sanday).

By inspection the first slack water is sharply defined at HW –2. The stream then sets NNE until a much less obvious slack water occurs between HW +4 and +5. The stream turns at about HW +4½, but rates are still between 1·2 and 1·7kn at springs (0·5 and 0·7kn at neaps).

The SSW-going stream reaches a max spring rate of 5·2kn at HW –5; neap rates are less than half these values.

There is considerable detail in these tables. Careful study enables accurate planning and timing for the transit of narrow waters and best use of the tidal streams.

4.7.3   Flood stream around UK

The main flood stream sets ENE up the English Channel, NE into the Bristol Channel and N up the W coasts of Ireland and Scotland (Fig 4(8)). The ebb stream is the reverse.

Two variations are worth noting:

The flood flows NE-N through St George's Channel. However the flood also sets SE through the North Channel and S into the Irish Sea. Both streams meet off the Isle of Man.

Off the E coasts of Scotland and England the stream sets S all the way from Orkney to the Thames Estuary, finally meeting the N-going stream which has curled round North Foreland and up towards London.

Fig 4(8) The main flood stream around the British Isles

4.7.4 Calculating tidal stream rates

The tidal stream rate at intermediate times can be calculated, assuming that it varies with the range of tide at Dover.

Example: Calculate the tidal stream rate off the north tip of Skye at 0420 UT on a day when the tide at Dover is:

UT	Ht (m)	
0328	1·4	By inspection the mean Range
0819	6·3	at Dover is:
1602	1·1	$\frac{(4·9 + 5·2 + 5·3)}{3} = 5·1m$
2054	6·4	

In 9.8.3 the hourly chartlet for HW Dover –4 gives mean Neap and Spring rates of 0·8 and 1·8 kn respectively.

On Fig 4(9) overleaf, from the horizontal Rates axis mark 08 on the horizontal blue Neaps line; likewise 18 on the Springs line. Join these two marks with a diagonal. From the range 5·1 on the vertical axis go horizontally to cut the diagonal just drawn. From this point go vertically to the Rates axis, top or bottom, and read off the predicted rate of 15 (1·5 knots).

4.7.5 Tidal streams in rivers

Tidal streams in rivers are influenced by the local topography of the river bed as well as solar and lunar forces. At or near Springs, in a river which is obstructed, for example by a bar, the time of HW gets later going up the river. The time of LW also gets later, but more rapidly so the duration of the flood becomes shorter, and duration of ebb becomes longer. At the entrance the flood stream starts at an interval after LW which increases with the degree of obstruction of the channel; this interval between local LW and the start of the flood increases with the distance up river. The ebb begins soon after local HW along the length of the river. Hence the duration of flood is less than that of the ebb and the difference increases with distance up river.

The flood stream is normally stronger than the ebb, and runs harder during the first half of the rise of tide. At Neaps the flood and ebb both start soon after local LW and HW respectively, and their durations and rates are about equal.

4.8 METEOROLOGICAL EFFECTS

Prolonged strong winds and unusually high/low pressure significantly affect tidal heights. Early or late times of HW or LW are principally caused by the wind. The effects of wind or pressure individually may not be great, but the combined effect, which is more likely, may be much greater.

4.8.1 Wind

Wind >Force 5 raises the sea level on a lee shore and lowers it on a windward, but there are wide variations due to topography. Strong on/offshore winds may affect the predicted times of HW or LW by up to 1 hour.

Strong winds blowing parallel to a coast tend to set up long waves, which travel along the coast. Sea level is raised at the crest of these waves (positive surge) and lowered in the troughs (negative surge). A storm surge is an unusually severe positive surge. Under exceptional conditions this can raise the height of HW by >1m; a negative surge can lower the height of LW by the same amount – clearly more serious for yachtsmen and other mariners.

The southern North Sea and the Thames Estuary are prone to such surges. In Jan 1953 a deep depression and an exceptionally severe and prolonged northerly storm caused a positive storm surge which raised sea level by almost 3m on the UK's E coast and by even more on the Dutch coast – with heavy loss of life.

4.8.2 Barometric pressure

Over a period of time and across a wide area sea levels are lowered by high pressure and raised by low. The former is of more practical concern to mariners. Mean sea level pressures are quoted in Admiralty Pilots: 1017mb, for example, along the UK south coast in July; 1014mb in January. 1013mb at Wick in July; 1007mb in January.

Intense minor depressions, line squalls or other abrupt changes in the weather can cause wave oscillations, a phenomenon known as a *seiche*. The wave period can vary from a few minutes up to two hours, with heights up to a metre – usually less, rarely more. Certain harbours, eg Wick and Fishguard, due to their shape or size, are particularly prone to *seiches* especially in winter.

4.8.3 Storm Warning Services

These warn of possible coastal flooding caused by abnormal meteorological conditions. A negative storm surge causes abnormally low tidal levels in the Dover Strait, Thames Estuary and Southern North Sea. 6–12 hrs warning is given, Sept–April, when tidal levels at Dover, Sheerness or Lowestoft are forecast to be >1m below predicted levels.

Warnings are broadcast by Navtex, HM Coastguard and the Channel Navigation Information Service (CNIS) on VHF and MF as normally used for navigation warnings.

4.9 PHASES OF THE MOON 2010 which principally determine Springs, Neaps and tide times (UT)

	New Moon ●				First Quarter ☽				Full Moon ○				Last Quarter ☾		
	d	h	m		d	h	m		d	h	m		d	h	m
Jan	15	07	11	Jan	23	10	53	Jan	30	06	18	Jan	07	10	39
Feb	14	02	51	Feb	22	00	42	Feb	28	16	38	Feb	05	23	48
Mar	15	21	01	Mar	23	11	00	Mar	30	02	25	Mar	07	15	42
Apr	14	12	29	Apr	21	18	20	Apr	28	12	18	Apr	06	09	37
May	14	01	04	May	20	23	43	May	27	23	07	May	06	04	15
June	12	11	15	June	19	04	29	June	26	11	30	June	04	22	13
July	11	19	40	July	18	10	11	July	26	01	37	July	04	14	35
Aug	10	03	08	Aug	16	18	14	Aug	24	17	05	Aug	03	04	59
Sept	08	10	30	Sept	15	05	50	Sept	23	09	17	Sept	01	17	22
Oct	07	18	44	Oct	14	21	27	Oct	23	01	37	Oct	01	03	52
Nov	06	04	52	Nov	13	16	39	Nov	21	17	27	Oct	30	12	46
Dec	05	17	36	Dec	13	13	59	Dec	21	08	13	Nov	28	20	36
												Dec	28	04	18

Fig 4(9) Graph for calculating tidal stream rates

Tidal rate graph

COMPUTATION OF RATES

TIDAL STREAM RATE (in tenths of a knot): assumed to vary with range of the tide at Dover

5

Communications

Fig 5(1) International Code of Signals: code flags, single letter meanings, phonetic alphabet and Morse code symbols

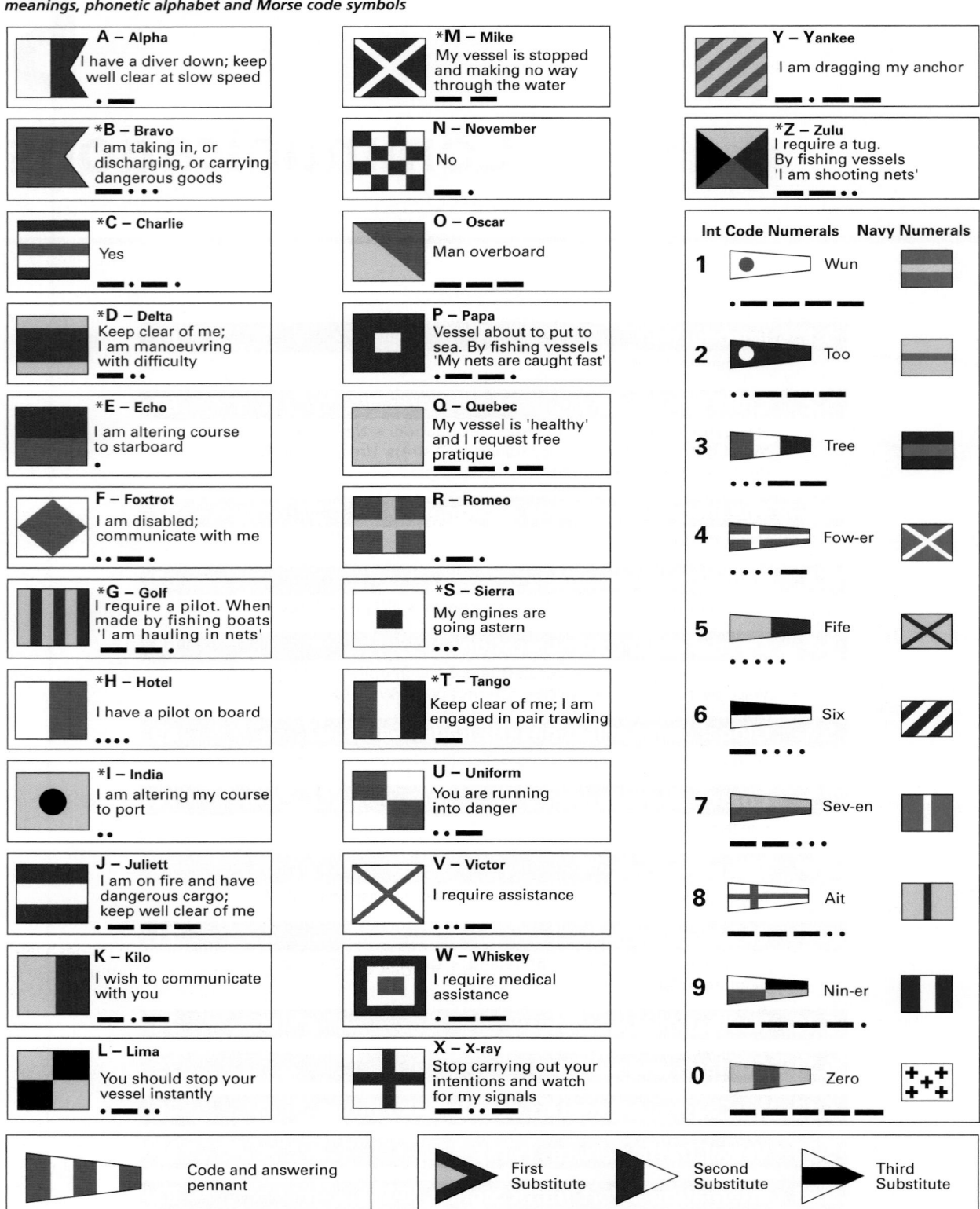

Signals marked * when made by sound may only be used in compliance with the Collision regulations Rules 34 and 35

5.1 INTRODUCTION

Communications are largely a means to an end, so this chapter concentrates on the various means by which mariners can communicate. But where the subject matter being communicated is more important than the means, it is dealt with under those subjects (cross references are given below). For example distress signals are best dealt with in Chapter 7 Safety. But coast radio stations, navigational warnings, Coastguard contact details, VTS (vessel traffic services, 5.22), IPTS (International Port Traffic Signals, 5.23) and flag etiquette (5.24) are all covered in this chapter.

5.2 CROSS REFERENCES

5.2.2 Weather information See Chapter 6.

5.2.3 Navtex
Navtex provides navigational and meteorological warnings and other Marine Safety Information (MSI), but is most often used by yachtsmen for obtaining weather bulletins; details are therefore in Chapter 6. Navtex is also referred to briefly in Chapter 7, as the MSI component of GMDSS.

5.2.4 Visual distress and emergency signals
Details of Distress signals, visual signals between shore and ships in distress, signals used by SAR aircraft, and directing signals used by aircraft are given in Chapter 7.

5.2.5 Distress, Urgency and Safety messages
There are agreed international procedures for passing R/T messages concerning vessels in Distress and SAR operations – or for lesser emergencies and medical assistance or situations where Urgency or Safety messages are appropriate. These are fully described in Chapter 7, together with the Global Maritime Distress and Safety System (GMDSS).

5.2.6 Port Operations
VHF channels for Port Operations are specified in Chapter 9 under individual harbours and marinas.

5.3 THE INTERNATIONAL CODE OF SIGNALS

Marine communication is rooted in the International Code of Signals (1987 edition published by IMO) which provides for safety of navigation and of persons, especially where there are language problems. The present Code came into force in 1969 and is available in nine languages: English, French, German, Greek, Italian, Japanese, Norwegian, Russian and Spanish. Ships, aircraft and shore stations can communicate with each other in these languages without knowing a foreign tongue, provided they have the relevant Code. The English language edition is published by HMSO.

5.3.1 Using the International Code
The Code can be used to convey information by: voice, using R/T or loud-hailer; the Morse code by flashing light and sound signals; alphabetical flags and numeral pendants; or by hand flags.

Signals consist of: single-letter signals which are urgent or much used; two-letter signals in the General Section; and three-letter signals starting with the letter 'M' in the Medical Section.

Fig 5(1) opposite shows the Code flags for letters and numerals, the alphanumeric phonetic alphabet, Morse code for letters and numerals, and the meanings of important or common single-letter signals.

Yachtsmen may also see or hear the following important two-letter signals (there are many others):

NC	I am in distress and require immediate assistance.
NE2	You should proceed with great caution; submarines are exercising in this area.
RY	You should proceed at slow speed when passing me (or vessels making signals).
YG	You appear to be contravening the rules of a Traffic Separation Scheme.

5.4 RADIO COMMUNICATIONS

5.4.1 Frequency bands
VHF radio (Marine band 156·00–174·00 MHz) is used by most vessels. VHF range is typically about 20M between yachts and up to 65M to a shore station depending on aerial heights. Use the formula $D_1 + D_2 = 1·17(\sqrt{H_1} + \sqrt{H_2})$ where D is the distance to the horizon in nautical miles and H is aerial height in feet. Actual observed ranges may be about 4% greater than the theoretical values in the formula. Use 1·22 instead of 1·17 to calculate the greater practical range.

Medium Frequency (MF) in the 1605–4200kHz band provides typical ranges of 100–300M. Transmissions are Single Sideband (SSB). SSB radio usually means a set able to receive and transmit in SSB over both MF and HF frequencies, although the set can probably transmit in other modes as well. Double sideband (DSB) transmissions are prohibited except for emergency transmissions on 2182 kHz, the international MF Distress frequency.

High Frequency (HF) radio, this frequency band has a global range capability and many ocean voyagers use 'the SSB' to communicate with others on the allocated marine and/or amateur (ham) frequencies.

Ultra High Frequency (UHF) radio with digital technologies is used for Satellite communications (see 5.6.3) and offers global or near global coverage.

5.4.2 Regulations
The regulations for using R/T communications are in the *Handbook for Marine Radio Communication* (Lloyd's of London Press). They are lengthy and form part of the syllabus and examination for certificates of competence.

Some of the more important stipulations are:

Operators must not divulge the contents of messages heard; distress calls have priority; Coast radio stations, or MRCCs as appropriate, control communications in their respective areas. Check that the channel is free before transmitting; unnecessary or superfluous messages are prohibited, as is bad language. In harbour a yacht may not use inter-ship channels except for safety; a radio log must be used to record all messages sent and received.

Communications between MRCCs and second parties are tape recorded, as are intercepted communications with a third party. The following statement is included at the request of the MCA:

'Radio & telephone calls to/from MRCCs are recorded for public safety, prevention/detection of crime and to maintain the operational standards of HM Coastguard'.

5.4.3 Radio Licences

- The **vessel** requires a Ship Radio Licence for any VHF, UHF, MF, HF, satellite or EPIRB equipment on board. It is valid 'for life' and is issued free of charge by: Ofcom, Riverside House, 2a Southwark Bridge Rd, London SE1 9HA. ☎ 020 7981 3000; 🖷 020 7981 3333. www.ofcom.org.uk.

  This allows the use of international maritime channels, Ch M for communications between yachts, marinas and clubs, and M2 for race control.

- The **person** in charge of a set requires a Certificate of Competence (Pt 1) and Authority to Operate (Pt 2). This will usually be the Short Range Certificate (SRC), incorporating VHF DSC procedures. The syllabus and conduct of examinations are the RYA's responsibility; see RYA booklet G26. The former Restricted Certificate of Competence (VHF only) is no longer issued, but remains valid for VHF-only radios.

  The Long Range Certificate (LRC) covers MF, HF, Satellite communications and EPIRBs.

- Citizen's Band (CB) and Amateur (Ham) Radio can be useful means of communication for other than safety matters, but only supplement maritime radio on VHF, MF or HF. CB no longer requires a licence in the UK, but Amateur Radio licences are issued by: The Radio Licensing Centre, PO Box 885, Bristol, BS99 5LG. ☎ 0117 925 8333.

5.4.4 R/T procedures

Communications between a vessel and a Coast radio station are controlled by the latter, except for Distress, Urgency or Safety messages. Between two vessels, the vessel which is called nominates the working channel.

Before making a call, decide exactly what you wish to say; it may help to write the message down. Speak slowly and distinctly. Names or important words can be repeated or spelled phonetically; see 5.4.5 for the use and meanings of common prowords.

Your position should be given as Lat/Long or the vessel's bearing and distance *from* a charted object, eg 'My position 225° Isle of May 4M' means you are 4M SW of the Isle of May (*not* 4M NE). Use the 360° True bearing notation and the 24 hours clock (0001–2359), specifying UT or LT.

5.4.5 Prowords

These simplify and expedite communications:

ACKNOWLEDGE	Have you received and understood?
CONFIRM	My version is … is that correct?
CORRECTION	An error has been made; the correct version is …
I SAY AGAIN	I repeat … (eg vital words)
I SPELL	What follows is spelled phonetically.
OUT	End of working.
OVER	I have completed this part of my message, and am inviting you to reply.
RECEIVED	Receipt acknowledged.
SAY AGAIN	Repeat your message (or part of it, ie: All after/before …).
STATION CALLING	Used when a station is unsure of the identity of the station which is calling.

5.5 COASTAL RADIO COMMUNICATIONS

5.5.1 VHF radio

VHF radio range is slightly better than the line of sight between the transmitting and receiving aerials (see 5.4.1). It always pays to fit a good aerial, as high as possible.

VHF sets may be **Simplex**, ie transmit and receive on the same frequency, so only one person can talk at a time. **Semi-Duplex** (most modern sets), transmit and receive on different frequencies, or **full Duplex**, ie simultaneous Semi-Duplex, so conversation is normal, but two aerials are needed.

Marine VHF frequencies are known by their international channel number (Ch), as shown below.

Channels are grouped according to three main purposes, but some have more than one purpose.

- *Public correspondence:* (via Coast radio stations). Ch 26, 27, 25, 24, 23, 28, 04, 01, 03, 02, 07, 05, 84, 87, 86, 83, 85, 88, 61, 64, 65, 62, 66, 63, 60, 82, 78, 81. All channels can be used for Duplex.
- *Inter-ship:* Ch 06*, 08*, 10, 13, 09, 72*, 73, 69, 77*, 15, 17. These are all Simplex channels. * for use in UK.
- *Port Operations:*
  Simplex: Ch 12, 14, 11, 13, 09, 68, 71, 74, 69, 73, 17, 15.
  Duplex: Ch 20, 22, 18, 19, 21, 05, 07, 02, 03, 01, 04, 78, 82, 79, 81, 80, 60, 63, 66, 62, 65, 64, 61, 84.

The following channels have one specific purpose:

Ch 0 (156·00 MHz): SAR ops, not available to yachts.

Ch 10 (156·50 MHz), **23** (161·750 MHz), **84** (161·825 MHz) and **86** (161·925 MHz): MSI broadcasts. The optimum channel number is stated on Ch 16 in the announcement prior to the broadcast itself.

Ch 13 (156·650 MHz): Inter-ship communications relating to safety of navigation; a possible channel for calling a merchant ship if no contact on Ch 16.

Ch 16 (156·80 MHz): Distress, Safety and calling. Ch 16, in parallel with DSC Ch 70, will be monitored by ships, CG rescue centres (and, in some areas, any remaining Coast radio stations) for Distress and Safety until further notice. Yachts should monitor Ch 16. After an initial call, stations concerned **must** switch to a working channel, except for Distress and Safety matters.

Ch 67 (156·375 MHz): Small craft safety channel used by all UK CG centres, accessed via Ch 16.

Ch 70 (156·525 MHz): Digital Selective Calling for Distress and Safety purposes under GMDSS.

Ch 80 (157·025 MHz): Primary working channel between yachts and UK marinas.

Ch M (157·85 MHz): Secondary working channel, formerly known as Ch 37, but no longer.

Ch M2 (161·425 MHz): for race control, with Ch M as stand-by. YCs may apply to use Ch M2.

5.5.2 MF radio

MF radios operate in the 1605–4200 kHz wavebands. Unlike VHF and HF, MF transmissions tend to follow the earth's curvature, which makes them suitable for direction-finding equipment.

For this reason, and because of their good range, the marine Distress frequency (2182 kHz) is in the MF band as is the DSC Distress alerting frequency 2187·5 kHz.

5.5.3 Wireless telephony (mobile/cellular phone)

Mobile phones are not suitable for emergency situations, except in extremis (see 7.5.5), but are often carried, in addition to VHF radio, for communicating with marinas. The digital GSM system also permits SMS text messaging as well as roaming between different countries. Many mobile phones now incorporate GPS receivers and mapping functionality.

Wireless telephony also has a definite role to play in data communication, allowing a PC to connect wirelessly to the Internet at a speed of 9.6kbps (thousand bits per second) in most areas when close to the shore; this is quite slow, but nevertheless sufficient for sending and receiving basic emails and browsing text-only websites.

Enhancements: GPRS (Global Packet Radio Service) works on mobile phone networks and boosts download rates to around 36–48kbps within about 5M of the more populated NW European coasts. So called Wireless Broadband mobile data services such as HSCSD and EDGE (aka 2·5 Generation) provide data rates up to 115kbps and 384kbps respectively, though currently only in urban and more populated areas. Emerging 3G (3rd Generation) standards promise even greater speeds, up to 14,000kbps (14 mbps) 'real soon now'.

These services are charged by the amount of data transmitted, not the duration of the call and therefore an 'always on' connection can be used. GPRS/G3/UMTS and EDGE all require compatible handsets and a suitable airtime contract with the phone company.

Availability of each service from base stations varies and range offshore cannot be relied upon, especially off sparsely populated coasts where only a limited service is provided.

5.5.4 Voice over IP (VOIP)

Internet Protocol, or IP, is the 'language' that drives the Internet, and VOIP (Voice over IP) is a system where voice communication is encoded and transmitted very efficiently as computer data. Free to join VOIP services such as Skype provide free voice communication between 'members', and also (for a small charge) with normal land-line telephones. VOIP will work over Wireless broadband, but network charges will be high if roaming, so broadband Internet connection is required, often available on the marina pontoons.

5.5.5 Wireless internet (Wi-Fi/Wi-MAX)

Wireless telephony services (5.5.3) are primarily geared-up for voice though they increasingly offer affordable data capability and may be used via an onboard PC (or Macintosh) to send and receive email, browse websites and download updates and chart corrections, in exactly the same way as from a home PC.

Wi-Fi, on the other hand, is an increasingly common wireless system, independent of the phone operators' networks, that provides broadband Internet access via 'hotspots', or 'wireless access points'. Increasingly marinas include Wi-Fi Internet access as part of their berthing fees, though paid-for access is also provided by specialist companies.

Even with special antennae, range is limited and this prevents Wi-Fi being useful to yachts while at sea, but speeds of up to 10,000kbps in the marina are typical and are perfectly suited to normal Internet use like web browsing and downloading Notices to Mariners or Almanac updates.

Wi-Max is an emerging (ie within 2 years) technology that *could* deliver Internet access at much higher speeds with ranges exceeding 10 miles offshore, actual ranges and indicative costs are not available at this stage.

[1] typical, **if** in coverage area [2] using VOIP [3] Likely to be expensive	Wired Broadband	Wi-Fi	Cellular GSM	Cellular GPRS/2-G	Cellular 3G	Wi-Max
Range offshore[1] (NM)	0	0-1	0-15	0-15	0-15	0-30
Voice communication	Y[2]	Y[2]	Y	Y	Y	Y[2]
Text messages	Y	Y	Y	Y	Y	Y
Light email traffic	Y	Y	Y[3]	Y	Y	Y
Text weather forecasts	Y	Y	Y[3]	Y	Y	Y
Heavy email traffic	Y	Y	×	Y[3]	Y	Y
Graphical weather forecasts	Y	Y	×	Y[3]	Y	Y
Full web browsing	Y	Y	×	Y[3]	Y	Y

5.6 GLOBAL COMMUNICATIONS (HF RADIO/SATCOMS)

Once out of range of VHF/MF, wireless telephony or wireless Internet service, the yachtsman's communications options are limited to MF/HF radio and satellite systems (Satcoms).

For voice communication, HF radio is free to use but requires an experienced operator to get the best out of it, whereas satcom systems operate much more like a domestic telephone, albeit with significant usage costs.

HF radio has a modest capability for digital data communication, and several operators provide low-cost (but slow) global email services. Satcom technology is itself digital and lends itself to data communication.

A yachtsman embarking on an extended offshore venture, for example an Atlantic 'circuit', would usually choose a mix of equipment. Though primarily for sensible reasons of redundancy, this also allows a choice of listening and transmitting, via terrestrial and satellite radio systems, to meet his needs at various times and in different circumstances.

A typical setup might include a fixed or handheld satcoms transceiver, a HF SSB transceiver and receiver as well as a digital satellite receiver. For data capability as well as voice, these would have to be interfaced to an on-board PC.

5.6.1 HF radio (SSB)

HF SSB radios use frequencies in the 4, 8, 12, 16 and 22 MHz bands (short wave) that are chosen to suit propagation conditions. HF SSB transceivers usually include MF frequencies as well; they are more expensive than MF-only and require more power, but can provide worldwide coverage – a good installation and correct operating techniques are essential for satisfactory results.

Whereas MF transmissions follow the curve of the earth, HF waves travel upwards and bounce off the ionosphere back to earth. Reception is better at night when the ionosphere is denser. The directional properties of HF transmissions are poor, so there is no HF Distress frequency.

Despite rapid growth in marine satellite communications, HF SSB remains a popular choice amongst long-distance cruisers, providing a cost-free voice (and limited email) capability. The system is often used like a telephone between groups of cruisers, organised into informal or more formal networks (nets), sometimes operating over vast distances.

Operators have the Long Range Certificate (LRC; see 5.4.3) or General Operators Certificate (GOC). To use Amateur (ham) bands (giving more frequencies and higher power, therefore range) operators must take the ham examination.

Using HF SSB radio for email requires a radio modem, often proprietary to the supplier of the email-over-radio system. Installation costs for the whole setup can be high (more than for some satcom systems) but despite the very slow speed of data communication and sometimes patchy voice operation, the nil or almost-nil operating costs appeal to many and SSB radio has a strong following amongst blue-water cruisers. Established suppliers include Sailmail and Globe Wireless.

HF SSB radio is also extensively used for receipt of weatherfax images, although a receive-only SSB radio (with an adequate, grounded antenna installation) may be used rather than a full transceiver. Though declining in popularity, several useful weatherfax transmitting stations remain, including Northwood, UK (see 6.5.1) and Offenbach, Germany.

5.6.2   Satellite Radio

Satellite radio is a receive-only digital radio broadcast signal transmitted via satellites. Services are subscription based, main providers being WorldSpace, XM Radio and Sirius. A digital decoding receiver is required (usually included with the subscription). Programming includes news, sport and music and some providers offer weather synopsis and forecast imagery, transmitted as a digital signal that is decoded using on board software.

5.6.3   Satellite Communications (Satcoms)

Satcoms offer simpler-to-operate and more reliable voice (and data) communications than HF SSB radio; they operate with either a dedicated ship installation or a standalone handheld terminal. Apart from the equipment purchase (and installation if necessary), ongoing costs usually include a monthly service fee and usage charges that will be related to either the amount of satellite time used, or the volume of data transmitted and received.

For two-way voice communications, the 'Ship Station' (aka 'Mobile Earth Station') transmits to a visible satellite that is simultaneously in sight of a 'Land Earth Station', eg Goonhilly, Cornwall. From there, the call is routed to its destination through the normal terrestrial wired telephone network.

The satellite 'constellations' have different architectures. Inmarsat for example has four geostationary (GEO) satellites, one each positioned over the Pacific and Indian oceans and two over the Atlantic. Because they are comparatively high up (19,400M/36,000km), each satellite has a large signal 'footprint', overlapping the next one and thus world-wide coverage is provided (although not in the polar regions above about 70°N and 70°S). Other systems employ many more Low Earth Orbit (LEO) satellites orbiting the Earth about (540M/1,000km) above the surface.

The smaller, low-data rate, handheld voice terminals incorporate an omni-directional antenna that works best with an unobstructed view of the satellite. Fixed installations use an external gyro-stabilised antenna (to keep it pointing at the satellite as the boat moves); more powerful systems that support higher data rates employ antenna radomes that are really too large for installation aboard a 10–15m yacht.

The GMDSS provides automatic distress, urgency and safety communications, with some systems (eg Inmarsat C) providing a red button that alerts a Maritime Rescue Coordination Centre (MRCC) when pressed.

There are several providers of satellite communications services, each offering an array of capabilities and services. Table 5 (1) below provides a useful summary of systems that might be used aboard a 10–20m yacht.

But note that this is a fast moving market place and you should check with manufacturers/retailers for up-to-date specifications and prices.

TABLE 5 (1)

System	Antenna	Satellites	Coverage	GMDSS	Phone (voice)	Fax	SMS text	Position tracking	Data rate
INMARSAT C	Omnidirectional	4 GEO	Global excepting polar regions	Yes	No	Yes	Yes	Yes (GPS)	Very low, uneconomic for email
INMARSAT Mini-M	Gyrostabilised 40cms diameter	4 GEO	Global excepting polar regions	No	Yes	Yes	No	No	2.4kbps
INMARSAT D+	Omnidirectional	4 GEO	Global excepting polar regions	No	No	No	No	Yes (GPS)	Very low, uneconomic for email
Fleet 33	Gyrostabilised 40cms diameter	4 GEO	Global excepting polar regions	No	Yes	Yes	Yes	No	9.6kbps uncompressed
Iridium	Omnidirectional	66 LEO	Global	No	Yes	Out only	Yes	No	Data kit required 2.4kbps (higher with compression)
Globalstar	Omnidirectional	40 LEO	Global excepting polar regions	No	Yes	Yes	Yes	To 10km	9.6kbps uncompressed, 38.6kbps compressed, 56k with data kit
Thuraya	Omnidirectional	1 GEO	Europe, N Africa & Middle East, India	No	Yes	Yes	Yes	Yes (GPS)	9.6kbps (144kbps possible with land *DSL receiver)

*DSL (Digital Subscriber Line) allows broadband Internet over normal copper telephone lines. It is used in the wireless/Satcoms arena to denote 'broadband-like speeds' over the wireless link and usually means speeds of 5 to 24mbps which is relatively fast for Satcoms.

5.7 COAST RADIO STATIONS (CRS)

In recent years many European nations have closed, or plan to close, their coast radio stations due in part to the popularity of mobile phones. The UK, France, Netherlands and Belgium have no CRS.

Ireland (but see 5.9.2), Denmark, Spain and Portugal still operate CRS. In Germany a commercial company, DP07 Seefunk, provides a limited link call service.

Details of national CRS are given below in 5.9.

5.7.1 Functions

CRS functions include:

- Control of ship-shore communications; see 5.4.4.
- Providing link calls; see 5.8. Note: The Coastguard, or foreign equivalent, *do not handle link calls*.
- Broadcasting at scheduled times traffic lists (messages awaiting ships at sea); navigational warnings (Chapter 3); weather bulletins and gale warnings (Chapter 6). Note: Do not transmit on a designated broadcast channel when a broadcast is scheduled.
- Handling Distress and Urgency calls in some countries.

5.7.2 Track Reports

A Track Report (TR) may be passed to a CRS or Coastguard centre, as appropriate, stating a yacht's point of departure, destination, ETA and number of people onboard. This is an obvious safety measure, especially in more remote regions, should a yacht subsequently become overdue. On arrival be sure to inform the local CRS or CG and ask that your TR be cancelled with the original CRS/CG.

5.8 LINK CALLS

5.8.1 Making a VHF link call

- Within range (up to 40M), select a 'clear' channel, ie no transmissions. A busy channel will have carrier noise, speech or the engaged signal (a series of pips).
- Call the CRS on a working channel related to the position of the yacht. Calls should state the calling channel and last at least 6 seconds in order to activate the response equipment at the CRS.

For example:

Bilbao Radio, this is Yacht Seabird, Yacht Seabird, Golf Oscar Romeo India Fower, Channel 27, Over.

A four-tone signal or pips indicate a temporary delay, but you will be answered when an operator is free.

- When the call is accepted you will hear pips, indicating that the channel has been engaged. Wait for the operator to speak. If no response, do not change channel since you may lose your turn.

  If the pips are not heard, the station's transmitter has not been activated or may be out of range. Try another station or call again when closer.

- The operator will request: Vessel's call sign (eg Golf Oscar Romeo India Fower), name, accounting code (see 5.8.2), type of message (eg telegram, telephone call) and the telephone number required (and in the case of a personal call the name of the person called).

5.8.2 Paying for a link call

Calls are accounted for worldwide by quoting an 'Accounting Authority Indicator Code' (AAIC). This must previously have been arranged with an ITU-recognised authority such as Cable and Wireless, who use GB 02 as

their AAIC. All CRS hold the complete ITU listing of ship stations and their AAICs.

5.8.3 MF link calls

Calls should be initiated on 2182 kHz or the nominated working frequency. The Coast station will allocate a working channel, and cue you into the system.

5.9 CRS BY COUNTRIES

5.9.1 The Channel Islands

St Peter Port and Jersey CRS are operated by the States of Guernsey and Jersey respectively. They handle Distress and Urgency situations as well as link calls.

St Peter Port Radio

VHF 20, **62** (link calls only), 16, **67** (for yacht safety messages; available on request Ch 16). MF 1764 kHz.

DSC Ch 70: **MMSI** 002320064.

Traffic lists: Vessels for which messages are held are called individually on Ch 16.

Jersey Coastguard

VHF **82**, 25 (link calls by charge card and for emergency purposes), 16, 67 (Small craft Distress and Safety working; pre-call on 16).

DSC Ch 70: **MMSI** 002320060.

Navigational warnings, weather bulletins and traffic lists are broadcast on Ch 25 & 82 at times in Chapters 3 and 6.

5.9.2 Republic of Ireland

The main CRS at Malin Head, Dublin and Valentia are co-located with Coastguard centres. Remote CRS sites, as listed below, ensure full coastal coverage in the three regions (NW, SE and SW Ireland). Callsign is station name and Radio.

All CRS guard Ch 16 (H24). Broadcasts are made on a working channel/frequency after pre-warning on Ch 16 and 2182 kHz. Ch 67 is only used for Safety messages. See Chapter 6 for times and details of gale warnings and weather bulletins.

Commercial link calls from ship to shore via CRS ceased to be available wef 1 January 2007, but Medico link calls are still available on both VHF and MF. Call CRS on a working channel; only call Ch 16 if in difficulty or emergency.

Ships should pass their intended voyage or position to Malin Head Coastguard, Dublin Coastguard or Valentia Coastguard, as appropriate. Update voyage details by TR.

The times at which Navigational warnings are broadcast is shown in 5.10.2.

NW Ireland (clockwise from the west)

Clifden Radio	26
Belmullet Radio	83
Donegal Bay Radio	02
Glen Head Radio	24
MALIN HEAD RADIO	23, 85
	MF: Tx 1677 kHz, Rx 2102

SE Ireland

Carlingford Radio	04
DUBLIN RADIO	(No MF) 83
Wicklow Head Radio	02
Rosslare Radio	23
Mine Head Radio	83

SW Ireland

Cork Radio	26
Mizen Head Radio	04
Bantry Radio	23
VALENTIA RADIO	24
	MF: Tx 1752 kHz, Rx 2096
Shannon Radio	28
Galway Radio	04

VHF and MF CRS

	VHF Ch	Tx MF	Rx
Skagen	04	**1758**	2045, 2102
Hirtshals	66		
Hanstholm	01		
Bovbjerg	02	**1767**	2045, 2111
Blåvand	23	**1734**	2045, 2078

HF RT. Lyngby Radio, in the course of normal working in the 4, 8, 12 & 16 MHz bands, *receives* calls from ships on the frequencies in *black italic*; and transmits on the paired frequencies in green. Ships may be directed to other paired frequencies as listed in ALRS Vol 1(1).

4116	4408	*16411*	17293
4137	4429	*16423*	17305
8216	8740	*16462*	17344
8246	8770	*22045*	22741
12257	13104	*22051*	22747
12269	13116	*22105*	22801
12296	13143	*25070*	26145
16408	17290	*25073*	26148

Fig 5(2) Irish coast radio stations

Fig 5(3) Danish coast radio stations

5.9.3 Denmark

All Danish VHF/MF CRS are remotely controlled by **Lyngby** and use the callsign *Lyngby Radio*.

The stations listed below monitor Ch 16 and DSC Ch 70, H24. Call on working frequencies, to keep Ch 16 clear. MF stations do not monitor 2182 kHz. Traffic lists are broadcast on all VHF channels every odd H+05.

5.9.4 Germany

DP07 – Seefunk, Estedeich 84, 21129 Hamburg. ☎ 040 23855782. 🖷 040 74134242. info@dp07.com www.dp07.com MMSI 002113100.

This company operates seven CRS on the North Sea coast and five on the Baltic coast as shown on Fig 5(4) and listed opposite. All CRS monitor Ch 16 and DSC Ch 70.

Fig 5(4) German coast radio stations

Nordfriesland	26	Baltic coast	
Elbe-Weser	24	**Kiel**	23
Hamburg	83	**Flensburg***	27
Bremerhaven	01	**Lübeck**	24
Bremen	25	**Rostock***	60
Accumersiel	28	**Arkona**	66
Borkum	61	* New channel planned	

Traffic Lists: Ch 16 every H and H+30; and at 0745, 0945, 1245, 1645 and 1945LT. Callsign is the name of the remote station; see panel in next column.

5.9.5 Belgium

OOSTENDE RADIO ☎ +32 59 702438. 📠 59 701339. rmd@mil.be DSC Ch 70 and 2187·5 kHz (H24). MMSI 002050480. MF: Tx 2484, Rx 3178 kHz.

Remote VHF stations:
Antwerpen Radio DSC Ch 70; MMSI 002050485.

Traffic lists: Ch 24 every H+05.	Ch 07, 24, 27
Zeebrugge	Ch 27, 63
Middelkerke (Oostende)	Ch 27, 85
De Panne (French border)	Ch 78, 85

5.9.6 Spain

CRS monitor (H24) Ch 16, 2182kHz and DSC (VHF & MF) so call initially on Ch 16, then switch to a working channel. Traffic lists are not broadcast on VHF, but passed on a working VHF channel; or broadcast on MF at every odd H +33, except 0133 and 2133.

North Spain
Remote stations controlled by Bilbao Comms Centre are:

Pasajes Radio		Ch 27
Machichaco Radio	*MF: Tx 1707; Rx 2132.*	No VHF
Bilbao Radio		Ch 26
Santander Radio		Ch 24
Cabo Peñas Radio	*MF: Tx 1677; Rx 2102.*	Ch 26
Navia Radio		Ch 60

North west Spain
Remote stations controlled by Coruña Comms Centre are:

Cabo Ortegal Radio		Ch 02
Coruña Radio	*MF: Tx 1698; Rx 2123.*	Ch 26
Finisterre Radio	*MF: Tx 1764; Rx 2108.*	Ch 22
Vigo Radio		Ch 65
La Guardia Radio		Ch 21

South west Spain
Remote stations controlled by Malaga Comms Centre include:

Chipiona Radio	*MF: Tx 1656; Rx 2081.*	No VHF
Cádiz Radio		Ch 26
Tarifa Radio	*MF: Tx 1704; Rx 2129.*	Ch 81

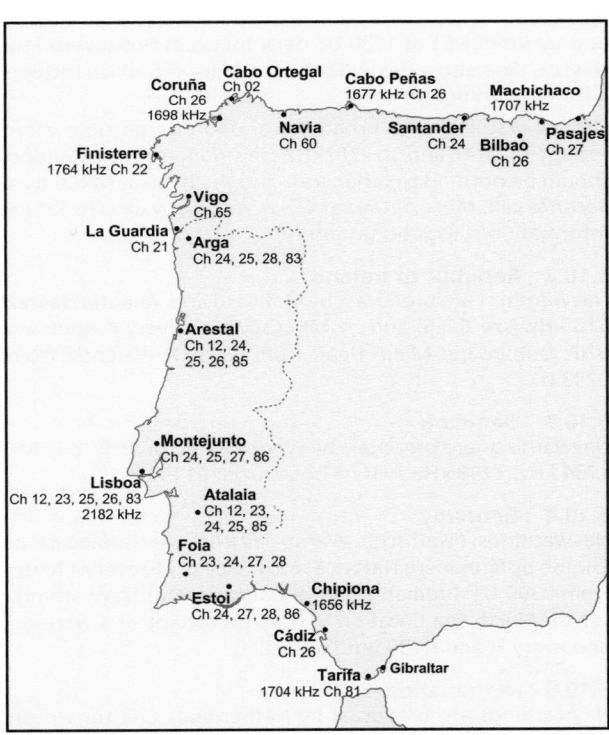

Fig 5(5) Spanish and Portuguese coast radio stations

5.9.7 Portugal

Lisboa Radio controls all remote stations. ☎ +351 214 190098, 📠 +351 214 199900. lisboa.radio@telecom.pt

All Coast radio stations monitor Ch 16 (H24). Callsign is the station name plus 'Radio'.

See Fig 5(5) for station names and VHF channels.

5.9.8 The Azores

All Coast radio stations monitor Ch 16 (H24) and are remotely controlled by Lisboa Radio. The following MF frequencies and VHF channels are used:

Flores Radio		23, 24, 25, 26
Faial Radio	MF: Tx & Rx 2182kHz.	24, 25, 26, 28
Pico Radio		23, 24, 26, 27
São Miguel Radio	MF: Tx & Rx 2182kHz.	23, 24, 25, 26, 27

5.10 NAVIGATIONAL WARNINGS

Navigational warnings are promulgated for 16 NavAreas (I-XVI) worldwide. An Area co-ordinator oversees each NavArea and handles inputs from national and other authorities. The 3 types of navigational warnings are:

NavArea warnings which deal with Oceanic matters and are transmitted by SafetyNet and Navtex at scheduled times in English and other languages.

Coastal warnings, up to 250M offshore, are issued by a national authority and broadcast in English or the local langauge by Navtex, SafetyNet or VHF Coast radio stations. These warnings cover navaids, lights, buoys, rocks, wrecks, naval exercises, SAR operations, cable laying, piracy etc.

Local warnings supplement the above for inshore waters and within port limits. They are issued by port, pilotage or CG authorities in English and/or the local language.

5.10.1 UK (NavArea I Co-ordinator)

After an announcement on Ch 16, HMCG broadcasts coastal navigational warnings (WZ) on receipt and every 12 hours at the same times and on the same frequencies as the Group A MSI broadcasts. See 6.4 and Table 6(1) for details. WZs are also broadcast by Navtex at the times shown at 6.3.3 – 6.3.5, and by SafetyNET at 1730 UT daily for areas not covered by Navtex. See also weekly *Notices to Mariners* which include a list of warnings in force.

Urgent warnings are broadcast as soon as possible after receipt on Ch 16 and on 2182kHz. New dangers to navigation should be notified to other craft and the nearest MRCC by a *Sécurité* call. More details at www. mcga.gov.uk (see Safety Information/Navigational Safety).

5.10.2 Republic of Ireland

Navwarnings are broadcast by Malin Hd and Valentia Navtex 518 kHz (see 6.3.5) and by MRCCs/MRSCs every 4 hours on VHF: Dublin and Malin Head from 0033 UT; Valentia from 0233 UT.

5.10.3 Denmark

Navwarnings are broadcast by Lyngby Radio on VHF and MF 1734 kHz, 1738 kHz every 4 hours from 0133 UT.

5.10.4 Germany

Navwarnings *(Nautische Warnnachricht)* are broadcast in English by Pinneberg Navtex 518 kHz (see 6.3.5) every 4 hours from 0300 UT. Bremen MRCC broadcasts vital Navwarnings for the North Sea Coast on VHF 16 on receipt of a warning and every H and H+30 until cancelled.

5.10.5 Netherlands

Navwarnings are broadcast by Netherlands Coastguard on Navtex 518 kHz (see 6.3.5) every 4 hours from 0230 UT, and in English on VHF Ch 23 or Ch 83 and MF 3673 kHz every 4 hours from 0333 UT.

5.10.6 Belgium

Navwarnings are broadcast by Oostende on Navtex 518 kHz (see 6.3.5); by Antwerpen, in English and Dutch, for the Schelde on VHF 24 on receipt and every H+55; and by Oostende, in English, on VHF 27 and MF 2761 kHz on receipt, every H+03 and H+33, and every 4 hours from 0233 UT.

Fig 5(6) UK Coastal (WZ) Navwarning areas 1–17. The area(s) for which each MRCC is responsible are in brackets.

5.10.7 France (NavArea II Co-ordinator)

Navwarnings are of two types: **Long-range** for NavArea II issued by SHOM and broadcast by SafetyNet.

AvurNavs include Coastal and Local warnings. They are issued by Cherbourg for the coast from the Belgian border to Mont St Michel, and by Brest from Mont St Michel to the Spanish border. They are broadcast by CROSS (Corsen) Navtex (see 6.3.5) in English every 4 hours from 0000 UT, and in French every 4 hours from 0040 UT. CROSS also broadcasts Navwarnings on VHF 79/80 after initial call on VHF 16 (see 6.20.1).

5.10.8 Spain (NavArea III Co-ordinator)

Long-range Navwarnings for NavArea III are broadcast by SafetyNet. **Coastal** warnings are broadcast in English and Spanish by Coast radio stations on Navtex 518 kHz (see 6.3.5) and on VHF; monitor VHF Ch 16 or MF 2182 kHz.

5.10.9 Portugal

Coastal Navwarnings (up to 200M offshore, inc the Azores) are broadcast in English on Navtex 518 kHZ (in Portuguese on 490 kHz) and by Radionaval stations on VHF Ch 11 and MF 2657 kHz, in English and Portuguese.

5.11 GUNFACTS AND SUBFACTS

5.11.1 Gunfacts

Gunfacts are warnings of intended naval firing practice, broadcast on Ch 16. They include gunnery and missile firings and underwater explosions. (For the latter only, broadcasts are made 1 hour, 30 mins and immediately before detonation.) They do not restrict the passage of any vessel. The onus for safety is on the firing warship. The broadcasts include:

- Time (LT) and approximate location of firings, with a declared safe distance in nautical miles.
- Whether illuminants, ie flares etc, are to be fired.

Gunfacts (S Coast) are issued from Plymouth for English Channel exercise areas (9.1.16 and 9.2.28). See 5.11.2 (Subfacts) for details.

Gunfacts (Ship) are issued by a nominated warship and cover activity in any UK areas. An initial announcement is made on VHF 16.

5.11.2 Subfacts

These are warnings of planned or known submarine activity.

Subfacts (South Coast) give details for the English Channel; see 9.1.16 and 9.2.28. They are broadcast on Navtex (see 6.3.3) and, after an announcement on Ch 16, by Brixham and Falmouth MRCCs every 4 hours from 0140 UT on VHF. The VHF channels are listed in Table 6(2).

Subfacts (Clyde) give details for the W coast of Scotland (see 9.8.22 and 9.9.19). They are broadcast on Navtex (see 6.3.3) and, after announcements on Ch 16, by Stornoway MRCC every 4 hours from 0410 UT; by Clyde MRCC every 4 hours from 0510 UT; and by Belfast CG every 4 hours from 0410 UT. The VHF channels are listed in Table 6(2).

NAVTEX also transmits Subfacts and Gunfacts twice daily: Niton (E) at 0440 and 1640 UT; Portpatrick (O) at 0620 and 1820 UT.

5.12 HM COASTGUARD – CONTACT DETAILS OF MRCCS

EASTERN REGION

PORTLAND COASTGUARD
50°36'N 02°27'W. DSC MMSI 002320012
Custom House Quay, Weymouth DT4 8BE.
☎ 01305 760439. 📠 01305 760451.
Area: Topsham to Chewton Bunney (50°44'N 01°42'W).

SOLENT COASTGUARD
50°48'N 01°12'W. DSC MMSI 002320011
44A Marine Parade West, Lee-on-Solent, PO13 9NR.
☎ 02392 552100. 📠 02392 554131.
Area: Chewton Bunney to Beachy Head.
Make routine initial calls on Ch 67 (H24) to avoid congestion on Ch 16.

DOVER COASTGUARD
50°08'N 01°20'E. DSC MMSI 002320010
Langdon Battery, Swingate, Dover CT15 5NA.
☎ 01304 210008. 📠 01304 225762.
Area: Beachy Head to Reculver Towers (51°23'N 01°12'E).
Operates Channel Navigation Information Service (CNIS); see 9.3.13.

THAMES COASTGUARD
51°51'N 01°17'E. MMSI 002320009
East Terrace, Walton-on-the-Naze CO14 8PY.
☎ 01255 675518. 📠 01255 679415.
Area: Reculver Towers to Southwold (52°19'N 01°40'E).

LONDON COASTGUARD
51°30'N 00°03'E. MMSI 002320063
Thames Barrier Navigation Centre, Unit 28,
34 Bowater Road, Woolwich, London SE18 5TF.
☎ 0208 3127380. 📠 0208 3098196.
Area: River Thames from Shell Haven Pt (N bank) and Egypt Bay (S bank) up-river to Teddington Lock.

YARMOUTH COASTGUARD
52°37'N 01°43'E. MMSI 002320008
Haven Bridge House, North Quay,
Great Yarmouth NR30 1HZ.
☎ 01493 851338. 📠 01493 331975.
Area: Southwold to Haile Sand Fort (SW of Spurn Hd).

†HUMBER COASTGUARD
54°06'N 00°11'W. MMSI 002320007
Lime Kiln Lane, Bridlington, Yorks E Riding YO15 2LX.
☎ 01262 672317. 📠 01262 400779.
Area: Haile Sand Fort to the Scottish border.

SCOTLAND & NORTHERN IRELAND REGION

FORTH COASTGUARD
56°17'N 02°35'W. MMSI 002320005
Fifeness, Crail, Fife KY10 3XN.
☎ 01333 450666. 📠 01333 450703.
Area: English border to Doonies Pt (57°01'N 02°10'W).

†ABERDEEN COASTGUARD
57°08'N 02°05'W. MMSI 002320004
Marine House, Blaikies Quay, Aberdeen AB11 5PB.
☎ 01224 592334. 📠 01224 575920.
Area: Doonies Pt to Cape Wrath, incl Pentland Firth.

†SHETLAND COASTGUARD
60°09'N 01°08'W. MMSI 002320001
Knab Road, Lerwick ZE1 0AX.
☎ 01595 692976. 📠 01595 693634.
Area: Orkney, Fair Isle and Shetland.

†*STORNOWAY COASTGUARD
58°12'N 06°22'W. MMSI 002320024
Battery Point, Stornoway, Isle of Lewis HS1 2RT.
☎ 01851 702013. 📠 01851 706796.
Area: Cape Wrath to Ardnamurchan Pt, Western Isles and St Kilda.

†*CLYDE COASTGUARD
55°58'N 04°48'W. MMSI 002320022
Navy Buildings, Eldon St, Greenock PA16 7QY.
☎ 01475 729988. 📠 01475 888095.
Area: Ardnamurchan Pt to Mull of Galloway inc islands.

*BELFAST COASTGUARD
54°40'N 05°40'W. MMSI 002320021
Bregenz House, Quay St, Bangor, Co Down BT20 5ED.
☎ 02891 463933. 📠 02891 469854.
Area: Carlingford Lough to Lough Foyle.

WESTERN REGION

LIVERPOOL COASTGUARD
53°30'N 03°03'W. MMSI 002320019
Hall Road West, Crosby, Liverpool L23 8SY.
☎ 0151 9313341. 🖷 0151 9320978
Area: Mull of Galloway to Queensferry (near Chester).

†HOLYHEAD COASTGUARD
53°19'N 04°38'W. MMSI 002320018
Prince of Wales Rd, Holyhead, Anglesey LL65 1ET.
☎ 01407 762051. 🖷 01407 761613
Area: Queensferry to Friog (1·6M S of Barmouth).

†MILFORD HAVEN COASTGUARD
51°42'N 05°03'W. MMSI 002320017
Gorsewood Drive, Hakin, Milford Haven, SA73 2HD.
☎ 01646 690909. 🖷 01646 697287.
Area: Friog to River Towy (11M N of Worms Head).

SWANSEA COASTGUARD
51°34'N 03°58'W. MMSI 002320016
Tutt Head, Mumbles, Swansea SA3 4EX.
☎ 01792 366534. 🖷 01792 368371.
Area: River Towy to Marsland Mouth (near Bude).

†*FALMOUTH COASTGUARD
50°09'N 05°03'W. MMSI 002320014
Pendennis Point, Castle Drive, Falmouth TR11 4WZ.
☎ 01326 317575. 🖷 01326 315610.
Area: Marsland Mouth (near Bude) to Dodman Point.

*BRIXHAM COASTGUARD
50°24'N 03°31'W. DSC MMSI 002320013
King's Quay, Brixham TQ5 9TW.
☎ 01803 882704. 🖷 01803 859562.
Area: Dodman Point to Topsham (River Exe).
NOTES: † Monitors DSC MF 2187.5 kHz.
* Broadcasts Gunfacts/Subfacts; see Chapter 3.
The 3 Regions above are Search and Rescue Regions.

5.13   CHANNEL ISLANDS

There is no Coastguard in the Channel Islands. The HMs at St Peter Port and St Helier direct SAR operations within the Northern and Southern areas respectively. The two Coast radio stations, *St Peter Port Radio* and *Jersey Coastguard*, provide communications on VHF and DSC.

Close liaison is maintained with French SAR authorities and a distress situation may be controlled by whichever is more appropriate. For example a British yacht in difficulty in French waters may be handled by St Peter Port or Jersey so as to avoid language problems; and vice versa for a French yacht.

ST PETER PORT RADIO (CRS)
49°27'·00N 02°32'00W. DSC MMSI 002320064
☎ 01481 720672. 🖷 01481 714177. VHF Ch 16, 67.
Area: The Channel Islands Northern area.

JERSEY COASTGUARD (CRS)
49°10'·90N 02°06'80W. DSC MMSI 002320060
☎ 01534 885505. 🖷 01534 499089. VHF Ch 16, 82.
Area: The Channel Islands Southern area.

5.13.1   Emergency VHF D/F

In the Channel Islands a yacht in distress should call on Ch 16; expect to be switched to Ch 67 for Guernsey or Ch 82 for Jersey. The emergency D/F sites, *from* which the true bearing of the yacht in distress is given, are: VHF D/F stations, ◉ RG.

Site	Lat/Long	Controlled via
Guernsey	49°26'.27N 02°35'.77W	*St Peter Port Radio*
Jersey	49°10'.85N 02°14'.30W	*Jersey Coastguard*

SEARCH AND RESCUE ABROAD

5.14   REPUBLIC OF IRELAND (ROI)

The Irish CG co-ordinates SAR operations around the coast of ROI via Dublin MRCC, Malin Head and Valentia MRSCs and remote sites. It may liaise with the UK and France during any rescue operation within 100M of the Irish coast. It is part of the Dept of Transport, Leeson Lane, Dublin 2. ☎ (01) 6620922; admin@irishcoastguard. The Irish EPIRB Registry is also at this address.

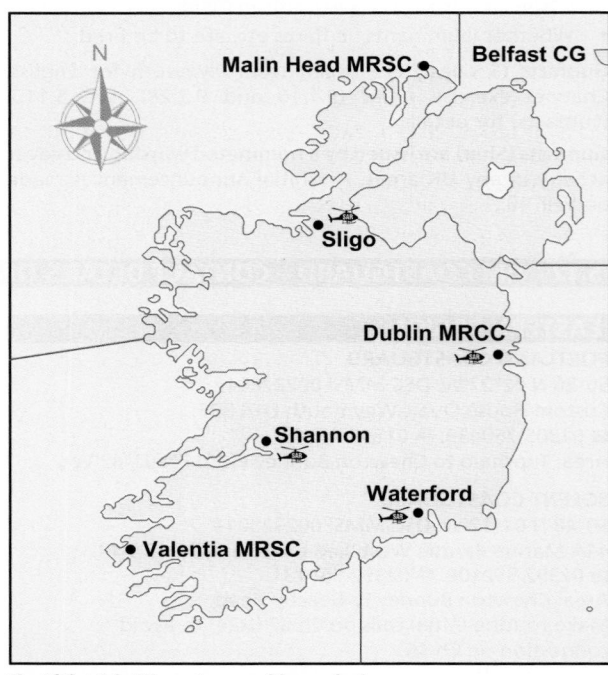

Fig 5(7) Irish CG centres and boundaries

The MRCC/MRSCs are co-located with the Coast radio stations of the same name and manned by the same staff. All stations keep watch H24 on VHF Ch 16 and DSC Ch 70. If ashore dial 999 or 112 in an emergency and ask for Marine Rescue.

Details of the MRCC/MRSCs are as follows:

DUBLIN (MRCC)
53°20'N 06°15W. DSC MMSI 002500300 (+2187·5 kHz).
☎ +353 1 662 0922/3; 🖷 +353 1 662 0795.
Area: Carlingford Lough to Youghal.

VALENTIA (MRSC)
51°56'N 10°21'W.DSC MMSI 002500200 (+2187·5 kHz).
☎ +353 669 476 109; 🖷 +353 669 476 289.
Area: Youghal to Slyne Head.

MALIN HEAD (MRSC)
55°22'N 07°20W. DSC MMSI 002500100 (+2187·5 kHz).
☎ +353 74 9370103; 🖷 +353 74 9370221.
Area: Slyne Head to Lough Foyle.

5.14.1   SAR resources

The Irish Coast Guard provides some 50 units around the coast and is on call H24. The RNLI maintains four stations around the coast and operates 42 lifeboats. Additionally, six community-run inshore rescue boats are available.

Helicopters, based at Dublin, Waterford, Shannon and Sligo, can respond within 15 to 45 minutes and operate to a radius of 200M. They are equipped with infrared search equipment and can uplift 30 survivors.

Military and civilian aircraft and vessels, together with the Garda and lighthouse service, can also be called upon.

Some stations provide specialist cliff climbing services. They are manned by volunteers, who are trained in first aid and equipped with inflatables, breeches buoys, cliff ladders etc. Their ☎ numbers (the Leader's residence) are given, where appropriate, under each port.

5.15 DENMARK

The national SAR agency is: Ministry of Defence, 42 Holmens Kanal,DK-1060 København K, Denmark.
☎ +45 339 23320; 📠 +45 333 20655.

The SAR coordinator is JRCC Denmark, ☎ +45 894 33099 switchboard; 📠 +45 894 33230; jrcc@sok.dk. JRCC Denmark has no direct communications with vessels in distress, but operates via two MRSCs and several Coast radio stations (CRS). MRSC Kattegat, ☎ +45 992 21520; 📠 +45 992 21538, covers the W coast of Denmark.

5.15.1 Lyngby Radio
This is the main Danish CRS and is DSC VHF/MF/HF equipped (☎ +45 666 34800; 📠 +45 458 82485, lyngby-radio@tdc.dk MMSI 002191000).

It operates through remote sites at Skagen, Hirtshals, Hantsholm, Bovbjerg and Blavand, all of which guard Ch 16 H24 and use callsign *Lyngby Radio*. Their VHF and MF frequencies are shown in Fig 5(8).

Fig 5(8) Danish Coastguard centres

There are at least 12 lifeboats stationed at the major harbours along this west facing coast. They are designed to double up as Pilot boats.

5.15.2 Firing practice areas
There are 4 such areas on the W coast as in Fig 5(8) and listed below. Firing times are broadcast daily by Danmarks Radio 1 at 1645 UT after the weather (5.16.2). Times are also available from the Range office by ☎ or Ch 16.

Ⓐ Tranum & Blokhus ☎ 982 35088 or call *Tranum*.

Ⓑ Nymindegab ☎ 752 89355 or call *Nymindegab*.

Ⓒ Oksbøl ☎ 765 41213 or call *Oksbøl*.

Ⓓ Rømø E ☎ 747 55219; Rømø W ☎ 745 41340 – or call *Fly Rømø*.

5.16 GERMANY
The national SAR agency is: *Deutsche Gesellschaft zur Rettung Schiffbrüchiger* (DGzRS), the German Sea Rescue Service. Werderstrasse 2, Hermann-Helms-Haus, D-28199 Bremen. mail@mrcc-bremen.de. ☎ 0421 537 070; 📠 421 537 0714.

DGzRS is responsible for coordinating SAR operations, supported by ships and SAR helicopters of the German Navy.

Bremen MRCC (☎ 0421 536870; 📠 0421 5368714; MMSI 002111240), using callsign *Bremen Rescue Radio,* maintains an H24 watch on Ch 16 and DSC Ch 70 via remote Coast radio stations at:

Blumenthal	Norderney
Borkum	Stade
Cuxhaven	Wangerooge
Helgoland	Westerhever
Kampen	

Bremen MRCC guarantees assistance, on request, to foreign MRCCs co-ordinating SAR measures for German vessels in foreign waters. An emergency ☎ 124 124 is available for mobile phone users.

There are 21 offshore lifeboats, LOA 23–44m, and 21 smaller <10m lifeboats, based at Borkum, Norderney, Langeoog, Wilhelmshaven, Bremerhaven, Cuxhaven, Helgoland, Amrum and List. There are also many inshore lifeboats.

Fig 5(9) German Coastguard radio stations

Fig 5(10) Netherlands Coastguard and Radio stations

5.17 THE NETHERLANDS

The national SAR agency is: SAR Commission Maritime, Ministry of Transport, Northsea Directorate, PO Box 5807, 2280 HV The Hague, Netherlands.

The Netherlands CG at Den Helder, co-located with the Navy HQ, coordinates SAR operations as the Dutch JRCC for A1 and A2 Sea Areas. (JRCC = Joint Rescue Coordination Centre – marine & aeronautical.) Callsign is *Netherlands Coastguard*, but *Den Helder Rescue* during SAR operations.

The JRCC keeps a listening watch H24 on DSC Ch 70, and MF DSC 2187·5 kHz (but not on 2182 kHz); MMSI 002442000.

Coastguard Operations can be contacted H24 via:

In emergency:
☎ +31 9000 111 or dial 112.

Operational telephone number:
☎ +31 223 542300. 🖷 +31 223 658358; ccc@kustwacht.nl If using a mobile phone, call 9000 111, especially if the International emergency number 112 is subject to delays.

Admin/info (HO):
☎ +31 223 658300. 🖷 +31 223 658303. info@kustwacht.nl PO Box 10000, 1780 CA Den Helder.

Remote CG stations are shown on Fig 5(10). Working channels are VHF 23 and 83.

5.17.1 Medical advice
Call initially on Ch 16, DSC Ch 70 or 2187·5 kHz (MMSI 002442000). Working chans are VHF Ch 23 & 83 or MF 2824 kHz (transmit), 2520 kHz (receive).

5.17.2 Resources
The Dutch Lifeboat Ass'n (KNRM) manages 26 lifeboat stations and 13 inshore lifeboat stations along the coast. The 60 lifeboats include 13m LOA water-jet, rigid inflatables capable of 36 kn. Helicopters, fixed wing aircraft and ships of the RNN can be called upon; also Air Force helicopters at Leeuwarden.

The area of activity extends across the Dutch Continental Shelf and into the Waddenzee, IJsselmeer and estuaries of Zuid Holland and Zeeland.

5.18 BELGIUM
The Belgian Coastguard coordinates SAR operations from Oostende MRCC, callsign *Coastguard Oostende*. The MRCC and *Oostende Radio* (Coast Radio Station) both keep listening watch H24 on Ch 16, 2182 kHz and DSC Ch 70 and 2187·5 kHz.

Coastguard stations

MRCC OOSTENDE
☎ +32 59 701000; 🖷 +32 59 703605. MMSI 002050480. mrcc@mrcc.be.

MRSC Nieuwpoort
☎ +32 58 233000; 🖷 +32 58 231575.

MRSC Zeebrugge
☎ +32 50 550801; 🖷 +32 50 547400. radartorenzeebrugge@vlaanderen.be.

RCC Brussels (Point of contact for COSPAS/SARSAT)
☎ +32 2 7200338; 🖷 +32 2 7524201. rcc@mil.be.

Coast Radio Stations

OOSTENDE Radio
☎ 50 558241; 🖷 50 558748. MMSI 002050480.
Ch 16, DSC Ch 70 and MF DSC 2187·5 kHz. rmd@mil.be

Antwerpen Radio (remotely controlled by Oostende CRS)
MMSI 002050485. Ch 16, DSC Ch 70.

5.18.1 Resources
Offshore and inshore lifeboats are based at Nieuwpoort, Oostende and Zeebrugge.

The Belgian Air Force provides helicopters from Koksijde near the French border. The Belgian Navy also participates in SAR operations as required.

5.19   FRANCE – CROSS

CROSS (Centres Régionaux Opérationnels de Surveillance et de Sauvetage) provide an all-weather presence H24 along the French coast in liaison with foreign CGs. CROSS is an MRCC. The main functions include:

- Co-ordinating SAR operations.
- Navigational surveillance.
- Broadcasting navigational warnings (5.10).
- Broadcasting weather information (6.19.1).
- Anti-pollution control.
- Marine and fishery surveillance.

All centres monitor VHF Ch 16 and DSC Ch 70 and co-ordinate SAR on Ch 15, 67, 68, 73; DSC Ch 70. They can be contacted by phone; (all centres also have Emergency ☎ 1616 for mobiles); via the National Gendarmerie, Affaires Maritimes or a Semaphore station.

CROSS also monitors the TSS in the Dover Strait, off Casquets and off Ouessant using, for example, callsign *Corsen Traffic*.

For medical advice call the appropriate CROSS which will contact a doctor or Service d'Aide Médicale Urgente (SAMU). ⚠ Note: SAMU (Ambulance) will respond more quickly to a medical emergency in a harbour or marina than calling a doctor. Simply dial 15.

5.19.1   CROSS locations/contact details

Any CROSS can be telephoned simply by dialling **1616**.

CROSS Gris-Nez   50°52'N 01°35'E
MMSI 002275100 ☎ 03·21·87·21·87; 📠 03·21·87·78·55
gris-nez@mrccfr.eu (Belgian border–Cap d'Antifer).

CROSS Jobourg   49°41'N 01°54'W
MMSI 002275200 ☎ 02·33·52·72·13; 📠 02·33·52·71·72
jobourg@mrccfr.eu (Cap d'Antifer–Mont St Michel).

CROSS Corsen   48°24'N 04°47'W
MMSI 002275300 ☎ 02·98·89·31·31; 📠 02·98·89·65·75
corsen@mrccfr.eu (Mont St Michel–Pointe de Penmarc'h).

CROSS Étel   47°39'N 03°12'W
MMSI 002275000 ☎ 02·97·55·35·35; 📠 02·97·55·49·34
etel@mrccfr.eu.

Area: Pointe de Penmarc'h to the Spanish border. CROSS Étel specialises in medical advice and also responds to COSPAS/SARSAT alerts

5.19.2   Lifeboats

Société National de Sauvetage en Mer (SNSM; the lifeboat service) comes under CROSS, which should be contacted even when ashore. SNSM tel nos are given in Chapter 9 for most ports. A hefty charge may be levied if a lifeboat is called out by a vessel which turns out to be not in distress.

Fig 5(11) CROSS centres

5.19.3 Semaphore (signal) stations

These keep visual, radar and radio watch (VHF Ch 16) around the coast and are manned by the French Navy. They relay emergency calls to CROSS and are equipped with VHF DF. They show gale warning signals, repeat forecasts and offer local weather reports. They are listed below.

Semaphore (Signal) stations

* H24. Remainder only operate sunrise to sunset.

*	Dunkerque	03·28·66·86·18
	Boulogne	03·21·31·32·10
	Ault	03·22·60·47·33
	Dieppe	02·35·84·23·82
*	Fécamp	02·35·28·00·91
*	La Hève	02·35·46·07·81
*	Le Havre	02·35·21·74·39
	Villerville	02·31·88·11·13
*	Port-en-Bessin	02·31·21·81·51
	St-Vaast	02·33·54·44·50
*	Barfleur	02·33·54·04·37
	Lévy	02·33·54·31·17
*	Le Homet	02·33·92·60·08
	La Hague	02·33·52·71·07
	Carteret	02·33·53·85·08
	Barneville Le Roc	02·33·50·05·85
	St-Cast	02·96·41·85·30
*	St Quay-Portrieux	02·96·70.42.18
	Bréhat	02·96·20·00·12
*	Ploumanac'h	02·96·91·46·51
	Batz	02·98·61·76·06
*	Brignogan	02·98·83·50·84
*	Ouessant Stiff	02·98·48·81·50
*	St-Mathieu	02·98·89·01·59
*	Portzic (Ch 08)	02·98·22·21·47
	Toulinguet	02·98·27·90·02
	Cap-de-la-Chèvre	02·98·27·09·55
*	Pointe-du-Raz	02·98·70·66·57
*	Penmarc'h	02·98·58·61·00
	Beg Meil	02·98·94·98·92
*	Port-Louis	02·97·82·52·10
	Étel Mât Fenoux	02·97·55·35·35
	Beg Melen (Groix)	02·97·86·80·13
	Talut (Belle-Île)	02·97·31·85·07
	St-Julien	02·97·50·09·35
	Piriac-sur-Mer	02·40·23·59·87
*	Chemoulin	02·40·91·99·00
	St-Sauveur (Yeu)	02·51·58·31·01
	Les Baleines (Ré)	05·46·29·42·06
	Chassiron (Oléron)	05·46·47·85·43
*	Pointe-de-Grave	05·56·09·60·03
	Cap Ferret	05·56·60·60·03
	Messanges	05·58·48·94·10
*	Socoa	05·59·47·18·54

5.19.4 Emergency VHF DF stations – France

A vessel in emergency can obtain its true bearing *from* a DF station. DF stations are remotely controlled by a semaphore (signal) station, a †Naval lookout station or a *CROSS all of which keep primary watch on Ch 16.

To obtain a true bearing from asterisked DF stations, call CROSS on Ch 16, 11 or 67.

Also available are seven continuously scanned frequencies from among Ch 1–29, 36, 39, 48, 50, 52, 55, 56 and 60–88.

HJ = Day service only.

VHF DF stations, marked ⊙ on Area maps, are listed below geographically from NE to W then S:

Dunkerque	51°03'.40N 02°20'.40E	H24
*Gris-Nez	50°52'.20N 01°35'.01E	H24
Boulogne	50°44'.00N 01°36'.00E	HJ
Ault	50°06'.50N 01°27'.50E	HJ
Dieppe	49°56'.00N 01°05'.20E	HJ
Fécamp	49°46'.10N 00°22'.20E	H24
La Hève	49°30'.60N 00°04'.20E	H24
Villerville	49°23'.20N 00°06'.50E	HJ
Port-en-Bessin	49°21'.10N 00°46'.30W	H24
Saint-Vaast	49°34'.50N 01°16'.50W	HJ
Barfleur	49°41'.90N 01°15'.90W	H24
Levy	49°41'.70N 01°28'.20W	HJ
†Homet	49°39'.50N 01°37'.90W	H24
*Jobourg	49°41'.50N 01°54'.50W	H24
La Hague	49°43'.60N 01°56'.30W	HJ
Carteret	49°22'.40N 01°48'.30W	HJ
Le Roc	48°50'.10N 01°36'.90W	HJ
Grouin (Cancale)	48°42'.60N 01°50'.60W	HJ
Saint-Cast	48°38'.60N 02°14'.70W	HJ
St-Quay-Portrieux	48°39'.30N 02°49'.50W	H24
Bréhat	48°51'.30N 03°00'.10W	HJ
Ploumanac'h	48°49'.50N 03°28'.20W	H24
Batz	48°44'.80N 04°00'.60W	HJ
Brignogan	48°40'.60N 04°19'.70W	H24
Creac'h (Ouessant)	48°27'.60N 05°07'.70W	HJ
*Creac'h (Ouessant)	48°27'.60N 05°07'.80W	H24
†Saint-Mathieu	48°19'.80N 04°46'.20W	H24
Toulinguet	48°16'.80N 04°37'.50W	HJ
Cap de la Chèvre	48°10'.20N 04°33'.00W	HJ
Pointe du Raz	48°02'.30N 04°43'.80W	H24
Penmarc'h	47°47'.90N 04°22'.40W	H24
Beg-Meil	47°51'.30N 03°58'.40W	HJ
Beg Melen	47°39'.20N 03°30'.10W	HJ
†Port-Louis	47°42'.60N 03°21'.80W	H24
*Etel	47°39'.80N 03°12'.00W	H24
Saint-Julien	47°29'.70N 03°07'.50W	HJ
Taillefer	47°21'.80N 03°09'.00W	HJ
Le Talut	47°17'.70N 03°13'.00W	HJ
Piriac	47°22'.50N 02°33'.40W	HJ
Chemoulin	47°14'.10N 02°17'.80W	H24
Saint-Sauveur	46°41'.70N 02°18'.80W	HJ
Les Baleines	46°14'.60N 01°33'.70W	HJ
Chassiron	46°02'.80N 01°24'.50W	HJ
La Coubre	45°41'.90N 01°13'.40W	H24
Pointe de Grave	45°34'.30N 01°03'.90W	HJ
Cap Ferret	44°37'.50N 01°15'.00W	HJ
Messanges	43°48'.80N 01°23'.90W	HJ
Socoa	43°23'.30N 01°41'.10W	H24

5.20 SPAIN

The Society for Maritime Rescue and Safety (Sociedad de Salvamento y Seguridad Maritima – SASEMAR) is the national agency for SAR operations (and the prevention of pollution); akin to MCA in the UK.

MRCC Madrid coordinates SAR operations via 3 MRCCs (Bilbao, Gijon and Finisterre) on the N coast and Tarifa MRCC on the SW coast – as listed below.

All Centres monitor (H24) VHF Ch 16, MF 2182 kHz and DSC Ch 70, 2187·5 kHz. They also broadcast weather as shown in Chapter 5 and Nav warnings, Chapter 3; but do *not* handle commercial link calls.

5.20.1 North and north west Spain
In N and NW Spain CG Centres do not keep continuous watch on Ch 16, so call on a working channel; see 5.9.6.

MADRID MRCC   MMSI 002241008
☎ 91 7559 132/3; 🖷 9I 5261440.

Bilbao MRCC
43°21'N 03°02'W   MMSI 002240996
☎ 944 839411; 🖷 944 83 9161.

Santander MRSC
43°28'N 03°43'W   MMSI 002241009
☎ 942 213 030; 🖷 942 213 638.

Gijón MRCC
43°34'N 05°42'W   MMSI 002240997
☎ 985 326050; 🖷 985 320908.

Finisterre MRCC
42°42'N 08°59'W   MMSI 002240993
☎ 981 767320; 🖷 981 767740.

Coruña MRSC
43°22'N 08°23'W   MMSI 002241022
☎ 981 209541; 🖷 981 209518.

Vigo MRSC
42°10'N 08°41'W   MMSI 002240998
☎ 986 222230; 🖷 986 228957.

5.20.2 South west Spain
Tarifa MRCC coordinates SAR in SW Spain and the Gibraltar Strait.

Tarifa MRCC
36°01'N 05°35'W   MMSI 002240994
☎ 956 684740; 🖷 956 680 606.

Huelva MRSC
37°13'N 07°07'W   MMSI 002241012
☎ 959 243000; 🖷 959 242103.

Cadiz MRSC
36°32'N 06°18'W   MMSI 002241011
☎ 956 214253; 🖷 956 226091.

Algeciras MRSC (controlled by Malaga MRCC)
36°08'N 05°26'W   MMSI 002241001
☎ 956 580930; 🖷 956 585402.

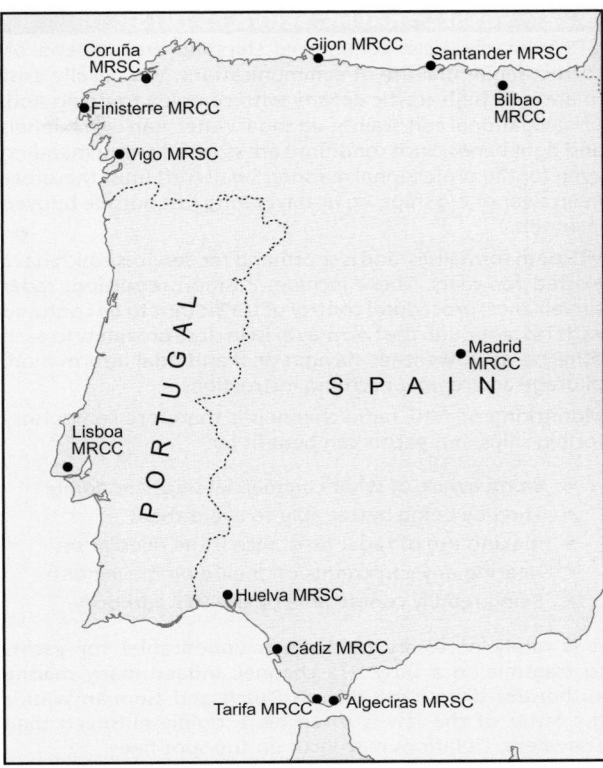

Fig 5(12) Spanish and Portuguese CG radio stations

5.21 PORTUGAL AND THE AZORES

The Portuguese Navy coordinates SAR in two regions, Lisboa and Santa Maria (Azores), via MRCCs at Lisboa and Ponta Delgada (Azores). A network of CRS maintains an H24 listening watch on all distress frequencies; see 5.9.7.

The Naval HQ (Estado Maior da Armada, 3 Divisao) is at: Rua do Arsenal, 1149-001 Lisboa, Portugal.

☎ 21 325 5498 (HO); 21 3217666 (H24). 🖷 21 347 9591.

5.21.1 Mainland

Lisboa MRCC
38°41'N 09°19'W   MMSI 002630100
☎ 21 4401919; 🖷 21 4401954. mrcc.lisboa@marinha.pt
Planned DSC Ch 70; 2187·5 kHz

5.21.2 Azores

Delgada MRCC
37°45'N 25°38'W   MMSI 002040100   VHF Ch 11
☎ +351 296 281777 (Emergency); 205227 (Ops);
mobile 917 777461; 🖷 296 205239
mrcc.delgada@mail.telepac.pt
Planned DSC Ch 70; 2187·5 kHz

Horta MRSC
38°32'N 28°38'W   MMSI 002040200   VHF Ch 11
DSC Ch 70; 2182 kHz

5.22 VESSEL TRAFFIC SERVICES (VTS)

VTS primarily assist commercial shipping and depend on correct sequential use of communications. VTS usually exist in areas of high traffic density with complex routeing and/or navigational constraints, eg shoal water, narrow channels and tight bends. Such conditions are stressful and demanding even for the professional mariner. Small craft must therefore keep clear of big ships, eg by navigating just outside buoyed channels.

VTS both formalises, and is shorthand for, services which have existed for years. These include: Position reporting; radar surveillance; procedural control of traffic (not to be confused with TSS, although the two may exist in close proximity to each other); traffic, weather, navigational and tidal information; pilotage advice; and berthing instructions.

Monitoring of VHF radio channels is therefore compulsory for big ships, but yachts can benefit by:

- Being aware of what commercial ships are doing
- Thereby being better able to avoid them
- Making use of radar assistance if the need arises
- Hearing any constraints on their own movements
- Being readily contactable by the VTS authority.

It is rarely necessary (and often undesirable) for yachts to transmit on a busy VTS channel; indeed many marine authorities discourage this. In Dutch and German waters the letter of the law is often more rigidly enforced than elsewhere; violations may incur on-the-spot fines.

VTS diagrams appear in the relevant geographic area of Chapter 9, with detailed notes in the harbour text.

5.23 INTERNATIONAL PORT TRAFFIC SIGNALS (IPTS)

The International system (IPTS) is now widely used on the Continent, but its universal adoption may take some years. Obsolescent national signals may occasionally be seen in a few minor ports. In some major ports, eg Calais, these important signals are the primary means of controlling traffic, thereby much reducing or even eliminating VHF radio 'chatter'.

- The main movement message always comprises three lights, vertically disposed. No additional light shall be added to the column carrying the main message.

  Thus the main message is always recognisable as IPTS, and not as lights of navigational significance. IPTS may also be used to control traffic at locks and bridges.

- Red lights indicate *Do not proceed*.

- Green lights indicate *Proceed, subject to the conditions stipulated*. Red and green lights are never displayed together, to avoid confusion.

- Signals may be omni-directional ie seen by all vessels simultaneously; or directional, ie seen only by vessels entering or by vessels leaving harbour.

- Signal 1 *Serious Emergency* must show at least 60 flashes/minute. All other signals may be fixed or slow occulting (useful when background glare is a problem). A mixture of fixed and occulting lights must not be used.

- Signal No 5 assumes that VHF, signal lamp, loud-hailer, auxiliary signal or other means of communication will specifically inform a vessel that she may proceed.

- Exemption signals. A single yellow light, displayed to the left of the column carrying main messages Nos 2 or

No	Lights		Main message
1		Flashing	Serious emergency – all vessels to stop or divert according to instructions
2		Fixed or Slow Occulting	Vessels shall not proceed (*Note:* Some ports may use an exemption signal, as in 2a below)
3			Vessels may proceed. One-way traffic
4			Vessels may proceed. Two-way traffic
5			A vessel may proceed only when she has received specific orders to do so. (*Note:* Some ports may use an exemption signal, as in 5a below)
	Exemption signals and messages		
2a		Fixed or Slow Occulting	Vessels shall not proceed, except that vessels which navigate outside the main channel need not comply with the main message
5a			A vessel may proceed when she has received specific orders to do so, except that vessels which navigate outside the main channel need not comply with the main message
	Auxiliary signals and messages		
	White and/or yellow lights, displayed with the main lights		Local meanings, as promulgated in local port orders

5 and level with the upper light, means *Vessels which can safely navigate outside the main channel need not comply with the main message*. This signal, shown as Nos 2a and 5a, is obviously important to small craft.

- Signals which are auxiliary to the main message may be devised by local authorities. Such auxiliary signals should show only white and/or yellow lights, and be displayed to the right of the column carrying the main message. Ports with complex entrances and much traffic may need many auxiliary signals, which will have to be documented. Smaller harbours with less traffic may only need the basic signals, such as Nos 2 and 3.

5.24 FLAG ETIQUETTE

Flags are still used to express identity – by national ensigns, club burgees, etc. Brief guidance on their use is given below and in *Reeds Maritime Flag Handbook* (ACN).

5.24.1 Ensign

A yacht's ensign is the national maritime flag corresponding to the nationality of her owner; Fig 5(13). Thus a British yacht should wear the Red Ensign unless she qualifies for a Special ensign (5.23.2). The national ensign should be kept clean and in good repair. It should normally be worn at the stern, but if this is not possible the nearest position should be used, eg at the peak in a gaff-rigged boat, at the mizzen masthead in a ketch or yawl, or about two-thirds up the leech of the mainsail. In harbour or at anchor the proper position is at the stern.

In British harbours by custom the ensign is hoisted at 0800 (0900 between 1 Nov and 14 Feb) or as soon after that time as people come on board; and lowered at sunset (or 2100 LT if earlier) or earlier if the crew is leaving the boat.

Abroad the ensign (and burgee) are increasingly left flying at all times, to identify nationality – even at night in harbour, unless the boat is unattended.

At sea the ensign must be worn when meeting other vessels, when entering or leaving foreign ports, or when approaching forts, Signal and CG stations – ie virtually at all times.

When racing the ensign should not be worn after the five minute gun. It should be hoisted on finishing or retiring.

5.24.2 Special ensigns

Members of certain clubs may apply for a permit to wear a special ensign (eg Blue Ensign, defaced Blue Ensign, or defaced Red Ensign). The yacht must either be registered under Part I of the Merchant Shipping Act 1995 and of at least 2 tons gross tonnage, or be registered on the Small Ships Register and of at least 7m LOA. The owner(s) must be British subjects, and the yacht must not be used for any professional, business or commercial purpose. Full details can be obtained from Secretaries of the clubs concerned. The permit must be carried on board.

A special ensign must only be worn when the owner is on board or ashore in the vicinity, and only when the yacht is flying the burgee (or a Flag Officer's flag) of the club concerned. When the yacht is sold, or the owner ceases to be a member of the club, the permit must be returned to the Secretary of the club.

5.24.3 Courtesy ensign

It is customary when abroad to fly a small maritime ensign of the country concerned at the starboard spreader. *A courtesy ensign must not be worn below any other flag on the same halyard.* Thus a club burgee, if usually flown at the starboard spreader, must be shifted to the port spreader when abroad, permitting the courtesy ensign to be close up at the starboard spreader. The correct courtesy flag for a foreign yacht in British waters is the Red Ensign. British yachts do not need to fly a courtesy flag in the Channel Islands.

5.24.4 Burgee

A burgee shows that a yacht is in the charge of a member of the club indicated, and does not necessarily indicate ownership. It should be flown at the masthead.

If this is impossible due to wind sensors, radio aerials etc, the burgee may be flown at the starboard spreader, but this should be avoided unless strictly necessary. A long bamboo cane can readily be hoisted to the masthead as a staff, keeping the burgee clear above sensors and aerials.

A yacht should not fly more than one burgee. A burgee is not flown when a yacht is racing. If the yacht is on loan, or is chartered, it is correct to use the burgee of the skipper or charterer – not that of the absent owner. Normal practice has been to lower the burgee at night, at the same time as the ensign, but nowadays many owners leave the burgee flying if they are on board or ashore in the vicinity.

5.24.5 Choice of burgee

An owner who is not a Flag Officer, and who belongs to more than one club, should normally fly the burgee (and if authorised the special ensign) of the senior club in the harbour where the yacht is lying. An exception may be if another club is staging a regatta or similar function.

5.24.6 Flag Officer's flag

Clubs authorise their Flag Officers to fly special swallow-tailed flags, with the same design as the club burgee and in place of it. The flags of a vice-commodore and a rear-commodore carry one and two balls respectively. A Flag Officer's flag is flown day and night while he is on board, or ashore nearby. A Flag Officer should fly his flag with the Red Ensign (or special ensign, where authorised) in preference to the burgee of some other club.

It is customary for a Flag Officer to be saluted (not more than once a day) by a yacht flying the burgee of that club.

5.24.7 House flag

An owner may fly his personal flag when he is on board in harbour. It must not conflict with the design of an existing flag. A house flag is normally rectangular, and is flown at the crosstrees in a sloop or cutter, at the mizzen masthead in a ketch or yawl, or at the foremast head in a schooner.

5.24.8 St George's Flag

This is predominantly a land flag, commonly misused afloat. It may only be flown at sea by admirals on duty and members of the Association of Dunkirk Little Ships (in conjunction with their burgee).

5.24.9 Q Flag

Vessels requiring customs' clearance should fly the yellow Q flag. This declares that 'my vessel is healthy and I request free pratique' ie to clear in and come ashore. This is not required for vessels from, and sailing within, the EU.

5.24.10 Salutes

Yachts should salute all Royal Yachts, and all warships of whatever nationality. A salute is made by dipping the ensign (only). The vessel saluted responds by dipping her ensign, and then re-hoisting it, whereupon the vessel saluting re-hoists hers.

5.24.11 Dressing ship

Dressing overall (as opposed to dressing with masthead flags) is normally only done in harbour to mark national festivals. The international code flags and pennants (Fig 5(1)) are flown in the following order from stem to masthead(s) to stern:

E, Q, p 3, G, p 8, Z, p 4, W, p 6, P, p 1, I, Code, T, Y, B, X, 1st Sub, H, 3rd Sub, D, F, 2nd Sub, U, A, O, M, R, p 2, J, p 0, N, p 9, K, p 7, V, p 5, L, C, S. (Total = 40).

Fig 5(13) Ensigns and flags

UK WHITE ENSIGN

UK BLUE ENSIGN

UK RED ENSIGN

AUSTRALIA

BASQUE FLAG

BELGIUM

BERMUDA

CANADA

CYPRUS

DENMARK

EU

FINLAND

FRANCE

GERMANY

GREECE

GUERNSEY

IRELAND

ISRAEL

ITALY

LIBERIA

MALTA

MONACO

MOROCCO

NETHERLANDS

NEW ZEALAND

NORWAY

PANAMA

POLAND

PORTUGAL

SOUTH AFRICA

SPAIN

SWEDEN

SWITZERLAND

TUNISIA

TURKEY

USA

Coastal/Inshore	2-day by Fax	5-day by Phone
North West	09065 222 351	09068 969 651
Clyde	09065 222 352	09068 969 652
Caledonia	09065 222 353	09068 969 653
Minch	09065 222 354	09068 969 654
Northern Ireland	09065 222 355	09068 969 655

Offshore	2-5 day by Fax	2-5 day by Phone
English Channel	09065 222 357	09068 969 657
S North Sea	09065 222 358	09068 969 658
Irish Sea	09065 222 359	09068 969 659
Biscay	09065 222 360	09068 969 660
NW Scotland	09065 222 361	09068 969 661
N North Sea	09065 222 362	09068 969 662

09066 CALLS COST 60P PER MIN. 09061 CALLS COST £1.50 PER MIN.

6

Weather

Weather

Beaufort scale – Sea states

6.1   SCALES AND TERMS

6.1.1   Beaufort wind scale and descriptions of the sea

Force	Wind speed			Description	Deep sea criteria	Probable mean (max) wave ht (m)
	(knots)	(km/h)	(m/sec)			
0	<1	0–2	0–0·5	Calm	Calm, glassy, like a mirror	–
1	1–3	2–6	0·3–1·5	Light air	Calm. Ripples like scales are formed	0·1 (0·1)
2	4–6	7–11	1·6–3·3	Light breeze	Small wavelets, still short but more pronounced, not breaking	0·1 (0·3)
3	7–10	13–19	3·4–5·4	Gentle breeze	Large wavelets, crests begin to break; glassy foam, perhaps a few white horses	0·6 (1)
4	11–16	20–30	5·5–7·9	Moderate breeze	Small waves becoming longer; fairly frequent white horses	1 (1·5)
5	17–21	31–39	8·0–10·7	Fresh breeze	Moderate waves, taking a more pronounced form; many white horses, perhaps some spray	2 (2·5)
6	22–27	41–50	10·8–13·8	Strong breeze	Large waves forming; white foam crests are extensive everywhere; probably some spray	3 (4)
7	28–33	52–61	13·9–17·1	Near gale	Sea heaps up; white foam from breaking waves begins to be blown in streaks	4 (5·5)
8	34–40	63–74	17·2–20·7	Gale	Moderately high waves of greater length; edge of crests break into spindrift; foam blown in well-marked streaks	5·5 (7·5)
9	41–47	76–87	20·8–24·4	Strong gale	High waves with tumbling crests; dense streaks of foam; spray may affect visibility	7 (10)
10	48–55	89–102	24·5–28·4	Storm	Very high waves with long overhanging crests; dense streaks of foam make the surface of sea white. Heavy, shock-like tumbling sea; visibility affected	9 (12·5)
11	56–63	104–117	28·5–32·6	Violent storm	Exceptionally high waves; sea completely covered with long white patches of foam; edges of wave crests blown into froth. Visibility affected	11·5 (16)
12	64 plus	118 plus	32·7 plus	Hurricane	Air filled with foam and spray; sea completely white with driving spray; visibility seriously affected	14 (—)

Notes

- The actual force exerted on a sail is proportional to the square of the windspeed and directly to the density. Thus a wind of Force 6 (say 25 knots) has more than three times the 'weight' of a wind of Force 4 (say 14 knots) – which is why even a small increase in windspeed, or gusts, have a significant effect on a sailing yacht. Temerature has a smaller effect; at 5°C the force of the wind is about 6% higher than at 20°C.

- The probable mean (maximum in brackets) wave heights shown in the table above are a guide to what may be expected in the open sea, away from land. In enclosed waters, or when near to land, with an offshore wind, wave heights will be smaller and the waves steeper – particularly with wind against tide.

Swell
The length and height in metres of swell waves are described and quantified as follows:

Length of Swell	
Short	0–100 m
Average	100–200
Long	over 200

Height of Swell	
Low	0–2 m
Moderate	2–4
Heavy	over 4

Fig 6(1) Typical sea states associated with various Beaufort wind forces

Wave height for a given wind strength depends upon the distance travelled (fetch), the length of time for which the wind has been blowing and any currents; see table opposite.

Sea states used in some forecasts are described relative to average wave heights, as follows:

Calm	0·1–0·5m
Slight	0·5–1·25m
Moderate	1·25–2·5m
Rough	2·5–4m
Very rough	4–6m

Photography
© *Crown* – Force 0, 11
© *GJ Simpson* – Force 1, 2, 7
© *IG MacNeil* – Force 3, 4, 5, 6
© *WAE Smith* – Force 8
© *JP Laycock* – Force 9
© *G Allen* – Force 10

Force 3   7–10kn   Gentle Breeze
Wave Ht 0.6m

Force 8   34–40kn   Gale
Wave Ht 5.5m

Force 4   11–16kn   Moderate Breeze
Wave Ht 1m

Force 9   41–47kn   Severe Gale
Wave Ht 7m

Force 0   0–1kn   Calm   Wave Ht 0m

Force 5   17–21kn   Fresh Breeze
Wave Ht 2m

Force 10   48–55kn   Storm
Wave Ht 9m

Force 1   1–3kn   Light Air
Wave Ht 0.1m

Force 6   22–27kn   Strong Breeze
Wave Ht 3m

Force 11   56–63kn   Violent Storm
Wave Ht 11.5m

Force 2   4–6kn   Light Breeze
Wave Ht 0.2m

Force 7   28–33kn   Near Gale
Wave Ht 4m

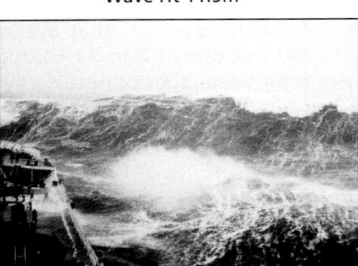

Force 12   64+kn   Hurricane
Wave Ht 14m

Barometric and temperature conversion scales

6.1.3 Terms used in weather bulletins
Speed of movement of pressure systems

Slowly	< 15 knots
Steadily	15–25 knots
Rather quickly	25–35 knots
Rapidly	35–45 knots
Very rapidly	> 45 knots

Visibility

Good	> 5 nautical miles
Moderate	2–5 nautical miles
Poor	1000 metres–2 nautical miles
Fog	Less than 1000 metres

Barometric pressure changes (tendency)

Rising or falling slowly: Pressure change of 0·1 to 1·5 hPa/mb in the preceding 3 hours.

Rising or falling: Pressure change of 1·6 to 3·5 hPa/mb in the preceding 3 hours.

Rising or falling quickly: Pressure change of 3·6 to 6 hPa/mb in the preceding 3 hours.

Rising or falling very rapidly: Pressure change of more than 6 hPa/mb in the preceding 3 hours.

Now rising (or falling): Pressure has been falling (rising) or steady in the preceding 3 hours, but at the time of observation was definitely rising (falling).

Gale warnings

A *Gale* warning means that average winds of at least F8 (34–40kn) or gusts up to 43–51kn are possible somewhere within the area, but not necessarily over the whole area.

Severe Gale means winds of at least F9 (41–47kn) or gusts reaching 52–60kn.

Storm means winds of F10 (48–55kn) or gusts of 61–68kn.

Violent Storm means winds of F11 (56–63kn) or gusts of 69kn or more.

Hurricane Force means winds of F12 (64kn or more).

Gale warnings remain in force until amended or cancelled ('gales now ceased'). If a gale persists for more than 24 hours the warning is re-issued.

Timing of gale warnings

Imminent:	Within 6 hrs from time of issue
Soon:	6–12 hrs from time of issue
Later:	More than 12 hrs from time of issue

Strong wind warnings
Issued, if possible 6 hrs in advance, when winds F6 or more are expected up to 5M offshore; valid for 12 hrs.

Wind

Wind direction: The direction from which the wind is blowing.

Winds becoming cyclonic: Indicates that there will be considerable changes in wind direction across the path of a depression within the forecast area.

Veering: A clockwise change in the wind direction, eg SW to W.

Backing: An anti-clockwise change in the wind direction, eg W to SW.

6.1.4 International storm warning signals
These signals are used in France, Spain, Portugal and The Netherlands (at certain hbrs; lights only, both by D & N). Elsewhere national signals may be shown; or none at all.

Day	Night	Meaning
		Strong wind (force 6–7)
		NW gale
		NE gale
		SW gale
		SE gale
		Hurricane force12, any direction
	Rectangular flags of any colour	Wind veering / Wind backing

6.1.5 Geostrophic scales
When interpreting a synoptic chart it often helps to be able to estimate the Beaufort wind Force; similarly the speed in knots at which warm, cold and occluded fronts are moving – hence when a warm front or a post-cold front clearance may arrive.

Three geostrophic scales are needed: one for wind Force, another for the movement of warm fronts and a third for cold and occluded fronts (which are assumed to move at the same speed). The scales that follow are calibrated for isobars at 2 hPa/mb intervals and are reasonably accurate between Latitudes 40° and 60°N.

Set your dividers between adjacent isobars, then read off from the left (high) end of the scale the wind Force or frontal speed. Or make a perspex scale and place it at 90° across the isobars.

Wind in Beaufort force

Warm front movement in knots

Cold front or Occlusion movement in knots

SOURCES OF WEATHER INFORMATION

Around the UK and along the coasts of NW and W Europe there is no shortage of weather information, both forecast and actual. From this it should be possible to compare your own analysis and outlook with those issued by professional forecasters.

The sources of this information are national Met Offices whose forecasts are disseminated by the following means: Broadcasts by national and local radio stations; Coastguard centres and Coast radio stations; Navtex; telephone recordings, fax messages, mobile text messages (SMS, MMS and WAP) and the Internet.

The contact details for the UK Meteorological Office are given in Chapter 1, 1.2.

At the BBC call ☎ 0370 010 0222 for useful information.

6.2   RADIO BROADCASTS IN THE UK

6.2.1   BBC Radio 4 shipping and other forecasts

Although not part of the GMDSS, for many the shipping forecast and its associated reports, as broadcast by BBC Radio 4, remain the principal source of weather data. Navtex broadcasts a more complete service, see 6.3 below. The main benefit of the shipping forecast is that it is updated 6 hourly. HM Coastguard broadcasts repeat as detailed in 6.4.1.

LT	Bands	Contents summary
0048	LW, MW, FM	Shipping, inshore waters forecast (between 2 sets of) coastal station reports
0520	LW, MW, FM	Shipping, coastal station reports, inshore waters forecast for all 17 areas
1201	LW only	Shipping
1754	LW, FM (Sat/Sun)	Shipping

Sea area **Trafalgar** is only included in the 0048 forecast.

Frequencies

LW   198 kHz

MW   Tyneside 603 kHz. London & N Ireland 720 kHz Redruth 756 kHz. Plymouth & Enniskillen 774 kHz Aberdeen 1449 kHz. Carlisle 1485 kHz

FM	England	92·4–94·6 MHz	
	Scotland	91·3–96·1 MHz	103·5–104·9 MHz
	Wales	92·8–96·1 MHz	103·5–104·9 MHz
	N Ireland	93·2–96·0 MHz	103·5–104·6 MHz
	Channel Islands		94·8 MHz

Contents of the Shipping forecast

Time of issue; summary of gale warnings in force at that time; a general synopsis of weather systems and their expected development and movement over the next 24 hours; sea area forecasts for the same 24 hours, including wind direction/force, weather and visibility in each; and an outlook for the following 24 hours.

Gale warnings for all affected areas are broadcast at the earliest break in Radio 4 programmes after receipt, as well as after the next news bulletin.

Weather reports from coastal stations follow the 0048 and 0520 shipping forecasts; see 6.2.4 and Fig 6(3). They include wind direction and force, present weather, visibility, and sea-level pressure and tendency, if available.

Shipping forecasts cover large sea areas, and rarely include the detailed variations that may occur near land. The Inshore waters forecast (below) can provide more specific information to mariners on coastal passages.

6.2.2   BBC Radio 4 Inshore waters forecast

A forecast for inshore waters (up to 12M offshore) in 17 areas around the UK and N Ireland, valid for 24 hrs, is broadcast after the 0048 and 0520 coastal station reports. It includes forecasts of wind direction and force, weather, visibility, sea state and an outlook for a further 24 hrs. It ends with a national inshore outlook for the next 3 days.

The 17 inshore areas (Fig 6(5)) are defined by the following places and headlands, clockwise around the UK:

Cape Wrath, Orkney, Rattray Hd, Berwick-upon-Tweed, Whitby, Gibraltar Point, N Foreland, Selsey Bill, Lyme Regis, Land's End, St David's Head, Great Ormes Head, Isle of Man, Mull of Galloway, Carlingford Lough, Lough Foyle, Mull of Kintyre, Ardnamurchan Pt and Shetland.

Strong Wind Warnings are issued by the Met Office when winds of Force 6 or more are expected up to 5M offshore.

Reports of actual weather. In the 0048 broadcast, a second set of coastal station reports are broadcast after the 0048 inshore waters forecast. As shown in Fig 6(3) these include:

Boulmer, *Bridlington*, Sheerness, St Catherine's Point*, *Scilly**, Milford Haven, Aberporth, Valley, Liverpool (Crosby), *Ronaldsway*, Larne, Machrihanish*, Greenock, *Stornoway*, *Lerwick*, Wick*, Aberdeen and Leuchars.

Asterisk* denotes an automatic station. Stations in italics also feature in the earlier 0048 and 0520 coastal reports.

6.2.3   BBC general (land) forecasts

Land area forecasts are broadcast by BBC Radio 4 on the frequencies in 6.2.1. They may include an outlook up to 48 hours beyond the shipping forecast, plus more details of frontal systems and coastal weather.

Land area forecasts – Wind strength

Wind descriptions used in land forecasts, with their Beaufort scale equivalents, are:

Calm:	0	Fresh:	5
Light:	1–3	Strong:	6–7
Moderate:	4	Gale:	8

Land area forecasts – Visibility

The following definitions apply to land forecasts:

Mist:	Visibility between 2000m and 1000m
Fog:	Visibility less than 1000m
Dense fog:	Less than 50m

6.2.4 UK Shipping forecast areas

Coastal Stations reporting actual weather

T	Tiree auto
St	Stornoway
L	Lerwick
F	Fife Ness
Br	Bridlington
S	Sandettié Auto
G	Greenwich Auto
J	Jersey
C	Channel Auto
Sc	Scilly Auto
V	Valentia
R	Ronaldsway
M	Malin Head

6.2.5   Shipping Forecast Record

SHIPPING FORECAST RECORD TIME/DAY/DATE ....

GENERAL SYNOPSIS	At 0048, 0520, 1201, 1754 UT/BST			
System	Present position	Movement	Forecast position	At

Gales	SEA AREA FORECAST	Wind (At first)	(Later)	Weather	Visibility
	VIKING				
	NORTH UTSIRE				
	SOUTH UTSIRE				
	FORTIES				
	CROMARTY				
	FORTH				
	TYNE				
	DOGGER				
	FISHER				
	GERMAN BIGHT				
	HUMBER				
	THAMES				
	DOVER				
	WIGHT				
	PORTLAND				
	PLYMOUTH				
	BISCAY				
	TRAFALGAR (0048)				
	FITZROY				
	SOLE				
	LUNDY				
	FASTNET				
	IRISH SEA				
	SHANNON				
	ROCKALL				
	MALIN				
	HEBRIDES				
	BAILEY				
	FAIR ISLE				
	FAEROES				
	S E ICELAND				

COASTAL REPORTS at .... UT BST	Wind Direction	Force	Weather	Visibility	Pressure	Change
Tiree auto (T)						
Stornoway (St)						
Lerwick (L)						
Fife Ness (F)						
Bridlington (Br)						
Sandettié auto (S)						

COASTAL REPORTS	Wind Direction	Force	Weather	Visibility	Pressure	Change
Greenwich auto (G)						
Jersey (J)						
Channel auto (C)						
Scilly auto (Sc)						
Valentia (V)						
Ronaldsway (R)						
Malin Head (M)						

Fig 6(2) Cloud types

Cirrus (Ci) Very high, silky-white clouds (mare's tails) consisting of ice-particles, associated with strong winds aloft. Often indicates the approach of a frontal system and deteriorating weather conditions. © *RK Pilsbury*

Nimbostratus (Ns) A low, dark grey, rain-bearing cloud mass obscuring the whole sky. Often follows Altostratus and the passing of a front. Steady rain, sleet or snow will set in, the base covering low hills. © *RK Pilsbury*

Cirrocumulus (Cc) Very high small white puffs in ripples, sometimes forming banks; the classic Mackerel sky. Thicker than Cirrus and formed by turbulence. Not usually associated with any particular weather. © *RK Pilsbury*

Stratus (St) Thin, grey, fog-like sheet of cloud as low as 1000 or even 500 feet. Dense Stratus can produce drizzle and poor visibility. It is usually associated with warm sector conditions. © *Crown*

Cirrostratus (Cs) A thin high whitish veil which does not blur the outline of the sun or moon; the only cloud to show a halo. If it thickens, it can indicate an approaching front or depression. © *CS Broomfield*

Stratocumulus (Sc) Dense, lumpy grey cloud below 5000 feet; persistent in winter with high pressure. If it thickens to form a solid grey layer across the sky, expect rain at any time. © *GA Watts*

Altocumulus (Ac) Essentially a greyish-white layer cloud with gaps between rounded globules of cumulus. If forming in bands, it may indicate an approaching front. © *CS Broomfield*

Cumulus (Cu) Fair weather cloud with vertical development due to rising warm air, especially over coasts. Plenty of blue sky but risk of gusty showers due to instability. Disappears by early evening. © *RK Pilsbury*

Altostratus (As) A medium level, sheet of blue-grey cloud like a layer of fog. The sun or moon may shine through it, without halo. Usually indicates that frontal rain can be expected in a few hours, turning to Ns. © *S Cornford*

Cumulonimbus (Cb) Large, dramatic convection cloud rising to great heights with huge tops, some anvil-shaped. Heavy rain and thundery squalls are likely. Down-currents produce sudden strong gusts, hazardous to yachts. © *Crown*

Fig 6(3) *Stations reporting actual weather via BBC Radio 4, telephone recordings or SMS*

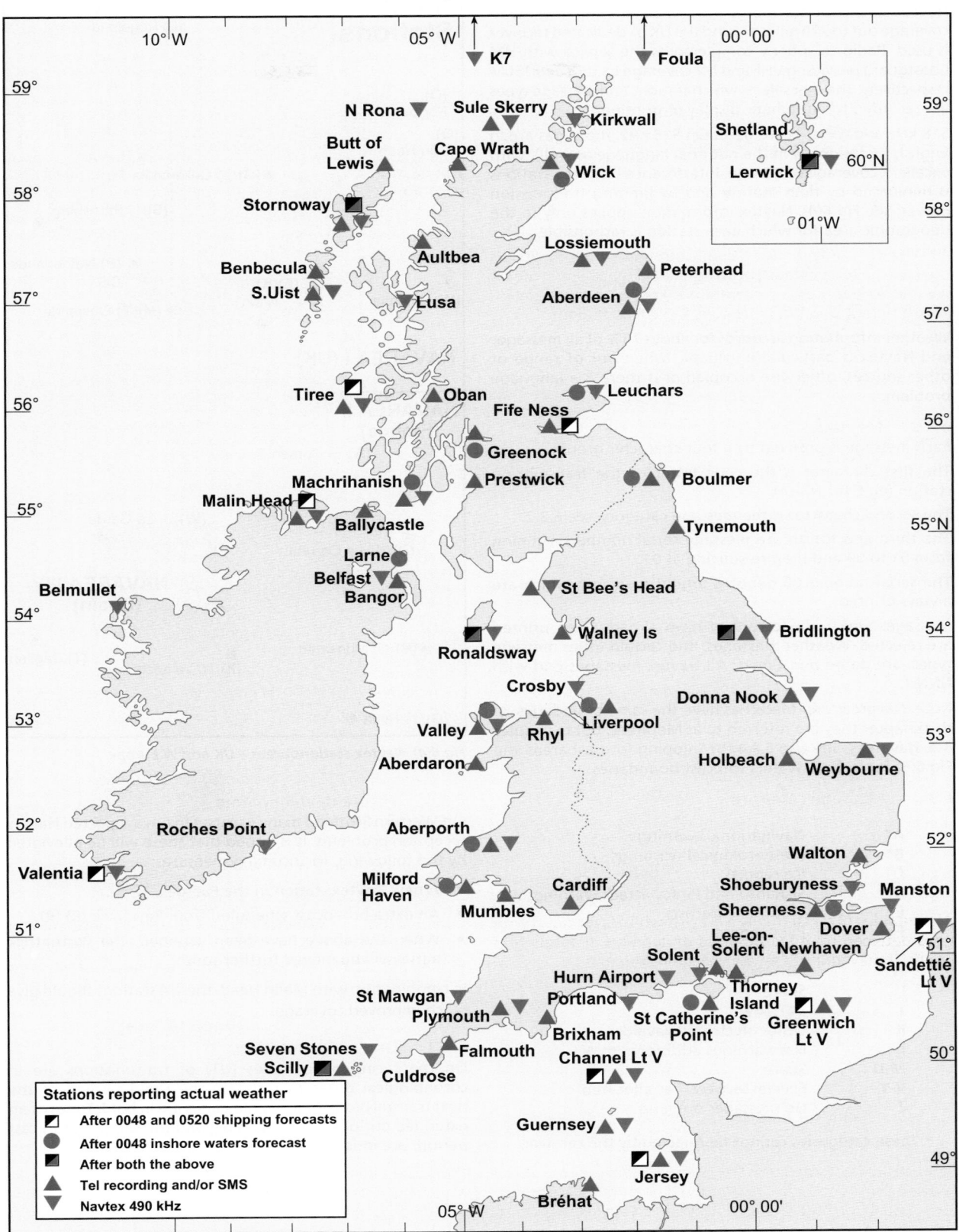

Weather

93

6.3 NAVTEX

Navtex is the prime method of disseminating MSI, with coverage out to 270 miles around the UK. A dedicated receiver is used. Radio telephony complements the service with HM Coastguard providing VHF and MF coverage to 30M and 150M respectively. The user selects which stations and message types are recorded for automatic display or printing.

518 kHz and 490 kHz are used. On 518 kHz, messages are in English (occasionally in the national language as well), with excellent coverage of Europe. Interference between stations is minimised by time sharing and by limiting transmission power; see Fig 6(4). Navtex information applies only to the geographic area for which each station is responsible.

490 kHz (for clarity shown in purple throughout this chapter) is used abroad for transmissions in the national language. In the UK it is used for inshore waters forecasts in English. 490 kHz stations have different identification letters to 518 kHz stations.

Weather information accounts for about 75% of all messages and Navtex is particularly valuable when out of range of other sources, otherwise occupied or if there is a language problem.

6.3.1 Messages

Each message is prefixed by a four-character group:

The first character is the code letter of the transmitting station (eg **E** for Niton).

The second character is the message category, see 6.3.2.

The third and fourth are message serial numbers, running from 01 to 99 and then re-starting at 01.

The serial number 00 denotes urgent messages which are always printed.

Messages which are corrupt or have already been printed are rejected. Weather messages, and certain other message types, are dated and timed. All Navtex messages end with NNNN.

Note: Navareas and Metareas have the same boundaries; in this chapter they are referred to as Metareas, but in chapter 3 as Navareas. See also 6.2.4 for Shipping forecast areas and Fig 6(5) for Inshore waters forecast boundaries.

6.3.2 Message categories

A*	Navigational warnings
B*	Meteorological warnings
C	Ice reports
D*	SAR info and Piracy attack warnings
E	Weather forecasts
F	Pilot service
G	AIS
H	LORAN
I	Spare
J	SATNAV
K	Other electronic Navaids
L	Navwarnings additional to **A**
M-U	Spare
V-Y	Special services – as allocated
Z	No messages on hand

* These categories cannot be rejected by the receiver.

Fig 6(4) Navtex stations/areas – UK and W Europe

6.3.3 Future developments

Off Western Scotland many yachtsmen have reported Navtex reception problems. It is hoped that these will be alleviated by the following, forthcoming measures:

• A new Navtex station in the Faeroes.

• An extra broadcast scheduled from Reykjavik (R) (R).

• When the above have been actioned, the Portpatrick aerial will be moved further south.

In combination with Malin Head, these 4 stations should give much improved coverage.

6.3.4 UK 518 kHz stations

On the facing page, times (UT) of transmissions are in chronological order to facilitate the rapid finding of the next transmission. Weather messages are in **bold**. Times of an extended outlook (2 or 3 days beyond the shipping forecast period) are in *italics*.

E –	**Niton**	*0040*	0440	**0840**	1240	1640	**2040**
	Thames clockwise to Fastnet, excluding Trafalgar.						
G –	**Cullercoats**	*0100*	0500	**0900**	1300	1700	**2100**
	Fair Isle clockwise to Thames, excluding N & S Utsire, Fisher and German Bight.						
O –	**Portpatrick**	*0220*	*0620*	1020	1420	**1820**	2220
	Lundy clockwise to SE Iceland.						

6.3.5 UK 490 kHz stations

These provide forecasts for UK inshore waters (to 12M offshore), a national 3 day outlook for inshore waters and, at times in bold, reports of actual weather at the places listed below in Notes 1–3. To receive these reports select 490 kHz and message category 'V' (6.3.2) on your Navtex receiver. Times (UT) of transmissions are listed in chronological order.
Actual Met data includes: Sea level pressure (mb), wind direction and speed (kn), weather, visibility (M), air and sea temperatures (°C), dewpoint temperature (°C) and mean wave height (m).

C –	**Portpatrick** St David's Head to Cape Wrath	0020	0420	0820	**1220**	**1620**	2020
	N Rona, Stornoway, S Uist, Lusa (Skye bridge), Tiree, Macrihanish, Belfast, Malin Head, Belmullet, St Bees Head, Ronaldsway, Crosby, Valley, Aberporth, Roches Point, Valentia, St Mawgan.						
I –	**Niton** The Wash to Colwyn Bay (Note 2)	0120	0520	**0920**	**1320**	1720	2120
	Sandettie Lt V, Greenwich Lt V, Solent, Hurn airport, Guernsey airport, Jersey airport, Portland, Channel Lt V, Plymouth, Culdrose, Seven Stones Lt V, St Mawgan and Roches Point (Cork).						
U –	**Cullercoats** Cape Wrath to North Foreland (3)	0320	0720	**1120**	**1520**	1920	2320
	Sandettie Lt V, Manston, Shoeburyness, Weybourne, Donna Nook or Bridlington, Boulmer, Leuchars, Aberdeen, Lossiemouth, Wick, Kirkwall, Lerwick, Foula, K7 Met buoy, Sule Skerry.						

6.3.6 Navtex coverage abroad

Selected Navtex stations in Metareas I to III, with their identity codes, are listed in chronological order of transmissions. Times of weather messages are shown in **bold**. Gale warnings are usually transmitted 4 hourly.

METAREA I (Co-ordinator – UK)	**Transmission times (UT)**					
K – **Niton** (Note 1)	0140	0540	0940	1340	1740	2140
L – **Rogaland**, Norway	**0150**	**0550**	**0950**	**1350**	1750	2150
L – Pinneberg, Hamburg (Note 5)	0150	0550	0950	1350	1750	2150
M – **Oostende**, Belgium (Note 2)	0200	0600	1000	1400	1800	2200
P – **Netherlands CG**, Den Helder	**0230**	**0630**	1030	**1430**	1830	2230
Q – **Malin Head**, Ireland (Note 3)	0240	**0640**	**1040**	1440	**1840**	**2240**
S – **Pinneberg**, Hamburg (Note 6)	**0300**	**0700**	**1100**	**1500**	**1900**	**2300**
T – **Oostende**, Belgium (Note 4)	0310	**0710**	1110	1510	**1910**	2310
W – **Valentia**, Ireland (Note 3)	0340	**0740**	**1140**	1540	**1940**	**2340**

Notes 1 In English, no weather; only Nav warnings for the French coast from Cap Gris Nez to Île de Bréhat.
2 No weather information, only Nav warnings for NavArea Juliett.
3 See 6.6 and Fig 6(6) for the Atlantic areas covered by 'Q' at 1040, 2240 and by 'W' at 1140, 2340.
4 Forecasts and strong wind warnings for Thames and Dover, plus nav info for the Belgian coast.
5 In German, weather and Nav warnings for German Bight (also W and S Baltic) at times in bold above
6 Weather broadcasts every 4 hours for the North Sea

METAREA II (Co-ordinator – France)	**Transmission times (UT)**					
A – **Corsen**, Le Stiff, France	**0000**	0400	0800	**1200**	1600	2000
D – **Coruña**, Spain	**0030**	0430	**0830**	1230	1630	**2030**
E – Corsen, Le Stiff, France (in French)	0040	0440	0840	1240	1640	2040
F – **Horta**, Azores, Portugal	**0050**	**0450**	**0850**	**1250**	**1650**	2050
G – Monsanto, Portugal (in Portuguese)	0100	0500	0900	1300	1700	2100
G – **Tarifa**, Spain (English & Spanish)	0100	0500	**0900**	1300	1700	**2100**
I – **Las Palmas**, Islas Canarias, Spain	0120	0520	**0920**	**1320**	**1720**	2120
J – Horta, Açores, Portugal (in Portuguese)	0130	0530	0930	1330	1730	2130
R – **Monsanto**, Portugal	**0250**	**0650**	**1050**	**1450**	**1850**	**2250**
T – Tarifa, Spain (in Spanish)	0310	0710	1110	1510	1910	2310
W – Coruña, Spain (in Spanish)	0340	0740	**1140**	1540	1940	2340

Fig 6(5) Inshore waters forecasts – Area boundaries used by the Coastguard

6.4   MSI BROADCASTS BY HM COASTGUARD

MRCC routinely broadcast Maritime Safety Information (MSI) every 3 hours at the times in Table 6(1) below.

Each broadcast contains one of 3 different Groups of MSI:

Group A, the full broadcast, contains the Shipping forecast, Inshore waters forecast (for local Areas as in Table 6(1)), Gale and strong wind warnings, and a Fisherman's 3 day forecast* see Note. **Times of 'A' broadcasts are in bold.**

Group B contains a new Inshore waters forecast, plus the previous outlook, and Gale warnings. 'B' broadcast times are in plain type.

Group C is a repeat of the Inshore waters forecast and Gale warnings (as per the previous Group A or B) plus any new Strong wind warnings. *'C' broadcast times are italicised.*

Notes

Fig 6(5) shows the boundaries of the 17 areas which are covered by Inshore waters forecasts. In the forecast these areas are referred to not by their numbers, but by their defining places/headlands, eg Whitby to Gibraltar Point.

‡ **Subfacts & Gunfacts** are broadcast by Falmouth, Brixham, Aberdeen (occas), Stornoway, Clyde and Belfast MRCC. See Chapter 5 for Nav (WZ) warnings and Subfacts & Gunfacts where appropriate.

*A **Fisherman's 3 day forecast** is broadcast (1 Oct–31 Mar) by MRCC which are MF equipped, except Tiree.

6.4.1   Actual weather

On request MRCC may report the actual weather in their vicinity. HM CG stresses that they are not qualified Met observers and such reports may be no more than a look out of the window or originate from passing ships and yachts.

TABLE 6(1)   Broadcasts of shipping and inshore waters forecasts by HM Coastguard

Coastguard	Shipping forecast areas	Inshore waters forecast areas	Broadcast Groups and local times							
South Coast			B	*C*	**A**	*C*	B	*C*	**A**	*C*
Falmouth‡	Portland, Plymouth, Sole, Shannon, Fastnet	8, 9	0110	*0410*	**0710**	*1010*	1310	*1610*	**1910**	*2210*
Brixham‡	Same as Falmouth CG	8, 9	0110	*0410*	**0710**	*1010*	1310	*1610*	**1910**	*2210*
Portland	Plymouth, Portland, Wight	6–8	0130	*0430*	**0730**	*1030*	1330	*1630*	**1930**	*2230*
Solent	Plymouth, Portland, Wight	6–8	0130	*0430*	**0730**	*1030*	1330	*1630*	**1930**	*2230*
Dover	Dover, Wight, Thames, Humber	5, 6	0110	*0410*	**0710**	*1010*	1310	*1610*	**1910**	*2210*
East Coast			B	*C*	**A**	*C*	B	*C*	**A**	*C*
Thames	Dover, Wight, Thames, Humber	5, 6	0110	*0410*	**0710**	*1010*	1310	*1610*	**1910**	*2210*
Yarmouth	Humber, Thames	4–5	0150	*0450*	**0750**	*1050*	1350	*1650*	**1950**	*2250*
Humber	Tyne, Dogger, Humber, German Bight	3–4	0150	*0450*	**0750**	*1050*	1350	*1650*	**1950**	*2250*
Forth	Tyne, Forth, Cromarty, Forties, Fair Isle	1, 2	0130	*0430*	**0730**	*1030*	1330	*1630*	**1930**	*2230*
Aberdeen‡	Same as Forth CG	1, 2	0130	*0430*	**0730**	*1030*	1330	*1630*	**1930**	*2230*
Shetland	Cromarty, Viking, Fair Isle, Faeroes	1, 17	0110	*0410*	**0710**	*1010*	1310	*1610*	**1910**	*2210*
West Coast			B	*C*	**A**	*C*	B	*C*	**A**	*C*
Stornoway‡	Rockall, Malin, Hebrides, Bailey, Fair Is, Faeroes, SE Iceland	16	0110	*0410*	**0710**	*1010*	1310	*1610*	**1910**	*2210*
Clyde‡	Rockall, Malin, Hebrides, Bailey	14, 15	0210	*0510*	**0810**	*1110*	1410	*1710*	**2010**	*2310*
Belfast‡	Irish Sea, Malin	12–14	0110	*0410*	**0710**	*1010*	1310	*1610*	**1910**	*2210*
Liverpool	Irish Sea	11, 12	0130	*0430*	**0730**	*1030*	1330	*1630*	**1930**	*2230*
Holyhead	Irish Sea	10, 11	0150	*0450*	**0750**	*1050*	1350	*1650*	**1950**	*2250*
Milford Haven	Lundy, Fastnet, Irish Sea	9, 10	0150	*0450*	**0750**	*1050*	1350	*1650*	**1950**	*2250*
Swansea	Lundy, Fastnet, Irish Sea	9, 10	0150	*0450*	**0750**	*1050*	1350	*1650*	**1950**	*2250*

Fig 6(6) Remote Coastguard transmitters

MRCC Stornoway ⬚ hrs
46 Butt of Lewis (+MF 1743kHz)
47 Portnaguran (Ullapool)
48 Forsnaval (W Lewis)
49 Melvaig (Loch Ewe)
50 Rodel (S Harris)
51 Clettreval (N Uist)
52 Skriag (Portree, Skye)
53 Drumfearn (SE Skye)
54 Barra
55 Arisaig (S of Mallaig)

MRCC Shetland ⬚ hrs
41 Wideford Hill (Kirkwall)
42 Fitfull Head (Sumburgh)
43 Lerwick (+MF 1770kHz)
44 Collafirth
45 Saxa Vord (Unst)

MRCC Aberdeen ⬚ hrs
36 Greg Ness (+MF 2226kHz)
37 Windyhead Hill
38 Rosemarkie (Cromarty)
39 Noss Head (Wick)
40 Durness (Loch Eriboll)

MRCC Forth ⬚ hrs
32 St Abbs/Cross Law
33 Craigkelly (Burntisland)
34 Fife Ness
35 Inverbervie

MRCC Clyde ⬚ hrs
56 Glengorm (N Mull)
57 Tiree (+MF 1883kHz)
58 Torosay (E Mull)
59 Clyde CG (Greenock)
60 S Knapdale (Loch Fyne)
61 Kilchiaran (W Islay)
62 Lawhill (Ardrossan)
63 Rhu Staffnish (Kintyre)

MRCC Humber ⬚ hrs
26 Easington (Spurn Head)
27 Flamborough Head (+MF 2226kHz)
28 Ravenscar
29 Hartlepool
30 Cullercoats (Blyth)
31 Newton

MRCC Belfast ⬚ hrs
64 Navar (Lower Lough Erne)
65 Limvady (Lough Foyle)
66 West Torr (Fair Head)
67 Black Mountain (Belfast)
68 Orlock Head (Bangor)
69 Slievemartin (Rostrevor)

MRCC Liverpool ⬚ hrs
70 Caldbeck (Carlisle)
71 Snaefell (Isle of Man)
72 Langthwaite (Lancaster)
73 Moel-y-Parc (N Wales)

MRCC Holyhead ⬚ hrs
74 Moel-y-Parc (N Wales)
75 South Stack (Holyhead)

MRCC Yarmouth ⬚ hrs
21 Lowestoft
22 Great Yarmouth
23 Trimingham (Cromer)
24 Langham (Blakeney)
25 Guy's Head (Wisbech)

MRCC Milford Haven ⬚ hrs
76 Blaenplwyf (Aberystwyth)
77 Dinas Head (Fishguard)
78 St Ann's
79 Monkstone (Tenby)

MRCC Thames ⬚ hrs
17 Shoeburyness
18 Bradwell (R Blackwater)
19 Walton-on-the-Naze
20 Bawdsey (R Deben)

MRCC Swansea ⬚ hrs
80 Mumbles
81 St Hilary (Barry)
82 Severn Bridges
83 Combe Martin
84 Hartland Point

MRCC Portland ⬚ hrs
10 Beer Head
11 Grove Pt (Portland Bill)

MRCC Falmouth ⬚ hrs
1 Trevose Head
2 St Mary's (Scilly)
3 Lizard (+MF 2226kHz)
4 Falmouth

MRCC Brixham ⬚ hrs
5 Fowey
6 Rame Head
7 East Prawle
8 Dartmouth
9 Berry Head

MRCC Solent ⬚ hrs
12 Needles
13 Boniface (Ventnor IoW)
14 Newhaven

MRCC Dover ⬚ hrs
15 Fairlight (Hastings)
16 Langdon (Dover)

Consult table 6(1) to find the transmission time(s) for the type (group A, B or C) of MSI broadcast and your location.

Map transmitter labels:
41 Ch 86 · 45 Ch 23 · 44 Ch 86 · 43 Ch 84 · 42 Ch 23 · 40 Ch 23 · 39 Ch 84 · 46 Ch 86 · 47 Ch 84 · 48 Ch 23 · 49 Ch 23 · 50 Ch 86 · 51 Ch 84 · 37 Ch 23 · 38 Ch 86 · 52 Ch 84 · 53 Ch 86 · 36 Ch 86 · 54 Ch 10 · 55 Ch 23 · 35 Ch 23 · 57 Ch 86 · 56 Ch 23 · 58 Ch 10 · 34 Ch 84 · 33 Ch 23 · 32 Ch 86 · 59 Ch 84 · 60 Ch 23 · 62 Ch 86 · 61 Ch 84 · 63 Ch 10 · 31 Ch 23 · 65 Ch 84 · 66 Ch 86 · 30 Ch 86 · 29 Ch 23 · 67 Ch 23 · 68 Ch 84 · 70 Ch 23 · 28 Ch 86 · 64 Ch 86 · 69 Ch 86 · 71 Ch 86 · 72 Ch 84 · 27 Ch 23 · 26 Ch 86 · 74 Ch 86 · 75 Ch 23 · 73 Ch 23 · 24 Ch 86 · 25 Ch 23 · 23 Ch 23 · 22 Ch 86 · 21 Ch 23 · 76 Ch 84 · 77 Ch 86 · 20 Ch 84 · 19 Ch 23 · 18 Ch 86 · 17 Ch 23 · 78 Ch 84 · 79 Ch 84 · 80 Ch 86 · 81 Ch 23 · 82 Ch 86 · 83 Ch 23 · 16 Ch 86 · 84 Ch 86 · 15 Ch 84 · 14 Ch 86 · 1 Ch 84 · 6 Ch 86 · 10 Ch 86 · 9 Ch 23 · 11 Ch 84 · 12 Ch 86 · 13 Ch 23 · 2 Ch 86 · 5 Ch 10 · 8 Ch 10 · 4 Ch 84 · 7 Ch 84 · 3 Ch 23

Coordinates: 59°, 58°, 57°, 56°, 55°N, 54°, 53°, 52°, 51°, 50° · 05° W · 00° 00' · 60°N · 01°W · Shetland

6.4.2 Remote transmitters

MSI broadcasts are transmitted via remote aerial sites selected to give optimum coverage. Figure 6(6) opposite shows their positions, and the VHF broadcast channel (one of Ch 10, 23, 84 or 86) to be used, which is also given in a prior announcement on Ch 16. Use Fig 6(6) in conjunction with table 6(1) on page 97 to reduce the risk of missing a broadcast. A useful tip is to pre-select Ch 16 on Dual watch with the relevant working channel; and/or verify the working channel by listening to the prior announcement.

MF frequencies (*kHz*), as identified in Fig 6(6), are also used for the broadcasts, primarily for the benefit of fishermen.

6.5 HF RADIO FACSIMILE BROADCASTS

Radio-Fax machines able to receive pictorial images, eg weather charts, are useful aboard yachts/other vessels and in marina offices. Isobaric charts (actual and forecast), sea and swell charts, satellite cloud images, sea temperature charts and wind charts are all of direct interest to the blue water yachtsman. For foreign stations see ALRS, Vol 3.

6.5.1 Northwood, London: HF Radio-Fax

Frequencies for the North Atlantic: 2618·5 kHz (2000–0600), 4610 & 8040 (H24), 11086·5 (0600–2000). Note: For military reasons this service may be withdrawn without notice.

Broadcast times UT. Items of interest to yachtsmen are shown below. The full schedule is broadcast at 0100 & 1300.

0000	1200	Surface analysis
0012	1212	24h surface prognosis
0036	1236	24h OAT & dewpoint contour
0100	1300	Schedule
0136	1336	Ocean fronts
0236	1436	Surface analysis
0300	1500	Surface analysis
0348	1548	Gale warning summary
0400	1600	Surface analysis
0412	1612	24h OAT & dewpoint contour
0436	1636	24h surface prognosis
0500	1700	Surface analysis
0512	1712	24h surface prognosis
0524	1724	48h surface prognosis
0548	1748	Gale warning summary
0612	1800	Surface analysis
0624	1812	24h surface prognosis
0712	1912	24h significant winds
0724	1924	48h surface prognosis
0736	1936	72h surface prognosis
0748	1948	96h surface prognosis
0800	2000	120h surface prognosis
0824	2024	48h significant winds
0836	2036	72h significant winds
0848	2048	96h significant winds contour
0900	2100	Surface analysis
1000	2200	Surface analysis
1012	2212	24h surface prognosis
1024	2224	24h reduced visibility prognosis
1048	2248	24h OAT & dewpoint contour
1100	2300	Surface analysis
1112	2312	24h surface prognosis
1124	2324	24h sea & swell prognosis
1148	2348	Gale warning summary

6.6 HIGH SEAS BULLETINS

In the N Atlantic part of MetArea 1, dotted outline in Fig 6(7), weather data is available from:

- SafetyNET which provides MSI to vessels in A3 sea areas. Goonhilly Coast Earth Station (CES) transmits Met data at 0930 & 2130 UT via the **AOR-E** and **AOR-W** satellites.

- Navtex. Malin Head (Q) and Valentia (W) cover the E Northern and E Central sections, as well as Sole, Shannon, Rockall and Bailey.

Fig 6(7) MetArea I – SafetyNET forecast areas

6.7 OTHER WEATHER SOURCES

6.7.1 Internet

The UK Met Office website www.metoffice.gov.uk/weather/marine/ posts Inshore waters forecasts and strong wind warnings (updated twice daily); Shipping forecasts and gale warnings (updated 4 times per day); High seas forecasts and storm warnings (updated twice daily).

Other UK and foreign Met Offices and weather authorities provide further information and are best equipped to produce the most authoritative and consistent forecasts. Their websites, e-mail and postal addresses are in Chapter 1.

Websites listed below may meet specific needs or situations:

www.xcweather.co.uk Aviation-orientated, wind 'snapshots', temp, weather at UK and weather buoys; 5 day forecasts.

www.franksweather.co.uk Authoritative, wide ranging coverage by retired senior forecaster and active yachtsman.

bbc.co.uk/weather/coast/ Atlantic pressure charts, actual and buoy observations, plus Shipping, coastal & inshore forecasts.

www.ecmwf.int/ European Centre for Medium-range Weather Forecasts. Draws on the expertise of its 28 member states.

www.sat.dundee.ac.uk/ Free, world-wide satellite imagery.

6.7.2 Talk to a forecaster

A UK Met Office forecaster will brief (approx 3 mins) by phone (H24) your special weather situation and a forecast for up to 5 days ahead.

Existing users call ☎ 08700 767 plus 888 for UK waters; or 818 for the Med and Canaries. New users in the UK call Customer Centre ☎ 0870 900 890; or from abroad call +44 1392 885 680. Cost £17 by major credit/debit cards. Open an account to benefit from bulk discounts, eg 1-14 calls £17 each; 20 calls £280, ie £14 each. www.metoffice.gov.uk/services/talkfc/index.html gives further details.

An alternative service is from WeatherwebMarine. Services include routing advice. Call 09061 991 189 from within the UK. Calls cost £1.50 per minute. Operates 8 am to 6 pm. From outside the UK call +44 8700 738 100, payment via credit card, costs £12.

6.7.3 Press

Some national and regional papers include a synoptic chart which can help to interpret the shipping forecast – although some data may be out of date by the time you read it.

6.7.4 Television

Most TV forecasts show a synoptic chart and satellite pictures – a useful guide. In remote areas a TV forecast in a bar or even shop window may be the only source of Met data.

Ceefax (BBC): p. 400 gives the weather index; p. 405 Met warnings; and p. 409 inshore waters forecasts.

Teletext (ITN): p.157 has shipping forecasts; p.158 inshore waters forecasts. Antiope is the equivalent French system.

6.7.5 Volmet

Volmet is a continuous broadcast of actual weather and/or forecasts for selected civil/military airfields. Reports contain wind direction/spd, vis, cloud amount/height, air/dewpoint temps, sea level pressure (QNH), any significant weather.

The aeronautical VHF band is used for short ranges, but not VHF marine band, so is of no use to mariners.

Long range HF SSB broadcasts include Shannon Volmet on: 3413 kHz (HN), 5505, 8957 kHz (H24) and 13264 kHz (HJ).

RAF Volmet (H24) on 5450 and 11253 kHz HF SSB includes coastal stations: Leuchars, Lossiemouth, Kinloss & Cardiff at H & H+30; and Culdrose, Belfast & Prestwick at H+07 & +37.

For further information on civilian Volmet contact the Civil Aviation Authority. For military Volmet contact No 1 AIDU, RAF Northolt, West End Road, Ruislip, Middlesex HA4 6NG.

6.8 MARINECALL WEATHER BY TELEPHONE

Marinecall provides a wide range of forecasts for UK and European waters. They are produced by the Met Office and disseminated via telephone recordings, fax, the internet, and by mobile phone.

> For further information contact:
> Marinecall Customer Services,
> iTouch (UK) Ltd,
> Avalon House,
> 57-63 Scrutton Street,
> London EC2A 4PF.
> ☎ 0871 200 3985 (M-F 0900-1700); 📠 0870 600 4229.
> www.marinecall.co.uk   marinecall@itouch.co.uk

Costs. 09068 calls cost 60p/min. 09065 faxes £1.50/min.

6.8 1 Operation

Dial ☎ 09068 96 96 + the required two digit area number on Fig 6(8), in green for inshore waters or red for offshore. These forecasts are updated up to 3 times a day and contain 5 main components as shown below:

- **Inshore and offshore forecasts for 48 hours**
- **Local waters forecast for days 1–5**
- **National forecast for days 6–10**
- **Outlook for one month ahead**

6.9 MARINECALL WEATHER ONLINE

Included are a 48 hours inshore and offshore forecast; a local area 1–5 day tabular forecast; a national forecast for days 6–10; plus synoptic charts valid for 48 hours and 2–5 days.

6.10 MARINECALL WEATHER BY FAX

Fax forecasts contain the same data as those listed under 6.9, but are updated thrice daily. The Advance forecast (📠 09065 @ £1.50/min) contains slightly more detail than the Standard forecast (📠 09060 @ £1/min). The Fax numbers in Fig 6(7) are for the Advance service.

To obtain a forecast dial 📠 09065 22 23 plus the 2-digit area number in Fig 6(7), either green for inshore waters or red for offshore. After dialling press the Start or Receive button to start the transmission; be prepared for a slight delay as the data is downloaded to your fax machine.

6.10.1 Marinecall FaxDirect

Discounts to regular users of the Advance service include, for example over 3 months: 1 fax per week costs £38.76 inc VAT; 3 faxes per week £102.23; and 7 faxes per week £211.50. Monthly and annual subscriptions are available.

6.11 EUROPEAN WEATHER BY TELEPHONE & FAX

Forecasts, updated 4 times/day, cover a 6 hr period and include wind speed/direction, cloud cover, temperature, visibility and significant weather for the European areas below. These forecasts are also available online; see 6.9.

For Tel forecasts dial ☎ 09064 700 + 3 digits below.

For Fax forecasts dial 📠 09065 501 + 3 digits below.

Area		☎	📠
NE France	(Dunkerque – Deauville)	421	611
N France	(Dives – St Quay-Portrieux)	422	612
N Brittany	(Lézardrieux – Douarnenez)	423	613
S Brittany	(Audierne – St Nazaire)	424	614
S Biscay	(Pornic – Capbreton)	425	615
N & W Spain	(Ribadesella – Camariñas)	426	616
Portugal	(Lisbon – Faro)	428	618
SW Spain	(Isla Cristina – Gibraltar)	427	617

Marinecall can be used from any landline or mobile network within the UK and Channel Islands. For international services join the Marinecall Club.

6.11.1 4-digit codes

Over 200 such codes give quicker, cheaper access to a required area or port by reducing the preamble.

They apply to Tel and Fax messages for UK and Europe. Dial ☎ 09068 96 96 or 🖾 09065 22 23, and the 2-digit area code, ie the offshore areas 57–62 shown in red in Fig 6(8).

Add the 4-digit code, eg 6360 for Oban, as soon as the call connects or you are prompted to do so.

6.11.2 Codes for Europe

For European coastal locations dial ☎ 09068 96 96 or 🖾 09065 22 23, and the 2-digit area code; add the 4-digit code as described above. For example for Dublin 59 2928 or for Les Sables d'Olonne 60 2964.

A selection of 2- and 4-digit area codes is listed in the table on the following page.

A full listing of 4-digit codes is in the Marinecall Handbook or visit www.marinecall.co.uk

Fig 6(8) Metcheck Inshore and offshore forecasts by telephone and fax

TABLE 6(2)   BROADCASTS OF SHIPPING AND INSHORE WATERS FORECASTS BY HM COASTGUARD

Area	Area code	dial ☎ 09068 96 96 or ▨ 09065 22 23, area code as shown + 4 digits		
Northern Ireland	59 + 4 digits:	Lough Foyle 6560; Larne 6564; Strangford Lough 6567	Portrush 6562; Bangor 6565;	Ballycastle 6563; Portavogie 6566;
Irish Republic	59 + 4 digits:	Carlingford Lough 2924; Mine Head 2926; **Note**: W coast locations are not covered	Dublin 2928; Baltimore 2927;	Wicklow Head 2925; Malin Head 6561;
West Denmark	58 + 4 digits:	Thyborøn 2938		
Netherlands/Belgium	58 + 4 digits:	West Terschelling 2940;	Westkapelle 2941;	Oostende 2939
North France	57 + 4 digits:	Dunkerque 2942; Dieppe 2911; St Malo 2914;	Calais 2909; Le Havre 2912; Ile de Bréhat 2915;	Le Touquet 2910; Cherbourg 2913; Ouessant 2916
West France	60 + 4 digits:	Pornic 2963; Royan 2966;	Sables d'Olonne 2964; Arcachon 2967;	La Rochelle 2965; Capbreton 2968.

6.12   SINGLE OBSERVER FORECASTING

Despite the many sources and ways of obtaining weather data, it is no bad thing – and may be essential – to draft your own forecast based largely on what you see and feel around you. Such a forecast may only be correct for up to 6 hrs, but with experience this may be extended to 12 hrs.

Initially you are most likely to be interested in forecasting:

*   Wind speed and direction; and
*   Visibility, both good and poor

Later you may wish to forecast the movement of Highs and Lows, with their attendant fronts and occlusions. This may be outside the scope of 'single observer forecasting', but the ability to construct a weather map, based on broadcast observations, and then to project it ahead for 12 or 24 hours is a most valuable string to your bow.

The main tools of your trade will be:

*   The barometer, logging carefully whether it is steady, rising or falling and at what hourly rate; see 6.1.3.
*   Actual wind direction and speed, noting any tendency to back or veer, increase or moderate; see 6.1.4.
*   The appearance of the sky, especially cloud types, their estimated heights and direction of movement; Fig 6(2).
*   When precipitation starts and ends may also provide valuable clues to frontal movement.

Instant Weather Forecasting or *The Weather Handbook* both by Alan Watts (ACN) are an excellent buy.

Compare your forecast with what actually happened. Analyse errors, learn the lessons and 'better luck next time'. Even the professionals get it wrong, spectacularly so.

6.13   CHANNEL ISLANDS (North to South)

6.13.1   Alderney
Alderney Radio Ch 74 can provide forecasts and reports on request; also available in the HM's office; see 9.19.7.

6.13.2   Weather broadcasts by commercial radio
BBC Radio Guernsey 93·2, 99·0 MHz; 1116 kHz broadcasts weather bulletins for the waters around Guernsey, Herm and Sark at 0630, 0730, 0830 LT Mon-Fri; 0730, 0830 LT Sat/Sun. They contain forecast, synopsis, coastal forecast, storm warnings and wind strength.

In the summer coastal reports are included from Jersey, Guernsey, Alderney, Cap de la Hague, Cherbourg, Dinard, Portland and Channel light vessel.

☎ 01481 200600. www.bbc.co.uk/guernsey guernsey@bbc.co.uk

BBC Radio Jersey 1026 kHz and 88·8 MHz broadcasts storm warnings on receipt; and a Shipping forecast for local waters at 0625 & 1825 LT Mon-Fri and 0625 & 0725 LT Sat/Sun.

Wind info for Jersey waters is broadcast live at 0725, 0825, 1725 LT Mon-Fri; and 0825 LT Sat/Sun.

www.bbc.co.uk/jersey jersey@bbc.co.uk ☎ 01534 870000.

6.13.3   Jersey Met
Provides marine forecasts updated 4 hourly for the area within 50°N, 03°W and the adjacent French coast. These are broadcast on VHF as in 6.13.4. The forecast includes the general situation, 24hr forecast for wind, weather, vis, sea state, swell, sea temperature, plus 2 & 4 day outlooks and St Helier tide times/heights. The quality of these forecasts for all the Channel Islands is generally excellent.

A recorded, chargeable version of the above can be obtained by calling ☎ 0900 665 0022 if in the CI or UK. From France call ☎ +44 1534 448787. From Guernsey only, call ☎ 06969 8800. For more detailed info and charge rates call ☎ +44 1534 745550, ▨ 746351; or visit www.jerseymet.gov.je

6.13.4   Weather broadcasts by Jersey Coastguard
Jersey Coastguard (formerly *Jersey Radio*) broadcasts gale warnings, synopsis, 24h forecast, outlook for next 24 hrs and reports from observation stations, at 0645, 0745, 0845 LT; 1245, 1845, 2245 UT and on request; on VHF Ch 25 and 82 (after prior announcement Ch 16). Gale warnings are also broadcast at 0307, 0907, 1507 & 2107 UT.

Jersey Coastguard is part of CG and SAR services at St Helier. www.coastalradio.org.uk/jersey.htm ☎ 01534 885505/04.

NATIONAL WEATHER INFORMATION ABROAD

6.14 REPUBLIC OF IRELAND (ROI)

Met Éireann (the Irish Met Office) is at Glasnevin Hill, Dublin 9, Ireland. ☎ 1 806 4250, 🖷 1 806 4250, www.met.ie. General forecasting division: ☎ 1 806 4255, 🖷 1 806 4275, forecasts@ met.ie (Charges may apply for individual forecasts.)

6.14.1 Irish Coast Radio Stations

CRS and their VHF channels are listed below (anti-clockwise from Malin Head) and shown on Fig 6(9). Weather bulletins for 30M offshore and the Irish Sea are broadcast on VHF at 0103, 0403, 0703, 1003, 1303, 1603, 1903 and 2203LT after an announcement on Ch 16. Bulletins include gale warnings, synopsis and a 24-hour forecast.

MALIN HEAD	23	Bantry	23
Glen Head	24	Mizen Head	04
Donegal Bay	02	Cork	26
Belmullet	83	Mine Head	83
Clifden	26	Rosslare	23
Galway	04	Wicklow Head	02
Shannon	28	DUBLIN	83
VALENTIA	24	Carlingford	04

Gale warnings are broadcast on receipt and at 0033, 0633, 1233 and 1833 UT, after an announcement on Ch 16.

MF Valentia Radio broadcasts forecasts for Shannon and Fastnet on 1752 kHz at 0833 & 2033 UT, and on request.

Gale warnings are broadcast on receipt and at 0303, 0903, 1503 and 2103 (UT) after an announcement on 2182 kHz.

Weather is not broadcast on MF by Malin Head or Dublin.

6.14.2 Weather by telephone

The latest sea area forecasts and gale warnings are available H24 from Weatherdial as recorded messages. Dial ☎ 1550 123 plus the following suffixes:

850 Munster; 851 Leinster; 852 Connaught; 853 Ulster; 854 Dublin (plus winds in Dublin Bay and HW times); 855 Coastal waters and Irish Sea.

6.14.3 Weather by fax

Similar information, plus isobaric, swell and wave charts and any Small craft warnings (>F6 up to 10M offshore; Apr–Sep inc) is available H24 by Weatherdial 🖷 1570 131 838 (from within ROI only). From the menu below select the required 4-digit product code (see code 0400 for full listing):

- 0015: Latest analysis chart
- 0016: Forecast valid for next 24 hrs
- 0017: Forecast valid for next 36 hrs
- 0018: Forecast valid for next 48 hrs
- 0021: Forecasts for coastal waters and Irish Sea
- 0031, 0032, 0033, 0034: Forecast (days 1–4) for sea and swell wave heights and periods
- 5-day forecasts (plain language, farming/national) 0001: Munster. 0002: Leinster. 0003: Connaught. 0004: Ulster. 0005: Dublin.

Sea Planners provide graphic forecasts for up to 5 days (updated at 0430 daily) of expected winds and waves at the following seven offshore positions:

0041: 53°N 05° 30′W.	0045: 54°N 11°W.
0042: 51°N 06°W.	0046: 55°N 10°W.
0043: 51°N 10°30′W.	0047: 56°N 08°W.
0044: 53°N 11°W.	

6.14.4 Radio Telefís Éireann (RTE) Radio 1

RTE Radio 1 broadcasts weather bulletins daily at 0602, 1253, 1650 & 2355LT on 252kHz (LW) Summerhill (15M W of Dublin airport) and FM (88·2–90·0MHz).

Bulletins contain a situation, forecast and coastal reports for Irish Sea and coastal waters. The forecast includes: wind, weather, vis, swell (if higher than 4m) and a 24 hrs outlook.

Gale warnings are included in hourly news bulletins on FM & MF.

Coastal reports include wind, weather, visibility, pressure, with pressure tendency over the last 3 hrs described as:

Steady	=	0–0·4 hPa change
Rising/falling slowly	=	0·5–1·9
Rising/falling	=	2·0–3·4
Rising/falling rapidly	=	3·5–5·9
Rising/falling very rapidly	=	> 6·0

Fig 6(9) shows the CRS, Met buoys M1–M5, provinces and headlands named in forecasts

6.15 WEST DENMARK

6.15.1 Gale warnings and forecasts are broadcast on receipt, on request and at 0133, 0533, 0933, 1333, 1733, 2133 UT, in Danish/**English** by remote CRS, callsign *Lyngby Radio:*

Areas, Fig 6(10)	VHF Channels
2 South Baltic	02, 04
3 West Baltic	01, 02, 03, 04, 07, 28
4 The Belts & the Sound	01, 02, 03, 04, 05, 07, 28, 65, 83
5 Kattegat	03, 04, 05, 07, 64, 65, 66, 83
6 Skagerrack	01, 02, 04, 64, 66
8 Fisher	01, 02, 23, 66
9 German Bight	02, 23

Areas 2–5 are north of the Kiel Canal and east of 10°E.
MF: Blåvand 1734 kHz, Skagen 1758 kHz, Skamlebæk 1704 kHz and Rønne 2586 kHz broadcast gale warnings for all areas in Danish/**English** on receipt.

Fig 6(10) Danish forecast areas

KEY:
2 S Baltic
3 W Baltic
4 The Belts and the Sound
5 Kattegat
6 Skagerrak
8 Fisher
9 German Bight

6.15.2 Danmarks Radio, Programme 1

Kalundborg (55°44′N 11°E) broadcasts on MW 1062 kHz:
• Gale warnings, weather reports and forecast for areas 2-6, 8, 9 & 22-25 (Faeroes) at 0545, 0845, 1145, 1745LT.
• A 5 day forecast for areas 2-6, 8 and 9 at 1145 & 1745LT.

6.15.3 Danmarks Meteorologiske Institut (DM)

provides marine forecasts in Danish, **English** and German on www.dmi.dk/dmi/index/

6.16 GERMANY

6.16.1 Deutscher Wetterdienst (DWD)

DWD (German weather service) provides Met info which is updated twice daily; more often for weather reports and text forecasts. SEEWIS (Marine weather information system) allows data to be accessed by telephone/modem and fed into an onboard computer.

DWD ☎ + 49 (0) 40 6690 1851. 🖷 + 49 (0) 40 6690 1946. www.dwd.de   seeschifffahrt@dwd.de.

6.16.2 Traffic Centres

Traffic Centres, Fig 6(11), broadcast local storm warnings, weather bulletins, visibility in German or **English** on request.

Traffic Centre	VHF Ch	Every
German Bight Traffic	80	H+00
Cuxhaven-Elbe Traffic	71 (outer Elbe)	H+35
Brunsbüttel-Elbe Traffic	68 (lower Elbe)	H+05
Kiel Kanal II (E-bound)	02	H+15 & H+45
Kiel Kanal III (W-bound)	03	H+20 & H+50
Bremerhaven-Weser Traffic	02, 04, 05, 07, 21, 22, 82	H+20
Bremen-Weser Traffic	19, 78, 81	H+30
Hunte Traffic	63	H+30
Jade Traffic	20, 63	H+10
Ems Traffic	15, 18, 20, 21	H+50

6.16.3 Coast Radio Stations

DP07 (Seefunk) operates commercial CRS, Fig 6(11), at:

Nordfriesland (Sylt)	Ch 26
Elbe-Weser	Ch 01, 24
Hamburg (Control centre)	Ch 83
Bremen	Ch 25
Accumersiel	Ch 28
Borkum	Ch 61

DP07 broadcasts (only in German): gale and strong wind warnings on receipt. At 0745Ⓐ, 0945, 1245, 1645 and 1945Ⓐ LT for Fisher, German Bight and Humber, DP07 broadcasts:

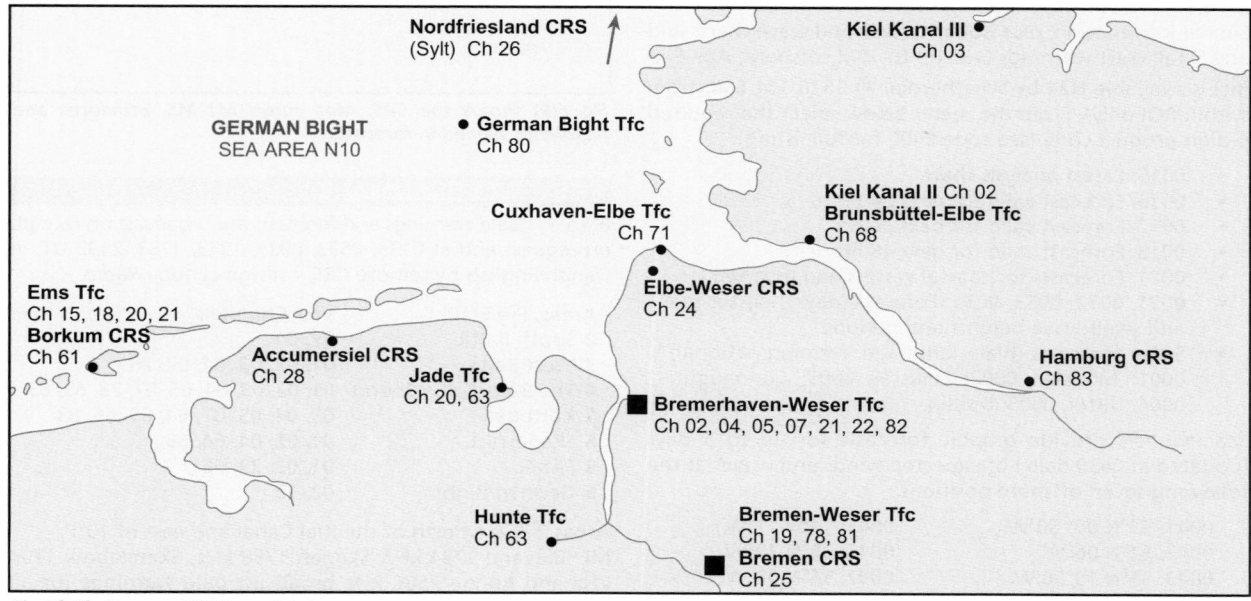

Fig 6(11) German MSI broadcasts

GERMAN BIGHT
SEA AREA N10

Nordfriesland CRS (Sylt) Ch 26

Kiel Kanal III Ch 03

German Bight Tfc Ch 80

Cuxhaven-Elbe Tfc Ch 71

Kiel Kanal II Ch 02
Brunsbüttel-Elbe Tfc Ch 68

Elbe-Weser CRS Ch 24

Ems Tfc Ch 15, 18, 20, 21
Borkum CRS Ch 61

Accumersiel CRS Ch 28

Jade Tfc Ch 20, 63

Bremerhaven-Weser Tfc Ch 02, 04, 05, 07, 21, 22, 82

Hamburg CRS Ch 83

Hunte Tfc Ch 63

Bremen-Weser Tfc Ch 19, 78, 81
Bremen CRS Ch 25

a synopsis, 12hr forecast, 24hrs outlook and coastal station reports. ⒶΑsummer only. Also a 4–5 day outlook for the North Sea (and Baltic) at 0945 and 1645.

6.16.4 Navtex
Pinneberg (S) in **English** on 518kHz and Pinneberg (L) in German on 490 kHz transmit Weather bulletins (and Nav warnings) for German Bight (area N10) at the times listed in 6.3.5.

6.16.5 Radio broadcasting
NDR 1 Welle Nord (FM)
A summary, outlook and wind forecast for the German Bight is broadcast after the news (0600–2200LT at H) and (0530–17300LT at H +30) by: **Sylt** 90·9 MHz; **Helgoland** 88·9 MHz; **Hamburg** 89·5 MHz; **Flensburg** 89·6 MHz; **Heide** 90·5 MHz; **Kiel** 91·3 MHz.

Radio Bremen (MW and FM)
Warnings of extreme weather conditions in German Bight, with potential for corresponding hazards, are broadcast after the news by: **Bremerhaven** 936 kHz; 89·3, 92·1, 95·4 & 100·8 MHz; and by **Bremen** 88·3, 93·8, 96·7 & 101·2 MHz.

6.16.6 HF Radio
Offenbach (Main) Programme 1 broadcasts in **English** on 4583, 7646 and 10100·8 kHz at 0005, 0020, 0305, 0320, 0535, 0550, 0835, 0850, 1135, 1150, 1435, 1450, 1735, 1750, 2035 and 2050 UT: Weather situation, 12 hour forecast and a

further 12 hours outlook for N Sea and Baltic.
At 0355,1530 UT: North Sea weather and 5 day forecasts in **English**. Note: Many other broadcasts are made H24.

6.16.7 Recorded telephone forecasts for yachtsmen
For wind forecast and outlook (1/4–30/9; only within Germany) call ☎ 0900 111 6050 plus two digits as follows:

00	Number for pleasure craft
54	Denmark
55	Netherlands, IJsselmeer, Maas and Schelde
59	Windline latest station reports

For year-round telephone weather synopsis, forecast and outlook, call ☎ 0900 111 6920 plus two digits as follows:

00	General maritime weather
21	North Sea and Baltic
22	German Bight, Fisher and SW North Sea

Call ☎ +49 (0)40 66901209 (H24) for the latest wind warnings (> F6) for individual North Sea areas. If no warning is in force, a wind forecast for the German Bight and W/S Baltic is given.

For **Fax** wind forecast and outlook (1/4–30/9; only within Germany) call 🖷 0900 100 1925 plus two digits as follows:

79	North Frisian Islands and Helgoland
80	R Elbe, Cuxhaven to Hamburg
81	Weser Estuary, Jade Bay and Helgoland
82	East Frisian Islands and Ems Estuary

6.17 THE NETHERLANDS

Fig 6(12) Netherlands MSI broadcasts

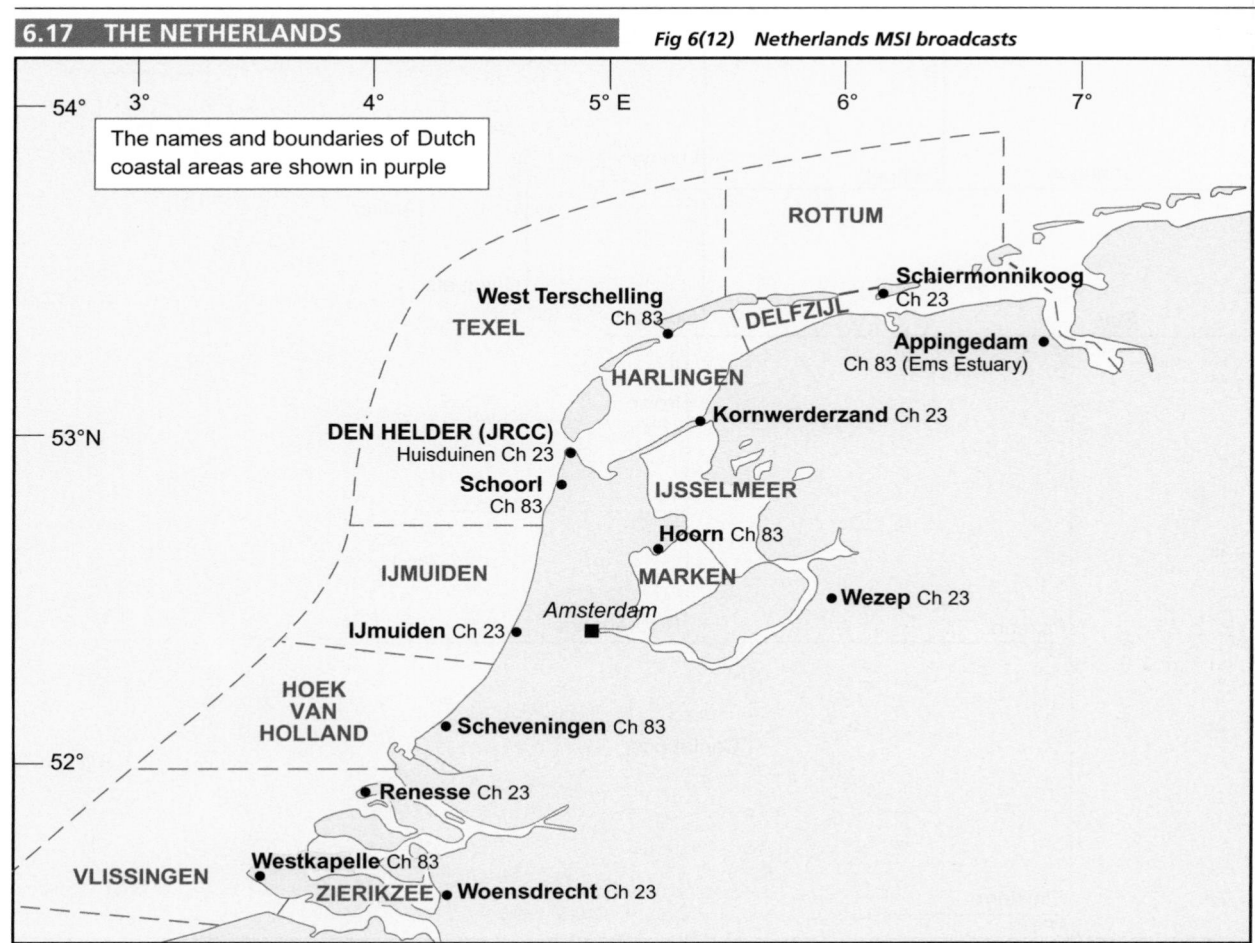

6.17.1 Netherlands Coastguard
VHF MSI broadcasts – Fig 6(12), NE to SW
Forecasts for 7 areas to 30M offshore and 3 inland waterways (IJsselmeer, Marken and Zierikzee) are broadcast in **English** and Dutch at 0805, 1305, 1905, 2305 LT on VHF as shown below, **without** prior announcement on Ch 16 or 70.

> **VHF Ch 23**: Schiermonnikoog, Kornwerderzand, Wezep, Huisduinen (Den Helder), IJmuiden, Renesse, Woensdrecht.
>
> **VHF Ch 83**: Appingedam, West Terschelling, Hoorn, Schoorl, Scheveningen, Westkapelle.
> All stations monitor Ch 16.

Gale warnings are broadcast 0333, 0733, 1133, 1533, 1933 and 2333UT and on receipt.
Ouddorp CG (51°48′N 03°52′E) broadcasts weather info Ch 74, 25 at H+30 and gives radar assistance on request H24.

MF weather broadcasts
Forecasts for Viking, Forties, Dogger, Fisher, German Bight, Humber, Thames and Dover are broadcast by Scheveningen in **English** at 0940 and 2140UT on 3673 kHz. Gale warnings for these areas are broadcast in **English** at 0333, 0733, 1133, 1533, 1933 and 2333UT and on receipt.

6.17.2 Radio Noord-Holland (FM)
Coastal forecasts for northern areas, gale warnings and wind strength are broadcast in Dutch, Mon–Fri at 0730, 0838, 1005, 1230 and 1705LT; Sat/Sun 1005, by:

Wieringermeer 93.9 MHz and **Haarlem** 97.6 MHz.

6.17.3 Omroep Zeeland (FM)
Coastal forecasts for southern areas, synopsis, gale warnings and wind strength are broadcast in Dutch, Mon–Fri at 0715, 0915, 1215 and 1715LT; Sat/Sun 1015, by:

Philippine 97.8 MHz and **Goes** 101.9 MHz.

6.18 BELGIUM
Coast Radio Stations
Oostende Radio, after prior notice on VHF 16, DSC 70 and 2182kHz, broadcasts in **English** and Dutch on VHF 27, MF 2256, 2376 and 2761 kHz: Strong wind warnings on receipt and after the next 2 silent periods. Forecasts for Thames, Dover and the Belgian coast at 0720 LT and 0820, 1720 UT.

Antwerpen Radio broadcasts in **English** and Dutch on VHF Ch 24 for the Schelde estuary: Gale warnings on receipt and at every H+55. Also strong wind warnings (F6+) on receipt and at every H+55.

6.19 FRANCE

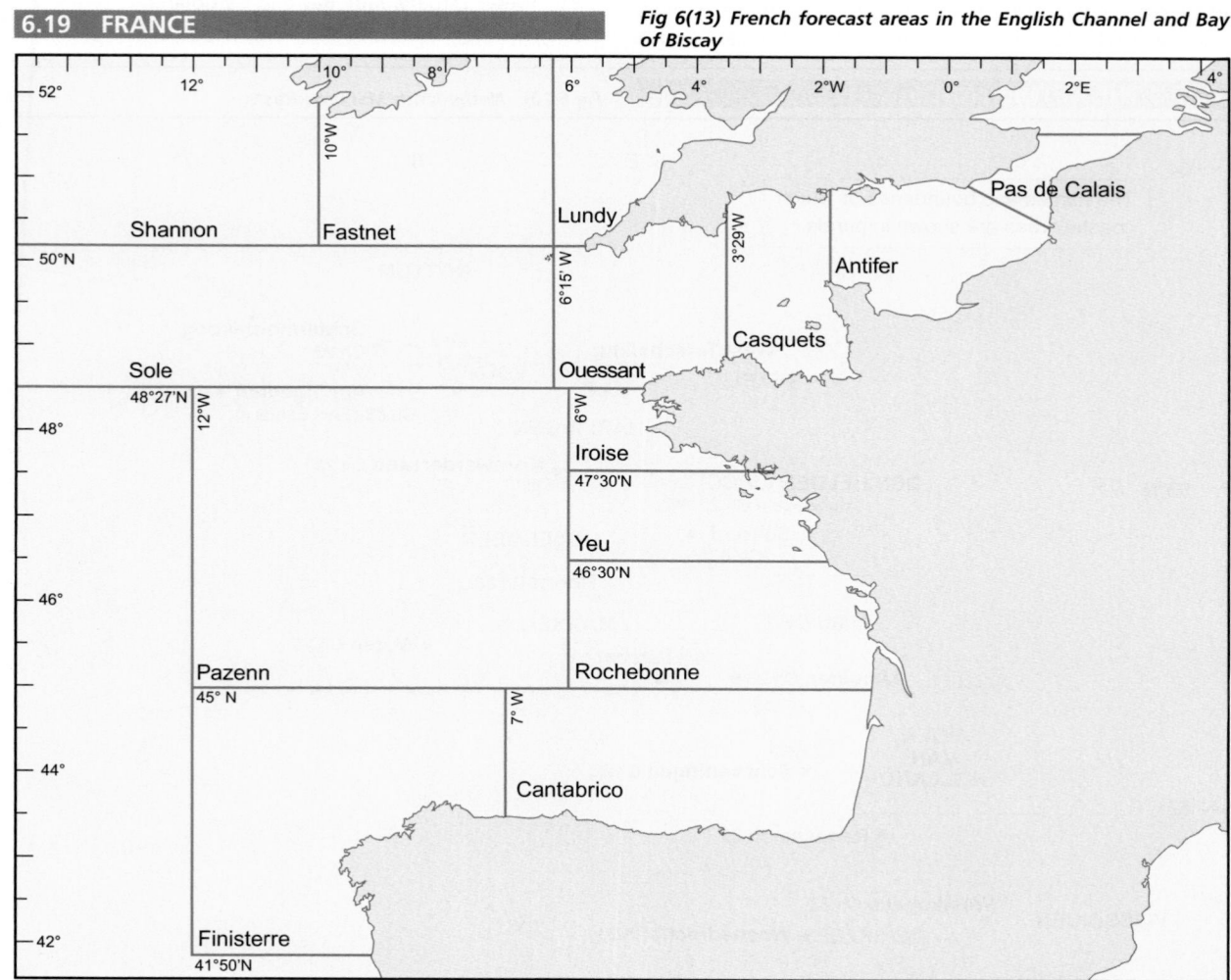

Fig 6(13) French forecast areas in the English Channel and Bay of Biscay

Fig 6(14) Weather broadcasts by CROSS on VHF

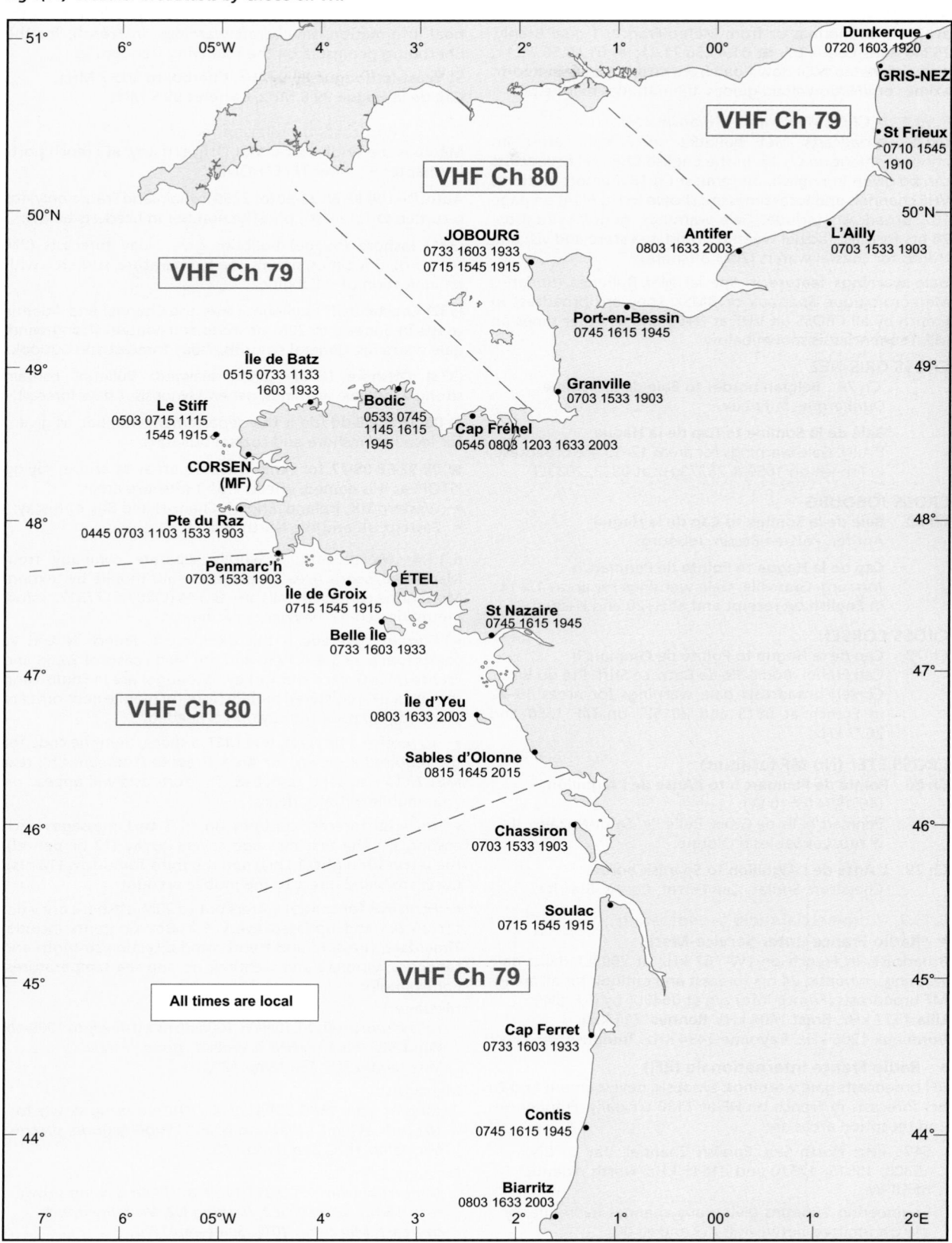

Le Guide Marine, a free annual booklet, summarises how forecasts and met warnings are broadcast or issued. It is available at marinas or from Météo-France, 1 quai Branly, 75340 Paris-Cedex 07. ☎ 01.45.56.71.71; ⊠ 01.45.56.71.11. marine@meteo.fr Or download from http://secours-meteo-fr.axime.com/FR/download/guides_thematiques/marine.pdf

6.19.1   CROSS VHF and MF broadcasts

CROSS broadcasts Met bulletins in French, after an announcement on Ch 16. In the English Channel broadcasts can be given in **English**, on request Ch 16. Remote stations, VHF channels and local times are shown in Fig 6(14) on page 107. Broadcasts include: Gale warnings, general situation, 24 hrs forecast (actual weather, wind, sea state and vis) and trends for coastal waters (20M offshore).

Gale warnings feature in Special Met Bulletins (*Bulletins Météorologique Spéciaux* or *BMS*). They are broadcast in French by all CROSS on VHF at H+03 and at other times on MF frequencies as shown below.

CROSS GRIS-NEZ

Ch 79   Belgian border to Baie de la Somme
Dunkerque. St Frieux.

Baie de la Somme to Cap de la Hague
L'Ailly. Gale warnings for areas 12–13 are broadcast in French on 1650 & 2677 kHz at 0833, 2033LT

CROSS JOBOURG

Ch 80   Baie de la Somme to Cap de la Hague
Antifer. Port-en-Bessin. Jobourg.

Cap de la Hague to Pointe de Penmarc'h
Jobourg. Granville. Gale warnings for areas 13–14 in **English** on receipt and at H+20 and H+50.

CROSS CORSEN

Ch 79   Cap de la Hague to Pointe de Penmarc'h
Cap Fréhel. Bodic. Ile de Batz. Le Stiff. Pte du Raz. Corsen broadcasts gale warnings for areas 13–22 in French at 0815 and 2015LT on MF 1650 and 2677 kHz.

CROSS ÉTEL (No MF facilities)

Ch 80   Pointe de Penmarc'h to l'Anse de l'Aiguillon
(46°15'N 01°10'W).
Penmarc'h. Ile de Groix. Belle Ile. Saint-Nazaire. Ile d'Yeu. Les Sables d'Olonne.

Ch 79   L'Anse de l'Aiguillon to Spanish border
Chassiron. Soulac. Cap Ferret. Contis. Biarritz.

6.19.2   Commercial radio broadcasting

• **Radio France (Inter-Service-Mer)**
Broadcasts in French on LW 162 kHz at 2003LT daily: gale warnings, synopsis, 24 hrs forecast and outlook for all areas. MF broadcasts (France Info) are at 0640LT by (NE–SW):
Lille 1377 kHz. **Brest** 1404 kHz. **Rennes** 711 kHz
Bordeaux 1206 kHz. **Bayonne** 1494 kHz. **Toulouse** 945 kHz.

• **Radio France Internationale (RFI)**
RFI broadcasts gale warnings, synopsis, development and 24 hrs forecasts in French on HF at 1130 UT daily. Frequencies and reception areas are:

6175 kHz: North Sea, English Channel, Bay of Biscay. 15300, 15515, 17570 and 21645 kHz: North Atlantic, E of 50°W.
Engineering bulletins giving any changes in frequency are transmitted between H+53 and H+00.

• **Radio France Cherbourg** broadcasts 7/7 at 0829 LT: Coastal forecast, gale warnings, visibility, wind strength, tidal information, small craft warnings, in French, for the Cherbourg peninsula on the following frequencies:
St Vaast-la-Hougue 85·0 MHz. **Cherbourg** 100·7 MHz. **Cap de la Hague** 99·8 MHz. **Carteret** 99·9 MHz.

6.19.3   Forecasts by telephone

Météo is the ☎ of a local Met Office, if any, at French ports in Chapter 9, under TELEPHONE.

Auto: Dial 08·92·68·32·50 (or 3250 in mainland France only) for recorded ☎ forecasts, plus the number in brackets below:

(331) Inshore (*rivage*) bulletins give 7-day forecasts (2M seaward), tide times, signals, sea temperature, surf etc – with an indication of reliability.

(332) Coastal (*côte*) bulletins cover the Channel and Atlantic coasts in 5 areas, to 20M offshore and contain strong wind/gale warnings, general synopsis, 7-day forecast and outlook.

(333) Offshore (*large*, 200M seaward) bulletins contain strong wind/gale warnings, general synopsis, 7 days forecast.

☎ 08·92·68·08·dd (dd is the *département* number, as given) for localised inshore and coastal bulletins.

☎ 08·92·68·08·77 for same offshore areas as above; saying 'STOP' as it is named, selects 1 of 3 offshore areas:
• Western UK, Ireland, English Channel and Bay of Biscay;
• Eastern UK and the North Sea.

6.19.4   Metmarine, a wholly separate company from Marinecall, sends Area forecasts to your mobile by texting. Metmarine contact details are: ☎ +44 (0)207 6177817; info@metmarine.com   www.metmarine.com

• Current coverage is the UK S coast, French N and W coasts (see 6.19.5 & 6.19.6) and the Med coasts of Spain and France (plus Greece and Turkey). Messages are in English and require a UK-registered mobile (foreign mobile networks are planned); no prior registration is needed.

• To receive a forecast, text MET, a space, then the code for the required area; eg, for Area 'Brest to Ploumanac'h', text MET FR13 and send to 80818. The forecasts will appear on your mobile without delay.

• An area forecast contains up to 3 text messages each costing £1: the first message covers Today (12 hr period), the second Tonight (12 hrs) and the third Tomorrow (12 hrs). Costs are billed direct to the mobile account.

• Forecasts for coastal waters out to 20M offshore are valid for 36 hrs and updated every 6 hours. Contents include: Time/date; pressure and trend; wind direction/strength and tendency; visibility and weather; air and sea temperatures. For example:

Message 1
Today from 0700 BST 10/9/08. 1008mb rising slowly to 1009mb. Wind NE2, backing NNE2. Visibility good, drizzle. Max temp 23°C. Sea temp 17°C.

Message 2
Tonight from 1900 BST 10/9/08. 1011mb rising slowly to 1012mb. Wind E1, backing NNE2. Visibility good, drizzle. Min temp 16°C. Sea temp 17°C.

Message 3
Tomorrow from 0700 BST 11/9/08. 1014mb rising slowly to 1016mb. Wind NNE2, backing N2. Visibility good, overcast. Min temp 20°C. Sea temp 17°C.

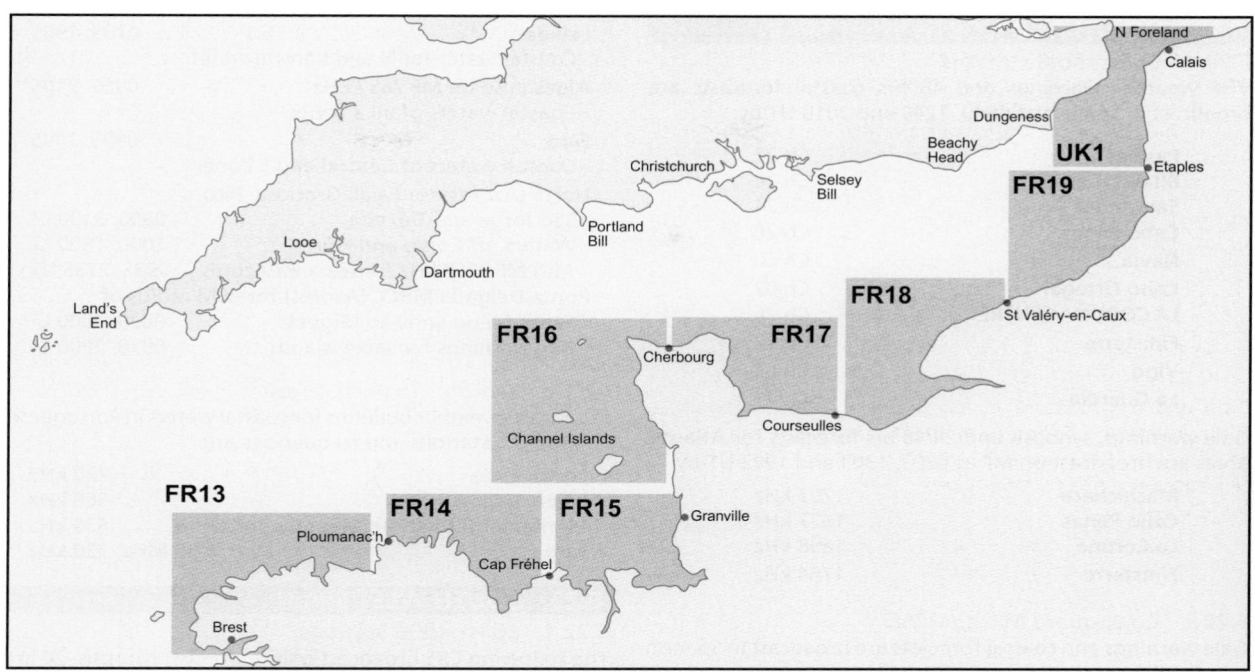

Fig 6(15) Forecast areas along the N coast of France

6.20.5 Metmarine forecasts by mobile phone

To request a forecast, text MET followed by a space before the code for the required area; then send it to 80818, whether you are in the UK or abroad. For example, to obtain Area 'Channel Islands to Cherbourg', text MET FR16 and send to 80818. The forecasts will appear on your mobile without delay.

The **N coast of France** is divided, west to east, into 7 Areas with codes and boundaries listed below and shown on Fig 6(15):

Code	Boundaries
FR13	Brest to Ploumanac'h
FR14	Ploumanac'h to Cap Fréhel
FR15	Cap Fréhel to Granville
FR16	Channel Islands to Cherbourg
FR17	Cherbourg to Courseulles
FR18	Courseulles to St Valéry-en-Caux
FR19	St Valéry-en-Caux to Étaples
UK1	Étaples to Calais

The **W coast of France** is divided, south to north, into 7 Areas with codes and boundaries listed below and shown on Fig 6(16).

Code	Boundaries
FR6	Spanish border to Arcachon
FR7	Arcachon to Pointe de Grave
FR8	Pointe de Grave to Les Sables d'Olonne
FR9	Les Sables d'Olonne to Pointe de Croisic
FR10	Pointe de Croisic to Lorient
FR11	Lorient to Pointe de Penmarc'h
FR12	Pointe de Penmarc'h to Brest

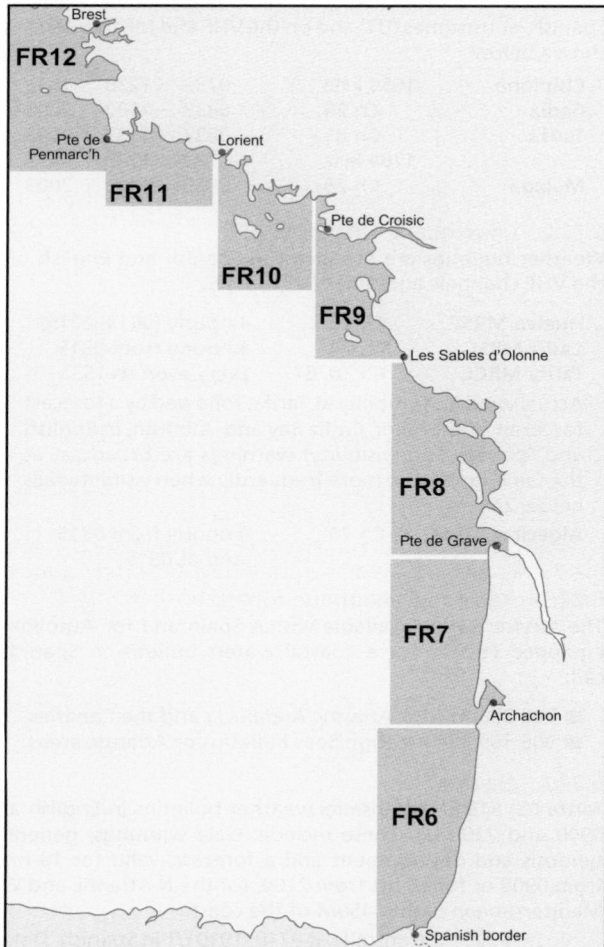

Fig 6(16) Forecast areas along the west coast of France

6.20 NORTH AND NORTH WEST SPAIN

6.20.1 Coast radio stations

VHF weather warnings and 48 hrs coastal forecasts are broadcast in Spanish at 0840, 1240 and 2010 UT by:

Pasajes	Ch 27
BILBAO CENTRE	Ch 26
Santander	Ch 24
Cabo Peñas	Ch 26
Navia	Ch 60
Cabo Ortegal	Ch 02
LA CORUÑA CENTRE	Ch 26
Finisterre	Ch 22
Vigo	Ch 65
La Guardia	Ch 21

Gale warnings, synopsis and 24/48 hrs forecasts for Atlantic areas are broadcast on MF at 0703, 1303 and 1903 UT by:

Machichaco	1707 kHz
Cabo Peñas	1677 kHz
La Coruña	1698 kHz
Finisterre	1764 kHz

6.20.2 Coastguard MRCC/MRSC

Gale warnings and coastal forecasts are broadcast in Spanish and **English** on receipt and as listed below:

Bilbao MRCC*	Ch 10	4 hrly from 0033, except 1633
Santander MRSC	Ch 74	0245, 0445, 0645, 0845,
		1045, 1445, 1845, 2245
Gijón MRCC	Ch 10	2 hrly (0215–2215)
Coruña MRSC	Ch 10	4 hrly from 0005
Finisterre MRCC	Ch 11	4 hrly from 0233
Vigo MRSC	Ch 10	4 hrly from 0015

*Bilbao also broadcasts High Seas gale warnings and forecasts at 0233, 0633, 1033, 1433, 1833 & 2233 UT.

6.20.3 Navtex

Coruna (D) 518 kHz transmits at 0830, 2030 UT. Coruna (W) 490 kHz transmits at 1140, 1940 UT in Spanish. Data for the next 18–36 hrs is valid to 450M offshore; see 6.3.5.

6.20.4 Radio Nacional de España (MW)

Broadcasts storm warnings, synopsis and 12 hrs or 18 hrs forecasts for Cantábrico and Galicia at 1100, 1400, 1800 & 2200 LT in Spanish. Stations/frequencies are:

San Sebastián	774 kHz	Bilbao	639 kHz
Santander	855 kHz	Oviedo	729 kHz
La Coruña	639 kHz		

6.20.5 Recorded telephone forecasts

This service is only available within Spain and for vessels equipped with Autolink. For a recorded weather bulletin in Spanish, call:

☎ 906 365 372 for the coasts of Cantábrico and Galicia.
☎ 906 365 374 for High Seas bulletins; Fig 6(18).

6.21 PORTUGAL AND THE AZORES

6.21.1 Radionaval Portugal weather broadcasts

Broadcasts in Portuguese and **English** are on Ch 11 at the times (UT) listed below. They contain: Storm, gale and poor visibility warnings; synopsis and 24 hrs forecasts for three coastal zones out to 20M offshore; see Fig 6(17):

Leixões	0705, 1905
Coastal waters of N and Central zones.	
Alges (also on MF 2657 kHz)	0905, 2105
Coastal waters of all 3 zones.	
Faro	0805, 2005
Coastal waters of Central and S Zones.	
Horta (Azores) for Faial, Graciosa, Pico,	
São Jorge and Terceira	0900, 2100 LT
Waters off Corvo and Flores	1000, 1900 LT
Also MF 2657 kHz for sea area Azores	0935, 2135 UT
Ponta Delgada MRCC (Azores) for 20M radius of	
Santa Maria and São Miguel	0830, 2000 LT
Nav warnings for same islands	0830, 2000 LT

6.21.2 Radiofusão Portuguesa

Broadcasts weather bulletins for coastal waters in Portuguese at 1100 UT. Stations and frequencies are:

Porto, Elvas	720 kHz
Viseu, Lisboa 1	666 kHz
Montemer (Coimbra), Miranda do Douro	630 kHz
Faro	97·6 MHz, 720 kHz

6.22 SOUTH WEST SPAIN

6.22.1 Coast radio stations

The following CRS broadcast gale warnings, synopsis, 24 hrs and 48 hrs forecasts for Atlantic and Mediterranean areas, in Spanish, at the times (UT) and on the VHF and MF frequencies shown below:

Chipiona	1656 kHz	0733	1233	1933
Cadiz	Ch 26	0833	1133	2003
Tarifa	Ch 81	0833	1133	2003
	1704 kHz	0733	1233	1933
Malaga	Ch 26	0833	1133	2003

6.22.2 Coastguard MRCC/MRSC

Weather bulletins are broadcast in Spanish and **English** on the VHF channels and times (UT) below:

Huelva MRSC	Ch 10	4 hourly (0415–2015)
Cadiz MRSC	Ch 74	4 hourly from 0315
Tarifa MRCC	Ch 10, 67	Every even H+15.

Actual wind and visibility at Tarifa, followed by a forecast for Strait of Gibraltar, Cádiz Bay and Alborán, in **English** and Spanish. Fog (visibility) warnings are broadcast at the same times, and more frequently when visibility falls below 2M.

Algeciras MRSC	Ch 74	4 hourly from 0315
		and at 0515.

6.22.3 Recorded telephone forecasts

The service is only available within Spain and for Autolink-equipped vessels. For a coastal waters bulletin in Spanish call:

☎ 906 365 373 for Atlantic Andalucia and the Canaries.
☎ 906 365 374 for High Seas bulletin for Atlantic areas.

6.22.4 Navtex

Tarifa (G) 518 kHz transmits weather bulletins in English at 0900 and 2100 UT. These include: Gale warnings, general synopsis and development and a forecast, valid for 18 hrs from 0900 or for 36 hrs from 2100, for the N Atlantic and W Mediterranean within 450M of the coast.

Tarifa (T) 490 kHz transmits at 0710, 1910 UT in Spanish. Data for the next 18–36 hrs is valid to 450M offshore; see 6.3.5.

Fig 6(17) Spain and Portugal: MSI broadcasts by CRS and MRCCs/MRSCs (all times UT)

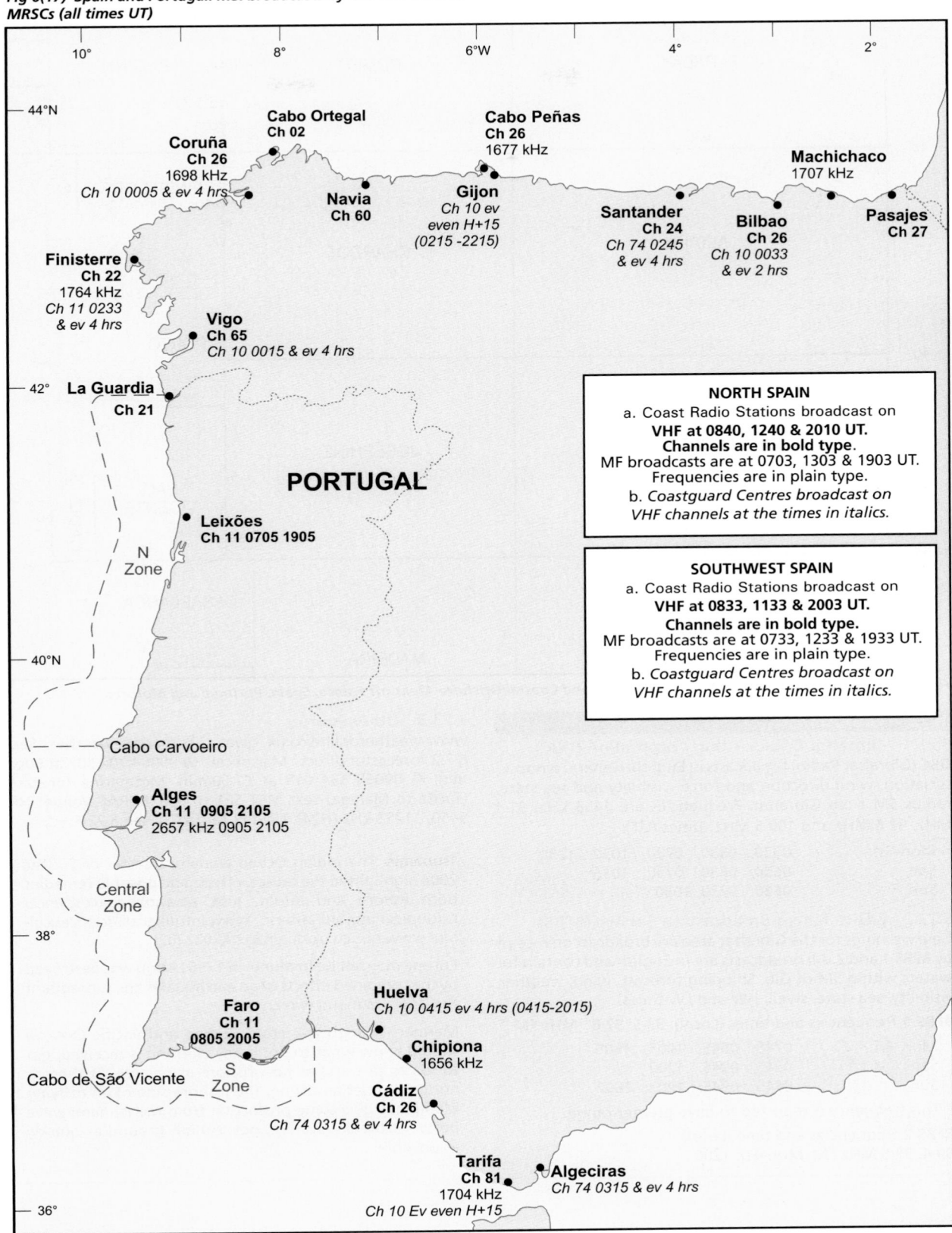

Map labels:

Cabo Ortegal
Ch 02

Cabo Peñas
Ch 26
1677 kHz

Coruña
Ch 26
1698 kHz
Ch 10 0005 & ev 4 hrs

Machichaco
1707 kHz

Navia
Ch 60

Gijon
Ch 10 ev even H+15 (0215 -2215)

Santander
Ch 24
Ch 74 0245 & ev 4 hrs

Bilbao
Ch 26
Ch 10 0033 & ev 2 hrs

Pasajes
Ch 27

Finisterre
Ch 22
1764 kHz
Ch 11 0233 & ev 4 hrs

Vigo
Ch 65
Ch 10 0015 & ev 4 hrs

La Guardia
Ch 21

PORTUGAL

N Zone

Leixões
Ch 11 0705 1905

Cabo Carvoeiro

Alges
Ch 11 0905 2105
2657 kHz 0905 2105

Central Zone

Cabo de São Vicente

Faro
Ch 11
0805 2005

S Zone

Huelva
Ch 10 0415 ev 4 hrs (0415-2015)

Chipiona
1656 kHz

Cádiz
Ch 26
Ch 74 0315 & ev 4 hrs

Tarifa
Ch 81
1704 kHz
Ch 10 Ev even H+15

Algeciras
Ch 74 0315 & ev 4 hrs

Boxes:

NORTH SPAIN
a. Coast Radio Stations broadcast on
VHF at 0840, 1240 & 2010 UT.
Channels are in bold type.
MF broadcasts are at 0703, 1303 & 1903 UT.
Frequencies are in plain type.
b. *Coastguard Centres broadcast on VHF channels at the times in italics.*

SOUTHWEST SPAIN
a. Coast Radio Stations broadcast on
VHF at 0833, 1133 & 2003 UT.
Channels are in bold type.
MF broadcasts are at 0733, 1233 & 1933 UT.
Frequencies are in plain type.
b. *Coastguard Centres broadcast on VHF channels at the times in italics.*

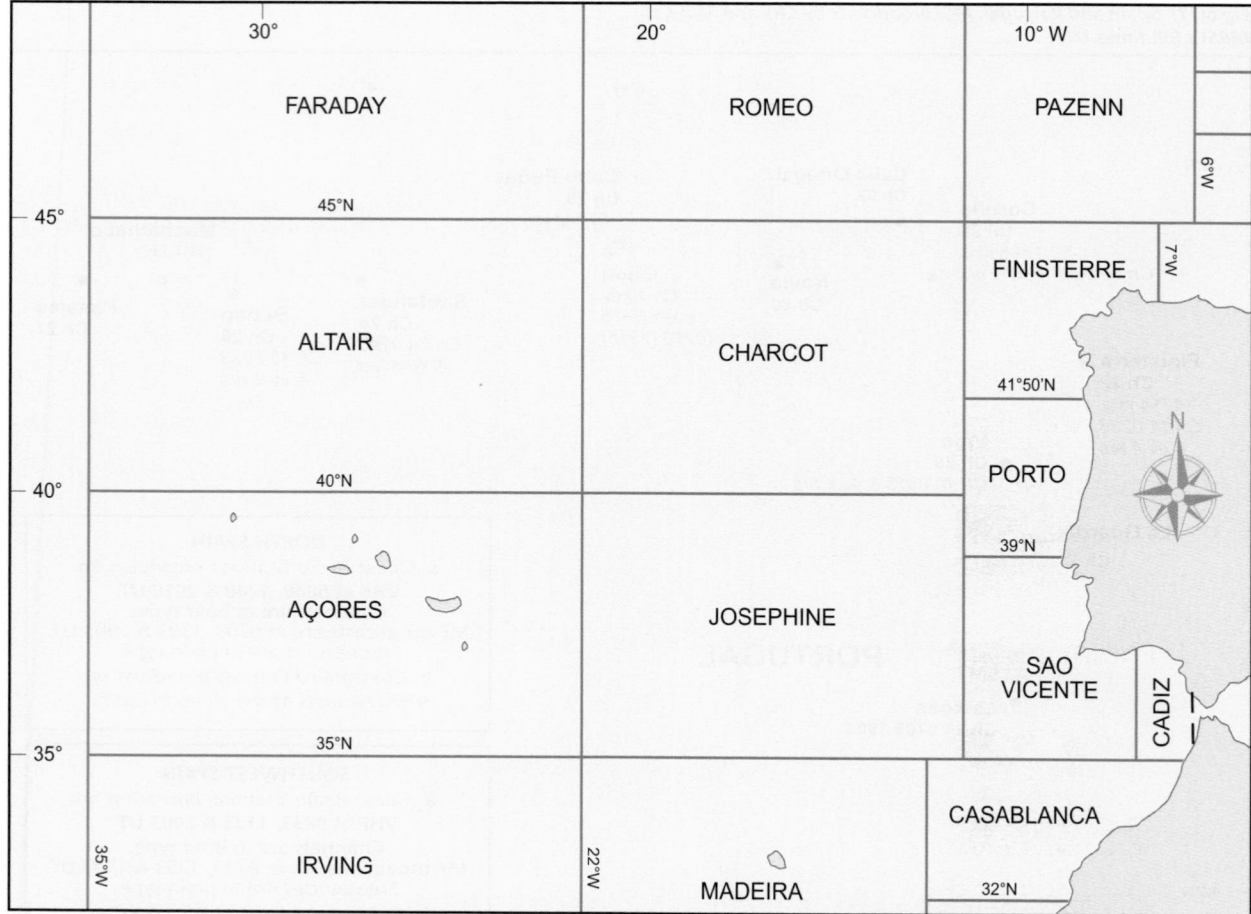

Fig 6(18) Forecast areas for Met Area II: High Seas and Coastal/Offshore Areas off France, Spain, Portugal and Morocco

6.23 GIBRALTAR

6.23.1 Gibraltar Broadcasting Corporation (GBC)

GBC (Gibraltar Radio) broadcasts in English: General synopsis, situation, wind direction and force, visibility and sea state, radius 5M from Gibraltar. Frequencies are 1458 kHz, 91·3 MHz, 92·6 MHz and 100·5 MHz. Times (UT):

Mon–Fri:	0530, 0630, 0730, 1030, 1230
Sat:	0530, 0630, 0730, 1030
Sun:	0630, 0730, 1030

6.23.2 British Forces Broadcasting Service (BFBS)

Gale warnings for the Gibraltar area are broadcast on receipt by BFBS 1 and 2. All broadcasts are in English and contain for waters within 5M of Gib: Shipping forecast, wind, weather, visibility, sea state, swell, HW and LW times.

BFBS 1 frequencies and times (Local): 93·5, 97·8* MHz FM.

Mon–Fri:	0745, 0845, 1005, 1605
Sat:	0845, 0945, 1202
Sun:	0845, 0945, 1202, 1602

* This frequency is reported to have greater range.

BFBS 2 frequencies and time (Local):
89·4, 99·5 MHz FM. Mon–Fri: 1200.

6.23.3 Other sources

www.weatheronline.co.uk gives Gib marine weather. See 6.7.2 forecaster direct. Marinecall ☎ 09064 702 507 at 60p/min; 🖷 09065 534 013 at £1.50/min. Metmarine forecast (Tarifa to Malaga) text MET SP1 to 80818. RAF Volmet HF 5450, 11253 kHz (H24). Navtex Tarifa (G), see 6.22.4.

Tsunamis. The Indian Ocean tsunami disaster of 26 Dec 2004 highlighted the causes, effects and possible remedies both ashore and afloat. Visit www.bbc.co.uk/science/hottopics/naturaldisasters; www.intute.ac.uk/sciences/cgi-bin/ www.bbc.co.uk/dna/h2g2/A3022282

Europe may not be immune. In 1755 Lisbon was destroyed by the combined effects of an earthquake, the subsequent fire and a tsunami wave.

Mariners in high risk areas (Indian and Pacific Oceans) should know what to do: if any warning is received, get to sea as fast and as far offshore as possible. If there is no time to get an offing, the inshore side of an offlying island may give some protection from the tsunami wave before it breaks. Ashore, get to high ground as quickly as possible.

7

Safety

Safety

TABLE 7(1) This is a precis of recommended safety equipment which should be carried, based on the categories in 7.2.1. A bullet (•) recommends that the item be carried, but the number, method or contents is left to the judgement of the skipper.

	CATEGORY	A	B	C	D
1	**Means of propulsion** (Sailing yachts only)				
1.2	A storm trisail or deep reef to reduce the mainsail area by at least 40%	•	•	•	
1.3	For engine starting, a battery isolated from all other electrical systems or hand cranking	•	•	•	
2	**Number of anchors**, with appropriate lengths/diameter of warp & chain or chain only	2+	2	2	1
3	**Bailing and bilge pumping**				
3.2	Buckets of 9–14 ltrs capacity with lanyard and strongly secured handle	2	2	2	
3.3	Hand bilge pumps discharging overboard and operable with all hatches closed	2	2	1	
3.4	Softwood bungs attached adjacent to all through-hull fittings (able to be closed)	•	•	•	•
4	**Detection equipment**				
4.1	Radar reflector properly mounted and with as large a radar cross-section as is reasonable	•	•	•	•
4.2	Fixed nav lights complying with IRPCS. 4.3 Foghorn. 4.4 Powerful torch ('steamer scarer')	•	•	•	•
	Motoring cone (sail only); anchor ball and light	•	•	•	
5	**Pyrotechnics** (in date)				
5.1	Hand-held red flares)	6	4	4	2
5.2	Buoyant orange smoke signals) to SOLAS standards	2	2		
5.3	Red parachute rockets)	12	4	2	
5.4	Hand-held orange smoke signals			2	2
5.5	Hand-held white flares (not available world-wide)	4	4	4	
6	**Fire fighting equipment**				
6.1	Fire blanket (BS EN 1869) for all yachts with cooking equipment	•	•	•	•
6.2	For yachts with a galley or carrying engine fuel: multi-purpose extinguishers of minimum fire rating 5A/34B to BS EN 3	3	2	1	1
6.3	Additionally, for yachts with both a galley and carrying engine fuel: multi-purpose extinguishers of minimum fire rating 5A/34B to BS EN 3	1	1	1	1
6.4	Additionally, for yachts with engines over 25hp, a fixed automatic or semi-automatic fire fighting system to discharge into the engine space	•	•	•	•
7	**Personal safety equipment for each crew member**				
7.1	Warm clothing, oilskins, seaboots and hat	•	•	•	•
7.2	Lifejacket or buoyancy aid (BS EN 395) 100 Newtons				1
7.3	Lifejacket (BS EN 396) 150 Newtons	1	1	1	
7.4	Lifejacket light. 7.5 Spray face cover	1	1		
7.6	Safety harness (for yachts with enclosed wheelhouse, one harness each for 50% of the crew)	1	1	1	
7.7	Immersion suit – per crew member	1			
7.8	Jackstays and cockpit clip-on strong points	•	•	•	
8	**Liferaft**				
8.1	Liferaft, designed solely for saving life, sufficient to carry all on board	1	1	1	
8.2	Emergency grab bag (see text for contents)	1	1	1	
9	**Man overboard recovery equipment**				
9.1	Horseshoe lifebelts fitted with drogue and self-igniting light	2	2	1	
9.2	Buoyant sling on floating line – may replace 1 horseshoe lifebelt if 2 are carried	1	1		
9.3	Buoyant heaving line, at least 30m long, with quoit	1	1	1	
9.4	Boarding ladder capable of rapid and secure attachment	1	1	1	
9.5	Dan buoy with a large flag	1	1		
10	**Radio**				
10.1	Radio receiver able to receive shipping forecasts on 198 kHz and local radio station forecasts	1	1	1	1
10.2	VHF Marine band radio telephone. 10.9 Waterproof hand-held VHF radio	1	1	1	1
10.3	Digital Selective Calling (DSC) controller to R&TTE directive standards. 10.6 Navtex	1	1	1	
10.4	Marine band HF/SSB radio and/or global SatCom system.	1			
10.5	406 MHz EPIRB. 10.7 SART	1			
10.8	Emergency VHF radio aerial with prepared deck mounting	1	1		
11	**Navigational equipment**				
11.2	Charts, tide tables and navigational publications of the cruising area and adjacent areas	•	•	•	
11.3	Steering compass, able to be lit at night.	1	1	1	1
11.4	Hand-bearing compass	•	•	•	
11.5	Navigational drawing instruments. 11.6 Barometer. 11.7 Lead line & echosounder	1	1	1	
11.8	Radio navigation system, eg GPS. 11.9 Watch or clock	1	1	1	1
11.10	Distance measuring log. 11.11 Binoculars	1	1	1	
11.12	Sextant and tables	1			
12	**First aid kit and manual** (see Chapter 8, 8.27 and 8.31)	1	1	1	1
13	**General equipment**				
13.1	Emergency tiller on all wheel-steered vessels	1	1	1	1
13.2	Towing warp. 13.10 Bosun's chair (sit harness BS EN 813 1997)	1	1	1	
13.3	Mooring warps and fenders	•	•	•	•
13.4	Waterproof torch	3	2	2	1
13.5	Rigid or inflatable tender	•	•	•	
13.6	Repair tools. 13.7 Spares for engine & electrics and bosun's bag of shackles and twine	•	•	•	•
13.8	Emergency water supply, isolated from main tanks		•	•	
13.9	Emergency repair materials		•	•	

7.1 THINK ABOUT SAFETY – IN FOG

It is evident that some commercial vessels at times substantially exceed what may be deemed a safe speed in reduced visibility and, for engineering reasons, may not immediately be able to reduce speed significantly. Small craft skippers should take this into account when deciding what avoiding action to take. Crossing close ahead of a large ship, even in good visibility, is inadvisable; in fog it becomes foolhardy because a small craft's radar (and/or operator) may not be able to resolve the large ship's course and speed with an acceptable degree of accuracy.

It is therefore essential to have an instinctive knowledge of Rule 19 (Conduct of vessels in restricted visibility), and to thoroughly familiarise yourself with your radar. Plenty of practice in good visibility will help to make sure that you are able to recognise potentially dangerous situations, as seen on radar, and to take the correct avoiding action.

7.1.1 Training

If you are new to radar, carefully read the manufacturer's handbook before attending an approved (eg RYA) radar course. Then go to sea with a knowledgeable mentor and apply what you have learned using your own radar set. Thereafter, as advised above, practise using your radar in good visibility whenever you can. A competent crew member in the cockpit helping you to relate what you see on the screen to reality – and for safety – is invaluable.

With experience, you should be able to track about three contacts simultaneously, determining if a close quarters situation is developing and/or if risk of collision exists. This requires careful plotting, preferably on a paper plotting sheet, of each contact at regular intervals. Keep plotting until each contact is finally clear.

7.1.2 Knowledge

What you decide largely depends on a thorough understanding of Rule 19. This rule is complex in that:

• It differs markedly from Rules 11–18 (Conduct of vessels in sight of one another) which clearly distinguish between stand-on and give-way vessels.

• It contains no such distinction; every vessel should keep clear of others.

• Rules 19d (i) & (ii) state what avoiding actions should *not* be taken, leaving the mariner to infer what more positive options are open to him. Simply stated, these boil down to:

Alter to starboard for all vessels *except* for those on or abaft your starboard beam.

7.2 SAFETY EQUIPMENT

Although non-commercial leisure craft of less than 13·7m LOA are not obliged to carry any specific life saving or firefighting equipment, SOLAS V requires *all* vessels to: plan each passage (see Chapter 3); carry a radar reflector if practicable; have access to a table of life-saving signals (Figs 7(1) and (2)); report serious hazards to navigation (if not already reported); respond to any distress signals. It is commonsense to carry more gear than the bare minimum. Table 7(1) offers a more detailed list.

7.2.1 Recommended safety equipment for seagoing vessels < 13·7m LOA

The minimum safety equipment to be carried depends on LOA, the area in which you are cruising and the risk of being caught out in heavy weather. Based on these parameters yachts are categorised as follows:

A Ocean Ocean passages of any length. LOA is likely to be longer than 10m.

B Offshore Yachts which make offshore passages of 50–500M around the UK and NW Europe. LOA is likely to be 8–13.7m.

C Inshore Coastal cruises by day/night, within 10M of land and 4 hours of a port of refuge. LOA is likely to be less than 8m.

D Sheltered In estuaries, inshore or inland waters, day only. Within 1 hour of a port of refuge. LOA is likely to be less than 6m.

Table 7(1) lists the equipment recommended for each of these four categories.

7.3 DEFINITIONS OF EMERGENCY

7.3.1 Distress (MAYDAY)

Distress applies to any situation where a vessel or person is in *grave and imminent danger and requires immediate assistance*. The radio prefix used with a Distress message is MAYDAY. A Distress call has priority over all other transmissions.

7.3.2 Urgency (PAN PAN)

Urgency applies to a *very urgent message concerning the safety of a vessel or person*. For example, for a vessel disabled but not sinking, or for an urgent medical problem. The radio prefix associated with an Urgency message is PAN PAN. An Urgency call has priority over all other transmissons except Distress.

7.3.3 Safety (SÉCURITÉ)

A Safety message is usually associated with a notification of a navigational hazard or meteorological warning. The radio prefix used with a Safety message is SÉCURITÉ.

7.4 DISTRESS SIGNALS BY RADIO

A distress call may only be made with the skipper's authority, and only if the boat or a person is in grave and imminent danger. A distress call may also be made on behalf of another vessel which is unable to make her own call. A man overboard will usually justify a Distress call.

7.4.1 MAYDAY calls

A MAYDAY call by voice should usually be sent on VHF Ch 16 or 2182 kHz, but any frequency may be used if help would thus be obtained more quickly. See 7.9.4 for Distress alerts on VHF DSC Ch 70 or MF DSC 2187·5 kHz.

Distress, Urgency and Safety messages from vessels at sea are free of charge. A Distress call has priority over all other transmissions. If you hear a MAYDAY call, immediately cease all transmissions that may interfere with the call, listen on the frequency concerned, and note down the details.

Brief your crew so they are all able to send a Distress message. The MAYDAY message format (next page) should be displayed near the radio. Before making the call:

• Check main battery switch ON
• Switch radio ON and select HIGH power (25 watts)
• Select VHF Ch 16 (or 2182 kHz for MF)
• Press and hold down the transmit button, and say slowly and distinctly:

- **MAYDAY MAYDAY MAYDAY**
- **THIS IS** ....
  (name of boat, spoken three times)
- **MAYDAY** ....
  (name of boat spoken once)
- **MY POSITION IS** ....
  (latitude and longitude, true bearing and distance .
  from a known point, or general location)
- **Nature of distress** ....
  (sinking, on fire etc)
- **Help required** ....
  (immediate assistance)
- **Number of persons on board** ....
- **Any other important, helpful information** ....
  (you are taking to the liferaft; distress rockets are ..
  being fired etc)
- **OVER**

On completion of the Distress message, release the transmit button and listen. The boat's position is of vital importance and should be repeated if time allows.

Vessels with GMDSS equipment should make a MAYDAY call by voice on Ch 16 *after* sending a DSC Distress alert on VHF Ch 70 or MF 2187·5 kHz; see 7.9.5.

7.4.2   MAYDAY acknowledgement
In coastal waters an immediate acknowledgement should be expected, as follows:

> **MAYDAY** ....
> (name of vessel sending the Distress message, spoken three times)
> **THIS IS** ....
> (name of station acknowledging, spoken three times)
> **RECEIVED MAYDAY**

If an acknowledgement is not received, check the set and repeat the Distress call.

If you hear a Distress message, write down the details and, if you can help, acknowledge accordingly – but only after giving an opportunity for the nearest Coastguard station or more suitable vessel to do so.

7.4.3   MAYDAY relay
If you hear a Distress message from a vessel, and it is not acknowledged, you should pass on the message as follows:

> **MAYDAY RELAY** ....
> (spoken three times)
> **THIS IS** ....
> (name of vessel re-transmitting the Distress message, spoken three times), followed by the intercepted message.

7.4.4   Control of MAYDAY traffic
A MAYDAY call imposes general radio silence until the vessel concerned or some other authority (eg the nearest Coastguard) cancels the Distress. If necessary the station controlling Distress traffic may impose radio silence as follows:

> **SEELONCE MAYDAY,** followed by its name or other identification, on the Distress frequency.
>
> If some other station nearby believes it necessary to do likewise, it may transmit:

SEELONCE DISTRESS, followed by its name or other identification.

7.4.5   Relaxing radio silence
When complete radio silence is no longer necessary on the frequency being used for Distress traffic, the controlling station may relax radio silence (indicating that restricted working may be resumed) as follows:

> **MAYDAY**
> **ALL STATIONS, ALL STATIONS, ALL STATIONS**
> **THIS IS** ....
> (name or callsign)
> Time ....
> Name of the vessel in distress..
> **PRUDONCE**

Normal working on a Distress frequency may then be resumed, having listened carefully before transmitting. Subsequent calls from the casualty should be prefixed by the Urgency signal (7.5.1).

If Distress working continues on other frequencies these will be identified. For example, PRUDONCE on 2182 kHz, but SEELONCE on VHF Ch 16.

7.4.6   Cancelling radio silence
When the problem is resolved, the Distress call must be cancelled by the co-ordinating station using the prowords SEELONCE FEENEE as follows:

> **MAYDAY**
> **ALL STATIONS, ALL STATIONS, ALL STATIONS**
> **THIS IS** ....
> (name or callsign)
> The time ....
> The name of the vessel in distress ....
> **SEELONCE FEENEE**

7.5   URGENCY AND SAFETY SIGNALS

7.5.1   PAN PAN – Urgency signal
The radio Urgency prefix, consisting of the words PAN PAN spoken three times, indicates that a vessel or station has a very urgent message concerning the safety of a ship or person. It may be used when urgent medical advice is needed (7.5.3).

This is an example of an Urgency call:

> **PAN PAN, PAN PAN, PAN PAN**
> **ALL STATIONS, ALL STATIONS, ALL STATIONS**
> **THIS IS YACHT SEABIRD, SEABIRD, SEABIRD**
> Two nine zero degrees Needles lighthouse two miles
> Dismasted and propeller fouled
> Anchor dragging and drifting east north east towards Shingles Bank
> Require urgent tow
> **OVER**

PAN PAN messages take priority over all traffic except Distress, and are sent on Ch 16 or 2182 kHz. They should be cancelled when the urgency is over.

If the message is long (eg a medical call) or communications traffic is heavy, it may be passed on a working frequency after an initial call on Ch 16 or 2182 kHz. At the end of the initial call you should indicate that you are switching to a working frequency.

If you hear an Urgency call react in the same way as for a Distress call.

7.5.2 SÉCURITÉ – Safety prefix
The word SÉCURITÉ (pronounced SAY-CURE-E-TAY), spoken three times, indicates that the station is about to transmit an important navigational or meteorological warning. Such messages usually originate from a CG Centre or a Coast Radio Station, and are transmitted on a working channel after an announcement on the distress/calling channel (Ch 16 or 2182 kHz).

Safety messages are usually addressed to 'All Stations', and are often transmitted at the end of the first available silence period. An example of a Sécurité message is:

SÉCURITÉ, SÉCURITÉ, SÉCURITÉ ....

THIS IS ....
(CG Centre or Coast Radio Station callsign, spoken three times)

ALL STATIONS ....
(spoken three times) followed by instructions to change channel, then the message.

7.5.3 Medical advice by R/T
Medical advice and help can be obtained via any UK and most European CG MRCC/MRSC; such calls are free. The initial call should be PAN PAN x 3 on Ch 16, or by DSC on Ch 70 or 2187·5 kHz. The Coastguard is always the first point of contact. See also Chapter 8 for further details.

7.5.4 Survival times
Average sea temperatures around the UK range from +5° to +15°C. If you fall overboard your chances of survival, unless quickly recovered, are not good.

- From 10°–16°C you will probably survive if wearing a lifejacket and rescued within 6 hours.
- At 10°C you may last for an hour or so, but this could become 4–8 hrs if also wearing a survival or wet suit.
- Below 10°C only 50% of people will survive for more than ONE hour; again a survival or wet suit would help to save your life.

7.5.5 Mobile telephones
When a vessel is in an emergency situation, using a mobile telephone to call the Coastguard on 999 (or 112) is no substitute for a radio call on VHF Ch 16 or Distress alerts on Ch 70 or 2187·5 kHz DSC. Mobiles should only be used as a last resort – in the event of radio failure, for example. They have limited coverage and are not monitored, unlike Ch 16 which the UK CG continues to monitor until further notice. Nor can emergency calls from a mobile phone be heard by nearby vessels which might be able to help. Mobiles may actually hamper on-scene SAR communications.

But, when all other means of communication have failed, mobiles have saved many lives, sometimes in bizarre circumstances. The Dutch and German CG even have an emergency phone number for mobile users to call when the CG and International emergency (112) lines are busy.

7.6 SOUND AND VISUAL DISTRESS SIGNALS
Annex IV of the IRPCS lists in full the recognised Distress signals. Those below, with notes on their use, are most relevant to yachts and small craft. Some are depicted in Fig 7(1) overleaf.

- Continuous sounding of any fog signalling apparatus.
  To avoid confusion, this is best done by repeatedly sending the letters SOS in Morse (··· ––– ···).
- An SOS signal made by any method.
  For a small craft the most likely methods are by fog horn or by flashing light.
- The International Code signal 'NC'.
  This can be made by hoisting the international code flags 'NC'. See Fig 7(1) and Chapter 5, Fig 5(1).
- A square flag with a ball, or anything resembling a ball, above or below it.
  This is not too difficult to contrive from any square flag, and a round fender or anchor ball.
- Slow and repeated raising/lowering of arms outstretched to each side.
  Raise and lower the arms together, above and below the horizontal; this is usually obvious inside a mile.
- A rocket parachute red flare or a hand-held red flare.
- An orange smoke signal.

By day orange smoke signals are more effective than flares, although the smoke disperses quickly in a strong wind.

If help is needed, but the boat is not in immediate danger, the proper signal is 'V' (Victor), meaning 'I require assistance'. This can be sent by light or sound in Morse code (···—), or hoist flag 'V'; see Fig 7(1).

7.6.1 Use of flares and other pyrotechnics
Fig 7(1) shows how flares are best used to attract attention and to communicate with SAR teams once help has arrived. SOLAS Reg V/29 requires this information to be on all sea-going boats; all crew members should know where to find it.

Flares serve two purposes:
- to raise the alarm, and
- to pinpoint the boat's position.

Within about three miles from land a red hand flare will do both; it is the most effective distress signal at night. At greater distances a red parachute rocket (which projects a suspended flare higher than 1,000ft (300m), burning for more than 40 seconds) is used to raise the alarm, but use red hand flares to pinpoint the boat's position.

Hold hand flares firmly, downwind of yourself. Rockets turn into wind: in normal conditions fire them vertically, but in strong winds aim about 15° downwind. Do not aim them into wind, or they will not gain altitude. If there is low cloud, fire rockets at 45° downwind, so that the flare burns under the cloud. Initially, fire two flares in succession.

Note: White flares are not distress signals, but are used to indicate your presence to another vessel on a collision course; or to acknowledge the sighting of a red flare. Boats which make night passages should carry at least four. When using them, shield your eyes to protect night vision.

7.6.2 Signals used by SAR aircraft
A searching aircraft normally flies at about 3,000–5,000ft, or below cloud, firing a green Very light every five or ten minutes and at each turning point.

Fig 7(1) Distress and life-saving signals

(1) Signals to be used by Ships, Aircraft or Persons in Distress

Fire rocket vertically

If windy fire 15° downwind

In low cloud fire at 45°

NEVER fire a parachute flare if a helicopter is approaching

WIND

NEVER fire into the wind

Handheld pinpoint flare shows exactly where you are - use inshore or in sight of other vessels

Orange smoke for use by day - especially in bright conditions

For use at night or in dull conditions to pinpoint position

Long range signal for use offshore

Floating orange smoke

Red hand flare

Red parachute rocket

Buoyant smoke

White pinpoint

White collision warning flare

Orange hand smoke

Handheld orange smoke

(2) Surface to Air Signals

Message	International Code of Signals		ICAO Visual Signals
'I require assistance'	'V' ▢	(· · · —)	V
'I require medical assistance' 'W'	▢	(· — —)	X
'No' or 'negative'	'N' ▦	(— ·)	N
'Yes' or 'affirmative'	'C' ▤	(— · — · ·)	Y
'Proceed in this direction'	↑		

(3) Air to Surface replies

'Message understood'

Drop a message   or   Rocking wings   or   Flash landing or navigation lights twice   or 'T' (—) or 'R' (· — ·) Morse code signal by light

'Message not understood - repeat'

Straight and level flight   Circling   or 'RPT' (· — · · — — · —) Morse code signal by light

(4) Air to Surface Direction Signals

Sequence of 3 manœuvres meaning proceed in this direction

(1) Circle vessel at least once

(2) Cross low ahead of vessel, rocking wings

(3) Overfly vessel and head in required direction

Your assistance is no longer required

Cross low astern of vessel rocking wings

Note: as an alternative to rocking wings, the aircraft engine pitch or volume may be varied

(5) Surface to Air replies

'Message understood - I will comply'

Change course or direction

or

'T' (—) Morse Code signal by light

or

Code and answering pennant 'Close up'

'I am unable to comply'

'N' (— ·) Morse Code signal by light

or

International flag 'N'

Fig 7(2)   Life-saving signals (Shore-to-Ship) (see 7.6.4)

Signals (1) to (4) may be indicated by a white flare, a rocket showing white stars on bursting, or an explosive sound signal.

(1) Landing signals for the guidance of small boats with crews or persons in distress

	Other signals	*Meaning*
Vertical motion of a white flag (or white light or flare by night) or of the arms	International Code letter **'K'** (— · —) by light or sound	**'This is the best place to land'** (An indication of direction may be given by a steady white light or flare at a lower level)
Horizontal motion of a white flag (or white light or flare by night) or of the arms extended horizontally	International Code letter **'S'** (· · ·) by light or sound	**'Landing here is highly dangerous'**
Horizontal motion of a white flag followed by 2. placing the white flag in the ground and 3. by carrying another white flag in the direction to be indicated. By night white lights or flares are used instead of white flags	1. Signalling the code letter **'S'** (· · ·), followed by the code letter **'R'** (· — ·) if the better landing place is more to the right in the direction of the approach, or 2, by the code letter **'L'** (· — · ·) if the better landing place is more to the left in the direction of approach	**'Landing here is highly dangerous. A more favourable location for landing is in the direction indicated'**

(2) Signals to be made in connection with the use of shore apparatus for life-saving

Signal	*Meaning*	**Signal**	*Meaning*
Vertical motion of a white flag (or white light or flare by night) or of the arms	**In general:** 'affirmative' Specifically: 'rocket line is held - tail block is made fast - hawser is made fast - man is in the breeches buoy - haul away'	**Horizontal** motion of a white flag (or white light or flare by night) or of the arms	**In general:** 'negative' Specifically: 'slack away - stop hauling'

(3) Replies from life-saving stations etc. to distress signals made by ships or persons

Pyrotechnic signals Orange smoke signal	White star rocket - three single signals fired at intervals of about one minute	**'You are seen - assistance will be given as soon as possible'**

(4) Signals to be used to warn a ship which is standing into danger

International Code signals **'U'**   or **'NF'**   } **'You are standing into danger'**

International Code signals **'U'** by light or sound · · —

(5) Signals used by Sub-Aqua divers

    'I am OK'   'I need assistance'

If a green flare is seen, a vessel in distress should take the following action:

- Wait for the green flare to die out.
- Fire one red flare.
- Fire another red flare some 20 seconds later. (The aircraft aligns itself on the transit of both flares.)
- Fire a third red flare when the aircraft is overhead, or if it appears to be going badly off course.

Other signals are shown in Fig 7(1).

7.6.3   Directing signals by aircraft
Fig 7(1) shows how an aircraft directs a vessel towards a ship or aircraft in distress; how it tells the vessel that its assistance is no longer required; and how the vessel may reply.

7.6.4   Shore to ship: visual signals
If no radio contact is possible, some of the signals shown in Figs 7(1) and (2) may be used to a vessel in distress or stranded off the UK coast. SOLAS V requires this information to be carried aboard in an accessible place which is known to all members of the crew before sailing.

NB: Rocket rescue equipment is no longer used by HM CG. Some larger vessels carry a line-throwing appliance requiring on-shore liaison before use.

7.7   HELICOPTER RESCUE
SAR helicopters in the UK are operated by HM Coastguard (Sumburgh, Stornoway, Portland and Lee-on-Solent), the Royal Navy (Prestwick and Culdrose) and the RAF (Lossiemouth, Boulmer, Valley, Leconfield, Wattisham and Chivenor).

Sea King SAR helicopters operated by the RN and RAF have a radius of action of 180–240M and can lift up to 18 survivors. The AW139 helicopters operated by HMCG have a radius of action of 180M and can lift 9 survivors or 2 stretchers. Both types are fully night capable.

7.7.1   Communications
SAR helicopters are generally fitted with VHF, FM & AM, UHF and HF SSB radios and can communicate with lifeboats on VHF FM, using callsign *Rescue nn*. Communications between ship and helicopter should normally be on VHF Ch 16 or 67; 2182 kHz SSB may also be available. If contact is difficult, communication can often be achieved through a Nimrod aircraft if on scene, or through a lifeboat or HM Coastguard.

When the helicopter is sighted by a vessel in distress, a flare (fired away from, not at, the helicopter), an orange smoke signal, dye marker or an Aldis lamp (not pointed directly at the helicopter) will assist recognition – very important if other vessels are in the vicinity. Cockpit dodgers with the yacht's name or sail number are useful aids to identification.

7.7.2   On the yacht
The helicopter will pass advice before it gets so close that communications become difficult because of the noise of its engines and rotors. Listen carefully and, if possible, do exactly as requested. You may be asked to keep the sails up in order to stabilise the yacht. If they are lowered, securely lash them and any loose gear. If possible remove items such as danbuoys or long aerials from the cockpit area.

If a crewman descends from the helicopter, he will take charge. Obey his instructions promptly. *Never* secure the winch wire to the yacht, and beware that it may carry a

dangerous static charge if it is not dipped (earthed) in the sea before handling.

7.7.3   Double lift
Survivors may be lifted by double lift in a strop, accompanied by the crewman in a canvas seat. Or it may be necessary, with no crewman, for a survivor to position himself in the strop. Put your head and shoulders through the strop so that the padded part is in the small of the back and the toggle is in front of the face. Pull the toggle down, as close to the chest as possible. When ready, give a thumbs-up sign with an extended arm, then place both arms close down by the side of the body to ensure that the strop does not slide up. Resist the temptation to hang on to the strop. On reaching the helicopter, do exactly as instructed by the crew. Injured persons can be lifted strapped into a special stretcher provided by the helicopter.

7.7.4   Hi-line
In some circumstances a 'Hi-line' technique may be used. This is a rope tail, attached to the helicopter winch wire by a weak link, and weighted at its lower end. When it is lowered to the yacht do not make it fast, but coil it down carefully. The helicopter pays out the winch wire and then moves to one side of the yacht and descends, while the yacht takes in the slack (keeping it outboard and clear of all obstructions) until the winch hook and strop are on board.

A helicopter crewman may be lowered with the strop. When ready to lift, the helicopter ascends and takes in the wire. Pay out the tail, keeping enough weight on it to keep it taut until the end is reached, then cast it off well clear of the yacht. But if a further lift is to be made the tail should be retained on board (not made fast) to facilitate recovery of the strop for the next lift.

When leaving a helicopter ashore, beware of the tail rotor which can be difficult to see. Obey all instructions given by the helicopter crew.

7.8   ABANDON SHIP
Do not abandon a yacht unless she is definitely sinking. A yacht is easier to find than a liferaft and provides better shelter. While she is still afloat use her resources (eg R/T for Distress calls) and put extra equipment in the liferaft or the dinghy (which should also be taken, if possible). Make all preparations.

The aim should be to board the liferaft without getting wet. Before boarding and cutting it adrift:

- Send a MAYDAY call or Distress alert, saying that the yacht is being abandoned, with position and number of people on board.
- Dress warmly with sweaters under oilskins, and life jacket on top. Take extra clothes.
- Fill any available containers with fresh water to about ¾ full, so that they will float.
- Collect additional food, tins and tin-opener.
- Collect navigational gear, EPIRB, SART, handheld VHF, torch, extra flares, bucket, length of line, first-aid kit, knife, fenders and any other equipment which might aid your survival.

Some items should already be in a survival bag – essential when a yacht is abandoned in a hurry. See *The Grab Bag Book* (ACN, £9.89).

Launch the liferaft on the lee side of the yacht, having first checked the painter is secured to a strongpoint. The painter may be up to 10m long; after about 3–4m give a sharp tug to activate the CO_2 bottle. If the liferaft inflates upside down, try to right it from the yacht. Keep the liferaft close alongside while boarding; release or cut the painter before the yacht sinks.

Once in the liferaft, plan for the worst: a long wait for rescue. Protection, location, water, food are your priorities – in that order. Always believe that you will survive. Read *The Sea Survival Manual* (ACN).

- Keep the inside of the raft as dry as possible. Huddle together for warmth. Close the openings as necessary, but keep a good lookout for shipping and aircraft.

- Stream the drogue if necessary for stability, or so as to stay near the original position.

- Take anti-seasickness pills.

- Ration fresh water to ½ litre per person per day; none in the first 24 hours. Do not drink sea water or urine. Collect rain water.

- Use flares sparingly, on the skipper's orders.

7.9   GMDSS

The Global Maritime Distress and Safety System (GMDSS) is a sophisticated, but complex, semi-automatic, third-generation communications system. Although not compulsory for yachts, its potential for saving life, particularly when far offshore and out of VHF range, is so great that every yachtsman should consider it. Equipment costs continue to fall. Training courses, leading to the award of the Short Range Certificate (SRC) of Competence, are widely available. The Long Range Certificate (LRC) covers MF, HF, SatCom, EPIRBs and SART.

Recommended reading:
- *ALRS, Vol 5* (UK Hydrographic Office)
- *GMDSS: a User's Handbook* (Bréhaut/ACN)
- *GMDSS for small craft* (Clemmetsen/Wiley)
- *Reeds VHF/DSC Handbook* (Fletcher/ACN)

7.9.1   Purpose
GMDSS enables a coordinated SAR operation to be mounted rapidly and reliably anywhere at sea. To this end, terrestrial and satellite communications and navigation equipment is used to alert SAR authorities ashore and ships in the vicinity to a Distress incident or Urgency situation. GMDSS also promulgates MSI (Maritime Safety Information); see 7.9.6.

7.9.2   Sea areas
For the purposes of GMDSS, the world's sea areas are divided into 4 categories (A1–4), defined mainly by the range of radio communications. These are:

A1   An area within R/T coverage of at least one VHF Coastguard or Coast radio station in which continuous VHF alerting is available via DSC. Range: 20–50M from the CG/CRS.

A2   An area, excluding sea area A1, within R/T coverage of at least one MF CG/CRS in which continuous DSC alerting is available. Range: approx 50–250M from the CG/CRS.

A3   An area between 70°N and 70°S, excluding sea areas A1 and A2, within coverage of HF or an Inmarsat satellite in which continuous alerting is available.

A4   An area outside sea areas A1, A2 and A3, ie the polar regions, within coverage of HF.

In each category certain types of radio equipment must be carried. In A1 areas VHF DSC; A2 areas MF or HF DSC; A3 areas SatCom; A4 MF/HF.

Most UK yachtsmen will operate in A1 areas where a simple VHF radio and a Navtex receiver will initially meet GMDSS requirements. As equipment becomes more affordable, yachtsmen may decide to fit more GMDSS equipment. This will become increasingly necessary as the present system for sending and receiving Distress calls is run down, however the CG will continue to keep a loudspeaker watch on VHF Ch 16 until further notice.

7.9.3   Functions
Regardless of the sea areas in which they operate, vessels complying with GMDSS must be able to perform certain functions:

- transmit ship-to-shore Distress alerts by two independent means
- receive shore-to-ship Distress alerts
- transmit and receive ship-to-ship Distress alerts
- transmit signals for locating incidents
- transmit and receive communications for SAR co-ordination
- transmit/receive maritime safety information eg navigation and weather warnings.

7.9.4   Distress alerts
A Distress alert is simply a Distress call using DSC. It is transmitted on Ch 70 and is automatically repeated five times. Whenever possible, a Distress alert should always include the last known position and time in UT. The position is normally entered automatically from an interfaced GPS, but can be entered manually if required. The nature of the distress can also be selected from the receiver's menu. The vessel's identity (MMSI number) is automatically included.

GMDSS requires participating ships to be able to send Distress alerts by two out of three independent means. These are:

- Digital Selective Calling (DSC) using terrestrial communications, ie VHF Ch 70, MF 2187·5 kHz, or HF distress and alerting frequencies in the 4, 6, 8, 12 and 16 MHz bands.

- EPIRBs (Emergency Position Indicating Radio Beacons), either float-free or manually released, using the Cospas/Sarsat satellites on 406 MHz with homing on 121·5 MHz. Both types transmit Distress messages which include the position and identification of the vessel in distress. See 7.11 for further details of EPIRBs.

- Inmarsat, via ship terminals.

7.9.5   Digital Selective Calling
DSC is an essential component of GMDSS. It is so called because information is sent by a burst of digital code; selective

Safety

because it can be addressed to a specific DSC-equipped vessel or to a selected group of vessels.

In all DSC messages every vessel and relevant shore station has a 9-digit identification number, or MMSI (Maritime Mobile Service Identity), which is in effect an automatic, electronic callsign.

DSC is used to transmit Distress alerts from ships, and to receive Distress acknowledgements from ships or shore stations. DSC is also used to send Urgency and Safety alerts; to relay Distress alerts; and for routine calling and answering. A thorough working knowledge is needed.

Using the procedures and switches applicable to your particular VHF/DSC radio, a VHF/DSC Distress alert might be sent as follows:

- Briefly press the (red, guarded) Distress button. The set automatically switches to Ch 70 (DSC Distress channel). Press again for 5 seconds to transmit a basic Distress alert with position and time. It then reverts to Ch l6.
- If time permits, select the nature of the distress from the menu, eg Collision, then press the Distress button for 5 seconds to send a full Distress alert.

A CG/CRS should automatically send a Distress acknowledgement on Ch 70 before replying on Ch 16. Ships in range should reply directly on Ch 16.

If a Distress acknowledgement is not received from a CG/CRS, the Distress alert will automatically be repeated every four minutes.

- When a DSC Distress acknowledgement has been received, or after about 15 seconds, the vessel in distress should transmit a MAYDAY message by voice on Ch 16 (see 7.4.1), including its MMSI.

NB: If a Distress alert is inadvertently transmitted, an All Stations DSC message cancelling the false alert (by date and time) must be sent at once.

7.9.6 Maritime Safety Information (MSI)
MSI consists of the vital navigational, weather and safety messages which traditionally were sent to vessels at sea by CRS in Morse, but by R/T on VHF and MF in more recent years – and now by GMDSS. For navigation and weather warnings see Chapters 5 and 6 respectively.

GMDSS transmits MSI in English by two independent but complementary means, Navtex and SafetyNet.

- Navtex on MF (518 kHz and 490 kHz) covers out to about 300 miles offshore, see 6.3).

- SafetyNet uses Inmarsat-C satellites to cover beyond MF range. Enhanced Group Calling (EGC) is a part of SafetyNet which enables MSI to be sent to selected groups of users in any of the four oceans.

7.10 SATELLITES FOR SAR
Inmarsat (International Maritime Satellite system) and COSPAS/SARSAT (joint Russian-USA satellite) provide satellite communications and alerts for SAR.

7.10.1 Inmarsat
Near-global communications are provided by four Inmarsat geostationary satellites, each positioned 19,300M above the four oceans (Pacific, Indian, East Atlantic & West Atlantic).

The polar regions, ie N of about 70°N and S of 70°S, are not covered.

7.10.2 COSPAS/SARSAT (C/S)
These Russian/US C/S satellites were specifically designed for SAR operations. They not only detect a 406 MHz Distress alert transmitted by an EPIRB, but also locate it with a high degree of accuracy. There are 10 ground receiving stations in 9 countries worldwide.

There are four geostationary satellites (GEOSAR) in a 24-hr orbit at 19,400M above the equator, ie apparently fixed in relation to the earth. Four more low earth orbit (LEOSAR) satellites, about 450M high, pass over both poles every 100 minutes. These 8 satellites give global coverage and receive 406 MHz signals. But coverage is not quite continuous due to possible delays in detection by the LEOSAR system; waiting time is greater in equatorial regions.

LEOSAR satellites calculate an EPIRB's position by Doppler effect. GEOSAR satellites cannot do this since there is no Doppler shift between beacon and satellite. However this problem is solved by newer (and dearer) EPIRBs which have a built-in GPS receiver to provide location directly and with continuous updating.

7.11 EPIRBs
These are best categorised by their frequencies:

- **406 MHz**. Specifically designed to be processed by C/S. They emit a powerful and frequency-stable signal which ensures proven success in detection and location. C/S has established its own beacon specification and issues type approvals.

- **121·5 MHz** (civilian aeronautical distress). These simple, inexpensive beacons were mainly used in conjunction with 406 MHz beacons for homing purposes. However their outdated technology was never designed to be detected by satellites. As a result they are no longer used at sea for satellite alerting. If you own a basic 121·5 MHz beacon, do not throw it away; it can still be detected at long range by overflying airliners/Nimrods and at short range by homing lifeboats and helicopters.

- **243·0 MHz** (military aeronautical distress). These too have been phased out since their limitations are similar to 121·5 MHz beacons.

Note: The Inmarsat-E (L-band EPIRBs) service ended in 2006.

EPIRBs can be hand-held or float-free. Hand-held are popular in small craft because of their smaller size and portability. Many have lanyards for securing them to a liferaft or person in the water; these must not be secured to the yacht. Float-free must be correctly installed so that they can indeed float free without snagging on a sinking vessel. Most modern EPIRBs have a built-in GPS and a 48 hrs battery life. Costs range from under £300 to more than £1000 for float-free, built-in GPS models.

7.11.1 Accuracy
All frequencies can be detected by C/S satellites. The processed positions are automatically passed to a Mission Control Centre (MCC) for assessment of any SAR action required; the UK MCC is co-located with the Aeronautical Rescue Coordination Centre (ARCC) at Kinloss, NE Scotland.

C/S location accuracy is normally better than 5 km on 406 MHz, but no better than 20 km on 121·5 and 243·0 MHz. Dedicated SAR aircraft can home on 121·5 MHz and 243·0 MHz, but not on 406 MHz. Typically a helicopter at 1000 feet can receive homing signals from about 30M range whilst fixed-wing aircraft at higher altitudes can home from about 60M. Best results will invariably be obtained from those 406 MHz EPIRBs with a built-in GPS receiver which transmits continuously updated positions.

7.11.2 Registration and false alerts

406 MHz EPIRBs transmit data which is uniquely coded to identify individual beacons. It is mandatory to register with the appropriate authority details of any 406 MHz EPIRBs fitted to a UK vessel.

Send UK registrations (and any subsequent changes) to: The EPIRB Registry, Falmouth MRCC, Pendennis Point, Castle Drive, Falmouth, Cornwall TR11 4WZ. ☎ 01326 211569; email: epirb @mcga.gov.uk, or register online (see www.mcga.gov.uk).

False alerts caused by inadvertent or incorrect use of EPIRBs put a significant burden on SAR Centres. The chances of false alerts coinciding with an actual distress situation are very real. As a result SAR forces could be delayed in responding to a genuine Distress alert, with possibly tragic results.

All GMDSS-qualified crew members should be trained in the proper use of the particular EPIRB onboard. Make sure that testing is adequately supervised; that the EPIRB is correctly installed and maintained; and that it is not activated if assistance is already available.

If an EPIRB is activated accidentally, make every effort to advise the nearest MRCC of the false alert as soon as possible.

7.11.3 SART

A SART (SAR transponder) is like a small portable Racon (3.11). When 'painted' by a search radar it transmits a series of pulses easily identifiable as blips on the radar screen. These enable accurate homing by searching ships, aircraft or helicopters. It operates on 9 GHz and will only respond to an X-Band (3cm) radar; not to an S-Band (10cm) radar.

It is often carried in liferafts to help ships and aircraft find survivors. For maximum range mount it as high as possible. At least 1m above sea level should give about 5M range from a ship's radar and up to 40M from an aircraft's. A SART lying on the floor of a liferaft will give a range of only 1·8M; 2·5M when standing upright on the floor and 2M when floating in the water – little better than visual search ranges.

7.12 GMDSS IN OPERATION

One picture is worth a thousand words. On this assumption and to illustrate the basic concept, the main agencies and equipment involved in a typical search and rescue operation controlled through GMDSS are shown pictorially below.

Fig 7(3) is of an early stage where Distress alerts have been transmitted by the vessel in distress – it could just as easily have been a yacht – and by its EPIRB. These have been received by satellites and will be relayed ashore to a Land Earth Station (LES), eg Goonhilly, and Mission Control Centre.

Fig 7(3) An early stage in a typical SAR operation. The wrecked ship and its EPIRB are transmitting Distress alerts which are received by CRS and by C/S.

Fig 7(4) A later stage in the same SAR operation. GMDSS is fully activated. Distress alerts have been relayed to a LES and a LUT; thence to MRCCs for SAR action. The lifeboat has been launched and is homing onto the SART signal from the liferaft. A passing ship has been diverted to the scene of action.

Two MRCCs and two CRS are also portrayed (not to scale). Notice that the EPIRB is communicating on 406 MHz with the COSPAS/SARSAT satellite.

Fig 7(4) shows a later stage with a lifeboat homing onto the SART and both terrestrial and satellite communications in full swing. SAR helicopters, other aircraft and ships have been omitted for clarity.

7.13 SEARCH AND RESCUE (SAR) – UK

Off the UK coast the lead authority for SAR operations is HM Coastguard (7.14), which initiates and co-ordinates all civil maritime SAR. HM CG can call upon: RNLI lifeboats; Ministry of Defence fixed wing aircraft and helicopters, together with other aircraft and ships which may be available. HM CG also provides SAR helicopters, emergency towing vessels at selected sites, and rescue teams to assist with coastal searches and other coastal incidents, including cliff and mud rescue.

7.13.1 Raising the alarm

If an incident afloat is seen from shore, dial 999 and ask for the Coastguard. You will be asked to report on the incident and possibly to stay in telephone contact for further communications.

If you receive a Distress signal at sea and are in a position to give realistic assistance, you are obliged to do so with all speed, unless or until you are specifically released.

When alerted, the Coastguard summons the most appropriate help, ie they may direct vessels in the vicinity of the distress, request the launch of an RNLI lifeboat or scramble a military or Coastguard SAR helicopter. Other vessels may be alerted

through Coastguard Rescue Centres, Coast radio stations abroad or by satellite communications.

7.14 HM COASTGUARD (HM CG), NCI & RNLI

The Maritime & Coastguard Agency (MCA), www.mcga.gov. uk, comprises HM Coastguard and the former Marine Safety Agency which has a regulatory and preventative role. HM Coastguard initiates and co-ordinates civil maritime SAR within the UK Search and Rescue Region (SRR).

The UK SRR is divided into 3 maritime SRRs (E, W and Scotland/NI), each sub-divided into 3 areas, which contain 2 districts.

Each area contains two Maritime Rescue Coordination Centres (MRCCs) in operational partnership. About 560 regular CG officers man the 18 MRCCs, plus London CG.

Within each area there are also Auxiliary CG rescue teams, grouped within sectors under the management of regular CG officers. Each team can respond to, assess, search and carry out cliff and mud rescues (depending on locations). Over 3,100 Auxiliary coastguards are on call to cover emergencies around the coastline.

The location and boundaries of MRCCs are shown in Fig 7(5), in Chapter 5 and on the area maps at the start of Areas 1–11 in Chapter 9. Under each port the ☎ of the nearest MRCC (or foreign equivalent) is given where possible.

E-mail addresses of all MRCCs have the Centre's name in front of coastguard@mcga.gov.uk, for example: milfordhavencoastguard@mcga.gov.uk

All centres monitor VHF Ch 16 and DSC Ch 70 H24. Broadcasts by HM Coastguard of navigation warnings, gale warnings and forecasts are in Chapters 5 and 6 respectively.

7.14.1 HM CG responsibilities

HM Coastguard is responsible for:

- Mobilising, organising and tasking adequate resources to respond to persons in distress at sea, or at risk of injury or death on the UK's cliffs or foreshore.

- Keeping an H24 radio watch on VHF, VHF DSC, MF and MF DSC at 19 MRCCs out to 150M offshore. This includes a loudspeaker watch on VHF Ch 16, but the primary means of Distress alerting in the marine VHF band should be via VHF DSC. SatCom extends cover to the whole UK SRR and worldwide.

  Note: HM CG no longer keeps a headset watch on Ch 16, only a loudspeaker watch. HM CG still monitors Ch 16 and 2182 kHz since, after a VHF/MF Distress alert, these Channels/frequencies are used to talk to a distressed vessel and to assist ships.

- Keeping watch on MF DSC 2187·5 kHz at selected stations, effectively from 30M–150M offshore.

  Note: The MCA have agreed with Denmark that Lyngby Radio relays any HF DSC alert messages to the UK, via Yarmouth MRCC.

- Providing medical advice from a doctor via telephone link call; and arranging medical assistance. Call initially on VHF DSC or MF DSC, or on Ch 16 or 2182 kHz. You will be switched to a working Channel/frequency.

- Rescuing people in distress or missing on the coastline. HM CG has search, cliff rescue and mud rescue capabilities at selected locations.

- Broadcasting MSI at four hourly intervals on VHF and MF. Broadcasts include WZ and local navigational warnings, gale warnings, local inshore forecasts and tidal surge warnings, Subfacts and Gunfacts, failure of electronic navigational aids and ice warnings (as appropriate). Skippers should listen to these scheduled broadcasts and avoid requesting individual repeats of forecasts.

  In the Dover Strait the Channel Navigation Information Service (CNIS) provides an H24 radar watch and a radio safety service for all shipping. TSS surveillance is conducted by Dover CG.

- Recording Traffic Reports (TRs) from yachts and other small craft either by phone or on VHF Ch 67. Include your ETD, ETA and number of persons onboard. The boat's safe arrival should be passed to the CG nearest to her destination, for relay to the departure CG. This avoids needless overdue action being taken . Equally the CG must be told of any change to the boat's planned movements.

However, be aware that overdue action is only taken if concern for the safety of the vessel is reported to HM CG.

Note: HM CG does not provide/accept telephone link calls.

Radio and phone calls to and from CG Centres are recorded for public safety, prevention and detection of crime.

7.14.2 CG66 Voluntary Safety Identification Scheme

This free scheme enables owners/skippers to register details of their vessel with HM CG for use in an emergency. If you get into difficulty, go missing or are overdue – and the initial information lacks detail – the CG66 has further details about your vessel to hand.

The CG66 may be completed on the MCA's website (see https://mcanet.mcga.gov.uk/public/cg66/) or it is available from MRCCs, RNLI boathouses or possibly at your sailing club or marina. Details are kept for two years, then destroyed if not renewed. The information is used solely for SAR and Prevention purposes.

Fig 7(5) HM CG centres and boundaries

7.14.3 Emergency VHF DF – UK

All MRCCs, except London CG, can give a boat in distress its true bearing *from* a D/F site. These are shown by the ⊙RG symbol on Admiralty charts and on the Area maps in this almanac. This service is *only for emergency use.* Call on Ch 16. Bearings will be passed on Ch 16 or 67, if in VHF range.

Site	Lat/Long	Controlled by CG
Trevose Head	50°32'.91N 05°01'.99W	Falmouth
Land's End	50°08'.18N 05°38'.23W	Falmouth
St Mary's, Scilly	49°55'.72N 06°18'.18W	Falmouth
Lizard Point	49°57'.86N 05°12'.46W	Falmouth
Rame Head	50°19'.03N 04°13'.18W	Brixham
East Prawle	50°13'.13N 03°42'.55W	Brixham
Berry Head	50°23'.97N 03°29'.05W	Brixham
Grove Point	50°32'.92N 02°25'.18W	Portland
Hengistbury Head	50°42'.94N 01°45'.60W	Portland
Boniface Down	50°36'.21N 01°12'.03W	Solent
Selsey	50°43'.83N 00°48'.24W	Solent
Newhaven	50°46'.94N 00°02'.99E	Solent
Fairlight	50°52'.23N 00°38'.74E	Dover
Langdon Battery	51°07'.96N 01°20'.56E	Dover
North Foreland	51°22'.53N 01°26'.73E	Dover
Shoeburyness	51°31'.38N 00°46'.50E	Thames
Bawdsey	51°59'.60N 01°25'.00E	Thames
Lowestoft	52°28'.60N 01°42'.20E	Yarmouth
Trimingham	52°54'.57N 01°20'.60E	Yarmouth
Skegness	53°09'.00N 00°21'.00E	Yarmouth
Easington	53°39'.13N 00°05'.90E	Humber
Flamborough Hd	54°07'.06N 00°05'.07W	Humber
Ravenscar	54°23'.83N 00°30'.68W	Humber
Hartlepool	54°41'.79N 01°10'.57W	Humber
Cullercoats	55°04'.40N 01°27'.80W	Humber
Newton	55°31'.01N 01°37'.10W	Humber
St Abbs (Crosslaw)	55°54'.46N 02°12'.33W	Forth
Fife Ness	56°16'.70N 02°35'.30W	Forth
Inverbervie	56°51'.10N 02°15'.65W	Forth
Windyheads Hill	57°38'.91N 02°14'.66W	Aberdeen
Dunnet Head	58°40'.29N 03°22'.59W	Aberdeen
Wideford Hill	58°59'.29N 03°01'.40W	Shetland
Compass Head	59°52'.05N 01°16'.30W	Shetland
Portnaguran	58°14'.80N 06°09'.81W	Stornoway
Rodel	57°44'.90N 06°57'.41W	Stornoway
Barra	57°00'.81N 07°30'.42W	Stornoway
Tiree	56°30'.62N 06°57'.68W	Clyde
Kilchiaran	55°45'.90N 06°27'.19W	Clyde
Law Hill	55°41'.76N 04°50'.46W	Clyde
West Torr	55°11'.70N 06°05'.20W	Belfast
Orlock Point	54°40'.41N 05°34'.97W	Belfast
Snaefell, I of Man	54°15'.84N 04°27'.66W	Liverpool
Great Ormes Hd	53°19'.97N 03°51'.21W	Holyhead
Rhiw	52°50'.00N 04°37'.82W	Holyhead
St Ann's Head	51°40'.97N 05°10'.52W	Milford Haven
Hartland Point	51°01'.22N 04°31'.40W	Swansea

7.14.4 National Coastwatch Institution (NCI)

The NCI is a charity dedicated to the safety of all mariners in UK coastal waters. Since 1994 it has re-introduced visual watch stations, usually by re-opening abandoned CG lookouts. Over long stretches of coastline volunteer NCI watchkeepers alone provide the vitally important visual watch link with HM CG, the RNLI and other SAR services. Many lives have been saved as a direct result of their actions.

NCI stations monitor VHF Ch 16. All passing small boats are logged to assist in the search for missing craft. By day NCI reports actual weather and sea states on request. In poor visibility some stations keep a radar watch to 20M offshore (Ⓡ = Radar equipped).

The NCI stations below were all operational in 2009. They are marked on the Area maps by ©, for Coastwatch.

For more details visit: www.nci.org.uk

Area 1		
Gwennap Head (Land's End) Ⓡ	01736	871351
Penzance	01736	367063
Bass Point (Lizard) Ⓡ	01326	290212
Nare Point (Helford River)	01326	231113
Portscatho (E of Fal; summer w/e only)	01872	580180
Charlestown Ⓡ	01726	817068
Polruan (Fowey) Ⓡ	01726	870291
Rame Head (Plymouth) Ⓡ	01752	823706
Prawle Point (Salcombe) Ⓡ	01548	511259
Froward Point (Dartmouth) Ⓡ	07976	505649
Teignmouth	01626	772377
Exmouth	01395	222492
Portland Bill Ⓡ	01305	860178
St Alban's Head Ⓡ	01929	439220
Area 2		
Peveril Pt (Swanage) Ⓡ	01929	422596
Lee on Solent	023	9255 6758
Gosport	023	9276 5194
Area 3		
Shoreham	07530	041733
Newhaven	01273	516464
Folkestone (Copt Pt)	01303	227132
Area 4		
Herne Bay (w/ends only)	01227	743208
Whitstable (w/ends only)	07932	968707
Holehaven (Canvey Island)	01268	696971
Southend (w/ends only)	07815	945210
Felixstowe	01394	670808
Gorleston (Great Yarmouth) Ⓡ	01493	440384
Area 5		
Mundesley (Norfolk) Ⓡ	01263	722399
Wells-next-the-sea (Norfolk) Ⓡ	01328	710587
Skegness Ⓡ	01754	610900
Hartlepool Ⓡ	01429	274931
Sunderland Life Brigade (Affiliate) Ⓡ	01915	672579
Berwick (Weekends 0830-1415)	07950	149865
Area 10		
Rossall Pt (Fleetwood)	01253	681378
Area 11		
Wooltack Point (St Brides Bay)	017817	871549
Worms Head (Gower)	01792	390167
Nells Point (Barry)	01446	420746
Boscastle (North Cornwall) Ⓡ	01840	250965
Stepper Point (Padstow) Ⓡ	07810	898041
St Agnes Head (N Cornwall)	01872	552073
St Ives Ⓡ	01736	799398
Cape Cornwall (Land's End) Ⓡ	01736	787890

7.14.5 Royal National Lifeboat Institution (RNLI)

The RNLI is a registered charity which saves life at sea. It provides, on call, a 24-hour lifeboat service up to 100M off the UK and Irish coasts. There are more than 230 lifeboat stations. Of these, four are on the River Thames, and another four are inland water stations. The RNLI also operates over 100 lifeguard units. All new lifeboats are capable of at least 25 knots.

When launched on service, lifeboats >10m keep watch on VHF and MF DSC as well as VHF Ch 16. They can also use alternative frequencies to contact other vessels, SAR aircraft, HM CG, Coast radio stations or other SAR agencies.

All lifeboats show a quick-flashing blue light when on operational service.

The RNLI actively promotes safety at sea by providing a free comprehensive safety service to members and the general public including advice, publications and demonstrations. The RNLI aims to save lives and prevent accidents by helping people be prepared through water safety awareness.

The RNLI Skippers' Handbook covers emergencies, seamanship, weather, first aid, navigation and engines.

For more details of how the RNLI can help you to be safer at sea, or to support the work of the RNLI, call the RNLI on 0845 122 6999, visit www.rnli.org.uk.

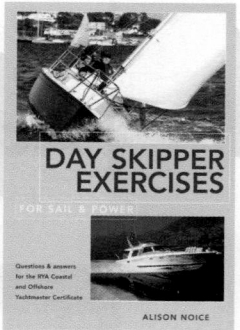

8

First Aid

First Aid

8.1 FIRST AID OBJECTIVES

The objectives of First Aid at sea are to:

- **Preserve life**
- **Prevent further damage**
- **Relieve pain and distress**
- **Deliver a live casualty ashore**

With any casualty be calm, reassuring and methodical. Try to examine the whole casualty if time and circumstances permit.

8.2 MEDICAL CARE ABROAD

For cruising in European waters it is advisable for each crew member to carry the European Health Insurance Card (EHIC) which entitles you to reduced-cost, sometimes free, medical treatment that becomes necessary while you are in the EU, Iceland, Liechtenstein and Norway. It is free and is available online, by phone or by post. See: *www.dh.gov.uk/ en/Policyandguidance/Healthadvicefortravellers/index.htm* for details. The EHIC has replaced the old E111, which is no longer valid.

A useful booklet *Health Advice for Travellers,* which gives details of how to claim in the 28 participating countries, is obtainable from Post Offices. A further 30+ countries have reciprocal health care agreements with the UK, but many others, including Turkey, the Americas, Canada, Caribbean, India, Middle East, Africa, Asia, Thailand, Japan, Hong Kong and the Pacific region (except Australia and New Zealand), do not. If cruising these areas private health insurance is strongly advised.

Yachtsmen cruising abroad may naturally be concerned about the risk of being given infected blood. Normally it is not possible to carry blood or plasma in a yacht. If a blood transfusion is essential, try to ensure that the blood used has been screened against HIV and Hepatitis B.

If you are cruising to distant destinations you may wish to take additional sterile needles and syringes, if you or a crewman are diabetic, for example. Seek advice from your doctor or local hospital before leaving. Syringes and needles are attractive to intravenous drug abusers so should be securely locked away.

8.3 MEDICAL ADVICE BY R/T

Medical advice can be obtained almost anywhere in European waters (and elsewhere) by making an all-stations 'PAN PAN' call or a DSC Urgency Alert to the Coastguard, or to a Coast Radio Station (CRS) in those countries where CRS still exist. You will be connected to a suitable medical authority – usually a doctor or the nearest hospital.

The Urgency signal 'PAN PAN' is always advised, especially abroad, because it is internationally understood and cuts through most language problems; see also 7.5.

Urgent help needed is shown in bold italic type against the more serious medical problems in the following pages and this implies a PAN PAN call. You should also recognise that as a layman you are not qualified to judge how serious the casualty's condition is – so get the best possible advice and/ or help as quickly as possible.

Be ready to give a detailed summary of the patient's symptoms – pulse rate, breathing rate, temperature, skin colour, conscious state (with reference to pupil size, responses to verbal command and to firm pinching); site and description of any pain, site and type of injury, amount of blood lost etc. See the Observation Form at 8.34.

If medical help is needed by way of a doctor coming aboard, or if a serious casualty has to be landed, the arrangements will be made by the Coastguard.

If you are sure that the situation is not urgent, you may wish to forewarn the port authority so that a doctor or paramedic can meet you on arrival. Such a call could be made in adequate time on the harbour's working channel.

8.4 ABC – EMERGENCY RESUSCITATION

Further advice is obtainable at: *www.resus.org.uk/pages/ guide.htm*

The immediate procedure for any collapsed or apparently unconscious person is:

> Assess whether or not the casualty is conscious. Carefully shake his shoulders and ask loudly 'What's happened?' or 'Are you all right?' or give a command such as 'Open your eyes'. An unconscious casualty will not respond.

A = Airway

Be aware of the risk of neck or spinal injury following a fall or head injury. If suspected, try to keep the head and neck still and in line, then lift the chin to maintain a clear airway rather than tilting the head. However, the priority must be to ensure the casualty is indeed beathing. Remove any visible obstruction from the casualty's mouth (leave well-fitting dentures in place). Listen at the mouth for breathing. Tilt the head backwards, using head tilt and chin lift to maintain a clear airway; Fig 8(1).

Fig 8(1) Ensuring a clear airway

If breathing, place casualty in recovery position; Fig 8(2). Check the area is clear of danger.

Fig 8(2) Recovery position

B = Breathing

If not breathing and the airway is clear, start mouth to mouth ventilation; Fig 8(3).

Fig 8(3) Mouth to mouth ventilation

Keeping the airway open, check whether the casualty is breathing normally by **looking** for chest movement, **listening** at the mouth for breathing sounds and **feeling** for breath on your cheek. Look, listen and feel for 10 seconds only before deciding that breathing is absent. If the casualty is not breathing and the airway is clear, mouth-to-mouth ventilation can be started, in conjunction with 'External chest compression'; see below. Kneel beside the casualty, maintain head tilt and chin lift, and pinch the nostrils. Take a deep breath and blow two full breaths into patient's mouth. Watch for rise and fall of chest.

C = Circulation

Assess the casualty for signs of circulation by looking, listening and feeling for normal breathing, coughing, movement or improvement in colour. Check for signs of circulation for no more than 10 seconds.

If there are no signs of a circulation or you are at all unsure, assume that the heart has stopped. This is called **cardiac arrest**. The casualty will be unconscious and may appear very pale, grey or bluish in colour. An artificial circulation will have to be provided by chest compression. If the circulation stops, the breathing will also stop. Casualties with cardiac arrest will need both rescue breathing and chest compression, a combination known as Cardio Pulmonary Resuscitation (**CPR**).

External chest compression

To start external chest compression, lay the casualty on a hard, flat surface if possible. Kneel beside casualty. The point at which pressure will be applied is the centre of the chest. (It is now considered a waste of valuable time for an

amateur first aider to search for the point of pressure by the 'rib margin' method.)

Place the heel of your first hand on top of the other hand and interlock your fingers.

Depress breastbone 4–5cm (1½–2in) then release; Fig 8(4).

With either one or two operators give 30 chest compressions and continue cycles of 2 breaths to 30 compressions; see Fig 8(5) and Fig 8(6). Use a compression rate of 100 per minute. Chest compression must always be combined with rescue breathing so after every 30 compressions, give 2 effective rescue breaths. *Do not stop.*

Action plan for the resuscitation of adults

Casualty is unconscious but is breathing normally:

- **Urgent help needed**
- Turn casualty into the recovery position
- Check for continued breathing

Fig 8(5) One operator

Fig 8(6) Two operators

Casualty is unconscious and not breathing:

- **Urgent help needed**
- Give 2 effective rescue breaths
- Check for signs of circulation

If no sign of a circulation, give 30 chest compressions and continue cycles of 2 breaths to 30 compressions.

If breathing restarts, place casualty in the recovery position.

Fig 8(4) Chest compression: body/hand position

Action plan for the resuscitation of children

Blow into both mouth and nose if necessary, but resuscitate at same rate as an adult. For external chest compression use gentle compression with one hand only, or just fingers for a baby; use a compression rate of up to 100 per minute, one breath every 5 compressions. In the case of a baby give up to 5 initial rescue breaths. Use a faster breathing rate (one inflation every 3 seconds) and smaller breaths.

Problems during resuscitation

It is unlikely that the casualty's pulse will return spontaneously without other more advanced techniques (especially *defibrillation*) so do not waste time by stopping CPR to check the circulation. Only stop and re-check if the casualty shows signs of life (movement or breathing). Otherwise, carry on until either the emergency services arrive, another rescuer can take over, or you are too exhausted to keep going.

Drowning (8.6) and Hypothermia (8.7)

Drowning and hypothermia casualties may exhibit all the signs of apparent death, yet may totally recover. Only abandon resuscitation if really necessary, and after thorough and repeated attempts have been made to warm the victim.

8.5   CHOKING

If blockage by some object is suspected, turn the casualty on his/her side and give up to 5 sharp back slaps with the flat of the hand between the shoulder blades. Check mouth and remove any obstruction.

If unsuccessful, wrap both your arms around the victim's waist from behind, and give 5 sharp upward thrusts with both fists into the abdomen above the navel but below the ribs so as to initiate coughing. Clear object from mouth.

In an unconscious adult administer abdominal thrusts with the victim lying on his back. Attempt mouth to mouth breathing. Do not give up.

Infants and small children should just be given 5 forceful blows on the back before proceeding to chest thrusts which are performed in the same way as chest compressions but should be sharper and performed at a slower rate, with each thrust trying to relieve the obstruction. Continue if no relief, with the sequence of 5 rescue breaths, 5 back blows and 5 chest thrusts.

8.6   DROWNING

The resuscitation of an apparently drowned person may be complicated by two factors:

- An acute (sudden) illness (8.9 and 8.10) – a stroke, accident or blow to the head, for example – may have precipitated the fall into the water.
- The time spent in the water may have produced marked hypothermia. The water around the UK is rarely warmer than 15°C (60°F).

During rescue and after resuscitation try to keep the head low so that vomit is not inhaled and water is able to drain from the mouth.

Treatment

A = Airway Clear airway: seaweed, dentures etc. See 8.4.

B = Breathing If not breathing start mouth to mouth ventilation as soon as possible and in the water if practicable. See 8.4.

C = Circulation If pulse is absent, start chest compression as soon as aboard. See 8.4.

- If stomach is bulging, turn casualty on to side to empty water, or he may vomit large quantities of water which could be inhaled.
- Prevent cooling. Remove wet clothes; wrap casualty in blankets to warm him/her.
- Continue resuscitation until the casualty revives or death is certain. Hypothermia may mimic death. Do not abandon resuscitation until the casualty has been warmed or signs of death persist despite attempts at warming.
- Once revived, put in the recovery position, Fig 8(2).
- Any person rescued from drowning may collapse in the next 24 hours as the lungs react to inhaled water. *Urgent help needed.*

8.7   HYPOTHERMIA

Lowered body temperature may follow immersion in the sea or prolonged exposure on deck.

Symptoms include: unreasonable behaviour followed by apathy and confusion; unsteady gait, stumbling; slurring of speech; pale, cold skin; slow, weak pulse; slow breathing; shivering. Hypothermia may lead to collapse, unconsciousness and, ultimately, death.

Treatment

A = Airway control; put in recovery position.

B = Breathing If not breathing, start mouth to mouth ventilation.

C = Circulation Be prepared to use chest compressions. Remove wet clothing. Avoid wind chill. Dry and wrap in blankets or sleeping bag plus warm hat and cover, if available, in foil survival bag. *Urgent help needed.* Give hot sweet drinks if conscious.

Do not give alcohol, rub the skin or place very hot objects against skin.

8.8   SHOCK

Shock can result from almost any accident or medical emergency and, depending upon the cause, may range in severity from a simple faint to near death. Shock occurs when the delivery of oxygen to the tissues is impaired because of inadequate or inefficient circulation of the blood. Possible causes include:

- Loss of blood: internal or external bleeding.
- Loss of fluid: diarrhoea, peritonitis, burns.
- Heart failure: heart attack.
- Lung failure: drowning.
- Brain failure: stroke, head injury.
- Illness: diabetes.

Signs and symptoms

Thirst, apathy, nausea, restlessness. Pale, cold, clammy skin, sweating. Rapid, weak pulse. Rapid, shallow breathing. Dull, sunken eyes, bluish lips; it can lead to collapse.

Treatment

- *ABC – airway, breathing, circulation* see 8.4.

- Control bleeding, if present.
- Lay the casualty flat; elevate legs to 20°.

Exceptions:
  i   Bleeding from mouth – use recovery position.
  ii Unconscious – use recovery position.
  iii Chest injury – sitting may be preferred.

- Splint any fractures; avoid movement.
- Keep reasonably warm; don't overheat.
- Relieve pain – give painkillers.

Exceptions:
  i   Head injury with impaired consciousness.
  ii Cases with severe breathing difficulty.

- Reassure the casualty.
- Do not let the casualty eat, drink, smoke or move unnecessarily. If he complains of thirst, moisten the lips with a little water.

Exception
Fluids may be life saving in cases of dehydration (diarrhoea, vomiting, severe burns, for example). Give half a cup of water at 15 minute intervals. Add a pinch of salt and a little sugar. Never give alcohol. Avoid fluids if severe abdominal pain or internal injury. *Never* attempt to give fluids by mouth to an unconscious person.

Collapse and signs of shock after an accident when external blood loss is slight or absent must suggest internal bleeding. Clues may be few. The casualty may cough or vomit blood, or pass blood in urine or from bowel. He/she may complain of worsening pain in abdomen or chest. *Urgent help needed.*

Medical illnesses, such as diabetes, severe infections or heart disease, may produce shock without giving many clues as to the cause. *Urgent help needed.*

8.9   ACUTE (SUDDEN) ILLNESS

Before a long passage be aware of any crew medical problems and record medication being taken. Seek medical advice on likely symptoms and treatment. Unless forewarned, diagnosis may be very difficult once at sea.

- *Abdominal pain (minor)*
  i   Upper abdomen, intermittent, burning, no tenderness, otherwise well. May follow large alcohol intake. Eased by milk or antacid; bland meals; no alcohol.
  ii More generalised, cramping or colicky pain, no tenderness, may have diarrhoea or vomiting. May be gastroenteritis or food poisoning. Take oral fluid with a pinch of salt added. Avoid dehydration. Seek advice.

- *Abdominal pain (major)* Severe abdominal pain, usually constant and generalised. Abdomen may be rigid or very tender to touch, fever may be present, rapid pulse rate, generally unwell, nausea and vomiting. Make the casualty comfortable; give pain relief (injection if possible). Give nothing to eat or drink. *Urgent help needed.*

- *Allergies* Mild cases may just have a rash which responds to calamine lotion and antihistamine tablets. Severe cases may collapse with breathing difficulty and require emergency ABC resuscitation. Seek advice.

- *Children* may become ill with alarming rapidity. Ear and throat infections are especially common. Children are also more susceptible to the effects of dehydration; if ill get them to drink copious fluids. Reduce drug dosage to a proportion of adult dose based on weight (average adult 70kg/155lb). Seek advice.

- *Constipation* Common at sea. Prevent by eating fruit, vegetables, bran and, if necessary, anti-constipation medication (eg senna preparations).

- *Convulsion* Casualty may be a known epileptic. **Do not** put anything in the mouth. Prevent injury. Place in recovery position; protect airway (he/she may still look very blue). After fit, allow him/her to sleep. *Urgent help needed.*

- *Diabetes* A diabetic may become unconscious if his/her blood sugar is too high or too low. For **hyper**glycaemia (too much sugar) insulin is needed. **Hypo**glycaemia (too little sugar) may be caused by too much insulin, unusual stress or exercise, or too little food. In either case, if rousable, first give sweets, sugar, soft drinks. If recovery not rapid, *Urgent help needed.*

- *Diarrhoea* Can become serious, especially in young children if much fluid is lost. Stop food, give plenty of fluid. Water is sufficient in most cases or, alternatively, add salt (1 teaspoon/litre) and sugar (4–5 teaspoons/litre) to water. Lomotil or Imodium tablets are very effective in adults.

- *Fever* May be associated with anything from common cold, appendicitis, heat stroke to an infected toe. Except for major abdominal problems, prescribe copious fluids, paracetamol or aspirin (not in the case of children) and antibiotics if infection is present. Seek advice.

- *Heart attack* Severe central 'crushing' chest pain; may spread to shoulders, neck or arms. Sweating, then bluish lips, then collapse. Breathing and heart may stop. Give one aspirin tablet 300mg, to be chewed not swallowed whole. Note that some casualties (diabetics, for example) may not experience the chest pains. *Urgent help needed.*
  i   Early symptoms; rest, reassure.
  ii If unconscious: recovery position; observe breathing and pulse.
  iii If breathing stops or pulse is absent, commence mouth to mouth ventilation and chest compression immediately and do not stop. See 8.4.

- *Heat stroke* Cool casualty by spraying with cold water or wrap the casualty in a cold wet sheet until their temperature falls to 38°C under the tongue; encourage drinking (one teaspoon of salt/half litre of water). If casualty stops sweating, has a rapid pounding pulse and is becoming unconscious, *urgent help needed.*

- *Seasickness* is basically an inner ear disturbance caused by motion. The condition is aggravated by fear, anxiety, fatigue and boredom. It may manifest itself as lethargy, dizziness or headache as well as nausea and vomiting. Most people know if they are vulnerable and should take preventative drugs.

Avoid strong food tastes and too much alcohol. Take small amounts of fluid and food frequently if you feel ill. Avoid fatigue; adequate sleep will often relieve the sick feeling. Keep warm. Stay on deck and concentrate on some task if possible – taking the helm can work wonders. Sick crew on deck must be secured by lifeline. Turn in if all else fails. Vomiting may cause serious loss of fluid.

No one remedy is suitable for every person. Try the various preparations until you find one that is effective with minimal side effects; most tend to cause a dry mouth and some tiredness. Tablets available over the counter include: Avomine (promethazine) and Stugeron (cinnarizine). Take the first tablet some hours before going to sea, and then regularly for as long as necessary. Take a tablet just before going to sleep if possible. Various preparations can be applied behind the ear or worn as a wrist band. Prolonged seasickness is serious – seek advice.

8.10   STROKE

Sudden unconsciousness, paralysis or weakness on one side of body, slurring of speech. Recognise a stroke by asking the victim to:

- Smile
- Speak
- Raise both arms
- Stick out tongue

If there is difficulty with *any one* of these tasks, or if the tongue goes to one side or the other, suspect a stroke.

Place in recovery position and check airway.

Urgent help needed – specialist treatment within 3 hours can reverse the effects of a stroke.

ACCIDENTS AND INJURIES

8.11   BITES AND STINGS

Injected poison from bites and stings usually only causes local swelling and discomfort, but some individuals may react severely. For insect stings, resuscitate if collapse occurs; otherwise give rest, painkillers, antihistamines (eg chlorpheniramine).

In warmer water, sea snakes and various sea stingers can inject deadly poison: prevent drowning, resuscitate if necessary. If sting is caused by jelly fish or Portuguese Man O'War etc, pour vinegar onto sting to reduce further poison release.

If the victim becomes weak and breathless, lightly compress the limb above the wound with a rolled up roller bandage to delay the spread of poison. **Do not** apply a tourniquet; this practice is out of date due to the danger of losing a limb. Start resuscitation. *Urgent help needed*.

Many large cities maintain a 24-hour poison information centre. Use the radio for advice.

8.12   BLEEDING – OPEN WOUND

Bleeding is often dramatic, but is almost always controllable.
Treatment

- Apply firm continuous direct pressure; bandage on a large pad. If bleeding continues, bandage more pads on top of initial pads; then press directly over wound for at least 10 minutes (blood takes this long to clot).
- Elevate if wound is on a limb.

- **Do not** apply a tourniquet. This practice is out of date and risks losing a limb.

8.13   BLEEDING – INTERNAL (CLOSED INJURY)

Follows fractured bones, crush injuries, or rupture of organs such as the liver or spleen. Treat for shock which may appear rapidly. *Urgent help needed*.

8.14   BURNS AND SCALDS
Treatment

- Move the victim into fresh air to avoid inhaling smoke.
- *ABC – Airway, Breathing, Circulation; see 8.4.*
- Stop further injury: dip the whole of the burnt part into cold water for 10–15 minutes. Seawater is excellent but may be very painful.
- Remove loose clothing only; do not pull off clothing stuck to the skin.
- Cover with sterile dressing. If skin is broken or blistered, use sterile paraffin gauze beneath the dressing. Separate burnt fingers with paraffin gauze. Never use adhesive dressings.
- Do not prick blisters or apply ointments.
- Elevate burnt limb and immobilise.
- Give strong painkillers.
- Treat for shock: give frequent and copious drinks of water.
- Start giving antibiotics for major burns.
- If burns are extensive or deep, *urgent help needed*.

Sunburn can be very severe. Best treated by keeping the skin cool by fanning or careful sponging with chilled water; give painkillers. For prevention keep well covered and only use sunscreen preparations with high protection factor, >20.

8.15   CHEST INJURY

May result in fractured ribs. These are very painful, and breathing may be uncomfortable and shallow. The fractured ribs may puncture the lung or, if a number of ribs are each broken in two places (eg after crush injury), then this part of the chest may move independently of the rest of the chest and seriously impair breathing.

Treatment

- *ABC – Airway, Breathing, Circulation; see 8.4.*
- Casualty may be more comfortable sitting up.
- Tape a plastic cover over any hole on 3 sides (top and both sides) if air is sucking in and out.
- Support any unstable chest segment with your hand.
- For fractured ribs prescribe rest and strong painkillers if necessary. Very painful.

Avoid tight strapping lest it restricts breathing even further. *Urgent help needed* for any case with impaired breathing.

8.16   CRUSH INJURIES

These injuries involve skin, underlying muscle and tendon and sometimes bone as well. Common in hands and fingers (from winches and anchor chains) and elsewhere when tissue is sandwiched. Bleeding may be slight, but bruising and swelling considerable and extremely painful. Keep affected part as cold as possible; elevate if a hand or foot and give painkillers. *Urgent help needed*.

8.17   CUTS AND WOUNDS

Often dramatic but only potentially serious if nerves, tendons or blood vessels are severed.

Treatment

- Clean thoroughly with antiseptic. Remove dirt or other foreign bodies from the wound.
- Small clean cuts can be closed using Steristrips. Skin must be dry. Use as many Steristrips as necessary to keep the skin edges together. Leave for 5 days at least.
- Larger deep cuts may require special suture techniques (stitches); apply a dressing and seek help. Do not try amateur surgery at sea.
- Ragged lacerations or very dirty wounds – do not attempt to close these; dead tissues may have to be trimmed away to prevent infection. Clean as well as possible, sprinkle antibiotic powder in wound and apply a dressing. Seek help.

If in doubt a wound is best left open and lightly covered to keep it clean and dry.

Fingers and toes

Blood may collect under the nail following an injury. Release the blood by piercing the nail with a red hot needle or paper clip. It will not hurt!

8.18   DENTAL PROBLEMS

Dental pain seems worse at sea; prevention is better than cure. It is advisable to see a dentist about 4 weeks before departing on a long voyage to allow time for any necessary treatment. If X-Rays are taken, keep them with you. Consider carrying a dental mirror, tongue spatula, pen torch, cotton wool rolls, tweezers and a ready-mixed temporary filling. Dentanurse is an emergency treatment pack which enables an amateur to make basic temporary repairs, eg replacing crowns, lost fillings. It contains zinc oxide and Eugenol.

Treatment

- Throbbing toothache, made worse by hot or cold or when bitten on. If a cavity is present, clean out and apply temporary filling. Take an anti-inflamatory painkiller.
- Dull toothache, tender to bite on; gum swollen or red with possible discharge. Treat as above but also take an antibiotic.
- Broken tooth or filling. Cover exposed surfaces with zinc oxide paste. Teeth which have been knocked out should be placed in a clean container with milk or moist gauze and taken to a dentist at the first opportunity for re-implantation. This can be attempted onboard. If the tooth is not re-implanted within 24 hours (preferably within 1 hour), chance of success is poor.
- Bleeding gums. Clean teeth more thoroughly. If accompanied by foul odour and metallic taste, use regular hot salt water rinses and antibiotics.
- Pain round wisdom tooth. Toothbrush to clean area; use hot salt water rinses; take antibiotics and painkillers.

8.19   EYE PROBLEMS

All eye injuries or illnesses are potentially serious. Never put old or previously opened ointment or drops into an eye; serious infection could result.

Treatment

- Foreign object. Flush the eye with clean water, pull the bottom lid out to inspect, remove object with a clean tissue. For objects under upper eyelid, ask casualty to grasp lashes and pull the upper lid over the lower lid. A proper eye-bath is very effective. Blinking under water may also remove the object. After removal of object, insert sterile antibiotic ointment inside pulled out lower lid. Cover with pad.
- Corrosive fluid. Flush continuously with water for 15 minutes. Give painkillers and chloramphenicol ointment; cover with pad. *Seek help as soon as possible*.
- Conjunctivitis. A sticky, weeping eye with yellow discharge. Chloramphenicol ointment 4 times a day.

8.20   FISH HOOK INJURY

Push the hook round until the point and barb appear. Cut off the point and barb and withdraw the hook. Dress the holes and give an antibiotic.

8.21   FRACTURES AND DISLOCATIONS

Fracture is a broken bone. Dislocation is a displaced joint. Both result from major trauma and will produce pain (which is worse on attempted movement), localised swelling, abnormal shape, and a grating feeling on movement (when a fracture is present). Blood vessels or nerves around the fracture or dislocation may also be damaged resulting in a cold, pale, or numb limb below the site of the injury.

Fractures of large bones such as the femur (upper leg) will result in major internal bleeding and may cause shock. When complications occur, *Urgent help needed*.

Early application of a splint and elevation of the injured limb where possible will reduce pain and minimise complications. Treat for shock and pain.

Specific fractures and dislocations

Cheek   Caused by a direct blow. Rarely serious but requires specialist care.

Jaw   Beware of associated brain or spinal injury. Remove blood and teeth fragments; leave loose teeth in place; protect broken teeth (see 8.18). Ensure airway is clear. Start regular antiseptic mouth washes and antibiotics. Support jaw with bandage over top of the head. Give only fluids by mouth.

Neck   May result from a direct blow, a fall or a whiplash type injury. If conscious, casualty may complain of pain, tingling, numbness or weakness in limbs below the injury. *Mishandling may damage the spinal cord, resulting in paralysis or death*. Avoid movement and support the head. Immobilise by wrapping a folded towel around the neck. If movement is necessary then lift the victim as one rigid piece, never allowing the neck to bend. *Urgent help needed*.

Nose   Control bleeding by pinching (8.25).

Ribs   See chest injury (8.15). Often very painful. Strapping is not advised.

Fig 8(7) Sling

Fig 8(8) Collar and cuff

Skull   See head injury (8.23).

Spine   Fracture of the spine may occur below the neck, also resulting in *paralysis or death*. Mishandling of the victim may greatly worsen the damage. Avoid movement if possible. Lift the casualty without allowing the spine to sag. *Urgent help needed*.

Upper limb

- **Collar bone (clavicle)**. Support arm in sling, Fig 8(7).
- **Dislocated shoulder**. If this has happened before, the casualty may remedy the dislocation himself; otherwise do not attempt to remedy it in case a fracture exists.
- **Upper arm (humerus)**. Support the arm with a collar and cuff inside the shirt as illustrated in Fig 8(8), ie tie a clove hitch around the wrist and loop the ends behind the neck.
- **Forearm and wrist**. Splint (eg with battens or wood). Do not bandage tightly. Elevate or support in a sling.
- **Fingers**. Elevate hand and, unless badly crushed, leave unbandaged; keep moving. If very wobbly, bandage to adjacent finger.

Lower limb

Thigh. Shock may be considerable. Splint by strapping to other leg with padding between the legs. Gently straighten the casualty's lower leg. If necessary apply traction at the ankle to help straighten the leg. Do not bandage too tightly.

Knee. Twisting injuries or falls damage the ligaments and cartilages of the knee. Very painful and swollen. Treat as for fracture.

Lower leg. Pad very well. Splint using oar, broom handle or similar pieces of wood.

Ankle. Fracture or severe sprain may be indistinguishable. Immobilise in neutral position with foot at right angles. Elevate the limb.

To be really effective a splint must be rigid and extend to the joints above and below the fracture. This is not always possible. The splint must be very well padded.

If the limb beyond the bandage or splint becomes swollen or discoloured, the bandage must be loosened to improve circulation. If you improvise a splint it is essential not to enclose the whole limb and risk cutting off the circulation (see 8.12, reference non-use of tourniquet).

As a general rule, if a fracture is suspected then seek advice.

Compound fractures

If a deep wound overlies the fracture, or the bone ends are visible, do not try to close the wound or replace the bone ends. Clean thoroughly with antiseptic and cover with a sterile dressing. Seek help. Start antibiotics if help is delayed.

8.22   FROSTBITE

Usually affects the extremities: toes, fingers, ears or nose. The affected part may be very painful, numb, stiff and discoloured. Warm gently (on someone else's back, for example).

Immersion in water less than 43°C (110°F); any higher temperature will cause more damage. Do not rub the affected part with anything.

8.23   HEAD INJURY

A blow to the head, with or without fracture, may result in immediate unconsciousness or more delayed effects.

Treatment

- Immediate unconsciousness, but quick recovery with slight drowsiness or headache. Prescribe rest and watch carefully.
- Immediate unconsciousness, no sign of recovery. Put in recovery position (beware of associated spine injury). Check airway. Observe the following and record every 10 minutes: pulse rate, breathing rate, pupil size (both sides), responses to verbal command, response to firm pinching. *Urgent help needed*.
- Delayed deterioration (either not unconscious immediately, or apparently recovering then worsening). Increasing drowsiness, change in mental state and eventually unconsciousness. Treat as above. *Urgent help needed*.

Scalp wounds may bleed profusely. Control with very firm pressure; cut away hair, and close using Steristrips if no fracture beneath. *If in doubt seek help*. Avoid giving drugs after head injury.

8.24   NAIL INJURIES

Nails can be torn or lifted off the underlying flesh and bleeding can be impressive. Do not try to remove the damaged nail which will support the underlying tissue or bone if it is also damaged. Treat as for any bleeding wound with a pad and a bandage wrapped around the finger.

Blood may collect under the nail following a blow. Release the blood by piercing the nail with a red hot needle or paper clip. It will not hurt!

8.25 NOSEBLEED

Lean forwards and pinch the soft part of the nose firmly for at least 10 minutes to allow the blood to clot. Do not blow nose or try to remove clot.

If bleeding continues repeat the pressure for longer than 10 minutes. If still bleeding after 30 minutes insert as much 50mm (2in) gauze bandage (moistened with water) into the nostrils as you can, using forceps to feed the bandage in. *Urgent help needed.*

8.26 POISONING

Poison may reach the body when swallowed, inhaled or injected through the skin (for bites and stings see 8.11).

Treatment

- *ABC – Airway, Breathing, Circulation;* see 8.4.
- Recovery position if unconscious.
- *Seek help.*

Swallowed poison
The poison container may give instructions or suggest antidote(s). For corrosive or petroleum products (acids, alkalis, bleach, detergent, petrol) *do not induce vomiting.* Administer copious fluids (eg milk).

For other substances (pills, medicines) *do not induce vomiting* – it is often ineffective and may cause further harm to the casualty. If collapsed or unconscious **urgent help needed**.

Inhaled poison
Poison may be inhaled from sources such as carbon monoxide or other exhaust fumes, bottled gas which has leaked into the bilge, or fire extinguisher gas. Carbon monoxide inhalation produces cherry red lips and skin. Move into fresh air at once. If breathing is absent, start resuscitation. **Urgent help needed**.

8.27 STRAINS AND SPRAINS

Torn ligaments, pulled muscles and other injuries. Rest the injured part; elevate if possible; apply ice packs (wrapped in a towel) if possible; administer painkillers. If in doubt, treat as a fracture and immobilise.

8.28 FIRST AID KIT

A made-up Offshore First Aid kit (below) costs about £50; a more comprehensive pre-packed kit might exceed £180. Prescriptions marked * are needed for three of the drugs listed in 8.29. Out of date drugs are potentially dangerous and should be destroyed. Special preparations are available for children. Stow the following suggested items in a readily accessible, clearly marked waterproof container:

Triangular bandage x 2 (doubles as bandage or sling)

Crepe bandage 75mm x 2

Gauze bandage 50mm x 2

Elastoplast 75mm x 1

Band Aids (or similar) various shapes and sizes

Wound dressings, 1 large, 1 medium

Sterile non-adhesive dressing (Melolin) x 5

Steristrips x 5 packs

Cotton wool

Scissors and forceps, good quality stainless steel

Safety pins

Thermometer

Disposable gloves

Antiseptic solution (eg Savlon)

Sunscreen with high protection factor

Antifungal powder or cream (athlete's foot)

Insect repellent (DEET, diethyltoluamide)

Individual choice of antiseasickness tablets

*Antibiotic eye ointment

Additional items for extended cruising

Do not forget vaccinations – a course may need to start as much as 6 months before departure.

Syringes 2ml x 2 (if carrying injections)

Dental kit – see 8.18.

Moisture cream (for cracked hands and lips)

8.29 DRUGS AND MEDICATION

Drug	Type/Use	Dose
Paracetamol 500mg tablets	painkiller	1–2 tablets every 4 hours
*Dihydrocodeine 30mg tablets	strong painkiller	1–2 tablets every 4 hours
Chlorpheniramine 4mg tablets	antihistamine	1 tablet every 8 hours
Aludrox	indigestion	1–2 before meals
Loperamide 2mg capsules	diarrhoea	Take 2 capsules initially followed by 1 after each loose stool, up to a maximum of 8 per day
Senokot tablets	constipation	2–4 tablets daily
Tetracycline 250mg	antibiotic	1 capsule 4 times daily
*Amoxycillin 250mg	antibiotic	250–500mg every 8 hours (beware penicillin allergy)
*Erythromycin 250mg	antibiotic	For penicillin-allergic adults 4 tablets daily
Cinnarizine 15mg tablets	seasickness	2 before voyage, then 1 every 8 hours

* denotes only available on prescription – may be a private one.

8.30 EMERGENCY CHILDBIRTH

A yacht is no place to give birth. Unless remaining within about one hour of harbour, a woman who is more than 32 weeks' pregnant should not even consider going to sea in a small boat. Before 30 weeks into the pregnancy, there should be no problem embarking on short offshore passages.

Although giving birth may be an entirely natural process, it is potentially fraught with danger – for both mother and baby – and should ideally be supervised by a midwife or other suitably qualified person. Labour may start with backache, regular pains in the abdomen, a show of blood-stained mucus and a gush of water from the birth canal. Such a situation clearly demands a PAN PAN call followed by rapid assessment and transfer to hospital by lifeboat or helicopter.

Should help not be available, the best advice is to stay calm, unhurried and let nature take its course.

8.31 INJECTIONS

A doctor's prescription is required for injections. Stringent regulations apply to injectable painkiller drugs, which are probably only warranted for long passages. It is safest to inject into the muscle on the outer part of the mid-thigh. Clean the area, then plunge the needle swiftly an inch or so through the skin, pull back on the plunger to ensure that a blood vessel has not been entered, then slowly complete the injection.

8.32 BOOKS ON FIRST AID

The books below give detailed advice. At least one should be on board and the crew should know where it is stowed:

First Aid at Sea by Douglas Justins & Colin Berry (Adlard Coles Nautical, £8.99). Recommended by the RORC.

Skipper's Medical Emergency Handbook by Briggs & Mackenzie (Adlard Coles Nautical, £13.99).

First Aid Manual of St John Ambulance, St Andrew's Ambulance Association and the British Red Cross (Dorling Kindersley, £12.99); Many colour illustrations.

8.33 NORMAL PHYSIOLOGICAL MEASUREMENTS

Pulse rate	Adults 60–80/minute
	Children up to 100/minute
Breathing	12–15/minute
Temperature	36·7°C (98·4°F)

8.34   OBSERVATION FORM

The information recorded by you on this form will be invaluable in helping doctors or paramedics to diagnose the problem and arrange the best possible treatment for your casualty. This is particularly important if there may be a significant time lapse between requesting medical help and the casualty reaching hospital.

- Keep photocopies of this form in your First Aid kit so as to preserve the original.
- Whilst awaiting help, record your observations by ticking

or annotating the various boxes at 10 minute intervals; trends can be important and will help doctors detect any improvement or deterioration in the casualty's condition.

- Continue recording observations until help arrives.
- If within radio range of shore attempt to pass the observations via the Coastguard to a medical authority; or ask a ship to relay.
- Before the casualty is taken off the yacht ensure that this form and personal documents are secured to him/her.

DATE ....   CASUALTY'S NAME ....   AGE ....   M/F ....

Times of observations @ 10 minute intervals:		10	20	30	40	50	60
EYES Observe for reactions whilst testing other responses	Open spontaneously						
	Open when spoken to						
	Open to painful stimulus						
	Nil response						
MOVEMENT Apply painful stimulus: Pinch ear lobe or skin on back of hand	Obeys commands						
	Responds						
	Nil response						
SPEECH Speak clearly and directly, close to the casualty's ear	Responds sensibly to queries						
	Seems confused						
	Uses inappropriate words						
	Incomprehensible sounds						
	Nil response						
PULSE (Beats per minute) Take adult's pulse at wrist or neck. Note rate and whether beats are: weak (w); strong (s); regular (reg) or irregular (irreg)	Over 110						
	101-110						
	91-100						
	81-90						
	71-80						
	61-70						
	Below 61						
BREATHING (Breaths per minute) Note rate and whether breathing is: quiet (q); noisy (n); easy (e); or difficult (d)	Over 40						
	31-40						
	21-30						
	11-20						
	Below 11						

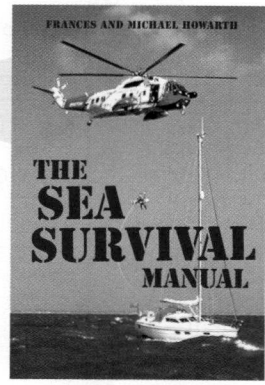

Harbours, Coasts and Tides

Map of areas • Area information • Harbour information • Distances across the English Channel, Irish Sea and the North Sea • Distances across the Bay of Biscay

9.0.1 MAP OF AREAS

Area	Page	Area	Page
1	149	14	649
2	203	15	665
3	257	16	701
4	281	17	747
5	337	18	797
6	371	19	819
7	401	20	845
8	437	21	883
9	473	22	913
10	503	23	947
11	533	24	981
12	569	25	1007
13	611		

9.0.2 AREA INFORMATION

The 25 geographic Areas are arranged as follows:

A map of the Area showing the positions of harbours, principal lights, emergency RDF stations, CG Centres with their boundaries, airports and ferry ports, magnetic variation and a distance table.

Tidal stream chartlets showing hourly rates and set.

Lights, buoys and waypoints listing characteristics of selected lights, their daytime appearance, fog signals, Racons and position. Arcs of visibility and alignment of sector/leading lights are true bearings as seen from seaward. Lights are white unless otherwise stated. Any colours are shown between the bearings of the relevant arcs (see 3.3).

Passage information is threaded between the harbours in each Area and briefly describes the coast, offlying dangers, tidal information, selected anchorages, recommended routes and any local weather patterns.

Special notes giving data specific to a country or area.

9.0.3 HARBOUR INFORMATION

Below the **harbour name**, the County or Unitary Council (or foreign equivalent) is given, followed by the lat/long of the harbour entrance for use as the final waypoint.

The **harbour ratings**, which are inevitably subjective, grade a port based on the following criteria:

Ease of access:

❀❀❀ *Can be entered in gales from most directions and at all states of tide, by day or night.*

❀❀ *Accessible in strong winds from most directions; possible tidal or pilotage constraints.*

❀ *Only accessible in calm, settled conditions by day with little or no swell; possible bar and difficult pilotage.*

Facilities available:

✇✇✇ *Good facilities for vessel and crew.*

✇✇ *Most domestic needs catered for, but limited boatyard facilities.*

✇ *Possibly some domestic facilities, but little else.*

Attractiveness:

✿✿✿ *An attractive place; well worth visiting.*

✿✿ *Average for this part of the coast.*

✿ *Holds no particular attraction.*

Chart numbers show Admiralty (AC), Imray, Stanford (Stan) and foreign charts, all smallest scale first, and Admiralty Leisure Folios (56XX). Some ACs are available as Leisure Editions (prefix: SC), printed on wet strength paper and with additional useful information on the back of each chart.

Tide tables and tidal curves are given for Standard Ports and the differences for Secondary Ports.

Harbour chartlets are based on Admiralty or relevant foreign charts.

Although great care has been taken to ensure that they accurately portray the harbour, *they are not intended to be used for navigation.* The publisher and editors disclaim any responsibility for resultant accidents or damage if they are so used. The largest scale official chart, properly corrected, should always be used.

Drying areas and the 5m depth contour are coloured as follows: Dries   <5m   >5m

Due to their scale, chartlets do not always cover the whole area referred to in the text nor do they show every depth, mark, feature or the approach waypoint (⊕).

Shelter assesses how protected a harbour is from wind, sea, surge and swell. It warns of access difficulties and advises on safe berths and anchorages.

Navigation gives the lat/long of an approach waypoint with its bearing and distance to the harbour entrance or next significant feature; some waypoints may be off the harbour chartlet. Approach channels, buoyage, speed limits and hazards are also described.

Access times, if quoted, are based on a nominal 1·5m draft, plus a safety margin, for an average tide, but must not be relied upon. Any significant swell may affect these times. Lock and bridge opening times are in local time.

Wrecks around the UK which are of archaeological or historic interest are protected by law. About 20 sites are listed under the nearest harbour or in Passage Information. Unauthorised interference, including anchoring and diving on such sites, may lead to a substantial fine.

Lights and Marks describe, in more detail than is shown on the chartlets, any unusual characteristics of marks, their appearance by day and features not listed elsewhere.

IPTS (International Port Traffic Signals) are in Chapter 5.

R/T lists VHF channels related to the port, marina or VTS. Callsigns, if not obvious, are in *italics*.

Telephone gives any area code in brackets (which is not repeated for individual telephone numbers unless different or additional codes apply). International calls from/to the UK are described in Special Notes, as are national numbers for marine emergencies abroad including Ambulance, Fire and Police. In the EU 112 is the main emergency number; in the UK it is 999.

Facilities describe man-made features: pontoons, ⚓s, quays, pile moorings, etc at harbours, YCs and marinas (see also the free **Reeds Marina Guide**) followed by commercial services. Most YCs usually welcome bona fide crews who belong to a recognised club and arrive by sea. Town facilities are listed, with rail, ferry and air links.

The overnight cost of a visitor's alongside berth (AB), *at the previous year's rates*, is the average charge per metre LOA (unless otherwise stated) during high season, usually June to Sept. It includes harbour dues, if applicable, and VAT. The cost of pile moorings, ⚓s or ⚓s where these are the norm, may also be given. Shore electricity is usually free abroad but extra in the UK.

The number of ❶ berths is a marina's estimate of how many visitors may be accommodated at any one time. It is always advisable to call the marina beforehand.

Slipways. Access and launch/recovery fees per day, eg Slip HW±2 (£6.00), are given in some harbours for craft <6·5m LOA.

FACILITIES FOR DISABLED PEOPLE

RYA Sailability operates under the RYA's auspices to open up sailing and its related benefits to disabled sailors. Facilities include car parking, wheelchair ramps to buildings and pontoons and purpose-built toilets and showers. Facilities for those with sight or hearing disabilities are becoming more widely available. Standard symbols (♿ ✇ ✇ ✇) are used in Chapter 9.

9.0.4 ENVIRONMENTAL GUIDANCE

- Comply with regulations for navigation and conduct within Marine Nature Reserves, Particularly Sensitive Sea Areas (PSSA) and National Water Parks.
- In principle never ditch rubbish at sea, keep it on board and dispose of it in harbour refuse bins.
- Readily degradable foodstuffs may be ditched at sea when >3M offshore (>12M in the English Channel).
- Foodstuffs and other materials which are not readily degradable should never be ditched at sea.
- Sewage. If you do not have a holding tank, only flush the onboard heads when well offshore. Consider fitting a holding tank as many countries now require them. Pump-out facilities (⚓) are shown in the text.
- Do not pump out holding tanks until >3M offshore.
- Do not discharge foul water into a marina, anchorage or moorings area and minimise on washing-up water.
- Deposit used engine oil and oily waste ashore at a recognised facility. Do not allow an automatic bilge pump to discharge oily bilge water overboard.
- Dispose of toxic waste, (eg some antifoulings, cleaning chemicals, old batteries) at an approved disposal facility.
- Row ashore whenever possible – to minimise noise, wash and disturbance. Land at recognised places.
- Respect wild birds, plants, fish and marine animals. Avoid protected nesting sites and breeding colonies.
- Do not anchor or dry out on vulnerable seabed species, eg soft corals, eel grass.

9.0.5 DISTANCES (M) ACROSS THE ENGLISH CHANNEL

Approximate distances in nautical miles are by the most direct route, avoiding dangers and allowing for TSS.

France/CI \ England	Longships	Falmouth	Fowey	Plymouth bkwtr	Salcombe	Dartmouth	Torbay	Exmouth	Weymouth	Poole Hbr Ent	Needles Lt Ho	Nab Tower	Littlehampton	Shoreham	Brighton	Newhaven	Eastbourne	Rye	Folkestone	Dover
Le Conquet	112	112	123	125	125	137	144	155	172	188	194	212	230	240	245	249	261	278	295	301
L'Aberwrac'h	102	97	106	107	105	117	124	135	153	168	174	192	211	219	224	228	239	257	275	280
Roscoff	110	97	101	97	91	100	107	117	130	144	149	165	184	193	197	200	211	229	246	252
Trébeurden	120	105	106	102	94	102	109	120	129	142	147	164	181	190	194	197	208	226	244	249
Tréguier	132	112	110	101	94	98	102	112	116	128	132	147	162	170	174	177	188	206	224	229
Lézardrieux	142	121	118	107	94	100	105	114	115	126	130	140	157	165	169	172	184	201	219	224
St Quay-Portrieux	159	137	135	124	111	115	121	129	127	135	135	146	162	171	174	178	189	207	225	230
St Malo	172	149	146	133	118	120	124	132	125	130	130	143	157	166	170	173	184	202	220	225
St Helier	155	130	123	108	93	95	100	108	99	104	104	115	132	140	144	147	158	176	194	199
St Peter Port	139	113	104	89	73	70	75	81	71	79	83	97	112	120	124	127	135	156	174	179
Braye (Alderney)	146	116	106	89	72	69	71	75	54	60	62	73	91	100	103	106	114	136	153	159
Cherbourg	168	138	125	107	92	87	88	93	66	64	63	68	81	90	92	96	102	122	140	145
St Vaast	194	164	150	132	116	111	112	116	83	76	72	71	80	87	88	90	96	115	132	138
Ouistreham	229	198	185	167	151	146	147	147	117	107	100	86	91	92	91	90	92	106	125	130
Deauville	236	205	192	174	158	153	154	154	122	111	104	88	89	88	87	85	87	101	120	125
Le Havre	231	200	187	169	153	148	148	148	118	105	97	82	82	83	82	79	80	94	115	120
Fécamp	242	212	197	179	163	157	157	157	120	105	96	75	71	68	65	62	62	72	90	95
Dieppe	268	237	222	204	188	180	180	180	142	125	117	91	80	75	70	64	63	60	70	75
Boulogne	290	258	242	224	208	198	195	191	153	135	127	97	81	71	66	59	47	33	28	25
Calais	305	272	257	239	223	213	210	209	168	150	141	111	96	86	81	74	62	43	26	22

9.0.6 DISTANCES (M) ACROSS THE IRISH SEA

Scotland / England / Wales / Ireland	Port Ellen (Islay)	Campbeltown	Troon	Portpatrick	Mull of Galloway	Kirkcudbright	Maryport	Fleetwood	Pt of Ayre (IOM)	Port St Mary (IOM)	Liverpool	Holyhead	Pwllheli	Fishguard	Milford Haven	Swansea	Avonmouth	Ilfracombe	Padstow	Longships
Tory Island	75	107	132	119	134	170	185	215	156	171	238	207	260	279	307	360	406	355	372	399
Malin Head	45	76	101	88	103	139	154	184	125	140	207	176	229	248	276	329	375	324	341	368
Lough Foyle	38	61	86	73	88	124	139	169	110	125	192	161	214	233	261	314	360	309	326	353
Portrush	31	50	76	64	80	116	131	161	102	117	184	153	206	225	253	306	352	301	318	345
Carnlough	42	35	57	32	45	81	96	126	67	78	149	115	168	187	215	268	314	363	280	307
Larne	51	39	58	24	37	72	88	118	58	70	141	106	159	178	206	259	305	254	271	298
Carrickfergus	64	48	65	26	34	69	85	115	55	66	138	101	154	173	201	254	300	249	266	293
Bangor	63	48	64	22	30	65	81	111	51	62	134	97	150	169	197	250	296	245	262	289
Strangford Loch	89	72	84	36	30	63	76	97	41	37	107	69	121	141	167	219	265	214	231	258
Carlingford Loch	117	100	112	64	60	90	103	112	70	51	118	67	111	124	149	202	248	197	214	241
Dun Laoghaire	153	136	148	100	93	119	126	120	93	69	119	56	82	94	109	162	208	157	174	201
Wicklow	170	153	165	117	108	133	140	127	108	83	123	56	67	71	90	143	189	138	155	182
Arklow	182	165	177	129	120	144	149	133	117	93	131	64	71	65	79	132	179	128	144	167
Rosslare	215	202	208	161	154	179	180	164	152	125	156	90	83	55	58	109	157	110	119	137
Tuskar Rock	216	203	209	162	155	179	182	165	152	126	152	91	82	48	51	105	150	103	112	130
Dunmore East	250	237	243	196	189	213	216	199	186	160	189	127	116	79	76	130	177	124	127	136
Youghal	281	268	274	227	220	244	247	230	217	191	220	158	147	110	103	156	200	148	139	138
Crosshaven	300	287	293	246	239	263	266	249	236	210	239	177	166	131	118	170	216	163	151	144
Baltimore	346	333	339	292	285	309	312	295	282	256	285	223	212	172	160	209	254	198	178	161
Fastnet Rock	354	341	347	300	293	317	320	303	290	264	293	231	220	181	169	216	260	207	185	170

NOTES

This Table applies to Areas 9–13, each of which also contains its own internal Distance Table. Approximate distances in nautical miles are by the most direct route, avoiding dangers and Traffic Separation Schemes.

9.0.7 DISTANCES (M) ACROSS THE NORTH SEA

Norway to France / UK	Bergen	Stavanger	Lindesnes	Skagen	Esjberg	Sylt (List)	Brunsbüttel	Helgoland	Bremerhaven	Willhelmshaven	Delfzijl	Den Helder	IJmuiden	Scheveningen	Roompotsluis	Vlissingen	Zeebrugge	Oostende	Nieuwpoort	Dunkerque
Lerwick	210	226	288	403	428	442	517	470	510	500	493	486	497	505	551	550	552	555	562	588
Kirkwall	278	275	323	438	439	452	516	467	507	497	481	460	473	481	515	514	516	519	526	545
Wick	292	283	323	437	428	440	498	449	489	479	458	433	444	451	485	484	486	489	496	514
Inverness	356	339	381	485	461	462	529	479	519	509	487	460	471	478	513	512	514	517	524	542
Fraserburgh	288	266	296	410	383	384	451	404	444	434	412	385	396	403	430	429	431	434	441	456
Aberdeen	308	279	298	411	371	378	433	382	432	412	386	353	363	369	401	400	402	405	412	426
Dundee	362	329	339	451	394	401	448	396	436	426	395	352	359	364	390	389	385	388	395	412
Port Edgar	391	355	362	472	409	413	457	405	445	435	401	355	361	366	391	390	386	389	396	413
Berwick	374	325	320	431	356	361	408	355	395	385	355	310	315	320	342	341	337	340	347	364
Hartlepool	409	353	340	440	340	331	367	312	352	342	302	241	243	247	266	265	261	264	271	288
Grimsby	463	395	362	452	324	318	342	291	332	325	288	187	182	185	199	198	190	191	201	198
Kings Lynn	485	416	379	466	330	333	343	292	344	336	283	184	183	183	197	195	187	188	198	195
Lowestoft	508	431	380	453	308	300	295	262	284	271	218	118	104	98	95	99	87	87	89	106
Harwich	540	461	410	483	330	331	320	287	309	296	243	147	126	114	94	100	84	77	80	80
Brightlingsea	558	479	428	501	348	349	338	305	327	314	261	165	144	105	108	106	92	88	86	87
Burnham/Crouch	567	488	437	510	357	358	347	314	336	323	270	174	151	112	109	115	99	92	93	95
London Bridge	620	543	490	560	400	408	395	361	382	374	320	222	199	149	153	149	134	125	126	114
Sheerness	580	503	450	520	360	367	353	319	340	334	280	180	157	109	113	109	94	85	86	74
Ramsgate	575	498	446	516	368	346	339	305	323	315	262	161	144	121	89	85	77	65	58	42
Dover	588	511	459	529	378	359	352	328	336	328	275	174	155	132	101	92	79	65	58	44

NOTES

This Table applies to Areas 3–7 and 14–17, each of which also contains its own internal Distance Table. Approximate distances in nautical miles are by the most direct route, while avoiding dangers and allowing for Traffic Separation Schemes.

9.0.8 DISTANCES (M) ACROSS THE BAY OF BISCAY

West France \ N & NW Spain	Bayona	Vigo	Sanxenxo	Vilagarcia	Muros	Cabo Finisterre	Camariñas	La Coruña	Ria de Cedeira	Cabo Ortegal	Ria de Vivero	Ria de Ribadeo	Cabo Peñas	Gijon	San Vicente de la B	Santander	Bilbao	Cabo Machichaco	Zumaya	Fuenterrabia
Le Conquet	453	453	449	442	402	382	374	340	321	305	308	306	286	293	300	300	311	308	322	330
Lampaul (Ushant)	450	450	446	439	399	379	366	336	315	303	307	306	290	296	306	311	320	317	331	337
Camaret	456	456	452	445	405	385	369	339	318	306	309	306	287	293	300	305	311	308	322	329
Brest (Moulin B)	463	463	459	452	412	392	379	347	326	313	315	314	294	300	307	309	320	315	329	336
Douarnenez	457	457	453	446	406	386	373	340	320	306	309	307	287	293	300	302	311	308	323	329
Audierne	450	450	443	437	397	377	356	324	304	290	291	289	268	273	279	283	288	284	298	304
Port-la-Forêt	459	459	452	445	405	385	367	331	309	297	298	292	270	273	276	273	277	273	285	290
Lorient entrance	463	463	456	449	409	389	375	340	319	304	304	295	266	269	264	261	264	258	270	274
Belle Ile (Le Palais)	462	462	455	448	408	388	370	334	311	297	296	287	255	257	249	244	245	238	250	254
La Trinité	471	471	464	457	417	397	382	348	326	312	311	300	267	269	260	256	257	249	260	247
Piriac	475	475	468	461	421	401	386	351	327	314	311	301	266	268	255	247	247	239	248	252
Pornichet	473	473	466	459	419	399	403	348	326	312	309	298	262	264	249	240	239	229	242	247
L'Herbaudière	468	468	461	454	414	394	380	344	320	306	293	291	253	254	238	230	227	220	228	233
Sables d'Olonne	471	471	464	457	417	397	379	342	318	304	300	284	243	242	217	205	197	187	195	199
La Rochelle	496	496	489	482	442	422	407	354	330	316	311	293	248	247	216	202	191	179	187	192
Royan/Port-Médoc*	492	492	485	478	438	418	404	353	327	313	307	287	237	235	198	181	170	158	166	146
Arcachon*	463	463	456	449	409	389	375	336	310	296	289	266	214	209	167	151	133	121	112	90
Capbreton	446	446	439	432	392	372	358	317	293	279	272	245	191	185	131	107	75	59	45	23
Anglet/Bayonne	442	442	435	428	388	368	354	313	289	275	267	242	188	181	126	103	70	54	35	16
Hendaye	434	434	427	420	380	360	346	305	281	267	258	232	179	172	115	92	60	44	23	0·6

NOTES

1. Approximate distances in nautical miles are by the most direct route, avoiding dangers and allowing for TSS. This Table can be read in conjunction with those in West France (9.20.2, 9.21.2, 9.22.2) and North Spain (9.23.2).

2. Yachts leaving Ireland for Longships use 9.0.6, if applicable; then use 9.0.5 for distances across the English Channel.

3. **Landes firing range** in SE Biscay (see 9.22.26 and AC 1104) extends 106M S from Pte de la Négade to Capbreton and up to 45M offshore. Distances are based on routes passing west of Landes range, except that from Royan/Port-Médoc* and Arcachon* the distances to Fuenterrabia and Zumaya are by the inshore route E of the range.
If this route is not available, add 25M to the tabulated distance from Royan/Port-Médoc to Fuenterrabia; add nil for Zumaya. From Arcachon add 44M and 16M to Fuenterrabia and Zumaya respectively, using the 8M wide, safe corridor extending 270°/39M from ATT-ARC buoy through the range. This corridor is also used in calculating distances from Arcachon to all headlands and destinations west of Zumaya.

South West England

Isles of Scilly to Anvil Point

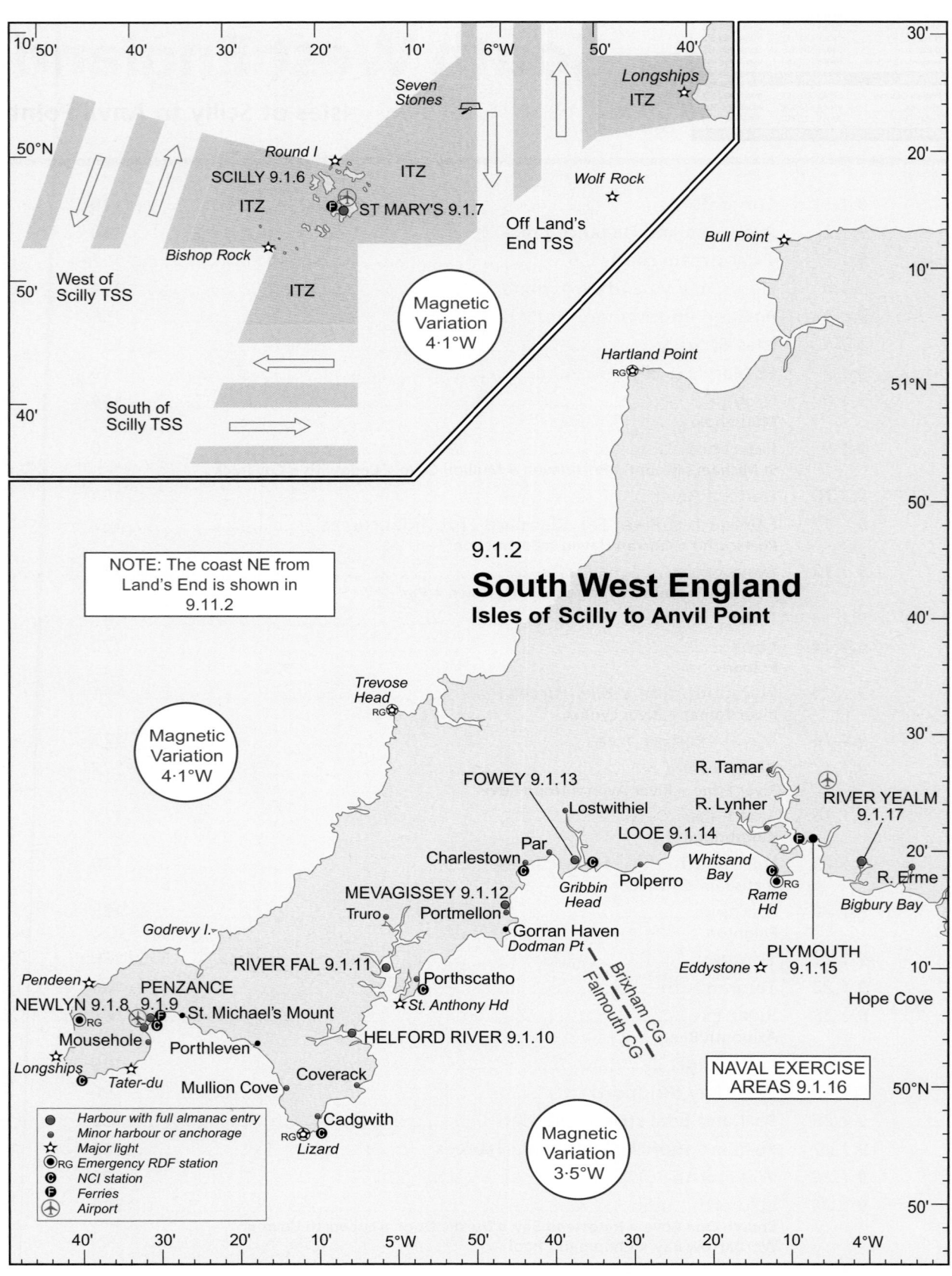

9.1.2

South West England
Isles of Scilly to Anvil Point

NOTE: The coast NE from Land's End is shown in 9.11.2

Longships ITZ

Seven Stones

Round I

SCILLY 9.1.6

ITZ

ITZ

ST MARY'S 9.1.7

Bishop Rock

ITZ

Off Land's End TSS

Wolf Rock

Magnetic Variation 4·1°W

West of Scilly TSS

South of Scilly TSS

Bull Point

Hartland Point
RG

Magnetic Variation 4·1°W

Trevose Head
RG

FOWEY 9.1.13

Lostwithiel

R. Tamar

R. Lynher

RIVER YEALM 9.1.17

Par

LOOE 9.1.14

Charlestown

Whitsand Bay

R. Erme

Gribbin Head

Polperro

Rame Hd

Bigbury Bay

MEVAGISSEY 9.1.12

Truro

Portmellon

Gorran Haven

Dodman Pt

Brixham CG

Falmouth CG

PLYMOUTH 9.1.15

Eddystone

Hope Cove

RIVER FAL 9.1.11

Porthscatho

St. Anthony Hd

NAVAL EXERCISE AREAS 9.1.16

Godrevy I.

Pendeen

PENZANCE 9.1.9

NEWLYN 9.1.8
RG

St. Michael's Mount

HELFORD RIVER 9.1.10

Mousehole

Porthleven

Longships

Tater-du

Mullion Cove

Coverack

Cadgwith
RG

Lizard

Magnetic Variation 3·5°W

Legend:
- ● Harbour with full almanac entry
- • Minor harbour or anchorage
- ☆ Major light
- ⊙RG Emergency RDF station
- Ⓒ NCI station
- Ⓕ Ferries
- ✈ Airport

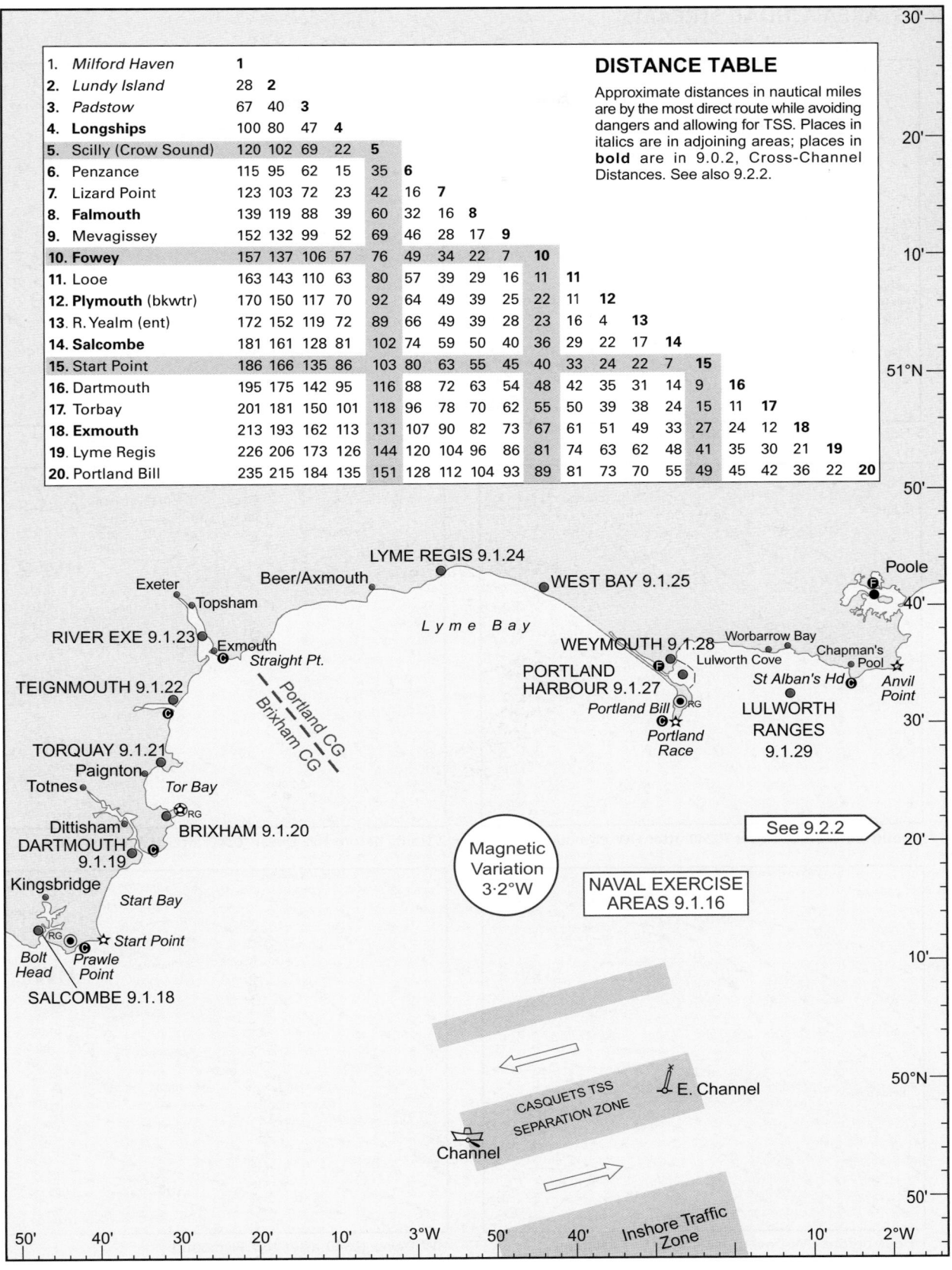

DISTANCE TABLE

Approximate distances in nautical miles are by the most direct route while avoiding dangers and allowing for TSS. Places in italics are in adjoining areas; places in **bold** are in 9.0.2, Cross-Channel Distances. See also 9.2.2.

1.	*Milford Haven*	**1**																		
2.	*Lundy Island*	28	**2**																	
3.	*Padstow*	67	40	**3**																
4.	**Longships**	100	80	47	**4**															
5.	Scilly (Crow Sound)	120	102	69	22	**5**														
6.	Penzance	115	95	62	15	35	**6**													
7.	Lizard Point	123	103	72	23	42	16	**7**												
8.	**Falmouth**	139	119	88	39	60	32	16	**8**											
9.	Mevagissey	152	132	99	52	69	46	28	17	**9**										
10.	**Fowey**	157	137	106	57	76	49	34	22	7	**10**									
11.	Looe	163	143	110	63	80	57	39	29	16	11	**11**								
12.	**Plymouth** (bkwtr)	170	150	117	70	92	64	49	39	25	22	11	**12**							
13.	R. Yealm (ent)	172	152	119	72	89	66	49	39	28	23	16	4	**13**						
14.	**Salcombe**	181	161	128	81	102	74	59	50	40	36	29	22	17	**14**					
15.	Start Point	186	166	135	86	103	80	63	55	45	40	33	24	22	7	**15**				
16.	Dartmouth	195	175	142	95	116	88	72	63	54	48	42	35	31	14	9	**16**			
17.	Torbay	201	181	150	101	118	96	78	70	62	55	50	39	38	24	15	11	**17**		
18.	**Exmouth**	213	193	162	113	131	107	90	82	73	67	61	51	49	33	27	24	12	**18**	
19.	Lyme Regis	226	206	173	126	144	120	104	96	86	81	74	63	62	48	41	35	30	21	**19**
20.	Portland Bill	235	215	184	135	151	128	112	104	93	89	81	73	70	55	49	45	42	36	22	**20**

9.1.3 AREA 1 TIDAL STREAMS

5 Hours before HW Dover (0040 after HW Plymouth)

4 Hours before HW Dover (0140 after HW Plymouth)

3 Hours before HW Dover (0240 after HW Plymouth)

2 Hours before HW Dover (0340 after HW Plymouth)

1 Hour before HW Dover (0440 after HW Plymouth)

HW Dover (0540 after HW Plymouth)

Eastward 9.2.3   Portland 9.1.26   Isle of Wight 9.2.17   Northward 9.11.3   Southward 9.20.3   Channel Is 9.19.3

1 Hour after HW Dover (0545 before HW Plymouth)

2 Hours after HW Dover (0445 before HW Plymouth)

3 Hours after HW Dover (0345 before HW Plymouth)

4 Hours after HW Dover (0245 before HW Plymouth)

5 Hours after HW Dover (0145 before HW Plymouth)

6 Hours after HW Dover (0045 before HW Plymouth)

9.1.4 LIGHTS, BUOYS AND WAYPOINTS

Bold print = light with a nominal range of 15M or more. CAPITALS = place or feature. *CAPITAL ITALICS* = light-vessel, light float or Lanby. *Italics* = Fog signal. ***Bold italics*** = Racon. Abbreviations are in Chapter 1.

ISLES OF SCILLY TO LAND'S END

Bishop Rock ☆ Fl (2) 15s 44m **20M**; part obsc 204°-211°, obsc 211°-233° and 236°-259°; Gy ○ twr with helo platform; ***Racon T, 18M, 254°-215°***; 49°52'·37N 06°26'·74W. Round Rk ⓘ 49°53'·10N 06°25'·19W. Old Wreck ⓘ VQ; 49°54'·26N 06°22'·81W.

ST AGNES and ST MARY'S

Peninnis Hd ☆ Fl 20s 36m **17M**; 231°-117° but part obsc 048°-083° within 5M; W○twr on B frame, B cupola; 49°54'·28N 06°18'·21W.
Spanish Ledge ⓘ Q (3) 10s; *Bell;* 49°53'·94N 06°18'·86W.
Bartholomew Ledges ⓘ QR 12m; 49°54'·37N 06°19'·89W.
N Bartholomew ⓐ Fl R 5s; 49°54'·49N 06°19'·99W.
Bacon Ledge ⓐ Fl (4) R 5s; 49°55'·22N 06°19'·26W.
Ldg lts 097·3°: Front, Iso RW (vert) 2s; W △, 49°55'·12N 06°18'·50W. Rear, Oc WR (vert) 10s; Or X on W bcn.
St Mary's Pool pier ⓕ Fl WRG 2s 5m 4M; 070°-R-100°-W-130°-G-070°; 49°55'·11N 06°19'·00W.
Crow Rock ⓘ Fl (2) 10s; 49°56'·26N 06°18'·49W.
Hats ⓘ VQ (6) + L Fl 10s; 49°56'·21N 06°17'·14W.

AROUND TRESCO, BRYHER and ST MARTIN'S

Tresco Flats, Hulman ⓘ Fl G 4s, 49°56'·29N 06°20'·31W.
Little Rag Ledge ⓘ Fl (2) R 5s, 49°56'·43N 06°20'·43W.
Bryher, Bar Quay ⓘ Q (3) 10s, 49°57'·37N 06°20'·84W.
Spencers Ledge ⓘ Q (6) + L Fl 15s; 49°54'·78N 06°22'·06W.
Steeple Rock ⓘ Q (9) 15s; 49°55'·46N 06°24'·24W.
Round Island ☆ Fl 10s 55m **18M**, also shown in reduced vis; 021°-288°; W○twr; *Horn (4) 60s;* ***Racon M, 10M;*** 49°58'·74N 06°19'·39W.
St Martin's, Higher Town quay ⓕ Fl R 5s, 49°57'·45N 06°16'·84W.

SCILLY TO LAND'S END

Seven Stones Lt V ⓐ Fl (3) 30s 12m **15M**; R hull; *Horn (3) 60s;* ***Racon O, 15M;*** 50°03'·63N 06°04'·32W.
Wolf Rock ☆ Fl 15s 34m **16M**; H24; *Horn 30s;* ***Racon T, 10M;*** 49°56'·72N 05°48'·57W.
Longships ☆ Fl (2) WR 10s 35m **W15M**, R11M; 189°-R-327°-W-189°; also shown in reduced vis; Gy ○ twr with helicopter platform; *Horn 10s;* 50°04'·01N 05°44'·81W.
Carn Base ⓘ Q (9) 15s; 50°01'·48N 05°46'·18W.
Runnel Stone ⓘ Q (6) + L Fl 15s; *Bell;* 50°01'·18N 05°40'·36W.

LAND'S END TO PLYMOUTH

Tater-du ☆ Fl (3) 15s 34m **20M**; 241°-072°; W○twr. FR 31m 13M, 060°-072° over Runnel Stone; *Horn (2) 30s;* 50°03'·14N 05°34'·67W.

NEWLYN

Low Lee ⓘ Q (3) 10s; 50°05'·56N 05°31'·38W.
S Pier ⓕ Fl 5s 10m 9M; W○ twr; 253°-336°; 50°06'·18N 05°32'·57W.
N Pier ⓕ FWG 4m 2M; 238°-G-248°, W over hbr; 50°06'·18N 05°32'·62W.

PENZANCE

S Pier ⓕ Fl WR 5s 11m **W17M**, R12M; 159°-R (unintens)-224°-R-268°-W-344·5°-R-shore; 50°07'·06N 05°31'·68W.
Mountamopus ⓘ Q (6) + L Fl 15s; 50°04'·62N 05°26'·25W.
Lizard ☆ Fl 3s 70m **26M**; H24; 250°-120°, partly visible 235°-250°; W 8-sided twr; *Horn 30s;* 49°57'·61N 05°12'·13W.
Manacle ⓘ Q (3) 10s; *Bell;* 50°02'·81N 05°01'·91W.

FALMOUTH

St Anthony Head ☆ Iso WR 15s 22m, **W16M**, R14M, H24; 295°-W-004°-R (over Manacles)-022°-W-172°; W 8-sided twr; *Horn 30s;* 50°08'·46N 05°00'·96W.
Black Rock Fl (2) 10s 3M; B IDM bcn twr; 50°08'·72N 05°02'·00W.

Black Rock ⓐ Fl R 2·5s; 50°08'·68N 05°01'·74W.
Castle ⓐ Fl G 2·5s; 50°08'·99N 05°01'·62W.
St Mawes ⓘ Q (6) + L Fl 15s; 50°09'·10N 05°01'·42W.
The Governor ⓘ VQ (3) 5s; 50°09'·15N 05°02'·40W.
West Narrows ⓐ Fl (2) R 10s; 50°09'·39N 05°02'·07W.
East Narrows ⓐ Fl (2) G 10s; 50°09'·43N 05°01'·90W.
The Vilt ⓐ Fl (4) G 15s; 50°09'·99N 05°02'·28W.
Northbank ⓐ Fl R 4s; 50°10'·34N 05°02'·26W.
St Just ⓐ QR; 50°10'·44N 05°01'·72W.
Mylor appr chan ⓐ Fl G 6s; 50°10'·79N 05°02'·70W. ⓐ Fl R 5s.
Messack ⓐ Fl G 15s; 50°11'·31N 05°02'·22W.
Carrick ⓐ Fl (2) G 10s; 50°11'·59N 05°02'·74W.
Pill ⓐ Fl (3) G 15s; 50°12'·05N 05°02'·40W.
Turnerware Bar ⓐ Fl G 5s; 50°12'·40N 05°02'·15W.
Inner Harbour
N Arm ⓕ QR 5m 3M; 50°09'·42N 05°03'·20W.
Visitors Yacht Haven ⓕ 2 FR (vert); 50°09'·27N 05°03'·91W.
Falmouth marina ⓘ VQ (3) 5s; 50°09'·91N 05°04'·99W.

DODMAN POINT and MEVAGISSEY

Naval gunnery targets SSE of Dodman Point:
'A' ⓐ Fl Y 10s; 50°08'·53N 04°46'·37W.
'B' ⓐ Fl Y 5s; 50°10'·30N 04°45'·00W.
'C' ⓐ Fl Y 2s; 50°10'·40N 04°47'·51W.

Gwineas ⓘ Q (3) 10s; *Bell;* 50°14'·48N 04°45'·40W.
Mevagissey, Victoria Pier ⓕ Fl (2) 10s 9m 12M; *Dia 30s;* 50°16'·15N 04°46'·92W.

FOWEY

Cannis Rock ⓘ Q (6) + L Fl 15s; *Bell;* 50°18'·38N 04°39'·95W.
Fowey ⓕ L Fl WR 5s 28m W11M, R9M; 284°-R-295°-W-028°-R-054°; W 8-sided twr, R lantern; 50°19'·63N 04°38'·83W.
St Catherine's Pt ⓕ Fl R 2·5s 15m 2M; 150°-295°; 50°19'·69N 04°38'·66W.
Lamp Rock ⓕ Fl G 5s 7m 2M; 088°-205°; 50°19'·70N 04°38'·38W.
Whitehouse Pt ⓕ Iso WRG 3s 11m W11M, R/G8M; 017°-G-022°-W-032°-R-037°; R col; 50°19'·98N 04°38'·28W.

POLPERRO, LOOE, EDDYSTONE and WHITSAND BAY

Udder Rock ⓘ VQ (6) + L Fl 10s; *Bell;* 50°18'·93N 04°33'·85W.
POLPERRO, W pier ⓕ FW 4m 4M; FR when hbr closed in bad weather; 50°19'·86N 04°30'·96W.
Spy House Pt ⓕ Iso WR 6s 30m 7M; W288°-060°, R060°-288°; 50°19'·81N 04°30'·69W.
LOOE, Ranneys ⓘ Q (6) + L Fl 15s; 50°19'·85N 04°26'·37W.
Mid Main ⓘ Q (3) 10s 2M; 50°20'·56N 04°26'·94W.
Banjo Pier ☆ Oc WR 3s 8m **W15M**, R12M; 207°-R267°- W-313°-R-332°; 50°21'·06N 04°27'·06W.
White Rock ⓕ Fl R 3s 5m 2M; 50°21'·03N 04°27'·09W.

Eddystone ☆ Fl (2) 10s 41m **17M**. Same twr, Iso R 10s 28m 8M; vis 110·5°-130·5° over Hand Deeps; Gy twr, helicopter platform; *Horn 30s;* ***Racon T, 10M;*** 50°10'·84N 04°15'·94W.
Hand Deeps ⓘ Q (9) 15s; 50°12'·68N 04°21'·10W.

PLYMOUTH

PLYMOUTH SOUND, WESTERN CHANNEL

Draystone ⓐ Fl (2) R 5s; 50°18'·85N 04°11'·07W.
Knap ⓐ Fl G 5s; 50°19'·56N 04°10'·02W.
Plymouth bkwtr W head, ⓕ Fl WR 10s 19m W12M, R9M; 262°-W-208°-R-262°; W ○ twr. Same twr, Iso 4s 12m 10M; vis 033°-037°; *Horn 15s;* 50°20'·07N 04°09'·52W.
Maker ⓕ Fl (2) WRG 10s 29m, W11M, R/G6M; 270°-G330°- W-004°-R-050°; W twr, R stripe; 50°20'·51N 04°10'·87W.
Queens Ground ⓐ Fl (2) R 10s; 50°20'·29N 04°10'·08W.
New Ground ⓐ Fl R 2s; 50°20'·47N 04°09'·43W.
Melampus ⓐ Fl R 4s; 50°21'·15N 04°08'·72W.

PLYMOUTH SOUND, EASTERN CHANNEL

Wembury Pt ⓕ Oc Y 10s 45m; occas; 50°19'·01N 04°06'·63W.

WGS84 DATUM
Plot waypoints on chart before use

West Tinker ⚓ VQ (9) 10s; 50°19'·25N 04°08'·64W.
East Tinker ⚓ Q (3) 10s; 50°19'·20N 04°08'·30W.
Whidbey ⚓ Oc (2) WRG 10s 29m, W8M, R/G6M, H24; 000°-G-137·5°-W-139·5°-R-159°; Or and W col; 50°19'·53N 04°07'·27W.
The Breakwater, E head ⚓ L Fl WR 10s 9m W8M, R6M; 190°-R-353°-W-001°-R-018°-W-190°; 50°20'·01N 04°08'·24W.
Staddon Pt ⚓ Oc WRG 10s 15m W8M, R/G5M; H24. 348°-G-038°-W-050°-R-090°; W structure, R bands; 50°20'·17N 04°07'·54W.
Withyhedge Dir ⚓ 070° (for W Chan): WRG 13m W13M, R/G5M; H24; 060°-FG-065°-Al WG (W phase increasing with brg) -069°-FW-071°-Al WR (R phase increasing with brg)-075°-FR-080°; W ▽, orange stripe on col. Same col, Fl (2) Bu 5s; vis 120°-160°; 50°20'·75N 04°07'·44W.

SMEATON PASS (W of Mount Batten and S of The Hoe)
Ldg lts 349°. Front, Mallard Shoal ⚓ Q WRG 5m W10M, R/G3M; W △, Or bands; 233°-G-043°- R-067°- G-087°-W-099°-R-108° (ldg sector); 50°21'·60N 04°08'·33W. Rear, 396m from front, Hoe ⚓ Oc G 1·3s 11m 3M, 310°-040°; W ▽, Or bands; 50°21'·81N 04°08'·39W.
S Mallard ⚓ VQ (6) + L Fl 10s; 50°21'·51N 04°08'·30W.
W Mallard ⚓ QG; 50°21'·57N 04°08'·36W.
S Winter ⚓ Q (6) + L Fl 15s; 50°21'·40N 04°08'·55W.
NE Winter ⚓ QR; 50°21'·54N 04°08'·50W.
NW Winter ⚓ VQ (9) 10s; 50°21'·55N 04°08'·70W.

ENTRANCE TO THE CATTEWATER
QAB (Queen Anne's Battery) ldg lts ⚓ 048·5°. Front, FR; Or/W bcn; 50°21'·84N 04°07'·84W. Rear, Oc R 8s 14m 3M; 139m NE.
Fishers Nose ⚓ Fl (3) R 10s 6m 4M; 50°21'·80N 04°08'·01W. Also F Bu ≠ 026·5° with F Bu 50°22'·00N 04°07'·86W, for Cobbler Chan.

DRAKE CHANNEL, THE BRIDGE and THE NARROWS
Asia ⚓ Fl (2) R 5s; 50°21'·47N 04°08'·85W. St Nicholas ⚓ QR; 50°21'·55N 04°09'·20W. N Drakes Is ⚓ Fl R 4s; 50°21'·52N 04°09'·38W. E Vanguard ⚓ QG; 50°21'·47N 04°09'·70W.
W Vanguard ⚓ Fl G 3s; 50°21'·49N 04°09'·98W.
Devils Point ⚓ QG 5m 3M; Fl 5s in fog; 50°21'·59N 04°10'·04W.
Battery ⚓ Fl R 2s; 50°21'·52N 04°10'·21W.
The Bridge Channel
No 1, ⚓ QG 4m; 50°21'·03N 04°09'·53W. No 2, ⚓ QR 4m. No 3, ⚓ Fl (3) G 10s 4m. No 4, ⚓ Fl (4) R 10s 4m; 50°21'·09N 04°09'·63W.
Mount Wise, Dir ⚓ 343°: WRG 7m W13M, R/G5M; H24. 331°-FG-338°-Al WG-342° (W phase increasing with brg)-FW-344°-Al WR-348° (R phase increasing with bearing)-FR-351°. In fog, 341·5°-FW-344·5°; 50°21'·96N 04°10'·33W.
Ocean Court Dir Q WRG 15m, W11M, R/G3M; 010°-G-080°-W-090°-R-100°; 50°21'·85N 04°10'·11W.

PLYMOUTH TO START POINT
RIVER YEALM Sand bar ⚓ Fl R 5s; 50°18'·59N 04°04'·12W.

SALCOMBE
Sandhill Pt Dir ⚓ 000°: Fl WRG 2s 27m W10M, R/G7M; 182·5°-G-357·5°-W-002·5°-R-182·5°; R/W ◊ on W mast, rear daymark; 50°13'·77N 03°46'·67W. Front daymark, Pound Stone R/W ⚓.
Bass Rk ⚓ QR; 50°13'·47N 03°46'·71W.
Wolf Rk ⚓ QG; 50°13'·53N 03°46'·58W.
Blackstone Rk ⚓ Q (2) G 8s 4m 2M; 50°13'·61N 03°46'·51W.
Ldg lts 042·5°, both Q 5/45m 8M. Front, 50°14'·53N 03°45'·31W.
Start Pt ☆ Fl (3) 10s 62m **25M**; 184°-068°. Same twr: FR 55m 12M; 210°-255° over Skerries Bank; *Horn 60s;* 50°13'·34N 03°38'·54W.

START POINT TO PORTLAND BILL
DARTMOUTH
Kingswear Dir ⚓ 328°: Iso WRG 3s 9m 8M; 318°-G-325°-W-331°-R-340°; W ○ twr; 50°20'·82N 03°34'·09W.
Mewstone ⚓ VQ (6) + L Fl 10s; 50°19'·92N 03°31'·89W.
West Rock ⚓ Q (6) + L Fl 15s; 50°19'·86N 03°32'·47W.
Homestone ⚓ QR; 50°19'·61N 03°33'·55W.

Castle Ledge ⚓ Fl G 5s; 50°19'·99N 03°33'·11W.
Checkstone ⚓ Fl (2) R 5s; 50°20'·45N 03°33'·81W.
Dir ⚓ 104·5°: FW 5m 9M; vis 102°-107°; 50°20'·65N 03°33'·80W.

BRIXHAM
Berry Head ☆ Fl (2) 15s 58m **19M**; vis 100°-023°; W twr; 03°29'·01W. R lts on radio mast 5·7M NW, inland of Paignton.

Victoria bkwtr ⚓ Oc R 15s 9m 6M; W twr; 50°24'·33N 03°30'·78W.
Fairway Dir ⚓ 159°: Iso WRG 5s 4m 6M; 145°-G-157°- W-161°-R-173°; 50°23'·83N 03°30'·57W.
No. 1 ⚓ Fl G; 50°24'·30N 03°30'·89W.
No. 2 ⚓ Fl R; 50°24'·32N 03°30'·83W.

PAIGNTON and TORQUAY
⚓ QG (May-Sep); 50°27'·42N 03°31'·80W, 85m off Haldon Pier.
Haldon Pier (E) ⚓ QG 9m 6M; 50°27'·43N 03°31'·73W.
Princess Pier (W) ⚓ QR 9m 6M; 50°27'·46N 03°31'·73W.

TEIGNMOUTH
Outfall ⚓ Fl Y 5s; 50°31'·97N 03°27'·77W, 288°/1·3M to hbr ent.
Bar ⚓ Fl G 2s; 50°32'·44N 03°29'·25W.
Trng wall, middle ⚓ Oc R 6s 4m 3M; 50°32'·33N 03°29'·93W.
The Point ⚓ Oc G 6s 3M & FG (vert); 50°32'·42N 03°30'·05W.

RIVER EXE to SIDMOUTH and AXMOUTH
Exe ⚓ Mo(A) 10s; 50°35'·92N 03°23'·75W.
No. 1 ⚓ 50°36'·07N 03°23'·78W.
No. 2 ⚓ 50°36'·03N 03°23'·91W.
Ldg lts 305°. Front, Iso 2s 6m 7M, 50°36'·99N 03°25'·34W. Rear, Q 12m 7M, 57m from front. No. 10 ⚓ Fl R 3s; 50°36'·73N 03°24'·77W.
No. 12 Warren Pt ⚓ 50°36'·91N 03°25'·41W.

Sidmouth ⚓ Fl R 5s 5m 2M; 50°40'·48'N 03°14'·43W.
Axmouth jetty ⚓ Fl G 4s 7m 2M; 50°42'·12N 03°03'·29W.

LYME REGIS
Outfall ⚓ Q (6) + L Fl 15s; 50°43'·17N 02°55'·66W.
Ldg lts 284°: Front, Victoria Pier ⚓ Oc WR 8s 6m, W9M, R7M; 284°-R-104°-W-284°; Bu col; 50°43'·19N 02°56'·17W. Rear, FG 8m 9M.

WEST BAY (BRIDPORT)
W pier root, Dir ⚓ 336°: F WRG 5m 4M; 165°-G-331°-W-341°-R-165°; 50°42'·62N 02°45'·89W.
W pier outer limit ⚓ Iso R 2s 5m 4M; 50°42'·51N 02°45'·83W.
E pier outer limit ⚓ Iso G 2s 5m 4M; 50°42'·53N 02°45'·80W.

PORTLAND BILL TO ANVIL POINT
Portland Bill lt ho ⚓ Fl (4) 20s 43m **25M**. vis 221°-244° (gradual change from 1 Fl to 4 Fl); 244°-117° (shows 4 Fl); 117°-141° (gradual change from 4 Fl to 1 Fl). W ○ twr; *Dia 30s;* 50°30'·85N 02°27'·39W. Same twr, FR 19m 13M; 271°-291° over Shambles.
W Shambles ⚓ Q (9) 15s; *Bell;* 50°29'·78N 02°24'·41W.
E Shambles ⚓ Q (3) 10s; *Bell;* 50°30'·78N 02°20'·08W.

PORTLAND HARBOUR
Outer Bkwtr Fort Head (N end) ⚓ QR 14m 5M; 013°-268°; 50°35'·11N 02°24'·87W.
NE Bkwtr (A Hd) ⚓ Fl 2·5s 22m **20M**; 50°35'·16N 02°25'·07W.
NE Bkwtr (B Hd) ⚓ Oc R 15s 11m 5M; 50°35'·65N 02°25'·88W.
N Arm (C Hd) ⚓ Oc G 10s 11m 5M; 50°35'·78N 02°25'·95W.

WEYMOUTH
Ldg lts 239·6°: both FR 5/7m 7M; Front 50°36'·46N 02°26'·87W, S Pier hd ⚓ Q 10m 9M; 50°36'·58N 02°26'·49W. IPTS 190m SW.

LULWORTH RANGE TO ANVIL POINT
Targets off St Alban's Hd: DZ 'A' ⚓ Fl Y 2s, 50°33'·34N 02°06'·52W.
DZ 'B' ⚓ Fl Y 10s, 50°32'·11N 02°05'·92W.
DZ 'C' ⚓ Fl Y 5s, 50°32'·76N 02°04'·56W.
Anvil Pt ☆ Fl 10s 45m **19M**; vis 237°-076° (H24); W ○ twr and dwelling; 50°35'·51N 01°57'·60W. Measured mile close west.

9.1.5   PASSAGE INFORMATION

See also: *Channel Havens* (ACN/Endean); *West Country Cruising Companion* (Wiley/Fishwick); *The Channel Cruising Companion* (NDL/Aslett & Featherstone); *Channel Pilot* (NP 27). More Passage information is threaded between the harbours in this Area. Notes on crossing the western part of the English Channel are after 9.1.25.

ISLES OF SCILLY TO LAND'S END

The 50 islands lie 21-31M WSW of Land's End, with many rocky outcrops and offlying dangers; see 9.1.6 and AC 34, 883. Care is needed particularly in poor visibility. No one anchorage gives shelter from all winds and swell, so be ready to move at short notice. Follow the approach transits on AC 34 because the tidal streams are difficult to predict with accuracy. They run harder off Points and over rocks, where overfalls may occur.

The **Seven Stones** rocks (lt F, fog sig, Racon; AC 1148) lie 16M W of Land's End; many of them dry, with ledges in between. **Wolf Rock** (lt ho, fog sig, Racon), 8M SSW of Land's End, is steep-to. The N/S lanes of the Land's End TSS are roughly defined by Seven Stones to the west and Wolf Rock to the east. Beware commercial vessels turning N near Wolf Rock to enter the N-bound lane of the TSS; and those leaving the S-bound lane.

▶*Between Scilly and Land's End (AC 1148) streams are rotatory, clockwise, setting W from HW Dover; N from HW + 2; NE from HW + 4; E from HW −6; SSE from HW − 4; and SW from HW − 2. Sp rates are about 1kn. From Mounts Bay to Scilly leave the Runnel Stone at HWD−2; a fair W-going tide lasts for only 3 hrs, with cross tides setting SW then NW to N. Consider arriving at dawn. For the return passage streams are a little less critical.◀*

LAND'S END

The peninsula (AC 1148, 1149, 777 and 2345) is always a critical tidal gate and often a dangerous lee shore. There are many inshore and offlying rocks but no ports of refuge. The main features are: Gwennap Head, with Runnel Stone buoy 1M to the S; Land's End and Longships reef 1M to the W; Cape Cornwall and The Brisons; Pendeen and The Wra. Further E see Area 11.

Passage between **Gwennap Head** and the Runnel Stone (0·5m; 7ca S) is not advised even in calm weather and at HW, due to rocks and uncharted wrecks closer inshore. These dangers are in the R sectors of Longships and Tater-du lts. From Gwennap Hd to Land's End, 2M NW, rocks extend up to 1½ca offshore, and depths are irregular causing a bad sea in strong winds over tide.

4 cables S of Land's End Armed Knight, a jagged 27m high rk, overlooks **Longships**. This is an extensive and very dangerous reef made up of Carn Bras, on which the lt ho stands, and other rky islets. About 5ca to the E and NE are Kettle's Bottom 5m and Shark's Fin 3·4m, both isolated and very dangerous drying rks. The ½M wide passage between Land's End and Kettle's Bottom is safe in calm, settled weather, but never at night. To clear Kettle's Bottom and Shark's Fin, keep the Brisons High summit just open W of Low summit brg 001°. In adverse weather navigate in the 3M wide ITZ, well W of Longships. ▶*Local streams exceed 4kn at Sp and are unpredictable.◀*

1M NNE of Land's End, after rounding Cowloe Rks and Little Bo 3·4m and Bo Cowloe 6m, the transit 150° of two bns on the cliffs E of Sennen Cove leads to an ⚓ in about 2m on the S side of **Whitesand Bay**, only safe in fair weather and offshore winds; avoid all underwater cables. Sennen ✠ twr (110m) is conspic, almost on the 150° transit.

Cape Cornwall (conspic ruined chy) is about 3M further N. It overlooks The Brisons, two rocky islets (27 and 22m, High and Low summits) about 5ca to SW. There is no safe passage inside The Brisons. The Vyneck rock 1·8m is 3 cables NW of Cape Cornwall.

3M NNE is **Pendeen Head** (lt ho) with the Wra (or Three Stone Oar), drying rocks, close N. Overfalls and a race extend up to 1½M W and SW of Pendeen; avoid except in calm weather and at slack water. A conspic TV mast is 1.5M S of Pendeen.

TIDAL STRATEGY FOR ROUNDING LAND'S END

The tidal stream chartlets and notes below are reproduced by kind permission of the Royal Cruising Club Pilotage Foundation, *Yachting Monthly* magazine in which they were first published and the author Hugh Davies.

▶*The chartlets referenced to HW Dover, illustrate tidal streams and inshore currents. Streams run hard around Land's End, setting N/S and E/W past it. It is truly a tidal gate, and one which favours a N-bound passage – with careful timing nearly 9½ hrs of fair tide can be carried, from HWD −3 to HWD +5. Use currents close inshore running counter to the tidal streams.*

Example N-bound: At HWD+1 the N-going flood starts off Gwennap and does not turn NE along the N Cornish coast until HWD+3, but as early as HWD−3 an inshore current is beginning to run N'ly. So, N-bound, use this by arriving off Runnel Stone at HWD−2 and then keep within ¼M of the shore. If abeam Brisons at HWD, the tide and current should serve for the next 6 or 7 hrs to make good St Ives, or even Newquay and Padstow.

Example S-bound: If S-bound from St Ives to Newlyn, aim to reach the Runnel Stone by HWD+5, ie with 2 hrs of E-going tide in hand for the remaining 9M to Newlyn. This would entail leaving St Ives 5 hrs earlier, at HWD, to make the 20M passage; buck a foul tide for the first 3 hrs but use an inshore S-going current, keeping as close inshore as prudent, but having to move offshore to clear the Wra and the Brisons. This timing would suit passages from S Wales and the Bristol Channel, going inshore of Longships if the weather suits.

From Ireland, ie Cork or further W, the inshore passage would not benefit. But plan to be off the Runnel Stone at HWD+5 if bound for Newlyn; or at HWD+3 if bound for Helford/Falmouth, with the W-going stream slackening and 5 hrs of fair tide to cover the remaining 20M past the Lizard.◀

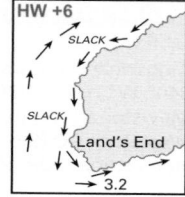

9.1.6 ISLES OF SCILLY

The Isles of Scilly consist of 48 islands and numerous rocky outcrops, covering an area approx 10M by 7M and lying 21–31M WSW of Land's End. Only St Mary's, St Martin's, Tresco, Bryher, St Agnes and Gugh are inhabited. The islands belong to the Duchy of Cornwall. There is a LB and CG Sector Base at St Mary's.

CHARTS AC *1148* (Scilly to Land's End), 34, 883 (both essential), 5603.8-13; Imray C7; Stanfords 2, 13.

TIDES Standard Port is Plymouth. Differences for St Mary's are given in 9.1.7. ▶*Tidal heights, times, and streams are irregular. See the 12 hourly tidal stream chartlets below and AC 34 for 5 tidal stream diamonds, all referred to HW Plymouth.*◀

SHELTER The Isles of Scilly are exposed to Atlantic swell and wind. Weather can be unpredictable and fast-changing. It is not a place for inexperienced navigators or poorly equipped yachts. Normal yacht ⬙s may drag on fine sand, even with plenty of scope, but holding is mostly good. That said, the islands are most attractive, interesting and rewarding. The following are some of the many ⬙s, anti-clockwise:

ST MARY'S Hugh Town Harbour. See 9.1.7.
Porth Cressa (S of Hugh Town). Beware of dangers on each side of ent and submarine cables. Good ⬙ (2m) in W/NW'lies, but exposed to swell from SE to SW.
Watermill Cove (NE corner of St Mary's). Excellent shelter in winds S to NW. ⬙ in approx 5m.
ST MARTIN'S, W end. Tean Sound needs careful pilotage, but attractive ⬙ in better weather. More suitable for shoal draft boats which can ⬙ or take the ground out of main tidal stream in chan. St Martin's Hotel ☎ 422092, stay@stmartinshotel.co.uk. 6 ⬙s £10 inc showers; D, FW, 🛒, ✉, R, Bar. Other fair weather ⬙s available.
ST HELEN'S POOL (S of St Helen's Is). Ent via St Helen's Gap to ⬙ in 1·5m–7m. Secure, but may be swell near HW; see chartlet.
OLD GRIMSBY SOUND. Old Grimsby Hbr comprises Green Porth & Raven's Porth, divided by a quay, both dry 2·3m. Beware cable in Green Porth. ⬙s 1½ca NE of quay in 2·5m; access more difficult than New Grimsby. Well sheltered in SW'lies but open to swell if wind veers N of W. Facilities: 7 ⬙s (R or Y) £15, L (quay), hotel, slip.
NEW GRIMSBY SOUND Appr (line G) between Tresco and Bryher, or with adequate rise of tide from the S across Tresco Flats. Good shelter except in NW'lies. Popular ⬙ between Hangman Is and the quay in 1·5–4·5m. Beware cables. 22 ⬙s, R or Y, £15 for <18m LOA, £30 for >18m; £5 to ⬙. Tresco HM ☎ 07778 601237. VHF Ch 08 for R, Bar, FW, 🛒, ✉. Ferry to St Mary's.
ST AGNES/GUGH The Cove, well sheltered from W and N winds, except when the sandbar between the islands covers near HWS with a strong NW wind. Beware cables.
Porth Conger, N of the sandbar, sheltered in S'lies except when the bar is covered. Facilities: L (two quays), ferry to St Mary's; in Middle Town (¾M), 🛒, ✉, R, Bar.

NAVIGATION See 9.1.2 for TSS to the E, S and W. If unable to identify approach ldg lines/marks, it is best to lie off. Many chans between islands have dangerous shallows, often with rky ledges. Some of the most used ldg lines, as on chartlet, include:

Line A. ⊕ 49°53′·55N 06°18′·00W. *North Carn of Mincarlo ≠ W extremity of Great Minalto 307·1°.* This is the usual approach to St Mary's Road, via St Mary's Sound. From the E or SE avoid Gilstone Rk (dries 4m) 3ca E of Peninnis Hd. Spanish Ledges, off Gugh, are marked by an ECM buoy; thence past Woolpack SCM bn, Bartholomew Ledges lt bcn and N Bartholomew PHM buoy Fl R 5s to ent St Mary's Road on 040·5° (see Line B).

Line B. ⊕ 49°54′·69N 06°20′·33W. *St Martin's daymark ≠ the top of Creeb 040·5°.* This clears Woodcock Ledge, breaks in bad weather.

Line C. ⊕ 49°52′·06N 06°21′·24W. *Summit of Castle Bryher ≠ gap between the summits of Great Smith 350·5°.* Via Smith Sound, between the drying rocks off St Agnes and Annet.

Line D. ⊕ 49°52′·40N 06°27′·80W. *Summit of Great Ganilly just open north of Bant's Carn 059°.* From the SW enter Broad Sound between Bishop Rk lt ho and Flemming's Ledge, 7ca to the N; pass between Round Rk NCM and Gunner SCM buoys to Old Wreck NCM By; beware Jeffrey Rk, close to port. Ldg marks are more than 7M off and at first not easy to see. See also Line C, Smith Sound.

Line E. ⊕ 49°54′·34N 06°27′·80W. *St Agnes Old lt ho ≠ Carn Irish 099·7°.* From WNW, passing close N of Crim Rocks and Gunners.

Line F. ⊕ 49°56′·34N 06°26′·46W. *St Agnes Old lt ho ≠ Tins Walbert bcn 127°.* The NW Passage is about 7ca wide with good ldg marks, but beware cross tide. A WCM lt buoy marks Steeple Rk (0·1m). Intercept Line D for St Mary's Road.

Line G. ⊕ 49°59′·00N 06°21′·96W. *Star Castle Hotel ≠ W side of Hangman Is 157°.* From the N, leads into New Grimsby Sound between Bryher and Tresco. Crossing Tresco Flats need adequate rise of tide (plan for max drying ht of 1·7m) and moderate vis.

Line H. ⊕ 49°55′·66N 06°14′·38W. *Summit of Samson Hill ≠ the NE extremity of Innisidgen 284·5°.* From the E or NE: Crow Snd can be rough in strong SE'lies, but, with sufficient rise of tide, is not difficult. From the NE pass close to Menawethan and Biggal Rk, avoiding Trinity Rk and the Ridge, which break in bad weather. Hats SCM buoy marks a shoal with an old boiler, (0·6m) on it. Maintain 284·5° between Bar Pt and Crow Bar (0·7m), pass N of Crow Rk IDM lt bn (for best water), then turn SSW for St Mary's.

Historic Wrecks (see 9.0.3) are at 49°52'·2N 06°26'·5W Tearing Ledge, 2ca SE of Bishop Rk Lt; and at 49°54'·30N 06°19'·89W, Bartholomew Ledges, 5ca N of Gugh.

LIGHTS AND MARKS See 9.1.4 for lts, including Seven Stones lt float, Wolf Rock lt ho and Longships lt ho. A working knowledge of the following daymarks and conspic features will greatly aid pilotage (from NE to SW):

St Martin's E end: Conical bcn twr (56m) with RW bands.

Round Is: roughly conical shaped, with W lt ho 19/55m high.

Tresco: Abbey & FS, best seen from S. Cromwell's Castle and Hangman Is from the NW.

Bryher: Watch Hill, stone bn (43m); rounded Samson Hill.

St Mary's: TV & radio masts (R lts) at N end, are visible from all over Scilly. Crow Rk IDM bn, 11m on rk drying 4·6m, at N.

St Agnes: Old lt ho, ○ W tr, visible from all directions.

Bishop Rk lt ho: Grey ○ tr, 44m; helo pad above lamp.

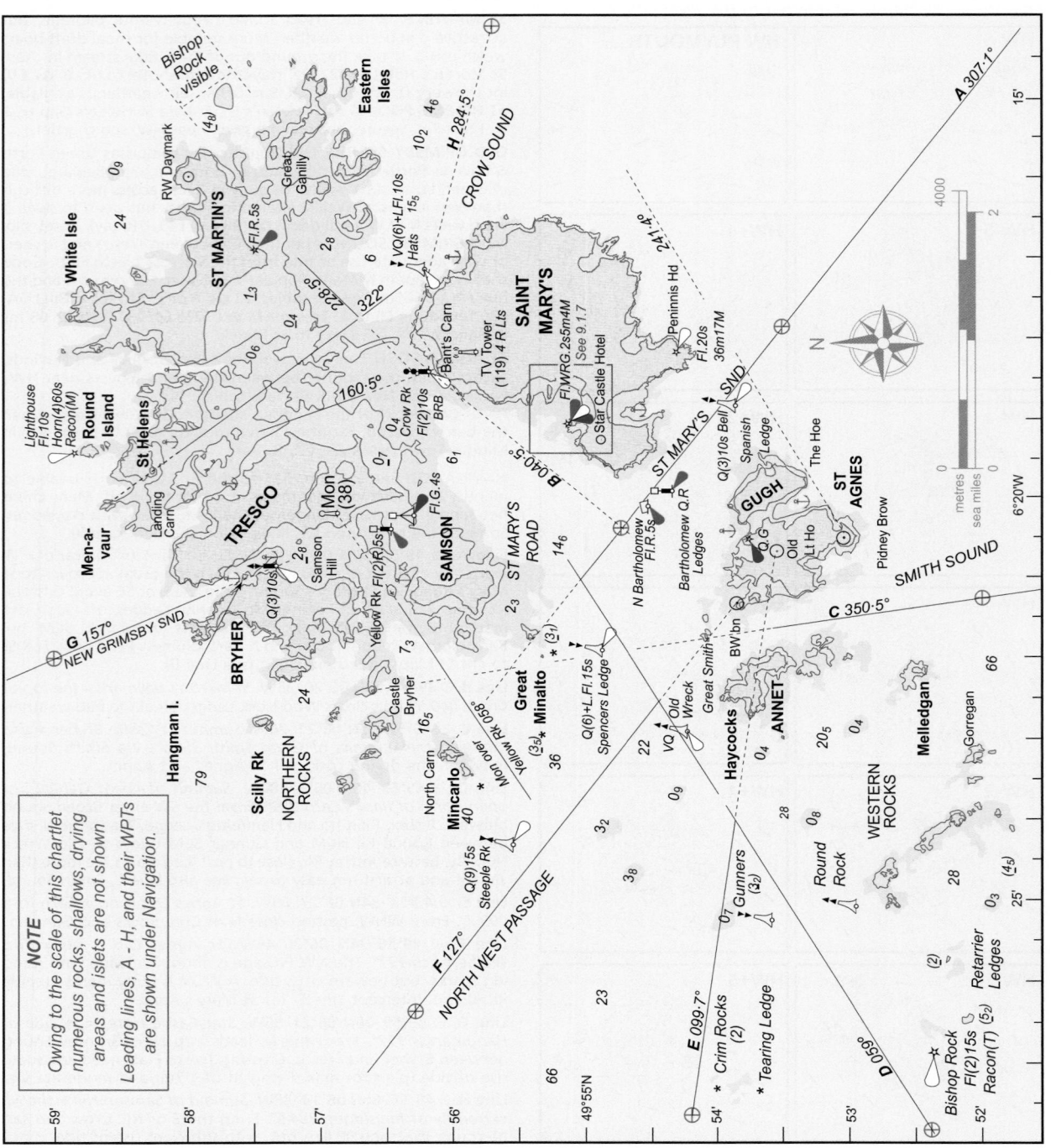

9.1.7 ST MARY'S

Isles of Scilly 49°55'·14N 06°18'·71W ❀❀❀◊◊❀❀❀☆

CHARTS AC 34, 883, 5603; Imray C7; Stanfords 2

TIDES –0630 Dover; ML 3·2; Duration 0600

Standard Port PLYMOUTH (→)

Times				Height (metres)			
High Water		Low Water		MHWS	MHWN	MLWN	MLWS
0000	0600	0000	0600	5·5	4·4	2·2	0·8
1200	1800	1200	1800				
Differences ST MARY'S							
–0035	–0100	–0040	–0025	+0·2	–0·1	–0·2	–0·1

SHELTER Good in St Mary's Hbr, except in W/NW gales when ⚓ in Porth Cressa may be more comfortable. Strictly no ⚓ in the apprs and Hbr limits (from Newman rock to Newford Is).

NAVIGATION WPT 49°53'·96N 06°18'·83W (abm Spanish Ledge ECM lt buoy) 307°/1·2M via St Mary's Sound to transit line B (040°). The 097·3° transit leads S of Bacon Ledge (0·3m) marked by PHM lt buoy. A charted 151° transit leads into the Pool between Bacon Ledge and the Cow and Calf (drying 0·6m and 1·8m). Pilotage is compulsory for yachts >30m LOA. Hbr speed limit 3kn. NB: Do not impede the ferry *Scillonian III* which arrives about 1200 and sails at 1630 Mon-Fri; Sat times vary with month. Also the blue-hulled cargo ship *Gry Maritha* thrice weekly.

LIGHTS AND MARKS See chartlet and 9.1.4. 097·3° ldg marks: W bcns; front, white △; rear, orange x; lts as chartlet. The R and G sectors of the Pierhead lt are not on the conventional sides of the W sector. Buzza Hill twr and power stn chy (48m) are conspic.

R/T *St Mary's Hbr* and Pilot Ch **14**, 16 (0800-1700LT). *Falmouth CG* covers Scilly and the TSS/ITZ off Land's End on Ch 16, 23. Call Falmouth CG if in emergency/gales/dragging ⚓.

TELEPHONE (Code 01720) MRCC (01326) 317575; Marinecall 09068 969648; Ⓗ 422392; Dr 422628; Police 08705 777444; Pilot 422078; Tourist Info 422536.

FACILITIES HM ☎ 422768 (H24 ansafone); Emergency out of hrs ☎ 07789 273626. hm@stmarys-harbour.co.uk; www.destination southwest.co.uk. HM holds mail if addressed c/o HM, St Mary's, Isles of Scilly TR21 0HU.
38 Y ⚓s lie in 6 trots close E of the LB ⌂ in 1·5-2·7m; 28 ⚓s are for <12m LOA and 10 for <18m. Fees: <12m LOA, £16, 4th night foc; <18m LOA, £22, 4th foc. 3 drying AB against hbr wall, also tender landing pontoon. FW at inner drying berth H24. D (hose), P (Sibleys ☎ 422431) at middle berth. Showers, Gas, Gaz, Slip, ✕, CH, ME, SM, El, @, Wi-Fi.
Hugh Town Essential shops, R, Bar, ACA, 🛒, ✉, Ⓑ, Ⓞ.
Mainland access: Ferry leaves Penzance 0915 Mon-Fri (not Sun) and 1630 St Mary's (Sat varies); booking ☎ 0845 710 5555. ✈ helicopter (☎ 422665 (tickets)) to Penzance; fixed wing (☎ 0345 105555) to St Just, Exeter, Newquay, Bristol, Southampton.

9.1.8 NEWLYN

Cornwall 50°06'·19N 05°32'·58W ❀❀◊◊◊◊❀❀☆

CHARTS AC 777, 2345, 5603; Imray C7, 2400.10; Stan 2

TIDES –0635 Dover; ML 3·2; Duration 0555

Standard Port PLYMOUTH (→)

Times				Height (metres)			
High Water		Low Water		MHWS	MHWN	MLWN	MLWS
0000	0600	0000	0600	5·5	4·4	2·2	0·8
1200	1800	1200	1800				
Differences NEWLYN							
–0040	–0110	–0035	–0025	+0·1	0·0	–0·2	0·0

SHELTER Good, but in SE'lies heavy swell enters hbr; access H24. FVs take priority. Good ⚓ in Gwavas Lake in offshore winds.

NAVIGATION WPT 50°06'·19N 05°31'·80W, 270°/0·5M to S pier. From NE, beware The Gear and Dog Rk 3½ca NE of hbr ent; from S, avoid Low Lee (1·1m) ECM buoy Q(3)10s and Carn Base (1·8m).

LIGHTS AND MARKS See chartlet and 9.1.4. Do not confuse S pier hd lt, Fl 5s, with Penzance pierhead lt, Fl WR 5s, 033°/1M. N pierhd lt: G sector (238°-248°) clears The Gear; W sector over hbr.

R/T *Newlyn Hbr* Ch 09 **12** 16 (M-F 0800-1700, Sat 0800-1200LT).

TELEPHONE (Code 01736) MRCC, Marinecall, Police, Ⓗ, Dr: as Penzance.

FACILITIES HM www.newlynharbour.co.uk ☎ 362523; non-HO ☎ 361017. SW of Mary Williams Pier finger pontoons are only for visiting yachts wishing to stay overnight. They are not long stay and preference will be given to FVs; yachtsmen may be asked to move and are strongly advised to pre-check with HM. 40 berths dredged 2m on NE pontoon are for <15m LOA; another 40 berths, dredged 0.75m or CD on SW pontoon, are for <10m LOA. 8-12m LOA £18.00/night; >12m £27.00.
Slip, D (cans), FW, C (6 ton), ME, ✕, SM, Gas, El, Ⓔ, CH.
Town Ⓞ, 🛒, R, Bar, ✉, Ⓑ (a.m only), bus to Penzance ⇌, ✈.

ADJACENT HARBOUR

MOUSEHOLE, Cornwall, **50°04'·97N 05°32'·26W**. ❀❀◊◊◊❀❀☆. AC 2345, 5603. HW +0550 on Dover; Tides as Newlyn; ML 3·2m; Duration 0600. Best appr from S, midway between St Clements Is and bkwtr. N pier lt, 2 FG (vert) = hbr open, summer; 3 FR (vert) = hbr closed (in winter). Ent 11m wide; hbr dries approx 2·4m, access HW±3. Shelter good except in NE and S or SE winds; protected by St Clements Is from E'lies. Ent is closed with timber baulks from Nov-Apr. HM ☎ (01736) 731897. Per night £10, multi hull £12. Facilities limited: FW, 🛒, Slip. Buses to Penzance.

9.1.9 PENZANCE

Cornwall 50°07′·09N 05°31′·68W ❀❀🌊🌊🌊🌊✿✿✿

CHARTS AC 777, 2345, 5603; Imray C7, 2400.10; Stan 2

TIDES –0635 Dover; ML 3·2; Duration 0550

Standard Port PLYMOUTH (⟶)

Times				Height (metres)			
High Water		Low Water		MHWS	MHWN	MLWN	MLWS
0000	0600	0000	0600	5·5	4·4	2·2	0·8
1200	1800	1200	1800				
Differences PENZANCE are the same as for Newlyn (9.1.8)							
PORTHLEVEN							
–0045	–0105	–0030	–0025	0·0	–0·1	–0·2	0·0
LIZARD POINT							
–0045	–0100	–0030	–0030	–0·2	–0·2	–0·3	–0·2

SHELTER Excellent in the wet dock; access HW –2 to +1. ⚓/dry out close N of wet dock or ⚓ E of hbr, but Mounts Bay is unsafe ⚓ in S or SE winds, which, if strong, also render the hbr ent dangerous.

NAVIGATION WPT 50°06′·77N 05°31′·06W, 306°/0·5M to S pier hd. Beware Gear Rk, IDM bcn Fl (2) 10s, 0·4M S. Western Cressar (4ca NE of ent) and Ryeman Rks are marked by unlit SCM bns. Hbr speed limit 5kn. 12 waiting buoys are S of S pier.

LIGHTS AND MARKS Hbr lts often hard to see against shore lts. No ldg lts/marks. IPTS 2 & 3, shown from FS at N side of dock gate, indicate gates open/shut, but may not be shown for yachts.

8 unlit Y spar buoy racing marks are laid, Apr-Sep, at: 50°07′·30N 05°31′·48W; 50°07′·11N 05°30′·33W; 50°06′·92N 05°29′·00W; 50°06′·63N 05°32′·03W; 50°06′·47N 05°31′·47W; 50°06′·33N 05°32′·48W; 50°05′·75N 05°29′·69W; 50°05′·58N 05°31′·36W.

R/T VHF Ch 09, **12**, 16 (HW –2 to HW +1, and office hrs).

TELEPHONE (Code 01736) HM 366113, in emergency 07967 240660; MRCC (01326) 317575; Marinecall 09068 969648; Police 08705 777444; Dr 363866; Ⓗ 362382.

FACILITIES Wet dock 50 Ⓥ, £1.70 (every 3rd night free). D by hose, C (3 ton), showers £1, Slip (dry dock), ME, El, CH, SM, ✕, Gas, Gaz. **Penzance SC** ☎ 364989, Bar, L, FW, R.
Town P cans, ⊙, 🛒, R, Bar, @, ✉, Ⓑ, ⇌, ✈.

MINOR HARBOURS AROUND MOUNTS BAY

ST MICHAEL'S MOUNT, Cornwall, **50°07′·17N 05°28′·67W**. AC 2345, 777, 5603. HW +0550 on Dover; Tides as Penzance; ML 3·2m; Duration 0550. Beware: Hogus Rks (5·5) 250m NW of hbr; Outer Penzeath Rk (0·4) 5ca W of hbr; and Maltman Rk (0·9) 1ca SSW of the Mount. Shelter good from N to SE, but only in fair wx. Unlit hbr dries 2·1; approx 3·3m at MHWS and 1·4m at MHWN. Dry out against W pier or ⚓ W of the hbr in 2-3m on sand, space for 6 boats. HM mob ☎ 07870 400282 or 07917 583284. **Facilities:** FW, R, café. Marazion, 3ca to N: R, Bar, 🛒, ✉; Mounts Bay SC.

PORTHLEVEN, Cornwall, **50°04′·92N 05°19′·13W**. ❀❀🌊🌊✿. AC 777, 2345, 5603. HW –0635 on Dover; ML 3·1m; Duration 0545. See 9.1.8. Hbr dries 2m above the old LB but has approx 2·3m in centre of ent; access HW±3. It is very exposed to W and SW. Beware rks round pier hd and Deazle Rks to W. Lt on S pier, FG 10m 4M, = hbr open. Inside hbr FG, 033°-067°, shown as required to vessels entering. Visitors berth on the quay 2m, E side of inner hbr. HM ☎ (01326) 574270. Facilities: **Inner Hbr** AB £8, FW, L, ME, P & D(cans). **Village** ✉, ⊙, R, Ⓑ, 🛒, Bar.

MULLION COVE, Cornwall, **50°00′·90N, 05°15′·54W**. ❀❀🌊✿✿✿. AC 777, 2345, 5603. Lizard HW –0630 on Dover, –0050 and –0·2m on HW Plymouth; ML 3·0m; Duration 0545. Porth Mellin hbr dries about 2·4m and is open to SW'lies. Due to lack of space, visiting boats may only stay in hbr briefly to load/unload. No lts. There is a slip on E side of hbr. ⚓ in Mullion Cove where shown on the chart and especially in lee of N end of Mullion Island in approx 4-5m, but best to ask local advice. NT owns the island and the hbr. HM ☎ (01326) 240222. Mullion village (1M) Bar, 🛒.

Historic Wrecks (see 9.0.3) are located at:
50°03′·44N 05°17′·16W (*St Anthony*), 2M SE of Porthleven.
50°02′·37N 05°16′·46W (*Schiedam*), 1·5M N of Mullion Is.
49°58′·54N 05°14′·51W, Rill Cove, 1·4M NW of Lizard Pt.
49°57′·49N 05°12′·98W (*Royal Anne*) The Stags, Lizard Pt.

LAND'S END TO FALMOUTH

Close E of Gwennap there is no anch off Porthcurno, due to cables (AC 777). Approaching Mount's Bay, the Bucks (3·3m) are 2ca ESE of Tater-du lt ho. Gull Rock (24m) is 9ca NE of Tater-du, close off the E point of Lamorna Cove. Little Heaver (dries) is 100m SW of Gull Rk, and Kemyel Rock (dries) is 1¾ca ENE.

Mousehole is a small drying hbr, sheltered from W and N, but exposed to E or S winds, when ent may be shut. Approach from SW side of St Clement's Is. In W winds there is good anchorage off the harbour.

Low Lee, a dangerous rock (1·1m) marked by ECM lt buoy, is 4ca NE of Penlee Pt. Carn Base (rk 1·8m) lies 3ca NNW of Low Lee. **Newlyn** is the only harbour in Mount's Bay safe to approach in strong onshore winds, but only near HW. From here to **Penzance** beware the unmarked Dog Rock (1·1m) and The Gear (1·9m, IDM lt bcn).

From Penzance to St Michael's Mount the head of the Bay is shoal, drying 4ca off in places. Danger rocks include Cressar, Long, Hogus and Outer Penzeath. Venton chimney on with pierheads of **St Michael's Mount** at 084° leads S of these dangers. This tiny hbr dries 2·1m, but is well sheltered, with anchorage about 1ca W of ent, see 9.1.9.

Two dangerous rocks, Guthen and Maltman (0·9m), lie 2ca W and S of St Michael's Mount. 1M SE is The Greeb (7m), with rocks between it and shore. The Bears (dry) lie 1¾ca E of The Greeb. The Stone (dries) is 5ca S of Cudden Pt, while offshore is Mountamopus shoal marked by a SCM lt buoy. Welloe Rk (0·8m) lies 5ca SW of Trewavas Head.

Porthleven is a small tidal harbour, entered between Great and Little Trigg Rocks and the pier on S side; closed in bad weather when approach is dangerous. In fair weather there is a good anchorage off Porth Mellin, about 1½ca NE of Mullion Is; Porth Mellin hbr (dries) is for temp use only. 2·5M W of Lizard Pt is The Boa, a rocky shoal (11m) on which the sea breaks in SW gales.

Lizard Point (lt ho, fog sig; AC 2345) is a bold, steep headland. Dangerous rocks, mostly drying, lie 7ca to 5ca from the lt ho in its SW quadrant. Either side of local LW these rocks are visible. 1M E and 1·5M NE of Lizard lt ho respectively, beware Vrogue (1·8m) and Craggan (1·5m) both dangerous sunken rocks.

A race extends 2–3M S, hazardous during the strength of the stream in either direction; it is worst in W'ly winds against W-going tide. Race conditions with short, heavy seas in westerlies may also exist SE of the Lizard. Pass at least 3M to seaward via 49°55′N 05°13′W. A shorter inner route which is rarely free of rough water may be taken, but go no further N than 49°56′·8N.

▶*In the race slack water occurs at about HW Plymouth –4 and the stream sets NE from HWP –3. The next slack water is at HWP +2½ and the stream sets SW from HWP +3; max springs rates reach 2-3kn. Outside the race the NE-going Channel flood starts at approx HWP –3¾ and the SW-going at HWP +3. Study NP 255 tidal stream atlas, Falmouth to Padstow inc Scilly.*◀

To await slack water, ⚓ (W to E) at: Kynance Cove, Housel Bay (3ca ENE of the lt ho and SSE of a conspic hotel), Parn Voose Cove (49°58'·4N 05°11'·1W), Cadgwith or Coverack.

N of Black Head rks extend at least 1ca offshore; a rk drying 1·6m lies off Chynhalls Pt (AC 1267). Coverack is a good anch in W'lies. WSW of Lowland Pt drying rks extend 2½ca offshore.

The Manacles (dry), 7½ca E and SE of Manacle Pt, are marked by ECM lt buoy and are in R sector of St Anthony Hd lt. ▶*Here the stream sets NE from HW Plymouth –0345, and SW from HW+ 0200, sp rates 1·25kn.*◀

There are no offshore dangers on courses NNW to Nare Pt and Helford River or N to Falmouth.

MINOR HARBOURS NORTH EAST OF THE LIZARD

CADGWITH, Cornwall, **49°59'·22N 05°10'·68W**. ✲✲✲☆⚓🛥☆☆☆. AC 154, 2345, 5603. HW –0625 on Dover; –0030 on Plymouth; –0·2m on Devonport; ML 3·0m. Use Differences Lizard Pt under 9.1.9. Hbr dries; it is divided by The Todden, a rky outcrop. Beware the extension of this, rks called The Mare; also beware Boa Rk to ESE which cover at quarter tide. ⚓ off The Mare in about 2–3m, but not recommended in on-shore winds. There are no lts. Many local FVs operate from here and are hauled up on the shingle beach. Facilities: ✉, Bar, R, shops at Ruan Minor (1M).

COVERACK, Cornwall, **50°01'·44N 05°05'·66W**. ✲✲✲☆⚓🛥☆☆☆. AC 154, 147, 5603. HW –0620 on Dover; ML 3·0m; Duration 0550. See 9.1.10. From the S beware the Guthens, off Chynhalls Pt; from the N, Davas and other rks off Lowland Pt, and to the NE Manacle Rks (ECM lt buoy). There are no lts. The tiny hbr dries and is full of small FVs. It has 3·3m at MHWS and 2·2m at MHWN. In good weather and off-shore winds it is better to ⚓ outside. HM ☎ (01326) 280679. Facilities: FW (hotel) D, P (cans) from garage (2M uphill), 🛒, ✉.

9.1.10 HELFORD RIVER

Cornwall **50°05'·79N 05·06'·06W** (Ent) ✲✲✲☆⚓🛥☆☆☆

CHARTS AC 154, 147, 5603; Imray C6, 2400.11; Stan 2, 23

TIDES –0615 Dover; ML 3·0; Duration 0550

Reference Port PLYMOUTH (→)

Times				Height (metres)			
High Water		Low Water		MHWS	MHWN	MLWN	MLWS
0000	0600	0000	0600	5·5	4·4	2·2	0·8
1200	1800	1200	1800				
Differences HELFORD RIVER (Entrance)							
–0030	–0035	–0015	–0010	–0·2	–0·2	–0·3	–0·2
COVERACK							
–0030	–0050	–0020	–0015	–0·2	–0·2	–0·3	–0·2

SHELTER Excellent, except in E'lies when an uncomfortable swell reaches west to Frenchman's Creek. Access by day only; no lights.

NAVIGATION WPT 50°05'·86N 05°04'·84W, 270°/1·9M to The Pool. From N beware August Rock marked by SHM buoy, Fl G 5s. From SE keep well off Nare Pt and Dennis Hd. At the entrance to Gillan harbour an ECM buoy marks Car Croc, a rock drying 1m, which is hit with monotonous regularity despite the buoy. A NCM buoy marks the Voose, a rky reef E of Bosahan Pt.

Beware an extensive drying mud bank N and W of Bar SHM buoy, which is partially obscured by 🛥s. Speed limit 6kn in the river.

The channel up to Gweek is buoyed but dries W of 05°10'·35W.

LIGHTS AND MARKS Marks as chartlet, all unlit.

R/T Moorings Officer and Water taxi Ch M. Ferry also acts as a water taxi, on request HO. Helford River SC Ch 80 M.

TELEPHONE (01326) Moorings Office: ☎ 250749 moorings@helford-river.com www.helfordrivermoorings.co.uk (local info); Ⓗ 572151; Marinecall 09068 969648; MRCC 317575; Police 08705 777444.

FACILITIES In The Pool 25 G 🛥s, marked 'Visitors' and with G pick-up buoys, are randomly numbered, not lettered (if requesting water taxi); see diagram. 🛥s £1.60/m (max LOA 14m); 7th night free. No prior reservations. Rafting is essential in high season. ⚓ only where marked on the chartlet, especially complying with the No Anch area E of Durgan Bay (due eelgrass beds). Yachts >15m ⚓ in Durgan Bay. No ⚓ in the river and creeks W of Porth Navas Creek due to oyster beds (local bye-law). Ditch rubbish ashore at the Helford River SC or the Ferryboat Inn (N bank).

N bank: Helford Passage Slip, FW. **Porth Navas YC** ☎ 340065, 🖂 251061, limited M, FW, R, Bar; www.portnavasyachtclub.co.uk.

S bank: Gillan Creek CH, FW, M. **Helford River SC** ☎ 231460, Slip, FW, R, Bar, 🗐. **Helford village** ✉, bus to Falmouth ⇌.

Gweek Quay ☎ 221657, 🖂 221685, info@gweek-quay.com M, FW, D (cans), CH, El, ⚒, ME, C (100 ton), BH, ✉.

9.1.11 FALMOUTH & RIVER FAL

Cornwall 50°08'·61N 05°01'·48W (Ent) ✿✿✿✿❄❄❄✿✿✿

CHARTS AC 154, 32, 18, *5602.3*; Imray C6, Y58; Stan 2, 23, L16

TIDES –0610 Dover; ML 3·0; Duration 0550.

SHELTER Excellent, depending on wind direction; see Facilities. Access H24 in any weather, although the ent, 1M wide and deep, is rough in fresh on-shore winds over the ebb.

NAVIGATION WPT 50°08'·00N 05°01'·74W, 000°/7ca to Black Rock PHM lt buoy; at night the E chan is advised. By day pass either side of Black Rk, (2·1m, IDM topmark, Fl (2) 10s) almost in mid-ent. Falmouth is a deep water port with sizeable commercial docks. Do not impede ships up to 90,000 tons nor ⚓ in prohib areas. Outside the buoyed chans large areas are quite shallow; care is needed below half tide.
Speed limits: 8kn in Falmouth inner hbr (ie W of the docks), the Penryn River and, N of Turnaware Bar, in the R Fal/Truro and offlying creeks.
5kn in St Mawes and the Percuil River, Mylor, Restronguet and St Just Creeks and Portscatho (50°10'·83N 04°58'·32W), 2 pages on.

LIGHTS AND MARKS See chartlet and 9.1.4. R sector of St Anthony Hd lt (H24) covers the Manacles Rocks.

R/T *Falmouth Hbr Radio* Ch **12** 14 (M-F 0800-1700). HM Truro and launch Ch 12. Visitors Yacht Haven and St Mawes Hbr: Ch 12. Pendennis and Falmouth marinas, Royal Cornwall YC: Ch **80**. RCYC launch Ch M. Mylor Yacht Harbour, Malpas Marine, St Mawes SC: Ch M (HO).

TELEPHONE (Code 01326, but Malpas & Truro 01872). MRCC 317575. Marinecall 09068 969648. Police 08705 777444. Dr 434800. 🏥 Falmouth 311841. 🏥 Truro (A&E) 250000. Port of Falmouth Sailing Ass'n ☎ 211555. Royal Cornwall YC (RCYC) ☎ 311105/312126 (Sec'y), M, Slip, FW, R, Bar. Falmouth Town SC ☎ 313662. Falmouth Watersports Ass'n ☎ 211223. Flushing SC ☎ 374043. Restronguet SC ☎ 374536.

FACILITIES from seaward, clockwise to St Just:
Falmouth Harbour Commissioners (FHC) ☎ 312285; www.falmouthport.co.uk; info@falmouthport.co.uk ⚓ £7/day; 21 G ⚓s (£13.50/day) off Prince of Wales pier.
Water taxi (Ocean Acqua Cab) ☎ 07970 242258; 0900-0100, 7/7.
Fuel: Barge, FW, D only, ☎ 07899 864001 or *Falmouth Industry* Ch 16, 0830-1630 7/7. Falmouth & Mylor marinas, Visitors' Yacht Haven.
Town 🛒, SM, Gaz, CH, ACA, R, Bar, ✉, Ⓑ, �₹, ✈ (Newquay).

Port Falmouth Marina A new marina is planned between Queen's Jetty and Duchy Wharf; it may be open in 2010.

Port Pendennis Marina 50°09'·15N 05°03'·70W. Outer hbr access H24; 45 + 20 ❶ in 3-4·5m, £2.65; max LOA 70m. Inner hbr 3m access HW±3 via ent gate/tfc lts. www.portpendennis.com ☎ 211211, ✉ 311116. marina@portpendennis.com ⚓s, YC, R, ▣, CH, tennis, @.

Visitors Yacht Haven (VYH) 50°09'·22N 05°03'·89W. ☎ 310991, ☎ 07815 955263, 0800-1900 in season. Ch 12. Access H24, max depth 1.4m on 235° ldg line, 2 orange △s. 100 AB, £2.50. **Short stay (2 hrs)** £6.00 all LOA. Visitors may ⚓ (£7/day) up to 200m E of VYH in 2-5m, £0.87. D&P, ▣, Wi-Fi.

Falmouth Marina 50°09'·90N 05°05'·02W up the Penryn River. Access H24, min depth 2m. In near appr, pass close N of outer pontoon, 2FR (vert), leaving ECM lt bn (hard to see) close to stbd.

Ignore unlit PHM & SHM buoys, close NE of ECM bn, which mark the Penryn R. Berth on J hammerhead/fuel berth, then as directed. A disused pipeline drying 1·8m crosses the marina E/W; adjacent depth gauge shows depth over it.
☎ 316620. ✉ 313939. 300+20 ❶, £2.55 (min £23); £1.30 for 4 hrs (min £11). D (H24), El, ME, CH, ✗, ▣, BH (30 ton), Wi-fi, C (25 ton), Gas/Gaz, SM, Bar, R, ♿, 🛒 (ATM). www.premiermarinas.com

Penryn/Flushing HM Penryn River ☎ 373352. Challenger Marine, www.challengermarine.co.uk, 50°10'·00N 05°05'·75W. ☎ 377222. 45 drying AB, £2.00. FW, El, P & D (cans 500m), ME, C (20 ton), ✗, SM, ACA, BY, CH.

Mylor Yacht Hbr 50°10'·74N 05°03'·14W, W bank of Carrick Road, is well sheltered in W'lies but exposed to E'lies. PHM and SHM lt buoys mark ent to the fairway to the Yacht Hbr, both are dredged 2m; access H24. Marina ☎ 372121. www.mylor.com; enquiries@mylor.com 140 AB + 40 ❶, Aug £3.40; 15 ⚓, Aug £2.30; other months £0.50 less. D, P, Slip, BH (35 ton), CH, Gas, Gaz, ✗, ME, El, Ⓔ, C (4 ton), Wi-Fi, 🛒, R, Bar, ▣.
Mylor YC ☎ 374391, Bar.

Mylor Pool has many moorings in 1m to 2·2m. Mylor Creek dries or is shoal, <1m.

St Mawes Hbr 50°09'·49N 05°00'·84W. Keep S of St Mawes SCM buoy marking Lugo Rk, 0·6m. 13 G ⚓s SE of the hbr, £2.00. ⚓ above Castle Pt £0.50 all LOA in excellent shelter except from SW winds, but beware many moorings and oyster beds, especially in Percuil River which dries above Percuil. HM ☎ 270553. www.stmawesharbour.co.uk FW, L, Slip, BY, ME, ✗, El, SM, Gas. St Mawes SC ☎ 270686, Bar; visitors welcome.

St Just, good ⚓ off the creek, except in strong W/SW'lies.

FACILITIES UP-RIVER TO TRURO See the chartlet overleaf.
Restronguet Creek 50°11'·53N 05°03'·56W, dries completely. Beware Carick Carlys Rk 0·8m, 3ca E of ent, marked by NCM & SCM posts. Moorings fill the pool (12·4m) so only space to ⚓ is outside. Pandora Inn ☎ 372678, pontoon dries 0·9m, ▣, 🛒, R, Bar.

River Fal/Truro River At N end of Carrick Roads beware strong tides and rips off Turnaware Point and Bar. *King Harry chain ferry has right of way over all passing vessels* except those with a pilot aboard. She shows the lts/marks of a vessel with limited manoeuvrability. Fl Y lts indicate her direction of travel.

HM Truro administers 4 ❶ pontoons, £10 all LOA: E of Channals Creek, N of Ruan Creek, off Woodbury Pt and at Malpas (max draft 1m).

A pontoon, W bank just S of King Harry ferry, is for tourist access to Trelissick House. Tenders may berth on the inshore side; yachts may berth outboard briefly for FW only.

Good ⚓s £5 off Tolcarne Creek, Channals Creek, Tolverne, Ruan Creek, Church Creek, Mopus Reach and Malpas. Smuggler's Cottage offers free ⚓s, if eating there.

Malpas Marine ☎ 271260. No facilities for visiting yachts

8ca NW of Malpas a flood barrier gate is usually open, 2 FR/FG (vert). Gate is shut HW ±2¼, and 3 Fl R lts shown, if HW >5·6m is forecast due to storm surge.

Truro 50°15'·72N 05°02'·85W. HW Truro, sp & nps, is approx HW Falmouth –0022 and –2·0m. Access HW ±2½. Drying AB (£10 all LOA) close SW of HM's office, ☎ 272130, www.portoftruro.co.uk Showers, AC, FW. ⚓ £5.00. **City** ≥, CH, Gas, all facilities.

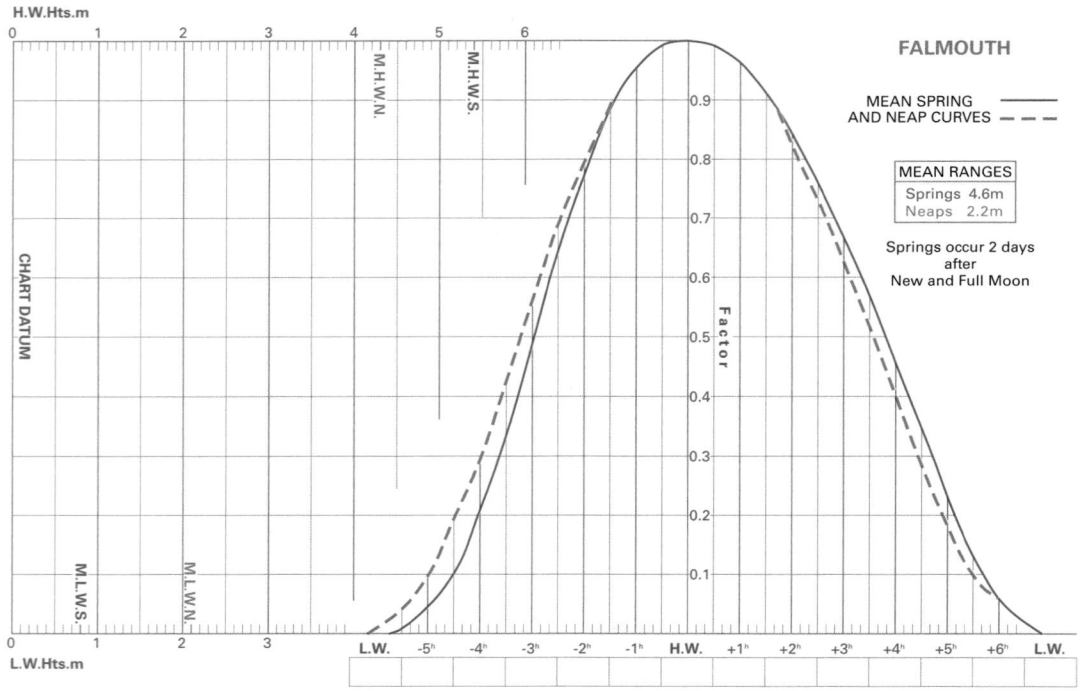

FALMOUTH

MEAN SPRING AND NEAP CURVES

MEAN RANGES
Springs 4.6m
Neaps 2.2m

Springs occur 2 days
after
New and Full Moon

FALMOUTH TO FOWEY

Porthscatho, 3M NNE of St Anthony Hd, is a safe anchorage in W'lies. Gull Rock (38m high) and The Whelps (dry 4·6m) lie 6ca E/SE of Nare Hd and may be passed inshore. In Veryan Bay beware Lath Rk (2·1m), 1·6M NE of Gull Rock.

On E side of Veryan Bay, Dodman Pt is a 110m rounded shoulder, with a conspic stone cross. Depths are irregular for 1M S, with heavy overfalls in strong winds over sp tide, when it is best to pass 2M off. 3 SPM lt buoys (targets) lie 2·3–4·8M SSE of Dodman Pt. For gunnery details, see below 9.1.12.

2·1M NE of Dodman Pt is Gwineas Rk (8m high) and Yaw Rk (0·9m), marked by ECM lt buoy. Passage inside Gwineas Rk is possible, but not advised in strong onshore winds or poor vis. **Gorran Haven**, 1M WSW of Gwineas Rk, a sandy cove with L-shaped pier which dries at sp, is a good anch in offshore winds. So too are **Portmellon** and **Mevagissey Bay**.

MINOR HARBOURS AND ANCHORAGES FROM ST ANTHONY HEAD TO MEVAGISSEY

PORTSCATHO, Cornwall, **50°10´·84N 04°58´·32W**. AC 1267, 154, 5602. HW −0600 on Dover, HW −0025 and −0·2m on Plymouth; ML 3·0m; Duration 0550. Small drying hbr, but in settled weather and off-shore winds pick up a ⚓ or ⚓ outside moorings in good holding. No lts. HM ☎ (01872) 580243. Facilities: ⛟, FW, R, Bar, Slip, P & D (cans), Ⓑ 1000-1230 Mon, Wed, Fri, ✉.

GORRAN HAVEN, Cornwall, **50°14´·49N 04°47´·16W**. AC 1267, 148, 5602. HW −0600 on Dover, HW −0010 and −0·1m on Plymouth. Shelter good with flat sand beach for drying out in off-shore wind; good ⚓ 100 to 500m E of harbour. Not suitable ⚓ when wind is in E. Beware Gwineas Rk and Yaw Rk marked by ECM lt buoy. Beware pot markers on appr. Fin keelers without legs should not ⚓ closer than 300m from hbr wall where depth is 1·8m at MLWS. Facilities: ⛟, Bar, R.

PORTMELLON, Cornwall, **50°15´·74N 04°46´·98W**. AC1267, 148, 5602. HW −0600 on Dover, HW −0010 and −0·1m on Plymouth; ML 3·1m; Duration 0600. Shelter good but only suitable as a temp ⚓ in settled weather and offshore winds. There are no lts. Facilities: Bar (serves food in summer).

SW England

TIME ZONE (UT)
For Summer Time add ONE hour in **non-shaded areas**

FALMOUTH LAT 50°09'N LONG 5°03'W
TIMES AND HEIGHTS OF HIGH AND LOW WATERS

Dates in red are **SPRINGS**
Dates in blue are **NEAPS**

YEAR **2010**

JANUARY

Time m	Time m
1 F 0511 5.5 / 1159 0.8 / 1744 5.3	**16** SA 0011 1.3 / 0539 5.2 / 1234 1.2 / 1801 5.0
2 SA 0019 0.8 / 0602 5.6 / 1249 0.7 / 1835 5.3	**17** SU 0045 1.2 / 0616 5.2 / 1306 1.2 / 1837 5.0
3 SU 0107 0.7 / 0652 5.7 / 1337 0.6 / 1925 5.3	**18** M 0115 1.3 / 0651 5.2 / 1334 1.2 / 1912 4.9
4 M 0153 0.7 / 0741 5.6 / 1422 0.6 / 2013 5.3	**19** TU 0140 1.3 / 0725 5.1 / 1400 1.3 / 1946 4.9
5 TU 0237 0.8 / 0829 5.5 / 1505 0.8 / 2059 5.1	**20** W 0205 1.4 / 0757 5.0 / 1425 1.4 / 2017 4.8
6 W 0319 1.0 / 0915 5.3 / 1548 1.1 / 2144 4.9	**21** TH 0230 1.5 / 0827 4.9 / 1451 1.5 / 2047 4.6
7 TH 0402 1.3 / 1003 5.1 / 1632 1.4 / ☽ 2233 4.7	**22** F 0259 1.5 / 0859 4.8 / 1523 1.6 / 2121 4.5
8 F 0449 1.6 / 1054 4.8 / 1722 1.7 / 2331 4.5	**23** SA 0336 1.7 / 0939 4.7 / 1605 1.8 / ☽ 2209 4.4
9 SA 0546 1.9 / 1157 4.5 / 1825 2.0	**24** SU 0426 1.9 / 1036 4.4 / 1704 2.0 / 2315 4.3
10 SU 0037 4.4 / 0700 2.1 / 1309 4.4 / 1946 2.1	**25** M 0543 2.1 / 1150 4.3 / 1838 2.1
11 M 0146 4.4 / 0828 2.1 / 1416 4.4 / 2103 2.0	**26** TU 0034 4.3 / 0727 2.1 / 1316 4.3 / 2006 1.9
12 TU 0247 4.6 / 0937 1.8 / 1515 4.5 / 2202 1.7	**27** W 0159 4.5 / 0848 1.8 / 1440 4.5 / 2119 1.6
13 W 0340 4.8 / 1031 1.6 / 1604 4.7 / 2250 1.5	**28** TH 0309 4.9 / 0956 1.4 / 1546 4.8 / 2222 1.3
14 TH 0424 5.0 / 1117 1.4 / 1647 4.8 / 2333 1.4	**29** F 0407 5.2 / 1055 1.0 / 1641 5.1 / 2318 0.9
15 F 0503 5.1 / 1157 1.3 / 1724 4.9 / ●	**30** SA 0459 5.5 / 1149 0.6 / 1732 5.3 / ○
	31 SU 0009 0.6 / 0549 5.7 / 1238 0.3 / 1823 5.4

FEBRUARY

Time m	Time m
1 M 0056 0.4 / 0639 5.8 / 1323 0.2 / 1910 5.5	**16** TU 0054 1.0 / 0632 5.2 / 1312 1.0 / 1850 5.0
2 TU 0139 0.3 / 0725 5.8 / 1405 0.3 / 1953 5.4	**17** W 0119 1.1 / 0705 5.2 / 1336 1.1 / 1922 5.0
3 W 0219 0.4 / 0809 5.6 / 1444 0.5 / 2033 5.3	**18** TH 0142 1.1 / 0734 5.1 / 1359 1.1 / 1949 4.9
4 TH 0256 0.7 / 0850 5.4 / 1520 0.9 / 2110 5.0	**19** F 0206 1.2 / 0801 5.0 / 1424 1.3 / 2015 4.8
5 F 0333 1.1 / 0927 5.0 / 1557 1.3 / ☽ 2145 4.7	**20** SA 0233 1.4 / 0829 4.8 / 1453 1.4 / 2043 4.7
6 SA 0412 1.5 / 1005 4.7 / 1637 1.7 / 2225 4.4	**21** SU 0308 1.5 / 0906 4.6 / 1531 1.6 / 2129 4.5
7 SU 0500 1.9 / 1055 4.3 / 1729 2.1 / 2336 4.2	**22** M 0353 1.8 / 1005 4.4 / 1624 1.9 / ☽ 2237 4.3
8 M 0605 2.2 / 1230 4.0 / 1845 2.3	**23** TU 0503 2.1 / 1123 4.2 / 1755 2.1
9 TU 0113 4.1 / 0752 2.3 / 1354 4.1 / 2041 2.2	**24** W 0003 4.3 / 0700 2.1 / 1255 4.2 / 1944 2.0
10 W 0225 4.3 / 0926 2.0 / 1458 4.3 / 2148 1.9	**25** TH 0137 4.4 / 0833 1.7 / 1428 4.4 / 2105 1.6
11 TH 0319 4.6 / 1018 1.6 / 1548 4.5 / 2236 1.5	**26** F 0253 4.8 / 0944 1.3 / 1534 4.8 / 2209 1.2
12 F 0404 4.9 / 1102 1.4 / 1629 4.7 / 2317 1.3	**27** SA 0352 5.2 / 1042 0.8 / 1627 5.1 / 2303 0.7
13 SA 0444 5.1 / 1140 1.2 / 1706 4.9 / 2353 1.1	**28** SU 0442 5.5 / 1132 0.4 / 1715 5.4 / ○ 2352 0.4
14 SU 0519 5.2 / 1215 1.0 / 1741 5.0 / ●	
15 M 0026 1.0 / 0556 5.2 / 1246 1.0 / 1817 5.0	

MARCH

Time m	Time m
1 M 0530 5.7 / 1219 0.2 / 1801 5.5	**16** TU 0530 5.2 / 1215 0.9 / 1751 5.1
2 TU 0037 0.2 / 0618 5.8 / 1302 0.1 / 1845 5.5	**17** W 0027 0.9 / 0606 5.2 / 1243 0.9 / 1825 5.1
3 W 0118 0.2 / 0703 5.7 / 1341 0.2 / 1926 5.5	**18** TH 0053 0.9 / 0640 5.2 / 1309 0.9 / 1855 5.1
4 TH 0156 0.3 / 0742 5.6 / 1418 0.4 / 2001 5.3	**19** F 0119 1.0 / 0711 5.1 / 1335 1.0 / 1923 5.0
5 F 0231 0.6 / 0819 5.3 / 1451 0.8 / 2031 5.1	**20** SA 0145 1.1 / 0738 5.0 / 1402 1.2 / 1950 4.9
6 SA 0305 1.0 / 0849 4.9 / 1524 1.3 / 2057 4.9	**21** SU 0214 1.2 / 0810 4.8 / 1432 1.4 / 2023 4.8
7 SU 0341 1.5 / 0917 4.5 / 1601 1.7 / ☽ 2130 4.5	**22** M 0250 1.4 / 0852 4.6 / 1511 1.6 / 2110 4.6
8 M 0425 1.9 / 0957 4.1 / 1650 2.2 / 2222 4.1	**23** TU 0337 1.7 / 0950 4.3 / 1606 1.9 / ☽ 2218 4.4
9 TU 0528 2.3 / 1126 3.8 / 1802 2.4	**24** W 0451 2.0 / 1108 4.1 / 1739 2.1 / 2344 4.3
10 W 0036 4.0 / 0700 2.4 / 1331 3.9 / 2005 2.4	**25** TH 0645 2.0 / 1245 4.1 / 1927 2.0
11 TH 0158 4.2 / 0903 2.1 / 1434 4.1 / 2123 2.0	**26** F 0119 4.5 / 0817 1.6 / 1415 4.5 / 2048 1.5
12 F 0253 4.5 / 0953 1.6 / 1522 4.5 / 2209 1.6	**27** SA 0235 4.8 / 0925 1.2 / 1516 4.8 / 2150 1.1
13 SA 0339 4.8 / 1034 1.4 / 1603 4.7 / 2249 1.3	**28** SU 0332 5.2 / 1021 0.7 / 1606 5.1 / 2242 0.7
14 SU 0418 5.0 / 1111 1.1 / 1640 4.9 / 2325 1.1	**29** M 0422 5.5 / 1110 0.4 / 1652 5.4 / 2329 0.4
15 M 0455 5.1 / 1145 1.0 / 1715 5.0 / ● 2357 1.0	**30** TU 0508 5.6 / 1155 0.2 / 1735 5.5 / ○
	31 W 0013 0.2 / 0553 5.7 / 1237 0.2 / 1818 5.5

APRIL

Time m	Time m
1 TH 0053 0.2 / 0636 5.6 / 1315 0.3 / 1855 5.4	**16** F 0027 0.9 / 0616 5.1 / 1244 0.9 / 1830 5.1
2 F 0131 0.4 / 0714 5.4 / 1351 0.6 / 1927 5.3	**17** SA 0059 0.9 / 0649 5.1 / 1315 1.0 / 1902 5.1
3 SA 0206 0.7 / 0747 5.1 / 1424 1.0 / 1954 5.1	**18** SU 0130 1.0 / 0724 5.0 / 1347 1.1 / 1934 5.0
4 SU 0240 1.1 / 0815 4.8 / 1456 1.4 / 2021 4.8	**19** M 0205 1.2 / 0802 4.8 / 1424 1.4 / 2015 4.9
5 M 0316 1.5 / 0844 4.4 / 1532 1.8 / 2056 4.5	**20** TU 0246 1.4 / 0848 4.6 / 1508 1.5 / 2104 4.7
6 TU 0359 1.9 / 0927 4.1 / 1620 2.2 / ☽ 2146 4.2	**21** W 0339 1.6 / 0946 4.4 / 1608 1.8 / ☽ 2209 4.5
7 W 0459 2.2 / 1036 3.8 / 1729 2.4 / 2308 4.0	**22** TH 0454 1.8 / 1102 4.2 / 1732 2.0 / 2330 4.5
8 TH 0617 2.3 / 1252 3.9 / 1855 2.4	**23** F 0629 1.8 / 1232 4.3 / 1905 1.8
9 F 0117 4.1 / 0801 2.1 / 1358 4.1 / 2029 2.1	**24** SA 0058 4.6 / 0752 1.5 / 1350 4.5 / 2021 1.5
10 SA 0216 4.4 / 0907 1.7 / 1446 4.4 / 2125 1.7	**25** SU 0210 4.8 / 0858 1.2 / 1449 4.8 / 2123 1.2
11 SU 0303 4.7 / 0951 1.5 / 1528 4.7 / 2208 1.5	**26** M 0307 5.1 / 0954 0.8 / 1540 5.1 / 2216 0.8
12 M 0345 4.9 / 1029 1.2 / 1607 4.9 / 2246 1.2	**27** TU 0357 5.3 / 1043 0.6 / 1626 5.3 / 2304 0.6
13 TU 0424 5.0 / 1105 1.0 / 1645 5.0 / 2321 1.0	**28** W 0443 5.4 / 1129 0.5 / 1708 5.4 / ○ 2348 0.5
14 W 0502 5.1 / 1139 0.9 / 1721 5.1 / ● 2355 0.9	**29** TH 0527 5.4 / 1211 0.5 / 1749 5.4
15 TH 0538 5.1 / 1212 0.9 / 1756 5.1	**30** F 0029 0.5 / 0610 5.3 / 1250 0.6 / 1826 5.3

Chart Datum is 2·62 metres below Ordnance Datum (Newlyn). HAT is 5·8 metres above Chart Datum; see 4.5.

TIME ZONE (UT)
For Summer Time add ONE hour in **non-shaded areas**

FALMOUTH   LAT 50°09'N   LONG 5°03'W
TIMES AND HEIGHTS OF HIGH AND LOW WATERS

Dates in red are SPRINGS
Dates in blue are NEAPS

YEAR 2010

MAY

Time	m	Time	m
1 0108	0.7	**16** 0044	0.9
0648	5.1	0635	5.0
SA 1327	0.9	SU 1302	1.0
1859	5.2	1846	5.2
2 0144	0.9	**17** 0124	0.9
0722	4.9	0716	5.0
SU 1401	1.2	M 1343	1.1
1927	5.0	1927	5.2
3 0220	1.2	**18** 0206	1.0
0752	4.7	0801	4.9
M 1435	1.5	TU 1426	1.3
1958	4.9	2012	5.1
4 0256	1.5	**19** 0253	1.2
0826	4.4	0841	4.7
TU 1511	1.7	W 1514	1.4
2035	4.6	2103	4.9
5 0338	1.8	**20** 0346	1.4
0910	4.2	0947	4.6
W 1556	2.0	TH 1610	1.5
2123	4.4	☽ 2203	4.8
6 0431	2.0	**21** 0450	1.5
1010	4.0	1055	4.5
TH 1654	2.2	F 1717	1.7
◑ 2225	4.2	2313	4.7
7 0535	2.1	**22** 0603	1.6
1139	4.0	1208	4.5
F 1803	2.3	SA 1833	1.7
2357	4.2		
8 0644	2.1	**23** 0029	4.7
1301	4.1	0717	1.5
SA 1914	2.1	SU 1317	4.6
		1946	1.5
9 0120	4.3	**24** 0139	4.8
0751	1.8	0825	1.4
SU 1358	4.3	M 1416	4.7
2019	1.9	2051	1.4
10 0216	4.5	**25** 0238	4.9
0848	1.6	0924	1.2
M 1445	4.6	TU 1510	4.9
2113	1.6	2148	1.2
11 0304	4.7	**26** 0331	5.0
0937	1.4	1016	1.0
TU 1529	4.8	W 1558	5.1
2200	1.4	2239	1.0
12 0349	4.9	**27** 0420	5.1
1021	1.2	1104	0.9
W 1611	4.9	TH 1643	5.2
2243	1.2	○ 2326	0.9
13 0432	5.0	**28** 0506	5.1
1103	1.1	1148	0.9
TH 1651	5.1	F 1724	5.2
2324	1.1		
14 0512	5.0	**29** 0010	0.9
1143	1.0	0548	5.0
F 1729	5.2	SA 1230	1.0
●		1802	5.2
15 0004	1.0	**30** 0051	1.0
0553	5.1	0628	4.9
SA 1223	1.0	SU 1308	1.1
1807	5.2	1837	5.2
		31 0128	1.1
		0704	4.8
		M 1344	1.3
		1910	5.1

JUNE

Time	m	Time	m
1 0204	1.3	**16** 0208	0.8
0738	4.7	0800	5.0
TU 1418	1.5	W 1426	1.0
1944	4.9	2011	5.3
2 0240	1.5	**17** 0254	0.9
0815	4.5	0850	4.9
W 1453	1.6	TH 1513	1.1
2021	4.8	2100	5.2
3 0316	1.6	**18** 0342	1.0
0856	4.4	0941	4.8
TH 1529	1.8	F 1601	1.3
2102	4.6	2152	5.0
4 0357	1.8	**19** 0433	1.2
0943	4.3	1036	4.7
F 1613	2.0	SA 1654	1.5
◑ 2150	4.5	◑ 2251	4.8
5 0447	1.9	**20** 0529	1.5
1038	4.2	1138	4.6
SA 1709	2.1	SU 1755	1.6
2247	4.3	2356	4.7
6 0545	2.0	**21** 0635	1.5
1144	4.2	1241	4.5
SU 1813	2.1	M 1905	1.7
2356	4.3		
7 0648	1.9	**22** 0105	4.6
1251	4.3	0747	1.6
M 1918	2.0	TU 1345	4.6
		2018	1.6
8 0109	4.4	**23** 0211	4.6
0749	1.8	0855	1.5
TU 1352	4.4	W 1443	4.7
2019	1.8	2124	1.5
9 0215	4.5	**24** 0309	4.7
0847	1.6	0954	1.5
W 1446	4.6	TH 1535	4.9
2116	1.5	2221	1.4
10 0311	4.7	**25** 0401	4.8
0941	1.4	1046	1.3
TH 1536	4.8	F 1623	5.0
2209	1.4	2311	1.2
11 0401	4.8	**26** 0448	4.8
1031	1.2	1133	1.2
F 1622	5.0	SA 1705	5.1
2259	1.2	○ 2356	1.1
12 0449	4.9	**27** 0530	4.9
1120	1.1	1216	1.2
SA 1707	5.2	SU 1744	5.1
● 2347	1.0		
13 0535	5.0	**28** 0038	1.1
1208	1.0	0610	4.9
SU 1751	5.3	M 1255	1.2
		1821	5.1
14 0034	0.8	**29** 0115	1.1
0624	5.1	0647	4.8
M 1255	0.9	TU 1330	1.2
1837	5.4	1855	5.1
15 0121	0.8	**30** 0149	1.2
0712	5.1	0722	4.8
TU 1341	0.9	W 1401	1.4
1923	5.4	1929	5.0

JULY

Time	m	Time	m
1 0220	1.3	**16** 0243	0.5
0758	4.7	0836	5.2
TH 1430	1.5	F 1459	0.7
2004	4.9	2048	5.4
2 0249	1.5	**17** 0325	0.8
0834	4.6	0922	5.0
F 1458	1.5	SA 1541	1.0
2039	4.8	2133	5.2
3 0318	1.5	**18** 0407	1.1
0912	4.5	1008	4.8
SA 1527	1.7	SU 1625	1.3
2117	4.6	◑ 2220	4.9
4 0352	1.7	**19** 0453	1.5
0953	4.4	1100	4.6
SU 1605	1.9	M 1716	1.6
◑ 2159	4.5	2320	4.5
5 0437	1.8	**20** 0550	1.7
1042	4.3	1205	4.4
M 1700	2.0	TU 1822	1.9
2253	4.4		
6 0542	1.9	**21** 0033	4.3
1143	4.2	0705	1.9
TU 1817	2.1	W 1315	4.4
2358	4.3	1947	2.0
7 0657	1.9	**22** 0148	4.3
1252	4.3	0831	1.9
W 1933	2.0	TH 1421	4.5
		2109	1.8
8 0118	4.3	**23** 0253	4.4
0806	1.8	0940	1.7
TH 1403	4.5	F 1517	4.7
2041	1.7	2210	1.5
9 0235	4.5	**24** 0347	4.6
0909	1.5	1034	1.5
F 1504	4.8	SA 1605	4.9
2142	1.5	2300	1.4
10 0336	4.7	**25** 0433	4.7
1008	1.4	1120	1.3
SA 1557	5.0	SU 1647	5.1
2240	1.2	2344	1.2
11 0431	4.9	**26** 0512	4.8
1104	1.1	1201	1.2
SU 1648	5.2	M 1725	5.2
● 2334	0.9	○	
12 0521	5.1	**27** 0023	1.0
1156	0.9	0550	4.9
M 1736	5.4	TU 1238	1.1
		1801	5.2
13 0025	0.6	**28** 0058	1.0
0613	5.2	0626	4.9
TU 1246	0.7	W 1311	1.1
1826	5.5	1836	5.2
14 0114	0.5	**29** 0128	1.1
0703	5.3	0701	4.9
W 1333	0.6	TH 1339	1.2
1915	5.6	1910	5.1
15 0200	0.4	**30** 0154	1.2
0751	5.3	0734	4.9
TH 1417	0.6	F 1402	1.3
2002	5.5	1941	5.0
		31 0217	1.3
		0806	4.8
		SA 1424	1.4
		2012	4.9

AUGUST

Time	m	Time	m
1 0240	1.4	**16** 0337	1.1
0837	4.7	0932	4.9
SU 1448	1.5	M 1555	1.4
2042	4.8	◑ 2143	4.8
2 0306	1.5	**17** 0418	1.5
0910	4.5	1015	4.6
M 1519	1.7	TU 1642	1.7
2118	4.6	2231	4.4
3 0342	1.7	**18** 0509	1.9
0951	4.4	1123	4.3
TU 1602	1.9	W 1744	2.1
◑ 2206	4.4		
4 0433	1.9	**19** 0004	4.1
1050	4.3	0624	2.2
W 1709	2.1	TH 1252	4.2
2313	4.2	1923	2.3
5 0601	2.1	**20** 0134	4.0
1204	4.3	0818	2.2
TH 1855	2.1	F 1404	4.3
		2101	2.0
6 0036	4.2	**21** 0240	4.2
0734	2.0	0928	1.9
F 1327	4.4	SA 1501	4.6
2016	1.8	2158	1.6
7 0210	4.4	**22** 0331	4.5
0848	1.7	1018	1.5
SA 1441	4.7	SU 1547	4.9
2125	1.5	2243	1.4
8 0319	4.7	**23** 0413	4.7
0952	1.4	1101	1.3
SU 1540	5.1	M 1627	5.1
2226	1.1	2323	1.1
9 0415	5.0	**24** 0450	4.9
1050	1.0	1139	1.1
M 1632	5.4	TU 1703	5.2
2321	0.7	○	
10 0506	5.2	**25** 0000	1.0
1143	0.7	0524	5.0
TU 1720	5.6	W 1215	1.0
●		1737	5.3
11 0011	0.4	**26** 0032	0.9
0555	5.4	0559	5.1
W 1232	0.4	TH 1245	1.0
1809	5.7	1812	5.3
12 0058	0.2	**27** 0100	1.0
0644	5.4	0633	5.1
TH 1317	0.3	F 1310	1.1
1858	5.7	1845	5.2
13 0141	0.2	**28** 0123	1.1
0729	5.5	0706	5.0
F 1358	0.4	SA 1332	1.2
1942	5.7	1916	5.1
14 0222	0.5	**29** 0144	1.2
0812	5.4	0736	4.9
SA 1437	0.6	SU 1353	1.3
2025	5.5	1945	5.0
15 0300	0.7	**30** 0206	1.3
0853	5.2	0803	4.8
SU 1515	0.9	M 1416	1.4
2104	5.1	2011	4.8
		31 0232	1.5
		0833	4.7
		TU 1447	1.5
		2044	4.6

Chart Datum is 2·62 metres below Ordnance Datum (Newlyn). HAT is 5·8 metres above Chart Datum; see 4.5.

FALMOUTH   LAT 50°09'N   LONG 5°03'W
TIMES AND HEIGHTS OF HIGH AND LOW WATERS

SW England

TIME ZONE (UT)
For Summer Time add ONE hour in **non-shaded areas**

Dates in red are **SPRINGS**
Dates in blue are **NEAPS**

YEAR 2010

SEPTEMBER

Time m	Time m
1 0306 1.6 / 0913 4.5 / W 1527 1.8 / ☽ 2135 4.4	**16** 0435 2.1 / 1020 4.3 / TH 1714 2.3 / 2327 3.9
2 0353 1.9 / 1014 4.3 / TH 1629 2.1 / 2245 4.2	**17** 0548 2.5 / 1225 4.1 / F 1855 2.4
3 0514 2.2 / 1132 4.3 / F 1827 2.2	**18** 0114 4.0 / 0755 2.4 / SA 1341 4.3 / 2041 2.1
4 0013 4.1 / 0712 2.1 / SA 1302 4.4 / 1959 1.9	**19** 0219 4.2 / 0904 2.0 / SU 1437 4.6 / 2133 1.7
5 0156 4.4 / 0832 1.7 / SU 1423 4.8 / 2110 1.5	**20** 0308 4.5 / 0951 1.6 / M 1521 4.9 / 2215 1.4
6 0306 4.7 / 0938 1.4 / M 1522 5.2 / 2210 1.0	**21** 0348 4.8 / 1032 1.4 / TU 1600 5.1 / 2253 1.2
7 0359 5.1 / 1034 0.9 / TU 1613 5.5 / 2302 0.6	**22** 0423 5.0 / 1109 1.1 / W 1637 5.2 / 2328 1.0
8 0447 5.3 / 1124 0.5 / W 1701 5.7 / ● 2350 0.3	**23** 0457 5.1 / 1142 1.0 / TH 1710 5.3 / ○ 2358 1.1
9 0532 5.5 / 1211 0.3 / TH 1748 5.8	**24** 0530 5.2 / 1213 1.0 / F 1745 5.3
10 0036 0.2 / 0619 5.6 / F 1254 0.2 / 1834 5.8	**25** 0026 1.0 / 0605 5.2 / SA 1239 1.1 / 1820 5.2
11 0117 0.2 / 0703 5.6 / SA 1334 0.3 / 1918 5.7	**26** 0051 1.1 / 0637 5.1 / SU 1303 1.2 / 1850 5.1
12 0156 0.4 / 0742 5.4 / SU 1412 0.6 / 1957 5.4	**27** 0115 1.2 / 0707 5.1 / M 1327 1.3 / 1919 5.0
13 0232 0.8 / 0819 5.2 / M 1449 1.0 / 2032 5.0	**28** 0140 1.3 / 0735 5.0 / TU 1354 1.4 / 1949 4.8
14 0307 1.3 / 0852 4.9 / TU 1527 1.5 / 2104 4.6	**29** 0208 1.5 / 0806 4.8 / W 1426 1.5 / 2026 4.6
15 0345 1.7 / 0926 4.6 / W 1612 1.9 / ☽ 2143 4.2	**30** 0244 1.7 / 0851 4.7 / TH 1509 1.8 / 2119 4.4

OCTOBER

Time m	Time m
1 0332 2.0 / 0951 4.5 / F 1613 2.1 / ☽ 2229 4.2	**16** 0514 2.5 / 1127 4.2 / SA 1805 2.4
2 0454 2.2 / 1109 4.4 / SA 1807 2.2 / 2358 4.2	**17** 0037 4.0 / 0648 2.5 / SU 1302 4.3 / 1951 2.2
3 0651 2.2 / 1240 4.5 / SU 1941 1.8	**18** 0144 4.2 / 0819 2.2 / M 1401 4.5 / 2051 1.9
4 0140 4.4 / 0814 1.8 / M 1403 4.8 / 2051 1.5	**19** 0233 4.5 / 0911 1.8 / TU 1447 4.8 / 2135 1.5
5 0246 4.8 / 0918 1.4 / TU 1502 5.2 / 2148 1.0	**20** 0313 4.8 / 0953 1.5 / W 1528 5.0 / 2213 1.4
6 0338 5.2 / 1012 0.9 / W 1553 5.5 / 2239 0.6	**21** 0351 5.0 / 1031 1.4 / TH 1606 5.1 / 2248 1.2
7 0424 5.4 / 1101 0.6 / TH 1640 5.7 / ● 2326 0.4	**22** 0427 5.1 / 1106 1.2 / F 1643 5.2 / 2321 1.1
8 0509 5.6 / 1147 0.4 / F 1724 5.7	**23** 0503 5.2 / 1139 1.1 / SA 1719 5.2 / ○ 2352 1.1
9 0010 0.3 / 0552 5.6 / SA 1230 0.4 / 1809 5.7	**24** 0537 5.3 / 1210 1.1 / SU 1755 5.2
10 0051 0.4 / 0634 5.6 / SU 1310 0.5 / 1851 5.5	**25** 0023 1.1 / 0612 5.3 / M 1240 1.2 / 1829 5.1
11 0130 0.7 / 0712 5.5 / M 1348 0.8 / 1930 5.3	**26** 0053 1.2 / 0644 5.2 / TU 1310 1.3 / 1902 5.0
12 0206 1.0 / 0747 5.2 / TU 1425 1.2 / 2003 4.9	**27** 0123 1.3 / 0716 5.1 / W 1343 1.4 / 1936 4.9
13 0241 1.5 / 0817 5.0 / W 1503 1.5 / 2034 4.6	**28** 0157 1.5 / 0754 5.0 / TH 1420 1.5 / 2019 4.7
14 0319 1.8 / 0851 4.7 / TH 1548 1.9 / ☽ 2113 4.2	**29** 0237 1.6 / 0840 4.8 / F 1507 1.7 / 2112 4.5
15 0407 2.2 / 0940 4.4 / F 1646 2.3 / 2220 4.0	**30** 0330 1.9 / 0939 4.7 / SA 1613 1.9 / ☽ 2219 4.4
	31 0446 2.1 / 1051 4.6 / SU 1745 2.0 / 2343 4.3

NOVEMBER

Time m	Time m
1 0623 2.1 / 1216 4.6 / M 1913 1.8	**16** 0039 4.2 / 0658 2.3 / TU 1302 4.4 / 1936 2.1
2 0111 4.5 / 0746 1.8 / TU 1334 4.9 / 2023 1.5	**17** 0141 4.4 / 0806 2.1 / W 1400 4.6 / 2035 1.8
3 0218 4.8 / 0851 1.5 / W 1436 5.1 / 2122 1.2	**18** 0230 4.6 / 0900 1.8 / TH 1448 4.8 / 2122 1.6
4 0312 5.1 / 0947 1.1 / TH 1528 5.4 / 2214 0.9	**19** 0313 4.9 / 0946 1.6 / F 1532 4.9 / 2205 1.5
5 0359 5.4 / 1037 0.8 / F 1617 5.5 / 2301 0.7	**20** 0356 5.0 / 1028 1.5 / SA 1614 5.1 / 2244 1.3
6 0444 5.5 / 1124 0.7 / SA 1703 5.5 / ● 2346 0.7	**21** 0435 5.2 / 1107 1.3 / SU 1655 5.1 / ○ 2323 1.2
7 0526 5.6 / 1207 0.7 / SU 1748 5.5	**22** 0512 5.3 / 1146 1.2 / M 1733 5.2
8 0028 0.7 / 0608 5.5 / M 1249 0.8 / 1830 5.3	**23** 0001 1.2 / 0550 5.3 / TU 1224 1.2 / 1813 5.1
9 0108 0.9 / 0647 5.4 / TU 1329 1.0 / 1908 5.1	**24** 0039 1.2 / 0628 5.3 / W 1303 1.2 / 1852 5.1
10 0145 1.2 / 0722 5.2 / W 1407 1.3 / 1942 4.9	**25** 0117 1.3 / 0707 5.3 / TH 1342 1.2 / 1933 5.0
11 0221 1.5 / 0754 5.0 / TH 1445 1.5 / 2016 4.6	**26** 0157 1.4 / 0749 5.2 / F 1425 1.4 / 2019 4.9
12 0258 1.8 / 0830 4.8 / F 1527 1.8 / 2056 4.4	**27** 0241 1.5 / 0836 5.1 / SA 1513 1.5 / 2109 4.7
13 0341 2.1 / 0915 4.6 / SA 1616 2.1 / ☽ 2150 4.2	**28** 0331 1.6 / 0931 4.9 / SU 1609 1.6 / ☽ 2209 4.6
14 0435 2.3 / 1015 4.4 / SU 1716 2.3 / 2310 4.1	**29** 0432 1.8 / 1034 4.8 / M 1717 1.7 / 2320 4.5
15 0543 2.4 / 1143 4.3 / M 1826 2.3	**30** 0546 1.9 / 1147 4.8 / TU 1834 1.7

DECEMBER

Time m	Time m
1 0033 4.6 / 0707 1.8 / W 1300 4.8 / 1948 1.6	**16** 0021 4.3 / 0655 2.3 / TH 1249 4.4 / 1928 2.1
2 0143 4.7 / 0819 1.6 / TH 1406 4.9 / 2053 1.5	**17** 0132 4.4 / 0801 2.1 / F 1358 4.5 / 2028 1.9
3 0243 5.0 / 0921 1.5 / F 1504 5.1 / 2149 1.3	**18** 0231 4.6 / 0900 1.8 / SA 1456 4.7 / 2123 1.6
4 0335 5.2 / 1015 1.2 / SA 1557 5.2 / 2240 1.1	**19** 0322 4.9 / 0952 1.6 / SU 1547 4.8 / 2213 1.5
5 0423 5.3 / 1105 1.1 / SU 1645 5.2 / ● 2327 1.1	**20** 0408 5.1 / 1041 1.4 / M 1633 5.0 / 2300 1.3
6 0507 5.4 / 1151 1.0 / M 1730 5.2	**21** 0451 5.2 / 1128 1.2 / TU 1717 5.1 / ○ 2346 1.2
7 0011 1.0 / 0549 5.4 / TU 1235 1.0 / 1813 5.1	**22** 0533 5.4 / 1213 1.0 / W 1802 5.2
8 0052 1.1 / 0629 5.4 / W 1316 1.1 / 1852 5.0	**23** 0030 1.1 / 0618 5.4 / TH 1258 0.9 / 1846 5.2
9 0130 1.3 / 0705 5.3 / TH 1353 1.2 / 1927 4.9	**24** 0114 1.0 / 0702 5.5 / F 1342 0.9 / 1931 5.2
10 0206 1.5 / 0738 5.1 / F 1429 1.5 / 2002 4.7	**25** 0157 1.0 / 0747 5.4 / SA 1426 1.0 / 2017 5.1
11 0240 1.6 / 0813 5.0 / SA 1505 1.6 / 2038 4.6	**26** 0240 1.1 / 0832 5.4 / SU 1509 1.1 / 2103 5.0
12 0314 1.8 / 0853 4.8 / SU 1542 1.8 / 2122 4.4	**27** 0324 1.3 / 0921 5.2 / M 1555 1.3 / 2152 4.8
13 0353 2.0 / 0938 4.6 / M 1625 2.0 / ☽ 2211 4.3	**28** 0412 1.5 / 1013 5.0 / TU 1646 1.5 / ☽ 2249 4.7
14 0442 2.2 / 1031 4.5 / TU 1719 2.1 / 2312 4.3	**29** 0508 1.7 / 1114 4.8 / W 1748 1.7 / 2355 4.6
15 0545 2.3 / 1136 4.4 / W 1823 2.2	**30** 0619 1.9 / 1224 4.6 / TH 1905 1.8
	31 0107 4.6 / 0743 1.9 / F 1338 4.6 / 2024 1.8

Chart Datum is 2·62 metres below Ordnance Datum (Newlyn). HAT is 5·8 metres above Chart Datum; see 4.5.

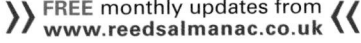

9.1.12 MEVAGISSEY

Cornwall **50°16'·16N 04°46'·93W** ❀⊛⚓⚓❁❁❁

CHARTS AC 1267, 148, 147, 5602; Imray C6, 2400.9; Stanfords 2, 23

TIDES –0600 Dover; ML 3·1; Duration 0600

Standard Port PLYMOUTH (⟶)

Times				Height (metres)			
High Water		Low Water		MHWS	MHWN	MLWN	MLWS
0000	0600	0000	0600	5·5	4·4	2·2	0·8
1200	1800	1200	1800				
Differences MEVAGISSEY							
–0015	–0020	–0010	–0005	–0·1	–0·1	–0·2	–0·1

SHELTER Exposed only to E'lies; if >F3 go to Fowey. Appr in strong SE'lies is dangerous. Access all tides.

NAVIGATION WPT 50°16'·16N 04°45'·98W, 270°/6ca to Victoria pier head. Beware rky ledges off N Quay. Speed limit 3kn.

LIGHTS AND MARKS As chartlet and 9.1.4. S Pier lt ho is conspic.

R/T HM Ch 16 14 (Summer 0900-2100. Winter 0900-1700); call on 16 for berth.

TELEPHONE (Code 01726) MRCC (01803) 882704; Marinecall 09068 969648; Police 0990 555999; Dr 843701.

FACILITIES HM meva.harbour@talk21.com ☎ 843305, home ☎ 842496. www.mevagisseyharbour.co.uk

Outer Hbr ❶ berth on Victoria Pier in about 2m, clear of D hose & pleasure boats at inner end; £12 all LOAs, short stay £1.00. 2 AB on seaward side of Victoria Pier, but beware lip projecting 0·7m. Bilge keelers/cats can dry out on sandy beach, SE side of W Quay. On request to HM: two fore & aft ⚓s off N Pier, rafting possible. A swinging ⚓ is available to seaward of Victoria Pier.

No ⚓ inside the hbr due to overcrowding and many FVs. ⚓ off is only advised in settled weather with no E in the wind.

Inner Hbr (dries 1·5m) is reserved for FVs, unless taking on FW. D, Slip, C (1 ton), BY, ✕, CH, ⚓. Shwr/WC on W Quay; key with carpark attendant.

Village 🍴, R, ⬚, @, Gas, Bar, Ice, ✉, Ⓑ (Jun-Sep 1000-1430, Oct-Jun 1000-1300), ⇌ (bus to St Austell), ✈ Newquay.

GUNNERY RANGE OFF DODMAN PT AND GRIBBIN HEAD

Naval gunnery practice takes place to seaward of Dodman Point and Gribbin Head, under the control of Flag Officer Sea Training (FOST), HMS Drake, Plymouth PL2 2BG. For info ☎ (01752) 557550 (H24) or call *FOST OPS* on VHF Ch 74, which is monitored by all warships in the exercise areas S of Plymouth.

Firing is by day only, approx 1-2 times per week, in a 2 hrs block, although actual firing only lasts about 15 mins. Planned firings are broadcast in Gunfacts (see 3.13) and Navtex. Advance details are also printed in local newspapers and are available from HMs at Fowey, Looe, Polperro and Mevagissey. Firings are not planned for 2 weeks at Christmas and 4 weeks in August.

Warships, from a position some 2·5 to 9M SSE of Gribbin Hd, fire WSW at 3 target ⚲s in danger areas D.006A and D.007A & B (see 9.1.15): **A** Fl Y 10s 50°08'·53N 04°46'·37W; **B** Fl Y 5s 50°10'·31N 04°45'·00W; and **C** Fl Y 2s 50°10'·41N 04°47'·51W, about 3·7M SSE of Dodman Pt.

If safety criteria cannot be met, eg due to vessels in the range area, firing will not take place. A helicopter provides range safety surveillance. A range safety boat will advise other craft of firings and may suggest a course alteration to clear the area. Yachts are legally entitled to transit the range area without undue delay.

MINOR HARBOURS BETWEEN MEVAGISSEY AND FOWEY

CHARLESTOWN, Cornwall, **50°19'·84N 04°45'·35W**. AC 1267, 148, 31. HW –0555 on Dover, –0010 on Plymouth; HW –0.1m on Plymouth; ML 3·1m; Duration 0605. HM ☎ 01726 70241, 🖷 61839, VHF Ch 14, 16 (HW –2, only when vessel expected). Still a china clay port, also home to square riggers for filming/publicity.
Enter the inner hbr via entry gate as agreed with HM, but only in W'lies. Ent dries and should only be attempted by day and in off-shore winds with calm weather. Gate fee £35, but free if within Square Sail's schedule. Hbr is shut in SE'lies. Waiting buoy 2ca S of hbr. Bkwtrs 2FG & 2FR(vert) 5m 1M. Ent sig: ● (night) = hbr shut. Facilities: www.square-sail.com; AB £3.12/m, FW, P & D (cans or pre-arranged tanker), C (8 ton), ME, SM, ✕, R, Bar, V at ✉.

PAR, Cornwall, **50°20'·61N 04°42'·06W**. AC 1267, 148, 31. HW –0555 on Dover; see 9.1.12. A china clay port, dries 1·2m; only in emergency for yachts. 4 chys are conspic 2½ca W of ent. Beware Killyvarder Rock (dries 2·4m) 3ca SE of ent, marked by unlit SHM bn. A mooring buoy Fl Y 5s is 130m ESE of the ent. Only enter by day, in calm weather with offshore winds. Entry sigs: R shape (day) or ● lt (night) = port closed/ship leaving. VHF Ch 12, 16 (by day, HW –2 to HW +1). Facilities: Bar, FW.

FOWEY TO PLYMOUTH

(AC 1267, 148, 1613) Gribbin Head has a conspic daymark, a 25m high ☐ twr with R & W bands. In bad weather the sea breaks on rks around the Head. Cannis Rock (4·3m) is 2½ca SE, marked by a SCM lt buoy.

Fowey is a fine natural harbour, accessible in most conditions although exposed to strong SSW'lies. 3M E of Fowey and 5ca offshore at E end of Lantivet Bay is Udder Rock (0·6m) marked by a SCM lt buoy. 1M ENE of this buoy Larrick Rock (4·3m) is 1½ca off Nealand Pt.

Polperro hbr dries, but the inlet is a good anchorage in offshore winds. Beware Polca Rock (1m) roughly in the approach. E of Polperro shoals lie 2½ca off Downend Point. A measured Mile lies between Polperro and **Looe**. The chan between Looe Island and Hannafore Point nearly dries; the charted Boat passage is not advised. The Ranneys (dry, marked by SCM lt buoy) are reefs extending 2½ca E and SE of Looe Island where there are overfalls in bad weather. In Whitsand Bay a buoyed artificial reef (the former *HMS Scylla*) lies 1·4M NW of Rame Head.

Eddystone rocks (AC 1613) lie 8M SSW of Rame Head. NE Rock (0·9m) and shoals are 280m NE. Close NW of the lt ho is the stump of the old lt ho. The sea can break on Hand Deeps (7m), rocks 3·4M NW of Eddystone, marked by a WCM light buoy.

9.1.13   FOWEY

Cornwall 50°19'·65N 04°38'·54W ❋❋❋🖰🖰🖰☆☆☆

CHARTS   AC 1267, 148, 31, 5602; Imray C6, 2400.7/8; Stanfords 2, 23

TIDES   –0540 Dover; ML 2·9; Duration 0605

Standard Port PLYMOUTH (→)

Times				Height (metres)			
High Water		Low Water		MHWS	MHWN	MLWN	MLWS
0000	0600	0000	0600	5·5	4·4	2·2	0·8
1200	1800	1200	1800				
Differences FOWEY							
–0010	–0015	–0010	–0005	–0·1	–0·1	–0·2	–0·2
LOSTWITHIEL							
+0005	–0010	Dries		–4·1	–4·1	Dries	
PAR							
–0010	–0015	–0010	–0005	–0·4	–0·4	–0·4	–0·2

SHELTER   Good, but exposed to S-SW winds. S-SW gales can cause heavy swell in the lower hbr and confused seas, especially on the ebb. Entry H24 at any tide in almost any conditions.

NAVIGATION WPT 50°19'·33N 04°38'·80W, 027°/7ca through hbr ent to Whitehouse Pt Dir lt in W sector. Appr in W sector of Fowey lt ho. 3M E of ent beware Udder Rk marked by SCM lt buoy. From SW beware Cannis Rk (4ca SE of Gribbin Hd) marked by SCM lt buoy. Entering hbr, keep well clear of Punch Cross Rks to stbd. Fowey is a busy commercial clay port. Speed limit 6kn. Give way to the Bodinnick–Caffa-Mill ferry.

Unmarked, mostly drying chan is navigable up to Golant (1M N of Wiseman's Pt), but moorings restrict ⚓ space. Access on the tide by shoal draft to Lerryn (1·6M) and Lostwithiel (3M) (18m power cables and 5·3m rail bridge).

LIGHTS AND MARKS See chartlet and 9.1.4. An unlit RW twr 33m on Gribbin Hd (1·3M WSW of hbr ent) is conspic from all sea directions, as is a white house 3ca E of hbr ent. Fowey lt ho is conspic. The W sector (022°-032°) of Whitehouse Pt dir lt leads safely through the 200m wide hbr ent. At the ent Lamp Rk lt and St Catherine's Point lt are both lamp boxes, only visible from within the hbr. At Whitehouse Pt a conspic radar and CCTV mast monitors traffic in the entrance.

R/T Call *Fowey Hbr Radio* Ch **12** 16 (HO). Hbr Patrol (0900-2000LT) Ch 12. Water taxi Ch 06. Pilots & Tugs Ch 09, 12.

TELEPHONE (Code 01726) HM 832471; MRCC (01803) 882704; NCI 870291 @ Polruan; Marinecall 09068 969648; Police 08452 777444; Ⓗ 832241; Dr 832451.

FACILITIES from seaward

Polruan Quay (E bank) short stay (2 hrs) pontoon, Slip, FW, C (3 ton), D (only fuel available by hose).

FOWEY All 🖰s are marked 'FHC VISITORS'. Berth/moor as directed by Hbr Patrol. **Ⓥ** pontoons are in situ May-Oct. Average overnight fees on 🖰/pontoon: £1.40/m, but £1.60/m on Mixtow Pill pontoon. Reductions for 3 or 7 days, except Jul/Aug.

Pont Pill, on the E side, offers double-berth fore and aft 🖰s and AB in 2m on two 36m floating pontoons; there is also a refuse barge and RNSA members' buoy.

Albert Quay HM's Office, L, FW, Wi-Fi. The 'T' shaped landing pontoon is for short stay (2 hrs) 🖰s and another 36m floating pontoon.

Berrills BY short stay (2 hrs) landing pontoon, 🖰 access, 250m N of Albert Quay, FW, ⚓, oil disposal.

Midway between Bodinnick and Mixtow Pill is a double-sided **Ⓥ** pontoon off the E bank.

Mixtow Pill (5ca upriver) is a quieter 135m,

shore-linked pontoon in 2·2m, **Ⓥ** on S side. Showers, FW, landing slip and boat storage ashore. BH (8.4 ton) by arrangement. A 🖰 is 30m N of Wiseman's Pt.

Royal Fowey YC ☎ 832245, FW, R, Bar, Showers.

Fowey Gallants SC ☎ 832335, Showers, Bar, R.

Services M, Gas, Gaz, CH, ACA, Ⓔ, BY, Slip, ME, El, ✕, C (7 ton).

Town R, Bar, ✉, Ⓑ, ➾ (bus to Par), ✈ (Newquay).

Fowey is the harbour of harbours. It ought to be a kingdom of its own. In Fowey all is courtesy, and good reason for the chance sailing man. For your provision, or your transport, or your mooring, you may pay no more than you should, and whatever you may need in gear is to be had at once. In Fowey there is security from all winds, good holding and, best of all, an air in which all other places may be forgotten.

So wrote Hilaire Belloc (*The cruise of the 'Nona'*) in 1925 and so it is today.

Daphne du Maurier lived at Bodinnick, across the river from Fowey. In other Cornish homes she wrote some of her most famous novels including *Jamaica Inn*, *Rebecca* and *Frenchman's Creek*. Kenneth Grahame (*Wind in the Willows*) and Sir Arthur Quiller-Couch both drew inspiration from Fowey in their writings.

MINOR HARBOUR BETWEEN FOWEY AND LOOE

POLPERRO, Cornwall, **50°19′·78N 04°30′·79W**. AC 1267, 148, 5602. HW –0554 on Dover; HW –0007 and –0.2m on Plymouth; ML 3·1m; Duration 0610.

Shelter Good.

Navigation WPT 50°19′·74N 04°30′·72W, 310°/2ca to inner basin. Beware The Raney, rocks W of ent, and rks to E. Both the inlet and the harbour are very small.

Lights See chartlet and 9.1.4. Spy House Pt shows W to seaward (288°-060°) with R sectors inshore. A FW lt on the W pier hd shows FR (black ball by day) when gate to inner Basin is shut.

Facilities Hbr dries about 2m; 3·3m depth at MHWS and 2·5m at MHWN. The ent is 9·8m wide (protected by gate in bad weather, but the inner basin remains tidal). Berth on E side of ent or pick up one of 4 moorings outside ent (£10-£15 depending on size); best to moor fore and aft to avoid swinging across the channel. HM on Fish Quay, ☎ (01503) 272809 or 'Girl Jane' 01503 272423; www.polperro.org AB £1.25. FW on quays. R, Bar, ✉.

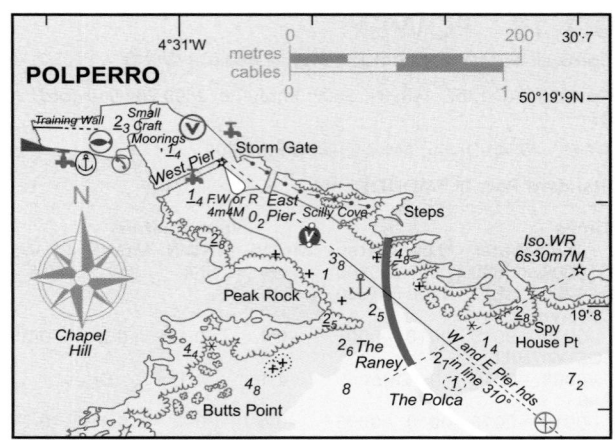

9.1.14 LOOE

Cornwall **50°21′·04N 04°27′·03W** ✿⊛⚓⚓✿✿

CHARTS AC 1267, 148, 147, 5602; Imray C6, 2400.7; Stanfords 2, 23

TIDES –0538 Dover; ML 3·0; Duration 0610

Standard Port PLYMOUTH (→)

Times				Height (metres)			
High Water		Low Water		MHWS	MHWN	MLWN	MLWS
0000	0600	0000	0600	5·5	4·4	2·2	0·8
1200	1800	1200	1800				
Differences LOOE							
–0010	–0010	–0005	–0005	–0·1	–0·2	–0·2	–0·2
WHITSAND BAY							
0000	0000	0000	0000	0·0	+0·1	–0·1	+0·2

SHELTER Good, but uncomfortable in strong SE winds. ⚓ in 2m E of the pier hd; no ⚓ in hbr.

NAVIGATION WPT 50°20′·68N 04°25′·60W, 290°/1·0M to hbr ent. Access approx HW ±1½. The outer chan has rky outcrops. At night appr in W sector (267°-313°) of Banjo Pier hd lt. Ent is

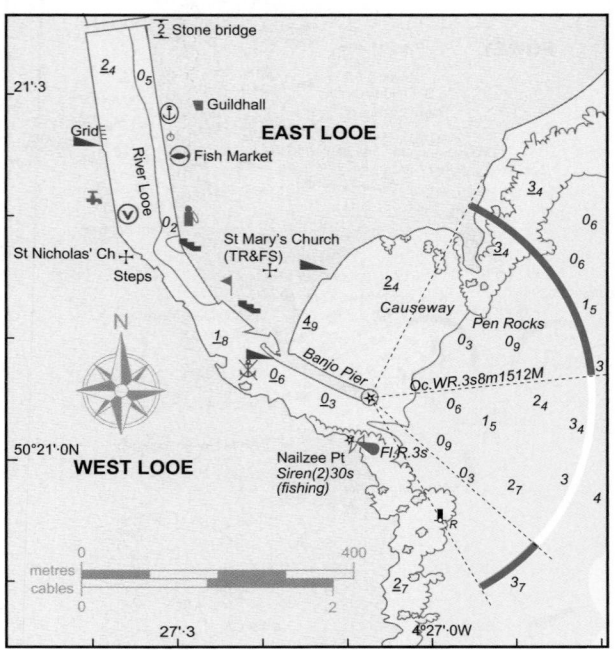

dangerous in strong SE'lies, when seas break heavily on the bar. From W, beware The Ranneys, reef extending 500m SE of Looe Is, marked by SCM buoy Q (6) + L Fl 15s. 3ca NE of hbr ent, avoid the Limmicks, rks extending 1½ca offshore. Do not attempt the rky passage between Looe Is and the mainland except with local knowledge and at HW. At sp, ebb tide runs up to 5kn. Speed limit 5 mph (sic) within the harbour.

LIGHTS AND MARKS See chartlet and 9.1.4. Looe Island (aka St George's Is) is conspic (45m), 8ca S of the ent. Mid Main ECM lt bcn is off Hannafore Pt, halfway between pier hd and Looe Is. Siren (2) 30s (fishing) at Nailzee Pt. No lts inside hbr.

R/T Ch 16 (occas).

TELEPHONE (Code 01503) CG 262138; MRCC (01803) 882704; Marinecall 09068 969648; Police 08705 777444; Dr 263195.

FACILITIES Ⓥ berth on W Quay, marked VISITORS, £12.00 all LOA, dries about 3·3m to firm, level sand; rafting is possible. HM ☎ 262839, mob 07918 7289550. Mon-Fri 0900-1700. www.looecornwall.com
W Quay Slip, P & D (cans), FW, ME, El, ✖ (Wood), Ⓔ, Gas.
E Quay For FVs, but access HW ±3 for D (hose), C (3 ton), Slip.
Looe SC ☎ 262559, L, R, Bar. www.looesailing club.co.uk
Town @, Wi-Fi, ☷, R, Bar, ⌕, ◎, ✉, Ⓑ, ⇌, ✈ (Plymouth).

PLYMOUTH TO START POINT

Rame Hd, on the W side of the entrance to **Plymouth Sound**, is a conspic conical headland, with a small chapel on top; rocks extend about 1ca off and wind-over-tide overfalls may be met 1·5M to seaward. Approaching Plymouth from the W, clear Rame Hd and Penlee Point by about 8ca, then steer NNE for the W end of the Breakwater.

At the SE entrance to Plymouth Sound, Great Mewstone (57m) is a conspic rocky islet 4ca off Wembury Pt. From the E keep at least 1M offshore until clear of the drying Mewstone Ledge, 2½ca SW of Great Mewstone. The Slimers, which dry, lie 2ca E of Mewstone. E and W Ebb Rocks (awash) lie 2½ca off Gara Point (AC 30). Wembury Bay gives access to the **River Yealm**. Between Gara Point and Stoke Point, 2·5M to the E, dangers extend up to 4ca offshore.

In Bigbury Bay beware Wells Rock (1m) and other dangers 5ca S of Erme Head. From Bolt Tail to Bolt Head keep 5ca offshore to clear Greystone Ledge, sunken rocks near Ham Stone (11m), and Gregory Rocks (2m) 5ca SE of Ham Stone. The Little Mew Stone (3m high) and Mew Stone lie below dramatic Bolt Head. Keep at least 3ca SE of the Mewstones before turning N for **Salcombe**. Overfalls occur off Prawle Point, 2·6M E of Bolt Head.

Naval exercise areas from the Isles of Scilly to Start Point are used by submarines and warships, especially near Plymouth. Yachts should try to stay clear.

9.1.15 PLYMOUTH

Devon **50°20'·04N 04°10'·07W** (W Chan) ✵✵✵❀❀❀❀❀❀❀
     50°20'·04N 04°08'·07W (E Chan)

CHARTS AC 1267, 1613, 5602, 1900, *30*, 1902, 1901, 1967, 871; Imray C14, C6; Stanfords 2, 22, L13

TIDES –0540 Dover; ML 3·3; Duration 0610
Standard Port PLYMOUTH (→)

Times				Height (metres)			
High Water		Low Water		MHWS	MHWN	MLWN	MLWS
0000	0600	0000	0600	5·5	4·4	2·2	0·8
1200	1800	1200	1800				
Differences BOVISAND PIER							
0000	–0020	0000	–0010	–0·2	–0·1	0·0	+0·1
TURNCHAPEL (Cattewater)							
0000	0000	+0010	–0015	0·0	+0·1	+0·2	+0·1
JUPITER POINT (R Lynher)							
+0010	+0005	0000	–0005	0·0	0·0	+0·1	0·0
ST GERMANS (R Lynher)							
0000	0000	+0020	+0020	–0·3	–0·1	0·0	+0·2
SALTASH (R Tamar)							
0000	+0010	0000	–0005	+0·1	+0·1	+0·1	+0·1
LOPWELL (R Tavy)							
No data		Dries	Dries	–2·6	–2·7	Dries	Dries
CARGREEN (R Tamar)							
0000	+0010	+0020	+0020	0·0	0·0	–0·1	0·0
COTEHELE QUAY (R Tamar)							
0000	+0020	+0045	+0045	–0·9	–0·9	–0·8	–0·4

NOTE: Winds from SE to W increase the flood and retard the ebb; vice versa in winds from the NW to E.

SHELTER Good to excellent in 4 major and some minor marinas; see Facilities for details. Around the Sound are ⚓s, sheltered according to the wind, in Cawsand Bay, Barn Pool (below

Mt Edgcumbe), N of Drake's Island, below The Hoe and in Jennycliff Bay. Also good shelter W of Cremyll and off the Hamoaze in the R Lynher and in the R Tamar/Tavy above Saltash; see next page.

Plymouth is a Naval Base (Devonport) and a commercial, ferry and fishing port. The whole hbr is under the QHM's jurisdiction, but Millbay and the Cattewater are controlled by ABP and Cattewater Commissioners.

Ferries Roscoff: 12/week; 5 Hrs; Brittany Ferries (www.brittany-ferries.co.uk); Santander: weekly; 19½ Hrs; Brittany Ferries.

NAVIGATION From the west: WPT 50°18'·81N 04°10'·90W (abeam Draystone PHM buoy), 035°/1·5M to W Bkwtr lt. From the east: WPT 50°18'·81N 04°08'·00W, 000°/1·2M to abeam E Bkwtr lt. The Sound can be entered via the W (main) or E Chans which are well lit/buoyed, but in strong W'lies the E Chan can be a hazardous lee shore for yachts. It is vital to keep well clear of the unlit Shag Stone. There are 3·2m patches NE of E Tinker ECM lt buoy. Yachts need not keep to the deep water chans. They must not impede the Torpoint chain ferries at 50°22'·50N 04°11'·30W. In Cattewater vessels <20m LOA keep clear of vessels >20m LOA.

The Bridge (short cut SW of Drake's Island) is marked by 2 PHM and 2 SHM lt bns (see 9.1.4), both with tide gauges showing height of tide above CD; least charted depth is 1·3m. There are drying rocky patches either side of the marked channel which is aligned 327°/147° with the LH (blue roof) of 3 conspic high-rise blocks (5ca NW of Mayflower marina). In the chan spring tides reach 346°/1·6kn at HW −4 and 150°/2·4kn at HW +4.

Speed limits: 10kn* N of Plymouth Bkwtr; 8kn in Cattewater; 4kn N of a line from Fisher's Nose to S side of QAB; 5kn in Sutton Hbr. *Vessels <15m LOA are exempt from the 10kn limit when more than 400m from the shore or in the access lane for water/jet skiers (Fisher's Nose to the W end of Mount Batten Bkwtr and from Royal Plymouth Corinthian YC to W Mallard buoy).

Historic Wrecks are at: 50°21'·73N 04°07'·70W (N of Mt Batten), 50°19'·00N 04°11'·64W and 50°18'·61N 04°12'·05W.

NAVAL ACTIVITY Call Devonport Ops ☎ 563777 Ext 2182/3. Naval Ops, ☎ 501182 (H24). www.qhmplymouth.org.uk contains much info of interest to mariners of every ilk and is worth visiting. It may well answer your question(s).
Warships have right of way in the main and DW channels; obey MOD Police. Keep >50m off berthed warships and 100m off berthed submarines).
Yachts should avoid impeding the safe passage of larger vessels.
Submarines: Do not pass within 200m or cross astern within 800m of any submarine under way. Submarines may secure to a buoy close N of the Breakwater, showing a Fl Y anti-collision lt.
Diving: Keep clear of Bovisand Pier, the Breakwater Fort and Raveness Pt when diving signals (Flag A) are displayed. Flag N flown from pier indicates steps temporarily occupied.

LIGHTS AND MARKS Principal daymarks: conical Rame Head to the W; Great Mew Stone & Staddon Heights to the E; The Breakwater; on The Hoe: Smeaton Tower (R/W bands) & the Naval War Memorial; and Ocean Court (a white bldg) overlooking The Narrows and Mayflower marina.

See chartlets and 9.1.4 for the many lts, some hard to see against shore lts. Dir WRG lts defining the main chans are shown H24** from: Whidbey (138·5°), Staddon Pt (044°), Withyhedge (070°), W Hoe bn (315°), Western King (271°), Millbay** (048·5°), Raveness (225°), Mount Wise (343°), and Ocean Court** (085°). ** Not H24

Notes: In fog W lts may, on request to Port Control, be shown from: Mallard (front ldg lt) Fl 5s; West Hoe bn F; Eastern King Fl 5s; Raveness Fl (2) 15s; Mount Wise F; Ocean Court Fl 5s.
Major lts in The Sound show QY if mains power fails. N of The Bkwtr, four large mooring buoys (C, D, E & F) have Fl Y lts.

> **Wind strength warning flags** (R & W vert stripes) are flown at Sutton lock, QAB and Mayflower marinas and at The Camber (HO only) to warn of excessive winds as follows:
> 1 wind flag = Force 5–7 (17–27kn).
> 2 wind flags = > Force 7 (>27kn).

R/T *Longroom Port Control* (H24). Monitor Ch 13, 14 or 16 underway. Mayflower & QAB marinas and Torpoint Yacht Hbr: Ch **80** M. Plymouth Yacht Haven: Ch **80**. *Sutton Lock,* for opening and marina: Ch **12** (H24). *Cattewater Hbr* Ch 14 (Mon-Fri, 0900-1700LT). *Millbay Docks* Ch 12 14 (only during ferry ops).

TELEPHONE (Code 01752) QHM 836952; DQHM 836485; Longroom Port Control 836528; Flagstaff Port Control 552413; Port surveyor 836962; Cattewater HM 665934; ABP Millbay 662191; ⊖ 0845 7231110; MRCC (01803) 882704; Marinecall 09068 969648; Police 08705 777444; Dr 663138; Ⓗ 668080.

FACILITIES **Marinas and Rivers from seaward (SE-NW):**

Plymouth Yacht Haven 50°21´·60N 04°07´·15W. ☎ 404231, 07721 498422 (1900-0800). plymouth@yachthavens.com www.yacht havens.com; 450 inc ♥, £3 inc AC. Access H24, dredged 2·25m, D (H24), ⚓, ⚒, BY, CH, ME, El, SM, Gas, Slip, mobile C (12 ton), BH (65 ton), Rigger, 🗑, ⬚, ♿, Wi-Fi, @, Bar, R.
Ferry ½ hrly from Mount Batten pier to the Barbican, 5 mins: daily 0700-2300, Ch M or ☎ 408590; 07930 838614.

Yacht Haven Quay, 50°21´·87N 04°06´·61W. ☎ 481190. Access H24 to pontoon in 1·2m, 2 FG (vert); C (above), ME, CH, El; Dry berths/ storage boatyard@yachthavenquay.com

Queen Anne's Battery (QAB) 50°21´·89N 04°07´·93W. ☎ 671142, mob 07740 806039. www.queenannesbattery.co.uk. 240+40 ♥, £3.20 <12.5m, £3.95 <18m, £4.40 > 18.1m. Short stay £7.85. P&D (0830-1830, 7/7), ME, El, ⚒, BH (25 ton), CH, Gas, Gaz, ⬚, SM, Slip, 🗑, Bar, YC, ATM, Wi-Fi. Extensive maintenance facilities.

Sutton Hbr 50°21´·98N 04°07´·96W. ☎ 204702. 467 AB inc ♥, £3.30 inc AC. www.suttonharbourmarina.com; marina@sutton-harbour.co.uk. West Pier and Guy's Quay marinas are mainly for locals (no shwrs). D, ⚓, @, Wi-Fi, ♿, Ice, ⬚. Nearby: CH, C, BH (25 ton), Slip, all maintenance/repairs, 🗑.
Lock operates H24, free. IPTS: sigs 1, 2 & 3. Call *Sutton Lock* Ch 12 for entry and allocation of a berth; secure to floating pontoons either side of lock. The lock retains CD +3·5m in the hbr; when rise of tide >3m, ie approx HW ±3, free-flow is in operation.

Mill Bay Village Marina ☎ 226785, Ch M. No ♥.

Mayflower Marina 50°21´·78N 04°10´·03W. ☎ 556633. 07840 116853. www.mayflowermarina.co.uk 396 AB inc 40 ♥, £2·80 (inc AC), £3·70/hr for 4 hrs max. 27m max LOA. 3·5m min depth, but 1·5m near BH and fuel berth. Max speed just fast enough to maintain steerage. D&P, ME, El, ⚒, C (1.5 ton), BH (33 ton), CH, Slip, Gas, Gaz, Divers, SM, BY, Wi-Fi, ⬚, R, Bar, ⬚.

Southdown Marina 50°21´·18N 04°11´·85W. ☎ 823084. Access HW±4. 35 pontoon AB in 2m inc ♥ £20 all LOA; or at drying quay; or ⚓s. Slip, D, C (20 ton), Wi-Fi, ⬚, Bar. www.southdownmarina.co.uk

Torpoint Yacht Hbr 50°22´·29N 04°11´·60W. ☎ 813658. Access H24, 2m. 70 AB, 100 M, ⚓s; pre-call for a ♥ berth, £2.03. Free water taxi, D, BY, C, ME, El, ⚒, SM, Wi-Fi. www.torpointyachtharbour.com

YACHT CLUBS **Royal Western YC of England** ☎ 660077, M, Bar, R. **Royal Plymouth Corinthian YC** ☎ 664327, VHF Ch M, M, R, Bar, Slip. **Plym YC** ☎ 404991. **RNSA** ☎ 567854. **Mayflower SC** ☎ 492566. **Torpoint Mosquito SC** ☎ 812508, R, Bar, visitors welcome. **Saltash SC** ☎ 845988.

LYNHER (or ST GERMANS) RIVER AC 871. This river flows into The Hamoaze about 0·8M SSW of the Tamar Bridge. On the tide it is navigable for some 4M inland. The chan, entered at Lynher PHM lt buoy 50°23´·78N 04°12´·83W, is marked by 2 more lt buoys in the first mile to Sandacre Pt and carries 2·5m up to Ince Castle. Caution: underwater cables/gaspipe, as charted. Thereafter it carries less than 1m or dries, except at Dandy Hole, a pool with 3-5m, 50°22´·54N 04°16´·29W. Here the navigable chan bends NW then dries completely; it is marked by small R and G posts.

Anchorages, amid local moorings, are: off Sand Acre Bay (N bank, beware foul ground); in 2·5-5m at the ent to Forder Lake (N bank opposite Jupiter Pt, where the pontoons are for naval use only); SE of Ince Pt and Castle in about 3m; and at Dandy Hole. St Germans Quay is private, but temp AB, M may be pre-arranged with Quay SC ☎ (01503) 250370. Facilities: 🗑, Bar, ✉ (½M).

RIVER TAMAR AC 871. The river is navigable on the tide for 12M via Calstock and Morwhellam to Gunnislake weir. Cargreen, 50°26´·55N 04°12´·25W, W bank 0·7M N of the Tavy, has many local moorings and ⚓ in 2·5-5m. Overhead cables, 0·4M S and 1M N of Cargreen, have 21m and 16m clearance (MHWS) respectively. Upstream the river S-bends, narrows and partly dries; above Halton Quay depths vary from 0·1m to > 2·5m. 4ca N of Cotehele Quay it turns 90° stbd to Calstock; possible AB, M, or ⚓ in 2m E of the viaduct (24m). **Tamar River SC** ☎ 362741. **Jubilee Green** (W bank, close N of Tamar Bridge), pontoon in ±3m, max LOA 10m. **Weir Quay SC** ☎ (01822) 840960, M. **Weir Quay BY** ☎ (01822) 840474, ⚓s, CH, ME, BH (20 ton), C (12 ton), Slip, ⚒, D, Gas, Wi-Fi, Victuals. **Calstock BY** ☎ (01822) 832502, access HW ±3, M, ME, SH, C (8 ton), BH (10 ton), P, D, 🛒, Bar, Ⓑ (Mon a.m.), ⚹.

TIME ZONE (UT)
For Summer Time add ONE hour in **non-shaded areas**

PLYMOUTH LAT 50°22'N LONG 4°11'W
TIMES AND HEIGHTS OF HIGH AND LOW WATERS

Dates in red are **SPRINGS**
Dates in blue are **NEAPS**

YEAR 2010

JANUARY

Day	Time	m	Time	m	Time	m	Time	m
1 F	0546	5.6	1209	0.8	1818	5.4		
2 SA	0029	0.8	0636	5.7	1259	0.7	1908	5.4
3 SU	0117	0.7	0725	5.8	1347	0.6	1957	5.4
4 M	0203	0.7	0813	5.7	1432	0.6	2044	5.4
5 TU	0247	0.8	0859	5.6	1515	0.8	2128	5.2
6 W	0329	1.0	0944	5.4	1558	1.1	2212	5.0
7 TH ☽	0412	1.3	1030	5.2	1642	1.4	2300	4.8
8 F	0459	1.7	1120	4.9	1732	1.8	2356	4.6
9 SA	0556	2.0	1223	4.6	1835	2.1		
10 SU	0104	4.5	0710	2.2	1337	4.5	1956	2.2
11 M	0215	4.5	0838	2.2	1446	4.5	2113	2.1
12 TU	0318	4.7	0947	1.9	1547	4.6	2212	1.8
13 W	0412	4.9	1041	1.7	1637	4.8	2300	1.6
14 TH	0457	5.1	1127	1.4	1721	4.9	2343	1.4
15 F ●	0537	5.2	1207	1.3	1759	5.0		
16 SA	0021	1.3	0614	5.3	1244	1.2	1835	5.1
17 SU	0055	1.2	0649	5.3	1316	1.2	1910	5.1
18 M	0125	1.3	0724	5.3	1344	1.2	1944	5.0
19 TU	0150	1.3	0757	5.2	1410	1.3	2017	5.0
20 W	0215	1.4	0828	5.1	1435	1.4	2047	4.9
21 TH	0240	1.5	0857	5.0	1501	1.5	2116	4.7
22 F	0309	1.6	0928	4.9	1533	1.7	2149	4.6
23 SA ☾	0346	1.8	1007	4.7	1615	1.9	2236	4.5
24 SU	0436	2.0	1103	4.5	1714	2.1	2341	4.4
25 M	0553	2.2	1216	4.4	1848	2.2		
26 TU	0101	4.4	0737	2.2	1344	4.4	2016	2.0
27 W	0228	4.6	0858	1.9	1510	4.6	2129	1.7
28 TH	0340	5.0	1006	1.4	1618	4.9	2232	1.3
29 F	0440	5.3	1105	1.0	1715	5.2	2328	0.9
30 SA ○	0533	5.6	1159	0.6	1807	5.4		
31 SU	0019	0.6	0623	5.8	1248	0.3	1856	5.5

FEBRUARY

Day	Time	m	Time	m	Time	m	Time	m
1 M	0106	0.4	0712	5.9	1333	0.2	1942	5.6
2 TU	0149	0.3	0757	5.9	1415	0.3	2024	5.5
3 W	0229	0.4	0840	5.7	1454	0.5	2103	5.4
4 TH	0306	0.7	0919	5.5	1530	0.9	2139	5.1
5 F ☽	0343	1.1	0955	5.1	1607	1.3	2213	4.8
6 SA	0422	1.5	1032	4.8	1647	1.8	2252	4.5
7 SU	0510	2.0	1121	4.4	1739	2.2		
8 M	0001	4.3	0615	2.3	1257	4.1	1855	2.4
9 TU	0141	4.2	0802	2.4	1423	4.2	2051	2.3
10 W	0255	4.4	0936	2.1	1529	4.4	2158	2.0
11 TH	0351	4.7	1028	1.7	1620	4.6	2246	1.6
12 F	0437	5.0	1112	1.4	1702	4.8	2327	1.3
13 SA	0518	5.2	1150	1.2	1740	5.0		
14 SU ●	0003	1.1	0554	5.3	1225	1.0	1815	5.1
15 M	0036	1.0	0630	5.3	1256	1.0	1850	5.1
16 TU	0104	1.0	0705	5.3	1322	1.0	1923	5.1
17 W	0129	1.1	0737	5.3	1346	1.1	1954	5.1
18 TH	0152	1.1	0806	5.2	1409	1.1	2020	5.0
19 F	0216	1.2	0832	5.1	1434	1.3	2045	4.9
20 SA	0243	1.4	0859	4.9	1503	1.4	2113	4.8
21 SU	0318	1.6	0935	4.7	1541	1.7	2157	4.6
22 M ☾	0403	1.9	1032	4.5	1634	2.0	2304	4.4
23 TU	0513	2.2	1148	4.3	1805	2.2		
24 W	0029	4.4	0710	2.2	1322	4.3	1954	2.1
25 TH	0205	4.5	0843	1.8	1458	4.5	2115	1.7
26 F	0324	4.9	0954	1.3	1606	4.9	2219	1.2
27 SA	0424	5.3	1052	0.8	1700	5.2	2313	0.7
28 SU ○	0516	5.6	1142	0.4	1750	5.5		

MARCH

Day	Time	m	Time	m	Time	m	Time	m
1 M	0002	0.4	0605	5.8	1229	0.1	1835	5.6
2 TU	0047	0.2	0651	5.9	1312	0.0	1918	5.6
3 W	0128	0.1	0735	5.8	1351	0.1	1958	5.6
4 TH	0206	0.3	0814	5.7	1428	0.4	2032	5.4
5 F	0241	0.6	0849	5.4	1501	0.8	2101	5.2
6 SA	0315	1.0	0918	5.0	1534	1.3	2126	4.9
7 SU ☽	0351	1.5	0945	4.6	1611	1.8	2158	4.6
8 M	0435	2.0	1025	4.2	1700	2.3	2249	4.2
9 TU	0538	2.4	1151	3.9	1812	2.5		
10 W	0103	4.1	0710	2.5	1359	4.0	2015	2.5
11 TH	0227	4.3	0913	2.2	1504	4.2	2133	2.1
12 F	0324	4.6	1003	1.7	1554	4.4	2219	1.7
13 SA	0411	4.9	1044	1.4	1636	4.8	2259	1.3
14 SU	0451	5.1	1121	1.1	1713	5.0	2335	1.1
15 M ●	0529	5.2	1155	1.0	1750	5.1		
16 TU	0007	1.0	0605	5.3	1225	0.9	1825	5.2
17 W	0037	0.9	0640	5.3	1253	0.9	1858	5.2
18 TH	0103	0.9	0713	5.3	1319	0.9	1928	5.2
19 F	0129	1.0	0743	5.2	1345	1.0	1955	5.1
20 SA	0155	1.1	0810	5.1	1412	1.2	2021	5.0
21 SU	0224	1.2	0841	4.9	1442	1.4	2053	4.9
22 M	0300	1.4	0921	4.7	1521	1.7	2139	4.7
23 TU ☾	0347	1.8	1014	4.4	1616	2.1	2245	4.5
24 W	0501	2.1	1134	4.2	1749	2.2		
25 TH	0009	4.4	0655	2.1	1312	4.2	1937	2.1
26 F	0147	4.6	0827	1.7	1444	4.6	2058	1.6
27 SA	0305	4.9	0935	1.2	1548	4.9	2200	1.1
28 SU	0404	5.3	1031	0.7	1639	5.2	2252	0.7
29 M	0455	5.6	1120	0.4	1726	5.5	2339	0.4
30 TU ○	0542	5.7	1205	0.2	1810	5.6		
31 W	0023	0.2	0627	5.8	1247	0.2	1851	5.6

APRIL

Day	Time	m	Time	m	Time	m	Time	m
1 TH	0103	0.2	0709	5.7	1325	0.3	1928	5.5
2 F	0141	0.4	0746	5.5	1401	0.6	1959	5.4
3 SA	0216	0.7	0818	5.2	1434	1.0	2025	5.2
4 SU	0250	1.1	0845	4.9	1506	1.4	2051	4.9
5 M	0326	1.6	0914	4.5	1542	1.9	2125	4.6
6 TU ☽	0409	2.0	0955	4.2	1630	2.3	2214	4.3
7 W	0509	2.3	1103	3.9	1739	2.5	2334	4.1
8 TH	0627	2.4	1319	4.0	1905	2.5		
9 F	0145	4.2	0811	2.2	1427	4.2	2039	2.2
10 SA	0246	4.5	0917	1.8	1517	4.5	2135	1.8
11 SU	0334	4.8	1001	1.5	1600	4.8	2218	1.5
12 M	0417	5.0	1039	1.2	1640	5.0	2256	1.2
13 TU	0457	5.1	1115	1.0	1719	5.1	2331	1.0
14 W ●	0536	5.2	1149	0.9	1756	5.2		
15 TH	0005	0.9	0613	5.2	1222	0.9	1830	5.2
16 F	0037	0.9	0649	5.2	1254	0.9	1903	5.2
17 SA	0109	0.9	0722	5.2	1325	1.0	1934	5.2
18 SU	0140	1.0	0756	5.1	1357	1.1	2006	5.1
19 M	0215	1.2	0833	4.9	1434	1.2	2045	5.0
20 TU	0256	1.4	0917	4.7	1518	1.6	2133	4.8
21 W ☾	0349	1.7	1014	4.5	1618	1.9	2236	4.6
22 TH	0504	1.9	1128	4.3	1742	2.1	2355	4.6
23 F	0639	1.9	1259	4.4	1915	1.9		
24 SA	0125	4.7	0802	1.6	1419	4.6	2031	1.6
25 SU	0239	4.9	0908	1.2	1520	4.9	2133	1.2
26 M	0338	5.2	1004	0.8	1612	5.2	2226	0.8
27 TU	0429	5.4	1053	0.6	1659	5.4	2314	0.6
28 W ○	0517	5.5	1139	0.5	1742	5.5	2358	0.5
29 TH	0602	5.5	1221	0.5	1823	5.5		
30 F	0039	0.5	0644	5.4	1300	0.6	1859	5.4

Chart Datum is 2·62 metres below Ordnance Datum (Newlyn). HAT is 5·9 metres above Chart Datum; see 4.5.

FREE monthly updates from
www.reedsalmanac.co.uk

PLYMOUTH LAT 50°22'N LONG 4°11'W
TIMES AND HEIGHTS OF HIGH AND LOW WATERS

TIME ZONE (UT)
For Summer Time add ONE hour in non-shaded areas

Dates in red are SPRINGS
Dates in blue are NEAPS

YEAR 2010

MAY				JUNE				JULY				AUGUST			
Time	m	Time	m	Time	m	Time	m	Time	m	Time	m	Time	m	Time	m
1 0118 0.7 0721 5.2 SA 1337 0.9 1931 5.3		**16** 0054 0.9 0708 5.1 SU 1312 1.0 1919 5.3		**1** 0214 1.3 0810 4.8 TU 1428 1.5 2015 5.0		**16** 0218 0.8 0831 5.1 W 1436 1.0 2042 5.4		**1** 0230 1.3 0829 4.8 TH 1440 1.5 2035 5.0		**16** 0253 0.5 0906 5.3 F 1509 0.7 2117 5.5		**1** 0250 1.4 0907 4.8 SU 1458 1.6 2112 4.9		**16** 0347 1.1 1000 5.0 M 1605 1.4 ◑ 2211 4.9	
2 0154 0.9 0754 5.0 SU 1411 1.2 1959 5.1		**17** 0134 0.9 0748 5.1 M 1353 1.1 1959 5.3		**2** 0250 1.5 0845 4.6 W 1503 1.7 2051 4.9		**17** 0304 0.9 0919 5.0 TH 1523 1.1 2129 5.3		**2** 0259 1.5 0904 4.7 F 1508 1.6 2109 4.9		**17** 0335 0.8 0950 5.1 SA 1551 1.0 2201 5.3		**2** 0316 1.6 0939 4.6 M 1529 1.8 2146 4.7		**17** 0428 1.6 1042 4.7 TU 1652 1.8 2258 4.5	
3 0230 1.2 0823 4.8 M 1445 1.5 2029 5.0		**18** 0216 1.1 0832 5.0 TU 1436 1.3 2043 5.2		**3** 0326 1.7 0925 4.5 TH 1539 1.9 2131 4.7		**18** 0352 1.1 1009 4.9 F 1611 1.3 2220 5.1		**3** 0328 1.6 0941 4.6 SA 1537 1.8 2145 4.7		**18** 0417 1.1 1035 4.9 SU 1635 1.3 ◑ 2247 5.0		**3** 0352 1.8 1019 4.5 TU 1612 2.0 ◑ 2233 4.5		**18** 0519 2.0 1148 4.4 W 1754 2.2	
4 0306 1.6 0856 4.5 TU 1521 1.8 2105 4.7		**19** 0303 1.2 0920 4.8 W 1524 1.4 2132 5.0		**4** 0407 1.9 1011 4.4 F 1623 2.1 ◑ 2218 4.6		**19** 0443 1.2 1103 4.8 SA 1704 1.5 ◑ 2317 4.9		**4** 0402 1.8 1021 4.5 SU 1615 2.0 ◑ 2227 4.6		**19** 0503 1.5 1126 4.7 M 1726 1.7 2345 4.6		**4** 0443 2.0 1116 4.4 W 1719 2.2 2339 4.3		**19** 0030 4.2 0634 2.3 TH 1319 4.3 1933 2.4	
5 0348 1.9 0939 4.3 W 1606 2.1 2151 4.5		**20** 0356 1.4 1015 4.7 TH 1620 1.6 ◑ 2230 4.9		**5** 0457 2.0 1105 4.3 SA 1719 2.2 2314 4.4		**20** 0539 1.5 1203 4.7 SU 1805 1.7		**5** 0447 1.9 1109 4.4 M 1710 2.1 2319 4.5		**20** 0600 1.8 1231 4.5 TU 1832 2.0		**5** 0611 2.2 1230 4.4 TH 1905 2.2		**20** 0202 4.1 0828 2.3 F 1433 4.4 2111 2.1	
6 0441 2.1 1037 4.1 TH 1704 2.3 ◑ 2252 4.3		**21** 0500 1.6 1121 4.6 F 1727 1.8 2339 4.8		**6** 0555 2.1 1209 4.3 SU 1823 2.2		**21** 0022 4.8 0645 1.6 M 1308 4.6 1915 1.8		**6** 0552 2.0 1208 4.3 TU 1827 2.2		**21** 0100 4.4 0715 2.0 W 1343 4.5 1957 2.1		**6** 0103 4.3 0744 2.1 F 1355 4.5 2026 1.9		**21** 0310 4.3 0938 2.0 SA 1532 4.7 2208 1.7	
7 0545 2.2 1204 4.1 F 1813 2.4		**22** 0613 1.6 1234 4.6 SA 1843 1.8		**7** 0022 4.4 0658 2.0 M 1318 4.4 1928 2.1		**22** 0133 4.7 0757 1.7 TU 1413 4.7 2028 1.7		**7** 0024 4.4 0707 2.0 W 1319 4.4 1943 2.1		**22** 0217 4.4 0841 2.0 TH 1451 4.6 2119 1.9		**7** 0239 4.5 0858 1.8 SA 1511 4.8 2135 1.5		**22** 0403 4.6 1028 1.6 SU 1619 5.0 2253 1.4	
8 0023 4.3 0654 2.2 SA 1328 4.2 1924 2.2		**23** 0056 4.8 0727 1.5 SU 1345 4.7 1956 1.6		**8** 0137 4.5 0759 1.9 TU 1421 4.5 2029 1.9		**23** 0240 4.7 0905 1.6 W 1513 4.8 2134 1.6		**8** 0146 4.4 0816 1.9 TH 1432 4.6 2051 1.8		**23** 0324 4.5 0950 1.8 F 1549 4.8 2220 1.6		**8** 0351 4.8 1002 1.4 SU 1612 5.2 2236 1.1		**23** 0446 4.8 1111 1.3 M 1700 5.2 2333 1.1	
9 0148 4.4 0801 1.9 SU 1427 4.4 2029 2.0		**24** 0207 4.9 0835 1.4 M 1446 4.8 2101 1.4		**9** 0244 4.6 0857 1.7 W 1517 4.7 2126 1.6		**24** 0340 4.8 1004 1.5 TH 1607 5.0 2231 1.4		**9** 0305 4.6 0919 1.6 F 1535 4.9 2152 1.5		**24** 0419 4.7 1044 1.5 SA 1638 5.0 2310 1.4		**9** 0448 5.1 1100 1.0 M 1705 5.5 2331 0.7		**24** 0524 5.0 1149 1.1 TU 1737 5.3 ○	
10 0246 4.6 0858 1.7 M 1516 4.7 2123 1.7		**25** 0308 5.0 0934 1.2 TU 1541 5.0 2158 1.2		**10** 0342 4.8 0951 1.4 TH 1608 4.9 2219 1.4		**25** 0434 4.9 1056 1.3 F 1656 5.1 2321 1.2		**10** 0408 4.8 1018 1.4 SA 1630 5.1 2250 1.2		**25** 0506 4.8 1130 1.3 SU 1721 5.2 2354 1.2		**10** 0540 5.3 1153 0.7 TU 1755 5.7 ●		**25** 0010 1.0 0559 5.1 W 1225 1.0 1812 5.4	
11 0335 4.8 0947 1.4 TU 1601 4.9 2210 1.4		**26** 0403 5.1 1026 1.0 W 1631 5.2 2249 1.0		**11** 0434 4.9 1041 1.2 F 1655 5.1 2309 1.2		**26** 0522 4.9 1143 1.2 SA 1739 5.2 ○		**11** 0504 5.0 1114 1.1 SU 1722 5.3 ● 2344 0.9		**26** 0547 4.9 1211 1.2 M 1800 5.3 ○		**11** 0021 0.4 0629 5.5 W 1242 0.4 1843 5.8		**26** 0042 0.9 0633 5.2 TH 1255 1.0 1845 5.4	
12 0421 5.0 1031 1.2 W 1644 5.1 2253 1.2		**27** 0453 5.2 1114 0.9 TH 1717 5.3 ○ 2336 0.9		**12** 0523 5.0 1130 1.1 SA 1741 5.3 ● 2357 1.0		**27** 0006 1.1 0605 5.0 SU 1226 1.2 1818 5.2		**12** 0556 5.2 1206 0.9 M 1811 5.5		**27** 0033 1.0 0624 5.0 TU 1248 1.1 1835 5.3		**12** 0108 0.2 0717 5.5 TH 1327 0.3 1930 5.8		**27** 0110 1.0 0706 5.2 F 1320 1.1 1918 5.3	
13 0505 5.1 1113 1.1 TH 1725 5.2 2334 1.1		**28** 0540 5.2 1158 0.9 F 1759 5.3		**13** 0610 5.1 1218 1.0 SU 1825 5.4		**28** 0048 1.1 0644 5.0 M 1305 1.2 1854 5.2		**13** 0035 0.6 0646 5.3 TU 1256 0.7 1859 5.6		**28** 0108 1.0 0659 5.0 W 1321 1.1 1909 5.3		**13** 0151 0.2 0801 5.6 F 1408 0.4 2014 5.8		**28** 0133 1.1 0738 5.1 SA 1342 1.2 1948 5.2	
14 0547 5.1 1153 1.0 F 1804 5.3 ●		**29** 0020 0.9 0622 5.1 SA 1240 1.0 1836 5.3		**14** 0044 0.8 0657 5.2 M 1305 0.9 1910 5.5		**29** 0125 1.1 0720 4.9 TU 1340 1.2 1928 5.2		**14** 0124 0.5 0735 5.4 W 1343 0.6 1947 5.7		**29** 0138 1.1 0733 5.0 TH 1349 1.2 1942 5.2		**14** 0232 0.4 0843 5.5 SA 1447 0.6 2055 5.6		**29** 0154 1.2 0808 5.0 SU 1403 1.3 2016 5.1	
15 0014 1.0 0627 5.2 SA 1233 1.0 1841 5.3		**30** 0101 1.0 0701 5.0 SU 1318 1.1 1910 5.3		**15** 0131 0.8 0744 5.2 TU 1351 0.9 1955 5.5		**30** 0159 1.2 0754 4.9 W 1411 1.4 2001 5.1		**15** 0210 0.4 0822 5.4 TH 1427 0.6 2033 5.6		**30** 0204 1.2 0806 5.0 F 1412 1.3 2013 5.1		**15** 0310 0.7 0922 5.3 SU 1525 0.9 2133 5.2		**30** 0216 1.3 0834 4.9 M 1426 1.4 2042 4.9	
								31 0227 1.3 0837 4.9 SA 1434 1.4 2043 5.0						**31** 0242 1.5 0903 4.8 TU 1457 1.6 2114 4.7	

Chart Datum is 2·62 metres below Ordnance Datum (Newlyn). HAT is 5·9 metres above Chart Datum; see 4.5.

» FREE monthly updates from «
www.reedsalmanac.co.uk

TIME ZONE (UT)
For Summer Time add ONE hour in **non-shaded areas**

PLYMOUTH LAT 50°22'N LONG 4°11'W
TIMES AND HEIGHTS OF HIGH AND LOW WATERS

Dates in red are **SPRINGS**
Dates in blue are NEAPS

YEAR 2010

SEPTEMBER

#	Time m	Time m	Time m	Time m	#	Time m	Time m	Time m	Time m
1	0316 1.7	0942 4.6	W 1537 1.9	◑ 2203 4.5	16	0445 2.2	1047 4.4	TH 1724 2.4	2352 4.0
2	0403 2.0	1041 4.4	TH 1639 2.2	2312 4.3	17	0558 2.6	1252 4.2	F 1905 2.5	
3	0524 2.3	1157 4.4	F 1837 2.3		18	0142 4.1	0805 2.5	SA 1409 4.4	2051 2.2
4	0039 4.2	0722 2.2	SA 1329 4.5	2009 2.0	19	0249 4.3	0914 2.1	SU 1507 4.7	2143 1.8
5	0225 4.5	0842 1.8	SU 1453 4.9	2120 1.5	20	0339 4.6	1001 1.7	M 1553 5.0	2225 1.4
6	0337 4.8	0948 1.4	M 1554 5.3	2220 1.0	21	0420 4.9	1042 1.4	TU 1633 5.2	2303 1.2
7	0432 5.2	1044 0.9	TU 1646 5.6	2312 0.6	22	0456 5.1	1119 1.1	W 1710 5.3	2338 1.0
8	0521 5.4	1134 0.5	W 1735 5.8	●	23	0531 5.2	1152 1.0	TH 1745 5.4	○
9	0000 0.3	0607 5.6	TH 1221 0.3	1822 5.9	24	0008 1.0	0605 5.3	F 1223 1.0	1819 5.4
10	0046 0.1	0652 5.7	F 1304 0.2	1907 5.9	25	0036 1.0	0639 5.3	SA 1249 1.1	1853 5.3
11	0127 0.2	0735 5.7	SA 1344 0.3	1950 5.8	26	0101 1.1	0710 5.2	SU 1313 1.2	1923 5.2
12	0206 0.4	0814 5.6	SU 1422 0.6	2028 5.5	27	0125 1.2	0739 5.2	M 1337 1.3	1951 5.1
13	0242 0.8	0849 5.3	M 1459 1.1	2102 5.1	28	0150 1.3	0807 5.1	TU 1404 1.4	2020 4.9
14	0317 1.3	0921 5.0	TU 1537 1.5	2133 4.7	29	0218 1.5	0837 4.9	W 1436 1.6	2056 4.7
15	0355 1.8	0954 4.7	W 1622 2.0	◑ 2211 4.3	30	0254 1.8	0920 4.8	TH 1519 1.9	2147 4.5

OCTOBER

#	Time m	Time m	Time m	Time m	#	Time m	Time m	Time m	Time m
1	0342 2.1	1019 4.6	F 1623 2.2	◑ 2256 4.3	16	0524 2.6	1152 4.3	SA 1815 2.5	
2	0504 2.3	1135 4.5	SA 1817 2.3		17	0104 4.1	0658 2.6	SU 1330 4.4	2001 2.3
3	0024 4.3	0701 2.3	SU 1307 4.6	1951 1.9	18	0212 4.3	0829 2.3	M 1430 4.6	2101 2.0
4	0208 4.5	0824 1.9	M 1432 4.9	2101 1.5	19	0303 4.6	0921 1.8	TU 1518 4.9	2145 1.6
5	0317 4.9	0928 1.4	TU 1533 5.3	2158 1.0	20	0345 4.9	1003 1.6	W 1600 5.1	2223 1.4
6	0410 5.3	1022 0.9	W 1625 5.6	2249 0.6	21	0423 5.1	1041 1.4	TH 1639 5.2	2258 1.2
7	0457 5.5	1111 0.6	TH 1713 5.8	● 2336 0.4	22	0500 5.3	1116 1.2	F 1717 5.3	2331 1.1
8	0543 5.7	1157 0.4	F 1759 5.8		23	0537 5.3	1149 1.1	SA 1754 5.3	○
9	0020 0.3	0626 5.7	SA 1240 0.4	1843 5.8	24	0002 1.1	0612 5.4	SU 1220 1.1	1829 5.3
10	0101 0.4	0707 5.7	SU 1320 0.5	1924 5.6	25	0033 1.1	0645 5.4	M 1250 1.2	1902 5.2
11	0140 0.7	0744 5.6	M 1358 0.8	2002 5.4	26	0103 1.3	0717 5.3	TU 1320 1.3	1934 5.1
12	0216 1.0	0818 5.3	TU 1435 1.2	2034 5.0	27	0133 1.3	0748 5.2	W 1353 1.4	2008 5.0
13	0251 1.5	0847 5.1	W 1513 1.6	2104 4.7	28	0207 1.5	0825 5.1	TH 1424 1.6	2049 4.8
14	0329 1.9	0920 4.8	TH 1558 2.0	◑ 2142 4.3	29	0247 1.7	0910 4.9	F 1517 1.8	2141 4.6
15	0417 2.3	1008 4.5	F 1656 2.4	2247 4.1	30	0340 2.0	1007 4.8	SA 1623 2.0	◑ 2246 4.5
					31	0456 2.2	1117 4.7	SU 1755 2.1	

NOVEMBER

#	Time m	Time m	Time m	Time m	#	Time m	Time m	Time m	Time m
1	0008 4.4	0633 2.2	M 1242 4.7	1923 1.9	16	0106 4.3	0708 2.4	TU 1330 4.5	1946 2.2
2	0139 4.6	0756 1.9	TU 1402 5.0	2033 1.5	17	0209 4.5	0816 2.2	W 1429 4.7	2045 1.9
3	0248 4.9	0901 1.5	W 1506 5.2	2132 1.2	18	0300 4.7	0910 1.9	TH 1519 4.9	2132 1.7
4	0343 5.2	0957 1.1	TH 1600 5.5	2224 0.9	19	0345 5.0	0956 1.7	F 1604 5.1	2215 1.5
5	0432 5.5	1047 0.8	F 1650 5.6	2311 0.7	20	0428 5.1	1038 1.5	SA 1647 5.2	2254 1.3
6	0518 5.6	1134 0.7	SA 1737 5.6	● 2356 0.7	21	0508 5.3	1117 1.3	SU 1729 5.2	○ 2333 1.2
7	0601 5.7	1217 0.7	SU 1822 5.6		22	0547 5.4	1156 1.2	M 1808 5.3	
8	0038 0.7	0642 5.6	M 1259 0.8	1903 5.4	23	0011 1.2	0624 5.4	TU 1234 1.2	1846 5.2
9	0118 0.9	0720 5.5	TU 1339 1.0	1940 5.2	24	0049 1.2	0701 5.4	W 1313 1.2	1925 5.2
10	0155 1.2	0754 5.3	W 1417 1.3	2014 5.0	25	0127 1.3	0739 5.4	TH 1352 1.2	2005 5.1
11	0231 1.5	0825 5.1	TH 1455 1.6	2046 4.7	26	0207 1.4	0820 5.3	F 1435 1.4	2049 5.0
12	0308 1.9	0906 4.9	F 1537 1.9	2125 4.5	27	0251 1.5	0906 1.5	SA 1523 1.5	2138 4.8
13	0351 2.2	0944 4.7	SA 1626 2.2	◑ 2218 4.3	28	0341 1.7	0959 5.0	SU 1619 1.7	◑ 2236 4.7
14	0445 2.4	1042 4.5	SU 1726 2.4	2336 4.2	29	0442 1.9	1101 4.9	M 1727 1.8	2345 4.6
15	0553 2.5	1208 4.4	M 1836 2.4		30	0556 2.0	1212 4.9	TU 1844 1.8	

DECEMBER

#	Time m	Time m	Time m	Time m	#	Time m	Time m	Time m	Time m
1	0100 4.7	0717 1.9	W 1327 4.9	1958 1.7	16	0048 4.4	0705 2.4	TH 1316 4.5	1938 2.2
2	0211 4.8	0829 1.7	TH 1435 5.0	2103 1.5	17	0200 4.5	0811 2.2	F 1427 4.6	2038 2.0
3	0313 5.1	0931 1.5	F 1535 5.2	2159 1.3	18	0301 4.7	0910 1.9	SA 1527 4.8	2133 1.7
4	0407 5.3	1025 1.2	SA 1629 5.3	2250 1.1	19	0354 5.0	1002 1.7	SU 1619 4.9	2223 1.5
5	0456 5.4	1115 1.1	SU 1719 5.3	● 2337 1.0	20	0441 5.2	1051 1.4	M 1706 5.1	2310 1.3
6	0541 5.5	1201 1.0	M 1805 5.3		21	0525 5.3	1138 1.2	TU 1752 5.2	○ 2356 1.2
7	0021 1.0	0623 5.5	TU 1245 1.0	1846 5.2	22	0608 5.5	1223 1.0	W 1836 5.3	
8	0102 1.1	0702 5.5	W 1326 1.1	1925 5.1	23	0040 1.1	0651 5.5	TH 1308 0.9	1919 5.3
9	0140 1.3	0737 5.4	TH 1403 1.2	1959 5.0	24	0124 1.0	0734 5.6	F 1352 0.9	2003 5.3
10	0216 1.5	0810 5.2	F 1439 1.5	2033 4.8	25	0207 1.0	0818 5.5	SA 1436 1.0	2047 5.2
11	0250 1.7	0844 5.1	SA 1515 1.7	2108 4.7	26	0250 1.1	0902 5.5	SU 1519 1.1	2132 5.1
12	0324 1.9	0922 4.9	SU 1552 1.9	2150 4.5	27	0334 1.3	0949 5.3	M 1605 1.3	2220 4.9
13	0403 2.1	1006 4.7	M 1635 2.1	◑ 2238 4.4	28	0422 1.5	1040 5.1	TU 1656 1.6	◑ 2315 4.7
14	0452 2.3	1058 4.6	TU 1729 2.2	2338 4.4	29	0518 1.8	1140 4.9	W 1758 1.8	
15	0555 2.4	1201 4.5	W 1833 2.3		30	0021 4.7	0629 2.0	TH 1251 4.7	1915 1.9
					31	0135 4.7	0753 2.0	F 1406 4.7	2034 1.9

Chart Datum is 2·62 metres below Ordnance Datum (Newlyn). HAT is 5·9 metres above Chart Datum; see 4.5.

》》 FREE monthly updates from 《《
www.reedsalmanac.co.uk

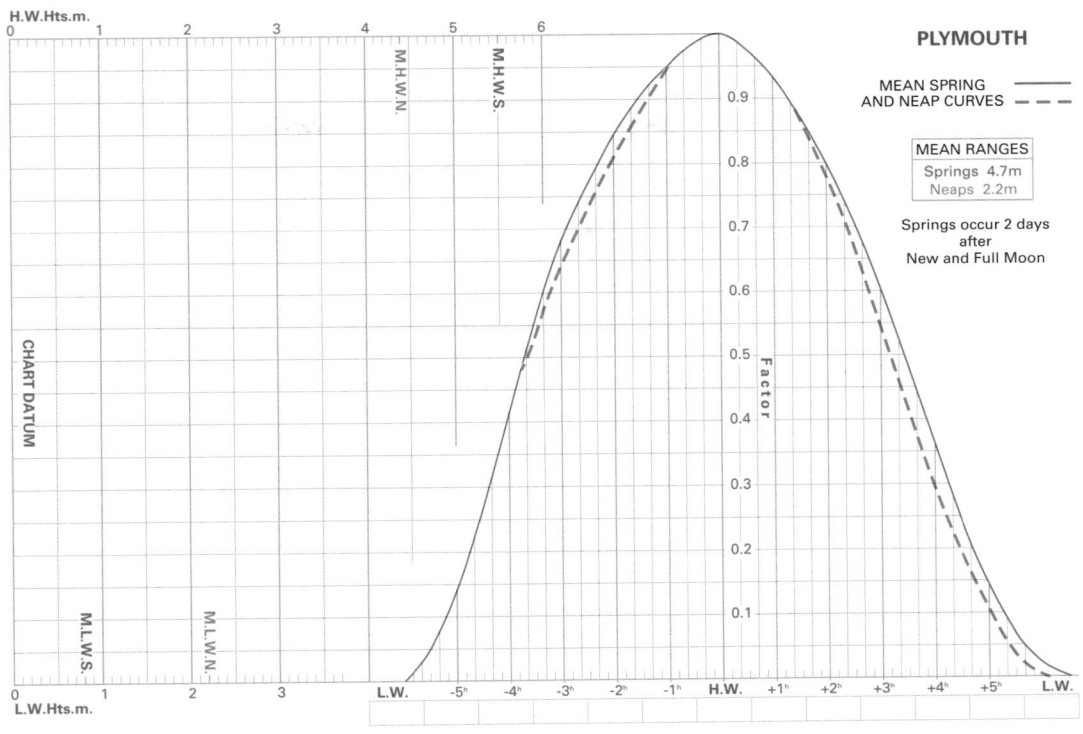

9.1.16 NAVAL EXERCISE AREAS (SUBFACTS and GUNFACTS)

Submarines and warships frequently exercise south of Plymouth and in the western part of the English Channel. Details of submarine activity and naval gunnery and missile firings are broadcast daily by HM Coastguard. See Chapter 3 for advice when sailing in areas of known submarine activity, and Chapter 6 for timings of daily broadcasts. Although the onus for safety is on the relevant naval vessels, if possible it is best to avoid areas where exercises are taking place.

9.1.17 RIVER YEALM

Devon 50°18'·58N 04°04'·13W (Ent) 🌊🌊⚓⚓☆☆☆☆

CHARTS AC *1613*, 1900, 30, 5602; Imray 2400.6; Stan 2, 22

TIDES 0522 Dover; ML 3·2; Duration 0615
Standard Port PLYMOUTH (◄—)

Times				Height (metres)			
High Water		Low Water		MHWS	MHWN	MLWN	MLWS
0000	0600	0000	0600	5·5	4·4	2·2	0·8
1200	1800	1200	1800				

Differences RIVER YEALM ENTRANCE
+0006	+0006	+0002	+0002	−0·1	−0·1	−0·1	−0·1

NOTE: Strong SW winds hold up the ebb and raise levels, as does the river if in spate.

SHELTER Very good inside. Ent easy except in strong SW/W'lies. ⚓ in Cellar Bay is open to SW-NW winds. No ⚓ in river.

NAVIGATION Outer WPT 50°18'·03N 04°05'·55W, 033°/7ca to the Inner WPT 50°18'·59N 04°04'·98W; thence 089°/5·5ca to sand bar. Clearing brgs of 010° and 030° on St Werburgh's ✠ twr avoid the drying Slimers and the W & E Ebb Rocks (which lie only 75m E of the 002° clearing brg shown on AC 30). Speed limit 6kn. Space in the hbr is limited and in wind-over-tide conditions, when moored yachts lie across the stream, larger vessels may find turning difficult. Vessels >18m LOA may not enter without the HM's prior permission.

LIGHTS AND MARKS Great Mewstone (57m) is conspic 1·5M to W of river ent; no passage between it and the coast. Ldg bns (W △, B stripe) in transit 089° clear Mouthstone Ledge, but not the sand bar. Two PHM buoys marking the S end of sand bar **must** be left to port on entry; the seaward buoy is Fl R 5s. When the second (eastern) buoy is **abaft** the beam (not before) turn NE toward bcn (W □, R stripe) high on N bank. From sand bar to Misery Pt, river carries only 1m at MLWS. Spit PHM buoy marks a drying spit.

TELEPHONE (Code 01752) HM 872533; MRCC 01803 882704; Marinecall 09068 969648; Dr 880567; Police 08452 777444.

R/T Water taxi Ch 08.

FACILITIES 1 ⚓ off Misery Pt and 2 off Warren Pt. Ⓥ pontoons in The Pool and 3ca up-river. Ⓥ pontoon, ⚓ & ⚓ £1.55. Shwrs, WC, FW, L, ⛽. **Yealm YC** ☎ 872291, FW, Bar. **Newton Ferrers** L, Slip, FW, 🛒, R, Bar, ⊠. **Noss Mayo** AB at Pope's Quay (dries), L, Slip, FW, R, Bar. **Bridgend** (Newton Creek) FW, ⛓. Fuel, Gas, Gaz at Yealmpton 3M.

ADJACENT ANCHORAGES IN BIGBURY BAY

RIVER ERME, Devon, 50°18'·15N 03°57'·67W. AC1613. HW −0525 on Dover; +0015 and −0·6m on HW Plymouth. Temp day ⚓ in 3m at mouth of drying river, open to SW. Access near HW, but only in offshore winds and settled weather. Beware Wells Rk (1m) 1M SE of ent. Appr from SW, clear of Edwards Rk. Ent between Battisborough Is and W. Mary's Rk (dries 1·1m) keeping to the W. No facilities. Two Historic Wrecks are at 50°18'·15N 03°57'·41W and 50°18'·41N 03°57'·19W on W side of the ent.

RIVER AVON, Devon, 50°16'·63N 03°53'·33W. AC1613. Tides as R Erme, above. Appr close E of conspic Burgh Is (⚓) & Murray's Rk, marked by bcn. Enter drying river HW −1, only in offshore winds and settled weather. Narrow chan hugs cliffy NW shore, then S-bends SE and N off Bantham. Local knowledge or a dinghy recce near LW would assist. Streams run hard, but able to dry out in good shelter clear of moorings. HM ☎ (01548) 561196. 🛒, ⊠, Bar at Bantham. Aveton Gifford accessible by dinghy, 2·5M.

HOPE COVE, Devon, 50°14'·65N 03°51'·78W. AC 1613. Tides as R Erme; ML 2·6m; Duration 0615. Popular day ⚓ in centre of cove, but poor holding and only in offshore winds. Appr with old LB ho in SE corner of the cove brg 130° and ⚓ WSW of the pier head, clear of moorings. Basse Rock extends 30m around the pier head. Off the S shore Goody Rock (dries 2·5m) is cleared by brgs of 060° on the pier head and 120° on the old LB ho. No lights. Facilities: very limited in village, good at Salcombe (4M bus).

9.1.18 SALCOMBE

Devon 50°14′·03N 03°46′·03W ❀❀❀⚓⚓⚓❁❁❁

CHARTS AC 1613, 1634, 28, 5602; Imray C6, 2400.1 & .5; Stanfords 2, 12, 22, L14

TIDES –0523 Dover; ML 3·1; Duration 0615

Standard Port PLYMOUTH (←——)

Times				Height (metres)			
High Water		Low Water		MHWS	MHWN	MLWN	MLWS
0100	0600	0100	0600	5·5	4·4	2·2	0·8
1300	1800	1300	1800				
Differences SALCOMBE							
0000	+0010	+0005	–0005	–0·2	–0·3	–0·1	–0·1
START POINT							
+0015	+0015	+0005	+0010	–0·1	–0·2	+0·1	+0·2

SHELTER Good, but fresh S'lies can cause uncomfortable swell off the town. Better shelter in The Bag at Ⓥ pontoon. ⚓s at Sunny Cove; off SE shore from YC start line to fuel barge (where poor holding has been reported); 200m W and 300m SSE of Salt Stone SHM bcn 50°15′·19N 03°45′·55W.

NAVIGATION WPT 50°12′·43N 03°46′·67W, 000°/1·3M to Sandhill Pt lt. Access HW±4½, but at springs this window applies only if swell height is <1m. The bar (least depth 0·7m) is not as dangerous as rumoured, but *should not be crossed on an ebb tide with strong onshore winds or swell*; if in doubt, call HM Ch 14 before approaching. The spring flood reaches 2·5kn. Speed limit 8kn but 6kn between Marine Hotel/racing start line and the Saltstone (approx 50°15′·2N 03°45′·5W); minimise wash; radar checks in force. In Jul/Aug within the hbr cruising yachts must motor, not sail. When dinghy racing in progress (Sat/Sun & regatta weeks: Fl Y lt at YC and warning Ch 14) yachts should use a fairway marked by Y SPM buoys close to the NW bank and straddling the start line. Two Historic Wrecks lie 1M WNW of Prawle Pt at 50°12′·74N 03°44′·40W & 50°12′·73N 03°44′·75W.

LIGHTS AND MARKS Outer 000° ldg marks, both R/W bcns (a conspic gabled house close N is more easily seen): front, Poundstone; rear, Sandhill Pt Dir lt 000°, stay in the W sector (357·5°-002·5°). Close W of ldg line beware Bass Rk (0·8m) marked by PHM lt buoy; and, close E, Wolf Rk (0·6m), marked by SHM lt buoy. When past Wolf Rk, leave Black Stone Rk (5m), G/W lt bcn, well to stbd and pick up inner ldg lts 042·5°, to make good the hbr ⊕ (under Title), which is abm the first ⚓.

R/T Ch 14 *Salcombe Hbr* or *Launch* (May to mid-Sep: daily 0600 -2100 (2200 Jul, Aug); rest of year: Mon-Fri 0900-1600). *Harbour taxi* Ch 12. *Fuel Barge* Ch 06. ICC HQ, *Egremont* Ch M.

TELEPHONE (Code 01548) MRCC (01803) 882704; Marinecall 09068 969648; Police 842107 (999 or 112); Dr 842284; Environment Agency (pollution report) 0800 807060.

FACILITIES HM 843791, 🖷 842033. Mid-May to mid-Sep: Mon-Thu 0900-1645 (1615 Fri-Sun). salcombe.harbour@southhams.gov.uk www.southhams.gov.uk
The Bag @ 50°14′·58N 03°45′·56W: pontoon for 150 Ⓥ. 21 ⚓s (orange <8m LOA, yellow >8m) are marked 'V'. Pontoon & ⚓ £1.80 (inc hbr dues £0.90/m). ⚓ £0.90/m.
Short stay pontoon (½ hour max, 0700-1900, for FW/stores) is E of HM's office in 0·9m.
Slip, Ⓔ, ME, El, C (15 ton), ✕, CH, SM, ACA, Ⓔ, Water Taxi, @. Public ⚓ & 🚽 in Batson Creek (Fishermens Quay). Wi-Fi **Fuel Barge** ☎ 07801 798862, 0900-1700 7/7 Jul-mid Sep.

Salcombe YC ☎ 842872/842593, L, R, Bar.
Island CC ☎ 531776 in *Egremont*, N of Ox Pt.
Town ▢, ✉, Ⓑ, Kingsbridge 🏥 852349 (A&E), ➤ (bus to Totnes). Plymouth ✈.

ADJACENT HARBOUR, 3M north
KINGSBRIDGE, 50°16′·88N 03°46′·52W. AC 28. HW = HW Salcombe +0005. Access HW±2½ for <2m draft/bilge keelers, max LOA 11m. The 3M chan is marked beyond Salt Stone SHM perch by R/W PHM poles with R can topmarks. 6ca N of Salt Stone a secondary chan marked by PHM buoys gradually diverges E into Balcombe Creek. There is a private ferry pontoon at New Quay, 3ca before the drying Kingsbridge basin.
Ⓥ AB on pontoon on W side of basin or on the wall N of the pontoon marked 'visitors' (drying 3·4m to soft mud). Best to pre-check berth availability with Salcombe HM; berthing fees and Hbr dues are payable. Facilities: Slip, SM. Police ☎ 08705 882704.
Town 🛒, R, Bar, ✉, Ⓑ, ▢, 🏥 852349 (A&E).

START POINT TO TEIGNMOUTH

(AC 1613, 1634, 3315) Start Point (lt ho, horn), 3·3M ENE of Prawle Point, is a long headland with a distinctive cock's comb spine, a W lt ho on the Point, and conspic radio masts to the WNW. Black Stone rock (6m high) is visible 2½ca SSE of the lt ho, with Cherrick Rocks (1m) 1ca further S; other drying rocks lie closer inshore. A race may extend 1M to the S and 1·6M to the E. In fair weather any overfalls can be avoided by passing close to seaward of rocks; there is no clear-cut inshore passage as such. In bad weather keep at least 2M off.

▶ *The NE-going flood begins at HW Plymouth −2; max 3·1kn springs @ HWP −1. The SW-going ebb begins at HWP +5; max 2·2kn springs @ HWP +6. But at HWP +4 it is possible to round Start Point close inshore using a back eddy. On both the flood and the ebb back eddies form between Start Point and Hallsands, 1M NW. Inshore the tide turns 30 minutes earlier.*◀

Skerries Bank (least depth 2·1m), on which the sea breaks in bad weather, lies from 9ca to 4·1M NE of Start Pt (AC 1634). In offshore winds there is a good anchorage in 3m 1ca off Hallsands (1M NW of Start). Between **Dartmouth** and **Brixham** rocks extend 5ca offshore.

Berry Head (lt), a bold, flat-topped headland (55m), gives a good radar return. ▶*Here the stream turns N at HW Plymouth −3, and S at HWP +3; max sp rates 3kn.*◀ In **Torbay** (AC 26) the more obvious dangers are steep-to, but beware the Sunker (awash at CD) 100m SW of Ore Stone, and Morris Rogue (0·8m) 5ca W of Thatcher Rock.

In westerlies Hope Cove, Anstey's Cove (beware the Three Brothers, rocks drying 0·6m, S side) and Babbacombe Bay are good ‡ages on sand. There are no offlying dangers from Long Quarry Point for 4M N to **Teignmouth** whose ent is dangerous in onshore winds. ▶*Off Teignmouth Bar the NNE-going stream begins at HW Plymouth −1½ and the SSW-going at HWP +5¼. In the ent the flood begins at HWP − 5½ and the ebb at HWP +¾. The spring ebb reaches 4–5kn off The Point.*◀

9.1.19 DARTMOUTH

Devon 50°20'·66N 03°33'·96W ❋❋❋❁♨♨♨✿✿✿

CHARTS AC 1613, 1634, 2253, 5602; Imray C5, 2400.1 & 4; Stanfords 2, 12, 22, L15

TIDES −0510 Dover; ML 2·8; Duration 0630

DARTMOUTH (⟶). The differences below are referred to Plymouth as Standard Port, not to Dartmouth.

Times				Height (metres)			
High Water		Low Water		MHWS	MHWN	MLWN	MLWS
0100	0600	0100	0600	5·5	4·4	2·2	0·8
1300	1800	1300	1800				
Differences GREENWAY QUAY (DITTISHAM)							
+0030	+0045	+0025	+0005	−0·6	−0·6	−0·2	−0·2
TOTNES							
+0030	+0040	+0115	+0030	−2·0	−2·1	Dries	Dries

SHELTER Excellent shelter inside the hbr and up-river.

NAVIGATION WPT 50°19'·53N 03°32'·83W, 328°/1·5M in the white sector of Kingswear Dir lt. Bayard's Cove Dir lt leads 293° to abeam Royal Dart YC where the main fairway opens. There is no bar and hbr access is H24, but ent can be difficult in strong

SE to SW winds. Speed limit 6kn from Castle Ledge buoy up-river to 1M below Totnes. *Caution: The Lower and Higher car ferries S and N of Dartmouth have right of way; give way early.*

LIGHTS AND MARKS as on the chartlet and/or 9.1.4. E of the ent, on Inner Froward Pt (167m) is a conspic daymark, obelisk (24·5m). Lateral and cardinal lt buoys mark all dangers to seaward of conspic Dartmouth Castle. Within hbr, all jetty/pontoon lts to the W are 2FR (vert); and 2FG (vert) to the E.

R/T HM: *Dartnav* VHF Ch 11 (summer, daily 0730-dusk). Darthaven, Dart and Noss marinas, Ch **80**. Fuel barge Ch 06. Water taxis: *Dartmouth water taxi* Ch 08 or ☎ 07770 628967 (run by Res Nova Inn, next to No 6 buoy). *Yacht taxi* (DHNA) Ch 69 or 11, ☎ 07970 346571, summer 0800-2300. *Greenway ferry* Ch 10 or ☎ 844010 (to Dittisham), daily 364/365.

TELEPHONE (Code 01803) HM 832337, 835220 (out of hours emergency); MRCC 882704; Police 08452 777444; Marinecall 09068 969648; Dr 832212; Ⓗ 832255.

FACILITIES **Dart Harbour & Navigation Authority** (DHNA), www.dartharbour.org.uk hm@dartharbour.org.uk ☎ 832337. 450+90 Ⓥ: Town jetty £2.26; S embankment £1.60; other pontoons, ♛s and ‡ £1.20; all inc Hbr dues (£0.60) & VAT. FW, Slip.

DHNA ❶ pontoons are marked by blue flags and ♛s are blue with black 'V'. Check availability with HM. The most likely ❶ berths from S to N are:

W bank: pontoon off Dartmouth YC (May-Sep). Town pontoon W side only, but E side 1700-0845 for larger yachts. N end of 2 pontoons just S of Dart marina (26'/8m max LOA).

E of fairway: The ❶ pontoon by Kingswear rail station is shared by DHNA and Darthaven marina; the former are for 2 hrs max. The 2 pontoons N of Fuel barge are for visitors.

Only space to ‡ is E of fairway and Nos 3A to 5 buoys, with HM's agreement. These large unlit mooring buoys (plus Nos 3, 5A and 6) in mid-stream are for commercial vessels/FVs; do not ‡ over their ground chains, as shown on AC 2253.

Darthaven Marina ☎ 752545. www.darthaven.co.uk 250+20 Ⓥ, £2.30 + hbr dues. ME, El, Ⓔ, Gas, Gaz, ▣, ✖, CH, BH (35 ton).

Dart Marina ☎ 832580. www. dartmarina.com. 100 +10 Ⓥs, £4.11+hbr dues. C (9 ton), R, ▣.

Noss Marina www.nossmarina.co.uk ☎ 835620, 07768 815872. 180 AB, £2.41 + dues. M, ME, El, ✖, C (15 ton), CH, Gas, Gaz, ▣, Wi-Fi.

YACHT CLUBS (visitors welcome): **Royal Dart YC** ☎ 752272, M, short stay pontoon, FW, Bar, R ☎ 752880. **Dartmouth YC** ☎ 832305, L, FW, Bar, R. **Royal Regatta**, last week Aug.

SERVICES **Fuel Barge** next to No 6 buoy, Ch 06, D, P; ☎ 07801 798861 summer 7/7 0900-1800; winter Mon, Wed, Fri 0900-1600.

Creekside BY (Old Mill Creek) ☎ 832649, Slip, dry dock, M, ME, ✖, El, C (14 ton), CH, ME (customer only), FW.

Dartside Quay (Galmpton Creek): ☎ 845445 CH, D, FW, L, M, C (13 ton), ME, ✖, BY, Slip, ⊏▷, BH (65, 16 ton), El, Ⓔ.

Town www.dartmouth-tourism.org.uk, SM, Wi-Fi, ▨ WC/showers, ▤, P (cans), R, Bar, ▣ (0800-2000 daily), ✉, Ⓑ, ⇌ ☎ 555872 (steam train in season to Paignton); bus to Totnes/Paignton, ✈ Exeter.

UP-RIVER TO DITTISHAM AND TOTNES

The R Dart is navigable by day (unlit above Stoney Ground) on the flood to Totnes bridge, about 5·5M above Dittisham. HW Totnes = HW Dartmouth +0015. Speed limit 6kn to S end of Home Reach, then 'Dead Slow', ie min steerage speed and no wash.

Directions: Use AC 2253 and DHNA annual Handbook. Leave Anchor Stone to port. From Dittisham brgs of 020° and 310° on successive Boat Houses lead between Lower Back and Flat Owers banks; or keep E of the latter. Up-river the 11 unlit buoys are numbered 1-11 in geographic sequence, contrary to the IALA system for lateral buoys, ie odd numbers to stbd, evens to port.

‡s/♛s/Berths: For ‡s above Anchor Stone, call *DartNav* Ch 11. Many ♛s (lt blue with black V) between Anchor Stone & Dittisham; no ‡. 4 ♛s off Stoke Gabriel by SHM bcn, QG.

Totnes all berths dry, access HW ±3. W bank: Baltic Wharf ☎ 867922, AB (visitors pre-call), AC, FW, BY, CH, BH (16 ton),

C (35 ton), ME. E bank: (visitors pre-call DHNA) for 5 AB at Steamer Quay, keep clear of ferry berths. Limited AB on soft mud in the W Arm N of Steam Packet Inn, ☎ 863880, AC, FW, R, Bar, ▣. **Totnes**: Usual amenities; mainline ⮂.

TIME ZONE (UT)
For Summer Time add ONE hour in **non-shaded areas**

DARTMOUTH LAT 50°21'N LONG 3°35'W
TIMES AND HEIGHTS OF HIGH AND LOW WATERS

Dates in red are **SPRINGS**
Dates in blue are NEAPS

YEAR 2010

JANUARY

Time	m	Time	m
1 0611	5.0	**16** 0020	1.1
1207	0.6	0639	4.7
F 1842	4.8	SA 1244	1.0
		1900	4.4
2 0028	0.6	**17** 0055	1.0
0659	5.1	0714	4.7
SA 1259	0.5	SU 1316	1.0
1932	4.8	1934	4.4
3 0118	0.5	**18** 0124	1.0
0747	5.2	0747	4.7
SU 1346	0.4	M 1344	1.0
2019	4.8	2007	4.4
4 0203	0.5	**19** 0149	1.1
0834	5.1	0819	4.6
M 1430	0.4	TU 1409	1.1
2105	4.8	2038	4.3
5 0245	0.6	**20** 0214	1.2
0920	5.0	0850	4.5
TU 1514	0.6	W 1433	1.2
2149	4.6	2108	4.2
6 0327	0.8	**21** 0238	1.3
1004	4.8	0918	4.4
W 1556	0.9	TH 1459	1.3
2232	4.4	2136	4.1
7 0410	1.1	**22** 0307	1.4
1048	4.6	0947	4.2
TH 1639	1.2	F 1530	1.5
◑ 2318	4.2	2208	4.0
8 0457	1.5	**23** 0343	1.6
1138	4.2	1025	4.1
F 1729	1.6	SA 1611	1.7
		◐ 2254	3.9
9 0012	4.0	**24** 0432	1.8
0553	1.8	1120	3.9
SA 1239	4.0	SU 1710	1.9
1833	1.9	2358	3.8
10 0119	3.9	**25** 0549	2.0
0709	2.0	1232	3.8
SU 1353	3.8	M 1842	2.0
1953	2.0		
11 0233	3.9	**26** 0116	3.8
0835	1.9	0732	2.0
M 1506	3.9	TU 1400	3.8
2110	1.9	2011	1.8
12 0338	4.1	**27** 0246	4.0
0945	1.7	0854	1.6
TU 1609	4.0	W 1528	4.0
2210	1.6	2126	1.5
13 0433	4.3	**28** 0401	4.4
1039	1.5	1004	1.2
W 1700	4.2	TH 1639	4.3
2259	1.4	2231	1.1
14 0520	4.5	**29** 0502	4.7
1125	1.2	1104	0.8
TH 1745	4.3	F 1737	4.6
2342	1.2	2327	0.7
15 0601	4.6	**30** 0557	5.0
1205	1.0	1158	0.4
F 1825	4.4	SA 1831	4.8
●		○	
		31 0018	0.4
		0648	5.2
		SU 1248	0.1
		1919	4.9

FEBRUARY

Time	m	Time	m
1 0106	0.2	**16** 0104	0.8
0736	5.3	0729	4.7
M 1332	0.0	TU 1322	0.8
2005	5.0	1946	4.5
2 0148	0.1	**17** 0129	0.8
0819	5.3	0800	4.7
TU 1414	0.1	W 1345	0.8
2046	4.9	2015	4.5
3 0228	0.2	**18** 0151	0.9
0901	5.1	0828	4.6
W 1452	0.3	TH 1408	0.9
2125	4.8	2042	4.4
4 0305	0.5	**19** 0214	1.0
0939	4.9	0853	4.4
TH 1528	0.7	F 1431	1.1
2200	4.5	2106	4.3
5 0341	0.9	**20** 0241	1.1
1014	4.5	0920	4.3
F 1604	1.1	SA 1501	1.2
◗ 2234	4.2	2134	4.1
6 0420	1.4	**21** 0315	1.3
1050	4.1	0954	4.1
SA 1644	1.6	SU 1537	1.5
2313	3.9	2216	4.0
7 0506	1.8	**22** 0400	1.6
1139	3.8	1049	3.8
SU 1735	2.0	M 1630	1.8
		◑ 2323	3.8
8 0019	3.7	**23** 0510	1.9
0611	2.1	1204	3.7
M 1311	3.5	TU 1800	2.0
1853	2.2		
9 0155	3.6	**24** 0045	3.8
0800	2.2	0705	2.0
TU 1441	3.5	W 1339	3.7
2048	2.1	1950	1.9
10 0312	3.8	**25** 0223	3.9
0932	1.9	0839	1.6
W 1549	3.7	TH 1516	3.9
2156	1.8	2112	1.5
11 0412	4.1	**26** 0345	4.3
1025	1.5	0952	1.1
TH 1642	4.0	F 1626	4.3
2244	1.4	2218	1.0
12 0459	4.4	**27** 0447	4.7
1110	1.2	1051	0.6
F 1726	4.2	SA 1723	4.6
2325	1.1	2313	0.5
13 0541	4.6	**28** 0541	5.0
1148	0.9	1142	0.2
SA 1804	4.4	SU 1815	4.9
		○	
14 0002	0.9		
0619	4.7		
SU 1224	0.8		
● 1841	4.5		
15 0036	0.8		
0654	4.7		
M 1255	0.7		
1914	4.5		

MARCH

Time	m	Time	m
1 0001	0.2	**16** 0006	0.7
0630	5.2	0629	4.7
M 1228	-0.1	TU 1225	0.7
1859	5.0	1849	4.6
2 0047	0.0	**17** 0037	0.7
0716	5.3	0704	4.7
TU 1312	-0.2	W 1253	0.7
1941	5.0	1921	4.6
3 0128	-0.1	**18** 0103	0.7
0758	5.2	0737	4.7
W 1351	-0.1	TH 1319	0.7
2020	5.0	1950	4.6
4 0205	0.1	**19** 0129	0.8
0836	5.1	0806	4.6
TH 1427	0.2	F 1343	0.8
2053	4.8	2016	4.5
5 0239	0.4	**20** 0153	0.8
0910	4.8	0833	4.4
F 1459	0.6	SA 1410	1.0
2123	4.6	2043	4.4
6 0312	0.8	**21** 0222	1.0
0939	4.4	0902	4.3
SA 1531	1.1	SU 1440	1.2
2148	4.3	2115	4.3
7 0347	1.3	**22** 0257	1.2
1006	4.0	0941	4.1
SU 1607	1.6	M 1519	1.5
◑ 2219	4.0	2200	4.1
8 0430	1.8	**23** 0344	1.6
1046	3.6	1037	3.8
M 1655	2.1	TU 1613	1.8
2311	3.6	◑ 2303	3.9
9 0532	2.2	**24** 0458	1.9
1213	3.3	1151	3.6
TU 1806	2.3	W 1746	2.0
10 0114	3.5	**25** 0025	3.8
0709	2.3	0651	1.9
W 1415	3.4	TH 1328	3.6
2011	2.3	1933	1.9
11 0243	3.7	**26** 0205	4.0
0908	2.0	0822	1.5
TH 1523	3.6	F 1502	3.9
2130	1.9	2055	1.4
12 0343	4.0	**27** 0326	4.3
1000	1.5	0933	1.0
F 1615	3.9	SA 1609	4.3
2217	1.5	2158	0.9
13 0431	4.3	**28** 0426	4.7
1042	1.2	1030	0.5
SA 1658	4.2	SU 1702	4.6
2258	1.1	2252	0.5
14 0513	4.5	**29** 0519	5.0
1120	0.9	1119	0.2
SU 1736	4.4	M 1751	4.9
2334	0.9	2339	0.2
15 0552	4.6	**30** 0607	5.1
1154	0.7	1204	0.0
M 1815	4.5	TU 1836	5.0
●		○	
		31 0022	0.0
		0653	5.1
		W 1247	-0.1
		1915	5.0

APRIL

Time	m	Time	m
1 0104	0.0	**16** 0037	0.7
0733	5.1	0712	4.6
TH 1325	0.1	F 1254	0.7
1951	4.9	1926	4.6
2 0140	0.2	**17** 0108	0.7
0809	4.9	0745	4.6
F 1400	0.4	SA 1325	0.8
2022	4.8	1956	4.6
3 0214	0.5	**18** 0139	0.8
0841	4.6	0818	4.4
SA 1431	0.8	SU 1356	1.0
2049	4.6	2028	4.5
4 0247	0.9	**19** 0213	1.0
0907	4.3	0854	4.3
SU 1503	1.2	M 1431	1.2
2114	4.3	2106	4.4
5 0322	1.4	**20** 0253	1.2
0935	3.9	0938	4.1
M 1538	1.7	TU 1516	1.4
2146	4.0	2153	4.2
6 0405	1.8	**21** 0346	1.5
1016	3.6	1034	3.9
TU 1626	2.0	W 1616	1.7
◗ 2235	3.7	◗ 2253	4.0
7 0504	2.1	**22** 0502	1.7
1126	3.3	1146	3.7
W 1733	2.3	TH 1740	1.8
8 0000	3.5	**23** 0011	4.0
0622	2.2	0635	1.6
TH 1334	3.4	F 1315	3.8
1901	2.3	1912	1.7
9 0158	3.6	**24** 0142	4.1
0807	2.0	0758	1.4
F 1444	3.6	SA 1438	4.0
2037	2.0	2029	1.4
10 0302	3.9	**25** 0259	4.3
0913	1.6	0905	1.0
SA 1537	3.9	SU 1541	4.3
2133	1.6	2132	1.0
11 0353	4.2	**26** 0400	4.6
0959	1.3	1002	0.6
SU 1621	4.2	M 1634	4.6
2217	1.3	2225	0.6
12 0438	4.4	**27** 0453	4.8
1048	1.0	1053	0.4
M 1702	4.4	TU 1723	4.8
2256	1.0	2314	0.4
13 0519	4.5	**28** 0543	4.9
1115	0.8	1138	0.3
TU 1742	4.5	W 1807	4.9
2331	0.8	○ 2357	0.3
14 0559	4.6	**29** 0628	4.9
1149	0.7	1220	0.3
W 1820	4.6	TH 1849	4.9
●			
15 0004	0.7	**30** 0039	0.3
0638	4.6	0709	4.8
TH 1221	0.7	F 1300	0.4
1854	4.6	1924	4.8

Chart Datum is 2·62 metres below Ordnance Datum (Newlyn). HAT is 5·3 metres above Chart Datum; see 4.5.

TIME ZONE (UT)
For Summer Time add ONE hour in **non-shaded areas**

DARTMOUTH   LAT 50°21'N   LONG 3°35W
TIMES AND HEIGHTS OF HIGH AND LOW WATERS

Dates in red are **SPRINGS**
Dates in blue are NEAPS

YEAR 2010

SW England

MAY

Time	m		Time	m
1 0118	0.5		**16** 0054	0.7
0745	4.6		0731	4.5
SA 1335	0.7		SU 1312	0.8
1955	4.7		1942	4.7
2 0153	0.7		**17** 0133	0.8
0817	4.4		0810	4.5
SU 1409	1.0		M 1352	0.9
2022	4.5		2021	4.7
3 0228	1.0		**18** 0215	0.9
0847	4.2		0853	4.4
M 1442	1.3		TU 1434	1.1
2051	4.3		2103	4.6
4 0303	1.4		**19** 0301	1.0
0919	3.9		0941	4.2
TU 1518	1.6		W 1523	1.3
2127	4.1		2152	4.4
5 0344	1.7		**20** 0354	1.2
1001	3.7		1035	4.1
W 1602	1.9		TH 1619	1.4
2212	3.9		◗ 2248	4.3
6 0436	1.9		**21** 0457	1.3
1058	3.5		1139	4.0
TH 1700	2.1		F 1725	1.6
◗ 2314	3.7		2357	4.2
7 0540	2.0		**22** 0609	1.4
1223	3.5		1251	3.9
F 1808	2.1		SA 1841	1.6
8 0043	3.7		**23** 0112	4.2
0650	1.9		0723	1.3
SA 1344	3.6		SU 1403	4.1
1920	2.0		1953	1.4
9 0204	3.8		**24** 0225	4.3
0758	1.7		0832	1.2
SU 1444	3.8		M 1507	4.2
2027	1.8		2059	1.4
10 0302	4.0		**25** 0329	4.4
0856	1.5		0932	1.0
M 1535	4.0		TU 1603	4.4
2121	1.5		2157	1.0
11 0354	4.2		**26** 0426	4.5
0946	1.2		1025	0.8
TU 1622	4.3		W 1654	4.6
2209	1.2		2249	0.8
12 0442	4.3		**27** 0518	4.6
1031	1.0		1114	0.7
W 1705	4.4		TH 1742	4.7
2253	1.0		○ 2336	0.7
13 0527	4.5		**28** 0605	4.6
1112	0.9		1158	0.7
TH 1748	4.6		F 1824	4.7
2334	0.9			
14 0611	4.5		**29** 0019	0.7
1152	0.8		0648	4.5
F 1828	4.7		SA 1240	0.8
●			1901	4.7
15 0013	0.8		**30** 0100	0.7
0652	4.6		0726	4.4
SA 1233	0.8		SU 1318	0.9
1904	4.7		1935	4.6
			31 0137	0.9
			0801	4.3
			M 1352	1.1
			2006	4.5

JUNE

Time	m		Time	m
1 0213	1.1		**16** 0217	0.6
0833	4.2		0853	4.5
TU 1426	1.3		W 1435	0.8
2038	4.4		2102	4.8
2 0247	1.3		**17** 0303	0.7
0907	4.0		0940	4.5
W 1500	1.5		TH 1522	0.9
2113	4.3		2149	4.7
3 0324	1.5		**18** 0350	0.8
0946	3.9		1029	4.3
TH 1536	1.7		F 1609	1.1
2153	4.1		2239	4.5
4 0405	1.6		**19** 0440	1.0
1032	3.7		1102	4.2
F 1621	1.8		SA 1702	1.3
◗ 2239	3.9		◗ 2334	4.3
5 0453	1.8		**20** 0536	1.3
1125	3.7		1220	4.1
SA 1715	2.0		SU 1802	1.5
2334	3.8			
6 0551	1.8		**21** 0039	4.2
1227	3.7		0643	1.4
SU 1818	2.0		M 1324	4.0
			1913	1.6
7 0041	3.8		**22** 0150	4.1
0654	1.8		0754	1.5
M 1334	3.7		TU 1431	4.1
1924	1.9		2025	1.5
8 0154	3.8		**23** 0259	4.1
0755	1.6		0902	1.4
TU 1438	3.9		W 1533	4.2
2027	1.7		2133	1.4
9 0302	4.0		**24** 0402	4.1
0854	1.5		1003	1.3
W 1536	4.1		TH 1629	4.3
2124	1.4		2230	1.2
10 0401	4.2		**25** 0457	4.2
0949	1.2		1055	1.1
TH 1628	4.3		F 1720	4.5
2217	1.2		2320	1.0
11 0455	4.3		**26** 0547	4.3
1041	1.0		1142	1.0
F 1717	4.5		SA 1804	4.6
2308	1.0		○	
12 0546	4.4		**27** 0005	0.9
1129	0.9		0631	4.3
SA 1804	4.7		SU 1224	0.9
● 2356	0.8		1844	4.6
13 0634	4.5		**28** 0048	0.9
1217	0.8		0709	4.3
SU 1850	4.8		M 1304	0.9
			1919	4.6
14 0044	0.6		**29** 0125	0.9
0720	4.6		0744	4.3
M 1305	0.7		TU 1338	1.0
1933	4.9		1952	4.6
15 0130	0.6		**30** 0158	1.0
0807	4.6		0817	4.2
TU 1350	0.7		W 1409	1.1
2017	4.9		2024	4.5

JULY

Time	m		Time	m
1 0228	1.1		**16** 0251	0.3
0851	4.2		0927	4.7
TH 1438	1.3		F 1508	0.5
2057	4.4		2137	4.9
2 0257	1.2		**17** 0332	0.5
0926	4.1		1009	4.5
F 1506	1.4		SA 1549	0.8
2131	4.3		2220	4.6
3 0327	1.4		**18** 0415	0.9
1001	4.0		1054	4.3
SA 1536	1.6		SU 1633	1.1
2205	4.1		◗ 2306	4.3
4 0400	1.5		**19** 0501	1.3
1041	3.8		1144	4.1
SU 1614	1.7		M 1725	1.5
◗ 2247	4.0			
5 0444	1.7		**20** 0001	4.0
1128	3.7		0557	1.6
M 1708	1.9		TU 1246	3.9
2337	3.8		1831	1.8
6 0547	1.8		**21** 0116	3.8
1225	3.7		0714	1.8
TU 1822	2.0		W 1359	3.8
			1955	1.9
7 0043	3.8		**22** 0236	3.8
0702	1.8		0840	1.8
W 1336	3.8		TH 1510	4.0
1938	1.8		2116	1.7
8 0205	3.8		**23** 0345	3.9
0811	1.7		0948	1.6
TH 1450	4.0		F 1611	4.2
2047	1.6		2218	1.4
9 0323	4.0		**24** 0442	4.0
0916	1.4		1043	1.3
F 1555	4.2		SA 1701	4.4
2150	1.3		2308	1.1
10 0428	4.2		**25** 0530	4.2
1016	1.1		1129	1.1
SA 1652	4.5		SU 1746	4.5
2249	1.0		2352	0.9
11 0525	4.4		**26** 0613	4.3
1113	0.9		1210	0.9
SU 1745	4.7		M 1825	4.6
● 2343	0.7		○	
12 0620	4.6		**27** 0032	0.8
1206	0.6		0650	4.4
M 1836	4.9		TU 1248	0.8
			1859	4.7
13 0035	0.4		**28** 0108	0.8
0709	4.7		0724	4.4
TU 1257	0.5		W 1320	0.9
1923	5.0		1933	4.7
14 0124	0.3		**29** 0137	0.8
0757	4.8		0756	4.4
W 1342	0.4		TH 1347	0.9
2008	5.1		2005	4.6
15 0209	0.2		**30** 0203	0.9
0843	4.8		0828	4.3
TH 1427	0.4		F 1411	1.1
2053	5.0		2036	4.5
			31 0226	1.1
			0858	4.2
			SA 1432	1.2
			2105	4.4

AUGUST

Time	m		Time	m
1 0248	1.2		**16** 0345	0.9
0928	4.1		1020	4.4
SU 1456	1.3		M 1603	1.2
2133	4.2		◗ 2231	4.2
2 0314	1.4		**17** 0425	1.4
0959	4.0		1102	4.0
M 1527	1.5		TU 1648	1.6
2205	4.0		2318	3.8
3 0348	1.6		**18** 0516	1.8
1038	3.9		1205	3.8
TU 1609	1.8		W 1751	2.0
◗ 2251	3.9			
4 0439	1.8		**19** 0045	3.6
1134	3.7		0632	2.1
W 1716	2.0		TH 1334	3.7
2357	3.7		1932	2.1
5 0605	2.0		**20** 0219	3.5
1245	3.7		0824	2.1
TH 1900	2.0		F 1451	3.8
			2107	1.9
6 0119	3.7		**21** 0329	3.7
0739	1.8		0936	1.8
F 1413	3.9		SA 1552	4.1
2021	1.7		2205	1.5
7 0256	3.9		**22** 0425	4.0
0854	1.5		1026	1.4
SA 1531	4.2		SU 1642	4.4
2132	1.3		2251	1.2
8 0411	4.2		**23** 0510	4.2
1000	1.2		1109	1.1
SU 1633	4.6		M 1723	4.6
2235	0.9		2331	0.9
9 0510	4.5		**24** 0549	4.4
1059	0.8		1148	0.9
M 1728	4.8		TU 1801	4.7
2330	0.5		○	
10 0603	4.7		**25** 0008	0.7
1152	0.4		0624	4.5
TU 1820	5.1		W 1223	0.8
●			1836	4.7
11 0020	0.2		**26** 0042	0.7
0653	4.9		0657	4.5
W 1242	0.2		TH 1254	0.8
1907	5.2		1909	4.7
12 0108	0.0		**27** 0110	0.8
0739	4.9		0730	4.5
TH 1327	0.1		F 1319	0.8
1953	5.2		1941	4.7
13 0151	0.0		**28** 0132	0.8
0823	5.0		0801	4.5
F 1408	0.1		SA 1340	0.9
2036	5.2		2010	4.6
14 0230	0.2		**29** 0153	1.0
0904	4.9		0829	4.4
SA 1446	0.4		SU 1402	1.1
2116	5.0		2038	4.4
15 0308	0.5		**30** 0215	1.1
0942	4.7		0855	4.3
SU 1524	0.7		M 1425	1.2
2153	4.6		2103	4.3
			31 0239	1.3
			0924	4.1
			TU 1454	1.4
			2135	4.1

Chart Datum is 2·62 metres below Ordnance Datum (Newlyn). HAT is 5·3 metres above Chart Datum; see 4.5.

TIME ZONE (UT)
For Summer Time add ONE hour in **non-shaded areas**

DARTMOUTH   LAT 50°21'N   LONG 3°35'W
TIMES AND HEIGHTS OF HIGH AND LOW WATERS

Dates in red are **SPRINGS**
Dates in blue are NEAPS

YEAR 2010

SEPTEMBER

Time	m	Time	m
1 0313	1.5	**16** 0440	2.1
1002	4.0	1110	3.7
W 1534	1.7	TH 1720	2.2
◗ 2221	3.9		
2 0359	1.8	**17** 0010	3.4
1059	3.8	0553	2.4
TH 1635	2.0	F 1304	3.6
2330	3.7	1904	2.3
3 0520	2.1	**18** 0157	3.4
1213	3.8	0657	2.3
F 1832	2.1	SA 1425	3.8
		2046	2.0
4 0055	3.6	**19** 0307	3.7
0717	2.0	0911	1.9
SA 1346	3.9	SU 1526	4.1
2004	1.8	2139	1.6
5 0241	3.9	**20** 0359	4.0
0839	1.6	0959	1.5
SU 1513	4.2	M 1614	4.4
2117	1.3	2222	1.2
6 0356	4.2	**21** 0442	4.3
0946	1.1	1041	1.1
M 1616	4.6	TU 1655	4.6
2218	0.8	2301	0.9
7 0453	4.6	**22** 0520	4.5
1043	0.7	1118	0.9
TU 1710	5.0	W 1732	4.7
2311	0.3	2336	0.8
8 0544	4.8	**23** 0555	4.6
1133	0.3	1151	0.8
W 1800	5.2	TH 1810	4.8
●		○	
9 0000	0.1	**24** 0007	0.8
0632	5.0	0630	4.7
TH 1220	0.1	F 1222	0.8
1847	5.3	1844	4.8
10 0046	-0.1	**25** 0036	0.8
0716	5.1	0702	4.7
F 1304	0.0	SA 1249	0.8
1931	5.3	1916	4.7
11 0127	0.0	**26** 0101	0.9
0757	5.1	0734	4.6
SA 1344	0.1	SU 1313	0.9
2012	5.1	1946	4.6
12 0205	0.2	**27** 0125	1.0
0836	4.9	0802	4.6
SU 1421	0.4	M 1336	1.0
2050	4.9	2013	4.5
13 0240	0.6	**28** 0148	1.1
0911	4.7	0828	4.4
M 1457	0.8	TU 1402	1.2
2124	4.5	2042	4.3
14 0315	1.1	**29** 0216	1.3
0942	4.4	0858	4.3
TU 1534	1.3	W 1434	1.4
2155	4.1	2117	4.1
15 0352	1.6	**30** 0251	1.5
1016	4.1	0940	4.1
W 1619	1.8	TH 1516	1.7
◗ 2233	3.7	2206	3.9

OCTOBER

Time	m	Time	m
1 0338	1.9	**16** 0518	2.4
1038	4.0	1208	3.7
F 1621	2.0	SA 1812	2.3
◗ 2314	3.7		
2 0501	2.1	**17** 0118	3.5
1151	3.9	0655	2.4
SA 1812	2.0	SU 1344	3.8
		1955	2.1
3 0040	3.7	**18** 0228	3.7
0657	2.0	0825	2.1
SU 1322	4.0	M 1447	4.0
1946	1.7	2056	1.8
4 0224	3.9	**19** 0321	4.0
0819	1.6	0918	1.7
M 1451	4.3	TU 1537	4.3
2057	1.2	2142	1.4
5 0337	4.3	**20** 0406	4.3
0925	1.1	1001	1.4
TU 1554	4.7	W 1620	4.5
2156	0.8	2221	1.2
6 0431	4.7	**21** 0445	4.5
1020	0.7	1040	1.1
W 1648	5.0	TH 1700	4.6
2248	0.4	2257	1.0
7 0521	4.9	**22** 0523	4.6
1110	0.4	1115	1.0
TH 1737	5.2	F 1740	4.7
● 2335	0.2	2330	0.9
8 0607	5.1	**23** 0600	4.7
1156	0.2	1148	0.9
F 1825	5.2	SA 1818	4.7
		○	
9 0019	0.1	**24** 0002	0.9
0651	5.1	0636	4.8
SA 1240	0.2	SU 1219	0.9
1907	5.2	1853	4.7
10 0101	0.2	**25** 0033	0.9
0731	5.1	0708	4.7
SU 1320	0.3	M 1250	1.0
1948	5.0	1925	4.6
11 0138	0.5	**26** 0103	1.0
0807	4.9	0739	4.7
M 1357	0.6	TU 1320	1.0
2024	4.7	1957	4.5
12 0214	0.8	**27** 0132	1.1
0840	4.7	0810	4.6
TU 1433	1.0	W 1351	1.2
2056	4.4	2030	4.4
13 0248	1.3	**28** 0205	1.3
0910	4.4	0846	4.5
W 1511	1.4	TH 1428	1.4
2127	4.1	2110	4.2
14 0325	1.7	**29** 0244	1.5
0942	4.1	0930	4.3
TH 1554	1.8	F 1515	1.6
◗ 2204	3.7	2201	4.0
15 0412	2.1	**30** 0336	1.8
1029	3.9	1025	4.2
F 1652	2.2	SA 1621	1.8
2311	3.5	◗ 2304	3.9
		31 0453	2.0
		1134	4.1
		SU 1751	1.9

NOVEMBER

Time	m	Time	m
1 0024	3.8	**16** 0120	3.7
0630	2.0	0704	2.2
M 1257	4.1	TU 1344	3.9
1918	1.7	1943	2.0
2 0155	4.0	**17** 0225	3.9
0751	1.7	0814	2.0
TU 1420	4.4	W 1445	4.1
2030	1.3	2042	1.7
3 0307	4.3	**18** 0318	4.1
0858	1.3	0909	1.7
W 1526	4.6	TH 1537	4.3
2130	0.9	2131	1.5
4 0403	4.6	**19** 0406	4.3
0955	0.9	0955	1.5
TH 1623	4.8	F 1624	4.4
2222	0.7	2213	1.3
5 0455	4.9	**20** 0449	4.5
1046	0.6	1038	1.2
F 1714	5.0	SA 1709	4.5
2311	0.5	2254	1.1
6 0543	5.0	**21** 0531	4.7
1133	0.5	1117	1.1
SA 1802	5.0	SU 1752	4.6
● 2355	0.5	○ 2332	1.0
7 0627	5.1	**22** 0612	4.8
1217	0.5	1155	1.0
SU 1847	5.0	M 1832	4.7
8 0038	0.5	**23** 0010	1.0
0706	5.0	0649	4.8
M 1259	0.6	TU 1234	1.0
1927	4.8	1910	4.6
9 0117	0.7	**24** 0049	1.0
0743	4.9	0724	4.8
TU 1337	0.8	W 1312	1.0
2004	4.6	1948	4.6
10 0153	1.0	**25** 0127	1.1
0816	4.7	0801	4.8
W 1415	1.1	TH 1351	1.0
2037	4.4	2027	4.5
11 0228	1.3	**26** 0206	1.2
0848	4.5	0841	4.7
TH 1453	1.4	F 1433	1.2
2109	4.1	2110	4.4
12 0305	1.7	**27** 0249	1.3
0922	4.3	0926	4.6
F 1533	1.7	SA 1521	1.3
2147	3.9	2158	4.2
13 0347	2.0	**28** 0339	1.5
1004	4.1	1017	4.4
SA 1623	2.0	SU 1617	1.5
◗ 2239	3.7	◗ 2254	4.1
14 0440	2.2	**29** 0439	1.7
1103	3.9	1118	4.3
SU 1723	2.2	M 1724	1.6
2356	3.6		
15 0547	2.3	**30** 0001	4.0
1226	3.8	0553	1.8
M 1833	2.1	TU 1228	4.2
		1841	1.6

DECEMBER

Time	m	Time	m
1 0116	4.1	**16** 0103	3.8
0714	1.7	0700	2.2
W 1344	4.3	TH 1332	3.9
1954	1.5	1934	2.0
2 0229	4.2	**17** 0216	3.9
0825	1.5	0807	2.0
TH 1455	4.4	F 1443	4.0
2100	1.3	2036	1.8
3 0333	4.3	**18** 0319	4.1
0929	1.2	0907	1.7
F 1557	4.5	SA 1545	4.2
2158	1.1	2131	1.5
4 0429	4.6	**19** 0414	4.3
1024	1.0	1001	1.5
SA 1653	4.7	SU 1639	4.3
2250	0.9	2221	1.3
5 0520	4.8	**20** 0503	4.6
1114	0.8	1050	1.2
SU 1744	4.7	M 1728	4.5
● 2336	0.8	2309	1.1
6 0606	4.9	**21** 0549	4.7
1200	0.8	1137	1.0
M 1831	4.7	TU 1815	4.6
		○ 2355	1.0
7 0020	0.8	**22** 0633	4.9
0649	4.9	1222	0.8
TU 1245	0.8	W 1859	4.7
1911	4.6		
8 0102	0.9	**23** 0040	0.9
0726	4.9	0714	4.9
W 1325	0.9	TH 1308	0.7
1949	4.5	1941	4.7
9 0138	1.0	**24** 0124	0.8
0801	4.8	0756	5.0
TH 1402	1.0	F 1351	0.7
2022	4.4	2024	4.7
10 0213	1.2	**25** 0206	0.8
0833	4.6	0839	4.9
F 1437	1.2	SA 1434	0.8
2055	4.2	2107	4.6
11 0246	1.5	**26** 0248	0.9
0907	4.5	0923	4.8
SA 1513	1.5	SU 1518	0.9
2130	4.1	2152	4.5
12 0321	1.7	**27** 0331	1.1
0944	4.3	1007	4.7
SU 1549	1.7	M 1603	1.1
2210	3.9	2239	4.3
13 0359	1.9	**28** 0420	1.3
1027	4.1	1058	4.5
M 1632	1.9	TU 1654	1.4
◗ 2258	3.8	◗ 2333	4.2
14 0447	2.1	**29** 0516	1.6
1118	3.9	1157	4.3
TU 1725	2.1	W 1755	1.6
2356	3.7		
15 0549	2.2	**30** 0038	4.0
1219	3.9	0627	1.8
W 1829	2.1	TH 1307	4.1
		1912	1.7
		31 0151	4.0
		0750	1.8
		F 1424	4.1
		2031	1.7

Chart Datum is 2·62 metres below Ordnance Datum (Newlyn). HAT is 5·3 metres above Chart Datum; see 4.5.

DARTMOUTH

MEAN SPRING ⎯⎯⎯⎯
AND NEAP CURVES ⎯ ⎯ ⎯

MEAN RANGES
Springs 4.3m
Neaps 1.8m

Springs occur 2 days
after
New and Full Moon

9.1.20 BRIXHAM

Devon 50°24'·31N 03°30'·85W
❋❋❋❋⚓⚓⚓🏨🏨

CHARTS AC *3315*, 1613, 1634, *5602*, 26; Imray C5, 2400.3; Stan 2, 12, 22

TIDES –0505 Dover; ML 2·9; Duration 0635. Use **TORQUAY** Differences on **PLYMOUTH**.

SHELTER Very good in marina; good at YC pontoon in SW corner of hbr, but outer hbr is dangerous in strong NW'lies. ⚓ NW of fairway or in Fishcombe and Elberry Coves W of the hbr; beware water skiers.

NAVIGATION WPT 50°24'·70N 03° 31'·09W, (3ca off chartlet), 159°/0·4M to hbr ent in W sector of Dir lt. No dangers; easy access H24. Inshore around Torbay controlled areas (May-Sep, mainly for swimmers) are marked by unlit Y SPM buoys; boats may enter with caution, speed limit 5kn.

LIGHTS AND MARKS Berry Hd, a conspic headland and good radar return, is 1·25M ESE of ent. Dir lt at SE end of hbr leads 159° into the fairway, which is marked by two pairs of lateral lt buoys. See chartlet and 9.1.4 for lt details.

R/T Marina Ch 80. YC and Water Taxi: *Shuttle* Ch M. Port HM Ch 14 (May-Sep 0800-1800LT; Oct-Apr 0900-1700, Mon-Fri). Brixham CG: Ch 16, 10, 67, 73.

TELEPHONE (01803) Port HM 853321; Pilot 882214; MRCC 882704; Marinecall 09068 969648; Police 08705 777444; Dr 855897; Ⓗ 882153.

FACILITIES Marina ☎ 882929, 07740 806034, www.brixhammarina.co.uk brixham@mdlmarinas.co.uk 500 inc Ⓥ: £3.20 < 12·5m, £3.90 <18m (electricity included); <4 hrs £7.85. Events pontoon (no AC) £2.20 < 12·5m, £2.55 >12·6m. D (0900-1800, Apr-Oct), ◎, Wi-Fi.
Brixham YC ☎ 853332, Ⓥ pontoon, M, L, Slip, FW, R, Bar. **Hbr Office** Slip, M each side of fairway, L, FW, C (4 ton), D. Town pontoon is exposed in NW'lies. **Town** CH, El, Ⓔ, ACA, ME, P (cans), R, Bar, ◎, ✉, Ⓑ, bus to Paignton ⇌, ✈ (Exeter).

BRIXHAM

MINOR HARBOUR 2·3M NW OF BRIXHAM
PAIGNTON, Devon, **50°25'·96N 03°33'·36W** 500m S of Paignton pier. AC 1613, 26. HW +0035 and –0·6m on Plymouth; Duration 0640; ML 2·9m. Hbr dries 1·3m, only suitable for max LOA 8·2m. A heavy swell enters in E'lies. Drying rks extend 180m ENE from E pier, ∡ QR, to Black Rk, ECM twr ∡ Q (3) 10s 5m 3M. In the appr chan *keep to port*. HM (summer only) ☎ (01803) 557812, VHF Ch 14. **Paignton SC** ☎ 525817. Facilities: M, ME, 🔧, Gas, CH, ACA.

9.1.21 TORQUAY

Devon **50°27'·45N 03°31'·73W** ❄❄❄🔱🔱🔱✿✿

CHARTS AC 3315, 1613, 5602, 26; Imray C5, 2400.1 & .3; Stanfords 2, 12, 22

TIDES –0500 Dover; ML 2·9; Duration 0640

Standard Port PLYMOUTH (←—)

Times				Height (metres)			
High Water		Low Water		MHWS	MHWN	MLWN	MLWS
0100	0600	0100	0600	5·5	4·4	2·2	0·8
1300	1800	1300	1800				
Differences TORQUAY							
+0025	+0045	+0010	0000	–0·6	–0·7	–0·2	–0·1

NOTE: There is often a stand of about 1 hour at HW

SHELTER Good, but some swell in hbr with strong SE'lies. ⚓s NW of Hope's Nose at Hope Cove, Anstey's Cove & Babbacombe Bay are well sheltered in W'lies. No ⚓ in hbr.

NAVIGATION WPT 50°27'·03N 03°31'·57W, 339°/0·40M to round SHM buoy 80m WSW of Haldon pier. Semi-blind ent; keep a good lookout. Access at all tides, but in strong SE winds backwash may make the narrow ent difficult. Hbr speed limit 5 knots.

Controlled areas (mainly for swimmers, May-Sep) close inshore around Torbay are marked by unlit Y SPM buoys; boats may enter with caution, speed limit 5 knots. Watch out for canoeists.

LIGHTS AND MARKS Ore Stone (32m rk) is conspic off Hope's Nose, 2·3M E of hbr ent. Many conspic white bldgs, but none unique. No ldg marks/lts. Lts may be hard to see against town lts.

R/T Marina Ch **80** (H24), M. *Torquay Harbour* Ch **14** 16 (May-Sep 0800-1800LT; Oct-Apr 0900-1700, M-F). *Torquay Fuel* Ch M.

TELEPHONE (Code 01803) MRCC 882704; Police 08705 777444; Marinecall 09068 969648; Dr 212429; Ⓗ 614567.

FACILITIES **Marina** ☎ 200210, 07764 175611. Wi-Fi, 🖥, ♿. www.torquaymarina.co.uk, 440 + 60 Ⓥ, £3.20 < 12·5m, £3.90 <18m, £4.40 <24m ; <4 hrs £7.85.

Town Dock HM 292429. 4 pontoons and a wavebreak replace moorings in SE part of the hbr. Limited Ⓥ berths on the W side of the wavebreak, £1.55/m/night, 4th night free. Call HM Ch 14.

Haldon Pier 96m Ⓥ pontoon in 2m, call HM Ch 14: AB/raft £1.55 (4th night free), AC (long lead), FW. Also used for events.

S Pier S side: D, P & LPG at fuel pontoon, call *Riviera Fuel* VHF Ch M, ☎ 294509, 07786 370324 (Apr-Sept, 0830-1900 Mon-Sat, 1000-1900 Sun); C (6 ton). N side: AB, FW.

Inner Hbr A wall, with sill/flapgate (11·6m wide), retains 1·0m– 2·8m inside. Above it a footbridge with lifting centre section

opens on request Ch 14 when the flapgate is down, approx HW –3½ to +3, 0700-2300 Apr-Sep. IPTS sigs 2 & 4 control ent/exit. Do not pass under the bridge when it is down. AB, FW.

Royal Torbay YC ☎ 292006, R, Bar.

Town ME, Gas, Gaz, 🖥, SM, Ⓔ, El, ✖, CH, ACA, 🛒, Bar, R, @, ✉, Ⓑ, ⇌, ✈ (Exeter or Plymouth).

9.1.22 TEIGNMOUTH

Devon **50°32'·37N 03°30'·00W** (Abeam The Point) ❄❄🔱🔱✿✿

CHARTS AC 3315, 26, 5601.2, 5602; Imray C5, 2400.1 & .3; Stanfords 2, 12, 22

TIDES –0450 Dover; ML 2·7; Duration 0625

Standard Port PLYMOUTH (←—)

Times				Height (metres)			
High Water		Low Water		MHWS	MHWN	MLWN	MLWS
0100	0600	0100	0600	5·5	4·4	2·2	0·8
1300	1800	1300	1800				
Differences TEIGNMOUTH (Approaches)							
+0020	+0050	+0025	0000	–0·9	–0·8	–0·2	–0·1
TEIGNMOUTH (New Quay)							
+0025	+0055	+0040	+0005	–0·8	–0·8	–0·2	+0·1

Tidal streams. At the hbr ent the flood starts HW Plymouth –5½ and the ebb at HWP +¾. Be aware that from about HW –3, as The Salty covers, the flood sets NW across it and a small back eddy flows S past the Ⓥ pontoons. HW slack occurs at approx HWP +½.

SHELTER Complete, but entry difficult or dangerous in strong onshore winds (NE-S) when surf forms on the bar. Access HW±3.

NAVIGATION WPT 50°32'·37N 03°29'·15W, 265°/5ca to trng wall lt (Oc R 6s) ≠ 2 white □s on seawall beyond. The E-W chan is dredged as the Bar, Pole and Spratt Sands shift frequently; AC 26 may not immediately show such shifts. Detailed pilotage and hbr notes are in the excellent website below. Where the channel crosses the bar depths are approx 0 to 0.5m below CD.

Appr chan is not well buoyed, contact HM for latest situation. Small buoys laid by Pilots near the appr chan, should not be relied upon. Beware rks off The Ness; and variable extent of The Salty, a bank of hard gravel/sand. Max speed 6kn over the ground; 5kn inside Y buoys off The Ness & Teignmouth beaches.

Clearance under Shaldon bridge is 2·9m at MHWS and approx 6·7m at MLWS; near its N end there is a 9m wide drawbridge section. Avoid a Historic wreck site (50°32'·95N 03°29'·24W; just off chartlet), close inshore ENE of Ch twr (see 9.0.3h).

LIGHTS AND MARKS The Ness, a 50m high red sandstone headland, and church tower are both conspic from afar. Close NE of the latter, just off N edge of chartlet, Teign Corinthian YC bldg (cream colour) is also conspic. A Y can buoy, Fl Y 5s, at 50°31'·97N 03°27'·78W marks the seaward end of outfall, 103° The Ness 1·3M. Ignore two FR (NNE of The Point); they are not ldg lts. N of The Point, two F Bu lts align 023°, but are not ldg lts.

WGS84 DATUM

SW England

R/T Ch **12** 16 (Mon-Fri 0900-1400)

TELEPHONE (Code 01626) MRCC (01803) 882704; Marinecall 09068 969648; Dr 774355; ⊞ 772161; Police 08705 777444.

FACILITIES HM ☎ 773165 (or 07796 178456 in emergency or out of hours); www.teignmouth-harbour.com; harbourmaster@teignmouth-harbour.com. In suitable weather up to 10 boats can raft on 2 detached 20m Ⓥ pontoons (Jubilee & Trafalgar) at 50°32'·62N 03°29'·96W in 2·5m; £1.10/m. Third pontoon (Newfoundland) is for local boats only. No ⚓ in hbr due to many moorings and strong tidal streams. In fair weather ⚓ approx 1·5ca SE of The Ness or Teignmouth Pier.

E Quay Polly Steps Slip (up to 10m).
Teign Corinthian YC ☎ 772734, ⚓ £8.00, M, Bar.

Services: ME, CH, El, Slip, BY, ✕, C (8 ton), Gas, Gaz, FW, CH, Ⓔ.

Town P & D (cans, 1M), L, FW, 🛒, R, 🖂, Bar, ⊠, Ⓑ, ⇌, ✈ (Exeter).

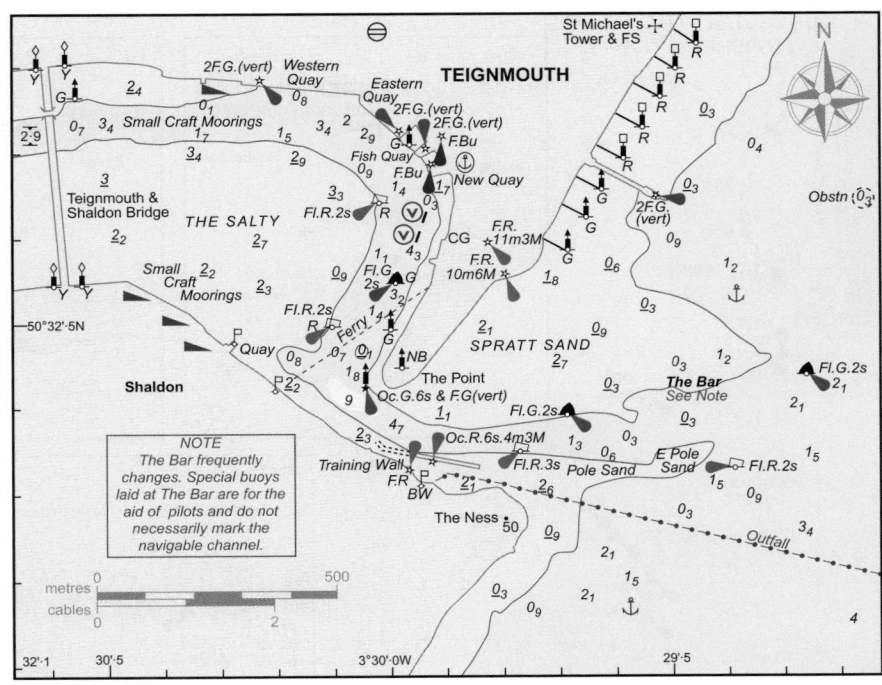

LYME BAY: TEIGNMOUTH TO PORTLAND BILL

From Teignmouth to Dawlish rocks extend 1ca offshore. Beware Dawlish Rock (2·1m) about 5ca off N end of town. Pole Sand (dries up to 3·5m) and Warren Sand on the W side of the **River Exe** estuary are liable to shift. Along the NE side of the channel, from Straight Pt to beyond Orcombe Point, drying rocks and shoals extend up to 2½ca offshore. A firing range at Straight Point has a danger zone extending 1·5M east and marked by 2 DZ lt buoys.

Lyme Bay curves 65M in a great arc N, E and SE from Start Pt to Portland Bill (AC 3315). ▶*Tides are weak, rarely more than 0·75kn. From west to east the tidal curve becomes progressively more distorted, especially on the rising tide. The rise is relatively fast for the 1st hr after LW; then slackens noticeably for the next 1½ hrs, before resuming the rapid rate of rise. There is often a stand at HW, not very noticeable at Start Point but lasting about 1½ hrs at Lyme Regis.*◀

Between Torbay and Portland there is no hbr accessible in strong onshore winds, and yachtsmen must take care not to be caught on a lee shore. There are no dangers offshore. In offshore winds there is a good anchorage NE of Beer Hd, the western-most chalk cliff in England. Golden Cap (186m and conspic) is 3·5M E of **Lyme Regis**. High Ground (3m) and Pollock (4m) are rocky patches 7ca offshore, respectively 1·5M W and 6ca SW of **West Bay** (Bridport).

From 6M SE of Bridport Chesil Beach runs SE for about 9M to the N end of the Isle of Portland. From a distance this peninsula looks like an island, with its distinctive wedge-shaped profile sloping down from 145m at the N to sea level at the Bill. Although mostly steep-to, an 18m high, white obelisk on the tip of the Bill warns of a rocky ledge extending about 50m S of the Bill. If the highest window on the lighthouse is seen above the top of the obelisk, you are clear of the outermost rk, but still very close inshore.

If heading up-Channel from Start Point, Dartmouth or Torbay time your departure to pass Portland Bill with a fair tide at all costs, especially at springs. If late, a temporary anchorage can be found close inshore at Chesil Cove, abeam the highest part of Portland.

9.1.23 RIVER EXE

Devon **50°36'·94N 03°25'·40W** (Abeam Exmouth) 🌐🌐⌂⌂⚘⚘

CHARTS AC 3315, 2290, 5601; Imray C5, 2400.1 &.2; Stanfords 2, 12, 22

TIDES −0445 Dover; ML 2·1; Duration 0625

Standard Port PLYMOUTH (⟵)

Times				Height (metres)			
High Water		Low Water		MHWS	MHWN	MLWN	MLWS
0100	0600	0100	0600	5·5	4·4	2·2	0·8
1300	1800	1300	1800				
Differences EXMOUTH (Approaches)							
+0030	+0050	+0015	+0005	−0·9	−1·0	−0·5	−0·3
EXMOUTH DOCK							
+0035	+0055	+0050	+0020	−1·5	−1·6	−0·9	−0·6
STARCROSS							
+0040	+0100	+0055	+0025	−1·4	−1·5	−0·8	−0·1
TURF LOCK							
+0045	+0100	+0034	no data	−1·6	−1·6	−1·2	−0·4
TOPSHAM							
+0045	+0105	No data		−1·5	−1·6	No data	

NOTE: In the appr chan the sp ebb reaches 3·3kn; with wind against tide a confused, breaking sea quickly builds. Off Warren Pt the flood stream runs at 3-4kn and the ebb can exceed 4½kn when the banks uncover.

SHELTER Good and up-river of Exmouth.

NAVIGATION WPT 50°35'·92N 03°23'·75W, Exe SWM buoy, 335°/6ca to No 7 SHM buoy.

Up to date AC 2290 is essential. Leave WPT at approx LW+2 (or when there is sufficient rise of the tide) when hazards can be seen and some shelter obtained, or at HW−1 or HW−2 to reach Exmouth or Topsham, respectively, at slack water.

The new (2008) approach channel, with a least depth of 0·4m, is well marked with PHM/SHM buoys, some of which are lit. Night entry is not advised. After No 10 PHM buoy do not cut the corner round Warren Point; turn to the SW after passing No 12

PHM buoy. Beware of the flood stream setting towards Exmouth and the moorings.

The estuary bed is sand/mud, free of rocks. Follow the curve of the channel rather than straight lines between the buoys; some bends are marked on the outside only. The estuary is an international conservation area.

LIGHTS AND MARKS See chartlet and 9.1.4. A caravan site is conspic close W of Straight Pt with red cliffs to W and NNE. Exmouth ⊕ tr and FS are conspic. At Exmouth the 305° ldg bcns are hard to see by day.

Caution: Firing range N of Straight Pt has a danger area to ESE, marked by 2 DZ SPM lt buoys (not the sewer outfall SPM buoy, Fl Y 5s, shown on chartlet). R flags are flown when the range is active (likely times 0800-1600, Mon-Fri); call *Straight Pt Range* VHF Ch 08 16. From the E, check also with safety launch.

R/T Exmouth Marina/bridge Ch 14. Water taxi, call *ExePlorer* Ch 37, M1. Port of Exeter Ch 12 16 (Mon-Fri: 0730-1730LT).

TELEPHONE (Code 01395) HM (01392) 274306; MRCC (01803) 882704; Marinecall 09068 969648; Police 08705 777444; Dr 273001; ⊞ 279684.

FACILITIES

EXMOUTH Marina, ☎ 269314. 172 AB + 5 **Ⓥ** in 2m; all LOA £12.00, max 13m; usually full of local boats, detached waiting pontoon 2ca SSW. Pontoon in ent chan is used by ferries/water taxi and for D. Pre-call Ch 14 for berth availability. Strong cross tides at ent. Footbridge lifts on request Ch 14 0800-1700; stays open HN. **Exe SC ☎** 264607, M (check if vacant).

Town P, ✕, CH, El, Ⓔ, ACA, SM, Gas, Gaz, 🖳, ◻, Bar, R, ✉, Ⓑ, ⇌.

🛟s £8.00 lie near No 15 SHM buoy, off Turf Lock and Topsham SC; call water taxi Ch M ☎ 07970 918418 for advice. ⚓ E of Starcross, 1ca SSE of No 19 buoy in 2·1m, ie clear of chan.

STARCROSS (01626) **Village** 🖳, Bar, ✉, Ⓑ, ⇌. **Starcross Garage ☎** 890225, P & D (cans), ME, Gas. **Starcross Fishing & Cruising Club ☎** 891996, call to check if 🛟 is vacant. **Starcross YC ☎** 890470.

TURF LOCK, 50°39'·88N 03°28'·06W, operates daily in working hours by prior arrangement with the lock keeper ☎ 274306.

Exeter Ship Canal (3·0m depth). Contact HM ☎ (below) or Ch 12 for non-tidal pontoon berths for **Ⓥ** in Turf Basin, £10.00 for 2 days (also laying up). 🛟s £8.80.

TOPSHAM (01392) Here the river carries about 0·4m. Best option is AB (pontoon in 1m at LW) at Trouts BY; or ⚓ in appr's, dry out at the Quay or find a mooring.

Town quay Drying AB £6.50 per day.

Topsham SC ☎ 877524, 2 🛟s, Slip, L, FW, Bar.

Trouts BY ☎ 873044. AB, <6m LOA £15; >6m £18 (+ £20 deposit for keys). M, D, Gas, Gaz, C, FW, ✕, CH. www.trouts boatyard.co.uk

Retreat BY ☎ 874720, (access HW±2), AB & M £1.00/m, D, FW, ME, C, CH, ✕. www.retreatboatyard.co.uk

Town P, CH, SM, ACA, R, 🖳, ◻, Bar, ✉, Ⓑ, ⇌.

EXETER See www.exeter.gov.uk river.canal@exeter.gov.uk. River & Canal Office, Haven Rd, Exeter EX2 8DU; hours 0730-1730 M-F, Sat/Sun as required. The HM is responsible for the whole River Exe and Exeter Canal. www.exe-estuary.org makes interesting reading. The City Basin accepts visitors and lay-ups by prior arrangement. **City** all facilities; CH, ME, ACA, @, ⇌, ✈.

TWO MINOR HARBOURS WEST OF LYME REGIS

BEER, Devon, **50°41'·64N 03°05'·22W**. **Beer Roads** is an ⚓age in 2-5m on sand, shingle and gravel sheltered by Beer Head from prevailing W'lies, but open to E-SW winds. Beer Head is 142m high, topped by a caravan site. Its chalk cliffs are white, becoming red sandstone to the E towards Seaton. A conspic radio/tel mast is above the centre of the beach. Church tower is conspic. Do not use the historic approach of the beach light ≠ church tower light. All beach lights are purely for illumination, not for navigation. Land on the open beach, as in centuries past; some traditional local boats are still hauled up the beach on skids.

Beer & Seaton are adjacent towns N and NNE of Beer Head: **Beer** Bar, R, 🖳, ✉, CH. **Seaton** Bar, R, P & D (cans), shops.

2·5M WSW of Beer Head and 8 cables offshore are the remains of the *MSC Napoli* wreck (50°40'·38N 03°09'·58W), marked by E, S and W cardinal buoys and a No Entry zone, radius 3 cables.

AXMOUTH, Devon, **50°42'·13N 03°03'·29W**, 1·85M ENE of Beer Head. AC 3315. HW –0455 on Dover; +0045 and –1·1m on Plymouth; ML 2·3m; Duration 0640. MHWS 4·3m, MHWN 3·2m.

A small drying hbr at the mouth of the R Axe for boats max draft 1·2m, LOA 8·5m (longer by prior arrangement), able to dry out. Appr chan to bar (dries 0·5m) often shifts about a NNE/SSW axis. A dinghy recce (best near LW) to view the access channel and a prior brief by HM/YC are advised. Enter only in settled weather from HW –2½ to +1½ nps; HW –2½ or –½ sp. After 7m wide ent and the pierhead SHM beacon, Fl G 4s 7m 2M, turn 90° to port inside; hug the hbr wall to stbd until into the mooring basin; moor as directed. The low bridge (2m clearance) just N of moorings is the head of navigation.

HM ☎ (01297) 22180/07939 044109. **Axe YC ☎** 20043: Slip, M, pontoon, BH (6 ton), Bar. Facilities: ME, CH, D (cans). Excellent

pilotage notes at www.axeyachtclub.co.uk are essential reading for first time visitors. **Seaton**, as above for victuals etc.

The chartlet is reproduced by kind permission of the Axe Yacht Club whose Commodore and others revised these notes.

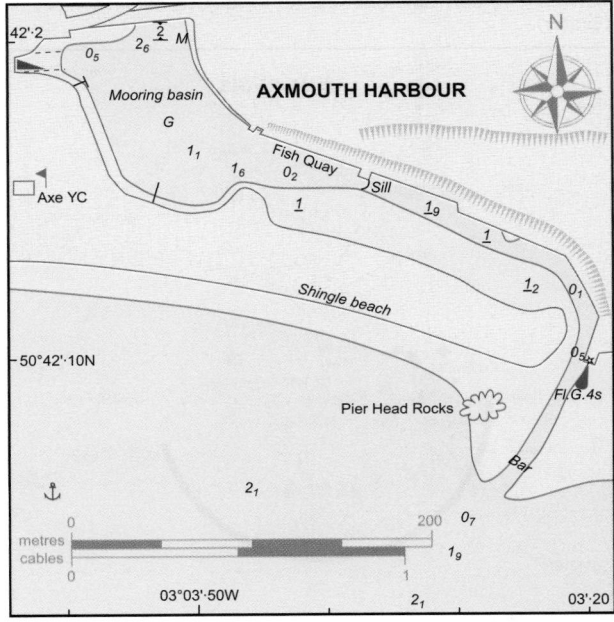

9.1.24 LYME REGIS

Dorset 50°43'·20N 02°56'·19W ✵✵✿✿✿✿✿

CHARTS AC 3315, 5601; Imray C5; Stanfords 2, 12, 22

TIDES −0455 Dover; ML 2·4; Duration 0700

Standard Port PLYMOUTH (←—)

Times				Height (metres)			
High Water		Low Water		MHWS	MHWN	MLWN	MLWS
0100	0600	0100	0600	5·5	4·4	2·2	0·8
1300	1800	1300	1800				
Differences LYME REGIS							
+0040	+0100	+0005	−0005	−1·2	−1·3	−0·5	−0·2

NOTE: Rise is relatively fast for the 1st hour after LW, but slackens for the next 1½ hrs, after which the rapid rate is resumed. There is often a stand of about 1½ hours at HW.

SHELTER Good in the hbr (dries up to 2.1m), but swell enters in strong E/SE winds when it may be best to dry inside the N Wall. The Cobb, a massive stone pier, protects the W and S sides of the hbr. In settled weather ⚓ as on the chartlet, clear of appr and ⚓s.

NAVIGATION WPT 50°43'·10N 02°55'·64W, 284°/0·35M to front ldg lt; best to be just inside W sector until hbr ent opens. Access about HW±2½, but craft drawing >1m may ground LW ±2 on a small sand bar outside the hbr mouth. A 70m rock extension to E end of The Cobb covers at half tide; it is marked by unlit PHM bcn. Beware many fishing floats and moorings.

LIGHTS AND MARKS The 284° ldg line & R/W sectors clear The Cobb extension. (Note: AC 3315 still, May 08, shows the former 296° ldg line.) R flag on Victoria Pier = Gale warning in force.

R/T Call Lyme Regis Hbr Radio Ch 14, 16.

TELEPHONE (Code 01297) MRCC (01305) 760439; Marinecall 09068 969647; Police (01305) 768970; Dr 445777.

FACILITIES HM m.poupard@westdorset-dc.gov.uk ☎/🖷 442137, mob 07870 240645. www.dorsetforyou/lymeregisharbour.com Dry out against Victoria Pier (0.3–1.3m) on clean, hard sand, max LOA 11m. AB 7–11m £14.00, >11m £20.00. A lightweight, 50m long pontoon has been installed against Victoria Pier.

8 R ⚓s lie ENE of hbr ent in 1·5-2m, £7.00. Slip, M, P & D (cans), ⚓ (mobile), ME, ✕, El, Ⓔ, CH, ACA (Axminster, 5M). SC ☎ 442373, FW, ⚒, R, Bar. **Power Boat Club** ☎ 07768 725959, R, Bar.

Town 🛒, R, Bar, Gas, Gaz, ✉, Ⓑ, 🏧, bus to Axminster ⇌, ✈ (Exeter).

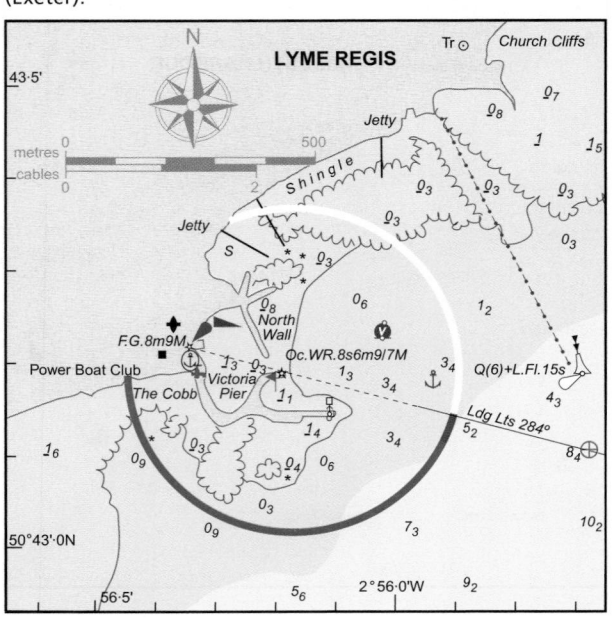

9.1.25 WEST BAY (BRIDPORT)

Dorset 50°42'·51N 02°45'·81W ✵✵✿✿✿✿✿✿

CHARTS AC 3315, 5601; Imray C5; Stanfords 2, 12, 22

TIDES −0500 Dover; ML 2·3; Duration 0650

Standard Port PLYMOUTH (←—)

Times				Height (metres)			
High Water		Low Water		MHWS	MHWN	MLWN	MLWS
0100	0600	0100	0600	5·5	4·4	2·2	0·8
1300	1800	1300	1800				
Differences BRIDPORT (West Bay)							
+0025	+0040	0000	0000	−1·4	−1·4	−0·6	−0·2
CHESIL BEACH							
+0040	+0055	−0005	+0010	−1·6	−1·5	−0·5	0·0
CHESIL COVE							
+0035	+0050	−0010	+0005	−1·5	−1·6	−0·5	−0·2

NOTE: Rise is relatively fast for first hr after LW; it then slackens for the next 1½ hrs, after which the rapid rise is resumed. There is often a stand of about 1½ hrs at HW.

SHELTER Access in W'lies and shelter in the outer hbr are improved by the new W pier, but the ent is exposed to SE'lies and swell/surge may affect the outer hbr in any wind direction.

NAVIGATION WPT 50°42'·05N 02°45'·49W, 336°/0·50M to ent in W sector of Dir lt. High Ground shoal 3m is 1·4M W of the ent. 3·7 and 4·6m shoals are SW & SE of hbr. SPM outfall buoy, Fl Y 5s, is 5ca SSW of ent.

LIGHTS AND MARKS See chartlet and 9.1.4 for lts. High cliffs are conspic close ESE of the hbr.

R/T Bridport Radio Ch 11 16.

TELEPHONE (Code 01308) MRCC (01305) 760439; Marinecall 09068 969647; Police (01305) 768970; Dr 421109.

FACILITIES HM ☎ 423222, mob 07870 240636, www.dorsetforyou/westbayharbour.com. **Outer hbr** is silted up to 0·5m below CD. Ⓥ pontoon is in front of the slipway, close W of ⚡ Fl R 8s. AB £14.50/night. Slip, AC, P & D (cans), ✕, ME.
Inner hbr dries, except for a pool scoured 2·7m by sluice water, and is full of FVs and local boats. The entry sill dries 0.1m.
Bridport (1½M N of the hbr) CH, 🛒, 🏧, R, Bar, ✉, Ⓑ, ⇌ (bus to Axminster), ✈ (Exeter).

PORTLAND RACE

South of the Bill lies Portland Race (AC 2255) in which severe and very dangerous sea states occur. Even in settled weather it should be carefully avoided by small craft, although at neaps it may be barely perceptible.

The Race occurs at the confluence of two strong tidal streams which at springs run S down each side of the Isle of Portland for almost 10 out of 12 hours. These streams meet the main E-W stream of the Channel, producing large eddies on either side of Portland Bill and a highly confused sea state with heavy overfalls in the Race. The irregular contours of the sea-bed, which shoals rapidly from depths of about 100m some 2M south of the Bill to as little as 10m on Portland Ledge 1M further N, greatly contribute to the violence of the Race. Portland Ledge strongly deflects the flow of water upwards, so that on the flood the Race lies SE of the Bill and vice versa on the ebb. Conditions deteriorate with wind-against-tide, especially at springs. In an E'ly gale against the flood stream the Race may spread eastward to The Shambles bank. The Race normally extends about 2M S of the Bill, but further S in bad weather.

The Race can be avoided by passing to seaward of it, ie 3–5M S of the Bill; or by using the inshore passage if conditions suit.

This passage offers relatively smooth water between 1ca and 3ca off the Bill (depending on wind). Do not use it in onshore winds >F4/5, nor at night under power due to pot floats and especially not at springs with wind against tide. From W or E, start close inshore at least 2M N of the Bill to utilise the S-going stream; hug the Bill to avoid being set into the Race.

▶ *The tidal stream chartlets at 9.1.26 which merit careful study show the approx hourly positions of the Race. They are referred to HW Plymouth, to HW Portland for those bound from/to Weymouth, and to HW Dover if passing S of the Race. See also the smaller scale chartlets at 9.1.3 and 9.2.3 and tidal diamonds 'A' on AC 2610 or 'R' on AC 2255.*

Timing is vital to catch 'slackish' water in the inshore passage and to enjoy a fair tide thereafter. The windows are as follows:

Westbound: HW Dover –1 to HW +2; HW Plymouth +5 to HW –5; or HW Portland +4 to HW –6. Timing is easier if starting from Portland Harbour, Weymouth or Lulworth Cove.

Eastbound: HW Dover +5 to HW –4; HW Plymouth –2 to HW +2; or HW Portland –3 to HW +1.◀

PORTLAND BILL TO ANVIL POINT

The buoyed Shambles bank lies 2–5M E of Portland Bill and is always best avoided, as is the gap between it and the Race (AC 2610). In bad weather the sea breaks heavily on it. E of **Weymouth** rocky ledges extend 3ca offshore as far as Lulworth Cove, which provides a reasonable anchorage in fine, settled weather and offshore winds; as do Worbarrow Bay and Chapman's Pool further E.

A firing range extends 5M offshore between Lulworth Cove and St Alban's Head. Yachts should avoid the range when it is active or pass through as quickly as possible. Beware Kimmeridge Ledges which extend over 5ca seaward. Three rarely used yellow naval target buoys (DZ A, B and C) lie on St Alban's Ledge.

St Alban's Head (107m) is bold and steep-to.

HW PLYMOUTH –1

Inshore Passage — St Alban's Head — 02.04

HW PLYMOUTH +0525

Inshore Passage — St Alban's Head — 04.07

A sometimes vicious race forms over **St Alban's Ledge**, a rocky dorsal ridge (least depth 8·5m) which extends 4M SW from St Alban's Hd. ▶*1M S of St Alban's Head the E-going flood starts at HW Plymouth –1, and the W-going ebb at HWP +0525; inshore max sp rates 4¾kn; see also diamond 'U' on AC 2610. Slack water lasts barely 30 mins. The race moves E on the flood and W on the ebb, which is more dangerous since overfalls extend 2½M further SW than on the flood. A back eddy sets almost continuously SSE down the W side of the Head.*◀

In settled weather and at neaps the race may be barely perceptible and can safely be crossed. Otherwise avoid it by passing to seaward via 50°31'·40N 02°07'·80W (thus clearing Lulworth Range); or by using the inshore passage very close inshore below St Alban's Head. This is at most 5ca wide and avoids the worst of the overfalls, but expect your decks to get wet. In onshore gales stay offshore.

The rugged, cliffy coastline between St Alban's Hd and Anvil Point (lt ho) is steep-to quite close inshore. Measured mile beacons stand either side of Anvil Pt lt ho; the track is 083·5°.

CROSSING THE ENGLISH CHANNEL, WESTERN PART

These notes cover cross-Channel passages from harbours between Scilly and Weymouth to French harbours between Ouessant and Île de Bréhat. See AC 2655, 2656; 9.2.5 for the central English Channel; and 9.0.6 for cross-Channel distances. Passage planning and SOLAS V requirements feature in Chapter 3.

The Western Channel differs from the central and eastern parts in that it is wider and its French hbrs are less easy to approach.

Distance is a major ingredient in any passage plan. Shortest is 88M (Salcombe-Bréhat or Trébeurden); longest 108M (Fowey-L'Aberwrac'h). Consider an average of 100M:

Time, therefore, at 5 knots is 20 hrs, or up to 30 hrs if the wind is southerly. Three things flow from that length of time:

- **Crew** strength and experience. A competent husband/wife team with/without kids can cope with 20 hrs, keeping individual watches, but might be rather stretched by 30 hrs to windward.

- **Weather.** A window of at least 24 hrs, preferably 48 hrs, is needed during which the forecast is: max wind F5 (approx, depending on direction); wind not N'ly, ie onshore along the Brittany coast; no fog on that coast nor in mid-Channel (haze Yes, fog No). In other words warm, settled anticyclonic weather with light E'lies. Pour a libation to the weather gods.

- **ETD and ETA.** This is part of the day/night equation. Some crews may prefer little or no night sailing, but that is not feasible in the Western Channel. In Jul/Aug it is darkish by 2230 and light again around 0430BST, so only 6 hrs of darkness intervenes. To avoid departing, arriving or crossing shipping lanes in the dark, leave the UK at 0900, cross the lanes in daylight and arrive at dawn.

Shipping lanes. Whilst not having to cross a TSS, it is as well to pencil in lines linking the lanes of the Casquets and Ushant TSS. From your ETA at the first 'lane' (5M wide), keep an above average lookout for an hour, then a lull between lanes, before a second hour of peak lookout. Give way early, do not expect big ships to give way to a small yacht; they may not even have seen you.

Destinations. North Brittany is not the easiest of coasts thanks to an abundance of offshore rocks which demand precise landfalls and careful pilotage. Fresh onshore winds will make the task difficult, as will fog. These two ingredients in combination may push the task beyond the skills and endurance of all but the more competent, experienced and large crews. Do not go.

Contingencies. There is no all-weather, all-tide, cast-iron port of refuge along the N Brittany coast. Hence the forecast weather window is crucial. If things are not going as planned, do not be too proud to turn back. If crossing near Longitude 3°W the Channel Islands are a possible diversion. Later consider heaving-to for a rest or to await a weather improvement. Bon Voyage!

9.1.26 PORTLAND TIDAL STREAMS

General Area 1: 9.1.3 and 9.2.3

TIME ZONE (UT)
For Summer Time add ONE hour in **non-shaded areas**

PORTLAND   LAT 50°34'N   LONG 2°26'W
TIMES AND HEIGHTS OF HIGH AND LOW WATERS

Dates in red are **SPRINGS**
Dates in blue are NEAPS

YEAR 2010

JANUARY

Time	m		Time	m
1 F 0646	2.2	**16** SA 0002	0.4
1149	0.3	0714	2.0
1921	2.0	1232	0.3
		1939	1.8
2 SA 0010	0.2	**17** SU 0041	0.3
0736	2.3	0748	2.0
1239	0.2	1309	0.3
2010	2.1	2011	1.8
3 SU 0058	0.2	**18** M 0116	0.3
0823	2.3	0820	2.0
1326	0.2	1343	0.2
2056	2.1	2041	1.8
4 M 0144	0.2	**19** TU 0147	0.3
0907	2.3	0850	1.9
1413	0.2	1409	0.3
2139	2.0	2109	1.7
5 TU 0228	0.2	**20** W 0210	0.3
0948	2.2	0918	1.8
1459	0.2	1430	0.3
2219	1.9	2135	1.6
6 W 0312	0.3	**21** TH 0231	0.4
1028	2.2	0943	1.7
1546	0.3	1452	0.3
2259	1.8	2200	1.5
7 TH 0358	0.5	**22** F 0255	0.4
1108	1.8	1007	1.6
1635	0.4	1520	0.4
☽ 2343	1.6	2230	1.5
8 F 0448	0.6	**23** SA 0327	0.5
1151	1.6	1038	1.5
1730	0.6	1600	0.4
		☽ 2312	1.4
9 SA 0035	1.5	**24** SU 0414	0.6
0549	0.7	1124	1.4
1245	1.5	1700	0.5
1832	0.7		
10 SU 0146	1.5	**25** M 0014	1.4
0706	0.8	0528	0.7
1358	1.4	1239	1.3
1943	0.7	1825	0.6
11 M 0307	1.5	**26** TU 0144	1.4
0835	0.8	0712	0.7
1528	1.4	1429	1.4
2054	0.7	2000	0.6
12 TU 0414	1.6	**27** W 0322	1.6
0943	0.7	0848	0.7
1638	1.5	1607	1.5
2151	0.6	2118	0.5
13 W 0508	1.7	**28** TH 0438	1.9
1031	0.6	0958	0.5
1734	1.6	1720	1.7
2238	0.6	2220	0.4
14 TH 0555	1.9	**29** F 0541	2.0
1113	0.5	1054	0.3
1821	1.7	1821	1.9
2321	0.5	2313	0.2
15 F 0636	2.0	**30** SA 0638	2.2
1153	0.4	1143	0.2
● 1903	1.7	1914	2.1
		○	
		31 SU 0002	0.1
		0728	2.3
		1230	0.0
		2000	2.2

FEBRUARY

Time	m		Time	m
1 M 0047	0.0	**16** TU 0056	0.1
0813	2.4	0806	2.0
1315	0.0	1318	0.1
2042	2.2	2025	1.9
2 TU 0130	0.0	**17** W 0126	0.1
0854	2.4	0836	2.0
1357	-0.1	1345	0.1
2121	2.1	2052	1.8
3 W 0211	0.0	**18** TH 0151	0.1
0932	2.3	0903	1.9
1438	0.0	1406	0.1
2156	2.0	2115	1.7
4 TH 0250	0.1	**19** F 0212	0.1
1006	2.0	0926	1.7
1517	0.2	1428	0.2
2229	1.8	2136	1.6
5 F 0328	0.3	**20** SA 0234	0.3
1038	1.8	0948	1.6
1557	0.3	1453	0.3
☽ 2301	1.6	2201	1.5
6 SA 0408	0.5	**21** SU 0301	0.3
1111	1.6	1015	1.5
1639	0.5	1525	0.4
2339	1.5	2236	1.5
7 SU 0459	0.7	**22** M 0340	0.5
1151	1.4	1054	1.4
1734	0.7	1613	0.5
		☽ 2330	1.4
8 M 0033	1.4	**23** TU 0445	0.6
0616	0.8	1205	1.3
1251	1.2	1747	0.7
1854	0.8		
9 TU 0209	1.3	**24** W 0056	1.4
0817	0.8	0651	0.7
1456	1.2	1359	1.3
2028	0.8	1948	0.7
10 W 0349	1.5	**25** TH 0249	1.5
0934	0.7	0845	0.6
1628	1.3	1556	1.4
2133	0.7	2111	0.5
11 TH 0449	1.6	**26** F 0420	1.7
1017	0.6	0952	0.4
1722	1.5	1710	1.7
2219	0.6	2210	0.3
12 F 0536	1.8	**27** SA 0527	2.0
1054	0.4	1043	0.2
1807	1.6	1807	1.9
2301	0.4	2300	0.1
13 SA 0619	1.9	**28** SU 0622	2.2
1132	0.3	1130	0.0
1848	1.8	1857	2.1
2341	0.3	○ 2346	0.0
14 SU 0658	2.0		
1209	0.2		
● 1924	1.8		
15 M 0019	0.2		
0733	2.1		
1246	0.1		
1955	1.9		

MARCH

Time	m		Time	m
1 M 0711	2.4	**16** TU 0708	2.0
1214	-0.1	1215	0.0
1941	2.2	1930	2.0
2 TU 0029	-0.1	**17** W 0027	0.1
0754	2.4	0742	2.1
1256	-0.2	1248	0.0
2020	2.3	2001	2.0
3 W 0110	-0.1	**18** TH 0059	0.1
0833	2.4	0814	2.0
1336	-0.2	1316	0.0
2056	2.2	2029	1.9
4 TH 0148	-0.1	**19** F 0125	0.1
0909	2.2	0843	1.9
1413	0.0	1341	0.1
2129	2.0	2052	1.8
5 F 0225	0.1	**20** SA 0150	0.1
0940	2.0	0907	1.8
1448	0.1	1406	0.2
2158	1.8	2114	1.7
6 SA 0259	0.2	**21** SU 0215	0.2
1008	1.7	0931	1.6
1520	0.3	1432	0.3
2225	1.6	2140	1.6
7 SU 0335	0.4	**22** M 0244	0.3
1036	1.5	1001	1.5
1551	0.5	1504	0.4
☽ 2255	1.5	2215	1.5
8 M 0418	0.6	**23** TU 0325	0.5
1113	1.3	1045	1.4
1629	0.7	1554	0.6
2340	1.3	☽ 2309	1.4
9 TU 0536	0.8	**24** W 0438	0.6
1210	1.2	1159	1.3
1800	0.8	1740	0.7
10 W 0057	1.3	**25** TH 0034	1.4
0756	0.8	0651	0.7
1432	1.1	1356	1.3
1953	0.8	1939	0.7
11 TH 0316	1.4	**26** F 0228	1.5
0914	0.7	0832	0.5
1612	1.3	1542	1.5
2104	0.7	2055	0.5
12 F 0420	1.6	**27** SA 0358	1.7
0951	0.5	0934	0.3
1659	1.5	1649	1.7
2151	0.5	2152	0.3
13 SA 0507	1.7	**28** SU 0503	2.0
1026	0.4	1024	0.1
1741	1.6	1743	1.9
2233	0.4	2240	0.2
14 SU 0550	1.9	**29** M 0558	2.2
1103	0.2	1109	0.0
1820	1.8	1831	2.1
2313	0.2	2325	0.0
15 M 0630	2.0	**30** TU 0646	2.3
1140	0.1	1152	-0.1
1856	1.9	1915	2.2
● 2352	0.1	○	
		31 W 0007	-0.1
		0730	2.3
		1233	-0.1
		1954	2.3

APRIL

Time	m		Time	m
1 TH 0048	-0.1	**16** F 0027	0.1
0809	2.3	0750	2.0
1311	-0.1	1245	0.1
2031	2.2	2004	2.0
2 F 0125	0.0	**17** SA 0059	0.1
0844	2.1	0822	1.9
1347	0.0	1317	0.2
2103	2.0	2032	1.9
3 SA 0201	0.1	**18** SU 0130	0.2
0915	1.9	0852	1.8
1419	0.2	1349	0.2
2130	1.9	2058	1.8
4 SU 0236	0.3	**19** M 0203	0.3
0941	1.7	0922	1.7
1449	0.4	1423	0.4
2153	1.7	2129	1.7
5 M 0311	0.4	**20** TU 0242	0.4
1008	1.4	0959	1.6
1515	0.6	1505	0.5
2220	1.5	2209	1.6
6 TU 0352	0.6	**21** W 0334	0.5
1045	1.3	1050	1.4
1543	0.7	1606	0.6
☽ 2259	1.4	☽ 2305	1.5
7 W 0504	0.7	**22** TH 0453	0.6
1143	1.1	1207	1.4
1657	0.9	1740	0.7
8 TH 0007	1.3	**23** F 0027	1.5
0657	0.8	0636	0.6
1325	1.0	1350	1.4
1905	0.9	1915	0.7
9 F 0155	1.3	**24** SA 0207	1.6
0824	0.7	0803	0.5
1531	1.3	1514	1.6
2022	0.7	2029	0.6
10 SA 0328	1.5	**25** SU 0328	1.7
0910	0.6	0905	0.3
1619	1.4	1618	1.8
2115	0.6	2126	0.4
11 SU 0422	1.6	**26** M 0433	1.9
0949	0.4	0957	0.2
1701	1.6	1713	1.9
2159	0.4	2216	0.3
12 M 0509	1.8	**27** TU 0529	2.0
1027	0.2	1043	0.1
1741	1.8	1802	2.1
2240	0.2	2302	0.2
13 TU 0553	1.9	**28** W 0620	2.1
1104	0.1	1127	0.0
1821	1.9	1848	2.2
2318	0.2	○ 2345	0.1
14 W 0635	2.0	**29** TH 0706	2.2
1140	0.1	1209	0.0
1858	2.0	1929	2.2
● 2354	0.1		
15 TH 0715	2.0	**30** F 0026	0.1
1213	0.1	0746	2.1
1933	2.0	1248	0.1
		2006	2.1

Chart Datum is 2·62 metres below Ordnance Datum (Newlyn). HAT is 2·5 metres above Chart Datum; see 4.5.

>> **FREE** monthly updates from <<
www.reedsalmanac.co.uk

PORTLAND LAT 50°34'N LONG 2°26'W

TIMES AND HEIGHTS OF HIGH AND LOW WATERS

YEAR **2010**

MAY

	Time	m		Time	m
1 SA	0105 0823 1324 2038	0.1 2.0 0.2 2.0	**16** SU	0038 0808 1300 2019	0.2 1.9 0.2 2.0
2 SU	0143 0854 1357 2105	0.2 1.8 0.3 1.9	**17** M	0119 0846 1342 2054	0.2 1.9 0.3 2.0
3 M	0219 0921 1428 2129	0.3 1.6 0.5 1.7	**18** TU	0201 0925 1426 2132	0.3 1.8 0.4 1.9
4 TU	0256 0949 1456 2156	0.5 1.4 0.6 1.6	**19** W	0248 1008 1515 2216	0.3 1.7 0.5 1.8
5 W	0336 1027 1526 2230	0.6 1.3 0.7 1.5	**20** TH	0343 1101 1613 2310	0.4 1.6 0.6 1.7
6 TH	0430 1119 1617 2325	0.7 1.2 0.8 1.4	**21** F	0450 1208 1723	0.5 1.5 0.7
7 F	0554 1234 1805	0.7 1.2 0.9	**22** SA	0019 0606 1324 1840	1.6 0.5 1.5 0.7
8 SA	0046 0716 1406 1930	1.4 0.7 1.3 0.8	**23** SU	0137 0723 1438 1953	1.6 0.5 1.6 0.6
9 SU	0213 0815 1517 2031	1.4 0.6 1.4 0.7	**24** M	0252 0829 1543 2056	1.7 0.4 1.7 0.5
10 M	0324 0902 1610 2119	1.5 0.4 1.6 0.5	**25** TU	0400 0927 1642 2151	1.8 0.4 1.8 0.5
11 TU	0421 0943 1657 2202	1.7 0.3 1.8 0.4	**26** W	0501 1018 1735 2241	1.8 0.3 2.0 0.4
12 W	0513 1023 1742 2242	1.8 0.3 1.9 0.3	**27** TH	0556 1105 1823 2327	1.9 0.3 2.0 0.3
13 TH	0602 1102 1825 2321	1.9 0.2 2.0 0.3	**28** F	0645 1148 1907	1.9 0.3 2.1
14 F	0647 1140 1906 2359	1.9 0.2 2.1 0.2	**29** SA	0010 0728 1229 1946	0.3 1.9 0.3 2.1
15 SA	0729 1220 1944	2.0 0.2 2.1	**30** SU	0051 0807 1308 2020	0.3 1.9 0.3 2.0
			31 M	0130 0840 1344 2048	0.3 1.8 0.4 1.9

JUNE

	Time	m		Time	m
1 TU	0208 0908 1417 2114	0.3 1.7 0.5 1.8	**16** W	0200 0930 1424 2139	0.2 1.9 0.3 2.0
2 W	0244 0937 1447 2142	0.4 1.5 0.6 1.7	**17** TH	0248 1013 1512 2222	0.2 1.8 0.4 1.8
3 TH	0318 1011 1515 2213	0.5 1.4 0.6 1.6	**18** F	0338 1059 1602 2308	0.3 1.8 0.4 1.8
4 F	0352 1053 1549 2252	0.5 1.4 0.7 1.5	**19** SA	0432 1149 1657 2359	0.4 1.7 0.5 1.7
5 SA	0436 1147 1643 2347	0.6 1.3 0.8 1.4	**20** SU	0532 1248 1801	0.4 1.6 0.6
6 SU	0541 1254 1806	0.6 1.3 0.8	**21** M	0059 0639 1356 1911	1.6 0.5 1.6 0.7
7 M	0103 0654 1408 1926	1.4 0.6 1.4 0.7	**22** TU	0211 0750 1508 2025	1.5 0.5 1.6 0.7
8 TU	0223 0757 1516 2027	1.4 0.5 1.5 0.7	**23** W	0327 0859 1614 2132	1.6 0.5 1.7 0.6
9 W	0333 0851 1614 2119	1.5 0.5 1.7 0.6	**24** TH	0437 0958 1712 2227	1.6 0.5 1.8 0.5
10 TH	0435 0941 1707 2207	1.6 0.4 1.8 0.5	**25** F	0538 1048 1804 2315	1.7 0.5 1.9 0.5
11 F	0531 1029 1757 2254	1.8 0.3 2.0 0.4	**26** SA	0631 1133 1850 2358	1.8 0.4 2.0 0.4
12 SA	0624 1117 1845 2341	1.9 0.3 2.1 0.3	**27** SU	0717 1214 1931	1.8 0.4 2.0
13 SU	0714 1205 1931	1.9 0.2 2.1	**28** M	0038 0756 1253 2006	0.3 1.8 0.3 2.0
14 M	0027 0802 1252 2015	0.2 2.0 0.2 2.1	**29** TU	0117 0829 1330 2036	0.3 1.8 0.3 2.0
15 TU	0114 0847 1338 2057	0.2 2.0 0.2 2.1	**30** W	0154 0856 1405 2103	0.3 1.8 0.4 1.9

JULY

	Time	m		Time	m
1 TH	0228 0923 1434 2130	0.3 1.7 0.4 1.8	**16** F	0237 1001 1457 2212	0.1 2.0 0.2 2.1
2 F	0255 0953 1457 2158	0.3 1.6 0.5 1.6	**17** SA	0322 1040 1541 2250	0.2 1.9 0.3 1.9
3 SA	0318 1024 1521 2225	0.4 1.5 0.5 1.5	**18** SU	0408 1120 1628 2331	0.2 1.7 0.5 1.7
4 SU	0345 1100 1554 2257	0.4 1.4 0.6 1.4	**19** M	0458 1208 1723	0.4 1.6 0.6
5 M	0425 1147 1645 2346	0.5 1.4 0.7 1.4	**20** TU	0018 0557 1311 1832	1.6 0.6 1.5 0.7
6 TU	0524 1253 1758	0.6 1.4 0.7	**21** W	0124 0713 1435 2002	1.4 0.7 1.5 0.8
7 W	0102 0638 1415 1922	1.3 0.6 1.4 0.7	**22** TH	0300 0840 1554 2124	1.4 0.7 1.6 0.7
8 TH	0239 0758 1531 2040	1.4 0.6 1.6 0.7	**23** F	0424 0945 1657 2218	1.5 0.6 1.7 0.6
9 F	0401 0909 1636 2144	1.5 0.5 1.7 0.5	**24** SA	0527 1034 1749 2301	1.6 0.6 1.8 0.5
10 SA	0508 1010 1735 2240	1.7 0.4 1.9 0.4	**25** SU	0619 1116 1835 2341	1.7 0.5 1.9 0.4
11 SU	0609 1104 1830 2331	1.8 0.3 2.1 0.3	**26** M	0703 1155 1915	1.8 0.5 2.0
12 M	0704 1155 1922	1.9 0.2 2.2	**27** TU	0019 0739 1234 1949	0.3 1.8 0.3 2.1
13 TU	0019 0754 1243 2009	0.2 2.1 0.1 2.3	**28** W	0057 0811 1311 2019	0.2 1.9 0.2 2.0
14 W	0106 0840 1329 2053	0.1 2.1 0.1 2.3	**29** TH	0133 0837 1345 2046	0.2 1.8 0.2 2.0
15 TH	0152 0922 1413 2133	0.1 2.1 0.1 2.2	**30** F	0204 0903 1413 2113	0.2 1.8 0.3 1.9
			31 SA	0228 0928 1433 2138	0.2 1.7 0.3 1.7

AUGUST

	Time	m		Time	m
1 SU	0246 0953 1452 2200	0.3 1.6 0.4 1.6	**16** M	0338 1048 1557 2300	0.3 1.8 0.4 1.7
2 M	0308 1019 1516 2223	0.4 1.5 0.5 1.5	**17** TU	0422 1128 1648 2340	0.5 1.6 0.6 1.5
3 TU	0339 1054 1554 2258	0.4 1.4 0.6 1.4	**18** W	0516 1224 1801	0.7 1.4 0.8
4 W	0426 1100 1656 2357	0.5 1.4 0.7 1.3	**19** TH	0040 0637 1407 1959	1.3 0.8 1.4 0.8
5 TH	0542 1305 1835	0.6 1.4 0.8	**20** F	0255 0828 1541 2121	1.3 0.8 1.5 0.8
6 F	0139 0725 1449 2020	1.3 0.7 1.5 0.7	**21** SA	0421 0931 1640 2204	1.4 0.7 1.6 0.6
7 SA	0335 0855 1612 2134	1.4 0.6 1.7 0.6	**22** SU	0514 1013 1728 2240	1.5 0.6 1.8 0.5
8 SU	0453 1000 1718 2230	1.6 0.4 1.9 0.4	**23** M	0558 1051 1811 2315	1.7 0.5 1.9 0.4
9 M	0556 1053 1815 2320	1.8 0.3 2.1 0.3	**24** TU	0637 1128 1849 2352	1.8 0.3 2.0 0.2
10 TU	0650 1141 1907	2.0 0.1 2.3	**25** W	0713 1207 1923	1.9 0.2 2.1
11 W	0006 0738 1228 1954	0.1 2.2 0.0 2.4	**26** TH	0029 0743 1244 1954	0.1 1.9 0.2 2.1
12 TH	0052 0822 1312 2036	0.0 2.2 0.0 2.4	**27** F	0104 0810 1318 2023	0.1 1.9 0.2 2.0
13 F	0135 0901 1354 2115	-0.1 2.2 0.0 2.3	**28** SA	0134 0837 1345 2050	0.1 1.9 0.2 1.9
14 SA	0217 0938 1434 2151	0.0 2.1 0.1 2.2	**29** SU	0156 0900 1405 2114	0.2 1.8 0.3 1.8
15 SU	0258 1015 1515 2225	0.1 2.0 0.2 1.9	**30** M	0215 0922 1422 2134	0.3 1.7 0.4 1.6
			31 TU	0235 0945 1444 2157	0.3 1.6 0.4 1.5

Chart Datum is 2·62 metres below Ordnance Datum (Newlyn). HAT is 2·5 metres above Chart Datum; see 4.5.

TIME ZONE (UT)
For Summer Time add ONE hour in **non-shaded areas**

PORTLAND LAT 50°34'N LONG 2°26'W
TIMES AND HEIGHTS OF HIGH AND LOW WATERS

Dates in red are SPRINGS
Dates in blue are NEAPS

YEAR 2010

SEPTEMBER

Day	Time m	Time m	Time m	Time m	Day	Time m	Time m	Time m	Time m
1	0301 0.4	1016 1.5	W 1517 0.5	☽ 2229 1.4	16	0429 0.8	1135 1.4	TH 1736 0.9	
2	0340 0.6	1104 1.4	TH 1613 0.7	2327 1.3	17	0004 1.2	0554 0.9	F 1325 1.4	1956 0.9
3	0458 0.7	1220 1.4	F 1816 0.8		18	0302 1.2	0800 0.9	SA 1518 1.5	2102 0.8
4	0112 1.3	0715 0.8	SA 1414 1.5	2014 0.7	19	0407 1.4	0903 0.8	SU 1612 1.6	2136 0.6
5	0324 1.4	0846 0.6	SU 1551 1.7	2123 0.5	20	0448 1.5	0942 0.7	M 1655 1.8	2207 0.5
6	0439 1.7	0946 0.4	M 1658 1.9	2215 0.3	21	0526 1.7	1019 0.5	TU 1735 1.9	2242 0.3
7	0537 1.9	1036 0.2	TU 1754 2.2	2302 0.1	22	0602 1.8	1057 0.4	W 1813 2.0	2319 0.2
8	0628 2.1	1122 0.1	W 1845 2.4	● 2347 0.0	23	0636 2.0	1135 0.3	TH 1848 2.1	○ 2355 0.2
9	0714 2.3	1206 0.0	TH 1931 2.4		24	0708 2.0	1212 0.2	F 1922 2.1	
10	0030 -0.1	0756 2.3	F 1249 -0.1	2012 2.4	25	0029 0.1	0739 2.0	SA 1245 0.2	1954 2.0
11	0112 -0.1	0835 2.3	SA 1330 0.0	2050 2.3	26	0058 0.2	0807 1.9	SU 1312 0.2	2023 1.9
12	0151 0.0	0910 2.2	SU 1409 0.1	2125 2.1	27	0123 0.2	0832 1.9	M 1335 0.3	2049 1.8
13	0229 0.2	0944 2.0	M 1447 0.3	2157 1.9	28	0145 0.3	0854 1.8	TU 1357 0.4	2111 1.7
14	0305 0.4	1015 1.8	TU 1528 0.5	2228 1.6	29	0207 0.4	0918 1.7	W 1421 0.5	2138 1.5
15	0342 0.6	1048 1.6	W 1618 0.7	☽ 2305 1.4	30	0234 0.5	0950 1.6	TH 1457 0.6	2215 1.4

OCTOBER

Day	Time m	Time m	Time m	Time m	Day	Time m	Time m	Time m	Time m
1	0313 0.7	1038 1.5	F 1601 0.7	☽ 2319 1.3	16	0500 1.0	1155 1.4	SA 1851 0.9	
2	0441 0.8	1155 1.5	SA 1816 0.8		17	0230 1.2	0652 1.0	SU 1420 1.4	2010 0.8
3	0111 1.3	0704 0.8	SU 1349 1.5	1958 0.7	18	0332 1.4	0812 0.9	M 1525 1.6	2051 0.6
4	0311 1.5	0827 0.7	M 1525 1.7	2101 0.5	19	0410 1.5	0901 0.6	TU 1608 1.7	2127 0.5
5	0418 1.7	0925 0.5	TU 1631 2.0	2152 0.3	20	0445 1.7	0943 0.6	W 1649 1.8	2204 0.4
6	0511 2.0	1014 0.3	W 1726 2.2	2238 0.1	21	0520 1.9	1023 0.5	TH 1730 1.9	2241 0.3
7	0600 2.2	1059 0.2	TH 1817 2.3	● 2322 0.0	22	0556 2.0	1101 0.4	F 1810 2.0	2317 0.2
8	0646 2.3	1143 0.1	F 1903 2.4		23	0632 2.1	1137 0.3	SA 1849 2.0	○ 2351 0.2
9	0005 0.0	0728 2.4	SA 1225 0.1	1945 2.3	24	0707 2.1	1210 0.3	SU 1926 2.0	
10	0046 0.0	0807 2.3	SU 1306 0.1	2024 2.2	25	0022 0.2	0739 2.1	M 1241 0.3	1959 1.9
11	0124 0.1	0843 2.2	M 1345 0.2	2059 2.0	26	0053 0.3	0808 2.0	TU 1310 0.4	2029 1.8
12	0159 0.3	0914 2.0	TU 1423 0.4	2130 1.8	27	0123 0.4	0834 2.0	W 1341 0.4	2057 1.7
13	0233 0.5	0942 1.8	W 1504 0.6	2159 1.6	28	0153 0.5	0903 1.9	TH 1415 0.5	2130 1.6
14	0305 0.7	1010 1.6	TH 1553 0.7	☽ 2235 1.4	29	0228 0.6	0939 1.7	F 1502 0.6	2215 1.5
15	0342 0.9	1048 1.5	F 1707 0.9	2331 1.2	30	0317 0.7	1028 1.6	SA 1616 0.7	☽ 2322 1.4
					31	0448 0.8	1141 1.6	SU 1759 0.7	

NOVEMBER

Day	Time m	Time m	Time m	Time m	Day	Time m	Time m	Time m	Time m
1	0105 1.4	0635 0.9	M 1322 1.6	1926 0.6	16	0150 1.3	0709 0.9	TU 1347 1.5	1953 0.7
2	0241 1.6	0756 0.7	TU 1452 1.7	2030 0.5	17	0303 1.5	0814 0.8	W 1501 1.6	2040 0.6
3	0347 1.8	0857 0.6	W 1559 1.9	2123 0.3	18	0351 1.7	0903 0.7	TH 1558 1.7	2121 0.5
4	0442 2.0	0949 0.5	TH 1656 2.1	2211 0.2	19	0435 1.8	0946 0.6	F 1648 1.8	2200 0.4
5	0531 2.1	1036 0.3	F 1749 2.2	2257 0.2	20	0517 2.0	1026 0.5	SA 1735 1.9	2238 0.3
6	0618 2.3	1121 0.3	SA 1838 2.2	● 2340 0.2	21	0559 2.1	1103 0.4	SU 1820 1.9	○ 2316 0.3
7	0702 2.3	1204 0.2	SU 1922 2.2		22	0640 2.1	1140 0.4	M 1903 2.0	2354 0.3
8	0021 0.2	0742 2.3	M 1246 0.3	2003 2.1	23	0718 2.2	1217 0.4	TU 1944 1.9	
9	0100 0.3	0818 2.2	TU 1326 0.3	2038 1.9	24	0033 0.3	0753 2.1	W 1256 0.4	2020 1.9
10	0136 0.4	0850 2.0	W 1406 0.4	2109 1.7	25	0113 0.4	0827 2.1	TH 1336 0.4	2057 1.8
11	0210 0.6	0916 1.9	TH 1446 0.6	2138 1.6	26	0153 0.5	0902 2.0	F 1420 0.5	2135 1.7
12	0242 0.7	0942 1.7	F 1531 0.7	2212 1.4	27	0237 0.6	0942 1.9	SA 1511 0.6	2222 1.6
13	0314 0.9	1015 1.6	SA 1628 0.8	☽ 2259 1.3	28	0329 0.7	1030 1.8	SU 1614 0.6	☽ 2321 1.6
14	0359 0.9	1104 1.5	SU 1743 0.8		29	0436 0.7	1131 1.7	M 1728 0.6	
15	0009 1.3	0539 1.0	M 1219 1.4	1856 0.8	30	0035 1.5	0554 0.8	TU 1248 1.7	1842 0.6

DECEMBER

Day	Time m	Time m	Time m	Time m	Day	Time m	Time m	Time m	Time m
1	0157 1.6	0713 0.8	W 1410 1.7	1951 0.5	16	0134 1.4	0701 0.9	TH 1349 1.4	1937 0.6
2	0309 1.7	0823 0.7	TH 1524 1.8	2051 0.5	17	0248 1.5	0811 0.8	F 1505 1.5	2030 0.6
3	0411 1.9	0923 0.6	F 1628 1.9	2145 0.4	18	0349 1.7	0905 0.7	SA 1610 1.6	2119 0.5
4	0505 2.0	1016 0.5	SA 1726 1.9	2235 0.4	19	0442 1.8	0952 0.6	SU 1706 1.7	2206 0.4
5	0555 2.1	1105 0.4	SU 1818 2.0	● 2321 0.3	20	0532 2.0	1036 0.5	M 1759 1.8	2252 0.4
6	0641 2.2	1150 0.4	M 1906 2.0		21	0619 2.1	1120 0.4	TU 1849 1.9	○ 2338 0.3
7	0004 0.3	0724 2.2	TU 1233 0.4	1948 1.9	22	0705 2.2	1205 0.3	W 1936 2.0	
8	0044 0.4	0801 2.2	W 1314 0.4	2025 1.9	23	0023 0.3	0748 2.2	TH 1249 0.3	2020 2.0
9	0121 0.4	0833 2.1	TH 1353 0.4	2056 1.8	24	0108 0.3	0829 2.2	F 1334 0.3	2101 1.9
10	0157 0.5	0900 1.9	F 1431 0.5	2123 1.6	25	0153 0.3	0909 2.1	SA 1419 0.3	2140 1.9
11	0229 0.6	0927 1.8	SA 1508 0.6	2153 1.5	26	0237 0.4	0948 2.0	SU 1506 0.3	2221 1.8
12	0257 0.7	0956 1.7	SU 1545 0.6	2230 1.4	27	0323 0.4	1030 1.9	M 1557 0.4	2305 1.7
13	0325 0.8	1031 1.6	M 1626 0.7	☽ 2317 1.4	28	0414 0.5	1116 1.8	TU 1654 0.5	2358 1.6
14	0406 0.8	1118 1.5	TU 1724 0.7		29	0514 0.7	1212 1.7	W 1758 0.6	
15	0018 1.3	0521 0.9	W 1228 1.4	1835 0.7	30	0104 1.6	0625 0.7	TH 1321 1.6	1908 0.6
					31	0224 1.6	0746 0.8	F 1446 1.6	2021 0.6

Chart Datum is 2·62 metres below Ordnance Datum (Newlyn). HAT is 2·5 metres above Chart Datum; see 4.5.

9.1.27 PORTLAND HARBOUR

Dorset 50°35'·72N 02°25'·91W (N Ship Chan) ❀❀❀⚓⚓✿

CHARTS AC 2610, 2255, 2268, 5601; Imray C5, C4; Stanfords 2, 12, 15

TIDES −0430 Dover; ML 1·0
Standard Port PORTLAND (→)

Times				Height (metres)			
High Water		Low Water		MHWS	MHWN	MLWN	MLWS
0100	0700	0100	0700	2·1	1·4	0·8	0·1
1300	1900	1300	1900				
LULWORTH COVE and MUPE BAY (Worbarrow Bay)							
+0005	+0015	−0005	0000	+0·1	+0·1	+0·2	+0·1

Double LWs occur between Portland and Lulworth Cove. Predictions are for the 1st LW. The 2nd LW occurs 3–4 hrs later.

SHELTER The large harbour is exposed to winds from the east/ northeast, but in westerlies the moorings and marina on the S side are partly sheltered by Chesil Beach and the Isle of Portland. ⚓ on W side of hbr in about 3m as on chartlet, or further N off Castle Cove SC.

NAVIGATION If approaching from the west inshore of Portland Race, see page 191 for timing details and 9.1.26 for tidal streams. WPT 50°35'·97N 02°25'·24W, 240°/0·5M to North Ship Channel (NSC), to be used by yachts; obey IPTS on 'C' Head. There is no need to call on VHF for clearance to enter if less than 20m LOA. East Ship Chan (ESC) is only for commercial vessels. South Ship Chan is permanently closed and blocked by overhead wires. 7ca SE of it a Noise range, marked by 4 Fl Y buoys, is a No ⚓ area. Beware: high speed ferries from/to Weymouth; rocky reef NE of Castle Cove SC; and shoals E of Small Mouth.

A 6kn harbour speed limit applies in the areas depicted and within 150m of any breakwater or harbour premises. Elsewhere vessels <10m LOA may exceed 12kn.

Approach to Weymouth & Portland National Sailing Academy (WPNSA) and Portland Marina. Craft >20m LOA must obtain permission from Portland Harbour Radio before entering or leaving the harbour. Small craft (<20m LOA) must use the Fairway and must use engines (if fitted) when proceeding to/ from NSC and the marina/WPNSA. From NSC head SW to the

SWM buoy (see chartlet) then S to the marina entrance, leaving the 2 PHM buoys to port. Obey IPTS on marina breakwater:

● (flashing) = Ent closed; await instructions from Marina Control (Ch 80)
● (fixed) = Ent closed; sailing fleet departing
● (fixed) = Ent closed; sailing fleet arriving

LIGHTS AND MARKS 'A' Hd lt ho is a conspic W twr. The white radome (145m) 8ca SE of the marina is a good daymark from afar.

R/T Monitor Ch **74** *Portland Hbr Radio* for commercial traffic. *Portland Marina* Ch 80.

TELEPHONE (Code 01305) MRCC 760439; Marinecall 09068 969647; Police 768970; Dorchester Ⓗ 824055; Ⓗ (A&E) 820341.

FACILITIES Portland Port owns the harbour which is a busy commercial port with an international bunkering station. Port Control ☎ 824044, www.portland-port.co.uk. Port and Harbour Dues (£0.70/m/day) apply to all vessels in Portland Inner Harbour; they are rigorously collected.

Castle Cove SC ☎ 783708, M, L, FW; **Services:** Slip, M, L, FW, ME, ✕, C, CH, El (mobile workshop).

The WPNSA at Osprey Quay will be the centre of the 2012 Sailing Olympics. A new rock breakwater enclosing 3 pontoons for keel boats has been completed, as has extensive land reclamation. ☎ 866000, admin@wpnsa.org.uk www.wpnsa.org.uk Temporary pontoon berths may be available for 1 or 2 nights by prior arrangement. The South West Regional Development Agency ☎ 01202 441920, www.southwestrda.org.uk is a major participant in this project.

Portland Marina The entrance, 50°34'·44N 02°27'·32W, is at the NW end of a 900m long stone breakwater which protects the marina from the N and E. 600 AB + ❶ berths on pontoons R, S & T , £2.75. Wifi, Tel & Sat TV, ▣, Bar, R, Helipad, D (inc bio-diesel) & P, ⚓, BH (50 and 320 ton), CH, ✕, Gaz, Rigger, Diver, Slip, ME, Ⓔ, El. Manager ☎ 08454 30 2012, mob 07977 586128; www.portlandmarina.co.uk; sales@portlandmarina.co.uk

The CG SAR helicopter is based next to the marina.

Castletown is SE of the marina. ✉, Ⓑ, Bar, R, 501 bus to Weymouth mainline ⇌, ✈ (Hurn).

Chartlet overleaf

PORTLAND HARBOUR *continued*

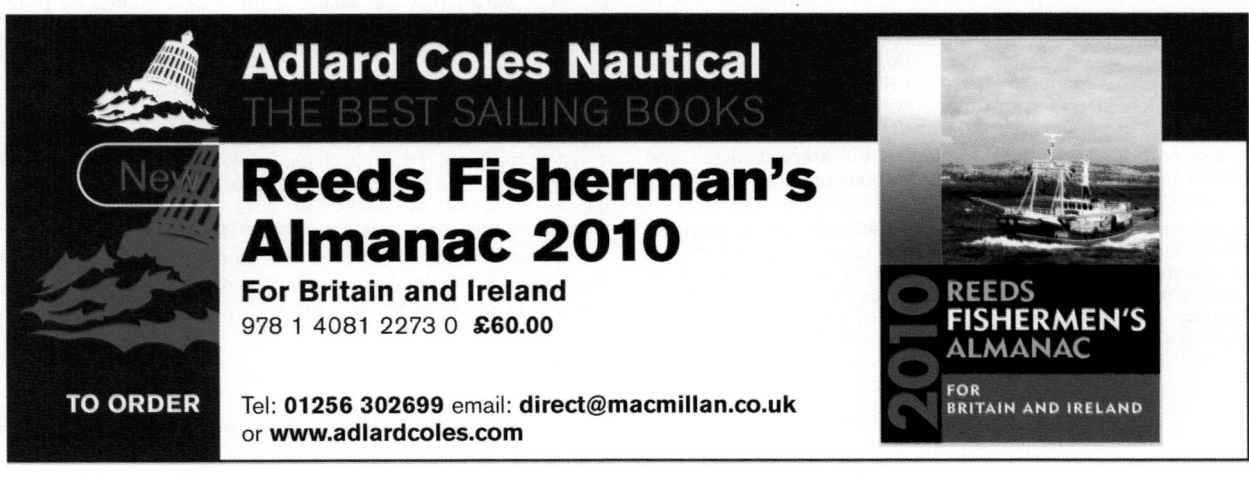

metres 0 1000
cables 0 5

Southlands

Castle Cove Sailing Club

Small Craft Moorings (April-Oct)

Wellworthy

Obstn

Small Mouth

Iso.G. 4s
Q.G

E Fleet

288°

Max 6 Kn

Shingle bank 13m

Chesil Beach

LFl.10s3m5M New Channel

Fl.R.4s

Fl(3)R.10s IPTS

Fl.G.3s

Sailing Academy

Portland Marina

Castletown

ISLE OF PORTLAND

Radome Conspic

Fairway

Iso.10s

Fl.R.3s

Northern Arm

2 F.R (Vert)

Max 6 Kn

'C'Head Oc.G.10s IPTS

'B'Head Oc.R.15s 11m5M

North Ship Channel

North Eastern Breakwater

'A'Head Fl.2·5s22m20M

East Ship Channel

Q.R. IPTS

Bn E

Obscd

210°

Max 6 Kn

Outer Breakwater

No unauthorised navigation

Fl.R.5s
Fl.G.5s
Fl.R.2s
2 F.R (vert)
2 F.R (vert)
VQ(3)5s
Q
F.R
F.R
Wk

'D'Head Oc.R.30s12m5M

South Ship Channel (CLOSED)

36'
50°35'N
34'

28'   27'   2°26'W   25'

9.1.28   WEYMOUTH

Dorset 50°36'·57N 02°26'·58W ✿✿✿✿✿✿✿✿✿

CHARTS AC 2610, 2255, 2268, *2172, 5601.4 & 8*; Imray C5, C4; Stanfords 2, 12, 15

TIDES –0438 Dover; ML 1·1

Standard Port PORTLAND (←)

Use Portland predictions and Note. Mean ranges are small: 0·6m at np and 2·0m at sp. NOTE: A LW stand lasts about 4 hrs at sp and 1 hr at nps. Due to an eddy, the tidal stream in Weymouth Roads is W-going at all times except for 2 hrs, HW –0510 to HW –0310.

SHELTER Good, but swell enters outer hbr and The Cove in strong E winds. It is feasible to ⚓ in Weymouth Bay, NE of hbr ent in about 3·5m, some way offshore due to shallow water and buoyed watersports areas inshore. See 9.1.26 for ⚓ at Portland.

NAVIGATION WPT 50°36'·69N 02°26'·23W, 240°/2ca to abeam S pierhd. The hbr lies deep in the NW corner of Weymouth Bay; do not confuse it with the N ent to Portland Hbr.
Hazards: A DG Range, (no ⚓ing), 500m SE of Weymouth S Pier and marked by 3 SPM buoys (one Fl Y 2s). See also 9.1.27 for a Noise Range close SE of Portland Hbr. If bound to/from the E, check whether Lulworth range is active. Info is available from HM, Portland CG, Range Control (9.1.28), YCs, local newspaper, or in monthly updates posted on www.reedsalmanac.co.uk.
Comply with IPTS. Hbr speed limit is 'Dead Slow'. High speed ferries berth on Commercial Pier. A rowing boat ferry crosses the fairway just E of the LB (see chartlet) and has right of way.

LIGHTS AND MARKS Conspic ✠ spire, 6ca NNW of hbr ent, is a useful daymark for finding the hbr ent.
Lts: see chartlet and 9.1.4. Portland 'A' Head lt ho is a conspic W twr 1·7M SE of hbr ent; it gives the best initial guidance at night.
Pierhead lts may be hard to see against shore lts.
Ldg lts 239·6°, 2 FR (H24), are 500m inside the pierhds; daymarks (same position) are R open ◊s on W poles; they are not visible until the hbr ent is opened.
IPTS sigs 1-3 & 5 are shown from a RW mast near the root of the S pier and must be obeyed. One additional signal, 2 ● over ● = Port closed (weather foul); do not enter the pierheads area. No signals = enter or leave with caution.

A LIFTING BRIDGE allows masted craft access to the marina.

Lifting times (LT): **15 Apr-15 Sep**, 0800, 1000, 1200, 1400, 1600, 1800, 2000; **plus 2100 Jun, Jul, Aug**.
16 Sep-14 Apr: 0800, 1000, 1200, 1400, 1600, 1800.
NOTE: Minimum of 1 hr's notice is required for all lifts 16 Sep-14 Apr: ☎ 838423 (ansafone), 789357 or Ch 12.

5 mins before lift times, craft should be visible to the bridge, and listening Ch 12 for any broadcasts; outbound vessels usually have priority. Waiting pontoons are on the S bank, E and W of the bridge. 3FR or 3FG (vert) on both sides of the bridge are tfc lts, not navigational lts, and must be obeyed at all times even when the bridge is down. Clearances beneath the bridge when down are approx 2·7m MHWS, 3·8m MHWN, 4·6m MLWN, 5·2m MLWS.

R/T *Weymouth Harbour* and *Weymouth Town Bridge* (at opening times): Ch 12 (0800-2000 in summer and when vessel due). *Weymouth Marina* Ch 80. Ch 60 for diesel.

TELEPHONE (Code 01305) MRCC 760439; Dr 774411; H Dorchester 251150; Marinecall 09068 969647; Police 767474.

FACILITIES from seaward:
Outer Harbour ☎ HM 838423; www.weymouth.gov.uk; berthingoffice@weymouth.gov.uk; AB £2.20 inc showers (£7.00 all LOA for <4 hrs), Wi-Fi, 🖴. AB/raft from seaward: If >10m LOA, Custom House Quay (N side, off RDYC). If <10m, in The Cove (S side) on ⓥ pontoons. In season rafting is the rule. **Weymouth SC** ☎ 785481, M, Bar. **Royal Dorset YC** ☎ 786258, M, R, Bar. The quays from The Cove to the bridge are for FVs and tourist boats.

Inner hbr No ⓥ berths at council pontoons close W of the bridge. **Weymouth Marina** Dredged 2·5m, well sheltered; call Ch 80 for a berth. ☎ 767576; www.weymouth-marina.co.uk; 290 inc ⓥ, £2.80 (£2.95 Fri/Sat/Sun & BH) inc showers. Short stay <4 hrs: £8 for <12m, £12 for >12m.

Fuel VHF Ch 60. No P in hbr. D, Mechanical Services (outer hbr jetty or by bowser) ☎ mob 07831 263524. Quayside Fuels (by bowser) ☎ mob 07747 182181 or 07977 337620.

Town P (cans), 🖴, CH, ✕, Gaz, Rigger, Diver, Slip, ME, Ⓔ, El, ⚒, R, Bar, ✉, Ⓑ. ⇌, ✈ (Bournemouth-Hurn). **Ferries** Condor Ferries (www.comdorferries.co.uk). Channel Islands: daily; 2-3½ Hrs; St Malo: 6/week; 8¼ Hrs.

9.1.29 LULWORTH RANGES

LULWORTH FIRING RANGES comprise an inner (D026) and an outer (D026B) sea danger area; the former is more likely to impact on yachts, so to speak. See chartlet above and AC 2610.

The inner area, shaded pink, extends 5·5M offshore. It runs from just E of Lulworth Cove coastwise to Kimmeridge Bay, thence seaward clockwise and back to just E of Lulworth. The Lat/Longs of boundary corners are shown.

The outer area extends 12M offshore and adjoins the seaward boundary of the inner as shown. It is rarely used.

INFORMATION Firing times and recorded range activity are available H24 primarily from Ansafone ☎ (01929) 404819; or secondarily, during office hours from Range Control ☎ (01929) 404712.

Times can also be obtained from Range Control and Range Safety Boats (Ch 08), Portland CG (Ch 16), the St Alban's Head National Coastwatch station ☎ (01929) 439220; and from local HMs, marinas, YCs and newspapers. Annual firing weekends and No Firing periods are given at www.reedsalmanac.co.uk in the Almanac's January Update.

NAVAL FIRING Warships may use the inner and outer areas, firing eastward from Adamant Shoal (50°33'N 02°19'W) at the 3 DZ target buoys (up to 3M SW of St Alban's Head), which should be avoided by at least 1M. Warships fly red flags and other vessels/helicopters may patrol the area.

ARMY FIRING takes place on the inner range most weekdays from 0930-1700 (1230 on Fri), often on Tues and Thurs nights for 3-4 hrs and for up to six weekends per year. There is NO firing in Aug and on Public Holidays. When firing is in progress red flags (at night Iso R 2s) are flown from St Alban's Head and Bindon Hill. However some red flags are flown whether or not firing is taking place; these mark the boundary of the range's land area.

REGULATIONS When the ranges are active the Range Safety boats will intercept yachts in the range and request them (Ch 08) to clear the range as quickly as possible.

However all the land danger area and the inner sea danger area are subject to The Lulworth Ranges Byelaws 1978 operative from 10 Nov 1978 – Statutory Instruments 1978 No 1663. A key passage states: *The Byelaws shall not apply to any vessel in the ordinary course of navigation, not being used for fishing, in the Sea Area and remaining in the Sea Area no longer than is reasonably necessary to pass through the Sea Area.*

Yachts should however make every reasonable effort to keep clear when firing is in progress. If on passage between Weymouth and Anvil Point, a track via 50°30'N 02°10'W just clips the SW corner of the inner range, avoids St Alban's Race and is only 3·3M longer than a direct track. See AC 2610 or *5601.4*.

The Range Safety boats, which are capable of 30kn, are based in Portland Harbour.

ANCHORAGES BETWEEN PORTLAND BILL AND ANVIL PT

Helpful to read *Inshore along the Dorset Coast* (Peter Bruce).

CHURCH OPE COVE, Dorset, **50°32´·26N 02°25´·64W**. AC 2255, 2268, *5601.8*. Tidal data as for Portland. A small cove on the E side of the Isle of Portland, about midway between the Bill and Portland Hbr. It is used by divers & completely open to the E, but could serve as a tempy ⚓ in about 3m off the shingle beach, to await a fair tide around the Bill.

RINGSTEAD BAY, Dorset, **50°37´·83N 02°20´·48W**. AC 2610, 5601. Tides as for Weymouth, 4M to WSW. Tempy ⚓ in 3-5m toward the E end of the bay. Ringstead Ledges, drying, define the W end of the bay. Rks on the E side restrict the effective width to about 3ca; easiest appr is from SE.

DURDLE DOOR, Dorset, **50°37´·27N 02°16´·58W**. AC 2610, 5601. Tides as for Lulworth Cove (see 9.1.26), 1M E. Durdle Door is a conspic rock archway. Close E of it Man o' War Cove offers ⚓ for shoal draft in settled weather. To the W, ⚓ may be found – with considerable caution – inside The Bull, Blind Cow, The Cow and The Calf which form part of a rocky reef.

LULWORTH COVE, Dorset, **50°37´·00N 02°14´·82W**. AC 2172, 5601. HW –0449 on Dover, see 9.1.26. Tides; ML 1·2m. Good shelter in fair weather and offshore winds, but ocasionally a squally katabatic wind may blow down from the surrounding cliffs at night. Heavy swell enters the Cove in S/SW winds; if strong the ⚓ becomes untenable. Enter the Cove slightly E of centre. 8kn speed limit. ⚓ in NE quadrant in 2·5m. Holding is poor. Local moorings, village and slip are on W side. Facilities: FW taps in car park and at slip, ✉, Bar, R, Slip, museum.

WORBARROW BAY, Dorset, **50°37´·03N 02°12´·08W**. AC 2172, 5601. Tides as Lulworth Cove/Mupe Bay, see 9.1.26. Worbarrow is a 1½M wide bay, close E of Lulworth Cove. It is easily identified from seaward by the V-shaped gap in the hills at Arish Mell, centre of bay just E of Bindon Hill. Bindon Hill also has a white chalk scar due to cliff falls. Caution: Mupe Rks at W end and other rks 1ca off NW side. ⚓s in about 3m sheltered from W or E winds at appropriate end. The bay lies within Lulworth Ranges (see overleaf); landing prohib at Arish Mell. No lights/facilities. Tyneham village, deserted since WW2, is close to the E.

CHAPMAN'S POOL, Dorset, **50°35´·53N 02°03´·93W**. AC 2172, 5601. Tidal data: interpolate between Mupe Bay (9.1.26) and Swanage (9.2.6). Chapman's Pool, like Brandy Bay and Kimmeridge Bay, is picturesque and comfortable when the wind is off-shore. ⚓ in depths of about 3m in centre of bay (to avoid tidal swirl). From here to St Alban's Hd the stream sets SSE almost continuously due to a back eddy. No lts. Facilities: village shop and 'Square & Compass' pub, ☎ 01929 439229, are at Worth Matravers (1.5M walk).

Central South England

Anvil Point to Selsey Bill

Central S England

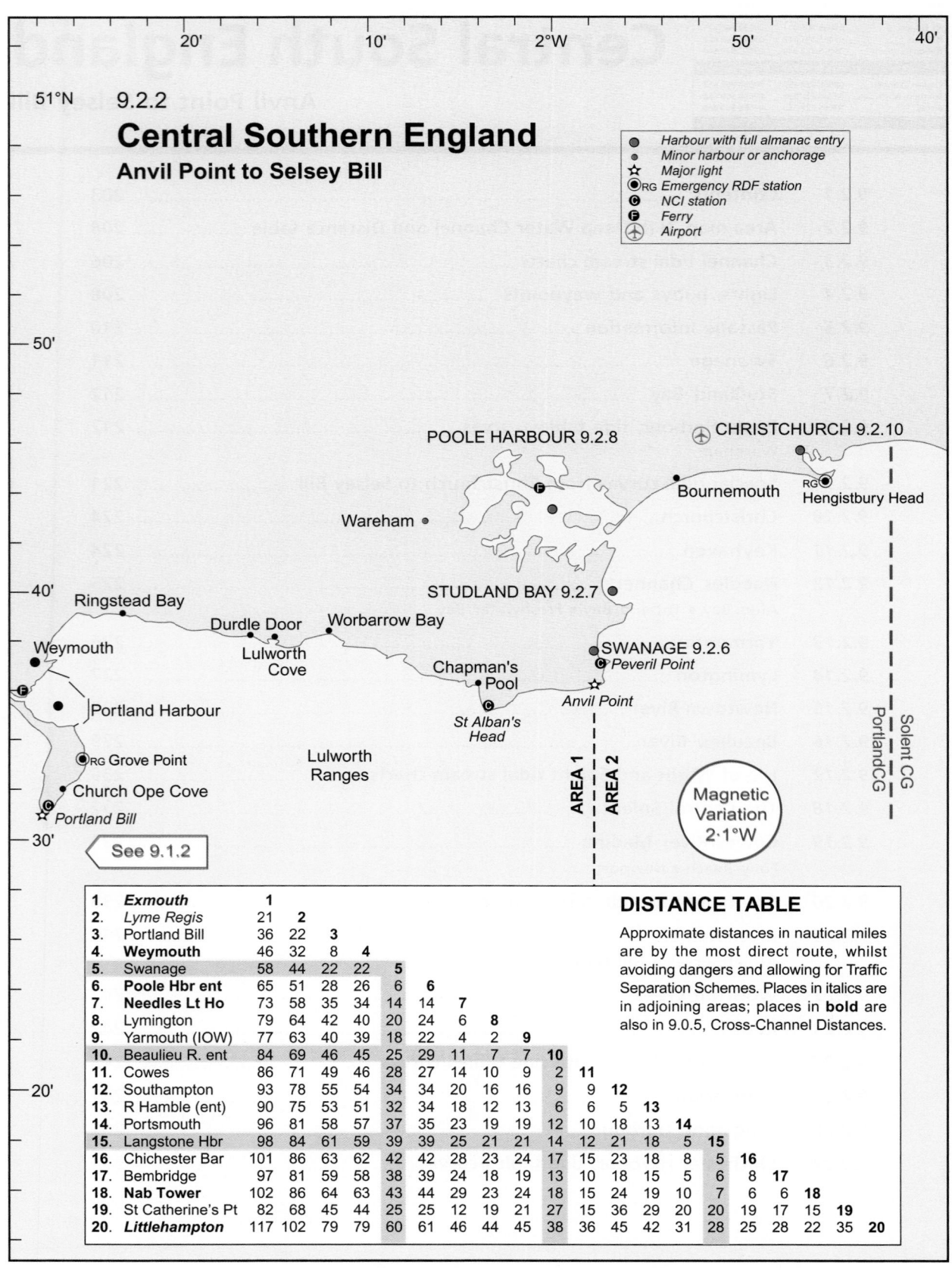

9.2.2

Central Southern England
Anvil Point to Selsey Bill

Symbol	Description
●	Harbour with full almanac entry
•	Minor harbour or anchorage
☆	Major light
●RG	Emergency RDF station
C	NCI station
F	Ferry
✈	Airport

POOLE HARBOUR 9.2.8

✈ CHRISTCHURCH 9.2.10

Bournemouth

RG Hengistbury Head

Wareham

STUDLAND BAY 9.2.7

Ringstead Bay

Durdle Door

Worbarrow Bay

Weymouth

Lulworth Cove

SWANAGE 9.2.6
C Peveril Point

Chapman's Pool

Portland Harbour

St Alban's Head

Anvil Point

RG Grove Point

Lulworth Ranges

Church Ope Cove

☆ Portland Bill

AREA 1 | AREA 2

Magnetic Variation 2·1°W

Solent CG | PortlandCG

See 9.1.2

DISTANCE TABLE

Approximate distances in nautical miles are by the most direct route, whilst avoiding dangers and allowing for Traffic Separation Schemes. Places in italics are in adjoining areas; places in **bold** are also in 9.0.5, Cross-Channel Distances.

		1	2	3	4	5	6	7	8	9	10	11	12	13	14	15	16	17	18	19	20
1.	*Exmouth*	1																			
2.	*Lyme Regis*	21	2																		
3.	Portland Bill	36	22	3																	
4.	**Weymouth**	46	32	8	4																
5.	Swanage	58	44	22	22	5															
6.	**Poole Hbr ent**	65	51	28	26	6	6														
7.	**Needles Lt Ho**	73	58	35	34	14	14	7													
8.	Lymington	79	64	42	40	20	24	6	8												
9.	Yarmouth (IOW)	77	63	40	39	18	22	4	2	9											
10.	Beaulieu R. ent	84	69	46	45	25	29	11	7	7	10										
11.	Cowes	86	71	49	46	28	27	14	10	9	2	11									
12.	Southampton	93	78	55	54	34	34	20	16	16	9	9	12								
13.	R Hamble (ent)	90	75	53	51	32	34	18	12	13	6	6	5	13							
14.	Portsmouth	96	81	58	57	37	35	23	19	19	12	10	18	13	14						
15.	Langstone Hbr	98	84	61	59	39	39	25	21	21	14	12	21	18	5	15					
16.	Chichester Bar	101	86	63	62	42	42	28	23	24	17	15	23	18	8	5	16				
17.	Bembridge	97	81	59	58	38	39	24	18	19	13	10	18	15	5	6	8	17			
18.	**Nab Tower**	102	86	64	63	43	44	29	23	24	18	15	24	19	10	7	6	6	18		
19.	St Catherine's Pt	82	68	45	44	25	25	12	19	21	27	15	36	29	20	20	19	17	15	19	
20.	*Littlehampton*	117	102	79	79	60	61	46	44	45	38	36	45	42	31	28	25	28	22	35	20

Central S England

SOUTHAMPTON 9.2.20

RIVER HAMBLE
9.2.21

PORTSMOUTH
HARBOUR
9.2.25

LANGSTONE
HARBOUR
9.2.26

CHICHESTER
HARBOUR
9.2.27

Ashlett
Creek

Hillhead

Calshot

Solent
MRCC

BEAULIEU RIVER 9.2.16

CENTRAL
SOLENT
9.2.18

LYMINGTON 9.2.14

Stansore Pt

COWES
9.2.19

Folly Reach

RYDE
9.2.23

Forts

KEYHAVEN
9.2.11

Selsey RG

Alum
Bay

Totland
Bay

Needles

Freshwater
Bay

NEEDLES CHAN
9.2.12

YARMOUTH 9.2.13

NEWTOWN RIVER
9.2.15

Newport

WOOTTON
CREEK
9.2.22

BEMBRIDGE
9.2.24

Sandown

Foreland

Nab Tower

See inset below

Magnetic
Variation
2·5°W

Ventnor

RG Boniface

St Catherine's Pt

See 9.3.2

Fl(3)G

Fl(3)R

St Helen's
Pilot boarding
area

Fl(2)G

Q

Q(6)+LFl.10s

BY

YB

Fl.G.5s

VTS SOUTHAMPTON
VHF CH 12

QHM PORTSMOUTH
VHF CH 11

St Helen's
Road

Fl(2)R

Fl.R.5s
Whis

Fl.Y.2·5s
N7

Nab Channel

CAUTION
*Southampton deep
draught vessels pilot
boarding area 4M S of
Nab Tower. Keep clear.*

Fl.Y.5s
N5

Fl.Y.15s
N3

BYB

Fl.Y.7·5s
N4

Nab Shoal

New Grounds

Fl.Y.10s
N1

Fl.Y.2·5s
N2

Q(3)10s
Bembridge
Ledge
BYB

Outer Nab Rk

Nab Tower
Fl.10s27m16M
Horn(2)30s
Racon(T)

Princessa Shoal

*NAB WEST
Southampton pilot
boarding area*

*NAB EAST
Southampton pilot
boarding area*

4

3

2

A N C H O R A G E S

8

7

NAB DEEP WATER CHANNEL
(see 9.2.5)

9.2.3 AREA 2 TIDAL STREAMS

5 Hours before HW Dover (0530 before HW Portsmouth)

4 Hours before HW Dover (0430 before HW Portsmouth)

3 Hours before HW Dover (0330 before HW Portsmouth)

2 Hours before HW Dover (0230 before HW Portsmouth)

1 Hour before HW Dover (0130 before HW Portsmouth)

HW Dover (0030 before HW Portsmouth)

Westward 9.1.3   Portland 9.1.26   Isle of Wight 9.2.17   Eastward 9.3.3   Southward 9.18.3   Channel Is 9.19.3

1 Hour after HW Dover (0030 after HW Portsmouth)

2 Hours after HW Dover (0130 after HW Portsmouth)

3 Hours after HW Dover (0230 after HW Portsmouth)

4 Hours after HW Dover (0330 after HW Portsmouth)

5 Hours after HW Dover (0430 after HW Portsmouth)

6 Hours after HW Dover (0530 after HW Portsmouth)

9.2.4 LIGHTS, BUOYS AND WAYPOINTS

Bold print = light with a nominal range of 15M or more. CAPITALS = place or feature. *CAPITAL ITALICS* = light-vessel, light float or Lanby. *Italics* = Fog signal. ***Bold italics*** = Racon. Abbreviations are in Chapter 1.

SWANAGE TO ISLE OF WIGHT

SWANAGE
Pier Hd ⚡ 2 FR (vert) 6m 3M; 50°36'·56N 01°56'·95W.
Peveril Ledge ⚓ QR; 50°36'·41N 01°56'·10W.

POOLE BAR and SWASH CHANNEL
Poole Bar (No. 1) ▲ QG; *Bell.*; 50°39·29N 01°55'·14W.
(Historic wreck) ⚓ Fl Y 5s; 50°39'·70N 01°54'·86W.
South Hook (No. 11) ⚓ 50°39'·70N 01°55'·20W.
No. 2 ⚓ Fl R 2s; 50°39'·23N 01°55'·24W.
No. 3 ▲ Fl G 3s; 50°39'·76N 01°55'·49W.
No. 4 ⚓ Fl R 2s; 50°39'·72N 01°55'·60W.
Training Bank ⚓ 2 FR (vert); 50°39'·82N 01°55'·86W.
No. 6 ⚓ Fl R 4s; 50°40'·14N 01°55'·91W.
No. 5 ▲ Fl G 5s; 50°40'·19N 01°55'·81W.
Hook Sands (No. 7) ▲ Fl G 3s; 50°40'·50N 01°56'·16W.
Channel (No. 8) ⚓ Fl R 2s; 50°40'·45N 01°56'·27W.
No. 10 ⚓ Fl R 4s; 50°40'·84N 01°56'·86W.
Swash (No. 9) ⚓ Q (9) 15s; 50°40'·88N 01°56'·70W.

EAST LOOE CHANNEL
East Hook ⚓ 50°40'·58W 01°55'·23W.
East Looe 1 ▲ Fl G 5s; 50°41'·09N 01°55'·82W.
East Looe 2 ⚓ Fl R 4s; 50°41'·07N 01°55'·83W.
East Looe 3 (Limit 10 knots) ▲ Fl G 3s; 50°41'·11N 01°56'·16W.
East Looe 4 (Limit 10 knots) ⚓ Fl R 2s; 50°41'·09N 01°56'·17W.
North Hook ⚓ Fl (2) R 5s; 50°41'·01N 01°56'·44W.

BROWNSEA ROADS
No. 12 ⚓ Q R; 50°40'·94N 01°57'·17W.
No.14 ⚓ Fl R 2s; 50°41'·03N 01°57'·32W.
N Haven ⚓ Q (9) 15s 5m; 50°41'·15N 01°57'·17W.
Brownsea ⚓ Q (3) 10s; 50°41'·14N 01°57'·39W.
Brownsea Island Dir lt 299°F WRG & 2FR(vert); 296·5°-G-297·8°-AltWG-298·8°-W-299·2°-AltWR-300·2°-R-301·5°; 50°41'·16N 01°57'·67W (only shown for commercial vessels); 2FR(vert); 301·5°-296·5° (shown H24).

MIDDLE SHIP CHANNEL
Bell (No. 15) ⚓ Q (6) + L Fl 15s; 50°41'·36N 01°57'·12W.
No. 16 ⚓ VQ R; 50°41'·43N 01°57'·25W.
No. 17 ▲ Fl G 3s; 50°41'·68N 01°57'·02W.
Aunt Betty (No. 22) ⚓ Q (3)10s; 50°41'·97N 01°57'·25W.
Diver (No. 25) ⚓ Q (9) 15s; 50°42'·29N 01°58'·32W.

NORTH CHANNEL
Salterns Marina Outer Bkwtr Hd ⚡ 2 FR (vert) 2M; Tfc sigs; 50°42'·23N 01°57'·10W.
Parkstone YC platform ⚡ Q 8m 1M; hut on dolphin; 50°42'·37N 01°58'·08W.
Stakes (No. 29) ⚓ Q (6) + L Fl 15s; 50°42'·43N 01°59'·00W.

POOLE BAY
Bournemouth Rocks ⚓ 50°42'·32N 01°53'·40W.
Lightwave ⚓ 50°41'·50N 01°51'·68W.
Christchurch Ledge ⚓ 50°41'·57N 01°41'·55W (Apr-Oct).
⚓ (x2) Fl (5) Y 20s; 50°37'·98N 01°43'·02W; (265° 2.6M from Needles F'wy)

WESTERN APPROACHES TO THE SOLENT

NEEDLES CHANNEL
Needles Fairway ⚓ L Fl 10s; *Whis*; 50°38'·24N 01°38'·98W.
SW Shingles ⚓ Fl R 2·5s; 50°39'·35N 01°37'·45W.
Bridge ⚓ VQ (9) 10s; ***Racon (T) 10M***; 50°39'·63N 01°36'·88W.

Needles 50°39'·73N 01°35'·50W; Oc (2) WRG 20s 24m **W17M,**

R14M, R13M G14M; ○ Twr, R band and lantern; vis: shore-R-300°-W-083°-R (unintens)-212°-W-217°-G-224° (H24). *Horn (2) 30s.*

Shingles Elbow ⚓ Fl (2) R 5s; 50°40'·37N 01°36'·05W.
Mid Shingles ⚓ Fl (3) R 10s; 50°41'·21N 01°34'·66W.
Warden ▲ Fl G 2·5s; *Bell*; 50°41'·48N 01°33'·55W.
NE Shingles ⚓ Q (3) 10s; 50°41'·96N 01°33'·41W.

Hurst Point ✦ 50°42'·48N 01°33'·03W; FL (4) WR 15s 23m W13M, R11M; W ○ Twr; vis:080°-W(unintens)-104°, 234°-W-244°-R-250°-W-053°. Same structure, Iso WRG 4s 19m **W21M, R18M, G17M**; vis: 038·8°-G-040·8°-W-041·8°-R- 043·8°; By day W7M, R5M, G5M.

NORTH CHANNEL
North Head ▲ Fl (3) G 10s; 50°42'·69N 01°35'·52W.

THE WESTERN SOLENT
Note: Numerous yellow yacht racing buoys are laid throughout the Solent (seasonal, Mar-Dec). Most, but not all, are lit Fl Y 4s.

SOLENT MARKS
Sconce ⚓ Q; *Bell*; 50°42'·53N 01°31'·43W.
Black Rock ▲ Fl G 5s; 50°42'·58N 01°30'·64W.
Lymington Bank ⚓ Fl (2) R 5s; *Bell*; 50°43'·10N 01°30'·85W.
Solent Bank ⚓ Fl (3) R 10s; 50°44'·23N 01°27'·37W.
Hamstead Ledge ▲ Fl (2) G 5s; 50°43'·87N 01°26'18W.
Newtown River ⚓ Fl R 4s; 50°43'·75N 01°24'·91W.
W Lepe ⚓ Fl R 5s; 50°45'·24N 01°24'·09W.
Salt Mead ▲ Fl (3) G 10s; 50°44'·51N 01°23'·04W.
Gurnard Ledge ▲ Fl (4) G 15s; 50°45'·51N 01°20'·59W.
E Lepe ⚓ Fl (2) R 5s; *Bell*; 50°45'·93N 01°21'·07W.
Lepe Spit ⚓ Q (6) + L Fl 15s; 50°46'·78N 01°20'·64W.
Gurnard ⚓ Q; 50°46'·22N 01°18'·84W.

YARMOUTH
East Fairway ⚓ Fl R 2s. 50°42'·64N 01°29'·88W.
Poole Belle ⚓ Fl Y; 50°42'·51N 01°30'·08W.
Pier Head, centre, ⚡ 2 FR (vert) 2M; G col. High intensity FW (occas); 50°42'·51N 01°29'·97W.
Ldg Lts 187·6° Front FG 5m 2M; 50°42'·36N 01°30'·06 W. Rear, 63m from front, FG 9m 2M; both W ◇.

LYMINGTON
Jack in the Basket ⚓ Fl R 2s 9m; 50°44'·27N 01°30'·57W.
Ldg Lts 319·5°. Front, FR 12m 8M; 50°45'·19N 01°31'·65W. vis: 309·5°-329·5°. Rear, 363m from front, FR 17m 8M.
Cross Boom No. 2 ⚓ Fl R 2s 4m 3M; R □ on pile; 50°44'·36N 01°30'·58W.
No. 1 ⚓ Fl G 2s 2m 3M; G △ on pile; 50°44'·41N 01°30'·48W.
Lymington Yacht Haven ldg lts 244°. Front FY 4m; R △; 50°45'·09N 01°31'·53W. Rear, 22m from front, FY 6m; R ▽.

BEAULIEU RIVER
Millennium Dir lt 334°. ⚡ Oc Q WRG 4s 13m W4M, R3M, G3M; vis: 321°-G-331°-W-337°-R-347°; 50°47'·12N 01°21'·90W.
Beaulieu Spit, E end ⚓ Fl R 5s 3M; R dolphin, W band; vis:277°-037°; 50°46'·85N 01°21'·76W.
No. 1 ⚓ 50°46'·91N 01°21'·70W.
No 2 ⚓ 50°46'·92N 01°21'·78W.

COWES
South Bramble ▲ Fl G 2·5s; 50°46'·98N 01°17'·72W.
Prince Consort ⚓ VQ; 50°46'·42N 01°17'·55W.
Prince Consort Shoal ▲ Fl (4) Y 10s; 50°46'·29N 01°17'·71W.
No. 1 ▲ Fl G 3s; 50°46'·07N 01°18'·03W.
No. 2 ⚓ QR; 50°46'·07N 01°17'·87W.
E. Cowes Bkwtr Hd ⚡ Fl R 3s 3M; 50°45'·88N 01°17'·52W.

CENTRAL SOLENT AND SOUTHAMPTON WATER
Note: Numerous yellow yacht racing buoys are laid throughout the Solent (seasonal, Mar-Dec). Most, but not all, are lit Fl Y 4s.

SOLENT MARKS
Lepe Spit ⚓ Q (6) + L Fl 15s; 50°46'·78N 01°20'·64W.

WGS84 DATUM

Plot waypoints on chart before use

NE Gurnard ≈ Fl (3) R 10s; 50°47'·06N 01°19'·42W.
W Bramble ⚓ VQ (9) 10s; *Bell*; **Racon (T) 3M**; 50°47'·20N 01°18'·65W.
Thorn Knoll ▲ Fl G 5s; 50°47'·50N 01°18'·44W.
Bourne Gap ≈ Fl R 3s; 50°47'·83N 01°18'·34W.
West Knoll ≈ Fl Y 2·5s; 50°47'·43N 01°17'·84W.
North Thorn ▲ QG; 50°47'·91N 01°17'·84W.
Stanswood Outfall ⚓ Iso R 10s 6m 5M; 4 FR Lts; 50°48'·26N 01°18'·82W.

CALSHOT REACH

East Knoll ▲ 50°47'·96N 01°16'·83W.
CALSHOT SPIT ⚓ Fl 5s 5m 10M; R hull, Lt Twr amidships; *Horn (2) 60s*; 50°48'·35N 01°17'·64W.
Calshot ⚓ VQ; *Bell* ; 50°48'·44N 01°17'·03W.
Castle Point ≈ IQ R 10s; 50°48'·71N 01°17'·67W.
Reach ▲ Fl (3) G 10s; 50°49'·05N 01°17'·65W .
Black Jack ≈ Fl (2) R 4s; 50°49'·13N 01°18'·09W.
Hook ⚓ QG; *Horn (1) 15s*; 50°49'·52N 01°18'·30W.
Coronation ▲ Fl Y 5s; 50°49'·55N 01°17'·62W.
Bald Head ▲ Fl G 2·5s; 50°49'·80N 01°18'·06W.

RIVER HAMBLE

Hamble Pt ⚓ Q (6) + L Fl 15s; 50°50'·15N 01°18'·66W.
Hamble Common Dir lt 351·7°, Oc (2) WRG 12s 5m W4M; R4M; G4M; vis: 348·7°-G-350·7°-W-352·7°-R-354·7°; 50°51'·00N 01°18'·84W.
Sailing Club Dir lt 028·9° ≼ Iso WRG 6s 5m W4M, R4M, G4M: vis: 025·9°-G-027·9°-W-029·9°-031·9°; 50°51'·10N 01°18'·34W.

SOUTHAMPTON WATER

Fawley Marine Terminal. SE end ≼ 2 FR (vert) 9m 10M; 50°50'·06N 01°19'·42W.
Greenland ▲ IQ G 10s; 50°51'·11N 01°20'·38W.
Cadland ≈ Fl R 3s; 50°51'·02N 01°20'·54W.
Lains Lake ≈ Fl (2) R 4s; 50°51'·59N 01°21'·65W.
Hound ▲ Fl (3) G 10s; 50°51'·68N 01°21'·52W.
Netley ▲ Fl G 3s; 50°52'·03N 01°21'·81W.
Deans Elbow ≈ Oc R 4s; 50°52'·16N 01°22'·76W.
NW Netley ▲ Fl G 7s; 50°52'·31N 01°22'·73W.
Weston Shelf ▲ Fl (3) G 15s; 50°52'·71N 01°23'·26W.

HYTHE

Hythe Pier Hd ≼ 2 FR (vert) 12m 5M; 50°52'·49N 01°23'·61W.
Hythe Marina Ent ⚓ Q (3) 10s; 50°52'·63N 01°23'·88W.
Hythe Knock ≈ Fl R 3s; 50°52'·83N 01°23'·81W.

SOUTHAMPTON and RIVER ITCHEN

Swinging Ground No. 1 ▲ Oc G 4s; 50°53'·00N 01°23'·44W.
E side. No. 1 ⚓ QG; 50°53'·15N 01°23'·40W.
No. 2 ⚓ Fl G 5s 2M; 50°53'·29N 01°23'·38W.
No. 3 ⚓ Fl G 7s; 50°53'·48N 01°23'·28W.
No. 4 ⚓ QG 4m 2M; 50°53'·62N 01°23'·16W.

SOUTHAMPTON and RIVER TEST

Queen Elizabeth II Terminal, S end ≼ 4 FG (vert) 16m 3M; 50°53'·00N 01°23'·71W.
Gymp ≈ QR; 50°53'·17N 01°24'·30W.
Town Quay Ldg Lts 329°, both FY 12/22m 3/2M (occas).
Gymp Elbow ≈ Oc R 4s; 50°53'·50N 01°24'·68W.
Dibden Bay ⚓ Q; 50°53'·70N 01°24'·92W.

THE EASTERN SOLENT

Note: Numerous yellow yacht racing buoys are laid throughout the Solent (seasonal, Mar-Dec). Most, but not all, are lit Fl Y 4s.

SOLENT MARKS

West Ryde Middle ⚓ Q (9) 15s; 50°46'·48N 01°15'·79W.
Norris ≈ Fl (3) R 10s; 50°45'·97N 01°15'·51W.
North Ryde Middle ≈ Fl (4) R 20s; 50°46'·61N 01°14'·31W.
South Ryde Middle ▲ Fl G 5s; 50°46'·13N 01°14'·16W.

Peel Bank ≈ Fl (2) R 5s; 50°45'·49N 01°13'·35W.
SE Ryde Middle ⚓ VQ (6)+L Fl 10s; 50°45'·93N 01°12'·10W.
NE Ryde Middle ≈ Fl (2) R 10s; 50°46'·21N 01°11'·88W.
Mother Bank ≈ Fl R 3s; 50°45'·49N 01°11'·21W.
Browndown ▲ Fl G 15s; 50°46'·57N 01°10'·95W.
Fort Gilkicker ≼ Oc G 10s 7M; 50°46'·43N 01°08'·47W.
N Sturbridge ⚓ VQ; 50°45'·33N 01°08'·23W.
Ryde Sands ⚓ Fl R 10s; 50°44'·54N 01°07'·19W.
Ryde Sands ⚓ L Fl R 12s; 50°44'·16N 01°05'·99W.
No Man's Land Fort; 50°44'·40N 01°05'·70W.
No Man's ≈ Iso R 2s; 50°44'·44N 01°05'·60W.
Horse Sand Fort ≼ Iso G 2s 21m 8M; 50°45'·01N 01°04'·34W.
Saddle ▲ VQ (3) G 10s; 50°45'·20N 01°04'·98W.

NORTH CHANNEL and HILLHEAD

Calshot ⚓ VQ; *Bell (1) 30s*; 50°48'·44N 01°17'·03W.
Hillhead ≈ Fl R 2·5s; 50°48'·07N 01°16'·00W.
E Bramble ⚓ VQ (3) 5s; 50°47'·23N 01°13'·64W.

WOOTTON CREEK

Wootton Beacon ⚓ Q 1M; (NB); 50°44'·53N 01°12'·13W.
Dir lt. Oc WRG 10s vis: 220·8°-G-224·3°-W-225·8°-R-230·8°; 50°44'·03N 01°12'·86W.

RYDE

Ryde Pier ≼, NW corner, N and E corner marked by 2 FR (vert). In fog FY from N corner, vis: 045°-165°, 200°-320°; 50°44'·34N 01°09'·72W.
Leisure Hbr E side ≼ 2 FR (vert) 7m 1M. FY 6m shown when depth of water in Hbr greater than 1m; 2 FY 6m when depth exceeds 1·5m; 50°43'·99N 01°09'·29W.

PORTSMOUTH APPROACHES

Horse Sand ▲ Fl G 2·5s; 50°45'·53N 01°05'·27W.
Outer Spit ⚓ Q (6) + L Fl 15s; 50°45'·58N 01°05'·50W.
Mary Rose ≈ Fl Y 5s; 50°45'·80N 01°06'·20W.
Boyne ▲ Fl G 5s; 50°46'·15N 01°05'·26W.
Spit Refuge ≈ Fl R 5s; 50°46'·15N 01°05'·46W.
Spit Sand Fort ≼ Fl R 5s; 18m 7M. 50°46'·24N 01°05'·94W.
Castle (NB)▲ Fl (2) G 6s; 50°46'·45N 01°05'·38W.
Southsea Castle N corner ≼ Iso 2s 16m 11M, W stone Twr, B band; vis: 337°-071°; 50°46'·69N 01°05'·33W.
Southsea Castle Dir lt 001·5° WRG 11m W13M, R5M, G5M; same structure; vis: 351·5°-FG-357·5°-Al WG (W phase incr with brg), 000°-FW-003°-AlWR(R phase incr with brg), 005·5°-FR-011·5°; 50°46'·69N 01°05'·33W.
Ridge ≈ Fl (2) R 6s; 50°46'·44N 01°05'·65W.
No. 1 Bar (NB) ▲ Fl (3) G 10s; 50°46'·77N 01°05'·81W.
No. 2 ≈ Fl (3) R 10s; 50°46'·69N 01°05'·97W.
No. 3 ▲ QG; 50°47'·08N 01°06'·24W.
No. 4 ≈ QR; 50°47'·01N 01°06'·36W.
BC Outer ⚓ Oc R 15s; 50°47'·32N 01°06'·68W.

PORTSMOUTH HARBOUR

Fort Blockhouse ≼ Dir lt 320°; WRG 6m W13M, R5M, G5M; vis: 310°- Oc G-316°-Al WG(W phase incr with brg), 318·5°-Oc-321·5°- Al WR (R phase incr with brg), 324°-Oc R-330°. 2 FR (vert) 20m E; 50°47'·37N 01°06'·74W.
Ballast ⚓ Fl R 2·5s; 50°47'·62N 01°06'·83W.
Hbr Ent Dir lt (NB) (Fuel Jetty) ≼ WRG 2m 1M; vis: 322·5°-Iso G 2s -330°-Al WG-332·5°-Iso 2s(main chan) -335°-Al WR-337·5°-Iso R 2s-345° (Small Boat Chan) H24; 50°47'·85N01°06'·98W.

EASTERN APPROACHES to THE SOLENT

Outer Nab 1 ⚓ VQ (9) 10s; 50°38'·18N 00°56'·88W.
Outer Nab 2 ⚓ VQ (3) 5s; 50°38'·43N 00°57'·70W.
Nab Tower ☆ 50°40'·08N 00°57'·15W; Fl 10s 27m **16M**, *Horn (2) 30s*; *Racon (T) 10M*.
N 2 ⚓ Fl Y 2·5s. 6M; 50°41'·03N 00°56'·74W.
N 1 ⚓ Fl Y (4)10s; 50°41'·26N 00°56'·52W.

Plot waypoints on chart before use

N 4 ⌀ Fl Y 7·5s; 50°41'·50N 00°57'·02W.
N 3 ⌀ Fl (3) Y 15s; 50°41'·63N 00°56'·74W.
N 5 ⌀ Fl Y 5s; 50°41'·99N 00°56'·97W.
N 7 ⌀ Fl Y 2·5s; 50°42'·35N 00°57'·20W.
New Grounds ⌀ VQ (3) 5s; 50°41'·84N 00°58'·49W.
Nab End ⌀ Fl R 5s; *Whis*; 50°42'·63N 00°59'·49W.
Dean Tail ⬥ Fl G 5s; 50°42'·99N 00°59'·17W.
Dean Tail S ⌀ Q (6) + L Fl 10s; 50°43'·04N 00°59'·57W.
Dean Tail N ⌀ Q; 50°43'·13N 00°59'·57W.
Horse Tail ⬥ Fl (2) G 10s; 50°43'·23N 01°00'·23W.
Nab East ⌀ Fl (2) R 10s; 50°42'·86N 01°00'·80W.
Dean Elbow ⬥ Fl (3) G 15s; 50°43'·69N 01°01'·88W.
St Helens ⌀ Fl (3) R 15s; 50°43'·36N 01°02'·41W.
Horse Elbow ⬥ QG; 50°44'·26N 01°03'·88W.
Cambrian Wreck ⟨ 50°44'·43N 01°03'·43W.
Warner ⌀ QR; *Whis*; 50°43'·87N 01°03'·99W.

BEMBRIDGE
St Helen's Fort ☆ (IOW) Fl (3) 10s 16m 8M; large ○ stone structure; 50°42'·30N 01°05'·05W.
Bembridge Tide Gauge ⌀ Fl Y 2s 1M; 50°42'·46N 01°05'·02W.

SOUTH EAST COAST of the ISLE OF WIGHT
St Catherine's Point ☆ 50°34'·54N 01°17'·87W; Fl 5s 41m **27M**; vis: 257°-117°; FR 35m **17M** (same Twr) vis: 099°-116°.
Ventnor Haven W Bwtr ⌀ 2 FR (vert) 3M; 50°35'·50N 01°12'·30W.
Sandown Pier Hd ⌀ 2 FR (vert) 7m 2M; 50°39'·05N 01°09'·18W.
W Princessa ⌀ Q (9) 15s; 50°40'·16N 01°03'·65W.
Bembridge Ledge ⌀ Q (3) 10s; 50°41'·15N 01°02'·81W

LANGSTONE and APPROACHES
Eastney Pt Fraser Trials Range ⌀ FR, Oc (2) Y 10s, and FY Lts (occas) when firing taking place; 50°47'·19N 01°02'·22W.

Winner ⟨; 50°45'·10N 01°00'·10W.
Roway Wk ⌀ Fl (2) 5s; 50°46'·11N 01°02'·28W.
Langstone Fairway ⌀ L Fl 10s; 50°46'·32N 01°01'·36W.
Eastney Pt Outfall ⌀ QR 2m 2M; 50°47'·23N 01°01'·68W.
East Milton ⌀ Fl (4) R 10s; 50°48'·16N 01°01'·76W.
NW Sinah ⬥ Fl G 5s; 50°48'·14N 01°01'·58W.

CHICHESTER ENTRANCE
West Pole (tripod) ⌀ Fl R 5s 14m 7M; 50°45'·45N 00°56'·59W.
Bar ⌀ Fl(2) R 10s 10m 4M; 50°46'·02N 00°56'·38W.
Eastoke ⌀ QR 2m 3M; 50°46'·66N 00°56'·16W.
West Winner ⌀ QG; Tide gauge. 50°46'·88N 00°55'·98W.

EMSWORTH CHANNEL
Fishery ⌀ Q (6) + L Fl 15s; 50°47'·38N 00°56'·07W.
NW Pilsey ⬥ Fl G 5s; 50°47'·50N 00°56'·20W.
Verner ⌀ Fl R 10s; 50°48'·20N 00°56'·63W.
Marker Pt ⌀ Fl (2) G 10s 8m; 50°48'·91N 00°56'·72W.
Emsworth ⌀ Q (6) + L Fl 15s; tide gauge; 50°49'·66N 00°56'·76W.

THORNEY CHANNEL
Camber ⌀ Q (6) + L Fl 15s; 50°47'·87N 00°54'·06W.
Pilsey ⌀ Fl (2) R 10s ; 50°47'·98N 00°54'·24W.
Thorney ⌀ Fl G 5s; 50°48'·20N 00°54'·28W.

CHICHESTER CHANNEL
NW Winner ⬥ Fl G 10s; 50°47'·19N 00°55'·92W.
N Winner ⬥ Fl (2) G 10s; 50°47'·31N 00°55'·83W.
Mid Winner ⬥ Fl (3) G 10s; 50°47'·38N 00°55'·69W.
Stocker ⌀ Fl (3) R 10s; 50°47'·46N 00°55'·54W.
East Head Spit ⬥ Fl (4) G 10s; 50°47'·41N 00°54'·90W.
Sandhead ⌀ Fl (4) R 10s; 50°47'·49N 00°54'·59W.
NE Sandhead ⌀ Fl R 10s; 50°47'·56N 00°54'·39W.
Chalkdock ⌀ Fl (2) G 10s; 50°48'·49N 00°53'·30W.

9.2.5 PASSAGE INFORMATION

Reference books include: Admiralty *Channel Pilot*; *Channel Cruising Companion* (Nautical Data Ltd/Featherstone & Aslett); *Channel Havens* (ACN/Endean); and *Solent Cruising Companion* (Nautical Data Ltd/Aslett). See 9.0.5 for distances across the Channel, and 9.3.5 and 9.18.5 for notes on cross-Channel passages.   Admiralty Leisure Folio 5601 covers Exmouth to Christchurch, and 5600 covers The Solent & Approaches.

More Passage Information is threaded between the harbours in this Area.

CROSSING THE ENGLISH CHANNEL – CENTRAL PART

(AC 2656) These notes cover the crossing (about 13 hrs) Weymouth/Poole/Solent to Channel Is/Cherbourg/Le Havre and should help in compiling a cross-Channel passage plan. Distances are tabulated in 9.0.5. Thorough planning is a requirement for a safe and efficient crossing. Refer to 3.1, Passage Planning.

• Study the meteorological situation several days before departure so that windows of opportunity may be predicted and bad weather avoided.

• Unless equipped with radar and competent in its use, do not consider the crossing if fog or poor visibility is forecast.

• Consider the forecast wind direction and likely shifts that may improve the probability of obtaining a good slant. Prevailing winds are SW/W, except in the spring when NE/E winds are equally likely. It is very advantageous to get well to windward and up-tide of the destination. For example, from the Needles it may be beneficial initially to proceed W'wards, working the tides to advantage.

• Choose the route, departure points and landfalls so that passage time out of sight of identifiable marks is minimised.

This reduces the risk of navigational errors, anxiety and fatigue. A landfall at night or dawn/dusk is frequently easier due to the additional range provided by lights.

• Consider tidal constraints at the points of departure and destination, and any tidal gates en route such as Hurst Narrows or the French coast between C Barfleur & C de la Hague. ▶ *Calculate the hourly direction/rate of tidal streams expected during the crossing so as to lay off the total drift angle required to make good the desired track. Rarely do 6 hrs of E-going tide cancel out 6 hrs of W-going (or vice versa); streams off the French coast are usually stronger. Note times and areas of races/overfalls and keep well clear.* ◀

• Consider actions to be taken if fog sets in as the risk of collision is much increased. Although one may be navigating electronically, if not equipped with radar it is 'blind navigation'.

• Cross on a heading as near 90° as practicable to the Traffic Routeing between the Casquets TSS and the Greenwich Meridian. Consider motoring to expedite such crossing.

• Keep a very sharp lookout particularly when in the Traffic Routeing area in mid-Channel. Ensure the crew is aware of the directions from which to expect approaching traffic. It is commonsense and good seamanship to alter course early in order to keep well clear of large ships since not all vessels required to give way to a sailing yacht will do so despite Rule 18 (a) (iv).

• Make use of additional navigational information such as soundings, noting when crossing distinctive seabed contours; the rising or dipping ranges of major lights; if equipped with radar, use clearly identifiable targets.

- Plan a harbour of refuge in case of fog, bad weather, accident or gear failure. For example, if unable to make Cherbourg in a strong SSW'ly and E-going tide, consider bearing away for St Vaast in the lee of the peninsula. Alternatively, heave to and stay at sea.

Departure and destination factors to be considered include:

Weymouth: The Shambles Bank and Portland Race both require a wide berth. Check the tidal streams for possible wind-over-tide conditions.

Poole: Leave on the ebb, but at springs with a S/SE wind beware short steep seas in the Swash Channel; off Handfast, Peveril and Anvil Pts overfalls occur with wind against tide.

Solent ports: Decide whether to leave via the Needles or Nab Tower. ▶The former usually requires a fair tide through Hurst Narrows (HW Portsmouth –0100 to +0430) which will dictate your ETD◀ The latter has no tidal gate, but is longer (unless bound to Le Havre and eastwards) and will give a less favourable slant if the wind is in the SW. In W'lies it offers better shelter initially in the lee of the IoW.

Braye (Alderney), whilst accessible at all times, presents a slight risk, especially at springs, of being swept past Alderney on a W-going tide. The yacht may then clew up in Guernsey, having negotiated the Swinge or the Alderney Race. Plan and monitor the track so as to approach from well up-tide. Braye Hbr is unsafe in fresh or strong E/NE'lies. See 9.19.5.

Cherbourg is accessible H24. On closing the coast, especially at springs, aim to be well up-tide and allow for a very large drift angle to maintain track. Harbours on the W side of the Cotentin (**Diélette** to **Granville**) are tidally constrained and exposed to the W but are good options in E'lies.

To the E, **Barfleur** dries; **St Vaast** is a safe anchorage if awaiting entry into the marina. Both are sheltered from the prevailing W'lies. **Le Havre** is a port of refuge although it always requires care due to the density of commercial shipping, shoal waters and strongish tidal streams.

SWANAGE TO CHRISTCHURCH BAY

(AC 2615) There is deep water quite close inshore between St Alban's Hd and Anvil Pt. ▶1M NE of Durlston Hd, Peveril Ledge runs 2½ca seaward, causing a significant race which extends nearly 1M eastwards, particularly on W-going stream against a SW wind. Proceeding towards the excellent shelter of Poole Harbour, overfalls may be met off Ballard Pt and Old Harry on the W-going stream.◀ Studland Bay (AC 2172) is a good anchorage especially in winds from the S and W.

Poole Bay offers good sailing in waters sheltered from the W and N, with no off-lying dangers. ▶ Tidal streams are weak N of a line between Handfast Pt and Hengistbury Hd and within Christchurch Bay. ◀Hengistbury Hd is a dark reddish headland S of Christchurch Hbr with a groyne extending 1ca S and Beerpan Rks a further 100m E of groyne. Beware lobster pots in this area. Christchurch Ledge extends 2·75M SE from Hengistbury Hd. ▶ The tide runs hard over the ledge at springs, and there may be overfalls. ◀

9.2.6   SWANAGE

Dorset 50°36'·70N 01°56'·55W ❀❀❀⚓⚓✿✿

CHARTS AC 5601, 2615, 2172; Imray C4; Stanfords 7, 12, 15.

TIDES HW Sp –0235 & +0125, Np –0515 & +0120 on Dover; ML 1·5
Standard Port POOLE HARBOUR (→)

Times				Height (metres)			
High Water		Low Water		MHWS	MHWN	MLWN	MLWS
—	—	0500	1100	2·2	1·7	1·2	0·6
—	—	1700	2300				
Differences SWANAGE							
—	—	–0045	–0055	–0·2	–0·1	0·0	–0·1

NOTE: From Swanage to Christchurch double HWs occur except at neaps. HW differences refer to the higher HW and are approximate.

SHELTER Good ⚓ in winds from SW to N, but bad in E/SE winds F4 and above due to swell which may persist for 6 hrs after a blow. Poole is nearest port of refuge. AB is feasible on S side of pier (open Apr-Oct) subject to wind and sea state; pleasure 'steamers' use the N side.

NAVIGATION WPT 50°36'·70N 01°56'·55W, 240°/0.3M to Pier Hd. From S beware Peveril Ledge and its Race which can be vicious with a SW wind against the main ebb. It is best to keep 1M seaward of Durlston Hd and Peveril Pt. On W side of Swanage Bay, keep clear of Tanville and Phippards Ledges, approx 300m offshore. To the S of the Pier are the ruins of an old pier.

LIGHTS AND MARKS 2 FR (vert) on the Pier difficult to see due to back scatter of street lights. Peveril Ledge PHM buoy is lit Q.R but may be hard to pick out.

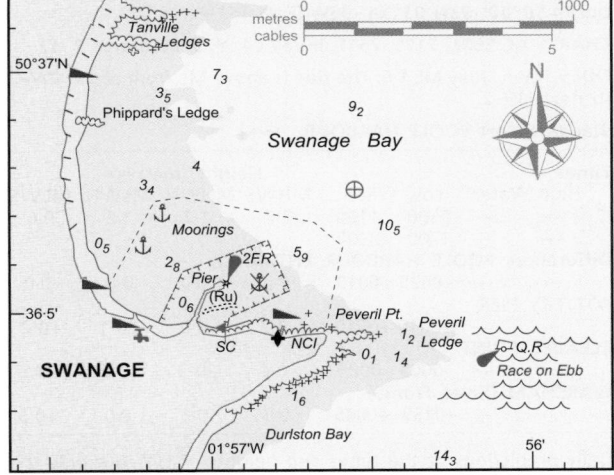

R/T None.

TELEPHONE (Code 01929) Pier 427058, mob 07801 616216; MRCC (01305) 760439; Marinecall 09066 526241; Police (01202) 855544; Dr 422231; Ⓗ 422202.

FACILITIES **Pier**, L, FW, AB £1, £3 for <3hrs; after 2100 gain access to pier from ashore via **Swanage SC** ☎ 422987, Slip, L, Bar, &; **Boat Park** (Peveril Pt), Slip, FW, L; **Services**: Diving. **Town** P & D (cans, 1½M), ⊞, R, Bar, ✉, Ⓑ, ⇌ (bus connection to Wareham), ✈ (Bournemouth International).

9.2.7 STUDLAND BAY

Dorset 50°38'·80N 01°55'·50W ✿✿✿✿☆☆☆

CHARTS AC 5601, 2175, 2172; Imray C4; Stanfords 7, 12, 15.

TIDES Approx as for Swanage (9.2.6).

SHELTER Good in winds from S, W and NW, but exposed to N and E. Best ⚓ in about 3m, 4ca WNW of Handfast Pt, but beware poor holding due to weed. Nearest port of refuge is Poole (9.2.8).

NAVIGATION No dangers except very close inshore; N end of bay is shallow. Beware unmarked Redend Rocks ESE of Redend Point. Sp limit 5kn in buoyed areas off beach. Beware of swimmers. PWCs not permitted to land on nor launch from beach.

LIGHTS AND MARKS See chartlet. Handfast Point and Old Harry Rock are conspicuous on approach to the bay.

R/T, TELEPHONE None

FACILITIES Village: FW at tap, 🛒, R, Bar, ✉, hotel, P&D (cans). No marine facilities.

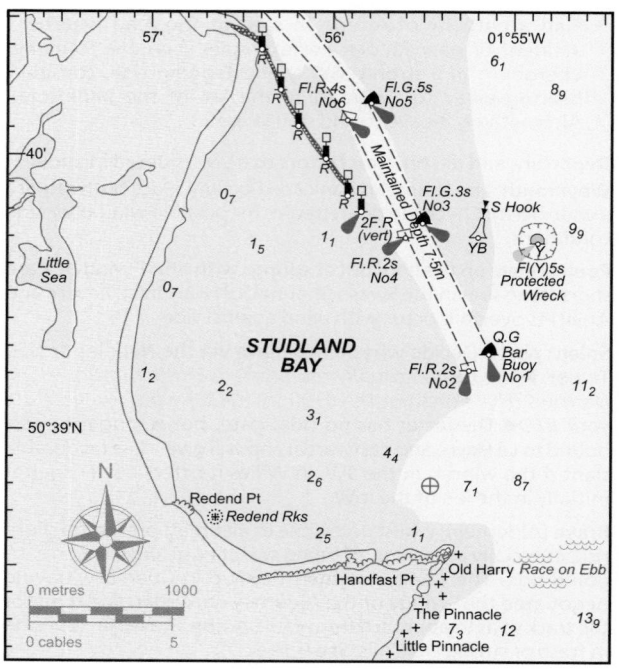

9.2.8 POOLE HARBOUR

Dorset 50°40'·93N 01°56'·96W (Ent) ✿✿✿✿⚓⚓⚓☆☆☆

CHARTS AC 5601, 2175, 2611; Imray C4, Y23; Stanfords 7, 12.

TIDES Town Quay ML 1·6. The tide is above ML from about LW+2 to next LW−2.

Standard Port POOLE HARBOUR (→)

Times				Height (metres)			
High Water		Low Water		MHWS	MHWN	MLWN	MLWS
—	—	0500	1100	2·2	1·7	1·2	0·6
—	—	1700	2300				
Differences POOLE HARBOUR ENTRANCE							
—	—	−0025	−0010	0·0	0·0	0·0	0·0
POTTERY PIER							
—	—	+0010	+0010	−0·2	0·0	+0·1	+0·2
CLEAVEL POINT							
—	—	−0005	−0005	−0·1	−0·2	0·0	−0·1
WAREHAM (River Frome)							
—	—	+0130	+0045	0·0	0·0	0·0	+0·3

Daily predictions of the times and heights of LW (but only the heights of HW) are for the Standard Port of **POOLE HARBOUR** (near the Ro-Ro terminal). Spring and neap curves are above. Intermediate predictions are simplified by use of the tidal curves on the next page. Double HWs occur except at neaps. The height of the 2nd HW is always about 1·8m; only the height of the 1st HW varies from springs to neaps.

Strong and continuous winds from E to SW may raise sea levels by as much as 0·2m; W to NE winds may lower levels by 0·1m. Barometric pressure can affect the tide by as much as 0·3m, see Chapter 4.

At Wareham the height of LW does not usually fall below 0·7m.

SHELTER An excellent harbour with a narrow entrance. Access in all conditions, but in E/SE gales the entrance can become very rough especially on the ebb. Yachts can berth alongside Poole Quay Boat Haven or on Poole Town Quay. The latter is very exposed in strong E/SE winds, and at busy periods yachts may be rafted up to 7 deep. Berths may be available, on request, in the marinas listed under Facilities. Good anchorages may be found wherever sheltered from the wind and clear of channels, moorings and shellfish beds, especially in South Deep, off Pottery Pier (W end of Brownsea Island) and off Shipstal Point, about 1·3M west of Pottery Pier. All are within a Quiet Area (see chartlet and speed limits). Craft must anchor clear of the buoyed fairway in South Deep and by Pottery Pier.

NAVIGATION WPT Poole Bar (No 1 SHM) Buoy, QG, 50°39'·29N 01°55'·14W, 328°/1·95M to Haven Hotel. In very strong SE-S winds the Bar is dangerous, especially on the ebb. Beware cross-Channel high speed ferries which operate through the area. In Studland Bay and close to training bank beware lobster pots. From Poole Bar to Shell Bay a **Boat Channel**, suitable for craft <3m draught, parallels the W side of the Swash Channel, close E of the Training Bank, and should be used whenever possible.

East Looe Approach Channel The well lit and buoyed channel, least depth 1·3m, is the recommended approach from the E when height of tide allows. It is liable to shift and the buoys moved accordingly. Check LNTMs from www.phc.co.uk; there may be less water than charted. The groynes to the N are marked by SHM beacons, the two most W'ly are lit, 2 FG (vert).

Within the harbour the two principal channels (Middle Ship and North) lead up to Poole Town Quay. Outside of these there are extensive shoal or drying areas.

Middle Ship Chan is dredged to 7·5m depth and 105m width for ferries and commercial shipping to/from the Continental Freight and Ferry Terminal. Small craft with a draught up to about 2m should use the **Boat Channel** which runs parallel to the main channel between the PHM buoys and the unlit beacons further S which mark the edge of the bank. Depth is 2·0m in this channel, but 1·5m closer to the stakes. Caution: When large ferries pass, a temporary but significant reduction in depth may be experienced; it is then prudent to keep close to the PHM buoys.

North Channel is no longer routinely dredged (least depth 2·8m in 2007) but remains usable for yachts and leisure craft; the best water is on the outside of channel bends.

Lulworth gunnery range (see 9.1.29). Prior to proceeding W all craft should check for activity, as shown in the HM's office and in the Updates to this Almanac.

LIGHTS AND MARKS See chartlet and 9.2.4 for main buoys, beacons and lights.

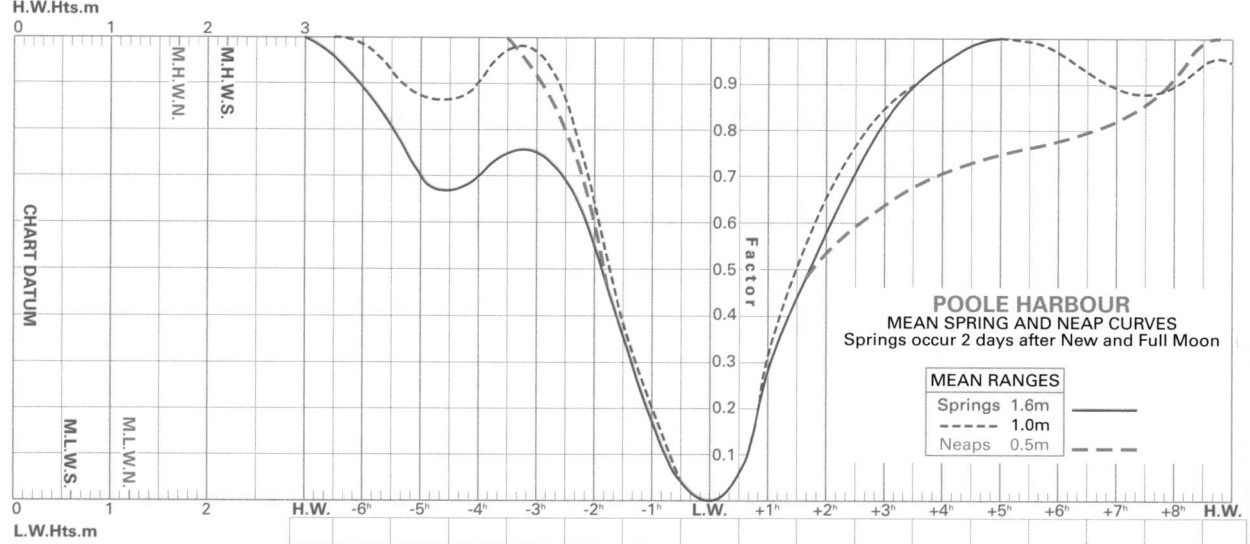

POOLE HARBOUR
MEAN SPRING AND NEAP CURVES
Springs occur 2 days after New and Full Moon

MEAN RANGES	
Springs	1.6m
-----	1.0m
Neaps	0.5m

Poole Bridge traffic lights, shown from bridge tower:
- ● = Do not approach bridge;
- ● (flashing) = Bridge lifting, proceed with caution;
- ● = Proceed.

Poole Bridge opens daily, only if vessels are waiting, at:

0530, 0630, 0730, 0930, 1030, 1230, 1430, 1630, 1730 (Sat, Sun and Bank Holidays only),1830, 1930, 2130, 2345.

Pleasure craft may pass when bridge is opened for commercial traffic. The bridge will not normally open weekday road traffic rush hours, 0730-0930 and 1630-1830.

Monitor Ch 14 for further information.

R/T *Poole Hbr Control* VHF Ch **14** 16 (H24). Poole Quay Boat Haven Ch 80; Salterns Marina Ch M 80; Parkstone Haven Ch M; Poole YC Haven (call *Pike*) Ch M; Dorset Yacht Co Ch M; Poole Bridge (call *PB*) Ch 14. Cobbs Quay (call *CQ Base*) Ch 80.

TELEPHONE (Code 01202) HM 440233, Harbour Control 440230; Poole Quay Boathaven 649488; Bridge 674115; MRCC (01305) 760439; Met (02392) 228844; Marinecall 09068 969647; Police 552099; Ⓗ 665511.

FACILITIES The following are some of the many facilities to be found in Poole Harbour. **Marinas** from seaward:

Salterns Marina ☎ 709971. 300, few Ⓥ, £3·70, max draft 2·5m. P & D (H24), C (5 ton), BH (45 T), ME, El, Ⓔ, ✕, CH, Gas, Gaz, 🛒, ✉, Bar, R, 🗑. Appr from North Channel near NC 7 SHM buoy, Fl G 3s.

Parkstone YC Haven ☎ 743610 (Parkstone YC). some Ⓥ berths, £2·75; dredged 2m. Access from North Channel near NC 11 SHM buoy, Fl G 3s. Approach chan, dredged 2·5m, is marked by PHM and SHM unlit buoys. Ldg daymarks 006°, both Y ◊s.

Poole Quay Boat Haven pooleboathaven@phc.co.uk ☎ 649488. 100 Ⓥ, max draft 3.0m, £3.31. Office open 0700-2200 Apr-Sep. **Town Quay** £1.70 (limited space). ME, El, Wi-fi, 🛠, 🗑, ♿.

Lake Yard Marina ☎ 674531. 56 AB + Ⓥ if space; 90 moorings and 🅰, £3.20 and £1.30. C (5 ton), BH (50 ton), Club bar/food; ent marked by 2FR (vert) and two 2FG (vert). Water taxi, weekends Apr-Oct.

Sunseeker International Marina (50) ☎ 685335, ✕, D, BH (30 ton), C (36 ton), ME, El, CH, 🛒, R, Bar.

Cobbs Quay Marina ☎ 674299. 850, some Ⓥ, £3·20. Slip, P, D, Gas, LPG, 🗑, SM, ME, El, Ⓔ, ✕, C (10 ton), CH, R, Bar.

Public Landing Places: Steps at Poole Quay. **Public Slip:** Baiter Harbourside Park, car/trailer parking – machine payment.

Fuel Poole Bay Fuels barge moored near Aunt Betty (No 22) ECM buoy, pbf.fuel@btconnect.com ☎ 07768 71511 (opening hrs only). Open subject to weather: Apr, Easter & w-ends only 0930-1630; May-Sep daily 0900-1800; Oct-Nov w-ends only 0930-dusk; Dec-Mar open by prior arrangement. P, D, Gas, Gaz, 🛒, Off licence. **Corrals** (S side of Poole Quay adjacent bridge) D.

YACHT CLUBS **Royal Motor YC** ☎ 707227, Wi-fi, M, Bar, R; **Parkstone YC** ☎ 743610 (Parkstone Haven); **Poole YC** ☎ 672687. **Services** A complete range of marine services is available; consult marina/HM for exact locations.

Town: All domestic facilities, ⇌, ✈ (Bournemouth 12M and Southampton by direct rail link). **Ferries:**

Cherbourg: 2-3/day; 4½ Hrs (HSS 2¼ hrs); Brittany (www. brittany-ferries.co.uk);

St Malo/Jersey/Guernsey: 2/day HSS; 2¾–4½ hrs; Condor (www. condorferries.co.uk);

REGULATIONS

The following speed limits are strictly enforced:

- **10kn** speed limit applies to the entire harbour.
- **8kn** speed limit applies within 200m of the beach from S Haven Pt NE'wards through E Looe Channel to Flag Head Chine.
- **6kn** speed limit applies from Stakes SCM past Poole Quay and Poole Bridge up to Cobbs Quay in Holes Bay. It is also an advisory speed limit within the S half of the harbour which is designated as a Quiet Area (see chartlet).
- **4kn** speed limit applies within the Poole Quay Boat Haven.

Exemptions The 10kn speed limit does not apply:

- From 1 Oct to 31 Mar to vessels in the North, Middle Ship and Wareham Channels only.
- To water-skiers within the water-ski area between Gold Pt and No 82 PHM buoy (Wareham Channel; see chartlet). Permits must be obtained from the HM.
- Personal Water Craft (PWC) operating in a designated area N of Brownsea Island must not enter the Quiet Area in the S of the harbour, nor linger in the harbour entrance. Permits must be obtained from the HM.

Sandbanks Chain Ferry *has right of way over all vessels not carrying a Pilot.* It exhibits a B ● above the control cabin when it is about to leave the slipway. A flashing white strobe light is exhibited in the leading direction when the engines are engaged. In fog it sounds 1 long and 2 short blasts every 2 mins. When stationary at night it shows a FW lt; in fog it rings a bell for 5s every 60s.

POOLE HARBOUR *continued*

QUIET AREA

That part of the Harbour, S of a line from Sandbanks via Brownsea Island to Shipstal Pt, is designated a Quiet Area. Respect others; no noise, no wash, please.

WAREHAM, Dorset, 50°41′·03N 02°06′·56W. AC 5601, 2611. HW −0030 (Np), +0320 (Sp) on Dover. LWs do not fall below 0·7m except under very low river flow conditions. **Shelter** Very good. Access approx HW±2 via narrow and winding chan and R Frome (see chartlet) but well marked by buoys and posts, lit to N of Gigger's Island; keep to the outside of all bends. Passage is unlit beyond Gigger's Island. There is a water-ski area between Gold Pt on the N side of the Arne peninsula and WH11/WH12 buoys. Beware prohib ⚓s (salmon holes) marked on the chart. Max draft 1·2m to Wareham Quay. Enforced 4kn speed limit in river.

Facilities: Ridge Wharf Yacht Centre (165+♥ £1·90) (½M upstream of R Frome ent) ☎ (01929) 552650; Access HW±2 approx, AB, M, FW, P, D, ME, El, Gas, BH (18 ton), Slip, ✕, CH; **Redcliffe YC** ☎ 551227 (½M below bridge); **Wareham Quay** AB, FW, R. **Town** P & D (cans), 🛒, Gas, R, Bar, ✉, ⑧, ⇌.

POOLE

See separate chartlet

POOLE BRIDGE OPENING TIMES
The bridge opens daily, only if vessels are waiting, at the following times:

0530, 0630, 0730, 0930, 1030, 1230, 1430, 1630, 1830, 1930, 2130 & 2345 (also at 1730 on Sat, Sun and Bank Holidays).

Pleasure craft may pass when bridge is opened for commercial traffic. Monitor Ch 14 for further information

Holes Bay

Sunseeker Marina

Poole Quay

Lifting Bridge
Poole YC

Ferry Terminal

Oyster Beds

Stakes

Upper Wych Ch

Pottery Pier

Brownsea Island

BOAT CHANNEL
A Boat Chan for pleasure craft and FVs up to 1.5m draft lies SW of the Middle Ship Channel

Furzey Island

Green Island

Cleavel Pt.

Goathorn Point

Avoid oyster beds in South Deep

Anchor clear of buoyed fairway in South Deep

Brands Bay

The Little Sea

HISTORIC WRECKS - VICINITY S HOOK
These sites are protected from unauthorised interference. See Admiralty Annual Notice to Mariners No 16

Harbourside Park

Baiter Pt

Parkstone Bay

PARKSTONE
Parkstone YC

Blue Lagoon

Poole Harbour YC

Salterns Marina

Middle Ship Channel

Boat Channel

Wych Channel

Blood Alley Lake

South Deep

Castle (conspic)

Stone Island

Brownsea Island

Studland Bay

Milkmaid Bank

Seasonal

Bar Sand

North Haven Point

SANDBANKS

Chain Ferry

North Channel

Whitley Lake

Jack Jones

Bell Buoy

RMYC

Shell Bay

South Haven Point

Swash Channel

Hook Sand

10kn Speed Limit

Training Bank

Boat Channel

Maintained Depth 7·5m

East Hook

BOAT CHANNEL
A Boat Chan for pleasure craft and FVs up to 3m draft lies on the SW side of the Swash Chan

Historic wrecks see note

S.Hook

Protected Wreck

Bar Buoy No1

HEIGHTS OF TIDE AT POOLE (TOWN QUAY)

The four curves below are an alternative to those shown on page 213. Although their accuracy should be regarded as approximate, they enable a speedy estimate to be made of the Height of Tide at hourly intervals after the time of LW at Poole Town Quay. The curves are drawn for LW heights above CD of: 0·3m, 0·6m (MLWS), 0·9m and 1·2m (MLWN). The small range of tide (neaps 0·4m; springs 1·5m) is immediately apparent, as is the HW stand at neaps and the double HWs at springs.

Note: All references to are to LW because at Poole the times and heights of LW are more sharply defined than those of HW. HW times and heights are complicated by a stand of tide at HW

at neaps and by double HWs at springs. The times of the two HWs cannot therefore be readily predicted with any accuracy.

Procedure:

- Extract time and height of the preceding LW from the Poole Harbour tide tables (⟶).

- Using the curve whose LW height is closest to the predicted height, note the time of LW and enter the curve at the number of hours after LW for the time required.

- Extract the estimated height of tide (above CD).

- For a more exact estimate, interpolate between the curves if appropriate.

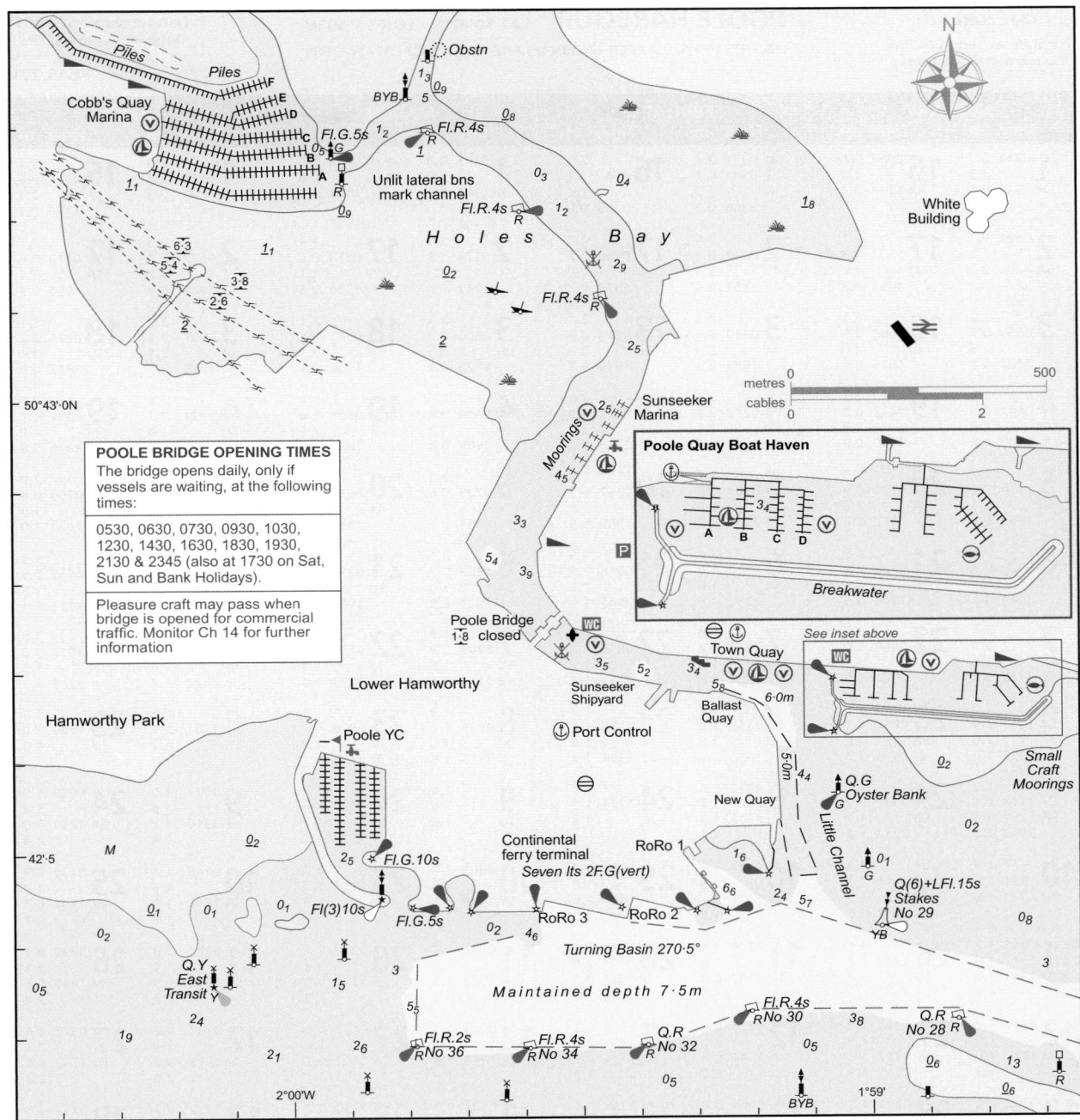

POOLE BRIDGE OPENING TIMES
The bridge opens daily, only if vessels are waiting, at the following times:

0530, 0630, 0730, 0930, 1030, 1230, 1430, 1630, 1830, 1930, 2130 & 2345 (also at 1730 on Sat, Sun and Bank Holidays).

Pleasure craft may pass when bridge is opened for commercial traffic. Monitor Ch 14 for further information

Poole Quay Boat Haven

SAFETY RECOMMENDATIONS

- Keep to the speed limits and be particularly aware of the wash you are creating. This can easily cause injury or damage to other craft and property.
- Look out for large ferries/commercial ships which are limited in their manoeuvrability and speed. Keep well clear and make your intentions obvious.
- Do not pass too close to other craft whether they are underway or moored.
- Be alert in the harbour entrance where the steam runs hard, and it is a particularly hazardous area with great potential for an accident.

- Proceed slowly in the vicinity Town Quay so as not to create a wash that can damage craft moored at the quayside.
- Before sailing check the tidal situation and comply with Passage planning requirements, see Chapter 3.1.
- Anticipate sailing craft manoeuvres, give them room to tack.
- Familiarise yourself with the Harbour, particularly its channels and navigation marks. Use the designated areas for their special use.
- Treat wildlife with care and consideration. Note that virtually all the intertidal mud area are Sites of Special Scientific Interest (SSSI) and Special Protection Areas for Birds.

Note - HW times are not shown because they cannot be predicted with reasonable accuracy. Approximate times can be gained using LW times and the Tidal Curves at the start of this section.

TIME ZONE (UT)
For Summer Time add ONE hour in **non-shaded** areas

POOLE HARBOUR   LAT 50°42'N   LONG 1°59'W
HEIGHTS OF HIGH WATER AND TIMES AND HEIGHTS OF LOW WATERS

Dates in red are SPRINGS
Dates in blue are NEAPS

YEAR 2010

JANUARY

Day	Time / m	Day	Time / m
1 F	0414 0.7 / 2.3 / 1645 0.6 / 2.3	16 SA	0457 0.8 / 2.0 / 1718 0.7
2 SA	0504 0.7 / 2.3 / 1734 0.5	17 SU	0531 0.8 / 2.1 / 2.0 / 1751 0.7
3 SU	0553 0.6 / 2.3 / 1822 0.4	18 M	0603 0.8 / 2.0 / 1821 0.7
4 M	0642 2.3 / 0.6 / 2.3 / 1909 0.5	19 TU	0633 0.8 / 2.0 / 1849 0.8
5 TU	0730 2.3 / 0.7 / 2.1 / 1956 0.6	20 W	0701 0.9 / 2.0 / 1917 0.8
6 W	0820 2.2 / 0.8 / 2.1 / 2044 0.7	21 TH	0732 0.9 / 2.0 / 1948 0.9
7 TH	0912 2.1 / 0.9 / 2.0 / 2135 0.8	22 F	0808 1.0 / 2.0 / 2027 0.9
8 F	1010 2.0 / 1.9 / 2233 1.0	23 SA	0854 1.1 / 1.9 / 2116 1.0
9 SA	1118 1.9 / 1.1 / 1.8 / 2342 1.2	24 SU	0952 1.2 / 1.8 / 2222 1.2
10 SU	1231 1.9 / 1.2 / 1.8	25 M	1111 1.2 / 1.8 / 2347 1.2
11 M	0055 1.2 / 1.9 / 1340 1.1 / 1.8	26 TU	1243 1.2 / 1.8
12 TU	0201 1.2 / 1.9 / 1437 1.0 / 1.9	27 W	0113 1.2 / 1.9 / 1357 1.0 / 1.9
13 W	0255 1.0 / 2.0 / 1524 0.9 / 2.0	28 TH	0221 1.0 / 2.0 / 1456 0.8 / 2.1
14 TH	0340 0.9 / 2.0 / 1605 0.8 / 2.0	29 F	0317 0.8 / 2.1 / 1548 0.6 / 2.2
15 F	0420 0.9 / 2.0 / 1642 0.8 / 2.1	30 SA	0408 0.7 / 2.3 / 1637 0.4 / 2.3
		31 SU	0456 0.5 / 2.3 / 1723 0.3

FEBRUARY

Day	Time / m	Day	Time / m
1 M	2.4 / 0542 0.4 / 2.3 / 1808 0.3	16 TU	2.1 / 0541 0.7 / 2.0 / 1758 0.6
2 TU	2.4 / 0627 0.4 / 2.3 / 1851 0.4	17 W	2.1 / 0608 0.7 / 2.0 / 1823 0.7
3 W	2.3 / 0710 0.5 / 2.2 / 1933 0.4	18 TH	2.1 / 0634 0.7 / 2.0 / 1849 0.7
4 TH	2.3 / 0753 0.6 / 2.1 / 2014 0.6	19 F	2.0 / 0702 0.8 / 1919 0.8
5 F	2.1 / 0837 0.8 / 2058 0.8	20 SA	2.0 / 0737 0.8 / 1.9 / 1955 0.8
6 SA	2.0 / 0927 1.0 / 1.8 / 2150 1.0	21 SU	1.9 / 0818 0.9 / 1.8 / 2041 0.9
7 SU	1.8 / 1031 1.2 / 1.6 / 2301 1.2	22 M	1.8 / 0913 1.1 / 1.7 / 2146 1.2
8 M	1.7 / 1155 1.3 / 1.6	23 TU	1.7 / 1035 1.2 / 1.6 / 2324 1.3
9 TU	0029 1.3 / 1.7 / 1318 1.2 / 1.7	24 W	1.7 / 1224 1.2 / 1.8
10 W	0147 1.2 / 1.8 / 1420 1.1 / 1.8	25 TH	0104 1.2 / 1.8 / 1345 0.9 / 1.9
11 TH	0244 1.1 / 1.9 / 1507 0.9 / 1.9	26 F	0214 0.9 / 1.9 / 1444 0.7 / 2.1
12 F	0326 0.9 / 2.0 / 1546 0.8 / 2.0	27 SA	0308 0.7 / 2.1 / 1534 0.6 / 2.2
13 SA	0403 0.8 / 2.0 / 1622 0.7 / 2.1	28 SU	0356 0.6 / 2.2 / 1621 0.4 / 2.3 ○
14 SU	0438 0.8 / 2.0 / 1656 0.7 / 2.1 ●		
15 M	0511 0.7 / 2.0 / 1729 0.6		

MARCH

Day	Time / m	Day	Time / m
1 M	0441 0.4 / 2.3 / 1705 0.3	16 TU	0444 0.7 / 2.0 / 1701 0.6
2 TU	0524 0.3 / 2.3 / 1747 0.3	17 W	0513 0.6 / 2.1 / 1730 0.6
3 W	0606 0.3 / 2.4 / 1828 0.3	18 TH	0541 0.6 / 2.1 / 1756 0.6
4 TH	0646 0.3 / 2.3 / 1906 0.4	19 F	0608 0.6 / 2.1 / 1824 0.7
5 F	0725 0.6 / 2.1 / 1944 0.4	20 SA	0638 0.7 / 2.0 / 1856 0.8
6 SA	0803 0.7 / 2.0 / 2023 0.9	21 SU	0714 0.8 / 2.0 / 1934 0.9
7 SU	0847 0.9 / 1.8 / 2112 1.1	22 M	0757 0.9 / 1.9 / 2023 1.0
8 M	0945 1.2 / 1.6 / 2225 1.3	23 TU	0854 1.0 / 1.8 / 2133 1.2
9 TU	1115 1.3 / 1.6	24 W	1020 1.2 / 1.7 / 2315 1.3
10 W	0003 1.4 / 1.5 / 1248 1.3 / 1.7	25 TH	1207 1.1 / 1.7 / 1.8
11 TH	0128 1.3 / 1.8 / 1353 1.2 / 1.8	26 F	0050 1.1 / 1.8 / 1326 0.9 / 1.9
12 F	0223 1.1 / 1.8 / 1440 1.0 / 1.9	27 SA	0157 0.9 / 1.9 / 1423 0.7 / 2.1
13 SA	0303 0.9 / 1.9 / 1518 0.8 / 2.0	28 SU	0250 0.7 / 2.1 / 1513 0.6 / 2.3
14 SU	0339 0.8 / 1553 0.7 / 2.1	29 M	0337 0.5 / 2.2 / 1558 0.4 / 2.3
15 M	0412 0.7 / 2.0 / 1628 0.7 / 2.1 ●	30 TU	0421 0.4 / 2.3 / 1641 0.3 / 2.4 ○
		31 W	0503 0.3 / 2.3 / 1723 0.3

APRIL

Day	Time / m	Day	Time / m
1 TH	2.3 / 0543 0.4 / 2.3 / 1802 0.4	16 F	2.1 / 0514 0.6 / 2.1 / 1730 0.7
2 F	2.3 / 0621 0.4 / 2.2 / 1839 0.6	17 SA	2.1 / 0546 0.6 / 2.1 / 1804 0.7
3 SA	2.2 / 0657 0.5 / 2.1 / 1916 0.7	18 SU	2.1 / 0621 0.7 / 2.1 / 1842 0.8
4 SU	2.1 / 0734 0.7 / 2.0 / 1955 0.9	19 M	2.0 / 0702 0.7 / 2.0 / 1926 0.9
5 M	1.9 / 0815 0.9 / 1.8 / 2043 1.1	20 TU	2.0 / 0750 0.8 / 1.9 / 2020 1.0
6 TU	1.8 / 0908 1.1 / 1.7 / 2151 1.3	21 W	1.9 / 0851 0.9 / 1.9 / 2131 1.1
7 W	1.6 / 1029 1.3 / 1.6 / 2324 1.4	22 TH	1.8 / 1012 1.0 / 1.8 / 2259 1.2
8 TH	1.5 / 1201 1.3 / 1.7	23 F	1.8 / 1140 1.0 / 1.9
9 F	0047 1.3 / 1.6 / 1310 1.2 / 1.8	24 SA	0023 1.0 / 1.8 / 1255 0.9 / 2.0
10 SA	0145 1.2 / 1.7 / 1359 1.0 / 1.9	25 SU	0130 0.9 / 1.9 / 1354 0.7 / 2.1
11 SU	0227 1.0 / 1.8 / 1440 0.9 / 2.0	26 M	0224 0.7 / 2.0 / 1445 0.6 / 2.2
12 M	0304 0.8 / 1.9 / 1518 0.8 / 2.0	27 TU	0312 0.6 / 2.1 / 1532 0.6 / 2.3
13 TU	0339 0.7 / 2.0 / 1553 0.7 / 2.1	28 W	0357 0.5 / 2.2 / 1616 0.5 / 2.3 ○
14 W	0412 0.7 / 2.0 / 1627 0.7 / 2.1 ●	29 TH	0440 0.5 / 2.2 / 1658 0.5 / 2.3
15 TH	0443 0.6 / 2.1 / 1659 0.7	30 F	2.3 / 0520 0.5 / 2.2 / 1737 0.6

Chart Datum: 1·40 metres below Ordnance Datum (Newlyn). HAT is 2·6 metres above Chart Datum; see 4.5

Note - HW times are not shown because they cannot be predicted with reasonable accuracy. Approximate times can be gained using LW times and the Tidal Curves at the start of this section.

POOLE HARBOUR   LAT 50°42'N   LONG 1°59'W
HEIGHTS OF HIGH WATER AND TIMES AND HEIGHTS OF LOW WATERS

TIME ZONE (UT)
For Summer Time add ONE hour in **non-shaded areas**

Dates in red are SPRINGS
Dates in blue are NEAPS

YEAR 2010

Central S England

MAY

Day	Time m	Day	Time m
1 SA	0559 2.2/0.6, 1816 2.1/0.7	16 SU	0530 2.1/0.6, 1750 2.1/0.7
2 SU	0635 2.1/0.7, 1853 2.1/0.8	17 M	0613 2.1/0.6, 1835 2.1/0.7
3 M	0712 2.0/0.8, 1933 2.0/0.9	18 TU	0659 2.1/0.7, 1924 2.1/0.8
4 TU	0752 1.9/0.9, 2019 1.9/1.1	19 W	0751 2.0/0.7, 2020 2.0/0.9
5 W	0839 1.8/1.0, 2116 1.8/1.2	20 TH	0850 2.0/0.8, 2123 2.0/1.0
6 TH	0941 1.6/1.2, 2229 1.7/1.3	21 F	0956 1.9/0.9, 2234 2.0/1.0
7 F	1058 1.6/1.2, 2346 1.7/1.3	22 SA	1108 1.9/0.9, 2348 2.0/1.0
8 SA	1210 1.6/1.2, 1.8	23 SU	1217 1.9/0.9, 2.0
9 SU	0050 1.2, 1306 1.6/1.1, 1.9	24 M	0056 0.9, 1320 1.9/0.8, 2.1
10 M	0139 1.0, 1353 1.8/1.0, 1.9	25 TU	0155 0.8, 1416 2.0/0.8, 2.1
11 TU	0221 0.9, 1435 1.9/0.9, 2.0	26 W	0248 0.7, 1506 2.0/0.7, 2.2
12 W	0300 0.8, 1515 1.9/0.8, 2.1	27 TH	0336 0.7, 1553 2.1/0.7, 2.2
13 TH	0337 0.7, 1553 2.0/0.8, 2.1	28 F	0421 0.6, 1637 2.1/0.7, 2.1
14 F	0414 0.7, 1631 2.1/0.7, 2.1	29 SA	0502 0.6, 1718 2.1/0.7
15 SA	0451 0.6, 1710 2.1/0.7	30 SU	0541 2.1/0.7, 1757 2.1/0.8
		31 M	0618 2.1/0.7, 1835 2.1/0.8

JUNE

Day	Time m	Day	Time m
1 TU	0654 2.0/0.8, 1913 2.0/0.9	16 W	0656 2.1/0.6, 1919 2.2/0.7
2 W	0731 1.9/0.9, 1954 1.9/1.0	17 TH	0746 2.1/0.6, 2011 2.1/0.8
3 TH	0811 1.9/0.9, 2038 1.9/1.1	18 F	0838 2.0/0.7, 2106 2.1/0.8
4 F	0856 1.8/1.0, 2130 1.8/1.2	19 SA	0933 2.0/0.8, 2206 2.0/0.9
5 SA	0951 1.7/1.2, 2232 1.8/1.3	20 SU	1034 1.9/0.9, 2312 2.0/1.0
6 SU	1054 1.6/1.2, 2338 1.8/1.2	21 M	1139 1.9/0.9, 2.0
7 M	1159 1.6/1.2, 1.8	22 TU	0021 1.0, 1247 1.9/1.0, 2.0
8 TU	0039 1.2, 1257 1.7/1.2, 1.9	23 W	0128 1.0, 1350 1.9/1.0, 2.0
9 W	0132 1.0, 1350 1.8/1.0, 2.0	24 TH	0228 0.9, 1446 1.9/0.9, 2.0
10 TH	0221 0.9, 1438 1.9/0.9, 2.0	25 F	0319 0.8, 1536 2.0/0.9, 2.1
11 F	0306 0.8, 1524 2.0/0.8, 2.1	26 SA	0405 0.8, 1621 2.0/0.8, 2.1
12 SA	0351 0.7, 1609 2.1/0.8, 2.1	27 SU	0447 0.7, 1702 2.1/0.8
13 SU	0436 0.6, 1655 2.1/0.7, 2.2	28 M	0525 0.7, 1740 2.1/0.8
14 M	0522 0.6, 1742 2.2/0.7	29 TU	0601 2.0/0.7, 1816 2.1/0.8
15 TU	0608 2.2/0.6, 1830 2.2/0.7	30 W	0635 2.0/0.7, 1851 2.0/0.9

JULY

Day	Time m	Day	Time m
1 TH	0708 2.0/0.8, 1926 2.0/0.9	16 F	0731 2.2/0.5, 1954 2.3/0.6
2 F	0740 1.9/0.9, 2000 2.0/1.0	17 SA	0818 2.1/0.6, 2043 2.2/0.7
3 SA	0814 1.9/0.9, 2039 1.9/1.0	18 SU	0906 2.0/0.7, 2136 2.1/0.9
4 SU	0855 1.8/0.9, 2124 1.9/1.2	19 M	1000 1.9/0.9, 2238 2.0/1.0
5 M	0944 1.8/1.1, 2222 1.8/1.2	20 TU	1105 1.8/1.0, 2351 1.9/1.1
6 TU	1047 1.7/1.2, 2332 1.8/1.2	21 W	1220 1.8/1.2, 1.9
7 W	1159 1.7/1.2, 1.8	22 TH	0108 1.1, 1333 1.8/1.2, 1.9
8 TH	0046 1.2, 1310 1.8/1.2, 1.9	23 F	0214 1.0, 1434 1.9/1.0, 2.0
9 F	0150 1.0, 1411 1.9/1.0, 2.0	24 SA	0306 0.9, 1524 2.0/1.0, 2.0
10 SA	0245 0.8, 1505 2.0/0.9, 2.1	25 SU	0350 0.8, 1606 2.0/0.9, 2.0
11 SU	0336 0.7, 1555 2.1/0.8, 2.1	26 M	0429 0.7, 1644 2.1/0.8, 2.0
12 M	0424 0.6, 1644 2.2/0.7, 2.2	27 TU	0506 0.7, 1720 2.1/0.8
13 TU	0512 0.5, 1732 2.3/0.6	28 W	0540 0.7, 1754 2.1/0.8
14 W	0559 2.3/0.4, 1819 2.3/0.6	29 TH	0612 2.0/0.7, 1825 2.1/0.8
15 TH	0645 2.3/0.4, 1907 2.3/0.6	30 F	0640 2.0/0.7, 1855 2.1/0.8
		31 SA	0707 2.0/0.8, 1924 2.0/0.9

AUGUST

Day	Time m	Day	Time m
1 SU	0736 1.9/0.8, 1956 2.0/0.9	16 M	0836 2.0/0.8, 2104 2.1/0.9
2 M	0811 1.9/0.9, 2036 1.9/1.0	17 TU	0927 1.9/1.0, 2204 1.9/1.1
3 TU	0854 1.9/1.1, 2128 1.9/1.2	18 W	1035 1.8/1.2, 2324 1.8/1.2
4 W	0954 1.7/1.2, 2239 1.8/1.2	19 TH	1200 1.6/1.3, 1.7
5 TH	1115 1.7/1.3, 1.8	20 F	0050 1.2, 1322 1.8/1.3, 1.8
6 F	0012 1.2, 1246 1.7/1.2, 1.8	21 SA	0200 1.1, 1423 1.9/1.2, 1.9
7 SA	0132 1.2, 1357 1.9/1.0, 2.0	22 SU	0250 0.9, 1509 2.0/1.0, 2.0
8 SU	0232 0.8, 1453 2.0/0.9, 2.1	23 M	0330 0.8, 1547 2.1/0.9, 2.0
9 M	0323 0.7, 1543 2.1/0.7, 2.2	24 TU	0406 0.7, 1622 2.1/0.8, 2.1
10 TU	0411 0.5, 1631 2.3/0.6, 2.3	25 W	0441 0.7, 1656 2.1/0.7, 2.1
11 W	0457 0.4, 1717 2.3/0.5, 2.3	26 TH	0514 0.6, 1728 2.1/0.7
12 TH	2.3, 0542 0.3, 1802 2.4/0.4	27 F	0544 0.7, 1756 2.1/0.7
13 F	2.3, 0626 0.3, 1846 2.4/0.4	28 SA	0611 0.7, 1823 2.1/0.8
14 SA	2.3, 0709 0.4, 1930 2.3/0.6	29 SU	0635 0.8, 1850 2.0/0.8
15 SU	2.2, 0752 0.6, 2015 2.2	30 M	0703 0.8, 1921 2.0/0.9
		31 TU	0736 0.9, 2000 1.9/1.0

Chart Datum: 1·40 metres below Ordnance Datum (Newlyn). HAT is 2·6 metres above Chart Datum; see 4.5

Note - HW times are not shown because they cannot be predicted with reasonable accuracy. Approximate times can be gained using LW times and the Tidal Curves at the start of this section.

TIME ZONE (UT)
For Summer Time add ONE hour in **non-shaded areas**

POOLE HARBOUR   LAT 50°42′N   LONG 1°59′W
HEIGHTS OF HIGH WATER AND TIMES AND HEIGHTS OF LOW WATERS

Dates in red are SPRINGS
Dates in blue are NEAPS

YEAR 2010

SEPTEMBER

Date	Time	m	m	Time	m	m
1 W	0818	1.9	1.1	◑ 2050	1.9	1.1
2 TH	0918	1.8	1.3	2204	1.8	1.3
3 F	1049	1.7	1.3	2351	1.7	1.2
4 SA	1233	1.7	1.3			1.8
5 SU	0117	1.0	1.9	1344	1.0	2.0
6 M	0216	0.8	2.1	1438	0.8	2.1
7 TU	0306	0.6	2.2	1526	0.7	2.3
8 W ●	0352	0.4	2.3	1612	0.5	2.3
9 TH	0436	0.3	2.4	1656	0.4	2.4
10 F	0520	0.3	2.4	1740	0.4	
11 SA	0602	2.4	0.4	1822	2.4	0.4
12 SU	0643	2.3	0.5	1903	2.3	0.6
13 M	0723	2.2	0.7	1945	2.2	0.7
14 TU	0806	2.1	0.8	2031	2.0	0.9
15 W	0857	1.9	1.1	◐ 2130	1.9	1.2
16 TH	1007	1.8	1.3	2253	1.7	1.3
17 F	1139	1.6	1.4			1.6
18 SA	0026	1.3	1.8	1304	1.3	1.8
19 SU	0136	1.2	1.9	1402	1.2	1.9
20 M	0224	1.0	2.0	1444	1.0	2.0
21 TU	0302	0.9	2.1	1520	0.9	2.0
22 W	0337	0.8	2.1	1553	0.8	2.1
23 TH ○	0411	0.7	2.1	1626	0.7	2.1
24 F	0443	0.7	2.1	1657	0.7	2.1
25 SA	0514	0.7	2.1	1726	0.7	
26 SU	0540	2.1	0.7	1752	2.1	0.7
27 M	0606	2.1	0.8	1820	2.1	0.8
28 TU	0635	2.1	0.8	1854	2.0	0.9
29 W	0711	2.0	0.9	1934	2.0	1.0
30 TH	0756	1.9	1.1	2027	1.9	1.1

OCTOBER

Date	Time	m	m	Time	m	m
1 F	0900	1.8	1.3	◑ 2144	1.8	1.2
2 SA	1035	1.8	1.3	2328	1.8	1.2
3 SU	1213	1.8	1.3			1.8
4 M	0052	1.0	1.9	1323	1.0	2.0
5 TU	0152	0.8	2.1	1416	0.8	2.1
6 W	0242	0.7	2.3	1504	0.7	2.3
7 TH ●	0328	0.5	2.4	1549	0.5	2.3
8 F	0412	0.4	2.4	1633	0.4	2.4
9 SA	0455	0.4	2.4	1716	0.4	
10 SU	0536	2.4	0.4	1757	2.4	0.5
11 M	0617	2.3	0.6	1838	2.3	0.6
12 TU	0657	2.2	0.7	1918	2.1	0.8
13 W	0740	2.1	0.9	2002	2.0	0.9
14 TH	0830	1.9	1.2	◑ 2057	1.8	1.2
15 F	0937	1.8	1.3	2212	1.7	1.3
16 SA	1104	1.7	1.4	2341	1.6	1.3
17 SU	1226	1.8	1.3			1.7
18 M	0053	1.2	1.9	1326	1.2	1.8
19 TU	0144	1.1	2.0	1409	1.0	1.9
20 W	0224	1.0	2.0	1445	0.9	2.0
21 TH	0301	0.9	2.1	1520	0.8	2.1
22 F	0337	0.8	2.1	1554	0.8	2.1
23 SA ○	0410	0.8	2.1	1626	0.7	2.1
24 SU	0442	0.8	2.1	1657	0.7	
25 M	0512	2.1	0.8	1727	2.1	0.7
26 TU	0543	2.1	0.8	1800	2.1	0.8
27 W	0617	2.1	0.9	1838	2.1	0.8
28 TH	0658	2.1	0.9	1922	2.0	0.9
29 F	0748	2.0	1.1	2018	1.9	1.0
30 SA	0854	1.9	1.2	◑ 2131	1.9	1.1
31 SU	1017	1.9	1.3	2257	1.8	1.1

NOVEMBER

Date	Time	m	m	Time	m	m
1 M	1142	1.9	1.2			1.9
2 TU	0016	1.0	2.0	1252	1.0	2.0
3 W	0120	0.9	2.1	1349	0.9	2.1
4 TH	0213	0.7	2.3	1440	0.7	2.2
5 F	0302	0.6	2.3	1527	0.6	2.3
6 SA ●	0347	0.6	2.4	1612	0.6	2.3
7 SU	0432	0.6	2.4	1656	0.6	
8 M	0514	2.3	0.6	1737	2.3	0.6
9 TU	0555	2.3	0.7	1817	2.2	0.7
10 W	0636	2.2	0.8	1857	2.1	0.8
11 TH	0718	2.1	1.0	1939	2.0	0.9
12 F	0805	2.0	1.1	2027	1.9	1.1
13 SA	0901	1.9	1.3	◑ 2125	1.8	1.2
14 SU	1011	1.8	1.4	2236	1.6	1.3
15 M	1126	1.8	1.4	2348	1.6	1.3
16 TU	1231	1.8	1.3			1.7
17 W	0049	1.2	1.9	1322	1.2	1.8
18 TH	0138	1.1	2.0	1405	1.0	1.9
19 F	0221	1.0	2.0	1445	0.9	2.0
20 SA	0300	0.9	2.1	1522	0.9	2.1
21 SU ○	0337	0.9	2.1	1558	0.8	2.1
22 M	0414	0.8	2.2	1634	0.7	2.1
23 TU	0450	0.8	2.2	1710	0.7	
24 W	0527	2.2	0.8	1749	2.1	0.7
25 TH	0608	2.2	0.8	1832	2.1	0.8
26 F	0654	2.1	0.9	1920	2.1	0.8
27 SA	0746	2.1	1.0	2014	2.0	0.9
28 SU ◑	0845	2.0	1.0	2116	1.9	0.9
29 M	0953	2.0	1.1	2224	1.9	1.0
30 TU	1106	2.0	1.1	2335	1.9	1.0

DECEMBER

Date	Time	m	m	Time	m	m
1 W	1217	2.0	1.0			1.9
2 TH	0043	0.9	2.1	1321	0.9	2.0
3 F	0144	0.9	2.2	1418	0.8	2.1
4 SA	0238	0.8	2.3	1509	0.8	2.1
5 SU ●	0328	0.8	2.3	1557	0.7	2.2
6 M	0415	0.7	2.3	1642	0.7	2.2
7 TU	0458	0.7	2.2	1724	0.7	
8 W	0539	2.2	0.8	1803	2.1	0.7
9 TH	0619	2.1	0.8	1840	2.1	0.8
10 F	0658	2.1	0.9	1918	2.0	0.9
11 SA	0738	2.0	1.0	1957	1.9	0.9
12 SU	0822	1.9	1.2	2040	1.8	1.0
13 M	0911	1.9	1.3	◑ 2130	1.8	1.2
14 TU	1011	1.8	1.3	2231	1.7	1.3
15 W	1119	1.8	1.3	2338	1.6	1.3
16 TH	1224	1.8	1.3			1.7
17 F	0042	1.2	1.9	1321	1.2	1.8
18 SA	0137	1.2	2.0	1409	1.0	1.9
19 SU	0226	1.0	2.0	1454	0.9	2.0
20 M	0310	0.9	2.1	1536	0.8	2.1
21 TU ○	0353	0.8	2.3	1618	0.7	2.1
22 W	0435	0.8	2.2	1701	0.7	
23 TH	0517	2.2	0.7	1744	2.2	0.6
24 F	0602	2.2	0.7	1828	2.2	0.6
25 SA	0648	2.2	0.8	1915	2.1	0.6
26 SU	0737	2.2	0.8	2003	2.1	0.7
27 M	0829	2.1	0.8	2055	2.0	0.8
28 TU	0926	2.1	0.9	2152	2.0	0.9
29 W	1031	2.0	1.0	2257	1.9	1.0
30 TH	1143	2.0	1.0			1.8
31 F	0009	1.0	2.0	1256	1.0	1.9

Chart Datum: 1·40 metres below Ordnance Datum (Newlyn). HAT is 2·6 metres above Chart Datum; see 4.5

9.2.9 SPECIAL TIDAL CURVES FROM CHRISTCHURCH TO SELSEY BILL

Due to the complex tidal patterns between Christchurch and Selsey Bill, **special curves** for each Secondary Port are used to obtain the most accurate values of times and heights. Because their LW points are more sharply defined than HW, *all times are referenced to LW*.

Critical curve. The spring and neap curves at harbours from Christchurch to Yarmouth differ considerably in shape and duration so a third, 'critical', curve is provided for the Portsmouth range at which the heights of the two HWs are equal for the port concerned. Interpolate between this critical curve and either the spring or neap curve as appropriate.

Note: Whilst the critical curve extends throughout the tidal range, the spring and neap curves stop at the higher HW. For example, with a Portsmouth range of 3·8m (near springs), at 7hrs after LW Lymington the factor should be referenced to the *next* LW. Had the Portsmouth range been 2·0m (near neaps), it should be referenced to the *previous* LW.

Example: Find the height of tide at Christchurch at 1420 on a day when the tidal predictions for Portsmouth are:

18
SA
0110	4·6
0613	1·1
1318	4·6
1833	1·0

Standard Port PORTSMOUTH

Times

High Water		Low Water		MHWS	MHWN	MLWN	MLWS
0000	0600	0500	1100	4·7	3·8	1·9	0·8
1200	1800	1700	2300				

Differences CHRISTCHURCH ENTRANCE

−0230	+0030	−0035	−0035	−2·9	−2·4	−1·2	−0·2

- On the tidal prediction form (see next column) complete fields 2-5, 8-10 (by interpolation) and thus 13-15.
- On the Christchurch tidal graph, plot the HW & LW heights (fields 14 & 15) and join them with a diagonal line.
- Time required (1420) is 3hr 38min before LW Christchurch (field 13); from this value go vertically towards the curves.
- Interpolate for the Portsmouth range (3·6m) between the spring curve (3·9m) and the critical curve (2·6m).
- Go horizontally to the diagonal; thence vertically to read off the height of tide at 1420: 1·6m.

STANDARD PORT ...Portsmouth... TIME/HEIGHT REQUIRED ...1420...

SECONDARY PORT ...Christchurch... DATE ...18 Nov... TIME ZONE ...0(UT)...

STANDARD PORT	TIME		HEIGHT		
	HW	LW	HW	LW	RANGE
	1	2 1833	3 4.6	4 1.0	5 3.6
Seasonal change	Standard Port		6	6	
DIFFERENCES	7	8 ~003S	9 −2.8	10 ~0.3	
Seasonal change	Standard Port		11	11	
SECONDARY PORT	12	13 1758	14 1.8	15 0.7	
Duration	16				

STANDARD PORT .... TIME/HEIGHT REQUIRED ....

SECONDARY PORT .... DATE .... TIME ZONE ....

STANDARD PORT	TIME		HEIGHT		
	HW	LW	HW	LW	RANGE
	1	2	3	4	5
Seasonal change	Standard Port		6	6	
DIFFERENCES	7	8	9	10	
Seasonal change	Standard Port		11	11	
SECONDARY PORT	12	13	14	15	
Duration	16				

Note*** At Tuckton LWs do not fall below 0·7m except under very low river flow conditions.

Note: From Christchurch to Yarmouth height differences always refer to the higher HW which should be used to obtain the range at the Secondary Port. HW time differences also refer to the higher HW, but are not required for this calculation.

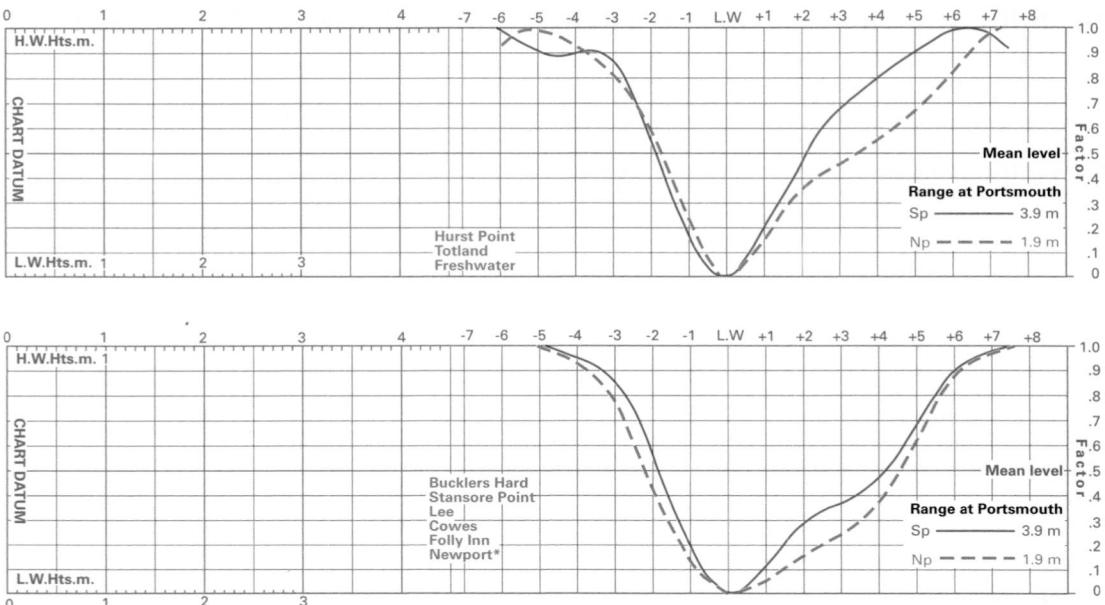

Note* Due to the constriction of the R Medina, Newport requires special treatment since the hbr dries 1·4m. The calculation should be made using the LW time and height differences for Cowes, and the HW height differences for Newport. Any calculated heights which fall below 1·4m should be treated as 1·4m.

ISLE OF WIGHT – SOUTH COAST

(AC 2045) From the Needles eastward to Freshwater Bay the cliffs can be approached to within 1ca, but beyond the E end of the chalk cliffs there are ledges off Brook and Atherfield which require at least 5ca offing. ▶ *The E-going stream sets towards these dangers. 4M SSW of the Needles the stream turns E x N at HW Portsmouth + 0500, and W at HW – 0030, sp rate 2kn St Catherine's lt ho is conspic. It is safe to pass 2ca off, but a race occurs off the point and can be very dangerous at or near sp against a strong wind, and particularly SE of the point on a W-going stream. St Catherine's should then be rounded at least 2M off. 1·25M SE of the point the stream turns E at HW Portsmouth +0520, and W at HW –0055, sp rate 3·75kn.* ◀

Rocks extend about 2½ca either side of Dunnose where a race occurs. In Sandown Bay anch off Shanklin or Sandown where the streams are weak inshore. ▶*Off the centre of the Bay they turn NE x E at HW Portsmouth +0500, and SW x W at HW –0100, sp rates 2 kn.* ◀ The Yarborough Monument is conspic above Culver Cliff. Whitecliff Bay provides an anch in winds between W and N. From here to Foreland (Bembridge Pt) the coast is fringed by a ledge of drying rocks extending up to 3ca offshore, and it is advisable to keep to seaward of Bembridge Ledge ECM lt buoy.

WESTERN APPROACHES TO THE SOLENT

(AC 2035) The Needles are distinctive rocks at the W end of the Isle of Wight. The adjacent chalk cliffs of High Down are conspic from afar, but the Lt Ho may not be seen by day until relatively close. Goose Rk, dries, is about 50m WNW of the Lt Ho, 100-150m WSW of which is a drying wreck. When rounding the Needles an offing of 1½ca will clear these. The NW side of Needles Chan is defined by the Shingles bank, parts of which dry and on which the sea breaks violently in the least swell. The SE side of the bank is fairly steep-to; the NW side shelves more gradually.

▶*The ENE-going flood runs from HW Portsmouth +0500 until HW –0130, sp rates 3.1kn at The Bridge , a reef which runs 8ca W of the Lt ho and is marked by WCM, and 3.9kn at Hurst. The WSW-going ebb runs from HW –0100 until HW +0430, sp rates 4.4kn at Hurst, 3.4kn WSW across the Shingles and at The Bridge. The Needles Chan is well marked and in fair weather presents no significant problems, but in a SW 4 or above over the ebb, breaking seas occur near The Bridge and SW Shingles. In bad weather broken water and overfalls extend along The Bridge. S to W gales against the ebb raise very dangerous breaking seas in the Needles Chan and approaches. The sea state can be at its worst shortly after LW when the flood has just begun. There is then no wind-over-tide situation, but a substantial swell is raised as a result of the recently turned stream.* ◀

In such conditions use the E route to the Solent, S of the IoW and via Nab Tower; or find shelter at Poole or Studland.

In strong winds the North Channel, N of the Shingles, is preferable to the Needles Channel. The two join S of Hurst Pt, where overfalls and tide rips may be met. Beware The Trap, a very shallow gravel shoal spit, 150m SE of Hurst Castle.

In E winds Alum Bay, with its coloured cliffs close NE of the Needles, is an attractive daytime anch but beware Long Rk (dries) in the middle of the bay, and Five Fingers Rock 1½ca SW of Hatherwood Pt on N side. Totland Bay is good anch in settled weather, but avoid Warden Ledge.

THE SOLENT

(AC 2035, 2036, 2037) Within the Solent there are few dangers in mid-chan. The most significant is Bramble Bank (dries) between Cowes and Calshot. The main shipping chan (buoyed) passes S and W of the Brambles, but yachts can use the North Chan to the NE of the Brambles at any state of tide. ▶ *Tidal streams are strong at sp, but principally follow the direction of the main chan.* ◀ A Precautionary Area between Cowes and Calshot provides priority and safety for large commercial shipping (See 9.2.17). There are many yacht racing buoys *(seasonal, Mar–Dec)* in the Solent and Southampton Water. Most are fitted with a Fl Y 4s light.

Several inshore spits, banks, rocks and ledges include: Pennington and Lymington Spits on the N shore; Black Rk 4ca W of entrance to Yarmouth ; Hamstead Ledge 8ca W of entrance to Newtown River and Saltmead Ledge 1·5M to E; Gurnard Ledge 1·5M W of Cowes; Lepe Middle and Beaulieu Spit, S and W of the ent to Beaulieu R; the shoals off Stone Pt, marked by Lepe Spit SCM buoy; Shrape Mud, which extends N from the breakwater of Cowes Hbr and along to Old Castle Pt; the shoals and isolated rks which fringe the island shore from Old Castle Pt to Ryde, including either side of the ent to Wootton Creek; and Calshot Spit which extends almost to the deep water chan into Southampton Water.

Southampton Water is a busy commercial waterway with large tankers, container ships, and frequent Ro-Ro and High Speed ferries. Yachts should monitor VHF Ch 12 (Southampton VTS) to ascertain shipping movements. Between the Fawley Marine Terminal and the BP jetty on the E side the channel is narrow for large vessels with little room for yachts to take refuge. N of this area there is adequate water for yachts close outboard of the main buoyed channel; the banks are of gently shelving soft mud, apart from foul ground between Hythe and Marchwood. At night, unlit marks and large mooring buoys may be hard to see against the many shore lights. Except in strong N'lies, Southampton Water and the R Test and Itchen provide sheltered sailing. The River Hamble is convenient, but somewhat crowded.

Depending on the wind direction, there are many good anchorages: in W winds on E side of Hurst, as close inshore as depth permits, NE of Hurst lt; in S winds, or in good weather, W of Yarmouth Harbour entrance, as near shore as possible; in winds between W and N in Stanswood Bay, about 1M NE of Stansore Pt. Just N of Calshot Spit there is shelter from SW and W, while Osborne Bay, 2M E of Cowes, is sheltered from winds between S and W; in E winds Gurnard Bay, to the W of Cowes, is preferable. Stokes Bay is well sheltered from the N, and at the E end of the IoW there is good anchorage in Priory Bay off Bembridge in winds from S, SW or W; but clear out if wind goes into E.

There are also places which shoal-draught boats can explore at the top of the tide such as Ashlett Creek between Fawley and Calshot, Eling up the R Test, and the upper reaches of the R Medina.

FLOOD The Needles Channel
Hurst Pt
3.2k   3.9k
The Shingles
2.5k
Needles
HW PORTSMOUTH –5

EBB The Needles Channel
2.5k
3.5k   Hurst Pt
4.4k
The Shingles
2.9k
Needles
HW PORTSMOUTH +3

9.2.10 CHRISTCHURCH

Dorset 50°43'·53N 01°44'·33W ❀⚓⚓❀❀

CHARTS AC 5601, 2035, 2172; Imray C4; Stanfords 7, 12, 24.

TIDES HW Sp –0210, Np, –0140 Dover; ML 1·2

Standard Port PORTSMOUTH (→)

Times				Height (metres)			
High Water		Low Water		MHWS	MHWN	MLWN	MLWS
0000	0600	0500	1100	4·7	3·8	1·9	0·8
1200	1800	1700	2300				
Differences BOURNEMOUTH							
–0240	+0055	–0050	–0030	–2·7	–2·2	–0·8	–0·3
CHRISTCHURCH (Entrance)							
–0230	+0030	–0035	–0035	–2·9	–2·4	–1·2	–0·2
CHRISTCHURCH (Quay)							
–0210	+0100	+0055	–2·9	–2·4	–1·0	0·0
CHRISTCHURCH (Tuckton bridge)							
–0205	+0110	+0110	+0105	–3·0	–2·5	–1·0	+0·1

NOTE: Double HWs occur, except near neaps; predictions are for the higher HW. Near neaps there is a stand; predictions are for mid-stand. Tidal levels are for inside the bar; outside, the tide is about 0·6m lower at springs. Water flow in Rivers Avon and Stour cause considerable variations from predicted heights. Tuckton LWs do not fall below 0·7m except under very low river flow conditions.

SHELTER Good in lee of Hengistbury Hd; elsewhere exposed to SW winds. R Stour navigable at HW up to Tuckton, and the R Avon up to the first bridge. Both are well sheltered. Most ⚓s in the hbr dry.

NAVIGATION WPT 50°43'·53N 01°43'·58W, 270°/0·5M to NE end of Mudeford Quay. Outer approach is marked by PHM and SHM buoys. The bar/chan lies approx 100m NE of The Run but is liable to shift. The entrance is difficult on the ebb which reaches 4-5kn in The Run. Best to enter or leave at HW/stand. Chan inside hbr is narrow and mostly shallow (approx 0·3m) with soft mud. No ⚓ in chan. No berthing at ferry jetty by Mudeford sandbank (beware frequent ferries between Mudeford Quay, The Run and Christchurch). Hbr speed limit 4kn. If fishing from any craft, local licence is obligatory. Beware groynes S of Hengistbury Hd, Beerpan, Yarranton/Clarendon Rks.

LIGHTS AND MARKS See chartlet and 9.2.4. Unlit chan buoys in hbr and apps are locally laid Apr-Oct inc; info from ☎ 483250.

R/T None.

TELEPHONE (Code 01202) HM 495061; MRCC (01305) 760439; Marinecall 09068 969647; Police 855544; Ⓗ 303626; Casualty 704167.

FACILITIES Elkins Boatyard ☎ 483141, AB £20; Rossiter Yachts ☎ 483250, AB £20; Christchurch SC (CSC) ☎ 483150, limited AB £10.50, monohulls only, max LOA 9m.
Services: M, L, D, P (cans), FW, El, ✕, CH, ACA, Gas, C (10 ton), Slip.
Town ✉, Ⓑ, ⇌, ✈ (Bournemouth).

9.2.11 KEYHAVEN

Hampshire 50°42'·85N 01°33'·26W ❀⚓⚓❀

CHARTS AC 5600, 2035, 2021; Imray C4, C3; Stanfords 7, 11, 12, 24, 25.

TIDES –0020, +0105 Dover; ML 2·0

Standard Port PORTSMOUTH (→)

Times				Height (metres)			
High Water		Low Water		MHWS	MHWN	MLWN	MLWS
0000	0600	0500	1100	4·7	3·8	1·9	0·8
1200	1800	1700	2300				
Differences HURST POINT							
–0115	–0005	–0030	–0025	–2·0	–1·5	–0·5	–0·1
TOTLAND BAY							
–0130	–0045	–0035	–0045	–2·2	–1·7	–0·4	–0·1
FRESHWATER BAY							
–0210	+0025	–0040	–0020	–2·1	–1·5	–0·4	0·0

NOTE: Double HWs occur at or near sp; predictions are for the first HW. Off springs there is a stand of about 2 hrs; predictions are then for mid-stand. See 9.2.9.

SHELTER Reasonable, but all moorings and ⚓s are exposed to winds across the marshland. The 'U' bend carries 2-2.5m but Keyhaven and Mount Lakes all but dry. The river gets very congested during the sailing season.

NAVIGATION WPT 50°42'·73N 01°32'·58W, 295°/0·40M to chan ent. Access HW ±4½. Ent difficult on ebb and should not be attempted in strong E winds. Bar is constantly changing, and North Pt is reported to be extending to the north. Leave chan SHM buoys well to stbd. Entrance is possible, with local knowledge, via Hawkers Lake (unmarked), approx 0.3m less water than main channel. Beware lobster pots. When approaching from the W beware the Shingles Bank over which seas break and which partly dries. At Hurst Narrows give The Trap a wide berth.

LIGHTS AND MARKS See 9.2.4, chartlet above and 9.2.12 for sectors of Hurst Point light. When NE of Hurst Point, two leading beacons (the rear is shorter than the front) lead 283° to R & G buoys at the the entrance to the buoyed channel.

R/T VHF Ch M (River Warden).

TELEPHONE (Code 01590) R. Warden 645695; Dr 643022; Ⓗ 677011; MRCC 02392 552100; Marinecall 09068 969647; Police 08450 454545.

FACILITIES Quay Slip, L; Keyhaven YC ☎ 642165, C, M, L (on beach), FW, Bar. ⚓, if available, £9/night. Hurst Castle SC ☎ (01590) 645589, M, L, FW. New Forest District Council (R.Warden), Slip, M.
Services W Solent Boat Builders ☎ 642080, Slip, ME, El, ✕, C (9 ton), CH.

Village Bar, R. Milford-on-Sea (1M): P, D, R, Bar, CH, 🛒, ✉ and Ⓑ, ⇌ (bus to New Milton), ✈ (Bournemouth)

9.2.12 NEEDLES CHANNEL

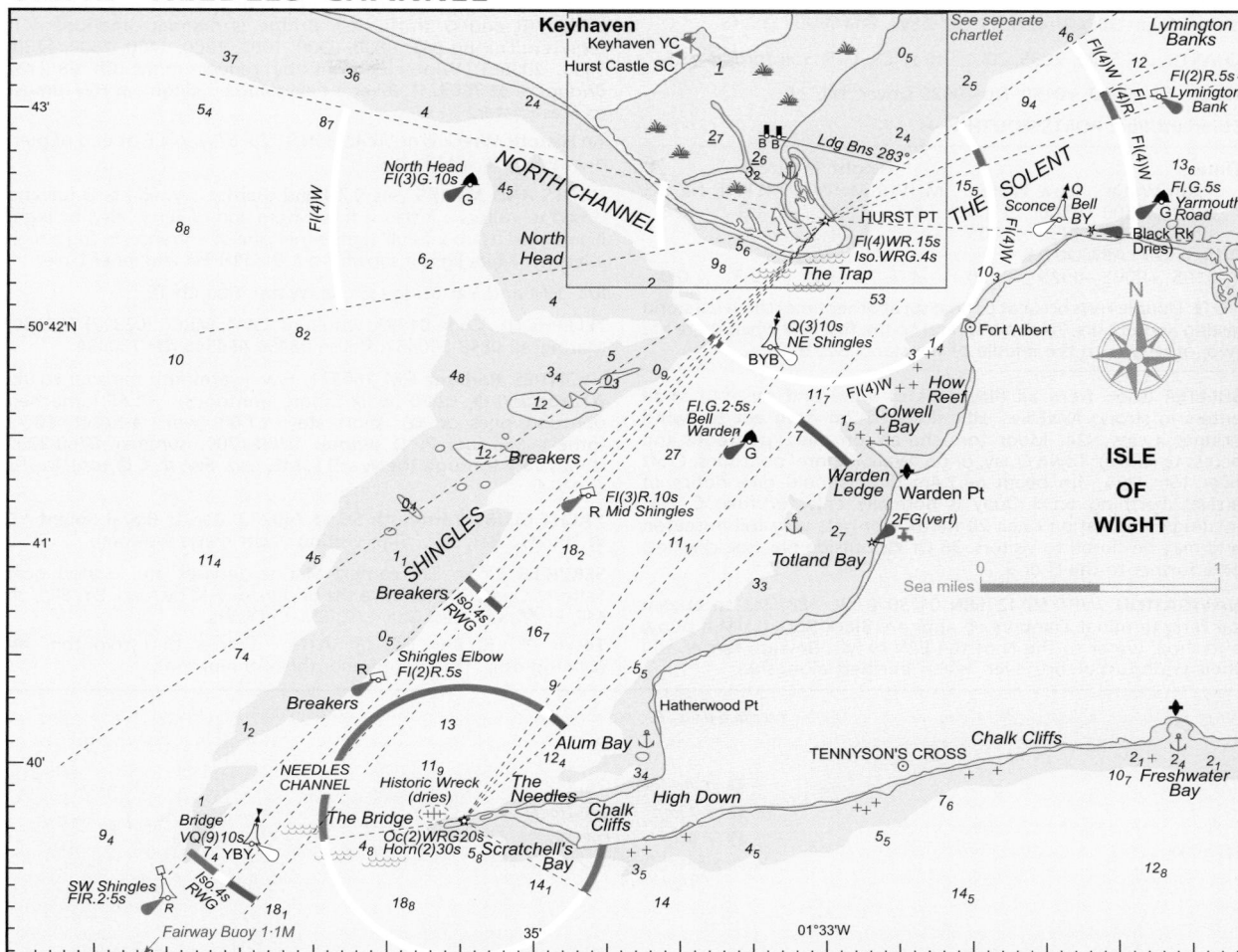

The Needles are distinctive rocks at the W end of the Isle of Wight (see AC 5600, 2035, 2021). By day the chalk cliffs of High Down are conspic from afar but the lt ho may not be seen by day until relatively close. Goose Rk, dries, is about 50m WNW of the Lt ho, 100-150m WSW of which is a drying wreck.

- The NW side of the Needles Chan is defined by the Shingles bank, parts of which dry and on which the sea breaks in the least swell. The SE side of the bank is fairly steep-to, the NW side is less defined. Dredgers work on the Pot Bank, 4ca S of Bridge WCM.

- On the ebb the stream sets very strongly (3-4kn) WSW across the Shingles. The Needles Chan is well lit and buoyed and in fair weather presents no significant problems. But even a SW Force 4 against the ebb will raise breaking seas near Bridge and SW Shingles buoys.

- In bad weather broken water and overfalls extend along The Bridge, a reef which runs 8ca W of the lt ho with its W extremity marked by Bridge WCM lt buoy, but in calm weather it is feasible to pass E of Bridge buoy to avoid the worst of the ebb stream. However, S to W gales against the ebb raise very dangerous breaking seas in the Needles Chan, here only 250m wide. The sea state can be at its worst shortly after LW when the flood has just begun. There is then no wind-over-tide situation, but a substantial swell is raised as a result of the recently turned stream. In such conditions consider using North Channel; the E route to the Solent, S of the IOW and via Nab Tower; or find shelter at Poole or Studland.

- In strong winds the North Channel, N of the Shingles, is preferable to the Needles Channel. The two join S off Hurst Point where overfalls and tide rips may be met. Beware The Trap, a shoal spit extending 150m SE of Hurst Castle.

ANCHORAGES BETWEEN THE NEEDLES AND YARMOUTH

ALUM BAY, 50°40'·10N 01°34'·33W. AC 5600, 2021. Tides as for Totland Bay. Very good shelter in E and S winds, but squally in gales. Distinctive white cliffs to S and multi-coloured cliffs and chairlift to E. Appr from due W of chairlift to clear Five Fingers Rk, to the N and Long Rk, a reef drying 0·9m at its E end, to the S. ⚓ in about 4m.

TOTLAND BAY, 50°40'·98N 01°32'·86W. AC 5600, 2035. Tides, see 9.2.9; ML 1·9m. Good shelter in E'lies in wide shelving bay between Warden Ledge (rks 4ca offshore) to the N, and Hatherwood Pt to the SW. Appr W of Warden SHM buoy Fl G 2·5s to ⚓ out of the stream in 2m between pier (2FG vert) and old LB house; good holding. Colwell Bay, to the N between Warden Pt and Fort Albert, is generally rocky and shallow.

ANCHORAGE EAST OF THE NEEDLES, SOUTH IOW

FRESHWATER BAY, 50°40'·07N 01°30'·61W. AC 5600, 2021. Tides see 9.2.9; ML 1·6m. Good shelter from the N, open to the S. The bay is 3·2M E of Needles Lt ho and 1·2M E of Tennyson's Cross. Conspic marks: Redoubt Fort on W side; a hotel on N side; Stag and Mermaid Rks to the E. The bay is shallow, with rocky drying ledges ¾ca either side and a rock (dries 0·1m) almost in the centre. Best to ⚓ in about 2m just outside the bay. 🛒, R, Bar, ✉.

9.2.13 YARMOUTH

Isle of Wight **50°42'·42N 01°30'·05W** ✿✿✿✿👐👐✿✿✿

CHARTS AC 5600, 2035, 2021; Imray C3, C15; Stanfords 24, 25.

TIDES Sp –0050, +0150, Np +0020 Dover; ML 2·0

Standard Port PORTSMOUTH (→)

Times				Height (metres)			
High Water		Low Water		MHWS	MHWN	MLWN	MLWS
0000	0600	0500	1100	4·7	3·8	1·9	0·8
1200	1800	1700	2300				
Differences YARMOUTH							
–0105	+0005	–0025	–0030	–1·7	–1·2	–0·3	0·0

NOTE: Double HWs occur at or near sp; at other times there is a stand lasting about 2 hrs. Predictions refer to the first HW when there are two; otherwise to the middle of the stand. See 9.2.9.

SHELTER Good from all directions of wind and sea, but swell enters in strong N/NE'lies. Hbr dredged 2m from ent to swing bridge; access H24. Moor fore-and-aft on piles, pontoons (no access to shore), Town Quay, or on 'Walk Ashore' pontoons. Craft over 15m LOA, 4m beam or 2·4m draft should give notice of arrival. Berthing on S Quay is normally only for fuel, C, FW, loading/embarkation (max 20 mins). Hbr gets very full in season and may be closed to visitors. 38 Or 🛥s outside hbr (see chartlet) or ⚓ further to the N or S.

NAVIGATION WPT 50°42'·58N 01°30'·01W, 188°/2ca to abeam car ferry terminal. Dangers on appr are Black Rock (SHM lt buoy) and shoal water to the N of the E/W bkwtr. Beware ferries and their wash/turbulence even when berthed alongside.

Caution: strong ebb in the ent at sp. Speed limits: 4kn in hbr and R Yar; 6kn in approaches. ⚓ prohib in hbr and beyond swing bridge (R and G traffic lts). Bridge is manned and opens if required: During BST: 0800, 0900, 1000, 1200, 1400, 1600, 1730, 1830, 2000LT; Winter months: by request only (Ch 68 (*Yar Bridge*) or ☎ 760321). River is navigable by dinghy at HW almost to Freshwater.

An **Historic Wreck** is at 50°42'·55N 01°29'·67W, 2ca E of end of pier; marked by Y SPM buoy.

LIGHTS AND MARKS See 9.2.4 and chartlet. When hbr is full and closed to visitors a R flag is flown from end of Ferry Jetty; by night illuminated 'Harbour Full' signs either side of entrance. In fog a high intensity white light is shown from the Pier Hd and inner E pier.

R/T HM and Yar Bridge Ch 68. Water Taxi Ch 15.

TELEPHONE (Code 01983, whole of IOW); MRCC (02392) 552100; Marinecall 0898 500457; Police 08450 454545; Dr 760434.

FACILITIES Harbour HM 760321, www.yarmouth-harbour.co.uk. Approx 250 🅥, £2·70 (walk ashore pontoons), £1·65 (detached pontoons/piles or 🛥), short stay: £1·00 (walk ashore), £0·72 (other). Slip,Fuel P, D (winter 0700-1700, summer 0700-2200 (times vary through the year)) L, ME, Gaz, FW, ⚓, C (5 ton), Ice, 🔲, ♿, Wi-fi.

YACHT CLUBS Yarmouth SC ☎ 760270, Bar, L; **Royal Solent YC** ☎ 760256, Bar, R, L, Slip; visiting yacht crews welcome.

SERVICES BY in SW corner; Marine Services are located near Salterns Quay, 500m above the bridge, or ½M by road. BY, Slip, ⚓, ME, El, ✖, CH, Gas, Gaz, LPG, SM, C, Divers.

Town 🛒, R, Bar, ✉, Ⓑ, ATM, Ferries to Lymington, ⇌ (Lymington), ✈ (Bournemouth/Southampton).

9.2.14 LYMINGTON

Hampshire 50°45'·13N 01·31'·40W ✿✿✿👙👙👙♻♻♻

CHARTS AC 5600, 2035, 2021; Imray C3, C15; Stanfords 11, 24, 25.

TIDES Sp –0040, +0100, Np +0020 Dover; ML 2·0

Standard Port PORTSMOUTH (→)

Times				Height (metres)			
High Water		Low Water		MHWS	MHWN	MLWN	MLWS
0000	0600	0500	1100	4·7	3·8	1·9	0·8
1200	1800	1700	2300				
Differences LYMINGTON							
–0110	+0005	–0020	–0020	–1·7	–1·2	–0·5	–0·1

NOTE: Double HWs occur at or near sp and on other occasions there is a stand lasting about 2 hrs. Predictions refer to the first HW when there are two. At other times they refer to the middle of the stand. See 9.2.9.

FACILITIES **HM Office** near Lymington Town SC.
Lymington Yacht Haven www.yachthavens.com ☎ 677071. 475+100 Ⓥ, £2.70. 2m depth, all tides access. P, D, BY, ME, El, ✖, C (25 ton), BH (50 ton), CH, Gas, Gaz, LPG, Wi-fi, ◻, ♿, ♒ (mobile).
Dan Bran Pontoon operated by Lymington Harbour Commisssioners (☎ 672014); reserved for rallies and other events.
Berthon Lymington Marina www.berthongroup.co.uk, ☎ 647405. 300+100 Ⓥ, £3.00. Slip, P, D, ME, El, ✖, SM, CH, BH (45 ton), C (80 ton), Gas, Gaz, Wi-fi, ◻, ♿.
Town Quay public pontoon, AB and many ⚓, £14/craft (9·5m-10·5m LOA), £6.50 for short stay; >15m LOA by arrangement with HM; M, WCs, Showers, Slip (see HM), FW, ♿, Ⓔ, SM.
Scrubbing grids (5) See HM for details.

YACHT CLUBS R Lymington YC, R, Bar, ♿. **Lymington Town SC**, R, Bar.

SERVICES M, FW, ME, El, ✖, C (16 ton), CH, Ⓔ, SM, ACA.
Town all facilities, ⇌, Ferries to Yarmouth, IoW, ✈ (Bournemouth or Southampton).

SHELTER Good above Short Reach. In off-shore winds there is good ⚓ off the mud flats outside river entrance.

NAVIGATION WPT 50°44'·23N 01°30'·36W, 319·5°/1·9ca to abeam Nos 1 and 2 piles. There are extensive but well marked mud banks around the entrance. River is accessible at all states of the tide. Min depth 2.2m in mid-chan from ent to Harbour Station; thence 1·7m to Town Quay. Speed limit 6kn; ⚓ in the river is prohibited.

All craft must give way to, and keep clear of, IoW ferries in the very narrow channel. Beware strong cross-tide at river entrance.

LIGHTS AND MARKS Ldg lts 319·5°, both FR 12/17m 8M. Ent marked by Jack-in-the-Basket, Fl R 2s, and by conspic YC starting platform, 60m E of No 1 bn, Fl G 2s. Narrow chan is marked by 8 PHM piles (five Fl R 2s),9 SHM piles (all Fl G 2s) and one lit PHM buoy (Fl R 2s) opposite No7 bcn. Two BW posts, Dir FW, on flats to SE of Cage Boom in line at 007·5° and two RW posts, Dir FW, on flats to SSE of Seymours Post in line at 187·5° ensure lateral separation of ferries passing in the river.

Harper's Post ECM bn, Q (3) 10s 5m 1M, and two FY ldg lts 244° mark the ent into Lymington Yacht Haven.

R/T Marinas VHF Ch **80** M (office hrs).

TELEPHONE (Code 01590) HM 672014; R Lymington YC 672677; Lymington Town SC 674514; Dr 0845 4647; Ⓗ 663000. Police 0845 045 4545; Marinecall 09068 505357; MRCC (023) 9255 2100.

9.2.15 NEWTOWN RIVER

Isle of Wight 50°43'·45N 01°24'·66W ✿✿✿✿✿✿✿✿

CHARTS AC 5600, 2035, 2036, 2021; Imray C3, C15; Stanfords 11, 24, 25.

TIDES Sp –0108, Np +0058, Dover; ML 2·3

Standard Port PORTSMOUTH (→)

Times				Height (metres)			
High Water		Low Water		MHWS	MHWN	MLWN	MLWS
0000	0600	0500	1100	4·7	3·8	1·9	0·8
1200	1800	1700	2300				
Differences YARMOUTH/NEWTOWN ENTRANCE							
–0105	+0005	–0025	–0030	–1·7	–1·2	–0·3	0·0

NOTE: Double HWs occur at or near springs; at other times there is a stand which lasts about 2 hrs. Predictions refer to the first HW when there are two. At other times they refer to the middle of the stand. See 9.2.9.

SHELTER 3½M E of Yarmouth, Newtown gives good shelter, but is exposed to N'ly winds. There are 5 W ⚓s in Clamerkin Lake and 20 W ⚓s in the main arm leading to Shalfleet Quay, R buoys are private; all are numbered; check with HM.

Do not ⚓ beyond boards showing 'Anchorage Limit' due to oyster beds. Fin keel boats can stay afloat from ent to Hamstead landing or to Clamerkin Limit Boards. If no room in river, good ⚓ in 3-5m W of ent, beware rky ledges SSE of Hamstead Ledge SHM lt buoy, and possible underwater obstns.

Public landing on E side of river at Newtown Quay by conspic black boathouse. Eastern peninsula out to Fishhouse Pt is a nature reserve; no landing.

NAVIGATION WPT 50°43'·83N 01°25'·18W, 130°/0·46M to ldg bn. Without local knowledge, best ent is from about HW –4, on the flood but while the mud flats are still visible.

From W, make good Hamstead Ledge SHM lt buoy, thence E to pick up ldg marks.

From E, keep N of Newtown gravel banks where W/SW winds over a sp ebb can raise steep breaking seas; leave PHM Fl R 4s buoy to port.

5kn speed limit in hbr is strictly enforced.

Inside the entrance many perches mark the mud banks. Near junction to Causeway Lake depth is only 0·9m and beyond this water quickly shoals.

At ent to Clamerkin Lake (1·2–1·8m) keep to SE to avoid gravel spit off W shore, marked by two SHM bcns; the rest of chan is marked by occas perches. Beware many oyster beds in Western Haven and Clamerkin Lake.

Rifle Range at top of Clamerkin Lake and in Spur Lake; R flags flown during firing.

High voltage power line across Clamerkin at 50°42'·81N 01°22'·66W has clearance of only 9m and no shore markings.

LIGHTS AND MARKS See 9.2.4 and chartlet. Conspic TV mast (152m) bearing about 150° (3·3M from hbr ent) provides initial approach track. In season a forest of masts inside the hbr are likely to be evident. The ldg bns, 130°, are on Fishhouse Pt on NE side of entrance. Front: RW pile with Y-shaped topmark; rear: R pile with W spherical topmark. Once inside, there are no lights.

R/T None.

TELEPHONE (Code 01983 for whole of IOW) HM 531424; MRCC (02392) 552100; Marinecall 09068 969647; Police 528000; Dr 08448 151428; Taxi 884353.

FACILITIES **Newtown Quay** M £1.22, ⚓ free of charge, L, FW. **Shalfleet Quay** Slip, M, L, AB(drying), dry waste facilities. **Lower Hamstead Landing** L, FW. **R. Seabroke** ☎ 531213, ✗. **Shalfleet Village** 🛒, Bar. **Newtown** ✉, Ⓑ (Yarmouth or Newport), ⇌ (bus to Yarmouth, ferry to Lymington), ✈ (Bournemouth or Southampton).

9.2.16 BEAULIEU RIVER

Hampshire 50°46'·89N 01°21'·72W (Ent) 🕸⚙◊◊◊✿✿✿

CHARTS AC 5600, 2036, 2021; Imray C3, C15; Stanfords 11, 24, 25.

TIDES –0100 and +0140 Dover; ML 2·4

Standard Port PORTSMOUTH (→)

Times				Height (metres)			
High Water		Low Water		MHWS	MHWN	MLWN	MLWS
0000	0600	0500	1100	4·7	3·8	1·9	0·8
1200	1800	1700	2300				
BUCKLERS HARD							
–0040	–0010	+0010	–0010	–1·0	–0·8	–0·2	–0·3
STANSORE POINT							
–0030	–0010	–0005	–0015	–0·7	–0·5	–0·3	–0·3

NOTE: Double HWs occur at or near springs; the 2nd HW is approx 1¾ hrs after the 1st. On other occasions there is a stand which lasts about 2 hrs. The predictions refer to the first HW when there are two, or to the middle of the stand. See 9.2.9.

SHELTER Very good above Needs Ore Pt in all winds. ⚓ possible in reach between Inchmery Ho and Needs Ore Pt, but for facilities proceed to Bucklers Hard Yacht Hbr (3·5M from entrance). No ⚓ E of Inchmery Ho or 1M either side of Bucklers Hard.

NAVIGATION WPT 50°46'·53N 01°21'·33W, 324°/4ca to abeam Beaulieu Spit Dn. Entrance possible LW±2. Speed limit of 5kn applies throughout the river. If possible proceed under power in the river.

Ldg marks at entrance 324° should be carefully aligned due to shoal water either side of ldg line. Possibly more water to NE of line. Seasonal (*Mar-Oct*) ⚓ 3·3ca SE of Beaulieu Spit Dn is nearly on ldg line and is a useful mark to start final approach to river. Beaulieu Spit Dn should be left approx 40m to port. At night keep in W sector of Millennium Bn (Lepe) until No 4 PHM Bn abeam. Many of the landing stages and slips shown on the chartlet and AC 2021 are privately owned and must not be used without permission. The river is navigable for about 2M above Bucklers Hard, but the uppermost reaches are best explored by dinghy. There are alongside drying berths at Beaulieu just below the weir.

LIGHTS AND MARKS See 9.2.4 and chartlet. Front ldg mark is red No 2 Bn, 0·7ca N of Beaulieu Spit Dn; the rear is W edge of Lepe Ho. The Old CG cottages and Boat House are conspic, approx 320m E of Lepe Ho. The river is clearly marked by R and G bns and perches. SHM bns 5, 9, 19 and 21 are all Fl G 4s; PHM bns 8,12 and 20 are Fl R 4s.

R/T None.

TELEPHONE (Code 01590) MRCC (023 92) 552100; Marinecall 09068 969647; Police 08450 454545; Dr 612451 or (02380) 845955; Ⓗ 0845 4647.

FACILITIES **Bucklers Hard Yacht Hbr,** ☎ 616200, www.beaulieu.co.uk 115+20 Ⓥ, £3.10, short stay from £9.50/craft; pile moorings from £9.50/night; detached pontoons £15/night, ⚓ in river £5. Fuel 0900-2000 P, D, ME, El, ⚒, C (1 ton), BH (26 ton), scrubbing grid (£23), SM, Gas, Gaz, CH, ▣, ♿, 🚿, R, Bar.

Royal Southampton YC (Gins Farm) ☎ 616213.

Village Ⓑ, 🛒 (☎ 616293), R, Bar, ✉ (Beaulieu), ATM, 🚌 (bus to Brockenhurst), ✈ (Bournemouth or Southampton).

9.2.17 ISLE OF WIGHT AND SOLENT TIDAL STREAMS

5 Hours before HW Portsmouth (0445 before HW Dover)

4 Hours before HW Portsmouth (0345 before HW Dover)

3 Hours before HW Portsmouth (0245 before HW Dover)

2 Hours before HW Portsmouth (0145 before HW Dover)

1 Hour before HW Portsmouth (0045 before HW Dover)

HW Portsmouth (0015 after HW Dover)

General Area 2: 9.2.3

1 Hour after HW Portsmouth (0115 after HW Dover)

2 Hours after HW Portsmouth (0215 after HW Dover)

3 Hours after HW Portsmouth (0315 after HW Dover)

4 Hours after HW Portsmouth (0415 after HW Dover)

5 Hours after HW Portsmouth (0515 after HW Dover)

6 Hours after HW Portsmouth (0615 after HW Dover)

9.2.18 THE CENTRAL SOLENT

CHARTS AC 5600, 2036.

Reference and websites *Solent Cruising Companion,* Aslett/ Wiley; *Solent Hazards,* Peter Bruce; *Solent Year Book* SCRA; *Yachtsman's Guide* ABP Southampton www.southampton vts.co.uk for detailed live port info including: shipping movements, VTS radar displays (Southampton to S of Nab Tr), webcams, tide & weather. See www.bramblemet.co.uk for live weather & tidal info at the Bramble Bk.

Vessel Traffic Service (VTS) See 5.10. **Southampton VTS** operates on VHF Ch **12** 14, advising Solent shipping between the Needles and Nab Tower including Southampton Water. VTS monitors and coordinates the safe passage of commercial ships. It includes a radar service on request. **QHM Portsmouth,** VHF Ch **11,** controls Portsmouth Harbour and its approaches N of a line from Gilkicker Pt to Outer Spit Buoy.

All small craft in the Solent are strongly advised to monitor VHF Ch 12 Southampton, and/or Ch 11 QHM Portsmouth.

Small Craft and Commercial Shipping Always consider the restricted field of vision from large ships at close quarters and their limited ability to manoeuvre at slow speeds with minimal under keel clearance in restricted waters. Smaller ships keeping clear of these vessels will be encountered outside the channel. Maintain a proper lookout, especially astern. If crossing the main fairway, try to do so at 90° to it. Southampton Hbr byelaw 2003/10 refers. Be aware of the frequent cross-Solent High Speed and Ro-Ro ferries.

The **Precautionary Area** is the potentially dangerous part of the Solent in which large vessels make tight turns into and out of the Thorn Channel leading to Southampton Water. It extends from just NW of Cowes to the Hook buoy N of Calshot Castle (see chartlet and AC 2036). This can be a very busy area. Be particularly alert when between East Lepe and Ryde Middle. Inbound ships pass Prince Consort NCM turning to *port* towards Gurnard NCM, before starting their critical turn to starboard into the Thorn Channel which is, for large ships, very narrow.

Clear Channel Vessels are over 150m LOA and require a clear and unimpeded passage ahead when transiting the Precautionary Area. Vessels may enter the Precautionary Area maintaining a safe distance astern of the 'clear channel vessel'.

Moving Prohibited Zone (MPZ) Any vessel over 150m LOA when in the Precautionary Area is enclosed by an MPZ which extends 1000m ahead of the vessel and 100m on either beam. Small craft under 20m LOA must remain outside the MPZ and use seaman-like anticipation of its route and sea-room required when turning.

Escort Towage for VLCCs From S of the Nab Tr VLCCs over 60,000dwt bound to and from Fawley Marine Terminal will have an escort tug secured to the stern by tow wire. Outwards, the escort tug may leave a tanker at Prince Consort. Use extreme caution when passing round the stern of a large tanker and do not pass between it and the escort tug.

Local Signals Clear Channel & MPZ vessels display a black cylinder by day or 3 all-round ● lts (vert) by night. They are normally preceded by a Harbour Patrol Launch (Ch 12 *Callsign SP*) exhibiting a flashing blue light. Southampton patrol launches have 'HARBOUR MASTER' painted on their superstructure. At night a fixed ● all-round lt is shown above the W masthead light.

Solent Coastguard See 7.14. The Maritime Rescue Control Centre (MRCC) at Lee-on-Solent, ☎ (02392) 552100, coordinates all SAR activities in the Solent District which is bounded by a line from Highcliffe S to mid-channel; E to the Greenwich Lt V; thence N to Beachy Hd. Due to the concentration of small craft in its area it is the busiest CG District in the UK. Solent CG keeps watch on VHF Ch 67/ 16. Uniquely, an initial call to *Solent Coastguard* should be made on Ch 67 and is only for essential traffic – not for radio checks which can sensibly be made with another station. Weather messages broadcast by Solent CG after announcement on Ch 16. See 6.4.

Solent Yacht Racing Buoys Numerous yellow yacht racing buoys are laid throughout the Solent (*seasonal, Mar-Dec*). Most, but not all, are lit Fl Y 4s.

9.2.19 COWES/RIVER MEDINA

Isle of Wight 50°46'·08N 01°17'·95W ✳✳✳✳⚓⚓⚓✿✿✿

CHARTS AC 5600, 2036, 2793; Imray C3, C15; Stanfords 11, 24, 25.

TIDES +0029 Dover; ML 2·7

Standard Port PORTSMOUTH (→)

Times				Height (metres)			
High Water		Low Water		MHWS	MHWN	MLWN	MLWS
0000	0600	0500	1100	4·7	3·8	1·9	0·8
1200	1800	1700	2300				
Differences COWES							
−0015	+0015	0000	−0020	−0·5	−0·3	−0·1	0·0
FOLLY INN							
−0015	+0015	0000	−0020	−0·6	−0·4	−0·1	+0·2
NEWPORT							
	No data		No data	−0·6	−0·4	+0·1	+0·8

NOTE: Double HWs occur at or near sp. At other times there is a stand of about 2 hrs. Times are for the middle of the stand. See 9.2.9.

SHELTER Excellent except outer hbr exposed to winds from N and NE. ⚓ prohib in hbr. 9 large ⚓s off The Green; pontoons S of chain ferry on both sides of river and in Folly Reach; see Facilities for marinas. Good ⚓ in Osborne Bay, 2M E, sheltered from SE to W but exposed to wash from large ships; no landing.

NAVIGATION WPT 50°46'·35N 01°18'·0W, 173°/2·7ca to mid chan between Nos 1 and 2 buoys. On the E side of the harbour entrance, the Shrape Mud extends to Old Castle Pt. R Medina navigable to Newport, but dries S of Folly Inn.

- Yachts must use the main chan near W shore and should motor.
- Beware strong tidal streams, particularly in vicinity of the chain ferry (4·5kn ebb at sp); no sailing through or ⚓ amongst moorings. Sp limit 6kn enforced in hbr.
- Beware frequent ferry movements, High-Speed to W Cowes, large Ro-Ro ferries to E Cowes, and commercial shipping.
- Ro-Ro ferries use thrust when manoeuvring at E Cowes causing considerable turbulence across the river. Hi-Speed ferries turn short round to stbd when appr Jubilee Pontoon.
- The Chain ferry (all round Fl W lt at fore-end) should give way to all traffic; it runs Mon-Sat: 0435-0005, Sun 0635-0005.

LIGHTS AND MARKS See 9.2.4 and chartlet.

R/T Monitor *Cowes Hbr Radio* VHF Ch **69**; and for hbr launches and HM's ⚓s. Yachts >30m LOA should advise arr/dep, and call *Chain Ferry* Ch 69 if passing. Marinas Ch 80. *Hbr Taxi* Ch 77. *Water Taxi* Ch 06. Casualties: (Ch 16/67/69) for ambulance at S end of Trinity Landing. Website: www.cowes.co.uk.

TELEPHONE (Code 01983, for all IOW) Cowes HM 293952, Folly HM (for ferry, berthing and moorings) 07884 400046; MRCC (02392) 552100; Weather Centre (02380) 228844; Marinecall 09068 505357; Police 08450 454545; Ⓗ 524081; Dr 294902; Water taxis 07050 344818 or 07831 331717/299033.

FACILITIES from seaward: **RYS Haven** (strictly members only). **Trinity Landing,** on The Parade, short stay on inner side only, pick-up/landing on outer side, call HM Ch 69. **Venture Quays** on E side of hbr N of ferry terminal, £1.00 (access to shore by water taxi only). **Marinas** from seaward:
Cowes Yacht Haven www.cowesyachthaven.com ☎ 299975; 35+200 Ⓥ, £2.90. ⚓, Gas, Gaz, El, Ⓔ,ME, ✗, SM, C (15 ton), BH (35 ton), Wi-fi, R, Ice, 🛒, 🗑.
Shepard's Wharf Marina ☎ 297821, www.shepards.co.uk, 30 + 100 Ⓥ, £2.30. El, Ⓔ, SM, ⛽, Bar, R. **UKSA** ☎ 294941, info@uksa.org, 5 Ⓥ, £3.30. ⚓, Bar, R.
East Cowes Marina www.eastcowesmarina.co.uk ☎ 293983. 200+130 Ⓥ, £2.95, 🛒, ⚓, Gas, Gaz, CH, Wi-fi, R, Bar. **Services** All marine services available. For details see *Port Handbook & Directory* (free from HM, Hbr Launches and Marinas).
FW at Marinas, Town Quay, Venture Quays, Trinity Landing, Whitegates pontoon and Folly Inn pontoon. **Fuel** Lallows BY (P, D); MST pontoon off Souters BY (P, D). **Scrubbing berths:** Town Quay, UKSA, Sealift, Folly Inn. **Town** All facilities.

YACHT CLUBS Royal Yacht Squadron ☎ 292191. **Royal Corinthian YC** ☎ 292608. **Royal London YC** ☎ 299727. **Island SC** ☎ 296621. **RORC** ☎ 295144 (Cowes Week only). **Cowes Corinthian YC** ☎ 296333. **E Cowes SC** www.eastcowessc.co.uk **Cowes Combined Clubs** ccc@cowesweek.co.uk ☎ 295744. Cowes Week is normally 1st full week in Aug.

FERRIES Red Funnel to/from Southampton: Car/pax – E Cowes; foot pax – W Cowes ☎ (02380) 334010, www.redfunnel.co.uk. **Chain Ferry** ☎ 293041, W/E Cowes.

RIVER MEDINA, FOLLY REACH TO NEWPORT
FOLLY REACH, 50°44'·03N 01°16'·99W. Above Medham ECM lt bn, there are depths of 1m to S Folly bcn. Ⓥ pontoons along W bank (£1·00). HM ☎ 07884 400046 and *Folly Launch* Ch 69. Folly Waterbus 07974 864627/*Waterbus* Ch 77. **Folly Inn** ⚓, ☎ 297171, AB (pontoon) £1.50, M, Slip, scrubbing berth.
Island Harbour Marina, (5ca S of Folly Inn), (96 + 120 Ⓥ), £2.95, ☎ 07929 797780, ⚓, BH (50 ton), D, Gas, Gaz, 🗑, ME, CH, BY, Slip, Bar, R. Ch 80 *Island Harbour Control.* Excellent shelter; approach via marked, dredged channel with waiting pontoon to stbd, withies to port. Access HW ±4 to lock (width 7·9m) 0600-2100 by arrangement (tfc lts). *Ryde* paddle steamer (in ruins) is conspic.
NEWPORT, 50°42'·21N 01°17'·43W. HM ☎ 525994. VHF Ch 69. Tides: See 9.2.9. Special treatment is required as the hbr dries 1·4m. Use the LW time and height differences for Cowes, and the HW height differences for Newport. Any calculated heights which fall below 1·4m should be treated as 1·4m. Above Island Hbr Marina the chan to Newport (1·2M) dries, but from HW Portsmouth −1½ to +2 it carries 2m or more. S from Folly Inn, the Hbr Authority is IWCC. Sp limit 6kn to Seaclose, S of Newport Rowing Club (NRC); thence 4kn to Newport. Buoyed and partially lit chan favours W bank; night appr not advised. Power lines have 33m clearance. 192° ldg marks/lts are W ◇ bns (lit) on E bank.
Odessa Boatyard ☎ 524337, odessa.boatyard@onwight.net, 75+5 Ⓥs pontoons downstream on W side, £1.00. ⚓, 🔧, FW, BY, C (6 ton), CH.
Newport Yacht Hbr ☎ 525994, 50 Ⓥs pontoons on the E/SE sides of the basin have 1·4m HW ±2, £1.66. Bilge keelers lie alongside pontoons (soft mud); fin keelers against quay wall (firm level bottom). Fender boards can be supplied. ⚓, 🔧, FW, BY, C (10 ton), R; Classic Boat Centre. **Town** P & D (cans), El, ✗, Slip, Gaz, Gas.

Continued overleaf

COWES HBR RADIO
VHF CH 69

01° 17'·5W
BY   VQ   *Prince Consort*

6_8

Fl.Y.5s
Trinity House

6_7

16_5

16_5

18'·0 16_5

⊕

Snowden
(Mar-Oct)
Y

Q.G
No1
G
2.FG(vert)
50°46'·0N
RYS   RYS Haven
RCYC   3x2.FG(vert)
RLYC   Trinity Landing

Q.R
No2
R

2_7

2_2

Small Craft Moorings

0_6

The
Shrape Mud

44'·0

The Parade

Iso2s3m6M
ISC

Fl.R.3s3M

Breakwater

1_4

No4
Fl(3)R5s
3_2

See separate
chartlet on
previous page

2.F.G(vert)
Ferry
Town Quay

2.F.G(vert)

2.F.G(vert)

Cowes
Yacht Haven

2.F.G
(vert)

Fl(2)R.5s
No6

2.F.R
(vert)x3

2.F.G
(vert)

CCYC

Shepards
Wharf
Marina

3

Venture
Quays

Ferry
Terminal
(RoRo)

COWES

Thetis
Wharf

2_8

45'·5

metres
cables
0   500
0   2

Souters
Shipyard

Chain
Ferry
See note

**EAST
COWES**

Hammer
Head Crane

DANGER - CHAIN FERRY
When the ferry is berthed, a
max depth of 1.7m below CD
exists over the chains in the
centre of the fairway. When the
chain ferry is underway, the
chains may rise to the surface.

East
Cowes
SC

Clarence
Yard

Unmarked lights on W bank
are 2FG(vert), and on
the E bank 2FR(vert)

UK Sailing
Academy

A

East
Cowes
Marina

45'·0

N

T

3_7

Power
Stn
Chimneys
Kingston Marine
Services

3_3

2_6

2_6
No8
Fl.R.2s

No10
R Fl.R.6s

1_8

1_1

Moorings

1_1

1_1

Folly Inn
Folly Point

Q.G
S.Folly
R

Unmarked lights on
the W bank are 2FG(vert),
and 2FR(vert) on the E bank.

G
R

0_1
G   R

2   2
Island Harbour
Marina

0_9

G   R

Power Cables (33)

50°43'·0N

1_1

N

NRC
R

Ldg Lts 192°

metres
cables
0   500
0   2

1_2
G   R
2F.R(Hor)

2F.R(Hor)

Odessa BY

NEWPORT

1_6

17'·5   01°17'·0W

Note Double HWs occur at Southampton.
The predictions are for the first HW.

TIME ZONE (UT)
For Summer Time add ONE hour in **non-shaded areas**

SOUTHAMPTON LAT 50°54′N LONG 1°24′W
TIMES AND HEIGHTS OF HIGH AND LOW WATERS

Dates in red are SPRINGS
Dates in blue are NEAPS

YEAR 2010

Central S England

JANUARY

Time	m	Time	m
1 0421	0.9	**16** 0502	1.1
1046	4.7	1123	4.4
F 1652	0.6	SA 1722	0.8
2315	4.7	2345	4.4
2 0512	0.7	**17** 0538	1.0
1133	4.8	1155	4.4
SA 1740	0.5	SU 1755	0.8
3 0002	4.7	**18** 0016	4.4
0600	0.7	0610	1.0
SU 1221	4.8	M 1227	4.4
1827	0.4	1825	0.8
4 0050	4.7	**19** 0049	4.3
0647	0.7	0639	1.1
M 1308	4.7	TU 1300	4.3
1913	0.5	1853	0.9
5 0138	4.7	**20** 0122	4.3
0735	0.8	0708	1.2
TU 1355	4.6	W 1333	4.2
1958	0.6	1920	1.1
6 0227	1.0	**21** 0156	4.2
0822	1.0	0738	1.3
W 1444	4.4	TH 1407	4.1
2045	0.9	1951	1.2
7 0319	4.4	**22** 0231	4.1
0912	1.2	0812	1.5
TH 1536	4.2	F 1444	4.0
◑ 2135	1.2	2029	1.4
8 0415	4.2	**23** 0312	4.0
1008	1.5	0856	1.7
F 1635	4.0	SA 1529	3.9
2233	1.5	◐ 2117	1.7
9 0518	4.0	**24** 0404	3.9
1115	1.7	0954	1.8
SA 1746	3.8	SU 1631	3.7
2342	1.7	2222	1.9
10 0630	4.0	**25** 0513	3.8
1229	1.8	1113	1.9
SU 1905	3.8	M 1751	3.7
		2349	1.9
11 0056	1.8	**26** 0634	3.9
0742	4.0	1242	1.8
M 1340	1.7	TU 1916	3.8
2016	3.9		
12 0202	1.7	**27** 0113	1.7
0843	4.1	0749	4.0
TU 1439	1.6	W 1357	1.5
2114	4.0	2027	4.0
13 0257	1.6	**28** 0222	1.4
0933	4.2	0852	4.3
W 1527	1.3	TH 1459	1.1
2200	4.2	2125	4.3
14 0343	1.4	**29** 0321	1.1
1014	4.3	0946	4.5
TH 1608	1.1	F 1553	0.7
2239	4.3	2216	4.5
15 0424	1.2	**30** 0413	0.7
1050	4.4	1035	4.7
F 1647	0.9	SA 1643	0.4
● 2313	4.3	○ 2303	4.7
		31 0502	0.5
		1121	4.8
		SU 1729	0.2
		2348	4.8

FEBRUARY

Time	m	Time	m
1 0549	0.3	**16** 0547	0.7
1205	4.9	1202	4.4
M 1814	0.1	TU 1802	0.7
2 0032	4.8	**17** 0020	4.4
0632	0.3	0614	0.8
TU 1249	4.8	W 1232	4.4
1855	0.2	1828	0.7
3 0116	4.8	**18** 0050	4.3
0714	0.4	0640	0.9
W 1332	4.7	TH 1303	4.3
1935	0.4	1853	0.9
4 0159	4.6	**19** 0121	4.3
0755	0.7	0707	1.0
TH 1416	4.5	F 1335	4.2
2015	0.7	1921	1.0
5 0243	4.4	**20** 0154	4.2
0837	1.0	0739	1.2
F 1501	4.2	SA 1409	4.1
◐ 2057	1.1	1955	1.3
6 0331	4.1	**21** 0231	4.1
0925	1.4	0818	1.4
SA 1553	3.9	SU 1451	3.9
2147	1.6	2039	1.5
7 0429	3.9	**22** 0319	3.9
1026	1.8	0912	1.7
SU 1701	3.6	M 1551	3.8
2259	1.9	◐ 2142	1.8
8 0546	3.7	**23** 0429	3.7
1152	2.0	1031	1.9
M 1835	3.6	TU 1716	3.6
		2317	2.0
9 0031	2.1	**24** 0600	3.7
0717	3.7	1216	1.8
TU 1320	1.9	W 1853	3.7
2003	3.7		
10 0151	1.9	**25** 0057	1.8
0830	3.8	0729	3.9
W 1425	1.7	TH 1342	1.5
2104	3.9	2011	4.0
11 0247	1.7	**26** 0211	1.4
0921	4.0	0837	4.2
TH 1512	1.4	F 1445	1.0
2148	4.1	2110	4.3
12 0330	1.4	**27** 0309	1.0
1000	4.2	0931	4.4
F 1551	1.1	SA 1538	0.6
2223	4.2	2200	4.6
13 0408	1.1	**28** 0400	0.6
1034	4.3	1019	4.7
SA 1628	0.9	SU 1626	0.2
2254	4.3	○ 2245	4.8
14 0443	0.9		
1104	4.4		
SU 1702	0.7		
● 2323	4.4		
15 0517	0.8		
1132	4.4		
M 1734	0.6		
2351	4.4		

MARCH

Time	m	Time	m
1 0447	0.3	**16** 0449	0.7
1102	4.8	1104	4.3
M 1711	0.0	TU 1705	0.6
2327	4.9	2320	4.4
2 0531	0.1	**17** 0519	0.6
1145	4.8	1133	4.4
TU 1753	0.0	W 1734	0.6
		2349	4.4
3 0009	4.9	**18** 0547	0.6
0612	0.1	1203	4.4
W 1226	4.8	TH 1801	0.7
1832	0.1		
4 0050	4.8	**19** 0019	4.4
0650	0.2	0614	0.7
TH 1307	4.7	F 1235	4.4
1909	0.3	1828	0.8
5 0130	4.6	**20** 0052	4.4
0728	0.5	0643	0.8
F 1348	4.4	SA 1309	4.3
1945	0.7	1857	1.0
6 0210	4.3	**21** 0126	4.3
0805	0.9	0716	1.0
SA 1431	4.2	SU 1346	4.2
2023	1.2	1934	1.2
7 0253	4.0	**22** 0205	4.1
0846	1.3	0757	1.3
SU 1520	3.8	M 1432	4.0
◑ 2109	1.7	2020	1.5
8 0345	3.7	**23** 0256	3.9
0941	1.8	0853	1.5
M 1625	3.6	TU 1535	3.8
2219	2.1	◐ 2127	1.8
9 0500	3.5	**24** 0408	3.7
1110	2.0	1015	1.8
TU 1804	3.5	W 1703	3.7
		2305	1.9
10 0005	2.2	**25** 0542	3.7
0644	3.5	1159	1.7
W 1250	2.0	TH 1838	3.8
1941	3.6		
11 0132	2.0	**26** 0042	1.7
0806	3.7	0710	3.9
TH 1359	1.8	F 1322	1.4
2041	3.9	1954	4.1
12 0226	1.7	**27** 0154	1.3
0858	3.9	0818	4.1
F 1445	1.4	SA 1424	0.9
2123	4.1	2051	4.4
13 0307	1.4	**28** 0251	0.9
0936	4.1	0911	4.4
SA 1524	1.1	SU 1516	0.5
2157	4.2	2139	4.6
14 0342	1.1	**29** 0340	0.5
1008	4.2	0958	4.6
SU 1559	0.9	M 1603	0.2
2226	4.3	2222	4.8
15 0416	0.9	**30** 0426	0.2
1037	4.3	1041	4.7
M 1633	0.7	TU 1647	0.1
● 2253	4.4	○ 2304	4.8
		31 0508	0.1
		1122	4.7
		W 1728	0.1
		2344	4.8

APRIL

Time	m	Time	m
1 0548	0.1	**16** 0520	0.6
1203	4.7	1138	4.4
TH 1807	0.2	F 1736	0.7
		2354	4.5
2 0023	4.7	**17** 0552	0.7
0625	0.3	1214	4.4
F 1243	4.5	SA 1808	0.8
1843	0.5		
3 0102	4.5	**18** 0030	4.4
0701	0.6	0626	0.8
SA 1324	4.3	SU 1252	4.3
1918	0.9	1843	1.0
4 0142	4.3	**19** 0109	4.3
0737	0.9	0705	0.9
SU 1407	4.1	M 1336	4.2
1955	1.3	1925	1.2
5 0223	4.0	**20** 0154	4.2
0815	1.3	0751	1.2
M 1455	3.8	TU 1428	4.0
2039	1.7	2018	1.5
6 0312	3.7	**21** 0250	4.0
0905	1.7	0851	1.4
TU 1557	3.6	W 1535	3.9
◑ 2145	2.1	◐ 2128	1.7
7 0418	3.5	**22** 0402	3.8
1022	2.0	1009	1.6
W 1722	3.5	TH 1656	3.8
2323	2.2	2255	1.8
8 0551	3.4	**23** 0527	3.8
1158	2.0	1137	1.5
TH 1855	3.6	F 1820	3.9
9 0049	2.1	**24** 0019	1.6
0719	3.5	0648	3.9
F 1311	1.8	SA 1254	1.3
1959	3.8	1930	4.2
10 0146	1.8	**25** 0128	1.3
0817	3.7	0754	4.1
SA 1402	1.5	SU 1355	1.0
2043	4.0	2026	4.4
11 0229	1.5	**26** 0225	0.9
0858	3.9	0847	4.3
SU 1444	1.3	M 1448	0.7
2119	4.2	2114	4.6
12 0307	1.2	**27** 0315	0.7
0932	4.1	0935	4.5
M 1522	1.0	TU 1536	0.5
2149	4.3	2159	4.7
13 0342	0.9	**28** 0401	0.5
1003	4.2	1019	4.5
TU 1558	0.8	W 1620	0.4
2219	4.4	○ 2240	4.7
14 0416	0.8	**29** 0444	0.4
1033	4.3	1101	4.5
W 1632	0.7	TH 1702	0.4
● 2249	4.4	2321	4.6
15 0449	0.6	**30** 0525	0.4
1105	4.4	1142	4.5
TH 1704	0.7	F 1742	0.6
2320	4.5		

Chart Datum: 2·74 metres below Ordnance Datum (Newlyn). HAT is 5·0 metres above Chart Datum; see 4.5

Note Double HWs occur at Southampton. The predictions are for the first HW.

SOUTHAMPTON LAT 50°54'N LONG 1°24'W
TIMES AND HEIGHTS OF HIGH AND LOW WATERS

TIME ZONE (UT)
For Summer Time add ONE hour in **non-shaded areas**

Dates in red are SPRINGS
Dates in blue are NEAPS

YEAR 2010

MAY

#	Time m	#	Time m
1 SA	0000 4.5 / 0602 0.5 / 1224 4.4 / 1820 0.8	**16** SU	0537 0.7 / 1200 4.4 / 1756 0.9
2 SU	0040 4.4 / 0639 0.7 / 1305 4.3 / 1857 1.1	**17** M	0017 4.5 / 0618 0.7 / 1245 4.4 / 1838 1.0
3 M	0119 4.2 / 0714 1.0 / 1348 4.1 / 1935 1.4	**18** TU	0102 4.4 / 0702 0.8 / 1334 4.3 / 1926 1.1
4 TU	0200 4.0 / 0752 1.3 / 1435 3.9 / 2018 1.7	**19** W	0152 4.3 / 0753 1.0 / 1429 4.2 / 2021 1.3
5 W	0246 3.8 / 0837 1.6 / 1528 3.8 / 2113 2.0	**20** TH	0249 4.1 / 0850 1.2 / 1531 4.1 / 2125 1.5
6 TH	0340 3.6 / 0935 1.8 / 1632 3.7 / 2227 2.1	**21** F	0354 4.0 / 0957 1.3 / 1641 4.1 / 2236 1.5
7 F	0448 3.5 / 1051 1.9 / 1746 3.7 / 2346 2.1	**22** SA	0506 3.9 / 1109 1.3 / 1753 4.1 / 2349 1.5
8 SA	0607 3.5 / 1206 1.9 / 1855 3.8	**23** SU	0619 4.0 / 1218 1.3 / 1900 4.2
9 SU	0049 1.9 / 0716 3.6 / 1307 1.7 / 1948 3.9	**24** M	0056 1.3 / 0725 4.1 / 1322 1.2 / 1958 4.3
10 M	0140 1.6 / 0808 3.8 / 1356 1.5 / 2031 4.1	**25** TU	0155 1.1 / 0823 4.2 / 1418 1.0 / 2050 4.4
11 TU	0223 1.4 / 0850 4.0 / 1439 1.2 / 2109 4.2	**26** W	0249 1.0 / 0914 4.3 / 1509 0.9 / 2137 4.5
12 W	0303 1.1 / 0928 4.1 / 1520 1.1 / 2144 4.4	**27** TH	0337 0.8 / 1001 4.3 / 1556 0.8 / 2221 4.5
13 TH	0342 0.9 / 1004 4.3 / 1559 0.9 / 2220 4.4	**28** F	0422 0.7 / 1046 4.3 / 1641 0.8 / 2303 4.5
14 F	0420 0.8 / 1041 4.4 / 1637 0.8 / 2257 4.5	**29** SA	0504 0.7 / 1128 4.3 / 1723 0.9 / 2342 4.4
15 SA	0458 0.7 / 1119 4.4 / 1716 0.8 / 2335 4.5	**30** SU	0544 0.7 / 1209 4.3 / 1803 1.0
		31 M	0021 4.3 / 0621 0.8 / 1250 4.2 / 1841 1.2

JUNE

#	Time m	#	Time m
1 TU	0101 4.2 / 0656 1.0 / 1330 4.2 / 1918 1.3	**16** W	0057 4.5 / 0700 0.6 / 1329 4.5 / 1925 0.9
2 W	0140 4.1 / 0731 1.2 / 1412 4.1 / 1957 1.5	**17** TH	0146 4.4 / 0749 0.7 / 1421 4.4 / 2016 1.0
3 TH	0221 3.9 / 0809 1.4 / 1456 4.0 / 2040 1.7	**18** F	0239 4.3 / 0840 0.9 / 1516 4.3 / 2110 1.2
4 F	0306 3.8 / 0853 1.6 / 1544 3.9 / 2131 1.9	**19** SA	0335 4.2 / 0935 1.1 / 1616 4.2 / 2209 1.3
5 SA	0357 3.7 / 0947 1.7 / 1639 3.8 / 2233 2.0	**20** SU	0437 4.0 / 1035 1.3 / 1720 4.2 / 2314 1.5
6 SU	0457 3.6 / 1051 1.8 / 1741 3.8 / 2339 1.9	**21** M	0546 3.9 / 1141 1.4 / 1826 4.1
7 M	0605 3.6 / 1159 1.8 / 1843 3.9	**22** TU	0022 1.5 / 0655 3.9 / 1249 1.5 / 1930 4.2
8 TU	0041 1.8 / 0710 3.7 / 1301 1.7 / 1939 4.0	**23** W	0128 1.4 / 0802 4.0 / 1352 1.4 / 2030 4.2
9 W	0135 1.6 / 0806 3.9 / 1355 1.5 / 2028 4.1	**24** TH	0228 1.3 / 0901 4.1 / 1449 1.3 / 2122 4.3
10 TH	0225 1.3 / 0854 4.1 / 1444 1.3 / 2113 4.3	**25** F	0320 1.1 / 0952 4.2 / 1541 1.2 / 2209 4.3
11 F	0311 1.1 / 0939 4.2 / 1531 1.1 / 2156 4.4	**26** SA	0407 1.0 / 1038 4.2 / 1627 1.1 / 2250 4.3
12 SA	0356 0.9 / 1022 4.3 / 1617 1.0 / 2239 4.5	**27** SU	0450 0.9 / 1118 4.3 / 1710 1.1 / 2329 4.3
13 SU	0441 0.7 / 1106 4.4 / 1703 0.9 / 2323 4.5	**28** M	0529 0.8 / 1156 4.3 / 1749 1.1
14 M	0527 0.6 / 1152 4.5 / 1749 0.8	**29** TU	0005 4.3 / 0605 0.8 / 1233 4.3 / 1826 1.1
15 TU	0009 4.6 / 0613 0.6 / 1240 4.5 / 1836 0.8	**30** W	0041 4.2 / 0638 0.9 / 1308 4.2 / 1900 1.2

JULY

#	Time m	#	Time m
1 TH	0117 4.1 / 0710 1.0 / 1344 4.2 / 1932 1.3	**16** F	0131 4.6 / 0735 0.5 / 1402 4.6 / 2000 0.7
2 F	0153 4.0 / 0741 1.2 / 1421 4.1 / 2005 1.5	**17** SA	0219 4.5 / 0820 0.7 / 1451 4.5 / 2047 1.0
3 SA	0231 3.9 / 0815 1.4 / 1500 4.0 / 2043 1.6	**18** SU	0309 4.3 / 0907 1.0 / 1544 4.3 / 2139 1.3
4 SU	0312 3.8 / 0854 1.6 / 1544 3.9 / 2129 1.8	**19** M	0405 4.1 / 1000 1.3 / 1643 4.1 / 2239 1.5
5 M	0400 3.7 / 0944 1.8 / 1636 3.8 / 2227 1.9	**20** TU	0511 3.9 / 1105 1.6 / 1752 4.0 / 2352 1.7
6 TU	0501 3.6 / 1049 1.9 / 1738 3.8 / 2337 1.9	**21** W	0630 3.8 / 1221 1.8 / 1908 3.9
7 W	0612 3.7 / 1204 1.9 / 1846 3.9	**22** TH	0108 1.7 / 0749 3.8 / 1337 1.8 / 2017 4.0
8 TH	0049 1.8 / 0723 3.8 / 1315 1.8 / 1950 4.0	**23** F	0216 1.6 / 0855 4.0 / 1440 1.6 / 2114 4.1
9 F	0152 1.5 / 0826 4.0 / 1416 1.5 / 2046 4.2	**24** SA	0310 1.4 / 0947 4.1 / 1531 1.4 / 2200 4.2
10 SA	0248 1.2 / 0919 4.2 / 1511 1.3 / 2137 4.4	**25** SU	0355 1.1 / 1030 4.2 / 1615 1.2 / 2239 4.3
11 SU	0340 0.9 / 1008 4.4 / 1603 1.0 / 2225 4.5	**26** M	0435 0.9 / 1106 4.3 / 1655 1.1 / 2313 4.3
12 M	0430 0.6 / 1055 4.5 / 1653 0.8 / 2311 4.6	**27** TU	0512 0.8 / 1138 4.3 / 1732 1.0 / 2345 4.3
13 TU	0518 0.5 / 1142 4.6 / 1741 0.6 / 2358 4.7	**28** W	0546 0.7 / 1209 4.3 / 1806 1.0
14 W	0605 0.3 / 1228 4.7 / 1828 0.6	**29** TH	0016 4.3 / 0617 0.8 / 1240 4.3 / 1836 1.0
15 TH	0044 4.7 / 0650 0.3 / 1315 4.7 / 1914 0.6	**30** F	0049 4.2 / 0645 0.9 / 1311 4.3 / 1903 1.1
		31 SA	0121 4.2 / 0711 1.0 / 1344 4.2 / 1930 1.2

AUGUST

#	Time m	#	Time m
1 SU	0154 4.1 / 0739 1.2 / 1417 4.1 / 2001 1.4	**16** M	0240 4.3 / 0838 1.0 / 1511 4.3 / 2106 1.3
2 M	0230 4.0 / 0812 1.4 / 1455 4.0 / 2039 1.6	**17** TU	0333 4.0 / 0927 1.5 / 1607 4.0 / 2205 1.7
3 TU	0311 3.8 / 0854 1.7 / 1540 3.9 / 2129 1.8	**18** W	0440 3.8 / 1033 1.9 / 1720 3.8 / 2324 1.9
4 W	0406 3.7 / 0952 1.9 / 1642 3.8 / 2240 1.9	**19** TH	0610 3.6 / 1203 2.1 / 1850 3.8
5 TH	0522 3.6 / 1114 2.0 / 1801 3.8	**20** F	0055 1.9 / 0741 3.7 / 1330 2.0 / 2007 3.9
6 F	0009 1.9 / 0648 3.7 / 1244 1.9 / 1919 3.9	**21** SA	0207 1.7 / 0847 4.0 / 1433 1.8 / 2103 4.1
7 SA	0129 1.6 / 0803 3.9 / 1358 1.7 / 2026 4.1	**22** SU	0257 1.5 / 0934 4.2 / 1518 1.5 / 2145 4.2
8 SU	0232 1.3 / 0903 4.2 / 1458 1.3 / 2121 4.4	**23** M	0337 1.2 / 1012 4.3 / 1557 1.3 / 2220 4.3
9 M	0327 0.9 / 0953 4.4 / 1551 0.9 / 2210 4.6	**24** TU	0413 0.9 / 1044 4.4 / 1632 1.0 / 2250 4.4
10 TU	0417 0.5 / 1040 4.6 / 1641 0.6 / 2256 4.7	**25** W	0448 0.8 / 1112 4.4 / 1706 0.9 / 2319 4.4
11 W	0505 0.3 / 1125 4.8 / 1728 0.4 / 2340 4.8	**26** TH	0520 0.7 / 1140 4.4 / 1738 0.9 / 2347 4.4
12 TH	0550 0.1 / 1209 4.8 / 1812 0.3	**27** F	0550 0.7 / 1207 4.4 / 1807 0.9
13 F	0024 4.8 / 0633 0.1 / 1253 4.8 / 1855 0.4	**28** SA	0017 4.3 / 0616 0.8 / 1237 4.4 / 1831 1.0
14 SA	0109 4.7 / 0714 0.3 / 1337 4.7 / 1937 0.6	**29** SU	0048 4.3 / 0640 1.0 / 1308 4.3 / 1856 1.1
15 SU	0153 4.6 / 0755 0.6 / 1422 4.5 / 2020 0.9	**30** M	0120 4.2 / 0706 1.2 / 1340 4.2 / 1925 1.3
		31 TU	0153 4.1 / 0738 1.4 / 1415 4.1 / 2001 1.5

Chart Datum: 2·74 metres below Ordnance Datum (Newlyn). HAT is 5·0 metres above Chart Datum; see 4.5

Note Double HWs occur at Southampton. The predictions are for the first HW.

TIME ZONE (UT)
For Summer Time add ONE hour in **non-shaded areas**

SOUTHAMPTON LAT 50°54'N LONG 1°24'W
TIMES AND HEIGHTS OF HIGH AND LOW WATERS

Dates in red are SPRINGS
Dates in blue are NEAPS

YEAR 2010

Central S England

SEPTEMBER

Time	m		Time	m
1 0233	4.0	**16**	0413	3.7
0818	1.7		1004	2.1
W 1459	4.0	TH	1649	3.7
◗ 2050	1.8		2254	2.1
2 0327	3.8	**17**	0548	3.6
0915	1.9		1143	2.2
TH 1602	3.8	F	1826	3.6
2201	2.0			
3 0449	3.7	**18**	0032	2.1
1042	2.1		0722	3.7
F 1729	3.8	SA	1313	2.1
2343	2.0		1946	3.8
4 0624	3.7	**19**	0143	1.9
1224	2.0		0824	4.0
SA 1857	3.9	SU	1410	1.9
			2039	4.0
5 0111	1.7	**20**	0230	1.6
0744	4.0		0908	4.2
SU 1342	1.6	M	1452	1.6
2007	4.2		2119	4.2
6 0217	1.2	**21**	0308	1.3
0844	4.3		0943	4.3
M 1442	1.2	TU	1528	1.3
2103	4.5		2152	4.3
7 0310	0.8	**22**	0343	1.0
0934	4.6		1013	4.4
TU 1534	0.8	W	1602	1.1
2151	4.7		2221	4.4
8 0359	0.4	**23**	0417	0.9
1019	4.8		1040	4.5
W 1622	0.5	TH	1635	0.9
● 2235	4.8	○	2249	4.4
9 0445	0.2	**24**	0449	0.8
1102	4.9		1107	4.5
TH 1707	0.3	F	1706	0.8
2318	4.9		2317	4.5
10 0528	0.1	**25**	0519	0.8
1145	4.9		1134	4.5
F 1751	0.2	SA	1735	0.9
			2346	4.5
11 0001	4.9	**26**	0547	0.9
0609	0.1		1204	4.4
SA 1228	4.9	SU	1802	0.9
1831	0.3			
12 0044	4.8	**27**	0018	4.4
0649	0.4		0613	1.0
SU 1310	4.7	M	1236	4.4
1911	0.6		1828	1.1
13 0127	4.6	**28**	0052	4.3
0728	0.7		0641	1.2
M 1353	4.5	TU	1310	4.3
1951	0.9		1859	1.2
14 0213	4.3	**29**	0128	4.2
0809	1.2		0714	1.4
TU 1439	4.2	W	1347	4.2
2035	1.4		1938	1.5
15 0305	4.0	**30**	0210	4.1
0857	1.6		0758	1.7
W 1534	3.9	TH	1434	4.0
◗ 2131	1.8		2028	1.7

OCTOBER

Time	m		Time	m
1 0309	3.9	**16**	0508	3.7
0858	1.9		1105	2.3
F 1541	3.9	SA	1738	3.6
◗ 2143	1.9		2342	2.1
2 0432	3.8	**17**	0637	3.8
1028	2.1		1229	2.2
SA 1709	3.8	SU	1901	3.7
2323	1.9			
3 0605	3.9	**18**	0055	2.0
1207	1.9		0741	4.0
SU 1837	4.0	M	1329	2.0
			1959	3.9
4 0049	1.6	**19**	0147	1.7
0722	4.1		0828	4.2
M 1322	1.6	TU	1413	1.7
1946	4.2		2042	4.1
5 0153	1.2	**20**	0228	1.5
0822	4.4		0905	4.3
TU 1421	1.2	W	1451	1.4
2041	4.5		2117	4.3
6 0247	0.8	**21**	0305	1.2
0911	4.7		0936	4.4
W 1512	0.8	TH	1527	1.2
2129	4.7		2149	4.4
7 0335	0.5	**22**	0341	1.0
0955	4.9		1006	4.5
TH 1559	0.5	F	1601	1.0
● 2213	4.9		2218	4.5
8 0420	0.3	**23**	0415	0.9
1038	4.9		1035	4.5
F 1643	0.4	SA	1634	0.9
2256	4.9	○	2249	4.5
9 0503	0.3	**24**	0448	0.9
1120	4.9		1105	4.6
SA 1726	0.3	SU	1706	0.9
2338	4.8		2321	4.5
10 0545	0.4	**25**	0520	1.0
1202	4.8		1138	4.5
SU 1807	0.5	M	1737	0.9
			2356	4.5
11 0021	4.7	**26**	0551	1.1
0624	0.6		1212	4.5
M 1244	4.7	TU	1809	1.0
1846	0.7			
12 0104	4.5	**27**	0033	4.4
0703	0.9		0624	1.2
TU 1327	4.4	W	1251	4.4
1925	1.0		1845	1.2
13 0150	4.3	**28**	0114	4.3
0744	1.3		0703	1.4
W 1412	4.2	TH	1333	4.3
2007	1.4		1928	1.4
14 0241	4.0	**29**	0202	4.2
0831	1.8		0751	1.6
TH 1504	3.9	F	1424	4.1
◗ 2058	1.8		2022	1.6
15 0345	3.8	**30**	0303	4.0
0935	2.1		0854	1.8
F 1611	3.7	SA	1530	4.0
2212	2.1	◗	2133	1.7
		31	0420	4.0
			1016	1.9
		SU	1650	3.9
			2259	1.7

NOVEMBER

Time	m		Time	m
1 0542	4.0	**16**	0637	3.9
1142	1.8		1232	2.1
M 1811	4.0	TU	1859	3.8
2 0018	1.5	**17**	0050	1.9
0655	4.2		0733	4.1
TU 1254	1.5	W	1325	1.8
1919	4.2		1954	4.0
3 0123	1.3	**18**	0141	1.7
0755	4.5		0819	4.2
W 1353	1.2	TH	1410	1.6
2016	4.4		2038	4.1
4 0217	1.0	**19**	0224	1.5
0846	4.7		0857	4.4
TH 1446	0.9	F	1450	1.4
2106	4.6		2116	4.3
5 0307	0.7	**20**	0305	1.3
0932	4.8		0933	4.5
F 1534	0.7	SA	1529	1.2
2152	4.7		2151	4.4
6 0354	0.6	**21**	0343	1.1
1016	4.9		1007	4.5
SA 1620	0.6	SU	1606	1.0
● 2236	4.7	○	2226	4.5
7 0438	0.6	**22**	0421	1.1
1058	4.8		1042	4.6
SU 1704	0.6	M	1643	0.9
2320	4.7		2303	4.5
8 0521	0.7	**23**	0458	1.0
1140	4.7		1119	4.6
M 1745	0.6	TU	1720	0.9
			2341	4.5
9 0003	4.6	**24**	0536	1.0
0602	0.9		1158	4.6
TU 1223	4.6	W	1759	0.9
1824	0.8			
10 0047	4.5	**25**	0023	4.5
0642	1.1		0615	1.1
W 1305	4.4	TH	1240	4.5
1903	1.1		1839	1.0
11 0132	4.3	**26**	0108	4.4
0723	1.4		0659	1.3
TH 1348	4.2	F	1326	4.4
1943	1.3		1925	1.1
12 0219	4.1	**27**	0158	4.3
0807	1.7		0749	1.4
F 1435	4.0	SA	1417	4.3
2027	1.6		2017	1.3
13 0312	4.0	**28**	0255	4.2
0900	2.0		0847	1.6
SA 1528	3.8	SU	1516	4.2
◗ 2122	1.9		2118	1.4
14 0415	3.8	**29**	0400	4.2
1009	2.2		0955	1.7
SU 1633	3.7	M	1624	4.1
2233	2.0		2227	1.5
15 0527	3.8	**30**	0511	4.2
1126	2.2		1108	1.7
M 1748	3.7	TU	1737	4.1
2347	2.0		2339	1.5

DECEMBER

Time	m		Time	m
1 0622	4.2	**16**	0625	3.9
1219	1.6		1226	2.0
W 1847	4.1	TH	1853	3.8
2 0046	1.4	**17**	0046	1.9
0725	4.4		0726	4.0
TH 1324	1.4	F	1325	1.8
1950	4.3		1954	3.9
3 0147	1.2	**18**	0142	1.8
0821	4.5		0818	4.2
F 1421	1.2	SA	1415	1.6
2046	4.4		2044	4.1
4 0242	1.1	**19**	0231	1.5
0912	4.6		0903	4.3
SA 1513	1.0	SU	1500	1.3
2136	4.5		2128	4.3
5 0332	1.0	**20**	0316	1.3
0959	4.7		0944	4.5
SU 1602	0.9	M	1544	1.1
● 2223	4.5		2209	4.4
6 0419	0.9	**21**	0400	1.1
1043	4.6		1025	4.6
M 1647	0.8	TU	1626	0.9
2308	4.5	○	2249	4.5
7 0503	0.9	**22**	0443	1.0
1125	4.6		1105	4.6
TU 1729	0.8	W	1709	0.8
2350	4.5		2331	4.6
8 0546	1.0	**23**	0526	0.9
1206	4.5		1147	4.7
W 1808	0.8	TH	1751	0.7
9 0032	4.4	**24**	0014	4.6
0625	1.1		0609	0.9
TH 1246	4.4	F	1231	4.6
1845	1.0		1834	0.7
10 0113	4.4	**25**	0100	4.6
0704	1.3		0654	0.9
F 1326	4.3	SA	1316	4.6
1921	1.1		1919	0.8
11 0154	4.3	**26**	0147	4.5
0743	1.5		0741	1.0
SA 1406	4.1	SU	1404	4.5
1957	1.4		2006	0.9
12 0237	4.1	**27**	0238	4.4
0824	1.7		0831	1.2
SU 1449	4.0	M	1455	4.3
2037	1.6		2056	1.1
13 0324	4.0	**28**	0333	4.3
0911	1.9		0927	1.4
M 1537	3.8	TU	1553	4.2
◗ 2126	1.8	◗	2153	1.3
14 0417	3.9	**29**	0435	4.2
1009	2.0		1031	1.6
TU 1634	3.7	W	1658	4.0
2228	2.0		2259	1.5
15 0518	3.9	**30**	0544	4.1
1118	2.1		1142	1.6
W 1742	3.7	TH	1812	4.0
2339	2.0			
		31	0011	1.6
			0655	4.2
		F	1256	1.6
			1926	4.0

Chart Datum: 2·74 metres below Ordnance Datum (Newlyn). HAT is 5·0 metres above Chart Datum; see 4.5

SOUTHAMPTON
MEAN SPRING AND NEAP CURVES
Springs occur 2 days after New and Full Moon

MEAN RANGES
Springs 4.0m
Neaps 1.9m

9.2.20 SOUTHAMPTON

Hampshire **50°52′·65N 01°23′·37W** ✦✦✦♦♦♦❀❀

CHARTS AC 5600, 2036, 2041; Imray C3, C15; Stanfords 11, 24.

TIDES HW (1st) −0001 Dover; ML 2·9

Standard Port SOUTHAMPTON (←)

Times				Height (metres)			
High Water		Low Water		MHWS	MHWN	MLWN	MLWS
0400	1100	0000	0600	4·5	3·7	1·8	0·5
1600	2300	1200	1800				
Differences REDBRIDGE							
−0020	+0005	0000	−0005	−0·1	−0·1	−0·1	−0·1

NOTE: At springs there are two separate HWs about 2 hrs apart; at neaps there is a long stand. Predictions are for the first HW when there are two, otherwise for the middle of the stand. See 9.2.9. NE gales and a high barometer may lower sea level by 0·6m.

SHELTER Good in most winds, although a choppy sea builds in SE winds >F4, when it may be best to shelter in marinas. Ⓥ berths available in Hythe, Ocean Village, Shamrock Quay and Kemp's Marinas. No specific yacht anchorages but temporary anchoring is permitted (subject to HM) off club moorings at Netley, Hythe, Weston and Marchwood in about 2m. Keep clear of all channels and Hythe Pier. Public moorings for larger yachts opposite Royal Pier near Gymp Elbow PHM buoy in 4m (contact HM); nearest landing is at Town Quay Marina.

NAVIGATION (See also 9.2.18) WPT 50°50′·0N 01°18′·6W, just S of Hamble Point SCM, to Weston Shelf SHM buoy 312°/4M. Main channels are well marked.

- For a Yachtsman's Guide see (www.southamptonvts.co.uk).
- Yachts should keep just outside the buoyed lit fairway and when crossing it should do so at 90°, abeam Fawley chy, at Cadland and Greenland buoys, abeam Hythe and abeam Town Quay.

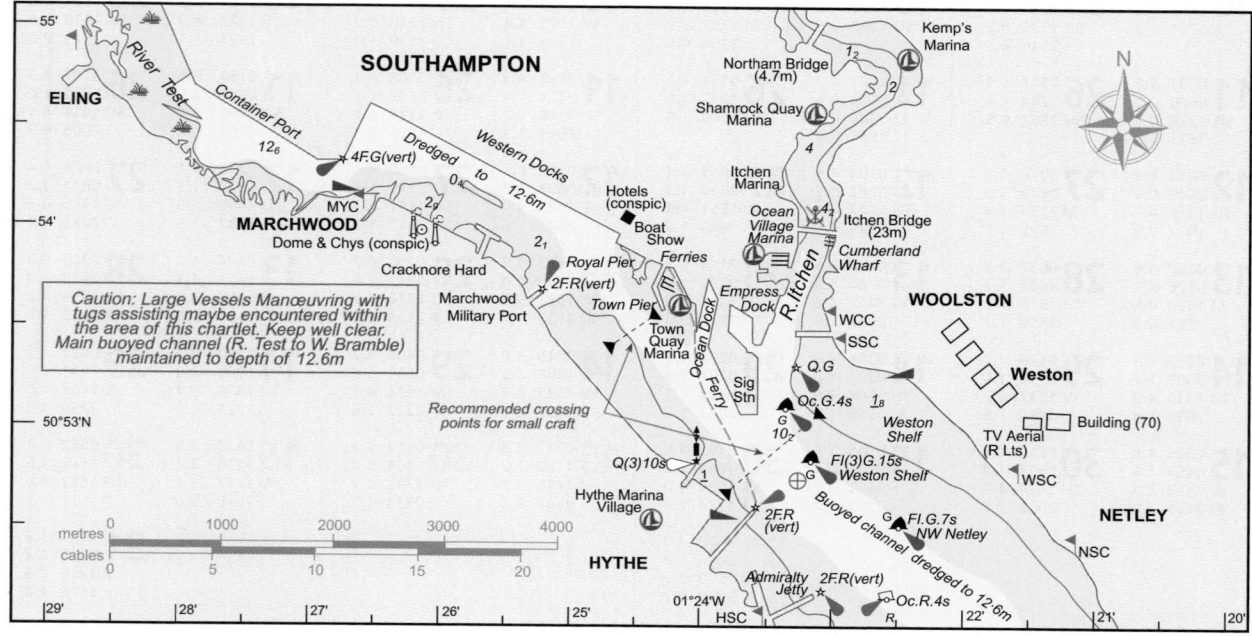

SOUTHAMPTON *continued*

- Caution: several large unlit mooring buoys off Hythe, both sides of the main chan, and elsewhere.
- Frequent hi-speed & Ro-Ro ferries operate through the area.
- Essential to keep clear of very large tankers operating from Fawley and commercial shipping from Southampton. See 9.2.16, Precautionary Area between Cowes and Calshot.

R Test There is foul ground at Marchwood and Royal Pier; extensive container port further upstream. Eling Chan dries.

R Itchen Care is necessary, particularly at night. Above Itchen Bridge the chan bends sharply to port and favours the W bank. There are unlit moorings in the centre of the river. Navigation above Northam Bridge (4·7m clearance) is not advisable. There is a speed limit of 6kn in both rivers N of a line Hythe Pier to Weston Shelf.

LIGHTS AND MARKS See 9.2.4. Main lights shown on chartlet. Fawley chimney (198m, R lts) is conspic by day and night.

Hythe Marina Village, close NW of Hythe Pier: appr chan marked by ECM lit Bn and PHM lit Bn.

Southampton Water divides into Rivers Test and Itchen at Dock Head which is easily identified by conspic silos and a high lattice mast showing traffic sigs which are mandatory for commercial vessels, but may be disregarded by yachts outside the main chans. Beware large ships manoeuvring off Dock Head, and craft leaving either river.

Ent to R Itchen marked by SHM Oc G 4s, beyond which piles with G lts mark E side of chan ldg to Itchen bridge (24·4m); a FW lt at bridge centre marks the main chan.

Above Itchen Bridge, marked by 2 FR (vert) and 2 FG (vert), the principal marks are: Crosshouse lit Bn; Chapel lit Bn.

Caution: 8 large unlit mooring buoys in middle of river.

R/T Vessel Traffic Services (VTS) Centre. Call: *Southampton VTS* Ch **12** 14 16 (H24). Traffic info for small craft broadcast on Ch 12 on the hour 0600-2200 Fri-Sun and Bank Holiday Mons from Easter to last weekend in Oct. From 1 June to 30 Sept broadcasts are every day at the same times.

Southampton Hbr Patrol Call: *Southampton Patrol* VHF Ch **12** 16, 01-28, 60-88 (H24). Marinas VHF Ch **80** M.

Fuel barges in R Itchen, call *Wyefuel* Ch 08.

TELEPHONE (Code 02380) HM ABP & VTS 330022, 339733 outside HO; MRCC 02392 552100; Weather Centre 228844; Marinecall 09068 969647; Police 08450 454545; Hythe Medical Centre ☎ 845955; Ⓗ ☎ 777222, R Soton YC ☎ 223352.

FACILITIES   Marinas:

Hythe Marina Village (210+ some ♥; 2·5m). Ch 80 (call ahead). ☎ 207073, £3·20, access H24; BH (30 ton), C (12 ton), P, D, Gas, Gaz, El, ME, ✖, CH, 🛒, R, Bar, SM, ♻, ♿, Wi-fi. IPTS at lock (2 ● over ○ = free flow) (lock width 8m; max LOA 18m). Waiting pontoon outside lock. Ferries from Hythe pier to Town Quay and Ocean Village.

Ocean Village Marina (450; ♥ welcome). Pre-book Ch 80, ☎ 229385, £3·20 <12·5m, £3·90 12.6-18m, £4.40 18.1-24m (all inc 🔌), access H24, CH, Slip, Gas, Gaz, Kos, ME, ✖, ♻, 🛒, R, Bar, Wi-fi, ♿.

Itchen Marina (50) ☎ 8063 1500; VHF Ch 12. D, BY, C (40 ton); No ♥ berths, but will assist a vessel in difficulty.

Shamrock Quay Marina (220+40♥). ☎ 229461. Pre-book Ch 80. £3·20 <12·5m, £3·90 >12·5m (all inc 🔌), access H24, BH (63 ton), C (12 ton), ME, El, ✖, SM, ♻, R, Bar, 🛒, Wi-fi, CH, Gas, Gaz, Kos.

Kemp's Marina (220; visitors welcome) ☎ 632323, £3.43, access HW±3½, C (5 ton), D, FW, Gas, ME.

Saxon Wharf Repair/refit for large yachts ☎ 339490.

Town Quay Marina (133 Annual B/holders only, no ♥) ☎ 234397, access H24 (2·6m); CH, ♻, R, Bar, ♿; marina ent is a dogleg between two floating wavebreaks (☆ 2 FR and ☆ 2 FG) which appear continuous from seaward. Beware adjacent fast ferries. Craft >20m LOA must get clearance from Southampton VTS to ent/dep Town Quay marina.

YACHT CLUBS
Royal Southampton YC ☎ 223352, Bar, R, M, FW, L, ♻, ♿; **Hythe SC** ☎ 846563; **Marchwood YC** ☎ 666141, Bar, M, C (10 ton), FW, L; **Netley SC** ☎ 454272; **Southampton SC** ☎ 446575; **Weston SC** ☎ 452527; **Eling SC** ☎ 863987.

Services CH, ACA, ✖, Rigging, Spars, SM, ME, El, Ⓔ. Note: D from Itchen Marine ☎ 8063 1500 above Itchen Bridge, nearest petrol by hose is from Hythe marina.

Hards at Hythe, Cracknore, Eling, Mayflower Park (Test), Northam (Itchen). Public landings at Cross House hard, Cross House slip, Block House hard (Itchen), Carnation public hard & Cowporters public hard.

City 🚂, R, Bar, Ⓑ, ✉, ⇌, ✈, Car ferry/Hi Speed Service for foot pax to IOW, ☎ 333042; ferry Town Quay, ☎ 840722, to Hythe.

Reference ABP publish a *Yachtsman's Guide to Southampton Water* obtainable from VTS Centre, Berth 37, Eastern Docks, Southampton SO1 1GG. Please send sae.

9.2.21   RIVER HAMBLE
Hampshire **50°51'·0N 01°18'·50W** ❀❀❀♨♨♨♿♿♿

CHARTS AC 5600, 2036, 2022; Imray C3, C15; Stanfords 11, 24.

TIDES +0020, −0010 Dover; ML 2·9

Standard Port SOUTHAMPTON (←)

Times				Height (metres)			
High Water		Low Water		MHWS	MHWN	MLWN	MLWS
0400	1100	0000	0600	4·5	3·7	1·8	0·5
1600	2300	1200	1800				
Differences WARSASH							
+0020	+0010	+0010	0000	0·0	+0·1	+0·1	+0·3
BURSLEDON							
+0020	+0020	+0010	+0010	+0·1	+0·1	+0·2	+0·2
CALSHOT CASTLE							
0000	+0025	0000	0000	0·0	0·0	+0·2	+0·3

NOTE: Double HWs occur at or near sp; at other times there is a stand of about 2 hrs. Predictions are for the first HW if there are two or for the middle of the stand. See 9.2.9. NE gales can decrease depths by 0·6m.

SHELTER Excellent, with ♥s berths at five main marinas, and at YCs, SCs, BYs and on some Hbr Authority pontoons. Jetty in front of B/W HM's Office Warsash has limited ♥s berths and some ♥s berths at Public Jetty on W bank near Bugle Inn car park. Pontoons at all marinas are lettered A, B et seq from the S end. In mid-stream between Warsash and Hamble Pt Marina is a clearly marked ♥ pontoon, between piles B1 to B7.

NAVIGATION WPT Hamble Point SCM buoy, 50°50'·15N 01°18'·66W, is in the centre of the W sector of Dir 352°, Oc (2) WRG 12s; Nos 1, 3, 5, piles are on the E edge of the G sector.

River can be very crowded and anchoring is prohibited. Unlit piles and buoys are a danger at night. Yachts may not use spinnakers above Warsash Maritime Centre jetty.

Bridge clearances: Road 4·0m; Rly 6·0m; M27 4·3m.

LIGHTS AND MARKS Dir ☆, Oc (2) WRG 12s, 351°-W-353°, leads 352° into river ent. and when midway between No 5 and 7 bns alter 028° in the white sector, 027°-W-029°, of Dir ☆, Iso WRG 6s. Piles Nos 1–10 (to either side of the above 352° and 028° tracks) are lit and fitted with radar refl.

Above Warsash, pontoons and jetties on the E side are marked by 2FG (vert) lts, and those on the W side by 2FR (vert) lts. Lateral piles are mostly Fl G 4s or Fl R 4s (see chartlet).

R/T Commercial and all vessels over 20m call: *Hamble Radio* Ch **68** (Apr-Sep: daily 0600-2200. Oct-Mar: daily 0700-1830). Marinas Ch **80** M. Water Taxi 02380 454512, Ch 77. See also 9.2.23 for VTS and info broadcasts.

TELEPHONE
HM ☎ 01489 576387, HM patrol mob 07718 146380/81/99; MRCC 02392 552100; Marinecall 09068 969647; Police 08450 454545; Seastart 0800 885500.

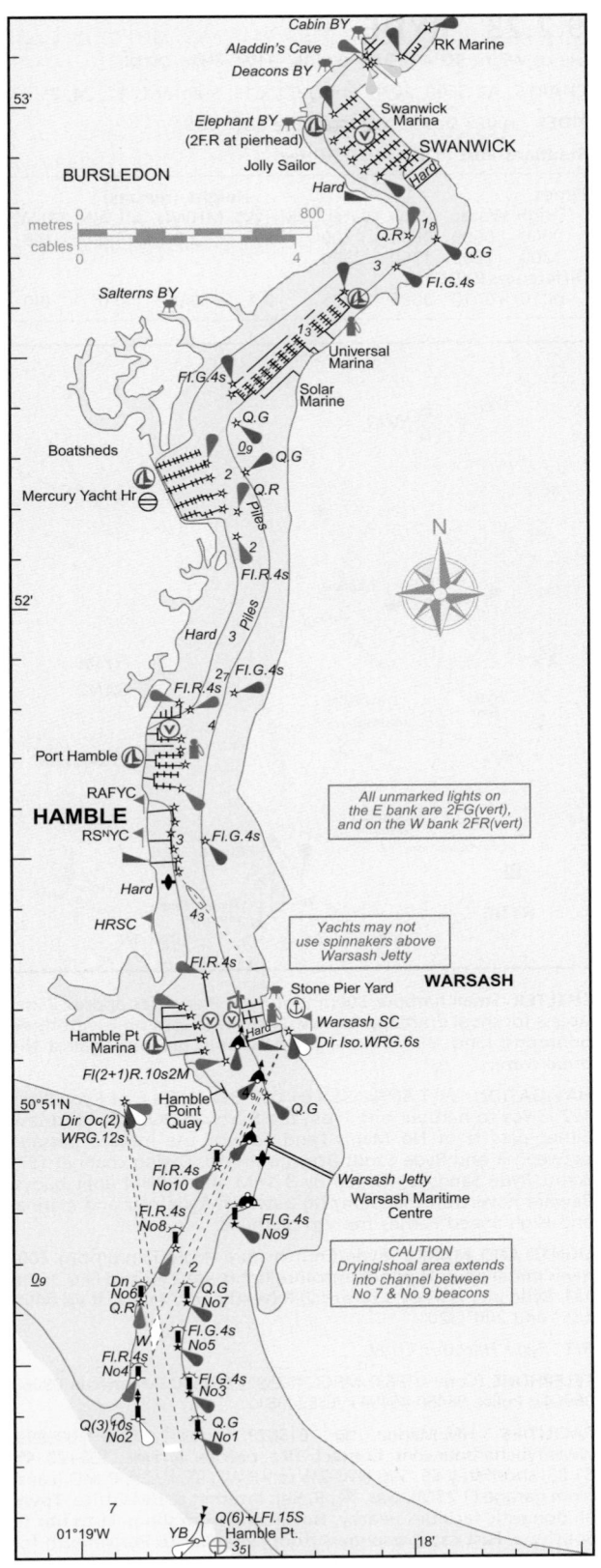

FACILITIES Marinas from seaward:

Hamble Pt Marina (220) ☎ 02380 452464, Wi-fi; pre-book Ch 80. Access H24; £3.20, short stay £7.85/craft, CH, BH (65 ton), C (7 ton), Ⓔ, El, Gas, Gaz, ME, ✕, ◻, YC, Bar, Wi-fi.

Stone Pier Yard (56) ☎ 01489 583813. Access H24; £2.00, FW, ◻, C (20 ton), CH, LPG, D, Gas, Gaz, ME, ✕, Wi-fi.

Port Hamble Marina (310+ Ⓥ) ☎ 02380 452741, Wi-fi; pre-book Ch 80. Access H24; £3.20, ◻, Bar, BH (60 ton), C (7 ton), CH, D, P, Ⓔ, Gas, Gaz, ✕, Slip, Wi-fi.

Mercury Yacht Hbr (346+ Ⓥ) ☎ 02380 455994; pre-book Ch 80. Access H24; £3.20, Bar, BH (20 ton), El, Slip, CH, D, Ⓔ, Gas, Gaz, ME, P, ✕, SM, ◻, ◻, Wi-fi.

Universal Marina (249+ Ⓥ) ☎ 01489 574272; pre-book Ch 80. Access H24; £3.10, short stay £8.00/craft; Bar/café, El, Gas, Gaz, ME, ✕, ◻; BH (80 ton), Wi-fi.

Swanwick Marina (380+ Ⓥ) ☎ 01489 884081 (after 1700, 01489 885262), £2.89, £0.88 <4hrs (min £5), BH (60 ton), C (12 ton), CH, D, Ⓔ, Gas, Gaz, ◻, ◻, ME, P, ✉, ✕, SM, @, Wi-fi, ◻.

The Hbr Authority jetty in front of the conspic B/W HM's Office at Warsash has limited AB (£2.00), also Ⓥ pontoons in mid-stream (both £1.50), ⚓, toilets ashore. Public Jetty on W bank near the Bugle Inn car park. See www.hants.gov.uk/hamble harbour.

YACHT CLUBS Hamble River SC ☎ 02380 452070; RAFYC ☎ 02380 452208, Bar, R, L; Royal Southern YC ☎ 02380 450300; Warsash SC ☎ 01489 583575.

SERVICES Wide range of marine services available; consult marina/HM for locations. CH, Ⓔ, BY, AB, C (12 ton), FW, Gas, Gaz, M, ME, R, ✕, Slip, SM; Riggers, BH (25 ton), ACA, Divers.✉ (Hamble, Bursledon, Warsash and Lower Swanwick); (Hamble, Bursledon, Sarisbury Green, Swanwick, Warsash); ⇌ (Hamble and Bursledon); ✈ (Southampton). *Hamble River Guide* available from HM.

Hards At Warsash, Hamble and Swanwick.

Slips at Warsash, Hamble, Bursledon & Lower Swanwick.

Maintenance piles at Warsash by HM's slipway; on W bank upriver of public jetty near Bugle; by slip opposite Swanwick Marina.

ADJACENT HARBOURS

ASHLETT CREEK, Hants, **50°50'·01N 01°19'·49W**. AC 5600, 2038, 2022. Tides approx as Calshot Castle (opposite). Small drying (2·1m) inlet across from R Hamble; best for shoal-draft vessels. Appr at HW close to Fawley Marine Terminal. Unlit chan, marked by 3 PHM buoys, 1 SHM buoy and 2 PHM bns, has four 90° bends. Ldg bns are hard to find; local knowledge desirable. Berth at drying quay. Facilities: AB, M, FW, Slip, Hard, Pub. **Esso SC.**

HILL HEAD, Hants, **50°49'·08N 01°14'·54W**. AC 5600, 2036, 2022. HW +0030 on Dover; see 9.2.25 LEE-ON-SOLENT diffs. Short term ⚓ for small craft at mouth of R Meon. Bar dries ¼M offshore. Ent dries 1·2m at MLWS. Appr on 030° towards Hill Head SC ho (W, conspic); Small hbr to W inside ent (very narrow due to silting) where small yachts can lie in soft mud alongside wall. Facilities: **Hill Head SC** ☎ (01329) 664843. **Hill Head village** ✉, CH, ◻, P & D (cans).

9.2.22 WOOTTON CREEK

Isle of Wight 50°44'·09N 01°12'·77W ❄❄⚓🌢🌸🌸🌸

CHARTS AC 5600, 2036, 2022; Imray C3, C15; Stanfords 11, 24, 25.

TIDES +0023 Dover; ML 2·8. Use RYDE differences. See 9.2.23; see also 9.2.9.

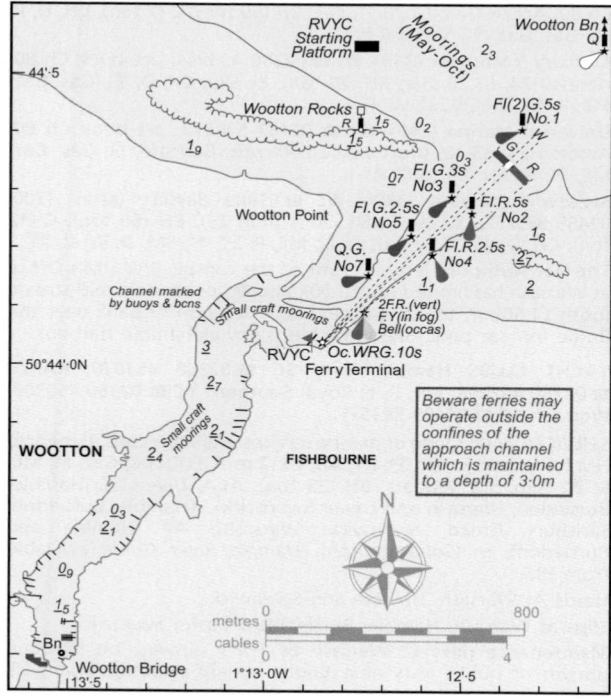

SHELTER Good except in strong N or E winds. Creek dries above the ferry terminal. ABs on RVYC pontoons (dry); No ⚓ in the fairway. Speed limit 5kn.

NAVIGATION WPT Wootton NCM Bn, Q, 50°44'·53N 01°12'·13W, 222°/6·3ca to ferry slip. Beware seasonal moorings (May-Oct) laid between the Starting Platform & No 1 bn. Large car ferries may operate outside the confines of the approach channel when proceeding to and from Fishbourne Ferry Terminal.

LIGHTS AND MARKS Entrance to approach channel due S of SE Ryde Middle SCM and 1·75M W of Ryde Pier. From the W, pass N of the Starting Platform & No 1 bn. The channel is marked by four SHM bns and two PHMs, all lit. Keep in W sector of Dir lt, Oc WRG 10s, 221°-G-224°-W-225½°-R-230½°. By ferry terminal, turn onto ldg marks on W shore △ ▽, which form a ◇ when in transit 270°.

R/T None.

TELEPHONE (Code 01983) Royal Victoria YC 882325; MRCC (023 92) 552100; Marinecall 09068 969647; Police 08450 454545; Dr 562955.

FACILITIES Fishbourne, **Royal Victoria YC**, Slip, AB £1.50/m (shortstay £5.00), FW, R, 🖳, Bar. **Village** Wootton Bridge P & D (cans), 🛒, 🍴, R,✉, Ⓑ (Ryde), ⇌ (ferry to Portsmouth), ✈ (Southampton).

9.2.23 RYDE

Isle of Wight 50°43'·98N 01°09'·31W ❄❄🌢⚓🌸🌸

CHARTS AC 5600, 2036; Imray C3, C15; Stanfords 11, 24, 25.

TIDES +0022 Dover; ML 2·8m. See also 9.2.9.

Standard Port PORTSMOUTH (⟶)

Times				Height (metres)			
High Water		Low Water		MHWS	MHWN	MLWN	MLWS
0000	0600	0500	1100	4·7	3·8	1·9	0·8
1200	1800	1700	2300				
Differences RYDE							
−0010	+0010	−0005	−0005	−0·1	0·0	0·0	0·0

SHELTER Small harbour 300m E of Ryde Pier; dries approx 2·3m. Access for shoal draft approx HW−2½ to +2. Berth on E'ly of three pontoons; long and fin keel yachts should dry out against the breakwater.

NAVIGATION WPT 50°44'·36N 01°09'·13W (2.7ca E of Ryde Pier), 197°/3·9ca to harbour ent. From the E beware Ryde Sand (dries). Either pass N of No Man's Land Fort or use inshore passage between it and Ryde Sands Bcns (lit PHMs). Drying channel 197° across Ryde Sands is marked by 3 SHM and 3 PHM unlit buoys. Beware hovercraft manoeuvring between Ryde pier and marina, and High Speed Ferries from/to pierhead.

LIGHTS AND MARKS Ryde Church spire (Holy Trinity) brg 200° gives initial appr. Harbour entrance lights are 2 FR and Fl G 3s 7m 1M. Ryde pier is lit by 3 sets of 2FR (vert) and a FY fog lt vis 045°-165° and 200°-320°.

R/T *Ryde Harbour* Ch 80.

TELEPHONE (Code 01983) MRCC (02392) 552100; Marinecall 09068 969647; Police 08450 454545; Ⓗ 524081.

FACILITIES **HM/Marina** ☎ 613879, mob 07970 009899, www.rydeharbour.com Contact HM before arrival. 100+70 Ⓥ, £1.35, short stay £5. Slip HW−2½ to +HW2, 🖥, 🖳, ✉, P & D (cans) from garage (1·25M), Gas, 🛒, R, Bar. Internet at HM Office. **Town** all domestic facilities nearby. Hovercraft from slip next to hbr to Southsea. Fast cat (passenger) from Ryde Pier to Portsmouth for mainland ⇌; ✈ Southampton.

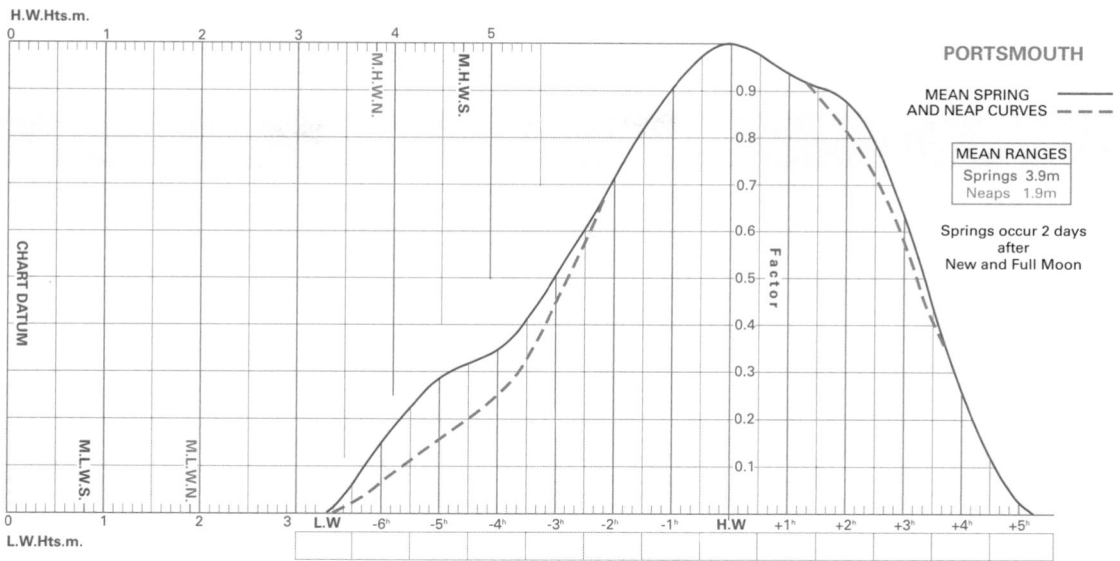

PORTSMOUTH

MEAN SPRING ——
AND NEAP CURVES - - -

MEAN RANGES
Springs 3.9m
Neaps 1.9m

Springs occur 2 days
after
New and Full Moon

9.2.24 BEMBRIDGE

Isle of Wight **50°41′·62N 01°06′·40W** ❄❄❄❄❄❄❄

CHARTS AC 5600, 2037, 2022; Imray C9, C3, C15; Stanfords 10, 24, 25.

TIDES +0020 Dover. See 9.2.9

Standard Port PORTSMOUTH (——)

Times				Height (metres)			
High Water		Low Water		MHWS	MHWN	MLWN	MLWS
0000	0600	0500	1100	4·7	3·8	1·9	0·8
1200	1800	1700	2300				

Differences BEMBRIDGE APPROACHES

–0010	–0005	0000	+0005	+0·1	+0·1	0·0	+0·1

BEMBRIDGE HARBOUR

+0020	0000	+0100	+0020	–1·5	–1·4	–1·3	–1·0

VENTNOR

–0025	–0030	–0025	–0030	–0·8	–0·6	–0·2	+0·2

SANDOWN

0000	+0005	+0010	+0025	–0·6	–0·5	–0·2	0·0

SHELTER Good, but approach difficult in strong N/NE winds. No access LW ±2½ for 1·5m draft; carefully check tide gauge which indicates depth over the bar. Speed limit 6kn. ❶ berths on pontoons at Duver Marina or Fisherman's Wharf; drying out facility on sand to port just inside hbr ent (⚓ F&A). No ⚓ in chan and hbr, but Priory Bay is sheltered ⚓ in winds from S to WNW (dries inshore but ½M off gives 1·5m).

NAVIGATION WPT tide gauge, Fl Y 2s, 50°42′·46N 01°05′·02W, approx 2ca E of ent to well-buoyed, but unlit chan. The bar, between Nos 6 and 10 buoys, almost dries. Avoid the gravel banks between St Helen's Fort, Nodes Pt and N to Seaview, by keeping to ent times above.

LIGHTS AND MARKS St Helen's Fort Fl (3) 10s 16m 8M; ⚓ within 1ca radius of Fort. Conspic W seamark on shore where chan turns S. Beware many unlit Y racing marks off Bembridge and Seaview (Mar-Oct).

R/T Hbr staff Ch 80; Hbr Launch Ch M.

TELEPHONE (Code 01983) HM 872828; MRCC (02392) 552100; Marinecall 09068 969647; Police 08450 454545; Dr 872614.

FACILITIES Duver Marina ☎ 872828. 40+100 ❶ £2.40. &, ▣. **Bembridge Marina** is for permanent berthholders only. **St Helen's Quay** FW, CH. **Brading Haven YC** ☎ 872289, Bar, R, FW. **Drying out area** £6 flat rate, FW. **Bembridge SC** ☎ 872686. **Services:** M, Slip, BY, P & D (cans), ME, El, ✕, Gas. **Town** 🛒, R, Bar, ✉, Ⓑ, ⇌ (Ryde), ✈ (So'ton).

HARBOUR ON S COAST ISLE OF WIGHT

VENTNOR HAVEN, 50°35′·53N 01°12′·50W. AC 2045. Bkwtrs to protect FVs. Very exposed to E to SSE. 8 ⚓ (in <F4; seasonal), ☎ 07976 009260 or VHF CH 17 for availability. ⚓ on quay, P & D (cans). **Town** All domestic facilities, some up a steep hill.

TIME ZONE (UT)
For Summer Time add ONE hour in **non-shaded areas**

PORTSMOUTH   LAT 50°48'N   LONG 1°07'W
TIMES AND HEIGHTS OF HIGH AND LOW WATERS

Dates in red are SPRINGS
Dates in blue are NEAPS

YEAR **2010**

JANUARY

Time	m	Time	m
1 0429	1.0	**16** 0512	1.2
1118	4.8	1152	4.4
F 1700	0.7	SA 1733	1.0
2352	4.8		
2 0519	0.9	**17** 0021	4.5
1207	4.8	0546	1.2
SA 1749	0.6	SU 1225	4.4
		1806	1.0
3 0042	4.9	**18** 0053	4.5
0608	0.8	0618	1.2
SU 1256	4.8	M 1258	4.4
1837	0.5	1836	1.0
4 0132	4.9	**19** 0125	4.5
0657	0.8	0648	1.2
M 1345	4.8	TU 1331	4.4
1924	0.6	1904	1.1
5 0220	4.8	**20** 0157	4.4
0745	0.9	0716	1.3
TU 1434	4.6	W 1404	4.3
2011	0.7	1932	1.1
6 0309	4.7	**21** 0230	4.4
0835	1.1	0747	1.4
W 1523	4.5	TH 1437	4.2
2059	1.0	2003	1.3
7 0358	4.6	**22** 0304	4.3
0927	1.3	0823	1.5
TH 1614	4.3	F 1513	4.1
☽ 2150	1.2	2042	1.4
8 0450	4.4	**23** 0343	4.2
1025	1.5	0909	1.7
F 1710	4.1	SA 1558	4.0
2248	1.5	☽ 2131	1.6
9 0550	4.2	**24** 0435	4.0
1133	1.7	1007	1.8
SA 1818	3.9	SU 1659	3.8
2357	1.8	2237	1.9
10 0659	4.1	**25** 0544	3.9
1246	1.8	1126	1.9
SU 1937	3.9	M 1822	3.8
11 0110	1.8	**26** 0002	1.9
0809	4.1	0706	4.0
M 1355	1.7	TU 1258	1.8
2050	4.0	1948	3.9
12 0216	1.8	**27** 0128	1.8
0911	4.2	0820	4.2
TU 1452	1.6	W 1412	1.5
2148	4.1	2100	4.3
13 0310	1.6	**28** 0236	1.5
1001	4.3	0922	4.4
W 1539	1.4	TH 1511	1.1
2235	4.3	2159	4.5
14 0355	1.4	**29** 0332	1.2
1043	4.4	1016	4.6
TH 1620	1.2	F 1603	0.8
2314	4.4	2252	4.7
15 0435	1.3	**30** 0423	0.9
1119	4.4	1107	4.8
F 1657	1.1	SA 1652	0.5
● 2349	4.5	○ 2341	4.9
		31 0511	0.6
		1156	4.9
		SU 1738	0.3

FEBRUARY

Time	m	Time	m
1 0029	5.0	**16** 0029	4.5
0557	0.5	0556	0.9
M 1244	4.9	TU 1238	4.4
1823	0.3	1813	0.8
2 0115	5.0	**17** 0059	4.5
0642	0.5	0623	1.0
TU 1330	4.9	W 1309	4.4
1906	0.4	1838	0.9
3 0159	4.9	**18** 0129	4.5
0725	0.6	0649	1.0
W 1415	4.7	TH 1340	4.4
1948	0.5	1904	1.0
4 0241	4.8	**19** 0158	4.4
0808	0.8	0717	1.1
TH 1458	4.6	F 1412	4.3
2029	0.8	1934	1.1
5 0323	4.6	**20** 0229	4.4
0852	1.1	0752	1.2
F 1543	4.3	SA 1446	4.2
◐ 2113	1.2	2010	1.3
6 0407	4.3	**21** 0305	4.2
0942	1.5	0833	1.4
SA 1632	4.0	SU 1528	4.0
2205	1.6	2056	1.6
7 0458	4.0	**22** 0353	4.0
1046	1.8	0928	1.7
SU 1735	3.7	M 1629	3.8
2316	1.9	◐ 2201	1.9
8 0608	3.8	**23** 0503	3.8
1210	2.0	1050	1.9
M 1907	3.7	TU 1759	3.7
		2339	2.0
9 0044	2.1	**24** 0634	3.8
0741	3.8	1239	1.8
TU 1333	1.9	W 1930	3.9
2036	3.8		
10 0202	1.9	**25** 0119	1.8
0855	3.9	0759	4.0
W 1435	1.7	TH 1400	1.4
2135	4.0	2046	4.2
11 0259	1.7	**26** 0229	1.4
0947	4.1	0906	4.3
TH 1522	1.4	F 1459	1.0
2220	4.2	2145	4.5
12 0341	1.4	**27** 0323	1.0
1028	4.3	1001	4.5
F 1601	1.2	SA 1549	0.7
2257	4.4	2236	4.7
13 0418	1.1	**28** 0411	0.7
1103	4.4	1051	4.7
SA 1637	1.0	SU 1636	0.4
2329	4.5	○ 2323	4.9
14 0453	1.1		
1135	4.4		
SU 1711	0.9		
● 2359	4.5		
15 0526	1.0		
1206	4.4		
M 1744	0.8		

MARCH

Time	m	Time	m
1 0456	0.5	**16** 0459	0.9
1139	4.9	1141	4.4
M 1720	0.2	TU 1716	0.8
2 0008	5.0	**17** 0000	4.5
0539	0.3	0528	0.8
TU 1225	4.9	W 1213	4.5
1802	0.2	1745	0.8
3 0052	5.0	**18** 0030	4.5
0621	0.3	0556	0.8
W 1310	4.9	TH 1246	4.5
1843	0.3	1811	0.8
4 0133	4.9	**19** 0100	4.5
0701	0.5	0623	0.8
TH 1352	4.8	F 1318	4.5
1921	0.5	1839	0.9
5 0211	4.8	**20** 0131	4.5
0740	0.7	0653	0.9
F 1433	4.6	SA 1352	4.4
1959	0.9	1911	1.1
6 0248	4.5	**21** 0203	4.4
0818	1.0	0729	1.1
SA 1514	4.3	SU 1429	4.3
2038	1.3	1949	1.3
7 0327	4.2	**22** 0241	4.2
0902	1.4	0812	1.3
SU 1600	4.0	M 1515	4.1
☽ 2127	1.7	2038	1.6
8 0412	3.9	**23** 0330	4.0
1000	1.8	0909	1.6
M 1700	3.7	TU 1618	3.9
2240	2.1	☽ 2148	1.9
9 0517	3.6	**24** 0441	3.8
1130	2.0	1035	1.8
TU 1836	3.6	W 1743	3.8
		2330	2.0
10 0018	2.2	**25** 0612	3.8
0705	3.5	1222	1.7
W 1303	2.0	TH 1914	3.9
2012	3.8		
11 0143	2.0	**26** 0105	1.7
0832	3.7	0739	4.0
TH 1408	1.8	F 1341	1.4
2110	4.0	2027	4.2
12 0238	1.7	**27** 0212	1.4
0924	4.0	0846	4.2
F 1455	1.5	SA 1438	1.0
2153	4.2	2125	4.5
13 0318	1.4	**28** 0305	1.0
1004	4.1	0941	4.5
SA 1533	1.2	SU 1528	0.7
2229	4.4	2214	4.8
14 0354	1.2	**29** 0352	0.6
1038	4.3	1031	4.7
SU 1608	1.0	M 1613	0.4
2300	4.5	2300	4.9
15 0427	1.0	**30** 0436	0.4
1109	4.4	1118	4.8
M 1643	0.9	TU 1656	0.2
● 2330	4.5	○ 2344	5.0
		31 0518	0.3
		1203	4.9
		W 1738	0.3

APRIL

Time	m	Time	m
1 0025	4.9	**16** 0001	4.6
0558	0.4	0529	0.8
TH 1247	4.8	F 1222	4.5
1817	0.5	1745	0.9
2 0105	4.9	**17** 0035	4.6
0636	0.5	0601	0.8
F 1329	4.7	SA 1258	4.5
1854	0.7	1819	1.0
3 0142	4.7	**18** 0109	4.5
0712	0.7	0636	0.9
SA 1409	4.5	SU 1337	4.5
1931	1.0	1857	1.1
4 0218	4.5	**19** 0146	4.4
0749	1.0	0717	1.0
SU 1450	4.3	M 1420	4.4
2010	1.3	1941	1.3
5 0255	4.2	**20** 0229	4.3
0830	1.4	0805	1.2
M 1535	4.0	TU 1511	4.2
2058	1.7	2035	1.5
6 0339	3.9	**21** 0322	4.1
0923	1.7	0906	1.4
TU 1631	3.8	W 1615	4.1
☽ 2206	2.1	◐ 2146	1.7
7 0437	3.6	**22** 0431	3.9
1044	2.0	1027	1.6
W 1752	3.7	TH 1732	4.0
2339	2.2	2314	1.8
8 0606	3.5	**23** 0553	3.9
1216	2.0	1155	1.5
TH 1926	3.8	F 1853	4.1
9 0102	2.0	**24** 0038	1.6
0746	3.6	0714	4.0
F 1325	1.8	SA 1310	1.3
2028	4.0	2001	4.3
10 0200	1.8	**25** 0145	1.3
0843	3.8	0820	4.2
SA 1414	1.5	SU 1409	1.0
2112	4.2	2058	4.6
11 0242	1.5	**26** 0239	1.0
0925	4.0	0917	4.5
SU 1455	1.3	M 1500	0.8
2149	4.3	2148	4.7
12 0319	1.2	**27** 0327	0.8
1001	4.2	1008	4.6
M 1533	1.1	TU 1547	0.7
2222	4.4	2235	4.8
13 0354	1.0	**28** 0412	0.6
1036	4.3	1056	4.7
TU 1608	1.0	W 1631	0.6
2255	4.5	○ 2319	4.9
14 0427	0.9	**29** 0455	0.6
1110	4.4	1142	4.7
W 1642	0.9	TH 1713	0.6
● 2328	4.5		
15 0458	0.8	**30** 0001	4.8
1146	4.5	0535	0.6
TH 1714	0.9	F 1226	4.7
		1752	0.7

Chart Datum: 2·73 metres below Ordnance Datum (Newlyn). HAT is 5·1 metres above Chart Datum; see 4.5

TIME ZONE (UT)
For Summer Time add ONE hour in **non-shaded areas**

PORTSMOUTH LAT 50°48′N LONG 1°07′W
TIMES AND HEIGHTS OF HIGH AND LOW WATERS

Dates in red are SPRINGS
Dates in blue are NEAPS

YEAR **2010**

Central S England

MAY

Date	Time m	Time m	Date	Time m	Time m
1 SA	0040 4.7 / 0614 0.7	1308 4.6 / 1831 0.9	**16** SU	0014 4.6 / 0545 0.8	1243 4.6 / 1805 1.0
2 SU	0117 4.6 / 0650 0.9	1348 4.5 / 1908 1.1	**17** M	0055 4.6 / 0628 0.8	1328 4.6 / 1850 1.0
3 M	0153 4.4 / 0727 1.1	1428 4.3 / 1948 1.4	**18** TU	0138 4.5 / 0714 0.9	1416 4.5 / 1939 1.2
4 TU	0231 4.2 / 0807 1.4	1512 4.1 / 2034 1.7	**19** W	0225 4.4 / 0806 1.0	1509 4.4 / 2035 1.3
5 W	0313 3.9 / 0854 1.6	1602 3.9 / 2131 1.9	**20** TH	0320 4.3 / 0905 1.2	1609 4.3 / 2138 1.5
6 TH	0405 3.7 / 0956 1.8	1704 3.8 / 2244 2.1	**21** F	0422 4.1 / 1011 1.3	1715 4.3 / 2249 1.5
7 F	0510 3.6 / 1113 1.9	1815 3.8	**22** SA	0532 4.1 / 1123 1.4	1825 4.3
8 SA	0001 2.0 / 0627 3.6	1225 1.8 / 1922 3.9	**23** SU	0003 1.5 / 0644 4.1	1232 1.3 / 1930 4.4
9 SU	0105 1.9 / 0737 3.7	1321 1.7 / 2015 4.1	**24** M	0111 1.4 / 0751 4.2	1335 1.2 / 2029 4.5
10 M	0154 1.6 / 0831 3.9	1408 1.5 / 2100 4.2	**25** TU	0210 1.2 / 0852 4.3	1431 1.1 / 2123 4.6
11 TU	0236 1.4 / 0916 4.1	1450 1.3 / 2140 4.3	**26** W	0303 1.0 / 0947 4.4	1521 1.0 / 2212 4.7
12 W	0315 1.2 / 0958 4.2	1530 1.2 / 2219 4.5	**27** TH	0351 0.9 / 1038 4.5	1608 1.0 / 2258 4.7
13 TH	0352 1.0 / 1039 4.4	1608 1.1 / 2257 4.5	**28** F	0436 0.8 / 1125 4.6	1652 0.9 / 2340 4.6
14 F	0429 0.9 / 1120 4.5	1646 1.0 / 2336 4.6	**29** SA	0517 0.8 / 1209 4.6	1733 1.0
15 SA	0506 0.8 / 1201 4.6	1725 1.0	**30** SU	0019 4.6 / 0556 0.9	1250 4.5 / 1812 1.1
			31 M	0056 4.5 / 0633 1.0	1330 4.5 / 1850 1.2

JUNE

Date	Time m	Time m	Date	Time m	Time m
1 TU	0132 4.4 / 0709 1.1	1408 4.4 / 1928 1.4	**16** W	0132 4.6 / 0711 0.7	1410 4.7 / 1934 1.0
2 W	0209 4.2 / 0746 1.3	1448 4.2 / 2009 1.6	**17** TH	0221 4.6 / 0801 0.8	1501 4.6 / 2026 1.1
3 TH	0249 4.1 / 0826 1.4	1531 4.1 / 2053 1.7	**18** F	0312 4.4 / 0853 0.9	1554 4.6 / 2121 1.2
4 F	0333 3.9 / 0911 1.6	1618 4.0 / 2145 1.9	**19** SA	0407 4.3 / 0948 1.1	1650 4.4 / 2221 1.3
5 SA	0423 3.8 / 1006 1.8	1712 3.9 / 2247 2.0	**20** SU	0507 4.2 / 1049 1.3	1751 4.4 / 2327 1.5
6 SU	0522 3.7 / 1109 1.8	1811 3.9 / 2353 1.9	**21** M	0613 4.1 / 1154 1.4	1856 4.3
7 M	0627 3.7 / 1214 1.8	1912 4.0	**22** TU	0036 1.5 / 0723 4.1	1302 1.5 / 2000 4.3
8 TU	0054 1.8 / 0732 3.8	1312 1.7 / 2008 4.1	**23** W	0143 1.5 / 0832 4.1	1405 1.5 / 2101 4.4
9 W	0147 1.6 / 0831 4.0	1405 1.5 / 2059 4.3	**24** TH	0243 1.3 / 0933 4.2	1501 1.4 / 2154 4.4
10 TH	0236 1.4 / 0923 4.2	1453 1.4 / 2146 4.4	**25** F	0334 1.2 / 1027 4.4	1551 1.3 / 2242 4.5
11 F	0321 1.2 / 1012 4.4	1539 1.2 / 2231 4.5	**26** SA	0420 1.1 / 1114 4.4	1636 1.2 / 2324 4.5
12 SA	0406 1.0 / 1059 4.5	1624 1.1 / 2315 4.6	**27** SU	0502 1.0 / 1156 4.5	1717 1.1
13 SU	0451 0.8 / 1145 4.6	1710 1.0 / 2359 4.7	**28** M	0002 4.5 / 0540 1.0	1235 4.5 / 1755 1.1
14 M	0537 0.7 / 1232 4.7	1757 0.9	**29** TU	0037 4.4 / 0616 1.0	1310 4.5 / 1831 1.2
15 TU	0044 4.7 / 0623 0.7	1321 4.7 / 1845 0.9	**30** W	0112 4.4 / 0650 1.0	1345 4.4 / 1906 1.3

JULY

Date	Time m	Time m	Date	Time m	Time m
1 TH	0147 4.3 / 0723 1.1	1420 4.4 / 1941 1.4	**16** F	0209 4.7 / 0746 0.6	1443 4.8 / 2009 0.8
2 F	0223 4.2 / 0755 1.3	1456 4.3 / 2015 1.5	**17** SA	0256 4.6 / 0833 0.8	1530 4.7 / 2058 1.0
3 SA	0300 4.1 / 0829 1.4	1534 4.2 / 2054 1.6	**18** SU	0345 4.4 / 0921 1.0	1619 4.5 / 2151 1.3
4 SU	0340 4.0 / 0910 1.6	1616 4.1 / 2139 1.8	**19** M	0438 4.2 / 1015 1.3	1714 4.3 / 2253 1.5
5 M	0427 3.9 / 0959 1.7	1707 4.0 / 2237 1.9	**20** TU	0541 4.0 / 1120 1.6	1819 4.1
6 TU	0525 3.8 / 1102 1.9	1809 4.0 / 2347 1.9	**21** W	0006 1.7 / 0659 3.9	1235 1.8 / 1935 4.1
7 W	0637 3.8 / 1214 1.9	1918 4.0	**22** TH	0123 1.7 / 0820 3.9	1348 1.8 / 2045 4.1
8 TH	0101 1.8 / 0751 3.9	1325 1.8 / 2022 4.2	**23** F	0229 1.6 / 0926 4.1	1449 1.6 / 2142 4.3
9 F	0205 1.5 / 0856 4.1	1426 1.5 / 2118 4.3	**24** SA	0321 1.4 / 1019 4.3	1539 1.5 / 2229 4.4
10 SA	0300 1.3 / 0952 4.3	1520 1.3 / 2209 4.5	**25** SU	0405 1.2 / 1102 4.4	1621 1.3 / 2309 4.4
11 SU	0351 1.0 / 1043 4.5	1610 1.1 / 2258 4.6	**26** M	0444 1.0 / 1141 4.5	1659 1.2 / 2344 4.4
12 M	0439 0.7 / 1132 4.7	1659 0.9 / 2345 4.7	**27** TU	0521 0.9 / 1215 4.5	1735 1.1
13 TU	0527 0.6 / 1221 4.8	1747 0.7	**28** W	0017 4.4 / 0555 0.9	1247 4.5 / 1809 1.1
14 W	0033 4.8 / 0614 0.5	1309 4.9 / 1834 0.7	**29** TH	0049 4.4 / 0627 0.9	1318 4.5 / 1840 1.1
15 TH	0121 4.8 / 0700 0.5	1357 4.9 / 1922 0.7	**30** F	0122 4.4 / 0655 1.0	1349 4.5 / 1910 1.2
			31 SA	0155 4.3 / 0722 1.1	1421 4.4 / 1939 1.3

AUGUST

Date	Time m	Time m	Date	Time m	Time m
1 SU	0227 4.2 / 0751 1.2	1453 4.3 / 2011 1.4	**16** M	0319 4.4 / 0851 1.1	1544 4.5 / 2119 1.3
2 M	0301 4.1 / 0826 1.4	1528 4.2 / 2051 1.6	**17** TU	0409 4.2 / 0942 1.5	1634 4.2 / 2219 1.7
3 TU	0342 4.0 / 0909 1.7	1612 4.1 / 2143 1.8	**18** W	0511 3.9 / 1050 1.9	1741 3.9 / 2339 1.9
4 W	0436 3.8 / 1009 1.9	1712 3.9 / 2254 1.9	**19** TH	0640 3.7 / 1215 2.1	1914 3.8
5 TH	0553 3.8 / 1130 2.0	1832 3.9	**20** F	0105 1.9 / 0812 3.9	1337 2.0 / 2034 4.0
6 F	0027 1.9 / 0721 3.8	1301 1.9 / 1951 4.0	**21** SA	0215 1.7 / 0916 4.1	1438 1.8 / 2130 4.2
7 SA	0147 1.6 / 0836 4.1	1412 1.6 / 2057 4.3	**22** SU	0305 1.4 / 1004 4.3	1524 1.5 / 2213 4.3
8 SU	0247 1.2 / 0936 4.4	1508 1.3 / 2151 4.5	**23** M	0345 1.2 / 1043 4.5	1602 1.3 / 2250 4.4
9 M	0338 0.9 / 1028 4.6	1558 1.0 / 2241 4.7	**24** TU	0421 1.0 / 1118 4.5	1637 1.1 / 2322 4.5
10 TU	0426 0.6 / 1117 4.8	1646 0.7 / 2329 4.8	**25** W	0456 0.9 / 1148 4.6	1711 1.0 / 2352 4.5
11 W	0512 0.4 / 1204 4.9	1732 0.6	**26** TH	0529 0.8 / 1217 4.6	1743 1.0
12 TH	0017 4.9 / 0557 0.3	1250 5.0 / 1817 0.5	**27** F	0023 4.5 / 0559 0.9	1247 4.6 / 1811 1.0
13 F	0104 4.9 / 0641 0.3	1335 5.0 / 1901 0.5	**28** SA	0054 4.5 / 0626 0.9	1316 4.5 / 1838 1.1
14 SA	0149 4.8 / 0724 0.5	1418 4.9 / 1945 0.7	**29** SU	0126 4.4 / 0650 1.1	1346 4.5 / 1905 1.2
15 SU	0234 4.7 / 0807 0.7	1501 4.7 / 2030 1.0	**30** M	0157 4.4 / 0718 1.2	1416 4.4 / 1936 1.3
			31 TU	0230 4.2 / 0751 1.4	1449 4.3 / 2015 1.5

Chart Datum: 2·73 metres below Ordnance Datum (Newlyn). HAT is 5·1 metres above Chart Datum; see 4.5

TIME ZONE (UT)
For Summer Time add ONE hour in **non-shaded areas**

PORTSMOUTH LAT 50°48′N LONG 1°07′W
TIMES AND HEIGHTS OF HIGH AND LOW WATERS

Dates in red are SPRINGS
Dates in blue are NEAPS

YEAR 2010

SEPTEMBER

Time	m		Time	m
1 0309	4.1	**16**	0444	3.9
0833	1.7		1022	2.0
W 1531	4.1		TH 1704	3.8
◑ 2105	1.7		2308	2.0
2 0404	3.9	**17**	0619	3.7
0933	2.0		1154	2.2
TH 1633	3.9		F 1851	3.7
2219	2.0			
3 0525	3.8	**18**	0041	2.0
1104	2.1		0752	3.9
F 1758	3.8		SA 1319	2.1
			2014	3.9
4 0006	1.9	**19**	0151	1.8
0659	3.8		0853	4.1
SA 1248	2.0		SU 1417	1.8
1927	4.0		2108	4.1
5 0132	1.6	**20**	0239	1.5
0819	4.1		0937	4.4
SU 1359	1.6		M 1459	1.5
2037	4.3		2148	4.3
6 0231	1.2	**21**	0317	1.3
0918	4.5		1014	4.5
M 1453	1.2		TU 1535	1.3
2132	4.5		2223	4.4
7 0321	0.8	**22**	0352	1.1
1008	4.7		1046	4.6
TU 1541	0.9		W 1608	1.1
2222	4.8		2253	4.5
8 0407	0.5	**23**	0426	0.9
1055	4.9		1116	4.6
W 1627	0.6		TH 1641	1.0
● 2309	4.9		○ 2323	4.5
9 0451	0.3	**24**	0458	0.9
1141	5.0		1144	4.6
TH 1711	0.5		F 1712	1.0
2355	5.0		2354	4.6
10 0535	0.3	**25**	0529	0.9
1225	5.1		1214	4.6
F 1755	0.4		SA 1741	1.0
11 0041	5.0	**26**	0026	4.6
0617	0.4		0555	1.0
SA 1308	5.0		SU 1244	4.6
1837	0.5		1807	1.0
12 0126	4.9	**27**	0058	4.5
0658	0.6		0621	1.1
SU 1350	4.9		M 1315	4.5
1918	0.7		1835	1.1
13 0209	4.7	**28**	0131	4.5
0738	0.9		0650	1.2
M 1430	4.7		TU 1346	4.4
2000	1.0		1909	1.3
14 0253	4.5	**29**	0206	4.4
0821	1.2		0726	1.4
TU 1511	4.4		W 1421	4.3
2046	1.4		1949	1.5
15 0342	4.2	**30**	0249	4.2
0912	1.7		0811	1.7
W 1559	4.1		TH 1506	4.1
◑ 2145	1.8		2042	1.7

OCTOBER

Time	m		Time	m
1 0347	4.0	**16**	0540	3.8
0915	2.0		1119	2.2
F 1609	3.9		SA 1801	3.7
◑ 2159	1.9		2356	2.1
2 0507	3.9	**17**	0711	3.9
1050	2.1		1241	2.1
SA 1734	3.9		SU 1934	3.8
2343	1.9			
3 0638	4.0	**18**	0108	1.9
1228	2.0		0812	4.1
SU 1903	4.0		M 1341	1.9
			2030	4.0
4 0107	1.6	**19**	0159	1.7
0755	4.2		0858	4.3
M 1338	1.6		TU 1424	1.6
2014	4.3		2112	4.2
5 0207	1.2	**20**	0239	1.5
0854	4.6		0935	4.4
TU 1431	1.2		W 1500	1.4
2110	4.6		2147	4.3
6 0257	0.9	**21**	0316	1.3
0944	4.8		1008	4.5
W 1519	0.9		TH 1535	1.2
2159	4.8		2220	4.5
7 0343	0.6	**22**	0352	1.1
1030	5.0		1039	4.6
TH 1604	0.6		F 1609	1.1
● 2247	4.9		2253	4.5
8 0427	0.5	**23**	0425	1.1
1115	5.1		1111	4.6
F 1648	0.6		SA 1641	1.0
2333	5.0		○ 2326	4.6
9 0510	0.4	**24**	0457	1.1
1159	5.1		1143	4.6
SA 1731	0.5		SU 1712	1.0
10 0019	5.0	**25**	0000	4.6
0551	0.5		0527	1.1
SU 1242	5.0		M 1216	4.6
1812	0.6		1742	1.0
11 0103	4.9	**26**	0036	4.6
0632	0.8		0558	1.2
M 1322	4.8		TU 1250	4.6
1853	0.8		1815	1.1
12 0146	4.7	**27**	0112	4.6
0712	1.0		0632	1.3
TU 1402	4.6		W 1325	4.5
1933	1.1		1853	1.2
13 0230	4.5	**28**	0152	4.5
0755	1.4		0713	1.4
W 1442	4.3		TH 1404	4.4
2017	1.4		1937	1.4
14 0318	4.2	**29**	0239	4.3
0845	1.8		0803	1.7
TH 1528	4.0		F 1453	4.2
◑ 2112	1.8		2033	1.6
15 0417	3.9	**30**	0338	4.2
0952	2.1		0909	1.9
F 1628	3.8		SA 1556	4.0
2227	2.0		◑ 2146	1.7
		31	0451	4.1
			1032	2.0
			SU 1712	4.0
			2312	1.7

NOVEMBER

Time	m		Time	m
1 0613	4.1	**16**	0003	2.0
1157	1.8		0706	4.0
M 1834	4.1		TU 1246	2.0
			1924	3.8
2 0031	1.5	**17**	0104	1.9
0725	4.4		0801	4.2
TU 1307	1.6		W 1337	1.8
1945	4.3		2019	4.0
3 0135	1.3	**18**	0153	1.7
0825	4.6		0845	4.3
W 1404	1.3		TH 1420	1.6
2044	4.5		2104	4.2
4 0228	1.0	**19**	0236	1.5
0917	4.8		0926	4.4
TH 1455	1.0		F 1500	1.4
2137	4.7		2144	4.3
5 0317	0.8	**20**	0315	1.4
1006	4.9		1003	4.5
F 1542	0.8		SA 1537	1.3
2226	4.8		2223	4.5
6 0402	0.7	**21**	0352	1.3
1052	5.0		1040	4.6
SA 1627	0.7		SU 1613	1.1
● 2314	4.9		○ 2301	4.6
7 0447	0.7	**22**	0429	1.2
1136	5.0		1117	4.7
SU 1711	0.7		M 1649	1.0
			2340	4.6
8 0000	4.9	**23**	0505	1.2
0529	0.8		1154	4.7
M 1219	4.9		TU 1725	1.0
1752	0.8			
9 0045	4.8	**24**	0019	4.7
0610	1.0		0542	1.2
TU 1259	4.7		W 1232	4.6
1832	0.9		1804	1.0
10 0128	4.7	**25**	0101	4.7
0651	1.2		0623	1.2
W 1338	4.5		TH 1312	4.6
1912	1.1		1847	1.1
11 0211	4.5	**26**	0145	4.6
0733	1.5		0709	1.3
TH 1418	4.3		F 1356	4.5
1954	1.4		1935	1.2
12 0256	4.3	**27**	0234	4.5
0820	1.7		0801	1.5
F 1501	4.1		SA 1446	4.4
2042	1.7		2029	1.3
13 0346	4.1	**28**	0330	4.4
0916	2.0		0900	1.6
SA 1552	3.9		SU 1543	4.2
◐ 2140	1.9		◐ 2131	1.4
14 0447	4.0	**29**	0433	4.3
1026	2.2		1008	1.7
SU 1655	3.7		M 1649	4.1
2251	2.0		2239	1.5
15 0558	3.9	**30**	0542	4.3
1141	2.2		1121	1.7
M 1812	3.7		TU 1801	4.1
			2350	1.5

DECEMBER

Time	m		Time	m
1 0652	4.4	**16**	0651	4.0
1232	1.6		1239	2.0
W 1914	4.2		TH 1914	3.8
2 0058	1.4	**17**	0057	1.9
0755	4.5		0750	4.1
TH 1336	1.4		F 1336	1.8
2019	4.4		2016	4.0
3 0159	1.3	**18**	0152	1.8
0852	4.7		0844	4.3
F 1433	1.2		SA 1424	1.6
2118	4.5		2110	4.2
4 0253	1.2	**19**	0241	1.6
0945	4.8		0931	4.4
SA 1524	1.1		SU 1509	1.4
2212	4.6		2157	4.4
5 0343	1.1	**20**	0325	1.4
1033	4.8		1014	4.6
SU 1612	0.9		M 1551	1.2
● 2301	4.7		2241	4.5
6 0430	1.0	**21**	0408	1.2
1118	4.8		1056	4.6
M 1657	0.9		TU 1633	1.0
2348	4.7		○ 2324	4.6
7 0513	1.0	**22**	0450	1.1
1201	4.7		1137	4.7
TU 1739	0.9		W 1716	0.9
8 0031	4.7	**23**	0007	4.7
0554	1.1		0532	1.0
W 1241	4.6		TH 1220	4.7
1818	1.0		1759	0.8
9 0113	4.6	**24**	0052	4.7
0634	1.2		0617	1.0
TH 1319	4.5		F 1304	4.7
1855	1.1		1843	0.8
10 0152	4.5	**25**	0138	4.7
0713	1.4		0703	1.0
F 1356	4.3		SA 1350	4.6
1933	1.3		1930	0.8
11 0231	4.4	**26**	0225	4.7
0753	1.6		0752	1.1
SA 1435	4.2		SU 1437	4.5
2012	1.4		2018	0.9
12 0312	4.2	**27**	0315	4.6
0837	1.8		0844	1.2
SU 1517	4.0		M 1529	4.4
2055	1.6		2110	1.1
13 0358	4.1	**28**	0409	4.5
0926	2.0		0941	1.4
M 1604	3.9		TU 1625	4.3
◐ 2145	1.8		◑ 2207	1.3
14 0449	4.0	**29**	0508	4.4
1026	2.1		1046	1.6
TU 1700	3.8		W 1728	4.1
2246	2.0		2312	1.5
15 0548	4.0	**30**	0615	4.3
1134	2.1		1158	1.6
W 1804	3.7		TH 1842	4.0
2353	1.9			
		31	0024	1.6
			0724	4.3
			F 1311	1.6
			1958	4.1

Chart Datum: 2·73 metres below Ordnance Datum (Newlyn). HAT is 5·1 metres above Chart Datum; see 4.5

9.2.25 PORTSMOUTH

Hampshire **50°47'·38N 01°06'·67W** (Entrance)

CHARTS AC 5600, 2037, 2625, 2631, 2629, 2628; Imray C9, C3, C15; Stanfords 11, 10.

TIDES +0020 Dover; ML 2·8

Standard Port PORTSMOUTH (←)

Times				Height (metres)			
High Water		Low Water		MHWS	MHWN	MLWN	MLWS
0500	1000	0000	0600	4·7	3·8	1·9	0·8
1700	2200	1200	1800				

Differences LEE-ON-THE-SOLENT
–0005 +0005 –0015 –0010   –0·2   –0·1   +0·1   +0·2

NOTE: Strong winds from NE to SE, coupled with a high barometer, may lower levels by 1m and delay times of HW and LW by 1hr; the opposite may occur in strong W'lies with low pressure.

SHELTER Excellent. This very large harbour affords shelter in some area from any wind. There are marinas at Gosport, Fareham and Portchester, plus several yacht pontoons/jetties and many swinging moorings. On the Portsmouth side, The Camber offers good shelter, but this is a busy commercial dock and often full; beware Isle of Wight car ferries berthing near the entrance.

Portsmouth is a major Naval Base and Dockyard Port; all vessels come under the authority of the Queen's Harbour Master (QHM). If over 20m LOA, QHM's permission (VHF Ch 11) must be obtained before entering, leaving or moving in the harbour. Fishing and ⚓ in main channels are prohibited.

NAVIGATION WPT No 4 Bar buoy, QR, 50°47'·01N 01°06'·36W, 330°/4·5ca to entrance. Beware strong tidal streams in the narrow entrance which is invariably very busy. Commercial shipping, cross-Channel ferries, warships, High Speed Ferries and small craft all operate within this area.

Approaches: From the W, yachts can use the Swashway Chan (to NW of Spit Sand Fort) which carries about 2m. The transit of the War Memorial and RH edge of block of flats (049·4°) indicates the deepest water, but need not be followed exactly except at LWS. The Inner Swashway (Round Tr brg approx 035°) carries only 0·3m; local knowledge required. Approaching inshore from the E, the submerged barrier, which extends from Southsea to Horse Sand Fort, should only be crossed via the unlit Inshore Boat Passage (0·9m) 1ca off the beach, marked by R & G piles; or via the lit Main Passage (min depth 1·2m), 7ca further S, marked by a G pile and a concrete dolphin.

- **The Small Boat Channel (SBC)** is *mandatory* for craft under 20m LOA when entering or leaving harbour. It runs just outside the W edge of the main dredged channel from abeam No 4 Bar buoy to Ballast Bcn PHM. A depth gauge, showing height above chart datum, is on BC4.

- Craft may not enter harbour on the E side of the main chan and must not enter the SBC on its E side; craft may enter or leave the SBC anywhere on its W side (beware Hamilton Bank, some of which dries).

- Engines (if fitted) must be used when in the SBC between No 4 Bar buoy and Ballast Bcn, *which should always be left to port*.

- If crossing to/from Gunwharf Quays or The Camber obtain approval from QHM (Ch 11) and then do so at 90° to the main channel N of Ballast Bcn.

- At night the SBC is covered by the Oc R sector (324°-330°) of the Dir WRG lt on Fort Blockhouse until close to the hbr ent. Thereafter the Iso R 2s sector (337·5°-345°) of the Dir WRG lt on the dolphin E of Gosport Marina leads 341° through the entrance to Ballast Bcn.

- If joining or leaving the SBC via the Inner Swashway, BC Outer Bn *must* be left to port.

- The SBC may be used even if the main channel is closed.

Speed limit is 10kn (through the water) within the harbour and within 1000 yds of the shore in any part of the Dockyard Port.

Exclusion zones: Do not approach within 50m of any MoD vessel or establishment, or within 100m of any submarine.

Yellow buoys (see chartlet above) are sometimes deployed to delineate the 50m zone. Some ships are protected by a zone of 250m while underway. They are escorted by armed vessels; listen to QHM on VHF 11 or 13 for details. If you fail to respond to warnings it will be assumed you have hostile intentions.

Historic wrecks (see 9.0.3) are: *Mary Rose* (sank 1545) at 50°45'·8N 01°06'·2W (5ca SSW of Spit Sand Fort), and *Invincible* (sank 1758) at 50°44'·36N 01°02'·32W (1·4M ESE of Horse Sand Fort). Both wrecks are marked by SPM buoys, Fl Y 5s.

Navigational piles should not be approached too closely as many are on steep-to mud banks; those lit in Portchester Lake may be difficult to see at night due to background lighting.

FOG ROUTINE

- Broadcast on VHF Ch **11** and **13,** Fog Routine comes into force when QHM considers that visibility is so low that normal shipping movements would be dangerous.

- Small craft may continue at the skipper's discretion, but with great caution, keeping well clear of the main and approach channels. Monitor VHF Ch **11** at all times.

- Be aware that the presence of radar echoes from small vessels within the main channel can cause much doubt and difficulty to the master of a large vessel.

- For their own safety, small craft are strongly advised not to proceed when fog routine is in force.

LIGHTS AND MARKS See 9.2.4 and chartlet. From S and E of the IoW Nab Tower is conspic about 9·5M SE of the harbour entrance. The entrance to the Eastern Solent is between Horse Sand Fort and No Man's Land Fort. Spit Sand Fort lies 160°/1·2M from the harbour entrance. All forts are conspic round stone structures.

St Jude's ✠ spire and Southsea Castle light house in transit 003° lead between Outer Spit SCM buoy and Horse Sand SHM buoy. At night keep in the W sector (000°-003°) of Southsea Castle Dir WRG lt, which also shows Iso 2s 16m 11M, vis 337°-071° (94°).

FIRING RANGE **Tipner Rifle Range**, N of Whale Island, danger area extends 2,500m from firing range. When firing is in progress, R flag or ● lt on Tipner Range FS indicates yachts should clear the range danger area or transit it as quickly as possible.

R/T Yachts should monitor Ch **11** (*QHM*) for traffic and navigational information. *Portsmouth Hbr Radio* (Commercial Port) Ch **14** (H24).

Haslar Marina and *Port Solent* Ch **80** M (H24). *Gosport Marina* call Ch **80** M (HO). Fareham Marine Ch M (summer 0900-1730). Gunwharf Quay Ch 80. **Naval activities** to the S/SE of Portsmouth and IOW may be advised by Solent CG Ch 67 or ☎ 9255 2100; or Naval Ops ☎ 9272 2008. Naval vessels use Ch 13. The positions and times of naval firings and underwater explosions are broadcast daily at 0800 and 1400LT Ch 06; preceded by a Securité call on Ch 16. Warnings of underwater explosions will also be broadcast on Ch 16 at 1 hour, at 30 mins and just before the detonation.

TELEPHONE (Code Portsmouth/Gosport 023) QHM 9272 3124; DQHM 9272 3794; Hbr Control (H24) 9272 3694; Commercial Docks 9229 7395; Camber Berthing Offices ☎ 9229 7395 Ext 310; MRCC 9255 2100; Marinecall 09068 969647; Weather Centre 8022 8844; Police 08450 454545; Ⓗ 822331; Dr Fareham Health Centre (01329) 282911.

FACILITIES **Marinas** from seaward:
Haslar Marina, ☎ 9260 1201. 580+ 50 Ⓥ at L/M pontoons, inboard of green light vessel (Mary Mouse), £2.95. Access H24. Bars & Rs; Gas, Gaz, CH, Wi-fi, @, ME, ⚓, Ⓔ, ▯, 🛒, Slip (upstream of Haslar bridge). All other moorings/pontoons in Haslar Creek are private.

Town Quay (Camber) ☎ 9283 3166, berth on wall, <12m £14.30, short stay (3hrs) £6.40, pay 'KB Boat Park'; no water/power.

Gunwharf Quays ☎ 9283 6732, Wi-fi, www.gunwharf-quays.com, FW, showers, ▯, ⅅ, Ⓥ £3.40 (winter £2.80), short stay £1.05/m, pre-booking essential (or try VHF 80 for short notice requirements). See 9.2.24 (Small Boat Channel).

Gosport Marina www.premiermarinas.com ☎ 9252 4811. 520 inc Ⓥ if berths available, £2.80, short stay £7.30/craft. P, D, CH, C (14 ton) Gas, Bar/R, Wi-fi, 🛒, ▯.

Endeavour Quay ☎ 9258 4200, fully equipped BY (no Ⓥ berths), BH (180 ton), C (16 ton), ⚓, El, ME, Ⓔ.

Royal Clarence Marina www.royalclarencemarina.org. ☎ 9252 3523, (130, Ⓥ space varies, up to 50m); < 12m £25.45/craft (winter £19.09), special rates for yacht rallies. Wi-fi, CH, R.

Port Solent Lock width 9m, portsolent@premiermarinas.com ☎ 9221 0765. 900 inc Ⓥ, £2·89, £1·08/m for <4hrs (min charge £9.30) , P, D, ME, El, Ⓔ, ⚓, BH (40 ton), SM, CH, 🛒, Wi-fi, R, Bar, Gas, Gaz, ▯, ♿.

Note: Portchester Lake is marked by lit and unlit piles. Unusually, PHMs are numbered 57 to 74 (from seaward), and SHMs 95 to 75. Beware unlit naval buoys at the S end. Do not delay crossing Tipner Range, S limit marked by piles 63/87 and N by 70/78.

Portchester Castle is conspic 5ca SSW of marina. Call marina Ch 80 when inbound passing pile 78. Pile B, Fl (4) G 10s, marks the waiting pontoon (see chartlet). Access H24 via chan dredged 1·5m to lock (43m x 9·1m); enter on 3 ● (vert) or on loudspeaker instructions.

Wicormarine (Portchester) ☎ (01329) 237112, www.wicormarine.co.uk, M, D, ME, ⚓, CH, ⅅ, BH (10 ton), C (7 ton), FW, El, Ⓔ, Gas, Gaz, 🛒, R.

Portsmouth Marine Engineering ☎ (01329) 232854, AB (drying), Ⓥ £15/night, showers, C (18 ton).

Upper Quay Marina (Access HW±3) ☎ (023) 9246 9855, 40 AB + Ⓥ by arrangement for short stay only, FW, AC.

TOWN CENTRES
PORTSMOUTH ✉, Ⓑ, CH, ACA, El, Ⓔ, ME, ⚓, BY, SM. ≋, ✈ (Southampton); **Ferries:**
Bilbao: 3/week; 34 Hrs; P&O (www.poferries.com);
Santander: weekly; 24 Hrs; Brittany;
Caen: 3/day; 6 Hrs (HSS 3¾ Hrs); Brittany (www.brittany-ferries.co.uk;
Cherbourg: up to 3/day; 4¾ Hrs (HSS 3 Hrs); Brittany;
St Malo: daily; 10¾; Brittany;
Le Havre: 2-3/day; 5½ Hrs; LD Lines (www.ldline.co.uk);
Channel Islands: 6/week; 7-10½ Hrs; Condor (www.condorferries.co.uk)
IoW: frequent car and passenger services to Ryde and Fishbourne.
Water Taxis between Gunwharf Quays, Historic Dockyard and RN Submarine Museum (Haslar Jetty, Gosport).

GOSPORT ✉, Ⓑ, CH, SM, ACA, El, Ⓔ, ME, ⚓, BY, ≋ (Portsmouth), ✈ (Southampton).
Gosport Hardway Marine ☎ 9258 0420 D, Gas, Gaz, CH.

FAREHAM (01329) ✉, Ⓑ, 🛒, Bar, ≋, ✈ (Southampton). Fareham Lake is well marked, but only partially lit up to Bedenham Pier and unlit thereafter. Chan dries 0·9m in final 5ca to Town Quay.

YACHT CLUBS
Royal Naval Sailing Association ☎ 9252 1100; **Royal Naval & Royal Albert YC** ☎ 9282 5924, M, Bar; **Portsmouth SC** ☎ 9282 0596; **Portchester SC** ☎ 9237 6375, ⚓ (close No71 bn; **Hardway SC** ☎ 92581875, Slip, M, L, FW, C (mast stepping only), AB; **Gosport CC** ☎ (01329) 47014 or (0860) 966390; **Fareham Sailing & Motor Boat Club** ☎ (01329) 280738.

EASTERN APPROACHES TO SOLENT

(AC 2045, 2036) Nab Tr (lt, fog sig), a conspic steel and concrete structure (28m) 4·5M E of Foreland, marks Nab Shoal for larger vessels and is of no direct significance to yachts. NW of Nab Tr the E approach to the Solent via Spithead presents few problems and is far safer in SW/W gales than the Needles Channel.

The main shipping chan is well buoyed and easy to follow, but there is plenty of water for yachts over New Grounds and Warner Shoal when approaching No Man's Land Fort and Horse Sand Fort. A submerged barrier lies N of the latter; the barrier to SW of the former has been demolished and therefore yachts may now pass safely SW of No Man's Land Fort; the Ryde Sand Bcns (both PHM and lit) mark the shallows to the SW. Ryde Sand dries extensively and is a trap for the unwary; so too is Hamilton Bank on the W side of the approach channel to Portsmouth.

Keep well clear of shipping manoeuvring in the Pilot Boarding Areas and using the Nab Deep Water Channel.

Langstone and Chichester Harbours have offlying sands which are dangerous in strong S'ly winds. E and W Winner flank the ent to Langstone Hbr. E and W Pole Sands, drying 1m, lie either side of the ent to Chichester Hbr. Bracklesham Bay is shallow, with a distinct inshore set at certain states of the tide. SE along a low-lying coast is Selsey Bill with extensive offshore rocks and shoals. Pass these to seaward via Owers SCM lt buoy or the Looe Chan, which in suitable conditions is much used by yachts on passage to/from points E of the Solent. Although lit, use with caution at night due to many lobster pot markers; dangerous in onshore gales as searoom is limited by extensive shoals on which the sea breaks.

Looe Channel: ▶ *the E-going flood runs from HW Portsmouth +0430 (HW Dover +0500) until HW Portsmouth –0130 (HW Dover –0100), at sp reaching 2.4kn near the Boulder and Street light buoys which mark its narrow western end; they may be hard to see. Max np rate is 1.2kn.*

The W-going ebb runs from HW Portsmouth –0130 (HW Dover –0100) until HW Portsmouth +0430 (HW Dover +0500), at springs reaching 2.6kn near Boulder and Street. Max neap rate is 1.3kn. ◀

Boulder SHM lt buoy is at the W ent to this chan, about 6M SE of Chichester Bar Bn. Medmery Bank, 3·7m, is 1M WNW of Boulder.

9.2.26 LANGSTONE HARBOUR

Hampshire 50°47'·23N 01°01'·54W (Ent) ❀❀♻♻♻❀❀

CHARTS AC 5600, 2037, 3418; Imray C3, Y33; Stanfords 11, 10.

TIDES +0022 Dover; ML 2·9

Standard Port PORTSMOUTH (←—)

Times				Height (metres)			
High Water		Low Water		MHWS	MHWN	MLWN	MLWS
0500	1000	0000	0600	4·7	3·8	1·9	0·8
1700	2200	1200	1800				
Differences LANGSTONE							
0000	–0015	0000	–0010	+0·1	+0·1	0·0	0·0
NAB TOWER							
+0015	0000	+0015	+0015	–0·2	0·0	+0·2	0·0
SELSEY BILL							
+0010	–0010	+0035	+0020	+0·5	+0·3	–0·1	–0·2

SHELTER Very good in marina (2·4m) to W inside ent, access HW±3 over tidal flap 1·6m CD; waiting pontoon. Ent is 7m wide. 6 Y ♻s on W side of harbour entrance, max LOA 9m. Or ⚓ out of the fairway in Russell's Lake or Langstone Chan (water ski area); or see HM (E side of ent). Hbr speed limit 10kn; 5kn in Southsea Marina channel.

NAVIGATION WPT 50°46'·31N 01°01'·36W, Langstone Fairway SWM Bcn 348°/9·4ca to QR light at ent (Eastney Pt).

Bar has about 1·2m. Ent chan lies between East and West Winner drying banks, which afford some protection. Appr is straightforward in most conditions, best from HW −3 to +1, but avoid entry against the ebb, esp at sp and in strong onshore winds. In strong S/SE winds do not attempt entry.

LIGHTS AND MARKS Ldg marks (concrete dolphins), or Fairway beacon in line with conspic chy, leads 344° just clear of East Winner. The entrance itself deepens and favours the W side. The narrow approach channel to Southsea Marina is marked by 5 SHM piles, only the first of which is lit, Fl G. There are 9 PHM piles; see chartlet for details.

R/T Harbour VHF Ch 12 16 (Summer 0830-1700 daily. Winter: Mon-Fri 0830-1700; Sat-Sun 0830-1300). Marina Ch 80 M.

TELEPHONE (Code 023) HM 9246 3419; MRCC 9255 2100; Marinecall 09068 969647; Police 0845 0454545; Dr 9246 5721.

FACILITIES **Southsea Marina,** ☎ 9282 2719, www.premier marinas.com; 300 AB, £1·96 (min charge £16); free electricity for 2 nights. Access HW±3; the lock (width 6·5m) has R/G sigs indicating if the sill is up or down; D, P, SM, CH, ME, BH (15 ton), C (6 ton), Gaz, Wi-fi, 🛒, Bar, R.

Hayling Pontoon (E side of ent), www.langstoneharbour.org.uk AB for D only (H24 with pre-payment tag available from HO Mon-Fri and summer w/ends), FW. Vacant mooring buoys in harbour may be available, £11.30/night.

Langstone SC ☎ 9248 4577, Slip, M, L, FW, Bar;

Eastney Cruising Association (ECA) ☎ 9273 4103,

6 ♻s craft under 9m (donation to RNLI), Bar, R, showers, visitors welcome; **Hayling Ferry SC; Locks SC** ☎ 9282 9833; **Tudor SC** (Hilsea) ☎ 9266 2002, Slip, M, FW, Bar.

Towns: ✉ (Eastney, Hayling), ⓑ (Havant, Hayling, Emsworth), ⇌ (bus to Havant), ✈ (Southampton).

9.2.27 CHICHESTER HARBOUR

W. Sussex **50°46′·86N 00°56′·06W** ❀❀◊◊◊❀❀❀

CHARTS AC 5600, 2045, 3418; Imray C9, C3, Y33; Stanfords 11, 10.

TIDES +0027 Dover; ML 2·8

Standard Port CHICHESTER (→)

Times				Height (metres)			
High Water		Low Water		MHWS	MHWN	MLWN	MLWS
0500	1000	0000	0600	4·9	4·0	1·9	0·9
1700	2200	1200	1800				
Differences NORTHNEY							
+0020	+0010	0000	+0005	0·0	−0·2	−0·2	−0·4
BOSHAM							
+0010	+0005	No data		0·0	−0·1	No data	
ITCHENOR							
+0005	0000	−0010	+0005	−0·1	−0·2	−0·2	−0·3
DELL QUAY							
+0015	+0010	No data		0·0	−0·1	No data	

SHELTER Excellent in all five main chans: Emsworth, Thorney, Chichester, Bosham, Itchenor Reach and Fishbourne. There are six yacht hbrs and marinas (see Facilities); also about 50 ⚓s at Emsworth and Itchenor. ⚓s in Thorney Chan off Pilsey Is; off E Head (uncomfortable in NE'lies); and in Chichester Chan off Chalkdock Pt. Harbour speed limit of 8kn; max fine £2,500.

NAVIGATION WPT 50°45'·32N 00°56'·60W, 013°/1·6M to entrance.
Best entry is HW −3 to +1, to avoid confused seas on the ebb, especially in onshore winds >F5. Leave West Pole Bn close to port; the chan N'ward is effectively only about 200m wide.

• Do not attempt entry in S'ly F6 or above. Bar is dredged 1·5m, but after gales depths may vary ±0·75m.

APPROACHES: From the W, Horse Sand Fort astern, bearing 265°, leads to the West Pole Bn. Closer in, transit 064° of Target NCM Bn with Cakeham Tr leads 1·3ca S of West Pole bn; thence alter 013° as Eastoke Pt opens to the E of West Pole and Bar bns. Leave both bns about 50m to port.

From the E/SE, via Looe Chan, keep W for 2M, then alter NW toward the West Pole Bn keeping Nab Tr astern brg 184° to clear shoals in Bracklesham Bay. Note: Historic Wrecks (see 9.0.3) lie 137°/1·2M and 095°/3·2M from West Pole Bn.

ENTRANCE Pass between Eastoke PHM lit bn and W Winner SHM lit bn (tide gauge). Three SHM lit buoys mark the edge of The Winner shoal, dries, to stbd of the ent. Near Fishery SCM lit buoy, depths may change and buoys may be moved accordingly. Here the chan divides: N towards Emsworth and ENE towards Chichester. Stocker's Sands, dries 1·9m, is marked by 3 PHM lt buoys. East Head SHM lit buoy, marks western end of recommended anchorage.

EMSWORTH CHANNEL Chan is straight, broad, deep and well marked/lit in the 2·5M reach to Emsworth SCM bn, Q (6) + L Fl 15s, where Sweare Deep forks NW to Northney. An unlit ECM bn marks channel to Sparkes Yacht Hbr. Pass close to Hayling Is SC pontoon on entering or leaving this chan to avoid shallow patch just S of bn.

THORNEY CHANNEL Strangers should go up at half-flood. Ent is at Camber SCM bn, Q (6) + L Fl 15s; pass between Pilsey and Thorney Lt bns, thereafter chan is marked by perches. Above Stanbury Pt chan splits, Prinsted Chan to port and Nutbourne Chan to stbd; both dry at N ends. Good ⚓ off Pilsey Island.

CHICHESTER CHANNEL runs up to Itchenor Reach and Bosham Chan. From NE Sandhead PHM buoy, Fl R 10s, Roman Transit bn in transit with Main Chan bn (see chartlet) and distant clump of trees leads to Chalkdock Bn, Fl (2) G 10s. Here alter 082° to Fairway buoy, Fl (3) G 10s; at Deep End SCM bn turn N into Bosham Chan, or ESE into Itchenor Reach, for Birdham Pool and Chichester Marina. ⚓ prohib in Itchenor Reach and Bosham Channel.

LIGHTS AND MARKS Approach marked by West Pole PHM tripod bn at 50°45'·45N 00°56'·59W; Bar PHM bn is 6ca N. E side of ent chan is marked by W Winner SHM lit pile with tide gauge;

and by 3 SHM buoys: NW Winner, N Winner, Mid Winner. All chans within the hbr are well marked by day. Emsworth Chan is well lit; Thorney Chan is partly lit; Bosham Chan is unlit. Itchenor Reach is unlit except for Birdham Pool and CYB entrance bns.

R/T *Chichester Hbr Radio* VHF Ch **14** 16 (Apr-Sep: 0830-1700; Sat 0900-1300) or Chichester Hbr Patrol (w/e's Apr-Sep). Northney Marina Ch **80** M. Chichester Marina Ch 80.

TELEPHONE (Code 01243) Chichester Harbour Office 512301, www.conservancy.co.uk, www.chimet.co.uk for current weather at Bar, Emsworth Harbour Office 376422; MRCC (02392) 552100; Marinecall 09068 969647; Police 0845 0454545; Ⓗ 787970.

FACILITIES

HAYLING ISLAND (Code 02392) **Sparkes Marina** ☎ 463572, mob 07770 365610.150 + 30 Ⓥ, £3.20 (inc elec). Access all tides via chan dredged 2m; pontoons have 1·6m. ME, El, P, D, M, Gas, Gaz, LPG, Ⓘ, ✗, C (25 ton), CH. From close N of Sandy Pt, appr on transit 277° of 2 x bns; thence alter S, past 3 PHM bns to marina.

Northney Marina ☎ 466321; pre-call Ch 80. 228+27 Ⓥ, £2·85, £8 <4hrs. Access all tides via chan 1m. D, P, LPG, El, ✗, CH, SM, ME, BH (35 ton), Ⓘ, Bar, R, Wi-fi; **Services:** Slip, BH (8 ton).

EMSWORTH CHANNEL Emsworth Yacht Hbr ☎ 377727. 200+20 Ⓥ, £2.75. Access HW±2 over 2·4m sill which maintains 1·5m inside, Slip, Gas, ME, El, ✗, P, D, BH (60 ton), C (20 ton). **Service jetty** (E of Emsworth SC) 50m long, ☆ 2FR (vert); access HW±4. Free for <2 hrs stay, FW. **Slips** at South St, Kings St, and Slipper Mill; contact the Warden ☎ 376422. Ferry £1 to moorings Ch 14 *Emsworth Mobile.* **Services:** ME, ✗, CH, El, ACA.

THORNEY CHANNEL Thornham Marina, ☎ 375335, ✉ 371522. 77+6 Ⓥ, £20/craft. Appr via drying chan, P & D (cans), ✗, ME, C (10 ton), BH (12 ton), CH, BY, Slip, R, Bar.

CHICHESTER CHANNEL/ITCHENOR REACH Hard available at all stages of the tide. There are berths for approx 40 yachts at Itchenor on both buoys and pontoons. £6.50 per night. **Services:** Slip (£2.50), P & D (cans), ✗, FW, M, El, Ⓔ, ME, showers in hbr office, 🚽. Ferry/Water taxi VHF Ch 08, ☎ 07970 378350, to Bosham and Birdham.

BOSHAM CHANNEL For moorings (200+) contact the Quaymaster ☎ 573336. ⚓ prohib in chan which mostly dries, access HW±2.
Bosham Quay Hard, L, FW, AB; **Services:** SM. EC Wed.

CHICHESTER LAKE Birdham Pool Marina ☎ 512310. 230+10 Ⓥ, £2·20. Enter chan at Birdham SHM bn, with depth gauge; access HW ±3 via lock (width 5m). Wi-fi, Slip, P, D, El, Ⓔ, ✗, CH, Gas, ME, SM, C (3 ton) R, Bar (Chichester YC ☎ 512916).

Chichester Marina ☎ 512731. 1000+50 Ⓥ, £2·45, £1.03/m for <4hrs (min £7.83). Enter chan at CM SHM lit pile, with depth gauge; 6kn speed limit. The well marked chan is dredged to CD but is reported (2008) to be silting; a waiting pontoon is outside the lock (width 7m). P, D, ME, El, Ⓔ, ✗, BH (40 ton), SM, CH, Wi-fi, 🛒, R, Bar, Gas, Gaz, LPG, Ⓘ, ♿.
Traffic sigs:
Q ⚪ (top of tr) = both gates open (free flow).
Lock sigs: ● = Wait; ● = Enter.
Call lock-keeper on Ch 80, ☎ 512731, H24 to book exit except during free-flow.
Services: Slip, P, D, ME, El, ✗, Gas, Gaz, LPG, CH, BY, BH (65 ton), 🛒, R, Bar, Ⓘ, ACA, SM, ♿.

FISHBOURNE CHANNEL Dell Quay: Possible drying berth against the Quay, apply to Hbr Office, public slip. **Services:** ✗, Slip, BH, M, L.

YACHT CLUBS

Bosham SC ☎ 572341; **Chichester YC** ☎ 512918, R, Bar, Ⓘ; **Chichester Cruiser and Racing Club** ☎ 371731; **Dell Quay SC** ☎ 785080; **Emsworth SC** ☎ 373065; **Emsworth Slipper SC** ☎ 372523; **Hayling Island SC** ☎ (02392) 463768; **Itchenor SC** ☎ 512400; **Mengham Rithe SC** ☎ (02392) 463337; **Thorney Island SC**; **W Wittering SC.**

Cobnor Activities Centre Trust (at Cobnor Pt) attracts many young people, inc disabled ♿, afloat. ☎ 01243 572791.

CHICHESTER HARBOUR

MEAN SPRING AND NEAP CURVES

MEAN RANGES
Springs 4.0m
Neaps 2.1m

Springs occur 2 days after New and Full Moon

CHICHESTER HARBOUR   LAT 50°47'N   LONG 0°56'W
TIMES AND HEIGHTS OF HIGH AND LOW WATERS

TIME ZONE (UT)
For Summer Time add ONE hour in **non-shaded areas**

Dates in red are SPRINGS
Dates in blue are NEAPS

YEAR 2010

JANUARY

Date	Time	m	Time	m	Time	m	Time	m
1 F	0429	1.1	1119	4.9	1656	0.8		
16 SA	0006	4.6	0514	1.3	1206	4.6	1735	1.1
2 SA	0000	4.9	0518	1.0	1209	5.0	1745	0.7
17 SU	0040	4.6	0550	1.2	1240	4.6	1810	1.0
3 SU	0053	4.9	0608	0.9	1300	5.0	1834	0.7
18 M	0112	4.6	0624	1.2	1313	4.6	1844	1.1
4 M	0145	5.0	0657	0.9	1352	4.9	1924	0.7
19 TU	0142	4.6	0658	1.3	1344	4.5	1917	1.1
5 TU	0236	4.9	0748	1.0	1445	4.8	2015	0.9
20 W	0213	4.5	0731	1.3	1416	4.4	1948	1.2
6 W	0326	4.8	0840	1.1	1539	4.6	2109	1.1
21 TH	0245	4.4	0803	1.5	1452	4.3	2020	1.4
7 TH	0416	4.7	0938	1.4	1634	4.4	2208	1.4 ◑
22 F	0323	4.3	0838	1.6	1536	4.1	2057	1.6
8 F	0507	4.5	1043	1.6	1731	4.2	2313	1.6
23 SA	0410	4.2	0923	1.8	1632	4.0	2147	1.8 ◑
9 SA	0603	4.3	1152	1.8	1835	4.0		
24 SU	0508	4.0	1026	1.9	1740	3.9	2258	2.0
10 SU	0022	1.8	0707	4.1	1305	1.8	1951	4.0
25 M	0617	4.0	1152	2.0	1858	3.9		
11 M	0133	1.9	0820	4.1	1412	1.7	2113	4.1
26 TU	0025	2.0	0733	4.1	1317	1.8	2016	4.1
12 TU	0233	1.8	0926	4.2	1503	1.6	2210	4.2
27 W	0144	1.8	0839	4.3	1421	1.5	2118	4.3
13 W	0320	1.7	1013	4.4	1545	1.4	2254	4.4
28 TH	0244	1.5	0933	4.6	1512	1.1	2210	4.6
14 TH	0400	1.5	1053	4.5	1623	1.2	2331	4.5
29 F	0334	1.2	1021	4.8	1559	0.8	2259	4.9
15 F	0438	1.4	1129	4.5	1700	1.1 ●		
30 SA	0421	0.9	1108	5.0	1646	0.6	2348	5.0 ○
31 SU	0508	0.7	1156	5.1	1732	0.4		

FEBRUARY

Date	Time	m	Time	m	Time	m	Time	m
1 M	0036	5.1	0554	0.6	1244	5.1	1818	0.4
16 TU	0047	4.7	0600	1.0	1251	4.7	1818	0.8
2 TU	0123	5.2	0640	0.6	1332	5.1	1904	0.5
17 W	0114	4.7	0632	1.0	1320	4.6	1849	0.9
3 W	0207	5.1	0725	0.7	1419	4.9	1950	0.7
18 TH	0142	4.7	0702	1.0	1350	4.6	1917	1.0
4 TH	0251	4.9	0811	0.9	1508	4.7	2036	1.0
19 F	0212	4.6	0731	1.1	1422	4.4	1946	1.1
5 F	0338	4.7	0859	1.2	1559	4.4	2127	1.4 ◑
20 SA	0243	4.4	0803	1.2	1459	4.2	2020	1.3
6 SA	0427	4.4	0958	1.6	1654	4.1	2233	1.7
21 SU	0323	4.2	0843	1.5	1550	4.0	2106	1.6
7 SU	0522	4.1	1118	1.9	1756	3.8	2355	2.0
22 M	0423	4.0	0939	1.7	1704	3.8	2215	1.9 ◑
8 M	0626	3.9	1243	2.0	1913	3.7		
23 TU	0540	3.9	1123	1.9	1828	3.8		
9 TU	0114	2.0	0745	3.8	1354	1.9	2102	3.8
24 W	0013	2.0	0702	3.9	1301	1.7	1954	4.0
10 W	0216	1.9	0918	3.9	1445	1.7	2205	4.1
25 TH	0135	1.7	0818	4.1	1406	1.4	2104	4.3
11 TH	0302	1.7	1013	4.2	1524	1.4	2248	4.3
26 F	0232	1.4	0919	4.5	1457	1.0	2158	4.6
12 F	0340	1.5	1049	4.4	1601	1.2	2321	4.5
27 SA	0320	1.0	1049	4.8	1543	0.7	2246	4.9
13 SA	0416	1.3	1120	4.5	1636	1.0	2350	4.6
28 SU	0405	0.7	1055	5.0	1628	0.4	2331	5.1 ○
14 SU	0452	1.1	1150	4.6	1711	0.9 ●		
15 M	0018	4.7	0526	1.0	1221	4.7	1745	0.8

MARCH

Date	Time	m	Time	m	Time	m	Time	m
1 M	0449	0.5	1141	5.1	1712	0.3		
16 TU	0500	0.9	1156	4.6	1716	0.8		
2 TU	0015	5.2	0533	0.4	1227	5.1	1755	0.3
17 W	0016	4.7	0532	0.8	1226	4.7	1748	0.8
3 W	0057	5.2	0616	0.4	1311	5.1	1838	0.4
18 TH	0045	4.7	0603	0.8	1257	4.7	1818	0.8
4 TH	0138	5.1	0658	0.6	1356	4.9	1920	0.6
19 F	0114	4.7	0632	0.8	1329	4.6	1847	0.9
5 F	0220	4.9	0738	0.8	1440	4.7	2000	1.0
20 SA	0144	4.6	0703	0.9	1402	4.5	1919	1.0
6 SA	0303	4.6	0818	1.1	1528	4.4	2040	1.4
21 SU	0216	4.5	0738	1.0	1440	4.3	1957	1.2
7 SU	0349	4.3	0902	1.5	1620	4.1	2131	1.7 ◑
22 M	0256	4.3	0820	1.2	1534	4.1	2045	1.5
8 M	0442	4.0	1013	1.8	1720	3.8	2312	2.1
23 TU	0358	4.0	0917	1.5	1647	3.9	2200	1.8 ◑
9 TU	0544	3.7	1205	2.0	1834	3.6		
24 W	0515	3.9	1104	1.7	1805	3.9	2357	1.9
10 W	0041	2.1	0704	3.6	1317	1.9	2029	3.7
25 TH	0635	3.9	1234	1.6	1929	4.0		
11 TH	0145	2.0	0858	3.7	1410	1.7	2144	4.0
26 F	0112	1.6	0755	4.1	1340	1.3	2044	4.3
12 F	0233	1.8	0955	4.0	1453	1.4	2224	4.2
27 SA	0210	1.3	0902	4.4	1433	1.0	2141	4.7
13 SA	0313	1.5	1029	4.2	1531	1.2	2254	4.4
28 SU	0259	0.9	0954	4.7	1520	0.7	2228	4.9
14 SU	0350	1.2	1057	4.4	1607	1.0	2321	4.6
29 M	0344	0.6	1040	4.9	1605	0.5	2310	5.1
15 M	0425	1.0	1126	4.5	1642	0.8	2349	4.7 ●
30 TU	0427	0.4	1125	5.0	1648	0.4	2351	5.1 ○
31 W	0510	0.4	1209	5.0	1731	0.4		

APRIL

Date	Time	m	Time	m	Time	m	Time	m
1 TH	0031	5.1	0551	0.5	1253	5.0	1811	0.6
16 F	0014	4.7	0531	0.8	1235	4.6	1746	0.9
2 F	0112	5.0	0630	0.6	1336	4.8	1851	0.8
17 SA	0048	4.6	0605	0.8	1312	4.6	1822	1.0
3 SA	0152	4.8	0709	0.8	1419	4.6	1928	1.1
18 SU	0123	4.6	0641	0.8	1352	4.5	1901	1.0
4 SU	0233	4.5	0746	1.1	1504	4.4	2007	1.4
19 M	0201	4.5	0723	0.9	1437	4.4	1946	1.2
5 M	0316	4.2	0827	1.4	1552	4.1	2053	1.7
20 TU	0249	4.3	0811	1.1	1534	4.3	2041	1.5
6 TU	0404	3.9	0922	1.7	1646	3.9	2208	2.0 ◑
21 W	0351	4.1	0915	1.4	1639	4.1	2203	1.7 ◑
7 W	0502	3.7	1105	1.9	1751	3.7	2355	2.1
22 TH	0500	4.0	1045	1.5	1747	4.1	2332	1.7
8 TH	0614	3.5	1226	1.9	1916	3.7		
23 F	0611	4.0	1202	1.4	1901	4.2		
9 F	0103	2.0	0748	3.6	1326	1.8	2047	3.8
24 SA	0041	1.5	0728	4.1	1307	1.3	2016	4.4
10 SA	0157	1.8	0905	3.8	1415	1.5	2136	4.1
25 SU	0141	1.3	0840	4.3	1404	1.1	2116	4.6
11 SU	0241	1.5	0947	4.1	1457	1.3	2210	4.3
26 M	0234	1.0	0937	4.5	1454	0.9	2204	4.8
12 M	0320	1.3	1021	4.3	1534	1.1	2241	4.5
27 TU	0321	0.8	1024	4.7	1541	0.7	2246	4.9
13 TU	0355	1.1	1053	4.4	1609	1.0	2312	4.6
28 W	0405	0.7	1108	4.8	1625	0.7	2326	4.9 ○
14 W	0428	1.0	1126	4.5	1642	0.9	2343	4.7 ●
29 TH	0447	0.6	1151	4.9	1707	0.8		
15 TH	0500	0.9	1200	4.6	1714	0.9		
30 F	0006	4.9	0527	0.7	1236	4.8	1747	0.9

Chart Datum: 2·73 metres below Ordnance Datum (Newlyn). HAT is 5·3 metres above Chart Datum; see 4.5

TIME ZONE (UT)
For Summer Time add ONE hour in **non-shaded areas**

CHICHESTER HARBOUR   LAT 50°47′N   LONG 0°56′W
TIMES AND HEIGHTS OF HIGH AND LOW WATERS

Dates in red are SPRINGS
Dates in blue are NEAPS

YEAR 2010

Central S England

MAY

Time	m		Time	m
1 0047	4.7	**16** 0024	4.6
0607	0.8	0543	0.9
SA 1319	4.7	SU 1259	4.6
1827	1.1	1804	1.1
2 0127	4.6	**17** 0107	4.6
0646	1.0	0628	0.9
SU 1401	4.5	M 1346	4.6
1906	1.3	1851	1.1
3 0208	4.4	**18** 0153	4.5
0725	1.2	0716	0.9
M 1444	4.4	TU 1436	4.5
1946	1.5	1943	1.2
4 0249	4.2	**19** 0245	4.4
0807	1.5	0810	1.0
TU 1528	4.2	W 1531	4.5
2032	1.7	2042	1.3
5 0333	4.0	**20** 0344	4.3
0859	1.6	0914	1.2
W 1615	4.0	TH 1628	4.4
2134	1.9	☽ 2153	1.5
6 0424	3.8	**21** 0445	4.2
1010	1.8	1025	1.3
TH 1708	3.9	F 1727	4.3
☽ 2259	2.0	2305	1.5
7 0521	3.7	**22** 0549	4.1
1128	1.9	1132	1.3
F 1811	3.8	SA 1831	4.3
8 0013	2.0	**23** 0010	1.4
0633	3.6	0657	4.1
SA 1233	1.8	SU 1235	1.3
1928	3.9	1941	4.4
9 0114	1.9	**24** 0112	1.3
0757	3.7	0812	4.2
SU 1328	1.7	M 1335	1.3
2033	4.0	2046	4.5
10 0204	1.7	**25** 0209	1.2
0855	3.9	0915	4.4
M 1415	1.6	TU 1431	1.2
2119	4.2	2137	4.6
11 0244	1.5	**26** 0300	1.0
0938	4.1	1006	4.5
TU 1454	1.4	W 1520	1.1
2157	4.4	2220	4.7
12 0318	1.3	**27** 0346	1.0
1016	4.3	1051	4.6
W 1528	1.3	TH 1605	1.1
2232	4.5	○ 2301	4.7
13 0351	1.1	**28** 0429	0.9
1054	4.4	1135	4.6
TH 1603	1.2	F 1648	1.1
2307	4.6	2342	4.6
14 0425	1.0	**29** 0510	1.0
1133	4.5	1219	4.6
F 1640	1.1	SA 1729	1.2
● 2344	4.6		
15 0502	0.9	**30** 0024	4.5
1215	4.6	0550	1.0
SA 1721	1.1	SU 1302	4.5
		1809	1.3
		31 0105	4.4
		0630	1.1
		M 1343	4.5
		1849	1.4

JUNE

Time	m		Time	m
1 0145	4.3	**16** 0142	4.6
0710	1.2	0710	0.8
TU 1423	4.4	W 1426	4.7
1930	1.5	1937	1.1
2 0225	4.2	**17** 0234	4.6
0751	1.3	0804	0.9
W 1503	4.3	TH 1517	4.7
2013	1.7	2033	1.1
3 0305	4.1	**18** 0329	4.5
0836	1.5	0901	1.0
TH 1544	4.2	F 1609	4.6
2102	1.8	2133	1.3
4 0350	4.0	**19** 0425	4.4
0928	1.7	1002	1.2
F 1628	4.1	SA 1702	4.5
☽ 2201	1.9	☽ 2237	1.4
5 0439	3.9	**20** 0523	4.2
1026	1.8	1105	1.3
SA 1716	4.0	SU 1758	4.4
2306	2.0	2341	1.5
6 0533	3.8	**21** 0625	4.1
1125	1.9	1208	1.5
SU 1812	4.0	M 1901	4.3
7 0007	1.9	**22** 0046	1.5
0637	3.8	0738	4.1
M 1221	1.8	TU 1312	1.5
1920	4.0	2010	4.3
8 0104	1.8	**23** 0150	1.4
0754	3.9	0853	4.2
TU 1313	1.8	W 1414	1.5
2024	4.1	2112	4.4
9 0153	1.7	**24** 0245	1.3
0854	4.1	0952	4.3
W 1402	1.7	TH 1506	1.4
2113	4.3	2201	4.4
10 0235	1.5	**25** 0333	1.2
0940	4.2	1041	4.4
TH 1447	1.5	F 1551	1.4
2154	4.4	2243	4.4
11 0316	1.3	**26** 0415	1.1
1024	4.4	1124	4.4
F 1532	1.4	SA 1633	1.3
2235	4.5	○ 2324	4.4
12 0358	1.1	**27** 0456	1.1
1109	4.5	1205	4.5
SA 1617	1.2	SU 1714	1.3
● 2318	4.6		
13 0443	0.9	**28** 0005	4.4
1156	4.6	0535	1.1
SU 1705	1.1	M 1244	4.5
		1753	1.3
14 0004	4.6	**29** 0045	4.4
0530	0.8	0614	1.1
M 1246	4.7	TU 1322	4.5
1754	1.1	1831	1.4
15 0052	4.7	**30** 0123	4.4
0619	0.8	0652	1.1
TU 1336	4.7	W 1358	4.5
1844	1.0	1909	1.4

JULY

Time	m		Time	m
1 0159	4.3	**16** 0214	4.8
0729	1.2	0746	0.7
TH 1433	4.4	F 1452	4.9
1946	1.5	2011	0.9
2 0235	4.3	**17** 0305	4.7
0806	1.4	0838	0.9
F 1508	4.3	SA 1541	4.7
2025	1.6	2106	1.1
3 0314	4.2	**18** 0358	4.5
0845	1.5	0934	1.1
SA 1547	4.2	SU 1631	4.5
2107	1.8	☽ 2207	1.4
4 0358	4.0	**19** 0453	4.3
0928	1.7	1037	1.4
SU 1631	4.1	M 1725	4.3
☽ 2158	1.9	2314	1.6
5 0448	3.9	**20** 0553	4.0
1020	1.8	1144	1.6
M 1720	4.0	TU 1824	4.1
2257	1.9		
6 0544	3.8	**21** 0025	1.7
1118	1.9	0703	3.9
TU 1818	4.0	W 1254	1.8
		1935	4.0
7 0000	1.9	**22** 0134	1.6
0651	3.8	0835	3.9
W 1220	1.9	TH 1400	1.7
1927	4.1	2054	4.1
8 0103	1.8	**23** 0232	1.5
0810	4.0	0949	4.1
TH 1323	1.8	F 1452	1.6
2033	4.2	2154	4.2
9 0202	1.5	**24** 0318	1.3
0911	4.2	1038	4.3
F 1422	1.6	SA 1536	1.5
2125	4.4	2236	4.3
10 0254	1.3	**25** 0358	1.2
1000	4.4	1117	4.4
SA 1515	1.4	SU 1615	1.3
2211	4.6	2312	4.4
11 0342	1.0	**26** 0436	1.1
1048	4.6	1150	4.5
SU 1604	1.1	M 1653	1.2
● 2257	4.7	○ 2348	4.5
12 0430	0.8	**27** 0514	1.0
1137	4.7	1223	4.6
M 1653	1.0	TU 1731	1.2
2344	4.8		
13 0519	0.7	**28** 0024	4.5
1226	4.8	0551	0.9
TU 1742	0.8	W 1256	4.6
		1807	1.2
14 0033	4.8	**29** 0059	4.5
0607	0.6	0627	1.0
W 1316	4.9	TH 1329	4.6
1831	0.8	1842	1.2
15 0124	4.8	**30** 0132	4.5
0657	0.6	0700	1.0
TH 1404	4.9	F 1359	4.5
1921	0.8	1914	1.3
		31 0203	4.4
		0731	1.2
		SA 1430	4.4
		1945	1.4

AUGUST

Time	m		Time	m
1 0237	4.3	**16** 0329	4.5
0801	1.3	0857	1.2
SU 1504	4.3	M 1558	4.5
2017	1.5	☽ 2126	1.4
2 0316	4.1	**17** 0424	4.2
0835	1.5	1000	1.5
M 1545	4.2	TU 1651	4.2
2057	1.7	2240	1.7
3 0404	4.0	**18** 0523	3.9
0920	1.7	1117	1.8
TU 1635	4.0	W 1751	3.9
☽ 2154	1.8		
4 0503	3.8	**19** 0001	1.8
1024	1.9	0632	3.8
W 1736	3.9	TH 1234	1.9
2313	1.9	1903	3.8
5 0612	3.8	**20** 0113	1.8
1147	2.0	0823	3.8
TH 1846	3.9	F 1339	1.9
		2051	3.8
6 0036	1.8	**21** 0209	1.6
0733	3.9	0944	4.0
F 1307	1.8	SA 1430	1.7
2001	4.1	2157	4.1
7 0145	1.5	**22** 0254	1.4
0846	4.1	1030	4.3
SA 1411	1.5	SU 1512	1.5
2102	4.4	2234	4.2
8 0240	1.2	**23** 0333	1.2
0941	4.4	1104	4.4
SU 1503	1.2	M 1551	1.3
2152	4.6	2301	4.4
9 0328	0.8	**24** 0411	1.0
1029	4.7	1131	4.6
M 1551	0.9	TU 1628	1.1
2238	4.8	○ 2330	4.5
10 0415	0.6	**25** 0447	0.9
1116	4.9	1158	4.6
TU 1638	0.7	W 1704	1.0
● 2325	4.9		
11 0502	0.4	**26** 0001	4.6
1203	5.0	0523	0.8
W 1725	0.6	TH 1228	4.7
		1739	1.0
12 0012	5.0	**27** 0033	4.6
0548	0.3	0556	0.8
TH 1251	5.1	F 1257	4.6
1811	0.5	1811	1.0
13 0101	5.0	**28** 0103	4.5
0635	0.4	0627	0.9
F 1336	5.1	SA 1325	4.6
1857	0.6	1841	1.1
14 0149	4.9	**29** 0132	4.5
0721	0.6	0655	1.0
SA 1422	5.0	SU 1353	4.5
1943	0.8	1908	1.2
15 0238	4.8	**30** 0203	4.4
0807	0.8	0723	1.2
SU 1509	4.8	M 1423	4.4
2031	1.1	1939	1.3
		31 0238	4.2
		0756	1.3
		TU 1500	4.2
		2017	1.5

Chart Datum: 2·73 metres below Ordnance Datum (Newlyn). HAT is 5·3 metres above Chart Datum; see 4.5

TIME ZONE (UT)
For Summer Time add ONE hour in **non-shaded areas**

CHICHESTER HARBOUR   LAT 50°47'N   LONG 0°56'W
TIMES AND HEIGHTS OF HIGH AND LOW WATERS

Dates in red are SPRINGS
Dates in blue are NEAPS

YEAR 2010

SEPTEMBER

Time m	Time m
1 0324 4.0 / 0838 1.6 / W 1552 4.0 / ☽2108 1.7	**16** 0457 3.9 / 1039 2.0 / TH 1720 3.8 / 2326 1.9
2 0431 3.9 / 0940 1.9 / TH 1703 3.9 / 2237 1.9	**17** 0603 3.7 / 1203 2.1 / F 1830 3.6
3 0545 3.8 / 1130 2.0 / F 1817 3.9	**18** 0037 1.9 / 0736 3.7 / SA 1308 2.0 / 2028 3.7
4 0018 1.8 / 0705 3.9 / SA 1254 1.8 / 1934 4.0	**19** 0135 1.7 / 0923 4.0 / SU 1400 1.8 / 2139 4.0
5 0126 1.5 / 0823 4.2 / SU 1355 1.5 / 2041 4.3	**20** 0222 1.5 / 1006 4.2 / M 1444 1.5 / 2213 4.2
6 0221 1.1 / 0922 4.5 / M 1446 1.1 / 2133 4.7	**21** 0303 1.2 / 1036 4.4 / TU 1524 1.3 / 2237 4.4
7 0309 0.7 / 1009 4.8 / TU 1533 0.7 / 2220 4.9	**22** 0342 1.0 / 1100 4.6 / W 1601 1.1 / 2305 4.5
8 0355 0.4 / 1054 5.1 / W 1618 0.5 / ●2305 5.1	**23** 0418 0.9 / 1127 4.7 / TH 1636 1.0 / ○2335 4.6
9 0440 0.3 / 1139 5.2 / TH 1702 0.4 / 2351 5.1	**24** 0453 0.9 / 1156 4.7 / F 1709 0.9
10 0525 0.3 / 1223 5.2 / F 1746 0.4	**25** 0005 4.6 / 0524 0.9 / SA 1224 4.7 / 1739 0.9
11 0038 5.1 / 0608 0.4 / SA 1308 5.1 / 1829 0.6	**26** 0035 4.6 / 0553 0.9 / SU 1252 4.6 / 1808 1.0
12 0126 5.0 / 0651 0.6 / SU 1353 5.0 / 1911 0.8	**27** 0105 4.5 / 0622 1.0 / M 1320 4.6 / 1838 1.0
13 0214 4.8 / 0733 0.9 / M 1439 4.7 / 1953 1.1	**28** 0137 4.4 / 0654 1.1 / TU 1351 4.4 / 1912 1.1
14 0304 4.5 / 0817 1.3 / TU 1527 4.4 / 2039 1.4	**29** 0214 4.3 / 0731 1.3 / W 1428 4.3 / 1952 1.3
15 0358 4.2 / 0909 1.7 / W 1620 4.1 / ☽2148 1.8	**30** 0303 4.1 / 0816 1.5 / TH 1524 4.1 / 2045 1.6

OCTOBER

Time m	Time m
1 0414 4.0 / 0921 1.8 / F 1642 3.9 / ☽2216 1.8	**16** 0533 3.8 / 1124 2.1 / SA 1754 3.7 / 2356 1.9
2 0528 3.9 / 1114 1.9 / SA 1756 3.9 / 2354 1.7	**17** 0644 3.8 / 1230 2.0 / SU 1914 3.7
3 0643 4.0 / 1232 1.7 / SU 1910 4.1	**18** 0055 1.8 / 0817 3.9 / M 1326 1.9 / 2041 3.9
4 0100 1.4 / 0758 4.3 / M 1332 1.4 / 2019 4.4	**19** 0147 1.6 / 0915 4.2 / TU 1415 1.6 / 2127 4.1
5 0156 1.1 / 0900 4.6 / TU 1424 1.0 / 2114 4.7	**20** 0232 1.4 / 0950 4.4 / W 1457 1.4 / 2201 4.3
6 0246 0.8 / 0948 4.9 / W 1511 0.7 / 2202 4.9	**21** 0312 1.3 / 1021 4.5 / TH 1534 1.2 / 2233 4.4
7 0332 0.6 / 1032 5.1 / TH 1556 0.5 / ●2246 5.0	**22** 0347 1.1 / 1051 4.6 / F 1607 1.1 / 2304 4.5
8 0416 0.4 / 1114 5.2 / F 1639 0.5 / 2332 5.1	**23** 0420 1.1 / 1121 4.7 / SA 1638 1.1 / ○2336 4.6
9 0500 0.5 / 1158 5.2 / SA 1722 0.5	**24** 0451 1.1 / 1151 4.7 / SU 1709 1.0
10 0019 5.0 / 0542 0.6 / SU 1242 5.0 / 1803 0.7	**25** 0010 4.6 / 0522 1.1 / M 1222 4.6 / 1741 1.0
11 0107 4.9 / 0624 0.8 / M 1326 4.9 / 1844 0.9	**26** 0045 4.5 / 0557 1.1 / TU 1255 4.6 / 1816 1.0
12 0155 4.7 / 0705 1.1 / TU 1411 4.6 / 1925 1.2	**27** 0123 4.5 / 0635 1.2 / W 1332 4.5 / 1857 1.1
13 0244 4.5 / 0747 1.4 / W 1459 4.3 / 2009 1.5	**28** 0206 4.4 / 0718 1.3 / TH 1415 4.4 / 1942 1.3
14 0336 4.2 / 0836 1.7 / TH 1551 4.1 / ☽2107 1.8	**29** 0301 4.3 / 0809 1.5 / F 1516 4.2 / 2040 1.5
15 0432 4.0 / 0951 2.0 / F 1649 3.8 / 2241 1.9	**30** 0408 4.2 / 0919 1.7 / SA 1629 4.1 / ☽2204 1.6
	31 0514 4.2 / 1052 1.8 / SU 1738 4.1 / 2326 1.6

NOVEMBER

Time m	Time m
1 0622 4.2 / 1204 1.6 / M 1847 4.2	**16** 0012 1.9 / 0703 4.0 / TU 1250 2.0 / 1932 3.8
2 0030 1.4 / 0731 4.4 / TU 1305 1.4 / 1956 4.4	**17** 0109 1.8 / 0809 4.1 / W 1345 1.8 / 2034 4.0
3 0129 1.2 / 0835 4.7 / W 1400 1.2 / 2056 4.6	**18** 0159 1.7 / 0900 4.3 / TH 1430 1.6 / 2120 4.2
4 0222 1.0 / 0926 4.9 / TH 1450 0.9 / 2145 4.8	**19** 0240 1.6 / 0940 4.5 / F 1506 1.5 / 2159 4.4
5 0310 0.9 / 1010 5.0 / F 1536 0.8 / 2231 4.9	**20** 0315 1.5 / 1015 4.6 / SA 1537 1.4 / 2235 4.5
6 0356 0.8 / 1052 5.1 / SA 1619 0.7 / ●2316 4.9	**21** 0347 1.4 / 1048 4.6 / SU 1609 1.2 / ○2311 4.5
7 0439 0.8 / 1134 5.0 / SU 1702 0.8	**22** 0422 1.3 / 1123 4.7 / M 1644 1.1 / 2350 4.6
8 0003 4.9 / 0521 0.9 / M 1219 4.9 / 1743 0.9	**23** 0500 1.2 / 1159 4.7 / TU 1723 1.1
9 0052 4.8 / 0604 1.1 / TU 1303 4.7 / 1825 1.1	**24** 0031 4.6 / 0541 1.2 / W 1240 4.7 / 1805 1.0
10 0140 4.6 / 0646 1.3 / W 1348 4.5 / 1907 1.2	**25** 0116 4.6 / 0626 1.2 / TH 1323 4.6 / 1851 1.1
11 0227 4.5 / 0729 1.5 / TH 1434 4.3 / 1952 1.5	**26** 0204 4.6 / 0715 1.3 / F 1411 4.5 / 1941 1.1
12 0315 4.3 / 0816 1.7 / F 1523 4.1 / 2044 1.7	**27** 0258 4.5 / 0809 1.4 / SA 1510 4.4 / 2039 1.3
13 0405 4.2 / 0916 2.0 / SA 1616 4.0 / ☽2154 1.9	**28** 0357 4.5 / 0914 1.5 / SU 1614 4.3 / ☽2148 1.4
14 0458 4.0 / 1036 2.1 / SU 1714 3.8 / 2309 1.9	**29** 0457 4.4 / 1027 1.6 / M 1718 4.3 / 2258 1.5
15 0557 4.0 / 1148 2.1 / M 1819 3.8	**30** 0559 4.4 / 1135 1.6 / TU 1823 4.3

DECEMBER

Time m	Time m
1 0002 1.5 / 0703 4.5 / W 1239 1.5 / 1931 4.3	**16** 0013 2.0 / 0710 4.1 / TH 1306 2.0 / 1943 3.9
2 0104 1.4 / 0808 4.6 / TH 1339 1.4 / 2037 4.5	**17** 0112 2.0 / 0813 4.2 / F 1401 1.9 / 2043 4.1
3 0202 1.3 / 0905 4.7 / F 1434 1.2 / 2133 4.6	**18** 0202 1.9 / 0904 4.3 / SA 1438 1.7 / 2130 4.3
4 0255 1.2 / 0952 4.8 / SA 1523 1.1 / 2222 4.7	**19** 0243 1.7 / 0945 4.5 / SU 1511 1.5 / 2212 4.4
5 0342 1.2 / 1035 4.9 / SU 1607 1.0 / ●2308 4.7	**20** 0323 1.6 / 1023 4.6 / M 1549 1.3 / 2252 4.5
6 0427 1.1 / 1117 4.8 / M 1650 1.0 / 2355 4.7	**21** 0404 1.4 / 1102 4.7 / TU 1629 1.1 / ○2335 4.6
7 0509 1.2 / 1201 4.8 / TU 1733 1.0	**22** 0448 1.2 / 1143 4.8 / W 1713 1.0
8 0041 4.7 / 0551 1.3 / W 1245 4.7 / 1814 1.1	**23** 0019 4.7 / 0534 1.1 / TH 1227 4.8 / 1759 0.9
9 0125 4.6 / 0633 1.3 / TH 1328 4.6 / 1856 1.2	**24** 0106 4.8 / 0621 1.0 / F 1313 4.8 / 1847 0.8
10 0207 4.6 / 0714 1.5 / F 1410 4.4 / 1937 1.4	**25** 0154 4.8 / 0710 1.0 / SA 1402 4.7 / 1936 0.9
11 0249 4.5 / 0757 1.6 / SA 1453 4.3 / 2021 1.5	**26** 0244 4.8 / 0801 1.1 / SU 1455 4.7 / 2028 1.0
12 0332 4.3 / 0843 1.8 / SU 1539 4.1 / 2110 1.7	**27** 0337 4.7 / 0856 1.2 / M 1553 4.5 / 2126 1.2
13 0417 4.2 / 0938 2.0 / M 1629 4.0 / ☽2208 1.9	**28** 0432 4.6 / 0959 1.4 / TU 1653 4.4 / ☽2230 1.4
14 0507 4.1 / 1046 2.1 / TU 1725 3.9 / 2311 2.0	**29** 0530 4.5 / 1107 1.6 / W 1755 4.2 / 2336 1.5
15 0604 4.0 / 1157 2.1 / W 1830 3.9	**30** 0631 4.4 / 1215 1.6 / TH 1905 4.2
	31 0044 1.6 / 0739 4.4 / F 1324 1.6 / 2020 4.2

Chart Datum: 2·73 metres below Ordnance Datum (Newlyn). HAT is 5·3 metres above Chart Datum; see 4.5

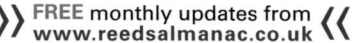
》》 FREE monthly updates from 《《
www.reedsalmanac.co.uk

Make a winning decision

Your choice of marine electronics is one of the most important decisions you will have to make as a boat owner, next to choosing the boat itself of course.

When you buy Raymarine equipment, you are buying into world-class performance, top-notch integration, and the latest proven design technologies. Years of research and development, and customer feedback have resulted in the 'simple-on-the-outside, sophisticated-on-the-inside' design philosophy that is behind all our intuitive easy-to-use equipment.

Worldwide support and warranty

That's why Raymarine has a worldwide network of product-trained distributors and service dealers and offers a comprehensive warranty to handle the unexpected… wherever you decide to go.

ADLARD COLES NAUTICAL
WEATHER FORECASTS
BY FAX & TELEPHONE

Coastal/Inshore	2-day by Fax	5-day by Phone
Mid Channel	09065 222 347	09068 969 647
Channel East	09065 222 346	09068 969 646
NE France	09065 501 611	09064 700 421
Anglia	09065 222 345	09068 969 645
East	09065 222 344	09068 969 644
National (3-5 day)	09065 222 340	09068 969 640
Offshore	**2-5 day by Fax**	**2-5 day by Phone**
English Channel	09065 222 357	09068 969 657
Southern North Sea	09065 222 358	09068 969 658
Northern North Sea	09065 222 362	09068 969 662

09064/68 CALLS COST 60P PER MIN. 09065 CALLS COST £1.50 PER MIN.

South East England

Selsey Bill to North Foreland

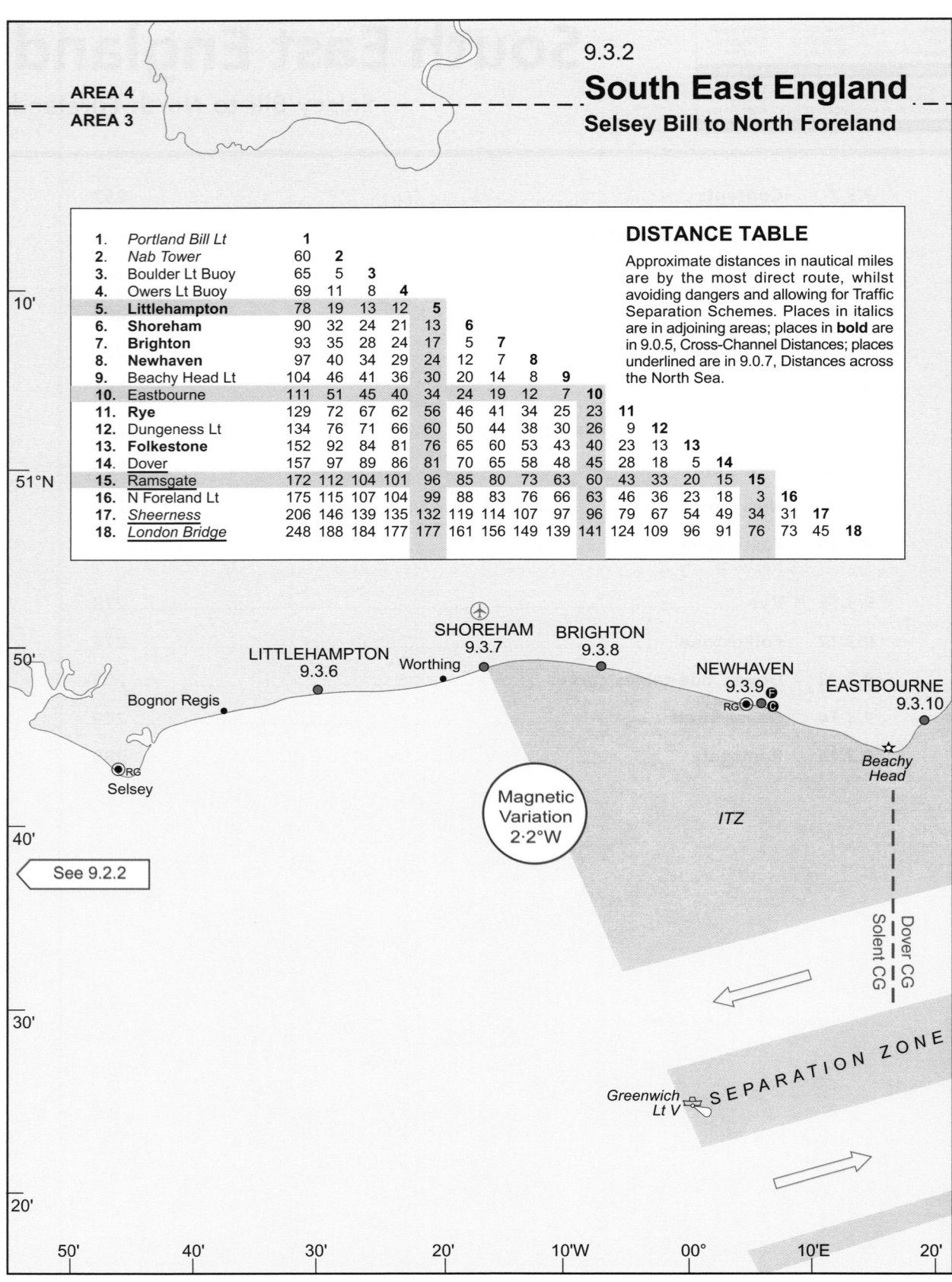

9.3.2
South East England
Selsey Bill to North Foreland

AREA 4
AREA 3

DISTANCE TABLE

Approximate distances in nautical miles are by the most direct route, whilst avoiding dangers and allowing for Traffic Separation Schemes. Places in italics are in adjoining areas; places in **bold** are in 9.0.5, Cross-Channel Distances; places underlined are in 9.0.7, Distances across the North Sea.

	1	2	3	4	5	6	7	8	9	10	11	12	13	14	15	16	17	18
1. *Portland Bill Lt*	**1**																	
2. *Nab Tower*	60	**2**																
3. Boulder Lt Buoy	65	5	**3**															
4. Owers Lt Buoy	69	11	8	**4**														
5. **Littlehampton**	78	19	13	12	**5**													
6. **Shoreham**	90	32	24	21	13	**6**												
7. **Brighton**	93	35	28	24	17	5	**7**											
8. **Newhaven**	97	40	34	29	24	12	7	**8**										
9. Beachy Head Lt	104	46	41	36	30	20	14	8	**9**									
10. Eastbourne	111	51	45	40	34	24	19	12	7	**10**								
11. **Rye**	129	72	67	62	56	46	41	34	25	23	**11**							
12. Dungeness Lt	134	76	71	66	60	50	44	38	30	26	9	**12**						
13. **Folkestone**	152	92	84	81	76	65	60	53	43	40	23	13	**13**					
14. Dover	157	97	89	86	81	70	65	58	48	45	28	18	5	**14**				
15. Ramsgate	172	112	104	101	96	85	80	73	63	60	43	33	20	15	**15**			
16. N Foreland Lt	175	115	107	104	99	88	83	76	66	63	46	36	23	18	3	**16**		
17. *Sheerness*	206	146	139	135	132	119	114	107	97	96	79	67	54	49	34	31	**17**	
18. *London Bridge*	248	188	184	177	177	161	156	149	139	141	124	109	96	91	76	73	45	**18**

SHOREHAM
9.3.7

BRIGHTON
9.3.8

LITTLEHAMPTON
9.3.6

Worthing

NEWHAVEN
9.3.9

EASTBOURNE
9.3.10

Bognor Regis

RG

Selsey

Beachy Head

Magnetic Variation 2·2°W

ITZ

See 9.2.2

Solent CG

Dover CG

Greenwich Lt V

SEPARATION ZONE

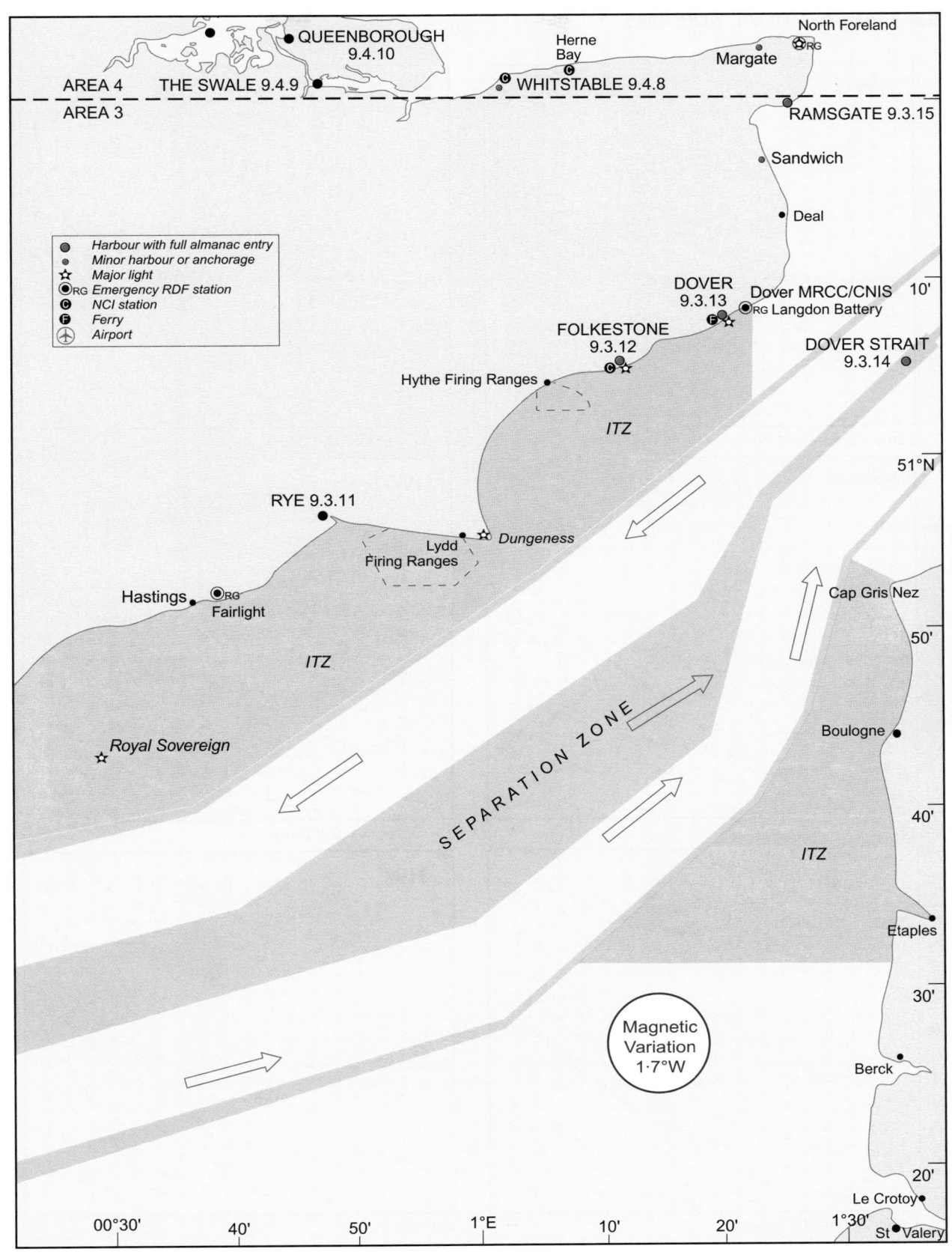

SE England

9.3.3 AREA 3 TIDAL STREAMS

5 Hours before HW Dover

4 Hours before HW Dover

3 Hours before HW Dover

2 Hours before HW Dover

1 Hour before HW Dover

HW Dover

Westward 9.2.3   Southward 9.17.3   Northward 9.4.3   Thames Estuary 9.4.6   Eastward 9.16.3

1 Hour after HW Dover

2 Hours after HW Dover

3 Hours after HW Dover

4 Hours after HW Dover

5 Hours after HW Dover

6 Hours after HW Dover

SE England

9.3.4 LIGHTS, BUOYS AND WAYPOINTS

Bold print = light with a nominal range of 15M or more. CAPITALS = place or feature. *CAPITAL ITALICS* = light-vessel, light float or Lanby. *Italics* = Fog signal. ***Bold italics*** = Racon. Abbreviations are in Chapter 1.

OWERS TO BEACHY HEAD

SELSEY BILL and THE OWERS
S Pullar ⚲ VQ (6) + L Fl 10s; 50°38'·84N 00°49'·29W.
Pullar ⚲ Q (9) 15s; 50°40'·47N 00°50'·09W.
Boulder ◣ Fl G 2·5s; 50°41'·56N 00°49'·09W.
Street ◣ QR; 50°41'·69N 00°48'·89W.
Owers ⚲ Q (6) + L Fl 15s; *Bell*; ***Racon (O) 10M***; 50°38'·59N 00°41'·09W.
E Borough Hd ⚲ Q (3) 10s *Bell;* 50°41'·54N 00°39'·09W.

LITTLEHAMPTON
West Pier Hd ⚲ QR 7m 6M; 50°47'·88N 00°32'·46W.
Training Wall Hd ⚲ QG 10m 2M; 50°47'·87N 00°32'·38W.
Ldg Lts 346°. Front, E Pier Hd ◣ FG 6m 7M; B col. Rear, 64m from front, Oc WY 7·5s 9m10M; W twr; vis: 290°-W-356°-Y-042°; 50°48'·09N 00°32'·51W.
Outfall ◌ Fl Y 5s; 50°46'·27N 00°30'·53W.
Littlehampton ◣ Fl (5) Y 20s 9m 5M; 50°46'·19N 00°29'·54W.

WORTHING and SHOREHAM
Outfall ⚲ Fl R 2·5s 3m; 50°48'·38N 00°20'·34W.
Express ⚲ Fl Y 5s; (Apr-Oct); 50°47'·28N 00°17'·09W.
W Bkwtr Head ◣ Fl R 5s 7m 7M; 50°49'·49N 00°14'·89W.
Ldg Lts 355°. Middle Pier Front, Oc 5s 8m 10M; W watch-house, R base; tidal Lts, tfc sigs; *Horn 20s*. **Rear**, 192m from front, Fl 10s 13m **15M**; Gy twr vis: 283°-103°; 50°49'·75N 00°14'·88W.
Outfall ⚲ 50°49'·47N 00°14'·39W.
Shoreham Outfall ⚲ Q (6) + L Fl 15s; 50°47'·88N 00°13'·72W.

BRIGHTON and BRIGHTON MARINA
Black Rk Ledge ⚲ Fl Y 4s; 50°48'·07N 00°06'·46W.
W Bkwtr Hd ◣ QR 10m 7M; W ○ structure, R bands; *Horn (2) 30s*; 50°48'·50N 00°06'·38W.
E Bkwtr Hd ◣ QG 8m 7M and Fl (4) WR 20s 16m W10M, R8M; W pillar, G bands; vis: 260°-R-295°-W-100°; 50°48'·47N 00°06'·37W.
Saltdean Outfall ◌ Fl Y 5s; 50°46'·72N 00°02'·13W.

NEWHAVEN
Bkwtr Head ◣ Oc (2) 10s 17m 12M; 50°46'·56N 00°03'·50E.
E Pier Hd ◣ Iso G 10s 12m 6M; W twr; 50°46'·81N 00°03'·59E.

OFFSHORE MARKS
CS 1 ⚲ Fl Y 2·5s; *Whis;* 50°33'·69N 00°03'·92W.
GREENWICH ⛟ 50°24'·54N 00°00'·10E; Fl 5s 12m **15M**; Riding light FW; R hull; ***Racon (M) 10M***; *Horn 30s* .
CS 2 ⚲Fl Y 5s; 50°39'·14N 00°32'·60E.
CS 3 ⚲Fl Y 10s; 50°52'·04N 01°02'·18E.

BEACHY HEAD TO DUNGENESS
Beachy Head ☆ 50°44'·03N 00°14'·49E; Fl (2) 20s 31m **20M**; W round twr, R band and lantern; vis: 248°-101°; (H24); *Horn 30s*.
Royal Sovereign ☆ Fl 20s 28m 12M; W ○ twr, R band on W cabin on col; *Horn (2) 30s*; 50°43'·45N 00°26'·09E.
Royal Sovereign ◣ QR; 50°44'·23N 00°25'·84E.

EASTBOURNE and SOVEREIGN HARBOUR
SH ⚲ L Fl 10s; 50°47'·40N 00°20'·71E.
Martello Tower ◣ Fl (3) 15s 12m 7M.; 50°47'·24N 00°19'·83E.
Dir lt 258°Fl WRG 5s 4m 1M; vis: 252·5°-G-256·5°-W-259·5°-R-262·5°; 50°47'·28N 00°19'·71E.
S Bkwtr Hd ◣ Fl (4) R 12s 3m 6M; 50°47'·30N 00°20'·03E.
St Leonard's Outfall ◌ Fl Y 5s; 50°49'·31N 00°31'·95E.

HASTINGS
Ldg Lts 356·3°. Front, FR 14m 4M; 50°51'·29N 00°35'·38E. Rear, West Hill, 357m from front, FR 55m 4M; W twr.

RYE
Rye Fairway , L Fl 10s; 50°54'·04N 00°48'·04E.
W Groyne Hd No. 2 ◣ Fl R 5s 7m 6M; 50°55'·58N 00°46'·55E.
E Arm Hd No. 1 ⚲ Q (9) 15s 7m 5M; G △; *Horn 7s*; 50°55'·73N 00°46'·46E.
Dungeness Outfall ◌ Q (6) + L Fl 15s; 50°54'·45N 00°58'·21E.
Dungeness ☆ 50°54'·81N 00°58'·56E; Fl 10s 40m **21M**; B ○ twr, W bands and lantern, floodlit; Part obsc 078°-shore; (H24). F RG 37m 10M (same twr); vis: 057°-R-073°-G-078°-196°-R-216°; *Horn (3) 60s*; FR Lts shown between 2·4M and 5·2M WNW when firing taking place. QR on radio mast 1·2M NW.

DUNGENESS TO NORTH FORELAND

FOLKESTONE
Hythe Flats Outfall ◌ Fl Y 5s; 51°02'·52N 01°05'·32E.
Breakwater Head ◣ Fl (2) 10s 14m **22M**; *Dia (4) 60s*. In fog Fl 2s; vis: 246°-306°, intens 271·5°-280·5°; 51°04'·56N 01°11'·69E.

DOVER
Admiralty Pier Extension Head ◣ 51°06'·69N 01°19'·66E; Fl 7·5s 21m **20M**; W twr; vis: 096°-090°, obsc in The Downs by S Foreland inshore of 226°; *Horn 10s;* Int Port Tfc sigs.
S Bkwtr W Hd ◣ 51°06'·78N 01°19'·80E; Oc R 30s 21m **18M**; W twr.
Knuckle ☆ 51°07'·04N 01°20'·49E; Fl (4) WR 10s 15m **W15M**, R13M; W twr; vis: 059°-R-239°-W-059°.
N Head ◣ Fl R 2·5s 11m 5M; 51°07'·20N 01°20'·61E.
Eastern Arm Hd ◣ Fl G 5s 12m 5M; *Horn (2) 30s*; Int port tfc sigs; 51°07'·31N 01°20'·59E.

OFFSHORE MARKS
Bullock Bank ⚲ VQ; 50°46'·94N 01°07'·60E.
Ridens SE ⚲ VQ (3) 5s; 50°43'·47N 01°18'·87E.
Colbart SW ⚲ VQ (6) + L Fl 10s; 50°48'·86N 01°16'·30E.
South Varne ⚲ Q (6) + L Fl 15s; 50°55'·64N 01°17'·30E.
Mid Varne ⚲ VQ(9)10s; 50°58'·94N 01°19'·88E.
East Varne ⚲ VQ(3)5s; 50°58'·22N 01°20'·90E.
Colbart N ⚲ VQ; 50°57'·45N 01°23'·29E
VARNE ⛟ 51°01'·29N 01°23'·90E; Fl R 5s 12m **15M**; ***Racon (T)10M***; *Horn 30s*.
CS 4 ⚲ Fl (4) Y 15s; 51°08'·62N 01°33'·92E.
CS 5 ⚲ Fl Y 2·5s; 51°27'·35N 01°52'·76E.
MPC ⚲ Fl Y 2·5s; ***Racon (O) 10M***; 51°06'·12N 01°38'·20E.
SW Goodwin ⚲ Q (6) + L Fl 15s; 51°08'·50N 01°28'·88E.
S Goodwin ◌ Fl (4) R 15s; 51°10'·60N 01°32'·26E.
SE Goodwin ◌ Fl (3) R 10s; 51°12'·99N 01°34'·45E
E GOODWIN ⛟ 51°13'·26N 01°36'·37E; Fl 15s 12m **23M**; R hull with lt twr amidships; ***Racon (T) 10M***; *Horn 30s*.
E Goodwin ⚲ Q (3) 10s; 51°15'·67N 01°35'·69E.
NE Goodwin ⚲ Q (3) 10s; ***Racon (M) 10M***. 51°20'·31N 01°34'·16E.

DEAL and THE DOWNS
Deal Bank ◌ QR; 51°12'·92N 01°25'·57E.
Goodwin Fork ⚲ Q (6) + L Fl 15s; *Bell;* 51°14'·33N 01°26'·86E.
Downs ◌ Fl (2) R 5s; *Bell;* 51°14'·50N 01°26'·22E.

GULL STREAM
W Goodwin ◣ Fl G 5s; 51°15'·61N 01°27'·38E.
S Brake ◌ Fl (3) R 10s; 51°15'·77N 01°26'·82E.
NW Goodwin ⚲ Q (9) 15s; *Bell;* 51°16'·65N 01°28'·50E.
Brake ◌ Fl (4) R 15s; *Bell;* 51°16'·98N 01°28'·19E.
N Goodwin ◣ Fl G 2·5s; 51°17'·91N 01°30'·20E.
Gull Stream ◌ QR; 51°18'·26N 01°29'·69E.
Gull ⚲ VQ (3) 5s; 51°19'·57N 01°31'·30E.
Goodwin Knoll ◣ Fl (2) G 5s; 51°19'·57N 01°32'·20E.

WGS84 DATUM
Plot waypoints on chart before use

RAMSGATE CHANNEL
B2 ◂ Fl (2) G 5s; 51°18'·26N 01°23'·93E.
W Quern ⌇Q (9) 15s; 51°18'·98N 01°25'·39E.

RAMSGATE
RA ⌇ Q(6) + L Fl 15s; 51°19'·60N 01°30'·13E.
E Brake ⌇ Fl R 5s; 51°19'·47N 01°29'·20E.
No. 1 ▴QG; 51°19'·56N 01°27'·29E.
No. 2 ⌇ Fl (4) R 10s; 51°19'·46N 01°27'·28E.
No. 3 ▴ Fl G 2·5s; 51°19'·56N 01°26'·61E.
No. 4 ⌇ QR; 51°19'·46N 01°26'·60E.
N Quern ⌇ Q; 51°19'·41N 01°26'·11E.
No. 5 ⌇ Q (6) + L Fl 15s; 51°19'·56N 01°25'·91E.
No. 6 ⌇ Fl (2) R 5s; 51°19'·46N 01°25'·91E.
South Bkwtr Hd ⌇ VQ R 10m 5M; 51°19'·46N 01°25'·41E.
N Bkwtr Hd ⌇ QG 10m 5M; 51°19'·56N 01°25'·47E.
Western Marine terminal Dir lt 270° ⌇, Oc WRG 10s 10m 5M; B △, Or stripe; vis: 259°-G-269°-W- 271°-R-281°; 51°19'·51N

01°24'·85E. Rear 493m from front Oc 5s 17m 5M; B ▽, Or stripe; vis: 263°-278°.

BROADSTAIRS and NORTH FORELAND
Broadstairs Knoll ⌇ Fl R 2·5s; 51°20'·88N 01°29'·48E.
Pier SE End ⌇ 2 FR (vert) 7m 4M; 51°21'·50N 01°26'·74E.
Elbow ⌇ Q; 51°23'·23N 01°31'·59E.

North Foreland ☆ 51°22'·49N 01°26'·70E; Fl (5) WR 20s 57m **W19M, R16M, R15M**; W 8-sided twr; vis: shore-W-150°-R(**16M**)-181°-R(**15M**)-200°-W-011°; H24.

OFFSHORE MARKS
F1 ⌇ Fl (4) Y 15s; 51°11'·21N 01°44'·91E.
South Falls ⌇ Q (6) + L Fl 15s; 51°13'·84N 01°43'·93E.
Mid Falls ⌇ Fl (3) R 10s; 51°18'·63N 01°46'·99E.
Inter Bank ⌇ Fl Y 5s; *Bell; **Racon (M)10M**;* 51°16'·47N 01°52'·23E.
F2 ⌇ Fl (4) Y 15s; 51°20'·41N 01°56'·19E.

9.3.5 PASSAGE INFORMATION

Reference books include: Admiralty *Channel Pilot*; *Channel Cruising Companion* (Nautical Data Ltd/Featherstone/Aslett). See 9.0.5 for cross-Channel distances. Admiralty Leisure Folio 5605 covers Chichester to Ramsgate including the Dover Strait.

More Passage Information is threaded between the harbours in this Area.

THE EASTERN CHANNEL

This area embraces the greatest concentration of commercial shipping in the world. In such waters the greatest danger is a collision with a larger vessel, especially in poor visibility. Even when coastal cruising it is essential to know the limits of the TSS and ITZ. For example, the SW-bound TSS lane from the Dover Strait passes only 3.5M off Dungeness. Radar surveillance of the Dover Strait is maintained at all times by the Channel Navigation Information Service (CNIS). In addition to the many large ships using the traffic lanes, ferries and hovercraft cross between English and continental ports; fishing vessels operate both inshore and offshore; in the summer months many yachts may be encountered; and static dangers such as lobster pots and fishing nets are concentrated in certain places.

▶ *Tidal streams and ranges are significantly affected by the weather. Although the rates of tidal streams vary with locality, they are greatest in the narrower parts of the Channel and off major headlands. In the Dover Strait spring rates can reach 4kn, but elsewhere in open water they seldom exceed 2kn.* ◀

N'ly winds, which may give smooth water and pleasant sailing off the English coast, can cause rough seas on the French coast. In strong S'lies the English coast between Isle of Wight and Dover is very exposed and shelter is hard to find. The Dover Strait has a funnelling effect, which can increase the wind speed and cause very rough seas.

ON PASSAGE UP CHANNEL

▶ *There are three tidal gates; the Looe, Beachy Head and Dungeness. These form a tidal sequence which can enable a reasonably fast yacht to carry a fair tide from Selsey Bill to Dover. Based on a mean speed over the ground of 7kn, transit the Looe at about slack water, HW Dover +0500 (HW Portsmouth +0430); Beachy Head will be passed at HW D –0100; Dungeness at HW D +0300 and Dover at HW +0530, only stemming the first of the ebb in the last hour. The down-Channel passage is less efficient and a stop at Sovereign Harbour or Brighton may be considered.* ◀

SELSEY BILL AND THE OWERS

(AC 1652) Selsey Bill is a low headland off which lie the Owers, groups of drying rocks and shoals extending 3M to the S and 5M to the SE. Just W and SW of Selsey, The Streets extend 1·25M seaward. 1·25M SSW of the Bill are The Grounds (or Malt Owers) and The Dries. 1M E of The Dries, and about 1·25M S of the lifeboat house on E side of Selsey Bill, is The Mixon, a group of rocks marked by a red lit ⌇ at the E end. Immediately S of these dangers is the Looe Chan. It is marked by buoys at the western end, where it is narrowest between Brake (or Cross) Ledge to the N and Boulder Bk to the S. In daylight, good visibility and moderate weather, it is a useful short cut. ▶ *The E-going stream begins at HW Portsmouth + 0430, and the W-going at HW Portsmouth –0135, spring rates 2·5kn.* ◀ Beware lobster pots in this area.

In poor visibility, bad weather or at night keep S of the Owers SCM lt buoy, 7M SE of Selsey Bill, marking SE end of the Outer Owers. ▶ *Much of the Outer Owers is less than 3m, and large parts virtually dry. A combination of tidal streams and strong winds produces heavy breaking seas and overfalls over a large area.* ◀

OWERS TO BEACHY HEAD

(AC 1652) The coast from Selsey Bill to Brighton is low, faced by a shingle beach and with few off-lying dangers. Bognor Rks (dry in places) extend 1·75M ESE from a point 1M W of the pier, and Bognor Spit extends another 0·5M further E and S. Middleton ledge are rks running 8ca offshore, about 2M E of Bognor pier, with depths of less than 1m. Shelley Rks lie 5ca S of Middleton ledge, with depths of less than 1m.

Winter Knoll, about 2·5M SSW of Littlehampton has depths of 2·1m. Kingston Rks, depth 2m, lie about 3·25M ESE of Littlehampton. An unlit outfall bn is 3ca off Goring-on-sea (2M W of Worthing pier). Grass Banks, an extensive shoal with 2m depth at W end, lie about 1M S of Worthing pier. Elbow shoal, with depth of 3·1m, lies E of Grass Banks.

Off Shoreham, Church Rks, with depth of 0·3m, lie 1·5M W of the hbr ent and 2½ca offshore. Jenny Rks, with depth 0·9m, are 1·25M E of the ent, 3ca offshore.

At Brighton the S Downs form the coastline, and high chalk cliffs are conspic from here to Beachy Head. There are no dangers more than 3ca offshore, until Birling Gap, where a rky ledge begins, on which is built Beachy Head lt ho. Head Ledge (dries) extends about 4ca S. Beware of fishing gear markers close inshore. ▶ *2M S of Beachy Hd the W-going stream begins at HW Dover +0030, and the E-going at HW Dover –0520, sp rates 2·25kn. In bad weather there are overfalls off the Head, which should then be given a berth of 2M.* ◀

9.3.6 LITTLEHAMPTON

W. Sussex **50°47´·87N 00°32´·43W** ❀⚓⚓✿✿

CHARTS AC 5605, 1652, 1991; Imray C12, C9; Stanfords 9, 30.

TIDES +0015 Dover; ML 2·8

Standard Port SHOREHAM (⟶)

Times				Height (metres)			
High Water		Low Water		MHWS	MHWN	MLWN	MLWS
0500	1000	0000	0600	6·3	4·8	1·9	0·6
1700	2200	1200	1800				
Differences **LITTLEHAMPTON (ENT)**							
+0010	0000	−0005	−0010	−0·4	−0·4	−0·2	−0·2
LITTLEHAMPTON (TARMAC)							
+0015	+0005	0000	+0045	−0·7	−0·7	−0·3	+0·2
ARUNDEL							
No data	+0120	No data		−3·1	−2·8	No data	
PAGHAM							
+0015	0000	−0015	−0025	−0·7	−0·5	−0·1	−0·1
BOGNOR REGIS							
+0010	−0005	−0005	−0020	−0·6	−0·5	−0·2	−0·1

NOTE: Tidal hts in hbr are affected by flow down R Arun. Tide seldom falls lower than 0·9m above CD.

SHELTER Good, but ent is dangerous in strong SE winds which cause swell up the hbr. The bar (0·8m) is rough in SW'lies. Visitors should berth initially at Town Quay, where marked, and then contact HM.

NAVIGATION WPT 50°47´·53N 00°32´·30W, 346°/0·6M to front ldg lt. Bar 5ca offshore.

- Hbr accessible from HW−3 to HW+2½ for approx 1·5m draft.
- The ebb runs fast (4–6 kn) at sp and yachts may have difficulty entering.
- From HW−1 to HW+4 a strong W-going tidal stream sets across the ent; keep to E side. Speed limit 6½kn.

On E side of ent chan a training wall which covers at half-tide is marked by 7 poles and lit bn at S end. The W pier is a long, prominent structure of wood piles; beware shoal ground within its arm. A tide gauge on end shows height of tide above CD. To obtain depth on the bar subtract 0·8m from indicated depth.

River Arun. A retractable footbridge (3·6m clearance MHWS; 9·4m above CD) 3ca above Town Quay gives access for masted craft to Littlehampton marina. It is opened by request to HM before 1630 previous day. The River Arun is navigable on the tide by small, unmasted craft for 24M.

LIGHTS AND MARKS High-rise bldg (38m) is conspic 0·4M NNE of hbr ent. A pile with small platform and ✯, Fl Y (5) 20s 5M, is 2·5M SE of hbr ent at 50°46´·1N 00°29´·5W.

Ldg lts 346°: Front FG on B column; Rear, lt ho Oc WY 7·5s at root of E bkwtr, 290°-W-356°-Y-042°. The Fl G 3s lt at Norfolk Wharf leads craft upstream, once inside hbr ent.

When Pilot boat with P1 at the bow displays the Pilot flag 'H' (WR vert halves) or ○ over ● lts, all boats keep clear of ent; large ship moving.

Footbridge sigs, from high mast to port: Fl G lt = open; Fl R lt = bridge moving Unlit = closed.

Bridge's retractable centre section (22m wide) has 2 FR (vert) to port and 2 FG (vert) to stbd at both upstream and downstream ends.

R/T HM VHF Ch 71 16 (0900-1700LT); Pilots Ch 71 16 when vessel due. Bridge Ch 71. Marinas Ch **80 M** (office hrs).

TELEPHONE (Code 01903) HM 721215, www.littlehampton.org.uk; MRCC (02392) 552100; Marinecall 09068 969646; Police 08456 070999; Dr 714113.

FACILITIES Town Quay, AB £20 <8m, £22 >8m, ⊞, FW, 🗑, ME, ✕; **Services**: ACA. Showers/toilets in hbr office. Slip (pay Hbr dues).

Littlehampton Sailing and Motor Club ☎ 715859, M, FW, Bar;

David Hillyard Ltd: ☎ 713327, hillyard@btclick.com; AB 6❶ £1.00; FW, ⊞, BY, ✕ (Wood), ME, Slip, C (50ton).

Arun YC (92+10 visitors), £10.00/yacht, ☎ 714533, (dries; access HW±3), M, ⊞, FW, Bar, Slip, R, Showers, ♿;

Littlehampton Marina, (120), £2.00, ☎ 713553, Slip, BH (12 ton), P, D, 🗑, R, Bar, ✕, ME, ♿;

Ship and Anchor Marina, about 2M up-river at Ford, (50+, some visitors) ☎ (01243) 551262, (access HW±4), Slip, FW, ME, ✕, CH, 🗑, R, Bar.

Town P, D, 🛒, R, Bar, ✉, Ⓑ, ⇌, ✈ (Shoreham).

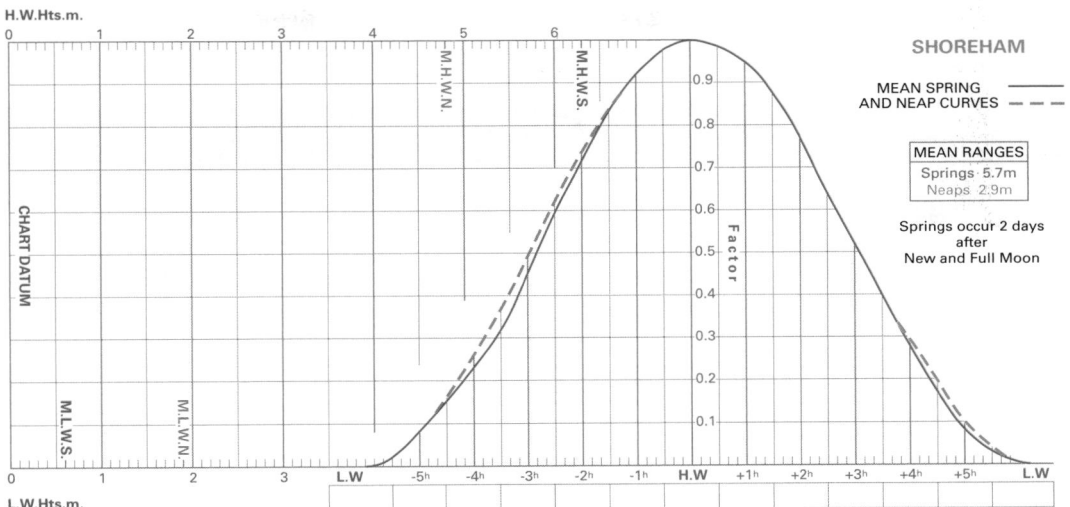

SHOREHAM

MEAN SPRING
AND NEAP CURVES

MEAN RANGES
Springs 5.7m
Neaps 2.9m

Springs occur 2 days
after
New and Full Moon

9.3.7 SHOREHAM

W. Sussex 50°49'·53N 00°14'·85W ✿✿♦♦✿✿

CHARTS AC 5605, 1652, 2044; Imray C12, C9; Stanfords 9, 30.

TIDES +0009 Dover; ML 3·3; Duration 0605

Standard Port SHOREHAM (→)

Times				Height (metres)			
High Water		Low Water		MHWS	MHWN	MLWN	MLWS
0500	1000	0000	0600	6·3	4·8	1·9	0·6
1700	2200	1200	1800				
Differences WORTHING							
+0010	0000	−0005	−0010	−0·1	−0·2	0·0	0·0

SHELTER Excellent, once through the lock and into The Canal. The shallow water (dredged 1·9m) at the ent can be very rough in strong on-shore winds and dangerous in onshore gales. Lady Bee and Aldrington (E end of The Canal) marinas, least depth 2m, both welcome visitors. They are managed by the Hbr Authority. Visitors are advised not to use the drying Western Arm if possible. Hbr speed limit = 4kn.

NAVIGATION WPT 50°49'·23N 00°14'·81W, 355°/0·52M to front ldg lt. From E beware Jenny Rks (0·9m) and, from the W, Church

Rks (0·3m). The Eastern Arm leads to Prince George Lock, the N'ly of two locks, which opens H24 @ H+30 for arrivals and H for departures; also, if not busy, at other times on request VHF Ch 14. Lock ent is 5·5m wide, pontoon inside on S wall; sill is 0·26m below CD, denying access only at about LWS±1. Lock will advise exact depth on Ch 14. Waiting space on S side of central lead-in pier. Commercial ships use Prince Philip lock; yachts to keep clear. A Ro-Ro ramp and terminal are on S side of lock.

LIGHTS AND MARKS Radio mast is conspic 170m N of High lt. SCM lit buoy, marks outfall diffusers, 157°/1·8M from hbr ent. Chimney 100m high, silver with blk top. 3F.R(hor) at top and 3F.R(hor) mid height. SYC yacht race signal mast on Shoreham Beach 00°16'·06W. Ldg lts 355°: front Oc 5s 8m 10M; rear High lt, Fl 10s 13m 15M.

Traffic Sigs IPTS (Sigs 2 and 5, Oc) are shown from Middle Pier. Note : ● Fl lt exempts small craft.
Oc R 3s (from LB ho, directed at E or W Arms) = No exit.

Lock Sigs (Comply strictly to avoid turbulence):
3 ● (vert) = do not approach lock.
● ○ ● (vert) = clear to approach lock.

R/T Call *Shoreham Hbr Radio* VHF Ch **14** 16 (H24) HM and lock. Lock will advise Lady Bee Marina of arrivals, 0830-1800 Mon-Sat; 1000-1400 Sun.

TELEPHONE (Code 01273) HM 598100; Locks 592366; MRCC (02392) 552100; Marinecall 09068 969646; Police 08456 070999; Ⓗ 455622; Dr 461101.

FACILITIES **Lady Bee Marina** (110+10 Ⓥ) ☎ 593801 (0900-1700), mob 07802 848915 (best to pre-book), £15·50/craft <12m inc FW & ⊡. Access as lock times, AB, P & D (cans), CH, ME, El, ✕, SM, R, 🛒, Slip. **Sussex YC** ☎ 464868, welcomes visitors, but has only one AB in The Canal, so prior notice advised; also a drying ½ tide pontoon in the Western Arm (limited Ⓥ), R, Bar, &.
Services: P & D on N side of W Arm HW±3; ACA.
Town Ⓞ, ✉, Ⓑ, ⇌, ✈.

TIME ZONE (UT)
For Summer Time add ONE hour in **non-shaded areas**

SHOREHAM LAT 50°50'N LONG 0°15'W
TIMES AND HEIGHTS OF HIGH AND LOW WATERS

Dates in red are SPRINGS
Dates in blue are NEAPS

YEAR 2010

JANUARY

Day	Time m	Time m	Time m	Time m
1 F	0506 0.9	1111 6.4	1733 0.6	2345 6.4
2 SA	0554 0.7	1200 6.5	1821 0.5	
3 SU	0034 6.5	0643 0.7	1250 6.5	1909 0.5
4 M	0123 6.5	0732 0.7	1338 6.4	1958 0.5
5 TU	0211 6.5	0821 0.8	1426 6.2	2047 0.7
6 W	0259 6.3	0912 0.9	1515 6.0	2138 0.9
7 TH	0347 6.0	1006 1.2	1607 5.6	2231 1.2
8 F	0440 5.7	1104 1.5	1704 5.3	2331 1.5
9 SA	0539 5.4	1211 1.7	1811 5.0	
10 SU	0041 1.8	0648 5.1	1322 1.8	1931 4.9
11 M	0152 1.9	0833 5.1	1427 1.7	2046 5.0
12 TU	0254 1.7	0909 5.3	1523 1.5	2144 5.3
13 W	0346 1.6	1001 5.5	1611 1.3	2231 5.6
14 TH	0431 1.4	1044 5.6	1653 1.1	2311 5.8
15 F	0511 1.2	1122 5.8	1731 1.0	2347 5.9
16 SA	0547 1.1	1156 5.9	1806 0.9	
17 SU	0020 6.0	0620 1.1	1226 5.9	1839 0.9
18 M	0049 6.0	0653 1.1	1254 5.8	1912 1.0
19 TU	0115 5.9	0725 1.1	1321 5.8	1944 1.0
20 W	0140 5.9	0756 1.2	1350 5.7	2012 1.1
21 TH	0209 5.8	0826 1.3	1422 5.6	2041 1.3
22 F	0244 5.6	0901 1.5	1500 5.4	2117 1.5
23 SA	0325 5.4	0945 1.7	1546 5.2	2205 1.7
24 SU	0416 5.2	1043 1.9	1646 4.9	2310 1.9
25 M	0526 5.0	1202 2.0	1820 4.8	
26 TU	0038 2.0	0703 5.0	1328 1.8	1948 5.0
27 W	0204 1.8	0818 5.3	1442 1.5	2056 5.4
28 TH	0311 1.4	0919 5.7	1541 1.1	2154 5.9
29 F	0406 1.0	1013 6.1	1633 0.7	2246 6.2
30 SA	0455 0.7	1103 6.4	1721 0.4	2336 6.5
31 SU	0542 0.5	1152 6.6	1808 0.3	

FEBRUARY

Day	Time m	Time m	Time m	Time m
1 M	0024 6.7	0629 0.4	1240 6.6	1854 0.2
2 TU	0109 6.8	0715 0.4	1325 6.6	1939 0.3
3 W	0152 6.7	0800 0.5	1408 6.4	2023 0.4
4 TH	0234 6.5	0844 0.7	1450 6.1	2106 0.7
5 F	0315 6.1	0929 1.0	1533 5.7	2150 1.2
6 SA	0400 5.6	1017 1.4	1623 5.2	2241 1.6
7 SU	0453 5.2	1119 1.8	1726 4.8	2353 2.0
8 M	0600 4.8	1249 2.1	1847 4.6	
9 TU	0126 2.2	0730 4.7	1406 2.0	2030 4.7
10 W	0237 2.0	0856 4.9	1506 1.7	2132 5.1
11 TH	0331 1.7	0949 5.3	1554 1.4	2217 5.5
12 F	0415 1.4	1031 5.6	1634 1.1	2255 5.7
13 SA	0452 1.2	1106 5.8	1710 0.9	2329 5.9
14 SU	0526 1.0	1138 5.9	1744 0.8	2359 6.0
15 M	0559 0.9	1205 5.9	1817 0.8	
16 TU	0024 6.0	0630 0.9	1230 5.9	1848 0.8
17 W	0047 6.0	0700 0.9	1256 5.9	1917 0.9
18 TH	0111 6.0	0727 1.0	1324 5.9	1941 0.9
19 F	0140 6.0	0754 1.0	1355 5.8	2008 1.1
20 SA	0213 5.9	0826 1.2	1430 5.7	2044 1.3
21 SU	0251 5.6	0908 1.4	1513 5.4	2131 1.6
22 M	0339 5.3	1004 1.7	1610 5.0	2235 1.9
23 TU	0445 4.9	1123 1.9	1743 4.7	
24 W	0010 2.1	0637 4.8	1304 1.9	1931 4.9
25 TH	0149 1.8	0803 5.1	1428 1.5	2044 5.4
26 F	0259 1.4	0908 5.6	1528 1.0	2143 5.9
27 SA	0353 0.9	1002 6.1	1617 0.6	2234 6.3
28 SU	0440 0.5	1051 6.4	1703 0.3	2321 6.6

MARCH

Day	Time m	Time m	Time m	Time m
1 M	0525 0.3	1138 6.6	1748 0.1	
2 TU	0006 6.8	0609 0.2	1223 6.7	1831 0.1
3 W	0048 6.8	0652 0.2	1305 6.6	1914 0.2
4 TH	0128 6.7	0734 0.4	1345 6.4	1954 0.4
5 F	0206 6.4	0814 0.6	1423 6.1	2033 0.8
6 SA	0243 6.0	0853 1.0	1503 5.7	2113 1.2
7 SU	0323 5.5	0935 1.4	1550 5.2	2158 1.7
8 M	0413 5.0	1027 1.9	1650 4.7	2301 2.2
9 TU	0520 4.6	1158 2.2	1807 4.4	
10 W	0058 2.3	0647 4.4	1340 2.1	2003 4.6
11 TH	0214 2.1	0833 4.7	1441 1.8	2108 5.0
12 F	0308 1.7	0927 5.1	1528 1.4	2152 5.4
13 SA	0350 1.4	1006 5.4	1607 1.1	2228 5.7
14 SU	0426 1.1	1040 5.7	1642 1.0	2300 5.9
15 M	0500 1.0	1110 5.8	1716 0.8	2328 6.0
16 TU	0532 0.9	1137 5.9	1749 0.8	2352 6.0
17 W	0604 0.8	1203 6.0	1821 0.8	
18 TH	0017 6.1	0634 0.8	1232 6.0	1849 0.8
19 F	0045 6.1	0701 0.8	1301 6.0	1915 0.9
20 SA	0115 6.0	0729 0.9	1333 5.9	1946 1.0
21 SU	0149 5.9	0804 1.0	1410 5.7	2025 1.2
22 M	0228 5.7	0848 1.3	1454 5.4	2114 1.5
23 TU	0317 5.3	0946 1.6	1554 5.0	2222 1.9
24 W	0426 4.8	1106 1.9	1735 4.7	2358 2.0
25 TH	0621 4.7	1247 1.8	1916 4.9	
26 F	0134 1.7	0747 5.1	1410 1.4	2028 5.4
27 SA	0241 1.3	0852 5.6	1508 0.9	2125 6.0
28 SU	0333 0.8	0945 6.0	1556 0.6	2214 6.4
29 M	0419 0.5	1033 6.4	1641 0.3	2259 6.6
30 TU	0503 0.3	1119 6.5	1724 0.2	2342 6.7
31 W	0546 0.2	1202 6.6	1807 0.2	

APRIL

Day	Time m	Time m	Time m	Time m
1 TH	0023 6.7	0628 0.3	1244 6.5	1847 0.4
2 F	0102 6.5	0708 0.4	1322 6.3	1927 0.6
3 SA	0138 6.3	0746 0.7	1400 6.0	2004 0.9
4 SU	0214 5.9	0824 1.0	1439 5.7	2043 1.3
5 M	0252 5.4	0904 1.4	1524 5.2	2128 1.7
6 TU	0340 5.0	0953 1.8	1622 4.8	2226 2.1
7 W	0446 4.5	1102 2.1	1731 4.6	
8 TH	0000 2.3	0602 4.4	1256 2.1	1856 4.6
9 F	0138 2.1	0738 4.5	1403 1.9	2023 4.9
10 SA	0233 1.8	0845 4.9	1452 1.6	2110 5.3
11 SU	0316 1.5	0927 5.2	1532 1.3	2147 5.6
12 M	0353 1.2	1000 5.5	1608 1.1	2219 5.8
13 TU	0427 1.0	1032 5.7	1644 1.0	2248 5.9
14 W	0501 0.9	1103 5.9	1718 0.9	2318 6.0
15 TH	0535 0.8	1136 6.0	1752 0.8	2349 6.1
16 F	0608 0.8	1209 6.0	1823 0.8	
17 SA	0021 6.1	0639 0.8	1243 6.0	1856 0.9
18 SU	0056 6.1	0714 0.8	1319 6.0	1933 1.0
19 M	0133 5.9	0754 0.9	1401 5.8	2017 1.2
20 TU	0217 5.6	0842 1.2	1450 5.5	2111 1.5
21 W	0310 5.3	0942 1.4	1556 5.2	2220 1.7
22 TH	0424 5.0	1058 1.6	1726 5.0	2347 1.8
23 F	0602 4.9	1228 1.6	1853 5.2	
24 SA	0110 1.6	0724 5.2	1343 1.3	2003 5.6
25 SU	0215 1.2	0828 5.5	1441 1.0	2059 5.9
26 M	0308 0.8	0922 5.9	1530 0.7	2149 6.2
27 TU	0355 0.6	1011 6.1	1616 0.5	2234 6.4
28 W	0440 0.4	1057 6.3	1700 0.5	2318 6.5
29 TH	0523 0.4	1141 6.3	1743 0.5	2359 6.4
30 F	0606 0.5	1222 6.3	1825 0.6	

Chart Datum: 3·27 metres below Ordnance Datum (Newlyn). HAT is 6·9 metres above Chart Datum; see 4.5

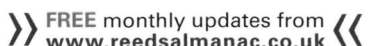

TIME ZONE (UT)
For Summer Time add ONE hour in **non-shaded areas**

SHOREHAM   LAT 50°50′N   LONG 0°15′W
TIMES AND HEIGHTS OF HIGH AND LOW WATERS

Dates in red are SPRINGS
Dates in blue are NEAPS

YEAR 2010

SE England

MAY

Day	Time	m	Day	Time	m
1 SA	0037	6.3	16 SU	0002	6.1
	0645	0.6		0623	0.7
	1302	6.1		1231	6.1
	1904	0.8		1843	0.9
2 SU	0114	6.0	17 M	0043	6.1
	0724	0.8		0705	0.8
	1340	5.9		1314	6.0
	1942	1.0		1927	0.9
3 M	0150	5.7	18 TU	0127	6.0
	0801	1.0		0751	0.8
	1419	5.7		1400	5.9
	2021	1.3		2016	1.1
4 TU	0229	5.4	19 W	0215	5.8
	0841	1.3		0842	1.0
	1503	5.3		1453	5.7
	2105	1.6		2111	1.2
5 W	0314	5.0	20 TH	0311	5.5
	0928	1.6		0940	1.2
	1554	5.0		1555	5.5
	2157	1.9		2215	1.4
6 TH	0413	4.7	21 F	0418	5.3
	1025	1.9		1048	1.3
	1654	4.8		1706	5.4
	2302	2.1		2328	1.5
7 F	0519	4.5	22 SA	0535	5.2
	1135	2.0		1201	1.4
	1758	4.8		1820	5.4
8 SA	0025	2.1	23 SU	0040	1.4
	0626	4.6		0651	5.2
	1257	1.9		1311	1.3
	1903	4.9		1929	5.6
9 SU	0139	1.9	24 M	0145	1.2
	0730	4.8		0758	5.4
	1359	1.7		1411	1.1
	2002	5.1		2029	5.8
10 M	0229	1.6	25 TU	0241	1.0
	0825	5.0		0857	5.6
	1447	1.5		1505	1.0
	2050	5.4		2122	6.0
11 TU	0312	1.4	26 W	0332	0.8
	0910	5.3		0949	5.8
	1528	1.3		1554	0.9
	2130	5.6		2211	6.1
12 W	0350	1.2	27 TH	0419	0.7
	0951	5.6		1037	6.0
	1608	1.1		1640	0.8
	2209	5.8		2256	6.1
13 TH	0428	1.0	28 F	0504	0.7
	1031	5.8		1123	6.0
	1646	1.0		1725	0.8
	2246	6.0		2338	6.1
14 F	0506	0.9	29 SA	0547	0.7
	1110	5.9		1205	6.0
	1724	0.9		1807	0.9
	2324	6.1			
15 SA	0544	0.8	30 SU	0018	6.0
	1150	6.0		0627	0.8
	1803	0.9		1246	6.0
				1846	1.0
			31 M	0056	5.9
				0706	0.9
				1324	5.9
				1923	1.1

JUNE

Day	Time	m	Day	Time	m
1 TU	0132	5.7	16 W	0123	6.1
	0743	1.0		0746	0.6
	1401	5.7		1358	6.2
	2001	1.3		2011	0.8
2 W	0209	5.5	17 TH	0212	6.0
	0821	1.2		0837	0.7
	1440	5.5		1449	6.1
	2042	1.5		2104	0.9
3 TH	0248	5.2	18 F	0305	5.8
	0903	1.4		0930	0.9
	1521	5.3		1542	5.9
	2127	1.7		2201	1.1
4 F	0333	5.0	19 SA	0401	5.6
	0950	1.6		1028	1.0
	1609	5.1		1639	5.7
	2219	1.8		2302	1.2
5 SA	0428	4.8	20 SU	0503	5.4
	1043	1.8		1131	1.2
	1704	5.0		1742	5.6
	2317	1.9			
6 SU	0531	4.7	21 M	0008	1.3
	1142	1.9		0611	5.2
	1804	4.9		1238	1.4
				1849	5.4
7 M	0020	1.9	22 TU	0114	1.4
	0633	4.7		0725	5.2
	1246	1.9		1343	1.4
	1903	5.0		1958	5.4
8 TU	0124	1.8	23 W	0216	1.3
	0732	4.9		0833	5.3
	1348	1.7		1443	1.4
	1958	5.2		2059	5.6
9 W	0221	1.6	24 TH	0313	1.2
	0826	5.2		0932	5.5
	1444	1.5		1537	1.3
	2049	5.5		2153	5.7
10 TH	0311	1.3	25 F	0403	1.1
	0916	5.4		1024	5.7
	1533	1.3		1626	1.2
	2135	5.7		2241	5.8
11 F	0357	1.1	26 SA	0450	1.0
	1010	5.7		1110	5.8
	1618	1.1		1710	1.1
	2220	5.9		2324	5.9
12 SA	0441	0.9	27 SU	0532	0.9
	1050	5.9		1152	5.9
	1703	1.0		1751	1.1
	2305	6.1			
13 SU	0526	0.8	28 M	0004	5.9
	1136	6.1		0611	0.9
	1748	0.9		1231	5.9
	2350	6.2		1829	1.1
14 M	0611	0.7	29 TU	0040	5.8
	1222	6.2		0648	0.9
	1834	0.8		1307	5.9
				1905	1.1
15 TU	0036	6.2	30 W	0114	5.7
	0657	0.6		0723	1.0
	1310	6.2		1340	5.8
	1921	0.8		1940	1.2

JULY

Day	Time	m	Day	Time	m
1 TH	0145	5.6	16 F	0202	6.3
	0759	1.1		0822	0.5
	1411	5.7		1434	6.4
	2016	1.3		2047	0.7
2 F	0216	5.4	17 SA	0249	6.1
	0835	1.2		0910	0.6
	1441	5.6		1520	6.2
	2054	1.4		2137	0.9
3 SA	0249	5.3	18 SU	0338	5.8
	0912	1.4		1001	0.8
	1514	5.4		1609	5.9
	2136	1.6		2232	1.2
4 SU	0328	5.1	19 M	0431	5.5
	0953	1.6		1057	1.3
	1555	5.2		1704	5.5
	2223	1.7		2334	1.5
5 M	0416	4.9	20 TU	0534	5.1
	1042	1.8		1204	1.6
	1648	5.0		1809	5.2
	2319	1.9			
6 TU	0522	4.8	21 W	0046	1.7
	1143	1.9		0651	4.9
	1800	5.0		1319	1.8
				1928	5.1
7 W	0025	1.9	22 TH	0157	1.7
	0642	4.8		0817	5.0
	1254	1.9		1427	1.7
	1912	5.0		2044	5.2
8 TH	0134	1.8	23 F	0259	1.5
	0749	5.0		0924	5.2
	1404	1.8		1525	1.6
	2015	5.3		2143	5.4
9 F	0238	1.5	24 SA	0351	1.3
	0849	5.3		1015	5.5
	1515	1.5		1613	1.3
	2111	5.6		2231	5.6
10 SA	0334	1.2	25 SU	0435	1.1
	0943	5.7		1059	5.8
	1558	1.2		1656	1.2
	2202	5.9		2312	5.8
11 SU	0423	0.9	26 M	0515	1.0
	1035	6.0		1138	5.9
	1647	0.9		1734	1.1
	2251	6.1		2349	5.9
12 M	0511	0.7	27 TU	0552	0.9
	1124	6.2		1213	6.0
	1739	0.7		1809	1.0
	2340	6.3			
13 TU	0558	0.5	28 W	0022	5.9
	1213	6.4		0626	0.9
	1822	0.6		1245	6.0
				1842	1.0
14 W	0027	6.4	29 TH	0051	5.8
	0646	0.4		0659	0.9
	1301	6.5		1313	5.9
	1909	0.5		1915	1.1
15 TH	0115	6.4	30 F	0117	5.8
	0734	0.4		0732	1.0
	1348	6.5		1336	5.9
	1958	0.6		1947	1.1
			31 SA	0142	5.7
				0803	1.1
				1401	5.8
				2019	1.2

AUGUST

Day	Time	m	Day	Time	m
1 SU	0211	5.6	16 M	0312	5.9
	0832	1.2		0929	1.0
	1431	5.7		1538	5.9
	2050	1.4		2156	1.3
2 M	0245	5.4	17 TU	0401	5.4
	0904	1.4		1020	1.5
	1508	5.5		1630	5.4
	2128	1.6		2256	1.7
3 TU	0327	5.2	18 W	0502	5.0
	0946	1.7		1129	1.9
	1554	5.2		1734	4.9
	2220	1.8			
4 W	0421	4.9	19 TH	0019	2.0
	1045	1.9		0621	4.7
	1656	4.9		1259	2.1
	2331	2.0		1901	4.7
5 TH	0547	4.7	20 F	0141	2.0
	1207	2.1		0806	4.8
	1832	4.9		1413	2.0
				2034	4.9
6 F	0056	1.9	21 SA	0244	1.7
	0722	4.9		0913	5.1
	1335	1.9		1511	1.7
	1951	5.1		2132	5.3
7 SA	0216	1.6	22 SU	0335	1.4
	0831	5.2		1001	5.5
	1448	1.6		1557	1.4
	2054	5.5		2216	5.6
8 SU	0318	1.2	23 M	0416	1.1
	0929	5.7		1040	5.8
	1543	1.2		1636	1.2
	2148	5.9		2254	5.8
9 M	0408	0.8	24 TU	0453	1.0
	1022	6.1		1116	6.0
	1632	0.8		1711	1.0
	2239	6.3		2328	5.9
10 TU	0455	0.5	25 W	0527	0.9
	1111	6.5		1148	6.1
	1719	0.6		1744	1.0
	2327	6.5		2357	6.0
11 W	0542	0.3	26 TH	0600	0.9
	1158	6.7		1216	6.1
	1805	0.4		1817	1.0
12 TH	0014	6.6	27 F	0022	5.9
	0627	0.2		0632	0.9
	1245	6.8		1239	6.0
	1851	0.4		1848	1.0
13 F	0100	6.6	28 SA	0046	5.9
	0713	0.3		0702	0.9
	1329	6.7		1301	6.0
	1937	0.4		1917	1.0
14 SA	0144	6.5	29 SU	0112	5.9
	0758	0.4		0729	1.0
	1411	6.6		1327	5.9
	2022	0.6		1943	1.1
15 SU	0227	6.3	30 M	0140	5.8
	0843	0.6		0755	1.2
	1453	6.3		1357	5.8
	2108	0.9		2012	1.3
			31 TU	0212	5.6
				0827	1.4
				1432	5.6
				2050	1.5

Chart Datum: 3·27 metres below Ordnance Datum (Newlyn). HAT is 6·9 metres above Chart Datum; see 4.5

TIME ZONE (UT)
For Summer Time add ONE hour in **non-shaded areas**

SHOREHAM LAT 50°50'N LONG 0°15'W
TIMES AND HEIGHTS OF HIGH AND LOW WATERS

Dates in red are **SPRINGS**
Dates in blue are NEAPS

YEAR **2010**

SEPTEMBER

Time	m		Time	m
1 0252	5.4	**16** 0434	4.9
0911	1.7	1051	2.1
W 1516	5.3	TH 1704	4.8
◗ 2141	1.8	2344	2.2
2 0344	5.0	**17** 0551	4.6
1011	2.0	1236	2.3
TH 1616	4.9	F 1830	4.6
2253	2.0		
3 0508	4.7	**18** 0117	2.2
1137	2.2	0743	4.7
F 1804	4.8	SA 1353	2.1
		2013	4.8
4 0029	2.0	**19** 0221	1.9
0703	4.8	0849	5.1
SA 1317	2.0	SU 1449	1.8
1934	5.0	2109	5.2
5 0159	1.7	**20** 0310	1.5
0815	5.3	0934	5.5
SU 1433	1.6	M 1532	1.5
2039	5.5	2151	5.6
6 0302	1.2	**21** 0350	1.2
0914	5.8	1012	5.8
M 1527	1.1	TU 1609	1.2
2134	6.0	2227	5.8
7 0351	0.8	**22** 0425	1.0
1005	6.3	1045	6.0
TU 1614	0.7	W 1643	1.0
2223	6.4	2258	6.0
8 0436	0.4	**23** 0459	0.9
1052	6.6	1115	6.1
W 1659	0.4	TH 1716	1.0
● 2310	6.6	○ 2325	6.0
9 0520	0.3	**24** 0532	0.9
1138	6.8	1141	6.1
TH 1743	0.3	F 1748	0.9
2355	6.7	2350	6.0
10 0604	0.2	**25** 0604	0.9
1221	6.9	1204	6.1
F 1828	0.3	SA 1820	1.0
11 0039	6.7	**26** 0017	6.0
0648	0.3	0633	1.0
SA 1304	6.8	SU 1230	6.1
1911	0.4	1848	1.0
12 0122	6.5	**27** 0045	6.0
0731	0.5	0659	1.1
SU 1345	6.6	M 1258	6.0
1954	0.6	1915	1.1
13 0203	6.3	**28** 0115	5.9
0813	0.8	0728	1.2
M 1425	6.2	TU 1330	5.9
2037	1.0	1946	1.2
14 0245	5.9	**29** 0148	5.8
0857	1.2	0804	1.4
TU 1507	5.7	W 1406	5.7
2122	1.4	2027	1.5
15 0334	5.4	**30** 0229	5.5
0945	1.7	0851	1.7
W 1558	5.2	TH 1451	5.3
◗ 2216	1.8	2120	1.8

OCTOBER

Time	m		Time	m
1 0324	5.1	**16** 0516	4.8
0954	2.0	1151	2.4
F 1554	4.9	SA 1748	4.6
◗ 2233	2.0		
2 0455	4.8	**17** 0036	2.2
1121	2.1	0645	4.8
SA 1745	4.8	SU 1318	2.2
		1926	4.7
3 0008	2.0	**18** 0144	2.0
0643	5.0	0806	5.1
SU 1258	2.0	M 1415	1.9
1915	5.1	2031	5.1
4 0137	1.7	**19** 0235	1.7
0756	5.4	0855	5.4
M 1411	1.5	TU 1459	1.6
2020	5.6	2114	5.4
5 0239	1.2	**20** 0316	1.4
0854	5.9	0933	5.7
TU 1505	1.0	W 1537	1.3
2114	6.0	2149	5.7
6 0328	0.8	**21** 0353	1.2
0943	6.4	1006	5.9
W 1551	0.6	TH 1612	1.1
2203	6.4	2220	5.9
7 0413	0.5	**22** 0428	1.1
1029	6.7	1035	6.0
TH 1635	0.4	F 1646	1.0
◑ 2249	6.6	2250	6.1
8 0456	0.4	**23** 0502	1.0
1113	6.8	1103	6.1
F 1719	0.3	SA 1720	1.0
2334	6.7	○ 2320	6.1
9 0540	0.4	**24** 0535	1.0
1156	6.8	1132	6.1
SA 1803	0.4	SU 1753	1.0
		2352	6.1
10 0017	6.6	**25** 0607	1.1
0623	0.5	1203	6.1
SU 1238	6.7	M 1824	1.0
1846	0.5		
11 0059	6.5	**26** 0024	6.1
0705	0.7	0637	1.1
M 1318	6.4	TU 1236	6.1
1928	0.7	1856	1.1
12 0140	6.2	**27** 0058	6.0
0747	1.0	0712	1.2
TU 1357	6.1	W 1311	5.9
2009	1.1	1932	1.2
13 0222	5.8	**28** 0136	5.9
0829	1.4	0752	1.4
W 1440	5.6	TH 1352	5.7
2052	1.5	2016	1.4
14 0310	5.4	**29** 0221	5.6
0916	1.8	0842	1.6
TH 1530	5.2	F 1441	5.4
◗ 2143	1.9	2111	1.6
15 0408	5.0	**30** 0319	5.3
1016	2.2	0946	1.8
F 1633	4.8	SA 1546	5.1
2253	2.2	◗ 2220	1.8
		31 0442	5.1
		1106	1.9
		SU 1720	5.0
		2345	1.8

NOVEMBER

Time	m		Time	m
1 0615	5.2	**16** 0039	2.1
1231	1.8	0647	5.0
M 1847	5.2	TU 1323	2.0
		1916	4.9
2 0106	1.6	**17** 0145	1.9
0727	5.5	0749	5.2
TU 1342	1.4	W 1416	1.8
1954	5.5	2014	5.1
3 0209	1.3	**18** 0234	1.7
0826	5.9	0837	5.5
W 1438	1.1	TH 1459	1.5
2050	5.9	2059	5.4
4 0302	0.9	**19** 0317	1.5
0918	6.3	0918	5.7
TH 1527	0.8	F 1539	1.3
2141	6.4	2138	5.7
5 0349	0.7	**20** 0356	1.3
1004	6.5	0955	5.9
F 1613	0.6	SA 1616	1.2
2228	6.4	2216	5.9
6 0434	0.6	**21** 0433	1.2
1049	6.6	1031	6.0
SA 1658	0.5	SU 1653	1.0
● 2314	6.5	○ 2254	6.0
7 0519	0.6	**22** 0510	1.1
1133	6.6	1106	6.1
SU 1742	0.6	M 1730	1.0
2358	6.5	2331	6.1
8 0602	0.7	**23** 0546	1.1
1215	6.5	1143	6.2
M 1826	0.7	TU 1806	0.9
9 0040	6.3	**24** 0009	6.1
0644	0.9	0622	1.1
TU 1255	6.2	W 1221	6.1
1907	0.9	1844	1.0
10 0122	6.1	**25** 0049	6.1
0725	1.1	0702	1.1
W 1335	6.0	TH 1302	6.0
1948	1.1	1925	1.0
11 0203	5.9	**26** 0131	6.0
0807	1.4	0747	1.2
TH 1417	5.6	F 1346	5.9
2029	1.4	2011	1.1
12 0248	5.6	**27** 0219	5.9
0851	1.7	0837	1.4
F 1503	5.3	SA 1436	5.7
2115	1.7	2104	1.3
13 0339	5.3	**28** 0314	5.7
0943	2.0	0936	1.5
SA 1559	4.9	SU 1536	5.4
◗ 2210	2.0	◗ 2206	1.5
14 0437	5.0	**29** 0421	5.5
1046	2.2	1045	1.6
SU 1703	4.7	M 1649	5.3
2317	2.1	2317	1.6
15 0540	4.9	**30** 0537	5.4
1208	2.2	1159	1.6
M 1809	4.7	TU 1808	5.3

DECEMBER

Time	m		Time	m
1 0030	1.5	**16** 0024	2.1
0650	5.5	0644	5.0
W 1308	1.5	TH 1305	2.0
1920	5.4	1914	4.9
2 0137	1.4	**17** 0132	2.0
0755	5.8	0742	5.2
TH 1410	1.2	F 1410	1.8
2024	5.6	2011	5.1
3 0236	1.2	**18** 0233	1.8
0852	6.0	0834	5.4
F 1504	1.0	SA 1502	1.6
2120	5.9	2102	5.4
4 0328	1.0	**19** 0323	1.6
0943	6.2	0921	5.7
SA 1555	0.9	SU 1548	1.3
2211	6.1	2149	5.7
5 0417	0.9	**20** 0407	1.4
1031	6.3	1005	5.9
SU 1642	0.8	M 1630	1.1
● 2259	6.2	2233	5.9
6 0503	0.9	**21** 0448	1.2
1116	6.3	1047	6.1
M 1727	0.7	TU 1711	0.9
2344	6.2	○ 2316	6.1
7 0547	0.9	**22** 0529	1.0
1159	6.2	1129	6.2
TU 1810	0.8	W 1753	0.8
		2358	6.2
8 0027	6.2	**23** 0611	0.9
0628	1.0	1211	6.3
W 1239	6.1	TH 1835	0.7
1851	0.9		
9 0107	6.1	**24** 0041	6.3
0708	1.1	0654	0.9
TH 1318	5.9	F 1255	6.3
1930	1.0	1918	0.7
10 0146	6.0	**25** 0126	6.3
0747	1.3	0739	0.9
F 1356	5.7	SA 1340	6.2
2008	1.2	2004	0.8
11 0225	5.7	**26** 0212	6.2
0826	1.5	0828	1.0
SA 1435	5.4	SU 1428	6.0
2048	1.4	2053	0.9
12 0305	5.5	**27** 0301	6.1
0909	1.7	0920	1.1
SU 1518	5.2	M 1519	5.8
2132	1.6	2147	1.1
13 0350	5.3	**28** 0355	5.8
0958	1.9	1019	1.3
M 1610	4.9	TU 1618	5.5
◗ 2222	1.9	◗ 2247	1.3
14 0443	5.1	**29** 0457	5.6
1054	2.0	1125	1.5
TU 1710	4.8	W 1725	5.3
2319	2.0	2354	1.5
15 0543	5.0	**30** 0606	5.4
1157	2.1	1235	1.6
W 1813	4.7	TH 1842	5.2
		31 0106	1.6
		0721	5.4
		F 1345	1.5
		1959	5.2

Chart Datum: 3·27 metres below Ordnance Datum (Newlyn). HAT is 6·9 metres above Chart Datum; see 4.5

9.3.8 BRIGHTON

E. Sussex **50°48'·53N 00°06'·38W** ✳✳✳✳✳✳✳✳

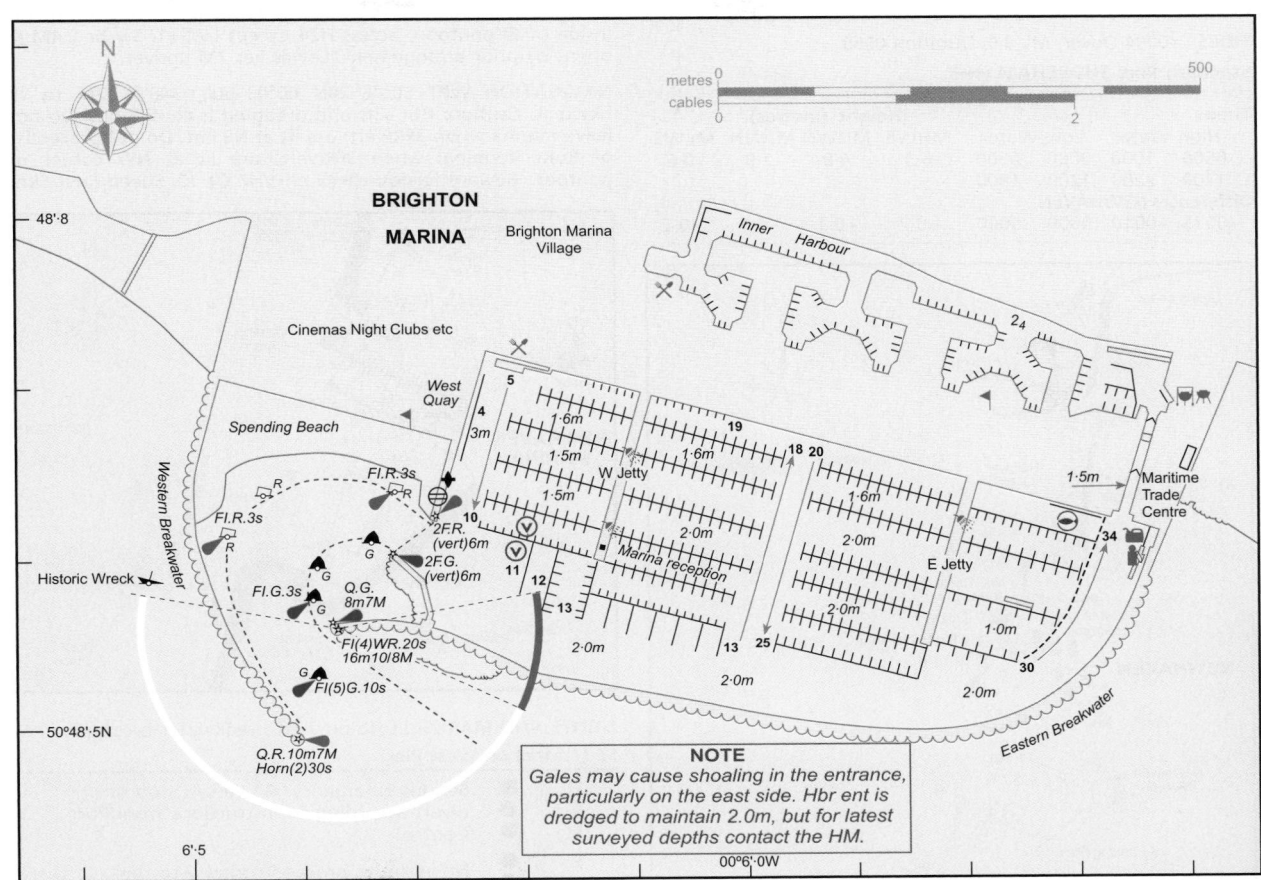

CHARTS AC 5605, 1652, 1991; Imray C12, C31, C9; Stanfords 9, 30.

TIDES +0004 Dover; ML 3·5; Duration 0605

Standard Port SHOREHAM (←)

Times				Height (metres)			
High Water		Low Water		MHWS	MHWN	MLWN	MLWS
0500	1000	0000	0600	6·3	4·8	1·9	0·6
1700	2200	1200	1800				
Differences BRIGHTON MARINA							
–0002	–0002	0000	0000	+0·2	+0·2	+0·1	+0·1

SHELTER Good in the marina under all conditions, but in strong S'ly winds confused seas can make the final appr very rough. Speed limit 5kn.

NAVIGATION WPT 50°48'·23N 00°06'·39W, 000°/0·26M to W bkwtr lt.

- Ent chan dredged 2·0m, but after gales shoaling occurs especially on E side; craft drawing >1·5m should keep to the W side of chan until past the second SHM buoy.
- In heavy weather, best appr is from SSE to avoid worst of the backlash from bkwtrs; beware shallow water E of ent in R sector of lt Fl (4) WR 20s.

W-going stream starts at Brighton HW–1½ and E-going at HW+4½. Inshore the sp rate reaches approx 1·5kn. A Historic Wreck (see 9.0.3) is at 50°48'·6N 00°06'·49W, immediately W of the marina's W bkwtr.

LIGHTS AND MARKS The marina is at the E end of the town, where white cliffs extend eastward. Daymark: conspic white

hospital block, brg 334° leads to ent. Six Y spar lt buoys (up to 2M offshore) used as racing buoys:

1. 50°48'·06N 00°06'·41W		2. 50°47'·61N 00°08'·43W	
3. 50°46'·61N 00°07'·00W		4. 50°47'·00N 00°15'·33W	
5. 50°48'·40N 00°19'·40W		6. 50°47'·40N 00°05'·00W	

A sewer outfall can buoy, Fl Y 5s is 1·1M off the coast. Navigational lts may be hard to see against shore glare:
E bkwtr Fl (4) WR 20s (intens) 16m 10/8M; vis 260°-R-295°-W-100°.
E bkwtr hd QG 8m 7M. W bkwtr hd, tr R/W bands, QR 10m 7M; Horn (2) 30s. Inner Hbr lock controlled by normal R/G lts, 0800-1800LT.

R/T Call: *Brighton Control* VHF Ch **M** 80 16 (H24).

TELEPHONE (Code 01273) HM 819919; MRCC (023 92) 552100; Marinecall 09068 969646; Police 08456 070999; Ⓗ 696955; Dr 686863.

FACILITIES **Brighton Marina** (1600 inc ⓥ) ☎ 819919, www. premiermarinas.com, £2·25, approx £1·00/m for < 4 hrs, Gas, Gaz, ▣, R, Bar, Wi-fi, BY, BH (60 ton), (35 ton), ⚓, ▣; Inner Hbr has least depth of 2·4m. Fuel pontoon (P, D, Gas): H24.

Brighton Marina YC ☎ 818711, Bar, R.

Services El, Ⓔ, ME, ✄, CH, ACA, Divers, Riggers, ▦, Superstore. Hbr Guides available from Hbr Office or by post.

Bus service from marina; timetable info ☎ 674881. Electric railway runs from marina to Palace Pier, Mar-Oct.

Town V, R, Bar, ✉, Ⓑ, ≈, ✈ (Shoreham).

9.3.9 NEWHAVEN

E. Sussex **50°46'·84N 00°03'·53E** ✵✵✵⚓⚓⚓✿✿

CHARTS AC 5605, 1652, 2154; Imray C31, C9, C12; Stanfords 9, 30.

TIDES +0004 Dover; ML 3·6; Duration 0550

Standard Port SHOREHAM (⟵)

Times				Height (metres)			
High Water		Low Water		MHWS	MHWN	MLWN	MLWS
0500	1000	0000	0600	6·3	4·8	1·9	0·6
1700	2200	1200	1800				
Differences NEWHAVEN							
–0015	–0010	0000	0000	+0·2	+0·1	–0·1	–0·2

SHELTER Good in all weathers, but in strong on-shore winds there is often a dangerous sea at the ent. Appr from the SW, to pass 50m off bkwtr hd to avoid heavy breaking seas on E side of dredged chan. At marina (mostly dredged to 1m), berth on inside of ❶ pontoon, access H24 except LWS±1. Sw br 0.4M N opens by prior arrangement. Lewes lies 7M upriver.

NAVIGATION WPT 50°46'·24N 00°03'·60E, 348°/0·32M to W bkwtr lt. Caution: Hbr silts and dredging is continuous. Do not leave marina when 3FR(vert) are lit at NE ent. Do not proceed S of RoRo terminal when 3FR(vert) are lit at NW corner of pontoon. Beware ferries; check on VHF Ch 12. Speed limit 5kn.

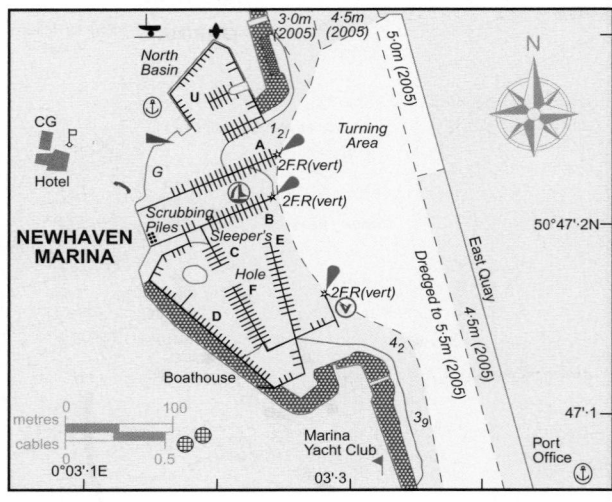

LIGHTS AND MARKS Lt Ho on west breakwater is conspic.

SS (Traffic) on West Pier

Fl	🔴	Serious emergency. All vessels stop or
Fl	🔴	divert according to instructions from Port
Fl	🔴	Control
F	🔴	No vessel to proceed contrary to this
F	🔴	signal
F	🔴	
F	🔴	
F	🔴	Small vessels may proceed. Two way traffic
F	⚪	
F	🔴	Proceed only when instructed by Port
F	⚪	Control. All other vessels keep clear
F	🔴	

R/T Port VHF Ch 12 16 (H24). Swing bridge opening Ch 12. Marina Ch 80 M (0800-1700).

TELEPHONE (Code 01273) HM 612868 (H24); Hbr Sig Stn 517922; MRCC (02392) 552100; Marinecall 09068 969646; Police 08456 070999; Dr 515076; Ⓗ 609411 (Casualty 696955).

FACILITIES Marina (280 +20 ❶) ☎ 513881, £2.15, D (HO,1ca N of marina ent), ME, El, ⚒, BH (18 ton), C (10 ton), CH, Gas, Gaz, Slip(☎ 612612 launch/recovery £17.50), 🛒, R, Bar, ▣, ♿; **Newhaven and Seaford SC** ☎ (01323) 890077, M, FW.

Town: ACA, SM, P, Ⓔ, 🛒, R, Bar, ✉, Ⓑ, ⇌, ✈ (Shoreham); **Ferries:** Dieppe; 2-3/day; 4 Hrs; LD Lines (www.ldlines.co.uk); Le Havre; daily (Summer); 6 Hrs; LD Lines.

9.3.10 EASTBOURNE

E. Sussex **50°47′·34N 00°19′·90E** ✳❀♨♨♨✿✿

CHARTS AC 536, 5605; Imray C31, C12, C8; Stanfords 9, 30.

TIDES –0005 Dover; ML 3·8; Duration 0540

Standard Port SHOREHAM (←)

Times				Height (metres)			
High Water		Low Water		MHWS	MHWN	MLWN	MLWS
0500	1000	0000	0600	6·3	4·8	1·9	0·6
1700	2200	1200	1800				
Differences EASTBOURNE							
–0010	–0005	+0015	+0020	+1·1	+0·6	+0·2	+0·1

SHELTER Very good, but in strong SE'lies the entrance may be hazardous and should be avoided at HW±1½. Access via buoyed channel (2m) and twin locks into inner basin (4m). The channel is prone to shoaling after gales and is dredged regularly. If uncertain of up-to-date situation, contact HM before entry.

NAVIGATION WPT 50°47′·37N 00°20′·81E, SWM buoy 'SH', L Fl 10s, 259°/0·45M to hbr ent. There are shoals to the NE in Pevensey Bay and from 2·5M SE toward Royal Sovereign lt (tide rips). From Beachy Hd, keep 0·75M offshore to clear Holywell Bank. 5kn speed limit in approach chan and Sovereign Harbour.

LIGHTS AND MARKS See 9.3.4 and chartlet. From E, by day R roofs are conspic. Dir lt, Fl WRG 5s leads 258° through appr channel. Large wreck on N side marked by 2 SHM lt buoys. Eastbourne pier, 2 FR, is 2M S of hbr ent; unlit PHM buoy is approx 5ca S.

R/T AND SAFETY RECOMMENDATIONS

- Monitor *Sovereign Harbour* VHF Ch **17** (H24) for nav info, lock status and berthing.

- Always follow IPTS (Sigs 2, 3 and 5) for locks entry.
- At busy periods obey instructions of Lock Keeper or Assistant on lock-side or directions by VHF.
- Locks close every H and H+30.
- Always approach locks with fenders (set about 1m above the waterline) and mooring lines rigged on both sides of craft. Secure to the pontoons as far to the front of the lock as possible. Set springs to reduce surging, particularly at LW.
- Switch off engines and radar whilst in lock.
- When secured alongside, assist other craft berthing.

TELEPHONE (Code 01323) HM 470099; MRCC (01304) 210008; Marinecall 09068 969646; Police 08456 070999; Dr470370; Ⓗ 417400.

FACILITIES Sovereign Harbour, 860 AB, ☎ 470099, www.premiermarinas.com £2·35, Wi-fi, D & P (H24), BH (50 tons), Gas, Gaz, ME, ✕, CH, ⚓, ▣, ♿, YC, Bar. R. including **Retail Park** with S/market and all domestic facilities. **Town** (2½M) all needs, ⇌, ✈ (Gatwick).

ADJACENT ANCHORAGE

HASTINGS, E Sussex, **50°50′·88N 00°35′·50E.** AC 536. Tides, see 9.3.11; ML 3·8m; Duration 0530. Strictly a settled weather ⚓ or emergency shelter. The stone breakwater is in disrepair and only protects FVs. Beware dangerous wreck 3ca SE of pier hd. Ldg lts 356°, both FR 14/55m 4M: front on W metal column; rear 357m from front, on 5-sided W tr on West Hill. Pier hd 2 FR (vert) 8m 5M from W hut; W bkwtr hd Fl R 2·5s 5m 4M; Fl G 5s 2m, 30m from head of No3 Groyne (E bkwtr). A Historic Wreck (*Amsterdam*; see 9.0.3) is about 2M W of pier, close inshore at 50°50′·7N 00°31′·65E. **Facilities**: ACA (St Leonards). Few marine services, but domestic facilities at Hastings and St Leonards. YC ☎ (01424) 420656.

EASTBOURNE

CROSSING THE EASTERN ENGLISH CHANNEL

See also 3.1 Passage Planning.

This section applies to crossings, ranging from the short (4–5 hrs) Dover Strait route to Boulogne or Calais to the moderate (10–15 hrs) ones from Brighton, Newhaven or Eastbourne to Dieppe and adjacent French ports. Distance tables are at 9.0.5. Routes cross the Dover Strait TSS where the SW-bound lane lies only 7M S of Beachy Head and 4.5M SE of Dover.

- Dover to Calais or Boulogne is only about 25M but crosses the most congested part of Dover Strait TSS.
- Plan to use the tidal streams to minimise crossing time and to be up-tide and to windward of the destination port when clear of the TSS.
- Always cross the TSS on a heading of 90° to the traffic flow, and minimise the time spent in the TSS. Be prepared to motor.
- When crossing the TSS, listen to the VHF broadcasts of navigational and traffic information made by CNIS. These include details of vessels which appear to be contravening Rule 10.
- Keep a very sharp lookout for ships in the traffic lanes and cross-Channel ferries. Ensure that the crew is aware of the directions from which to expect traffic in the TSS.
- Unless equipped with radar, and you are competent in its operation, do not attempt the crossing if fog or poor visibility is forecast. Even with radar, navigate with extreme caution.
- A Voluntary Separation Scheme (VSS) is in use to help ferries safely cross the Dover TSS. It is not a formal separation scheme and is not shown on official charts, but small craft should be aware of its existence. Most cross-Channel ferries can be expected to be using the VSS but high speed ferries are not included in the scheme. The VSS is bounded by the following points:
    1) 51°05'·35N 01°28'·00E
    2) 51°00'·10N 01°40'·00E
    3) 50°59'·30N 01°39'·10E
    4) 51°04'·70N 01°26'·80E

A separation line extends from a point midway between points 2 and 3 above to 1M W of CA6 buoy. Parallel to and 1·5M to the E of this zone a further separation line extends from 51°06'·40N 01°29'·90E to 51°01'·20N 01°41'·60E. Calais to Dover ferries keep to the W of this line; ferries to and from Dover and Dunkerque keep to the E.

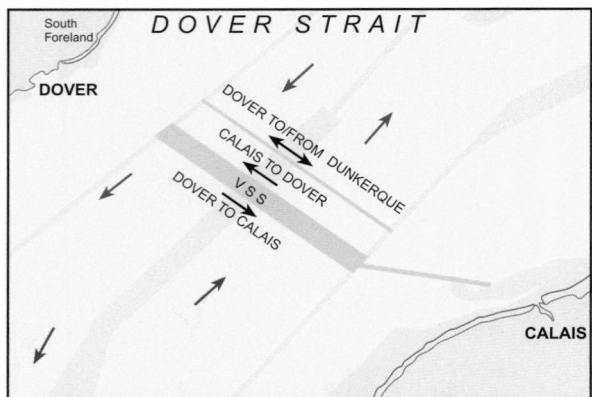

BEACHY HEAD TO DUNGENESS

(AC 536) Royal Sovereign lt tr is 7·4M E of Beachy Head. The extensive Royal Sovereign shoals lie from 3M NW of the tr to 1·5M N of it, and have a minimum depth of 3·5m. ▶ *There are*

strong eddies over the shoals at sp, and the sea breaks on them in bad weather. ◀

On the direct course from the Royal Sovereign to Dungeness there are no dangers. Along the coast in Pevensey B and Rye B there are drying rky ledges or shoals extending 5ca offshore in places. These include Boulder Bank near Wish tr, S of Eastbourne; Oyster Reef off Cooden; Bexhill Reef off Bexhill-on-Sea; Bopeep Rks off St Leonards; and the shoals at the mouth of R Rother, at the entrance to Rye. There are also banks 2–3M offshore, on which the sea builds in bad weather.

Avoid the firing range danger area between Rye and Dungeness (lt, fog sig, RC). The nuclear power station is conspic at S extremity of the low-lying spit. The point is steep-to on SE side. ▶ *2M SE of Dungeness the NE-going flood starts at HW Dover –0100, max sp rate 1.9kn. The SW-going ebb starts at HW Dover +0430, max spring rate 2.1kn.* ◀

DUNGENESS TO NORTH FORELAND

(AC 1892, 1828) From Dungeness to Folkestone the coast forms a bay. Beware Roar bank, depth 2·7m, E of New Romney: otherwise there are no off-lying dangers apart from Hythe firing range. Good anch off Sandgate in offshore winds.
▶ *Off Folkestone the E-going stream starts at HW Dover – 0155, sp rate 2kn; the W-going at HW Dover + 0320, sp rate 1·5kn.* ◀

Passing Dover and S Foreland keep 1M offshore. Do not pass too close to Dover as the many ferries leave at speed and there can be considerable backwash. It is advisable to call Dover Port Control (Ch 74) to identify yourself before passing the hbr entrances. 8M S of Dover in the TSS is the Varne, a shoal 7M long, with least depth 3·3m and heavy seas in bad weather, marked by Lanby and 3 buoys. ▶ *Between S and N Foreland the N-going stream begins at about HW Dover – 0150, and the S-going at about HW Dover + 0415.* ◀

The Goodwin Sands are drying, shifting shoals, extending about 10M from S to N, and 5M from W to E at their widest part. The E side is relatively steep-to, but large areas dry up to 3m. The sands are well marked by lit buoys. Kellett Gut is an unmarked chan about 5ca wide, running SW/NE through the middle of the sands, but it is not regularly surveyed and is liable to change. The Gull Stream (buoyed) leads from The Downs, inside Goodwin Sands and outside Brake Sands to the S of Ramsgate. The Ramsgate chan leads inside the Brake Sands and Cross Ledge.

LYDD FIRING RANGES

Off Lydd, centred on 50°54'N 00°53'E, a Sea Danger Area extends 3M offshore and stretches E from Rye Fairway buoy to a N/S line approx 1·5M W of Dungeness lt ho. When firing takes places, about 300 days p.a. 0830–1630LT (often to 2300), R flags/R lts are displayed ashore and a Range Safety Craft may be on station. Call Lydd Ranges Ch 06 13 16 72 **73** or ☎ 01303 225518, 🖷 225519.

Radar fixes may also be obtained by VHF. Vessels may legally transit through the Sea Danger Area, but should not enter or remain in it for other purposes. If possible vessels should transit S of Stephenson Shoal.

HYTHE FIRING RANGES

(Centred on 51°02'N 01°03'E) have a Sea Danger Area extending 2M offshore, from Hythe to Dymchurch (approx 5M and 8M WSW of Folkestone hbr). Vessels may legally transit through the Sea Danger Area, but should not enter or remain in it for other purposes. When firing takes place, about 300 days pa 0830–1630LT (often to 2300), R flags/R lts are displayed ashore and a Range Safety Craft may be on station.

Radar fixes may also be obtained by VHF. Call *Hythe Ranges* Ch 06 13 16 **73** or ☎ 01303 225879, 🖷 225924 or 225861 for 24H pre-recorded message.

9.3.11 RYE

E. Sussex 50°55'·60N 00°46'·58E ❁❁◊◊❀❀❀❀

CHARTS AC 5605, 536, 1991; Imray C31, C12, C8; Stanfords 9, 30.

TIDES ML 2·0; Duration 3·25hrs sp, 5hrs nps

Standard Port DOVER (⟶)

Times				Height (metres)			
High Water		Low Water		MHWS	MHWN	MLWN	MLWS
0000	0600	0100	0700	6·8	5·3	2·1	0·8
1200	1800	1300	1900				
Differences RYE (approaches)							
+0005	–0010	No data		+1·0	+0·7	No data	
RYE HARBOUR							
+0005	–0010	Dries		–1·4	–1·7	Dries	
HASTINGS							
0000	–0010	–0030	–0030	+0·8	+0·5	+0·1	–0·1

SHELTER Very good in R Rother which dries completely to soft mud. Rye Bay is exposed to prevailing SW'lies with little shelter, when there is good ⌕ in lee of Dungeness (6M to E). In N'lies ⌕ 5ca N of the Rye Fairway buoy.

Rye Hbr is a small village, ¾M inside ent on W bank, used by commercial shipping. Berth initially on Admiralty Jetty (E bank) and see HM for AB or M. No ⌕. Max speed 6kn.

Rye Town (a Cinque Port) is 2M up river. Enter via Rock Channel for ❷ AB along NE side of Strand Quay.

NAVIGATION WPT Rye Fairway SWM lt buoy, 50°54'·04N 00°48'·02E, 330°/1·8M to W Arm tripod lt.

- Bar dries 2·75m about 2ca offshore and needs care when wind >F6 from SE to SW. Also shoals E and W of ent with ground swell or surf; narrow ent (42m) and chan (30m).
- Enter HW –2 to HW +2; flood runs 4·5kn (max HW –2 to HW –1).
- Depth of water over the bar can be judged by day from horizontal timbers at base of West Arm tripod structure (approx 2ca N of the bar) these are set at 1·5, 3 and 4·5m above CD.

For information on Lydd and Hythe Firing Ranges see 9.3.5.

LIGHTS AND MARKS W Arm lt Fl R 5s 7m 6M, wooden tripod, radar reflector. E Arm hd, Q (9) 15s 7m 5M; Horn 7s, G △. On E Pier a floodlit 'Welcome to Rye' sign may be helpful. Rock Chan ent marked by a QR and QG lt buoy.

IPTS (Sigs 2 & 5 only) are shown to seaward (3M) from HM's office and up-river (1M) from HM's office.

R/T VHF Ch 14 (0900-1700LT, HW±2 or when vessel due). To avoid cargo ships monitor Ch 14 before arr/dep.

TELEPHONE (Code 01797) HM 225225; MRCC (01304) 210008; Marinecall 09068 969646; Police 08456 6070999; Dr 222031; Ⓗ 222109.

FACILITIES (from seaward) **Admiralty Jetty** Slip, M, L, FW; **Rye Hbr** Slip HW±3 (launching £10), ME, El, BY, ✗, CH, C (15 ton), C (3 ton), Slip (26 ton), Ⓔ, ACA; **Rye Hbr SC** (Sec'y) ☎ 223376. **Rye Town, Strand Quay** AB approx £1·00, wood fendering posts against solid wall with numbered ladders. M, P & D (cans), FW, ⟐, Showers, &; **Town** ✉, Ⓑ, ☰, ⇌, ✈ (Lydd). Note: A Historic Wreck (*Anne*; see 9.0.3) is about 4M WSW of Rye, close inshore at 50°53'·42N 00°41'·91E.

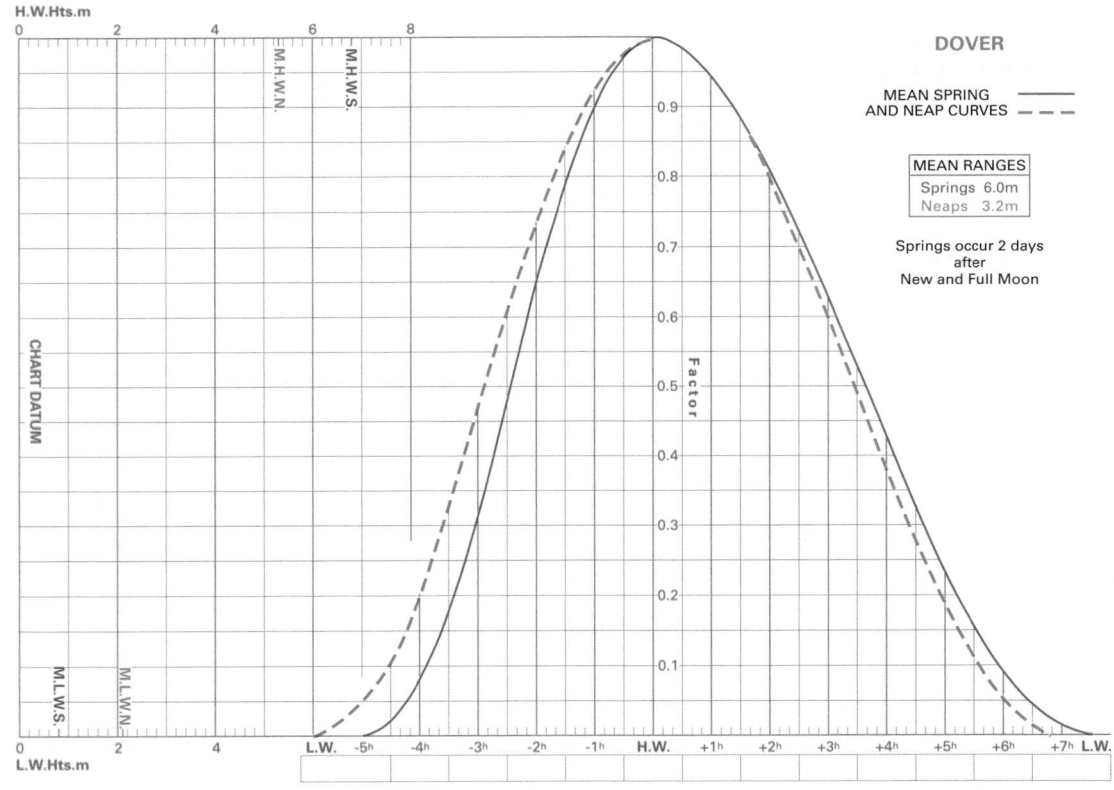

DOVER

MEAN SPRING ─────
AND NEAP CURVES ─ ─ ─

| MEAN RANGES |
| Springs 6.0m |
| Neaps 3.2m |

Springs occur 2 days
after
New and Full Moon

9.3.12 FOLKESTONE

Kent **51°04'·59N 01°11'·67E** ❀❀⬙⬙❁❁

CHARTS AC 5605, 1892, 1991; Imray C12, C8; Stanfords 20, 9.

TIDES −0010 Dover; ML 3·9; Duration 0500
Standard Port DOVER (⟶)

Times				Height (metres)			
High Water		Low Water		MHWS	MHWN	MLWN	MLWS
0000	0600	0100	0700	6·8	5·3	2·1	0·8
1200	1800	1300	1900				
Differences FOLKESTONE							
−0020	−0005	−0010	−0010	+0·4	+0·4	0·0	−0·1
DUNGENESS							
−0010	−0015	−0020	−0010	+1·0	+0·6	+0·4	+0·1

SHELTER Good except in strong E-S winds when seas break at the hbr ent.

NAVIGATION WPT 51°04'·33N 01°11'·89E, 330°/0·26M to bkwtr hd lt. Depth gauge on hd of E Pier. Beware drying Mole Hd Rks and Copt Rks to stbd of the ent; from/to the NE, keep well clear of the latter due to extended sewer outfall pipe. Inner Hbr, dries 1·7m, has many FVs and local shoal draft boats. For Lydd firing ranges see 9.3.5.

LIGHTS AND MARKS Hotel block is conspic at W end of Inner Hbr. Ldg lts 295° at old ferry terminal, FR and FG (occas).

R/T *Folkestone Port Control* Ch 15, 16.

TELEPHONE (Code 01303) Folkestone Hbr Co Ltd/HM 254597 (H24); MRCC (01304) 210008; Marinecall 09068 969646; Police 850055.

FACILITIES Access approx HW±2. Berth on **Inner S Quay** £15/craft for AB (fender board needed) or ⚓. Slip (free), FW.

For F&A mooring contact **Folkestone Y & MB Club** ☎ 251574, D, FW, Slip, M, Bar, ♿.

Town P & D (cans, 100m), 🛒, R, Bar, ✉, Ⓑ, ➤, ✈ (Lydd).

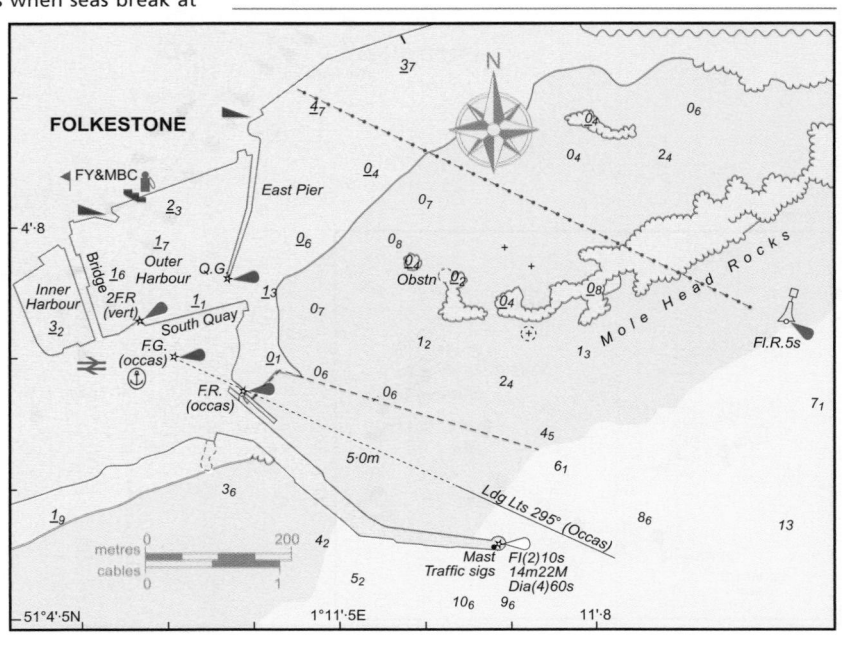

9.3.13 DOVER

Kent   **51°06'·74N 01°19'·73E** (W ent) 🌸🌸🌸🌊🌊🌊☆☆
        51°07'·25N 01°20'·61E (E ent)

CHARTS AC 5605,1892, 1828, 1698; Imray C30, C12, C8; Stanfords 9, 20.

TIDES 0000 Dover; ML 3·7; Duration 0505

Standard Port DOVER (➔)

Times				Height (metres)			
High Water		Low Water		MHWS	MHWN	MLWN	MLWS
0000	0600	0100	0700	6·8	5·3	2·1	0·8
1200	1800	1300	1900				
Differences DEAL							
+0010	+0020	+0010	+0005	−0·6	−0·3	0·0	0·0

SHELTER The Outer Hbr ⚓ is tenable in offshore winds, but exposed to winds from NE through S to SW; in gales a heavy sea builds up. Small craft must not be left unattended at ⚓ in Outer Hbr. Very good in marina.

NAVIGATION Advise Port Control of intentions when 2M off. WPT from SW, 51°06'·18N 01°19'·67E, 000°/0·5M to Admiralty Pier lt ho. WPT from NE, 51°07'·30N 01°21'·41E, 270°/0·5M to S end Eastern Arm. Beware lumpy seas/overfalls outside the bkwtrs and the frequent ferries and high speed craft using both ents. Strong tides across ents and high walls make ent under sail slow and difficult; use of engine is very strongly recommended. Inside the W ent do not pass between NCM buoy, Q (marking wreck) and the S bkwtr.

Note: A Historic wreck (see 9.0.3) is adjacent to the Eastern Arm bkwtr at 51°07'·6N 01°20'·7E (see chartlet). There are 4 more Historic wrecks on the Goodwin Sands.

• **Specific permission** to ent/leave the hbr via E or W ent must first be obtained from Port Control on Ch **74**; advise if you have no engine. Comply with any VHF instructions from Port Control or hbr patrol launch.

• Clearance for small/slow craft is not normally given until within 200m of ent. Visitors are welcomed and usually escorted by hbr launch to the marina.

• **If no VHF:** Stay safe distance clear of either ent, make visual contact (Aldis lamp) with Port Control (E Arm) who may direct Hbr launch to assist/escort in. Q lt from Port Control twr or patrol launch = keep clear of ent you are approaching.

LIGHTS AND MARKS As per 9.3.4 and chartlet. **IPTS** (for all vessels) are shown for the E ent by Port Control (conspic twr) at S end of E Arm; and for W ent, from the head of Admiralty Pier.

R/T Call *Dover Port Control* (also Hbr launch) Ch **74**, 12, 16 for clearance to enter. Request clearance to leave hbr as soon as clear of the marina. *Dover Marina* Ch 80, only within marina. *Dover Coastguard* Ch **69** 16 80, gives TSS surveillance. Chan Nav Info Service (CNIS) broadcasts tfc/ nav/weather/tidal info Ch 11 at H+40; also, if vis < 2M, at H+55.

TELEPHONE (Code 01304) HM 240400 ext 4520, Duty HM mob 07836 262713; Port Control 240400 ext 5530; MRCC 210008; Marinecall 09068 969646; Police 240055; Ⓗ 201624.

FACILITIES 3 berthing options in the marina, ☎ 241663:
• Tidal hbr, E of waiting pontoon (1·5m), access H24. 112 AB on 3 pontoons (C, B, A) in 2·5m, £2.30. Mostly for single night stop.
• Granville Dock, gate open approx HW−3½ to +4½, 132 AB, £2.05.
• Wellington Dock. Gate and swing bridge open HW ±2 nps and approx HW−1½ to HW+1½ or 2½ sp, depending on range; 161 AB, £1.85. In the final appr, especially near LW, stay in deep water as defined by the W sector (324°-333°) of the F WR lt, 2 unlit SHM poles and a G conical buoy. IPTS are shown, plus a small Fl ● lt 5 mins before Wellington bridge is swung open.

Services: 370 inc ♥ www.doverport.co.uk @ (Marina Office), C, Slip, D, 🚿, LPG, Gas, Gaz, ⊘, BH (50 ton), ME, El, ✗, SM, CH, ACA, Ⓔ (H24). **Royal Cinque Ports YC** ☎ 206262, www.rcpyc.co.uk, FW, Bar. **White Cliffs M and YC** ☎ 211666, www.wcmyc.co.uk

Town: D & P (H24 cans), 🛒, R, Bar, ✉, Ⓑ, ⇌. **Ferries:** Very frequent services to Dunkerque, Calais and Boulogne; also to Dieppe (6/week).

TIME ZONE (UT)
For Summer Time add ONE hour in **non-shaded areas**

DOVER LAT 51°07'N LONG 1°19'E
TIMES AND HEIGHTS OF HIGH AND LOW WATERS

Dates in red are SPRINGS
Dates in blue are NEAPS

YEAR 2010

JANUARY

Day	Time	m		Day	Time	m
1 F	0608 / 1100 / 1838 / 2327	1.0 / 6.7 / — / 6.8		**16** SA	0648 / 1152 / 1858	1.3 / 6.2 / 1.4
2 SA	0702 / 1148 / 1930	0.8 / 6.8 / 0.9		**17** SU	0007 / 0719 / 1223 / 1927	6.5 / 1.3 / 6.2 / 1.3
3 SU	0013 / 0754 / 1236 / 2018	6.9 / 0.7 / 6.8 / 0.9		**18** M	0038 / 0749 / 1252 / 1957	6.5 / 1.2 / 6.2 / 1.3
4 M	0101 / 0843 / 1325 / 2103	7.0 / 0.6 / 6.7 / 0.9		**19** TU	0105 / 0819 / 1317 / 2028	6.4 / 1.3 / 6.1 / 1.3
5 TU	0148 / 0928 / 1414 / 2144	6.9 / 0.7 / 6.5 / 1.0		**20** W	0129 / 0851 / 1341 / 2100	6.4 / 1.3 / 6.1 / 1.4
6 W	0238 / 1012 / 1506 / 2226	6.8 / 0.9 / 6.3 / 1.2		**21** TH	0156 / 0923 / 1410 / 2133	6.4 / 1.4 / 6.0 / 1.5
7 TH ◐	0329 / 1057 / 1601 / 2312	6.5 / 1.1 / 6.0 / 1.5		**22** F	0229 / 0957 / 1447 / 2209	6.2 / 1.6 / 5.9 / 1.7
8 F	0424 / 1147 / 1703	6.2 / 1.5 / 5.7		**23** SA ◑	0311 / 1037 / 1533 / 2253	6.1 / 1.8 / 5.7 / 2.0
9 SA	0006 / 0527 / 1245 / 1814	1.9 / 5.8 / 1.8 / 5.4		**24** SU	0404 / 1128 / 1635 / 2353	5.8 / 2.0 / 5.4 / 2.2
10 SU	0111 / 0641 / 1349 / 1928	2.1 / 5.6 / 2.0 / 5.4		**25** M	0517 / 1243 / 1820	5.5 / 2.2 / 5.2
11 M	0222 / 0759 / 1457 / 2036	2.1 / 5.6 / 2.0 / 5.5		**26** TU	0124 / 0657 / 1414 / 1947	2.3 / 5.5 / 2.1 / 5.4
12 TU	0335 / 0907 / 1607 / 2133	2.0 / 5.7 / 1.8 / 5.8		**27** W	0249 / 0812 / 1528 / 2050	2.0 / 5.7 / 1.8 / 5.8
13 W	0440 / 1002 / 1704 / 2219	1.7 / 5.9 / 1.7 / 6.0		**28** TH	0358 / 0914 / 1634 / 2144	1.6 / 6.1 / 1.4 / 6.2
14 TH	0531 / 1044 / 1749 / 2258	1.5 / 6.1 / 1.5 / 6.3		**29** F	0501 / 1008 / 1737 / 2234	1.2 / 6.4 / 1.1 / 6.6
15 F ●	0612 / 1120 / 1826 / 2333	1.4 / 6.2 / 1.4 / 6.4		**30** SA ○	0602 / 1057 / 1834 / 2320	0.9 / 6.7 / 0.8 / 6.9
				31 SU	0658 / 1143 / 1926	0.6 / 6.8 / 0.6

FEBRUARY

Day	Time	m		Day	Time	m
1 M	0003 / 0748 / 1227 / 2010	7.1 / 0.4 / 6.9 / 0.5		**16** TU	0012 / 0728 / 1225 / 1937	6.5 / 1.1 / 6.3 / 1.1
2 TU	0047 / 0832 / 1309 / 2048	7.2 / 0.3 / 6.8 / 0.6		**17** W	0036 / 0757 / 1247 / 2006	6.5 / 1.1 / 6.3 / 1.1
3 W	0130 / 0912 / 1352 / 2124	7.1 / 0.4 / 6.7 / 0.7		**18** TH	0059 / 0827 / 1310 / 2036	6.5 / 1.1 / 6.3 / 1.2
4 TH	0214 / 0949 / 1436 / 2159	6.9 / 0.6 / 6.4 / 1.0		**19** F	0125 / 0856 / 1339 / 2107	6.5 / 1.2 / 6.3 / 1.3
5 F ◑	0259 / 1026 / 1524 / 2237	6.6 / 1.0 / 6.1 / 1.4		**20** SA	0157 / 0927 / 1415 / 2140	6.5 / 1.4 / 6.2 / 1.5
6 SA	0348 / 1108 / 1619 / 2323	6.2 / 1.5 / 5.7 / 1.9		**21** SU	0237 / 1003 / 1459 / 2221	6.3 / 1.6 / 5.9 / 1.8
7 SU	0445 / 1201 / 1725	5.7 / 2.0 / 5.3		**22** M ◑	0326 / 1050 / 1556 / 2318	5.9 / 1.9 / 5.5 / 2.1
8 M	0027 / 0557 / 1310 / 1845	2.2 / 5.3 / 2.3 / 5.1		**23** TU	0434 / 1200 / 1743	5.4 / 2.2 / 5.1
9 TU	0146 / 0731 / 1425 / 2013	2.4 / 5.2 / 2.3 / 5.2		**24** W	0046 / 0644 / 1345 / 1932	2.3 / 5.3 / 2.2 / 5.3
10 W	0308 / 0902 / 1541 / 2119	2.2 / 5.4 / 2.1 / 5.6		**25** TH	0225 / 0806 / 1510 / 2039	2.1 / 5.6 / 1.9 / 5.8
11 TH	0423 / 0956 / 1646 / 2205	1.9 / 5.7 / 1.8 / 5.9		**26** F	0341 / 0908 / 1621 / 2134	1.6 / 6.0 / 1.4 / 6.2
12 F	0517 / 1034 / 1734 / 2242	1.5 / 6.0 / 1.5 / 6.2		**27** SA	0449 / 1001 / 1726 / 2222	1.1 / 6.4 / 1.0 / 6.7
13 SA	0558 / 1105 / 1810 / 2315	1.3 / 6.1 / 1.4 / 6.4		**28** SU ○	0551 / 1048 / 1821 / 2306	0.7 / 6.7 / 0.7 / 7.0
14 SU ●	0632 / 1132 / 1841 / 2345	1.2 / 6.2 / 1.3 / 6.5				
15 M	0700 / 1159 / 1909	1.1 / 6.3 / 1.2				

MARCH

Day	Time	m		Day	Time	m
1 M	0645 / 1130 / 1909 / 2348	0.4 / 6.9 / 0.5 / 7.2		**16** TU	0632 / 1129 / 1842 / 2341	1.1 / 6.3 / 1.1 / 6.5
2 TU	0732 / 1210 / 1950	0.2 / 7.0 / 0.4		**17** W	0702 / 1154 / 1912	1.0 / 6.4 / 1.0
3 W	0028 / 0812 / 1249 / 2025	7.2 / 0.2 / 6.9 / 0.4		**18** TH	0005 / 0732 / 1218 / 1943	6.5 / 1.0 / 6.4 / 1.0
4 TH	0108 / 0848 / 1328 / 2058	7.1 / 0.3 / 6.8 / 0.6		**19** F	0030 / 0802 / 1244 / 2013	6.6 / 1.0 / 6.5 / 1.1
5 F	0149 / 0921 / 1409 / 2130	6.9 / 0.6 / 6.5 / 1.0		**20** SA	0058 / 0831 / 1314 / 2044	6.6 / 1.1 / 6.5 / 1.2
6 SA	0230 / 0954 / 1453 / 2204	6.6 / 1.1 / 6.2 / 1.4		**21** SU	0132 / 0903 / 1352 / 2119	6.5 / 1.3 / 6.3 / 1.4
7 SU ◑	0316 / 1030 / 1545 / 2244	6.1 / 1.6 / 5.7 / 1.9		**22** M	0213 / 0940 / 1439 / 2203	6.3 / 1.6 / 6.0 / 1.7
8 M	0412 / 1118 / 1648 / 2347	5.6 / 2.1 / 5.3 / 2.3		**23** TU ◑	0304 / 1029 / 1540 / 2301	5.9 / 1.9 / 5.5 / 2.0
9 TU	0522 / 1233 / 1805	5.1 / 2.5 / 5.0		**24** W	0420 / 1139 / 1739	5.4 / 2.2 / 5.2
10 W	0115 / 0654 / 1356 / 1938	2.5 / 5.0 / 2.5 / 5.1		**25** TH	0030 / 0636 / 1328 / 1914	2.2 / 5.3 / 2.2 / 5.4
11 TH	0240 / 0844 / 1512 / 2053	2.3 / 5.2 / 2.2 / 5.5		**26** F	0207 / 0753 / 1452 / 2021	1.9 / 5.6 / 1.8 / 5.8
12 F	0355 / 0934 / 1617 / 2140	1.9 / 5.6 / 1.8 / 5.8		**27** SA	0322 / 0855 / 1603 / 2116	1.5 / 6.0 / 1.4 / 6.3
13 SA	0450 / 1010 / 1705 / 2216	1.5 / 5.9 / 1.5 / 6.1		**28** SU	0431 / 0946 / 1705 / 2204	1.0 / 6.4 / 1.0 / 6.7
14 SU	0530 / 1038 / 1743 / 2247	1.3 / 6.1 / 1.3 / 6.3		**29** M	0532 / 1031 / 1758 / 2247	0.6 / 6.7 / 0.7 / 7.0
15 M ●	0603 / 1103 / 1813 / 2315	1.2 / 6.2 / 1.2 / 6.4		**30** TU ○	0624 / 1111 / 1844 / 2328	0.4 / 6.8 / 0.5 / 7.1
				31 W	0708 / 1149 / 1923	0.3 / 6.9 / 0.5

APRIL

Day	Time	m		Day	Time	m
1 TH	0007 / 0747 / 1226 / 1959	7.1 / 0.3 / 6.9 / 0.6		**16** F	0707 / 1151 / 1921	1.0 / 6.5 / 1.0
2 F	0046 / 0822 / 1305 / 2032	7.0 / 0.5 / 6.7 / 0.8		**17** SA	0005 / 0740 / 1223 / 1954	6.6 / 1.0 / 6.5 / 1.0
3 SA	0125 / 0854 / 1345 / 2104	6.8 / 0.8 / 6.5 / 1.1		**18** SU	0039 / 0813 / 1259 / 2029	6.6 / 1.1 / 6.5 / 1.1
4 SU	0206 / 0924 / 1428 / 2136	6.4 / 1.3 / 6.2 / 1.4		**19** M	0117 / 0848 / 1342 / 2109	6.5 / 1.3 / 6.3 / 1.3
5 M	0251 / 0955 / 1518 / 2213	6.0 / 1.7 / 5.8 / 1.9		**20** TU	0203 / 0929 / 1435 / 2156	6.2 / 1.5 / 6.0 / 1.6
6 TU	0346 / 1036 / 1617 / 2309	5.5 / 2.2 / 5.4 / 2.3		**21** W ◑	0302 / 1021 / 1546 / 2258	5.8 / 1.8 / 5.7 / 1.8
7 W	0452 / 1151 / 1726	5.1 / 2.5 / 5.1		**22** TH	0433 / 1134 / 1721	5.5 / 2.1 / 5.5
8 TH	0040 / 0609 / 1320 / 1846	2.5 / 5.0 / 2.5 / 5.1		**23** F	0024 / 0617 / 1310 / 1846	1.9 / 5.5 / 2.0 / 5.6
9 F	0201 / 0752 / 1432 / 2006	2.3 / 5.1 / 2.3 / 5.4		**24** SA	0147 / 0732 / 1426 / 1954	1.7 / 5.7 / 1.7 / 5.9
10 SA	0307 / 0851 / 1532 / 2058	2.0 / 5.5 / 1.9 / 5.7		**25** SU	0257 / 0832 / 1533 / 2051	1.4 / 6.0 / 1.4 / 6.3
11 SU	0401 / 0928 / 1621 / 2136	1.6 / 5.8 / 1.6 / 6.0		**26** M	0404 / 0923 / 1634 / 2140	1.0 / 6.3 / 1.1 / 6.6
12 M	0444 / 0957 / 1702 / 2208	1.4 / 6.0 / 1.4 / 6.2		**27** TU	0505 / 1008 / 1729 / 2225	0.8 / 6.5 / 0.9 / 6.8
13 TU	0522 / 1025 / 1737 / 2237	1.2 / 6.2 / 1.2 / 6.3		**28** W ○	0558 / 1049 / 1816 / 2307	0.6 / 6.6 / 0.8 / 6.9
14 W ●	0558 / 1054 / 1812 / 2306	1.1 / 6.3 / 1.1 / 6.4		**29** TH	0642 / 1127 / 1857 / 2347	0.6 / 6.7 / 0.7 / 6.8
15 TH	0633 / 1123 / 1847 / 2335	1.0 / 6.4 / 1.0 / 6.5		**30** F	0722 / 1206 / 1935	0.7 / 6.7 / 0.8

Chart Datum: 3·67 metres below Ordnance Datum (Newlyn). HAT is 7·3 metres above Chart Datum; see 4.5

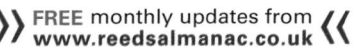

》》 **FREE** monthly updates from 《《
www.reedsalmanac.co.uk

TIME ZONE (UT)
For Summer Time add ONE hour in **non-shaded areas**

DOVER LAT 51°07′N LONG 1°19′E
TIMES AND HEIGHTS OF HIGH AND LOW WATERS

Dates in red are SPRINGS
Dates in blue are NEAPS

YEAR **2010**

MAY

	Time	m		Time	m
1 SA	0027 0757 1246 2010	6.7 0.9 6.6 1.0	**16** SU	0725 1210 1943	1.0 6.5 1.0
2 SU	0106 0829 1326 2043	6.5 1.1 6.5 1.2	**17** M	0028 0803 1254 2023	6.5 1.1 6.5 1.1
3 M	0147 0859 1409 2115	6.3 1.4 6.2 1.5	**18** TU	0114 0844 1343 2108	6.4 1.2 6.4 1.2
4 TU	0231 0928 1455 2151	5.9 1.7 5.9 1.8	**19** W	0206 0930 1440 2200	6.2 1.4 6.2 1.3
5 W	0322 1005 1547 2239	5.6 2.0 5.6 2.1	**20** TH	0309 1024 1544 2301	6.0 1.6 5.8 1.5
6 TH	0421 1100 1647 2350	5.3 2.3 5.4 2.3	**21** F	0425 1131 1654	5.8 1.8 5.9
7 F	0527 1224 1753	5.1 2.4 5.3	**22** SA	0011 0546 1244 1808	1.6 5.7 1.8 5.9
8 SA	0106 0638 1338 1901	2.2 5.1 2.3 5.4	**23** SU	0120 0700 1352 1920	1.5 5.7 1.7 6.0
9 SU	0210 0743 1438 1959	2.0 5.3 2.1 5.6	**24** M	0225 0802 1456 2021	1.4 5.9 1.5 6.2
10 M	0304 0831 1529 2043	1.8 5.6 1.8 5.8	**25** TU	0330 0856 1600 2115	1.2 6.1 1.3 6.3
11 TU	0353 0909 1616 2121	1.5 5.8 1.6 6.0	**26** W	0434 0944 1659 2204	1.1 6.2 1.2 6.4
12 W	0439 0945 1700 2157	1.3 6.1 1.4 6.2	**27** TH	0530 1028 1749 2250	1.0 6.4 1.1 6.5
13 TH	0523 1020 1742 2232	1.2 6.2 1.2 6.4	**28** F	0618 1110 1834 2332	1.0 6.4 1.0 6.5
14 F	0605 1055 1823 2309	1.1 6.4 1.1 6.5	**29** SA	0659 1150 1915	1.0 6.5 1.0
15 SA	0646 1131 1903 2347	1.0 6.5 1.0 6.5	**30** SU	0012 0735 1230 1952	6.4 1.2 6.5 1.1
			31 M	0052 0809 1310 2026	6.3 1.3 6.4 1.3

JUNE

	Time	m		Time	m
1 TU	0131 0839 1350 2059	6.1 1.5 6.3 1.4	**16** W	0112 0848 1340 2113	6.5 1.0 6.7 0.9
2 W	0212 0908 1430 2132	5.9 1.6 6.1 1.6	**17** TH	0204 0934 1431 2202	6.4 1.1 6.6 1.0
3 TH	0255 0942 1513 2211	5.7 1.8 5.9 1.8	**18** F	0300 1021 1526 2253	6.2 1.2 6.4 1.1
4 F	0343 1024 1600 2300	5.5 2.0 5.7 2.0	**19** SA	0400 1113 1624 2348	6.0 1.4 6.2 1.3
5 SA	0438 1117 1655	5.3 2.1 5.5	**20** SU	0506 1211 1728	5.8 1.6 6.0
6 SU	0001 0539 1225 1755	2.0 5.2 2.2 5.4	**21** M	0047 0618 1314 1839	1.4 5.7 1.7 5.9
7 M	0107 0641 1335 1855	2.0 5.3 2.2 5.5	**22** TU	0150 0727 1420 1950	1.5 5.7 1.7 5.9
8 TU	0209 0736 1438 1949	1.9 5.4 2.0 5.7	**23** W	0255 0830 1527 2055	1.6 5.8 1.6 6.0
9 W	0307 0824 1534 2037	1.7 5.7 1.7 5.9	**24** TH	0404 0925 1633 2151	1.5 5.9 1.5 6.1
10 TH	0401 0909 1626 2123	1.5 5.9 1.5 6.1	**25** F	0507 1014 1730 2240	1.4 6.1 1.3 6.2
11 F	0453 0952 1716 2207	1.3 6.2 1.3 6.3	**26** SA	0558 1057 1818 2322	1.3 6.3 1.2 6.3
12 SA	0542 1035 1803 2252	1.2 6.4 1.1 6.5	**27** SU	0641 1136 1900	1.3 6.4 1.2
13 SU	0629 1118 1850 2337	1.1 6.5 1.0 6.6	**28** M	0000 0718 1215 1937	6.3 1.3 6.5 1.2
14 M	0716 1203 1937	1.0 6.6 0.9	**29** TU	0037 0751 1252 2010	6.2 1.4 6.5 1.2
15 TU	0023 0802 1251 2025	6.6 1.0 6.7 0.9	**30** W	0113 0819 1328 2040	6.1 1.4 6.4 1.3

JULY

	Time	m		Time	m
1 TH	0147 0846 1401 2109	6.0 1.5 6.3 1.4	**16** F	0150 0924 1413 2149	6.6 0.8 6.9 0.6
2 F	0219 0917 1431 2142	5.9 1.5 6.1 1.5	**17** SA	0239 1004 1502 2232	6.5 1.0 6.7 0.9
3 SA	0252 0952 1505 2220	5.7 1.7 5.9 1.7	**18** SU	0331 1046 1554 2318	6.2 1.2 6.4 1.2
4 SU	0329 1032 1547 2304	5.6 1.9 5.8 1.8	**19** M	0428 1136 1652	5.9 1.6 6.0
5 M	0419 1121 1642	5.4 2.1 5.6	**20** TU	0012 0534 1237 1800	1.6 5.6 1.9 5.7
6 TU	0001 0530 1226 1752	2.0 5.3 2.2 5.5	**21** W	0116 0651 1348 1923	1.9 5.4 2.0 5.5
7 W	0114 0645 1346 1903	2.1 5.3 2.2 5.5	**22** TH	0226 0808 1502 2045	1.9 5.5 2.0 5.6
8 TH	0226 0748 1457 2006	1.9 5.5 2.0 5.7	**23** F	0341 0913 1618 2148	1.9 5.7 1.8 5.8
9 F	0329 0843 1558 2101	1.7 5.8 1.6 6.0	**24** SA	0452 1003 1719 2236	1.7 6.0 1.5 6.0
10 SA	0428 0934 1653 2153	1.4 6.1 1.3 6.3	**25** SU	0545 1045 1807 2313	1.5 6.2 1.3 6.2
11 SU	0523 1022 1747 2242	1.2 6.4 1.1 6.5	**26** M	0626 1122 1847 2346	1.4 6.4 1.2 6.3
12 M	0618 1109 1841 2330	1.0 6.7 0.9 6.7	**27** TU	0701 1157 1920	1.3 6.5 1.2
13 TU	0711 1154 1933	0.9 6.8 0.7	**28** W	0018 0729 1231 1948	6.3 1.3 6.5 1.2
14 W	0016 0759 1240 2022	6.7 0.8 7.0 0.6	**29** TH	0048 0754 1301 2014	6.2 1.3 6.5 1.2
15 TH	0103 0844 1326 2107	6.7 0.8 7.0 0.5	**30** F	0116 0819 1327 2041	6.2 1.3 6.4 1.2
			31 SA	0139 0849 1350 2111	6.1 1.4 6.3 1.3

AUGUST

	Time	m		Time	m
1 SU	0202 0921 1418 2143	6.0 1.5 6.2 1.5	**16** SU	0300 1017 1525 2246	6.3 1.2 6.4 1.3
2 M	0233 0955 1454 2220	5.9 1.7 6.0 1.7	**17** TU	0354 1102 1621 2337	5.9 1.7 5.9 1.8
3 TU	0314 1035 1542 2305	5.7 1.9 5.8 2.0	**18** W	0459 1203 1729	5.5 2.1 5.5
4 W	0409 1128 1648	5.4 2.2 5.5	**19** TH	0045 0616 1321 1858	2.2 5.3 2.3 5.3
5 TH	0011 0553 1252 1830	2.2 5.2 2.3 5.4	**20** F	0203 0747 1446 2042	2.3 5.3 2.2 5.4
6 F	0148 0724 1424 1949	2.2 5.4 2.1 5.6	**21** SA	0327 0900 1609 2141	2.1 5.6 1.9 5.8
7 SA	0304 0827 1534 2050	1.9 5.7 1.8 6.0	**22** SU	0439 0949 1707 2223	1.8 6.0 1.5 6.0
8 SU	0409 0909 1635 2144	1.6 6.1 1.3 6.3	**23** M	0527 1027 1751 2256	1.5 6.3 1.3 6.2
9 M	0508 1010 1733 2233	1.2 6.5 1.0 6.6	**24** TU	0606 1101 1826 2324	1.4 6.5 1.2 6.3
10 TU	0606 1055 1830 2318	1.0 6.9 0.7 6.8	**25** W	0637 1133 1854 2351	1.3 6.6 1.2 6.4
11 W	0659 1139 1922	0.8 7.1 0.5	**26** TH	0701 1203 1918	1.3 6.6 1.1
12 TH	0002 0745 1223 2008	6.9 0.6 7.2 0.3	**27** F	0017 0725 1230 1944	6.3 1.2 6.5 1.1
13 F	0045 0826 1306 2049	6.9 0.6 7.2 0.4	**28** SA	0041 0752 1251 2011	6.3 1.2 6.5 1.2
14 SA	0127 0902 1350 2127	6.8 0.7 7.1 0.5	**29** SU	0100 0821 1312 2040	6.3 1.3 6.5 1.3
15 SU	0212 0938 1436 2204	6.6 0.9 6.8 0.9	**30** M	0124 0851 1340 2110	6.3 1.4 6.4 1.4
			31 TU	0155 0924 1416 2144	6.2 1.6 6.2 1.7

Chart Datum: 3·67 metres below Ordnance Datum (Newlyn). HAT is 7·3 metres above Chart Datum; see 4.5

SE England

TIME ZONE (UT)
For Summer Time add ONE hour in **non-shaded areas**

DOVER LAT 51°07'N LONG 1°19'E
TIMES AND HEIGHTS OF HIGH AND LOW WATERS

Dates in red are SPRINGS
Dates in blue are NEAPS

YEAR 2010

SEPTEMBER

Day	Time m	Day	Time m
1 W ☽	0236 5.9 / 1002 1.9 / 1501 5.9 / 2226 2.0	**16** TH	0428 5.5 / 1131 2.3 / 1701 5.4
2 TH	0329 5.6 / 1052 2.2 / 1604 5.5 / 2326 2.3	**17** F	0014 2.5 / 0542 5.2 / 1257 2.5 / 1829 5.1
3 F	0507 5.2 / 1208 2.4 / 1816 5.3	**18** SA	0141 2.6 / 0714 5.3 / 1428 2.3 / 2025 5.4
4 SA	0113 2.4 / 0705 5.3 / 1358 2.2 / 1937 5.6	**19** SU	0304 2.3 / 0833 5.6 / 1546 1.9 / 2118 5.7
5 SU	0244 2.1 / 0811 5.8 / 1513 1.8 / 2039 6.0	**20** M	0409 1.9 / 0922 6.0 / 1639 1.6 / 2157 6.0
6 M	0351 1.6 / 0905 6.2 / 1617 1.3 / 2131 6.4	**21** TU	0456 1.6 / 1000 6.3 / 1720 1.3 / 2227 6.2
7 TU	0452 1.2 / 0953 6.7 / 1717 0.9 / 2218 6.8	**22** W	0533 1.4 / 1032 6.5 / 1752 1.2 / 2253 6.4
8 W ●	0547 0.9 / 1037 7.0 / 1812 0.6 / 2301 7.0	**23** TH ○	0603 1.3 / 1102 6.6 / 1819 1.1 / 2318 6.4
9 TH	0637 0.7 / 1120 7.2 / 1902 0.4 / 2342 7.0	**24** F	0628 1.2 / 1130 6.6 / 1845 1.2 / 2343 6.4
10 F	0721 0.6 / 1201 7.3 / 1946 0.3	**25** SA	0655 1.2 / 1154 6.6 / 1913 1.2
11 SA	0021 7.0 / 0800 0.6 / 1243 7.3 / 2024 0.4	**26** SU	0006 6.4 / 0724 1.2 / 1217 6.5 / 1943 1.2
12 SU	0102 6.9 / 0836 0.7 / 1325 7.1 / 2100 0.7	**27** M	0028 6.4 / 0755 1.2 / 1241 6.5 / 2013 1.3
13 M	0145 6.7 / 0911 1.0 / 1409 6.8 / 2135 1.1	**28** TU	0055 6.4 / 0826 1.4 / 1312 6.5 / 2043 1.5
14 TU	0232 6.3 / 0948 1.4 / 1458 6.3 / 2213 1.6	**29** W	0129 6.3 / 0859 1.6 / 1349 6.3 / 2118 1.7
15 W ☾	0326 5.9 / 1031 1.9 / 1554 5.8 / 2302 2.1	**30** TH	0212 6.1 / 0939 1.8 / 1436 5.9 / 2202 2.0

OCTOBER

Day	Time m	Day	Time m
1 F ☽	0308 5.7 / 1031 2.1 / 1543 5.5 / 2301 2.3	**16** SA	0506 5.4 / 1225 2.5 / 1750 5.1
2 SA	0458 5.3 / 1147 2.3 / 1803 5.4	**17** SU	0104 2.7 / 0624 5.3 / 1348 2.4 / 1934 5.3
3 SU	0045 2.4 / 0641 5.5 / 1334 2.2 / 1920 5.6	**18** M	0221 2.4 / 0745 5.6 / 1458 2.1 / 2036 5.6
4 M	0221 2.1 / 0748 5.9 / 1451 1.7 / 2021 6.1	**19** TU	0323 2.1 / 0841 5.9 / 1551 1.7 / 2116 5.9
5 TU	0329 1.6 / 0843 6.3 / 1555 1.2 / 2113 6.5	**20** W	0411 1.8 / 0921 6.2 / 1633 1.5 / 2147 6.1
6 W	0428 1.2 / 0931 6.8 / 1654 0.9 / 2158 6.8	**21** TH	0450 1.5 / 0955 6.3 / 1708 1.3 / 2214 6.3
7 TH ●	0522 0.9 / 1015 7.1 / 1748 0.6 / 2240 7.0	**22** F	0523 1.4 / 1024 6.5 / 1740 1.2 / 2242 6.4
8 F	0611 0.7 / 1057 7.2 / 1837 0.5 / 2319 7.0	**23** SA ○	0555 1.3 / 1052 6.5 / 1813 1.2 / 2309 6.5
9 SA	0654 0.7 / 1139 7.2 / 1920 0.5 / 2358 7.0	**24** SU	0627 1.2 / 1120 6.5 / 1846 1.2 / 2336 6.5
10 SU	0734 0.7 / 1220 7.2 / 1958 0.7	**25** M	0701 1.2 / 1148 6.6 / 1919 1.2
11 M	0039 6.9 / 0811 0.9 / 1302 6.9 / 2033 0.9	**26** TU	0004 6.6 / 0734 1.2 / 1219 6.6 / 1951 1.3
12 TU	0122 6.7 / 0847 1.1 / 1345 6.6 / 2108 1.3	**27** W	0037 6.5 / 0808 1.3 / 1254 6.5 / 2025 1.5
13 W	0208 6.4 / 0924 1.5 / 1434 6.2 / 2144 1.8	**28** TH	0116 6.4 / 0845 1.5 / 1335 6.3 / 2102 1.7
14 TH ☾	0300 6.0 / 1005 1.9 / 1530 5.7 / 2227 2.2	**29** F	0204 6.2 / 0928 1.7 / 1427 6.0 / 2149 1.9
15 F	0359 5.6 / 1101 2.3 / 1634 5.3 / 2337 2.6	**30** SA ☾	0306 5.8 / 1022 2.0 / 1543 5.6 / 2249 2.2
		31 SU	0438 5.6 / 1137 2.1 / 1738 5.5

NOVEMBER

Day	Time m	Day	Time m
1 M	0020 2.3 / 0607 5.7 / 1308 2.0 / 1854 5.7	**16** TU	0119 2.5 / 0641 5.5 / 1354 2.2 / 1928 5.4
2 TU	0149 2.0 / 0717 6.0 / 1421 1.6 / 1956 6.0	**17** W	0223 2.3 / 0743 5.7 / 1449 2.0 / 2020 5.6
3 W	0256 1.7 / 0815 6.3 / 1525 1.3 / 2048 6.4	**18** TH	0317 2.0 / 0831 5.9 / 1538 1.7 / 2059 5.9
4 TH	0357 1.4 / 0906 6.6 / 1626 1.0 / 2135 6.6	**19** F	0403 1.8 / 0909 6.1 / 1623 1.5 / 2134 6.1
5 F	0454 1.1 / 0952 6.9 / 1722 0.8 / 2218 6.8	**20** SA	0445 1.5 / 0944 6.3 / 1704 1.4 / 2207 6.3
6 SA ●	0544 0.9 / 1036 7.0 / 1812 0.8 / 2259 6.9	**21** SU	0525 1.4 / 1018 6.4 / 1745 1.3 / 2240 6.4
7 SU	0630 0.9 / 1119 7.0 / 1855 0.8 / 2340 6.9	**22** M	0604 1.3 / 1053 6.5 / 1824 1.2 / 2314 6.5
8 M	0712 0.9 / 1201 6.9 / 1935 0.9	**23** TU	0642 1.2 / 1128 6.6 / 1901 1.2 / 2350 6.6
9 TU	0021 6.8 / 0751 1.0 / 1243 6.7 / 2011 1.2	**24** W	0721 1.2 / 1206 6.6 / 1939 1.3
10 W	0104 6.7 / 0829 1.2 / 1326 6.4 / 2045 1.5	**25** TH	0029 6.6 / 0759 1.2 / 1247 6.5 / 2016 1.4
11 TH	0148 6.4 / 0906 1.5 / 1413 6.1 / 2119 1.8	**26** F	0114 6.5 / 0841 1.3 / 1333 6.3 / 2058 1.5
12 F	0236 6.2 / 0944 1.8 / 1505 5.8 / 2155 2.1	**27** SA	0204 6.4 / 0927 1.4 / 1427 6.1 / 2145 1.7
13 SA ☾	0328 5.9 / 1030 2.1 / 1603 5.5 / 2245 2.4	**28** SU ☾	0302 6.2 / 1021 1.6 / 1534 5.9 / 2242 1.9
14 SU	0427 5.6 / 1134 2.3 / 1707 5.3	**29** M	0410 6.0 / 1125 1.7 / 1657 5.7 / 2353 2.0
15 M	0001 2.6 / 0532 5.4 / 1248 2.4 / 1819 5.2	**30** TU	0525 5.9 / 1236 1.7 / 1817 5.7

DECEMBER

Day	Time m	Day	Time m
1 W	0108 1.9 / 0639 6.0 / 1345 1.6 / 1924 5.9	**16** TH	0106 2.4 / 0638 5.4 / 1346 2.1 / 1922 5.4
2 TH	0217 1.8 / 0744 6.1 / 1450 1.5 / 2022 6.1	**17** F	0217 2.3 / 0736 5.6 / 1447 1.9 / 2013 5.6
3 F	0323 1.6 / 0842 6.3 / 1556 1.3 / 2114 6.3	**18** SA	0317 2.0 / 0825 5.8 / 1543 1.7 / 2058 5.8
4 SA	0426 1.4 / 0934 6.5 / 1658 1.2 / 2202 6.4	**19** SU	0410 1.7 / 0910 6.0 / 1634 1.5 / 2139 6.1
5 SU ●	0522 1.2 / 1022 6.6 / 1751 1.1 / 2246 6.6	**20** M	0458 1.5 / 0953 6.3 / 1721 1.3 / 2219 6.3
6 M	0611 1.1 / 1107 6.6 / 1837 1.1 / 2328 6.7	**21** TU ○	0543 1.3 / 1035 6.4 / 1806 1.2 / 2300 6.5
7 TU	0656 1.1 / 1149 6.6 / 1917 1.2	**22** W	0628 1.1 / 1116 6.6 / 1850 1.1 / 2341 6.7
8 W	0008 6.7 / 0737 1.1 / 1230 6.5 / 1954 1.4	**23** TH	0712 1.0 / 1159 6.6 / 1933 1.1
9 TH	0050 6.6 / 0815 1.2 / 1311 6.3 / 2028 1.5	**24** F	0023 6.8 / 0757 1.0 / 1243 6.6 / 2016 1.1
10 F	0130 6.5 / 0851 1.4 / 1352 6.1 / 2058 1.6	**25** SA	0108 6.8 / 0842 1.0 / 1328 6.5 / 2058 1.2
11 SA	0211 6.3 / 0924 1.6 / 1436 5.9 / 2128 1.8	**26** SU	0156 6.7 / 0927 1.0 / 1418 6.4 / 2142 1.3
12 SU	0254 6.1 / 0958 1.8 / 1523 5.6 / 2204 2.0	**27** M	0246 6.6 / 1014 1.1 / 1513 6.2 / 2229 1.4
13 M ☾	0339 5.8 / 1040 2.0 / 1616 5.4 / 2250 2.2	**28** TU ☾	0342 6.4 / 1105 1.3 / 1615 5.9 / 2324 1.7
14 TU	0432 5.6 / 1133 2.1 / 1718 5.3 / 2350 2.4	**29** W	0445 6.1 / 1203 1.5 / 1728 5.7
15 W	0534 5.4 / 1239 2.2 / 1822 5.2	**30** TH	0028 1.9 / 0556 5.9 / 1308 1.7 / 1846 5.6
		31 F	0138 1.9 / 0712 5.8 / 1416 1.7 / 1956 5.7

9.3.14 DOVER STRAIT
For orientation only – due to scale not all lights and buoys are shown

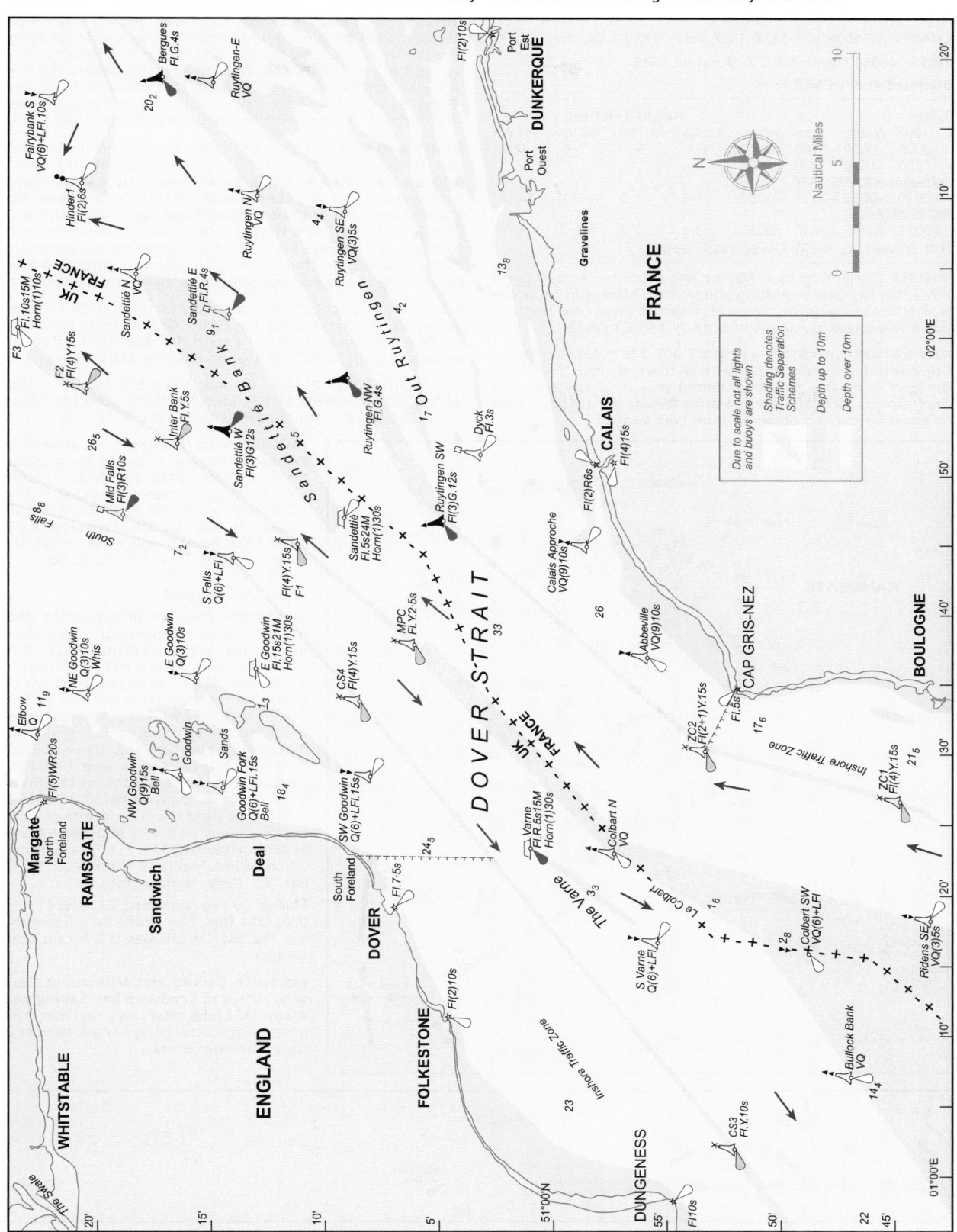

9.3.15 RAMSGATE

Kent 51°19′·51N 01°25′·50E ※※※◊◊◊✿✿✿

CHARTS AC 5605, 323, 1828, 1827; Imray C30, C8, C1; Stan 9, 5, 20.

TIDES +0030 Dover; ML 2·7; Duration 0530

Standard Port DOVER (◄─)

Times				Height (metres)			
High Water		Low Water		MHWS	MHWN	MLWN	MLWS
0000	0600	0100	0700	6·8	5·3	2·1	0·8
1200	1800	1300	1900				
Differences RAMSGATE							
+0030	+0030	+0017	+0007	−1·6	−1·3	−0·7	−0·2
RICHBOROUGH							
+0015	+0015	+0030	+0030	−3·4	−2·6	−1·7	−0·7

HW Broadstairs = HW Dover +0037 approx.

SHELTER Options: (a) Inner Marina, min depth 3m. Access approx HW ±2 via flap gate and lifting bridge; (b) W Marina, in 3m, access H24; (c) E Marina, in 2m, access H24. Larger vessels can berth on outer wavebreak pontoons of both W and E marinas.

NAVIGATION WPT 51°19′·43N 01°27′·70E, 270°/1·45M to S bkwtr. Commercial shipping uses the well-marked main E-W chan dredged 7·5m. *Due to silting, depths may be significantly less than shown; parts of Eastern Marina almost dry at LWS.* Latest information may be obtained from Port Control.

For ent/dep yachts must use the Recommended Yacht Track on the S side of the main buoyed chan. Ent/dep under power, or advise Port Control if unable to motor. Ent/dep Royal Hbr directly; cross the turning basin without delay *keeping close to the W Pier to avoid shoal patch alongside E Pier.* Holding area to the S of the S bkwtr must be used by yachts to keep the hbr ent clear for freight vessels. Beware Dike Bank to the N and Quern Bank close S of the chan. Cross Ledge and Brake shoals are further S. Speed limit 5kn. See www.portoframsgate.co.uk

LIGHTS AND MARKS Ldg lts 270°: front Dir Oc WRG 10s 10m 5M; rear, Oc 5s 17m 5M. N bkwtr hd = QG 10m 5M; S bkwtr hd = VQ R 10m 5M. At E Pier, **IPTS** (Sigs 2 and 3) visible from seaward and from within Royal Hbr, control appr into hbr limits (abeam Nos 1 & 2 buoys) and ent/exit to/from Royal Hbr. In addition a Fl Orange lt = ferry is under way; no other vessel may enter Hbr limits from seaward or leave Royal Hbr. Ent to inner marina controlled by separate IPTS to stbd of ent. Siren sounded approx 10 mins before gate closes; non-opening indicated by red ball or light.

R/T Listen and contact *Ramsgate Port Control* on Ch 14 when intending to enter or leave Royal Hbr. Only when in Royal Hbr call *Ramsgate Marina* Ch 80 for a berth. Ramsgate Dock Office can be called on Ch 14 for information on Inner Marina Lock.

TELEPHONE (Code 01843) Marina Office 572110, Hbr Office 572100; Broadstairs HM 861879; MRCC (01304) 210008; Marinecall 09068 500 455/456; Police 231055; Dr 852853; Ⓗ 225544.

FACILITIES Note: No animals are allowed in Ramsgate Harbour, including the marinas. **Marinas** (510+300Ⓥ) £2.30, ☎ 572100, portoframsgate@ thanet.gov.uk, D, P, FW, ⚓D, BH (40 ton), Ⓔ, ME, El, ✕, Slip £28/craft <5tons, CH, ACA, Gaz, SM, Ⓖ; **Royal Hbr** P & D (0600-2200). **Royal Temple YC** ☎ 591766, Bar. **Town:** Gas, Gaz, ⚒, R, Bar, ✉, Ⓑ, ⇌.

ADJACENT HARBOUR

SANDWICH, Kent, **51°16′·83N 01°21′·20E.** AC 1827 1828. Richborough differences above; ML 1·4m; Duration 0520. HW Sandwich Town quay is HW Richborough +1. Access HW ±1 at sp for draft 2m to reach Sandwich; arrive off ent at HW Dover. Visitors should seek local knowledge before arriving by day; night ent definitely not advised. The chan is marked by small lateral buoys and beacons. Visitors' berths on S bank of the River Stour at Town Quay ☎ (01304) 612162. Limited turning room before the swing bridge (opens 1H notice ☎ 01304 620644 or Mobile 0860 378792), 1·7m clearance when closed. Facilities: Slip HW±2; ⚒, R, Bar, ✉, Ⓑ, ⇌, ✈ (Manston).

Marina (50 + some visitors), £2.20, ☎ 613783 (max LOA 18m, 2·1m draft), BH (15 ton), ✕, Slip, FW, SM, CH, ME, Gas; D & P (cans from garage).

Sandwich Sailing and Motorboat Club ☎ 617650 and **Sandwich Bay Sailing and Water Ski Clubs** offer some facilities. The port is administered by Sandwich Port & Haven Commissioners.

ADLARD COLES NAUTICAL
WEATHER FORECASTS
BY FAX & TELEPHONE

Coastal/Inshore	2-day by Fax	5-day by Phone
Channel East	09065 222 346	09068 969 646
NE France	09065 501 611	09064 700 421
Anglia	09065 222 345	09068 969 645
East	09065 222 344	09068 969 644
North East	09065 222 343	09068 969 643
National (3-5 day)	09065 222 340	09068 969 640

Offshore	2-5 day by Fax	2-5 day by Phone
English Channel	09065 222 357	09068 969 657
Southern North Sea	09065 222 358	09068 969 658
Northern North Sea	09065 222 362	09068 969 662

09064/68 CALLS COST 60P PER MIN. 09065 CALLS COST £1.50 PER MIN.

East England

North Foreland to Great Yarmouth

E England

9.4.2

East England
North Foreland to Great Yarmouth

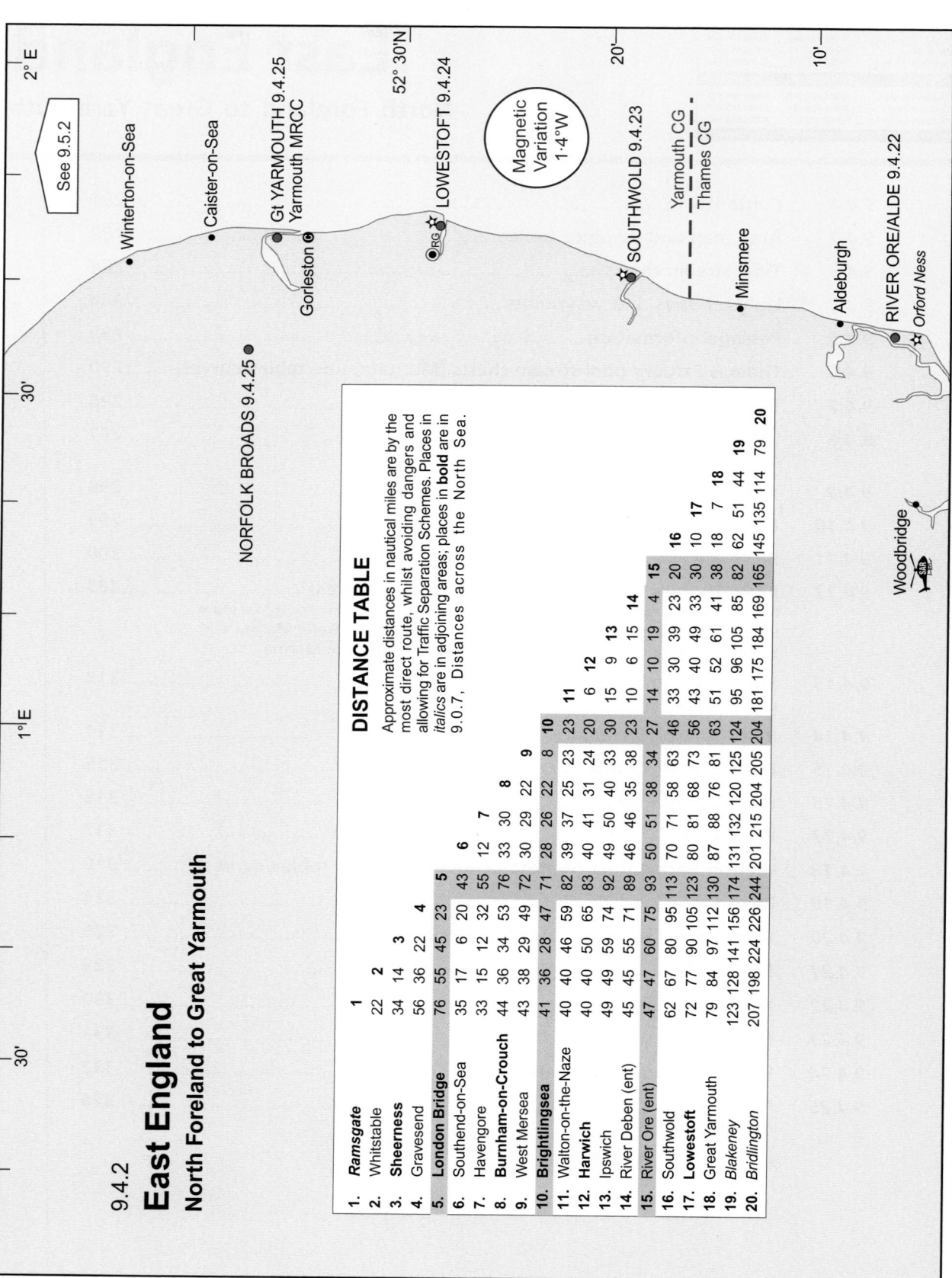

See 9.5.2

Winterton-on-Sea

Caister-on-Sea

Gt YARMOUTH 9.4.25
Yarmouth MRCC

Gorleston

NORFOLK BROADS 9.4.25

52° 30'N

R'G'

LOWESTOFT 9.4.24

Magnetic
Variation
1·4°W

SOUTHWOLD 9.4.23

Yarmouth CG
Thames CG

Minsmere

20'

Aldeburgh

RIVER ORE/ALDE 9.4.22
Orford Ness

Woodbridge

10'

2° E

1° E

30'

30'

DISTANCE TABLE

Approximate distances in nautical miles are by the most direct route, whilst avoiding dangers and allowing for Traffic Separation Schemes. Places in *italics* are in adjoining areas; places in **bold** are in 9.0.7. Distances across the North Sea.

	1	2	3	4	5	6	7	8	9	10	11	12	13	14	15	16	17	18	19	20
1. *Ramsgate*	1																			
2. Whitstable	22	2																		
3. **Sheerness**	34	14	3																	
4. Gravesend	56	36	22	4																
5. **London Bridge**	76	55	45	23	5															
6. Southend-on-Sea	35	17	6	20	43	6														
7. Havengore	33	15	12	32	55	12	7													
8. **Burnham-on-Crouch**	44	36	34	53	76	33	30	8												
9. West Mersea	43	38	29	49	72	30	29	22	9											
10. **Brightlingsea**	41	36	28	47	71	28	26	22	8	10										
11. Walton-on-the-Naze	40	40	46	59	82	39	37	25	23	23	11									
12. **Harwich**	40	40	50	65	83	40	41	31	24	20	6	12								
13. Ipswich	49	49	59	74	92	49	50	40	33	30	15	9	13							
14. River Deben (ent)	45	45	55	71	89	46	46	35	38	23	10	6	15	14						
15. **River Ore (ent)**	47	47	60	75	93	50	51	38	34	27	14	10	19	4	15					
16. Southwold	62	67	80	95	113	70	71	58	63	46	33	30	39	23	20	16				
17. **Lowestoft**	72	77	90	105	123	80	81	68	73	56	43	40	49	33	30	10	17			
18. Great Yarmouth	79	84	97	112	130	87	88	76	81	63	51	52	61	41	38	18	7	18		
19. *Blakeney*	123	128	141	156	174	131	132	120	125	124	95	96	105	85	82	62	51	44	19	
20. *Bridlington*	207	198	224	226	244	201	215	204	205	204	181	175	184	169	165	145	135	114	79	20

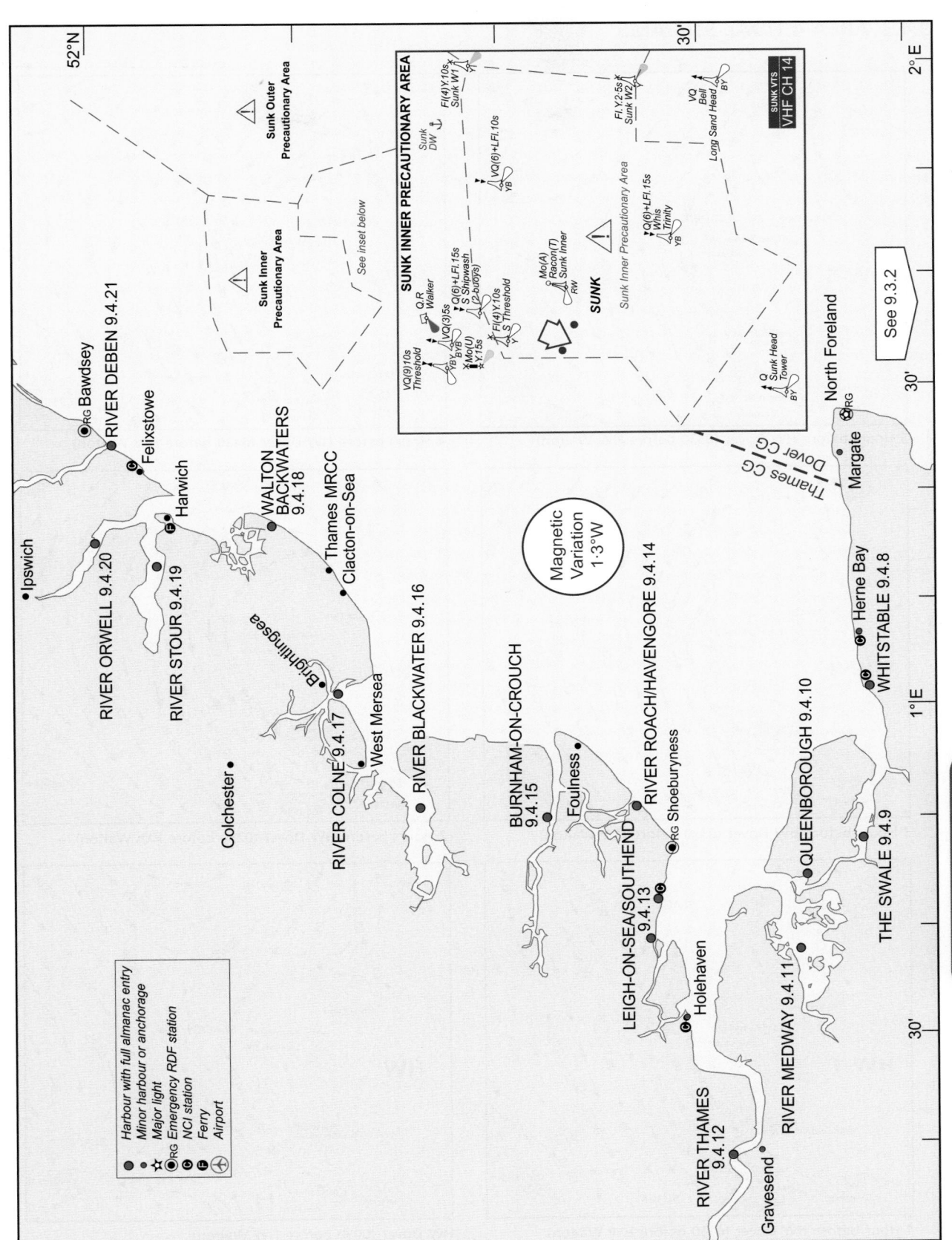

52°N

RIVER DEBEN 9.4.21

Bawdsey

Felixstowe

Harwich

Ipswich

RIVER ORWELL 9.4.20

RIVER STOUR 9.4.19

WALTON
BACKWATERS
9.4.18

Thames MRCC

Clacton-on-Sea

Brightlingsea

Colchester

West Mersea

RIVER COLNE 9.4.17

RIVER BLACKWATER 9.4.16

BURNHAM-ON-CROUCH
9.4.15

Foulness

RIVER ROACH/HAVENGORE 9.4.14

Shoeburyness

LEIGH-ON-SEA/SOUTHEND
9.4.13

Holehaven

RIVER THAMES
9.4.12

Gravesend

RIVER MEDWAY 9.4.11

QUEENBOROUGH 9.4.10

THE SWALE 9.4.9

WHITSTABLE 9.4.8

Herne Bay

Margate

North Foreland

Thames CG
Dover CG

See 9.3.2

Magnetic
Variation
1·3°W

1°E

30'

Sunk Outer
Precautionary Area

Sunk Inner
Precautionary Area

See inset below

SUNK INNER PRECAUTIONARY AREA

30'

Fl(4)Y.10s
Sunk W1

Sunk
DW

Fl(4)Y.10s
Sunk W2

VQ(6)+LFl.10s
YB

VQ
Bell
BY
Long Sand Head

VQ(6)+LFl.10s
YB

Q.R
Walker

VQ(3)5s
BYB

Q(6)+LFl.15s
S Shipwash
(2-buoys)

Mo(U)
Y.15s

Fl(4)Y.10s
S Threshold
Y

Mo(A)
Racon(T)
Sunk Inner
RW

Q(6)+LFl.15s
Whis
Trinity
YB

VQ(9)10s
Threshold
BY

Mo(U)
Y.15s

SUNK

Sunk Inner Precautionary Area

Q
Sunk Head
Tower
BY

Sunk VTS
VHF CH 14

2°E

Harbour with full almanac entry
Minor harbour or anchorage
Major light
Emergency RDF station
NCI station
Ferry
Airport

9.4.3 AREA 4 TIDAL STREAMS

5 Hours before HW Dover (0530 before HW Walton)

4 Hours before HW Dover (0430 before HW Walton)

3 Hours before HW Dover (0330 before HW Walton)

2 Hours before HW Dover (0230 before HW Walton)

1 Hour before HW Dover (0130 before HW Walton)

HW Dover (0030 before HW Walton)

Southward 9.3.3   Thames Estuary 9.4.6   Northward 9.5.3   Eastward 9.16.3

1 Hour after HW Dover (0030 after HW Walton)

2 Hours after HW Dover (0130 after HW Walton)

3 Hours after HW Dover (0230 after HW Walton)

4 Hours after HW Dover (0330 after HW Walton)

5 Hours after HW Dover (0430 after HW Walton)

6 Hours after HW Dover (0530 after HW Walton)

E England

9.4.4 LIGHTS, BUOYS AND WAYPOINTS

Bold print = light with a nominal range of 15M or more. CAPITALS = place or feature. *CAPITAL ITALICS* = light-vessel, light float or Lanby. *Italics* = Fog signal. ***Bold italics*** = Racon. Abbreviations are in Chapter 1.

IMPORTANT NOTE. Regular changes are made to Thames Estuary buoyage. Check Notices to Mariners for the latest information.

THAMES ESTUARY – SOUTHERN

(Direction of buoyage generally East to West)

APPROACHES to THAMES ESTUARY

Foxtrot 3 ⌐ 51°24'·20N 02°00'·40E; Fl 10s 12m **15M**; *Racon (T) 10M*; *Horn 10s.*
Falls Hd ⌑ Q; 51°28'·23N 01°49'·89E.
Drill Stone ⌑ Q (3) 10s; 51°25'·88N 01°42'·89E.
Thanet Offshore Windfarm Met ⌑ Fl (5) Y 20s; 51°25'·53N 01°38'·60E.
NE Spit ⌑ VQ (3); *Racon (T) 10M*; 5s; 51°27'·93N 01°29'·89E.
East Margate ⌐ Fl R 2·5s; 51°27'·03N 01°26'·40E.
Elbow ⌑ Q; 51°23'·23N 01°31'·59E.
Foreness Pt Outfall ⌐ Fl R 5s; 51°24'·61N 01°26'·02E.
Longnose ⌐ 51°24'·15N 01°26'·08E.
Longnose Spit ⌑ Fl R 2·5s 5m 2M; 51°23'·93N 01°25'·68E.

MARGATE and GORE CHANNEL

SE Margate ⌑ Q (3) 10s; 51°24'·05N 01°20'·40E.
S Margate ⌑ Fl G 2·5s; 51°23'·83N 01°16'·65E.
Hook Spit ⌃ QG; 51°24'·08N 01°12'·18E.
E Last ⌐ QR; 51°24'·07N 01°11'·92E.

HERNE BAY

Beltinge Bay Bn ⌑ Fl Y 5s; 51°22'·73N 01°08'·63E.
Landing Stage ⌑ Q 18m 4M, (isolated); 51°22'·91N 01°06'·89E.
N Pier Hd ⌑ 2 FR (vert); 51°22'·43N 01°07'·27E.

WHITSTABLE

Whitstable Street ⌐; 51°24'·00N 01°01'·54E. (See The Swale.)
Oyster ⌐ Fl (2) R 10s; 51°22'·14N 01°01'·16E.
W Quay Dn ⌑ Fl G 5s 2m.
S Quay ⌑ Dir lt 122°; Dir Fl WRG 3s 7m: vis: 117·5°-G-120·5°-W-123·5°-R-126·5°; 51°21'·76N 01°01·70E.

THE SWALE

Whitstable Street ⌐ Fl R 2s; 51°24'·00N 01°01'·54E.
Columbine ⌃ Fl G 2s; 51°24'·26N 01°01'·34E.
Columbine Spit ⌃ Fl (3) G 10s; 51°23'·86N 01°00'·03E.
Ham Gat ⌃ Q G; 51°23'·08N 00°58'·32E.
Pollard Spit ⌐ Q R; 51°22'·98N 00°58'·57E.
Sand End ⌃ Fl G 5s; 51°21'·43N 00°55'·90E.
Receptive Point ⌃ Fl G 10s; 51°20'·86N 00°54'·41E.
Queenborough Spit ⌑ Q (3) 10s; 51°25'·81N 00°43'·93E.
South Oaze ⌐ Fl R 2s; 51°21'·34N 00°56'·01E.

QUEENS CHANNEL and FOUR FATHOMS CHANNEL

E Margate ⌐ Fl R 2·5s; 51°27'·03N 01°26'·40E.
Spaniard ⌑ Q (3) 10s; 51°26'·23N 01°04'·00E.
Spile ⌃ Fl G 2·5s; 51°26'·43N 00°55'·70E.

PRINCES CHANNEL

Tongue Sand E ⌑ VQ (3) 5s; 51°29'·48N 01°22'·21E.
Tongue Sand N ⌑ Q; 51°29'·68N 01°22'·03E.
Princes Outer ⌑ VQ (6) + L Fl 10s; 51°28'·89N 01°20'·43E.
Princes North ⌃ Q G; 51°29'·25N 01°18'·35E.
Princes South ⌐ Q R; 51°28'·74N 01°18'·26E.
Princes No.1 ⌃ Fl (4) G 15s; 51°29'·23N 01°16'·02E.
Princes No.2 ⌐ Fl (2) R 5s; 51°28'·81N 01°13'·08E.
Princes No.3 ⌃ Fl (2) G 5s; 51°29'·33N 01°13'·10E.
Princes No.4 ⌐ Fl (3) R 10s; 51°28'·83N 01°09'·90E.
Princes No.5 ⌃ Fl (3) G 10s; 51°29'·39N 01°10'·00E.
Princes Mid ⌑ Fl Y 5s; 51°29'·19N 01°09'·00E.

Shivering Sand Twr N ⌑ Q; 51°30'·01N 01°04'·76E.
Shivering Sand Twr S ⌑ Q (6) + L Fl 15s; *Bell*; 51°29'·75N 01°04'·83E.
Princes No.8 ⌐ Fl (2) R 5s; 51°29'·15N 01°03'·87E.
Princes Inner ⌑ Fl Y 2·5s; 51°29'·59N 01°03'·47E.

FOULGER'S GAT and KNOB CHANNEL

The N Edinburgh Channel is not buoyed. Fisherman's Gat is a commercial ship channel; Foulger's Gat, suitable for leisure craft, is marked at each end with SWMs.

Long Sand Inner ⌐ Mo 'A' 15s; 51°38'·80N 01°25'·60E.
Long Sand Outer ⌐ L Fl 10s; 51°35'·90N 01°26'·00E.
Shingles Patch ⌑ Q; 51°33'·01N 01°15'·37E.
N Shingles ⌐ Fl R 2·5s; 51°32'·79N 01°14'·25E.
Tizard ⌑ Q (6) + L Fl 15s; 51°32'·93N 01°12'·90E.
Mid Shingles ⌐ Fl (2) R 5s; 51°31'·96N 01°11'·98E.
NE Knob ⌃ QG; 51°32'·03N 01°10'·00E.
NW Shingles ⌑ VQ; 51°31'·26N 01°09'·73E.
SE Knob ⌃ Fl G 5s; 51°30'·89N 01°06'·41E.
Knob ⌑ Iso 5s; *Bell*; 51°30'·69N 01°04'·28E.

OAZE DEEP

Oaze Deep ⌃ Fl (2) G 5s; 51°30'·03N 01°00'·70E.
Red Sand Trs N ⌐ Fl (3) R 10s; *Bell*; 51°28'·73N 00°59'·32E.
N Oaze ⌐ QR; 51°30'·03N 00°57'·65E.
Oaze ⌑ Fl (4) Y 10s; 51°29'·06N 00°56'·93E.
W Oaze ⌑ Iso 5s; 51°29'·06N 00°55'·43E.
Oaze Bank ⌃ Q G 5s; 51°29'·36N 00°56'·95E.
Cant ⌑ (unlit); 51°27'·77N 00°53'·36E.
East Cant ⌐ QR; 51°28'·53N 00°55'·60E.

MEDWAY, SHEERNESS

Medway ⌑ Mo (A) 6s; 51°28'·83N 00°52'·81E.
No. 1 ⌃ Fl G 2·5s; 51°28'·55N 00°50'·50E.
No. 2 ⌑ Q; 51°28'·33N 00°50'·52E.
No. 7 ⌃ Fl G 10s; 51°27'·91N 00°47'·52E.
No. 9 ⌃ Fl G 5s; 51°27'·74N 00°46'·61E.
No. 11 ⌃ Fl (3) G 10s; 51°27'·51N 00°45'·80E.
Grain Hard ⌃ Fl G 5s; 51°26'·98N 00°44'·17E.
Isle of Grain ☆ Q WRG 20m W13M, R7M, G8M; R & W ◇ on R twr; vis 220°-R-234°- G-241°-W-013°; 51°26'·70N 00°43'·38E.
Queenborough Spit ⌑ Q (3) 10s; 51°25'·81N 00°43'·93E.

RIVER THAMES

SEA REACH, NORE and YANTLET

No. 1 ⌑ Fl Y 2·5s; *Racon (T) 10M*; 51°29'·45N 00°52'·57E.
No. 2 ⌑ Iso 5s; 51°29'·40N 00°49'·75E.
No. 3 ⌐ L Fl 10s; 51°29'·33N 00°46'·54E.
No. 4 ⌑ Fl Y 2·5s; 51°29'·61N 00°44'·18E.
No. 5 ⌐ Iso 5s; 51°29'·95N 00°41'·44E.
No. 6 ⌑ Iso 2s; 51°30'·03N 00°39'·83E.
No. 7 ⌑ Fl Y 2·5s; *Racon (T) 10M*; 51°30'·10N 00°37'·04E.
Nore Swatch ⌐ Fl (4) R 15s; 51°28'·28N 00°45'·55E.
Mid Swatch ⌃ Fl G 5s; 51°28'·68N 00°44'·16E.
W Nore Sand ⌐ Fl (3) R 10s; 51°29'·41N 00°40'·85E.
East Blyth ⌐ Fl (2) R 10s; 51°29'·72N 00°37'·80E.
Mid Blyth ⌑ Q; 51°30'·08N 00°32'·38E.

LEIGH-ON-SEA and SOUTHEND-ON-SEA

Leigh ⌃; 51°31'·07N 00°42'·56E.
Southend Pier E End ⌑ 2 FG (vert) 7m; *Horn Mo (N) 30s, Bell (1)*
SE Leigh ⌑ Q (6) + L Fl 15s; 51°29'·42N 00°47'·07E.

GRAVESEND

Shornmead ⌑ Fl (2) WR 10s 12m 11/7M , W11M, W7M, R11M; vis 070°-W-084°-R(Intens)-089°-W(Intens) -094°-W - 250°; 51°26'·92N 00°26'·24E.

Northfleet Upper ☆ Oc WRG 10s 30m **W16M**, R12M, G12M; vis:126°- R - 149°- W - 159°- G - 268° - W -279°; 51°26'·93N 00°20'·06E.

WGS84 DATUM
Plot waypoints on chart before use

THAMES TIDAL BARRIER
Span B (51°29'·73N 00°02'·23E) is used for small craft/yachts Eastbound and Span G (51°29'·91N 00°02'·21E) is used for small craft/yachts Westbound. Spans B, C, D, E, F & G are navigable. Spans C to F are for larger vessels. All spans display a F GR ⚡. A Green → indicates span open for navigation. A Red X indicates span closed to navigation. In low visibility F lights are shown either side of those spans which are displaying a Green →.

THAMES ESTUARY – NORTHERN

KENTISH KNOCK
Kentish Knock ⚪ Q (3) 10s; *Whis*; 51°38'·08N 01°40·43E.
S Knock ⚪ Q (6) + L Fl 15s; *Bell*; 51°34'·13N 01°34'·29E.

KNOCK JOHN CHANNEL
No. 7 ⚐ Fl (4) G 15s; 51°32'·03N 01°06'·40E.
No. 5 ⚐ Fl (3) G 10s; 51°32'·49N 01°07'·75E.
No. 4 ⚑ QR 10s; 51°32'·33N 01°07'·90E.
No. 2 ⚑ Fl (3) R 10s; 51°33'·11N 01°09'·85E.
No. 3 ⚪ Q (6) + L Fl 15s; 51°33'·23N 01°09'·70E.
No. 1 ⚐ Fl G 5s; 51°33'·75N 01°10'·72E.
Knock John ⚑ Fl (2) R 5s; 51°33'·61N 01°11'·37E.

BLACK DEEP
No. 12 ⚑ Fl (4) R 15s; 51°33'·83N 01°13'·50E.
No. 11 ⚐ Fl (3) G 10s; 51°34'·33N 01°13'·40E.
No. 10 ⚑ Fl (3) R 10s; 51°34'·74N 01°15'·60E.
No. 9 ⚪ Q (6) + L Fl 15s; 51°35'·13N 01°15'·09E.
No. 8 ⚪ Q (9) 15s; 51°36'·36N 01°20'·43E.
No. 7 ⚐ QG; 51°37'·08N 01°17'·69E.
No. 6 ⚑ Fl R 2·5s; 51°38'·53N 01°24'·41E.
No. 5 ⚪ VQ (3) 5s; 51°39'·53N 01°23'·00E.
No. 4 ⚑ Fl (2) R 5s; 51°41'·42N 01°28'·49E.
Long Sand Bcn ⚓ ; 51°41'·48N 01°29'·49E.
No. 3 ⚐ Fl (3) G 15s; 51°42'·41N 01°26'·48E.
No. 1 ⚐ Fl G 5s, 51°44'·03N 01°28'·09E.
No. 2 ⚑ Fl (4) R 15s; 51°45'·63N 01°32'·20E.
Sunk Head Tower ⚪ Q; *Whis*; 51°46'·63N 01°30'·51E.
Black Deep ⚑ QR.51°47'·50N 01°35'·64E.
Trinity ⚪ Q (6) + L Fl 15s; *Whis*; 51°49'·03N 01°36'·39E.
Long Sand Head ⚪ VQ; *Bell*; 51°47'·90N 01°39'·42E.

FISHERMANS GAT
Outer Fisherman ⚪ Q (3) 10s; 51°33'·89N 01°25'·01E.
Fisherman No. 1 ⚐ Fl G 2·5s; 51°34'·53N 01°23'·57E.
Fisherman No. 2 ⚑ Fl R 2·5s; 51°34'·35N 01°23'·01E.
Fisherman No. 3 ⚐ Fl G 5s; 51°34'·72N 01°22'·94E.
Fisherman No. 4 ⚑ Fl (2) R 5s; 51°35'·25N 01°21'·35E.
Fisherman No. 5 ⚐ Fl (2) G 5s; 51°35'·52N 01°21'·75E.
Inner Fisherman ⚑ Q R; 51°36'·07N 01°19'·87E.

BARROW DEEP
SW Barrow ⚪ Q(6) + L Fl 15s; *Bell*; 51°32'·29N 01°00'·31E.
Barrow No. 14 ⚑ Fl R 2·5s; 51°31'·83N 01°00'·43E.
Barrow No. 13 ⚐ Fl (2) G 5s; 51°32'·82N 01°03'·07E.
Barrow No. 12 ⚑ Fl (2) R 5s; 51°32'·77N 01°04'·13E.
Barrow No.11 ⚐ Fl (3) G 10s; 51°34'·08N 01°06'·70E.
Barrow No. 9 ⚪ VQ (3) 5s; 51°35'·34N 01°10'·30E.
Barrow No. 8 ⚑ Fl (2) R 5s; 51°35'·03N 01°11'·40E.
Barrow No. 6 ⚑ Fl (4) R 15s; 51°37'·30N 01°14'·69E.
Barrow No. 5 ⚐ Fl G 10s; 51°40'·03N 01°16'·20E.
Barrow No. 4 ⚪ VQ (9) 10s; 51°39'·88N 01°17'·48E.
Barrow No. 3 ⚪ Q (3) 10s; *Racon (M)10M*; 51°42'·02N 01°20'·24E.
Barrow No. 2 ⚑ Fl (2) R 5s; 51°41'·98N 01°22'·89E.

WEST SWIN and MIDDLE DEEP
Blacktail (W) ⚓ ; 51°31'·46N 00°55'·19E.
Maplin ⚐ Q G; *Bell*; 51°33'·66N 01°01'·59E.

W Swin ⚑ QR; 51°33'·40N 01°01'·97E.
Maplin Edge ⚐ Fl G 2.5s; 51°35'·33N 01°03'·64E.
Maplin Bank ⚑ Fl (3) R 10s; 51°35'·50N 01°04'·70E.

EAST SWIN and KING'S CHANNEL
NE Maplin ⚐ Fl G 5s; *Bell*; 51°37'·43N 01°04'·90E.
W Hook Middle ⚑ 51°39'·18N 01°07'·97E.
S Whitaker ⚐ Fl (2) G 10s; 51°40'·23N 01°09'·05E.
N Middle ⚪ Q; 51°41'·03N 01°11'·88E.
W Sunk ⚪ Q (9) 15s; 51°44'·33N 01°25'·80E.
Gunfleet Spit ⚪ Q (6) + L Fl 15s; *Bell*; 51°45'·33N 01°21'·70E.

WHITAKER CHANNEL and RIVER CROUCH
Whitaker ⚪ Q (3) 10s; *Bell*; 51°41'·43N 01°10'·51E.
Whitaker No. 6 ⚪ Q; 51°40'·69N 01°08'·06E.
Swin Spitway ⚪ Iso 10s; *Bell*; 51°41'·95N 01°08'·35E.
Ron Pipe ⚑ 51°40'·51N 01°03'·62E.
Swallow Tail ⚐ 51°40'·51N 01°04'·70E.
Ridge ⚑ Fl R 10s; 51°40'·13N 01°04'·87E.
Foulness ⚑ Fl (2) R 10s; 51°39'·85N 01°03'·81E.
Sunken Buxey ⚪ Q; 51°39'·54N 01°00'·59E.
Buxey No. 1 ⚪ VQ (6) + L Fl 10s; 51°39'·18N 01°01'·01E.
Buxey No. 2 ⚪ Q; 51°38'·98N 01°00'·15E.
Outer Crouch ⚪ Q (6) + L Fl 15s; 51°38'·38N 00°58'·48E.

GOLDMER GAT and WALLET
NE Gunfleet ⚪ Q (3) 10s; 51°49'·93N 01°27'·79E.
Wallet No. 2 ⚑ Fl R 5s; 51°48'·88N 01°22'·99E.
Wallet No. 4 ⚑ Fl (4) R 10s; 51°46'·53N 01°17'·23E.
Wallet Spitway ⚪ L Fl 10s; *Bell*; 51°42'·86N 01°07'·30E.
Knoll ⚪ Q; 51°43'·88N 01°05'·07E.
Eagle ⚐ QG; 51°44'·13N 01°03'·82E.
N Eagle ⚪ Q; 51°44'·71N 01°04'·32E.
NW Knoll ⚑ Fl (2) R 5s; 51°44'·35N 01°02'·17E.
Colne Bar ⚐ Fl (2) G 5s; 51°44'·61N 01°02'·57E.
Bench Head ⚐ Fl (3) G 10s; 51°44'·69N 01°01'·10E.

RIVER BLACKWATER
The Nass ⚪ VQ (3) 5s 6m 2M; 51°45'·83N 00°54'·83E.
Thirslet ⚐ Fl (3) G 10s; 51°43'·73N 00°50'·39E.
No. 1 ⚐ ; 51°43'·44N 00°48'·02E.

RIVER COLNE and BRIGHTLINGSEA
Inner Bench Head No. 2 ⚑ Fl (2) R 5s; 51°45'·96N 01°01'·74E.
Colne Pt No. 1 ⚐ Fl G 3s; 51°46'·01N 01°01'·92E.
No. 8 ⚑ Fl R 3s; 51°46'·90N 01°01'·30E.
No. 9 ⚐ Fl G 3s; 51°47'·36N 01°01'·07E.
Ldg lts 041°. Front, FR 7m 4M; W □, R stripe on post; vis: 020°-080°; 51°48'·39N 01°01'·20E. Rear, 50m from front, FR 10m 4M; W □, R stripe on post. FR lts are shown on 7 masts between 1·5M and 3M NW when firing occurs.

WALTON BACKWATERS
Pye End ⚑ L Fl 10s; 51°55'·03N 01°17'·90E.
No. 2 ⚑ Fl (2) 5s; 51°54'·62N 01°16'·80E.
Crab Knoll No. 3 ⚐ Fl G 5s; 51°54'·41N 01°16'·41E.

HARWICH APPROACHES
(Direction of buoyage North to South)

MEDUSA CHANNEL
Medusa ⚐ Fl G 5s; 51°51'·23N 01°20'·35E.
Stone Banks ⚑ FlR 5s; 51°53'·19N 01°19'·23E.
Pennyhole ⚑ ; 51°53'·55N 01°18'·00E (Mar–Sep).

CORK SAND and ROUGH SHOALS
S Cork ⚪ Q (6) + L Fl 15s; 51°51'·33N 01°24'·09E.
Roughs Tower SE ⚪ Q (3) 10s; 51°53'·64N 01°28'·94E.
Roughs Tower NW ⚪ Q (9) 15s; 51°53'·61N 01°29'·06E.
Cork Sand ⚪ Fl (3) R 10s; 51°55'·51N 01°25'·42E.

Lights etc – Passage information

HARWICH CHANNEL

Sunk Inner ⌐ Iso 3s 11m 12M, *Racon T*; *Horn 30s*; 51°51'·03N 01°34'·89E.
S Threshold ↙ Fl (4) Y 10s; 51°52'·20N 01°33'·14E.
S Shipwash ↙↙ 2 By(s) Q (6) + L Fl 15s; 51°52'·71N 01°33'·97E.
Outer Tidal Bn ↙ Mo (U) 15s 2m 3M; 51°52'·85N 01°32'·34E.
E Fort Massac ↙ VQ (3) 5s; 51°53'·36N 01°32'·79E.
W Fort Massac ↙ VQ (9) 10s; 51°53'·36N 01°32'·49E.
Walker ⌐ QR; 51°53'·79N 01°33'·90E.
N Threshold ↙ Fl Y 5s; 51°54'·49N 01°33'·47E.
SW Shipwash ↙ Q (9)15s; 51°54'·75N 01°34'·21E.
Haven ↙ Mo (A) 5s; 51°55'·76N 01°35'·56E.
W Shipwash ⌐ Fl (2) R 10s; 51°57'·12N 01°35'·89E.
NW Shipwash ⌐ Fl R 5s; 51°58'·98N 01°37'·01E.
Harwich App (HA) ↙ Iso 5s; 51°56'·75N 01°30'·66E.
Cross ↙ Fl (3) Y 10s; 51°56'·23N 01°30'·48E.
Harwich Chan No. 1 ⌐ Fl Y 2·5s; *Racon (T)10M*; 51°56'·13N 01°27'·06E.
Harwich Chan No. 3 ⌐ Fl (3) Y 10s; 51°56'·04N 01°25'·54E.
Harwich Chan No. 5 ⌐ Fl (5) Y 10s; 51°55'·96N 01°24'·01E.
Harwich Chan No. 7 ⌐ Fl (3) Y 10s; 51°55'·87N 01°22'·49E.
S Bawdsey ↙ Q (6) + L Fl 15s; *Whis*; 51°57'·23N 01°30'·19E.
Washington ▲ QG; 51°56'·52N 01°26'·59E.
Felixstowe Ledge ▲ Fl (3) G 10s; 51°56'·30N 01°23'·72E.
Wadgate Ledge ↙ Fl (4) G 15s; 51°56'·16N 01°21'·99E.
Platters ↙ Q (6) + L Fl 15s; 51°55'·64N 01°20'·97E.
Rolling Ground ▲ QG; 51°55'·55N 01°19'·75E.
Beach End ▲ Fl (2) G 5s; 51°55'·62N 01°19'·21E.
Cork Sand Yacht Bn ↙ VQ 2M; 51°55'·21N 01°25'·20E.
Rough ↙ VQ; 51°55'·19N 01°31'·00E.
Pitching Ground ⌐ Fl (4) R 15s; 51°55'·43N 01°21'·05E.
Inner Ridge ⌐ QR; 51°55'·38N 01°20'·20E.
Deane ⌐ L Fl R 6s; 51°55'·36N 01°19'·28E.
Landguard ↙ Q; 51°55'·45N 01°18'·84E.

RIVERS STOUR AND ORWELL

RIVER STOUR and HARWICH

Shotley Spit ↙ Q (6) + L Fl 15s; 51°57'·21N 01°17'·69E.
Shotley Marina Lock E side Dir lt 339·5° 3m 1M (uses Moiré pattern); Or structure; 51°57'·46N 01°16'·60E.
Guard ⌐ Fl R 5s; *Bell*; 51°57'·07N 01°17'·86E.

RIVER ORWELL and IPSWICH

Suffolk Yacht Harbour. Ldg lts Front Iso Y 1M; 51°59'·73N 01°16'·09E. Rear Oc Y 4s 1M.

HARWICH TO ORFORDNESS

FELIXSTOWE, R DEBEN and WOODBRIDGE HAVEN

Woodbridge Haven ⌐ Mo(A)15s; 51°58'·20N 01°23'·85E.
Deben ⌐; 51°59'·30N 01°23'·53E.

RIVERS ORE and ALDE

Orford Haven ⌐ L Fl 10s; *Bell*. 52°01'·62N 01°28'·00E.

OFFSHORE MARKS

S Galloper ↙ Q (6) L Fl 15s; *Racon (T)10M*; 51°43'·98N 01°56'·43E.
N Galloper ↙ Q; 51°49'·84N 01°59'·99E.
S Inner Gabbard ↙ Q (6) + L Fl 15s. 51°49'·92N 01°51'·89E.
N Inner Gabbard ↙ Q; 51°59'·20N 01°56'·00E.
Outer Gabbard ↙ Q (3) 10s; *Racon (O)10M*; 51°57'·83N 02°04'·19E.
NHR-SE ▲ Fl G 5s; 51°45'·39N 02°39'·89E.

SHIPWASH and BAWDSEY BANK

E Shipwash ↙ VQ (3) 5s; 51°57'·08N 01°37'·89E.
NW Shipwash ⌐ Fl R 5s; 51°58'·98N 01°37'·01E.
N Shipwash ↙ Q 7M; *Racon (M) 10M*; *Bell*; 52°01'·73N 01°38'·27E.
S Bawdsey ↙ Q (6) + L Fl 15s; *Whis*; 51°57'·23N 01°30'·22E.
Mid Bawdsey ▲ Fl (3) G 10s; 51°58'·88N 01°33'·59E.
NE Bawdsey ▲ Fl G 10s; 52°01'·73N 01°36'·09E.

CUTLER and WHITING BANKS

Cutler ▲ QG; 51°58'·51N 01°27'·48E.
SW Whiting ↙ Q (6) + L Fl 10s; 52°00'·96N 01°30'·69E.
Whiting Hook ⌐ Fl R 10s; 52°02'·98N 01°31'·82E.
NE Whiting ↙ Q (3) 10s; 52°03'·61N 01°33'·32E.

ORFORDNESS TO WINTERTON

(Direction of buoyage is South to North)
Orford Ness ☆ 52°05'·03N 01°34'·46E; Fl 5s 28m **20M**; W ○ twr, R bands. F WRG 14m **W17M**, R13M, **G15M** (same twr). vis: R shore-210°, 038°-R-047°-G-shore; *Racon (T) 18M*.
FR 13m 12M vis: 026°- 038° over Whiting Bank.
Aldeburgh Ridge ⌐ QR; 52°06'·72N 01°36'·95E.

SOUTHWOLD

Southwold ☆ 52°19'·63N 01°40'·89E; Fl (4) WR 20s 37m **W16M, R12M**, R14M; vis 204°-R (intens)- 215°-W-001°.

LOWESTOFT and APPR VIA STANFORD CHANNEL

E Barnard ↙ Q (3) 10s; 52°25'·14N 01°46'·38E.
Newcome Sand ↙ QR; 52°26'·28N 01°46'·97E.
S Holm ↙ VQ (6) + L Fl 10s; 52°27'·05N 01°47'·15E.
Stanford ⌐ Fl R 2·5s; 52°27'·35N 01°46'·67E.
SW Holm ▲ Fl (2) G 5s; 52°27'·87N 01°46'·99E.
Claremont Pier ⌐ Fl R 5s 5m 3M; 52°27'·89N 01°44'·87E.
Outer Hbr S Pier Hd ⌐ Oc R 5s 12m 6M; *Horn (4) 60s*; Tfc sigs; 52°28'·29N 01°45'·36E.
N Newcome ⌐ Fl (4) R 15s; 52°28'·39N 01°46'·37E.
Lowestoft ☆ 52°29'·22N 01°45'·35; Fl 15s 37m **23M**; W twr; part obscd 347°- shore;

LOWESTOFT NORTH ROAD and CORTON ROAD

Lowestoft Ness SE ↙ Q (6) + L Fl 15s; 52°28'·84N 01°46'·25E.
Lowestoft Ness N ↙ VQ (3) 5s; *Bell*; 52°28'·89N 01°46'·23E.
W Holm ▲ Fl (3) G 10s; 52°29'·80N 01°47'·09E.
NW Holm ▲ Fl (4) G 15s; 52°31'·93N 01°46'·70E.

GREAT YARMOUTH APPROACH via HOLM CHANNEL

E Newcome ⌐ Fl (2) R 5s; 52°28'·51N 01°49'·21E.
Corton ↙ Q (3) 10s; *Whis*; 52°31'·13N 01°51'·39E.
E. Holm ⌐ Fl (3) R 10s; 52°30'·64N 01°49'·72E.
S Corton ↙ Q (6) + L Fl 15s; *Bell*; 52°32'·70N 01°49'·50E.
NE Holm ⌐ Fl R 2·5s; 52°32'·30N 01°48'·20E.
Holm ▲ Fl G 2·5s; 52°33'·53N 01°47'·96E.
Holm Sand ↙ Q. 52°33'·36N 01°46'·85E.

GREAT YARMOUTH and GORLESTON

W Corton ↙ Q (9) 15s; 52°34'·59N 01°46'·62E.
Brush Sector ⌐ Dir Oc WRG 10s 7m 1M; 248·5°-G-250·5°-Alt GW-252·5°-W-257·5°-R-258·5°; metal framework tower; 52°34'·30N 01°44'·00E.
Gorleston South Pier Hd ⌐ Fl R 3s 11m 11M; vis: 235°-340°; *Horn (3) 60s*; 52°34'·33N 01°44'·28E.
N Pier Hd ⌐ QG 8m 6M; vis: 176°-078°; 52°34'·38N 01°44'·38E.

9.4.5 PASSAGE INFORMATION

Reference books include: *East Coast Rivers* – latest edition 2004 (NDL/Harber) from the Swale to Lowestoft. The Admiralty NP 28 *Dover Strait Pilot* and NP54 *North Sea (West) Pilot*. The area is well covered by Admiralty Leisure Folios: 5606 covers the Thames Estuary from Ramsgate to Tower Bridge, 5607 the northern Thames Estuary to Orford Ness, and 5614 from Orford Ness northwards.

More Passage Information is threaded between the harbours of this Area.

THE THAMES ESTUARY

(AC 1183, 1975) To appreciate the geography of the Thames Estuary there is a well-known analogy between its major sandbanks and the fingers and thumb of the left hand, out-stretched palm-down: With the thumb lying E over Margate Sand, the index finger covers Long Sand; the middle finger represents Sunk Sand and the third finger delineates West and East Barrow; the little finger points NE along Buxey and Gunfleet Sands.

The intervening channels are often intricate, but the main ones, in sequence from south to north, are:

- between the Kent coast and thumb – Four Fathoms, Horse, Gore and South Chans; sometimes known as the overland route due to relatively shallow water.
- between thumb and index finger – Queens and Princes Chans leading seaward to Knock Deep.
- between index and middle fingers – Knob Chan leading to Knock Deep via the Edinburgh Chans across Long Sand and the Shingles. Knock John Chan and Black Deep, the main shipping channels which are restricted to vessels drawing more than 6m.
- between middle and third fingers – Barrow Deep.
- between third and little fingers – W and E Swin, Middle Deep and Whitaker Chan leading seaward to King's Chan.
- between little finger and the Essex coast – The Wallet and Goldmer Gat.

The sandbanks shift constantly in the Thames Estuary. Up-to-date charts showing the latest buoyage changes are essential, but it is unwise to put too much faith in charted depths over the banks; a reliable echosounder is vital. The main chans carry much commercial shipping and are well buoyed and lit, but this is not so in lesser chans and swatchways which are convenient for yachtsmen, particularly when crossing the estuary from N to S, or vice versa. Unlit, unmarked minor chans should be used with great caution, which could indeed be the hallmark of all passage-making in the Thames Estuary. Good visibility is needed to pick out buoys/marks, and to avoid shipping.

CROSSING THE THAMES ESTUARY

▶ *Study the tides carefully and understand them, so as to work the streams to best advantage and to ensure sufficient depth at the times and places where you expect to be, or might be later. In principle it is best to make most of the crossing on a rising tide, ie departing N Foreland or the vicinity of the Whitaker buoy at around LW. The stream runs 3kn at sp in places, mostly along the chans but sometimes across the intervening banks. With wind against tide a short, steep sea is raised, particularly in E or NE winds.* ◀

Making N from N Foreland to Orford Ness or beyond (or vice versa) it may be preferable to keep to seaward of the main banks, via Kentish Knock and Long Sand Head buoys, thence to N Shipwash lt buoy 14M further N.

Bound NW from N Foreland it is approximately 26M to the Rivers Crouch, Blackwater or Colne. A safe route is through either the Princes Channel or Fisherman's Gat, thence S of the Tizard,

Knob and West Barrow banks to the West Swin, before turning NE into Middle Deep and the East Swin. This is just one of many routes which could be followed, depending on wind direction, tidal conditions and confidence in electronic aids in the absence of marks.

A similar, well-used route in reverse, ie to the SE, lies via the Wallet Spitway, to the Whitaker lt buoy, through Barrow Swatchway to SW Sunk bn; thence via the N Edinburgh Chan, toward the E Margate lt buoy keeping E of Tongue Sand tr. Beware shoal waters off Barrow and Sunk Sands.

London VTS can give navigational help to yachts on VHF Ch 69; Thames CG at Walton-on-the-Naze can also assist. *London VTS* has radar coverage between the Naze and Margate, eastward to near the Dutch coast.

NORTH FORELAND TO LONDON BRIDGE

N Foreland has a conspic lt ho (AC 1828), with buoys offshore. ▶ *From HW Dover –0120 to +0045 the stream runs N from The Downs and W into Thames Estuary. From HWD + 0045 to + 0440 the N-going stream from The Downs meets the E-going stream from Thames Estuary, which in strong winds causes a bad sea. From HWD –0450 to –0120 the streams turn W into Thames Estuary and S towards The Downs. If bound for London, round N Foreland against the late ebb in order to carry a fair tide from Sheerness onward.* ◀

For vessels drawing less than 2m the most direct route from North Foreland to the Thames and Medway is via South Chan, Gore Chan, Horse Chan, Kentish Flats, Four Fathom Chan and Cant; but it is not well marked particularly over the Kentish Flats. Beware of Kentish Flats wind farm (30 turbines) with submarine cables to Herne Bay. An alternative, deeper route is East of Margate Sand and the Tongue, via the Princes Channel to the Oaze Deep. The N & S Edinburgh Channels are unmarked but navigable with caution. ▶ *W-going streams begin at approx HW Sheerness –0600 and E-going at HW Sheerness +0030.* ◀

Margate or Whitstable afford little shelter for yachts. The Swale provides an interesting inside route S of the Isle of Sheppey with access to Sheerness and the R Medway. If sailing from N Foreland to the Thames, Queenborough offers the first easily accessible, all-tide, deep-water shelter. The Medway Chan is the main appr to Sheerness from the Warp and the Medway Fairway buoy.

CROSSING FROM THAMES/ORWELL TO BELGIUM OR THE NETHERLANDS

(ACs 1408, 1406, 1610, 1630, 1872, 1183) Up to date charts are *essential*. The southern North Sea is an extremely busy area with several large and complex Traffic Separation Schemes and associated Precautionary Areas which should be avoided if at all possible. Where practicable, navigate outside the schemes using any available ITZs, and always cross a TSS on a heading at 90° to the traffic flow in accordance with the Collision Regulations. However, from the Thames to Zeebrugge the most direct route crosses the Nord Hinder South TSS in the vicinity of F3 light float which is a focal point for dense crossing traffic. The very busy area around West Hinder would then have to be negotiated. A longer but much safer route (or if bound for Dunkerque, Oostende or Nieuwpoort) via S Falls, Sandettié and Dyck minimises time spent in the TSS.

From the Orwell (or adjacent rivers) to the Netherlands, it may be best to pass north of the Sunk Inner and Sunk Outer TSS/ Precautionary Areas before setting course for Hoek van Holland. From S Shipwash make for N Inner Gabbard before setting course for NHR-S to cross the North Hinder TSS to NHR-SE, then pass S of the Maas-West TSS leaving MW1, MW3 and MW5 buoys to port before shaping up for MV-N buoy.

▶ *Care must be taken throughout with the tidal streams, which may be setting across the yacht's track.* ◀ The whole area is relatively shallow, and in bad weather seas are steep and short. *(See also Area 16.)*

9.4.6 THAMES ESTUARY TIDAL STREAMS

Due to very strong rates of tidal streams in some areas, eddies may occur. Where possible, some indication of these is shown, but in many areas there is insufficient information or eddies are unstable.

5 Hours before HW Sheerness (0335 before HW Dover)

4 Hours before HW Sheerness (0235 before HW Dover)

3 Hours before HW Sheerness (0135 before HW Dover)

2 Hours before HW Sheerness (0035 before HW Dover)

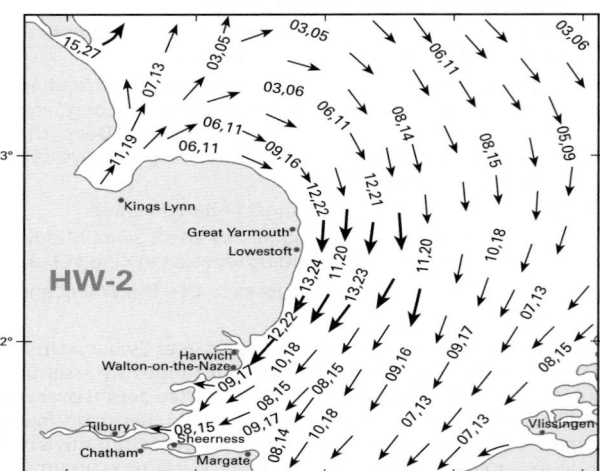

1 Hour before HW Sheerness (0025 after HW Dover)

HW Sheerness (0125 after HW Dover)

Due to very strong rates of tidal streams in some areas, eddies may occur. Where possible, some indication of these is shown, but in many areas there is insufficient information or eddies are unstable.

1 Hour after HW Sheerness (0225 after HW Dover)

2 Hours after HW Sheerness (0325 after HW Dover)

3 Hours after HW Sheerness (0425 after HW Dover)

4 Hours after HW Sheerness (0525 after HW Dover)

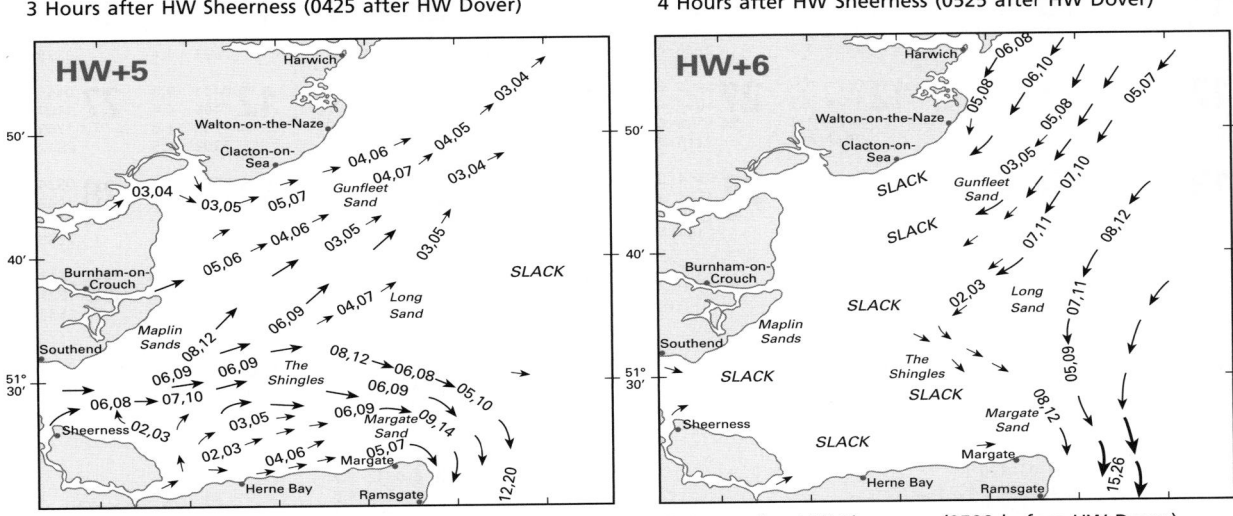

5 Hours after HW Sheerness (0600 before HW Dover)

6 Hours after HW Sheerness (0500 before HW Dover)

E England

291

MARGATE LAT 51°23'N LONG 1°23'E
TIMES AND HEIGHTS OF HIGH AND LOW WATERS

Dates in red are SPRINGS
Dates in blue are NEAPS

YEAR 2010

JANUARY

Time	m		Time	m
1 0612	0.6	**16**	0020	4.5
1203	4.8		0651	0.7
F 1819	0.8	SA 1244	4.4
			1850	0.8
2 0024	4.7	**17**	0052	4.6
0700	0.5		0724	0.7
SA 1253	4.9	SU 1315	4.5
1906	0.8		1918	1.0
3 0112	4.8	**18**	0127	4.6
0748	0.3		0752	0.6
SU 1344	4.9	M 1350	4.5
1954	0.8		1945	1.0
4 0200	4.8	**19**	0202	4.6
0835	0.3		0820	0.6
M 1436	4.6	TU 1425	4.4
2042	0.9		2016	1.0
5 0249	4.8	**20**	0236	4.6
0922	0.3		0850	0.7
TU 1530	4.7	W 1459	4.3
2128	0.9		2051	1.0
6 0337	4.6	**21**	0307	4.5
1009	0.4		0923	0.7
W 1623	4.6	TH 1529	4.2
2216	1.0		2128	1.1
7 0426	4.7	**22**	0337	4.4
1100	0.6		0958	0.8
TH 1715	4.4	F 1600	4.1
◑ 2307	1.2		2208	1.2
8 0519	4.5	**23**	0415	4.3
1157	0.8		1036	1.0
F 1811	4.2	SA 1642	4.0
		◒ 2259	1.3
9 0004	1.3	**24**	0506	4.2
0620	4.3		1125	1.1
SA 1259	1.0	SU 1741	3.9
1911	4.0		
10 0113	1.4	**25**	0007	1.4
0736	4.1		0609	4.0
SU 1401	1.1	M 1235	1.3
2019	4.0		1905	3.9
11 0242	1.4	**26**	0123	1.4
0849	4.1		0727	4.0
M 1504	1.2	TU 1409	1.3
2129	4.1		2022	4.0
12 0353	1.2	**27**	0255	1.3
0953	4.2		0857	4.1
TU 1605	1.2	W 1523	1.2
2227	4.2		2135	4.1
13 0447	1.0	**28**	0412	1.0
1049	4.2		1007	4.4
W 1656	1.2	TH 1626	1.0
2311	4.3		2239	4.4
14 0534	0.8	**29**	0510	0.7
1135	4.3		1104	4.6
TH 1739	1.1	F 1722	0.9
2348	4.4		2330	4.6
15 0614	0.7	**30**	0601	0.5
1212	4.4		1155	4.8
F 1817	1.1	SA 1811	0.8
●		○	
		31	0016	4.8
			0648	0.3
		SU 1245	4.9
			1857	0.7

FEBRUARY

Time	m		Time	m
1 0101	4.9	**16**	0106	4.7
0733	0.2		0724	0.6
M 1334	5.0	TU 1326	4.5
1941	0.7		1926	0.9
2 0146	5.0	**17**	0140	4.7
0817	0.2		0751	0.6
TU 1422	4.9	W 1359	4.5
2023	0.7		1957	0.8
3 0231	5.0	**18**	0211	4.7
0858	0.2		0821	0.6
W 1508	4.8	TH 1427	4.5
2105	0.8		2030	0.9
4 0315	5.0	**19**	0238	4.6
0937	0.4		0852	0.6
TH 1552	4.6	F 1452	4.4
2147	0.9		2103	1.0
5 0358	4.8	**20**	0305	4.5
1018	0.6		0923	0.8
F 1636	4.4	SA 1522	4.3
◑ 2232	1.1		2137	1.1
6 0445	4.5	**21**	0341	4.4
1104	0.9		0958	0.9
SA 1726	4.1	SU 1602	4.2
2324	1.2		2222	1.2
7 0541	4.2	**22**	0431	4.3
1206	1.2		1044	1.1
SU 1825	3.9	M 1657	4.0
		◒ 2332	1.3
8 0028	1.4	**23**	0535	4.1
0658	4.0		1156	1.3
M 1318	1.4	TU 1824	3.8
1936	3.8		
9 0213	1.5	**24**	0053	1.4
0823	3.9		0702	3.9
TU 1434	1.5	W 1341	1.4
2100	3.9		1957	3.9
10 0336	1.3	**25**	0237	1.2
0938	4.0		0845	4.1
W 1553	1.4	TH 1505	1.3
2207	4.1		2121	4.1
11 0435	1.0	**26**	0356	0.9
1042	4.2		0956	4.4
TH 1647	1.3	F 1613	1.1
2255	4.3		2226	4.4
12 0521	0.9	**27**	0454	0.6
1128	4.3		1053	4.6
F 1728	1.2	SA 1708	0.9
2332	4.4		2316	4.7
13 0558	0.7	**28**	0544	0.4
1201	4.4		1143	4.8
SA 1803	1.1	SU 1755	0.8
		○ 2359	4.9
14 0004	4.5		
0630	0.7		
SU 1228	4.4		
● 1833	1.0		
15 0034	4.6		
0658	0.6		
M 1255	4.5		
1859	0.9		

MARCH

Time	m		Time	m
1 0629	0.2	**16**	0010	4.6
1229	4.9		0626	0.6
M 1838	0.7	TU 1230	4.5
			1835	0.9
2 0042	5.0	**17**	0041	4.7
0710	0.1		0652	0.6
TU 1315	4.9	W 1259	4.6
1920	0.6		1905	0.8
3 0125	5.1	**18**	0113	4.7
0750	0.2		0721	0.5
W 1358	4.9	TH 1328	4.6
2001	0.6		1938	0.8
4 0208	5.1	**19**	0143	4.7
0826	0.3		0752	0.6
TH 1439	4.7	F 1355	4.5
2041	0.7		2012	0.8
5 0249	5.0	**20**	0212	4.6
0902	0.5		0823	0.6
F 1517	4.6	SA 1424	4.5
2121	0.8		2046	0.9
6 0330	4.8	**21**	0244	4.6
0938	0.7		0855	0.8
SA 1555	4.4	SU 1458	4.4
2202	1.0		2122	1.0
7 0413	4.5	**22**	0323	4.5
1019	1.0		0932	1.0
SU 1641	4.1	M 1541	4.2
◑ 2250	1.2		2210	1.1
8 0505	4.2	**23**	0414	4.3
1116	1.4		1023	1.2
M 1741	3.9	TU 1638	4.0
2352	1.4	◒ 2318	1.2
9 0624	3.9	**24**	0521	4.1
1234	1.6		1144	1.4
TU 1855	3.7	W 1806	3.9
10 0138	1.5	**25**	0039	1.2
0755	3.8		0659	4.0
W 1401	1.7	TH 1325	1.4
2024	3.8		1938	3.9
11 0311	1.3	**26**	0225	1.1
0915	3.9		0833	4.2
TH 1534	1.5	F 1446	1.3
2136	4.0		2103	4.2
12 0411	1.1	**27**	0336	0.8
1018	4.2		0941	4.5
F 1627	1.3	SA 1554	1.1
2227	4.2		2205	4.5
13 0456	0.9	**28**	0433	0.5
1102	4.3		1037	4.7
SA 1707	1.1	SU 1647	0.9
2306	4.4		2254	4.7
14 0531	0.8	**29**	0521	0.3
1136	4.4		1125	4.8
SU 1740	1.0	M 1733	0.8
2340	4.5		2337	4.9
15 0601	0.7	**30**	0603	0.2
1203	4.5		1208	4.8
M 1809	0.9	TU 1815	0.6
●		○	
		31	0018	5.0
			0642	0.2
		W 1249	4.8
			1857	0.6

APRIL

Time	m		Time	m
1 0101	5.1	**16**	0044	4.7
0719	0.3		0653	0.6
TH 1329	4.8	F 1257	4.6
1939	0.6		1920	0.7
2 0144	5.1	**17**	0118	4.7
0756	0.4		0726	0.6
F 1408	4.7	SA 1330	4.6
2020	0.6		1957	0.7
3 0225	4.9	**18**	0154	4.7
0831	0.6		0800	0.7
SA 1444	4.6	SU 1406	4.5
2059	0.8		2036	0.8
4 0305	4.7	**19**	0233	4.6
0905	0.9		0837	0.8
SU 1520	4.4	M 1446	4.4
2139	0.9		2118	0.8
5 0346	4.4	**20**	0317	4.5
0943	1.2		0921	1.0
M 1603	4.2	TU 1535	4.3
2223	1.1		2210	0.9
6 0435	4.1	**21**	0411	4.3
1034	1.5		1019	1.2
TU 1659	4.0	W 1638	4.1
◑ 2320	1.3	◒ 2314	1.0
7 0547	3.8	**22**	0521	4.2
1152	1.7		1142	1.4
W 1809	3.8	TH 1755	4.0
8 0047	1.5	**23**	0035	1.0
0719	3.7		0655	4.1
TH 1315	1.6	F 1306	1.4
1937	3.8		1916	4.1
9 0227	1.3	**24**	0205	0.8
0835	3.9		0814	4.3
F 1452	1.6	SA 1421	1.2
2055	4.0		2037	4.3
10 0328	1.1	**25**	0311	0.6
0936	4.1		0919	4.5
SA 1552	1.4	SU 1528	1.1
2149	4.2		2139	4.5
11 0414	0.9	**26**	0406	0.5
1023	4.3		1014	4.6
SU 1634	1.2	M 1622	0.9
2231	4.4		2228	4.7
12 0451	0.8	**27**	0453	0.4
1100	4.4		1101	4.6
M 1708	1.0	TU 1709	0.8
2308	4.6		2312	4.8
13 0521	0.7	**28**	0534	0.4
1131	4.4		1142	4.7
TU 1739	0.9	W 1753	0.7
2340	4.6	○ 2355	4.9
14 0550	0.7	**29**	0613	0.4
1159	4.5		1221	4.7
W 1810	0.8	TH 1837	0.6
●			
15 0011	4.6	**30**	0038	5.0
0620	0.6		0651	0.5
TH 1227	4.6	F 1301	4.7
1843	0.8		1920	0.6

Chart Datum: 2·5 metres below Ordnance Datum (Newlyn). HAT is 5·2 metres above Chart Datum; see 4.5

›› FREE monthly updates from **‹‹**
www.reedsalmanac.co.uk

| TIME ZONE (UT) |
| For Summer Time add ONE hour in **non-shaded areas** |

MARGATE LAT 51°23'N LONG 1°23'E
TIMES AND HEIGHTS OF HIGH AND LOW WATERS

Dates in red are SPRINGS
Dates in blue are NEAPS

YEAR 2010

MAY

	Time m		Time m
1 SA	0121 4.9 / 0729 0.6 / 1340 4.6 / 2002 0.6	**16** SU	0059 4.7 / 0706 0.7 / 1314 4.6 / 1946 0.6
2 SU	0203 4.8 / 0806 0.8 / 1417 4.5 / 2042 0.7	**17** M	0141 4.7 / 0746 0.8 / 1357 4.6 / 2030 0.6
3 M	0243 4.6 / 0840 1.0 / 1455 4.4 / 2120 0.9	**18** TU	0227 4.7 / 0830 0.9 / 1444 4.5 / 2117 0.7
4 TU	0324 4.3 / 0916 1.2 / 1537 4.3 / 2200 1.0	**19** W	0316 4.6 / 0920 1.0 / 1536 4.4 / 2209 0.7
5 W	0410 4.1 / 1000 1.4 / 1627 4.1 / 2250 1.2	**20** TH	0413 4.4 / 1021 1.2 / 1635 4.3 / 2310 0.7
6 TH	0508 3.9 / 1106 1.6 / 1725 3.9 / 2358 1.3	**21** F	0524 4.3 / 1130 1.2 / 1740 4.3
7 F	0625 3.8 / 1222 1.7 / 1831 3.9	**22** SA	0025 0.8 / 0638 4.3 / 1240 1.3 / 1849 4.3
8 SA	0122 1.3 / 0739 3.8 / 1334 1.6 / 1950 3.9	**23** SU	0139 0.7 / 0747 4.3 / 1349 1.2 / 2004 4.4
9 SU	0226 1.2 / 0842 4.0 / 1446 1.5 / 2059 4.1	**24** M	0241 0.7 / 0850 4.4 / 1458 1.1 / 2109 4.5
10 M	0317 1.0 / 0934 4.1 / 1543 1.3 / 2148 4.2	**25** TU	0336 0.6 / 0948 4.4 / 1558 1.0 / 2202 4.6
11 TU	0401 0.9 / 1016 4.3 / 1628 1.1 / 2228 4.4	**26** W	0424 0.7 / 1037 4.5 / 1648 0.9 / 2250 4.7
12 W	0440 0.8 / 1052 4.4 / 1707 1.0 / 2305 4.5	**27** TH	0507 0.7 / 1120 4.5 / 1735 0.7 / ○ 2335 4.7
13 TH	0517 0.8 / 1125 4.5 / 1746 0.9 / 2341 4.6	**28** F	0549 0.7 / 1159 4.5 / 1821 0.6
14 F	0553 0.7 / 1157 4.5 / 1825 0.8 / ●	**29** SA	0020 4.7 / 0629 0.8 / 1239 4.6 / 1905 0.6
15 SA	0018 4.7 / 0629 0.7 / 1234 4.6 / 1905 0.7	**30** SU	0103 4.7 / 0709 0.8 / 1318 4.6 / 1948 0.6
		31 M	0144 4.6 / 0747 0.9 / 1357 4.5 / 2027 0.7

JUNE

	Time m		Time m
1 TU	0224 4.5 / 0821 1.0 / 1435 4.5 / 2102 0.8	**16** W	0222 4.8 / 0828 0.8 / 1440 4.7 / 2112 0.4
2 W	0303 4.3 / 0853 1.2 / 1515 4.4 / 2138 0.9	**17** TH	0315 4.7 / 0919 0.9 / 1531 4.7 / 2202 0.5
3 TH	0345 4.2 / 0932 1.3 / 1559 4.3 / 2218 1.0	**18** F	0412 4.6 / 1012 1.0 / 1623 4.6 / 2257 0.5
4 F	0433 4.0 / 1021 1.4 / 1648 4.1 / ◑ 2307 1.1	**19** SA	0512 4.4 / 1108 1.1 / 1718 4.5 / ◐
5 SA	0528 3.9 / 1122 1.5 / 1740 4.0	**20** SU	0000 0.6 / 0611 4.3 / 1208 1.2 / 1819 4.4
6 SU	0013 1.2 / 0627 3.9 / 1230 1.6 / 1835 4.0	**21** M	0106 0.7 / 0713 4.2 / 1313 1.2 / 1928 4.4
7 M	0124 1.2 / 0728 3.9 / 1336 1.5 / 1936 4.0	**22** TU	0207 0.8 / 0816 4.2 / 1427 1.2 / 2039 4.4
8 TU	0222 1.1 / 0827 4.0 / 1443 1.4 / 2042 4.1	**23** W	0305 0.9 / 0920 4.2 / 1537 1.1 / 2140 4.4
9 W	0315 1.1 / 0922 4.1 / 1546 1.2 / 2141 4.2	**24** TH	0359 1.0 / 1018 4.3 / 1634 1.0 / 2235 4.4
10 TH	0404 1.0 / 1011 4.3 / 1638 1.0 / 2230 4.4	**25** F	0449 1.0 / 1106 4.3 / 1724 0.8 / 2324 4.5
11 F	0449 0.9 / 1057 4.4 / 1725 0.9 / 2316 4.5	**26** SA	0534 1.0 / 1147 4.4 / 1810 0.7 / ○
12 SA	0531 0.9 / 1137 4.5 / 1809 0.7 / ●	**27** SU	0009 4.5 / 0615 1.0 / 1225 4.5 / 1853 0.6
13 SU	0000 4.7 / 0612 0.8 / 1220 4.6 / 1853 0.6	**28** M	0050 4.5 / 0655 0.9 / 1301 4.6 / 1933 0.6
14 M	0045 4.8 / 0654 0.8 / 1304 4.7 / 1938 0.5	**29** TU	0127 4.5 / 0731 1.0 / 1338 4.6 / 2009 0.7
15 TU	0132 4.8 / 0740 0.8 / 1352 4.7 / 2025 0.5	**30** W	0203 4.5 / 0803 1.0 / 1415 4.6 / 2041 0.7

JULY

	Time m		Time m
1 TH	0240 4.4 / 0832 1.0 / 1453 4.5 / 2111 0.8	**16** F	0305 4.8 / 0905 0.8 / 1515 4.9 / 2143 0.3
2 F	0319 4.3 / 0906 1.1 / 1532 4.4 / 2144 0.8	**17** SA	0356 4.7 / 0951 0.9 / 1602 4.8 / 2230 0.5
3 SA	0359 4.2 / 0946 1.2 / 1611 4.3 / 2222 0.9	**18** SU	0446 4.5 / 1039 1.0 / 1652 4.7 / ◑ 2322 0.7
4 SU	0441 4.0 / 1033 1.3 / 1654 4.2 / ◑ 2306 1.1	**19** M	0539 4.3 / 1133 1.1 / 1748 4.5
5 M	0530 3.9 / 1128 1.4 / 1743 4.1	**20** TU	0024 0.9 / 0636 4.1 / 1235 1.3 / 1856 4.3
6 TU	0001 1.2 / 0627 3.9 / 1234 1.5 / 1839 4.0	**21** W	0130 1.1 / 0741 4.0 / 1359 1.3 / 2014 4.2
7 W	0118 1.3 / 0730 3.9 / 1345 1.4 / 1945 4.0	**22** TH	0237 1.2 / 0856 4.0 / 1523 1.2 / 2125 4.2
8 TH	0231 1.2 / 0834 4.0 / 1506 1.3 / 2059 4.1	**23** F	0344 1.2 / 1004 4.1 / 1625 1.0 / 2229 4.3
9 F	0331 1.1 / 0937 4.2 / 1612 1.1 / 2204 4.3	**24** SA	0441 1.2 / 1056 4.3 / 1716 0.8 / 2322 4.4
10 SA	0425 1.0 / 1034 4.3 / 1706 0.8 / 2257 4.5	**25** SU	0526 1.1 / 1137 4.4 / 1800 0.7
11 SU	0515 0.9 / 1124 4.5 / 1754 0.6 / ● 2346 4.7	**26** M	0004 4.4 / 0605 1.0 / 1211 4.5 / ○ 1838 0.6
12 M	0601 0.8 / 1209 4.6 / 1841 0.5	**27** TU	0038 4.5 / 0640 1.0 / 1243 4.6 / 1913 0.6
13 TU	0034 4.8 / 0647 0.8 / 1255 4.8 / 1927 0.3	**28** W	0108 4.5 / 0713 0.9 / 1317 4.6 / 1944 0.6
14 W	0123 4.9 / 0733 0.7 / 1342 4.9 / 2013 0.3	**29** TH	0140 4.5 / 0741 0.9 / 1352 4.7 / 2012 0.6
15 TH	0214 4.9 / 0819 0.7 / 1429 4.9 / 2058 0.2	**30** F	0214 4.5 / 0809 0.9 / 1428 4.6 / 2040 0.7
		31 SA	0249 4.4 / 0842 0.9 / 1502 4.6 / 2110 0.7

AUGUST

	Time m		Time m
1 SU	0320 4.3 / 0917 1.0 / 1533 4.4 / 2144 0.8	**16** M	0413 4.4 / 1010 0.9 / 1623 4.7 / ◑ 2240 0.8
2 M	0350 4.2 / 0956 1.2 / 1607 4.3 / 2220 1.0	**17** TU	0502 4.2 / 1100 1.1 / 1717 4.4 / 2338 1.1
3 TU	0426 4.0 / 1042 1.3 / 1652 4.2 / ◑ 2304 1.2	**18** W	0600 4.0 / 1201 1.3 / 1829 4.1
4 W	0518 3.9 / 1144 1.4 / 1749 4.0	**19** TH	0052 1.4 / 0708 3.9 / 1337 1.4 / 1954 4.0
5 TH	0008 1.3 / 0638 3.8 / 1258 1.4 / 1901 4.0	**20** F	0213 1.5 / 0833 3.9 / 1510 1.2 / 2113 4.1
6 F	0145 1.4 / 0757 3.9 / 1429 1.3 / 2031 4.1	**21** SA	0336 1.4 / 0946 4.1 / 1614 1.0 / 2222 4.2
7 SA	0303 1.2 / 0912 4.1 / 1550 1.0 / 2145 4.3	**22** SU	0432 1.2 / 1038 4.3 / 1704 0.8 / 2313 4.4
8 SU	0406 1.1 / 1018 4.3 / 1647 0.8 / 2242 4.6	**23** M	0514 1.1 / 1119 4.4 / 1743 0.7 / 2351 4.5
9 M	0501 0.9 / 1110 4.5 / 1737 0.5 / 2333 4.8	**24** TU	0549 1.0 / 1152 4.5 / 1817 0.6 / ○
10 TU	0549 0.8 / 1155 4.7 / 1824 0.3 / ●	**25** W	0019 4.5 / 0621 0.9 / 1222 4.6 / 1847 0.6
11 W	0020 4.9 / 0633 0.7 / 1239 4.9 / 1909 0.2	**26** TH	0044 4.5 / 0650 0.9 / 1253 4.7 / 1914 0.6
12 TH	0108 4.9 / 0717 0.6 / 1323 5.0 / 1952 0.1	**27** F	0113 4.5 / 0718 0.8 / 1326 4.7 / 1939 0.6
13 F	0156 4.9 / 0800 0.6 / 1408 5.1 / 2033 0.2	**28** SA	0144 4.5 / 0747 0.8 / 1359 4.7 / 2008 0.6
14 SA	0243 4.7 / 0843 0.7 / 1452 5.0 / 2113 0.3	**29** SU	0214 4.5 / 0819 0.8 / 1429 4.6 / 2038 0.7
15 SU	0328 4.6 / 0925 0.8 / 1536 4.9 / 2154 0.5	**30** M	0239 4.4 / 0853 0.9 / 1457 4.5 / 2109 0.8
		31 TU	0306 4.2 / 0927 1.0 / 1529 4.4 / 2142 1.0

Chart Datum: 2·5 metres below Ordnance Datum (Newlyn). HAT is 5·2 metres above Chart Datum; see 4.5

E England

» FREE monthly updates from «
www.reedsalmanac.co.uk
293

WGS84 DATUM

TIME ZONE (UT)
For Summer Time add ONE hour in **non-shaded areas**

MARGATE LAT 51°23'N LONG 1°23'E
TIMES AND HEIGHTS OF HIGH AND LOW WATERS

Dates in red are SPRINGS
Dates in blue are NEAPS

YEAR 2010

SEPTEMBER

Time	m		Time	m
1 0343	4.1		**16** 0521	3.9
1008	1.2		1052	1.3
W 1614	4.2		TH 1804	4.0
◗ 2223	1.2			
2 0433	4.0		**17** 0014	1.6
1109	1.3		0634	3.8
TH 1713	4.1		F 1312	1.4
2327	1.4		1932	3.9
3 0550	3.8		**18** 0143	1.7
1226	1.4		0803	3.8
F 1831	3.9		SA 1447	1.2
			2053	4.0
4 0111	1.5		**19** 0317	1.5
0725	3.8		0916	4.0
SA 1404	1.3		SU 1550	1.0
2014	4.0		2159	4.2
5 0239	1.3		**20** 0411	1.3
0851	4.0		1009	4.3
SU 1528	0.9		M 1639	0.8
2128	4.3		2246	4.4
6 0347	1.1		**21** 0452	1.1
0959	4.3		1050	4.4
M 1626	0.6		TU 1716	0.7
2226	4.6		2322	4.5
7 0442	0.9		**22** 0527	1.0
1050	4.6		1125	4.5
TU 1716	0.4		W 1747	0.6
2316	4.8		2351	4.5
8 0529	0.7		**23** 0558	0.9
1154	4.8		1156	4.6
W 1802	0.2		TH 1814	0.6
●			○	
9 0001	4.9		**24** 0016	4.5
0613	0.6		0626	0.8
TH 1216	5.0		F 1226	4.7
1844	0.1		1839	0.6
10 0045	4.9		**25** 0043	4.6
0655	0.6		0654	0.8
F 1259	5.1		SA 1257	4.7
1924	0.1		1907	0.6
11 0129	4.9		**26** 0111	4.6
0738	0.6		0725	0.7
SA 1343	5.1		SU 1329	4.7
2003	0.2		1937	0.6
12 0213	4.8		**27** 0138	4.5
0820	0.6		0759	0.8
SU 1427	5.0		M 1359	4.6
2042	0.4		2008	0.7
13 0254	4.6		**28** 0206	4.4
0902	0.7		0833	0.8
M 1510	4.8		TU 1430	4.5
2120	0.7		2039	0.9
14 0335	4.4		**29** 0238	4.3
0946	0.9		0908	0.9
TU 1555	4.6		W 1506	4.4
2203	1.0		2113	1.0
15 0422	4.2		**30** 0317	4.2
1034	1.1		0952	1.0
W 1648	4.3		TH 1553	4.2
◖ 2258	1.3		2158	1.2

OCTOBER

Time	m		Time	m
1 0409	4.0		**16** 0550	3.8
1052	1.2		1229	1.3
F 1653	4.1		SA 1901	3.8
◗ 2306	1.4			
2 0527	3.8		**17** 0055	1.8
1207	1.2		0717	3.8
SA 1817	4.0		SU 1406	1.3
			2016	3.9
3 0049	1.5		**18** 0237	1.6
0658	3.9		0836	3.9
SU 1344	1.1		M 1509	1.1
1956	4.1		2118	4.1
4 0212	1.3		**19** 0338	1.4
0824	4.1		0931	4.2
M 1503	0.8		TU 1558	0.9
2108	4.4		2207	4.3
5 0322	1.1		**20** 0421	1.2
0933	4.4		1015	4.3
TU 1601	0.5		W 1636	0.8
2205	4.7		2246	4.4
6 0419	0.9		**21** 0457	1.0
1025	4.7		1053	4.4
W 1651	0.3		TH 1708	0.7
2254	4.8		2318	4.5
7 0506	0.7		**22** 0530	0.9
1108	4.9		1126	4.6
TH 1735	0.2		F 1738	0.7
● 2337	4.9		2345	4.5
8 0550	0.6		**23** 0601	0.8
1150	5.0		1156	4.6
F 1816	0.2		SA 1807	0.7
			○	
9 0017	4.9		**24** 0010	4.6
0633	0.5		0632	0.8
SA 1234	5.1		SU 1228	4.6
1855	0.3		1837	0.8
10 0059	4.8		**25** 0039	4.6
0717	0.5		0706	0.7
SU 1318	5.1		M 1301	4.6
1934	0.4		1909	0.7
11 0140	4.7		**26** 0110	4.6
0800	0.5		0741	0.6
M 1403	4.9		TU 1336	4.6
2013	0.6		1942	0.8
12 0221	4.6		**27** 0144	4.5
0843	0.7		0819	0.7
TU 1446	4.7		W 1413	4.5
2051	0.9		2017	0.9
13 0301	4.4		**28** 0222	4.4
0925	0.8		0859	0.8
W 1531	4.5		TH 1455	4.4
2132	1.2		2057	1.1
14 0345	4.2		**29** 0305	4.3
1011	1.0		0946	0.9
TH 1622	4.2		F 1544	4.3
◖ 2223	1.5		2148	1.2
15 0441	4.0		**30** 0400	4.1
1106	1.2		1043	1.0
F 1734	3.9		SA 1645	4.2
2335	1.7		◗ 2259	1.4
			31 0513	4.0
			1152	1.0
			SU 1808	4.1

NOVEMBER

Time	m		Time	m
1 0025	1.4		**16** 0113	1.7
0630	4.0		0728	3.8
M 1321	0.9		TU 1406	1.2
1932	4.2		2025	4.0
2 0141	1.3		**17** 0233	1.6
0749	4.2		0842	4.0
TU 1433	0.7		W 1459	1.1
2041	4.4		2119	4.1
3 0251	1.1		**18** 0335	1.4
0901	4.4		0933	4.1
W 1531	0.5		TH 1546	1.0
2139	4.6		2204	4.3
4 0351	1.0		**19** 0420	1.2
0956	4.6		1015	4.3
TH 1622	0.4		F 1626	0.9
2229	4.7		2241	4.4
5 0443	0.8		**20** 0459	1.0
1043	4.8		1052	4.4
F 1707	0.4		SA 1704	0.9
2312	4.7		2312	4.4
6 0529	0.7		**21** 0536	0.8
1127	4.9		1127	4.5
SA 1748	0.4		SU 1738	0.8
● 2352	4.7		○ 2342	4.5
7 0614	0.6		**22** 0612	0.8
1212	4.9		1202	4.6
SU 1829	0.5		M 1812	0.8
8 0033	4.7		**23** 0015	4.6
0659	0.5		0649	0.7
M 1258	4.9		TU 1240	4.6
1910	0.6		1847	0.8
9 0115	4.7		**24** 0052	4.6
0744	0.5		0728	0.6
TU 1342	4.8		W 1320	4.7
1950	0.8		1924	0.8
10 0156	4.6		**25** 0132	4.6
0827	0.6		0809	0.6
W 1426	4.6		TH 1403	4.6
2029	1.0		2005	0.9
11 0236	4.5		**26** 0214	4.5
0908	0.8		0853	0.6
TH 1509	4.4		F 1449	4.6
2107	1.2		2051	1.0
12 0319	4.3		**27** 0302	4.4
0950	0.9		0940	0.7
F 1556	4.1		SA 1539	4.4
2151	1.4		2144	1.2
13 0408	4.1		**28** 0356	4.3
1038	1.1		1033	0.7
SA 1654	3.9		SU 1639	4.3
◖ 2251	1.6		◗ 2248	1.3
14 0504	3.9		**29** 0457	4.3
1141	1.2		1136	0.8
SU 1807	3.8		M 1751	4.2
			2357	1.3
15 0001	1.7		**30** 0603	4.2
0608	3.8		1251	0.8
M 1300	1.3		TU 1902	4.2
1920	3.8			

DECEMBER

Time	m		Time	m
1 0105	1.3		**16** 0110	1.6
0713	4.2		0711	3.9
W 1400	0.7		TH 1359	1.2
2008	4.3		2006	3.9
2 0215	1.2		**17** 0224	1.5
0827	4.3		0822	3.9
TH 1459	0.7		F 1455	1.2
2109	4.4		2106	4.0
3 0324	1.1		**18** 0334	1.3
0929	4.5		0927	4.1
F 1553	0.7		SA 1547	1.1
2204	4.5		2158	4.2
4 0422	0.9		**19** 0427	1.1
1022	4.6		1017	4.2
SA 1642	0.7		SU 1633	1.0
2252	4.5		2243	4.3
5 0513	0.8		**20** 0512	0.9
1111	4.7		1101	4.4
SU 1727	0.7		M 1715	1.0
● 2335	4.6		2322	4.5
6 0601	0.6		**21** 0554	0.8
1158	4.7		1143	4.5
M 1811	0.8		TU 1754	0.9
			○	
7 0017	4.6		**22** 0000	4.6
0647	0.6		0634	0.6
TU 1243	4.7		W 1225	4.7
1853	0.8		1833	0.9
8 0058	4.6		**23** 0041	4.7
0731	0.6		0716	0.5
W 1327	4.6		TH 1309	4.8
1934	0.9		1915	0.8
9 0138	4.6		**24** 0124	4.7
0813	0.6		0759	0.4
TH 1408	4.5		F 1354	4.8
2012	1.1		1959	0.8
10 0217	4.5		**25** 0209	4.7
0851	0.7		0844	0.4
F 1448	4.4		SA 1442	4.7
2045	1.2		2047	0.9
11 0257	4.4		**26** 0256	4.7
0927	0.8		0929	0.4
SA 1529	4.2		SU 1532	4.6
2120	1.3		2136	1.0
12 0339	4.3		**27** 0345	4.6
1004	0.9		1016	0.5
SU 1615	4.1		M 1626	4.5
2203	1.4		2229	1.1
13 0425	4.2		**28** 0437	4.5
1048	1.1		1110	0.6
M 1706	3.9		TU 1726	4.3
◖ 2257	1.6		◗ 2325	1.2
14 0516	4.0		**29** 0534	4.4
1145	1.2		1214	0.7
TU 1803	3.8		W 1828	4.2
15 0002	1.6		**30** 0027	1.3
0610	3.9		0639	4.3
W 1256	1.3		TH 1323	0.9
1904	3.8		1931	4.1
			31 0138	1.3
			0755	4.2
			F 1427	1.0
			2039	4.1

Chart Datum: 2·5 metres below Ordnance Datum (Newlyn). HAT is 5·2 metres above Chart Datum; see 4.5

》》 FREE monthly updates from 《《
www.reedsalmanac.co.uk

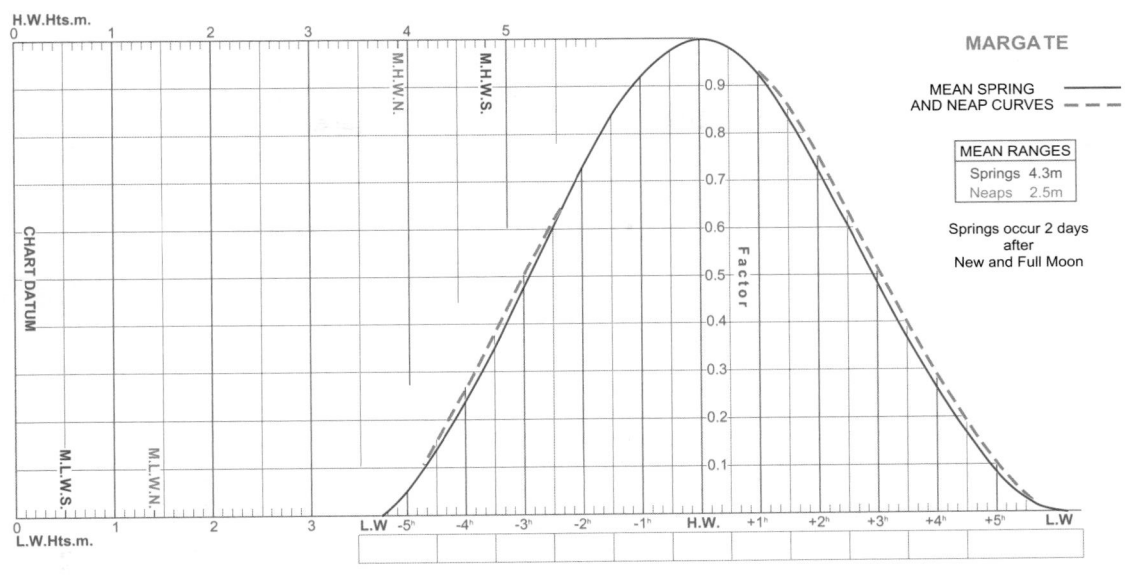

MARGATE

MEAN SPRING
AND NEAP CURVES

MEAN RANGES
Springs 4.3m
Neaps   2.5m

Springs occur 2 days
after
New and Full Moon

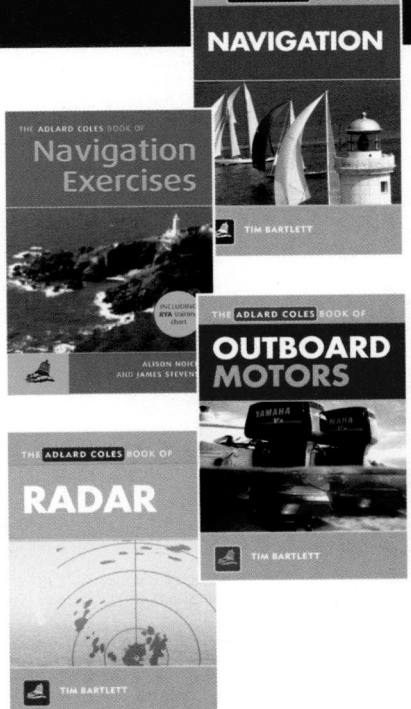
E England

295

9.4.7 THAMES ESTUARY

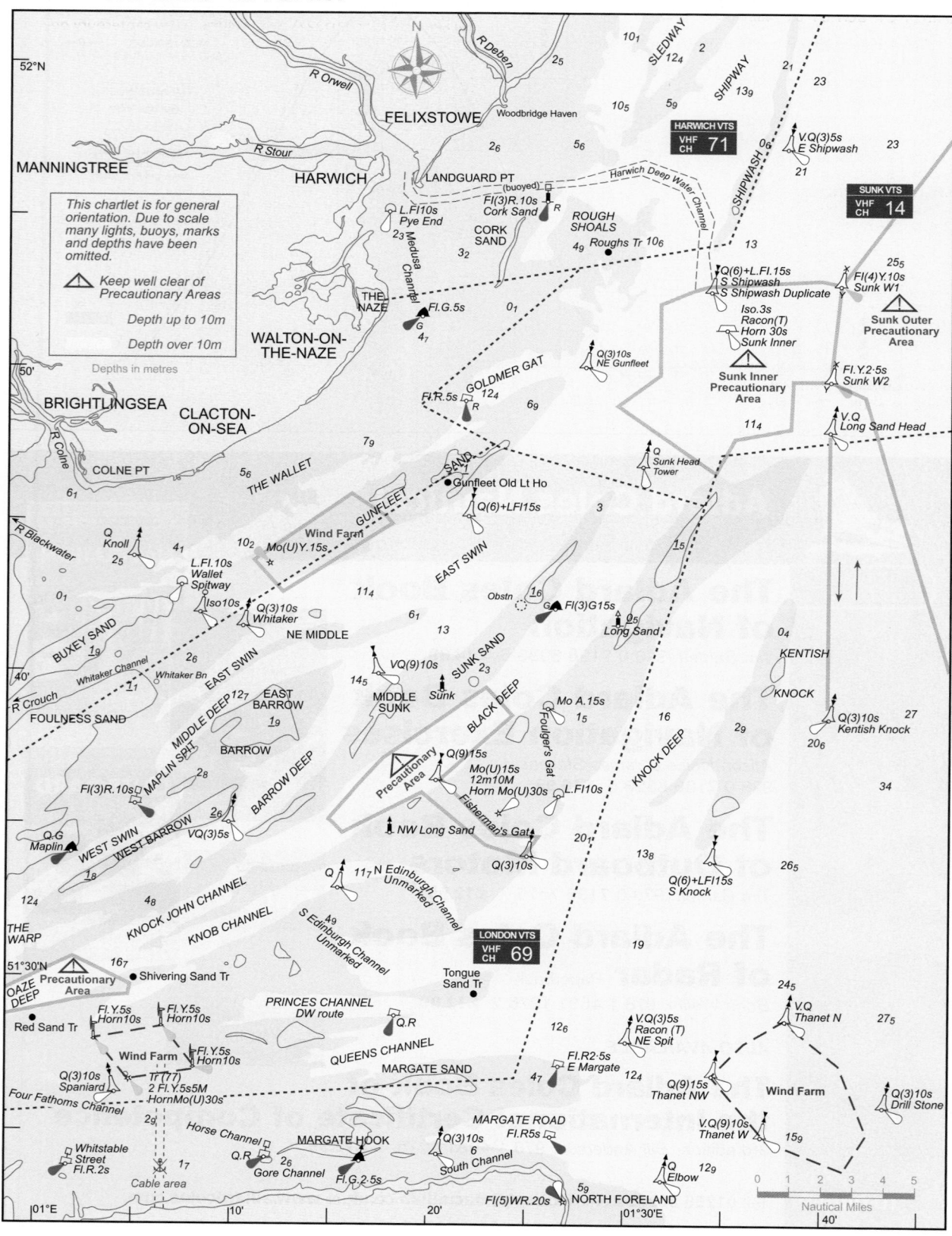

This chartlet is for general orientation. Due to scale many lights, buoys, marks and depths have been omitted.

△ Keep well clear of Precautionary Areas

Depth up to 10m

Depth over 10m

Depths in metres

9.4.8 WHITSTABLE

Kent **51°21'·86N 01°01'·46E** ❀❀🌢🌢🌣🌣

CHARTS AC 5606, 1607, 2571; Imray C1; Stanfords 5, 8.

TIDES +0135 Dover; ML 3·0; Duration 0605

Standard Port MARGATE (←—)

Times				Height (metres)			
High Water		Low Water		MHWS	MHWN	MLWN	MLWS
0100	0700	0100	0700	4·8	3·9	1·4	0·5
1300	1900	1300	1900				
Differences HERNE BAY							
+0034	+0022	+0015	+0032	+0·6	+0·4	+0·1	0·0
WHITSTABLE APPROACHES							
+0042	+0029	+0025	+0050	+0·6	+0·6	+0·1	0·0

SHELTER Good, except in strong winds from NNW to NE. Hbr dries up to 0·4m; access HW±1 for strangers. Yacht berths are limited since priority is given to commercial shipping. Fender board needed against piled quays or seek a mooring to NW of hbr (controlled by YC).

NAVIGATION WPT 51°22'·65N 01°01'·10E, 345°/0·83M to W Quay dolphin. From E keep well seaward of Whitstable Street, a hard drying sandspit, which extends 1M N from the coast; shoals a further 1M to seaward are marked by Whitstable Street NCM lt buoy. From W avoid Columbine and Pollard Spits.

Appr (not before half flood) via Oyster PHM lt buoy to harbour entrance or in W sector of Dir lt.

LIGHTS AND MARKS Off head of W Quay on a dolphin, ⚡ Fl G 5s, covers the approaches. At the head of the hbr a Dir lt, Fl WRG 3s 7m, leads 122° into hbr ent.

R/T Call *Whitstable Harbour Radio* VHF Ch **09** 12 16 (Mon–Fri:

0830–1700 LT. Other times: HW –3 to HW+1). Tidal info is available on request.

TELEPHONE (Code 01227) HM 274086, www.canterbury.gov.uk, MRCC (01255) 675518; Marinecall 09068 969645; Police 770055; Dr 594400.

FACILITIES Hbr ☎ 274086, AB £10.00, FW, D.
Whitstable YC ☎ 272942, M, R, Slip HW ±3, L, FW, Bar.
Services: ME, C, CH, ACA, SM, Gas, Ⓔ.
Town: ▣, P, 🛒, R, Bar, ✉, Ⓑ, ⇌, ✈ Lydd/Manston.

MINOR HARBOURS WEST OF NORTH FORELAND
MARGATE, Kent, 51°23'·43N 01°22'·65E. AC 5606,1 827, 1828, 323; Imray Y7, C1; Stanfords 5, 8. HW+0045 on Dover; ML 2·6; Duration 0610; Standard Port (←—). Small hbr drying 3m, inside bkwtr (Stone Pier) FR 17m 4M; exposed to NW'lies. Appr's: from E, via Longnose NCM buoy, keeping about 5ca offshore; from N, via Margate PHM lt buoy; from W via Gore Chan and S Chan to SE Margate ECM lt buoy. Facilities: Margate YC ☎ (01843) 292602, Ⓒ, Bar.

Town, 10 Slips all HW±2, check suitability with Foreshore Office ☎ (01843) 577529, D & P (cans), R, 🛒, Bar, ✉, Ⓑ, ⇌, ✈ Manston.

HERNE BAY, Kent, 51°22'·40N 01°07'·22E. AC 5606, 1607. Tides see 9.4.8. Close E of Pavillion (old pier), 400m long bkwtr 'Neptunes Arm' gives well sheltered drying ⚓'ge for craft <8m. Exposed to strong NE'lies at HW springs when Thames Barrier closed as seas may then top the bkwtr. 3 Slips (HW±2½ to HW±3). Foreshore Mngr ☎ (01227) 266719. Herne Bay SC ☎ (01227) 375650. Lts: QW 8m 4M is 6ca offshore (former pier hd); bkwtr hd 2FR (vert); pier hd 2FG (vert); R bn on B dolphin, Fl Y 5s, is approx 1M ENE of bkwtr hd. Reculvers twrs are conspic 3M to the E.

Town, D & P (cans), Ⓔ, R, 🛒, Bar, ✉, Ⓑ, ▣, ⇌, ✈ Lydd/Manston.

9.4.9 THE SWALE

Kent ✿✿⚓⚓⚓✿✿

CHARTS AC 5606, 2482, 2571, 2572, 1834, 3683; Imray Y18, C1; Stanford

TIDES Queenborough +0130 Dover; Harty Ferry +0120 Dover; ML (Harty Ferry) 3·0; Duration 0610. Faversham HW differences are –0·2m on Sheerness; no other data.

Standard Port SHEERNESS (→)

Times				Height (metres)			
High Water		Low Water		MHWS	MHWN	MLWN	MLWS
0200	0800	0200	0700	5·8	4·7	1·5	0·6
1400	2000	1400	1900				
Differences R. SWALE (Grovehurst Jetty)							
–0007	0000	0000	+0016	0·0	0·0	0·0	–0·1

Grovehurst Jetty is close N of the ent to Milton Creek.

SHELTER Excellent in the Swale, the 14M chan between the Isle of Sheppey and the N Kent coast, from Shell Ness in the E to Queenborough in the W. Yachts can enter the drying creeks of Faversham, Oare, Conyer, and Milton. Beware wrecks at ent to Faversham Creek. Many moorings line the chan from Faversham to Conyer Creeks. See 9.4.10 for Queenborough, all-tide access.

NAVIGATION E ent WPT: Whitstable Street lit PHM, 51°24′·00N 01°01′·54E, at ent to well marked buoyed chan. Speed limit 8kn. The middle section from 1·5M E of Conyer Creek to 0·5M E of Milton Creek is narrowed by drying mudbanks and carries least depths of 0·4m. At Milton Creek direction of buoyage changes. There are numerous oyster beds in the area. Kingsferry Bridge (see opposite) opens for masted craft on request, but subject to railway trains; temp anchs off SW bank. The power lines crossing SE of the br have a clearance of 30m. **W ent** is marked by Queenborough Spit ECM buoy, Q (3) 10s, 1M S of Garrison Pt, at 51°25′·81N 00°43′·93E.

LIGHTS AND MARKS See chartlet and 9.4.4. In W Swale the following lights intended for large coasters using the narrow chan:

No 5 Bn Oc WRG 6s; vis: 161°-G-166°-W-167°-R-172°. Round Loden Hope bend: two Q WG and one Q WRG on bns; keep in G sectors. See 9.4.10 chartlet. Horse Reach ldg lts 113°: front QG 7m 5M; rear Fl G 3s 10m 6M. Dir lt 098°, VQ (4) R 5s 6m 5M. Kingsferry Bridge: Dir WRG, 142°-G-147°-W-148°-R-153° 9m. Lts on bridge: two x 2 FG (vert) on SW buttresses; two x 2 FR (vert) on NE. Road bridge has a vertical clearance of 28m.

Kingsferry Bridge traffic sigs:

No lts	= Bridge down (3·35m MHWS).
Al Q ●/●	= Centre span lifting.
F ●	= Bridge open (29m MHWS).
Q ●	= Centre span lowering. Keep clear.
Q ○	= Bridge out of action.

Request bridge opening on VHF Ch 10 (or Ch 74 if no response).

R/T Call: *Medway VTS* VHF Ch **74** 16 22 (H24); Kingsferry Bridge Ch 10 (H24).

TELEPHONE (Code 01795) HM (Medway Ports Ltd) 596593; MRCC (01255) 675518; Marinecall 09068 969645; Police 477055; Dr or Ⓗ via Medway Navigation Service 663025.

FACILITIES FAVERSHAM: Services: BY, AB £5, M, ⬚⬚, FW, Ⓔ, ME, El, ⚒, C (40 ton), SM, D, C (25 ton).

Town 🛒, R, Bar, Gas, ✉, Ⓑ, ⇌, ✈ Gatwick.

OARE CREEK: Services: AB, M, C (8 ton), ME, El, ⚒, CH; **Hollow Shore Cruising Club,** Bar.

CONYER CREEK: Swale Marina ☎ 521562; AB(dredged 2m) £13/craft, FW, ⬚⬚, D, P, Gas, BH (30 ton), ME, ⚒, C (30ton), Slip, 🛢, 🗑; **Conyer CC. Conyer Marina** ☎ 521711 AB £7.50, CH, SM, Rigging, BY, ME, ⚒, El, Ⓔ, Slip, D.

MILTON CREEK (Sittingbourne): **Crown Quay** M, FW.

Town 🛒, R, Bar, ✉, Ⓑ, ⇌, ✈ (Gatwick); also the Dolphin Yard Sailing Barge Museum.

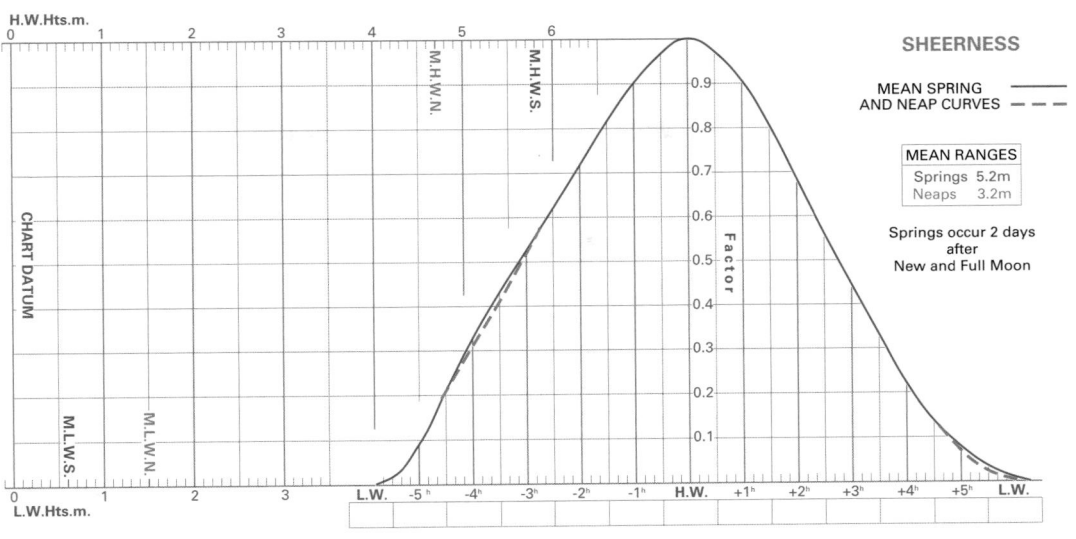

SHEERNESS

MEAN SPRING AND NEAP CURVES

MEAN RANGES
Springs 5.2m
Neaps 3.2m

Springs occur 2 days after New and Full Moon

9.4.10 QUEENBOROUGH

Kent (Isle of Sheppey) 51°25'·04N 00°44'·19E ✿✿✿🌑🌑🌑🌑✿✿

CHARTS AC 5606, 1834, 2572, 3683; Imray C1, Y18; Stanford 8.

TIDES Use 9.4.11 Sheerness, 2M to the N. +0130 Dover; ML 3·0; Duration 0610

SHELTER Good, except near HW in strong N'ly winds. The first deep-water refuge W of N Foreland, accessible at all tides from Garrison Pt (9.4.11); or from the Swale (9.4.9) on the tide. An all-tide pontoon/jetty (5m depth at end) on E bank is for landing/short stay only; both sides of the jetty are foul. 2 pairs Gy 🅥s (raft up to 6 craft <10m each) on E side, N & S of all-tide landing & the hard/drying causeway; also single visitors Y 🅥s Nos 14-26 for craft <10m, with HM's permission craft >10m berth on W side of Concrete Lighter. When 🅥s are full the hbr controller will offer spare buoys. Smaller R buoys (numbered) are for locals. ⚓ is discouraged due to commercial traffic. Speed limit 8kn.

NAVIGATION WPT: see 9.4.11 for appr via Garrison Pt. Enter the river at Queenborough Spit ECM buoy, Q (3) 10s, 51°25'·75N 00°43'·93E. The chan narrows between drying banks and moorings. See 9.4.9 if approaching from the Swale.

LIGHTS AND MARKS Lights as chartlet. Note: No 5 Bn Dir Oc WRG 6s, vis 161°-G-166°-W-167°-R-172°, on river bend covers the appr chan. All-tide landing 2 FR (vert). Concrete lighter Fl G 3s.

R/T Monitor *Medway VTS* VHF Ch **74** for tfc info. Call Ch 08 *Sheppey One* (Q'boro HM) for berths, also water taxi at weekends only (£1.20 to landing).

TELEPHONE (Code 01795) HM ☎ 662051; MRCC (01255) 675518; Marinecall 09068 969645; Police 477055; Dr 583828; Ⓗ (01634) 830000 (Gillingham).

FACILITIES HM/Hbr Controller, 🅥 £9 <11m, inc 2 tokens for all-tide-landing turnstile, FW on all-tide landing jetty.

Queenborough YC Wed, Fri, Sat evenings, Sat, Sun lunchtimes, M, R, Bar, ♿, 🚿, 📶;

The Creek ☎ 07974 349018, (HW±1½) Slip, Scrubbing berth (FW, ⟲, D (cans)).

Services: Slip, BY, ME, El, 🔧, C (10 ton), Gas

Town P & D (cans), 🛒, R, Bar, ✉, ⇌, ✈ (Gatwick).

9.4.11 RIVER MEDWAY (SHEERNESS TO ROCHESTER)

Kent 51°27'·03N 00°44'·50E (Off Garrison Pt) ✿✿✿◊◊◊◊✿✿✿

CHARTS AC 5606, 1835, 1834, 1185, 2482, 3683; Imray C1, Y18; Stanfords 5, 8.

TIDES +0130 Dover; ML 3·1; Duration 0610

Standard Port SHEERNESS (→)

Times				Height (metres)			
High Water		Low Water		MHWS	MHWN	MLWN	MLWS
0200	0800	0200	0700	5·8	4·7	1·5	0·6
1400	2000	1400	1900				
Differences BEE NESS							
+0002	+0002	0000	+0005	+0·2	+0·1	0·0	0·0
BARTLETT CREEK							
+0016	+0008	No data		+0·1	0·0	No data	
DARNETT NESS							
+0004	+0004	0000	+0010	+0·2	+0·1	0·0	−0·1
CHATHAM (Lock Approaches)							
+0010	+0012	+0012	+0018	+0·3	+0·1	−0·1	−0·2
UPNOR							
+0015	+0015	+0015	+0025	+0·2	+0·2	−0·1	−0·1
ROCHESTER (STROOD PIER)							
+0018	+0018	+0018	+0028	+0·2	+0·2	−0·2	−0·3
WOULDHAM							
+0030	+0025	+0035	+0120	−0·2	−0·3	−1·0	−0·3
NEW HYTHE							
+0035	+0035	+0220	+0240	−1·6	−1·7	−1·2	−0·3
ALLINGTON LOCK							
+0050	+0035	No data		−2·1	−2·2	−1·3	−0·4

NOTE: Sheerness tidal predictions are given below.

SHELTER There are 4 marinas down-river of Rochester Bridge and 5 above. Sheerness is solely a commercial hbr. See 9.4.10 for Queenborough and access to/from The Swale. Lower reaches of the Medway are exposed to strong NE winds, but Stangate and Half Acre Creeks are secure in all winds and give access to lesser creeks. There are good ⚓s in Sharfleet Creek; from about HW−4 it is possible to go via the 'back-door' into Half Acre Creek. Speed limit is 6kn W of Folly Pt (Hoo Island).

NAVIGATION WPT 51°28'·80N 00°52'·92E, Medway SWM buoy, 253°/4·5M to No 11 SHM buoy, then follow recommended route 240°/1M to Grain Hard SHM buoy. The wreck of the *Richard Montgomery* is visible 2M NE of estuary ent and a Military Wreck depth 2₂ in Kethole Reach. There is a huge area to explore, although much of it dries to mud. Some minor creeks are buoyed. The river is well buoyed/marked up to Rochester and is tidal up to Allington Lock (21·6M). Above Rochester bridge the river shoals appreciably and in the upper reaches there is only about 1m at LW; access approx HW±3.

Bridge Clearances (HAT), going up-river:

Rochester	5·4m
Medway (M2)	16·2m
New Hythe (footbridge)	10·7m
Aylesford (pedestrian)	2·3m
Aylesford (road)	2·7m
Maidstone bypass (M20)	8·9m

LIGHTS AND MARKS See 9.4.4 and chartlet for details of most lts. NB: not all buoys are shown due to small scale. Isle of Grain lt Q WRG 20m 13/7/8M 220°-R-234°-G-241°-W-013°. Power stn chy (242m) Oc and FR lts. Tfc Sigs: Powerful lt, Fl 7s, at Garrison Pt

means large vessel under way: if shown up river = inbound; if to seaward = outbound.

R/T Call: *Medway VTS* VHF Ch **74** 16 (H24). Monitor Ch 74 underway and Ch 16 at ⚓. Radar assistance is available on request Ch 22. Ch **80** M for marinas: Gillingham, Hoo (H24), Chatham Maritime (H24), Medway Bridge (0900-1700LT) and Port Medway (0800-2000LT). Link calls via Thames Radio Ch 02, 83.

TELEPHONE (Codes 01795 Sheerness; 01634 Medway) HM (01795) 596593; MRCC (01255) 675518; Marinecall 0891-500455; Police (01634) 827055, (01795) 661451; Dr via Medway Navigation Service (01795) 663025.

FACILITIES (☎ code 01634, unless otherwise stated) All moorings are run by YCs or marinas. Landing (only) at Ship Pier and Town Quay (Rochester). Slips at Commodores Hard, and Gillingham.

Marinas from seaward to Rochester Bridge:

Gillingham Marina (252+12🅥s) ☎ 280022, pre-book. £2·00 locked basin (access via lock (width 6m) HW±4½), £1·40 tidal basin HW±2, P, ME, El, Ⓔ, ✕, Gas, Gaz, CH, BH (65 ton), ⚓, C (1 ton), BY, 🛒. Note: effects of cross-tide, esp. the ebb, off the lock ent are reduced by a timber baffle at 90° to the stream (close W of the lock). An angled pontoon deflects the stream and is also the fuel berth; the outboard end is lit by 2FR (vert). **Medway Pier Marine** ☎ 851113, D, FW, Slip, C (6 ton), BY, Ⓔ; **Hoo Marina** (120 AB inc 🅥) £2·35, ☎ 250311,🅾, ✕, ✕, ME, SM, CH, El, Ⓔ, D (cans), C (16 ton), access to W basin HW±2½; HW±3 to E basin (via sill 1m above CD); an unlit WCM buoy marks chan ent; 4 waiting buoys in river. **Chatham Maritime Marina** – see inset on previous page – ☎ 899200, (300 AB), access via lock H24 and sill 1.3m below CD (1.5m at MLWS), £3.20. C(15T), P, D, 🅾, Wi-fi. **Victory Marina** ☎ 07785 971797, 🅥, FW, ▭.

Marinas (Up-river from Rochester Bridge)
Medway Bridge Marina (160+4 visitors) ☎ 843576, £1.20, Slip, D, P, ME, El, Ⓔ, ✕, C (3 ton), BH (10 ton), Gas, 🛒, R, Bar; **Port Medway Marina** (50) ☎ 720033, BH (16 ton), C, ⚓; **Cuxton Marina** (150+some 🅥) ☎ 721941, Slip, ME, El, Ⓔ, ✕, BH (12 ton), CH; **Elmhaven Marina** (60) ☎ 240489, ME, El, ✕, C; **Allington Lock** operates HW−3 to +2, ☎ (01622) 752864. **Allington Marina** (120) ☎ (01622) 752057, above the lock; CH, ME, El, ✕, P, D, Slip, C (10 ton), FW, Gas, Gaz.

YACHT CLUBS Sheppey YC (Sheerness) ☎ 663052; **Lower Halstow YC** ☎ (01227) 458554; **Medway Cruising Club** (Gillingham) ☎ 856489, Bar, M, L, FW; **Hoo Ness YC** ☎ (01634) 250052, Bar, R, M, L, FW; **Hundred of Hoo SC** ☎ (01634) 250102; **Medway Motor Cruising Club** ☎ 827194; **Medway Motor YC** ☎ 01622 737647; **Medway YC** (Upnor) ☎ 718399; **Upnor SC** ☎ 718043; **Royal Engineers YC** ☎ 844555; **RNSA** (Medway) ☎ (01634) 200970; **Rochester CC** ☎ 841350, Bar, R, M, FW, L, 🅾; **Strood YC** ☎ 718261, Bar, M, C (1·5 ton), FW, L, Slip.

Towns: All facilities R, 🛒, 🅾, ✉, ⇌, ✈ (Gatwick).

GILLINGHAM MARINA

HOO MARINA

TIME ZONE (UT)
For Summer Time add ONE
hour in **non-shaded areas**

SHEERNESS   LAT 51°27'N   LONG 0°45'E
TIMES AND HEIGHTS OF HIGH AND LOW WATERS

Dates in red are **SPRINGS**
Dates in blue are **NEAPS**

YEAR 2010

JANUARY

Time	m		Time	m
1 0020	5.6		**16** 0101	5.4
0639	0.7		0719	0.9
F 1243	5.9		SA 1327	5.5
1857	0.8		1912	1.1
2 0107	5.7		**17** 0133	5.5
0733	0.5		0751	0.8
SA 1333	6.0		SU 1359	5.5
1945	0.8		1944	1.0
3 0152	5.8		**18** 0203	5.5
0824	0.4		0822	0.8
SU 1421	6.1		M 1431	5.5
2031	0.8		2017	1.0
4 0237	5.9		**19** 0233	5.5
0913	0.3		0852	0.8
M 1509	6.0		TU 1502	5.5
2115	0.8		2049	1.0
5 0322	5.8		**20** 0304	5.5
0959	0.3		0922	0.8
TU 1556	5.9		W 1534	5.4
2157	0.9		2121	1.1
6 0408	5.7		**21** 0336	5.4
1043	0.5		0951	0.9
W 1645	5.7		TH 1607	5.3
2239	1.1		2152	1.2
7 0456	5.6		**22** 0409	5.3
1127	0.7		1018	1.0
TH 1737	5.4		F 1644	5.1
☽ 2324	1.2		2224	1.3
8 0550	5.4		**23** 0448	5.2
1215	0.9		1049	1.2
F 1833	5.2		SA 1727	5.0
			☾ 2304	1.4
9 0018	1.4		**24** 0536	5.0
0651	5.2		1133	1.3
SA 1313	1.2		SU 1823	4.8
1935	5.0			
10 0126	1.5		**25** 0003	1.6
0801	5.0		0640	4.8
SU 1421	1.3		M 1241	1.5
2043	4.9		1936	4.7
11 0243	1.5		**26** 0130	1.6
0915	4.9		0804	4.8
M 1528	1.4		TU 1429	1.5
2151	4.9		2057	4.8
12 0359	1.4		**27** 0310	1.5
1024	5.1		0928	5.0
TU 1630	1.4		W 1551	1.3
2252	5.1		2209	5.1
13 0507	1.2		**28** 0425	1.2
1122	5.2		1039	5.3
W 1723	1.3		TH 1657	1.1
2342	5.2		2312	5.4
14 0600	1.1		**29** 0532	0.8
1210	5.4		1140	5.6
TH 1803	1.2		F 1755	0.9
15 0024	5.3		**30** 0005	5.6
0642	0.9		0633	0.6
F 1251	5.5		SA 1234	5.9
● 1839	1.1		○ 1847	0.8
			31 0053	5.8
			0726	0.3
			SU 1322	6.1
			1935	0.7

FEBRUARY

Time	m		Time	m
1 0138	6.0		**16** 0141	5.6
0814	0.1		0800	0.7
M 1407	6.2		TU 1405	5.6
2018	0.6		1958	0.8
2 0220	6.1		**17** 0210	5.6
0858	0.1		0831	0.7
TU 1451	6.1		W 1435	5.6
2059	0.6		2031	0.8
3 0302	6.1		**18** 0240	5.6
0939	0.2		0900	0.7
W 1534	6.0		TH 1505	5.5
2136	0.7		2100	0.9
4 0344	6.0		**19** 0310	5.6
1016	0.4		0926	0.8
TH 1617	5.7		F 1537	5.4
2211	0.9		2126	1.0
5 0427	5.7		**20** 0342	5.5
1054	0.7		0946	1.0
F 1701	5.4		SA 1611	5.3
☽ 2248	1.1		2151	1.1
6 0514	5.4		**21** 0419	5.3
1127	1.0		1009	1.1
SA 1750	5.1		SU 1651	5.1
2333	1.3		2228	1.2
7 0611	5.1		**22** 0505	5.1
1216	1.3		1051	1.3
SU 1849	4.8		M 1742	4.9
			☾ 2325	1.4
8 0037	1.5		**23** 0607	4.9
0724	4.8		1200	1.5
M 1330	1.6		TU 1855	4.6
2002	4.6			
9 0210	1.6		**24** 0054	1.5
0850	4.7		0734	4.8
TU 1454	1.7		W 1358	1.6
2123	4.6		2026	4.7
10 0342	1.5		**25** 0249	1.4
1009	4.9		0908	4.9
W 1606	1.6		TH 1531	1.4
2232	4.9		2148	5.0
11 0457	1.2		**26** 0411	1.1
1108	5.1		1026	5.3
TH 1704	1.4		F 1640	1.2
2324	5.1		2254	5.3
12 0549	1.0		**27** 0523	0.7
1155	5.3		1127	5.7
F 1748	1.2		SA 1741	0.9
			2347	5.7
13 0006	5.3		**28** 0622	0.4
0627	0.9		1218	6.0
SA 1233	5.5		SU 1832	0.7
1823	1.1		○	
14 0041	5.4			
0700	0.8			
SU 1306	5.5			
● 1855	1.0			
15 0112	5.5			
0731	0.7			
M 1336	5.6			
1926	0.9			

MARCH

Time	m		Time	m
1 0033	5.9		**16** 0044	5.5
0711	0.2		0702	0.7
M 1304	6.1		TU 1307	5.6
1917	0.6		1903	0.8
2 0116	6.1		**17** 0114	5.6
0755	0.1		0733	0.7
TU 1347	6.2		W 1336	5.7
1958	0.5		1936	0.8
3 0157	6.2		**18** 0143	5.7
0835	0.1		0804	0.6
W 1427	6.1		TH 1406	5.7
2037	0.5		2010	0.8
4 0238	6.1		**19** 0214	5.7
0912	0.2		0835	0.7
TH 1507	6.0		F 1437	5.6
2113	0.6		2041	0.9
5 0318	6.0		**20** 0246	5.6
0944	0.5		0901	0.8
F 1546	5.7		SA 1509	5.5
2145	0.8		2107	0.9
6 0359	5.8		**21** 0320	5.6
1013	0.8		0922	1.0
SA 1625	5.4		SU 1544	5.4
2218	1.0		2135	1.0
7 0443	5.4		**22** 0400	5.4
1046	1.1		0949	1.1
SU 1708	5.1		M 1625	5.1
☽ 2258	1.2		2214	1.1
8 0537	5.0		**23** 0449	5.2
1130	1.5		1037	1.3
M 1801	4.7		TU 1718	4.9
2355	1.5		☾ 2315	1.3
9 0649	4.6		**24** 0554	5.0
1240	1.8		1152	1.6
TU 1917	4.4		W 1831	4.7
10 0138	1.7		**25** 0049	1.4
0820	4.5		0720	4.8
W 1419	1.9		TH 1342	1.7
2048	4.4		2003	4.7
11 0319	1.5		**26** 0236	1.2
0944	4.7		0853	5.0
TH 1538	1.7		F 1510	1.4
2203	4.7		2126	5.0
12 0431	1.2		**27** 0357	0.9
1044	5.1		1008	5.4
F 1638	1.4		SA 1619	1.2
2257	5.0		2231	5.4
13 0521	1.0		**28** 0506	0.6
1128	5.3		1107	5.7
SA 1722	1.2		SU 1719	0.9
2338	5.3		2323	5.7
14 0559	0.9		**29** 0601	0.4
1205	5.5		1156	5.9
SU 1759	1.1		M 1809	0.7
15 0013	5.4		**30** 0009	5.9
0632	0.8		0647	0.2
M 1237	5.5		TU 1241	6.0
● 1831	0.9		○ 1853	0.6
			31 0052	6.1
			0729	0.2
			W 1322	6.1
			1935	0.5

APRIL

Time	m		Time	m
1 0133	6.1		**16** 0117	5.7
0807	0.2		0736	0.7
TH 1401	6.0		F 1340	5.7
2014	0.5		1949	0.8
2 0214	6.1		**17** 0152	5.7
0841	0.4		0810	0.8
F 1439	5.9		SA 1413	5.6
2050	0.6		2025	0.8
3 0255	5.9		**18** 0228	5.7
0913	0.6		0842	0.9
SA 1516	5.6		SU 1448	5.6
2123	0.8		2059	0.8
4 0336	5.7		**19** 0307	5.6
0942	0.9		0912	1.0
SU 1553	5.4		M 1527	5.4
2155	1.0		2136	0.9
5 0419	5.3		**20** 0352	5.5
1013	1.2		0950	1.2
M 1632	5.0		TU 1611	5.2
2231	1.2		2222	1.0
6 0509	4.9		**21** 0445	5.3
1055	1.5		1042	1.4
TU 1720	4.7		W 1707	5.0
☽ 2322	1.5		☾ 2325	1.1
7 0615	4.6		**22** 0551	5.1
1157	1.8		1155	1.5
W 1830	4.4		TH 1819	4.8
8 0053	1.6		**23** 0052	1.2
0737	4.5		0712	5.0
TH 1333	1.9		F 1325	1.6
1958	4.4		1943	4.9
9 0238	1.5		**24** 0220	1.0
0900	4.6		0834	5.2
F 1456	1.8		SA 1444	1.4
2117	4.6		2100	5.1
10 0345	1.3		**25** 0334	0.8
1003	4.9		0944	5.4
SA 1556	1.5		SU 1550	1.2
2215	4.9		2203	5.4
11 0437	1.1		**26** 0440	0.6
1050	5.2		1042	5.7
SU 1644	1.3		M 1650	1.0
2259	5.2		2257	5.6
12 0519	0.9		**27** 0534	0.5
1128	5.4		1131	5.8
M 1725	1.1		TU 1742	0.8
2336	5.4		2344	5.8
13 0555	0.8		**28** 0619	0.5
1202	5.5		1215	5.9
TU 1801	1.0		W 1828	0.7
			○	
14 0010	5.5		**29** 0028	5.9
0629	0.8		0659	0.5
W 1234	5.6		TH 1257	5.9
● 1836	0.9		1912	0.6
15 0044	5.6		**30** 0112	6.0
0702	0.7		0737	0.5
TH 1307	5.7		F 1336	5.8
1913	0.8		1953	0.6

Chart Datum: 2·90 metres below Ordnance Datum (Newlyn). HAT is 6·3 metres above Chart Datum; see 4.5

》 **FREE** monthly updates from 《
www.reedsalmanac.co.uk

TIME ZONE (UT)
For Summer Time add ONE hour in **non-shaded areas**

SHEERNESS   LAT 51°27'N   LONG 0°45'E
TIMES AND HEIGHTS OF HIGH AND LOW WATERS

Dates in red are **SPRINGS**
Dates in blue are **NEAPS**

YEAR 2010

MAY

Day	Time	m	Day	Time	m
1 SA	0154 / 0812 / 1414 / 2032	5.9 / 0.6 / 5.7 / 0.7	**16** SU	0135 / 0751 / 1356 / 2016	5.7 / 0.8 / 5.7 / 0.7
2 SU	0236 / 0845 / 1451 / 2107	5.8 / 0.8 / 5.5 / 0.8	**17** M	0217 / 0830 / 1436 / 2059	5.8 / 0.9 / 5.6 / 0.7
3 M	0318 / 0915 / 1527 / 2138	5.5 / 1.1 / 5.3 / 1.0	**18** TU	0301 / 0910 / 1519 / 2145	5.7 / 1.0 / 5.5 / 0.7
4 TU	0400 / 0947 / 1604 / 2211	5.3 / 1.3 / 5.1 / 1.2	**19** W	0350 / 0955 / 1607 / 2235	5.6 / 1.1 / 5.3 / 0.8
5 W	0446 / 1026 / 1649 / 2256	5.0 / 1.5 / 4.8 / 1.4	**20** TH	0445 / 1047 / 1702 / 2335	5.5 / 1.3 / 5.2 / 0.8
6 TH ☽	0541 / 1119 / 1746	4.7 / 1.7 / 4.6	**21** F	0547 / 1149 / 1807	5.3 / 1.4 / 5.1
7 F	0000 / 0645 / 1230 / 1859	1.5 / 4.6 / 1.9 / 4.5	**22** SA	0044 / 0657 / 1300 / 1919	0.9 / 5.2 / 1.4 / 5.1
8 SA	0133 / 0757 / 1355 / 2014	1.5 / 4.6 / 1.8 / 4.6	**23** SU	0156 / 0808 / 1411 / 2030	0.8 / 5.3 / 1.3 / 5.2
9 SU	0246 / 0902 / 1502 / 2118	1.4 / 4.8 / 1.6 / 4.8	**24** M	0304 / 0915 / 1516 / 2134	0.8 / 5.4 / 1.2 / 5.3
10 M	0342 / 0956 / 1556 / 2210	1.2 / 5.0 / 1.4 / 5.0	**25** TU	0407 / 1014 / 1618 / 2231	0.8 / 5.5 / 1.1 / 5.5
11 TU	0430 / 1042 / 1644 / 2255	1.0 / 5.2 / 1.2 / 5.3	**26** W	0502 / 1106 / 1716 / 2323	0.8 / 5.6 / 1.0 / 5.6
12 W	0513 / 1123 / 1727 / 2336	1.0 / 5.4 / 1.0 / 5.4	**27** TH ○	0550 / 1153 / 1807	0.8 / 5.6 / 0.8
13 TH	0554 / 1202 / 1809	0.9 / 5.6 / 0.9	**28** F	0011 / 0631 / 1237 / 1854	5.7 / 0.8 / 5.6 / 0.7
14 F ●	0015 / 0632 / 1240 / 1851	5.5 / 0.8 / 5.6 / 0.8	**29** SA	0058 / 0710 / 1317 / 1938	5.7 / 0.8 / 5.6 / 0.7
15 SA	0055 / 0711 / 1318 / 1933	5.6 / 0.8 / 5.7 / 0.7	**30** SU	0141 / 0747 / 1356 / 2018	5.7 / 0.9 / 5.6 / 0.7
			31 M	0223 / 0821 / 1432 / 2054	5.6 / 1.0 / 5.5 / 0.8

JUNE

Day	Time	m	Day	Time	m
1 TU	0303 / 0853 / 1508 / 2126	5.5 / 1.1 / 5.3 / 0.9	**16** W	0257 / 0908 / 1513 / 2149	5.9 / 0.9 / 5.7 / 0.4
2 W	0342 / 0925 / 1543 / 2157	5.3 / 1.3 / 5.2 / 1.1	**17** TH	0346 / 0953 / 1600 / 2237	5.8 / 0.9 / 5.6 / 0.5
3 TH	0423 / 1001 / 1622 / 2234	5.1 / 1.4 / 5.0 / 1.1	**18** F	0438 / 1039 / 1651 / 2327	5.7 / 1.1 / 5.5 / 0.6
4 F ☽	0506 / 1045 / 1708 / 2320	4.9 / 1.5 / 4.9 / 1.3	**19** SA ☾	0533 / 1130 / 1747	5.5 / 1.2 / 5.4
5 SA ☾	0555 / 1137 / 1802	4.8 / 1.7 / 4.7	**20** SU	0021 / 0633 / 1228 / 1850	0.7 / 5.4 / 1.3 / 5.3
6 SU	0017 / 0652 / 1240 / 1906	1.4 / 4.7 / 1.7 / 4.7	**21** M	0122 / 0737 / 1333 / 1958	0.8 / 5.3 / 1.4 / 5.2
7 M	0127 / 0755 / 1353 / 2014	1.4 / 4.7 / 1.7 / 4.7	**22** TU	0227 / 0843 / 1442 / 2106	1.0 / 5.2 / 1.3 / 5.2
8 TU	0238 / 0857 / 1501 / 2116	1.3 / 4.9 / 1.5 / 4.9	**23** W	0331 / 0946 / 1551 / 2211	1.0 / 5.2 / 1.2 / 5.3
9 W	0339 / 0954 / 1600 / 2213	1.2 / 5.1 / 1.3 / 5.1	**24** TH	0432 / 1045 / 1658 / 2310	1.1 / 5.3 / 1.1 / 5.4
10 TH	0432 / 1046 / 1654 / 2304	1.1 / 5.3 / 1.1 / 5.3	**25** F	0525 / 1137 / 1755	1.1 / 5.4 / 1.0
11 F	0521 / 1136 / 1744 / 2352	1.0 / 5.5 / 1.0 / 5.5	**26** SA ○	0002 / 0610 / 1223 / 1844	5.5 / 1.1 / 5.5 / 0.8
12 SA ●	0608 / 1218 / 1834	0.9 / 5.6 / 0.8	**27** SU	0049 / 0650 / 1305 / 1928	5.5 / 1.0 / 5.5 / 0.8
13 SU	0038 / 0652 / 1302 / 1922	5.7 / 0.9 / 5.7 / 0.7	**28** M	0131 / 0727 / 1342 / 2007	5.6 / 1.0 / 5.5 / 0.8
14 M	0124 / 0737 / 1345 / 2011	5.8 / 0.8 / 5.7 / 0.5	**29** TU	0210 / 0801 / 1417 / 2041	5.6 / 1.1 / 5.5 / 0.8
15 TU	0210 / 0823 / 1428 / 2100	5.9 / 0.8 / 5.7 / 0.4	**30** W	0246 / 0834 / 1449 / 2112	5.5 / 1.1 / 5.4 / 0.9

JULY

Day	Time	m	Day	Time	m
1 TH	0321 / 0905 / 1522 / 2140	5.4 / 1.1 / 5.4 / 0.9	**16** F	0333 / 0940 / 1545 / 2223	6.0 / 0.8 / 5.9 / 0.3
2 F	0355 / 0939 / 1556 / 2211	5.3 / 1.2 / 5.3 / 1.0	**17** SA	0420 / 1021 / 1630 / 2305	5.9 / 0.9 / 5.8 / 0.5
3 SA	0431 / 1014 / 1632 / 2246	5.2 / 1.3 / 5.2 / 1.1	**18** SU ☽	0509 / 1103 / 1720 / 2349	5.6 / 1.1 / 5.6 / 0.7
4 SU ☾	0511 / 1054 / 1714 / 2326	5.0 / 1.5 / 5.0 / 1.2	**19** M	0602 / 1152 / 1818	5.4 / 1.2 / 5.4
5 M	0556 / 1141 / 1804	4.9 / 1.6 / 4.9	**20** TU	0041 / 0702 / 1254 / 1926	1.0 / 5.1 / 1.4 / 5.1
6 TU	0016 / 0652 / 1242 / 1908	1.4 / 4.8 / 1.7 / 4.8	**21** W	0147 / 0809 / 1412 / 2042	1.2 / 5.0 / 1.5 / 5.0
7 W	0125 / 0800 / 1402 / 2023	1.5 / 4.8 / 1.7 / 4.8	**22** TH	0259 / 0921 / 1534 / 2157	1.4 / 5.0 / 1.4 / 5.1
8 TH	0248 / 0909 / 1520 / 2134	1.4 / 4.9 / 1.5 / 5.0	**23** F	0408 / 1028 / 1650 / 2302	1.4 / 5.1 / 1.2 / 5.3
9 F	0356 / 1013 / 1625 / 2238	1.3 / 5.2 / 1.2 / 5.2	**24** SA	0508 / 1124 / 1750 / 2354	1.3 / 5.3 / 1.0 / 5.4
10 SA	0455 / 1110 / 1724 / 2334	1.1 / 5.4 / 1.0 / 5.5	**25** SU	0555 / 1211 / 1837	1.2 / 5.4 / 0.9
11 SU ●	0548 / 1201 / 1821	1.0 / 5.6 / 0.8	**26** M ○	0038 / 0634 / 1251 / 1915	5.5 / 1.2 / 5.5 / 0.8
12 M	0026 / 0638 / 1249 / 1914	5.7 / 0.9 / 5.7 / 0.6	**27** TU	0117 / 0708 / 1325 / 1949	5.6 / 1.1 / 5.6 / 0.8
13 TU	0114 / 0727 / 1334 / 2005	5.9 / 0.8 / 5.8 / 0.4	**28** W	0151 / 0741 / 1357 / 2020	5.6 / 1.0 / 5.6 / 0.8
14 W	0201 / 0814 / 1417 / 2054	6.1 / 0.7 / 5.9 / 0.2	**29** TH	0223 / 0813 / 1427 / 2049	5.6 / 1.0 / 5.6 / 0.8
15 TH	0247 / 0858 / 1501 / 2139	6.1 / 0.7 / 6.0 / 0.2	**30** F	0254 / 0844 / 1457 / 2117	5.5 / 1.0 / 5.6 / 0.8
			31 SA	0325 / 0915 / 1527 / 2145	5.5 / 1.1 / 5.5 / 0.9

AUGUST

Day	Time	m	Day	Time	m
1 SU	0356 / 0945 / 1559 / 2213	5.3 / 1.2 / 5.4 / 1.1	**16** M ☽	0438 / 1034 / 1652 / 2311	5.6 / 1.1 / 5.7 / 0.9
2 M	0430 / 1016 / 1635 / 2242	5.2 / 1.4 / 5.2 / 1.2	**17** TU	0526 / 1118 / 1747 / 2357	5.3 / 1.3 / 5.3 / 1.3
3 TU	0510 / 1053 / 1718 / 2321	5.0 / 1.5 / 5.0 / 1.4	**18** W ☾	0624 / 1217 / 1857	5.0 / 1.5 / 5.0
4 W	0559 / 1145 / 1816	4.9 / 1.6 / 4.9	**19** TH	0105 / 0735 / 1347 / 2021	1.6 / 4.8 / 1.6 / 4.8
5 TH	0021 / 0706 / 1305 / 1935	1.6 / 4.7 / 1.7 / 4.8	**20** F	0230 / 0856 / 1523 / 2144	1.7 / 4.8 / 1.5 / 5.0
6 F	0200 / 0828 / 1446 / 2101	1.6 / 4.8 / 1.6 / 4.9	**21** SA	0348 / 1010 / 1642 / 2249	1.6 / 5.0 / 1.2 / 5.3
7 SA	0327 / 0944 / 1602 / 2216	1.5 / 5.1 / 1.3 / 5.2	**22** SU	0451 / 1107 / 1737 / 2339	1.4 / 5.3 / 1.0 / 5.5
8 SU	0433 / 1049 / 1709 / 2318	1.2 / 5.4 / 0.9 / 5.6	**23** M	0537 / 1151 / 1818	1.3 / 5.4 / 0.9
9 M	0531 / 1143 / 1810	1.0 / 5.7 / 0.7	**24** TU ○	0019 / 0613 / 1229 / 1852	5.6 / 1.2 / 5.6 / 0.8
10 TU ●	0011 / 0624 / 1231 / 1903	5.9 / 0.9 / 5.9 / 0.4	**25** W	0055 / 0646 / 1301 / 1922	5.6 / 1.1 / 5.6 / 0.8
11 W	0100 / 0713 / 1316 / 1952	6.1 / 0.8 / 6.0 / 0.2	**26** TH	0125 / 0717 / 1331 / 1951	5.7 / 1.0 / 5.7 / 0.8
12 TH	0145 / 0758 / 1358 / 2037	6.2 / 0.7 / 6.1 / 0.1	**27** F	0154 / 0748 / 1359 / 2020	5.7 / 1.0 / 5.7 / 0.7
13 F	0229 / 0840 / 1440 / 2119	6.2 / 0.7 / 6.2 / 0.1	**28** SA	0223 / 0820 / 1428 / 2049	5.7 / 1.0 / 5.7 / 0.8
14 SA	0312 / 0920 / 1522 / 2158	6.1 / 0.7 / 6.1 / 0.3	**29** SU	0252 / 0851 / 1458 / 2116	5.6 / 1.0 / 5.6 / 0.9
15 SU	0354 / 0957 / 1605 / 2234	5.9 / 0.9 / 5.9 / 0.6	**30** M	0323 / 0918 / 1529 / 2140	5.5 / 1.2 / 5.5 / 1.1
			31 TU	0355 / 0944 / 1604 / 2202	5.3 / 1.3 / 5.4 / 1.3

E England

Chart Datum: 2·90 metres below Ordnance Datum (Newlyn). HAT is 6·3 metres above Chart Datum; see 4.5

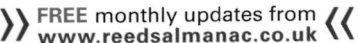

TIME ZONE (UT)
For Summer Time add ONE hour in **non-shaded areas**

SHEERNESS LAT 51°27'N LONG 0°45'E
TIMES AND HEIGHTS OF HIGH AND LOW WATERS

Dates in red are SPRINGS
Dates in blue are NEAPS

YEAR 2010

SEPTEMBER

Time	m		Time	m
1 0432	5.2		**16** 0545	4.9
1016	1.4		1145	1.6
W 1647	5.2		TH 1829	4.9
◖ 2237	1.4			
2 0519	5.0		**17** 0023	1.8
1106	1.6		0657	4.6
TH 1743	5.0		F 1324	1.7
2338	1.6		1955	4.7
3 0624	4.8		**18** 0158	1.9
1227	1.7		0824	4.6
F 1901	4.8		SA 1503	1.6
			2120	4.9
4 0123	1.8		**19** 0319	1.8
0752	4.7		0941	4.9
SA 1421	1.6		SU 1616	1.3
2035	4.9		2224	5.2
5 0302	1.6		**20** 0421	1.5
0918	5.0		1039	5.2
SU 1543	1.2		M 1707	1.1
2156	5.3		2312	5.5
6 0411	1.3		**21** 0508	1.3
1026	5.4		1122	5.4
M 1652	0.8		TU 1746	0.9
2259	5.7		2351	5.6
7 0511	1.0		**22** 0545	1.2
1120	5.7		1159	5.6
TU 1753	0.6		W 1819	0.9
2352	6.0			
8 0605	0.9		**23** 0024	5.7
1208	6.0		0617	1.1
W 1845	0.3		TH 1231	5.7
●			○ 1848	0.8
9 0038	6.2		**24** 0054	5.7
0652	0.7		0649	1.0
TH 1252	6.2		F 1300	5.7
1930	0.2		1918	0.8
10 0122	6.2		**25** 0122	5.7
0736	0.7		0722	0.9
F 1334	6.3		SA 1330	5.8
2013	0.2		1948	0.8
11 0204	6.2		**26** 0151	5.7
0817	0.6		0755	0.9
SA 1415	6.3		SU 1400	5.7
2052	0.3		2018	0.9
12 0245	6.1		**27** 0221	5.7
0856	0.7		0827	1.0
SU 1457	6.2		M 1431	5.7
2128	0.5		2047	1.0
13 0325	5.9		**28** 0253	5.6
0932	0.9		0856	1.1
M 1540	5.9		TU 1505	5.6
2200	0.8		2111	1.2
14 0407	5.6		**29** 0326	5.4
1008	1.1		0923	1.2
TU 1626	5.6		W 1542	5.4
2234	1.2		2136	1.3
15 0451	5.2		**30** 0404	5.2
1048	1.3		0957	1.3
W 1719	5.2		TH 1628	5.3
◖ 2317	1.5		2215	1.5

OCTOBER

Time	m		Time	m
1 0452	5.0		**16** 0616	4.6
1051	1.5		1244	1.7
F 1726	5.0		SA 1917	4.7
◖ 2321	1.7			
2 0557	4.8		**17** 0109	2.0
1213	1.6		0738	4.6
SA 1843	4.9		SU 1422	1.6
			2037	4.8
3 0059	1.8		**18** 0234	1.9
0723	4.8		0856	4.7
SU 1400	1.4		M 1529	1.4
2014	5.0		2143	5.0
4 0235	1.6		**19** 0337	1.7
0849	5.0		0956	5.0
M 1521	1.1		TU 1622	1.2
2133	5.4		2233	5.3
5 0344	1.3		**20** 0427	1.4
0958	5.4		1043	5.3
TU 1630	0.8		W 1704	1.0
2235	5.7		2313	5.5
6 0445	1.1		**21** 0508	1.2
1053	5.7		1121	5.5
W 1729	0.5		TH 1739	1.0
2327	6.0		2347	5.6
7 0539	0.9		**22** 0545	1.1
1141	6.0		1156	5.6
TH 1819	0.4		F 1812	0.9
●				
8 0013	6.1		**23** 0019	5.7
0626	0.8		0619	1.1
F 1234	6.1		SA 1229	5.7
1903	0.3		○ 1843	0.9
9 0057	6.2		**24** 0051	5.7
0711	0.6		0655	0.9
SA 1309	6.2		SU 1302	5.7
1944	0.4		1916	0.9
10 0138	6.1		**25** 0123	5.7
0753	0.7		0731	0.9
SU 1352	6.2		M 1335	5.7
2022	0.5		1949	0.9
11 0218	6.0		**26** 0155	5.7
0833	0.7		0806	0.9
M 1435	6.0		TU 1411	5.7
2057	0.7		2021	1.0
12 0258	5.8		**27** 0229	5.6
0911	0.9		0841	1.0
TU 1518	5.8		W 1448	5.7
2129	1.0		2053	1.1
13 0338	5.5		**28** 0306	5.5
0946	1.1		0917	1.1
W 1604	5.5		TH 1530	5.5
2202	1.3		2127	1.3
14 0419	5.2		**29** 0347	5.3
1024	1.3		0958	1.2
TH 1656	5.1		F 1619	5.4
◖ 2242	1.6		2212	1.5
15 0509	4.9		**30** 0437	5.1
1115	1.5		1053	1.3
F 1800	4.8		SA 1718	5.2
2340	1.9		◖ 2315	1.6
			31 0540	4.9
			1208	1.3
			SU 1831	5.1

NOVEMBER

Time	m		Time	m
1 0038	1.7		**16** 0127	2.0
0658	4.9		0751	4.6
M 1338	1.2		TU 1427	1.5
1951	5.2		2041	4.8
2 0202	1.6		**17** 0240	1.8
0818	5.1		0857	4.8
TU 1454	1.0		W 1524	1.4
2105	5.4		2138	5.0
3 0311	1.4		**18** 0337	1.6
0926	5.4		0952	5.0
W 1600	0.8		TH 1613	1.2
2207	5.6		2226	5.2
4 0412	1.2		**19** 0426	1.3
1024	5.7		1039	5.3
TH 1659	0.7		F 1656	1.1
2300	5.8		2307	5.4
5 0509	1.0		**20** 0510	1.2
1115	5.9		1121	5.4
F 1750	0.6		SA 1735	1.0
2348	5.9		2346	5.6
6 0600	0.8		**21** 0551	1.0
1202	6.0		1200	5.6
SA 1834	0.6		SU 1812	1.0
●			○	
7 0032	5.9		**22** 0023	5.6
0648	0.7		0630	0.9
SU 1248	6.1		M 1239	5.6
1915	0.6		1849	0.9
8 0114	5.9		**23** 0100	5.7
0733	0.7		0711	0.9
M 1333	6.0		TU 1317	5.7
1953	0.7		1926	0.9
9 0155	5.8		**24** 0137	5.7
0815	0.7		0753	0.8
TU 1418	5.9		W 1357	5.8
2029	0.9		2005	1.0
10 0235	5.7		**25** 0214	5.6
0854	0.9		0835	0.9
W 1502	5.7		TH 1439	5.7
2102	1.2		2043	1.0
11 0314	5.4		**26** 0254	5.6
0930	1.1		0918	0.9
TH 1547	5.4		F 1524	5.7
2134	1.4		2125	1.1
12 0354	5.2		**27** 0338	5.4
1004	1.2		1005	0.9
F 1634	5.1		SA 1614	5.5
2211	1.6		2211	1.3
13 0438	5.0		**28** 0428	5.3
1046	1.4		1056	1.0
SA 1726	4.9		SU 1710	5.4
◖ 2259	1.8		◖ 2306	1.4
14 0532	4.8		**29** 0525	5.2
1144	1.6		1158	1.0
SU 1827	4.7		M 1814	5.2
15 0004	1.9		**30** 0010	1.5
0638	4.6		0632	5.1
M 1312	1.6		TU 1308	1.1
1935	4.7		1924	5.2

DECEMBER

Time	m		Time	m
1 0123	1.5		**16** 0119	1.8
0745	5.2		0747	4.7
W 1419	1.0		TH 1411	1.5
2033	5.3		2032	4.7
2 0233	1.4		**17** 0236	1.7
0854	5.3		0854	4.8
TH 1526	1.0		F 1518	1.4
2137	5.4		2133	4.9
3 0339	1.3		**18** 0340	1.5
0957	5.5		0954	5.0
F 1627	0.9		SA 1613	1.3
2235	5.5		2227	5.2
4 0442	1.1		**19** 0434	1.3
1054	5.6		1047	5.2
SA 1722	0.9		SU 1701	1.2
2326	5.6		2316	5.4
5 0540	0.9		**20** 0524	1.1
1146	5.7		1136	5.4
SU 1809	0.9		M 1746	1.1
●				
6 0013	5.7		**21** 0000	5.5
0632	0.8		0611	0.9
M 1236	5.8		TU 1221	5.6
1850	0.9		○ 1828	1.0
7 0058	5.7		**22** 0043	5.6
0719	0.7		0658	0.8
TU 1322	5.8		W 1305	5.7
1930	0.9		1911	0.9
8 0139	5.7		**23** 0124	5.7
0803	0.7		0745	0.6
W 1406	5.7		TH 1348	5.8
2006	1.0		1954	0.8
9 0218	5.6		**24** 0205	5.7
0843	0.8		0832	0.5
TH 1448	5.6		F 1432	5.9
2040	1.1		2038	0.9
10 0255	5.5		**25** 0246	5.7
0917	1.0		0919	0.5
F 1529	5.4		SA 1517	5.9
2111	1.3		2120	0.9
11 0332	5.3		**26** 0330	5.7
0947	1.1		1004	0.6
SA 1608	5.2		SU 1605	5.7
2144	1.4		2203	1.0
12 0409	5.2		**27** 0416	5.6
1019	1.2		1049	0.7
SU 1650	5.0		M 1655	5.6
2223	1.5		2248	1.2
13 0451	5.0		**28** 0506	5.5
1058	1.3		1136	0.8
M 1735	4.9		TU 1750	5.3
◖ 2310	1.7		◖ 2339	1.3
14 0540	4.8		**29** 0604	5.3
1149	1.4		1232	1.0
TU 1828	4.7		W 1852	5.2
15 0007	1.8		**30** 0041	1.4
0639	4.7		0711	5.2
W 1254	1.5		TH 1339	1.1
1928	4.6		2000	5.1
			31 0155	1.4
			0824	5.1
			F 1450	1.2
			2108	5.1

Chart Datum: 2·90 metres below Ordnance Datum (Newlyn). HAT is 6·3 metres above Chart Datum; see 4.5

》》 FREE monthly updates from 《《
www.reedsalmanac.co.uk

9.4.12 RIVER THAMES

Canvey Island to Teddington lock. See 9.4.13 for Southend and Leigh-on-Sea.

CHARTS AC 5606, 1185,1186, 2151, 3337, 2484, 3319. Imray C1, C2, Y18, 2100 Series. Stanfords 5, 8.

Publications. The Port of London Authority (PLA), London River House, Royal Pier Road, Gravesend, Kent DA12 2BG, ☎ 01474 562200, publish (or download free from www. portoflondon. co.uk) *A Pleasure Users Guide; General Directions; Permanent Notices to Mariners; Port of London River Byelaws; Tide Tables* and a *Port Handbook.*

HARBOURS IN SEA REACH and GRAVESEND REACH

HOLEHAVEN CREEK, Essex, **51°30´·57N 00°33´·16E.** AC 2484, 1186. HW +0140 on Dover; use differences for CORYTON, see 9.4.13; ML 3·0m; Duration 0610. Shelter is good, but beware swell from passing traffic. Keep to Canvey Is side on ent. Temp ⚓ in lee of Chainrock jetty or call PLA ☎ 01474 562462 for possible mooring. 5ca N of ent an overhead oil pipe crosses chan with 11m clearance, plus 2 FY lts (horiz). 2 FG (vert) on all jetty heads, plus Chainrock SHM buoy Fl G 5s. FW from Lobster Smack pub, P & D from Canvey Village (1M); all other facilities on Canvey Is.

Small craft crossing routes. To clear tanker berths off Holehaven, Coryton and Thames Haven yachts should navigate as follows:
Inward from north: Keep close to SHM buoys & bcns. At W Leigh Middle ensure the fairway is clear, then cross to the S side of Yantlet Channel. Make for E Blyth buoy before turning onto the inward track, so as to clear outward vessels passing close to the PHM buoys. It is safe to pass close S of Mid Blyth, W Blyth and Lower Hope buoys. When safe, cross to the N side in Lower Hope Reach as quickly as possible.
Outward to north, as above in reverse, but cross to the N side between Sea Reach Nos 4 & 5 buoys.
Inward from the south: Keep well south of Yantlet Channel, crossing to the N side in Lower Hope Reach as described above.

> Caution: In Gravesend Reach beware 6 groynes off the N bank, WSW of Coalhouse Pt, which project almost into the fairway. Outer ends marked by SHM beacons, Fl G 2·5s. *No passage exists inshore of the groynes.*
>
> A light, Iso 6s, on Tilbury Cargo Jetty (51°27´·06N 00°20´·95E) is shown when vessels are manoeuvring off Tilbury Dock locks or for a berth in Northfleet Hope. *Proceed with caution.*

GRAVESEND, Kent, **51°26´·61N 00°22´·92E.** AC 1186, 2151. HW +0150 on Dover; ML 3·3m; Duration 0610. Use Tilbury diffs overleaf. ⚓ E of Clubb's Jetty close to S shore, but remote from town. There are 2 Øs off **Gravesend SC** ☎ 01474 533974, www.gravesendsailing club.co.uk, opposite Tilbury Power Station. Ø nearest club dries; Ø downriver in 2m. Larger PLA Øs are just upriver, £14/night. **Embankment Marina** ☎ 01474 535700, www.theembankmentmarina.co.uk, Ch 80. Lock into Canal Basin HW −1 to HW Tilbury by arrangement: 1 Apr-31 Oct, 0800-2000; Winter 1000-1600. Lock closes at local HW. Out of hours openings up to HW by arrangement with lock keeper. D, Gaz, Bar, M, Ⓔ, ME, El, ✕, slip.
Town Tourist info ☎ (01474) 337600, Ⓔ, ME, El, ✕, P & D, BH (70 ton) at Denton Wharf, R, 🛒.

Thurrock YC 51°28´·28N 00°19´·47E at Grays, ☎ 01375 373720. 1 Ø, D, P (2M), Bar, R (occas). M-F 1000-1500; Thu 2000-2300.

9.4.12A THAMES TIDAL BARRIER

51°29´·91N 00°02´·21E (Span G)

CHARTS AC 5606, 2484 and 3337.

DESCRIPTION Located at Woolwich Reach, it protects London from floods. There are 9 piers between which gates can be rotated upwards from the river bed to form a barrier. The piers are numbered 1-9 from N to S; the spans are lettered A-K from S to N (see diagram). A, H, J & K are not navigable. C-F, with depth 5·8m and 61m wide, are for larger ships. Spans B and G, with 1·25m, are for small craft/yachts which should lower sail and use engine: W-bound via G and E-bound via B (51°29´·73N 00°02´·24E).

LIGHTS AND SIGNALS To the E at Barking Creek (N bank),to the W at Blackwall Stairs (N bank) and Blackwall Pt (S bank), noticeboards and lights indicate:
Fl ⚪ = Barrier is about to close.
Fl ● = Barrier closing; all vessels must stop.
Short textual messages may also be displayed.
On the Barrier piers:
● lts laid out as arrows = span indicated is open to traffic.
● lts in St Andrew's cross layout = barrier or span closed.
3 ● in ▽ layout on spans A, H, J and K = No passage.

SPANS OPEN TO NAVIGATION In reduced visibility, spans open to navigation are marked by high intensity lts and racons (T). Information will be included in routine broadcasts by *London VTS* on VHF Ch **14** at H + 15 and H + 45.

CONTROL AND COMMUNICATIONS The Thames Barrier Navigation Centre controls all traffic in a Zone from Margaret Ness (51°30´·5N 00°05´·56E) to Blackwall Point (51°30´·3N 00°00´·2E), using the callsign *London VTS,* VHF Ch **14,** 22, 16.
Inbound yachts and small craft should call *London VTS* to obtain clearance to proceed through the Barrier when passing Margaret Ness (51°30´·54N 00°05´·50E).
Outbound yachts and small craft should call *London VTS* to obtain clearance to proceed through the Barrier when passing Blackwall Point (51°30´·30N 00°00´·18E).
Non-VHF craft should, if possible, pre-notify the Barrier Control ☎ 020 8855 0315; then observe all visual signals, proceed with caution keeping clear of larger vessels and use spans B or G as appropriate. Call before and after transiting the Barrier.

NAVIGATION Sailing craft should transit the Barrier under power, not sail. When all spans are closed, keep 200m clear to avoid turbulence.

It is dangerous to transit a closed span, as the gate may be semi-raised.

Small craft should not navigate between Thames Refinery Jetty and Gulf Oil Island, unless intending to transit the Barrier.

On N side of river (Spans E and F) a cross-tide component is reported; expect to lay-off a compensating drift angle.

TESTING
The Barrier is completely closed for testing once a month for about 3hrs, LW ±1½. Call ☎ 0208 3054188, and see Reeds Almanac monthly updates, for details. In Sept/Oct an annual closure lasts about 10 hrs, LW to LW; this may affect passage plans.

CANVEY ISLAND TO CRAYFORDNESS (AC 1185, 1186, 2484, 2151)

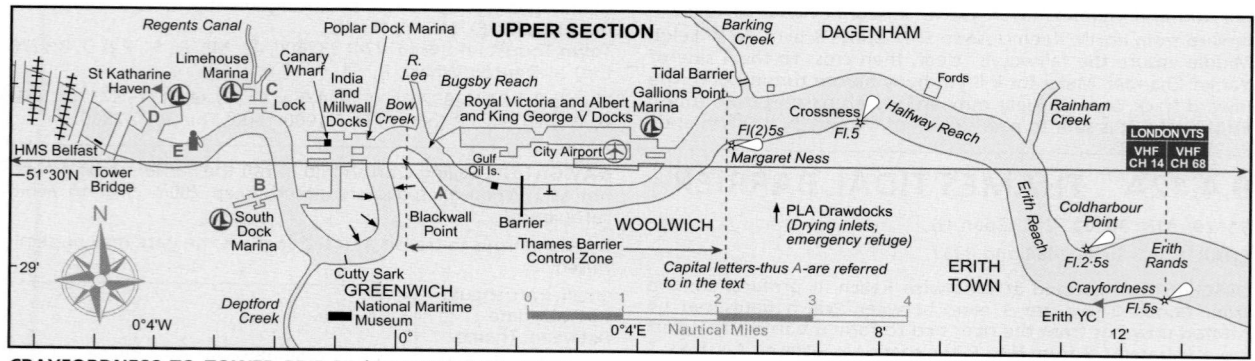

CRAYFORDNESS TO TOWER BRIDGE (AC 2484, 2151, 3337)

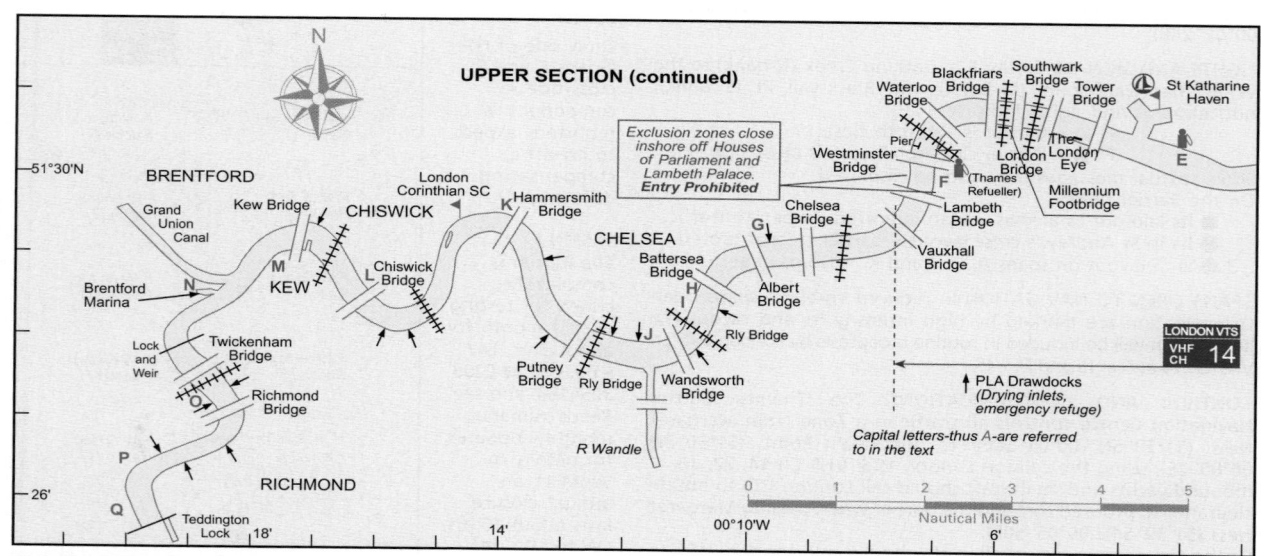

TOWER BRIDGE TO TEDDINGTON (AC 3319)

Tide Boards, showing height of tide above CD, are at Lower Pool (Met Police Boatyard), King's Reach (Temple Stairs), Nine Elms Reach (Cringle Wharf) and Battersea Reach (Plantation Wharf).

TIDES The river is tidal up to Teddington. +0252 Dover; ML 3·6; Duration 0555.

Standard Port LONDON BRIDGE (⟶)

Times				Height (metres)			
High Water		Low Water		MHWS	MHWN	MLWN	MLWS
0300	0900	0400	1100	7·1	5·9	1·3	0·5
1500	2100	1600	2300				
Differences TILBURY							
−0055	−0040	−0050	−0115	−0·7	−0·5	+0·1	0·0
WOOLWICH (GALLIONS POINT)							
−0020	−0020	−0035	−0045	−0·1	0·0	+0·2	0·0
ALBERT BRIDGE							
+0025	+0020	+0105	+0110	−0·9	−0·8	−0·7	−0·4
HAMMERSMITH BRIDGE							
+0040	+0035	+0205	+0155	−1·4	−1·3	−1·0	−0·5
KEW BRIDGE							
+0055	+0050	+0255	+0235	−1·8	−1·8	−1·2	−0·5
TEDDINGTON (RICHMOND) LOCK							
+0105	+0055	+0325	+0305	−2·2	−2·2	−1·3	−0·5

Above Putney the ht of LW may be below CD if the water flow over Teddington Weir is reduced; prior warnings are broadcast by London VTS. If the Thames Barrier (previous page) is closed, water levels will vary greatly from predictions.

SHELTER Very good in marinas. PLA Drawdocks, arrowed, are drying inlets offering emergency refuge, but subject to wash.

NAVIGATION WPT 51°29′·62N 00°44′·17E, Sea Reach No 4 buoy, 276°/6·8M to abm Holehaven Creek and 37·8M to Tower Bridge.
Speed limits. Minimise wash. 8kn speed limit applies inshore of Southend-on-sea, at Coryton and Thurrock when gas tankers are berthed, in all creeks and above Wandsworth Bridge.

Keep at least 60m clear of oil/gas jetties at Canvey Island, Coryton, Thames Haven, Thurrock, Purfleet and Dagenham. Pleasure craft should always keep clear of commercial vessels, including tug/barge tows.

Sea Reach, keep well S of the main chan to clear tankers turning abeam Canvey Is and Shellhaven.

Lower Hope Reach, hold the NW bank until Ovens SHM; long groynes extend from the N bank for the next 2M. Tilbury Landing Stage is used by the Gravesend ferry and cruise liners.

Northfleet Hope, beware ships/tugs turning into Tilbury Docks; container berths and a grain terminal are close up-river.

Above **Gravesend** keep to stbd side of channel – do not cut corners.

Above **Cherry Garden Pier** (Wapping), vessels > 40m LOA and tugs/tows always have priority. Very heavy traffic/frequent River Ferries from/to Greenwich, Tower of London and Westminster. Police and PLA launches are always willing to assist.

At **Richmond** a half-tide lock and a weir with overhead sluice gates give access up-river. 3 R discs (3 Ⓡ lts at night) in a ▽ show when the sluice gates are down (closed) and maintaining at least 1·72m between Richmond and Teddington bridges. The half-tide lock, on the Surrey bank, must then be used.

At other times (approx HW ±2) two Ⓨ lights at each arch = weir open to navigation. Pass freely below the 3 central arches.

Teddington lock marks the end of the tidal Thames (semi-tidal above Richmond). Red/green lights indicate which of the launch or barge locks is in operation.

LIGHTS AND MARKS See 9.4.4 and chartlets. Glare from shore lts can make navigation by night difficult or even hazardous.

R/T London VTS operates from Centres at Gravesend and the Thames Barrier, dividing the estuary/river into three sectors. Routine MSI broadcasts are made at the times shown below.

Sector 1: Outer limits – Sea Reach No 4 buoy. Ch **69**, H +15, H +45.

Sector 2: Sea Reach 4 – Crayfordness. Ch **68**, H and H +30.

Sector 3: Crayfordness – Teddington. Ch **14**, H +15 and H +45.

PLA launches *Thames Patrol* Ch 69, 68, 14. Police launches *Thames Police* Ch 14. Do not use tug Channels 8, 10, 13, 36, 72, 77. For marina VHF see overleaf.

EMERGENCY In emergency call *London Coastguard* Ch 16, 67, co-located with London VTS at the Thames Barrier Navigation Control and covering from Canvey Island to Teddington.

Thames Coastguard covers the area to seaward of Canvey Island. The RNLI operates four LB stations at Gravesend, Victoria Embankment (Waterloo Br), Chiswick and Teddington.

TELEPHONE Port of London Authority (PLA): General enquiries 01474 562200. www.portoflondon.co.uk. HM lower district (01474) 562200. Port Controller Gravesend (01474) 560311. HM upper district 020 7743 7912. Thames Barrier Centre 0208 8550315. London CG londoncoastguard@mcga.gov.uk 0208 3127380. Thames CG (01255) 675518. Metropolitan Police, Marine Support Unit 0207 2754421. Tower Bridge 0207 9403984. Richmond lock 0208 9400634; Teddington lock 0208 9408723.

BRIDGES Craft approaching a bridge against the tide give way to those approaching with the tide. All bridges above Tower Bridge are fixed. Clearances (m) above HAT are as follows:

Dartford (QEII)	53	Chelsea	6·1
Tower (closed)	8·1	Albert	4·4
Tower (open)	42	Battersea road	5·0
London	8·4	Battersea rail	5·5
Cannon St	6·6	Wandsworth	5·3
Southwark	6·8	Fulham	6·3
Millennium	8·9	Putney	4·9
Blackfriars rail	6·6	Hammersmith	3·0
Blackfriars road	6·4	Barnes	4·9
Waterloo	8·0	Chiswick	6·1
Charing Cross	6·5	Kew rail	5·1
Westminster	4·9	Kew road	4·7
Lambeth	5·9	Richmond foot	4·7
Vauxhall	5·1	Twickenham	8·5*
Victoria Railway	5·5	Richmond rail	7·9*
		Richmond road	7·9*

* Above maintained water level.

Tower Bridge fog horn sounds a 10s blast every 20s when bascules are open for shipping; standby signal is a bell 30s. A ▽ of R discs (● lts) below a bridge span = this arch closed.

On bridge arches between Tower and Wandsworth bridges high intensity white signal lts are electronically triggered by one or more large vessels approaching a bridge. Iso W 4s means a single large vessel, VQ a second large vessel, nearing the same bridge. Other vessels keep clear of that arch.

FACILITIES Marinas See overleaf for Gallions Point, Poplar Dock, South Dock, Limehouse, St Katharine Haven, Chelsea Harbour and Brentford Dock. Other marinas and YCs (Bold red letters in brackets appear on chartlets):

Greenwich YC (A) ☎ 0844 736 5846; VHF Ch M. FW, ⌗, ME.

West India Dock ☎ 020 7517 5500; group bookings only (min 6 boats).

Westminster Petroleum Ltd (F) (Fuel barge). Call *Thames Refueller* (moored off Houses of Parliament from Easter to mid-Oct) VHF Ch 14, ☎ 07831 110681, D, Gas, CH, L.

Chelsea Yacht & Boat Co (H) ☎ 020 7352 1427, M, Gas;

Hurlingham YC (J) ☎ 020 8788 5547, M, CH, ME, FW, El, ✕; **Dove Marina (K)**.

Chiswick Pier, ☎ 0208 7422713, £0.95m, long pontoon, 2FG (vert). All tide access, max draft 1·4m. FW, ⟥, ⚓. Visitors welcome.

Chiswick Quay Marina (L) (50) ☎ 0208 9948743, Access HW±2 via lock, M, FW, BY, M, ME, El, ✕.

Kew Marina (M) ☎ 020 8940 8364, M, CH, D, P, Gas, SM;

(O), Richmond Slipway BY, CH, D, Gas, M, FW, ME, El, ✕.

(P) Eel Pie Island BY, CH, ⟥, ME, M, Gas, C (6 ton), ✕, El, FW; **(Q) Swan Island Hbr**, D, M, ME, El, ✕, FW, Gas, Slip, AB, C (30 ton), CH.

Piers where landing may be possible, by prior arrangement. Call London River Services ☎ 0207 9412400 for: Greenwich, Tower Millennium, Embankment, Bankside, Festival, Westminster, Millbank, Blackfriars and Waterloo.

(G) Cadogan 0208 7482715, give 24 hrs notice. Chiswick 0208 7422713. Dove 0208 7482715. St Katharine 0207 4880555. Putney 0207 3781211. 0207 9302062 for Kew Pier and Richmond Lndg Stage.

MARINAS ON THE TIDAL THAMES, from seaward to Brentford

GALLIONS POINT MARINA, 51°30'·30N 00°04'·66E in entry basin for Royal Albert Dock. ☎ 020 7476 7054, www.gallionspoint marina.co.uk. Ch M/80, when vessel expected. Access via lock (width 7·6m) HW±5; Locking £5 each way; H24 security, AB £12/yacht, Showers, 🚽, ♒, Gas, P & D (by arrangement), ME. 2 x ☆s 2FG (vert) on river pier. 8m depth in basin. DLR from N Woolwich to central London, until 0030. Woolwich ferry & foot tunnel 15 mins walk. ✈ (City) is adjacent.

POPLAR DOCK MARINA, 51°30'·07N 00°00'·50W (lock ent). AC 484, 3337. Tides: India & Millwall Docks ent. 4·5M below Tower Bridge. Canary Wharf twr (244m) is conspic 4ca W of marina. Lock (200m x 24m) opens 0700-1700LT at HW for outbound and HW-1 to HW+1 for arrivals, foc, but OT £20. Least width 12·1m into marina. **Marina** ☎ 020 7308 9930. VHF Ch 13 (H24). **Facilities:** Slip, Bar, R, 🚿, ♒, ⊘, 🅿; Dr ☎ 020 7237 1078; 🅗 ☎ 020 7955 5000; Police ☎ 252 2836. ≋, Blackwall DLR, Canary Wharf Tube, ✈ City.

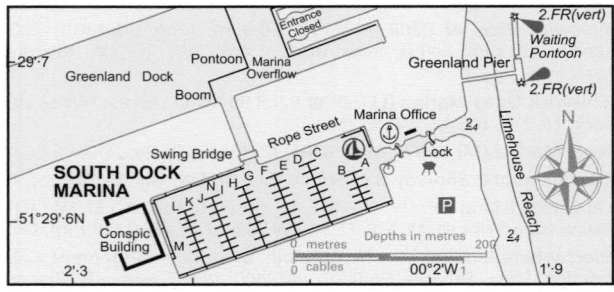

SOUTH DOCK MARINA (B), 51°29'·65N 00°01'·97W. AC 2484, 3337. Tides as for Surrey Dock Greenland Ent. 1·1M above Greenwich, 2·5M below Tower Bridge. Baltic Quay building at SW end of marina is conspic with five arched rooftops. Waiting pontoon at Greenland Pier. Approx access via lock (width 6·4m)

HW-2½ to HW+1½ for 2m draft. **Marina** ☎ 020 7252 2244, (250 + ♥, £15 <15m, £20 >15.5m). VHF Ch **M** 80. **Facilities:** ME, ✗, El, CH, C (20 ton), Bar, R, 🚿, ⊘, ♒, Dr ☎ 237 1078; 🅗 ♒ ☎ 020 7955 5000; Police ☎ 020 7252 2836. ≋, Surrey Quays and Canada Water tube, ✈ City Airport.

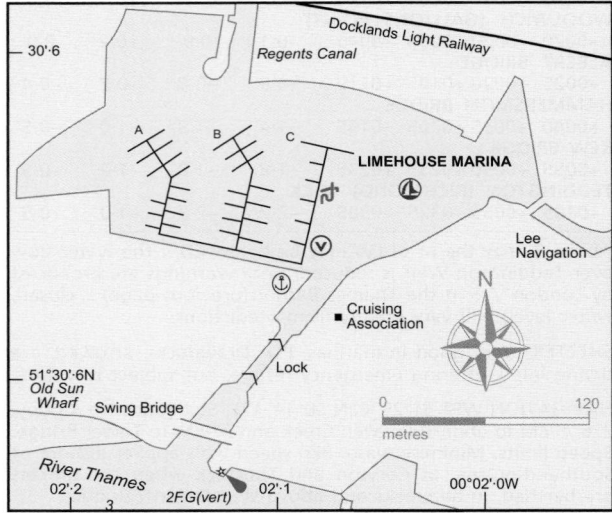

LIMEHOUSE MARINA (C), 51°30'·57N 00°02'·27W. Entry HW±3 via swing bridge/lock (width 8m), 0800-1800LT daily Apr-Sep; 0800-1600 Oct-Mar; other times by prior arrangement (24hrs notice) to BW Lock control ☎ 0207 3089930, beware cross-tide at lock cut, mid flood/ebb. **Marina** ☎ 0207 3089930, www.bwml.co.uk. Waiting pontoon in lock entrance is accessible outside LW±2. Call VHF Ch 80 *Limehouse Marina*. **Facilities:** (90 berths, from £25/craft ♥) H24 security, ♒, ⚓, ♒, ⊘, Bar, ≋, DLR; also entry to Regents Canal and Lee Navigation.

ST KATHARINE HAVEN, (D) 51°30'·36N 00°04'·35W. AC 3337, 3319. HW +0245 on Dover. Tides as London Bridge. Beware of cross tide at mid-flood/ebb. Good shelter under all conditions. Tower Bridge and the Tower of London are uniquely conspic, close up-river. Six Y waiting buoys are close downstream of ent in 0.1–1.9m. Or berth on inshore side of St Katharine Pier, 30m upriver of ent, but limited berthing/shore access, only suitable for shoal draft. Pleasure launches berth on S side of pier.
St Katharine Haven Ch 80 M. Lock (41m x 12·5m with 2 small lifting bridges), access HW –2 to HW +1½, season 0600-2030, winter 0800-1800LT; other times by prior arrangement. R/G tfc lts at ent. Lock is shut Tues and Wed, Nov to Feb.
Facilities: (100 + 50 ♥, usually in Centre Basin or East Dock; give 1 week's notice in season) ☎ 0207 2645312, www.skdocks.co.uk; £25·80/yacht, ✗, ♒, @, Wi-fi, YC, Bar, R, 🚿, ⊖, ⊘. **Fuel Barge (E)** is 400m downstream of lock ent. ☎ 0207 4811774; VHF Ch 14 *Heiko*. D & Gas, Mon-Fri 0630-1430. W/ends Apr-Oct, HW±2, not open before 0600 & not after 1800.

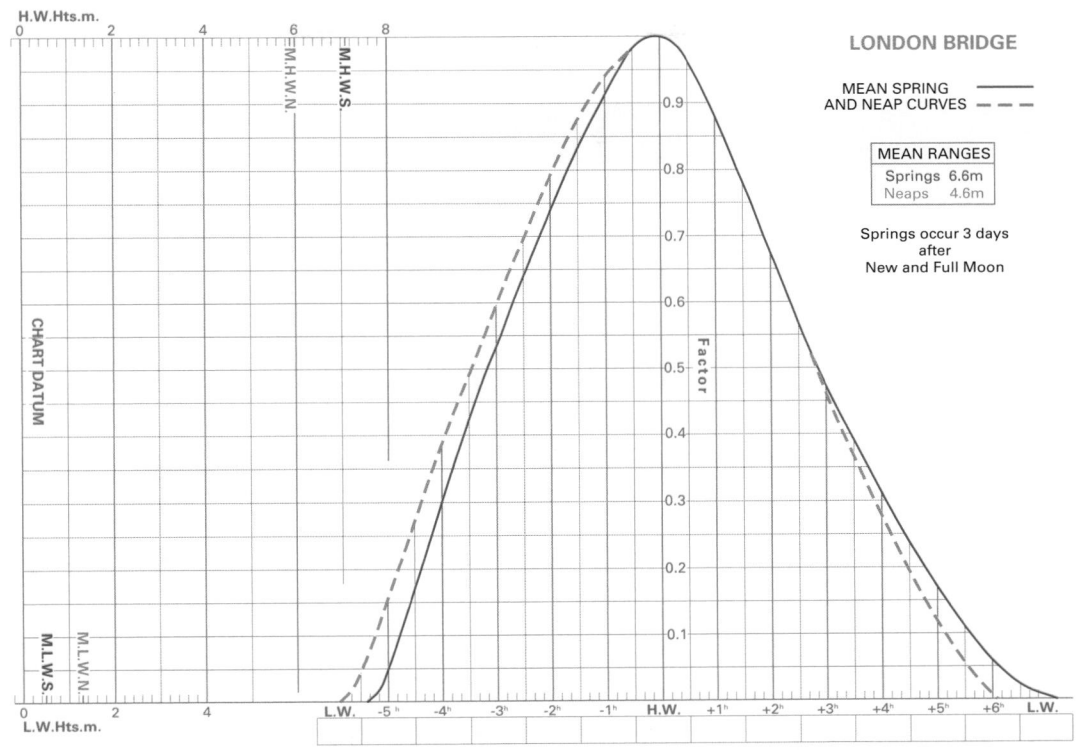

LONDON BRIDGE

MEAN SPRING ——————
AND NEAP CURVES – – – – –

MEAN RANGES
Springs 6.6m
Neaps 4.6m

Springs occur 3 days
after
New and Full Moon

BRENTFORD DOCK
MARINA

CHELSEA HARBOUR, (I) London, **51°28´·48N 00°10´·82W.** AC 3319. Tides: see Albert Bridge. Good shelter in all conditions, 5M above Tower Bridge, reached via 14 fixed bridges. Battersea railway bridge is 120m upstream. Belvedere Tower (80m high with tide ball) is conspic, next to the lock and bascule bridge. Max sizes for lock: LOA 24m, beam 5·5m, draft 1·8m. Lock opens when 2·5m water above sill; tide gauge outside, access HW np ±30mins/HW sp±1½, R/G tfc lts. Limited waiting berths and shore access on Chelsea Hbr Pier (1·7m) close upriver. **Marina,** 50+10 ⓥ £15.00. ☎ 0207 225 9100, mobile ☎ 07770 542783. VHF Ch 80. Bar, R, Ⓑ, ▫, showers, ⚿, ♿, ⚓, 🛒.

BRENTFORD DOCK MARINA (N). **51°28´·92N 00°18´·05W,** 1100m beyond Kew bridge. AC 3319. Tides, see Kew Bridge. 60 AB inc ⓥ, £18·94 for all LOA. ☎ 020 8232 8941, mobile 07970 143 987. No VHF. Access HW±2½ via lock 4·8m x 9·8m (longer LOA during freeflow); 15m waiting pontoon. **Facilities:** El, ME, Bar, R, ⚿, ✕; Gunnersbury & Ealing tubes. Ent to Grand Union Canal via lock is nearby: M, AB.

TIME ZONE (UT)
For Summer Time add ONE hour in **non-shaded areas**

LONDON BRIDGE LAT 51°30'N LONG 0°05'W
TIMES AND HEIGHTS OF HIGH AND LOW WATERS

Dates in red are SPRINGS
Dates in blue are NEAPS

YEAR **2010**

JANUARY

Time	m		Time	m
1 0141	6.7		**16** 0222	6.5
0827	0.6		0859	0.8
F 1400	7.1		SA 1444	6.6
2041	1.0		2101	1.2
2 0231	6.8		**17** 0256	6.6
0925	0.4		0933	0.8
SA 1451	7.3		SU 1518	6.7
2133	0.9		2136	1.1
3 0317	6.9		**18** 0328	6.6
1017	0.2		1006	0.8
SU 1540	7.3		M 1549	6.6
2220	0.8		2208	1.1
4 0402	7.0		**19** 0358	6.6
1102	0.1		1036	0.7
M 1629	7.3		TU 1618	6.6
2303	0.8		2238	1.1
5 0447	7.0		**20** 0427	6.6
1143	0.1		1102	0.8
TU 1717	7.2		W 1647	6.6
2343	0.9		2307	1.2
6 0532	6.9		**21** 0457	6.5
1221	0.2		1122	0.9
W 1806	6.9		TH 1719	6.4
			2333	1.3
7 0024	1.0		**22** 0529	6.4
0619	6.7		1144	0.9
TH 1301	0.4		F 1755	6.3
◗ 1857	6.6			
8 0107	1.2		**23** 0003	1.3
0712	6.5		0607	6.3
F 1344	0.7		SA 1217	0.9
1950	6.4		◑ 1837	6.1
9 0157	1.4		**24** 0041	1.4
0812	6.3		0654	6.1
SA 1434	1.0		SU 1259	1.1
2051	6.1		1931	5.8
10 0302	1.6		**25** 0132	1.6
0920	6.1		0754	5.9
SU 1533	1.3		M 1354	1.3
2203	5.9		2044	5.7
11 0421	1.6		**26** 0240	1.7
1029	6.0		0924	5.9
M 1645	1.4		TU 1524	1.5
2314	5.9		2207	5.8
12 0533	1.4		**27** 0444	1.5
1136	6.1		1044	6.2
TU 1756	1.4		W 1705	1.4
			2326	6.1
13 0013	6.0		**28** 0559	1.1
0637	1.2		1152	6.6
W 1236	6.3		TH 1821	1.2
1853	1.3			
14 0104	6.2		**29** 0033	6.4
0733	1.0		0711	0.8
TH 1325	6.5		F 1255	6.9
1941	1.2		1934	1.0
15 0146	6.4		**30** 0129	6.7
0820	0.9		0823	0.4
F 1407	6.6		SA 1350	7.2
● 2023	1.2		○ 2037	0.9
			31 0218	7.0
			0920	0.1
			SU 1441	7.4
			2129	0.8

FEBRUARY

Time	m		Time	m
1 0303	7.1		**16** 0306	6.8
1007	-0.1		0945	0.7
M 1528	7.5		TU 1524	6.8
2214	0.7		2152	1.0
2 0347	7.3		**17** 0336	6.8
1049	-0.1		1015	0.6
TU 1613	7.4		W 1552	6.8
2254	0.7		2223	1.0
3 0428	7.3		**18** 0404	6.8
1125	0.0		1042	0.6
W 1657	7.2		TH 1620	6.7
2329	0.7		2251	1.0
4 0509	7.2		**19** 0432	6.8
1157	0.2		1059	0.7
TH 1739	6.9		F 1650	6.6
			2315	1.1
5 0002	0.9		**20** 0504	6.7
0551	6.9		1118	0.8
F 1228	0.5		SA 1724	6.4
◗ 1821	6.4		2340	1.2
6 0036	1.1		**21** 0541	6.5
0636	6.6		1147	0.9
SA 1301	0.8		SU 1804	6.1
1906	6.2			
7 0113	1.3		**22** 0014	1.3
0728	6.3		0624	6.3
SU 1343	1.2		M 1226	1.0
1956	5.9		◑ 1853	5.9
8 0202	1.6		**23** 0102	1.4
0835	5.9		0722	6.1
M 1440	1.4		TU 1319	1.3
2104	5.6		2005	5.6
9 0324	1.8		**24** 0207	1.6
0952	5.7		0851	5.9
TU 1558	1.8		W 1452	1.7
2239	5.6		2134	5.6
10 0459	1.6		**25** 0415	1.5
1112	5.8		1020	6.1
W 1729	1.6		TH 1643	1.5
2351	5.8		2305	6.0
11 0615	1.3		**26** 0543	1.1
1221	6.2		1136	6.5
TH 1832	1.4		F 1811	1.2
12 0044	6.2		**27** 0017	6.4
0714	1.0		0704	0.6
F 1311	6.5		SA 1243	6.9
1921	1.4		1924	1.0
13 0127	6.4		**28** 0112	6.8
0759	0.8		0811	0.2
SA 1350	6.6		SU 1337	7.2
2005	1.1		○ 2024	0.8
14 0203	6.6			
0838	0.6			
SU 1424	6.7			
● 2044	1.1			
15 0235	6.7			
0913	0.7			
M 1455	6.7			
2119	1.1			

MARCH

Time	m		Time	m
1 0159	7.1		**16** 0207	6.7
0902	0.0		0843	0.7
M 1424	7.4		TU 1426	6.7
2113	0.7		2055	1.0
2 0242	7.3		**17** 0238	6.9
0947	-0.1		0917	0.6
TU 1508	7.4		W 1455	6.8
2156	0.6		2130	0.9
3 0323	7.4		**18** 0308	6.9
1025	-0.1		0947	0.6
W 1550	7.4		TH 1524	6.8
2234	0.6		2203	0.8
4 0403	7.4		**19** 0338	7.0
1058	0.1		1014	0.6
TH 1630	7.4		F 1554	6.8
2307	0.7		2233	0.9
5 0443	7.3		**20** 0409	6.9
1125	0.4		1036	0.7
F 1708	6.9		SA 1626	6.6
2335	0.8		2300	1.0
6 0522	7.0		**21** 0443	6.8
1150	0.7		1057	0.8
SA 1744	6.5		SU 1700	6.4
			2325	1.1
7 0002	1.0		**22** 0521	6.7
0602	6.6		1126	1.0
SU 1220	1.0		M 1741	6.2
◗ 1822	6.1		2359	1.1
8 0034	1.2		**23** 0607	6.4
0650	6.2		1206	1.2
M 1258	1.4		TU 1833	5.9
1908	5.8		◑	
9 0118	1.5		**24** 0046	1.2
0754	5.8		0708	6.1
TU 1355	1.8		W 1305	1.5
2010	5.5		1944	5.7
10 0228	1.8		**25** 0154	1.5
0915	5.6		0837	6.0
W 1516	2.0		TH 1443	1.7
2152	5.4		2112	5.7
11 0419	1.7		**26** 0358	1.4
1042	5.7		1002	6.2
TH 1659	1.8		F 1630	1.6
2317	5.7		2245	6.0
12 0541	1.3		**27** 0530	0.9
1155	6.1		1121	6.6
F 1803	1.4		SA 1756	1.2
			2355	6.5
13 0014	6.1		**28** 0647	0.5
0641	1.0		1225	7.0
SA 1244	6.4		SU 1904	0.9
1854	1.2			
14 0058	6.4		**29** 0049	6.9
0728	0.8		0748	0.2
SU 1323	6.6		M 1317	7.2
1939	1.1		2001	0.8
15 0134	6.6		**30** 0135	7.1
0808	0.8		0837	0.0
M 1356	6.7		TU 1402	7.3
● 2019	1.1		○ 2050	0.8
			31 0217	7.3
			0919	0.1
			W 1443	7.3
			2132	0.6

APRIL

Time	m		Time	m
1 0257	7.4		**16** 0240	7.0
0955	0.2		0916	0.7
TH 1523	7.2		F 1459	6.8
2210	0.6		2141	0.8
2 0337	7.4		**17** 0314	7.0
1024	0.4		0947	0.7
F 1601	7.1		SA 1533	6.7
2241	0.7		2215	0.7
3 0417	7.3		**18** 0350	7.0
1050	0.6		1016	0.8
SA 1637	6.8		SU 1608	6.6
2307	0.8		2247	0.8
4 0455	6.9		**19** 0428	6.9
1115	0.9		1046	0.9
SU 1712	6.4		M 1646	6.4
2332	1.0		2318	0.9
5 0535	6.5		**20** 0510	6.7
1144	1.2		1122	1.1
M 1748	6.1		TU 1730	6.2
			2356	0.9
6 0003	1.2		**21** 0601	6.5
0620	6.1		1209	1.3
TU 1223	1.5		W 1825	6.0
◗ 1832	5.8		●	
7 0045	1.4		**22** 0045	1.1
0719	5.7		0708	6.3
W 1317	1.8		TH 1314	1.5
1931	5.5		1935	5.9
8 0146	1.7		**23** 0155	1.2
0836	5.5		0827	6.2
TH 1432	2.0		F 1434	1.6
2056	5.4		2056	5.9
9 0328	1.7		**24** 0344	1.1
0955	5.6		0945	6.4
F 1609	1.9		SA 1613	1.5
2227	5.6		2221	6.2
10 0448	1.4		**25** 0506	0.8
1111	6.0		1101	6.6
SA 1722	1.5		SU 1731	1.1
2330	6.0		2329	6.6
11 0550	1.1		**26** 0617	0.5
1204	6.3		1203	6.9
SU 1816	1.3		M 1835	0.9
12 0018	6.4		**27** 0023	6.9
0642	0.9		0716	0.4
M 1246	6.5		TU 1254	7.0
1903	1.1		1932	0.8
13 0058	6.6		**28** 0109	7.4
0728	0.8		0805	0.4
TU 1320	6.6		W 1338	7.0
1946	1.0		○ 2022	0.7
14 0133	6.8		**29** 0152	7.2
0807	0.8		0846	0.5
W 1353	6.7		TH 1419	7.0
● 2026	0.9		2106	0.6
15 0207	6.9		**30** 0233	7.3
0843	0.7		0921	0.6
TH 1426	6.8		F 1459	7.0
2104	0.8		2144	0.6

Chart Datum: 2·90 metres below Ordnance Datum (Newlyn). HAT is 7·6 metres above Chart Datum; see 4.5

FREE monthly updates from
www.reedsalmanac.co.uk

TIME ZONE (UT)
For Summer Time add ONE hour in **non-shaded areas**

LONDON BRIDGE   LAT 51°30'N   LONG 0°05'W
TIMES AND HEIGHTS OF HIGH AND LOW WATERS

Dates in red are **SPRINGS**
Dates in blue are **NEAPS**

YEAR 2010

MAY

Time	m		Time	m
1 0314	7.3		**16** 0256	7.1
0951	0.7		0927	0.8
SA 1537	6.9		SU 1520	6.7
2216	0.7		2201	0.6
2 0355	7.1		**17** 0337	7.1
1019	0.9		1005	0.9
SU 1612	6.7		M 1600	6.6
2243	0.8		2239	0.6
3 0434	6.8		**18** 0420	7.0
1047	1.1		1045	0.9
M 1647	6.4		TU 1642	6.5
2310	1.0		2318	0.6
4 0514	6.4		**19** 0508	6.9
1119	1.3		1128	1.1
TU 1722	6.1		W 1729	6.4
2341	1.1			
5 0556	6.1		**20** 0000	0.7
1156	1.5		0602	6.7
W 1805	5.9		TH 1218	1.2
			◖ 1823	6.3
6 0019	1.3		**21** 0052	0.8
0649	5.8		0706	6.5
TH 1245	1.8		F 1314	1.3
◗ 1859	5.7		1926	6.2
7 0112	1.5		**22** 0201	0.9
0753	5.6		0814	6.5
F 1347	1.9		SA 1423	1.4
2008	5.6		2039	6.2
8 0233	1.6		**23** 0320	0.8
0900	5.7		0924	6.5
SA 1503	1.9		SU 1546	1.4
2128	5.6		2154	6.4
9 0349	1.4		**24** 0430	0.7
1008	5.8		1035	6.6
SU 1621	1.7		M 1700	1.2
2237	5.9		2259	6.6
10 0450	1.2		**25** 0538	0.7
1110	6.1		1137	6.7
M 1724	1.4		TU 1804	1.1
2331	6.2		2356	6.7
11 0545	1.1		**26** 0640	0.7
1159	6.3		1230	6.7
TU 1818	1.2		W 1903	0.9
12 0017	6.5		**27** 0046	6.8
0637	1.0		0730	0.8
W 1242	6.5		TH 1317	6.7
1908	1.1		○ 1955	0.8
13 0058	6.7		**28** 0132	6.9
0725	0.9		0813	0.8
TH 1322	6.6		F 1400	6.7
1955	0.9		2042	0.7
14 0137	6.9		**29** 0215	7.0
0809	0.9		0850	0.9
F 1401	6.7		SA 1440	6.7
● 2039	0.8		2123	0.7
15 0216	7.0		**30** 0258	7.0
0849	0.8		0925	0.9
SA 1440	6.7		SU 1518	6.7
2121	0.7		2158	0.7
			31 0340	6.9
			0957	1.0
			M 1555	6.6
			2228	0.8

JUNE

Time	m		Time	m
1 0419	6.7		**16** 0417	7.2
1030	1.1		1047	0.8
TU 1629	6.4		W 1639	6.8
2257	0.9		2328	0.3
2 0457	6.5		**17** 0506	7.1
1103	1.3		1131	0.9
W 1704	6.3		TH 1725	6.7
2328	1.0			
3 0536	6.2		**18** 0011	0.3
1138	1.4		0558	7.0
TH 1743	6.1		F 1217	1.0
			1815	6.6
4 0002	1.1		**19** 0057	0.4
0618	6.0		0654	6.8
F 1219	1.5		SA 1306	1.1
◗ 1827	6.0		◖ 1911	6.6
5 0042	1.2		**20** 0148	0.6
0709	5.9		0752	6.6
SA 1305	1.7		SU 1403	1.3
1921	5.8		2014	6.5
6 0132	1.3		**21** 0246	0.7
0805	5.8		0856	6.5
SU 1401	1.8		M 1512	1.4
2026	5.7		2122	6.4
7 0241	1.4		**22** 0347	0.9
0906	5.8		1004	6.3
M 1510	1.8		TU 1625	1.3
2138	5.8		2228	6.4
8 0350	1.4		**23** 0454	1.0
1009	5.9		1110	6.3
TU 1628	1.6		W 1733	1.2
2241	6.1		2330	6.5
9 0451	1.2		**24** 0601	1.1
1110	6.1		1209	6.4
W 1734	1.3		TH 1836	1.0
2335	6.4			
10 0550	1.1		**25** 0027	6.5
1205	6.4		0658	1.1
TH 1831	1.1		F 1306	6.4
			1934	0.9
11 0025	6.6		**26** 0119	6.7
0645	1.0		0746	1.1
F 1255	6.6		SA 1346	6.5
1925	0.9		○ 2024	0.8
12 0112	6.9		**27** 0205	6.8
0739	1.0		0829	1.1
SA 1341	6.7		SU 1427	6.6
● 2018	0.7		2108	0.7
13 0158	7.0		**28** 0248	6.8
0829	0.9		0907	1.1
SU 1427	6.7		M 1504	6.6
2109	0.6		2145	0.7
14 0244	7.1		**29** 0327	6.8
0916	0.9		0943	1.1
M 1511	6.8		TU 1540	6.6
2158	0.4		2217	0.8
15 0330	7.2		**30** 0404	6.7
1002	0.8		1017	1.1
TU 1555	6.8		W 1614	6.6
2244	0.3		2248	0.8

JULY

Time	m		Time	m
1 0438	6.6		**16** 0455	7.3
1050	1.2		1128	0.7
TH 1646	6.5		F 1711	7.1
2317	0.8			
2 0511	6.4		**17** 0004	0.0
1122	1.2		0542	7.1
F 1719	6.4		SA 1208	0.8
2345	0.9		1756	6.9
3 0546	6.3		**18** 0041	0.2
1154	1.3		0631	6.8
SA 1754	6.3		SU 1249	1.0
			◖ 1845	6.8
4 0010	1.0		**19** 0120	0.5
0624	6.1		0722	6.5
SU 1227	1.5		M 1334	1.2
◗ 1834	6.1		1942	6.5
5 0042	1.1		**20** 0206	0.8
0709	5.9		0820	6.2
M 1307	1.6		TU 1431	1.4
1923	5.9		2047	6.3
6 0123	1.2		**21** 0302	1.2
0805	5.8		0928	6.0
TU 1358	1.7		W 1546	1.5
2028	5.8		2156	6.2
7 0222	1.4		**22** 0411	1.4
0912	5.8		1042	6.0
W 1513	1.7		TH 1703	1.4
2149	5.9		2307	6.2
8 0353	1.4		**23** 0529	1.4
1024	5.9		1149	6.1
TH 1653	1.5		F 1815	1.1
2256	6.2			
9 0509	1.3		**24** 0014	6.4
1132	6.2		0634	1.3
F 1759	1.1		SA 1246	6.3
2355	6.6		1918	0.9
10 0614	1.1		**25** 0110	6.6
1232	6.5		0727	1.2
SA 1900	0.8		SU 1333	6.5
			2010	0.7
11 0051	6.9		**26** 0155	6.7
0717	1.0		0812	1.1
SU 1325	6.7		M 1412	6.6
● 2004	0.6		○ 2052	0.7
12 0143	7.1		**27** 0234	6.8
0819	0.9		0852	1.1
M 1414	6.8		TU 1448	6.7
2104	0.4		2128	0.7
13 0233	7.3		**28** 0310	6.8
0914	0.9		0928	1.1
TU 1500	7.0		W 1521	6.7
2157	0.1		2200	0.7
14 0321	7.4		**29** 0343	6.8
1003	0.7		1001	1.0
W 1544	7.1		TH 1552	6.8
2243	0.0		2230	0.7
15 0408	7.4		**30** 0413	6.6
1047	0.7		1033	1.0
TH 1627	7.1		F 1623	6.7
2325	-0.1		2258	0.7
			31 0442	6.6
			1103	1.2
			SA 1651	6.6
			2321	0.8

AUGUST

Time	m		Time	m
1 0510	6.5		**16** 0012	0.4
1130	1.2		0600	6.7
SU 1721	6.5		M 1224	0.9
2338	0.9		◗ 1814	6.8
2 0542	6.3		**17** 0045	0.7
1155	1.3		0645	6.4
M 1755	6.3		TU 1301	1.2
			1906	6.5
3 0002	1.0		**18** 0125	1.1
0619	6.0		0737	6.0
TU 1227	1.4		W 1348	1.4
1836	6.1		2011	6.1
4 0038	1.1		**19** 0219	1.5
0707	5.8		0844	5.7
W 1311	1.5		TH 1502	1.6
1931	5.9		2126	5.9
5 0128	1.3		**20** 0332	1.7
0816	5.6		1012	5.7
TH 1412	1.7		F 1635	1.5
2055	5.8		2245	6.0
6 0246	1.6		**21** 0506	1.6
0940	5.7		1128	5.9
F 1611	1.6		SA 1757	1.2
2220	6.1			
7 0433	1.5		**22** 0001	6.3
1102	6.0		0614	1.3
SA 1732	1.1		SU 1227	6.3
2329	6.5		1900	0.9
8 0551	1.2		**23** 0055	6.6
1211	6.4		0706	1.1
SU 1842	0.8		M 1313	6.5
			1948	0.7
9 0033	6.9		**24** 0137	6.8
0704	1.0		0752	1.1
M 1307	6.7		TU 1351	6.7
1955	0.4		○ 2028	0.6
10 0129	7.2		**25** 0213	6.8
0811	0.9		0831	1.0
TU 1357	7.0		W 1424	6.8
● 2055	0.1		2102	0.6
11 0219	7.4		**26** 0245	6.8
0906	0.8		0907	1.0
W 1442	7.2		TH 1455	6.8
2144	-0.1		2133	0.6
12 0305	7.5		**27** 0314	6.8
0953	0.6		0940	1.0
TH 1525	7.3		F 1525	6.9
2228	-0.2		2203	0.6
13 0350	7.5		**28** 0342	6.8
1036	0.6		1012	0.9
F 1606	7.4		SA 1554	6.9
2307	-0.2		2230	0.6
14 0434	7.3		**29** 0409	6.7
1114	0.6		1041	1.0
SA 1647	7.3		SU 1621	6.8
2341	0.1		2251	0.8
15 0517	7.1		**30** 0437	6.6
1149	0.7		1107	1.1
SU 1729	7.1		M 1650	6.6
			2307	0.9
			31 0507	6.4
			1129	1.2
			TU 1724	6.5
			2329	1.0

E England

Chart Datum: 2·90 metres below Ordnance Datum (Newlyn). HAT is 7·6 metres above Chart Datum; see 4.5

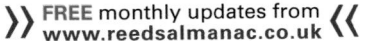

TIME ZONE (UT)
For Summer Time add ONE hour in **non-shaded areas**

LONDON BRIDGE LAT 51°30′N LONG 0°05′W
TIMES AND HEIGHTS OF HIGH AND LOW WATERS

Dates in red are SPRINGS
Dates in blue are NEAPS

YEAR 2010

SEPTEMBER

Time	m	Time	m
1 W 0542 / 1157 / 1805 ◐	6.1 / 1.3 / 6.3	**16** TH 0046 / 0653 / 1310 / 1937	1.4 / 5.8 / 1.4 / 5.9
2 TH 0003 / 0627 / 1239 / 1856	1.1 / 5.9 / 1.4 / 6.1	**17** F 0139 / 0756 / 1418 / 2054	1.7 / 5.5 / 1.7 / 5.7
3 F 0051 / 0732 / 1337 / 2015	1.4 / 5.6 / 1.5 / 5.9	**18** SA 0254 / 0932 / 1603 / 2218	2.0 / 5.5 / 1.6 / 5.8
4 SA 0208 / 0900 / 1526 / 2149	1.7 / 5.6 / 1.6 / 6.0	**19** SU 0439 / 1056 / 1728 / 2335	1.8 / 5.8 / 1.2 / 6.2
5 SU 0405 / 1033 / 1711 / 2307	1.6 / 5.9 / 1.1 / 6.5	**20** M 0547 / 1156 / 1828	1.4 / 6.2 / 0.9
6 M 0535 / 1148 / 1827	1.3 / 6.4 / 0.7	**21** TU 0028 / 0638 / 1243 / 1914	6.6 / 1.1 / 6.5 / 0.7
7 TU 0014 / 0649 / 1245 / 1938	6.9 / 1.0 / 6.8 / 0.3	**22** W 0109 / 0723 / 1321 / 1954	6.7 / 1.0 / 6.7 / 0.7
8 W 0110 / 0754 / 1333 / 2035 ●	7.2 / 0.8 / 7.1 / 0.0	**23** TH 0143 / 0804 / 1353 / 2029 ○	6.8 / 1.0 / 6.8 / 0.7
9 TH 0158 / 0848 / 1417 / 2122	7.4 / 0.7 / 7.3 / -0.1	**24** F 0213 / 0840 / 1424 / 2101	6.8 / 1.0 / 6.9 / 0.7
10 F 0243 / 0934 / 1459 / 2204	7.5 / 0.6 / 7.5 / -0.1	**25** SA 0242 / 0914 / 1454 / 2131	6.8 / 0.9 / 6.9 / 0.7
11 SA 0326 / 1016 / 1540 / 2240	7.4 / 0.5 / 7.5 / 0.0	**26** SU 0310 / 0947 / 1523 / 2158	6.8 / 0.8 / 6.9 / 0.7
12 SU 0407 / 1052 / 1621 / 2311	7.3 / 0.6 / 7.4 / 0.3	**27** M 0339 / 1018 / 1553 / 2220	6.8 / 0.9 / 6.9 / 0.8
13 M 0447 / 1125 / 1702 / 2339	7.0 / 0.7 / 7.1 / 0.7	**28** TU 0408 / 1045 / 1625 / 2240	6.6 / 1.0 / 6.8 / 0.9
14 TU 0526 / 1155 / 1744	6.6 / 0.9 / 6.8	**29** W 0440 / 1109 / 1701 / 2305	6.4 / 1.1 / 6.6 / 1.1
15 W 0008 / 0606 / 1227 / 1832 ◑	1.0 / 6.2 / 1.2 / 6.3	**30** TH 0516 / 1138 / 1743 / 2340	6.2 / 1.2 / 6.4 / 1.2

OCTOBER

Time	m	Time	m
1 F 0602 / 1220 / 1837 ◐	5.9 / 1.2 / 6.2	**16** SA 0104 / 0714 / 1338 / 2016	1.9 / 5.5 / 1.6 / 5.6
2 SA 0030 / 0706 / 1318 / 1956	1.5 / 5.7 / 1.4 / 6.0	**17** SU 0212 / 0837 / 1512 / 2134	2.1 / 5.4 / 1.7 / 5.7
3 SU 0155 / 0830 / 1501 / 2124	1.8 / 5.6 / 1.5 / 6.1	**18** M 0347 / 1007 / 1635 / 2253	2.0 / 5.6 / 1.4 / 6.0
4 M 0341 / 1004 / 1650 / 2243	1.7 / 5.9 / 1.4 / 6.5	**19** TU 0506 / 1113 / 1737 / 2350	1.6 / 6.0 / 1.1 / 6.3
5 TU 0516 / 1120 / 1805 / 2351	1.3 / 6.4 / 0.6 / 6.9	**20** W 0600 / 1202 / 1828	1.3 / 6.3 / 0.9
6 W 0626 / 1217 / 1913	1.0 / 6.8 / 0.3	**21** TH 0032 / 0647 / 1243 / 1911	6.5 / 1.1 / 6.6 / 0.8
7 TH 0046 / 0728 / 1306 / 2008 ●	7.2 / 0.8 / 7.1 / 0.1	**22** F 0108 / 0730 / 1318 / 1950	6.6 / 1.0 / 6.7 / 0.8
8 F 0134 / 0822 / 1350 / 2054	7.3 / 0.7 / 7.3 / 0.1	**23** SA 0139 / 0809 / 1351 / 2025 ○	6.7 / 0.9 / 6.8 / 0.8
9 SA 0218 / 0910 / 1432 / 2134	7.3 / 0.6 / 7.4 / 0.2	**24** SU 0210 / 0846 / 1423 / 2057	6.8 / 0.9 / 6.9 / 0.8
10 SU 0300 / 0951 / 1514 / 2209	7.3 / 0.6 / 7.5 / 0.4	**25** M 0242 / 0922 / 1456 / 2127	6.8 / 0.8 / 7.0 / 0.8
11 M 0340 / 1028 / 1556 / 2238	7.1 / 0.6 / 7.3 / 0.7	**26** TU 0314 / 0956 / 1530 / 2155	6.7 / 0.8 / 6.9 / 0.9
12 TU 0419 / 1059 / 1637 / 2305	6.8 / 0.7 / 7.0 / 0.9	**27** W 0347 / 1027 / 1606 / 2224	6.6 / 0.8 / 6.9 / 1.0
13 W 0456 / 1127 / 1719 / 2335	6.5 / 0.9 / 6.6 / 1.2	**28** TH 0422 / 1101 / 1646 / 2256	6.4 / 0.9 / 6.8 / 1.1
14 TH 0533 / 1158 / 1806 ◑	6.1 / 1.2 / 6.2	**29** F 0501 / 1131 / 1732 / 2337	6.3 / 1.0 / 6.6 / 1.3
15 F 0013 / 0616 / 1238 / 1904	1.5 / 5.8 / 1.4 / 5.8	**30** SA 0550 / 1215 / 1830 ◐	6.1 / 1.1 / 6.3
		31 SU 0033 / 0653 / 1313 / 1944	1.5 / 5.9 / 1.2 / 6.2

NOVEMBER

Time	m	Time	m
1 M 0149 / 0808 / 1449 / 2102	1.7 / 5.9 / 1.2 / 6.3	**16** TU 0238 / 0902 / 1529 / 2144	2.0 / 5.5 / 1.5 / 5.7
2 TU 0318 / 0934 / 1622 / 2217	1.6 / 6.1 / 0.9 / 6.5	**17** W 0400 / 1014 / 1631 / 2251	1.9 / 5.8 / 1.3 / 5.9
3 W 0449 / 1049 / 1733 / 2325	1.4 / 6.4 / 0.6 / 6.9	**18** TH 0507 / 1112 / 1727 / 2344	1.6 / 6.1 / 1.2 / 6.2
4 TH 0558 / 1148 / 1840	1.1 / 6.7 / 0.5	**19** F 0601 / 1159 / 1819	1.3 / 6.3 / 1.1
5 F 0021 / 0659 / 1239 / 1935	6.9 / 0.9 / 7.0 / 0.4	**20** SA 0026 / 0650 / 1241 / 1906	6.4 / 1.1 / 6.6 / 1.0
6 SA 0110 / 0755 / 1325 / 2022 ●	7.0 / 0.8 / 7.1 / 0.5	**21** SU 0105 / 0736 / 1320 / 1948 ○	6.6 / 1.0 / 6.7 / 1.0
7 SU 0154 / 0844 / 1409 / 2103	7.0 / 0.7 / 7.2 / 0.6	**22** M 0143 / 0819 / 1358 / 2027	6.7 / 0.9 / 6.9 / 1.0
8 M 0237 / 0927 / 1453 / 2137	7.0 / 0.6 / 7.3 / 0.7	**23** TU 0221 / 0900 / 1436 / 2104	6.7 / 0.8 / 6.9 / 1.0
9 TU 0318 / 1005 / 1536 / 2208	6.9 / 0.6 / 7.2 / 0.9	**24** W 0259 / 0940 / 1515 / 2140	6.7 / 0.7 / 7.0 / 1.0
10 W 0357 / 1037 / 1619 / 2238	6.7 / 0.8 / 6.9 / 1.1	**25** TH 0336 / 1018 / 1556 / 2218	6.6 / 0.7 / 7.0 / 1.0
11 TH 0433 / 1106 / 1700 / 2310	6.4 / 0.9 / 6.5 / 1.3	**26** F 0415 / 1055 / 1639 / 2300	6.5 / 0.7 / 6.9 / 1.1
12 F 0509 / 1136 / 1743 / 2347	6.2 / 1.1 / 6.2 / 1.6	**27** SA 0457 / 1133 / 1728 / 2345	6.4 / 0.7 / 6.7 / 1.2
13 SA 0549 / 1213 / 1833 ◑	5.9 / 1.3 / 5.9	**28** SU 0545 / 1218 / 1825 ◑	6.3 / 0.8 / 6.6
14 SU 0031 / 0638 / 1303 / 1932	1.8 / 5.7 / 1.5 / 5.7	**29** M 0037 / 0642 / 1314 / 1929	1.4 / 6.2 / 0.9 / 6.4
15 M 0128 / 0743 / 1414 / 2036	2.0 / 5.5 / 1.6 / 5.6	**30** TU 0137 / 0748 / 1431 / 2038	1.5 / 6.1 / 1.0 / 6.4

DECEMBER

Time	m	Time	m
1 W 0252 / 0904 / 1546 / 2149	1.6 / 6.2 / 0.9 / 6.4	**16** TH 0235 / 0907 / 1523 / 2139	2.0 / 5.6 / 1.5 / 5.7
2 TH 0418 / 1018 / 1655 / 2258	1.5 / 6.3 / 0.9 / 6.5	**17** F 0400 / 1016 / 1628 / 2245	1.9 / 5.8 / 1.5 / 5.9
3 F 0528 / 1120 / 1803 / 2358	1.2 / 6.5 / 0.8 / 6.6	**18** SA 0512 / 1114 / 1728 / 2344	1.6 / 6.1 / 1.3 / 6.2
4 SA 0632 / 1216 / 1902	1.0 / 6.7 / 0.8	**19** SU 0610 / 1205 / 1824	1.2 / 6.3 / 1.2
5 SU 0050 / 0730 / 1306 / 1952 ●	6.6 / 0.9 / 6.8 / 0.9	**20** M 0035 / 0704 / 1253 / 1916	6.4 / 1.0 / 6.6 / 1.1
6 M 0137 / 0822 / 1353 / 2035	6.7 / 0.7 / 6.9 / 0.9	**21** TU 0122 / 0755 / 1337 / 2005 ○	6.6 / 0.8 / 6.8 / 1.2
7 TU 0220 / 0909 / 1439 / 2113	6.7 / 0.7 / 7.0 / 1.0	**22** W 0206 / 0845 / 1422 / 2051	6.7 / 0.7 / 7.0 / 1.0
8 W 0301 / 0949 / 1523 / 2147	6.7 / 0.7 / 7.0 / 1.1	**23** TH 0249 / 0934 / 1506 / 2136	6.7 / 0.5 / 7.1 / 1.0
9 TH 0340 / 1023 / 1605 / 2220	6.6 / 0.8 / 6.8 / 1.2	**24** F 0330 / 1021 / 1550 / 2220	6.8 / 0.4 / 7.2 / 0.9
10 F 0417 / 1052 / 1644 / 2253	6.5 / 0.9 / 6.5 / 1.3	**25** SA 0411 / 1104 / 1635 / 2304	6.8 / 0.4 / 7.1 / 0.9
11 SA 0451 / 1122 / 1722 / 2327	6.3 / 1.0 / 6.3 / 1.4	**26** SU 0452 / 1144 / 1722 / 2346	6.7 / 0.4 / 7.0 / 1.0
12 SU 0526 / 1153 / 1801	6.2 / 1.1 / 6.1	**27** M 0537 / 1224 / 1813	6.7 / 0.5 / 6.8
13 M 0003 / 0606 / 1229 / 1846 ◑	1.5 / 6.0 / 1.2 / 5.9	**28** TU 0030 / 0626 / 1309 / 1908 ◑	1.1 / 6.5 / 0.6 / 6.6
14 TU 0044 / 0654 / 1311 / 1938	1.7 / 5.8 / 1.4 / 5.8	**29** W 0120 / 0724 / 1402 / 2009	1.3 / 6.4 / 0.8 / 6.4
15 W 0133 / 0753 / 1410 / 2035	1.9 / 5.7 / 1.5 / 5.7	**30** TH 0220 / 0832 / 1504 / 2116	1.5 / 6.3 / 1.0 / 6.2
		31 F 0340 / 0946 / 1613 / 2229	1.5 / 6.2 / 1.2 / 6.1

Chart Datum: 2·90 metres below Ordnance Datum (Newlyn). HAT is 7·6 metres above Chart Datum; see 4.5

》》 FREE monthly updates from 《《
www.reedsalmanac.co.uk

9.4.13 SOUTHEND-ON-SEA/LEIGH-ON-SEA

Essex 51°31´·07N 00°42´·57E ❀❀❀❀❀❀

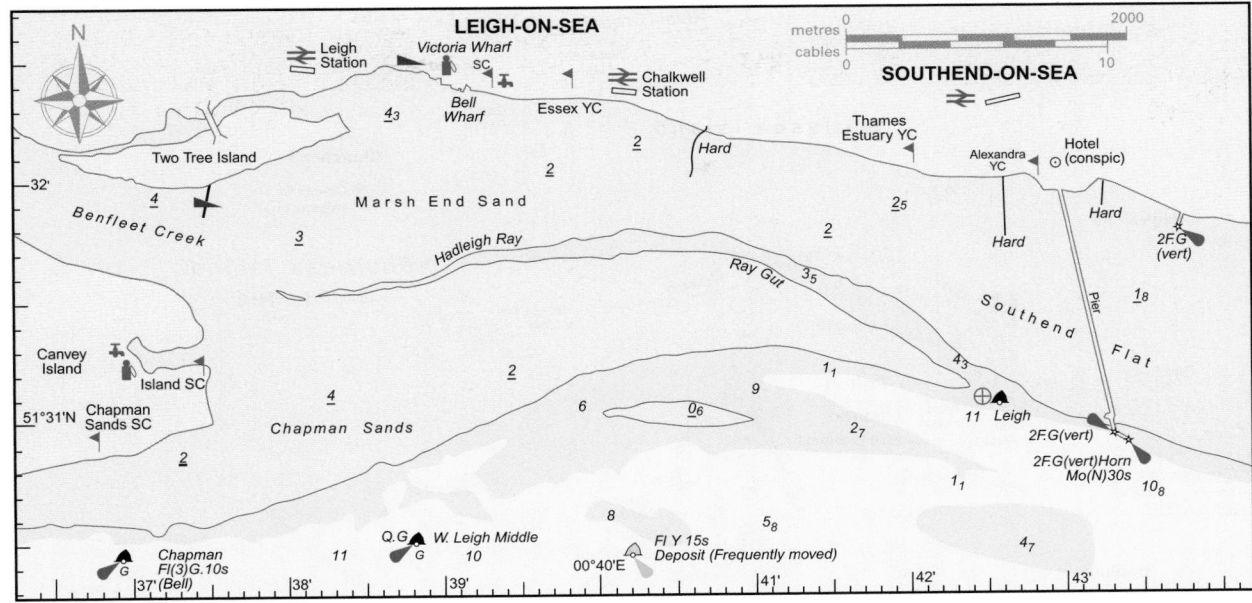

CHARTS AC 5606, 1183, 1185; Imray C1, C2, Y18; Stanfords 5, 8.

TIDES +0125 Dover; ML 3·0; Duration 0610

Standard Port SHEERNESS (←→)

Times				Height (metres)			
High Water		Low Water		MHWS	MHWN	MLWN	MLWS
0200	0800	0200	0700	5·8	4·7	1·5	0·6
1400	2000	1400	1900				
Differences SOUTHEND-ON-SEA							
−0005	−0005	−0005	−0005	0·0	0·0	−0·1	−0·1
CORYTON							
+0005	+0010	+0010	+0010	+0·4	+0·3	0·0	0·0

SHELTER The whole area dries soon after half ebb, except Ray Gut (0·4–4·8m) which leads to Leigh Creek and Hadleigh Ray, either side of Two Tree Island, thence to Benfleet Creek where the limit of W navigation is the Tidal Barrier just above Benfleet YC; all are buoyed, but echo-sounder is essential. Craft can take the ground alongside Bell Wharf or Victoria Wharf. It is also possible to secure at the end of Southend Pier to collect stores, FW. NOTE: Southend-on-Sea and Leigh-on-Sea are both part of the lower PLA Area and an 8kn speed limit is enforced in inshore areas.

NAVIGATION WPT 51°31´·07N 00°42´·57E, Leigh SHM buoy, at ent to Ray Gut; this SHM buoy can be left close to port on entering Ray Gut, since there is now more water NE of it than to the SW. Appr from Shoeburyness, keep outside the W Shoebury SHM buoy, Fl G 2·5s.

Beware some 3000 small boat moorings 1M either side of Southend Pier. Speed limit in Canvey Island/Hadleigh Ray areas is 8kn.

LIGHTS AND MARKS Pier lts as on chartlet.

R/T Port Control London: *London VTS* VHF Ch 68 inward from Sea Reach No4, *London VTS* VHF Ch 69 seaward from Sea Reach No4,

TELEPHONE (Code 01702) HM ☎ 215620; HM Leigh-on-Sea 710561; MRCC (01255) 675518; Essex Police Marine Section (01268) 775533; Marinecall 09068 969645; Police 431212; Dr 225500; Ⓗ 348911.

FACILITIES
SOUTHEND-ON-SEA: Southend Pier ☎ 215620, AB (craft not to be unattended), 24hrs free then £10/night <35' LOA, £17/night >35', M, L. Alexandra YC ☎ 340363, Bar, FW; Thorpe Bay YC ☎ 587563, Bar, L, Slip, R, FW; Thames Estuary YC ☎ 345967; Halfway YC ☎ 582025, pre-book 1 ⚓, FW; Town CH, ACA, Ⓔ, 🛒, R, Bar, ✉, Ⓑ, ⇌, ✈.

LEIGH-ON-SEA: Essex YC ☎ 478404, FW, Bar; Leigh on Sea SC ☎ 476788, FW, Bar; Bell Wharf, AB 24hrs free then £9/night; Victoria Wharf AB 24hrs free then £9/night, D, SM, Slip (Two Tree Is HW±2½); Town: ME, El, ✗, C, CH, SM.

CANVEY ISLAND: (Code 01268) Services: Slip, M, D, FW, ME, El, ✗, C, Gas, CH, Access HW±2; Island YC ☎ 683729; Benfleet YC (on S side of Benfleet Creek on Canvey Island) ☎ 792278, Access HW±2½, M, Slip, FW, D (by day), CH, ME, El, ✗, C, Bar, 🛒, 🅿.

SHOEBURYNESS TO RIVER COLNE

(Charts 1185, 1975) Maplin and Foulness Sands extend nearly 6M NE from Foulness Pt, the extremity being marked by Whitaker bn. On N side of Whitaker chan leading to R. Crouch and R Roach lies Buxey Sand, inshore of which is the Ray Sand chan (dries), a convenient short cut between R. Crouch and R. Blackwater with sufficient rise of tide.

To seaward of Buxey Sand and the Spitway, Gunfleet Sand extends 10M NE, marked by buoys and dries in places. ▶ *A conspic disused lt tr stands on SE side of Gunfleet Sand, about 6M SSE of the Naze tr, and here the SW-going (flood) stream begins*

about HW Sheerness + 0600, and the NE-going stream at about HW Sheerness – 0030, sp rates 2kn. ◀

The Rivers Blackwater and Colne share a common estuary which is approached from the NE via NE Gunfleet lt buoy; thence along Goldmer Gat and the Wallet towards Knoll and Eagle lt buoys. For the Colne turn NNW via Colne Bar buoy towards Inner Bench Hd buoy keeping in mid-chan. For R Blackwater, head WNW for NW Knoll and Bench Hd buoys. From the S or SE, make for the Whitaker ECM buoy, thence through the Spitway, via Swin Spitway and Wallet Spitway buoys to reach Knoll buoy and deeper water.

9.4.14 RIVER ROACH/HAVENGORE

Essex **51°36'·98N 00°52'·14E** (Branklet SPM buoy), R Roach ✿✿✿🌢 ✿✿✿. **51°33'·62N 00°50'·52E**, Havengore Bridge ✿🌢✿

CHARTS AC 5607, 1185, 3750; Imray C1, Y17; Stanfords 5, 4.

TIDES +0110 Dover; ML 2·7; Duration 0615

Standard Port WALTON-ON-THE-NAZE (→)

Times				Height (metres)			
High Water		Low Water		MHWS	MHWN	MLWN	MLWS
0000	0600	0500	1100	4·2	3·4	1·1	0·4
1200	1800	1700	2300				
Differences ROCHFORD							
+0050	+0040	Dries		−0·8	−1·1	Dries	

SHELTER Good. The Roach gives sheltered sailing and access to a network of secluded creeks, including Havengore (the 'backdoor' from the Crouch to the Thames Estuary). No AB available in the area. ⚓s behind sea-walls can be found for all winds at: Quay Reach (often more protected than the Crouch), Paglesham Reach, West Reach, Barling Reach and Yokes Fleet. An ⚓ light is essential due to freighters H24. Speed limit 8kn. Crouch Hbr Authority controls R Roach and Crouch, out to Foulness Pt.

NAVIGATION Normal access H24 to the Roach is from R Crouch (see 9.4.15 for WPT from seaward); the ent between Branklet SPM buoy and Nase Pt is narrowed by mudbanks. Unlit buoys up-river to Barling Ness, above which few boats go. To exit at Havengore Creek, appr via Middleway and Narrow Cuts to reach the bridge before HW.

Entry via **Havengore Creek** is possible in good weather, with great care and adequate rise of tide (max draft 1·5m at HW sp). Shoeburyness Range is usually active Mon-Fri 0600-1700LT; give 24hrs notice to Range Officer by ☎. Subsequent clearance on VHF by Havengore lifting bridge (☎ HW±2, HJ); no passage unless bridge raised. Least water is over the shifting bar, just inside creek ent. From the S, cross Maplin Sands at HW −1 from S Shoebury SHM buoy, leaving Pisces wreck (conspic, 1M from ent) to port.

LIGHTS AND MARKS Unlit, but night entry to R Roach may be possible.

R/T VHF Ch 72 16 is worked by Range Officer (*Shoe Base*) (HO); Radar Control (*Shoe Radar*) (HO); & Bridge keeper (*Shoe Bridge*) (HW±2 by day). Radar guidance may be available.

TELEPHONE (Code 01702 Southend) Crouch HM ☎ (01621) 783602; Range Officer 383211; Havengore Br 383436; Swing Br to Potton I. ☎ 219491; Marinecall 09068 969645; MRCC (01255) 675518; Dr 218678.

FACILITIES **Paglesham** (East End) FW, D, slip, El, ME (from BY), ✕, Bar; **Gt Wakering:** Slip, P, D, FW, ME, El, ✕, C, CH (from BY); at Rochford Wakering YC ☎ 530926, M, L, Bar. **Towns** Gt Wakering & Rochford; 🛒, R, Bar, ✉ (Great Wakering and Barling); most facilities, Ⓑ and ⇌ in Rochford and Shoeburyness, ✈ (Southend).

9.4.15 BURNHAM-ON-CROUCH

Essex 51°37′·50N 00°48′·23E (Yacht Hbr) ⚓⚓⚓♻♻♻🌸🌸

CHARTS AC 5607, 1183, 1975, 3750; Imray C1, Y17; Stanfords 1, 19, 5, 4.

TIDES +0115 Dover; ML 2·5; Duration 0610.

Standard Port WALTON-ON-THE-NAZE (→)

Times				Height (metres)			
High Water		Low Water		MHWS	MHWN	MLWN	MLWS
0000	0600	0500	1100	4·2	3·4	1·1	0·4
1200	1800	1700	2300				
Differences WHITAKER BEACON							
+0022	+0024	+0033	+0027	+0·6	+0·5	+0·2	+0·1
HOLLIWELL POINT							
+0034	+0037	+0100	+0037	+1·1	+0·9	+0·3	+0·1
BURNHAM-ON-CROUCH							
+0050	+0035	+0115	+0050	+1·0	+0·8	−0·1	−0·2
NORTH FAMBRIDGE							
+0115	+0050	+0130	+0100	+1·1	+0·8	0·0	−0·1
HULLBRIDGE							
+0115	+0050	+0135	+0105	+1·1	+0·8	0·0	−0·1
BATTLESBRIDGE							
+0120	+0110	Dries		−1·8	−2·0	Dries	

SHELTER River is exposed to most winds. Cliff Reach (off W edge of lower chartlet) is sheltered from SW'lies. ⚓ prohib in fairway but possible just E or W of the moorings.

NAVIGATION WPT 51°39′·79N 01°02′·50E, S Buxey SHM lit buoy. Appr from East Swin, or the Wallet via Spitway and N Swallow SWM, into the Whitaker Chan.

Near Sunken Buxey seas can be hazardous with strong wind over tide. Ray Sand Chan (dries 1·7m), usable on the tide by shoal draft boats as a short cut from/to the Blackwater. Shoeburyness Artillery ranges lie E and S of Foulness Pt, clear of fairway. R Crouch is navigable to Battlesbridge, 10M beyond Burnham. No landing on Foulness (limited access) and Bridgemarsh Is (up-river). Keep N of Wallasea Wetlands (opposite and down-river of Burnham) which are marked with PHM bcns.

LIGHTS AND MARKS There are few landmarks to assist entering, but Whitaker Chan and the river are lit/buoyed to 0·5M W of Essex Marina. From Sunken Buxey NCM lit buoy, the spire of St Mary's ♔ (difficult to identify) leads 233° to Outer Crouch SCM lit buoy; thence steer 240° past Foulness Pt into the river. There is a 2·2M unlit gap between Inner Crouch SWM lit buoy, and Horse Shoal NCM lit buoy.

R/T VHF Ch 80 for: Crouch HM Launch (0900-1700LT, w/e); Essex Marina; Burnham Yacht Harbour; W Wick Marina (1000-1700), also Ch M.

TELEPHONE (Code Maldon 01621) HM 783602; MRCC (01255) 675518; Marinecall 09068 969645; Police 773663; Dr 782054.

FACILITIES There are five marinas or yacht hbrs. Speed limit in moorings is 8kn.

BURNHAM Burnham Yacht Hbr, ☎ 782150, Access H24, (350) £2.10, some ⚓s, Wi-fi, D, ME, El, ✕, BH (30 ton), BY, CH, ◻, R, Bar, Slip (£10), ♿. **Royal Corinthian YC** ☎ 782105, AB, FW, M, L, R, Bar. **Royal Burnham YC** ☎ 782044, FW, L, R, Bar. **Crouch YC** ☎ 782252, L, R, Bar. **Services:** AB, BY, C (15 ton), D, P, FW, ME, El, ✕, M, Slip, CH, ACA, Gas, SM, Gaz. **Town** 🍴, R, Bar, ✉, Ⓑ, ⇌, ✈ (Southend).

WALLASEA ISLAND. Essex Marina (400) ☎ (01702) 258531, £2.00, BY, Gas, Bar, C (13 ton), BH (40 ton), CH, D, P, LPG, El, M, ME, R, ✕, Slip. Ferry to Burnham Town Hard at w/ends in season, ☎ 258870. **Essex YC.** ACA.

FAMBRIDGE Fambridge Yacht Haven (170 + ❻) LOA < 10m: £12/night; LOA > 10m: £17/night, ⚓s £7/£12, ☎ 740370, Access HW±5, Wi-fi, M, ✕, ME, BY, BH (25ton), C (5 ton), El, Slip (£6-£15), Gas, Gaz, ◻, showers, YC, Bar, 🍴. ❻ pontoon (with electricity and water) at former Fambridge Yacht Station, £5/night.

Brandy Hole Yacht Stn (120) ☎ (01702) 230248, L, M, ME, ✕, Slip, Gas, Gaz, Bar, BY, D, Access HW±4.

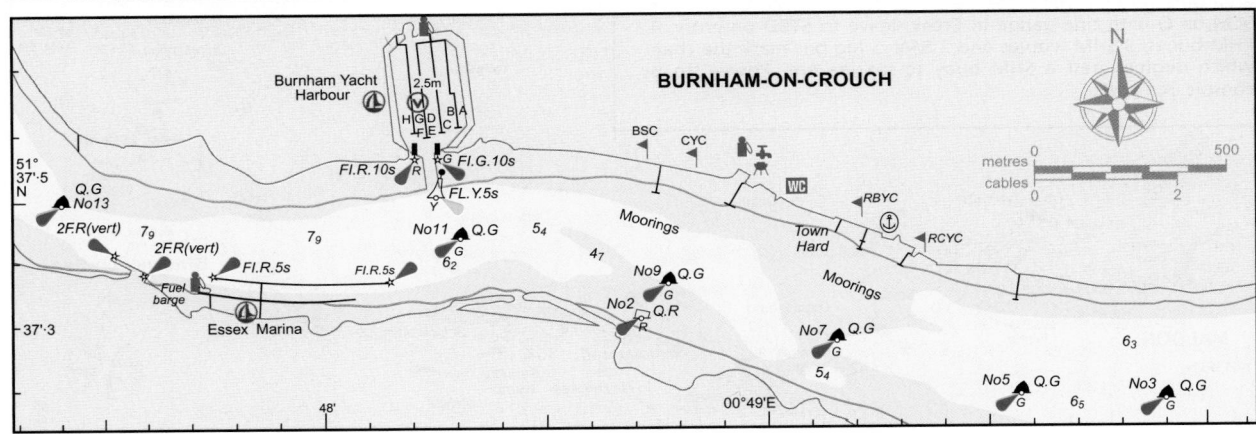

9.4.16 RIVER BLACKWATER

Essex 51°45'·33N 00°54'·90E ✸✸✸✧✧✧✧✿✿✿

CHARTS AC 5607, 1183, 1975, 3741; Imray C1, Y17, 2000 Series; Stanfords 5, 6.

TIDES Maldon +0130 Dover; ML 2·8; Duration 0620)

Standard Port WALTON-ON-THE-NAZE (→)

Times				Height (metres)			
High Water		Low Water		MHWS	MHWN	MLWN	MLWS
0000	0600	0500	1100	4·2	3·4	1·1	0·4
1200	1800	1700	2300				
Differences SUNK HEAD							
0000	+0002	−0002	+0002	−0·3	−0·3	−0·1	−0·1
WEST MERSEA							
+0035	+0015	+0055	+0010	+0·9	+0·4	+0·1	+0·1
BRADWELL							
+0035	+0023	+0047	+0004	+1·0	+0·8	+0·2	0·0
OSEA ISLAND							
+0057	+0045	+0050	+0007	+1·1	+0·9	+0·1	0·0
MALDON							
+0107	+0055	No data		−1·3	−1·1	No data	

SHELTER Good, as appropriate to wind. ⚓ restricted by oyster beds and many moorings.

NAVIGATION WPT Knoll NCM, Q, 51°43'·88N 01°05'·07E, 287°/6·7M to Nass bn, ECM VQ (3) 5s. Speed limit 8kn W of Osea Is.

WEST MERSEA Avoid oyster beds between Cobmarsh and Packing Marsh Is and in Salcott Chan. ⚓ in Mersea Quarters, access approx HW±1½. There is a pontoon for landing (limited waiting); also pile moorings in Ray Chan.

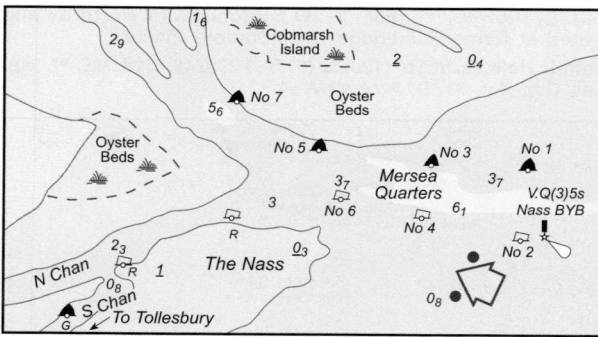

TOLLESBURY FLEET Proceed via S Chan up Woodrolfe Creek. A tide gauge shows depth over marina ent sill (approx 2·4m at MHWS and 1·4m at MHWN). Speed limits: Tollesbury Fleet S Chan 8kn; Woodrolfe Creek upper reaches 4kn.

BRADWELL No dangers, but only suitable for small craft and area gets very crowded; see below under Lts & Marks. Ent has SCM bn Q with tide gauge in Creek; leave to **STBD** on entry. 4 PHM buoys, 3 SHM withies and 2 B/W △ ldg bns mark the chan which doglegs past a SHM buoy to marina ent. Power stn is conspic 7ca NNE.

MALDON From S of Osea Is, 'The Doctor', No 3 SHM buoy on with Blackwater SC lt, Iso G 5s, lead 300° approx up the chan; or No 3 and No 8 buoys in line at 305°.

LIGHTS AND MARKS See chartlets and 9.4.4.

R/T Bradwell and Tollesbury Marinas Ch **80** M (HO). Blackwater Marina Ch M, 0900-2300. Heybridge Lock Ch 80 HW −2+1. Clark and Carter launch: call CC1.

TELEPHONE Codes: 01621 Maldon. 01206 Colchester/W Mersea. R. Bailiff 875837, Mobile 0860 456802. MRCC (01255) 675518. Marinecall 09068 969645. Police: Colchester 762212; W Mersea 382930. Dr 854118; W Mersea 382015.

FACILITIES **WEST MERSEA** (01206). W Mersea YC 382947, Bar, launch service call YC 1. **Town** P, D, FW, ME, El, CH, ▣, R, Bar, ✉, Ⓑ, ⚅ (bus to Colchester, Ⓗ ☎ 01206-853535), ✈ (Southend/Stansted).

TOLLESBURY (01621). Tollesbury Marina (220+20 Ⓥ) ☎ 869202, £1·75, marina@woodrolfe.demon.co.uk Access HW±1½, Slip, D, BH (20 ton), Gas, Gaz, LPG, El, ME, ✖, C (5 ton), CH, R, Bar, Wi-fi, ▣. Tollesbury Cruising Club ☎ 869561, Bar, R, M. **Village** P, ▥, R, Bar, ✉, Ⓑ (Tues, Thurs 1000-1430), ⚅ (bus to Witham), ✈ (Southend or Cambridge).

BRADWELL (01621). Bradwell Marina (300, some Ⓥ) ☎ 776235, £1·70, short stay £1.00/hr. Slip, D, P, ME, El, ✖, BH (16 ton), CH, R, Bar, Access HW±4½, approx 2m. Bradwell Quay YC ☎ 776539, M, FW, Bar, L, Slip. **Town** ✉, ⚅ (bus/taxi to Southminster), ✈ (Southend).

MAYLANDSEA (01621). Blackwater Marina (230) ☎ 740264, £10/craft, Slip, D, ✖, CH, R, Bar; Access HW±2. 150 moorings (£5/craft) in chan. Taxi to Southminster ⚅.

MALDON (01621). **Maldon Quay** Beyond No 8 buoy, the chan which shifts and carries 0·2m, is lit and buoyed. Access near HW; pontoons dry to soft mud. HM/River bailiff ☎ 856487, Mobile 07818 013723; M, P, D, FW, AB < 8m £8, > 8m £10, Slip. **Maldon Little Ship Club** ☎ 854139, Bar. **Services:** Slip, D, ✖, CH, M, ACA, SM, ME, El, Ⓔ. **Town** ✉, Ⓑ, ⚅ (bus to Chelmsford, Ⓗ ☎ (01245) 440761), ✈ (Southend, Cambridge or Stansted).

HEYBRIDGE BASIN (01621). **Lock** ☎ 853506, opens HW −1 to HW approx. A SHM buoy opposite the lock marks the deep water ent. Access to Chelmer & Blackwater Canal (not navigable). **Blackwater SC** ☎ 853923, L, FW. **Services:** at CRS Marine ☎ 854684, Mobile 07850 543873 (pontoon outside lock), Slip, D, L, M, FW, ME, El, ✖, C. Bus to Heybridge/Maldon.

9.4.17   RIVER COLNE

Essex **51°47'·98N 01°00'·60E** (Brightlingsea) 🌊🌊🌊🌊🌊

CHARTS AC 5607, 1183, 1975, 3741; Imray C1, Y17, 2000 Series; Stanfords 5, 6.

TIDES +0050 Dover; ML 2·5; Duration 0615

Standard Port WALTON-ON-THE-NAZE (→)

Times				Height (metres)			
High Water		Low Water		MHWS	MHWN	MLWN	MLWS
0000	0600	0500	1100	4·2	3·4	1·1	0·4
1200	1800	1700	2300				
Differences BRIGHTLINGSEA							
+0025	+0021	+0046	+0004	+0.8	+0.4	+0.1	0.0
COLCHESTER							
+0035	+0025	Dries		0.0	−0.3	Dries	
CLACTON-ON-SEA							
+0012	+0010	+0025	+0008	+0.3	+0.1	+0.1	+0.1

SHELTER Suitable shelter can be found from most winds, but outer hbr is exposed to W'lies. In the creek S of Cindery Island are moorings (as shown) and long pontoons in about 1·5m, with possible AB for Ⓥs. ⚓ prohib in Brightlingsea Hbr, but there are ⚓s to the NW of Mersea Stone Pt and in Pyefleet Chan, E of Pewit Island. R Colne is navigable for 4·5m draft to Wivenhoe, where the river dries; and to The Hythe, Colchester (3m draft).

NAVIGATION WPT Colne Bar By, SHM Fl (2) G 5s, 51°44'·61N 01°02'·57E, 340°/3·6M to Mersea Stone. See also 9.4.16. Extensive mud and sand banks flank the ent chan. Large coasters use the Brightlingsea chans. The ent to Brightlingsea Creek is narrow at LW and carries about 1m.

A flood barrier 2ca below Wivenhoe church is normally open (30m wide) allowing unrestricted passage; keep to stbd, max speed 5kn. Tfc lts on N pier are 3FR (vert), vis up/downstream. When lit, they indicate the barrier gates are shut; see also LIGHTS AND MARKS.

Speed limits in approaches and up-river: No13–15By(s) = 8kn; No15–18By(s) = no spd limit; No18–34By(s) = 8kn; No 34 – Colchester = 5kn; Brightlingsea Harbour = 4kn.

LIGHTS AND MARKS Well buoyed/lit up to Wivenhoe. Bateman's Tr (conspic) by Westmarsh Pt. Ldg lts/marks 041° for Brightlingsea: both FR 7/10m 4M; dayglo W ☐, R stripes on posts; adjusted to suit the chan. Then Spit SCM lt buoy, and chan lt buoys SHM, PHM, plus NCM bn Q where chan is divided by Cindery Is. Pyefleet Chan and other creeks are unlit.

The flood barrier is marked by 2FR/FG (vert) on both sides and there are bns, QR/QG, up/downstream on the river banks.

R/T *Brightlingsea Harbour Radio* VHF Ch 68.

TELEPHONE HM (Brightlingsea) (01206) 302200, mob 07952 734814; MRCC (01255) 675518; Marinecall 09068 969645; Police (01255) 221312; Dr 302522.

FACILITIES

BRIGHTLINGSEA: Town Hard ☎ (01206) 302200, L, FW, Pontoon moorings £9 up to 26ft, £10 up to 36ft, £11 over 36ft, ⚓ afloat near NCM opposite Town Hard, Slip £8; @ Brightlingsea Wireless 07719 096369 and Colne Community College (HO Term time) **Colne YC** ☎ 302594, L, FW, R, Bar.

Brightlingsea SC Slip, Bar; **Services:** M, L, FW, ME, El, Ⓔ, ✖, CH supply P & D (cans HO), ACA, P & D (cans), Gas, SM, BY, C, Slip. **Town** FW, ME, El, ✖, C (mobile), CH, 🛒, R, Bar, ✉, Ⓑ, ⇌ (bus to Wivenhoe or Colchester), ✈ (Southend or Stansted).

WIVENHOE: Wivenhoe SC. AB (pontoons 10 Ⓥ drying berths), **Village** P, 🛒, Bar, ✉, ⇌.

ROWHEDGE: Quay AB(drying) some Ⓥ.

RIVER COLNE TO HARWICH

(Chart 1975, 1593) 4M SW of the Naze tr at Hollands Haven a conspic radar tr (67m, unlit) is an excellent daymark. From the S, approach Walton and Harwich via the Medusa chan about 1M E of Naze tr. At N end of this chan, 1M off Dovercourt, Pye End buoy marks chan SSW to Walton Backwaters. Harwich and Landguard Pt are close to the N. Making Harwich from the SE beware the drying Cork Sand, which lies N/S.

Sunk Inner SWM buoy, 11M E of The Naze, marks the outer apprs to Harwich, an extensive and well sheltered hbr accessible at all times (chart *2693*).

- Harwich, Felixstowe Docks and Ipswich are referred to collectively as the Haven Ports.
- Small craft should give plenty of sea room to shipping manoeuvring to board/disembark Pilots in the Sunk Inner Precautionary Area, see chartlet at 9.4.7.
- The Harwich DW channel begins 1·5M NNW of Sunk Inner buoy and runs N between Rough and Shipwash shoals, then W past the Cork Sand PHM lt buoy. Constantly used by commercial shipping, approach should be via the recommended track for yachts.

Approaching from NE and 2M off the ent to R. Deben, beware Cutler shoal, with least depth of 1·2m, marked by SHM buoy on E side; Wadgate Ledge and the Platters are about 1·5M ENE of Landguard Point. ▶ *S of Landguard Point the W-going (flood) stream begins at HW Harwich + 0600, and the E-going stream at HW Harwich, sp rates about 1·5kn. Note: HW Harwich is never more than 7 mins after HW Walton; LW times are about 10 mins earlier.* ◀

HARWICH TO ORFORD NESS

(Chart 2052) Shipwash shoal, buoyed and with a drying patch, runs NNE from 9M E of Felixstowe to 4M SSE of Orford Ness. Inshore of this is Shipway Chan, then Bawdsey Bank, buoyed with depths of 2m, on which the sea breaks in E'ly swell.

The Sledway Chan lies between Bawdsey Bank and Whiting Bank (buoyed) which is close SW of Orford Ness, and has depths less than 1m. Hollesley Chan, about 1M wide, runs inshore W and N of this bank. In the SW part of Hollesley B is the ent to Orford Haven and the R Ore/Alde. ▶ *There are overfalls S of Orford Ness on both the ebb and flood streams. 2M E of Orford Ness the SW-going stream begins at HW Harwich +0605, sp rate 2·5kn; the NE-going stream begins at HW Harwich – 0010, sp rate 3kn.* ◀

Note: The direction of local buoyage becomes S to N off Orford Ness (52°05'N).

ORFORD NESS TO GREAT YARMOUTH

(Chart 1543) N of Orford Ness seas break on Aldeburgh Ridge (1.3m), but the coast is clear of offlying dangers past Aldeburgh and Southwold, as far as Benacre Ness, 5M S of Lowestoft. Sizewell power stn is a conspic 3 bldg 1·5M N of Thorpe Ness. Keep 1·5M offshore to avoid fishing floats.

▶ *Lowestoft is best approached from both S and E by the buoyed/lit Stanford chan, passing E of Newcome Sand and SW of Holm Sand; beware possible strong set across hbr ent.* ◀ From the N, approach through Cockle Gatway, Caister Road, Yarmouth Road, passing Great Yarmouth (beware of prohibited area N of harbour entrance); then proceed S through Gorleston, Corton and Lowestoft North Roads (buoyed). ▶ *1M E of hbr ent, the S-going stream begins at HW Dover –0600, and the N-going at HW Dover, sp rates 2·6kn.* ◀ Scroby Sands Wind Farm consists of 30 turbines centred on 52°39'·00N 01°47'·00E. Each turbine is 61m high, with 80m diameter blades and clearance height of 18m and six of the perimeter ones are lit. Vessels to keep well clear and not enter the area.

In the approaches to Great Yarmouth from seaward the banks are continually changing; use the buoyed chans which, from N and S, are those described in the preceding paragraph. But from the E the shortest approach is via Corton ECM lt buoy and the Holm Channel leading into Gorleston Road. ▶ *The sea often breaks on North Scroby, Middle Scroby and Caister Shoal (all of which dry), and there are heavy tide rips over parts of Corton and South Scroby Sands, Middle and South Cross Sands, and Winterton Overfalls.* ◀

▶ *1M NE of ent to Gt Yarmouth the S-going stream begins at HW Dover –0600, and the N-going at HW Dover – 0015, sp rates 2·3kn. Breydon Water (tidal) affects streams in the Haven; after heavy rain the out-going stream at Brush Quay may exceed 5kn.* ◀ About 12M NE of Great Yarmouth lie Newarp Banks, on which the sea breaks in bad weather.

WALTON ON THE NAZE

MEAN SPRING ——————
AND NEAP CURVES – – – –

MEAN RANGES
Springs 3.8m
Neaps   2.3m

Springs occur 2 days
after
New and Full Moon

9.4.18 WALTON BACKWATERS

Essex **51°54'·57N 01°16'·79E** (No 2 PHM buoy) ✲✲⚓⚓⚓⚓❀❀

CHARTS AC 5607, 2052, 2695; Imray C1, Y16, 2000 Series; Stanfords 5, 6.

TIDES +0030 Dover; ML 2·2; Duration 0615. Walton is a Standard Port. Predictions are for Walton Pier, ie to seaward. Time differences for Bramble Creek (N of Hamford Water) are +10, –7, –5, +10 mins; height differences are all +0·3m.

SHELTER Good in all weather, but ent not advised if a big sea is running from the NE. Good ⚓s in Hamford Water (clear of Oakley Creek) and in N end of Walton Chan, 2ca S of Stone Pt on E side.

NAVIGATION From S, appr via Medusa Chan; from N and E via the Harwich recomended yacht track. WPT Pye End SWM buoy, L Fl 10s, 51°55'·05N 01°17'·89E, 234°/1·1M to Crab Knoll SHM at chan ent. NB this stretch carries only 0·9m. Beware lobster pots off the Naze and Pye Sands and oyster beds in the Backwaters. Buoys may be moved to suit channel changes.
At narrow ent to Walton Chan leave NCM buoy to stbd, and 3 PHM buoys close to port; after a SHM Fl G 10s buoy abeam Stone Pt best water is on E side.

LIGHTS AND MARKS Naze Tr (49m) is conspic 3M S of Pye End buoy. 2M NNE at Felixstowe, cranes and Y flood lts are conspic D/N.

R/T Titchmarsh Marina Ch 80, 0800-2000 in season.

TELEPHONE (Code 01255) HM 851899; MRCC 675518; Marinecall 09068 969645; Police 851212; ⊞ 421145.

FACILITIES
Titchmarsh Marina 420 inc **Ⓥ**, £1.60. ☎ 672185. Access HW±5 over sill 1·3m. Pontoons lettered A-H from ent, dredged 1·3m; or on adjacent pontoons in the Twizzle. D, Gas, Gaz, LPG, ME, CH, El, C (10 ton), BH (35 ton), Slip, R, Bar, Wi-fi. **Walton & Frinton YC,** ☎ 675526/678161, R, Bar. **Yacht Basin** (60) run by YC; appr dries. AB (long stay), ⊞, Slip, M, D, C (½ ton), El.
Town P, SM, 🛒, R, Bar, ✉, ⚉, ✈ (Southend/Cambridge/Stansted).

<table>
<tr><td>TIME ZONE (UT)
For Summer Time add ONE
hour in non-shaded areas</td></tr>
</table>

WALTON-ON-THE-NAZE LAT 51°51'N LONG 1°17'E
TIMES AND HEIGHTS OF HIGH AND LOW WATERS

Dates in red are **SPRINGS**
Dates in blue are **NEAPS**

YEAR 2010

JANUARY

Time	m		Time	m
1 0540 F 1146 1755	0.4 4.3 0.7	**16** 0008 SA 0625 1226 1827	4.0 0.5 4.0 0.9
2 0018 SA 0631 1236 1842	4.2 0.3 4.4 0.7	**17** 0041 SU 0657 1301 1857	4.0 0.5 4.0 0.9
3 0106 SU 0720 1326 1928	4.3 0.2 4.5 0.7	**18** 0113 M 0725 1336 1925	4.1 0.5 4.0 0.9
4 0153 M 0809 1415 2014	4.3 0.1 4.4 0.8	**19** 0146 TU 0753 1410 1953	4.1 0.5 4.0 0.9
5 0239 TU 0857 1504 2100	4.3 0.1 4.3 0.9	**20** 0218 W 0822 1443 2024	4.0 0.5 3.9 0.9
6 0324 W 0945 1553 2148	4.2 0.2 4.1 0.9	**21** 0250 TH 0852 1516 2058	4.0 0.6 3.8 1.0
7 0412 TH 1035 1644 2240	4.1 0.4 3.9 1.0	**22** 0322 F 0925 1552 2138	3.9 0.6 3.7 1.1
8 0504 F 1128 1739 2339	3.9 0.5 3.7 1.1	**23** 0400 SA 1004 1636 2227	3.8 0.8 3.6 1.2
9 0607 SA 1225 1845	3.8 0.8 3.5	**24** 0447 SU 1056 1732 2333	3.7 0.9 3.5 1.2
10 0050 SU 0718 1336 2004	1.2 3.6 0.9 3.5	**25** 0549 M 1209 1841	3.6 1.0 3.4
11 0209 M 0830 1452 2113	1.1 3.6 1.0 3.6	**26** 0103 TU 0711 1336 1959	1.2 3.5 1.1 3.5
12 0320 TU 0933 1550 2207	1.0 3.7 1.1 3.7	**27** 0234 W 0834 1458 2120	1.0 3.6 1.0 3.6
13 0420 W 1026 1637 2253	0.8 3.8 1.0 3.8	**28** 0338 TH 0944 1602 2224	0.8 3.9 0.9 3.9
14 0510 TH 1111 1718 2332	0.7 3.9 1.0 3.9	**29** 0436 F 1043 1656 2317	0.5 4.1 0.8 4.1
15 0551 F 1149 1754	0.6 3.9 0.9	**30** 0529 SA 1136 1744	0.3 4.3 0.7
		31 0005 SU 0619 1225 1829	4.3 0.1 4.5 0.7

FEBRUARY

Time	m		Time	m
1 0051 M 0706 1312 1912	4.4 0.0 4.5 0.6	**16** 0052 TU 0657 1312 1903	4.2 0.4 4.1 0.7
2 0135 TU 0751 1357 1953	4.5 0.0 4.5 0.6	**17** 0123 W 0724 1344 1932	4.2 0.4 4.1 0.7
3 0217 W 0832 1442 2035	4.5 0.1 4.4 0.7	**18** 0153 TH 0751 1414 2003	4.2 0.4 4.0 0.8
4 0259 TH 0912 1525 2117	4.4 0.2 4.1 0.8	**19** 0222 F 0820 1445 2035	4.1 0.5 3.9 0.8
5 0341 F 0952 1604 2202	4.3 0.4 3.9 0.9	**20** 0252 SA 0850 1518 2110	4.0 0.6 3.8 0.9
6 0426 SA 1036 1658 2254	4.0 0.7 3.7 1.0	**21** 0328 SU 0926 1559 2156	4.0 0.6 3.7 1.0
7 0523 SU 1129 1756	3.7 1.0 3.4	**22** 0413 M 1015 1651 2258	3.9 0.9 3.5 1.1
8 0000 M 0638 1243 1921	1.2 3.5 1.2 3.3	**23** 0512 TU 1129 1801	3.7 1.1 3.4
9 0140 TU 0802 1423 2046	1.2 3.4 1.3 3.4	**24** 0029 W 0639 1315 1933	1.2 3.5 1.2 3.4
10 0304 W 0914 1529 2146	1.1 3.5 1.2 3.6	**25** 0212 TH 0818 1444 2105	1.0 3.6 1.1 3.6
11 0410 TH 1010 1618 2233	0.9 3.7 1.1 3.8	**26** 0320 F 0932 1546 2208	0.7 3.9 0.9 3.9
12 0457 F 1055 1658 2313	0.7 3.8 1.0 3.9	**27** 0420 SA 1031 1638 2300	0.4 4.1 0.8 4.1
13 0532 SA 1132 1732 2348	0.6 3.9 0.9 4.0	**28** 0513 SU 1121 1725 2346	0.2 4.3 0.7 4.4
14 0603 SU 1206 1804	0.5 4.0 0.8		
15 0020 M 0630 1240 1834	4.1 0.4 4.0 0.8		

MARCH

Time	m		Time	m
1 0601 M 1207 1808	0.0 4.5 0.6	**16** 0558 TU 1212 1808	0.5 4.1 0.7
2 0029 TU 0644 1251 1849	4.5 0.0 4.5 0.6	**17** 0023 W 0625 1244 1838	4.2 0.4 4.1 0.7
3 0111 W 0724 1334 1930	4.6 0.0 4.4 0.6	**18** 0055 TH 0652 1315 1910	4.2 0.4 4.1 0.6
4 0151 TH 0801 1414 2009	4.6 0.1 4.3 0.7	**19** 0125 F 0720 1346 1942	4.2 0.4 4.0 0.7
5 0230 F 0835 1454 2049	4.5 0.3 4.1 0.7	**20** 0155 SA 0749 1418 2015	4.2 0.5 4.0 0.7
6 0309 SA 0910 1535 2130	4.3 0.6 3.9 0.8	**21** 0228 SU 0822 1452 2052	4.1 0.6 3.9 0.8
7 0352 SU 0951 1618 2217	4.0 0.8 3.6 0.9	**22** 0306 M 0901 1533 2138	4.0 0.8 3.7 0.9
8 0446 M 1042 1710 2317	3.7 1.1 3.4 1.1	**23** 0353 TU 0953 1626 2241	3.9 1.0 3.6 1.0
9 0602 TU 1155 1829	3.4 1.4 3.2	**24** 0455 W 1112 1736	3.7 1.2 3.4
10 0103 W 0731 1346 2008	1.2 3.3 1.5 3.3	**25** 0023 TH 0630 1306 1918	1.0 3.5 1.3 3.4
11 0236 TH 0847 1458 2113	1.1 3.5 1.3 3.5	**26** 0153 F 0803 1423 2044	0.8 3.7 1.1 3.6
12 0346 F 0945 1550 2203	0.9 3.7 1.2 3.7	**27** 0300 SA 0915 1523 2146	0.6 3.9 0.9 3.9
13 0431 SA 1029 1630 2244	0.7 3.8 1.0 3.9	**28** 0400 SU 1013 1614 2237	0.3 4.2 0.8 4.2
14 0503 SU 1106 1704 2319	0.6 3.9 0.9 4.0	**29** 0453 M 1102 1701 2322	0.2 4.3 0.7 4.4
15 0531 M 1140 1737 2352	0.5 4.0 0.8 4.1	**30** 0538 TU 1146 1744	0.1 4.4 0.6
		31 0004 W 0618 1227 1826	4.5 0.1 4.4 0.5

APRIL

Time	m		Time	m
1 0044 TH 0655 1307 1907	4.6 0.2 4.3 0.5	**16** 0025 F 0621 1248 1848	4.2 0.5 4.1 0.6
2 0123 F 0729 1346 1947	4.6 0.3 4.2 0.5	**17** 0059 SA 0651 1323 1923	4.2 0.5 4.1 0.6
3 0202 SA 0802 1424 2026	4.4 0.5 4.1 0.6	**18** 0134 SU 0724 1358 2000	4.2 0.6 4.0 0.6
4 0242 SU 0836 1502 2105	4.2 0.7 3.9 0.7	**19** 0212 M 0802 1436 2042	4.2 0.7 3.9 0.7
5 0325 M 0915 1543 2148	3.9 1.0 3.7 0.9	**20** 0255 TU 0847 1521 2132	4.0 0.9 3.7 0.7
6 0418 TU 1004 1633 2244	3.6 1.2 3.4 1.0	**21** 0347 W 0946 1616 2241	3.9 1.1 3.6 0.8
7 0530 W 1116 1742	3.4 1.4 3.3	**22** 0457 TH 1114 1730	3.7 1.2 3.5
8 0018 TH 0651 1258 1916	1.2 3.3 1.5 3.4	**23** 0018 F 0623 1247 1901	0.8 3.7 1.2 3.5
9 0146 F 0806 1415 2027	1.1 3.4 1.4 3.4	**24** 0131 SA 0742 1356 2017	0.6 3.8 1.1 3.7
10 0258 SA 0906 1511 2121	0.9 3.6 1.2 3.6	**25** 0236 SU 0852 1456 2119	0.5 3.9 0.9 4.0
11 0348 SU 0953 1555 2205	0.8 3.8 1.0 3.8	**26** 0336 M 0951 1549 2211	0.4 4.1 0.8 4.2
12 0424 M 1032 1632 2243	0.7 3.9 0.9 3.9	**27** 0428 TU 1040 1637 2257	0.3 4.2 0.7 4.3
13 0454 TU 1107 1707 2318	0.6 4.0 0.8 4.1	**28** 0513 W 1123 1722 2339	0.3 4.2 0.6 4.4
14 0523 W 1141 1741 2351	0.5 4.0 0.7 4.1	**29** 0553 TH 1204 1807	0.3 4.2 0.5
15 0552 TH 1214 1815	0.5 4.1 0.6	**30** 0019 F 0629 1243 1850	4.4 0.4 4.2 0.5

Chart Datum: 2·16 metres below Ordnance Datum (Newlyn). HAT is 4·6 metres above Chart Datum; see 4.5

WALTON-ON-THE-NAZE LAT 51°51′N LONG 1°17′E
TIMES AND HEIGHTS OF HIGH AND LOW WATERS

TIME ZONE (UT)
For Summer Time add ONE hour in **non-shaded areas**

Dates in red are SPRINGS
Dates in blue are NEAPS

YEAR 2010

MAY

Time	m	Time	m
1 SA 0059 0704 1321 1931	4.4 0.6 4.1 0.5	**16** SU 0040 0631 1308 1912	4.3 0.6 4.1 0.5
2 SU 0140 0738 1359 2009	4.3 0.7 4.0 0.6	**17** M 0122 0710 1350 1955	4.3 0.7 4.0 0.5
3 M 0221 0812 1437 2047	4.1 0.9 3.9 0.7	**18** TU 0207 0754 1434 2043	4.2 0.8 3.9 0.5
4 TU 0305 0849 1517 2127	3.9 1.0 3.7 0.8	**19** W 0256 0847 1522 2140	4.1 0.9 3.8 0.5
5 W 0356 0934 1605 2218	3.6 1.2 3.6 0.9	**20** TH 0354 0952 1619 2250	4.0 1.1 3.8 0.6
6 TH 0456 1036 1704 2332	3.5 1.4 3.4 1.0	**21** F 0458 1106 1724	3.9 1.1 3.7
7 F 0604 1202 1817	3.4 1.5 3.3	**22** SA 0000 0605 1219 1836	0.5 3.8 1.1 3.7
8 SA 0048 0711 1321 1930	1.0 3.4 1.4 3.4	**23** SU 0105 0715 1326 1946	0.5 3.8 1.1 3.8
9 SU 0154 0814 1424 2029	1.0 3.5 1.3 3.6	**24** M 0209 0825 1428 2049	0.5 3.9 1.0 3.9
10 M 0250 0906 1514 2119	0.9 3.7 1.1 3.7	**25** TU 0310 0927 1525 2145	0.5 3.9 0.9 4.1
11 TU 0336 0951 1557 2202	0.8 3.8 0.9 3.9	**26** W 0404 1019 1617 2235	0.5 4.0 0.7 4.1
12 W 0415 1031 1637 2242	0.7 3.9 0.8 4.1	**27** TH 0451 1105 1706 2319	0.6 4.0 0.6 4.2
13 TH 0450 1109 1715 2320	0.7 4.0 0.7 4.1	**28** F 0533 1146 1754	0.6 4.1 0.5
14 F 0523 1147 1753 2359	0.6 4.0 0.6 4.2	**29** SA 0001 0613 1226 1839	4.2 0.7 4.1 0.5
15 SA 0556 1227 1832	0.6 4.1 0.6	**30** SU 0043 0651 1304 1922	4.2 0.8 4.1 0.5
		31 M 0124 0725 1341 1959	4.1 0.9 4.0 0.6

JUNE

Time	m	Time	m
1 TU 0206 0758 1419 2034	4.0 1.0 3.9 0.6	**16** W 0206 0800 1433 2046	4.3 0.8 4.1 0.3
2 W 0248 0831 1458 2109	3.9 1.0 3.8 0.7	**17** TH 0256 0851 1520 2139	4.3 0.9 4.1 0.3
3 TH 0333 0910 1541 2151	3.7 1.1 3.7 0.8	**18** F 0348 0945 1610 2235	4.1 0.9 4.0 0.3
4 F 0421 0957 1629 2243	3.6 1.2 3.6 0.9	**19** SA 0442 1042 1705 2333	4.0 1.0 4.0 0.4
5 SA 0513 1057 1723 2348	3.5 1.3 3.5 0.9	**20** SU 0540 1145 1807	3.9 1.1 3.9
6 SU 0609 1211 1825	3.4 1.4 3.5	**21** M 0033 0643 1251 1914	0.5 3.8 1.1 3.8
7 M 0052 0707 1327 1928	1.0 3.4 1.3 3.5	**22** TU 0137 0755 1400 2021	0.6 3.7 1.0 3.8
8 TU 0152 0806 1420 2027	1.0 3.5 1.2 3.6	**23** W 0244 0904 1505 2123	0.7 3.7 0.9 3.9
9 W 0247 0902 1520 2119	0.9 3.7 1.0 3.8	**24** TH 0345 1002 1605 2218	0.8 3.8 0.8 4.0
10 TH 0337 0953 1607 2208	0.8 3.8 0.8 3.9	**25** F 0435 1051 1659 2307	0.8 3.9 0.7 4.0
11 F 0421 1041 1652 2255	0.8 3.9 0.7 4.0	**26** SA 0520 1134 1748 2350	0.9 4.0 0.6 4.1
12 SA 0503 1127 1737 2341	0.8 4.0 0.6 4.2	**27** SU 0600 1214 1832	0.8 4.0 0.5
13 SU 0544 1213 1822	0.7 4.1 0.5	**28** M 0031 0637 1251 1910	4.1 0.9 4.0 0.5
14 M 0028 0627 1300 1908	4.3 0.7 4.1 0.4	**29** TU 0110 0712 1326 1944	4.1 0.9 4.0 0.5
15 TU 0117 0712 1346 1956	4.4 0.7 4.2 0.3	**30** W 0149 0743 1401 2015	4.0 0.9 4.0 0.5

JULY

Time	m	Time	m
1 TH 0228 0813 1437 2046	3.9 0.9 4.0 0.6	**16** F 0242 0836 1503 2119	4.4 0.7 4.4 0.2
2 F 0306 0845 1514 2118	3.8 1.0 3.9 0.6	**17** SA 0329 0922 1548 2207	4.2 0.8 4.3 0.3
3 SA 0344 0922 1552 2156	3.7 1.1 3.8 0.7	**18** SU 0417 1012 1637 2257	4.0 0.9 4.1 0.5
4 SU 0425 1006 1635 2240	3.6 1.2 3.7 0.9	**19** M 0509 1107 1733 2354	3.8 1.0 3.9 0.7
5 M 0511 1059 1725 2336	3.5 1.3 3.6 1.0	**20** TU 0609 1213 1842	3.6 1.1 3.8
6 TU 0605 1207 1826	3.4 1.3 3.5	**21** W 0101 0724 1334 1956	0.9 3.5 1.1 3.7
7 W 0046 0706 1334 1935	1.0 3.5 1.3 3.5	**22** TH 0221 0843 1451 2106	1.0 3.6 1.0 3.7
8 TH 0158 0813 1444 2041	1.0 3.5 1.1 3.6	**23** F 0327 0945 1558 2206	1.0 3.7 0.8 3.8
9 F 0304 0921 1540 2141	1.0 3.7 0.9 3.8	**24** SA 0420 1037 1654 2255	1.0 3.8 0.7 3.9
10 SA 0401 1020 1632 2237	0.9 3.8 0.7 4.0	**25** SU 0504 1120 1739 2337	1.0 3.9 0.6 4.0
11 SU 0451 1112 1722 2328	0.8 4.0 0.5 4.2	**26** M 0542 1158 1817	0.9 4.0 0.5
12 M 0538 1200 1811	0.8 4.1 0.3	**27** TU 0015 0617 1233 1849	4.0 0.9 4.1 0.5
13 TU 0018 0623 1248 1859	4.4 0.7 4.3 0.2	**28** W 0051 0650 1306 1919	4.1 0.8 4.1 0.5
14 W 0107 0707 1334 1946	4.5 0.7 4.4 0.1	**29** TH 0127 0720 1339 1947	4.0 0.8 4.1 0.5
15 TH 0155 0751 1419 2033	4.5 0.7 4.4 0.1	**30** F 0201 0750 1411 2015	4.0 0.8 4.1 0.5
		31 SA 0235 0820 1443 2043	3.9 0.8 4.0 0.6

AUGUST

Time	m	Time	m
1 SU 0307 0853 1515 2114	3.8 0.9 3.9 0.7	**16** M 0347 0941 1605 2215	4.0 0.8 4.1 0.6
2 M 0341 0929 1550 2149	3.7 1.0 3.8 0.8	**17** TU 0435 1032 1700 2308	3.7 0.9 3.9 0.9
3 TU 0421 1013 1632 2235	3.6 1.1 3.7 1.0	**18** W 0532 1136 1812	3.5 0.9 3.6
4 W 0512 1112 1729 2341	3.5 1.2 3.6 1.1	**19** TH 0022 0652 1310 1933	1.2 3.4 1.1 3.5
5 TH 0616 1235 1846	3.4 1.3 3.5	**20** F 0157 0820 1436 2049	1.3 3.4 1.0 3.6
6 F 0113 0733 1412 2010	1.2 3.4 1.1 3.6	**21** SA 0307 0924 1550 2150	1.2 3.6 0.8 3.8
7 SA 0241 0856 1516 2121	1.1 3.6 0.8 3.8	**22** SU 0401 1016 1643 2238	1.1 3.8 0.7 3.9
8 SU 0344 1001 1613 2221	0.9 3.8 0.6 4.0	**23** M 0443 1059 1721 2318	1.0 3.9 0.5 4.0
9 M 0436 1055 1706 2313	0.8 4.0 0.4 4.3	**24** TU 0519 1135 1753 2353	0.9 4.0 0.5 4.0
10 TU 0523 1143 1755	0.7 4.2 0.2	**25** W 0552 1208 1821	0.8 4.1 0.4
11 W 0002 0606 1229 1842	4.4 0.6 4.4 0.1	**26** TH 0026 0623 1239 1847	4.1 0.7 4.1 0.4
12 TH 0049 0649 1313 1926	4.5 0.6 4.5 0.0	**27** F 0059 0654 1310 1914	4.1 0.7 4.2 0.4
13 F 0135 0731 1356 2009	4.5 0.6 4.5 0.1	**28** SA 0131 0724 1341 1940	4.0 0.7 4.1 0.5
14 SA 0219 0813 1437 2049	4.4 0.6 4.5 0.2	**29** SU 0202 0755 1410 2008	4.0 0.7 4.1 0.6
15 SU 0303 0856 1519 2130	4.2 0.7 4.3 0.4	**30** M 0231 0826 1440 2036	3.9 0.8 4.0 0.7
		31 TU 0302 0900 1513 2109	3.8 0.9 3.9 0.8

Chart Datum: 2·16 metres below Ordnance Datum (Newlyn). HAT is 4·6 metres above Chart Datum; see 4.5

TIME ZONE (UT)
For Summer Time add ONE hour in **non-shaded areas**

WALTON-ON-THE-NAZE   LAT 51°51'N   LONG 1°17'E
TIMES AND HEIGHTS OF HIGH AND LOW WATERS

Dates in red are SPRINGS
Dates in blue are NEAPS

YEAR 2010

SEPTEMBER

Time	m		Time	m
1 0339	3.6		**16** 0453	3.4
0940	1.0		1105	1.0
W 1554	3.8		TH 1744	3.5
◑ 2152	1.0		2342	1.4
2 0427	3.5		**17** 0614	3.3
1036	1.1		1241	1.1
TH 1649	3.6		F 1908	3.4
2257	1.2			
3 0532	3.4		**18** 0123	1.4
1156	1.2		0746	3.3
F 1808	3.5		SA 1410	1.0
			2025	3.5
4 0042	1.3		**19** 0238	1.3
0659	3.3		0853	3.5
SA 1345	1.0		SU 1528	0.8
1947	3.6		2126	3.7
5 0219	1.2		**20** 0333	1.2
0834	3.5		0946	3.7
SU 1453	0.7		M 1618	0.7
2102	3.8		2212	3.9
6 0321	1.0		**21** 0415	1.0
0939	3.8		1028	3.9
M 1551	0.5		TU 1652	0.6
2203	4.1		2250	4.0
7 0413	0.8		**22** 0451	0.9
1032	4.1		1104	4.0
TU 1645	0.3		W 1720	0.5
2254	4.3		2324	4.0
8 0500	0.7		**23** 0524	0.8
1119	4.3		1136	4.1
W 1734	0.1		TH 1747	0.5
● 2341	4.4		○ 2356	4.1
9 0543	0.6		**24** 0556	0.7
1203	4.5		1207	4.1
TH 1818	0.0		F 1813	0.5
10 0026	4.5		**25** 0028	4.1
0625	0.5		0627	0.7
F 1246	4.6		SA 1238	4.2
1900	0.0		1839	0.5
11 0109	4.5		**26** 0059	4.1
0708	0.5		0659	0.6
SA 1328	4.6		SU 1309	4.2
1939	0.2		1906	0.5
12 0152	4.4		**27** 0129	4.0
0749	0.5		0730	0.7
SU 1408	4.5		M 1339	4.1
2016	0.3		1933	0.6
13 0233	4.2		**28** 0200	3.9
0831	0.6		0803	0.7
M 1450	4.3		TU 1411	4.0
2053	0.6		2003	0.7
14 0315	3.9		**29** 0232	3.8
0915	0.7		0837	0.8
TU 1534	4.1		W 1447	4.0
2135	0.8		2039	0.9
15 0359	3.7		**30** 0309	3.7
1003	0.8		0919	0.9
W 1629	3.8		TH 1530	3.8
◑ 2227	1.1		2126	1.1

OCTOBER

Time	m		Time	m
1 0357	3.5		**16** 0528	3.3
1014	0.9		1202	1.0
F 1626	3.7		SA 1831	3.4
◑ 2233	1.3			
2 0501	3.4		**17** 0035	1.5
1139	1.0		0659	3.3
SA 1749	3.5		SU 1324	1.0
			1946	3.5
3 0024	1.3		**18** 0154	1.4
0633	3.3		0809	3.4
SU 1320	0.9		M 1440	0.9
1925	3.6		2048	3.6
4 0152	1.2		**19** 0254	1.2
0807	3.5		0904	3.6
M 1426	0.6		TU 1535	0.8
2039	3.9		2136	3.8
5 0253	1.0		**20** 0340	1.1
0912	3.8		0949	3.8
TU 1526	0.4		W 1612	0.7
2140	4.1		2216	3.9
6 0346	0.8		**21** 0419	0.9
1006	4.1		1027	3.9
W 1620	0.2		TH 1642	0.6
2231	4.3		2251	4.0
7 0434	0.7		**22** 0454	0.8
1053	4.3		1102	4.0
TH 1708	0.1		F 1711	0.6
● 2317	4.4		2324	4.0
8 0519	0.6		**23** 0528	0.7
1136	4.5		1135	4.1
F 1751	0.1		SA 1739	0.6
			○ 2356	4.1
9 0001	4.4		**24** 0602	0.6
0603	0.5		1207	4.1
SA 1219	4.5		SU 1807	0.6
1831	0.2			
10 0043	4.4		**25** 0028	4.1
0646	0.5		0635	0.6
SU 1300	4.5		M 1240	4.2
1909	0.3		1834	0.6
11 0124	4.3		**26** 0102	4.1
0729	0.5		0709	0.6
M 1341	4.4		TU 1314	4.1
1946	0.6		1904	0.7
12 0204	4.1		**27** 0136	4.0
0812	0.5		0744	0.6
TU 1423	4.2		W 1351	4.1
2022	0.8		1939	0.8
13 0244	3.9		**28** 0212	3.9
0854	0.6		0823	0.6
W 1509	4.0		TH 1431	4.0
2103	1.0		2021	0.9
14 0327	3.7		**29** 0252	3.8
0940	0.8		0908	0.7
TH 1604	3.7		F 1518	3.9
◑ 2153	1.2		2112	1.1
15 0417	3.5		**30** 0341	3.6
1038	0.9		1007	0.8
F 1714	3.4		SA 1619	3.7
2303	1.5		◑ 2223	1.3
			31 0446	3.5
			1135	0.8
			SU 1739	3.6

NOVEMBER

Time	m		Time	m
1 0001	1.3		**16** 0055	1.5
0611	3.5		0710	3.4
M 1254	0.7		TU 1331	1.0
1859	3.7		1954	3.5
2 0119	1.2		**17** 0203	1.3
0735	3.6		0811	3.5
TU 1358	0.5		W 1431	0.9
2011	3.9		2049	3.6
3 0222	1.0		**18** 0258	1.2
0842	3.9		0902	3.6
W 1457	0.4		TH 1521	0.8
2114	4.0		2135	3.8
4 0318	0.8		**19** 0343	1.0
0938	4.1		0946	3.8
TH 1553	0.3		F 1601	0.8
2208	4.2		2215	3.9
5 0409	0.7		**20** 0424	0.8
1027	4.2		1026	3.9
F 1642	0.3		SA 1637	0.7
2255	4.2		2252	4.0
6 0457	0.6		**21** 0502	0.7
1112	4.4		1104	4.0
SA 1726	0.4		SU 1709	0.7
● 2339	4.3		○ 2329	4.0
7 0544	0.5		**22** 0539	0.6
1155	4.4		1141	4.1
SU 1809	0.4		M 1740	0.7
8 0020	4.3		**23** 0006	4.1
0631	0.4		0616	0.6
M 1238	4.4		TU 1220	4.2
1848	0.6		1811	0.7
9 0101	4.2		**24** 0045	4.1
0716	0.4		0655	0.5
TU 1321	4.3		W 1300	4.2
1926	0.7		1847	0.7
10 0141	4.1		**25** 0125	4.1
0759	0.5		0735	0.5
W 1404	4.1		TH 1342	4.2
2002	0.9		1928	0.8
11 0220	3.9		**26** 0206	4.0
0840	0.6		0818	0.5
TH 1450	3.9		F 1427	4.1
2040	1.1		2015	0.9
12 0301	3.8		**27** 0249	3.9
0922	0.7		0908	0.5
F 1541	3.7		SA 1519	4.0
2123	1.2		2110	1.0
13 0347	3.6		**28** 0339	3.8
1011	0.8		1008	0.5
SA 1638	3.5		SU 1617	3.9
◑ 2221	1.4		◑ 2218	1.2
14 0444	3.4		**29** 0437	3.7
1116	0.9		1117	0.6
SU 1742	3.4		M 1722	3.8
2336	1.5		2332	1.2
15 0555	3.3		**30** 0546	3.7
1225	1.0		1224	0.5
M 1850	3.4		TU 1830	3.8

DECEMBER

Time	m		Time	m
1 0043	1.2		**16** 0056	1.4
0701	3.7		0703	3.4
W 1326	0.5		TH 1326	1.0
1940	3.8		1943	3.4
2 0150	1.1		**17** 0207	1.3
0810	3.8		0807	3.5
TH 1428	0.5		F 1427	1.0
2048	3.9		2043	3.6
3 0252	0.9		**18** 0303	1.1
0912	4.0		0902	3.6
F 1528	0.6		SA 1521	0.9
2148	4.0		2136	3.7
4 0349	0.8		**19** 0352	0.9
1006	4.1		0952	3.8
SA 1622	0.6		SU 1607	0.9
2239	4.0		2223	3.8
5 0443	0.6		**20** 0437	0.8
1055	4.2		1038	3.9
SU 1711	0.6		M 1648	0.8
● 2324	4.1		2308	4.0
6 0534	0.5		**21** 0520	0.6
1141	4.2		1122	4.1
M 1755	0.7		TU 1726	0.8
			○ 2351	4.1
7 0006	4.1		**22** 0602	0.5
0622	0.4		1206	4.2
TU 1225	4.2		W 1805	0.8
1837	0.8			
8 0046	4.1		**23** 0035	4.2
0708	0.4		0645	0.4
W 1307	4.2		TH 1252	4.3
1915	0.9		1845	0.7
9 0125	4.1		**24** 0119	4.2
0749	0.5		0729	0.3
TH 1350	4.1		F 1338	4.3
1949	1.0		1929	0.8
10 0203	4.0		**25** 0203	4.2
0826	0.5		0814	0.3
F 1432	3.9		SA 1425	4.3
2022	1.0		2016	0.8
11 0241	3.9		**26** 0247	4.1
0901	0.6		0902	0.3
SA 1515	3.8		SU 1513	4.2
2057	1.1		2105	0.9
12 0321	3.8		**27** 0332	4.1
0938	0.7		0953	0.3
SU 1601	3.6		M 1604	4.0
2138	1.2		2159	1.0
13 0405	3.6		**28** 0420	4.0
1023	0.8		1049	0.5
M 1649	3.5		TU 1658	3.9
◑ 2230	1.3		◑ 2258	1.1
14 0456	3.5		**29** 0517	3.9
1119	0.9		1149	0.5
TU 1743	3.4		W 1757	3.7
2336	1.4			
15 0556	3.4		**30** 0004	1.1
1223	1.0		0626	3.8
W 1842	3.4		TH 1252	0.7
			1906	3.6
			31 0118	1.1
			0741	3.7
			F 1400	0.8
			2024	3.6

Chart Datum: 2·16 metres below Ordnance Datum (Newlyn). HAT is 4·6 metres above Chart Datum; see 4.5

》》 **FREE** monthly updates from 《《
www.reedsalmanac.co.uk

9.4.19 & 20 RIVERS STOUR AND ORWELL

9.4.19 RIVER STOUR

Essex/Suffolk **51°57'·06N 01°17'·77E** (Guard PHM buoy)

❀❀❀❀♨♨♨ ❁❁❁

CHARTS AC 5607, 2052, 2693, 1491, 1594; Imray C1, Y16, 2000 Series; Stanfords 5, 6.

TIDES Harwich +0050 Dover; ML 2·1; Duration 0630

Standard Port HARWICH (⟶)

Times				Height (metres)			
High Water		Low Water		MHWS	MHWN	MLWN	MLWS
0000	0600	0000	0600	4·0	3·4	1·1	0·4
1200	1800	1200	1800				
Differences MISTLEY							
+0032	+0027	−0010	−0012	0·0	0·0	−0·1	−0·1

SHELTER Good at Shotley Marina; access (H24) via chan dredged 2m, outer limits lit, to lock. Enter only on F.G tfc lt. AB also at Halfpenny Pier (H24), Mistley, Manningtree (both dry). No yachts at Parkeston Quay. ⚓s off Wrabness Pt, Holbrook Creek and Stutton Ness.

NAVIGATION WPT Cork Sand Yacht Bn, 51°55'·21N 01°25'·20E.

• Keep clear of commercial shipping/HSS. Outside the hbr, yachts should cross the DW chan at 90° between Rolling Ground and Platters buoys. See 9.4.5. Stay clear of the DW chan (Y lit SPMs) using Recommended Yacht Track, running S and W of DW chan to beyond Harwich. High Speed Craft operate in this area and may generate large waves causing serious impact on small craft particularly in shallow waters.

• **Caution:** Bkwtr, ESE of Blackman's Hd, covers at HW; marked by PHM lit Bn, only 5ca W of main chan. The Guard Shoal (0·8m), about 2ca S of Guard PHM, lies close to the Recommended Yacht Track. R Stour is well marked; sp limit 8kn. Beware 'The Horse' 4ca NE and drying bank 1½ca NW of Wrabness Pt. From Mistley Quay local knowledge needed for the narrow, tortuous chan to Manningtree.

Special local sound signals
Commercial vessels may use these additional signals:

Four short and rapid blasts followed by one short blast	} = I am turning short around to stbd.
Four short and rapid blasts followed by two short blasts	} = I am turning short around to port.
One prolonged blast	= I am leaving dock, quay or ⚓.

LIGHTS AND MARKS The R Stour to Mistley Quay is lit. At Cattawade, 8M up river, a conspic chy leads 270° through the best water up to Harkstead Pt. Shotley Marina: a Dir lt at lock indicates the dredged chan (2·0m) by Inogen (or Moiré) visual marker lt which is a square, ambered display; a vert B line indicates on the appr centre line 339°. If off the centre line, arrows indicate the direction to steer to regain it.

R/T *Harwich VTS* Ch **71** 11 14 16 (H24). Yachts should monitor Ch 71 for tfc info, but not transmit. Weather, tidal info and possibly

help in poor vis may be available on request. The Hbr Patrol launch listens on Ch 11. Hbr Radar Ch 20. Shotley Marina Ch **80** (lock master).

TELEPHONE (Code 01255) Harwich HM 243030; Hbr Ops 243000; Marinecall 09068 226455; MRCC 675518; Police 0300 3334444; Dr 201299; Ⓗ 201200.

FACILITIES HARWICH Halfpenny Pier Available Apr–Oct, no reservations. Free 0900-1600; overnight: £1·00/m up to 20m, £30 > 20m, max stay 72hrs, FW, showers. **Town** P, D, ME, SM, Gas, El, ✕, 🛒, R, Bar, ✉, Ⓑ, ⇌, ✈ (Cambridge). **Ferries:** Hook of Holland: 2/day; 6¼ Hrs; Stena (www.stenaline.co.uk); Esbjerg: 3/week; 18 Hrs; DFDS Seaways (dfdsseaways.com).

SHOTLEY (01473) **Shotley Marina** (350, visitors welcome) ☎ 788982 H24, sales@shotleymarina.co.uk, £2.20, access H24 via lock (width 7m); Wi-fi, D(H24), 🖥, ♿, ME, El, Ⓔ, ✕, BH (40 ton), C, 🛒, BY, CH, SM, Wi-fi, Bar, R, Gas, Gaz, Ferries to Harwich; **Shotley SC** ☎ 787500, Slip, FW, Bar.

WRABNESS: M, FW, 🛒.

MANNINGTREE, AB (drying), FW. **Stour SC** ☎ (01206) 393924, M (drying but free), FW, Bar, showers. **Town** P & D (cans), 🛒, Gas.

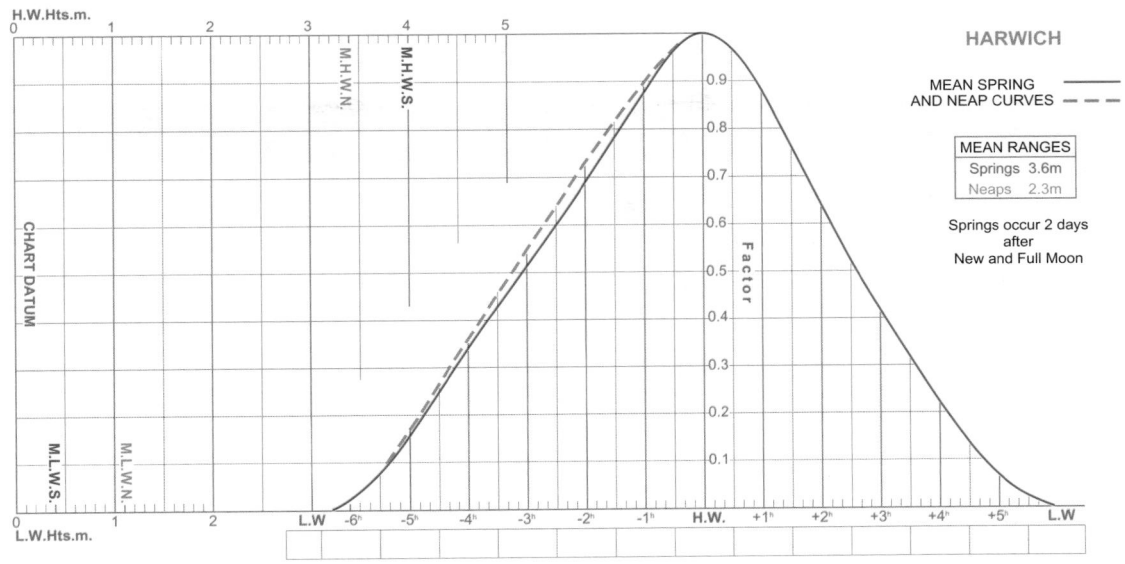

HARWICH

MEAN SPRING ———
AND NEAP CURVES − − −

MEAN RANGES
Springs 3.6m
Neaps 2.3m

Springs occur 2 days
after
New and Full Moon

9.4.20 RIVER ORWELL

Suffolk 51°57'·06N 01°17'·77E (Guard PHM by) 🌊🌊🌊⚓⚓⚓⭐⭐⭐

CHARTS AC 5607, 2052, 2693, 1491; Imray C1, Y16, 2000 Series; Stanfords 5, 6. A *Yachting Guide to Harwich Harbour and its Rivers* has much useful info; it can be obtained free from Harwich Haven Authority, The Quay, Harwich CO12 3HH; ☎ (01255) 243030.

TIDES Pin Mill +0100 Dover; Ipswich +0115 Dover; ML 2·4; Duration 0555

Standard Port HARWICH (→)

Times				Height (metres)			
High Water		Low Water		MHWS	MHWN	MLWN	MLWS
0000	0600	0000	0600	4·0	3·4	1·1	0·4
1200	1800	1200	1800				
Differences IPSWICH							
+0015	+0025	0000	+0010	+0·2	0·0	−0·1	−0·1

SHELTER Good. Ent and river well marked, but many unlit moorings line both banks. ⚓s above Shotley Pt on W side, or off Pinmill. No yacht facilities at Felixstowe. Ⓥ's (pre-book) at Suffolk Yacht Hbr, Woolverstone Marina, Ipswich Dock (via Prince Philip Lock) and Fox's Marina (Ipswich) all accessible H24 as is Ipswich Haven – call *Ipswich Port Radio* Ch 68 before arrival, then call *Neptune Marina* or *Ipswich Port Marina*.

NAVIGATION Appr/ent from seaward as in 9.4.19. WPT Shotley Spit SCM buoy, Q (6)+L Fl 15s, 51°57'·21N 01°17'·68E, at river ent.

- Keep clear of the many large ships, ferries from/to Harwich, Felixstowe and Ipswich, especially container ships turning between Trinity container terminal, Shotley Spit and Guard buoys.
- 6kn speed limit in R Orwell. Ipswich Dock ent closed when tide >4.6m above CD. Ipswich New Cut entrance, *Velocity Control Structure is raised from seabed when required with the top of it just below sea level*; 3 FR (vert) = no passage.

LIGHTS AND MARKS Suffolk Yacht Hbr appr marked by four bns and ldg lts: front Iso Y; rear Oc Y 4s.
A14 bridge lts: Centre FY (clearance 38m)
No 9 Pier 2 FR (vert) } shown up and
No 10 Pier 2 FG (vert) } down stream.
● and ● tfc lts control ent to Ipswich Dock (H24).
Ipswich New Cut: 3 FR (vert) when closed to navigation.

R/T Call: *Ipswich Port Radio* and *Ipswich Lock Control* VHF Ch 68 (H24). Once above Shotley Pt or anywhere in the area, monitor Ch 68 continuously in fog. Suffolk Yacht Hbr, Woolverstone Marina, Fox's Marina: Ch 80 M. Neptune Marina: Ch M, 80 (0800-1730LT), Ipswich Haven Marina Ch M 80.

TELEPHONE (Code 01473) Orwell Navigation Service 211066 (also Ipswich HM and Port Radio); MRCC (01255) 675518; Marinecall 09068 226455; Police 613500; Ⓗ 712233.

FACILITIES
LEVINGTON Suffolk Yacht Hbr (SYH) Ch 80 (550+Ⓥ £2.19) ☎ 659240, info@syharbour.co.uk, slip (launching £12.50), &,P & D (0815-1750), ME, El, Ⓔ, ✕, C (15 ton), BH (10/60 ton), CH, 🛒, Gas, Gaz, LPG, SM, Wi-fi, 🚿, &, ⊛, Access H24; **Haven Ports YC** ☎ 659658, R, Bar. **Town** ✉, Ⓑ (Felixstowe), ⇌ (bus to Ipswich), ✈ (Cambridge/Norwich).

PIN MILL King's Boatyard 780258 M (£6.50/night), Slip, L, CH, C (6 ton), ✕, ME, El, FW, Bar, R; **Pin Mill SC** ☎ 780271; Facilities at Ipswich.

WOOLVERSTONE Marina 345+Ⓥ, £2.70 (inc electricity). ☎ 780206 (H24), Mob 07803 968209. D (0800-1800), BY, ME, El, Gas, Gaz, 🚿, &, Wi-fi, C (20 ton), SM, CH, Slip, 🛒, R. **Royal Harwich YC** ☎ 780319, AB, R, Bar. **Town** Chelmondiston: ✉, 🛒.

IPSWICH Fox's Marina 75 + some Ⓥ £1.98. Ch 80, ☎ 689111. D (0800-1730), BY, Gas, Gaz, BH (44/70 ton), C (7 ton), P, ME, El, Ⓔ, ✕, CH, ACA, SM, Rigger, Wi-fi, &, Bar.

Prince Philip Lock gives H24 access to **Neptune Marina** 150+Ⓥ £2.18, ☎ 215204; and to **Ipswich Haven Marina** 270+Ⓥ ☎ 236644, £2.10. Both are near city centre. Services: D (0800-1700 Neptune; 0800-1900 Haven), ✕, ME, C, BH, BY, El, Ⓔ, Gas, Gaz, 🚿, R, Bar, Wi-fi. **Orwell YC** ☎ 602288, Slip, FW, Bar. **City** ✉, Ⓑ, P (cans), ⇌, ✈ (Cambridge/Norwich).

HARWICH — LAT 51°57'N LONG 1°17'E
TIMES AND HEIGHTS OF HIGH AND LOW WATERS

TIME ZONE (UT)
For Summer Time add ONE hour in **non-shaded areas**

Dates in red are **SPRINGS**
Dates in blue are **NEAPS**

YEAR 2010

JANUARY

Time	m		Time	m
1 0519	0.5	**16**	0009	3.8
1148	4.1		0608	0.6
F 1737	0.6	SA 1234	3.7
			1804	0.9
2 0014	4.0	**17**	0044	3.8
0608	0.3		0640	0.6
SA 1239	4.2	SU 1308	3.7
1821	0.6		1836	0.8
3 0101	4.1	**18**	0113	3.7
0656	0.2		0708	0.6
SU 1328	4.2	M 1337	3.7
1905	0.6		1907	0.8
4 0147	4.1	**19**	0141	3.7
0743	0.1		0737	0.6
M 1406	4.1	TU 1406	3.7
1949	0.7		1940	0.8
5 0233	4.0	**20**	0212	3.7
0831	0.2		0810	0.6
TU 1505	4.0	W 1440	3.7
2035	0.8		2014	0.8
6 0320	3.9	**21**	0246	3.7
0919	0.3		0844	0.6
W 1554	3.9	TH 1518	3.6
2122	0.9		2051	0.9
7 0408	3.8	**22**	0324	3.7
1012	0.4		0922	0.7
TH 1646	3.7	F 1601	3.6
☽ 2214	1.0		2132	0.9
8 0502	3.7	**23**	0407	3.6
1111	0.6		1004	0.8
F 1741	3.5	SA 1651	3.4
2320	1.1	☽ 2221	1.1
9 0603	3.5	**24**	0500	3.4
1219	0.8		1056	0.9
SA 1843	3.3	SU 1750	3.3
			2323	1.2
10 0042	1.2	**25**	0607	3.3
0710	3.4		1208	1.0
SU 1324	0.9	M 1854	3.2
1949	3.3			
11 0156	1.1	**26**	0044	1.2
0819	3.4		0719	3.3
M 1424	1.0	TU 1334	1.1
2054	3.3		2002	3.3
12 0300	1.0	**27**	0205	1.1
0923	3.5		0832	3.4
TU 1519	1.0	W 1447	1.0
2153	3.5		2113	3.4
13 0357	0.8	**28**	0317	0.9
1020	3.6		0943	3.6
W 1608	0.9	TH 1548	0.8
2244	3.6		2217	3.6
14 0447	0.7	**29**	0419	0.6
1110	3.7		1045	3.8
TH 1651	0.9	F 1640	0.7
2329	3.7		2312	3.9
15 0531	0.6	**30**	0511	0.3
1154	3.8		1139	4.1
F 1730	0.9	SA 1726	0.6
●		○		
		31	0001	4.0
			0558	0.1
		SU 1228	4.2
			1808	0.5

FEBRUARY

Time	m		Time	m
1 0047	4.1	**16**	0055	3.7
0643	0.0		0641	0.5
M 1314	4.2	TU 1315	3.7
1850	0.5		1845	0.7
2 0131	4.2	**17**	0121	3.7
0726	0.0		0710	0.5
TU 1359	4.2	W 1341	3.7
1931	0.5		1916	0.7
3 0213	4.2	**18**	0147	3.8
0808	0.0		0740	0.5
W 1442	4.1	TH 1411	3.7
2012	0.6		1947	0.7
4 0255	4.1	**19**	0218	3.8
0851	0.2		0811	0.5
TH 1525	3.9	F 1446	3.7
2055	0.7		2022	0.7
5 0337	3.9	**20**	0252	3.8
0936	0.4		0845	0.6
F 1609	3.6	SA 1526	3.6
☽ 2139	0.8		2101	0.8
6 0424	3.7	**21**	0333	3.7
1027	0.7		0925	0.7
SA 1656	3.4	SU 1612	3.4
2233	1.0		2147	0.9
7 0519	3.5	**22**	0422	3.5
1134	0.9		1014	0.9
SU 1751	3.2	M 1708	3.2
		☽ 2245	1.1
8 0000	1.2	**23**	0527	3.3
0632	3.2		1118	1.1
M 1250	1.1	TU 1817	3.1
1907	3.0			
9 0133	1.1	**24**	0005	1.1
0757	3.2		0648	3.2
TU 1357	1.2	W 1307	1.2
2028	3.1		1933	3.1
10 0244	1.0	**25**	0147	1.0
0907	3.3		0814	3.3
W 1457	1.1	TH 1435	1.1
2132	3.3		2054	3.3
11 0344	0.8	**26**	0308	0.8
1005	3.5		0933	3.5
TH 1549	1.0	F 1536	0.9
2224	3.5		2201	3.6
12 0433	0.6	**27**	0409	0.4
1053	3.7		1033	3.8
F 1633	0.9	SA 1625	0.7
2310	3.7		2254	3.9
13 0514	0.5	**28**	0458	0.2
1137	3.8		1124	4.1
SA 1711	0.8	SU 1709	0.5
2350	3.8	○ 2342	4.1
14 0548	0.5			
1215	3.8			
SU 1744				
●				
15 0025	3.8			
0615	0.5			
M 1249	3.7			
1814	0.7			

MARCH

Time	m		Time	m
1 0542	0.0	**16**	0542	0.5
1210	4.2		1220	3.8
M 1750	0.4	TU 1748	0.7
2 0026	4.2	**17**	0028	3.7
0623	-0.1		0610	0.5
TU 1253	4.2	W 1248	3.7
1830	0.4		1819	0.6
3 0108	4.3	**18**	0055	3.7
0702	-0.1		0640	0.4
W 1335	4.2	TH 1314	3.7
1910	0.4		1851	0.6
4 0148	4.2	**19**	0122	3.8
0741	0.0		0711	0.4
TH 1415	4.0	F 1343	3.8
1949	0.4		1924	0.5
5 0228	4.2	**20**	0153	3.8
0820	0.2		0742	0.5
F 1453	3.9	SA 1418	3.7
2028	0.5		1959	0.6
6 0308	4.0	**21**	0229	3.8
0900	0.5		0818	0.6
SA 1532	3.6	SU 1456	3.6
2109	0.7		2040	0.6
7 0351	3.7	**22**	0311	3.7
0945	0.8		0900	0.7
SU 1613	3.4	M 1540	3.4
☽ 2157	0.9		2127	0.8
8 0443	3.4	**23**	0402	3.5
1046	1.1		0949	0.9
M 1701	3.2	TU 1635	3.2
2320	1.1	☽ 2226	0.9
9 0554	3.1	**24**	0509	3.3
1215	1.3		1053	1.2
TU 1810	3.0	W 1748	3.1
			2349	1.0
10 0109	1.1	**25**	0634	3.2
0735	3.1		1254	1.3
W 1330	1.3	TH 1913	3.1
1956	3.0			
11 0221	1.0	**26**	0138	0.9
0845	3.2		0803	3.3
TH 1432	1.2	F 1418	1.1
2103	3.2		2033	3.3
12 0320	0.8	**27**	0254	0.6
0941	3.5		0917	3.6
F 1525	1.0	SA 1516	0.9
2156	3.5		2137	3.6
13 0407	0.6	**28**	0351	0.3
1029	3.7		1014	3.9
SA 1608	0.9	SU 1604	0.6
2242	3.6		2230	3.9
14 0445	0.5	**29**	0438	0.1
1111	3.8		1102	4.1
SU 1645	0.8	M 1648	0.5
2322	3.7		2317	4.1
15 0515	0.5	**30**	0520	0.0
1149	3.8		1147	4.2
M 1717	0.7	TU 1729	0.4
● 2357	3.7	○		
		31	0001	4.2
			0558	0.0
		W 1229	4.2
			1809	0.3

APRIL

Time	m		Time	m
1 0043	4.2	**16**	0027	3.8
0637	0.1		0613	0.5
TH 1309	4.1	F 1247	3.8
1849	0.3		1830	0.5
2 0123	4.2	**17**	0100	3.8
0714	0.2		0646	0.5
F 1347	4.0	SA 1321	3.8
1928	0.4		1906	0.5
3 0203	4.1	**18**	0135	3.9
0751	0.4		0721	0.5
SA 1423	3.8	SU 1357	3.8
2006	0.5		1945	0.5
4 0243	3.9	**19**	0216	3.8
0828	0.6		0800	0.6
SU 1459	3.6	M 1437	3.7
2045	0.6		2028	0.5
5 0327	3.7	**20**	0302	3.7
0909	0.9		0844	0.8
M 1539	3.4	TU 1523	3.5
2132	0.8		2119	0.6
6 0417	3.4	**21**	0358	3.5
1002	1.2		0936	1.0
TU 1627	3.2	W 1620	3.3
☽ 2246	1.0	☽ 2221	0.8
7 0521	3.1	**22**	0506	3.4
1130	1.4		1042	1.2
W 1729	3.0	TH 1735	3.2
			2350	0.8
8 0035	1.0	**23**	0627	3.3
0658	3.0		1233	1.2
TH 1254	1.4	F 1856	3.2
1904	3.0			
9 0145	0.9	**24**	0120	0.7
0812	3.2		0745	3.4
F 1358	1.3	SA 1351	1.1
2022	3.2		2007	3.4
10 0241	0.8	**25**	0229	0.5
0908	3.4		0851	3.6
SA 1451	1.1	SU 1449	0.9
2118	3.4		2108	3.6
11 0327	0.7	**26**	0324	0.3
0956	3.6		0947	3.8
SU 1534	0.9	M 1539	0.7
2205	3.5		2202	3.8
12 0403	0.6	**27**	0411	0.2
1038	3.7		1037	4.0
M 1611	0.8	TU 1625	0.5
2246	3.6		2251	4.0
13 0434	0.5	**28**	0454	0.2
1115	3.8		1122	4.0
TU 1645	0.7	W 1709	0.4
2323	3.7	○ 2337	4.1
14 0506	0.5	**29**	0534	0.2
1147	3.8		1205	4.0
W 1720	0.6	TH 1751	0.4
● 2356	3.7			
15 0540	0.5	**30**	0020	4.1
1217	3.8		0612	0.3
TH 1755	0.5	F 1245	4.0
			1832	0.4

Chart Datum: 2·02 metres below Ordnance Datum (Newlyn). HAT is 4·4 metres above Chart Datum; see 4.5

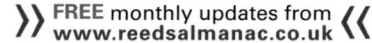

TIME ZONE (UT)
For Summer Time add ONE hour in **non-shaded areas**

HARWICH LAT 51°57'N LONG 1°17'E
TIMES AND HEIGHTS OF HIGH AND LOW WATERS

Dates in red are SPRINGS
Dates in blue are NEAPS

YEAR **2010**

MAY

Time	m	Time	m
1 0102	4.1	**16** 0043	3.9
0650	0.4	0629	0.6
SA 1322	3.9	SU 1305	3.8
1912	0.4	1855	0.4
2 0143	4.0	**17** 0125	3.9
0726	0.6	0708	0.6
SU 1358	3.8	M 1345	3.8
1950	0.5	1938	0.4
3 0224	3.8	**18** 0211	3.9
0803	0.8	0750	0.7
M 1434	3.7	TU 1429	3.7
2029	0.6	2026	0.4
4 0307	3.6	**19** 0301	3.8
0841	1.0	0837	0.8
TU 1514	3.5	W 1518	3.6
2114	0.8	2119	0.5
5 0355	3.4	**20** 0358	3.7
0928	1.2	0930	1.0
W 1601	3.4	TH 1617	3.5
2215	0.9	☾ 2221	0.5
6 0449	3.2	**21** 0502	3.6
1034	1.3	1034	1.1
TH 1658	3.2	F 1725	3.4
☽ 2334	1.0	2337	0.6
7 0556	3.1	**22** 0611	3.5
1156	1.4	1159	1.1
F 1806	3.1	SA 1834	3.4
8 0045	0.9	**23** 0052	0.5
0714	3.1	0718	3.5
SA 1306	1.3	SU 1316	1.1
1919	3.1	1938	3.5
9 0141	0.9	**24** 0157	0.5
0818	3.3	0821	3.6
SU 1402	1.2	M 1418	0.9
2023	3.3	2038	3.6
10 0228	0.8	**25** 0254	0.4
0910	3.4	0919	3.7
M 1449	1.0	TU 1513	0.8
2116	3.4	2135	3.8
11 0311	0.7	**26** 0344	0.4
0954	3.6	1011	3.8
TU 1531	0.9	W 1604	0.6
2202	3.5	2228	3.9
12 0352	0.6	**27** 0429	0.4
1034	3.7	1100	3.9
W 1612	0.7	TH 1652	0.5
2244	3.6	○ 2317	3.9
13 0433	0.6	**28** 0512	0.5
1111	3.8	1144	3.9
TH 1653	0.6	F 1737	0.5
2324	3.7		
14 0512	0.5	**29** 0004	3.9
1148	3.8	0552	0.6
F 1733	0.5	SA 1226	3.9
●		1820	0.4
15 0003	3.8	**30** 0048	3.9
0551	0.5	0630	0.7
SA 1226	3.9	SU 1304	3.8
1813	0.5	1902	0.5
		31 0129	3.8
		0707	0.8
		M 1339	3.8
		1941	0.5

JUNE

Time	m	Time	m
1 0209	3.7	**16** 0207	4.0
0742	0.9	0744	0.7
TU 1415	3.7	W 1426	3.9
2017	0.6	2022	0.2
2 0249	3.6	**17** 0258	4.0
0819	1.0	0830	0.8
W 1453	3.6	TH 1515	3.8
2056	0.7	2113	0.3
3 0331	3.5	**18** 0351	3.9
0901	1.1	0920	0.8
TH 1536	3.5	F 1607	3.7
2142	0.7	2209	0.3
4 0416	3.4	**19** 0446	3.7
0951	1.2	1015	1.0
F 1626	3.4	SA 1704	3.6
☽ 2236	0.8	☾ 2311	0.5
5 0506	3.3	**20** 0546	3.6
1051	1.2	1122	1.0
SA 1722	3.3	SU 1806	3.6
2336	0.9		
6 0601	3.2	**21** 0018	0.6
1157	1.3	0647	3.5
SU 1821	3.2	M 1238	1.1
		1908	3.5
7 0035	0.9	**22** 0124	0.6
0700	3.3	0750	3.5
M 1301	1.2	TU 1348	1.0
1921	3.3	2012	3.6
8 0132	0.8	**23** 0223	0.7
0801	3.3	0851	3.5
TU 1358	1.1	W 1451	0.9
2020	3.3	2114	3.6
9 0225	0.8	**24** 0318	0.7
0859	3.5	0949	3.6
W 1451	1.0	TH 1548	0.7
2117	3.5	2212	3.7
10 0316	0.7	**25** 0408	0.7
0951	3.6	1042	3.7
TH 1541	0.8	F 1640	0.6
2209	3.6	2305	3.8
11 0404	0.7	**26** 0453	0.8
1039	3.7	1129	3.8
F 1629	0.7	SA 1728	0.5
2258	3.8	○ 2353	3.8
12 0450	0.6	**27** 0535	0.8
1125	3.8	1212	3.8
SA 1716	0.5	SU 1812	0.5
● 2345	3.9		
13 0534	0.6	**28** 0037	3.8
1210	3.9	0614	0.8
SU 1802	0.4	M 1252	3.8
		1852	0.5
14 0031	4.0	**29** 0118	3.8
0617	0.6	0649	0.8
M 1255	3.9	TU 1326	3.8
1847	0.3	1928	0.5
15 0119	4.0	**30** 0155	3.7
0700	0.6	0723	0.9
TU 1339	3.9	W 1358	3.7
1934	0.2	1959	0.5

JULY

Time	m	Time	m
1 0228	3.6	**16** 0244	4.1
0757	0.9	0815	0.6
TH 1431	3.7	F 1459	4.0
2031	0.6	2055	0.1
2 0303	3.6	**17** 0331	4.0
0834	0.9	0900	0.7
F 1509	3.7	SA 1545	3.9
2108	0.6	2143	0.3
3 0341	3.5	**18** 0421	3.8
0915	1.0	0949	0.8
SA 1551	3.6	SU 1636	3.8
2151	0.7	☾ 2238	0.5
4 0425	3.5	**19** 0514	3.6
1002	1.1	1047	1.0
SU 1639	3.5	M 1733	3.6
☽ 2241	0.8	2342	0.7
5 0515	3.4	**20** 0613	3.4
1052	1.2	1202	1.1
M 1733	3.4	TU 1839	3.5
2340	0.9		
6 0610	3.3	**21** 0051	0.9
1203	1.2	0719	3.3
TU 1833	3.3	W 1322	1.1
		1950	3.4
7 0044	0.9	**22** 0157	0.9
0709	3.3	0828	3.3
W 1311	1.2	TH 1433	1.0
1934	3.3	2059	3.5
8 0147	0.9	**23** 0256	1.0
0812	3.4	0931	3.5
TH 1414	1.1	F 1537	0.8
2038	3.4	2200	3.6
9 0247	0.9	**24** 0349	0.9
0915	3.5	1026	3.6
F 1514	0.9	SA 1631	0.6
2140	3.6	2253	3.8
10 0343	0.8	**25** 0436	0.9
1014	3.7	1114	3.8
SA 1611	0.7	SU 1718	0.5
2239	3.8	2340	3.9
11 0434	0.7	**26** 0518	0.9
1107	3.8	1157	3.8
SU 1703	0.5	M 1759	0.5
● 2332	4.0	○	
12 0521	0.6	**27** 0023	3.9
1157	4.0	0555	0.9
M 1752	0.3	TU 1236	3.9
		1835	0.5
13 0021	4.1	**28** 0102	3.8
0605	0.6	0629	0.8
TU 1244	4.0	W 1310	3.8
1838	0.2	1905	0.5
14 0110	4.2	**29** 0134	3.7
0648	0.6	0700	0.8
W 1329	4.1	TH 1338	3.8
1924	0.1	1931	0.5
15 0157	4.2	**30** 0202	3.7
0731	0.6	0731	0.8
TH 1414	4.1	F 1406	3.8
2009	0.1	2000	0.6
		31 0231	3.7
		0805	0.8
		SA 1437	3.8
		2033	0.6

AUGUST

Time	m	Time	m
1 0305	3.7	**16** 0349	3.8
0841	0.9	0922	0.8
SU 1513	3.7	M 1603	3.9
2109	0.7	☽ 2203	0.6
2 0346	3.6	**17** 0437	3.5
0921	1.0	1015	1.0
M 1554	3.6	TU 1658	3.6
2150	0.8	2306	0.9
3 0433	3.5	**18** 0533	3.3
1007	1.1	1132	1.1
TU 1644	3.5	W 1810	3.4
2239	0.9		
4 0528	3.3	**19** 0022	1.1
1107	1.2	0646	3.2
W 1747	3.3	TH 1303	1.2
2349	1.1	1933	3.3
5 0630	3.3	**20** 0132	1.2
1225	1.3	0805	3.2
TH 1856	3.3	F 1418	1.0
		2044	3.4
6 0114	1.1	**21** 0234	1.2
0736	3.3	0910	3.4
F 1344	1.2	SA 1522	0.8
2007	3.3	2144	3.6
7 0225	1.1	**22** 0329	1.1
0847	3.4	1005	3.6
SA 1455	0.9	SU 1616	0.7
2120	3.5	2235	3.8
8 0326	0.9	**23** 0416	1.0
0954	3.6	1052	3.8
SU 1557	0.7	M 1659	0.5
2224	3.8	2320	3.9
9 0419	0.6	**24** 0457	0.9
1050	3.9	1135	3.9
M 1651	0.4	TU 1736	0.5
2318	4.1	○	
10 0505	0.6	**25** 0001	3.9
1140	4.1	0532	0.8
TU 1738	0.2	W 1213	3.9
●		1807	0.5
11 0006	4.2	**26** 0037	3.9
0548	0.6	0604	0.8
W 1226	4.2	TH 1245	3.9
1822	0.0	1833	0.5
12 0053	4.3	**27** 0107	3.8
0630	0.5	0633	0.8
TH 1310	4.3	F 1311	3.8
1904	0.0	1858	0.6
13 0137	4.3	**28** 0131	3.7
0711	0.5	0704	0.8
F 1352	4.3	SA 1336	3.8
1946	0.0	1927	0.6
14 0221	4.2	**29** 0157	3.8
0753	0.5	0736	0.8
SA 1433	4.2	SU 1403	3.8
2028	0.1	1957	0.6
15 0304	4.0	**30** 0229	3.8
0836	0.6	0810	0.8
SU 1516	4.1	M 1436	3.8
2113	0.3	2030	0.7
		31 0307	3.7
		0847	0.9
		TU 1515	3.7
		2107	0.8

F England

Chart Datum: 2·02 metres below Ordnance Datum (Newlyn). HAT is 4·4 metres above Chart Datum; see 4.5

TIME ZONE (UT)
For Summer Time add ONE hour in **non-shaded areas**

HARWICH   LAT 51°57'N   LONG 1°17'E
TIMES AND HEIGHTS OF HIGH AND LOW WATERS

Dates in red are SPRINGS
Dates in blue are NEAPS

YEAR 2010

SEPTEMBER
Time m / Time m

1 0351 3.5 / 0931 1.0 / W 1601 3.6 / ◗ 2153 1.0
16 0448 3.3 / 1003 1.0 / TH 1741 3.3 / 2351 1.4

2 0445 3.3 / 1026 1.1 / TH 1704 3.4 / 2252 1.2
17 0606 3.1 / 1243 1.2 / F 1913 3.2

3 0552 3.2 / 1143 1.2 / F 1823 3.2
18 0106 1.4 / 0737 3.2 / SA 1355 1.0 / 2022 3.4

4 0042 1.3 / 0706 3.2 / SA 1322 1.2 / 1944 3.3
19 0209 1.3 / 0841 3.4 / SU 1456 0.9 / 2119 3.6

5 0208 1.2 / 0823 3.3 / SU 1439 0.9 / 2104 3.6
20 0303 1.2 / 0935 3.6 / M 1547 0.7 / 2208 3.8

6 0309 1.0 / 0932 3.6 / M 1542 0.6 / 2207 3.9
21 0350 1.0 / 1022 3.8 / TU 1629 0.6 / 2252 3.9

7 0400 0.8 / 1028 3.9 / TU 1633 0.3 / 2259 4.1
22 0430 0.9 / 1104 3.9 / W 1703 0.6 / 2332 4.0

8 0445 0.6 / 1116 4.1 / W 1718 0.1 / ● 2345 4.3
23 0504 0.8 / 1142 3.9 / TH 1731 0.6 / ○

9 0527 0.5 / 1201 4.3 / TH 1800 0.0
24 0006 3.9 / 0534 0.8 / F 1214 3.8 / 1757 0.6

10 0029 4.3 / 0608 0.4 / F 1244 4.4 / 1839 0.0
25 0035 3.8 / 0605 0.7 / SA 1240 3.8 / 1825 0.6

11 0112 4.3 / 0649 0.4 / SA 1325 4.4 / 1919 0.1
26 0058 3.8 / 0637 0.7 / SU 1305 3.9 / 1855 0.6

12 0153 4.2 / 0730 0.5 / SU 1406 4.3 / 1959 0.3
27 0125 3.8 / 0710 0.7 / M 1335 3.9 / 1926 0.7

13 0233 4.0 / 0812 0.6 / M 1447 4.1 / 2041 0.5
28 0157 3.8 / 0744 0.7 / TU 1409 3.9 / 1959 0.7

14 0314 3.8 / 0856 0.7 / TU 1532 3.9 / 2127 0.8
29 0233 3.8 / 0823 0.8 / W 1449 3.8 / 2038 0.9

15 0357 3.5 / 0948 1.0 / W 1626 3.6 / ◗ 2227 1.1
30 0315 3.6 / 0908 0.9 / TH 1537 3.6 / 2125 1.1

OCTOBER
Time m / Time m

1 0406 3.4 / 1003 1.0 / F 1639 3.4 / ◗ 2223 1.3
16 0516 3.2 / 1213 1.1 / SA 1839 3.2

2 0516 3.2 / 1118 1.1 / SA 1800 3.3
17 0031 1.5 / 0652 3.2 / SU 1321 1.0 / 1948 3.3

3 0006 1.4 / 0639 3.2 / SU 1304 1.0 / 1926 3.4
18 0136 1.4 / 0801 3.3 / M 1418 0.9 / 2045 3.5

4 0145 1.3 / 0758 3.4 / M 1419 0.8 / 2043 3.6
19 0231 1.2 / 0857 3.5 / TU 1507 0.8 / 2135 3.7

5 0245 1.0 / 0904 3.6 / TU 1519 0.5 / 2143 3.9
20 0317 1.1 / 0945 3.7 / W 1548 0.7 / 2218 3.9

6 0336 0.8 / 0959 3.9 / W 1609 0.3 / 2234 4.1
21 0356 0.9 / 1028 3.8 / TH 1621 0.7 / 2257 3.9

7 0422 0.6 / 1048 4.1 / TH 1653 0.2 / ● 2320 4.3
22 0431 0.8 / 1106 3.8 / F 1651 0.7 / 2331 3.9

8 0505 0.5 / 1134 4.3 / F 1734 0.1
23 0505 0.8 / 1139 3.8 / SA 1723 0.6 / ○

9 0003 4.3 / 0546 0.4 / SA 1218 4.3 / 1813 0.2
24 0000 3.9 / 0539 0.7 / SU 1210 3.8 / 1756 0.7

10 0045 4.2 / 0628 0.4 / SU 1300 4.3 / 1852 0.3
25 0028 3.9 / 0614 0.7 / M 1300 3.9 / 1829 0.7

11 0125 4.1 / 0710 0.5 / M 1341 4.2 / 1932 0.5
26 0059 3.9 / 0650 0.7 / TU 1314 3.9 / 1902 0.7

12 0203 4.0 / 0751 0.6 / TU 1424 4.1 / 2012 0.7
27 0133 3.9 / 0727 0.7 / W 1353 3.9 / 1938 0.8

13 0242 3.8 / 0835 0.7 / W 1509 3.8 / 2054 1.0
28 0211 3.8 / 0808 0.7 / TH 1436 3.8 / 2020 0.9

14 0322 3.6 / 0926 0.8 / TH 1601 3.5 / ◗ 2147 1.3
29 0253 3.6 / 0855 0.8 / F 1527 3.7 / 2108 1.1

15 0410 3.4 / 1044 1.1 / F 1709 3.3 / 2309 1.5
30 0344 3.5 / 0951 0.9 / SA 1629 3.5 / ◗ 2206 1.3

31 0451 3.3 / 1105 0.9 / SU 1745 3.4 / 2330 1.4

NOVEMBER
Time m / Time m

1 0615 3.3 / 1238 0.9 / M 1904 3.5
16 0044 1.4 / 0659 3.2 / TU 1325 1.0 / 1956 3.3

2 0111 1.3 / 0703 3.4 / TU 1350 0.7 / 2014 3.7
17 0144 1.3 / 0803 3.3 / W 1413 0.9 / 2050 3.5

3 0215 1.1 / 0833 3.7 / W 1450 0.5 / 2114 3.9
18 0233 1.2 / 0858 3.5 / TH 1456 0.8 / 2136 3.7

4 0308 0.9 / 0930 3.9 / TH 1541 0.4 / 2206 4.0
19 0315 1.0 / 0945 3.6 / F 1536 0.8 / 2217 3.8

5 0357 0.7 / 1021 4.0 / F 1626 0.3 / 2254 4.1
20 0356 0.9 / 1027 3.7 / SA 1615 0.7 / 2254 3.9

6 0443 0.6 / 1109 4.2 / SA 1709 0.3 / ● 2339 4.2
21 0436 0.8 / 1106 3.8 / SU 1654 0.7 / ○ 2329 3.9

7 0528 0.5 / 1155 4.2 / SU 1750 0.4
22 0516 0.7 / 1144 3.9 / M 1733 0.7

8 0021 4.1 / 0611 0.5 / M 1240 4.2 / 1829 0.5
23 0005 3.9 / 0556 0.6 / TU 1222 3.9 / 1810 0.7

9 0101 4.0 / 0654 0.5 / TU 1323 4.1 / 1908 0.7
24 0042 3.9 / 0636 0.6 / W 1302 4.0 / 1847 0.8

10 0139 3.9 / 0737 0.6 / W 1406 4.0 / 1947 0.9
25 0120 3.9 / 0718 0.5 / TH 1344 4.0 / 1926 0.8

11 0217 3.8 / 0820 0.7 / TH 1450 3.8 / 2026 1.1
26 0200 3.8 / 0801 0.6 / F 1431 3.9 / 2009 0.9

12 0256 3.7 / 0907 0.8 / F 1538 3.6 / 2111 1.3
27 0244 3.7 / 0849 0.6 / SA 1522 3.8 / 2057 1.0

13 0342 3.5 / 1005 0.9 / SA 1632 3.4 / ◗ 2210 1.4
28 0335 3.6 / 0943 0.6 / SU 1621 3.6 / ◗ 2152 1.1

14 0437 3.3 / 1119 1.0 / SU 1738 3.2 / 2330 1.5
29 0436 3.5 / 1048 0.7 / M 1727 3.5 / 2259 1.2

15 0544 3.2 / 1228 1.0 / M 1853 3.2
30 0549 3.4 / 1204 0.7 / TU 1836 3.5

DECEMBER
Time m / Time m

1 0026 1.2 / 0658 3.5 / W 1316 0.7 / 1942 3.6
16 0033 1.3 / 0654 3.3 / TH 1309 1.0 / 1934 3.3

2 0139 1.1 / 0803 3.6 / TH 1418 0.6 / 2044 3.7
17 0135 1.2 / 0757 3.3 / F 1405 0.9 / 2035 3.4

3 0240 0.9 / 0903 3.7 / F 1513 0.6 / 2140 3.8
18 0231 1.1 / 0856 3.4 / SA 1456 0.9 / 2131 3.6

4 0335 0.8 / 0959 3.9 / SA 1602 0.6 / 2232 3.9
19 0322 0.9 / 0950 3.6 / SU 1545 0.8 / 2220 3.7

5 0426 0.6 / 1051 4.0 / SU 1648 0.6 / ● 2319 3.9
20 0411 0.8 / 1039 3.7 / M 1632 0.8 / 2305 3.8

6 0514 0.5 / 1140 4.0 / M 1731 0.6
21 0457 0.6 / 1125 3.8 / TU 1715 0.7 / ○ 2348 3.9

7 0003 4.0 / 0600 0.5 / TU 1227 4.0 / 1811 0.7
22 0542 0.5 / 1209 4.0 / W 1757 0.7

8 0045 3.9 / 0644 0.6 / W 1310 4.0 / 1850 0.8
23 0031 3.9 / 0626 0.4 / TH 1254 4.0 / 1836 0.7

9 0123 3.9 / 0726 0.5 / TH 1352 3.9 / 1927 0.9
24 0113 3.9 / 0710 0.4 / F 1339 4.0 / 1917 0.7

10 0159 3.8 / 0806 0.6 / F 1433 3.7 / 2003 1.0
25 0155 3.9 / 0754 0.3 / SA 1425 4.0 / 2000 0.8

11 0236 3.7 / 0843 0.7 / SA 1513 3.6 / 2041 1.1
26 0239 3.9 / 0840 0.3 / SU 1514 3.9 / 2045 0.8

12 0316 3.6 / 0923 0.8 / SU 1555 3.5 / 2125 1.2
27 0326 3.8 / 0928 0.4 / M 1606 3.8 / 2134 0.9

13 0402 3.5 / 1011 0.9 / M 1641 3.4 / ◗ 2219 1.3
28 0418 3.7 / 1022 0.5 / TU 1702 3.6 / ◗ 2229 1.0

14 0454 3.4 / 1108 0.9 / TU 1734 3.3 / 2324 1.3
29 0518 3.6 / 1126 0.6 / W 1803 3.5 / 2340 1.1

15 0553 3.3 / 1209 1.0 / W 1832 3.3
30 0626 3.5 / 1239 0.7 / TH 1909 3.4

31 0104 1.1 / 0734 3.5 / F 1348 0.8 / 2015 3.4

Chart Datum: 2·02 metres below Ordnance Datum (Newlyn). HAT is 4·4 metres above Chart Datum; see 4.5

》》 FREE monthly updates from 《《
www.reedsalmanac.co.uk

9.4.21 RIVER DEBEN

Suffolk **51°59'·38N 01°23'·58E** (Felixstowe Ferry) ⊛♦♦♦✿✿✿

CHARTS AC 5607, 2052, 2693; Imray C1, C28, Y16, 2000 Series; Stan 3, 5, 6.

TIDES Woodbridge Haven +0025 Dover; Woodbridge +0105 Dover; ML 1·9; Duration 0635

Standard Port WALTON-ON-THE-NAZE (←—)

Times				Height (metres)			
High Water		Low Water		MHWS	MHWN	MLWN	MLWS
0100	0700	0100	0700	4·2	3·4	1·1	0·4
1300	1900	1300	1900				
Differences FELIXSTOWE PIER (51° 57'N 1° 21'E)							
–0005	–0007	–0018	–0020	–0·5	–0·4	0·0	0·0
BAWDSEY							
–0016	–0020	–0030	–0032	–0·8	–0·6	–0·1	–0·1
WOODBRIDGE HAVEN (Entrance)							
0000	–0005	–0020	–0025	–0·5	–0·5	–0·1	+0·1
WOODBRIDGE (Town)							
+0045	+0025	+0025	–0020	–0·2	–0·3	–0·2	0·0

SHELTER Good in Tide Mill Yacht Hbr (TMYH) Woodbridge. ⚓s upriver, clear of moorings: N of Horse Sand; off Ramsholt, The Rocks, Waldringfield, The Tips, Methersgate, Kyson Pt and Woodbridge.

NAVIGATION WPT 51°58'·20N 01°23'·85E Woodbridge Haven SWM buoy (off chartlet to the S), thence NNW'ly leaving W Knoll PHM to port to Mid Knoll SHM and then head north upriver to the entrance.

Chartlet depicts the ent at latest survey, but depths can change significantly and the buoyage is adjusted as required. Visit *www.eastcoastrivers.com* for essential info (including sketch chartlet and aerial photos) and call *Odd Times* Ch 08 or telephone HM/Asst HM (see below).

Cross the shifting shingle bar HW–4 to HW depending on draft. Best to enter after half-flood, and leave on the flood. The ent is only 1ca wide and in strong on-shore winds gets dangerously choppy; channel is well buoyed/marked. Keep to the W shore until PHM opposite the SC, then move E of Horse Sand. No commercial traffic. 8kn max speed N of Green Reach.

LIGHTS AND MARKS See 9.4.4 and chartlets.

R/T Pilotage for river ent, call *Odd Times* Ch 08 or HM on mobile.

TELEPHONE (Code 01394) HM 270106, mob 07803 476621; Asst HM 07860 191768; MRCC (01255) 675518; Marinecall 09068 969645; Police (01473) 613500.

FACILITIES

FELIXSTOWE FERRY (01394) Quay Slip, M, L, FW, ME, El, ⚒, CH, 🛒, R, Bar; Felixstowe Ferry SC ☎ 272466; BY ☎ 282173, M (200), Gas, Slip £10.

RAMSHOLT HM ☎ 07930 304061. M, FW, Bar.

WALDRINGFIELD AC 2693. Possibly some ⚓ for <11m by prior arrangement with HM or Secretary Waldringfield Fairway Committee, ☎ 01394 276004 or 07810 233445. Craft >11m should anchor at the Rocks (NW of Prettyman's Pt) or upriver at The Tips. Waldringfield SC ☎ 736633, Bar (Wed and Sat evenings only). Services BY, C, Slip.

WOODBRIDGE (01394) **Tide Mill Yacht Hbr**, 200+Ⓥ (max 24m) £2. info@tidemillyachtharbour.co.uk; ☎ 385745. Ent by No 26 PHM buoy. Depth over sill, dries 1·5m, is 1·6m @ MHWN and 2·5m MHWS, with very accurate tide gauge and 6 waiting buoys. D, L, ME, El, ⚒, C (18 ton), 🛢, 🛒, ⊙, FW, Gas/Gaz, 🍴, CH, C, M, ACA, Wi-fi; **Woodbridge Cruising Club**, ☎ 386737. **Deben YC**. Town P, D, CH, 🛒, R, Bar, ✉, Ⓑ, ⇌, ✈ (Cambridge, Norwich).

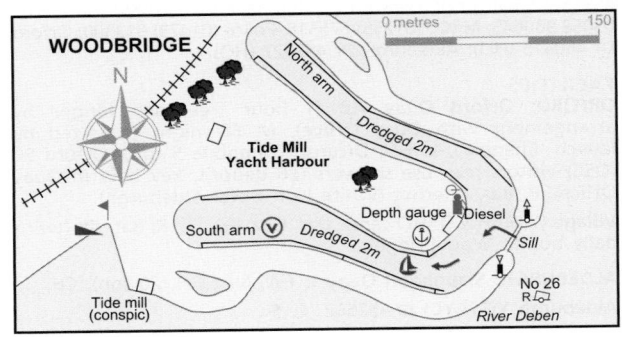

9.4.22 RIVER ORE/ALDE

Suffolk 52°02'·13N 01°27'·49E (Ent) ❀◊◊◊❁❁❁

CHARTS AC 5607, 1543, 2052, 2693, 2695; Imray C28, 2000 Series; Stanfords 3, 5, 6.

TIDES Ent. +0015 Dover Slaughden Quay +0155 Dover; ML1·6; Duration 0620

Standard Port WALTON-ON-THE-NAZE (←—)

Times				Height (metres)			
High Water		Low Water		MHWS	MHWN	MLWN	MLWS
0100	0700	0100	0700	4·2	3·4	1·1	0·4
1300	1900	1300	1900				
Differences ORFORD HAVEN BAR							
−0026	−0030	−0036	−0038	−1·0	−0·8	−0·1	0·0
ORFORD QUAY							
+0040	+0040	+0055	+0055	−1·4	−1·1	0·0	+0·2
SLAUGHDEN QUAY							
+0105	+0105	+0125	+0125	−1·3	−0·8	−0·1	+0·2
IKEN CLIFF							
+0130	+0130	+0155	+0155	−1·3	−1·0	0·0	+0·2

SHELTER Good shelter within the river, but the entrance should not be attempted in strong E/ESE onshore winds and rough seas or at night. Good ⚓s as shown and at Iken; also between Martello Tr and Slaughden Quay. Landing on Havergate Island bird sanctuary, is prohib. Visitors' moorings at Orford have small pick-up buoys marked V. Possible use of private mooring via Upson's BY at Slaughden.

NAVIGATION WPT Orford Haven SWM buoy, 52°01'·62N 01°28'·00E, may be moved as required. For latest position call Thames CG ☎ (01255) 675518.

Chartlet is based on surveys carried out in 2009, but depths can change significantly. It is essential to obtain the latest plan of entrance and directions. For regularly updated local information, including chartlet and aerial photos, see *www.eastcoast rivers.com*. For latest info call Small Craft Deliveries: ☎ (01394) 387672, sales@scd-charts.co.uk; or local marinas or chandlers.

- The bar (approx 0·5m) shifts after onshore gales and is dangerous in rough or confused seas. These result from tidal streams offshore running against those within the shingle banks. Sp ebb reaches 6kn.
- Without local info do not enter before half flood or at night. For a first visit, appr at about LW+2½ in settled conditions and at nps.
- Beware Horse Shoal close WNW of N Weir Pt and shoals S & SW of Dove Pt (SW tip of Havergate Island).

R Ore (re-named R Alde between Orford and Slaughden Quay) is navigable up to Snape. The upper reaches are shallow and winding, and marked by withies with red and green topmarks. Shellfish beds on the E bank centred on 52°08'·0N 01°35'·6E.

LIGHTS AND MARKS As chartlet. Ent and river are unlit. Shingle Street, about 2ca S of ent, is identified by Martello tr 'AA', CG Stn, terrace houses and DF aerial. Up-river, Orford Ch and Castle are conspic; also Martello Tr 'CC', 3ca S of Slaughden Quay.

R/T Call *Chantry* on Ch 08.

TELEPHONE (Codes 01394 Orford; 01728 Aldeburgh) Hbr Office 459950; Small Craft Deliveries (pilotage info) 382655; Marinecall 09068 969645; MRCC (01255) 675518; Police (01473) 613500; Orford Dr 450315 (HO); Aldeburgh Dr 452027 (HO).

FACILITIES
ORFORD: Orford Quay AB (1 hour free, any longer by arrangement with Quay Office), M £8/ night (collected by launch 'Chantry'), L, FW, D(cans), C (mobile 5 ton), Orford SC (OSC) visitors may use showers (£6 deposit, key held in Quay Office), R, Bar, Internet (White Lion Hotel Aldeburgh).

Village (¼M) P & D (HO cans), Gas, Gaz, ✉, ☕, R, Bar, ⇌ (twice daily bus to Woodbridge).

ALDEBURGH: Slaughden Quay L, FW, Slip, BH (20 ton), CH;
Aldeburgh YC (AYC) ☎ 452562, ⚓, ✕.

Slaughden SC (SSC). **Services:** M (via Upson's BY if any vacant) £5, ✕, Slip, D, ME, BY, Gas, Gaz, P.
Town (¾M) P, ☕, R, Bar, ✉, Ⓑ, ⇌ (bus to Wickham Market), ✈ (Norwich).

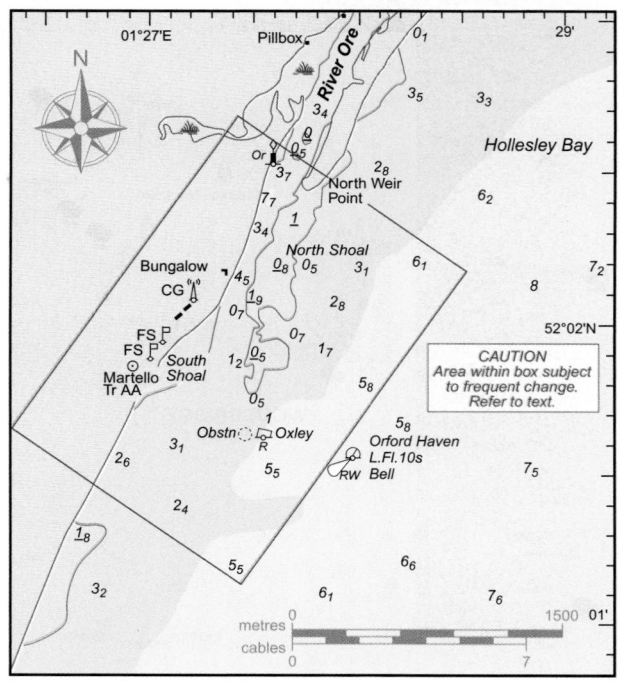

9.4.23 SOUTHWOLD

Suffolk 52°18'·78N 01°40'·54E ❀❀❀✿✿✿✿✿✿

CHARTS AC 5614, 1543, *2695*; Imray C29, C28; Stanfords 3.

TIDES –0105 Dover; ML 1·5; Duration 0620

Standard Port LOWESTOFT (→)

Times				Height (metres)			
High Water		Low Water		MHWS	MHWN	MLWN	MLWS
0300	0900	0200	0800	2·4	2·1	1·0	0·5
1500	2100	1400	2000				
Differences SOUTHWOLD							
+0105	+0105	+0055	+0055	0·0	0·0	–0·1	0·0
MINSMERE SLUICE							
+0110	+0110	+0110	+0110	0·0	–0·1	–0·2	–0·2
ALDEBURGH (seaward)							
+0130	+0130	+0115	+0120	+0·3	+0·2	–0·1	–0·2
ORFORD NESS							
+0135	+0135	+0135	+0125	+0·4	+0·6	–0·1	0·0

NOTE: HW time differences (above) for Southwold apply up the hbr. At the ent mean HW is HW Lowestoft +0035.

SHELTER Good, but the ent is dangerous in strong winds from N through E to S. Visitors berth on a staging 6ca from the ent, on N bank near to the Harbour Inn. If rafted, shore lines are essential due to current.

NAVIGATION WPT 52°18'·09N 01°41'·69E, 315°/1M to N Pier lt.

- Enter on the flood since the ebb runs up to 6kn. Some shoals are unpredictable; a sand and shingle bar, extent/depth variable, lies off the hbr ent and a shoal builds inside N Pier. Obtain details of appr chans from HM before entering (Ch 12 or ☎ 724712).
- Enter between piers in midstream. When chan widens keep close to The Knuckle (2 FG vert), turn stbd towards LB House; keep within 3m of quay wall until it ends, then resume midstream.

- **Caution** Rowing ferry (which has right of way at all times) 3ca and unlit low footbridge 7.5ca upstream of ent.

LIGHTS AND MARKS See 9.4.4 and chartlet. Walberswick ✠ in line with N Pier lt = 268°. Hbr ent opens on 300°. 3 FR (vert) at N pier = port closed. Lt ho, W ○ tr, in Southwold town, 0·86M NNE of hbr ent.

R/T *Southwold Port Radio* Ch **12** 16 09 (as reqd).

TELEPHONE (Code 01502) HM 724712; MRCC (01493) 851338; Marinecall 09068 969645; Police (01986) 855321; Dr 722326; Ⓗ 723333.

FACILITIES Hbr AB 20-30ft £14.50, FW, D (cans) also by bowser 100 litres min, BY, CH, ME, ✕, Slip HW±3 (Hbr dues £5.95), BH (20 ton). **Southwold SC; Town** (¾M), Gas, Gaz, Kos, R, 🛒, ✉, Ⓑ, ≽ (bus to Brampton/Darsham), ✈ (Norwich).

E England

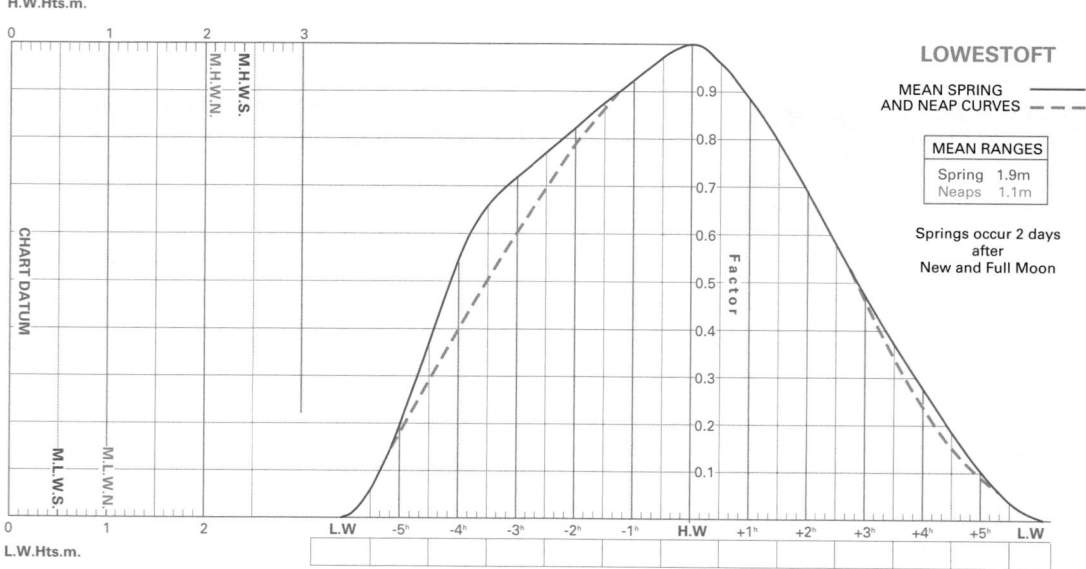

H.W.Hts.m.

LOWESTOFT

MEAN SPRING ———
AND NEAP CURVES – – –

MEAN RANGES
Spring 1.9m
Neaps 1.1m

Springs occur 2 days
after
New and Full Moon

L.W.Hts.m.

9.4.24 LOWESTOFT

Suffolk 52°28'·31N 01°45'·39E ✸✸✸✸◊◊◊◊✿✿✿

CHARTS AC 5614, 1535, 1543; Imray C28, C29; Stanfords 3.

TIDES –0133 Dover; ML 1·6; Duration 0620

SHELTER Good; accessible H24. Wind over tide, especially on the ebb, can make the entrance lively. Fairway is dredged 4·7m. Yacht Basin in SW corner of Outer Hbr is run by RN&S YC with 2 to 2·5m; no berthing on N side of S Pier. Lowestoft Haven Marina 1.5M upriver with additional 47 berths in Hamilton Dock.

NAVIGATION Call on Ch 14 for permission to enter or leave hbr. Sands continually shift and buoys are moved to suit. Beware shoals and drying areas; do not cross banks in bad weather, nor at mid flood/ebb. Speed limit in harbour is 4 kn.
From S, WPT is E Barnard ECM buoy, Q (3) 10s, 52°25'·15N 01°46'·36E; thence via Stanford Chan E of Newcome Sand QR, Stanford Fl R 2.5s and N Newcome Fl (4) R 15s, all PHM buoys. S Holm SCM, VQ (6)+L Fl 10s, and SW Holm SHM, Fl (2) G 5s, buoys mark the seaward side of this channel.
From E, WPT is Corton ECM buoy, Q (3) 10s Whis, 52°31'·14N 01°51'·37E; then via Holm Chan (buoyed) into Corton Road. Or approach direct to S Holm SCM buoy for Stanford Channel.
From N, appr via Yarmouth, Gorleston and Corton Roads.

Bridge to Inner Hbr (Lake Lothing and Lowestoft CC) lifts at the following times (20 mins notice required): every day at 0300, 0500, 0700, 0945, 1115, 1430, 1600, 1800 (W/Es + BHs only), 1900, 2100 and 2400. Small craft may pass under the bridge (clearance 2·2m) at any time but call on VHF Ch 14. Craft waiting for bridge opening must do so on pontoon at E end of Trawl Dock.

LIGHTS AND MARKS N Newcome PHM lt buoy bears 082°/6ca from hbr ent. Lowestoft lt ho, Fl 15s 37m 23M, is 1M N of hbr ent.

Tfc Sigs: Comply with IPTS (only Nos 2 and 5 are shown) on S pierhead; also get clearance on VHF Ch 14 when entering or leaving, due to restricted vis in appr and ent.

Bridge Sigs (on N bank each side of bridge):
● = bridge operating, keep 150m clear.
● = vessels may pass through bridge channel.

Yacht Basin tfc sigs on E arm (only visible from inside):
3 FR (vert) = no exit; GWG (vert) = proceed on instruction.

R/T *Lowestoft Hbr Control* (ABP) VHF Ch **14** 16 11 (H24). *Lowestoft Haven Marina* Ch **80**, 37. *Oulton Broad YS and Mutford Lock Control* Ch 73, 9, 14. Pilot Ch 14. RN & SYC Ch 14, 80.

TELEPHONE (Code 01502) HM & Bridge Control 572286; Mutford Bridge and Lock 531778 (+Ansafone, checked daily at 0830, 1300 & 1730); Oulton Broad Yacht Stn 574946; MRCC (01493) 851338; Pilot 572286 ext 243; Marinecall 09068 969645; Police (01986) 835100; H 01493 452452.

FACILITIES Royal Norfolk & Suffolk YC ☎ 566726, www.rnsyc.net, £1·95 inc YC facilities, ⊅, Slip, R, Bar, WiFi; **Lowestoft Cruising Club** ☎ 07913 391950, www.lowestoftcruisingclub.co.uk. AB (max 13m) £1.40, ⊡, FW, Slip (emergency only); **Lowestoft Haven Marina** ☎ 580300, www. lowestofthavenmarina.co.uk, 140 AB, £1.95 (+ 47 AB in Hamilton Dock, £2.15). **Services:** @, BH (70 tons), ME, El, ⚒, D, Gas, Gaz, ▣, ⬓, Ⓔ, ACA. **Town** 🛒, R, CH, ACA, Bar, ✉, Ⓑ, ⇌, ✈ (Norwich).

Entry to the Broads: See also 9.4.25 & www.norfolkbroads.com. Passage to Oulton Broad from Lake Lothing is via two bridges and Mutford Lock (width 5·9m). The lock is available 0800-1200 and 1300-1730 daily; 0800-1200 and 1300-1930 at weekends/ Bank Holidays; 0900-1200 only 1 Nov to 31 Mar. Charge is £10/ day. Booking 24 hours in advance is recommended, ☎ 01502 531778 or Ch 14. Oulton Broad Yacht Station ☎ (01502) 574946. From Oulton Broad, access into the R Waveney is via Oulton Dyke.

LOWESTOFT   LAT 52°28'N   LONG 1°45'E
TIMES AND HEIGHTS OF HIGH AND LOW WATERS

TIME ZONE (UT)
For Summer Time add ONE hour in **non-shaded areas**

Dates in red are **SPRINGS**
Dates in blue are **NEAPS**

YEAR 2010

JANUARY

Time	m		Time	m
1 0322	0.7	**16**	0415	0.7
0930	2.5		1027	2.3
F 1538	0.8	SA 1605	1.0
2143	2.6		2213	2.6
2 0416	0.5	**17**	0450	0.7
1022	2.6		1059	2.3
SA 1626	0.8	SU 1633	1.0
2227	2.7		2245	2.6
3 0507	0.4	**18**	0521	0.7
1111	2.6		1128	2.3
SU 1712	0.8	M 1702	1.0
2313	2.8		2319	2.6
4 0556	0.3	**19**	0552	0.7
1200	2.5		1158	2.3
M 1756	0.9	TU 1734	1.0
2358	2.8		2354	2.6
5 0643	0.3	**20**	0623	0.7
1249	2.4		1231	2.2
TU 1838	1.0	W 1809	1.1
6 0045	2.7	**21**	0031	2.5
0730	0.4		0655	0.8
W 1342	2.3	TH 1306	2.2
1921	1.1		1847	1.1
7 0134	2.7	**22**	0109	2.5
0821	0.6		0730	0.9
TH 1447	2.2	F 1346	2.2
◑ 2008	1.2		1929	1.1
8 0229	2.6	**23**	0150	2.4
0919	0.7		0812	0.9
F 1604	2.2	SA 1434	2.1
2107	1.2	◐ 2019	1.2
9 0338	2.4	**24**	0239	2.3
1026	0.9		0906	1.0
SA 1707	2.2	SU 1542	2.1
2236	1.3		2122	1.3
10 0459	2.4	**25**	0344	2.3
1132	1.0		1025	1.1
SU 1805	2.2	M 1710	2.1
2359	1.2		2253	1.2
11 0613	2.3	**26**	0516	2.2
1233	1.1		1145	1.1
M 1901	2.3	TU 1811	2.2
12 0109	1.1	**27**	0013	1.1
0729	2.3		0629	2.3
TU 1329	1.1	W 1246	1.0
1950	2.3		1903	2.3
13 0209	0.9	**28**	0116	0.9
0828	2.3		0733	2.4
W 1419	1.1	TH 1342	1.0
2031	2.4		1952	2.4
14 0257	0.8	**29**	0216	0.7
0913	2.3		0832	2.5
TH 1500	1.1	F 1436	0.9
2108	2.5		2039	2.5
15 0338	0.8	**30**	0313	0.5
0952	2.4		0924	2.5
F 1535	1.1	SA 1527	0.8
● 2141	2.5	○ 2125	2.7
		31	0405	0.3
			1010	2.6
		SU 1614	0.8
			2210	2.8

FEBRUARY

Time	m		Time	m
1 0453	0.2	**16**	0453	0.6
1055	2.6		1058	2.3
M 1657	0.7	TU 1642	0.8
2254	2.8		2255	2.6
2 0537	0.2	**17**	0523	0.6
1139	2.5		1127	2.3
TU 1737	0.8	W 1713	0.8
2339	2.9		2329	2.6
3 0620	0.2	**18**	0552	0.7
1222	2.4		1158	2.3
W 1817	0.8	TH 1746	0.9
4 0024	2.8	**19**	0003	2.5
0702	0.4		0621	0.7
TH 1308	2.3	F 1233	2.3
1856	0.9		1821	0.9
5 0111	2.7	**20**	0040	2.5
0746	0.6		0654	0.8
F 1357	2.2	SA 1310	2.2
◑ 1941	1.0		1901	1.0
6 0204	2.5	**21**	0120	2.4
0836	0.9		0732	0.9
SA 1459	2.1	SU 1354	2.2
2035	1.1		1949	1.1
7 0316	2.3	**22**	0209	2.3
0943	1.1		0822	1.0
SU 1618	2.1	M 1450	2.1
2203	1.2	● 2051	1.1
8 0449	2.2	**23**	0316	2.2
1106	1.2		0934	1.2
M 1725	2.1	TU 1611	2.1
2343	1.1		2226	1.1
9 0614	2.2	**24**	0503	2.2
1217	1.3		1119	1.2
TU 1832	2.2	W 1733	2.2
			2355	1.0
10 0058	1.0	**25**	0623	2.3
0732	2.2		1229	1.1
W 1321	1.2	TH 1834	2.3
1930	2.3		
11 0157	0.9	**26**	0101	0.8
0823	2.3		0729	2.4
TH 1410	1.2	F 1329	1.0
2013	2.3		1927	2.4
12 0241	0.8	**27**	0202	0.6
0902	2.3		0824	2.4
F 1448	1.1	SA 1424	0.9
2048	2.4		2016	2.5
13 0319	0.7	**28**	0258	0.4
0935	2.3		0910	2.5
SA 1519	1.0	SU 1512	0.8
2118	2.5	○ 2103	2.7
14 0352	0.6			
1004	2.3			
SU 1546	0.9			
● 2149	2.5			
15 0424	0.6			
1031	2.3			
M 1613	0.9			
2221	2.6			

MARCH

Time	m		Time	m
1 0347	0.2	**16**	0350	0.6
0951	2.5		0959	2.4
M 1556	0.7	TU 1548	0.8
2149	2.8		2154	2.5
2 0431	0.1	**17**	0420	0.6
1032	2.5		1026	2.4
TU 1637	0.6	W 1620	0.8
2233	2.9		2229	2.6
3 0513	0.2	**18**	0451	0.6
1113	2.5		1057	2.4
W 1716	0.6	TH 1653	0.7
2318	2.8		2304	2.5
4 0553	0.3	**19**	0521	0.6
1154	2.4		1129	2.4
TH 1755	0.7	F 1727	0.8
			2339	2.5
5 0003	2.7	**20**	0552	0.7
0631	0.5		1204	2.3
F 1235	2.3	SA 1802	0.8
1834	0.8		
6 0051	2.6	**21**	0016	2.4
0711	0.7		0625	0.8
SA 1317	2.2	SU 1242	2.3
1918	0.9		1842	0.9
7 0145	2.4	**22**	0100	2.4
0754	1.0		0705	0.9
SU 1405	2.2	M 1327	2.2
◑ 2012	1.0		1932	0.9
8 0304	2.2	**23**	0154	2.3
0849	1.2		0756	1.1
M 1510	2.1	TU 1421	2.2
2138	1.1	● 2038	1.0
9 0438	2.1	**24**	0309	2.2
1037	1.4		0906	1.2
TU 1633	2.1	W 1532	2.1
2323	1.0		2215	1.0
10 0602	2.2	**25**	0503	2.2
1159	1.4		1056	1.3
W 1744	2.1	TH 1656	2.2
			2339	0.8
11 0032	0.9	**26**	0618	2.3
0715	2.2		1211	1.2
TH 1302	1.3	F 1803	2.3
1851	2.3		
12 0128	0.8	**27**	0043	0.6
0803	2.3		0718	2.4
F 1348	1.2	SA 1311	1.1
1941	2.3		1859	2.4
13 0211	0.8	**28**	0142	0.5
0839	2.3		0807	2.4
SA 1424	1.1	SU 1404	0.9
2016	2.3		1951	2.5
14 0248	0.7	**29**	0236	0.3
0909	2.3		0849	2.5
SU 1453	1.0	M 1451	0.8
2047	2.4		2039	2.7
15 0320	0.6	**30**	0323	0.3
0934	2.3		0928	2.5
M 1520	0.9	TU 1534	0.7
● 2120	2.5	○ 2127	2.8
		31	0406	0.2
			1008	2.5
		W 1615	0.6
			2213	2.8

APRIL

Time	m		Time	m
1 0446	0.3	**16**	0420	0.6
1047	2.5		1029	2.4
TH 1656	0.6	F 1634	0.7
2259	2.7		2241	2.5
2 0524	0.5	**17**	0454	0.7
1126	2.4		1104	2.4
F 1736	0.6	SA 1712	0.7
2346	2.6		2320	2.4
3 0602	0.7	**18**	0529	0.7
1205	2.4		1141	2.4
SA 1817	0.7	SU 1752	0.7
4 0035	2.4	**19**	0002	2.4
0638	0.9		0606	0.9
SU 1245	2.3	M 1221	2.4
1901	0.8		1836	0.7
5 0132	2.3	**20**	0051	2.3
0717	1.1		0649	1.0
M 1328	2.2	TU 1308	2.3
1953	0.9		1930	0.8
6 0253	2.1	**21**	0151	2.2
0803	1.3		0742	1.2
TU 1421	2.2	W 1402	2.2
◑ 2113	1.0	● 2038	0.8
7 0417	2.1	**22**	0317	2.2
0918	1.4		0849	1.3
W 1530	2.1	TH 1507	2.2
2250	1.0		2204	0.8
8 0531	2.1	**23**	0456	2.2
1123	1.4		1026	1.3
TH 1646	2.1	F 1622	2.2
2352	0.9		2318	0.7
9 0640	2.2	**24**	0602	2.3
1224	1.4		1143	1.2
F 1751	2.1	SA 1732	2.3
10 0044	0.8	**25**	0019	0.6
0730	2.2		0658	2.3
SA 1311	1.2	SU 1244	1.1
1846	2.2		1830	2.4
11 0129	0.8	**26**	0117	0.5
0807	2.3		0744	2.4
SU 1347	1.1	M 1338	1.0
1931	2.3		1925	2.5
12 0207	0.7	**27**	0209	0.4
0836	2.3		0825	2.4
M 1417	1.0	TU 1427	0.8
2010	2.4		2017	2.6
13 0241	0.7	**28**	0256	0.4
0901	2.3		0904	2.5
TU 1448	0.9	W 1513	0.7
2048	2.4	○ 2108	2.6
14 0313	0.6	**29**	0339	0.4
0927	2.4		0944	2.5
W 1521	0.8	TH 1557	0.6
● 2125	2.5		2157	2.6
15 0346	0.6	**30**	0419	0.5
0957	2.4		1023	2.5
TH 1557	0.7	F 1639	0.5
2203	2.5		2246	2.5

Chart Datum: 1·50 metres below Ordnance Datum (Newlyn). HAT is 2·9 metres above Chart Datum; see 4.5

E England

LOWESTOFT LAT 52°28'N LONG 1°45'E
TIMES AND HEIGHTS OF HIGH AND LOW WATERS

TIME ZONE (UT)
For Summer Time add ONE hour in **non-shaded areas**

Dates in red are **SPRINGS**
Dates in blue are NEAPS

YEAR 2010

MAY

Time	m		Time	m
1 0458	0.7		**16** 0433	0.7
1102	2.5		1043	2.5
SA 1721	0.6		SU 1703	0.6
2335	2.4		2308	2.4
2 0534	0.8		**17** 0514	0.8
1141	2.4		1123	2.5
SU 1803	0.6		M 1749	0.6
			2356	2.4
3 0025	2.3		**18** 0556	0.9
0609	1.0		1206	2.4
M 1219	2.4		TU 1838	0.6
1847	0.7			
4 0120	2.2		**19** 0049	2.3
0645	1.1		0642	1.0
TU 1300	2.3		W 1254	2.4
1936	0.8		1932	0.6
5 0228	2.1		**20** 0150	2.3
0725	1.3		0732	1.1
W 1346	2.3		TH 1347	2.4
2038	0.9		◖ 2034	0.6
6 0342	2.1		**21** 0311	2.2
0814	1.4		0831	1.2
TH 1441	2.2		F 1445	2.4
◗ 2201	0.9		2145	0.6
7 0447	2.1		**22** 0436	2.2
0929	1.5		0945	1.3
F 1545	2.2		SA 1552	2.4
2306	0.9		2252	0.6
8 0548	2.1		**23** 0537	2.3
1125	1.4		1106	1.2
SA 1655	2.2		SU 1703	2.4
2357	0.9		2353	0.6
9 0642	2.2		**24** 0631	2.3
1217	1.3		1212	1.1
SU 1754	2.2		M 1806	2.4
10 0041	0.8		**25** 0049	0.6
0723	2.2		0719	2.3
M 1258	1.2		TU 1311	1.0
1846	2.4		1904	2.4
11 0121	0.8		**26** 0142	0.6
0755	2.3		0802	2.4
TU 1336	1.1		W 1406	0.9
1933	2.3		2002	2.5
12 0158	0.7		**27** 0231	0.6
0825	2.3		0843	2.4
W 1414	0.9		TH 1457	0.7
2016	2.3		○ 2057	2.5
13 0236	0.7		**28** 0315	0.7
0856	2.4		0923	2.5
TH 1454	0.7		F 1544	0.6
2058	2.4		2149	2.5
14 0314	0.7		**29** 0357	0.7
0929	2.4		1003	2.5
F 1536	0.7		SA 1628	0.6
● 2140	2.4		2239	2.4
15 0353	0.7		**30** 0435	0.8
1005	2.5		1043	2.5
SA 1618	0.6		SU 1711	0.6
2223	2.4		2326	2.3
			31 0511	0.9
			1120	2.5
			M 1752	0.6

JUNE

Time	m		Time	m
1 0012	2.3		**16** 0548	0.9
0543	1.0		1154	2.6
TU 1157	2.5		W 1834	0.4
1832	0.7			
2 0058	2.2		**17** 0042	2.4
0617	1.1		0632	1.0
W 1235	2.4		TH 1240	2.6
1913	0.7		1924	0.4
3 0146	2.1		**18** 0136	2.3
0653	1.2		0718	1.1
TH 1317	2.4		F 1329	2.6
1959	0.8		2017	0.5
4 0244	2.1		**19** 0242	2.2
0735	1.3		0808	1.1
F 1403	2.3		SA 1422	2.5
◗ 2051	0.9		◖ 2117	0.6
5 0351	2.1		**20** 0402	2.2
0824	1.3		0907	1.2
SA 1455	2.3		SU 1524	2.5
2157	0.9		2222	0.6
6 0450	2.1		**21** 0506	2.2
0925	1.4		1025	1.2
SU 1556	2.2		M 1638	2.4
2300	0.9		2325	0.7
7 0542	2.1		**22** 0602	2.2
1055	1.4		1144	1.2
M 1705	2.2		TU 1748	2.4
2351	0.9			
8 0628	2.2		**23** 0024	0.8
1203	1.3		0654	2.3
TU 1805	2.2		W 1252	1.0
			1855	2.4
9 0036	0.9		**24** 0120	0.9
0710	2.3		0743	2.4
W 1255	1.1		TH 1354	0.9
1858	2.2		2001	2.4
10 0120	0.8		**25** 0212	0.9
0749	2.3		0827	2.4
TH 1343	1.0		F 1449	0.8
1948	2.3		2059	2.4
11 0203	0.8		**26** 0259	0.9
0826	2.4		0908	2.5
F 1430	0.9		SA 1537	0.7
2037	2.3		○ 2148	2.4
12 0247	0.8		**27** 0341	0.9
0905	2.4		0947	2.5
SA 1518	0.7		SU 1620	0.6
● 2125	2.4		2232	2.4
13 0332	0.8		**28** 0418	1.0
0944	2.5		1024	2.6
SU 1607	0.6		M 1659	0.6
2213	2.4		2312	2.3
14 0418	0.8		**29** 0451	1.0
1026	2.6		1100	2.6
M 1656	0.5		TU 1736	0.6
2302	2.5		2350	2.3
15 0503	0.8		**30** 0521	1.0
1109	2.6		1134	2.6
TU 1745	0.4		W 1811	0.6
2351	2.4			

JULY

Time	m		Time	m
1 0026	2.2		**16** 0023	2.5
0551	1.0		0616	0.9
TH 1210	2.5		F 1222	2.8
1845	0.7		1904	0.3
2 0101	2.2		**17** 0111	2.4
0624	1.1		0658	0.9
F 1248	2.5		SA 1309	2.7
1920	0.8		1952	0.5
3 0138	2.1		**18** 0204	2.3
0702	1.1		0743	1.0
SA 1329	2.4		SU 1359	2.6
1958	0.8		◗ 2044	0.6
4 0222	2.1		**19** 0313	2.2
0746	1.2		0836	1.1
SU 1413	2.4		M 1501	2.5
◗ 2042	0.9		2147	0.8
5 0321	2.1		**20** 0428	2.2
0837	1.3		0951	1.2
M 1504	2.3		TU 1623	2.4
2139	1.0		2258	1.0
6 0439	2.1		**21** 0530	2.2
0941	1.3		1124	1.2
TU 1610	2.2		W 1743	2.3
2252	1.0			
7 0537	2.2		**22** 0004	1.1
1110	1.3		0629	2.3
W 1727	2.2		TH 1241	1.1
2355	1.0		1902	2.3
8 0628	2.2		**23** 0107	1.1
1220	1.2		0726	2.3
TH 1830	2.2		F 1349	0.9
			2010	2.3
9 0048	1.0		**24** 0203	1.1
0715	2.3		0813	2.4
F 1316	1.0		SA 1442	0.8
1927	2.3		2059	2.4
10 0138	0.9		**25** 0249	1.1
0759	2.4		0853	2.5
SA 1410	0.9		SU 1526	0.7
2023	2.4		2139	2.4
11 0227	0.9		**26** 0328	1.0
0842	2.5		0929	2.6
SU 1504	0.7		M 1604	0.6
● 2115	2.4		○ 2216	2.4
12 0317	0.8		**27** 0401	1.0
0925	2.6		1003	2.6
M 1557	0.5		TU 1640	0.6
2204	2.5		2249	2.4
13 0406	0.8		**28** 0430	1.0
1008	2.7		1036	2.6
TU 1646	0.4		W 1713	0.6
2251	2.5		2320	2.3
14 0452	0.8		**29** 0457	1.0
1052	2.8		1109	2.6
W 1734	0.3		TH 1743	0.6
2337	2.5		2350	2.3
15 0535	0.8		**30** 0526	1.0
1137	2.8		1143	2.6
TH 1820	0.3		F 1813	0.7
			31 0020	2.3
			0557	1.0
			SA 1219	2.6
			1842	0.8

AUGUST

Time	m		Time	m
1 0054	2.3		**16** 0128	2.3
0633	1.1		0720	1.0
SU 1256	2.5		M 1339	2.6
1915	0.8		◖ 2008	0.8
2 0132	2.2		**17** 0223	2.3
0713	1.1		0813	1.1
M 1336	2.4		TU 1445	2.5
1953	0.9		2107	1.0
3 0216	2.2		**18** 0339	2.2
0801	1.2		0928	1.2
TU 1422	2.3		W 1619	2.3
2040	1.0		2231	1.2
4 0314	2.2		**19** 0453	2.2
0859	1.3		1112	1.1
W 1522	2.3		TH 1744	2.3
2146	1.1		2349	1.3
5 0441	2.2		**20** 0559	2.3
1023	1.3		1230	1.0
TH 1653	2.2		F 1906	2.3
2316	1.2			
6 0547	2.2		**21** 0057	1.3
1151	1.2		0703	2.3
F 1810	2.3		SA 1336	0.9
			2004	2.4
7 0022	1.1		**22** 0152	1.2
0642	2.3		0753	2.4
SA 1255	1.0		SU 1424	0.8
1915	2.3		2045	2.4
8 0118	1.1		**23** 0234	1.2
0731	2.4		0831	2.5
SU 1353	0.8		M 1504	0.7
2013	2.4		2120	2.4
9 0211	1.0		**24** 0307	1.1
0818	2.5		0904	2.6
M 1449	0.6		TU 1539	0.7
2103	2.5		○ 2151	2.4
10 0303	0.9		**25** 0337	1.0
0903	2.7		0935	2.6
TU 1541	0.4		W 1611	0.6
● 2149	2.6		2219	2.4
11 0350	0.8		**26** 0404	0.9
0947	2.8		1007	2.7
W 1629	0.2		TH 1641	0.6
2232	2.6		2246	2.4
12 0434	0.8		**27** 0432	0.9
1031	2.9		1041	2.7
TH 1714	0.2		F 1710	0.7
2315	2.6		2314	2.4
13 0516	0.8		**28** 0501	0.9
1116	2.9		1115	2.7
F 1757	0.2		SA 1738	0.7
2357	2.5		2345	2.4
14 0556	0.8		**29** 0533	0.9
1200	2.9		1149	2.6
SA 1839	0.4		SU 1806	0.8
15 0041	2.4		**30** 0018	2.4
0636	0.9		0607	1.0
SU 1247	2.8		M 1225	2.5
1921	0.6		1837	0.9
			31 0055	2.3
			0646	1.1
			TU 1304	2.4
			1913	1.0

Chart Datum: 1·50 metres below Ordnance Datum (Newlyn). HAT is 2·9 metres above Chart Datum; see 4.5

>> **FREE** monthly updates from <<
www.reedsalmanac.co.uk

LOWESTOFT LAT 52°28'N LONG 1°45'E
TIMES AND HEIGHTS OF HIGH AND LOW WATERS

TIME ZONE (UT) — For Summer Time add ONE hour in non-shaded areas

Dates in red are SPRINGS · Dates in blue are NEAPS

YEAR 2010

SEPTEMBER

Day	Readings (Time, m)	Day	Readings (Time, m)
1 W	0137 2.3 / 0732 1.1 / 1351 2.4 / ◑1959 1.1	16 TH	0247 2.3 / 0912 1.1 / 1613 2.3 / 2156 1.4
2 TH	0229 2.3 / 0830 1.2 / 1452 2.3 / 2100 1.2	17 F	0407 2.3 / 1055 1.1 / 1733 2.3 / 2328 1.4
3 F	0339 2.2 / 0953 1.2 / 1634 2.2 / 2237 1.3	18 SA	0518 2.3 / 1206 1.0 / 1849 2.3
4 SA	0505 2.3 / 1129 1.1 / 1759 2.3 / 2359 1.2	19 SU	0035 1.4 / 0623 2.3 / 1305 0.9 / 1943 2.4
5 SU	0608 2.4 / 1235 0.9 / 1904 2.4	20 M	0127 1.3 / 0718 2.4 / 1352 0.8 / 2022 2.4
6 M	0059 1.2 / 0701 2.5 / 1334 0.7 / 1959 2.5	21 TU	0206 1.2 / 0757 2.5 / 1431 0.8 / 2054 2.4
7 TU	0153 1.0 / 0750 2.6 / 1429 0.5 / 2045 2.6	22 W	0238 1.1 / 0830 2.6 / 1505 0.7 / 2121 2.4
8 W	0243 0.9 / 0837 2.8 / 1519 0.3 / ●2127 2.6	23 TH	0307 1.0 / 0903 2.6 / 1536 0.7 / ○2146 2.5
9 TH	0329 0.8 / 0923 2.9 / 1606 0.2 / 2208 2.6	24 F	0335 0.9 / 0937 2.7 / 1605 0.7 / 2212 2.5
10 F	0412 0.7 / 1008 3.0 / 1649 0.2 / 2249 2.6	25 SA	0405 0.9 / 1012 2.7 / 1634 0.7 / 2241 2.5
11 SA	0454 0.7 / 1054 3.0 / 1730 0.3 / 2330 2.6	26 SU	0437 0.9 / 1047 2.6 / 1703 0.7 / 2313 2.5
12 SU	0535 0.7 / 1140 2.9 / 1810 0.5	27 M	0511 0.9 / 1123 2.6 / 1734 0.8 / 2347 2.5
13 M	0012 2.5 / 0616 0.8 / 1229 2.7 / 1850 0.7	28 TU	0547 0.9 / 1159 2.5 / 1806 0.9
14 TU	0056 2.4 / 0702 0.9 / 1323 2.6 / 1934 1.0	29 W	0024 2.4 / 0626 1.0 / 1241 2.4 / 1843 1.0
15 W	0145 2.3 / 0755 1.0 / 1437 2.4 / ◑2026 1.2	30 TH	0107 2.4 / 0713 1.0 / 1331 2.3 / 1931 1.2

OCTOBER

Day	Readings (Time, m)	Day	Readings (Time, m)
1 F	0159 2.3 / 0813 1.1 / 1437 2.3 / ◑2032 1.3	16 SA	0312 2.3 / 1023 1.0 / 1706 2.3 / 2249 1.5
2 SA	0302 2.3 / 0937 1.1 / 1628 2.3 / 2200 1.4	17 SU	0426 2.3 / 1129 1.0 / 1814 2.3 / 2356 1.5
3 SU	0421 2.3 / 1108 1.0 / 1747 2.4 / 2333 1.3	18 M	0530 2.3 / 1223 0.9 / 1910 2.3
4 M	0532 2.4 / 1212 0.8 / 1847 2.4	19 TU	0047 1.4 / 0625 2.4 / 1310 0.9 / 1950 2.4
5 TU	0034 1.2 / 0629 2.5 / 1309 0.6 / 1937 2.5	20 W	0128 1.3 / 0711 2.4 / 1350 0.8 / 2021 2.4
6 W	0128 1.1 / 0720 2.7 / 1403 0.5 / 2021 2.6	21 TH	0202 1.2 / 0751 2.5 / 1424 0.8 / 2047 2.5
7 TH	0218 1.0 / 0810 2.8 / 1453 0.4 / ●2102 2.6	22 F	0233 1.1 / 0829 2.5 / 1456 0.8 / 2112 2.5
8 F	0305 0.8 / 0858 2.9 / 1539 0.3 / 2142 2.7	23 SA	0305 1.0 / 0907 2.6 / 1527 0.8 / ○2140 2.5
9 SA	0350 0.7 / 0946 2.9 / 1621 0.4 / 2223 2.6	24 SU	0339 0.9 / 0944 2.6 / 1600 0.8 / 2211 2.6
10 SU	0433 0.7 / 1035 2.9 / 1702 0.5 / 2304 2.6	25 M	0416 0.8 / 1022 2.6 / 1633 0.8 / 2245 2.6
11 M	0517 0.7 / 1123 2.8 / 1742 0.7 / 2345 2.6	26 TU	0453 0.8 / 1101 2.5 / 1707 0.9 / 2321 2.5
12 TU	0600 0.7 / 1214 2.6 / 1821 0.9	27 W	0533 0.9 / 1141 2.5 / 1744 1.0
13 W	0027 2.5 / 0646 0.8 / 1312 2.4 / 1901 1.1	28 TH	0001 2.5 / 0616 0.9 / 1227 2.4 / 1825 1.1
14 TH	0113 2.4 / 0740 0.9 / 1427 2.3 / ◑1948 1.3	29 F	0045 2.5 / 1321 2.3 / 1913 1.2
15 F	0206 2.4 / 0852 1.0 / 1553 2.3 / 2052 1.5	30 SA	0136 2.4 / 0807 0.9 / 1429 2.3 / ◑2012 1.3
		31 SU	0236 2.4 / 0924 0.9 / 1614 2.3 / 2126 1.4

NOVEMBER

Day	Readings (Time, m)	Day	Readings (Time, m)
1 M	0344 2.4 / 1042 0.8 / 1726 2.4 / 2257 1.4	16 TU	0432 2.3 / 1137 1.0 / 1822 2.3 / 2354 1.5
2 TU	0456 2.5 / 1145 0.7 / 1823 2.4	17 W	0533 2.3 / 1224 1.0 / 1907 2.3
3 W	0003 1.3 / 0557 2.6 / 1242 0.6 / 1912 2.5	18 TH	0040 1.3 / 0626 2.4 / 1305 0.9 / 1941 2.4
4 TH	0100 1.1 / 0653 2.7 / 1335 0.6 / 1956 2.5	19 F	0120 1.2 / 0714 2.4 / 1342 0.9 / 2010 2.4
5 F	0153 1.0 / 0746 2.7 / 1425 0.5 / 2037 2.6	20 SA	0158 1.1 / 0758 2.4 / 1417 0.9 / 2039 2.5
6 SA	0243 0.8 / 0838 2.8 / 1512 0.5 / ●2118 2.6	21 SU	0236 1.0 / 0840 2.5 / 1453 0.8 / ○2111 2.5
7 SU	0331 0.7 / 0930 2.8 / 1556 0.6 / 2159 2.7	22 M	0316 0.9 / 0921 2.6 / 1531 0.8 / 2146 2.6
8 M	0418 0.7 / 1021 2.7 / 1637 0.7 / 2241 2.6	23 TU	0358 0.8 / 1003 2.5 / 1610 0.8 / 2222 2.6
9 TU	0503 0.6 / 1112 2.6 / 1716 0.9 / 2322 2.6	24 W	0442 0.8 / 1046 2.5 / 1650 0.9 / 2301 2.6
10 W	0548 0.6 / 1204 2.5 / 1755 1.0	25 TH	0526 0.7 / 1132 2.5 / 1731 1.0 / 2343 2.6
11 TH	0003 2.6 / 0633 0.8 / 1259 2.4 / 1832 1.2	26 F	0613 0.7 / 1220 2.4 / 1814 1.1
12 F	0046 2.5 / 0723 0.8 / 1403 2.3 / 1912 1.3	27 SA	0028 2.6 / 0703 0.7 / 1314 2.4 / 1901 1.2
13 SA	0132 2.4 / 0821 0.9 / 1518 2.2 / ◑1959 1.5	28 SU	0118 2.5 / 0759 0.7 / 1416 2.3 / ◑1953 1.3
14 SU	0224 2.4 / 0935 1.0 / 1625 2.2 / 2100 1.5	29 M	0212 2.5 / 0903 0.7 / 1542 2.3 / 2054 1.3
15 M	0325 2.3 / 1043 1.0 / 1726 2.2 / 2253 1.5	30 TU	0312 2.5 / 1012 0.7 / 1657 2.3 / 2211 1.3

DECEMBER

Day	Readings (Time, m)	Day	Readings (Time, m)
1 W	0422 2.5 / 1117 0.7 / 1755 2.4 / 2329 1.3	16 TH	0442 2.3 / 1134 1.1 / 1809 2.2 / 2344 1.4
2 TH	0531 2.5 / 1215 0.7 / 1846 2.4	17 F	0546 2.3 / 1221 1.0 / 1853 2.3
3 F	0032 1.1 / 0631 2.6 / 1310 0.7 / 1932 2.5	18 SA	0038 1.3 / 0641 2.3 / 1304 1.0 / 1932 2.4
4 SA	0132 1.0 / 0730 2.6 / 1402 0.7 / 2015 2.5	19 SU	0125 1.1 / 0731 2.3 / 1345 1.0 / 2009 2.4
5 SU	0228 0.9 / 0828 2.6 / 1450 0.8 / ●2058 2.6	20 M	0211 1.0 / 0819 2.4 / 1427 0.9 / 2046 2.5
6 M	0320 0.7 / 0924 2.6 / 1535 0.8 / 2140 2.6	21 TU	0257 0.9 / 0906 2.4 / 1510 0.9 / ○2124 2.6
7 TU	0408 0.6 / 1015 2.6 / 1617 0.9 / 2222 2.6	22 W	0345 0.7 / 0952 2.5 / 1554 0.9 / 2204 2.6
8 W	0454 0.6 / 1104 2.5 / 1656 1.0 / 2303 2.6	23 TH	0433 0.6 / 1038 2.5 / 1638 0.9 / 2246 2.7
9 TH	0537 0.6 / 1151 2.4 / 1732 1.1 / 2342 2.6	24 F	0520 0.5 / 1124 2.5 / 1721 0.9 / 2329 2.7
10 F	0619 0.7 / 1237 2.3 / 1805 1.1	25 SA	0607 0.5 / 1210 2.5 / 1804 1.0
11 SA	0020 2.6 / 0700 0.8 / 1324 2.2 / 1839 1.2	26 SU	0013 2.7 / 0654 0.5 / 1259 2.4 / 1847 1.0
12 SU	0100 2.5 / 0743 0.9 / 1416 2.2 / 1918 1.3	27 M	0059 2.7 / 0743 0.6 / 1351 2.3 / 1933 1.1
13 M	0144 2.5 / 0832 0.9 / 1522 2.1 / ◑2003 1.4	28 TU	0149 2.6 / 0836 0.6 / 1455 2.2 / ◑2024 1.2
14 TU	0233 2.4 / 0931 1.0 / 1626 2.1 / 2057 1.4	29 W	0244 2.6 / 0939 0.7 / 1619 2.2 / 2129 1.2
15 W	0331 2.3 / 1038 1.1 / 1721 2.2 / 2217 1.5	30 TH	0354 2.5 / 1047 0.8 / 1723 2.2 / 2257 1.2
		31 F	0512 2.5 / 1151 0.9 / 1819 2.3

Chart Datum: 1·50 metres below Ordnance Datum (Newlyn). HAT is 2·9 metres above Chart Datum; see 4.5

E England

9.4.25 GREAT YARMOUTH

Norfolk **52°34'·36N 01°44'·39E** ❀❀⚓❀❀

CHARTS AC 5614, 1543, 1535, 1534; Imray C29, C28; Stanfords 3.

TIDES –0210 Dover; ML 1·5; Duration 0620

Standard Port LOWESTOFT (←—)

Times				Height (metres)			
High Water		Low Water		MHWS	MHWN	MLWN	MLWS
0300	0900	0200	0800	2·4	2·1	1·0	0·5
1500	2100	1400	2000				
Differences GORLESTON (To be used for Great Yarmouth)							
–0035	–0035	–0030	–0030	0·0	0·0	0·0	0·0
CAISTER-ON-SEA							
–0120	–0120	–0100	–0100	0·0	–0·1	0·0	0·0
WINTERTON-ON-SEA							
–0225	–0215	–0135	–0135	+0·8	+0·5	+0·2	+0·1

• Rise of tide occurs mainly during 3.5 hours after LW. From HW Lowestoft –3 until HW the level is usually within 0·3m of predicted HW. Flood tide runs until about HW +15 and ebb until about LW +25. See also NAVIGATION.

SHELTER Excellent on Town Hall Quay, close S of Haven Bridge; ⚓ prohib in hbr which is a busy commercial port.

NAVIGATION WPT 52°34'·43N 01°45'·56E, 264°/1M to front ldg lt.

• Access is H24, subject to clearance, but small craft must not attempt ent in strong SE winds which cause dangerous seas, especially on the ebb. Except at local slack water, which occurs at HW+1½ and LW+1¾, tidal streams at the ent are strong.
• On the flood, the stream eddies NW past S pier, thence up-river; a QY tidal lt on S pier warns of this D/N. Beware being set onto the N pier.
• Temporary shoaling may occur in the ent during strong E'lies, with depths 1m less than those charted.
• Beware strong tidal streams that sweep through the Haven Bridge. Proceed slowly past Bure Marine.
• Outer harbour is for commercial vessels only.

LIGHTS AND MARKS See 9.4.4 and chartlet. Note: Tfc Sigs and the tidal QY are co-located with the Main lt on a R brick bldg, W lower half floodlit, at S pier. W sector (252·5°-257·5°) of Brush Sector Light leads to harbour entrance. Ent and bend marked by five x 2 FG and seven x 2FR (all vert).

TRAFFIC SIGNALS Port operations advise on Ch 12, this should always be heeded. **Inbound:** now IALA sigs on S pier: 3 Fl ● = hbr closed; 3F ● = do not proceed; 3 F ● = vessels may proceed, oneway; ● ○ ● = proceed only when told to; **Outbound:** 3 ● (vert) = no vessel to go down river south of LB shed. Haven and Breydon bridges: 3 ● (vert) = passage prohib.

R/T *Yarmouth Radio* Ch **12** (H24). *Breydon Bridge* Ch **12** (OH).

TELEPHONE (Code 01493) HM 335511; MRCC 851338; Marinecall 09068 969645; Police 336200; Breydon Bridge 651275.

FACILITIES Town Hall Quay (50m stretch) AB £15/yacht, then £7 for successive days. **Bure Marine** Cobholm ☎ 656996, H24. (Marina planned 2007). FW, El, ⚓, BH, C, Slip. **Burgh Castle Marina** (top of Breydon Water 5M) (90+10 visitors) ☎ 780331, £16, Slip, D, ⚓, ME, El, ✕, ◻, Gas, CH, ☷, R, Bar, Access HW ±4 (1m), diving ACA; **Goodchild Marine Services** (top of Breydon Water 5M) (27+6✔ £12.50) ☎ 782301, D, FW, ME, El, C (32 tons, including mast stepping), ⚓, Access 6ft at LW; **Services:** AB, L, M, ✕, SM, ACA. **Town** P, D, CH, ☷, R, Bar, ✉, Ⓑ, ⇌, ✈ (Norwich).

Entry to the Broads: Pass up R Yare at slack LW, under Haven Bridge (1·8m HAT) thence to Breydon Water via Breydon Bridge (4·0m) or to R Bure. Both bridges lift in co-ordination to pass small craft in groups. All br lifts on request to Hbr Office (01493) 335503 during office hrs. Weekend and bank holiday lifts to be requested working afternoon before. Call the Bridge Officer on VHF Ch 12. R Bure has two fixed bridges (2·3m MHWS).

NORFOLK BROADS: The Broads comprise about 120 miles of navigable rivers and lakes in Norfolk and Suffolk. The main rivers (Bure, Yare and Waveney) are tidal, flowing into the sea at Great Yarmouth. The N Broads have a 2·3m headroom limit. Br clearances restrict cruising to R Yare (Great Yarmouth to Norwich, but note that 3M E of Norwich, Postwick viaduct on S bypass has 10.7m HW clearance) and River Waveney (Lowestoft to Beccles). The Broads may be entered also at Lowestoft (9.4.24). Broads Navigation Authority ☎ (01603) 610734.

Tidal data on the rivers and Broads is based on the time of LW at Yarmouth Yacht Stn (mouth of R Bure), which is LW Gorleston +0100 (see TIDES). Add the differences below to time of LW Yarmouth Yacht Stn to get local LW times:

R Bure		R Waveney		R Yare	
Acle Bridge	+0230	Berney Arms	+0100	Reedham	+0130
Horning	+0300	St Olaves	+0130	Cantley	+0200
Potter Heigham	+0300	Oulton Broad	+0300	Norwich	+0300

LW at Breydon (mouth of R Yare) is LW Yarmouth Yacht Stn +0100. Tide starts to flood on Breydon Water whilst still ebbing from R Bure. Max draft is 1·8m; 2m with care. Tidal range 0·6m to 1·8m.

Licences (compulsory) are obtainable from: The Broads Authority, 18 Colegate, Norwich NR3 1BQ, ☎ 01603-610734; the Info Centre, Yarmouth Yacht Stn or the River Inspectors. *Hamilton's Guide to the Broads* is recommended. www.hamilton publications.com.

ADLARD COLES NAUTICAL
WEATHER FORECASTS
BY FAX & TELEPHONE

Coastal/Inshore	2-day by Fax	5-day by Phone
Anglia	09065 222 345	09068 969 645
East	09065 222 344	09068 969 644
North East	09065 222 343	09068 969 643
Scotland East	09065 222 342	09068 969 642
National (3-5 day)	09065 222 340	09068 969 640

Offshore	2-5 day by Fax	2-5 day by Phone
English Channel	09065 222 357	09068 969 657
Southern North Sea	09065 222 358	09068 969 658
Northern North Sea	09065 222 362	09068 969 662
North West Scotland	09065 222 361	09068 969 661

09068 CALLS COST 60P PER MIN. 09065 CALLS COST £1.50 PER MIN.

North East England
Winterton to Berwick-upon-Tweed

NE England

DISTANCE TABLE

Approximate distances in nautical miles are by the most direct route, whilst avoiding dangers and allowing for Traffic Separation Schemes. Places in *italics* are in adjoining areas; places in **bold** are in 9.0.7, Distances across the North Sea.

	1	2	3	4	5	6	7	8	9	10	11	12	13	14	15	16	17	18	19	20
1. *Great Yarmouth*	**1**																			
2. Blakeney	44	**2**																		
3. **King's Lynn**	85	42	**3**																	
4. Boston	83	39	34	**4**																
5. Humber Lt Buoy	82	45	55	54	**5**															
6. **Grimsby**	99	54	61	58	17	**6**														
7. Hull	113	68	75	72	31	14	**7**													
8. Bridlington	114	79	87	83	35	44	58	**8**												
9. Scarborough	130	96	105	98	50	59	81	20	**9**											
10. Whitby	143	101	121	114	66	75	88	35	16	**10**										
11. River Tees (ent)	166	122	138	135	87	96	118	56	37	21	**11**									
12. **Hartlepool**	169	126	140	137	89	98	122	58	39	24	4	**12**								
13. Seaham	175	137	151	145	100	106	133	66	47	33	15	11	**13**							
14. Sunderland	180	142	156	149	105	110	138	70	51	36	20	16	5	**14**						
15. Tynemouth	183	149	163	154	112	115	145	75	56	41	27	23	12	7	**15**					
16. Blyth	190	156	171	162	120	123	153	83	64	49	35	31	20	15	8	**16**				
17. Amble	203	170	185	176	126	143	157	102	81	65	46	42	32	27	21	14	**17**			
18. Holy Island	225	191	196	198	148	166	180	126	104	88	68	65	54	50	44	37	22	**18**		
19. **Berwick-on-Tweed**	232	200	205	205	157	166	189	126	107	91	82	78	67	61	55	47	31	9	**19**	
20. Eyemouth	240	208	213	213	165	174	197	134	115	99	90	86	75	69	63	55	39	17	8	**20**

9.5.2 North East England
Blakeney to Berwick-upon-Tweed

Magnetic Variation 3·1°W

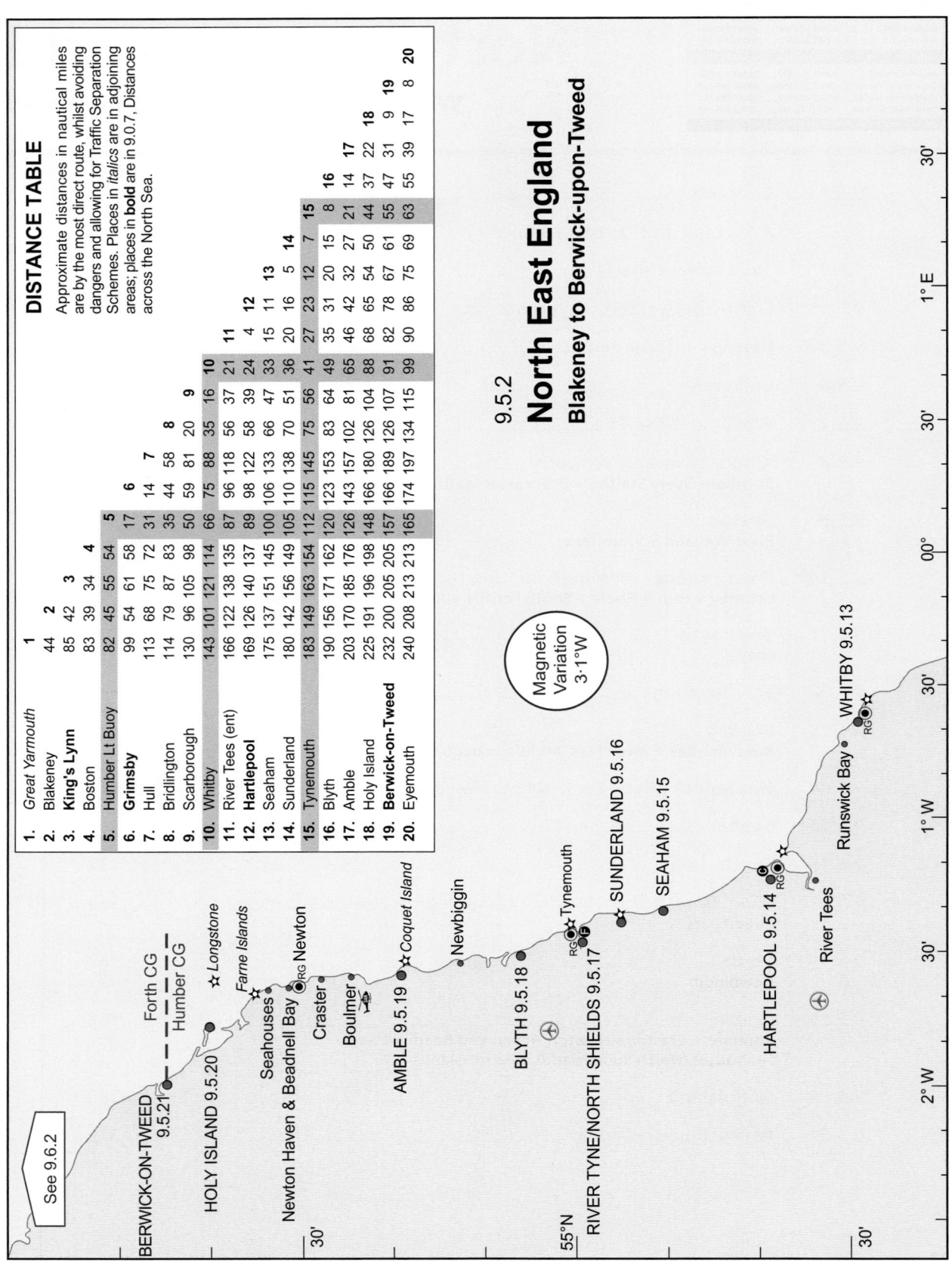

See 9.6.2

BERWICK-ON-TWEED 9.5.21

Forth CG
Humber CG

HOLY ISLAND 9.5.20

☆ Longstone

Farne Islands

Seahouses

Newton Haven & Beadnell Bay ●RG Newton

Craster

Boulmer

AMBLE 9.5.19 ☆ Coquet Island

Newbiggin

BLYTH 9.5.18

RG☆ Tynemouth
RIVER TYNE/NORTH SHIELDS 9.5.17 RG

SUNDERLAND 9.5.16

SEAHAM 9.5.15

HARTLEPOOL 9.5.14 RG

River Tees

Runswick Bay ●

WHITBY 9.5.13 ☆ RG

30'

1°E

00°

1°W

2°W

55°N

30'

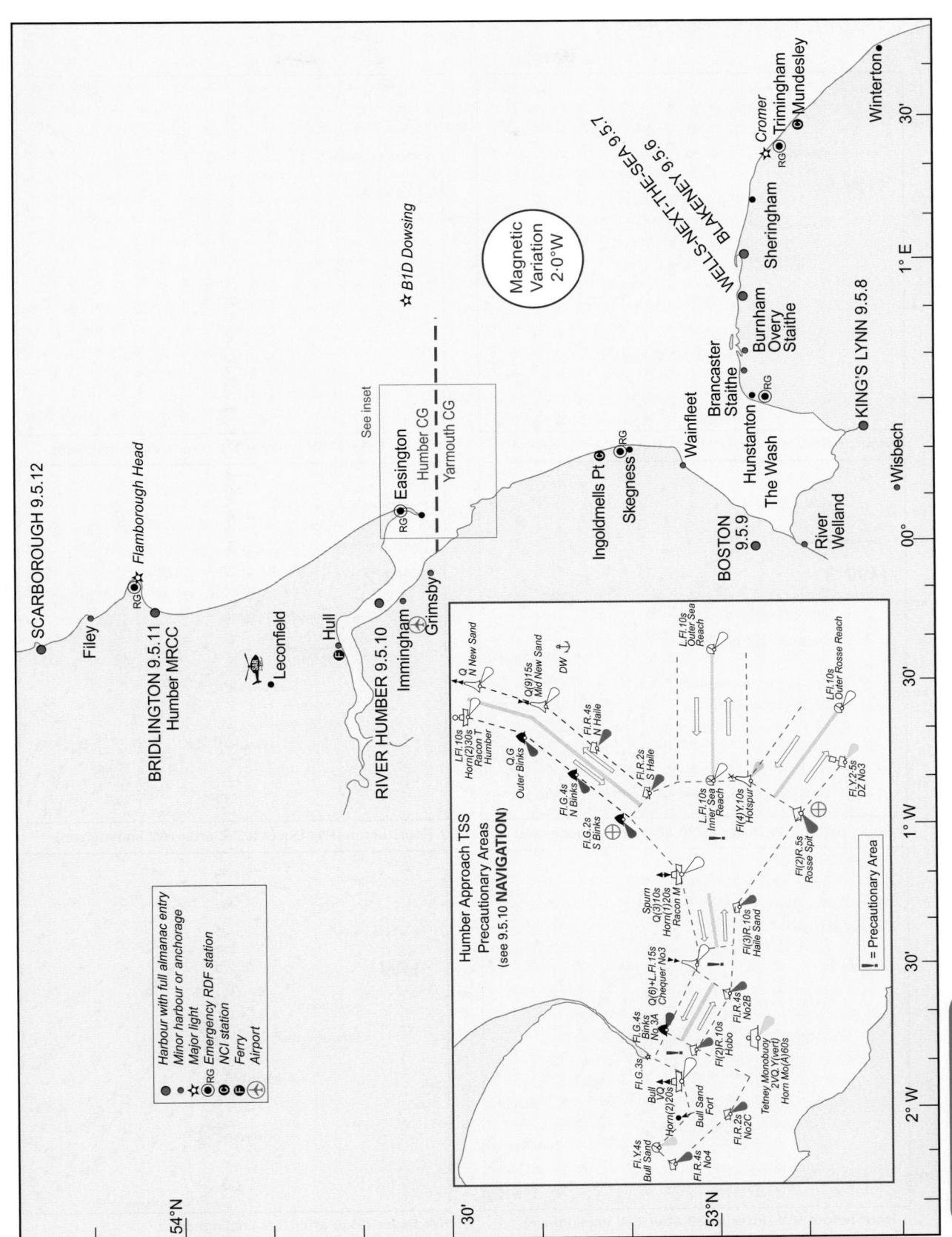

9.5.3 AREA 5 TIDAL STREAMS

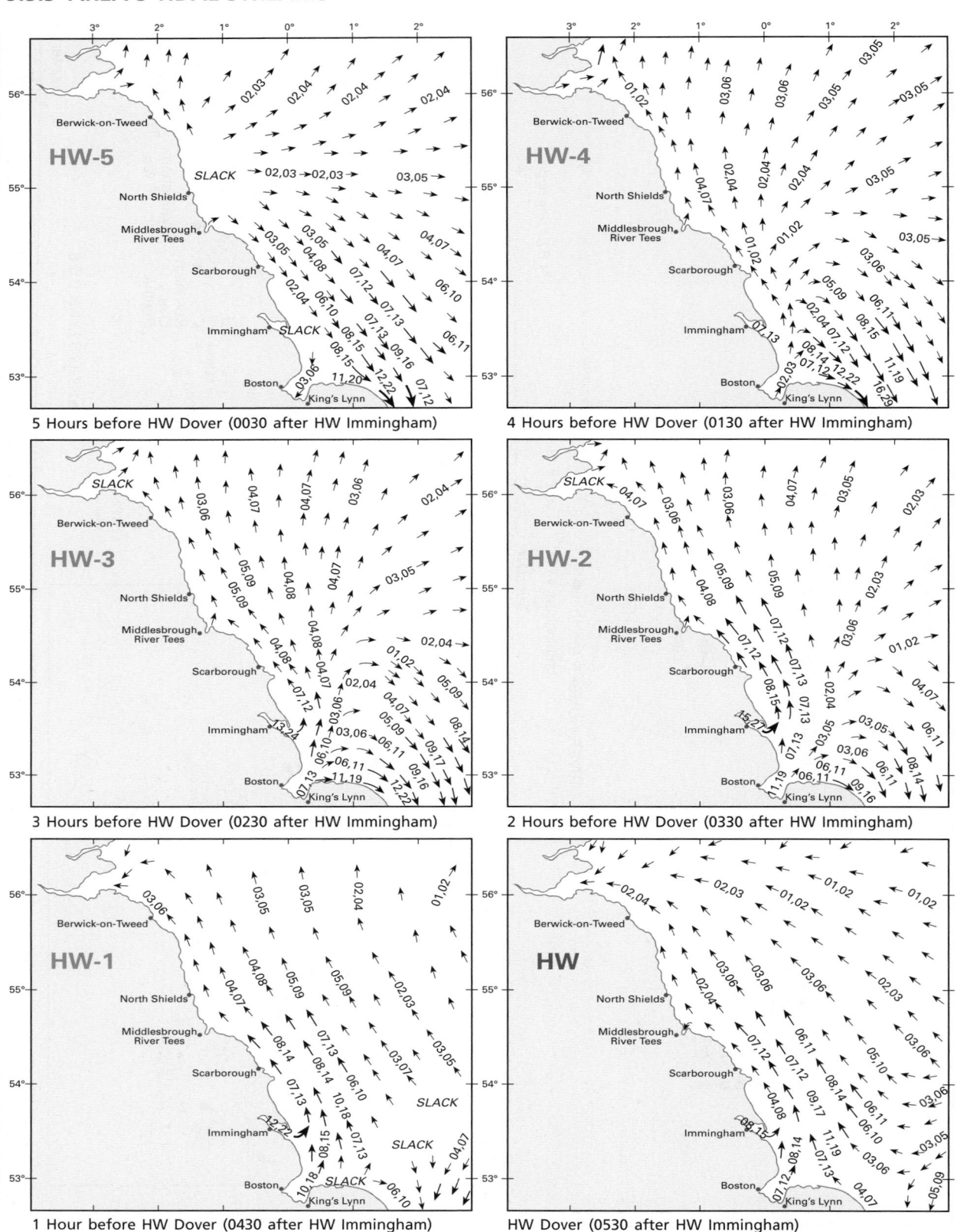

5 Hours before HW Dover (0030 after HW Immingham)

4 Hours before HW Dover (0130 after HW Immingham)

3 Hours before HW Dover (0230 after HW Immingham)

2 Hours before HW Dover (0330 after HW Immingham)

1 Hour before HW Dover (0430 after HW Immingham)

HW Dover (0530 after HW Immingham)

Northward 9.6.3   Southward 9.4.3

HW+1

1 Hour after HW Dover (0555 before HW Immingham)

HW+2

2 Hours after HW Dover (0455 before HW Immingham)

HW+3

3 Hours after HW Dover (0355 before HW Immingham)

HW+4

4 Hours after HW Dover (0255 before HW Immingham)

HW+5

5 Hours after HW Dover (0155 before HW Immingham)

HW+6

6 Hours after HW Dover (0055 before HW Immingham)

9.5.4 LIGHTS, BUOYS AND WAYPOINTS

Bold print = light with a nominal range of 15M or more. CAPITALS = place or feature. *CAPITAL ITALICS* = light-vessel, light float or Lanby. *Italics* = Fog signal. ***Bold italics*** = Racon. Abbreviations are in Chapter 1.

GREAT YARMOUTH TO THE WASH

(Direction of buoyage ⇧ South to North)

YARMOUTH and CAISTER ROADS/COCKLE GATEWAY
SW Scroby ⬩ Fl G 2·5s; 52°35'·82N 01°46'·26E.
Scroby Elbow ⬩ Fl (2) G 5s; *Bell*; 52°37'·35N 01°46'·10E.
Yarmouth Outfall ⬟ Q R; 52°37'·58N 01°45'·70E.
Mid Caister ⬟ Fl (2) R 5s; *Bell*; 52°38'·99N 01°45'·66E.
NW Scroby ⬩ Fl (3) G 10s; 52°40'·36N 01°46'·31E.
N Caister ⬟ Fl (3) R 10s; 52°40'·77N 01°45'·65E.
Hemsby ⬟ Fl R 2·5s; 52°41'·80N 01°46'·00E.
N Scroby ⚐ VQ; 52°41'·39N 01°46'·47E.
Cockle ⚐ VQ (3) 5s; *Bell*; 52°44'·03N 01°43'·59E.

OFFSHORE ROUTE
Cross Sand ⚐ L Fl 10s 6m 5M; ***Racon (T)10M***; 52°37'·03N 01°59'·14E.
E Cross Sand ⬟ Fl (4) R 15s; 52°38'·55N 01°53'·55E.
NE Cross Sand ⚐ VQ (3) 5s; 52°44'·22N 01°53'·80E.
Smith's Knoll ⚐ Q (6) + L Fl 15s 7M; ***Racon (T) 10M***; 52°43'·52N 02°17'·89E.
S Winterton Ridge ⚐ Q (6) + L Fl 15s; 52°47'·21N 02°03'·44E.
E Hammond Knoll ⚐ Q (3) 10s; 52°52'·32N 01°58'·64E.
Hammond Knoll ⚐ Q (9) 15s; 52°49'·68N 01°57'·54E.
Newarp ⚐ L Fl 10s 7M; ***Racon (O) 10M***; 52°48'·37N 01°55'·69E.
S Haisbro ⚐ Q (6) + L Fl 15s; *Bell*; 52°50'·82N 01°48'·29E.
Mid Haisbro ⬩ Fl (2) G 5s; 52°54'·22N 01°41'·59E.
N Haisbro ⚐ Q; ***Racon (T) 10M***; 53°00'·22N 01°32'·29E.
Happisburgh ☆ Fl (3) 30s 41m 14M; 52°49'·21N 01°32'·18E.

(Direction of buoyage ⇧ East to West)

CROMER
Cromer ☆ 52°55'·45N 01°19'·01E; Fl 5s 84m **21M**; W 8-sided twr; vis: 102°-307° H24; ***Racon (O) 25M***.
Tayjack Wk ⬟ Fl R 2·5s; 52°57'·61N 01°15'·37E.
E Sheringham ⚐ Q (3) 10s; 53°02'·21N 01°14'·84E.
W Sheringham ⚐ Q (9) 15s; 53°02'·95N 01°06'·72E.

BLAKENEY
Blakeney Fairway (SWM) ⬟; 52°59'·31N 00°57'·83E (approx).
Blakeney Overfalls ⬟ Fl (2) R 5s; *Bell;* 53°03'·01N 01°01'·37E.

WELLS-NEXT-THE-SEA/BRANCASTER STAITHE
Wells Leading Buoy ⬩ Fl(2) R 5s; 52°59'·80N 00°50'·49E.
Bridgirdle ⬟ Fl R 2·5s; 53°01'·73N 00°43'·95E.

APPROACHES TO THE WASH
S Race ⚐ Q (6) + L Fl 15s; *Bell*; 53°07'·81N 00°57'·34E.
E Docking ⬟ Fl R 2·5s; 53°09'·82N 00°50'·39E.
N Race ⬩ Fl G 5s; *Bell.*; 53°14'·98N 00°43'·87E.
N Docking ⚐ Q; 53°14'·82N 00°41'·49E.
Scott Patch ⚐ VQ (3) 5s; 53°11'·12N 00°36'·39E.
S Inner Dowsing ⚐ Q (6) + L Fl 15s; *Bell*; 53°12'·12N 00°33'·69E.
Boygrift Tower ⚐ Fl (2) 10s 12m 5M; 53°17'·63N 00°19'·24E.
Burnham Flats ⚐ Q (9) 15s; *Bell*; 53°07'·53N 00°34'·89E.

THE WASH
West Ridge ⚐ Q (9) 15s; 53°19'·06N 00°44'·47E.
N Well ⚐ L Fl 10s; *Bell*; ***Racon (T) 10M***; 53°03'·02N 00°27'·90E.
Roaring Middle ⬩ L Fl 10s 7m 8M; 52°58'·64N 00°21'·08E.

CORK HOLE/KING'S LYNN
Sunk ⚐ Q (9) 15s; 52°56'·29N 00°23'·40E.
Seal Sand ⚐ Q; *Bell*; 52°56'·00N 00°20'·00E.

WISBECH CHANNEL/RIVER NENE
Beacons are moved as required.
Masts on W side of River Nene to Wisbech carry FG Lts and those on E side QR or FR Lts.

FREEMAN CHANNEL
Boston Roads ⬟ L Fl 10s; 52°57'·66N 00°16'·04E.
Boston No. 1 ⬩ Fl G 3s; 52°57'·88N 00°15'·16E.
Alpha ⬟ Fl R 3s; 52°57'·65N 00°14'·99E.
No. 3 ⬩ Fl G 6s; 52°58'·08N 00°14'·07E.
No. 5 ⬩ Fl G 3s; 52°58'·51N 00°12'·72E.
Freeman Inner ⚐ Q (9) 15s; 52°58'·59N 00°11'·36E.
Delta ⬟ Fl R 6s; 52°58'·38N 00°11'·25E.

BOSTON LOWER ROAD
Boston No. 7 ⬩ Fl G 3s; 52°58'·62N 00°10'·00E.
Boston No. 9 ⬩ Fl G 3s; 52°57'·58N 00°08'·36E.
Black Buoy ⬟ Fl (2) R 6s; 52°56'·82N 00°07'·74E.
Tabs Head ⚐ Q WG 4m 1M; R □ on W mast; vis: W shore - 251°-G - shore; 52°56'·00N 00°04'·91E.

BOSTON, NEW CUT AND RIVER WITHAM
Ent N side, Dollypeg ⚐ QG 4m 1M; B △ on Bn; 52°56'·13N 00°05'·03E.
New Cut ⚐ Fl G 3s; △ on pile; 52°55'·98N 00°04'·67E.
New Cut Ldg Lts 240°. Front, No. 1, F 5m 5M; 52°55'·85N 00°04'·40E. Rear, 90m from front, F 8m 5M.

WELLAND CUT/RIVER WELLAND
SE side ⚐ Iso R 2s; NW side Iso G 2s. Lts QR (to port) and QG (to stbd) mark the chan upstream; 52°55'·72E 00°04'·68E.

(Direction of buoyage ⇧ North to South)

BOSTON DEEP/WAINFLEET ROADS
Scullridge ⬩; 52°59'·76N 00°13'·86E.
Friskney ⬩; 53°00'·59N 00°16'·76E.
Long Sand ⬩; 53°01'·27N 00°18'·30E.
Pompey ⬩; 53°02'·19N 00°19'·26E.
Swatchway ⬩; 53°03'·81N 00°19'·70E.
Off Ingoldmells Point ⚐ Fl Y 5s 22m 5M; Mast; *Mo (U) 30s*; 53°12'·49N 00°25'·85E.

THE WASH TO THE RIVER HUMBER

(Direction of buoyage ⇧ South to North)

Dudgeon ⚐ Q (9) 15s 7M; ***Racon (O) 10M***; 53°16'·62N 01°16'·90E.
E Dudgeon ⚐ Q (3) 10s; 53°19'·72N 00°58'·69E.
Mid Outer Dowsing ⬩ Fl (3) G 10s; 53°24'·82N 01°07'·79E.
N Outer Dowsing ⚐ Q; 53°33'·52N 00°59'·59E; ***Racon (T) 10M.***

B.1D Platform Dowsing ⬒ 53°33'·68N 00°52'·63E; Fl (2) 10s 28m **22M**; *Morse (U) R 15s 28m 3M; Horn (2) 60s*.

RIVER HUMBER APPROACHES
W Ridge ⚐ Q (9) 15s; 53°19'·04N 00°44'·50E.
Inner Dowsing ⚐ Q (3) 10s 7M; ***Racon (T) 10M***; *Horn 60s*; 53°19'·10N 00°34'·80E.
Protector ⬟ Fl R 2·5s; 53°24'·84N 00°25'·12E.
DZ No. 4 ⬟ Fl Y 5s; 53°27'·15N 00°19'·06E.
DZ No. 3 ⬟ Fl Y 2·5s 53°29'·30N 00°19'·21E.
Rosse Spit ⬟ Fl (2) R 5s 53°30'·56N 00°16'·60E.
Haile Sand No. 2 ⬟ Fl (3) R 10s; 53°32'·42N 00°13'·18E.

Humber ⬩ G lt float L Fl 10s 7M; *Horn (2) 30s*; ***Racon (T) 7M***; 53°38'·70N 00°21'·24E.
N Binks ⬩ Fl G 4s; 53°36'·01N 00°18'·28E.
S Binks ⬩ Fl G 2s 53°34'·74N 00°16'·55E.

SPURN ⬩ Q (3) 10s 10m 8M; *Horn 20s*; ***Racon (M) 5M***; 53°33'·56N 00°14'·20E.
SE CHEQUER ⬩ VQ (6) + L Fl 10s 6m 6M; *Horn 30s* 53°33'·38N 00°12'·55E.

WGS84 DATUM
Plot waypoints on chart before use

Chequer No. 3 ⚓ Q (6) + L Fl 15s; 53°33'·07N 00°10'·63E.
No 2B ⚓ Fl R 4s; 53°32'·33N 00°09'·10E.
Tetney ⚓ 2 VQ Y (vert); *Horn Mo (A)60s*; QY on 290m floating hose; 53°32'·35N 00°06'·76E.

RIVER HUMBER/GRIMSBY/HULL
Binks No. 3A ⚓ Fl G 4s; 53°33'·92N 00°07'·43E.
Spurn Pt ⚓ Fl G 3s 11m 5M; 53°34'·37N 00°06'·47E.
BULL ⚓ VQ 8m 6M; *Horn (2) 20s*; 53°33'·54N 00°05'·70E.
Bull Sand ⚓ Q R ; 53°34'·45N 00°03'·69E.
North Fort ⚓ Q; 53°33'·80N 00°04'·19E.
South Fort ⚓ Q (6) + L Fl 15s; 53°33'·65N 00°03'·96E.
Haile Sand Fort ⚓ Fl R 5s 21m 3M; 53°32'·07N 00°01'·99E.
Haile Chan No. 4 ⚓ Fl R 4s; 53°33'·64N 00°02'·84E.
Middle No. 7 ⚓ VQ (6) + L Fl 10s; *Horn 20s*; 53°35'·80N 00°01'·50E.
Grimsby Royal Dock ent E side ⚓ Fl (2) R 6s 10m 8M; Dn; 53°35'·08N 00°04'·04W.
Killingholme Lts in line 292°. Front, Iso R 2s 10m 14M. 53°38'·78N 00°12'·96W. Rear, 219m from front, F WRG 22m 3M; vis: 289·5°-G-290·5°-G/W-291·5°-W-292·5°-R/W-293·5° (H24).

RIVER HUMBER TO WHITBY
Canada & Giorgios Wreck ⚓ VQ (3) 5s; 53°42'·37N 00°07'·16E.

BRIDLINGTON
SW Smithic ⚓ Q (9) 15s; 54°02'·41N 00°09'·21W.
N Pier Hd ⚓ Fl 2s 12m 9M; *Horn 60s*; (Tidal Lts) Fl R or Fl G; 54°04'·77N 00°11'·19W.
N Smithic ⚓ VQ; *Bell*; 54°06'·22N 00°03'·90W.
Flamborough Hd ☆ 54°06'·98N 00°04'·96W; Fl (4) 15s 65m **24M**; W ○ twr; *Horn (2) 90s* .

FILEY/SCARBOROUGH/WHITBY
Filey Brigg ⚓ Q (3) 10s; *Bell*; 54°12'·74N 00°14'·60W.
Scarborough E Pier Hd ⚓ QG 8m 3M; 54°16'·88N 00°23'·36W.
Scarborough Pier ⚓ Iso 5s 17m 9M; W ○ twr; vis: 219°- 039° (tide sigs); *Dia 60s*; 54°16'·91N 00°23'·40W.
Whitby ⚓ Q; *Bell*; 54°30'·33N 00°36'·58W.
Whitby High ☆ 54°28'·67N 00°34'·10W; Ling Hill Fl WR 5s 73m **18M**, R16M; W 8-sided twr and dwellings; vis: 128°-R-143°-W- 319°.

WHITBY TO THE RIVER TYNE
RUNSWICK/REDCAR
Salt Scar ⚓ 54°38'·12N 01°00'·12W VQ; *Bell*.
Luff Way Ldg Lts 197°. Front, on Esplanade, FR 8m 7M; vis: 182°-212°; 54°37'·10N 01°03'·71W. Rear, 115m from front, FR 12m 7M; vis: 182°-212°.
High Stone. Lade Way Ldg Lts 247°. Front, Oc R 2·5s 9m 7M; 54°37'·15N 01°03'·92W. Rear, 43m from front, Oc R 2·5s 11m 7M; vis: 232°-262°.

TEES APPROACHES/HARTLEPOOL
Tees Fairway ⚓ Iso 4s 8m 8M; *Racon (B) unknown range*; *Horn (1) 5s*; 54°40'·94N 01°06'·48W .
Bkwtr Hd S Gare ☆ 54°38'·85N 01°08'·27W; Fl WR 12s 16m **W20M, R17M**; W ○ twr; vis: 020°-W-274°-R-357°; Sig Stn; *Horn 30s*.
Ldg Lts 210·1° Front, FR 18m 13M; 54°37'·22N 01°10'·20W. **Rear**, 560m from front, FR 20m **16M**.
Longscar ⚓ Q (3) 10s; *Bell*; 54°40'·86N 01°09'·89W.
The Heugh ☆ 54°41'·79N 01°10'·56W; Fl (2) 10s 19m**19M** ; W twr.

Hartlepool Marina Lock Dir Lt 308° Dir Fl WRG2s 6m 3M; vis: 305·5°-G-307°-W-309°-R-310·5°; 54°41'·45N 01°11'·92W.

SEAHAM/SUNDERLAND
Seaham N Pier Hd ⚓ Fl G 10s 12m 5M; W col, B bands; *Dia 30s*; 54°50'·26N 01°19'·26W.
Sunderland Roker Pier Hd ☆ 54°55'·28N 01°21'·15W; Fl 5s 25m **23M**; W □ twr, 3 R bands and cupola: vis: 211°- 357°; *Siren 20s*.
Old N Pier Hd ⚓ QG 12m 8M; metal column; *Horn 10s*; 54°55'·13N 01°21'·61W.
DZ ⚓ 54°57'·04N 01°18'·90W and ⚓ 54°58'·61N 01°19'·90W; both Fl Y 2·5s.

TYNE ENTRANCE/NORTH SHIELDS
Ent North Pier Hd ☆ 55°00'·88N 01°24'·18W; Fl (3) 10s 26m **26M**; Gy □ twr, W lantern; *Horn 10s* .
Herd Groyne Hd Ldg Lt 249°, Oc RG 10s 13m, R11M, G11M; R pile structure, R&W lantern; vis: 224°-G-246·5°, 251·5°-R-277°; FR (unintens) 080°-224°. Same structure Dir Oc 10s 14m **19M**; vis: 246·5°-W-251·5°; *Bell (1) 5s*; 55°00'·49N 01°25'·44W.

RIVER TYNE TO BERWICK-UPON-TWEED
CULLERCOATS and BLYTH
Cullercoats Ldg Lts 256°. Front, FR 27m 3M; 55°02'·06N 01°25'·91W. Rear, 38m from front, FR 35m 3M.
Blyth Ldg Lts 324°. Front ⚓ F Bu 11m 10M; 55°07'·42N 01°29'·82W. Rear ⚓, 180m from front, F Bu 17m 10M. Both Or ⚓ on twr.
Blyth Fairway ⚓ Fl G 3s; *Bell*;55°06'·59N 01°28'·60W.
Blyth E Pier Hd ☆ 55°06'·98N 01°29'·21W; Fl (4) 10s 19m **21M**, W twr; same structure FR 13m 13M, vis:152°-249°; Horn (3) 30s.

COQUET ISLAND, AMBLE and WARKWORTH
Coquet ☆ 55°20'·03N 01°32'·39W; Fl (3) WR 20s 25m **W19M, R15M**; W □ twr, turreted parapet, lower half Gy; vis: 330°-R-140°-W-163°-R-180°-W-330°; sector boundaries are indeterminate and may appear as Alt WR; *Horn 30s*.
Amble N Pier Head ⚓ Fl G 6s 12m 6M; 55°20'·39N 01°34'·25W.

SEAHOUSES, BAMBURGH and FARNE ISLANDS
N Sunderland ⚓ Fl R 2·5s; 55°34'·62N 01°37'·12W.
Bamburgh Black Rocks Point ☆ 55°36'·99N 01°43'·45W; Oc(2) WRG 8s 12m **W14M**, R11M, G11M; W bldg; vis: 122°-G-165°-W-175°-R-191°-W- 238°-R- 275°-W- 289°-G-300°.
Inner Farne ⚓ Fl (2) WR 15s 27m W10M, R7M; W ○ twr; vis: 119°-R - 280° - W -119°; 55°36'·92N 01°39'·35W.
Longstone ☆ **W side** 55°38'·62N 01°36'·65W; Fl 20s 23m **24M**; R twr, W band; *Horn (2) 60s*.
Swedman ⚓ Fl G 2·5s; 55°37'·65N 01°41'·63W.

HOLY ISLAND
Ridge ⚓ Q (3) 10s; 55°39'·70N 01°45'·97W.
Plough Rock ⚓ Q (9) 15s; 55°40'·24N 01°46'·00W.
Old Law E Bn ⚓ (Guile Pt) Oc WRG 6s 9m 4M; vis: 180·5°-G-258·5°-W-261·5°-R-shore.
Heugh ⚓ Oc WRG 6s 24m 5M; vis: 135°-G-308°-W-311-R- shore; 55°40'·09N 01°47'·99W.
Plough Seat ⚓ QR; 55°40'·37N 01°44'·97W.
Goldstone ⚓ QG; 55°40'·25N 01°43'·64W.

BERWICK-UPON-TWEED
Bkwtr Hd ⚓ Fl 5s 15m 6M; vis: 201°-009°, (obscured 155°-201°); W ○ twr, R cupola and base; FG (same twr) 8m 1M; vis 009°-G-155°; 55°45'·88N 01°59'·06W.

9.5.5 PASSAGE INFORMATION

For directions and pilotage refer to *Tidal Havens of the Wash and Humber* (Imray/Irving) which carefully documents the hbrs of this little-frequented cruising ground. N from R Humber see the Royal Northumberland YC's Sailing Directions, Humber to Rattray Head. The Admiralty *North Sea (West) Pilot* covers the whole coast. *North Sea Passage Pilot* (Imray/Navin) goes as far N as Cromer and across to Den Helder. Admiralty Leisure Folio 5614 covers the area Orford Ness to Whitby.

More Passage Information is threaded between the harbours of this Area.

NORTH SEA PASSAGES

See 9.0.7 for distances across the North Sea. There is further Passage Information in Area 4 for the southern North Sea, in Area 6 for crossing to Norway and the Baltic, and in Area 16 for crossings from the Frisian Islands, German Bight, Belgium and the Netherlands.

OIL AND GAS INSTALLATIONS

See 3.14. Any craft going offshore in the N Sea is likely to encounter oil or gas installations. These are shown on Admiralty charts, where scale permits; the position of mobile rigs is updated in weekly NMs. Safety zones of radius 500m are established round all permanent platforms, mobile exploration rigs, and tanker loading moorings, as described in the Annual Summary of Admiralty Notices to Mariners No 20. Some of these platforms are close together or inter-linked. Unauthorised vessels, including yachts, must not enter these zones except in emergency or due to stress of weather.

Platforms show a main lt, Fl Mo (U) 15s 15M. In addition secondary lts, Fl Mo (U) R 15s 2M, synchronised with the main lt, may mark projections at each corner of the platform if not marked by a W lt. The fog signal is Horn Mo (U) 30s. See the Admiralty List of Lights and Fog Signals, Vol A.

9.5.6 BLAKENEY

Norfolk **52°59'·19N 00°57'·90E** (ent shifts)   ❀⚓⚓❀❀❀

CHARTS AC 1190, 108; Imray C28; Stanfords 19, 3.

TIDES –0445 Dover; ML Cromer 2·8; Duration 0530; Zone 0 (UT)

Standard Port IMMINGHAM (→)

Times				Height (metres)			
High Water		Low Water		MHWS	MHWN	MLWN	MLWS
0100	0700	0100	0700	7·3	5·8	2·6	0·9
1300	1900	1300	1900				
Differences BLAKENEY BAR (approx 52°59'N 00°59'E)							
+0035	+0025	+0030	+0040	−1·6		−1·3	No data
BLAKENEY (approx 52°57'N 01°01'E)							
+0115	+0055	No data		−3·9	−3·8		No data
CROMER							
+0050	+0030	+0050	+0130	−2·1	−1·7	−0·5	−0·1

SHELTER Very good. Entry, sp HW ±2, nps HW ±1½. No access in fresh on-shore winds when conditions at the ent deteriorate very quickly, especially on the ebb. Moorings in The Pit area dry out.

NAVIGATION WPT 53°00'·00N 00°58'·20E, approx 225°/1M to Fairway RW buoy which is moved as required.

- Hjordis lit IDM buoy marks large dangerous wreck, close E of entrance.
- The bar is shallow, shifts often and the channel is marked by unlit SHM and PHM buoys, relaid each spring.
- Strangers are best advised to follow local boats in. Beware mussel lays, drying, off Blakeney Spit. Speed limit 8kn.

LIGHTS AND MARKS Conspic marks: Blakeney and Langham churches; a chimney on the house on Blakeney Point neck; TV mast (R lts) approx 2M S of entrance.

R/T None.

TELEPHONE (Code 01263) MRCC (01493) 851338; Marinecall 09068 969645; Dr 740314.

FACILITIES Quay AB (Free), Slip, M, D, FW, C (15 ton); Services: CH (Stratton Long) ☎ 740362, AB, BY, M, P & D (cans), FW, ME, El, ⚒, SM, Gaz, AC. Village 🛒, R, Bar, ⊠, Ⓑ, ⇌ (Sheringham), ✈ (Norwich).

NORTH NORFOLK COAST

(Charts 1503, 108) The coast of N Norfolk is unfriendly in bad weather, with no hbr accessible when there is any N in the wind. The hbrs all dry, and seas soon build up in the entrances or over the bars, some of which are dangerous even in a moderate breeze and an ebb tide. But in settled weather and moderate offshore winds it is a peaceful area to explore, particularly for boats which can take the ground. At Blakeney and Wells chans shift almost every year, so local knowledge is essential and may best be acquired in advance from the HM, or possibly by following a friendly FV of suitable draft.

Haisborough Sand (buoyed) lies parallel to and 8M off the Norfolk coast at Happisburgh lt ho, with depths of less than 1m in many places, and drying 0·4m near the mid-point. The shoal is steep-to, on its NE side in particular, and there are tidal eddies. Even a moderate sea or swell breaks on the shallower parts. There are dangerous wks near the S end. Haisborough Tail and Hammond Knoll (with wk depth 1.6m) lie to the E of S end of Haisborough Sand. Newarp lt F is 5M SE. Similar banks lie parallel to and up to 60M off the coast.

▶ *The streams follow the generally NW/SE direction of the coast and offshore chans. But in the outer chans the stream is somewhat rotatory: when changing from SE-going to NW-going it sets SW, and when changing from NW-going to SE-going it sets NE, across the shoals. Close S of Haisborough Sand the SE-going stream begins at HW Immingham −0030; the NW-going at HW Immingham +0515, sp rates up to 2·5kn. It is possible to carry a fair tide from Gt Yarmouth to the Wash.* ◀

▶ *If proceeding direct from Cromer to the Humber, pass S of Sheringham Shoal (buoyed) where the ESE-going stream begins at HW Immingham −0225, and the WNW-going at +0430.* ◀ Proceed to NE of Blakeney Overfalls and Docking Shoal, and to SW of Race Bank, so as to fetch Inner Dowsing lt tr (lt, fog sig). Thence pass E of Protector Overfalls, and steer for Rosse Spit buoy at SE ent to R Humber.

THE WASH

(Charts 108,1200) The Wash is formed by the estuaries of the rivers Great Ouse, Nene, Welland and Witham; it is an area of shifting sands, most of which dry. Important features are the strong tidal streams, the low-lying shore, and the often poor vis. Watch the echo sounder carefully, because buoys may have been moved to accommodate changes in the channel. ▶*Near North Well, the in-going stream begins at HW Immingham −0430, and the out-going at HW Immingham +0130, sp rates about 2kn. The in-going stream is usually stronger than the out-going, but its duration is less. Prolonged NE winds cause an in-going current, which can increase the rate and duration of the in-going stream and raise the water level at the head of the estuary. Do not attempt entry to the rivers too early on the flood, which runs hard in the rivers.* ◀

North Well SWM lt buoy and Roaring Middle lt F are the keys to entering the Wash from N or E. But from the E it is also possible to appr via a shallow route N of Stiffkey Overfalls and Bridgirdle PHM buoy; thence via Sledway and Woolpack PHM lt buoy to North Well and into Lynn Deeps. Near north end of Lynn Deeps there are overfalls over Lynn Knock at sp tides. Approach King's Lynn via the buoyed/lit Bulldog chan. For R Nene (Wisbech) follow the Wisbech Chan. Boston and R Welland are reached via Freeman Chan, westward from Roaring Middle; or via Boston Deep, all lit.

The NW shore of The Wash is fronted by mudflats extending 2–3M offshore and drying more than 4m; a bombing range is marked by Y bns and buoys. Wainfleet Swatchway should only be used in good vis; the buoyed chan shifts constantly, and several shoals (charted depths unreliable) off Gibraltar Pt obstruct access to Boston Deep. In an emergency Wainfleet offers good shelter (dries).

9.5.7 WELLS-NEXT-THE-SEA

Norfolk **52°59'·30N 00°49'·75E** (ent shifts) ❁❀◈◊◊◊♔♔♔

CHARTS AC 1190, 108; Imray C28, Y9; Stanfords 19, 3.

TIDES −0445 Dover; ML 1·2 Duration 0540

Standard Port IMMINGHAM (⟶)

Times				Height (metres)			
High Water		Low Water		MHWS	MHWN	MLWN	MLWS
0100	0700	0100	0700	7·3	5·8	2·6	0·9
1300	1900	1300	1900				

Differences WELLS BAR (approx 52°59'N 00°49'E)
| +0020 | +0020 | +0020 | +0020 | −1·3 | −1·0 | No data | |

WELLS-NEXT-THE-SEA (approx 52°58'N 00°51'E)
| +0035 | +0045 | +0340 | +0310 | −3·8 | −3·8 | Not below CD | |

NOTE: LW time differences at Wells are for the end of a LW stand which lasts about 4 hrs at sp and about 5 hrs at nps.

SHELTER Good, but ent difficult in strong on-shore winds (N'lies) for small craft. Max draft 3m at sp. Access from HW−2 to HW+2, but best on the flood. Quay berths mostly dry, pontoon berths at W end of Town Quay.

NAVIGATION WPT Wells Leading Buoy, 52°59'·80N 00°50'·49E. Ent varies in depth and position; buoys are altered to suit. Initially keep to W side of chan to counter E-going tide at HW−2; and to E side of chan from No 12 PHM lt buoy to Quay.

Obtain HM's advice, Hbr Launch often available to escort visitors into hbr & up to Quay. Spd limits: No 6 buoy to Quay 8kn; above this 5kn. See www.wellsharbour.co.uk for latest harbour chart.

LIGHTS AND MARKS As plan. Temp buoys may be laid when chan changes. A pine plantation is conspic W of hbr ent; ditto white LB ho with R roof.

R/T Call 'Wells Harbour' Ch 12 16 before entering, listens HW−2 to HW+2 and when vessels expected.

TELEPHONE (Code 01328 Fakenham) HM 711646, mob 07775 507284, DHM mob 07881824912; MRCC (01493) 851338; Marinecall 09068 969645; Police (01493) 336200; Dr 710741; Ⓗ 710097.

FACILITIES **Main Quay** AB (£13/yacht), ⚓ drying (£12/craft), ⚓ (£5/craft), ⌂, Showers, ⓦⒸ, ▣, FW, ME, El, ✕, BH (7·5 ton), C (25 ton mobile), CH, 🛒, R, Bar; **E Quay** Slips (£6/craft/day), M, L; **Wells SC** ☎ 710622, Slip, Bar; **Services:** Ⓔ, ACA, SM, LB. **Town**: P(cans) & D (Hbr fueling stn HW-2 to HW+3; supply up to 500 galls), Gas, ▣, 🛒, R, Bar, ✉, Ⓑ, ⇌ (bus to Norwich/King's Lynn), ✈ (Norwich).

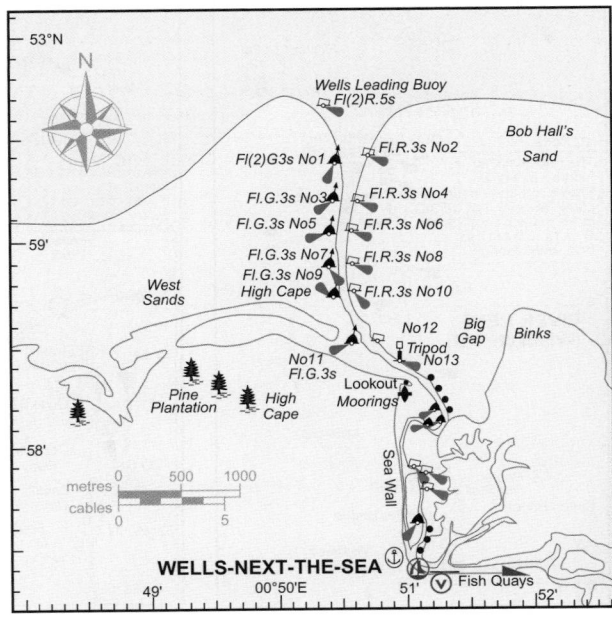

WELLS-NEXT-THE-SEA

9.5.8 KING'S LYNN AND WISBECH

Norfolk 52°49´·72N 00°21´·14E (W Stones Bn) ⊛⊛⊛🚢☆☆

CHARTS AC 1190, 108, 1200, 5614. Imray Y9

TIDES −0443 Dover, +0030 Immingham; ML 3·6; Duration 0340;

Standard Port IMMINGHAM (→)

Times				Height (metres)			
High Water		Low Water		MHWS	MHWN	MLWN	MLWS
0100	0700	0100	0700	7·3	5·8	2·6	0·9
1300	1900	1300	1900				
Differences KING'S LYNN							
+0030	+0030	+0305	+0140	−0·5	−0·8	−0·8	+0·1
OUTER WESTMARK KNOCK							
+0010	+0015	+0040	+0020	−0·2	−0·5	−0·6	−0·4
WISBECH CUT							
+0020	+0010	+0120	+0055	−0·3	−0·7	−0·4	No data
WISBECH							
+0055	+0040	Dries		−0·2	−0·6	Dries	
BURNHAM OVERY STAITHE							
+0045	+0055	No data		−5·0	−4·9	No data	
HUNSTANTON							
+0010	+0020	+0105	+0025	+0·1	−0·2	−0·1	0·0
WEST STONES							
+0025	+0025	+0115	+0040	−0·3	−0·4	−0·3	+0·2

SHELTER Port is well sheltered; entry only recommended HW−3. A busy commercial and fishing port with limited facilities. River moorings available from local clubs; keep clear of FV moorings.

NAVIGATION WPT Sunk WCM 52° 56´.29N 00° 23´.40E follow Bulldog chan buoyed/lit apprs to King's Lynn. From there to Denver Sluice (ent to inland routes) 6 bridges span river, min cl 9·15m less ht of tide at King's Lynn above Dock sill. Allow 1½H for passage. The sand banks regularly shift and extend several miles into the Wash; buoyage is altered accordingly. Contact HM a

week beforehand for latest info or see www.portauthority kingslynn.fsnet.co.uk.

LIGHTS AND MARKS See 9.5.4 and chartlet.

R/T Call: *Kings Lynn Hbr Radio* Ch **14** 11 (M-F: 0800-1730 LT. Other times: HW −4 to HW+1.) (ABP) Ch **14** 16 11 (HW−2½ to HW).

TELEPHONE HM ☎ 01553 773411 **Docks** ☎ 01553 691555.

FACILITIES AB £42 (9m LOA/48 hrs), FW, C (32 ton); **Services**: CH, ✕, ME, El, Ⓔ, D. **Town** P, D, 🛒, R, Bar, ✉, Ⓑ, ⇌, ✈ (Norwich). **Note**: 24M up the Great Ouse river, Ely Marina ☎ (01353) 664622, Slip, M, P, D, FW, ME, El, ✕, C (10 ton), CH. Lock half-way at Denver Sluice ☎ (01366) 382340/VHF Ch 73, and low bridges beyond.

WISBECH Cambridgeshire 52°40´·02N 00°09´·55E ⊛⊛🚢☆☆

SHELTER Excellent shelter in river with Wisbech Yacht Harbour pontoon berths and shower/toilet facilities immediately below Freedom Bridge in Wisbech town. Vessels of 4·8m draft can reach Wisbech at sp (3·4m at nps), but depths vary. Ent to inland waterways above Wisbech to Peterborough, Oundle, Northampton. Mast lift out service available.

NAVIGATION WPT Roaring Middle NCM Lt Flt 52° 58´.64N 00° 21´.08E 220°/7M to Wisbech No 1 SHM Fl G 5s. Monitor Ch 09 and call HM when you reach Holbeach RAF No 4 ECM to check commercial traffic and opening of Cross Keys Sw Br in river. Red flags and lights shown when Firing Range in use. Ent to R Nene from The Wash well marked with lit buoys/bns from Wisbech No 1 Fl G 5s. Best ent HW−3. 🚢s for waiting at Holbeach RAF No 4 ECM. Cross Keys Sw Br in river opens by request given notice. Waiting pontoon 0.5M downstream from bridge thence 6M to Wisbech with FG lts to stbd. Call HM and Cross Keys Sw Br HW±3. 24H prior notice of visit recommended. Departure best at HW, unless draught >3m; if so, aim to clear Kerr NCM by HW+3. For local pilotage notes ☎ Hbr Office or visit www.fenland.gov.uk.

LIGHTS AND MARKS See 9.5.4 and chartlet.

R/T HM *Wisbech Harbour* Ch **09**.

TELEPHONE Code (01945) HM 588059 (Hbr Office 24H); Cross Keys Swing Bridge 01406 350364; MRCC (01493) 851338;Marinecall 09068 969645; Police (01354) 652561; Dr 582133; Ⓗ 585781.

FACILITIES **Yacht Hbr** (102AB + 15Ⓥ), £0.90, min charge £5, FW, ⬚, El. D (barge). **Town** P (cans), CH, Bar, R, 🛒, Gas.

ADJACENT HARBOURS

BURNHAM OVERY STAITHE, Norfolk, 52°58´·95N 00°46´·55E ⊛☆☆☆. AC 1190, 108. HW −0420 on Dover. See 9.5.8. Small drying hbr; ent chan has 0·3m MLWS. ⚓ off the Staithe only suitable in good weather. No lts. Scolt Hd is conspic to W and Gun Hill to E; Scolt Hd Island is conspic 3M long sandbank which affords some shelter. Chan varies constantly and buoys are moved to suit. Local knowledge advisable. Facilities: (01328) **Burnham Overy Staithe SC** ☎ 738348, M, L; **Services**: CH, M, ME, ✕, Slip, FW; **Burnham Market** EC Wed; Bar, P and D (cans), R, 🛒.

BRANCASTER STAITHE, Norfolk, 52°59´·02N 00°37´·65E ⊛☆☆☆. AC 1190, 108. HW −0425 on Dover; as Burnham. Small drying hbr, dangerous to enter except by day in settled weather. Spd limit 6kn. Appr from due N. Conspic golf club house with lt, Fl 5s 8m 3M, is 0·5M S of chan ent and Fairway buoy. Beware wk shown on chart. Sandbanks shift; buoys changed to suit. Scolt Hd conspic to E. Local knowledge or Pilot advised. Possible ⚓ in The Hole. HM ☎ (01485) 210638. Facilities: **Brancaster Staithe SC** ☎ 210249, R, Bar; **Services**: BY, CH, El, FW, P & D (cans), ME, R, ✕, Bar, 🛒.

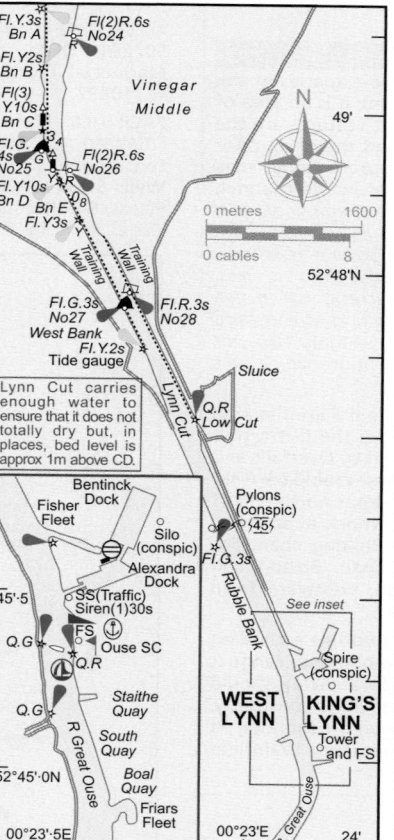

9.5.9 BOSTON

Lincs **52°56'·00N 00°04'·92E** (Tabs Head bn) ✸✳🔱✿✿

CHARTS AC 108, 1200, 5614; Imray Y9.

TIDES –0415 Dover; ML 3·3; Duration Flood 0500, Ebb 0700

Standard Port IMMINGHAM (⟶)

Times				Height (metres)			
High Water		Low Water		MHWS	MHWN	MLWN	MLWS
0100	0700	0100	0700	7·3	5·8	2·6	0·9
1300	1900	1300	1900				
Differences BOSTON							
0000	+0010	+0140	+0050	–0·5	–1·0	–0·9	–0·5
TABS HEAD (WELLAND RIVER)							
0000	+0005	+0125	+0020	+0·2	–0·2	–0·2	–0·2
SKEGNESS							
+0010	+0015	+0030	+0020	–0·4	–0·5	–0·1	0·0
INNER DOWSING LIGHT TOWER							
0000	0000	+0010	+0010	–0·9	–0·7	–0·1	+0·3

SHELTER Very good. Except in emergency berthing in the Dock is prohib wthout HM permission. Yachts secure just above Dock ent and see HM. The port is administered by Port of Boston Ltd.

Yachts capable of lowering masts can pass through the Grand Sluice (**24 hrs notice required**) into fresh water. Sluice dimensions 16m x 9m and opens twice a tide at approx HW±2 . It leads into the R Witham Navigation which goes 31M to Lincoln. Marina is to stbd immediately beyond the sluice. British Waterways have 50 moorings, with FW and ⬆⃝, beyond Grand Sluice.

NAVIGATION WPT Boston Rds SWM lt buoy, 52°57'·63N 00°16'·03E, 280°/0·7M to Freeman Chan ent. Thence Bar Chan is well marked, but liable to change. SW of Clay Hole a new chan has formed which dries 0·6m at entr; it is marked by SHM lt buoys Nos 11N, 13N, and 15. Tabs Head marks the ent to the river; it should be passed not earlier than HW–3 to enable the Grand Sluice to be reached before the start of the ebb. Beware rocky bottom within 100m of the Sluice. On reaching Boston

Dock, masts should be lowered to negotiate swing bridge (cannot always be opened) and three fixed bridges. Chan through town is un-navigable at LW.

LIGHTS AND MARKS St Boltoph's ch tr (the Boston Stump) is conspic from afar. New Cut and R Witham are marked by bns with topmarks. FW lts mark ldg lines: three pairs going upstream and six pairs going downstream.

R/T All vessels between No 9 buoy and Grand Sluice must listen Ch 12. Call: *Boston Port Control* VHF Ch 12 (Mon-Fri 0800-1700 LT & HW –2½ to HW +1½). Ch 11 used by dock staff as required. *Grand Sluice* Ch 74.

TELEPHONE (Code 01205) HM 362328; Dock office 365571; Grand Sluice Control 364864 (not always manned but has answerphone) mob 07712 010920; MRCC (01493) 851338; Marinecall 09068 969645; Police 366222; 🏥 364801.

FACILITIES **Boston Marina** (48 + some ✔) ☎ 364420, £5 per night any size inc ⬆⃝, access HW±2; FW, D, CH, ACA, C in dock, see HM (emergency); **Grand Sluice** showers and toilets; **BWB** moorings: 1st night free, then £5·00. **Services**: El, ME, ✗, Gas. **Town** Thurs; 🛒, R, Bar, ✉, ⓑ, ⇌, ✈ (Humberside).

ADJACENT HARBOURS

RIVER WELLAND, Lincolnshire, **52°56'·00N 00°04'·92E** (Tabs Head bn). AC 1190, 1200. At Welland Cut HW –0440 on Dover; ML 0·3m; Duration 0520. See 9.5.9. At Tabs Head bn HW ±3, ent Welland Cut which is defined by training walls and lt bns. Beware sp flood of up to 5kn. Berth 6M up at **Fosdyke Yacht Haven** ☎ 01205 260240. (50 + 6✔ 2m depth); ⬆⃝, Showers, 🚻, D, FW, ME, BH (50 ton – only one between R. Humber & Lowestoft), R, 🗑.

WAINFLEET, Lincolnshire, **53°04'·79N 00°19'·89E** (chan ent). AC 108. Skegness HW +0500 on Dover. See 9.5.9 (Skegness). ML 4·0m; Duration 0600. Shelter good, but emergency only. Drying channel starts close S of Gibraltar Point. Channel through saltings marked by posts with radar reflectors and lateral topmarks. Enter HW ±1½. No lts. Facilities: M, AB (larger boats at fishing jetties, smaller at YC), FW at Field Study Centre on stbd side of ent. All shore facilities at Skegness (3½ miles).

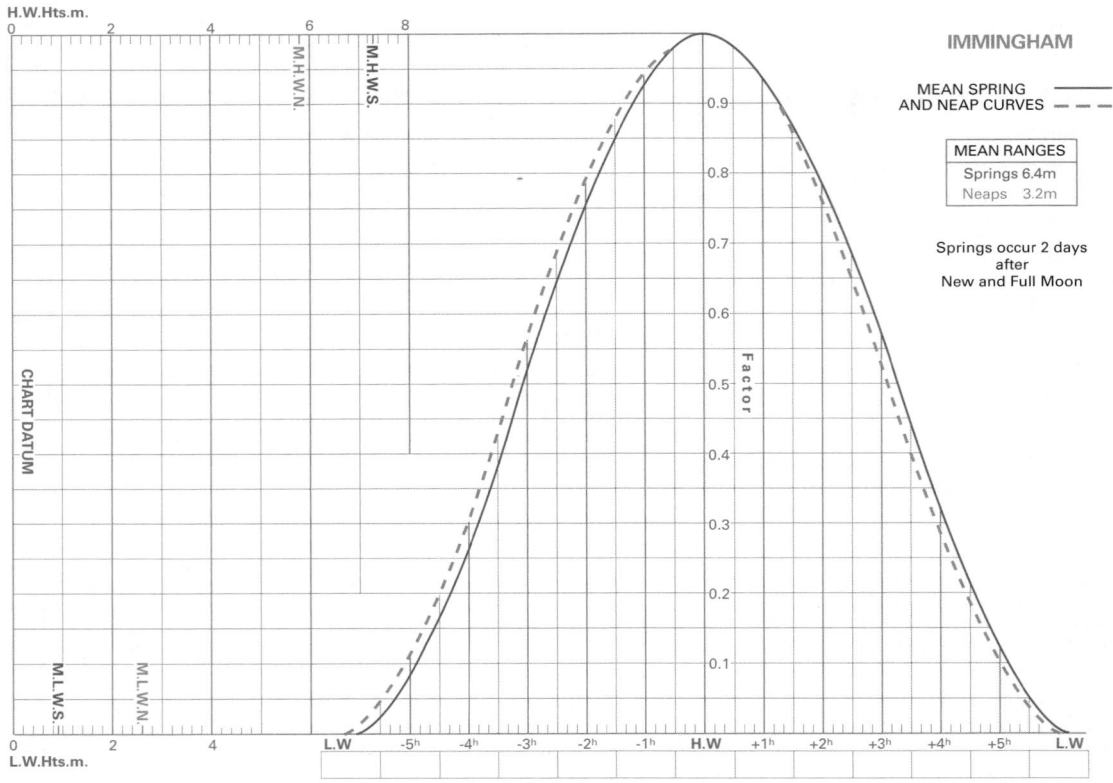

IMMINGHAM

MEAN SPRING
AND NEAP CURVES

MEAN RANGES	
Springs	6.4m
Neaps	3.2m

Springs occur 2 days
after
New and Full Moon

THE WASH TO THE RIVER HUMBER

(Charts 108, 107) Inner Dowsing is a narrow N/S sandbank with a least depth of 1·2m, 8M offshore between Skegness and Mablethorpe. There are overfalls off the W side of the bank at the N end. Inner Dowsing lt float (fog sig) is 1M NE of the bank.

In the outer approaches to The Wash and R. Humber there are many offlying banks, but few of them are of direct danger to yachts. The sea however breaks on some of them in bad weather, when they should be avoided. Fishing vessels may be encountered, and there are many oil/gas installations offshore.

RIVER HUMBER

(Charts 109, 1188, 3497) The Humber is formed by the Ouse and the Trent, which meet 13M above Kingston-upon-Hull. The river is commercially important and gives access to these rivers and inland waterways; it also drains most of Yorkshire and the Midlands. Where the Humber estuary reaches the sea between Northcoates Pt and Spurn Hd it is 4M wide. A VTS scheme is in operation to regulate commercial shipping in the Humber, Ouse and Trent and provide full radar surveillance. Yachts are advised to monitor the appropriate Humber VTS frequency.

Approaching from the S, a yacht should make good Rosse Spit and then Haile Sand No 2, both PHM lt buoys, before altering westward leading SW of Bull Ch.

If bound to/from the N, avoid The Binks, a shoal (dries 1·6m in places) extending 3M E from Spurn Hd, with a rough sea when wind is against tide. Depths offshore are irregular and subject to frequent change; it would be best to round the S Binks SPM buoy, unless in calm conditions and with local knowledge.

Haile Sand and Bull Sand Forts are both conspic to the SW of Spurn Head; beyond them it is advisable to keep just outside one of the buoyed chans, since shoals are liable to change. Hawke Chan (later Sunk) is the main dredged chan to the N. Haile Chan favours the S side and Grimsby. Bull Chan takes a middle course before merging with Haile Chan. There are good yachting facilities at Grimsby and Hull. ⌁ inside Spurn Head.

▶ *Streams are strong, even fierce at sp; local info suggests that they are stronger than shown in Tidal Streams based upon NP 251 (Admiralty Tidal Stream Atlas). 5ca S of Spurn Hd the flood sets NW from about HW Immingham –0520, sp rate 3·5kn; the ebb sets SE from about HW Immingham, sp rate 4kn. The worst seas are experienced in NW gales against a strong flood tide. 10M E of Spurn Hd the tidal streams are not affected by the river; relative to HW Immingham, the S-going stream begins at –0455, and the N-going at +0130. Nearer the entrance the direction of the S-going stream becomes more W'ly, and that of the N-going stream more E'ly.* ◀

TIME ZONE (UT)
For Summer Time add ONE hour in **non-shaded areas**

IMMINGHAM LAT 53°38'N LONG 0°11'W
TIMES AND HEIGHTS OF HIGH AND LOW WATERS

Dates in red are SPRINGS
Dates in blue are NEAPS

YEAR 2010

JANUARY

Time	m	Time	m
1 F	0558 7.1 / 1213 1.3 / 1814 7.3	**16** SA	0043 1.4 / 0642 6.6 / 1245 1.7 / 1840 7.0
2 SA	0049 0.8 / 0649 7.3 / 1301 1.2 / 1857 7.5	**17** SU	0118 1.4 / 0713 6.6 / 1319 1.7 / 1913 7.0
3 SU	0138 0.6 / 0737 7.3 / 1346 1.2 / 1941 7.6	**18** M	0150 1.4 / 0743 6.6 / 1348 1.7 / 1944 7.0
4 M	0225 0.6 / 0824 7.2 / 1430 1.3 / 2025 7.5	**19** TU	0219 1.5 / 0812 6.6 / 1416 1.7 / 2014 6.9
5 TU	0312 0.7 / 0911 7.0 / 1513 1.5 / 2111 7.4	**20** W	0245 1.6 / 0841 6.5 / 1445 1.8 / 2044 6.8
6 W	0359 0.9 / 1001 6.7 / 1558 1.7 / 2201 7.1	**21** TH	0312 1.7 / 0913 6.3 / 1515 2.0 / 2116 6.6
7 TH	0447 1.3 / 1054 6.4 / 1647 2.1 / ☾ 2258 6.7	**22** F	0343 1.8 / 0948 6.2 / 1551 2.2 / 2156 6.4
8 F	0539 1.7 / 1152 6.1 / 1743 2.4	**23** SA	0421 2.0 / 1031 5.9 / 1637 2.4 / ☽ 2245 6.2
9 SA	0002 6.3 / 0637 2.1 / 1253 5.9 / 1851 2.6	**24** SU	0514 2.3 / 1126 5.7 / 1742 2.6 / 2348 6.0
10 SU	0113 6.1 / 0743 2.3 / 1357 5.8 / 2014 2.6	**25** M	0625 2.5 / 1244 5.6 / 1903 2.7
11 M	0227 6.0 / 0850 2.4 / 1500 6.0 / 2128 2.4	**26** TU	0112 5.9 / 0745 2.5 / 1416 5.7 / 2025 2.5
12 TU	0338 6.0 / 0949 2.3 / 1557 6.2 / 2227 2.1	**27** W	0246 6.0 / 0903 2.3 / 1528 6.1 / 2143 2.1
13 W	0438 6.2 / 1040 2.1 / 1645 6.5 / 2317 1.8	**28** TH	0400 6.4 / 1011 2.0 / 1625 6.6 / 2250 1.5
14 TH	0527 6.4 / 1126 2.0 / 1727 6.7	**29** F	0501 6.8 / 1110 1.6 / 1716 7.0 / 2348 1.0
15 F	0002 1.6 / 0607 6.5 / 1208 1.8 / ● 1805 6.9	**30** SA	0554 7.1 / 1202 1.2 / 1802 7.4 / ○
		31 SU	0040 0.6 / 0642 7.4 / 1250 1.0 / 1845 7.7

FEBRUARY

Time	m	Time	m
1 M	0127 0.3 / 0726 7.5 / 1333 0.9 / 1927 7.8	**16** TU	0129 1.2 / 0717 6.7 / 1330 1.5 / 1921 7.1
2 TU	0211 0.2 / 0807 7.4 / 1415 0.9 / 2009 7.8	**17** W	0157 1.3 / 0744 6.7 / 1356 1.5 / 1949 7.0
3 W	0252 0.4 / 0847 7.2 / 1454 1.1 / 2050 7.6	**18** TH	0221 1.4 / 0811 6.7 / 1422 1.5 / 2017 7.0
4 TH	0332 0.8 / 0927 6.9 / 1532 1.4 / 2134 7.2	**19** F	0244 1.5 / 0839 6.6 / 1449 1.7 / 2048 6.8
5 F	0411 1.3 / 1009 6.5 / 1610 1.8 / ◐ 2223 6.7	**20** SA	0308 1.6 / 0910 6.4 / 1520 1.8 / 2124 6.6
6 SA	0453 1.9 / 1059 6.1 / 1655 2.3 / 2323 6.1	**21** SU	0341 1.9 / 0949 6.1 / 1602 2.1 / 2211 6.3
7 SU	0543 2.4 / 1201 5.7 / 1754 2.7	**22** M	0429 2.2 / 1041 5.8 / 1704 2.5 / ● 2314 5.9
8 M	0040 5.7 / 0653 2.8 / 1315 5.5 / 1935 2.9	**23** TU	0542 2.6 / 1154 5.6 / 1832 2.6
9 TU	0207 5.5 / 0822 2.9 / 1428 5.6 / 2115 2.6	**24** W	0047 5.7 / 0716 2.7 / 1344 5.6 / 2005 2.5
10 W	0327 5.7 / 0932 2.6 / 1533 6.0 / 2214 2.2	**25** TH	0240 5.9 / 0845 2.5 / 1507 6.0 / 2132 2.0
11 TH	0430 6.0 / 1024 2.3 / 1625 6.3 / 2302 1.8	**26** F	0354 6.3 / 0958 2.0 / 1607 6.6 / 2239 1.3
12 F	0516 6.3 / 1109 2.0 / 1708 6.6 / 2344 1.5	**27** SA	0452 6.8 / 1056 1.5 / 1658 7.1 / 2334 0.8
13 SA	0552 6.5 / 1150 1.8 / 1745 6.8	**28** SU	0542 7.2 / 1146 1.1 / 1744 7.5 / ○
14 SU	0022 1.4 / 0622 6.6 / 1228 1.6 / ● 1819 7.0		
15 M	0058 1.3 / 0650 6.7 / 1301 1.5 / 1850 7.0		

MARCH

Time	m	Time	m
1 M	0022 0.4 / 0625 7.4 / 1232 0.8 / 1827 7.8	**16** TU	0028 1.2 / 0620 6.7 / 1236 1.4 / 1823 7.0
2 TU	0107 0.1 / 0705 7.5 / 1315 0.7 / 1908 7.9	**17** W	0101 1.2 / 0648 6.8 / 1306 1.4 / 1854 7.1
3 W	0148 0.2 / 0742 7.5 / 1354 0.7 / 1948 7.8	**18** TH	0129 1.2 / 0715 6.8 / 1334 1.3 / 1924 7.1
4 TH	0226 0.4 / 0817 7.3 / 1431 0.9 / 2028 7.6	**19** F	0155 1.3 / 0743 6.8 / 1401 1.4 / 1954 7.0
5 F	0301 0.8 / 0852 7.0 / 1505 1.2 / 2108 7.1	**20** SA	0218 1.4 / 0811 6.7 / 1430 1.5 / 2026 6.9
6 SA	0335 1.4 / 0928 6.5 / 1539 1.7 / 2153 6.5	**21** SU	0245 1.6 / 0843 6.6 / 1503 1.6 / 2105 6.6
7 SU	0409 2.0 / 1009 6.1 / 1618 2.2 / ◐ 2249 5.9	**22** M	0319 1.9 / 0923 6.3 / 1547 1.9 / 2154 6.2
8 M	0454 2.6 / 1107 5.6 / 1713 2.6	**23** TU	0409 2.3 / 1015 5.9 / 1652 2.3 / ◑ 2303 5.8
9 TU	0014 5.4 / 0559 3.0 / 1254 5.4 / 1842 2.9	**24** W	0523 2.7 / 1131 5.6 / 1821 2.4
10 W	0147 5.3 / 0748 3.1 / 1357 5.5 / 2054 2.7	**25** TH	0052 5.6 / 0659 2.8 / 1321 5.7 / 1954 2.2
11 TH	0306 5.5 / 0909 2.8 / 1505 5.8 / 2150 2.2	**26** F	0232 5.9 / 0828 2.5 / 1443 6.1 / 2115 1.7
12 F	0407 5.9 / 1001 2.4 / 1558 6.2 / 2235 1.8	**27** SA	0340 6.4 / 0938 2.0 / 1543 6.6 / 2218 1.1
13 SA	0450 6.2 / 1045 2.0 / 1641 6.5 / 2315 1.5	**28** SU	0434 6.8 / 1034 1.5 / 1634 7.1 / 2310 0.7
14 SU	0524 6.5 / 1125 1.7 / 1717 6.8 / 2353 1.3	**29** M	0521 7.2 / 1124 1.1 / 1721 7.5 / 2358 0.4
15 M	0554 6.6 / 1202 1.5 / ● 1751 6.9	**30** TU	0602 7.3 / 1210 0.8 / 1806 7.7 / ○
		31 W	0041 0.3 / 0640 7.4 / 1253 0.7 / 1848 7.7

APRIL

Time	m	Time	m
1 TH	0122 0.4 / 0715 7.4 / 1332 0.7 / 1928 7.6	**16** F	0100 1.2 / 0648 6.9 / 1312 1.2 / 1902 7.0
2 F	0158 0.6 / 0749 7.2 / 1409 0.9 / 2008 7.3	**17** SA	0130 1.3 / 0719 6.9 / 1345 1.2 / 1937 7.0
3 SA	0231 1.1 / 0822 7.0 / 1442 1.2 / 2047 6.9	**18** SU	0200 1.4 / 0751 6.9 / 1419 1.3 / 2015 6.8
4 SU	0303 1.6 / 0855 6.6 / 1515 1.6 / 2130 6.3	**19** M	0232 1.6 / 0827 6.7 / 1459 1.5 / 2100 6.5
5 M	0336 2.1 / 0933 6.2 / 1553 2.1 / 2224 5.8	**20** TU	0312 1.9 / 0911 6.4 / 1549 1.8 / 2155 6.2
6 TU	0419 2.6 / 1024 5.8 / 1647 2.5 / ◐ 2347 5.3	**21** W	0405 2.3 / 1007 6.1 / 1657 2.0 / 2311 5.8
7 W	0520 3.0 / 1150 5.5 / 1806 2.8	**22** TH	0518 2.6 / 1124 5.9 / 1817 2.0
8 TH	0116 5.3 / 0651 3.2 / 1318 5.5 / 2007 2.6	**23** F	0051 5.8 / 0643 2.6 / 1258 6.0 / 1937 1.8
9 F	0229 5.5 / 0828 2.9 / 1427 5.7 / 2109 2.3	**24** SA	0211 6.1 / 0804 2.4 / 1413 6.3 / 2049 1.5
10 SA	0327 5.8 / 0925 2.5 / 1521 6.1 / 2155 1.9	**25** SU	0314 6.4 / 0910 2.0 / 1514 6.7 / 2148 1.1
11 SU	0412 6.1 / 1010 2.1 / 1604 6.4 / 2236 1.6	**26** M	0407 6.7 / 1007 1.6 / 1608 7.0 / 2241 0.9
12 M	0447 6.4 / 1051 1.8 / 1641 6.6 / 2315 1.4	**27** TU	0454 7.0 / 1058 1.2 / 1658 7.2 / 2329 0.7
13 TU	0518 6.6 / 1129 1.6 / 1717 6.8 / 2352 1.3	**28** W	0535 7.1 / 1146 1.0 / 1745 7.3 / ○
14 W	0547 6.7 / 1205 1.4 / 1752 6.9 / ●	**29** TH	0014 0.7 / 0613 7.2 / 1231 0.9 / 1829 7.3
15 TH	0027 1.2 / 0617 6.8 / 1239 1.3 / 1827 7.0	**30** F	0055 0.8 / 0650 7.2 / 1313 0.9 / 1912 7.2

Chart Datum: 3·90 metres below Ordnance Datum (Newlyn). HAT is 8·0 metres above Chart Datum; see 4.5.

NE England

IMMINGHAM LAT 53°38'N LONG 0°11'W
TIMES AND HEIGHTS OF HIGH AND LOW WATERS

TIME ZONE (UT)
For Summer Time add ONE hour in **non-shaded areas**

Dates in red are **SPRINGS**
Dates in blue are **NEAPS**

YEAR 2010

MAY

Time	m	Time	m
1 SA	0132 1.0 / 0724 7.1 / 1351 1.0 / 1952 7.0	**16** SU	0110 1.3 / 0702 7.0 / 1334 1.1 / 1929 7.0
2 SU	0206 1.3 / 0758 6.9 / 1425 1.3 / 2032 6.6	**17** M	0147 1.4 / 0740 7.0 / 1416 1.1 / 2013 6.8
3 M	0239 1.7 / 0832 6.7 / 1500 1.6 / 2114 6.2	**18** TU	0227 1.5 / 0821 6.9 / 1502 1.2 / 2103 6.6
4 TU	0312 2.1 / 0909 6.3 / 1556 2.0 / 2203 5.8	**19** W	0312 1.8 / 0908 6.7 / 1556 1.4 / 2201 6.3
5 W	0353 2.5 / 0956 6.0 / 1629 2.3 / 2309 5.5	**20** TH	0405 2.1 / 1005 6.5 / 1658 1.5 / ☽ 2314 6.1
6 TH	0447 2.8 / 1103 5.7 / 1733 2.5 / ☾	**21** F	0510 2.3 / 1115 6.3 / 1805 1.6
7 F	0027 5.3 / 0556 3.0 / 1223 5.6 / 1846 2.5	**22** SA	0030 6.1 / 0621 2.3 / 1231 6.3 / 1913 1.5
8 SA	0136 5.4 / 0715 2.9 / 1332 5.7 / 1959 2.3	**23** SU	0139 6.2 / 0733 2.2 / 1341 6.4 / 2018 1.4
9 SU	0234 5.7 / 0825 2.7 / 1429 5.9 / 2057 2.1	**24** M	0241 6.3 / 0839 2.0 / 1445 6.6 / 2117 1.3
10 M	0322 5.9 / 0920 2.3 / 1517 6.1 / 2146 1.8	**25** TU	0336 6.5 / 0940 1.8 / 1543 6.7 / 2211 1.3
11 TU	0402 6.2 / 1007 2.0 / 1600 6.4 / 2230 1.6	**26** W	0425 6.7 / 1035 1.5 / 1638 6.8 / 2302 1.2
12 W	0438 6.4 / 1050 1.8 / 1642 6.6 / 2313 1.5	**27** TH	0509 6.8 / 1126 1.3 / 1729 6.9 / ○ 2348 1.2
13 TH	0514 6.6 / 1132 1.5 / 1723 6.8 / 2353 1.3	**28** F	0550 6.9 / 1214 1.2 / 1817 6.9
14 F	0550 6.8 / 1213 1.3 / 1805 6.9 / ●	**29** SA	0031 1.3 / 0631 7.0 / 1258 1.1 / 1900 6.8
15 SA	0032 1.3 / 0626 6.9 / 1254 1.2 / 1846 7.0	**30** SU	0111 1.4 / 0705 7.0 / 1338 1.2 / 1941 6.7
		31 M	0147 1.5 / 0740 6.9 / 1415 1.3 / 2020 6.5

JUNE

Time	m	Time	m
1 TU	0220 1.8 / 0815 6.7 / 1450 1.5 / 2057 6.2	**16** W	0223 1.3 / 0816 7.2 / 1503 0.8 / 2102 6.9
2 W	0254 2.0 / 0851 6.5 / 1526 1.8 / 2137 6.0	**17** TH	0308 1.5 / 0904 7.1 / 1553 0.9 / 2156 6.7
3 TH	0331 2.3 / 0932 6.3 / 1608 2.0 / 2224 5.7	**18** F	0358 1.7 / 0956 6.9 / 1647 1.1 / 2256 6.4
4 F	0415 2.5 / 1021 6.0 / 1657 2.2 / ☽ 2320 5.6	**19** SA	0452 1.9 / 1056 6.7 / 1744 1.3 / ☽ 2358 6.3
5 SA	0508 2.7 / 1121 5.8 / 1752 2.3	**20** SU	0553 2.1 / 1202 6.5 / 1844 1.5
6 SU	0022 5.5 / 0609 2.8 / 1226 5.8 / 1851 2.3	**21** M	0101 6.1 / 0659 2.2 / 1310 6.4 / 1946 1.7
7 M	0124 5.6 / 0713 2.7 / 1328 5.8 / 1951 2.2	**22** TU	0203 6.1 / 0809 2.2 / 1418 6.3 / 2048 1.8
8 TU	0221 5.8 / 0817 2.5 / 1426 6.0 / 2050 2.1	**23** W	0303 6.2 / 0917 2.1 / 1524 6.3 / 2146 1.8
9 W	0313 6.0 / 0917 2.3 / 1520 6.2 / 2145 1.9	**24** TH	0358 6.4 / 1018 1.8 / 1626 6.4 / 2240 1.7
10 TH	0400 6.3 / 1011 2.0 / 1611 6.4 / 2236 1.7	**25** F	0446 6.5 / 1112 1.6 / 1722 6.5 / 2329 1.7
11 F	0445 6.5 / 1103 1.6 / 1701 6.7 / 2325 1.5	**26** SA	0530 6.7 / 1202 1.4 / 1810 6.6 / ○
12 SA	0527 6.8 / 1152 1.3 / 1750 6.9 / ●	**27** SU	0013 1.6 / 0610 6.9 / 1247 1.3 / 1851 6.6
13 SU	0011 1.4 / 0609 7.0 / 1241 1.1 / 1838 7.0	**28** M	0054 1.6 / 0648 6.9 / 1328 1.3 / 1929 6.6
14 M	0056 1.3 / 0651 7.1 / 1328 0.9 / 1925 7.1	**29** TU	0131 1.6 / 0724 6.9 / 1404 1.3 / 2003 6.5
15 TU	0139 1.3 / 0733 7.2 / 1415 0.8 / 2012 7.0	**30** W	0204 1.7 / 0758 6.9 / 1437 1.4 / 2035 6.4

JULY

Time	m	Time	m
1 TH	0236 1.8 / 0832 6.7 / 1508 1.6 / 2107 6.2	**16** F	0257 1.2 / 0851 7.5 / 1538 0.6 / 2136 6.9
2 F	0308 2.0 / 0906 6.5 / 1541 1.8 / 2142 6.1	**17** SA	0340 1.4 / 0938 7.2 / 1625 1.0 / 2226 6.6
3 SA	0343 2.2 / 0944 6.3 / 1618 1.9 / 2223 5.9	**18** SU	0427 1.7 / 1031 6.9 / 1714 1.4 / ☽ 2320 6.3
4 SU	0424 2.4 / 1028 6.1 / 1701 2.1 / ☽ 2312 5.8	**19** M	0519 2.1 / 1132 6.5 / 1809 1.8
5 M	0514 2.5 / 1121 5.9 / 1754 2.3	**20** TU	0020 6.0 / 0622 2.4 / 1242 6.1 / 1913 2.2
6 TU	0012 5.6 / 0614 2.7 / 1226 5.8 / 1854 2.3	**21** W	0126 5.9 / 0741 2.5 / 1358 6.0 / 2023 2.3
7 W	0123 5.7 / 0722 2.6 / 1337 5.8 / 2000 2.3	**22** TH	0232 5.9 / 0902 2.4 / 1514 6.0 / 2128 2.3
8 TH	0230 5.8 / 0831 2.5 / 1447 6.0 / 2106 2.2	**23** F	0334 6.1 / 1008 2.1 / 1624 6.1 / 2224 2.1
9 F	0329 6.1 / 0939 2.1 / 1550 6.3 / 2208 1.9	**24** SA	0427 6.4 / 1102 1.7 / 1718 6.3 / 2313 1.9
10 SA	0422 6.5 / 1042 1.7 / 1648 6.6 / 2304 1.7	**25** SU	0513 6.6 / 1150 1.5 / 1802 6.5 / 2357 1.8
11 SU	0510 6.8 / 1139 1.3 / 1742 6.9 / ● 2356 1.4	**26** M	0553 6.9 / 1232 1.3 / 1838 6.6 / ○
12 M	0556 7.1 / 1232 0.9 / 1832 7.1	**27** TU	0037 1.6 / 0629 7.0 / 1311 1.2 / 1910 6.6
13 TU	0044 1.2 / 0639 7.4 / 1321 0.6 / 1919 7.3	**28** W	0114 1.6 / 0704 7.0 / 1346 1.2 / 1939 6.6
14 W	0130 1.1 / 0723 7.5 / 1408 0.4 / 2005 7.3	**29** TH	0146 1.6 / 0736 7.0 / 1416 1.3 / 2007 6.6
15 TH	0213 1.1 / 0806 7.6 / 1453 0.4 / 2050 7.2	**30** F	0215 1.7 / 0807 6.9 / 1444 1.4 / 2035 6.5
		31 SA	0242 1.8 / 0838 6.8 / 1510 1.6 / 2104 6.4

AUGUST

Time	m	Time	m
1 SU	0311 1.9 / 0909 6.6 / 1537 1.8 / 2137 6.2	**16** M	0357 1.6 / 1004 6.9 / 1637 1.6 / ☾ 2238 6.3
2 M	0343 2.1 / 0944 6.4 / 1610 2.0 / 2216 6.0	**17** TU	0443 2.1 / 1103 6.3 / 1727 2.2 / 2338 5.9
3 TU	0425 2.4 / 1029 6.1 / 1656 2.3 / ☽ 2307 5.7	**18** W	0543 2.5 / 1218 5.9 / 1836 2.7
4 W	0523 2.6 / 1128 5.9 / 1801 2.5	**19** TH	0050 5.7 / 0719 2.8 / 1343 5.7 / 2002 2.8
5 TH	0021 5.6 / 0638 2.7 / 1253 5.7 / 1919 2.6	**20** F	0205 5.7 / 0854 2.5 / 1507 5.8 / 2113 2.6
6 F	0153 5.7 / 0758 2.6 / 1426 5.9 / 2038 2.4	**21** SA	0312 6.0 / 0956 2.1 / 1616 6.1 / 2208 2.3
7 SA	0305 6.0 / 0918 2.2 / 1539 6.2 / 2149 2.1	**22** SU	0407 6.4 / 1045 1.8 / 1704 6.3 / 2254 2.0
8 SU	0403 6.5 / 1029 1.7 / 1640 6.6 / 2249 1.7	**23** M	0451 6.7 / 1129 1.5 / 1742 6.6 / 2336 1.8
9 M	0453 6.9 / 1127 1.1 / 1733 7.0 / 2341 1.4	**24** TU	0530 6.9 / 1209 1.3 / 1814 6.7 / ○
10 TU	0539 7.3 / 1219 0.6 / 1821 7.3 / ●	**25** W	0015 1.6 / 0605 7.1 / 1246 1.2 / 1842 6.8
11 W	0029 1.1 / 0623 7.6 / 1307 0.3 / 1905 7.5	**26** TH	0051 1.5 / 0638 7.1 / 1319 1.2 / 1909 6.8
12 TH	0114 0.9 / 0706 7.8 / 1351 0.2 / 1947 7.5	**27** F	0122 1.5 / 0710 7.1 / 1348 1.3 / 1935 6.8
13 F	0157 0.8 / 0748 7.9 / 1433 0.3 / 2027 7.4	**28** SA	0150 1.5 / 0740 7.0 / 1414 1.4 / 2002 6.7
14 SA	0237 0.9 / 0831 7.7 / 1514 0.6 / 2107 7.1	**29** SU	0215 1.6 / 0808 6.9 / 1437 1.5 / 2028 6.6
15 SU	0317 1.2 / 0915 7.4 / 1554 1.1 / 2149 6.7	**30** M	0241 1.8 / 0837 6.8 / 1459 1.7 / 2058 6.4
		31 TU	0310 2.0 / 0910 6.5 / 1527 2.0 / 2133 6.2

Chart Datum: 3·90 metres below Ordnance Datum (Newlyn). HAT is 8·0 metres above Chart Datum; see 4.5.

》》 FREE monthly updates from 《《
www.reedsalmanac.co.uk

IMMINGHAM LAT 53°38'N LONG 0°11'W
TIMES AND HEIGHTS OF HIGH AND LOW WATERS

TIME ZONE (UT)
For Summer Time add ONE hour in **non-shaded areas**

Dates in red are **SPRINGS**
Dates in blue are **NEAPS**

YEAR 2010

SEPTEMBER

Time	m		Time	m
1 0348	2.2		**16** 0507	2.6
0953	6.2		1158	5.6
W 1609	2.3		TH 1751	3.0
◗ 2220	5.9			
2 0446	2.5		**17** 0016	5.6
1052	5.9		0655	2.9
TH 1716	2.7		F 1326	5.5
2330	5.6		1935	3.1
3 0608	2.7		**18** 0136	5.7
1226	5.6		0834	2.6
F 1847	2.8		SA 1446	5.7
			2050	2.9
4 0119	5.6		**19** 0244	6.0
0737	2.6		0932	2.2
SA 1415	5.8		SU 1550	6.0
2017	2.6		2143	2.5
5 0241	6.0		**20** 0339	6.4
0904	2.1		1017	1.8
SU 1528	6.3		M 1635	6.4
2132	2.2		2228	2.1
6 0341	6.6		**21** 0423	6.7
1013	1.5		1058	1.5
M 1626	6.8		TU 1711	6.6
2231	1.7		2308	1.8
7 0431	7.1		**22** 0501	6.9
1109	0.9		1136	1.3
TU 1716	7.2		W 1742	6.8
2322	1.3		2347	1.6
8 0518	7.5		**23** 0536	7.0
1158	0.5		1212	1.2
W 1802	7.4		TH 1810	6.9
●			○	
9 0009	1.0		**24** 0022	1.5
0601	7.8		0608	7.1
TH 1244	0.2		F 1246	1.2
1842	7.6		1836	6.9
10 0053	0.8		**25** 0054	1.5
0644	8.0		0640	7.1
F 1327	0.2		SA 1316	1.3
1921	7.6		1903	6.9
11 0135	0.7		**26** 0122	1.5
0727	8.0		0712	7.1
SA 1407	0.4		SU 1342	1.4
1958	7.5		1930	6.9
12 0214	0.9		**27** 0149	1.5
0808	7.7		0742	7.0
SU 1444	0.8		M 1406	1.5
2035	7.2		1958	6.8
13 0252	1.2		**28** 0217	1.7
0851	7.3		0812	6.8
M 1520	1.3		TU 1430	1.7
2113	6.8		2027	6.6
14 0329	1.6		**29** 0248	1.8
0938	6.8		0847	6.6
TU 1558	1.9		W 1501	2.0
2157	6.3		2103	6.4
15 0410	2.1		**30** 0328	2.1
1037	6.1		0933	6.2
W 1643	2.5		TH 1544	2.4
◗ 2255	5.9		2151	6.1

OCTOBER

Time	m		Time	m
1 0427	2.4		**16** 0607	2.8
1037	5.9		1255	5.5
F 1651	2.7		SA 1840	3.3
◗ 2301	5.8			
2 0551	2.6		**17** 0058	5.7
1220	5.7		0752	2.7
SA 1822	2.9		SU 1407	5.6
			2009	3.0
3 0047	5.8		**18** 0206	5.9
0720	2.4		0852	2.3
SU 1400	5.9		M 1507	5.9
1954	2.7		2107	2.6
4 0212	6.2		**19** 0302	6.3
0843	1.9		0938	2.0
M 1509	6.4		TU 1555	6.3
2108	2.2		2153	2.2
5 0313	6.7		**20** 0348	6.5
0948	1.4		1019	1.7
TU 1604	6.8		W 1633	6.5
2206	1.8		2235	1.9
6 0405	7.2		**21** 0426	6.8
1042	0.9		1057	1.5
W 1653	7.2		TH 1705	6.7
2257	1.3		2313	1.7
7 0452	7.5		**22** 0502	6.9
1131	0.6		1135	1.4
TH 1736	7.4		F 1735	6.9
● 2344	1.0		2349	1.6
8 0538	7.8		**23** 0537	7.0
1216	0.4		1210	1.4
F 1816	7.5		SA 1804	7.0
			○	
9 0029	0.8		**24** 0024	1.5
0622	7.9		0612	7.1
SA 1259	0.5		SU 1243	1.4
1854	7.5		1834	7.0
10 0112	0.8		**25** 0056	1.5
0706	7.8		0647	7.1
SU 1338	0.7		M 1312	1.4
1930	7.4		1904	7.0
11 0152	0.9		**26** 0128	1.5
0748	7.5		0722	7.0
M 1415	1.0		TU 1341	1.6
2006	7.2		1935	6.9
12 0229	1.2		**27** 0201	1.5
0831	7.1		0758	6.9
TU 1449	1.5		W 1412	1.7
2042	6.9		2008	6.8
13 0305	1.6		**28** 0237	1.7
0917	6.6		0838	6.6
W 1524	2.1		TH 1448	2.0
2122	6.4		2047	6.6
14 0345	2.1		**29** 0322	1.9
1014	6.0		0928	6.3
TH 1605	2.6		F 1534	2.3
◗ 2215	6.0		2137	6.3
15 0440	2.5		**30** 0423	2.1
1133	5.6		1035	6.0
F 1705	3.1		SA 1637	2.7
2335	5.7		◗ 2245	6.1
			31 0539	2.2
			1209	5.9
			SU 1759	2.8

NOVEMBER

Time	m		Time	m
1 0015	6.1		**16** 0112	5.9
0659	2.1		0743	2.5
M 1333	6.1		TU 1413	5.8
1923	2.6		2007	2.9
2 0137	6.3		**17** 0211	6.0
0813	1.8		0841	2.3
TU 1439	6.4		W 1505	6.0
2035	2.3		2105	2.5
3 0240	6.7		**18** 0302	6.2
0916	1.4		0929	2.0
W 1535	6.7		TH 1548	6.3
2136	1.9		2152	2.2
4 0336	7.0		**19** 0346	6.5
1011	1.1		1013	1.8
TH 1624	7.0		F 1625	6.5
2230	1.5		2235	2.0
5 0428	7.3		**20** 0428	6.7
1101	0.9		1055	1.7
F 1709	7.2		SA 1700	6.7
2320	1.2		2316	1.7
6 0517	7.5		**21** 0508	6.8
1148	0.8		1134	1.6
SA 1750	7.4		SU 1735	6.9
●			○ 2355	1.5
7 0007	1.0		**22** 0549	6.9
0604	7.5		1212	1.5
SU 1232	0.9		M 1811	7.0
1829	7.4			
8 0052	1.0		**23** 0034	1.4
0650	7.4		0629	7.0
M 1312	1.1		TU 1248	1.5
1906	7.3		1845	7.1
9 0133	1.1		**24** 0113	1.3
0734	7.2		0709	7.0
TU 1350	1.3		W 1324	1.5
1943	7.2		1920	7.1
10 0212	1.3		**25** 0153	1.3
0816	6.9		0751	6.9
W 1424	1.7		TH 1401	1.6
2019	6.9		1958	7.0
11 0249	1.6		**26** 0235	1.4
0900	6.5		0836	6.7
TH 1458	2.1		F 1441	1.8
2057	6.6		2040	6.9
12 0328	2.0		**27** 0322	1.6
0950	6.1		0927	6.5
F 1537	2.5		SA 1528	2.1
2143	6.3		2129	6.7
13 0415	2.3		**28** 0418	1.7
1054	5.7		1029	6.3
SA 1627	2.9		SU 1625	2.3
◗ 2246	6.0		◗ 2230	6.5
14 0517	2.6		**29** 0523	1.8
1206	5.5		1143	6.1
SU 1733	3.1		M 1733	2.5
			2343	6.4
15 0002	5.8		**30** 0631	1.8
0630	2.6		1255	6.1
M 1313	5.6		TU 1848	2.5
1852	3.1			

DECEMBER

Time	m		Time	m
1 0058	6.4		**16** 0105	5.8
0739	1.8		0725	2.5
W 1401	6.3		TH 1401	5.7
2000	2.3		1952	2.8
2 0207	6.6		**17** 0208	5.9
0843	1.6		0827	2.4
TH 1501	6.5		F 1457	6.0
2107	2.1		2056	2.6
3 0310	6.7		**18** 0304	6.1
0941	1.5		0924	2.2
F 1555	6.7		SA 1546	6.2
2206	1.8		2153	2.2
4 0408	6.9		**19** 0356	6.4
1035	1.4		1016	1.9
SA 1643	6.9		SU 1630	6.5
2301	1.5		2244	1.9
5 0503	7.0		**20** 0445	6.6
1124	1.3		1103	1.7
SU 1728	7.1		M 1712	6.8
● 2351	1.3		2333	1.6
6 0554	7.1		**21** 0532	6.8
1210	1.3		1148	1.6
M 1809	7.2		TU 1752	7.0
			○	
7 0038	1.2		**22** 0019	1.3
0640	7.1		0617	7.0
TU 1252	1.4		W 1231	1.5
1848	7.2		1831	7.2
8 0122	1.2		**23** 0104	1.1
0723	7.0		0701	7.1
W 1330	1.5		TH 1313	1.4
1925	7.2		1910	7.3
9 0201	1.3		**24** 0148	1.0
0804	6.8		0745	7.1
TH 1405	1.7		F 1354	1.4
2001	7.0		1950	7.3
10 0237	1.5		**25** 0233	1.0
0843	6.5		0830	7.0
F 1438	2.0		SA 1436	1.5
2037	6.8		2032	7.3
11 0312	1.7		**26** 0318	1.1
0922	6.2		0917	6.8
SA 1513	2.2		SU 1520	1.7
2115	6.6		2118	7.1
12 0349	2.0		**27** 0406	1.2
1004	6.0		1009	6.6
SU 1552	2.5		M 1608	1.9
2200	6.3		2211	6.9
13 0433	2.2		**28** 0459	1.5
1055	5.7		1108	6.3
M 1640	2.7		TU 1704	2.2
◗ 2255	6.0		◗ 2313	6.6
14 0525	2.4		**29** 0558	1.7
1155	5.6		1213	6.1
TU 1739	2.9		W 1809	2.4
2359	5.9			
15 0624	2.5		**30** 0023	6.4
1259	5.6		0703	1.9
W 1845	2.9		TH 1320	6.1
			1924	2.4
			31 0137	6.3
			0811	2.0
			F 1426	6.1
			2041	2.3

Chart Datum: 3·90 metres below Ordnance Datum (Newlyn). HAT is 8·0 metres above Chart Datum; see 4.5.

NE England

FREE monthly updates from
www.reedsalmanac.co.uk

9.5.10 RIVER HUMBER

S bank: NE and N Lincolnshire
N bank: E Riding of Yorks and City of Kingston-upon-Hull
Hull marina: **53°44'·24N 00°20'·15W** ✿✿❀❀❀❀❀❀❀

CHARTS AC 1190, 109, 3497, 1188, 5614; Imray C29; ABP (local)

TIDES –0510 Immingham, –0452 Hull, Dover; ML 4·1; Duration 0555

Standard Port IMMINGHAM (←—)

Times				Height (metres)			
High Water		Low Water		MHWS	MHWN	MLWN	MLWS
0100	0700	0100	0700	7·3	5·8	2·6	0·9
1300	1900	1300	1900				
Differences BULL SAND FORT							
–0020	–0030	–0035	–0015	–0·4	–0·3	+0·1	+0·2
GRIMSBY							
–0012	–0012	–0015	–0015	–0·2	–0·1	0·0	+0·2
HULL (ALBERT DOCK)							
+0019	+0019	+0033	+0027	+0·3	+0·1	–0·1	–0·2
HUMBER BRIDGE							
+0027	+0022	+0049	+0039	–0·1	–0·4	–0·7	–0·6
BURTON STATHER (R Trent)*							
+0105	+0045	+0335	+0305	–2·1	–2·3	–2·3	Dries
KEADBY (R Trent)*							
+0135	+0120	+0425	+0410	–2·5	–2·8	Dries	
BLACKTOFT (R Ouse)†							
+0100	+0055	+0325	+0255	–1·6	–1·8	–2·2	–1·1
GOOLE (R Ouse)†							
+0130	+0115	+0355	+0350	–1·6	–2·1	–1·9	–0·6

NOTE: Daily predictions for Immingham are given above.

* Normal river level at Burton Stather is about 0·1m below CD, and at Keadby 0·1m to 0·2m below CD.

† Heights of LW can increase by up to 0·3m at Blacktoft and 0·6m at Goole when river in spate. HW hts are little affected.

SHELTER R Humber is the estuary of R Ouse and R Trent. The estuary has strong tidal streams: a strong NW'ly against a spring flood of 3-4kn causes a short steep sea, as does a SE'ly over the ebb stream. Off Hull Marina it can be very choppy with fresh winds over spring tidal streams.

Anchorages. ⚓ inside Spurn Hd only with winds from NE to ESE. ⚓ close off Haile Sand Fort only in fair weather. Immingham should be used by yachts only in emergency. If unable to reach Hull on the tide, in S to W winds there is a good ⚓ off the SW bank 8ca above N Killingholme Oil jetty, well out of main chan. In N'lies ⚓ off Hawkin's Pt, N of S9 buoy.

Marinas at Hull, S Ferriby and the docks at Goole are all entered by lock access HW±3, and Grimsby also by lock HW±2. S Ferriby should not be attempted without up-to-date ABP charts for the ever-changing buoyed chan above Hull. Waiting pontoon at S Ferriby outside the Hope & Anchor pub.

Do not attempt entry to Winteringham (HW±½ MHWS with draft 1.5m) or Brough Havens (HW±1) without contacting Humber Yawl Club for details of approach channel and mooring availability. Both dry to soft mud. Winteringham is prone to bad silting, but is dredged.

NAVIGATION Note TSS on chartlet 9.5.2 and on AC 109.
From S, WPT 53°30'·50N 00°16'·50E, 1ca SW of Rosse Spit PHM buoy, Fl (2) R 5s. Thence make Haile Sand No 2, then via No 2B, Tetney monobuoy and No 2C into Haile Chan.

From N, WPT 53°34'·74N 00°16'·55E, S Binks SHM buoy, Fl G 2s. Thence passing N of Spurn Lt Float, SE Chequer and Chequer No 3 to make Binks 3A; then enter the estuary to the S of Spurn Hd outside Bull Chan. Best arrival at LW. Sp tides are fierce: 4·4kn ebb off Spurn Head and Immingham. There is a big ship ⚓ S of Spurn Hd. Keep clear of large commercial vessels using Hawke (8·4m) and Sunk (8·8m) Chans; these are marked by S1-S9 SHM buoys, all Fl G 1·5s (S8 is a SHM bn, Fl G 1·5s with tide gauge); and by P2-P9 PHM buoys, all Fl R 1·5s. Foul Holm Chan off Immingham is recommend for small craft.

For **Grimsby,** the lock into Fish Docks is 255°/1·35M from Lower Burcom No 6 Lt Float, Fl R 4s.

Off **Kingston-upon-Hull** a tidal eddy and streams can be rotatory, ie the flood makes W up Hull Roads for ¾hr whilst the ebb is already running down-river over Skitter Sand on the opposite bank (reaches 2½kn at sp). Humber Bridge (conspic) has 29m clearance.

LIGHTS AND MARKS The Humber is well buoyed/lit. At Grimsby a conspic tr (94m with 'minaret' on top) is 300m W of Fish Dock lock. IPTS control entry to Grimsby, Immingham, Killingholme, Hull and Goole.

R/T Advise *VTS Humber* on Ch 14 (or ☎ 01482 212191) posn and intentions on appr from seaward of Clee Ness lt float; listen on Ch 14 or 12 when W of the float up to Gainsborough (R Trent) and Goole (R Ouse). Weather, nav & tidal information is broadcast on Ch 12/14 every odd H+03; more detailed info, including height of tide, is available on request.

Other VHF stns: *Grimsby Docks Radio* Ch **74** (H24) 18 79 call *Humber Cruising* for marina staff or *Fishdock Island* for lock keeper. *Immingham Docks Radio* Ch 19 68 (H24). R Hull Port Ops Service call *Drypool Radio* Ch 22 (Mon-Fri HW–2 to HW+1; Sat 0900-1100 LT). *Hull Marina*, Ch M **80** (H24); *Albert Dock Radio* Ch 09. *Ferriby Sluice* (Lock) Ch 74. Humber YC, Ch M (if racing). *Goole Docks Radio* Ch 14 (H24) 09 19. Boothferry Bridge Ch 09 (H24). Selby Railway and Toll Bridges Ch 09. Br Waterways locks Ch 74. *Brough and Winteringham Havens, Humber Yawl Club* Ch M.

TELEPHONE (Codes: Grimsby 01472; Hull 01482) Humber HM 01482 327171 controls whole estuary/river, see www.humber.com

GRIMSBY Port Director 327171; MRCC (01262) 672317; Marinecall 09068 969644; Police (01482) 881111.

HULL Marina ☎ 609960; lock 330508; MRCC (01262) 672317; ⊖ 782107; Marinecall 09068 969644; Police 26111; Dr contact Humber VTS 212191.

FACILITIES

TETNEY HAVEN N Lincs. Humber Mouth YC ☎ (01472) 812063, drying moorings. **GRIMSBY** (01472; NE Lincs) **Grimsby and Cleethorpes YC** ☎ 356678 (tel for berthing, enter via ABP Royal Dock), Bar, R, M, FW, 🔲. **Fish Docks** entered by lock 300m E of conspic tr. Access HW±3(£10 locking fee for ♥), with R/G tfc lts, but enter free of charge HW±2 after authorisation by *Fish Dock Island*,Ch 74, when both gates open for free flow. In No 2 Fish Dock is: **Meridian Quay Marina** (run by Humber Cruising Association), call *Fish Dock Island* Ch 74) ☎ (01472) 268424, www.hca grimsby.co.uk, 200 berths + 30 ♥ AB, £1.45 inc ⚡, D, BH (35ton), bar, 🔲, Wi-fi. **Town** all facilities, ACA.

HULL (01482; Kingston-upon-Hull) **Hull Marina** ☎ 609960, (312 + 20 ♥ £1.94), access HW±3 via lock (width 8·5m) 150m to the E. Beware no shelter from adverse weather/sea conditions (from W through S to E) when waiting outside lock in river, but waiting pontoon, dries, in basin. Marina office open 0900-1700 daily; D, P, CH, Gas, ⊖, ♿, 🔩, ME, El, ⚒, BH (50 ton), C (2 ton), 🔲, SM, ACA, 🏴, Wi-fi. **City** All facilities. **Ferries:** Rotterdam and Zeebrugge; daily; 10 Hrs; P&O (www.poferries.com).

SOUTH FERRIBY N Lincs. **South Ferriby Marina** (100+20 ♥ £15/ yacht/60hrs inc lock fee) VHF 80, ☎ (01652) 635620; access HW±3, D, P (cans), ME, El, ⚒, C (30 ton), CH, Gas, Gaz, 🔩. **Village** 🏴, Bar. S Ferriby Sluice VHF 74: 0730-1600, or ☎ 01652 635219.

BROUGH HAVEN E Riding of Yorkshire, **Humber Yawl Club** ☎ (01482) 667224, Slip, FW, Bar, limited AB; entry HW±1½.

WINTERINGHAM HAVEN N Lincs (belongs to Humber Yawl Club) ☎ (01724) 734452; access HW±1. BH (10 ton), ✉.

GOOLE BOATHOUSE (☎ 01405 763985) and **VIKING MARINA** (☎ 01405 765737) are both situated off the Aire and Calder Canal. Access via the commercial lock for Goole Docks (Ch 14). Limited ♥ £5.00 (Goole Boathouse) or £6.00 (Viking Marina) any size, D, FW, Gas, El. Other facilities include Dry Dk, Slip, CH, ♿. Take the flood up the River Humber, follow the buoyed channel past Hull, Brough and when approaching Trent Falls Apex alter course to stbd and follow the River Ouse to Goole.

NABURN (R Ouse, 4M S of York and 80M above Spurn Pt). **Naburn Marina** (300+50 ♥ £1.00) ☎ (01904) 621021; CH, P, D, FW, showers, 🚻, 🔩, ⚡ (£2.00), ⚒, ME, BH (16 ton), R.

Hull Marina 10·5M

7A
Fl.G.1·3s
Hawkin's Point
Sunk Sand

Q(6)+LFl15s
YB
11
Fl.R.1·5s
S9
P9
S8
Tanker Channel
S7
Sunk Channel
S6
P8
P7

Fl(3)Y.9s
Fl(2)R.6s
Burcom Sand
0₂
Fl.Y.5s
0₂
0₆
S5
P5
Hawke
S4
P6
Channel
P4
S3
No5A
Fl.G.2s
P3

Trinity Sand

VQ(6)LFl.10s
Horn 20s
Middle No7
YB
R
Fl.R.4s Bell
Lower Burcom
2
No4B
Fl.R.2s
Q(6)+LFl15s
S. Shoal
10
Fl(2)R.10s
No4A
Clee Ness
7
Bull Channel
Fl.G.4s
No5
S2
P2
S1
Moorings
BYB
Hawke
VQ(3)5s
Fl.G3s11m5M
Spurn Point Bn

Sand hills 6 to 10m high

Oc G
Grimsby
Road
Sewer
Chimney
(conspic)
(Red Lts)
Alexandra
Dock
Marina
bridge (3.2m)
Fish Dock
GRIMSBY
Water Tower
(conspic)
2F.R(vert)
Pier
Clee Ness Sand
0₉
2₉
Q.R
Bull Sand
15
Spurn Head
Fl.G.4s
Binks
No3A
BY
Delta
L.Fl.10s
RW
Haile Channel
Fl.R.4s
No4
Q(6)+
LFl.15s
Bull Sand Fort
Q
Bull
7
VQ8m6M
Horn(2)20s
Hobo
Fl(2)R.10s
Charlie
L.Fl.10s
RW

VTS Humber
Ch12 | Ch14

Fl.R5s
21m3M
4
No2C
R Fl.R2s
13
Tetney Monobuoy
6
2VQ.Y(vert)
HornMo(A)60s
05'
No2B
Fl.R4s
R

Haile Sand Fort
HMYC
Marked channel
Moorings
Tetney Haven

Inset: GRIMSBY DOCK

Oc.G.2s
Oc.G.2s
Fl(2)R.6sDn
Hydraulic Tower
(conspic)
Iso.G4s
Iso.R.4s
Horn20s
RoRo
No1 Fish Dock
Fl.Y.2.5s
GRIMSBY DOCK
Royal Dock
6·8m
North Quay
6-8m
No3 Fish Dock
Meridian Quay Marina
East Quay
West Quay
Union Dock
RoRo
No2 Fish Dock
Swing Footbridge
South Quay

05' 01'W 00' 01'E

38'
53°36'N
34'
32'

Kingston-Upon-Hull
Hull Marina
See inset
Fl.R.4s
Fl.R.4s
Fl.R.4s
R
Q.R
G
Fl.G.1·3s
Fl.R.4s
RIVER HUMBER
2₉
0₃
Fl.R.4s
Skitter Sand
2₃
3₃
1₁
1₁
Skitter Ness
Fl.R.4s
1₆
Fl.G.2s
Fl.R.4s
0₇
9
Hessle
Continued at inset
Fl.G.4s
G
Humber Bridge
2₉ G
Fl.G.2s
Changing depths
29
Fl.R.2s R
Fl.R.
New Holland
Barton-upon-Humber
Halton Flat
1₇
Fl.R.4s
VQ(9)10s
R
G
Fl.G.2s
YBY
Fl.G.4s
G
3₄
Fl.R.2s
0₂
Brickworks
Q.G
Humber Sea Terminal RoRo
Q.R
R
3₉
1₅
Foul Holme Channel (Buoyed)
Fl.G.4s
G
5₁
1₇
Fl.G.2s
Iso.R.4s21m
Killingholme
High Light
Iso.R.2s10m
Killingholme S
Low Light
Fl.G.4s
Iso.2s RW
Fl.R.2s
3
Fl(3)G.9s
Humber Intrnl Terminal
Fl.G.4s
Fl.G(2+1)10s
Fl.G.4s
Immingham
2Q.R (vert)
Fl(2)R.6s R
Immingham Dock
2Q.R (vert)
Fl.R.1·5s R
Fl.Y.4s

Inset: HULL MARINA

00°20'·5W
20'·2
Railway Dock
City centre ¼ mile
Marina Recreation Centre
53°44'·3N
44'·4
Services
HULL MARINA
Humber Dock
Lock
Albert Dock Ent
Beware commercial shipping
2F.G

Inset (lower left)

Broomfleet Spire
Brough
Humber YC
North Ferriby
Continued overleaf
53°40'N
Whitton Ness
Brough Sand
Redcliffe Middle Sand
Chowder Ness
Silo (conspic)
Chimney (conspic)
Humber Bridge
53°48'N
Winteringham Haven (Humber YC)
Winteringham
Read's I
Barton-upon-Humber
Note: Sand banks constantly changing
South Ferriby
Continuation not at same scale
00°27'W

45'
40'
38'
25' 20' 15' 00°10'W

RIVER HUMBER TO HARTLEPOOL

(Charts 107, 121, 129, 134) Air gunnery and bombing practice is carried out 3M off Cowden, 17M S of Bridlington. The range is marked by 6 SPM buoys; 3 seaward ones Fl Y 10s, the 3 inner ones Fl Y 2s or 5s. Bridlington Bay (chart 1882) is clear of dangers apart from Smithic Shoals (marked by N and S cardinal lt buoys), about 3M off Bridlington, seas break on these shoals in strong N or E winds even at HW.

Flamborough Head (lt, fog sig, RG) is a steep, W cliff with conspic lt ho on summit. The lt may be obsc by cliffs when close inshore. An old lt ho, also conspic, is 2½ca WNW. ▶ *Tides run hard around the Head which, in strong winds against a sp tide, is best avoided by 2M.* ◀ From here the coast runs NW, with no offshore dangers until Filey Brigg where rky ledges extend 5ca ESE, marked by an ECM lt buoy. There is anch in Filey B in N or offshore winds. NW of Filey Brigg beware Old Horse Rks and foul ground 5ca offshore; maintain this offing past Scarborough to Whitby High lt. Off Whitby beware Whitby Rk and The Scar (dry in places) to E of hbr, and Upgang Rks (dry in places) 1M to WNW; swell breaks heavily on all these rocks.

From Whitby to Hartlepool there are no dangers more than 1M offshore. Runswick B (AC 1612), 5M NW of Whitby, provides anch in winds from S and W but is dangerous in onshore winds. 2½M further NW the little hbr of Staithes is more suitable for yachts which can take the ground, but only in good weather and offshore winds.

Redcliff, dark red and 205m high, is a conspic feature of this coast which, along to Hunt Cliff, is prone to landslides and is fringed with rky ledges which dry for about 3ca off. There is a conspic radio mast 4ca SSE of Redcliff. Off Redcar and Coatham

beware Salt Scar and West Scar, drying rky ledges lying 1– 8ca offshore. Other ledges lie close SE and S of Salt Scar which has NCM lt buoy. Between R. Tees and Hartlepool beware Long Scar, detached rky ledge (dries 2m) with extremity marked by ECM lt buoy. Tees and Hartlepool Bays are exposed to strong E/SE winds. The R. Tees and Middlesbrough are highly industrialised. At Hartlepool there is a centre specialising in the maintenance and restoration of Tall Ships.

HARTLEPOOL TO COQUET ISLAND

(Charts 134, 152, 156) From The Heugh an offing of 1M clears all dangers until past Seaham and approaching Sunderland (2.40), where White Stones, rky shoals with depth 1·8m, lie 1·75M SSE of Roker Pier lt ho, and Hendon Rk, depth 0·9m, lies 1·25M SE of the lt ho. 1M N of Sunderland is Whitburn Steel, a rky ledge with less than 2m over it; a dangerous wreck (buoyed) lies 1ca SE of it. A firing range at Souter Pt is marked by R flags (R lts) when active.

The coast N of Tynemouth is foul, and on passage to Blyth it should be given an offing of 1M. St Mary's Island (with disused conspic lt ho) is 3·5M N of Tynemouth, joined to the mainland by a causeway. The tiny drying harbour of Seaton Sluice, 1M NW of St Mary's Island, is accessible only in offshore winds via a narrow entrance.

Proceeding N from Blyth, keep well seaward of The Sow and Pigs rks, and set course to clear Newbiggin Pt and Beacon Pt by about 1M. Newbiggin church spire is prominent from N and S, and NW of Beacon Pt are conspic chys of aluminium smelter and power stn. 2M NNW of Beacon Pt is Snab Pt where rks extend 3ca seaward. Further offshore Cresswell Skeres, rky patches with depth 3m, lie about 1·5M NNE of Snab Pt.

9.5.11 BRIDLINGTON

E Riding of Yorkshire 54°04'·78N 00°11'·21W ✿✿⬨⬨✿✿

CHARTS AC 1191, 1190, 129, 121, 1882, *5614*; Imray C29.

TIDES +0553 Dover; ML 3·6; Duration 0610

Standard Port RIVER TEES (→)

Times				Height (metres)			
High Water		Low Water		MHWS	MHWN	MLWN	MLWS
0000	0600	0000	0600	5·5	4·3	2·0	0·9
1200	1800	1200	1800				
Differences BRIDLINGTON							
+0100	+0050	+0055	+0050	+0·6	+0·4	+0·3	+0·2
FILEY BAY							
+0042	+0042	+0047	+0034	+0·3	+0·6	+0·4	+0·1

SHELTER Good, except in E, SE and S winds. Hbr dries completely to soft black mud; access HW±3 (for draft of 2·7m). Visitors normally berth on S pier or near HM's Office. A marina is planned but agreement not yet reached.

NAVIGATION WPT SW Smithic WCM, Q (9) 15s, 54°02'·41N 00°09'·21W, 333°/2·6M to ent. Close-in appr is with N pier hd lt on brg 002° to keep W of drying patch (The Canch). Beware bar, 1m at MLWN, could dry out at MLWS.

LIGHTS AND MARKS Hbr is 4M WSW of Flamborough Hd lt, Fl (4) 15s 65m 24M. Y racing marks are laid in the Bay, Apr-Oct. Tidal sigs, by day from S pier: R flag = >2·7m in hbr; No flag = < 2·7m. At night from N pier: Fl ● = >2·7m in hbr; Fl ● = < 2·7m.

R/T Call on VHF Ch 16, then Ch 12, 67 for working.

TELEPHONE (Code 01262) HM 670148/9, mobile 0860 275150; MRCC 672317; Marinecall 09068 969644; Police (01482) 881111; Ⓗ 673451.

FACILITIES S Pier FW, AB £2.80 /sq m/week or £15/yacht <3days, D (tank/hose ☎ 500227), C (5 ton), BH (70 ton), Slip; M, see HM; **Royal Yorks YC** ☎ 672041, L, FW, R, Bar. **Town** P (cans), CH, ME, El, ⬚, R, Bar, ✉, Ⓑ, ⇌, ✈ (Humberside).

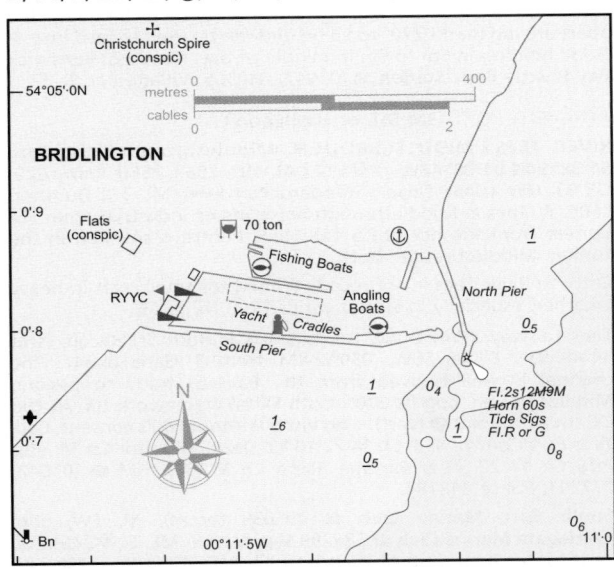

ADJACENT ANCHORAGE (7M SE of Scarborough)
FILEY, N Yorkshire, 54°12'·80N 00°16'·20W, AC 1882, 129. HW +0532 on Dover; ML 3·5m; Duration 0605. See 9.5.11. Good ⚓ in winds from S to NNE in 4 – 5m on hard sand. Lt on cliff above CG Stn, G metal column, FR 31m 1M vis 272°-308°. Filey Brigg, a natural bkwtr, is marked by ECM buoy, Q(3)10s, Bell. Beware Old Horse Rks, 2M WNW of Filey Brigg, foul ground extending ½M offshore. An unmarked Historic Wreck (see 9.0.3) lies at 54°11'·51N 00°13'·48W. Facilities: ⬚, R, Bar, L, Ⓗ ☎ (01723) 68111, ✉, Ⓑ, ⇌.

9.5.12 SCARBOROUGH

N. Yorkshire 54°16'·88N 00°23'·36W ✿✿⬨⬨✿✿✿

CHARTS AC 1191, 129, 1612, 5614; Imray C29.

TIDES +0527 Dover; ML 3·5; Duration 0615

Standard Port RIVER TEES (→)

Times				Height (metres)			
High Water		Low Water		MHWS	MHWN	MLWN	MLWS
0000	0600	0000	0600	5·5	4·3	2·0	0·9
1200	1800	1200	1800				
Differences SCARBOROUGH							
+0040	+0040	+0030	+0030	+0·2	+0·3	+0·3	0·0

SHELTER Good in E Hbr, access HW±3 via narrow (10m) ent by E pier, but not in strong E/SE'lies. 5 ♥ pontoon berths, (max LOA 10.3m, draft 1.8m), in the SW corner of E Hbr, just below lt ho; 4 ♥ drying AB on Old Pier just N of the drawbridge; ♥ AB on SE side of pontoons in Old Harbour, dredged to 2m. In winter months access to East Hbr is via the drawbridge only.

NAVIGATION WPT 54°16'·50N 00°22'·00W, 302°/0·83M to E pier lt. Appr from the E to avoid Ramsdale Scar, rky shoal 0·9m. Keep careful watch for salmon nets E & SE of ent. Beware rks extending approx 20m SW of E pier head. Give Castle Headland close N of hbr a wide berth due to coastal defences.

LIGHTS AND MARKS Lt ho (conspic), Iso 5s, Dia 60s, on Vincent Pier is shown by night or B ● by day when there is more than 3·7m over bar in entrance. Other lts as shown on chartlet.

R/T Call *Scarborough Port Control* VHF Ch 12 16 (H24). Watchkeeper will offer guidance to approaching visitors.

TELEPHONE (Code 01723) HM (HO) ☎ 373530; www.scarboroughbc.gov.uk; Port Control 373877; CG 372323; MRCC (01262) 672317; Marinecall 09068 969644; Police 500300; Ⓗ 368111.

FACILITIES **East Harbour** AB £10/night, pontoon berth £23/night <10m LOA, M, FW, ⬚, D, C (4 ton), Slip; **Scarborough YC** ☎ 373821, AB, Slip, M*, FW, ME, El, ⬚; **Services** ME, El, ✖, CH, P & D (cans), Ⓔ. **Town** P, D, Slip (£11·50) ⬚, R, Bar, ✉, Ⓑ, ⇌, ✈ (Humberside).

9.5.13 WHITBY

N. Yorkshire 54°29'·65N 00°36'·78W 🌊🏴⚓⚓⚓⚓🌸🌸🌸

CHARTS AC 129, 134, 1612, 5614; Imray C29, C24.

TIDES +0500 Dover; ML 3·3; Duration 0605

Standard Port RIVER TEES (→)

Times				Height (metres)			
High Water		Low Water		MHWS	MHWN	MLWN	MLWS
0000	0600	0000	0600	5·5	4·3	2·0	0·9
1200	1800	1200	1800				
Differences WHITBY							
+0015	+0030	+0020	+0005	+0·1	0·0	−0·1	−0·1

SHELTER Good, except in lower hbr in strong NW to NE winds.

NAVIGATION WPT 54°30'·21N 00°36'·96W, 169°/0·57M to ent. The harbour can be entered safely under most conditions except during N-NE gales when the approach is dangerous due to breaking seas and entry should not be attempted.

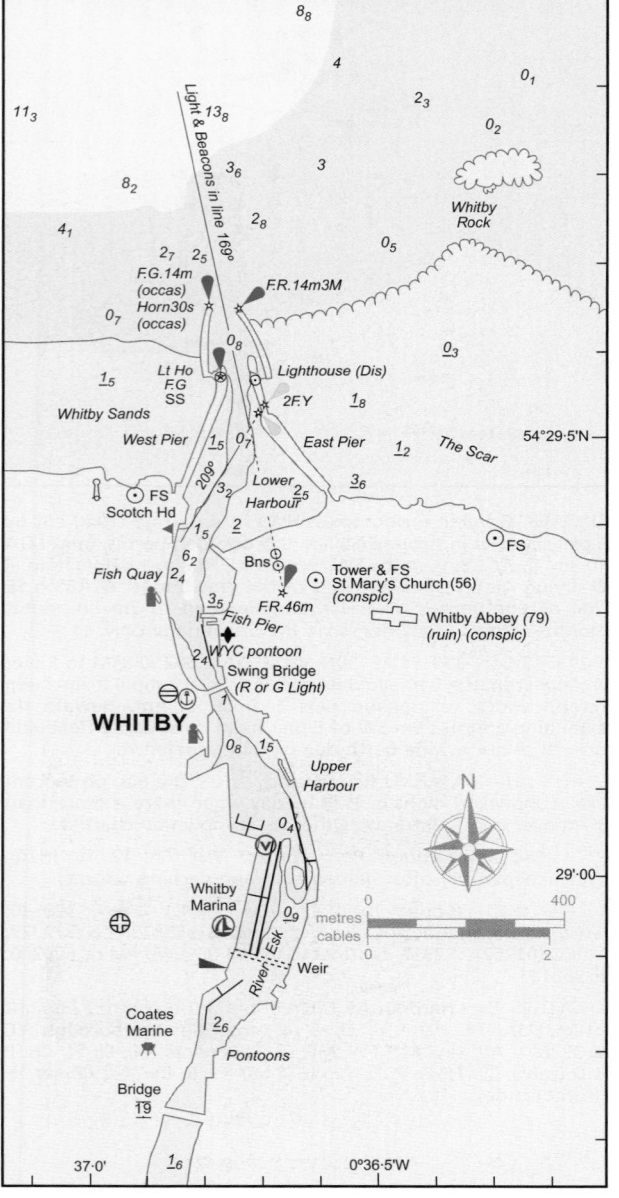

• From the SE beware Whitby Rk; leave Whitby NCM lit buoy to port.
• Beware strong set to E from HW –2 to HW, when nearing piers.

Vessels >37m LOA must embark pilot; via HM.

Access HW±4 for approx 2m draft. Bridge opens on request HW±2 every H and H+30. Additional openings at w/e and BH: May-Sep 0930 and1730; Aug 1300 (irrespective of tides). FG lts = open; FR lts = shut. Wait on pontoon at Fish Pier if necessary. If alongside Fish Quay or FVs, craft must not be left unattended.

LIGHTS AND MARKS See 9.5.4 and chartlet. Ruins of Whitby Abbey are to the E of the entrance. Whitby High Lt ho (white 8-sided tower) is 2M ESE of harbour entrance.

Leading lines for entering hbr:
FR lt and 2 bns (W △ and W ○ with B stripe), seen between the outer pierheads (FR and FG), lead 169° into hbr. Maintain this line until bns on E pier (two FY lts) are abeam. Thence keep these same bns in transit astern bearing 209°.

R/T Hbr and Marina VHF Ch **11** 16 12 (H24). Whitby Bridge Ch **11** 16 06 (listens on Ch 16 HW–2 to HW+2).

TELEPHONE (Code 01947) HM/Watchkeepers ☎ 602354/602272, www.yorkshireports.co.uk; MRCC (01262) 672317; Marinecall 09068 969644/453; Police (01653) 692424; Dr 820888.

FACILITIES Whitby Marina (dredged 1.5m) is 2ca beyond swing bridge; visitor berths at seaward end of long pontoon. ☎ 600165. 240+10 Ⓥ, £1.82; D (cans), Slip, ME, El, ✕, C, CH, BH, ACA, SM, Gas, Gaz. **Whitby YC** ☎ 07786 289393, M, L, Bar.

Fish Quay D (in commercial quantities only, ☎ 602255), C (1 ton).

Town All domestic facilities, R, Bar, ⇌, ✈ (Teesside).

ADJACENT ANCHORAGE (5M WNW of Whitby)

RUNSWICK BAY, N. Yorkshire, **54°32'·11N 00°44'·20W**. AC 1612. HW +0505 on Dover: Differences on R Tees are approx as Whitby; ML 3·1m; Duration 0605. Good shelter in all winds from SSE thru W to NW. Enter bay at 225° keeping clear of many rks at base of cliffs. Two W posts (2FY by night when required by lifeboat) 18m apart are ldg marks 270° to LB ho and can be used to lead into ⚓. Good holding in 6m to 9m in middle of bay. Facilities: **Runswick Bay Rescue Boat Station** ☎ (01947) 840965. **Village** Bar, R, 🛒.

ADJACENT PORT (3M SSE of Hartlepool)

RIVER TEES / MIDDLESBROUGH, Middlesbrough / Stockton, **54°38'·94N 01°08'·48W**. 🌊⚓⚓🌸. AC 152, 2567, 2566; Imray C29; OS 93. HW +0450 Dover; Standard Port (→). ML 3·1; Duration 0605. R. Tees & Middlesbrough are a major industrial area. 5M upriver from the hbr ent a Tall Ships Centre is planned in the former Middlesbrough Dock.

Entry to River Tees is not recommended for small craft in heavy weather, especially in strong winds from NE to SE.

Tees Fairway SWM buoy, Iso 4s 9m 8M, Horn 5s, Racon, is at 54°40'·93N 01°06'·38W, 030°/2·4M from S Gare bkwtr. The channel is well buoyed from the Fairway buoy to beyond Middlesbrough. Ldg lts 210°, both FR on framework trs. At Old CG stn a Q lt, or 3 ● (vert), = no entry without HM's consent. Call: Tees Port Control VHF Ch **14** 22 16 12 (H24). Monitor Ch 14; also info Ch 14 22. Tees Barrage Radio Ch M (37). HM ☎ (01642) 277201; Police 248184.

South Gare Marine Club ☎ 491039 (occas), M, FW, Slip; **Castlegate Marine Club** ☎ 583299 Slip, M, FW, ME, El, ✕, CH, 🛒; **Tees Motor Boat Club** M; **Services**: El, ME, Ⓔ, ACA. **City** All domestic facilities, ⇌, ✈. Hartlepool marina (9.5.14) lies 3M to the NNW with all yacht facilities.

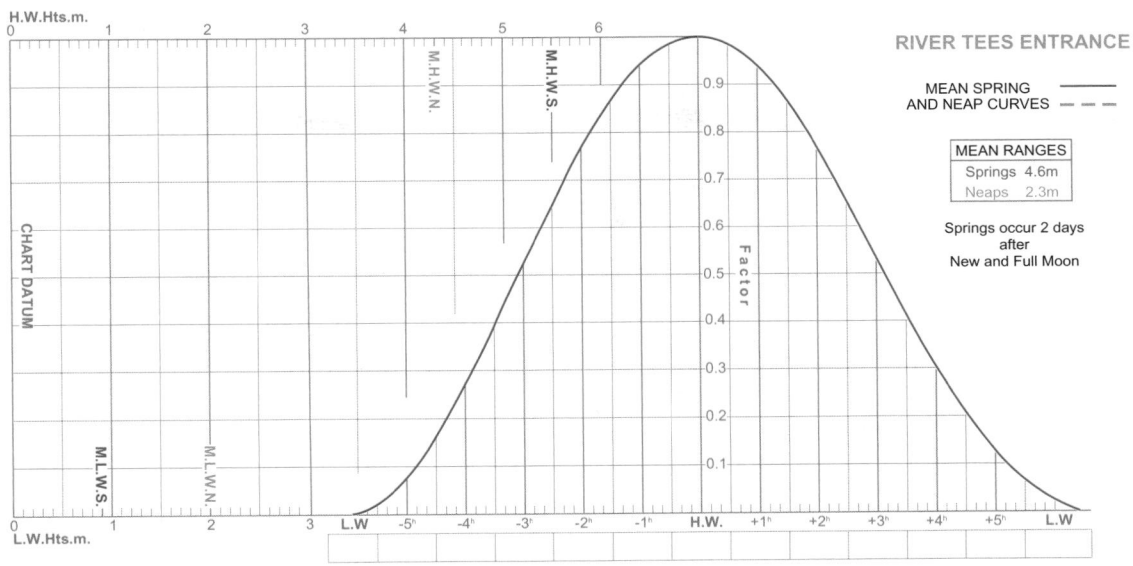

RIVER TEES ENTRANCE

MEAN SPRING
AND NEAP CURVES

MEAN RANGES
Springs 4.6m
Neaps 2.3m

Springs occur 2 days
after
New and Full Moon

TIME ZONE (UT)
For Summer Time add ONE hour in **non-shaded areas**

RIVER TEES LAT 54°38'N LONG 0°09'W
TIMES AND HEIGHTS OF HIGH AND LOW WATERS

Dates in red are **SPRINGS**
Dates in blue are **NEAPS**

YEAR 2010

JANUARY

Time	m		Time	m
1 0333	5.3		**16** 0420	4.9
0952	1.1		1022	1.4
F 1552	5.5		SA 1621	5.2
2223	0.6		2250	1.1
2 0424	5.5		**17** 0454	5.0
1040	1.0		1053	1.4
SA 1638	5.6		SU 1652	5.2
2312	0.4		2322	1.0
3 0513	5.5		**18** 0526	5.0
1126	1.0		1125	1.4
SU 1724	5.7		M 1723	5.2
			2352	1.1
4 0000	0.3		**19** 0557	4.9
0602	5.4		1156	1.4
M 1212	1.1		TU 1757	5.2
1810	5.7			
5 0047	0.4		**20** 0023	1.2
0651	5.3		0630	4.9
TU 1258	1.2		W 1229	1.5
1858	5.5		1831	5.1
6 0135	0.6		**21** 0055	1.3
0742	5.1		0707	4.7
W 1344	1.5		TH 1304	1.7
1949	5.3		1909	4.9
7 0224	1.0		**22** 0132	1.4
0835	4.8		0748	4.6
TH 1436	1.7		F 1344	1.8
◐ 2045	5.0		1953	4.8
8 0320	1.3		**23** 0214	1.6
0933	4.6		0837	4.4
F 1537	2.0		SA 1432	2.0
2148	4.7		◑ 2045	4.6
9 0423	1.7		**24** 0307	1.8
1036	4.4		0935	4.3
SA 1650	2.1		SU 1536	2.2
2300	4.5		2150	4.4
10 0536	1.9		**25** 0417	2.0
1146	4.4		1042	4.2
SU 1813	2.1		M 1658	2.1
			2305	4.4
11 0017	4.4		**26** 0537	2.0
0648	1.9		1153	4.3
M 1255	4.5		TU 1819	1.9
1924	1.9			
12 0128	4.5		**27** 0022	4.5
0747	1.8		0653	1.8
TU 1351	4.6		W 1300	4.6
2019	1.6		1930	1.5
13 0222	4.6		**28** 0132	4.8
0833	1.7		0758	1.5
W 1437	4.8		TH 1359	4.9
2104	1.4		2031	1.1
14 0306	4.8		**29** 0231	5.1
0913	1.6		0853	1.3
TH 1515	5.0		F 1451	5.3
2142	1.2		2125	0.7
15 0345	4.9		**30** 0324	5.3
0948	1.5		0943	1.0
F 1549	5.1		SA 1538	5.6
● 2217	1.1		○ 2214	0.3
			31 0412	5.5
			1029	0.8
			SU 1623	5.8
			2300	0.1

FEBRUARY

Time	m		Time	m
1 0458	5.6		**16** 0459	5.1
1112	0.7		1101	1.1
M 1708	5.9		TU 1658	5.3
2344	0.1		2324	0.9
2 0543	5.6		**17** 0527	5.1
1154	0.8		1131	1.2
TU 1751	5.9		W 1728	5.3
			2352	1.0
3 0026	0.2		**18** 0557	5.0
0627	5.4		1201	1.2
W 1234	0.9		TH 1800	5.2
1835	5.7			
4 0108	0.5		**19** 0023	1.1
0711	5.2		0630	4.9
TH 1315	1.2		F 1234	1.4
1921	5.4		1835	5.1
5 0151	0.9		**20** 0058	1.3
0757	4.8		0707	4.7
F 1358	1.5		SA 1310	1.5
◒ 2012	5.0		1917	4.9
6 0238	1.4		**21** 0137	1.5
0849	4.5		0752	4.5
SA 1452	1.8		SU 1354	1.8
2113	4.6		2009	4.6
7 0336	1.9		**22** 0226	1.8
0950	4.2		0849	4.3
SU 1606	2.1		M 1455	2.0
2227	4.3		◑ 2117	4.4
8 0455	2.2		**23** 0336	2.1
1104	4.1		1002	4.2
M 1747	2.2		TU 1624	2.1
2354	4.1		2240	4.2
9 0626	2.2		**24** 0510	2.1
1227	4.2		1123	4.2
TU 1913	2.0		W 1759	1.9
10 0115	4.3		**25** 0005	4.4
0731	2.1		0638	1.9
W 1334	4.4		TH 1240	4.5
2009	1.7		1918	1.4
11 0211	4.5		**26** 0121	4.7
0818	1.9		0746	1.6
TH 1421	4.7		F 1342	4.9
2051	1.4		2019	0.9
12 0252	4.7		**27** 0219	5.1
0856	1.6		0839	1.2
F 1459	4.9		SA 1434	5.3
2126	1.2		2110	0.5
13 0328	4.8		**28** 0308	5.4
0930	1.4		0926	0.9
SA 1532	5.1		SU 1520	5.7
2158	1.0		○ 2156	0.3
14 0400	5.0			
1002	1.3			
SU 1602	5.2			
● 2228	0.9			
15 0430	5.0			
1032	1.2			
M 1630	5.3			
2257	0.9			

MARCH

Time	m		Time	m
1 0353	5.6		**16** 0400	5.1
1009	0.7		1005	1.1
M 1603	5.9		TU 1603	5.2
2239	0.0		2226	0.8
2 0436	5.6		**17** 0427	5.1
1050	0.6		1035	1.0
TU 1645	5.9		W 1630	5.3
2320	0.0		2254	0.8
3 0517	5.6		**18** 0455	5.1
1130	0.6		1105	1.0
W 1727	5.9		TH 1700	5.3
2359	0.2		2323	0.9
4 0558	5.4		**19** 0526	5.1
1207	0.7		1136	1.0
TH 1810	5.7		F 1733	5.2
			2355	1.0
5 0037	0.6		**20** 0559	5.0
0638	5.2		1210	1.2
F 1246	1.0		SA 1811	5.1
1854	5.3			
6 0116	1.1		**21** 0030	1.2
0720	4.8		0636	4.8
SA 1326	1.3		SU 1248	1.3
1943	4.9		1855	4.9
7 0158	1.6		**22** 0110	1.5
0806	4.5		0720	4.6
SU 1415	1.7		M 1334	1.6
◑ 2042	4.4		1951	4.6
8 0250	2.1		**23** 0200	1.9
0905	4.2		0819	4.3
M 1528	2.1		TU 1438	1.8
2157	4.1		◑ 2102	4.3
9 0412	2.4		**24** 0312	2.1
1022	4.0		0935	4.2
TU 1715	2.2		W 1610	1.9
2328	4.0		2227	4.2
10 0553	2.4		**25** 0453	2.2
1151	4.1		1059	4.3
W 1848	2.0		TH 1744	1.6
			2353	4.4
11 0051	4.1		**26** 0621	1.9
0704	2.2		1218	4.6
TH 1304	4.3		F 1900	1.2
1943	1.7			
12 0146	4.4		**27** 0105	4.7
0830	1.6		0725	1.6
F 1353	4.6		SA 1321	5.0
2024	1.4		1958	0.8
13 0226	4.6		**28** 0200	5.0
0830	1.6		0816	1.2
SA 1432	4.8		SU 1412	5.3
2058	1.2		2047	0.4
14 0301	4.8		**29** 0246	5.3
0904	1.4		0902	0.9
SU 1505	5.0		M 1457	5.6
2129	1.0		2132	0.2
15 0332	5.0		**30** 0329	5.5
0935	1.2		0945	0.6
M 1535	5.2		TU 1540	5.8
● 2159	0.9		○ 2214	0.1
			31 0410	5.5
			1026	0.5
			W 1622	5.8
			2254	0.2

APRIL

Time	m		Time	m
1 0449	5.5		**16** 0427	5.2
1105	0.6		1041	0.9
TH 1704	5.7		F 1637	5.7
2332	0.5		2257	0.9
2 0528	5.3		**17** 0500	5.1
1143	0.7		1116	0.9
F 1747	5.4		SA 1715	5.2
			2333	1.0
3 0008	0.8		**18** 0536	5.0
0606	5.1		1154	1.0
SA 1222	0.9		SU 1758	5.0
1832	5.1			
4 0046	1.2		**19** 0011	1.2
0646	4.9		0616	4.9
SU 1303	1.3		M 1238	1.2
1920	4.7		1848	4.8
5 0124	1.7		**20** 0055	1.5
0730	4.6		0704	4.7
M 1351	1.6		TU 1330	1.4
2017	4.3		1947	4.6
6 0212	2.1		**21** 0149	1.6
0824	4.3		0804	4.5
TU 1458	1.9		W 1437	1.5
◑ 2128	4.0		◑ 2057	4.4
7 0327	2.4		**22** 0304	2.1
0937	4.1		0918	4.4
W 1630	2.1		TH 1601	1.6
2250	3.9		2216	4.3
8 0503	2.5		**23** 0435	2.1
1103	4.1		1038	4.5
TH 1759	1.9		F 1722	1.4
			2333	4.5
9 0008	4.0		**24** 0553	1.9
0619	2.3		1152	4.7
F 1218	4.2		SA 1832	1.1
1859	1.7			
10 0106	4.3		**25** 0040	4.7
0712	2.0		0656	1.6
SA 1312	4.5		SU 1255	5.0
1943	1.5		1930	0.8
11 0149	4.5		**26** 0135	5.0
0754	1.7		0749	1.2
SU 1354	4.7		M 1348	5.2
2020	1.2		2021	0.6
12 0225	4.7		**27** 0222	5.2
0830	1.4		0837	1.0
M 1430	4.9		TU 1435	5.4
2054	1.0		2106	0.5
13 0257	4.9		**28** 0304	5.3
0903	1.2		0921	0.8
TU 1502	5.0		W 1519	5.5
2124	0.9		○ 2149	0.5
14 0327	5.0		**29** 0345	5.3
0935	1.0		1003	0.7
W 1532	5.2		TH 1603	5.5
● 2154	0.8		2229	0.6
15 0356	5.1		**30** 0423	5.3
1008	0.9		1044	0.7
TH 1603	5.2		F 1646	5.4
2224	0.8		2307	0.8

Chart Datum: 2·85 metres below Ordnance Datum (Newlyn). HAT is 6·1 metres above Chart Datum; see 4.5.

》》 **FREE** monthly updates from 《《
www.reedsalmanac.co.uk

TIME ZONE (UT)
For Summer Time add ONE hour in **non-shaded areas**

RIVER TEES LAT 54°38′N LONG 0°09′W
TIMES AND HEIGHTS OF HIGH AND LOW WATERS

Dates in red are **SPRINGS**
Dates in blue are NEAPS

YEAR 2010

MAY

Time	m	Time	m
1 SA 0501 / 1124 / 1730 / 2344	5.2 / 0.8 / 5.2 / 1.1	**16** SU 0442 / 1103 / 1706 / 2319	5.2 / 0.8 / 5.2 / 1.1
2 SU 0540 / 1204 / 1815	5.1 / 1.0 / 4.9	**17** M 0523 / 1148 / 1755	5.1 / 0.8 / 5.1
3 M 0021 / 0619 / 1247 / 1901	1.4 / 4.9 / 1.2 / 4.6	**18** TU 0003 / 0607 / 1237 / 1847	1.3 / 5.1 / 0.9 / 4.9
4 TU 0059 / 0702 / 1334 / 1953	1.7 / 4.7 / 1.5 / 4.4	**19** W 0051 / 0657 / 1332 / 1944	1.5 / 4.9 / 1.1 / 4.7
5 W 0144 / 0752 / 1430 / 2053	2.0 / 4.5 / 1.7 / 4.1	**20** TH 0147 / 0755 / 1435 / 2049	1.7 / 4.8 / 1.2 / 4.6
6 TH 0245 / 0853 / 1540 / 2202	2.3 / 4.3 / 1.9 / 4.0	**21** F 0255 / 0902 / 1544 / 2157	1.9 / 4.7 / 1.2 / 4.5
7 F 0403 / 1006 / 1653 / 2310	2.4 / 4.2 / 1.9 / 4.1	**22** SA 0409 / 1013 / 1653 / 2306	1.9 / 4.7 / 1.2 / 4.5
8 SA 0518 / 1118 / 1758	2.3 / 4.2 / 1.8	**23** SU 0519 / 1123 / 1800	1.8 / 4.8 / 1.1
9 SU 0011 / 0618 / 1218 / 1850	4.2 / 2.1 / 4.4 / 1.6	**24** M 0010 / 0624 / 1228 / 1901	4.7 / 1.6 / 4.9 / 1.0
10 M 0101 / 0707 / 1307 / 1934	4.4 / 1.8 / 4.6 / 1.4	**25** TU 0108 / 0722 / 1326 / 1955	4.8 / 1.4 / 5.1 / 0.9
11 TU 0142 / 0750 / 1349 / 2013	4.6 / 1.6 / 4.7 / 1.2	**26** W 0158 / 0815 / 1417 / 2043	5.0 / 1.2 / 5.2 / 0.9
12 W 0218 / 0828 / 1427 / 2048	4.8 / 1.3 / 4.9 / 1.1	**27** TH 0243 / 0902 / 1505 / 2127	5.1 / 1.0 / 5.2 / 0.9
13 TH 0253 / 0905 / 1504 / 2123	5.0 / 1.1 / 5.1 / 1.0	**28** F 0325 / 0947 / 1550 / 2208	5.1 / 0.9 / 5.2 / 1.0
14 F 0327 / 0943 / 1541 / 2200	5.1 / 1.0 / 5.2 / 0.9	**29** SA 0404 / 1029 / 1634 / 2247	5.2 / 0.9 / 5.1 / 1.1
15 SA 0403 / 1022 / 1622 / 2238	5.2 / 0.9 / 5.2 / 1.0	**30** SU 0441 / 1110 / 1717 / 2325	5.1 / 0.9 / 5.0 / 1.3
		31 M 0519 / 1151 / 1759	5.1 / 1.0 / 4.9

JUNE

Time	m	Time	m
1 TU 0001 / 0557 / 1231 / 1842	1.5 / 5.0 / 1.2 / 4.7	**16** W 0000 / 0559 / 1235 / 1841	1.1 / 5.4 / 0.6 / 5.2
2 W 0039 / 0638 / 1313 / 1926	1.6 / 4.9 / 1.4 / 4.5	**17** TH 0048 / 0648 / 1326 / 1934	1.3 / 5.3 / 0.7 / 5.0
3 TH 0118 / 0722 / 1358 / 2014	1.8 / 4.7 / 1.6 / 4.3	**18** F 0139 / 0742 / 1420 / 2030	1.4 / 5.2 / 0.9 / 4.8
4 F 0205 / 0812 / 1448 / 2107	2.0 / 4.5 / 1.7 / 4.2	**19** SA 0235 / 0841 / 1519 / 2130	1.6 / 5.0 / 1.1 / 4.7
5 SA 0303 / 0909 / 1545 / 2206	2.2 / 4.4 / 1.8 / 4.2	**20** SU 0338 / 0946 / 1621 / 2233	1.8 / 4.8 / 1.2 / 4.5
6 SU 0409 / 1012 / 1646 / 2305	2.2 / 4.3 / 1.9 / 4.2	**21** M 0445 / 1054 / 1728 / 2338	1.8 / 4.7 / 1.4 / 4.5
7 M 0514 / 1115 / 1746	2.2 / 4.3 / 1.8	**22** TU 0555 / 1204 / 1835	1.8 / 4.7 / 1.4
8 TU 0001 / 0613 / 1214 / 1840	4.3 / 2.0 / 4.4 / 1.6	**23** W 0042 / 0702 / 1311 / 1935	4.6 / 1.6 / 4.8 / 1.4
9 W 0053 / 0705 / 1306 / 1929	4.5 / 1.8 / 4.6 / 1.5	**24** TH 0139 / 0801 / 1408 / 2027	4.7 / 1.4 / 4.9 / 1.4
10 TH 0139 / 0753 / 1355 / 2015	4.7 / 1.5 / 4.8 / 1.3	**25** F 0228 / 0852 / 1458 / 2112	4.9 / 1.2 / 4.9 / 1.3
11 F 0222 / 0839 / 1441 / 2059	4.9 / 1.2 / 5.0 / 1.2	**26** SA 0311 / 0937 / 1543 / 2153	5.0 / 1.2 / 5.0 / 1.3
12 SA 0304 / 0924 / 1526 / 2143	5.0 / 1.0 / 5.1 / 1.1	**27** SU 0350 / 1018 / 1624 / 2231	5.1 / 1.0 / 5.0 / 1.3
13 SU 0346 / 1010 / 1613 / 2228	5.2 / 0.8 / 5.2 / 1.0	**28** M 0426 / 1057 / 1703 / 2307	5.1 / 1.0 / 5.0 / 1.3
14 M 0429 / 1057 / 1701 / 2313	5.3 / 0.7 / 5.3 / 1.0	**29** TU 0501 / 1134 / 1740 / 2341	5.1 / 1.0 / 4.9 / 1.4
15 TU 0513 / 1145 / 1750	5.4 / 0.6 / 5.3	**30** W 0536 / 1210 / 1817	5.1 / 1.1 / 4.8

JULY

Time	m	Time	m
1 TH 0015 / 0613 / 1245 / 1854	1.5 / 5.0 / 1.2 / 4.7	**16** F 0034 / 0632 / 1309 / 1913	1.0 / 5.6 / 0.5 / 5.2
2 F 0050 / 0651 / 1321 / 1933	1.6 / 4.9 / 1.4 / 4.6	**17** SA 0119 / 0721 / 1357 / 2004	1.2 / 5.4 / 0.7 / 5.0
3 SA 0128 / 0734 / 1400 / 2017	1.8 / 4.8 / 1.6 / 4.5	**18** SU 0208 / 0815 / 1449 / 2058	1.4 / 5.2 / 1.1 / 4.7
4 SU 0211 / 0821 / 1445 / 2107	1.9 / 4.6 / 1.7 / 4.3	**19** M 0304 / 0917 / 1548 / 2159	1.7 / 4.9 / 1.5 / 4.5
5 M 0304 / 0915 / 1540 / 2203	2.1 / 4.4 / 1.9 / 4.2	**20** TU 0412 / 1027 / 1617 / 2306	1.9 / 4.6 / 1.7 / 4.4
6 TU 0410 / 1017 / 1644 / 2304	2.2 / 4.3 / 1.9 / 4.2	**21** W 0532 / 1146 / 1814	1.9 / 4.5 / 1.8
7 W 0519 / 1123 / 1750	2.1 / 4.4 / 1.9	**22** TH 0020 / 0652 / 1303 / 1922	4.4 / 1.8 / 4.5 / 1.8
8 TH 0005 / 0624 / 1229 / 1853	4.3 / 1.9 / 4.5 / 1.7	**23** F 0126 / 0756 / 1404 / 2016	4.6 / 1.6 / 4.7 / 1.7
9 F 0104 / 0724 / 1329 / 1950	4.5 / 1.6 / 4.7 / 1.5	**24** SA 0218 / 0846 / 1451 / 2100	4.8 / 1.3 / 4.8 / 1.6
10 SA 0157 / 0819 / 1423 / 2043	4.8 / 1.3 / 5.0 / 1.3	**25** SU 0301 / 0928 / 1532 / 2138	5.0 / 1.2 / 4.9 / 1.4
11 SU 0245 / 0911 / 1514 / 2132	5.1 / 0.9 / 5.2 / 1.1	**26** M 0337 / 1005 / 1609 / 2213	5.1 / 1.0 / 5.0 / 1.4
12 M 0331 / 1000 / 1603 / 2219	5.3 / 0.6 / 5.4 / 1.0	**27** TU 0410 / 1039 / 1643 / 2246	5.2 / 1.0 / 5.0 / 1.3
13 TU 0416 / 1049 / 1651 / 2305	5.5 / 0.4 / 5.5 / 0.9	**28** W 0441 / 1111 / 1715 / 2317	5.2 / 1.0 / 5.0 / 1.3
14 W 0501 / 1136 / 1738 / 2350	5.7 / 0.3 / 5.5 / 0.9	**29** TH 0512 / 1142 / 1747 / 2347	5.2 / 1.1 / 5.0 / 1.3
15 TH 0546 / 1222 / 1826	5.7 / 0.3 / 5.4	**30** F 0545 / 1212 / 1819	5.2 / 1.1 / 4.9
		31 SA 0019 / 0618 / 1243 / 1853	1.4 / 5.1 / 1.3 / 4.8

AUGUST

Time	m	Time	m
1 SU 0052 / 0656 / 1318 / 1932	1.6 / 4.9 / 1.4 / 4.7	**16** M 0138 / 0748 / 1416 / 2023	1.3 / 5.2 / 1.3 / 4.7
2 M 0129 / 0737 / 1358 / 2018	1.7 / 4.8 / 1.7 / 4.5	**17** TU 0230 / 0849 / 1513 / 2123	1.6 / 4.8 / 1.8 / 4.4
3 TU 0214 / 0827 / 1448 / 2112	1.9 / 4.6 / 1.9 / 4.3	**18** W 0341 / 1003 / 1628 / 2235	2.0 / 4.4 / 2.1 / 4.2
4 W 0313 / 0929 / 1553 / 2216	2.1 / 4.4 / 2.1 / 4.2	**19** TH 0515 / 1132 / 1757 / 2358	2.1 / 4.3 / 2.2 / 4.3
5 TH 0432 / 1043 / 1711 / 2326	2.2 / 4.3 / 2.1 / 4.3	**20** F 0645 / 1255 / 1909	1.9 / 4.4 / 2.1
6 F 0554 / 1200 / 1828	2.0 / 4.4 / 1.9	**21** SA 0111 / 0747 / 1353 / 2001	4.5 / 1.6 / 4.6 / 1.9
7 SA 0035 / 0704 / 1311 / 1933	4.5 / 1.6 / 4.7 / 1.7	**22** SU 0202 / 0833 / 1436 / 2042	4.8 / 1.4 / 4.8 / 1.7
8 SU 0136 / 0805 / 1409 / 2029	4.8 / 1.2 / 5.0 / 1.4	**23** M 0243 / 0910 / 1513 / 2117	5.0 / 1.2 / 5.0 / 1.5
9 M 0227 / 0858 / 1500 / 2118	5.2 / 0.8 / 5.3 / 1.1	**24** TU 0317 / 0943 / 1546 / 2149	5.2 / 1.0 / 5.1 / 1.3
10 TU 0314 / 0947 / 1547 / 2204	5.5 / 0.4 / 5.5 / 0.8	**25** W 0348 / 1013 / 1616 / 2219	5.3 / 1.0 / 5.1 / 1.2
11 W 0358 / 1034 / 1633 / 2248	5.8 / 0.2 / 5.7 / 0.7	**26** TH 0416 / 1042 / 1645 / 2249	5.3 / 0.9 / 5.2 / 1.2
12 TH 0442 / 1118 / 1717 / 2331	5.9 / 0.1 / 5.7 / 0.7	**27** F 0445 / 1110 / 1713 / 2318	5.3 / 1.0 / 5.1 / 1.2
13 F 0525 / 1201 / 1802	6.0 / 0.2 / 5.6	**28** SA 0514 / 1138 / 1743 / 2348	5.3 / 1.1 / 5.1 / 1.3
14 SA 0012 / 0609 / 1244 / 1846	0.8 / 5.8 / 0.4 / 5.4	**29** SU 0546 / 1208 / 1816	5.2 / 1.2 / 5.0
15 SU 0053 / 0656 / 1328 / 1933	1.0 / 5.6 / 0.8 / 5.1	**30** M 0020 / 0620 / 1242 / 1853	1.4 / 5.1 / 1.4 / 4.8
		31 TU 0056 / 0700 / 1320 / 1936	1.6 / 4.9 / 1.6 / 4.6

Chart Datum: 2·85 metres below Ordnance Datum (Newlyn). HAT is 6·1 metres above Chart Datum; see 4.5.

NE England

TIME ZONE (UT)
For Summer Time add ONE hour in **non-shaded areas**

RIVER TEES LAT 54°38'N LONG 0°09'W
TIMES AND HEIGHTS OF HIGH AND LOW WATERS

Dates in red are SPRINGS
Dates in blue are NEAPS

YEAR 2010

SEPTEMBER

Day	Time m			Day	Time m		
1 W	0137 1.8	0750 4.6	1407 1.9 / ◗ 2029 4.4	**16** TH	0314 2.0	0940 4.3	1556 2.4 / 2201 4.2
2 TH	0234 2.0	0855 4.4	1513 2.2 / 2137 4.2	**17** F	0455 2.1	1112 4.2	1730 2.4 / 2328 4.2
3 F	0358 2.1	1015 4.3	1643 2.3 / 2255 4.3	**18** SA	0625 1.9	1234 4.3	1843 2.3
4 SA	0532 2.0	1140 4.4	1810 2.1	**19** SU	0042 4.5 / 0723 1.7	1329 4.5	1934 2.0
5 SU	0010 4.5 / 0649 1.6	1254 4.7	1917 1.7	**20** M	0134 4.7 / 0806 1.4	1410 4.8	2014 1.7
6 M	0114 4.9 / 0749 1.1	1352 5.1	2010 1.4	**21** TU	0214 5.0 / 0841 1.2	1445 5.0	2048 1.5
7 TU	0206 5.3 / 0840 0.6	1441 5.4	2058 1.0	**22** W	0249 5.1 / 0912 1.1	1517 5.1	2120 1.3
8 W	0252 5.7 / 0927 0.3	1526 5.6	● 2143 0.8	**23** TH	0319 5.3 / 0942 1.0	1546 5.2	○ 2151 1.2
9 TH	0336 5.9 / 1011 0.1	1609 5.8	2225 0.6	**24** F	0348 5.3 / 1010 1.0	1613 5.2	2220 1.1
10 F	0418 6.0 / 1054 0.1	1652 5.8	2306 0.6	**25** SA	0416 5.3 / 1037 1.0	1641 5.2	2250 1.1
11 SA	0501 6.0 / 1135 0.2	1734 5.6	2347 0.7	**26** SU	0445 5.3 / 1105 1.0	1710 5.2	2321 1.2
12 SU	0546 5.8 / 1216 0.5	1817 5.4		**27** M	0517 5.2 / 1137 1.2	1744 5.1	2354 1.3
13 M	0027 0.9 / 0632 5.5	1258 1.0	1900 5.1	**28** TU	0553 5.1 / 1211 1.4	1820 4.9	
14 TU	0111 1.3 / 0723 5.1	1343 1.5	1948 4.7	**29** W	0031 1.5 / 0635 4.9	1250 1.7	1903 4.7
15 W	0202 1.6 / 0824 4.6	1438 2.0	◗ 2047 4.4	**30** TH	0115 1.7 / 0728 4.6	1338 2.0	1957 4.5

OCTOBER

Day	Time m			Day	Time m		
1 F	0214 1.9	0835 4.4	1445 2.3 / ◗ 2107 4.3	**16** SA	0415 2.1	1035 4.1	1645 2.5 / 2242 4.3
2 SA	0340 2.0	0956 4.3	1621 2.3 / 2227 4.4	**17** SU	0541 2.0	1152 4.2	1800 2.4 / 2356 4.4
3 SU	0513 1.8	1121 4.4	1747 2.1 / 2343 4.6	**18** M	0642 1.8	1250 4.5	1855 2.1
4 M	0627 1.4	1234 4.8	1853 1.8	**19** TU	0052 4.6 / 0726 1.5	1334 4.7	1938 1.8
5 TU	0048 5.0 / 0726 1.0	1331 5.1	1946 1.4	**20** W	0137 4.8 / 0804 1.4	1411 4.9	2015 1.6
6 W	0141 5.4 / 0816 0.6	1418 5.4	2034 1.0	**21** TH	0214 5.0 / 0837 1.2	1443 5.1	2049 1.4
7 TH	0228 5.7 / 0902 0.3	1502 5.6	● 2118 0.8	**22** F	0248 5.1 / 0909 1.1	1513 5.2	2122 1.2
8 F	0312 5.9 / 0946 0.2	1544 5.7	2201 0.6	**23** SA	0319 5.2 / 0938 1.0	1542 5.3	○ 2153 1.1
9 SA	0356 5.9 / 1028 0.3	1625 5.7	2243 0.6	**24** SU	0350 5.3 / 1007 1.0	1612 5.3	2226 1.1
10 SU	0440 5.9 / 1109 0.5	1707 5.6	2324 0.7	**25** M	0421 5.3 / 1038 1.1	1644 5.3	2300 1.1
11 M	0525 5.6 / 1149 0.8	1748 5.4		**26** TU	0457 5.2 / 1113 1.2	1719 5.2	2337 1.2
12 TU	0006 0.9 / 0612 5.3	1230 1.2	1830 5.1	**27** W	0538 5.1 / 1150 1.4	1758 5.0	
13 W	0051 1.2 / 0703 4.9	1313 1.7	1916 4.8	**28** TH	0018 1.3 / 0624 4.9	1232 1.7	1843 4.9
14 TH	0141 1.6 / 0802 4.5	1404 2.1	◗ 2011 4.5	**29** F	0106 1.5 / 0719 4.7	1322 2.0	1937 4.7
15 F	0248 1.9 / 0913 4.2	1517 2.4	2121 4.3	**30** SA	0207 1.7 / 0825 4.5	1428 2.2	◗ 2044 4.6
				31 SU	0325 1.7 / 0940 4.4	1556 2.3	2159 4.6

NOVEMBER

Day	Time m			Day	Time m		
1 M	0446 1.6	1057 4.5	1716 2.1 / 2313 4.7	**16** TU	0541 1.9	1155 4.3	1802 2.3 / 2357 4.5
2 TU	0557 1.3	1206 4.8	1822 1.8	**17** W	0636 1.8	1246 4.5	1854 2.0
3 W	0018 5.0 / 0657 1.0	1304 5.1	1918 1.5	**18** TH	0050 4.6 / 0720 1.6	1329 4.7	1937 1.8
4 TH	0115 5.3 / 0750 0.8	1353 5.3	2009 1.2	**19** F	0135 4.8 / 0759 1.4	1407 4.9	2017 1.5
5 F	0206 5.5 / 0838 0.6	1438 5.5	2056 0.9	**20** SA	0215 4.9 / 0835 1.3	1441 5.1	2054 1.3
6 SA	0253 5.6 / 0922 0.6	1521 5.5	● 2141 0.8	**21** SU	0252 5.1 / 0908 1.2	1514 5.2	2130 1.2
7 SU	0339 5.6 / 1005 0.7	1602 5.5	2225 0.8	**22** M	0329 5.1 / 0943 1.2	1549 5.3	2208 1.1
8 M	0424 5.6 / 1047 0.8	1643 5.5	2308 0.8	**23** TU	0406 5.2 / 1019 1.2	1625 5.3	2247 1.0
9 TU	0510 5.4 / 1127 1.1	1724 5.4	2351 1.0	**24** W	0447 5.2 / 1058 1.3	1704 5.3	2328 1.0
10 W	0557 5.1 / 1207 1.4	1805 5.2		**25** TH	0531 5.1 / 1139 1.4	1745 5.2	
11 TH	0035 1.2 / 0646 4.9	1248 1.7	1849 5.0	**26** F	0013 1.1 / 0619 5.0	1224 1.6	1831 5.1
12 F	0123 1.5 / 0738 4.6	1334 2.1	1937 4.7	**27** SA	0103 1.2 / 0713 4.9	1314 1.8	1923 5.0
13 SA	0217 1.7 / 0838 4.3	1431 2.3	◗ 2036 4.5	**28** SU	0200 1.3 / 0813 4.7	1414 2.0	◗ 2023 4.9
14 SU	0322 1.9 / 0945 4.2	1543 2.5	2145 4.4	**29** M	0304 1.4 / 0918 4.6	1526 2.1	2130 4.8
15 M	0434 2.0 / 1053 4.2	1658 2.4	2255 4.4	**30** TU	0413 1.4 / 1027 4.6	1639 2.0	2240 4.8

DECEMBER

Day	Time m			Day	Time m		
1 W	0521 1.3	1133 4.7	1748 1.9 / 2348 4.9	**16** TH	0527 2.0	1145 4.3	1758 2.2 / 2356 4.4
2 TH	0626 1.2	1235 4.9	1852 1.6	**17** F	0627 1.9	1239 4.5	1855 2.0
3 F	0051 5.1 / 0725 1.1	1330 5.1	1949 1.4	**18** SA	0058 4.5 / 0718 1.7	1327 4.7	1944 1.7
4 SA	0149 5.2 / 0817 1.0	1419 5.2	2041 1.2	**19** SU	0143 4.7 / 0803 1.5	1410 4.9	2029 1.5
5 SU	0241 5.3 / 0904 1.0	1504 5.3	● 2129 1.0	**20** M	0229 4.9 / 0845 1.4	1451 5.1	2112 1.2
6 M	0330 5.3 / 0948 1.1	1546 5.4	2214 0.9	**21** TU	0312 5.1 / 0926 1.3	1531 5.3	○ 2155 1.0
7 TU	0416 5.3 / 1030 1.1	1626 5.4	2257 0.9	**22** W	0355 5.2 / 1008 1.2	1611 5.4	2238 0.8
8 W	0500 5.2 / 1110 1.3	1705 5.2	2338 1.0	**23** TH	0439 5.3 / 1050 1.2	1652 5.5	2323 0.7
9 TH	0544 5.0 / 1148 1.5	1744 5.3		**24** F	0525 5.3 / 1133 1.2	1734 5.5	
10 F	0019 1.1 / 0626 4.9	1226 1.7	1824 5.1	**25** SA	0008 0.7 / 0611 5.2	1218 1.3	1819 5.5
11 SA	0059 1.3 / 0710 4.7	1304 1.9	1906 4.9	**26** SU	0055 0.7 / 0701 5.1	1304 1.4	1907 5.4
12 SU	0141 1.5 / 0756 4.5	1346 2.1	1953 4.7	**27** M	0144 0.9 / 0753 5.0	1354 1.6	2000 5.2
13 M	0227 1.7 / 0847 4.3	1438 2.3	◗ 2047 4.5	**28** TU	0238 1.1 / 0850 4.8	1453 1.8	◗ 2101 5.0
14 TU	0321 1.9 / 0945 4.2	1542 2.4	2148 4.4	**29** W	0339 1.3 / 0952 4.6	1600 1.9	2209 4.8
15 W	0423 2.0 / 1045 4.2	1652 2.4	2253 4.3	**30** TH	0446 1.5 / 1059 4.6	1715 2.0	2321 4.7
				31 F	0558 1.6 / 1207 4.6	1831 1.8	

Chart Datum: 2·85 metres below Ordnance Datum (Newlyn). HAT is 6·1metres above Chart Datum; see 4.5.

9.5.14 HARTLEPOOL

Hartlepool 54°41'·26N 01°11'·90W (West Hbr ent) ✹✹♒♒♒❀❀

CHARTS AC 152, 2567, 2566; Imray C24.

TIDES +0437 Dover; ML 3·0; Duration 0600

Standard Port RIVER TEES (←)

Times				Height (metres)			
High Water		Low Water		MHWS	MHWN	MLWN	MLWS
0000	0600	0000	0600	5·5	4·3	2·0	0·9
1200	1800	1200	1800				
Differences HARTLEPOOL							
−0004	−0004	−0006	−0006	−0·1	−0·1	−0·2	−0·1
MIDDLESBROUGH							
0000	+0002	0000	−0003	+0·1	+0·2	+0·1	−0·1

SHELTER Excellent in marina (5m). Strong E/SE winds raise broken water and swell in the bay, making ent channel hazardous, but possible. In such conditions, ask marina's advice.

NAVIGATION WPT 54°40'·86N 01°09'·90W, Longscar ECM buoy, 295°/1·06M to W Hbr ent. (For Victoria Hbr, 308°/0·65M to Nos 1/ 2 buoys.) From S, beware Longscar Rks, 4ca WSW of WPT. Note: Tees Fairway SWM buoy, (54°40'·94N 01°06'·47W) is 2M E of Longscar ECM buoy and may assist the initial landfall. Speed limit 4kn in W Hbr and Marina.

LIGHTS AND MARKS Steetly Works chimney, 1·4M NW of marina ent, and St Hilda's Church tower on The Heugh, are both prominent. Dir lt Fl WRG leads 308° to marina lock, between W Hbr outer piers, Oc R and Oc G, and inner piers, FR and FG; bright street lts on S pier.

Lock sigs: ● = Proceed; ● = Wait; ● ● = Lock closed.

Dir lt, Iso WRG, leads 325° via lit buoyed chan to Victoria Hbr.

R/T Marina Ch **M**, 80. *Tees Port Control* info Ch 14, 22 (H24). *Hartlepool Dock Radio* Ch 12, only for ship docking.

TELEPHONE (Code 01429) MRCC 01262 672317; Tees Port Authority (01642) 277205; Marinecall 09068 969643; ⊖ (0191) 257 9441; Police 221151; Dr 272679.

FACILITIES

Hartlepool Marina Access HW±3 via chan dredged to CD and lock (max beam 8.5m) H24, over tidal cill 0.8m below CD. ☎ 865744, www.hartlepool-marina.com, 500+100 Ⓥ, £2. D (H24), LPG, BY, El, ME, CH, SM, ✕, ▣, ♿, ⚓, BH (40 and 300 tons), Wi-fi, C (13 tons), Gas, Gaz.

Victoria Hbr (commercial dock, not normally for yachts), access H24. Call *Tees Port Control* Ch 14 for short-stay.

Tees & Hartlepool YC ☎ 233423, Bar, Slip.

Town P (cans), 🛒 (H24), R, Bar, ✉, Ⓑ, ⇌, ✈ (Teesside).

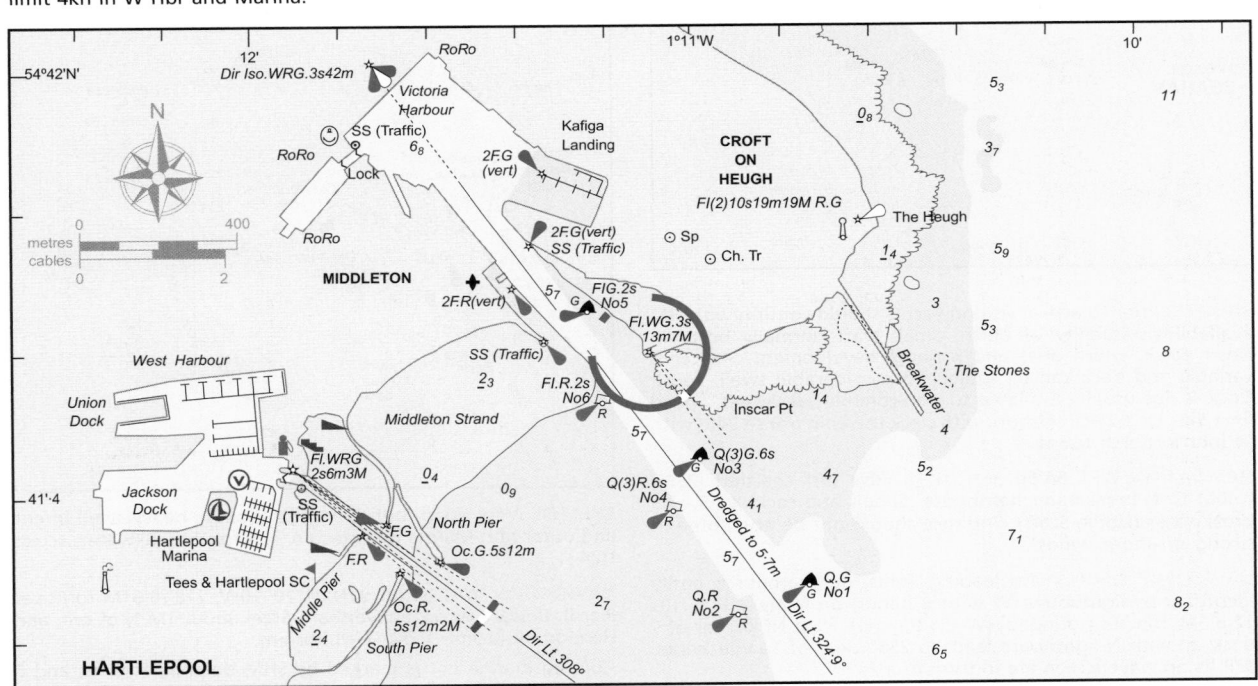

HARTLEPOOL TO SOUTHERN NETHERLANDS

(Charts 2182A, 1191, 1190, 1503, 1408, 1610, 3371, 110) From abeam Whitby the passage can, theoretically, be made on one direct course, but this would conflict with oil/gas activities and platforms including Rough and Amethyst fields off Humber, Hewett off Cromer and very extensive fields further offshore. Commercial, oil-rig support and fishing vessels may be met S of Flamborough Hd and particularly off NE Norfolk where it is advisable to follow an inshore track.

After passing Flamborough Hd, Dowsing B1D, Dudgeon lt buoy and Newarp lt F, either:

Proceed SE'ly to take departure from the Outer Gabbard; thence cross N Hinder South TSS at right angles before heading for Roompotsluis via Middelbank and subsequent buoyed chan.

Or set course ESE from the vicinity of Cross Sand lt buoy and Smith's Knoll, so as to cross the N/S deep-water traffic routes to the E. Thence alter SE towards Hoek van Holland, keeping N of Maas Approaches TSS.

HARTLEPOOL TO THE GERMAN BIGHT

(Charts 2182A, 1191, 266, 1405) Taking departure eastward from abeam Whitby High lt, skirt the SW Patch off Dogger Bank, keeping clear S of Gordon Gas Field and then N of German Bight W Approach TSS. Thence head for the Elbe or Helgoland; the latter may also serve as a convenient haven in order to adjust the passage for Elbe tides and streams, without greatly increasing passage distance. ▶ *Tidal streams are less than 1kn away from the coast and run E/W along much of the route.* ◀

9.5.15 SEAHAM

Durham 54°50'·24N 01°19'·28W ✳🚩🏵

CHARTS AC 152, 1627; Imray C24.

TIDES +0435 Dover; ML 3·0; Duration 0600

Standard Port RIVER TEES (←—)

Times				Height (metres)			
High Water		Low Water		MHWS	MHWN	MLWN	MLWS
0000	0600	0000	0600	5·5	4·3	2·0	0·9
1200	1800	1200	1800				
Differences SEAHAM							
–0015	–0015	–0015	–0015	–0·3	–0·2	0·0	–0·2

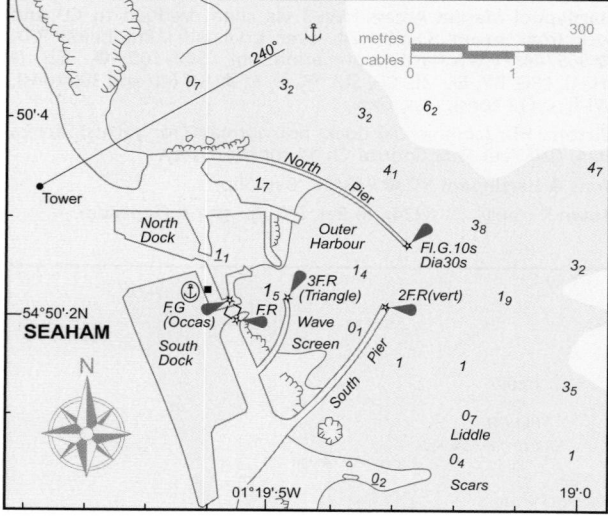

SHELTER Prior to arrival visiting yachts should confirm with HM availability/suitability of berth. Small craft normally berth in North Dock, which dries and is under development. Shelter is variable and dock can be subject to considerable swell. South Dock is not usually available to non-commercial vessels. Speed limit 5kn. Or ⚓ 2½ca offshore with clock tower in transit 240° with St John's church tower.

NAVIGATION WPT 54°50'·36N 01°18'·60W (off chartlet), 256°/0·40M to N breakwater lighthouse. Shoals and rocks to S of S breakwater (Liddle Scars). Entrance should not be attempted in strong on-shore winds.

LIGHTS AND MARKS No leading lights, but harbour is easily identified by lighthouse (W with B bands) on N pier, Fl G 10s 12m 5M, Dia 30s (sounded HW–2½ to +1½). FS at NE corner of S dock on with N lighthouse leads in 256° clear of Tangle Rocks. 3FR lts on wave screen are in form of a △.

Traffic sigs at S Dock: ● = Vessels enter: ● = Vessels leave.

R/T VHF Ch **12** 16 06 0800–1700 (Mon-Fri).

TELEPHONE (Code 0191) HM 07786 565205; Admin Office 5161700; MRCC 01262 672317; Marinecall 09068 969643; Police 0345 6060365; Dr 5812332.

FACILITIES S Dock (Seaham Hbr Dock Co) ☎ 516 1700, AB £5 but normally no charge for the odd night, L, FW, C (40 ton), AB; **N Dock** M. **Town** (½M) P, D, FW, ME, El, CH (5M), 🛒, R, Bar, ✉, Ⓑ, ⇌, ✈ (Teesside or Newcastle).

9.5.16 SUNDERLAND

Tyne and Wear 54°55'·23N 01°21'·15W ✳✳✳🚩🚩🏵🏵

CHARTS AC 152, 1627; Imray C24.

TIDES +0430 Dover; ML 2·9; Duration 0600; Zone 0 (UT)

Standard Port RIVER TEES (←—)

Times				Height (metres)			
High Water		Low Water		MHWS	MHWN	MLWN	MLWS
0000	0600	0000	0600	5·5	4·3	2·0	0·9
1200	1800	1200	1800				
Differences SUNDERLAND							
–0017	–0017	–0016	–0016	–0·3	–0·1	0·0	–0·1

SHELTER Very good, but strong E'lies cause heavy swell in ent and outer hbr. Marina is protected by a fixed breakwater; access H24.

NAVIGATION WPT 54°55'·21N 01°20'·10W, 278°/0·61M to Roker Pier lt. Beware wreck at Whitburn Steel about 1M N of ent, and Hendon Rk (0·9m), 1·2M SE of hbr ent.

Appr to marina ent is marked by SHM dolphin, Fl G 5s, and E jetty, Fl (2) G 10s. Close (4m) SSW of end of pontoon D, beware substantial obst'n (1·6m) in surrounding depth 2·1m, see chartlet.

LIGHTS AND MARKS 3 Fl ● at Pilot Stn (Old N Pier) = danger in harbour; no entry/departure.

R/T Sunderland Marina Ch M, 80. Port VHF Ch **14** (H24); tide and visibility reports on request.

TELEPHONE (Code 0191) HM 567 2626 (HO), 567 0161 (OT); MRCC 01262 672317; ⊖ (0191) 257 9441; Marinecall 09068 969643; Police 454 7555; Ⓗ 565 6256.

FACILITIES Sunderland Marina 120 pontoon berths in 2·1m, max LOA 13m; and 110 moorings. ☎ 5144721. **Ⓥ** (if available) £2.05/m; M £10/craft, ♿, D (H24), Slip, FW, ⚓.

Sunderland YC ☎ 567 5133, FW, AB, Bar, Slip (dinghy).

Wear Boating Association ☎ 567 5313, AB. **Town** P (cans), Gas, Gaz, CH, El, ME, SM, 🛒, R, Bar, ✉, 🖂, Ⓑ, ⇌, ✈ (Newcastle).

9.5.17   R TYNE/NORTH SHIELDS

Tyne and Wear **55°00′·89N 01°24′·10W** ✿✿⊛⚓⚓✿✿

CHARTS AC 152, 1191, 1934; Imray C24.

TIDES +0430 Dover; ML 3·0; Duration 0604

Standard Port NORTH SHIELDS (→)

Times				Height (metres)			
High Water		Low Water		MHWS	MHWN	MLWN	MLWS
0200	0800	0100	0800	5·0	3·9	1·8	0·7
1400	2000	1300	2000				
Differences NEWCASTLE-UPON-TYNE							
+0003	+0003	+0008	+0008	+0·3	+0·2	+0·1	+0·1

SHELTER Good in all weather. Access H24, but in strong E and NE winds appr may be difficult for smaller craft due to much backwash off the piers. Confused seas can build at the ent in severe weather, and a large steep swell can break dangerously when meeting an ebb tide up to half a mile inside the harbour. In emergency or as a refuge yachts may berth on Fish Quay; contact HM.

NAVIGATION WPT 55°01′·01N 01°22′·32W, 258°/1·1M to hbr ent. From S, no dangers. From N, beware Bellhues Rk (approx 1M N of hbr and ¾M off shore); give N pier a wide berth. Dredged chan in Lower Hbr is buoyed. 6kn speed limit in the river west of Herd Groyne Lt Ho.

Proceed up/down river under power keeping to the starboard side. Tacking across the channel is not permitted. The 7 bridges at Newcastle have least clearance above HAT of 23m, or 3·7m when Millennium Bridge is closed.

LIGHTS AND MARKS See 9.5.4 and chartlet.

R/T *Tyne VTS* Ch **12**, 11 (H24). Royal Quays marina Ch 80. St Peter's Marina Ch **80** M.

TELEPHONE (Code 0191) HM 2570407; Tyne VTS 2572080; MRCC 01262 672317; Marinecall 09068 969643; Met 2326453; Police 2146555; Doctor via Tyne VTS; Ⓗ (Tynemouth) 2596660; Ⓗ (Newcastle) 2325131.

FACILITIES Notes: A conservancy fee (£10) may be levied by the Port Authority on all visiting craft. Craft waiting to enter the marinas should do so outside the fairway.

Royal Quays Marina 54°59′·79N 01°26′·84W, in former Albert Edward Dock, is 2M upriver from pierheads. ☎ 2728282; 302 berths inc Ⓥ, 7·9m depth; £2·15. S lock (42.5m x 7·5m) departures H and H+30; arrivals H+15 and H+45, or on request at quiet times. H24. Waiting pontoon outside lock. BY, BH (30 ton), D, P (H24), FW, ▢, Bar, El, Gas, Gaz, 🛒, Wi-fi. **St Peter's Marina** 54°57′·94N 01°34′·35W, 8M upriver, and 1M E of city. ☎ 2654472; 140 + 20 Ⓥ, £2.27. Access approx HW±3½ over sill, 0·8m below CD, which retains 2·5m within. Tfc lts at ent. D&P on pontoon outside ent in 2m, ▢. **Services.** Slip, ME, ✕, C, ACA, Ⓔ. **Millennium Bridge** in city centre, limited pontoon berthing; pre-book ☎ 2211363.

City. All amenities, ⇌ (Newcastle/S Shields), ✈ (Newcastle). **Ferries:** Ijmuiden; daily; 16 hrs; DFDS (www.dfdsseaways.co.uk).

ADJACENT HARBOUR

CULLERCOATS, Tyne & Wear, **55°02′·08N 01°25′·81W.** AC 1191. +0430 Dover. Tides as 9.5.17. Small drying hbr 1·6M N of R Tyne ent. Appr on ldg line 256°, two bns (FR lts), between drying rks. An occas fair weather ⚓ or dry against S pier. Facilities at Tynemouth.

RIVER TYNE/NORTH SHIELDS   LAT 55°01′N   LONG 1°26′W

TIMES AND HEIGHTS OF HIGH AND LOW WATERS

TIME ZONE (UT)
For Summer Time add ONE hour in **non-shaded areas**

Dates in red are **SPRINGS**
Dates in blue are **NEAPS**

YEAR 2010

JANUARY

Day	Time	m	Time	m	Time	m	Time	m
1 F	0320	5.1	0939	1.0	1536	5.2	2210	0.6
2 SA	0409	5.2	1026	1.0	1620	5.3	2259	0.4
3 SU	0458	5.2	1111	1.0	1705	5.4	2347	0.4
4 M	0546	5.2	1156	1.1	1752	5.3		
5 TU	0035	0.5	0636	5.0	1241	1.2	1841	5.2
6 W	0124	0.7	0727	4.7	1328	1.4	1934	5.0
7 TH	0215	1.0	0822	4.5	1420	1.6	2033	4.8
8 F	0311	1.3	0921	4.3	1523	1.9	2139	4.5
9 SA	0415	1.6	1026	4.2	1640	2.0	2253	4.3
10 SU	0525	1.8	1135	4.2	1802	1.9		
11 M	0009	4.3	0635	1.8	1242	4.3	1914	1.8
12 TU	0117	4.3	0734	1.8	1337	4.4	2010	1.6
13 W	0212	4.4	0821	1.7	1423	4.6	2054	1.4
14 TH	0256	4.6	0901	1.5	1502	4.8	2133	1.2
15 F	0334	4.6	0936	1.4	1536	4.9	2207	1.1
16 SA	0408	4.7	1008	1.3	1608	4.9	2239	1.0
17 SU	0441	4.7	1039	1.3	1639	5.0	2310	1.0
18 M	0512	4.7	1109	1.3	1710	5.0	2340	1.0
19 TU	0544	4.6	1140	1.3	1743	4.9		
20 W	0012	1.1	0616	4.5	1212	1.4	1816	4.8
21 TH	0045	1.2	0651	4.4	1245	1.6	1852	4.7
22 F	0121	1.4	0729	4.3	1323	1.7	1933	4.5
23 SA	0201	1.6	0815	4.2	1410	1.9	2024	4.3
24 SU	0253	1.8	0912	4.0	1515	2.1	2128	4.2
25 M	0404	1.9	1023	4.0	1641	2.1	2248	4.1
26 TU	0527	1.9	1142	4.1	1807	1.9		
27 W	0012	4.2	0644	1.7	1253	4.3	1920	1.5
28 TH	0124	4.5	0748	1.5	1349	4.7	2019	1.1
29 F	0221	4.8	0841	1.2	1438	5.0	2111	0.7
30 SA	0311	5.1	0929	1.0	1522	5.3	2159	0.3
31 SU	0357	5.3	1013	0.8	1606	5.5	2246	0.1

FEBRUARY

Day	Time	m	Time	m	Time	m	Time	m
1 M	0442	5.3	1056	0.7	1649	5.6	2330	0.1
2 TU	0526	5.2	1137	0.8	1733	5.5		
3 W	0014	0.3	0610	5.1	1217	0.9	1818	5.4
4 TH	0057	0.6	0655	4.8	1259	1.1	1906	5.1
5 F	0140	1.0	0743	4.5	1344	1.4	2000	4.7
6 SA	0229	1.4	0837	4.3	1440	1.8	2104	4.3
7 SU	0328	1.8	0940	4.1	1558	2.0	2221	4.1
8 M	0445	2.1	1056	3.9	1737	2.0	2350	4.0
9 TU	0613	2.1	1217	4.0	1904	1.9		
10 W	0106	4.1	0721	2.0	1321	4.2	2000	1.6
11 TH	0202	4.3	0809	1.8	1409	4.5	2042	1.4
12 F	0243	4.4	0846	1.6	1447	4.7	2116	1.2
13 SA	0318	4.6	0919	1.4	1519	4.8	2147	1.0
14 SU	0348	4.7	0950	1.2	1548	4.9	2217	0.9
15 M	0417	4.7	1019	1.1	1617	5.0	2246	0.8
16 TU	0446	4.8	1047	1.1	1646	5.0	2314	0.8
17 W	0514	4.7	1116	1.1	1716	5.0	2343	0.9
18 TH	0544	4.7	1145	1.2	1747	4.9		
19 F	0013	1.0	0614	4.6	1217	1.3	1821	4.8
20 SA	0044	1.2	0649	4.4	1251	1.4	1900	4.6
21 SU	0120	1.4	0731	4.3	1335	1.7	1950	4.4
22 M	0208	1.7	0826	4.1	1438	1.9	2056	4.1
23 TU	0321	2.0	0941	3.9	1609	2.0	2226	4.0
24 W	0501	2.0	1112	4.0	1748	1.8		
25 TH	0000	4.2	0630	1.8	1232	4.3	1906	1.4
26 F	0113	4.5	0735	1.5	1332	4.6	2005	0.9
27 SA	0208	4.8	0826	1.2	1420	5.0	2056	0.5
28 SU	0255	5.1	0912	0.9	1504	5.3	2142	0.2

MARCH

Day	Time	m	Time	m	Time	m	Time	m
1 M	0338	5.3	0954	0.7	1546	5.5	2226	0.0
2 TU	0420	5.3	1034	0.6	1628	5.6	2307	0.1
3 W	0500	5.2	1114	0.6	1710	5.5	2347	0.3
4 TH	0541	5.1	1152	0.7	1755	5.3		
5 F	0026	0.6	0622	4.8	1232	1.0	1841	5.0
6 SA	0105	1.1	0705	4.6	1315	1.3	1933	4.6
7 SU	0148	1.5	0754	4.3	1407	1.6	2034	4.2
8 M	0242	2.0	0855	4.0	1520	1.9	2151	3.9
9 TU	0402	2.3	1014	3.8	1706	2.0	2323	3.8
10 W	0544	2.3	1143	3.9	1840	1.9		
11 TH	0044	3.9	0657	2.1	1254	4.1	1935	1.6
12 F	0139	4.2	0745	1.8	1343	4.4	2015	1.3
13 SA	0218	4.4	0822	1.6	1421	4.6	2048	1.1
14 SU	0251	4.5	0854	1.3	1453	4.7	2119	0.9
15 M	0320	4.7	0924	1.1	1522	4.9	2148	0.8
16 TU	0348	4.8	0954	1.0	1550	5.0	2216	0.7
17 W	0416	4.8	1023	0.9	1619	5.0	2245	0.7
18 TH	0444	4.8	1052	0.9	1649	5.0	2314	0.8
19 F	0513	4.8	1122	1.0	1722	4.9	2344	1.0
20 SA	0545	4.7	1155	1.1	1758	4.8		
21 SU	0015	1.2	0620	4.5	1233	1.3	1841	4.6
22 M	0053	1.4	0704	4.4	1320	1.5	1935	4.3
23 TU	0144	1.7	0800	4.1	1426	1.7	2046	4.1
24 W	0302	2.0	0918	4.0	1557	1.7	2218	4.0
25 TH	0445	2.0	1049	4.0	1732	1.5	2347	4.2
26 F	0612	1.8	1209	4.3	1847	1.2		
27 SA	0056	4.5	0715	1.5	1309	4.7	1945	0.8
28 SU	0149	4.8	0805	1.1	1358	5.0	2034	0.4
29 M	0233	5.0	0849	0.8	1441	5.3	2119	0.2
30 TU	0314	5.2	0931	0.6	1524	5.4	2201	0.2
31 W	0354	5.2	1012	0.5	1606	5.5	2241	0.3

APRIL

Day	Time	m	Time	m	Time	m	Time	m
1 TH	0433	5.2	1051	0.6	1649	5.3	2319	0.5
2 F	0512	5.0	1131	0.7	1734	5.1	2356	0.8
3 SA	0552	4.8	1210	0.9	1821	4.8		
4 SU	0033	1.2	0633	4.6	1253	1.2	1911	4.4
5 M	0113	1.6	0719	4.3	1342	1.5	2009	4.1
6 TU	0203	2.0	0816	4.0	1448	1.8	2119	3.8
7 W	0316	2.3	0928	3.9	1619	1.9	2241	3.7
8 TH	0454	2.3	1052	3.8	1751	1.8		
9 F	0001	3.8	0613	2.1	1208	4.0	1851	1.6
10 SA	0059	4.0	0706	1.9	1302	4.2	1934	1.4
11 SU	0140	4.3	0746	1.6	1343	4.4	2010	1.2
12 M	0215	4.5	0821	1.4	1418	4.6	2042	1.0
13 TU	0246	4.6	0854	1.2	1449	4.7	2114	0.9
14 W	0316	4.7	0925	1.0	1520	4.9	2144	0.8
15 TH	0345	4.8	0957	0.9	1553	4.9	2216	0.8
16 F	0415	4.8	1030	0.9	1627	4.9	2248	0.9
17 SA	0447	4.8	1105	0.9	1704	4.9	2321	1.0
18 SU	0523	4.8	1143	0.9	1746	4.7	2358	1.2
19 M	0603	4.6	1226	1.1	1835	4.6		
20 TU	0042	1.5	0650	4.5	1320	1.2	1933	4.3
21 W	0139	1.7	0749	4.3	1427	1.4	2046	4.2
22 TH	0255	1.9	0904	4.2	1549	1.4	2208	4.1
23 F	0426	1.9	1027	4.2	1711	1.3	2326	4.2
24 SA	0544	1.7	1141	4.4	1821	1.0		
25 SU	0030	4.5	0646	1.5	1242	4.7	1918	0.7
26 M	0123	4.7	0739	1.2	1333	4.9	2008	0.6
27 TU	0208	4.9	0825	0.9	1420	5.1	2053	0.5
28 W	0250	5.0	0909	0.7	1504	5.2	2135	0.5
29 TH	0329	5.1	0952	0.6	1548	5.2	2215	0.6
30 F	0408	5.0	1033	0.6	1633	5.1	2253	0.8

Chart Datum: 2·60 metres below Ordnance Datum (Newlyn). HAT is 5·7 metres above Chart Datum; see 4.5.

RIVER TYNE/NORTH SHIELDS   LAT 55°01'N   LONG 1°26'W

TIMES AND HEIGHTS OF HIGH AND LOW WATERS

TIME ZONE (UT)
For Summer Time add ONE hour in **non-shaded areas**

Dates in red are SPRINGS
Dates in blue are NEAPS

YEAR **2010**

MAY

Date	Time m	Time m	Time m	Time m		Date	Time m	Time m	Time m	Time m
1 SA	0447 4.9	1114 0.7	1718 4.9	2330 1.1		16 SU	0428 4.9	1054 0.8	1654 4.9	2308 1.0
2 SU	0527 4.8	1154 0.9	1804 4.6			17 M	0508 4.9	1138 0.8	1741 4.8	2352 1.2
3 M	0006 1.4	0607 4.6	1236 1.1	1851 4.3		18 TU	0553 4.8	1226 0.8	1833 4.6	
4 TU	0046 1.7	0651 4.4	1321 1.4	1944 4.1		19 W	0040 1.4	0643 4.7	1321 0.9	1932 4.5
5 W	0131 1.9	0742 4.2	1416 1.6	2043 3.9		20 TH	0136 1.6	0741 4.5	1423 1.0	2038 4.3
6 TH	0230 2.1	0843 4.0	1524 1.7	2149 3.8		21 F	0242 1.7	0848 4.4	1533 1.1	2148 4.3
7 F	0348 2.2	0953 3.9	1639 1.8	2258 3.8		22 SA	0357 1.8	1000 4.4	1643 1.1	2257 4.3
8 SA	0507 2.1	1103 3.9	1746 1.7			23 SU	0510 1.7	1110 4.5	1750 1.0	
9 SU	0000 3.9	0610 2.0	1205 4.1	1839 1.5		24 M	0000 4.4	0614 1.5	1215 4.6	1849 0.9
10 M	0051 4.1	0700 1.7	1255 4.3	1922 1.3		25 TU	0056 4.6	0713 1.3	1311 4.7	1942 0.9
11 TU	0132 4.3	0741 1.5	1337 4.4	2001 1.2		26 W	0144 4.7	0805 1.1	1403 4.8	2030 0.9
12 W	0208 4.5	0820 1.3	1415 4.6	2038 1.2		27 TH	0228 4.8	0852 0.9	1441 4.9	2113 0.9
13 TH	0242 4.7	0857 1.1	1452 4.7	2114 0.9		28 F	0310 4.9	0937 0.8	1537 4.9	2154 1.0
14 F	0316 4.8	0934 0.9	1530 4.8	2150 0.9		29 SA	0349 4.9	1020 0.8	1621 4.8	2232 1.1
15 SA	0351 4.9	1013 0.8	1611 4.9	2228 0.9		30 SU	0428 4.9	1100 0.8	1705 4.7	2309 1.2
						31 M	0507 4.8	1139 0.9	1747 4.5	2344 1.4

JUNE

Date	Time m	Time m	Time m	Time m		Date	Time m	Time m	Time m	Time m
1 TU	0546 4.7	1218 1.1	1830 4.4			16 W	0544 5.0	1223 0.5	1827 4.8	
2 W	0021 1.6	0626 4.6	1258 1.2	1914 4.2		17 TH	0033 1.2	0632 5.0	1314 0.6	1920 4.7
3 TH	0102 1.7	0710 4.4	1342 1.4	2002 4.0		18 F	0123 1.3	0726 4.9	1409 0.8	2018 4.5
4 F	0148 1.9	0800 4.3	1433 1.5	2055 3.9		19 SA	0219 1.5	0826 4.7	1508 0.9	2119 4.4
5 SA	0245 2.0	0856 4.1	1531 1.7	2153 3.9		20 SU	0323 1.6	0931 4.6	1611 1.1	2223 4.3
6 SU	0352 2.1	0957 4.0	1634 1.7	2253 3.9		21 M	0433 1.7	1040 4.5	1717 1.2	2328 4.3
7 M	0501 2.0	1101 4.0	1735 1.6	2352 4.0		22 TU	0545 1.6	1151 4.5	1823 1.3	
8 TU	0604 1.9	1159 4.1	1830 1.5			23 W	0030 4.4	0652 1.5	1257 4.5	1921 1.3
9 W	0044 4.2	0657 1.7	1254 4.3	1919 1.4		24 TH	0125 4.5	0752 1.3	1354 4.6	2013 1.3
10 TH	0130 4.4	0746 1.4	1343 4.5	2005 1.2		25 F	0213 4.6	0843 1.1	1445 4.6	2058 1.2
11 F	0212 4.6	0831 1.2	1429 4.6	2049 1.1		26 SA	0256 4.8	0929 1.0	1530 4.7	2138 1.2
12 SA	0252 4.8	0915 0.9	1514 4.8	2132 1.0		27 SU	0336 4.8	1009 0.9	1611 4.7	2215 1.2
13 SU	0333 4.9	1000 0.7	1600 4.9	2216 1.0		28 M	0413 4.9	1047 0.9	1650 4.7	2250 1.2
14 M	0414 5.0	1046 0.6	1647 5.0	2301 1.0		29 TU	0448 4.9	1122 0.9	1726 4.6	2323 1.3
15 TU	0457 5.0	1134 0.5	1736 4.9	2346 1.0		30 W	0524 4.8	1156 1.0	1803 4.5	2356 1.4

JULY

Date	Time m	Time m	Time m	Time m		Date	Time m	Time m	Time m	Time m
1 TH	0600 4.7	1231 1.1	1840 4.4			16 F	0017 0.9	0615 5.3	1257 0.4	1858 4.9
2 F	0031 1.5	0638 4.6	1308 1.2	1919 4.2		17 SA	0102 1.1	0705 5.1	1345 0.6	1949 4.6
3 SA	0109 1.6	0719 4.5	1348 1.4	2003 4.1		18 SU	0151 1.3	0800 4.9	1437 1.0	2046 4.4
4 SU	0153 1.8	0804 4.3	1434 1.5	2052 4.0		19 M	0248 1.5	0903 4.6	1537 1.3	2148 4.2
5 M	0245 1.9	0857 4.2	1528 1.7	2148 3.9		20 TU	0359 1.7	1014 4.4	1646 1.6	2257 4.2
6 TU	0351 2.0	0958 4.1	1632 1.8	2251 4.0		21 W	0521 1.8	1133 4.2	1800 1.7	
7 W	0505 2.0	1105 4.1	1740 1.7	2356 4.1		22 TH	0008 4.2	0642 1.7	1249 4.3	1908 1.7
8 TH	0615 1.8	1214 4.2	1843 1.6			23 F	0111 4.4	0747 1.4	1350 4.4	2002 1.6
9 F	0055 4.3	0716 1.6	1318 4.4	1940 1.4		24 SA	0203 4.5	0837 1.2	1439 4.5	2046 1.5
10 SA	0147 4.5	0811 1.2	1412 4.6	2031 1.2		25 SU	0245 4.7	0919 1.1	1520 4.6	2124 1.3
11 SU	0233 4.8	0901 0.9	1501 4.9	2119 1.0		26 M	0322 4.8	0955 0.9	1556 4.7	2157 1.2
12 M	0317 5.0	0949 0.6	1549 5.1	2205 0.9		27 TU	0355 4.9	1028 0.8	1629 4.7	2229 1.2
13 TU	0400 5.2	1036 0.3	1635 5.2	2249 0.8		28 W	0427 5.0	1059 0.8	1701 4.7	2300 1.2
14 W	0443 5.3	1123 0.2	1722 5.2	2333 0.8		29 TH	0459 5.0	1129 0.8	1732 4.6	2330 1.2
15 TH	0528 5.4	1209 0.2	1810 5.0			30 F	0531 4.9	1200 0.9	1804 4.6	
						31 SA	0001 1.3	0604 4.8	1232 1.1	1838 4.4

AUGUST

Date	Time m	Time m	Time m	Time m		Date	Time m	Time m	Time m	Time m
1 SU	0034 1.4	0640 4.7	1306 1.3	1915 4.3		16 M	0123 1.2	0734 4.9	1404 1.2	2010 4.4
2 M	0111 1.6	0720 4.5	1344 1.5	1957 4.2		17 TU	0217 1.5	0837 4.5	1501 1.6	2112 4.2
3 TU	0155 1.8	0807 4.3	1432 1.7	2050 4.0		18 W	0330 1.8	0953 4.2	1615 1.9	2226 4.1
4 W	0254 2.0	0907 4.2	1536 1.9	2157 4.0		19 TH	0504 1.9	1119 4.0	1742 2.0	2346 4.1
5 TH	0415 2.0	1023 4.0	1657 1.9	2313 4.0		20 F	0635 1.7	1240 4.1	1857 1.9	
6 F	0541 1.9	1147 4.1	1817 1.8			21 SA	0056 4.3	0738 1.5	1341 4.3	1949 1.8
7 SA	0026 4.2	0655 1.6	1301 4.4	1922 1.6		22 SU	0148 4.5	0824 1.3	1425 4.5	2030 1.6
8 SU	0126 4.5	0755 1.2	1358 4.7	2016 1.3		23 M	0228 4.7	0901 1.1	1501 4.6	2104 1.4
9 M	0215 4.9	0846 0.7	1447 5.0	2104 1.0		24 TU	0302 4.9	0933 0.9	1533 4.7	2135 1.3
10 TU	0259 5.2	0934 0.4	1533 5.2	2148 0.8		25 W	0333 5.0	1002 0.8	1602 4.8	2205 1.1
11 W	0341 5.4	1020 0.1	1617 5.3	2231 0.6		26 TH	0402 5.0	1031 0.8	1631 4.8	2234 1.1
12 TH	0424 5.6	1105 0.0	1700 5.3	2313 0.6		27 F	0431 5.1	1059 0.8	1700 4.8	2302 1.1
13 F	0507 5.6	1148 0.1	1744 5.2	2354 0.7		28 SA	0501 5.0	1128 0.9	1729 4.7	2332 1.2
14 SA	0553 5.5	1231 0.4	1829 5.0			29 SU	0533 4.9	1157 1.0	1800 4.6	
15 SU	0036 0.9	0641 5.2	1316 0.7	1917 4.7		30 M	0003 1.3	0607 4.8	1228 1.2	1834 4.5
						31 TU	0038 1.5	0645 4.6	1303 1.5	1914 4.3

Chart Datum: 2·60 metres below Ordnance Datum (Newlyn). HAT is 5·7 metres above Chart Datum; see 4.5.

NE England

RIVER TYNE/NORTH SHIELDS

LAT 55°01'N LONG 1°26'W

TIMES AND HEIGHTS OF HIGH AND LOW WATERS

YEAR 2010

TIME ZONE (UT)
For Summer Time add ONE hour in **non-shaded areas**

Dates in red are **SPRINGS**
Dates in blue are NEAPS

SEPTEMBER

Time	m		Time	m
1 0120	1.7	**16**	0305	1.8
0732	4.4		0931	4.0
W 1347	1.7	TH 1542	2.2
☽ 2005	4.2		2152	4.0
2 0219	1.9	**17**	0444	1.9
0834	4.1		1059	3.9
TH 1453	2.0	F 1718	2.3
2114	4.0		2318	4.1
3 0343	2.0	**18**	0616	1.8
0958	4.0		1221	4.1
F 1627	2.1	SA 1835	2.1
2240	4.0		
4 0518	1.8	**19**	0030	4.2
1130	4.1		0715	1.6
SA 1758	1.9	SU 1318	4.3
			1925	1.9
5 0001	4.3	**20**	0123	4.5
0636	1.5		0757	1.3
SU 1245	4.4	M 1400	4.5
1905	1.6		2004	1.6
6 0104	4.6	**21**	0202	4.7
0736	1.0		0831	1.1
M 1341	4.8	TU 1434	4.6
1958	1.3		2037	1.4
7 0153	5.0	**22**	0235	4.9
0827	0.6		0902	1.0
TU 1428	5.1	W 1504	4.8
2044	1.0		2108	1.2
8 0237	5.3	**23**	0305	5.0
0914	0.3		0931	0.9
W 1511	5.3	TH 1532	4.9
● 2127	0.7	○ 2138	1.1
9 0319	5.6	**24**	0334	5.1
0958	0.1		0959	0.8
TH 1553	5.4	F 1600	4.9
2208	0.6		2207	1.0
10 0401	5.7	**25**	0403	5.1
1041	0.0		1027	0.8
F 1634	5.4	SA 1628	4.9
2249	0.6		2236	1.0
11 0444	5.7	**26**	0434	5.0
1122	0.2		1056	0.9
SA 1716	5.3	SU 1657	4.9
2330	0.7		2307	1.1
12 0530	5.5	**27**	0506	4.9
1203	0.5		1126	1.1
SU 1759	5.0	M 1728	4.8
			2339	1.2
13 0012	0.9	**28**	0542	4.8
0618	5.2		1157	1.3
M 1245	1.0	TU 1803	4.6
1843	4.8		
14 0058	1.2	**29**	0016	1.4
0711	4.8		0622	4.6
TU 1330	1.4	W 1233	1.5
1934	4.5		1843	4.5
15 0152	1.5	**30**	0101	1.6
0815	4.4		0713	4.4
W 1425	1.9	TH 1319	1.8
☽ 2036	4.2		1936	4.3

OCTOBER

Time	m		Time	m
1 0202	1.8	**16**	0405	1.9
0819	4.2		1022	3.9
F 1429	2.1	SA 1633	2.4
☽ 2047	4.1		2232	4.1
2 0326	1.8	**17**	0532	1.9
0944	4.1		1140	4.0
SA 1605	2.2	SU 1752	2.2
2214	4.1		2347	4.2
3 0458	1.7	**18**	0634	1.7
1112	4.2		1239	4.2
SU 1735	2.0	M 1848	2.0
2334	4.4		
4 0614	1.3	**19**	0043	4.4
1223	4.5		0718	1.5
M 1842	1.7	TU 1323	4.4
			1929	1.7
5 0037	4.7	**20**	0126	4.6
0713	0.9		0754	1.3
TU 1319	4.8	W 1359	4.6
1934	1.3		2005	1.5
6 0128	5.1	**21**	0202	4.7
0803	0.6		0826	1.1
W 1405	5.1	TH 1431	4.7
2020	1.0		2038	1.3
7 0213	5.4	**22**	0234	4.9
0849	0.3		0857	1.0
TH 1447	5.3	F 1501	4.9
● 2103	0.8		2110	1.2
8 0256	5.6	**23**	0306	5.0
0933	0.2		0927	1.0
F 1527	5.4	SA 1530	4.9
2146	0.6	○ 2141	1.1
9 0339	5.6	**24**	0338	5.0
1015	0.3		0958	1.0
SA 1608	5.4	SU 1600	5.0
2228	0.6		2214	1.1
10 0424	5.6	**25**	0411	5.0
1056	0.5		1029	1.0
SU 1648	5.3	M 1630	5.0
2310	0.7		2248	1.1
11 0510	5.3	**26**	0446	4.9
1135	0.8		1101	1.2
M 1730	5.1	TU 1704	4.9
2353	0.9		2324	1.1
12 0559	5.0	**27**	0526	4.8
1216	1.2		1136	1.3
TU 1814	4.8	W 1741	4.8
13 0039	1.2	**28**	0006	1.3
0652	4.6		0611	4.7
W 1259	1.7	TH 1217	1.6
1902	4.6		1825	4.6
14 0131	1.5	**29**	0055	1.4
0753	4.3		0704	4.5
TH 1350	2.0	F 1308	1.8
☽ 2000	4.3		1919	4.5
15 0238	1.8	**30**	0156	1.5
0903	4.0		0811	4.3
F 1501	2.3	SA 1415	2.0
2112	4.1	☽ 2027	4.3
		31	0312	1.6
			0929	4.2
		SU 1541	2.1
			2146	4.3

NOVEMBER

Time	m		Time	m
1 0433	1.5	**16**	0528	1.8
1047	4.3		1142	4.1
M 1704	2.0	TU 1751	2.2
2302	4.5		2348	4.2
2 0544	1.2	**17**	0624	1.7
1155	4.5		1235	4.2
TU 1811	1.7	W 1844	1.9
3 0007	4.8	**18**	0040	4.4
0645	1.0		0708	1.5
W 1252	4.8	TH 1318	4.4
1906	1.4		1927	1.7
4 0102	5.0	**19**	0124	4.5
0737	0.8		0747	1.4
TH 1340	5.0	F 1356	4.6
1956	1.1		2006	1.5
5 0151	5.2	**20**	0203	4.7
0825	0.6		0823	1.3
F 1423	5.2	SA 1430	4.8
2043	0.9		2043	1.3
6 0238	5.4	**21**	0240	4.8
0909	0.6		0858	1.2
SA 1505	5.3	SU 1503	4.9
● 2128	0.8	○ 2119	1.2
7 0323	5.4	**22**	0317	4.9
0952	0.7		0933	1.1
SU 1545	5.4	M 1536	5.0
2212	0.7		2156	1.1
8 0410	5.3	**23**	0354	5.0
1033	0.9		1009	1.1
M 1626	5.2	TU 1611	5.0
2255	0.8		2235	1.0
9 0457	5.1	**24**	0435	5.0
1112	1.1		1047	1.2
TU 1707	5.1	W 1648	5.0
2338	1.0		2317	1.0
10 0545	4.9	**25**	0518	4.9
1151	1.4		1127	1.3
W 1750	4.9	TH 1729	5.0
11 0022	1.2	**26**	0002	1.0
0634	4.6		0605	4.8
TH 1232	1.7	F 1211	1.5
1835	4.7		1814	4.9
12 0110	1.4	**27**	0052	1.1
0727	4.3		0658	4.6
F 1317	2.0	SA 1301	1.7
1925	4.4		1906	4.7
13 0204	1.7	**28**	0148	1.2
0825	4.1		0758	4.5
SA 1412	2.2	SU 1359	1.8
☽ 2025	4.2	☽ 2007	4.6
14 0308	1.8	**29**	0252	1.3
0930	4.0		0906	4.4
SU 1525	2.3	M 1509	1.9
2134	4.1		2116	4.6
15 0421	1.9	**30**	0402	1.3
1038	3.9		1015	4.4
M 1644	2.3	TU 1625	1.9
2244	4.1		2228	4.6

DECEMBER

Time	m		Time	m
1 0511	1.3	**16**	0516	1.9
1123	4.5		1134	4.0
W 1736	1.8	TH 1746	2.1
2337	4.7		2344	4.2
2 0615	1.2	**17**	0616	1.8
1223	4.6		1231	4.2
TH 1840	1.6	F 1845	2.0
3 0040	4.8	**18**	0042	4.3
0713	1.1		0707	1.7
F 1317	4.8	SA 1319	4.4
1937	1.3		1935	1.7
4 0136	5.0	**19**	0133	4.5
0805	1.0		0753	1.5
SA 1405	4.9	SU 1402	4.6
2029	1.1		2019	1.5
5 0228	5.1	**20**	0218	4.6
0851	1.0		0835	1.4
SU 1448	5.1	M 1440	4.8
● 2117	1.0		2101	1.2
6 0316	5.1	**21**	0301	4.8
0935	1.1		0916	1.2
M 1530	5.1	TU 1518	5.0
2202	0.9	○ 2143	1.0
7 0402	5.0	**22**	0343	5.0
1015	1.1		0956	1.1
TU 1610	5.1	W 1556	5.1
2245	0.9		2226	0.8
8 0446	4.9	**23**	0425	5.0
1054	1.3		1038	1.1
W 1650	5.1	TH 1636	5.2
2326	1.0		2310	0.7
9 0530	4.8	**24**	0510	5.0
1131	1.4		1120	1.1
TH 1729	5.0	F 1717	5.2
			2355	0.7
10 0005	1.1	**25**	0556	5.0
0612	4.6		1203	1.2
F 1207	1.6	SA 1802	5.1
1809	4.8		
11 0045	1.3	**26**	0042	0.7
0656	4.4		0644	4.8
SA 1245	1.8	SU 1248	1.4
1852	4.6		1850	5.1
12 0126	1.5	**27**	0132	0.9
0742	4.2		0737	4.7
SU 1327	2.0	M 1338	1.5
1939	4.4		1944	4.9
13 0213	1.7	**28**	0227	1.1
0833	4.1		0836	4.5
M 1419	2.1	TU 1435	1.7
☽ 2033	4.3	☽ 2046	4.7
14 0308	1.8	**29**	0328	1.3
0930	4.0		0940	4.4
TU 1523	2.2	W 1545	1.8
2134	4.2		2156	4.6
15 0411	1.9	**30**	0436	1.4
1032	4.0		1048	4.3
W 1637	2.3	TH 1703	1.8
2239	4.1		2311	4.5
		31	0547	1.5
			1156	4.4
		F 1819	1.7

Chart Datum: 2·60 metres below Ordnance Datum (Newlyn). HAT is 5·7 metres above Chart Datum; see 4.5.

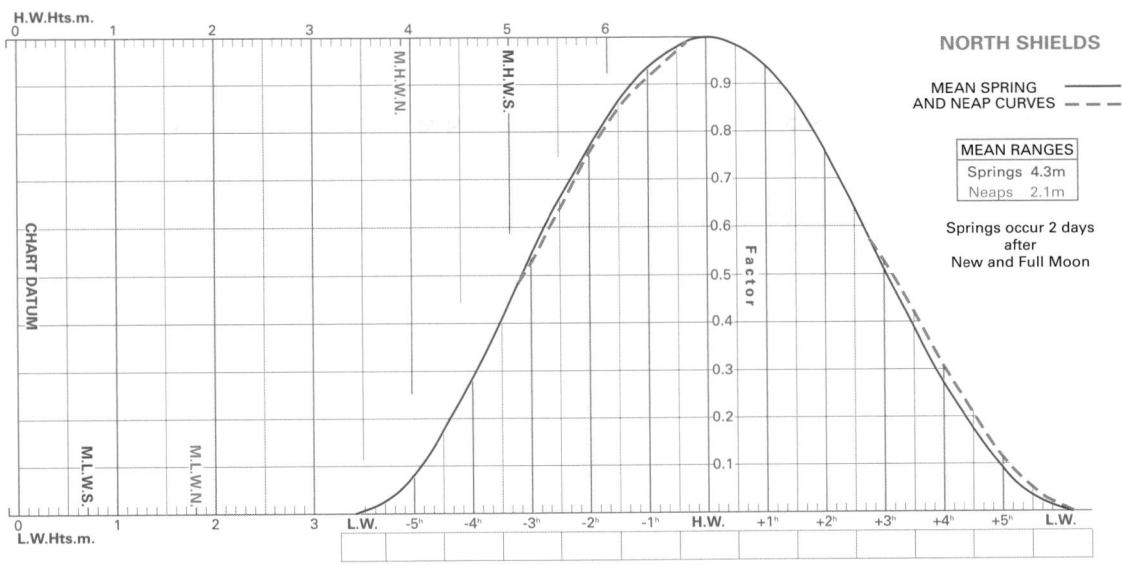

NORTH SHIELDS

MEAN SPRING ———
AND NEAP CURVES - - - - -

MEAN RANGES
Springs 4.3m
Neaps 2.1m

Springs occur 2 days after
New and Full Moon

9.5.18 BLYTH

Northumberland **55°06'·98N 01° 29'·27W** ❀❀❀♦♦✿✿

CHARTS AC 152, 156, 1626; Imray C24.

TIDES +0430 Dover; ML 2·8; Duration 0558

Standard Port NORTH SHIELDS (←—)

Times				Height (metres)			
High Water		Low Water		MHWS	MHWN	MLWN	MLWS
0200	0800	0100	0800	5·0	3·9	1·8	0·7
1400	2000	1300	2000				
Differences BLYTH							
+0005	−0007	−0001	+0009	0·0	0·0	−0·1	+0·1

SHELTER Very good. Access H24 but at LW in strong SE winds, seas break across ent.

NAVIGATION WPT Fairway SHM buoy, Fl G 3s, Bell, 55°06'·58N 01°28'·60W, 320°/0·53M to E pier lt. From N, beware The Pigs, The Sow and Seaton Sea Rks and 2 wind turbines on North Spit (1·2M N of hbr ent) centred on 55°08'·16N 01°29'·41W. No dangers from S. See RNYC Sailing Directions, £28·75 inc P&P, from RNYC, House Yacht Tyne, S Hbr, Blyth NE24 3PB (see website below).

LIGHTS AND MARKS 9 wind turbines are conspic on E pier also Blyth E Pier Hd, W twr on S end. Outer ldg lts 324°, Or ◊ on framework trs. Inner ldg lts 338°, front W 6-sided tr; rear W △ on mast. See chartlet and 9.5.4 for lt details.

R/T Call: *Blyth Hbr Control* Ch **12** 11 (H24) for clearance to enter or depart.

TELEPHONE (Code 01670) Port HM 352678; MRCC 01262 672317; Marinecall 09068 969643; Police (01661) 872555.

FACILITIES **R Northumberland YC** ☎ 353636, www.rnyc.org.uk hon.sec@rnyc.org.uk In SE part of South Hbr, E side of Middle Jetty, Ⓥ berth on N side of RNYC pontoons in 4·4m least depth. 75 AB £1.50, D (cans), C (1½ ton for trailer sailers), BH (20 ton), ME (www.millermarine.co.uk), Bar. **South Hbr** ☎ 352678, FW, C (50 ton). **Town** @ Town Library (HO), P (cans), D (07836 677730), 🛒, R, Bar, ✉, Ⓑ, Gas, Gaz, bus to Newcastle ⇌, ✈.

ADJACENT ANCHORAGE

NEWBIGGIN, Northumberland, **55°10'·75N 01°30'·10W**. AC 156. Tides approx as for Blyth, 3·5M to the S. Temp, fair weather

⚓ in about 4m in centre of the bay, off the the conspic sculptures on the breakwater; sheltered from SW to N winds. Caution: offlying rky ledges to N and S. Conspic church on N side of bay; bkwtr lt Fl G 10s 4M. Facilities: **SC** (dinghies). **Town** 🛒, R, Bar.

9.5.19 AMBLE

Northumberland **55°20'·37N 01°34'·25W** ✿⊛♦♦♦✿✿

CHARTS AC 156, 1627; Imray C24.

TIDES +0412 Dover; ML 3·1; Duration 0606

Standard Port NORTH SHIELDS (←—)

Times				Height (metres)			
High Water		Low Water		MHWS	MHWN	MLWN	MLWS
0200	0800	0100	0800	5·0	3·9	1·8	0·7
1400	2000	1300	2000				
Differences AMBLE							
–0013	–0013	–0016	–0020	0·0	0·0	+0·1	+0·1
COQUET ISLAND							
–0010	–0010	–0020	–0020	+0·1	+0·1	0·0	+0·1

SHELTER The Hbr (alias Warkworth Hbr) is safe in all winds. But ent is dangerous in strong N to E winds or in swell, when heavy seas break on Pan Bush shoal and on the bar at hbr ent, where least depth is 0·8m. ⚓ in Coquet Road or NNE of North Pier.

NAVIGATION WPT 55°21'·00N 01°33'·10W, 225° to hbr ent, 0·9M. Ent recommended from NE, passing N and W of Pan Bush. The S-going stream sets strongly across ent. Once inside the N bkwtr, beware drying banks to stbd, ie on N side of channel;

keep close (15m) to S quays. 4kn speed limit in hbr.

- In NE'ly gales broken water can extend to Coquet Island, keep E of island and go to Blyth where appr/ent may be safer.
- Coquet Chan (min depth 0·3m) is not buoyed and is only advised with caution, by day, in good vis/weather, slight sea state and with adequate rise of tide, ie HW–2.

LIGHTS AND MARKS Coquet Island lt ho, (conspic) W□tr, turreted parapet, lower half grey. Sector boundaries are indeterminate and may appear as Al WR. Horn 30s. See chartlet and 9.5.4.

R/T Amble Marina Ch **80** (7/7, 0900-1700). HM Ch 16, works Ch 14 (Mon-Fri 0900-1700 LT). Coquet YC Ch M (occas).

TELEPHONE (Code 01665) HM ☎ 710306; MRCC (01262) 672317; local CG 710575; Police (01661) 872555; Marinecall 09068 969643; Ⓗ (01670) 521212.

FACILITIES Amble Marina is about 5ca from hbr ent. Tidal gauge shows depth over sill; access approx HW±4 between PHM buoy and ECM bn, both unlit. Pontoons are 'A' to 'F' from sill; Ⓥ berth on 'B' initially. 200+40 Ⓥ, £2·20. ☎ 712168, marina@amble.co.uk, BY, C, D, BH (50 ton), ME, El, ⚒, Ⓔ, SM, R, Bar, 🛒, CH, ⬚, ♿, Gas, Gaz. **Hbr** D, AB. **Coquet YC** ☎ 711179 Slip, Bar, M, FW, L.

Town 🛒, R, Bar, ✉, ⇌ (Alnmouth), ✈ (Newcastle).

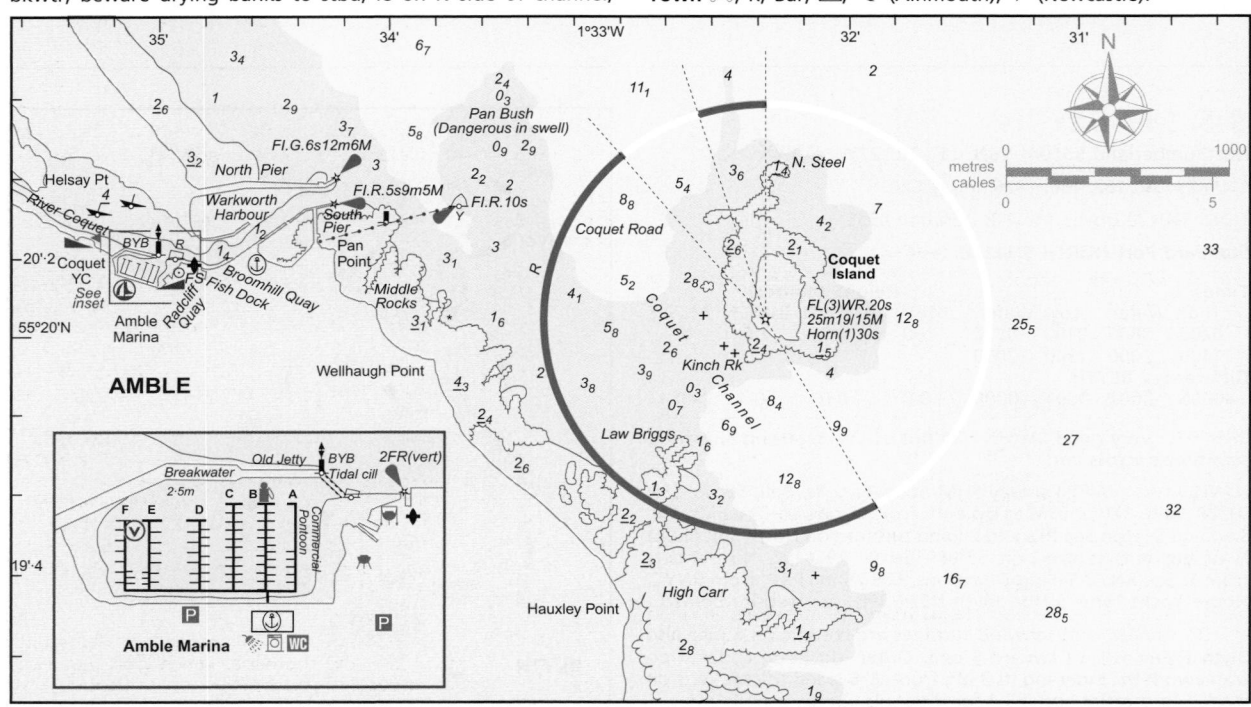

HBRS AND ANCHORAGES BETWEEN AMBLE AND HOLY ISLAND

BOULMER, Northumberland, **55°25'·00N 01°33'·90W**. AC 156. Tides approx as for Amble, 4·6M to the S. A small haven almost enclosed by N and S Rheins, rky ledges either side of the narrow (30m) ent, Marmouth; only advised in settled offshore weather. 2 FW bns (lit when req'd by LB or FVs) lead approx 257° through the ent, leaving close to stbd a bn on N Rheins. ⚓ just inside in about 1·5m or dry out on sand at the N end. Few facilities: Pub, ✉ in village. Alnwick is 4M inland.

CRASTER, Northumberland, **55°28'·40N 01°35'·30W**. AC 156. Tidal differences: interpolate between Amble (9.5.19) and N Sunderland (9.5.20). Strictly a fair weather ⚓ in offshore winds, 1M S of the conspic Dunstanburgh Castle (ru). The ent, 40m wide, is N of Muckle Carr and S of Little Carr which partly covers and has a bn on its S end. ⚓ in about 3·5m just inshore of these 2 rocky outcrops; or berth at the E pier on rk/sand inside the tiny drying hbr. Facilities: 🛒, R, Bar.

NEWTON HAVEN and BEADNELL BAY, Northumberland, **55°30'·90N 01° 36'·70W**. AC 156. HW +0342 on Dover; Tidal differences: interpolate between Amble (9.5.19) and N Sunderland (9.5.20). ML 2·6m; Duration 0625. A safe ⚓ in winds from NNW to SE via S but susceptible to swell. Ent to S of Newton PHM buoy and Newton Pt. Beware Fills Rks. ⚓ between Fills Rks and Low Newton by the Sea in 4/5m. A very attractive ⚓ with no lts, marks or facilities except a pub. Further ⚓ S of Beadnell Pt (1M N of Newton Pt) in 4–6m; small, fishing hbr whose wall is newly rebuilt; Beadnell SC. Village 0·5M.

SEAHOUSES (North Sunderland), Northumberland, **55°35'·04N 01°38'·91W**. AC 1612. HW +0340 on Dover; ML No data; Duration 0618. See 9.5.20. Good shelter except in on-shore winds when swell makes outer hbr berths (0·7m) very uncomfortable and dangerous. Access HW±3. Inner hbr has excellent berths but usually full of FVs. Beware The Tumblers (rks) to the W of ent and rks protruding NE from bkwtr hd Fl R 2·5s 6m; NW pier hd

FG 11m 3M; vis 159°-294°, on W tr; traffic sigs; Siren 90s when vessels expected. Good facilities. When it is dangerous to enter, a ● is shown over the FG lt (or R flag over a Bu flag) on NW pier hd.

FARNE ISLANDS, Northumberland, **55°37′·15N 01°39′·37W**. AC 160, 156, 111. HW +0345 on Dover; ML 2·6m; Duration 0630. See 9.5.20. The islands are a NT nature reserve in a beautiful area; they should only be attempted in good weather. Landing is only allowed on Farne Is, Staple Is and Longstone. In the inner group, ⚓ in The Kettle on the NE side of Inner Farne; near the Bridges (connecting Knocks Reef to West Wideopen); or to the S of West Wideopen. In the outer group, ⚓ in Pinnacle Haven (between Staple Is/Brownsman). Beware turbulence over Knivestone and Whirl Rks and eddy S of Longstone during NW tidal streams. Lts and marks: Black Rocks Pt, Oc (2) WRG 8s 12m 14/11M;122°-G-165°-W-175°-R-191°-W-238°-R-275°-W-289°-G-300°. Bamburgh Castle is conspic 6ca to the SE. Farne Is lt ho at SW Pt, Fl (2) WR 15s

27m 8/6M; W ○ tr; 119°-R-280°-W-119°. Longstone Fl 20s 23m 24M, R tr with W band (conspic), RC, horn (2) 60s. Caution: reefs extend about 7ca seaward. No facilities.

NATIONAL NATURE RESERVE (Holy Island) A National Nature Reserve (NNR) extends from Budle Bay (**55°37′N 01°45′W**, close to Black Rocks Point lt ho) along the coast to Cheswick Black Rocks, 3M SE of Berwick-upon-Tweed. The NNR extends seaward from the HW shoreline to the drying line; it includes Holy Island and the adjacent islets.

Visiting craft are asked to respect two constraints:

- Landing is prohibited on the small island of Black Law (55°39′·68N 01°47′·50W) from April to August inclusive.
- Boats should not be landed or recovered anywhere in the NNR except at the designated and buoyed watersports zone on the SE side of Budle Bay.

COQUET ISLAND TO FARNE ISLANDS

(Chart 156) Coquet Is (lt, fog sig) lies about 5ca offshore at SE end of Alnmouth B, and nearly 1M NNE of Hauxley Pt, off which dangerous rks extend 6ca offshore, drying 1·9m. On passage, normally pass 1M E of Coquet Is in the W sector of the lt. Coquet chan may be used in good vis by day; but it is only 2ca wide, not buoyed, has least depth of 0·9m near the centre. ▶*The stream runs strongly: S-going from HW Tyne –0515 and N-going from HW Tyne + 0045.* ◀ In S or W winds, there are good anchs in Coquet Road, W and NW of the Island.

Amble (Warkworth) Hbr ent is about 1M W of Coquet Is, and 1·5M SE of Warkworth Castle (conspic). 4ca NE and ENE of ent is Pan Bush, rky shoal with least depth of 0·9m on which dangerous seas can build in any swell. The bar has varying depths, down to less than 1m. The entrance is dangerous in strong winds from N/E when broken water may extend to Coquet Is. Once inside, the hbr is safe.

Between Coquet Is and the Farne Is, 19M to N, keep at least 1M offshore to avoid various dangers. To seaward, Craster Skeres lie 5M E of Castle Pt, and Dicky Shad and Newton Skere lie 1·75M and 4·5M E of Beadnell Pt; these are three rky banks on which the sea breaks heavily in bad weather.

FARNE ISLANDS

(Charts 111, 160) The coast between N Sunderland Pt (Snook) and Holy Island, 8M NW, has fine hill (Cheviots) scenery fronted by dunes and sandy beaches. The Farne Is and offlying shoals extend 4·5M offshore, and are a mini-cruising ground well worth visiting in good weather. The islands are a bird sanctuary, owned and operated by the National Trust, with large colonies of sea birds and grey seals. The R Northumberland YC's Sailing Directions (see 9.5.18) are useful; AC 111 is essential.

Inner Sound separates the islands from the mainland. In good conditions it is a better N/S route than keeping outside the whole group; but the stream runs at 3kn at sp, and with strong wind against tide there is rough water. If course is set outside Farne Is, pass 1M E of Longstone (lt, fog sig) to clear Crumstone

Rk 1M to S, and Knivestone (dries 3·6m) and Whirl Rks (depth 0·6m) respectively 5 and 6ca NE of Longstone lt ho. The sea breaks on these rks.

The islands, rks and shoals are divided by Staple Sound, running NW/SE, into an inner and outer group. The former comprises Inner Farne, W and E Wideopens and Knock's Reef. Inner Farne (lt) is the innermost Is; close NE there is anch called The Kettle, sheltered except from NW, but anch out of stream close to The Bridges connecting Knock's Reef and W Wideopen. 1M NW of Inner Farne Is and separated by Farne Sound, which runs NE/SW, lies the Megstone, a rk 5m high. Beware Swedman reef (dries 0·5m), marked by SHM buoy 4ca WSW of Megstone.

The outer group of Islands comprises Staple and Brownsman Islands, N and S Wamses, the Harcars and Longstone. There is occas anch between Staple and Brownsman Is. ▶ *Piper Gut and Crafords Gut may be negotiated in calm weather and near HW, stemming the S-going stream.* ◀

HOLY ISLAND TO BERWICK

(Charts 1612, 111, 160) ▶ *Near the Farne Is and Holy Is the SE-going stream begins at HW Tyne –0430, and the NW-going at HW Tyne +0130. Sp rates are about 2.5kn in Inner Sound, 4kn in Staple Sound and about 3.5kn 1M NE of Longstone, decreasing to seaward. There is an eddy S of Longstone on NW-going stream.* ◀

Holy Is (or Lindisfarne) lies 6M WNW of Longstone, and is linked to mainland by a causeway covered at HW. There is a good anch on S side (chart 1612) with conspic daymarks and dir lts. The castle and a W obelisk at Emmanuel Head are also conspic. ▶ *The stream runs strongly in and out of hbr, W-going from HW Tyne + 0510, and E-going from HW Tyne –0045. E of Holy Is, Goldstone chan runs N/S between Goldstone Rk (dries) SHM buoy on E side and Plough Seat Reef and Plough Rk (both dry) on W side, with PHM buoy.* ◀

Berwick Bay has some offlying shoals. Berwick-upon-Tweed is easily visible against the low shoreline, which rises again to high cliffs further north. The hbr entrance is restricted by a shallow bar, dangerous in onshore winds.

9.5.20 HOLY ISLAND

Northumberland 55°39′·57N 01°46′·81W ✿✿◐△✿✿✿✿

TIDES +0344 Dover; ML No data; Duration 0630

Standard Port NORTH SHIELDS (←—)

Times				Height (metres)			
High Water		Low Water		MHWS	MHWN	MLWN	MLWS
0200	0800	0100	0800	5·0	3·9	1·8	0·7
1400	2000	1300	2000				
Differences HOLY ISLAND							
–0043	–0039	–0105	–0110	–0·2	–0·2	–0·3	–0·1
NORTH SUNDERLAND (Seahouses)							
–0048	–0044	–0058	–0102	–0·2	–0·2	–0·2	0·0

CHARTS AC 111, 1612; Imray C24.

SHELTER Good S of The Heugh in 3-6m, but ⚓ is uncomfortable in fresh W/SW winds esp at sp flood, and foul in places; trip-line advised. Better shelter in The Ouse on sand/mud if able to dry out; but not in S/SE winds. For detailed information for trailer sailers see www.dca.uk.com.

NAVIGATION WPT 55°39′·76N 01°44′·88W, 260°/1·55M to Old Law E bn. From N identify Emmanuel Hd, conspic W △ bn, then appr via Goldstone Chan leaving Plough Seat PHM buoy to stbd. From S, clear Farne Is thence to WPT. Outer ldg bns lead 260° close past Ridge ECM and Triton SHM buoys. Possible overfalls in chan across bar (1·6m) with sp ebb up to 4kn. Inner ldg marks lead 310° to ⚓. Inshore route, round Castle Pt via Hole Mouth and The Yares, may be more sheltered, but is not for strangers.

Continued overleaf

HOLY ISLAND *continued*

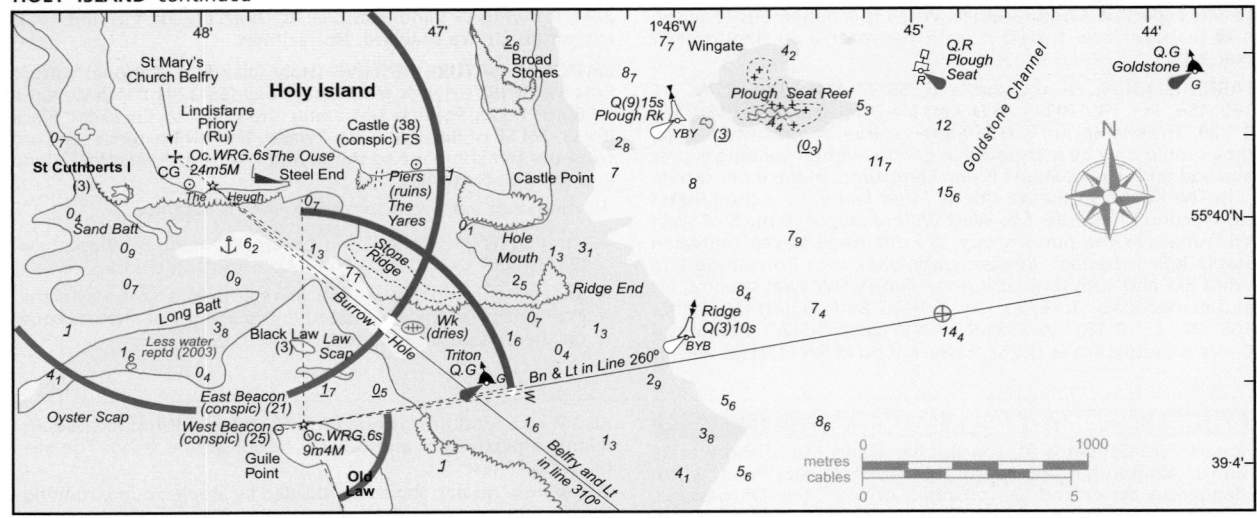

LIGHTS AND MARKS See 9.5.4 and chartlet. Outer leading marks/lts are Old Law beacons (conspic), 2 reddish obelisks 21/25m on 260°; E beacon has directional light, Oc WRG 6s. Inner leading marks/lights are The Heugh tower, B △, on with St Mary's church belfry 310°. The Heugh has directional light, Oc WRG 6s. Directional lights Oc WRG are aligned on 263° and 309·5° respectively.

R/T None.

TELEPHONE (Code 01289) HM 389248; MRCC 01262 672317; Marinecall 09068 969643.

FACILITIES Limited. FW on village green, Slip (contact HM prior to launching) £2/day or £5/week, R, Bar, limited 🍴, P & D from Beal (5M); bus (occas) to Berwick. Note Lindisfarne is ancient name; Benedictine Abbey (ruins) and Castle (NT) are worth visiting. Causeway to mainland, covers at HW, is useable by vehicles approx HW+3½ to HW-2.

9.5.21 BERWICK-UPON-TWEED

Northumberland 55°45'·87N 01°59'·05W ❀❀🐚🐚🏵🏵

CHARTS AC 111, 160, 1612; Imray C24.

TIDES +0348 Dover; ML 2·5; Duration 0620

Standard Port NORTH SHIELDS (◄—)

Times				Height (metres)			
High Water		Low Water		MHWS	MHWN	MLWN	MLWS
0200	0800	0100	0800	5·0	3·9	1·8	0·7
1400	2000	1300	2000				
Differences BERWICK-UPON-TWEED							
−0053	−0053	−0109	−0109	−0·3	−0·1	−0·5	−0·1

SHELTER Good shelter or ⚓ except in strong E/SE winds. AB may be available in Tweed Dock (no dock gates) which is primarily used by commercial shipping. If possible contact HM beforehand to avoid disappointment. Alternative temporary AB possible at W end of Fish Jetty (1·2m).

NAVIGATION WPT 55°45'·62N 01°58'·0W, 294°/0·65M to breakwater lighthouse.

- On-shore winds and ebb tides cause very confused seas over the bar (0·6m). Access HW±4 at springs. From HW−2 to HW+1 strong flood tide sets S across the entrance; keep well up to breakwater.
- The sands at the mouth of the Tweed shift so frequently that local knowledge is essential to enter the harbour.

Town Hall Spire and Lt ho in line at 294°. Keep close to breakwater to avoid Sandstell Point. When past PHM buoy and S of Crabwater Rk, keep Spittal Bns (Or ▽ on B Or Bn) in line brg 207°; best water may be further W. Berwick Bridge (first/lowest) has about 3m clearance.

LIGHTS AND MARKS See 9.5.4 and chartlet.

R/T HM VHF Ch 12 16 (0800-1700).

TELEPHONE (Code 01289) HM 307404; MRCC 01333 450666; Marinecall 09068 969643/236; Police 01661 872555; Dr 307484.

FACILITIES **Tweed Dock** ☎ 307404, AB £8.00, M, P(cans), D(cans), FW, Showers, ME, El, 🔧, C (Mobile 3 ton), Slip, SM. **Town** P, 🍴, R, Bar, ✉, Ⓑ, ⇌ and ✈ (Newcastle or Edinburgh).

ADLARD COLES NAUTICAL
WEATHER FORECASTS
BY FAX & TELEPHONE

Coastal/Inshore	2-day by Fax	5-day by Phone
East	09065 222 344	09068 969 644
North East	09065 222 343	09068 969 643
Scotland East	09065 222 342	09068 969 642
Scotland North	09065 222 341	09068 969 641
National (3-5 day)	09065 222 340	09068 969 640

Offshore	2-5 day by Fax	2-5 day by Phone
English Channel	09065 222 357	09068 969 657
Southern North Sea	09065 222 358	09068 969 658
Northern North Sea	09065 222 362	09068 969 662
North West Scotland	09065 222 361	09068 969 661

09068 CALLS COST 60P PER MIN. 09065 CALLS COST £1.50 PER MIN.

South East Scotland

Eyemouth to Rattray Head

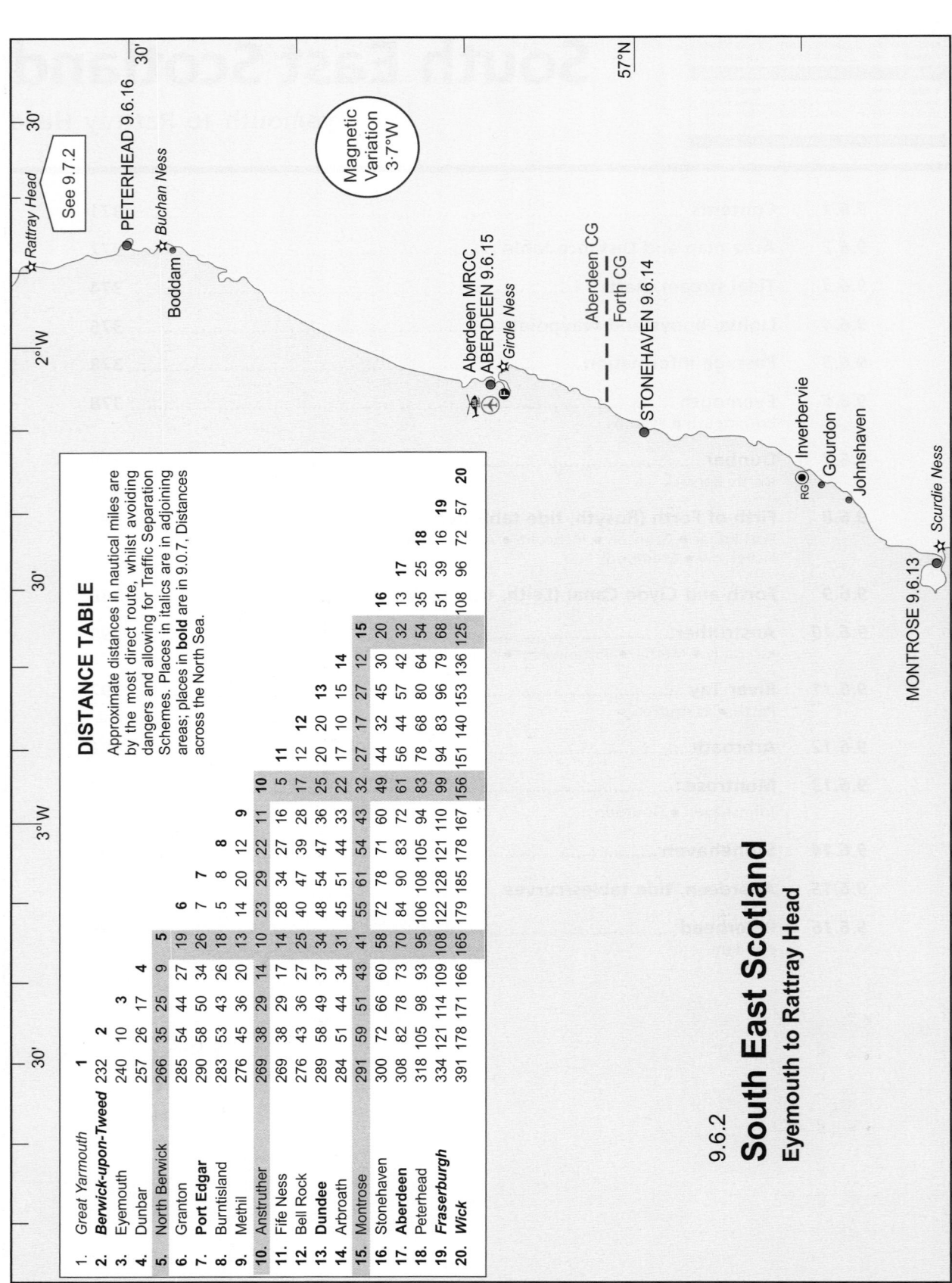

DISTANCE TABLE

Approximate distances in nautical miles are by the most direct route, whilst avoiding dangers and allowing for Traffic Separation Schemes. Places in italics are in adjoining areas; places in **bold** are in 9.0.7. Distances across the North Sea.

		1	2	3	4	5	6	7	8	9	10	11	12	13	14	15	16	17	18	19	20
1.	*Great Yarmouth*	**1**																			
2.	*Berwick-upon-Tweed*	232	**2**																		
3.	Eyemouth	240	10	**3**																	
4.	Dunbar	257	26	17	**4**																
5.	North Berwick	266	35	25	9	**5**															
6.	Granton	285	54	44	27	19	**6**														
7.	**Port Edgar**	290	58	50	34	26	7	**7**													
8.	Burntisland	283	53	43	26	18	5	8	**8**												
9.	Methil	276	45	36	20	13	14	20	12	**9**											
10.	Anstruther	269	38	29	14	10	23	29	22	11	**10**										
11.	Fife Ness	269	38	29	17	14	28	34	27	16	5	**11**									
12.	Bell Rock	276	43	36	27	25	40	47	39	28	17	12	**12**								
13.	**Dundee**	289	58	49	37	34	48	54	47	36	25	20	20	**13**							
14.	Arbroath	284	51	44	34	31	45	51	44	33	22	17	10	15	**14**						
15.	Montrose	291	59	51	43	41	55	61	54	43	32	27	17	27	12	**15**					
16.	Stonehaven	300	72	66	60	58	72	78	71	60	49	44	32	45	30	20	**16**				
17.	**Aberdeen**	308	82	78	73	70	84	90	83	72	61	56	44	57	42	32	13	**17**			
18.	Peterhead	318	105	98	93	95	106	108	105	94	83	78	68	80	64	54	35	25	**18**		
19.	*Fraserburgh*	334	121	114	109	108	122	128	121	110	99	94	83	96	79	68	51	39	16	**19**	
20.	*Wick*	391	178	171	166	165	179	185	178	167	156	151	140	153	136	125	108	96	72	57	**20**

9.6.2

South East Scotland

Eyemouth to Rattray Head

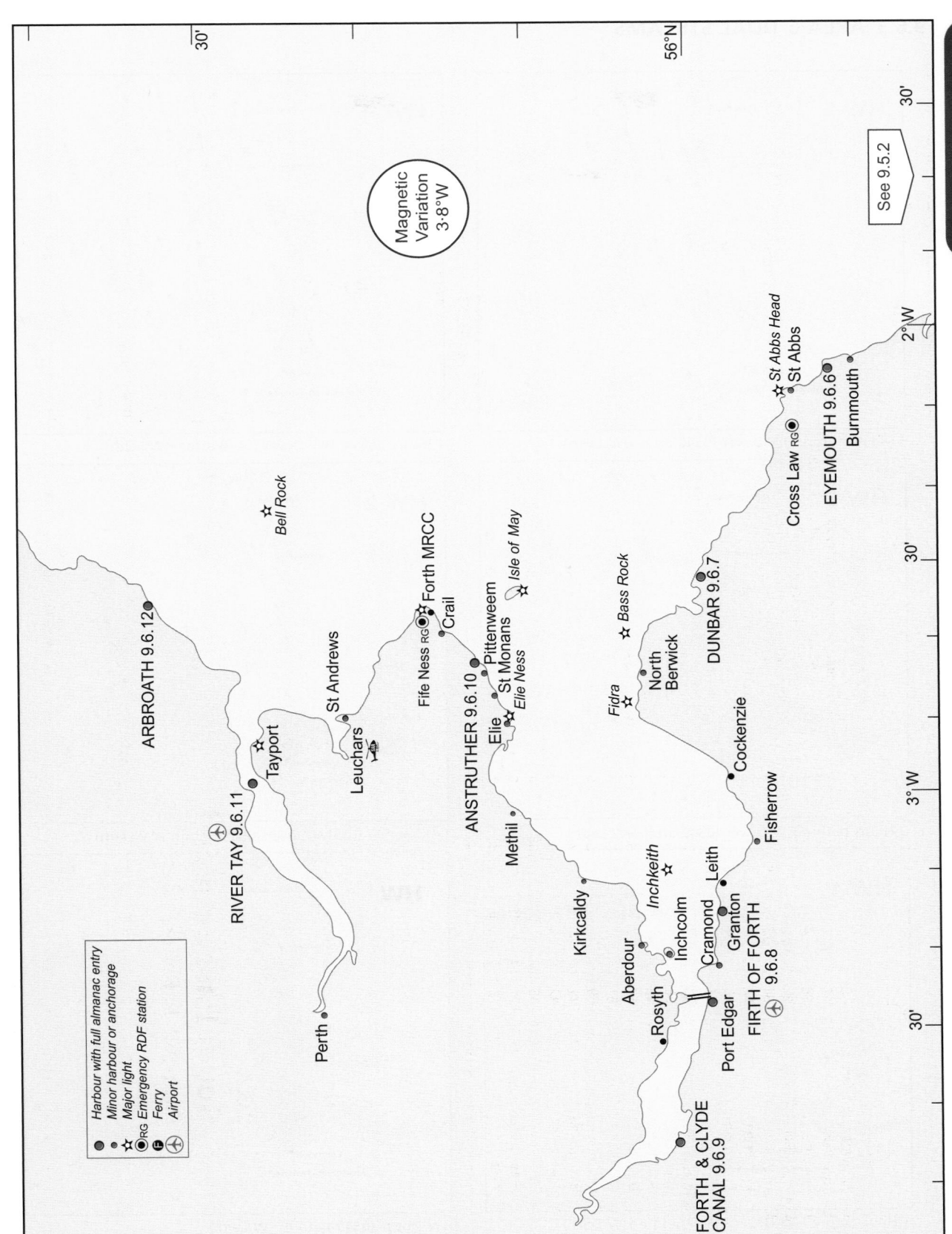

Magnetic Variation 3·8°W

See 9.5.2

St Abbs Head
St Abbs
Cross Law RG
EYEMOUTH 9.6.6
Burnmouth

Bell Rock

Forth MRCC
Fife Ness RG
Crail

Isle of May

Pittenweem
St Monans
Elie Ness

Bass Rock

DUNBAR 9.6.7

ARBROATH 9.6.12

St Andrews

ANSTRUTHER 9.6.10
Elie

Leuchars

Tayport

RIVER TAY 9.6.11

Methil

North Berwick

Fidra

Cockenzie

Fisherrow

Kirkcaldy

Inchkeith

Leith

Aberdour

Inchcolm
Cramond
Granton
FIRTH OF FORTH
9.6.8

Perth

Rosyth

Port Edgar

FORTH & CLYDE
CANAL 9.6.9

Harbour with full almanac entry
Minor harbour or anchorage
Major light
RG Emergency RDF station
Ferry
Airport

9.6.3 AREA 6 TIDAL STREAMS

5 Hours before HW Dover (0340 after HW Leith)

4 Hours before HW Dover (0440 after HW Leith)

3 Hours before HW Dover (0540 after HW Leith)

2 Hours before HW Dover (0545 before HW Leith)

1 Hour before HW Dover (0445 before HW Leith)

HW Dover (0345 before HW Leith)

Northward 9.7.3   Southward 9.5.3

HW+1

Peterhead

Aberdeen

57°

Dundee

56°

Leith

Eyemouth

Berwick-on-Tweed

1 Hour after HW Dover (0245 before HW Leith)

HW+2

Peterhead

Aberdeen

57°

Dundee

56°

Leith

Eyemouth

Berwick-on-Tweed

2 Hours after HW Dover (0145 before HW Leith)

HW+3

Peterhead

Aberdeen

57°

Dundee

56°

Leith

Eyemouth

Berwick-on-Tweed

3 Hours after HW Dover (0045 before HW Leith)

HW+4

Peterhead

Aberdeen

57°

Dundee

SLACK

56°

Leith

Eyemouth

Berwick-on-Tweed

4 Hours after HW Dover (0015 after HW Leith)

HW+5

Peterhead

SLACK

Aberdeen

57°

Dundee

56°

Leith

Eyemouth

Berwick-on-Tweed

5 Hours after HW Dover (0115 after HW Leith)

HW+6

Peterhead

Aberdeen

57°

Dundee

SLACK   SLACK

56°

Leith

Eyemouth

Berwick-on-Tweed

6 Hours after HW Dover (0215 after HW Leith)

9.6.4 LIGHTS, BUOYS AND WAYPOINTS

Bold print = light with a nominal range of 15M or more. CAPITALS = place or feature. *CAPITAL ITALICS* = light-vessel, light float or Lanby. *Italics* = Fog signal. ***Bold italics*** = Racon. Abbreviations are in Chapter 1.

BERWICK-UPON-TWEED TO BASS ROCK

BURNMOUTH
Ldg lts 241°. Front, FR 29m 4M; 55°50'·53N 02°04'·25W. Rear, 45m from front, FR 35m 4M. Both on W posts (unclear by day).

EYEMOUTH
Blind Buss ⚓ Q; 55°52'·80N 02°05'·25E.
Ldg Lts 174°. Front, W Bkwtr Hd ⚡, FG 9m 6M; 55°52'·47N 02°05'·29W. Rear, elbow 55m from front, FG 10m 6M.

ST ABBS to DUNBAR and BASS ROCK
St Abbs Hd ☆ 55°54'·96N 02°08'·29W; Fl 10s 68m **26M**; W twr; ***Racon (T) 18M***.
Barns Ness Tower (Lt ho disused 36m); 55°59'·22N 02°26'·76W.
Bayswell Hill Ldg Lts 198°. Front, Oc G 6s 15m 3M; W △ on Or col; 188°-G(intens)-208°; 56°00'·25N 02°31'·21W. Rear, Oc G 6s 22m 3M; ▽ on Or col; synch with front,188°-G(intens)-208°.
Bass Rock, S side, ☆ Fl (3) 20s 46m 10M; W twr; vis: 241°-107°; 56°04'·61N 02°38'·48W.

FIRTH OF FORTH AND SOUTH SHORE
(Direction of buoyage East to West)

NORTH BERWICK
Outfall ⚓ Fl Y; 56°04'·29N 02°40'·89W.
Fidra ☆ 56°04'·39N 02°47'·13W; Fl (4) 30s 34m **24M**; W twr; obsc by Bass Rock, Craig Leith and Lamb Island.

PORT SETON, COCKENZIE, FISHERROW and S CHANNEL
Port Seton, E Pier Hd ⚡ Iso WR 4s 10m W9M, R6M; vis: shore - R - 105°- W - 225°- R - shore; *Bell (occas);* 55°58'·40N 02°57'·23W.
Fisherrow E Pier Hd ⚡ Oc 6s 5m 6M; 55°56'·79N 03°04'·11W.
Narrow Deep ⚓ Fl (2) R 10s; 56°01'·46N 03°04'·59W.
Herwit ▲ Fl (3) G 10s; 56°01'·05N 03°06'·52W.
North Craig ⚓ Q (3) 10s 56°01'·02N 03°03'·52W.
Craigh Waugh ⚓ Fl (2) 10s;56°00'·26N 03°04'·47W.
Diffuser Hds (Outer) ⚓ 55°59'·81N 03°07'·84W.

LEITH and GRANTON
Leith Approach ⚓ Fl R 3s; 55°59'·95N 03°11'·51W .
East Bkwtr Hd ⚡ Iso R 4s 7m 9M; 55°59'·48N 03°10'·94W.
GrantonE Pier Head ⚡ Fl R 2s 5m 6M; 55°59'·28N 03°13'·27W.

NORTH CHANNEL and MIDDLE BANK
Inchkeith Fairway ⚓ Iso 2s; ***Racon (T) 5M***; 56°03'·49N 03°00'·10W.
No. 1 ▲ Fl G 9s; 56°03'·22N 03°03'·71W.
No. 2 ⚓ Fl R 9s; 56°02'·90N 03°03'·72W.
No. 3 ▲ Fl G 6s; 56°03'·22N 03°06'·10W.
No. 4 ⚓ Fl R 6s; 56°02'·89N 03°06'·11W.
No. 5 ▲ Fl G 3s; 56°03'·18N 03°07'·88W.
No. 6 ⚓ Fl R 3s; 56°03'·05N 03°08'·44W.
No. 8 ⚓ Fl R 9s 56°02'·95N 03°09'·62W.
Inchkeith ☆ 56°02'·01N 03°08'·17W; Fl 15s 67m **22M**; stone twr.
Pallas Rock ⚓ VQ (9) 10s 56°01'·50N 03°09'·30W.
East Gunnet ⚓ Q (3) 10s; 56°01'·41N 03°10'·38W.
West Gunnet ⚓ Q (9) 15s 56°01'·34N 03°11'·06W.
No. 7 ▲ QG; ***Racon (T) 5M***; 56°02'·80N 03°10'·97W.
No. 9 ▲ Fl G 6s; 56°02'·32N 03°13'·48W.
No. 10 ⚓ Fl R 6s; 56°02'·07N 03°13'·32W.

No. 11 ▲ Fl G 3s 56°02'·08N 03°15'·26W.
No. 12 ⚓ Fl R 3s; 56°01'·78N 03°15'·15W.
No. 13 ▲ Fl G 9s; 56°01'·77N 03°16'·94W.
No. 14 ⚓ Fl R 9s; 56°01'·52N 03°16'·82W.
Oxcars ☆ Fl (2) WR 7s 16m W13M, R12M; W twr, R band; vis: 072°-W-087°- R-196°-W-313°-R-072°; 56°01'·36N 03°16'·84W.
Inchcolm E Pt ☆ Fl (3) 15s 20m 10M; Gy twr; part obsc by land 075°-145·5°; 56°01'·72N 03°17'·83W.
No. 15 ▲ Fl G 6s; 56°01'·39N 03°18'·95W.

MORTIMER'S DEEP
Hawkcraig Point Ldg Lts 292°. Front, Iso 5s 12m 14M; W twr; vis: 282°-302°; 56°03'·03N 03°17'·07W. Rear, 96m from front, Iso 5s 16m 14M; W twr; vis: 282°-302°.
Inchcolm S Lts in line 066°. Front, 84m from rear, Q 7m 7M; W twr; vis: 062·5°-082·5°; 56°01'·78N 03°18'·28W. Common Rear, Iso 5s 11m 7M; W twr; vis: 062·5°-082·5°; 56°01'·80N 03°18'·13W. N Lts in line 076·7°. Front, 80m from rear, Q 7m 7M; W twr; vis: 062·5°-082·5°.

APPROACHES TO FORTH BRIDGES
No. 17 ▲ Fl G 3s; 56°01'·23N 03°19'·84W.
No. 16 ⚓ Fl R 3s; 56°00'·87N 03°19'·60W.
No. 19 ▲ Fl G 9s; 56°00'·71N 03°22'·47W.
Beamer Rk ⚡ Fl 3s 6m 9M; W twr, R top; 56°00'·28N 03°24'·74W.

PORT EDGAR
W Bkwtr Hd ⚡ Fl R 4s 4m 8M; 55°59'·86N 03°24'·78W. W blockhouse.

FIRTH OF FORTH – NORTH SHORE (INWARD)

BURNTISLAND
W Pier Outer Hd ⚡ Fl (2) R 6s 7m; W twr; 56°03'·22N 03°14'·26W.
E Pier Outer Hd ⚡ Fl (2) G 6s 7m 5M; 56°03'·24N 03°14'·17W.

ABERDOUR, BRAEFOOT BAY and INCHCOLM
Hawkcraig Pt ⚡ (see **MORTIMER'S DEEP** above).
Braefoot Bay Terminal, W Jetty. Ldg Lts 247·3°. **Front**, Fl 3s 6m **15M**; W △ on E dolphin; vis: 237·2°-257·2°; 56°02'·16N 03°18'·71W; 4 dolphins with 2 FG (vert). **Rear**, 88m from front, Fl 3s 12m **15M**; W ▽ on appr gangway; vis: 237·2°-257·2°; synch with front.

INVERKEITHING BAY
St David's ⚓ Fl G 5s 3m 7M; Or □, on pile; 56°01'·37N 03°22'·29W.
Channel ▲ QG; 56°01'·43N 03°23'·02W.

HM NAVAL BASE, ROSYTH
Main Chan Dir lt 323·5°. Bn 'A' Oc WRG 7m 4M; R □ on W post with R bands; vis: 318°-G-321°-321°-W-326°-R-328° (H24); 56°01'·19N 03°25'·61W.
Dir lt 115°, Bn 'C' Oc WRG 6s 7m 4M; W ▽ on W Bn; vis: 110°- R -113° W -116·5° - G -120°; 56°00'·61N 03°24'·25W.
S Arm Jetty Hd ⚡ L Fl (2) WR 12s 5m W9M; R6M; vis: 010°-W-280°-R-010°; 56°01'·09N 03°26'·58W.

RIVER FORTH

ROSYTH to GRANGEMOUTH
Dhu Craig ▲ Fl G 5s; 56°00'·74N 03°27'·23W.
Blackness ⚓ QR; 56°01'·06N 03°30'·30W.
Tancred Bank ⚓ Fl (2) R 10s; 56°01'·58N 03°31'·91W.
Dods Bank ⚓ Fl R 3s; 56°02'·03N 03°34'·07W.
Bo'ness ⚓ Fl R 10s; 56°02'·23N 03°35'·38W.
Torry ⚡ Fl G 10s 5m 7M; G ○ structure; 56°02'·46N 03°35'·28W.
Bo'ness Bcns ◊ 2 QR 3m 2M; 56°01'·85N 03°36'·22W.
Bo'ness Hbr ⚓; 56°01'·26N 03°36'·46W.

GRANGEMOUTH
Grangemouth App No. 1 ⚓ Fl (3) 10s 4m 6M;56°02'·12N 03°38'·10W.
Hen & Chickens ▲ Fl (3) G 10s; 56°02'·35N 03°38'·08W.

WGS84 DATUM
Plot waypoints on chart before use

FIRTH OF FORTH – NORTH SHORE (OUTWARD)
KIRKCALDY and METHIL
Kirkcaldy E. Pier Hd ⚡Fl WG 10s 12m 8M; vis: 156°-G-336°-W-156°; 56°06'·78N 03°08'·90W.
Methil Outer Pier Hd ⚡ Oc G 6s 8m 5M; W twr; vis: 280°-100°; 56°10'·76N 03°00'·48W

ELIE and ST MONANS
Elie Ness ☆ 56°11'·04N 02°48'·77W; Fl 6s 15m **18M**; W twr.

St Monans Bkwtr Hd ⚡ Oc WRG 6s 5m W7M, R4M, G4M; vis: 282°-G-355°-W-026°-R-038°; 56°12'·20N 02°45'·94W.

PITTENWEEM and ANSTRUTHER EASTER
Pittenweem, Ldg Lts 037° Middle Pier Hd. Front, FR 4m 5M. Rear, FR 8m 5M. Both Gy Cols, Or stripes; 56°12'·69N 02°43'·69W.
Pittenweem, E Bkwtr Hd ⚡ Fl (2) RG 5s 9m R9M, G6M; vis: 265°-R-345°-G-055°; *Horn 90s (occas);* 56°12'·63N 02°43'·74W.
Anstruther, Ldg Lts 019°. Front FG 7m 4M; 56°13'·28N 02°41'·76W. Rear, 38m from front, FG 11m 4M, (both W masts).

MAY I, CRAIL, ST ANDREWS and FIFE NESS to MONTROSE
Isle of May ☆ 56°11'·12N 02°33'·46W(Summit); Fl (2) 15s 73m **22M**; ☐ twr on stone dwelling.

Crail, Ldg Lts 295°. Front, FR 24m 6M (not lit when hbr closed); 56°15'·46N 02°37'·84W. Rear, 30m from front, FR 30m 6M.
Fife Ness ☆ 56°16'·74N 02°35'·19W; Iso WR 10s 12m **W21M, R20M**; W bldg; vis: 143°-W-197°-R-217°-W-023°.
N Carr ⚡ Q (3) 10s 3m 5M; 56°18'·05N 02°32'·94W.
Bell Rk ☆ 56°26'·08N 02°23'·21W; Fl 5s 28m **18M**; *Racon (M) 18M*.
St Andrews N Bkwtr Bn ⚡ Fl G 3M 56°20'·36N 02°46'·77W.

RIVER TAY, TAYPORT, DUNDEE and PERTH
Tay Fairway ⚓ L Fl 10s; *Bell;* 56°28'·30N 02°36'·60W.
Middle ⚓ Fl G 3s; 56°27'·93N 02°38'·26W.
Middle ⚓ Fl (2) R 6s 56°27'·65N 02°38'·23W.
Abertay N ⚡ Q (3) 10s; *Racon (T) 8M;* 56°27'·39N 02°40'·36W.
Abertay S (Elbow) ⚓ Fl R 6s 56°27'·13N 02°39'·83W.
Tayport High Lt Ho ☆ 56°27'·17N 02°53'·96W; Dir lt 269°; Iso WRG3s 24m **W22M, R17M, G16M**; W twr; vis: 267°-G-268°-W-270°-R-271°.

ARBROATH
Ldg lts 299·2°. Front , FR 7m 5M; W col; 56°33'·29N 02°35'·16W. Rear, 50m from front, FR 13m 5M; W col.

MONTROSE
Scurdie Ness ☆ 56°42'·10N 02°26'·24W; Fl (3) 20s 38m **23M**; W twr; *Racon (T) 14-16M.*

Outer Ldg Lts 271·5°; Front, FR 11m 5M; W twin pillars, R bands; 56°42'·21N 02°27'·41W; Rear, 272m from front, FR 18m 5M; W twr, R cupola.
Inner Ldg Lts 265°; Front FG 21m 5M; Rear FG 33m 5M.

MONTROSE TO RATTRAY HEAD
JOHNSHAVEN and GOURDON HARBOUR
Johnshaven, Ldg Lts 316°. Front,FR 5m; 56°47'·62N 02°20'·26W. Rear, 85m from front, FG 20m; shows R when unsafe to enter hbr.
Gourdon Hbr, Ldg Lts 358°. Front, FR 5m 5M; W twr; shows G when unsafe to enter; *Siren (2) 60s* (occas); 56°49'·69N 02°17'·24W. Rear, 120m from front, FR 30m 5M; W twr.
Todhead Lighthouse (disused), white tower, 13m.

STONEHAVEN to GIRDLE NESS
Outer Pier Hd ⚡ Iso WRG 4s 7m W11M, R7M, G8M; vis: 214°-G-246°-W-268°-R-280°; 56°57'·59N 02°12'·00W.

Girdle Ness ☆ Fl (2) 20s 56m **22M**; obsc by Greg Ness when brg more than about 020°; *Racon (G) 25M;* 57°08'·34N 02°02'·91W.

ABERDEEN
Fairway ⚓ Mo (A) 5s; *Racon (T) 7M;* 57°09'·31N 02°01'·95W.
Torry Ldg lts 235·7°. Front, FR or G 14m 5M; R when ent safe, FG when dangerous to navigation; vis: 195°-279°; 57°08'·37N 02°04'·51W. Rear, 205m from front, FR 19m 5M; W twr; vis: 195°-279°.
S Bkwtr Hd ⚡ Fl (3) R 8s 23m 7M; 57°08'·69N 02°03'·34W.
N Pier Hd ⚡ Oc WR 6s 11m 9M; W twr; vis: 145°-W-055°-R-145°; 57°08'·74N 02°03'·69W. In fog FY 10m (same twr) vis: 136°-336°; *Bell (3) 12s.*

PETERHEAD and RATTRAY HEAD
Buchan Ness ☆ Fl 5s 40m **28M**; W twr, R bands; *Racon (O) 14-16M;* 57°28'·23N 01°46'·51W.
Kirktown Ldg lts 314°. Front, FR 13m 8M; R mast, Or △ on R mast; 57°30'·22N 01°47'·21W. Rear, 91m from front, FR 17m 8M.
S Bkwtr Hd ⚡ Fl (2) R 12s 24m 7M; 57°29'·79N 01°46'·54W.
N Bkwtr Hd ⚡Iso RG 6s 19m 11M; W tripod; vis: 171°-R-236°-G-171°; *Horn 30s;* 57°29'·84N 01°46'·32W .
Rattray Hd ☆ 57°36'·61N 01°49'·03W; Fl (3) 30s 28m **24M**; W twr; *Racon (M) 15M.*

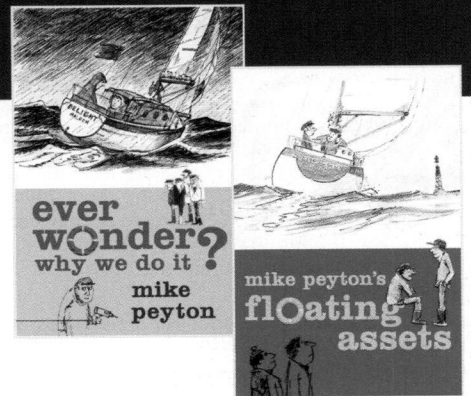

9.6.5 PASSAGE INFORMATION

For these waters refer to the Admiralty *North Sea (West) Pilot*; R Northumberland YC's *Sailing Directions Humber to Rattray Head*, and the *Forth Yacht Clubs Association Pilot Handbook*, which covers the Firth of Forth in detail.

A '*Rover Ticket*', £30 from Aberdeenshire and Moray Councils allows berthing (subject to availability) for one week from the date of arrival at the first harbour. Scheme includes; Johnshaven, Gourdon, Stonehaven, Rosehearty, Banff, Portsoy, Cullen, Portknockie, Findochty, Hopeman and Burghead. More Passage Information is threaded between the harbours of this Area.

BERWICK-UPON-TWEED TO BASS ROCK

(AC 160,175) From Berwick-upon-Tweed to the Firth of Forth there is no good hbr which can be approached with safety in strong onshore winds. So, if on passage with strong winds from N or E, plan accordingly and keep well to seaward. In late spring and early summer fog (haar) is likely in onshore winds.

The coast N from Berwick is rocky with cliffs rising in height to Burnmouth, then diminishing gradually to Eyemouth. Keep 5ca offshore to clear outlying rks. Burnmouth, although small, has more alongside space than Eyemouth, which is a crowded fishing hbr. 2·1M NW is St Abbs Hbr, with temp anchorage in offshore winds in Coldingham B close to the S.

St Abbs Hd (lt) is a bold, steep headland, 92m high, with no offlying dangers. ▶ *The stream runs strongly round the Hd, causing turbulence with wind against tide; this can be largely avoided by keeping close inshore. The ESE-going stream begins at HW Leith −0345, and the WNW-going at HW Leith +0240.* ◀ There is a good anch in Pettico Wick, on NW side of Hd, in S winds, but dangerous if the wind shifts onshore. There are no off-lying dangers between St Abbs Hd and Fast Castle Hd, 3M WNW. Between Fast Castle Hd and Barns Ness, about 8M NW, is the attractive little hbr of Cove; but it dries and should only be approached in ideal conditions.

Torness Power Station (conspic, lt on bkwtr) is 1·75M SE of Barns Ness (lt) which lies 2·5M ESE of Dunbar and is fringed with rks; tidal streams as for St Abb's Hd. Conspic chys are 7½ca WSW inland of Barns Ness. Between here and Dunbar keep at least 2½ca offshore to clear rky patches. Sicar Rk (7·9m depth) lies about 1·25M ENE of Dunbar, and sea breaks on it in onshore gales.

The direct course from Dunbar to Bass Rk (lt) is clear of all dangers; inshore of this line beware Wildfire Rks (dry) on NW side of Bellhaven B. In offshore winds there is anch in Scoughall Road. Great Carr is ledge of rks, nearly covering at HW, 1M ESE of Gin Hd, with Carr bn (stone tr surmounted by cross) at its N end. Drying ledges of rks extend 1M SE of Great Carr, up to 3ca offshore. Keep at least 5ca off Carr bn in strong onshore winds. Tantallon Castle (ruins) is on cliff edge 1M W of Great Car. Bass Rk (lt) lies 1·25M NNE of Gin Hd, and is a sheer, conspic rk (115m) with no offlying dangers; landing difficult due to swell.

9.6.6 EYEMOUTH

Borders **55°52'·52N 02°05'·29W** ❀⊕⟡⟡⟐✿✿✿

CHARTS AC 160, 1612; Imray C24.

TIDES +0330 Dover; ML No data; Duration 0610

Standard Port LEITH (→)

Times				Height (metres)			
High Water		Low Water		MHWS	MHWN	MLWN	MLWS
0300	0900	0300	0900	5·6	4·4	2·0	0·8
1500	2100	1500	2100				
Differences EYEMOUTH							
−0005	+0007	+0012	+0008	−0·4	−0·3	0·0	+0·1

SHELTER Good in all weathers except uncomfortable surge in N over F5. Busy FV hbr which encourages yachtsman to visit. Berth as directed by HM. The options are:

- Middle Quay (100m pontoon), depth 0.9m bottom soft mud.
- On the W wall of the N-pointing jetty by the LB;
- On W wall of the centre jetty W of Gunsgreen House (conspic).
- ⚓ in bay only in offshore winds.

NAVIGATION WPT 55°52'·80N 02°05'·34W, 174°/3ca to E bkwtr lt.

- Entry should not be attempted in strong N to E winds. F.R (occas) lt ● or R flag = unsafe to enter indicates unsafe to enter bay or hbr.
- Caution, the entrance is 17m wide and is maintained to 2m depth with soundings taken monthly due to frequent sand movement and silting.
- Appr can be made N or S of Hurkars; from the N, beware Blind Buss 1·2m, marked by NCM lit buoy about 200m ENE of WPT.
- From the S, approach on 250° midway between Hurkars and Hettle Scar (no ldg marks).
- Approaching vessels are advised to contact HM for latest information.

LIGHTS AND MARKS St. Abbs Hd lt ho Fl 10s 68m 26M is 3M NW. Ldg lts 174° both FG 9/10m 6M, orange columns on W pier.

R/T VHF Ch 16 **12** (HO). Advisable to listen to VHF Ch 6 for FVs entering/leaving port.

TELEPHONE (Code 01890) HM 750223, Mobile 07885 742505; MRCC (01333) 450666; Marinecall 09068 969642; Police 750217; Dr 750599, Ⓗ (0131) 536 1000.

FACILITIES **Hbr** AB (quay) £12/yacht, AB (pontoon) £17/yacht (any LOA +7 days for the price of 5), FW, D (in Gunsgreen Basin),

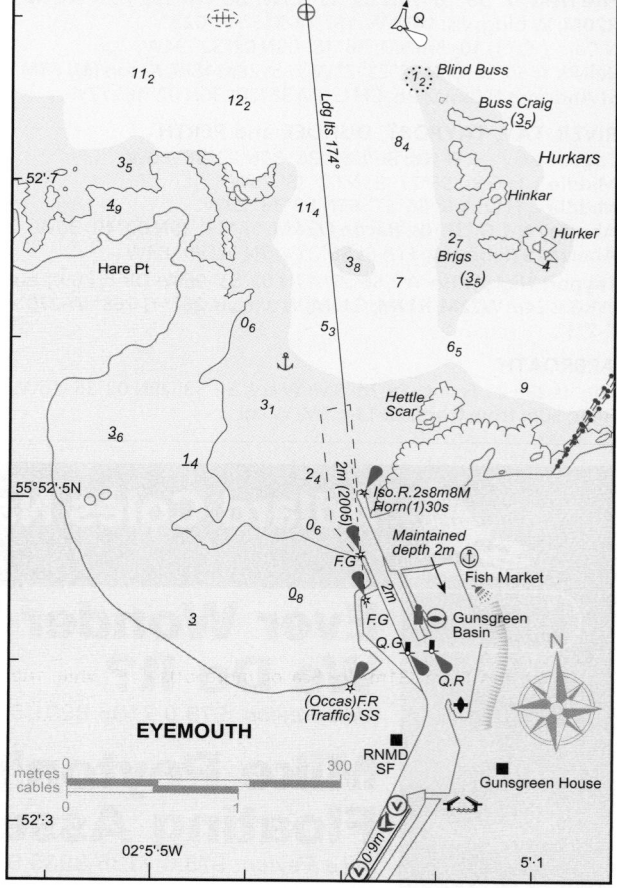

EYEMOUTH

Slip, BY, ME, ✕, El, C (12 ton mobile), Ⓔ. See www.eyemouthharbour.org.

Town LB, P, CH, 🛒, R, Bar, ✉, ▣, Gas, Gaz, Ⓑ, Wi-fi at public library. ⇌ (bus to Berwick-on-Tweed and Edinburgh), ✈ (Edinburgh).

ADJACENT HARBOURS

BURNMOUTH, Borders, **55°50′·61N 02°04′·10W**. AC 160. HW +0315 on Dover, –0025 on Leith; Duration 0615. Use Eyemouth tides 9.6.6. From S beware Quarry Shoal Rks; and E & W Carrs from N. 2 W posts (unclear by day, FR 29/35m 4M) 45m apart, lead 253° to close N of the hbr; as hbr mouth opens, enter on about 185° with outer hbr ent in line with 2FG (vert). Min depth at ent at LWS is 0·6m. Shelter is good especially in inner hbr (dries). With on-shore winds, swell makes outer hbr uncomfortable. HM (018907) 81283 (home). Facilities: AB £7 (all LOA), FW, limited 🛒.

ST ABBS, Borders, **55°54′·10N 02°07′·74W**. AC 175. HW +0330 on Dover, –0017 on Leith; HW –0·6m on Leith; Duration 0605. Ldg line (about 228°) S face of Maw Carr on village hall (conspic R roof) leads SW until the hbr ent opens to port and the 2nd ldg line (about 167°) can be seen 2FR 4/8m 1M, or Y LB ho visible thru' ent. On E side of ent chan, beware Hog's Nose and on W side the Maw Carr. Shelter good. In strong on-shore winds outer hbr suffers from waves breaking over E pier. Inner hbr (dries) is best but often full of FVs. Access HW±3. HM (0775 1136758) directs visitors. Facilities: AB £10 (all LOA), Slip (launching £10), FW, ⏻, at quay, R, ✉, 🛒, more facilities & bar at Coldingham.

9.6.7 DUNBAR

East Lothian **56°00′·39N 02°31′·09W** ❄❀♨♨✿✿✿

CHARTS AC 175, 734; Imray C23, C27.

TIDES +0330 Dover; ML 3·0; Duration 0600

Standard Port LEITH (→)

Times				Height (metres)			
High Water		Low Water		MHWS	MHWN	MLWN	MLWS
0300	0900	0300	0900	5·6	4·4	2·0	0·8
1500	2100	1500	2100				
Differences DUNBAR							
–0005	+0003	+0003	–0003	–0·3	–0·3	0·0	+0·1
FIDRA							
–0001	0000	–0002	+0001	–0·2	–0·2	0·0	0·0

SHELTER Outer (Victoria) Hbr is subject to surge in strong NW to NE winds. N side dries; berth below castle and contact HM. Keep steps clear. Inner (Old or Cromwell) Hbr dries and is safe in strong onshore conditions; entry is through a bridge, lifted on request to HM.

NAVIGATION WPT 56°00′·60N 02°31′·49W, 132°/3ca to hbr ent, preferable entry in marginal conditions.

- Entry is dangerous in heavy on-shore swell with no access in strong winds from NW to E.
- Beware Wallace's Head Rock, Half Ebb Rock (2₁m), 1½ca from ent. and Outer Buss 4ca E of ent.
- Min depth at ent 0·5m, but may be much less in abnormal circumstances.
- Keep to port on entry to avoid rockfall off castle.

LIGHTS AND MARKS Church and Castle ruin both conspic. From NE, ldg lts, Oc G 6s 15/22m 3M, synch, intens 188°-208°, 2 W △ on Or cols, lead 198° through the outer rks to the Roads; thence narrow ent opens with QR brg 132°. From NW, appr on brg 132° between bns on Wallaces Head and Half Ebb Rk.

R/T None.

TELEPHONE (Code 01368) HM 865404, Mobile 07958754858;

DUNBAR

MRCC (01333) 450666; Police 862718; Dr 863704; Ⓗ (0131) 536 1000.

FACILITIES **Quay** AB £10 (£15 over 12m LOA), Slip, FW, D (quayside), P (cans); **N Wall** M, AB; **Inner Hbr** Slip, AB; **Services** ME, Gas, Gaz. **Town** LB, P, ⏻, 🛒, R, Bar, ✉, Ⓑ, ⇌, ✈ Edinburgh.

ADJACENT HARBOUR

NORTH BERWICK, East Lothian, **56°03′·74N 02°43′·04W**. AC 734. Fidra HW +0344 on Dover; ML 3·0m; Duration 0625. See 9.6.7 Fidra. Shelter good with winds from S to W but dangerous with on-shore winds. Ent is 8m wide. Hbr dries. From E or W, from position 0·25M S of Craigleith, steer S for Plattock Rks, thence SSW 40m off bkwtr before turning 180° port into hbr. Bkwtr lt F WR 7m 3M, R to seaward, W over hbr; not lit when bad weather closes hbr. Beware Maiden Rks (bn) 100m NW of this lt. Facilities: AB £5.70, P & D (cans), FW on pier, CH, Wi-fi at public library. HM ☎ (01620) 893333, Mob 0776 467373. **East Lothian YC** ☎ (01620) 892698, M, ⚓s, Bar. **Town** 🛒, Gas, Ⓑ, ✉, ⇌ and bus Edinburgh.

FIRTH OF FORTH – SOUTH SHORE

(Chart 734, 735) Westward of Bass Rk, Craigleith (51m), Lamb Is (24m) and Fidra (31m) lie 5ca or more offshore, while the coast is generally foul. Craigleith is steep-to, and temporary anchorage can be found on SE and SW sides; if passing inshore of it keep well to N side of chan. N Berwick hbr (dries) lies S of Craigleith, but is unsafe in onshore winds. Between Craigleith and Lamb Is, beware drying rks up to 3ca from land. Lamb Is is 1·5M WNW of N Berwick and has a rky ledge extending 2½ca SW. Fidra Is (lt) is a bird reserve, nearly connected to the shore by rky ledges, and should be passed to the N; passage and anchorage on S side are tricky. Anchor on E or W sides, depending on wind, in good weather.

In the bay between Fidra and Edinburgh some shelter can be found in SE winds in Aberlady Bay and Gosford Bay. The best anchorage is SW of Craigielaw Pt. Port Seton is a drying fishing harbour 7½ca E of the conspic chys of Cockenzie Power

Station; the E side of the hbr can be entered HW ±3, but not advisable in strong onshore winds. Cockenzie (dries) is close to power station; beware Corsik Rk 400m to E. Access HW ±2·5, but no attractions except boatyard.

There are no dangers on the direct course from Fidra to Inchkeith (lt), which stands between the buoyed deep water chans. Rks extend 7½ca SE from Inchkeith, and 5ca off the W side where there is a small hbr below the lt ho; landing is forbidden without permission. N Craig and Craig Waugh (least depth 0·2m) are buoyed shoals 2·5M SE from Inchkeith lt ho.

▶*In N Chan, close to Inchkeith the W-going (flood) stream begins about HW Leith –0530, and the E-going at HW Leith +0030, sp rates about 1kn. The streams gather strength towards the Forth bridges, where they reach 2·25kn and there may be turbulence.*◀

Leith is wholly commercial; Granton has yacht moorings in the E hbr; Port Edgar is a major yacht hbr close W of Forth Road

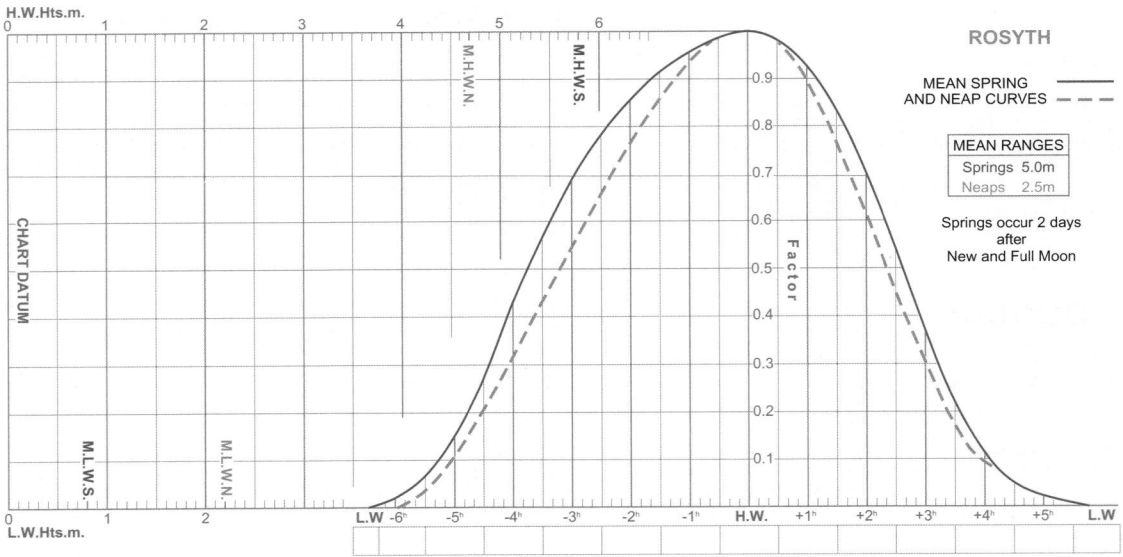

ROSYTH

MEAN SPRING ——————
AND NEAP CURVES ― ― ― ―

MEAN RANGES	
Springs	5.0m
Neaps	2.5m

Springs occur 2 days
after
New and Full Moon

Bridge. Hound Point oil terminal is an artificial 'island-jetty' almost in mid-stream, connected to the shore by underwater pipeline (no ⚓). Yachts may pass the terminal on either side at least 30m off keeping well clear of manoeuvring ships.

▶ *Tidal streams are quite weak in the outer part of the Firth. Apart from the stream of the Tay, which attains 5kn in most places, the coastwise tidal streams between Fife Ness and Arbroath are weak.*

Northbound. *Leave before HW (Dover +0400) to be at N Carr at Dover +0600. Bound from Forth to Tay aim to arrive at Abertay By at LW slack (Dover –0200).*

Southbound. *Leave before LW (Dover –0200) to be at Bass Rk at HW Dover. Similar timings if bound from Tay to Forth, leave late in ebb to pick up early flood off St Andrews to N Carr and into Forth.*◀

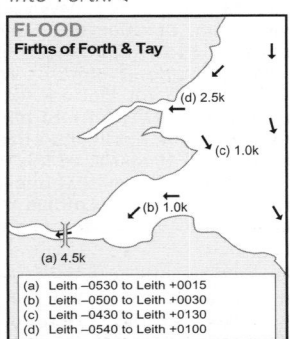

FLOOD
Firths of Forth & Tay

(d) 2.5k
(c) 1.0k
(b) 1.0k
(a) 4.5k

(a) Leith –0530 to Leith +0015
(b) Leith –0500 to Leith +0030
(c) Leith –0430 to Leith +0130
(d) Leith –0540 to Leith +0100

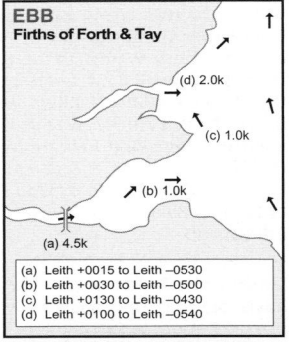

EBB
Firths of Forth & Tay

(d) 2.0k
(c) 1.0k
(b) 1.0k
(a) 4.5k

(a) Leith +0015 to Leith –0530
(b) Leith +0030 to Leith –0500
(c) Leith +0130 to Leith –0430
(d) Leith +0100 to Leith –0540

RIVER FORTH TO KINCARDINE

(AC 736, 737, 738) The main shipping chan under the N span of the rail bridge is busy with commercial traffic for Grangemouth and Rosyth. W of Beamer Rk the Firth widens as far as Bo'ness (small drying hbr) on the S shore where the chan narrows between drying mudbanks. Charlestown (N bank) dries, but is a secure hbr. Grangemouth is industrially conspicuous. Beware of gas carriers, tankers and other cargo vessels; there are no facilities for yachts. Few yachts go beyond Kincardine swing bridge, clearance 9m, which is no longer opened.

FIRTH OF FORTH – NORTH SHORE

(AC 734, 190) From Burntisland the N shore of Firth of Forth leads E to Kinghorn Ness. 1M SSW of Kinghorn Ness Blae Rk (SHM lt buoy) has least depth of 4·1m, and seas break on it in E gales.

▶ *Rost Bank lies halfway between Kinghorn Ness and Inchkeith, with tide rips at sp tides or in strong winds.* ◀

From Kinghorn Ness to Kirkcaldy, drying rks lie up to 3ca offshore. Kirkcaldy Hbr is effectively closed, but yachts can enter inner dock near HW by arrangement; ent is dangerous in strong E'lies, when seas break a long way out.

Between Kirkcaldy and Methil the only dangers more than 2ca offshore are The Rockheads, extending 4ca SE of Dysart, and marked by 2 SHM buoys. Largo B is anch, well sheltered from N and E, but avoid gaspipes near E side. Close SW of Elie, beware W Vows (dries) and E Vows (dries, bn). There is anch close W of Elie Ness (9.6.8). Ox Rk (dries 2m) lies 5ca ENE of Elie Ness, and 2½ca offshore; otherwise there are no dangers more than 2ca offshore past St Monance, Pittenweem and Anstruther, but in bad weather the sea breaks on Shield Rk 4ca off Pittenweem. From Anstruther to Crail and on to Fife Ness keep 3ca offshore to clear Caiplie Rk and other dangers.

May Island (lt) lies about 5M S of Fife Ness; its shores are bold except at NW end where rks extend 1ca off. Anch near N end at E or W Tarbert, on lee side according to winds; in good weather it is possible to land. Lt ho boats use Kirkhaven, close SE of lt ho.

FORTH TO NORWAY AND BALTIC

(AC 2182B, 2182C) Heading ENE'ly from the Firth of Forth the main hazards result from offshore industrial activities and their associated traffic. Particularly in summer months oil/gas exploration, movement of drilling rigs and pipe laying create potentially hazardous situations for small craft. Rig movements and many of the more intense activities are published in Notices to Mariners, but even so it is wise to avoid the gas and oil fields where possible and never to approach within 500m of installations. There are TSS to be avoided off the S and SW coast of Norway. Strong currents and steep seas may be experienced in the approaches to the Skagerrak.

TIME ZONE (UT)
For Summer Time add ONE hour in **non-shaded areas**

ROSYTH LAT 56°01'N LONG 3°27'W
TIMES AND HEIGHTS OF HIGH AND LOW WATERS

Dates in red are **SPRINGS**
Dates in blue are NEAPS

YEAR 2010

JANUARY
Time m	Time m
1 0234 5.8 / 0823 1.2 / F 1501 5.9 / 2108 0.7	**16** 0317 5.3 / 0829 1.4 / SA 1535 5.5 / 2048 1.1
2 0325 5.9 / 0913 1.1 / SA 1549 6.0 / 2159 0.5	**17** 0352 5.3 / 0905 1.2 / SU 1607 5.5 / 2123 1.0
3 0415 6.0 / 0958 1.0 / SU 1639 6.0 / 2246 0.4	**18** 0427 5.3 / 0938 1.2 / M 1639 5.4 / 2156 1.0
4 0506 5.9 / 1040 1.1 / M 1729 6.0 / 2327 0.5	**19** 0503 5.3 / 1007 1.3 / TU 1715 5.3 / 2224 1.1
5 0556 5.8 / 1119 1.2 / TU 1818 5.8 / 2250 1.2	**20** 0542 5.2 / 1031 1.4 / W 1754 5.2 / 2250 1.2
6 0001 0.7 / 0646 5.6 / W 1201 1.4 / 1908 5.6	**21** 0623 5.1 / 1058 1.5 / TH 1834 5.1 / 2320 1.3
7 0038 1.0 / 0737 5.3 / TH 1248 1.7 / ◗ 2000 5.3	**22** 0705 4.9 / 1133 1.7 / F 1916 4.9 / 2357 1.5
8 0125 1.4 / 0832 5.0 / F 1344 2.0 / 2058 5.1	**23** 0750 4.8 / 1215 1.9 / SA 2003 4.8 / ◖
9 0228 1.8 / 0933 4.8 / SA 1457 2.2 / 2205 4.9	**24** 0043 1.8 / 0839 4.6 / SU 1310 2.2 / 2058 4.7
10 0429 2.0 / 1040 4.7 / SU 1716 2.2 / 2313 4.8	**25** 0142 2.1 / 0938 4.6 / M 1615 2.3 / 2204 4.7
11 0555 2.0 / 1145 4.8 / M 1836 2.0	**26** 0449 2.2 / 1045 4.7 / TU 1717 2.0 / 2315 4.8
12 0016 4.9 / 0651 1.9 / TU 1246 5.0 / 1932 1.7	**27** 0546 1.9 / 1152 4.9 / W 1815 1.6
13 0113 5.0 / 0734 1.8 / W 1338 5.2 / 2016 1.5	**28** 0022 5.1 / 0639 1.6 / TH 1255 5.3 / 1914 1.2
14 0201 5.1 / 0807 1.7 / TH 1423 5.3 / 2051 1.4	**29** 0122 5.5 / 0735 1.3 / F 1351 5.6 / 2015 0.7
15 0241 5.2 / 0759 1.5 / F 1501 5.4 / ● 2106 1.3	**30** 0217 5.8 / 0828 1.0 / SA 1443 5.9 / ○ 2108 0.4
	31 0307 6.0 / 0916 0.8 / SU 1532 6.1 / 2153 0.1

FEBRUARY
Time m	Time m
1 0356 6.1 / 0958 0.7 / M 1621 6.2 / 2232 0.1	**16** 0401 5.4 / 0918 1.0 / TU 1619 5.5 / 2134 0.8
2 0445 6.1 / 1035 0.7 / TU 1709 6.2 / 2305 0.2	**17** 0437 5.4 / 0948 1.0 / W 1653 5.5 / 2200 0.9
3 0533 5.9 / 1107 0.8 / W 1755 6.0 / 2331 0.5	**18** 0514 5.3 / 1010 1.1 / TH 1730 5.4 / 2222 1.0
4 0619 5.7 / 1135 1.1 / TH 1841 5.7	**19** 0554 5.2 / 1032 1.2 / F 1808 5.2 / 2249 1.1
5 0000 1.0 / 0706 5.3 / F 1211 1.5 / ◗ 1929 5.3	**20** 0634 5.1 / 1102 1.4 / SA 1848 5.1 / 2323 1.4
6 0041 1.5 / 0755 5.0 / SA 1300 1.9 / 2022 4.9	**21** 0717 4.9 / 1141 1.6 / SU 1933 4.9
7 0139 2.0 / 0852 4.6 / SU 1415 2.3 / 2130 4.6	**22** 0007 1.7 / 0805 4.7 / M 1233 2.0 / ◗ 2027 4.7
8 0306 2.4 / 1004 4.5 / M 1712 2.4 / 2247 4.5	**23** 0104 2.1 / 0902 4.5 / TU 1348 2.2 / 2133 4.6
9 0540 2.4 / 1118 4.6 / TU 1833 2.0 / 2357 4.6	**24** 0429 2.3 / 1011 4.6 / W 1703 1.9 / 2250 4.7
10 0639 2.2 / 1223 4.8 / W 1925 1.7	**25** 0531 2.0 / 1125 4.8 / TH 1804 1.5
11 0055 4.8 / 0721 1.9 / TH 1318 5.1 / 2006 1.5	**26** 0002 5.1 / 0626 1.6 / F 1232 5.2 / 1905 1.0
12 0143 5.0 / 0754 1.7 / F 1402 5.3 / 2039 1.3	**27** 0105 5.4 / 0721 1.2 / SA 1331 5.6 / 2003 0.5
13 0221 5.2 / 0730 1.5 / SA 1439 5.4 / 2057 1.2	**28** 0158 5.8 / 0813 0.9 / SU 1423 6.0 / ○ 2051 0.2
14 0255 5.3 / 0805 1.2 / SU 1513 5.5 / ● 2026 1.0	
15 0328 5.4 / 0843 1.0 / M 1545 5.5 / 2102 0.8	

MARCH
Time m	Time m
1 0247 6.0 / 0858 0.6 / M 1512 6.2 / 2131 0.0	**16** 0301 5.4 / 0818 0.9 / TU 1520 5.5 / 2036 0.8
2 0334 6.1 / 0939 0.5 / TU 1559 6.3 / 2207 0.0	**17** 0335 5.5 / 0854 0.8 / W 1554 5.5 / 2108 0.7
3 0420 6.1 / 1016 0.5 / W 1645 6.2 / 2237 0.2	**18** 0410 5.5 / 0925 0.9 / TH 1630 5.5 / 2134 0.8
4 0506 5.9 / 1047 0.7 / TH 1730 6.0 / 2301 0.6	**19** 0448 5.4 / 0948 1.0 / F 1707 5.4 / 2157 0.9
5 0550 5.6 / 1111 1.0 / F 1815 5.7 / 2326 1.1	**20** 0527 5.3 / 1010 1.1 / SA 1746 5.3 / 2224 1.1
6 0635 5.3 / 1137 1.4 / SA 1900 5.2	**21** 0608 5.1 / 1040 1.2 / SU 1827 5.1 / 2259 1.4
7 0001 1.6 / 0719 4.9 / SU 1219 1.8 / ◗ 1950 4.8	**22** 0652 4.9 / 1121 1.5 / M 1913 4.9 / 2344 1.7
8 0055 2.2 / 0811 4.6 / M 1347 2.2 / 2057 4.4	**23** 0741 4.7 / 1216 1.8 / TU 2007 4.7 / ◗
9 0231 2.6 / 0926 4.3 / TU 1659 2.4 / 2221 4.3	**24** 0045 2.2 / 0838 4.6 / W 1536 2.0 / 2114 4.6
10 0514 2.6 / 1050 4.4 / W 1811 2.0 / 2334 4.4	**25** 0406 2.3 / 0949 4.6 / TH 1646 1.7 / 2232 4.7
11 0614 2.3 / 1156 4.6 / TH 1859 1.7	**26** 0511 1.9 / 1104 4.9 / F 1748 1.2 / 2346 5.1
12 0032 4.7 / 0655 2.0 / F 1304 4.9 / 1937 1.5	**27** 0607 1.5 / 1211 5.2 / SA 1848 0.8
13 0119 4.9 / 0725 1.7 / SA 1334 5.2 / 2008 1.3	**28** 0046 5.4 / 0701 1.1 / SU 1309 5.6 / 1941 0.4
14 0156 5.2 / 0703 1.4 / SU 1412 5.3 / 1926 1.1	**29** 0139 5.7 / 0751 0.8 / M 1402 5.9 / 2027 0.2
15 0229 5.3 / 0739 1.1 / M 1446 5.5 / ● 2000 0.9	**30** 0227 5.9 / 0837 0.6 / TU 1451 6.1 / ○ 2106 0.1
	31 0312 6.0 / 0918 0.4 / W 1538 6.1 / 2140 0.2

APRIL
Time m	Time m
1 0357 5.9 / 0955 0.5 / TH 1623 6.0 / 2210 0.5	**16** 0345 5.5 / 0902 0.8 / F 1608 5.5 / 2108 0.8
2 0441 5.8 / 1027 0.7 / F 1708 5.8 / 2234 0.8	**17** 0424 5.5 / 0929 0.9 / SA 1647 5.5 / 2135 0.9
3 0524 5.5 / 1050 1.0 / SA 1752 5.5 / 2255 1.3	**18** 0505 5.4 / 0956 1.0 / SU 1729 5.4 / 2207 1.1
4 0606 5.2 / 1135 1.1 / SU 1836 5.1 / 2323 1.7	**19** 0549 5.2 / 1031 1.2 / M 1813 5.2 / 2246 1.4
5 0648 4.9 / 1146 1.7 / M 1924 4.7	**20** 0635 5.0 / 1118 1.4 / TU 1901 5.0 / 2337 1.8
6 0004 2.2 / 0734 4.6 / TU 1318 2.1 / ◗ 2023 4.4	**21** 0725 4.8 / 1222 1.6 / W 1956 4.8 / ●
7 0150 2.6 / 0840 4.4 / W 1501 2.2 / 2147 4.2	**22** 0050 2.2 / 0824 4.7 / TH 1512 1.7 / 2102 4.7
8 0329 2.6 / 1013 4.4 / TH 1726 2.1 / 2300 4.4	**23** 0334 2.2 / 0935 4.8 / F 1624 1.4 / 2217 4.8
9 0523 2.4 / 1119 4.5 / F 1814 1.8 / 2358 4.6	**24** 0444 1.9 / 1047 5.0 / SA 1727 1.1 / 2326 5.1
10 0606 2.1 / 1212 4.8 / SA 1852 1.6	**25** 0543 1.5 / 1150 5.3 / SU 1824 0.8
11 0044 4.9 / 0604 1.7 / SU 1257 5.0 / 1915 1.4	**26** 0024 5.4 / 0638 1.2 / M 1247 5.6 / 1916 0.6
12 0123 5.1 / 0634 1.4 / M 1337 5.2 / 1856 1.2	**27** 0117 5.6 / 0730 0.9 / TU 1341 5.7 / 2002 0.5
13 0158 5.3 / 0712 1.2 / TU 1415 5.4 / 1932 1.0	**28** 0206 5.7 / 0817 0.7 / W 1431 5.8 / ○ 2042 0.5
14 0233 5.4 / 0751 0.9 / W 1452 5.5 / ● 2008 0.8	**29** 0252 5.6 / 0859 0.6 / TH 1519 5.8 / 2116 0.6
15 0308 5.5 / 0829 0.8 / TH 1529 5.5 / 2040 0.8	**30** 0337 5.7 / 0937 0.7 / F 1605 5.8 / 2146 0.8

Chart Datum: 2·95 metres below Ordnance Datum (Newlyn). HAT is 6·4 metres above Chart Datum; see 4.5

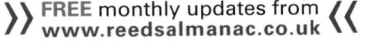

TIME ZONE (UT)
For Summer Time add ONE hour in **non-shaded areas**

ROSYTH LAT 56°01'N LONG 3°27'W
TIMES AND HEIGHTS OF HIGH AND LOW WATERS

Dates in red are **SPRINGS**
Dates in blue are **NEAPS**

YEAR 2010

MAY

Day	Time m	Time m	Day	Time m	Time m
1 SA	0420 5.6 / 1010 0.8 / 1649 5.6 / 2210 1.1		**16** SU	0405 5.5 / 0918 0.8 / 1631 5.6 / 2123 1.0	
2 SU	0501 5.4 / 1034 1.0 / 1732 5.3 / 2230 1.4		**17** M	0449 5.5 / 0953 0.9 / 1716 5.5 / 2201 1.2	
3 M	0542 5.2 / 1051 1.3 / 1815 5.1 / 2257 1.7		**18** TU	0535 5.3 / 1036 1.0 / 1803 5.4 / 2247 1.4	
4 TU	0622 4.9 / 1126 1.6 / 1859 4.8 / 2333 2.0		**19** W	0624 5.2 / 1131 1.1 / 1853 5.2 / 2343 1.7	
5 W	0705 4.7 / 1222 1.9 / 1948 4.5		**20** TH ☽	0717 5.1 / 1251 1.3 / 1948 5.0	
6 TH ☽	0028 2.3 / 0757 4.5 / 1408 2.0 / 2050 4.3		**21** F	0056 1.9 / 0815 5.0 / 1436 1.3 / 2049 4.9	
7 F	0231 2.5 / 0913 4.4 / 1529 2.1 / 2206 4.3		**22** SA	0235 2.0 / 0920 5.0 / 1551 1.3 / 2156 4.9	
8 SA	0348 2.4 / 1027 4.5 / 1637 1.9 / 2307 4.5		**23** SU	0405 1.8 / 1026 5.1 / 1658 1.2 / 2301 5.1	
9 SU	0445 2.1 / 1123 4.7 / 1721 1.7 / 2357 4.7		**24** M	0515 1.6 / 1127 5.3 / 1759 1.1	
10 M	0527 1.8 / 1212 4.9 / 1753 1.5		**25** TU	0000 5.2 / 0617 1.4 / 1225 5.4 / 1853 1.0	
11 TU	0041 5.0 / 0605 1.6 / 1257 5.1 / 1827 1.3		**26** W	0056 5.4 / 0713 1.2 / 1321 5.5 / 1941 1.0	
12 W	0122 5.2 / 0645 1.3 / 1341 5.3 / 1903 1.2		**27** TH ○	0147 5.5 / 0803 1.0 / 1414 5.6 / 2021 1.0	
13 TH	0202 5.4 / 0725 1.1 / 1423 5.4 / 1940 1.0		**28** F	0235 5.5 / 0846 0.9 / 1503 5.6 / 2056 1.0	
14 F ●	0242 5.5 / 0806 0.9 / 1505 5.5 / 2015 1.0		**29** SA	0320 5.5 / 0925 0.9 / 1548 5.5 / 2125 1.1	
15 SA	0323 5.5 / 0843 0.8 / 1547 5.6 / 2049 1.0		**30** SU	0402 5.4 / 0957 0.9 / 1631 5.4 / 2149 1.2	
			31 M	0443 5.3 / 1020 1.0 / 1712 5.3 / 2212 1.4	

JUNE

Day	Time m	Day	Time m
1 TU	0521 5.2 / 1038 1.2 / 1752 5.1 / 2239 1.6	**16** W	0524 5.6 / 1108 0.7 / 1752 5.6 / 2253 1.2
2 W	0600 5.0 / 1108 1.4 / 1832 4.9 / 2311 1.8	**17** TH	0614 5.6 / 1158 0.8 / 1842 5.5 / 2344 1.4
3 TH	0640 4.9 / 1145 1.6 / 1913 4.7 / 2350 2.0	**18** F	0706 5.5 / 1246 0.9 / 1933 5.3
4 F ☽	0726 4.7 / 1232 1.8 / 1959 4.6	**19** SA ☽	0039 1.6 / 0759 5.3 / 1340 1.1 / 2028 5.1
5 SA	0041 2.2 / 0817 4.6 / 1345 2.0 / 2052 4.5	**20** SU	0141 1.7 / 0858 5.2 / 1451 1.4 / 2129 5.0
6 SU	0236 2.3 / 0918 4.6 / 1533 2.0 / 2154 4.5	**21** M	0256 1.9 / 1000 5.1 / 1620 1.5 / 2232 4.9
7 M	0356 2.2 / 1022 4.6 / 1633 1.9 / 2256 4.6	**22** TU	0444 1.9 / 1103 5.1 / 1734 1.5 / 2335 5.0
8 TU	0451 2.0 / 1120 4.8 / 1720 1.8 / 2352 4.8	**23** W	0605 1.7 / 1205 5.2 / 1835 1.5
9 W	0538 1.8 / 1214 5.0 / 1802 1.6	**24** TH	0034 5.1 / 0707 1.5 / 1304 5.2 / 1925 1.4
10 TH	0043 5.0 / 0622 1.5 / 1306 5.2 / 1841 1.4	**25** F	0130 5.3 / 0800 1.3 / 1358 5.3 / 2006 1.4
11 F	0131 5.2 / 0706 1.2 / 1355 5.4 / 1920 1.3	**26** SA	0220 5.4 / 0844 1.1 / 1447 5.4 / 2040 1.3
12 SA ●	0217 5.4 / 0753 1.0 / 1442 5.5 / 2001 1.1	**27** SU	0305 5.4 / 0920 1.0 / 1530 5.4 / 2103 1.3
13 SU	0302 5.6 / 0840 0.8 / 1528 5.7 / 2042 1.0	**28** M	0345 5.4 / 0947 1.0 / 1610 5.3 / 2125 1.2
14 M	0348 5.6 / 0928 0.7 / 1615 5.7 / 2123 1.0	**29** TU	0423 5.4 / 0957 1.0 / 1648 5.3 / 2153 1.3
15 TU	0435 5.7 / 1017 0.6 / 1703 5.7 / 2206 1.1	**30** W	0459 5.3 / 1018 1.0 / 1724 5.2 / 2221 1.3

JULY

Day	Time m	Day	Time m
1 TH	0535 5.2 / 1045 1.2 / 1801 5.1 / 2248 1.5	**16** F	0557 5.9 / 1146 0.4 / 1822 5.7 / 2332 1.1
2 F	0613 5.1 / 1114 1.3 / 1840 4.9 / 2319 1.6	**17** SA	0646 5.8 / 1220 0.7 / 1910 5.5
3 SA	0655 4.9 / 1146 1.5 / 1921 4.8 / 2356 1.8	**18** SU ☽	0016 1.3 / 0736 5.5 / 1300 1.1 / 2001 5.2
4 SU ☽	0739 4.8 / 1224 1.7 / 2006 4.7	**19** M	0107 1.6 / 0831 5.3 / 1354 1.5 / 2058 4.9
5 M	0041 2.1 / 0828 4.7 / 1312 1.9 / 2057 4.6	**20** TU	0212 2.0 / 0933 5.0 / 1517 1.9 / 2203 4.8
6 TU	0140 2.2 / 0925 4.6 / 1415 2.1 / 2155 4.6	**21** W	0414 2.1 / 1042 4.9 / 1713 2.0 / 2311 4.8
7 W	0419 2.2 / 1028 4.7 / 1653 2.0 / 2300 4.7	**22** TH	0605 1.9 / 1148 4.9 / 1823 1.9
8 TH	0516 2.0 / 1133 4.8 / 1742 1.8	**23** F	0016 4.9 / 0708 1.6 / 1250 5.0 / 1914 1.8
9 F	0003 4.9 / 0606 1.6 / 1233 5.1 / 1828 1.4	**24** SA	0114 5.1 / 0759 1.4 / 1344 5.2 / 1955 1.6
10 SA	0100 5.1 / 0657 1.3 / 1328 5.3 / 1914 1.4	**25** SU	0204 5.3 / 0840 1.2 / 1430 5.3 / 2025 1.5
11 SU ●	0152 5.4 / 0752 1.0 / 1419 5.6 / 2002 1.2	**26** M ○	0247 5.4 / 0912 1.0 / 1510 5.3 / 2028 1.3
12 M	0241 5.7 / 0848 0.7 / 1508 5.8 / 2049 1.0	**27** TU	0324 5.5 / 0932 1.0 / 1545 5.4 / 2055 1.2
13 TU	0329 5.9 / 0940 0.4 / 1556 5.9 / 2133 0.9	**28** W	0358 5.5 / 0922 0.9 / 1619 5.3 / 2129 1.1
14 W	0418 6.0 / 1027 0.3 / 1645 6.0 / 2214 0.8	**29** TH	0432 5.4 / 0951 0.9 / 1653 5.3 / 2159 1.1
15 TH	0507 6.0 / 1116 0.3 / 1734 5.9 / 2253 0.9	**30** F	0506 5.4 / 1018 1.0 / 1729 5.2 / 2224 1.3
		31 SA	0543 5.3 / 1041 1.1 / 1807 5.1 / 2249 1.4

AUGUST

Day	Time m	Day	Time m
1 SU	0623 5.1 / 1108 1.3 / 1847 5.0 / 2319 1.6	**16** M ◐	0709 5.6 / 1228 1.3 / 1931 5.2
2 M	0704 5.0 / 1141 1.5 / 1929 4.8 / 2357 1.8	**17** TU	0037 1.7 / 0802 5.2 / 1323 1.8 / 2025 4.8
3 TU	0749 4.8 / 1222 1.8 / 2014 4.7	**18** W	0146 2.1 / 0907 4.8 / 1442 2.2 / 2134 4.6
4 W	0045 2.1 / 0839 4.7 / 1315 2.1 / 2107 4.6	**19** TH	0424 2.3 / 1023 4.7 / 1700 2.3 / 2251 4.6
5 TH	0152 2.3 / 0942 4.6 / 1629 2.3 / 2213 4.6	**20** F	0604 2.0 / 1135 4.7 / 1810 2.2 / 2359 4.8
6 F	0458 2.1 / 1054 4.7 / 1724 2.0 / 2324 4.8	**21** SA	0700 1.6 / 1237 4.9 / 1859 1.9
7 SA	0552 1.7 / 1203 5.0 / 1814 1.7	**22** SU	0056 5.1 / 0745 1.4 / 1329 5.1 / 1937 1.7
8 SU	0030 5.1 / 0647 1.2 / 1250 5.4 / 1903 1.4	**23** M	0144 5.3 / 0822 1.2 / 1411 5.3 / 2001 1.5
9 M	0127 5.5 / 0745 0.8 / 1357 5.7 / 1954 1.1	**24** TU ○	0224 5.5 / 0851 1.1 / 1446 5.4 / 1948 1.3
10 TU ●	0218 5.8 / 0840 0.4 / 1446 6.0 / 2043 0.8	**25** W	0259 5.6 / 0820 1.0 / 1518 5.4 / 2024 1.1
11 W	0307 6.1 / 0928 0.1 / 1534 6.1 / 2127 0.6	**26** TH	0331 5.6 / 0848 0.9 / 1549 5.5 / 2101 1.0
12 TH	0355 6.2 / 1010 0.0 / 1622 6.1 / 2206 0.6	**27** F	0403 5.5 / 0920 0.8 / 1622 5.4 / 2133 1.0
13 F	0444 6.3 / 1048 0.1 / 1709 6.1 / 2241 0.7	**28** SA	0437 5.5 / 0948 0.9 / 1657 5.4 / 2158 1.1
14 SA	0532 6.1 / 1121 0.4 / 1756 5.9 / 2313 0.9	**29** SU	0513 5.4 / 1009 1.1 / 1735 5.3 / 2220 1.3
15 SU	0620 5.9 / 1150 0.8 / 1843 5.6 / 2350 1.3	**30** M	0551 5.3 / 1033 1.2 / 1814 5.1 / 2247 1.5
		31 TU	0632 5.1 / 1105 1.5 / 1855 4.9 / 2323 1.7

Chart Datum: 2·95 metres below Ordnance Datum (Newlyn). HAT is 6·4 metres above Chart Datum; see 4.5

SE Scotland

ROSYTH LAT 56°01′N LONG 3°27′W
TIMES AND HEIGHTS OF HIGH AND LOW WATERS

TIME ZONE (UT)
For Summer Time add ONE hour in **non-shaded areas**

Dates in red are SPRINGS
Dates in blue are NEAPS

YEAR 2010

SEPTEMBER

Time	m		Time	m
1 0715	4.9	**16**	0128	2.1
1146	1.8		0841	4.7
W 1939	4.8	TH	1416	2.5
◗			2104	4.5
2 0010	2.0	**17**	0424	2.3
0805	4.7		1003	4.5
TH 1239	2.2	F	1636	2.6
2030	4.6		2229	4.6
3 0116	2.3	**18**	0545	2.0
0907	4.6		1117	4.6
F 1606	2.4	SA	1746	2.3
2135	4.6		2337	4.8
4 0439	2.0	**19**	0636	1.7
1023	4.7		1217	4.9
SA 1704	2.1	SU	1832	2.1
2251	4.8			
5 0536	1.5	**20**	0032	5.1
1139	5.0		0717	1.4
SU 1755	1.8	M	1306	5.1
			1908	1.8
6 0002	5.2	**21**	0117	5.3
0632	1.1		0752	1.3
M 1242	5.4	TU	1345	5.3
1844	1.4		1844	1.6
7 0101	5.6	**22**	0155	5.5
0728	0.6		0817	1.2
TU 1335	5.8	W	1419	5.4
1935	1.0		1916	1.3
8 0153	6.0	**23**	0229	5.5
0820	0.3		0740	1.0
W 1423	6.1	TH	1449	5.5
● 2024	0.7	○	1954	1.1
9 0242	6.2	**24**	0302	5.6
0906	0.0		0815	0.9
TH 1510	6.2	F	1520	5.6
2108	0.5		2032	1.0
10 0330	6.4	**25**	0335	5.6
0946	0.0		0849	0.9
F 1556	6.2	SA	1553	5.5
2148	0.5		2105	1.0
11 0418	6.3	**26**	0409	5.6
1021	0.2		0916	0.9
SA 1642	6.1	SU	1628	5.5
2222	0.6		2132	1.1
12 0506	6.2	**27**	0446	5.5
1052	0.5		0939	1.1
SU 1728	5.8	M	1705	5.4
2251	0.9		2155	1.2
13 0554	5.9	**28**	0525	5.3
1121	1.0		1005	1.3
M 1814	5.5	TU	1745	5.2
2323	1.3		2223	1.4
14 0642	5.5	**29**	0606	5.2
1157	1.6		1038	1.5
TU 1901	5.1	W	1827	5.0
			2300	1.6
15 0010	1.7	**30**	0651	5.0
0735	5.0		1120	1.9
W 1255	2.1	TH	1912	4.8
◗ 1952	4.8		2350	1.9

OCTOBER

Time	m		Time	m
1 0742	4.8	**16**	0250	2.3
1217	2.3		0932	4.5
F 2004	4.7	SA	1516	2.6
◗			2156	4.5
2 0309	2.2	**17**	0506	2.1
0843	4.7		1045	4.6
SA 1539	2.4	SU	1702	2.5
2108	4.7		2303	4.7
3 0418	1.8	**18**	0556	1.8
0959	4.8		1143	4.8
SU 1641	2.1	M	1751	2.2
2225	4.9		2357	4.9
4 0517	1.4	**19**	0637	1.6
1117	5.1		1231	5.0
M 1733	1.7	TU	1820	1.9
2337	5.2			
5 0612	1.0	**20**	0041	5.2
1219	5.5		0710	1.5
TU 1823	1.3	W	1312	5.2
			1813	1.6
6 0036	5.6	**21**	0121	5.3
0706	0.6		0637	1.3
W 1312	5.8	TH	1347	5.4
1913	1.0		1847	1.4
7 0129	6.0	**22**	0157	5.5
0756	0.4		0708	1.2
TH 1400	6.1	F	1419	5.5
● 2003	0.7		1926	1.1
8 0218	6.2	**23**	0233	5.6
0841	0.2		0744	1.0
F 1447	6.2	SA	1452	5.6
2048	0.6	○	2004	1.0
9 0307	6.3	**24**	0308	5.6
0921	0.3		0818	1.0
SA 1532	6.1	SU	1527	5.6
2128	0.6		2039	1.0
10 0355	6.2	**25**	0345	5.6
0956	0.5		0848	1.1
SU 1618	6.0	M	1603	5.6
2203	0.7		2110	1.1
11 0443	6.0	**26**	0424	5.5
1027	0.9		0915	1.2
M 1703	5.7	TU	1642	5.4
2229	1.0		2137	1.2
12 0531	5.7	**27**	0505	5.4
1052	1.3		0944	1.3
TU 1747	5.4	W	1722	5.3
2256	1.3		2209	1.3
13 0619	5.3	**28**	0548	5.3
1124	1.8		1021	1.6
W 1832	5.1	TH	1806	5.1
2341	1.7		2250	1.5
14 0710	5.0	**29**	0635	5.1
1219	2.2		1107	1.9
TH 1920	4.8	F	1853	5.0
◖			2346	1.7
15 0102	2.1	**30**	0727	4.9
0812	4.6		1211	2.2
F 1343	2.6	SA	1946	4.8
2026	4.6	◗		
		31	0236	1.9
			0827	4.8
		SU	1502	2.3
			2050	4.8

NOVEMBER

Time	m		Time	m
1 0350	1.6	**16**	0440	2.1
0940	4.9		1053	4.6
M 1610	2.1	TU	1629	2.3
2204	5.0		2307	4.7
2 0451	1.3	**17**	0530	1.9
1052	5.1		1145	4.8
TU 1707	1.8	W	1710	2.1
2313	5.3		2357	4.9
3 0548	1.1	**18**	0546	1.8
1154	5.4		1230	5.1
W 1800	1.4	TH	1745	1.8
4 0012	5.6	**19**	0041	5.1
0642	0.8		0607	1.6
TH 1248	5.7	F	1310	5.3
1853	1.2		1821	1.5
5 0107	5.8	**20**	0123	5.3
0733	0.7		0640	1.4
F 1339	5.9	SA	1348	5.4
1946	0.9		1900	1.3
6 0159	6.0	**21**	0204	5.5
0819	0.6		0716	1.3
SA 1427	6.0	SU	1426	5.5
● 2033	0.8	○	1940	1.2
7 0249	6.0	**22**	0244	5.6
0859	0.7		0752	1.2
SU 1513	5.9	M	1504	5.6
2115	0.8		2019	1.1
8 0337	6.0	**23**	0324	5.6
0935	0.9		0826	1.2
M 1558	5.8	TU	1544	5.6
2151	0.9		2055	1.0
9 0424	5.8	**24**	0406	5.6
1006	1.2		0900	1.2
TU 1642	5.6	W	1626	5.6
2214	1.1		2130	1.0
10 0511	5.6	**25**	0449	5.5
1027	1.5		0936	1.3
W 1724	5.4	TH	1707	5.5
2235	1.3		2208	1.1
11 0557	5.3	**26**	0535	5.4
1053	1.8		1017	1.5
TH 1806	5.2	F	1752	5.3
2314	1.6		2253	1.2
12 0644	5.0	**27**	0623	5.3
1133	2.1		1107	1.7
F 1848	4.9	SA	1841	5.2
			2352	1.4
13 0009	1.9	**28**	0716	5.2
0735	4.7		1211	2.0
SA 1242	2.4	SU	1934	5.1
◖ 1936	4.7	◗		
14 0137	2.1	**29**	0116	1.5
0837	4.5		0812	5.1
SU 1412	2.6	M	1346	2.1
2047	4.6		2034	5.1
15 0308	2.2	**30**	0306	1.5
0950	4.5		0917	5.1
M 1528	2.5	TU	1523	2.0
2208	4.6		2141	5.1

DECEMBER

Time	m		Time	m
1 0417	1.4	**16**	0412	2.1
1024	5.1		1037	4.6
W 1634	1.9	TH	1632	2.3
2248	5.2		2258	4.7
2 0521	1.3	**17**	0504	2.0
1126	5.3		1137	4.8
TH 1738	1.7	F	1719	2.0
2350	5.4		2355	4.9
3 0621	1.2	**18**	0545	1.8
1225	5.5		1229	5.0
F 1841	1.4	SA	1802	1.8
4 0048	5.6	**19**	0047	5.1
0715	1.1		0621	1.7
SA 1320	5.6	SU	1317	5.3
1938	1.2		1843	1.5
5 0143	5.7	**20**	0135	5.3
0803	1.1		0659	1.5
SU 1411	5.7	M	1401	5.4
● 2028	1.1		1926	1.3
6 0235	5.7	**21**	0220	5.5
0844	1.1		0738	1.3
M 1458	5.7	TU	1444	5.6
2111	1.0	○	2010	1.0
7 0322	5.7	**22**	0304	5.6
0920	1.2		0818	1.2
TU 1543	5.7	W	1526	5.7
2147	1.0		2053	0.9
8 0407	5.6	**23**	0348	5.7
0949	1.3		0858	1.2
W 1624	5.6	TH	1610	5.7
2209	1.1		2134	0.8
9 0451	5.5	**24**	0434	5.7
1008	1.4		0938	1.2
TH 1704	5.4	F	1654	5.7
2219	1.2		2216	0.8
10 0533	5.3	**25**	0521	5.7
1031	1.6		1021	1.2
F 1741	5.3	SA	1741	5.7
2250	1.4		2259	0.8
11 0614	5.1	**26**	0610	5.6
1100	1.8		1107	1.4
SA 1818	5.1	SU	1829	5.6
2327	1.6		2347	1.0
12 0655	4.9	**27**	0700	5.4
1137	2.0		1200	1.6
SU 1859	4.9	M	1919	5.4
13 0010	1.8	**28**	0041	1.2
0739	4.7		0752	5.2
M 1224	2.3	TU	1300	1.8
◖ 1946	4.7	◗	2013	5.3
14 0104	2.0	**29**	0143	1.4
0830	4.6		0849	5.1
TU 1358	2.5	W	1411	2.0
2042	4.6		2115	5.1
15 0258	2.2	**30**	0309	1.7
0930	4.5		0953	5.0
W 1533	2.4	TH	1544	2.0
2150	4.6		2222	5.0
		31	0452	1.7
			1059	5.0
		F	1725	1.9
			2329	5.1

Chart Datum: 2·95 metres below Ordnance Datum (Newlyn). HAT is 6·4 metres above Chart Datum; see 4.5

9.6.8 FIRTH OF FORTH

E and W Lothian/City of Edinburgh/Fife

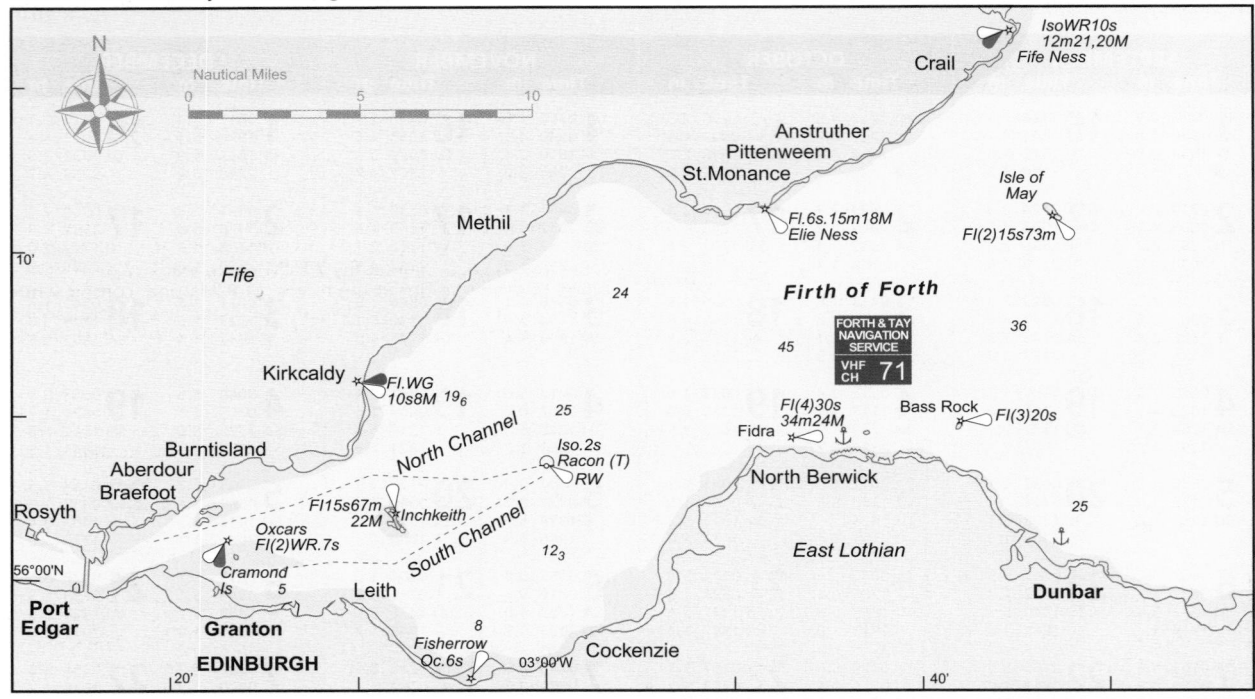

CHARTS AC 734, 735, 736, 737, 741; Imray C23, C27.

TIDES +0350 (Granton) Dover; ML 3·3; Duration 0620

Standard Port LEITH (→)

Times				Height (metres)			
High Water		Low Water		MHWS	MHWN	MLWN	MLWS
0300	0900	0300	0900	5·6	4·4	2·0	0·8
1500	2100	1500	2100				
Differences COCKENZIE							
−0007	−0015	−0013	−0005	−0·2	0·0	No data	

GRANTON: Same as LEITH

SHELTER Granton mostly dries but is open to violent swell in N'lies. Pontoons on E side of Middle Pier in about 2m and RFYC welcomes visitors. Pilot launches berth at seaward end. W hbr is planned for development as a marina. Port Edgar Marina offers good shelter, except for a surge at LW esp in E winds, but prone to silting. Caution: strong tidal streams. Do not enter E of wavebreak; 3kn sp limit. Leith is purely commercial. Rosyth should only be used in emergency. Forth Navigation Service controls the Firth of Forth, Granton Hbr and all commercial impounded docks.

NAVIGATION WPT Granton 56°00′·00N 03°13′·31W, 180°/0·72M to ent. WPT Port Edgar 56°N 03°24′·3W, 244°/3ca to W bkwtr.

- Beware Hound Pt terminal; Forth Railway and Road Bridges; vessels bound to/from Rosyth and Grangemouth especially in local fog (haar). 12kn speed limit W of Forth Rly Bridge.
- On N shore, no vessel may enter Mortimer's Deep (Braefoot gas terminal) without approval from Forth Navigation Service.
- Protected chan runs from Nos 13 & 14 buoys (NNW of Oxcars) under the bridges (N of Inch Garvie and Beamer Rk), to Rosyth. When activated (occas) via Forth Ports plc, other vessels must clear the chan for Rosyth traffic.

LIGHTS AND MARKS See 9.6.4 and chartlets. Granton: R flag with W diagonal cross (or ● lt) on signal mast at middle pier hd = Entry prohib.

R/T Call *Forth Navigation* (at Grangemouth) Ch **71** (calling and short messages, H24) 16; **20** 12 will be requested if necessary. Traffic, nav and weather info available on request. Leith Hbr

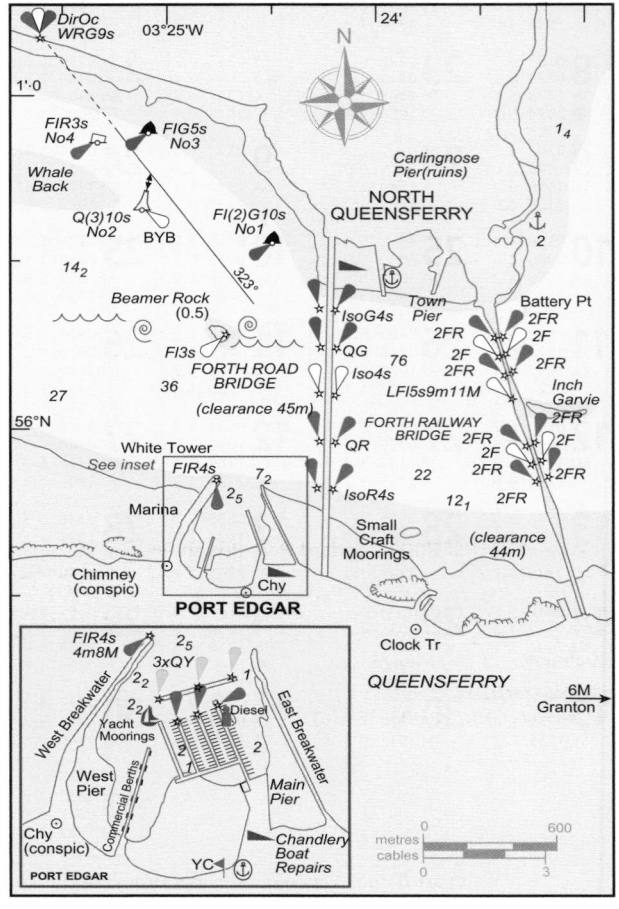

Radio Ch 12. Granton marina, call *Boswell* Ch M. Port Edgar Marina Ch M 80 (Apr-Sept 0900-1930; Oct-Mar 0900-1630 LT). Rosyth Dockyard, call *QHM* Ch 74 13 73 (Mon-Fri: 0730-1700). Grangemouth Docks Ch 14 (H24).

TELEPHONE (Code 0131) Forth Navigation Service 5558700; QHM Rosyth (01383) 425050; MRCC (01333) 450666; Weather (0141) 2483451; Marinecall 09068 969642; Police (S Queensferry) 3311798; ⊞ Edinburgh Royal Infirmary 2292477; Flag Officer Scotland/Northern Ireland (01436) 674321 ext 3206, for Naval activities off N and E Scotland; Forth Yacht Clubs Ass'n 5523452.

FACILITIES
GRANTON Extensive development of the W hbr is proposed. HM via Leith, ☎ 555 8866, Access HW±3½, FW, Slip; **Royal Forth YC** ☎ 552 3006, Slip, M, L, FW, C (5 ton), D, El, Bar; **Forth Corinthian YC** ☎ 552 5939, Slip, M, L, Bar; **Services:** Gas, Gaz, ✕, CH, ME. **Town** D, P, 🛒, R, Bar, ✉, Ⓑ, ⇌, ✈ (Buses to Edinburgh).

ROSYTH Dockyard and ferry port; no facilities for yachts except in emergency. **Ferries:** Zeebrugge; 3/week; 17 Hrs; Superfast (www.superfast.com).

Standard Port ROSYTH (←)

Times				Height (metres)			
High Water		Low Water		MHWS	MHWN	MLWN	MLWS
0300	1000	0300	0900	5·8	4·7	2·2	0·8
1500	2200	1500	2100				
Differences GRANGEMOUTH							
+0015	+0010	−0050	−0045	0·0	−0·1	−0·2	−0·2
KINCARDINE							
+0015	+0030	−0030	−0030	0·0	−0·2	−0·5	−0·3

SOUTH QUEENSFERRY Standard Port Rosyth (←)
Port Edgar Marina (301+8 visitors) ☎ 331 3330, admin.PE@ edinburghleisure.co.uk, £1.90, Access H24, Wi-fi, M, Slip, CH, ME, D, C (5 ton) on N end of main pier, El, Ⓔ, ME, ✕, SM, Gas, Gaz, FW, R; Port Edgar YC, Bar. **Town** P, 🛒, R, Bar, ✉, Ⓑ, ⇌ (Dalmeny), ✈ Edinburgh.

GRANGEMOUTH: Standard Port Rosyth (←). HM ☎ 01324 498566 (H24); Port Office ☎ 498597 (HO). VHF Ch 14 16. Commercial port.

FIRTH OF FORTH
MINOR HARBOURS AND ANCHORAGES ON THE S SHORE
FISHERROW, East Lothian, **55°56′·79N 03°04′·09W.** AC 734, 735. HW +0345 on Dover, −0005 on Leith; HW −0·1m on Leith; ML 3·0m; Duration 0620. Shelter good except in NW winds. Mainly a pleasure craft hbr, dries 5ca offshore. Appr dangerous in on-shore winds. Access HW±2. High-rise block (38m) is conspic 9ca W of hbr. E pier lt, Oc 6s 5m 6M on metal framework tr. Berth on E pier. HM ☎ (0131) 665 5900; **Fisherrow YC** FW.

Town 🛒, P & D from garage, R, Bar, Ⓑ, ✉, SM.

CRAMOND, City of Edinburgh, **55°59′·80N 03°17′·49W.** AC 736. Tides as Leith (see 9.6.8). Cramond Island, approx 1M offshore, is connected to the S shore of the Firth by a drying causeway. A chan, marked by 7 SHM posts, leads W of Cramond Island to Cramond hbr at the mouth of R Almond, conspic white houses. Access HW±2; AB free or ⚓ off the Is. Seek local advice from: **Cramond Boat Club** ☎ (0131) 336 1356, FW, M, Bar. **Village** 🛒, R, Pub, Bus.

MINOR HARBOURS AND ANCHORAGES ON THE N SHORE
INCHCOLM, Fife, **56°01′·85N 03°17′·89W.** AC 736. Tides see 9.6.8. Best ⚓ in 4m, N of abbey (conspic); appr from NW or ESE, to land at pier close E (small fee). Meadulse Rks (dry) on N side. Ends of island foul. At SE end, lt Fl (3) 15s, obsc 075°-145°. No facilities. ☎ 0131-244 3101. Keep clear of large ships under way in Mortimer's Deep.

ABERDOUR, Fife, **56°03′·00N 03°17′·49W.** AC 735, 736. HW +0345 on Dover; +0005 on Leith; HW 0·5m on Leith; ML 3·3m; Duration 0630. See 9.6.8. Good shelter except in SE winds when a swell occurs. The ⚓ between The Little Craigs and the disused pier is good but exposed to winds from E to SW. Temp berths £2 are available in hbr (dries) alongside the quay wall. Beware Little Craigs (dries 2·2m) and outfall 2ca N marked by bn. There are no lts/ marks. Facilities: FW (tap on pier), P, R, 🛒, Bar in village; **Aberdour BC** ☎ (01592) 202827.

ELIE, Fife, **56°11′·20N 02°49′·29W.** AC 734. HW +0325 on Dover, −0015 on Leith; HW −0·1m on Leith; ML 3·0m; Duration 0620; Elie B provides good shelter from N winds for small craft but local knowledge is needed. Hbr dries; 3 short term waiting buoys available. Beware ledge off end of pier which dries. From E beware Ox Rk (dries 1m) 5M ENE of Elie Ness; from W beware rks off Chapel Ness, W Vows, E Vows (surmounted by cage bn) and Thill Rk, marked by PHM Fl(4)R.10s buoy. Lt: Elie Ness Fl 6s 15m 18M, W tr. HM (01333) 330051; AB (3) drying £5, M, ⬠, FW, CH, SC, Slip. Police 592100. Dr ☎ 330302; **Services:** P & D (tanker), Gas, Gaz. El. In Elie & Earlsferry: R, 🛒, Bar, ✉, Ⓑ.

ST MONANS, Fife, **56°12′·25 N 02°45′·94W.** AC 734. HW +0335 on Dover, −0020 on Leith; HW −0·1m on Leith; ML 3·0m; Duration 0620. Shelter good except in strong SE to SW winds when scend occurs in the hbr (dries). Berth alongside E pier until contact with HM. From NE keep at least 2½ca from coast. Bkwtr hd Oc WRG 6s 5m 7/4M; E pier hd 2 FG (vert) 6m 4M. W pier hd 2 FR (vert)6m4M. **Facilities** HM ☎ 07836 703014 if no reply, 01333 310836 (Anstruther HM assists); AB £15.29 then £10.37 thereafter, FW, ⬠, El; **Services:** Gas, P & D (tanker), AC. Police ☎ (01333) 592100. **Village** R, Bar, 🛒, ✉, Ⓑ.

9.6.9 FORTH AND CLYDE CANAL

Lowland Carron River Ent. 51°02'·30N 03°41·46W ✿✿✿✿✿

These notes are for the convenience of those entering the canal at Grangemouth. Refer to 9.9.21 for the W entrance at Bowling Sea Lock, R Clyde.

CHARTS AC 737, 741; Imray C27; BWS *Skipper's Guide* Forth & Clyde and Union Canal essential. Obtain from British Waterways Scotland, Lowland Canals, Rosebank House, Camelon, Main Street, Falkirk. FK1 4DS. ☎ (01324) 671217 or www.scottish canals.co.uk

TIDES Carron River +0325 Dover, 0030 Leith.

SHELTER Carron Sea Lock operates HW–4 to HW+1½, 0800-2000 and daylight hours. Temporary berthing at Grangemouth YC or at nearby Refuge Posts. Temporary ‡s close WNW of Carron PHM and close SSW of Carron Bn SHM dependent on depth.

NAVIGATION Carron River entrance approached from Grangemouth Roads via Small Craft Recommended Tracks close N of Ship Manoeuvring Area.

- Canal passage has to be booked in advance, call *Carron Sea Lock* VHF Ch74, ☎ (01324)483034/07810 0794468.
- The canal is about 30M long with 39 locks. Allow a minimum of 21 hours underway for a passage to Bowling Sea Lock. Transit of the canal can be achieved in 2 days by reaching the Summit Pound at Lock 20 Wyndford on the first day.
- Canal can take vessels 20m LOA, 6m beam, 1.8m draft (add 0.1m/4inches to draft for freshwater), mast ht 3.0m. Masts should be unstepped before passing through Kerse Bridge

which is equipped with air draft gauges calibrated for the canal dimensions.

- Mast craneage at Port Edgar or BWS mast crane pontoon near Grangemouth YC.
- Vessels should have a reliable engine and be capable of a minimum speed through the water of 4kn against adverse conditions. Ebb tide attains rates of up to 6kn in Carron River after heavy rainfall. 4mph speed limit throughout the canal.
- Access via Falkirk Wheel to Union Canal and Edinburgh, refer to BWS *Skipper's Guide*.

LOCKS Carron Sea Lock and 9.9.21 Bowling Sea Lock are operated by BW Staff. At other locks BW Staff available to assist. 5 day passage licence costs £5/m and £4/m return including access to the Falkirk Wheel, Union Canal and Edinburgh.

LIGHTS AND MARKS Carron River channel is marked by lighted By PHM & Bn SHM and unlit By(s) PHM & SHM. Bkwtr/Training Bank to W & N of channel marked with Bn(s) & Bol(s).

BOAT SAFETY SCHEME BWS *Skipper's Guide* refers. At Carron Sea Lock transient/visiting craft staying no more than 28 days will be subject to a Dangerous Boat Check of gas and fuel systems. Also required to complete a boat condition declaration and provide evidence of insurance for £1M third party liability.

R/T Call *Carron Sea Lock* VHF Ch **74**.

TELEPHONE Carron Sea Lock (01324) 483034/07810794468. British Waterways Lowlands Canals (01324) 671271.

FACILITIES Carron Sea Lock ⚓ ,P,🛢, 🚻, ⛽, Slip. **Falkirk Wheel (on Forth & Clyde)** FW, P, D, 🛢, 🚻, ⛽. For details throughout the canal refer to BWB *Skipper's Guide* (using maps).

TIME ZONE (UT)
For Summer Time add ONE hour in **non-shaded areas**

LEITH LAT 55°59'N LONG 3°11'W
TIMES AND HEIGHTS OF HIGH AND LOW WATERS

Dates in red are **SPRINGS**
Dates in blue are NEAPS

YEAR 2010

SE Scotland

JANUARY

Day	Time m	Time m	Time m	Time m	Day	Time m	Time m	Time m	Time m
1 F	0228 5.6	0830 1.1	1448 5.7	2104 0.6	**16** SA	0318 5.2	0847 1.3	1524 5.3	2124 1.1
2 SA	0316 5.8	0920 1.0	1532 5.8	2155 0.4	**17** SU	0350 5.2	0919 1.3	1555 5.3	2151 1.0
3 SU	0403 5.8	1007 0.9	1618 5.9	2244 0.3	**18** M	0422 5.2	0950 1.2	1627 5.3	2219 1.0
4 M	0450 5.8	1052 1.0	1705 5.8	2331 0.4	**19** TU	0455 5.1	1021 1.3	1659 5.2	2247 1.1
5 TU	0539 5.6	1135 1.2	1755 5.7		**20** W	0529 5.0	1048 1.4	1733 5.1	2314 1.3
6 W	0017 0.7	0631 5.3	1217 1.4	1849 5.4	**21** TH	0606 4.9	1114 1.6	1808 5.0	2342 1.4
7 TH	0103 1.0	0726 5.0	1301 1.7	◗1951 5.2	**22** F	0645 4.7	1143 1.8	1848 4.8	
8 F	0153 1.4	0827 4.8	1400 2.0	2058 4.9	**23** SA	0016 1.6	0729 4.6	◑1226 2.0	1935 4.7
9 SA	0257 1.8	0931 4.6	1519 2.1	2205 4.7	**24** SU	0105 1.9	0824 4.4	1335 2.2	2037 4.5
10 SU	0414 2.0	1036 4.6	1644 2.1	2314 4.7	**25** M	0219 2.1	0933 4.4	1520 2.2	2159 4.5
11 M	0526 2.0	1143 4.6	1801 1.9		**26** TU	0408 2.1	1048 4.5	1658 2.0	2319 4.6
12 TU	0021 4.7	0624 1.9	1245 4.8	1902 1.7	**27** W	0537 1.9	1159 4.7	1810 1.7	
13 W	0119 4.9	0707 1.8	1334 5.0	1947 1.5	**28** TH	0029 5.0	0639 1.6	1259 5.1	1911 1.2
14 TH	0205 5.0	0742 1.6	1415 5.1	2024 1.3	**29** F	0127 5.3	0733 1.3	1348 5.4	2007 0.7
15 F	0244 5.1	0815 1.5	●1451 5.2	2056 1.1	**30** SA	0216 5.6	0822 1.0	○1433 5.7	2057 0.3
					31 SU	0302 5.8	0908 0.7	1517 6.0	2144 0.1

FEBRUARY

Day	Time m	Time m	Time m	Time m	Day	Time m	Time m	Time m	Time m
1 M	0346 5.9	0952 0.6	1601 6.1	2229 0.0	**16** TU	0356 5.2	0933 1.0	1604 5.4	2159 0.8
2 TU	0431 5.8	1034 0.7	1646 6.0	2311 0.2	**17** W	0427 5.2	1001 1.0	1634 5.3	2223 0.9
3 W	0516 5.6	1111 0.8	1733 5.8	2349 0.5	**18** TH	0459 5.1	1023 1.1	1705 5.2	2242 1.1
4 TH	0603 5.3	1144 1.1	1823 5.5		**19** F	0533 5.0	1041 1.3	1739 5.1	2301 1.2
5 F	0024 1.0	0652 5.0	1216 1.5	◗1918 5.1	**20** SA	0609 4.9	1107 1.5	1818 5.0	2330 1.5
6 SA	0058 1.5	0747 4.7	1303 1.8	2022 4.7	**21** SU	0651 4.7	1145 1.7	1905 4.7	
7 SU	0149 2.0	0849 4.4	1426 2.2	2132 4.5	**22** M	0013 1.8	0741 4.5	◑1245 2.0	2005 4.5
8 M	0324 2.3	0958 4.3	1627 2.2	2249 4.4	**23** TU	0126 2.1	0849 4.3	1438 2.2	2128 4.4
9 TU	0503 2.3	1115 4.4	1805 2.0		**24** W	0349 2.3	1017 4.4	1645 2.0	2258 4.5
10 W	0009 4.5	0612 2.2	1230 4.6	1902 1.7	**25** TH	0526 2.0	1137 4.6	1803 1.5	
11 TH	0110 4.7	0656 1.9	1322 4.8	1942 1.5	**26** F	0014 4.9	0627 1.6	1240 5.0	1902 1.0
12 F	0153 4.9	0729 1.7	1401 5.0	2013 1.2	**27** SA	0111 5.3	0718 1.2	1330 5.5	1955 0.5
13 SA	0228 5.1	0759 1.4	1435 5.2	2040 1.1	**28** SU	0159 5.6	0804 0.8	1414 5.8	○2041 0.2
14 SU	0259 5.2	0830 1.2	1505 5.3	●2105 0.9					
15 M	0327 5.2	0902 1.1	1534 5.4	2132 0.8					

MARCH

Day	Time m	Time m	Time m	Time m	Day	Time m	Time m	Time m	Time m
1 M	0242 5.8	0849 0.6	1456 6.0	2125 -0.1	**16** TU	0259 5.2	0839 1.0	1507 5.4	2105 0.8
2 TU	0324 5.9	0931 0.4	1540 6.1	2207 0.0	**17** W	0328 5.3	0911 0.9	1537 5.4	2133 0.8
3 W	0407 5.8	1011 0.5	1624 6.0	2245 0.2	**18** TH	0358 5.3	0939 0.9	1608 5.4	2156 0.9
4 TH	0450 5.6	1047 0.7	1710 5.8	2319 0.6	**19** F	0430 5.2	1001 0.9	1641 5.3	2212 1.0
5 F	0534 5.3	1115 1.0	1758 5.4	2346 1.1	**20** SA	0504 5.1	1019 1.1	1718 5.2	2231 1.2
6 SA	0619 5.0	1141 1.3	1851 5.0		**21** SU	0541 5.0	1046 1.3	1759 5.0	2302 1.5
7 SU	0011 1.6	0709 4.7	1224 1.8	◗1951 4.6	**22** M	0623 4.8	1127 1.5	1849 4.8	2348 1.8
8 M	0058 2.1	0809 4.4	1338 2.1	2058 4.3	**23** TU	0714 4.5	1235 1.8	◑1951 4.5	
9 TU	0231 2.5	0918 4.2	1614 2.2	2216 4.2	**24** W	0114 2.2	0823 4.4	1441 2.0	2113 4.4
10 W	0434 2.5	1038 4.2	1747 2.0	2345 4.3	**25** TH	0343 2.3	0955 4.4	1635 1.7	2241 4.6
11 TH	0544 2.2	1200 4.4	1839 1.7		**26** F	0506 2.0	1114 4.7	1746 1.3	2354 4.9
12 F	0047 4.6	0629 1.9	1255 4.7	1916 1.5	**27** SA	0604 1.6	1216 5.1	1843 0.8	
13 SA	0129 4.8	0703 1.6	1335 4.9	1945 1.2	**28** SU	0049 5.3	0653 1.2	1306 5.5	1933 0.5
14 SU	0202 5.0	0735 1.4	1408 5.1	2012 1.0	**29** M	0136 5.5	0740 0.8	●1350 5.8	2018 0.2
15 M	0231 5.1	0807 1.1	1438 5.3	●2038 0.9	**30** TU	0218 5.7	0824 0.5	1434 6.0	○2101 0.1
					31 W	0259 5.7	0908 0.4	1518 6.0	2141 0.2

APRIL

Day	Time m	Time m	Time m	Time m	Day	Time m	Time m	Time m	Time m
1 TH	0342 5.7	0948 0.5	1603 5.9	2218 0.5	**16** F	0330 5.3	0917 0.9	1545 5.4	2131 0.9
2 F	0424 5.5	1025 0.7	1650 5.6	2249 0.9	**17** SA	0404 5.3	0948 0.9	1622 5.3	2155 1.1
3 SA	0507 5.3	1055 1.0	1737 5.3	2311 1.3	**18** SU	0440 5.2	1016 1.0	1703 5.2	2220 1.3
4 SU	0550 5.0	1120 1.3	1827 4.9	2337 1.7	**19** M	0520 5.0	1052 1.2	1748 5.1	2257 1.6
5 M	0638 4.7	1159 1.7	1922 4.5		**20** TU	0606 4.9	1146 1.4	1841 4.9	2357 1.9
6 TU	0022 2.1	0733 4.4	1303 2.0	2023 4.3	**21** W	0700 4.7	1306 1.6	◗1944 4.7	
7 W	0142 2.5	0839 4.2	1534 2.2	2132 4.1	**22** TH	0142 2.1	0810 4.5	1443 1.6	2102 4.6
8 TH	0347 2.5	0952 4.2	1659 2.0	2253 4.2	**23** F	0322 2.1	0935 4.6	1612 1.4	2220 4.7
9 F	0457 2.3	1109 4.3	1753 1.8		**24** SA	0435 1.9	1048 4.8	1719 1.1	2328 4.9
10 SA	0004 4.4	0545 2.0	1211 4.6	1832 1.5	**25** SU	0532 1.5	1149 5.1	1815 0.9	
11 SU	0049 4.7	0626 1.7	1255 4.8	1904 1.3	**26** M	0023 5.2	0623 1.2	1241 5.4	1905 0.6
12 M	0124 4.9	0702 1.4	1331 5.0	1933 1.1	**27** TU	0110 5.4	0712 0.9	1328 5.6	1951 0.5
13 TU	0155 5.1	0737 1.2	1404 5.2	2003 0.9	**28** W	0154 5.5	0800 0.7	1414 5.7	○2034 0.5
14 W	0226 5.2	0811 1.0	1437 5.3	●2033 0.9	**29** TH	0236 5.6	0846 0.6	1500 5.7	2114 0.6
15 TH	0258 5.3	0845 0.9	1510 5.3	2103 0.8	**30** F	0319 5.5	0929 0.6	1546 5.6	2150 0.8

Chart Datum: 2·90 metres below Ordnance Datum (Newlyn). HAT is 6·3 metres above Chart Datum; see 4.5

TIME ZONE (UT)
For Summer Time add ONE hour in **non-shaded areas**

LEITH   LAT 55°59′N   LONG 3°11′W
TIMES AND HEIGHTS OF HIGH AND LOW WATERS

Dates in red are **SPRINGS**
Dates in blue are NEAPS

YEAR 2010

MAY

Time	m	Time	m
1 0401 / 1007 / SA 1632 / 2220	5.4 / 0.8 / 5.4 / 1.1	**16** 0344 / 0943 / SU 1607 / 2156	5.3 / 0.8 / 5.4 / 1.1
2 0443 / 1039 / SU 1718 / 2244	5.2 / 1.0 / 5.1 / 1.5	**17** 0424 / 1028 / M 1652 / 2239	5.3 / 0.9 / 5.4 / 1.3
3 0526 / 1107 / M 1805 / 2313	5.0 / 1.3 / 4.9 / 1.8	**18** 0507 / 1117 / TU 1741 / 2328	5.2 / 1.0 / 5.2 / 1.5
4 0610 / 1142 / TU 1854 / 2356	4.8 / 1.6 / 4.6 / 2.0	**19** 0556 / 1212 / W 1834	5.1 / 1.1 / 5.0
5 0701 / 1233 / W 1947	4.5 / 1.8 / 4.4	**20** 0026 / 0651 / TH 1314 / ◑ 1935	1.7 / 4.9 / 1.2 / 4.9
6 0058 / 0758 / TH 1351 / ◑ 2044	2.3 / 4.4 / 2.0 / 4.2	**21** 0135 / 0757 / F 1426 / 2044	1.9 / 4.8 / 1.3 / 4.8
7 0231 / 0901 / F 1545 / 2147	2.4 / 4.3 / 2.0 / 4.2	**22** 0250 / 0901 / SA 1540 / 2155	1.9 / 4.8 / 1.3 / 4.8
8 0357 / 1006 / SA 1647 / 2251	2.3 / 4.3 / 1.9 / 4.3	**23** 0359 / 1021 / SU 1645 / 2259	1.8 / 4.9 / 1.2 / 4.9
9 0454 / 1108 / SU 1733 / 2347	2.1 / 4.4 / 1.7 / 4.5	**24** 0459 / 1123 / M 1743 / 2356	1.6 / 5.1 / 1.1 / 5.0
10 0541 / 1201 / M 1812	1.8 / 4.6 / 1.5	**25** 0555 / 1218 / TU 1837	1.4 / 5.2 / 1.0
11 0034 / 0623 / TU 1247 / 1848	4.7 / 1.6 / 4.8 / 1.3	**26** 0046 / 0649 / W 1310 / 1924	5.2 / 1.2 / 5.3 / 1.0
12 0114 / 0702 / W 1329 / 1923	5.0 / 1.3 / 5.0 / 1.1	**27** 0133 / 0741 / TH 1359 / ○ 2008	5.3 / 1.0 / 5.4 / 0.9
13 0152 / 0741 / TH 1408 / 1959	5.1 / 1.1 / 5.2 / 1.0	**28** 0218 / 0829 / F 1447 / 2048	5.3 / 0.8 / 5.4 / 1.0
14 0229 / 0820 / F 1446 / ● 2036	5.3 / 1.0 / 5.3 / 1.0	**29** 0301 / 0913 / SA 1532 / 2124	5.3 / 0.8 / 5.4 / 1.1
15 0306 / 0900 / SA 1526 / 2115	5.3 / 0.8 / 5.4 / 1.0	**30** 0343 / 0952 / SU 1616 / 2155	5.3 / 0.9 / 5.2 / 1.3
		31 0424 / 1025 / M 1659 / 2223	5.2 / 1.0 / 5.1 / 1.5

JUNE

Time	m	Time	m
1 0503 / 1053 / TU 1740 / 2254	5.1 / 1.2 / 4.9 / 1.6	**16** 0456 / 1119 / W 1730 / 2329	5.5 / 0.6 / 5.5 / 1.2
2 0544 / 1124 / W 1823 / 2332	4.9 / 1.4 / 4.7 / 1.8	**17** 0545 / 1208 / TH 1822	5.4 / 0.7 / 5.3
3 0628 / 1204 / TH 1908	4.8 / 1.6 / 4.5	**18** 0018 / 0638 / F 1301 / 1918	1.4 / 5.3 / 0.9 / 5.1
4 0020 / 0715 / F 1255 / ◑ 1956	2.0 / 4.6 / 1.7 / 4.4	**19** 0110 / 0738 / SA 1357 / ◑ 2020	1.6 / 5.1 / 1.1 / 4.9
5 0122 / 0809 / SA 1358 / 2050	2.2 / 4.5 / 1.9 / 4.3	**20** 0211 / 0846 / SU 1501 / 2125	1.7 / 5.0 / 1.3 / 4.8
6 0237 / 0907 / SU 1512 / 2147	2.2 / 4.4 / 1.9 / 4.3	**21** 0319 / 0954 / M 1608 / 2229	1.8 / 4.9 / 1.4 / 4.8
7 0350 / 1007 / M 1621 / 2245	2.2 / 4.4 / 1.8 / 4.5	**22** 0428 / 1059 / TU 1713 / 2330	1.7 / 4.9 / 1.5 / 4.8
8 0450 / 1106 / TU 1716 / 2342	2.0 / 4.5 / 1.7 / 4.6	**23** 0534 / 1202 / W 1812	1.6 / 4.9 / 1.5
9 0542 / 1203 / W 1804	1.8 / 4.7 / 1.5	**24** 0028 / 0636 / TH 1300 / 1902	4.9 / 1.4 / 5.0 / 1.4
10 0034 / 0629 / TH 1255 / 1849	4.8 / 1.5 / 4.9 / 1.4	**25** 0120 / 0732 / F 1352 / 1947	5.1 / 1.2 / 5.1 / 1.3
11 0122 / 0714 / F 1342 / 1933	5.1 / 1.3 / 5.1 / 1.2	**26** 0206 / 0820 / SA 1438 / ○ 2026	5.2 / 1.1 / 5.2 / 1.3
12 0205 / 0801 / SA 1427 / ● 2019	5.2 / 1.0 / 5.3 / 1.1	**27** 0249 / 0902 / SU 1520 / 2101	5.2 / 1.0 / 5.2 / 1.3
13 0246 / 0850 / SU 1511 / 2106	5.4 / 0.8 / 5.5 / 1.0	**28** 0328 / 0938 / M 1559 / 2132	5.3 / 0.9 / 5.2 / 1.3
14 0328 / 0939 / M 1556 / 2154	5.5 / 0.6 / 5.6 / 1.0	**29** 0405 / 1008 / TU 1636 / 2202	5.2 / 0.9 / 5.1 / 1.3
15 0411 / 1029 / TU 1642 / 2242	5.5 / 0.5 / 5.6 / 1.1	**30** 0441 / 1034 / W 1713 / 2234	5.2 / 1.0 / 5.0 / 1.4

JULY

Time	m	Time	m
1 0517 / 1102 / TH 1750 / 2307	5.1 / 1.2 / 4.9 / 1.5	**16** 0528 / 1152 / F 1802 / 2356	5.7 / 0.4 / 5.5 / 1.1
2 0555 / 1135 / F 1829 / 2343	5.0 / 1.3 / 4.7 / 1.7	**17** 0619 / 1236 / SA 1854	5.6 / 0.7 / 5.2
3 0635 / 1213 / SA 1912	4.8 / 1.5 / 4.6	**18** 0038 / 0714 / SU 1322 / ◑ 1950	1.4 / 5.3 / 1.1 / 4.9
4 0026 / 0719 / SU 1258 / ◑ 1959	1.9 / 4.7 / 1.7 / 4.5	**19** 0129 / 0819 / M 1417 / 2053	1.6 / 5.0 / 1.5 / 4.7
5 0122 / 0809 / M 1353 / 2053	2.1 / 4.5 / 1.9 / 4.4	**20** 0240 / 0928 / TU 1531 / 2159	1.9 / 4.8 / 1.8 / 4.6
6 0234 / 0910 / TU 1503 / 2154	2.2 / 4.4 / 2.0 / 4.4	**21** 0406 / 1039 / W 1650 / 2307	1.9 / 4.7 / 1.9 / 4.6
7 0353 / 1017 / W 1622 / 2257	2.2 / 4.4 / 1.9 / 4.5	**22** 0529 / 1151 / TH 1758	1.8 / 4.7 / 1.9
8 0504 / 1123 / TH 1730 / 2359	2.0 / 4.6 / 1.8 / 4.7	**23** 0014 / 0641 / F 1255 / 1850	4.8 / 1.6 / 4.8 / 1.7
9 0603 / 1226 / F 1827	1.7 / 4.8 / 1.6	**24** 0112 / 0734 / SA 1347 / 1932	4.9 / 1.3 / 5.0 / 1.6
10 0055 / 0657 / SA 1322 / 1918	5.0 / 1.3 / 5.1 / 1.3	**25** 0157 / 0815 / SU 1429 / 2006	5.1 / 1.1 / 5.1 / 1.4
11 0145 / 0749 / SU 1411 / ● 2008	5.2 / 1.0 / 5.4 / 1.1	**26** 0236 / 0850 / M 1505 / ○ 2039	5.2 / 1.0 / 5.2 / 1.3
12 0230 / 0842 / M 1457 / 2057	5.5 / 0.6 / 5.6 / 0.9	**27** 0311 / 0920 / TU 1539 / 2110	5.3 / 0.9 / 5.2 / 1.2
13 0313 / 0932 / TU 1541 / 2145	5.7 / 0.3 / 5.8 / 0.8	**28** 0344 / 0946 / W 1611 / 2141	5.3 / 0.9 / 5.2 / 1.1
14 0356 / 1021 / W 1627 / 2230	5.8 / 0.2 / 5.8 / 0.8	**29** 0416 / 1011 / TH 1643 / 2211	5.3 / 0.9 / 5.1 / 1.2
15 0441 / 1107 / TH 1714 / 2314	5.8 / 0.2 / 5.7 / 0.9	**30** 0449 / 1037 / F 1717 / 2240	5.3 / 1.0 / 5.0 / 1.3
		31 0523 / 1103 / SA 1753 / 2306	5.1 / 1.1 / 4.9 / 1.5

AUGUST

Time	m	Time	m
1 0558 / 1130 / SU 1831 / 2335	5.0 / 1.3 / 4.8 / 1.7	**16** 0005 / 0649 / M 1244 / ◑ 1919	1.3 / 5.3 / 1.3 / 4.9
2 0637 / 1202 / M 1913	4.8 / 1.6 / 4.6	**17** 0050 / 0753 / TU 1331 / 2021	1.6 / 4.9 / 1.8 / 4.6
3 0013 / 0722 / TU 1246 / ◑ 2003	1.9 / 4.6 / 1.8 / 4.5	**18** 0205 / 0904 / W 1455 / 2130	2.0 / 4.6 / 2.2 / 4.5
4 0117 / 0819 / W 1355 / 2106	2.1 / 4.5 / 2.1 / 4.4	**19** 0358 / 1019 / TH 1634 / 2245	2.1 / 4.5 / 2.3 / 4.5
5 0255 / 0932 / TH 1537 / 2219	2.2 / 4.4 / 2.2 / 4.4	**20** 0538 / 1140 / F 1749	1.9 / 4.5 / 2.1
6 0434 / 1051 / F 1710 / 2330	2.1 / 4.5 / 2.0 / 4.6	**21** 0000 / 0641 / SA 1247 / 1838	4.7 / 1.6 / 4.7 / 1.9
7 0547 / 1203 / SA 1813	1.7 / 4.8 / 1.7	**22** 0058 / 0725 / SU 1335 / 1914	4.9 / 1.4 / 4.9 / 1.7
8 0033 / 0646 / SU 1304 / 1905	5.0 / 1.3 / 5.2 / 1.4	**23** 0142 / 0759 / M 1412 / 1944	5.1 / 1.2 / 5.1 / 1.4
9 0126 / 0740 / M 1354 / 1954	5.3 / 0.8 / 5.5 / 1.0	**24** 0217 / 0828 / TU 1444 / ○ 2015	5.3 / 1.0 / 5.2 / 1.2
10 0210 / 0831 / TU 1438 / ● 2041	5.7 / 0.4 / 5.8 / 0.8	**25** 0249 / 0853 / W 1513 / 2046	5.4 / 0.9 / 5.3 / 1.1
11 0253 / 0918 / W 1522 / 2127	5.9 / 0.1 / 5.9 / 0.6	**26** 0318 / 0918 / TH 1542 / 2117	5.4 / 0.8 / 5.3 / 1.0
12 0336 / 1004 / TH 1606 / 2211	6.1 / -0.1 / 5.9 / 0.5	**27** 0348 / 0943 / F 1612 / 2147	5.4 / 0.8 / 5.2 / 1.0
13 0421 / 1047 / F 1651 / 2252	6.1 / 0.0 / 5.8 / 0.7	**28** 0419 / 1008 / SA 1644 / 2211	5.4 / 0.9 / 5.2 / 1.2
14 0507 / 1128 / SA 1737 / 2329	6.0 / 0.3 / 5.5 / 0.9	**29** 0452 / 1029 / SU 1718 / 2232	5.3 / 1.1 / 5.1 / 1.3
15 0556 / 1206 / SU 1825	5.7 / 0.8 / 5.2	**30** 0526 / 1048 / M 1754 / 2255	5.1 / 1.3 / 4.9 / 1.5
		31 0605 / 1113 / TU 1834 / 2329	4.9 / 1.5 / 4.7 / 1.7

Chart Datum: 2·90 metres below Ordnance Datum (Newlyn). HAT is 6·3 metres above Chart Datum; see 4.5

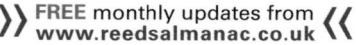

TIME ZONE (UT)
For Summer Time add ONE hour in **non-shaded areas**

LEITH   LAT 55°59'N   LONG 3°11'W
TIMES AND HEIGHTS OF HIGH AND LOW WATERS

Dates in red are SPRINGS
Dates in blue are NEAPS

YEAR 2010

SEPTEMBER

Time	m		Time	m
1 W 0650	4.7	**16** TH 0136	2.1
1151	1.8	0839	4.5
1922	4.6	1417	2.4
◗		2101	4.4
2 TH 0024	2.0	**17** F 0355	2.2
0746	4.5	0954	4.4
1257	2.2	1612	2.5
2025	4.4	2217	4.4
3 F 0216	2.2	**18** SA 0524	1.9
0900	4.4	1117	4.4
1513	2.3	1724	2.3
2146	4.4	2333	4.6
4 SA 0417	2.0	**19** SU 0620	1.7
1026	4.5	1224	4.7
1656	2.1	1810	2.0
2305	4.7		
5 SU 0535	1.6	**20** M 0031	4.8
1143	4.8	0659	1.4
1758	1.7	1310	4.9
		1845	1.7
6 M 0010	5.0	**21** TU 0114	5.1
0632	1.1	0729	1.2
1244	5.2	1345	5.1
1847	1.3	1916	1.5
7 TU 0103	5.4	**22** W 0149	5.2
0724	0.7	0755	1.1
1332	5.6	1415	5.2
1934	1.0	1948	1.2
8 W 0147	5.8	**23** TH 0220	5.4
0812	0.3	0820	0.9
1416	5.9	1443	5.3
● 2019	0.7	○ 2020	1.1
9 TH 0229	6.1	**24** F 0250	5.4
0857	0.0	0846	0.9
1458	6.0	1511	5.3
2104	0.5	2052	1.0
10 F 0313	6.2	**25** SA 0320	5.4
0941	0.0	0912	0.9
1541	6.0	1541	5.3
2147	0.4	2121	1.0
11 SA 0358	6.2	**26** SU 0352	5.4
1022	0.1	0936	1.0
1625	5.8	1613	5.3
2228	0.6	2146	1.1
12 SU 0444	6.0	**27** M 0425	5.3
1100	0.5	0956	1.1
1704	5.5	1647	5.2
2304	0.9	2207	1.3
13 M 0534	5.6	**28** TU 0501	5.2
1134	1.0	1014	1.3
1757	5.2	1723	5.0
2337	1.3	2231	1.4
14 TU 0628	5.2	**29** W 0542	5.0
1204	1.6	1041	1.6
1849	4.9	1804	4.9
		2308	1.7
15 W 0019	1.7	**30** TH 0630	4.8
0729	4.8	1121	1.9
1248	2.1	1853	4.7
◗ 1950	4.6		

OCTOBER

Time	m		Time	m
1 F 0010	1.9	**16** SA 0321	2.2
0727	4.6	0918	4.3
1233	2.3	1526	2.6
◗ 1956	4.5	2138	4.4
2 SA 0207	2.1	**17** SU 0443	2.0
0841	4.5	1033	4.4
1501	2.4	1637	2.4
2119	4.5	2249	4.5
3 SU 0401	1.9	**18** M 0537	1.8
1005	4.6	1142	4.6
1633	2.1	1727	2.1
2240	4.8	2349	4.7
4 M 0514	1.5	**19** TU 0617	1.6
1120	4.9	1231	4.8
1733	1.7	1807	1.8
2344	5.1		
5 TU 0611	1.0	**20** W 0036	5.0
1219	5.3	0648	1.4
1822	1.4	1308	5.0
		1843	1.6
6 W 0036	5.5	**21** TH 0114	5.1
0701	0.6	0715	1.2
1307	5.6	1340	5.2
1908	1.0	1918	1.3
7 TH 0122	5.9	**22** F 0147	5.3
0747	0.3	0743	1.1
1351	5.8	1410	5.3
● 1954	0.7	1952	1.2
8 F 0206	6.1	**23** SA 0220	5.4
0832	0.2	0812	1.0
1433	5.9	1441	5.4
2040	0.5	○ 2026	1.1
9 SA 0251	6.1	**24** SU 0254	5.4
0915	0.2	0841	1.0
1516	5.9	1513	5.4
2125	0.5	2059	1.0
10 SU 0337	6.1	**25** M 0328	5.4
0955	0.5	0909	1.1
1559	5.7	1547	5.4
2207	0.7	2130	1.1
11 M 0425	5.8	**26** TU 0404	5.4
1032	0.8	0935	1.2
1644	5.5	1622	5.3
2245	1.0	2200	1.2
12 TU 0515	5.5	**27** W 0443	5.3
1103	1.3	1000	1.4
1731	5.2	1700	5.2
2319	1.3	2233	1.4
13 W 0608	5.1	**28** TH 0527	5.1
1128	1.8	1032	1.7
1821	4.9	1743	5.0
2357	1.7	2320	1.5
14 TH 0706	4.8	**29** F 0616	5.0
1210	2.2	1120	2.0
1920	4.7	1833	4.9
◗			
15 F 0103	2.0	**30** SA 0032	1.7
0809	4.5	0714	4.8
1326	2.5	1250	2.2
2027	4.5	◗ 1935	4.7
		31 SU 0201	1.8
		0824	4.7
		1437	2.3
		2054	4.7

NOVEMBER

Time	m		Time	m
1 M 0333	1.7	**16** TU 0432	2.0
0942	4.8	1034	4.4
1559	2.1	1635	2.3
2212	4.9	2251	4.6
2 TU 0444	1.4	**17** W 0519	1.9
1052	5.0	1132	4.6
1700	1.8	1725	2.1
2316	5.2	2345	4.7
3 W 0542	1.1	**18** TH 0559	1.7
1151	5.3	1219	4.8
1753	1.5	1808	1.8
4 TH 0010	5.5	**19** F 0032	4.9
0633	0.8	0633	1.5
1242	5.5	1300	5.0
1842	1.1	1847	1.6
5 F 0100	5.7	**20** SA 0114	5.1
0721	0.7	0707	1.4
1327	5.7	1338	5.2
1931	0.9	1925	1.4
6 SA 0146	5.9	**21** SU 0153	5.2
0806	0.6	0741	1.3
1410	5.8	1414	5.4
● 2020	0.7	○ 2003	1.2
7 SU 0233	5.9	**22** M 0231	5.4
0850	0.7	0816	1.2
1454	5.8	1450	5.4
2107	0.7	2041	1.1
8 M 0321	5.8	**23** TU 0309	5.4
0930	0.9	0852	1.2
1538	5.7	1526	5.5
2151	0.8	2121	1.0
9 TU 0409	5.6	**24** W 0348	5.5
1006	1.1	0930	1.3
1623	5.5	1603	5.4
2231	1.0	2204	1.0
10 W 0458	5.4	**25** TH 0430	5.4
1035	1.5	1009	1.4
1708	5.3	1644	5.4
2305	1.3	2250	1.1
11 TH 0547	5.1	**26** F 0516	5.3
1101	1.8	1052	1.6
1755	5.0	1729	5.3
2337	1.6	2340	1.2
12 F 0638	4.8	**27** SA 0605	5.2
1139	2.1	1143	1.8
1847	4.8	1819	5.1
13 SA 0022	1.9	**28** SU 0036	1.4
0732	4.6	0700	5.0
1236	2.4	1247	2.0
◗ 1945	4.6	◗ 1916	5.0
14 SU 0138	2.1	**29** M 0142	1.5
0831	4.4	0803	4.9
1400	2.5	1402	2.1
2048	4.5	2027	4.9
15 M 0328	2.1	**30** TU 0256	1.5
0932	4.4	0914	4.8
1532	2.5	1518	2.0
2151	4.5	2141	5.0

DECEMBER

Time	m		Time	m
1 W 0407	1.4	**16** TH 0401	2.1
1022	4.9	1026	4.5
1625	1.9	1633	2.3
2248	5.1	2248	4.5
2 TH 0509	1.3	**17** F 0504	2.0
1124	5.1	1125	4.6
1725	1.6	1730	2.1
2348	5.3	2347	4.7
3 F 0606	1.2	**18** SA 0554	1.8
1218	5.3	1219	4.8
1822	1.4	1818	1.8
4 SA 0043	5.4	**19** SU 0040	4.9
0633	1.1	0637	1.7
1308	5.4	1308	5.1
1917	1.2	1902	1.5
5 SU 0134	5.5	**20** M 0129	5.1
0745	1.1	0718	1.5
1355	5.5	1351	5.3
● 2009	1.0	1946	1.3
6 M 0223	5.6	**21** TU 0212	5.3
0829	1.1	0800	1.3
1439	5.6	1432	5.4
2057	0.9	○ 2030	1.0
7 TU 0311	5.6	**22** W 0254	5.5
0909	1.1	0843	1.2
1523	5.5	1510	5.5
2141	0.9	2116	0.8
8 W 0356	5.5	**23** TH 0335	5.6
0944	1.3	0927	1.1
1606	5.4	1550	5.6
2219	1.0	2203	0.7
9 TH 0441	5.3	**24** F 0418	5.6
1013	1.5	1012	1.2
1648	5.3	1631	5.6
2249	1.2	2250	0.7
10 F 0524	5.1	**25** SA 0503	5.6
1040	1.6	1056	1.2
1729	5.2	1716	5.6
2315	1.4	2337	0.8
11 SA 0607	4.9	**26** SU 0550	5.4
1113	1.8	1139	1.4
1812	5.0	1803	5.5
2347	1.6		
12 SU 0651	4.7	**27** M 0024	0.9
1155	2.0	0640	5.2
1859	4.8	1225	1.6
		1856	5.3
13 M 0031	1.8	**28** TU 0114	1.2
0739	4.5	0737	5.0
1249	2.2	1320	1.8
◗ 1951	4.6	◗ 1958	5.1
14 TU 0128	2.0	**29** W 0213	1.4
0831	4.4	0842	4.8
1400	2.4	1430	1.9
2048	4.5	2111	5.0
15 W 0240	2.1	**30** TH 0324	1.6
0928	4.4	0951	4.8
1523	2.4	1549	2.0
2148	4.5	2223	4.9
		31 F 0438	1.7
		1057	4.8
		1704	1.8
		2331	5.0

Chart Datum: 2·90 metres below Ordnance Datum (Newlyn). HAT is 6·3 metres above Chart Datum; see 4.5

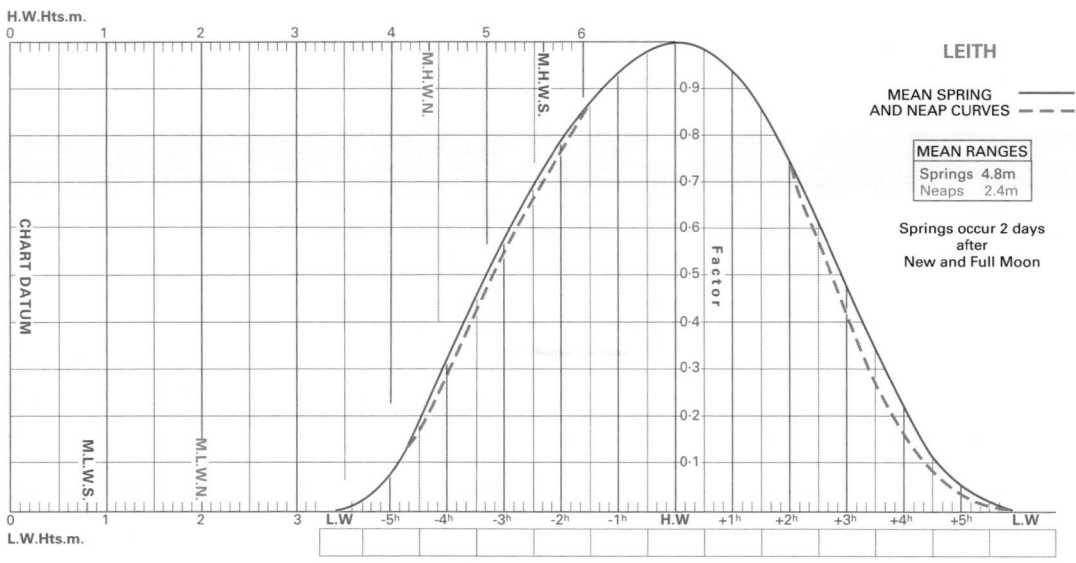

9.6.10 ANSTRUTHER

Fife 56°13'·15N 02°41'·82W ✿✿⚓⚓⚓✿✿✿

CHARTS AC 175, 734; Imray C23, C27.

TIDES +0315 Dover; ML 3·1; Duration 0620

Standard Port LEITH (←—)

Times				Height (metres)			
High Water		Low Water		MHWS	MHWN	MLWN	MLWS
0300	0900	0300	0900	5·6	4·4	2·0	0·8
1500	2100	1500	2100				
Differences ANSTRUTHER EASTER							
−0018	−0012	−0006	−0008	−0·3	−0·2	0·0	0·0

SHELTER Good, but dangerous to enter in strong E to S winds. Hbr dries; access approx HW±2. Pontoon berths for bilge keel craft only, drying out soft mud.

NAVIGATION WPT 56°12'·59N 02°42'·20W, 019° to ent, 0·60M. Beware FVs and creels in the area. Do not go N of W Pier Lt due to rks extending N & W across the mouth of Dreel Burn.

LIGHTS AND MARKS Conspic tr on W pier. Ldg lts 019°, both FG 7/11m 4M. Pier lts as chartlet. Horn (3) 60s in conspic tr.

R/T Call *Anstruther Hbr* VHF Ch 11 16 (HO) or Forth CG 16 (OT).

TELEPHONE (Code 01333) HM ☎ 310836 (HO); MRCC 450666; Marinecall 09068 969642; Police: 08456 005702, St Andrews

592100; Dr 310352; Ⓗ St Andrews 01334 472327, Kirkaldy 01592 643355;⊖ 0800 595000.

FACILITIES Harbour: wall AB (22 + 8Ⓥ); for 10m LOA: entry £15.29 then £10.37 per day; pontoons (no fin keels, 100 + 8 Ⓥ,check availability with HM) £17.85 then £10.28 per day; Slip, FW, ⬚, ⬚, Shwrs 0800-2100; **Services:** D (tanker ☎ 730622), Marine engineer (☎ 01382 541848), ACA, Gas, Gaz,El, Ⓔ, LB. **Town** D, P, SM (☎ 01383 622444), SC (☎ 313492) ⬚, R, Bar, ✉, Ⓑ, ⇌ (bus Cupar or Leuchars), ✈ Edinburgh/Dundee.

ADJACENT HARBOURS AND ANCHORAGE

KIRKCALDY, Fife, **56°06'·80N 03°08'·96W**. AC 741. HW +0345 on Dover, −0005 on Leith; HW −0·1m on Leith; ML 3·2m; Duration 0620. See 9.6.10. Shelter good except in strong E winds; an emergency refuge. Officially the hbr is closed (no commercial tfc, but some local FVs) and not manned; depths may be less than charted due to silting. The only hbr light is on E Pier head, Fl WG 10s 12m 8M. Small craft should contact Forth Ports Authority ☎ (01333) 426725, Forth Navigation Ch 71 (H24) or Methil Docks Radio Ch 16 14 for advice.

METHIL, Fife, **56°10'·75N 03°00'·55W**. AC 734,741. HW +0330 Dover; −0020 and −0·1 on Leith; ML 3m; Duration 0615. Commercial port unsuitable for leisure/small craft; infrastructure unsafe. Dangerous to enter in bad weather; in emergency call Forth Navigation Ch 71 (H24) or Forth Coastguard Ch 16.

PITTENWEEM, Fife, **56°12'·60N 02°43'·79W**. AC 734. HW +0325 Dover; −0015 and −0·1m on Leith; ML 3m; Duration 0620. Busy fishing hbr, dredged 1-2m, access all tides, but not in onshore winds; seek advice before entering at LW springs. Yachts not encouraged; contact HM for berth at W end of inner hbr, but only for emergency use. Outer hbr dries to rock; is only suitable for temp stop in calm weather. Appr 037° on ldg marks/lts, W cols, both FR 3/8m 5M. Rks to port marked by bn, QR 3m 2M, and 3 unlit bns. E bkwtr lt Fl (2) RG 5s 9m 9/6M, 265°-R-345°-G-055°. **R/T** VHF Ch 11 (0700-2100, Mon-Fri) or Forth CG Ch 16 (other times). HM ☎ (01333) 312591. Facilities: FW, CH, D & P (tanker) (☎ 730622), Gas, ⬚, Bar.

CRAIL, Fife, **56°15'·35N 02°37'·29W**. AC 175. HW +0320 on Dover, −0020 on Leith; HW −0·2m on Leith; ML 3·0m; Duration 0615. Good shelter but only for boats able to take the ground alongside. Appr between S pier and bn on rks to S following ldg line 295°, two W concrete pillars with FR lts, 24/30m 6M. Turn 150° to stbd for ent. Call Forth CG on VHF Ch 16 before entering. HM ☎ (01333) 450820. Facilities: AB, entry £15.29/craft then £10.37/day, El, FW, ⟨D⟩, Slip, P. **Village** Bar, R, 🍴, ✉, Ⓑ.

ISLE OF MAY, Fife, 56°11′·40N 02°33′·69W. AC 734. HW +0325 on Dover, −0025 on Leith. In settled weather only, and depending on the wind, ⚓ at E or W Tarbert in 4m; landing at Altarstanes. Near the SE tip there is a tiny hbr at Kirkhaven, with narrow, rky ent; yachts can moor fore-and-aft to rings in rks, in about 1-1·5m.

SDs are needed. Beware Norman Rk to N of Island, and Maiden Hair Rk to S. At the summit, a 3 tr on stone ho, Fl (2) 15s 73m 22M. The island, owned by Scottish Natural Heritage (☎ 01334 654038), is a bird/seal-colony sanctuary. Sensitive seasons: (a) breeding birds April to September; (b) breeding seals October to January (c) moulting seals January to March. Land only at Alterstanes or Kirkhaven 0900-1700 UT (not Tuesdays). No overnight accommodation or camping. Avoid marked out areas to minimise disturbance to wildlife and ongoing conservation experiments. Island warden is in residence Easter to September. Contact on VHF CH 16 or 6, or on first landing.

FIFE NESS TO MONTROSE

(AC 190) Fife Ness is fringed by rky ledges, and a reef extends 1M NE to N Carr Rk (dries 1·4m, marked by bn). In strong onshore winds keep to seaward of N Carr ECM lt buoy. From here keep 5ca offshore to clear dangers entering St Andrews B, where there is anch; the little hbr dries, and should not be approached in onshore winds.

Northward from Firth of Forth to Rattray Hd the coast is mostly rky and steep-to, and there are no out-lying dangers within 2M of the coast except those off R Tay and Bell Rk. But in an onshore blow there are few safe havens; both yachts and crews need to be prepared for offshore cruising rather than coast-crawling.

R Tay (AC 1481) is approached from the NE via Fairway buoy; it is dangerous to cut corners from the S. The Bar, NE of Abertay lt buoy, is dangerous in heavy weather, particularly in strong onshore wind or swell. Abertay Sands extend nearly 4M E of Tentsmuir Pt on S side of chan (buoyed); Elbow is a shoal extension eastward. Gaa Sands, running 1·75M E of Buddon Ness, are marked by Abertay lt buoy (Racon) on N side of chan. Passage across Abertay and Gaa Sands is very dangerous. The estuary is shallow, with many shifting sandbanks; Tayport is a good passage stop and best yacht hbr (dries) in the Tay. ▶ S of

Buddon Ness the W-going (flood) stream begins about HW Aberdeen − 0400, and the E-going at about HW Aberdeen + 0230, sp rates 2kn. ◀

Bell Rk (lt, Racon) lies about 11·5M E of Buddon Ness. ▶ 2M E of Bell Rk the S-going stream begins HW Aberdeen − 0220, and the N-going at HW Aberdeen + 0405, sp rates 1kn. W of Bell Rk the streams begin earlier. ◀

N from Buddon Ness the coast is sandy. 1·25M SW of Arbroath beware Elliot Horses, rky patches with depth 1·9m, which extend about 5ca offshore. Between Whiting Ness and Scurdie Ness, 9·5M NNE, the coast is clear of out-lying dangers, but is mostly fringed with drying rks up to 1ca off. In offshore winds there is temp anch in SW of Lunan B, off Ethie Haven.

Scurdie Ness (lt, Racon) is conspic on S side of ent to Montrose. Scurdie Rks (dry) extend 2ca E of the Ness. On N side of chan Annat Bank dries up to about 5ca E of the shore, opposite Scurdie Ness (AC 1438). ▶ The in-going stream begins at HW Aberdeen − 0500, and the outgoing at HW Aberdeen + 0115; both streams are very strong, up to 7kn at sp, and there is turbulence off the ent on the ebb. The ent is dangerous in strong onshore winds, with breaking seas extending to Scurdie Ness on the ebb. In marginal conditions the last quarter of the flood is best time to enter. ◀

9.6.11 RIVER TAY

Fife/Angus Tayport (56°27'·10N 02°52'·87W) ❀❀❀❀❀❀❀

CHARTS AC 190, 1481; Imray C23.

TIDES +0401 (Dundee) Dover; ML 3·1; Duration 0610

Standard Port ABERDEEN (→)

Times				Height (metres)			
High Water		Low Water		MHWS	MHWN	MLWN	MLWS
0000	0600	0100	0700	4·3	3·4	1·6	0·6
1200	1800	1300	1900				
Differences BAR							
+0100	+0100	+0050	+0110	+0·9	+0·8	+0·3	+0·1
DUNDEE							
+0140	+0120	+0055	+0145	+1·1	+0·9	+0·3	+0·1
NEWBURGH							
+0215	+0200	+0250	+0335	−0·2	−0·4	−1·1	−0·5
PERTH							
+0220	+0225	+0510	+0530	−0·9	−1·4	−1·2	−0·3

NOTE: At Perth LW time differences give the start of the rise, following a LW stand of about 4 hours.

SHELTER Good in Tay Estuary, but ent is dangerous in strong E/SE winds or on-shore swell. **Tayport** best place for yachts on passage, access HW±4. Hbr partly dries except W side of NE pier; S side has many yacht moorings. **Dundee** commercial dock (Camperdown), gates open HW−2 to HW by request (fee £6 – Fl R lt = no ent/exit). Docks no longer used commercially. Possible moorings off Royal Tay YC. ⚓s as chartlet: the ⚓ off the city is exposed/landing difficult. Off S bank good shelter at Woodhaven and ⚓s from Wormit BC. There are other ⚓s up-river at Balmerino, Newburgh and Inchyra.

NAVIGATION WPT Tay Fairway SWM buoy, 56°28'·30N 02°36'·60W, 239°/1M to Middle Bar buoys. Chan is well buoyed, least depth 5·2m. Keep N of Larick, a conspic disused lt bn.

> Beware strong tidal streams. No passage across Abertay or Gaa Sands; charted depths are unreliable.

LIGHTS AND MARKS See 9.6.4 and chartlet. 'Abertay' ECM buoy(Racon), at E end of Gaa Sands is a clear visual mark.

R/T *Forth & Tay Navigation Service* VHF Ch 71; *Dundee Hbr Radio* VHF Ch 12 16 (H24); local nav warnings, weather, vis and tides on request. Royal Tay YC, Ch M.

TELEPHONE (Code 01382): Forth & Tay Navigation Service (01324) 498584; HM (Dundee) 224121; HM (Perth) (01738) 624056; MRCC (01333) 450666; Marinecall 09068 969642; Tayport Boatowners' Association 553679; Police (Tayport) 542222, (Dundee) 223200; Dr 221953; Ⓗ 223125.

FACILITIES N BANK: Camperdown Dock, AB £19 all LOA, £38 for week; FW, ME, El, C (8 ton); **Victoria Dock**, AB, FW, ME, C (8 ton); **Royal Tay YC** (Broughty Ferry) ☎ 477516, ⚓s free, R, Bar; **Services:** CH, M, L, ME, El, ✗, C (2 ton), ACA. **Dundee City** P, D, CH, 🛒, R, Bar, ✉, Ⓑ, ⛽, ✈.

S BANK: Tayport Hbr AB £6.80, Slip, L, FW, AC; **Wormit Boating Club** ☎ 541400 ⚓s free, Slip, L, FW, 🛒.

ADJACENT HARBOURS

PERTH, Perth & Kinross, 56°22'·89N 03°25'·74W. AC 1481; OS 53, 58. Tides, see 9.6.12. FYCA Pilot Handbook needed. Leave Tay Rly bridge about HW Dundee −2 to carry the tide for 16·5M to Perth. Keep clear of coasters which have to travel at speed and are constrained by their draft. Lit chan favours S bank for 9M to Newburgh where caution req'd due to mudbanks mid-stream; keep S of Mugdrum Is. Up-river, power cables clearance 33m and Friarton Bridge 26m. Keep S of Willow Is, past gasworks to Hbr on W bank. Hbr has approx 1·5m. See HM, ☎ (01738) 624056, for berth. VHF Ch 09 16. FW, D & P (cans), all city amenities, ⛽, ✈.

ST ANDREWS, Fife, 56°20'·32N 02°46'·79W. AC 190. HW −0015 Leith. Small drying hbr 7M S of Tay Estuary /8M NW of Fife Ness. In strong onshore winds breaking seas render appr/ent impossible. Appr at HW±2 on 270°, N bkwtr bn in transit with conspic cathedral tr; no lights. A recce by dinghy is useful. Keep about 10m S of the bkwtr for best water. 8m wide ent to inner hbr (drying 2·5m) has lock gates, usually open, and sliding footbridge; berth on W side. Facilities: FW, SC; all amenities of university town, inc golf course.

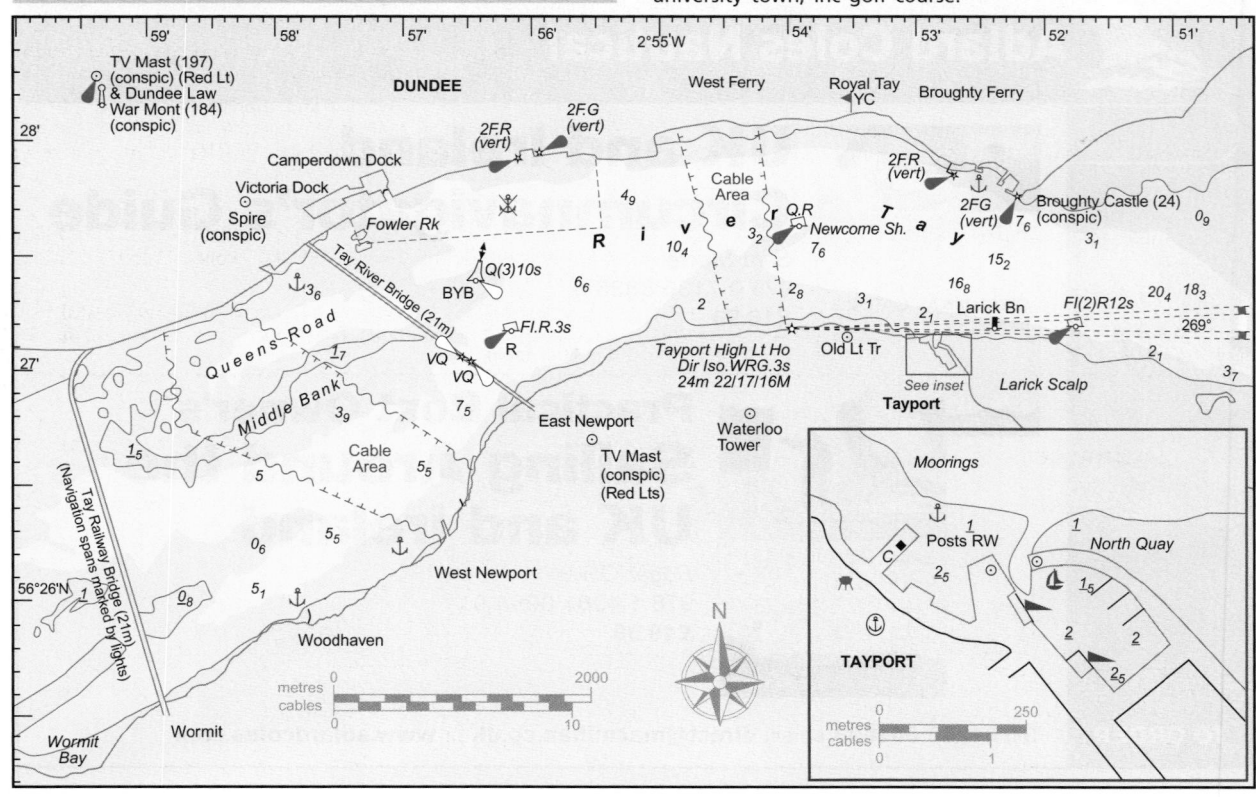

9.6.12 ARBROATH

Angus 56°33'·22N 02°34'·99W ✹✹♒♒♣♣

CHARTS AC 190, 1438; Imray C23.

TIDES +0317 Dover; ML 2·9; Duration 0620

Standard Port ABERDEEN (⟶)

Times				Height (metres)			
High Water		Low Water		MHWS	MHWN	MLWN	MLWS
0000	0600	0100	0700	4·3	3·4	1·6	0·6
1200	1800	1300	1900				
Differences ARBROATH							
+0056	+0037	+0034	+0055	+1·0	+0·8	+0·4	+0·2

SHELTER Good, especially in Inner Basin with lock gates, afloat pontoon berths with 2.5m depth maintained. Ent can be dangerous in moderate SE swell. Inside the entrance, turn to starboard and then to starboard again.

NAVIGATION WPT 56°32'·98N 02°34'·21W, 299°/0·5M to ent.

Entry should not be attempted LW±2½. Beware Knuckle rks to stbd and Cheek Bush rks to port on entering.

LIGHTS AND MARKS Ldg lts 299°, both FR 7/13m 5M, or twin trs of St Thomas' ✠ visible between N pier lt ho and W bkwtr bn. Hbr entry sigs: Fl G 3s on E pier = Entry safe. Same lt shows FR when hbr closed, entry dangerous. Siren (3) 60s at E pier lt is occas, for FVs. Inner Basin Lock Gates, FR = closed, FG = open >2.5m over sill.

R/T Ch 11 16.

TELEPHONE (Code 01241) HM 872166; MRCC (01224) 592334 MRCC 01333 452000; Marinecall 09068 969642; Police 872222; Dr 876836.

FACILITIES Inner Basin 59 inc ✔, £19/craft, Showers, 🚽, Pier AB £13/craft, Slip, FW; Services: BY, Slip, L, ME, El, ⚒, C (8 ton) Ⓔ, M, Gas, CH. Town P, D, 🛒, R, Bar, ✉, Ⓑ, ⇌, ✈ (Dundee).

9.6.13 MONTROSE

Angus 56°42'·19N 02°26'·60W ✹✹♒♒♣♣

CHARTS AC 190, 1438; Imray C23.

TIDES +0320 Dover; ML 2·9; Duration 0645

Standard Port ABERDEEN (⟶)

Times				Height (metres)			
High Water		Low Water		MHWS	MHWN	MLWN	MLWS
0000	0600	0100	0700	4·3	3·4	1·6	0·6
1200	1800	1300	1900				
Differences MONTROSE							
+0055	+0055	+0030	+0040	+0·5	+0·4	+0·2	0·0

SHELTER Good; yachts are welcome in this busy commercial port. Contact HM for AB, usually available, but beware wash from other traffic. Double mooring lines advised due to strong tidal streams (up to 6kn).

NAVIGATION WPT 56°42'·18N 02°25'·11W, 271°/1·25M to front ldg lt. Beware Annat Bank to N and Scurdie Rks to S of ent chan. In quiet weather best access is LW to LW+1, but in strong onshore winds only safe access would be from HW –2 to HW.

Ent is dangerous with strong onshore winds against any ebb tide when heavy overfalls develop.

LIGHTS AND MARKS See 9.6.4 and chartlet two sets of ldg lts: Outer 271·5°, both FR 11/18m 5M, front W twin pillars, R bands; rear W tr, R cupola. Inner 265°, both FG 21/33m 5M, Orange △ front and ▽ rear.

R/T VHF Ch 12 16 (H24).

TELEPHONE (Code 01674) HM 672302; MRCC (01333) 450666; Marinecall 09068 969642; Police 01307 302200; Dr 672554.

FACILITIES N Quay ☎ 672302, AB £6.50, D (by tanker via HM), FW, ME, El, C (1½ to 40 ton), CH, Gas. Town 🛒, R, P, Bar, ✉, Ⓑ, ⇌, ✈ (Aberdeen).

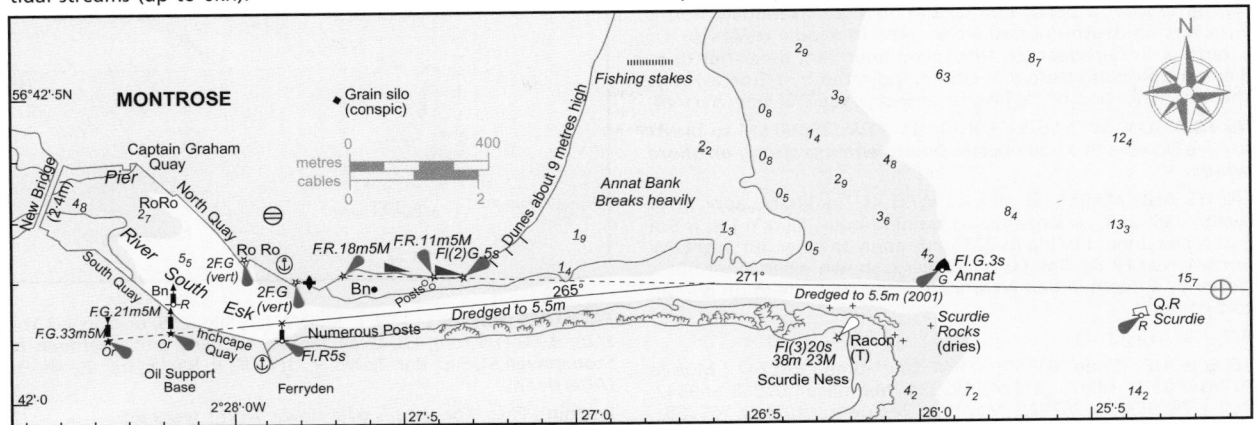

MONTROSE TO ABERDEEN

(AC 210) N from Montrose the coast is sandy for 5M to Milton Ness, where there is anch on S side in N winds. Johnshaven, 2M NE, is a small hbr (dries) with tight entrance, which should not be approached with onshore wind or swell. 5ca NE, off Brotherton Cas, drying rks extend 4ca offshore. Gourdon has a small hbr (mostly dries) approached on ldg line between rky ledges; inner hbr has storm gates. Outside the hbr rks extend both sides of entrance, and the sea breaks heavily in strong E winds. Keep a sharp lookout for lobster pot dan buoys between Montrose and Stonehaven.

North to Inverbervie the coast is fringed with rky ledges up to 2ca offshore. Just N of Todhead Pt is Catterline, a small B which forms a natural anch in W winds, but open to E. Downie Pt, SE of Stonehaven, should be rounded 1ca off. The Bay is encumbered by rky ledges up to 2ca from shore and exposed to the E; anch 6ca E of Bay Hotel or berth afloat in outer hbr.

From Garron Pt to Girdle Ness the coast is mostly steep-to. Fishing nets may be met off headlands during fishing season. Craigmaroinn and Seal Craig (dry) are parts of reef 3ca offshore SE of Portlethen, a fishing village with landing sheltered by rks. Cove B has a very small fishing hbr, off which there is anch in good weather; Mutton Rk (dries 2·1m) lie 1½ca offshore. From Cove to Girdle Ness keep 5ca offshore, avoiding Hasman Rks (dries 3·4m) 1ca off Altens.

Greg Ness and Girdle Ness (lt, Racon), at SE corner of Aberdeen Bay, are fringed by rks. Girdlestone is a rocky patch, depth less than 2m, 2ca ENE of lt ho. A drying patch lies 2ca SE of lt ho. ▶ *Off Girdle Ness the S-going stream begins at HW Aberdeen –0430, and the N-going at HW Aberdeen + 0130, sp rates 2·5kn. A race forms on S-going stream.* ◀

HARBOURS SOUTH OF STONEHAVEN

JOHNSHAVEN, Aberdeenshire, 56°47'·60N 02°20'·07W. AC 210. HW +0245 on Dover; +0045 and +0·4m on Aberdeen; ML 2·7m; Duration 0626. Very small, attractive drying hbr 6·5M N of Montrose.

Ent impossible in strong onshore winds; strictly a fair weather visit with great caution. Even in calm weather swell is a problem inside the hbr.

Appr from 5ca SE at HW±2½. Conspic W shed at N end of hbr. Ldg marks/lts on 316°: front, R structure with FR 5m; rear is G structure, 20m up the hill and 85m from front, with FG (FR when entry unsafe). Transit leads between rky ledges to very narrow (20m) ent. Turn 90° port into Inner Basin (dries 2·5m) and berth on outer wall or secure to mooring chains, rigged NE/SW. HM ☎ (01561) 362262 (home). Facilities: Slip, AB, ⬦, C (5 ton), FW, 🛒, R, ME, Bar, ✉. Bus to Montrose/Aberdeen.

Berthing Fees: *For details of Rover Ticket see 9.6.5.*

GOURDON, Aberdeenshire, 56°49'·49N 02°17'·21W. AC 210. HW +0240 on Dover; +0035 on Aberdeen; HW +0·4m on Aberdeen; ML 2·7m; Duration 0620. Shelter good in inner W hbr (dries about 2m; protected by storm gates); access from about mid-flood. E (or Gutty) hbr is rky, with difficult access. Beware rky ledges marked by bn and extending 200m S from W pier end. **A dangerous rk dries on the ldg line** about 1½ca S of pier heads. Ldg marks/lts 358°, both FR 5/30m 5M, 2 W trs; front lt shows G when not safe to enter. W pier hd Fl WRG 3s 5m 9/7M, vis 180°-G-344°-W-354°-R-180°. Essential to keep in W sector until R Ldg Lts are aligned. E bkwtr hd Q 3m 7M. HM ☎ (01569) 762741 (part-time, same as 9.6.14). Facilities: Slip, FW from standpipe, D, ME, ⬦, M, 🛒, R, Bar.

Berthing Fees: *For details of Rover Ticket see 9.6.5.*

9.6.14 STONEHAVEN

Aberdeenshire 56°57'·57N 02°12'·02W ✿✿✿♦✿✿

CHARTS AC 210, 1438; Imray C23.

TIDES +0235 Dover; ML 2·6; Duration 0620

Standard Port ABERDEEN (→)

Times				Height (metres)			
High Water		Low Water		MHWS	MHWN	MLWN	MLWS
0000	0600	0100	0700	4·3	3·4	1·6	0·6
1200	1800	1300	1900				
Differences STONEHAVEN							
+0013	+0008	+0013	+0009	+0·2	+0·2	+0·1	0·0

SHELTER Good, especially from offshore winds. Berth in Outer hbr on W side of bkwtr (3m to 2m) or N wall; sandbank forms with varying depths (not <0.6m to date) in middle to W side. Or ⚓ outside in fair weather. Hbr speed limit 3kn. Inner hbr dries 3·4m and in bad weather is closed, indicated by FG(occas) lt as shown. Do not go S of ldg line, to clear rks close E of inner hbr wall.

NAVIGATION WPT 56°57'·69N 02°11'·11W, 258°/0·5M to bkwtr lt. Give Downie Pt a wide berth. *Do not enter in strong on-shore winds.*

LIGHTS AND MARKS N pier Iso WRG 4s 7m 11/7M; appr in W sector, 246°-268°. A large yellow training buoy, Fl(4) Y 12s, is 5ca E of N pier. Inner hbr ldg lts 273° only apply to inner hbr: front FW 6m 5M; rear FR 8m 5M. FG on SE pier is shown when inner hbr is closed by a boom in bad weather. Conspic monument on hill top to S of hbr.

R/T HM VHF Ch 11.

TELEPHONE (Code 01569) HM (part-time) 762741, Mobile 07741050210; MRCC (01224) 592334; Marinecall 09068 969642; Police 762963; Dr 762945; Maritime Rescue Institute ☎ 765768.

FACILITIES Hbr AB £14.99, L, M, FW, ⬦, Slip (£15, or craft < 3.1m £10), ⬦, C (1·5 ton), LB, D by tanker, Fri early am; **Aberdeen & Stonehaven SC** Slip, Bar. **Town** P, Gas, 🛒, R, Bar, Ⓗ, ✉, Ⓑ, ⇌, ✈ (Aberdeen).

Berthing Fees: *For details of a Rover Ticket see 9.6.5.*

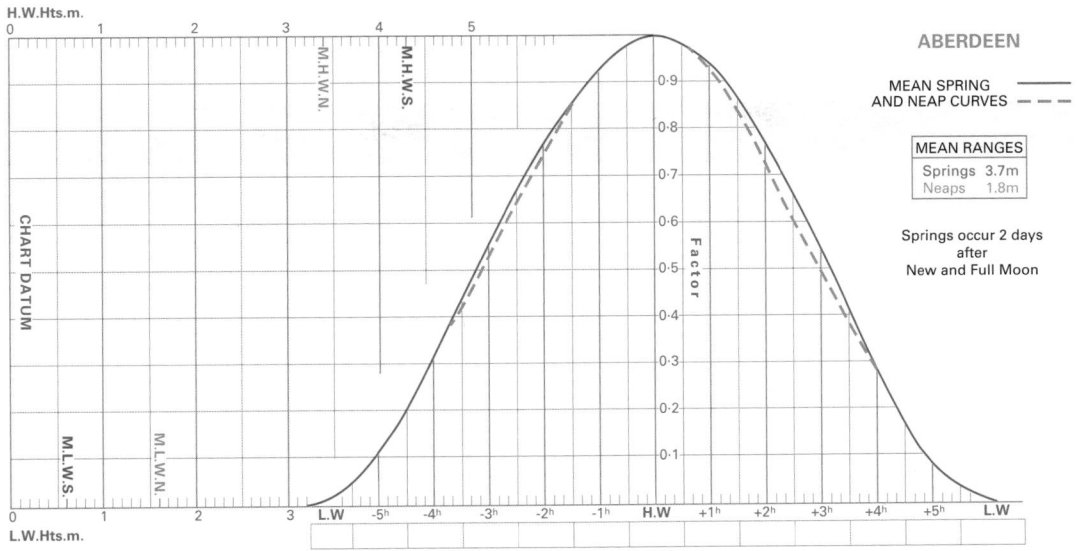

ABERDEEN

MEAN SPRING ───────
AND NEAP CURVES ─ ─ ─ ─

MEAN RANGES
Springs 3.7m
Neaps 1.8m

Springs occur 2 days
after
New and Full Moon

9.6.15 ABERDEEN

Aberdeenshire **57°08'·70N 02°03'·59W** ✿✿✿✿✿✿

CHARTS AC 210, 1446; Imray C23.

TIDES +0231 Dover; ML 2·5; Duration 0620

SHELTER Good in hbr; open at all tides, but do not enter in strong NE/ESE winds. Call Aberdeen VTS when 3M off for permission to enter VTS area and berthing availability.

Yachts are not encouraged in this busy commercial port, but usually lie on N side of Albert Basin alongside floating linkspan.

⚓ in Aberdeen Bay gives some shelter from S and W winds. Peterhead is 25M to N; Stonehaven is 13M S.

NAVIGATION WPT Fairway SWM buoy, Mo (A) 5s, Racon, 57°09'·31N 02°01'·96W, 236°/1M to hbr ent. Give Girdle Ness a berth of at least ¼M (more in bad weather). Do not pass close round pier hds. Strong tidal streams and, with river in spate, overfalls. Chan dredged to 6m on ldg line.

LIGHTS AND MARKS Ldg lts 236° (FR = port open; FG = port closed). Traffic sigs at root of N pier:

● = Entry prohib
● = Dep prohib
● & ● = Port closed

R/T Aberdeen VTS VHF Ch **12** 16 (H24).

TELEPHONE (Code 01224) VTS 597000; MRCC 592334; Weather 722334; Marinecall 09068 969642/0839 406189; Police 0845 600 5700.

FACILITIES Services: AB £18/craft for up to 5 days , El, Ⓔ, ME, ACA. **City** all amenities, ⇌, ✈. **Ferries:** Kirkwall and Lerwick (www. northlinkferries.co.uk).

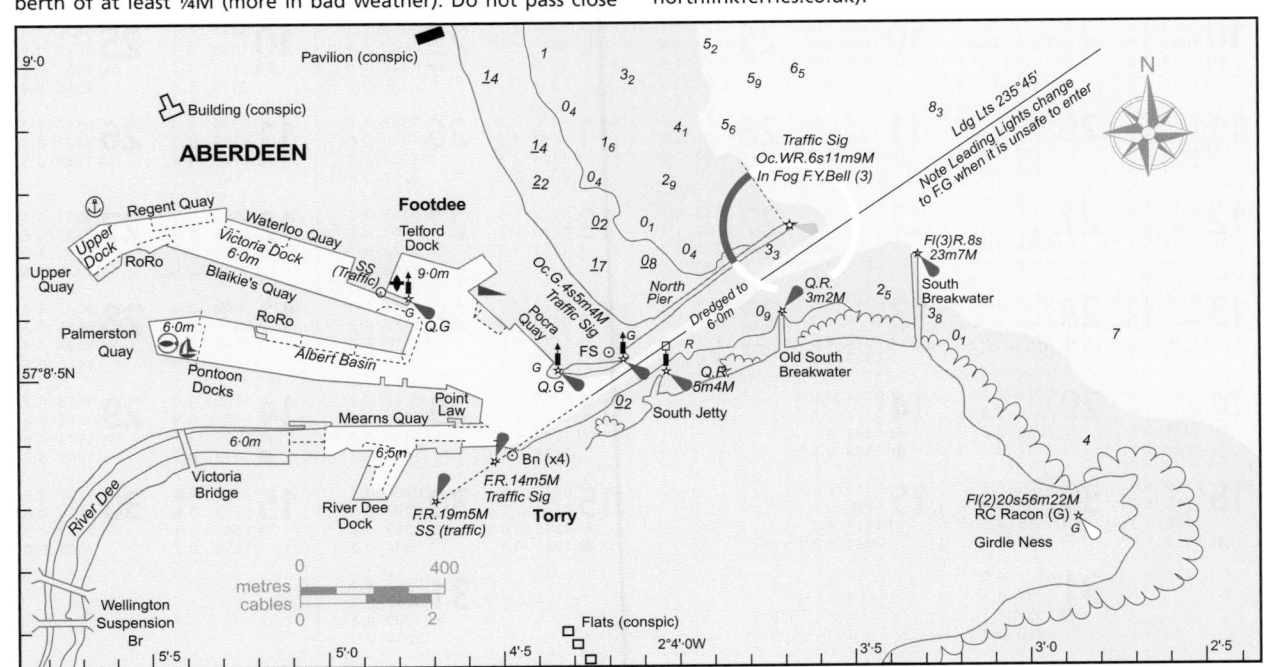

ABERDEEN   LAT 57°09'N   LONG 2°05'W
TIMES AND HEIGHTS OF HIGH AND LOW WATERS

TIME ZONE (UT)
For Summer Time add ONE hour in **non-shaded areas**

Dates in red are **SPRINGS**
Dates in blue are NEAPS

YEAR **2010**

JANUARY

Day	Time	m	Day	Time	m
1 F	0114	4.3	**16** SA	0203	4.0
	0714	1.0		0746	1.2
	1329	4.4		1402	4.2
	1945	0.6		2015	0.9
2 SA	0203	4.4	**17** SU	0236	4.0
	0801	0.9		0818	1.2
	1413	4.5		1433	4.2
	2033	0.4		2047	0.9
3 SU	0252	4.5	**18** M	0307	4.0
	0846	0.9		0848	1.2
	1459	4.6		1504	4.2
	2121	0.4		2117	0.9
4 M	0341	4.4	**19** TU	0339	3.9
	0931	1.0		0919	1.2
	1546	4.6		1535	4.2
	2210	0.5		2148	1.0
5 TU	0431	4.2	**20** W	0412	3.8
	1017	1.1		0950	1.3
	1635	4.5		1609	4.1
	2300	0.6		2221	1.1
6 W	0522	4.0	**21** TH	0447	3.7
	1106	1.3		1024	1.4
	1729	4.3		1646	4.0
	2352	0.9		2257	1.2
7 TH	0617	3.8	**22** F	0527	3.6
	1200	1.5		1103	1.6
	1828	4.1		1729	3.8
				2339	1.4
8 F	0048	1.2	**23** SA	0615	3.5
	0715	3.7		1152	1.7
	1303	1.7		1821	3.7
	1933	3.8			
9 SA	0152	1.4	**24** SU	0032	1.6
	0821	3.6		0713	3.4
	1417	1.8		1259	1.8
	2048	3.7		1927	3.5
10 SU	0305	1.6	**25** M	0141	1.7
	0931	3.6		0822	3.4
	1543	1.8		1422	1.9
	2206	3.6		2045	3.5
11 M	0418	1.7	**26** TU	0303	1.7
	1037	3.7		0937	3.5
	1654	1.6		1548	1.7
	2312	3.7		2206	3.6
12 TU	0514	1.6	**27** W	0422	1.6
	1131	3.8		1045	3.7
	1747	1.4		1659	1.4
				2317	3.8
13 W	0006	3.8	**28** TH	0525	1.4
	0559	1.5		1141	4.0
	1216	3.9		1756	1.0
	1830	1.3			
14 TH	0051	3.9	**29** F	0014	4.1
	0638	1.4		0616	1.1
	1255	4.1		1230	4.2
	1908	1.1		1846	0.7
15 F	0129	3.9	**30** SA	0105	4.3
	0713	1.3		0703	0.9
	1329	4.1		1315	4.5
	1943	1.0		1933	0.4
			31 SU	0151	4.5
				0747	0.8
				1359	4.7
				2019	0.2

FEBRUARY

Day	Time	m	Day	Time	m
1 M	0236	4.5	**16** TU	0240	4.0
	0830	0.7		0824	1.0
	1442	4.7		1439	4.3
	2104	0.2		2049	0.8
2 TU	0320	4.4	**17** W	0308	4.0
	0911	0.7		0853	1.0
	1526	4.7		1509	4.2
	2148	0.3		2118	0.8
3 W	0404	4.3	**18** TH	0338	3.9
	0952	0.9		0922	1.1
	1612	4.6		1541	4.2
	2232	0.6		2147	1.0
4 TH	0450	4.1	**19** F	0410	3.9
	1035	1.1		0954	1.2
	1701	4.3		1616	4.0
	2317	0.9		2219	1.1
5 F	0538	3.8	**20** SA	0446	3.7
	1123	1.3		1029	1.3
	1756	4.0		1657	3.9
				2257	1.3
6 SA	0007	1.3	**21** SU	0529	3.6
	0632	3.6		1115	1.5
	1222	1.6		1747	3.7
	1901	3.7		2347	1.5
7 SU	0106	1.6	**22** M	0626	3.5
	0737	3.4		1219	1.7
	1338	1.8		1856	3.5
	2019	3.5			
8 M	0224	1.9	**23** TU	0100	1.8
	0853	3.4		0741	3.4
	1522	1.8		1349	1.8
	2148	3.4		2022	3.4
9 TU	0358	1.9	**24** W	0237	1.8
	1012	3.5		0905	3.4
	1643	1.7		1529	1.6
	2303	3.5		2152	3.5
10 W	0500	1.8	**25** TH	0409	1.7
	1115	3.6		1023	3.6
	1736	1.4		1646	1.3
	2357	3.6		2306	3.8
11 TH	0546	1.6	**26** F	0513	1.4
	1201	3.8		1123	3.9
	1817	1.2		1742	0.9
12 F	0037	3.8	**27** SA	0002	4.1
	0622	1.4		0602	1.1
	1239	4.0		1213	4.2
	1851	1.1		1830	0.5
13 SA	0112	3.9	**28** SU	0049	4.3
	0656	1.3		0646	0.8
	1312	4.1		1257	4.5
	1923	0.9		1916	0.2
14 SU	0142	4.0			
	0727	1.1			
	1342	4.2			
	1953	0.8			
15 M	0212	4.0			
	0756	1.0			
	1411	4.2			
	2021	0.8			

MARCH

Day	Time	m	Day	Time	m
1 M	0132	4.4	**16** TU	0142	4.0
	0728	0.6		0730	0.9
	1339	4.7		1344	4.2
	1959	0.1		1951	0.7
2 TU	0213	4.5	**17** W	0209	4.0
	0808	0.5		0758	0.9
	1421	4.8		1413	4.2
	2040	0.1		2019	0.7
3 W	0254	4.4	**18** TH	0238	4.0
	0847	0.6		0827	0.9
	1504	4.7		1444	4.2
	2121	0.3		2048	0.8
4 TH	0334	4.3	**19** F	0307	4.0
	0927	0.7		0858	0.9
	1549	4.5		1517	4.1
	2201	0.6		2117	0.9
5 F	0416	4.1	**20** SA	0340	3.9
	1008	0.9		0930	1.0
	1636	4.2		1555	4.0
	2242	1.0		2150	1.1
6 SA	0501	3.8	**21** SU	0416	3.8
	1054	1.2		1008	1.1
	1730	3.9		1638	3.8
	2327	1.4		2229	1.3
7 SU	0551	3.6	**22** M	0500	3.7
	1148	1.5		1057	1.3
	1833	3.5		1732	3.6
				2322	1.5
8 M	0023	1.8	**23** TU	0557	3.5
	0653	3.4		1205	1.5
	1303	1.7		1846	3.5
	1950	3.3			
9 TU	0143	2.0	**24** W	0041	1.8
	0810	3.3		0715	3.4
	1455	1.8		1337	1.5
	2122	3.2		2011	3.4
10 W	0331	2.0	**25** TH	0223	1.8
	0937	3.3		0840	3.4
	1622	1.6		1514	1.4
	2242	3.3		2139	3.5
11 TH	0438	1.8	**26** F	0353	1.6
	1047	3.5		1000	3.6
	1713	1.4		1627	1.0
	2334	3.5		2250	3.8
12 F	0523	1.6	**27** SA	0453	1.3
	1135	3.7		1101	3.9
	1752	1.2		1722	0.7
				2343	4.0
13 SA	0012	3.7	**28** SU	0542	1.0
	0559	1.4		1150	4.2
	1213	3.8		1810	0.4
	1825	1.0			
14 SU	0045	3.8	**29** M	0027	4.2
	0631	1.2		0624	0.8
	1245	4.0		1235	4.4
	1855	0.9		1853	0.2
15 M	0114	3.9	**30** TU	0108	4.3
	0701	1.0		0705	0.6
	1315	4.1		1318	4.6
	1923	0.8		1934	0.2
			31 W	0147	4.4
				0745	0.5
				1400	4.6
				2014	0.3

APRIL

Day	Time	m	Day	Time	m
1 TH	0226	4.3	**16** F	0209	4.1
	0825	0.5		0805	0.8
	1443	4.5		1422	4.1
	2053	0.5		2022	0.8
2 F	0305	4.2	**17** SA	0242	4.1
	0905	0.6		0840	0.8
	1528	4.3		1500	4.1
	2131	0.8		2056	0.9
3 SA	0345	4.0	**18** SU	0317	4.0
	0947	0.8		0918	0.9
	1616	4.0		1542	4.0
	2210	1.1		2133	1.1
4 SU	0428	3.8	**19** M	0357	3.9
	1031	1.1		1002	1.0
	1709	3.7		1630	3.8
	2254	1.5		2219	1.3
5 M	0515	3.6	**20** TU	0444	3.7
	1124	1.4		1056	1.1
	1809	3.4		1730	3.6
	2347	1.8		2317	1.5
6 TU	0614	3.4	**21** W	0544	3.5
	1231	1.6		1205	1.2
	1919	3.2		1843	3.5
7 W	0100	2.0	**22** TH	0035	1.7
	0725	3.3		0659	3.5
	1404	1.7		1329	1.2
	2039	3.2		2000	3.5
8 TH	0238	2.0	**23** F	0206	1.7
	0846	3.2		0817	3.5
	1539	1.6		1452	1.1
	2159	3.2		2119	3.6
9 F	0358	1.9	**24** SA	0325	1.6
	1001	3.3		0932	3.7
	1634	1.4		1601	0.9
	2255	3.4		2225	3.7
10 SA	0447	1.7	**25** SU	0426	1.3
	1055	3.5		1035	3.9
	1714	1.2		1657	0.7
	2335	3.6		2318	3.9
11 SU	0526	1.4	**26** M	0517	1.1
	1136	3.7		1127	4.1
	1749	1.0		1745	0.5
12 M	0009	3.7	**27** TU	0002	4.1
	0559	1.2		0602	0.8
	1211	3.8		1214	4.3
	1819	0.9		1829	0.5
13 TU	0040	3.9	**28** W	0043	4.2
	0630	1.0		0645	0.7
	1243	4.0		1258	4.4
	1849	0.8		1910	0.5
14 W	0109	4.0	**29** TH	0123	4.2
	0701	0.9		0726	0.6
	1315	4.1		1343	4.4
	1919	0.7		1949	0.6
15 TH	0139	4.0	**30** F	0201	4.2
	0732	0.8		0808	0.6
	1348	4.1		1427	4.3
	1950	0.7		2028	0.8

Chart Datum: 2·25 metres below Ordnance Datum (Newlyn). HAT is 4·8 metres above Chart Datum; see 4.5

TIME ZONE (UT)
For Summer Time add ONE hour in **non-shaded areas**

ABERDEEN LAT 57°09'N LONG 2°05'W
TIMES AND HEIGHTS OF HIGH AND LOW WATERS

Dates in red are **SPRINGS**
Dates in blue are **NEAPS**

YEAR 2010

SE Scotland

MAY

Time	m	Time	m
1 SA 0240 4.1 / 0849 0.7 / 1513 4.1 / 2106 1.0		**16** SU 0222 4.1 / 0829 0.7 / 1449 4.1 / 2044 0.9	
2 SU 0320 4.0 / 0931 0.8 / 1600 3.9 / 2145 1.2		**17** M 0302 4.1 / 0914 0.7 / 1536 4.0 / 2128 1.1	
3 M 0401 3.9 / 1014 1.0 / 1650 3.6 / 2227 1.5		**18** TU 0346 4.0 / 1003 0.8 / 1629 3.9 / 2217 1.2	
4 TU 0446 3.7 / 1102 1.2 / 1743 3.4 / 2315 1.7		**19** W 0436 3.9 / 1058 0.8 / 1728 3.7 / 2315 1.4	
5 W 0539 3.5 / 1158 1.4 / 1842 3.3		**20** TH 0535 3.8 / 1202 0.9 / 1833 3.6	
6 TH 0015 1.9 / 0639 3.4 / 1307 1.5 / 1945 3.2		**21** F 0023 1.5 / 0642 3.7 / 1312 1.0 / 1940 3.6	
7 F 0132 1.9 / 0746 3.3 / 1423 1.5 / 2055 3.2		**22** SA 0137 1.6 / 0752 3.7 / 1423 1.0 / 2050 3.6	
8 SA 0250 1.9 / 0856 3.3 / 1532 1.5 / 2157 3.3		**23** SU 0249 1.5 / 0902 3.7 / 1530 0.9 / 2155 3.7	
9 SU 0354 1.7 / 0959 3.4 / 1623 1.3 / 2246 3.5		**24** M 0355 1.4 / 1008 3.9 / 1629 0.9 / 2250 3.8	
10 M 0441 1.5 / 1049 3.6 / 1703 1.2 / 2326 3.6		**25** TU 0452 1.2 / 1106 4.0 / 1721 0.8 / 2338 3.9	
11 TU 0521 1.3 / 1131 3.7 / 1739 1.0		**26** W 0543 1.0 / 1157 4.1 / 1808 0.8	
12 W 0002 3.8 / 0557 1.1 / 1210 3.8 / 1813 0.9		**27** TH 0022 4.0 / 0629 0.8 / 1246 4.1 / 1850 0.8	
13 TH 0037 3.9 / 0633 1.0 / 1248 4.0 / 1849 0.9		**28** F 0103 4.1 / 0713 0.7 / 1332 4.1 / 1930 0.9	
14 F 0110 4.0 / 0716 0.8 / 1326 4.0 / 1925 0.8		**29** SA 0143 4.1 / 0756 0.7 / 1417 4.0 / 2009 1.0	
15 SA 0145 4.1 / 0748 0.7 / 1406 4.1 / 2004 0.9		**30** SU 0222 4.1 / 0837 0.7 / 1501 3.9 / 2047 1.1	
		31 M 0301 4.0 / 0916 0.8 / 1544 3.8 / 2124 1.4	

JUNE

Time	m	Time	m
1 TU 0340 3.9 / 0956 0.9 / 1628 3.7 / 2203 1.4		**16** W 0337 4.2 / 0959 0.5 / 1622 4.0 / 2211 1.1	
2 W 0421 3.8 / 1037 1.1 / 1712 3.5 / 2244 1.5		**17** TH 0427 4.2 / 1051 0.6 / 1716 3.9 / 2302 1.2	
3 TH 0505 3.7 / 1122 1.2 / 1800 3.4 / 2331 1.7		**18** F 0521 4.1 / 1147 0.7 / 1813 3.8 / 2359 1.3	
4 F 0555 3.5 / 1214 1.4 / 1852 3.3		**19** SA 0621 3.9 / 1246 0.8 / 1913 3.7	
5 SA 0029 1.8 / 0650 3.4 / 1312 1.5 / 1948 3.3		**20** SU 0103 1.4 / 0725 3.8 / 1350 1.0 / 2017 3.6	
6 SU 0135 1.8 / 0750 3.4 / 1414 1.5 / 2049 3.3		**21** M 0213 1.5 / 0834 3.8 / 1456 1.1 / 2123 3.6	
7 M 0243 1.8 / 0853 3.4 / 1515 1.4 / 2148 3.4		**22** TU 0326 1.5 / 0946 3.7 / 1604 1.2 / 2225 3.7	
8 TU 0345 1.7 / 0955 3.4 / 1610 1.4 / 2240 3.5		**23** W 0434 1.3 / 1052 3.8 / 1702 1.2 / 2319 3.8	
9 W 0438 1.5 / 1050 3.6 / 1658 1.2 / 2325 3.7		**24** TH 0532 1.2 / 1149 3.8 / 1752 1.2	
10 TH 0525 1.3 / 1138 3.7 / 1742 1.1		**25** F 0007 3.9 / 0621 1.0 / 1240 3.9 / 1836 1.1	
11 F 0006 3.9 / 0608 1.1 / 1224 3.9 / 1825 1.0		**26** SA 0050 4.0 / 0705 0.9 / 1326 3.9 / 1916 1.1	
12 SA 0046 4.0 / 0652 0.9 / 1309 4.0 / 1908 0.9		**27** SU 0130 4.1 / 0746 0.8 / 1407 3.9 / 1953 1.1	
13 SU 0126 4.1 / 0736 0.7 / 1355 4.1 / 1952 0.9		**28** M 0207 4.1 / 0823 0.8 / 1446 3.9 / 2029 1.1	
14 M 0208 4.2 / 0822 0.5 / 1442 4.2 / 2037 0.9		**29** TU 0243 4.1 / 0859 0.8 / 1523 3.8 / 2103 1.2	
15 TU 0251 4.2 / 0910 0.5 / 1531 4.1 / 2123 1.0		**30** W 0318 4.0 / 0934 0.8 / 1600 3.8 / 2137 1.2	

JULY

Time	m	Time	m
1 TH 0354 4.0 / 1009 0.9 / 1637 3.7 / 2212 1.3		**16** F 0410 4.4 / 1033 0.4 / 1653 4.1 / 2240 1.0	
2 F 0432 3.9 / 1045 1.1 / 1717 3.6 / 2250 1.4		**17** SA 0500 4.3 / 1122 0.6 / 1745 3.9 / 2331 1.2	
3 SA 0513 3.7 / 1125 1.2 / 1801 3.5 / 2334 1.6		**18** SU 0556 4.1 / 1215 0.9 / 1841 3.7	
4 SU 0600 3.6 / 1212 1.4 / 1850 3.4		**19** M 0029 1.4 / 0658 3.9 / 1315 1.2 / 1943 3.6	
5 M 0028 1.7 / 0653 3.5 / 1307 1.5 / 1945 3.3		**20** TU 0139 1.5 / 0810 3.7 / 1424 1.4 / 2052 3.5	
6 TU 0134 1.8 / 0754 3.4 / 1410 1.6 / 2048 3.4		**21** W 0303 1.6 / 0930 3.6 / 1543 1.5 / 2203 3.6	
7 W 0246 1.8 / 0901 3.4 / 1517 1.6 / 2152 3.5		**22** TH 0425 1.5 / 1045 3.6 / 1650 1.5 / 2306 3.7	
8 TH 0356 1.6 / 1011 3.5 / 1622 1.5 / 2250 3.6		**23** F 0526 1.3 / 1146 3.7 / 1741 1.4 / 2356 3.8	
9 F 0457 1.4 / 1113 3.7 / 1718 1.3 / 2340 3.8		**24** SA 0614 1.1 / 1235 3.8 / 1824 1.3	
10 SA 0550 1.1 / 1207 3.9 / 1809 1.1		**25** SU 0039 4.0 / 0655 1.0 / 1316 3.9 / 1901 1.2	
11 SU 0026 4.0 / 0638 0.8 / 1257 4.1 / 1855 1.0		**26** M 0116 4.1 / 0731 0.8 / 1351 3.9 / 1935 1.1	
12 M 0110 4.2 / 0725 0.5 / 1344 4.2 / 1940 0.8		**27** TU 0150 4.1 / 0805 0.8 / 1425 3.9 / 2007 1.1	
13 TU 0154 4.4 / 0811 0.3 / 1431 4.3 / 2025 0.8		**28** W 0222 4.2 / 0836 0.8 / 1457 3.9 / 2038 1.1	
14 W 0238 4.5 / 0858 0.2 / 1517 4.3 / 2109 0.8		**29** TH 0253 4.2 / 0906 0.8 / 1528 3.9 / 2109 1.1	
15 TH 0323 4.5 / 0945 0.2 / 1605 4.2 / 2153 0.9		**30** F 0325 4.1 / 0937 0.9 / 1600 3.8 / 2140 1.2	
		31 SA 0358 4.0 / 1008 1.0 / 1634 3.7 / 2213 1.3	

AUGUST

Time	m	Time	m
1 SU 0435 3.9 / 1042 1.1 / 1712 3.6 / 2250 1.4		**16** 0531 4.1 / 1142 1.1 / 1806 3.7 / 2359 1.4	
2 M 0516 3.8 / 1121 1.3 / 1757 3.5 / 2336 1.6		**17** TU 0635 3.8 / 1240 1.5 / 1909 3.5	
3 TU 0605 3.6 / 1209 1.5 / 1851 3.4		**18** W 0111 1.6 / 0750 3.5 / 1354 1.7 / 2022 3.4	
4 W 0037 1.7 / 0707 3.6 / 1314 1.7 / 1956 3.4		**19** TH 0249 1.7 / 0918 3.4 / 1527 1.8 / 2142 3.5	
5 TH 0157 1.8 / 0821 3.4 / 1434 1.7 / 2109 3.4		**20** F 0418 1.5 / 1038 3.5 / 1638 1.7 / 2250 3.6	
6 F 0323 1.7 / 0942 3.5 / 1556 1.6 / 2220 3.6		**21** SA 0516 1.3 / 1137 3.6 / 1727 1.6 / 2341 3.8	
7 SA 0437 1.4 / 1054 3.7 / 1702 1.4 / 2318 3.8		**22** SU 0600 1.1 / 1221 3.8 / 1807 1.4	
8 SU 0534 1.1 / 1152 3.9 / 1754 1.2		**23** M 0021 4.0 / 0636 1.0 / 1257 3.9 / 1840 1.2	
9 M 0007 4.1 / 0623 0.7 / 1242 4.2 / 1840 0.9		**24** TU 0055 4.1 / 0709 0.9 / 1328 4.0 / 1912 1.1	
10 TU 0053 4.4 / 0709 0.4 / 1328 4.4 / 1924 0.7		**25** W 0126 4.2 / 0739 0.8 / 1357 4.0 / 1942 1.0	
11 W 0135 4.6 / 0754 0.1 / 1412 4.5 / 2006 0.6		**26** TH 0156 4.2 / 0807 0.7 / 1426 4.0 / 2011 1.0	
12 TH 0218 4.7 / 0839 0.1 / 1455 4.5 / 2048 0.6		**27** F 0225 4.3 / 0835 0.8 / 1454 4.0 / 2040 1.0	
13 F 0302 4.7 / 0923 0.1 / 1539 4.4 / 2130 0.7		**28** SA 0255 4.2 / 0903 0.8 / 1524 4.0 / 2109 1.1	
14 SA 0347 4.6 / 1007 0.4 / 1624 4.2 / 2213 0.9		**29** SU 0327 4.1 / 0932 0.9 / 1556 3.9 / 2141 1.1	
15 SU 0436 4.4 / 1052 0.7 / 1712 4.0 / 2302 1.1		**30** M 0402 4.0 / 1003 1.1 / 1631 3.8 / 2216 1.3	
		31 TU 0442 3.8 / 1039 1.3 / 1712 3.7 / 2259 1.5	

Chart Datum: 2·25 metres below Ordnance Datum (Newlyn). HAT is 4·8 metres above Chart Datum; see 4.5

TIME ZONE (UT)
For Summer Time add ONE hour in **non-shaded areas**

ABERDEEN   LAT 57°09'N   LONG 2°05'W
TIMES AND HEIGHTS OF HIGH AND LOW WATERS

Dates in red are **SPRINGS**
Dates in blue are NEAPS

YEAR 2010

SEPTEMBER

Day	Time	m		Day	Time	m
1 W ☽	0531 / 1125 / 1805 / 2359	3.7 / 1.5 / 3.5 / 1.7		**16** TH	0047 / 0730 / 1322 / 1949	1.6 / 3.4 / 2.0 / 3.4
2 TH	0635 / 1232 / 1916	3.5 / 1.8 / 3.4		**17** F	0230 / 0858 / 1502 / 2112	1.7 / 3.4 / 2.0 / 3.5
3 F	0123 / 0756 / 1404 / 2036	1.8 / 3.4 / 1.9 / 3.4		**18** SA	0400 / 1019 / 1616 / 2224	1.6 / 3.5 / 1.9 / 3.6
4 SA	0300 / 0922 / 1538 / 2153	1.6 / 3.5 / 1.8 / 3.6		**19** SU	0454 / 1115 / 1703 / 2315	1.4 / 3.6 / 1.7 / 3.8
5 SU	0419 / 1038 / 1645 / 2256	1.3 / 3.7 / 1.5 / 3.9		**20** M	0535 / 1155 / 1741 / 2354	1.2 / 3.8 / 1.5 / 3.9
6 M	0516 / 1135 / 1736 / 2346	0.9 / 4.0 / 1.2 / 4.2		**21** TU	0609 / 1228 / 1815	1.0 / 3.9 / 1.3
7 TU	0604 / 1223 / 1820	0.6 / 4.3 / 0.9		**22** W	0027 / 0639 / 1258 / 1845	4.1 / 0.9 / 4.0 / 1.1
8 W ●	0030 / 0649 / 1306 / 1902	4.5 / 0.3 / 4.5 / 0.7		**23** TH ○	0058 / 0707 / 1326 / 1914	4.2 / 0.8 / 4.1 / 1.0
9 TH	0113 / 0732 / 1348 / 1943	4.7 / 0.1 / 4.6 / 0.6		**24** F	0128 / 0735 / 1354 / 1943	4.3 / 0.8 / 4.1 / 1.0
10 F	0156 / 0815 / 1429 / 2024	4.8 / 0.1 / 4.5 / 0.5		**25** SA	0157 / 0803 / 1422 / 2013	4.3 / 0.8 / 4.1 / 1.0
11 SA	0239 / 0856 / 1510 / 2105	4.8 / 0.2 / 4.4 / 0.6		**26** SU	0228 / 0831 / 1452 / 2043	4.2 / 0.9 / 4.1 / 1.0
12 SU	0325 / 0938 / 1553 / 2149	4.6 / 0.5 / 4.0 / 0.8		**27** M	0301 / 0900 / 1523 / 2116	4.2 / 1.0 / 4.0 / 1.1
13 M	0414 / 1021 / 1639 / 2236	4.4 / 0.9 / 4.0 / 1.1		**28** TU	0338 / 0932 / 1559 / 2152	4.0 / 1.2 / 3.9 / 1.3
14 TU	0509 / 1109 / 1732 / 2333	4.0 / 1.3 / 3.8 / 1.4		**29** W	0420 / 1009 / 1640 / 2238	3.9 / 1.4 / 3.8 / 1.4
15 W ◐	0614 / 1206 / 1835	3.7 / 1.7 / 3.6		**30** TH	0511 / 1058 / 1734 / 2341	3.7 / 1.6 / 3.6 / 1.6

OCTOBER

Day	Time	m		Day	Time	m
1 F ☽	0619 / 1208 / 1847	3.5 / 1.8 / 3.5		**16** SA	0147 / 0820 / 1413 / 2027	1.7 / 3.3 / 2.1 / 3.5
2 SA	0106 / 0740 / 1344 / 2008	1.6 / 3.5 / 1.9 / 3.5		**17** SU	0319 / 0939 / 1535 / 2140	1.7 / 3.4 / 2.0 / 3.6
3 SU	0239 / 0904 / 1516 / 2125	1.5 / 3.6 / 1.8 / 3.7		**18** M	0417 / 1036 / 1628 / 2236	1.5 / 3.6 / 1.8 / 3.7
4 M	0355 / 1018 / 1622 / 2229	1.2 / 3.8 / 1.5 / 4.0		**19** TU	0458 / 1118 / 1708 / 2318	1.3 / 3.7 / 1.6 / 3.9
5 TU	0452 / 1113 / 1712 / 2321	0.9 / 4.1 / 1.2 / 4.3		**20** W	0533 / 1153 / 1743 / 2354	1.2 / 3.9 / 1.4 / 4.0
6 W	0541 / 1159 / 1757	0.6 / 4.3 / 0.9		**21** TH	0605 / 1224 / 1816	1.1 / 4.0 / 1.2
7 TH ●	0007 / 0625 / 1242 / 1839	4.5 / 0.4 / 4.5 / 0.7		**22** F	0027 / 0634 / 1254 / 1846	4.1 / 1.0 / 4.1 / 1.1
8 F	0051 / 0708 / 1322 / 1921	4.7 / 0.3 / 4.5 / 0.6		**23** SA ○	0100 / 0703 / 1323 / 1918	4.2 / 0.9 / 4.2 / 1.0
9 SA	0134 / 0749 / 1402 / 2002	4.8 / 0.3 / 4.5 / 0.6		**24** SU	0132 / 0733 / 1353 / 1950	4.2 / 0.9 / 4.2 / 1.0
10 SU	0219 / 0830 / 1443 / 2045	4.7 / 0.5 / 4.4 / 0.7		**25** M	0206 / 0804 / 1425 / 2024	4.2 / 1.0 / 4.2 / 1.0
11 M	0306 / 0911 / 1525 / 2129	4.5 / 0.8 / 4.3 / 0.9		**26** TU	0242 / 0837 / 1459 / 2100	4.2 / 1.1 / 4.1 / 1.1
12 TU	0356 / 0953 / 1609 / 2217	4.2 / 1.2 / 4.1 / 1.1		**27** W	0322 / 0913 / 1536 / 2142	4.1 / 1.2 / 4.1 / 1.2
13 W	0451 / 1038 / 1700 / 2311	3.9 / 1.5 / 3.8 / 1.4		**28** TH	0408 / 0954 / 1620 / 2232	3.9 / 1.4 / 3.9 / 1.3
14 TH ◐	0553 / 1132 / 1800	3.6 / 1.8 / 3.6		**29** F	0502 / 1046 / 1715 / 2334	3.8 / 1.6 / 3.8 / 1.4
15 F	0019 / 0702 / 1243 / 1910	1.6 / 3.4 / 2.1 / 3.5		**30** SA ☽	0610 / 1155 / 1824	3.6 / 1.8 / 3.7
				31 SU	0051 / 0724 / 1321 / 1940	1.4 / 3.6 / 1.9 / 3.7

NOVEMBER

Day	Time	m		Day	Time	m
1 M	0213 / 0840 / 1444 / 2054	1.3 / 3.7 / 1.8 / 3.8		**16** TU	0313 / 0939 / 1533 / 2142	1.7 / 3.5 / 1.9 / 3.6
2 TU	0325 / 0950 / 1551 / 2200	1.1 / 3.8 / 1.6 / 4.0		**17** W	0408 / 1031 / 1625 / 2234	1.5 / 3.6 / 1.8 / 3.7
3 W	0424 / 1046 / 1646 / 2256	0.9 / 4.1 / 1.3 / 4.3		**18** TH	0450 / 1112 / 1707 / 2318	1.4 / 3.8 / 1.6 / 3.9
4 TH	0516 / 1134 / 1734 / 2345	0.7 / 4.2 / 1.1 / 4.5		**19** F	0527 / 1149 / 1745 / 2357	1.3 / 3.9 / 1.4 / 4.0
5 F	0602 / 1217 / 1819	0.6 / 4.4 / 0.9		**20** SA	0601 / 1223 / 1820	1.2 / 4.1 / 1.2
6 SA ●	0032 / 0645 / 1259 / 1903	4.6 / 0.6 / 4.4 / 0.8		**21** SU ○	0034 / 0634 / 1256 / 1856	4.1 / 1.1 / 4.2 / 1.1
7 SU	0118 / 0727 / 1339 / 1947	4.6 / 0.7 / 4.5 / 0.7		**22** M	0111 / 0709 / 1330 / 1933	4.2 / 1.1 / 4.2 / 1.0
8 M	0205 / 0808 / 1420 / 2030	4.5 / 0.8 / 4.4 / 0.8		**23** TU	0149 / 0745 / 1405 / 2012	4.2 / 1.1 / 4.3 / 0.9
9 TU	0252 / 0848 / 1501 / 2114	4.3 / 1.1 / 4.3 / 0.9		**24** W	0230 / 0823 / 1442 / 2053	4.2 / 1.1 / 4.3 / 0.9
10 W	0341 / 0929 / 1545 / 2200	4.1 / 1.3 / 4.1 / 1.1		**25** TH	0313 / 0904 / 1522 / 2138	4.1 / 1.2 / 4.2 / 1.0
11 TH	0433 / 1012 / 1631 / 2249	3.9 / 1.6 / 4.0 / 1.3		**26** F	0401 / 0948 / 1608 / 2228	4.0 / 1.4 / 4.1 / 1.0
12 F	0527 / 1059 / 1724 / 2344	3.7 / 1.8 / 3.8 / 1.5		**27** SA	0455 / 1039 / 1701 / 2325	3.9 / 1.5 / 4.0 / 1.1
13 SA ◐	0625 / 1156 / 1824	3.5 / 2.0 / 3.6		**28** SU ◐	0555 / 1139 / 1803	3.8 / 1.7 / 3.9
14 SU	0049 / 0727 / 1307 / 1928	1.6 / 3.4 / 2.1 / 3.5		**29** M	0031 / 0700 / 1251 / 1911	1.2 / 3.7 / 1.7 / 3.9
15 M	0202 / 0835 / 1424 / 2037	1.7 / 3.4 / 2.1 / 3.5		**30** TU	0141 / 0808 / 1405 / 2021	1.2 / 3.7 / 1.7 / 3.9

DECEMBER

Day	Time	m		Day	Time	m
1 W	0250 / 0916 / 1516 / 2130	1.2 / 3.8 / 1.6 / 4.0		**16** TH	0255 / 0930 / 1527 / 2138	1.7 / 3.5 / 1.9 / 3.5
2 TH	0355 / 1018 / 1620 / 2234	1.1 / 3.9 / 1.4 / 4.1		**17** F	0356 / 1026 / 1626 / 2237	1.7 / 3.6 / 1.8 / 3.7
3 F	0452 / 1111 / 1716 / 2330	1.0 / 4.1 / 1.2 / 4.2		**18** SA	0447 / 1113 / 1714 / 2327	1.6 / 3.8 / 1.6 / 3.8
4 SA	0543 / 1158 / 1807	1.0 / 4.2 / 1.1		**19** SU	0531 / 1154 / 1757	1.4 / 3.9 / 1.4
5 SU ●	0021 / 0628 / 1242 / 1853	4.3 / 1.0 / 4.3 / 0.9		**20** M	0012 / 0611 / 1233 / 1838	3.9 / 1.3 / 4.1 / 1.1
6 M	0110 / 0711 / 1323 / 1937	4.3 / 1.0 / 4.4 / 0.8		**21** TU ○	0055 / 0652 / 1311 / 1919	4.1 / 1.2 / 4.2 / 0.9
7 TU	0157 / 0751 / 1404 / 2020	4.3 / 1.0 / 4.4 / 0.8		**22** W	0137 / 0732 / 1349 / 2002	4.2 / 1.1 / 4.3 / 0.8
8 W	0242 / 0831 / 1444 / 2102	4.2 / 1.2 / 4.3 / 0.9		**23** TH	0220 / 0814 / 1429 / 2046	4.3 / 1.1 / 4.4 / 0.7
9 TH	0326 / 0909 / 1524 / 2142	4.1 / 1.3 / 4.2 / 1.0		**24** F	0305 / 0856 / 1511 / 2131	4.3 / 1.1 / 4.4 / 0.7
10 F	0410 / 0947 / 1605 / 2223	3.9 / 1.5 / 4.1 / 1.2		**25** SA	0351 / 0939 / 1556 / 2218	4.2 / 1.2 / 4.4 / 0.7
11 SA	0455 / 1026 / 1648 / 2306	3.8 / 1.6 / 3.9 / 1.3		**26** SU	0440 / 1025 / 1645 / 2309	4.1 / 1.3 / 4.3 / 0.8
12 SU	0541 / 1110 / 1736 / 2353	3.6 / 1.8 / 3.8 / 1.5		**27** M	0533 / 1117 / 1740	4.0 / 1.4 / 4.2
13 M ◐	0631 / 1202 / 1829	3.5 / 1.9 / 3.6		**28** TU ☽	0005 / 0631 / 1217 / 1841	1.0 / 3.8 / 1.6 / 4.0
14 TU	0048 / 0726 / 1307 / 1928	1.6 / 3.6 / 2.0 / 3.5		**29** W	0107 / 0734 / 1325 / 1950	1.2 / 3.7 / 1.7 / 3.9
15 W	0150 / 0827 / 1418 / 2032	1.7 / 3.4 / 2.0 / 3.5		**30** TH	0214 / 0842 / 1441 / 2105	1.3 / 3.7 / 1.7 / 3.8
				31 F	0326 / 0951 / 1600 / 2219	1.4 / 3.7 / 1.6 / 3.9

Chart Datum: 2·25 metres below Ordnance Datum (Newlyn). HAT is 4·8 metres above Chart Datum; see 4.5

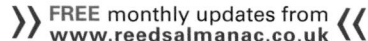

ABERDEEN TO RATTRAY HEAD

(AC 213) From Aberdeen there are few offshore dangers to Buchan Ness. Drums Links Firing Range lies 8¾M N of Aberdeen; red flags and lights are shown when firing is taking place. R Ythan, 1·75M SSW of Hackley Hd, is navigable by small craft, but chan shifts constantly. 3M North is the very small hbr of Collieston (mostly dries), only accessible in fine weather. 4·75M NNE of Hackley Head lie The Skares, rks (marked by PHM lt buoy) extending 3½ca from S point of Cruden B, where there is anch in offshore winds. On N side of Cruden B is Port Erroll (dries 2·5m).

Buchan Ness (lt, fog sig, Racon) is a rky peninsula. 2ca N is Meikle Mackie islet, close W of which is the small hbr of Boddam (dries). 3ca NE of Meikle Mackie is The Skerry, a rk 6m high on S side of Sandford B; rks on which the sea breaks extend 2ca NNE. The chan between The Skerry and the coast is foul with rks

and not advised. Peterhead is easy to enter in almost all conditions and is an excellent passage port with marina at SW corner of the Bay.

Rattray Bay has numerous submarine pipelines leading ashore to St Fergus Gas Terminal.

For notes on offshore oil/gas installations, see 3.14 and 9.5.5.

Rattray Hd (with lt, fog sig on The Ron, rk 2ca E of Hd) has rky foreshore, drying for 2ca off. Rattray Briggs is a detached reef, depth 0·2m, 2ca E of lt ho. Rattray Hard is a rky patch, depth 10·7m, 1·5M ENE of lt ho, which raises a dangerous sea during onshore gales. ▶ *Off Rattray Hd the S-going stream begins at HW Aberdeen – 0420, and the N-going at HW Aberdeen + 0110, sp rates 3kn. In normal conditions keep about 1M E of Rattray Hd, but pass 5M off in bad weather, preferably at slack water.* ◀ Conspic radio masts with red lights lie 2·5M WNW and 2·2M W of lighthouse.

9.6.16 PETERHEAD

Aberdeenshire **57°29´·81N 01°46´·42W** ✵✵✵❀◊◊❀❀

CHARTS AC 213, 1438; Imray C23.

TIDES +0140 Dover; ML 2·3; Duration 0620

Standard Port ABERDEEN (←—)

Times				Height (metres)			
High Water		Low Water		MHWS	MHWN	MLWN	MLWS
0000	0600	0100	0700	4·3	3·4	1·6	0·6
1200	1800	1300	1900				
Differences PETERHEAD							
–0035	–0045	–0035	–0040	–0·3	–0·2	0·0	+0·1

SHELTER Good in marina (2·8m). A useful passage hbr, also a major fishing and oil/gas industry port. Access any weather/tide.

NAVIGATION WPT 57°29´·44N 01°45´·75W, 314°/0·5M to ent. No dangers. 5kn speed limit in Bay; 4kn in marina. Chan between marina bkwtr and SHM lt buoy is <30m wide.

LIGHTS AND MARKS Power stn chy (183m) is conspic 1·25M S of ent, with Fl W lts H24. Ldg marks 314°, front △, rear ▽ on cols; lts as chartlet. Marina E bkwtr ✫ Fl R 4s 6m 2M; W bkwtr hd, QG 5m 2M; vis 185°-300°. Buchan Ness ✫ Fl 5s 40m 28M is 1·6M S of entr.

R/T All vessels, including yachts, **must** call *Peterhead Harbour Radio* VHF Ch **14** for clearance to enter/depart the Bay.

TELEPHONE (Code 01779) Marina Manager (Bay Authority: www.peterheadport.co.uk) 477868; Hr Control (H24) 483630; MRCC (01224) 592334; Marinecall 09068 969642; Police 472571; Dr 474841; Ⓗ 472316.

FACILITIES Peterhead Bay Marina ☎ 477868, 150 AB £11 up to 6m LOA, + £1 per m thereafter (7 days for price of 5), max LOA 20m; access all tides, 2·3m at ent. Pontoons are 'E' to 'A' from ent. Gas, CH; D from bowser at end of Princess Royal jetty (✫ Oc WRG 4s); R, 🍴 and Ⓦ at caravan site. **Peterhead SC** ☎ (01358) 751340 (Sec); **Services:** Slip, ME, El, Ⓔ, ✖, C, Gas. **Town** P, 🍴, R, ✉, bus to Aberdeen for ⇌ & ✈.

ADJACENT HARBOUR

BODDAM, Aberdeenshire, **57°28´·47N 01°46´·56W**.
AC 213. HW +0145 on Dover; Tides as 9.6.16. Good shelter in the lee of Meikle Mackie, the island just N of Buchan Ness, Fl 5s 40m 28M Horn (3) 60s. Inner hbr dries/unlit. Beware rks around Meikle Mackie and to the SW of it. Appr from 1½ca NW of The Skerry. Yachts on S side of outer hbr. All facilities at Peterhead, 2M N.

PETERHEAD

ADLARD COLES NAUTICAL
WEATHER FORECASTS
BY FAX & TELEPHONE

Coastal/Inshore	2-day by Fax	5-day by Phone
North East	09065 222 343	09068 969 643
Scotland East	09065 222 342	09068 969 642
Scotland North	09065 222 341	09068 969 641
Minch	09065 222 354	09068 969 654
National (3-5 day)	09065 222 340	09068 969 640
Offshore	2-5 day by Fax	2-5 day by Phone
Southern North Sea	09065 222 358	09068 969 658
Northern North Sea	09065 222 362	09068 969 662
North West Scotland	09065 222 361	09068 969 661
Irish Sea	09065 222 359	09068 969 659

09068 CALLS COST 60P PER MIN. 09065 CALLS COST £1.50 PER MIN.

AREA 7 – NE Scotland

NE Scotland

North East Scotland

Rattray Head to Cape Wrath
including Orkney and Shetland Islands

Contents

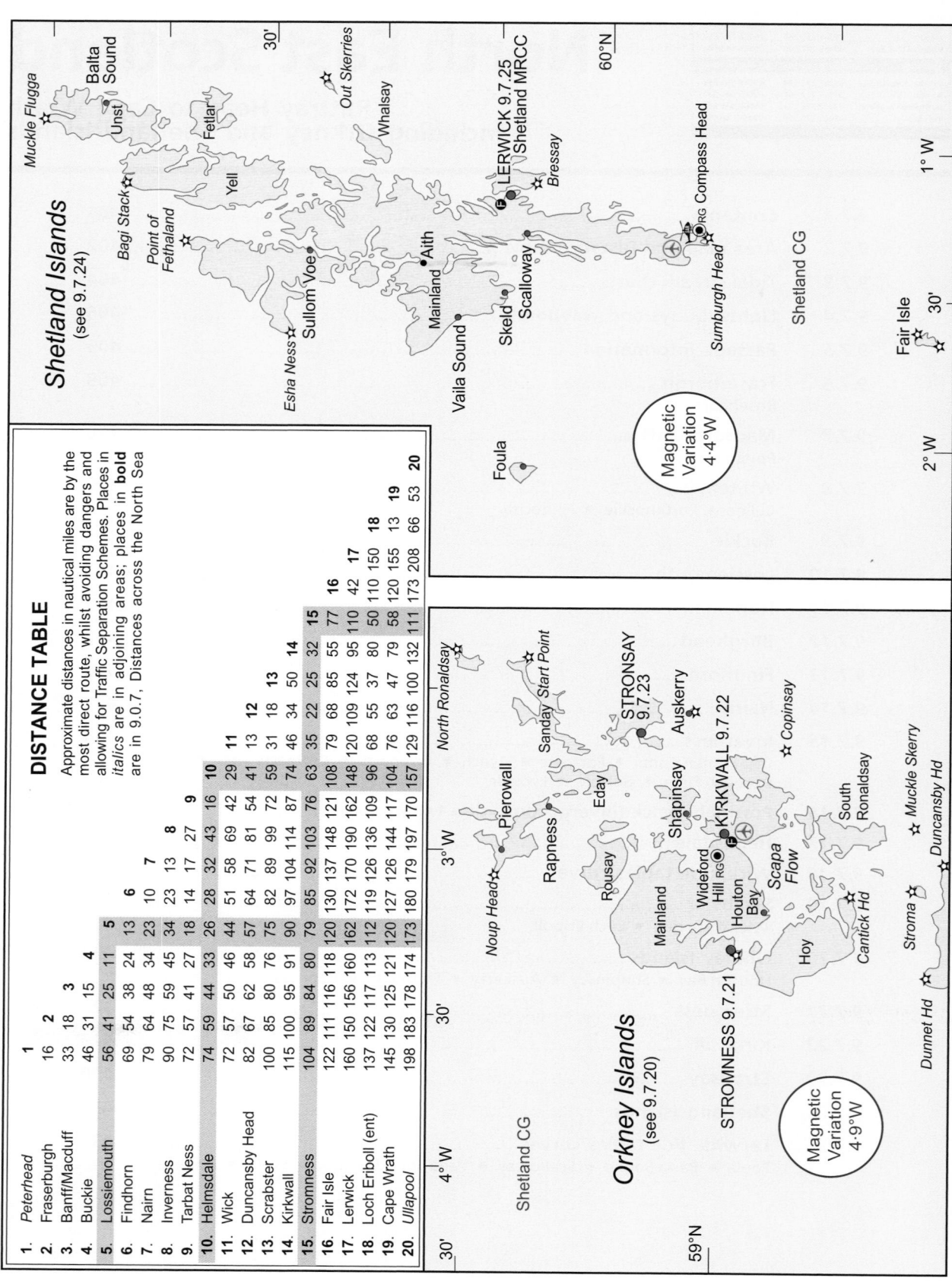

Shetland Islands
(see 9.7.24)

Orkney Islands
(see 9.7.20)

STROMNESS 9.7.21
KIRKWALL 9.7.22
STRONSAY 9.7.23
LERWICK 9.7.25 Shetland MRCC

Magnetic Variation 4·4°W (Shetland)

Magnetic Variation 4·9°W (Orkney)

DISTANCE TABLE

Approximate distances in nautical miles are by the most direct route, whilst avoiding dangers and allowing for Traffic Separation Schemes. Places in *italics* are in adjoining areas; places in **bold** are in 9.0.7, Distances across the North Sea

	1	2	3	4	5	6	7	8	9	10	11	12	13	14	15	16	17	18	19	20
1. *Peterhead*	**1**																			
2. Fraserburgh	16	**2**																		
3. Banff/Macduff	33	18	**3**																	
4. Buckie	46	31	15	**4**																
5. Lossiemouth	56	41	25	11	**5**															
6. Findhorn	69	54	38	24	13	**6**														
7. Nairn	79	64	48	34	23	10	**7**													
8. Inverness	90	75	59	45	34	23	13	**8**												
9. Tarbat Ness	72	57	41	27	18	14	17	27	**9**											
10. Helmsdale	74	59	44	33	26	28	32	43	16	**10**										
11. Wick	72	57	50	46	44	51	58	69	42	29	**11**									
12. Duncansby Head	82	67	62	58	57	64	71	81	54	41	13	**12**								
13. Scrabster	100	85	80	76	75	82	89	99	72	59	31	18	**13**							
14. Kirkwall	115	100	95	91	90	97	104	114	87	74	46	34	50	**14**						
15. Stromness	104	89	84	80	79	85	92	103	76	63	35	22	25	32	**15**					
16. Fair Isle	122	111	116	118	120	130	137	148	121	108	79	68	85	55	77	**16**				
17. Lerwick	160	150	156	160	162	172	170	190	162	148	120	109	124	95	110	42	**17**			
18. Loch Eriboll (ent)	137	122	117	113	112	119	126	136	109	96	68	55	37	80	50	110	150	**18**		
19. Cape Wrath	145	130	125	121	120	127	126	144	117	104	76	63	47	79	58	120	155	13	**19**	
20. Ullapool	198	183	178	174	173	180	179	197	170	157	129	116	100	132	111	173	208	66	53	**20**

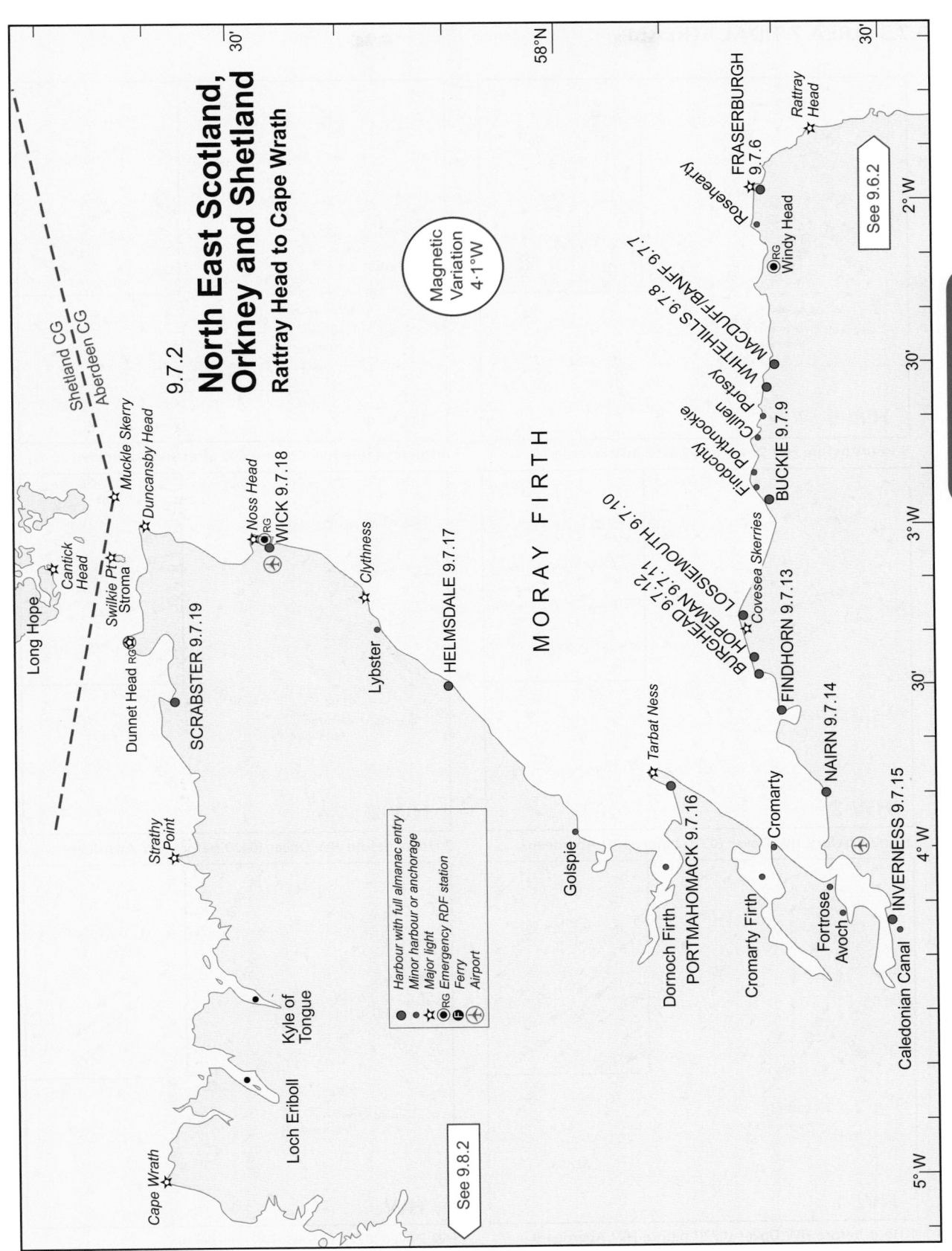

9.7.2

North East Scotland, Orkney and Shetland
Rattray Head to Cape Wrath

Magnetic Variation 4·1°W

See 9.6.2

See 9.8.2

FRASERBURGH 9.7.6

Rattray Head

Rosehearty

Windy Head RG

MACDUFF/BANFF 9.7.7

WHITEHILLS 9.7.8

Findochty
Portknockie
Cullen
Portsoy

BUCKIE 9.7.9

Covesea Skerries

LOSSIEMOUTH 9.7.10

HOPEMAN 9.7.11

BURGHEAD 9.7.12

FINDHORN 9.7.13

NAIRN 9.7.14

Cromarty

Fortrose
Avoch

INVERNESS 9.7.15

Caledonian Canal

Cromarty Firth

PORTMAHOMACK 9.7.16

Dornoch Firth

Tarbat Ness

Golspie

MORAY FIRTH

Clythness

Lybster

HELMSDALE 9.7.17

WICK 9.7.18
RG
Noss Head

SCRABSTER 9.7.19

Duncansby Head

Dunnet Head RG

Muckle Skerry

Swilkie Pt
Stroma
RG

Cantick Head

Long Hope

Shetland CG
Aberdeen CG

Strathy Point

Kyle of Tongue

Loch Eriboll

Cape Wrath

Harbour with full almanac entry
Minor harbour or anchorage
Major light
Emergency RDF station
Ferry
Airport
● ● ☆ ◉RG 🚢 ✈

NE Scotland

403

9.7.3 AREA 7 TIDAL STREAMS

5 Hours before HW Dover (0500 after HW Aberdeen)

4 Hours before HW Dover (0600 after HW Aberdeen)

3 Hours before HW Dover (0520 before HW Aberdeen)

2 Hours before HW Dover (0420 before HW Aberdeen)

1 Hour before HW Dover (0320 before HW Aberdeen)

HW Dover (0220 before HW Aberdeen)

Southward 9.6.3   Westward 9.8.3

HW+1
1 Hour after HW Dover (0120 before HW Aberdeen)

HW+2
2 Hours after HW Dover (0020 before HW Aberdeen)

HW+3
3 Hours after HW Dover (0040 after HW Aberdeen)

HW+4
4 Hours after HW Dover (0140 after HW Aberdeen)

HW+5
5 Hours after HW Dover (0240 after HW Aberdeen)

HW+6
6 Hours after HW Dover (0340 after HW Aberdeen)

NE Scotland

9.7.4 LIGHTS, BUOYS AND WAYPOINTS

Bold print = light with a nominal range of 15M or more. CAPITALS = place or feature. *CAPITAL ITALICS* = light-vessel, light float or Lanby. *Italics* = Fog signal. ***Bold italics*** = Racon. Abbreviations are in Chapter 1.

RATTRAY HEAD TO INVERNESS

Rattray Hd ☆ 57°36'·61N 01°49'·03W Fl (3) 30s 28m **24M**; W twr; ***Racon (M) 15M***; *Horn (2) 45s.*

FRASERBURGH
Fraserburgh Ldg lt 291°; Iso R 2s 12m 9M; 57°41'·57N 02°00'·13W. Rear, 75m from front, Iso R 2s 17m 9M.
Fraserburgh, Balaclava Bkwtr Head ⚓ Fl (2) G 8s 26m 6M; dome on W twr; vis: 178°-326°; 57°41'·51N 01°59'·70W.

Kinnaird Hd ☆ 57°41'·87N 02°00'·26W Fl 5s 25m **22M**; vis: 092°-297°.

MACDUFF, BANFF and WHITEHILLS
Macduff Pier Hd ⚓ Fl (2) WRG 6s 12m W9M, R7M; W twr; vis: shore-G-115°-W-174°-R-210°; 57°40'·25N 02°30'·02W.
Macduff Ldg Lts 127°, Front FR 44m 3M; 57°40'·12N 02°29'·75W. Rear, 60m from front, FR 55m 3M; both Or △ on mast.
Banff Ldg Lts 295°, Front Fl R 4s; 57°40·30N 02°31·36W. Rear, QR; both vis: 210°-345°.
Whitehills Pier Hd ⚓ 57°40'·80N 02°34'·88W Fl WR 3s 7m W9M, R6M; W twr; vis: 132°-R-212°-W-245°.

PORTSOY and FINDOCHTY
Portsoy Pier Ldg Lts 173°, Front Fl G 4s 20m 3M; post; 57°41'·09N 02°41'·40W; Rear Q G 22m 3M; R △ on BW post.
Findochty Middle Pier Ldg Lts 166°, Front FR 6m 3M; 57°41'·90N 02°54'·20W. Rear FR 10m 3M.

BUCKIE
West Muck ⚓ QR 5m 7M; tripod; 57°41'·06N 02°58'·01W.
N Pier 60m from Hd ☆ 57°40'·9N 02°57'·5W Oc R 10s 15m **15M** W twr.

LOSSIEMOUTH, HOPEMAN and BURGHEAD
Lossiemouth S Pier Hd ⚓ Fl R 6s 11m 5M; *Siren 60s;* 57°43'·42N 03°16'·69W.
Covesea Skerries ☆ 57°43'·47N 03°20'·45W Fl WR 20s 49m **W24M, R20M**; W twr; vis: 076° - W - 267° - R - 282°.
Hopeman Ldg Lts 081°, Front,FR 3m; 57°42'·71N 03°26'·18W. Rear, 10m from front, FR 4m.
Burghead N Bkwtr Hd ⚓ Oc 8s 7m 5M; 57°42'·09N 03°30'·03W.

FINDHORN, NAIRN and INVERNESS FIRTH
Findhorn Landfall ⚓ LF 10s 57°43'·00 N 03°38'·94W.
Nairn E Pier Hd ⚓ Oc WRG 4s 6m 5M; 8-sided twr; vis: shore-G-100°-W-207°-R-shore; 57°35'·62N 03°51'·65W
Riff Bank E ⚓ Fl Y 10s 3m 5M 57°38'·38N 03°58'·18W.

SOUTH CHANNEL
Riff Bank S ⚓ Q (6) + L Fl 15s; 57°36'·73N 04°00'·97W.
Chanonry ☆ 57°34'·44N 04°05'·57W Oc 6s 12m **15M**; W twr; vis: 148°-073°.
Munlochy ⚓ L Fl 10s; 57°32'·91N 04°07'·65W .
Petty Bank ⚓ Fl R 5s 57°31'·58N 04°08'·98W.
Meikle Mee ⚓ Fl G 3s 57°30'·26N 04°12'·02W.
Longman Pt ⚓ Fl WR 2s 7m W5M, R4M; vis: 078°-W-258°-R-078°; 57°29'·99N 04°13'·31W.
Craigton Point ⚓ Fl WRG 4s 6m W11M, R7M, G7M; vis: 312° - W - 048° - R - 064° - W - 085°- G - shore; 57°30'·05N 04°14'·09W.
Bridge Centre , Or △; ***Racon (K) 6M***; 57°29'·97N 04°13'·79W.

INVERNESS and CALEDONIAN CANAL
R. Ness Outer ⚓ QR 3m 4M; 57°29'·83N 04°13'·93W.

Emb'kmt H'd ⚓ Fl G 2s 8m 4M; G f'work twr; 57°29'·72N 04°14'·25W.

Clachnaharry, S Tr'ng Wall Hd ⚓ Iso G 4s 5m 2M; tfc sigs; 57°29'·43N 04°15'·86W.

INVERNESS TO DUNCANSBY HEAD

CROMARTY FIRTH and INVERGORDON
Fairway ⚓ L Fl 10s; ***Racon (M) 5M***; 57°39'·96N 03°54'·19W.
Cromarty Bank ⚓ Fl (2) G 10s; 57°40'·66N 03°56'·78W.
Buss Bank ⚓ Fl R 3s 57°40'·97N 03°59'·54W.
Cromarty - The Ness (Lt ho disused W tr 13m); 57°40'·98N 04°02'·20W
Nigg Oil Terminal Pier Hd ⚓ Oc G 5s 31m 5M; Gy twr, floodlit; 57°41'·54N 04°02'·60W.

DORNOCH FIRTH to LYBSTER
Tarbat Ness ☆ 57°51'·88N 03°46'·76W Fl (4) 30s 53m **24M**; W twr, R bands; ***Racon (T) 14-16M***.
Lybster, S Pier Hd ⚓ Oc R 6s 10m 3M; 58°17'·79N 03°17'·41W.
Clyth Ness ☆ Fl (2) 30s 45m 14M; 58°18'·64N 03°12'·74W.

WICK
S Pier Hd ⚓ Fl WRG 3s 12m W12M, R9M, G9M; W 8-sided twr; vis: 253°-G-270°-W-286°-R-329°; *Bell (2) 10s* (occas); 58°26'·34N 03°04'·73W.

Dir lt 288·5° F WRG 9m W10M, R7M, G7M; col, N end of bridge; vis: 283·5°-G-287·2°-W-289·7°-R-293·5°; 58°26'·54N 03°05'·34W

Noss Hd ☆ 58°28'·71N 03°03'·09W Fl WR 20s 53m **W25M, R21M**; W twr; vis: shore-R-191°-W-shore.

DUNCANSBY HEAD TO CAPE WRATH
Duncansby Hd ☆ 58°38'·65N 03°01'·58W Fl 12s 67m **22M**; W twr; ***Racon (T)***.

Pentland Skerries ☆ 58°41'·41N 02°55'·49W Fl (3) 30s 52m **23M**; W twr.

Lother Rock ⚓ Fl 2s 13m 6M; ***Racon (M) 10M***; 58°43'·79N 02°58'·69W.
Swona ⚓ Fl 8s 17m 9M; vis: 261°-210°; 58°44'·25N 03°04'·24W.
Swona N Hd ⚓ Fl (3) 10s 16m 10M; 58°45'·11N 03°03'·10W.
Stroma ☆, Swilkie Point 58°41'·75N 03°07'·01W Fl (2) 20s 32m **26M**; W twr.

Dunnet Hd ☆ 58°40'·28N 03°22'·60W Fl (4) 30s 105m **23M**.

THURSO, SCRABSTER and CAPE WRATH
Thurso Ldg Lts 195°. Front, FG 5m 4M; Gy post; 58°35'·96N 03°30'·76W. Rear, FG 6m 4M; Gy mast.
Scrabster Q. E. Pier Hd ⚓ Fl (2) 4s 8m 8M 58°36'·66N 03°32'·31W.
Strathy Pt ☆ 58°36'·04N 04°01'·12W Fl 20s 45m **26M**; W twr on W dwelling. F.R. on chy 100° 8·5M.
Sule Skerry ☆ 59°05'·09N 04°24'·38W Fl (2) 15s 34m **21M**; W twr; ***Racon (T)***.
North Rona ☆ 59°07'·27N 05°48'·91W Fl (3) 20s 114m **24M**.
Sula Sgeir ⚓ Fl 15s 74m 11M; □ structure; 59°05'·61N 06°09'·57W.
Loch Eriboll, White Hd ⚓ Fl WR10s 18m W13M, R12M; W twr and bldg; vis: 030°-W-172°-R-191°-W-212°; 58°31'·01N 04°38'·90W.
Cape Wrath ☆ 58°37'·54N 04°59'·94W Fl (4) 30s 122m **22M**; W twr.

ORKNEY ISLANDS
Tor Ness ☆ 58°46'·78N 03°17'·86W Fl 5s 21m **17M**; W twr.

Cantick Hd (S Walls, SE end) ☆ 58°47'·23N 03°07'·88W Fl 20s 35m 13M; W twr.

SCAPA FLOW and APPROACHES
Long Hope, S Ness Pier Hd ⚓ Fl WRG 3s 6m W7M, R5M, G5M; vis:

WGS84 DATUM
Plot waypoints on chart before use

082°-G- 242°-W- 252°-R-082; 58°48'·05N 03°12'·35W.
Hoxa Head ⚓ Fl WR 3s 15m W9M, R6M; W twr; vis: 026°-W-163°-R-201°-W-215°; 58°49'·31N 03°02'·09W.
Nevi Skerry ⚓ Fl (2) 6s 7m 6M; 58°50'·67N 03°02'·70W.
Rose Ness ⚓ 58°52'·33N 02°49'·97W Fl 6s 24m 8M; W twr.
Barrel of Butter ⚓ Fl (2) 10s 6m 7M; 58 53'·40N 03°07'·62E.
Cava ⚓ Fl WR 3s 11m W10M, R8M; W ○ twr; vis: 351°-W-143°-196°-W-251°-R-271°-R-298°; 58°53'·21N 03°10'·70W .
Houton Bay Ldg Lts 316°. Front ⚓ Fl G 3s 8m. Rear ⚓, 200m from front, FG 16m; vis: 312°- 320°; 58°54'·97N 03°11'·56W.

CLESTRAN SOUND and HOY SOUND
Graemsay Is Hoy Sound Low ☆ Ldg Lts 104°. **Front,** 58°56'·42N 03°18'·60W Iso 3s 17m **15M**; W twr; vis: 070°-255°. **High Rear,** 1·2M from front, Oc WR 8s 35m **W20M, R16M**; W twr; vis: 097°-R-112°-W-163°-R-178°-W-332°; obsc on Ldg line within 0·5M.
Skerry of Ness ⚓ Fl WG 4s 7m W7M, G4M; vis: shore -W-090°- G-shore; 58°56'·95N 03°17'·83W.

STROMNESS
Ldg Lts 317°. Front, FR 29m 11M; post on W twr; 58°57'·61N 03°18'·15W. Rear, 55m from front, FR 39m 11M; vis: 307°-327°; H24.

AUSKERRY
Copinsay ☆ 58°53'·77N 02°40'·35W Fl (5) 30s 79m **21M**; W twr.
Auskerry ☆ 59°01'·51N 02°34'·34W Fl 20s 34m **20M**; W twr.

Helliar Holm, S end ⚓ Fl WRG 10s 18m W14M, R11M, G11M; W twr; vis: 256°-G-276°-W-292°-R-098°-W-116°-G-154°; 59°01'·13N 02°54'·09W.
Balfour Pier Shapinsay ⚓ Fl (2) WRG 5s 5m W3M, R2M, G2M; vis: 270°-G-010°-W-020°-R-090°; 59°01'·86N 02°54'·49W.

KIRKWALL
Thieves Holm, ⚓ Q.R8M; 59°01'·09N 02°56'·21W.

Pier N end ☆ 58°59'·29N 02°57'·72W Iso WRG 5s 8m **W15M**, R13M, G13M; W twr; vis: 153°-G-183°-W-192°-R-210°.

WIDE FIRTH
Linga Skerry ⚓ Q (3) 10s; 59°02'·39N 02°57'·56W.
Boray Skerries ⚓ Q (6) + L Fl 15s; 59°03'·65N 02°57'·66W.
Skertours ⚓ Q; 59°04'·11N 02°56'·72W.
Galt Skerry ⚓ Q; 59°05'·21N 02°54'·20W.
Brough of Birsay ☆ 59°08'·19N 03°20'·41W Fl (3) 25s 52m **18M**.

Papa Stronsay NE end, The Ness Fl(4)20s 8m 9M; W twr; 59°09'·34N 02°34'·93W.

SANDAY ISLAND and NORTH RONALDSAY
Quiabow ◣ Fl (2) G 12s; 59°09'·82N 02°36'·30W.
Start Pt ☆ 59°16'·69N 02°22'·71W Fl (2) 20s 24m **18M**.

Kettletoft Pier Hd ⚓ Fl WRG 3s 7m W7M, R5M, G5M; vis: 351°-W-011°-R-180°-G-351°; 59°13'·80N 02°35'·86W.

N Ronaldsay ☆ NE end, 59°23'·34N 02°22'·91W Fl 10s 43m **24M**; R twr, W bands; *Racon (T) 14-17M.*

EDAY and EGILSAY
Calf Sound ⚓ Fl (3) WRG 10s 6m W8M, R6M, G6M; W twr; vis: shore-R-215°-W-222°-G-301°-W-305°; 59°14'·21N 02°45'·82W.
Backaland Pier ⚓ 59°09'·43N 02°44'·88W Fl R 3s 5m 4M; vis: 192°-250°.
Egilsay Graand ⚓ Q (6) + L Fl 15s; 59°06'·86N 02°54'·42W.

WESTRAY and PIEROWALL
Noup Head ☆ 59°19'·86N 03°04'·23W Fl 30s 79m **20M**; W twr; vis: about 335°-282° but partially obsc 240°-275°.

Pierowall E Pier Head ⚓ Fl WRG 3s 7m W11M, R7M, G7M; vis: 254°-G-276°-W-291°-R-308°-G-215°; 59°19'·35N 02°58'·53W.
Papa Westray, Moclett Bay Pier Head ⚓ Fl WRG 5s 7m W5M, R3M, G3M; vis: 306°-W-341°-W-040°-R-074°; 59°19'·60N 02°53'·52W.

FAIR ISLE
Skadan South ☆, 59°30'·84N 01°39'·16W Fl (4) 30s 32m **22M**; W twr; vis: 260°-146°, obsc inshore 260°-282°.

Skroo ☆ N end 59°33'·13N 01°36'·58W Fl (2) 30s 80m **22M**; W twr; vis: 086·7°-358°.

MAINLAND, SOUTH
Sumburgh Head ☆ 59°51'·21N 01°16'·58W Fl (3) 30s 91m **23M**.
Mousa, Perie Bard ⚓ Fl 3s 20m 10M; 59°59'·84N 01°09'·51W.

BRESSAY and LERWICK
Bressay, Kirkabister Ness ☆ 60°07'·20N 01°07'·29W; Fl (2) 20s 32m **23M**.
Maryfield Ferry Terminal ⚓ Oc WRG 6s 5m 5M; vis: W008°-R013°-G-111°-008°; 60°09'·43N 01°07'·45W.

North Ness ⚓ Iso WG 4s 4m 5M; vis: shore-W-158°-G-216°-W-301°; 60°09'·57N 01°08'·77W

Loofa Baa ⚓ Q (6) + L Fl 15s 4m 5M; 60°09'·72N 01°08'·79W.
Soldian Rock ⚓ Q (6) + L Fl 15s 60°12'·51N 01°04'·73W.
N ent Dir lt 215°, Oc WRG 6s 27m 8M; Y △, Or stripe; vis: 211°-R-214°-W-216°-G-221°; 60°10'·47N 01°09'·53W.

Rova Hd ⚓ 60°11'·46N 01°08'·60W Fl (3) WRG 18s 12m W12M, R9M, G9M; W twr; vis: 090°-R-182°-W-191°-G-213°-R-241°-W-261·5°-G-009°-R-040°. Same structure and synchronised: Fl (3) WRG 18s 14m **W16M**, R13M, G13M; vis: 176·5°-R-182°-W-191°-G-196·5°.
Dales Voe ⚓ Fl (2) WRG 8s 5m W4M, R3M, G3M; vis: 220°-G-227°-W-233°-R-240°; 60°11'·79N 01°11'·23W.
Hoo Stack ⚓ Fl (4) WRG 12s 40m W7M, R5M, G5M; W pylon; vis: 169°-R-180°-W-184°-G-193°-W-169°. Same structure, Dir lt 182°. Fl (4) WRG 12s 33m W9M, R6M, G6M; vis: 177°- R-180°-W-184°-W-187°; synch with upper lt; 60°14'·96N 01°05'·38W.
Mull (Moul) of Eswick ⚓ Fl WRG 3s 50m W9M, R6M, G6M; W twr; vis: 028°-R-200°-W-207°-G-018°-W-028°; 60°15'·74N 01°05'·90W.
Inner Voder ⚓ Q (9) 15s; 60°16'·43N 01°05'·18W.

WHALSAY and SKERRIES
Symbister Ness ⚓ Fl (2) WG 12s 11m W8M, G6M; W twr; vis: shore-W-203°-G-shore; 60°20'·43N 01°02'·29W.
Suther Ness ⚓ Fl WRG 3s 10m W10M, R8M, G7M; vis: shore -W-038°-R-173°-W-206°-G-shore; 60°22'·12N 01°00'·20W.
Bound Skerry ☆ 60°25'·47N 00°43'·72W Fl 20s 44m **20M**; W twr.
South Mouth. Ldg Lts 014°. Front, FY3m 2M; 60°25'·33N 00°45'·01W. Rear, FY 12m 2M.
Muckle Skerry ⚓ Fl (2) WRG 10s 15m W7M, R5M, G5M; W twr; vis: 046°-W-192°-R-272°-G-348°-W-353°-R-046°; 60°26'·41N 00°51'·84W.

YELL SOUND
S ent, Lunna Holm ⚓ Fl (3) WRG 15s 19m W10M,R7M,G7M; W○twr; vis: shore-R-090°-W-094°-G-209°-W-275°-R-shore; 60°27'·34N 01°02'·52W.

Firths Voe ☆, N shore 60°27'·21N 01°10'·63W Oc WRG 8s 9m **W15M**, R10M, G10M; W twr; vis: 189°-W-194°-G-257°-W-261°-R-339°-W-066°.
Linga Is. Dir lt 150° ⚓ Q (4) WRG 8s 10m W9M, R9M, G9M; vis: 145°-R-148°-W-152°-G-155°. Q (4) WRG 8s 10m W7M, R4M, G4M; same structure; vis: 052°-R-146°, 154°-G-196°-W-312°; synch; 60°26'·80N 01°09'·13W.
The Rumble Bn ⚓ R Bn; Fl 10s 8m 4M; *Racon (O)*; 60°28'·16N 01°07'·26W.
Yell, Ulsta Ferry Term. Bkwtr Hd ⚓ Oc RG 4s 7m R5M, G5M; vis: shore-G-354°, 044°-R-shore. Same structure; Oc WRG 4s 5m W8M, R5M, G5M; vis: shore-G-008°-W-036°-R-shore; 60°29'·74N 01°09'·52W.

Toft Ferry Terminal ☆,Dir lt 241° (H24); Dir Oc WRG 10s 8m **W16M**, R10M, G10M; vis: 236° -G-240°-W-242°-R-246°; By day W2M, R1M, G1M. 60°27'·96N 01°12'·34W.

NE Scotland

Ness of Sound, W side ⚓ Fl (3) WRG 12s 18m W9M, R6M, G6M; vis: shore-G-345°-W-350°-R-160°-W-165°-G-shore;60°31'·34N 01°11'·28W.

Brother Is. Dir lt 329°. Fl (4) WRG 8s 16m W10M, R7M, G7M; vis: 323·5°-G-328°-W-330°-R-333·5°; 60°30'·95N 01°14'·11W.

Mio Ness ⚓ Q (2) WR 10s 12m W7M, R4M; W ○ twr; vis: 282° - W - 238° - R - 282°; 60°29'·66N 01°13'·68W.

Tinga Skerry ⚓ Q (2) G 10s 9m 5M. W ○ twr; 60°30'·48N 01°14'·86W.

YELL SOUND, NORTH ENTRANCE

Bagi Stack ⚓ Fl (4) 20s 45m 10M; 60°43'·53N 01°07'·54W.

Gruney Is ⚓ Fl WR 5s 53m W8M, R6M; W twr; vis: 064°-R-180°-W-012°; *Racon (T) 14M*; 60°39'·15N 01°18'·17W.

Pt of Fethaland ☆ 60°38'·05N 01°18'·70W Fl (3) WR 15s 65m **W24M, R20M**; vis 080°-R-103°-W-160°-206°-W-340°.

Muckle Holm ⚓ Fl (4) 10s 32m 10M 60°34'·83N 01°16'·01W.

Little Holm ⚓ Iso 4s 12m 6M; W twr; 60°33'·42N 01°15'·88W.

Outer Skerry ⚓ Fl 6s 12m 8M; 60°33'·04N 01°18'·32W.

Quey Firth ⚓ Oc WRG 6s 22m W12M, R8M, G8M; W twr; vis: shore (through S & W)-W-290°-G-327°-W-334°-W-shore; 60°31'·43N 01°19'·58W.

Lamba, S side ⚓Fl WRG 3s 30m W8M, R5M, G5M; W twr; vis: shore-G-288°-W-293°-R-327°-W-044°-R-140°-W-shore. Dir lt 290·5° Fl WRG 3s 24m W10M, R7M, G7M; vis: 285·5°-G-288°-W-293°-W-295·5°; 60°30'·73N 01°17'·84W .

SULLOM VOE

Gluss Is ☆ Ldg Lts 194·7° (H24). **Front**, 60°29'·77N 01°19'·44W F 39m **19M**; □ on Gy twr; H24. **Rear**, 0·75M from front, F 69m **19M**; □ on Gy twr.; H24. Both Lts 9M by day.

Little Roe ⚓ Fl (3) WR 10s 16m W5M, R4M; W structure, Or band; vis: 036°-R-095·5°-W-036°; 60°29'·99N 01°16'·46W.

Skaw Taing ⚓ Ldg Lts 150·5°. Front, Oc WRG 5s 21m W8M, R5M, G5M; Or and W structure; vis: 049°-W-078°-G-147°-W-154°-R-169°-W-288°; 60°29'·10N 01°16'·86W. Rear, 195m from front, Oc 5s 35m 8M; vis: W145°-156°.

Ness of Bardister ⚓ Oc WRG 8s 20m W9M, R6M, G6M; Or &W structure; vis: 180·5°- W-240°- R-310·5°- W-314·5°- G-030·5°; 60°28'·19N 01°19'·63W.

Fugla Ness. Lts in line 212·3°. Rear, 60°27'·25N 01°19'·74W Iso 4s 45m 14M. Common front 60°27'·45N 01°19'·57W Iso 4s 27m 14M; synch with rear Lts. Lts in line 203°. Rear, 60°27'·26N 01°19'·81W Iso 4s 45m 14M.

Sella Ness ☆ Dir lt 133·5° 60°26'·76N 01°16'·66W Oc WRG 10s 19m **W16M**, R3M, G3M; vis: 123·5° -G- 130·5°-Al WG(white phase increasing with brg)-132·5°-W-134·5°-Al WR(R phase inc with brg)-136·5°-R-143·5°; H24. By day Oc WRG 10s 19m W2M, R1M,G1M as above.

EAST YELL, UNST and BALTA SOUND

Whitehill ⚓ Fl WR 3s 24m W9M, R6M; vis: shore-W-163°-R-211°-W-352°-R-shore.

Balta Sound ⚓Fl WR 10s 17m 10M, R7M; vis: 249°-W-008°-R-058°-W-154°; 60°44'·48N 00°47'·56W.

Holme of Skaw ⚓ Fl 5s 8m 8M; 60°49'·87N 00°46'·33W.

Muckle Flugga ☆ 60°51'·32N 00°53'·14W Fl (2) 20s 66m **22M**.

Yell. Cullivoe Bkwtr Hd ⚓Fl (2) WRG 10s 3m 4M; vis: 080°-G- 294°-W-355°-R-080°; 60°41'·91N 00°59'·66W.

Head of Mula ⚓Fl WRG 5s 48m W10M, G7M, R7M; metal framework twr; vis: 292°-G-357°-W-002°-R-157°-W-161·5; 60°44'·48N 00°47'·56W.

MAINLAND, WEST

Esha Ness ☆ 60°29'·34N 01°37'·65W Fl 12s 61m **25M**.

Ness of Hillswick ⚓ Fl (4) WR 15s 34m W9M, R6M; vis: 217°-W-093°-R-114°; 60°27'·21N 01°29'·80W.

Muckle Roe, Swarbacks Minn ⚓ Fl WR 3s 30m W9M, R6M; vis: 314°-W-041°-R-075°-W-137°; 60°20'·98N 01°27'·07W.

W Burra Firth Outer ⚓ Oc WRG 8s 27m W9M, R7M, G7M; vis: 136°-G-142°-W-150°-R-156°. H24; 60°17'·79N 01°33'·56W.

W Burra Firth Inner ☆ 60°17'·78N 01°32'·17W F WRG 9m **W15M**, R9M, G9M; vis: 095°-G-098°-W-102°-105°; H24.

Ve Skerries ⚓ Fl (2) 20s 17m 11M; W twr; *Racon (T) 15M*; 60°22'·36N 01°48'·78W.

Papa Stour Housa Voe Dir lt 228° ⚓ F WRG 2m W9M, R7M, G7M; vis: 219°- G-226°- W-230°-R-239°; 60°19'·58N 01°40'·47W.

Rams Head ⚓ Fl WRG 8s 16m W9M, R6M; G6M; W house; vis: 265°-G-355°-W-012°-R-090°-W-136°, obsc by Vaila I when brg more than 030°; 60°11'·96N 01°33'·47W.

North Havra ⚓Fl(3) WRG 12s 24m W11M, R8M, G8M; W twr; vis: 001°-G-053·5°-W-060·5°-R-182°, 274°- G-334°-W-337·5°-R -001°; 60°09'·85N 01°20'·31W.

SCALLOWAY

Bullia Skerry ⚓ Fl 5s 5m 5M; steel pillar & platform 60°06'·55N 01°21'·57W.

Point of the Pund ⚓ Fl WRG 5s 20m W7M, R5M, G5M; W twr; vis: 350°-R-090°-G-111°-R-135°-W-140°-G-177°, 267°-W-350°; 60°07'·99N 01°18'·31W.

Whaleback Skerry ⚓ Q; 60°07'·95N 01°18'·90W.

Blacks Ness Pier SW corner ⚓Oc WRG 10s 10m W11M, G8M, R8M; vis: 052°-G-063·5°-W-065·5°-R-077°; 60°08'·02N 01°16'·59W.

Fugla Ness ⚓ Fl (2) WRG 10s 20m W10M, R7M, G7M; W twr; vis: 014°-G-032°-W-082°-R-134°-W-shore; 60°06'·38N 01°20'·85W.

FOULA

South Ness ☆ 60°06'·75N 02°03'·87W Fl (3) 15s 36m **18M**; W twr; vis: obscured 123°-221°.

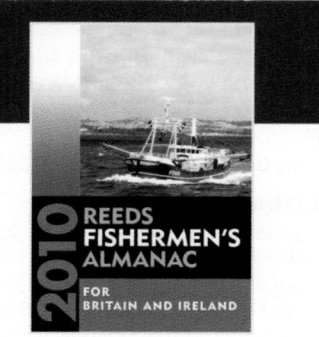

9.7.5 PASSAGE INFORMATION

Refer to the *N Coast of Scotland Pilot*; the CCC's SDs (3 vols) for N and NE coasts of Scotland; Orkney; and Shetland.

A 'Rover Ticket', £25 from Aberdeenshire and Moray Councils, allows berthing (subject to availability) for one week from arrival at the first harbour. The scheme includes: Johnshaven, Gourdon, Stonehaven, Rosehearty, Banff, Portsoy, Cullen, Portknockie, Findochty, Hopeman and Burghead.

Orkney Marinas charge on a sliding scale (based on 10m LOA): £17·50/day or £80/week. In harbours without a marina, berthing on a pier costs £14 for 4 days or £28 for 14 days. This scheme covers all marinas and piers in the Orkney Islands except St Margaret's Hope (9.7.20) which is independently run.

More Passage Information is threaded between the harbours in this Area.

MORAY FIRTH: SOUTH COAST

(AC 115, 222, 223) Crossing the Moray Firth from Rattray Hd (lt, fog sig) to Duncansby Hd (lt, Racon) heavy seas may be met in strong W winds. Most hbrs in the Firth are exposed to NE-E winds. For oil installations, see 9.5.5; the Beatrice Field is 20M S of Wick. ▶ *Tidal streams attain 3kn at sp close off Rattray Hd, but 5M NE of the Head the NE-going stream begins at HW Aberdeen + 0140, and the SE-going stream at HW Aberdeen – 0440, sp rates 2kn. Streams are weak elsewhere in the Moray Firth, except in the inner part.* ◀

In late spring/early summer fog (haar) is likely in onshore winds. In strong winds the sea breaks over Steratan Rk and Colonel Rk, respectively 3M E and 1M ENE of Fraserburgh. Rosehearty firing range is N & W of Kinnairds Hd (lt); tgt buoys often partially submerged. Banff B is shallow; N of Macduff beware Collie Rks. Banff hbr dries, and should not be approached in fresh NE-E winds, when seas break well offshore; Macduff is a possible alternative.

From Meavie Pt to Scar Nose dangers extend up to 3ca from shore in places. Beware Caple Rk (depth 0·2m) 7½ca W of Logie Hd. Spey B is clear of dangers more than 7½ca from shore; anch here, but only in offshore winds. Beware E Muck (dries) 5ca SW of Craigenroan, an above-water rky patch 5ca SW of Craig Hd, and Middle Muck and W Muck in approach to Buckie. Findochty & Portknockie are 2 and 3.5M ENE. Halliman Skerries (dry; bn) lie 1·5M WNW of Lossiemouth. Covesea Skerries (dry) lie 5ca NW of their lt ho.

The area to the SW of a line between Helmsdale and Lossiemouth is an EU Special Area of Conservation to protect a vulnerable population of bottlenose dolphins. Mariners are advised to proceed at a safe, constant speed through the area and avoid disturbing the dolphins.

Inverness Firth is approached between Nairn and S Sutor. In heavy weather there is a confused sea with overfalls on Guillam Bank, 9M S of Tarbat Ness. The sea also breaks on Riff Bank (S of S Sutor) which dries in places. Chans run both N and S of Riff Bank. ▶ *Off Fort George, on E side of ent to Inverness Firth (AC1078), the SW-going stream begins HW Aberdeen + 0605, sp rate 2·5kn; the NE-going stream begins at HW Aberdeen – 0105, sp rate 3·5kn. There are eddies and turbulence between Fort George and Chanonry Pt when stream is running hard. Tidal streams in the Inverness Firth and approaches are not strong, except in the Cromarty Fifth Narrows, the Fort George Narrows and the Kessock Road, including off the entrance to the Caledonian Canal.*◀

There is a firing range between Nairn and Inverness marked, when in operation, by flags at Fort George. Much of Inverness Firth is shallow, but a direct course from Chanonry Pt to Kessock Bridge, via Munlochy SWM and Meikle Mee SHM lt buoys, carries a least depth of 2·1m. Meikle Mee bank dries 0·2m.

9.7.6 FRASERBURGH

Aberdeenshire 57°41'·50N 01°59'·79W ✲❋♨♨❀❀

CHARTS AC 115, 222, 1462; Imray C23.

TIDES +0120 Dover; ML 2·3; Duration 0615

Standard Port ABERDEEN (◀——)

Times				Height (metres)			
High Water		Low Water		MHWS	MHWN	MLWN	MLWS
0000	0600	0100	0700	4·3	3·4	1·6	0·6
1200	1800	1300	1900				
Differences FRASERBURGH							
–0105	–0115	–0120	–0110	–0·6	–0·5	–0·2	0·0

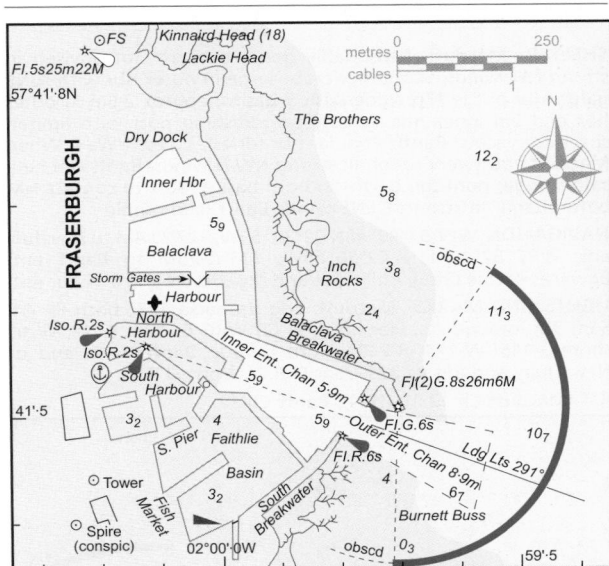

SHELTER A safe refuge, but ent is dangerous in NE/SE gales. A very busy fishing hbr; yachts are not encouraged but may find a berth in S Hbr (3.2m). FVs come and go H24.

NAVIGATION WPT 57°41'·30N 01°58'·80W, 291°/0·57M to ent. The Outer Ent Chan is maintained to 8·9m and Inner Ent Chan 5·9m. Good lookout on entering/leaving. Yachts can enter under radar control in poor vis.

LIGHTS AND MARKS Kinnairds Hd lt ho, Fl 5s 25m 22M, is 0·45M NNW of ent. Cairnbulg Briggs bn, Fl (2) 10s 9m 6M, is 1·8M ESE of ent. Ldg lts 291°: front Iso R 2s 12m 9M; rear Iso R 2s 17m 9M.

R/T Call on approach VHF Ch 12 16 (H24) for directions/berth.

TELEPHONE (Code 01346) Port Office 515858; Watch Tr 515926; MRCC (01224) 592334; Marinecall 09068 969641; Police 513121; Dr 518088.

FACILITIES Port ☎ 515858, AB £10 (in S Hbr) any LOA, Slip, P (cans), D, FW, CH, ME, El, ⚒, C (30 ton & 70 ton mobile), SM, 🛒, R, Bar; **Town** ✉, Ⓑ, ⇌, ✈ (bus to Aberdeen).

ADJACENT HARBOURS
ROSEHEARTY, Aberdeen, **57°42'·08N 02°06'·87W**. ✲❋♨❀❀. AC 222, 213. HW Aberdeen –1. E pier and inner hbr dry, but end of W pier is accessible at all tides. Ent exposed in N/E winds; in E/SE winds hbr can be uncomfortable. Ldg marks B/W now (2001) lit on approx 220°; rks E of ldg line. When 30m from pier, steer midway between ldg line and W pier. Port Rae, close to E, has unmarked rks; local knowledge req'd. AB £10 any LOA. *For details of Rover berthing ticket see 9.7.5.* **Town** 🛒, R, Bar, ✉. Firing range: for info ☎ (01346) 571634; see also 9.7.5. **Pennan Bay**, 5M W: ⚓ on sand between Howdman (2·9m) and Tamhead (2·1m) rks, 300m N of hbr (small craft only). **Gardenstown** (Gamrie Bay). Appr from E of Craig Dagerty rk (4m, conspic). Access HW±3 to drying hbr or ⚓ off.

NE Scotland

9.7.7   MACDUFF/BANFF

Aberdeenshire Macduff 57°40'·25N 02°30'·03W
Banff   57°40'·22N 02°31'·27W

CHARTS   AC 115, 222, 1462; Imray C23.

TIDES + 0055 Dover; ML 2·0; Duration 0615

Standard Port ABERDEEN (←—)

Times				Height (metres)			
High Water		Low Water		MHWS	MHWN	MLWN	MLWS
0200	0900	0400	0900	4·3	3·4	1·6	0·6
1400	2100	1600	2100				
Differences BANFF							
–0100	–0150	–0150	–0050	–0·4	–0·2	–0·1	+0·2

SHELTER   Macduff: Reasonably good, but ent not advised in strong NW winds. Slight/moderate surge in outer hbr with N/NE gales. Hbr ent is 17m wide with 3 basins; approx 2·6m in outer hbr and 2m inner hbr. A busy cargo/fishing port with limited space for yachts. **Banff**: Popular hbr (dries); access HW±4. When Macduff ent is very rough in strong NW/N winds, Banff can be a safe refuge; pontoon berths in both basins. Best to contact HM beforehand. In strong E/ENE winds Banff is unusable.

NAVIGATION WPT 57°40'·48N 02°30'·59W, 127°/0·4M to **Macduff** ent. WPT 57°40'·11N 02°30'·85W, 115°/0·25M to **Banff** ent. Beware Feachie Craig, Collie Rks and rky coast N and S of hbr ent.

LIGHTS AND MARKS   Macduff: Ldg lts/marks 127° both FR 44/55m 3M, orange △s. Pier hd lt, Fl (2) WRG 6s 12m 9/7M, W tr; shore-G-115°-W-174°-R-210°, Horn (2) 20s. **Banff**: Fl 4s end of New Quay and ldg lts 295° rear Fl R 2s, front Fl R 4s.

R/T Macduff Ch 12 16 (H24); **Banff** Ch 12.

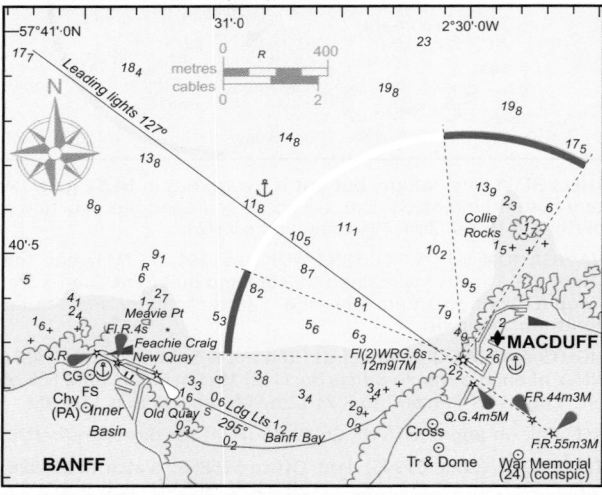

TELEPHONE (Code 01261) HM (**Macduff**) 832236, Watch tr 833962; HM (**Banff**) 815544; MRCC (01224) 592334; Marinecall 09068 969641; Police 812555; Dr (**Banff**) 812027.

FACILITIES Macduff: Hbr £10 any LOA, Slip, P (cans), D, FW, ME, El, ✕, CH. **Town** ⬚, R, Bar, ✉, ⇌ (bus to Keith). **Banff: Hbr** £10 any LOA, *for details of Rover berthing ticket see 9.7.5;* ❷ in marina (www.banffmarina.com) in Inner Hbr; FW, ⬓, Slip, toilet block; **Banff SC**: showers. **Town**, P, D, ⬚, R, Bar, ⇌, Ⓑ, ✈ (Aberdeen).

ADJACENT HARBOURS

PORTSOY, Aberdeenshire, **57°41'·34N 02°41'·59W**. ❀❀⚓⚓✿✿✿. AC 222. HW +0047 on Dover; –0132 and Ht –0·3m on Aberdeen. Small drying hbr; ent exposed to NW/NE'lies. New Hbr to port of ent partially dries; Inner Hbr dries to clean sand. Ldg lts 173°, front Fl G 4s 20m 3M, metal post; rear Q G 22m 3M, R △ on BW post. HM ☎ (01261) 815544. Facilities: few but hosts Scottish Traditional Boat Festival late June/early July. AB £10, *for details of Rover berthing ticket see 9.7.5.*, FW, Slip, ⬚, R, Bar, ✉. **Sandend Bay**, 1·7M W (57°41'N 02°44'·5W). ⚓ on sand E of hbr.

9.7.8   WHITEHILLS

Aberdeenshire **57°40'·80N 02°34'·87W** ❀❀⚓⚓✿✿✿

CHARTS   AC 115, 222; Imray C23.

TIDES +0050 Dover; ML 2·4; Duration 0610

Standard Port ABERDEEN (←—)

Times				Height (metres)			
High Water		Low Water		MHWS	MHWN	MLWN	MLWS
0200	0900	0400	0900	4·3	3·4	1·6	0·6
1400	2100	1600	2100				
Differences WHITEHILLS							
–0122	–0137	–0117	–0127	–0·4	–0·3	+0·1	+0·1

SHELTER Safe. In strong NW/N winds beware surge in the narrow ent and outer hbr, when ent is best not attempted. See HM for vacant pontoon berth.

NAVIGATION WPT 57°41'·98N 02°34'·89W, 180°/1·2M to bkwtr lt. Reefs on S side of chan marked by 2 rusty/white SHM bns. Beware fishing floats. Narrow entrance dredged to 1·8m, Outer Hbr pontoon berths 2.2m and Inner Hbr 1.5m–1·8m.

LIGHTS AND MARKS Fl WR 3s on pier hd, vis 132°-R-212°-W-245°; approach in R sector.

R/T Whitehills Hbr Radio VHF Ch **14** 16.

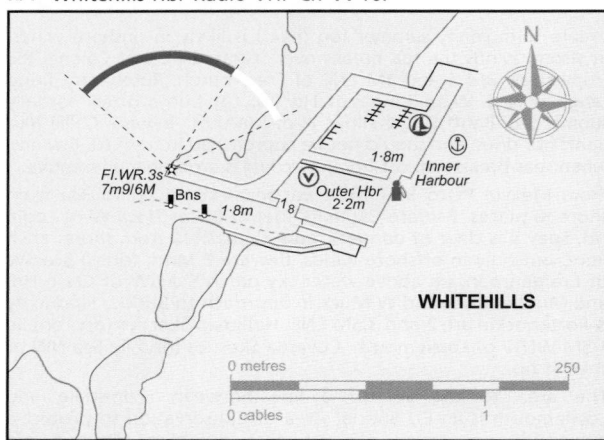

TELEPHONE (Code 01261) HM/Marina ☎ 861291, mobile 07906 135786, www.whitehillsharbour.co.uk; MRCC (01224) 592334; Marinecall 09068 969641; Police Banff 812555; Dr 812027.

FACILITIES Marina (47 + ❷), £15 (decreasing to £30/3nights), Quayside £12, @,Wi-fi, D, ◻, ME, El, CH; **Town** ⬚, R, Bar, ✉, ⇌ (bus to Keith), ✈ (Aberdeen).

ADJACENT HARBOURS

CULLEN, Moray, **57°41'·63N 02°49'·29W**. ❀⚓⚓✿✿. AC 222. HW +0045 on Dover, HW –0135 & –0·3m on Aberdeen; Duration 0555; ML 2·4m. Shelter good, but ent hazardous in strong W/N winds. Appr on 180° toward conspic viaduct and W bn on N pier. Caple Rk, 0·2m, is 5ca NE of hbr. Access HW ±2 approx. Small drying unlit hbr, best for shoal draft. Moor S of Inner jetty if < 1m draft. Beware moorings across inner basin ent. Pontoons in inner hbr (1·8m at HW Np). *For details of Rover berthing ticket see 9.7.5.* HM ☎ (01261) 842477 (home, part-time). **Town** ⬚,R,Bar, ✉.

PORTKNOCKIE, Moray, **57°42'·28N 02°51'·79W**. ❀❀⚓✿✿✿. AC 222. HW +0045 on Dover; –0135 and ht –0·3m Aberdeen; ML 2·3m; Duration 0555; access H24. Good shelter in one of the safest hbrs on S side of Moray Firth, but scend is often experienced; care needed in strong NW/N winds. FW ldg lts, on white-topped poles, lead approx 151°, to ent. Orange street lts surround the hbr. Limited ABs on N Quay; most of inner hbr dries. HM ☎ (01542) 840833 (home, p/time); Facilities: Slip, AB; *for details of Rover berthing ticket see 9.7.5.*, FW, ✕; Dr ☎ 840272. **Town** Ⓑ, P & D, ✉, ⬚, Bar.

ADJACENT HARBOUR (2M ENE of BUCKIE)

FINDOCHTY, Moray, **57°41'·94N 02°54'·29W**. AC 222. HW +0045 on Dover, HW −0135 & ht −0·2m on Aberdeen; ML 2·3m; Duration 0550. Ent is about 2ca W of conspic church belfry. 1ca N of ent, leave Beacon Rock (3m high) to stbd. Ldg lts, FR, lead approx 166° into Outer Basin which dries 0·2m and has many rky outcrops; access HW ±2 for 1·5m draft. Ent faces N and is 20m wide; unlit white bn at hd of W pier. Good shelter in inner basin for 100 small craft/yachts on 3 pontoons (the 2 W'ly pontoons dry); possible AB on Sterlochy Pier in 2m; Slip (£10) *for details of Rover berthing ticket see 9.7.5*. HM ☎ (01542) 832560 (home, part-time), mob 07900 920445. **Town** 🛒, R, Bar, ✉, Ⓑ.

9.7.9 BUCKIE

Moray **57°40'·84N 02°57'·63W** ❄❄❄♤♤♤♧♧

CHARTS AC 115, 222, 1462; Imray C23.

TIDES +0040 Dover; ML 2·4; Duration 0550

Standard Port ABERDEEN (⟵)

Times				Height (metres)			
High Water		Low Water		MHWS	MHWN	MLWN	MLWS
0200	0900	0400	0900	4·3	3·4	1·6	0·6
1400	2100	1600	2100				
Differences BUCKIE							
−0130	−0145	−0125	−0140	−0·2	−0·2	0·0	+0·1

SHELTER Good in all weathers.

In strong NNW to NE winds there is a dangerous swell over the bar at hbr ent, which is 24m wide.

Access H24. Berth in No 4 basin as directed by HM.

NAVIGATION WPT 57°41'·3N 02°59'·0W, 125°/0·8M to ent. The recommended track from the WPT is 128° until the 2F.R (vert) and Oc.R. 10s on the N breakwater are in line (096°), thence to the hbr ent. Beware W Muck (QR 5m tripod, 2M), Middle Muck and E Muck Rks, 3ca off shore.

LIGHTS AND MARKS The Oc R 10s 15m 15M, W tr on N bkwtr, 2FG(vert) in line 120° with Iso WG 2s 20m 16/12M, W tr, R top, leads clear of W Muck. Entry sigs on N pier: 3 ● lts = hbr closed. Traffic is controlled by VHF.

R/T VHF Ch 12 16 (H24).

TELEPHONE (Code 01542) HM 831700; MRCC (01224) 592334; Marinecall 09068 969641; Police 08450 6005 700; Dr 831555.

FACILITIES No 4 Basin AB £10.58 or £5.29 <12hrs, 🛢, FW; **Services:** D & P (delivery), BY, ME, EI, ✗, CH, Slip, BH (50 tons), C (15 ton), Gas. **Town** 🛒, Bar, Ⓑ, ✉, ▣ at Strathlene caravan site 1·5M E, ≠ (bus to Elgin), ✈ (Aberdeen or Inverness).

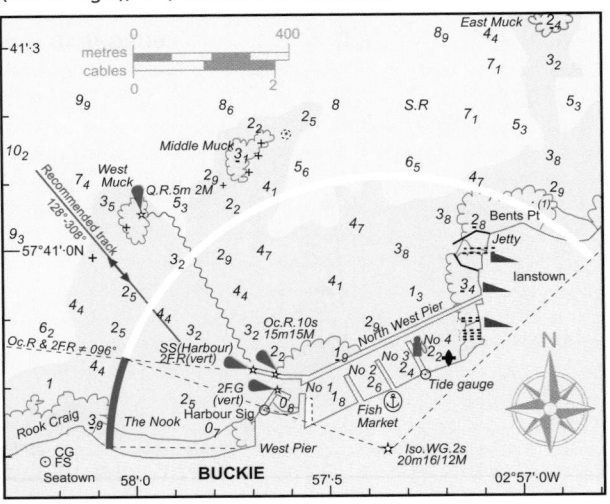

9.7.10 LOSSIEMOUTH

Moray **57°43'·41N 03°16'·63W** ❄⊛♧♤♧♧♧♧

CHARTS AC 223, 1462; Imray C23.

TIDES +0040 Dover; ML 2·3; Duration 0605

Standard Port ABERDEEN (⟵)

Times				Height (metres)			
High Water		Low Water		MHWS	MHWN	MLWN	MLWS
0200	0900	0400	0900	4·3	3·4	1·6	0·6
1400	2100	1600	2100				
Differences LOSSIEMOUTH							
−0125	−0200	−0130	−0130	−0·2	−0·2	0·0	0·0

SHELTER Very good in winds from SSE to NW. Pontoon berths in both basins, dredged 2m; access HW±4.

• In N to SE winds >F6 appr can be dangerous, with swell tending to break across hbr mouth and in outer hbr. Residual swell from E to SE can be particularly hazardous.

• Near ent, beware current from R Lossie setting in N'ly direction, causing confused water in N to SE winds at sp.

• Chan and Basins are prone to silting; a vessel drawing 2m would have little clearance at LWS ±2.

NAVIGATION WPT 57°43'·38N 03°16'·09W, 277°/0·3M to ent. Rks to N and S of hbr ent; appr from E.

LIGHTS AND MARKS Covesea Skerries, W lt ho, Fl WR 20s 49m 24M, is 2M W of the hbr ent. Ldg lts 292°, both FR 5/8m; S pier hd Fl R 6s 11m 5M. Traffic sigs: B ● at S pier (● over Fl R 6s) = hbr shut.

R/T VHF Ch 12 16 HO.

TELEPHONE (Code 01343) HM ☎ 813066, mob 07796790481; MRCC (01224) 592334; Marinecall 09068 969641; Police 0845 6005 700; Dr 812277.

FACILITIES Marina (85 + some ♥), ☎ 813066, £20/craft, ▣, ♿; **Hbr Slip** (£5), ME, EI, ✗, C, BH, CH, @, SM ☎ 07989 956698, harbourmaster@lossiemarina.fsnet.co.uk; **Hbr Service Stn** ☎ 813001, Mon-Fri 0800-2030, Sat 0800-1930, Sun 0930-1900, P & D cans, Gas. **Town** 🛒, R, Bar, ✉, Ⓑ, ≠ (bus to Elgin), ✈ (Inverness).

9.7.11 HOPEMAN

Moray 57°42'·70N 03°26'·31W ❀❀⊛⍋⍋❀❀

CHARTS AC 223, 1462; Imray C23.

TIDES +0050 Dover; ML 2·4; Duration 0610;

Standard Port ABERDEEN (←—)

Times				Height (metres)			
High Water		Low Water		MHWS	MHWN	MLWN	MLWS
0200	0900	0400	0900	4·3	3·4	1·6	0·6
1400	2100	1600	2100				
Differences HOPEMAN							
–0120	–0150	–0135	–0120	–0·2	–0·2	0·0	0·0

SHELTER Once in Inner Basin, shelter good from all winds; but hbr dries, access HW ± 2 (for 1·5m draft). Ent is difficult in winds from NE to SE. A popular yachting hbr with AB.

NAVIGATION WPT 57°42'·66N, 03°26'·59W, 083° to ent, 0·17M.

> Dangerous rks lie off hbr ent. Do not attempt entry in heavy weather. Beware lobster pot floats E and W of hbr (Mar-Aug).

LIGHTS AND MARKS See 9.7.4 and chartlet.

R/T Call *Burghead Radio* Ch 14 (HX).

TELEPHONE (Code 01343) HM ☎ 835337 (part-time); MRCC (01224) 592334; Marinecall 09068 969641; Police 830222; Dr 543141.

FACILITIES Hbr AB £9, *for details of Rover Ticket see 9.7.5*, FW, Slip.
Services: CH, ME, Gas, ✗, El, P (cans).
Town 🛒, R, Bar, ✉, Ⓑ, 🚌 (bus to Elgin), ✈ (Inverness).

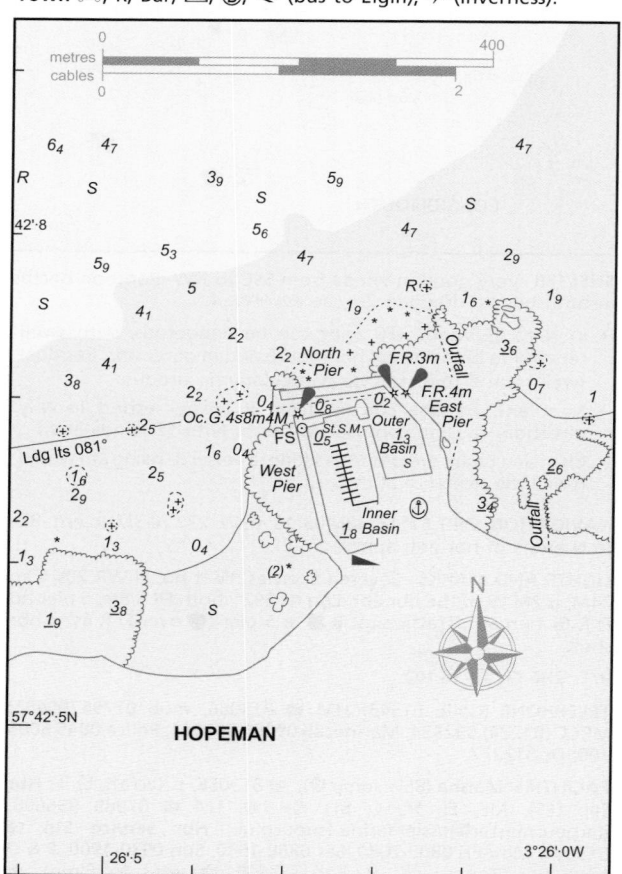

9.7.12 BURGHEAD

Moray 57°42'·06N 03°30'·02W ❀❀⍋⍋⍋❀❀

CHARTS AC 223, 1462; Imray C23.

TIDES +0035 Dover; ML 2·4; Duration 0610

Standard Port ABERDEEN (←—)

Times				Height (metres)			
High Water		Low Water		MHWS	MHWN	MLWN	MLWS
0200	0900	0400	0900	4·3	3·4	1·6	0·6
1400	2100	1600	2100				
Differences BURGHEAD							
–0120	–0150	–0135	–0120	–0·2	–0·2	0·0	0·0

SHELTER One of the few Moray Firth hbrs accessible in strong E winds. 0·6m depth in ent chan and 1·4m in hbr. Go alongside where available and contact HM. Can be very busy with FVs.

NAVIGATION WPT 57°42'·28N 03°30'·39W, 137°/0·28M to N pier lt QR. Access HW ±4. Chan is variable due to sand movement. Advisable to contact HM if entering at LW. 3kn speed limit.

LIGHTS AND MARKS No ldg lts but night ent is safe after identifying the N pier lts: QR 3m 5M and Oc 8s 7m 5M.

R/T Call *Burghead Radio* VHF Ch **14** 12 (HO and when vessel due).

TELEPHONE (Code 01343) HM 835337; MRCC (01224) 592334; Marinecall 09068 969641; Dr 812277.

FACILITIES Hbr AB £9, *for details of Rover Ticket see 9.7.5*, FW, AB, C (50 ton mobile), L, Slip, BY, ✗.
Town Bar, ✉, 🛒, Ⓑ, 🚌 (bus to Elgin), ✈ (Inverness).

9.7.13   FINDHORN

Moray 57°39'·64N 03°37'·47W ❀❀👁👁☆☆☆

CHARTS AC 223; Imray C23.

TIDES +0110 Dover; ML 2·5; Duration 0615

Standard Port ABERDEEN (←)

Times				Height (metres)			
High Water		Low Water		MHWS	MHWN	MLWN	MLWS
0200	0900	0400	0900	4·3	3·4	1·6	0·6
1400	2100	1600	2100				
Differences FINDHORN							
–0120	–0150	–0135	–0130	0·0	–0·1	0·0	+0·1

SHELTER ⚓ in pool off boatyard or off N pier or dry out alongside, inside piers and ask at YC; or pick up Y ⚓ off N pier.

> Do not attempt entry in strong NW/NE winds or with big swell running; expect breakers/surf either side of ent.

NAVIGATION WPT 57°43'·00N 03°38'·94W, SWM Landfall Buoy. Access HW±2. 100m SE of the Landfall Buoy there is 1 Y waiting ⚓ in 4m. From WPT, the bar is marked (Fl R marker) and thence by Fl R or G buoys all of which are moved to suit the channel into the bay, and may be lifted Nov to early Apr. Once past The Ee, turn port inside G buoys. The S part of Findhorn Bay dries extensively.

LIGHTS AND MARKS Unlit. There is a windsock on FS by The Ee. Boatyard building is conspic.

R/T VHF Ch M *Chadwick Base* (when racing in progress). Findhorn BY: Ch 80.

TELEPHONE (Code 01309) Fairways Committee (via BY) 690099; MRCC (01224) 592334; Findhorn Pilot (Derek Munro) 690802, mob 07747 840916; Marinecall 09068 969641; Police 0845 6005000700; Dr 678866/678888; Findhorn BY 690099.

FACILITIES **Royal Findhorn YC** ☎ 690247, M, ⚓ (free), FW, Bar; **Services:** BY, L, M, ⧉, FW, Slip, C (16 ton), P & D (cans), El, ME, CH, ACA, Gas, ✗.

Town 🍴, R, Bar, ✉, Ⓑ, ⇌ (Forres), ✈ (Inverness).

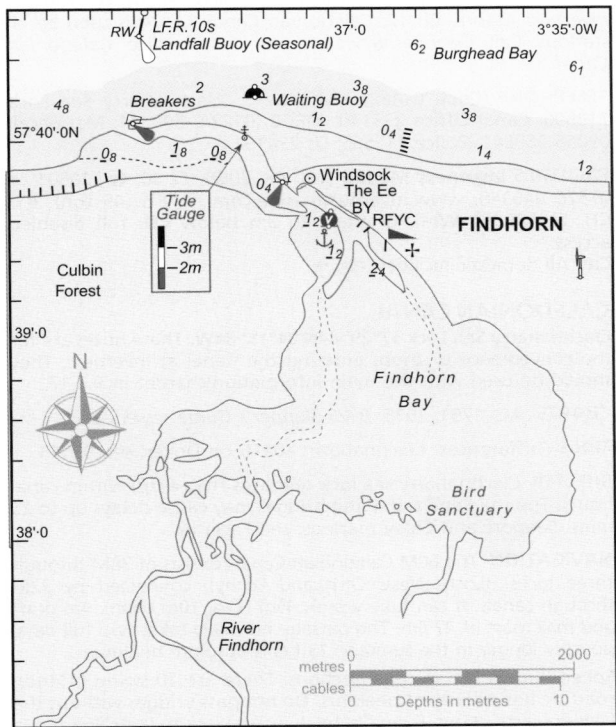

9.7.14   NAIRN

Highland 57°35'·61N 03°51'·65W ❀❀👁👁☆☆

CHARTS AC 223, 1462; Imray C23.

TIDES +0110 Dover; ML 2·2; Duration 0615

Standard Port INVERGORDON (→)

Times				Height (metres)			
High Water		Low Water		MHWS	MHWN	MLWN	MLWS
0100	0700	0000	0700	4·3	3·3	1·6	0·7
1300	1900	1200	1900				
Differences NAIRN							
+0005	–0015	0000	–0015	0·0	0·0	0·0	0·0
McDERMOTT BASE							
+0015	–0005	+0015	0000	–0·1	0·0	+0·1	+0·2

SHELTER Good, but entry difficult in fresh NNE'ly. Pontoons in hbr with ❶ berths. Best entry HW ± 1½. No commercial shipping.

NAVIGATION WPT 57°35'·88N 03°51'·89W, 155°/0·3M to ent. The approach dries to 100m off the pierheads. Inside, the best water is to the E side of the river chan.

LIGHTS AND MARKS Lt ho on E pier hd, Oc WRG 4s 6m 5M, vis shore-G-100°-W-207°-R-shore. Keep in W sector.

R/T None. Ch M (weekends only).

TELEPHONE (Code 01667) Hbr Office 456008; MRCC (01224) 592334; Doctor and Clinic 452096; Marinecall 09068 500451; Police 452222; Dr 453421.

FACILITIES **Nairn Basin** AB £15.28 - 48hrs, Slip (launching £6), AC (110 volts), P(cans), D; **Nairn SC** ☎ 453897, Bar.

Town 🍴, R, Bar, ✉, Ⓑ, ⇌, ✈ (Inverness).

MORAY FIRTH: NORTH WEST COAST

(AC 115) Cromarty Firth (AC 1889, 1890) is entered between the North and South Sutors, both fringed by rks, some of which dry.

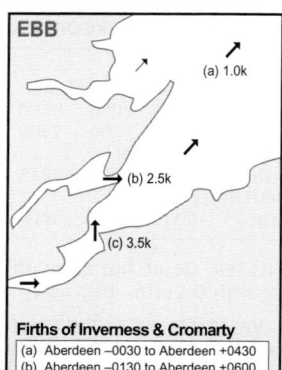

Firths of Inverness & Cromarty (FLOOD)
(a)	Aberdeen +0430 to Aberdeen −0030
(b)	Aberdeen +0600 to Aberdeen −0130
(c)	Aberdeen +0430 to Aberdeen −0030

Firths of Inverness & Cromarty (EBB)
(a)	Aberdeen −0030 to Aberdeen +0430
(b)	Aberdeen −0130 to Aberdeen +0600
(c)	Aberdeen −0030 to Aberdeen +0430

▶ *Off the entrance the in-going stream starts at HW Aberdeen + 0600, and the out-going at HW Aberdeen – 0130, sp rates 1·5 kn, stronger in the narrows between Nigg and Cromarty* ◀ Buss Bank buoy, Fl R 3s, marks the entrance, and there are good sheltered anchorages within the firth. Keep 100m clear of the Nigg Oil Terminal on the north side. A buoyed deep-water channel runs to Invergordon; outside the channel there are shallows and drying banks. Beware large ships and tugs using Invergordon.

The coast NE to Tarbat Ness (lt) is fringed with rocks. Beware Three Kings (dries) about 3M NE of N Sutor. ▶ *Culloden Rk, a shoal with depth of 1·8m, extends 2½ca NE of Tarbat Ness, where stream is weak.* ◀

Beware salmon nets between Tarbat Ness and Portmahomack. Dornoch Firth is shallow, with shifting banks, and in strong E'lies the sea breaks heavily on the bar E of Dornoch Pt.

At Lothbeg Pt, 5M SW of Helmsdale, a rocky ledge extends 5ca offshore. Near Berriedale, 7M NE of Helmsdale, The Pinnacle, a detached rk 61m high, stands close offshore. The Beatrice oil field lies on Smith Bank, 28M NE of Tarbat Ness, and 11M off Caithness coast. Between Dunbeath and Lybster there are no dangers more than 2ca offshore. Clyth Ness (lt) is fringed by detached and drying rks. From here to Wick the only dangers are close inshore. There is anch in Sinclair's B in good weather, but Freswick B further N is better to await the tide in Pentland Firth (beware wreck in centre of bay). Stacks of Duncansby and Baxter Rk (depth 2·7m) lie 1M and 4ca S of Duncansby Hd.

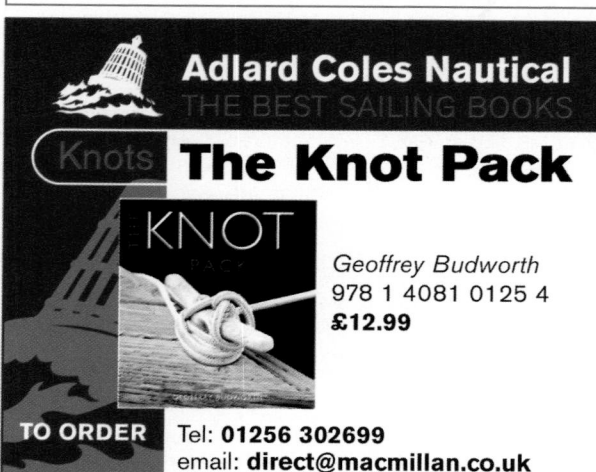
9.7.15 INVERNESS

Highland 57°29'·73N 04°14'·17W ❁❁⚓⚓⚓✿✿

CHARTS AC 223, 1077, 1078; Imray C23.

TIDES +0100 Dover; ML 2·7; Duration 0620

Standard Port INVERGORDON (⟶)

Times				Height (metres)			
High Water		Low Water		MHWS	MHWN	MLWN	MLWS
0100	0700	0000	0700	4·3	3·3	1·6	0·7
1300	1900	1200	1900				
Differences INVERNESS							
+0010	+0015	+0015	+0010	+0·3	+0·2	+0·1	+0·1
FORTROSE							
0000	+0010	+0010	−0010	0·0+0·1		No data	
CROMARTY							
−0005	0000	0000	−0005	0·0	0·0	0·0	0·0
DINGWALL							
+0020	+0015	No data		0·0	+0·1	No data	

SHELTER Good in all weathers. Berth at Inverness Marina (2.5m at CD) or at one of the 2 marinas in the Caledonian Canal, entrance to which can be difficult in strong tidal streams. The sea lock is normally available HW±4 in canal hours; the gates cannot be opened LW±2.

NAVIGATION WPT Meikle Mee SHM By Fl G 3s, 57°30'·25N 04°12'·03W, 250°/0·74M to Longman Pt bn. Inverness Firth is deep from Chanonry Pt to Munlochy SWM buoy, but shoal (2·1m) to Meikle Mee buoy. Meikle Mee partly dries. Beware bird rafts S of Avoch (off chartlet). Tidal streams are strong S of Craigton Pt (E-going stream at sp exceeds 5kn). Ent to R Ness is narrow, dredged to 3m CD. For the entrance to the Caledonian Canal, keep to N Kessock bank until clear of unmarked shoals on S bank. Care must be taken to avoid Carnarc Pt W of R mouth.

LIGHTS AND MARKS Longman Pt bn Fl WR 2s 7m 5/4M, vis 078°-W-258°-R-078°. Craigton Pt lt, Fl WRG 4s 6m 11/7M vis 312°-W-048°-R-064°-W-085°-G-shore. Caledonian Canal ent marked by QR and Iso G 4s on ends of training walls.

R/T Call: *Inverness Hbr Office* VHF Ch 12 (Mon-Fri: 0800 -1700 LT). *Inverness Marina* Ch 12. Caledonian Canal: Ch 74 is used by all stations. Call: *Clachnaharry Sea Lock*; or for office: *Caledonian Canal.*

TELEPHONE (Code 01463) HM 715715; Clachnaharry Sea Lock 713896; Canal Office 233140; MRCC (01224) 592334; Marinecall 09068 969641; Police 715555; Dr 234151.

FACILITIES Inverness Marina (150 inc 20❶), £2.00, ☎ 220501 or 07526 446348, www.invernessmarina.com, D, BH (45 ton), BY, CH, El, ME, ▣, Wi-fi, dredged to 3m below CD, full disabled access.
City All domestic facilities, ⇌, ✈.

CALEDONIAN CANAL

Clachnaharry Sea Lock 57°29'·44N 04°15'·84W. These notes are for the convenience of those entering the Canal at Inverness. They should be used with the main information/chartlet in 9.8.17.

CHARTS AC 1791, 1078. *BWB Skipper's Guide* essential.

TIDES Differences: Clachnaharry +0116 on Dover; see 9.7.15.

SHELTER Clachnaharry sea lock operates HW±4 (sp) within canal hours. The road and rail swing bridges may cause delays up to 25 mins. Seaport and Caley marinas: see Facilities.

NAVIGATION The 60M Caledonian Canal consists of 38M through three lochs, (Lochs Ness, Oich and Lochy), connected by 22M through canals. It can take vessels 45m LOA, 10m beam, 4m draft and max mast ht 27·4m. The passage normally takes two full days, possibly longer in the summer; 13 hrs is absolute minimum.

Speed limit is 5kn in canal sections. There are 10 swing bridges; road tfc has priority at peak hrs. Do not pass bridges without the keeper's instructions. From Clachnaharry sea lock to Loch Ness (Bona Ferry lt ho) is approx 7M, via Muirtown and Dochgarroch locks.

LOCKS   All 29 locks are manned and operate early May to early Oct, 0800-1800LT daily. Dues: see 9.8.17. For regulations and *BWS Skipper's Guide* apply: Canal Manager, Muirtown Wharf, Inverness IV3 5LS, ☎ (01463) 233140. www. scottishcanals.co.uk

LIGHTS AND MARKS   Chans are marked by posts, cairns and unlit buoys, PHM on the NW side of the chan and SHM on the SE side.

BOAT SAFETY SCHEME   Visiting vessels will be checked for apparent dangerous defects eg leaking gas or fuel, damaged electrical cables, taking in water, risk of capsize. £1M 3rd party insurance is required. For details see 9.8.17.

R/T   Sea locks and main lock flights operate VHF Ch 74 (HO).

TELEPHONE   Clachnaharry sea lock (01463) 713896; Canal Office, Inverness (01463) 233140.

FACILITIES   **Seaport Marina** (20+ 20♥), ☎ (01463) 725500, ⬚, FW, D, El, ME, ✗, Gas, Gaz, ▣, C (40 ton), ⚓, ♿. **Caley Marina** (25+25 ♥ £1.50) ☎ (01463) 236539, CH, D, ME, El, ✗, C (20 ton), ACA, Wi-fi.

MINOR HARBOURS IN INVERNESS FIRTH

FORTROSE, Highland, **57°34'·71N 04°08'·04W**. AC 1078. Tides 9.7.15. HW +0055 on Dover; ML 2·5m; Duration 0620. Small drying unlit hbr, soft silt bottom, well protected by Chanonry Ness to E; access HW±2, limited space. Follow ldg line 296°, Broomhill Ho (conspic on hill to NW) in line with school spire until abeam SPM buoy; then turn W to avoid Craig an Roan rks (1·8m) ESE of ent. Chanonry Pt lt, Oc 6s 12m 15M, obscd 073°-shore. HM ☎ (01381) 620311; Dr ☎ 620909. Facilities: AB £5, 4 ⚓, L, M, P, D, Slip, scrubbing grid, Gas, R, 🛒, ✉, Ⓑ; **Chanonry SC** (near pier) ☎ 01381 621973.

AVOCH, Highland, **57°34'·03N 04°09'·94W**. AC 1078. Tides as Fortrose (1·25M to the ENE). Hbr dries, mostly on the N side, but is bigger than Fortrose; access HW±2. Small craft may stay afloat at nps against the S pier (2FR (vert)). AB may be available on drying pontoons; one ⚓ (max 35ft LOA) off hbr ent. HM ☎ (mobile) 07779 833951. **Facilities**: AB £7, FW, ⬚. **Village**: ✉, 🛒, R, Bar, P & D (cans), ME.

MINOR HARBOURS FROM CROMARTY FIRTH TO WICK

CROMARTY FIRTH, Highland, 57°41'·18N 04°02'·09W. AC 1889, 1890. HW +0100 on Dover –0135 on Aberdeen; HW height 0.0m on Aberdeen; ML 2·5m; Duration 0625. See 9.7.15. Excellent hbr extending 7·5M W, past Invergordon, then 9M SW. Good shelter always available, depending on wind direction. Beware rks and reefs round N and S Sutor at the ent; many unlit oil rig mooring buoys. *Cromarty Firth Port Control* VHF Ch 11 16 13 (H24) ☎ (01349) 852308.

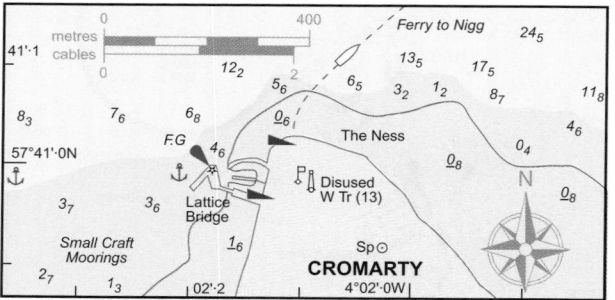

CROMARTY HARBOUR, Highland. **57°41'·00N 04°02'·35W.** Approach from WPT 57°41'·10N 04°02'·50W, 142°/1.3ca to entrance. When inside hbr beware of set towards lattice bridge. Sheltered from N through E to S. Approx 20 AB on 50m central pontoon, £1·00/m. 2 🅰 2ca W of S pier hd, or ⚓ in approx 6m with good holding but exposed to the W. Harbour administered by Cromarty Harbour Trust, www.cromartyharbour.org. HM ☎ (01381) 600493 (office not normally manned) or call Ch M/16. D, 🛢, ⬆ available in harbour. **Cromarty Boat Club**, www.cromartyboatclub.org, 2 🅰 in 0·5m to 1·5m; showers, 🚻, ☐ (owned by Boat Club; key held at Royal Hotel). ✉, 🛒. Local ferry to Nigg.

Invergordon West Harbour Highland. **57°41'·12N 04°10'·05W.** AB on pontoons, Bar, C (3 ton), D, FW, ✉, P, R, 🛒, Gas, L. Dinghy landing at Invergordon Boat Club (1·5M W), ☎ (01863) 766710.

DORNOCH FIRTH, Highland. **57°51'·28N 03°59'·39W.** AC 115, 223. HW +0115 on Dover; ML 2·5m; Duration 0605; see 9.7.16. Excellent shelter but difficult ent. There are many shifting sandbanks, especially near the ent, from N edge of Whiteness Sands to S edge of Gizzen Briggs. ⚓s in 7m ¾M ESE of Dornoch Pt (sheltered from NE swell by Gizzen Briggs); in 7m 2ca SSE of Ard na Cailc; in 3·3m 1M below Bonar Bridge. Firth extends 15M inland, but AC coverage ceases ¼M E of Ferry Pt. The A9 road bridge, 3·3M W of Dornoch Pt, with 11m clearance, has 3 spans lit on both sides; span centres show Iso 4s, N bank pier Iso G 4s, S bank pier Iso R 4s and 2 midstream piers QY. Tarbat Ness lt ho Fl (4) 30s 53m 24M. Fl R 5s lt shown when Tain firing range active. Very limited facilities at Ferrytown and Bonar Bridge. MRCC ☎ 01224 592334. **Dornoch:** 🛒, P, ✉, Dr, Ⓑ, R, Bar.

GOLSPIE, Highland, 57°58'·71N 03°56'·79W. AC 223. HW +0045 on Dover; ML 2·3m; Duration 068. See 9.7.16. Golspie pier projects 60m SE across foreshore with arm projecting SW at the hd, giving shelter during NE winds. Beware The Bridge, a bank (0·3m to 1·8m) running parallel to the shore ¼M to seaward of pier hd. Seas break heavily over The Bridge in NE winds. There are no lts. To enter, keep Duke of Sutherland's Memorial in line 316° with boathouse SW of pier, until church spire in village is in line 006° with hd of pier, then keep on those marks. Hbr gets very congested; good ⚓ off pier. HM ☎ 01431 821692. **Town** Bar, D, Dr, Ⓗ, L, M, P, Gas, ✉, R, ⚓, 🛒, Ⓑ.

LYBSTER, Highland, 58°17'·72N 03°17'·39W. AC 115. HW +0020 on Dover; HW –0150 sp, –0215 np; HW ht –0·6m on Aberdeen; ML 2·1m; Duration 0620. Excellent shelter in SW inner hbr; AB on W side of pier in about 1·2m. Most of hbr dries to sand/mud and is much used by FVs; no bollards on N wall. Appr on about 350°. Beware rks close on E side of ent; narrow (10m) ent is difficult in strong E to S winds. Min depth 2·5m in ent. S pier hd, Oc R 6s 10m 3M, occas in fishing season. AB £7.00 per week, FW on W quay. Showers/laundry at Waterlines Visitor Centre, 01593 721520. **Town** Bar, D, P, R, 🛒.

9.7.16 PORTMAHOMACK

Highland 57°50'·25N 03°50'·00W ✿✿⚓✿✿

CHARTS AC 115, 223; Imray C23.

TIDES +0035 Dover; ML 2·5; Duration 0600

Standard Port ABERDEEN (⟵)

Times				Height (metres)			
High Water		Low Water		MHWS	MHWN	MLWN	MLWS
0300	0800	0200	0800	4·3	3·4	1·6	0·6
1500	2000	1400	2000				
Differences PORTMAHOMACK							
–0120	–0210	–0140	–0110	–0·2	–0·1	+0·1	+0·1
MEIKLE FERRY (Dornoch Firth)							
–0100	–0140	–0120	–0055	+0·1	0·0	–0·1	0·0
GOLSPIE							
–0130	–0215	–0155	–0130	–0·3	–0·3	–0·1	0·0

SHELTER Good, but uncomfortable in SW/NW winds. Hbr dries, access only at HW, but good ⚓ close SW of pier.

NAVIGATION WPT 57°53'·00N 03°50'·00W, 180°/2.7M to 1ca W of hbr ent. Beware Curach Rks which lie from 2ca SW of pier to the shore. Rks extend N and W of the pier. Beware lobster pot floats and salmon nets N of hbr. Tain firing & bombing range is about 3M to the W, S of mouth of Dornoch Firth; R flags, R lts, shown when active.

LIGHTS AND MARKS Tarbert Ness lt ho Fl (4) 30s 53m 24M, W twr R bands, is 2·6M to NE of hbr. Pier hd 2 FR (vert) 7m 5M.

R/T None.

TELEPHONE (Code 01862) HM 871705; MRCC (01224) 592334; Marinecall 09068 969641; Dr 892759.

FACILITIES Hbr, AB <5m £9, 5-7m £12, 7-10m £16, some drying pontoon berths, M, L, FW. Showers, 🚻. **Town** R, 🛒, Bar, ✉, ⚓ (bus to Tain), ✈ (Inverness).

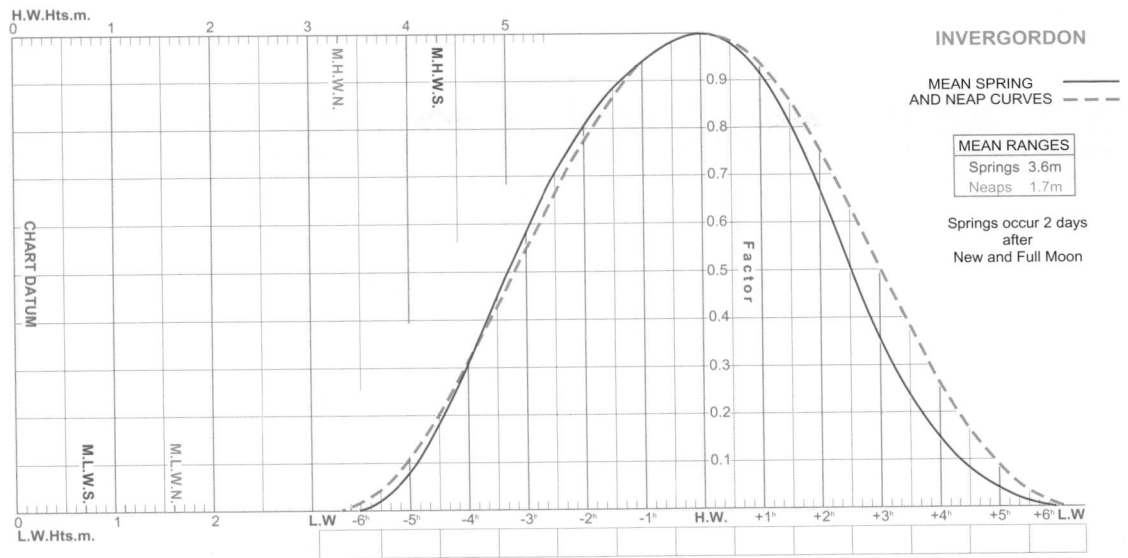

INVERGORDON

MEAN SPRING
AND NEAP CURVES

MEAN RANGES
Springs 3.6m
Neaps 1.7m

Springs occur 2 days
after
New and Full Moon

TIME ZONE (UT)
For Summer Time add ONE
hour in **non-shaded areas**

INVERGORDON
LAT 57°41'N   LONG 4°10'W
TIMES AND HEIGHTS OF HIGH AND LOW WATERS

Dates in red are **SPRINGS**
Dates in blue are **NEAPS**

YEAR 2010

JANUARY

	Time	m		Time	m
1 F	0611 1211 1846	1.0 4.5 0.5	**16** SA	0039 0611 1236 1904	3.9 1.2 4.2 0.9
2 SA	0040 0659 1259 1934	4.4 1.0 4.6 0.4	**17** SU	0111 0647 1310 1933	3.9 1.1 4.2 0.9
3 SU	0132 0742 1347 2021	4.4 1.0 4.7 0.3	**18** M	0143 0720 1344 2002	3.9 1.1 4.1 0.9
4 M	0221 0823 1435 2107	4.4 1.0 4.6 0.4	**19** TU	0214 0747 1415 2028	3.8 1.2 4.0 1.0
5 TU	0310 0859 1523 2152	4.3 1.1 4.5 0.6	**20** W	0244 0759 1445 2045	3.7 1.3 3.9 1.1
6 W	0356 0933 1610 2237	4.1 1.3 4.3 0.9	**21** TH	0315 0813 1516 2046	3.6 1.4 3.8 1.3
7 TH	0442 1011 1659 2328	3.9 1.5 4.1 1.2	**22** F	0350 0841 1553 2106	3.5 1.5 3.7 1.4
8 F	0531 1100 1754	3.7 1.7 3.8	**23** SA	0431 0921 1639 2149	3.4 1.6 3.6 1.6
9 SA	0042 0626 1207 1903	1.5 3.5 1.9 3.6	**24** SU	0523 1028 1738	3.3 1.8 3.4
10 SU	0214 0732 1455 2022	1.6 3.5 1.8 3.6	**25** M	0035 0631 1316 1855	1.7 3.3 1.8 3.4
11 M	0319 0845 1559 2140	1.6 3.5 1.6 3.6	**26** TU	0157 0746 1443 2019	1.6 3.4 1.5 3.5
12 TU	0413 0952 1653 2242	1.6 3.7 1.4 3.7	**27** W	0300 0855 1548 2132	1.5 3.6 1.2 3.7
13 W	0455 1045 1736 2329	1.6 3.9 1.2 3.8	**28** TH	0406 1000 1651 2241	1.3 3.9 0.9 4.0
14 TH	0522 1127 1810	1.5 4.0 1.1	**29** F	0508 1101 1745 2341	1.1 4.2 0.5 4.3
15 F	0006 0540 1202 1838	3.9 1.4 4.1 1.0	**30** SA	0600 1156 1833	0.9 4.5 0.2
			31 SU	0032 0644 1245 1918	4.4 0.8 4.7 0.1

FEBRUARY

	Time	m		Time	m
1 M	0120 0724 1332 2001	4.5 0.7 4.8 0.1	**16** TU	0118 0704 1321 1935	4.0 0.9 4.2 0.7
2 TU	0205 0802 1418 2042	4.5 0.7 4.8 0.2	**17** W	0147 0735 1352 2004	3.9 0.9 4.1 0.8
3 W	0248 0836 1503 2121	4.4 0.8 4.6 0.5	**18** TH	0216 0754 1422 2025	3.9 1.0 4.0 1.0
4 TH	0330 0908 1547 2200	4.2 1.0 4.4 0.9	**19** F	0246 0744 1453 1957	3.8 1.1 3.9 1.1
5 F	0411 0942 1633 2239	3.9 1.3 4.0 1.3	**20** SA	0319 0805 1529 2019	3.7 1.2 3.8 1.3
6 SA	0454 1026 1726 2333	3.6 1.6 3.7 1.7	**21** SU	0358 0840 1613 2059	3.5 1.4 3.6 1.5
7 SU	0544 1136 1831	3.4 1.8 3.4	**22** M	0448 0929 1710 2157	3.4 1.6 3.4 1.8
8 M	0139 0646 1435 1953	1.9 3.3 1.8 3.3	**23** TU	0554 1253 1829	3.3 1.7 3.3
9 TU	0259 0754 1545 2127	1.8 3.4 1.6 3.4	**24** W	0133 0712 1423 2000	1.7 3.3 1.4 3.4
10 W	0357 0906 1640 2233	1.8 3.5 1.4 3.5	**25** TH	0248 0826 1533 2122	1.6 3.6 1.1 3.6
11 TH	0442 1018 1723 2317	1.6 3.7 1.2 3.7	**26** F	0357 0935 1636 2234	1.3 3.9 0.7 4.0
12 F	0511 1107 1755 2352	1.5 3.9 1.0 3.8	**27** SA	0455 1041 1728 2330	1.0 4.2 0.3 4.3
13 SA	0525 1144 1817	1.3 4.1 0.9	**28** SU	0542 1138 1814	0.8 4.6 0.0
14 SU	0021 0554 1217 1839	3.9 1.1 4.2 0.8			
15 M	0050 0629 1249 1906	4.0 1.0 4.2 0.7			

MARCH

	Time	m		Time	m
1 M	0017 0624 1227 1856	4.5 0.6 4.8 -0.1	**16** TU	0022 0607 1222 1835	4.0 0.9 4.2 0.7
2 TU	0101 0702 1313 1935	4.6 0.5 4.9 0.0	**17** W	0050 0642 1255 1907	4.1 0.8 4.2 0.7
3 W	0142 0738 1357 2013	4.5 0.5 4.8 0.2	**18** TH	0120 0715 1328 1938	4.0 0.8 4.2 0.7
4 TH	0222 0812 1440 2049	4.4 0.7 4.6 0.6	**19** F	0150 0741 1401 2002	4.0 0.9 4.1 0.9
5 F	0301 0845 1524 2123	4.2 0.9 4.3 1.0	**20** SA	0222 0730 1435 1928	3.9 1.0 4.0 1.1
6 SA	0341 0917 1610 2151	3.9 1.2 3.9 1.4	**21** SU	0256 0745 1514 1954	3.7 1.1 3.8 1.2
7 SU	0423 0955 1701 2229	3.6 1.5 3.5 1.8	**22** M	0337 0821 1600 2037	3.6 1.3 3.6 1.5
8 M	0511 1118 1804	3.4 1.8 3.3	**23** TU	0429 0918 1700 2142	3.4 1.5 3.4 1.8
9 TU	0104 0612 1412 1921	2.0 3.3 1.7 3.1	**24** W	0534 1238 1817	3.3 1.5 3.3
10 W	0235 0719 1519 2103	1.9 3.3 1.5 3.2	**25** TH	0110 0649 1407 1947	1.8 3.4 1.2 3.4
11 TH	0333 0825 1613 2211	1.8 3.4 1.3 3.4	**26** F	0242 0802 1517 2113	1.6 3.6 0.9 3.6
12 F	0418 0932 1656 2252	1.6 3.6 1.1 3.6	**27** SA	0346 0911 1617 2221	1.3 3.9 0.5 4.0
13 SA	0448 1031 1726 2325	1.5 3.8 1.0 3.8	**28** SU	0438 1019 1707 2313	1.0 4.2 0.3 4.3
14 SU	0505 1113 1745 2354	1.3 4.0 0.9 3.9	**29** M	0522 1118 1751 2357	0.7 4.5 0.1 4.4
15 M	0532 1148 1806	1.1 4.1 0.7	**30** TU	0602 1207 1831	0.6 4.7 0.0
			31 W	0038 0640 1252 1910	4.5 0.5 4.7 0.1

APRIL

	Time	m		Time	m
1 TH	0117 0716 1336 1946	4.5 0.5 4.6 0.4	**16** F	0053 0655 1305 1914	4.1 0.8 4.2 0.8
2 F	0156 0752 1419 2019	4.3 0.6 4.4 0.7	**17** SA	0127 0728 1342 1942	4.1 0.8 4.1 1.0
3 SA	0234 0826 1503 2046	4.1 0.9 4.1 1.1	**18** SU	0202 0754 1422 1922	4.0 0.9 4.0 1.1
4 SU	0313 0857 1549 2050	3.9 1.1 3.8 1.5	**19** M	0241 0741 1505 1949	3.9 1.1 3.8 1.3
5 M	0355 0922 1634 2119	3.7 1.4 3.4 1.8	**20** TU	0325 0905 1556 2039	3.7 1.2 3.6 1.3
6 TU	0443 1133 1738 2237	3.4 1.7 3.2 2.0	**21** W	0419 1051 1656 2248	3.6 1.3 3.5 1.8
7 W	0541 1337 1845	3.3 1.6 3.1	**22** TH	0521 1223 1808	3.5 1.2 3.4
8 TH	0158 0645 1442 2002	2.0 3.3 1.5 3.2	**23** F	0031 0629 1346 1930	1.8 3.5 1.0 3.5
9 F	0256 0748 1534 2117	1.8 3.4 1.3 3.3	**24** SA	0224 0739 1455 2053	1.6 3.7 0.8 3.7
10 SA	0340 0846 1615 2207	1.6 3.5 1.2 3.5	**25** SU	0326 0848 1554 2158	1.3 3.9 0.6 3.9
11 SU	0411 0941 1642 2244	1.5 3.7 1.1 3.7	**26** M	0417 0956 1645 2249	1.1 4.1 0.4 4.1
12 M	0436 1029 1703 2317	1.3 3.9 1.0 3.9	**27** TU	0502 1057 1729 2334	0.8 4.3 0.3 4.3
13 TU	0506 1112 1731 2349	1.1 4.0 0.8 4.0	**28** W	0543 1148 1809	0.7 4.5 0.4
14 W	0542 1152 1805	1.0 4.1 0.7	**29** TH	0014 0622 1233 1846	4.3 0.6 4.5 0.5
15 TH	0021 0619 1229 1841	4.1 0.8 4.2 0.7	**30** F	0053 0700 1317 1920	4.3 0.6 4.4 0.7

Chart Datum: 2·10 metres below Ordnance Datum (Local). HAT is 5·0 metres above Chart Datum; see 4.5

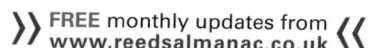

INVERGORDON LAT 57°41'N LONG 4°10'W
TIMES AND HEIGHTS OF HIGH AND LOW WATERS

TIME ZONE (UT)
For Summer Time add ONE hour in **non-shaded areas**

Dates in red are **SPRINGS**
Dates in blue are NEAPS

YEAR 2010

NE Scotland

MAY

Time m	Time m
1 0131 4.2 / 0737 0.7 / SA 1400 4.2 / 1951 1.0	**16** 0108 4.1 / 0722 0.7 / SU 1329 4.2 / 1932 1.0
2 0209 4.1 / 0814 0.9 / SU 1444 3.9 / 2011 1.2	**17** 0148 4.1 / 0805 0.8 / M 1414 4.1 / 2000 1.2
3 0248 3.9 / 0850 1.1 / M 1529 3.7 / 2013 1.5	**18** 0232 4.0 / 0853 0.8 / TU 1503 3.9 / 2020 1.3
4 0330 3.7 / 0901 1.3 / TU 1617 3.4 / 2047 1.7	**19** 0320 3.9 / 0948 0.9 / W 1556 3.8 / 2121 1.5
5 0417 3.5 / 1056 1.5 / W 1709 3.2 / 2142 1.9	**20** 0412 3.9 / 1050 1.0 / TH 1652 3.7 / ◑ 2232 1.6
6 0510 3.4 / 1236 1.6 / TH 1806 3.1 / ◑ 2316 2.0	**21** 0508 3.8 / 1159 1.0 / F 1754 3.6 / 2342 1.6
7 0608 3.3 / 1345 1.5 / F 1907 3.2	**22** 0610 3.7 / 1317 1.0 / SA 1904 3.6
8 0201 1.9 / 0708 3.3 / SA 1435 1.4 / 2008 3.3	**23** 0143 1.6 / 0716 3.8 / SU 1429 0.9 / 2020 3.6
9 0248 1.7 / 0804 3.4 / SU 1512 1.1 / 2103 3.5	**24** 0300 1.4 / 0825 3.9 / M 1530 0.8 / 2127 3.8
10 0325 1.5 / 0856 3.6 / M 1541 1.2 / 2151 3.6	**25** 0356 1.2 / 0935 4.0 / TU 1623 0.8 / 2223 3.9
11 0359 1.3 / 0946 3.7 / TU 1615 1.1 / 2233 3.8	**26** 0446 1.0 / 1038 4.1 / W 1709 0.8 / 2310 4.1
12 0437 1.2 / 1035 3.9 / W 1655 1.0 / 2313 4.0	**27** 0530 0.9 / 1132 4.2 / TH 1749 0.8 / ○ 2353 4.2
13 0518 1.0 / 1121 4.0 / TH 1737 0.9 / 2351 4.1	**28** 0610 0.8 / 1219 4.2 / F 1824 0.9
14 0559 0.9 / 1204 4.1 / F 1817 0.9 / ●	**29** 0032 4.2 / 0650 0.7 / SA 1302 4.1 / 1857 1.0
15 0029 4.1 / 0641 0.8 / SA 1246 4.2 / 1856 0.9	**30** 0110 4.1 / 0728 0.8 / SU 1344 4.0 / 1927 1.1
	31 0148 4.1 / 0807 0.9 / M 1426 3.8 / 1948 1.2

JUNE

Time m	Time m
1 0226 3.9 / 0846 1.0 / TU 1508 3.7 / 1956 1.4	**16** 0226 4.3 / 0856 0.5 / W 1500 4.1 / 2050 1.1
2 0307 3.8 / 0919 1.2 / W 1551 3.5 / 2025 1.5	**17** 0314 4.3 / 0944 0.6 / TH 1550 4.0 / 2129 1.2
3 0349 3.6 / 0911 1.3 / TH 1634 3.4 / 2109 1.6	**18** 0403 4.2 / 1034 0.7 / F 1640 3.9 / 2214 1.4
4 0433 3.5 / 1002 1.4 / F 1720 3.2 / ◑ 2207 1.8	**19** 0454 4.0 / 1128 0.9 / SA 1732 3.7 / ◑ 2306 1.5
5 0521 3.4 / 1122 1.5 / SA 1812 3.2 / 2323 1.8	**20** 0549 3.9 / 1236 1.1 / SU 1830 3.6
6 0616 3.3 / 1302 1.5 / SU 1909 3.2	**21** 0011 1.6 / 0653 3.8 / M 1358 1.2 / 1939 3.6
7 0137 1.8 / 0715 3.4 / M 1357 1.5 / 2006 3.4	**22** 0233 1.5 / 0804 3.7 / TU 1507 1.2 / 2051 3.6
8 0233 1.6 / 0812 3.5 / TU 1443 1.4 / 2059 3.5	**23** 0339 1.4 / 0919 3.7 / W 1604 1.2 / 2155 3.7
9 0319 1.5 / 0906 3.6 / W 1530 1.2 / 2149 3.7	**24** 0435 1.2 / 1026 3.8 / TH 1653 1.2 / 2248 3.9
10 0406 1.3 / 1000 3.8 / TH 1621 1.1 / 2237 3.9	**25** 0523 1.0 / 1122 3.9 / F 1733 1.2 / 2334 4.0
11 0456 1.1 / 1053 3.9 / F 1712 1.0 / 2324 4.0	**26** 0605 0.9 / 1209 4.0 / SA 1806 1.1 / ○
12 0545 0.9 / 1144 4.1 / SA 1800 1.0 / ●	**27** 0014 4.1 / 0643 0.8 / SU 1250 3.9 / 1835 1.1
13 0008 4.2 / 0633 0.7 / SU 1233 4.2 / 1846 0.9	**28** 0052 4.1 / 0718 0.8 / M 1328 3.9 / 1904 1.1
14 0053 4.3 / 0720 0.6 / M 1321 4.2 / 1929 1.0	**29** 0129 4.1 / 0751 0.8 / TU 1406 3.8 / 1932 1.1
15 0139 4.3 / 0808 0.5 / TU 1411 4.2 / 2011 1.0	**30** 0205 4.0 / 0823 0.9 / W 1443 3.7 / 1954 1.2

JULY

Time m	Time m
1 0241 3.9 / 0851 1.0 / TH 1519 3.6 / 2011 1.3	**16** 0301 4.6 / 0925 0.3 / F 1534 4.2 / 2115 1.0
2 0316 3.8 / 0859 1.1 / F 1553 3.5 / 2039 1.4	**17** 0347 4.4 / 1008 0.6 / SA 1618 4.0 / 2153 1.2
3 0349 3.6 / 0920 1.2 / SA 1627 3.4 / 2119 1.5	**18** 0435 4.2 / 1054 0.9 / SU 1704 3.8 / ◑ 2239 1.4
4 0425 3.5 / 1003 1.4 / SU 1705 3.3 / ◑ 2212 1.7	**19** 0527 3.9 / 1151 1.2 / M 1756 3.6 / 2342 1.6
5 0509 3.4 / 1109 1.5 / M 1756 3.3 / 2331 1.8	**20** 0630 3.7 / 1327 1.5 / TU 1859 3.5
6 0606 3.3 / 1250 1.6 / TU 1901 3.3	**21** 0213 1.7 / 0746 3.5 / W 1448 1.5 / 2013 3.5
7 0141 1.7 / 0718 3.4 / W 1403 1.5 / 2008 3.4	**22** 0328 1.6 / 0908 3.5 / TH 1550 1.5 / 2128 3.6
8 0245 1.5 / 0828 3.5 / TH 1458 1.4 / 2108 3.6	**23** 0429 1.3 / 1020 3.6 / F 1642 1.4 / 2230 3.8
9 0340 1.3 / 0931 3.7 / F 1554 1.3 / 2204 3.8	**24** 0519 1.1 / 1115 3.8 / SA 1722 1.4 / 2319 4.0
10 0437 1.0 / 1032 3.9 / SA 1654 1.1 / 2259 4.1	**25** 0559 0.9 / 1159 3.9 / SU 1749 1.3 / 2359 4.1
11 0532 0.8 / 1130 4.1 / SU 1748 1.0 / ● 2350 4.3	**26** 0630 0.8 / 1236 3.9 / M 1810 1.2 / ○
12 0623 0.5 / 1223 4.3 / M 1836 0.9	**27** 0034 4.2 / 0657 0.8 / TU 1309 3.9 / 1840 1.1
13 0039 4.5 / 0711 0.3 / TU 1313 4.4 / 1920 0.8	**28** 0107 4.2 / 0724 0.7 / W 1341 3.9 / 1912 1.0
14 0127 4.6 / 0757 0.2 / W 1401 4.4 / 2001 0.8	**29** 0140 4.2 / 0752 0.8 / TH 1412 3.9 / 1942 1.0
15 0214 4.6 / 0841 0.2 / TH 1448 4.4 / 2039 0.9	**30** 0212 4.1 / 0819 0.8 / F 1442 3.8 / 2003 1.1
	31 0241 3.9 / 0839 1.0 / SA 1509 3.7 / 2013 1.2

AUGUST

Time m	Time m
1 0310 3.8 / 0846 1.1 / SU 1538 3.6 / 2035 1.4	**16** 0414 4.2 / 1020 1.1 / M 1636 3.8 / ◐ 2217 1.4
2 0342 3.6 / 0900 1.3 / M 1614 3.5 / 2110 1.5	**17** 0506 3.8 / 1112 1.5 / TU 1725 3.6 / 2326 1.7
3 0423 3.5 / 0932 1.5 / TU 1700 3.3 / 2208 1.7	**18** 0609 3.5 / 1300 1.8 / W 1825 3.4
4 0515 3.4 / 1130 1.7 / W 1801 3.3	**19** 0203 1.7 / 0729 3.4 / TH 1434 1.8 / 1939 3.4
5 0057 1.8 / 0627 3.3 / TH 1332 1.7 / 1919 3.3	**20** 0317 1.5 / 0902 3.4 / F 1537 1.7 / 2101 3.6
6 0219 1.5 / 0756 3.4 / F 1437 1.5 / 2031 3.5	**21** 0416 1.3 / 1012 3.6 / SA 1628 1.6 / 2213 3.8
7 0320 1.3 / 0910 3.6 / SA 1537 1.4 / 2134 3.8	**22** 0504 1.1 / 1102 3.8 / SU 1706 1.5 / 2302 4.0
8 0421 0.9 / 1018 3.9 / SU 1640 1.1 / 2235 4.1	**23** 0541 0.9 / 1141 3.9 / M 1728 1.3 / 2339 4.1
9 0518 0.6 / 1116 4.2 / M 1734 0.9 / 2331 4.4	**24** 0607 0.8 / 1215 4.0 / TU 1744 1.1 / ○
10 0608 0.2 / 1211 4.4 / TU 1820 0.7 / ●	**25** 0009 4.2 / 0626 0.8 / W 1244 4.0 / 1814 1.0
11 0022 4.7 / 0653 0.0 / W 1258 4.6 / 1902 0.6	**26** 0039 4.3 / 0650 0.7 / TH 1312 4.1 / 1848 0.9
12 0109 4.8 / 0736 -0.1 / TH 1343 4.6 / 1941 0.6	**27** 0110 4.2 / 0718 0.7 / F 1339 4.0 / 1921 0.9
13 0156 4.9 / 0818 0.0 / F 1427 4.5 / 2018 0.7	**28** 0140 4.2 / 0748 0.8 / SA 1406 3.9 / 1948 1.0
14 0241 4.8 / 0859 0.3 / SA 1510 4.3 / 2054 0.9	**29** 0210 4.1 / 0813 0.9 / SU 1433 3.8 / 1953 1.1
15 0327 4.5 / 0939 0.7 / SU 1552 4.1 / 2132 1.1	**30** 0240 3.9 / 0812 1.0 / M 1503 3.7 / 2000 1.3
	31 0314 3.8 / 0810 1.3 / TU 1540 3.6 / 2030 1.4

Chart Datum: 2·10 metres below Ordnance Datum (Local). HAT is 5·0 metres above Chart Datum; see 4.5

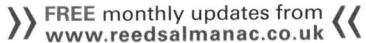

TIME ZONE (UT)
For Summer Time add ONE hour in **non-shaded areas**

INVERGORDON   LAT 57°41'N   LONG 4°10'W
TIMES AND HEIGHTS OF HIGH AND LOW WATERS

Dates in **red** are **SPRINGS**
Dates in blue are **NEAPS**

YEAR 2010

SEPTEMBER

Day	Time m	Time m	Time m	Time m		Day	Time m	Time m	Time m	Time m
1 W	0356 3.6	0843 1.5	1625 3.4	◐ 2118 1.7		16 TH	0548 3.4	1236 2.0	1755 3.5	
2 TH	0449 3.4	0935 1.7	1726 3.3			17 F	0147 1.7	0707 3.3	1414 2.0	1906 3.4
3 F	0033 1.7	0601 3.3	1307 1.8	1844 3.4		18 SA	0256 1.5	0845 3.4	1514 1.8	2024 3.6
4 SA	0159 1.5	0733 3.4	1424 1.6	2000 3.6		19 SU	0351 1.3	0951 3.6	1603 1.7	2140 3.8
5 SU	0303 1.1	0856 3.6	1528 1.4	2108 3.9		20 M	0437 1.1	1037 3.8	1640 1.5	2230 4.0
6 M	0403 0.8	1006 4.0	1626 1.1	2211 4.2		21 TU	0512 1.0	1113 4.0	1701 1.3	2305 4.1
7 TU	0458 0.4	1104 4.3	1716 0.9	2310 4.6		22 W	0533 1.0	1144 4.1	1717 1.2	2336 4.2
8 W	0547 0.1	1153 4.5	1759 0.6 ●			23 TH	0549 0.8	1212 4.2	1748 1.0 ○	
9 TH	0001 4.8	0631 0.0	1237 4.7	1840 0.5		24 F	0006 4.3	0615 0.8	1239 4.2	1823 0.9
10 F	0048 4.9	0712 0.0	1320 4.7	1918 0.5		25 SA	0038 4.3	0647 0.7	1306 4.2	1858 0.9
11 SA	0134 4.9	0752 0.1	1401 4.6	1956 0.6		26 SU	0110 4.2	0719 0.8	1334 4.1	1928 1.0
12 SU	0219 4.8	0831 0.5	1442 4.4	2033 0.8		27 M	0142 4.1	0747 1.0	1404 4.0	1944 1.1
13 M	0304 4.5	0909 0.9	1524 4.1	2112 1.1		28 TU	0216 4.0	0739 1.2	1436 3.9	1940 1.3
14 TU	0352 4.1	0946 1.3	1607 3.9	2200 1.5		29 W	0254 3.9	0741 1.4	1515 3.7	2010 1.4
15 W	0445 3.7	1031 1.7	1656 3.6	◐ 2330 1.7		30 TH	0339 3.7	0818 1.6	1603 3.6	2108 1.6

OCTOBER

Day	Time m	Time m	Time m	Time m		Day	Time m	Time m	Time m	Time m
1 F	0434 3.5	0916 1.9	1704 3.5 ◐			16 SA	0114 1.7	0632 3.3	1337 2.1	1830 3.5
2 SA	0013 1.6	0546 3.4	1234 1.9	1818 3.5		17 SU	0221 1.5	0755 3.3	1439 1.9	1938 3.5
3 SU	0138 1.4	0714 3.4	1411 1.7	1933 3.7		18 M	0315 1.4	0907 3.5	1527 1.8	2041 3.7
4 M	0243 1.0	0839 3.7	1515 1.5	2042 4.0		19 TU	0359 1.3	0955 3.7	1604 1.6	2133 3.9
5 TU	0342 0.7	0949 4.0	1608 1.2	2147 4.3		20 W	0430 1.2	1032 3.9	1627 1.4	2216 4.0
6 W	0436 0.4	1044 4.3	1655 0.9	2246 4.6		21 TH	0447 1.1	1105 4.1	1651 1.2	2255 4.2
7 TH	0524 0.2	1131 4.6	1738 0.7	● 2339 4.8		22 F	0508 1.0	1210 4.3	1724 1.1	2333 4.2
8 F	0607 0.1	1214 4.7	1819 0.6			23 SA	0541 0.9	1205 4.3	1801 1.0 ○	
9 SA	0026 4.9	0648 0.2	1255 4.7	1858 0.6		24 SU	0008 4.3	0618 0.9	1236 4.3	1838 1.0
10 SU	0112 4.8	0727 0.4	1335 4.6	1937 0.7		25 M	0044 4.3	0654 1.0	1307 4.2	1912 1.0
11 M	0157 4.6	0804 0.8	1415 4.4	2016 0.9		26 TU	0120 4.2	0725 1.1	1341 4.1	1943 1.1
12 TU	0243 4.3	0839 1.1	1456 4.1	2058 1.2		27 W	0158 4.1	0728 1.3	1416 4.0	2004 1.2
13 W	0332 4.0	0907 1.5	1539 3.9	2150 1.5		28 TH	0240 3.9	0730 1.4	1457 3.9	2055 1.3
14 TH	0424 3.7	0923 1.9	1628 3.7	◐ 2332 1.7		29 F	0328 3.8	0813 1.6	1547 3.7	2226 1.4
15 F	0523 3.4	1040 2.1	1725 3.5			30 SA	0425 3.6	0941 1.9	1647 3.7	◐ 2350 1.4
						31 SU	0532 3.5	1145 1.9	1754 3.7	

NOVEMBER

Day	Time m	Time m	Time m	Time m		Day	Time m	Time m	Time m	Time m
1 M	0109 1.3	0650 3.6	1338 1.8	1905 3.8		16 TU	0222 1.6	0752 3.4	1436 1.9	1950 3.6
2 TU	0218 1.0	0812 3.7	1451 1.5	2015 4.0		17 W	0302 1.5	0848 3.6	1516 1.7	2043 3.7
3 W	0319 0.8	0922 4.0	1547 1.3	2122 4.2		18 TH	0328 1.4	0936 3.8	1549 1.5	2131 3.9
4 TH	0413 0.6	1018 4.2	1636 1.1	2224 4.4		19 F	0351 1.3	1017 4.0	1623 1.4	2217 4.0
5 F	0501 0.5	1106 4.4	1721 0.8	2319 4.4		20 SA	0428 1.2	1056 4.1	1702 1.2	2301 4.1
6 SA	0545 0.5	1150 4.5	1803 0.7 ●			21 SU	0511 1.1	1133 4.2	1742 1.1	○ 2342 4.2
7 SU	0007 4.6	0626 0.6	1231 4.6	1844 0.7		22 M	0553 1.1	1210 4.3	1823 1.0	
8 M	0053 4.6	0704 0.8	1311 4.5	1925 0.8		23 TU	0023 4.2	0634 1.1	1246 4.3	1905 1.0
9 TU	0138 4.4	0740 1.0	1350 4.3	2007 0.9		24 W	0104 4.2	0712 1.2	1324 4.3	1947 1.0
10 W	0224 4.2	0811 1.3	1430 4.2	2051 1.1		25 TH	0146 4.2	0742 1.3	1404 4.2	2032 1.0
11 TH	0311 3.9	0821 1.6	1513 4.0	2143 1.4		26 F	0232 4.0	0749 1.4	1448 4.1	2123 1.1
12 F	0401 3.7	0837 1.8	1559 3.8	2253 1.6		27 SA	0323 3.9	0833 1.6	1537 4.0	2220 1.1
13 SA	0452 3.5	0927 2.0	1651 3.6 ◐			28 SU	0416 3.8	0952 1.7	1631 3.9	◑ 2321 1.2
14 SU	0014 1.7	0548 3.3	1045 2.1	1749 3.5		29 M	0514 3.7	1102 1.8	1730 3.9	
15 M	0126 1.7	0649 3.3	1341 2.0	1850 3.5		30 TU	0030 1.2	0619 3.6	1211 1.8	1836 3.8

DECEMBER

Day	Time m	Time m	Time m	Time m		Day	Time m	Time m	Time m	Time m
1 W	0145 1.2	0731 3.7	1416 1.7	1947 3.9		16 TH	0140 1.7	0744 3.4	1421 1.8	1957 3.5
2 TH	0252 1.1	0845 3.8	1524 1.4	2059 4.0		17 F	0226 1.6	0840 3.6	1510 1.7	2052 3.6
3 F	0350 1.0	0949 4.0	1620 1.2	2207 4.2		18 SA	0308 1.5	0930 3.8	1555 1.5	2143 3.8
4 SA	0442 1.0	1042 4.2	1709 1.0	2305 4.3		19 SU	0353 1.4	1018 3.9	1641 1.3	2233 4.0
5 SU	0527 0.9	1128 4.3	1754 0.9	● 2355 4.3		20 M	0444 1.3	1104 4.1	1728 1.1	2321 4.1
6 M	0608 1.0	1211 4.4	1836 0.8			21 TU	0535 1.2	1147 4.3	1814 0.9 ○	
7 TU	0040 4.3	0645 1.1	1251 4.4	1917 0.8		22 W	0007 4.2	0623 1.1	1230 4.4	1900 0.8
8 W	0124 4.2	0718 1.2	1329 4.3	1958 0.9		23 TH	0053 4.3	0706 1.1	1313 4.4	1945 0.7
9 TH	0207 4.0	0747 1.3	1408 4.2	2038 1.0		24 F	0140 4.3	0747 1.1	1356 4.4	2030 0.7
10 F	0249 3.9	0801 1.4	1447 4.1	2117 1.2		25 SA	0227 4.2	0824 1.2	1441 4.4	2116 0.7
11 SA	0332 3.7	0814 1.6	1528 3.9	2151 1.4		26 SU	0315 4.1	0859 1.3	1527 4.3	2201 0.8
12 SU	0414 3.5	0852 1.7	1611 3.7	2200 1.6		27 M	0402 4.0	0939 1.4	1615 4.2	2249 1.0
13 M	0459 3.4	0944 1.9	1658 3.6	◑ 2302 1.7		28 TU	0451 3.8	1029 1.5	1707 4.0	◑ 2346 1.2
14 TU	0548 3.3	1053 2.0	1753 3.5			29 W	0545 3.7	1129 1.7	1807 3.8	
15 W	0036 1.7	0645 3.3	1306 2.0	1856 3.4		30 TH	0102 1.3	0647 3.6	1250 1.7	1920 3.7
						31 F	0227 1.4	0800 3.6	1506 1.6	2042 3.8

Chart Datum: 2·10 metres below Ordnance Datum (Local). HAT is 5·0 metres above Chart Datum; see 4.5

9.7.17 HELMSDALE

Highland **58°06'·83N 03°38'·89W** ✿❀🌸🌸🌸

CHARTS AC 115, 1462; Imray C23.

TIDES +0035 Dover; ML 2·2; Duration 0615

Standard Port WICK (→)

Times				Height (metres)			
High Water		Low Water		MHWS	MHWN	MLWN	MLWS
0000	0700	0200	0700	3·5	2·8	1·4	0·7
1200	1900	1400	1900				
Differences HELMSDALE							
+0025	+0015	+0035	+0030	+0·4	+0·3	+0·1	0·0

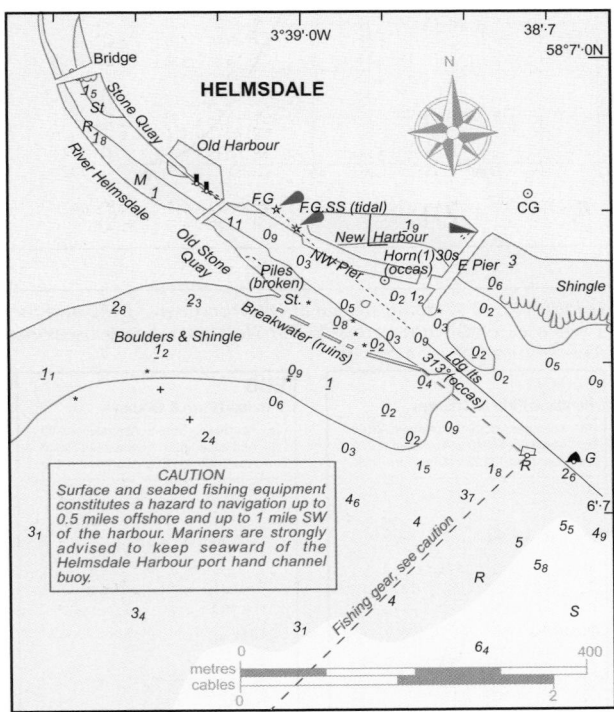

CAUTION
Surface and seabed fishing equipment constitutes a hazard to navigation up to 0.5 miles offshore and up to 1 mile SW of the harbour. Mariners are strongly advised to keep seaward of the Helmsdale Harbour port hand channel buoy.

SHELTER Good, except in strong E/SE'lies. AB on NW pier, approx 1m. 80m of pontoon berths through HM. Limited depths at LWS.

NAVIGATION WPT 58°06'·59N 03°38'·39W, 313°/0·35M to ent; ldg marks are black masts with Or □ topmarks.

- Surface and seabed fishing gear, hazardous to navigation, extends up to 0.5M offshore and 1.0M SW of hbr.
- Essential to pass seaward of Hbr Chan PHM.
- Beware spate coming down river after heavy rain. Shoals both sides of chan and bar build up when river in spate.

LIGHTS AND MARKS See 9.7.4 and chartlet.

R/T VHF Ch 13 16.

TELEPHONE (Code 01431) HM 821692 (Office), 821386 (Home); MRCC (01224) 592334; Police 821222; Marinecall 09068 969641; Dr 821221, or 821225 (Home).

FACILITIES Hbr AB <5m £9, 5m-7m £12, 7m-10m £16, M (See HM), FW, Slip. **Town** P, D, Gas, 🛒, R, Bar, ✉, Ⓑ (Brora), ⇌.

9.7.18 WICK

Highland **58°26'·38N 03°04'·72W** ✿❀❀🌸🌸

CHARTS AC 115, 1462; Imray C23, C68.

TIDES +0010 Dover; ML 2·0; Duration 0625. Wick is a Standard Port. Daily tidal predictions are given below.

Standard Port WICK (→)

Times				Height (metres)			
High Water		Low Water		MHWS	MHWN	MLWN	MLWS
0000	0700	0200	0700	3·5	2·8	1·4	0·7
1200	1900	1400	1900				
Differences DUNCANSBY HEAD							
–0115	–0115	–0110	–0110	–0·4	–0·4	No data	

SHELTER Good, except in strong NNE to SSE winds, to await right conditions for W-bound passage through the Pentland Firth (see 9.7.5). Berth where directed in the Outer Harbour, 2·4m, or in marina in Inner Harbour, 2·0m. NB: The River Hbr (commercial) is leased and must not be entered without prior approval.

NAVIGATION WPT 58°26'·18N 03°03'·39W, 284°/0·72M to S pier. From the N, open up hbr ent before rounding North Head so as to clear drying Proudfoot Rks.

Hbr ent is dangerous in strong E'lies as craft have to turn 90° to port at the end of S pier.

On S side of bay, unlit bn, 300m ENE of LB slip, marks end of ruined bkwtr.

LIGHTS AND MARKS S pier lt, Fl WRG 3s 12m 12/9M, 253°-G-270°-W-286°-R-329°, Bell (2) 10s (fishing). Ldg lts, both FR 5/8m, lead 234° into outer hbr. Traffic signals:

B ● (●) at CG stn on S Head = hbr closed by weather.
B ● (●) at S pier head = caution; hbr temp obstructed.

R/T VHF Ch 14 16 (Mon-Fri 0800-1700).

TELEPHONE (Code 01955) HM 602030; MRCC (01224) 592334; Police 603551; Ⓗ 602434, 602261.

FACILITIES Poss temporary AB on pontoons in Outer Harbour. **Wick Marina** (Inner Harbour) 70 inc 15 Ⓥ dredged to 2·0m; £15/craft up to 10m; max 25m LOA; BH; shower block 50m from marina. **Fish Jetty** D, FW, CH; **Services**: ME, El, 🔧, Slip, Gas, C (15/100 ton). **Town** P, 🛒, R, Bar, ✉, Ⓑ, ⇌, ✈.

PENTLAND FIRTH

(AC 2162, 2581) ▶ *This potentially dangerous chan should only be attempted with moderate winds (less than F4), good vis, no swell and a fair np tide. In such conditions it presents few problems. A safe passage depends on a clear understanding of tidal streams and correct timing. The Admiralty Tidal Stream Atlas for Orkney and Shetland (NP 209) gives large scale vectors and is essential. Even in ideal conditions the races off Duncansby Hd, Swilkie Pt (N end of Stroma), and Rks of Mey (Merry Men of Mey) must be avoided as they are always dangerous to small craft. Also avoid the Pentland Skerries, Muckle Skerry, Old Head, Lother Rock (S Ronaldsay), and Dunnet Hd on E-going flood. For passages across the Firth see CCC SDs for Orkney.* ◀

At E end the Firth is entered between Duncansby Hd and Old Hd (S Ronaldsay), between which lie Muckle Skerry and the Pentland Skerries. Near the centre of Firth are the Islands of Swona (N side) and Stroma (S side). Outer Sound (main chan, 2·5M wide) runs between Swona and Stroma; Inner Sound (1·5M wide) between Stroma and the mainland. Rks of Mey extend about 2ca N of St John's Pt. The W end of the Firth is between Dunnet Hd and Tor Ness (Hoy).

▶*Tide flows strongly around and through the Orkney Islands. The Pentland Firth is a dangerous area for all craft, tidal flows reach 12 knots between Duncansby Head and S Ronaldsay. W of Dunnet Hd and Hoy is less violent. There is little tide within Scapa Flow. Tidal streams reach 8-9kn at sp in the Outer Sound, and 9-12kn between Pentland Skerries and Duncansby Hd. The resultant dangerous seas, very strong eddies and violent races should be avoided by yachts at all costs.*

The E-going stream begins at HW Aberdeen + 0500, and the W-going at HW Aberdeen − 0105. **Duncansby Race** extends ENE towards Muckle Skerry on the SE-going stream, but by HW Aberdeen − 0440 it extends NW from Duncansby Hd. Note: HW at Muckle Skerry is the same time as HW Dover. A persistent race off **Swilkie Pt**, at N end of Stroma, **is very dangerous with a strong W'ly wind over a W-going stream. The most dangerous and extensive race in the Firth is Merry Men of Mey**. It forms off

St John's Pt on W-going stream at HW Aberdeen − 0150 and for a while extends right across to Tor Ness with heavy breaking seas even in fine weather. ◀

FLOOD
Pentland Firth & Orkneys

(a)	Aberdeen +0500 to Aberdeen −0105
(b)	Aberdeen +0340 to Aberdeen −0220
(c)	Aberdeen +0400 to Aberdeen −0150

EBB
Pentland Firth & Orkneys

(a)	Aberdeen −0105 to Aberdeen +0500
(b)	Aberdeen −0220 to Aberdeen +0340
(c)	Aberdeen −0150 to Aberdeen +0400

Passage Westward: This is the more difficult direction due to prevailing W winds. ▶ *Freswick B, 3·5M S of Duncansby Hd, is a good waiting anch; here an eddy runs N for 9 hrs. Round Duncansby Hd close in at HW Aberdeen −0220, as the ebb starts to run W. Take a mid-course through the Inner Sound to appr the Rks of Mey from close inshore. Gills Bay is a temp anch if early; do not pass Rks of Mey until ebb has run for at least 2 hrs. Pass 100m N of the Rks (awash).* ◀

Passage Eastward: ▶ *With a fair wind and tide, no race forms and the passage is easier. Leave Scrabster at local LW+1 so as to be close off Dunnet Hd not before HW Aberdeen +0340 when the E-going flood starts to make. If late, give the Hd a wide berth. Having rounded the Rks of Mey, steer S initially to avoid being set onto the rky S tip of Stroma, marked by unlit SCM bn.* ◀ Then keep mid-chan through the Inner Sound and maintain this offing to give Duncansby Hd a wide berth.

TIME ZONE (UT)
For Summer Time add ONE hour in **non-shaded areas**

WICK LAT 58°26'N LONG 3°05'W
TIMES AND HEIGHTS OF HIGH AND LOW WATERS

Dates in red are **SPRINGS**
Dates in blue are NEAPS

YEAR 2010

NE Scotland

JANUARY

Day	Time	m	Day	Time	m
1 F	0459	1.0	16 SA	0530	1.1
	1123	3.7		1155	3.5
	1732	0.6		1802	0.9
	2356	3.6			
2 SA	0545	0.9	17 SU	0027	3.2
	1210	3.8		0601	1.1
	1820	0.4		1228	3.5
				1833	0.8
3 SU	0046	3.6	18 M	0059	3.2
	0629	0.9		0632	1.1
	1257	3.8		1259	3.5
	1908	0.4		1904	0.8
4 M	0135	3.6	19 TU	0131	3.2
	0713	0.9		0702	1.1
	1343	3.8		1330	3.4
	1957	0.5		1934	0.9
5 TU	0224	3.4	20 W	0202	3.1
	0758	1.0		0733	1.1
	1431	3.7		1403	3.4
	2047	0.6		2006	1.0
6 W	0313	3.3	21 TH	0235	3.0
	0844	1.2		0806	1.2
	1522	3.5		1438	3.3
	2141	0.8		2040	1.1
7 TH	0405	3.1	22 F	0313	2.9
	0936	1.3		0842	1.4
	1618	3.4		1518	3.1
	☽ 2241	1.1		2119	1.2
8 F	0500	3.0	23 SA	0359	2.9
	1043	1.5		0928	1.5
	1720	3.2		1608	3.0
	2347	1.3		☾ 2212	1.4
9 SA	0602	2.9	24 SU	0456	2.8
	1206	1.6		1035	1.6
	1830	3.0		1712	2.9
				2331	1.5
10 SU	0100	1.4	25 M	0605	2.8
	0710	2.9		1216	1.6
	1337	1.5		1829	2.9
	1948	3.0			
11 M	0209	1.4	26 TU	0057	1.5
	0819	3.0		0719	2.9
	1448	1.4		1343	1.5
	2058	3.0		1950	2.9
12 TU	0303	1.4	27 W	0212	1.4
	0917	3.1		0829	3.0
	1539	1.3		1452	1.2
	2153	3.1		2103	3.1
13 W	0346	1.3	28 TH	0313	1.2
	1004	3.3		0929	3.3
	1620	1.1		1547	0.9
	2238	3.1		2204	3.3
14 TH	0423	1.3	29 F	0404	1.1
	1045	3.4		1022	3.5
	1657	1.0		1636	0.6
	2318	3.2		2256	3.5
15 F	0457	1.2	30 SA	0449	0.9
	1121	3.4		1110	3.7
	1730	0.9		1722	0.4
	● 2354	3.2		○ 2345	3.6
			31 SU	0532	0.8
				1156	3.9
				1806	0.2

FEBRUARY

Day	Time	m	Day	Time	m
1 M	0031	3.7	16 TU	0034	3.2
	0613	0.7		0608	0.9
	1241	3.9		1236	3.5
	1850	0.2		1835	0.7
2 TU	0116	3.6	17 W	0102	3.2
	0653	0.7		0637	0.9
	1326	3.9		1305	3.5
	1933	0.3		1904	0.7
3 W	0159	3.5	18 TH	0131	3.2
	0733	0.8		0706	0.9
	1410	3.8		1336	3.4
	2016	0.5		1932	0.8
4 TH	0242	3.3	19 F	0202	3.1
	0814	1.0		0737	1.0
	1456	3.6		1409	3.3
	2101	0.8		2003	1.0
5 F	0327	3.1	20 SA	0236	3.0
	0858	1.2		0812	1.1
	1547	3.3		1448	3.2
	�ö 2151	1.1		2039	1.1
6 SA	0417	2.9	21 SU	0318	2.9
	0955	1.4		0853	1.3
	1646	3.0		1536	3.0
	2255	1.4		2124	1.3
7 SU	0516	2.8	22 M	0411	2.8
	1126	1.5		0953	1.4
	1800	2.8		1640	2.8
				☾ 2239	1.5
8 M	0018	1.6	23 TU	0522	2.7
	0628	2.8		1146	1.5
	1321	1.5		1805	2.8
	1930	2.7			
9 TU	0149	1.6	24 W	0032	1.5
	0751	2.8		0646	2.8
	1440	1.4		1327	1.3
	2048	2.8		1935	2.8
10 W	0251	1.5	25 TH	0159	1.4
	0858	3.0		0806	2.9
	1529	1.2		1440	1.0
	2142	2.9		2053	3.0
11 TH	0334	1.4	26 F	0302	1.2
	0947	3.1		0911	3.2
	1607	1.1		1534	0.7
	2224	3.0		2152	3.3
12 F	0409	1.3	27 SA	0350	1.0
	1027	3.3		1005	3.5
	1640	0.9		1620	0.4
	2301	3.1		2242	3.5
13 SA	0440	1.1	28 SU	0432	0.8
	1103	3.4		1052	3.7
	1710	0.8		1703	0.2
	2334	3.2		○ 2327	3.6
14 SU	0510	1.0			
	1135	3.4			
	1739	0.7			
	●				
15 M	0004	3.2			
	0539	0.9			
	1206	3.5			
	1807	0.7			

MARCH

Day	Time	m	Day	Time	m
1 M	0512	0.6	16 TU	0514	0.8
	1137	3.9		1139	3.4
	1745	0.1		1737	0.6
2 TU	0010	3.6	17 W	0004	3.2
	0551	0.5		0542	0.8
	1221	3.9		1209	3.4
	1825	0.2		1805	0.6
3 W	0051	3.6	18 TH	0033	3.2
	0630	0.5		0612	0.7
	1304	3.9		1240	3.4
	1905	0.3		1833	0.7
4 TH	0130	3.5	19 F	0102	3.2
	0709	0.6		0643	0.8
	1347	3.7		1313	3.3
	1944	0.6		1903	0.8
5 F	0210	3.3	20 SA	0134	3.2
	0748	0.8		0716	0.8
	1431	3.4		1348	3.2
	2023	0.9		1935	0.9
6 SA	0250	3.1	21 SU	0209	3.1
	0830	1.0		0752	1.0
	1519	3.1		1430	3.1
	2105	1.2		2013	1.1
7 SU	0336	2.9	22 M	0250	3.0
	0922	1.3		0837	1.1
	1616	2.8		1521	2.9
	◖ 2202	1.5		2101	1.3
8 M	0432	2.8	23 TU	0344	2.8
	1053	1.5		0943	1.2
	1731	2.6		1628	2.8
	2331	1.7		◖ 2221	1.5
9 TU	0546	2.7	24 W	0456	2.7
	1254	1.5		1138	1.3
	1907	2.6		1755	2.7
10 W	0119	1.7	25 TH	0018	1.5
	0713	2.7		0622	2.8
	1417	1.3		1312	1.1
	2028	2.7		1925	2.8
11 TH	0228	1.6	26 F	0142	1.4
	0829	2.8		0743	2.9
	1505	1.2		1421	0.8
	2120	2.8		2039	3.0
12 F	0311	1.4	27 SA	0242	1.1
	0920	3.0		0849	3.2
	1541	1.0		1514	0.6
	2200	2.9		2134	3.2
13 SA	0345	1.2	28 SU	0328	0.9
	1001	3.1		0943	3.4
	1612	0.9		1559	0.3
	2234	3.1		2221	3.4
14 SU	0416	1.1	29 M	0410	0.7
	1036	3.2		1031	3.6
	1641	0.7		1640	0.2
	2306	3.1		2304	3.5
15 M	0445	0.9	30 TU	0450	0.5
	1108	3.3		1116	3.7
	1709	0.7		1720	0.2
	● 2335	3.2		○ 2344	3.5
			31 W	0529	0.5
				1159	3.8
				1759	0.3

APRIL

Day	Time	m	Day	Time	m
1 TH	0023	3.5	16 F	0004	3.3
	0608	0.5		0550	0.7
	1242	3.7		1218	3.3
	1837	0.4		1807	0.7
2 F	0102	3.4	17 SA	0038	3.3
	0648	0.6		0625	0.7
	1325	3.5		1255	3.3
	1914	0.7		1841	0.8
3 SA	0139	3.3	18 SU	0112	3.2
	0728	0.7		0703	0.7
	1408	3.2		1336	3.2
	1951	1.0		1918	0.9
4 SU	0218	3.1	19 M	0151	3.1
	0810	0.9		0746	0.8
	1455	3.0		1422	3.0
	2030	1.3		2001	1.1
5 M	0301	2.9	20 TU	0236	3.0
	0903	1.1		0838	0.9
	1551	2.7		1517	2.9
	2120	1.5		2056	1.3
6 TU	0354	2.8	21 W	0331	2.9
	1022	1.3		0954	1.0
	1701	2.5		1626	2.7
	◖ 2240	1.7		◖ 2220	1.4
7 W	0503	2.6	22 TH	0442	2.8
	1202	1.4		1129	1.0
	1826	2.5		1747	2.7
				2357	1.4
8 TH	0020	1.7	23 F	0602	2.8
	0623	2.6		1249	0.9
	1331	1.3		1906	2.8
	1947	2.6			
9 F	0145	1.6	24 SA	0113	1.3
	0741	2.7		0717	2.9
	1425	1.1		1355	0.7
	2043	2.7		2014	2.9
10 SA	0234	1.4	25 SU	0214	1.1
	0839	2.8		0822	3.1
	1504	1.0		1448	0.5
	2124	2.8		2108	3.1
11 SU	0312	1.2	26 M	0303	0.9
	0923	3.0		0918	3.3
	1536	0.9		1534	0.4
	2200	3.0		2155	3.2
12 M	0344	1.0	27 TU	0347	0.7
	1000	3.1		1008	3.4
	1607	0.7		1615	0.4
	2232	3.1		2238	3.3
13 TU	0415	0.9	28 W	0429	0.6
	1035	3.2		1055	3.5
	1636	0.7		1655	0.4
	2303	3.2		○ 2319	3.4
14 W	0446	0.8	29 TH	0510	0.5
	1108	3.3		1140	3.5
	1705	0.6		1734	0.5
	● 2333	3.2		2358	3.4
15 TH	0517	0.7	30 F	0552	0.5
	1142	3.3		1223	3.4
	1735	0.6		1812	0.7

Chart Datum: 1·71 metres below Ordnance Datum (Newlyn). HAT is 4·0 metres above Chart Datum; see 4.5

WICK LAT 58°26'N LONG 3°05'W
TIMES AND HEIGHTS OF HIGH AND LOW WATERS

TIME ZONE (UT) For Summer Time add ONE hour in **non-shaded areas**

Dates in red are **SPRINGS**
Dates in blue are **NEAPS**

YEAR 2010

MAY

Day	Time m				Day	Time m			
1 SA	0036 3.4	0633 0.6	1307 3.3	1849 0.9	16 SU	0018 3.3	0614 0.6	1244 3.3	1827 0.8
2 SU	0114 3.3	0714 0.7	1350 3.1	1926 1.1	17 M	0058 3.3	0658 0.6	1329 3.2	1911 0.9
3 M	0152 3.1	0757 0.9	1435 2.9	2005 1.3	18 TU	0141 3.2	0748 0.6	1419 3.1	1959 1.1
4 TU	0234 3.0	0846 1.0	1526 2.7	2050 1.4	19 W	0229 3.2	0845 0.7	1516 2.9	2055 1.2
5 W	0322 2.8	0947 1.1	1625 2.5	2152 1.5	20 TH	0324 3.1	0954 0.8	1620 2.8	◑ 2206 1.3
6 TH	0421 2.7	1101 1.2	1733 2.5	◐ 2312 1.6	21 F	0429 3.0	1109 0.8	1728 2.8	2325 1.3
7 F	0529 2.6	1216 1.2	1844 2.5		22 SA	0539 3.0	1219 0.8	1837 2.8	
8 SA	0032 1.5	0638 2.6	1323 1.1	1947 2.6	23 SU	0037 1.3	0648 3.0	1324 0.7	1941 2.9
9 SU	0138 1.4	0741 2.7	1412 1.0	2036 2.7	24 M	0143 1.1	0754 3.1	1421 0.7	2039 3.0
10 M	0227 1.3	0833 2.8	1452 0.9	2117 2.9	25 TU	0239 1.0	0855 3.2	1509 0.7	2129 3.1
11 TU	0307 1.1	0918 2.9	1527 0.8	2153 3.0	26 W	0329 0.9	0950 3.2	1553 0.7	2215 3.2
12 W	0344 1.0	0959 3.1	1601 0.8	2229 3.1	27 TH	0415 0.7	1040 3.3	1634 0.7	○ 2257 3.3
13 TH	0419 0.8	1039 3.2	1635 0.7	2304 3.2	28 F	0459 0.7	1126 3.3	1714 0.8	2337 3.3
14 F	0455 0.7	1119 3.2	1710 0.7	● 2340 3.3	29 SA	0541 0.6	1210 3.2	1752 0.9	
15 SA	0534 0.6	1200 3.3	1747 0.7		30 SU	0016 3.3	0622 0.6	1252 3.1	1829 1.0
					31 M	0054 3.3	0702 0.7	1333 3.0	1906 1.1

JUNE

Day	Time m				Day	Time m			
1 TU	0132 3.2	0742 0.8	1414 2.9	1943 1.2	16 W	0133 3.4	0745 0.4	1414 3.2	1952 0.9
2 W	0211 3.1	0824 0.9	1458 2.8	2023 1.3	17 TH	0221 3.4	0838 0.5	1506 3.1	2042 1.0
3 TH	0253 3.0	0909 1.0	1545 2.6	2108 1.4	18 F	0313 3.3	0937 0.6	1602 3.0	2139 1.1
4 F	0340 2.9	1003 1.1	1638 2.6	◐ 2206 1.5	19 SA	0411 3.2	1040 0.7	1700 2.9	◐ 2247 1.2
5 SA	0434 2.8	1104 1.2	1736 2.5	2318 1.5	20 SU	0513 3.1	1145 0.8	1802 2.8	
6 SU	0534 2.7	1208 1.2	1836 2.6		21 M	0000 1.3	0619 3.0	1252 0.9	1906 2.8
7 M	0029 1.5	0636 2.7	1308 1.1	1934 2.7	22 TU	0115 1.2	0730 3.0	1355 1.0	2010 2.9
8 TU	0133 1.4	0737 2.7	1401 1.1	2026 2.8	23 W	0224 1.1	0839 3.0	1451 1.0	2107 3.0
9 W	0227 1.2	0833 2.8	1447 1.0	2113 2.9	24 TH	0321 1.0	0935 3.0	1538 1.0	2157 3.1
10 TH	0314 1.1	0925 3.0	1529 0.9	2156 3.1	25 F	0410 0.9	1031 3.1	1620 1.0	2242 3.2
11 F	0357 0.9	1014 3.1	1610 0.9	2238 3.2	26 SA	0453 0.8	1116 3.1	1659 1.0	○ 2323 3.3
12 SA	0439 0.7	1101 3.2	1652 0.8	● 2320 3.3	27 SU	0533 0.7	1158 3.1	1736 1.0	
13 SU	0523 0.6	1147 3.3	1735 0.8		28 M	0001 3.3	0610 0.7	1237 3.1	1811 1.0
14 M	0003 3.4	0608 0.5	1235 3.3	1819 0.8	29 TU	0038 3.3	0646 0.7	1314 3.0	1846 1.0
15 TU	0047 3.5	0655 0.4	1324 3.3	1905 0.8	30 W	0113 3.3	0720 0.7	1350 3.0	1919 1.1

JULY

Day	Time m				Day	Time m			
1 TH	0147 3.2	0755 0.8	1426 2.9	1953 1.1	16 F	0207 3.6	0819 0.3	1446 3.2	2019 0.9
2 F	0223 3.1	0831 0.9	1504 2.8	2030 1.2	17 SA	0255 3.5	0909 0.5	1535 3.1	2108 1.0
3 SA	0302 3.0	0910 1.0	1545 2.7	2112 1.3	18 SU	0347 3.3	1005 0.8	1627 2.9	◐ 2208 1.2
4 SU	0345 2.9	0957 1.1	1633 2.6	◐ 2206 1.4	19 M	0446 3.1	1109 1.0	1725 2.8	2327 1.3
5 M	0436 2.8	1056 1.2	1729 2.6	2321 1.5	20 TU	0554 2.9	1219 1.2	1831 2.8	
6 TU	0537 2.7	1203 1.3	1831 2.7		21 W	0056 1.3	0712 2.8	1335 1.3	1943 2.8
7 W	0039 1.5	0644 2.7	1310 1.3	1935 2.8	22 TH	0221 1.2	0831 2.8	1440 1.3	2050 3.0
8 TH	0149 1.3	0753 2.8	1411 1.2	2034 2.9	23 F	0320 1.1	0933 2.9	1529 1.2	2143 3.1
9 F	0249 1.2	0858 2.9	1505 1.1	2128 3.1	24 SA	0405 0.9	1023 3.0	1609 1.2	2228 3.2
10 SA	0340 0.9	0955 3.1	1554 1.0	2217 3.3	25 SU	0444 0.8	1105 3.1	1645 1.1	2308 3.3
11 SU	0427 0.7	1047 3.3	1640 0.9	● 2303 3.4	26 M	0518 0.7	1143 3.1	1718 1.0	○ 2344 3.4
12 M	0513 0.5	1136 3.4	1724 0.8	2349 3.6	27 TU	0551 0.7	1217 3.1	1750 0.9	
13 TU	0559 0.3	1224 3.5	1808 0.7		28 W	0017 3.4	0622 0.6	1250 3.1	1821 0.9
14 W	0034 3.7	0644 0.2	1312 3.4	1851 0.7	29 TH	0049 3.4	0652 0.7	1321 3.1	1852 0.9
15 TH	0120 3.7	0731 0.2	1359 3.4	1935 0.8	30 F	0121 3.3	0722 0.7	1352 3.0	1922 1.0
					31 SA	0152 3.3	0753 0.8	1424 3.0	1955 1.1

AUGUST

Day	Time m				Day	Time m			
1 SU	0226 3.2	0825 0.9	1459 2.9	2030 1.2	16 M	0323 3.3	0926 1.0	1552 3.0	◑ 2135 1.2
2 M	0304 3.0	0902 1.1	1541 2.8	2113 1.3	17 TU	0421 3.1	1028 1.3	1649 2.9	2302 1.4
3 TU	0350 2.9	0948 1.3	1633 2.7	◑ 2214 1.5	18 W	0532 2.8	1148 1.5	1759 2.8	
4 W	0449 2.8	1059 1.4	1737 2.7	2352 1.5	19 TH	0048 1.4	0659 2.8	1319 1.5	1919 2.8
5 TH	0603 2.7	1228 1.4	1850 2.8		20 F	0217 1.3	0824 2.8	1429 1.5	2032 2.9
6 F	0120 1.4	0723 2.8	1346 1.4	2002 2.9	21 SA	0311 1.1	0923 2.9	1516 1.4	2127 3.1
7 SA	0231 1.2	0839 2.9	1450 1.2	2104 3.1	22 SU	0351 1.0	1008 3.0	1553 1.2	2210 3.2
8 SU	0326 0.9	0940 3.1	1541 1.0	2157 3.3	23 M	0425 0.8	1046 3.1	1625 1.1	2247 3.3
9 M	0414 0.6	1033 3.3	1626 0.9	2246 3.6	24 TU	0455 0.7	1119 3.2	1655 1.0	○ 2320 3.4
10 TU	0458 0.3	1121 3.5	1708 0.7	● 2332 3.7	25 W	0524 0.7	1151 3.2	1725 0.9	2352 3.5
11 W	0542 0.2	1207 3.6	1750 0.6		26 TH	0553 0.6	1220 3.2	1755 0.9	
12 TH	0017 3.9	0625 0.1	1252 3.6	1831 0.6	27 F	0022 3.5	0621 0.6	1249 3.2	1824 0.9
13 F	0102 3.9	0708 0.2	1335 3.5	1912 0.6	28 SA	0052 3.4	0649 0.7	1318 3.2	1853 0.9
14 SA	0146 3.8	0752 0.3	1418 3.4	1953 0.8	29 SU	0122 3.3	0717 0.8	1348 3.1	1924 1.0
15 SU	0233 3.6	0836 0.6	1503 3.2	2039 1.0	30 M	0155 3.2	0747 1.0	1421 3.0	1958 1.1
					31 TU	0233 3.1	0821 1.1	1501 2.9	2038 1.3

Chart Datum: 1·71 metres below Ordnance Datum (Newlyn). HAT is 4·0 metres above Chart Datum; see 4.5

>> **FREE** monthly updates from <<
www.reedsalmanac.co.uk

WICK LAT 58°26'N LONG 3°05'W
TIMES AND HEIGHTS OF HIGH AND LOW WATERS

TIME ZONE (UT)
For Summer Time add ONE hour in **non-shaded areas**

Dates in red are **SPRINGS**
Dates in blue are **NEAPS**

YEAR 2010

NE Scotland

SEPTEMBER

Time	m	Time	m
1 0319	3.0	**16** 0511	2.7
0903	1.3	1112	1.7
W 1550	2.8	TH 1725	2.8
◗ 2134	1.4		
2 0418	2.8	**17** 0031	1.4
1008	1.5	0641	2.7
TH 1655	2.8	F 1253	1.7
2321	1.5	1848	2.8
3 0537	2.7	**18** 0158	1.3
1200	1.6	0805	2.7
F 1816	2.8	SA 1407	1.6
		2004	2.9
4 0101	1.4	**19** 0248	1.1
0705	2.8	0900	2.9
SA 1329	1.5	SU 1453	1.4
1934	2.9	2100	3.1
5 0214	1.1	**20** 0325	1.0
0824	3.0	0942	3.0
SU 1434	1.3	M 1528	1.3
2041	3.2	2142	3.2
6 0308	0.8	**21** 0356	0.9
0925	3.2	1018	3.1
M 1523	1.0	TU 1559	1.1
2136	3.4	2218	3.3
7 0354	0.5	**22** 0425	0.8
1015	3.4	1050	3.2
TU 1606	0.8	W 1628	1.0
2224	3.7	2251	3.4
8 0437	0.3	**23** 0453	0.7
1101	3.6	1118	3.3
W 1647	0.7	TH 1658	0.9
● 2310	3.9	○ 2322	3.5
9 0519	0.1	**24** 0521	0.7
1144	3.7	1149	3.3
TH 1727	0.7	F 1728	0.8
2355	4.0	2353	3.5
10 0601	0.1	**25** 0549	0.7
1226	3.7	1217	3.3
F 1808	0.5	SA 1757	0.8
11 0039	3.9	**26** 0024	3.4
0641	0.3	0617	0.8
SA 1308	3.6	SU 1247	3.3
1848	0.6	1828	0.9
12 0124	3.8	**27** 0057	3.4
0722	0.5	0646	0.9
SU 1348	3.4	M 1318	3.3
1930	0.8	1900	1.0
13 0210	3.5	**28** 0132	3.3
0803	0.8	0717	1.0
M 1431	3.3	TU 1352	3.2
2014	1.0	1936	1.1
14 0259	3.2	**29** 0211	3.1
0848	1.2	0752	1.2
TU 1518	3.1	W 1431	3.1
2110	1.2	2019	1.2
15 0358	3.0	**30** 0259	3.0
0946	1.5	0836	1.4
W 1614	2.9	TH 1521	3.0
◗ 2241	1.4	2120	1.3

OCTOBER

Time	m	Time	m
1 0401	2.8	**16** 0605	2.6
0944	1.6	1158	1.8
F 1627	2.9	SA 1805	2.8
◗ 2307	1.4		
2 0522	2.8	**17** 0114	1.4
1140	1.6	0724	2.7
SA 1749	2.9	SU 1323	1.7
		1919	2.9
3 0040	1.2	**18** 0209	1.2
0649	2.8	0823	2.8
SU 1307	1.5	M 1416	1.5
1908	3.0	2019	3.0
4 0151	1.0	**19** 0249	1.1
0804	3.0	0907	3.0
M 1410	1.3	TU 1455	1.4
2015	3.2	2105	3.1
5 0245	0.7	**20** 0321	1.0
0903	3.2	0943	3.1
TU 1500	1.1	W 1528	1.2
2111	3.5	2144	3.3
6 0331	0.5	**21** 0351	0.9
0952	3.4	1016	3.2
W 1543	0.9	TH 1600	1.1
2201	3.7	2219	3.3
7 0413	0.3	**22** 0420	0.8
1036	3.6	1047	3.3
TH 1624	0.7	F 1631	1.0
● 2248	3.9	2252	3.4
8 0454	0.3	**23** 0449	0.8
1118	3.7	1118	3.4
F 1705	0.6	SA 1703	0.9
2333	3.9	○ 2326	3.5
9 0535	0.3	**24** 0519	0.8
1159	3.7	1148	3.4
SA 1746	0.6	SU 1735	0.9
10 0018	3.8	**25** 0000	3.4
0614	0.5	0549	0.9
SU 1240	3.6	M 1220	3.4
1828	0.6	1808	0.9
11 0103	3.7	**26** 0037	3.4
0654	0.7	0621	1.0
M 1320	3.5	TU 1254	3.4
1911	0.8	1845	0.9
12 0149	3.4	**27** 0116	3.3
0734	1.0	0657	1.1
TU 1401	3.3	W 1331	3.3
1957	1.0	1926	1.0
13 0239	3.2	**28** 0159	3.2
0816	1.3	0737	1.2
W 1447	3.2	TH 1413	3.2
2053	1.2	2014	1.1
14 0336	2.9	**29** 0250	3.0
0907	1.6	0826	1.4
TH 1541	3.0	F 1504	3.1
◗ 2212	1.4	2119	1.2
15 0445	2.7	**30** 0353	2.9
1024	1.8	0934	1.6
F 1648	2.9	SA 1608	3.0
2347	1.4	◗ 2251	1.2
		31 0509	2.9
		1113	1.6
		SU 1725	3.0

NOVEMBER

Time	m	Time	m
1 0013	1.1	**16** 0106	1.4
0626	2.9	0727	2.8
M 1235	1.5	TU 1319	1.7
1839	3.1	1923	2.9
2 0121	1.0	**17** 0159	1.3
0737	3.1	0820	2.9
TU 1340	1.4	W 1412	1.5
1946	3.3	2018	3.0
3 0218	0.8	**18** 0239	1.2
0836	3.2	0902	3.1
W 1433	1.2	TH 1455	1.4
2046	3.5	2104	3.1
4 0306	0.6	**19** 0315	1.1
0926	3.4	0940	3.2
TH 1520	1.0	F 1532	1.2
2139	3.6	2145	3.2
5 0349	0.6	**20** 0348	1.0
1011	3.5	1014	3.3
F 1604	0.8	SA 1607	1.1
2228	3.7	2224	3.3
6 0431	0.6	**21** 0421	1.0
1054	3.6	1049	3.4
SA 1647	0.7	SU 1643	1.0
● 2315	3.7	○ 2303	3.4
7 0512	0.6	**22** 0454	1.0
1136	3.7	1124	3.5
SU 1731	0.7	M 1719	0.9
		2342	3.4
8 0001	3.7	**23** 0529	1.0
0552	0.8	1200	3.5
M 1217	3.6	TU 1757	0.9
1814	0.7		
9 0047	3.5	**24** 0023	3.4
0631	1.0	0606	1.0
TU 1257	3.5	W 1238	3.5
1859	0.8	1838	0.8
10 0133	3.3	**25** 0106	3.4
0711	1.2	0647	1.1
W 1338	3.4	TH 1318	3.5
1944	1.0	1923	0.9
11 0220	3.1	**26** 0152	3.3
0751	1.4	0731	1.2
TH 1421	3.3	F 1402	3.4
2033	1.1	2013	0.9
12 0311	2.9	**27** 0244	3.2
0835	1.6	0820	1.3
F 1509	3.1	SA 1453	3.3
2132	1.3	2113	1.0
13 0409	2.8	**28** 0342	3.1
0931	1.7	0919	1.5
SA 1606	3.0	SU 1551	3.2
◗ 2243	1.4	◗ 2225	1.0
14 0513	2.7	**29** 0448	3.0
1046	1.8	1035	1.5
SU 1712	2.9	M 1659	3.2
2358	1.4	2339	1.0
15 0622	2.7	**30** 0556	3.0
1207	1.8	1154	1.5
M 1820	2.9	TU 1808	3.2

DECEMBER

Time	m	Time	m
1 0047	1.0	**16** 0049	1.4
0702	3.0	0716	2.8
W 1305	1.4	TH 1316	1.7
1916	3.3	1920	2.9
2 0148	1.0	**17** 0148	1.4
0805	3.2	0813	2.9
TH 1408	1.3	F 1416	1.5
2022	3.3	2020	3.0
3 0242	0.9	**18** 0237	1.3
0900	3.3	0901	3.1
F 1503	1.1	SA 1505	1.4
2121	3.4	2112	3.1
4 0330	0.9	**19** 0319	1.2
0950	3.4	0943	3.2
SA 1553	1.0	SU 1547	1.2
2215	3.5	2200	3.3
5 0414	0.9	**20** 0358	1.2
1035	3.5	1024	3.4
SU 1639	0.9	M 1627	1.0
● 2304	3.5	2244	3.3
6 0455	0.9	**21** 0436	1.1
1118	3.6	1104	3.5
M 1723	0.8	TU 1707	0.9
2350	3.5	○ 2328	3.4
7 0536	1.0	**22** 0516	1.0
1159	3.6	1144	3.6
TU 1806	0.8	W 1749	0.7
8 0034	3.4	**23** 0012	3.5
0614	1.1	0556	1.0
W 1239	3.6	TH 1226	3.7
1847	0.8	1831	0.6
9 0117	3.3	**24** 0058	3.5
0651	1.2	0638	1.0
TH 1318	3.5	F 1308	3.7
1928	0.9	1916	0.6
10 0159	3.2	**25** 0144	3.4
0728	1.3	0722	1.0
F 1358	3.4	SA 1352	3.6
2008	1.0	2004	0.7
11 0241	3.0	**26** 0232	3.3
0805	1.4	0807	1.1
SA 1439	3.3	SU 1440	3.6
2051	1.2	2055	0.8
12 0327	2.9	**27** 0323	3.2
0846	1.5	0856	1.3
SU 1524	3.1	M 1532	3.4
2139	1.3	2154	0.9
13 0417	2.8	**28** 0419	3.1
0937	1.6	0955	1.4
M 1615	3.0	TU 1632	3.3
◗ 2238	1.4	◗ 2301	1.0
14 0514	2.7	**29** 0520	3.0
1045	1.7	1110	1.5
TU 1714	2.9	W 1738	3.2
2344	1.4		
15 0615	2.7	**30** 0011	1.2
1203	1.7	0625	3.0
W 1817	2.9	TH 1232	1.5
		1850	3.1
		31 0121	1.2
		0734	3.2
		F 1351	1.4
		2006	3.2

Chart Datum: 1·71 metres below Ordnance Datum (Newlyn). HAT is 4·0 metres above Chart Datum; see 4.5

Scrabster – Orkney Islands

WGS84 DATUM

9.7.19   SCRABSTER

Highland 58°36'·61N 03°32'·61W ✿✿✿⚓⚓✿✿✿

CHARTS AC 1954, 2162, 1462; Imray C68.

TIDES -0240 Dover; ML 3·2; Duration 0615

Standard Port WICK (←)

Times				Height (metres)			
High Water		Low Water		MHWS	MHWN	MLWN	MLWS
0200	0700	0100	0700	3·5	2·8	1·4	0·7
1400	1900	1300	1900				
Differences SCRABSTER							
-0255	-0225	-0240	-0230	+1·5	+1·2	+0·8	+0·3
GILLS BAY							
-0150	-0150	-0202	-0202	+0·7	+0·7	+0·6	+0·3
STROMA							
-0115	-0115	-0110	-0110	-0·4	-0·5	-0·1	-0·2
LOCH ERIBOLL (Portnancon)							
-0340	-0255	-0315	-0255	+1·6	+1·3	+0·8	+0·4
KYLE OF DURNESS							
-0350	-0350	-0315	-0315	+1·1	+0·7	+0·4	-0·1
SULE SKERRY (59°05'N 04°24'W)							
-0320	-0255	-0315	-0250	+0·4	+0·3	+0·2	+0·1
RONA (59°08'N 05°49'W)							
-0410	-0345	-0330	-0340	-0·1	-0·2	-0·2	-0·1

SHELTER Very good except for swell in NW and N winds. Yachts usually lie in the Inner (0·9–1·2m) or Centre Basins (0·9–2·7m). ⚓ is not advised.

- A good hbr to await the right conditions for E-bound passage through Pentland Firth (see 9.7.5).
- Beware floating creel lines in W of hbr.

NAVIGATION WPT 58°36'·58N 03°32'·09W, 278°/0·25M to E pier lt. Can be entered H24 in all weathers. Beware FVs and the Orkney ferries.

LIGHTS AND MARKS No ldg marks/lts but entry is simple once the conspic ice plant tr and/or pier lts have been located. Do not confuse hbr lts with the shore lts of Thurso.

R/T Call HM VHF Ch 12 16 (H24) for berthing directions, before entering hbr. From the W reception is very poor due to masking by Holborn Head.

TELEPHONE (Code 01847) HM 892779, Mobile 07803 290366, www.scrabster.co.uk; MRCC (01224) 592334; Marinecall 09068 969641; Police 893222; Dr 893154.

FACILITIES Hbr AB £8.00 (£35/week), FW, D, P (cans), ME, El, C (15, 30 & 99 ton mobiles), Slip, CH, ⛽; **Pentland Firth YC** M, R, Bar, Showers (keys held by Duty HM). **Thurso** ⚒, R, Bar, ⊠, Ⓑ, ⇌, ✈ (Wick). **Ferries**: Stromness; 3/day; 1½ Hrs; Northlink (www.northlinkferries.co.uk). Faroe Islands (Torshavn); weekly (seasonal); 12 Hrs; Smyril (www.smyril.co.uk). Bergen; weekly (seasonal); 16 Hrs; Smyril.

ANCHORAGES BETWEEN SCRABSTER AND CAPE WRATH

KYLE OF TONGUE, Highland, **58°31'·97N 04°22'·67W** (ent). AC 2720, 1954. HW +0050 on Ullapool; HW ht –0·4m; see 9.7.19. The Kyle runs about 7M inland.

- *Entry (see 9.7.5) should not be attempted in strong N winds.*

⚓ at Talmine (W of Rabbit Is) protected from all but NE winds; at Skullomie Hr, protected from E'lies; off Mol na Coinnle, a small bay on SE side of Eilean nan Ron, protected from W and N winds; off S of Rabbit Is, protected from W to N winds. No ldg lts/marks. Facilities: Limited ⛒ at Talmine (½M from slip) or at Coldbachie (1½M from Skullomie).

LOCH ERIBOLL, Highland, **58°32'·58N 04°37'·48W**. AC 2076. HW – 0345 on Dover; ML 2·7m. See 9.7.19. Enter between Whiten Hd and Klourig Is in W sector of White Hd lt. See 9.7.4.

In SW winds fierce squalls funnel down the loch.

Yachts can enter Rispond Hbr, access approx HW ± 3, and dry out alongside; no lts/marks and very limited facilities. Good ⚓s at: Rispond Bay on W side of loch, ent good in all but E winds, in approx 5m; off Portnancon in 5·5m; at the head of the loch; Camus an Duin and in bays to N and S of peninsula at Heilam on E side of loch. Beware numerous marine farms in the S half of the loch.

PENTLAND FIRTH TO CAPE WRATH

(AC 1954) Dunnet B, S of Dunnet Hd (lt) gives temp anch in E or S winds, but dangerous seas enter in NW'lies. On W side of Thurso B is Scrabster sheltered from S and W. ▶ *Between Holborn Hd and Strathy Pt the E-going stream begins at HW Ullapool –0150, and the W-going at HW Ullapool + 0420, sp rates 1·8kn. Close to Brims Ness off Ushat Hd the sp rate is 3kn, and there is often turbulence.*◀

SW of Ushat Hd the Dounreay power stn is conspic, near shore. Dangers extend 2½ca seaward off this coast.▶ *Along E side of Strathy Pt (lt) an eddy gives almost continuous N-going stream, but there is usually turbulence off the Pt where this eddy meets the main E or W stream.*◀ Several small bays along this coast give temp anch in offshore winds, but should not be used or approached with wind in a N quarter.

Kyle of Tongue is entered from E through Caol Raineach, S of Eilean nan Ron, or from N between Eilean Iosal and Cnoc Glass. There is no chan into the kyle W of Rabbit Is, to which a drying spit extends 0·5M NNE from the mainland shore. Further S there is a bar across entrance to inner part of kyle. There are anchs on SE side of Eilean nan Ron, SE side of Rabbit Is, off Skullomie, or S of Eilean Creagach off Talmine. Approach to the latter runs close W of Rabbit Islands, but beware rks to N and NW of them.

Loch Eriboll (AC 2076) provides secure anchs, but in strong winds violent squalls blow down from mountains. Eilean Cluimhrig lies on W side of entrance; the E shore is fringed with rks up to 2ca offshore. At White Hd (lt) the loch narrows to 6ca. There are chans W and E of Eilean Choraidh. Best anchs in Camas an Duin (S of Ard Neackie) or in Rispond B close to entrance (but not in E winds, and beware Rispond Rk which dries).

The coast to C Wrath is indented, with dangers extending 3ca off the shore and offlying rks and Is. Once a yacht has left Loch Eriboll she is committed to a long and exposed passage until reaching Loch Inchard. The Kyle of Durness is dangerous if the wind or sea is onshore. ▶ *Give Cape Wrath a wide berth when wind-against-tide which raises a severe sea.*◀ A firing exercise area extends 8M E of C. Wrath, and 4M offshore. When in use, R flags or pairs of R lts (vert) are shown from E and W limits, and yachts should keep clear.

ORKNEY ISLANDS

(AC 2249, 2250) The Islands are mostly indented and rocky, but with sandy beaches especially on NE sides. ▶*Pilotage is easy in good vis, but in other conditions great care is needed since tides run strongly. For details refer to **Clyde Cruising Club's Orkney Sailing Directions** and the **Admiralty Tidal Atlas NP 209**. When cruising in Orkney it is essential to understand and use the tidal streams to the best advantage, avoiding the various tide races and overfalls, particularly near sp.*◀

A good engine is needed since, for example, there are many places where it is dangerous to get becalmed. Swell from the Atlantic or North Sea can contribute to dangerous sea conditions, or penetrate to some of the anchorages. During summer months winds are not normally unduly strong, and can be expected to be Force 7 or more on about two days a month. But in winter the wind reaches this strength for 10-15 days per month, and gales can be very severe in late winter and early spring. Cruising conditions are best near midsummer, when of course the hours of daylight are much extended.

Stronsay Firth and Westray Firth run SE/NW through the group. The many good anchs include: Deer Sound (W of Deer Ness); B of Firth, B of Isbister, and off Balfour in Elwick B (all leading from Wide Firth); Rysa Sound, B of Houton, Hunda Sound (in Scapa Flow); Rousay Sound; and Pierowall Road (Westray). Plans for some of these are on AC 2622. There is a major oil terminal and prohibited area at Flotta, on the S side of Scapa Flow.

▶ *Tide races or dangerous seas occur at the entrances to most of the firths or sounds when the stream is against strong winds. This applies particularly to Hoy Sound, Eynhallow Sound, Papa Sound (Westray), Lashy Sound, and North Ronaldsay Firth. Also off Mull Head, over Dowie Sand, between Muckle Green Holm and War Ness (where violent turbulence may extend right across the firth), between Faraclett Head and Wart Holm, and off Sacquoy Hd. Off War Ness the SE-going stream begins at HW Aberdeen + 0435, and the NW-going at HW Aberdeen – 0200, sp rates 7kn.* ◀

9.7.20 ORKNEY ISLANDS

The Orkney Islands number about 70, of which some 24 are inhabited. They extend 5 to 50M NNE from Duncansby Hd, are mostly low-lying, but Hoy in the SW of the group reaches 475m (1560ft). Coasts are rocky and much indented, but there are many sandy beaches. A passage with least width of about 3M runs NW/SE through the group. The islands are separated from Scotland by the Pentland Firth, a very dangerous stretch of water. The principal island is Mainland (or Pomona) on which stands Kirkwall, the capital. For inter island ferries see www.orkneyferries.co.uk.

Severe gales blow in winter and early spring. The climate is mild but windy, and very few trees grow. There are LBs at Longhope, Stromness and Kirkwall.

CHARTS AC 2162, 2250 and 2249, at medium scale. For larger scale charts, see under individual hbrs. Imray C68.

TIDES Wick (9.7.18) is the Standard Port. Tidal streams are strong, particularly in Pentland Firth and in the islands' firths and sounds.

SHELTER/MARINA CHARGES There are piers (fender board advised) at all main islands. See 9.7.5 for details of berthing charges in marinas or on piers throughout the Orkney Islands (except St Margaret's Hope). Some of the many ‡s are listed below:

MAINLAND Scapa Bay: good except in S winds. No yacht berths alongside pier due to heavy hbr traffic. Only ents to Scapa Flow are via Hoy Snd, Hoxa Snd or W of Flotta.
St Marys (Holm/Ham): **58°53'·80N 02°54'·50W**; N side of Kirk Sound; ‡ in B of Ayre or berth E side of Pier, HW±4. P & D (cans), ✉, Bar, R, Bus to Kirkwall & Burwick Ferry.

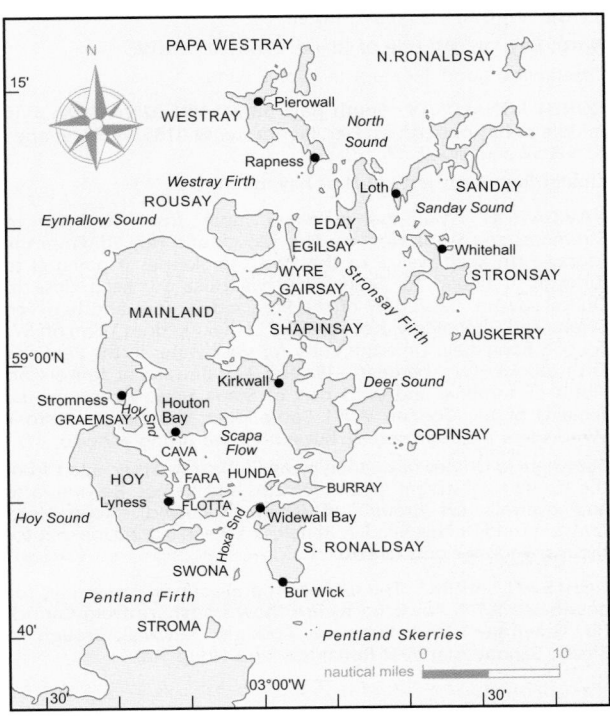

Kirk Sound (E ent): ⚓ N of Lamb Holm; beware fish cages.
Deer Sound: ⚓ in Pool of Mirkady or off pier on NW side of sound; very good shelter, no facilities.
Hunda Sound: good ⚓ in all winds.

SOUTH RONALDSAY/BURRAY St Margaret's Hope/Water Sound: ☀🏪⚓♨🏩. Ldg Lts, F.G, 174°. ⚓ in centre of bay; or AB £7/day at pier (but limited space and keep clear of ferry berth on S side of pier), beware salmon farm. HM ☎ 01856 831440, mob 07879 688040; Dr 831206. FW, P & D (cans), 🛒, R, Bar, ✉, Bus Kirkwall, Vehicle ferry to Gill's Bay/Caithness.

Widewall Bay: ⚓ sheltered except SW'lies.

FLOTTA 58°50'·20N 03°07'·90W; berth on Sutherland Pier, SW of oil terminal. HM ☎ 01856 701411. P & D (cans), 🛒, ✉.

HOY Long Hope: 58°48'·07N 03°12'·25W; ⚓ E of Pier, used by ferry, or berth on pier (safest at slack water). 2 ⚓'s < 18 tonnes close to Pier. ☎ 01856 701263; Dr 701209. Facilities: FW, P & D (cans), ✉, 🛒, Bar.

Lyness: 58°50'·20N 03°11'·40W; berth on Pier; avoid disused piles; ⚓ in Ore Bay. HM ☎ 01856 791387. FW, P & D (cans), Bar, ✉. Beware fish cages.

Pegal Bay: good ⚓ except in strong W winds.

ROUSAY Wyre Sound: 59°09'·40N 02°44'·70W; ⚓ E of Rousay Pier or berth on it ✉, 🛒, R. Piermaster ☎ 01856 821261.

EDAY Fersness Bay: good holding, sheltered from S winds. Dr ☎ 01857 622243.

Backaland Bay: 59°09'·40N 02°44'·70W: berth on Pier clear of ferry; Piermaster ☎ 01856 622282; or ⚓ to NW. Beware cross tides. FW, P & D, 🛒, ✉.

Calf Sound: ⚓ in Carrick B; good shelter from SW-NW'lies.

PAPA WESTRAY Bay of Moclett 58°21'·40N 02°26'·30W: Good ⚓ but open to S. Pier . Piermaster ☎ 01857 644259;

South Wick: ⚓ off the old pier or ESE of pier off Holm of Papa. Backaskaill: P & D (cans), 🛒, ✉.

SANDAY Loth Bay: 59°11'·50N 02°41'·80W; berth on Pier clear of ferry. Piermaster ☎ 01857 600227; Beware strong tides.

Kettletoft Bay: 59°13'·90N 02°35'·80W; ⚓ in bay or berth on Pier, very exposed to SE'lies. HM ☎ (01857) 600227, Dr 600221; P & D (cans), FW, Gas, ✉, Ⓑ, 🛒, hotel.

North Bay: on NW side of island, exposed to NW.

Otterswick: good ⚓ except in N or E winds.

NORTH RONALDSAY South Bay: 58°21'·40N 02°26'·30W; ⚓ in middle of bay or berth on Pier. Piermaster ☎ 01857 633239; open to S & W and swell. 🛒, ✉.

Linklet Bay: ⚓ off jetty at N of bay, open to E.

NAVIGATION From the mainland, appr from Scrabster to Stromness and Scapa Flow via Hoy Mouth and Hoy Sd. From the Moray Firth keep well E of the Pentland Skerries if going N to Kirkwall. If bound for Scapa Flow via Hoxa Sd, keep close to Duncansby Hd, passing W of the Pentland Skerries and between Swona and S Ronaldsay. Keep clear of Lother Rk (dries 1·8m) off SW tip of S Ronaldsay. Time this entry for slack water in the Pentland Firth (about HW Aberdeen –1¾ and +4). Beware of tankers off Flotta oil terminal and in S part of Scapa Flow, where are the remains of the German WW1 Battle Fleet; classified as Historic Wrecks (see 9.0.3) protected, but authorised diving allowed.

Elsewhere in Orkney navigation is easy in clear weather, apart from the strong tidal streams in all the firths and sounds. Beware races and overfalls off Brough of Birsay (Mainland), Noup Head (Westray) and Dennis Head (N Ronaldsay). Keep a good lookout for the many lobster pots (creels).

LIGHTS AND MARKS The main hbrs and sounds are well lit; for details see 9.7.4. Powerful lts are shown offshore from Cantick Hd, Graemsay Island, Copinsay, Auskerry, Kirkwall, Brough of Birsay, Sanday Island, N Ronaldsay and Noup Hd.

R/T Orkney Hbrs Navigation Service (call: *Orkney Hbr Radio*, Ch 09 11 20 16 (H24)) covers Scapa Flow and apprs, Wide Firth, Shapinsay Sound and Kirkwall Bay.

TELEPHONE Area Code for islands SW of Stronsay and Westray Firths is 01856; islands to the NE are 01857.

MEDICAL SERVICES Doctors are available at Kirkwall, Stromness, Rousay, Hoy, Shapinsay, Eday, S and N Ronaldsay, Stronsay, Sanday and Westray (Pierowall); Papa Westray is looked after by Westray. The only hospital (and dentist) are at Kirkwall. Serious cases are flown to Aberdeen (1 hour).

MARINE FARMS Fish cages/farms approx 30m x 50m may be found anywhere in sheltered waters within anchoring depths. Some are well buoyed, others are marked only by poles. Too many to list but the following will show the scale of the operations:

Beware **salmon cages** (may be marked by Y buoys/lts) at:

Kirkwall Bay	Toy Ness (Scapa Flow)
Rysa Sound	St Margaret's Hope
Bring Deeps	Backaland Bay (Eday)
Pegal Bay (Hoy)	Hunda Sound
Lyrawa Bay	Kirk Sound
Ore Bay (Hoy)	Carness Bay
Widewall Bay (S Ronaldsay)	Bay of Ham
	Bay of London (Eday)

Beware **oysters and longlines** at:

Widewall Bay	Bay of Firth
Swanbister Bay	Damsay Sound
Water Sound	Millburn Bay (Gairsay)
Hunda Sound	Pierowall
Deer Sound	Bay of Skaill (Westray)
Inganess Bay	Longhope

MINOR HARBOURS IN THE ORKNEY ISLANDS

HOUTON BAY, Mainland, 58°54'·85N 03°11'·33W. AC 35, 2568. HW –0140 on Dover, –0400 on Aberdeen; HW ht +0·3m on Kirkwall; ML 1·8m; Duration 0615. ⚓ in the bay in approx 5·5m at centre, sheltered from all winds. Ent is to the E of Holm of Houton; ent chan dredged 3·5m for 15m each side of ldg line. Keep clear of shipping/ferries plying to Flotta. Ldg lts 316°: front Fl G 3s 8m, rear FG 16m; both R △ on W pole, B bands. Ro Ro terminal in NE corner marked by Iso R 4s with SHM Fl G on edge of ldg line. Bus to Kirkwall; Slip close E of piers. Yachtsmen may contact M.Grainger ☎ 01856 811397 for help.

SHAPINSAY, Orkney Islands, 59°01'·97N 02°54'·10W. AC 2249, 2584. HW –0015 on Dover, –0330 on Aberdeen; HW ht –1·0m on Aberdeen. Good shelter in Elwick Bay off Balfour on SW end of island in 2·5-3m. Enter bay passing W of Helliar Holm which has lt Fl WRG 10s on S end. Keep mid-chan. Balfour Pier lt Q WRG 5m 3/2M; vis 270°-G-010°-W-020°-R-090°. Piermaster ☎ 01856 711358; Tides in The String reach 5kn at sp. Facilities: FW, P & D (cans), ✉, shop, Bar.

AUSKERRY, Orkney Islands, 59°02'·02N 02°34'·65W. AC 2250. HW –0010 on Dover, –0315 on Aberdeen, HW ht -1m on Aberdeen. Small island at ent to Stronsay Firth with small hbr on W side. Safe ent and good shelter except in SW winds. Ent has 3·5m; 1·2m alongside pier. Yachts can lie secured between ringbolts at ent and the pier. Auskerry Sound and Stronsay Firth are dangerous with wind over tide. Auskerry lt at S end, Fl 20s 34m 18M, W tr. No facilities.

PIEROWALL, Westray, 59°19'·32N 02°58'·51W. AC 2250, 2622. HW –0135 on Dover; ML 2·2m; Duration 0620. See 9.7.23. The bay is a good ⚓ in 2-7m and well protected. Marina pontoons in deep water alongside pier at Gill Pt. From S, beware Skelwick Skerry rks, and from the N the rks extending approx 1ca off Vest Ness. The N ent via Papa Sound needs local knowledge; tide race on the ebb. A dangerous tide race runs off Mull Hd at the N of Papa Westray. Lights: E Pier Hd Fl WRG 3s 7m 11/7M. W Pier Hd 2 FR (vert) 4/6m 3M. VHF Ch 16. HM ☎ (01857) 677216. **Marina** ☎ 07810 465784 AB £15/craft, FW, ⚡. Facilities: P & D (cans), Gas, Bar, ✉, Ⓑ, R, 🛒. Dr ☎ (01857) 677209.

RAPNESS: 58°14'·90N 02°51'·50W, berth on Pier clear of Ro-Ro. Piermaster ☎ 01857 677212; Open to SSW.

9.7.21 STROMNESS

Orkney Islands, Mainland 58°57'·78N 03°17'·72W ❀❀❀❀❀❀❀❀❀❀

CHARTS AC 2249, 2568; Imray C68.

TIDES -0145 Dover; ML 2·0; Duration 0620

Standard Port WICK (←—)

Times				Height (metres)			
High Water		Low Water		MHWS	MHWN	MLWN	MLWS
0000	0700	0200	0700	3·5	2·8	1·4	0·7
1200	1900	1400	1900				
Differences STROMNESS							
–0225	–0135	–0205	–0205	+0·1	–0·1	0·0	0·0
ST MARY'S (Scapa Flow)							
–0140	–0140	–0140	–0140	–0·2	–0·2	0·0	–0·1
BURRAY NESS (Burray)							
+0005	+0005	+0015	+0015	–0·2	–0·3	–0·1	–0·1
WIDEWALL BAY (S Ronaldsay)							
–0155	–0155	–0150	–0150	+0·1	–0·1	–0·1	–0·3
BUR WICK (S Ronaldsay)							
–0100	–0100	–0150	–0150	–0·1	–0·1	+0·2	+0·1
MUCKLE SKERRY (Pentland Firth)							
–0025	–0025	–0020	–0020	–0·9	–0·8	–0·4	–0·3

SHELTER Very good. Northern Lights Board have sole use of pier near to ldg lts. Marina in N of hbr; or ⚓ where shown.

NAVIGATION WPT 58°56'·93N 03°17'·00W, 317°/0·9M to front ldg lt.

- Entry from the W should not be attempted with strong wind against tide due to heavy overfalls.
- If entering against the ebb, stand on to avoid being swept onto Skerry of Ness.
- Tides in Hoy Sound are >7kn at springs. No tidal stream in hbr.

LIGHTS AND MARKS For Hoy Sound, ldg lts 104° on Graemsay Is: front Iso 3s 17m 15M, W tr; rear Oc WR 8s 35m 20/16M, ldg sector is 097°-R-112°. Skerry of Ness, Fl WG 4s 7m 7/4M; shore-W-090°-G-shore. Hbr ldg lts 317°, both FR 29/39m 11M (H24), W trs, vis 307°-327°. Stromness Marina ent. Fl(2)R 5s.

R/T VHF Ch 14 16 (0900-1700 LT). (See also 9.7.22.)

TELEPHONE (Code 01856) HM 850744; Fuel 851286; MRCC 01595 692976; Marinecall 09068 969641; Police 850222; Dr 850205; Dentist 850658.

FACILITIES Stromness Marina: ☎ 07810 465825, 10Ⓥ £14.50/craft, ⏍, FW, Showers, 🚻, ⚒, El, Ⓔ, ME, C (mobile, 30 ton), P & D (0800-2100 ☎ 8851286), Slip. Town FW, D, 🏪, R, Bar, Gas, ✉, ◎, Ⓑ, 🚂 (Ferries to Scrabster, bus to Thurso), ✈ (Kirkwall). Yachtsmen may contact for help/advice: Orkney Marinas ☎ 879600 or Piermaster ☎ 850744.

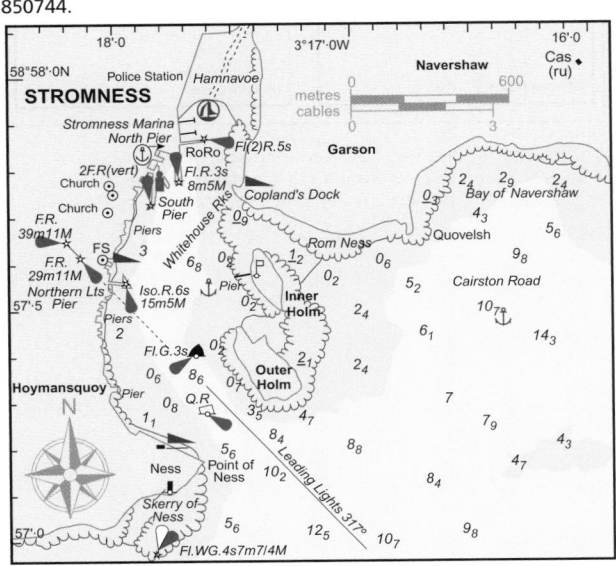

9.7.22 KIRKWALL

Orkney Islands, Mainland 58°59'·30N 02°57'·70W ❀❀❀❀❀❀❀❀❀❀

CHARTS AC 2250, 2249, 2584, 1553; Imray C68.

TIDES –0045 Dover; ML 1·8; Duration 0620

Standard Port WICK (←—)

Times				Height (metres)			
High Water		Low Water		MHWS	MHWN	MLWN	MLWS
0000	0700	0200	0700	3·5	2·8	1·4	0·7
1200	1900	1400	1900				
Differences KIRKWALL							
–0042	–0042	–0041	–0041	–0·5	–0·4	–0·1	–0·1
DEER SOUND							
–0040	–0040	–0035	–0035	–0·3	–0·3	–0·1	–0·1
TINGWALL							
–0200	–0125	–0145	–0125	–0·4	–0·4	–0·1	–0·1

SHELTER Good except in N winds or W gales when there is a surge at the ent. Berth in marina on E of main pier, or SW end of main pier in inner hbr (very full in Jun/Jul). Safe ⚓ between pier and Crow Ness Pt. RoRo terminal in NW of bay.

NAVIGATION WPT 59°01'·37N 02°57'·10W, 188°/2·2M to pier hd lt. Appr in W sector of pier hd lt. Bay is shoal to SW.

LIGHTS AND MARKS See 9.7.4 and chartlet. Appr with St Magnus Cathedral (conspic) brg about 185°.

R/T Kirkwall Hbr Radio VHF Ch 14 16 (0800-1700 LT). Orkney Hbrs Navigation Service, call: VTS Orkney Ch 09 11 20 16 (0915–1715).

TELEPHONE (Code 01856) HM 872292; Port Office 873636; Fuel 873105; MRCC (01595) 692976; Weather 873802; Marinecall 09068 969641; Police 872241; Dr 888000 (Ⓗ).

FACILITIES Kirkwall Marina ☎ 879600 (berths 07810 465835), 71 inc Ⓥ £14.50/craft. Pier P & D (HO ☎ 873105), FW, CH, C (mob, 25 ton); N and E Quays M; Orkney SC ☎ 872331, M, L, C, AB (£15/4days), Slip. Town @ Library & Support Training Orkney (HO) P, D, ME, El, ⚒, CH, 🏪, Gas, R, Bar, Ⓑ, ◎, ✉, Ferries to Scrabster, Aberdeen and Shetland see 9.0.4, ✈.

9.7.23 STRONSAY

Orkney Islands, Stronsay 59°08'·57N 02°36'·01W ❄❄❄❄❄❄❄

CHARTS AC 2250, 2622; Imray C68.

TIDES As Dover; ML 1·7; Duration 0620

Standard Port WICK (←)

Times				Height (metres)			
High Water		Low Water		MHWS	MHWN	MLWN	MLWS
0000	0700	0200	0700	3·5	2·8	1·4	0·7
1200	1900	1400	1900				
Differences WHITEHALL (Stronsay)							
–0030	–0030	–0025	–0030	–0·1	0·0	+0·2	+0·2
LOTH (Sanday)							
–0052	–0052	–0058	–0058	–0·1	0·0	+0·3	+0·4
EGILSAY (Rousay Sound)							
–0125	–0125	–0125	–0125	–0·1	0·0	+0·2	+0·1
KETTLETOFT PIER (Sanday)							
–0030	–0025	–0025	–0025	0·0	0·0	+0·2	+0·2
RAPNESS (Westray)							
–0205	–0205	–0205	–0205	+0·1	0·0	+0·2	0·0
PIEROWALL (Westray)							
–0150	–0150	–0145	–0145	+0·2	0·0	0·0	–0·1

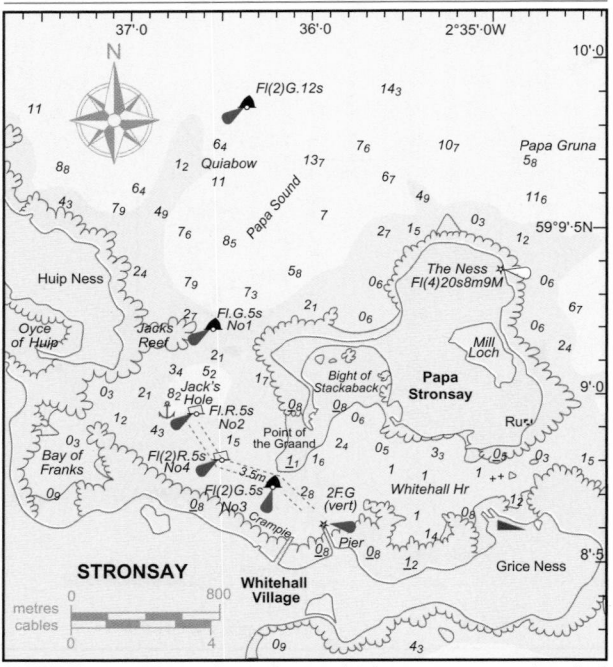

SHELTER Good from all winds. Good ⚓ between seaward end of piers, or berth on outer end of W pier and contact HM. The extended E pier head is berth for Ro-Ro ferry. There are many other sheltered ⚓s around the bay.

NAVIGATION WPT 59°09'·82N 02°36'·31W, Quiabow SHM lt buoy, 189°/6·5ca to No 1 lt buoy. 800m NE of Huip Ness is Quiabow, a submerged rk. Jack's Reef extends 400m E from Huip Ness, and is marked by No 1 SHM lt buoy. A bank extends 350m SW from Papa Stronsay. Crampie Shoal is in mid-chan, marked by No 3 buoy. The buoyed chan to Whitehall pier is dredged 3·5m. Spit to E of Whitehall pier extends 400m N. The E ent is narrow and shallow and should not be attempted.

LIGHTS AND MARKS See chartlet.

R/T See Kirkwall.

TELEPHONE (Code 01857) Piermaster 616317; MRCC (01595) 692976; Marinecall 09068 969641; Police (01856) 872241; Dr 616321.

FACILITIES **W Pier** M, L, AB; **Main (E) Pier** M, L, FW, AB clear of ferry. **Village (Whitehall)** P, D, 🛒, Bar, ✉, Ⓑ, ⇆ (Ferry to Scrabster, bus to Thurso), ✈.

SHETLAND ISLANDS

(AC 3281, 3282, 3283) ▶ *These Islands mostly have bold cliffs and are relatively high, separated by narrow sounds through which the tide runs strongly, so that in poor vis great care is needed. Avoid sp tides, swell and wind against tide conditions. The tidal flow around the Shetland Islands rotates as the cycle progresses. When the flood begins, at –0400 HW Dover, the tidal flow is to the E, at HW Dover it is S, at Dover +0300 it is W, and at –0600 Dover it is N.◀*

Although there are many secluded and attractive anchs, remember that the weather can change very quickly, with sudden shifts of wind. Also beware salmon fisheries and mussel rafts (unlit) in many Voes, Sounds and hbrs. Lerwick is the busy main port and capital; other hbrs are Scalloway, Vaila Sound and Balta Sound. Refer to the CCC's *Shetland Sailing Directions.*

▶ *Coming from the S, beware a most violent and dangerous race (roost) off Sumburgh Hd (at S end of Mainland) on both streams. Other dangerous areas include between Ve Skerries and Papa Stour; the mouth of Yell Sound with strong wind against N-going stream; and off Holm of Skaw (N end of Unst). Tidal streams run mainly NW/SE and are not strong except off headlands and in the major sounds; the Admiralty Tidal Atlas NP 209 gives detail. The sp range is about 2m.◀*

The 50M passage from Orkney can conveniently be broken by a stop at Fair Isle (North Haven). ▶ *Note that races form off both ends of the Is, especially S (Roost of Keels).◀*

Recommended Traffic Routes: NW-bound ships pass to the NE (no closer than 10M to Sumburgh Hd) or SW of Fair Isle; SE-bound ships pass no closer than 5M off N Ronaldsay (Orkney). Lerwick to Bergen, Norway, is about 210M.

FLOOD	EBB
Shetland Islands	**Shetland Islands**
(a) Dover –0410 to Dover +0020	(a) Dover +0050 to Dover –0410
(b) Dover –0400 to Dover +0030	(b) Dover +0130 to Dover –0500
(c) Dover –0530 to Dover +01 00	(c) Dover +01 00 to Dover –0530
(d) Dover –0400 to Dover –0200	(d) Dover +0200 to Dover +0500

9.7.24 SHETLAND ISLANDS

The Shetland Islands number about 100 islands, holms and rks with fewer than 20 inhabited. Lying 90 to 150M NNE of the Scottish mainland, the biggest island is Mainland with Lerwick (9.7.25), the capital, on the E side. Scalloway, the only other town and old capital, is on the W side. At the very S is Sumburgh airport, with other airstrips at Baltasound, Scalsta and Tingwall. Two offlying islands of the Shetland group are Fair Isle, 20M SSW of Sumburgh Hd and owned by the NT for Scotland, and Foula, 12M WSW of Mainland. There are LBs at Lerwick and Aith. The MRCC is at Lerwick, ☎ (01595) 692976, with an Auxilliary Stn at Fair I.
CHARTS AC: medium scale 3281, 3282, 3283; larger scale 3271, 3272, 3292, 3293, 3294, 3295, 3297, 3298.
TIDES Standard Port Lerwick. Tidal streams run mostly N-S or NW-SE; in open waters to the E and W they are mostly weak. Rates >6kn can cause dangerous disturbances at the N and S extremities of the islands and in the two main sounds (Yell Sound and BlueMull/Colgrave Sounds). Keep 3M off Sumburgh Head to clear a dangerous race (Röst) or pass close inshore.
SHELTER Weather conditions are bad in winter; yachts should only visit Apr–Sept. Around mid-summer it is daylight H24. Some small marinas are asterisked* below (see www.visitshetland.com); they may have room for visitors. Of the many ⌕s, the following are safe to enter in most conditions:
MAINLAND (anti-clockwise from Sumburgh Head)
Grutness Voe: 1·5M N of Sumburgh Hd, a convenient passage ⌕, open to NE. Beware 2 rocks awash in mid-ent.
Pool of Virkie*: 59°53'N 01°17W; Close N of Grutness Voe. Ness Boating Club Marina ☎ 01950 477260, AB (pontoon 1❶< 1m £10/craft/week, slip, ⌖, FW, toilet. Shallow and narrow/entrance, otherwise ⌕ Grutness Voe.
Cat Firth: excellent shelter, ⌕ in approx 6m. Facilities: ✉ (Skellister), FW, ⬚ (both at Lax Firth).
Grunna Voe: off S side of Dury Voe, good shelter and holding, ⌕ in 5-10m; beware prohib ⌕ areas. Facilities: ⬚, FW, ✉ (Lax Firth).
Whalsay*: 60°20'·60N 01°01'·60W; Fishing hbr with small marina at Symbister welcomes visitors. FW, D, AB (pontoon or pier 20❶s) £7.17/craft/4 days, ⌖, ME, FW, D, P, toilet/showers, ⬚, R, Bar, ✉.
Out Skerries*: 60°25'N 00°45'W; Pier (£2/craft/night); Small Boat Marina (£7.17/craft/4 days). ⌖, FW, D (by arrangement), toilet/showers, ⬚, ✉. Good ⌕ at Bruray.
South of Yell Sound: Tides –0025 on Lerwick. W of Lunna Ness, well protected ⌕s with good holding include: Boatsroom Voe, W Lunna Voe (small hotel, FW), Colla Firth* and Dales Voe. No facilities.
Sullom Voe: Tides –0130 on Lerwick. 6·5M long deep water voe, partly taken over by the oil industry. ⌕ S of the narrows. Facilities at Brae: FW, ⬚, ✉, D, ME, El, ✗, Bar.
Hamna Voe: Tides –0200 on Lerwick; very good shelter. Ldg line 153° old house on S shore with prominent rock on pt of W shore 3ca within ent. Almost land-locked; ⌕ in 6m approx, but bottom foul with old moorings. Facilities: ✉ (0.5M), Vs, D (1.5M), L (at pier).
Ura Firth: NE of St Magnus Bay, ⌕ off Hills Wick on W side or in Hamar Voe (no facilities) on E side, which has excellent shelter/good holding in all weathers. Facilities: **Hills Wick** FW, ✉, D, ME, El, ✗, ⬚, R, Bar.
Busta Voe: N of Swarbacks Minn; AB ❶s at Delting Boating Club's 52-berth marina. ☎ 01806 522479.
Olna Firth: NE of Swarbacks Minn, beware rk 1ca off S shore which dries. ⌕ in firth, 4-8m or in Gon Firth or go alongside pier at Voe. Facilities: (Voe) FW, ⬚, D, ✉, Bar.
Swarbacks Minn*: a large complex of voes and isles SE of St Magnus Bay. Best ⌕ Uyea Sound or Aith Voe, both well sheltered and good holding. No facilities.
Aith Voe*: 60°17·3'N 01°22·3W; Good shelter from all directions. FW, D, AB depth LW 1.2m (pontoon2 ❶s) otherwise ⌕ on Pier access H24, ⌖, FW, slip, ME, ✗, toilet/showers (leisure centre), R, Bar, ✉.
Vaila Sound: on SW of Mainland, ent via Easter Sound (do not attempt Wester Sound); very good shelter, ⌕ N of Salt Ness in 4-5m in mud. See WALLS* overleaf: FW, ⬚, ✉.
Gruting Voe*: HW –0150 on Lerwick, ⌕ in main voe or in Seli, Scutta or Browland* voes. Facilities: ⬚ and ✉ at Bridge of Walls (head of Browland Voe).
Hamna Voe*: 60°06·3'N 01°20·3W (West Burra) Entered between Fugla Ness and Alta Ness. Open to the NW; good shelter in small marina. Limited facilities in small village.
YELL **Mid Yell Voe***: 60°36'N 01°03·4W; tides –0040 on Lerwick,

enter via S Sd or Hascosay Sd, good ⌕ in wide part of voe 2·5-10m. Berth at marina £5/week or Pier £7.17/4 days/craft. Facilities: ✉, FW at pier on S side, D, ⬚, ME, ✗, El.
Basta Voe: good ⌕ above shingle bank in 5-15m; good holding in places. Facilities: FW, ⬚, Hotel, ✉.
Blue Mull Sound/Cullivoe*: 60°42'N 00°59'·7W; Hbr with small craft marina depth 1.2m AB £5/craft/day. FW, D, AB pier 20❶s £7.17/craft/4 days, ⌖, ME, FW, D, P,toilet/showers, ⬚, R, Bar, ✉. ⌕ off pier and slip. D, FW, ⬚.
Burra Voe*: 60°29'·8N 01°02'·4W; Entrance to voe has 2.5m bar. Good ⌕ at head of voe. AB at small marina £5/visit or on Pier £12/visit , FW, toilets ⌖, ⬚, Bar ✉.
FOULA: **Ham Voe** on E side has tiny hbr/pier, unsafe in E'ly; berth clear of mailboat. Avoid Hoevdi Grund, 2M ESE.
NAVIGATION A careful lookout must be kept for marine farms, mostly marked by Y buoys and combinations of Y lts. Clyde CC's *Shetland Sailing Directions and Anchorages* are essential for visitors. Local magnetic anomalies may be experienced.
Note: There are two Historic Wrecks (*Kennemerland* and *Wrangels Palais*) on Out Skerries at 60°25'·2N 00°45'·0W and 60°25'·5N 00°43'·3W (see 9.0.3).
LIGHTS AND MARKS See 9.7.4. Powerful lighthouses at Fair I, Sumburgh Hd, Kirkabister Ness, Bound Skerry, Muckle Flugga, Pt of Fethaland, Esha Ness and Foula.
R/T For Port Radio services see 9.7.25. No Coast Radio Station.
TELEPHONE (Code 01595; 01806 for Sullom Voe) MRCC 692976; Sullom Voe Port Control (01806) 242551, ⚏ 242237; Weather 692239; Forecaster (01806) 242069; Sumburgh Airport (01950) 460654.
FACILITIES All stores obtainable in Lerwick and   Scalloway. Elsewhere in Shetland there is little available and yachts should be well provisioned for extended offshore cruising.

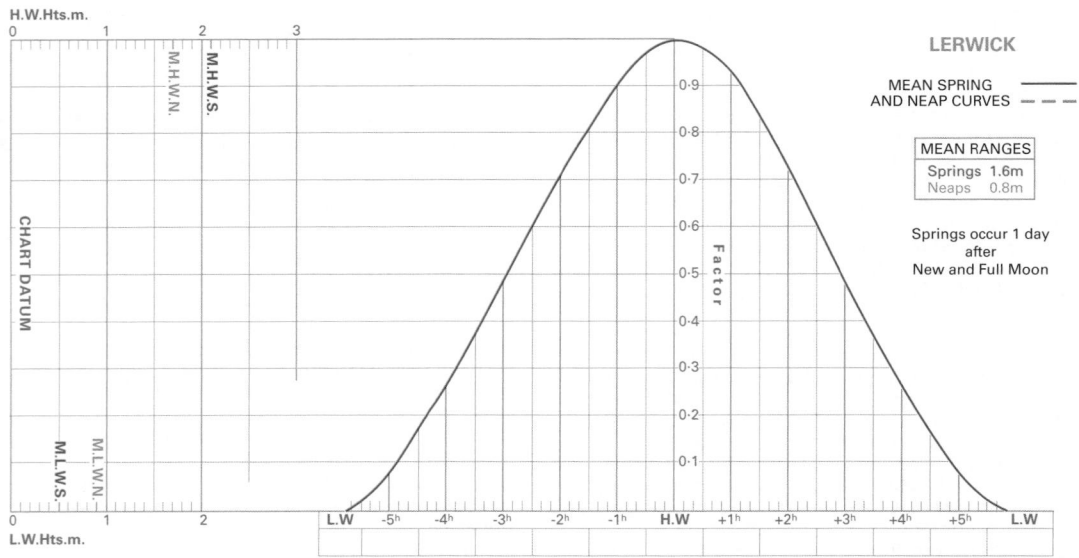

H.W.Hts.m.

LERWICK

MEAN SPRING
AND NEAP CURVES

MEAN RANGES
Springs 1.6m
Neaps 0.8m

Springs occur 1 day
after
New and Full Moon

9.7.25 LERWICK

Shetland Is, Mainland 60°09'·26N 01°08'·42W ❁❁❁♨♨❀❀

CHARTS AC 3283, 3272, 3271.

TIDES –0001 Dover; ML 1·4; Duration 0620

Standard Port LERWICK (←—)

Times				Height (metres)			
High Water		Low Water		MHWS	MHWN	MLWN	MLWS
0000	0600	0100	0800	2·1	1·7	0·9	0·5
1200	1800	1300	2000				
Differences FAIR ISLE							
–0006	–0015	–0031	–0037	+0·1	0·0	+0·1	+0·1
SUMBURGH (Grutness Voe)							
+0006	+0008	+0004	–0002	–0·3	–0·3	–0·2	–0·1
DURY VOE							
–0015	–0015	–0010	–0010	0·0	–0·1	0·0	–0·2
BURRA VOE (YELL SOUND)							
–0025	–0025	–0025	–0025	+0·2	+0·1	0·0	–0·1
BALTA SOUND							
–0055	–0055	–0045	–0045	+0·2	+0·1	0·0	–0·1
BLUEMULL SOUND							
–0135	–0135	–0155	–0155	+0·5	+0·2	+0·1	0·0
SULLOM VOE							
–0135	–0125	–0135	–0120	0·0	0·0	–0·2	–0·2
HILLSWICK (URA FIRTH)							
–0220	–0220	–0200	–0200	–0·1	–0·1	–0·1	–0·1
SCALLOWAY							
–0150	–0150	–0150	–0150	–0·5	–0·4	–0·3	0·0
FOULA (23M West of Scalloway)							
–0140	–0130	–0140	–0120	–0·1	–0·1	0·0	0·0

SHELTER Good. HM allocates berths in Small Dock or Albert Dock. FVs occupy most alongside space. ⚓ prohib for about 2ca off the waterfront. Gremista marina in N hbr, is mainly for local boats, and is about 1M from the town.

NAVIGATION WPT 60°05'·97N 01°08'·62W, 010°/3·5M to Maryfield lt, in W sector. From S, Bressay Sound is clear of dangers. From N, WPT 60°11'·60N 01°07'·88W, 215°/1·34M to N ent Dir lt (Oc WRG 6s, 214°-W-216°). Beware Soldian Rk (dries), Nive Baa (0·6m), Green Holm (10m) and The Brethren (two rocks 2m and 1·5m).

LIGHTS AND MARKS Kirkabister Ness, Fl (2) 20s 32m 23M; Cro of Ham, Fl 3s 3M; Maryfield, Oc WRG 6s, 008°-W-013°; all on Bressay. Twageos Pt, L Fl 6s 8m 6M. Loofa Baa SCM lt bn, as on chartlet. 2 SHM lt buoys mark Middle Ground in N Hbr.

R/T *Lerwick Harbour* VHF Ch **12** 16 (H24) for Vessel Information

Service. Other stns: *Sullom Voe Hbr Radio* broadcasts traffic info and local forecasts on request Ch **14** 12 20 16 (H24).

TELEPHONE (Code 01595) HM 692991; MRCC 692976; Weather 692239; Police 692110; Dr 693201.

FACILITIES Hbr Slip, M, P, D, L, FW, ME, ✕, Gas; **Lerwick Hbr Trust** ☎ 692991, 🅥 pontoons £0.60, ⬡, M, FW, D, P, 🅢 ramps/toilet; **Lerwick Boating Club** ☎ 692407, L, C, Bar, ⓞ; **Services:** ME, El, Ⓔ, ✕, Slip, BY, CH, SM, Gas, ACA. **Town** 🛒, R, Bar, ✉, Ⓑ, @, **Ferries:** Aberdeen via Kirkwall; daily; overnight; North Link (www.northlinkferries.co.uk), ✈. See www.shetland.news.co.uk and www.lerwickboating.co.uk.

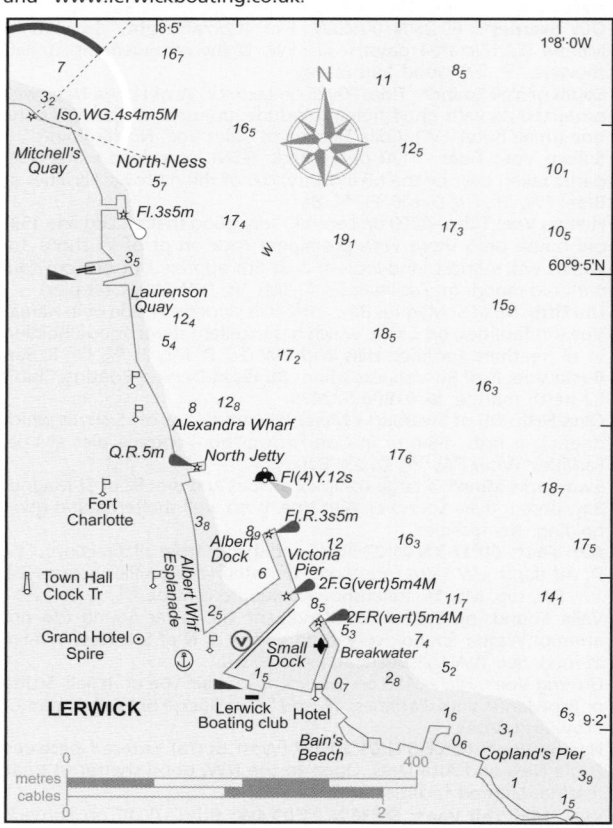

TIME ZONE (UT)
For Summer Time add ONE hour in **non-shaded areas**

LERWICK LAT 60°09'N LONG 1°08'W

TIMES AND HEIGHTS OF HIGH AND LOW WATERS

Dates in red are **SPRINGS**
Dates in blue are **NEAPS**

YEAR 2010

NE Scotland

JANUARY

Time	m	Time	m
1 0442 1057 F 1714 2336	0.7 2.3 0.4 2.3	**16** 0518 1133 SA 1749	0.8 2.2 0.6
2 0529 1145 SA 1801	0.7 2.4 0.3	**17** 0006 0549 SU 1205 1819	2.0 0.8 2.2 0.6
3 0027 0614 SU 1233 1848	2.3 0.7 2.4 0.3	**18** 0039 0619 M 1236 1850	2.0 0.8 2.2 0.6
4 0117 0658 M 1321 1936	2.2 0.7 2.4 0.3	**19** 0110 0649 TU 1306 1921	2.0 0.8 2.1 0.6
5 0205 0744 TU 1410 2025	2.1 0.7 2.3 0.4	**20** 0141 0721 W 1337 1954	1.9 0.8 2.1 0.7
6 0252 0831 W 1501 2117	2.0 0.8 2.2 0.6	**21** 0214 0756 TH 1413 2030	1.9 0.9 2.0 0.8
7 0342 0923 TH 1555 ☽ 2217	1.9 0.9 2.1 0.8	**22** 0253 0836 F 1456 2112	1.8 0.9 1.9 0.8
8 0436 1029 F 1658 2330	1.8 1.0 1.9 0.9	**23** 0339 0925 SA 1547 ☽ 2204	1.8 1.0 1.8 0.9
9 0539 1203 SA 1813	1.8 1.0 1.8	**24** 0434 1033 SU 1650 2316	1.7 1.1 1.8 1.0
10 0046 0651 SU 1327 1931	1.0 1.8 1.0 1.8	**25** 0541 1210 M 1807	1.7 1.1 1.7
11 0151 0757 M 1432 2040	1.0 1.9 0.9 1.8	**26** 0044 0659 TU 1330 1934	1.0 1.8 1.0 1.8
12 0245 0854 TU 1523 2135	1.0 2.0 0.8 1.9	**27** 0155 0809 W 1433 2044	1.0 1.9 0.8 1.9
13 0330 0942 W 1605 2219	0.9 2.1 0.8 2.0	**28** 0254 0906 TH 1527 2143	0.9 2.0 0.6 2.1
14 0409 1022 TH 1643 2258	0.9 2.1 0.7 2.0	**29** 0345 0957 F 1616 2236	0.7 2.2 0.4 2.2
15 0445 1059 F 1716 ● 2333	0.9 2.2 0.6 2.0	**30** 0432 1046 SA 1702 ○ 2325	0.6 2.3 0.4 2.2
		31 0515 1133 SU 1746	0.5 2.4 0.1

FEBRUARY

Time	m	Time	m
1 0011 0557 M 1219 1829	2.3 0.5 2.5 0.1	**16** 0011 0554 TU 1211 1820	2.0 0.6 2.2 0.5
2 0056 0638 TU 1304 1913	2.2 0.5 2.4 0.2	**17** 0039 0623 W 1239 1849	2.0 0.6 2.1 0.5
3 0138 0720 W 1348 1957	2.1 0.5 2.3 0.4	**18** 0106 0655 TH 1309 1920	1.9 0.6 2.1 0.6
4 0220 0803 TH 1434 2042	2.0 0.6 2.2 0.6	**19** 0137 0728 F 1343 1954	1.9 0.7 2.0 0.7
5 0303 0850 F 1524 ☽ 2132	1.9 0.8 2.0 0.8	**20** 0212 0807 SA 1423 2033	1.9 0.8 1.9 0.8
6 0350 0949 SA 1621 2237	1.8 0.9 1.8 1.0	**21** 0254 0853 SU 1513 2121	1.8 0.9 1.8 0.9
7 0448 1130 SU 1740	1.7 1.0 1.7	**22** 0348 0956 M 1619 ☽ 2229	1.7 1.0 1.7 1.0
8 0010 0609 M 1313 1916	1.1 1.7 1.0 1.6	**23** 0456 1133 TU 1742	1.7 1.0 1.6
9 0132 0734 TU 1423 2032	1.1 1.7 0.9 1.7	**24** 0018 0623 W 1311 1922	1.0 1.7 0.9 1.7
10 0231 0838 W 1513 2123	1.0 1.8 0.8 1.8	**25** 0143 0749 TH 1419 2035	1.0 1.8 0.7 1.8
11 0317 0926 TH 1552 2203	1.0 1.9 0.7 1.9	**26** 0243 0850 F 1513 2131	0.8 2.0 0.5 2.0
12 0354 1005 F 1626 2238	0.9 2.0 0.6 1.9	**27** 0331 0941 SA 1559 2220	0.7 2.1 0.3 2.1
13 0427 1040 SA 1655 2310	0.8 2.1 0.5 2.0	**28** 0414 1029 SU 1643 ○ 2305	0.5 2.3 0.1 2.2
14 0457 1113 SU 1724 ● 2341	0.7 2.1 0.5 2.0		
15 0526 1143 M 1752	0.6 2.2 0.5		

MARCH

Time	m	Time	m
1 0455 1114 M 1725 2348	0.4 2.4 0.1 2.2	**16** 0458 1114 TU 1720 2338	0.5 2.1 0.4 2.0
2 0535 1158 TU 1806	0.3 2.4 0.1	**17** 0528 1143 W 1749	0.5 2.1 0.4
3 0028 0615 W 1241 1846	2.2 0.3 2.4 0.2	**18** 0006 0558 TH 1213 1819	2.0 0.5 2.1 0.4
4 0107 0656 TH 1324 1927	2.1 0.4 2.3 0.4	**19** 0034 0631 F 1245 1851	2.0 0.5 2.0 0.5
5 0145 0738 F 1408 2008	2.0 0.5 2.1 0.6	**20** 0105 0707 SA 1320 1926	1.9 0.6 2.0 0.6
6 0224 0824 SA 1455 2052	1.9 0.7 1.9 0.8	**21** 0140 0748 SU 1403 2006	1.9 0.6 1.9 0.7
7 0308 0921 SU 1550 ☽ 2149	1.8 0.8 1.7 1.0	**22** 0221 0837 M 1456 2056	1.8 0.7 1.7 0.9
8 0401 1059 M 1706 2327	1.7 0.9 1.5 1.1	**23** 0315 0942 TU 1606 ☽ 2207	1.7 0.8 1.6 1.0
9 0518 1247 TU 1856	1.6 0.9 1.5	**24** 0428 1117 W 1734	1.6 0.8 1.6
10 0103 0703 W 1359 2011	1.1 1.6 0.8 1.7	**25** 0003 0558 TH 1253 1912	1.0 1.6 0.7 1.6
11 0208 0810 TH 1448 2058	1.0 1.7 0.7 1.7	**26** 0126 0727 F 1359 2019	0.9 1.7 0.5 1.8
12 0253 0858 F 1525 2135	0.9 1.8 0.6 1.8	**27** 0223 0829 SA 1452 2111	0.7 1.9 0.3 1.9
13 0329 0937 SA 1556 2208	0.8 1.9 0.5 1.8	**28** 0310 0920 SU 1537 2157	0.6 2.1 0.2 2.0
14 0400 1012 SU 1625 2240	0.7 2.0 0.5 1.9	**29** 0352 1007 M 1620 2240	0.4 2.2 0.1 2.1
15 0429 1044 M 1652 ● 2310	0.6 2.1 0.4 2.0	**30** 0433 1052 TU 1700 ○ 2320	0.3 2.3 0.1 2.1
		31 0513 1136 W 1740 2358	0.3 2.3 0.1 2.1

APRIL

Time	m	Time	m
1 0554 1219 TH 1819	0.3 2.2 0.3	**16** 0536 1150 F 1752	0.4 2.0 0.4
2 0035 0635 F 1302 1858	2.1 0.3 2.1 0.5	**17** 0007 0613 SA 1227 1827	2.0 0.4 2.0 0.5
3 0112 0718 SA 1346 1938	2.0 0.4 1.9 0.7	**18** 0041 0653 SU 1308 1907	2.0 0.4 1.9 0.6
4 0151 0804 SU 1433 2020	1.9 0.6 1.7 0.9	**19** 0119 0738 M 1356 1951	1.9 0.5 1.8 0.7
5 0233 0900 M 1525 2111	1.8 0.7 1.6 1.0	**20** 0204 0832 TU 1456 2046	1.8 0.6 1.7 0.8
6 0323 1023 TU 1632 2238	1.7 0.8 1.5 1.1	**21** 0302 0938 W 1606 ☽ 2159	1.7 0.6 1.6 0.9
7 0427 1158 W 1812	1.6 0.8 1.4	**22** 0415 1105 TH 1726 2340	1.7 0.6 1.6 0.9
8 0015 0610 TH 1313 1926	1.1 1.5 0.8 1.5	**23** 0539 1228 F 1850	1.7 0.5 1.6
9 0127 0727 F 1407 2016	1.0 1.6 0.7 1.6	**24** 0058 0700 SA 1333 1953	0.8 1.7 0.4 1.7
10 0216 0818 SA 1446 2056	0.9 1.7 0.6 1.7	**25** 0157 0803 SU 1426 2044	0.7 1.9 0.3 1.8
11 0254 0900 SU 1518 2131	0.8 1.8 0.5 1.8	**26** 0245 0856 M 1512 2130	0.5 2.0 0.3 1.9
12 0326 0936 M 1547 2204	0.7 1.9 0.5 1.9	**27** 0329 0945 TU 1555 2212	0.4 2.1 0.2 2.0
13 0357 1010 TU 1616 2235	0.6 1.9 0.4 1.9	**28** 0412 1032 W 1636 ○ 2252	0.3 2.1 0.3 2.2
14 0429 1043 W 1647 ● 2305	0.5 2.0 0.4 2.0	**29** 0454 1117 TH 1716 2330	0.3 2.1 0.3 2.1
15 0502 1116 TH 1719 2335	0.4 2.0 0.4 2.0	**30** 0536 1201 F 1755	0.3 2.0 0.4

Chart Datum: 1·22 metres below Ordnance Datum (Local). HAT is 2·5 metres above Chart Datum; see 4.5

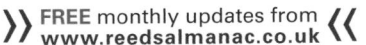

TIME ZONE (UT)
For Summer Time add ONE
hour in **non-shaded areas**

LERWICK   LAT 60°09'N   LONG 1°08'W
TIMES AND HEIGHTS OF HIGH AND LOW WATERS

Dates in red are **SPRINGS**
Dates in blue are **NEAPS**

YEAR **2010**

MAY		JUNE		JULY		AUGUST	
1 0008 2.0 0618 0.3 SA 1245 1.9 1834 0.6	**16** 0600 0.4 1217 1.9 SU 1813 0.5	**1** 0107 1.9 0731 0.5 TU 1353 1.7 1933 0.8	**16** 0107 2.1 0726 0.2 W 1355 1.9 1937 0.6	**1** 0123 1.9 0742 0.5 TH 1403 1.7 1942 0.8	**16** 0144 2.2 0756 0.2 F 1425 1.9 2005 0.6	**1** 0200 1.9 0813 0.7 SU 1435 1.8 2022 0.8	**16** 0300 2.0 0905 0.7 M 1526 1.8 ◗ 2124 0.8
2 0046 2.0 0702 0.4 SU 1328 1.9 1913 0.7	**17** 0027 2.0 0644 0.4 M 1306 1.9 1857 0.6	**2** 0146 1.9 0814 0.6 W 1435 1.6 2014 0.8	**17** 0158 2.0 0817 0.3 TH 1447 1.8 2027 0.7	**2** 0158 1.9 0818 0.6 F 1440 1.7 2019 0.8	**17** 0233 2.1 0845 0.4 SA 1512 1.8 2053 0.7	**2** 0240 1.8 0852 0.8 M 1518 1.7 2108 0.8	**17** 0357 1.8 1005 0.9 TU 1621 1.7 2251 0.9
3 0125 1.9 0749 0.5 M 1414 1.7 1955 0.8	**18** 0111 2.0 0733 0.4 TU 1359 1.8 1946 0.7	**3** 0228 1.8 0900 0.6 TH 1519 1.6 2100 0.9	**18** 0251 2.0 0911 0.4 F 1540 1.7 2121 0.7	**3** 0237 1.8 0858 0.7 SA 1520 1.6 2102 0.9	**18** 0325 2.0 0939 0.5 SU 1602 1.7 ◗ 2151 0.8	**3** 0328 1.8 0939 0.9 TU 1609 1.7 ◗ 2210 1.0	**18** 0510 1.7 1134 1.0 W 1734 1.7
4 0207 1.8 0840 0.6 TU 1502 1.6 2043 0.9	**19** 0201 1.9 0828 0.4 W 1457 1.7 2041 0.8	**4** 0312 1.7 0951 0.7 F 1608 1.5 ◗ 2159 0.9	**19** 0348 1.9 1012 0.5 SA 1637 1.7 ◗ 2225 0.8	**4** 0320 1.7 0943 0.7 SU 1606 1.6 ◗ 2156 0.9	**19** 0423 1.9 1043 0.7 M 1700 1.7 2313 0.9	**4** 0427 1.7 1042 0.9 W 1709 1.7 2343 1.0	**19** 0039 0.9 0645 1.6 TH 1301 1.1 1902 1.7
5 0254 1.7 0942 0.7 W 1556 1.5 2148 1.0	**20** 0259 1.8 0930 0.5 TH 1559 1.7 ◗ 2145 0.8	**5** 0403 1.6 1050 0.7 SA 1704 1.5 2310 0.9	**20** 0450 1.8 1122 0.6 SU 1739 1.6 2345 0.8	**5** 0410 1.7 1039 0.8 M 1659 1.6 2312 1.0	**20** 0533 1.8 1202 0.8 TU 1809 1.7	**5** 0537 1.6 1212 1.0 TH 1823 1.7	**20** 0154 0.8 0806 1.7 F 1406 1.0 2011 1.8
6 0348 1.6 1052 0.8 TH 1706 1.4 ◗ 2308 1.0	**21** 0405 1.8 1042 0.5 F 1706 1.6 2304 0.8	**6** 0500 1.6 1151 0.7 SU 1812 1.5	**21** 0600 1.8 1232 0.6 M 1844 1.7	**6** 0509 1.6 1148 0.8 TU 1802 1.6	**21** 0047 0.8 0655 1.7 W 1317 0.9 1922 1.7	**6** 0105 0.9 0704 1.7 F 1328 0.9 1939 1.8	**21** 0250 0.7 0902 1.8 SA 1455 0.9 2104 1.9
7 0453 1.5 1201 0.7 F 1826 1.5	**22** 0516 1.7 1157 0.5 SA 1817 1.6	**7** 0019 0.9 0609 1.6 M 1248 0.7 1913 1.6	**22** 0102 0.8 0712 1.8 TU 1335 0.7 1945 1.7	**7** 0030 0.9 0618 1.6 W 1253 0.8 1910 1.7	**22** 0201 0.8 0811 1.7 TH 1418 0.9 2026 1.8	**7** 0209 0.8 0819 1.8 SA 1429 0.8 2039 1.9	**22** 0332 0.7 0944 1.8 SU 1535 0.8 2146 2.0
8 0021 1.0 0622 1.5 SA 1302 0.7 1924 1.5	**23** 0023 0.8 0630 1.8 SU 1303 0.5 1920 1.7	**8** 0118 0.9 0719 1.6 TU 1339 0.7 2001 1.7	**23** 0207 0.7 0818 1.8 W 1430 0.7 2041 1.8	**8** 0133 0.9 0734 1.7 TH 1351 0.8 2009 1.8	**23** 0259 0.7 0914 1.8 F 1509 0.8 2120 1.9	**8** 0303 0.6 0917 1.9 SU 1521 0.7 2131 2.1	**23** 0407 0.6 1021 1.9 M 1609 0.7 2223 2.1
9 0121 0.9 0727 1.6 SU 1350 0.7 2009 1.6	**24** 0128 0.7 0736 1.8 M 1359 0.4 2014 1.8	**9** 0208 0.8 0813 1.7 W 1425 0.7 2045 1.8	**24** 0302 0.6 0918 1.8 TH 1518 0.7 2131 1.9	**9** 0228 0.7 0836 1.8 F 1444 0.8 2100 1.9	**24** 0346 0.6 1002 1.9 SA 1552 0.7 2205 2.0	**9** 0351 0.4 1009 2.0 M 1607 0.6 2219 2.2	**24** 0438 0.5 1054 2.0 TU 1641 0.7 ○ 2256 2.1
10 0208 0.8 0814 1.7 M 1429 0.6 2048 1.6	**25** 0222 0.6 0834 1.9 TU 1448 0.4 2103 1.9	**10** 0253 0.7 0902 1.8 TH 1508 0.6 2127 1.9	**25** 0351 0.5 1010 1.9 F 1602 0.7 2216 2.0	**10** 0318 0.6 0931 1.9 SA 1534 0.7 2148 2.0	**25** 0425 0.5 1043 1.9 SU 1630 0.7 2244 2.1	**10** 0437 0.2 1058 2.1 TU 1651 0.5 ● 2306 2.3	**25** 0508 0.5 1126 2.0 W 1711 0.6 2328 2.1
11 0247 0.7 0856 1.7 TU 1505 0.5 2124 1.8	**26** 0311 0.5 0927 1.9 W 1533 0.5 2148 1.9	**11** 0337 0.6 0948 1.9 F 1551 0.6 2208 2.0	**26** 0435 0.5 1056 1.9 SA 1643 0.7 ○ 2258 2.0	**11** 0406 0.4 1023 2.0 SU 1622 0.6 ● 2235 2.1	**26** 0501 0.5 1120 1.9 M 1704 0.7 ○ 2320 2.1	**11** 0521 0.1 1144 2.2 W 1733 0.4 2352 2.4	**26** 0536 0.5 1155 2.0 TH 1740 0.6 2357 2.1
12 0324 0.6 0935 1.8 W 1540 0.5 2159 1.9	**27** 0357 0.4 1018 2.0 TH 1615 0.5 ○ 2230 2.0	**12** 0420 0.5 1035 1.9 SA 1634 0.6 ● 2250 2.1	**27** 0516 0.4 1138 1.9 SU 1722 0.7 2336 2.0	**12** 0453 0.3 1113 2.1 M 1707 0.5 2322 2.2	**27** 0534 0.4 1154 1.9 TU 1737 0.7 2353 2.1	**12** 0604 0.1 1229 2.2 TH 1815 0.4	**27** 0604 0.5 1224 2.0 F 1809 0.6
13 0401 0.5 1013 1.9 TH 1616 0.5 2234 2.0	**28** 0441 0.4 1105 2.0 F 1656 0.5 2310 2.0	**13** 0505 0.4 1123 2.0 SU 1719 0.5 2334 2.1	**28** 0554 0.4 1216 1.9 M 1759 0.7	**13** 0539 0.2 1203 2.1 TU 1752 0.5	**28** 0606 0.4 1226 1.9 W 1808 0.6	**13** 0037 2.4 0647 0.1 F 1313 2.1 1856 0.4	**28** 0025 2.1 0633 0.5 SA 1251 2.0 1840 0.6
14 0439 0.4 1052 2.0 F 1653 0.5 ● 2310 2.0	**29** 0524 0.4 1149 1.9 SA 1736 0.6 2349 2.0	**14** 0550 0.3 1213 2.0 M 1804 0.6	**29** 0013 2.0 0631 0.4 TU 1253 1.8 1833 0.7	**14** 0009 2.3 0624 0.1 W 1251 2.1 1835 0.5	**29** 0025 2.1 0637 0.5 TH 1258 1.9 1838 0.6	**14** 0123 2.3 0731 0.3 SA 1355 2.0 1940 0.5	**29** 0055 2.1 0703 0.6 SU 1321 1.9 1914 0.7
15 0518 0.4 1133 2.0 SA 1732 0.5 2347 2.0	**30** 0607 0.4 1231 1.9 SU 1816 0.7	**15** 0019 2.1 0637 0.2 TU 1304 2.0 1849 0.6	**30** 0049 2.0 0707 0.5 W 1328 1.8 1908 0.7	**15** 0057 2.3 0710 0.1 TH 1338 2.0 1919 0.5	**30** 0055 2.0 0707 0.5 F 1328 1.8 1910 0.7	**15** 0210 2.2 0816 0.5 SU 1439 1.9 2027 0.7	**30** 0128 2.0 0736 0.7 M 1354 1.9 1951 0.8
	31 0028 2.0 0649 0.4 M 1312 1.8 1854 0.7			**31** 0126 2.0 0739 0.6 SA 1400 1.8 1943 0.7		**31** 0207 1.9 0813 0.8 TU 1434 1.8 2036 0.9	

Chart Datum: 1·22 metres below Ordnance Datum (Local). HAT is 2·5 metres above Chart Datum; see 4.5

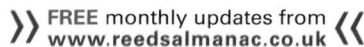

TIME ZONE (UT)
For Summer Time add ONE hour in **non-shaded areas**

LERWICK   LAT 60°09'N   LONG 1°08'W
TIMES AND HEIGHTS OF HIGH AND LOW WATERS

Dates in red are SPRINGS
Dates in blue are NEAPS

YEAR **2010**

NE Scotland

SEPTEMBER
Time	m		Time	m
1 0255	1.8	**16**	0447	1.6
0857	0.9		1103	1.2
W 1525	1.8	TH	1658	1.7
◑ 2136	1.0			
2 0356	1.7	**17**	0021	0.9
0959	1.0		0629	1.6
TH 1629	1.0	F	1237	1.2
2306	1.0		1835	1.7
3 0512	1.7	**18**	0134	0.9
1142	1.1		0747	1.7
F 1747	1.7	SA	1343	1.1
			1946	1.8
4 0044	0.9	**19**	0226	0.8
0647	1.7		0837	1.8
SA 1313	1.0	SU	1432	1.0
1915	1.8		2037	1.9
5 0151	0.7	**20**	0306	0.7
0805	1.8		0915	1.8
SU 1414	0.9	M	1510	0.9
2020	2.0		2118	2.0
6 0245	0.5	**21**	0339	0.6
0901	2.0		0950	1.9
M 1503	0.7	TU	1543	0.8
2112	2.1		2154	2.1
7 0332	0.3	**22**	0408	0.6
0950	2.1		1022	2.0
TU 1547	0.6	W	1613	0.7
2159	2.3		2227	2.1
8 0416	0.2	**23**	0436	0.5
1036	2.2		1053	2.1
W 1629	0.5	TH	1642	0.6
● 2245	2.4	○	2258	2.2
9 0459	0.1	**24**	0503	0.5
1120	2.3		1122	2.1
TH 1710	0.4	F	1712	0.6
2330	2.5		2327	2.2
10 0540	0.1	**25**	0532	0.5
1202	2.2		1150	2.1
F 1752	0.4	SA	1742	0.6
			2356	2.2
11 0015	2.5	**26**	0601	0.6
0621	0.2		1217	2.1
SA 1243	2.2	SU	1815	0.6
1833	0.4			
12 0100	2.4	**27**	0027	2.1
0703	0.4		0632	0.6
SU 1323	2.1	M	1247	2.1
1917	0.5		1850	0.7
13 0147	2.2	**28**	0103	2.0
0746	0.6		0705	0.7
M 1405	2.0	TU	1321	2.0
2005	0.7		1930	0.8
14 0237	2.0	**29**	0143	2.0
0833	0.8		0744	0.9
TU 1451	1.9	W	1401	1.9
2103	0.8		2017	0.9
15 0334	1.8	**30**	0234	1.8
0930	1.0		0831	1.0
W 1545	1.8	TH	1453	1.8
◑ 2236	0.9		2118	0.9

OCTOBER
Time	m		Time	m
1 0340	1.7	**16**	0548	1.6
0936	1.1		1153	1.2
F 1601	1.8	SA	1750	1.7
◑ 2245	0.9			
2 0459	1.7	**17**	0054	0.9
1120	1.1		0703	1.7
SA 1723	1.8	SU	1305	1.1
			1906	1.8
3 0022	0.8	**18**	0149	0.9
0632	1.7		0756	1.7
SU 1253	1.0	M	1357	1.0
1851	1.8		1959	1.9
4 0129	0.7	**19**	0230	0.8
0746	1.9		0837	1.8
M 1352	0.9	TU	1437	0.9
1956	2.0		2042	2.0
5 0222	0.5	**20**	0303	0.7
0840	2.0		0913	1.9
TU 1441	0.8	W	1511	0.8
2049	2.2		2120	2.0
6 0309	0.4	**21**	0333	0.7
0927	2.1		0947	2.0
W 1525	0.6	TH	1542	0.7
2137	2.3		2154	2.1
7 0353	0.3	**22**	0401	0.6
1011	2.2		1019	2.1
TH 1607	0.5	F	1613	0.7
● 2223	2.4		2227	2.1
8 0435	0.2	**23**	0431	0.6
1053	2.3		1049	2.1
F 1648	0.4	SA	1646	0.6
2308	2.5	○	2300	2.2
9 0516	0.3	**24**	0501	0.6
1133	2.3		1119	2.2
SA 1731	0.4	SU	1720	0.6
2354	2.4		2333	2.2
10 0557	0.4	**25**	0533	0.7
1213	2.3		1150	2.2
SU 1814	0.4	M	1755	0.6
11 0040	2.3	**26**	0008	2.1
0638	0.6		0607	0.7
M 1253	2.2	TU	1223	2.2
1859	0.5		1834	0.7
12 0128	2.1	**27**	0048	2.1
0720	0.8		0645	0.8
TU 1334	2.1	W	1300	2.1
1948	0.7		1917	0.7
13 0218	2.0	**28**	0133	2.0
0805	1.0		0727	0.9
W 1420	2.0	TH	1342	2.0
2046	0.8		2007	0.8
14 0313	1.8	**29**	0228	1.9
0859	1.1		0818	1.0
TH 1513	1.9	F	1436	1.9
◑ 2207	0.9		2108	0.8
15 0418	1.7	**30**	0334	1.8
1020	1.2		0923	1.1
F 1618	1.8	SA	1544	1.9
2340	1.0	◑	2226	0.8
		31	0447	1.8
			1051	1.1
		SU	1701	1.9
			2353	0.8

NOVEMBER
Time	m		Time	m
1 0608	1.8	**16**	0050	0.9
1221	1.0		0704	1.7
M 1822	1.9	TU	1306	1.1
			1910	1.8
2 0100	0.7	**17**	0140	0.9
0718	1.9		0753	1.8
TU 1324	0.9	W	1355	1.0
1929	2.0		2000	1.9
3 0156	0.6	**18**	0219	0.8
0813	2.0		0834	1.9
W 1416	0.8	TH	1435	0.9
2025	2.2		2043	2.0
4 0245	0.5	**19**	0253	0.8
0900	2.1		0911	2.0
TH 1503	0.7	F	1512	0.8
2116	2.3		2122	2.0
5 0330	0.4	**20**	0327	0.8
0945	2.2		0946	2.1
F 1547	0.6	SA	1548	0.8
2204	2.3		2200	2.1
6 0412	0.4	**21**	0401	0.7
1027	2.3		1020	2.2
SA 1631	0.5	SU	1624	0.7
● 2252	2.4	○	2238	2.1
7 0454	0.5	**22**	0436	0.7
1108	2.3		1054	2.2
SU 1715	0.5	M	1702	0.6
2339	2.3		2317	2.2
8 0535	0.6	**23**	0513	0.7
1149	2.3		1130	2.2
M 1800	0.5	TU	1742	0.6
			2358	2.1
9 0026	2.2	**24**	0552	0.8
0616	0.7		1208	2.2
TU 1230	2.2	W	1824	0.6
1845	0.6			
10 0113	2.1	**25**	0042	2.1
0658	0.9		0633	0.8
W 1312	2.2	TH	1249	2.2
1933	0.7		1910	0.6
11 0200	1.9	**26**	0131	2.0
0742	1.0		0719	0.9
TH 1356	2.1	F	1335	2.1
2026	0.8		2000	0.6
12 0249	1.8	**27**	0225	2.0
0830	1.1		0809	1.0
F 1445	2.0	SA	1428	2.1
2126	0.9		2056	0.7
13 0342	1.7	**28**	0324	1.9
0930	1.2		0907	1.0
SA 1538	1.9	SU	1529	2.0
◑ 2235	0.9	◑	2200	0.7
14 0446	1.7	**29**	0427	1.8
1045	1.2		1015	1.1
SU 1642	1.8	M	1637	2.0
2347	1.0		2316	0.7
15 0602	1.7	**30**	0535	1.8
1201	1.2		1138	1.0
M 1804	1.8	TU	1750	2.0

DECEMBER
Time	m		Time	m
1 0028	0.7	**16**	0034	1.0
0644	1.9		0658	1.8
W 1253	1.0	TH	1304	1.1
1901	2.0		1906	1.8
2 0130	0.7	**17**	0128	1.0
0743	2.0		0751	1.8
TH 1354	0.9	F	1358	1.0
2003	2.1		2003	1.8
3 0223	0.7	**18**	0214	0.9
0836	2.1		0835	1.9
F 1447	0.8	SA	1444	0.9
2100	2.2		2051	1.9
4 0311	0.7	**19**	0257	0.9
0924	2.1		0916	2.1
SA 1535	0.7	SU	1526	0.9
2154	2.2		2136	2.0
5 0355	0.7	**20**	0338	0.8
1010	2.2		0955	2.1
SU 1621	0.6	M	1608	0.7
● 2244	2.2		2221	2.1
6 0438	0.7	**21**	0419	0.8
1053	2.3		1035	2.2
M 1706	0.5	TU	1649	0.6
2331	2.2	○	2305	2.1
7 0520	0.7	**22**	0500	0.8
1134	2.3		1116	2.3
TU 1750	0.5	W	1732	0.5
			2350	2.2
8 0015	2.1	**23**	0542	0.7
0600	0.8		1158	2.3
W 1215	2.3	TH	1815	0.5
1833	0.6			
9 0058	2.1	**24**	0037	2.2
0640	0.9		0625	0.7
TH 1255	2.2	F	1242	2.3
1916	0.6		1900	0.4
10 0139	2.0	**25**	0125	2.1
0720	0.9		0709	0.8
F 1335	2.1	SA	1328	2.3
1959	0.7		1947	0.5
11 0220	1.9	**26**	0214	2.0
0759	1.0		0755	0.8
SA 1416	2.0	SU	1418	2.2
2043	0.8		2037	0.5
12 0303	1.8	**27**	0305	2.0
0842	1.1		0844	0.9
SU 1459	1.9	M	1511	2.1
2131	0.9		2132	0.6
13 0349	1.7	**28**	0359	1.9
0933	1.1		0941	1.0
M 1547	1.9	TU	1610	2.0
◑ 2228	1.0	◑	2236	0.7
14 0443	1.7	**29**	0459	1.8
1042	1.2		1053	1.0
TU 1641	1.8	W	1718	2.0
2332	1.0		2352	0.8
15 0550	1.7	**30**	0607	1.8
1159	1.2		1224	1.0
W 1751	1.8	TH	1835	1.9
		31	0104	0.9
			0715	1.9
		F	1339	0.9
			1949	1.9

Chart Datum: 1·22 metres below Ordnance Datum (Local). HAT is 2·5 metres above Chart Datum; see 4.5

OTHER HARBOURS IN THE SHETLAND ISLANDS

BALTA SOUND, Unst, **60°44'·32N 00°48'·12W**. AC 3293. HW –0105 on Dover; ML 1·3; Duration 0640. See 9.7.25. Balta Sound is a large almost landlocked inlet with good shelter from all winds. Beware fish farms and bad holding on kelp. Safest and main entry is via S Chan between Huney Is and Balta Is; inner chan marked by two PHM lt buoys. N Chan is deep but narrow; keep to Unst shore. ‡ off Sandisons Wharf (2FG vert) in approx 6m or enter marina close W (one **Ⓥ**, very shallow); pier has Oc WRG 10s 5m 2M, 272°-G-282°-W-287°-R-297°. VHF Ch 16; 20 (HO or as required). Facilities: BY, FW, D, El, ME, ✕; Hotel by pier. **Baltasound village**, Bar, R, 🛒, ✉.

FOULA, Shetland Islands, **60°08'·02N 02°02'·92W** (Ham Voe). AC 3283. HW –0150 on Dover; ML 1·3m. See 9.7.25. Foula is 12M WSW of Mainland. Highest ground is 416m. S Ness lt ho, Fl (3) 15s, is at the S tip. Beware Foula Shoal (7·6m) and Hœvdi Grund (1·4m), respectively 4·3M E and 2M SE of Ham Voe.

Ham Voe is a narrow inlet on the E coast with a quay; rks on both sides. Two R ▲ ldg marks, approx 270°, are hard to see. ☆ 2 FG (vert) on pierhead. Berthing or landing is only possible in settled weather with no swell. Take advice from mail boat skipper out of Walls and call Foula, ☎ (01595) 753222. Small ✈. No other facilities.

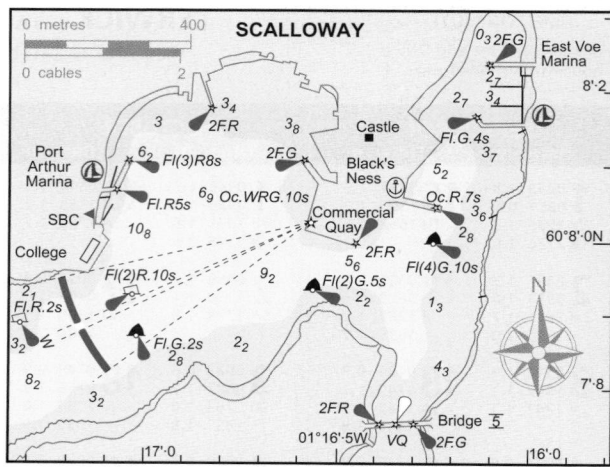

SCALLOWAY, Mainland, **60°08'·02N 01°16'·59W**. AC 3294. HW –0200 on Dover; ML 0·9m; Duration 0620. See 9.7.25. A busy fishing port; good shelter and ‡ in all weathers. Care is needed negotiating the islands in strong SW'lies. The N Chan is easier and safer than the S Chan, both are well lit and marked. Castle and warehouse (both conspic) lead 054° through S Chan. Dir Oc WRG 10s on hbr quay leads 064·5° into hbr. Hbr lts as chartlet. **Ⓥ** pontoon in 3m off SBC is best option; marina close N or new marina in E Voe (though mostly full of local boats). ‡s in hbr 6–10m or in Hamna Voe (W Burra). Call *Scalloway Hbr Radio* VHF Ch **12** 09 16 (Mon-Fri 0600-1800; Sat 0600-1230LT). Piermaster ☎ (01595) 880574. **Facilities: Scalloway Boat Club** (SBC) ☎ 880409 welcomes visitors; AB (free), Bar. **Town** Slip, P, D, FW, SM, BY, CH, C, El, ME, ✕, ✉, R, 🛒, Bar.

VAILA SOUND (WALLS), Mainland, **60°13'·65N 01°33'·87W**. AC 3295. Tides approx as Scalloway (above); see 9.7.25. Appr to E of Vaila island (do not attempt Wester Sound) in the W sector (355°-012°) of Rams Head lt, Fl WRG 8s 16m 9/6M. Gruting Voe lies to the NE. Enter Easter Sound and go N for 1·5M, passing E of Linga islet, to Walls at the head of Vaila Voe. Navigate by echo sounder. Beware fish farms. Temporary AB on Bayhaa pier (covers). Close E of this, AB £1 on pontoon of Peter Georgeson. **Marina**: Sec ☎ (01595) 809273, FW. **Walls Regatta Club** welcomes visitors; showers, Bar, Slip. **Village**: P & D (cans), 🛒, ✉.

SKELD, Mainland, **60°09'·65N 01°27'·W**. AC 3283, 3294. Tides approx as Scalloway (above); see 9.7.25. Appr from Skelda Voe. 1M S of ent which is subject to heavy seas and swell in strong S'lies. Beware Braga Rk (dries 2m) and drying rock 1ca S of it. At E of ent also Snap Rk (dries 3.5m) with isolated rocks inshore. **Marina** offers good shelter as virtually landlocked, welcomes visitors; 8**Ⓥ** £10/craft/week; James Scott ☎ (01595) 860287, FW, ⌐Ⓓ, showers, P & D (cans), Bus to Lerwick 2/daily.

FAIR ISLE, Shetland Islands, **59°32'·37N 01°36'·21W** (North Haven). AC 3299. HW –0030 on Dover; ML 1·4m; Duration 0620. See 9.7.25 Good shelter in North Haven, except in NE winds. AB on pier or ‡ in approx 2m. Beware strong cross-tides in the apprs; beware also rocks all round Fair Isle, particularly in S Haven and South Hbr which are not recommended. Ldg marks 199° into North Haven: front, Stack of N Haven (only visible as a dark 'tooth' sticking up from the jumble of blocks which form the bkwtr) in transit with conspic summit of Sheep Craig (rear). Dir lt into N Haven, Oc WRG 8s 10m 6M, vis 204°-G-208°-W-211°-R-221°. Other lts: At N tip, Skroo Fl (2) 30s 80m **22M**, vis 086·7°-358°, Horn (3) 45s. At S tip, Skadan Fl (4) 30s 31m **22M**, vis 260°-146°, but obscd close inshore from 260°-282°, Horn (2) 60s. **Facilities**: 🛒, ✉ at N Shriva, ✈ and a bi-weekly mail boat (*Good Shepherd*) to Shetland.

ADLARD COLES NAUTICAL
WEATHER FORECASTS
BY FAX & TELEPHONE

Coastal/Inshore	2-day by Fax	5-day by Phone
Scotland North	09065 222 341	09068 969 641
Minch	09065 222 354	09068 969 654
Caledonia	09065 222 353	09068 969 653
Clyde	09065 222 352	09068 969 652
National (3-5 day)	09065 222 340	09068 969 640

Offshore	2-5 day by Fax	2-5 day by Phone
Southern North Sea	09065 222 358	09068 969 658
Northern North Sea	09065 222 362	09068 969 662
North West Scotland	09065 222 361	09068 969 661
Irish Sea	09065 222 359	09068 969 659

09068 CALLS COST 60P PER MIN. 09065 CALLS COST £1.50 PER MIN.

North West Scotland

Cape Wrath to Crinal Canal

NW Scotland

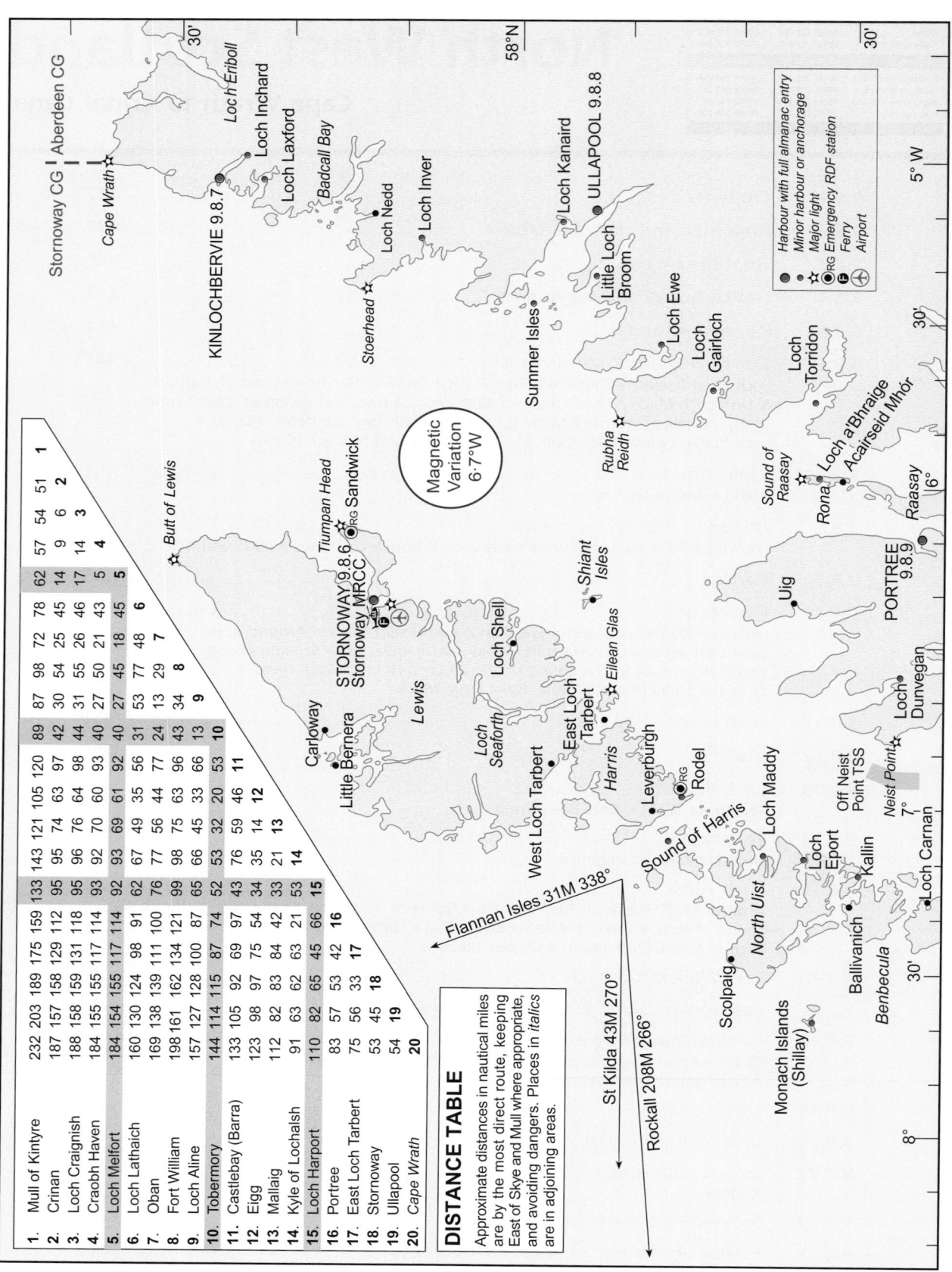

Stornoway CG | Aberdeen CG

Map labels: Cape Wrath · Loch Eriboll · Loch Inchard · Loch Laxford · KINLOCHBERVIE 9.8.7 · Badcall Bay · Loch Nedd · Loch Inver · Stoerhead · Loch Kanaird · ULLAPOOL 9.8.8 · Summer Isles · Little Loch Broom · Loch Ewe · Loch Gairloch · Loch Torridon · Rubha Reidh · Loch a'Bhraige · Acairseid Mhór · Sound of Raasay · Rona · Raasay · PORTREE 9.8.9 · Uig · Loch Dunvegan · Neist Point · Off Neist Point TSS · Butt of Lewis · Tiumpan Head · Sandwick RG · STORNOWAY 9.8.6 · Stornoway MRCC · Loch Shell · Shiant Isles · Lewis · Carloway · Little Bernera · Loch Seaforth · West Loch Tarbert · East Loch Tarbert · Harris · Eilean Glas · Leverburgh · Rodel RG · Sound of Harris · Loch Maddy · Loch Eport · Kallin · Loch Carnan · North Uist · Ballivanich · Benbecula · Scolpaig · Monach Islands (Shillay)

Magnetic Variation 6·7°W

Flannan Isles 31M 338°
St Kilda 43M 270°
Rockall 208M 266°

Grid: 58°N · 5°W · 30' · 8° · 7° · 6°

Legend:
- ● Harbour with full almanac entry
- • Minor harbour or anchorage
- ☆ Major light
- ⓡ RG Emergency RDF station
- Ⓛ Ferry
- ✈ Airport

DISTANCE TABLE

	Distances (nautical miles, as printed left → right)	No.
Mull of Kintyre	232 203 189 175 159 133 143 121 105 120 89 87 98 72 78 62 57 54 51	**1**
Crinan	187 157 158 129 112 95 95 74 63 97 42 30 54 25 45 14 9 6	**2**
Loch Craignish	188 158 159 131 118 96 96 76 64 98 44 31 55 26 46 17 14	**3**
Craobh Haven	184 155 155 117 114 93 92 70 60 93 40 27 50 21 43 5	**4**
Loch Melfort	184 154 155 117 114 92 93 69 61 92 40 27 45 18 45	**5**
Loch Lathaich	160 130 124 98 91 62 67 49 35 56 31 53 77 48	**6**
Oban	169 138 139 111 100 76 77 56 44 77 24 13 29	**7**
Fort William	198 161 162 134 121 99 98 75 63 96 43 34	**8**
Loch Aline	157 127 128 100 87 65 66 45 33 66 13	**9**
Tobermory	144 114 115 87 74 52 53 32 20 53	**10**
Castlebay (Barra)	133 105 92 69 97 43 76 59 46	**11**
Eigg	123 98 98 75 54 34 35 14	**12**
Mallaig	112 82 83 84 42 33 21	**13**
Kyle of Lochalsh	91 63 62 63 21 53	**14**
Loch Harport	110 82 65 45 66	**15**
Portree	83 57 53 42	**16**
East Loch Tarbert	75 56 33	**17**
Stornoway	53 45	**18**
Ullapool	54	**19**
Cape Wrath		**20**

Approximate distances in nautical miles are by the most direct route, keeping East of Skye and Mull where appropriate, and avoiding dangers. Places in *italics* are in adjoining areas.

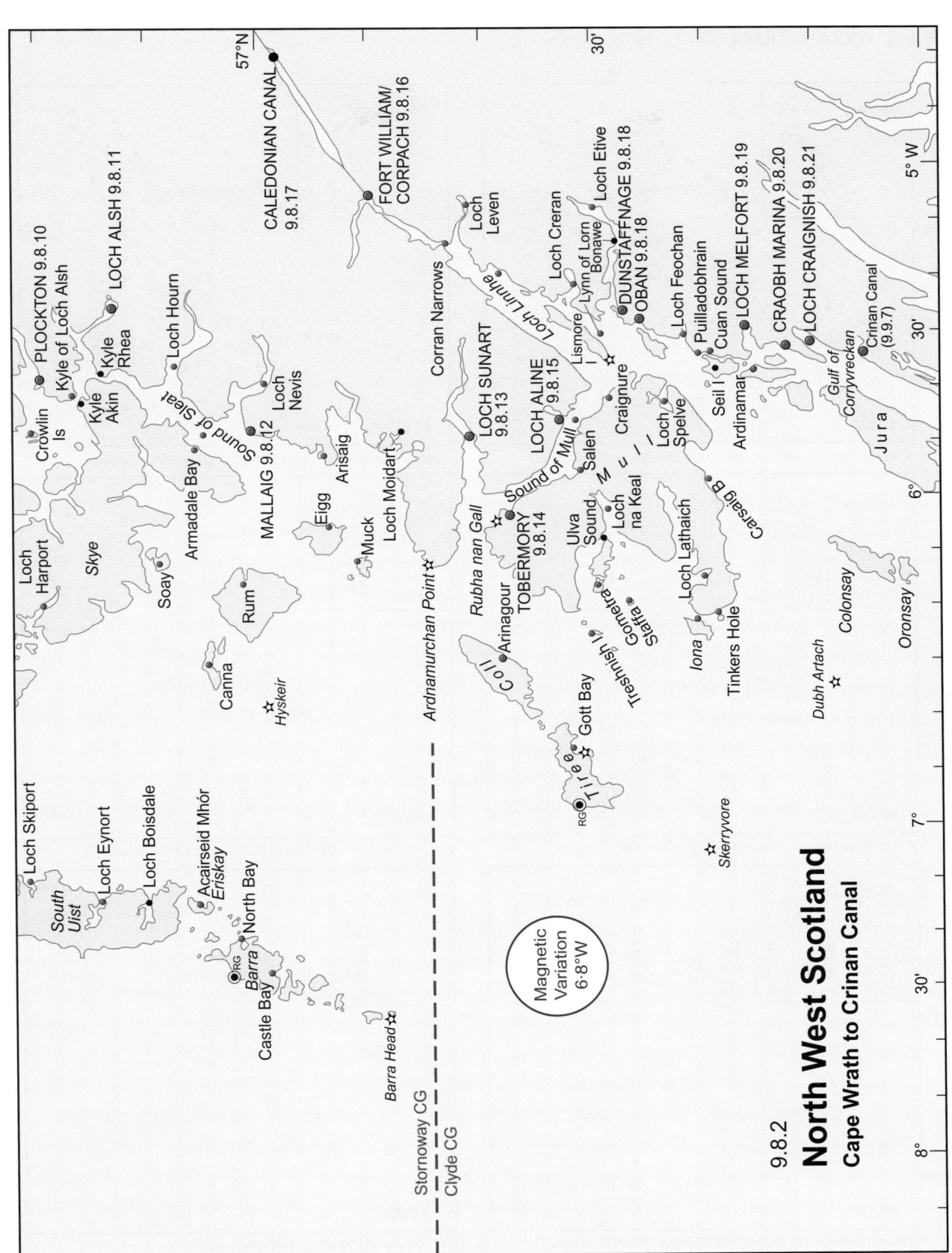

PLOCKTON 9.8.10
Kyle of Loch Alsh
LOCH ALSH 9.8.11
Kyle Akin
Kyle Rhea
Loch Hourn
Crowlin Is
Loch Nevis
Loch Harport
Sound of Sleat
Skye
Armadale Bay
Arisaig
MALLAIG 9.8.12
Eigg
Loch Moidart
Soay
Muck
Rum
Canna
Hyskeir

CALEDONIAN CANAL 9.8.17
FORT WILLIAM/ CORPACH 9.8.16
Corran Narrows

Loch Linnhe
LOCH SUNART 9.8.13
LOCH ALINE 9.8.15
Sound of Mull
Lismore I
Salen
Craignure
M u l l
TOBERMORY 9.8.14
Ardnamurchan Point
Rubha nan Gall
Arinagour
Ulva Sound
Loch na Keal
Gometra
Staffa
Loch Lathaich
Iona
Tinkers Hole

Loch Leven
Loch Creran
Loch Etive
Bonawe
Lynn of Lorn
DUNSTAFFNAGE 9.8.18
OBAN 9.8.18
Loch Feochan
Puilladobhrain
Cuan Sound
Seil I
Loch Spelve
Ardinamar
Carsaig B
Loch Melfort 9.8.19
CRAOBH MARINA 9.8.20
LOCH CRAIGNISH 9.8.21
Crinan Canal (9.9.7)
Gulf of Corryvreckan
J u r a

C o l l
Tiree
Gott Bay
Treshnish I
RG
Dubh Artach
Colonsay
Oronsay

Skerryvore

Loch Skiport
Loch Eynort
Loch Boisdale
Acairseid Mhór
Eriskay
South Uist
Barra North Bay
Castle Bay
RG
Barra Head

Stornoway CG
Clyde CG

Magnetic Variation 6·8°W

9.8.2
North West Scotland
Cape Wrath to Crinan Canal

57°N
30'
5° W
30'
6°
7°
30'
8°

9.8.3 AREA 8 TIDAL STREAMS

5 Hours before HW Dover (0050 before HW Ullapool)

4 Hours before HW Dover (0010 after HW Ullapool)

3 Hours before HW Dover (0110 after HW Ullapool)

2 Hours before HW Dover (0210 after HW Ullapool)

1 Hour before HW Dover (0310 after HW Ullapool)

HW Dover (0410 after HW Ullapool)

Eastward 9.7.3   Southward 9.9.3   Mull of Kintyre 9.9.10

1 Hour after HW Dover (0510 after HW Ullapool)

2 Hours after HW Dover (0615 before HW Ullapool)

3 Hours after HW Dover (0515 before HW Ullapool)

4 Hours after HW Dover (0415 before HW Ullapool)

5 Hours after HW Dover (0315 before HW Ullapool)

6 Hours after HW Dover (0215 before HW Ullapool)

9.8.4 LIGHTS, BUOYS AND WAYPOINTS

Bold print = light with a nominal range of 15M or more. CAPITALS = place or feature. *CAPITAL ITALICS* = light-vessel, light float or Lanby. *Italics* = Fog signal. ***Bold italics*** = Racon. Abbreviations are in Chapter 1.

CAPE WRATH TO LOCH TORRIDON

Cape Wrath ☆ 58°37'·54N 04°59'·99W Fl (4) 30s 122m **22M**; W twr.

LOCH INCHARD and LOCH LAXFORD

Kinlochbervie Dir lt 327° ☆. 58°27'·49N 05°03'·08W WRG 15m **16M**; vis: 326°-FG-326·5°-Al GW-326·75°-FW-327·25°-Al RW-327·5°-FR-328°.

Creag Mhòr Dir lt 147°; Iso WRG 2s 16m 4M; vis: 136·5°-R -146·5°-W-147·5°-G-157·5°; 58°26'·99N 05°02'·45W.

Stoer Head ☆ 58°14'·43N 05°24'·07W Fl 15s 59m **24M**; W twr.

LOCH INVER, SUMMER ISLES and ULLAPOOL

Soyea I ⚓ Fl (2) 10s 34m 6M; 58°08'·56N 05°19'·67W.

Glas Leac ⚓ Fl WRG 3s 7m 5M; vis: 071°- W-078°-R-090°-G-103°-W-111°, 243°-W-247°-G-071°; 58°08'·68N 05°16'·36W.

Rubha Cadail ⚓ Fl WRG 6s 11m W9M, R6M, G6M; W twr; vis: 311°-G-320°-W-325°-R-103°-W-111°-G-118°-W-127°-R-157°-W-199°; 57°55'·51N 05°13'·40W.

Ullapool Pt ⚓ Iso R G 4s 8m 6M; W twr; vis: 258°-108°; 57°53'·59N 05°09'·93W.

Cailleach Head ⚓ Fl (2) 12s 60m 9M; W twr; vis: 015°-236°; 57°55'·81N 05°24'·23W.

LOCH EWE and LOCH GAIRLOCH

Fairway ⚓ L Fl 10s; 57°51'·98N 05°40'·09W.

Rubha Reidh ☆ 57°51'·52N 05°48'·72W Fl (4) 15s 37m **24M**.

Glas Eilean ⚓ Fl WRG 6s 9m W6M, R4M; vis: 080°-W-102°-R-296°-W-333°-G-080°; 57°42'·79N 05°42'·42W.

OUTER HEBRIDES – EAST SIDE

LEWIS

Butt of Lewis ☆ 58°30'·89N 06°15'·84W Fl 5s 52m **25M**; R twr; vis: 056°-320°.

Tiumpan Head ☆ 58°15'·66N 06°08'·29W Fl (2) 15s 55m **25M**; W twr.

Broad Bay Tong Anch. Ldg Lts 320°, Oc R 8s 8m 4M; 58°14'·48N 06°19'·98W. Rear, 70m from front, Oc R 8s 9m 4M.

STORNOWAY

Arnish Point ☆ Fl WR 10s 17m W9M, R7M; W ○ twr; vis: 088°-W-198°-R-302°-W-013°; 58°11'·50N 06°22'·16W.

Sandwick Bay, NW side ⚓ Oc WRG 6s 10m 9M; vis: 334°-G-341°-W-347°-R-354°; 58°12'·20N 06°22'·11W.

No. 1 Pier SW corner ⚓ Q WRG 5m 11M; vis: shore-G-335°-W-352°-R-shore; 58°12'·36N 06°23'·43W.

Creed Estuary ⚓ Iso WRG 10s 24m 5M; vis: 277°-G-282°-W-290°-R-295°; 58°12'·03N 06°23'·47W.

No. 3 Pier ⚓ Q (2) G 10s 7m 2M 58°12'·31N 06°23'·28W.

Glumaig Hbr ⚓ Iso WRG 3s 8m 3M; 58°11'·27N 06°22'·9W; grey framework twr; vis: 150°-G-174°-W-180°-R-205°.

LOCH ERISORT, LOCH SHELL and EAST LOCH TARBERT

Shiants ⚓ QG; 57°54'·57N 06°25'·70W.

Sgeir Inoe ⚓ Fl G 6s; ***Racon (M) 5M;*** 57°50'·93N 06°33'·93W.

Eilean Glas (Scalpay) ☆ 57°51'·41N 06°38'·55W Fl (3) 20s 43m **23M**; W twr, R bands; ***Racon (T) 16-18M.***

Sgeir Graidach ⚓ Q (6) + L Fl 15s; 57°50'·36N 06°41'·37W.

Sgeir Ghlas ⚓ Iso WRG 4s 9m W9M, R6M, G6M; W ○ twr; vis: 282°-G-319°-W-329°-R-153°-W-164°-G-171°; 57°52'·36N 06°45'·24W.

Tarbert ⚓ 57°53'·82N 06°47'·93W Oc WRG 6s 10m 5M

SOUND OF HARRIS, LEVERBURGH and BERNERAY

Fairway ⚓ L Fl 10s; 57°40'·35N 07°02'·15W.

No.1 ⚓ QG; 57°41'·20N 07°02'·67W.

No. 3 ⚓ Fl G 5s; 57°41'·86N 07°03'·44W.

No. 4 ⚓ Fl R 5s; 57°41'·76N 07°03'·63W.

Suilven ⚓ Fl (3)R 10s; 57°41'·68N 07°04'·36W.

Cabbage ⚓ Fl (2) R 6s; ***Racon (T) 5M (3cm);*** 57°42'·13N 07°03'·96W.

Leverburgh Ldg Lts 014·7°. Front, Q 10m 4M 57°46'·23N 07°02'·04W. Rear, Oc 3s 12m 4M.

Jane's Tower ⚓ Q (2) G 5s 6m 4M; vis: obscured 273°-318°; 57°45'·76N 07°02'·12W.

Leverburgh Reef ⚓ Fl R 2s 4m 57°45'·97N 07°01'·86W.

Leverburgh Pier Hd ⚓ Oc WRG 8s 5m 2M; Gy col; vis: 305°-G-059°-W-066°-R-125°; 57°46'·01N 07°01'·62W.

NORTH UIST

Fairway ⚓ L Fl 10s; 57°40'·23N 07°01'·39W.

Vallay Island ⚓ Fl WRG 3s 4m 8M; vis: 206°-W-085°-G-140°-W-145°-R-206°; 57°39'·69N 07°26'·42W.

Griminish Hbr Ldg Lts 183°. Front, QG 6m 4M; 57°39'·38N 07°26'·75W. Rear, 110m from front, QG 7m 4M.

LOCH MADDY and GRIMSAY

Weaver's Pt ⚓ 57°36'·49N 07°06'·00W Fl 3s 24m 7M; W hut.

Glas Eilean Mòr ⚓ 57°35'·95N 07°06'·70W Fl (2) G 4s 8m 5M.

Vallaquie I ⚓ Fl (3) WRG 8s 11m W7M, R5M, G5M; W pillar; vis: shore-G -205°-W-210°-R-240°-G-254°-W-257°-R-shore; 57°35'·50N 07°09'·40W.

Lochmaddy Ldg Lts 298°. Front, Ro-Ro Pier 2 FG (vert) 8m 4M. Rear, 110m from front, Oc G 8s 10m 4M; vis: 284°-304°; 57°35'·76N 07°09'·36W.

Grimsay No. 1 ⚓ Fl (2) R 8s; 57°28'·26N 07°11'·82W.

SOUTH UIST and LOCH CARNAN

Landfall ⚓ L Fl 10s; 57°22'·27N 07°11'·52W.

Ldg Lts 222°. Front Fl R 2s 7m 5M; W ◇ on post; 57°22'·00N 07°16'·34W. Rear, 58m from front, Iso R 10s 11m 5M; W ◇ on post.

Ushenish ☆ (S Uist) 57°17'·89N 07°11'·58W Fl WR 20s 54m **W19M, R15M**; W twr; vis: 193°-W-356°-R-018°.

LOCH BOISDALE

MacKenzie Rk ⚓ Fl (3) R 15s 3m 4M; 57°08'·24N 07°13'·71W.

Calvay E End ⚓ Fl (2) WRG 10s 16m W7M, R4M, G4M; W twr; vis: 111°-W-190°-G-202°-W-286°-R-111°; 57°08'·53N 07°15'·38W.

Gasay I ⚓ Fl WR 5s 10m W7M, R4M; W twr; vis: 120°-W-284°-R-120°; 57°08'·93N 07°17'·39W.

Ro-Ro Jetty Head ⚓ Iso RG 4s 8m 2M; vis: shore-G-283°-R-shore; 2 FG (vert) 8m 3M on dn; 57°09'·12N 07°18'·22W.

LUDAIG and ERISKAY

Ludaig Bwtr ⚓ 2 FR (vert) 6m 3M; 57°06'·17N 07°19'·49W.

Acairseid Mhor Ldg Lts 285°. Front, Oc R 6s 9m 4M; 57°03'·89N 07°17'·25W. Rear, 24m from front, Oc R 6s 10m 4M.

BARRA, CASTLEBAY and VATERSAY SOUND

Drover Rocks ⚓ Q (6) + L Fl 15s; 57°04'·08N 07°23'·54W.

Binch Rock ⚓ Q (6) + L Fl 15s; 57°01'·60N 07°17'·12W.

Curachan ⚓ Q (3) 10s; 56°58'·56N 07°20'·51W.

Ardveenish ⚓ Oc WRG 6m 9/6M; vis: 300°-G-304°-W-306°-R-310°; 57°00'·21N 07°24'·43W.

Bo Vich Chuan ⚓ Q (6) + L Fl 15s; ***Racon (M) 5M;*** 56°56'·15N 07°23'·31W.

Channel Rk ⚓ Fl WR 6s 4m W6M, R4M; vis: 121·5°-W-277°-R-121·5°; 56°56'·24N 07°28'·94W.

Sgeir a Scape ⚓ Fl (2) G 8s; 56°56'·25N 07°27'·21W.

Rubha Glas. Ldg Lts 295°. Front ⚓ FBu 9m 6M; Or △ on W twr; 56°56'·77N 07°30'·64W. Rear, 457m from front, FBu 15m 6M; Or ▽ on W twr; vis: 15° and 8° respectively either side of ldg line.

Barra Hd ☆ 56°47'·11N 07°39'·26W Fl 15s 208m **18M**; W twr; obsc by islands to NE.

OUTER HEBRIDES – WEST SIDE

Flannan I ☆, Eilean Mór Fl (2) 30s 101m **20M**; W twr; 58°17'·32N 07°35'·23W, obsc in places by Is to W of Eilean Mór.

Rockall ⚓ Fl 15s 19m 8M (unreliable); 57°35'·76N 13°41'·27W.

WGS84 DATUM
Plot waypoints on chart before use

Gasker Lt ⚡ Fl (3) 10s 38m 10M; 57°59'·05N 07°17'·20W.
Whale Rock ↯ Q (3) 10s 5m 5M; *Racon (T)*; 57°54'·40N 07°59.91W.
Haskeir I ⚡ 57°41'·98N 07°41.36W Fl 20s 44m **23M**; W twr; *Racon (M) 17–15M.*
Monach Isles ☆ Fl (2) 15s 47m **18M**; R brick twr; 57°31'·55N 07°41'·68W.

EAST LOCH ROAG
Aird Laimishader Carloway ⚡ Fl 6s 63m 8M; W hut; obsc on some brgs; 58°17'·06N 06°49'·50W.
Ardvanich Pt ⚡ Fl G 3s 4m 2M; 58°13'·48N 06°47'·68W.
Tidal Rk ⚡ Fl R 3s 2m 2M (synch with Ardvanich Pt above); 58°13'·45N 06°47'·57W.
Grèinam ⚡ Fl WR 6s 8m W8M, R7M; W Bn; vis: R143°-169°, W169°-143°; 58°13'·30N 06°46'·16W.

NORTH UIST and SOUTH UIST
Vallay I ⚡ Fl WRG 3s 8M; vis: 206°-W-085°-G-140°-W-145°-R-206°; 57°39'·70N 07°26'·34W.
Falconet twr ⚡ FR 25m 8M (3M by day); shown 1hr before firing, changes to Iso R 2s 15 min before firing until completion; 57°22'·04N 07°23'·58W.

ST KILDA
Ldg Lts 270°. Front, Oc 5s 26m 3M; 57°48'·32N 08°34'·31W. Rear, 100m from front, Oc 5s 38m 3M; synch.

LOCH TORRIDON TO MALLAIG
LITTLE MINCH and W SKYE
Eugenie Rock t Q 6 + LF 15s; 57°46'·47N 06°27'·28W.
Eilean Troddday ⚡ Fl (2) WRG 10s 52m W12M, R9M, G9M; W Bn; vis: W062°-R088°-130°-W-322°-G-062°; 57°43'·64N 06°17'·89W.
Uig, Edward Pier Hd ⚡ 57°35'·09N 06°22'·29W Iso WRG 4s 9m W7M, R4M, G4M; vis: 180-W-006°-G-050°-W-073°-R-180°.
Waternish Pt ⚡ Fl 20s 21m 8M; W twr; 57°36'·48N 06°37'·99W.
Loch Dunvegan, Uiginish Pt ⚡ Fl WRG 3s 16m W7M,R5M,G5M; W metal-framed Twr; vis: 041°-G-132°-W-145°-R-148°-W-253°-R-263°-W-273°-G-306°, obsc by Fiadhairt Pt when brg > 148°; 57°26'·84N 06°36'·53W.
Neist Point ☆ 57°25'·41N 06°47'·30W Fl 5s 43m **16M**; W twr.
Loch Harport, Ardtreck Pt ⚡ 57°20'·38N 06°25'·80W Fl 6s 18m 9M; small W twr.

RONA, LOCH A'BHRAIGE and INNER SOUND
Na Gamhnachain ↯ Q; 57°35'·89N 05°57'·71W.
Rona NE Point ☆ 57°34'·68N 05°57'·56W Fl 12s 69m **19M**; W twr; vis: 050°-358°.
Loch A'Bhraige, Sgeir Shuas ⚡ Fl R 2s 6m 3M; vis: 070°-199°; 57°35'·02N 05°58'·61W.
Ldg Lts 136·5°. Front, ↯ Q WRG 3m W4M, R3M; vis: 135°-W- 138°-R-318°-G-135°; 57°34'·41N 05°58'·09W. Rear, ↯ Iso 6s 28m 5M.
Ru Na Lachan ⚡ Oc WR 8s 21m 10M; twr; vis: 337°-W-022°- R-117°-W-162°; 57°29'·02N 05°52'·15W.

SOUND OF RAASAY, PORTREE and CROWLIN ISLANDS
Sgeir Mhór ↯ Fl G 5s; 57°24'·57N 06°10'·53W.
Eilean Beag ⚡ Fl 6s 32m 6M; W Bn; 57°21'·21N 05°51'·42W.

RAASAY and LOCH SLIGACHAN
Suisnish ⚡ 2 FG (vert) 8m 2M; 57°19'·87N 06°03'·91W.
Eyre Point ⚡ Fl WR 3s 6m W9M, R6M; W twr; vis: 215°-W-266°-R-288°-W-063°; 57°20'·01N 06°01'·29W.

KYLEAKIN and KYLE OF LOCH ALSH
Carragh Rk ▲ Fl (2) G 12s; *Racon (T) 5M*; 57°17'·18N 05°45'·36W.
Bow Rk ◌ Fl (2) R 12s; 57°16'·71N 05°45'·85W.
Fork Rks ▲ Fl G 6s; 57°16'·85N 05°44'·93W.
Black Eye Rk ◌ Fl R 6s; 57°16'·72N 05°45'·31W.
Eileanan Dubha East ⚡ Fl (2) 10s 9m 8M; vis: obscured 104°-146°; 57°16'·56N 05°42'·32W.
8 Metre Rock ⚡ Fl G 6s 5m 4M; 57°16'·60N 05°42'·69W.
String Rock ◌ Fl R 6s; 57°16'·50N 05°42'·89W.

Sgeir-na-Caillich ⚡ Fl (2) R 6s 3m 4M; 57°15'·59N 05°38'·90W.

SOUND OF SLEAT
Kyle Rhea ⚡ Fl WRG 3s 7m W8M, R5M, G5M; W Bn; vis: shore-R-219°-W-228°-G-338°-W-346°-R-shore; 57°14'·22N 05°39'·93W.
Sandaig I, NW point ⚡ Fl 6s 13m 8M; W twr; 57°10'·05N 05°42'·29W.
Ornsay, SE end ☆ 57°08'·59N 05°46'·88W Oc 8s 18m **15M**; W twr; vis: 157°-030°.
Pt. of Sleat ⚡ Fl 3s 20m9M; W twr; 57°01'·08N06°01'·08W.

MALLAIG and LOCH NEVIS ENTRANCE
Sgeir Dhearg ▲ QG; 57°00'·74N 05°49'·50W.
Northern Pier E end ⚡ Iso WRG 4s 6m W9M, R6M, G6M; Gy twr; vis: 181°-G-185°-W-197°-R-201°. Fl G 3s 14m 6M; same structure; 57°00'·47N 05°49'·50W.
Sgeir Dhearg ⚡ 57°00'·63N 05°49'·61W Fl (2) WG 8s 6m 5M; Gy Bn; vis: 190°-G-055°-W-190°.

CANNA and RUM
Canna, E end Sanday Is ⚡ Fl 10s 32m 9M; W twr; vis: 152°-061°; 57°02'·82N 06°28'·02W.
Loch Screesort ↯ Q; 57°00'·79N 06°14'·61W.

HYSKEIR, EIGG, MUCK and ARISAIG
Humla ▲ Fl G 6s 3m 4M 57°00'·46N 06°37'·39W.
Hyskeir ☆ 56°58'·14N 06°40'·87W Fl (3) 30s 41m **24M**; W twr. *Racon (T) 14-17M.*
SE point Eigg (Eilean Chathastail) ⚡ Fl 6s 24m 8M; W twr; vis: 181°-shore; 56°52'·25N 06°07'·28W.
Eigg, Sgeir nam Bagh (Ferry Terminal) ⚡ Dir 245°; Fl WRG 3s 9m W14, R11, G11; H24; steel pole; vis: 242·5°-G-244°-W-246°-R-247·5°. 2FR(vert) on same structure; 56°52'·80N 06°07'·60W.
Isle of Muck (Port Mor) ⚡ Dir Fl WRG 3s 7m W14, R11, G11, by day W1, R1, G1; steel twr; vis: 319·5°-G-321°-W-323°-R-324·5°; 56°49'·96N 06°13'·64W.
Bogha Ruadh⚡ Fl G 5s 4m 3M; 56°49'·56N 06°13'·05W.
Bo Faskadale ▲ Fl (3) G 18s; 56°48'·18N 06°06'·37W.
Ardnamurchan ☆ 56°43'·63N 06°13'·58W Fl (2) 20s 55m **24M**; Gy twr; vis: 002°-217°.
Cairns of Coll, Suil Ghorm ⚡ Fl 12s 23m 10M; W twr; 56°42'·26N 06°26'·75W.

TIREE, COLL and ARINAGOUR
Loch Eatharna, Bogha Mór ▲ Fl G 6s; 56°36'·65N 06°30'·90W.
Roan Bogha ↯ Q (6) + L Fl 15s 3m 5M; 56°32'·23N 06°40'·18W.
Placaid Bogha ▲ Fl G 4s; 56°33'·22N 06°44'·06W.
Scarinish ☆, S side of ent 56°30'·01N 06°48'·27W Fl 3s 11m **16M**; W □ twr; vis: 210°-030°.
Cairn na Burgh More (Treshnish Is), Fl (3) 15s 36m 8M; solar panels on framework tr; 56°31'·05N 06°22'·95W.
Gott Bay Ldg Lts 286·5°. Front FR 8m; 56°30'·61N 06°47'·82W. Rear 30m from front FR 11m.
Cairn na Burgh More (Treshnish Is), Fl (3) 15s 36m 8M; solar panels on framework tr; 56°31'·05N 06°22'·95W.
Skerryvore ☆ Fl 10s 46m **23M**; Gy twr; *Racon (M) 18M*. 56°19'·36N 07°06'·88W

LOCH NA LÀTHAICH (LOCH LATHAICH)
Eileanan na Liathanaich, SE end ⚡ Fl WR 6s 12m W8M, R6M; vis: R088°- W108°-088°; 56°20'·56N 06°16'·38W.
Loch Eatharna, Pier Head ⚡ Dir Oc WRG 7s 6m 2M; vis: 316°-G-322°-W-328°-R-334°; 56°36'·86N 06°31'·29W.
Dubh Artach ☆ 56°07'·94N 06°38'·08W Fl (2) 30s 44m **20M**; Gy twr, R band.

SOUND OF MULL
LOCH SUNART, TOBERMORY and LOCH ALINE
Ardmore Pt ⚡ Fl (2) 10s 18m 13M; 56°39'·37N 06°07'·70W.
New Rks ▲ Fl G 6s 56°39'·05N 06°03'·30W.

Rubha nan Gall ☆ 56°38'·33N 06°04'·00W Fl 3s 17m **15M**; W twr.
Eileanan Glasa (Dearg Sgeir) ≼ 56°32'·25N 05°54'·80W Fl 6s 7m 8M; W ○ twr.
Fiunary Spit ▲ 56°32'·66N 05°53'·17W Fl G 6s.
Lochaline Ldg Lts 356°. Front, F 2m; 56°32'·39N 05°46'·49W. Rear, 88m from front, F 4m; both H24.

Ardtornish Pt ≼ Fl (2) WRG 10s 8m W8M, R6M, G6M; W twr; vis: G shore- 302°-W-308°-R-342°-W-057°-R-095°-W-108°-G-shore; 56°31'·10N 05°45'·23W.

Craignure Ldg Lts 240·9°. Front, FR 10m; 56°28'·26N 05°42'·28W. Rear, 150m from front, FR 12m; vis: 225·8°-255·8°.

MULL TO CALEDONIAN CANAL AND OBAN

Lismore ☆, SW end 56°27'·34N 05°36'·45W Fl 10s 31m **17M**; W twr; vis: 237°-208°.

Lady's Rk ⌶ Fl 6s 12m 5M; 56°26'·92N 05°37'·05W.
Duart Pt ≼ Fl (3) WR 18s 14m W5M, R3M; vis: 162°-W-261°-R-275°-W-353°-R-shore; 56°26'·84N 05°38'·77W.

LOCH LINNHE

Corran Shoal ≋ QR 56°43'·69N 05°14'·39W.
Ent W side, Corran Pt ≼ Iso WRG 4s 12m W10M, R7M, G7M; W twr; vis: shore-R-195°-W-215°-G-020-W-030°-R-shore;56°43'·25N 05°14'·54W.
Corran Narrows NE ≼Fl 5s 4m 4M; W twr; vis: S shore-214°; 56°43'·62N 05°13'·90W .
Clovullin Spit ≋ Fl (2) R 15s; 56°42'·29N 05°15'·56W.
Cuil-cheanna Spit ▲ Fl G 6s; 56°41'·17N 05°15'·72W.

FORT WILLIAM and CALEDONIAN CANAL

Corpach, Caledonian Canal Lock ent ≼ Iso WRG 4s 6m 5M; W twr; vis: G287°- W310°- R335°-030°; 56°50'·52N 05°07'·44W.

LYNN OF LORN

Sgeir Bhuidhe Appin ⌶ Fl (2) WR 7s 8m W9M R6M; W Bn; vis: W013·5°- R184°-220°; 56°33'·63N 05°24'·65W.
Appin Point ▲ Fl G 6s; 56°32'·69N 05°25'·97W.
Dearg Sgeir, off Aird's Point ⌶ Fl WRG 2s 2m W3M, R1M, G1M; vis: 196°-R-246°-W-258°-G-041°-W-058°-R-093°-W-139°; 56°32'·20N 05°25'·22W.
Rubha nam Faoileann (Eriska) ⌶ QG 2m 2M; G col; vis 128°-329°; 56°32'·20N 05°24'·11W.

DUNSTAFFNAGE BAY/OBAN

N spit of Kerrera ≼ Fl R 3s 9m 5M; W col, R bands; 56°25'·49N 05°29'·56W.
Dunollie ≼ Fl (2) WRG 6s 6m W8M, R6M, G6M; vis: 351°-G- 020°-W-047°-R-120°-W-138°-G-143°; 56°25'·37N 05°29'·05W.
Corran Ledge ⌿ VQ (9) 10s; 56°25'·19N 05°29'·11W.

OBAN TO LOCH CRAIGNISH

Kerrera Sound, Dubha Sgeirean ≼ Fl (2) 12s 7m 5M; W ○ twr; 56°22'·81N 05°32'·27W.
Bogha Nuadh ⌿ Q (6) + LFl 15s; 56°21'·69N 05°37'·88W.
Bono Rock ⌿ Q (9) 15s; 56°16'·21N 05°41'·22W.
Fladda ≼ Fl (2) WRG 9s 13m W11M, R9M, G9M; W twr; vis: 169°-R-186°-W-337°-G-344°-W-356°-R-026°; 56°14'·89N 05°40'·83W.
Dubh Sgeir (Luing) ≼Fl WRG 6s 9m W6M, R4M. G4M; W twr; vis: W000°- R010°- W025°- G199°-000°; *Racon (M) 5M*; 56°14'·76N 05°40'·20W.
The Garvellachs, Eileach an Naoimh, SW end ≼ Fl 6s 21m 9M; W Bn; vis: 240°-215°; 56°13'·04N 05°49'·06W.

LOCH MELFORT and CRAOBH HAVEN

Melfort Pier ≼ Dir FR 6m 3M; (Apr -Nov); 56°16'·14N 05°30'·19W.
▲ 56°12'·88N 05°33'·59W.
Craobh Marina Bkwtr Hd ≼ Iso WRG 5s 10m, W5M, R3M, G3M; vis:114°-G-162°-W-183°-R-200°; 56°12'·78N 05°33'·52W.

9.8.5 PASSAGE INFORMATION

It is essential to carry large scale charts and current Pilot Books: Admiralty *W Coast of Scotland Pilot*; Clyde Cruising Club's *Sailing Directions, Pt 2 Kintyre to Ardnamurchan* and *Pt 3 Ardnamurchan to Cape Wrath*; and the *Yachtsman's Pilot to W Coast of Scotland ; Vol 2 Crinan to Canna, Vol 3 The Western Isles, Vol 4 Skye & NW Scotland* (Lawrence/Imray).

Scotland's west coast provides splendid, if boisterous, sailing and matchless scenery. In summer the long daylight hours and warmth of the Gulf Stream compensate for the lower air temperatures and higher wind speeds experienced when depressions run typically north of Scotland. Inshore winds are often unpredictable, due to geographical effects of lochs, mountains and islands offshore; calms and squalls can alternate rapidly.

Good anchors, especially on kelp/weed, are essential. ⚓s are listed but it should not be assumed that these will always be available. Particularly in N of area, facilities are very dispersed. A *'Rover Ticket'* from Highland Council allows berthing for 15 days; the scheme includes: Kinlochbervie, Lochinver, Gairloch, Kyle of Lochalsh, Kyleakin, Portree and Uig. VHF communications with shore stations may be limited by high ground. Beware ever more fish farms in many inlets. Local magnetic anomalies occur in Kilbrannan Sound, Passage of Tiree, Sound of Mull, Canna, and East Loch Roag. Submarines exercise throughout these waters.

More Passage Information is threaded between the harbours in this Area.

OUTER HEBRIDES

(AC 1785, 1794, 1795) The E sides of these Is have many good, sheltered anchs, but W coasts give little shelter. The CCC's *Outer Hebrides SDs* or *The Western Isles* (Imray) are advised.

▶ *The Minches and Sea of the Hebrides can be very rough, particularly in the Little Minch between Skye and Harris, and around Shiant Is where tide runs locally 4kn at sp, and heavy overfalls can occur. The NE going stream on both shores begins at HW Ullapool -0340 (HW Dover +0430), with the strongest flow from mid channel to the Skye coast. There is a W going counter tide E of Vaternish Pt.*

The SW going stream on both shores begins at HW Ullapool +0240 (HW Dover –0130), with the strongest flow from mid channel to the Skye coast, sp rates 2·5kn. The E going stream in Sound of Scalpay runs at up to 2k.The E going flood and W going ebb in Sound of Scalpay run at up to 2k.◀

▶ *Sound of Harris. The behaviour of tidal streams is complicated and varies from day to night, springs to neaps, and winter to summer. In the NE part of the Sound, at springs, the stream sets SE from Ullapool +0535 to –0035. At neaps, in the summer, the stream sets SE during the day and NW during the night. To the SW of the Sound, the NW stream starts at Ullapool –0545; the SE stream starts at Ullapool +0025. The approximate maximum rates are as shown. For more detailed information refer to the Admiralty West Coast of Scotland Pilot.◀*

From N to S, the better harbours in Outer Hebrides include:

Lewis. Stornoway; Loch Grimshader (beware Sgeir a'Chaolais, dries in entrance); Loch Erisort; Loch Odhairn; Loch Shell. Proceeding S from here, or to E Loch Tarbert beware Sgeir Inoe (dries 2·3m) 3M ESE of Eilean Glas lt ho at SE end of Scalpay.

Harris. E Loch Tarbert; Loch Scadaby; Loch Stockinish; Loch Finsby; W Loch Tarbert; Loch Rodel (🅰). A well marked ferry chan connects Leverburgh (South Harris) to Berneray.

N Uist. Loch Maddy (🅰); Loch Eport, Kallin Hbr (🅰).

S Uist. Loch Carnan (🅰); Loch Skiport; Loch Eynort; Loch Boisdale (🅰).

Barra. Castlebay (🅰), and Berneray, on N side, E of Shelter Rk.

Activity at the Hebrides Range, S. Uist ☎ (01870) 604441, is broadcast daily at 0950LT and Mon-Fri 1100-1700LT on VHF Ch **12** (Ch 73 in emergency) and on MF 2660 kHz.

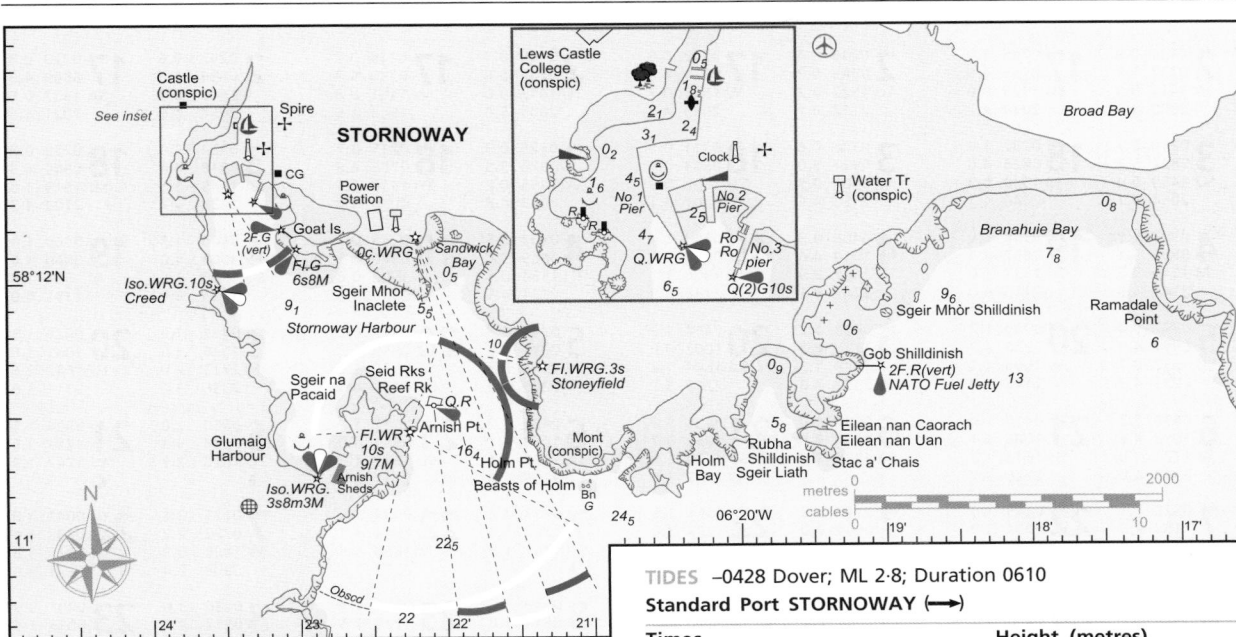

9.8.6   STORNOWAY

Lewis (Western Isles) **58°11'·58N 06°21'·82W** ❄❄❄⚓⚓⚓🏵🏵

CHARTS AC 1785, 1794, 2529; Imray C67.

SHELTER Good. A small marina, max LOA 12m, at the N end of the Inner Hbr, beyond the LB berth, has depths 1·4–3·3m. Or AB for larger boats on adjacent Cromwell St Quay, close S; or lie alongside FVs in the inner hbr. Visitors should report to HM. Ferries use W side No 3 pier, and commercial vessels on Nos 1 and 2 Piers. S'ly swells can make anchoring uncomfortable.

⚓s as on chartlet at: Poll nam Portan on the W side of inner chan, opposite No 1 Pier; Glumaig Hbr is best ⚓, and in bay NW of Goat Island (Eilean na Gobhail).

NAVIGATION WPT 58°09'·98N 06°20'·87W, 343°/2·3M to Oc WRG lt. Reef Rk, N of Arnish Pt on W side of ent, is marked by PHM buoy, QR. At the E side of ent an unlit G bn marks the Beasts of Holm, a rky patch off Holm Pt, on which is a conspic memorial. A local magnetic anomaly exists over a small area in mid-hbr, 1·75ca N of Seid Rks PHM bn.

LIGHTS AND MARKS Arnish sheds are conspic 3ca SW of Arnish Pt lt, W sector 302°-013° covers ent. Then in turn follow W sectors of: Sandwick Bay lt (close E of water tr, 3 power stn chys; all conspic), then Creed Estuary, Iso WRG 10s, across the harbour, and finally No 1 Pier, Q WRG.

R/T VHF Ch 12 16 (H24).

TELEPHONE (Code 01851) HM 702688; MRCC 702013; ⊖ 703626; Marinecall 09068 969654; Police 702222; Dr 703145.

FACILITIES **Marina** 27 berths, inc 8 🅥, £9.40 via HM Ch 12; FW. **Nos 1 & 2 Piers** FW, C (10 ton), CH, AB, Slip, P. **No3 Pier** AB(E side), FW, C (Mobile10+ ton), D(road tanker) **Services:** ACA, ME, El, ✖. **Town** P (cans), D, El, 🛒, 🅾, R, Bar, Gas, ✉, Ⓑ, ⇌ (Ferry to Ullapool, bus to Garve), ✈.

TIDES –0428 Dover; ML 2·8; Duration 0610
Standard Port STORNOWAY (→)

Times				Height (metres)			
High Water		Low Water		MHWS	MHWN	MLWN	MLWS
0100	0700	0300	0900	4·8	3·7	2·0	0·7
1300	1900	1500	2100				

East side of Outer Hebrides, N to S
Differences LOCH SHELL (Harris)

–0013	0000	0000	–0017	0·0	–0·1	–0·1	0·0

EAST LOCH TARBERT (Harris)

–0025	–0010	–0010	–0020	+0·2	0·0	+0·1	+0·1

LOCH MADDY (N Uist)

–0044	–0014	–0016	–0030	0·0	–0·1	–0·1	0·0

LOCH CARNAN (S Uist)

–0050	–0010	–0020	–0040	–0·3	–0·5	–0·1	–0·1

LOCH SKIPORT (S Uist)

–0100	–0025	–0024	–0024	–0·2	–0·4	–0·3	–0·2

LOCH BOISDALE (S Uist)

–0055	–0030	–0020	–0040	–0·7	–0·7	–0·3	–0·2

BARRA (North Bay)

–0103	–0031	–0034	–0048	–0·6	–0·5	–0·2	–0·1

CASTLE BAY (Barra)

–0115	–0040	–0045	–0100	–0·5	–0·6	–0·3	–0·1

BARRA HEAD (Berneray)

–0115	–0040	–0045	–0055	–0·8	–0·7	–0·2	+0·1

West side of Outer Hebrides, N to S
CARLOWAY (W Lewis)

–0040	+0020	–0035	–0015	–0·6	–0·5	–0·4	–0·1

LITTLE BERNERA (W Lewis)

–0021	–0011	–0017	–0027	–0·5	–0·6	–0·4	–0·2

WEST LOCH TARBERT (W Harris)

–0015	–0015	–0046	–0046	–1·1	–0·9	–0·5	0·0

SCOLPAIG (W North Uist)

–0033	–0033	–0040	–0040	–1·0	–0·9	–0·5	0·0

SHILLAY (Monach Islands)

–0103	–0043	–0047	–0107	–0·6	–0·7	–0·7	–0·3

BALIVANICH (W Benbecula)

–0103	–0017	–0031	–0045	–0·7	–0·6	–0·5	–0·2

TIME ZONE (UT)
For Summer Time add ONE hour in **non-shaded areas**

STORNOWAY   LAT 58°12'N   LONG 6°23'W
TIMES AND HEIGHTS OF HIGH AND LOW WATERS

Dates in red are **SPRINGS**
Dates in blue are **NEAPS**

YEAR 2010

JANUARY

Day	Time	m	Day	Time	m
1 F	0050 / 0652 / 1327 / 1923	0.9 / 5.0 / 0.7 / 4.8	16 SA	0132 / 0724 / 1358 / 1945	1.0 / 4.6 / 1.0 / 4.2
2 SA	0135 / 0737 / 1414 / 2009	0.8 / 5.1 / 0.5 / 4.8	17 SU	0205 / 0755 / 1429 / 2014	1.0 / 4.6 / 0.9 / 4.2
3 SU	0219 / 0822 / 1459 / 2054	0.7 / 5.2 / 0.4 / 4.7	18 M	0237 / 0826 / 1500 / 2044	1.0 / 4.6 / 0.9 / 4.1
4 M	0303 / 0908 / 1545 / 2141	0.7 / 5.1 / 0.5 / 4.5	19 TU	0308 / 0857 / 1532 / 2115	1.0 / 4.5 / 1.0 / 4.0
5 TU	0347 / 0957 / 1632 / 2233	0.9 / 4.9 / 0.7 / 4.3	20 W	0340 / 0930 / 1606 / 2148	1.2 / 4.3 / 1.1 / 3.9
6 W	0433 / 1053 / 1721 / 2333	1.2 / 4.6 / 1.0 / 4.0	21 TH	0415 / 1006 / 1643 / 2228	1.4 / 4.1 / 1.3 / 3.7
7 TH	0525 / 1158 / 1816	1.5 / 4.3 / 1.3	22 F	0453 / 1051 / 1725 / 2321	1.6 / 3.9 / 1.5 / 3.6
8 F	0042 / 0624 / 1311 / 1918	3.8 / 1.7 / 4.0 / 1.6	23 SA	0539 / 1150 / 1814	1.8 / 3.8 / 1.7
9 SA	0156 / 0738 / 1428 / 2033	3.7 / 1.9 / 3.8 / 1.8	24 SU	0032 / 0635 / 1301 / 1914	3.5 / 2.0 / 3.7 / 1.8
10 SU	0308 / 0906 / 1541 / 2150	3.7 / 2.0 / 3.7 / 1.8	25 M	0148 / 0750 / 1418 / 2029	3.5 / 2.0 / 3.7 / 1.9
11 M	0410 / 1024 / 1643 / 2250	3.8 / 1.8 / 3.8 / 1.7	26 TU	0303 / 0920 / 1536 / 2150	3.7 / 1.9 / 3.8 / 1.7
12 TU	0500 / 1123 / 1731 / 2338	4.0 / 1.6 / 3.8 / 1.5	27 W	0411 / 1038 / 1644 / 2258	4.0 / 1.6 / 4.0 / 1.5
13 W	0541 / 1209 / 1811	4.2 / 1.4 / 3.9	28 TH	0508 / 1138 / 1739 / 2352	4.3 / 1.2 / 4.3 / 1.2
14 TH	0019 / 0618 / 1250 / 1844	1.3 / 4.4 / 1.2 / 4.0	29 F	0557 / 1230 / 1827	4.7 / 0.8 / 4.6
15 F	0057 / 0652 / 1325 / 1916	1.2 / 4.5 / 1.1 / 4.1	30 SA	0039 / 0641 / 1316 / 1910	0.8 / 5.0 / 0.4 / 4.8
			31 SU	0124 / 0723 / 1400 / 1951	0.6 / 5.3 / 0.2 / 4.9

FEBRUARY

Day	Time	m	Day	Time	m
1 M	0205 / 0804 / 1441 / 2031	0.4 / 5.4 / 0.1 / 4.9	16 TU	0214 / 0757 / 1432 / 2012	0.7 / 4.7 / 0.7 / 4.3
2 TU	0246 / 0845 / 1522 / 2112	0.4 / 5.3 / 0.2 / 4.7	17 W	0242 / 0825 / 1501 / 2039	0.8 / 4.6 / 0.7 / 4.2
3 W	0326 / 0927 / 1604 / 2155	0.6 / 5.0 / 0.5 / 4.4	18 TH	0311 / 0853 / 1532 / 2107	0.9 / 4.4 / 0.9 / 4.1
4 TH	0408 / 1014 / 1647 / 2245	0.9 / 4.6 / 0.9 / 4.1	19 F	0343 / 0924 / 1606 / 2138	1.1 / 4.2 / 1.1 / 3.9
5 F	0453 / 1113 / 1734 / 2352	1.2 / 4.2 / 1.3 / 3.8	20 SA	0417 / 1002 / 1644 / 2219	1.3 / 4.0 / 1.3 / 3.7
6 SA	0544 / 1234 / 1830	1.6 / 3.8 / 1.7	21 SU	0458 / 1059 / 1729 / 2327	1.6 / 3.7 / 1.6 / 3.5
7 SU	0117 / 0651 / 1404 / 1947	3.5 / 2.0 / 3.5 / 2.0	22 M	0551 / 1227 / 1828	1.9 / 3.6 / 1.8
8 M	0209 / 0837 / 1526 / 2127	3.5 / 2.1 / 3.5 / 2.1	23 TU	0109 / 0710 / 1400 / 1953	3.5 / 2.0 / 3.5 / 2.0
9 TU	0350 / 1019 / 1635 / 2237	3.6 / 2.0 / 3.5 / 1.9	24 W	0239 / 0905 / 1526 / 2134	3.6 / 1.9 / 3.7 / 1.8
10 W	0445 / 1118 / 1724 / 2325	3.9 / 1.7 / 3.7 / 1.6	25 TH	0355 / 1029 / 1634 / 2245	3.9 / 1.5 / 4.0 / 1.5
11 TH	0527 / 1200 / 1759	4.1 / 1.4 / 3.8	26 F	0454 / 1126 / 1726 / 2338	4.3 / 1.0 / 4.4 / 1.1
12 F	0005 / 0602 / 1235 / 1828	1.4 / 4.3 / 1.2 / 4.0	27 SA	0542 / 1214 / 1810	4.8 / 0.6 / 4.7
13 SA	0041 / 0634 / 1307 / 1856	1.1 / 4.5 / 1.0 / 4.1	28 SU	0023 / 0624 / 1258 / 1850	0.7 / 5.1 / 0.2 / 4.9
14 SU	0114 / 0703 / 1336 / 1921	0.9 / 4.6 / 0.8 / 4.3			
15 M	0145 / 0731 / 1404 / 1946	0.8 / 4.7 / 0.7 / 4.3			

MARCH

Day	Time	m	Day	Time	m
1 M	0106 / 0704 / 1338 / 1928	0.4 / 5.3 / 0.0 / 5.0	16 TU	0118 / 0703 / 1333 / 1918	0.8 / 4.7 / 0.7 / 4.5
2 TU	0146 / 0742 / 1417 / 2005	0.3 / 5.4 / 0.0 / 5.0	17 W	0146 / 0729 / 1401 / 1943	0.7 / 4.7 / 0.6 / 4.5
3 W	0225 / 0820 / 1455 / 2042	0.3 / 5.3 / 0.2 / 4.8	18 TH	0215 / 0756 / 1430 / 2010	0.7 / 4.6 / 0.6 / 4.4
4 TH	0303 / 0859 / 1534 / 2121	0.5 / 5.0 / 0.5 / 4.5	19 F	0245 / 0826 / 1502 / 2038	0.8 / 4.5 / 0.8 / 4.3
5 F	0343 / 0941 / 1614 / 2205	0.8 / 4.5 / 0.9 / 4.2	20 SA	0317 / 0859 / 1535 / 2110	0.9 / 4.3 / 1.0 / 4.1
6 SA	0425 / 1033 / 1657 / 2305	1.2 / 4.1 / 1.4 / 3.8	21 SU	0352 / 0941 / 1613 / 2152	1.2 / 4.0 / 1.3 / 3.9
7 SU	0513 / 1200 / 1747	1.6 / 3.6 / 1.9	22 M	0435 / 1044 / 1658 / 2303	1.4 / 3.7 / 1.6 / 3.6
8 M	0038 / 0614 / 1340 / 1902	3.6 / 2.0 / 3.4 / 2.2	23 TU	0531 / 1220 / 1759	1.7 / 3.5 / 1.9
9 TU	0206 / 0808 / 1506 / 2056	3.5 / 2.2 / 3.3 / 2.3	24 W	0052 / 0701 / 1353 / 1934	3.6 / 1.9 / 3.5 / 2.0
10 W	0320 / 1002 / 1618 / 2213	3.6 / 2.0 / 3.4 / 2.0	25 TH	0222 / 0855 / 1515 / 2118	3.7 / 1.7 / 3.7 / 1.9
11 TH	0419 / 1058 / 1705 / 2302	3.8 / 1.7 / 3.6 / 1.7	26 F	0337 / 1012 / 1618 / 2226	4.0 / 1.3 / 4.0 / 1.5
12 F	0503 / 1136 / 1737 / 2341	4.0 / 1.5 / 3.8 / 1.4	27 SA	0435 / 1106 / 1707 / 2317	4.4 / 0.9 / 4.4 / 1.1
13 SA	0538 / 1209 / 1805	4.2 / 1.2 / 4.0	28 SU	0522 / 1152 / 1749	4.8 / 0.5 / 4.7
14 SU	0016 / 0609 / 1239 / 1830	1.2 / 4.4 / 1.0 / 4.2	29 M	0002 / 0603 / 1234 / 1827	0.8 / 5.0 / 0.3 / 4.9
15 M	0049 / 0637 / 1307 / 1854	0.9 / 4.6 / 0.8 / 4.4	30 TU	0044 / 0642 / 1314 / 1904	0.5 / 5.2 / 0.2 / 5.0
			31 W	0124 / 0719 / 1351 / 1940	0.4 / 5.2 / 0.2 / 5.0

APRIL

Day	Time	m	Day	Time	m
1 TH	0203 / 0757 / 1429 / 2016	0.4 / 5.0 / 0.4 / 4.8	16 F	0150 / 0735 / 1403 / 1948	0.8 / 4.6 / 0.7 / 4.6
2 F	0242 / 0836 / 1506 / 2054	0.6 / 4.7 / 0.7 / 4.6	17 SA	0223 / 0809 / 1437 / 2021	0.8 / 4.5 / 0.8 / 4.5
3 SA	0322 / 0918 / 1545 / 2138	0.9 / 4.4 / 1.1 / 4.3	18 SU	0259 / 0849 / 1513 / 2100	0.9 / 4.3 / 1.0 / 4.3
4 SU	0404 / 1008 / 1626 / 2233	1.3 / 4.0 / 1.6 / 4.0	19 M	0340 / 0940 / 1554 / 2151	1.1 / 4.0 / 1.3 / 4.0
5 M	0451 / 1126 / 1713 / 2356	1.6 / 3.6 / 2.0 / 3.7	20 TU	0429 / 1051 / 1642 / 2311	1.3 / 3.8 / 1.6 / 3.8
6 TU	0550 / 1304 / 1820	2.0 / 3.3 / 2.3	21 W	0534 / 1217 / 1747	1.5 / 3.6 / 1.9
7 W	0121 / 0725 / 1428 / 2008	3.6 / 2.2 / 3.3 / 2.4	22 TH	0041 / 0703 / 1339 / 1921	3.8 / 1.6 / 3.6 / 2.0
8 TH	0236 / 0913 / 1541 / 2132	3.6 / 2.1 / 3.4 / 2.2	23 F	0201 / 0833 / 1453 / 2051	3.9 / 1.5 / 3.8 / 1.8
9 F	0338 / 1015 / 1631 / 2225	3.8 / 1.8 / 3.6 / 1.9	24 SA	0311 / 0945 / 1555 / 2157	4.1 / 1.2 / 4.0 / 1.5
10 SA	0427 / 1057 / 1706 / 2307	4.0 / 1.6 / 3.8 / 1.6	25 SU	0410 / 1039 / 1644 / 2250	4.4 / 0.9 / 4.3 / 1.2
11 SU	0505 / 1132 / 1734 / 2344	4.2 / 1.3 / 4.0 / 1.4	26 M	0459 / 1126 / 1726 / 2337	4.6 / 0.7 / 4.5 / 1.0
12 M	0538 / 1203 / 1800	4.3 / 1.1 / 4.3	27 TU	0542 / 1208 / 1805	4.8 / 0.6 / 4.7
13 TU	0017 / 0606 / 1232 / 1824	1.1 / 4.5 / 0.9 / 4.4	28 W	0021 / 0621 / 1249 / 1841	0.8 / 4.9 / 0.5 / 4.8
14 W	0048 / 0634 / 1301 / 1850	1.0 / 4.6 / 0.8 / 4.6	29 TH	0103 / 0700 / 1328 / 1918	0.7 / 4.8 / 0.6 / 4.8
15 TH	0118 / 0703 / 1331 / 1918	0.8 / 4.6 / 0.7 / 4.6	30 F	0144 / 0739 / 1406 / 1956	0.7 / 4.7 / 0.7 / 4.7

Chart Datum: 2·71 metres below Ordnance Datum (Newlyn). HAT is 5·5 metres above Chart Datum; see 4.5

FREE monthly updates from
www.reedsalmanac.co.uk

TIME ZONE (UT)
For Summer Time add ONE hour in **non-shaded areas**

STORNOWAY LAT 58°12'N LONG 6°23'W
TIMES AND HEIGHTS OF HIGH AND LOW WATERS

Dates in red are SPRINGS
Dates in blue are NEAPS

YEAR 2010

MAY

	Time	m		Time	m
1 SA	0225	0.8	**16** SU	0210	0.8
	0820	4.5		0803	4.5
	1443	1.0		1421	0.9
	2035	4.6		2015	4.6
2 SU	0306	1.0	**17** M	0253	0.9
	0903	4.2		0850	4.3
	1522	1.3		1501	1.0
	2119	4.4		2100	4.5
3 M	0349	1.3	**18** TU	0339	1.0
	0952	3.9		0945	4.1
	1602	1.6		1545	1.2
	2211	4.1		2157	4.3
4 TU	0435	1.6	**19** W	0433	1.1
	1053	3.6		1049	3.9
	1648	1.9		1636	1.5
	2315	3.9		2306	4.1
5 W	0528	1.8	**20** TH	0536	1.3
	1209	3.4		1200	3.8
	1745	2.1		1740	1.7
6 TH	0025	3.8	**21** F	0021	4.0
	0635	2.0		0646	1.3
	1329	3.3		1312	3.7
	1904	2.3		1857	1.8
7 F	0137	3.7	**22** SA	0133	4.0
	0758	2.0		0759	1.3
	1444	3.4		1422	3.8
	2031	2.2		2015	1.7
8 SA	0242	3.7	**23** SU	0241	4.1
	0912	1.9		0909	1.2
	1543	3.5		1526	3.9
	2135	2.1		2124	1.6
9 SU	0338	3.9	**24** M	0343	4.2
	1004	1.7		1009	1.1
	1625	3.8		1619	4.1
	2223	1.8		2223	1.4
10 M	0422	4.0	**25** TU	0437	4.3
	1045	1.5		1100	1.0
	1657	4.0		1704	4.3
	2304	1.6		2315	1.2
11 TU	0500	4.2	**26** W	0524	4.4
	1121	1.3		1146	0.9
	1725	4.2		1745	4.5
	2340	1.4			
12 W	0534	4.3	**27** TH	0003	1.1
	1155	1.1		0607	4.4
	1754	4.4		1229	0.9
				1824	4.6
13 TH	0016	1.2	**28** F	0049	1.0
	0607	4.4		0648	4.4
	1230	1.0		1310	0.9
	1825	4.5		1902	4.6
14 F	0052	1.0	**29** SA	0133	1.0
	0643	4.5		0729	4.3
	1306	0.9		1349	1.0
	1858	4.6		1941	4.6
15 SA	0130	0.9	**30** SU	0214	1.0
	0721	4.5		0809	4.2
	1342	0.8		1427	1.1
	1935	4.6		2021	4.6
			31 M	0255	1.1
				0850	4.1
				1505	1.3
				2102	4.4

JUNE

	Time	m		Time	m
1 TU	0335	1.2	**16** W	0336	0.7
	0933	3.9		0937	4.5
	1544	1.4		1539	1.0
	2146	4.3		2147	4.6
2 W	0417	1.4	**17** TH	0426	0.7
	1019	3.7		1032	4.1
	1625	1.7		1637	1.2
	2236	4.1		2246	4.4
3 TH	0501	1.6	**18** F	0519	0.9
	1111	3.5		1132	3.9
	1712	1.9		1722	1.4
	2330	3.9		2352	4.2
4 F	0549	1.7	**19** SA	0618	1.1
	1211	3.4		1238	3.8
	1807	2.1		1825	1.6
5 SA	0028	3.8	**20** SU	0101	4.1
	0643	1.8		0721	1.3
	1319	3.4		1347	3.7
	1910	2.2		1936	1.7
6 SU	0129	3.7	**21** M	0212	4.0
	0743	1.9		0829	1.4
	1429	3.5		1455	3.8
	2020	2.1		2052	1.7
7 M	0230	3.7	**22** TU	0320	3.9
	0847	1.8		0939	1.4
	1526	3.6		1556	3.9
	2123	2.0		2203	1.6
8 TU	0326	3.8	**23** W	0421	4.0
	0945	1.7		1039	1.3
	1610	3.8		1648	4.1
	2216	1.8		2303	1.5
9 W	0416	3.9	**24** TH	0514	4.0
	1035	1.5		1131	1.3
	1648	4.0		1732	4.2
	2302	1.6		2356	1.3
10 TH	0502	4.1	**25** F	0601	4.0
	1120	1.3		1216	1.2
	1726	4.3		1813	4.4
	2347	1.4			
11 F	0546	4.3	**26** SA	0043	1.2
	1203	1.2		0642	4.1
	1804	4.5		1258	1.1
				1850	4.5
12 SA	0032	1.1	**27** SU	0125	1.0
	0630	4.4		0720	4.1
	1246	1.0		1336	1.1
	1844	4.6		1927	4.6
13 SU	0118	0.9	**28** M	0204	1.0
	0714	4.5		0756	4.1
	1329	0.9		1413	1.0
	1925	4.8		2003	4.6
14 M	0203	0.7	**29** TU	0240	1.0
	0800	4.5		0831	4.1
	1411	0.8		1448	1.1
	2009	4.8		2039	4.5
15 TU	0249	0.6	**30** W	0315	1.0
	0847	4.5		0906	4.0
	1454	0.9		1523	1.2
	2056	4.7		2116	4.4

JULY

	Time	m		Time	m
1 TH	0350	1.1	**16** F	0405	0.4
	0943	3.9		1005	4.4
	1559	1.4		1609	0.9
	2156	4.2		2218	4.7
2 F	0427	1.3	**17** SA	0452	0.7
	1023	3.7		1059	4.1
	1637	1.6		1657	1.2
	2240	4.0		2319	4.3
3 SA	0507	1.4	**18** SU	0543	1.0
	1111	3.6		1203	3.9
	1720	1.8		1751	1.5
	2330	3.8			
4 SU	0551	1.6	**19** M	0031	4.0
	1205	3.5		0641	1.4
	1809	2.0		1315	3.7
				1858	1.7
5 M	0026	3.7	**20** TU	0149	3.8
	0640	1.7		0751	1.6
	1306	3.5		1429	3.7
	1906	2.1		2025	1.9
6 TU	0126	3.6	**21** W	0307	3.7
	0737	1.8		0914	1.7
	1411	3.5		1539	3.8
	2013	2.1		2155	1.8
7 W	0230	3.7	**22** TH	0416	3.7
	0842	1.8		1027	1.7
	1515	3.7		1637	3.9
	2126	2.0		2302	1.6
8 TH	0336	3.8	**23** F	0512	3.8
	0951	1.7		1121	1.5
	1612	3.9		1722	4.1
	2231	1.7		2353	1.4
9 F	0437	3.9	**24** SA	0556	3.9
	1052	1.5		1205	1.3
	1702	4.2		1801	4.3
	2328	1.4			
10 SA	0531	4.2	**25** SU	0035	1.2
	1144	1.3		0632	4.0
	1748	4.5		1245	1.2
				1836	4.5
11 SU	0019	1.1	**26** M	0113	1.0
	0619	4.4		0705	4.1
	1233	1.0		1321	1.0
	1831	4.7		1909	4.6
12 M	0107	0.8	**27** TU	0146	0.9
	0705	4.6		0735	4.1
	1317	0.8		1355	0.9
	1914	5.0		1941	4.6
13 TU	0153	0.5	**28** W	0218	0.8
	0749	4.7		0805	4.2
	1400	0.7		1427	0.9
	1957	5.1		2011	4.6
14 W	0237	0.3	**29** TH	0248	0.8
	0833	4.7		0834	4.1
	1442	0.6		1458	1.0
	2040	5.1		2042	4.5
15 TH	0321	0.3	**30** F	0318	0.9
	0917	4.6		0905	4.0
	1525	0.7		1528	1.2
	2127	4.9		2114	4.3
			31 SA	0350	1.0
				0938	3.9
				1601	1.4
				2150	4.1

AUGUST

	Time	m		Time	m
1 SU	0426	1.2	**16** M	0508	1.2
	1016	3.8		1129	4.0
	1637	1.6		1720	1.5
	2231	3.9			
2 M	0505	1.4	**17** TU	0007	3.9
	1104	3.6		0602	1.6
	1720	1.8		1248	3.7
	2328	3.7		1825	1.9
3 TU	0550	1.7	**18** W	0135	3.7
	1207	3.5		0715	1.9
	1812	2.0		1408	3.7
				2009	2.1
4 W	0037	3.6	**19** TH	0258	3.6
	0644	1.8		0856	2.1
	1319	3.5		1523	3.7
	1919	2.1		2156	2.0
5 TH	0153	3.6	**20** F	0413	3.6
	0828	1.8		1015	1.9
	1434	3.6		1623	3.9
	2049	2.0		2259	1.7
6 F	0312	3.7	**21** SA	0508	3.7
	0918	1.9		1107	1.7
	1545	3.8		1709	4.1
	2213	1.8		2342	1.4
7 SA	0422	3.9	**22** SU	0546	3.9
	1033	1.7		1148	1.5
	1643	4.2		1745	4.4
	2314	1.4			
8 SU	0518	4.2	**23** M	0018	1.2
	1129	1.3		0615	4.0
	1732	4.6		1226	1.2
				1816	4.5
9 M	0005	0.9	**24** TU	0051	1.0
	0605	4.5		0643	4.2
	1217	1.0		1259	1.0
	1816	4.9		1846	4.7
10 TU	0051	0.6	**25** W	0120	0.9
	0649	4.8		0709	4.3
	1301	0.7		1331	0.9
	1858	5.2		1914	4.7
11 W	0135	0.2	**26** TH	0148	0.8
	0730	4.9		0735	4.4
	1343	0.5		1400	0.9
	1938	5.4		1941	4.7
12 TH	0216	0.1	**27** F	0215	0.8
	0810	5.0		0801	4.4
	1423	0.4		1428	0.9
	2019	5.3		2008	4.6
13 F	0257	0.1	**28** SA	0243	0.8
	0851	4.8		0828	4.3
	1504	0.5		1457	1.0
	2101	5.1		2037	4.4
14 SA	0338	0.3	**29** SU	0314	1.0
	0935	4.6		0856	4.2
	1545	0.8		1528	1.2
	2148	4.8		2106	4.2
15 SU	0421	0.7	**30** M	0348	1.2
	1025	4.3		0927	4.0
	1630	1.1		1601	1.5
	2246	4.3		2141	4.0
			31 TU	0424	1.4
				1006	3.8
				1640	1.7
				2234	3.8

Chart Datum: 2·71 metres below Ordnance Datum (Newlyn). HAT is 5·5 metres above Chart Datum; see 4.5

NW Scotland

TIME ZONE (UT)
For Summer Time add ONE hour in **non-shaded areas**

STORNOWAY LAT 58°12'N LONG 6°23'W
TIMES AND HEIGHTS OF HIGH AND LOW WATERS

Dates in red are **SPRINGS**
Dates in blue are **NEAPS**

YEAR 2010

SEPTEMBER
Time m

1	0507 1.7 / 1113 3.6 / W 1730 2.0 ☽	16	0117 3.6 / 0640 2.2 / TH 1341 3.8 / 1951 2.2
2	0006 3.6 / 0602 1.9 / TH 1246 3.6 / 1843 2.1	17	0241 3.5 / 0831 2.3 / F 1456 3.8 / 2143 2.1
3	0136 3.5 / 0718 2.1 / F 1409 3.7 / 2031 2.1	18	0359 3.6 / 0952 2.1 / SA 1558 4.0 / 2239 1.8
4	0259 3.7 / 0858 2.0 / SA 1525 3.9 / 2200 1.7	19	0450 3.8 / 1042 1.9 / SU 1644 4.2 / 2317 1.6
5	0408 4.0 / 1016 1.7 / SU 1625 4.3 / 2258 1.3	20	0523 3.9 / 1122 1.6 / M 1720 4.4 / 2350 1.3
6	0501 4.3 / 1110 1.4 / M 1715 4.7 / 2346 0.8	21	0551 4.1 / 1158 1.4 / TU 1752 4.6
7	0546 4.7 / 1157 1.0 / TU 1758 5.1	22	0020 1.1 / 0616 4.3 / W 1232 1.2 / 1820 4.7
8	0029 0.4 / 0627 5.0 / W 1240 0.7 / ● 1838 5.4	23	0048 1.0 / 0641 4.5 / TH 1303 1.0 / ○ 1846 4.8
9	0111 0.2 / 0707 5.1 / TH 1321 0.5 / 1917 5.5	24	0115 0.9 / 0704 4.6 / F 1331 0.9 / 1912 4.8
10	0151 0.1 / 0745 5.2 / F 1401 0.4 / 1956 5.4	25	0142 0.8 / 0729 4.6 / SA 1400 1.0 / 1939 4.7
11	0230 0.2 / 0824 5.0 / SA 1441 0.6 / 2037 5.2	26	0211 0.9 / 0756 4.5 / SU 1429 1.1 / 2008 4.6
12	0310 0.5 / 0906 4.8 / SU 1522 0.8 / 2121 4.8	27	0242 1.0 / 0824 4.4 / M 1500 1.2 / 2039 4.3
13	0351 0.9 / 0954 4.4 / M 1605 1.4 / 2218 4.3	28	0316 1.2 / 0855 4.2 / TU 1535 1.4 / 2117 4.1
14	0435 1.4 / 1058 4.1 / TU 1655 1.7 / 2346 3.9	29	0352 1.4 / 0935 4.0 / W 1615 1.7 / 2217 3.8
15	0527 1.9 / 1221 3.9 / W 1759 2.1 ☽	30	0436 1.7 / 1046 3.8 / TH 1708 1.9 / 2356 3.6

OCTOBER
Time m

1	0533 2.0 / 1226 3.7 / F 1830 2.1 ☽	16	0205 3.5 / 0745 2.5 / SA 1413 3.9 / 2053 2.2
2	0125 3.6 / 0657 2.2 / SA 1349 3.8 / 2018 2.0	17	0320 3.6 / 0910 2.3 / SU 1517 4.0 / 2156 2.0
3	0243 3.8 / 0839 2.1 / SU 1503 4.1 / 2140 1.6	18	0414 3.8 / 1005 2.1 / M 1608 4.2 / 2238 1.8
4	0348 4.1 / 0953 1.8 / M 1603 4.5 / 2235 1.2	19	0450 4.0 / 1049 1.8 / TU 1648 4.3 / 2313 1.5
5	0440 4.5 / 1046 1.4 / TU 1653 4.8 / 2322 0.8	20	0520 4.2 / 1126 1.6 / W 1722 4.5 / 2344 1.3
6	0524 4.8 / 1133 1.1 / W 1736 5.2	21	0547 4.4 / 1200 1.4 / TH 1752 4.6
7	0004 0.5 / 0604 5.0 / TH 1217 0.8 / ● 1816 5.4	22	0013 1.2 / 0611 4.5 / F 1233 1.2 / 1819 4.7
8	0045 0.4 / 0642 5.2 / F 1259 0.6 / 1856 5.4	23	0042 1.0 / 0636 4.7 / SA 1303 1.1 / ○ 1847 4.7
9	0125 0.4 / 0721 5.2 / SA 1340 0.6 / 1935 5.3	24	0112 1.0 / 0704 4.7 / SU 1334 1.1 / 1918 4.7
10	0204 0.5 / 0800 5.1 / SU 1421 0.8 / 2016 5.0	25	0144 1.0 / 0733 4.7 / M 1407 1.1 / 1951 4.6
11	0244 0.8 / 0841 4.9 / M 1502 1.0 / 2102 4.6	26	0217 1.0 / 0805 4.6 / TU 1442 1.2 / 2028 4.4
12	0324 1.2 / 0929 4.6 / TU 1546 1.4 / 2158 4.2	27	0253 1.2 / 0842 4.4 / W 1521 1.4 / 2115 4.2
13	0407 1.6 / 1030 4.3 / W 1636 1.7 / 2319 3.8	28	0332 1.5 / 0929 4.2 / TH 1606 1.6 / 2220 3.9
14	0457 2.0 / 1148 4.0 / TH 1738 2.1 ☾	29	0417 1.7 / 1042 4.0 / F 1705 1.7 / 2346 3.8
15	0045 3.6 / 0604 2.4 / F 1303 3.9 / 1910 2.3	30	0517 2.0 / 1208 3.9 / SA 1825 1.8 ☽
		31	0105 3.8 / 0640 2.1 / SU 1325 4.0 / 1952 1.8

NOVEMBER
Time m

1	0218 3.9 / 0809 2.0 / M 1435 4.2 / 2108 1.5	16	0323 3.7 / 0915 2.2 / TU 1520 4.0 / 2146 1.9
2	0321 4.1 / 0922 1.8 / TU 1537 4.5 / 2206 1.2	17	0410 3.9 / 1007 2.0 / W 1608 4.1 / 2229 1.8
3	0414 4.4 / 1019 1.5 / W 1629 4.7 / 2255 1.0	18	0446 4.1 / 1050 1.8 / TH 1648 4.3 / 2305 1.6
4	0500 4.7 / 1108 1.2 / TH 1715 4.9 / 2339 0.8	19	0516 4.3 / 1128 1.6 / F 1722 4.4 / 2339 1.4
5	0542 4.9 / 1154 1.0 / F 1758 5.0	20	0544 4.5 / 1203 1.4 / SA 1756 4.5
6	0021 0.7 / 0621 5.0 / SA 1239 0.9 / 1839 5.1	21	0012 1.2 / 0613 4.6 / SU 1239 1.3 / ○ 1829 4.6
7	0103 0.7 / 0700 5.1 / SU 1323 0.9 / 1920 4.9	22	0048 1.1 / 0644 4.7 / M 1316 1.1 / 1905 4.6
8	0143 0.9 / 0741 5.0 / M 1406 1.0 / 2003 4.7	23	0124 1.0 / 0719 4.7 / TU 1354 1.1 / 1944 4.6
9	0223 1.1 / 0823 4.9 / TU 1449 1.1 / 2048 4.5	24	0201 1.1 / 0756 4.7 / W 1434 1.1 / 2027 4.5
10	0303 1.3 / 0909 4.7 / W 1533 1.4 / 2139 4.2	25	0240 1.2 / 0838 4.6 / TH 1517 1.1 / 2115 4.3
11	0346 1.6 / 1001 4.4 / TH 1620 1.6 / 2240 3.9	26	0321 1.3 / 0928 4.5 / F 1605 1.2 / 2214 4.1
12	0432 2.0 / 1103 4.2 / F 1713 1.9 / 2352 3.7	27	0408 1.5 / 1030 4.3 / SA 1701 1.4 / 2323 3.9
13	0528 2.2 / 1209 4.1 / SA 1817 2.1 ☽	28	0505 1.7 / 1141 4.2 / SU 1806 1.5 ☽
14	0107 3.6 / 0642 2.4 / SU 1316 4.0 / 1934 2.2	29	0034 3.9 / 0614 1.9 / M 1253 4.2 / 1916 1.5
15	0220 3.6 / 0806 2.4 / M 1422 3.9 / 2050 2.1	30	0143 3.9 / 0731 1.9 / TU 1402 4.2 / 2028 1.5

DECEMBER
Time m

1	0249 4.0 / 0845 1.8 / W 1508 4.3 / 2133 1.3	16	0316 3.7 / 0908 2.2 / TH 1515 3.8 / 2130 1.9
2	0348 4.2 / 0951 1.6 / TH 1607 4.4 / 2229 1.2	17	0404 3.9 / 1006 2.0 / F 1608 3.9 / 2222 1.8
3	0438 4.4 / 1048 1.4 / F 1659 4.5 / 2319 1.1	18	0443 4.1 / 1054 1.8 / SA 1654 4.1 / 2307 1.6
4	0524 4.6 / 1140 1.2 / SA 1746 4.6	19	0518 4.3 / 1138 1.6 / SU 1736 4.2 / 2349 1.4
5	0004 1.0 / 0606 4.8 / SU 1229 1.1 / ● 1829 4.6	20	0554 4.5 / 1221 1.3 / M 1817 4.4
6	0047 1.0 / 0647 4.9 / M 1314 1.0 / 1912 4.6	21	0030 1.2 / 0631 4.7 / TU 1303 1.1 / ○ 1858 4.5
7	0129 1.0 / 0727 4.9 / TU 1357 1.0 / 1953 4.5	22	0110 1.0 / 0709 4.8 / W 1345 0.9 / 1939 4.6
8	0209 1.1 / 0807 4.8 / W 1439 1.1 / 2034 4.3	23	0151 0.9 / 0749 4.9 / TH 1428 0.8 / 2021 4.6
9	0248 1.2 / 0848 4.7 / TH 1519 1.2 / 2115 4.2	24	0231 0.9 / 0831 4.9 / F 1511 0.7 / 2105 4.5
10	0327 1.4 / 0931 4.6 / F 1600 1.4 / 2158 4.0	25	0313 1.0 / 0916 4.8 / SA 1556 0.8 / 2154 4.3
11	0408 1.6 / 1017 4.4 / SA 1642 1.6 / 2247 3.8	26	0357 1.1 / 1007 4.6 / SU 1645 0.9 / 2250 4.1
12	0453 1.9 / 1109 4.2 / SU 1728 1.8 / 2346 3.6	27	0447 1.3 / 1108 4.4 / M 1738 1.1 / 2354 3.9
13	0544 2.1 / 1206 4.0 / M 1820 1.9 ☽	28	0543 1.5 / 1216 4.2 / TU 1838 1.3 ☽
14	0055 3.5 / 0645 2.2 / TU 1308 3.8 / 1919 2.0	29	0104 3.8 / 0650 1.7 / W 1329 4.1 / 1945 1.5
15	0211 3.6 / 0756 2.3 / W 1412 3.8 / 2026 2.0	30	0216 3.8 / 0807 1.8 / TH 1442 4.0 / 2100 1.5
		31	0324 3.9 / 0928 1.7 / F 1551 4.0 / 2209 1.5

Chart Datum: 2·71 metres below Ordnance Datum (Newlyn). HAT is 5·5 metres above Chart Datum; see 4.5

>> **FREE** monthly updates from <<
www.reedsalmanac.co.uk

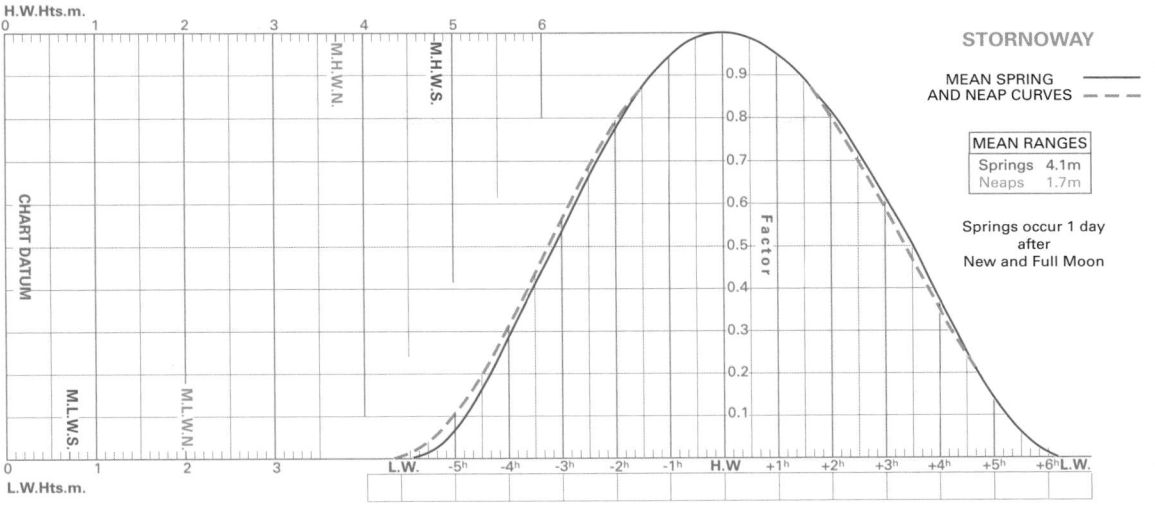

STORNOWAY

MEAN SPRING ——————
AND NEAP CURVES – – – –

| MEAN RANGES |
| Springs 4.1m |
| Neaps 1.7m |

Springs occur 1 day
after
New and Full Moon

HARBOURS AND ANCHORAGES ON THE EAST SIDE OF THE OUTER HEBRIDES, from N to S:

Visitor moorings mentioned in this section are inspected annually, have pick up buoys, can take yachts <15tons, and there is no charge <7days. Refer to www.w-isles.gov.uk/harbour master.

LOCH SHELL, Lewis, **57°59'·98N 06°25'·07W**. AC 1794. HW –0437 on Dover; ML 2·7m. See 9.8.6. Pass S of Eilean Iuvard; beware rks to W of Is. ⚓ in Tob Eishken, 2½M up loch on N shore (beware rk awash on E side of ent), or at head of loch (exposed to E winds; dries some distance). **Facilities:** ✉/Stores at Lemreway.

SHIANT ISLANDS, Lewis, **57°53'·68N 06°21'·37W**. AC 1794, 1795. Tides as Loch Shell 9.8.6. Beware strong tidal streams and overfalls in Sound of Shiant. Strictly a fair weather ⚓ ; in W winds ⚓ E of Mol Mor, isthmus between Garbh Eileen (159m) and Eileen an Tighe. In E winds ⚓ W of Mol Mor. No lights or facilities.

EAST LOCH TARBERT, Harris, **57°49'·98N 06°41'·07W**. AC 2905. HW –0446 on Dover; ML 3·0m; Duration 0605. See 9.8.6. Appr via Sound of Scalpay; beware Elliot Rk (2m) 2½ca SSW of Rubha Crago. A bridge (20m clearance) at 57°52'·80N 06°41'·73W joins Scalpay to Harris. Bridge lts: Centre Oc 6s; N side Iso G 4s 35m; S side Iso R 4s 35m. Eilean Glas lt ho at E end of Scalpay, Fl (3) 20s 43m 23M; W tr, R bands. In Sound of Scalpay, stream sets W from HW +3, and E from HW –3. ⚓ off Tarbert WSW of steamer pier in about 2·5m. ☎ (01589) 502444. Facilities: Bar, D, Dr, FW, P, ✉, R, 🛒, ferry to Uig. Alternatively Scalpay N Hbr gives good shelter. Beware rk 5ca off Aird an Aiseig, E side of ent. SHM buoy marks wk off Coddem; 5ca E of the buoy is a rk, depth 1·1m. Ldg Lt Oc WRG 6s 10m 5M. Both piers have 2FG (vert) lts; ⚓ 7ca N, in about 3m. **Facilities:** FW at pier, ✉, 🛒, Ferry to Harris.

SOUND OF HARRIS, **57°43'N 06°58'W**. Passages through this difficult Sound are detailed in the *W Coast of Scotland Pilot*. The Stanton and Outer Stromay Chans off the Harris shore are the most feasible for yachts. AC 2802 shows the ferry routes from Leverburgh to Berneray.

LOCH RODEL, Harris. AC 2802. 3 🅰s at **57°44'·2N 06°57'·4W** in Poll an Tigh-mhàil; enter from SW past jetties. No lts.

LOCH MADDY, North Uist, **57°35'·98N 07°06'·07W**. AC 2825. HW –0500 on Dover. See 9.8.6. With strong wind against tide there can be bad seas off ent. Appr clear, but from S beware submerged rk ½ca N of Leacnam Madadh. Lts: Weaver's Pt Fl 3s 21m 7M; Glas Eilean Mor Fl (2) G 4s 8m 5M; Rubna Nam Pleac Fl R 4s 7m 5M. Inside loch: Ruigh Liath QG 6m 5M; Vallaquie Is Dir

Fl (3) WRG 8s. Ferry pier ldg lts 298°: front 2FG(vert) 4M; rear Oc G 8s 10m 4M, vis 284°-304°. 2 🅰s Bagh Aird nam Madadh; 2 🅰s W of and 4 🅰s SW of ferry pier ☎ (01870) 602425; 2 🅰s E of Oronsay. ⚓s: clear S of ferry pier; NE of Vallaquie Is; Charles Hbr; Oronsay (⚓ not advised due to moorings), tidal berth on private pier; Sponish Hbr; Loch Portain. VHF Ch 12 16. Port Manager ☎ (01876) 5003337 (day), 5003226 (night). **Facilities:** Lochmaddy, Shop, Ⓑ, Gas, ✉, P, D, FW; Loch Portain ✉, Shop.

LOCH EPORT, North Uist, **57°33'·45N 07°08'·12W**. AC 2825, but not the head of loch. Tides, approx as L Maddy; 3kn sp stream. On the S side of ent are rks, some drying. The ent proper is clean but very narrow (about 100m) for 5ca, then widens. Follow the charted clearing line 082°. Best ⚓s are: Bàgh a' Bhiorain (S of chan; line up cairn and Bu boulder on 129°); and Acairseid Lee (N bank) E or W of Deer Is. 🛒, R, Bar, ✉ at Clachan, hd of loch.

KALLIN, Grimsay. **57°28'·9N 07°12'·2W**. AC 2904. 1 🅰 in NE of hbr. 3 chan lt buoys and 2 FR (vert) on hbr bkwtr. ☎ (01870) 602425.

LOCH CARNAN, South Uist, **57°22'·03N 07°16'·39W**. AC 2825. Tides, see 9.8.6. SWM buoy, L Fl 10s, at 57°22'·30N 07°11'·57W is almost 2M E of app chan proper, marked by Nos 1 and 2 buoys, Fl G 2·5s and Fl R 2s, at 57°22'·45N 07°14'·90W. Round No 3 PHM buoy, Fl R 5s, between Gasay and Taigh Iamain, then pick up ldg lts 222° to Sandwick Quay; front Fl R 2s, rear Iso R 10s, both 5M, W ◇s on posts. Power stn and 2 chys are conspic close to SE of quay. ☎ (01870) 602425 for permission to berth on the quay (MoD property). There is ⚓ or 2 🅰s about 2ca WNW of the quay in deep water. ☎ (01870) 610238. The passage S of Gasay is unmarked and needs careful pilotage. FW, D available.

LOCH SKIPPORT, South Uist, **57°19'·98N 07°13'·67W**. AC 2904, 2825. HW –0602 on Dover; see 9.8.6. Easy ent 3M NNE of Hecla (604m). No lights, but 2¼M SSE is Usinish lt ho Fl WR 20s 54m 19/15M. ⚓s at: Wizard Pool in 7m; beware Float Rk, dries 2·3m; on N side of Caolas Mor in 7m; Bagh Charmaig in 5m. Linne Arm has narrow ent, many fish farms and poor holding. No facilities.

LOCH EYNORT, South Uist, **57°13'·13N 07°16'·87W**. AC 2825. Tides: interpolate between Lochs Skipport and Boisdale, see 9.8.6. ⚓s in the outer loch at Cearcdal Bay and on the N side just before the narrows are exposed to the E. The passage to Upper L Eynort is very narrow and streams reach 5-7kn; best not attempted unless local fishermen offer guidance. Good ⚓ inside at Bàgh Lathach.

Continued overleaf

LOCH BOISDALE, South Uist, **57°08'·78N 07°16'·07W**. AC 2770. HW –0455 on Dover; ML 2·4m; Duration 0600. See 9.8.6. Good shelter except in SE gales when swell runs right up the 2M loch. From N, appr between Rubha na Cruibe and Calvay Is; ldg line 245°: Hollisgeir (0·3m) on with pier (ru). From S beware Clan Ewan Rk, dries 1·2m, and McKenzie Rk (2·4m), marked by PHM lt buoy Fl (3) R 15s. Chan to Boisdale Hbr lies N of Gasay Is; beware rks off E end. ⚓ off pier in approx 4m, or SW of Gasay Is in approx 9m. 4 ⚓s NE of pier ☎ (01870) 602425. There are fish cages W of Rubha Bhuailt. Lts: E end of Calvay Is Fl (2) WRG 10s 16m 7/4M. Gasay Is Fl WR 5s 10m 7/4M. N side of loch, opp Gasay Is, Fl G 6s. Ro-Ro terminal Iso RG 4s 8m 2M; and close SE, Fl (2) R 5s. See 9.8.4. ☎ (0187) 700288. **Facilities:** Bar, FW (on pier), P, ✉, R, Ferry to mainland.

ACAIRSEID MHÓR, Eriskay, ⊕ **57°03'·78N 07°16'·35W**. AC 2770. Tides approx as for North Bay (Barra), see 9.8.6. Ben Scrien (183m) is conspic, pointed peak N of hbr. Ldg lts 285°, both Oc R 6s 9/10m 4M, W △ ▽ on orange posts, lead for 0·5M from the above lat/long between two drying rks into the outer loch. A SHM buoy, Fl G 6s, marks a rk drying 3m. Possible AB on pontoon; 2 ⚓s (perhaps submerged at HW) are at 57°03'·95N 07°17'·40W on S side of inner loch, opp pier, 2 FG (vert). ☎ (01870) 602425. 🛒, R, Bar, ✉ at Haun, 1·5M at N end of island.

NORTH BAY, Barra, **57°00'·11N 07°24'·67W**. AC 2770. Tides see 9.8.6. Well marked approach to inlet sheltered from S and W winds. WPT 56°58'·68N 07°20'·31W is about 200m NE of Curachan ECM buoy, Q (3) 10s, and in the white sector (304°-306°) of Ardveenish dir ☆ 305°, Oc WRG 3s, 2·5M to the WNW. ⚓ 1ca WNW of Black Island or in N part of Bay Hirivagh where there are ⚓s; or tempy AB on the quay in 4·5m. FW, Bar, 🛒, bus to Castlebay.

CASTLEBAY, Barra, **56°56'·78N 07°29'·67W**. AC 2769. HW –0525 on Dover; ML 2·3m; Duration 0600. See 9.8.6. Very good shelter & holding. Best ⚓ in approx 8m NW of Kiessimul Castle (on an island); NE of castle are rks. About 20 ⚓s lie to W of the pier; they may be encroaching on the recommended anchorage NW of Kiessimul Castle. ☎ (01870) 602425. Or ⚓ in Vatersay Bay in approx 9m. W end of Vatersay Sound is closed by a causeway. Beware rks NNW of Sgeir Dubh a conspic W/G tr, Q(3)G 6s 6m 5M, which leads 283° in transit with Sgeir Liath bn. Chan Rk, 2ca to the S, is marked by Fl WR 6s 4m 6/4M. Close-in ldg lts 295°, both FBu 6M on W framework trs: front 9m Or △ on Rubha Glas; rear, 457m from front, 15m Or ▽, vis: 15° and 8° respectively either side of ldg line. ☎ (01871) 810306. **Facilities:** Bar, D, FW, P, ✉, R, 🛒, Ferry to mainland.

TIDES

Standard Port STORNOWAY (⟵)

Times				Height (metres)			
High Water		Low Water		MHWS	MHWN	MLWN	MLWS
0100	0700	0300	0900	4·8	3·7	2·0	0·7
1300	1900	1500	2100				
Differences FLANNAN ISLES							
–0026	–0016	–0016	–0026	–0·9	–0·7	–0·6	–0·2
VILLAGE BAY (St Kilda)							
–0040	–0040	–0045	–0045	–1·4	–1·2	–0·8	–0·3
ROCKALL							
–0055	–0055	–0105	–0105	–1·8	–1·5	–0·9	–0·2

FLANNAN ISLES, Western Isles, centred on **58°17'·28N 07°35'·27W** (Eilean Mór). AC 2524, 2721. Tides, as above. Uninhabited group of several rky islets, 18M WNW of Gallan Head (Lewis). The main islet is Eilean Mór where landing can be made on SW side in suitable conditions. Lt ho, Fl (2) 30s 101m 20M, is a 23m high W tr on NE tip of Eilean Mór; the lt is obscured by islets to the W which are up to 57m high. No recommended ⚓s and the few charted depths are by lead-line surveys.

ST KILDA, Western Isles, **57°48'·28N 08°33'·07W**. AC 2721, 2524. Tides at Village Bay, Hirta: HW –0510 on Dover; ML 1·9m; Duration 0615; see above. A group of four isles and three stacks, the main island is Hirta from which the Army withdrew in April 1998 after 30 years. The facility is now manned by a civilian company, Qinetiq ☎ (01870) 604443, based at South Uist. Hirta is owned by National Trust for Scotland and leased to Scottish National Heritage who employ a Seasonal Warden, ☎ 01870 604628. ⚓ in Village Bay, SE-facing, in approx 5m about 1·5ca off the pier. Ldg lts 270°, both Oc 5s 26/38m 3M. If wind is between NE and SSW big swells enter the bay; good holding, but untenable if winds strong. Levenish Is (55m) is 1·5M E of Hirta with offlying rks. Call *Kilda Radio* VHF Ch 16 **12** 73 (HJ) for permission to land; ☎ (01870) 604406 (HO), 604612 (OT).

Alternative ⚓ at Glen Bay on N side is only safe in S & E winds. Facilities: FW from wells near landings.

ROCKALL, **57°35'·7N 13°41'·2W**. AC 1128, 2524. Tides, as above. A 19m high granite rock, 200M W of N Uist. Best access by helicopter. Lt, Fl 15s 13M, is often extinguished for long periods due to weather damage. Helen's Reef, 1·4m, on which the sea breaks is 2M ENE.

MONACH ISLANDS (Heisker Is), centred on **57°31'·28N 07°38'·07W**. AC 2721, 2722. Tides, see 9.8.6 Shillay. The group lies 5M SW of N Uist and 8M WNW of Benbecula. The 5 main islands (W-E) are Shillay, Ceann Iar, Shivinish, Ceann Ear and Stockay; all uninhabited. Many rky offliers from NW through N to SE of the group. On Shillay there is a conspic red brick lt ho, Fl (2) 15s. ⚓s at: E of lt ho; Croic Hbr, bay N of Shivinish; and S Hbr on W side of Shivinish.

CAPE WRATH TO ULLAPOOL

(AC 1785, 1794) C Wrath (lt, fog sig) is a steep headland (110m). ▶ *To N of it the E-going stream begins at HW Ullapool – 0350, and W-going at HW Ullapool + 0235, sp rates 3kn. Eddies close inshore cause almost continuous W-going stream E of Cape, and N-going stream SW of it. Where they meet is turbulence, with dangerous seas in bad weather.* ◀ Duslic Rk, 7ca NE of lt ho, dries 3·4m. 6M SW of C Wrath, islet of Am Balg (45m)is foul for 2ca around.

There are anchorages in Loch Inchard (AC 2503), the best shelter being in Kinlochbervie on N shore; also good anchs among Is along S shore of Loch Laxford, entered between Ardmore Pt and Rubha Ruadh. Handa Is to WSW is a bird sanctuary. Handa Sound is navigable with care, but beware Bogha Morair in mid-chan and associated overfalls. ▶ *Tide turns 2hrs earlier in the Sound than offshore. Strong winds against tide raise a bad sea off Pt of Stoer.* ◀ The best shelter is 8M S at Loch Inver (AC 2504), with good anch off hotel near head of loch. Anchorages to the N of Loch Inver may be found at Kylesku, Culkein Drumbeg, Drumbeg, Loch Nedd and Loch Roe. To the S lies Enard Bay.

9.8.7 KINLOCHBERVIE

Highland 58°27'·26N 05°02'·78W ✿✿✿✿⚓⚓✿✿

CHARTS AC 1954, 1785, 2503; Imray C67.

TIDES –0400 Dover; ML 2·7; Duration 0610

Standard Port ULLAPOOL (→)

Times				Height (metres)			
High Water		Low Water		MHWS	MHWN	MLWN	MLWS
0000	0600	0300	0900	5·2	3·9	2·1	0·7
1200	1800	1500	2100				
Differences LOCH BERVIE							
+0020	+0010	+0010	+0020	–0·4	–0·3	–0·2	0·1
LOCH LAXFORD							
+0015	+0015	+0005	+0005	–0·3	–0·4	–0·2	0·0
BADCALL BAY							
+0005	+0005	+0005	+0005	–0·7	–0·5	–0·5	+0·2
LOCH NEDD							
0000	0000	0000	0000	–0·3	–0·2	–0·2	0·0
LOCH INVER							
–0005	–0005	–0005	–0005	–0·2	0·0	0·0	+0·1

SHELTER Very good in Kinlochbervie Hbr off the N shore of Loch Inchard. A useful passage port, only 14.5 track miles S of Cape Wrath. It is an active FV port, but yachts AB on pontoon (contact HM for details); NE side is shoal/foul. If full, ⚓ at Loch Clash, open to W; landing jetty in 2·7m. Other ⚓s at: Camus Blair on S shore, 5ca SW of hbr ent, and up the loch at L Sheigra, Achriesgill Bay and 5ca short of the head of the loch.

NAVIGATION WPT 58°27'·34N 05°05'·08W (at mouth of Loch Inchard), 100°/1·3M to hbr ent. The sides of the loch are clean, but keep to N side of Loch Inchard to clear Bodha Ceann na Saile NCM and rk (3m depth) almost in mid-chan.

LIGHTS AND MARKS From offshore in good vis Ceann Garbh, a conspic mountain 900m (6M inland), leads 110° toward ent of Loch Inchard. Rubha na Leacaig, Fl (2) 10s 30m 8M, marks N side of loch ent. Dir ✩ WRG (H24) 15m 16M, Y framework tr (floodlit) leads 327° into hbr; see 9.8.4 for vis sectors. The 25m wide ent chan (and hbr) is dredged 4m and marked by 2 PHM poles, Fl R 4s and QR, and by a SHM pole, Fl G 4s. On S shore of loch Creag Mhòr, Dir Oc lt WRG 2.8s 16m 9M, is aligned 147°/327° with hbr ent chan; see 9.8.4.

R/T VHF Ch **14** 16 HX. Ch 06 is used by FVs in the Minches.

TELEPHONE (Code 01971) HM ☎ 521235, mob 07901 514350; MRCC (01851) 702013; ⊖ (0141) 887 9369 (H24); Marinecall 09068 969654; Police 521222; Dr 502002.

FACILITIES AB (pontoon) £1.50<10m for 48hrs, FW, D at FV quay, P (cans), Gas, CH, ME, ⊠, Bar, 🍴, R, Showers (Mission & Hbr Office), ⛽. In summer, bus to Inverness.

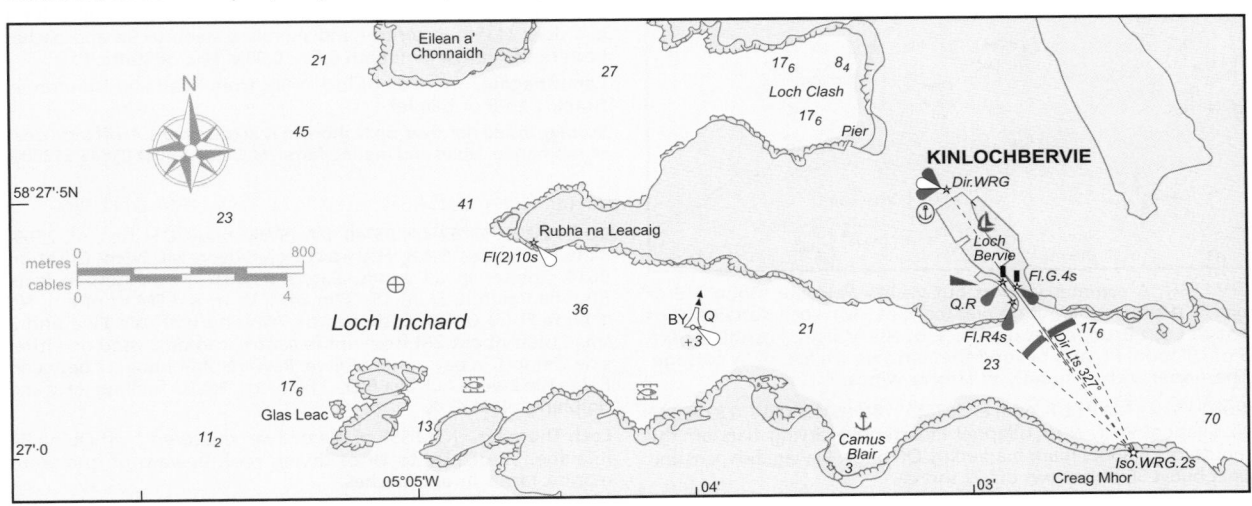

⚓ & HBR BETWEEN KINLOCHBERVIE AND ULLAPOOL

LOCH LAXFORD Highland, **58°24'·78N 05°07'·18W**. AC 2503. HW –0410 on Dover. ML 2·7m. See 9.8.7. Ent between Rubha Ruadh and Ardmore Pt, 1M ENE, clearly identified by 3 isolated mountains (N-S) Ceann Garbh, Ben Arkle and Ben Stack. The many ⚓s in the loch include: Loch a'Chadh-fi, on N/NE sides of islet (John Ridgeway's Adventure School on Pt on W side of narrows has moorings); Bagh nah-Airde Beag, next bay to E, (beware rk 5ca off SE shore which covers at MHWS); Weaver's Bay on SW shore, 3M from ent (beware drying rk off NW Pt of ent); Bagh na Fionndalach Mor on SW shore (4-6m); Fanagmore Bay on SW shore (beware head of bay foul with old moorings). Beware many fish farming cages. Facilities: none, nearest stores at Scourie (5M).

LOCH INVER Highland, **58°08'·98N 05°15'·08W**. AC 2504. HW –0433 on Dover; ML 3·0m. See 9.8.7. Good shelter in all weathers at head of loch in busy fishing hbr on S side. Appr N or S of Soyea Is, Fl (2) 10s 34m 6M; beware rock drying 1·7m about 50m off Kirkaig Point (S side of ent). Glas Leac, a small islet 7ca WSW of hbr, may be passed on either side. Its ✩, Fl WRG 3s, has 3 WRG sectors (see 9.8.4) covering the chans N and S of Soyea Is and into the hbr. The church, hotel (S side) and white ho (N side) are all conspic. A 22-berth marina is between the breakwater (QG) and the first FV pier. Or, in W'ly gales, ⚓ in the lee of bkwtr in about 8m; or where HM directs. Other ⚓s on S shore of Loch Inver. VHF Ch 12 16.

HM ☎ (01571) 844247; mob 07958 734610. Health Centre 01571 844452. **Facilities:** FW, P, D, ⛽, showers (Leisure Centre), CH, 🍴, ⊠, Gas.

9.8.8 ULLAPOOL

Highland 57°53'·70N 05°09'·38W ✸✸✸✿✿✿✿✿

CHARTS AC 1794, 2500, 2501, 2509; Imray C67.

TIDES –0415 Dover; ML 3·0; Duration 0610

Standard Port ULLAPOOL (→)

Times				Height (metres)			
High Water		Low Water		MHWS	MHWN	MLWN	MLWS
0000	0600	0300	0900	5·2	3·9	2·1	0·7
1200	1800	1500	2100				
Differences SUMMER ISLES (Tanera Mor)							
–0005	–0005	–0010	–0010	–0·1	+0·1	0·0	+0·1
LOCH EWE (Mellon Charles, 57°51'N 05°38'W)							
–0005	–0010	–0005	–0005	–0·5	–0·5	–0·5	0·5
LOCH GAIRLOCH							
–0020	–0020	–0010	–0010	0·0	+0·1	–0·3	–0·1

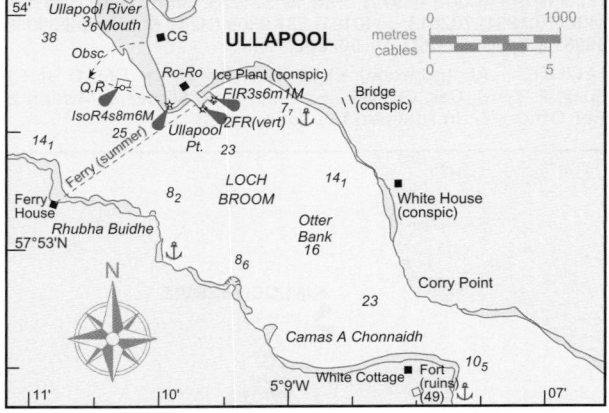

SHELTER A commercial port but yachts welcome. Good ⚓ E of pier, 8 🔩 or possible AB on pier (consult HM). Loch Kanaird (N of ent to Loch Broom) has good ⚓ E of Isle Martin. Possible ⚓s 6ca S of Ullapool Pt, and beyond the narrows 3ca ESE of W cottage. The upper loch is squally in strong winds.

NAVIGATION WPT L Broom ent 57°55'·78N 05°15'·08W, 129°/3.5M to Ullapool Pt lt. N of Ullapool Pt extensive drying flats off the mouth of Ullapool R are marked by QR buoy. Beware fish pens and unlit buoys SE of narrows off W shore.

LIGHTS AND MARKS Rhubha Cadail, N of L. Broom ent, Fl WRG 6s 11m 9/6M. Cailleach Hd, W of ent, Fl (2) 12s 60m 9M. Ullapool Pt Iso R 4s 8m 6M; grey mast, vis 258°-108°.

R/T Ullapool Harbour Ch 14 16 (H24).

TELEPHONE (Code 01854) HM 612724, mob 07734 004843; CG (non-emergency) 613076; ⊖ (0141) 887 9369; Marinecall 09068 969654; Police 612017; Dr Dr 08454 242424; Dentist 613289 or 612660.

FACILITIES Pier D, FW, CH; Loch Broom SC Services: Gas, ME & GRP repairs Mobile Marine Services ☎ 633719, mob 07866 516067, El, ℗, El, ⚒ A.Morgan ☎ 666383; Town D & P (cans 0700-2100), @ at Captains Cabin, Library and Ceilidh Place Hotel, all domestic facilities, showers at swimming pool, 🛒, R, Bar, ⇌ (bus to Garve). Daily buses to Inverness (✈)(no Sunday bus services. Ferries: Stornoway; 2-3/day; 2¾ Hrs; Calmac (www.calmac.co.uk).

ADJACENT ANCHORAGES

LOCH KANAIRD, 57°56'·60'N 05°12'·20'W. AC 2500. HW –0425 Dover; See 9.8.8; streams are weak and irreg. Situated E of the entrance to Loch Broom, S of the Summer Is and protected by Isle Martin. Good ⚓s (tripping line recommended) ENE of Sgeir Mhor or E of Isle Martin, N of Rubha Beag (also AB on pontoon). Beware cables and marine farms. Ent from S (1ca wide) between two rocky spits, leading line E extremity of Isle Martin in transit

with dark streak on cliff behind brg 000°. Ent from N, deep and clear of dangers. Facilities: Ardmair Boat Centre ☎ P.Fraser (01854) 612054, M, FW, showers, some repairs. Isle Martin, Landing permitted (voluntary donation to Trust, ☎ (01854) 612531).

SUMMER ISLES, 58°01'N 05°25'W. AC 2509, 2501. HW –0425 Dover; See 9.8.8; streams are weak and irregular. In the N apps to Loch Broom some 30 islands and rks, the main ones being Eilean Mullagrach, Isle Ristol, Glas-leac Mor, Tanera Beg, Eilean a' Char, Eilean Fada Mor. Beware rocks at S end of Horse Sound. ⚓s:

Isle Ristol, ⚓ to S of drying causeway and clear of moorings; beware landings frequented by local FVs. Close to slip is lt Fl G 3s. Facilities: 🛒 (at Polbain 2M).

Tanera Beg, ⚓ in the chan to the E inside Eilean Fada Mor.

Tanera Mor, on E side, ⚓ in bay to N off pier or in W corner off stone jetty; beware many moorings and fish pens. Also poss ⚓ close NW of Is and close E of Eilean na Saille, but N of drying rock. Facilities: ☎ (01854) 622272 B Wilder for M, showers, FW, Tea Room.

Badentarbat Bay, Temp'y ⚓ NW part of bay ESE of pier which is busy with marina farm activity. Beware N part of bay is shoal. Suitable for Achiltibuie or Polbain on mainland. Facilities: 🛒, R, Gas, FW, D (emerg) ☎ (01854) 622261.

LITTLE LOCH BROOM, 57°54'·98N 05°24'·68W. AC 2500. HW –0415 Dover as per Ullapool, see 9.8.8; streams are weak (approx 1kn). Between Loch Broom and Gruinard Bay, entered S of Cailleach Hd it is deep (115m in centre) and shoreline steep to. In approaches beware of Ardross Rk (depth 0.6m) 0.38M ENE of Stattic Pt.

Camusnagaul, on S side of loch 1.6M from head and Dundonnel Hotel, ⚓ to E of hamlet.

Scoraig, inside narrows on N shore in N'ly conditions, ⚓ off jetty clear of submarine cables and marine farm. ⚒ C.Dawson ☎ 01845 613380.

⚓s BETWEEN LITTLE LOCH BROOM AND LOCH GAIRLOCH

LOCH EWE, 57°52'·0N 05°40'·0W (SWM buoy, L Fl 10s). AC 2509, 3146. Tides: See 9.8.8; HW –0415 on Dover; ML 2·6m; Duration 0610. Shelter in all winds. Easy ent with no dangers in loch. Rhubha Reidh lt, Fl (4) 15s 37m 24M, W tr, is 4·5M W of ent. No 1 buoy Fl (3) G 10s. Loch approx 7M long with Isle Ewe and 2 small islets about 2M from ent in centre; can be passed on either side. Temp ⚓ in bay of Isle of Ewe. Beware unlit buoy A2 between E side Isle Ewe & Aultbea Pier, 2 FG (vert). NATO fuelling jetty and dolphins, all Fl G 4s.

Loch Thurnaig, 1.7M SSE of Isle of Ewe, sheltered ⚓ off Ob na Bà Rùaidhe, SE of pier to W of drying reef. Beware of numerous marine farms in approaches.

Aultbea: ⚓ off Aultbea Hotel on E shore or in NW'lies close of pier. N part of bay is shoal. Facilities: Dr, P, ✉, R, 🛒, Bar.

Poolewe Bay ⚓ in SW part of bay in 3·5m, at head of loch: Boor Rks(3m) with drying rocks extending 1ca NW lie off W shore about 9ca NW of Poolewe. Facilities: FW, D, L on pier, P (at garage), ✉, R, Bar, 🛒, Gas.

Inverewe Gdns on NE side of bay, ⚓ to SW of Jetty at Port na Cloiche Gile.

LOCH GAIRLOCH, 57°43'N 05°45'W. AC 228, 2528. HW –0440 on Dover. See 9.8.8. A wide loch facing W. Ent clear of dangers but Submarine Exercise Area (see 9.8.22) to S of Longa Is. Quite heavy seas enter in bad weather. Lts: Glas Eilean Fl WRG 6s 9m 6/4M, Gairloch Pier Hd, QR 9m. HM ☎ (01445) 712140.

Badachro, good shelter SW of Eilean Horrisdale on SW side of loch but busy with FVs and local craft. Also ⚓'ge to NNW of Sgeir Dhubh Bheag SSE of Eilean Horrisdale, passage to S of this island is possible with caution. R, Bar, (Bad Inn HM ☎ (01445) 741255 for M availability.

Loch Shieldaig, at SE end of the loch with many moorings for local craft, if congested ⚓ to SSW of Eilean an t-Sabhail. Beware marine farms.

Flowerdale Bay, ⚓ in approx 6m near Gairloch pier or berth on pontoons (2m depth N side, 3m S side) at pier. HM ☎ (01445) 712140. VHF Ch 16 (occas). Gairloch Pier: AB fees charged. P (cans), D, FW, SC, Hotel, Bar, Showers, Gas, 🛒, CH, ✉.

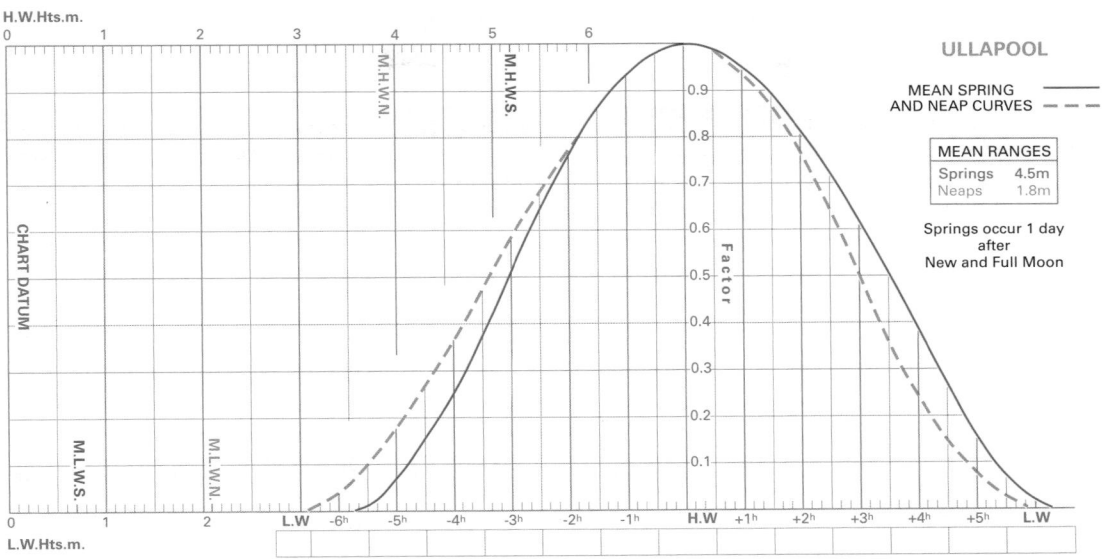

ULLAPOOL

MEAN SPRING AND NEAP CURVES

MEAN RANGES
Springs 4.5m
Neaps 1.8m

Springs occur 1 day after New and Full Moon

9.8.9 PORTREE

Skye (Highland) 57°24'·73N 06°11'·07W ✿✿✿✿♦♦✿✿✿

CHARTS AC 2209, 2534; Imray C66.

TIDES –0445 Dover; ML no data; Duration 0610

Standard Port ULLAPOOL (→)

Times				Height (metres)			
High Water		Low Water		MHWS	MHWN	MLWN	MLWS
0000	0600	0300	0900	5·2	3·9	2·1	0·7
1200	1800	1500	2100				
Differences PORTREE (Skye)							
–0025	–0025	–0025	–0025	+0·1	–0·2	–0·2	0·0
SHIELDAIG (Loch Torridon)							
–0020	–0020	–0015	–0015	+0·4	+0·3	+0·1	0·0
LOCH A'BHRAIGE (Rona)							
–0020	0000	–0010	0000	–0·1	–0·1	–0·1	–0·2
PLOCKTON							
+0005	–0025	–0005	–0010	+0·5	+0·5	+0·5	+0·2
LOCH SNIZORT (Uig Bay, Skye)							
–0045	–0020	–0005	–0025	+0·1	–0·4	–0·2	0·0
LOCH DUNVEGAN (Skye)							
–0105	–0030	–0020	–0040	0·0	–0·1	0·0	0·0
LOCH HARPORT (Skye)							
–0115	–0035	–0020	–0100	–0·1	–0·1	0·0	+0·1
SOAY (Camus nan Gall)							
–0055	–0025	–0025	–0045	–0·4	–0·2	No data	
KYLE OF LOCHALSH							
–0040	–0020	–0005	–0025	+0·1	0·0	0·0	–0·1
DORNIE BRIDGE (Loch Alsh)							
–0040	–0010	–0005	–0020	+0·1	–0·1	0·0	0·0
GLENELG BAY (Kyle Rhea)							
–0105	–0035	–0035	–0055	–0·4	–0·4	–0·9	–0·1
LOCH HOURN							
–0125	–0050	–0040	–0110	–0·2	–0·1	–0·1	+0·1

SHELTER Secure in all but strong S to SW'lies, when Camas Bàn is more sheltered. In the NW of the bay there are 8 ⚓s for <15 tons. Short stay pontoon on pier.

NAVIGATION WPT 57°24'·58N 06°10'·07W, 275°/0·72M to pier. From the S, avoid rks off An Tom Pt (1·5M to E, off chartlet).

LIGHTS AND MARKS Only lts are a SHM buoy Fl G 5s marking Sgeir Mhór, 2 FR (vert) 6m 4M (occas) on the pier and a SPM buoy Fl Y 5s.

R/T VHF Ch 16 12 (occas).

TELEPHONE (Code 01478) HM ☎ 612926; Moorings 612341; MRCC (01851) 702013; ⊜ (0141) 887 9369; Marinecall 09068 969654; Police 612888; Dr 612013; Ⓗ 612704.

FACILITIES Pier AB £14, D (cans), L, FW. Town P, ⚒, Gas, Gaz, ▣, R, Bar, ✉, Ⓑ, bus to Kyle of Lochalsh, ⇌.

TIME ZONE (UT)
For Summer Time add ONE hour in **non-shaded areas**

ULLAPOOL   LAT 57°54'N   LONG 5°10'W
TIMES AND HEIGHTS OF HIGH AND LOW WATERS

Dates in red are **SPRINGS**
Dates in blue are **NEAPS**

YEAR 2010

JANUARY

Time	m		Time	m
1 0058	1.1	**16** 0142	1.4
0657	5.4	0809	5.0
F 1332	0.9	SA 1405	1.2
1929	5.3	1955	4.8
2 0144	0.9	**17** 0214	1.3
0741	5.6	0801	5.1
SA 1418	0.7	SU 1436	1.2
2015	5.3	2023	4.8
3 0229	0.9	**18** 0245	1.3
0826	5.6	0830	5.1
SU 1505	0.6	M 1507	1.2
2103	5.3	2051	4.7
4 0314	0.9	**19** 0316	1.4
0913	5.5	0901	5.0
M 1551	0.7	TU 1538	1.3
2152	5.1	2121	4.6
5 0359	1.1	**20** 0347	1.5
1003	5.3	0933	4.9
TU 1639	0.9	W 1610	1.4
2244	4.8	2154	4.5
6 0446	1.3	**21** 0420	1.7
1058	5.0	1010	4.7
W 1728	1.2	TH 1645	1.6
2342	4.5	2232	4.3
7 0538	1.6	**22** 0457	1.9
1201	4.7	1052	4.5
TH 1822	1.6	F 1724	1.8
◑		2320	4.1
8 0047	4.3	**23** 0541	2.1
0636	2.0	1147	4.3
F 1314	4.4	SA 1812	2.0
1925	1.9	◐	
9 0201	4.2	**24** 0028	4.0
0748	2.2	0639	2.3
SA 1435	4.2	SU 1304	4.1
2041	2.1	1914	2.2
10 0317	4.2	**25** 0156	4.0
0913	2.3	0801	2.4
SU 1553	4.2	M 1428	4.1
2159	2.1	2038	2.2
11 0421	4.3	**26** 0316	4.1
1032	2.1	0934	2.3
M 1655	4.3	TU 1547	4.2
2301	2.0	2203	2.1
12 0512	4.5	**27** 0423	4.4
1131	1.9	1048	1.9
TU 1743	4.4	W 1653	4.5
2350	1.8	2308	1.7
13 0554	4.7	**28** 0517	4.7
1217	1.7	1145	1.5
W 1823	4.6	TH 1746	4.8
14 0031	1.6	**29** 0000	1.4
0629	4.9	0603	5.1
TH 1257	1.5	F 1235	1.0
1856	4.7	1832	5.2
15 0108	1.5	**30** 0048	1.0
0702	5.0	0645	5.5
F 1332	1.4	SA 1321	0.6
● 1927	4.8	○ 1916	5.4
		31 0132	0.7
		0727	5.7
		SU 1405	0.3
		1958	5.5

FEBRUARY

Time	m		Time	m
1 0214	0.6	**16** 0221	1.1
0809	5.8	0804	5.2
M 1448	0.3	TU 1440	0.9
2040	5.4	2021	4.9
2 0256	0.6	**17** 0250	1.1
0851	5.7	0832	5.1
TU 1530	0.4	W 1508	1.0
2123	5.2	2048	4.8
3 0338	0.7	**18** 0319	1.2
0935	5.4	0902	5.0
W 1611	0.7	TH 1538	1.1
2208	4.9	2118	4.7
4 0420	1.0	**19** 0350	1.3
1023	5.0	0936	4.8
TH 1654	1.1	F 1610	1.3
2258	4.6	2152	4.5
5 0505	1.4	**20** 0424	1.6
1120	4.6	1015	4.6
F 1740	1.6	SA 1646	1.5
◑		2233	4.3
6 0001	4.3	**21** 0505	1.8
0556	1.9	1106	4.3
SA 1235	4.2	SU 1729	1.8
1835	2.0	2332	4.1
7 0119	4.0	**22** 0558	2.1
0703	2.3	1225	4.0
SU 1407	3.9	M 1828	2.1
1955	2.4	◐	
8 0246	4.0	**23** 0110	3.9
0844	2.4	0720	2.3
M 1538	3.9	TU 1406	3.9
2137	2.4	2001	2.3
9 0402	4.1	**24** 0248	4.0
1023	2.3	0914	2.2
TU 1645	4.0	W 1533	4.1
2249	2.2	2147	2.1
10 0457	4.3	**25** 0405	4.3
1123	2.0	1036	1.8
W 1734	4.2	TH 1642	4.4
2337	1.9	2255	1.7
11 0538	4.6	**26** 0501	4.7
1205	1.7	1132	1.3
TH 1809	4.4	F 1733	4.8
		2346	1.3
12 0016	1.7	**27** 0547	5.1
0612	4.8	1220	0.8
F 1241	1.5	SA 1816	5.2
1839	4.6		
13 0051	1.4	**28** 0031	0.8
0642	5.0	0627	5.5
SA 1313	1.2	SU 1304	0.4
1906	4.7	○ 1856	5.4
14 0123	1.2		
0710	5.1		
SU 1343	1.1		
● 1931	4.8		
15 0153	1.1		
0737	5.2		
M 1412	1.0		
1955	4.9		

MARCH

Time	m		Time	m
1 0114	0.5	**16** 0126	1.0
0707	5.7	0709	5.1
M 1345	0.1	TU 1341	0.8
1934	5.5	1926	4.9
2 0154	0.4	**17** 0154	0.9
0746	5.8	0736	5.1
TU 1424	0.1	W 1409	0.8
2013	5.5	1951	4.9
3 0234	0.4	**18** 0223	0.9
0826	5.6	0804	5.1
W 1503	0.3	TH 1438	0.8
2052	5.3	2018	4.9
4 0314	0.5	**19** 0253	1.0
0908	5.3	0836	5.0
TH 1542	0.6	F 1508	0.9
2133	5.0	2049	4.8
5 0354	0.9	**20** 0325	1.1
0952	4.9	0911	4.8
F 1621	1.1	SA 1541	1.1
2218	4.6	2124	4.6
6 0436	1.3	**21** 0401	1.4
1045	4.4	0954	4.5
SA 1703	1.6	SU 1618	1.4
2315	4.2	2207	4.3
7 0524	1.8	**22** 0443	1.6
1201	4.0	1052	4.2
SU 1753	2.1	M 1703	1.8
◑		2309	4.1
8 0036	3.9	**23** 0539	1.9
0626	2.2	1220	3.9
M 1338	3.7	TU 1804	2.1
1908	2.4	◐	
9 0209	3.8	**24** 0051	3.9
0811	2.4	0707	2.1
TU 1514	3.7	W 1355	3.9
2108	2.5	1944	2.3
10 0331	3.9	**25** 0226	4.0
1003	2.3	0900	2.0
W 1623	3.8	TH 1518	4.0
2226	2.3	2129	2.0
11 0430	4.1	**26** 0342	4.3
1100	2.0	1017	1.6
TH 1710	4.1	F 1624	4.4
2314	1.9	2235	1.6
12 0512	4.4	**27** 0439	4.7
1139	1.7	1112	1.1
F 1745	4.3	SA 1713	4.7
2352	1.6	2325	1.2
13 0546	4.6	**28** 0524	5.0
1213	1.4	1158	0.7
SA 1813	4.5	SU 1754	5.1
14 0025	1.4	**29** 0009	0.8
0615	4.8	0605	5.4
SU 1244	1.1	M 1240	0.3
1838	4.7	1832	5.3
15 0057	1.2	**30** 0052	0.5
0642	5.0	0644	5.5
M 1313	0.9	TU 1320	0.2
● 1902	4.8	○ 1910	5.4
		31 0132	0.4
		0724	5.5
		W 1359	0.2
		1947	5.4

APRIL

Time	m		Time	m
1 0212	0.4	**16** 0158	0.9
0804	5.4	0741	5.0
TH 1436	0.4	F 1411	0.8
2025	5.2	1955	4.9
2 0251	0.6	**17** 0231	0.9
0845	5.0	0818	4.8
F 1514	0.8	SA 1444	0.9
2104	4.9	2029	4.8
3 0331	0.9	**18** 0307	1.0
0930	4.6	0900	4.7
SA 1552	1.2	SU 1520	1.1
2148	4.6	2110	4.6
4 0413	1.3	**19** 0348	1.2
1022	4.2	0951	4.4
SU 1633	1.6	M 1602	1.4
2240	4.2	2201	4.4
5 0500	1.7	**20** 0436	1.5
1134	3.8	1059	4.1
M 1721	2.0	TU 1651	1.7
2354	4.0	2311	4.2
6 0558	2.1	**21** 0538	1.7
1300	3.6	1221	4.0
TU 1828	2.4	W 1758	2.0
◑		◐	
7 0119	3.8	**22** 0040	4.0
0726	2.3	0704	1.8
W 1429	3.6	TH 1341	4.0
2016	2.5	1930	2.1
8 0242	3.8	**23** 0202	4.1
0911	2.2	0836	1.7
TH 1543	3.7	F 1455	4.1
2143	2.3	2100	1.9
9 0346	4.0	**24** 0314	4.3
1016	2.0	0948	1.4
F 1633	3.9	SA 1558	4.3
2236	2.0	2206	1.6
10 0433	4.2	**25** 0412	4.6
1059	1.7	1044	1.0
SA 1710	4.1	SU 1648	4.6
2316	1.7	2259	1.2
11 0510	4.4	**26** 0501	4.9
1135	1.4	1131	0.8
SU 1739	4.4	M 1731	4.9
2351	1.4	2346	0.9
12 0542	4.6	**27** 0544	5.1
1208	1.2	1215	0.6
M 1806	4.6	TU 1810	5.1
13 0024	1.2	**28** 0029	0.7
0611	4.8	0625	5.2
TU 1239	1.0	W 1256	0.5
1831	4.8	○ 1848	5.2
14 0056	1.0	**29** 0112	0.6
0639	4.9	0706	5.1
W 1309	0.8	TH 1335	0.6
● 1856	4.9	1926	5.2
15 0127	0.9	**30** 0153	0.6
0709	5.0	0747	5.0
TH 1339	0.8	F 1413	0.7
1924	4.9	2004	5.0

Chart Datum: 2·75 metres below Ordnance Datum (Newlyn). HAT is 5·9 metres above Chart Datum; see 4.5

ULLAPOOL LAT 57°54'N LONG 5°10'W
TIMES AND HEIGHTS OF HIGH AND LOW WATERS

TIME ZONE (UT)
For Summer Time add ONE hour in **non-shaded areas**

Dates in red are SPRINGS
Dates in blue are NEAPS

YEAR 2010

MAY

	Time	m		Time	m
1 SA	0233 0830 1451 2044	0.8 4.7 1.0 4.8	**16** SU	0217 0810 1428 2021	0.9 4.8 0.9 4.9
2 SU	0314 0915 1530 2126	1.0 4.4 1.3 4.6	**17** M	0259 0859 1510 2108	0.9 4.7 1.1 4.8
3 M	0356 1006 1611 2215	1.3 4.1 1.6 4.3	**18** TU	0345 0956 1556 2203	1.0 4.5 1.3 4.6
4 TU	0441 1104 1657 2314	1.6 3.9 1.9 4.1	**19** W	0437 1100 1649 2310	1.2 4.3 1.5 4.4
5 W	0533 1211 1753	1.8 3.7 2.2	**20** TH	0538 1208 1752	1.4 4.2 1.7
6 TH ◑	0024 0638 1324 1911	3.9 2.0 3.6 2.3	**21** F	0023 0649 1317 1907	4.3 1.5 4.1 1.8
7 F	0137 0757 1438 2036	3.8 2.1 3.6 2.3	**22** SA	0135 0803 1425 2024	4.3 1.5 4.1 1.8
8 SA	0244 0909 1538 2142	3.9 2.0 3.8 2.1	**23** SU	0243 0912 1529 2132	4.3 1.4 4.3 1.6
9 SU	0340 1005 1623 2231	4.0 1.8 4.0 1.9	**24** M	0346 1013 1623 2232	4.5 1.2 4.5 1.4
10 M	0425 1048 1659 2312	4.2 1.5 4.2 1.6	**25** TU	0441 1106 1710 2325	4.6 1.1 4.7 1.2
11 TU	0503 1126 1730 2349	4.4 1.3 4.4 1.4	**26** W	0530 1153 1753	4.7 1.0 4.9
12 W	0538 1202 1800	4.6 1.1 4.6	**27** TH ○	0012 0614 1237 1832	1.0 4.8 0.9 5.0
13 TH	0025 0612 1237 1830	1.2 4.7 1.0 4.8	**28** F	0058 0657 1318 1911	0.9 4.8 1.0 5.0
14 F ●	0101 0648 1313 1903	1.0 4.8 0.9 4.9	**29** SA	0140 0739 1357 1950	0.9 4.7 1.0 4.9
15 SA	0138 0727 1350 1940	0.9 4.8 0.9 4.9	**30** SU	0221 0820 1435 2028	1.0 4.5 1.2 4.8
			31 M	0300 0901 1513 2107	1.1 4.4 1.3 4.7

JUNE

	Time	m		Time	m
1 TU	0340 0943 1552 2149	1.2 4.2 1.5 4.5	**16** W	0341 0947 1550 2156	0.7 4.7 1.1 4.9
2 W	0421 1027 1633 2235	1.4 4.0 1.7 4.3	**17** TH	0431 1043 1640 2253	0.9 4.6 1.2 4.7
3 TH	0504 1118 1719 2328	1.6 3.9 1.9 4.1	**18** F	0524 1143 1735 2357	1.0 4.4 1.5 4.6
4 F ◑	0553 1216 1813	1.8 3.7 2.1	**19** SA ◑	0622 1246 1837	1.2 4.2 1.6
5 SA	0030 0648 1321 1918	4.0 1.9 3.7 2.2	**20** SU	0105 0725 1353 1946	4.4 1.4 4.2 1.8
6 SU	0136 0751 1426 2030	3.9 1.9 3.7 2.2	**21** M	0215 0835 1500 2059	4.3 1.6 4.2 1.8
7 M	0238 0856 1524 2134	3.9 1.9 3.9 2.1	**22** TU	0326 0944 1603 2210	4.3 1.6 4.3 1.7
8 TU	0334 0953 1613 2227	4.0 1.8 4.1 1.9	**23** W	0430 1045 1656 2311	4.3 1.5 4.5 1.5
9 W	0423 1043 1654 2314	4.2 1.6 4.3 1.6	**24** TH	0525 1138 1742	4.4 1.4 4.7
10 TH	0508 1128 1732 2358	4.4 1.4 4.5 1.4	**25** F	0004 0611 1225 1823	1.4 4.5 1.3 4.8
11 F	0551 1211 1810	4.6 1.2 4.8	**26** SA ○	0050 0653 1306 1901	1.2 4.5 1.2 4.9
12 SA ●	0041 0634 1253 1849	1.1 4.7 1.0 4.9	**27** SU	0131 0731 1344 1937	1.1 4.6 1.2 4.9
13 SU	0124 0719 1336 1931	0.9 4.8 1.0 5.0	**28** M	0210 0806 1421 2011	1.1 4.5 1.2 4.9
14 M	0208 0806 1419 2015	0.8 4.9 0.9 5.1	**29** TU	0246 0840 1456 2045	1.1 4.5 1.3 4.8
15 TU	0254 0855 1504 2103	0.7 4.8 0.9 5.0	**30** W	0321 0913 1531 2119	1.1 4.4 1.4 4.7

JULY

	Time	m		Time	m
1 TH	0356 0948 1606 2156	1.2 4.3 1.5 4.5	**16** F	0413 1016 1622 2227	0.6 4.8 1.0 5.0
2 F	0432 1026 1644 2238	1.4 4.1 1.7 4.3	**17** SA	0459 1110 1710 2327	0.8 4.6 1.2 4.7
3 SA	0510 1111 1725 2327	1.5 4.0 1.9 4.2	**18** SU ◑	0550 1212 1805	1.2 4.3 1.6
4 SU ◑	0553 1207 1814	1.7 3.9 2.1	**19** M	0036 0647 1322 1910	4.4 1.6 4.1 1.9
5 M	0028 0642 1315 1915	4.0 1.9 3.8 2.2	**20** TU	0153 0757 1436 2031	4.1 1.9 4.1 2.0
6 TU	0136 0744 1423 2029	3.9 2.0 3.8 2.2	**21** W	0316 0920 1548 2159	4.0 2.0 4.2 2.0
7 W	0244 0855 1527 2143	3.9 2.0 4.0 2.1	**22** TH	0428 1033 1647 2307	4.1 1.9 4.4 1.8
8 TH	0348 1003 1623 2245	4.0 1.9 4.2 1.8	**23** F	0523 1129 1733 2359	4.2 1.7 4.6 1.5
9 F	0446 1101 1711 2338	4.2 1.7 4.5 1.5	**24** SA	0607 1214 1812	4.4 1.5 4.7
10 SA	0537 1152 1755	4.5 1.4 4.8	**25** SU	0041 0642 1254 1846	1.3 4.5 1.4 4.9
11 SU ●	0026 0623 1239 1837	1.1 4.8 1.1 5.0	**26** M ○	0119 0714 1329 1918	1.2 4.6 1.2 5.0
12 M	0113 0709 1324 1920	0.8 5.0 0.9 5.3	**27** TU	0153 0743 1403 1948	1.0 4.7 1.2 5.0
13 TU	0158 0754 1408 2003	0.5 5.1 0.7 5.4	**28** W	0224 0811 1434 2017	1.0 4.7 1.1 5.0
14 W	0243 0839 1452 2048	0.4 5.1 0.7 5.4	**29** TH	0255 0839 1505 2047	1.0 4.6 1.2 4.9
15 TH	0328 0926 1536 2136	0.4 5.1 0.8 5.2	**30** F	0325 0908 1536 2119	1.0 4.5 1.3 4.7
			31 SA	0357 0940 1608 2154	1.2 4.4 1.5 4.6

AUGUST

	Time	m		Time	m
1 SU	0430 1016 1644 2235	1.4 4.2 1.7 4.3	**16** M ◐	0516 1136 1734	1.3 4.4 1.6
2 M	0506 1101 1725 2327	1.6 4.1 1.9 4.1	**17** TU	0010 0609 1252 1838	4.2 1.8 4.1 2.0
3 TU ◐	0549 1203 1817	1.8 3.9 2.2	**18** W	0139 0722 1415 2010	3.9 2.2 4.0 2.2
4 W	0040 0645 1329 1931	3.9 2.1 3.8 2.3	**19** TH	0309 0902 1533 2155	3.9 2.3 4.1 2.1
5 TH	0205 0803 1449 2107	3.9 2.2 3.9 2.2	**20** F	0422 1023 1633 2301	4.0 2.1 4.3 1.9
6 F	0323 0933 1558 2225	4.0 2.1 4.1 1.9	**21** SA	0514 1116 1718 2346	4.2 1.9 4.5 1.5
7 SA	0430 1043 1654 2323	4.2 1.8 4.5 1.5	**22** SU	0552 1158 1754	4.4 1.6 4.7
8 SU	0524 1137 1740	4.5 1.4 4.9	**23** M	0023 0623 1234 1825	1.4 4.5 1.4 4.9
9 M	0012 0609 1225 1821	1.0 4.9 1.1 5.2	**24** TU	0057 0650 1307 1853	1.2 4.7 1.2 5.0
10 TU ●	0058 0652 1309 1902	0.6 5.2 0.7 5.5	**25** W	0127 0716 1338 1921	1.0 4.8 1.1 5.1
11 W	0141 0733 1351 1943	0.3 5.4 0.5 5.7	**26** TH	0156 0740 1407 1948	0.9 4.8 1.1 5.1
12 TH	0223 0815 1433 2025	0.1 5.4 0.4 5.7	**27** F	0225 0806 1436 2016	0.9 4.8 1.1 5.0
13 F	0305 0857 1515 2109	0.2 5.3 0.5 5.4	**28** SA	0253 0832 1505 2045	1.0 4.8 1.2 4.9
14 SA	0347 0943 1558 2158	0.4 5.0 0.8 5.1	**29** SU	0322 0901 1536 2118	1.1 4.6 1.3 4.7
15 SU	0430 1034 1643 2255	0.8 4.7 1.2 4.7	**30** M	0353 0934 1609 2156	1.3 4.5 1.6 4.5
			31 TU	0428 1014 1648 2246	1.5 4.3 1.8 4.2

Chart Datum: 2·75 metres below Ordnance Datum (Newlyn). HAT is 5·9 metres above Chart Datum; see 4.5

TIME ZONE (UT)
For Summer Time add ONE hour in **non-shaded areas**

ULLAPOOL LAT 57°54'N LONG 5°10'W
TIMES AND HEIGHTS OF HIGH AND LOW WATERS

Dates in red are **SPRINGS**
Dates in blue are **NEAPS**

YEAR 2010

SEPTEMBER

Day	Time m	Time m	Time m	Time m
1 W ◐	0509 1.8	1109 4.0	1738 2.1	
2 TH	0003 3.9	0602 2.1	1245 3.9	1853 2.4
3 F	0142 3.8	0725 2.3	1421 3.9	2043 2.3
4 SA	0307 4.0	0913 2.1	1537 4.2	2208 1.9
5 SU	0415 4.3	1027 1.8	1634 4.6	2305 1.4
6 M	0507 4.7	1119 1.4	1720 5.0	2353 0.9
7 TU	0550 5.3	1205 1.0	1801 5.4	
8 W ●	0036 0.5	0630 5.4	1248 0.6	1840 5.7
9 TH	0118 0.2	0709 5.5	1329 0.4	1920 5.8
10 F	0159 0.1	0748 5.5	1410 0.4	2001 5.7
11 SA	0239 0.2	0828 5.4	1451 0.5	2043 5.4
12 SU	0319 0.5	0911 5.1	1533 0.8	2130 5.0
13 M	0400 1.0	0958 4.8	1617 1.2	2227 4.5
14 TU	0444 1.5	1059 4.4	1707 1.7	2348 4.1
15 W ◐	0535 2.0	1221 4.1	1811 2.1	
16 TH	0121 3.8	0648 2.4	1349 4.0	1949 2.3
17 F	0252 3.8	0838 2.5	1509 4.1	2138 2.2
18 SA	0403 3.9	1002 2.3	1609 4.2	2239 2.0
19 SU	0452 4.1	1052 2.0	1653 4.5	2320 1.7
20 M	0528 4.4	1132 1.7	1728 4.7	2355 1.4
21 TU	0556 4.6	1207 1.5	1758 4.9	
22 W	0026 1.2	0622 4.7	1239 1.3	1825 5.0
23 TH ○	0056 1.0	0646 4.9	1310 1.1	1852 5.1
24 F	0125 0.9	0710 5.0	1339 1.1	1919 5.1
25 SA	0153 0.9	0735 5.0	1408 1.1	1947 5.1
26 SU	0221 1.0	0801 4.9	1437 1.1	2017 5.0
27 M	0251 1.1	0830 4.8	1509 1.3	2052 4.8
28 TU	0323 1.3	0904 4.7	1544 1.5	2132 4.5
29 W	0358 1.5	0945 4.4	1625 1.8	2227 4.2
30 TH	0441 1.8	1043 4.2	1717 2.0	2352 4.0

OCTOBER

Day	Time m	Time m	Time m	Time m
1 F ◐	0537 2.2	1220 4.0	1836 2.2	
2 SA	0127 3.9	0704 2.4	1356 4.1	2024 2.1
3 SU	0247 4.1	0852 2.2	1511 4.3	2145 1.8
4 M	0353 4.4	1003 1.8	1609 4.7	2242 1.3
5 TU	0445 4.8	1055 1.4	1656 5.1	2329 0.9
6 W	0528 5.1	1141 1.0	1738 5.4	
7 TH ●	0012 0.5	0606 5.4	1225 0.7	1818 5.7
8 F	0054 0.3	0645 5.6	1307 0.5	1858 5.7
9 SA	0134 0.3	0723 5.6	1348 0.5	1940 5.6
10 SU	0214 0.5	0803 5.4	1430 0.6	2023 5.3
11 M	0253 0.8	0844 5.2	1512 0.9	2110 4.9
12 TU	0334 1.2	0930 4.8	1557 1.3	2207 4.4
13 W	0417 1.6	1026 4.5	1646 1.7	2322 4.1
14 TH ◐	0507 2.1	1142 4.2	1747 2.1	
15 F	0047 3.8	0614 2.4	1307 4.0	1911 2.3
16 SA	0214 3.8	0751 2.5	1426 4.0	2048 2.3
17 SU	0326 3.9	0919 2.4	1530 4.2	2156 2.1
18 M	0417 4.1	1015 2.1	1617 4.4	2241 1.8
19 TU	0455 4.3	1058 1.9	1655 4.6	2318 1.6
20 W	0525 4.5	1134 1.6	1727 4.8	2351 1.4
21 TH	0552 4.7	1208 1.4	1757 4.9	
22 F	0022 1.2	0617 4.9	1240 1.3	1825 5.0
23 SA ○	0053 1.1	0642 5.0	1311 1.2	1854 5.1
24 SU	0123 1.0	0709 5.1	1342 1.1	1925 5.1
25 M	0153 1.1	0738 5.1	1415 1.2	1959 5.0
26 TU	0226 1.1	0810 5.0	1450 1.3	2038 4.8
27 W	0301 1.3	0848 4.8	1528 1.5	2125 4.6
28 TH	0340 1.5	0934 4.6	1613 1.7	2226 4.3
29 F	0426 1.8	1036 4.4	1710 1.9	2345 4.1
30 SA ◐	0525 2.1	1202 4.2	1826 2.0	
31 SU	0106 4.1	0647 2.3	1327 4.1	1956 1.9

NOVEMBER

Day	Time m	Time m	Time m	Time m
1 M	0220 4.2	0819 2.2	1439 4.4	2112 1.7
2 TU	0325 4.5	0931 1.9	1540 4.7	2212 1.3
3 W	0419 4.8	1028 1.5	1632 5.0	2302 1.0
4 TH	0505 5.1	1117 1.2	1718 5.3	2348 0.8
5 F	0546 5.3	1203 0.9	1801 5.4	
6 SA ●	0031 0.7	0625 5.4	1248 0.8	1843 5.4
7 SU	0113 0.7	0705 5.5	1331 0.8	1927 5.3
8 M	0153 0.7	0745 5.4	1414 0.9	2011 5.1
9 TU	0233 1.1	0826 5.2	1457 1.1	2057 4.8
10 W	0314 1.4	0910 4.9	1541 1.4	2148 4.5
11 TH	0356 1.7	0959 4.7	1627 1.7	2246 4.2
12 F	0443 2.0	1057 4.4	1719 2.0	2352 3.9
13 SA ●	0538 2.3	1206 4.2	1821 2.2	
14 SU	0106 3.8	0648 2.5	1320 4.1	1935 2.3
15 M	0222 3.8	0810 2.5	1430 4.1	2048 2.2
16 TU	0325 4.0	0921 2.4	1528 4.2	2148 2.0
17 W	0412 4.2	1014 2.1	1614 4.4	2234 1.8
18 TH	0449 4.4	1057 1.9	1653 4.6	2313 1.6
19 F	0521 4.6	1135 1.7	1728 4.7	2348 1.5
20 SA	0551 4.8	1211 1.5	1802 4.9	
21 SU ○	0023 1.3	0620 5.0	1247 1.4	1835 5.0
22 M	0058 1.2	0650 5.1	1323 1.2	1911 5.0
23 TU	0133 1.2	0724 5.1	1400 1.2	1951 5.0
24 W	0210 1.2	0801 5.1	1439 1.2	2034 4.9
25 TH	0249 1.3	0843 5.0	1522 1.3	2124 4.8
26 F	0331 1.4	0931 4.9	1610 1.4	2221 4.6
27 SA	0419 1.7	1029 4.7	1704 1.6	2326 4.4
28 SU ●	0515 1.9	1138 4.6	1808 1.7	
29 M	0036 4.3	0623 2.0	1253 4.5	1920 1.8
30 TU	0146 4.3	0739 2.1	1405 4.5	2033 1.7

DECEMBER

Day	Time m	Time m	Time m	Time m
1 W	0253 4.4	0854 2.0	1512 4.6	2139 1.6
2 TH	0354 4.6	0959 1.8	1612 4.8	2237 1.4
3 F	0446 4.9	1057 1.5	1706 4.9	2328 1.2
4 SA	0532 5.1	1148 1.3	1754 5.1	
5 SU ●	0015 1.1	0614 5.2	1237 1.1	1838 5.1
6 M	0058 1.1	0654 5.3	1321 1.1	1921 5.1
7 TU	0140 1.1	0734 5.3	1404 1.1	2003 5.0
8 W	0219 1.2	0813 5.2	1445 1.2	2043 4.8
9 TH	0258 1.4	0852 5.1	1525 1.3	2124 4.6
10 F	0337 1.6	0932 4.9	1606 1.5	2205 4.4
11 SA	0418 1.8	1014 4.6	1648 1.7	2251 4.2
12 SU	0501 2.0	1103 4.4	1733 1.9	2346 4.0
13 M ●	0550 2.3	1204 4.2	1825 2.1	
14 TU	0054 3.9	0650 2.4	1313 4.1	1926 2.2
15 W	0207 3.9	0803 2.5	1421 4.1	2035 2.2
16 TH	0314 4.0	0916 2.4	1523 4.2	2139 2.1
17 F	0407 4.2	1015 2.2	1616 4.3	2232 2.0
18 SA	0450 4.4	1104 2.0	1702 4.5	2317 1.8
19 SU	0527 4.7	1147 1.7	1743 4.7	2359 1.5
20 M	0602 4.9	1228 1.5	1823 4.9	
21 TU ○	0039 1.4	0637 5.1	1309 1.3	1902 5.0
22 W	0119 1.2	0714 5.2	1350 1.1	1944 5.1
23 TH	0159 1.1	0754 5.3	1432 1.0	2027 5.1
24 F	0240 1.1	0836 5.3	1515 0.9	2114 5.0
25 SA	0323 1.1	0922 5.3	1601 1.0	2203 4.9
26 SU	0409 1.3	1012 5.1	1649 1.2	2259 4.7
27 M	0458 1.5	1110 4.9	1742 1.4	
28 TU ◐	0001 4.5	0554 1.8	1218 4.7	1842 1.6
29 W	0109 4.4	0659 2.0	1331 4.5	1951 1.8
30 TH	0221 4.3	0816 2.1	1448 4.4	2107 1.9
31 F	0332 4.4	0935 2.0	1602 4.5	2218 1.8

Chart Datum: 2·75 metres below Ordnance Datum (Newlyn). HAT is 5·9 metres above Chart Datum; see 4.5

ULLAPOOL TO LOCH TORRIDON

(AC 1794, 2210) The Summer Isles (AC 2501), 12M NW of the major fishing port of Ullapool, offer some sheltered anchorages and tight approaches. The best include the bay on E side of Tanera Mor; off NE of Tanera Beg (W of Eilean Fada Mor); and in Caolas Eilean Ristol, between the island and mainland.

Loch Ewe (AC 3146) provides good shelter and easy access. Best anchorages are in Poolewe Bay (beware Boor Rks off W shore) and in SW corner of Loch Thuirnaig (entering, keep close to S shore to avoid rocks extending from N side). Off Rubha Reidh (lt) seas can be dangerous.

▶ *The NE-going stream begins at HW Ullapool –0335; the SW-going at HW Ullapool +0305. Sp rates 3kn, but slacker to SW of point.* ◀

Longa Is lies N of ent to Loch Gairloch (AC 2528). The channel N of it is navigable but narrow at E end. Outer loch is free of dangers, but exposed to swell. Best anchorage is on S side of loch in Caolas Bad a' Chrotha, W of Eilean Horrisdale.

Entering L Torridon (AC 2210) from S or W beware Murchadh Breac (dries 1·5m) 3ca NNW of Rubha na Fearna. Best anchorages are SW of Eilean Mor (to W of Ardheslaig); in Loch a 'Chracaich, 7ca further SE; E of Shieldaig Is; and near head of Upper L Torridon. ▶ *Streams are weak except where they run 2-3kn in narrows between L Shieldaig and Upper L Torridon.* ◀

SKYE TO ARDNAMURCHAN

(AC 1795, 2210, 2209, 2208, 2207) Skye and the islands around it provide many good and attractive anchorages, of which the most secure are: Acairseid Mhor on the W side of Rona; Portree (9.8.9); Isleornsay; Portnalong, near the entrance to Loch Harport, and Carbost at the head; Loch Dunvegan; and Uig Bay in Loch Snizort. ⚓s at Stein (Loch Dunvegan), Portree, Acairseid Mhor (Rona), Churchton Bay (Raasay) and Armadale Bay (S tip).

▶*Tides are strong off Rubha Hunish at N end of Skye, and heavy overfalls occur with tide against fresh or strong winds.*◀ Anchorage behind Fladday Is near the N end of Raasay can be squally and uncomfortable; and Loch Scavaig (S. Skye, beneath the Cuillins) more so, though the latter is so spectacular as to warrant a visit in fair weather. Soay Is has a small, safe harbour on its N side, but the bar at entrance almost dries at LW springs.

Between N Skye and the mainland there is the choice of Sound of Raasay or Inner Sound. **The direction of buoyage in both Sounds is Northward.** In the former, coming S from Portree, beware Sgeir Chnapach (3m) and Ebbing Rk (dries 2·9m), both NNW of Oskaig Pt. Beware McMillan's Rk (0·4m depth) in mid-channel, marked by SHM lt buoy. ▶ *At the Narrows (chart 2534) the SE-going stream begins at HW Ullapool –0605, and the NW-going at HW Ullapool +0040; sp rate 1·4kn in mid-chan, but more near shoals each side.* ◀

The channel between Scalpay and Skye narrows to 2.5ca with drying reefs each side and least depth 0·1m. ▶ *Here the E-going stream begins at HW Ullapool +0550, and W-going at HW Ullapool –0010, sp rate 1kn.* ◀

Inner Sound, which is a Submarine exercise area, is wider and easier than Sound of Raasay; the two are connected by Caol Rona and Caol Mor, respectively N and S of Raasay. Dangers extend about 1M N of Rona, and Cow Is lies off the mainland 8M to S; otherwise approach from N is clear to Crowlin Is, which should be passed to W. There is a good anch between Eilean Mor and Eilean Meadhonach.

A torpedo range in the Inner Sound does not normally restrict passage, but vessels may be requested to keep to the E side of the Sound if the range is active. Range activity is broadcast at 0800 and 1800LT first on VHF Ch 16 and then on Ch 8, and is indicated by Red Flags flown at the range building at

Applecross, by all range vessels and at the naval pier at Kyle of Lochalsh, ☎ (01599) 534262.

Approaching Kyle Akin (AC 2540) from W, beware dangerous rks to N, off Bleat Is (at S side of entrance to Loch Carron); on S side of chan, Bogha Beag (dries 1·2m) and Black Eye Rk (depth 3·2m), respectively 6ca and 4ca W of bridge. Pass at least 100m N or S of Eileanan Dubha in Kyle Akin. On S side of chan String Rk (dries) is marked by PHM lt buoy.

Kyle Rhea connects Loch Alsh with NE end of Sound of Sleat. ▶ *The tidal streams are very strong: N-going stream begins HW Ullapool +0600, sp rate 6-7kn; S-going stream begins at HW Ullapool, sp rate 8kn. N-going stream in Kyle Rhea begins HW Dover +0140 (HW Ullapool +0555) and runs for 6 hours. The E-going stream in Kyle Akin begins (Sp) HW Dover +0350 (HW Ullapool –0415). (Nps) HW Dover –0415 (HW Ullapool).*

 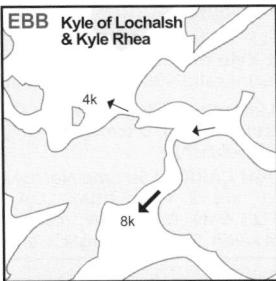

S-going stream in Kyle Rhea begins HW Dover –0415 (HW Ullapool) and runs for 6 hours. The W-going stream in Kyle Akin begins (Sp) HW Dover –0015 (HW Ullapool +0400). (Nps) HW Dover +0140 (HW Ullapool +0555). Eddies form both sides of the Kyle and there are dangerous overfalls off S end in fresh S'ly winds on S-going stream. ◀ Temp anch in Sandaig Bay, 3M to SW.

The Sound of Sleat widens to 4M off Point of Sleat and is exposed to SW winds unless Eigg and Muck give a lee. Mallaig is a busy fishing and ferry hbr, convenient for supplies. Further S the lochs require intricate pilotage. 6M NE of Ardnamurchan Pt (lt, fog sig) are Bo Faskadale rks, drying 0·5m and marked by SHM lt buoy, and Elizabeth Rock with depth of 0·7m. ▶ *Ardnamurchan Pt is an exposed headland onto which the ebb sets. With onshore winds, very heavy seas extend 2M offshore and it should be given a wide berth. Here the N-going stream begins at HW Oban –0525, and the S-going at HW Oban +0100, sp rates 1·5kn.* ◀

THE SMALL ISLES

(AC 2207, 2208) These consist of Canna, Rum, Eigg and Muck. The hbrs at Eigg (SE end), Rhum (Loch Scresort) and Canna (between Canna and Sanday) are all exposed to E'lies; Canna has best shelter and is useful for the Outer Hebrides. Dangers extend SSW from Canna: at 1M Jemina Rk (depth 1·5m) and Belle Rk (depth 3·6m); at 2M Humla Rk (5m high), marked by buoy and with offlying shoals close W of it; at 5M Hyskeir (lt, fog sig), the largest of a group of small islands; and at 7M Mill Rks (with depths of 1·8m).

▶ *The tide runs hard here, and in bad weather the sea breaks heavily up to 15M SW of Canna. Between Skerryvore and Neist Pt the stream runs generally N and S, starting N-going at HW Ullapool +0550, and S-going at HW Ullapool –0010. It rarely exceeds 1kn, except near Skerryvore, around headlands of The Small Isles, and over rks and shoals.* ◀

1M off the N side of Muck are Godag Rks, some above water but with submerged dangers extending 2ca further N. Most other dangers around the Small Isles are closer inshore, but there are banks on which the sea breaks heavily in bad weather. A local magnetic anomaly exists about 2M E of Muck.

9.8.10 PLOCKTON

Highland 57°20´·52N 05°38´·47W ❀❀❀❀❀❀❀❀

CHARTS AC 2209, 2528; Imray C66.

TIDES −0435 Dover; ML 3·5m; Duration 0600; See 9.8.9

SHELTER Good, exposed only to N/NE'lies. 9 Y ⚓s or ⚓ in centre of bay in approx 3·5m. Inner part of bay shoals and dries to the SW.

NAVIGATION WPT 57°21´·16N 05°39´·44W; thence towards Bogha Dubh Sgeir PHM bn, between Cat Is disused Lt ho and Sgeir Golach PHM Bcn and High Stone (1m) to the N. Hawk (0.1m) will be cleared when Duncraig Castle bears 158°. Alter S to the ⚓. Beware Plockton Rks (3·1m) on E side of bay.

LIGHTS AND MARKS See 9.8.4 and chartlet. Old lt ho (13m) on Cat Is is conspic, as is Duncraig Castle. Plockton Rks marked by lit PHM Bcn.

R/T None.

TELEPHONE HM (01599) 534589, 🖷 534167, Mobile 07802 367253 (at Kyle of Lochalsh); MRCC (01851) 702013; ⊖ (0141) 887 9369; Marinecall 09068 969654; Police/Dr via HM.

FACILITIES Village FW, M £5, L at 50m dinghy pontoon (H24 except MLWS), D (cans), CH, 🖷, R, Bar, ✉, ⚕, airstrip, (bus to Kyle of Lochalsh).

LOCH CARRON Strome Narrows are not buoyed or lit. At head of loch are 3 Y ⚓s (max LOA 14m) in 3m off drying jetty at 57°23´·95N 05°29´·0W; call ☎ 01520 722321. Appr on 328° between Sgeir Chreagach and Sgeir Fhada.

PLOCKTON

ANCHORAGES AROUND OR NEAR SKYE

LOCH TORRIDON Highland, **57°36´N 05°49´W**. AC 2210. Tides, see 9.8.9. Three large lochs: ent to outer loch (Torridon) is 3M wide, with isolated Sgeir na Trian (2m) almost in mid-chan; ⚓s on SW side behind Eilean Mór and in L Beag. L Sheildaig is middle loch with good ⚓ and 2 ⚓s (up to 10 tons) between the Is and village. 1M to the N, a 2ca wide chan leads into Upper L Torridon; many fish cages and prone to squalls. Few facilities, except Shieldaig: FW, 🖷, R, Bar, ✉, Garage.

LOCH A'BHRAIGE Rona (Highland), **57°34´·6N 05°57´·9W**. AC 2479, 2534. HW −0438 on Dover; ML 2·8m; Duration 0605. See 9.8.9. A good ⚓ in NW of the island, safe except in NNW winds. Beware rks on NE side up to 1ca off shore. Hbr in NE corner of loch head. Ldg lts 137°, see 9.8.4. Facilities: jetty, FW and a helipad, all owned by MOD (DRA). Before ent, call Rona Range Control VHF Ch 13.

Acarseid Mhór is ⚓ on W of Rona. One ⚓ £12, ☎ 07831 293963. App S of Eilean Garbh marked by W arrow. SD sketch of rks at ent is necessary. FW (cans), showers. At **Churchton Bay**, SW tip of Raasay, there are 4 HIE ⚓s; ☎ (01478) 612341; Slip, showers, R, ⚕.

LOCH DUNVEGAN 4 ⚓s off Stein, **57°30´·9N 06°34´·5W**. 3 ⚓s off Dunvegan, 57°26´·3N 06°35´·2W. Fuel, FW, R. ☎ (01478) 612341.

LOCH HARPORT Skye (Highland), **57°20´·6N 06°25´·8W**. AC 1795. HW −0447 (sp), −0527 (np) on Dover. See 9.8.9. On E side of Loch Bracadale, entered between Oronsay Is and Ardtreck Pt (W lt ho, Fl 6s 18m 9M). SW end of Oronsay has conspic rk pillar, called The Castle; keep ¼M off-shore here and off E coast of Oronsay which is joined to Ullinish Pt by drying reef. ⚓ Oronsay Is, N side of drying reef (4m), or on E side, but beware rk (dries) 0·5ca off N shore of Oronsay. Fiskavaig Bay 1M S of Ardtreck (7m); Loch Beag on N side of loch, exposed to W winds; Port na Long E of Ardtreck, sheltered except from E winds (beware fish farm); 1 ⚓ off the distillery and 2 ⚓ off The Old Inn at Carbost on SW shore. Facilities: (Carbost) 🖷, Bar, R, P (garage), ✉, FW. (Port na Long) Bar, FW, 🖷.

SOAY HARBOUR Skye (Highland), **57°09´·5N 06°13´·4W**. AC 2208. Tides see 9.8.9. Narrow inlet on NW side of Soay; enter from Soay Sound above half flood to clear bar, dries 0·6m. Appr on 135° from 5ca out to avoid reefs close each side of ent. Cross bar slightly E of mid-chan, altering 20° stbd for best water; ent is 15m wide between boulder spits marked by W poles with Or tops. ⚓ in 3m mid-pool or shoal draft boats can enter inner pool. Good shelter and holding. Camas nan Gall (poor holding); no other facilities.

ARMADALE BAY Skye (Highland), 4M NW of Mallaig. AC 2208. 6 ⚓s £12 at **57°04´·0N 05°53´·6W**, ☎ (01471) 844216. Bay is sheltered from SE to N winds but subject to swell in winds from N to SE. From S, beware the Eilean Maol & Sgorach rocks. Ferry pier, Oc R 6s 6m 6M, with conspic W shed. Facilities, Skye Yachts ☎ 01471 844216, M (£12), FW at pontoon or by hose to charter M's, D, 🖷 (not Sat pm or Sun), showers, Gas, free pontoon for tenders, ferry to Mallaig for ⚕. Ardvasar ¾ mile: Slip HW±3 at BY (launching/parking £5), P (cans) (not Sun), showers, WC; Gaz at ¼ mile; R, Bar.

CROWLIN ISLANDS Highland, **57°21´·1N 05°50´·6W**. AC 2209, 2498. HW −0435 on Dover, −0020 on Ullapool; HW +0·3m on Ullapool. See 9.8.8. ⚓ between Eilean Meadhonach and Eilean Mor, appr from N, keep E of Eilean Beg. Excellent shelter in strong N winds. There is an inner ⚓ with 3½m but ent chan dries. Eilean Beg lt ho Fl 6s 32m 6M, W tr. No facilities.

ANCHORAGES IN THE SOUND OF SLEAT (see also 9.8.9)

SOUND OF SLEAT There are ⚓s at: **Glenelg Bay** (57°12´·57N 05°37´·95W) SW of pier out of the tide, but only moderate holding. Usual facilities in village. At **Sandaig Bay** (57°10´·0N 05°41´·4W), exposed to SW. Sandaig Is are to NW of the bay; beware rks off Sgeir nan Eun. Eilean Mór has lit Fl 6s. At **Isleornsay Hbr** (57°09´N 05°48´W) 2ca N of pier, 2FR (vert) and floodlit. Give drying N end of Ornsay Is a wide berth. Lts: SE tip of Ornsay, Oc 8s 18m 15M, W tr; N end, Fl R 6s 8m 4M. Facilities: FW, ✉, Hotels. 5 ⚓s at Duisdale (NW corner).

LOCH HOURN Highland, **57°08´N 05°42´W**. AC 2208, 2541. Tides see 9.8.9. Ent is S of Sandaig Is and opposite Isle Ornsay, Skye. Loch extends 11M inland via 4 narrows to Loch Beag; it is scenically magnificent, but violent squalls occur in strong winds. Sgeir Ulibhe, drying 2·1m, bn, lies almost in mid-ent; best to pass S of it to clear Clansman Rk, 2·1m, to the N. ⚓s on N shore at Eilean Ràrsaidh and Camas Bàn, within first 4M. For pilotage further E, consult SDs. Facilities at Arnisdale (Camas Bàn): FW, 🖷, R, Bar, ✉. Doune Marine (01687 462667) FW, D.

LOCH NEVIS Highland, **57°02´·2N 05°43´·3W**. AC 2208, 2541. HW −0515 on Dover. See 9.8.9. Beware rks Bogha cas Sruth (dries 1·8m), Bogha Don and Sgeirean Glasa both marked by bns. ⚓ NE of Eilean na Glaschoille, good except in S winds; or 9 Or ⚓s off Inverie, £5 (free if dining), 10m max LOA. Call Old Forge VHF Ch 16, 12; FW, Bar, R, showers, ⚕. In strong winds expect violent unpredictable squalls. Enter the inner loch with caution, and ⚓ N or SE of Eilean Maol.

ANCHORAGES IN THE SMALL ISLES

CANNA The Small Isles, **57°03´·3N 06°29´·4W**. AC 1796, 2208. HW −0457 (Sp), −0550 (Np) on Dover; HW −0035 and −0·4m on Ullapool; Duration 0605. Good shelter, except in strong E'lies, in hbr between Canna and Sanday Is but holding is poor due to kelp. Appr along Sanday shore, keeping N of Sgeir a' Phuirt, dries

4·6m. Ldg marks as in SDs. ‡ in 3–4m W of Canna pier, off which beware drying rky patch. ‡ Lt is advised due to FVs. Conspic W lt bn, Fl 10s 32m 9M, vis 152°-061°, at E end of Sanday Is. Magnetic anomaly off NE Canna. Facilities: FW, shower at farm, R(☎01687 462937) with limited ☷, ✉, Note: NT manage island.

RUM The Small Isles, **57°00′·1N 06°15′·7W**. AC 2207, 2208. HW −0500 on Dover; −0035 and −0·3m on Ullapool; ML 2·4m; Duration 0600. SNH owns Is. The mountains (809m) are unmistakable. Landing is only allowed at L Scresort on E side; no dogs beyond village limit. Beware drying rks 1ca off N point of ent and almost 3ca off S point. The head of the loch dries 2ca out; ‡ off slip on S side or further in, to NE of jetty. Hbr is open to E winds/swell. Facilities: ✉, FW, ☷ (limited), R, Bar, ferry to Mallaig.

EIGG HARBOUR The Small Isles, **56°52′·6N 06°07′·6W**. AC 2207. HW −0523 on Dover. See 9.8.12. Entering from N or E use Sgeir nam Bagh (Ferry Terminal) Dir lt 245° Fl WRG 3s, leads between Garbh

Sgeir Bn Fl (2) G 10s & Flod Sgeir Bn Fl R 5s. An Sgùrr is a conspic 391m high peak/ridge brg 281°/1·3M from Sgeir nam Bagh. Most of hbr dries, but good ‡ 1ca NE of Galmisdale Pt pier, except in NE winds when yachts should go through the narrows and ‡ in South Bay in 6–8m; tide runs hard in the narrows. Also ‡ in 2·5m at Poll nam Partan, about 2ca N of Flod Sgeir. SE point of Eilean Chathastail Fl 6s 24m 8M, vis 181°-shore, W tr. VHF Ch 08 *Eigg Hbr*. HM ☎ via (01687) 482428. FW, repairs. **Pierhead** Showers, ✉, R, ☷, Gas. **Cleadale village** (2M to N) Bar.

MUCK The Small Isles, **56°49′·8N 06°13′·3W**. AC 2207. Tides approx as Eigg, 9.8.12. Port Mór at SE end is the main hbr, with a deep pool inside offlying rks, but open to S'lies. Approach: Dir lt Fl WRG 3s vis 1M by day leads between Dubh Sgeir (Fl(2) R 10s) and Bogha Ruadh (Fl G 5s) rks; see 9.8.4. ‡ towards the NW side of inlet; NE side has drying rks. To N of Is, Bagh a' Ghallanaich is ‡ protected from S. Few facilities.

9.8.11 LOCH ALSH

Highland **57°16′·68N 05°42′·87W** ❀❀❀♠♠✿✿✿

CHARTS AC 2540; Imray C66.

TIDES −0450 Dover; ML 3·0m; Duration 0555; See 9.8.9

SHELTER **Kyle of Lochalsh:** AB on Railway Pier, with FVs, or on 40m L-shaped pontoon (seasonal), close W of Railway Pier; or ‡ off the hotel there in 11m. **Kyle Akin:** 3 free ♠s are subject to tidal stream. Lit pontoon on NW side of hbr, shoal on N side.

‡s, safe depending on winds, are (clockwise from Kyle): Avernish B, (2ca N of Racoon Rk) in 3m clear of power cables, open to SW; NW of Eilean Donnan Cas (conspic); in Ratagan B at head of L Duich in 7m; in Totaig B facing Loch Long ent in 3·5m; on S shore in Ardintoul B in 5·5m; at head of Loch na Béiste in 7m close inshore and W of fish cages.

NAVIGATION WPT (from Inner Sound) 57°16′·98N 05°45′·77W, 123°/0·75M to bridge. Chan to bridge is marked by 2 PHM and 2 SHM lt buoys. Bridge to Skye, 29m clearance, is lit Oc 6s in centre of main span, Iso R 4s on S pier and Iso G4s on N pier. The secondary NE span is lit, but has only 3.7m clearance.

LIGHTS AND MARKS See chartlet. Direction of buoyage is N in Kyle Rhea, thence E up Loch Alsh; but W through Kyle Akin and the bridge, ie SHMs are on N side of chan.

R/T VHF Ch 11 16.

TELEPHONE (Code 01599) HM 534589, Mobile 07802 367253; MRCC (01851) 702013; ⊜ (0141) 887 9369; Marinecall 09068 969654; Police, Dr, Ⓗ : via HM. Skye br ☎ 534844.

FACILITIES **Kyle of Lochalsh:** AB pontoon, £14 (second day free), FW, D (Fish pier via HM), P (cans), ME, Ⓔ, CH, ✉, Ⓑ, R, Bar, ☷, Gas, ⇌ (useful railhead), Bus to Glasgow & Inverness; buses

every ½hr to/from Kyleakin. **Kyleakin:** ☎ 534167 or VHF Ch 11, 120m AB (£14/craft) depth varies from 3m to drying, M, FW, ☷, R, Bar.

9.8.12 MALLAIG

Highland **57°00′·47N 05°49′·47W** ❀❀❀♠♠♠✿✿

CHARTS AC 2208, 2541; Imray C65, C66.

TIDES −0515 Dover; ML 2·9; Duration 0605

Standard Port OBAN (→)

Times				Height (metres)			
High Water		Low Water		MHWS	MHWN	MLWN	MLWS
0000	0600	0100	0700	4·0	2·9	1·8	0·7
1200	1800	1300	1900				
Differences MALLAIG							
+0017	+0017	+0017	+0017	+1·0	+0·7	+0·3	+0·1
INVERIE BAY (Loch Nevis)							
+0030	+0020	+0035	+0020	+1·0	+0·9	+0·2	0·0
BAY OF LAIG (Eigg)							
+0015	+0030	+0040	+0005	+0·7	+0·6	−0·2	−0·2
LOCH MOIDART							
+0015	+0015	+0040	+0020	+0·8	+0·6	−0·2	−0·2
LOCH EATHARNA (Coll)							
+0025	+0010	+0015	+0025	+0·4	+0·3	No data	
GOTT BAY (Tiree)							
0000	+0010	+0005	+0010	0·0	+0·1	0·0	0·0

SHELTER Good in SW'lies but open to N. Access H24. ‡ in SE part of hbr or find a berth on Fish Pier. No ♠s. Hbr is often full of FVs; also Skye ferry.

Continued overleaf

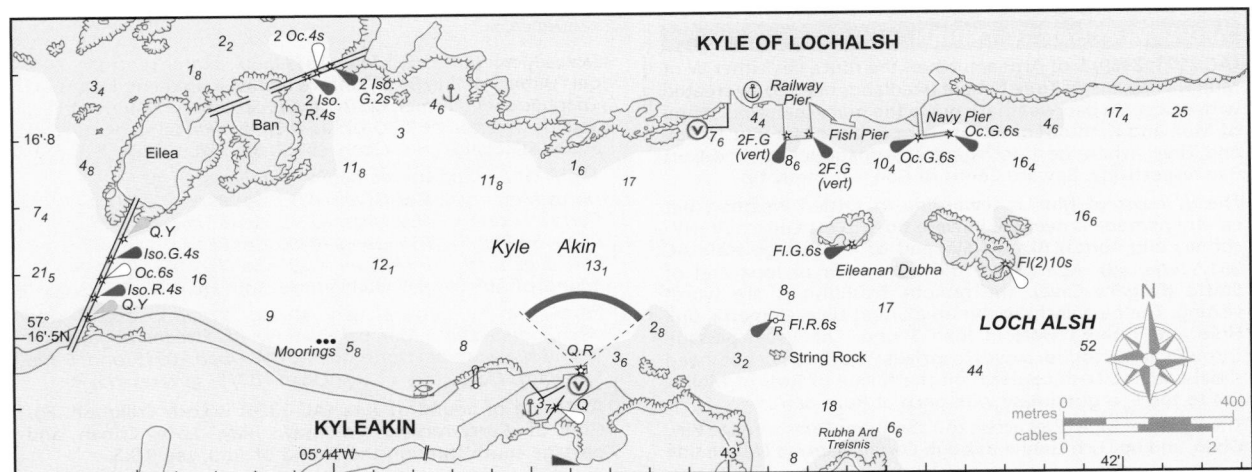

NW Scotland

MALLAIG *continued*

NAVIGATION WPT 57°00′·75N 05°49′·40W, 191°/0·3m to Steamer Pier lt, passing E of Sgeir Dhearg lt bn. The former W chan is now permanently closed to navigation.

LIGHTS AND MARKS As chartlet & 9.8.4. Town lts may obscure Sgeir Dhearg lt. Outer Hbr Pier Hds floodlit. IPTS (3 FR vert at pier hd) when ferries manoeuvring, no other traffic allowed except by HM's permission.

R/T Call: *Mallaig Hbr Radio* VHF Ch 09 16 (HO).

TELEPHONE (Code 01687) HM 462154, outside office hrs 462411; MRCC (01851) 702013; ⊜ (0141) 887 9369; Marinecall 09068 969654; Police 462177.

FACILITIES **Hbr** AB £6 whenever alongside for FW/fuel/stores (⌁ is free), M, P (cans), D, FW, ME, El, ✕, C (mobile 10 ton), CH, Ⓔ, ACA, Slip; a busy FV hbr, yacht berths may be provided at a later date near root of the Fish Pier. **Town** Dr 462202. 🛒, R, Gas, Gaz, Bar, ✉, Ⓑ, ⇌.

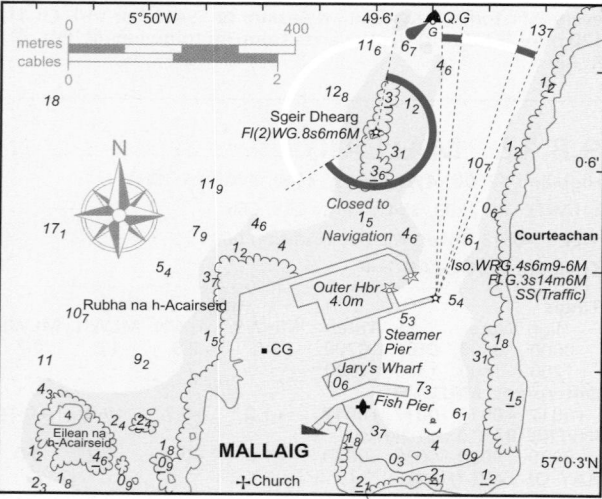

ADJACENT ANCHORAGE

ARISAIG, (Loch nan Ceall), Highland, **56°53′·64N 05°55′·77W** (ent). AC 2207. HW −0515 on Dover; +0030 and +0·9m on Oban. S side of ent is identifiable by W mark on Rubh' Arisaig. SDs essential. S Chan is winding, but marked by 8 perches; each must be identified. Appr HW±4 to avoid strongest streams LW±1½. Caution: many unmarked rks; no lts. Sheltered ⌁ at head of loch, clear of moorings. Call **Arisaig Marine** ☎ (01687) 450224, VHF Ch 16, M; few 🅰s, C (10 ton), CH, D & FW at ferry pier (HW), P (cans), El, ME, ✕, Slip. **Village** FW at hotel, Bar, ✉, R, Gas, 🛒, ⇌.

ARDNAMURCHAN TO CRINAN

(AC 2171, 2169) S of Ardnamurchan the route lies either W of Mull via Passage of Tiree (where headlands need to be treated with respect in bad weather); or via the more sheltered Sound of Mull and Firth of Lorne. The former permits a visit to Coll and Tiree, where best anchs are at Arinagour (🅰s) and Gott Bay respectively. Beware Cairns of Coll, off the N tip.

The W coast of Mull is rewarding in settled weather, but careful pilotage is needed. Beware tide rip off Caliach Pt (NW corner) and Torran Rks off SW end of Mull (large scale AC 2617 required). Apart from the attractions of Iona and of Staffa (Fingal's Cave), the remote Treshnish Is are worth visiting. The best anchs in this area are at Ulva, Gometra, Bull Hole and Tinker's Hole in Iona Sound. The usual passage through Iona Sound avoids overfalls W of Iona, but heed shoal patches. Loch Lathaich on the N side of Ross of Mull is 5M to the E; a good base with anch at Bunessan.

The Sound of Mull gives access to Tobermory, Dunstaffnage Bay, Oban, and up Loch Linnhe through Corran Narrows (where tide runs strongly) to Fort William and to Corpach for the Caledonian Canal. Apart from these places, there are dozens of lovely anchs in the sheltered lochs inside Mull, as for example in Loch Sunart with 🅰s at Kilchoan.

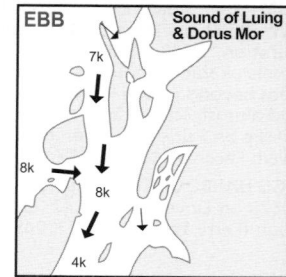

▶ *Firth of Lorne: the N-going stream begins at HW Oban +0430 (HW Dover −0100). The W-going stream in the Sound of Mull begins at HW Oban −0550 (HW Dover +0105). The ingoing tides at Lochs Feochan, Etive and Creran begin at HW Oban −0350, +0430 and +0600.*

The S-going stream in the Firth of Lorne begins at HW Oban −0155 (HW Dover +0500). The E-going stream in the Sound of Mull begins at HW Oban −0025 (HW Dover +0555).◀

On the mainland shore Puilladobhrain is a sheltered anch. Cuan Sound is a useful short cut to Loch Melfort, and Craobh Marina. Good shelter, draft permitting, in Ardinamar B, SW of Torsa.

Sound of Luing (AC 2326) between Fladda (lt), Lunga and Scarba on the W side, and Luing and Dubh Sgeir (lt) on the E side, is the normal chan to or from Sound of Jura, despite dangers at the N end and strong tidal streams. ▶ *The N- and W-going flood begins at HW Oban + 0430; the S- and E-going ebb at HW Oban −0155. Sp rates are 2·5kn at S end of Sound, increasing to 6kn or more in Islands off N entrance, where there are eddies, races and overfalls.* ◀

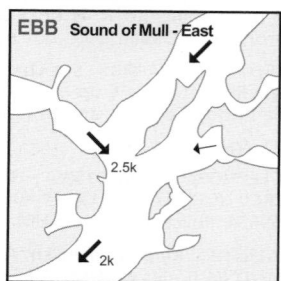

▶ *The N- or W-going stream begins in the following sequence:*

Dorus Mor:	HW Oban +0330. Sp: 8kn.
Corryvreckan:	HW Oban +0410. Sp: 8.5kn.
Cuan Sound:	HW Oban +0420. Sp: 6kn.
Sound of Jura:	HW Oban +0400. Sp: 4kn.
Sound of Luing:	HW Oban +0430. Sp: 7kn.

The S- or E-going stream begins as follows:

Dorus Mor:	HW Oban −0215. Sp: 8kn.
Corryvreckan:	HW Oban −0210. Sp: 8.5kn.
Cuan Sound:	HW Oban −0200. Sp: 6kn.
Sound of Jura:	HW Oban −0205. Sp: 4kn.
Sound of Luing:	HW Oban −0155. Sp: 7kn.

From the N, beware very strong streams, eddies and whirlpools in Dorus Mór, off Craignish Pt. Streams begin to set W and N away from Dorus Mór at HW Oban +0345, and E and S towards Dorus Mór at HW Oban −0215, sp rates 7kn.◀

At N end of Sound of Jura (AC 2326) is Loch Craignish. For Gulf of Corryvreckan, Colonsay, Islay, Loch Crinan and passage south through the Sound of Jura, see 9.9.5.

9.8.13 LOCH SUNART

Highland 56°39'·49N 06°00'·07W ❄✿⚓⚓✿✿

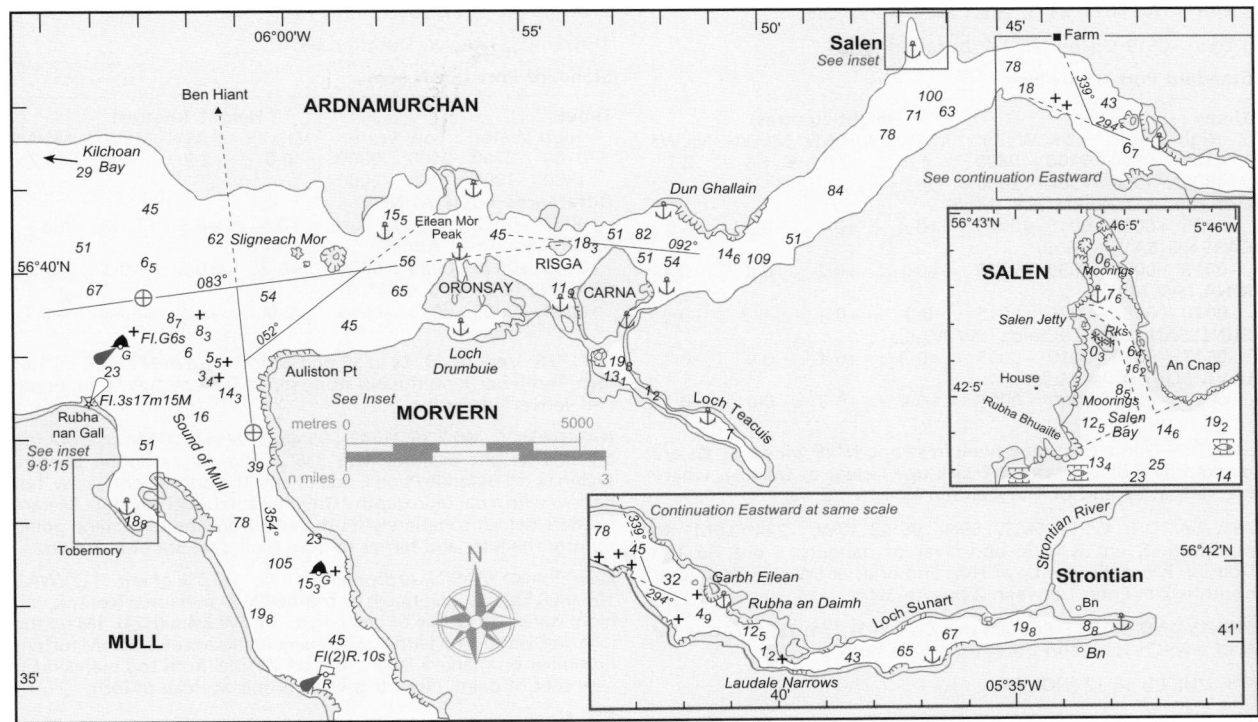

CHARTS AC 5611, 2171, 2392, 2394; Imray C65.

TIDES Salen –0500 Dover; ML 2·0

Standard Port OBAN (⟶)

Times				Height (metres)			
High Water		Low Water		MHWS	MHWN	MLWN	MLWS
0100	0700	0100	0800	4·0	2·9	1·8	0·7
1300	1900	1300	2000				
Differences SALEN (Loch Sunart)							
–0015	+0015	+0010	+0005	+0·6	+0·5	–0·1	–0·1

SHELTER 8 ⚓s at Kilchoan Bay (56°41'·5N 06°07'·3W); ☎ (01972) 510209. ⚓s in Loch Drumbuie (S of Oronsay) sheltered in all winds; in Sailean Mór (N of Oronsay) convenient and easy ent; between Oronsay and Carna; in Loch Teacuis (very tricky ent); E of Carna; Salen Bay, with ⚓s and jetty, open only to SSE (see facilities); Garbh Eilean (NW of Rubha an Daimh), and E of sand spit by Strontian R.

NAVIGATION **West WPT**, 56°39'·69N 06°03'·07W, 083°/3·7M to Creag nan Sgarbh (NW tip of Orinsay). **South WPT**, 56°38'·00N 06°00'·65W, 1M S of Auliston Pt; there are extensive rky reefs, The Stirks W of this pt. AC 2394 and detailed directions are needed to navigate the 17M long loch, particularly in its upper reaches. Beware Ross Rk, S of Risga; Broad Rk, E of Risga; Dun Ghallain Rk; shoals extending 3ca NNW from Eilean mo Shlinneag off S shore; drying rock 1ca W of Garbh Eilean and strong streams at sp in Laudale Narrows. Fish farms on both sides of the loch.

LIGHTS AND MARKS Unlit. Transits as on the chart: from W WPT, Risga on with N tip of Oronsay at 083°; N pt of Carna on with top of Risga 092°. From S WPT, Ben Hiant bearing 354°, thence Eilean Mor Peak at 052°. Further up the loch, 339° and 294°, as on chartlet, are useful. Many other transits are shown on AC 2394.

R/T None, except under Salen Bay opposite.

TELEPHONE (Code 01967) MRCC (01475) 729014; ⊖ (0141) 887 9369; Marinecall 09068 969653; Dr 431231.

FACILITIES **Salen Bay** jetty (56°42'·39N 05°46'·17W). ☎ 01967 431333. VHF Ch 16 (occas). Access HW±2 to jetty, keeping on E side of ent to avoid a drying reef on W side; two R ⚓s (15 ton) £10 (other moorings are private); ⚓ buoy advised as bottom is generally foul. L (£2 unless on ⚓), FW, D by hose, ⛽, Slip, SM, ME, El, CH, Gas, Gaz, Diver, ⬚, ▦, R, Bar. **Acharacle** (2½M), P, 🛒, ✉, ⑧ (Tues/Wed, mobile), ⇌ (bus to Loch Ailort/Fort William), ✈ (Oban). **Strontian** FW, P, 🛒, hotel, ✉, Gas, Gaz, Bar. Bus to Fort William.

ANCHORAGES IN COLL AND TIREE (Argyll and Bute)

ARINAGOUR, Loch Eatharna, Coll, **56°37'·0N 06°31'·2W**. AC 5611, 2171, 2474. HW –0530 on Dover; ML 1·4m; Duration 0600; see 9.8.12. Good shelter except with SE swell or strong winds from ENE to SSW. Enter at SHM buoy, Fl G 6s, marking Bogha Mòr. Thence NW to Arinagour ferry pier, 2 FR(vert) 10m and Dir Oc WRG 7s. Beware McQuarrie's Rk (dries 2·9m) 1ca E of pier hd and unmarked drying rks further N on E side of fairway. Ch and hotel are conspic ahead. Continue N towards old stone pier; ⚓ S of it or pick up a buoy. Six ⚓s on W side of hbr, between the two piers. Also ⚓ E of Eilean Eatharna. Piermaster ☎ (01879) 230347; VHF Ch 31. **Facilities**: HIE Trading Post ☎ 230349, M, D, FW, Gas, ▦, CH, R. **Village** ⬚, FW, P, ✉, Ferry to Oban (⇌).

GOTT BAY, Tiree, **56°30'·74N 06°48'·07W**. AC 5611, 2474. Tides as 9.8.12; HW –0540 on Dover. HM ☎ (01879) 230337, VHF Ch 31. Adequate shelter in calm weather, but exposed in winds ENE to S. (in which case use Wilson hbr in Balephetrish Bay 1M W, Ldg lts F.G/Oc.G). The bay, at NE end of island, can be identified by conspic latticed tr at Scarinish about 8ca SW of ent, with lt Fl 3s 11m 16M close by (obscd over hbr). Appr on NW track, keeping to SW side of bay which is obstructed on NE side by Soa Is and drying rks. The ferry pier at S side of ent has FR ldg lts 286½°. ⚓ 1ca NW of pier head in 3m on sand; L at pier. Facilities: P & D (cans), Gas, ▦, R, Bar, ✉ at Scarinish (½M), Ferry to Oban (⇌).

9.8.14 TOBERMORY

Mull (Argyll and Bute) 56°37'·19N 06°03'·87W ✹✹✹✿⚓⚓✿✿✿

CHARTS AC 5611, 2171, 2390, 2474; Imray C65.

TIDES –0519 Dover; ML 2·4; Duration 0610

Standard Port OBAN (→)

Times				Height (metres)			
High Water		Low Water		MHWS	MHWN	MLWN	MLWS
0100	0700	0100	0800	4·0	2·9	1·8	0·7
1300	1900	1300	2000				
Differences TOBERMORY (Mull)							
+0025	+0010	+0015	+0025	+0·4	+0·4	0·0	0·0
CARSAIG BAY (S Mull)							
–0015	–0005	–0030	+0020	+0·1	+0·2	0·0	–0·1
IONA (SW Mull)							
–0010	–0005	–0020	+0015	0·0	+0·1	–0·3	–0·2
BUNESSAN (Loch Lathaich, SW Mull)							
–0015	–0015	–0010	–0015	+0·3	+0·1	0·0	–0·1
ULVA SOUND (W Mull)							
–0010	–0015	0000	–0005	+0·4	+0·3	0·0	–0·1

SHELTER Good, but some swell in strong N/NE winds. 22 ⚓s are marked by a blue ⚬ with a Y pick-up. ⚓ clear of fairway, where marked; at SE end of The Doirlinn.

NAVIGATION WPT 56°37'·59N 06°03'·17W, 224°/0·5M to moorings. N ent is wide and clear of dangers. S ent via The Doirlinn is only 80m wide at HW, and dries at LW; at HW±2 least depth is 2m. Enter between 2 bns on 300°.

LIGHTS AND MARKS Rhubha nan Gall, Fl 3s 17m 15M, W tr is 1M N of ent. Ch spire and hotel turret are both conspic.

R/T VHF Ch 16 12 (HO), M.

TELEPHONE (Code 01688) Piermaster 302017; MRCC (01475) 729014; Local CG 302200; Marinecall 09068 969653; Police 302016; Dr 302013.

FACILITIES Cal-Mac Pier, only short stay AB for P, D; landing stage FW £2; Western Isles YC ☎ 302371; Services: ⚓ £9 <8m £12 >8m or, 10 nights/£70-£90, ME, CH, ACA, Gaz, Gas, Divers. Town FW, P, Dr, 🛒, R, Bar, ✉, Ⓑ, ⇌ (ferry to Oban), ✈ (grass strip; helipad on golf course).

SOUND OF MULL (Mull, 56°31'·44N 05°56'·82W). Beware drying rocks 6ca E of the bay; ent on SE side. Salen Jetty, ⚓s £10. Landing from yacht at ⚓ £1 per person/H24. FW, D. Village, 🛒, ME, Ⓔ, CH, R, Dr, ✉. Land at jetty in SW corner.

CRAIGNURE, (Mull, 56°28'·37N 05°42'·25W) ldg lts 241°, both FR 10/12m. Facilities: 🛒, Bar, ✉, Gas, Ferry to Oban. Tides, see 9.8.15.

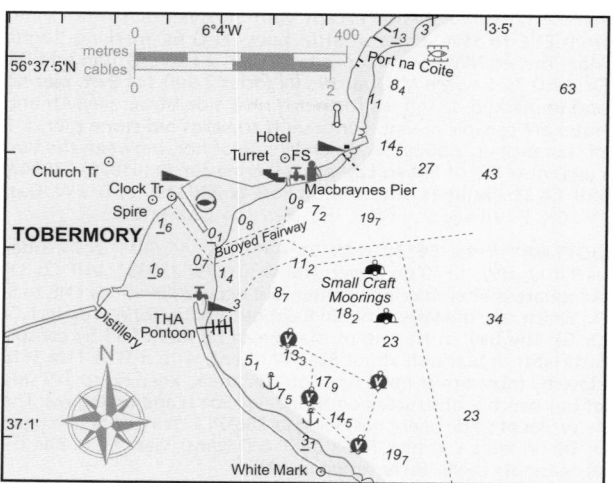

9.8.15 LOCH ALINE

Highland 56°32'·09N 05°46'·47W ✹✹✹✿⚓ ✿✿✿

CHARTS AC 5611, 2390; Imray C65.

TIDES –0523 Dover; Duration 0610

Standard Port OBAN (→)

Times				Height (metres)			
High Water		Low Water		MHWS	MHWN	MLWN	MLWS
0100	0700	0100	0800	4·0	2·9	1·8	0·7
1300	1900	1300	2000				
Differences LOCH ALINE							
+0012	+0012	No data		+0·5	+0·3	No data	
SALEN (Sound of Mull)							
+0045	+0015	+0020	+0030	+0·2	+0·2	–0·1	0·0
CRAIGNURE (Sound of Mull)							
+0030	+0005	+0010	+0015	0·0	+0·1	–0·1	–0·1

SHELTER Very good. ⚓s in SE end of loch and in N and E part of loch. Temp berth on the old stone slip in the ent on W side, depth and ferries permitting.

NAVIGATION WPT 56°31'·49N 05°46'·37W, 176°/0·9M to front ldg bn. Bns (bright orange) lead 356°, 100m W of Bogha Lurcain, drying rk off Bolorkle Pt on E side of ent. The buoyed ent is easy, but narrow with a bar (min depth 2·1m); stream runs 2½kn at sp. Beware coasters (which completely fill the ent) from the sand mine going to/from the jetty and ferries to/from Mull. Last 5ca of loch dries.

LIGHTS AND MARKS Ardtornish Pt lt ho, 1M SSE of ent, Fl (2) WRG 10s 7m 8/5M. Lts and buoys as chartlet. War memorial (conspic, 9m high) stands on W side of ent. Ldg lts are FW 2/4m (H24). 1M up the loch on E side a Y bn with Y ● topmark marks a reef, and ½M further up similar bn marks a larger reef on W side. Both top marks need new coat of paint. Clock tr is very conspic at head of loch.

R/T None.

TELEPHONE (Code 01967) MRCC (01475) 729014; ⊜ (0141) 887 9369; Marinecall 09068 969653; Ⓗ (01631) 563727; Dr 421252.

FACILITIES Village FW at pier, P & D, Gas, 🛒, R, Bar, P, ✉, (Ⓑ, ⇌, ✈ at Oban), Ferry to Fishnish Bay (Mull).

ANCHORAGES on WEST and SOUTH COASTS OF MULL (Anti-clockwise from the north. SDs essential) (See AC *5611*)

TRESHNISH ISLES 56°29'N 06°31'W. AC 2652. The main Is (N to S) are: Cairn na Burgh, Fladda, Lunga, Bac Mòr and Bac Beag. Tides run hard and isles are exposed to swell, but merit a visit in calm weather. Appr with caution on ldg lines as in CCC SDs; temp ⚓ off Lunga's N tip in 4m.

STAFFA 56°25'·96N 06°20'·34W. AC 2652. Spectacular isle with Fingal's Cave, but same caveats as above. Very temp ⚓ off SE tip where there is landing; beware unmarked rks.

GOMETRA 56°28'·85N 06°23'W. AC 2652. Tides as 9.8.14. The narrow inlet between Gometra and Ulva Is offers sheltered ⚓, except in S'lies. Appr on 020° between Staffa and Little Colonsay, or N of the former. Beware rks drying 3·2m, to stbd and 5ca S of ent. Inside, E side is cleaner.

LOCH NA KEAL 56°26'N 06°18'W (ent). AC 2652. Tides in 9.8.14. Appr S of Geasgill Is and N of drying rks off **Inch Kenneth**; E of this Is and in **Sound of Ulva** are sheltered ⚓s, except in S'lies. Beware MacQuarrie's Rk, dries 0·8m.

LOCH LATHAICH Mull, **56°19'·29N 06°15'·47W**. AC 2617. HW – 0545 on Dover; ML 2·4. See 9.8.14. Excellent shelter with easy access; good base for cruising W Mull. Eilean na Liathanaich (a group of islets) lie off the ent, marked by a W bn at the E end, Fl WR 6s 12m 8/6M, R088°-108°, W108°-088°. Keep to W side of loch and ⚓ off Bendoran BY in SW, or SE of Eilean Ban off the pier in approx 5m. **Facilities:** (Bunessan) Shop, ✉, Bar, R, FW.

SOUND OF IONA 56°19'·45N 06°23'·12W. AC 2617. Tides see 9.8.14. From N, enter in mid-chan; from S keep clear of Torran Rks. Cathedral brg 012° closes the Iona shore past 2 SHM buoys and SCM buoy. Beware a bank 0·1m in mid-sound, between cathedral and Fionnphort; also tel cables and ferries. ⚓ S of ferry close in to Iona, or in Bull Hole. Consult SDs. Crowded in season; limited facilities.

TINKER'S HOLE Ross of Mull, **56°17'·49N 06°23'·07W**. AC 2617. Beware Torran Rks, reefs extending 5M S and SW of Erraid. Usual app from S, avoiding Rankin's Rks, drying 0·8m, and rk, dries 2·3m, between Eilean nam Muc and Erraid. Popular ⚓ in mid-pool between Eilean Dubh and Erraid.

CARSAIG BAY Ross of Mull, **56°19'·19N 05°59'·07W**. Tides see 9.8.14. AC 2386. Temp, fair weather ⚓s to N of Gamhnach Mhòr, reef 2m high, or close into NW corner of bay. Landing at stone quay on NE side. No facilities.

LOCH SPELVE Mull, **56°23'N 05°41'W**. AC 2387. Tides as Oban. Landlocked water, prone to squalls off surrounding hills. Ent narrows to ½ca due to shoal S side and drying rk N side, 56°23'·24N 05°41'·95W, ☆ FlG 5s 3m 2M, G pole. CCC SDs give local ldg lines. ⚓s in SW and NW arms, clear of fish farms. Pier at Croggan; no facilities.

ANCHORAGES ALONG LOCH LINNHE
(AC 5611, 2378, 2379, 2380)

LYNN OF LORN 56°33'N 05°25'·2W. At NE end are ⚓s off **Port Appin**, clear of ferry and cables (beware Appin Rks); and in **Airds Bay**, open to SW. At NW tip of Lismore, **Port Ramsey** offers good ⚓s between the 3 main islets. **Linnhe Marina** ☎ 01631 730401 offers pontoon and mooring berths.

LOCH CRERAN 56°32'·14N 05°25'·22W. Tides 9.8.16. Ent at Airds Pt, Dir lt 050°, Fl WRG 2s, W vis 041-058°. Chan turns 90° stbd with streams of 4kn. Sgeir Callich, rky ridge extends NE to SHM By, Fl G 3s; ⚓ W of it. ⚓s (max LOA 7m) off Barcaldine; also ⚓s max LOA 9m off Creagan Inn, ☎ (01631) 573250. Bridge has 12m clearance. Beware of extensive marine farms in loch.

LOCH LEVEN 56°42'N 05°12'W. (See inset 9.8.16.) Tides 9.8.16. Fair weather ⚓s in Ballachulish Bay, at Kentallen B (deep), Onich and off St Brides on N shore. App bridge (17m clnce) on 114°; 4ca ENE of br are moorings and ⚓ at Poll an Dùnan, entered W of perch. Facilities at Ballachulish: Hotels, 🛒, R, ✉, Ⓑ. Loch is navigable 7M to Kinlochleven.

CORRAN NARROWS 56°43'·27N 05°14'·34W. AC 2372. Sp rate 6kn. Well buoyed; Corran Pt lt ho, Iso WRG 4s, and lt bn 5ca NE. ⚓ 5ca NW of Pt, off Camas Aiseig pier/slip.

9.8.16 FORT WILLIAM/CORPACH

Highland 56°48'·99N 05°07'·07W (off Fort William)

CHARTS AC 5611, 2372, 2380; Imray C65, C23.

TIDES –0535 Dover; ML 2·3; Duration 0610

Standard Port OBAN (→)

Times				Height (metres)			
High Water		Low Water		MHWS	MHWN	MLWN	MLWS
0100	0700	0100	0800	4·0	2·9	1·8	0·7
1300	1900	1300	2000				
Differences CORPACH							
0000	+0020	+0040	0000	0·0	0·0	–0·2	–0·2
LOCH EIL (Head)							
+0025	+0045	+0105	+0025		No data		No data
CORRAN NARROWS							
+0007	+0007	+0004	+0004	+0·4	+0·4	–0·1	0·0
LOCH LEVEN (Head)							
+0045	+0045	+0045	+0045		No data		No data
LOCH LINNHE (Port Appin)							
–0005	–0005	–0030	0000	+0·2	+0·2	+0·1	+0·1
LOCH CRERAN (Barcaldine Pier)							
+0010	+0020	+0040	+0015	+0·1	+0·1	0·0	+0·1
LOCH CRERAN (Head)							
+0015	+0025	+0120	+0020	–0·3	–0·3	–0·4	–0·3

SHELTER Exposed to winds SW thro' N to NE. ⚓s off Fort William pier; in Camus na Gall; SSW of Eilean A Bhealaidh; and off Corpach Basin, where there is also a waiting pontoon; or inside the canal where it is more sheltered. The sea lock is normally available HW±4 during canal hrs. For Caledonian Canal see 9.8.17.

NAVIGATION Corpach WPT 56°50'·29N 05°07'·07W, 315°/0.32M to lock ent.

Beware McLean Rk, dries 0·3m, buoyed, 8ca N of Fort William. Lochy Flats dry 3ca off the E bank. In Annat Narrows at ent to Loch Eil streams reach 5kn.

LIGHTS AND MARKS Iso WRG 4s lt is at N jetty of sea-lock ent, W310°-335°. A long pier/viaduct off Ft William is unlit.

R/T Call: *Corpach Lock* VHF Ch **74** 16 (during canal hours).

TELEPHONE (Code 01397) HM 772249; MRCC (01475) 729014; ⊖ 702948; Marinecall 09068 969653; Police 702361; Dr 703136.

FACILITIES **Fort William:** Pier ☎ 703881, AB; **Services:** Slip, L, CH, ACA. **Town:** P, ME, El, ⚒, YC, 🛒, R, Bar, Ⓗ, ✉, Ⓑ, ➤. **Corpach:** **Corpach Basin** ☎ 772249, AB, L, FW, D; **Lochaber YC** ☎ 703576, M, FW, L, Slip; **Services:** ME, El, ⚒, D (cans), M, CH, Slip, Divers. **Village:** P, 🛒, R, Bar, ✉, Ⓑ, ➤.

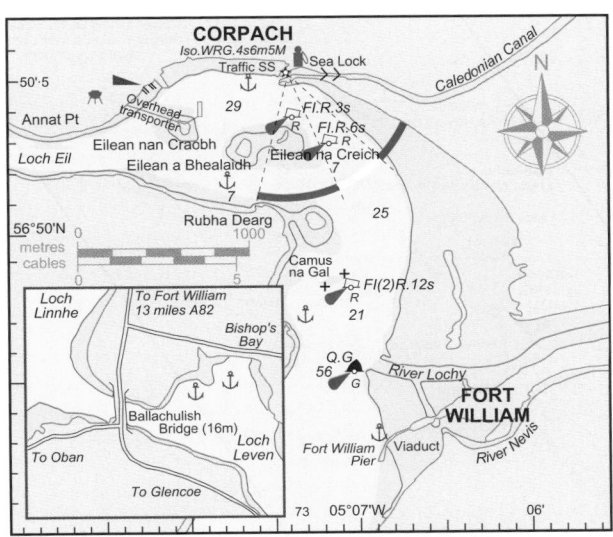

9.8.17 CALEDONIAN CANAL

Highland ❀❀❀♒♒♒✿✿✿

CHARTS AC 1791; Imray C23; *BWB Skippers Guide*

TIDES Tidal differences: Corpach –0455 on Dover; See 9.8.16. Clachnaharry: +0116 on Dover; See 9.7.15.

SHELTER Corpach is at the SW ent of the Caledonian Canal, see 9.8.16; the sea locks at both ends do not open LW±2 at springs. For best shelter transit the sea lock and lie above the double lock. Numerous pontoons along the canal; cost is included in the canal dues. For Inverness see 9.7.15.

NAVIGATION The 60M canal consists of 38M through 3 lochs, (Lochs Lochy, Oich and Ness), connected by 22M of canal. Loch Oich is part of a hydro-electric scheme which may vary the water level. The passage normally takes two full days, possibly longer in the summer; absolute minimum is 14 hrs. Speed limit is 5kn in the canal sections. There are 10 swing bridges; road traffic has priority at peak hrs. Do not pass bridges without the keeper's instructions.

LOCKS There are 29 locks: 14 between Loch Linnhe (Corpach), via Lochs Lochy and Oich up to the summit (106ft above sea level); and 15 locks from the summit down via Loch Ness to Inverness.

2005 information

Hours: Winter Mon-Fri 0900-1600
Spring Mon-Sun 0830-1730
Summer Mon-Sun 0800-1730
Autumn Mon-Sun 0830-1730

Dues payable at Corpach: transit/lock fee Outward £16 per metre for 8 day passage or less; Return £12 per metre. £20 per metre is charged for a 2 week sojourn. For regulations and useful booklet *BWS Skipper's Guide* apply: Canal Manager, Canal Office, Seaport Marina, Muirtown Wharf, Inverness IV3 5LE, ☎ (01463) 233140, or download from: www.waterscape.com

LIGHTS AND MARKS See 9.8.16 and 9.7.15 for ent lts. Channel is marked by posts, cairns and unlit buoys, PHM on the NW side of the chan and SHM on the SE side.

BOAT SAFETY SCHEME BWS, who operate the Caledonian and Crinan Canals, require compulsory safety and seaworthiness checks for craft based on these waterways. Transient/visiting craft will be checked for apparent dangerous defects, for example: leaking gas or fuel, damaged electrical cables, taking in water, risk of capsize. £1M 3rd party insurance is required. For details contact: Boat Safety Scheme, Willow Grange, Church Road, Watford WD1 3QA. ☎ 01923 226422.

R/T Sea locks and main lock flights operate VHF Ch **74** (HO).

TELEPHONE Corpach Sea Lock/Basin (01397) 772249; Canal Office, Inverness (01463) 233140; Clachnaharry Sea Lock (01463) 713896.

FACILITIES For details see *BWS Skipper's Guide* (using maps).
– Corpach see 9.8.16.
– Banavie (Neptune's Staircase; one-way locking takes 1½ hrs) 🛢, 60m jetty, FW, 🛒, ✉, ♂, ♿.
– Gairlochy AB, R.
– NE end of Loch Lochy 🛒, M, AB, R.
– Great Glen Water Park D, FW, AB, ♿, 🛒, Gas, Gaz, R.
– Invergarry L, FW, AB.
– Fort Augustus AB, FW, D, P, ME, El, 🛒, ✉, ♿, ♂, Dr, Bar.
– Urquhart B. (L. Ness) FW, 🛢, AB £6, 3m depth, 🛒, Bar.
– Dochgarroch FW, 🛢, P, ♿, 🛒.
At Inverness (9.7.15):
– Caley Marina (25+25 visitors) ☎ (01463) 236539, FW, CH, D, ME, El, ⚒, 🛢, C (20 ton), ACA.
– Seaport Marina (20 + 20 Ⓥ), £6 all LOA, ☎ (01463) 239475, FW, 🛢, D, El, ME, ⚒, Gas, Gaz, 🗑, ♂, ♿, C (40 ton). www.scottishcanals.co.uk.

TIME ZONE (UT)
For Summer Time add ONE
hour in **non-shaded areas**

OBAN LAT 56°25'N LONG 5°29'W
TIMES AND HEIGHTS OF HIGH AND LOW WATERS

Dates in red are **SPRINGS**
Dates in blue are NEAPS

YEAR 2010

JANUARY		FEBRUARY		MARCH		APRIL	
Time m	Time m	Time m	Time m	Time m	Time m	Time m	Time m

JANUARY

1 0543 4.0 / 1216 0.9 / F 1814 4.0 — **16** 0023 1.1 / 0621 4.0 / SA 1249 1.3 / 1833 3.8

2 0019 0.6 / 0627 4.2 / SA 1322 1.0 / 1856 4.0 — **17** 0058 1.1 / 0655 4.0 / SU 1322 1.3 / 1905 3.8

3 0105 0.5 / 0710 4.2 / SU 1350 0.8 / 1937 3.9 — **18** 0131 1.1 / 0728 4.0 / M 1354 1.3 / 1935 3.8

4 0152 0.5 / 0754 4.1 / M 1437 0.9 / 2020 3.7 — **19** 0201 1.2 / 0759 4.0 / TU 1425 1.4 / 2002 3.7

5 0239 0.6 / 0839 3.9 / TU 1524 1.0 / 2105 3.5 — **20** 0227 1.3 / 0828 3.8 / W 1452 1.5 / 2029 3.6

6 0328 0.7 / 0925 3.7 / W 1613 1.3 / 2153 3.3 — **21** 0252 1.4 / 0858 3.6 / TH 1521 1.6 / 2100 3.4

7 0419 1.0 / 1016 3.4 / TH 1708 1.5 / ☽ 2250 3.1 — **22** 0321 1.6 / 0931 3.5 / F 1559 1.7 / 2137 3.3

8 0515 1.3 / 1118 3.2 / F 1810 1.7 — **23** 0401 1.7 / 1014 3.3 / SA 1652 1.9 / ◑ 2223 3.1

9 0010 3.0 / 0618 1.5 / SA 1251 3.0 / 1922 1.8 — **24** 0458 1.9 / 1114 3.1 / SU 1803 1.9 / 2328 3.0

10 0139 3.0 / 0731 1.7 / SU 1431 3.0 / 2043 1.8 — **25** 0621 1.9 / 1310 3.0 / M 1920 1.9

11 0251 3.1 / 0853 1.7 / M 1553 3.1 / 2146 1.7 — **26** 0122 3.0 / 0753 1.9 / TU 1503 3.2 / 2033 1.7

12 0346 3.3 / 1004 1.6 / TU 1627 3.2 / 2233 1.5 — **27** 0309 3.2 / 0925 1.6 / W 1602 3.4 / 2137 1.3

13 0429 3.5 / 1056 1.5 / W 1656 3.4 / 2312 1.4 — **28** 0408 3.5 / 1034 1.3 / TH 1648 3.7 / 2233 1.0

14 0507 3.7 / 1137 1.4 / TH 1727 3.6 / 2348 1.2 — **29** 0455 3.9 / 1126 0.9 / F 1729 3.9 / 2322 0.6

15 0545 3.9 / 1214 1.3 / F 1800 3.7 / ● — **30** 0538 4.1 / 1211 0.7 / SA 1807 4.0 / ○

31 0008 0.4 / 0619 4.3 / SU 1255 0.5 / 1844 4.1

FEBRUARY

1 0053 0.2 / 0659 4.3 / M 1336 0.5 / 1922 4.0 — **16** 0108 0.9 / 0705 4.0 / TU 1327 1.0 / 1910 3.9

2 0137 0.2 / 0738 4.2 / TU 1416 0.6 / 1959 3.9 — **17** 0133 1.0 / 0732 3.9 / W 1353 1.1 / 1934 3.8

3 0220 0.3 / 0817 4.0 / W 1456 0.8 / 2037 3.7 — **18** 0154 1.1 / 0757 3.8 / TH 1414 1.2 / 1958 3.7

4 0304 0.6 / 0855 3.7 / TH 1538 1.1 / 2116 3.5 — **19** 0215 1.2 / 0823 3.7 / F 1440 1.3 / 2027 3.6

5 0350 0.9 / 0935 3.4 / F 1624 1.4 / ◗ 2200 3.2 — **20** 0244 1.3 / 0854 3.5 / SA 1516 1.5 / 2102 3.4

6 0439 1.2 / 1021 3.1 / SA 1718 1.7 / 2259 3.1 — **21** 0322 1.5 / 0933 3.3 / SU 1606 1.7 / 2145 3.2

7 0537 1.6 / 1129 2.8 / SU 1826 1.9 — **22** 0416 1.7 / 1030 3.0 / M 1718 1.8 / ◑ 2247 3.0

8 0049 2.8 / 0650 1.8 / M 1514 2.7 / 2002 1.9 — **23** 0553 1.9 / 1230 2.8 / TU 1848 1.8

9 0231 2.9 / 0841 1.9 / TU 1623 2.9 / 2132 1.8 — **24** 0056 2.9 / 0746 1.8 / W 1459 3.0 / 2010 1.6

10 0341 3.1 / 1006 1.7 / W 1653 3.1 / 2223 1.5 — **25** 0303 3.2 / 0926 1.5 / TH 1555 3.3 / 2122 1.3

11 0419 3.3 / 1052 1.5 / TH 1654 3.3 / 2302 1.3 — **26** 0359 3.5 / 1027 1.1 / F 1639 3.6 / 2219 0.9

12 0454 3.6 / 1128 1.4 / F 1716 3.5 / 2336 1.1 — **27** 0443 3.9 / 1114 0.8 / SA 1716 3.8 / 2308 0.5

13 0529 3.8 / 1159 1.2 / SA 1745 3.7 — **28** 0523 4.2 / 1156 0.5 / SU 1751 4.0 / ○ 2353 0.2

14 0008 1.0 / 0603 4.0 / SU 1229 1.1 / ● 1816 3.8

15 0039 0.9 / 0635 4.0 / M 1258 1.0 / 1845 3.9

MARCH

1 0602 4.3 / 1235 0.4 / M 1825 4.1 — **16** 0010 0.8 / 0608 4.0 / TU 1227 0.9 / 1816 3.8

2 0036 0.1 / 0639 4.3 / TU 1313 0.4 / 1859 4.1 — **17** 0038 0.8 / 0637 4.0 / W 1255 0.9 / 1840 3.8

3 0118 0.1 / 0715 4.2 / W 1350 0.5 / 1934 4.0 — **18** 0102 0.8 / 0703 3.9 / TH 1320 0.9 / 1904 3.8

4 0159 0.3 / 0758 4.0 / TH 1427 0.7 / 2009 3.8 — **19** 0125 0.9 / 0728 3.8 / F 1344 1.0 / 1931 3.7

5 0240 0.5 / 0824 3.7 / F 1505 1.0 / 2044 3.5 — **20** 0150 1.0 / 0756 3.6 / SA 1414 1.1 / 2002 3.6

6 0323 0.9 / 0859 3.3 / SA 1548 1.3 / 2123 3.3 — **21** 0222 1.2 / 0830 3.4 / SU 1453 1.3 / 2039 3.4

7 0409 1.3 / 0937 3.0 / SU 1640 1.6 / ◗ 2212 3.0 — **22** 0304 1.4 / 0912 3.2 / M 1543 1.5 / 2126 3.2

8 0506 1.7 / 1028 2.7 / M 1746 1.8 / 2355 2.8 — **23** 0405 1.6 / 1014 2.9 / TU 1656 1.6 / ◑ 2235 3.0

9 0619 1.9 / 1455 2.5 / TU 1917 1.9 — **24** 0555 1.8 / 1239 2.7 / W 1826 1.6

10 0210 2.8 / 0834 1.9 / W 1603 2.7 / 2106 1.7 — **25** 0051 2.9 / 0746 1.7 / TH 1439 2.9 / 1949 1.5

11 0322 3.0 / 0952 1.7 / TH 1627 2.9 / 2159 1.5 — **26** 0242 3.2 / 0912 1.4 / F 1534 3.2 / 2101 1.1

12 0358 3.3 / 1031 1.5 / F 1628 3.2 / 2238 1.3 — **27** 0337 3.6 / 1008 1.0 / SA 1617 3.5 / 2158 0.8

13 0431 3.5 / 1103 1.3 / SA 1650 3.4 / 2312 1.1 — **28** 0421 3.9 / 1052 0.7 / SU 1654 3.8 / 2247 0.5

14 0504 3.7 / 1131 1.1 / SU 1719 3.6 / 2342 0.9 — **29** 0501 4.1 / 1132 0.5 / M 1727 3.9 / 2333 0.2

15 0537 3.9 / 1159 0.9 / M 1749 3.8 / ● — **30** 0539 4.2 / 1209 0.4 / TU 1801 4.1 / ○

31 0015 0.2 / 0614 4.2 / W 1247 0.4 / 1835 4.1

APRIL

1 0057 0.2 / 0650 4.1 / TH 1323 0.5 / 1909 4.0 — **16** 0033 0.8 / 0636 3.9 / F 1251 0.8 / 1839 3.8

2 0138 0.4 / 0724 3.9 / F 1359 0.7 / 1944 3.9 — **17** 0104 0.9 / 0706 3.7 / SA 1323 0.8 / 1911 3.7

3 0218 0.7 / 0757 3.6 / SA 1438 1.0 / 2019 3.6 — **18** 0138 1.0 / 0740 3.6 / SU 1359 0.9 / 1948 3.6

4 0259 1.1 / 0831 3.3 / SU 1520 1.3 / 2059 3.3 — **19** 0218 1.1 / 0821 3.4 / M 1443 1.1 / 2031 3.5

5 0346 1.4 / 0908 2.9 / M 1611 1.5 / 2147 3.1 — **20** 0310 1.3 / 0911 3.1 / TU 1537 1.3 / 2125 3.3

6 0441 1.7 / 0957 2.7 / TU 1714 1.8 / ◗ 2305 2.8 — **21** 0423 1.5 / 1019 2.9 / W 1646 1.4 / 2239 3.1

7 0551 1.9 / 1324 2.5 / W 1830 1.8 — **22** 0556 1.6 / 1225 2.8 / TH 1805 1.4

8 0130 2.8 / 0741 1.9 / TH 1453 2.6 / 2013 1.8 — **23** 0031 3.1 / 0729 1.5 / F 1407 2.9 / 1923 1.3

9 0241 3.0 / 0910 1.8 / F 1525 2.8 / 2119 1.6 — **24** 0209 3.3 / 0845 1.3 / SA 1504 3.2 / 2033 1.1

10 0323 3.2 / 0952 1.5 / SA 1547 3.1 / 2201 1.3 — **25** 0308 3.5 / 0940 1.0 / SU 1549 3.4 / 2132 0.8

11 0358 3.4 / 1024 1.3 / SU 1615 3.3 / 2236 1.2 — **26** 0354 3.7 / 1025 0.8 / M 1627 3.6 / 2224 0.6

12 0432 3.6 / 1053 1.1 / M 1646 3.5 / 2306 1.0 — **27** 0436 3.9 / 1106 0.7 / TU 1701 3.8 / 2310 0.5

13 0505 3.8 / 1122 0.9 / TU 1716 3.7 / 2335 0.9 — **28** 0514 4.0 / 1144 0.6 / W 1737 3.9 / ○ 2355 0.5

14 0538 3.9 / 1151 0.8 / W 1745 3.8 / ● — **29** 0551 4.0 / 1221 0.6 / TH 1812 4.0

15 0004 0.8 / 0608 3.9 / TH 1221 0.8 / 1811 3.8 — **30** 0037 0.5 / 0627 3.9 / F 1258 0.7 / 1848 3.9

Chart Datum: 2·10 metres below Ordnance Datum (Newlyn). HAT is 4·5 metres above Chart Datum; see 4.5

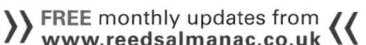

OBAN LAT 56°25'N LONG 5°29'W
TIMES AND HEIGHTS OF HIGH AND LOW WATERS

Dates in red are SPRINGS
Dates in blue are NEAPS

YEAR **2010**

MAY		JUNE		JULY		AUGUST	
Time m	Time m	Time m	Time m	Time m	Time m	Time m	Time m

MAY

1 0119 0.7 / 0702 3.7 / SA 1336 0.9 / 1925 3.8
16 0053 0.9 / 0654 3.7 / SU 1308 0.7 / 1901 3.8

2 0159 1.0 / 0737 3.5 / SU 1519 1.1 / 2002 3.6
17 0137 0.9 / 0734 3.6 / M 1351 0.8 / 1944 3.7

3 0241 1.2 / 0813 3.2 / M 1458 1.3 / 2043 3.4
18 0226 1.0 / 0820 3.4 / TU 1439 0.9 / 2032 3.6

4 0326 1.5 / 0853 3.0 / TU 1545 1.5 / 2130 3.2
19 0321 1.2 / 0913 3.2 / W 1532 1.0 / 2128 3.4

5 0418 1.7 / 0941 2.8 / W 1639 1.7 / 2230 3.0
20 0426 1.3 / 1016 3.0 / TH 1633 1.1 / 2234 3.3

6 0519 1.9 / 1053 2.6 / TH 1741 1.8 / 2359 2.9
21 0540 1.4 / 1144 2.9 / F 1740 1.2 / 2358 3.2

7 0633 1.9 / 1313 2.6 / F 1852 1.8
22 0658 1.4 / 1321 2.9 / SA 1852 1.2

8 0138 3.0 / 0751 1.8 / SA 1417 2.8 / 2006 1.7
23 0128 3.2 / 0810 1.3 / SU 1427 3.1 / 2001 1.1

9 0234 3.1 / 0849 1.6 / SU 1457 3.0 / 2103 1.6
24 0235 3.4 / 0909 1.2 / M 1518 3.3 / 2104 1.0

10 0316 3.3 / 0931 1.4 / M 1533 3.4 / 2145 1.4
25 0329 3.5 / 0958 1.1 / TU 1601 3.5 / 2200 0.9

11 0354 3.5 / 1007 1.2 / TU 1608 3.4 / 2221 1.2
26 0414 3.6 / 1041 1.0 / W 1639 3.7 / 2251 0.9

12 0432 3.6 / 1041 1.1 / W 1642 3.5 / 2257 1.1
27 0456 3.7 / 1129 0.8 / TH 1717 3.8 / ○ 2337 0.9

13 0508 3.7 / 1116 0.9 / TH 1715 3.7 / 2333 1.0
28 0534 3.7 / 1200 0.9 / F 1756 3.9

14 0543 3.8 / 1151 0.8 / F 1748 3.7 / ●
29 0021 0.9 / 0611 3.6 / SA 1239 0.9 / 1833 3.9

15 0012 0.9 / 0617 3.8 / SA 1228 0.7 / 1823 3.8
30 0103 1.0 / 0648 3.6 / SU 1318 1.0 / 1911 3.8

31 0144 1.2 / 0724 3.5 / M 1357 1.1 / 1949 3.7

JUNE

1 0225 1.3 / 0801 3.3 / TU 1437 1.2 / 2029 3.6
16 0225 0.8 / 0816 3.5 / W 1430 0.6 / 2029 3.8

2 0307 1.5 / 0840 3.2 / W 1519 1.4 / 2111 3.4
17 0316 0.9 / 0905 3.3 / TH 1520 0.7 / 2120 3.6

3 0351 1.6 / 0922 3.0 / TH 1603 1.6 / 2157 3.2
18 0412 1.1 / 0959 3.2 / F 1614 0.9 / 2215 3.4

4 0441 1.7 / 1010 2.9 / F 1651 1.7 / ◐ 2251 3.1
19 0512 1.3 / 1104 3.0 / SA 1713 1.1 / ◐ 2321 3.3

5 0536 1.8 / 1059 2.8 / SA 1744 1.8 / 2358 3.0
20 0619 1.4 / 1226 3.0 / SU 1818 1.2

6 0635 1.8 / 1229 2.8 / SU 1840 1.8
21 0043 3.1 / 0729 1.4 / M 1345 3.0 / 1926 1.3

7 0116 3.1 / 0735 1.8 / M 1347 2.9 / 1940 1.8
22 0204 3.1 / 0838 1.4 / TU 1449 3.1 / 2036 1.3

8 0223 3.2 / 0830 1.6 / TU 1443 3.0 / 2039 1.6
23 0311 3.2 / 0936 1.4 / W 1542 3.3 / 2142 1.3

9 0316 3.3 / 0919 1.4 / W 1530 3.2 / 2134 1.5
24 0405 3.3 / 1025 1.3 / TH 1626 3.5 / 2238 1.2

10 0403 3.5 / 1004 1.2 / TH 1613 3.4 / 2225 1.3
25 0449 3.4 / 1108 1.2 / F 1706 3.7 / 2327 1.2

11 0446 3.6 / 1046 1.0 / F 1655 3.6 / 2313 1.1
26 0528 3.5 / 1147 1.1 / SA 1745 3.8 / ○

12 0528 3.7 / 1129 0.8 / SA 1735 3.7 / ●
27 0010 1.2 / 0604 3.5 / SU 1226 1.0 / 1822 3.9

13 0000 0.9 / 0608 3.7 / SU 1212 0.7 / 1816 3.8
28 0051 1.2 / 0639 3.6 / M 1304 1.0 / 1859 3.9

14 0048 0.8 / 0649 3.7 / M 1256 0.6 / 1858 3.9
29 0130 1.2 / 0713 3.6 / TU 1340 1.1 / 1935 3.8

15 0135 0.8 / 0731 3.6 / TU 1342 0.6 / 1943 3.9
30 0207 1.3 / 0747 3.5 / W 1416 1.1 / 2011 3.7

JULY

1 0243 1.4 / 0821 3.4 / TH 1451 1.3 / 2046 3.6
16 0259 0.7 / 0845 3.6 / F 1502 0.5 / 2101 3.8

2 0320 1.5 / 0854 3.3 / F 1525 1.4 / 2122 3.5
17 0346 0.9 / 0931 3.4 / SA 1552 0.7 / 2148 3.5

3 0359 1.6 / 0929 3.2 / SA 1601 1.6 / 2201 3.3
18 0438 1.2 / 1025 3.1 / SU 1645 1.0 / ◐ 2242 3.2

4 0442 1.7 / 1009 3.1 / SU 1643 1.7 / ◑ 2246 3.2
19 0536 1.4 / 1135 3.0 / M 1745 1.3 / 2356 3.0

5 0534 1.8 / 1059 2.9 / M 1736 1.8 / 2346 3.1
20 0645 1.6 / 1307 2.9 / TU 1854 1.5

6 0633 1.8 / 1207 2.9 / TU 1839 1.9
21 0141 2.9 / 0807 1.6 / W 1430 3.0 / 2013 1.6

7 0120 3.0 / 0736 1.7 / W 1348 2.9 / 1949 1.8
22 0327 2.9 / 0923 1.6 / TH 1536 3.2 / 2136 1.6

8 0245 3.1 / 0838 1.6 / TH 1503 3.1 / 2101 1.6
23 0431 3.1 / 1017 1.4 / F 1620 3.4 / 2237 1.5

9 0346 3.3 / 0935 1.3 / F 1558 3.3 / 2209 1.4
24 0456 3.2 / 1100 1.2 / SA 1657 3.6 / 2322 1.3

10 0436 3.5 / 1026 1.1 / SA 1645 3.6 / 2306 1.1
25 0523 3.4 / 1138 1.1 / SU 1734 3.8

11 0521 3.7 / 1114 0.8 / SU 1729 3.8 / ● 2356 0.9
26 0000 1.2 / 0553 3.5 / M 1214 1.0 / ○ 1808 3.9

12 0603 3.8 / 1159 0.5 / M 1812 4.0
27 0036 1.1 / 0625 3.7 / TU 1248 0.9 / 1843 4.0

13 0043 0.7 / 0642 3.8 / TU 1245 0.4 / 1853 4.1
28 0109 1.1 / 0656 3.7 / W 1320 0.9 / 1915 4.0

14 0129 0.6 / 0722 3.8 / W 1330 0.3 / 1935 4.1
29 0142 1.1 / 0726 3.7 / TH 1351 1.0 / 1947 3.9

15 0213 0.6 / 0803 3.7 / TH 1416 0.3 / 2017 4.0
30 0214 1.2 / 0754 3.6 / F 1419 1.2 / 2016 3.8

31 0244 1.3 / 0821 3.5 / SA 1445 1.3 / 2045 3.6

AUGUST

1 0314 1.5 / 0850 3.4 / SU 1512 1.5 / 2115 3.5
16 0403 1.2 / 0946 3.2 / M 1618 1.1 / ◐ 2200 3.1

2 0347 1.6 / 0921 3.3 / M 1547 1.7 / 2152 3.3
17 0458 1.5 / 1048 3.0 / TU 1716 1.4 / 2304 2.8

3 0435 1.7 / 1007 3.1 / TU 1636 1.8 / 2242 3.1
18 0606 1.7 / 1237 2.8 / W 1826 1.7 / ◑ 2242

4 0541 1.8 / 1105 2.9 / W 1752 1.9
19 0142 2.7 / 0738 1.8 / TH 1424 2.9 / 2003 1.8

5 0009 2.9 / 0656 1.8 / TH 1256 2.9 / 1921 1.9
20 0400 2.8 / 0909 1.6 / F 1540 3.1 / 2142 1.7

6 0236 3.0 / 0810 1.7 / F 1454 3.1 / 2053 1.7
21 0442 3.0 / 1004 1.4 / SA 1612 3.3 / 2232 1.5

7 0342 3.2 / 0916 1.4 / SA 1552 3.4 / 2208 1.4
22 0450 3.2 / 1045 1.2 / SU 1641 3.6 / 2309 1.4

8 0430 3.5 / 1012 1.0 / SU 1638 3.7 / 2302 1.0
23 0503 3.4 / 1121 1.0 / M 1713 3.8 / 2341 1.2

9 0512 3.7 / 1101 0.7 / M 1719 4.0 / 2348 0.7
24 0531 3.6 / 1154 0.9 / TU 1747 4.0 / ○

10 0550 3.9 / 1146 0.4 / TU 1800 4.2 / ●
25 0011 1.1 / 0601 3.8 / W 1225 0.8 / 1818 4.0

11 0030 0.5 / 0626 4.0 / W 1230 0.2 / 1838 4.3
26 0042 1.0 / 0630 3.8 / TH 1255 0.9 / 1849 4.1

12 0112 0.4 / 0703 4.0 / TH 1314 0.1 / 1917 4.3
27 0112 1.0 / 0657 3.9 / F 1322 1.0 / 1918 4.0

13 0153 0.5 / 0740 3.9 / F 1357 0.3 / 1956 4.1
28 0141 1.1 / 0722 3.8 / SA 1346 1.1 / 1944 3.9

14 0234 0.6 / 0819 3.7 / SA 1441 0.4 / 2034 3.8
29 0207 1.2 / 0747 3.7 / SU 1407 1.3 / 2009 3.7

15 0316 0.9 / 0900 3.5 / SU 1528 0.7 / 2115 3.5
30 0231 1.3 / 0814 3.5 / M 1432 1.4 / 2037 3.5

31 0303 1.5 / 0847 3.4 / TU 1506 1.6 / 2112 3.3

Chart Datum: 2·10 metres below Ordnance Datum (Newlyn). HAT is 4·5 metres above Chart Datum; see 4.5

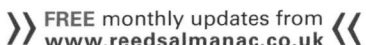

TIME ZONE (UT)
For Summer Time add ONE hour in **non-shaded areas**

OBAN LAT 56°25'N LONG 5°29'W
TIMES AND HEIGHTS OF HIGH AND LOW WATERS

Dates in red are **SPRINGS**
Dates in blue are **NEAPS**

YEAR **2010**

SEPTEMBER

Day	Time	m	Time	m	Time	m	Time	m
1 W ◖	0348	1.7	0929	3.2	1554	1.8	2200	3.0
2 TH	0457	1.8	1027	3.0	1724	2.0	2331	2.8
3 F	0625	1.8	1235	2.9	1915	2.0		
4 SA	0233	2.9	0747	1.6	1447	3.2	2055	1.7
5 SU	0331	3.2	0858	1.3	1539	3.5	2200	1.3
6 M	0416	3.5	0955	1.0	1621	3.9	2247	0.9
7 TU	0454	3.8	1044	0.6	1700	4.1	2329	0.6
8 W ●	0529	4.0	1128	0.3	1739	4.3		
9 TH	0009	0.4	0603	4.1	1212	0.1	1816	4.4
10 F	0048	0.4	0638	4.1	1254	0.1	1852	4.3
11 SA	0126	0.4	0714	4.0	1336	0.2	1929	4.1
12 SU	0205	0.6	0751	3.9	1419	0.5	2005	3.8
13 M	0246	0.9	0829	3.6	1504	0.9	2042	3.5
14 TU	0331	1.2	0912	3.3	1553	1.3	2122	3.1
15 W ◑	0424	1.5	1009	3.1	1651	1.6	2215	2.7
16 TH	0531	1.7	1210	2.9	1803	1.9		
17 F	0208	2.6	0702	1.8	1410	3.0	2000	2.0
18 SA	0340	2.8	0842	1.7	1517	3.1	2129	1.8
19 SU	0415	3.0	0938	1.5	1547	3.4	2210	1.6
20 M	0416	3.2	1019	1.3	1615	3.6	2242	1.4
21 TU	0433	3.4	1055	1.1	1646	3.8	2311	1.2
22 W	0501	3.6	1127	1.0	1718	4.0	2339	1.0
23 TH ○	0532	3.8	1156	0.9	1750	4.1		
24 F	0009	0.9	0600	3.9	1224	0.9	1820	4.1
25 SA	0039	0.9	0626	3.9	1251	1.0	1847	4.0
26 SU	0107	1.0	0651	3.9	1315	1.1	1913	3.9
27 M	0133	1.1	0717	3.8	1338	1.3	1940	3.7
28 TU	0201	1.2	0747	3.7	1406	1.4	2010	3.5
29 W	0236	1.4	0822	3.5	1444	1.6	2048	3.3
30 TH	0322	1.6	0906	3.3	1540	1.8	2141	3.0

OCTOBER

Day	Time	m	Time	m	Time	m	Time	m
1 F ◖	0430	1.7	1011	3.1	1723	2.0	2323	2.8
2 SA	0557	1.8	1224	3.0	1913	1.9		
3 SU	0212	2.9	0720	1.6	1423	3.3	2040	1.6
4 M	0308	3.2	0833	1.3	1515	3.6	2138	1.3
5 TU	0353	3.5	0931	1.0	1557	3.9	2223	0.9
6 W	0430	3.8	1021	0.6	1636	4.2	2304	0.7
7 TH ●	0503	4.0	1107	0.4	1713	4.3	2343	0.5
8 F	0537	4.1	1151	0.3	1751	4.4		
9 SA	0021	0.5	0612	4.2	1234	0.3	1827	4.3
10 SU	0059	0.6	0649	4.1	1316	0.5	1902	4.1
11 M	0138	0.7	0726	4.0	1359	0.8	1938	3.8
12 TU	0219	1.0	0805	3.7	1443	1.1	2014	3.4
13 W	0303	1.2	0848	3.5	1531	1.5	2053	3.1
14 TH ◑	0355	1.5	0941	3.2	1628	1.8	2142	2.8
15 F	0457	1.7	1112	3.0	1737	2.0		
16 SA	0100	2.6	0615	1.9	1330	3.0	1917	2.0
17 SU	0237	2.7	0753	1.8	1432	3.2	2047	1.9
18 M	0313	2.9	0859	1.6	1511	3.4	2131	1.7
19 TU	0332	3.2	0945	1.4	1543	3.6	2204	1.5
20 W	0358	3.4	1022	1.3	1614	3.8	2234	1.3
21 TH	0428	3.6	1054	1.2	1647	3.9	2304	1.1
22 F	0500	3.8	1123	1.1	1720	4.0	2334	1.0
23 SA ○	0530	3.9	1152	1.1	1751	4.0		
24 SU	0006	1.0	0557	3.9	1222	1.1	1820	4.0
25 M	0037	1.0	0625	3.9	1252	1.2	1849	3.9
26 TU	0108	1.0	0656	3.8	1322	1.3	1921	3.7
27 W	0142	1.1	0730	3.7	1358	1.4	1957	3.5
28 TH	0222	1.3	0810	3.6	1444	1.6	2042	3.3
29 F	0311	1.4	0900	3.4	1548	1.8	2140	3.1
30 SA ◑	0413	1.6	1007	3.3	1719	1.9	2308	2.9
31 SU	0530	1.6	1148	3.2	1851	1.8		

NOVEMBER

Day	Time	m	Time	m	Time	m	Time	m
1 M	0134	3.0	0648	1.5	1344	3.4	2010	1.6
2 TU	0237	3.2	0801	1.3	1443	3.6	2108	1.3
3 W	0324	3.5	0903	1.1	1530	3.9	2156	1.1
4 TH	0403	3.7	0957	0.8	1611	4.1	2238	0.9
5 F	0438	3.9	1045	0.7	1650	4.2	2318	0.8
6 SA ●	0514	4.1	1131	0.6	1728	4.2	2357	0.7
7 SU	0552	4.2	1215	0.7	1806	4.1		
8 M	0036	0.8	0629	4.1	1259	0.8	1842	3.9
9 TU	0116	0.9	0708	4.0	1342	1.0	1919	3.7
10 W	0157	1.1	0748	3.9	1426	1.3	1956	3.5
11 TH	0241	1.3	0830	3.7	1512	1.6	2035	3.2
12 F	0328	1.5	0918	3.4	1603	1.8	2121	3.0
13 SA ◑	0422	1.7	1018	3.2	1702	2.0	2222	2.8
14 SU	0523	1.8	1153	3.1	1812	2.1		
15 M	0030	2.8	0634	1.9	1335	3.2	1928	2.0
16 TU	0200	2.9	0753	1.8	1426	3.3	2030	1.9
17 W	0242	3.1	0855	1.7	1505	3.5	2115	1.7
18 TH	0318	3.3	0940	1.6	1541	3.6	2152	1.5
19 F	0354	3.5	1016	1.5	1617	3.8	2227	1.3
20 SA	0429	3.6	1050	1.4	1653	3.9	2302	1.2
21 SU ○	0503	3.8	1124	1.3	1729	3.9	2337	1.0
22 M	0536	3.9	1200	1.2	1802	3.9		
23 TU	0012	1.0	0609	3.9	1238	1.2	1836	3.9
24 W	0050	1.0	0644	3.9	1317	1.2	1912	3.8
25 TH	0130	1.0	0723	3.9	1401	1.3	1953	3.6
26 F	0213	1.1	0807	3.8	1450	1.4	2039	3.4
27 SA	0302	1.2	0857	3.6	1548	1.6	2133	3.2
28 SU ◖	0357	1.3	0957	3.5	1657	1.7	2240	3.1
29 M	0502	1.4	1111	3.4	1813	1.7		
30 TU	0015	3.0	0612	1.4	1248	3.4	1928	1.6

DECEMBER

Day	Time	m	Time	m	Time	m	Time	m
1 W	0151	3.1	0724	1.4	1407	3.5	2034	1.5
2 TH	0251	3.3	0833	1.3	1505	3.6	2128	1.3
3 F	0338	3.6	0934	1.1	1553	3.8	2215	1.2
4 SA	0419	3.8	1028	1.0	1635	3.9	2258	1.1
5 SU ●	0459	3.9	1117	1.0	1715	3.9	2339	1.0
6 M	0538	4.1	1203	1.0	1753	3.9		
7 TU	0020	1.0	0617	4.1	1247	1.1	1830	3.8
8 W	0100	1.0	0656	4.1	1329	1.2	1906	3.7
9 TH	0140	1.1	0735	4.0	1411	1.4	1943	3.6
10 F	0221	1.2	0814	3.8	1451	1.6	2020	3.5
11 SA	0302	1.4	0855	3.7	1534	1.7	2058	3.3
12 SU	0346	1.6	0939	3.5	1620	1.9	2141	3.1
13 M ◑	0433	1.7	1030	3.3	1712	2.0	2233	3.0
14 TU	0524	1.9	1136	3.2	1811	2.0	2344	3.0
15 W	0622	2.0	1303	3.2	1912	2.0		
16 TH	0118	3.0	0726	2.0	1416	3.3	2012	1.9
17 F	0228	3.1	0832	1.9	1509	3.4	2105	1.7
18 SA	0319	3.3	0932	1.7	1554	3.6	2151	1.5
19 SU	0404	3.5	1021	1.6	1635	3.7	2233	1.3
20 M ●	0444	3.7	1105	1.4	1715	3.8	2314	1.1
21 TU	0523	3.8	1148	1.2	1753	3.9	2354	0.9
22 W	0602	3.9	1230	1.1	1830	3.9		
23 TH	0035	0.8	0639	4.0	1313	1.0	1906	3.9
24 F	0118	0.7	0719	4.0	1357	1.0	1945	3.8
25 SA	0202	0.7	0801	4.0	1443	1.1	2028	3.6
26 SU	0249	0.8	0847	3.8	1532	1.2	2115	3.4
27 M	0339	0.9	0937	3.7	1627	1.4	2208	3.3
28 TU ◖	0435	1.1	1035	3.5	1729	1.6	2315	3.1
29 W	0538	1.3	1151	3.3	1840	1.7		
30 TH	0047	3.1	0649	1.4	1329	3.2	1954	1.7
31 F	0215	3.2	0803	1.5	1449	3.3	2103	1.6

Chart Datum: 2·10 metres below Ordnance Datum (Newlyn). HAT is 4·5 metres above Chart Datum; see 4.5

NW Scotland

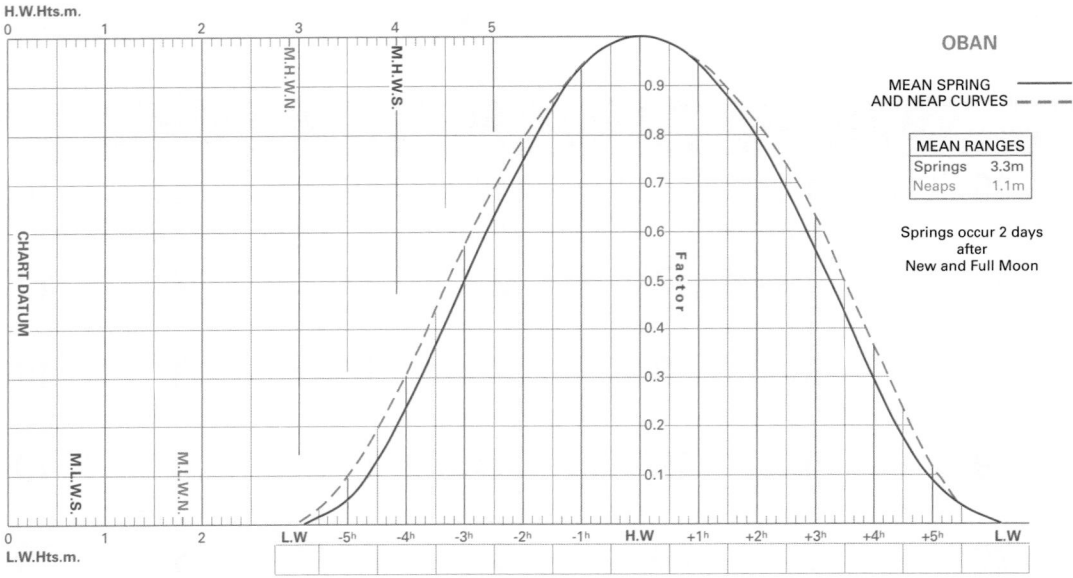

OBAN

MEAN SPRING ———
AND NEAP CURVES - - - -

MEAN RANGES	
Springs	3.3m
Neaps	1.1m

Springs occur 2 days
after
New and Full Moon

9.8.18 DUNSTAFFNAGE/OBAN

DUNSTAFFNAGE BAY, Argyll and Bute, **56°27'·04N 05°25'·97W**.
⚓⚓⚓♻♻♻✿✿✿

CHARTS AC 2171, 2387, 2388, 1790, 5611; Imray C65.

TIDES –0530 Dover; ML 2·4; Duration 0610

Standard Port OBAN (←—)

Times				Height (metres)			
High Water		Low Water		MHWS	MHWN	MLWN	MLWS
0100	0700	0100	0800	4·0	2·9	1·8	0·7
1300	1900	1300	2000				
Differences DUNSTAFFNAGE BAY							
+0005	0000	0000	+0005	+0·1	+0·1	+0·1	+0·1
CONNEL							
+0020	+0005	+0010	+0015	–0·3	–0·2	–0·1	+0·1
BONAWE							
+0150	+0205	+0240	+0210	–2·0	–1·7	–1·3	–0·5

SHELTER Good at marina in SE side of bay, little room to ⚓, within the bay the tidal stream is rotary but sets mainly E through the marina.

NAVIGATION Entered between Rubha Garbh and Eilean Mór. No navigational hazards, spd limit 4kn in bay/⚓. Do not approach marina through moorings, use buoyed fairway. W and SW sides of bay dry.

LIGHTS AND MARKS See 9.8.4 and chartlet.

R/T Call *Dunstaffnage Marina* VHF Ch M.

TELEPHONE Marinecall 09068 969653; ⊖ 08457231110; MRCC (01475) 729988; Police 510500; Dr 563175.

FACILITIES **Dunstaffnage Marina**, (Code 01631) 566555, 150 inc 10♥ AB £2.00, Wi-fi, D (0830-2000 summer), Gas, Slip (launching H24 except LWS ±2hrs, £9.00 each way) BH (18 ton), CH, C (masting), ME, BY, ▢, SM, R, Bar; Facilities: P (cans, ¾M), 🛒 (½M), Bus, ≈ Oban (2M), Glasgow (✈) 2-3hrs and Connel (airstrip).

OBAN, Argyll and Bute **56°24'·99N 05°29'·07W**
⚓⚓⚓♻♻♻✿✿

CHARTS and TIDES As Dunstaffnage

SHELTER Good shelter in bay except in strong SW/NW winds, but Oban Marina in Ardantrive Bay (Kerrera) is well sheltered from all directions. The only ⚓s convenient for town are in deep water off the Esplanade and NW of Sailing Club, beware of moorings. Alternatively ⚓ at N end of Kerrera to S of Rubh'a Chruidh Is or Horseshoe Bay and Little Horseshoe Bay, Kerrera Sound.

NAVIGATION WPT (N) 56°25'·85N 05°30'·0W, 132°/0·7M to Dunollie lt; **WPT (S)** 56°22'N 05°33'W, 035°/1M to 1·5ca E of Sgeirean Dubha, thence through Kerrera Sound to Oban Bay. Ferry Rks (56°24'·0N) can be passed on either side. Note the direction of the buoyage is **NE**, thus pass to the E'ward of PHM unlit buoy or to W'ward of the SHM QG buoy. The N'ly SHM buoy must be passed to the W'ward. In Oban Bay beware Sgeir Rathaid, buoyed, in middle of the bay; also ferries running to/from Railway Pier.

LIGHTS AND MARKS See 9.8.4 and Oban chartlet.

R/T Call: *North Pier* Ch 12 16 (0900-1700). For Railway Pier, call *CalMac* Ch 06 12 16. **Oban Marina**, call *Oban Yachts* Ch 80.

☎ (Code 01631) Pier 562892; Marinecall 09068 969653; ⊖ 08457231110; MRCC (01475) 729988; Police 510500; Dr 563175.

FACILITIES **Oban Marina** (Ardantrive Bay) www.obanmarina.com ☎ 01631 565333; 94 AB £2.00; 33 ♥s £15/day. D (0800-1800), Gas/Gaz, ▢, Bar, R, Wi-fi, 🅻(limited), 🍴, BH (50T), SM, Ⓔ, El. Free water taxi (2 hourly, 0800-1800) to/from Oban.

ARDANTRIVE BAY, KERRERA Argyll and Bute **56°25'·15N 05°29'·80W** ❀❀❀❀⚓☆☆☆ AC 1790. HW -0530 on Dover. **Oban Yachts Marina,** www.obanyachts.com, VHF Ch80/16, ☎ 565333. 56 AB (pontoons,inc 30❤) £2.20, 30❤s £1.95; D, FW, Gas, ⌦, ▣, Showers, 🚾, ME, BY, ✕, C (masting), CH, Slip, BH (16 ton), marina water taxi 0800-2200 in season, (call *Oban Yachts* Ch 80 for timetable); 10min crossing to Oban. For Town facilities see previous page.

N Pier 562892, L, FW, C (15 ton mobile) via Piermaster; **Rly Pier,** L, Slip, D (H24, ☎ 562849), FW, CH; **Services:** Slip, ACA, Gas, ME, El, divers. **Town** P (cans, ½M), all facilities, Ⓗ, ⇋, Glasgow (✈) 2-3hrs & Connel (airstrip) 3M, Ferry to Inner & Outer Hebrides.

ANCHORAGES ON MAINLAND SHORE OF FIRTH OF LORN
LOCH FEOCHAN, Argyll and Bute, **56°21'·39N 05°29'·77W.** AC 5611, 2387. HW = HW Oban; flood runs 4 hrs, ebb for 8 hrs. Caution: strong streams off Ardentallan Pt. Good shelter, 5M S of Oban and 1·5M SE of Kerrera. Best appr at local slack LW = LW Oban +0200. Narrow buoyed channel, ⚓ off pier, or moor off **Ardoran Marine** ☎ (01631) 566123, 🖷 566611; 4 ❤s £10 <11m, D, FW, ME, CH, Slip, Showers.

PUILLADOBHRAIN, Argyll and Bute, **56°19'·47N 05°35'·22W.** AC 5611, 2386/2387. Tides as Oban. Popular ⚓ on the SE shore of the Firth of Lorne, approx 7M S of Oban, sheltered by the islets to the W of it. At N end of Ardencaple Bay identify Eilean Dùin (18m) and steer SE keeping 1½ca off to clear a rk awash at its NE tip. Continue for 4ca between Eilean nam Beathach, with Orange drum on N tip, and Dun Horses rks drying 2·7m. Two W cairns on E side of Eilean nam Freumha lead approx 215° into the

inner ⚓ in about 4m. Landing at head of inlet. Nearest facilities: Bar, ☎, at Clachan Br (½M); ☎, ⊠ at Clachan Seil.

CUAN SOUND, Argyll and Bute, **56°15'·84N 05°37'·47W.** AC 2386, 2326. Tides see 9.8.19 SEIL SOUND. Streams reach 6kn at sp; N-going makes at HW Oban +0420, S-going at HW Oban −2. The Sound is a useful doglegged short cut from Firth of Lorne to Lochs Melfort and Shuna, but needs care due to rks and tides. There are ⚓s at either end to await the tide. At the 90° dogleg, pass close N of Cleit Rk onto which the tide sets; it is marked by a Y △ perch. The chan is only ¾ca wide here due to rks off Seil. Overhead cables (35m) cross from Seil to Luing. There are ⚓s out of the tide to the S of Cleit Rk. No lts/facilities. See CCC SDs.

ARDINAMAR, Luing/Torsa, **56°14'·92N 05°37'·04W.** AC 2326. HW −0555 on Dover; ML 1·7m; see 9.8.19 SEIL SOUND. A small cove and popular ⚓ between Luing and Torsa, close W of ent to L. Melfort. Appr on brg 290°. Narrow, shallow (about 1m CD) ent has drying rks either side, those to N marked by 2 SHM perches. Keep about 15m S of perches to ⚓ in 2m in centre of cove; S part dries. Few facilities: 🛒, ⊠, ☎, at Cullipool 1·5M WNW. Gas at Cuan Sound ferry 2M NNW.

9.8.19 LOCH MELFORT

Argyll and Bute **56°14'·59N 05°34'·07W** ❀❀❀❄❄❄❄❄❀❀❀

CHARTS AC 5611, 2169, 2326; Imray C65.

TIDES Loch Shuna –0615 Dover; ML Loch Melfort 1·7; Duration Seil Sound 0615

Standard Port OBAN (←)

Times				Height (metres)			
High Water		Low Water		MHWS	MHWN	MLWN	MLWS
0100	0700	0100	0800	4·0	2·9	1·8	0·7
1300	1900	1300	2000				
Differences LOCH MELFORT							
–0055	–0025	–0040	–0035	–1·2	–0·8	–0·5	–0·1
SEIL SOUND							
–0035	–0015	–0040	–0015	–1·3	–0·9	–0·7	–0·3

SHELTER Good at Kilmelford Yacht Haven in Loch na Cille; access at all tides for 3m draft, W lts at end of pier and along its length. Or lt at Melfort Pier (Fearnach Bay at N end of loch): pier/pontoon in 2m, but chan to inner hbr dries; good ⚓ in N winds. ⚓'ge sheltered from S to W at Kames Bay clear of moorings, rks and marine farms. ⚓'ge N of Arduaine denied to small craft due extensive marine farm activity (2005).

NAVIGATION WPT 56°13'·90N 05°34'·80W, 000°/3·5ca to Eilean Gamhna. Pass either side of Eilean Gamhna. 8ca NE lies Campbell Rk (1·8m). A rk drying 1m lies 1½ca ESE of the FS on Eilean Coltair. The S side of L Melfort is mostly steep-to, except in Kames Bay. At Loch na Cille, beware drying reef ¾ca off NE shore (PHM perch), and rk near S shore (SHM perch); boats may obscure perches.

LIGHTS AND MARKS A Dir FR ☆ 6m 3M on Melfort pier (also depth gauge) and a Dir FG ☆ close NE on the shore are not ldg lts, nor do they form a safe transit. Approach on a N'ly track keeping them an equal angle off each bow.

R/T Kilmelford VHF Ch **80** M (HO).

TELEPHONE (Code 01852) MRCC (01475) 729014; ⊖ (0141) 887 9369; Police (01631) 510500; Marinecall 09068 969653; Ⓗ (01631) 567500.

FACILITIES **Kilmelford Yacht Haven** ☎ 200248, 🖳 200343, £16/craft (any LOA), D (Mon-Sat 0800-2000), FW, 🔲,BH (20 ton), Slip HW±4, ME, El, ✕, Gas, 🔧 village (¾M); **Melfort Pier** ☎ 200333, AB or 🛢 £12/day, Slip, @. Village (1¼M) 🍴, Bar, ✉.

[Chart of Loch Melfort with soundings, Melfort Pier and Harbour, Fearnach Bay, Loch na Cille, Kilmelford Yacht Haven, Sgeir na Ceàrdaich, and compass rose]

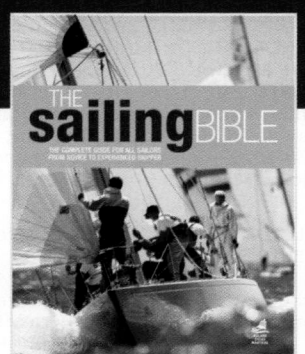

9.8.20 CRAOBH MARINA (L SHUNA)

Argyll & Bute **56°12′·80N 05°33′·54W** ✿✿✿✿✿✿✿✿✿

CHARTS AC 5611, 2169, 2326; Imray C65.

TIDES HW Loch Shuna –0100 Oban; –0615 Dover; Seil Sound Duration 0615, ML 1·4. For tidal figures see 9.8.19.

SHELTER Very good. Craobh (pronounced Croove) Marina (access H24) on SE shore of Loch Shuna is enclosed by N and S causeways between islets. The ent is between 2 bkwtrs on the N side. In the marina, a shoal area S of the E bkwtr is marked by 9 PHM and 2 SHM buoys. A Y perch in W corner of hbr marks a spit; elsewhere ample depth. There are ⚓s in Asknish Bay 1M to the N, and in the bays E of Eilean Arsa and at Bàgh an Tigh-Stòir, S of Craobh.

NAVIGATION WPT 56°13′·01N 05°33′·57W, 173°/2ca to ent. Tidal streams in Loch Shuna are weak. Beware fish farm 2ca N of Shuna, lobster pots in appr's and unmarked rks (dr 1·5m) 4ca NNE of ent. An unlit SHM buoy marks a rk (1m) 150m NNW of the W bkwtr. 1M N of marina, Eich Donna, an unmarked reef (dr 1·5m), lies between Eilean Creagach and Arduaine Pt.

LIGHTS AND MARKS The W sector, 162°-183°, of Dir Lt, Iso WRG 5s 10m 5/3M, on E bkwtr hd leads 172° between the close-in rks above. Multi coloured marina buildings are conspic.

R/T VHF Ch M, 80 (summer 0830-2000; winter 0830-1800).

TELEPHONE (Code 01852) HM 500222; MRCC (01475) 729014; ⊖ (0141) 887 9369; Marinecall 09068 969653; Police (01546) 602222; Ⓗ (01546) 602323.

FACILITIES **Craobh Marina** (200+50 Ⓥ) ☎ 500222; £2.00, D, SM,

BY, CH, Slip (launch/recovery £3.70/m), BH (15 ton), C (12 ton), Gas, Gaz, ME, El, ⚒, R, SC, Ⓔ, ⧫, Divers. **Village** ⌖, Bar, Ⓑ (Fri), ⊠ (Kilmelford), ⇌ (Oban by bus), ✈ (Glasgow).

9.8.21 LOCH CRAIGNISH

Argyll and Bute **56°07′·99N 05°35′·07W** (Ardfern) ✿✿✿✿✿✿✿✿✿

CHARTS AC 5611, 2169, 2326; Imray C65, C63.

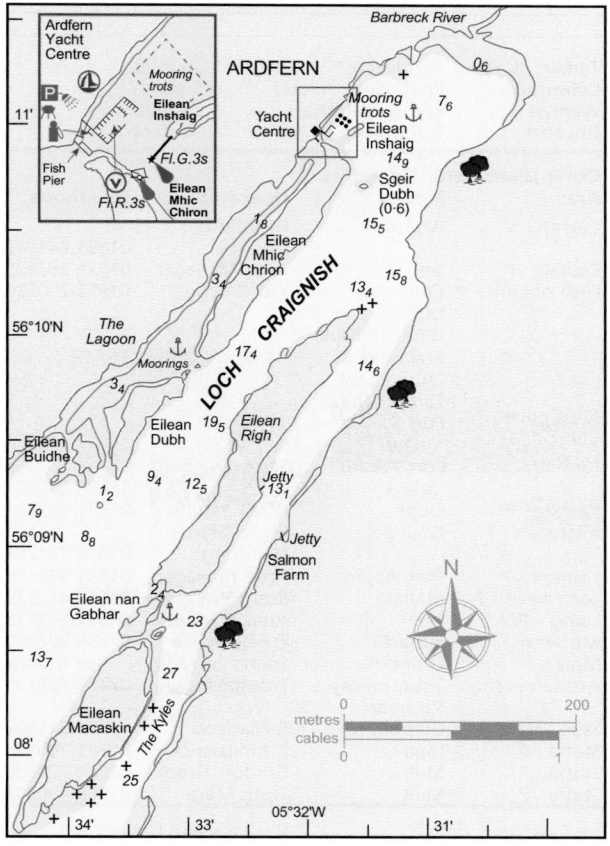

TIDES +0600 Dover; ML (Loch Beag)1·2; Duration (Seil Sound) 0615

Standard Port OBAN (←→)

Times				Height (metres)			
High Water		Low Water		MHWS	MHWN	MLWN	MLWS
0100	0700	0100	0800	4·0	2·9	1·8	0·7
1300	1900	1300	2000				
Differences LOCH BEAG (Sound of Jura)							
–0110	–0045	–0035	–0045	–1·6	–1·2	–0·8	–0·4

NOTE: HW Ardfern is approx HW Oban –0045; times/heights much affected by local winds and barometric pressure

SHELTER Good at Ardfern, 56°11′·0N 05°31′·8W, access H24; ⚓s at:
• Eilean nan Gabhar; appr from E chan and ⚓ E of island.
• Eilean Righ; midway up the E side of the island.
• Eilean Dubh in the 'lagoon' between the Is and mainland.
• Beware squalls in E'lies, especially on E side of loch.

NAVIGATION See 9.8.5. WPT 56°07′·59N 05°35′·37W (off chartlet) between Dorus Mór and Liath-sgier Mhòr.

Beware: strong tidal streams (up to 8kn) in Dorus Mór see 9.8.5; a reef extending 1ca SSW of the SE chain of islands; rk 1½ca SSW of Eilean Dubh; fish cages especially on E side of loch; a drying rock at N end of Ardfern ⚓ with a rock awash ¼ca E of it. (These 2 rks are more S'ly of little islets close to mainland.) The main fairway is free from hazards, except for Sgeir Dhubh, an unmarked rk 3½ca SSE of Ardfern, with a reef extending about ½ca all round. Ardfern is 1ca W of Eilean Inshaig.

LIGHTS AND MARKS Ent to Ardfern Yacht Centre marked by PHM buoy, Fl R 3s, and end of floating breakwater, Fl G 3s, which extends 90m SW from Eilean Inshaig.

R/T Ardfern Yacht Centre VHF Ch 80 M (office hrs).

TELEPHONE (Code 01852) HM (Yacht Centre) 500247, www.ardfernyacht.co.uk, MRCC (01475) 729014; Marinecall 09068 969653; ⊖ (0141) 887 9369; Dr (01546) 602921; Ⓗ (01546) 602449.

FACILITIES **Ardfern Yacht Centre** (87+20 AB; 80+12Ⓥ) AB £1.95, M £1.30, Wi-fi, D (HO), BH (20 ton), Slip (HW±3, £1.50/m inc parking), ME, El, ⚒, SM, ACA, C (12 ton), CH, ⧫, Gas, Gaz. **Village** R, ⌖, Ⓑ (Fri), ⊠ , ⇌ (Oban), Bar, ✈ (Glasgow).

9.8.22 SUBMARINE EXERCISE AREAS (SUBFACTS)

Details of submarine activity in the Exercise Areas north of Mull are broadcast by MRCCs on a specified VHF Ch after an initial announcement on Ch 16 at the following times:

Stornoway 0710 1910 UT
Clyde 0810 2010 UT

The areas are referred to by the names given below, rather than by the numbers indicated on the chartlet. For Areas 22–81 (South of Mull), see page 472.

General information on SUBFACTS is also broadcast twice daily at 0620 & 1820 UT on Navtex. Stornoway and Clyde MRCCs will provide SUBFACTS on request; call on Ch 16.

A 'Fisherman's hotline' (☎ (01436) 677201) is available on a 24 hour basis and may be used for any queries relating to SUBFACTS from any mariner.

Submarines on the surface and at periscope depth always listen on Ch 16.

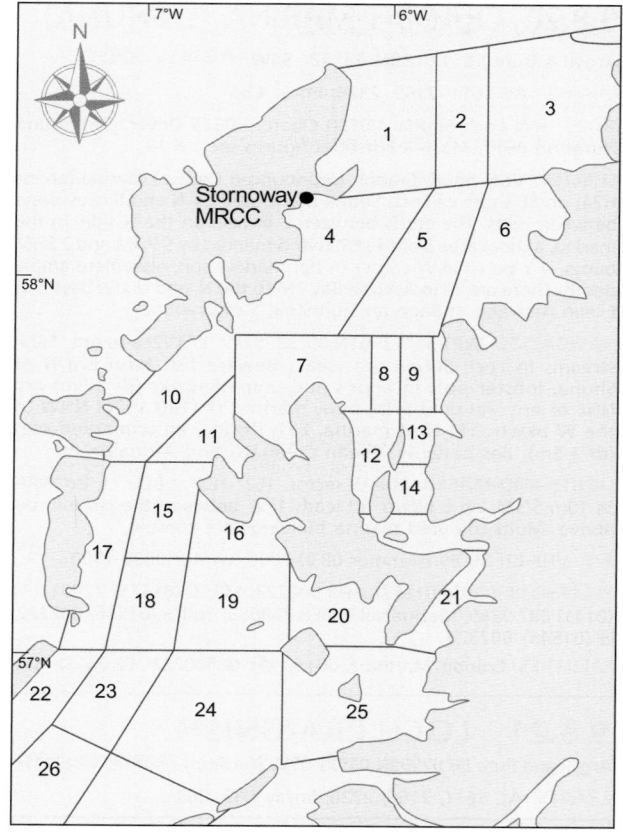

1	Tiumpan	14	Raasay
2	Minch North	15	Neist
3	Stoer	16	Bracadale
4	Shiant	17	Ushenish
5	Minch South	18	Hebrides North
6	Ewe	19	Canna
7	Troddaw	20	Rhum
8	Rona West	21	Sleat
9	Rona North	22	Barra
10	Lochmaddy	23	Hebrides Central
11	Dunvegan	24	Hawes
12	Portree	25	Eigg
13	Rona South	26	Hebrides South

9.8.23 FERRIES

Many ferries ply between mainland and island harbours. This summary may prove useful when plans or crews change in remote places. It covers Areas 8 and 9. The major operator is Caledonian MacBrayne: Head Office, The Ferry Terminal, Gourock PA19 1QP. For reservations: ☎ 08000 665000; www.calmac.co.uk. Many routes are very short and may not be pre-bookable; seasonal routes are marked *.

From	To	Time	Remarks
Area 8			
Berneray	Leverburgh	1¼	
Ullapool	Stornoway	2¾ hrs	
Uig (Skye)	Tarbert (Harris)	1¾ hrs	Not Sun
Uig	Lochmaddy (N Uist)	1¾ hrs	
Oban	Castlebay/Lochboisdale	5-7 hrs	
Sconser (Skye)	Raasay	15 mins	Not Sun
Mallaig*	Armadale (Skye)	20 mins	
Mallaig	Eigg-Muck-Rum-Canna	Varies	Not Sun
Oban	Coll-Tiree	Varies	Not Thurs
Tobermory	Kilchoan	35 mins	
Fionnphort	Iona	5 mins	
Lochaline	Fishnish (Mull)	15 mins	
Oban	Craignure (Mull)	45 mins	
Oban	Lismore	50 mins	Not Sun
Areas 8/9			
Oban	Colonsay	2¼ hrs	Sun/W/Fri
Area 9			
Kennacraig	Port Askaig/Colonsay	Varies	Wed
Kennacraig	Port Ellen	2h 10m	
Kennacraig	Port Askaig	2 hrs	
Tayinloan	Gigha	20 mins	
Ardrossan	Brodick	55 mins	
Claonaig	Lochranza (Arran)	30 mins	
Largs	Cumbrae Slip	10 mins	

Tarbert (L Fyne)	Portavadie*	25 mins
Colintraive	Rhubodach (Bute)	5 mins
Wemyss Bay	Rothesay (Bute)	35 mins
Gourock	Dunoon	20 mins

Other Island Ferry Operators

Area	From	Operator	Telephone
Corran - V	Ardgour	Highland Council	01855 841243
Easdale - P	Seil	Area Manager	01631 562125
Firth of Lorn - P	Colonsay	K & C Byrne	01951 200320
	Uisken (Ross of Mull)		
	Scalasaig (Colonsay)		
	Tarbert (Jura)		
	Port Askaig (Islay)		
Jura - V	Port Askaig (Islay)	Serco Denholm	01496 840681
Kerrara - P	Oban	Oban Yachts	01631 565333
Kilgregan - P	Gourock	Clyde Marine Motoring	01475 721281
Lismore - P	Port Appin	Area Manager	01631 562125
Loch Nevis - P	Mallaig	Bruce Watt	01687 462233
Luing - P/V	Seil	Area Manager	01631 562125
Morvern	Sunart	Pre-book via	01688 302851
Mull	Drimnin	Sound of Mull	or mobile
Ardnamurchan	Tobermoray	Transport	07799 608199
	Kilchoan		
Skye - V	Gleneig	R Macleod	01599 511302
Staffa - P	Iona	D Kirkpatrick	01681 700373
Staffa - P	Mull	Gordon Grant	01681 700338
Staffa - P	Mull	Turus Mara	01688 400242

P = Passenger only   V = Cars and Passengers

ADLARD COLES NAUTICAL
WEATHER FORECASTS
BY FAX & TELEPHONE

Coastal/Inshore	2-day by Fax	5-day by Phone
Minch	09065 222 354	09068 969 654
Caledonia	09065 222 353	09068 969 653
Clyde	09065 222 352	09068 969 652
North West	09065 222 351	09068 969 651
National (3-5 day)	09065 222 340	09068 969 640
Offshore	2-5 day by Fax	2-5 day by Phone
Southern North Sea	09065 222 358	09068 969 658
Northern North Sea	09065 222 362	09068 969 662
North West Scotland	09065 222 361	09068 969 661
Irish Sea	09065 222 359	09068 969 659

09068 CALLS COST 60P PER MIN. 09065 CALLS COST £1.50 PER MIN.

South West Scotland

Crinal Canal to Mull of Galloway

SW Scotland

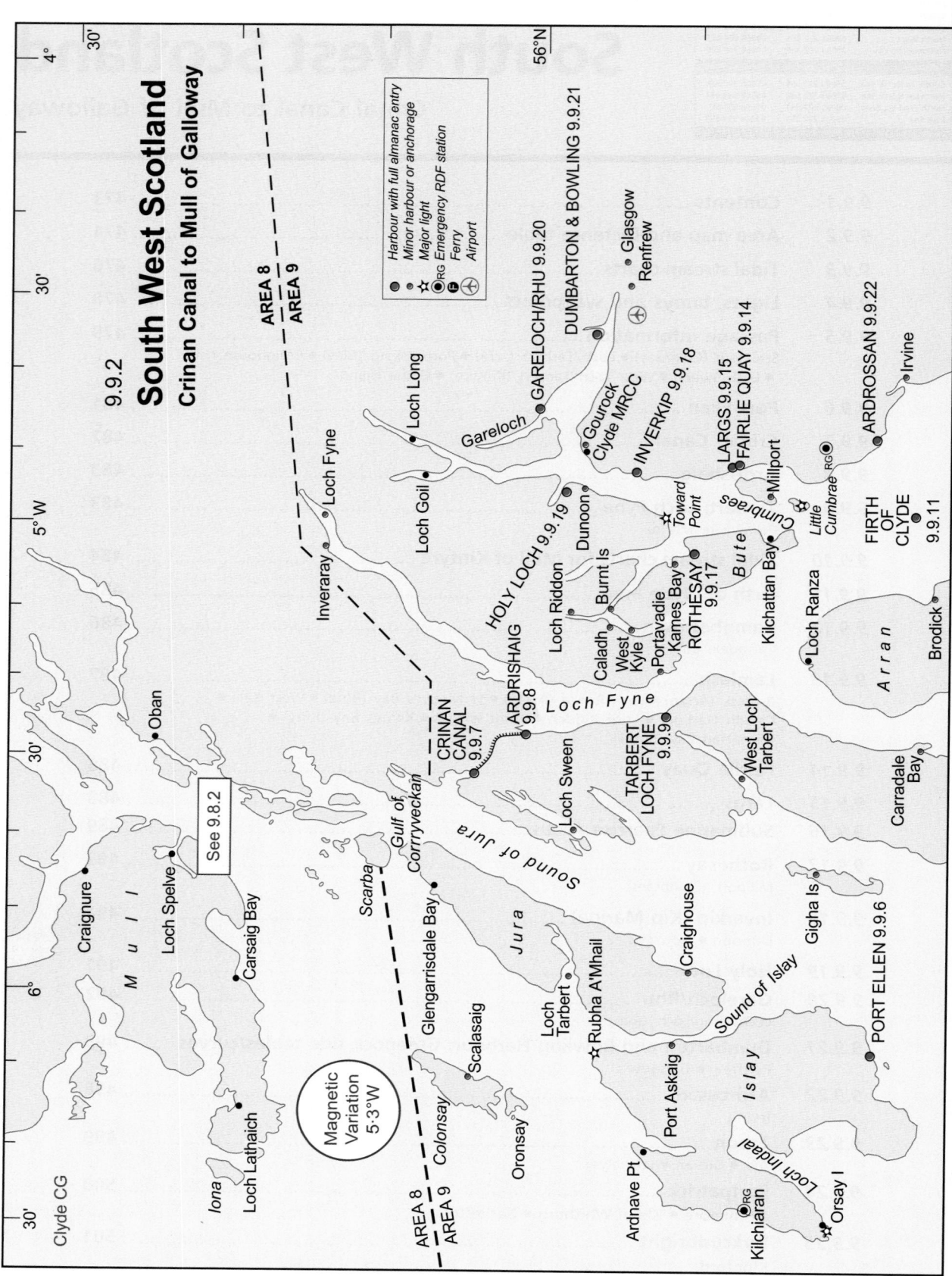

9.9.2

South West Scotland
Crinan Canal to Mull of Galloway

AREA 8
AREA 9

Harbour with full almanac entry
Minor harbour or anchorage
Major light
RG Emergency RDF station
Ferry
Airport

56°N

Loch Long

GARELOCH/RHU 9.9.20

DUMBARTON & BOWLING 9.9.21

Glasgow
Renfrew

Loch Fyne

Gareloch

Gourock
Clyde MRCC

INVERKIP 9.9.18

ARDROSSAN 9.9.22

Irvine

Loch Goil

Toward
Point

LARGS 9.9.15
FAIRLIE QUAY 9.9.14

Millport

Cumbrae RG

Little
Cumbrae

FIRTH
OF
CLYDE
9.9.11

HOLY LOCH 9.9.19

Dunoon

Loch Riddon

Burnt Is

Cumbraes

Bute

Kilchattan Bay

ARDRISHAIG
9.9.8

Caladh
West
Kyle
Portavadie

Kames Bay
ROTHESAY
9.9.17

Loch Ranza

Brodick

CRINAN
CANAL
9.9.7

Corryveckan

Loch Sween

Loch Fyne

TARBERT
LOCH FYNE
9.9.9

West Loch
Tarbert

Arran

Oban

Gulf of

See 9.8.2

Scarba

Glengarrisdale Bay

Jura

Sound of Jura

Craighouse

Carradale
Bay

Craignure

Mull

Loch Spelve

Carsaig Bay

Colonsay

Scalasaig

Loch
Tarbert

Rubha A'Mhail

Gigha Is.

PORT ELLEN 9.9.6

Iona

Loch Lathaich

Oronsay

Port Askaig

Islay

Sound of Islay

Loch Indaal

Magnetic
Variation
5·3°W

AREA 8
AREA 9

Ardnave Pt

Kilchiaran RG

Orsay I

Clyde CG

Inveraray

4°

30'

30'

5°W

30'

6°

30'

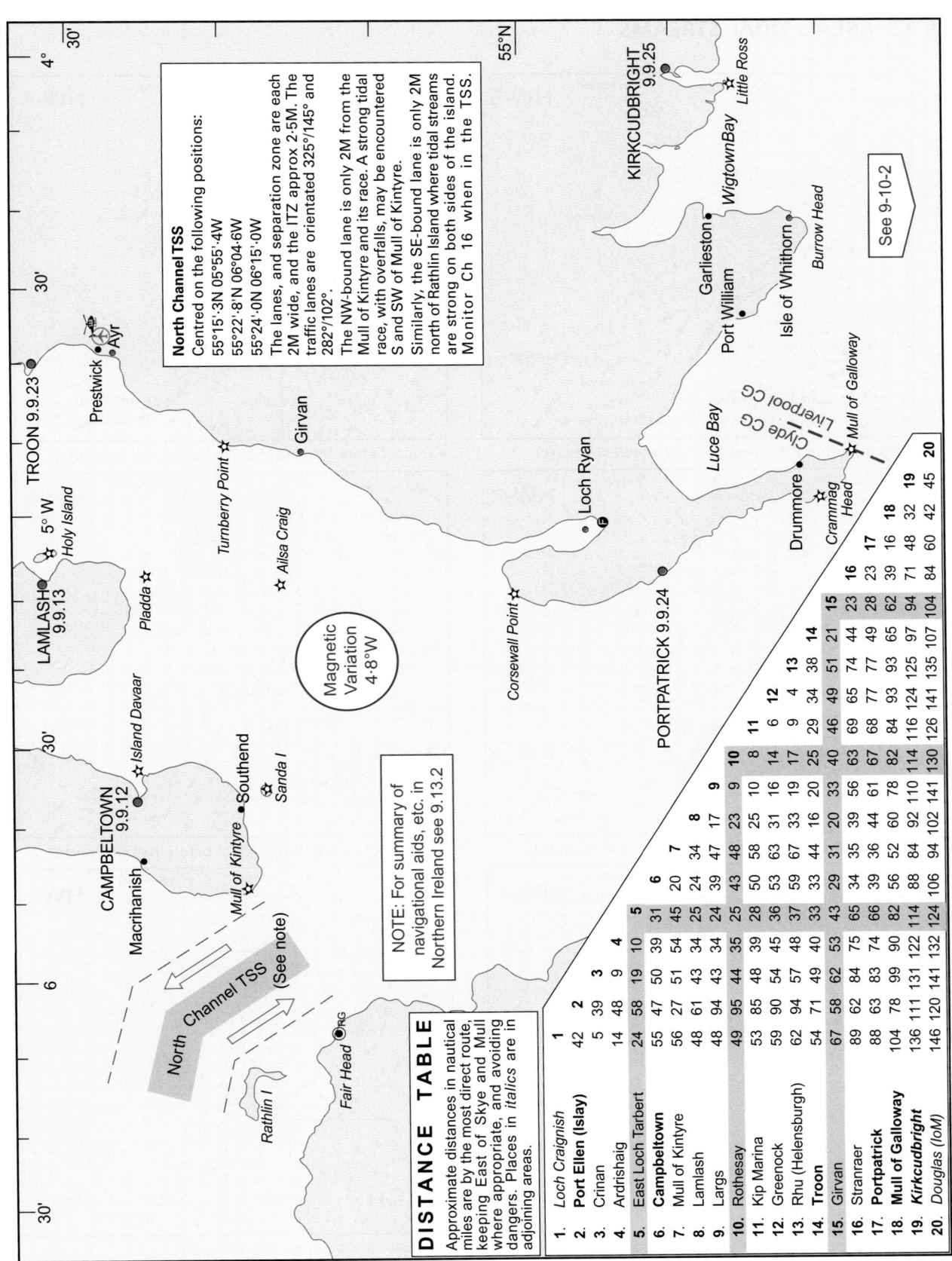

North Channel TSS

Centred on the following positions:

55°15'·3N 05°55'·4W
55°22'·8N 06°04·6W
55°24'·0N 06°15'·0W

The lanes, and separation zone are each 2M wide, and the ITZ approx 2·5M. The traffic lanes are orientated 325°/145° and 282°/102°.

The NW-bound lane is only 2M from the Mull of Kintyre and its race. A strong tidal race, with overfalls, may be encountered S and SW of Mull of Kintyre.

Similarly, the SE-bound lane is only 2M north of Rathlin Island where tidal streams are strong on both sides of the island. Monitor Ch 16 when in the TSS.

See 9-10-2

Magnetic Variation 4·8°W

NOTE: For summary of navigational aids, etc. in Northern Ireland see 9.13.2

DISTANCE TABLE

Approximate distances in nautical miles are by the most direct route, keeping East of Skye and Mull where appropriate, and avoiding dangers. Places in *italics* are in adjoining areas.

No.	Place	1	2	3	4	5	6	7	8	9	10	11	12	13	14	15	16	17	18	19	20
1.	*Loch Craignish*	1																			
2.	**Port Ellen (Islay)**	42	2																		
3.	Crinan	5	39	3																	
4.	Ardrishaig	14	48	9	4																
5.	East Loch Tarbert	24	58	19	10	5															
6.	**Campbeltown**	55	47	50	39	31	6														
7.	Mull of Kintyre	56	27	51	54	45	20	7													
8.	Lamlash	48	61	43	34	25	24	34	8												
9.	Largs	48	94	43	34	24	39	47	17	9											
10.	Rothesay	49	95	44	35	25	43	48	23	9	10										
11.	Kip Marina	53	85	48	39	28	50	58	25	10	8	11									
12.	Greenock	59	90	54	45	36	53	63	31	16	14	6	12								
13.	Rhu (Helensburgh)	62	94	57	48	37	59	67	33	19	17	9	4	13							
14.	**Troon**	54	71	49	40	33	33	44	16	20	25	29	34	38	14						
15.	Girvan	67	58	62	53	43	29	31	20	33	40	46	49	51	21	15					
16.	Stranraer	89	62	84	75	65	34	35	39	56	63	69	74	77	44	23	16				
17.	**Portpatrick**	88	63	83	74	66	39	36	44	61	67	68	77	93	49	28	23	17			
18.	**Mull of Galloway**	104	78	99	90	82	56	52	60	78	82	93	93	125	65	62	39	16	18		
19.	*Kirkcudbright*	136	111	131	122	114	88	84	92	110	116	124	125	135	97	94	71	48	32	19	
20.	*Douglas (IoM)*	146	120	141	132	124	106	94	102	141	141	130	126	135	107	104	84	60	42	45	20

Map labels: TROON 9.9.23, Prestwick, Ayr, LAMLASH 9.9.13, Holy Island, 5°W, Pladda, Island Davaar, CAMPBELTOWN 9.9.12, Macrihanish, Southend, Sanda I, Mull of Kintyre, North Channel TSS (See note), Fair Head, Rathlin I, Turnberry Point, Ailsa Craig, Girvan, Loch Ryan, Corsewall Point, PORTPATRICK 9.9.24, Luce Bay, Drummore, Crammag Head, Mull of Galloway, Clyde CG, Liverpool CG, Port William, Garlieston, Wigtown Bay, Isle of Whithorn, Burrow Head, KIRKCUDBRIGHT 9.9.25, Little Ross

SW Scotland

9.9.3 AREA 9 TIDAL STREAMS

5 Hours before HW Dover (0605 after HW Greenock)

4 Hours before HW Dover (0520 before HW Greenock)

3 Hours before HW Dover (0420 before HW Greenock)

2 Hours before HW Dover (0320 before HW Greenock)

1 Hour before HW Dover (0220 before HW Greenock)

HW Dover (0120 before HW Greenock)

Northward 9.8.3   Mull of Kintyre 9.9.10   Irish Sea 9.10.3   Northern Ireland 9.13.3

1 Hour after HW Dover (0020 before HW Greenock)

2 Hours after HW Dover (0040 after HW Greenock)

3 Hours after HW Dover (0140 after HW Greenock)

4 Hours after HW Dover (0240 after HW Greenock)

5 Hours after HW Dover (0340 after HW Greenock)

6 Hours after HW Dover (0440 after HW Greenock)

SW Scotland

9.9.4 LIGHTS, BUOYS AND WAYPOINTS

Bold print = light with a nominal range of 15M or more. CAPITALS = place or feature. *CAPITAL ITALICS* = light-vessel, light float or Lanby. *Italics* = Fog signal. ***Bold italics*** = Racon. Abbreviations are in Chapter 1.

COLONSAY TO ISLAY
COLONSAY
Scalasaig, Rubha Dubh ⚡ Fl (2) WR 10s 8m W8M, R6M; W bldg; vis: shore-R- 230°-W-337°-R-354°; 56°04'·01N 06°10'·90W.

SOUND OF ISLAY
Rhubh' a Mháil (Ruvaal) ☆ 55°56'·18N 06°07'·46W Fl (3) 15s 45m **19M**; W twr.

Carragh an t'Struith ⚡ Fl 3s 8m 9M; W twr; vis: 354°-180°; 55°52'·30N 06°05'·78W.

Carraig Mòr ⚡ Fl (2) WR 6s 7m W8M, R6M; W twr; vis: shore-R-175°-W-347°-R-shore; 55°50'·42N 06°06'·13W.

McArthur's Hd ⚡ Fl (2) WR 10s 39m W14M, R11M; W twr; W in Sound of Islay from NE coast,159°-R-244°-W-E coast of Islay; 55°45'·84N 06°02'·90W.

PORT ELLEN and LOCH INDAAL
Carraig Fhada ⚡ Fl WRG 3s 20m W8M, R6M, G6M; W☐ twr; vis: W shore- 248°-G-311°-W-340°-R-shore; 55°37'·22N 06°12'·71W.

Rubh'an Dùin ⚡ Fl (2) WR 7s 15m W11M, R8M; W twr; vis: shore-R-218°-W-249°-R-350°-W-shore; 55°44'·70N 06°22'·28 W.

Orsay Is, **Rhinns of Islay** ☆ 55°40'·40N 06°30'·84W Fl 5s 46m **24M**; W twr; vis: 256°-184°.

JURA TO MULL OF KINTYRE
SOUND OF JURA, CRAIGHOUSE, L SWEEN and GIGHA
Na Cùiltean ⚡ Fl 10s 9m 9M; 55°48'·64N 05°54'·90W.
Gamhna Gigha ⚡ Fl (2) 6s 7m 5M; 55°43'·78N 05°41'·08W.

WEST LOCH TARBERT
Dunskeig Bay ⚡ Q (2) 10s 11m 8M; 55°45'·22N 05°35'·00W.
Eileen Tráighe (off S side) ↓ Fl (2) R 5s 5m 3M; R post; 55°45'·37N 05°35'·75W.

MULL OF KINTYRE
Mull of Kintyre ☆ 55°18'·64N 05°48'·25W Fl (2) 20s 91m **24M**; W twr on W bldg; vis: 347°-178°.

CRINAN CANAL and ARDRISHAIG
Crinan, E of lock ent ⚡ Fl WG 3s 8m 4M; W twr, R band; vis: shore-W-146°-G-shore; 56°05'·48N 05°33'·37W.

Ardrishaig Bkwtr Hd ⚡ L Fl WRG 6s 9m 4M; vis: 287°-G-339°-W-350°-R-035°; 56°00'·76N 05°26'·59W.

LOCH FYNE TO SANDA ISLAND
EAST LOCH TARBERT
Eilean na Beithe ⚡ Fl WRG 3s 7m 5M; vis: G036°- W065°- R078°-106°; 55°52'·68N 05°19'·62W.

Skipness range ⚡ Iso R 8s 7m 10M; Y ◇ on bldg; vis 292·2°-312·2°. Oc (2) Y 10s **24M** when range in use (occas); 55°46'·72N 05°19'·06W.

KILBRANNAN SOUND, CRANNAICH and CARRADALE BAY
Port Crannaich Bkwtr Hd ⚡ Fl R 10s 5m 6M; vis: 099°-279°; 55°35'·60N 05°27'·84W.

CAMPBELTOWN LOCH to SANDA ISLAND
Davaar N Pt ☆ 55°25'·69N 05°32'·42W Fl (2) 10s 37m **23M**; W twr; vis: 073°-330°.

Sanda Island ☆ 55°16'·50N 05°35'·01W Fl 10s 50m **15M**; W twr.
Patersons Rock ⚡ Fl (3) R 18s; 55°16'·90N 05°32'·48W.

KYLES OF BUTE TO RIVER CLYDE
KYLES OF BUTE and CALADH
Ardlamont Point No. 47 ⚡ W Fl R 4s; 55°49'·59N 05°11'·76.

Ardmaleish Point No. 41 ↓ Q (3) 10s; 55°53'·02N 05°04'·70W.
Bogany Point No. 36 ⚡ Fl R 4s; 55°50'·78N 05°01'·41W.

FIRTH OF CLYDE
Toward Pt ☆ 55°51'·73N 04°58'·79W Fl 10s 21m **22M**; W twr.
No. 34 ⚡ 55°51'·44N 04°59'·11W.
Skelmorlie ↓ Iso 5s; 55°51'·65N 04°56'·34W.

WEMYSS and INVERKIP
Cowal ↓ L Fl 10s; 55°56'·00N 04°54'·83W.
The Gantocks ↓ Fl R 6s 12m 6M; ○ twr; 55°56'·45N 04°55'·08W.

DUNOON
Cloch Point ⚡ Fl 3s 24m 8M; W ○ twr, B band, W dwellings; 55°56'·55N 04°52'·74W.

LOCH LONG and LOCH GOIL
Loch Long ↓ Oc 6s; 55°59'·15N 04°52'·42W.
Baron's Pt No. 3 ⚡ Oc (2) Y 10s 5m 3M; 55°59'·18N 04°51'·12W.
Ravenrock Pt ⚡ Fl 4s 12m 10M; W twr on W col. Dir lt 204°, WRG 9m (same twr); vis: 201·5°-F R-203°-Al WR(W phase incr with brg)-203·5°-FW-204·5°-Al WG(G phase incr with brg)-205°-FG-206·5°; 56°02'·14N 04°54'·39W.
Port Dornaige ⚡ Fl 6s 8m 11M; W col; vis: 026°-206°; 56°03·75N 04°53'·65W.
Rubha Ardnahein ⚡ Fl R 5s 3m 3M; vis: 132°-312°; 56°06'·15N 04°53'·60W.
The Perch, Ldg Lts 318° Front, F WRG 3m 5M; vis: 311°-G-317°-W-320°-R-322°. Same structure, Fl R 3s 3m 3M; vis: 187°-322°; 56°06'·90N 04°54'·31W. Rear, 700m from front, F 7m 5M; vis: 312°-322·5°.
Cnap Pt ⚡ Ldg Lts 031°. Front, Q 8m 10M; W col; 56°07'·40N 04°49'·97W. Rear, 87m from front F 13m; R line on W twr.

GOUROCK
Ashton ↓ Iso 5s; 55°58'·10N 04°50'·65W.
Rosneath Patch ↓ Fl (2) 10s 5m 10M; 55°58'·52N 04°47'·45W.

ROSNEATH, RHU NARROWS and GARELOCH
Ldg Lts 356°. **Front, No. 7N** ↓ 56°00'·05N 04°45'·36W Dir lt 356°. WRG 5m **W16M**, R13M, G13M; vis: 353°-Al WG- 355°-FW-357°-Al WR-000°-FR-002°.
Dir lt 115° WRG 5m **W16M**, R13M, G13M; vis: 111°-Al WG-114°-FW- 116°-Al WR-119°-FR-121°. Passing lt Oc G 6s 6m 3M; G △ on G pile . Rear, Ardencaple Castle Centre ⚡ 56°00'·54N 04°45'·43W 2 FG (vert) 26m 12M; twr on Castle NW corner; vis: 335°-020°.
No. 8N Lt Bn ↓ 55°59'·09N 04°44'·21W Dir lt 080° WRG 4m; **W16M**, R13M,G13M;vis: 075°-FG-077·5°-Al WG-079·5°-FW-080·5°-AltWR-082·5°-FR-085°. **Dir lt 138°** WRG 4m **W16M**, R13M, G13M; vis: 132°-FG-134°-Al WG- FW137°-139°-Al WR-142°. Passing lt Fl Y 3s 6m 3M.
Gareloch No. 1 Lt Bn ⚡ VQ (4) Y 5s 9m; Y 'X' on Y structure; 55°59'·12N 04°43'·89W.
No. 3 N Lt Bn ↓ 56°00'·07N 04°46'·72W Dir lt 149° WRG 9m **W16M**, R13M, G13M F & Al; vis: 144°-FG-145°-Al WG-148°-FW-150°-Al WR-153°-FR-154°. Passing lt Oc R 8s 9m 3M.
Rosneath DG Jetty ⚡ 2 FR (vert) 5M; W col; vis: 150°-330°; 56°00'·39N 04°47'·51W.
Rhu Pt ↓ Q (3) WRG 6s 9m W10M, R7M, G7M; vis: 270°-G-000°-W-114°-R-188°; 56°00'·95N 04°47'·19W.
Dir lt 318° WRG **W16M**, R13M,G13M; vis: 315°-Al WG-317°-F-319°-Al WR-321°-FR-325°.
Limekiln No. 2N Lt Bn ↓ 56°00'·67N 04°47'·64W Dir lt 295° WRG 5m **W16M**, R13M, G13M F & Al; R ☐ on R Bn; vis: 291°-Al WG-294°-FW- 296°-Al WR-299°-FR-301°.
Mambeg Dir lt 331°, Q (4) WRG 8s 10m 14M; vis: 328·5°-G-330°-W-332°-R-333°; H24; 56°03'·74N 04°50'·47W.

GREENOCK and PORT GLASGOW
Anchorage Lts in line 196°. Front, FG 7m 12M; Y col; 55°57'·62N 04°46'·58W. Rear, 32m from front, FG 9m 12M. Y col.
Lts in line 194·5°. Front, FG 18m; 55°57'·45N 04°45'·91W. Rear, 360m from front, FG 33m.

Steamboat Quay, W end ≴ FG 12m 12M; B&W chequered col; vis 210°-290°; 55°56'·25N 04°41'·44W. From here to Glasgow Lts on S bank are Fl G and Lts on N bank are Fl R.

CLYDE TO MULL OF GALLOWAY

LARGS and FAIRLIE
Approach ℺ L Fl 10s; 55°46'·40N 04°51'·85W.
Fairlie Patch ▲ Fl G 1·5s; 55°45'·38N 04°52'·34W.

MILLPORT and GREAT CUMBRAE
Ldg Lts 333°. Pier Head front, 55°45'·04N 04°55'·85W FR 7m 5M. Rear, 137m from front, FR 9m 5M.
Mountstuart ⌀ L Fl 10s; 55°48'·00N 04°57'·57W.
Runnaneun Pt (Rubha'n Eun) ≴ Fl R 6s 8m 12M; W twr; 55°43'·79N 05°00'·23W.
Little Cumbrae Is, Cumbrae Elbow ≴ Fl 6s 28m 14M; W twr; vis: 334°-193°; 55°43'·22N 04°58'·06W.

ARDROSSAN
Approach Dir lt 055°, WRG 15m W14M, R11M, G11M; vis: 050°-F G-051·2°-Alt WG(W phase inc with Brg)- 053·8°-FW-056·2°-Alt WR(R phase inc with brg)-058·8°-FR-060°; 55°38'·66N 04°49'·22W. Same structure FR 13m 6M; vis: 325°-145°.
Lt ho Pier Hd ≴ Iso WG 4s 11m 9M; W twr; vis: 035°-W-317°-G-035°; 55°38'·47N 04°49'·57W.

IRVINE
Ldg Lts 051°. Front, FG 10m 5M; 55°36'·40N 04°41'·57W. Rear, 101m from front, FR 15m 5M; G masts, both vis: 019°-120°.

TROON
Troon Approach ⌀ Fl R 2s 4m 3M; 55°33'·06N 04°41'·35W.
W Pier Hd ≴ Fl (2) WG 5s 11m 9M; W twr; vis: 036°-G-090°-W-036°; 55°33'·07N 04°41'·02W.
Lady I ≴ Fl 2s 19m 11M; W Tr R vert stripes; *Racon (T) 13-11M*; 55°31'·63N 04°44'·05W.

ARRAN, RANZA, LAMLASH and BRODICK
Pillar Rk Pt ☆ (Holy Island), 55°31'·04N 05°03'·67W Fl (2) 20s 38m **25M**; W ☐ twr.
Holy I SW end ≴ Fl G 3s 14m 10M; W twr; vis: 282°-147°; 55°30'·73N 05°04'·21W.
Pladda ☆ 55°25'·50N 05°07'·12W Fl (3) 30s 40m **17M**; W twr.

AYR and AILSA CRAIG
S Pier Hd ≴ Q 7m 7M; R twr; vis: 012°-161°. Also FG 5m 5M; vis: 012°-082°; 55°28'·17N 04°38'·74W.

Ldg Lts 098°. Front, FR 10m 5M; Tfc sigs; 55°28'·15N 04°38'·38W. Rear, 130m from front Oc R 10s 18m 9M.
Turnberry Point ☆, near castle ruins 55°19'·56N 04°50'·71W Fl 15s 29m **24M**; W twr.
Ailsa Craig ☆ 55°15'·12N 05°06'·52W Fl 4s 18m **17M**; W twr; vis: 145°-028°.

GIRVAN
S Pier Hd ≴ 2 FG (vert) 8m 4M; W twr; 55°14'·72N 04°51'·90W.

LOCH RYAN and STRANRAER
Milleur Point ⌀ Q; 55°01'·28N 05°05'·66W.
Forbes Shoal ⌀ QR; 54°59'·47N 05°02'·96W.
Loch Ryan W ▲ QG; 54°59'·23N 05°03'·24W.
Cairn Pt ≴ Fl (2) R 10s 14m 12M; W twr; 54°58'·46N 05°01'·85W.
Cairnryan ≴ Fl R 5s 5m 5M; 54°57'·77N 05°00'·99W.
Stranraer No.1 ⌀ Oc G 6s; 54°56'·67N 05°01'·32W.
No. 3 ⌀ QG; 54°55'·87N 05°01'·60W.
No. 5 ⌀ Fl G 3s; 54°55'·08N 05°01'·86W.
E Pier Hd ≴ 2 FR (vert) 9m; 54°54'·61N 05°01'·60W.
Corsewall Point ☆ 55°00'·41N 05°09'·58W Fl (5) 30s 34m **22M**; W twr; vis: 027°-257°.
Black Head Old Lighthouse (disused); W tower, 22m; 54°51'·70N 05°08'·80W.

PORTPATRICK
Ldg Lts 050·5°. Front, FG (occas); 54°50'·50N 05°07'·02W. Rear, 68m from front, FG 8m (occas).
Crammag Hd ☆ 54°39'·90N 04°57'·92W Fl 10s 35m **18M**; W twr.
Mull of Galloway ☆, SE end 54°38'·08N 04°51'·45W Fl 20s 99m **28M**; W twr; vis: 182°-105°.

MULL OF GALLOWAY and WIGTOWN BAY
Port William Ldg Lts 105°. Front, Pier Hd Fl G 3s 7m 3M; 54°45'·66N 04°35'·28W. Rear, 130m from front, FG 10m 2M.
Whithorn Ldg Lts 335°. Front, Oc R 8s 7m 7M; Or ♦; 54°42'·01N 04°22'·05W. Rear, 35m from front, Oc R 8s 9m 7M; Or ♦, synch.
Little Ross ≴ Fl 5s 50m 12M; W twr; obsc in Wigtown B when brg more than 103°; 54°45'·93N 04°05'·10W.

KIRKCUDBRIGHT BAY and KIPPFORD
Little Ross NNE end of Is ≴ Fl (2) 5s 21m 5M; Stone bcn; 54°46'·06N 04°05'·02W.
Hestan I, E end ≴ Fl (2) 10s 42m 9M; 54°49'·95N 03°48'·53W.

9.9.5 PASSAGE INFORMATION

Conditions in the SW of Scotland are generally less rugged south of Mull. Some of the remarks at the start of 9.8.5 are equally applicable to this area. The area is covered by Admiralty Leisure Folios 5610, 5611 and, to the south, 5613. Refer to the Clyde Cruising Club's SDs, Admiralty *West Coast of Scotland Pilot* and to *Yachtsman's Pilot to the W Coast of Scotland, Clyde to Colonsay* (Imray/Lawrence). Submarines exercise throughout these waters; see Subfacts for information on active areas.

More Passage Information is threaded between the harbours of this Area.

Some of the following more common *Gaelic* terms may help with navigation: *Acairseid*: anchorage. *Ailean*: meadow. *Aird, ard*: promontory. *Aisir, aisridh*: passage between rocks. *Beag*: little. *Beinn*: mountain. *Bo, boghar, bodha*: rock. *Cala*: harbour. *Camas*: channel, bay. *Caol*: strait. *Cladach*: shore, beach. *Creag*: cliff. *Cumhamn*: narrows. *Dubh, dhubh*: black. *Dun*: castle. *Eilean, eileanan*: island. *Garbh*: rough. *Geal, gheal*: white. *Glas, ghlas*: grey, green. *Inis*: island. *Kyle*: narrow strait. *Linn, Linne*: pool. *Mor, mhor*: large. *Mull*: promontory. *Rinn, roinn*: point. *Ruadh*: red, brown. *Rubha, rhu*: cape. *Sgeir*: rock. *Sruth*: current. *Strath*: river valley. *Tarbert*: isthmus. *Traigh*: beach. *Uig*: bay.

CORRYVRECKAN TO CRINAN

(AC 2326, 2343) ▶ *Between Scarba and Jura is the Gulf of Corryvreckan (AC 2343) which is best avoided, and should never be attempted by small craft except at slack water and in calm conditions. (In any event the Sound of Luing is always a safer and not much longer alternative.) The Gulf has a least width of 6ca and is free of dangers apart from its very strong tides which, in conjunction with a very uneven bottom, cause extreme turbulence. This is particularly dangerous with strong W winds over a W-going (flood) tide which spews out several miles to seaward of the gulf, with overfalls extending 5M from the W of ent (The Great Race). Keep to the S side of the gulf to avoid the worst turbulence and the whirlpool known as The Hag, caused by depths of only 29m, as opposed to more than 100m in the fairway.*

The W-going stream in the gulf begins at HW Oban + 0410, and the E-going at HW Oban – 0210. Sp rate W-going is 8·5kn, and E-going about 6kn. The range of tide at sp can vary nearly 2m between the E end of the gulf (1·5m) and the W end (3·4m), with HW 30mins earlier at the E end. Slack water occurs at HW Oban +0400 and –0230 and lasts almost 1 hr at nps, but only 15 mins at sps. On the W-going (flood) stream eddies form both sides of the gulf, but the one on the N (Scarba) shore is more important. Where this eddy meets the main stream off Camas nam Bairneach there is violent turbulence, with heavy overfalls extending W at the division of the eddy and the main stream.

◄ There are temp anchs with the wind in the right quarter in Bàgh Gleann a' Mhaoil in the SE corner of Scarba, and in Bàgh Gleann nam Muc at N end of Jura but the latter has rks in approaches E and SW of Eilean Beag.

SE of Corryvreckan is Loch Crinan, which leads to the Crinan Canal. Beware Black Rk, 2m high and 2ca N of the canal sea lock, and dangers extending 100m from the rock.

WEST OF JURA TO ISLAY

(AC 2481, 2168) The W coasts of Colonsay and Oronsay (AC 2169) are fringed with dangers up to 2M offshore. The two islands are separated by a narrow chan which dries and has an overhead cable (10m). There are HIE ⚓s at Scalasaig.

The Sound of Islay presents no difficulty; hold to the Islay shore, where all dangers are close in. ▶ *The N-going stream begins at HW Oban + 0440, and the S-going at HW Oban – 0140. Main flood begins HW Oban +0545. Streams turn approx 1 hr earlier in Gigha Sd and at Kintyre and Jura shores. S going stream for 9hrs close inshore between Gigha and Machrihanish starting HW Oban –0530.*

Main ebb begins HW Oban –0015. Streams turn 1 hr earlier in Gigha Sd, Kintyre and Jura shores. Overfalls off McArthur's Hd. The sp rates are 2·5kn at N entrance and 1·5kn at S entrance, but reaching 5kn in the narrows off Port Askaig.◄ There are anchs in the Sound, but holding ground is mostly poor. The best places are alongside at Port Askaig, or at anch off the distillery in Bunnahabhain B, 2·5M to N. ▶ *There are overfalls off McArthur's Hd (Islay side of S entrance) during the S-going stream.* ◄

The N coast of Islay and Rhinns of Islay are very exposed. In the N there is anch SE of Nave Island at entrance to Loch Gruinart; beware Balach Rks which dry, just to N. ▶ *To the SW off Orsay (lt), Frenchman's Rks and W Bank there is a race and overfalls which should be cleared by 3M. Here the NW-going stream begins at HW Oban + 0530, and the SE-going at HW Oban – 0040; sp rates are 6-8kn inshore, but decrease to 3kn 5M offshore.* ◄ Loch Indaal gives some shelter; beware rks extending from Laggan Pt on E side of ent. Off the Mull of Oa there are further overfalls. Port Ellen, the main hbr on Islay, has HIE ⚓s; there are some dangers in approach, and it is exposed to S; see AC 2474.

SOUND OF JURA TO GIGHA

(AC 2397, 2396, 2168) From Crinan to Gigha the Sound of Jura is safe if a mid-chan course is held. Ruadh Sgeir (lt) are rocky ledges in mid-fairway, about 3M W of Crinan. Loch Sween (AC 2397) can be approached N or SE of MacCormaig Islands, where there is an attractive anch on NE side of Eilean Mor, but exposed to NE. Coming from N beware Keills Rk and Danna Rk. Sgeirean a Mhain is a rk in fairway 1·5M NE of Castle Sween (conspic on SE shore). Anch at Tayvallich, near head of loch on W side.

W Loch Tarbert (AC 2477) is long and narrow, with good anchs and lts near ent, but unmarked shoals. On entry give a berth of at least 2½ca to Eilean Traighe off N shore, E of Ardpatrick Pt. Dun Skeig, an isolated hill, is conspic on S shore. Good anch near head of loch, 1M by road from E Loch Tarbert, Loch Fyne.

On W side of Sound, near S end of Jura, are The Small Is (AC 2396) across the mouth of Loch na Mile. Beware Goat Rk (dries 0·3m) 1.5ca off s'most Is, Eilean nan Gabhar, behind which is good anch. Also possible to go alongside Craighouse Pier (HIE ⚓). Another anch is in Lowlandman's B, about 3M to N, but exposed to S winds; Ninefoot Rks with depth of 2·4m and ECM lt buoy lie off ent. Skervuile (lt) is a reef to the E, in middle of the Sound.

S of W Loch Tarbert, and about 2M off the Kintyre shore, is Gigha Is (AC 2475). Good anchs on E side in Druimeyon B and Ardminish B (HIE ⚓s), respectively N and S of Ardminish Pt. Outer and Inner Red Rks (least depth 2m) lie 2M SW of N end of Gigha Is. Dangers extend 1M W off S end of Gigha Is. Gigalum Is and Cara Is are off the S end. Gigha Sound needs very careful pilotage, since there are several dangerous rks, some buoyed/lit, others not. ▶ *The N-going stream begins at HW Oban + 0430, and S-going at HW Oban – 0155, sp rates 1·3kn.* ◄

HARBOURS AND ANCHORAGES IN COLONSAY, JURA, ISLAY AND THE SOUND OF JURA

SCALASAIG, Colonsay, 56°04'·14N 06°10'·86W. AC 2169. HW +0542 on Dover; ML 2·2m. See 9.9.6. Conspic monument ½M SW of hbr. Beware group of rks N of pier hd marked by bn. 2 HIE ♦ berths on N side of pier, inner end approx 2·5m. Inner hbr to SW of pier is safe, but dries. Ldg lts 262°, both FR 8/10m on pier. Also ⚓ clear of cable in **Loch Staosnaig**; SW of Rubha Dubh lt, Fl (2) WR 10s 8m 8/6M; shore-R-230°-W-337°-R-354°. Facilities: D, P, ▦ (all at ✉), FW, Hotel ☎ (01951) 200316, Dr (0951) 200328.

LOCH TARBERT, W Jura, 55°57'·69N 06°00'·06W. AC 2169, 2481. Tides as Rubha A'Mhàil (N tip of Islay). See 9.9.6. HW –0540 on Dover; ML 2·1m; Duration 0600. Excellent shelter inside the loch, but subject to squalls in strong winds; ⚓ outside in Glenbatrick Bay in approx 6m in S winds, or at Bagh Gleann Righ Mor in approx 2m in N winds. To enter inner loch via Cumhann Beag, there are four pairs of ldg marks (W stones) at approx 120°, 150°, 077°, and 188°, the latter astern, to be used in sequence; pilot book required. There are no facilities.

PORT ASKAIG, Islay, 55°50'·87N 06°06'·26W. AC 2168, 2481. HW +0610 on Dover; ML 1·2m. See 9.9.6. Hbr on W side of Sound of Islay. ⚓ close inshore in 4m or secure to ferry pier. Beware strong tide/eddies. ☆ FR at LB. Facilities: FW (hose on pier), Gas, P, R, Hotel, ▦, ✉, ferries to Jura and Kintyre. Other ⚓s in the Sound at: Bunnahabhain (2M N); Whitefarland Bay, Jura, opp Caol Ila distillery; NW of Am Fraoch Eilean (S tip of Jura); Aros Bay, N of Ardmore Pt.

CRAIGHOUSE, SE Jura, 55°49'·99N 05°56'·31W. AC 2168, 2481, 2396. HW +0600 on Dover; ML 0·5m; Duration 0640 np, 0530 sp. See 9.9.6. Good shelter, but squalls occur in W winds. Enter between lt bn on SW end of Eilean nan Gabhar, Fl 5s 7m 8M vis 225°-010°, and unlit bn close SW. There are 8 HIE ⚓s N of pier (☎ (01496) 810332), where yachts may berth alongside; or ⚓ in 5m in poor holding at the N end of Loch na Mile. Facilities: very limited, Bar, FW, ✉, R, ▦, Gas, P & D (cans). **Lowlandman's Bay** is 1M further N, with ECM buoy, Q (3) 10s, marking Nine Foot Rk (2·4m) off the ent. ⚓ to SW of conspic houses, off stone jetty.

LOCH SWEEN, Argyll and Bute, 55°55'·69N 05°41'·26W. AC 2397. HW +0550 on Dover; ML 1·5m; Duration = 0610. See 9.9.7 Carsaig Bay. Off the ent to loch, **Eilean Mòr** (most SW'ly of MacCormaig Isles) has tiny ⚓ on N side in 3m; local transit marks keep clear of two rks, 0·6m and 0·9m. Inside the loch, beware Sgeirean a'Mhain, a rk in mid-chan to S of Taynish Is, 3M from ent. Good shelter in Loch a Bhealaich (⚓ outside **Tayvallich** in approx 7m on boulders) or enter inner hbr to ⚓ W of central reef. There are no lts. Facilities: Gas, Bar, ✉, FW (⚓ by ✉), R, ▦. Close to NE are ⚓s at **Caol Scotnish** and **Fairy Is**, the former obstructed by rks 3ca from ent.

WEST LOCH TARBERT, Argyll and Bute, (Kintyre), 55°45'N 05°36'W. AC 2476. Tides as Gigha Sound, 9.9.6. Good shelter. Ent is S of Eilean Traighe, Fl (2) R 5s, and NW of Dun Skeig, Q (2) 10s, where there is also conspic conical hill (142m). Loch is lit for 5M by 3 bns, QG, QR and QG in sequence, up to Kennacraig ferry pier, 2FG (vert). PHM buoy, QR, is 2½ca NW of pier. Caution: many drying rks and fish farms outside the fairway and near head of loch. ⚓s are NE of Eilean Traighe (beware weed and ferry wash); near Rhu Pt, possible ⚓s; NE of Eilean dà Gallagain, and at loch hd by pier (ru). Tarbert (9.9.9) is 1·5M walk/bus.

GIGHA ISLAND, Argyll and Bute, **55°40´·6N 05°44´·0W**. AC 2168, 2475. HW +0600 on Dover; ML 0·9m; Duration 0530. See 9.9.6. Main ⚓ is **Ardminish Bay**: 12 HIE ⚓s in the centre. Reefs extend off both points, the S'ly reef marked by an unlit PHM buoy. Kiln Rk (dries 1·5m) is close NE of the old ferry jetty. **Druimyeon Bay** is more sheltered in E'lies, but care needed

entering from S. ⚓s sheltered from winds in Kilnaughton Bay, Port Mór (S-W), Bàgh na Dòirlinne (SE-S), W Tarbert Bay (NE). Caolas Gigalum (⚓ 50m SE of pier) is safe in all but NE-E winds. Beware many rks in Gigha Sound. Lts: Fl (2) 6s, on Gamhna Gigha (off NE tip); WCM buoy Fl (9) 15s marks Gigalum Rks, at S end of Gigha. **Ardminish** ☎ (01583) 505254: FW, Gas, P & D (cans), 🅿, ✉, Bar, R, 🛒.

9.9.6 PORT ELLEN

Islay (Argyll and Bute) **55°37´·29N 06°12´·26W** ✿✿⚓⚓✿✿✿

CHARTS AC 2168, 2476; Imray C64

TIDES HW +0620 np, +0130 sp on Dover; ML 0·6. Sea level is much affected by the weather, rising by 1m in S/E gales; at nps the tide is sometimes diurnal and range negligible.

Standard Port OBAN (←)

Times				Height (metres)			
High Water		Low Water		MHWS	MHWN	MLWN	MLWS
0100	0700	0100	0800	4·0	2·9	1·8	0·7
1300	1900	1300	2000				
Differences PORT ELLEN (S Islay)							
−0530	−0050	−0045	−0530	−3·1	−2·1	−1·3	−0·4
SCALASAIG (E Colonsay)							
−0020	−0005	−0015	+0005	−0·1	−0·2	−0·2	−0·2
GLENGARRISDALE BAY (N Jura)							
−0020	−0010	0000	0000	−0·4	−0·2	0·0	−0·2
CRAIGHOUSE (SE Jura)							
−0230	−0250	−0150	−0230	−3·0	−2·4	−1·3	−0·6
RUBHA A'MHÀIL (N Islay)							
−0020	+0005	−0015		−0·3	−0·1	−0·3	−0·1
ARDNAVE POINT (NW Islay)							
−0035	+0010	0000	−0025	−0·4	−0·2	−0·3	−0·1
ORSAY ISLAND (SW Islay)							
−0110	−0110	−0040	−0040	−1·4	−0·6	−0·5	−0·2
BRUICHLADDICH (Islay, Loch Indaal)							
−0105	−0035	−0110	−0110	−1·8	−1·3	−0·4	+0·1
PORT ASKAIG (Sound of Islay)							
−0110	−0030	−0020	−0020	−1·9	−1·4	−0·8	−0·3
GIGHA SOUND (Sound of Jura)							
−0450	−0210	−0130	−0410	−2·5	−1·6	−1·0	−0·1
MACHRIHANISH							
−0520	−0350	−0340	−0540	Mean range 0·5 metres.			

SHELTER Good shelter on pontoons (3m at MLWS), but in S winds swell sets into the bay. 10 HIE ⚓s to W of Rubha Glas; adjacent rks marked by 3 bcns with reflective topmarks. In W'lies ⚓ in Kilnaughton Bay, N of Carraig Fhada lt ho; or 4M ENE at Loch-an-t-Sàilein.

NAVIGATION WPT 55°36´·69N 06°12´·06W, 326°/0·63M to Carraig Fhada lt ho. Beware Otter Rk 4M SE of hbr, rks on both sides of ent and in NE corner of bay. Keep close to pier.

LIGHTS AND MARKS On W side 10 Radio masts (103m) and Carraig Fhada lt ho (conspic), Fl WRG 3s 20m 8/6M; keep in W sector until past the SHM lt buoy. Sgeir nan Ròn Bn Fl R 5s, Ro-Ro Pier 2 FG (vert) and Marina pontoon Fl G 4s. Limits of dredged area around Ro-Ro Pier and pontoon area marked by buoys.

TELEPHONE Moorings (01496)300301/mob 07732191333; MRCC (01475) 729988.

FACILITIES Marina (30 inc ⓥ – welcome, ⚓ in bay), ☎ 300301 for fuel and assistance, dredged to 3m, £12<10m, £14 >10m, D, Slip; **Village** Bar, FW, ✉, R, 🛒, Gas.

MULL OF KINTYRE

(AC 2126, 2199, 2798) From Crinan to Mull of Kintyre is about 50M. Passage round the Mull of Kintyre within 2 or 3 miles of the coast requires great care. Races exist S and SW of the Mull, and fresh to strong S winds cause dangerous breaking seas especially during E-going (flood) tidal streams. Best to keep at least 3 miles offshore and S of Sanda Island. ▶ *In Sanda Sound the W-going stream starts HW Dover −0110, and the E-going stream starts HW Dover +0500. Sp rates 5kn. Close W of the Mull the N-going stream starts at HW Dover −0130, and the S-going stream at HW Dover +0430. Sp rates 5kn. Careful timing is needed, especially W-bound.* ◀ The Traffic Separation Scheme in the North Channel, is only 2M W of the Mull and limits sea-room in the ITZ.

Sanda Sound separates Sanda Island and its rocks and islets from Kintyre. On the mainland shore beware Macosh Rks (dry, PHM lt buoy), forming part of Barley Ridges, 2ca offshore; and Arranman's Barrels, drying and submerged, marked by PHM lt buoy. Sanda Is provides useful stopping point while waiting for the tide. Beware Paterson's Rk (9ca E, dries). There is good anchorage on N side in Sanda Roads. Approach with Boat Ho bearing 155°; beware strong TS across entrance, and drying rocks in middle of bay. See Plan on AC 2126.

MULL OF KINTYRE TO UPPER LOCH FYNE

(AC 2126, 2383, 2381, 2382). ▶ *Once E of Mull of Kintyre, tidal conditions and pilotage much improve.* ◀ Campbeltown is entered N of Island Davaar (lt). 1·5M N off lt ho is Otterard Rk (depth 3·8m), with Long Rk (dries 1·1m) 5ca W of it; only Otterard Rock is buoyed. ▶ *E of Island Davaar tide runs 3kn at sp, and there are overfalls.* ◀

Kilbrannan Sound runs 21M from Island Davaar to Skipness Pt, where it joins Inchmarnock Water, Lower Loch Fyne and Bute Sound. ▶ *There are few dangers apart from overfalls on Erins Bank, 10M S of Skipness, on S-going stream.* ◀ Good anch in Carradale Bay, off Torrisdale Castle. ▶ *There are overfalls off Carradale Pt on S-going stream.* ◀

Lower L Fyne (AC 2381) is mainly clear of dangers to East L Tarbert. On E shore beware rks off Ardlamont Pt; 4M to NW is Skate Is which is best passed to W. 3M S of Ardrishaig beware Big Rk (depth 2·1m). Further N, at entrance to Loch Gilp (mostly dries), note shoals (least depth 1·5m) round Gulnare Rk, PHM lt buoy; also Duncuan Is with dangers extending SW to Sgeir Sgalag (depth 0·6m), buoyed.

Where Upper L Fyne turns NE (The Narrows) it is partly obstructed by Otter Spit (dries 0·9m), extending 8ca WNW from E shore and marked by lt bn. The stream runs up to 2kn here. A buoyed/lit rk, depth less than 2m, lies about 7ca SW of Otter Spit bn. In Upper L Fyne (AC 2382) off Minard Pt, the chan between rks and islands in the fairway is buoyed/lit.

9.9.7 CRINAN CANAL

Argyll and Bute 56°05'·50N 05°33'·38W Crinan ❀❀⌀⌀✿✿✿

CHARTS AC 2326, 2320; Imray C65.

TIDES −0608 Dover; ML 2·1; Duration 0605; HW Crinan is at HW Oban −0045

Standard Port OBAN (←—→)

Times				Height (metres)			
High Water		Low Water		MHWS	MHWN	MLWN	MLWS
0100	0700	0100	0800	4·0	2·9	1·8	0·7
1300	1900	1300	2000				
Differences CARSAIG BAY (56°02'N 05°38'W)							
−0105	−0040	−0050	−0050	−2·1	−1·6	−1·0	−0·4

NOTE: In the Sound of Jura, S of Loch Crinan, the rise of tide occurs mainly during the 3½ hrs after LW; the fall during the 3½ hrs after HW. At other times the changes in level are usually small and irregular.

SHELTER Complete shelter in canal basin; yachts are welcome. Good shelter in Crinan Hbr (E of Eilean da Mheinn) but full of moorings. Except in strong W/N winds, ⌀ E of the canal ent, clear of fairway. Gallanach Bay on N side of L Crinan has good holding in about 3m.

NAVIGATION WPT 56°05'·70N 05°33'·64W, 146°/0·27M to Fl WG 3s lt. Beware Black Rock (2m high) in appr NE of ldg line 146° to dir Fl WG 3s lt. Off NW corner of chartlet, no ⌀ in a nearly rectangular shellfish bed, 6ca by 6ca. SPM lt buoys mark each corner: Fl (4) Y 12s at the NE and NW corners, Fl Y 6s at the SW and SE corners; the latter being about 100m NE of Black Rock.

CANAL Canal is 9M long with 15 locks and 7 opening bridges. Least transit time is 5 to 6 hrs, observing 4kn speed limit. Entry at all tides. Max LOA: 26·82m, 6·09m beam, 2·89m draft (add 0.10m to your salt water draft), mast 28.95m. Vessels NW-bound have right of way. **Lock hrs**: The canal operates 7 days a week during the summer but during the winter periods of closure or partial closure can be expected. Contact the Canal Office for current operating schedule. The lock can be turbulent; have ready long warps and plenty of fenders. The canal is normally closed from Christmas to the New Year. Do not pump out bilge water or toilets in the canal. Contact canal staff if reqd.

BOAT SAFETY SCHEME Transit craft liable to safety checks on gas, fuel, electrics; £1M 3rd party insurance required. Resident craft subject to full safety checks. See 9.8.17.

LIGHTS AND MARKS Crinan Hotel is conspic W bldg. A conspic chy, 3ca SW of hotel, leads 187° into Crinan Hbr. E of sea-lock: Dir Fl WG 3s 8m 4M, vis 114°-W-146°-G-280°. Ent: 2 FG (vert) and 2FR (vert).

R/T VHF Ch **74** 16 only at sea locks.

TELEPHONE (Code 01546) Sea lock 830285; Canal HQ 603210; MRCC (01475) 729988; Marinecall 09068 500463; Police 702201; Dr 462001.

FACILITIES Canal HQ ☎ 603210, www.waterscape.com. All fees are under review; contact office for details. M, L, FW, *Skippers Guide* is essential reading; **Sea Basin** AB (overnight rate available). **Services:** BY, D, Slip, ME, El, ✕, Gas, ACA, C (5 ton), ▣, CH, P (cans), ▦, R, Bar. Use shore toilets, not yacht heads, whilst in canal. **Village** ✉, Ⓑ (Ardrishaig), ⇌ (Oban), ✈ (Glasgow or Macrihanish). There is a wintering park, plus BY and CH, at Cairnbaan for yachts <10m LOA.

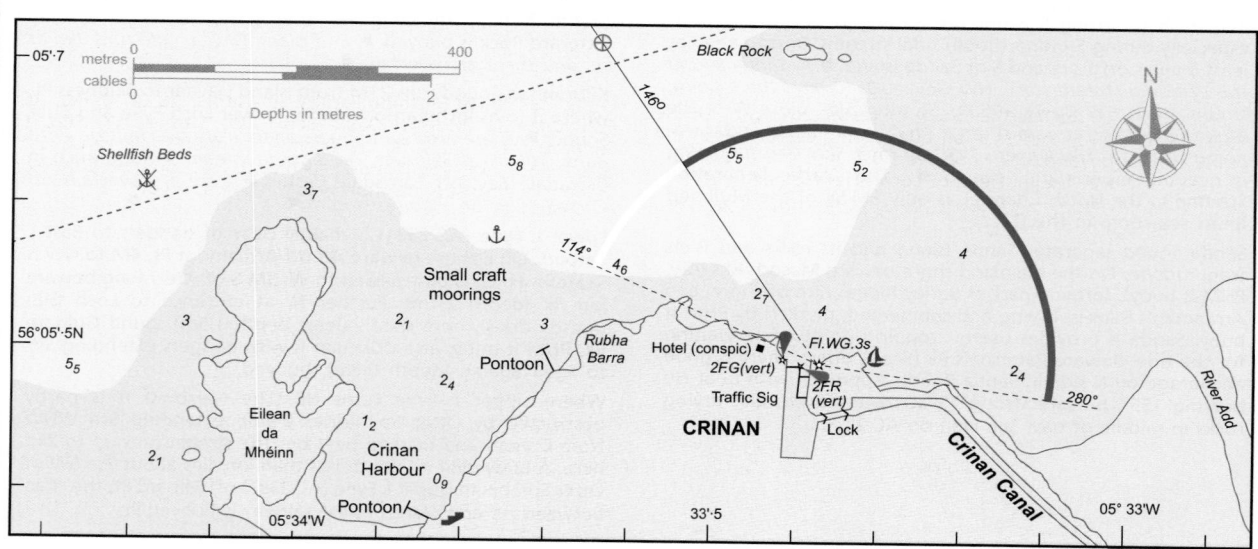

9.9.8 ARDRISHAIG

Argyll and Bute 56°00'·78N 05°26'·62W ❀⊛♋♋✿✿

CHARTS AC 5610, 2131, 2381; Imray C63.

TIDES +0120 Dover; ML 1·9; Duration 0640

Standard Port GREENOCK (→)

Times				Height (metres)			
High Water		Low Water		MHWS	MHWN	MLWN	MLWS
0000	0600	0000	0600	3·4	2·8	1·0	0·3
1200	1800	1200	1800				
Differences ARDRISHAIG							
+0006	+0006	-0015	+0020	0·0	0·0	+0·1	-0·1
INVERARAY							
+0011	+0011	+0034	+0034	-0·1	+0·1	-0·5	-0·2

SHELTER Hbr is sheltered except from strong E'lies; do not berth on pier or ⊥ due to commercial vessels H24. Sea lock into the Crinan Canal is usually left open, however, a waiting pontoon has been installed outside the lock, with restricted depth, for use in fair weather only. Access at all tides. Complete shelter in the canal basin, or beyond lock No 2; see 9.9.7. Also ⊥ 2ca N of hbr, off the W shore of L Gilp. Head of Loch dries for nearly 1M.

NAVIGATION WPT No 48 PHM lt buoy, 56°00'·18N 05°26'·31W, 345°/0·6M to bkwtr lt. Dangerous drying rocks to E of appr chan are marked by No 49 Fl.G.5s SHM buoy.

LIGHTS AND MARKS Conspic W Ho on with block of flats leads 315°between Nos 48 and 49 buoys. Bkwtr lt, L Fl WRG 6s, W339°-350°. Pier is floodlit. Other lights as plan.

R/T VHF Ch 74 16.

TELEPHONE (Code 01546) HM 603210; Sea lock 602458; MRCC (01475) 729988; Marinecall 09068 969652; Police 702201; Dr 462001.

FACILITIES Pier/Hbr ☎ 603210, AB (fees under review), Slip, FW; Sea Lock ☎ 602458; Crinan Canal www.scottishcanals.co.uk/crinan/index.html, AB, M, L, FW, R, Bar; dues, see 9.9.7. Services: BY, ME, El, ✗, CH, D (cans), Gas. Village P & D (cans), ⬛, R, Bar, ✉, Ⓑ, ⇌ (bus to Oban), ✈ (Glasgow or Campbeltown).

9.9.9 TARBERT, LOCH FYNE

Also known as East Loch Tarbert

Argyll and Bute 55°52'·05N 05°24'·22W ❀⊛⊛♋♋♋✿✿

CHARTS AC 5610, 2131, 2381; Imray C63.

TIDES +0120 Dover; ML 1·9; Duration 0640

Standard Port GREENOCK (→)

Times				Height (metres)			
High Water		Low Water		MHWS	MHWN	MLWN	MLWS
0000	0600	0000	0600	3·4	2·8	1·0	0·3
1200	1800	1200	1800				
Differences EAST LOCH TARBERT							
-0005	-0005	0000	-0005	+0·2	+0·1	0·0	0·0

TARBERT

SHELTER Very good in all weathers but gets crowded. Access H24. 120 Ⓥ AB on pontoons; only use Fish Quay if directed by HM. See also Portavadie Marina, below.

NAVIGATION WPT 55°52'·02N 05°23'·03W, 270°/0·7M to Fl R 2·5s lt. Ent is very narrow. Cock Isle divides the ent in half: Main hbr to the S, Buteman's Hole to the N, where ⊥s are fouled by heavy moorings and lost chains. Speed limit 3kn.

LIGHTS AND MARKS Outer ldg lts 252° to S ent: Fl R 2·5s on with Cock Is lt QG. Inner ldg line 239°: same QG, G column, on with conspic ✠ tr. Note: The W sector, 065°-078°, of Eilean na Beithe ☆, Fl WRG 3s 7m 5M (on E shore of Lower Loch Fyne), could be used to position for the initial appr to Tarbert.

R/T Call VHF Ch 14 (0900-1700LT).

TELEPHONE (Code 01880) HM 820344, tarberthbour@btconnect.com; MRCC (01475) 729988; Marinecall 09068 969652; Police 820200; Ⓗ (01546) 602323.

FACILITIES Yacht Berthing Facility 99 visitors, AB £2.10, FW, AC; Fish Quay D (Mon-Fri 0800-1800), FW; Tarbert YC Slip, L; Services: SM, ▣, ACA, ✗, CH. Town P & D (0800-1800 cans), Gas, Gaz, L, ⬛, R, Bar, ✉, Ⓑ, Wi-fi, ⇌ (bus to Glasgow), ✈ (Glasgow/Campbeltown). See also Portavadie Marina, below.

PORTAVADIE MARINA (55°52'·23N 05°18'·98W)
3M east of Tarbert; ☎ (01700) 811075, www.portavadie marina.com, 230 inc Ⓥ, £1.80; D, BH (18 ton), Gas, Gaz, Wi-fi, ▣. Entrance marked by Fl R 2s and Fl (2) G 8s lights. Local shops at Kames (2.5M).

ANCHORAGES IN LOCH FYNE
• Beware discarded wires on seabed throughout the area.
In Lower L Fyne there is a ⚓ at Kilfinan Bay, ☎ (01700) 821201. In Upper Loch Fyne: 4 ⚓ for patrons of the Oyster Bar at Inverary, ⊥ SSW of pier in 4m or dry out NW of the pier; FW (on pier), ✉, ⬛, R, Bar, Gas, bus to Glasgow. On NW bank at Port Ann, Loch Gair and Minard Bay; and on SE bank at Otter Ferry, Strachur Bay (5 ⚓s off Creggans Inn, ☎ (01369) 860279) and St Catherine's.

9.9.10 TIDAL STREAMS AROUND THE MULL OF KINTYRE

9.9.11 FIRTH OF CLYDE AREA

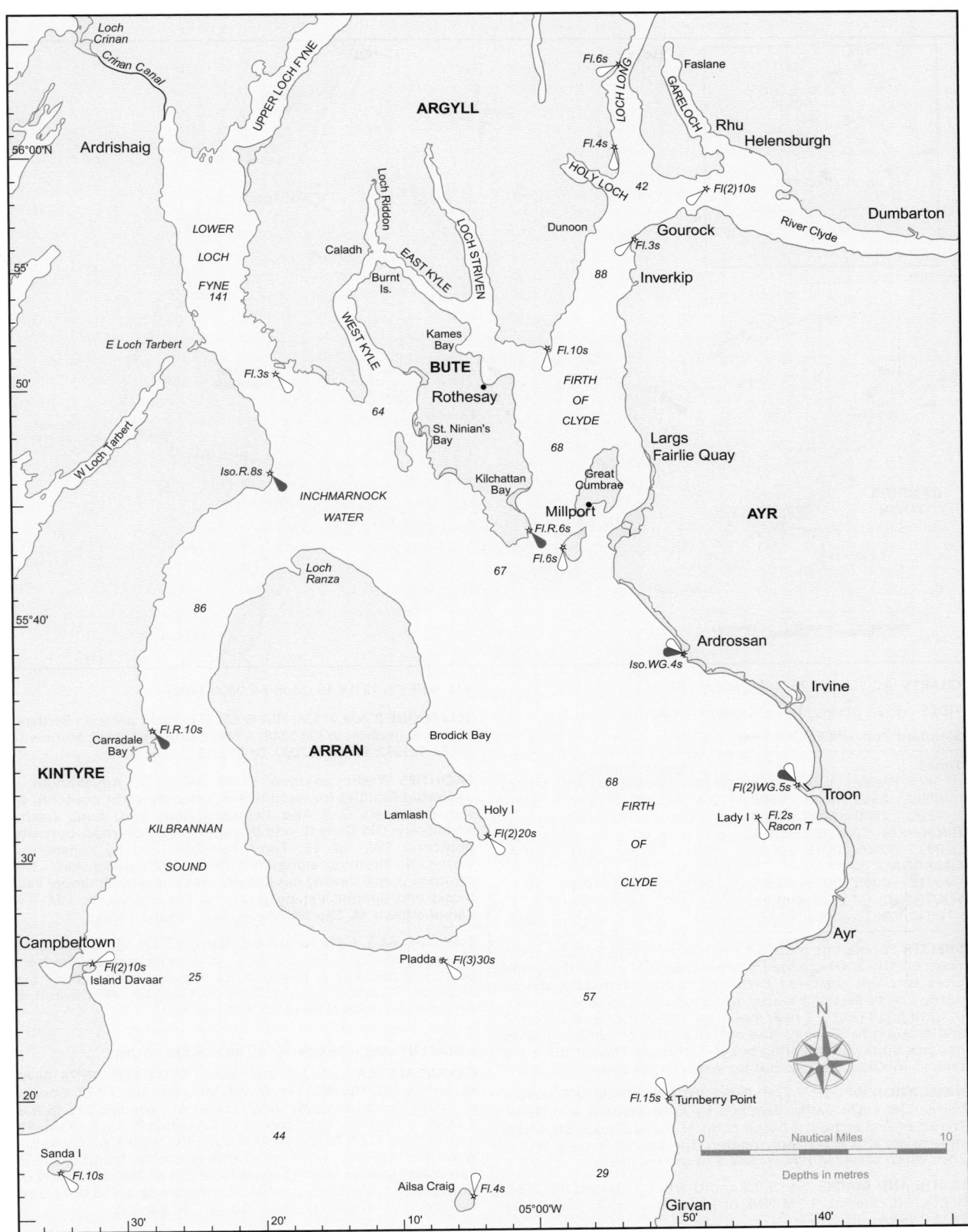

9.9.12 CAMPBELTOWN

Argyll & Bute 55°25'·90N 05°32'·56W Hbr ent ✿✿✿✿☆☆☆☆☆

CHARTS AC 5610, 2126, 1864; Imray C63;.

TIDES +0125 Dover; ML 1·8; Duration 0630

Standard Port GREENOCK (→)

Times				Height (metres)			
High Water		Low Water		MHWS	MHWN	MLWN	MLWS
0000	0600	0000	0600	3·4	2·8	1·0	0·3
1200	1800	1200	1800				
Differences CAMPBELTOWN							
−0025	−0005	−0015	+0005	−0·5	−0·3	+0·1	+0·2
CARRADALE BAY							
−0015	−0005	−0005	+0005	−0·3	−0·2	+0·1	+0·1
SOUTHEND, (Mull of Kintyre)							
−0030	−0010	+0005	+0035	−1·3	−1·2	−0·5	−0·2

SHELTER Good, but gusts off the hills in strong SW'lies. Yacht pontoon (10+20♥) dredged 3·0m is close NW of Old Quay and gives excellent sheltered berthing. Yachts >12m LOA should notify ETA to Berthing Master by ☎ (below). Excellent ⚓ close E of front ldg lt (240°); ⚓ near moorings NNE of the hbr is cluttered and exposed to SE winds: use only in settled conditions and do not pick up private mooring buoys. S of Island Davaar there is a temp ⚓ in Kildalloig Bay, but no access to the loch.

NAVIGATION WPT 55°26'·24N 05°31'·61W, 240°/1·4M to first chan buoys. The ent is easily identified by radio masts N and NE of Trench Pt and conspic lt ho on N tip of Island Davaar off which streams are strong (4kn sp). Caution: The Dhorlin, a bank drying 2·5m which covers at HW, is close S of the ldg line.

LIGHTS AND MARKS See 9.9.5 and chartlet. Otterard Rk (3·8m depth, off chartlet, 1·5M NNE of Island Davaar), is marked by ECM lt buoy.

R/T VHF Ch 12 13 16 (Mon-Fri 0900-1700).

TELEPHONE (Code 01586) HM ☎ 552552; Yacht pontoon Berthing Master ☎ (mobile) 07798 524821; MRCC (01475) 729988; Marinecall 09068 969652; Police 862000; Dr 552105.

FACILITIES Yacht pontoon £1·40, FW, ⊕; **Aqualibrium** – dedicated facilities for yacht crews, opposite yacht pontoon: @, showers, toilets, ▣, R. Also swimming pool, gym, sauna, creche and library. **Old Quay** D (and by cans from across road, opposite pontoon), FW, AB, LB; **Ferry Terminal** used by commercial vessels. No berthing alongside without HM's permission. The attached public slipway has a drying out berth (with timber keel blocks and upright leaning posts) for FVs and yachts, FW, ⊕; **Campbeltown SC** Slip (dinghies), Bar, regular racing.

Town ME, ACA, C (10 ton), P & D (cans), El, CH, Ⓔ, Gas, Gaz, 🛒 (2 supermarkets), R, Bar, ✉, Ⓑ, ▣, Ⓗ, ⬆ toilet about 100m from yacht pontoon, key at Tourist office or police station (H24). Bus 3/day to Glasgow, ✈ twice daily to Glasgow, ⇌ (nearest is Arrochar, 90 miles N by road). Car hire/taxi.

ADJACENT ANCHORAGE IN KILBRANNAN SOUND

CARRADALE BAY, Argyll and Bute, **55°34'·40N 05°28'·66W**. AC 5610, 2131, HW+0115 on Dover. ML 1·8m. See 9.9.12. Good ⚓ in 7m off Torrisdale Castle in SW corner of Carradale Bay. In N & E winds ⚓ in NE corner of bay, W of Carradale Pt 3ca E of this Pt, a PHM buoy Fl (2) R 12s marks Cruban Rk. With S & SE winds a swell sets into bay, when good shelter can be found 1M N in **Carradale Harbour** (Port Crannaich); if full of FVs, ⚓ 100m N of Hbr. Bkwtr lt, Fl R 10s 5m 6M. Piermaster ☎ (01583) 431228. Facilities: FW on pier, D (cans), Gas, 🛒, R, Bar, ✉.

9.9.13 LAMLASH

Isle of Arran, N Ayrshire **55°32'·00N 05°07'·06W**
⊛⊛⊛☆☆☆☆☆☆☆

CHARTS AC 5610, 2131, 2220, 1864; Imray C63.

TIDES +0115 Dover; ML no data; Duration 0635

Standard Port GREENOCK (→)

Times				Height (metres)			
High Water		Low Water		MHWS	MHWN	MLWN	MLWS
0000	0600	0000	0600	3·4	2·8	1·0	0·3
1200	1800	1200	1800				
Differences LAMLASH							
−0016	−0036	−0024	−0004	−0·2	−0·2	No data	
BRODICK BAY							
−0013	−0013	−0008	−0008	−0·2	−0·1	0·0	+0·1
LOCH RANZA							
−0015	−0005	−0010	−0005	−0·4	−0·3	−0·1	0·0

SHELTER Very good in all weathers. Lamlash is a natural hbr with sheltered anchorages as follows: off Lamlash except in E'lies – depth may be 20m but shoals rapidly to the W; off Kingscross Point, good except in strong N/NW winds; off the NW of Holy Island in E'lies. ⚓ off Lamlash Pier. Dry out against pier if in need of repairs. See also Brodick 5M N, and Loch Ranza 14M N (RH col).

NAVIGATION WPT 55°32'·63N 05°03'·06W, 270°/1M to N Chan buoy (Fl R 6s).

Beware: submarines exercise frequently in this area (see 9.9.16), and also wreck of landing craft (charted) off farmhouse on Holy Is.

LIGHTS AND MARKS See 9.9.5 and chartlet.

R/T None.

TELEPHONE (Code 01770) MRCC (01475) 729988; Marinecall 09068 969652; Police 302573; Ⓗ 600777.

FACILITIES Lamlash Old Pier Slip (£3–£5), L, FW, CH, ✕; **Arran YC** 25 ⚓ £10 via: ☎ 01770 600333. **Village** (Lamlash/Brodick); ME, P & D (cans), Bar, R, 🍴, ✉, ⇌ (bus to Brodick, Ferry to Ardrossan), ✈ (Glasgow or Prestwick).

OTHER HARBOURS ON ARRAN (See AC 5610)

BRODICK, Arran, **55°35'·50N 05°08'·66W**. AC 2131, 2220, 1864. HW +0115 on Dover; ML 1·8m; Duration 0635. See 9.9.13. Shelter is good except in E winds. ⚓ W of ferry pier in 3m; on NW side just below the Castle in 4·5m, or further N off Merkland Pt in 3-4m. Also 5 ⚓s. There are no navigational dangers but the bay is in a submarine exercise area; see 9.9.16. Only lts are 2FR (vert) 9/7m 4M on pier hd and Admiralty buoy, Fl Y 2s, 5ca N of pier. Facilities: Ⓑ, Bar, P & D (cans), FW (at pier hd), ME, ✉, R, 🍴. Ferry to Ardrossan.

LOCH RANZA, Arran, **55°42'·60N 05°17'·96W**. AC 2131, 2383, 2221. HW +0120 on Dover; ML 1·7m; Duration 0635. See 9.9.13. Good shelter, but swell enters loch with N'lies. The 850m mountain 4M to S causes fierce squalls in the loch with S winds. Beware Screda Reef extending SW off Newton Pt. 12 ⚓s. ⚓ in 5m off castle (conspic); holding is suspect in soft mud. Dinghy landing pontoon at Lochranza. 2F.G lts on RoRo pier at Coillemore. S shore dries. Facilities: Bar, FW at ferry slip, ✉, R, 🍴. Ferry to Claonaig.

HARBOURS AND ANCHORAGES AROUND BUTE
(Clockwise from Garroch Head, S tip of Bute) (See AC 5610)

ST NINIAN'S BAY, Bute, **55°48'·15N 05°07'·86W**. AC 2221, 2383. Inchmarnock Is gives some shelter from the W, but Sound is exposed to S'lies. At S end, beware Shearwater Rk, 0·9m, almost in mid-sound. ⚓ in about 7m, 2ca E of St Ninian's Pt; beware drying spit to S of this Pt. Or ⚓ off E side of Inchmarnock, close abeam Midpark Farm.

WEST KYLE, Bute, **55°54'N 05°12'·7W**. AC1906. Tides, see 9.9.17. (Tighnabruaich). On W bank PHM buoys, each Fl R 4s, mark Ardlamont Pt, Carry Pt and Rubha Ban; N of which are two Fl Y buoys (fish farms). ⚓ close off Kames or Tighnabruaich, where space allows; or in Black Farland Bay (N of Rubha Dubh). Some ⚓s off Kames and Royal Hotels, maintained by them on a 'use at own risk basis': Kames Hotel ☎ (01700) 811489; Kyles of Bute Hotel 811350; Royal Hotel 811239; and Tighnabruaich Hotel 811615. Facilities: FW, D (cans), BY, 🍴.

CALADH HARBOUR, Argyll and Bute, **55°56'·00N, 05°11'·73W**. AC 1906. HW (Tighnabruaich) +0015 on Dover; ML 2·1m. See 9.9.17. Perfectly sheltered natural hbr on W side of ent to Loch Riddon. Enter Caladh Hbr to N or S of Eilean Dubh; keep to the middle of the S passage. When using the N ent, keep between R and G bns to clear a drying rk marked by perch. ⚓ in the middle of hbr clear of moorings. No facilities/stores; see West Kyle above.

LOCH RIDDON, Argyll and Bute, **55°57'N 05°11'·6W**. AC 1906. Tides, see 9.9.17. Water is deep for 1·3M N of Caladh and shore is steep-to; upper 1·5M of loch dries. ⚓ on W side close N of Ormidale pier; on E side at Salthouse; off Eilean Dearg (One Tree Is); and at NW corner of Fearnoch Bay.

BURNT ISLANDS, Bute, **55°55'·76N 05°10'·39W**. AC 1906. Tides, see 9.9.17. The three islands (Eilean Mor, Fraoich and Buidhe) straddle the East Kyle. There are 2 channels: North, between Buidhe and the other 2 islets, is narrow, short and marked by 2 SHM buoys (the NW'ly one is Fl G 3s), and one PHM buoy, Fl R 2s. South chan lies between Bute and Fraoich/Mor; it is unlit, but marked by one PHM and two SHM buoys. Depths may be less than charted. A SHM buoy, Fl G 3s, is off Rubha a' Bhodaich, 4ca ESE. Direction of buoyage is to SE. Sp streams reach 5kn in N Chan and 3kn in S Chan. ⚓ in Wreck Bay, Balnakailly Bay or in the lee of Buidhe and Mor in W'lies; also W of Colintraive Pt, clear of ferry and cables. There are 6 ⚓s off the hotel, ☎ (01700) 841207.

KAMES BAY, Bute, **55°51'·7N 05°04'·81W**. AC 1906, 1867. Tides as Rothesay. Deep water bay, but dries 2ca off head of loch and 1ca off NW shore. AB in marina, 55 inc ❻, £1·85/m, on S side of bay at Port Bannatyne. P & D in cans, CH, Gas, BY, BH (25 ton). ⚓ off Port Bannatyne (clear of moorings) W of unmarked ruined jetty. Beware drying rks 1ca off Ardbeg Pt. No lts. Facilities: BY, FW, Gas, 🍴, Bar, ✉.

KILCHATTAN BAY, Bute, **55°45'N 05°01'·1W**. AC 1907. Bay is deep, but dries 3ca off the W shore. Temp ⚓s only in offshore winds: off the village on SW side, or on N side near Kerrytonlia Pt. 4 ⚓s for hotel guests. Rubh' an Eun Lt, Fl R 6s, is 1·1M to SSE. Facilities: FW, 🍴, ✉, bus Rothesay.

9.9.14 FAIRLIE QUAY

N Ayrshire 55°46'·07N 04°51'·78W ❀⚓❀❀

CHARTS AC 5610, 2131, 1907, 1867; Imray C63, 2900 Series.

TIDES +0105 Dover; ML 1·9; Duration 0640

Standard Port GREENOCK (→)

Times				Height (metres)			
High Water		Low Water		MHWS	MHWN	MLWN	MLWS
0000	0600	0000	0600	3·4	2·8	1·0	0·3
1200	1800	1200	1800				
Differences MILLPORT							
−0005	−0025	−0025	−0005	0·0	−0·1	0·0	0·1

SHELTER Access H24 with at least 2.6m at berths. Poor shelter; pontoon subject to swell in fresh conditions and wash from passing vessels. Craft should not be left unsupervised unless calm settled weather is forecast. Cumbrae Island gives shelter from westerlies; Largs Channel is open to S or N winds.

NAVIGATION WPT 55°46'·08N 04°51'·84W. From S beware Hunterston Sands, Southannan Sands and outfalls from Hunterston Power Stn (conspic).

LIGHTS AND MARKS Lts as on chartlet. Fairlie Quay, 2 FG (vert) N & S ends of Pier.

R/T *Fairlie Quay Marina* Ch 80 M (H24).

TELEPHONE (Code 01475) Fairlie Quay 568267; MRCC 729988; Dr 673380; Ⓗ 733777; Marinecall 09068 969652; Police 674651.

FACILITIES **Fairlie Quay** Some Ⓥ £12/yacht, Fuel H24: D, SM, BY, ME, El, ⚒, BH (80 ton), CH, Gas. **Fairlie YC; Town** 🛒, R, Bar, ⊠, Ⓑ, ⇌ (Fairlie & Largs; 50 mins to Glasgow), ✈.

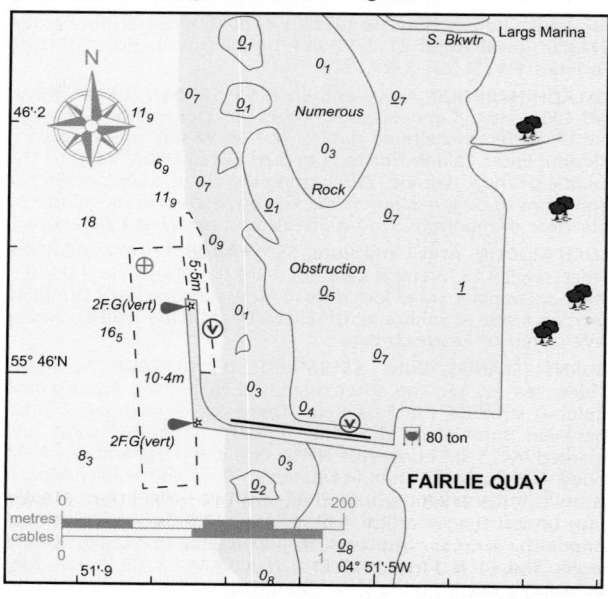

FAIRLIE QUAY

9.9.15 LARGS

N Ayrshire 55°46'·40N 04°51'·84W ❀❀⚓⚓⚓❀❀

CHARTS AC 5610, 2131, 1907, 1867; Imray C63, 2900 Series.

TIDES +0105 Dover; ML 1·9; Duration 0640

Standard Port GREENOCK (→)

Times				Heights (metres)			
High Water		Low Water		MHWS	MHWN	MLWN	MLWS
0000	0600	0000	0600	3·4	2·8	1·0	0·3
1200	1800	1200	1800				
Differences MILLPORT							
−0005	−0025	−0025	−0005	0·0	−0·1	0·0	+0·1

SHELTER Excellent in Largs Yacht Haven, access all tides (2·5m in ent; 3m deep berths). 7 pontoons; Ⓥ on 'C/D'. Cumbrae Is gives shelter from W'lies; Largs Chan is open to S or N winds.

NAVIGATION WPT 55°46'·40N 04°51'·84W, SWM lt buoy, off ent. From S beware Hunterston Sands, Southannan Sands and outfalls from Hunterston Power Stn (conspic). From the S bkwtr to Fairlie Quay is a restricted, no ⚓ area.

LIGHTS AND MARKS 'Pencil' monument (12m) conspic 4ca N of ent. Lts as on chartlet. Largs Pier, 2 FG (vert) when vessel expected.

R/T *Largs Yacht Haven* Ch 80 M (H24).

TELEPHONE (Code 01475) Largs Yacht Haven 675333; www.yachthavens.com; Largs SC 670000; MRCC 729988; Dr 673380; Ⓗ 733777; Marinecall 09068 969652; Police 674651.

FACILITIES **Largs Yacht Haven** (755, some Ⓥ), £2.58, Wi-fi, Fuel H24: D, P, 🛢, SM, BY, C (17 ton), ME, El, ⚒, ⚓, BH (70 ton), Divers, Ⓔ,CH, 🅾, Ice, Gas, Gaz, Slip (access H24), Bar, R.**Town** 🛒, R, Bar, ⊠, Ⓑ, ⇌ (dep Largs every H −10; 50 mins to Glasgow), ✈.

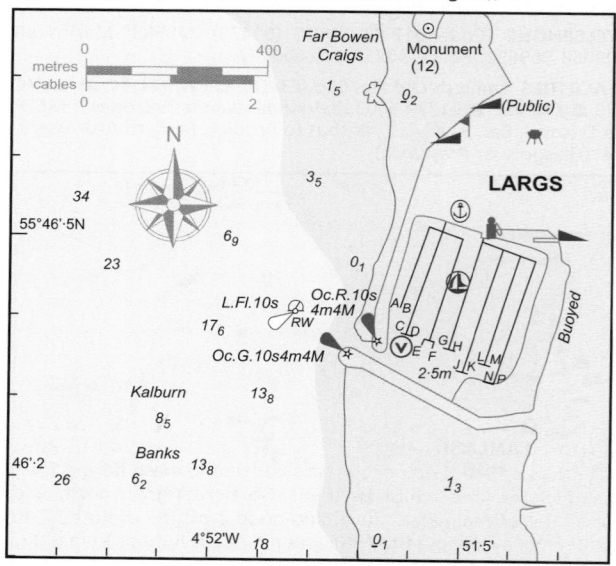

LARGS

ARRAN, BUTE AND FIRTH OF CLYDE

(AC1906, 1907) Arran's mountains tend to cause squalls or calms, but there are good anchorages at Lamlash, Brodick and Loch Ranza. Sannox Rock (depth 1·5m) is 2½ca off Arran coast 8M N of Lamlash. 1ca off W side of Inchmarnock is Tra na-h-uil, a rock drying 1·5m. In Inchmarnock Sound, Shearwater Rk (depth 0·9m) lies in centre of S entrance.

The Kyles of Bute are attractive channels N of Bute, and straightforward apart from the Burnt Islands where it is best to take the north channel, narrow but well buoyed, passing between Eilean Buidhe and Eilean Fraoich/Eilean Mor. ▶Spring

stream may reach 5kn.◀ Caladh Hbr is a beautiful anchorage 7ca NW of Burnt Is.

The N lochs in Firth of Clyde are less attractive. Loch Goil is worth a visit; Loch Long is squally with few anchs but no hidden dangers; Gareloch has Rhu Marina, Faslane submarine base and small craft moorings at the northern end. ▶ *Navigation in Firth of Clyde is easy since tidal streams are weak, seldom exceeding 1kn.* ◀ Channels are well marked; but beware unlit moorings commercial and naval shipping. There are marinas on the mainland at Largs, Holy Loch, Portavadie and Inverkip. Rothesay Hbr on E Bute, and Kilchattan B (anch 6M to S) are both sheltered from SSE to WNW.

9.9.16 SUBMARINE EXERCISE AREAS

Submarines on the surface and at periscope depth keep a constant listening watch on Ch 16. Submarines on the surface will comply strictly with IRPCS; submarines at periscope depth will not close to within 1500 yds of a FV without her express agreement. See 3.13.1 for more guidance.

Details of submarine activity in the Exercise Areas between Barra and the Isle of Man are broadcast by MRCCs on a specified VHF Ch after an initial announcement on Ch 16 at the following times:

Stornoway	0710	1910 UT
Clyde	0810	2010 UT
Belfast	0710	1910 UT

The areas are referred to by the names given in the table on the right, rather than by the numbers indicated on the chartlet on Page 490. For Areas 1–26 (North of Mull), see 9.8.22.

General information on SUBFACTS is also broadcast twice daily at 0620 & 1820 UT on Navtex. Stornoway and Clyde MRCCs will provide SUBFACTS on request; call on Ch 16.

A 'Fisherman's hotline' (☎ (01436) 677201) is available on a 24 hour basis and may be used for any queries relating to SUBFACTS from any mariner.

22	Barra	52	Boyle
23	Hebrides Central	53	Orsay
24	Hawes	54	Islay
25	Eigg	55	Otter
26	Hebrides South	56	Gigha
27	Ford	57	Earadale
28	Tiree	58	Lochranza
29	Staffa	59	Davaar
30	Mackenzie	60	Brodick
31	Mull	61	Irvine
32	Linnhe	62	Lamlash
33	Jura Sound	63	Ayr
34	Fyne	64	Skerries
35	Minard	65	Rathlin
36	Tarbert	66	Kintyre
37	Skipness	67	Sanda
38	West Kyle	68	Stafnish
39	Striven	69	Pladda
40	East Kyle	70	Turnberry
41	Goil	71	Torr
42	Long	72	Mermaid
43	Cove	73	Ailsa
44	Gareloch	74	Maiden
45	Rosneath	75	Corsewall
46	Cumbrae	76	Ballantrae
47	Garroch	77	Magee
48	Laggan	78	Londonderry
49	Blackstone	79	Beaufort
50	Place	80	Ardglass
51	Colonsay	81	Peel

9.9.17 ROTHESAY

Isle of Bute, Argyll and Bute **55°50′·32N 05°03′·08W**
❀❀❀☆☆❀☆

CHARTS AC 5610, 2131, 1907, 1906, 1867; Imray C63, 2900 Series;.

TIDES +0100 Dover; ML 1·9; Duration 0640

Standard Port GREENOCK (→)

Times				Height (metres)			
High Water		Low Water		MHWS	MHWN	MLWN	MLWS
0000	0600	0000	0600	3·4	2·8	1·0	0·3
1200	1800	1200	1800				
Differences ROTHESAY BAY							
−0020	−0015	−0010	−0002	+0·2	+0·2	+0·2	+0·2
RUBHA BHODACH (Burnt Is)							
−0020	−0010	−0007	−0007	−0·2	−0·1	+0·2	+0·2
TIGHNABRUAICH							
+0007	−0010	−0002	−0015	0·0	+0·2	+0·4	+0·5

SHELTER Good in Outer and Inner Harbours, and on pontoons S of West Arm, but beware of very strong easterly flow towards the rocks on the E side of the harbour due to wash during ferry manoeuvres (and whilst berthed). No berthing on north and east faces of Main Pier. 20 ⚓, and good ⚓ off Isle of Bute SC, in Rothesay Bay. Exposed to N/NE when Kyles of Bute or Kames Bay offer better shelter.

NAVIGATION WPT 55°51′·00N 05°02′·76W, 194°/0·69M to Outer hbr ent. From E keep 1ca off Bogany Pt PHM buoy, Fl R 4s. Call HM for bridge openings to Inner Harbour.

LIGHTS AND MARKS Lts as chartlet, hard to see against shore lts. Conspicuous church spire leads 190° to outer hbr; at night beware large, unlit Admiralty buoy 'MK' on this bearing 5½ca from harbour. 3½ca N of hbr is Rothesay 'A' mooring buoy, Fl Y 2s.

R/T Bute Berthing Ch 16 **M**; Rothesay Harbour Ch **16**.

TELEPHONE (Code 01700) HM 503842; Bute Berthing Co 07799

724225; MRCC (01475) 729988; Marinecall 09068 969652; Police 894000; Dr 503985; ⊞ 503938.

FACILITIES 60 Ⓥ AB (Bute Berthing Co) £14 for 8m LOA, £19 for 11m LOA, ⬚, Slip, L, FW, ME, 🔧; showers/toilets on Rothesay Pier; D by arrangement week days only (min 200 galls). ⚓s £7/night. **Town** P & D (closes 1800), @ (0900-1700) 🛒, R, Bar, ⊠, Ⓑ, ⇌ (Ferry to Wemyss Bay), ✈ (Glasgow).

GREAT CUMBRAE ISLAND

MILLPORT, Great Cumbrae, N Ayrshire, **55°45′·00N 04°55′·82W**. AC 5610, 1867, 1907. HW +0100 on Dover; ML 1·9m; Duration 0640. See 9.9.17. Good shelter, except in S'lies. ⚓ in approx 3m S of pier or E of the Eileans. 12 ⚓s 1½ca SSE of pier. Ldg marks: pier hd on with ✠ twr 333°; or ldg lts 333°, both FR 7/9m 5M, between the Spoig and the Eileans, QG. Unmarked, drying rk is close E of ldg line. HM ☎ (01475) 530826. **Town** CH, Bar, Gas, D, P, FW, ⊠, R, Slip, 🛒. Possible temporary AB on pontoon belonging to SportScotland off NE of island (approx 55°47′·1N 04°53′·8W) in 3.5m–4.5m; no services.

SUBMARINE EXERCISE AREA MAP

9.9.18 INVERKIP (KIP MARINA)

Inverclyde 55°54'·50N 04°53'·00W ✵✵✵☆☆☆✿✿✿

CHARTS AC 5610, 2131, 1907; Imray C63, 2900 Series.

TIDES +0110 Dover; ML 1·8; Duration 0640

Standard Port GREENOCK (⟶)

Times				Height (metres)			
High Water		Low Water		MHWS	MHWN	MLWN	MLWS
0000	0600	0000	0600	3·4	2·8	1·0	0·3
1200	1800	1200	1800				
Differences WEMYSS BAY							
−0005	−0005	−0005	−0005	0·0	0·0	+0·1	+0·1

SHELTER Excellent inside marina. Chan and marina are dredged 3·5m; accessible H24. Inverkip Bay is exposed to SW/NW winds.

NAVIGATION WPT 55°54'·49N 04°52'·95W, Kip SHM buoy, Fl G 5s, at ent to buoyed chan; beware shifting bank to the N.

LIGHTS AND MARKS SHM 55°54'·55N 04°54'·47W Fl G 1·06M 093° to entr which is ½M N of conspic chmy (238m). SPM buoy marks sewer outfall off Ardgowan Pt. From Kip SHM buoy, 3 SHM and 3 PHM buoys mark 365m long appr chan.

R/T *Kip Marina* Ch **80** M (H24). *Clydeport Estuary Radio* VHF Ch **12** 16 (H24). Info on weather and traffic available on request.

TELEPHONE (Code 01475) MRCC 729988; Marinecall 09068 969652; Police 521222; Dr 520248; Ⓗ 33777.

FACILITIES Kip Marina ☎ 521485, www.scottishmarinas.co.uk; (700 + Ⓥ) £2.15, £12 <5hrs), Wi-fi, D, P (cans), ✕, C, ME, El, Ⓔ, SM, CH, Diver, BH (50 ton), 🛒, R, Bar, 🄌, Gas, Gaz, YC. **Town** ✉ Ⓑ (Gourock), ⇌, ✈ (Glasgow).

ADJACENT ANCHORAGE

DUNOON, Argyll and Bute, **55°56'·70N 04°55'·20W**. AC 5610, 2131, 1907, 1994. Use Greenock tides. Temp ⚓ in West or East Bays (S and N of Dunoon Pt). The former is open to the S; the latter more shoal. Six HIE ⚓s (free, but condition uncertain) in each bay; call ☎ (01369) 703785. The Gantocks, drying rks 3ca SE of Dunoon Pt, have W ○ bn tr, Fl R 6s 12m 6M. 2FR (vert) on ferry pier. Facilities: P & D (cans), 🛒, R, Bar, ✉, Gas, ferry to Gourock. 3 ⚓s off Inellan, 3·7M S of Dunoon, ☎ (01369) 830445.

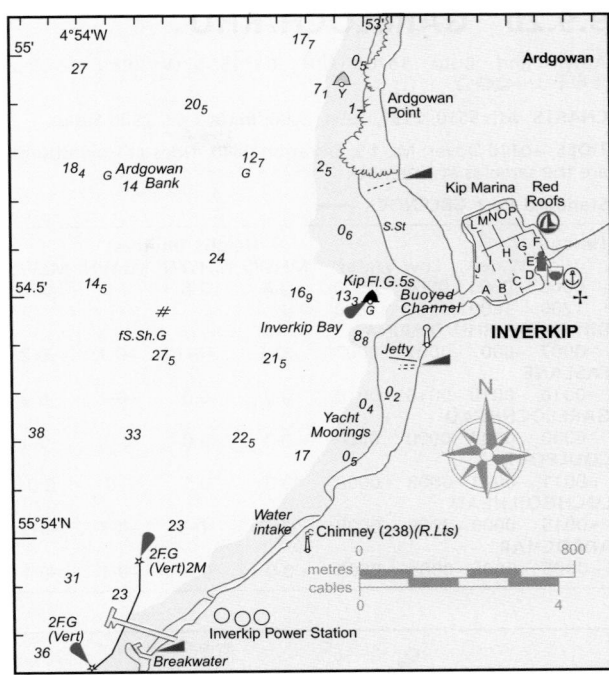

ANCHORAGE IN THE UPPER FIRTH OF CLYDE

GOUROCK, Inverclyde, **55°58'·00N 04°49'·00W**. AC 5610, 2131, 1994, Imray C63, 2900 Series; OS 63. Use Greenock tides. ⚓ in West Bay, beware of moorings. It is exposed in NW/NE'lies. Beware foul ground in Gourock Bay. No navigational dangers, but much shipping and ferries in the Clyde. The S edge of the Firth of Clyde recommended channel lies 2ca N of Kempock Pt. The pier at the S end of Gourock Bay is disused and unsafe. Facilities: Royal Gourock YC ☎ 632983 M, L, FW, ME, Slip, 🛒, R, Bar. Services: SM. Town: P, D (cans) 🛒, R, Bar, ✉, Ⓑ, ⇌, Ferry (to Dunoon) ✈ (Glasgow).

9.9.19 HOLY LOCH

Argyll **55°59'·03N 04°56'·82W** ✵✵✵☆☆☆✿✿✿

CHARTS AC 5610, 2131, 1994; Imray C63, 2900 Series.

TIDES +0122 Dover; ML 2·0; Duration 0640

Standard Port GREENOCK (⟶)

SHELTER Good, but exposed to to E/NE.

NAVIGATION WPT 55°59'·03N 04°55'·75W 270° to marina ent 0.60M. No offshore dangers. Holy Loch is controlled by QHM Clyde but navigation is not restricted; keep well clear of ferries when entering or leaving the loch.

LIGHTS AND MARKS No 30 SCM 55°58'·75N 04°53'·82W off Strone Pt. 2FR at SE end of pier. Marina floodlit.

R/T *Holy Loch Marina* Ch **80** M.

TELEPHONE (Code 01369) MRCC (01475) 729988; Marinecall 09068 969652; Police 702222; Dr 703279; Ⓗ 704341.

FACILITIES Marina (270 + Ⓥ in 3m) £2.00, short stay £5. ☎ 701800, www.holylochmarina.co.uk, D, P, C, BH (25 ton), BY, CH, Gas, Wi-fi, 🄌 ✕. Possible AB on breakwater pontoon for larger yachts in depth >5m, but open to the E. **Holy Loch SC** ☎ 702707.

Sandbank (town) PO, 🛒. Ferries from Sandbank to Gourock connecting with trains and coaches to Glasgow Airport.

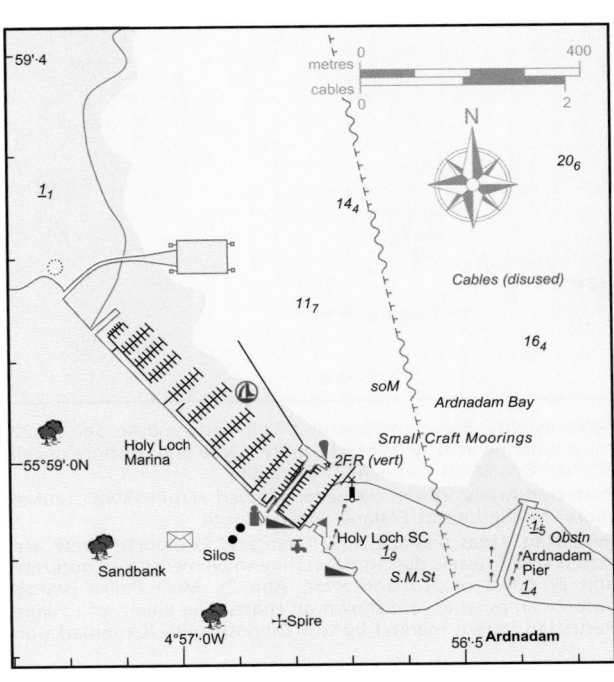

9.9.20 GARELOCH/RHU

Argyll and Bute 56°00'·70N 04°46'·57W (Rhu Marina)

CHARTS AC 5610, 2131, 1994, 2000; Imray C63, 2900 Series.

TIDES +0110 Dover; ML 1·9; Duration 0640. Tides at Helensburgh are the same as at Greenock.

Standard Port GREENOCK (→)

Times				Height (metres)			
High Water		Low Water		MHWS	MHWN	MLWN	MLWS
0000	0600	0000	0600	3·4	2·8	1·0	0·3
1200	1800	1200	1800				
Differences RHU MARINA							
−0007	−0007	−0007	−0007	−0·1	−0·1	−0·1	−0·2
FASLANE							
−0010	−0010	−0010	−0010	0·0	0·0	−0·1	−0·2
GARELOCHHEAD							
0000	0000	0000	0000	0·0	0·0	0·0	−0·1
COULPORT							
−0011	−0011	−0008	−0008	0·0	0·0	0·0	0·0
LOCHGOILHEAD							
+0015	0000	−0005	−0005	−0·2	−0·3	−0·3	−0·3
ARROCHAR							
−0005	−0005	−0005	−0005	0·0	0·0	−0·1	−0·1

BYELAWS Loch Long and Gareloch are Dockyard Ports under the jurisdiction of the Queen's Harbour Master. All submarines and other warships at anchor or underway have an Exclusion Zone around them enforced by MOD Police.

SHELTER Rhu Marina is entered between low, floating wavebreaks on its S and W sides, not easy to find at night; beware cross-tides. On E/SE sides a rock bkwtr 1m above MHWS protects from strong SE'lies. Helensburgh Pier is a temp'y drying berth, rather exposed, used by occas steamers. ↓ E of marina or in Rosneath Bay. Moorings N of the narrows at Stroul B & Clynder; and at the head of the loch. Clyde Naval Base at Faslane must be avoided by yachts.

NAVIGATION WPT 55°59'·29N 04°45'·26W, 356°/1·3M to bn No 7. Beaches between Cairndhu Pt and Helensburgh Pier are strewn with large boulders above/below MLWS. Gareloch ent is via Rhu Narrows. Beware submerged breakwater between new break-water and Fl G SHM buoy S of marina entrance. There are large unlit MoD buoys and barges off W shore of Gareloch; for Garelochhead keep to W shore until well clear of Faslane Naval Base.

LIGHTS AND MARKS Ldg/dir lts into Gareloch 356°, 318°, 295°, 329° and 331°. Conspic ✠ tr at Rhu.

R/T VHF Ch 16. Rhu Marina Ch 80 M (H24 in season).

TELEPHONE (Code 01436) Marina 820238; Queen's HM 674321; MRCC (01475) 729014; Marinecall 09068 969652; Police 672141; Ⓗ (01389) 754121; Dr 672277.

FACILITIES Rhu Marina (200) ☎ 820238, AB £2.20 (£11 for 5Hrs), @, D, M, BH (35 ton), CH, ME, El, Slip, M, C hire, Gas, Gaz, Wi-fi; Royal Northern and Clyde YC ☎ 820322. Possible ⚓s, L, R, Bar; Helensburgh SC ☎ 672778 Slip (dinghies) L, FW; Town (1M) all services, ⇌, ✈ (Glasgow). DRB Marine (Rosneath) ☎ 831231, no AB but some ⚓s, BH (40 ton), Slip, Wi-fi (ashore only).

Naval activity: Beware submarines from Faslane Base. See 9.9.22 for submarine activity (Subfacts) in the Clyde and offshore or call FOSNNI Ops ☎ (01436) 674321 Ext 3206.

Protected Areas: Vessels are never allowed within 150m of naval shore installations at Faslane and Coulport.

Restricted Areas (Faslane, Rhu Chan and Coulport): These are closed to all vessels during submarine movements (see opposite and W Coast of Scotland Pilot, App 2). MoD Police patrols enforce areas which are shown on charts. The S limit of Faslane Restricted area is marked by two Or posts with X topmarks on

Shandon foreshore. The W limit is marked by Iso WRG 4s, vis W356°-006°, at Gareloch Oil fuel depot N jetty. The following signals are shown when restrictions are in force:

Entrance to Gareloch
Day & Night: ● ● ● (vert), supplemented by R flag with W diagonal bar.

Faslane and Coulport
Day & Night: ● ● ● (vert), supplemented by International Code pendant over pendant Nine.

LOCH LONG/LOCH GOIL, Argyll and Bute, approx 56°00′N 04°52′·5W to 56°12′·00N 04°45′·00W. AC *5610*, 3746. Tides: See 9.9.20 for differences. ML 1·7m; Duration 0645.

SHELTER Loch Long is about 15M long. Temp ⚓s (south to north)at: Cove, Blairmore (not in S'lies), Ardentinny, Portincaple, Coilessan (about 1M S of Ardgartan Pt), and near head of loch (Arrochar) on either shore. In Loch Goil ⚓ at Swines Hole and off Carrick Castle (S of the pier, in N'lies a swell builds). Avoid ⚓ near Douglas Pier. The head of the loch is crowded with private/dinghy moorings, and is either too steep-to or too shallow to ⚓. The loch is frequently closed to navigation due to the trial range half way down.

LIGHTS Coulport Jetty, 2FG (vert) each end and two Fl G 12s on N jetty; Port Dornaige Fl 6s 8m 11M, vis 026°-206°; Dog Rock (Carraig nan Ron) Fl 2s 11M; Finnart Oil Terminal has FG lts and ldg lts 031° QW/FW on Cnap Pt. Upper Loch Long is unlit. Loch Goil ent is marked by 2 PHM buoys (Fl R 3s and QR), a SHM buoy (QG) and ldg lts 318°: front (The Perch) Dir FWRG and Fl R 3s; rear FW. Rubha Ardnahein Fl R5s.

FACILITIES Loch Long (Cove), Cove SC, FW, Bar; ▭, FW (pier); (Portincaple) shops, hotel, ⊠, FW; (Ardentinny) shop, ▭, R, hotel, M; (Blairmore) shops, ⊠, Slip, FW; (Arrochar) shops, hotel, FW, Gas, ⊠. Loch Goil (Carrick Castle) has one blue ⚓ (£10/night, max 15 ton) ⊠, ▦, shop; (Lochgoilhead) has a store, ⊠, FW, Gas.

9.9.21 DUMBARTON (SANDPOINT) AND BOWLING HARBOUR

Dunbartonshire 55°56′·50N 04°34′·27W ❋❋❋⚓✿

CHARTS AC 5610, 2131, 1994, 2007: BW Skipper's Guide for Forth and Clyde Canal, BW Skipper's Brief for Lowland Canals; Imray 63, 2900 Series.

TIDES +0122 Dover; ML 2·0; Duration 0640

Standard Port GREENOCK (⟶)

Times				Height (metres)			
High Water		Low Water		MHWS	MHWN	MLWN	MLWS
0000	0600	0000	0600	3·4	2·8	1·0	0·3
1200	1800	1200	1800				
Differences PORT GLASGOW (55°56′·10N 04°40′·50W)							
+0010	+0005	+0010	+0020	+0·2	+0·1	0·0	0·0
DUMBARTON							
+0015	+0010	+0020	+0040	+0·4	+0·3	+0·1	0·0
BOWLING							
+0020	+0010	+0030	+0055	+0·6	+0·5	+0·3	+0·1
RENFREW							
+0025	+0015	+0035	+0100	+0·9	+0·8	+0·5	+0·2
GLASGOW							
+0025	+0015	+0035	+0105	+1·3	+1·2	+0·6	+0·4

SHELTER Good at Dumbarton (Sandpoint Marina) and Bowling Hbr 3M further east. Hbrs are controlled by Clyde Port Authority.

NAVIGATION WPT 55°57′·61N 04°45′·96W, No 1 SHM buoy, 2ca NNW of Clydeport container terminal (conspic blue cranes). No navigational dangers, but much shipping and ferries in the Clyde. Keep just inboard of chan lateral marks as depths shoal rapidly outboard. For Dumbarton cross the river at 90° abeam No 39 SHM buoy. Depths in R Leven may be less than charted. For Bowling Hbr cross abeam No 45 SHM buoy. Follow ldg marks as charted.

LIGHTS AND MARKS The R Clyde is well buoyed/lit.

R/T Call *Clydeport Estuary Radio* Ch **12** 16 (H24) when abm No 1 buoy E-bound. Weather and traffic info on request. Marina Ch M. Bowling lockkeeper Ch 74, HW±2.

TELEPHONE (Codes: Greenock 01475; Glasgow 0141, followed by 7 digit Tel No): HM 725775; Estuary Control 726221; British Waterways Board 332 6936; MRCC 729988; Police 01389 822000; Dr 634617; Marinecall 09068 969652; ⊞ 01389 754121.

FACILITIES Sandpoint Marina 55°56′·48N 04°34′·07W. ☎ 01389 762396/731500. Limited visitors berths, £10 per night. VHF Ch M. BH (40 ton), Slip, BY, D (can), CH ☎ 01389 742438. **Town** ▭, R, Bar, ⑧, ⊠, ⇌ 30 mins to Glasgow.

Bowling Basin 55°55′·8N 04°29′·0W, W end of Forth & Clyde Canal, see 9.6.9. ☎ 01389 877969. Lock access HW±2 to Basin and Canal. For lock hrs call VHF Ch 74 asap for latest schedule. *Skipper's Brief* essential obtain from www.scottishcanals.co.uk. **Facilities** AB £30/night, FW, Showers, ▦, D by prior notice, C (mast), Wi-fi. **Town** P&D (cans), ▭, R, Bar, ⊠, ⑧, ⇌ .

There are no yachting facilities on R Clyde E of Bowling Basin.

GLASGOW 55°55′·94N 04°34′·25W; Clyde Yacht Clubs Association is at 8 St James St, Paisley. ☎ 8878296. Clyde Cruising Club is at Suite 408, Pentagon Centre, 36 Washington Street, Glasgow G3 8AZ, ☎ 221 2774. **Services:** ACA, CH.

GREENOCK

MEAN SPRING ————
AND NEAP CURVES – – –

MEAN RANGES
Springs 3.1m
Neaps 1.8m

Springs occur 2 days
after
New and Full Moon

FIRTH OF CLYDE TO MULL OF GALLOWAY

(AC 2131, 2126, 2199, 2198) Further S the coast is less inviting, with mostly commercial hbrs until reaching Ardrossan and Troon, NW of which there are various dangers: beware Troon Rk (depth 5·6m, but sea can break), Lappock Rk (dries 0·6m, marked by bn), and Mill Rk (dries 0·4m, buoyed). Lady Isle (lt, racon), shoal to NE, is 2M WSW of Troon.

► There is a severe race off Bennane Hd (8M SSE of Ailsa Craig, conspic) when tide is running strongly.◄ Loch Ryan offers little for yachtsmen but there is anch S of Kirkcolm Pt, inside the drying spit which runs in SE direction 1·5M from the point. There is also a useful anch in Lady Bay, sheltered except from NE. Portpatrick is a useful passage hbr, but not in onshore winds.

► *North Channel South* (9.13.5 for N.Chan N): *Irish coast – the S-going flood begins HW Belfast –0600 (HW Dover +0610). Counter tide off Donaghadee and Island Magee for last 3 hrs of flood. Scottish coast between Corsewall Pt and Mull of Galloway – HW Greenock +0310 (HW Dover +0430). Sp rate off Corsewall Pt is 2–3kn, increasing to 5kn off and S of Black Hd.*

Races occur off Copeland Is. Morroch B, Money Hd Mull of Logan and Mull of Galloway.

Irish coast – N-going ebb begins at HW Belfast (HW Dover – 0015). Scottish coast – HW Greenock –0250 (HW Dover –0130). Races off Copeland Is and Mull of Galloway. Flood begins 2 hrs early close inshore N of Mull of Galloway. A race SSE of Crammag Hd is bad if wind against tide. Mull of Galloway (lt) is a high (82m), steep-to headland with a **dangerous race extending nearly 3M to S.** *On E-going stream it extends NNE into Luce B; on W-going stream it extends SW and W. Give the race a wide berth, or pass close inshore at slack water nps and calm weather. SW wind >F4 against W-going stream, do not attempt inshore route.*◄

SCOTLAND – SW COAST

The Scares, two groups of rocks, lie at the mouth of Luce Bay which elsewhere is clear more than 3ca offshore; but the whole bay is occupied by a practice bombing range, marked by 12 DZ SPM lt buoys. Good anch at E Tarbert B to await the tide around the Mull of Galloway, or good shelter in drying hbr of Drummore. Off Burrow Hd there is a bad race in strong W winds with W-going tide. Luce Bay Firing Range (D402/403) lies at the NW end. For info on activity ☎ (01776) 888792. In Wigtown B the best anch is in Isle of Whithorn B, but exposed to S. It is also possible to dry out in Garlieston.

A tank firing range, between the E side of ent to Kirkcudbright Bay and Abbey Hd, 4M to E, extends 14M offshore. If unable to avoid the area, cross it at N end close inshore. For information contact the Range safety boat 'Gallovidian' on VHF Ch 16, 73. The range operates 0900-1600LT Mon-Fri, but weekend and night firing may also occur.

See 9.10.5 for continuation E into Solway Firth and S into the Irish Sea. For notes on crossing the Irish Sea, see 9.13.5.

TIME ZONE (UT)
For Summer Time add ONE hour in **non-shaded areas**

GREENOCK   LAT 55°57'N   LONG 4°46'W
TIMES AND HEIGHTS OF HIGH AND LOW WATERS

Dates in red are SPRINGS
Dates in blue are NEAPS

YEAR 2010

JANUARY

Time m	Time m
1 0019 3.4 / 0539 0.5 / F 1225 3.7 / 1800 0.3	**16** 0100 3.1 / 0617 0.7 / SA 1313 3.6 / 1843 0.5
2 0111 3.4 / 0627 0.4 / SA 1311 3.8 / 1848 0.2	**17** 0133 3.2 / 0649 0.7 / SU 1345 3.6 / 1914 0.5
3 0202 3.4 / 0715 0.4 / SU 1357 3.9 / 1936 0.1	**18** 0206 3.2 / 0719 0.7 / M 1416 3.6 / 1946 0.5
4 0251 3.4 / 0804 0.4 / M 1443 3.9 / 2025 0.2	**19** 0239 3.2 / 0751 0.7 / TU 1447 3.6 / 2018 0.5
5 0339 3.4 / 0853 0.4 / TU 1528 3.9 / 2116 0.4	**20** 0312 3.2 / 0826 0.7 / W 1521 3.5 / 2053 0.6
6 0425 3.3 / 0944 0.5 / W 1615 3.8 / 2209 0.4	**21** 0346 3.2 / 0904 0.7 / TH 1556 3.4 / 2133 0.6
7 0512 3.2 / 1039 0.7 / TH 1703 3.6 / ◑ 2307 0.6	**22** 0422 3.2 / 0946 0.8 / F 1635 3.3 / 2219 0.7
8 0601 3.1 / 1139 0.8 / F 1754 3.4	**23** 0500 3.1 / 1033 0.9 / SA 1718 3.1 / ◐ 2312 0.8
9 0011 0.7 / 0657 3.0 / SA 1249 0.9 / 1850 3.2	**24** 0543 3.0 / 1129 1.1 / SU 1812 3.0
10 0124 0.9 / 0808 2.9 / SU 1403 1.0 / 2009 3.0	**25** 0015 1.0 / 0636 2.9 / M 1236 1.1 / 1923 2.8
11 0232 0.9 / 0925 3.0 / M 1510 0.9 / 2142 3.0	**26** 0128 1.0 / 0754 2.9 / TU 1355 1.1 / 2055 2.9
12 0331 0.9 / 1027 3.2 / TU 1605 0.7 / 2248 3.0	**27** 0245 0.9 / 0923 3.0 / W 1512 0.9 / 2218 3.0
13 0421 0.9 / 1117 3.4 / W 1652 0.6 / 2339 3.1	**28** 0348 0.7 / 1031 3.2 / TH 1612 0.5 / 2320 3.2
14 0505 0.8 / 1200 3.5 / TH 1733 0.5	**29** 0440 0.5 / 1125 3.4 / F 1702 0.3
15 0022 3.1 / 0543 0.8 / F 1239 3.6 / ● 1809 0.5	**30** 0013 3.3 / 0527 0.3 / SA 1214 3.6 / ○ 1747 0.1
	31 0104 3.4 / 0613 0.2 / SU 1301 3.7 / 1832 0.0

FEBRUARY

Time m	Time m
1 0152 3.4 / 0658 0.2 / M 1346 3.8 / 1917 -0.1	**16** 0144 3.2 / 0652 0.6 / TU 1355 3.5 / 1916 0.4
2 0237 3.4 / 0743 0.2 / TU 1431 3.9 / 2002 0.0	**17** 0213 3.2 / 0721 0.5 / W 1424 3.5 / 1944 0.4
3 0318 3.4 / 0829 0.2 / W 1513 3.9 / 2048 0.1	**18** 0243 3.3 / 0755 0.5 / TH 1456 3.5 / 2018 0.4
4 0357 3.4 / 0916 0.3 / TH 1555 3.8 / 2135 0.3	**19** 0313 3.3 / 0832 0.5 / F 1530 3.4 / 2057 0.4
5 0435 3.3 / 1004 0.4 / F 1636 3.6 / ◑ 2225 0.5	**20** 0346 3.3 / 0914 0.5 / SA 1606 3.3 / 2142 0.6
6 0514 3.1 / 1059 0.6 / SA 1719 3.3 / 2324 0.8	**21** 0421 3.2 / 1000 0.7 / SU 1646 3.1 / 2235 0.8
7 0559 3.0 / 1210 0.8 / SU 1807 3.0	**22** 0501 3.1 / 1056 0.8 / M 1736 2.9 / ◑ 2338 0.9
8 0045 1.0 / 0656 2.8 / M 1337 0.9 / 1906 2.7	**23** 0551 2.9 / 1203 1.0 / TU 1846 2.7
9 0210 1.1 / 0848 2.8 / TU 1451 0.9 / 2135 2.6	**24** 0054 1.0 / 0701 2.8 / W 1327 0.9 / 2037 2.7
10 0314 1.1 / 1009 3.0 / W 1548 0.7 / 2244 2.8	**25** 0225 1.0 / 0853 2.9 / TH 1454 0.7 / 2214 2.9
11 0406 0.9 / 1101 3.2 / TH 1634 0.5 / 2330 2.9	**26** 0334 0.7 / 1015 3.1 / F 1557 0.4 / 2312 3.1
12 0449 0.8 / 1144 3.4 / F 1714 0.4	**27** 0426 0.4 / 1110 3.4 / SA 1646 0.1
13 0009 3.0 / 0526 0.7 / SA 1222 3.5 / 1749 0.3	**28** 0001 3.3 / 0511 0.2 / SU 1159 3.5 / ○ 1729 -0.1
14 0043 3.1 / 0558 0.6 / SU 1256 3.5 / ● 1820 0.4	
15 0114 3.1 / 0626 0.6 / M 1326 3.5 / 1849 0.4	

MARCH

Time m	Time m
1 0048 3.4 / 0554 0.1 / M 1245 3.7 / 1811 -0.2	**16** 0046 3.1 / 0558 0.5 / TU 1259 3.3 / 1818 0.3
2 0132 3.4 / 0637 0.0 / TU 1330 3.8 / 1853 -0.1	**17** 0115 3.2 / 0622 0.5 / W 1328 3.3 / 1843 0.3
3 0213 3.4 / 0720 0.0 / W 1413 3.8 / 1935 -0.1	**18** 0143 3.3 / 0651 0.4 / TH 1359 3.4 / 1913 0.3
4 0250 3.4 / 0802 0.0 / TH 1453 3.8 / 2018 0.1	**19** 0212 3.3 / 0726 0.3 / F 1432 3.4 / 1950 0.3
5 0325 3.4 / 0845 0.1 / F 1532 3.6 / 2101 0.3	**20** 0243 3.4 / 0805 0.3 / SA 1508 3.4 / 2032 0.4
6 0359 3.3 / 0931 0.3 / SA 1610 3.4 / 2147 0.6	**21** 0316 3.4 / 0849 0.4 / SU 1545 3.3 / 2119 0.5
7 0436 3.2 / 1023 0.5 / SU 1651 3.1 / ◑ 2240 0.9	**22** 0352 3.3 / 0938 0.5 / M 1627 3.1 / 2213 0.7
8 0518 3.0 / 1133 0.8 / M 1737 2.8 / 2357 1.2	**23** 0432 3.2 / 1036 0.7 / TU 1718 2.9 / ◐ 2318 0.9
9 0610 2.8 / 1310 0.9 / TU 1833 2.5	**24** 0523 3.0 / 1146 0.8 / W 1831 2.7
10 0141 1.2 / 0741 2.6 / W 1424 0.8 / 2120 2.5	**25** 0037 1.0 / 0634 2.8 / TH 1313 0.8 / 2036 2.7
11 0250 1.1 / 0942 2.8 / TH 1521 0.6 / 2224 2.7	**26** 0206 0.9 / 0830 2.8 / F 1436 0.5 / 2201 2.9
12 0342 0.9 / 1035 3.1 / F 1607 0.4 / 2305 2.9	**27** 0315 0.7 / 0954 3.1 / SA 1537 0.2 / 2254 3.1
13 0425 0.7 / 1117 3.2 / SA 1646 0.3 / 2341 3.0	**28** 0407 0.4 / 1050 3.3 / SU 1625 0.0 / 2340 3.3
14 0501 0.6 / 1154 3.3 / SU 1720 0.3	**29** 0452 0.2 / 1138 3.5 / M 1708 -0.1
15 0014 3.1 / 0532 0.5 / M 1228 3.3 / ● 1751 0.3	**30** 0024 3.3 / 0534 0.0 / TU 1225 3.6 / ○ 1748 -0.1
	31 0106 3.4 / 0615 -0.1 / W 1309 3.6 / 1828 -0.1

APRIL

Time m	Time m
1 0144 3.4 / 0655 -0.1 / TH 1351 3.6 / 1909 0.1	**16** 0112 3.3 / 0626 0.3 / F 1334 3.3 / 1849 0.3
2 0219 3.4 / 0736 0.0 / F 1431 3.6 / 1950 0.2	**17** 0144 3.4 / 0704 0.3 / SA 1411 3.3 / 1930 0.4
3 0253 3.4 / 0818 0.1 / SA 1509 3.4 / 2032 0.4	**18** 0218 3.5 / 0746 0.3 / SU 1451 3.3 / 2016 0.4
4 0328 3.4 / 0902 0.2 / SU 1547 3.2 / 2117 0.6	**19** 0254 3.5 / 0833 0.3 / M 1532 3.2 / 2107 0.5
5 0405 3.2 / 0953 0.5 / M 1628 3.0 / 2207 0.9	**20** 0333 3.4 / 0926 0.4 / TU 1619 3.0 / 2204 0.7
6 0447 3.0 / 1101 0.7 / TU 1715 2.7 / ◑ 2313 1.2	**21** 0416 3.3 / 1027 0.5 / W 1715 2.9 / ◑ 2309 0.8
7 0538 2.8 / 1232 0.8 / W 1812 2.5	**22** 0509 3.1 / 1139 0.6 / TH 1833 2.7
8 0053 1.3 / 0651 2.6 / TH 1346 0.7 / 1957 2.4	**23** 0023 0.9 / 0625 2.9 / F 1258 0.5 / 2020 2.7
9 0209 1.2 / 0852 2.7 / F 1443 0.6 / 2137 2.6	**24** 0141 0.8 / 0806 2.9 / SA 1411 0.4 / 2133 2.9
10 0306 1.0 / 0955 2.9 / SA 1530 0.4 / 2223 2.8	**25** 0248 0.6 / 0927 3.1 / SU 1510 0.2 / 2226 3.1
11 0351 0.8 / 1039 3.1 / SU 1610 0.3 / 2301 3.0	**26** 0343 0.4 / 1024 3.3 / M 1600 0.1 / 2313 3.2
12 0428 0.6 / 1117 3.2 / M 1645 0.3 / 2337 3.1	**27** 0431 0.2 / 1114 3.4 / TU 1644 0.0 / 2356 3.3
13 0459 0.6 / 1152 3.2 / TU 1717 0.3	**28** 0514 0.1 / 1201 3.5 / W 1725 0.1 / ○
14 0010 3.1 / 0526 0.5 / W 1226 3.2 / ● 1744 0.3	**29** 0037 3.4 / 0555 0.0 / TH 1246 3.5 / 1805 0.1
15 0042 3.2 / 0554 0.4 / TH 1259 3.2 / 1814 0.3	**30** 0116 3.4 / 0635 0.0 / F 1329 3.4 / 1846 0.3

SW Scotland

Chart Datum: 1·62 metres below Ordnance Datum (Newlyn). HAT is 4·0 metres above Chart Datum; see 4.5.

TIME ZONE (UT)
For Summer Time add ONE hour in **non-shaded areas**

GREENOCK   LAT 55°57'N   LONG 4°46'W
TIMES AND HEIGHTS OF HIGH AND LOW WATERS

Dates in red are SPRINGS
Dates in blue are NEAPS

YEAR 2010

MAY

Time	m		Time	m
1 SA	0152 3.4 / 0715 0.1 / 1409 3.3 / 1927 0.4		**16** SU	0121 3.5 / 0649 0.2 / 1355 3.3 / 1917 0.4
2 SU	0227 3.4 / 0756 0.1 / 1448 3.2 / 2010 0.5		**17** M	0159 3.6 / 0735 0.2 / 1440 3.2 / 2007 0.4
3 M	0302 3.4 / 0840 0.3 / 1527 3.1 / 2054 0.7		**18** TU	0240 3.6 / 0824 0.2 / 1526 3.2 / 2100 0.5
4 TU	0340 3.3 / 0930 0.4 / 1609 2.9 / 2143 0.9		**19** W	0322 3.5 / 0919 0.3 / 1617 3.1 / 2156 0.6
5 W	0421 3.1 / 1029 0.6 / 1657 2.8 / 2238 1.0		**20** TH	0409 3.4 / 1020 0.3 / 1716 2.9 / ☽ 2257 0.7
6 TH	0510 2.9 / 1141 0.7 / 1753 2.6 / ☽ 2345 1.2		**21** F	0504 3.2 / 1127 0.4 / 1828 2.9
7 F	0612 2.8 / 1252 0.7 / 1902 2.6		**22** SA	0002 0.7 / 0612 3.1 / 1235 0.4 / 1946 2.9
8 SA	0102 1.2 / 0733 2.7 / 1353 0.6 / 2019 2.6		**23** SU	0111 0.7 / 0735 3.1 / 1342 0.4 / 2055 2.9
9 SU	0210 1.1 / 0854 2.8 / 1444 0.5 / 2123 2.8		**24** M	0217 0.6 / 0854 3.1 / 1442 0.3 / 2153 3.0
10 M	0303 0.9 / 0949 2.9 / 1527 0.4 / 2213 2.9		**25** TU	0318 0.5 / 0956 3.2 / 1535 0.3 / 2244 3.2
11 TU	0346 0.8 / 1033 3.1 / 1606 0.4 / 2255 3.1		**26** W	0410 0.3 / 1050 3.3 / 1622 0.3 / 2330 3.3
12 W	0422 0.6 / 1112 3.1 / 1641 0.4 / 2333 3.2		**27** TH	0456 0.2 / 1139 3.3 / 1706 0.3 / ○
13 TH	0456 0.5 / 1150 3.2 / 1714 0.3		**28** F	0013 3.3 / 0539 0.1 / 1226 3.3 / 1748 0.4
14 F ●	0008 3.3 / 0530 0.4 / 1230 3.2 / 1750 0.3		**29** SA	0054 3.4 / 0620 0.1 / 1310 3.2 / 1829 0.5
15 SA	0044 3.4 / 0607 0.3 / 1312 3.2 / 1831 0.3		**30** SU	0131 3.4 / 0659 0.2 / 1351 3.1 / 1910 0.5
			31 M	0206 3.4 / 0739 0.2 / 1430 3.1 / 1951 0.6

JUNE

Time	m		Time	m
1 TU	0242 3.4 / 0821 0.3 / 1510 3.0 / 2034 0.7		**16** W	0229 3.7 / 0815 0.1 / 1523 3.2 / 2048 0.4
2 W	0319 3.4 / 0906 0.4 / 1551 2.9 / 2117 0.8		**17** TH	0314 3.6 / 0908 0.1 / 1614 3.1 / 2141 0.4
3 TH	0358 3.2 / 0955 0.5 / 1636 2.9 / 2204 0.8		**18** F	0401 3.6 / 1004 0.2 / 1708 3.1 / 2236 0.5
4 F	0441 3.1 / 1051 0.6 / 1724 2.8 / ☽ 2254 1.0		**19** SA	0453 3.4 / 1104 0.3 / 1804 3.0 / ☽ 2335 0.6
5 SA	0531 2.9 / 1151 0.7 / 1816 2.8 / 2350 1.0		**20** SU	0550 3.3 / 1206 0.4 / 1905 2.9
6 SU	0629 2.8 / 1251 0.7 / 1913 2.8		**21** M	0039 0.6 / 0656 3.1 / 1311 0.4 / 2011 2.9
7 M	0054 1.1 / 0734 2.8 / 1348 0.6 / 2014 2.8		**22** TU	0147 0.7 / 0815 3.0 / 1415 0.5 / 2118 3.0
8 TU	0159 1.0 / 0843 2.8 / 1439 0.6 / 2115 2.9		**23** W	0254 0.6 / 0930 3.0 / 1514 0.5 / 2218 3.1
9 W	0257 0.9 / 0943 2.9 / 1525 0.5 / 2209 3.0		**24** TH	0353 0.5 / 1032 3.1 / 1606 0.5 / 2310 3.2
10 TH	0346 0.7 / 1034 3.0 / 1608 0.4 / 2255 3.1		**25** F	0443 0.4 / 1126 3.1 / 1653 0.5 / 2356 3.3
11 F	0429 0.6 / 1121 3.1 / 1649 0.4 / 2338 3.3		**26** SA	0528 0.3 / 1215 3.1 / 1737 0.6 / ○
12 SA ●	0511 0.4 / 1208 3.2 / 1732 0.4		**27** SU	0038 3.4 / 0609 0.2 / 1259 3.0 / 1816 0.6
13 SU	0020 3.4 / 0553 0.3 / 1256 3.2 / 1818 0.3		**28** M	0116 3.4 / 0647 0.2 / 1338 3.0 / 1854 0.6
14 M	0102 3.4 / 0638 0.2 / 1344 3.2 / 1906 0.3		**29** TU	0151 3.5 / 0723 0.3 / 1415 3.0 / 1931 0.6
15 TU	0145 3.6 / 0725 0.1 / 1433 3.2 / 1956 0.3		**30** W	0225 3.4 / 0759 0.3 / 1451 3.0 / 2009 0.6

JULY

Time	m		Time	m
1 TH	0259 3.4 / 0837 0.4 / 1528 3.0 / 2047 0.6		**16** F	0303 3.8 / 0847 0.0 / 1559 3.2 / 2118 0.2
2 F	0333 3.3 / 0918 0.4 / 1607 3.0 / 2127 0.7		**17** SA	0348 3.7 / 0938 0.1 / 1644 3.2 / 2210 0.3
3 SA	0410 3.2 / 1002 0.5 / 1647 3.0 / 2210 0.8		**18** SU ◑	0434 3.6 / 1033 0.2 / 1730 3.1 / 2305 0.5
4 SU	0451 3.1 / 1051 0.6 / 1730 2.9 / ☽ 2257 0.9		**19** M	0522 3.3 / 1133 0.4 / 1819 3.0
5 M	0539 2.9 / 1146 0.7 / 1816 2.9 / 2352 1.0		**20** TU	0008 0.6 / 0615 3.1 / 1242 0.6 / 1919 2.9
6 TU	0636 2.8 / 1246 0.7 / 1910 2.8		**21** W	0121 0.7 / 0724 2.9 / 1354 0.8 / 2042 2.8
7 W	0055 1.1 / 0743 2.8 / 1348 0.7 / 2014 2.8		**22** TH	0236 0.7 / 0911 2.8 / 1459 0.8 / 2158 3.0
8 TH	0206 1.0 / 0857 2.8 / 1447 0.7 / 2122 2.9		**23** F	0340 0.6 / 1027 2.8 / 1555 0.7 / 2256 3.1
9 F	0312 0.8 / 1005 2.9 / 1541 0.6 / 2223 3.1		**24** SA	0432 0.4 / 1122 2.9 / 1643 0.7 / 2343 3.3
10 SA	0408 0.6 / 1102 3.0 / 1630 0.4 / 2314 3.3		**25** SU	0516 0.3 / 1208 3.0 / 1725 0.6
11 SU ●	0456 0.3 / 1154 3.1 / 1717 0.3		**26** M ○	0025 3.4 / 0554 0.2 / 1249 3.0 / 1802 0.6
12 M	0001 3.4 / 0540 0.1 / 1246 3.2 / 1803 0.3		**27** TU	0102 3.4 / 0629 0.2 / 1323 3.0 / 1835 0.6
13 TU	0047 3.6 / 0626 0.0 / 1336 3.2 / 1851 0.2		**28** W	0135 3.5 / 0702 0.3 / 1354 3.0 / 1907 0.6
14 W	0133 3.7 / 0711 -0.1 / 1426 3.2 / 1939 0.2		**29** TH	0205 3.5 / 0733 0.3 / 1425 3.1 / 1938 0.6
15 TH	0218 3.7 / 0759 -0.1 / 1513 3.2 / 2028 0.2		**30** F	0235 3.4 / 0804 0.3 / 1458 3.1 / 2013 0.5
			31 SA	0307 3.4 / 0838 0.4 / 1531 3.1 / 2049 0.6

AUGUST

Time	m		Time	m
1 SU	0340 3.3 / 0915 0.5 / 1606 3.1 / 2129 0.6		**16** M ◐	0411 3.6 / 0958 0.4 / 1650 3.2 / 2234 0.5
2 M	0417 3.2 / 0957 0.6 / 1644 3.1 / 2214 0.7		**17** TU	0454 3.3 / 1056 0.6 / 1734 3.0 / 2339 0.7
3 TU	0458 3.0 / 1049 0.7 / 1727 3.0 / ☽ 2306 0.9		**18** W	0541 3.0 / 1213 0.9 / 1828 2.9
4 W	0549 2.9 / 1150 0.8 / 1818 2.9		**19** TH	0101 0.8 / 0639 2.7 / 1338 1.0 / 2000 2.8
5 TH	0008 1.0 / 0657 2.7 / 1301 0.9 / 1923 2.8		**20** F	0220 0.8 / 0909 2.6 / 1445 1.0 / 2142 2.9
6 F	0124 1.0 / 0822 2.7 / 1417 0.8 / 2042 2.9		**21** SA	0323 0.6 / 1024 2.7 / 1541 0.8 / 2239 3.2
7 SA	0245 0.9 / 0949 2.8 / 1521 0.7 / 2156 3.1		**22** SU	0414 0.4 / 1112 2.9 / 1627 0.7 / 2325 3.3
8 SU	0350 0.6 / 1053 3.0 / 1614 0.5 / 2255 3.3		**23** M	0456 0.3 / 1152 3.0 / 1707 0.6
9 M	0440 0.2 / 1145 3.1 / 1701 0.3 / 2345 3.5		**24** TU ○	0005 3.4 / 0533 0.2 / 1227 3.0 / 1741 0.6
10 TU ●	0525 0.0 / 1235 3.2 / 1746 0.2		**25** W	0041 3.5 / 0605 0.3 / 1257 3.1 / 1811 0.6
11 W	0032 3.6 / 0608 -0.1 / 1323 3.3 / 1831 0.1		**26** TH	0112 3.5 / 0635 0.3 / 1326 3.1 / 1837 0.6
12 TH	0119 3.7 / 0651 -0.2 / 1409 3.3 / 1917 0.1		**27** F	0140 3.4 / 0702 0.4 / 1354 3.2 / 1905 0.5
13 F	0204 3.8 / 0735 -0.1 / 1452 3.3 / 2003 0.1		**28** SA	0209 3.4 / 0729 0.4 / 1424 3.2 / 1937 0.5
14 SA	0247 3.8 / 0821 0.0 / 1532 3.3 / 2050 0.1		**29** SU	0239 3.4 / 0800 0.4 / 1455 3.3 / 2014 0.5
15 SU	0329 3.8 / 0908 0.1 / 1611 3.3 / 2140 0.3		**30** M	0313 3.4 / 0836 0.5 / 1529 3.3 / 2054 0.6
			31 TU	0348 3.3 / 0919 0.6 / 1605 3.3 / 2140 0.7

Chart Datum: 1·62 metres below Ordnance Datum (Newlyn). HAT is 4·0 metres above Chart Datum; see 4.5.

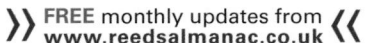

| TIME ZONE (UT) |
| For Summer Time add ONE hour in **non-shaded areas** |

GREENOCK LAT 55°57'N LONG 4°46'W
TIMES AND HEIGHTS OF HIGH AND LOW WATERS

Dates in red are SPRINGS
Dates in blue are NEAPS

YEAR **2010**

SEPTEMBER

Time m	Time m
1 0426 3.1 / 1010 0.8 / W 1646 3.1 / ◑ 2232 0.9	**16** 0515 2.9 / 1141 1.1 / TH 1750 2.9
2 0514 2.9 / 1111 1.0 / TH 1736 3.0 / 2336 1.0	**17** 0043 0.9 / 0613 2.6 / F 1316 1.2 / 1914 2.8
3 0622 2.7 / 1227 1.1 / F 1842 2.9	**18** 0158 0.9 / 0858 2.5 / SA 1423 1.1 / 2114 2.9
4 0055 1.0 / 0758 2.7 / SA 1354 1.0 / 2009 2.9	**19** 0258 0.7 / 1004 2.7 / SU 1518 1.0 / 2212 3.2
5 0225 0.8 / 0943 2.8 / SU 1504 0.8 / 2135 3.1	**20** 0347 0.5 / 1047 2.9 / M 1604 0.8 / 2257 3.4
6 0331 0.5 / 1043 3.1 / M 1557 0.5 / 2236 3.4	**21** 0428 0.3 / 1123 3.1 / TU 1642 0.6 / 2336 3.5
7 0421 0.2 / 1131 3.2 / TU 1643 0.3 / 2327 3.6	**22** 0505 0.3 / 1154 3.2 / W 1715 0.6
8 0505 0.0 / 1216 3.3 / W 1727 0.1 / ●	**23** 0010 3.5 / 0536 0.3 / TH 1224 3.2 / ○ 1742 0.6
9 0014 3.7 / 0546 -0.1 / TH 1301 3.4 / 1809 0.1	**24** 0042 3.5 / 0605 0.4 / F 1253 3.3 / 1807 0.6
10 0101 3.8 / 0627 -0.1 / F 1343 3.4 / 1852 0.0	**25** 0111 3.5 / 0631 0.4 / SA 1322 3.3 / 1834 0.6
11 0145 3.8 / 0710 -0.1 / SA 1422 3.4 / 1936 0.1	**26** 0141 3.5 / 0658 0.5 / SU 1351 3.4 / 1907 0.5
12 0228 3.8 / 0753 0.1 / SU 1500 3.4 / 2022 0.4	**27** 0214 3.5 / 0730 0.5 / M 1423 3.5 / 1945 0.5
13 0308 3.7 / 0837 0.3 / M 1536 3.4 / 2109 0.3	**28** 0249 3.4 / 0809 0.5 / TU 1458 3.5 / 2028 0.6
14 0348 3.5 / 0924 0.6 / TU 1615 3.3 / 2203 0.5	**29** 0326 3.3 / 0854 0.7 / W 1534 3.4 / 2115 0.7
15 0429 3.2 / 1019 0.9 / W 1658 3.1 / ◑ 2313 0.8	**30** 0406 3.2 / 0946 0.9 / TH 1615 3.3 / 2210 0.8

OCTOBER

Time m	Time m
1 0454 3.0 / 1048 1.1 / F 1705 3.1 / ◑ 2316 1.0	**16** 0011 0.9 / 0556 2.7 / SA 1236 1.4 / 1835 2.9
2 0603 2.8 / 1206 1.2 / SA 1812 3.0	**17** 0124 0.9 / 0746 2.6 / SU 1348 1.3 / 2023 3.0
3 0037 1.0 / 0746 2.7 / SU 1333 1.1 / 1942 3.0	**18** 0223 0.8 / 0919 2.8 / M 1445 1.1 / 2132 3.1
4 0203 0.8 / 0927 2.9 / M 1443 0.8 / 2111 3.2	**19** 0312 0.6 / 1005 3.0 / TU 1532 0.9 / 2219 3.3
5 0308 0.5 / 1023 3.2 / TU 1537 0.6 / 2214 3.4	**20** 0355 0.5 / 1043 3.2 / W 1611 0.8 / 2259 3.4
6 0358 0.2 / 1109 3.4 / W 1623 0.3 / 2305 3.6	**21** 0432 0.4 / 1117 3.3 / TH 1644 0.7 / 2335 3.4
7 0442 0.0 / 1152 3.5 / TH 1706 0.2 / ● 2353 3.7	**22** 0505 0.4 / 1150 3.4 / F 1713 0.7
8 0523 0.0 / 1234 3.5 / F 1748 0.1	**23** 0008 3.5 / 0535 0.5 / SA 1221 3.4 / ○ 1740 0.7
9 0039 3.8 / 0604 0.0 / SA 1315 3.5 / 1830 0.1	**24** 0042 3.5 / 0603 0.5 / SU 1252 3.5 / 1810 0.6
10 0124 3.8 / 0645 0.1 / SU 1353 3.6 / 1912 0.1	**25** 0116 3.5 / 0633 0.6 / M 1324 3.6 / 1845 0.6
11 0207 3.7 / 0728 0.3 / M 1430 3.6 / 1956 0.2	**26** 0153 3.5 / 0710 0.6 / TU 1358 3.7 / 1925 0.6
12 0247 3.6 / 0811 0.5 / TU 1507 3.5 / 2043 0.4	**27** 0231 3.5 / 0752 0.7 / W 1435 3.7 / 2010 0.6
13 0327 3.4 / 0857 0.8 / W 1546 3.4 / 2136 0.6	**28** 0312 3.4 / 0840 0.8 / TH 1514 3.6 / 2059 0.7
14 0409 3.2 / 0949 1.0 / TH 1630 3.2 / ◑ 2245 0.8	**29** 0355 3.2 / 0933 0.9 / F 1556 3.5 / 2156 0.8
15 0457 2.9 / 1059 1.3 / F 1722 3.1	**30** 0447 3.1 / 1034 1.1 / SA 1647 3.4 / ◑ 2303 0.9
	31 0554 2.9 / 1147 1.2 / SU 1753 3.2

NOVEMBER

Time m	Time m
1 0019 0.9 / 0728 2.9 / M 1305 1.1 / 1915 3.2	**16** 0136 0.9 / 0759 2.8 / TU 1356 1.3 / 2027 3.1
2 0135 0.7 / 0856 3.0 / TU 1414 0.9 / 2041 3.3	**17** 0230 0.8 / 0904 3.0 / W 1450 1.2 / 2129 3.2
3 0240 0.5 / 0954 3.2 / W 1512 0.7 / 2148 3.5	**18** 0316 0.7 / 0955 3.1 / TH 1534 1.0 / 2216 3.3
4 0333 0.4 / 1042 3.4 / TH 1602 0.5 / 2242 3.6	**19** 0356 0.6 / 1038 3.3 / F 1612 0.9 / 2258 3.3
5 0419 0.2 / 1127 3.5 / F 1647 0.3 / 2331 3.7	**20** 0433 0.6 / 1117 3.4 / SA 1646 0.8 / 2336 3.4
6 0503 0.2 / 1209 3.6 / SA 1730 0.2 / ●	**21** 0507 0.6 / 1152 3.5 / SU 1718 0.7 / ○
7 0019 3.7 / 0544 0.3 / SU 1250 3.6 / 1812 0.2	**22** 0015 3.4 / 0540 0.6 / M 1226 3.6 / 1752 0.7
8 0105 3.7 / 0626 0.4 / M 1329 3.7 / 1854 0.3	**23** 0055 3.4 / 0616 0.6 / TU 1302 3.7 / 1830 0.6
9 0149 3.6 / 0708 0.5 / TU 1407 3.7 / 1937 0.3	**24** 0136 3.4 / 0656 0.6 / W 1340 3.8 / 1912 0.6
10 0230 3.5 / 0751 0.7 / W 1445 3.6 / 2023 0.5	**25** 0218 3.4 / 0741 0.7 / TH 1419 3.8 / 1959 0.5
11 0311 3.3 / 0836 0.9 / TH 1525 3.5 / 2113 0.6	**26** 0302 3.4 / 0830 0.7 / F 1501 3.8 / 2049 0.6
12 0354 3.2 / 0924 1.1 / F 1608 3.4 / 2211 0.8	**27** 0349 3.3 / 0922 0.8 / SA 1546 3.7 / 2145 0.6
13 0441 3.0 / 1019 1.2 / SA 1657 3.2 / ◑ 2321 0.9	**28** 0441 3.2 / 1019 0.9 / SU 1636 3.6 / ◑ 2246 0.7
14 0537 2.8 / 1128 1.4 / SU 1756 3.1	**29** 0541 3.1 / 1123 1.0 / M 1735 3.4 / 2353 0.7
15 0033 0.9 / 0644 2.8 / M 1248 1.4 / 1908 3.0	**30** 0656 3.0 / 1232 1.0 / TU 1845 3.4

DECEMBER

Time m	Time m
1 0102 0.7 / 0815 3.1 / W 1342 1.0 / 2004 3.3	**16** 0134 1.0 / 0755 3.0 / TH 1346 1.3 / 2018 3.0
2 0209 0.6 / 0921 3.2 / TH 1447 0.8 / 2119 3.4	**17** 0230 0.9 / 0900 3.0 / F 1448 1.2 / 2125 3.1
3 0308 0.6 / 1016 3.3 / F 1543 0.6 / 2220 3.5	**18** 0320 0.8 / 0957 3.2 / SA 1538 1.1 / 2222 3.2
4 0400 0.5 / 1104 3.5 / SA 1632 0.5 / 2314 3.5	**19** 0403 0.8 / 1045 3.3 / SU 1620 0.9 / 2310 3.3
5 0447 0.5 / 1150 3.6 / SU 1717 0.4 / ●	**20** 0443 0.7 / 1126 3.5 / M 1659 0.7 / 2355 3.3
6 0004 3.5 / 0530 0.5 / M 1233 3.7 / 1800 0.3	**21** 0522 0.6 / 1205 3.6 / TU 1738 0.6 / ○
7 0052 3.5 / 0613 0.6 / TU 1313 3.7 / 1842 0.3	**22** 0040 3.4 / 0602 0.6 / W 1245 3.7 / 1818 0.5
8 0136 3.4 / 0655 0.7 / W 1352 3.7 / 1923 0.4	**23** 0125 3.4 / 0644 0.6 / TH 1325 3.8 / 1902 0.4
9 0217 3.4 / 0735 0.8 / TH 1429 3.7 / 2005 0.3	**24** 0210 3.4 / 0730 0.5 / F 1408 3.9 / 1948 0.3
10 0257 3.3 / 0817 0.8 / F 1507 3.6 / 2049 0.6	**25** 0255 3.4 / 0817 0.5 / SA 1451 3.9 / 2036 0.3
11 0338 3.2 / 0858 0.9 / SA 1547 3.5 / 2136 0.7	**26** 0341 3.3 / 0906 0.6 / SU 1536 3.8 / 2128 0.4
12 0421 3.1 / 0943 1.0 / SU 1630 3.4 / 2229 0.8	**27** 0428 3.3 / 0959 0.7 / M 1623 3.7 / 2223 0.5
13 0507 3.0 / 1031 1.2 / M 1716 3.3 / ◑ 2328 0.9	**28** 0519 3.2 / 1055 0.8 / TU 1714 3.6 / ◑ 2323 0.6
14 0557 3.0 / 1127 1.3 / TU 1809 3.1	**29** 0616 3.1 / 1159 0.9 / W 1812 3.4
15 0031 1.0 / 0652 2.9 / M 1235 1.4 / 1909 3.0	**30** 0029 0.7 / 0725 3.0 / TH 1310 0.9 / 1920 3.2
	31 0141 0.8 / 0843 3.0 / F 1423 0.9 / 2049 3.2

SW Scotland

Chart Datum: 1·62 metres below Ordnance Datum (Newlyn). HAT is 4·0 metres above Chart Datum; see 4.5.

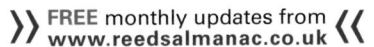

》 FREE monthly updates from 《
www.reedsalmanac.co.uk

9.9.22 ARDROSSAN

N Ayrshire 55°38'·50N 04°49'·61W ❀❀♦♦♦❀❀

CHARTS AC 5610, 2126, 2221, 2491, 1866; Imray C63.

TIDES +0055 Dover; ML 1·9; Duration 0630

Standard Port GREENOCK (←)

Times				Height (metres)			
High Water		Low Water		MHWS	MHWN	MLWN	MLWS
0000	0600	0000	0600	3·4	2·8	1·0	0·3
1200	1800	1200	1800				
Differences ARDROSSAN							
−0020	−0010	−0010	−0010	−0·2	−0·2	+0·1	+0·1
IRVINE							
−0020	−0020	−0030	−0010	−0·3	−0·3	−0·1	0·0

SHELTER Good in marina (formerly Eglinton Dock), access at all tides over sill, 5·2m least depth. A storm gate is fitted; max acceptable beam is 8·6m (28ft). Strong SW/NW winds cause heavy seas in the apprs and the hbr may be closed in SW gales. Ferries berth on both sides of Winton Pier.

NAVIGATION WPT 55°38'·13N 04°50'·55W, 055°/0·65M to hbr ent. From the W/NW keep clear of low-lying Horse Isle (conspic W tower on its S end) ringed by drying ledges. The passage between Horse Isle and the mainland is obstructed by unmarked drying rks and should not be attempted. Be aware of following dangers: From the S/SE, Eagle Rk 3ca S of hbr ent, marked by SHM buoy, Fl G 5s. 3ca SE of Eagle Rk lies unmarked Campbell Rk (0·2m). W Crinan Rk (1·1m) is 300m W of hbr ent, marked by PHM buoy, Fl R 4s.

LIGHTS AND MARKS Dir lt WRG 15m W14M, R/G11M (see 9.9.4); W sector leads 055° to hbr ent between lt ho and detached bkwtr. Lt ho Iso WG 4s 11m 9M, 317°-G-035°, W elsewhere. On S end of detached bkwtr, Fl R 5s 7m 5M.

Traffic Signals, shown H24 from control twr at ent to marina:

3 F ● lts (vert) = hbr and marina closed; no entry/exit for commercial and pleasure vessels.

3 F ● lts (vert) = marina open, hbr closed; pleasure craft may enter/exit the marina, no commercial movements.

2 F ● lts over 1 F ● = hbr open, marina closed; in severe weather marina storm gate is closed. Commercial vessels may enter/exit hbr, subject to approval by Hbr Control on VHF. Pleasure craft must clear the approach channel, ferry turning area (between the detached bkwtr and Winton Pier) and the outer basin. Yachts may not manoeuvre under sail alone until seaward of the outer breakwater.

R/T *Clyde Marina* VHF Ch **80** M. *Hbr Control* Ch 12 14 16 (H24).

TELEPHONE (Code 01294) Marina 607077, www. clyde marina.com; Ardrossan Hbr 469468; MRCC (01475) 729988; Marinecall 09068 969652; Police 404500; Dr 463011.

FACILITIES Clyde Marina (252 inc 50 ♥) £2.35, short stay £10<4hrs, access H24, Marina Office hrs 0900-1800, Wi-fi, D, ME, El, Ⓔ, CH, BH (50 ton), R. **Town** 🍴, R, Bar, ▣, Gas, ✉, Ⓑ, Wi-fi. ⇌, ✈ (Prestwick/Glasgow). Ferry to Brodick (Arran).

HARBOUR BETWEEN ARDROSSAN AND TROON

IRVINE, N Ayrshire, **55°36'·17N 04°42'·07W.** AC 2126, 2220, 1866. HW +0055 on Dover. Tides: see 9.9.22.

- Do not attempt ent in heavy onshore weather.
- Good shelter once across the bar (0·5m CD); access approx HW ±3½ for 1·4m draft.

The IB-B SPM buoy, Fl Y 3s, is 1·15M from hbr ent, close NW of ldg line. 5 blocks of flats and chys are conspic ENE of ent. Ldg lts 051°: front, FG 10m 5M; rear, FR 15m 5M. The S ent groyne is lit, Fl G 3s; groynes inside the ent have unlit perches. White Pilot tr with mast is conspic 3ca inside ent. Visitors' pontoons on N side or on S side at visitors' quay (2·2m). ⚓ prohib. VHF Ch 12 (0800-1600 Tues and Thurs; 0800-1300 Wed). HM ☎ (01294) 487286, 🖷 487111. Berths available above opening footbridge which opens at 5 mins notice ☎ 08708 403123 or VHF Ch 12 (call *Irvine Bridge*). Facilities: **Quay** AB < 5m £4, >5m <10m £6, >10m <15m £9, FW, Slip, C (3 ton), Showers, SM. **Town** P & D (cans, 1·5km), Gas, 🍴, R, ⇌, ✈ (Prestwick).

9.9.23 TROON

S Ayrshire **55°33'·10N 04°40'·97W** ✴⚓🏴🏴🏵🏵

CHARTS AC 5610, 2126, 2220, 1866; Imray C63.

TIDES +0050 Dover; ML 1·9; Duration 0630

Standard Port GREENOCK (←)

Times				Height (metres)			
High Water		Low Water		MHWS	MHWN	MLWN	MLWS
0000	0600	0000	0600	3·4	2·8	1·0	0·3
1200	1800	1200	1800				
Differences TROON							
–0025	–0025	–0020	–0020	–0·2	–0·2	0·0	0·0
AYR							
–0025	–0025	–0030	–0015	–0·4	–0·3	+0·1	+0·1
GIRVAN							
–0025	–0040	–0035	–0010	–0·3	–0·3	–0·1	0·0
LOCH RYAN (Stranraer)							
–0030	–0025	–0010	–0010	–0·2	–0·1	0·0	+0·1

SHELTER Complete in marina (2·4m at ent, 1·6m at SE end); speed limit 5kn. *Strong SW/NW winds cause heavy seas in the harbour approaches.*

NAVIGATION WPT 55°33'·20N 04°42'·00W, 103°/0·6M to W pier lt. Appr in sector SW to NW. Beware Lady Isle, Fl (4) 30s 19m 8M, W bn, 2·2M SW; Troon Rock (5·6m, occas breaks) 1·1M W; Lappock Rock (0·6m, bn with G barrel topmark) 1·6M NNW; Mill Rock (0·4m) ½M NNE of hbr ent, marked by unlit PHM buoy. Beware wash from high speed ferries in approaches.

LIGHTS AND MARKS No ldg lts. Traffic signals VQ.Y. occas when Fast Ferries arriving/departing. 14m SE of W pier hd lt, Fl (2) WG 5s, there is a floodlit dolphin, W with dayglow patches. A SHM lt buoy, FG, marks the chan in the ent to marina.

R/T HM Ch 14. Marina Ch **80** M (H24).

TELEPHONE (Code 01292) HM 281687; Troon CC 311865; Troon YC 316770. MRCC (01475) 729988; Marinecall 09068 969652; Police 313100; Dr 313593; Ⓗ 610555 (Ayr).

FACILITIES Troon Yacht Haven (300+50 ❻), £2.35, access all tides. ☎ 315553, www.yachthavens.com ❻ berths on pontoon A, first to stbd. AB for LOA 36m x 3m draft at hammerheads. Wi-fi, D (H24), ME, El, Ⓔ, CH, ✗, SM (daily pick-up), BH (50 ton), C (20 ton), Slip, 🛒, R ☎ 311523, Bar, ▣, Gas, Gaz. **Town** ✉, Ⓑ, ⇌, ✈ (Prestwick/Glasgow). Fast RoRo ferry to Belfast.

HARBOURS ON THE FIRTH OF CLYDE SOUTH OF TROON

AYR, S Ayrshire, **55°28'·22N 04°38'·78W**. AC 5610, 2126, 2220, 1866. HW +0050 on Dover; ML 1·8m. Duration 0630. See 9.9.23. After heavy rains large amounts of debris may be washed down the R Ayr. From the W, hbr ent lies between conspic gasholder to the N and townhall spire to the S. Outer St Nicholas SHM buoy, Fl G 2s, warns of shoals and Rk (0·8m) 150m S of ent. Ldg lts 098°: front, by Pilot Stn, FR 10m 5M R tr, also tfc sigs; rear (130m from front), Oc R 10s 18m 9M. N bkwtr hd, QR 9m 5M. S pier hd, Q 7m 7M, vis 012°-161°, and FG 5m 5M, same structure, vis 012°-082°, over St Nicholas Rk. Tfc sigs (near front ldg lt): 2 ● (vert) = hbr closed to incoming traffic. HM ☎ (01292) 281687; VHF Ch 14 16. **Ayr Y & CC** at S dock, limited AB on pontoon on N side of hbr (access key, £10 deposit) from Ship Inn). M. **Services:** ✗, ME, El, CH. **Town** Ⓑ, Bar, Gas, P & D, FW, ✉, R, ⇌, 🛒.

GIRVAN, S Ayrshire, **55°14'·77N 04°51'·87W**. AC 2199, 1866. HW +0043 on Dover; ML 1·8m; Duration 0630. See 9.9.23. Good shelter at inner hbr for 16 yachts on 60m pontoon (1·7m) beyond LB. Coasters and FVs berth on adjacent quay. No access LW±2 over bar 1·5m. Beware Girvan Patch, 1·7m, 4ca SW of ent, and Brest Rks, 3·5M N of hbr extending 6ca offshore. Ch spire (conspic) brg 104° leads between N bkwtr, Fl R 4s 5m 2M, and S pier, 2 FG (vert) 8m 4M. Inner N groyne, Iso 4s 3m 4M. Tfc sigs at root of S pier: 2 B discs (hor), at night 2 ● (hor) = hbr shut. VHF Ch 12 16 (HO). HM ☎ (01465) 713648; FW, Slip. **Town** Ⓑ, ✉, 🛒, R, ⇌, P & D (cans).

ANCHORAGES WITHIN LOCH RYAN
(See chartlet on next page)

LOCH RYAN, Dumfries and Galloway, **55°01'N 05°05'W**. AC 2198, 1403. HW (Stranraer) +0055 on Dover; ML 1·6m; Duration 0640. See tides 9.9.23. See adjacent chartlet. Very good shelter except in strong NW winds. Ent between Milleur Pt and Finnarts Pt. Beware The Beef Barrel rock, 1m high 6ca SSE of Milleur Pt, and The Spit running 1·5M to SE from W shore opposite Cairn Pt lt ho Fl (2) R10s 14m 12M. **Lights:** Cairnryan ferry terminal Fl R 5s 5m 5M; Stranraer, centre pier hd 2FBu (vert), E pier hd 2FR (vert). ⚓s in Lady Bay, 1·3M SSE of Milleur Pt, but exposed to heavy wash from HSS; in The Wig in 3m (avoid weed patches); or off Stranraer 3ca NW of W Pier hd. Larger yachts berth on NE side of E pier, by arrangement with HM, VHF Ch **14** (H24) or ☎ (01776) 702460. Area W of W Pier has been dredged and new pontoons are being installed (2008). Facilities (Stranraer): Ⓑ, Bar, D, FW, P, ✉, R, ⇌, 🛒.

TROON

9.9.24 PORTPATRICK

Dumfries and Galloway 54°50'·42N 05°07'·18W

CHARTS AC 2724, 2198; Imray C62.

TIDES +0032 Dover; ML 2·1; Duration 0615

Standard Port LIVERPOOL (→)

Times				Heights (metres)			
High Water		Low Water		MHWS	MHWN	MLWN	MLWS
0000	0600	0200	0800	9·3	7·4	2·9	0·9
1200	1800	1400	2000				
Differences PORTPATRICK							
+0018	+0026	0000	−0035	−5·5	−4·4	−2·0	−0·6

SHELTER Good in tiny Inner harbour, but entrance is difficult in strong SW/NW winds.

NAVIGATION WPT 54°50'·00N 05°08'·07W, 055°/0·7M to ent. Ent to outer hbr by short narrow chan with hazards either side, including rky shelf covered at HW. Beware cross tides off ent, up to 3kn springs. Barrel buoy (a mooring buoy) marks end of Half Tide Rk; do not cut inside.

LIGHTS AND MARKS Old Lt Ho (W tower, 22m) on Black Head is 1·6M north of entrance. Ldg lts 050°, FG (H24) 6/8m: Front on sea wall; rear on bldg; 2 vert orange stripes by day. Conspic features include: TV mast 1M NE, almost on ldg line; large hotel on cliffs about 1½ca NNW of hbr ent; Dunskey Castle (ru) 4ca SE of hbr.

R/T None.

TELEPHONE (Code 01776) HM 810355; MRCC (01475) 729988; Marinecall 09068 969652; Police 702112; Ⓗ 702323; RNLI Coxswain (for local advice) 07771 741717.

FACILITIES Hbr Slip (small craft), AB £12, M, FW, L. **Village** P (cans), D (bulk tanker), Gas, ⛟, R, Bar, ✉, Ⓑ (Stranraer), ⇌ (bus to Stranraer), ✈ (Prestwick).

HARBOURS FROM MULL OF GALLOWAY TO WIGTOWN BAY

DRUMMORE, Dumfries and Galloway, **54°41'·57N 04°53'·49W.** AC 2094, 5613. HW +0040m on Dover; ML 3.3m; Duration 0610. Recently acquired from MOD by Drummore Hbr Trust ☎ 01557 330337. Good shelter from all conditions in small drying harbour convenient for awaiting weather/tidal conditions for rounding Mull of Galloway westbound. Temp'y ⚓ 5.5ca NNE of hbr ent in 4m. Access HW ±0245; approach entrance heading 140° from 1ca off. Depth in hbr varies due to silting but suitable for craft of <1.3m draft. Berth on pier (fender board required with fenders). Facilities FW, Slip, P (cans), Gas, ⛟, R, Bar, ✉, ⇌ (bus to Stranraer), ✈ (Carlisle).

ISLE OF WHITHORN, Dumfries and Galloway, **54°41'·91N 04°21'·88W.** AC 1826, 2094, 5613. HW +0035 on Dover; ML 3·7m; Duration 0545. See 9.9.25. Shelter good but hbr dries, having approx 2·5m at HW±3. On W side of ent beware the Skerries ledge. St Ninian's Tr (Fl WR 3s 20m 6/4M viz: 310°-W-005°-R-040°; W ☐ tr) is conspic at E side of ent. E pier hd has QG 4m 5M; ldg lts 335°, both Oc R 8s 7/9m 7M, synch, Or masts and ◇. HM ☎ (01988) 500468, www.isleofwhithorn.com; Facilities: AB on quay £4.83/yacht, 2 Slips (launching £1.00), P, D (by arrangement with HM), FW, ME, ⚒, CH, ⛟, Bar, ✉, VHF Ch 08 (occas).

GARLIESTON, Dumfries and Galloway, **54°47'·36N 04°21'·83W.** AC 1826, 2094, 5613. HW +0035 on Dover; ML no data; Duration 0545. See 9.9.25. Hbr affords complete shelter but dries. Access (2m) HW±3. Pier hd lt 2FR (vert) 5m 3M. Beware rky outcrops in W side of bay marked by a perch. HM ☎ (01988) 600295, Mobile 07734 073422. Facilities: M £3, FW, AC on quay, Slip. **Town:** ⛟, ME, P, D. ⚓s NE or W of Hestan Is to await tide. VHF: Ch M call *Kippford Startline* (YC) HW±2 in season. Ch 16 *Kippford Slipway* (Pilotage). Facilities: **Solway YC** (01556) 600221, www.thesyc.com; AB, ⚡, FW, M; **Services:** AB £6, M, Slip, D (cans), CH, Gaz, BY *Kippford Slipway Ltd*(01556) 620249, ME. **Town** P, SM, ⛟, ✉, Bar, Slip.

NW England, IoM & N Wales

Mull of Galloway to Bardsey Island

NW Englamd

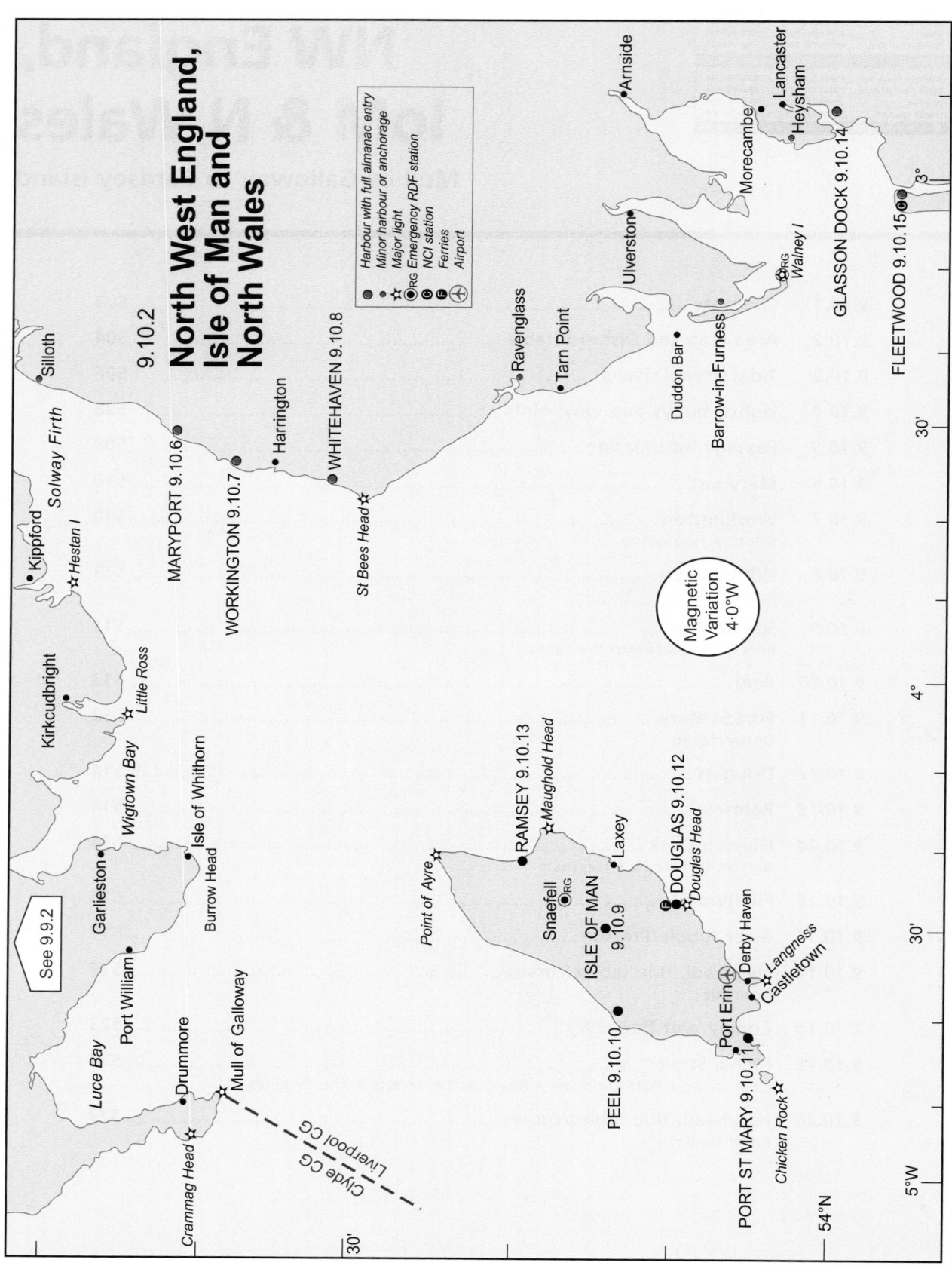

North West England, Isle of Man and North Wales

9.10.2

Harbour with full almanac entry
Minor harbour or anchorage
Major light
RG Emergency RDF station
NCI station
Ferries
Airport

Magnetic Variation 4.0°W

See 9.9.2

Silloth
Solway Firth
Kippford
Hestan I
Kirkcudbright
Little Ross
Garlieston
Wigtown Bay
Isle of Whithorn
Burrow Head
Port William
Luce Bay
Drummore
Mull of Galloway
Crammag Head

Clyde CG
Liverpool CG

Point of Ayre
RAMSEY 9.10.13
Maughold Head
Snaefell
RG
Laxey
ISLE OF MAN
9.10.9
DOUGLAS 9.10.12
Douglas Head
PEEL 9.10.10
Derby Haven
Langness
Castletown
Port Erin
PORT ST MARY 9.10.11
Chicken Rock

Harrington
MARYPORT 9.10.6
WORKINGTON 9.10.7
WHITEHAVEN 9.10.8
St Bees Head

Ravenglass
Tarn Point
Duddon Bar
Barrow-in-Furness
Ulverston
Walney I
RG
GLASSON DOCK 9.10.14
FLEETWOOD 9.10.15
Arnside
Lancaster
Heysham
Morecambe

54°N
30'
5°W
30'
4°
30'
3°

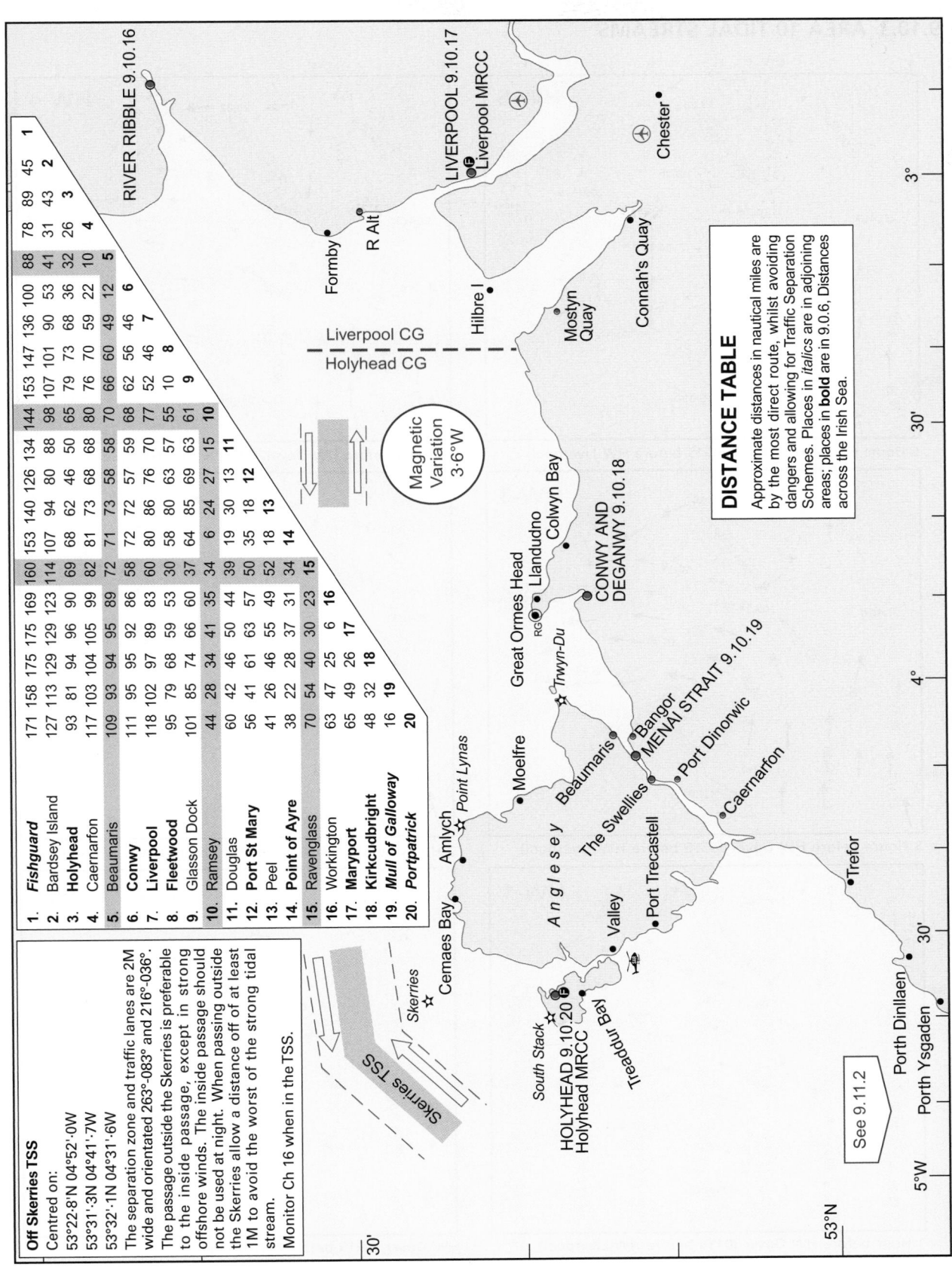

Off Skerries TSS

Centred on:
53°22'·8N 04°52'·0W
53°31'·3N 04°41'·7W
53°32'·1N 04°31'·6W

The separation zone and traffic lanes are 2M wide and orientated 263°-083° and 216°-036°. The passage outside the Skerries is preferable to the inside passage, except in strong offshore winds. The inside passage should not be used at night. When passing outside the Skerries allow a distance off of at least 1M to avoid the worst of the strong tidal stream.

Monitor Ch 16 when in the TSS.

DISTANCE TABLE

Approximate distances in nautical miles are by the most direct route, whilst avoiding dangers and allowing for Traffic Separation Schemes. Places in *italics* are in adjoining areas; places in **bold** are in 9.0.6. Distances across the Irish Sea.

Distance table (nautical miles). Figures preceding each **bold** index are the distances from that place to the places listed below it.

#	Place	Distances
1	*Fishguard*	171 158 175 175 169 160 153 147 153 144 134 126 140 153 160 169 175 175 158
2	Bardsey Island	127 113 129 123 114 107 101 90 98 88 80 62 72 71 58 86 83 60
3	**Holyhead**	93 81 94 96 90 69 68 79 73 65 80 46 57 62 68 59 89
4	Caernarfon	117 103 104 105 99 82 81 73 70 80 68 68 73 76 66 49 12
5	**Beaumaris**	109 93 94 95 89 72 71 58 60 70 58 58 58 73 72 60 12
6	Conwy	111 95 95 92 86 58 72 72 57 59 59 57 76 80 86 58
7	Liverpool	118 102 97 89 83 60 77 76 70 63 69 85 84 46
8	Fleetwood	95 79 68 59 53 30 52 55 10
9	Glasson Dock	101 85 74 66 60 37 64 61 63 57 10
10	Ramsey	44 28 34 41 35 34 6 24 27 15
11	Douglas	60 42 46 50 44 39 19 30 13
12	**Port St Mary**	56 41 61 63 57 49 52 18
13	Peel	41 26 46 55 49 52 34
14	**Point of Ayre**	38 22 28 37 31 34
15	*Ravenglass*	70 54 40 30 23
16	Workington	63 47 25 6
17	**Maryport**	65 49 26
18	Kirkcudbright	48 32
19	*Mull of Galloway*	16
20	*Portpatrick*	

Magnetic Variation 3·6°W

Skerries TSS

See 9.11.2

Map labels:

RIVER RIBBLE 9.10.16

LIVERPOOL 9.10.17
Liverpool MRCC
Liverpool CG
Holyhead CG

Formby
R Alt
Chester
Hilbre I
Mostyn Quay
Connah's Quay

Great Ormes Head
RG Llandudno
Colwyn Bay
CONWY AND DEGANWY 9.10.18
Trwyn-Du

Point Lynas
Moelfre
Amlwch
Cemaes Bay
Anglesey
Beaumaris
Bangor
MENAI STRAIT 9.10.19
The Swellies
Port Dinorwic
Caernarfon
Port Trecastell
Valley
South Stack
HOLYHEAD 9.10.20
Holyhead MRCC
Treaddur Bay

Trefor
Porth Dinllaen
Porth Ysgaden

5°W   30'   4°   30'   3°
53°N   30'

9.10.3 AREA 10 TIDAL STREAMS

5 Hours before HW Dover (0515 before HW Liverpool)

4 Hours before HW Dover (0415 before HW Liverpool)

3 Hours before HW Dover (0315 before HW Liverpool)

2 Hours before HW Dover (0215 before HW Liverpool)

1 Hour before HW Dover (0115 before HW Liverpool)

HW Dover (0015 before HW Liverpool)

Northward 9.9.3   Southward 9.11.3   North Ireland 9.13.3   Mull of Kintyre 9.9.10   South Ireland 9.12.3

1 Hour after HW Dover (0045 after HW Liverpool)

2 Hours after HW Dover (0145 after HW Liverpool)

3 Hours after HW Dover (0245 after HW Liverpool)

4 Hours after HW Dover (0345 after HW Liverpool)

5 Hours after HW Dover (0445 after HW Liverpool)

6 Hours after HW Dover (0545 after HW Liverpool)

NW England

9.10.4 LIGHTS, BUOYS AND WAYPOINTS

Blue print = light with a nominal range of 15M or more. CAPITALS = place or feature. *CAPITAL ITALICS* = light-vessel, light float or Lanby. *Italics* = Fog signal. ***Bold italics*** = Racon. Abbreviations are in Chapter 1.

SOLWAY FIRTH TO BARROW-IN-FURNESS

SILLOTH and MARYPORT
Two Feet Bank ⟨ Q (9) 15s; 54°42'·90N 03°47'·10W.
Groyne Hd ⊀ 2 FG (vert) 4m 4M; Fl Bu tfc signals close by; 54°52'·14N 03°23'·93W.
Maryport S Pier Hd ⊀.Fl 1·5s 10m 6M; 54°43'·07N 03°30'·64W.

WORKINGTON and HARRINGTON
N Workington ⟨ Q; 54°40'·10N 03°38'·18W.
S Workington ⟨ VQ (6) + L Fl 10s; 54°37'·01N 03°38'·58W.
South Pier ⊀ Fl 5s 11m 5M; R bldg; 54°39'·12N 03°34'·67W.
Ldg Lts 131·8°. Front, FR 10m 3M; 54°38'·92N 03°34'·19W. Rear, 134m from front, FR 12m 3M.

WHITEHAVEN
W Pier Hd ⊀ Fl G 5s 16m 8M; W ○ twr; 54°33'·17N 03°35'·92W.
N Pier Hd ⊀ 2 FR (vert) 8m 5M; W ○ twr; 54°33'·17N 03°35'·75W.
Saint Bees Hd ☆ 54°30'·81N 03°38'·23W Fl (2) 20s 102m **18M**; W○ twr; obsc shore-340°.

RAVENGLASS
Blockhouse ⊀ FG; (Eskdale Range); 54°20'·16N 03°25'·34W.
Selker ▲ Fl (3) G 10s; *Bell;* 54°16'·14N 03°29'·58W.

BARROW-IN-FURNESS
Lightning Knoll ⊙ L Fl 10s; 53°59'·83N 03°14'·28W.
Halfway Shoal ⟨ QR 19m 10s; R&W chequer Bn; ***Racon (B) 10M***; 54°01'·46N 03°11'·88W.
Isle of Walney ☆ 54°02'·92N 03°10'·64W Fl 15s 21m **23M**; stone twr; obsc 122°-127° within 3M of shore.
Walney Chan Ldg Lts 040·7°. No.1 Front ⟨, Q 7m 10M; B Pile; 54°03'·19N 03°09'·22W. No. 2 Rear ⟨, 0·61M from front, Iso 2s 13m 10M; Pile.
Rampside Sands Ldg Lts 005·1°. No. 3 Front ⟨, Q 9m 10M; W ○ twr; 54°04'·41N 03°09'·79W. No. 4 Rear ⟨, 0·77M from front, Iso 2s 14m 6M; R col, W face.

ISLE OF MAN

Whitestone Bank ⟨ Q (9) 15s; 54°24'·58N 04°20'·41W.
Point of Ayre ☆ 54°24'·94N 04°22'·13W Fl (4) 20s 32m **19M**; W twr, two R bands, ***Racon (M) 13-15M***.
Low Lt ⊀ 54°25'·03N 04°21'·86W Fl 3s 10m 8M; R twr, lower part W, on B Base; part obsc 335°-341°.

PEEL
Peel Bkwtr Hd ⊀ Oc 7s 11m 6M; W twr; 54°13'·67N 04°41'·69W.

PORT ERIN and PORT ST MARY
Ldg Lts 099·1°. Front, 54°05'·23N 04°45'·57W FR 10m 5M; W twr, R band. Rear, 39m from front, FR 19m 5M; W col, R band.
Calf of Man Lighthouse (disused), white 8-sided tower.
Chicken Rk ⊀ Fl 5s 38m **21M**; twr; 54°02'·27N 04°50'·32W.
Alfred Pier Hd ⊀ Oc R 10s 8m 6M; W twr, R band; 54°04'·33N 04°43'·82W.

CASTLETOWN and DERBY HAVEN
Dreswick Pt ⊀ Fl (2) 30s 23m 12M; W twr; 54°03'·29N 04°37'·45W.
New Pier Hd ⊀ Oc R 15s 8m 5M; 54°04'·33N 04°38'·97W.
Derby Haven, Bkwtr SW end ⊀ Iso G 2s 5m 5M; W twr, G band; 54°04'·58N 04°37'·06W.

DOUGLAS
Douglas Head ☆ 54°08'·60N 04°27'·95W Fl 10s 32m **24M**; W twr; obsc brg more than 037°. FR Lts on radio masts 1 and 3M West.
No. 1 ▲ Q (3) G 5s; 54°09'·04N 04°27'·68W.

Princess Alexandra Pier Hd ⊀ Fl R 5s 16m 8M; R mast; *Whis (2) 40s;* 54°08'·84N 04°27'·85W.
Ldg Lts 229·3°, Front ⟨, Oc 10s 9m 5M; W △ R border on mast; 54°08'·72N 04°28'·25W. Rear ⟨, 62m from front, Oc 10s 12m 5M; W ▽ on R border; synch with front.
Victoria Pier Hd ⊀ Iso G 10s 10m 3M; W col; vis: 225°-327°; Intnl Port Tfc Signals; 54°08'·84N 04°28'·08W.
Conister Rk Refuge twr Q 3M; vis: 234°-312°; 54°09'·03N 04°28'·12W.

LAXEY to RAMSEY
Laxey Pier Hd ⊀ Oc R 3s 7m 5M; W twr, R band; obsc when brg less than 318°; 54°13'·50N 04°23'·43W.
Maughold Head ☆ 54°17'·72N 04°18'·58W Fl (3) 30s 65m **21M**.
Bahama ⟨ VQ (6) + L Fl 10s; 54°20'·01N 04°08'·57W.
Queens Pier Dn ⊀ Fl R 5s; 54°19'·28N 04°21'·95W.
King William Bank ⟨ Q (3) 10s; 54°26'·01N 04°00'·08W.

BARROW TO RIVERS MERSEY AND DEE

MORECAMBE
Lightning Knoll ⊙ L Fl 10s; 53°59'·84N 03°14'·28W.
Morecambe ⟨ Q (9) 15s; 53°52'·01N 03°24'·10W.
Lune Deep ⟨ Q (6) + L Fl 15s; ***Racon (T);*** 53°56'·07N 03°12·9W.
Lts in line about 090°. Front, FR 10m 2M; G mast; 54°04'·41N 02°52'·63W. Rear, 140m from front, FR 14m 2M; G mast.

HEYSHAM
SW Quay Ldg Lts 102·2°. Front ⟨, both F Bu 11/14m 2M; Or & B ♦ on masts; 54°01'·91N 02°55'·22W.

RIVER LUNE, GLASSON DOCK and FLEETWOOD
R Lune ⟨ Q (9) 15s; 53°58'·63N 03°00'·03W.
Fairway No. 1(Fleetwood) ⟨ 53°57'·67N 03°02'·03W Q; *Bell*.
Fleetwood Esplanade Ldg Lts 156°. Front, Iso G 2s 14m 9M; 53°55'·71N 03°00'·56W. Rear, 320m from front, Iso G 4s 28m 9M. Both vis on Ldg line only. (H24) (chan liable to change).

RIVER RIBBLE
Gut ⊙ L Fl 10s; 53°41'·74N 03°08'·98W.
Perches show Fl R on N side, and Fl G on S side of chan.
S side, 14¼M Perch ⊀ Fl G 5s 6m 3M; 53°42'·75N 03°04'·90W.
Jordan's Spit ⟨ Q (9) 15s; 53°35'·76N 03°19'·28W.
FT ⟨ Q; 53°34'·56N 03°13'·20W.

RIVER MERSEY and LIVERPOOL
Bar ⌐ Fl.5s 12M; ***Racon (T) 10M;*** 53°32'·01N 03°20'·98W.
Q1 ⋛ VQ; 53°31'·00N 03°16'·72W.
Q2 ⋛ VQ R; 53°31'·47N 03°14'·95W.
Q3 ▲ Fl G 3s; 53°30'·95N 03°15'·10W.
BT ▲ Fl (3) G 9s; 53°30'·41N 03°17'·61W.
Formby ⌐ Iso 4s 11m 6M; R hull, W stripes; 53°31'·13N 03°13'·50W.
C4 ⌐ Fl R 3s; 53°31'·82N 03°08'·51W.
Crosby ⋛ Oc 5s 11m 8M; R hull, W stripes; 53°30'·72N 03°06'·29W.
C14 ⌐ Fl R 3s; R hull; 53°29'·91N 03°05'·34W.
Brazil ▲ QG; G hull; 53°26'·84N 03°02'·24W.

RIVER DEE, MOSTYN and CONNAH'S QUAY
HE1 ⟨ Q (9) 15s; 53°26'·33N 03°18'·08W.
HE2 ⟨ Q (3) 10s; 53°25'·13N 03°13'·07W.
Mostyn Dir Lt 174°. ⊀ 53°19'·33N 03°16'·12W Iso WRG 2s 16m 7M vis: 174·8°-G-176·8°-W-177·8°-R-179·8°; H24.

WALES – NORTH COAST AND INNER PASSAGE

South Hoyle Outer ⌐ Fl R 2·5s; 53°21'·47N 03°24'·70W.
Prestatyn ▲ QG; 53°21'·51N 03°28'·51W.
Inner Passage ⌐ Fl R 5s; 53°21'·91N 03°31'·95W.
Mid Patch Spit ⌐ QR; 53°22'·25N 03°32'·67W.
North Hoyle Wind Farm (30 turbines, see 9.10.5) centred on 53°25'·00N 03°27'·00W. NW, NE, SW, SE extremities (F.R Lts) Fl Y 2.5s 5M Horn Mo (U) 30s.

WGS84 DATUM
Plot waypoints on chart before use

Mast ⚡ Mo (U) 15s 12m 10M & 2FR (vert); Horn Mo (U) 30s; Mast (80); 53°28'·84N 03°30'·50W.
W Constable ⚓ Q (9) 15s; *Racon (M) 10M;* 53°23'·14N 03°49'·26W.
N Constable ⚓ VQ; 53°23'·76N 03°41'·42W.

RHYL, LLANDUDNO and CONWY
River Clwyd Outfall ⚓ 53°19'·59N 03°30'·63W.
Llandudno Pier Hd ⚡ 2 FG (vert) 8m 4M; 53°19'·90N 03°49'·51W.
Great Ormes Hd Lt Ho, (unlit); 53°20'·56N 03°52'·17W.
Conwy Fairway ⚓ L Fl 10s; 53°17'·95N 03°55'·58W.
C2 ⚓ Fl (2) R 10s; 53°17'·64N 03°54'·71W.
Conway R ent S side ⚡ Fl WR 5s 5m 2M; vis: 076°-W-088°-R- 171°-W-319°-R-076°; 53°18'·07N 03°50'·86W.

ANGLESEY
Point Lynas ☆ 53°24'·98N 04°17'·35W Oc 10s 39m **18M**; W castellated twr; vis: 109°-315°; *Horn 45s;* H24.

AMLWCH to HOLYHEAD BAY
Main Bkwtr ⚡ Fl G 15s 11m 3M; W mast; vis: 141°-271°; 53°25'·02N 04°19'·91W.
Furlong ⚓ Fl G 2·5s; 53°25'·41N 04°30'·47W.
Archdeacon Rock ⚓ Q; 53°26'·71N 04°30'·87W.
Victoria Bank ⚓ VQ; 53°25'·61N 04°31'·37W.
Coal Rk ⚓ Q (6) + L Fl 15s; 53°25'·91N 04°32'·79W.
Ethel Rk ⚓ VQ; 53°26'·64N 04°33'·67W.
The Skerries ☆ 53°25'·27N 04°36'·55W Fl (2) 15s 36m **20M**; W ○ twr, R band; *Racon (T) 25M.* Iso R 4s 26m 10M; same twr; vis: 233°-253°; *Horn (2) 60s.* H24 in periods of reduced visibility.
Langdon ⚓ Q (9) 15s; 53°22'·74N 04°38'·74W.
Bolivar ⚓ Fl G 2·5s; 53°21'·51N 04°35'·33W.
Wk ⚓ Fl (2) R 10s; 53°20'·43N 04°36'·60W.

HOLYHEAD to SOUTH STACK
Bkwtr Head ⚡ Fl (3) G 10s 21m 14M; W □ twr, B band; Fl Y vis: 174°-226°; *Siren 20s;* 53°19'·31N 04°37'·16W.

Spit ⚓ Fl G 3s; 53°19'·79N 04°37'·15W.
South Stack ☆ 53°19'·31N 04°41'·98W Fl 10s 60m **24M**; (H24); W ○ twr; obsc to N by N Stack and part obsc in Penrhos bay; *Horn 30s.* Fog Det lt vis: 145°-325°.

Ten Feet Bank ⚓ QR; 53°19'·47N 04°02'·82W.
Dinmor ⚓ QG; 53°19'·34N 04°03'·32W.
Trwyn-Du ⚡ Fl 5s 19m 12M; W ○ castelled twr, B bands; vis: 101°-023°; *Bell (1) 30s,* sounded continuously; 53°18'·77N 04°02'·44W. FR on radio mast 2M SW.

APPROACHES to BEAUMARIS and BANGOR
(Direction of buoyage ↺ NE to SW)
Perch Rock ⚓ Fl R 5s; 53°18'·73N 04°02'·09W.

PORT DINORWIC and CAERNARFON
Port Dinorwic Pier Hd ⚡ 53°11'·18N 04°12'·64W F WR 5m 2M; vis: 225°-R- 357°-W-225°.
(Direction of buoyage ↺ SW to NE)
Caernarfon N Pier Hd ⚡ 2 FG (vert) 5m 2M; 53°08'·72N 04°16'·56W.
Abermenai Point ⚡ Fl WR 3·5s 6m 3M; W mast; vis: 065°-R-245°-W-065°; 53°07'·62N 04°19'·72W.
C1 ⚓ Fl G 5s; 53°07'·27N 04°24'·85W.
C2 ⚓ Fl R 10s; 53°07'·38N 04°24'·87W.
Llanddwyn I ⚡Fl WR 2·5s 12m W7M, R4M; W twr; vis: 280°-R-015°-W-120°; 53°08'·05N 04°24'·79W .

PORTH DINLLÄEN
CG Stn ⚡ FR when firing taking place 10M N; 52°56'·82N 04°33'·89W.
Careg y Chwislen ⚓ 52°56'·99N 04°33'·51W.

Bardsey I ☆ 52°44'·97N 04°48'·02W Fl (5) 15s 39m **26M**; W □ twr, R bands; obsc by Bardsey Is 198°-250° and in Tremadoc B when brg < 260°; *Horn Mo (N) 45s;* (H24 in poor vis).

9.10.5 PASSAGE INFORMATION

For detailed directions covering these waters and harbours refer to the Admiralty Pilot *W Coast of England and Wales; Lundy and Irish Sea Pilot* (Taylor/Imray). Admiralty Leisure Folio 5609 covers North West Wales from Aberystwyth to Colwyn Bay including Menai Strait; Folio 5613 covers Great Ormes Head to the Mull of Galloway including the Isle of Man.

More Passage Information is threaded between the harbours of this Area.

(AC 1346) Between Abbey Hd and St Bees Hd lies the Solway Firth, most of which is encumbered by shifting sandbanks. The *Solway SDs* are essential. Off the entrances to the Firth, and in the approaches to Workington beware shoals over which strong W winds raise a heavy sea. There are navigable, buoyed chans as far as Annan on the N shore, but buoys are laid primarily for the aid of Pilots. ▶ *Local knowledge is required, particularly in the upper Firth, where streams run very strongly in the chans when the banks are dry, and less strongly over the banks when covered. In Powfoot chan for example the in-going stream begins at HW Liverpool – 0300, and the outgoing at HW Liverpool + 0100, sp rates up to 6kn.* ◀

Between Silloth and Walney Is are Maryport, Workington, Harrington, Whitehaven, and Ravenglass. A windfarm is under construction (2008) approximately 7M WNW of Maryport. South along the Cumbrian coast past St Bees Hd to Walney Is there are no dangers more than 2M offshore, but no shelter except, possibly, in Ramsey bay, IoM.

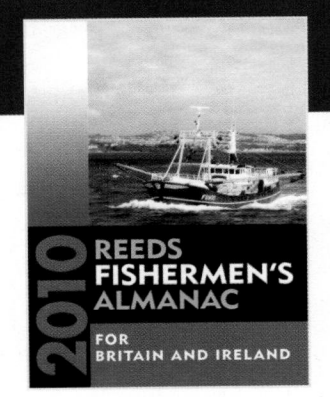
NW England

9.10.6 MARYPORT

Cumbria **54°43'·03N 03°30'·38W** ❀❀❀❀❀❀

CHARTS AC 1826, 1346, 2013, 5613; Imray C62.

TIDES +0038 Dover; ML no data; Duration 0550

Standard Port LIVERPOOL (⟶)

Times				Height (metres)			
High Water		Low Water		MHWS	MHWN	MLWN	MLWS
0000	0600	0200	0800	9·3	7·4	2·9	0·9
1200	1800	1400	2000				
Differences MARYPORT							
+0017	+0032	+0020	+0005	−0·7	−0·8	−0·4	0·0
SILLOTH							
+0030	+0040	+0045	+0055	−0·1	−0·3	−0·6	−0·1

SHELTER Good in marina, access HW ±2½ nps over sill 1·75m; at other times Workington is a refuge. Elizabeth Basin dries 2m, access HW±1½; commercial, not used by yachts.

NAVIGATION WPT 54°43'·09N 03°32'·47W, 090°/1M to S pier. Overfalls at ent with W/SW winds over ebb. At HW−3 1·8m over bar at ent and in river chan; mud banks cover HW −2.

LIGHTS AND MARKS See 9.10.4 and chartlet. SHM bn Fl G 5s marks outfall 6ca SW of S pier.

R/T Port VHF Ch 12 16. Marina (H24) Ch 12 16.

TELEPHONE (Code 01900) HM 817440; Hbr Authority 604351; CG 812782; MRCC (0151) 931 3341; Marinecall 09068 969651; Police 602422; Dr 815544; Ⓗ 812634.

FACILITIES Maryport Marina (201 inc Ⓥ £14.69/craft inc ⚡), ☎ 814431, www.maryportmarina.com, BY, BH, El, CH, ▣, ME, Slip (±3HW), D, P, (fresh fish from Fisherman's Co-op); **Maryport Yachting Ass'n** ☎ 64964. **Town** P, D, ME, 🛒, R, Bar, ✉, Ⓑ, ⇌, ✈ (Newcastle).

9.10.7 WORKINGTON

Cumbria **54°39'·03N 03°34'·38W** ❀❀❀

CHARTS AC 1826, 1346, 2013, 5613; Imray C62.

TIDES +0025 Dover; ML 4·5; Duration 0545

Standard Port LIVERPOOL (⟶)

Times				Height (metres)			
High Water		Low Water		MHWS	MHWN	MLWN	MLWS
0000	0600	0200	0800	9·3	7·4	2·9	0·9
1200	1800	1400	2000				
Differences WORKINGTON							
+0020	+0020	+0020	+0010	−1·2	−1·1	−0·3	0·0

SHELTER Good; ent and chan to Prince of Wales Dock are dredged 1·8m. Berth where you can (free in tidal harbour); no ⚓ in Turning Basin. Lock (HW±1½) into PoW Dock 1·8m (for coasters). Low (1·8m) fixed railway bridge across ent to inner tidal hbr.

NAVIGATION WPT 54°39'·59N 03°35'·38W, 131°/1M to front ldg lt.

• Tide sets strongly across ent. In periods of heavy rain a strong freshet from R Derwent may be encountered in the hbr ent.

LIGHTS AND MARKS Workington Bank, least depth 5·5m, is 2M W of hbr ent; and is marked by NCM and SCM lt buoys (see 9.10.4). A SHM buoy, Fl G 5s, 1·3M NW of hbr ent is a mark for English Chan. Ldg lts 132°, both FR 10/12m 3M, on W pyramidal trs with R bands. Two sets of F Bu lts in line mark NE and SW edges of chan.

• There are 16 wind-turbines between ¾M and 2M NE of hbr ent.

R/T VHF Ch 14 16 (HW−2½ to HW+2 approx).

TELEPHONE (Code 01900) HM 602301; MRCC (0151) 931 3341; Marinecall 09068 969651; Police 602422; Dr 64866; Ⓗ 602244.

FACILITIES Dock D, FW, ME, El; **Vanguard SC** ☎ 01228 674238, M, FW. **Town** P, 🛒, R, Bar, ✉, Ⓑ, ⇌, ✈ (Carlisle).

MINOR HARBOUR 10M NNE OF MARYPORT

SILLOTH, Cumbria, **54°52'·16N 03°23'·86W**. AC 1826, 1346, 2013, 5613. HW −0050 on Dover; ML no data; Duration 0520. See 9.10.6. Appr via English or Middle Chans, approx 8M long, requires local knowledge. Beware constantly shifting chans and banks. Yachts are not encouraged. ⚓ SW of ent in about 4m off Lees Scar, Fl G 10s 11m 2M; exposed to SW winds. Outer hbr dries; lock into New Dock (note sill 1.2 above CD), which is mainly commercial. East Cote Dir lt 052° FG 15m 12M; vis 046°-058°, intens 052°. Ldg lts, both F, 115°. Groyne 2 FG (vert). Tfc sigs on mast at New Dock: must receive permission from Port Authority before proceeding. VHF Ch 16 12 (HW−2½ to HW+1½). HM ☎ (016973) 31358. Facilities: FW, Ⓑ, Bar, ✉, R, 🛒.

MINOR HARBOUR 2M S OF WORKINGTON

HARRINGTON, Cumbria, **54°36'·77N 03°34'·29W**. AC 1826, 1346, 2013, 5613. HW +0025 on Dover; Duration 0540; Use Diff's Workington 9.10.7. Good shelter in small hbr only used by local FVs and yachts; dries 3ca offshore. Ent difficult in strong W winds. Berth on N wall of inner hbr (free). Call ☎ (01946) 823741 Ext 148 for moorings. Limited facilities. **SC**.

9.10.8　WHITEHAVEN

Cumbria **54°33'·18N 03°35'·82W** ✴✴✴✴✿✿✿✿✿

CHARTS AC 1826, 1346, 2013, 5613; Imray C62.

TIDES +0015 Dover; ML 4·5; Duration 0550

Standard Port LIVERPOOL (→)

Times				Height (metres)			
High Water		Low Water		MHWS	MHWN	MLWN	MLWS
0000	0600	0200	0800	9·3	7·4	2·9	0·9
1200	1800	1400	2000				
Differences WHITEHAVEN							
+0005	+0015	+0010	+0005	−1·3	−1·1	−0·5	+0·1
TARN POINT (54°17'N 03°25'W)							
+0005	+0005	+0010	0000	−1·0	−1·0	−0·4	0·0
DUDDON BAR (54°09'N 03°20'W)							
+0003	+0003	+0008	+0002	−0·8	−0·8	−0·3	0·0

SHELTER Very good, entry safe in most weathers. One of the more accessible ports of refuge in NW England, with a new marina in the inner hbr. Appr chan across the outer hbr is dredged to 1·0m above CD giving access approx HW±4. Sea lock (30m x 13.7m), with sill at CD, maintains 7m within inner hbr. Queen's Dock (from which the lock gates have been decommissioned) and N Hbr remain for commercial and FV use.

NAVIGATION WPT 54°33'·34N 03°36'·21W, 133°/4½ca to W pier hd. There are no hazards in the offing. Hold closer to the North Pier, and beware stone bar at end of W Pier.

LIGHTS AND MARKS Several tall chimneys are charted within 1·5M S of hbr. St Bees Head Lt ho is 2·7M SSW of hbr ent. SHM bn, Fl G 2·5s, 4½ca S of W pierhead marks sewer outfall. IPTS sigs 1-3 shown from N side of lock ent to seaward only at present: priority to inward bound vessels.

R/T HM VHF Ch 12 16 (as for access times).

TELEPHONE (Code 01946)HM 692435, 🖹 691135; Sealock 694672; MRCC (0151) 931 3341; Police 692616; Marinecall 09068 969651.

FACILITIES Marina (200 inc Ⓥ) ☎ 692435, office@whitehaven-harbour.co.uk, <12m £15, <12m £8 on quay wall, contact HM, D, Gas, BY, CH, ME, Ⓔ, El, ✕, BH, Slip, 🗑. **SC. Town** Market days Thurs, Sat; P (cans), Bar, Ⓑ, ✉, R, 🛒, ⇌.

MINOR HARBOUR BETWEEN ST BEES HD AND MORECAMBE BAY
RAVENGLASS, Cumbria, **54°20'·00N 03°26'·80W** (drying line). AC 1346, 1826, 5613. HW +0020 on Dover; ML no data; Duration 0545. See 9.10.8 (Tarn Pt). Large drying hbr, into which R's Mite, Irt and Esk flow; approx 2·5m in ent at HW−2. Sellafield power stn with WCM lt buoy and outfall buoys are 5M NNW. FG ✩ (occas) on blockhouse at S side of ent. *Solway Sailing Directions* with pilotage notes by Ravenglass Boating Ass'n, local knowledge advisable. From N beware Drigg Rk and from S Selker Rks, SHM lt buoy, 5M SSW of ent. Firing range D406 close S at Eskmeals; Mon-Thur 0800-1600LT (1500 Fri). When in use R flags flown, R lts at night; *Eskmeals Gun Range* VHF Ch 16 13, ☎ (01229) 717631 Ext 245/6. **Village:** FW, Slip, Bar, 🛒, ✉.

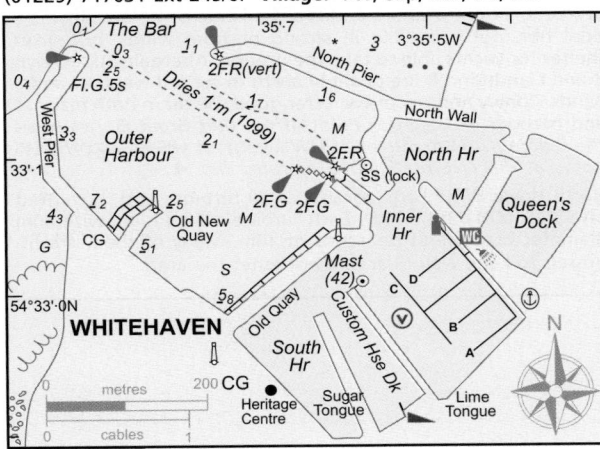

9.10.9　ISLE OF MAN

Charts AC Irish Sea 1826, 1411; 2094 (small scale); 2696 (ports), 5613 (Folio). Imray, C26, Y70.

The Isle of Man is one of the British Islands, set in the Irish Sea roughly equidistant from England, Scotland, Wales and Ireland but it is not part of the UK. It has a large degree of self-government. Lights are maintained by the Northern Lighthouse Board. Manx harbours are administered by the IOM Government.

Distances See 9.10.2 for distances between ports in Area 10 and 9.0.7 for distances across the Irish Sea, North Channel and St George's Channel.

Harbours and anchorages Most of the harbours are on the E and S sides, but a visit to the W coast with its characteristic cliffs is worth while. The four main harbours are described in an anti-clockwise direction from Peel on the W coast to Ramsey in the NE. There are good ⚓s at: Port Erin in the SW, Castletown and Derby Haven in the SE, and Laxey Bay in the E. All IOM harbours charge the same overnight berthing rate, £1.02/m (multi-hulls £1.53/m).

R/T If contact with local Harbour Offices cannot be established on VHF, vessels should call *Douglas Hbr Control* Ch **12** 16 for urgent messages or other info.

Coastguard Call Liverpool MRCC Ch 16 67 86; the Snaefell (IoM) aerial is linked to Liverpool by land line.

Customs The IOM is under the same customs umbrella as the rest of the UK, and there are no formalities on arriving from or returning to the UK.

Weather Forecasts can be obtained direct from the forecaster at Ronaldsway Met Office ☎ 0900 6243 3200, H24. **Douglas Hbr Control** (9.10.16) can supply visibility and wind info on request.

MINOR HARBOURS IN THE ISLE OF MAN

PORT ERIN, Isle of Man, **54°05'·31N 04°46'·34W**. AC 2094, 2696, 5613. HW −0020 on Dover; ML 2·9m; Duration 0555. See 9.10.15. From S and W, Milner's Twr on Bradda Hd is conspic. Ldg lts, both FR 10/19m 5M, lead 099° into the bay. Beware the ruined bkwtr (dries 2·9m) extending N from the SW corner, marked by an unlit SHM buoy. A small hbr on the S side dries 0·8m. Raglan Pier (E arm of hbr), Oc G 5s 8m 5M. Two ⚓s W of Raglan Pier. Good ⚓ in 3-8m N of Raglan Pier, but exposed to W'lies. Call Port St. Mary Harbour (VHF Ch 12) ☎ 833205

CASTLETOWN BAY, Isle of Man, **54°03'·51N 04°38'·57W**. AC 2094, 2696, 5613. HW +0025 on Dover; ML 3·4m; Duration 0555. The bay gives good shelter except in SE to SW winds. From the E, keep inside the race off Dreswick Pt, or give it a wide berth. Beware Lheeah-rio Rks in W of bay, marked by PHM buoy, Fl R 3s, Bell. Hbr dries 3·1m to level sand. Access HW±2½. Berth in outer hbr or go via swing footbridge (manually opened) into inner hbr below fixed bridge. ⚓ between Lheeah-rio Rks and pier in 3m; or NW of Langness Pt. Lts: Langness lt, on Dreswick Pt, Fl (2) 30s 23m 12M. Hbr S (New) Pier, Oc R 15s 8m 5M; Inner S pier (Irish Quay), Oc R 4s 5m 5M, vis 142°-322°. 150m NW is swing bridge marked by 2 FR (hor). N pier, Oc G 4s 3m (W metal post on concrete column). VHF Ch 12 16 (when vessel due). HM ☎ 823549; Dr 823597. Facilities: **Outer hbr** Slip, L, C (mobile), AB; **Irish Quay** AB, C, FW; **Inner hbr** AB, C, FW; **Town** P, D, Gas, ME.

LAXEY, Isle of Man, **54°13'·46N 04°23'·32W**. AC 2094, 5613. HW +0025 on Dover; +0010 and −2·0m on Liverpool; ML 4m; Duration 0550. The bay gives good shelter in SW to N winds. 2 yellow ⚓s (seasonal) are close E of hbr ent; 2 more are 1M S in Garwick Bay. ⚓ about 2ca S of pier hds or in Garwick Bay. The hbr dries 3·0m to rk and is only suitable for small yachts; access HW±3 for 1·5m draft. Beware rks on N side of the narrow ent. Keep close to pier after entering to avoid training wall on NE side. AB on inside of pier; inner basin is full of local boats. Pier hd lt Oc R 3s 7m 5M, obsc when brg <318°. Bkwtr hd lt Oc G 3s 7m. Harbour Office ☎ 861663. Facilities: FW, R, ✉, Ⓑ, Bar.

NW England

ISLE OF MAN

(Charts 2094, 2696, 5613) For general pilotage information, tidal streams and hbr details of IOM, see *IOM Sailing Directions, Tidal Streams and Anchorages*, published by Hunter Publications. For notes on crossing the Irish Sea, see 9.13.5.

There are four choices when rounding S of IoM:

In bad weather, or at night, keep S of Chicken Rk. In good conditions, pass between Chicken Rk and Calf of Man. With winds of <Force 3 and a reliable engine giving >5kn, and only by day use Calf Sound between Calf of Man and IoM, passing W of Kitterland Is but E of Thousla Rk, which is marked by lt bn and is close to Calf of Man shore. Little Sound, a minor chan, runs E of Kitterland Is.

▶ *The stream runs strongly through Calf Sound, starting N-going at HW Liverpool – 0145, and S-going at HW Liverpool + 0345, sp rates 3·5kn. W of Calf of Man the stream runs N and S, but changes direction off Chicken Rk and runs W and E between Calf of Man and Langness Pt 6M to E. Overfalls extend E from Chicken Rk on E-going stream, which begins at HW Liverpool + 0610, and N from the rk on W-going stream, which begins at HW Liverpool.*

Off Langness Pt (lt) the Skerranes (dry) extend 1ca SW, and tidal stream runs strongly, with eddies and a race. E side of Langness peninsula is foul ground, over which a dangerous sea can build in strong winds. Here the NE-going stream begins at HW Liverpool +0545, and the SW-going at HW Liverpool –0415, sp rates 2·25kn. ◀

There is an anchorage in Derby Haven, N of St Michael's Is, but exposed to the E. From here to Douglas and on to Maughold Hd (lt), there are no dangers more than 4ca offshore. ▶ *Near the coast the SW-going stream runs for 9 hours and the NE-going for 3 hours, since an eddy forms during the second half of the main NE-going stream. Off Maughold Hd the NE-going stream begins at HW Liverpool +0500, and the SW-going at HW Liverpool –0415.*◀

SE, E and NW of Pt of Ayre are dangerous banks, on which seas break in bad weather. These are Whitestone Bk (least depth 2·0m), Bahama Bk (1·5m), Ballacash Bk (2·7 m), King William Bks (3·3m), and Strunakill Bk (6·7m).

▶ *E-going stream at Point of Ayre begins HW Liverpool –0600 (HW Dover –0545). Counter tide inside banks E of Point. In Ramsey Bay the S-going tide runs for 3 hours from Liverpool +0515 (Dover +0530).*

W-going stream at Point of Ayre begins HW Liverpool (HW Dover +0015). Counter tide inside banks W of Point. In Ramsey Bay the N going tide runs for 9 hours from Liverpool –0345 (Dover –0330).◀

The W coast of IOM has few pilotage hazards. A spit with depth of 1·4m runs 2ca offshore from Rue Pt. Jurby Rk (depth 2·7m) lies 3ca off Jurby Hd. Craig Rk (depth 4 m) and shoals lie 2·5M NNE of Peel.

BARROW TO CONWY

(AC 2010, 1981, 1978, 5613) Ent to Barrow-in-Furness (AC 3164) is about 1M S of Hilpsford Pt at S end of Walney Island where the lt ho is prominent. ▶*The stream sets across the narrow chan, which is well marked but shallow in patches.*◀ W winds cause rough sea in the ent. Moorings and anch off Piel and Roa Islands, but space is limited. ▶ *Stream runs hard on ebb. Coming from the S it is possible with sufficient rise of tide to cross the sands between Fleetwood and Barrow.* ◀

Barrow Wind Farm, consisting of 30 turbines, is marked by FR and Fl Y lights on all structures. The site is centred approx 7·6M SSW of Barrow-in-Furness.

Lune Deep, 2M NW of Rossall Pt, is ent to Morecambe B (chart 2010), and gives access to the ferry/commercial port of Heysham, Glasson Dock, and Fleetwood; it is well buoyed. ▶ *Streams run 3·5kn at sp.*◀ Most of Bay is encumbered with drying sands, intersected by chans which are subject to change. S of Morecambe B, beware shoals and drying outfall (2·0m) extending 3M W of Rossall Pt. Further S, R. Ribble gives access via a long drying chan to the marina at Preston.

Queen's Chan and Crosby Chan (AC 1951 &1978) are entered E of the Bar Lat Buoy SWM. They are well buoyed, dredged and preserved by training banks, and give main access to R Mersey and Liverpool. Keep clear of commercial shipping. From the N the old Formby chan is abandoned, but possible near HW. Towards HW in moderate winds a yacht can cross the training bank (level varies between 2m and 3m above CD) E of Great Burbo Bk, if coming from the W, Rock Chan, which is unmarked and dries in parts, may also be used but beware wrecks.

In good weather at nps, the Dee Estuary (AC 1953, 1978) is accessible for boats able to take the ground. But most of estuary dries and banks extend 6M seaward. Chans shift, and buoys are moved as required. ▶ *Stream runs hard in chans when banks are dry.* ◀ Main ent is Welsh Chan, but if coming from N, Hilbre Swash runs W of Hilbre Is.

Sailing W from the Dee on the ebb, it is feasible to take the Inner Passage (buoyed) S of West Hoyle Spit, which gives some protection from onshore winds at half tide or below. Rhyl is a tidal hbr, not accessible in strong onshore winds, but gives shelter for yachts able to take the ground. Abergele Rd, Colwyn B and Llandudno B are possible anchs in settled weather and S winds. Conwy and Deganwy offer good shelter in both marinas and harbour. ▶ *Between Point of Ayr and Great Ormes Head the E-going stream begins at HW Liverpool +0600, and the W-going at HW Liverpool –0015, sp rates 3kn.* ◀

North Hoyle Wind Farm consists of 30 turbines and is centred on 53°25'·00N 03°27'·00W. Each turbine is 58m high, with 80m diameter blades and clearance of 18m. Many of them are lit. Vessels to keep well clear and not enter the area.

9.10.10   PEEL

Isle of Man 54°13'·61N 04°41'·68W ✿❀♨♨✿✿✿

CHARTS AC 2094, 2696, 5613; Imray C62; Y70.

TIDES +0005 Dover; ML 2·9; Duration 0545

Standard Port LIVERPOOL (→)

Times				Height (metres)			
High Water		Low Water		MHWS	MHWN	MLWN	MLWS
0000	0600	0200	0700	9·3	7·4	2·9	0·9
1200	1800	1400	1900				
Differences PEEL							
+0005	+0005	–0015	–0025	–4·1	–3·1	–1·4	–0·5

SHELTER Good, except in strong NW to NE winds when ent should not be attempted. 4 Y ⚓s (seasonal) off S groyne in about 2m. Fin keelers may be able to berth on N bkwtr in 5m. A new (2009) 120-berth marina is in the Inner Harbour. Approach dries 1·4m; access approx HW±2 when flapgate lowered and through swing bridge. Maintained depth 2·5m.

NAVIGATION WPT 54°13'·97N 04°41'·43W, 200°/0·42M to groyne lt. When close in, beware groyne on S side of hbr ent, submerged at half tide.

LIGHTS AND MARKS Power stn chy (80m, grey with B top) at S end of inner hbr is conspic from W and N; chy brg 203° leads to hbr ent. Groyne lt and Clock Tr (conspic) in transit 200° are almost on same line. Peel Castle and 2 twrs are conspic on St Patrick's Isle to NW of hbr. Ldg lts in transit 207° on Groyne Fl R 5s 4m. Traffic sigs for Inner Hbr.

R/T *Peel Hbr* VHF Ch **12** 16 (HW±2, HO for Swing Bridge – other times call *Douglas Hbr Control* Ch 12 for remote bridge opening).

TELEPHONE (Code 01624) Harbour Office ☎ 842338, Mobile 07624 495036; MRCC 0151-931 3341; Weather 0900 6243 322; Marinecall 09068 969651; Police 697327; Dr 843636.

FACILITIES **Outer Hbr**, AB see 9.10.9; **Marina** 102 AB inc ♥, £1.53; access via flapgate; M, Slip, FW, D, ME, El, ⚒, C (mobile); **Peel Sailing and Cruising Club** ☎ 842390, Showers (key from Harbour Office), R, 🚽, Bar; **Services:** Gas, BY, CH, ACA. **Town** P (cans), 🍴, R, Bar, ✉, Ⓑ, ⇌ (bus to Douglas (and ferry)), ✈ Ronaldsway. Facilities: Bar, D, P, FW, R, Slip, 🛒.

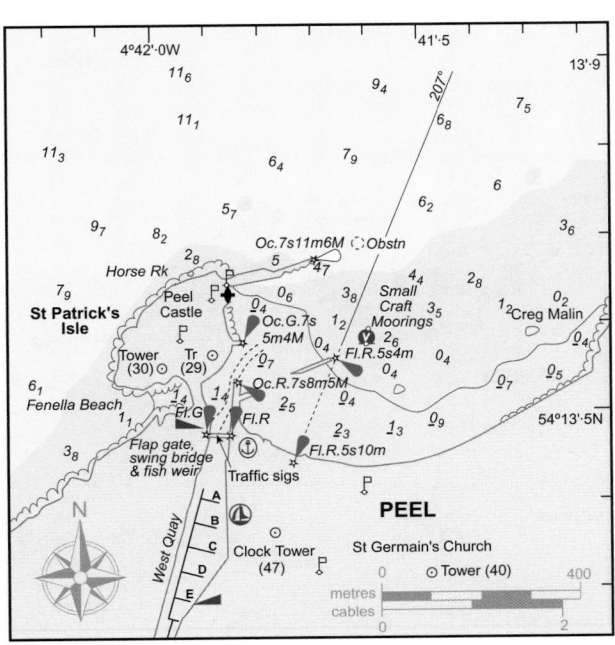

PEEL

9.10.11   PORT ST MARY

Isle of Man 54°04'·43N 04°43'·73W ✿❀♨♨✿✿

CHARTS AC 2094, 2696, 5613; Imray C62; Y70.

TIDES +0020 Dover; ML 3·2; Duration 0605

Standard Port LIVERPOOL (→)

Times				Height (metres)			
High Water		Low Water		MHWS	MHWN	MLWN	MLWS
0000	0600	0200	0700	9·3	7·4	2·9	0·9
1200	1800	1400	1900				
Differences PORT ST MARY							
+0005	+0015	–0010	–0030	–3·4	–2·6	–1·3	–0·4
CALF SOUND							
+0005	+0005	–0015	–0025	–3·2	–2·6	–0·9	–0·3
PORT ERIN							
–0005	+0015	–0010	–0050	–4·1	–3·2	–1·3	–0·5

SHELTER Very good except in E or SE winds. ⚓ S of Gansey Pt, but poor holding. 5 yellow ⚓s (seasonal) between Alfred Pier and Little Carrick.

NAVIGATION WPT 54°04'·21N 04°43'·37W, 295°/0·3M to Alfred Pier lt. Rocky outcrops to SE of pier to 2ca offshore. Beware lobster/crab pots, especially between Calf Island and Langness Pt.

LIGHTS AND MARKS Alfred Pier, Oc R 10s 8m 6M. Inner pier, Oc R 3s 8m 5M; both lts on W trs + R band, in transit 295° lead clear S of The Carrick Rk, in centre of bay, which is marked by IDM bn, Q (2) 5s 6m 3M. A conspic TV mast (133m), 5ca WNW of hbr, in transit with Alfred Pier lt leads 290° towards the hbr and also clears The Carrick rock.

R/T Call *Port St Mary Hbr* VHF Ch 12 16 (when vessel due or through Douglas Hbr Control Ch 12).

TELEPHONE (Code 01624) HM 833205; MRCC 0151 931 3341; Weather 0900 6243 322, Marinecall 09068 969651; Police 697327; Dr 832226.

FACILITIES **Alfred Pier** AB see 9.10.9, Slip, D, L, FW, C (mobile); **Inner Hbr** dries 2·4m on sand; AB, Slip, D, L, FW; **Isle of Man YC** ☎ 832088, FW, Showers, Bar; **Services:** ME, CH, D, El, SM. **Town** CH, 🍴, R, Bar, ✉, Ⓑ, ⇌ (bus to Douglas, qv for ferries), ✈ Ronaldsway.

MINOR HARBOUR EAST OF CASTLETOWN

DERBY HAVEN, Isle of Man, **54°04'·65N 04°36'·45W**. Tides & charts as above. Rather remote bay exposed only to NE/E winds. ⚓ in centre of bay, NW of St Michael's Island, in 3-5m. A detached bkwtr on NW side of the bay gives shelter to craft able to dry out behind it. Lts: Iso G 2s on S end of bkwtr. Aero FR (occas) at Ronaldsway airport, NW of bay. Facilities: at Castletown (1½M) or Port St Mary.

Isle of Man

9.10.12 DOUGLAS

Isle of Man **54°08'·87N 04°27'·96W** ❀❀❀⚓⚓✿✿✿

CHARTS AC 2094, 2696, 5613; Imray C62; Y70.

TIDES +0009 Dover; ML 3·8; Duration 0600

Standard Port LIVERPOOL (⟶)

Times				Height (metres)			
High Water		Low Water		MHWS	MHWN	MLWN	MLWS
0000	0600	0200	0700	9·3	7·4	2·9	0·9
1200	1800	1400	1900				
Differences DOUGLAS							
+0005	+0015	–0015	–0025	–2·4	–2·0	–0·5	–0·1

SHELTER Good except in NE winds. Very heavy seas run in during NE gales. Outer hbr: Victoria and King Edward VIII piers are for commercial vessels/ferries. At inner end of Battery Pier in summer about 18 boats can raft up on pontoon; untenable in NE/E winds. Complete shelter in inner hbr, with possible pontoon berths, flagpate lowers on the flood and rises on the ebb at 4·4m above CD, lifting bridge opens every ½H subject to tide/road traffic conditions (request opening on VHF Ch12).

NAVIGATION WPT 54°09'·01N 04°27'·67W (abeam No 1 SHM buoy, Q (3) G 5s), 229°/0·47M to front ldg lt. Appr from NE of No 1 buoy (to avoid overfalls E of Princess Alexandra Pier) and await port entry sig, or call on VHF Ch 12. There is no bar. Keep clear of large vessels and ferries. Beware concrete step at end of dredged area (◇ mark on King Edward VIII Pier) and cill at ent to inner hbr.

LIGHTS AND MARKS Douglas Head Fl 10s 32m 24M. Ldg lts 229°, both Oc 10s 9/12m 5M, synch; front W △; rear W ▽, both on R border. IPTS Nos 2, 3 and 5 shown from mast on Victoria Pier. Dolphin at N end of Alexandra Pier 2FR (vert).

R/T *Douglas Hbr Control* VHF Ch **12** 16 (H24); also broadcasts nav warnings for IoM ports and coastal waters on Ch 12 including weather and tidal info on request.

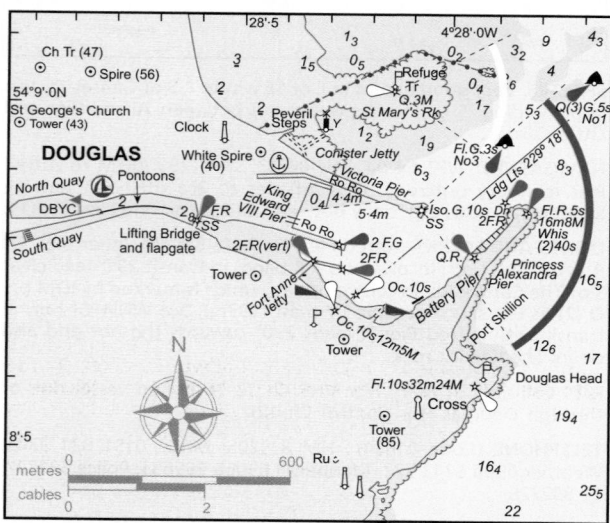

TELEPHONE (Code 01624) Hr Control 686628 (H24); MRCC 0151-931 3341; Weather 0900 6243 322, Marinecall 09068 969651; Police 697327; ⊞ 650000.

FACILITIES Outer Hbr AB see 9.10.9, M, FW at pontoon, D, ME, El, ✕, C (mobile), Slip; **Inner Hbr (Pontoons and N and S Quays)** (110); ❶ according to space (no reservations), M, ⇱, FW, ME, C, El, ✕, CH, Slip; **Douglas Bay YC** ☎ 673965, Bar, Slip, L, showers 0930-2300. **Services:** P (cans), D, CH, ACA, El, Divers, Gas, Gaz, Kos. **Town** www.gov.im, 🍴, R, Bar, ✉, Ⓑ, 🖰, ✈ Ronaldsway. **Ferries:** Liverpool; 16/week; 2½ Hrs; IoM Steam Packet (www.steam-packet.com). Heysham; 16/week; 3½ Hrs; Steam Packet. Also to Dublin and Belfast.

9.10.13 RAMSEY

Isle of Man **54°19'·44N 04°22'·49W** ❀❀⚓⚓✿✿

CHARTS AC 2094, 2696, 5613; Imray C62; Y70.

TIDES +0020 Dover; ML 4·2; Duration 0545

Standard Port LIVERPOOL (⟶)

Times				Height (metres)			
High Water		Low Water		MHWS	MHWN	MLWN	MLWS
0000	0600	0200	0700	9·3	7·4	2·9	0·9
1200	1800	1400	1900				
Differences RAMSEY							
+0005	+0015	–0005	–0015	–1·9	–1·5	–0·6	0·0

SHELTER Very good except in strong NE winds. Hbr dries 1·8m–6m. Access and ent only permitted HW –2½ to HW +2. Berth on Town quay (S side) or as directed by HM on entry. 4 yellow ⚓s are close NW of Queen's Pier hd (seasonal). Note: Landing on Queen's Pier is prohibited.

NAVIGATION WPT 54°19'·44N 04°21'·89W, 270°/0·37M to ent. The foreshore dries out 1ca to seaward of the pier hds.

LIGHTS AND MARKS No ldg lts/marks. Relative to hbr ent, Pt of Ayre, Fl (4) 20s 32m 19M, is 5·5M N; Maughold Hd, Fl (3) 30s 65m 21M, is 3M SE; Albert Tr (□ stone tr 14m, on hill 130m) is conspic 7ca S; and Snaefell (617m) bears 220°/5M. Inside the hbr an Iso G 4s, G SHM post, marks the S tip of Mooragh Bank; it is not visible from seaward. 2FR (hor) on each side mark the centre of swing bridge.

R/T *Ramsey Hbr* VHF Ch **12** 16 (0800-1600LT and when a vessel is due); Other times call *Douglas Hbr Control* Ch **12**.

TELEPHONE (Code 01624) Harbour Office 812245, mob 07624 460304; MRCC 0151 931 3341; Weather 0900 6243 322, Marinecall 09068 969651; Police 812234; Dr 813881; ⊞ 811811.

FACILITIES Outer Hbr: E Quay ☎ 812245, strictly for commercial vessels (frequent movements H24), no AB for yachts, FW; **Town Quay** (S side) AB see 9.10.9, ⇱, FW. **Inner Hbr, W Quay** AB, ⇱, FW, Slip (Grid); **N Quay** AB, D, FW; **Shipyard Quay** Slip; **Old Hbr** AB, Slip, M; **Manx S&CC:** ☎ 813494 AB; **Services:** P (cans) from garages, D, ME, El, Ⓔ, ✕, ☒. **Town** 🍴, R, Gas, Gaz, Kos, Bar, @ in Library, 🖰, ✉, Ⓑ, ≈ (bus to Douglas, which see for ferries), ✈ Ronaldsway.

9.10.14 GLASSON DOCK

Lancashire 53°59'·98N 02°50'·93W ✿✿⌾⌾⌾⌾✿✿

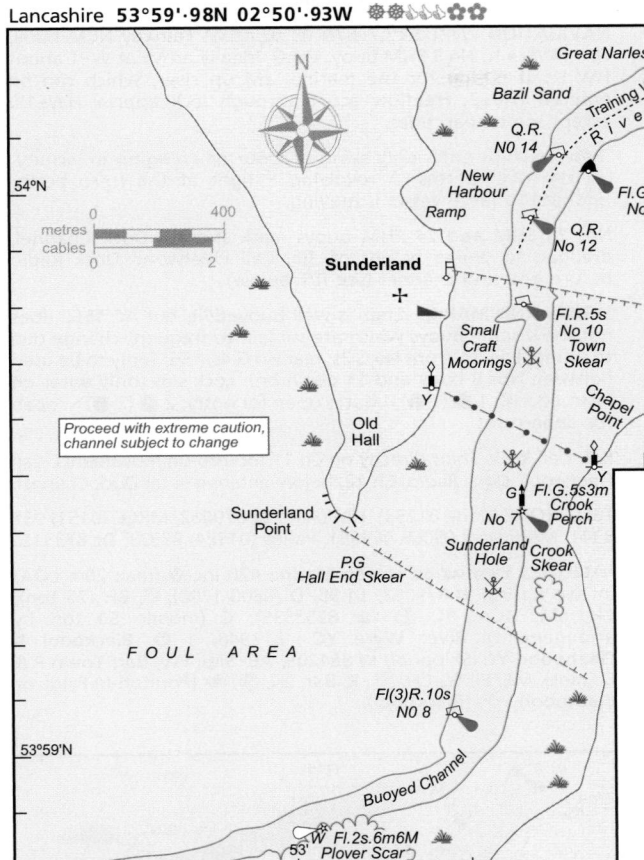

CHARTS AC 1826, 1552, 2010, 5613; Imray C62.

TIDES +0020 Dover; ML No data; Duration 0535

Standard Port LIVERPOOL (→)

Times				Height (metres)			
High Water		Low Water		MHWS	MHWN	MLWN	MLWS
0000	0600	0200	0700	9·3	7·4	2·9	0·9
1200	1800	1400	1900				
Differences BARROW-IN-FURNESS (Ramsden Dock)							
+0015	+0015	+0015	+0015	0·0	−0·3	+0·1	+0·2
ULVERSTON							
+0020	+0040	No data		0·0	−0·1	No data	
ARNSIDE							
+0100	+0135	No data		+0·5	+0·2	No data	
MORECAMBE							
+0005	+0010	+0030	+0015	+0·2	0·0	0·0	+0·2
HEYSHAM							
+0005	+0005	+0015	0000	+0·1	0·0	0·0	+0·2
GLASSON DOCK							
+0020	+0030	+0220	+0240	−2·7	−3·0	No data	
LANCASTER							
+0110	+0030	Dries out		−5·0	−4·9	Dries out	

NOTE: At Glasson Dock LW time differences give the end of a LW stand which lasts up to 2 hrs at sp.

SHELTER Very good in marina (lock width 9m); also sheltered ⌁ in R Lune to await sea lock, opens HW−1 to HW (Liverpool) (but daylight hrs only Nov-Mar) into Glasson Dock. Inner lock/swing bridge lead into BWB basin.

NAVIGATION WPT 53°58'·63N 03°00'·03W (R Lune WCM buoy), 4·2M to Plover Scar. Leave WPT at HW−1½ via buoyed/lit chan which is subject to frequent change. For latest info call Port Commission (☎ 01524 751724). ⌁ is prohibited between Sutherland Pt and No 10 PHM lt buoy. Beyond this a training wall, marked by PHM lt buoys/bn, extends to lock ent. R Lune is navigable to Lancaster.

- *It is dangerous to proceed downriver later than HW +1.*

LIGHTS AND MARKS Plover Scar, Fl 2s, on with Cockersand, FW, leads 084° up to Nos 2/3 buoys; then follow buoyed chan which shifts.
Tfc Sigs at E side of lock from estuary
- ● = lock manned, but shut
- ● = lock open, clear to enter

Tfc Sigs inside dock
- ● = Gate closed or vessel(s) entering dock
- ● = Gate open. Vessels may leave

R/T VHF Ch 16 69 (HW−1½ to HW Liverpool).

TELEPHONE (Code 01524) HM 751724, 🖷 753601; MRCC 0151 931 3341; Marinecall 09068 969651; Police 63333; Ⓗ 765944.

FACILITIES Glasson Basin Marina (240 + 20 Ⓥ) £12.00/craft) ☎ 751491, www.BWML.co.uk. Slip, D (0830-1630), ME, El, Ⓔ, ✕, BH (35 ton), CH, ⌁; **Glasson SC** ☎ 751089 Slip, M, C; **Lune CC** Access HW±2. **Town** P (cans), 🛒, R, Bar, ✉, Ⓑ (Lancaster), ⇌ (bus to Lancaster 4M), ✈ (Blackpool).

ADJACENT HARBOURS IN MORECAMBE BAY

BARROW-IN-FURNESS, Cumbria, 54°05'·64N 03°13'·44W. AC 1826, 2010, 3164, 5613. HW +0030 on Dover. ML 5·0m; Duration 0530. Good shelter but open to SE winds. Drying moorings off Piel and Roa Islands or ⌁ clear of fairway. Marks/lts: Walney Island Lt ho (conspic stone tr), Fl 15s 21m 23M (obsc 122°-127° within 3M of shore). Directions: From Lightning Knoll lt buoy, ldg lts, front Q 7m 10M; rear (6ca from front), Iso 2s 13m 10M (lattice structures) lead 041°/3·7M past Halfway Shoal bn, QR 16m 10M with RY chequers, Racon, to Bar lt buoy (abeam Walney Island lt ho). Inner Channel ldg lts, front Q 9m 10M, rear Iso 2s 14m 6M, lead 005° past Piel ls with least charted depth 1·7m. Piel ls, conspic ruined castle, slip and moorings on E side. Roa ls, 5ca N, has jetty at S end and moorings on E & W sides. Slip (Roa ls Boat Club ☎ (01229) 825291). Causeway joins to mainland. Commercial docks, 3M NW at Barrow, reached via buoyed/lit Walney Chan, dredged to 2·5m, which must be kept clear. HM (Barrow) ☎ (01229) 822911; VHF *Barrow Port Control* Ch 12 16 (H24). Facilities: Hotel at Rampside, 🛒.

HEYSHAM, Lancashire, 54°02'·01N 02°55'·96W. AC 1826, 2010, 1552, 5613. HW +0015 on Dover; ML 5·1m; Duration 0545. See 9.10.14. Good shelter, but yachts not normally accepted without special reason. Beware high speed ferries and oil rig supply ships. Ldg lts 102°, both F Bu 11/14m 2M, Y+B ◇ on masts. S jetty lt 2 FG (vert), Siren 30s. S pier hd ,Oc G 7·5s 9m 6M. N pier hd, 2FR (vert) 11m, obsc from seaward. Ent sigs: R flag or ● = no entry; no sig = no dep; 2 R flags or 2 ● = no ent or dep. VHF Ch 14 74 16 (H24). HM ☎ (01524) 852373. Facilities: Bar, FW, R, 🛒 at Morecambe (2M).

9.10.15 FLEETWOOD

Lancashire 53°55'·49N 03°00'·15W ✿✿✿⚓⚓⚓✿✿

CHARTS AC 1826, 2010, 1552, 5613; Imray C62.

TIDES +0015 Dover; ML 5.2; Duration 0530

Standard Port LIVERPOOL (⟶)

Times				Height (metres)			
High Water		Low Water		MHWS	MHWN	MLWN	MLWS
0000	0600	0200	0700	9·3	7·4	2·9	0·9
1200	1800	1400	1900				
Differences WYRE LIGHTHOUSE							
–0010	–0010	+0005	0000	–0·1	–0·1	No data	
FLEETWOOD							
–0008	–0008	–0003	–0003	–0·1	–0·1	+0·1	+0·3
BLACKPOOL							
–0015	–0005	–0005	–0015	–0·4	–0·4	–0·1	+0·1

SHELTER Excellent in Fleetwood Haven Marina. Sheltered ⚓ off Knott End pier on E bank to await tide. Passage up-river to

Skippool (5M) needs local knowledge and shoal draft; access HW±1.5 hrs (if ht of tide is >8·5m).

NAVIGATION WPT 53°57'·67N 03°02'·05W, Fairway NCM buoy, Q, 134°/3ca to No 3 SHM buoy, VQ.G. Ideally arrive at WPT about HW–1½ if bound for the marina, 3M up river, which can be entered HW±2. Freeflow access through lock approx HW±1½ except some neap tides.

> Beware ships entering/leaving harbour or swinging in vicinity of the river berths. A revolving Y light at the ro-ro berth indicates a large vessel is moving.

Nos 23 SHM and 24 PHM buoys mark start of Dock Channel, dredged to drying height of 3m. Call Fleetwood Dock Radio before entering channel (see R/T below).

LIGHTS AND MARKS Chan is well buoyed/lit, but AC 1552 does not show some buoys which are subject to frequent change due to silting. Ldg lts, front Iso G 2s; rear Iso G 4s, 156° (only to be used between Nos 8 buoy and 11 perch bn). Lock sigs (only enter on instructions): 1 ● (1 ●) = Gates open for entry; 2 ● (2 ●) = open for departures.

R/T Call *RoRo Ships* directly on Ch 11 for info on movements. Call *Fleetwood Dock Radio*, Ch 12, before entering enter Dock Channel.

TELEPHONE (Code 01253) HM (ABP) ☎ 879062; MRCC (0151) 931 3341; Marinecall 09068 969651; Police (01524) 63333; Dr 873312.

FACILITIES Fleetwood Haven Marina 420 inc Ⓥ (max 20m LOA) in two basins, ☎ 879062, £1.96, D (0800-1700), 🅟, BH (75 ton), CH, SM, ACA, ⚒, Ⓔ (☎ 8253535), C (mobile 50 ton by arrangement). **River Wyre YC** 811948, 1 Ⓥ. **Blackpool & Fleetwood YC** (Skippool) ☎ 884205, AB, Slip, FW, Bar; **Town** P & D (cans), ME, El, ⚒, CH, 🛒, R, Bar, ✉, Ⓑ, ≠ (Poulton-le-Fylde or Blackpool), ✈ (Blackpool).

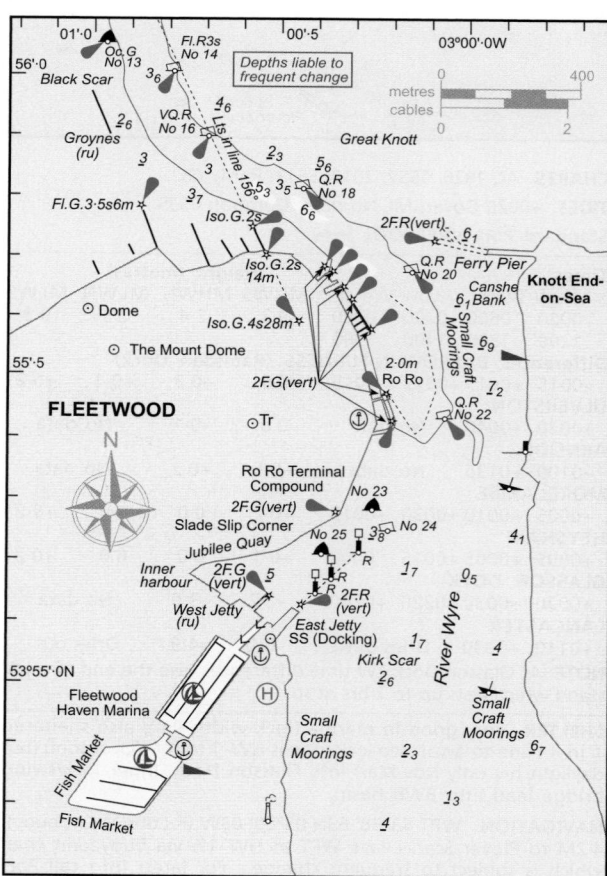

9.10.16 RIVER RIBBLE/PRESTON

Lancashire 53°43´·51N 03°00´·08W ❀❀⚓⚓⚘⚘

CHARTS AC 1826, 1981, 5613; Imray C62.

TIDES +0013 Dover; ML No data; Duration 0520

Standard Port LIVERPOOL (⟶)

Times				Height (metres)			
High Water		Low Water		MHWS	MHWN	MLWN	MLWS
0000	0600	0200	0700	9·3	7·4	2·9	0·9
1200	1800	1400	1900				
Differences PRESTON							
+0010	+0010	+0335	+0310	−4·0	−4·1	−2·8	−0·8

LW time differences give the end of a LW stand lasting 3½ hrs.

SOUTHPORT							
−0020	−0010	No data		−0·3	−0·3	No data	
FORMBY							
−0015	−0010	−0020	−0020	−0·3	−0·1	0·0	+0·1

SHELTER Good in Preston Marina (5m depth) 15M upriver. Possible drying berths on the N bank at Lytham or Freckleton, or 2M up R Douglas access HW±1.

NAVIGATION WPT **A** 53°41´·75N 03°08´·90W, Gut SWM lt buoy. The chartlet shows only the outer 6M of the estuary. The seaward 2·5M of the Gut chan is silted up. Best water is now via South Gut chan (liable to shift), navigable HW±2.

Leave WPT **A** at HW Liverpool −2. Track 105°/2·9M to WPT **B** 53°40´·96N 03°04´·22W; thence 032°/0·9M to WPT **C** 53°41´·70N 03°03´·43W; thence 026°/1·8M to WPT **D** 53°43´·29N 03°02´·10W.

Enter Gut Chan via the gap, leaving 11½M perch 100m to port. The river trends 080° between training walls 3m, marked by lit perches. The remaining 15M is straightforward but night appr not advised.

Shortcut if draught < 2m: from WPT **A** track 090°/3·2M to WPT **C**. Then 026°/1·8M to WPT **D** and the transit of the 11½M SCM lt perch with conspic W twr.

LIGHTS AND MARKS 14½M perch is the most seaward chan mark. Up-river of 11½M perch there is a PHM buoy and perch (off chartlet), both Fl R 5s. 4 SHM perches, Fl G 5s, lead to 5M perch, Fl (2) G 10s, marking mouth of unlit R Douglas. 3M and 2M perches are Fl G 5s; 1M perch is Fl G 10s. Warton airfield beacon, Mo (WQ) G 9s occas, is N abeam 6M perch, Fl G 5s.

R/T At Preston, for locks call *Riversway* Ch **16** 14 (HW −1½ to +2); Marina Ch 80 (HO); Douglas BY Ch 16 when vessel due.

TELEPHONE (Code 01772) Preston locks 726871; MRCC (0151) 9313341; Marinecall 09068 969651; Police 203203; Ⓗ 710408.

FACILITIES Waiting berth for 2m draft outside storm gates which are usually open. Tfc lts at lock into marina; see plan below. Lock in HW−1 to +2, 0700-2100 Apr-Sep (Oct-Mar by arrangement with 24Hrs notice). Swing bridge opens in unison with locks.

Preston Marina ☎ 733595, www.prestonmarina. co.uk, £1·60, D, CH, ME, ⚒, Gas, C (25 ton, 45 ton by arrangement), R, 🛒, ACA, ♿.

Douglas BY, ☎ 812462, mob 07740 780899, AB, £0·70, C (20 ton), CH, D, FW, ⚒, Slip, ME.

Freckleton BY ☎ 632439, mob 07957 820881, AB, £5/yacht, slip, FW, CH, ME.

Ribble Cruising Club ☎ (01253) 739983.

TIME ZONE (UT)
For Summer Time add ONE hour in **non-shaded areas**

LIVERPOOL (GLADSTONE DOCK) LAT 53°27'N LONG 3°01'W
TIMES AND HEIGHTS OF HIGH AND LOW WATERS

Dates in red are SPRINGS
Dates in blue are NEAPS

YEAR 2010

JANUARY

Day	Time	m	Day	Time	m
1 F	0539 / 1110 / 1815 / 2338	1.4 / 9.5 / 1.1 / 9.5	16 SA	0610 / 1145 / 1838	2.0 / 9.0 / 1.8
2 SA	0629 / 1158 / 1905	1.2 / 9.7 / 0.8	17 SU	0007 / 0641 / 1218 / 1908	8.7 / 1.9 / 9.1 / 1.8
3 SU	0027 / 0715 / 1246 / 1953	9.6 / 1.1 / 9.8 / 0.7	18 M	0038 / 0711 / 1250 / 1937	8.7 / 1.9 / 9.1 / 1.7
4 M	0115 / 0801 / 1334 / 2039	9.5 / 1.2 / 9.8 / 0.8	19 TU	0108 / 0743 / 1321 / 2008	8.6 / 1.9 / 8.9 / 1.8
5 TU	0203 / 0846 / 1422 / 2125	9.3 / 1.4 / 9.5 / 1.1	20 W	0138 / 0815 / 1352 / 2039	8.5 / 2.1 / 8.8 / 2.0
6 W	0251 / 0931 / 1511 / 2212	8.9 / 1.8 / 9.2 / 1.6	21 TH	0209 / 0849 / 1424 / 2113	8.3 / 2.4 / 8.5 / 2.3
7 TH	0341 / 1019 / 1604 / 2303	8.5 / 2.2 / 8.7 / 2.1	22 F	0243 / 0926 / 1501 / 2150	8.1 / 2.7 / 8.2 / 2.6
8 F	0436 / 1114 / 1704	8.1 / 2.6 / 8.2	23 SA	0324 / 1008 / 1547 / 2236	7.8 / 3.0 / 7.9 / 2.9
9 SA	0002 / 0540 / 1220 / 1814	2.6 / 7.7 / 3.0 / 7.8	24 SU	0417 / 1104 / 1650 / 2342	7.5 / 3.3 / 7.6 / 3.2
10 SU	0111 / 0654 / 1337 / 1930	2.9 / 7.6 / 3.1 / 7.7	25 M	0531 / 1226 / 1812	7.3 / 3.4 / 7.5
11 M	0221 / 0806 / 1452 / 2040	2.9 / 7.7 / 2.9 / 7.8	26 TU	0111 / 0657 / 1358 / 1935	3.2 / 7.4 / 3.1 / 7.7
12 TU	0324 / 0907 / 1556 / 2137	2.8 / 8.1 / 2.7 / 8.0	27 W	0232 / 0814 / 1511 / 2047	2.8 / 7.9 / 2.6 / 8.2
13 W	0417 / 0955 / 1648 / 2223	2.5 / 8.4 / 2.4 / 8.3	28 TH	0337 / 0917 / 1615 / 2147	2.3 / 8.5 / 1.9 / 8.7
14 TH	0500 / 1036 / 1730 / 2301	2.3 / 8.7 / 2.1 / 8.5	29 F	0436 / 1010 / 1713 / 2240	1.7 / 9.1 / 1.2 / 9.2
15 F	0538 / 1112 / 1806 / 2335	2.1 / 8.9 / 1.9 / 8.6	30 SA	0529 / 1059 / 1805 / 2328	1.3 / 9.6 / 0.7 / 9.6
			31 SU	0618 / 1146 / 1853	0.9 / 10.0 / 0.3

FEBRUARY

Day	Time	m	Day	Time	m
1 M	0013 / 0703 / 1231 / 1937	9.8 / 0.7 / 10.1 / 0.2	16 TU	0014 / 0652 / 1226 / 1914	8.8 / 1.5 / 9.2 / 1.4
2 TU	0058 / 0746 / 1315 / 2019	9.7 / 0.7 / 10.1 / 0.4	17 W	0042 / 0722 / 1255 / 1943	8.8 / 1.5 / 9.1 / 1.5
3 W	0140 / 0826 / 1357 / 2059	9.5 / 0.9 / 9.8 / 0.8	18 TH	0110 / 0753 / 1323 / 2013	8.7 / 1.7 / 9.0 / 1.7
4 TH	0222 / 0906 / 1441 / 2139	9.1 / 1.3 / 9.3 / 1.4	19 F	0138 / 0824 / 1353 / 2042	8.6 / 1.9 / 8.7 / 2.0
5 F	0305 / 0947 / 1527 / 2221	8.6 / 1.9 / 8.7 / 2.2	20 SA	0209 / 0856 / 1428 / 2114	8.4 / 2.3 / 8.5 / 2.3
6 SA	0353 / 1034 / 1621 / 2313	8.1 / 2.6 / 8.0 / 2.8	21 SU	0246 / 0933 / 1512 / 2155	8.1 / 2.7 / 8.1 / 2.8
7 SU	0454 / 1137 / 1733	7.6 / 3.1 / 7.4	22 M	0336 / 1025 / 1612 / 2257	7.7 / 3.1 / 7.6 / 3.2
8 M	0026 / 0613 / 1305 / 1903	3.3 / 7.2 / 3.4 / 7.1	23 TU	0451 / 1147 / 1741	7.3 / 3.3 / 7.3
9 TU	0153 / 0740 / 1435 / 2027	3.4 / 7.3 / 3.2 / 7.3	24 W	0032 / 0629 / 1332 / 1916	3.3 / 7.3 / 3.1 / 7.5
10 W	0307 / 0850 / 1545 / 2127	3.1 / 7.7 / 2.8 / 7.7	25 TH	0207 / 0755 / 1454 / 2035	3.0 / 7.8 / 2.4 / 8.0
11 TH	0404 / 0940 / 1636 / 2210	2.7 / 8.2 / 2.4 / 8.1	26 F	0320 / 0901 / 1601 / 2136	2.3 / 8.4 / 1.7 / 8.7
12 F	0447 / 1024 / 1715 / 2245	2.3 / 8.6 / 2.0 / 8.4	27 SA	0421 / 1003 / 1658 / 2226	1.7 / 9.1 / 0.9 / 9.3
13 SA	0522 / 1054 / 1748 / 2316	2.0 / 8.9 / 1.8 / 8.6	28 SU	0514 / 1043 / 1748 / 2310	1.1 / 9.7 / 0.4 / 9.7
14 SU	0553 / 1125 / 1817 / 2346	1.8 / 9.1 / 1.6 / 8.8			
15 M	0623 / 1156 / 1846	1.6 / 9.2 / 1.4			

MARCH

Day	Time	m	Day	Time	m
1 M	0601 / 1127 / 1833 / 2353	0.6 / 10.0 / 0.1 / 9.8	16 TU	0557 / 1128 / 1817 / 2345	1.5 / 9.1 / 1.3 / 8.9
2 TU	0644 / 1209 / 1915	0.4 / 10.2 / 0.0	17 W	0629 / 1157 / 1848	1.3 / 9.2 / 1.2
3 W	0033 / 0724 / 1251 / 1953	9.8 / 0.4 / 10.0 / 0.3	18 TH	0013 / 0700 / 1227 / 1917	8.9 / 1.3 / 9.1 / 1.3
4 TH	0113 / 0802 / 1331 / 2029	9.6 / 0.7 / 9.7 / 0.8	19 F	0042 / 0731 / 1257 / 1947	8.9 / 1.4 / 9.0 / 1.5
5 F	0151 / 0839 / 1411 / 2105	9.2 / 1.2 / 9.2 / 1.5	20 SA	0111 / 0803 / 1330 / 2017	8.8 / 1.7 / 8.8 / 1.8
6 SA	0230 / 0917 / 1453 / 2141	8.7 / 1.8 / 8.5 / 2.3	21 SU	0144 / 0836 / 1408 / 2050	8.6 / 2.0 / 8.5 / 2.2
7 SU	0315 / 1000 / 1544 / 2226	8.1 / 2.5 / 7.7 / 3.0	22 M	0224 / 0914 / 1455 / 2133	8.2 / 2.4 / 8.1 / 2.7
8 M	0412 / 1059 / 1654 / 2336	7.5 / 3.2 / 7.1 / 3.6	23 TU	0317 / 1009 / 1559 / 2236	7.8 / 2.8 / 7.6 / 3.1
9 TU	0532 / 1232 / 1831	7.1 / 3.5 / 6.8	24 W	0436 / 1133 / 1729	7.4 / 3.1 / 7.3
10 W	0120 / 0704 / 1409 / 2004	3.7 / 7.1 / 3.3 / 7.0	25 TH	0010 / 0612 / 1314 / 1901	3.3 / 7.4 / 2.8 / 7.5
11 TH	0242 / 0820 / 1518 / 2104	3.4 / 7.5 / 2.9 / 7.5	26 F	0145 / 0735 / 1435 / 2018	2.9 / 7.9 / 2.2 / 8.1
12 F	0338 / 0912 / 1607 / 2145	2.9 / 8.0 / 2.4 / 8.0	27 SA	0258 / 0840 / 1540 / 2116	2.3 / 8.5 / 1.5 / 8.7
13 SA	0421 / 0952 / 1645 / 2219	2.4 / 8.4 / 2.0 / 8.3	28 SU	0359 / 0933 / 1636 / 2204	1.6 / 9.1 / 0.9 / 9.2
14 SU	0455 / 1026 / 1717 / 2249	2.0 / 8.7 / 1.7 / 8.6	29 M	0451 / 1020 / 1724 / 2247	1.1 / 9.6 / 0.4 / 9.6
15 M	0527 / 1103 / 1748 / 2317	1.7 / 9.0 / 1.4 / 8.8	30 TU	0538 / 1128 / 1807 / 2328	0.7 / 9.9 / 0.3 / 9.7
			31 W	0620 / 1145 / 1847	0.5 / 9.9 / 0.3

APRIL

Day	Time	m	Day	Time	m
1 TH	0007 / 0700 / 1226 / 1924	9.7 / 0.5 / 9.7 / 0.6	16 F	0637 / 1201 / 1853	1.3 / 9.1 / 1.3
2 F	0046 / 0738 / 1306 / 1959	9.5 / 0.8 / 9.4 / 1.1	17 SA	0017 / 0712 / 1237 / 1926	9.0 / 1.4 / 9.0 / 1.5
3 SA	0123 / 0815 / 1345 / 2033	9.2 / 1.3 / 8.9 / 1.8	18 SU	0052 / 0747 / 1315 / 2000	8.9 / 1.6 / 8.8 / 1.8
4 SU	0201 / 0852 / 1426 / 2107	8.7 / 1.9 / 8.3 / 2.5	19 M	0131 / 0825 / 1359 / 2038	8.7 / 1.9 / 8.5 / 2.1
5 M	0244 / 0932 / 1514 / 2147	8.2 / 2.5 / 7.6 / 3.1	20 TU	0217 / 0910 / 1452 / 2126	8.4 / 2.2 / 8.1 / 2.6
6 TU	0339 / 1026 / 1619 / 2247	7.6 / 3.1 / 7.0 / 3.6	21 W	0315 / 1009 / 1559 / 2230	8.0 / 2.5 / 7.7 / 2.9
7 W	0452 / 1150 / 1747	7.2 / 3.4 / 6.7	22 TH	0432 / 1129 / 1720 / 2354	7.7 / 2.6 / 7.6 / 3.0
8 TH	0028 / 0617 / 1323 / 1917	3.8 / 7.1 / 3.3 / 6.9	23 F	0555 / 1254 / 1842	7.8 / 2.4 / 7.7
9 F	0155 / 0732 / 1430 / 2021	3.5 / 7.3 / 2.9 / 7.3	24 SA	0118 / 0709 / 1408 / 1952	2.7 / 8.1 / 2.0 / 8.2
10 SA	0254 / 0828 / 1521 / 2106	3.1 / 7.8 / 2.5 / 7.8	25 SU	0229 / 0813 / 1512 / 2050	2.2 / 8.6 / 1.5 / 8.6
11 SU	0339 / 0912 / 1602 / 2142	2.6 / 8.2 / 2.1 / 8.2	26 M	0331 / 0907 / 1607 / 2138	1.7 / 9.0 / 1.1 / 9.0
12 M	0418 / 0949 / 1656 / 2214	2.1 / 8.5 / 1.8 / 8.5	27 TU	0424 / 0955 / 1656 / 2222	1.3 / 9.3 / 0.9 / 9.3
13 TU	0453 / 1023 / 1712 / 2244	1.8 / 8.8 / 1.5 / 8.7	28 W	0512 / 1040 / 1740 / 2303	1.0 / 9.5 / 0.8 / 9.4
14 W	0528 / 1056 / 1746 / 2314	1.5 / 9.0 / 1.3 / 8.9	29 TH	0556 / 1123 / 1820 / 2343	0.9 / 9.5 / 0.9 / 9.4
15 TH	0602 / 1128 / 1820 / 2344	1.4 / 9.0 / 1.3 / 9.0	30 F	0637 / 1204 / 1857	0.9 / 9.3 / 1.1

Chart Datum: 4·93 metres below Ordnance Datum (Newlyn). HAT is 10·5 metres above Chart Datum; see 4.5.

>> FREE monthly updates from <<
www.reedsalmanac.co.uk

TIME ZONE (UT)
For Summer Time add ONE hour in **non-shaded areas**

LIVERPOOL (GLADSTONE DOCK)   LAT 53°27'N   LONG 3°01'W
TIMES AND HEIGHTS OF HIGH AND LOW WATERS

Dates in red are **SPRINGS**
Dates in blue are **NEAPS**

YEAR 2010

MAY

Time	m		Time	m
1 0021	9.3		**16** 0658	1.3
0716	1.2		1223	9.0
SA 1245	9.0		SU 1911	1.5
1932	1.5			
2 0059	9.0		**17** 0040	9.1
0754	1.5		0740	1.4
SU 1324	8.6		M 1308	8.9
2006	2.0		1951	1.7
3 0138	8.7		**18** 0126	8.9
0831	2.0		0824	1.6
M 1404	8.1		TU 1357	8.7
2040	2.5		2034	2.0
4 0220	8.3		**19** 0217	8.7
0910	2.5		0914	1.8
TU 1450	7.7		W 1452	8.4
2117	3.0		2125	2.3
5 0310	7.8		**20** 0315	8.4
0956	2.9		1012	2.0
W 1545	7.2		TH 1554	8.1
2207	3.4		◑ 2226	2.5
6 0412	7.4		**21** 0422	8.2
1058	3.2		1119	2.1
TH 1655	6.9		F 1702	7.9
◑ 2319	3.7		2335	2.6
7 0523	7.3		**22** 0531	8.2
1215	3.2		1228	2.1
F 1810	6.9		SA 1813	8.0
8 0044	3.6		**23** 0046	2.5
0632	7.3		0639	8.3
SA 1326	3.0		SU 1337	1.9
1918	7.2		1920	8.1
9 0152	3.3		**24** 0155	2.3
0732	7.6		0744	8.5
SU 1423	2.7		M 1440	1.8
2012	7.5		2020	8.4
10 0246	2.8		**25** 0259	2.0
0823	7.9		0842	8.7
M 1511	2.3		TU 1537	1.6
2055	7.9		2112	8.7
11 0332	2.4		**26** 0357	1.8
0906	8.2		0934	8.8
TU 1555	2.0		W 1628	1.5
2133	8.3		2159	8.9
12 0415	2.0		**27** 0449	1.5
0946	8.5		1021	8.9
W 1635	1.7		TH 1714	1.4
2208	8.6		○ 2242	9.1
13 0457	1.7		**28** 0536	1.4
1024	8.7		1106	8.9
TH 1715	1.5		F 1756	1.5
2243	8.8		2323	9.1
14 0537	1.5		**29** 0619	1.4
1101	8.9		1148	8.8
F 1754	1.4		SA 1834	1.6
● 2320	9.0			
15 0618	1.4		**30** 0002	9.1
1141	9.0		0659	1.5
SA 1832	1.4		SU 1229	8.7
2358	9.1		1910	1.8
			31 0041	8.9
			0737	1.7
			M 1307	8.5
			1944	2.1

JUNE

Time	m		Time	m
1 0119	8.7		**16** 0121	9.3
0813	2.0		0824	1.1
TU 1345	8.2		W 1352	9.0
2018	2.4		2032	1.6
2 0158	8.5		**17** 0211	9.2
0848	2.2		0913	1.2
W 1425	7.9		TH 1443	8.8
2053	2.7		2121	1.8
3 0242	8.2		**18** 0304	8.9
0926	2.5		1003	1.5
TH 1510	7.6		F 1537	8.5
2135	3.0		2212	2.0
4 0331	7.8		**19** 0401	8.7
1011	2.7		1058	1.7
F 1602	7.3		SA 1636	8.2
◑ 2226	3.3		◑ 2309	2.3
5 0427	7.6		**20** 0502	8.4
1105	2.9		1157	2.0
SA 1702	7.1		SU 1740	8.0
2328	3.4			
6 0529	7.4		**21** 0013	2.5
1209	3.0		0607	8.2
SU 1806	7.1		M 1303	2.2
			1847	8.0
7 0038	3.3		**22** 0123	2.5
0630	7.5		0715	8.1
M 1316	2.9		TU 1409	2.2
1907	7.3		1952	8.1
8 0146	3.1		**23** 0233	2.4
0728	7.7		0821	8.2
TU 1417	2.7		W 1511	2.2
2002	7.7		2051	8.3
9 0245	2.7		**24** 0337	2.2
0821	7.9		0919	8.3
W 1511	2.3		TH 1607	2.1
2051	8.0		2143	8.5
10 0338	2.3		**25** 0434	2.0
0910	8.3		1010	8.4
TH 1601	2.0		F 1655	2.0
2135	8.4		2228	8.8
11 0428	2.0		**26** 0524	1.8
0934	8.6		1056	8.6
F 1647	1.8		SA 1738	1.9
2218	8.8		○ 2310	8.9
12 0516	1.6		**27** 0607	1.7
1041	8.8		1136	8.6
SA 1732	1.6		SU 1817	1.9
● 2301	9.0		2348	9.0
13 0603	1.4		**28** 0646	1.7
1127	9.0		1214	8.6
SU 1817	1.4		M 1852	1.9
2346	9.2			
14 0650	1.2		**29** 0024	8.9
1213	9.2		0721	1.7
M 1902	1.3		TU 1249	8.5
			1925	2.0
15 0032	9.3		**30** 0100	8.9
0737	1.1		0753	1.8
TU 1302	9.1		W 1323	8.4
1946	1.4		1956	2.1

JULY

Time	m		Time	m
1 0135	8.7		**16** 0155	9.6
0824	2.0		0859	0.8
TH 1357	8.2		F 1423	9.1
2029	2.3		2106	1.3
2 0212	8.5		**17** 0242	9.4
0856	2.1		0943	1.1
F 1434	8.0		SA 1511	8.8
2105	2.6		2151	1.7
3 0250	8.2		**18** 0332	8.9
0932	2.4		1029	1.7
SA 1513	7.7		SU 1603	8.4
2146	2.8		◑ 2241	2.2
4 0333	7.9		**19** 0429	8.4
1014	2.6		1123	2.2
SU 1559	7.5		M 1703	8.0
◑ 2233	3.1		2341	2.6
5 0423	7.6		**20** 0535	8.0
1104	2.9		1228	2.6
M 1655	7.3		TU 1814	7.7
2333	3.3			
6 0524	7.5		**21** 0055	2.9
1209	3.0		0651	7.7
TU 1802	7.3		W 1342	2.8
			1929	7.7
7 0047	3.3		**22** 0216	2.8
0632	7.5		0808	7.7
W 1324	3.0		TH 1453	2.7
1911	7.5		2037	8.0
8 0202	3.0		**23** 0329	2.6
0739	7.7		0912	7.9
TH 1432	2.7		F 1554	2.5
2014	7.8		2132	8.3
9 0307	2.6		**24** 0428	2.3
0841	8.0		1004	8.2
F 1531	2.3		SA 1644	2.3
2109	8.3		2218	8.6
10 0405	2.1		**25** 0516	2.0
0936	8.5		1046	8.4
SA 1625	1.9		SU 1726	2.1
2200	8.8		2256	8.9
11 0459	1.6		**26** 0556	1.8
1027	8.9		1122	8.6
SU 1716	1.6		M 1802	1.9
● 2247	9.2		○ 2331	9.0
12 0552	1.2		**27** 0630	1.7
1116	9.2		1155	8.7
M 1806	1.3		TU 1833	1.8
2334	9.5			
13 0642	0.8		**28** 0004	9.1
1203	9.4		0659	1.6
TU 1853	1.1		W 1226	8.7
			1903	1.8
14 0021	9.7		**29** 0037	9.0
0729	0.6		0728	1.6
W 1250	9.5		TH 1257	8.6
1938	1.0		1933	1.9
15 0108	9.8		**30** 0108	8.9
0814	0.6		0756	1.7
TH 1337	9.4		F 1327	8.5
2023	1.1		2004	2.0
			31 0140	8.8
			0826	1.9
			SA 1357	8.3
			2036	2.2

AUGUST

Time	m		Time	m
1 0211	8.5		**16** 0302	8.9
0857	2.1		0957	1.9
SU 1430	8.1		M 1529	8.4
2111	2.5		◐ 2212	2.3
2 0246	8.2		**17** 0355	8.2
0932	2.5		1047	2.6
M 1507	7.8		TU 1627	7.9
2151	2.9		2312	2.9
3 0328	7.9		**18** 0504	7.6
1014	2.8		1154	3.1
TU 1555	7.5		W 1743	7.5
◐ 2242	3.2			
4 0425	7.5		**19** 0034	3.2
1112	3.1		0631	7.3
W 1702	7.3		TH 1321	3.3
2355	3.4		1908	7.5
5 0542	7.3		**20** 0206	3.1
1234	3.3		0759	7.4
TH 1828	7.3		F 1440	3.1
			2023	7.8
6 0125	3.2		**21** 0321	2.7
0706	7.4		0905	7.7
F 1359	3.0		SA 1542	2.7
1945	7.7		2119	8.2
7 0242	2.7		**22** 0417	2.3
0820	7.9		0952	8.1
SA 1507	2.5		SU 1630	2.4
2050	8.3		2201	8.6
8 0347	2.1		**23** 0459	2.0
0922	8.5		1029	8.4
SU 1607	1.9		M 1708	2.1
2144	8.9		2236	8.9
9 0445	1.4		**24** 0534	1.7
1014	9.0		1101	8.7
M 1701	1.4		TU 1740	1.9
2233	9.4		○ 2308	9.1
10 0538	0.8		**25** 0604	1.6
1102	9.5		1130	8.8
TU 1752	1.0		W 1809	1.7
● 2318	9.9		2339	9.2
11 0627	0.4		**26** 0632	1.5
1147	9.7		1159	8.9
W 1839	0.7		TH 1838	1.6
12 0003	10.1		**27** 0009	9.2
0712	0.2		0659	1.5
TH 1231	9.8		F 1227	8.8
1922	0.6		1907	1.7
13 0048	10.1		**28** 0039	9.1
0755	0.3		0727	1.5
F 1314	9.7		SA 1255	8.8
2004	0.8		1938	1.8
14 0131	9.9		**29** 0108	8.9
0835	0.6		0756	1.7
SA 1357	9.4		SU 1323	8.6
2044	1.1		2009	2.0
15 0215	9.5		**30** 0137	8.7
0915	1.2		0826	2.0
SU 1441	8.9		M 1353	8.4
2126	1.6		2042	2.4
			31 0210	8.4
			0858	2.4
			TU 1428	8.1
			2118	2.8

Chart Datum: 4·93 metres below Ordnance Datum (Newlyn). HAT is 10·5 metres above Chart Datum; see 4.5.

NW England

| TIME ZONE (UT) |
| For Summer Time add ONE hour in **non-shaded areas** |

LIVERPOOL (GLADSTONE DOCK) LAT 53°27'N LONG 3°01'W

TIMES AND HEIGHTS OF HIGH AND LOW WATERS

Dates in red are **SPRINGS**
Dates in blue are **NEAPS**

YEAR 2010

SEPTEMBER

Time	m		Time	m
1 0251	8.0	**16**	0435	7.3
0937	2.8		1119	3.5
W 1514	7.8	TH	1712	7.4
◑ 2206	3.1			
2 0347	7.6	**17**	0015	3.4
1032	3.2		0607	7.0
TH 1622	7.4	F	1256	3.7
2320	3.4		1841	7.4
3 0509	7.3	**18**	0147	3.3
1156	3.4		0625	7.0
F 1757	7.3	SA	1418	3.4
			1957	7.7
4 0059	3.2	**19**	0257	2.8
0643	7.4		0843	7.6
SA 1332	3.2	SU	1518	2.9
1923	7.7		2052	8.2
5 0222	2.6	**20**	0348	2.4
0804	7.9		0928	8.1
SU 1446	2.6	M	1603	2.5
2031	8.4		2133	8.6
6 0329	1.9	**21**	0428	2.0
0906	8.6		1002	8.4
M 1548	1.9	TU	1639	2.2
2125	9.1		2208	8.9
7 0427	1.2	**22**	0501	1.8
0957	9.2		1033	8.7
TU 1643	1.3	W	1710	1.9
2213	9.7		2240	9.1
8 0519	0.6	**23**	0531	1.6
1042	9.6		1101	8.9
W 1732	0.9	TH	1740	1.7
● 2257	10.1	○	2310	9.2
9 0606	0.3	**24**	0559	1.5
1125	9.9		1129	9.0
TH 1818	0.6	F	1810	1.6
2341	10.2		2340	9.2
10 0649	0.2	**25**	0628	1.5
1207	9.9		1157	9.0
F 1900	0.6	SA	1842	1.6
11 0023	10.2	**26**	0010	9.2
0729	0.3		0658	1.5
SA 1248	9.8	SU	1225	8.9
1941	0.7		1913	1.7
12 0106	9.9	**27**	0040	9.0
0808	0.8		0728	1.7
SU 1329	9.4	M	1254	8.8
2020	1.2		1946	2.0
13 0148	9.4	**28**	0111	8.8
0846	1.4		0759	2.0
M 1410	9.0	TU	1325	8.6
2101	1.8		2019	2.3
14 0233	8.7	**29**	0147	8.5
0925	2.2		0832	2.4
TU 1456	8.4	W	1403	8.3
2147	2.4		2057	2.7
15 0325	8.0	**30**	0231	8.1
1012	2.9		0913	2.8
W 1554	7.8	TH	1452	7.9
◑ 2246	3.1		2147	3.0

OCTOBER

Time	m		Time	m
1 0330	7.7	**16**	0529	7.0
1010	3.2		1214	3.9
F 1603	7.6	SA	1758	7.4
◑ 2303	3.2			
2 0453	7.4	**17**	0107	3.4
1133	3.4		0656	7.1
SA 1736	7.5	SU	1336	3.6
			1912	7.6
3 0039	3.1	**18**	0213	3.0
0625	7.5		0804	7.5
SU 1307	3.2	M	1436	3.2
1900	7.9		2010	8.0
4 0200	2.5	**19**	0304	2.6
0743	8.1		0851	7.9
M 1422	2.6	TU	1522	2.8
2007	8.5		2056	8.4
5 0306	1.8	**20**	0345	2.3
0844	8.7		0927	8.3
TU 1524	1.9	W	1601	2.4
2102	9.2		2133	8.7
6 0403	1.2	**21**	0421	2.0
0934	9.3		0959	8.6
W 1619	1.4	TH	1636	2.1
2150	9.7		2208	8.9
7 0454	0.7	**22**	0454	1.8
1018	9.7		1029	8.8
TH 1708	1.0	F	1709	1.8
● 2234	10.0		2240	9.1
8 0540	0.5	**23**	0527	1.6
1101	9.9		1059	9.0
F 1754	0.8	SA	1743	1.7
2318	10.1	○	2312	9.1
9 0622	0.5	**24**	0559	1.6
1142	9.9		1129	9.1
SA 1837	0.7	SU	1818	1.7
			2344	9.1
10 0000	10.0	**25**	0633	1.6
0702	0.7		1159	9.1
SU 1222	9.7	M	1853	1.7
1918	0.9			
11 0043	9.6	**26**	0018	9.0
0741	1.2		0706	1.8
M 1303	9.4	TU	1233	9.0
1959	1.4		1928	1.9
12 0125	9.1	**27**	0055	8.9
0818	1.8		0740	2.0
TU 1343	9.0	W	1310	8.8
2040	1.9		2006	2.2
13 0209	8.5	**28**	0136	8.6
0856	2.5		0817	2.4
W 1428	8.5	TH	1352	8.5
2125	2.6		2049	2.5
14 0259	7.9	**29**	0224	8.3
0940	3.2		0901	2.7
TH 1524	7.9	F	1445	8.2
◑ 2222	3.1		2142	2.7
15 0404	7.3	**30**	0325	7.9
1042	3.7		1000	3.1
F 1636	7.5	SA	1554	7.9
2343	3.4	◑	2255	2.9
		31	0441	7.7
			1116	3.2
		SU	1716	7.9

NOVEMBER

Time	m		Time	m
1 0017	2.7	**16**	0112	3.2
0601	7.8		0700	7.3
M 1239	3.0	TU	1337	3.5
1832	8.1		1915	7.7
2 0132	2.3	**17**	0208	2.9
0715	8.2		0758	7.6
TU 1352	2.6	W	1431	3.1
1939	8.6		2008	8.0
3 0237	1.8	**18**	0256	2.6
0817	8.7		0843	8.0
W 1455	2.1	TH	1517	2.7
2036	9.1		2054	8.3
4 0335	1.4	**19**	0338	2.3
0909	9.1		0922	8.3
TH 1552	1.6	F	1559	2.4
2126	9.4		2134	8.6
5 0426	1.1	**20**	0418	2.1
0955	9.4		0957	8.7
F 1643	1.3	SA	1639	2.1
2213	9.7		2211	8.8
6 0513	1.0	**21**	0456	1.9
1038	9.6		1031	8.9
SA 1731	1.1	SU	1719	1.9
● 2258	9.7	○	2248	9.0
7 0557	1.0	**22**	0534	1.7
1120	9.7		1106	9.1
SU 1816	1.1	M	1759	1.7
2342	9.6		2325	9.1
8 0638	1.2	**23**	0612	1.7
1201	9.6		1142	9.2
M 1900	1.2	TU	1839	1.7
9 0025	9.3	**24**	0004	9.1
0717	1.6		0650	1.7
TU 1242	9.3	W	1220	9.2
1941	1.6		1919	1.7
10 0108	8.9	**25**	0046	9.0
0755	2.1		0729	1.9
W 1323	9.0	TH	1302	9.1
2023	2.0		2002	1.8
11 0150	8.4	**26**	0131	8.8
0832	2.6		0813	2.1
TH 1406	8.6	F	1348	8.9
2105	2.5		2048	2.0
12 0236	7.9	**27**	0221	8.6
0912	3.1		0857	2.4
F 1455	8.2	SA	1441	8.7
2153	2.9		2141	2.2
13 0330	7.5	**28**	0317	8.3
1001	3.5		0952	2.6
SA 1555	7.8	SU	1542	8.4
◑ 2254	3.3	◑	2242	2.4
14 0436	7.2	**29**	0421	8.1
1110	3.8		1055	2.8
SU 1703	7.5	M	1650	8.3
			2349	2.4
15 0005	3.4	**30**	0531	8.0
0549	7.1		1206	2.8
M 1230	3.8	TU	1800	8.3
1812	7.5			

DECEMBER

Time	m		Time	m
1 0058	2.3	**16**	0058	3.3
0642	8.1		0650	7.3
W 1317	2.7	TH	1329	3.5
1908	8.5		1913	7.6
2 0206	2.1	**17**	0201	3.0
0747	8.4		0751	7.6
TH 1425	2.4	F	1431	3.1
2010	8.7		2010	7.8
3 0307	1.9	**18**	0256	2.7
0844	8.7		0847	7.9
F 1528	2.1	SA	1524	2.7
2107	8.9		2100	8.2
4 0402	1.7	**19**	0345	2.4
0935	9.0		0927	8.4
SA 1624	1.8	SU	1612	2.3
2159	9.1		2146	8.5
5 0452	1.6	**20**	0430	2.1
1022	9.3		1008	8.7
SU 1715	1.5	M	1659	2.0
● 2246	9.2		2229	8.8
6 0537	1.5	**21**	0514	1.8
1106	9.4		1048	9.0
M 1803	1.4	TU	1745	1.7
2331	9.2	○	2311	9.0
7 0620	1.6	**22**	0557	1.6
1147	9.4		1129	9.3
TU 1847	1.5	W	1830	1.4
			2353	9.2
8 0013	9.0	**23**	0640	1.5
0659	1.8		1211	9.4
W 1227	9.3	TH	1915	1.3
1928	1.7			
9 0054	8.8	**24**	0038	9.3
0736	2.1		0723	1.5
TH 1306	9.1	F	1256	9.5
2006	1.9		2000	1.3
10 0132	8.5	**25**	0124	9.2
0811	2.4		0806	1.6
F 1345	8.8	SA	1341	9.4
2043	2.3		2045	1.4
11 0211	8.2	**26**	0211	9.0
0845	2.7		0851	1.8
SA 1426	8.5	SU	1430	9.2
2119	2.6		2131	1.6
12 0253	7.9	**27**	0301	8.7
0923	3.1		0938	2.1
SU 1513	8.1	M	1521	8.9
2159	2.9		2221	1.9
13 0341	7.5	**28**	0355	8.4
1009	3.4		1030	2.4
M 1606	7.8	TU	1619	8.6
◑ 2248	3.1	◑	2317	2.2
14 0438	7.3	**29**	0457	8.1
1106	3.6		1131	2.6
TU 1706	7.5	W	1725	8.3
2349	3.3			
15 0543	7.2	**30**	0022	2.4
1217	3.7		0606	7.9
W 1810	7.5	TH	1242	2.8
			1837	8.1
		31	0134	2.5
			0718	8.0
		F	1359	2.7
			1950	8.2

Chart Datum: 4·93 metres below Ordnance Datum (Newlyn). HAT is 10·5 metres above Chart Datum; see 4.5.

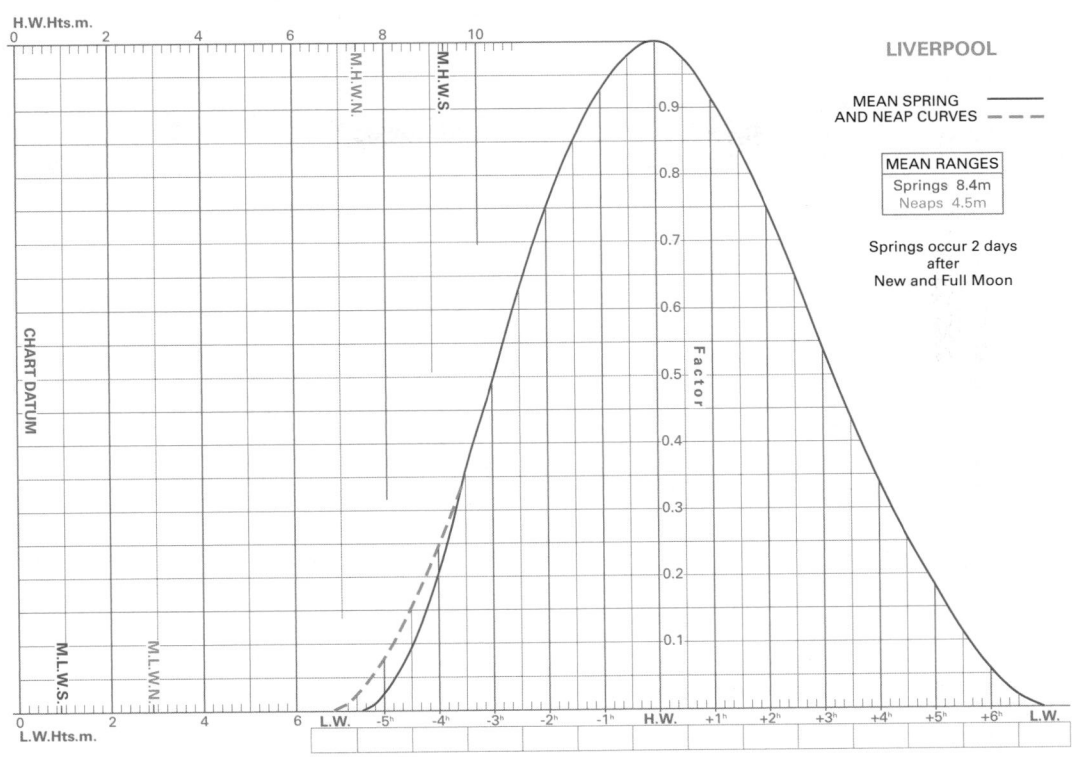

LIVERPOOL

MEAN SPRING
AND NEAP CURVES

MEAN RANGES
Springs 8.4m
Neaps 4.5m

Springs occur 2 days
after
New and Full Moon

9.10.17 LIVERPOOL

Merseyside **53°24'·22N 03°00'·28W** (Liver Bldg) 🌸🌸🌸💧💧🌸🌸

CHARTS AC 1826, 1978, 1951, 3490, 5613; Imray C62.

TIDES +0015 Dover; ML 5·2; Duration 0535

Standard Port LIVERPOOL (GLADSTONE DOCK) (←→)

Times				Height (metres)			
High Water		Low Water		MHWS	MHWN	MLWN	MLWS
0000	0600	0200	0700	9·3	7·4	2·9	0·9
1200	1800	1400	1900				

Differences EASTHAM (River Mersey)

+0010	+0010	+0009	+0009	+0·3	+0·1	−0·1	−0·3

HALE HEAD (River Mersey)

+0030	+0025	No data		−2·4	−2·5	No data	

WIDNES (River Mersey)

+0040	+0045	+0400	+0345	−4·2	−4·4	−2·5	−0·3

FIDDLER'S FERRY (River Mersey)

+0100	+0115	+0540	+0450	−5·9	−6·3	−2·4	−0·4

HILBRE ISLAND (River Dee)

−0015	−0012	−0010	−0015	−0·3	−0·2	+0·2	+0·4

MOSTYN DOCKS (River Dee)

−0020	−0015	−0020	−0020	−0·8	−0·7	No data	

CONNAH'S QUAY (River Dee)

0000	+0015	+0355	+0340	−4·6	−4·4	Dries	

CHESTER (River Dee)

+0105	+0105	+0500	+0500	−5·3	−5·4	Dries	

COLWYN BAY

−0020	−0020	No data		−1·5	−1·3	No data	

LLANDUDNO

−0020	−0020	−0035	−0040	−1·7	−1·4	−0·7	−0·3

NOTE: LW time differences at Connah's Quay give the end of a LW stand lasting about 3¾hrs at sp and 5hrs at nps. A bore occurs in the R Dee at Chester.

SHELTER Good at marinas in Brunswick/Coburg docks and in Canning/Albert Docks. Fair weather ⚓ on the SW side of river. In strong NW'lies there is swell on the bar. Wind against tide causes steep, breaking seas in outer reaches of River Mersey. Inside, the buoyed chan is safe; elsewhere local knowledge and great caution needed as the whole area (R Dee, R Mersey to R Alt and N to Morecambe Bay) is littered with sandbanks.

NAVIGATION WPT 53°32'·02N 03°20'·98W, Bar SWM lt buoy, 111°/2·8M to Q1 NCM lt F. From Q1 to marina is 15·5M via Queen's and Crosby Chans. Both chans have training banks which cover and it is unwise to navigate between the floats/buoys and the trng banks. Sp tidal streams exceed 5kn within the river.

Leeds and Liverpool Canal (BWB) gives access to E Coast, ent at Stanley Dock. Max draft 1·0m, air draft 2·2m, beam 4·3m, LOA 18·3m. Liverpool to Goole 161M, 103 locks.

Manchester Ship Canal, ent at Eastham Locks, leads 31M to Salford Quays or R Weaver for boatyards at Northwich. Obtain licence from MSC Co ☎ 0151 327 1461.

R Dee: WPT 53°25'·13N 03°13'·17W, Hilbre Swash HE2 ECM buoy, Q (3) 10s, (chan shifts). From the W use Welsh Chan. The Dee estuary mostly dries.

LIGHTS AND MARKS Bar SWM lt buoy, L Fl 10s Racon. Keep 5ca clear of SPM, 5ca W of Bar lt float. Formby SWM lt F, Iso 4s, is at the ent to Queen's Chan which is marked by PHM lt Flts and SHM buoys, and 3 NCM buoys, numbered Q1-Q12. Crosby Chan is similarly marked, C1-C23. From Crosby SWM lt F, Oc 5s, the track up-river is approx 145°. The Liver Bldg (twin spires) and Port of Liverpool Bldg (dome) are conspic on the E bank opposite Birkenhead Docks.

R/T Monitor *Mersey Radio* VHF Ch **12** 16 (H24). Local nav and gale warnings are broadcast on receipt on Ch 12. Traffic movements, nav warnings and weather reports are broadcast on Ch 09 at HW−3 and −2. Radar Ch 18 covers a radius of 20M and in poor vis can offer continuous fixing. *Liverpool Marina* Ch **M**. Eastham Locks Ch 07 (H24). Manchester Ship Canal Ch 14.

NW England

TELEPHONE (Code 0151) Port Ops 949 6134/5; MRCC 931 3341; Marinecall 09068 969651; Police 709 6010; ⊞ 709 0141.

FACILITIES Liverpool Marina entrance is 1M S of the Liver Bldg, abeam Pluckington Bank WCM buoy. **IPTS** (sigs 2, 3 & 5) from conspic black control bldg at lock ent. Access approx HW ±2¼ sp, ±1½ nps, 0600-2200 Mar-Oct, via Brunswick Dock lock (width 8m); pontoons inside, min depth 3·5m; night locking by arrangement. www.liverpoolmarina.co.uk ☎ 7076777, (0600-2200 Mar–Oct). 350 AB + 50 ♥, £2.42. D, P (½M), BH (60 ton), Slip, CH, SM, Ⓦ, ⟨, Bar, R (☎ 7076888).

Albert Dock ☎ 7096558; access HW–2 to HW via Canning Dock, but not on every tide. VHF Ch M when ent manned, AB, FW, AC.

Royal Mersey YC ☎ 6453204, Slip, M, P, D, L, FW, R, Bar.

W Kirby SC ☎ 6255579, AB (at HW), Slip, M (in Dee Est), L, FW, C (30ton), Bar.

Hoylake SC ☎ 6322616, Slip, M, FW, Bar; **Services:** CH, SM, ME, El, ✕, ACA, Ⓔ.

City all facilities, ⇌, ✈.

ADJACENT ANCHORAGE

RIVER ALT, Merseyside, **53°31′·42N 03°03′·80W**. AC 1978, 1951, 5613. HW –0008 on Dover. Good shelter but only for LOA <8·5m x 1·2m draft on a HW of at least 8m. Mersey E training wall can be crossed HW±2. Ent to chan (shifts frequently) is E of C14 PHM lt float, thence marked by locally-laid Y Fairway buoy and perches on the training wall. Unsafe to ⚓ in R Alt; pick up a free mooring off the SC and contact club. Local knowledge advised. Facilities very limited. **Blundellsands SC** ☎ (0151) 929 2101 (occas), Slip, L (at HW), FW, Bar.

9.10.18 CONWY AND DEGANWY

Conwy **53°17'·48N 03°50'·23W** (marina) ⬡⬡⬡⬡⬡⬡
Deganwy **53°17'·41N 03°49'·66W** (marina) ⬡⬡⬡⬡⬡⬡

CHARTS AC 5609, 1826, 1977, 1978, 1463; Imray C52; Stan 27

TIDES –0015 Dover; ML 4·3; Duration 0545

Standard Port HOLYHEAD (→)

Times				Height (metres)			
High Water		Low Water		MHWS	MHWN	MLWN	MLWS
0000	0600	0500	1100	5·6	4·4	2·0	0·7
1200	1800	1700	2300				
Differences CONWY							
+0025	+0035	+0120	+0105	+2·3	+1·8	+0·6	+0·4

NOTE: HW Conwy is approx HW Liverpool –0040 sp and –0020 nps.

SHELTER Good, except in NW gales.

NAVIGATION WPT Fairway buoy, 53°17'·95N 03°55'·58W, 120°/6·5ca to No 2 PHM. Access HW±2; if Conwy Sands (to the N) are covered, there is enough water in chan for a 2m draught boat. A bar, dries 1·0m, forms at The Scabs adjacent to No 6 PHM.

After No C2 PHM buoy the channel up to Deganwy is marked by lt buoys (even Nos = PHM, odd Nos = SHM) in sequence: C1, C4, then paired buoys C3 and C6, C5 and C8, C7 and C10, C9 and C12, C11 and C14. C16 (unlit) at narrows into R Conwy. 10kn speed limit above Perch lt bcn. Sp ebb up to 5kn.

North Deep, a buoyed inshore passage (close SW of Gt Orme's Hd to Deganwy Point), is only advised with local knowledge.

Beware: unlit Beacons Jetty (close N of Conwy marina); unlit moorings off Deganwy; and five unlit pontoons between Bodlondeb Pt and the road/rail bridge.

LIGHTS AND MARKS Penmaenmawr SPM outfall buoy (SW of No 2 buoy) is not a channel mark. The 4 towers of Conwy castle and the 2 adjacent bridge towers are conspic.

R/T HM Ch **14**. Summer 0900-1700LT daily; winter, same times Mon-Fri). Conwy Marina, pre-call Ch 80 (H24) for a berth. Deganwy Quay Ch 80. N Wales CC launch Ch M, water taxi.

TELEPHONE (Code 01492) HM 596253. MRCC (01407) 762051. Marinecall 09068 969650. Police 517171. Dr 592424.

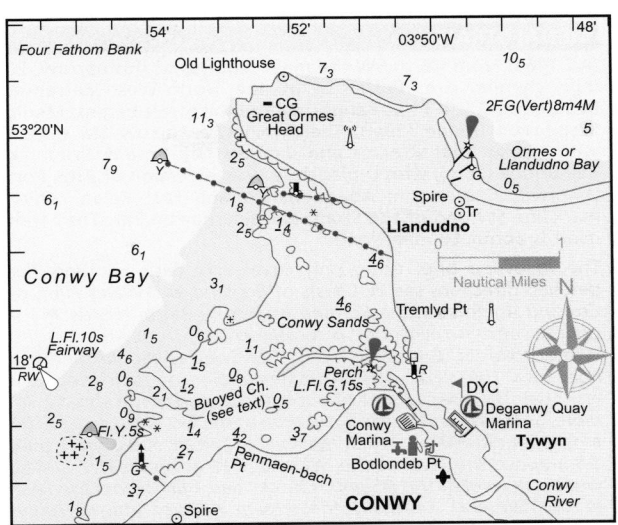

FACILITIES Conwy Marina Access when height of tide above CD exceeds 3·5m, ie approx HW ±3¼. Gate times are on an electronic noticeboard. Waiting pontoon outside. Obey R/G entry lts. ☎ 593000. www.quaymarinas.com, 505 AB inc Ⓥ, £2.25m; < 5hrs, £10. D & P (0700-2200), BH (30 ton), BY, ✕, ⚓, CH, Gas, SM, Wi-fi, ▣, R, Bar.

Harbour Between Bodlondeb Pt and Conwy bridge contact HM for: Pontoon AB £13; Town Quay AB dries (12·3m max LOA, short stay for loading); and 🅐's. D (Town Quay/pontoon HW±2, call Ch 14 to confirm), FW, ▣. Slip HW±3 at Beacons Jetty £18/day.

Deganwy Quay Marina Keep close to 3 PHM lt buoys marking the appr channel (see lower chartlet). Min depth in chan is 2·5m when marina gate open. Access when height of tide above CD exceeds 4m, ie approx HW ±3¼. www.deganwyquay.com/marina ☎ 576888. deganwymarina@tiscali.co.uk 200 AB inc Ⓥ, £3.30. ▣, ✕, ME, El, Ⓔ, Slip, BH (20 ton).

Conwy YC (Deganwy) ☎ 583690, Slip, M, L, FW, R, Bar.

N Wales Cruising Club (in Conwy) ☎ 593481, AB, M, FW, Bar. **Services**: ME, Gas, Gaz, ✕, El, Ⓔ.

Town P & D (cans), 🛒, R, Bar, ✉, Ⓑ, ⇌, ✈ (Liverpool).

MENAI STRAIT

(AC 1464) From NE to SW the main features of this narrow, 20 mile channel are: Puffin Is, at the North-West Entrance; Beaumaris; Garth Pt at Bangor, where the Strait begins; Menai Suspension Bridge (29m); The Swellies, a narrow 1M stretch with strong tidal streams and dangers mid-stream; Britannia Rail Bridge (26m), with cables close W at elevation of 21m; Port Dinorwic; Caernarfon; Abermenai Pt and Fort Belan, which mark the SW end of the Strait; and Caernarfon Bar. The Strait itself is about 10 miles long.

The following brief notes only cover very basic pilotage. For detailed directions see *W Coasts of England and Wales Pilot*, or *Cruising Anglesey and adjoining waters* by Ralph Morris. ▶ *For tidal streams 'Arrowsmiths' is recommended, from Arrowsmiths, Winterstoke Rd, Bristol, BS3 2NT. The Swellies should be taken near local HW slack, and an understanding of tidal streams is essential. The tide is about 1 hour later, and sp range about 2·7m more, at the NE end of the Strait than at the SW end. Levels differ most at about HW +1, when the level at the NE end is more than 1·8m above the level at the SW end; and at about HW − 0445, when the level at the NE end is more than 1·8m below the level at the SW end. Normally the stream runs as follows (times referred to HW Holyhead). HW −0040 to HW +0420: SW between Garth Pt and Abermenai Pt. HW +0420 to HW +0545: outwards from about The Swellies, ie NE towards Garth Pt and SW towards Abermenai Pt. HW +0545 to HW −0040: NE between Abermenai Pt and Garth Pt. Sp rates are generally about 3kn,* **but more in narrows, eg 5kn off Abermenai Pt, 6kn between the bridges, and 8kn at The Swellies.** *The timings and rates of streams may be affected by strong winds in either direction.* ◀ **Note: Direction of buoyage becomes NE off Caernarfon.**

From SW to NE, arrive at the Swellies early (HW Holyhead − 0130) to take the last of the E-going tidal stream. Better to arrive too early, and wait, than too late and risk not making it through the narrows before the stream turns to the W. Approach the S arch of Britannia Bridge keeping the white pyramid in line with the centre of the arch. Once through the bridge, head for a point midway between the pyramid and Price's Point. When the pyramid is abeam, look astern and keep the white leading marks (beneath the S arch of the bridge) in line. When Price's Point is abeam, turn to starboard to pass 20-30m S of Swelly Perch rock, then head just S of the Anglesey (ie N) pillar of the Menai Suspension Bridge until clear of the Platters (cottage abeam to starboard). Then head for the centre of the bridge.

From the NE, pilotage is the reverse of the above, and timing is not quite so critical. If too early, passage will be slow until the stream turns; but if too late you may have difficulty with the strong, but favourable, stream.

▶ *Caernarfon Bar is impassable even in moderately strong winds against the ebb, and the narrows at Abermenai Pt demand a fair tide, or slackish water, since the tide runs strongly here. Going seaward on first of the ebb, when there is water over the banks, it may not be practicable to return to the Strait if conditions on the bar are bad.* ◀

Then it is best to anchor near Mussel Bank buoy and await slack water before returning. Leaving Abermenai Pt on the last of the ebb means banks to seaward are exposed and there is little water in the channel or over the bar.

ANGLESEY TO BARDSEY ISLAND

(AC 1977, 1970, 1971) On N coast of Anglesey a race extends 5ca off Pt Lynas (lt, fog sig, RC) on the E-going stream. Amlwch is a small harbour (partly dries) 1·5M W of Pt Lynas. A drying rock lies 100m offshore on W side of approach, which should not be attempted in strong onshore winds. From here to Carmel Hd beware E Mouse (and shoals to SE), Middle Mouse, Harry Furlong's Rocks (dry), Victoria Bank (least depth

1·8m), Coal Rock (awash), and W Mouse (with dangers to W & SW). The outermost of these dangers is 2M offshore. There are overfalls and races at headlands and over the many rocks and shoals along this coast.

The simplest passage, or at night or in bad weather, is to pass 1M off Skerries, in the TSS ITZ. In good conditions by day and at slack water, Carmel Hd can be rounded close inshore; but beware short, steep, breaking seas here in even moderate winds against tide. Holyhead (port of refuge), access H24 in all weathers, within New Harbour; beware fast ferries.

▶ *Between Carmel Hd and The Skerries the NE-going stream begins at HW Holyhead +0550, and the SW-going at HW Holyhead −0010, sp rates 5kn. 1M NW of Skerries the stream turns 0130 later, and runs less strongly.* **Flood tide close to the coast runs at over 5kn springs,** *and at about 2.5kn 7 miles offshore. The brief period of slack water offshore is HW Dover −0100 (HW L'pool −0115). Slack water lasts longer in Holyhead Bay.*

Ebb tide close to the coast runs at over 5k springs, *and at about 2.5kn 7 miles offshore. Slack water is 5 hours after HW Dover (4¾ hours after HW L'pool). There is no significant counter tide in Holyhead Bay, but the ebb starts first there, giving about 9 hours W-going tide N of the harbour.* ◀

▶ *Races occur off N Stack and (more severe) off S Stack, up to 1·5M offshore on NNE-going stream which begins at HW Holyhead −0605, sp rate 5kn. Races do not extend so far on SSW-going stream which begins at HW Holyhead +0020, sp rate 5kn.* ◀

The W coast of Anglesey is rugged with rks, some drying, up to 1·5M offshore. There are races off Penrhyn Mawr and Rhoscolyn Hd. Pilot's Cove, E of Llanddwyn Is, is good anch to await the right conditions for Menai Strait.

On the Lleyn Peninsula Porth Dinllaen is good anch, but exposed to N and NE. Braich y Pwll is the steep, rky point at end of Lleyn Peninsula (AC 1971). About 1M N of it and up to 1M offshore lie The Tripods, a bank on which there are o'falls and a bad sea with wind against tide.

▶ *Bardsey Sound, 1·5M wide, can be used by day in moderate winds.* **Stream reaches 6kn at sp, and passage should be made at slack water,** *Holyhead −0015 HW or +0035 LW.* ◀

Avoid Carreg Ddu on N side and Maen Bugail Rock (dries 4·1m) on S side of Sound, where there are dangerous races. If passing outside Bardsey Is make a good offing to avoid overfalls which extend 1·5M W and 2·5M S of the island. Turbulence occurs over Bastram Shoal, Devil's Tail and Devil's Ridge, which lie SSE and E of Bardsey Island.

FLOOD Bardsey Sound

The tide turns to the NW or NE (flood) as follows:
(a): Milford Haven +0130;
(b): Milford Haven −0030;
(c): Milford Haven −0100.
These times are approximate.

EBB Bardsey Sound

The tide turns to the SW or SE (ebb) as follows:
(a): Milford Haven −0430;
(b): Milford Haven +0530;
(c): Milford Haven +0500.
These times are approximate.

NOTE: There is a strong eddy down tide off Bardsey Island and overfalls throughout the area.

9.10.19 MENAI STRAIT

Gwynedd/Isle of Anglesey

CHARTS AC 5609, 1464, Imray C52; Stanfords 27. NOTE: The definitive Pilot book is *Cruising Anglesey and adjoining waters* by Ralph Morris.

TIDES Beaumaris –0025 Dover; ML Beaumaris 4·2; Duration 0540
Standard Port HOLYHEAD (→)

Times				Height (metres)			
High Water		Low Water		MHWS	MHWN	MLWN	MLWS
0000	0600	0500	1100	5·6	4·4	2·0	0·7
1200	1800	1700	2300				
Differences BEAUMARIS							
+0025	+0010	+0055	+0035	+2·0	+1·6	+0·5	+0·1
MENAI BRIDGE							
+0030	+0010	+0100	+0035	+1·7	+1·4	+0·3	0·0
PORT DINORWIC							
–0015	–0025	+0030	0000	0·0	0·0	0·0	+0·1
CAERNARFON							
–0030	–0030	+0015	–0005	–0·4	–0·4	–0·1	–0·1
FORT BELAN							
–0040	–0015	–0025	–0005	–1·0	–0·9	–0·2	–0·1
LLANDDWYN ISLAND							
–0115	–0055	–0030	–0020	–0·7	–0·5	–0·1	0·0

Sketch showing the relationship of Caernarfon, Port Dinorwic, The Swellies, Bangor, and Beaumaris in the Menai Strait.

SOUTH WEST ENTRANCE – CAERNARFON BAR

NAVIGATION WPT 53°06´·70N 04°25´·40W, 6ca WSW of C1 SHM. A dangerous sea can build in even a moderate breeze against tide, especially if a swell is running. Bar Chan should not be used at any time other than HW-3 to HW+3. Caernarfon Bar shifts often and unpredictably.

LIGHTS AND MARKS See 9.10.4 and chartlet. **Direction of buoyage changes at Caernarfon.**

CAERNARFON 53°08´·51N 04°16´·83W ❀❀♦♦♦♧♧♧♧

SHELTER Good in Victoria Dock marina, access HW±2 via gates, trfc lts; pontoons at SW end in 2m. Or in river hbr (S of conspic castle), dries to mud/gravel, access HW±3 via swing bridge; for opening sound B (—···). ‡ off Foel Ferry, with local knowledge; or temp ‡ in fair holding off Abermenai Pt, sheltered from W'lies, but strong streams. ⚓ waiting 1½ca SW of C9.

R/T Victoria Dock marina VHF Ch 80. Port Ch 14 16 (HJ).

TELEPHONE (Code 01286) HM 672118, Mobile 07786 730865; Police 673333; Ⓗ 01248 384384; Dr (emergency) 01248 384001.

FACILITIES **Dock** £1·80 **River** £13·50/craft, 0700-2300 (Summer), FW, Slip, C (2 ton), ⊞, ME, El, Ⓔ, ♒; **Caernarfon SC** ☎ (01248) 672861, L, Bar; **Royal Welsh YC** ☎ (01248) 672599, Bar; **Town** P (cans), ✉, Ⓑ.

PORT DINORWIC 53°11´·23N 04°13´·70W

TELEPHONE (Code 01248) Marina 671500; MRCC (01407) 762051; Dr 670423.

FACILITIES Port Dinorwic Marina (231 berths in fresh water) ♥ £21/craft. Call *Dinorwic Marina* VHF Ch 80 M (HO)3 ⚓ 1ca NE of lock. **Tidal basin** dries at sp; lock (width 9·7m) opens HW±2. ☎ 671500, D, P (cans), ⛽, CH, SM; Pier hd F WR 5m 2M, vis R225°- W357°-225°. **Services:** SM, ME, El, ✖, Slip, C, CH. Dinas Boatyard ☎ 671642 all BY facilities. **Town** Ⓔ, ✉ (Bangor or Caernarfon), Ⓑ, ⚒ (Bangor), ✈ (Liverpool). **Plas Menai** (between Port Dinorwic and Caernarfon), the Sport Council for Wales Sailing and Sports Centre: ☎ 670964. *Menai Base* Ch 80 M; day moorings only; ♿.

NORTH EAST ENTRANCE

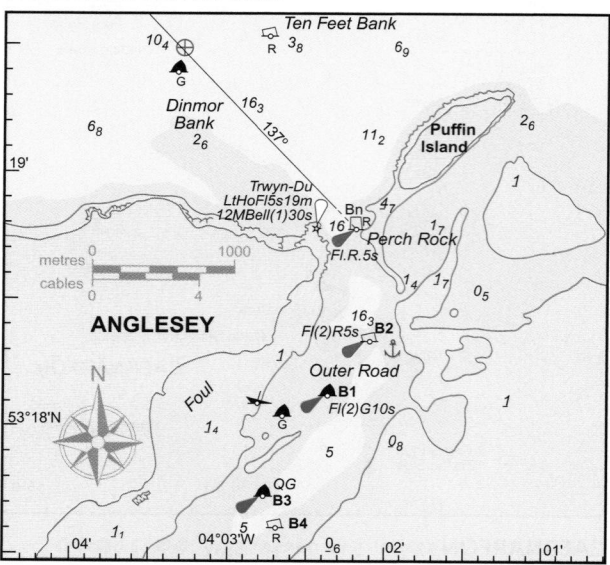

NAVIGATION WPT 53°19′·48N 04°03′·28W, 137°/1M to Perch Rk PHM Bn.

- In N'ly gales seas break on Ten Feet Bank.
- In N Strait keep to buoyed chan, nearer Anglesey.
- Night pilotage not advised due to many unlit buoys/moorings.

LIGHTS AND MARKS See 9.10.4. and chartlet. At NE end of Strait, Trwyn-Du Lt ho and Conspic tr on Puffin Is. Chan is laterally buoyed, some lit. Beaumaris pier has FWG sectored lt.

MENAI BRIDGE/BEAUMARIS 53°15′·66N 04°05′·38W

SHELTER Reasonable off Beaumaris except from NE winds. ⚓ S of B10 PHM buoy or call YCs for mooring. At Menai Bridge, call HM VHF Ch 69 16 for mooring or temp'y berth on St George's Pier (S of which a marina is planned).

TELEPHONE (Code 01248) HM Menai 712312, mobile 07990 531595; MRCC (01407) 762051; Marinecall 09068 969650; Police (01286) 673333; Dr (emergency) 01248 384001.

FACILITIES St George's Pier (Fl G 10s) L at all tides; **Royal Anglesey YC** ☎ 810295, Slip, M, L, R, Bar, P; **North West Venturers YC** ☎ 810023, M, L, FW, water taxi at w/ends only; **Menai Bridge SC. Services:** Slip, P & D (cans), FW, ME, BH (20 ton), ⚒, C (2 ton), CH, El, Ⓔ, Gas. **Both towns** ⊠, Ⓑ, ⇌ (bus to Bangor), ✈ (Liverpool).

BANGOR 53°14′·46N 04°07′·58W

SHELTER Good, except in E'lies, at Dickies BY or Port Penrhyn dock (both dry; access HW±2).

R/T Dickies VHF Ch 09 M 16 (0930-1730), all year.

TELEPHONE (Code 01248) Penrhyn HM 352525; MRCC (01407) 762051; Police (01286) 673333; Dr (emergency) 384001.

FACILITIES Services: Slip, D, P (cans), FW, ME, El, ⚒, C, CH, Ⓔ, SM, BH (30 ton), Gas, Gaz, ACA; **Port Penrhyn**, Slip, AB, D. **Town** ⊠, Ⓑ, ⇌, ✈ (Chester).

THE SWELLIES 53°13′·14N 04°10′·46W

NAVIGATION

- The passage should only be attempted at slack HW, which is about −0100 HW Holyhead.
- The shallow rky narrows between the bridges are dangerous for yachts at other times, when the stream can reach 8kn.
- At slack HW there is 3m over The Platters and the outcrop off Price Pt, which can be ignored.
- For shoal-draft boats passage is also possible at slack LW nps, but there are depths of 0·5m close E of Britannia Bridge.
- The bridges and power cables have a least clearance of 21m at MHWS. Night passage is not recommended.

LIGHTS AND MARKS See 9.10.4. and chartlet. Britannia Bridge, E side, ldg lts 231°, both FW (shown Apr-Sep). Bridge lts, both sides: Centre span Iso 5s 27m 3M; S end, FR 21m 3M; N end, FG 21m 3M.

WGS84 DATUM

9.10.20 HOLYHEAD

Isle of Anglesey 53°19'·72N 04°37'·07W ✿✿✿✿👍👍👍✿✿

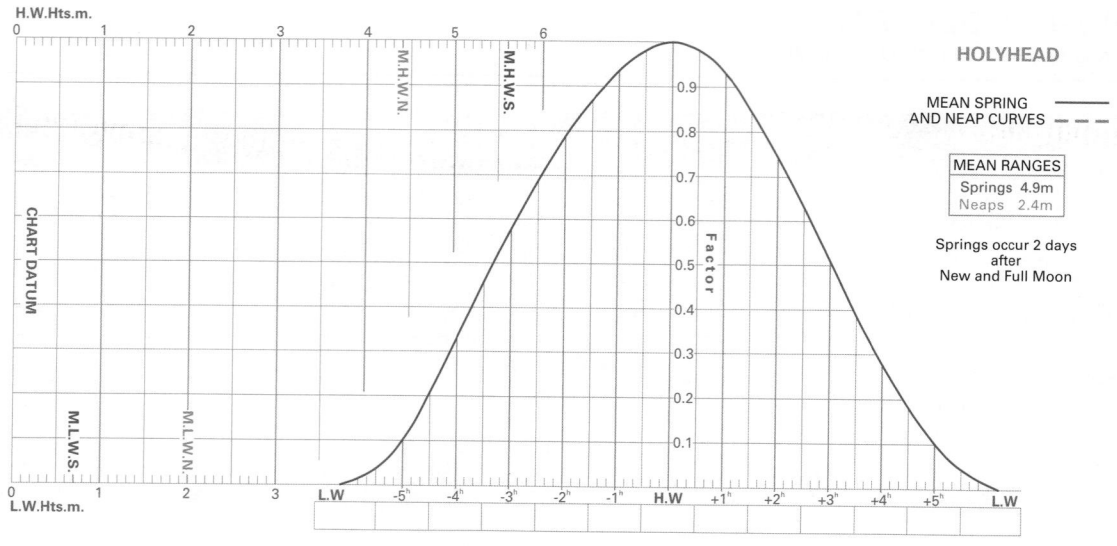

HOLYHEAD

MEAN SPRING ———
AND NEAP CURVES - - - -

MEAN RANGES
Springs 4.9m
Neaps 2.4m

Springs occur 2 days
after
New and Full Moon

HOLYHEAD *continued*

CHARTS AC 5609, 1826, 1970, 1977, 1413, 2011; Imray C61, C52; Stanfords 27.

TIDES –0035 Dover; ML 3·2; Duration 0615

Standard Port HOLYHEAD (→)

Times				Height (metres)			
High Water		Low Water		MHWS	MHWN	MLWN	MLWS
0000	0600	0500	1100	5·6	4·4	2·0	0·7
1200	1800	1700	2300				
Differences TRWYN DINMOR (W of Puffin Is)							
+0025	+0015	+0050	+0035	+1·9	+1·5	+0·5	+0·2
MOELFRE (NE Anglesey)							
+0025	+0020	+0050	+0035	+1·9	+1·4	+0·5	+0·2
AMLWCH (N Anglesey)							
+0020	+0010	+0035	+0025	+1·6	+1·3	+0·5	+0·2
CEMAES BAY (N Anglesey)							
+0020	+0025	+0040	+0035	+1·0	+0·7	+0·3	+0·1
TREARDDUR BAY (W Anglesey)							
–0045	–0025	–0015	–0015	–0·4	–0·4	0·0	+0·1
PORTH TRECASTELL (SW Anglesey)							
–0045	–0025	–0005	–0015	–0·6	–0·6	0·0	0·0
TREFOR (Lleyn peninsula)							
–0115	–0100	–0030	–0020	–0·8	–0·9	–0·2	–0·1
PORTH DINLLAEN (Lleyn peninsula)							
–0120	–0105	–0035	–0025	–1·0	–1·0	–0·2	–0·2
PORTH YSGADEN (Lleyn peninsula)							
–0125	–0110	–0040	–0035	–1·1	–1·0	–0·1	–0·1
BARDSEY ISLAND							
–0220	–0240	–0145	–0140	–1·2	–1·2	–0·5	–0·1

SHELTER Good in marina, least depth 2m, but temp'y visitors berths on E side of floating bwtr are exposed to fresh E'lies. Alternatively ⚓ or use Y ⚓ off HSC; drying AB on bkwtr in emergency only; or in Fish Dock. Strong NE winds raise an uncomfortable sea.

NAVIGATION WPT 53°20'·12N 04°37'·27W, 165°/0·28M to Bkwtr Lt ho. Small craft should leave Spit SHM buoy to starboard then use the main fairway to New Harbour keeping well clear of commercial shipping. Beware numerous fishing markers close to the breakwater. No anchoring in the fairways.

Frequent HSS and Ro-Ro ferries to and from Dun Laoghaire comply with a mini-TSS at the hbr ent by entering within 100-500m of bkwtr hd for Ro-Ro terminals in New Hbr or the Inner Hbr; outbound ferries pass within 2½ca WSW of Clipera PHM buoy, Fl(4) R 15s. Yachts should keep well clear.

LIGHTS AND MARKS Ldg marks 165°: bkwtr lt ho on with chy (127m, grey + B top; R lts); chy and Holyhead Mountain (218m) are conspic from afar. Cranes on aluminium jetty conspic closer to.

Inner hbr tfc sigs from old lt ho at E end of Admiralty pier:
● = Ent is impracticable. ○ = Ent is clear.

R/T *Holyhead Marina* and *Holyhead SC*: Ch **M**. Monitor *Holyhead* Ch 14 16 (H24) for ferry traffic. Broadcast of local nav info/ warnings 1200UT daily on Ch 14.

TELEPHONE (Code 01407) Marina 764242; Port Control 763071; MRCC 762051; Marinecall 09068 969650; Police (01286) 673333; Dr via MRCC.

FACILITIES Holyhead Marina ☎ 764242, mob 07714 292990, www.holyheadmarina.co.uk, £2.50, ❼ 21 approx, D (0800-1800), Gas, Gaz, BY, CH, ME, Ⓔ, El, ✗, BH (14 tons), Slip, R. **Holyhead SC (HSC)** ☎ 762526, M £8.00, L, FW, launch (call Ch M: 0900-2100, Fri/Sat to 2330), Slip, R (Wed, Fri, Sat, Sun only), Bar ☎ 762496. **Fish Dock** ☎ 760139 AB on pontoons, but little room, FW, D by hose. **Inner Hbr** ☎ 762304, used by Stena HSS; not advised for yachts. **Services:** BY, ACA, CH, ME, El, ✗, C (100 ton), BH, Slip, Ⓔ. **Town** P, 🛒, R, Bar, 🏧, ✉, Ⓑ, ⇌, ✈ (Liverpool/Manchester). Ferry/ HSS to Dun Laoghaire and Dublin.
Trearddur Bay (3M south) M (small craft only), L; **BY** ☎ 860501, D, FW, ✗, CH. **Village** P, 🛒, R, Bar.

MINOR HARBOUR ON THE LLEYN PENINSULA

PORTH DINLLAEN, Gwynedd, **52°56'·68N 04°33'·66W**. AC 1971, 1512. HW –0240 on Dover; ML 2·5m; Duration 0535. See 9.10.20. Shelter good in S to W winds but strong NNW to NNE winds cause heavy seas in the bay. Beware Carreg-y-Chad (1·8m) 0·75M SW of the point, and Carreg-y-Chwislen (dries, with unlit IDM Bn) 2ca ENE of the point. From N, Garn Fadryn (369m) brg 182° leads into the bay. Best ⚓ 1ca S of LB ho in approx 2m. HM ☎ (01758) 720276; CG ☎ 01407 762051. Facilities: Bar, 🛒 by landing stage. At Morfa Nefyn (1M), Bar, P, R, 🛒.

See 9.11.6 for Bardsey Island and Aberdaron Bay anchorages.

TIME ZONE (UT)
For Summer Time add ONE hour in **non-shaded areas**

HOLYHEAD   LAT 53°19'N   LONG 4°37'W
TIMES AND HEIGHTS OF HIGH AND LOW WATERS

Dates in red are **SPRINGS**
Dates in blue are **NEAPS**

YEAR 2010

JANUARY

	Time m		Time m
1	0405 0.9 / 1021 5.8 / F 1637 0.7 / 2250 5.7	**16**	0448 1.3 / 1057 5.5 / SA 1712 1.1 / 2320 5.2
2	0452 0.8 / 1107 6.0 / SA 1725 0.5 / 2338 5.7	**17**	0519 1.2 / 1129 5.6 / SU 1743 1.1 / 2351 5.2
3	0538 0.7 / 1154 6.0 / SU 1813 0.4	**18**	0550 1.2 / 1201 5.5 / M 1814 1.1
4	0026 5.7 / 0625 0.8 / M 1242 6.0 / 1902 0.5	**19**	0022 5.1 / 0622 1.3 / TU 1234 5.5 / 1846 1.2
5	0115 5.5 / 0713 1.0 / TU 1331 5.9 / 1953 0.7	**20**	0055 5.1 / 0655 1.4 / W 1308 5.4 / 1920 1.3
6	0205 5.3 / 0803 1.2 / W 1423 5.6 / 2046 1.0	**21**	0129 4.9 / 0730 1.5 / TH 1344 5.2 / 1956 1.5
7	0259 5.0 / 0859 1.5 / TH 1519 5.3 / ☽ 2145 1.4	**22**	0206 4.8 / 0809 1.7 / F 1423 5.0 / 2038 1.6
8	0400 4.8 / 1002 1.8 / F 1624 5.0 / 2251 1.7	**23**	0249 4.6 / 0857 2.0 / SA 1511 4.8 / ☽ 2130 1.9
9	0510 4.6 / 1115 2.0 / SA 1739 4.8	**24**	0346 4.5 / 0959 2.1 / SU 1614 4.6 / 2237 2.0
10	0001 1.9 / 0623 4.6 / SU 1231 2.0 / 1857 4.7	**25**	0504 4.4 / 1119 2.2 / M 1738 4.5 / 2357 2.0
11	0110 1.9 / 0731 4.8 / M 1342 1.9 / 2004 4.8	**26**	0629 4.5 / 1241 2.0 / TU 1901 4.7
12	0210 1.8 / 0827 5.0 / TU 1441 1.7 / 2058 4.9	**27**	0111 1.8 / 0739 4.8 / W 1350 1.6 / 2008 4.9
13	0300 1.7 / 0912 5.2 / W 1527 1.5 / 2141 5.0	**28**	0214 1.5 / 0835 5.2 / TH 1448 1.2 / 2104 5.3
14	0340 1.5 / 0951 5.3 / TH 1606 1.3 / 2217 5.1	**29**	0307 1.1 / 0923 5.5 / F 1538 0.8 / 2152 5.5
15	0416 1.4 / 1025 5.5 / F 1640 1.2 / ● 2250 5.2	**30**	0354 0.8 / 1008 5.9 / SA 1625 0.4 / ○ 2238 5.8
		31	0438 0.6 / 1053 6.1 / SU 1710 0.2 / 2322 5.8

FEBRUARY

	Time m		Time m
1	0522 0.4 / 1137 6.2 / M 1755 0.1	**16**	0525 1.0 / 1136 5.6 / TU 1746 0.9 / 2354 5.3
2	0006 5.8 / 0605 0.4 / TU 1222 6.2 / 1839 0.3	**17**	0555 1.0 / 1207 5.5 / W 1815 1.0
3	0050 5.6 / 0649 0.6 / W 1307 6.0 / 1924 0.6	**18**	0024 5.2 / 0626 1.1 / TH 1239 5.4 / 1845 1.1
4	0135 5.4 / 0735 0.9 / TH 1354 5.6 / 2012 1.0	**19**	0056 5.1 / 0658 1.2 / F 1312 5.3 / 1919 1.2
5	0221 5.1 / 0825 1.3 / F 1444 5.2 / ◔ 2104 1.4	**20**	0130 5.0 / 0735 1.4 / SA 1349 5.1 / 1958 1.5
6	0314 4.8 / 0923 1.7 / SA 1544 4.8 / 2207 1.9	**21**	0209 4.8 / 0820 1.7 / SU 1434 4.8 / 2047 1.7
7	0421 4.5 / 1037 2.0 / SU 1704 4.4 / 2324 2.1	**22**	0301 4.6 / 0920 1.9 / M 1536 4.6 / ◑ 2155 2.0
8	0545 4.4 / 1205 2.2 / M 1840 4.3	**23**	0417 4.4 / 1046 2.1 / TU 1709 4.4 / 2327 2.1
9	0046 2.2 / 0710 4.5 / TU 1329 2.0 / 1958 4.5	**24**	0558 4.4 / 1219 1.9 / W 1846 4.5
10	0156 2.0 / 0813 4.7 / W 1431 1.8 / 2051 4.7	**25**	0053 1.9 / 0718 4.7 / TH 1335 1.5 / 1957 4.9
11	0247 1.8 / 0859 5.0 / TH 1515 1.5 / 2130 4.9	**26**	0159 1.5 / 0818 5.1 / F 1433 1.0 / 2051 5.2
12	0326 1.5 / 0935 5.2 / F 1550 1.3 / 2202 5.0	**27**	0252 1.1 / 0906 5.6 / SA 1522 0.6 / 2137 5.5
13	0359 1.3 / 1007 5.4 / SA 1620 1.1 / 2230 5.1	**28**	0337 0.7 / 0950 5.9 / SU 1606 0.2 / ○ 2219 5.8
14	0428 1.1 / 1036 5.5 / SU 1649 1.0 / ● 2257 5.2		
15	0456 1.0 / 1106 5.6 / M 1717 0.9 / 2325 5.3		

MARCH

	Time m		Time m
1	0419 0.4 / 1033 6.1 / M 1649 0.0 / 2300 5.9	**16**	0429 0.9 / 1038 5.5 / TU 1646 0.8 / 2256 5.3
2	0500 0.2 / 1116 6.2 / TU 1731 0.1 / 2341 5.8	**17**	0458 0.8 / 1108 5.6 / W 1715 0.8 / 2325 5.4
3	0542 0.3 / 1159 6.1 / W 1813 0.2	**18**	0528 0.8 / 1140 5.5 / TH 1745 0.8 / 2356 5.3
4	0022 5.7 / 0624 0.4 / TH 1243 5.9 / 1854 0.6	**19**	0600 0.9 / 1212 5.4 / F 1816 1.0
5	0104 5.5 / 0708 0.8 / F 1327 5.5 / 1938 1.0	**20**	0028 5.3 / 0633 1.1 / SA 1247 5.3 / 1850 1.1
6	0147 5.2 / 0755 1.2 / SA 1414 5.1 / 2026 1.5	**21**	0103 5.1 / 0712 1.3 / SU 1327 5.1 / 1931 1.4
7	0235 4.8 / 0850 1.6 / SU 1510 4.6 / ◔ 2124 2.0	**22**	0145 4.9 / 0800 1.5 / M 1415 4.8 / 2023 1.7
8	0336 4.5 / 1002 2.0 / M 1629 4.2 / 2244 2.3	**23**	0239 4.7 / 0904 1.8 / TU 1522 4.5 / ◑ 2134 2.0
9	0500 4.3 / 1135 2.2 / TU 1816 4.1	**24**	0356 4.5 / 1031 1.9 / W 1658 4.4 / 2308 2.1
10	0015 2.4 / 0636 4.3 / W 1303 2.1 / 1938 4.3	**25**	0535 4.5 / 1202 1.7 / TH 1833 4.5
11	0131 2.2 / 0745 4.6 / TH 1405 1.8 / 2029 4.5	**26**	0034 1.9 / 0655 4.8 / F 1316 1.3 / 1940 4.9
12	0222 1.9 / 0832 4.8 / F 1448 1.5 / 2106 4.8	**27**	0139 1.5 / 0755 5.2 / SA 1412 0.9 / 2031 5.2
13	0301 1.6 / 0908 5.1 / SA 1522 1.2 / 2136 5.0	**28**	0230 1.0 / 0844 5.5 / SU 1500 0.5 / 2115 5.5
14	0332 1.3 / 0939 5.3 / SU 1551 1.0 / 2203 5.1	**29**	0315 0.7 / 0928 5.8 / M 1543 0.3 / 2156 5.7
15	0401 1.1 / 1009 5.4 / M 1619 0.9 / ● 2229 5.2	**30**	0356 0.4 / 1011 6.0 / TU 1625 0.2 / ○ 2236 5.8
		31	0438 0.3 / 1054 6.0 / W 1705 0.2 / 2316 5.8

APRIL

	Time m		Time m
1	0520 0.3 / 1137 5.9 / TH 1746 0.4 / 2357 5.7	**16**	0503 0.8 / 1115 5.5 / F 1718 0.9 / 2331 5.4
2	0602 0.5 / 1220 5.6 / F 1827 0.8	**17**	0539 0.9 / 1151 5.4 / SA 1753 1.0
3	0037 5.5 / 0646 0.8 / SA 1304 5.3 / 1909 1.2	**18**	0008 5.4 / 0617 1.0 / SU 1232 5.2 / 1833 1.1
4	0119 5.2 / 0732 1.2 / SU 1349 4.9 / 1954 1.6	**19**	0048 5.2 / 0702 1.1 / M 1317 5.0 / 1918 1.4
5	0205 4.9 / 0824 1.6 / M 1442 4.5 / 2048 2.0	**20**	0135 5.0 / 0755 1.3 / TU 1411 4.8 / 2015 1.7
6	0259 4.6 / 0930 1.9 / TU 1554 4.2 / ◔ 2200 2.3	**21**	0233 4.8 / 0901 1.5 / W 1521 4.6 / ◔ 2126 1.9
7	0413 4.3 / 1053 2.1 / W 1730 4.0 / 2329 2.4	**22**	0347 4.7 / 1022 1.6 / TH 1649 4.5 / 2251 1.9
8	0541 4.3 / 1215 2.0 / TH 1855 4.2	**23**	0513 4.7 / 1142 1.4 / F 1810 4.6
9	0045 2.3 / 0656 4.5 / F 1320 1.8 / 1950 4.4	**24**	0008 1.8 / 0627 4.9 / SA 1250 1.2 / 1914 4.9
10	0142 2.0 / 0749 4.7 / SA 1407 1.6 / 2029 4.7	**25**	0112 1.4 / 0728 5.2 / SU 1346 0.9 / 2006 5.1
11	0223 1.7 / 0830 4.9 / SU 1443 1.3 / 2101 4.9	**26**	0205 1.1 / 0819 5.4 / M 1435 0.7 / 2051 5.4
12	0257 1.4 / 0904 5.1 / M 1515 1.1 / 2129 5.1	**27**	0251 0.8 / 0906 5.6 / TU 1519 0.5 / 2132 5.5
13	0328 1.2 / 0936 5.3 / TU 1544 1.0 / 2157 5.2	**28**	0335 0.6 / 0950 5.7 / W 1601 0.5 / ○ 2213 5.6
14	0358 1.0 / 1007 5.4 / W 1614 0.9 / ● 2226 5.3	**29**	0418 0.6 / 1034 5.7 / TH 1643 0.6 / 2254 5.7
15	0430 0.9 / 1040 5.5 / TH 1645 0.8 / 2258 5.4	**30**	0502 0.6 / 1118 5.6 / F 1724 0.8 / 2335 5.6

Chart Datum: 3·05 metres below Ordnance Datum (Newlyn). HAT is 6·3 metres above Chart Datum; see 4.5.

N Wales

TIME ZONE (UT)
For Summer Time add ONE hour in **non-shaded areas**

HOLYHEAD   LAT 53°19′N   LONG 4°37′W
TIMES AND HEIGHTS OF HIGH AND LOW WATERS

Dates in **red** are **SPRINGS**
Dates in **blue** are **NEAPS**

YEAR 2010

MAY

Time	m	Time	m
1 0545 1201 SA 1804	0.7 5.4 1.0	**16** 0525 1138 SU 1739 2355	0.8 5.4 1.0 5.5
2 0016 0628 SU 1245 1845	5.4 0.9 5.1 1.3	**17** 0609 1223 M 1824	0.9 5.3 1.1
3 0057 0713 M 1328 1928	5.2 1.2 4.8 1.6	**18** 0040 0658 TU 1314 1913	5.4 0.9 5.1 1.3
4 0140 0801 TU 1417 2017	5.0 1.5 4.5 1.9	**19** 0131 0754 W 1410 2010	5.2 1.1 4.9 1.5
5 0228 0856 W 1515 2116	4.7 1.8 4.3 2.2	**20** 0228 0856 TH 1515 2115	5.1 1.2 4.7 1.7
6 0328 1002 TH 1629 2228	4.5 1.9 4.1 2.3	**21** 0334 1005 F 1628 2227	5.0 1.3 4.7 1.7
7 0438 1114 F 1746 2343	4.4 2.0 4.2 2.3	**22** 0447 1115 SA 1740 2338	4.9 1.3 4.7 1.7
8 0550 1219 SA 1851	4.4 1.9 4.3	**23** 0557 1220 SU 1844	5.0 1.2 4.8
9 0045 0651 SU 1312 1939	2.1 4.6 1.7 4.5	**24** 0042 0700 M 1319 1939	1.5 5.1 1.1 5.0
10 0134 0741 M 1355 2017	1.9 4.8 1.5 4.8	**25** 0140 0756 TU 1411 2028	1.3 5.2 1.0 5.2
11 0215 0823 TU 1433 2052	1.6 4.9 1.3 5.0	**26** 0231 0847 W 1459 2112	1.1 5.3 0.9 5.3
12 0252 0901 W 1508 2125	1.4 5.1 1.1 5.1	**27** 0320 0935 TH 1543 2155	0.9 5.4 0.9 5.5
13 0328 0938 TH 1543 2159	1.1 5.2 1.0 5.3	**28** 0405 1020 F 1625 2237	0.9 5.3 0.9 5.5
14 0405 1016 F 1619 2235	1.0 5.3 0.9 5.4	**29** 0449 1104 SA 1706 2318	0.9 5.3 1.0 5.5
15 0443 1055 SA 1658 2313	0.9 5.4 0.9 5.5	**30** 0532 1146 SU 1746 2357	0.9 5.1 1.2 5.4
		31 0613 1227 M 1825	1.0 5.0 1.3

JUNE

Time	m	Time	m
1 0036 0653 TU 1307 1904	5.3 1.2 4.8 1.5	**16** 0032 0652 W 1306 1905	5.6 0.6 5.3 1.0
2 0116 0735 W 1348 1947	5.1 1.4 4.6 1.7	**17** 0122 0744 TH 1359 1957	5.5 0.7 5.1 1.2
3 0158 0821 TH 1434 2034	4.9 1.5 4.5 1.9	**18** 0215 0840 F 1455 2054	5.4 0.9 5.0 1.4
4 0245 0911 F 1528 2128	4.8 1.7 4.3 2.1	**19** 0313 0940 SA 1558 2157	5.2 1.1 4.8 1.5
5 0340 1007 SA 1630 2231	4.6 1.8 4.2 2.2	**20** 0417 1044 SU 1705 2306	5.1 1.2 4.7 1.6
6 0443 1108 SU 1736 2336	4.5 1.9 4.3 2.2	**21** 0526 1150 M 1812	5.0 1.4 4.7
7 0547 1208 M 1837	4.5 1.8 4.4	**22** 0014 0636 TU 1254 1915	1.6 4.9 1.4 4.8
8 0036 0646 TU 1302 1928	2.0 4.6 1.7 4.6	**23** 0120 0741 W 1353 2010	1.5 4.9 1.4 5.0
9 0130 0740 W 1351 2014	1.8 4.8 1.5 4.8	**24** 0220 0838 TH 1446 2059	1.4 5.0 1.3 5.1
10 0217 0828 TH 1435 2055	1.6 4.9 1.3 5.0	**25** 0312 0928 F 1532 2143	1.2 5.0 1.3 5.3
11 0302 0913 F 1517 2135	1.3 5.1 1.2 5.3	**26** 0359 1012 SA 1614 2224	1.1 5.1 1.2 5.4
12 0345 0957 SA 1600 2217	1.0 5.3 1.0 5.4	**27** 0440 1053 SU 1652 2302	1.0 5.1 1.2 5.4
13 0429 1042 SU 1643 2300	0.8 5.4 0.9 5.6	**28** 0518 1130 M 1728 2339	1.0 5.1 1.2 5.4
14 0515 1128 M 1729 2345	0.7 5.4 0.9 5.6	**29** 0555 1206 TU 1803	1.0 5.0 1.2
15 0603 1216 TU 1816	0.6 5.4 0.9	**30** 0014 0630 W 1241 1838	5.4 1.1 4.9 1.3

JULY

Time	m	Time	m
1 0050 0706 TH 1316 1915	5.3 1.2 4.8 1.5	**16** 0105 0724 F 1337 1935	5.8 0.5 5.4 0.9
2 0127 0744 F 1354 1955	5.1 1.3 4.7 1.7	**17** 0154 0814 SA 1427 2027	5.7 0.7 5.1 1.1
3 0206 0824 SA 1435 2039	5.0 1.5 4.6 1.9	**18** 0247 0909 SU 1523 2126	5.4 1.1 4.9 1.4
4 0250 0909 SU 1524 2129	4.8 1.7 4.4 2.0	**19** 0347 1011 M 1628 2235	5.1 1.4 4.7 1.7
5 0342 1002 M 1624 2230	4.6 1.8 4.3 2.1	**20** 0458 1121 TU 1742 2352	4.8 1.7 4.6 1.8
6 0444 1104 TU 1733 2339	4.5 1.9 4.4 2.1	**21** 0619 1233 W 1856	4.6 1.8 4.7
7 0555 1210 W 1841	4.5 1.9 4.5	**22** 0108 0735 TH 1341 2000	1.8 4.6 1.7 4.8
8 0047 0702 TH 1313 1940	2.0 4.6 1.7 4.7	**23** 0216 0836 F 1438 2051	1.6 4.7 1.6 5.0
9 0148 0802 F 1409 2031	1.7 4.8 1.5 5.0	**24** 0308 0924 SA 1523 2134	1.4 4.9 1.4 5.2
10 0242 0855 SA 1459 2117	1.4 5.0 1.3 5.3	**25** 0351 1004 SU 1601 2211	1.2 5.0 1.3 5.4
11 0330 0943 SU 1545 2201	1.1 5.3 1.0 5.5	**26** 0427 1038 M 1635 2244	1.1 5.1 1.2 5.4
12 0417 1029 M 1630 2246	0.7 5.4 0.8 5.8	**27** 0500 1110 TU 1707 2317	1.0 5.1 1.1 5.5
13 0503 1115 TU 1715 2331	0.4 5.6 0.7 5.9	**28** 0531 1140 W 1738 2349	1.0 5.1 1.1 5.5
14 0549 1201 W 1801	0.3 5.6 0.6	**29** 0602 1210 TH 1810	1.0 5.1 1.2
15 0017 0636 TH 1249 1847	5.9 0.3 5.5 0.7	**30** 0021 0633 F 1243 1843	5.4 1.1 5.0 1.3
		31 0055 0706 SA 1316 1917	5.3 1.2 4.9 1.4

AUGUST

Time	m	Time	m
1 0130 0741 SU 1352 1955	5.1 1.4 4.8 1.7	**16** 0219 0837 M 1449 ◗ 2057	5.4 1.2 5.0 1.5
2 0207 0820 M 1432 2040	4.9 1.6 4.6 1.9	**17** 0318 0937 TU 1552 2208	4.9 1.7 4.7 1.8
3 0252 0907 TU 1523 ◑ 2137	4.7 1.8 4.5 2.1	**18** 0434 1052 W 1713 2334	4.6 2.0 4.5 2.0
4 0350 1009 W 1634 2251	4.5 2.0 4.4 2.2	**19** 0608 1214 TH 1839	4.4 2.1 4.6
5 0509 1126 TH 1759	4.4 2.1 4.4	**20** 0059 0732 F 1329 1948	1.9 4.5 2.0 4.8
6 0014 0634 F 1244 1913	2.1 4.5 1.9 4.7	**21** 0207 0831 SA 1425 2038	1.7 4.7 1.8 5.0
7 0126 0745 SA 1349 2011	1.7 4.7 1.6 5.0	**22** 0256 0913 SU 1508 2117	1.5 4.8 1.5 5.2
8 0225 0841 SU 1442 2100	1.3 5.0 1.3 5.4	**23** 0333 0946 M 1542 2150	1.3 5.0 1.3 5.4
9 0315 0929 M 1529 2144	0.9 5.3 0.9 5.7	**24** 0405 1016 TU 1613 ○ 2220	1.1 5.1 1.2 5.5
10 0400 1013 TU 1613 ● 2227	0.5 5.6 0.6 6.0	**25** 0434 1043 W 1641 2250	1.0 5.2 1.1 5.5
11 0444 1056 W 1656 2311	0.2 5.8 0.4 6.1	**26** 0502 1111 TH 1710 2320	0.9 5.2 1.0 5.6
12 0528 1139 TH 1739 2356	0.1 5.8 0.4 6.2	**27** 0530 1139 F 1740 2351	0.9 5.2 1.1 5.5
13 0613 1224 F 1824	0.2 5.7 0.5	**28** 0600 1209 SA 1811	1.0 5.2 1.2
14 0041 0657 SA 1309 1910	6.0 0.4 5.5 0.7	**29** 0023 0630 SU 1241 1843	5.4 1.1 5.1 1.3
15 0128 0745 SU 1356 1959	5.7 0.8 5.2 1.1	**30** 0056 0702 M 1315 1919	5.2 1.3 5.0 1.5
		31 0132 0739 TU 1353 2002	5.0 1.5 4.8 1.8

Chart Datum: 3·05 metres below Ordnance Datum (Newlyn). HAT is 6·3 metres above Chart Datum; see 4.5.

TIME ZONE (UT)
For Summer Time add ONE hour in **non-shaded areas**

HOLYHEAD   LAT 53°19'N   LONG 4°37'W
TIMES AND HEIGHTS OF HIGH AND LOW WATERS

Dates in red are SPRINGS
Dates in blue are NEAPS

YEAR 2010

SEPTEMBER

Time	m	Time	m
1 0215	4.8	**16** 0412	4.4
0825	1.8	1022	2.3
W 1441	4.6	TH 1641	4.5
◑ 2059	2.0	2313	2.1
2 0313	4.5	**17** 0552	4.3
0927	2.1	1149	2.4
TH 1551	4.4	F 1812	4.5
2218	2.2		
3 0438	4.4	**18** 0038	2.0
1053	2.2	0715	4.4
F 1726	4.4	SA 1306	2.2
2350	2.1	1923	4.7
4 0616	4.5	**19** 0144	1.8
1221	2.0	0810	4.6
SA 1849	4.7	SU 1401	1.9
		2012	5.0
5 0107	1.7	**20** 0230	1.5
0729	4.8	0849	4.9
SU 1330	1.7	M 1442	1.7
1950	5.1	2050	5.2
6 0206	1.2	**21** 0305	1.3
0824	5.1	0920	5.0
M 1423	1.3	TU 1515	1.4
2039	5.5	2122	5.4
7 0255	0.7	**22** 0335	1.1
0910	5.5	0947	5.2
TU 1509	0.9	W 1545	1.2
2123	5.9	2152	5.5
8 0339	0.4	**23** 0403	1.0
0952	5.7	1013	5.3
W 1551	0.5	TH 1613	1.1
● 2205	6.1	○ 2221	5.6
9 0421	0.1	**24** 0430	1.0
1033	5.9	1040	5.4
TH 1633	0.3	F 1641	1.0
2248	6.3	2251	5.6
10 0503	0.1	**25** 0458	1.0
1115	5.9	1109	5.4
F 1716	0.3	SA 1711	1.1
2332	6.2	2322	5.5
11 0546	0.2	**26** 0527	1.0
1157	5.8	1139	5.4
SA 1759	0.5	SU 1743	1.1
		2354	5.4
12 0017	6.0	**27** 0558	1.2
0630	0.5	1211	5.3
SU 1241	5.6	M 1817	1.3
1845	0.7		
13 0104	5.7	**28** 0029	5.3
0715	1.0	0632	1.3
M 1327	5.3	TU 1246	5.2
1934	1.1	1854	1.5
14 0154	5.2	**29** 0107	5.1
0805	1.4	0711	1.6
TU 1417	5.0	W 1326	5.0
2032	1.6	1939	1.7
15 0252	4.8	**30** 0153	4.8
0905	1.9	0759	1.8
W 1519	4.7	TH 1417	4.8
◑ 2144	2.0	2039	1.9

OCTOBER

Time	m	Time	m
1 0255	4.6	**16** 0513	4.2
0904	2.1	1108	2.5
F 1528	4.6	SA 1725	4.6
◑ 2200	2.1	2357	2.1
2 0423	4.4	**17** 0636	4.4
1031	2.2	1224	2.4
SA 1701	4.6	SU 1838	4.7
2330	1.9		
3 0558	4.6	**18** 0101	1.9
1158	2.1	0732	4.6
SU 1823	4.9	M 1322	2.1
		1932	4.9
4 0044	1.5	**19** 0150	1.7
0708	4.9	0813	4.8
M 1306	1.7	TU 1406	1.9
1924	5.2	2013	5.1
5 0142	1.1	**20** 0228	1.5
0802	5.2	0846	5.0
TU 1359	1.3	W 1442	1.6
2014	5.6	2048	5.3
6 0231	0.7	**21** 0300	1.3
0847	5.6	0915	5.2
W 1445	0.9	TH 1513	1.4
2059	5.9	2120	5.4
7 0315	0.4	**22** 0329	1.2
0928	5.8	0943	5.3
TH 1528	0.6	F 1543	1.2
● 2142	6.1	2151	5.5
8 0357	0.3	**23** 0358	1.1
1009	5.9	1011	5.4
F 1611	0.4	SA 1614	1.1
2226	6.2	○ 2223	5.5
9 0439	0.3	**24** 0428	1.1
1051	6.0	1041	5.5
SA 1654	0.4	SU 1647	1.1
2311	6.1	2257	5.5
10 0522	0.5	**25** 0500	1.1
1133	5.9	1114	5.5
SU 1739	0.6	M 1721	1.2
2356	5.9	2332	5.5
11 0605	0.8	**26** 0534	1.2
1217	5.7	1149	5.5
M 1825	0.9	TU 1759	1.2
12 0043	5.5	**27** 0011	5.3
0649	1.2	0612	1.3
TU 1302	5.4	W 1228	5.3
1914	1.2	1840	1.4
13 0133	5.1	**28** 0054	5.1
0737	1.6	0655	1.6
W 1351	5.1	TH 1312	5.2
2010	1.6	1930	1.6
14 0229	4.7	**29** 0145	4.9
0833	2.1	0746	1.8
TH 1448	4.8	F 1406	5.0
◑ 2117	2.0	2031	1.7
15 0342	4.4	**30** 0248	4.7
0945	2.4	0851	2.0
F 1601	4.6	SA 1513	4.9
2238	2.2	◑ 2146	1.8
		31 0408	4.6
		1010	2.1
		SU 1635	4.8
		2305	1.7

NOVEMBER

Time	m	Time	m
1 0532	4.7	**16** 0002	2.1
1130	2.0	0634	4.5
M 1752	5.0	TU 1227	2.3
		1835	4.7
2 0015	1.4	**17** 0057	1.9
0640	5.0	0725	4.7
TU 1237	1.7	W 1319	2.1
1855	5.3	1926	4.9
3 0114	1.1	**18** 0142	1.7
0735	5.2	0805	4.9
W 1333	1.4	TH 1403	1.9
1948	5.6	2010	5.1
4 0205	0.9	**19** 0221	1.6
0822	5.5	0840	5.1
TH 1422	1.1	F 1440	1.6
2037	5.8	2048	5.2
5 0252	0.7	**20** 0256	1.4
0906	5.7	0913	5.3
F 1508	0.8	SA 1516	1.4
2123	5.9	2124	5.4
6 0336	0.6	**21** 0330	1.3
0948	5.8	0945	5.4
SA 1553	0.7	SU 1551	1.3
● 2209	6.0	○ 2201	5.4
7 0419	0.7	**22** 0404	1.2
1031	5.9	1019	5.5
SU 1638	0.7	M 1628	1.2
2255	5.8	2238	5.4
8 0502	0.8	**23** 0440	1.2
1114	5.8	1056	5.6
M 1724	0.8	TU 1707	1.1
2341	5.6	2318	5.5
9 0545	1.1	**24** 0519	1.2
1157	5.7	1135	5.6
TU 1810	1.0	W 1749	1.1
10 0026	5.4	**25** 0000	5.4
0628	1.4	0600	1.3
W 1241	5.5	TH 1218	5.6
1857	1.3	1834	1.2
11 0114	5.0	**26** 0047	5.3
0713	1.7	0646	1.4
TH 1326	5.3	F 1304	5.4
1947	1.6	1924	1.3
12 0203	4.7	**27** 0138	5.1
0802	2.0	0737	1.6
F 1416	5.0	SA 1356	5.3
2043	1.9	2021	1.4
13 0302	4.5	**28** 0237	4.9
0900	2.3	0837	1.8
SA 1514	4.8	SU 1456	5.2
◑ 2147	2.1	◑ 2125	1.5
14 0412	4.3	**29** 0344	4.8
1009	2.5	0944	1.9
SU 1622	4.6	M 1605	5.1
2257	2.1	2235	1.5
15 0528	4.3	**30** 0458	4.8
1123	2.5	1056	1.9
M 1732	4.6	TU 1717	5.1
		2343	1.4

DECEMBER

Time	m	Time	m
1 0607	4.9	**16** 0620	4.5
1205	1.8	1221	2.3
W 1825	5.2	TH 1831	4.7
2 0046	1.3	**17** 0049	2.0
0707	5.1	0717	4.7
TH 1307	1.5	F 1318	2.1
1926	5.4	1929	4.8
3 0142	1.2	**18** 0140	1.8
0801	5.3	0805	4.9
F 1403	1.3	SA 1408	1.9
2021	5.5	2018	5.0
4 0234	1.1	**19** 0225	1.7
0849	5.5	0846	5.1
SA 1455	1.1	SU 1452	1.6
2111	5.6	2102	5.1
5 0321	1.0	**20** 0306	1.4
0934	5.7	0924	5.3
SU 1544	1.0	M 1533	1.3
● 2159	5.6	2143	5.3
6 0405	1.0	**21** 0346	1.2
1017	5.8	1003	5.5
M 1630	0.9	TU 1615	1.1
2245	5.6	○ 2225	5.4
7 0448	1.1	**22** 0426	1.1
1100	5.8	1042	5.7
TU 1714	1.0	W 1656	0.9
2329	5.4	2307	5.5
8 0529	1.2	**23** 0508	1.0
1141	5.7	1123	5.8
W 1757	1.1	TH 1740	0.8
		2351	5.5
9 0011	5.3	**24** 0551	1.0
0609	1.3	1207	5.8
TH 1222	5.6	F 1825	0.8
1838	1.2		
10 0052	5.1	**25** 0036	5.5
0649	1.5	0635	1.0
F 1302	5.4	SA 1253	5.8
1920	1.4	1912	0.8
11 0133	4.9	**26** 0125	5.4
0731	1.8	0723	1.2
SA 1343	5.2	SU 1341	5.6
2004	1.6	2003	1.0
12 0216	4.7	**27** 0216	5.2
0816	2.0	0815	1.4
SU 1428	5.0	M 1434	5.5
2052	1.8	2059	1.2
13 0306	4.5	**28** 0314	5.0
0907	2.2	0914	1.6
M 1519	4.8	TU 1534	5.3
◑ 2146	2.0	◑ 2202	1.4
14 0406	4.4	**29** 0419	4.8
1007	2.4	1021	1.8
TU 1620	4.7	W 1643	5.1
2247	2.1	2310	1.5
15 0514	4.4	**30** 0531	4.8
1115	2.4	1135	1.8
W 1726	4.6	TH 1758	5.0
2351	2.1		
		31 0019	1.6
		0642	4.9
		F 1247	1.8
		1910	5.0

Chart Datum: 3·05 metres below Ordnance Datum (Newlyn). HAT is 6·3 metres above Chart Datum; see 4.5.

N Wales

South Wales & Bristol Channel

Bardsey Island to Land's End

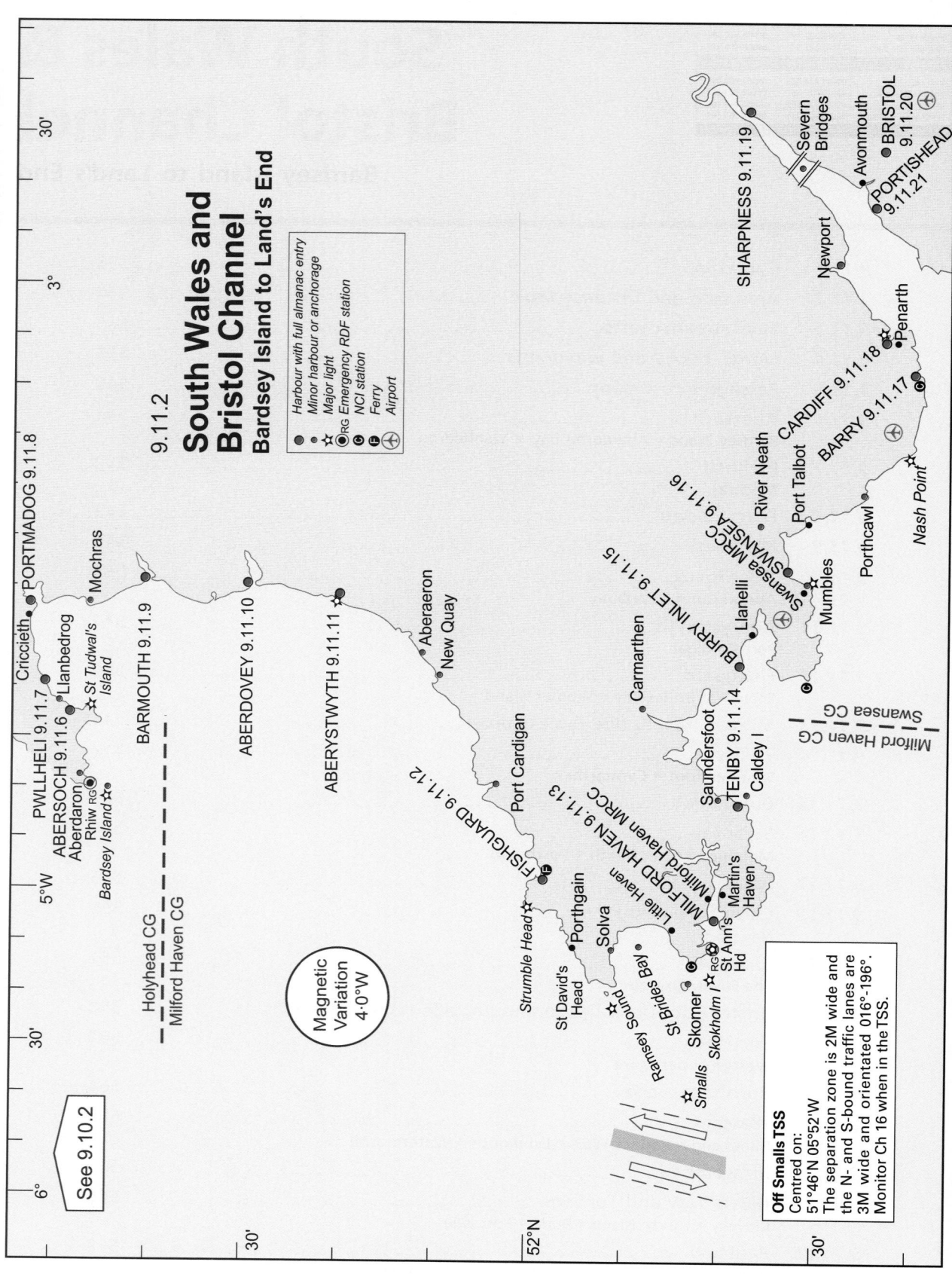

South Wales and Bristol Channel

Bardsey Island to Land's End

9.11.2

Harbour with full almanac entry
Minor harbour or anchorage
Major light
RG Emergency RDF station
NCI station
Ferry
Airport

PORTMADOG 9.11.8
Mochras
Criccieth
Llanbedrog
PWLLHELI 9.11.7
St Tudwal's Island
ABERSOCH 9.11.6
Aberdaron
Rhiw RG
Bardsey Island

BARMOUTH 9.11.9

ABERDOVEY 9.11.10

ABERYSTWYTH 9.11.11

Aberaeron
New Quay

Port Cardigan

FISHGUARD 9.11.12

Strumble Head
St David's Head
Porthgain
Solva
St Brides Bay
Ramsey Sound
Skomer
Smalls
Skokholm I
St Ann's Hd
Little Haven
MILFORD HAVEN MRCC
Martin's Haven
MILFORD HAVEN 9.11.13

Carmarthen

Saundersfoot
TENBY 9.11.14
Caldey I

Llanelli
BURRY INLET 9.11.15

Mumbles
Swansea MRCC
SWANSEA 9.11.16
River Neath
Port Talbot
Porthcawl
Nash Point

BARRY 9.11.17
CARDIFF 9.11.18
Penarth
Newport
SHARPNESS 9.11.19
Severn Bridges
Avonmouth
BRISTOL 9.11.20
PORTISHEAD 9.11.21

Milford Haven CG
Swansea CG

Holyhead CG
Milford Haven CG

See 9.10.2

Magnetic Variation 4·0°W

Off Smalls TSS
Centred on:
51°46'N 05°52'W
The separation zone is 2M wide and the N- and S-bound traffic lanes are 3M wide and orientated 016°-196°. Monitor Ch 16 when in the TSS.

5°W
6°
30'
30'
30'
52°N
30'
30'
3°

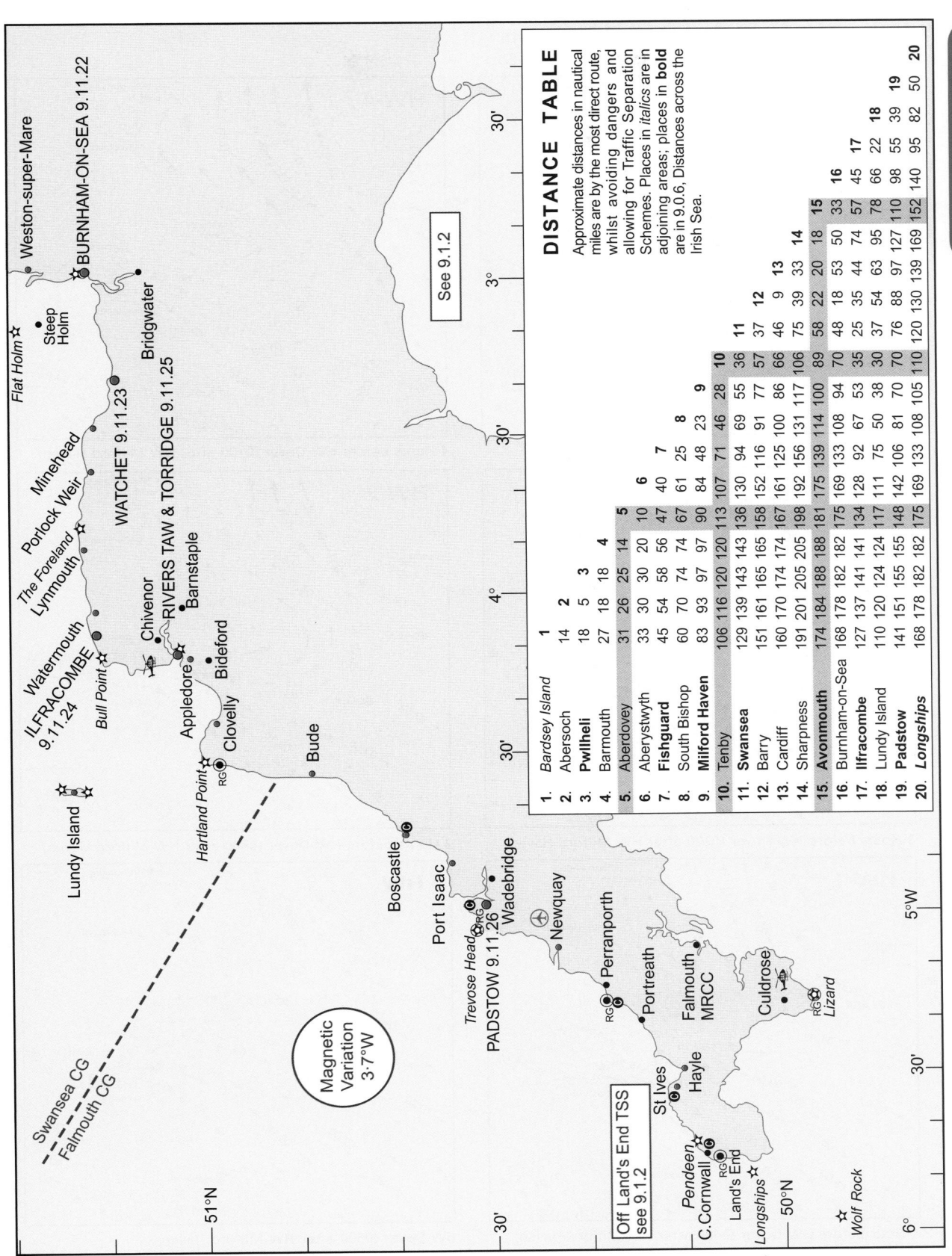

See 9.1.2

Magnetic Variation 3·7°W

Off Land's End TSS see 9.1.2

DISTANCE TABLE

Approximate distances in nautical miles are by the most direct route, whilst avoiding dangers and allowing for Traffic Separation Schemes. Places in *italics* are in adjoining areas; places in **bold** are in 9.0.6, Distances across the Irish Sea.

	1	2	3	4	5	6	7	8	9	10	11	12	13	14	15	16	17	18	19	20
1. *Bardsey Island*	1																			
2. Abersoch	14	2																		
3. **Pwllheli**	18	5	3																	
4. Barmouth	27	18	18	4																
5. **Aberdovey**	31	26	25	14	5															
6. Aberystwyth	33	30	30	20	10	6														
7. **Fishguard**	45	54	58	56	47	40	7													
8. South Bishop	60	70	74	74	67	61	25	8												
9. **Milford Haven**	83	93	97	97	90	84	48	23	9											
10. **Tenby**	106	116	120	120	113	107	71	46	28	10										
11. **Swansea**	129	139	143	143	136	130	94	69	55	36	11									
12. Barry	151	161	165	165	158	152	116	91	77	57	37	12								
13. Cardiff	160	170	174	174	167	161	125	100	86	66	46	9	13							
14. Sharpness	191	201	205	205	198	192	156	131	117	106	75	39	33	14						
15. **Avonmouth**	174	184	188	188	181	175	139	114	100	89	58	22	20	18	15					
16. Burnham-on-Sea	168	178	182	182	175	169	133	108	94	70	48	18	53	50	33	16				
17. Ilfracombe	127	137	141	141	134	128	92	67	53	35	25	35	44	74	57	45	17			
18. Lundy Island	110	120	124	124	117	111	75	50	38	30	37	54	63	95	78	66	22	18		
19. **Padstow**	141	151	155	155	148	142	106	81	70	70	76	88	97	127	110	95	55	39	19	
20. *Longships*	168	178	182	182	175	169	133	108	105	110	120	130	139	169	152	140	95	82	50	20

Weston-super-Mare
BURNHAM-ON-SEA 9.11.22
Flat Holm
Steep Holm
Bridgwater
Minehead
Porlock Weir
WATCHET 9.11.23
The Foreland
Lynmouth
RIVERS TAW & TORRIDGE 9.11.25
Barnstaple
Watermouth
ILFRACOMBE 9.11.24
Chivenor
Bull Point
Bideford
Appledore
Clovelly
Lundy Island
Hartland Point
Bude
Boscastle
Port Isaac
Wadebridge
Newquay
Perranporth
Portreath
Falmouth MRCC
Culdrose
Lizard
Trevose Head
PADSTOW 9.11.26
St Ives
Hayle
Pendeen
C. Cornwall
Land's End
Longships
Wolf Rock

Swansea CG
Falmouth CG

51°N
50°N
30'
30'
6°
5°W
4°
3°
30'

9.11.3 AREA 11 TIDAL STREAMS

5 Hours before HW Dover (HW Milford Haven)

4 Hours before HW Dover (0100 after HW Milford Haven)

3 Hours before HW Dover (0200 after HW Milford Haven)

2 Hours before HW Dover (0300 after HW Milford Haven)

1 Hour before HW Dover (0400 after HW Milford Haven)

HW Dover (0500 after HW Milford Haven)

Southward 9.1.3   Northward 9.10.3   South Ireland 9.12.3

1 Hour after HW Dover (0600 after HW Milford Haven)

2 Hours after HW Dover (0525 before HW Milford Haven)

3 Hours after HW Dover (0425 before HW Milford Haven)

4 Hours after HW Dover (0325 before HW Milford Haven)

5 Hours after HW Dover (0225 before HW Milford Haven)

6 Hours after HW Dover (0125 before HW Milford Haven)

9.11.4 LIGHTS, BUOYS AND WAYPOINTS

Bold print = light with a nominal range of 15M or more. CAPITALS = place or feature. *CAPITAL ITALICS* = light-vessel, light float or Lanby. *Italics* = Fog signal. ***Bold italics*** = Racon. Abbreviations are in Chapter 1.

CARDIGAN BAY (see also 9.10.4)

Bardsey I ☆ 52°45'·00N 04°47'·98W Fl (5) 15s 39m **26M**; W☐ twr, R bands; obsc by Bardsey I 198°-250° and in Tremadoc B when brg less than 260°; *Horn Mo(N) 45s*.

St Tudwal's ≰ Fl WR 15s 46m W14, R10M; vis: 349°-W-169°-R-221°-W-243°-R-259°-W-293°-R-349°; obsc by East I 211°-231°; 52°47'·92N 04°28'·30W.

PWLLHELI and PORTHMADOG

Pwllheli App ↙ Iso 2s; 52°53'·02N 04°23'·07W.
Porthmadog Fairway ↘ L Fl 10s; 52°52'·97N 04°11'·18W.

BARMOUTH and ABERDOVEY

Diffuser ↙ Fl Y 5s; 52°43'·19N 04°05'·38W.
Barmouth Outer ↙ L Fl 10s; 52°42'·62N 04°04'·83W.
Aberdovey Outer ↘ Iso 4s; 52°32'·00N 04°05'·56W.
Cynfelyn Patches, Patches ↙ Q (9) 15s; 52°25'·83N 04°16'·41W.

ABERYSTWYTH, ABERAERON and NEW QUAY

Aberystwyth S Bkwtr Hd ≰ Fl (2) WG 10s 12m 10M; vis: 030°-G-053°-W-210°; 52°24'·40N 04°05'·52W.
Ldg Lts 133°. Front, FR 4m 5M; 52°24'·37N 04°05'·39W. Rear, 52m from front, FR 7m 6M.
Aberaeron N Pier ≰ Fl (4) WRG 15s 10m 6M; vis: 050°-G-104°-W-178°-R-232°; 52°14'·61N 04°15'·87W.
Carreg Ina ↙ Q; 52°13'·25N 04°20'·75W.
New Quay Pier Hd ≰ Fl WG 3s 12m W8M, G5M; G △; vis: 135°-W-252°-G-295; 52°12'·95N 04°21'·35W.

CARDIGAN and FISHGUARD

Cardigan Channel ↙ Fl (2) 5s; 52°06'·44N 04°41'·43W.
Fishguard N Bkwtr Hd ≰ Fl G 4·5s 18m 13M; *Bell (1) 8s;* 52°00'·76N 04°58'·23W.
Strumble Head ☆ 52°01'·79N 05°04'·43W Fl (4) 15s 45m **26M**; vis: 038°-257°; (H24).

BISHOPS and SMALLS

South Bishop ☆ 51°51'·14N 05°24'·74W Fl 5s 44m **16M**; W ○ twr; *Horn (3) 45s;* ***Racon (O)10M;*** (H24).
The Smalls ☆ 51°43'·27N 05°40'·19W Fl (3) 15s 36m **18M**; ***Racon (T);*** *Horn (2) 60s.* Same twr, Iso R 4s 33m 13M; vis: 253°-285° over Hats & Barrels Rk; both Lts shown H24 in periods of reduced visibility.
Skokholm I ☆, 51°41'·64N 05°17'·22W Fl WR 10s 54m **W18M, R15M**; vis: 301°-W-154°-R-301°; partially obsc 226°-258°.

WALES – SOUTH COAST – BRISTOL CHANNEL

MILFORD HAVEN

St Ann's Head ☆ 51°40'·87N 05°10'·42W Fl WR 5s 48m **W18M, R17M, R14M**; W 8-sided twr; vis: 233°-W-247°-R-285°-R(intens)- 314°-R-332°-W131°, partially obscured between 124°-129°; *Horn (2) 60s.*
W Blockhouse Point ↙ Ldg Lts 022·5°. Front, F 54m 13M; B stripe on W twr; vis: 004·5°-040·5°; intens on lead. By day 10M; vis: 004·5°-040·5°; ***Racon (Q);*** 51°41'·31N 05°09'·56W.
Watwick Point Common Rear ☆, 0·5M from front, F 80m **15M**; vis: 013·5°-031·5°. By day 10M; vis: 013·5°-031·5°; ***Racon (Y).***
W Blockhouse Point ↙ Q WR 21m W9M, R7M; R lantern on W base: vis: 220°-W-250°-R-020°-W-036°-R-049°; 51°41'·31N 05°09'·56W.
Dale Fort ≰ Fl (2) WR 5s 20m W5M, R3M; vis: 222°-R-276°-W-019°; 51°42'·16N 05°09'·01W.
Gt Castle Hd ↙ F WRG 27m W5M, R3M, G3M; vis: 243°-R-281°-G-299°-W-029°; also Dir WRG (040°) 038·25°-G-039°-Al WG-039·5°-W-

040·5°-AlWR-041°-R-041·75°; 51°42'·67N 05°07'·07W (not used in conjunction with the following front light) also Ldg Lts 039·7° **Front**, Oc 4s 27m **15M**; vis: 031·2°-048·2°. **Rear**, 890m from front. 05°06'·60W Oc 8s 53m **15M** (by day 10M) vis: 031·2°-048·2°.
St Ann's ↘ Fl R 2·5s; 51°40'·25N 05°10'·51W.
Mid Channel Rks ↙ Q (9) 15s; 51°40'·18N 05°10'·14W.
Sheep ↖ QG; 51°40'·06N 05°08'·31W.
Millbay ↘ Fl (2) R 5s; 51°41'·05N 05°09'·45W.
W Chapel ↖ Fl G 10s; 51°40'·98N 05°08'·67W.
E Chapel ↘ Fl R 5s; 51°40'·87N 05°08'·15W.
Rat ↖ Fl G 5s; 51°40'·80N 05°07'·86W.
Angle ↙ VQ; 51°41'·63N 05°08'·27W.
Thorn Rock ↙ Q (9) 15s; 51°41'·53N 05°07'·76W.
Turbot Bank ↙ VQ (9) 10s; 51°37'·41N 05°10'·08W.
ODAS Fl(5) Y 20s; 51°36'·70N 05°08'·70W
St Gowan ↙ Q (6) + L Fl 15s, ***Racon (T) 10M;*** 51°31'·93N 04°59'·77W.

TENBY to SWANSEA BAY

Caldey I ≰ Fl (3) WR 20s 65m W13M, R9M; vis: R173°- W212°-R088°-102°; 51°37'·90N 04°41'·08W.
Woolhouse ↙ Q (6) + L Fl 15s; 51°39'·35N 04°39'·69W.
Burry Port Inlet ≰ 51°40'·62N 04°15'·06W Fl 5s 7m **15M**.
W. Helwick (W HWK) ↙ (9) 15s; ***Racon (T) 10M;*** *Whis;* 51°31'·40N 04°23'·65W Q.
E. Helwick ↙ VQ (3) 5s; *Bell;* 51°31'·80N 04°12'·68W.

SWANSEA BAY and SWANSEA

Ledge ↙ VQ (6) + L Fl 10s; 51°29'·93N 03°58'·77W.
Mixon ↘ Fl (2) R 5s; *Bell;* 51°33'·12N 03°58'·78W.
Outer Spoil Gnd ↘ Fl Y 2·5s; 51°32'·11N 03°55'·73W.
Grounds ↙ VQ (3) 5s; 51°32'·81N 03°53'·47W.
Mumbles ☆ 51°34'·01N 03°58'·27W Fl (4) 20s 35m **15M**; W twr; *Horn (3) 60s.*
SW Inner Green Grounds ↙ Q (6) + L Fl 15s; *Bell;* 51°34'·06N 03°57'·03W.
Lts in line 020°. Jetty Head Front, Oc G 4s 5m 2M; 51°36'·55N 03°55'·52W. Rear, 260m from front, FG 6M.

SWANSEA BAY, RIVER NEATH and PORT TALBOT

Neath App Chan ↖ Fl G 5s; 51°35'·71N 03°52'·83W.
Cabenda ↙ VQ (6) + L Fl 10s; ***Racon (Q);*** 51°33'·36N 03°52'·23W.
Ldg Lts 059·8° (occas). Front, Oc R 3s 12m 6M; 51°34'·92N 03°48'·10W. Rear, 400m from front, Oc R 6s 32m 6M.

BRISTOL CHANNEL – NORTH SHORE (EASTERN PART)

W Scar ↙ Q (9) 15s, Bell, ***Racon (T) 10M;*** 51°28'·31N 03°55'·57W.
South Scar (S SCAR) ↙ Q (6) + L Fl 15s; 51°27'·61N 03°51'·58W.
E. Scarweather ↙ Q (3) 10s; *Bell;* 51°27'·98N 03°46'·76W.

PORTHCAWL

Fairy ↙ Q (9) 15s; *Bell;* 51°27'·86N 03°42'·07W.
Porthcawl Bkwtr Hd ≰ 51°28'·39N 03°41'·98W F WRG 10m W6M, R4M, G4M; vis: 302°-G-036°-W-082°-R-122°.
W Nash ↙ VQ (9) 10s; *Bell;* 51°25'·99N 03°45'·95W.
Nash ☆ 51°24'·03N 03°33'·06W Fl (2) WR 15s 56m **W21M, R16M**; vis: 280°-R-290°-W-100°-R-120°-W-128°.
Breaksea ↙ L Fl 10s; ***Racon (T) 10M;*** 51°19'·88N 03°19'·08W.

BARRY

W Bkwtr Hd ≰ Fl 2·5s 12m 10M; 51°23'·46N 03°15'·52W.
N. One Fathom ↙ Q; 51°20'·94N 03°12'·17W.
Mackenzie ↘ QR; 51°21'·75N 03°08'·24W.
Flat Holm ☆, SE Pt 51°22'·54N 03°07'·14W Fl (3) WR 10s 50m **W15M, R12M**; W ○ twr; vis: 106°-R-140°-W-151°-R-203°-W-106°; (H24).

CARDIFF and PENARTH ROADS

Lavernock Outfall ↘ Fl Y 5s; 51°23'·95N 03°09'·50W.
Ranie ↘ Fl (2) R 5s; 51°24'·23N 03°09'·39W.

WGS84 DATUM
Plot waypoints on chart before use

S Cardiff ⚓ Q (6) + L Fl 15s; *Bell;* 51°24'·18N 03°08'·57W.
Mid Cardiff ▲ Fl (3) G 10s; 51°25'·60N 03°08'·09W.
Cardiff Spit ≈ QR; 51°24'·57N 03°07'·12W.
N Cardiff ▲ QG; 51°26'·52N 03°07'·19W.

PENARTH and CARDIFF
Wrach Chan Dir lt 348·5°. Oc WRG 10s 5m; W3M, R3M, G3M;
vis: 344·5°-G-347°-W-350°-R-352°; H24; 51°27'·16N 03°09'·75W.
Outer Wrach ⚓ Q (9) 15s; 51°26'·20N 03°09'·46W.
Tail Patch ▲ QG; 51°23'·53N 03°03'·65W.
Hope ⚓ Q (3) 10s; 51°24'·84N 03°02'·68W.
NW Elbow ⚓ VQ (9) 10s; *Bell;* 51°26'·28N 02°59'·93W.
EW Grounds ⚓ L Fl 10s 7M; *Bell; **Racon (T) 7M;*** 51°27'·12N 02°59'·95W.

NEWPORT DEEP, RIVER USK and NEWPORT
Newport Deep ▲ Fl (3) G 10s; *Bell;* 51°29'·36N 02°59'·12W.
East Usk ☆ 51°32'·40N 02°58'·01W; Fl(2) WRG 10s 11m W11M, R10M,
G10M; vis: 284°-W-290° -obscured shore-324°-R- 017°-W-037°-G-
115°-W-120°. Also Oc WRG 10s 10m W11M, R9M, G9M; vis: 018°-G-
022°-W-024°-R-028°.
Julians Pill Ldg Lts 062°. Front, FG 5m 4M; 51°33'·30N 02°57'·94W.
Rear, 61m from front, FG 8m 4M.

BRISTOL CHANNEL – SOUTH SHORE (EASTERN PART)
BRISTOL DEEP
N Elbow ▲ QG; *Bell;* 51°26'·97N 02°58'·65W.
S Mid Grounds ⚓ VQ (6) + L Fl 10s; 51°27'·62N 02°58'·68W.
E Mid Grounds ≈ Fl R 5s; 51°27'·75N 02°54'·98W.
Clevedon ⚓ VQ; 51°27'·39N 02°54'·93W.
Welsh Hook ⚓ Q (9) + L Fl 15s; 51°28'·53N 02°51'·86W.
Avon ▲ Fl G 2·5s; 51°27'·92N 02°51'·73W.
Black Nore Point ☆ 51°29'·09N 02°48'·05W Fl (2) 10s 11m **17M**;
obsc by Sand Pt when brg less than 049°; vis: 044°-243°.
Newcome ≈ 51°30'·01N 02°46'·71W Fl (3) R 10s.
Denny Shoal ⚓ VQ (6) + L Fl 10s; 51°30'·15N 02°45'·45W.
Firefly ▲ Fl (2) G 5s; 51°29'·96N 02°45'·35W.
Portishead Point ☆ 51°29'·68N 02°46'·42W Q (3) 10s 9m **16M**; B
twr, W base; vis: 060°-262°; *Horn 20s.*

PORTISHEAD
Pier Hd ⚡ Iso G 2s 5m 3M; 51°29'·69N 02°45'·27W.
Seabank. Lts in line 086·8°. Front, IQ 13m 5M; vis: 070·3°-103·3°; by
day 1M vis: 076·8°-096·8°; 51°30'·07N 02°43'·81W. Dir WG 6m 5M;
vis: 089·7°-FG-090·6°-AltWG-090·8°-FW-093·6°. Rear, 500m from
front, IQ 16m 5M; vis: 070·3°-103·3°; by day 1M, vis: 076·8°-096·8°.
Knuckle Lts in line 099·6°, Oc G 5s 6m 6M; 51°29'·94N 02°43'·67W.
Rear, 165m from front, FG 13m 6M; vis: 044°-134°.

AVONMOUTH
Royal Edward Dock N Pier Hd ⚡ Fl 4s 15m 10M; vis: 060°-228·5°;
51°30'·49N 02°43'·09W.
King Road Ldg Lts 072·4°. N Pier Hd ⚡ Front, Oc R 5s 5m 9M; W
obelisk, R bands; vis: 062°-082°; 51°30'·49N 02°43'·09W. Rear ⚡,
546m from front, QR 15m 10M; vis: 066°- 078°.

RIVER AVON, CUMBERLAND BASIN and AVON BRIDGE
S Pier Hd ⚡ Oc RG 30s 9m 10M and FBu 4m 1M; vis: 294°-R-036°-
G-194°; 51°30'·37N 02°43'·10W. *Bell(1) 10s.*
Ldg Lts 127·2°. Front ⚓, Iso R 2s 6m 3M, vis: 010°-160°; 51°30'·10N
02°42'·59W. Rear ⚓, Iso R 2s 10m 3M, vis: 048°-138°.

BRISTOL CHANNEL (SOUTH SHORE)
WESTON-SUPER-MARE
Pier Hd ⚡ 2 FG (vert) 6m; 51°20'·88N 02°59'·26W.
E Culver ⚓ Q (3) 10s; 51°18'·00N 03°15'·44W.
W Culver ⚓ VQ (9) 10s; 51°17'·37N 03°18'·68W.
Gore ≈ Iso 5s; *Bell;* 51°13'·94N 03°09'·79W.

BURNHAM-ON-SEA and RIVER PARRETT
Ent ⚡ Fl 7·5s 7m 12M; vis: 074°-164°; 51°14'·89N 03°00'·36W;

Dir lt 076°. F WRG 4m W12M, R10M, G10M; vis: 071°-G-075°-W-077°-R-
081°.
DZ No. 1 ⚓ Fl Y 2·5s; 51°15'·28N 03°09'·49W.
DZ No. 2 ⚓ Fl Y 10s; 51°13'·77N 03°17'·19W.
DZ No. 3 ⚓ Fl Y 5s; 51°15'·52N 03°14'·98W.

WATCHET, MINEHEAD and PORLOCK WEIR
Watchet W Bkwtr Hd ⚡ Oc G 3s 9m 9M; 51°11'·03N 03°19'·74W.
Watchet E Pier ⚡ 2 FR (vert) 3M; 51°11'·01N 03°19'·72W.
Minehead Bkwtr Hd ⚡ Fl(2) G 5s 4M; vis: 127°-262°; 51°12'·81N 03°28'·36W.
Lynmouth Foreland ☆ 51°14'·73N 03°47'·21W Fl (4) 15s 67m **18M**;
W ○ twr; vis: 083°-275°; (H24).

LYNMOUTH and WATERMOUTH
River Training Arm ⚡ 2 FR (vert) 6m 5M; 51°13'·90N 03°49'·83W.
Harbour Arm ⚡ 2 FG (vert) 6m 5M; 51°13'·92N 03°49'·84W.
Sand Ridge ▲ Q G; 51°15'·01N 03°49'·77W.
Copperas Rock ▲ Fl G 2·5s; 51°13'·78N 04°00'·60W.
Watermouth ⚡ Oc WRG 5s 1m 3M; W △; vis: 149·5°-G-151·5°-W-
154·5°-R-156·5°; 51°12'·93N 04°04'·60W.

ILFRACOMBE to BAGGY POINT
Ldg Lts 188°. Front, Oc 10s 8m 3M; 51°12'·53N 04°06'·65W. Rear,
Oc 10s 6m 3M.

Horseshoe ⚓ Q; 51°15'·02N 04°12'·96W.
Bull Point ☆ 51°11'·94N 04°12'·09W Fl (3) 10s 54m **20M**; W ○ twr,
obscd shore-056°. Same twr; FR 48m 12M; vis: 058°-096°.
Morte Stone ▲ Fl G 5s; 51°11'·30N 04°14'·95W.
Baggy Leap ▲ Fl G 10s; 51°08'·92N 04°16'·97W.

BIDEFORD, RIVERS TAW and TORRIDGE
Bideford Fairway ⚓ L Fl 10s; *Bell;* 51°05'·25N 04°16'·25W.
Bideford Bar ▲ Q G; 51°04'·89N 04°14'·62W.
Instow ☆ Ldg Lts 118°. **Front**, 51°03'·62N 04°10'·66W Oc 6s 22m
15M; vis: 103·5°-132°. **Rear**, 427m from front, Oc 10s 38m **15M**; vis:
103°-132·5°; (H24).
Crow Pt ⚡ Fl WR 2. 5s 8m W6M R5M; vis: 225°-R-232°-W-237°-R-358°-
W-015°-R-045°; 51°03'·96N 04°11'·39W.

LUNDY
Near North Point ☆ 51°12'·10N 04°40'·65W Fl 15s 48m **17M**; vis:
009°-285°.

South East Point ☆ 51°09'·72N 04°39'·37W Fl 5s 53m **15M**;
vis: 170°-073°; *Horn 25s.*

Hartland Point ☆ 51°01'·29N 04°31'·59W Fl (6) 15s 37m **25M**;
(H24); *Horn 60s.*

NORTH CORNWALL
BUDE, PADSTOW and NEWQUAY
Compass Point twr 50°49'·71N 04°33'·42W.
Stepper Point (Padstow) ⚡ L Fl 10s 12m 4M; 50°34'·12N
04°56'·72W.
Trevose Head ☆ 50°32'·94N 05°02'·13W Fl 7·5s 62m **21M**;
Horn (2) 30s.
North Pier Hd (Newquay) ⚡ 2 FG (vert) 5m 2M; 50°25'·07N
05°05'·19W.

HAYLE and ST IVES
The Stones ⚓ Q; 50°15'·64N 05°25'·51W.
Godrevy I ⚡ Fl WR 10s 37m W12M, R9M; vis: 022°-W-101°-R-145°-
W-272°; 50°14'·54N 05°24'·04W.
Hayle App ≈ QR; 50°12'·26N 05°26'·30W.
Lts in line 180°. Front, F 17m 4M; 50°11'·50N 05°26'·18W. Rear,
110m from front, F 23m 4M.
St Ives App ▲ 50°12'·85N 05°28'·42W

Pendeen ☆ 50°09'·90N 05°40'·32W Fl (4) 15s 59m **16M**; vis: 042°-
240°; in bay between Gurnard Hd and Pendeen it shows to coast;
Horn 20s.

539

9.11.5 PASSAGE INFORMATION

For directions on this coast refer to the Admiralty *W Coasts of England and Wales Pilot*; *Lundy and Irish Sea Pilot* (Imray/Taylor). The area is well covered by Admiralty Leisure Folios. For additional tidal information east of Ilfracombe/Swansea see *Arrowsmith's Bristol Channel Tide Tables* from J.W. Arrowsmith Ltd ☎ (0117) 9667545.

It is useful to know some Welsh words with navigational significance. *Aber:* estuary. *Afon:* river. *Bach, bychan, fach:* little. *Borth:* cove. *Bryn:* hill. *Careg, craig:* rock. *Coch, goch:* red. *Dinas:* fort. *Ddu:* black. *Fawr, Mawr:* big. *Ffrydiau:* tiderip. *Llwyd:* grey. *Moel:* bare conical hill. *Mor:* sea. *Morfa:* sandy shore. *Mynydd:* mountain. *Penrhyn:* headland. *Porth:* cove. *Ynys, Ynysoedd:* island(s).

There is more Passage Information threaded between the harbours in this Area.

CARDIGAN BAY

(AC 1971, 1972, 1973) Harbours are mostly on a lee shore, and/or have bars which make them dangerous to approach in bad weather. Abersoch and Pwllheli offer best shelter from the prevailing westerlies. There may be overfalls off Trwyn Cilan, SW of St Tudwal's Is (lit). In N part of the bay there are three major dangers to coasting yachts: St Patrick's Causeway (Sarn Badrig) runs 12M SW from Mochras Pt. It is mostly large loose stones, and dries (up to 1·5m) for much of its length. In strong winds the sea breaks heavily at all states of tide. The outer end is marked by a WCM light buoy. At the inner end there is a channel about 5ca offshore, which can be taken with care at half tide.

Sarn-y-Bwch runs 4M WSW from Pen Bwch Pt. It is consists of rocky boulders, drying in places close inshore and with least depth 0·3m over 1M offshore. There is a WCM buoy off the W end. NW of Aberystwyth, Sarn Cynfelyn and Cynfelyn Patches extend 6·5M offshore, with depths of 1·5m in places. A WCM buoy is at the outer end. Almost halfway along the bank is Main Channel, 3ca wide, running roughly N/S but not marked.

Aberporth Range occupies much of Cardigan B. Beware targets and buoys, some unlit. Range activity is broadcast on VHF Ch 16, 0800-1600LT Mon-Fri or ☎ (01239) 813462.

If on passage N/S through St George's Chan (ie not bound for Cardigan B or Milford Haven) the easiest route, and always by night, is W of the Bishops and the Smalls, noting the TSS. If bound to/from Milford Haven or Cardigan Bay, passage inside both the Smalls and Grassholm is possible.

RAMSEY SOUND, THE BISHOPS, THE SMALLS TO MILFORD HAVEN

(AC 1478, 1482) The Bishops and the Clerks are islets and rocks 2·5M W and NW of Ramsey Island, a bird sanctuary SSW of St David's Head. N Bishop is the N'ly of the group, 3ca ENE of which is Bell Rock (depth 1·9m). S Bishop (Lt, fog sig) is 3M to the SSW.

Between South Bishop and Ramsey Island the dangers include Daufraich with offlying dangers to the E and heavy overfalls; Llech Isaf and Llech Uchaf drying rocks are further ENE. Carreg Rhoson and offlying dangers are between Daufraich and N Bishop. The navigable routes between most of these islets and rocks trend NE/SW. Use only by day, in good visibility and with local knowledge. The N/S route close W of Ramsey Island is considered easier than Ramsey Sound.

▶ 2M W of The Bishops the S-going stream begins at Milford Haven +0400, and the N-going at Milford Haven –0230, sp rates 2kn. Between The Bishops and Ramsey Is the SW-going stream begins at Milford Haven +0330, and the NE-going at Milford Haven –0300, **sp rates 5kn.** Ramsey Sound should be taken at slack water. The S-going stream begins at Milford Haven +0300, and the N-going at Milford Haven –0330, **sp rates 6kn at The Bitches,** where the channel is narrowest (2ca), decreasing N and S. ◀

FLOOD SW Wales

The tide turns to the S or SE (Bristol Channel flood) as follows:
(a): Milford Haven +0330;
(b) & (c): Milford Haven +0400;
(d): Milford Haven +0200.

EBB SW Wales

The tide turns to the N or NW (Bristol Channel ebb) as follows:
(a): Milford Haven –0300;
(b) & (c): Milford Haven –0230 ;
(d): Milford Haven –0430.

The Bitches are rocks up to 4m high and extending 2ca from E side of Ramsey Island. Other dangers are: Gwahan and Carreggafeiliog, both 3m high at N end of Sound, to W and E; Horse Rock (dries 0·9m) almost in mid-channel about 5ca NNE of The Bitches, with associated overfalls; Shoe Rock (dries 3m) at SE end of channel; and rocks extending 5ca SSE from S end of Ramsey Island.

St Brides Bay provides an anchorage in settled weather/ offshore winds. It is also a regular anchorage for tankers, but is a trap in westerlies. Solva is a little hbr with shelter for boats able to take the ground, or anchor behind Black Rk (dries 3·6m) in the middle of the entrance.

The Smalls Lt, where there is a Historic Wreck (see 9.0.3) is 13M W of the Welsh mainland (Wooltack Pt). 2M and 4M E of The Smalls are the Hats and Barrels, rocky patches on which the sea breaks.

▶ 7M E of The Smalls is Grassholm Island with a race either end and strong tidal eddies so that it is advisable to pass about 1M off. The chan between Barrels and Grassholm is 2·5M wide, and here the S-going stream begins at Milford Haven + 0440, and the N-going at Milford Haven – 0135, sp rates 5kn.◀

Five miles of clear water lie between Grassholm and Skomer Is/ Skokholm Is to the E. But Wildgoose Race, which forms W of Skomer and Skokholm is very dangerous, so keep 2M W of these two Islands.

To E of Skomer Island Midland Island, and between here and Wooltack Point is Jack Sound, least width about 1ca. Do not attempt it without AC 1482, detailed pilotage directions, and only at slack water neaps. ▶ Correct timing is important. The S-going stream begins at Milford Haven +0200, and the N-going at Milford Haven –0430, sp rates 6-7kn. ◀ Rocks which must be identified include, from N to S: On E side of chan off Wooltack Pt, Tusker Rock (2m), steep-to on its W side; and off Anvil Point, The Cable (2·4m), The Anvil and Limpet Rocks (3·7m). On the W side lie the Crabstones (3·7m) and the Blackstones (1·5m).

9.11.6 ABERSOCH

Gwynedd 52°49'·29N 04°29'·20W (⚓) ✤✤⚓⚓✿✿

CHARTS AC 5609, 1410, 1411, 1971, 1512; Imray C61, C52; Stanfords 27.

TIDES –0315 Dover; ML 2·5; Duration 0520; Zone 0 (UT)

Standard Port MILFORD HAVEN (→)

Times				Height (metres)			
High Water		Low Water		MHWS	MHWN	MLWN	MLWS
0100	0800	0100	0700	7·0	5·2	2·5	0·7
1300	2000	1300	1900				
Differences ST TUDWAL'S ROADS							
+0155	+0145	+0240	+0310	–2·2	–1·9	–0·7	–0·2
ABERDARON							
+0210	+0200	+0240	+0310	–2·4	–1·9	–0·6	–0·2

SHELTER There are few moorings for visitors. Apply to HM or SC. ⚓ in St Tudwal's Roads clear of moored yachts; sheltered from SSE through S to NE.

NAVIGATION WPT 52°48'·52N 04°26'·13W, 293°/2·4M to YC jetty. There are no navigational dangers, but steer well clear of the drying rks to the E of East Island; Carred y Trai buoy FlR 2·5s is 2ca E of these rks (just off chartlet). St Tudwal's islands themselves are fairly steep-to, except at N ends. St Tudwal's Sound is clear of dangers.

LIGHTS AND MARKS The only It is on St Tudwal's West Island, Fl WR 15s 46m 14/10M (see chartlet and 9.11.4).

R/T S Caernarfon YC Ch 80 M.

TELEPHONE (Code 01758) HM 712203; MRCC (01407) 762051; Marinecall 09068 969650; Police (01286) 673333; Dr 612535.

FACILITIES **South Caernarvonshire YC** ☎ 712338, Slip, M, L, FW, R, Bar (May-Sept), D, **Abersoch Power Boat Club** ☎ 812027. **Services** BY, Slip, ME, El, ✕, ACA, CH, P, C (12 ton), LPG. **Town** CH, 🛒, R, Bar, ✉, Ⓑ, ⩫ (Pwllheli), ✈ (Chester).

ADJACENT ANCHORAGES

BARDSEY ISLAND – YNYS ENNLI, Gwynedd, **52°45'·00N 04°47'·40W**. AC 5609, 1410, 1411, 1971. HW –0240 on Dover, see 9.10.20. Lights and Marks see 9.11.4. ⚓ in settled conditions only, is useful on passage N when awaiting tide through Bardsey Sound, see 9.10.5. ⚓ to W of Pen Cristin in approach to Henllwyn Cove in 4m. Sheltered in winds from WSW through N to NE but may be subject to swell at times. Possible with caution for smaller craft to anchor in the cove but beware of isolated rocks and shoals. Landing at jetty in rocks at cove marked by small boathouse at top of slip. Island is of historical interest with ruined abbey and religious settlement since 6th century. Now run as managed farm and nature reserve, see 9.0.3 Environmental Guidance.

ABERDARON BAY, Gwynedd, **52°47'·75N 04°42'·82W**. AC 5609, 1410, 1411, 1971, 5609. HW –0240 on Dover, see 9.10.20 Bardsey Is. In settled conditions only, is useful on passage N when awaiting tide through Bardsey Sound, see 9.10.5. In SE appr to bay are 2 islets Ynys Gwylan-fawr and Ynys Gwylan-bâch with a deep water passage between them, also passage between Ynys Gwylan-fawr and Trwyn Gwningaer (shore). ⚓ 4ca SSW of church in 5-10m, limited protection and subject to swell at times but sheltered in winds from W through N to NE. Do not leave craft unattended due to poor holding ground. Dinghy landing with care on shingle beach at Porth Meudwy, W side of bay. **Village** limited facilities: FW, R, Bar, ✉, ⩫ (Pwllheli).

LLANBEDROG, Gwynedd, **52°51'·14N 04°28'·09W**. AC 5609, 1410, 1411, 1971, 1512. HW –0245 on Dover, see 9.11.6 (St Tudwal's Roads). Good ⚓ N of Trwyn Llanbedrog (steep sided headland 131m) 1.0ca ENE of Bcn PHM in 2-3m. Beach has numerous conspicuous bathing huts. Sheltered in winds from N through W to SW. ⚓ well clear of local craft moorings as they have a long scope. Dinghy landing near boathouse. **Village** limited facilities: P & D (cans ½M), FW, R, Bar, ⩫ (Pwllheli).

9.11.7 PWLLHELI

Gwynedd 52°53′·23N 04°23′·75W ✿✿✿⊛♒♒♒✿✿✿

CHARTS AC 1410, 1971, 1512; Imray C61, C52; Stanfords 27

TIDES −0315 Dover; ML 2·6; Duration 0510

Standard Port MILFORD HAVEN (→)

Times				Height (metres)			
High Water		Low Water		MHWS	MHWN	MLWN	MLWS
0100	0800	0100	0700	7·0	5·2	2·5	0·7
1300	2000	1300	1900				
Differences PWLLHELI							
+0210	+0150	+0245	+0320	−2·0	−1·8	−0·6	−0·2
CRICCIETH							
+0210	+0155	+0255	+0320	−2·0	−1·8	−0·7	−0·3

SHELTER Good in hbr and marina. Drying moorings in inner hbr (SW and NW bights).

NAVIGATION WPT 52°53′·02N 04°23′·07W, SWM lt buoy 299°/ 0·47M to QG lt at head of Training Arm.

- Ent is safe in most winds, but in strong E to SW winds sea breaks on offshore shoals.
- Ent subject to silting and bar and hbr chan are dredged but only to 0·6m below CD; 3 tide gauges. Max tidal stream 2kn.
- No ⚓ in hbr; 4kn speed limit.

LIGHTS AND MARKS See 9.11.4 and chartlet. Gimblet Rock (30m) is conspic conical rock 3ca SW of ent.

R/T Marina: Ch 80 M H24. HM: VHF Ch 12 16 (0900-1715).

TELEPHONE (Code 01758) HM 704081, mob 07879 433145; MRCC (01407) 762051; Ⓗ Bangor (A&E) 01248 384384; Marinecall 09068 969650; Police (01286) 673333; Dr 701457.

FACILITIES Marina ☎ 701219, www.hafanpwllheli.co.uk; 400 AB, £2.88, £12.21 <4hrs. Pontoon numbers are 4–12 from S–N. Pile berths on S side of appr chan. Wi-fi, P&D, LPG, BH (40 ton), C, Slip, 🚿, ♿, ⚓; Boat Club ☎ 612271, Slip, FW.
Pwllheli SC pwllhelisailingclub@btinternet.com ☎ 614442.
Services: BY, ME, Gas, Gaz, ✗, CH, ACA, C (14 ton), El, Ⓔ, SM.
Town 🍴, R, Bar, ✉, Ⓑ, ➡, ✈ (Chester).

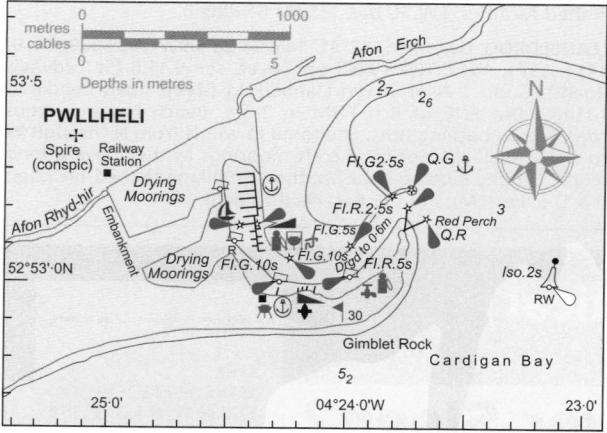

ADJACENT HARBOUR

MOCHRAS, Gwynedd, 52°49′·57N 04°07′·77W. AC 1971, 1512. HW −0245 on Dover. Small yacht hbr in drying Mochras lagoon on SE side of Shell Is. Bar, about 2ca seaward. Appr advised HW±2. 3 grey posts, R topmarks, mark NE side of chan. Ebb tide runs strongly in the narrow ent between the sea wall and Shell Is (lt Fl WRG 4s, 079°-G-124°-W-134°-R-179°; Mar-Nov); at sp beware severe eddies inside. Inside ent, buoyed chan runs WSW to Shell Island Yacht Hbr ☎ 01341 241453. Facilities: M, FW, Slip, R, Bar, shwrs. Shifting chan, marked by posts and buoys, runs NE to Pensarn, where permanent moorings limit space. Drying AB, ⇌.

9.11.8 PORTHMADOG

Gwynedd 52°55′·32N 04°07′·77W ⊛♒♒♒✿✿✿

CHARTS AC 1410, 1971, 1512,; Imray C61, C51; Stanfords 27.

TIDES −0247 Dover; ML no data; Duration 0455

Standard Port MILFORD HAVEN (→)

Times				Height (metres)			
High Water		Low Water		MHWS	MHWN	MLWN	MLWS
0100	0800	0100	0700	7·0	5·2	2·5	0·7
1300	2000	1300	1900				
Differences PORTHMADOG							
+0235	+0210	No data		−1·9	−1·8		No data

SHELTER Inner hbr (N of Cei Ballast): Good all year round; visitors' drying AB adjacent Madoc YC or afloat rafted on moored yachts off YC. Outer hbr: Summer only, exposed to S winds. Speed limit 6kn in hbr upstream of No 8 buoy.

NAVIGATION WPT Fairway SWM buoy, 52°52′·97N 04°11′·09W, 041°/1·9M to conspic white Ho at W side of ent.

- Chan shifts and may divide. Bar changes frequently, but is near to No 3 and 4 buoys; dries approx 0·3m.
- In SW'lies, waves are steep-sided and close, especially on the ebb.
- Latest info from HM on request. Advise entering HW±1½.

LIGHTS AND MARKS Fairway buoy RW, L Fl 10s. Chan marker buoys (14) Nos 1–9 lit (May-Oct), have R/G reflective tops marks and W reflective numbers. Moel-y-Gest is conspic hill (259m) approx 1M WNW of hbr. Harlech Castle (ru) is about 3M SE of appr chan.

R/T HM Ch 12 16 (HO and when vessel due). Madoc YC Ch M.

TELEPHONE (Code 01766) HM 512927, mobile (07879) 433147; MRCC (01407) 762051; Pilot 530684; Hbr Authority Gwynedd Council (01758) 704066; Marinecall 09068 969650; Police (01286) 673333; Dr 512284.

FACILITIES Hbr (265 berths) ☎ 512927, £7.00 all craft; D, FW, C, Slip access HW±4 (launching £10); Madoc YC ☎ 512976, AB, M, FW, Bar; Porthmadog SC ☎ 513546, AB, M, FW, Slip; Services: CH, ACA, ✗, D(quay), D & P (cans), C (8 ton), M, BY, El, Pilot. Town ✉, Ⓑ, ➡, ✈ (Chester).

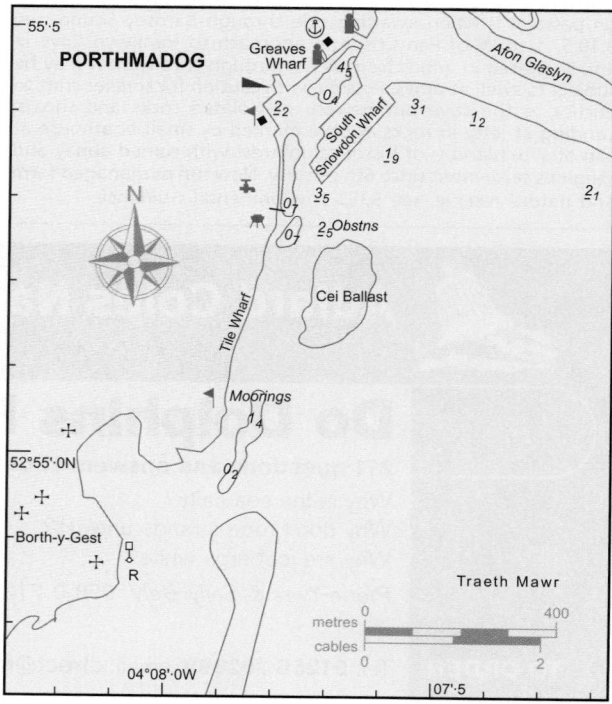

9.11.9 BARMOUTH

Gwynedd **52°42'·97N 04°03'·07W** ☀☀⌂⌂⌂⌂

CHARTS AC 5609, 1410, 1971, 1484; Imray C61, C51; Stanfords 27.

TIDES –0305 Dover; ML 2·6; Duration 0515

Standard Port MILFORD HAVEN (→)

Times				Height (metres)			
High Water		Low Water		MHWS	MHWN	MLWN	MLWS
0100	0800	0100	0700	7·0	5·2	2·5	0·7
1300	2000	1300	1900				
Differences BARMOUTH							
+0215	+0205	+0310	+0320	–2·0	–1·7	–0·7	0·0

SHELTER Good. Entry HW±2½ safe, but impossible with strong SW'lies. Exposed ⌂ W of Barmouth Outer buoy in 6 to 10m. Serious silting reported. In hbr there are 5 ⚓s; secure as directed by HM, because of submarine cables and strong tidal streams. A Ⓥ berth is marked at W end of quay, dries at half-tide. Drying ⚓ inside Penrhyn Pt.

NAVIGATION WPT, Barmouth Outer SWM buoy, 52°42'·72N 04°05'·02W, 082°/0·8M to Y perch lt, QR. Appr from SW between St Patrick's Causeway (Sarn Badrig) and Sarn-y-Bwch. Barmouth can be identified by Cader Idris, a mountain 890m high, 5M ESE. Fegla Fawr, a rounded hill, lies on S side of hbr.

- The Bar, 0·75M W of Penrhyn Pt, with min depth 0·3m is subject to constant change. Chan is marked by buoys (see below) fitted with radar reflectors and reflective tape and moved as required.
- Spring ebb runs 3–5kn.
- The estuary and river (Afon Mawddach) are tidal and can be navigated for about 7M above rly br (clearance approx 5·5m); but chan is not buoyed, and sandbanks move constantly – local knowledge essential.

LIGHTS AND MARKS Outer SWM L Fl 10s; Bar SHM Fl G; No2 PHM Fl R. Inner PHM not lit. Y perch QR 4m 5M on R framework tr, marks S end of stony ledge extending 3ca SW from Ynys y Brawd across N Bank. Ynys y Brawd groyne, SE end, marked by lit bn, Fl R 5s 5M. NW end of rly bridge 2 FR (hor).

R/T Call *Barmouth Hbr* VHF Ch **12** 16 (Apr-Sep 0900-1700 later for HW; Oct-Mar 0900-1600); wind and sea state are available.

TELEPHONE (Code 01341) HM 280671 mob 07795 012747; MRCC (01407) 762051; Marinecall 09068 969650; Police (01286) 673333; Dr 280521. Local information www.barmouthwebcam.co.uk

FACILITIES Quay £9.00/yacht (inc electricity), M (incl 3 drying ⚓) contact HM in advance if deep water ⚓ required, D, FW, 2 Slips (HW±3, £12/day); Merioneth YC ☎ 280000; Services: CH, ACA. **Town** P, D, 🛒, R, Bar, ✉, @, Ⓑ, ⇌, ✈ (Chester), Ferry to Penrhyn Pt. **Fairbourne** ✉, 🛒, ⇌, Ferry to Barmouth.

9.11.10 ABERDOVEY

Gwynedd **52°32'·57N 04°02'·72W** (Jetty) ☀☀⌂⌂⌂⌂

CHARTS AC 5609, 1410, 1972, 1484; Imray C61, C51; Stanfords 27.

TIDES –0320 Dover; ML 2·6; Duration 0535. For differences see 9.11.11.

SHELTER Good except in strong W/SW winds. Berth on jetty in 3m; to the E there is heavy silting.

NAVIGATION WPT Aberdovey Outer SWM buoy, 52°32'·00N 04°05'·56W, 093°/0.43M to Bar buoy.

- Bar and channel constantly shift and are hazardous below half-tide; buoys moved accordingly.
- Enter the channel at gateway between Bar SHM and PHM Fl R 5s. Visitors should call HM on VHF before entering.

LIGHTS AND MARKS See 9.11.4 and chartlet. No daymarks. Lts may be unreliable. Submarine cables (prohib ⚓s) marked by bns with R ◇ topmarks.

R/T Call *Aberdovey Hbr* VHF Ch 12 16.

TELEPHONE (Code 01654) HM 767626, mobile 07879 433148; MRCC (01646) 690909; Marinecall 09068 969650; Police (01286) 673333; Dr 710414; Ⓗ 710411.

FACILITIES **Jetty** AB £7.00 <9m, £10.50 >9m; M, FW; **Wharf** Slip, AB, L, FW, C; **Dovey YC** ☎ 767607, Bar, Slip(launching £4.50 if engine <10hp), L, FW; **Services:** BY, ME, El, ⚒, CH, ACA, Ⓔ. **Town** P & D (cans), ME, El, CH, 🛒, R, Bar, ✉, Ⓑ, ⇌, ✈ (Chester).

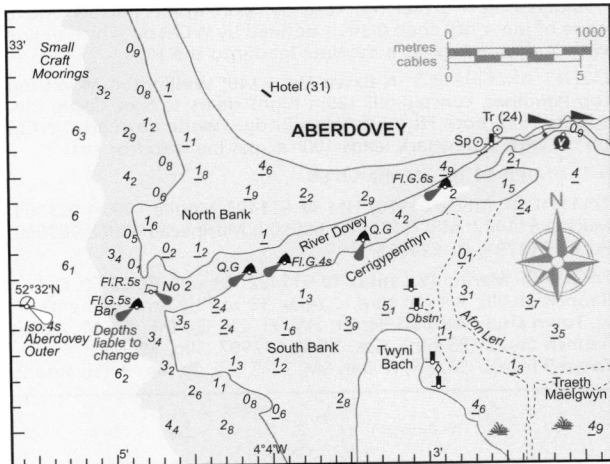

OTHER HARBOURS IN SOUTH PART OF CARDIGAN BAY

ABERAERON, Ceredigion, **52°14'·62N 04°15'·94W**. AC 1410, 1972, 1484. HW –0325 on Dover; +0140 and –1·9m on Milford Haven; ML 2·7m; Duration 0540. A small, popular drying hbr at the mouth of the R Aeron; access HW±1½. Short drying piers extend each side of river ent. In strong NW'lies there is little shelter. AB £8/craft on NW wall, only in calm conditions. Foul ground with depths of 1·5m extend 3ca offshore to SW of Aberaeron. Beware Carreg Gloyn (0·3m) 4ca WSW of hbr, and Sarn Cadwgan (1·8m) shoals 5ca N of the hbr ent. Lts (see 9.11.4 for sectors): N pier Fl (4) WRG 15s 10m 6M. S pier Fl (3) G 10s 11m 6M. VHF **14** 16. HM ☎ (01545) 571645; FW, D (from fishermen). **YC** ☎ 570077. **Town** P.

NEW QUAY, Ceredigion, **52°12'·92N 04°21'·22W**. AC 1410, 1972, 1484. HW –0335 on Dover; Duration 0540; see 9.11.11. Good shelter in offshore winds, but untenable in NW'lies. On E side of bay Carreg Ina, rks drying 1·3m, are marked by NCM buoy, Q. Two Y bns mark a sewer outfall running 7ca NNW from Ina Pt. The hbr (dries 1·6m) is protected by a pier with lt, Fl WG 3s 12m 8/5M; 135°-W-252°-G-295°. Groyne extends 80m SSE of pierhd to a SHM bn; close ENE of which is a ECM bn, Q (3) 10s. VHF Ch **14** 16. HM ☎ (01545) 560368. MRCC (01646) 690909; Dr ☎ 560203; YC ☎ 560516. Facilities: FW, D (from fishermen), slip (£6). **Town** P (3M), ✉, R, Bar.

9.11.11 ABERYSTWYTH

Ceredigion **52°24'·42N 04°05'·47W** ✿✿✿✿✿✿✿✿✿✿

CHARTS AC 5609, 5620, 1410, 1972, 1484; Imray C61, C51; Stanfords 27.

TIDES –0330 Dover; ML 2·7; Duration 0540

Standard Port MILFORD HAVEN (⟶)

Times				Height (metres)			
High Water		Low Water		MHWS	MHWN	MLWN	MLWS
0100	0800	0100	0700	7·0	5·2	2·5	0·7
1300	2000	1300	1900				
Differences ABERDOVEY							
+0215	+0200	+0230	+0305	–2·0	–1·7	–0·5	0·0
ABERYSTWYTH							
+0145	+0130	+0210	+0245	–2·0	–1·7	–0·7	0·0
NEW QUAY							
+0150	+0125	+0155	+0230	–2·1	–1·8	–0·6	–0·1
ABERPORTH							
+0135	+0120	+0150	+0220	–2·1	–1·8	–0·6	–0·1

SHELTER Good, in marina (1·7m) on E side of chan; or dry against Town Quay. Access approx HW±3 (HW±2 for strangers).

NAVIGATION WPT 52°24'·83N 04°06'·22W,133/0·6M° to ent. Appr dangerous in strong on-shore winds. The Bar, close off S pier hd, has 0·7m least depth. From N, beware Castle Rks, in R sector of N bkwtr lt; also rks drying 0·5m W of N bkwtr and boulders below S pier hd. Turn 90° port inside narrow ent. E edge of inner hbr chan 0·3m is defined by WCM bn which in line with Y daymark gives a daytime lead into the Hbr.

LIGHTS AND MARKS N Bkwtr Hd ≠ 140° Wellington Mon't (on top Pendinas, conspic hill 120m high) clears to S of Castle Rks. Ldg lts 133°, both FR on Ystwyth Bridge, white daymarks. WCM bn on with Y daymark leads 100° across bar into hbr ent.

R/T HM Ch **14** 16. Marina Ch 80.

TELEPHONE (Code 01970) HM ☎ 611433 Mobile 07974 023965; Marina 611422; MRCC (01646) 690909; Marinecall 09068 969650; Police 612791; Dr 624855.

FACILITIES Marina (Y Lanfa), ☎ 611422. 88 + 15 🅥, £2.60. D, Slip (launch £8.00), BH (10 ton), C (max 15 ton by arrangement), ⚓, 🅖. **Town Quay** AB £6.50/craft, FW, El, CH, Ⓔ, ME, ✕, M, 2 Slips (launch £6), C (25 ton), Gas. **YC** ☎ 612907, Slip, M, Bar. **Town** P (cans), CH, 🛒, R, Bar, SM, 🅖, 🅞, ✉, Ⓑ, ⇌, ✈ (Swansea).

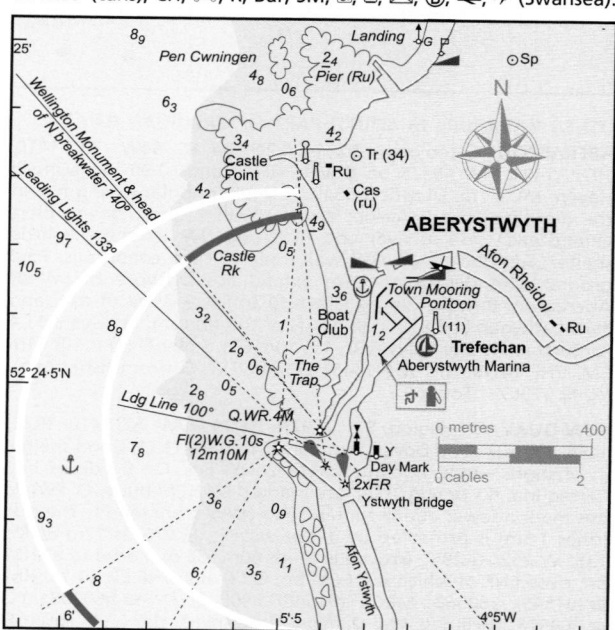

MINOR HARBOUR, 12M NE of Fishguard

PORT CARDIGAN, Ceredigion, **52°07'·02N 04°42'·07W**. AC 1973, 1484. HW –0405 on Dover; ML 2·4m; Duration 0550. Shelter is good, but ent dangerous in strong N/NW winds. Large scale charts are essential; see www.afon-teifi-fairways.com for up to date advice or telephone Mooring Master (see below) before entering. The bar has 0·5m or less. ⚓ near Hotel (conspic) on E side of ent. Chan is usually close to E side; IDM bn, Fl (2) 5s, should be left to stbd when clear of the bar. From Pen-yr-Ergyd to Bryn-Du chan is marked with lit mid channel markers but shifts constantly. St Dogmaels has ⚓ or a 🅐 via Mooring Master ☎ (01329) 621437 mob 07774 126342. Or ⚓ in pools off Pen-yr-Ergyd. Short stay pontoons in the Teifi; possible 🅐s off Teifi Boating Club. **Moorings**: administered by Afon Teifi Fairway Committee, Mooring Master ☎ (01239) 613966, mob 07799 284206. **Teifi Boating Club** ☎ 613846, FW, Bar; **Services:** ME, ✕. **Town** Ⓑ, 🛒, CH, P&D (cans), FW, ME, Bar, R.

9.11.12 FISHGUARD

Pembrokeshire **52°00'·12N 04°58'·40W**
Commercial Hbr ✿✿✿✿✿✿✿; Lower Hbr ✿✿✿✿✿✿

CHARTS AC 5620, 1178, 1410, 1973, 1484; Imray C61, C51, C60; Stanfords 27.

TIDES –0400 Dover; ML 2·6; Duration 0550

Standard Port MILFORD HAVEN (⟶)

Times				Height (metres)			
High Water		Low Water		MHWS	MHWN	MLWN	MLWS
0100	0800	0100	0700	7·0	5·2	2·5	0·7
1300	2000	1300	1900				
Differences FISHGUARD							
+0115	+0100	+0110	+0135	–2·2	–1·8	–0·5	+0·1
PORT CARDIGAN							
+0140	+0120	+0220	+0130	–2·3	–1·8	–0·5	0·0
CARDIGAN (Town)							
+0220	+0150	No data		–2·2	–1·6	No data	
PORTHGAIN							
+0055	+0045	+0045	+0100	–2·5	–1·8	–0·6	0·0
RAMSEY SOUND							
+0030	+0030	+0030	+0030	–1·9	–1·3	–0·3	0·0
SOLVA							
+0015	+0010	+0035	+0015	–1·5	–1·0	–0·2	0·0
LITTLE HAVEN							
+0010	+0010	+0025	+0015	–1·1	–0·8	–0·2	0·0
MARTIN'S HAVEN							
+0010	+0010	+0015	+0015	–0·8	–0·5	+0·1	+0·1
SKOMER IS							
–0005	–0005	+0005	+0005	–0·4	–0·1	0·0	0·0

SHELTER Good, except in strong NW/NE winds. Beware large swell, especially in N winds. No ⚓, except SW of ferry quay. Good holding in most of the bay. At Lower town ⚓ off Saddle or Castle Points in 2m. Strong S'lies funnel down the hbr.

NAVIGATION WPT 52°01'·02N 04°57'·57W, 237°/0·48M to N bkwtr lt. *Keep at least 1ca clear of N bkwtr head; beware of ferries and High-Speed SeaCats manoeuvring.*

LIGHTS AND MARKS See 9.11.4 and chartlet. Strumble Hd Lt ho, Fl (4) 15s 45m 26M, is approx 4M WNW of hbr. The SHM (bn) at Aber Gwaun is very small.

R/T HM Ch **14** 16. Goodwick Marine Ch M (occas).

TELEPHONE (Code 01348) Commercial Hbr Supervisor 404425; MRCC (01646) 690909; Marinecall 09068 969650; Police 873073; Dr 872802.

FACILITIES Fishguard (Lower town) dries 3·2m; access HW±1, limited AB. 15 🅐 (drying, max 5 tons), FW, 🅟. HM (Lower hbr) ☎ 873369; mob 07775 523846. Slip, BY, ✕, FW, D (cans) from Goodwick Marine, ME, ACA, Slip, CH, El.

Fishguard Bay YC, FW, Bar, 🅖.

Town P & D (cans), 🛒, R, Gas, Bar, ✉, 🅞, @, Ⓑ, ⇌, ✈ (Cardiff), Ferry to Rosslare.

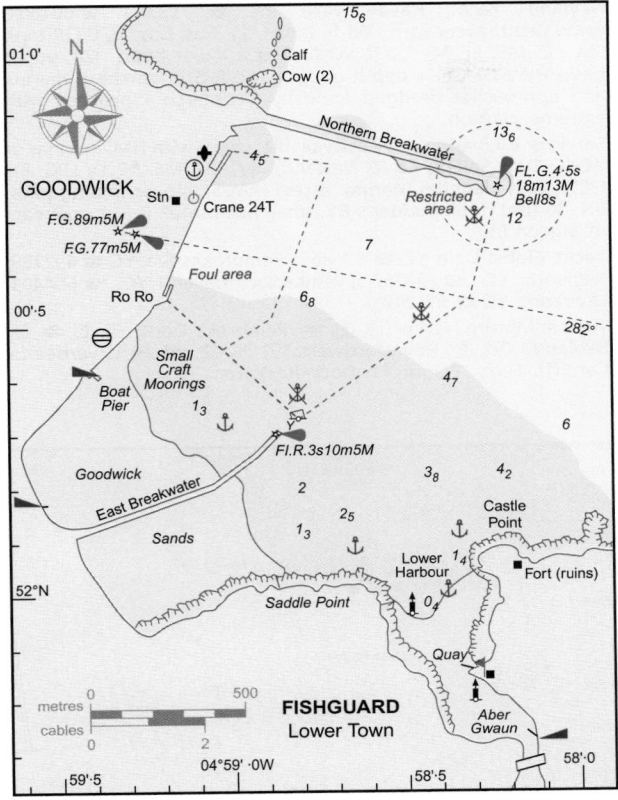

9.11.13 MILFORD HAVEN

Pembrokeshire **51°40'·13N 05°08'·16W** ✪✪✪♻♻♻☆☆

CHARTS AC 5620, 1410, 1178, 1478, 2878, 3273/4/5; Imray C60, C13; Stanfords 27.

TIDES –0500 Dover; ML 3·8; Duration 0605

Standard Port MILFORD HAVEN (→)

Times				Height (metres)			
High Water		Low Water		MHWS	MHWN	MLWN	MLWS
0100	0800	0100	0700	7·0	5·2	2·5	0·7
1300	2000	1300	1900				
Differences DALE ROADS							
–0005	–0005	–0008	–0008	0·0	0·0	0·0	–0·1
NEYLAND							
+0002	+0010	0000	0000	0·0	0·0	0·0	0·0
HAVERFORDWEST							
+0010	+0025	Dries out		–4·8	–4·9	Dries out	
LLANGWM (Black Tar)							
+0010	+0020	+0005	0000	+0·1	+0·1	0·0	–0·1

SHELTER Very good in various places round the hbr, especially in Milford Marina and Neyland Yacht Haven. ⚓s in Dale Bay; off Chapel Bay and Angle Pt on S shore; off Scotch Bay, E of Milford marina; and others beyond Pembroke Dock. Free pontoons (May-Oct) include: Dale Bay, Gelliswick Bay; waiting pontoons off Milford Dock and Hobbs Pt (for Pembroke Dock); and drying pontoons at Dale Beach, Hazelbeach, Neyland and Burton; mainly intended for tenders. It is possible to dry out safely at inshore areas of Dale, Sandy Haven and Angle Bay, depending on weather.

NAVIGATION West Channel WPT 51°40'·21N 05°10'·28W. **East Channel** WPT 51°40'·12N 05°08'·67W.

- The tide sets strongly across the ent to the Haven particularly at sp. In bad weather avoid passing over Mid Chan Rks and St Ann's Hd shoal, where a confused sea and swell will be found (see AC 3273). Give St Ann's Head a wide berth especially on the ebb, when East Chan by Sheep Island is better.
- Beware large tankers entering/departing the Haven and ferries moving at high speed in the lower Haven. Caution: Only 15m clearance below cables between Thorn Is and Thorn Pt.
- Milford Haven Port Authority has a jetty, Port Control and offices near Hubberston Pt. Their launches have G hulls and W upperworks with 'PILOT' in black letters and fly a Pilot flag while on patrol; Fl Bu lt at night. Their instructions must be obeyed. No vessel may pass within 100m of any terminal or any tanker, whether at ⚓ or under way.

River Cleddau is navigable 6M to Picton Pt, at junction of West and East arms, at all tides for boats of moderate draught. Clearance under Cleddau Bridge above Neyland is 37m; and 25m under power cable 1M upstream. Chan to Haverfordwest has 2m at HW and clearances of only 6m below cables and bridge; only feasible for shoal draft/lifting keel and unmasted craft.

Firing Ranges to the S and SE, see 9.11.14 and AC 1076.

LIGHTS AND MARKS See 9.11.4 and chartlets. The ldg lts are specifically for VLCCs entering/leaving hbr and proceeding to/from the oil refineries. The Haven is very well buoyed and lit as far as Cleddau bridge.

Milford Dock ldg lts 348°, both F.Bu, with W ○ daymarks. Dock entry sigs on E side of lock: 2 FG (vert) = gates open, vessels may enter. VHF Ch 18 is normally used for ent/exit by day and night.

R/T Monitor *Milford Haven Port Control* Ch 12 (H24) while underway in the Haven. *Milford Haven Patrol* launches Ch11/12 (H24). To lock in to Milford Dock marina call *Pierhead*, Ch 18, for clearance, then call *Milford Marina*, Ch M, for a berth. Neyland Yacht Haven Ch 80/M.

Broadcasts: Local forecasts on Ch 12 14 at 0300, 0900, 1500 and 2100 (all UT). Nav warnings follow on Ch14. Gale warnings issued on receipt Ch 12 14. Expected shipping movements for next 24

HARBOURS IN ST BRIDES BAY (See AC 5620)

SOLVA, Pembrokeshire, **51°52'02N 05°11'·67W**. AC 1478. HW –0450 on Dover; ML 3·2m; Duration 0555. See 9.11.12. Good shelter for small boats that can take the ground; access HW±3. Avoid in strong S winds. Black Scar, Green Scar and The Mare are rks 5ca S. Ent via SSE side; best water near Black Rk in centre of ent. Beware stone spit at Trwyn Caws on W just inside ent. There are 9 Or ⚓s drying on hard sand (£6.00), drying/rafting ABs for <9·5m LOA; or ⚓ behind the rk in approx 3m. Yachts can go up to the quay (£7.50) Facilities: showers, 🚿, Bar, R in village. FW on quay, Slip (launching £5). HM (01437) 721703 mob 07974 020139, VHF Ch 16 8, M, CH. **Solva Boat Owners Assn** ☎ 721489 mob 07974 020139.

ST BRIDES BAY, Pembrokeshire, **51°49'02N 05°10'·07W**. AC 1478. HW (Little Haven) –0450 on Dover; ML 3·2m; Duration 0555. See 9.11.12. A SPM buoy, Fl (5) Y 20s, is midway between Ramsey and Skomer islands at 51°48'·2N 05°20'·0W. Keep at least 100m offshore 1/9-28/2 to avoid disturbing seals, and ditto nesting sea birds 1/3-31/7. Many good ⚓s, especially between Little Haven and Borough Head in S or E winds or between Solva and Dinas Fawr in N or E winds. In W'lies boats should shelter in Solva (above), Skomer (below) or Pendinas Bach. Tankers anchor in mouth of B. For apprs from the N or S see 9.11.5. Facilities: (Little Haven) CH, 🚿, R, Bar, FW (cans).

SKOMER, Pembrokeshire, **51°44'·42N 05°16'·77W**. AC 1478, 2878. HW –0455 Dover. See 9.11.12. The island is a National Nature Reserve (fee payable to Warden on landing) and also a Marine Nature Reserve, extending to Marloes Peninsula. Keep at least 100m offshore 1/9-28/2 to avoid disturbing seals and ditto nesting sea birds 1/3-31/7. There is a 5kn speed limit within 100m of the island. ⚓ in S Haven (N Haven ⚓ due to eel grass). Enter N Haven close to W shore, and land on W side of bay on beach or at steps. In N Haven pick up ⚓s provided or ⚓ to seaward of them. No access to the island from S Haven. For Jack Sound see 9.11.5. There are no lts, marks or facilities. For info, Marine Conservation Officer ☎ (01646) 636736.

hours on Ch 12, 0800–0830, 2000–2030LT and on request. Tide hts and winds on request. Bcsts on Ch 16 67 at 0335 then every 4 hrs to 2335.

TELEPHONE (Code 01646) Lock 696310; Port Ctrl 696136/7; MRCC 690909; Marinecall 09068 969649; Police (01437) 763355; Ⓗ Haverfordwest (01437) 764545; Dr 690674.

FACILITIES Marinas/Berthing (from seaward):
Dale Bay 🛒, FW, R, Slip, Pontoon, YC.

Milford Haven Port Authority jetty ☎ 696133 (occas use by visitors with approval from HM), AB, FW.

Milford Marina (280) ☎ 696312, Pierhead ☎ 696310; £2·05. VHF Ch 14 M. Lock hrs: ent HW–4, exit –3½, free flow HW –2¼ to HW– ¼, ent +1½, exit +1¾, ent +2¾, exit +3¼; waiting pontoon or shelter in lock, 3·5m water at MLWS. D (H24), C, BH (16 ton), CH, El, ME, ✖, Ⓔ, D, Gas, Gaz, 🛒, R, Bar, Ice, ▣, ♿, ✉, Ⓑ,Wi-fi.

Lawrenny Yacht Station (100) ☎ 651212/651065, ⚓ £5, L, FW, BY, CH, D, P, ✖, C (15 ton), ME, Slip (launching £5.00), ▣, Bar, R, 🛒, ♿, ✉, Gas.

Neyland Yacht Haven (420 inc Ⓥ, £2.06) ☎ 601601, www.yachthavens.com ; Wi-fi, D, CH, Ⓔ, Gas, Gaz, ▣, C (20 ton), SM, SC, ME, El, ✖, R, 🛒, Wi-fi; Access lower basin H24, upper basin HW±3½ (sill + depth gauges and R/G lit perches); marina and approaches dredged annually Oct/March – proceed with extreme caution.

Services: All marine services available; check with HM, marinas or YC/SC. **Dale Sailing Co** (@ Neyland), BY, CH, ME, ✖, D, LPG, BH (35T). **East Llannion Marine**: access HW±3, Slip, scrubbing piles, BH (30 ton), fuel. **Rudder's BY**, small but useful, is just upstream of Burton Pt.

Yacht Clubs: Dale YC ☎ 636362; Pembrokeshire YC ☎ 692799; Neyland YC ☎ 600267; Pembroke Haven YC ☎ 684403; Lawrenny YC ☎ 651212.

Towns: Milford Haven, ✉, Ⓑ, ⇌. Pembroke Dock; ✉, Ⓑ, ⇌, Ⓗ. Neyland, ✉, Ⓑ. Haverfordwest, ✉, Ⓗ, Ⓑ, ⇌, ✈ (Swansea or Cardiff). Ferry: Pembroke Dock–Rosslare.

MILFORD HAVEN *continued*

TIME ZONE (UT)
For Summer Time add ONE hour in **non-shaded areas**

MILFORD HAVEN LAT 51°42'N LONG 5°03'W
TIMES AND HEIGHTS OF HIGH AND LOW WATERS

Dates in red are **SPRINGS**
Dates in blue are **NEAPS**

YEAR 2010

JANUARY

Day	Time	m	Time	m	Time	m	Time	m
1 F	0011	1.0	0614	7.1	1240	0.8	1842	7.1
16 SA	0049	1.4	0654	6.7	1309	1.3	1910	6.4
2 SA	0058	0.8	0702	7.3	1328	0.6	1930	7.2
17 SU	0121	1.3	0726	6.7	1341	1.2	1941	6.5
3 SU	0145	0.7	0750	7.4	1416	0.5	2017	7.1
18 M	0151	1.3	0757	6.7	1412	1.2	2011	6.4
4 M	0231	0.7	0837	7.4	1503	0.6	2103	7.0
19 TU	0221	1.3	0828	6.6	1442	1.3	2041	6.3
5 TU	0317	0.9	0924	7.2	1549	0.9	2150	6.7
20 W	0251	1.4	0859	6.5	1513	1.5	2112	6.2
6 W	0403	1.2	1011	6.8	1636	1.3	2237	6.3
21 TH	0322	1.6	0931	6.3	1546	1.7	2145	6.0
7 TH	0452	1.5	1101	6.4	1727	1.7	2330	5.9
22 F	0356	1.7	1007	6.0	1621	1.9	2223	5.7
8 F	0547	1.9	1157	6.0	1825	2.1		
23 SA	0435	2.2	1049	5.7	1705	2.2	2312	5.4
9 SA	0031	5.6	0652	2.2	1304	5.6	1936	2.3
24 SU	0526	2.4	1146	5.5	1806	2.5		
10 SU	0144	5.5	0811	2.4	1418	5.5	2053	2.3
25 M	0019	5.3	0643	2.6	1303	5.3	1933	2.5
11 M	0258	5.5	0926	2.3	1532	5.6	2159	2.2
26 TU	0146	5.3	0821	2.5	1431	5.4	2101	2.3
12 TU	0405	5.8	1028	2.1	1633	5.8	2252	1.9
27 W	0309	5.6	0942	2.1	1546	5.8	2211	1.8
13 W	0458	6.1	1117	1.8	1722	6.0	2335	1.7
28 TH	0416	6.1	1045	1.5	1649	6.3	2308	1.3
14 TH	0541	6.4	1159	1.6	1802	6.2		
29 F	0513	6.7	1140	1.0	1742	6.8	2359	0.8
15 F	0013	1.5	0619	6.6	1236	1.4	1837	6.4
30 SA	0604	7.2	1230	0.5	1831	7.2		
31 SU	0047	0.5	0651	7.5	1317	0.2	1916	7.4

FEBRUARY

Day	Time	m	Time	m	Time	m	Time	m
1 M	0132	0.3	0736	7.7	1401	0.2	2000	7.4
16 TU	0129	1.0	0733	6.8	1347	0.9	1946	6.6
2 TU	0215	0.3	0819	7.6	1443	0.3	2042	7.2
17 W	0158	1.0	0802	6.8	1416	1.0	2014	6.6
3 W	0257	0.5	0902	7.4	1524	0.6	2123	6.9
18 TH	0226	1.1	0831	6.7	1445	1.2	2042	6.4
4 TH	0337	0.8	0943	7.0	1604	1.1	2204	6.5
19 F	0256	1.3	0900	6.5	1514	1.4	2113	6.2
5 F	0418	1.3	1026	6.4	1645	1.6	2249	6.0
20 SA	0326	1.6	0933	6.2	1547	1.7	2148	6.0
6 SA	0504	1.9	1114	5.8	1734	2.2	2343	5.5
21 SU	0402	1.9	1012	5.9	1626	2.0	2232	5.6
7 SU	0603	2.4	1215	5.3	1843	2.6		
22 M	0449	2.2	1105	5.5	1721	2.4	2336	5.3
8 M	0058	5.2	0729	2.7	1342	5.0	2020	2.7
23 TU	0602	2.5	1225	5.2	1853	2.6		
9 TU	0231	5.2	0906	2.6	1514	5.1	2141	2.5
24 W	0111	5.2	0755	2.5	1408	5.2	2040	2.4
10 W	0350	5.5	1015	2.2	1621	5.5	2238	2.1
25 TH	0249	5.5	0926	2.0	1533	5.7	2155	1.8
11 TH	0443	5.9	1104	1.9	1707	5.9	2321	1.7
26 F	0402	6.1	1032	1.4	1636	6.3	2253	1.2
12 F	0525	6.3	1143	1.5	1745	6.2	2357	1.4
27 SA	0458	6.7	1125	0.8	1727	6.9	2343	0.7
13 SA	0601	6.5	1217	1.3	1818	6.4		
28 SU	0547	7.3	1213	0.3	1813	7.3		
14 SU	0030	1.2	0633	6.7	1249	1.1	1849	6.5
15 M	0100	1.1	0704	6.8	1319	1.0	1918	6.6

MARCH

Day	Time	m	Time	m	Time	m	Time	m
1 M	0029	0.3	0632	7.6	1257	0.1	1856	7.5
16 TU	0034	1.0	0635	6.8	1250	0.9	1849	6.7
2 TU	0112	0.1	0715	7.7	1339	0.0	1937	7.5
17 W	0103	0.9	0704	6.9	1319	0.9	1917	6.8
3 W	0153	0.1	0756	7.6	1418	0.2	2016	7.3
18 TH	0132	0.9	0734	6.8	1349	0.9	1946	6.7
4 TH	0232	0.3	0835	7.3	1455	0.6	2054	7.0
19 F	0202	1.0	0803	6.7	1418	1.0	2016	6.6
5 F	0310	0.7	0914	6.9	1531	1.1	2132	6.5
20 SA	0232	1.1	0835	6.5	1449	1.3	2048	6.4
6 SA	0347	1.3	0953	6.3	1607	1.7	2213	6.0
21 SU	0305	1.4	0910	6.3	1523	1.6	2125	6.1
7 SU	0428	1.9	1036	5.7	1649	2.2	2301	5.4
22 M	0343	1.7	0951	6.0	1604	1.9	2211	5.7
8 M	0521	2.4	1131	5.1	1751	2.7		
23 TU	0433	2.1	1048	5.5	1703	2.2	2318	5.4
9 TU	0013	5.0	0646	2.8	1303	4.7	1939	2.9
24 W	0550	2.4	1211	5.1	1836	2.5		
10 W	0158	5.0	0837	2.7	1448	4.9	2114	2.6
25 TH	0055	5.3	0741	2.3	1353	5.2	2021	2.3
11 TH	0322	5.3	0949	2.3	1556	5.3	2212	2.2
26 F	0231	5.6	0908	1.9	1515	5.7	2135	1.7
12 F	0416	5.7	1038	1.9	1641	5.7	2255	1.8
27 SA	0341	6.2	1012	1.3	1615	6.3	2232	1.2
13 SA	0457	6.1	1116	1.5	1718	6.1	2331	1.4
28 SU	0437	6.8	1104	0.7	1705	6.8	2322	0.7
14 SU	0533	6.5	1149	1.2	1750	6.4		
29 M	0525	7.2	1150	0.4	1750	7.2		
15 M	0003	1.2	0604	6.7	1221	1.0	1820	6.6
30 TU	0006	0.3	0609	7.5	1233	0.2	1831	7.4
31 W	0049	0.2	0651	7.5	1313	0.2	1911	7.4

APRIL

Day	Time	m	Time	m	Time	m	Time	m
1 TH	0129	0.2	0731	7.4	1351	0.4	1949	7.2
16 F	0107	0.9	0707	6.8	1323	0.9	1921	6.8
2 F	0207	0.5	0809	7.1	1427	0.8	2027	6.9
17 SA	0141	1.0	0741	6.7	1357	1.0	1955	6.7
3 SA	0244	0.9	0847	6.6	1502	1.2	2104	6.5
18 SU	0216	1.1	0817	6.5	1432	1.2	2032	6.5
4 SU	0321	1.4	0925	6.1	1537	1.7	2144	6.0
19 M	0254	1.3	0858	6.3	1512	1.5	2115	6.2
5 M	0401	1.9	1006	5.6	1616	2.2	2230	5.5
20 TU	0338	1.6	0946	5.9	1559	1.9	2208	5.9
6 TU	0451	2.4	1058	5.1	1712	2.7	2334	5.1
21 W	0435	1.9	1047	5.5	1701	2.2	2317	5.6
7 W	0607	2.7	1217	4.7	1846	2.9		
22 TH	0552	2.1	1206	5.3	1828	2.3		
8 TH	0109	5.0	0746	2.7	1400	4.8	2025	2.7
23 F	0042	5.6	0724	2.0	1333	5.4	1956	2.1
9 F	0235	5.2	0903	2.4	1512	5.1	2130	2.3
24 SA	0206	5.8	0841	1.7	1448	5.8	2107	1.7
10 SA	0333	5.6	0956	2.0	1601	5.6	2216	1.9
25 SU	0313	6.2	0944	1.3	1547	6.3	2205	1.2
11 SU	0418	6.0	1037	1.6	1640	5.9	2254	1.6
26 M	0410	6.6	1037	0.9	1638	6.7	2256	0.9
12 M	0455	6.3	1113	1.3	1724	6.3	2329	1.3
27 TU	0459	6.9	1123	0.7	1724	6.9	2341	0.6
13 TU	0530	6.5	1146	1.1	1746	6.5		
28 W	0545	7.1	1206	0.6	1807	7.1		
14 W	0002	1.1	0602	6.7	1218	1.0	1817	6.7
29 TH	0024	0.6	0627	7.1	1247	0.6	1847	7.1
15 TH	0034	1.0	0634	6.8	1250	0.9	1848	6.8
30 F	0106	0.6	0707	7.0	1325	0.8	1926	7.0

Chart Datum: 3·71 metres below Ordnance Datum (Newlyn). HAT is 7·8 metres above Chart Datum; see 4.5.

TIME ZONE (UT)
For Summer Time add ONE hour in **non-shaded areas**

MILFORD HAVEN   LAT 51°42′N   LONG 5°03′W
TIMES AND HEIGHTS OF HIGH AND LOW WATERS

Dates in red are **SPRINGS**
Dates in blue are NEAPS

YEAR 2010

MAY

Time	m	Time	m
1 0145 0.8 / 0747 6.7 / SA 1402 1.0 / 2004 6.7		**16** 0125 1.0 / 0726 6.7 / SU 1342 1.0 / 1943 6.8	
2 0223 1.1 / 0825 6.4 / SU 1438 1.4 / 2043 6.4		**17** 0207 1.0 / 0809 6.6 / M 1424 1.1 / 2027 6.7	
3 0301 1.5 / 0903 6.0 / M 1514 1.8 / 2122 6.0		**18** 0251 1.2 / 0855 6.4 / TU 1509 1.4 / 2115 6.5	
4 0341 1.8 / 0944 5.6 / TU 1553 2.1 / 2207 5.7		**19** 0340 1.4 / 0947 6.1 / W 1559 1.6 / 2210 6.2	
5 0427 2.2 / 1031 5.2 / W 1641 2.4 / 2300 5.4		**20** 0437 1.6 / 1046 5.8 / TH 1659 1.9 / ◐ 2313 6.0	
6 0526 2.5 / 1132 5.0 / TH 1751 2.7 / ◑		**21** 0544 1.7 / 1152 5.7 / F 1811 1.9	
7 0010 5.2 / 0641 2.5 / F 1252 4.9 / 1913 2.7		**22** 0022 5.9 / 0657 1.8 / SA 1304 5.7 / 1925 1.9	
8 0130 5.2 / 0755 2.4 / SA 1409 5.0 / 2026 2.5		**23** 0135 6.0 / 0808 1.7 / SU 1414 5.8 / 2034 1.7	
9 0236 5.4 / 0857 2.2 / SU 1507 5.4 / 2122 2.2		**24** 0241 6.1 / 0912 1.5 / M 1515 6.1 / 2136 1.5	
10 0327 5.7 / 0947 1.9 / M 1552 5.7 / 2209 1.8		**25** 0341 6.3 / 1008 1.3 / TU 1610 6.3 / 2230 1.3	
11 0410 6.0 / 1029 1.6 / TU 1632 6.1 / 2249 1.6		**26** 0434 6.5 / 1058 1.2 / W 1700 6.6 / 2319 1.1	
12 0450 6.3 / 1108 1.3 / W 1709 6.4 / 2328 1.3		**27** 0523 6.6 / 1143 1.1 / TH 1746 6.7 / ○	
13 0528 6.5 / 1146 1.1 / TH 1746 6.6		**28** 0004 1.0 / 0608 6.6 / F 1225 1.1 / 1828 6.8	
14 0006 1.1 / 0606 6.6 / F 1224 1.0 / ● 1823 6.8		**29** 0047 1.0 / 0650 6.6 / SA 1305 1.1 / 1909 6.7	
15 0045 1.0 / 0645 6.7 / SA 1302 1.0 / 1902 6.8		**30** 0128 1.1 / 0730 6.4 / SU 1343 1.3 / 1948 6.6	
		31 0206 1.3 / 0808 6.3 / M 1420 1.4 / 2026 6.4	

JUNE

Time	m	Time	m
1 0244 1.5 / 0845 6.0 / TU 1455 1.7 / 2104 6.2		**16** 0248 0.8 / 0851 6.7 / W 1504 1.0 / 2112 6.8	
2 0321 1.7 / 0923 5.8 / W 1531 1.9 / 2143 5.9		**17** 0337 1.0 / 0940 6.5 / TH 1553 1.2 / 2202 6.6	
3 0401 1.9 / 1003 5.5 / TH 1612 2.1 / 2227 5.7		**18** 0428 1.2 / 1032 6.2 / F 1646 1.4 / 2256 6.4	
4 0446 2.1 / 1049 5.3 / F 1701 2.4 / ◑ 2317 5.5		**19** 0524 1.4 / 1128 6.0 / SA 1744 1.7 / ◑ 2355 6.1	
5 0540 2.3 / 1144 5.1 / SA 1802 2.5		**20** 0625 1.7 / 1230 5.8 / SU 1850 1.8	
6 0016 5.3 / 0643 2.4 / SU 1249 5.1 / 1911 2.5		**21** 0100 5.9 / 0731 1.8 / M 1338 5.7 / 1959 1.9	
7 0123 5.3 / 0748 2.3 / M 1358 5.2 / 2017 2.4		**22** 0208 5.9 / 0839 1.8 / TU 1445 5.8 / 2108 1.8	
8 0226 5.5 / 0848 2.1 / TU 1457 5.5 / 2116 2.1		**23** 0314 5.9 / 0943 1.8 / W 1547 6.0 / 2210 1.7	
9 0322 5.7 / 0942 1.9 / W 1548 5.8 / 2209 1.8		**24** 0416 6.0 / 1038 1.6 / TH 1643 6.3 / 2304 1.5	
10 0411 6.0 / 1031 1.6 / TH 1634 6.2 / 2257 1.5		**25** 0509 6.1 / 1127 1.5 / F 1732 6.4 / 2351 1.4	
11 0458 6.3 / 1117 1.3 / F 1719 6.5 / 2343 1.2		**26** 0556 6.3 / 1210 1.4 / SA 1816 6.5 / ○	
12 0544 6.5 / 1202 1.1 / SA 1804 6.7 / ●		**27** 0034 1.3 / 0637 6.3 / SU 1250 1.3 / 1855 6.6	
13 0028 1.0 / 0630 6.7 / SU 1247 1.0 / 1849 6.9		**28** 0113 1.2 / 0715 6.3 / M 1327 1.3 / 1932 6.6	
14 0114 0.9 / 0716 6.8 / M 1332 0.9 / 1935 7.0		**29** 0149 1.3 / 0751 6.3 / TU 1401 1.4 / 2007 6.5	
15 0201 0.8 / 0803 6.8 / TU 1417 0.9 / 2023 7.0		**30** 0224 1.3 / 0824 6.2 / W 1434 1.5 / 2042 6.4	

JULY

Time	m	Time	m
1 0257 1.4 / 0858 6.0 / TH 1506 1.6 / 2116 6.2		**16** 0322 0.6 / 0923 6.8 / F 1537 0.8 / 2144 7.0	
2 0331 1.6 / 0932 5.9 / F 1540 1.8 / 2152 6.0		**17** 0407 0.9 / 1009 6.5 / SA 1623 1.2 / 2231 6.6	
3 0407 1.8 / 1009 5.7 / SA 1618 2.0 / 2231 5.8		**18** 0454 1.3 / 1058 6.1 / SU 1713 1.6 / ◑ 2323 6.2	
4 0447 2.0 / 1050 5.4 / SU 1702 2.2 / ◑ 2317 5.5		**19** 0547 1.8 / 1154 5.8 / M 1813 1.9	
5 0536 2.2 / 1141 5.3 / M 1759 2.4		**20** 0024 5.7 / 0652 2.1 / TU 1302 5.5 / 1927 2.2	
6 0013 5.4 / 0638 2.4 / TU 1245 5.2 / 1911 2.5		**21** 0137 5.5 / 0810 2.3 / W 1419 5.5 / 2049 2.2	
7 0122 5.3 / 0750 2.4 / W 1359 5.3 / 2027 2.4		**22** 0255 5.4 / 0925 2.2 / TH 1533 5.7 / 2159 2.0	
8 0234 5.4 / 0900 2.2 / TH 1507 5.6 / 2134 2.1		**23** 0406 5.6 / 1026 1.9 / F 1634 6.0 / 2255 1.8	
9 0339 5.7 / 1001 1.8 / F 1607 6.0 / 2233 1.7		**24** 0501 5.9 / 1115 1.7 / SA 1722 6.3 / 2341 1.5	
10 0436 6.1 / 1056 1.5 / SA 1700 6.4 / 2326 1.3		**25** 0545 6.1 / 1157 1.5 / SU 1803 6.5	
11 0528 6.5 / 1146 1.1 / SU 1750 6.8 / ●		**26** 0020 1.3 / 0622 6.3 / M 1234 1.3 / ○ 1839 6.6	
12 0015 0.9 / 0618 6.8 / M 1234 0.8 / 1838 7.1		**27** 0055 1.2 / 0657 6.4 / TU 1308 1.2 / 1912 6.7	
13 0104 0.6 / 0705 7.0 / TU 1321 0.6 / 1925 7.3		**28** 0128 1.1 / 0729 6.4 / W 1339 1.2 / 1944 6.7	
14 0151 0.5 / 0752 7.1 / W 1407 0.5 / 2012 7.3		**29** 0159 1.1 / 0759 6.4 / TH 1409 1.2 / 2015 6.6	
15 0237 0.5 / 0838 7.0 / TH 1452 0.6 / 2058 7.2		**30** 0229 1.2 / 0828 6.3 / F 1438 1.3 / 2045 6.5	
		31 0259 1.4 / 0858 6.2 / SA 1509 1.5 / 2116 6.3	

AUGUST

Time	m	Time	m
1 0330 1.6 / 0930 6.0 / SU 1541 1.8 / 2150 6.0		**16** 0421 1.4 / 1025 6.2 / M 1641 1.6 / ◑ 2250 6.0	
2 0404 1.8 / 1005 5.7 / M 1617 2.1 / 2229 5.7		**17** 0509 2.0 / 1118 5.7 / TU 1738 2.2 / 2348 5.5	
3 0443 2.1 / 1048 5.5 / TU 1703 2.3 / ◑ 2318 5.4		**18** 0613 2.4 / 1228 5.3 / W 1859 2.5	
4 0536 2.4 / 1147 5.2 / W 1810 2.6		**19** 0109 5.1 / 0746 2.6 / TH 1358 5.2 / 2036 2.5	
5 0028 5.2 / 0655 2.5 / TH 1309 5.0 / 1945 2.6		**20** 0243 5.1 / 0913 2.5 / F 1522 5.5 / 2151 2.2	
6 0156 5.2 / 0826 2.4 / F 1436 5.4 / 2110 2.2		**21** 0357 5.5 / 1015 2.1 / SA 1621 5.9 / 2243 1.9	
7 0316 5.6 / 0940 2.0 / SA 1547 5.9 / 2216 1.7		**22** 0447 5.8 / 1101 1.7 / SU 1705 6.3 / 2324 1.5	
8 0420 6.1 / 1039 1.5 / SU 1644 6.5 / 2311 1.1		**23** 0527 6.2 / 1138 1.5 / M 1743 6.5 / 2359 1.3	
9 0514 6.6 / 1130 1.0 / M 1736 7.0		**24** 0601 6.4 / 1212 1.3 / TU 1816 6.7 / ○	
10 0001 0.7 / 0603 7.0 / TU 1219 0.6 / ● 1823 7.4		**25** 0031 1.1 / 0632 6.5 / W 1243 1.1 / 1847 6.8	
11 0049 0.3 / 0649 7.3 / W 1305 0.3 / 1908 7.6		**26** 0102 1.0 / 0701 6.6 / TH 1313 1.1 / 1916 6.8	
12 0134 0.2 / 0733 7.4 / TH 1349 0.2 / 1953 7.6		**27** 0130 1.0 / 0730 6.6 / F 1341 1.1 / 1945 6.8	
13 0217 0.2 / 0816 7.3 / F 1431 0.4 / 2036 7.5		**28** 0159 1.1 / 0757 6.6 / SA 1409 1.2 / 2014 6.6	
14 0258 0.5 / 0858 7.1 / SA 1513 0.7 / 2119 7.1		**29** 0227 1.2 / 0825 6.4 / SU 1438 1.4 / 2043 6.4	
15 0339 0.9 / 0940 6.7 / SU 1555 1.1 / 2202 6.6		**30** 0257 1.5 / 0855 6.2 / M 1509 1.6 / 2114 6.2	
		31 0328 1.7 / 0928 6.0 / TU 1543 2.0 / 2151 5.8	

Chart Datum: 3·71 metres below Ordnance Datum (Newlyn). HAT is 7·8 metres above Chart Datum; see 4.5.

TIME ZONE (UT)
For Summer Time add ONE hour in **non-shaded areas**

MILFORD HAVEN

LAT 51°42'N   LONG 5°03'W

TIMES AND HEIGHTS OF HIGH AND LOW WATERS

Dates in red are **SPRINGS**
Dates in blue are NEAPS

YEAR 2010

SEPTEMBER

Day	Time m	Time m	Time m	Time m		Day	Time m	Time m	Time m	Time m
1 W	0404 2.1	1009 5.7	1626 2.3	◗ 2239 5.5		16 TH	0537 2.7	1156 5.2	1832 2.7	
2 TH	0455 2.4	1107 5.3	1732 2.6	2351 5.2		17 F	0041 4.9	0719 2.9	1334 5.1	2017 2.7
3 F	0615 2.7	1234 5.2	1919 2.6			18 SA	0223 5.0	0852 2.6	1459 5.4	2130 2.4
4 SA	0130 5.1	0803 2.5	1414 5.4	2053 2.2		19 SU	0335 5.4	0952 2.2	1556 5.9	2219 1.8
5 SU	0300 5.6	0922 2.0	1530 6.0	2200 1.6		20 M	0422 5.8	1036 1.8	1638 6.3	2257 1.6
6 M	0404 6.2	1022 1.4	1627 6.6	2254 1.0		21 TU	0500 6.2	1112 1.5	1714 6.6	2331 1.3
7 TU	0457 6.7	1112 0.9	1717 7.2	2342 0.5		22 W	0532 6.4	1144 1.3	1747 6.7	•
8 W	0544 7.2	1159 0.5	1803 7.6	●		23 TH	0002 1.1	0602 6.6	1215 1.1	○ 1817 6.8
9 TH	0028 0.2	0627 7.5	1244 0.2	1847 7.8		24 F	0032 1.1	0631 6.7	1245 1.1	1846 6.9
10 F	0111 0.1	0710 7.6	1326 0.2	1929 7.7		25 SA	0101 1.0	0659 6.8	1313 1.1	1915 6.9
11 SA	0152 0.2	0751 7.4	1407 0.3	2011 7.5		26 SU	0130 1.1	0728 6.7	1343 1.2	1945 6.7
12 SU	0232 0.5	0831 7.1	1448 0.7	2052 7.1		27 M	0159 1.2	0757 6.6	1413 1.3	2015 6.6
13 M	0310 1.0	0912 6.7	1528 1.2	2133 6.5		28 TU	0229 1.4	0828 6.4	1445 1.6	2048 6.3
14 TU	0350 1.6	0955 6.2	1612 1.8	2219 5.8		29 W	0302 1.7	0903 6.2	1521 1.9	2127 5.9
15 W	0434 2.2	1045 5.7	1707 2.4	◗ 2315 5.3		30 TH	0341 2.1	0946 5.8	1608 2.3	2219 5.5

OCTOBER

Day	Time m	Time m	Time m	Time m		Day	Time m	Time m	Time m	Time m
1 F	0435 2.4	1047 5.5	1718 2.6	◗ 2335 5.2		16 SA	0003 4.9	0634 2.9	1252 5.2	1932 2.8
2 SA	0557 2.7	1216 5.3	1904 2.5			17 SU	0139 5.0	0809 2.8	1415 5.4	2048 2.5
3 SU	0113 5.2	0744 2.5	1354 5.6	2034 2.1		18 M	0253 5.3	0913 2.4	1515 5.7	2140 2.1
4 M	0240 5.7	0901 2.0	1508 6.1	2139 1.5		19 TU	0344 5.7	0959 2.1	1601 6.1	2221 1.8
5 TU	0343 6.3	1000 1.4	1605 6.7	2232 1.0		20 W	0424 6.1	1038 1.7	1639 6.4	2257 1.5
6 W	0434 6.8	1050 0.9	1654 7.2	2320 0.6		21 TH	0458 6.4	1112 1.5	1714 6.6	2330 1.3
7 TH	0520 7.2	1137 0.5	1740 7.5	●		22 F	0530 6.6	1145 1.3	1746 6.8	
8 F	0004 0.4	0603 7.5	1221 0.3	1823 7.7		23 SA	0001 1.2	0601 6.7	1217 1.2	○ 1817 6.8
9 SA	0046 0.3	0645 7.5	1303 0.4	1906 7.6		24 SU	0033 1.1	0631 6.8	1249 1.2	1849 6.8
10 SU	0127 0.5	0726 7.4	1345 0.6	1947 7.3		25 M	0104 1.1	0703 6.8	1321 1.2	1922 6.8
11 M	0206 0.8	0807 7.1	1425 0.9	2028 6.8		26 TU	0137 1.2	0736 6.8	1355 1.3	1957 6.6
12 TU	0244 1.3	0847 6.7	1506 1.4	2109 6.3		27 W	0211 1.4	0811 6.6	1432 1.6	2035 6.3
13 W	0323 1.8	0930 6.2	1549 1.9	2153 5.8		28 TH	0249 1.7	0851 6.3	1514 1.8	2119 6.0
14 TH	0406 2.3	1019 5.7	1642 2.4	◗ 2247 5.3		29 F	0333 2.0	0940 6.0	1606 2.1	2215 5.7
15 F	0504 2.7	1123 5.3	1758 2.8			30 SA	0430 2.3	1043 5.8	1715 2.3	◗ 2328 5.5
						31 SU	0547 2.5	1203 5.6	1845 2.3	

NOVEMBER

Day	Time m	Time m	Time m	Time m		Day	Time m	Time m	Time m	Time m
1 M	0052 5.5	0718 2.3	1327 5.8	2006 2.0		16 TU	0150 5.1	0811 2.7	1419 5.5	2044 2.4
2 TU	0211 5.8	0832 2.0	1439 6.2	2111 1.6		17 W	0251 5.4	0910 2.4	1513 5.8	2134 2.1
3 W	0314 6.2	0933 1.5	1538 6.7	2206 1.2		18 TH	0339 5.8	0957 2.1	1558 6.1	2217 1.8
4 TH	0408 6.7	1026 1.1	1630 7.0	2256 0.9		19 F	0420 6.1	1038 1.8	1638 6.3	2255 1.6
5 F	0456 7.0	1115 0.8	1718 7.2	2341 0.7		20 SA	0457 6.4	1115 1.6	1715 6.5	2332 1.4
6 SA	0541 7.2	1200 0.7	1803 7.3	●		21 SU	0533 6.6	1152 1.4	1752 6.7	○
7 SU	0024 0.7	0624 7.3	1244 0.7	1846 7.2		22 M	0008 1.3	0608 6.8	1229 1.3	1829 6.8
8 M	0105 0.8	0706 7.2	1326 0.9	1928 7.0		23 TU	0045 1.2	0645 6.9	1307 1.2	1907 6.8
9 TU	0145 1.1	0748 7.0	1407 1.1	2009 6.7		24 W	0123 1.2	0723 6.9	1346 1.2	1948 6.7
10 W	0224 1.4	0829 6.7	1448 1.5	2050 6.3		25 TH	0202 1.3	0805 6.8	1428 1.3	2031 6.5
11 TH	0303 1.8	0911 6.3	1530 1.9	2132 5.8		26 F	0244 1.5	0849 6.6	1514 1.5	2118 6.3
12 F	0344 2.2	0956 5.9	1617 2.3	2219 5.5		27 SA	0331 1.7	0940 6.4	1605 1.7	2212 6.0
13 SA	0432 2.5	1048 5.6	1714 2.6	◗ 2317 5.2		28 SU	0425 1.9	1037 6.2	1706 1.9	◗ 2314 5.8
14 SU	0537 2.8	1154 5.4	1826 2.7			29 M	0530 2.1	1143 6.0	1817 2.0	
15 M	0032 5.0	0657 2.8	1311 5.3	1940 2.6		30 TU	0023 5.7	0644 2.1	1255 6.0	1930 2.0

DECEMBER

Day	Time m	Time m	Time m	Time m		Day	Time m	Time m	Time m	Time m
1 W	0136 5.8	0758 2.0	1405 6.1	2039 1.8		16 TH	0140 5.2	0801 2.7	1412 5.4	2035 2.4
2 TH	0243 6.1	0905 1.8	1510 6.3	2140 1.6		17 F	0245 5.4	0906 2.4	1511 5.6	2133 2.2
3 F	0342 6.4	1004 1.5	1608 6.6	2234 1.4		18 SA	0339 5.7	1001 2.1	1602 5.9	2222 1.9
4 SA	0436 6.6	1057 1.3	1701 6.7	2323 1.2		19 SU	0426 6.1	1048 1.8	1648 6.2	2306 1.6
5 SU	0525 6.9	1145 1.1	1749 6.8	●		20 M	0509 6.4	1131 1.5	1732 6.5	2348 1.3
6 M	0008 1.1	0611 7.0	1231 1.0	1834 6.8		21 TU	0551 6.7	1214 1.3	1815 6.7	○
7 TU	0050 1.1	0654 7.0	1313 1.1	1916 6.7		22 W	0030 1.1	0633 6.9	1257 1.1	1857 6.9
8 W	0130 1.2	0735 6.9	1354 1.2	1955 6.6		23 TH	0113 1.0	0716 7.1	1340 0.9	1941 6.9
9 TH	0208 1.4	0814 6.7	1433 1.4	2034 6.3		24 F	0155 1.0	0800 7.1	1424 0.9	2026 6.8
10 F	0245 1.6	0852 6.5	1510 1.7	2111 6.1		25 SA	0239 1.0	0845 7.0	1509 1.0	2112 6.7
11 SA	0321 1.9	0931 6.2	1549 1.9	2150 5.8		26 SU	0324 1.2	0932 6.9	1555 1.2	2159 6.4
12 SU	0359 2.2	1012 5.9	1630 2.2	2233 5.5		27 M	0412 1.4	1022 6.6	1646 1.5	2251 6.2
13 M	0443 2.4	1059 5.7	1720 2.4	◗ 2323 5.3		28 TU	0505 1.7	1117 6.3	1743 1.8	◗ 2350 5.9
14 TU	0540 2.6	1155 5.4	1821 2.6			29 W	0607 2.0	1219 6.0	1850 2.0	
15 W	0026 5.1	0649 2.7	1302 5.3	1929 2.6		30 TH	0057 5.7	0720 2.1	1331 5.9	2004 2.1
						31 F	0211 5.7	0837 2.1	1444 5.9	2117 2.0

Chart Datum: 3·71 metres below Ordnance Datum (Newlyn). HAT is 7·8 metres above Chart Datum; see 4.5.

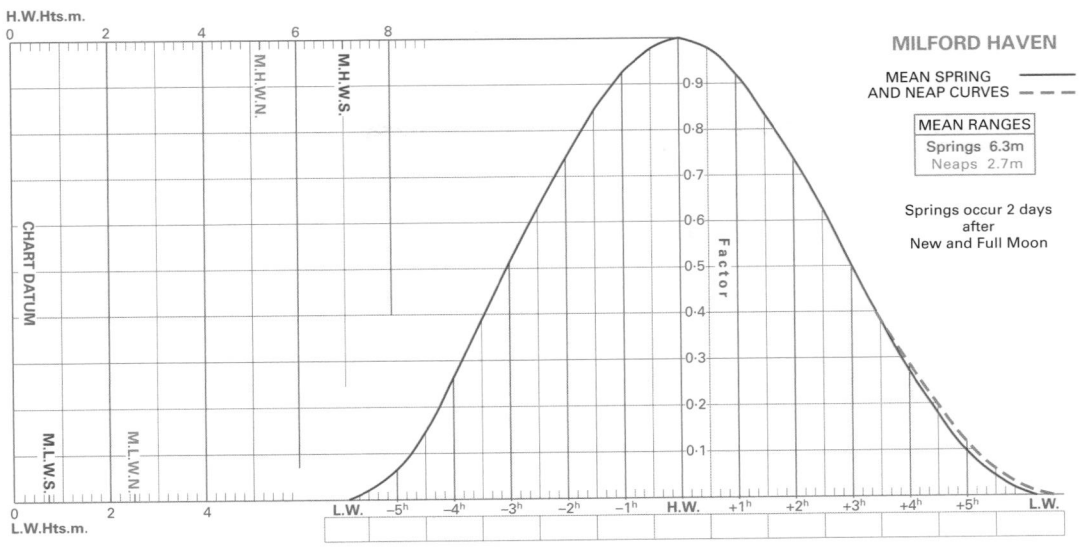

MILFORD HAVEN

MEAN SPRING ——
AND NEAP CURVES – – –

MEAN RANGES
Springs 6.3m
Neaps 2.7m

Springs occur 2 days
after
New and Full Moon

MILFORD HAVEN TO MUMBLES HEAD

(AC 1179, 1076) Milford Haven is a long natural, all-weather harbour with marinas beyond the oil terminals. Beware Turbot Bank (WCM lt buoy) 3M S of the entrance. Crow Rk (dries 5·5m) is 5ca SSE of Linney Hd, and The Toes are dangerous submerged rocks close W and SE of Crow Rock. There is a passage inshore of these dangers. There are overfalls on St Gowan Shoals which extend 4M SW of St Govan's Hd, and the sea breaks on the shallow patches in bad weather. There are firing areas from Linney Hd to Carmarthen Bay.

Caldey Is (lit) lies S of Tenby. Off its NW pt is St Margaret's Is connected by a rocky reef. Caldey Sound, between St Margaret's Is and Giltar Pt (AC 1482), is buoyed, but beware Eel Spit near W end of Caldey Is where there can be a nasty sea with wind against tide, and Woolhouse Rocks (dry 3·6m) 1ca NE of Caldey Is. Saundersfoot harbour (dries) is 2M N of Tenby, with an anchorage well sheltered from N and W but subject to swell. Streams are weak here. Carmarthen Bay has no offshore dangers for yachts, other than the extensive drying sands at head of the bay and on its E side off Burry Inlet.

S of Worms Head, Helwick Sands (buoyed at each end) extend 7M W from Port Eynon Pt; least depth of 1·3m is near their W end. Stream sets NE/SW across the sands. There is a narrow channel inshore, close to Port Eynon Pt.

▶ *Between here and Mumbles Hd the stream runs roughly along coast, sp rates 3kn off headlands, but there are eddies in Port Eynon Bay and Oxwich Bay (both yacht anchorages), and overfalls SSE of Oxwich Pt.* ◀

FIRING RANGES – LINNEY HEAD TO BURRY INLET

For daily info on all range firing times call *Milford Haven CG* Ch 16/67 or ☎ 01646 690909.

Castlemartin Range Danger Area extends 12M WNW from Linney Hd, thence in an anti-clockwise arc to a point 12M S of St Govan's Hd. The exact Danger Area operative on any one day depends on the ranges/ammunition used; it is primarily a tank range. When firing is in progress R flags are flown (Fl R lts at night) along the coast from Freshwater West to Linney Head to St Govan's Head. Yachts are requested to keep clear of ranges when active.

Firing takes place on weekdays 0900–1630, exceptionally to 1700. Night firing takes place on Mon to Thurs, up to 2359, depending on the hours of darkness. In Jan only small arms are usually fired and the danger area is reduced.

Days/times of firing are published locally and can be obtained by VHF from *Castlemartin Range* Ch 16 or ☎ 01646 662367 (H24 answering service); Range safety launches Ch 16 or 12; and Milford Haven CG Ch 16. Also from the Range Office ☎ (01646) 662287 or Warren Tower 01646 662336.

Manorbier Range (further E) covers a sector arc radius 12M centred on Old Castle Head; E/W extent is approximately between St Govan's Hd and Caldey Is (see AC Q6402). It is usually active Mon-Fri 0900-1700LT, occasionally Sat and Sun, and is primarily a surface to air missile range, but active areas depend on the weapons in use on any given day. On firing days warnings are broadcast on Ch 16, 73 at 0830, 1430 and on completion; red flags are flown either side of Old Castle Hd. Yachts on passage should either keep 12M offshore or transit close inshore via Stackpole Hd, Trewent Pt, Priest's Nose and Old Castle Hd. Firing days/times are available from local HMs and YCs. For further info call: *Manorbier Range Control* Ch 16, 73 (also manned by Range safety launches); *Milford Haven CG* Ch 16; or Range Control ☎ (01834) 871282 ext 209, ✉ 871283.

Penally Range (further E at Giltar Pt) is for small arms only and seldom interferes with passage through Caldey Sound. Info ☎ (01834) 843522.

Pendine Range (between Tenby and Burry Inlet) is a MOD range for testing explosive devices. It is usually possible to steer the rhumb line course from Tenby to Worms Hd without interference. Info ☎ (01994) 453243. Broadcasts on VHF Ch 16, 73 at 0900 and 1400LT. Range active 0800-1615.

Pembrey Range (approx 5M NW of Burry Inlet) is used for bombing practice by the RAF. Info ☎ (01554) 891224.

9.11.14 TENBY

Pembrokeshire 51·40'·42N 04°41'·93W ❀❀⚓⚓♕♕♕

CHARTS AC 5620, 1179, 1076, 1482; Imray C60; Stanfords 14.

TIDES −0510 Dover; ML 4·5; Duration 0610

Standard Port MILFORD HAVEN (←)

Times				Height (metres)			
High Water		Low Water		MHWS	MHWN	MLWN	MLWS
0100	0800	0100	0700	7·0	5·2	2·5	0·7
1300	2000	1300	1900				
Differences TENBY							
−0015	−0010	−0015	−0020	+1·4	+1·1	+0·5	+0·2
STACKPOLE QUAY (7M W of Caldey Island)							
−0005	+0025	−0010	−0010	+0·9	+0·7	+0·2	+0·3

SHELTER Good, but hbr dries up to 5m; access HW±2½. Sheltered ⚓s, depending on wind direction, to NE in Tenby Roads, in Lydstep Haven (2·5M SW), and around Caldey Is as follows: Priory

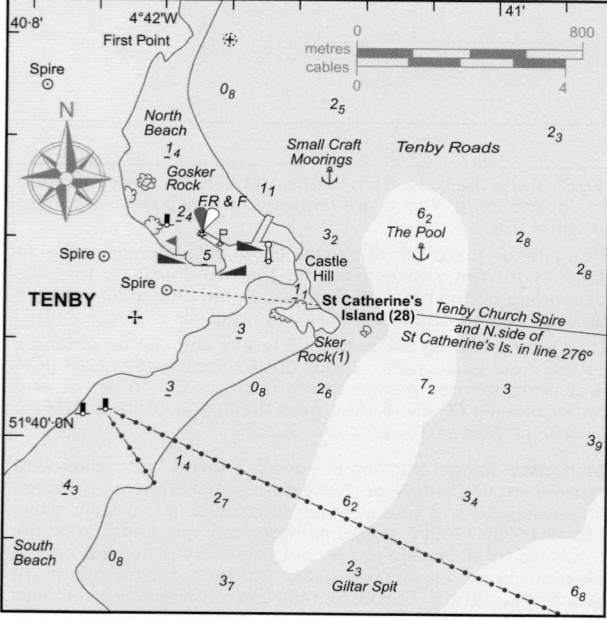

MUMBLES HEAD TO CARDIFF

(AC 1165, 1182) Off Mumbles Hd (Lt, fog sig) beware Mixon Shoal (dries 0·3m), marked by PHM buoy. In good conditions pass N of shoal, 1ca off Mumbles Hd. Anch N of Mumbles Hd, good holding but exposed to swell. At W side of Swansea Bay, Green Grounds, rky shoals, lie in appr's to Swansea.

Scarweather Sands, much of which dry (up to 3·3m) with seas breaking heavily, extend 7M W from Porthcawl (9.11.16) and are well buoyed (AC 1161). There is a chan between the sands and coast to E, but beware Hugo Bank (dries 2·6m) and Kenfig Patches (0·5m) with o'falls up to 7ca offshore between Sker Pt and Porthcawl.

Bay to the N but shallow, Jone's Bay (NE), Drinkim Bay (E) or Sandtop Bay (W).

NAVIGATION WPT 51°40'·02N 04°38'·08W, 279°/2·2M to monument on Castle Hill. The ⊕ WPT (off chartlet) is 2ca W of DZ2 SPM lit buoy. Beware Woolhouse Rks (3·6m) 1·5M SExE of the Hbr, marked by lit SCM buoy; and Sker Rk (1m high) closer in off St Catherine's Island (28m). From the W, Caldey Sound is navigable with care between Eel Pt SHM and Giltar Spit PHM lit buoys. Approaching Tenby Roads, keep outside the line of mooring buoys. For adjacent Firing ranges, see overleaf. Caldey Island is private and no landing without permission from the Abbot.

LIGHTS AND MARKS See 9.11.4 and chartlet. Church spire transit N side of St Catherine's Is 276°. FR 7m 7M on pier hd. Inside hbr, FW 6m 1M marks landing steps PHM beacon (unlit) marks outcrop from Gosker Rk on beach close N of hbr ent. Hbr is floodlit.

R/T Ch 16, 80 (listening during HO).

TELEPHONE (Code 01834) HM ☎ 842717 (end May-end Sept), Mobile 07977 609947; MRCC (01646) 690909; Marinecall 09068 969649; Police (01437) 763355 ; Dr 844161; Ⓗ 842040.

FACILITIES Hbr AB, Slip (up to 4·2m). Town P & D (cans), ▣, CH, 🛒, R, Bar, Gas, ✉, Ⓑ, ⇌, ✈ (Swansea; and a small airfield at Haverfordwest).

OTHER ADJACENT HARBOURS (See AC 5620)
SAUNDERSFOOT, Pembrokeshire, 51°42'·60N 04°41'·76W. AC 1179, 1076, 1482. HW −0510 on Dover; ML 4·4m; Duration 0605. See 9.11.14. A half-tide hbr with good shelter, but there may be a surge in prolonged E winds. On appr, beware buoys marking restricted area (power boats, etc) between Coppett Hall Pt and Perry's Pt. AB may be available (see HM), or moorings in the middle. Pier hd lt Fl R 5s 6m 7M on stone cupola. VHF: HM 11 16. HM ☎ (01834) 812094/(Home 831389). Facilities: 6 AB, CH, FW (on SW wall), Slip, P & D (cans), ME, BH. Town 🛒, R, Bar, ✉, Ⓑ, ⇌ (Tenby/Saundersfoot).

CARMARTHEN, Carmarthenshire, 51°46'·27N 04°22'·53W. AC 1179, 1076. HW −0455 on Dover. See 9.11.15. R Towy & Taf dry; access HW±2. Beware Carmarthen Bar in S winds F4 and over with strong sp streams. Nav info is available from Carmarthen Bar Navigation Committee ☎ (01267) 231250 or YC's. Appr on N'ly hdg toward Wharley Pt, leaving DZ8 & 9 buoys 5ca to stbd. Chan shifts frequently and is unmarked so local knowledge reqd unless conditions ideal. ⚓ in mid-stream or ⚓s at R Towy YC off Ferryside (7M below Carmarthen) or R Towey Boat Club 1M N on W bank. Access for both HW±2. 4 power lines cross in last 2·5M before Carmarthen, clearance 7·4m. R Towy YC ☎ (01267) 238356, M, FW, Bar. R Towy BC ☎ (01267) 238316. Town Ⓑ, Bar, Gas, ✉, 🛒, ⇌, ✈ (Cardiff).

Nash Sands extend 7·5M WNW from Nash Pt. Depths vary and are least at inshore end (dries 3m), but Nash Passage, 1ca wide, runs close inshore between E Nash ECM buoy and ledge off Nash Pt. ▶ On E-going stream there are heavy overfalls off Nash Pt and at W end of Nash Sands. Between Nash Pt and Breaksea Pt the E-going stream begins at HW Avonmouth + 0535, and the W-going at HW Avonmouth −0035, sp rates 3kn. Off Breaksea Pt there may be overfalls.◀

From Rhoose Pt to Lavernock Pt the coast is fringed with foul ground. Lavernock Spit extends 1·75M S of Lavernock Pt, and E of the spit is main chan to Cardiff; the other side of the chan being Cardiff Grounds, a bank drying 5·4m which lies parallel with the shore and about 1·5M from it.

9.11.15 BURRY INLET

Carmarthenshire 51°40'·52N 04°14'·93W (Burry Port) ✴✴✴△△✿

CHARTS AC 5620, 5608 1179, 1076, 1167; Imray C59, C60; Stanfords 14.

TIDES –0500 Dover; ML 4·7; Duration 0555

Standard Port MILFORD HAVEN (←)

Times				Height (metres)			
High Water		Low Water		MHWS	MHWN	MLWN	MLWS
0100	0800	0100	0700	7·0	5·2	2·5	0·7
1300	2000	1300	1900				
Differences BURRY PORT							
+0003	+0003	+0007	+0007	+1·6	+1·4	+0·5	+0·4
LLANELLI							
–0003	–0003	+0150	+0020	+0·8	+0·6	No data	
FERRYSIDE							
0000	–0010	+0220	0000	–0·3	–0·7	–1·7	–0·6
CARMARTHEN							
+0010	0000	Dries		–4·4	–4·8	Dries	

SHELTER Good in Burry Port via lock with flapgate controlled by R/G lts. Access HW±2 over sill depth 2m. Pontoons for visitors. Sp tides run hard. Note: If bad weather precludes access, see 9.11.14 for ⚓s around Caldey Island, especially in W'lies. Call Hbr Office (01554 835691 mob 07817 395710). Visitors welcome but few facilities.

NAVIGATION WPT 51°36'·37N 04°24'·38W, 087°/3·3M to Burry Holms, thence 4·5M to Burry Port.

Carmarthen Bar, extending from the R Towy entrance SE to Burry Holms, should not be attempted in W winds >F5 nor at night. Best entry is close NW of Burry Holms at HW–2; thence track 018° with Worms Hd on a transit astern (198°) between Burry Holms and Limekiln Pt. When Whiteford lighthouse (disused) bears about 082°, alter to approx 050° into deeper water and steer to leave the Barrel Post at least 1½ ca to port as a large sand bank has formed to E of it.

Near approaches to the harbour are marked by a buoyed channel (3·2m) access HW±2. Barrel Post now marks W end of new sandbank, only to be used as reference point – do not round close to. E end of this bank marked by unlit buoy PHM. Approach from here on NW'ly heading, channel marked by 3 pairs unlit buoys PHMs & SHMs beyond which 2 unlit PHMs in near appr to lock/flapgate. Chan is liable to shift. Before appr, check Firing Range activity (contact HM or Pendine Range Control, see above).

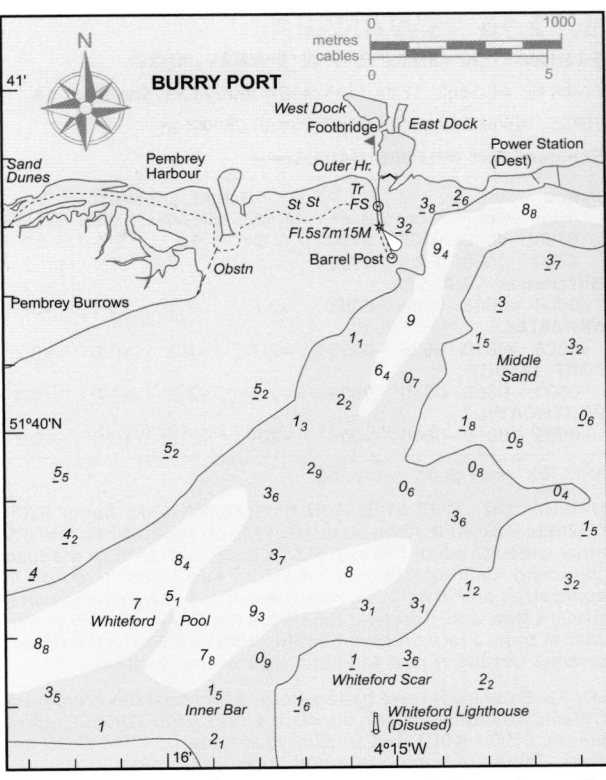

LIGHTS AND MARKS Whiteford lt ho is conspic, but no longer lit. On head of W bkwtr is Barrel post; 1½ca N is conspic old lt ho (W tr, R top) Fl 5s 7m 15M, and flagstaff.

R/T Ch M (Hbr Office), 18.

TELEPHONE (Code 01554); HM 835691, mob 07817 395710; MRCC (01792) 366534; Pendine Range (01994) 453243 Ext 240; Marinecall 09068 969649; Police 0845 3302000; Dr 832240.

FACILITIES Slip, M, L, CH; **E Pier** (small craft only): Slip; **Burry Port YC** Bar; **Services**: D, ME, El, ✂, C, Gas. **Town** P, D, CH, 🛒, R, Bar, ✉, ⑧, ⇌, ✈ (Cardiff).

SEVERN ESTUARY

(AC 1176, 1166) Near the centre of Bristol Chan, either side of the buoyed fairway, are the islands of Flat Holm (Lt, fog sig) and Steep Holm. 7M SW of Flat Holm lies Culver Sand (0·9m), 3M in length, with W and ECM bys. Monkstone Rk (Lt, dries) is 2M NW of the buoyed chan to Avonmouth and Bristol. Extensive drying banks cover the N shore of the estuary, beyond Newport and the Severn bridges (AC 1176).

▶ The range of tide in the Bristol Chan is exceptionally large, 12·2m sp and 6·0m np, and tidal streams are very powerful, particularly above Avonmouth. Between Flat Holm and Steep Holm the E-going stream begins at HW Avonmouth – 0610, sp 3kn, and the W-going at HW Avonmouth + 0015, sp 4kn. ◀

The ent to the R Avon is just to the S of Avonmouth S Pier Hd. Bristol City Docks lie some 6M up-river. Approach the ent via King Road and the Newcombe and Cockburn lt buoys and thence via the Swash chan into the Avon. The ent dries at LW but the river is navigable at about half tide. ▶ Tidal streams are strong in the approaches to Avonmouth, up to 5kn at sp. The tide is also strong in the R. Avon which is best entered no earlier than HW Avonmouth – 0200. ◀

From Avonmouth it is 16M to Sharpness which yachts should aim to reach at about HW Avonmouth. ▶ Spring streams can run 8kn at the Shoots, and 6kn at the Severn bridges. At the Shoots the flood begins at HW Avonmouth –0430 and the ebb at HW Avonmouth + 0045. The Severn Bore can usually be seen if Avonmouth range is 13·5m or more. ◀

9.11.16 SWANSEA

Swansea 51°36'·43N 03°55'·67W ✱✱✱✱♒♒♒♒♧♧♧

CHARTS AC 5608, 1179, 1165, 1161; Imray C59; Stanfords 14.

TIDES –0500 Dover; ML 5·2; Duration 0620

Standard Port MILFORD HAVEN (←—)

Times				Height (metres)			
High Water		Low Water		MHWS	MHWN	MLWN	MLWS
0100	0800	0100	0700	7·0	5·2	2·5	0·7
1300	2000	1300	1900				
Differences SWANSEA							
+0004	+0006	–0006	–0003	+2·6	+2·1	+0·7	+0·3
MUMBLES							
+0005	+0010	–0020	–0015	+2·3	+1·7	+0·6	+0·2
PORT TALBOT							
0000	+0005	–0010	–0005	+2·8	+2·2	+1·0	+0·4
PORTHCAWL							
+0005	+0010	–0010	–0005	+2·9	+2·3	+0·8	+0·3

SHELTER Very good in marina.

NAVIGATION WPT 51°35'·53N 03°56'·08W (SHM buoy) 020°/ 0·92M to E bkwtr lt. Keep seaward of Mixon Shoal. When N of SW Inner Green Grounds (SWIGG) SCM lt buoy keep to W of dredged chan and clear of commercial ships. *Yachts must motor in approaches and in harbour,* max speed 4kn. In Swansea Bay tidal streams flow anti-clockwise for 9½ hrs (Swansea HW –3½ to +6), with at times a race off Mumbles Hd. From HW–6 to –3 the stream reverses, setting N past Mumbles Hd towards Swansea.

LOCKS Enter via R Tawe barrage lock, which operates on request HW±4½ (co-ordinated with the marina lock), 0700-2200BST; out of season, 0700-1900UT, but to 2200 at w/ends. Lock fee £2.40 per week. There are pontoons in both locks.

Yachts usually exit Tawe barrage lock at H+00, and enter at H+30. Locks are closed when ht of tide falls to 1·5m above CD, usually at MLWS. At sp, do not enter river until LW+1½. Two large Or holding buoys below barrage in mid-stream; also, at W side of barrage lock, a landing pontoon (dries, foul ground).

LIGHTS AND MARKS See 9.11.4 and chartlet. Mumbles Hd, Fl (4) 20s35m16M, is 3M SSW of hbr ent. A conspic TV mast (R lts) NNE of hbr is almost aligned with the fairway. Ldg lts 020° mark E side of chan dredged 3m. When N of Swansea Middle West (QR) and Swansea Middle East (QG) chan buoys stay inside dredged chan. Barrage lock lit by 2FR/FG (vert) to seaward.

Port Traffic sigs are conspic at W side of ent to King's Dock; there are 9 lts, ●, arranged in a 3 x 3 frame. Yachts arriving must obey the middle lt in left column:

- ● = Do not enter the river; hold SW of W Pier.
- ● = Yachts may enter the river, keeping to mid-chan, then to W of holding buoys.

Lock Master will advise on tfc movements Ch 18.
Lock sigs for barrage and marina locks alike are:

- ●●] = Lock closed. Do not proceed
- ● = Wait
- ● = Enter with caution
- ●●] = Free flow operating; proceed with caution

R/T Barrage, *Tawe Lock* Ch 18. *Swansea Marina* Ch 80. For commercial docks call *Swansea Docks Radio* VHF Ch14 (H24).

TELEPHONE (Code 01792) HM 653787; Barrage 456014; MRCC 366534; Police 456999; Marinecall 09068 969649; ⊞ 205666; Dr 653452; DVLA (for SSR) 783355.

FACILITIES Swansea Marina (340+50 ♥) ☎ 470310, £1·85, Lock width 9m; D (no P), C (1 ton), BH (25 ton), ⚓, Gas, Gaz, Ice, CH, ME, ACA, SM, El, Ⓔ, ✕, ▢, ▨, Bar, R.
Swansea Yacht & Sub Aqua Club (SY & SAC) ☎ 654863, No visitors, M, L, FW, C (5 ton static), R, Bar. **City** 🛒, R, Bar, ✉, Ⓑ, ⇌, ✈.

ADJACENT HARBOURS AND ANCHORAGES

Mumbles, 51°34'·2N 03°58'·2W. Good ⚓ in W'lies 5ca N of Mumbles Hd lt ho. **Bristol Chan YC** ☎ (01792) 366000, Slip, M; **Mumbles YC** ☎ 369321, Slip, M, L, FW, C (hire).

R Neath, 51°37'·88N 03°49'·97W. Ent over bar HW±2½ via 1·5M chan, marked/lit training wall to stbd. Tfc info from *Neath Pilot* VHF Ch 77, if on stn. **Monkstone Marina,** W bank just S of bridge, dries 4m: AB, 2 Y ⚓s, D, FW, Slip, BH (15 ton), R, Bar, Visitors welcome. **Monkstone C & SC,** ☎ (01792) 812229; VHF Ch M (occas).

PORTHCAWL, Bridgend, 51°28'·48N 03°42'·02W. AC 1165, 1169. HW –0500 on Dover; ML 5·3m. See 9.11.16. A tiny drying hbr (access HW±2) protected by bkwtr running SE from Porthcawl Pt. Beware rk ledge (dries) W of bkwtr. Porthcawl lt ho, F WRG (see 9.11.4) in line 094° with St Hilary radio mast (QR & FR) leads through Shord chan. Tidal streams can reach 6kn at sp off end of bkwtr. 3 ⚓s or ⚓ approx 3ca SSE of lt ho. HM ☎ (01656) 782756. Facilities: **Porthcawl Hbr B C** ☎ 782342. **Town** P & D (cans), CH, 🛒, R, Bar, ✉, Ⓑ, ⇌ (Bridgend), ✈ (Cardiff).

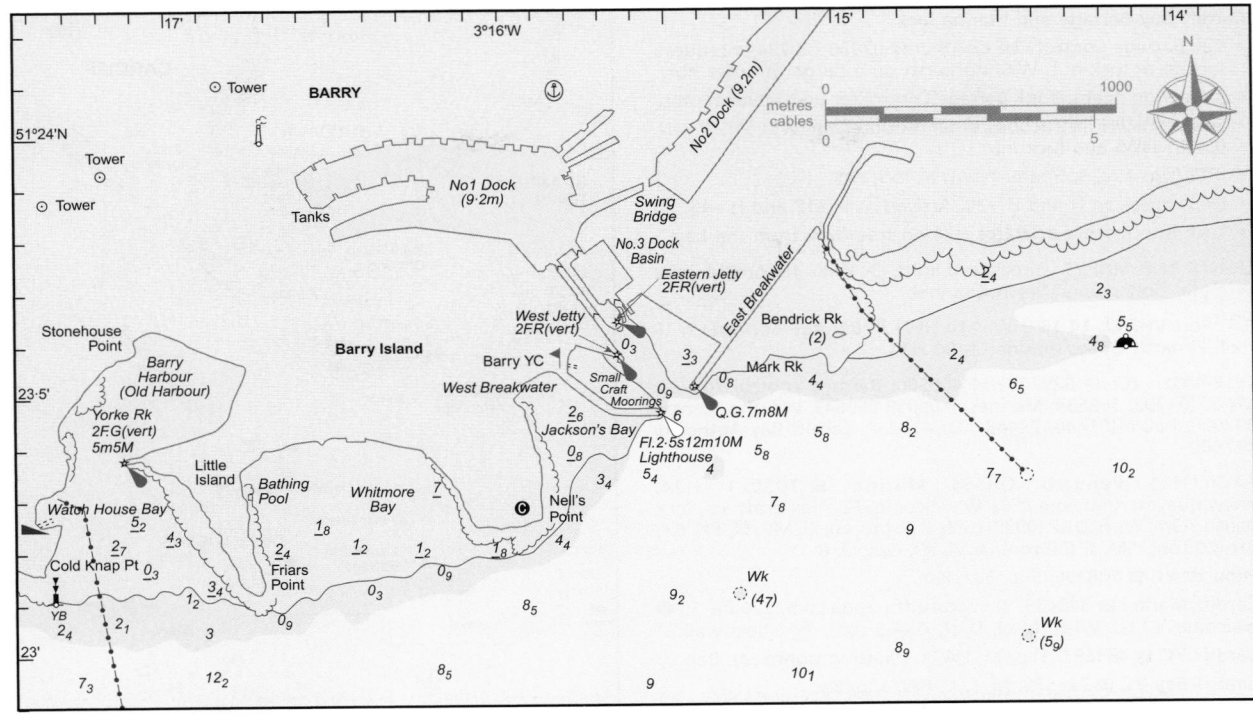

9.11.17 BARRY

Vale of Glamorgan **51°23'·48N 03°15'·45W** ✲✲✲☆☆☆☆☆

CHARTS AC 5608, 1179, 1152, 1182; Imray C59; Stanfords 14.

TIDES −0423 Dover; ML 6·1; Duration 0630

Standard Port BRISTOL (AVONMOUTH) (→)

Times				Height (metres)			
High Water		Low Water		MHWS	MHWN	MLWN	MLWS
0600	1100	0300	0800	13·2	9·8	3·8	1·0
1800	2300	1500	2000				
Differences BARRY							
−0025	−0025	−0130	−0045	−1·6	−1·0	−0·2	0·0
FLAT HOLM							
−0015	−0015	−0035	−0035	−1·4	−1·0	−0·5	0·0
STEEP HOLM							
−0020	−0020	−0040	−0040	−1·7	−1·1	−0·5	−0·4

SHELTER Good, but in strong E/SE winds avoid Barry; No 1 Dock is not available for pleasure craft. Access H24 to the Outer hbr. No AB or ⚓, but Barry YC administers all moorings and welcomes visitors. Temporary mooring may be available from Bristol Pilots on request.

NAVIGATION WPT 51°23'·03N 03°15'·08W, 332°/0·53M to ent. Beware heavy commercial traffic. Approaching from E keep well out from the shore. Strong tidal stream across ent.

LIGHTS AND MARKS Welsh Water Barry West PHM buoy, Fl R 5s, and Merkur PHM buoy, Fl R 2·5s, lie respectively 217°/1·5M and 191°/1·65M from hbr ent. W bkwtr Fl 2·5s 10M. E bkwtr QG 8M.

R/T *Barry Radio* VHF Ch **11** 10 16 (HW−4 to HW+3); tidal info on request. *Bristol Pilot* via Ch 16 may advise on vacant moorings.

TELEPHONE HM 0870 609 6699; MRCC (01792) 366534; Marinecall 09068 969649; Police 01446 734451; Dr 01446 739543.

FACILITIES **Barry YC** (130) ☎ 735511, access HW±3½, Slip, M, Bar, FW, D, Gas, ME, El, ✂, SM.
Town P (cans, 1M away), CH, 🛒, R, Bar, ✉, Ⓑ, ⇌, ✈ (Cardiff).

9.11.18 CARDIFF (PENARTH)

Vale of Glamorgan **51°26'·74N 03°09'·92W** (marina) ✲✲☆☆☆☆☆☆

CHARTS AC 5608, 1179, 1176, 1182; Imray C59; Stanfords 14.

TIDES −0425 Dover; ML 6·4; Duration 0610

Standard Port BRISTOL (AVONMOUTH) (→)

Times				Height (metres)			
High Water		Low Water		MHWS	MHWN	MLWN	MLWS
0600	1100	0300	0800	13·2	9·8	3·8	1·0
1800	2300	1500	2000				
Differences CARDIFF							
−0015	−0015	−0100	−0030	−1·0	−0·5	0·0	0·0
NEWPORT							
−0020	−0010	0000	−0020	−1·1	−0·9	−0·6	−0·6
CHEPSTOW (River Wye)							
+0020	+0020	No data		No data		No data	

NOTE: At Newport the ht of LW does not normally fall below MLWS. Tidal hts are based on a minimum river flow; max flow may raise ht of LW by as much as 0·3m.

SHELTER Very good in marinas. See above for barrage locks. Waiting trot berths in outer hbr; or ⚓ off Penarth seafront in W'lies; in E'lies cramped ⚓ off Alexandra Dock ent in 2m.

NAVIGATION WPT 51°24'·03N 03°08'·81W (2½ca SW of S Cardiff SCM lt buoy), 349°/2·9M to barrage locks.

The outer approaches from W or SW are via Breaksea lt float and N of One Fathom Bk. Keep S of Lavernock Spit SCM lt buoy and NW of Flat Holm and Wolves NCM lt buoy drying rk. From NE, drying ledges and shoals extend >1M offshore. From E, appr via Monkstone Lt ho and S Cardiff SCM buoy. Ranny Spit (dries 0·4m) is 3½ca to the W, and Cardiff Grounds (dries 5·4m) 3½ca to the E.

The Wrach Chan is buoyed/lit and dredged 1·2m; it passes 1½ca E of Penarth Hd. The locks appr chan, buoyed, is dredged 0·7m below CD.

Do not impede merchant ships, especially those entering/leaving Alexandra Dock.

Cardiff Bay Barrage and Marina lock

- Call *Barrage Control* VHF Ch 18 or ☎ 02920 700234 to request lock-in or lock-out. Waiting berth on a barge in outer hbr.
- If entering near LW ask Barrage Control for up-to-date depths.
- Subject to VHF instructions, enter the outer hbr (Wpt 51°26'·71N 03°09'·84W) and lock in.
- IPTS (sigs 1, 2, 3, 5) are shown at lock ent.
- Departures on H and H +30. Arrivals at H +15 and H +45.
- Lock into marina operates H24 on free-flow from the bay.

LIGHTS AND MARKS Directional light, Oc WRG 10s 5m3M, on a W metal post marks Wrach Channel.

R/T Port VHF Ch **14** 16 (HW–4 to HW+3). *Barrage Control* Ch 18 H24. Penarth Quays marina Ch 80 H24.

TELEPHONE (Code 02920) HM 400500; Barrage control 700234; MRCC (01792) 366534; Marinecall 09068 969649; Weather Centre 397020; Police (01446) 734451; Dr 415258; Cardiff Bay Authority 877900.

FACILITIES Penarth Quays Marina ☎ 705021 H24, www.quaymarinas.com 350+ Ⓥ welcome, £2, max draft 3m, lock width 7·3m; Wi-fi, D&P (0930-1630, E pontoon), El, ME, ✕, CH, BY, BH (20 ton), SM, C (20 ton), ACA, Ⓔ, Gas, ⚋, R.

Penarth YC ☎ 708196, Slip, FW, Bar.

Cardiff Marina ☎ 343459, www.cardiffmarina.com, 320 inc 50 Ⓥ welcome, £1.60, Wi-fi (free), D, ⚓, C (4·5 ton), 🛒 (short walk).

Cardiff YC ☎ 463697, Slip, M, FW, L (floating pontoon), Bar.

Cardiff Bay YC ☎ 226575, M, L, C, FW, Slip, Bar.

City 🛒, R, Bar, ✉, Ⓑ, ⇌, ✈ (15 mins).

ADJACENT HARBOUR

NEWPORT, Newport, **51°32'·95N 02°59'·13W**. AC 5608, 1179, 1152, 1176. HW –0425 on Dover; ML 6·0m; Duration 0620. See 9.11.18. A commercial port controlled by ABP, but a safe shelter for yachts. Enter R Usk over bar (approx 0·5m) E of West Usk buoy, QR Bell) and follow buoyed and lit chan to S Lock ent; turn NE (ldg lts 062°) for yacht moorings on S side between power stn pier and YC. Beware overhead cables in Julian's Pill, clearance 3·8m.

Lights, see 9.11.4. East Usk lt ho Fl (2) WRG 10s. Ldg lts 062°, both FG. Alexandra Dock, S lock W pier head 2 FR (vert) 9/7m 6M. E pier head 2 FG (vert) 9/7m 6M.

Port VHF, *Newport Radio*, and VTS: Ch 09, **71**, 74 (HW ±4). HM (ABP) ☎ 0870 609 6699. Facilities: CH, El, ME, ✕, Ⓔ. **Newport and Uskmouth SC** Bar, M. **Town** all facilities.

THE SEVERN BRIDGES (AC 1166) The Second Severn Crossing (37m clearance), from 51°34'·88N 02°43'·80W to 51°34'·14N 02°39'·82W, is 4M upriver from Avonmouth and 3M below the Severn Bridge.

The following brief directions, coupled with strong tidal streams and shifting banks, emphasise the need for local knowledge.

Going upriver, pass both bridges at about HW Avonmouth –1¾ (see also 9.11.19); max sp stream is 8kn at The Shoots and 6kn at the Severn Bridge, setting across the channel when the banks are covered.

Redcliffe F Bu ldg lts in transit with Charston Rock lt lead 013° through The Shoots, a narrow passage between English Stones (6·2m) and the rocky ledges (5·1m) off the Welsh shore. 5ca S of the Second Crossing, the chan is marked by Lower Shoots WCM bcn and Mixoms PHM bcn.

No vessel may navigate between the shore and the nearer Tower of the 2nd Crossing, except in emergency.

4ca N of the 2nd Crossing, leave the 013° transit before passing Old Man's Hd WCM bcn and Lady Bench PHM bcn. From abeam Charston Rk, keep Chapel Rk, Fl 2·6s, brg 050° until the E twr of Severn Bridge bears 068°; maintain this brg until Lyde Rk, QWR, bears about 355°, when alter 010° to transit the bridge (36m clearance) close to rks drying 1m.

Radar Warning. In certain conditions and tidal states, radar displays may show misleading echoes in the vicinity of the 2nd Severn Crossing. *Racon (O)* is at centre span of crossing.

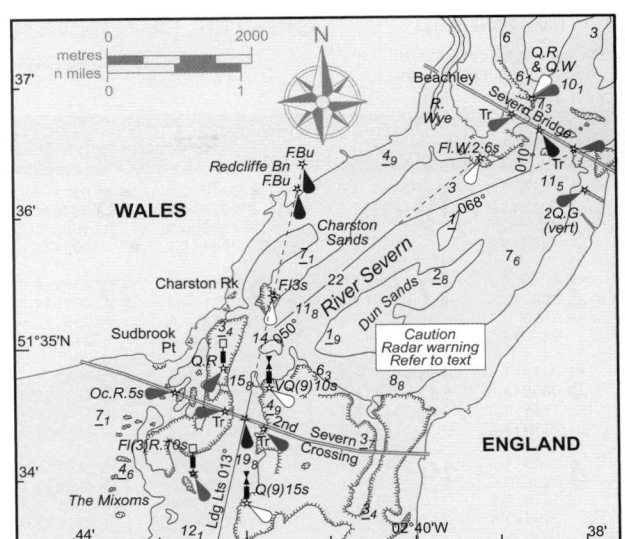

9.11.19 SHARPNESS

Gloucestershire 51°43'·03N 02°29'·08W ✳❄⚓⚓❁❁

CHARTS AC 5608, 1166, Imray C59; Stanfords 14.

TIDES –0315 Dover; Duration 0415. Note: The tidal regime is irregular and deviates from Avonmouth curve.

Standard Port BRISTOL (AVONMOUTH) (→)

Times				Height (metres)			
High Water		Low Water		MHWS	MHWN	MLWN	MLWS
0000	0600	0000	0700	13·2	9·8	3·8	1·0
1200	1800	1200	1900				
Differences SUDBROOK (Second Severn Crossing)							
+0010	+0010	+0025	+0015	+0·2	+0·1	–0·1	+0·1
BEACHLEY/AUST (Severn Bridge)							
+0010	+0015	+0040	+0025	–0·2	–0·2	–0·5	–0·3
INWARD ROCKS (River Severn)							
+0020	+0020	+0105	+0045	–1·0	–1·1	–1·4	–0·6
NARLWOOD ROCKS							
+0025	+0025	+0120	+0100	–1·9	–2·0	–2·3	–0·8
WHITE HOUSE							
+0025	+0025	+0145	+0120	–3·0	–3·1	–3·6	–1·0
BERKELEY							
+0030	+0045	+0245	+0220	–3·8	–3·9	–3·4	–0·5
SHARPNESS DOCK							
+0035	+0050	+0305	+0245	–3·9	–4·2	–3·3	–0·4
WELLHOUSE ROCK							
+0040	+0055	+0320	+0305	–4·1	–4·4	–3·1	–0·2

SHELTER Very good. The sea lock into the commercial dock is generally open HW–2 to HW but this depends on commercial shipping movements. The advice is plan your passage to arrive no sooner than HW–1 and no later than HW. For more detailed information on lock fees, canal licences and the passage from Avonmouth contact the HM at Sharpness on 01453 811862. The fog signal on Sharpness Point is available on request to Sharpness Radio on VHF channel 13 or 01453 511968.

NAVIGATION WPT 51°42'·83N 02°29'·28W, 028°/2ca to ent.

• Use transits shown on AC 1166. Request pilot notes from Sharpness HM in good time.
• Leave King Road, Avonmouth (17M downriver) not before HW Sharpness –3, to be off Hbr ent about HW –½. Stem strong flood S of F Bu lt; beware tidal eddy.
• Do not proceed above the Severn Bridge except HW±2. There is a 5H flood and a 7H ebb.

LIGHTS AND MARKS Lights as chartlet, but night passage not advised without local knowledge/pilot (07774 226143).

R/T Call *Sharpness Radio* VHF Ch 13 (HW –6 to +1) for lock. Gloucester and Sharpness Canal Ch 74 for bridges (no locks). Call *Bristol VTS* VHF Ch 12 when passing reporting points inwards/ outwards: E/W Grounds PHM, Welsh Hook SCM and at Lower Shoots Bcn.

TELEPHONE (Code 01453) Pierhead 511968 (HW–5 to HW+1); HM 811862/64 (HO), 811863; Police (01452) 521201; 810777.

FACILITIES Sharpness Marina ☎ 811476. 170 inc 2 ♥, £8 all LOA. El, D, ✕, CH, Gas, ME, C. **Town** D (above Fretherne Bridge), 🛒, R, Bar, ✉, ⓑ (Berkeley), ➜ (Stonehouse), ✈ (Bristol). Gloucester: D, ACA.

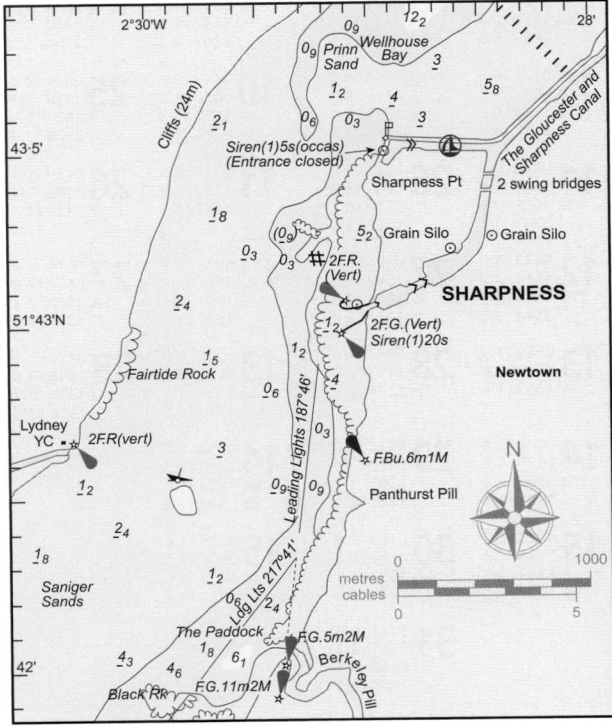

BRISTOL (AVONMOUTH)   LAT 51°30'N   LONG 2°44'W
TIMES AND HEIGHTS OF HIGH AND LOW WATERS

TIME ZONE (UT)
For Summer Time add ONE hour in **non-shaded areas**

Dates in red are **SPRINGS**
Dates in blue are **NEAPS**

YEAR 2010

JANUARY

Time m	Time m
1 0136 1.5 / 071313.3 / F 1407 1.4 / 194413.3	**16** 0211 1.8 / 074912.5 / SA 1433 1.9 / 201012.2
2 0229 1.2 / 080213.7 / SA 1500 1.1 / 203313.5	**17** 0252 1.9 / 082512.5 / SU 1512 2.0 / 204412.1
3 0319 1.0 / 085013.8 / SU 1548 1.0 / 211913.5	**18** 0325 2.1 / 085812.3 / M 1543 2.1 / 211412.0
4 0403 1.0 / 093613.8 / M 1630 1.0 / 220413.4	**19** 0349 2.3 / 092812.1 / TU 1606 2.3 / 214211.9
5 0442 1.2 / 102113.5 / TU 1708 1.3 / 224612.9	**20** 0406 2.3 / 095511.9 / W 1626 2.3 / 220911.7
6 0518 1.5 / 110412.9 / W 1742 1.7 / 232912.3	**21** 0429 2.3 / 102311.7 / TH 1652 2.3 / 223911.5
7 0554 2.0 / 115012.2 / TH 1817 2.3 ◗	**22** 0500 2.4 / 105711.4 / F 1725 2.5 / 231611.2
8 001511.5 / 0633 2.6 / F 124311.4 / 1858 2.9	**23** 0536 2.7 / 113911.0 / SA 1805 2.9 ◖
9 011210.7 / 0722 3.2 / SA 135010.7 / 1953 3.5	**24** 000210.7 / 0621 3.2 / SU 123410.4 / 1857 3.4
10 022710.3 / 0832 3.7 / SU 150410.3 / 2117 3.9	**25** 010410.2 / 0723 3.8 / M 134710.1 / 2014 3.6
11 034010.3 / 1003 3.7 / M 161310.5 / 2242 3.6	**26** 022510.0 / 0901 3.9 / TU 151910.2 / 2159 3.6
12 044310.7 / 1114 3.2 / TU 171310.9 / 2344 3.0	**27** 040010.5 / 1042 3.4 / W 164411.0 / 2321 2.9
13 053911.3 / 1210 2.6 / W 180511.4	**28** 051311.6 / 1157 2.5 / TH 174812.0
14 0036 2.4 / 062611.9 / TH 1301 2.2 / 185111.9	**29** 0026 2.0 / 061012.6 / F 1301 1.7 / 184312.9
15 0125 1.9 / 070912.3 / F 1349 1.9 / ● 193312.1	**30** 0126 1.4 / 070213.5 / SA 1359 1.1 / ○ 193313.6
	31 0221 0.8 / 075114.1 / SU 1452 0.6 / 202014.0

FEBRUARY

Time m	Time m
1 0310 0.4 / 083714.4 / M 1538 0.3 / 210414.1	**16** 0311 1.7 / 083612.5 / TU 1528 1.8 / 205112.3
2 0353 0.3 / 092114.4 / TU 1617 0.4 / 214514.0	**17** 0338 2.0 / 090512.4 / W 1551 2.0 / 211812.2
3 0429 0.5 / 100114.0 / W 1649 0.8 / 222313.5	**18** 0352 2.1 / 093012.3 / TH 1605 2.1 / 214312.1
4 0458 1.0 / 103913.4 / TH 1714 1.4 / 225812.7	**19** 0407 2.0 / 095812.1 / F 1625 2.0 / 221212.0
5 0523 1.6 / 111612.4 / F 1739 2.1 ◗ 233411.7	**20** 0433 2.0 / 103011.8 / SA 1654 2.0 / 224711.7
6 0552 2.4 / 115611.3 / SA 1810 2.8	**21** 0506 2.3 / 111011.3 / SU 1729 2.5 / 233011.1
7 001610.7 / 0630 3.2 / SU 124910.2 / 1854 3.7	**22** 0546 2.8 / 120010.6 / M 1816 3.2 ◖
8 0122 9.8 / 0728 4.0 / M 1419 9.5 / 2003 4.4	**23** 002710.3 / 0641 3.6 / TU 1311 9.9 / 1925 3.9
9 0304 9.5 / 0903 4.4 / TU 1547 9.6 / 2207 4.3	**24** 0148 9.8 / 0815 4.1 / W 1454 9.8 / 2134 3.9
10 041910.0 / 1050 3.8 / W 165310.3 / 2322 3.4	**25** 033910.2 / 1030 3.5 / TH 163110.7 / 2308 3.0
11 051910.9 / 1150 2.9 / TH 174711.1	**26** 045911.4 / 1148 2.4 / F 173711.9
12 0016 2.5 / 060811.7 / F 1241 2.1 / 183211.8	**27** 0014 1.9 / 055712.6 / SA 1250 1.4 / 182913.0
13 0105 1.9 / 065112.3 / SA 1329 1.7 / 191212.2	**28** 0112 1.1 / 064813.6 / SU 1344 0.7 / ○ 191613.8
14 0152 1.6 / 072912.6 / SU 1414 1.6 / ● 194912.4	
15 0235 1.6 / 080412.6 / M 1454 1.6 / 202212.4	

MARCH

Time m	Time m
1 0205 0.4 / 073414.3 / M 1434 0.2 / 200114.3	**16** 0207 1.5 / 073512.6 / TU 1427 1.6 / 195212.5
2 0252 0.1 / 081814.6 / TU 1518 0.0 / 204214.4	**17** 0245 1.6 / 080812.6 / W 1502 1.6 / 202312.5
3 0333 0.0 / 085914.5 / W 1555 0.3 / 212014.1	**18** 0315 1.8 / 083812.5 / TH 1527 1.9 / 205012.4
4 0406 0.4 / 093614.0 / TH 1623 0.8 / 215513.5	**19** 0332 2.0 / 090512.4 / F 1542 1.9 / 211812.4
5 0432 1.0 / 101113.3 / F 1642 1.5 / 222712.7	**20** 0347 1.9 / 093512.3 / SA 1601 1.9 / 214912.2
6 0452 1.6 / 104312.2 / SA 1702 2.1 / 225811.7	**21** 0412 1.9 / 101012.0 / SU 1630 2.0 / 222511.9
7 0516 2.3 / 111711.1 / SU 1730 2.9 ◗ 233310.6	**22** 0445 2.1 / 105011.4 / M 1705 2.4 / 230911.2
8 0552 3.2 / 1159 9.9 / M 1809 3.7	**23** 0525 2.7 / 114110.6 / TU 1752 3.2 ◖
9 0026 9.5 / 0645 4.1 / TU 1325 9.0 / 1915 4.6	**24** 000610.4 / 0621 3.5 / W 1253 9.8 / 1901 3.9
10 0230 9.1 / 0814 4.6 / W 1518 9.1 / 2119 4.6	**25** 0131 9.9 / 0800 4.0 / TH 1442 9.8 / 2121 3.9
11 0352 9.6 / 1023 4.0 / TH 1626 9.9 / 2257 3.6	**26** 032410.3 / 1017 3.3 / F 161510.8 / 2249 2.8
12 045210.6 / 1124 2.9 / F 172010.9 / 2350 2.6	**27** 044011.5 / 1128 2.2 / SA 171712.0 / 2352 1.7
13 054111.5 / 1214 2.1 / SA 180411.7	**28** 053712.7 / 1226 1.2 / SU 180813.1
14 0038 1.9 / 062212.2 / SU 1301 1.6 / 184312.2	**29** 0048 0.9 / 062613.6 / M 1319 0.6 / 185313.8
15 0124 1.6 / 070012.5 / M 1346 1.4 / ● 191912.5	**30** 0139 0.4 / 071114.1 / TU 1407 0.2 / ○ 193614.1
	31 0225 0.1 / 075414.3 / W 1452 0.2 / 201614.1

APRIL

Time m	Time m
1 0306 0.2 / 0834 14.1 / TH 1526 0.5 / 2053 13.8	**16** 0245 1.7 / 081112.5 / F 1459 1.7 / 202512.6
2 0340 0.6 / 0911 13.6 / F 1554 1.1 / 2127 13.2	**17** 0311 1.8 / 084512.5 / SA 1523 1.8 / 205812.6
3 0405 1.2 / 0945 12.8 / SA 1612 1.7 / 2159 12.4	**18** 0334 1.8 / 092012.4 / SU 1548 1.8 / 213412.4
4 0425 1.8 / 1016 11.9 / SU 1631 2.3 / 2228 11.5	**19** 0402 1.8 / 095812.0 / M 1619 2.0 / 221412.0
5 0449 2.4 / 1047 10.9 / M 1659 2.9 / 2302 10.5	**20** 0437 2.1 / 104211.5 / TU 1657 2.4 / 230111.3
6 0524 3.1 / 1126 9.8 / TU 1736 3.6 ◗ 2351 9.6	**21** 0521 2.6 / 113610.7 / W 1747 3.1 ◖
7 0616 3.9 / 1235 9.0 / W 1838 4.4	**22** 000010.6 / 0622 3.3 / TH 124810.2 / 1903 3.7
8 0143 9.0 / 0737 4.4 / TH 1435 8.9 / 2019 4.6	**23** 012510.3 / 0804 3.5 / F 142510.2 / 2059 3.5
9 0312 9.5 / 0917 4.0 / F 1546 9.7 / 2212 3.9	**24** 030110.7 / 0946 2.9 / SA 154711.0 / 2218 2.6
10 0412 10.3 / 1041 3.2 / SA 1640 10.6 / 2312 2.9	**25** 041211.6 / 1056 2.1 / SU 164911.9 / 2321 1.8
11 0502 11.1 / 1135 2.4 / SU 1726 11.4	**26** 051012.5 / 1154 1.4 / M 174012.8
12 0001 2.2 / 0545 11.8 / M 1224 1.8 / 1806 12.0	**27** 0016 1.1 / 055913.1 / TU 1247 0.9 / 182613.3
13 0048 1.8 / 0625 12.2 / TU 1309 1.6 / 1844 12.4	**28** 0108 0.7 / 064513.5 / W 1335 0.7 / ○ 190913.6
14 0132 1.6 / 0702 12.5 / W 1351 1.5 / ● 1919 12.5	**29** 0155 0.6 / 072913.5 / TH 1419 0.8 / 194913.5
15 0211 1.6 / 0737 12.5 / TH 1429 1.6 / 1953 12.6	**30** 0238 0.7 / 081013.3 / F 1457 1.1 / 202813.2

Chart Datum: 6·50 metres below Ordnance Datum (Newlyn). HAT is 14·7 metres above Chart Datum; see 4.5.

TIME ZONE (UT)
For Summer Time add ONE hour in **non-shaded areas**

BRISTOL (AVONMOUTH)   LAT 51°30'N   LONG 2°44'W
TIMES AND HEIGHTS OF HIGH AND LOW WATERS

Dates in red are **SPRINGS**
Dates in blue are **NEAPS**

YEAR 2010

MAY

Time m	Time m
1 SA 0314 1.1 / 0848 12.9 / 1528 1.5 / 2104 12.7	**16** SU 0255 1.6 / 0830 12.6 / 1511 1.6 / 2046 12.8
2 SU 0343 1.6 / 0924 12.3 / 1550 2.0 / 2137 12.1	**17** M 0330 1.6 / 0912 12.5 / 1545 1.7 / 2127 12.6
3 M 0406 2.0 / 0956 11.6 / 1611 2.4 / 2209 11.4	**18** TU 0406 1.8 / 0956 12.2 / 1621 1.9 / 2212 12.2
4 TU 0432 2.5 / 1029 10.8 / 1639 2.8 / 2243 10.6	**19** W 0446 2.0 / 1043 11.8 / 1703 2.2 / 2301 11.8
5 W 0507 2.9 / 1107 10.1 / 1716 3.3 / 2328 9.9	**20** TH 0533 2.3 / 1135 11.3 / 1755 2.7 / ◑ 2359 11.3
6 TH 0555 3.4 / 1200 9.5 / 1809 3.9 ◑	**21** F 0632 2.7 / 1238 10.9 / 1903 3.0
7 F 0040 9.4 / 0700 3.8 / 1321 9.2 / 1926 4.2	**22** SA 0011 11.0 / 0746 2.8 / 1356 10.7 / 2024 3.0
8 SA 0212 9.5 / 0814 3.8 / 1444 9.5 / 2049 4.0	**23** SU 0230 11.1 / 0905 2.7 / 1510 11.0 / 2140 2.6
9 SU 0318 10.0 / 0927 3.4 / 1546 10.2 / 2206 3.4	**24** M 0338 11.4 / 1016 2.4 / 1614 11.5 / 2245 2.2
10 M 0413 10.7 / 1037 2.8 / 1639 10.9 / 2310 2.7	**25** TU 0438 11.9 / 1118 2.0 / 1709 12.1 / 2343 1.7
11 TU 0501 11.3 / 1135 2.3 / 1725 11.6	**26** W 0532 12.3 / 1213 1.6 / 1759 12.5
12 W 0002 2.2 / 0545 11.8 / 1226 1.9 / 1807 12.1	**27** TH 0036 1.4 / 0620 12.6 / 1304 1.4 / ○ 1844 12.8
13 TH 0050 1.9 / 0627 12.2 / 1313 1.7 / 1847 12.5	**28** F 0126 1.3 / 0706 12.7 / 1351 1.4 / 1927 12.8
14 F 0135 1.4 / 0708 12.4 / 1356 1.6 / ● 1926 12.7	**29** SA 0212 1.3 / 0749 12.5 / 1433 1.6 / 2008 12.7
15 SA 0216 1.6 / 0749 12.6 / 1435 1.6 / 2006 12.8	**30** SU 0253 1.5 / 0830 12.3 / 1509 1.9 / 2046 12.4
	31 M 0328 1.9 / 0908 11.9 / 1538 2.2 / 2122 12.0

JUNE

Time m	Time m
1 TU 0356 2.2 / 0943 11.5 / 1601 2.5 / 2156 11.5	**16** W 0414 1.4 / 0953 12.8 / 1629 1.5 / 2209 12.9
2 W 0423 2.4 / 1015 11.1 / 1628 2.7 / 2229 11.0	**17** TH 0456 1.5 / 1039 12.5 / 1710 1.7 / 2257 12.5
3 TH 0455 2.6 / 1050 10.7 / 1702 2.9 / 2307 10.6	**18** F 0538 1.7 / 1126 12.1 / 1754 2.0 / 2347 12.1
4 F 0534 2.9 / 1130 10.3 / 1744 3.2 / ◑ 2353 10.2	**19** SA 0623 2.0 / 1218 11.6 / 1843 2.3 ◑
5 SA 0623 3.1 / 1220 10.0 / 1838 3.5	**20** SU 0045 11.5 / 0714 2.4 / 1320 11.1 / 1943 2.7
6 SU 0054 9.9 / 0721 3.3 / 1324 9.8 / 1945 3.7	**21** M 0153 11.2 / 0816 2.8 / 1429 10.9 / 2055 2.9
7 M 0205 10.0 / 0826 3.3 / 1435 10.0 / 2058 3.6	**22** TU 0302 11.0 / 0931 3.0 / 1537 10.9 / 2208 2.9
8 TU 0311 10.3 / 0934 3.1 / 1542 10.5 / 2210 3.2	**23** W 0407 11.1 / 1042 3.0 / 1640 11.2 / 2313 2.5
9 W 0412 10.8 / 1043 2.7 / 1641 11.1 / 2315 2.6	**24** TH 0507 11.4 / 1144 2.5 / 1735 11.7
10 TH 0507 11.4 / 1144 2.2 / 1733 11.8	**25** F 0010 2.1 / 0600 11.7 / 1238 2.1 / 1824 12.1
11 F 0012 2.1 / 0557 11.9 / 1238 1.9 / 1820 12.4	**26** SA 0103 1.8 / 0649 12.0 / 1329 1.9 / ○ 1910 12.3
12 SA 0104 1.8 / 0645 12.2 / 1329 1.6 / ● 1906 12.8	**27** SU 0152 1.7 / 0734 12.1 / 1415 1.8 / 1952 12.4
13 SU 0155 1.6 / 0733 12.6 / 1417 1.5 / 1952 13.0	**28** M 0238 1.7 / 0816 12.1 / 1457 1.9 / 2032 12.3
14 M 0244 1.4 / 0820 12.8 / 1504 1.4 / 2038 13.1	**29** TU 0318 1.9 / 0854 11.9 / 1531 2.1 / 2108 12.1
15 TU 0331 1.4 / 0907 12.8 / 1547 1.4 / 2124 13.1	**30** W 0350 2.1 / 0927 11.7 / 1557 2.3 / 2140 11.8

JULY

Time m	Time m
1 TH 0416 2.3 / 0958 11.5 / 1619 2.4 / 2211 11.5	**16** F 0451 0.9 / 1025 13.2 / 1703 1.1 / 2241 13.2
2 F 0441 2.3 / 1027 11.3 / 1644 2.5 / 2241 11.2	**17** SA 0526 1.2 / 1107 12.7 / 1737 1.5 / 2325 12.6
3 SA 0510 2.4 / 1059 11.0 / 1716 2.6 / 2316 10.9	**18** SU 0559 1.7 / 1150 12.0 / 1814 2.1 ◑
4 SU 0546 2.6 / 1137 10.7 / 1756 2.9 / ◑ 2359 10.5	**19** M 0013 11.7 / 0636 2.4 / 1241 11.2 / 1857 2.8
5 M 0631 2.9 / 1225 10.3 / 1847 3.3	**20** TU 0113 10.9 / 0724 3.1 / 1348 10.5 / 2000 3.5
6 TU 0055 10.2 / 0727 3.3 / 1327 10.1 / 1955 3.7	**21** W 0228 10.3 / 0836 3.7 / 1505 10.2 / 2132 3.7
7 W 0207 10.1 / 0839 3.4 / 1443 10.1 / 2118 3.6	**22** TH 0342 10.3 / 1012 3.7 / 1616 10.5 / 2250 3.3
8 TH 0324 10.3 / 0958 3.2 / 1600 10.6 / 2237 3.1	**23** F 0448 10.6 / 1121 3.1 / 1717 11.1 / 2351 2.6
9 F 0433 10.9 / 1110 2.6 / 1704 11.4 / 2344 2.4	**24** SA 0545 11.2 / 1218 2.5 / 1809 11.8
10 SA 0535 11.7 / 1212 2.1 / 1800 12.2	**25** SU 0044 2.1 / 0634 11.7 / 1310 2.0 / 1855 12.3
11 SU 0044 1.9 / 0629 12.3 / 1311 1.7 / ● 1851 12.9	**26** M 0134 1.7 / 0718 12.1 / 1358 1.7 / ○ 1936 12.5
12 M 0143 1.5 / 0720 12.9 / 1407 1.3 / 1940 13.4	**27** TU 0221 1.6 / 0759 12.2 / 1442 1.7 / 2015 12.6
13 TU 0238 1.2 / 0810 13.2 / 1459 1.1 / 2028 13.7	**28** W 0303 1.6 / 0834 12.2 / 1520 1.8 / 2048 12.4
14 W 0329 0.9 / 0858 13.4 / 1545 0.9 / 2114 13.7	**29** TH 0338 1.8 / 0906 12.0 / 1549 2.1 / 2119 12.2
15 TH 0413 0.8 / 0943 13.4 / 1626 0.9 / 2159 13.6	**30** F 0404 2.1 / 0934 11.9 / 1607 2.3 / 2146 11.9
	31 SA 0422 2.2 / 1000 11.7 / 1622 2.4 / 2212 11.6

AUGUST

Time m	Time m
1 SU 0442 2.2 / 1027 11.5 / 1647 2.4 / 2241 11.3	**16** M 0527 1.9 / 1118 12.0 / 1739 2.2 / ◑ 2338 11.6
2 M 0510 2.4 / 1059 11.2 / 1720 2.6 / 2318 10.9	**17** TU 0556 2.7 / 1201 11.0 / 1815 3.1
3 TU 0546 2.7 / 1141 10.7 / 1800 3.1 ◑	**18** W 0029 10.4 / 0636 3.5 / 1305 10.0 / 1909 4.0
4 W 0007 10.4 / 0633 3.2 / 1236 10.2 / 1856 3.7	**19** TH 0158 9.6 / 0741 4.3 / 1441 9.6 / 2054 4.4
5 TH 0115 9.9 / 0743 3.7 / 1352 9.9 / 2027 4.0	**20** F 0324 9.6 / 0950 4.3 / 1557 10.0 / 2234 3.8
6 F 0245 9.9 / 0921 3.7 / 1527 10.2 / 2210 3.5	**21** SA 0431 10.2 / 1104 3.4 / 1659 10.9 / 2334 2.8
7 SA 0413 10.6 / 1047 3.1 / 1644 11.2 / 2329 2.7	**22** SU 0527 11.0 / 1159 2.5 / 1750 11.7
8 SU 0520 11.5 / 1157 2.3 / 1745 12.3	**23** M 0024 2.0 / 0614 11.8 / 1248 1.8 / 1834 12.4
9 M 0034 1.8 / 0616 12.5 / 1259 1.6 / 1837 13.2	**24** TU 0112 1.5 / 0656 12.3 / 1335 1.5 / ○ 1914 12.8
10 TU 0134 1.2 / 0707 13.2 / 1357 1.0 / ● 1926 13.8	**25** W 0158 1.3 / 0733 12.5 / 1420 1.4 / 1950 12.8
11 W 0228 0.7 / 0755 13.7 / 1448 0.6 / 2013 14.2	**26** TH 0240 1.4 / 0807 12.4 / 1459 1.6 / 2022 12.6
12 TH 0317 0.4 / 0841 14.0 / 1533 0.4 / 2057 14.3	**27** F 0316 1.6 / 0838 12.3 / 1529 1.9 / 2052 12.4
13 F 0359 0.4 / 0923 13.9 / 1612 0.5 / 2139 14.1	**28** SA 0343 2.0 / 0905 12.1 / 1548 2.2 / 2117 12.1
14 SA 0434 0.6 / 1003 13.6 / 1645 0.9 / 2219 13.5	**29** SU 0358 2.2 / 0929 11.9 / 1558 2.3 / 2142 11.9
15 SU 0503 1.2 / 1040 12.9 / 1712 1.5 / 2257 12.7	**30** M 0412 2.2 / 0955 11.8 / 1618 2.3 / 2210 11.6
	31 TU 0437 2.3 / 1027 11.5 / 1648 2.5 / 2246 11.2

Chart Datum: 6·50 metres below Ordnance Datum (Newlyn). HAT is 14·7 metres above Chart Datum; see 4.5.

TIME ZONE (UT) For Summer Time add ONE hour in **non-shaded areas**

BRISTOL (AVONMOUTH) LAT 51°30'N LONG 2°44'W
TIMES AND HEIGHTS OF HIGH AND LOW WATERS

Dates in red are **SPRINGS**
Dates in blue are **NEAPS**

YEAR 2010

SEPTEMBER

Time m	Time m
1 W 0510 2.6 / 1107 10.9 / 1724 3.0 / ☽ 2333 10.5	**16** TH 0556 3.8 / 1223 9.6 / 1831 4.3
2 TH 0552 3.2 / 1200 10.3 / 1814 3.7	**17** F 0125 9.1 / 0659 4.7 / 1419 9.3 / 2008 4.8
3 F 0038 9.8 / 0654 3.9 / 1317 9.8 / 1938 4.3	**18** SA 0302 9.2 / 0929 4.7 / 1533 9.8 / 2213 4.0
4 SA 0217 9.6 / 0852 4.1 / 1506 10.0 / 2157 3.8	**19** SU 0407 10.0 / 1042 3.6 / 1633 10.8 / 2309 2.9
5 SU 0359 10.4 / 1034 3.3 / 1629 11.1 / 2320 2.7	**20** M 0500 10.9 / 1133 2.6 / 1723 11.7 / 2357 2.0
6 M 0506 11.6 / 1144 2.2 / 1729 12.4	**21** TU 0546 11.8 / 1220 1.8 / 1806 12.4
7 TU 0021 1.6 / 0600 12.7 / 1244 1.3 / 1820 13.5	**22** W 0043 1.5 / 0625 12.3 / 1306 1.4 / 1843 12.8
8 W 0117 0.9 / 0648 13.6 / 1338 0.7 / ● 1907 14.2	**23** TH 0128 1.3 / 0701 12.6 / 1349 1.4 / ○ 1919 12.8
9 TH 0208 0.4 / 0734 14.1 / 1428 0.3 / 1952 14.5	**24** F 0209 1.3 / 0735 12.6 / 1429 1.6 / 1952 12.7
10 F 0255 0.2 / 0817 14.3 / 1512 0.2 / 2035 14.5	**25** SA 0246 1.6 / 0806 12.5 / 1501 1.9 / 2022 12.5
11 SA 0335 0.3 / 0858 14.1 / 1549 0.5 / 2115 14.1	**26** SU 0315 1.9 / 0834 12.3 / 1523 2.2 / 2049 12.3
12 SU 0409 0.8 / 0936 13.6 / 1620 1.0 / 2153 13.4	**27** M 0332 2.2 / 0901 12.1 / 1535 2.3 / 2116 12.1
13 M 0433 1.5 / 1012 12.8 / 1644 1.7 / 2229 12.4	**28** TU 0347 2.2 / 0929 12.0 / 1556 2.3 / 2147 11.8
14 TU 0453 2.2 / 1046 11.8 / 1707 2.5 / 2305 11.2	**29** W 0412 2.3 / 1003 11.7 / 1625 2.5 / 2225 11.3
15 W 0518 3.0 / 1125 10.7 / 1740 3.3 / ☾ 2349 10.0	**30** TH 0445 2.6 / 1045 11.1 / 1703 2.9 / 2311 10.6

OCTOBER

Time m	Time m
1 F 0527 3.2 / 1139 10.4 / 1752 3.7 / ☽	**16** SA 0035 9.1 / 0625 4.6 / 1343 9.3 / 1923 4.6
2 SA 0018 9.8 / 0628 4.0 / 1256 9.9 / 1915 4.3	**17** SU 0225 9.1 / 0804 4.8 / 1458 9.7 / 2120 4.3
3 SU 0159 9.6 / 0832 4.2 / 1448 10.2 / 2142 3.8	**18** M 0330 9.8 / 1001 4.0 / 1555 10.5 / 2230 3.3
4 M 0341 10.5 / 1016 3.3 / 1608 11.3 / 2259 2.6	**19** TU 0423 10.7 / 1056 3.0 / 1646 11.4 / 2320 2.4
5 TU 0446 11.7 / 1122 2.4 / 1707 12.5 / 2358 1.6	**20** W 0509 11.5 / 1144 2.3 / 1729 12.0
6 W 0538 12.8 / 1219 1.3 / 1758 13.5	**21** TH 0006 1.8 / 0549 12.1 / 1229 1.8 / 1809 12.5
7 TH 0051 0.8 / 0625 13.6 / 1311 0.7 / ● 1844 14.1	**22** F 0051 1.5 / 0626 12.5 / 1313 1.6 / 1846 12.6
8 F 0141 0.4 / 0709 14.1 / 1400 0.4 / 1928 14.4	**23** SA 0133 1.5 / 0702 12.6 / 1353 1.7 / ○ 1921 12.7
9 SA 0226 0.4 / 0751 14.2 / 1444 0.4 / 2011 14.3	**24** SU 0211 1.6 / 0736 12.6 / 1429 1.9 / 1955 12.6
10 SU 0307 0.6 / 0831 13.9 / 1523 0.7 / 2051 13.8	**25** M 0244 1.8 / 0808 12.5 / 1457 2.1 / 2027 12.4
11 M 0340 1.1 / 0910 13.4 / 1554 1.3 / 2129 13.1	**26** TU 0309 2.0 / 0839 12.4 / 1519 2.2 / 2059 12.0
12 TU 0405 1.8 / 0946 12.6 / 1619 2.0 / 2204 12.1	**27** W 0332 2.2 / 0913 12.2 / 1544 2.3 / 2135 11.9
13 W 0425 2.5 / 1020 11.7 / 1643 2.6 / 2239 11.0	**28** TH 0400 2.3 / 0951 11.9 / 1617 2.6 / 2217 11.5
14 TH 0451 3.1 / 1057 10.7 / 1716 3.4 / ☾ 2320 10.0	**29** F 0435 2.6 / 1036 11.4 / 1657 2.9 / 2306 10.9
15 F 0527 3.9 / 1151 9.7 / 1804 4.2	**30** SA 0520 2.8 / 1130 10.8 / 1750 3.5 / ☽
	31 SU 0009 10.3 / 0623 3.7 / 1244 10.4 / 1911 3.9

NOVEMBER

Time m	Time m
1 M 0138 10.1 / 0807 3.9 / 1421 10.6 / 2106 3.5	**16** TU 0231 9.6 / 0825 4.2 / 1505 10.1 / 2108 3.8
2 TU 0311 10.7 / 0942 3.2 / 1539 11.4 / 2225 2.7	**17** W 0332 10.2 / 0946 3.7 / 1559 10.7 / 2221 3.1
3 W 0417 11.6 / 1050 2.3 / 1639 12.3 / 2326 1.9	**18** TH 0424 10.9 / 1052 3.0 / 1647 11.3 / 2319 2.5
4 TH 0511 12.5 / 1148 1.6 / 1732 13.1	**19** F 0509 11.6 / 1144 2.4 / 1731 11.9
5 F 0020 1.2 / 0559 13.2 / 1241 1.0 / 1820 13.6	**20** SA 0008 2.0 / 0551 12.1 / 1232 2.1 / 1813 12.3
6 SA 0110 0.9 / 0644 13.6 / 1331 0.8 / ● 1905 13.8	**21** SU 0054 1.8 / 0631 12.5 / 1316 1.9 / ○ 1853 12.5
7 SU 0157 0.8 / 0727 13.7 / 1417 0.8 / 1948 13.7	**22** M 0137 1.7 / 0709 12.7 / 1358 1.9 / 1932 12.6
8 M 0239 1.0 / 0808 13.5 / 1458 1.1 / 2030 13.3	**23** TU 0217 1.7 / 0747 12.8 / 1437 1.9 / 2011 12.6
9 TU 0316 1.5 / 0848 13.1 / 1533 1.6 / 2110 12.7	**24** W 0253 1.8 / 0826 12.7 / 1512 2.0 / 2051 12.5
10 W 0344 2.0 / 0926 12.5 / 1602 2.2 / 2147 11.9	**25** TH 0326 2.0 / 0905 12.6 / 1547 2.1 / 2132 12.3
11 TH 0407 2.6 / 1002 11.7 / 1628 2.7 / 2222 11.1	**26** F 0401 2.1 / 0948 12.4 / 1623 2.3 / 2215 12.0
12 F 0433 3.0 / 1039 11.0 / 1700 3.2 / 2300 10.4	**27** SA 0439 2.4 / 1033 12.0 / 1705 2.5 / 2303 11.5
13 SA 0508 3.5 / 1124 10.2 / 1743 3.7 / ☾ 2349 9.7	**28** SU 0524 2.7 / 1125 11.5 / 1755 2.9 / ☽ 2358 11.1
14 SU 0556 4.0 / 1232 9.7 / 1842 4.0	**29** M 0620 3.1 / 1227 11.1 / 1858 3.2
15 M 0107 9.3 / 0704 4.4 / 1401 9.7 / 1952 4.1	**30** TU 0107 10.7 / 0733 3.3 / 1345 11.0 / 2019 3.2

DECEMBER

Time m	Time m
1 W 0229 10.8 / 0858 3.2 / 1502 11.2 / 2141 3.0	**16** TH 0211 9.8 / 0827 4.0 / 1453 10.1 / 2109 3.6
2 TH 0341 11.2 / 1013 2.8 / 1608 11.7 / 2250 2.5	**17** F 0323 10.2 / 0943 3.7 / 1557 10.5 / 2222 3.2
3 F 0441 11.8 / 1116 2.2 / 1706 12.3 / 2349 2.0	**18** SA 0425 10.8 / 1053 3.1 / 1653 11.2 / 2325 2.6
4 SA 0534 12.4 / 1212 1.7 / 1758 12.7	**19** SU 0517 11.5 / 1152 2.5 / 1743 11.8
5 SU 0042 1.6 / 0622 12.9 / 1305 1.4 / 1846 12.9	**20** M 0019 2.1 / 0604 12.2 / 1245 2.1 / ● 1829 12.3
6 M 0131 1.4 / 0707 13.1 / 1354 1.4 / 1931 13.0	**21** TU 0109 1.8 / 0648 12.7 / 1335 1.8 / ○ 1915 12.6
7 TU 0217 1.4 / 0751 13.1 / 1439 1.5 / 2015 12.8	**22** W 0157 1.6 / 0732 13.0 / 1424 1.7 / 2000 12.8
8 W 0258 1.7 / 0832 12.9 / 1519 1.7 / 2056 12.5	**23** TH 0243 1.6 / 0816 13.2 / 1510 1.7 / 2045 12.9
9 TH 0333 2.0 / 0911 12.5 / 1552 2.1 / 2133 12.0	**24** F 0326 1.6 / 0900 13.2 / 1552 1.6 / 2128 12.9
10 F 0359 2.4 / 0948 12.0 / 1619 2.4 / 2206 11.6	**25** SA 0406 1.6 / 0944 13.1 / 1631 1.7 / 2211 12.8
11 SA 0423 2.7 / 1022 11.5 / 1647 2.7 / 2239 11.1	**26** SU 0444 1.7 / 1027 12.9 / 1708 1.8 / 2254 12.4
12 SU 0452 2.9 / 1057 11.0 / 1721 2.9 / 2315 10.6	**27** M 0522 2.0 / 1113 12.5 / 1748 2.1 / 2340 11.9
13 M 0528 3.2 / 1139 10.5 / 1803 3.2 / ☾ 2359 10.1	**28** TU 0605 2.3 / 1204 11.9 / 1833 2.5 / ☽
14 TU 0615 3.6 / 1232 10.1 / 1855 3.5	**29** W 0033 11.3 / 0656 2.8 / 1306 11.3 / 1928 3.0
15 W 0057 9.8 / 0714 3.9 / 1342 9.9 / 1958 3.7	**30** TH 0142 10.8 / 0804 3.3 / 1422 10.9 / 2046 3.4
	31 F 0302 10.6 / 0931 3.4 / 1537 10.9 / 2214 3.3

Chart Datum: 6·50 metres below Ordnance Datum (Newlyn). HAT is 14·7 metres above Chart Datum; see 4.5.

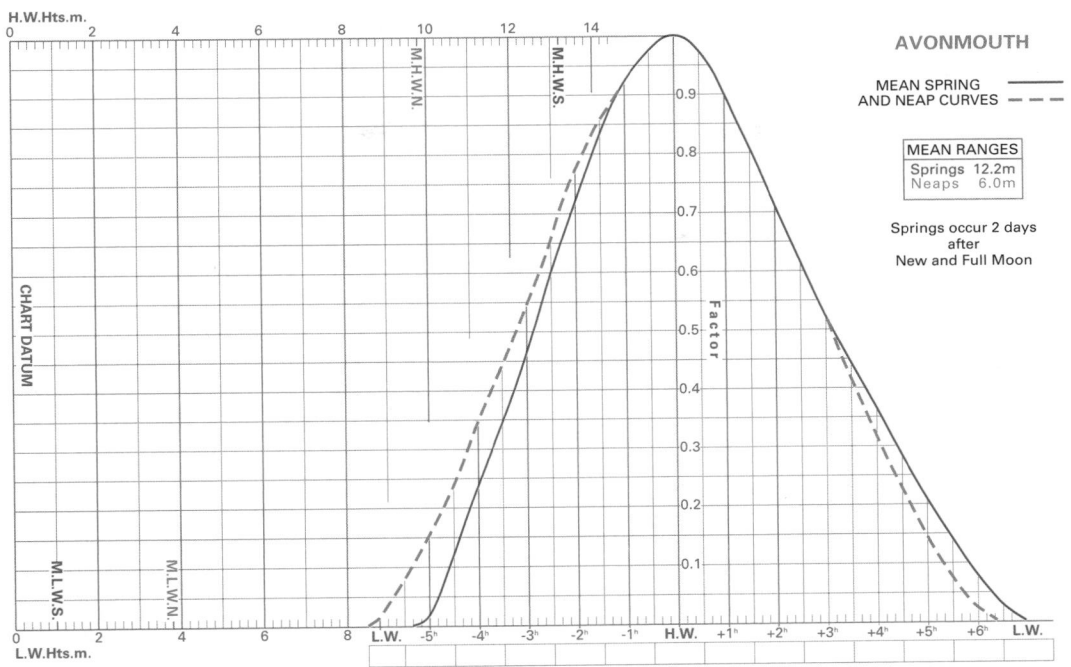

AVONMOUTH

MEAN SPRING ———
AND NEAP CURVES – – –

MEAN RANGES
Springs 12.2m
Neaps 6.0m

Springs occur 2 days
after
New and Full Moon

9.11.20   BRISTOL (CITY DOCKS)

Ent to R Avon **51°30'·44N 02°43'·31W** ✲✲⚓⚓⚓✿✿✿

CHARTS AC 5608, 1179, 1176, 1859; Imray C59; Stanfords 14.

TIDES –0410 on Dover; ML 7·0; Duration 0620. NB very large range
Standard Port BRISTOL (AVONMOUTH) (⟵)

Times				Height (metres)			
High Water		Low Water		MHWS	MHWN	MLWN	MLWS
0200	0800	0300	0800	13·2	9·8	3·8	1·0
1400	2000	1500	2000				
Differences SHIREHAMPTON (R Avon, 51°29'N 02°41'W)							
0000	0000	+0035	+0010	–0·7	–0·7	–0·8	0·0
SEA MILLS (R Avon, 51°29'N 02°39'W)							
+0005	+0005	+0105	+0030	–1·4	–1·5	–1·7	–0·1
CUMBERLAND BASIN (Ent)							
+0010	+0010	Dries		–2·9	–3·0		Dries

SHELTER Excellent in Bristol Floating Harbour. Avonmouth and Royal Portbury Docks are prohib to yachts, except in emergency. If early/late on the tide, ⚓ as close inshore as depth allows in Portishead Pool between Portishead Dock and Royal Portbury Dock, but avoid in onshore winds.

NAVIGATION **From the south and west**: from Avon SHM buoy (51°27'·92N 02°51'·73W) stay well clear to the S of the Bristol Deep shipping channel and use the *Inshore Route* (see chartlet), passing close to Portishead Pt. If using the *Offshore Route* to the north, cross the shipping channel immediately E of Denny Shoal SCM Buoy (51°30'·15N 02°45'·45W) and Firefly SHM Buoy.

From the north: use the *Inshore Route*, passing close to the entrance to Avonmouth Docks but keeping clear of disused fuel pier 2ca NE.

- Beware large ships transiting and turning in the main channel.
- Beware ships and tugs leaving the docks at any time.
- When on passage up/down the Severn estuary without stopping at Bristol or Portishead, use the *Offshore Route*.

Entering R Avon keep N of shallows (Swatch Bank) between Royal Portbury Dock and Avonmouth Docks. Speed limit 6kn in river.

LIGHTS AND MARKS Ldg lts 127°, both Iso R 2s, to R Avon ent abeam S pier lt, Oc RG 30s. St George ldg lts 173°, both Oc G 5s, front R/Or post, rear W/Or post, clear Swash Bank (dries). Upriver, G or R ✩s mark the outside of bends.

Entry signals to Bristol Hbr may be shown from E bank, 1½ and 2½ca S of Clifton Suspension Bridge: ● = continue with caution; ● = stop and await orders.

LOCKS Floating Harbour (approx 7M upriver) is accessed via Entrance Lock into Cumberland Basin and Junction Lock into Floating Hbr. Aim to reach the Ent lock no later than HW –0015; waiting pontoon (dries). Ent lock opens approx HW –2½, –1½ and –¼hr for arrivals; departures approx 15 mins after these times. Plimsoll swing bridge opens in unison with lock, except weekday rush hours 0800-0900 and 1700-1800.

Junction lock is always open, unless ht of HW is >9·6m ('stopgate' tide) when it closes; read special instructions. If you miss the last lock-in, call Ch 12 for advice. Options: dry out in soft mud at pontoons, or on N Wall (bow abreast ladder No 4 Survey Mark; no nearer the lock gate). Other areas are foul.

BRIDGES Prince St Bridge usually opens H+15, 0915-2215 summer, by arrangement in winter; pre-notify Bridgemaster ☎ 9299338, Ch 73 or sound ·—·(R). Redcliffe Bridge, pre-arrange same ☎. Clearances above HAT: St Augustine's Reach 1·8m & 0·7m; Prince St 0·7m; Redcliffe 2·1m; Bristol 2·6m. The R Avon leads to Netham lock ☎ 9776590, Keynsham, Bath and the Kennett & Avon canal.

R/T VTS Areas: *Severn VTS* Ch 69, W of Brean Down/Flatholm/ Steepholm; *Bristol VTS* Ch 12, East of *Severn VTS* area. *Bristol VTS* is friendly and helpful and will, on request, advise big ship movements and other MSI. If no radio, ☎ 0117 982 2257.

R/T procedures for R Avon and Bristol City Docks
- When inbound, call *Bristol VTS* with intentions at Welsh Hook PHM buoy and abeam Portishead Pt.
- This also applies to craft bound for Portishead marina.
- In R Avon at Nelson Point call *Bristol VTS* again, low power, confirming inbound to City Docks.
- At Black Rks (1M to run) call *City Docks Radio* Ch 14, 11 low power, (HW–3 to HW+1) for locking instructions.
- For berth: *Bristol Hbr* Ch 73, or Bristol Marina Ch 80 M.
- Departure procedure is the reverse.

Top Chart

Maintain listening watch on VHF Ch12 - Bristol VTS.

Denny Shoal (constantly changing)

S.Sh.G

Spoil Ground

Lts in line 127°

AVONMOUTH

2F.G(vert)
Oil Jetty (disused)
Kings Rd (Rear) Q.R.15m10M
Or.W

Fl.10M
Ldg Oc.R.9M

Cockburn Fl.R
R

KING ROAD
Changeable depths
Ldg R Lts 072°26'

Oc.RG.10M &
F.Bu.1M
Bell(1)10s
SS

2F.G (vert)
2F.R(vert)

F.R
F.R
Fl.R.2s

Obstn
Obstn

Avonmouth Docks (11m)

Fl.R.5s 5m3M

Iso. R.2s

Swash Channel

"Training Wall" Wharf Pt

Ldg Lts 173°17'

Iso.R.2s 10m3M
Or W

VQ(6)+LFl.10s
Denny Shoal
YB

Firefly Fl(2)G

Outer Fl.G.5s

Fl.G
LFl.G

Seabank(Front) IQ.10s13m5M

Seabank(Rear) IQ.16m5M

W Bldgs

Ship unloaders

Nelson Pt Fl.R.3s3M

Lts in line 099°34'

Obstn

Knuckle Oc.G.5s6m6M

F.G.13m6M

St George Oc.G.5s6m

Oc.G.5s9m

Portishead Pool

Obstn

Fl(3)G.15s Inner
M

Royal Portbury Dock Maintained depth 14.5m

Conveyor

Culverts (disused)

Iso.G

Obstns

Oc.G.10M

Oc.G.10M

N

Portishead Quays Marina

Portishead Dock

metres 0 — 100
cables 0 — 0.5

Facilities

TELEPHONE (Bristol code 0117) Severn VTS 0845 6018870; Bristol VTS 982 2257; Dock Master (Cumberland Basin) 9273633; Bristol weather centre 927 9298; Swansea MRCC (01792) 366534; Marinecall 0891 500459; Police 9277777; ⊞ 923 0000.

FACILITIES from seaward. **Portishead CC**, at Crockerne Pill, SW bank, 5ca upstream of the M5 motorway bridge; ☎ 01275 373988, www.portisheadcruisingclub.org.uk. Drying ⚓ (soft mud), Slip, grid (£5/day).

Bristol Hbr HM, Underfall Yard, Cumberland Rd, Bristol BS1 6XG. ☎ 9031484, www.bristol-city.gov.uk/bristolharbour Approx 40 Ⓥ AB near ent to St Augustine's Reach, £2.60 inc licence fee. FW, D, ⛽, ⚓, Slip (launching £9), CH, Gas, 🛒, R, Bar; ferries ply between various landing stages around the hbr.

Baltic Wharf Leisure Centre contact HM ☎ 9031484, Slip, L, Bar.

Bristol Marina ☎ 9213198. www.bristolmarina.co.uk Access HW–3 to +1. 100 AB, inc about 5 Ⓥ (20m max LOA), £1.97. D, ⚓, BY, El, Ⓔ, ME, ✂, Gas, Gaz, SM, Wi-fi (some berths), Slip (£1.97/m), CH, C (9 & 12 ton), BH (50 ton), ♿, 🔲.

Bathurst Basin Shower block.

Cabot CC ☎ 9268318, AB, M, FW, Bar.

City All domestic facilities, ACA, 🚆, ✈.

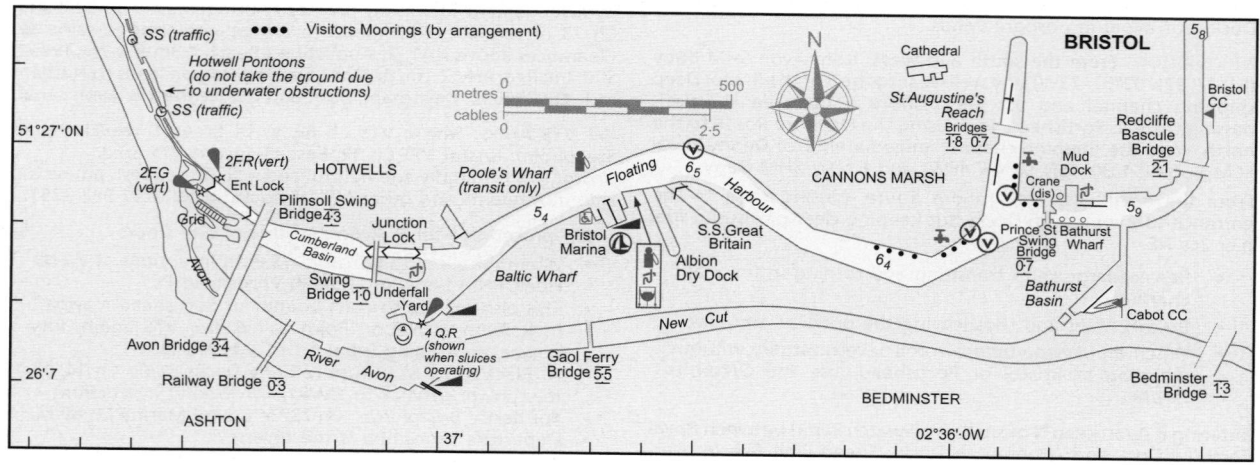

Bottom Chart (Bristol)

SS (traffic)

●●●● Visitors Moorings (by arrangement)

Hotwell Pontoons (do not take the ground due to underwater obstructions)

SS (traffic)

N

Cathedral

St.Augustine's Reach
Bridges 1.8 0.7

BRISTOL

Bristol CC

51°27'·0N

2F.R(vert)
Ent Lock

2F.G (vert)
Grid

HOTWELLS

Plimsoll Swing Bridge 4.3
Junction Lock
Cumberland Basin

Swing Bridge 1.0

Underfall Yard

Avon Bridge 3.4

Railway Bridge 0.3

ASHTON

River Avon

4 Q.R (shown when sluices operating)

Gaol Ferry Bridge 5.5

Poole's Wharf (transit only)

Floating Harbour

Bristol Marina

Baltic Wharf

Albion Dry Dock

S.S.Great Britain

New Cut

metres 0 — 500
cables 0 — 2.5

CANNONS MARSH

6.5

6.4

Crane (dis)

Mud Dock

Prince St Swing Bridge 0.7

Bathurst Wharf

Bathurst Basin

BEDMINSTER

Cabot CC

Redcliffe Bascule Bridge 2.1

5.9

Bedminster Bridge 1.3

26'·7

37'

02°36'·0W

9.11.21 PORTISHEAD

Somerset 51°29'·56N 02°45'·41W ✿✿✿✿✿✿✿✿

CHARTS AC 5608, 1176, 1859; Imray C59; Stanfords 14.

TIDES –0405 Dover; ML 6·8

Standard Port BRISTOL (AVONMOUTH) (←—)

Times				Height (metres)			
High Water		Low Water		MHWS	MHWN	MLWN	MLWS
0200	0800	0300	0800	13·2	9·8	3·8	1·0
1400	2000	1500	2000				
Differences PORTISHEAD							
–0002	0000	No data		–0·1	–0·1	No data	
CLEVEDON							
–0010	–0020	–0025	–0015	–0·4	–0·2	+0·2	0·0
ST THOMAS HEAD							
0000	0000	–0030	–0030	–0·4	–0·2	+0·1	+0·1
ENGLISH AND WELSH GROUNDS							
–0008	–0008	–0030	–0030	–0·5	–0·8	–0·3	0·0
WESTON-SUPER-MARE							
–0020	–0030	–0130	–0030	–1·2	–1·0	–0·8	–0·2

SHELTER Good in marina. Access by lock 9m x 40m x 3·5m draft (5·5m by prior arrangement) HW ±4½ (nps) ±3¾ (sp). **Ⓥ**'s available in marina. ‡ 1ca NE of pier hd (sheltered from SE to W) to await the tide for marina or Sharpness.

NAVIGATION WPT 51°29'·96N 02°45'·35W, Firefly SHM lt buoy, 168°/500m to pier hd. Firefly Rks (0·9m) are close W of the 168° appr track. Appr's dry to mud and are exposed to N/NE winds. Close inshore a W-going eddy begins at HW –3 whilst the flood is still making E.

LIGHTS AND MARKS Portishead Pt, Q (3) 10s9m 16M, is 7ca W of Portishead pierhd, Iso G 2s 5m 3M. Lock ent has 2FG(vert) and 2FR(vert) lts.

R/T See 9.11.20. Monitor *Bristol VTS* Ch **12** for shipping movements. Portishead Quays Marina VHF Ch 80 24H.

TELEPHONE (Code 01275) MRCC (01792) 366534; Marinecall 09068 969649; Police 08454 567000; Health centre 08444 773283; Ⓗ (Clevedon) 01179 872212.

FACILITIES Marina (200+**Ⓥ**), £1·65 (min charge £16.50), ☎ 841941, www.quaymarinas.com; Wi-fi, BH (35 ton), Slip, P & D, El, ME, CH, BY, SM, Gas, 🅿. **Portishead Cruising Club** ☎ 373988, Bar Town ✉, Ⓑ, ⇌, ✈ (Bristol). 3M to Junction 19 of M5.

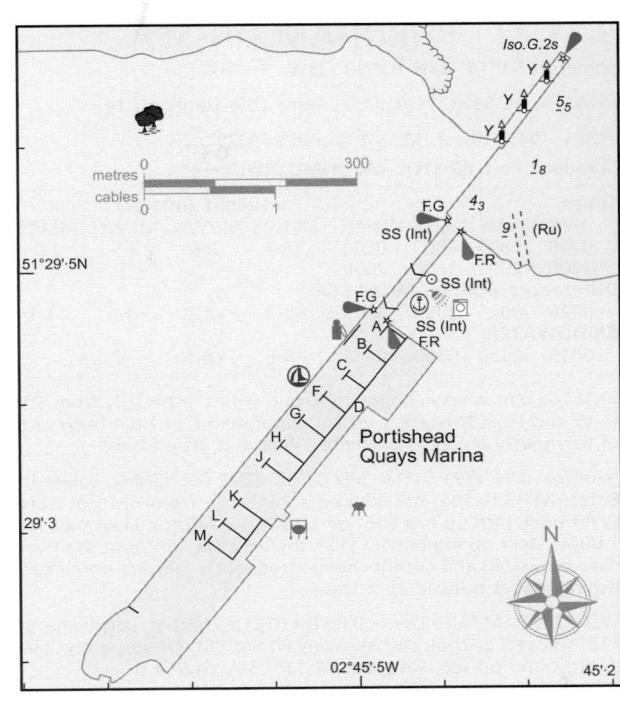

Portishead Quays Marina

ADJACENT HARBOUR

WESTON-SUPER-MARE, Somerset, **51°21'·03N 02°59'·28W**. AC 5608, 1179, 1176,1152. HW –0435 on Dover; Duration 0655; ML 6·1m. See 9.11.21. Good shelter, except in S'lies, in Knightstone Hbr (dries) at N end of bay; access HW±1½. Causeway at ent marked by bn. Grand Pier hd 2 FG (vert) 6/5m. Or ‡ in good weather in R Axe (dries), entry HW±2. Facilities: **Weston Bay YC** (located on beach) ☎ 01934 413366, M (lower R Axe), dry out on beach, FW, Bar, VHF Ch 80; **Services**: AB, CH, El, D, BH (10 ton), FW, Slip, ME, ✖; **Uphill Boat Centre** ☎ 01934 418617 AB, slip, Gas, Gaz; **Town** Bar, Ⓑ, FW, P, ✉, R, ⇌, 🛒.

AVONMOUTH TO HARTLAND POINT

(AC 1152, 1165) From Avonmouth to Sand Pt, the part-drying English Grounds extend 3M off the S shore. Portishead Quays Marina offers good shelter. Extensive mud flats fill the bays S to Burnham-on-Sea. Westward, the S shore of Bristol Chan is cleaner than N shore. But there is less shelter since the approaches to harbours such as Watchet, Minehead, Porlock Weir and Watermouth dry out.

▶ In bad weather dangerous overfalls occur NW and NE of Foreland Pt. 5M to W there is a race off Highveer Pt. Between Ilfracombe and Bull Point the E-going stream begins at HW Milford Haven + 0540, and the W-going at HW Milford Haven – 0025, sp rates 3kn. Overfalls occur up to 1·5M N of Bull Pt and over Horseshoe Rks, which lie 3M N. There is a dangerous race off Morte Pt, 1·5M to W of Bull Pt. ◀

Shelter is available under the lee of Lundy Island; but avoid bad races to NE (White Horses), NW (Hen and Chickens), and SE; also overfalls over NW Bank. ▶ W of Lundy streams are moderate, but strong around the island and much stronger towards the Bristol Channel proper. ◀

Proceeding WSW from Rivers Taw/Torridge, keep 3M off to avoid the race N of Hartland Pt (Lt, fog sig, conspic radome). There is shelter off Clovelly in S/SW winds.

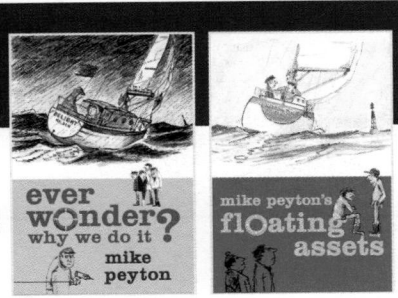

9.11.22 BURNHAM-ON-SEA

Somerset 51°14'·23N 03°00'·33W ✿⚓✿✿

CHARTS AC 5608, 1179, 1152; Imray C59; Stanfords 14.

TIDES –0435 Dover; ML 5·4; Duration 0620
Standard Port BRISTOL (AVONMOUTH) (←)

Times				Height (metres)			
High Water		Low Water		MHWS	MHWN	MLWN	MLWS
0200	0800	0300	0800	13·2	9·8	3·8	1·0
1400	2000	1500	2000				
Differences BURNHAM-ON-SEA							
–0020	–0025	–0030	0000	–2·3	–1·9	–1·4	–1·1
BRIDGWATER							
–0015	–0030	+0305	+0455	–8·6	–8·1	Dries	

SHELTER Ent is very choppy in strong winds, especially from SW to W and from N to NE. ⚓ in 4m about 40m E of No 1 buoy or S of town jetty or, for best shelter, ✓/⚓ in R Brue (dries).

NAVIGATION WPT 51°15'·32N 03°08'·22W, 095°/5M to Lower lt. Enter HW –3 to HW; not advised at night. Or from ½M S of Gore SWM buoy pick up brg 076° on Low lt ho. Approx 1½M past No 1 buoy, steer on ldg line/lts 112°; thence alter 180° into the river chan but banks and depths change frequently. Beware unmarked fishing stakes outside appr chan.

LIGHTS AND MARKS Lower lt ho Dir 076° as chartlet. Ldg lts/marks 112° (moved as chan shifts): front FR 6m 3M, Or stripe on ☐ W background on sea wall; rear FR 12m 3M, church tr.

R/T HM and Pilot VHF Ch 08 16 (when vessel expected).

TELEPHONE (Code 01278) HM 01938 822666, mob 0772 773469; harbour.master@ sedgemoor.gov.uk; Marinecall 09068 969649; Police 0845 456 7000; Ⓗ 782262.

FACILITIES **Burnham-on-Sea MB&SC** ☎ 781500, M, two drying pontoon berths in River Brue (£8), L, Bar; FW, D, 🛒. **Services:** ME, El, 🔧, ACA (Bridgwater). **Town** Gas, ✉, Ⓑ, ≠ (Highbridge), ✈ (Bristol). Note: No access to Bridgwater marina from sea/R Parrett.

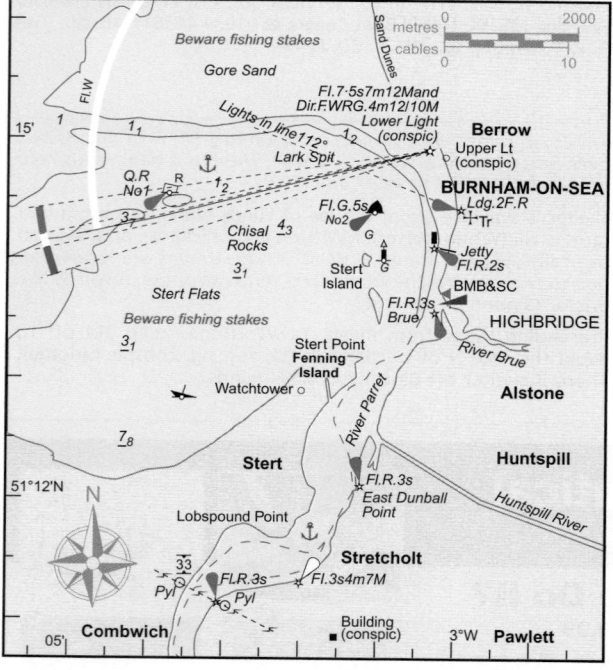

9.11.23 WATCHET

Somerset 51°11'·03N 03°19'·72W ✿⚓✿✿

CHARTS AC 5608, 1179, 1152, 1160; Imray C59; Stanfords 14.

TIDES –0450 Dover; ML 5·9; Duration 0655
Standard Port BRISTOL (AVONMOUTH) (←)

Times				Height (metres)			
High Water		Low Water		MHWS	MHWN	MLWN	MLWS
0200	0800	0300	0800	13·2	9·8	3·8	1·0
1400	2000	1500	2000				
Differences HINKLEY POINT							
–0020	–0025	–0100	–0040	–1·7	–1·4	–0·2	–0·2
WATCHET							
–0035	–0050	–0145	–0040	–1·9	–1·5	+0·1	+0·1
MINEHEAD							
–0037	–0052	–0155	–0045	–2·6	–1·9	–0·2	0·0
PORLOCK BAY							
–0045	–0055	–0205	–0050	–3·0	–2·2	–0·1	–0·1
LYNMOUTH							
–0055	–0115	No data		–3·6	–2·7	No data	

SHELTER Good, but open to N and E winds. Outer hbr (controlled by HM on VHF) dries 6·5m, but has about 6m depth at MHWS; access approx HW±2½. Marina entered through a dropping sill gate (width 7m) which is open when the tide level is at or above CD +6.92m (retained water level). Min clearance over the gate is 2.5m. Approx gate opening times HW ±2½H sp, HW ±1½H np.

NAVIGATION WPT 51°12'·03N 03°18'·88W, 208°/1.1M to hbr ent. Rks/mud dry 5ca to seaward. Beware tidal streams 4-5kn at sp offshore and around W pier hd. Movement through the marina entrance is controlled by stop/go R/G lts. Entrance max width 8m. Min retained water depths vary 1.5–3.0m. Marina subject to constant silting and some berths may not be accessible at all times. 3kn speed limit in marina.

LIGHTS AND MARKS Two unlit radio masts (206m) bearing 208° 1·6M from hbr ent are conspic approach marks. Hinkley Pt nuclear power stn is conspic 7·5M to the E. W pier hd Oc G 3s 9m 9M on Red (R) tr. E pier hd 2 FR (vert) 3M.

R/T Outer Harbour VHF Ch 16 10 12 14; Marina VHF Ch 80.

TELEPHONE (Code 01984) HM 634562, mob 07739 958441; Watchet Boat Owners Association (01643) 702569; MRCC (01792) 366534; Marinecall 09068 969649; Police 0845 456 7000.

FACILITIES **Outer Harbour** 6 drying AB on W wall, £2, also used by commercial shipping. **Watchet Harbour Marina** ☎ 631264, www.watchet-harbour-marina.com, AB (250 inc ✓) £2·54 inc ⌁, D, 🚿, CH, Gaz, ACA, BY, C (20 ton). **Town** ✉, Ⓑ, 🛒, R, Bar. At Williton (2M): Gas, D & P (cans); Ⓗ (Minehead 8M), ≠ (Taunton 18M), ✈ (Bristol).

HARBOURS ON THE SOUTH SHORE OF THE BRISTOL CHANNEL

MINEHEAD, Somerset, **51°12´·79N 03°28´·37W**. AC 1179, 1165, 1160. HW –0450 on Dover. ML 5·7m. See 9.11.23. Small hbr, dries 7·5m; access HW±2. Good shelter within pier curving E and then SE, over which seas may break in gales at MHWS; exposed to E'lies. Best appr from N or NW; beware The Gables, shingle bank (dries 3·7m) about 5ca ENE of pier. Keep E of a sewer outfall which passes ½ca E of pierhd and extends 1¾ca NNE of it; outfall is protected by rk covering, drying 2·8m and N end marked by SHM Bn QG 6m 7M. There are 3 pairs of fore and aft R ⚓s at hbr ent just seaward of 3 posts or drying alongside berth, £2, at inner end of pier. Hbr gets very crowded. Holiday camp is conspic 6ca SE. Pierhd lt Fl (2) G 5s 4M, vis 127°-262°. VHF Ch 16 12 14 (occas). HM ☎ (01984) 634562, Mob 07739 958441; **Facilities: Hbr** FW, Slip (launching £7.00). **Town** D, P, El, Gas, ME, ✕, R, Bar, 🛒, ✉, Ⓑ, ⇌ (Taunton).

PORLOCK WEIR, Somerset, **51°13´·17N 03°37´·64W**. AC 1179, 1165, 1160. HW –0500 on Dover; ML 5·6m. See 9.11.23. Access HW±1½. Ent chan (250°), about 15m wide marked by withies (3 PHM and 1 SHM), between shingle bank/wood pilings to stbd and sunken wooden wall to port is difficult in any seas. A small pool (1m) just inside ent is for shoal draft boats; others dry out on pebble banks. Or turn 90° stbd, via gates (but opening bridge usually closed),

into inner drying dock with good shelter. No lts. HM ☎ 01643 863187 (not local). **Porlock Weir SC**. Facilities: FW and limited 🛒.

LYNMOUTH, Devon, **51°14'·16N 03°49'·79W**. AC 1160,1165. HW–0515 on Dover. See 9.11.23. Tiny hbr, dries approx 5m; access HW±1, but not with particularly low Nps, but only in settled offshore weather. Appr from Sand Ridge SHM lt buoy, 1·6M W of Foreland Pt and 9ca N of hbr ent. The narrow appr chan between drying boulder ledges is marked by 7 unlit posts. After first 2 posts keep 10m away from next SH post then next 2PH posts keep to middle of ent. Hbr ent is between piers, 2FR/FG lts, on W side of river course. Berth on E pier, which covers (beware) at MHWS. Resort facilities. Admin by Council ☎ 01598 752384.

WATERMOUTH, Devon, **51°13'·03N 04°04'·6W**. AC 1179, 1165. HW –0525 on Dover; ML 4·9m; Duration 0625. Use 9.11.24. Good shelter in drying hbr, but heavy surge runs in strong NW winds. Access HW±3 at sp; only as far as inner bkwtr at np. Dir lt 153° Oc WRG 5s 1m, W sector 151·5°-154·5°, W △ on structure, 1½ca inside ent on S shore. Bkwtr, covered at high tide, has Y poles along its length and a G pole with conical topmark at the end. 9 Y ⚓s with B handles £6.50. HM ☎ (01271) 865422. Facilities: **Hbr** D (cans), FW (cans), CH, C (12 ton), Slip; **YC**, Bar. **Combe Martin** 1½M all facilities.

9.11.24 ILFRACOMBE

Devon **51°12'·65N 04°06'·65W** ✦✦⚓⚓♨♨

CHARTS AC 5608, *1179, 1165,* 1160; Imray C59; Stanfords 14.

TIDES –0525 Dover; ML 5·0; Duration 0625

Standard Port MILFORD HAVEN (←—)

Times				Height (metres)			
High Water		Low Water		MHWS	MHWN	MLWN	MLWS
0100	0700	0100	0700	7·0	5·2	2·5	0·7
1300	1900	1300	1900				
Differences ILFRACOMBE							
–0016	–0016	–0041	–0031	+2·3	+1·8	+0·6	+0·3
LUNDY ISLAND							
–0025	–0025	–0020	–0035	+0·9	+0·7	+0·3	+0·1

SHELTER Good except in NE/E winds. SW gales can cause surge in hbrs, which dry. 8 ⚓s in outer hbr, access HW±3. Or ⚓ clear of pier. Visitors AB on N snd S walls of Inner Hbr, access HW±2 or dry out on chains off foot of N Pier.

NAVIGATION WPT 51°13'·23N 04°06'·67W, 180°/0·55M to pier hd. From E, beware Copperas Rks (4M to E), and tiderips on Buggy Pit, 7ca NE of ent. On entry keep toward Pier to clear drying ledges and lobster keep-pots obstructing Hbr ent on SE side.

LIGHTS AND MARKS See 9.11.4 and chartlet.

R/T Call: *Ilfracombe Hbr* VHF Ch 12 16 (when manned).

TELEPHONE (Code 01271) HM 862108 mob 07775 532606; MRCC (01792) 366534; Marinecall 09068 969649; Police 08705 777444; Dr 863119.

FACILITIES Hbr AB and ⚓s £1·18 (inc use of showers), M, D, ⛽,(S Quay), FW, CH, Slip(launching £16·50/week), ME, El, ✕; **Ilfracombe YC** ☎ 863969, M, 🖥, Bar, C (35 ton, as arranged) **Town** 🛒, R, Bar, ✉, Ⓑ, bus to Barnstaple (⇌), ✈ (Exeter).

HARTLAND POINT TO LAND'S END

(AC 1156, 1149) The N coast of Cornwall and SW approaches to Bristol Chan are very exposed. Yachts need to be sturdy and well equipped since, if bad weather develops, no shelter may be at hand.

Bude dries, and is not approachable in W winds; only accessible in calm weather or offshore winds. Boscastle is a tiny hbr (dries) 3M NE of Tintagel Hd. Only approach in good weather or offshore winds; anch off or dry out alongside.

Padstow can be a refuge, but in strong NW winds the sea breaks on bar and prevents entry. Off Trevose Hd beware Quies Rks which extend 1M to W. From here S the coast is relatively clear to Godrevy Is, apart from Bawden Rks 1M N of St Agnes Hd. Newquay B is good anch in offshore winds, and the hbr (dries) is sheltered but uncomfortable in N winds. Off Godrevy Is are The Stones, drying rky shoals extending 1·5M offshore, marked by NCM lt buoy.

In St Ives Bay (AC 1168), Hayle is a commercial port (dries); seas break heavily on bar at times, especially with a ground swell. ▶ Stream is strong, so enter just before HW. ◀ The bottom is mostly sand. St Ives (dries) gives shelter from winds E to SW, but is very exposed to N; there is sometimes a heavy breaking sea if there is ground swell.

From St Ives to Land's End coast is rugged and exposed. There are o'falls SW of Pendeen Pt. Vyneck Rks lie awash about 3ca NW of C Cornwall. The Brisons are two high rky islets 5ca SW of C Cornwall, with rky ledges inshore and to the S. The Longships group of rks is about 1M W of Land's End. The inshore passage (001° on Brisons) is about 4ca wide with unmarked drying rks on the W side; only to be considered in calm weather and beware of fishing gear marker buoys.

For Isles of Scilly, South Cornwall and Tides, see 9.1.5.

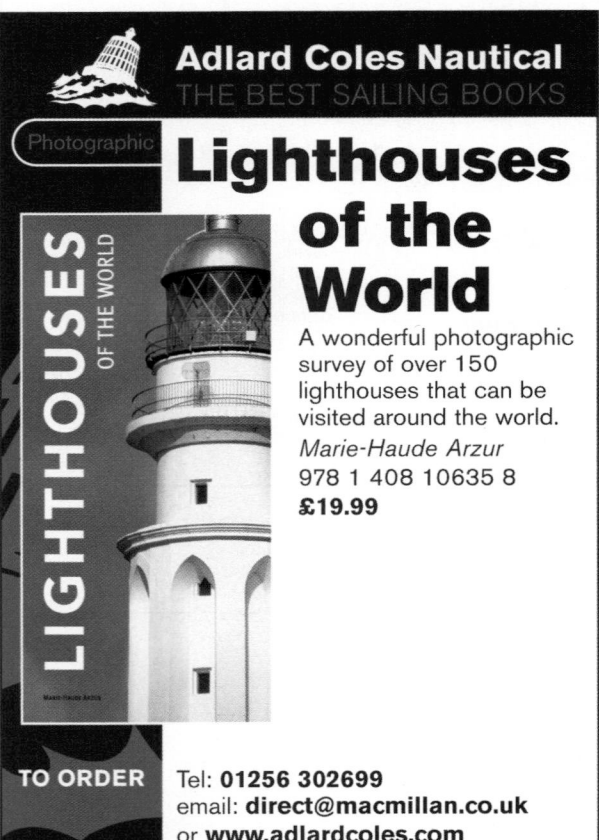
9.11.25 RIVERS TAW and TORRIDGE

Devon **51°04'·37N 04°12'·88W** ✵✺⚓⚓✿✿✿

CHARTS AC 5608, 1179, 1164, 1160; Imray C58; Stanfords 14.

TIDES –0525 (Appledore) Dover; ML 3·6; Duration 0600

Standard Port MILFORD HAVEN (←—)

Times				Height (metres)			
High Water		Low Water		MHWS	MHWN	MLWN	MLWS
0100	0700	0100	0700	7·0	5·2	2·5	0·7
1300	1900	1300	1900				
Differences APPLEDORE							
–0020	–0025	+0015	–0045	+0·5	0·0	–0·9	–0·5
YELLAND MARSH (R Taw)							
–0010	–0015	+0100	–0015	+0·1	–0·4	–1·2	–0·6
FREMINGTON (R Taw)							
–0010	–0015	+0030	–0030	–1·1	–1·8	–2·2	–0·5
BARNSTAPLE (R Taw)							
0000	–0015	–0155	–0245	–2·9	–3·8	–2·2	–0·4
BIDEFORD (R Torridge)							
–0020	–0025	0000	0000	–1·1	–1·6	–2·5	–0·7
CLOVELLY							
–0030	–0030	–0020	–0040	+1·3	+1·1	+0·2	+0·2

SHELTER Very well protected, but ent is dangerous in strong on-shore winds and/or swell. Yachts can ⚓ or pick up RNLI buoy (please donate to RNLI, Boathouse ☎ 473969) in Appledore Pool N of Skern Pt where spring stream can reach 5kn. Bideford quay dries to hard sand; used by commercial shipping.

NAVIGATION WPT 51°05'·43N 04°16'·11W, 118°/0·9M to Bar.

Bar and sands constantly shift; buoys are moved occasionally to comply. For advice on bar contact Bideford HM. Least depths over bar 0·1 and 0·4m. Estuary dries and access is only feasible from HW–2 to HW. Night entry not advised for strangers. Once tide is ebbing, breakers quickly form between Bideford Bar SHM lt buoy and Middle Ridge SHM lt buoy. Hold the ldg line 118° only up to Outer Pulley where chan deviates stbd toward Pulley buoy and Grey Sand Hill, thence to Appledore Pool. 2M passage to Bideford is not difficult. Barnstaple (7M): seek local advice or take pilot.

LIGHTS AND MARKS See 9.11.4 and chartlet. Ldg marks are W trs, lit H24. R Torridge: Lt QY at E end of Bideford bridge, 2FR vert & 2FG vert indicate preferred chan; then SHM bn, QG, on W bank.

R/T *2 Rivers Port/Pilots* VHF Ch 12 16 (From HW–2 occasional).

TELEPHONE Appledore/Bideford: Code 01237. Appledore HM 474569; Bideford HM/Pilot 475834, mob 07967 333725; Dr 474994. Instow/Barnstaple: Code 01271. Dr 372672 Common Nos: MRCC (01792) 366534; Marinecall 09068 969649; Police 08705 777444.

FACILITIES

APPLEDORE: no AB; slips at town quay. **Services:** CH, D, El, Ⓔ, BY, C (70 tons), Slip, ME, ⚒.

BIDEFORD: some AB (contact HM), FW, 🛒, R, Gas, Bar. Ferry to Lundy Is.

INSTOW: North Devon YC, ☎ 860367, FW, Slip, R, Bar; **Services:** AB and a few moorings, £5 via Instow Marine ☎ 861081, CH, D, ME, M, Ⓔ, C (4 ton). **Town** R, FW, Bar.

BARNSTAPLE: AB (free for short stay), 🛒, Bar, Gas. FW: limited facilities; P & D: small quantities in cans.

Towns ✉ (all four), Ⓑ (Barnstaple, Bideford), ⇌ (Barnstaple), ✈ (Exeter).

CLOVELLY, Devon, **51°00'·18N 04°23'·77W** ✵⚓⚓✿✿✿. AC 1164. Tides see above. HW –0524 on Dover. Tiny drying hbr, 5M E of Hartland Pt, is sheltered from S/SW winds; useful to await the tide into Bideford or around Hartland Pt. Some AB (max LOA 12m) £7 on pier, access only near HW; or ⚓ off in 5m. Lt Fl G 5s 5m 5M on hbr wall. HM ☎ (01237) 431761. Facilities: Slip, FW, ✉, limited 🛒, P, D.

RIVERS TAW & TORRIDGE *continued*

ISLAND IN BRISTOL CHANNEL, 10M NNW of Hartland Pt

LUNDY ISLAND, Devon, **51°09´·83N 04°39´·27W**. AC 5608, *1179, 1164*. HW –0530 on Dover; ML 4·3m; Duration 0605. See 9.11.24. Shore Office ☎ 01237 470074, Island ☎ 01237 431831. Beware bad tide races, esp on E-going flood, off the N and SE tips of the island; and to the SW on the W-going ebb. A violent race forms over Stanley Bank 3M NE of the N tip. Shelter good in lee of island's high ground (145m). In SSW to NW winds, usual ⚓ is close inshore to NW of SE Pt and Rat Island, clear of ferry. In N'lies ⚓ in The Rattles, small bay on S side. In E'lies Jenny's Cove is safe if no W'ly swell. Lts: NW Pt, Fl 15s 48m 17M, vis 009°-285°, W ○ tr. On SE Pt, Fl 5s 53m 15M, vis 170°-073°, W ○ tr, horn 25s. Two Historic Wrecks (see 9.0.3) lie on the E side of island, at 51°11´N 04°39´·4W, and 4ca further E. Facilities: Landing by the ⚓ off SE end of island or using N side of jetty to disembark passengers only, boats may not remain alongside; £5.00/person landing fee. The waters around Lundy are a Marine Nature Reserve. **Lundy Co**: Gas, Bar, limited stores, ✉.

MINOR HARBOURS ON THE NW COAST OF CORNWALL

BUDE, Cornwall, **50°49´·93N 04°33´·37W**. AC 5608, 1156. HW – 0540 on Dover. Duration 0605. See 9.11.26. Limited shelter in drying hbr, access HW±2 in daylight, quiet weather, no swell conditions but sea-lock gives access to canal basin with 2m. Conspic W radar dish aerials 3·3M N of hbr. Outer ldg marks 075°, front W spar with Y ◇ topmark, rear W flagstaff; hold this line until inner ldg marks in line at 131°, front W pile, rear W spar, both with Y △ topmarks. There are no lts. VHF Ch 16 12 (when vessel expected). Advise HM of ETA with 24H notice ☎ (01288) 353111; FW on quay; **Town** (½M); Ⓑ, Bar, ✉, R, 🛒, Gas.

BOSCASTLE, Cornwall, **50°41´·48N 04°42·17W**. AC 5608, 1156. HW –0543 on Dover; see 9.11.26. A tiny, picturesque hbr, almost a land-locked cleft in the cliffs. Access HW±2, but not in onshore winds when swell causes surge inside. An E'ly appr, S of Meachard Rk (37m high, 2ca NW of hbr), is best. 2 short bkwtrs at ent; moor bows-on to drying S quay. HM ☎ 01840 250453.

9.11.26 PADSTOW

Cornwall 50°32'·51N 04°56'·17W ❄❄❄🐚🐚✿✿✿

CHARTS AC 5608, 1156, 1168; Imray C58; Stanfords 13.

TIDES –0550 Dover; ML 4·0; Duration 0600

Standard Port MILFORD HAVEN (←)

Times				Height (metres)			
High Water		Low Water		MHWS	MHWN	MLWN	MLWS
0100	0700	0100	0700	7·0	5·2	2·5	0·7
1300	1900	1300	1900				
Differences BUDE							
–0040	–0040	–0035	–0045	+0·7	+0·6	No data	
BOSCASTLE							
–0045	–0010	–0110	–0100	+0·3	+0·4	+0·2	+0·2
PADSTOW							
–0055	–0050	–0040	–0050	+0·3	+0·4	+0·1	+0·1
WADEBRIDGE (R Camel)							
–0052	–0052	+0235	+0245	–3·8	–3·8	–2·5	–0·4
NEWQUAY							
–0100	–0110	–0105	–0050	0·0	+0·1	0·0	–0·1
PERRANPORTH							
–0100	–0110	–0110	–0050	–0·1	0·0	0·0	+0·1
ST IVES							
–0050	–0115	–0105	–0040	–0·4	–0·3	–0·1	+0·1
CAPE CORNWALL							
–0130	–0145	–0120	–0120	–1·0	–0·9	–0·5	–0·1

NOTE: At Wadebridge LW time differences give the start of the rise, following a LW stand of about 5 hours.

SHELTER Good in inner hbr 3m+, access via tidal gate HW±2 sp, ±1½ nps via tidal gate. If too late for gate, moor in the Pool or ⚓ close N in 1·5m LWS. Drying moorings available for smaller craft. Good AB at Wadebridge 4.5M up R Camel.

NAVIGATION WPT 50°34'·56N 04°56'·07W, 044°/ 0·6Mto Stepper Pt. From SW, beware Quies Rks, Gulland Rk, The Hen, Gurley Rk,

Chimney Rks and a wreck 5ca W of Stepper Pt (all off the chartlet). From N, keep well off Newland Island and its offlying reef.

- Best appr HW–2½, do not try LW±1½; least depth on the bar is 0·5m at MLWS. Waiting ⚓s in Port Quin Bay in lee of Rumps Pt and Mother Ivey's Bay 3M WSW Stepper Pt.
- Shifting banks in estuary require care and a rising tide (ditto the drying R Camel to Wadebridge, 4M). In doubt, consult HM.
- Identify/align 180° the first 2 chan buoys before entry. In strong onshore winds or heavy ground swell, seas can break on Doom Bar and in the adjacent chan.
- S of St Saviour's Pt the chan lies very close to W shore.

LIGHTS AND MARKS See 9.11.4 and chartlet.

R/T VHF Ch 12 16 (Mon-Fri 0800–1700 and HW+2). Water taxi.

TELEPHONE (Codes 01841; 01208 = Wadebridge) HM 532239; padstowharbour@btconnect.com; MRCC (01326) 317575; Marinecall 09068 500 458; Police 08705 777444; Dr 532346.

FACILITIES Hbr ☎ 532239, AB £1.40, 🛢, Slip(£3.50/£5.00 depends on engine hp), M, FW, El, C (60 ton), D, Gas, Gaz, ME, 🔧, showers, 🧺, R, Bar, Wi-fi; **Rock SC** ☎ (01208) 862431, Slip; **Ferry 1** to Rock, also on request as water taxi, ☎ (01326) 317575 or VHF Ch 12 16. **Services**: BY, C, ME, CH, Slip, L, 🔧. **Town** 🅿, FW, ⊠, ®, 🚌 (bus to Bodmin Parkway), ✈ (Newquay/Plymouth). **Wadebridge** HM as Padstow; AB only; **Town** 🧺, R, Bar, ⊠, ®, Wi-fi in Tourist Information Centre.

MINOR HBRS BETWEEN BOSCASTLE AND LAND'S END

PORT ISAAC, Cornwall, **50°35'·75N 04°49'·57W**. AC 1156, 1168. HW –0548 on Dover; ML 4·0m. Small drying hbr, access HW±2. Conspic ✠ tr bears 171°/1·3M. Rks close E of 50m wide ent between short bkwtrs. HM ☎ 01208 880321, mob 07855 429422; 🧺, R, Bar, ⊠, LB.

NEWQUAY, Cornwall, **50°25'·06N 05°05'·19W**. AC 1149, 1168. HW –0604 on Dover; ML 3·7m; see 9.11.26. Ent to drying hbr ('The Gap') between two walls, is 23m wide. Beware Old Dane Rk and Listrey Rk outside hbr towards Towan Hd. Swell causes a surge in the hbr. Enter HW±2 but not in strong onshore winds. Berth as directed by HM. Lts: N pier 2 FG (vert) 2M; S pier 2 FR (vert) 2M. VHF Ch 08 16 14. HM ☎ (01637) 872809 mob 07737 387217. Facilities: Gas, Gaz, CH. **Town**: FW, Slip, D, 🧺, R, Bar. Note: Shoal draft boats can dry out in Gannel Creek, close S of Newquay, but only in settled weather. Beware causeway bridge half way up creek.

PORTREATH, Cornwall, **50°15'·88N 05°17'·57W**. AC 1149. HW –0600 on Dover. Conspic W daymark (38m) at E side of ent to small drying hbr, access HW±2. Gull Rk (23m) is 3ca W of ent and Horse Rk is close N. Keep close to pier on W side of chan. AB in either of 2 basins, both dry. 🧺, R, Bar, ⊠.

HAYLE, Cornwall, **50°11'·84N 05°26'·19W** (Chan ent) ❄🐚✿. AC 1149, 1168. HW –0605 on Dover; ML 3·6m; Duration 0555. See 9.11.26. Drying hbr gives very good shelter, but is not advised for yachts. In ground swell dangerous seas break on the bar, drying 2·7m; approx 4m at ent @ MHWS. Cross the bar in good weather HW±1. Charted aids do not necessarily indicate best water. Ldg marks/lts 180°: both W □ R horiz band, ☆ FW 17/23m 4M. PHM buoy, QR is about 7ca N of the front ldg lt. Training wall on W side of ent chan is marked by 5 lit perches, all Oc G 4s. The hbr is divided by long central island (about 700m long, with lt bn QG at NW end) which should be left to stbd. Follow the SE arm of hbr to Hayle; the S arm leads to Lelant Quay. HM ☎ (01736) 754043, AB £5. Facilities: ®, Bar, FW (can), 🚌, R, 🧺, Gas, P & D (cans).

ST IVES, Cornwall, **50°12'·79N 05°28'·67W** ❄❄🐚🐚✿✿✿. AC 1149, 1168. HW –0610 on Dover; ML 3·6m; Duration 0555. See 9.11.26. Drying hbr with about 4·5m @ MHWS. Good shelter except in on-shore winds when heavy swell works in. 🅰s and ⚓ in 3m between the hbr and Porthminster Pt to S and drying Or 🅰s in hbr. From the NW beware Hoe Rk off St Ives Hd, and from SE The Carracks. Keep E of SHM buoy about 1½ ca ENE of E pier. Lts: E pier hd 2 FG (vert) 8m 5M. W pier hd 2 FR (vert) 5m 3M. VHF Ch 12 16 (occas). HM ☎ (01736) 795018. Facilities: 🅰s £12.13; **E Pier** FW. **Town** Gas, Gaz, ®, 🔧, Bar, ⊠, R, 🧺, 🚂.

South Ireland

Malahide clockwise to Liscannor Bay

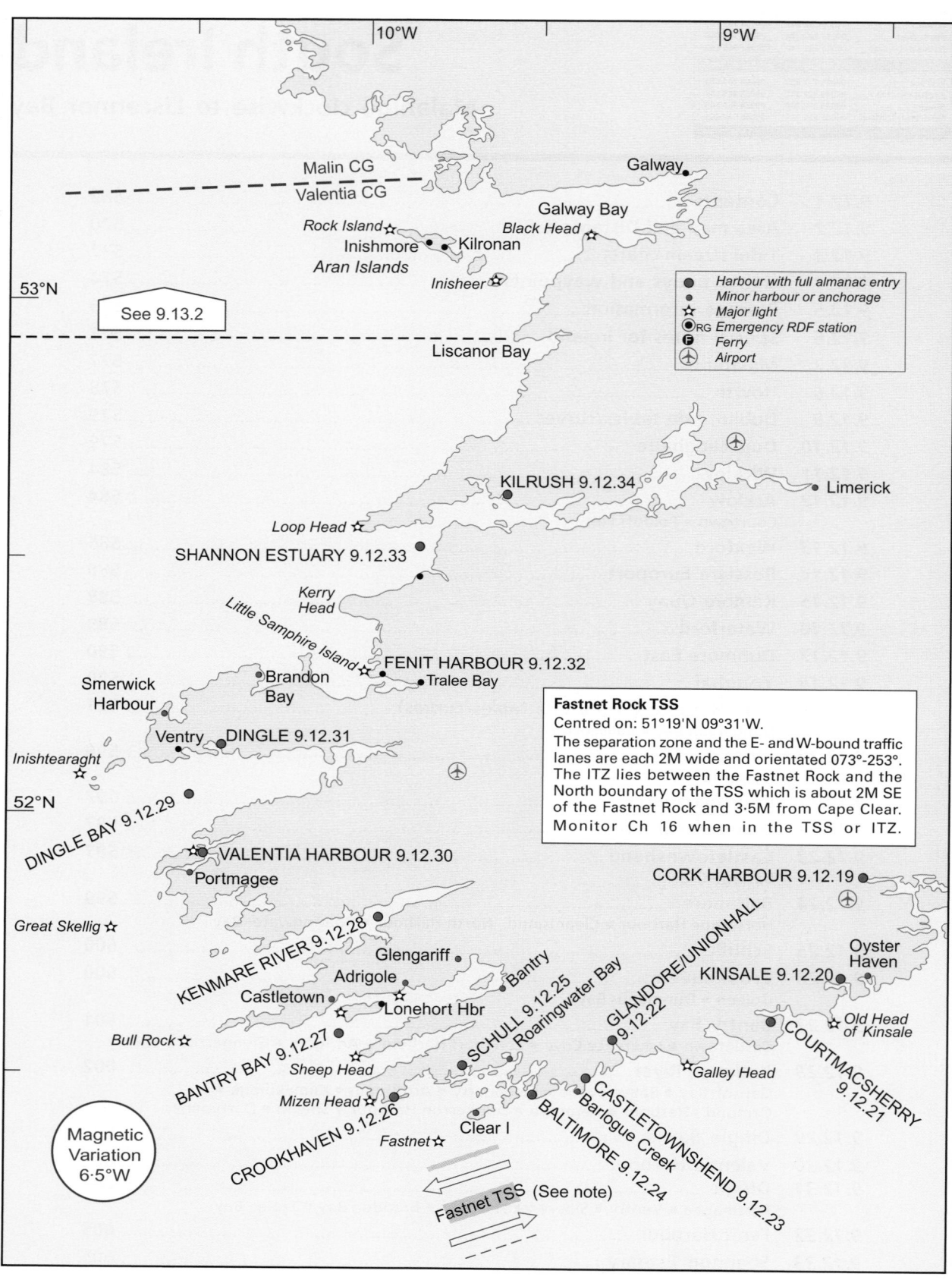

10°W

9°W

Malin CG

Valentia CG

Galway

Galway Bay

Rock Island ☆

Black Head ☆

Inishmore

Kilronan

Aran Islands

Inisheer ☆

53°N

See 9.13.2

Liscanor Bay

●	Harbour with full almanac entry
•	Minor harbour or anchorage
☆	Major light
⊙RG	Emergency RDF station
Ⓕ	Ferry
✈	Airport

KILRUSH 9.12.34

Limerick

Loop Head ☆

SHANNON ESTUARY 9.12.33

Kerry Head

Little Samphire Island

Smerwick Harbour

Brandon Bay

FENIT HARBOUR 9.12.32

Tralee Bay

Inishtearaght

Ventry

DINGLE 9.12.31

Fastnet Rock TSS
Centred on: 51°19'N 09°31'W.
The separation zone and the E- and W-bound traffic lanes are each 2M wide and orientated 073°-253°. The ITZ lies between the Fastnet Rock and the North boundary of the TSS which is about 2M SE of the Fastnet Rock and 3·5M from Cape Clear. Monitor Ch 16 when in the TSS or ITZ.

52°N

DINGLE BAY 9.12.29

VALENTIA HARBOUR 9.12.30

Portmagee

CORK HARBOUR 9.12.19

Great Skellig ☆

Oyster Haven

KENMARE RIVER 9.12.28

Glengariff

Bantry

KINSALE 9.12.20

Adrigole

Castletown

Old Head of Kinsale

Lonehort Hbr

SCHULL 9.12.25

Roaringwater Bay

GLANDORE/UNIONHALL 9.12.22

COURTMACSHERRY 9.12.21

Bull Rock ☆

BANTRY BAY 9.12.27

Sheep Head

Galley Head ☆

Mizen Head ☆

CASTLETOWNSHEND 9.12.23

Barlogue Creek

Magnetic Variation 6·5°W

CROOKHAVEN 9.12.26

Clear I

BALTIMORE 9.12.24

Fastnet ☆

Fastnet TSS (See note)

		1																		
1.	*Carlingford Lough*	1																		
2.	Howth	39	2																	
3.	**Dun Laoghaire**	48	8	3																
4.	**Wicklow**	63	25	21	4															
5.	**Arklow**	75	37	36	15	5														
6.	**Tuskar Rock**	113	73	70	52	37	6													
7.	**Rosslare**	108	70	66	47	34	8	7												
8.	**Dunmore East**	139	101	102	84	69	32	32	8											
9.	**Youghal**	172	134	133	115	100	63	65	34	9										
10.	**Crosshaven**	192	154	155	137	122	85	85	59	25	10									
11.	**Kinsale**	202	164	168	150	135	98	95	69	35	17	11								
12.	**Baltimore**	239	201	196	177	164	128	132	102	70	54	42	12							
13.	**Fastnet Rock**	250	212	207	189	174	137	144	112	78	60	49	10	13						
14.	Bantry	281	243	241	223	208	171	174	146	112	94	83	42	34	14					
15.	Darrynane	283	245	240	221	208	172	176	146	114	98	86	44	39	38	15				
16.	Valentia	295	257	252	242	227	184	188	165	131	113	102	56	48	55	16	16			
17.	Dingle	308	270	265	246	233	197	201	171	139	123	111	69	61	63	29	13	17		
18.	Kilrush	361	323	318	299	286	250	254	224	192	176	164	122	114	116	82	66	64	18	
19.	*Galway*	366	362	357	339	324	287	291	262	228	210	199	159	150	155	119	103	101	76	19
20.	*Slyne Head*	317	351	346	328	313	276	283	251	217	199	188	153	139	144	113	97	95	75	49	20

DISTANCE TABLE

Approximate distances in nautical miles are by the most direct route, whilst avoiding dangers and allowing for Traffic Separation Schemes. Places in *italics* are in adjoining areas; places in **bold** are in 9.0.6, Distances across the Irish Sea.

9.12.2

South Ireland
Malahide clockwise to Liscanor Bay

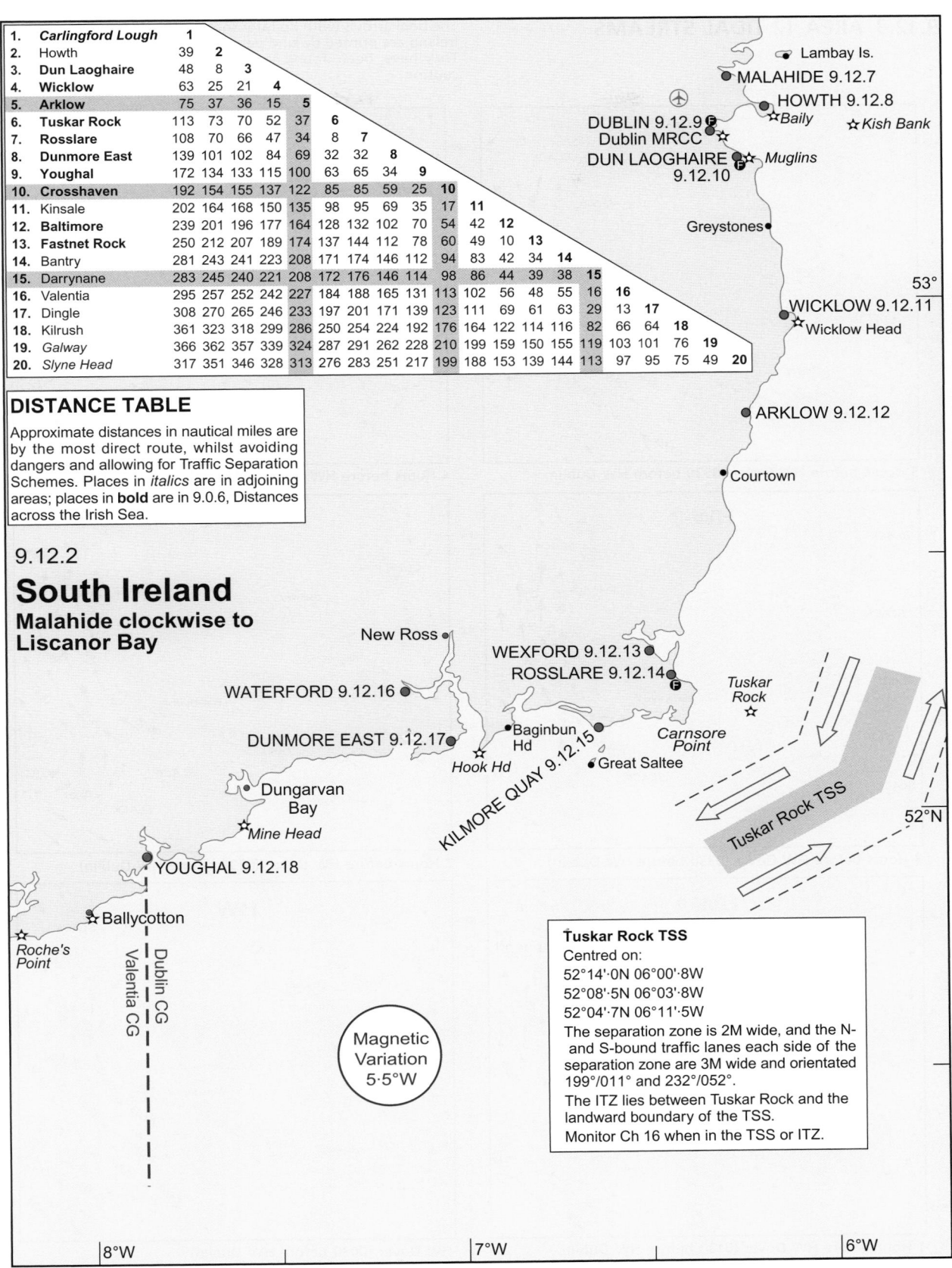

Tuskar Rock TSS

Centred on:
52°14'·0N 06°00'·8W
52°08'·5N 06°03'·8W
52°04'·7N 06°11'·5W
The separation zone is 2M wide, and the N- and S-bound traffic lanes each side of the separation zone are 3M wide and orientated 199°/011° and 232°/052°.
The ITZ lies between Tuskar Rock and the landward boundary of the TSS.
Monitor Ch 16 when in the TSS or ITZ.

Magnetic Variation 5·5°W

9.12.3 AREA 12 TIDAL STREAMS

The tidal arrows (with no rates shown) off the S and W coasts of Ireland are printed by kind permission of the Irish Cruising Club. They have been found accurate, but should be used with caution.

5 Hours before HW Dover (0530 before HW Dublin)

4 Hours before HW Dover (0430 before HW Dublin)

3 Hours before HW Dover (0330 before HW Dublin)

2 Hours before HW Dover (0230 before HW Dublin)

1 Hour before HW Dover (0130 before HW Dublin)

HW Dover (0030 before HW Dublin)

Northward 9.13.3   South Irish Sea 9.11.3

The tidal arrows (with no rates shown) off the S and W coasts of Ireland are printed by kind permission of the Irish Cruising Club. They have been found accurate, but should be used with caution.

1 Hour after HW Dover (0030 after HW Dublin)

2 Hours after HW Dover (0130 after HW Dublin)

3 Hours after HW Dover (0230 after HW Dublin)

4 Hours after HW Dover (0330 after HW Dublin)

5 Hours after HW Dover (0430 after HW Dublin)

6 Hours after HW Dover (0530 after HW Dublin)

S Ireland

9.12.4 LIGHTS, BUOYS AND WAYPOINTS

Bold print = light with a nominal range of 15M or more. CAPITALS = place or feature. *CAPITAL ITALICS* = light-vessel, light float or Lanby. *Italics* = Fog signal. ***Bold italics*** = Racon. Abbreviations are in Chapter 1.

LAMBAY ISLAND TO TUSKAR ROCK
MALAHIDE and LAMBAY ISLAND
Taylor Rks ⚓ Q; 53°30'·21N 06°01'·87W.
Malahide approach ⚓ L Fl 10s; 53°27'·12N 06°06'·87W.

HOWTH
Rowan Rocks ⚓ Q (3) 10s; 53°23'·88N 06°03'·27W.
E Pier Hd ⚡ Fl (2) WR 7·5s 13m W12M, R9M; W twr; vis: W256°-R295°-256°; 53°23'·66N 06°04'·03W.

Baily ☆ 53°21'·70N 06°03'·14W Fl 15s 41m **26M**; twr. Fog Det Lt VQ.

Rosbeg E ⚓ Q (3) 10s; 53°21'·02N 06°03'·45W.
Rosbeg S ⚓ Q (6) + L Fl 15s; 53°20'·22N 06°04'·17W.

PORT OF DUBLIN
Dublin Bay ⚓ Mo (A) 10s; ***Racon (M);*** 53°19'·92N 06°04'·64W.
No. 1 ⚓ Fl (3) G 5s; 53°20'·30N 06°05'·56W.
No. 3 ⚓ IQ G; 53°20'·57N 06°06'·76W.
No. 4 ⚓ IQ R; 53°20'·48N 06°06'·93W.
No. 5 ⚓ Fl G 2s; 53°20'·64N 06°08'·60W.
No. 6 ⚓ Fl R 2s; 53°20'·56N 06°08'·75W.

Great S Wall Hd Poolbeg ☆ Fl R 4s 20m 10M *(synchro with N.Bull)*; R ◯ twr; *Horn (2) 60s*; 53°20'·53N 06°09'·08W
N Bull ☆ Fl G 4s 15m 10M; G ◯ twr; 53°20'·70N 06°08'·98W.
N Bank ☆ 53°20'·69N 06°10'·59W Oc G 8s 10m **16M**; G ☐ twr.

DUN LAOGHAIRE
E Bkwtr Hd ⚡ Fl (2) R 8s 16m **17M**; twr, R lantern; 53°18'·15N 06°07'·62W. *Horn 30s.* Fog Det Lt VQ.

Outfall ⚓ Fl Y 5s; 53°18'·41N 06°08'·35W.
Muglins ⚡Fl R 5s 14m 11M; 53°16'·52N 06°04'·58W.

OFFSHORE MARKS
Bennett Bank ⚓ Q (6) + L Fl 15s; 53°20'·17N 05°55'·11W.

Kish Bank ☆ 53°18'·64N 05°55'·48W Fl (2) 20s 29m **22M**; W twr, R band; ***Racon (T) 15M***; *Horn (2) 30s.* Fog Det Lt VQ.
N Kish ⚓ VQ; 53°18'·56N 05°56'·44W.
E Kish ⚓ Fl (2) R 10s; 53°14'·35N 05°53'·56W.
E Codling ⚓ Fl (4) R 10s; 53°08'·54N 05°47'·11W.
W Codling ⚓ Fl G 10s; 53°06'·97N 05°54'·51W.
S Codling ⚓ VQ (6) + L Fl 10s; 53°04'·74N 05°49'·76W.
Breaches Shoal ⚓ Fl (2) R 6s; 53°05'·67N 05°59'·81W.
North India ⚓ Q; 53°03'·12N 05°53'·46W.
South India ⚓ Q (6) + L Fl 15s; 53°00'·36N 05°53'·31W.

CODLING LANBY ⚓ 53°03'·02N 05°40'·76W Fl 4s 12m **15M**; tubular structure on By; ***Racon (G)10M***; *Horn 20s.*

WICKLOW to ARKLOW
Wicklow ⚓ Fl (4) Y 10s; 52°59'·54N 06°01'·29W.
E Pier Hd ⚡ Fl WR 5s 11m 6M; W twr, R base and cupola; vis: 136°-R-293°-W-136°; 52°58'·99N 06°02'·07W.
W Packet Quay Hd ⚡ Fl WG 10s 5m 6M; vis: 076°-G-256°-W-076°; 52°58'·88N 06°02'·08W.

Wicklow Head ☆ 52°57'·95N 05°59'·89W Fl (3) 15s 37m **23M**; W twr.

Horseshoe ⚓ Fl R 3s; 52°56'·62N 05°59'·31W.
N Arklow ⚓ Q; 52°53'·86N 05°55'·21W.
Arklow Bank Wind Farm from 52°48'·47N 05°56'·57W to 52°46'·47N 05°57'·11W, N and S Turbines Fl Y 5s14m 10M + Fl W Aero lts. AIS transmitters. Other turbines Fl Y 5s. See 9.12.5.

ARKLOW to WEXFORD
S Pier Hd ⚡ Fl WR 6s 11m 13M; twr; vis: R shore- W223°- R350°-shore; 52°47'·61N 06°08'·22W.
Roadstone Bkwtr Hd ⚡ QY; 52°46'·65N 06°08'·23W.
S Arklow ⚓ VQ (6) + L Fl 10s; 52°40'·82N 05°59'·21W.

ARKLOW LANBY ⚓ 52°39'·52N 05°58'·16W Fl (2) 12s 12m **15M**; ***Racon (O)10M***; *Horn Mo (A) 30s.*
No. 2 Glassgorman ⚓ Fl (4) R 10s; 52°44'·52N 06°05'·36W.
No. 1 Glassgorman ⚓ Fl (2) R 6s; 52°39'·08N 06°07'·42W.
N Blackwater ⚓ Q; 52°32'·22N 06°09'·51W.
No. 6 Rusk ⚓ Fl R 3s; 52°32'·65N 06°10'·41W.
No. 4 Rusk ⚓ Fl (2) R 5s; 52°31'·07N 06°10'·86W.
No. 2 Rusk ⚓ Fl (2) R 5s; 52°28'·64N 06°12'·61W.
No. 1 Rusk ⚓ Fl (2) G 5s; 52°28'·54N 06°11'·80W.
W Blackwater ⚓ Fl G 6s; 52°25'·87N 06°13'·56W.
SE Blackwater ⚓ Fl R 10s; 52°25'·64N 06°09'·66W.
S Blackwater ⚓ Q (6) + L Fl 15s; 52°22'·76N 06°12'·87W.
North Long ⚓ Q; 52°21'·44N 06°17'·04W.
West Long ⚓ QG; 52°18'·18N 06°17'·96W.
Lucifer ⚓ VQ (3) 5s; 52°17'·02N 06°12'·67W.

ROSSLARE
S Long ⚓ VQ (6) + L Fl 10s; 52°14'·84N 06°15'·64W.
Splaugh ⚓ Fl (2) R 6s; 52°14'·37N 06°16'·76W.
South Holdens ⚓ Fl G 3s; 52°15'·14N 06°17'·24W. (Synch with Calmines)
Calmines ⚓ Fl R 3s; 52°15'·01N 06°17'·77W. (Synch with S Holdens)
W Holdens ⚓ Fl (3) G 10s; 52°15'·77N 06°18'·74W.
Rosslare Pier Hd ⚡ Oc WRG 5s 15m W13M, R10M, G10M; R twr; vis:098°-G-188°-W-208°-R-246°-G-283°-W-286°-R-320°; 52°15'·43N 06°20'·29W.
Ballygeary ⚡Oc WR 1·7s 7m 4M vis: shore-R-152°-W-200°-W(unintens)-205°; 52°15'·25N 06°20'·48W .

TUSKAR ROCK TO OLD HEAD OF KINSALE
Tuskar ☆ 52°12'·17N 06°12'·42W Q (2) 7·5s 33m **24M**; W twr; *Horn (4) 45s*, ***Racon (T) 18M***.
S Rock ⚓ Q (6) + L Fl 15s; 52°10'·80N 06°12'·84W.
Fundale ⚓ Fl (2) R 10s; 52°11'·04N 06°19'·78W.
Barrels ⚓ Q (3) 10s; 52°08'·32N 06°22'·05W.

KILMORE
Kilmore Quay SWM ⚓ Iso 10s; (Apr-Sep); 52°09'·20N 06°35'·30W.
Kilmore Bkwtr Hd ⚡ Q RG 7m 5M; vis: 269°-R-354°-G-003°-R-077°; 52°10'·20N 06°35'·15W.
Ldg lts 007·9°, Front 52°10'·37N 06°35'·08W Oc 4s 3m 6M. Rear, 100m from front, Oc 4s 6m 6M; sync with front.
Coningbeg ⚓ Q(6)+LFl 15s, Racon, AIS; 52°03'·20N 06°38'·57W.
'M5' ODAS 35 ⚓ 51°41'·40N 06°42'·24W; Fl (5) Y 20s.

WATERFORD
Hook Hd ☆ 52°07'·32N 06°55'·85W Fl 3s 46m **23M**; W twr, two B bands; ***Racon (K) 10M vis 237°-177°***; *Horn (2) 45s*. Fog Det Lt VQ.
Waterford ⚓ Fl R 3s. Fl (3) R 10s; 52°08'·95N 06°57'·00W.
Duncannon Dir lt ⚡ F WRG 13m 10M, white tower on fort, 359·5°-FG-001·2°-Alt GW-001·7°-FW-002·4°-Alt WR-002·9°-FR-004·5°; 52°13'·23N 06°56'·25W; Oc WR 4s 13m W 9M R 7M on same tower, 119°-R-149°-W-172°.
Passage Pt ⚡ Fl WR 5s 7m W6M, R5M; R pile structure; vis: W shore- R127°-302°; 52°14'·26N 06°57'·77W.
Cheek Pt ⚡ Q WR 6m 5M; W mast; vis: W007°-R289°-007°; 52°16'·12N 06°59'·38W.
Sheagh ⚡ Fl R 3s 29m 3M; Gy twr; vis: 090°-318°; 52°16'·29N 06°59'·34W.
Snowhill Point Ldg lts 255°. Front, Fl WR 2·5s 5m 3M; vis: W222°-R020°- W057°-107°; 52°16'·39N 07°00'·91W. Rear, Flour Mill, 750m from front, Q 12m 5M.

WGS84 DATUM
Plot waypoints on chart before use

Queen's Chan Ldg lts 098°. Front, QR 8m 5M; B twr, W band; vis: 030°-210°;52°15'·32N 07°02'·38W. Rear, 550m from front, Q 15m 5M; W mast.

Beacon Quay ⚓ Fl G 3s 9m; vis: 255°-086°; 52°15'·50N 07°04'·21W.

Cove ⚓ Fl WRG 6s 6m 2M; W twr; vis: R111°- G161°- W234°-111°; 52°15'·05N 07°05'·16W.

Smelting Ho Pt ⚓ Q 8m 3M; W mast; 52°15'·15N 07°05'·27W.

Ballycar ⚓ Fl RG 3s 5m; vis: G127°- R212°-284°; 52°15'·06N 07°05'·51W.

DUNMORE EAST
East Pier Head ☆ 52°08'·93N 06°59'·37W Fl WR 8s 13m **W17M**, R13M; Gy twr, vis: W225°- R310°-004°.

W Wharf ⚓ Fl G 2s 6m 4M; vis: 165°-246°; 52°08'·97N 06°59'·45W.

DUNGARVAN
Ballinacourty Point ⚓ Fl (2) WRG 10s 16m W10M, R8M, G8M; W twr; vis: G245°- W274°- R302°- W325°-117°; 52°04'·69N 07°33'·18W.

Helvick ⚓ Q (3) 10s; 52°03'·61N 07°32'·25W.

Mine Head ☆ 51°59'·52N 07°35'·25W Fl (4) 30s 87m **20M**; W twr, B band; vis: 228°-052°.

YOUGHAL
Bar Rocks ⚓ Q (6) + L Fl 15s; 51°54'·85N 07°50'·05W.

Blackball Ledge ⚓ 51°55'·34N 07°48'·53W Q (3) 10s.

W side of ent ☆ 51°56'·57N 07°50'·53W Fl WR 2·5s 24m **W17M**, R13M; W twr; vis: W183°- R273°- W295°- R307°- W351°-003°.

BALLYCOTTON
Ballycotton ☆ 51°49'·52N 07° 59'·09W Fl WR 10s 59m **W22M, R18M**; B twr, within W walls, B lantern; vis: W238°- R048°-238°; *Horn (4) 90s*. Fog Det Lt VQ.

The Smiths ⚓ Fl (3) R 10s; 51°48'·62N 08°00'·71W.

Power ⚓ Q (6) + L Fl 15s; 51°45'·59N 08°06'·67W.

CORK
Cork ⚓ L Fl 10s; *Racon (T) 7M*; 51°42'·92N 08°15'·60W.

Daunt Rock ⚓ Fl (2) R 6s; 51°43'·52N 08°17'·65W.

Fort Davis Ldg lts 354·1°. Front, 51°48'·82N 08°15'·80W Dir WRG 29m **17M**; vis: FG351·5°-AlWG352·25°-FW353°-AlWR355°-FR355·75°-356·5°. Rear, Dognose Quay, 203m from front, Oc 5s 37m 10M; Or 3, synch with front.

Roche's Point ☆ 51°47'·59N 08°15'·29W Fl WR 3s 30m **W20M, R16M**; vis: Rshore- W292°- R016°- 033°, W (unintens) 033°- R159°- shore.

Outer Hbr Rk E2 ⚓ Fl R 2·5s; 51°47'·52N 08°15'·67W.

Chicago Knoll E1 ⚓ Fl G 5s; 51°47'·66N 08°15'·54W.

W1 ⚓ Fl G 10s; 51°47'·69N 08°16'·05W.

W2 ⚓ Fl R 10s; 51°47'·69N 08°16'·34W.

White Bay Ldg lts 034·6°. Front, Oc R 5s 11m 5M; W hut; 51°48'·53N 08°15'·22W. Rear, 113m from front, Oc R 5s 21m 5M; W hut; synch with front.

Spit Bank Pile ⚓ Iso WR 4s 10m W10M, R7M; W house on R piles; vis: R087°- W196°- R221°- 358°; 51°50'·72N 08°16'·45W.

KINSALE and OYSTER HAVEN
Bulman ⚓ Q (6) + L Fl 15s; 51°40'·14N 08°29'·74W.

Charle's Fort ⚓ Fl WRG 5s 18m W9M, R6M, G7M; vis: G348°- W358°- R004°-168°; H24; 51°41'·74N 08°29'·97W.

OLD HEAD OF KINSALE TO MIZEN HEAD
Old Head of Kinsale ☆, S point 51°36'·28N 08°32'·03W Fl (2) 10s 72m **20M**; B twr, two W bands; *Horn (3) 45s*.

COURTMACSHERRY
Barrel Rock ⚓ 51°37'·01N 08°37'·30W.

Black Tom ⚓ Fl G 5s; 51°36'·41N 08°37'·95W.

Wood Pt (Land Pt) ⚓ Fl (2) WR 5s 15m 5M; vis: W315°- R332°-315°; 51°38'·16N 08°41'·00W.

Galley Head ☆ summit 51°31'·80N 08°57'·19W Fl (5) 20s 53m **23M**; W twr; vis: 256°-065°.

GLANDORE and CASTLETOWNSHEND
Reen Point ⚓ Fl WRG 10s 9m W5M, R3M, G3M; W twr; vis: Gshore- W338°- R001°-shore; 51°30'·98N 09°10'·50W.

Kowloon Bridge ⚓ Q (6) + L Fl 15s; 51°27'·58N 09°13'·75W.

BALTIMORE and FASTNET
Barrack Pt ⚓ Fl (2) WR 6s 40m W6M, R3M; vis: R168°- W294°-038°; 51°28'·33N 09°23'·65W.

Loo Rock ⚓ Fl G 3s; 51°28'·43N 09°23'·45W.

Fastnet ☆, W end 51°23'·35N 09°36'·19W Fl 5s 49m **27M**; Gy twr, *Horn (4) 60s, Racon (G) 18M*. Fog Det Lt VQ.

SCHULL and LONG ISLAND CHANNEL
Ldg lts 346° Front, Oc 5s 5m 11M, W mast; 51°31'·68N 09°32'·43W. Rear, 91m from front, Oc 5s 8m11M; W mast.

CROOKHAVEN
Rock Is Pt ⚓ L Fl WR 8s 20m W13M, R11M; W twr; vis: W over Long Is B to 281°-R-340°; inside harbour 281°-R-348°- towards N shore; 51°28'·59N 09°42'·29W.

MIZEN HEAD TO DINGLE BAY
Mizen Head ☆ 51°27'·00N 09°49'·24W Iso 4s 55m **15M**; vis: 313°-133°.

Sheep's Hd ☆ 51°32'·60N 09°50'·95W Fl (3) WR 15s 83m **W18M, R15M**; W bldg; vis: 007°-R-017°-W-212°.

BANTRY BAY, CASTLETOWN BEARHAVEN, WHIDDY ISLE, BANTRY and GLENGARIFF
Roancarrigmore ☆ 51°39'·19N 09°44'·83W Fl WR 3s 18m **W18M**, R14M; W □ twr, B band; vis: 312°-W-050°-R-122°-R (unintens)-242°-R-312°. Reserve lt W8M, R6M obsc 140°-220°.

Ardnakinna Pt ☆ 51°37'·11N 09°55'·08W Fl (2) WR 10s 62m **W17M**, R14M; W ○ twr; vis: 319°-R- 348°-W- 066°-R-shore.

Castletown Dir lt 024° ⚓ Oc WRG 5s 4m W14M, R11M, G11M; W hut, R stripe; vis: 020·5°-G-024°-W-024·5°-R-027·5°; 51°38'·79N 09°54'·30W.

Castletown Ldg lts 010°. Front, Oc 3s 4m 1M; W col, R stripe; vis: 005°-015°; 51°39'·16N 09°54'·40W. Rear, 80m from front, Oc 3s 7m 1M; W with R stripe; vis: 005°-015°.

Bull Rock ☆ 51°35'·51N 10°18'·08W Fl 15s 83m **21M**; W twr; vis: 220°-186°.

KENMARE RIVER, DARRYNANE and BALLYCROVANE
Darrynane Ldg lts 034°. Front, Oc 3s 10m 4M; 51°45'·90N 10°09'·20W. Rear, Oc 3s 16m 4M.

Skelligs Rock ☆ 51°46'·12N 10°32'·51W Fl (3) 15s 53m **19M**; W twr; vis: 262°-115°; part obsc within 6M 110°-115°.

VALENTIA and PORTMAGEE
Fort (Cromwell) Point ☆ 51°56'·02N 10°19'·27W Fl WR 2s 16m **W17M, R15M**; W twr; vis: 304°-R-351°,102°-W-304°; obsc from seaward by Doulus Head when brg more than 180°.

Ldg lts 141°. Front, Oc WRG 4s 25m W11M, R8M, G8M; W twr, R stripe; vis:134°-G-140°-W-142°-R-148°; 51°55'·52N 10°18'·41W. Rear, 122m from front, Oc 4s 43m 5M; vis:128°-157·5° synch with front.

DINGLE BAY TO LOOP HEAD
DINGLE BAY, VENTRY and DINGLE
Ldg lts 182° Oc 3s. Front 52°07'·41N 10°16'·59W, rear 100m behind.

Inishtearaght ☆, W end Blasket Islands 52°04'·55N 10°39'·68W Fl (2) 20s 84m **19M**; W twr; vis: 318°-221°; *Racon (O)*.

BRANDON BAY, TRALEE BAY and FENIT HARBOUR
Little Samphire Is ☆ 52°16'·26N 09°52'·91W Fl WRG 5s 17m **W16M**, R13M, G13M; Bu ○ twr; vis: 262°-R-275°, 280-R-090°-G-140°-W-152°-R-172°.

Great Samphire I ⚓ QR 15m 3M; vis: 242°-097°; 52°16'·15N 09°51'·82W.

Fenit Hbr Pier Hd ⚓ 2 FR (vert) 12m 3M; vis: 148°-058°; 52°16'·24N 09°51'·55W.

SHANNON ESTUARY

Ballybunnion ⚓ VQ; *Racon (M) 6M*; 52°32'·52N 09°46'·93W.
Kilstiffin ⚓ Fl R 3s; 52°33'·80N 09°43'·83W.

Kilcredaune Head ☆ Fl 6s 41m **15M**; W twr; 52°34'·79N 09°42'·58W; obsc 224°-247° by hill within 1M.

Tail of Beal ⚓ Q (9) 15s; 52°34'·39N 09°40'·75W.
Carrigaholt ⚓ Fl (2) R 6s; 52°34'·92N 09°40'·51W.
Beal Spit ⚓ VQ (9) 10s; 52°34'·82N 09°39'·98W.
Beal Bar ⚓ Q; 52°35'·18N 09°39'·23W.
Doonaha ⚓ Q (3) R 5s; 52°35'·46N 09°38'·50W.
Letter Point ⚓ Fl R 7s; 52°35'·44N 09°35'·89W.
Asdee ⚓ Fl R 5s; 52°35'·09N 09°34'·55W.
Rineanna ⚓ QR; 52°35'·59N 09°31'·24W.
North Carraig ⚓ Q; 52°35'·60N 09°29'·76W.

Scattery Is, Rineanna Pt ⚓ Fl (2) 8s 15m 10M; W twr; vis: 208°-092°; 52°36'·32N 09°31'·03W.

KILRUSH

Marina Ent Chan Ldg lts 355°. Front, Oc 3s; 52°37'·99N 09°30'·27W. Rear, 75m from front, Oc 3s.

Tarbert Is N Point ⚓ Q WR 4s 18m W14M, R10M; W ○ twr; vis: W069°- R277°- W287°-339°; 52°35'·52N 09°21'·83W.

Tarbert (Ballyhoolahan Pt) Ldg lts 128·2° ⚓. Front, Iso 3s 13m 3M; △ on W twr; vis: 123·2°-133·2°; 52°34'·35N 09°18'·80W. Rear, 400m from front, Iso 5s 18m 3M; G stripe on W Bn.

Garraunbaun Pt ⚓ Fl (3) WR 10s 16m W8M, R5M; W □ col, vis: R shore - W072°- R242°- shore; 52°35'·62N 09°13'·94W.

Rinealon Pt ⚓ Fl 2·5s 4m 7M; B col, W bands; vis: 234°-088°; 52°37'·12N 09°09'·82W.

FOYNES

W Chan Ldg lts 107·9° (may be moved for changes in chan). Front, Oc 4s 34m 12M; 52°36'·91N 09°06'·59W . Rear, Oc 4s 39m 12M.

RIVER SHANNON

Beeves Rock ⚓Fl WR 5s 12m W12M, R9M; vis: 064·5°-W-091°-R-238°-W-265°-W(unintens)-064·5°; 52°39'·01N 09°01'·35W .
North Channel Ldg lts 093°. Front, Tradree Rock Fl R 2s 6m 5M; W Trs; vis: 246°-110°; 52°41'·00N 08°49'·87W. Rear 0·65M from front, Iso 6s 14m 5M; W twr, R bands; vis: 327°-190°.

N side, Ldg lts 061°. Front, 52°40'·72N 08°45'·27W, Crawford Rock 490m from rear, Fl R 3s 6m 5M. Crawford No. 2, Common Rear, Iso 6s 10m 5M; 52°40'·85N 08°44'·88W.
Ldg lts 302·1°, Flagstaff Rock, 670m from rear, Fl R 7s 7m 5M; 52°40'·66N 08°44'·40W.
Ldg lts 106·5°. Meelick Rk, Front Iso 4s 6m 3M; 52°40'·25N 08°42'·36W . Meelick No. 2, rear 275m from front Iso 6s 9m 5M; both W pile structures.

LOOP HEAD

Loop Head ☆ 52°33'·68N 09°55'·96W Fl (4) 20s 84m **23M**.

9.12.5 PASSAGE INFORMATION

The latest editions of the Irish Cruising Club (www.irish cruisingclub.com) Sailing Directions are strongly recommended for all Irish waters. Particularly useful on the W coast where other information is scarce, they are published in two volumes: *E and N coasts of Ireland* and *S and W coasts of Ireland*. See also *Cruising Cork and Kerry* (Graham Swanson/Imray). For notes on crossing the Irish Sea, see 9.13.5; and for Distances across it see 9.0.6.

More Passage Information is threaded between the harbours of this Area.

9.12.6 SPECIAL NOTES FOR IRELAND

Céad Míle Fáilte! One hundred thousand Welcomes!
Lifejackets: It is compulsory to wear lifejackets in Irish waters on all craft of <7m LOA. Children under 16 years must wear a lifejacket or personal flotation device at all times on deck when underway. Every vessel, irrespective of size, must carry a lifejacket or personal flotation device for each person on board. These regulations are mandatory.

Ordnance Survey map numbers refer to the Irish OS maps, scale 1:50,000 or 1¼ inch to 1 mile, which cover the whole island, including Ulster, in 89 sheets.

Irish Customs: First port of call should preferably be at Customs posts in one of the following hbrs: Dublin, Dun Laoghaire, Waterford, New Ross, Cork, Ringaskiddy, Bantry, Foynes, Limerick, Galway, Sligo and Killybegs. Yachts may, in fact, make their first call anywhere and if no Customs officer arrives within a reasonable time, the skipper should inform the nearest Garda (Police) station of the yacht's arrival. Only non-EC members should fly flag Q or show ● over ○ lts on arrival. Passports are not required by UK citizens. All current Northern Ireland 5 and 6 digit telephone numbers have become 8 digits **028 90**12 3456.

Telephone: To call the **Republic of Ireland (RoI)** from the UK, dial **00 - 353**, then the area code (given in UK ☎ directories and below) minus the initial 0, followed by the ☎ number. To call UK from the RoI: dial 00-44, followed by the area code minus the initial 0, then the number.

Salmon drift nets: Use of these is decreasing but may be encountered along the S and W coasts, off headlands and islands during the summer, especially May–Jul. They may be 1½ to 3M long and difficult to see. FVs may give warnings on VHF Ch 16, 06, 08.

Liquefied petroleum gas: In RoI LPG is supplied by Kosan, a sister company of Calor Gas Ltd, but the bottles have different connections, and the smallest bottle is taller than the normal Calor one fitted in most yachts. Calor Gas bottles can be filled in most larger towns. Camping Gaz is widely available. The abbreviation Kos indicates where Kosan gas is available.

Information: The Irish Cruising Club publishes 2 highly recommended books of Sailing Directions, one for the S and W coasts of Ireland, the other for the N and E coasts. All three are distributed by Imray. See also *Cruising Cork and Kerry* by Graham Swanson (Imray.com & Amazon). All three available from: Irish Sailing Association, 3 Park Road, Dun Laoghaire, Co Dublin, ☎ (01) 2800239, 🖷 2807558; or the Irish Tourist Board, 150 New Bond St, London W1Y 0AQ, ☎ (020 7) 518 0800.

Useful websites:

Commissioners of Irish Lights	www.cil.ie
Irish Sailing Association	www.sailing.ie
Irish Tourist Board	www.discoverireland.com
Irish Met Service Sea Area Forecast	www.met.ie/forecasts/sea-area.asp

Currency is the Euro (€), cash is most readily available from ATMs. VAT is 21·5%.

Access by air: There are airports in RoI at Dublin, Waterford, Cork, Kerry, Shannon, Galway, Connaught, Sligo and Donegal/Carrickfin. See also Ferries in 9.0.5.

Northern Ireland: Belfast CG (MRCC) is at Bangor, Co Down, ☎ (028 91) 463933. HM Customs (⊖) should be contacted H24 on ☎ (028 90) 358250 at the following ports, if a local Customs Officer is not available: Belfast, Warrenpoint, Kilkeel, Ardglass, Portavogie, Larne, Londonderry, Coleraine. Northern Ireland's main airport is Belfast (Aldergrove).

9.12.7 MALAHIDE

Dublin 53°27'·20N 06°08'·90W ❀❀✿♦♦♦✿✿✿

CHARTS AC 1468, 633, 5621; Imray C61, C62.

TIDES +0030 Dover; ML 2·4; Duration 0615

Standard Port DUBLIN (NORTH WALL) (→)

Times				Height (metres)			
High Water		Low Water		MHWS	MHWN	MLWN	MLWS
0000	0700	0000	0500	4·1	3·4	1·5	0·7
1200	1900	1200	1700				
Differences MALAHIDE							
+0002	+0003	+0009	+0009	+0·1	–0·2	–0·4	–0·2

SHELTER Excellent in marina, dredged approx 2·3m. Access HW±4. Visitors berth on pontoon F. ⚓ between marina and Grand Hotel on S edge of fairway, clear of moorings.

NAVIGATION WPT: SWM LFl 10s 53°27'·12N 06°06'·87W. The approach channel lies between drying sandbanks. It is strongly recommended that visiting yachtsmen obtain up-to-date information by ☎ or VHF from the marina on the latest depths and buoyage and refer this to AC 633. The channel is marked by PHM and SHM perches which are lit.

Entry not advised in strong onshore winds against the ebb. The flood reaches 3kn sp, and the ebb 3½kn. Speed limit 10kn in fairway and 4kn in marina.

LIGHTS AND MARKS The marina and apartment blocks close S of it are visible from the WPT. The Grand Hotel is no longer conspic from seaward, due to trees and bldgs.

R/T Marina, *Call sign Malahide Marina*, Ch **M** 80 (H24). MYC, call *Yacht Base* Ch M (occas).

TELEPHONE (Code 01) Marina 8454129; MRCC 6620922/3; ⊖ 8746571; Police 666 4600; Dr 845 5994; Ⓗ 837 7755.

FACILITIES Marina (349) ☎ 8454129, Ⓥ (20) €3·90, ⫫Ⓓ (€6·50) D(hose H24), P(cans H24), Wi-fi, Gas, BH (30 ton), BY, R, Bar, Ice, Ⓘ, Ⓦⓒ, showers **Malahide YC** ☎ 8453372, Slip (for craft <5.5m, launching HW ±2), Scrubbing posts for <10m LOA; **Services:** Ⓔ, ✕, Kos. **Town** Ⓘ, ⊠, Ⓑ, ⇌, ✈ (Dublin).

MALAHIDE TO TUSKAR ROCK

(AC 1468, 1787) Malahide, 4M from both Lambay Is and Howth, can be entered in most weather via a channel which constantly shifts through drying sandbanks. Ireland's Eye, a rky island which rises steeply to a height of 99m, lies about 7½ca N of Howth with reefs running SE and SW from Thulla Rk at its SE end. Ben of Howth, on N side of Dublin Bay, is steep-to, with no dangers more than 1ca offshore.

Rosbeg Bank lies on the N side of Dublin Bay. Burford Bank, on which the sea breaks in E gales, and Kish Bank lie offshore in the approaches. ▶ *The N-going stream begins at HW Dublin – 0600, and the S-going at HW Dublin, sp rates 3kn.* ◀

From Dublin to Carnsore Pt as a cruising area, hbr facilities are being improved. The shallow offshore banks cause dangerous overfalls and dictate the route which is sheltered from the W winds. ▶ *Tidal streams run mainly N and S, but the N-going flood sets across the banks on the inside, and the S-going ebb sets across them on the outside.* ◀

Leaving Dublin Bay, yachts normally use Dalkey Sound, but with a foul tide or light wind it is better to use Muglins Sound. Muglins (lt) is steep-to except for a rk about 1ca WSW of the lt. Beware Leac Buidhe (dries) 1ca E of Clare Rk. The inshore passage is best as far as Wicklow.

Thereafter yachts may either route offshore, passing east of Arklow Bank and its Lanby to fetch Tuskar Rock or Greenore Pt, or keep inshore of Arklow Bank, avoiding Glassgorman Banks. Stay E of the Blackwater Bank to Lucifer ECM buoy then pass W of Tuskar Rock to round Carnsore Pt to the SW. Avoid the Rusk Channel except in settled weather. Arklow is safe in offshore winds; Wexford has a difficult entrance. Rosslare lacks yacht facilities, but provides good shelter to wait out a SW'ly blow.

Arklow Bank Wind Farm, 7 miles east of Arklow, has 7 wind turbines, each 72.8m high with 104m diameter blades. They are lit, N'most and S'most are fitted with AIS transmitters.

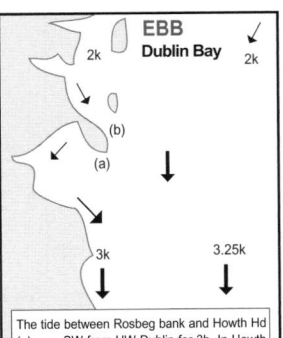

9.12.8 HOWTH

Dublin 53°23'·60N 06°04'·00W ✸✸✸✸♒♒♒♒♒✿✿✿

CHARTS AC 1468, 1415, 5621; Imray C61, C62.

TIDES +0025 Dover; ML 2·4; Duration 0625

Standard Port DUBLIN (NORTH WALL) (⟶)

Times				Height (metres)			
High Water		Low Water		MHWS	MHWN	MLWN	MLWS
0000	0700	0000	0500	4·1	3·4	1·5	0·7
1200	1900	1200	1700				
Differences HOWTH							
–0007	–0005	+0001	+0005	0·0	–0·1	–0·2	–0·2

SHELTER Excellent in marina, available at all tides and in almost any conditions. After a severe ENE'ly storm, expect a dangerous scend in the app chan. Caution: many moorings in E part of outer hbr. No ent to FV basin for yachts. Inside the inner hbr keep strictly to chan to avoid drying shoals either side and a substantial wavebreak (gabion). Marina depth 2·2m. R PHM posts mark the outer limit of dredging around the marina. 4kn speed limit. There is a fair weather ⚓ in 2-3m at Carrigeen Bay, SW side of Ireland's Eye.

NAVIGATION WPT Howth SHM buoy, Fl G 5s, 53°23'·72N 06°03'·53W, 251°/0·27M to E pier lt. From the S beware Casana Rk

4ca S of the Nose of Howth and Puck's Rks extending about 50m off the Nose. Ireland's Eye is 0·6M N of hbr, with the Rowan Rks SE and SW from Thulla, marked by Rowan Rks ECM, and S Rowan SHM lt buoys. The usual approach passes S of Ireland's Eye, but beware many lobster pots between the Nose of Howth and the hbr, and rocks off both pier hds. Howth Sound has 2·4m min depth; give way to FVs (constrained by draft) in the Sound and hbr entrance. 2·5m in marina approach channel.

LIGHTS AND MARKS Baily lt ho, Fl 15s 41m 26M, is 1·5M S of Nose of Howth. Disused lt ho on E pier is conspic. E pier lt, Fl (2) WR 7·5s 13m 12/9M; 256°-W-295°, R elsewhere. W sector leads safely to NE pierhead which should be rounded 50m off. Ent to FV Basin has QR and Fl G 3s. The chan to marina is marked by 8 R & G floating perches (some lit) with W reflective tape (2 bands = port, 1 = stbd).

R/T Marina Ch M 80 (H24). HM VHF Ch 16 11 (Mon-Fri 0700–2300LT; Sat/Sun occas).

TELEPHONE (Code 01) HM 832 2252; MRCC 6620922/3; ⊜ 8746571; Police 666 4900; Dr 832 3191; Ⓗ 837 7755.

FACILITIES Howth Marina (350 inc Ⓥ) ☎ 8392777, www.hyc.ie; €2.75, Wi-fi, M, D (H24), P(cans), Slip(H24), C (15 ton), ⛽, ◻, ♿. **Howth YC** ☎ 832 2141, Scrubbing posts <20m LOA, R (☎ 839 2100), Bar (☎ 8320606), ◻, ⛽. **Howth Boat Club** (no facilities). **Services:** LB, Gas, Kos, ME, SM, CH, El, Ⓔ. **Town** ✉, Ⓑ, ◻, ⇌, ✈ (Dublin).

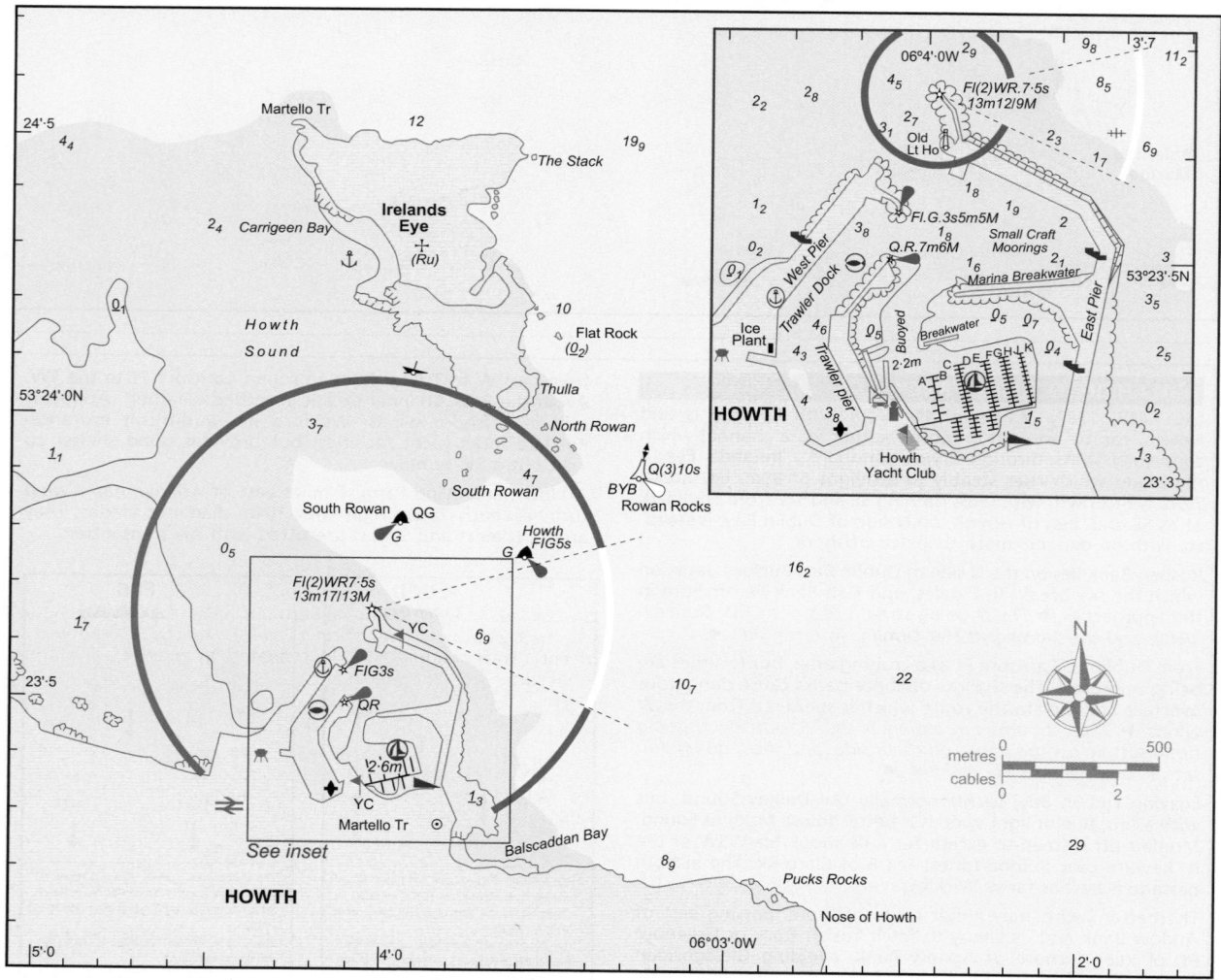

9.12.9 DUBLIN

Dublin 53°20'·85N 06°14'·80W ✿✿✿⚓⚓✿✿✿

CHARTS AC 1468, 1415, 1447, 5621; Imray C61, C62.

TIDES +0042 Dover; ML 2·4; Duration 0640

Standard Port DUBLIN (NORTH WALL) (→)

Times				Height (metres)			
High Water		Low Water		MHWS	MHWN	MLWN	MLWS
0000	0700	0000	0500	4·1	3·4	1·5	0·7
1200	1900	1200	1700				
Differences DUBLIN BAR and DUN LAOGHAIRE							
–0006	–0001	–0002	–0003	0·0	0·0	0·0	+0·1
GREYSTONES (53°09'N 06°04'W)							
–0008	–0008	–0008	–0008	–0·5	–0·4	No data	

SHELTER Dublin Port, excellent on N side 1ca below Matt Talbot Br on pontoons and Poolbeg YBC Marina, S of Alexandra Basin W.

NAVIGATION Dublin Port WPT 53°20'·50N 06°06'·71W, 275°/1·35M to hbr ent. Accessible H24, but the ent to R Liffey is rough in >E'ly F5 against ebb tide.

Note that Bull Wall covers 0.6 to 2.7m at HW. For clearance to enter call *Dublin Port Radio* Ch 12. Beware of shipping; small craft must keep outside fairway buoys. E Link Lifting Br (2·2m closed) opens 1100, 1500 and 2100, or on request HO and Bank Holidays. Call 00 353 1 855 5779.

LIGHTS AND MARKS Entance, N. Bull Lt Fl G 4s 15m 10M synchro with Gt. S. Wall Hd Poolbeg Lt Fl R 4s 20m 10M. Poolbeg power stn 2 R/W chimneys (VQ R) are conspic from afar.

R/T Call *Dublin Port Radio* Ch **12** 13 16 (H24). Lifting bridge (call *Eastlink*) Ch 12. *Poolbeg Marina* Ch **37** 12 16. Dublin Coast Radio Stn 16 67 83.

TELEPHONE (Code 00 353 1) HM Dublin 8748771; MRCC 6620922/3; Coast/Cliff Rescue Service 2803900; ⊖ 2803992; Weather 1550 123855; Police (Dublin) 6668000; Dr 2859244; Ⓗ 2806901.

FACILITIES Dublin City Moorings ☎ 818 3300, mobile 086856 8113, 20 Ⓥ's AB in 3·3m,€3.25, FW, ⌁, Showers. **Poolbeg YBC Marina** ☎ 6604681, www.poolbegmarina.ie, 35 Ⓥs for 20m max LOA in 2.4m,€3.80, D, FW, ⌁, Showers, ◻, Slip, Bar, R. **Dublin City,** all needs, @ at library, ⇌, ✈. **Ferries:** Holyhead; 4/day; 3¼ hrs; Irish Ferries (www.irishferries.com). Liverpool; 2/day; 8 hrs; P&O (www.poferries.co.uk).

9.12.10 DUN LAOGHAIRE

Dublin (Port ent) 53°18'·16N 06°07'·68W ✿✿✿⚓⚓✿✿

CHARTS AC 1468, 1415, 1447, 5621; Imray C61, C62.

TIDES +0042 Dover; ML 2·4; Duration 0640

Standard Port DUBLIN (NORTH WALL) (→)

Times				Height (metres)			
High Water		Low Water		MHWS	MHWN	MLWN	MLWS
0000	0700	0000	0500	4·1	3·4	1·5	0·7
1200	1900	1200	1700				
Differences DUBLIN BAR and DUN LAOGHAIRE							
–0006	–0001	–0002	–0003	0·0	0·0	0·0	+0·1
GREYSTONES (53°09'N 06°04'W)							
–0008	–0008	–0008	–0008	–0·5	–0·4	No data	

SHELTER Excellent. Breakwaters within main hbr protect 800+ berth marina from ferry wash. Ⓥ berths on end of pontoons or as directed. Additional berths inside Western Marina Breakwater. All YCs advertise ⚓s and/or pontoon berths.

NAVIGATION Dun Laoghaire is accessible H24, WPT 53°18'·40N 06°07'·00W, 240° 0·47M to ent. Keep clear of coasters, ferries/HSS, which turn off St Michael's Pier. Beware drying rocks approx 10m off E Pier Hd. See chartlet overleaf.

TSS: Two TSS ½M long, one at either end of the Burford Bank lead to/from an anti-clockwise circular TSS radius 2·3ca centred on Dublin Bay SWM lt buoy,(53°19'·90N 06°04'·58W, 2·5M NE of Dun Laoghaire/2·75M ESE of Dublin Port). Do not impede large vessels and keep clear of the TSS and fairway.

LIGHTS AND MARKS On Ro Ro Berth 2 x Fl.W = 'Large vessel under way; small craft keep clear of No 1 Fairway' (extends 600m seaward of ent). Traffic signals (Fl W) repeated at head of E Marina Breakwater when large vessels underway.

R/T Dun Laoghaire Hbr VHF Ch **14** 16 (H24); Marina Ch **M**; YCs Ch M. Dublin Coast Radio Stn 16 67 83.

TELEPHONE (Code 00 353 1) HM Dun Laoghaire 2801130; MRCC 6620922/3; Coast/Cliff Rescue Service 2803900; ⊖ 2803992; Weather 1550 123855; Police 6665000; Dr 2859244; Ⓗ 2806901.

FACILITIES Dun Laoghaire Hbr Marina ☎ 2020040, hal@dlmarina.com, www.dlmarina.com, (800 AB inc 20Ⓥ) €4.00, BH, D&P, ◻, ♿, Wi-fi. **Yacht Clubs** (E to W): **National YC** ☎ 2805725, ◫ 2807837, Slip, M, L, C (12 ton), FW, D, R, Bar; **Royal St George YC** ☎ 2801811, ◫ 2843002, Boatman ☎ 2801208; AB by prior agreement, €3.00, Slip, M, D, L, FW, C (5 ton), R, Bar; **Royal Irish YC** ☎ 2809452, ◫ 2809723, Slip, M, D, L, FW, C (5 ton), R, Bar; **Dun Laoghaire Motor YC** ☎ 2801371, ◫ 2800870, Slip, FW, AB, Bar, R. **Services** SM, CH, ACA, ✖, Ⓔ, El, Gas. **Irish National SC** ☎ 28444195. HSS to Holyhead.

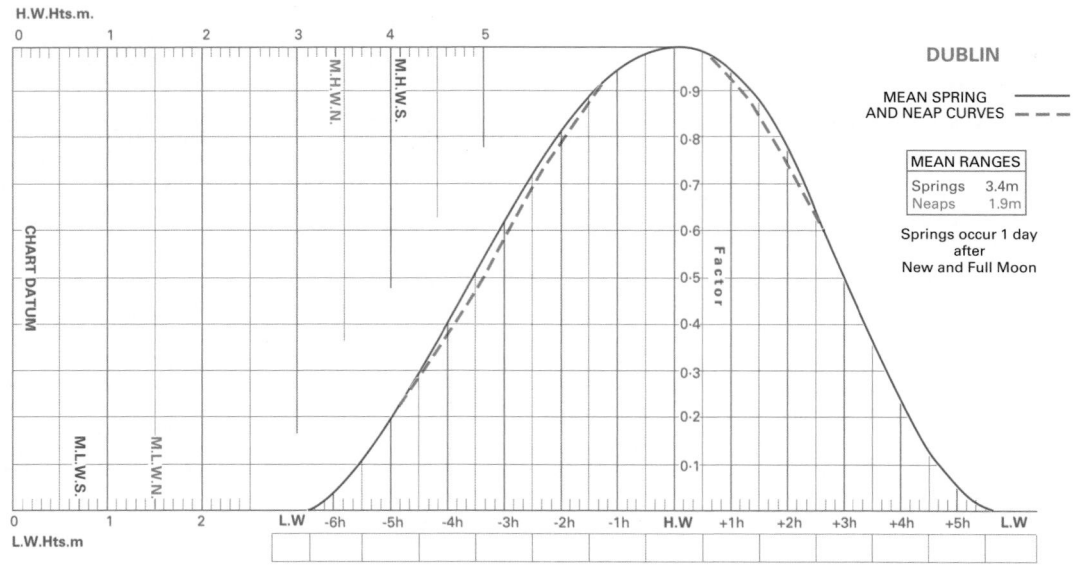

DUBLIN

MEAN SPRING
AND NEAP CURVES

MEAN RANGES
Springs   3.4m
Neaps   1.9m

Springs occur 1 day
after
New and Full Moon

H.W.Hts.m.

CHART DATUM

Factor

M.H.W.N.
M.H.W.S.

M.L.W.S.
M.L.W.N.

L.W.Hts.m.

L.W -6h -5h -4h -3h -2h -1h H.W +1h +2h +3h +4h +5h L.W

9'·0

Fl.Y.5s
06°8'·0W

Sewer

Race
start
hut

Western Marina Breakwater

Yacht
moorings

West Pier

Yacht
moorings

Fl(2)G.8s
11m7M

Fl(2)R.8s16m17M
Horn(1)30s
Fog Det Lt VQ

Anemometer

Yacht
Moorings

Boyd Obelisk

Fairway
No 1

53°18'·0N

2F.R(vert)

Q.R

2F.R(Vert)
11m2M

Traders
Wharf

Eastern Marina Breakwater

2F.G(vert)
Fl.G.4s
F'way No 2

Fl.R.5s

2F.G
(vert)

NB
NC
ND
NE
NF
NG
NH
NJ
NK
NL

Fl.W Traffic Sigs displayed
when large power driven
vessels manoeuvring

2F.G(vert)

SB
SC
SD
SE
SF
SG
SH
SJ
SK

Traffic
Signals Fl.W

Car Ferry Pier

East Pier

Fl.R.3s
9m1M

Inner
Harbour
Moorings

Old
Harbour

Old Quay

Moorings

Turret

Royal Irish
YC

Dun Laoghaire
Hbr Marina

INSC
Dun Laoghaire
Motor Yacht
Club

Bandstand

DUN LAOGHAIRE

Moorings

Moorings

East
Pier
Berth

Clock Tr
(Disused)

Royal
St George YC

Scotsman's Bay

N

Spire

National
YC

Spire

17'·5

metres
cables
400

DUBLIN (NORTH WALL)   LAT 53°21'N   LONG 6°13'W
TIMES AND HEIGHTS OF HIGH AND LOW WATERS

TIME ZONE (UT)
For Summer Time add ONE hour in **non-shaded areas**

Dates in red are **SPRINGS**
Dates in blue are **NEAPS**

YEAR 2010

S Ireland

JANUARY

Time	m	Time	m
1 0451 0.8 / 1133 4.3 / F 1723 0.4		**16** 0007 3.7 / 0542 1.0 / SA 1211 4.0 / 1811 0.9	
2 0003 4.1 / 0535 0.7 / SA 1219 4.4 / 1809 0.3		**17** 0036 3.7 / 0612 1.0 / SU 1242 4.0 / 1841 0.9	
3 0051 4.1 / 0620 0.7 / SU 1306 4.4 / 1859 0.3		**18** 0106 3.7 / 0642 1.0 / M 1314 4.0 / 1910 0.9	
4 0140 4.1 / 0708 0.8 / M 1356 4.4 / 1950 0.4		**19** 0139 3.7 / 0713 1.0 / TU 1350 3.9 / 1940 0.9	
5 0232 4.0 / 0759 0.9 / TU 1449 4.3 / 2044 0.5		**20** 0215 3.6 / 0747 1.0 / W 1428 3.9 / 2014 0.9	
6 0327 3.8 / 0855 1.0 / W 1545 4.1 / 2140 0.7		**21** 0254 3.6 / 0826 1.1 / TH 1510 3.8 / 2053 1.0	
7 0426 3.7 / 0955 1.2 / TH 1645 4.0 / ◑ 2239 1.0		**22** 0338 3.5 / 0909 1.2 / F 1554 3.7 / 2136 1.1	
8 0529 3.6 / 1100 1.4 / F 1752 3.8 / 2343 1.2		**23** 0427 3.4 / 0959 1.4 / SA 1644 3.5 / ◐ 2227 1.3	
9 0636 3.5 / 1211 1.5 / SA 1902 3.6		**24** 0525 3.3 / 1100 1.5 / SU 1744 3.4 / 2332 1.4	
10 0053 1.3 / 0741 3.5 / SU 1328 1.5 / 2012 3.6		**25** 0635 3.3 / 1218 1.5 / M 1858 3.4	
11 0206 1.4 / 0845 3.6 / M 1441 1.4 / 2119 3.6		**26** 0052 1.5 / 0749 3.4 / TU 1335 1.4 / 2015 3.4	
12 0307 1.4 / 0942 3.7 / TU 1539 1.3 / 2217 3.6		**27** 0207 1.4 / 0852 3.6 / W 1441 1.1 / 2121 3.6	
13 0356 1.3 / 1030 3.8 / W 1625 1.1 / 2302 3.6		**28** 0307 1.1 / 0946 3.9 / TH 1537 0.8 / 2216 3.8	
14 0436 1.2 / 1109 3.9 / TH 1704 1.0 / 2338 3.7		**29** 0357 0.9 / 1034 4.1 / F 1626 0.5 / 2304 4.0	
15 0511 1.1 / 1141 4.0 / F 1739 0.9 / ●		**30** 0441 0.7 / 1119 4.3 / SA 1711 0.2 / ○ 2349 4.1	
		31 0523 0.5 / 1203 4.4 / SU 1755 0.1	

FEBRUARY

Time	m	Time	m
1 0033 4.1 / 0604 0.5 / M 1248 4.5 / 1840 0.1		**16** 0036 3.7 / 0613 0.8 / TU 1246 4.0 / 1834 0.7	
2 0117 4.1 / 0648 0.5 / TU 1334 4.4 / 1926 0.2		**17** 0105 3.7 / 0641 0.8 / W 1320 3.9 / 1902 0.7	
3 0203 4.0 / 0734 0.6 / W 1423 4.3 / 2015 0.4		**18** 0139 3.7 / 0713 0.8 / TH 1357 3.9 / 1936 0.8	
4 0251 3.8 / 0825 0.8 / TH 1515 4.1 / 2106 0.7		**19** 0217 3.7 / 0751 0.9 / F 1438 3.8 / 2015 0.8	
5 0343 3.7 / 0921 1.0 / F 1611 3.8 / ☽ 2200 1.0		**20** 0259 3.6 / 0833 1.0 / SA 1522 3.7 / 2058 1.0	
6 0442 3.5 / 1023 1.3 / SA 1717 3.6 / 2259 1.3		**21** 0346 3.5 / 0923 1.1 / SU 1612 3.5 / 2149 1.2	
7 0552 3.4 / 1133 1.4 / SU 1832 3.4		**22** 0442 3.3 / 1024 1.3 / M 1712 3.3 / ◐ 2253 1.4	
8 0010 1.5 / 0704 3.4 / M 1301 1.5 / 1948 3.3		**23** 0552 3.2 / 1146 1.4 / TU 1831 3.3	
9 0139 1.6 / 0815 3.4 / TU 1428 1.4 / 2103 3.4		**24** 0022 1.5 / 0718 3.3 / W 1314 1.3 / 1958 3.3	
10 0252 1.5 / 0919 3.6 / W 1527 1.3 / 2205 3.4		**25** 0149 1.4 / 0831 3.5 / TH 1427 1.0 / 2107 3.6	
11 0341 1.3 / 1010 3.7 / TH 1611 1.1 / 2248 3.5		**26** 0255 1.1 / 0849 3.5 / F 1525 0.6 / 2203 3.8	
12 0419 1.2 / 1050 3.8 / F 1646 0.9 / 2320 3.6		**27** 0345 0.8 / 1019 4.1 / SA 1613 0.3 / 2249 4.0	
13 0452 1.0 / 1122 3.9 / SA 1717 0.8 / 2346 3.6		**28** 0427 0.6 / 1104 4.3 / SU 1656 0.1 / ○ 2331 4.1	
14 0521 0.9 / 1150 3.9 / SU 1745 0.8 / ●		
15 0011 3.7 / 0548 0.8 / M 1217 4.0 / 1810 0.7		

MARCH

Time	m	Time	m
1 0507 0.4 / 1146 4.4 / M 1737 0.0		**16** 0520 0.7 / 1150 3.9 / TU 1736 0.6	
2 0011 4.1 / 0546 0.3 / TU 1229 4.4 / 1818 0.0		**17** 0004 3.7 / 0544 0.6 / W 1218 3.9 / 1759 0.6	
3 0051 4.1 / 0627 0.3 / W 1312 4.3 / 1901 0.2		**18** 0033 3.8 / 0612 0.6 / TH 1252 3.9 / 1829 0.6	
4 0132 4.0 / 0711 0.4 / TH 1358 4.2 / 1945 0.4		**19** 0107 3.8 / 0645 0.6 / F 1331 3.9 / 1905 0.7	
5 0216 3.9 / 0759 0.6 / F 1447 3.9 / 2033 0.7		**20** 0147 3.8 / 0725 0.7 / SA 1413 3.8 / 1946 0.8	
6 0303 3.7 / 0853 0.9 / SA 1541 3.7 / 2124 1.1		**21** 0230 3.7 / 0810 0.8 / SU 1500 3.7 / 2032 1.0	
7 0357 3.5 / 0953 1.1 / SU 1646 3.4 / ☽ 2221 1.4		**22** 0319 3.6 / 0904 1.0 / M 1552 3.5 / 2127 1.2	
8 0506 3.3 / 1101 1.3 / M 1802 3.2 / 2328 1.6		**23** 0415 3.4 / 1001 1.1 / TU 1656 3.3 / ◐ 2236 1.4	
9 0626 3.3 / 1226 1.5 / TU 1921 3.1		**24** 0527 3.3 / 1133 1.2 / W 1818 3.3	
10 0057 1.7 / 0740 3.3 / W 1401 1.4 / 2040 3.2		**25** 0004 1.5 / 0653 3.3 / TH 1258 1.1 / 1942 3.3	
11 0224 1.6 / 0848 3.5 / TH 1501 1.2 / 2141 3.3		**26** 0130 1.4 / 0808 3.5 / F 1410 0.8 / 2051 3.5	
12 0316 1.4 / 0942 3.6 / F 1544 1.0 / 2222 3.5		**27** 0236 1.1 / 0909 3.8 / SA 1507 0.5 / 2146 3.8	
13 0354 1.1 / 1023 3.7 / SA 1618 0.9 / 2252 3.6		**28** 0326 0.8 / 1001 4.0 / SU 1554 0.3 / 2232 3.9	
14 0426 0.9 / 1056 3.8 / SU 1647 0.8 / 2319 3.6		**29** 0410 0.5 / 1047 4.2 / M 1637 0.1 / 2312 4.0	
15 0454 0.8 / 1124 3.9 / M 1713 0.7 / ● 2342 3.7		**30** 0450 0.4 / 1129 4.3 / TU 1717 0.1 / ○ 2349 4.0	
		31 0529 0.3 / 1211 4.2 / W 1757 0.2	

APRIL

Time	m	Time	m
1 0026 4.0 / 0609 0.3 / TH 1254 4.2 / 1837 0.3		**16** 0004 3.8 / 0546 0.6 / F 1229 3.9 / 1803 0.6	
2 0106 4.0 / 0653 0.4 / F 1339 4.0 / 1920 0.4		**17** 0042 3.9 / 0624 0.6 / SA 1310 3.8 / 1841 0.7	
3 0148 3.9 / 0740 0.6 / SA 1426 3.8 / 2005 0.8		**18** 0124 3.8 / 0708 0.6 / SU 1356 3.8 / 1926 0.8	
4 0233 3.7 / 0833 0.8 / SU 1519 3.6 / 2055 1.1		**19** 0211 3.8 / 0759 0.7 / M 1447 3.7 / 2017 1.0	
5 0324 3.6 / 0931 1.0 / M 1620 3.3 / 2150 1.4		**20** 0303 3.7 / 0859 0.9 / TU 1544 3.5 / 2118 1.2	
6 0427 3.4 / 1034 1.2 / TU 1731 3.1 / ☽ 2254 1.6		**21** 0402 3.6 / 1008 1.0 / W 1650 3.4 / ☽ 2228 1.4	
7 0546 3.3 / 1147 1.3 / W 1846 3.1		**22** 0513 3.5 / 1123 1.0 / TH 1806 3.4 / 2347 1.4	
8 0008 1.7 / 0701 3.3 / TH 1313 1.3 / 1958 3.1		**23** 0631 3.5 / 1238 0.9 / F 1922 3.4	
9 0134 1.6 / 0807 3.4 / F 1419 1.2 / 2057 3.3		**24** 0103 1.3 / 0743 3.7 / SA 1345 0.7 / 2027 3.6	
10 0235 1.4 / 0902 3.5 / SA 1505 1.0 / 2141 3.4		**25** 0208 1.1 / 0846 3.8 / SU 1442 0.5 / 2123 3.7	
11 0317 1.2 / 0946 3.6 / SU 1540 0.9 / 2215 3.5		**26** 0302 0.9 / 0941 4.0 / M 1532 0.4 / 2211 3.8	
12 0351 1.0 / 1022 3.7 / M 1610 0.8 / 2245 3.6		**27** 0349 0.7 / 1030 4.1 / TU 1617 0.3 / 2253 3.9	
13 0421 0.8 / 1053 3.8 / TU 1636 0.7 / 2310 3.7		**28** 0433 0.5 / 1115 4.1 / W 1659 0.3 / ○ 2330 4.0	
14 0448 0.7 / 1121 3.8 / W 1701 0.7 / ● 2334 3.8		**29** 0515 0.5 / 1158 4.1 / TH 1738 0.4	
15 0515 0.6 / 1152 3.8 / TH 1729 0.6		**30** 0007 4.0 / 0556 0.5 / F 1240 4.0 / 1817 0.6	

Chart Datum: 0·20 metres above Ordnance Datum (Dublin). HAT is 4·5 metres above Chart Datum; see 4.5.

TIME ZONE (UT)
For Summer Time add ONE hour in **non-shaded areas**

DUBLIN (NORTH WALL) LAT 53°21'N LONG 6°13'W
TIMES AND HEIGHTS OF HIGH AND LOW WATERS

Dates in red are **SPRINGS**
Dates in blue are **NEAPS**

YEAR 2010

MAY

Day	Time m	Time m	Time m	Time m	Day	Time m	Time m	Time m	Time m
1 SA	0045 3.9	0639 0.5	1323 3.8	1858 0.7	16 SU	0022 4.0	0610 0.6	1256 3.9	1825 0.8
2 SU	0126 3.9	0726 0.6	1409 3.7	1942 0.9	17 M	0108 4.0	0658 0.6	1345 3.8	1913 0.9
3 M	0210 3.8	0816 0.8	1458 3.5	2030 1.1	18 TU	0158 3.9	0753 0.6	1439 3.7	2008 1.0
4 TU	0259 3.7	0910 0.9	1553 3.4	2123 1.3	19 W	0253 3.9	0854 0.7	1537 3.6	2108 1.1
5 W	0355 3.5	1007 1.1	1655 3.2	2222 1.5	20 TH	0352 3.8	0959 0.8	1640 3.6	2213 1.2
6 TH	0502 3.4	1109 1.2	1803 3.1	2325 1.6	21 F	0458 3.8	1106 0.8	1748 3.5	2322 1.3
7 F	0614 3.3	1214 1.3	1907 3.1		22 SA	0608 3.7	1213 0.8	1856 3.5	
8 SA	0032 1.6	0719 3.3	1318 1.2	2004 3.2	23 SU	0032 1.2	0717 3.8	1317 0.6	2000 3.6
9 SU	0136 1.5	0814 3.4	1411 1.1	2052 3.4	24 M	0138 1.2	0822 3.8	1416 0.7	2058 3.7
10 M	0227 1.3	0902 3.5	1453 1.0	2133 3.5	25 TU	0237 1.0	0921 3.9	1510 0.7	2150 3.8
11 TU	0308 1.1	0943 3.6	1527 0.9	2206 3.6	26 W	0330 0.9	1016 3.9	1558 0.7	2235 3.8
12 W	0343 1.0	1019 3.7	1559 1.0	2236 3.7	27 TH	0419 0.8	1104 3.9	1642 0.7	2315 3.9
13 TH	0415 0.8	1053 3.8	1630 0.7	2306 3.8	28 F	0504 0.7	1147 3.9	1723 0.7	2351 3.9
14 F	0449 0.7	1130 3.8	1705 0.7	2342 3.9	29 SA	0547 0.7	1227 3.8	1801 0.8	
15 SA	0527 0.6	1211 3.9	1743 0.7		30 SU	0028 3.9	0629 0.7	1307 3.7	1840 0.9
					31 M	0107 3.9	0712 0.8	1349 3.6	1920 1.0

JUNE

Day	Time m	Time m	Time m	Time m	Day	Time m	Time m	Time m	Time m
1 TU	0149 3.9	0758 0.8	1433 3.5	2004 1.1	16 W	0145 4.1	0742 0.5	1426 3.9	1953 0.9
2 W	0233 3.8	0845 0.9	1520 3.4	2052 1.2	17 TH	0238 4.1	0840 0.5	1521 3.8	2050 1.0
3 TH	0320 3.7	0935 1.0	1611 3.3	2144 1.4	18 F	0335 4.0	0940 0.6	1619 3.7	2150 1.1
4 F	0413 3.5	1027 1.1	1708 3.2	2240 1.5	19 SA	0437 4.0	1041 0.7	1721 3.6	2253 1.2
5 SA	0512 3.4	1121 1.2	1809 3.2	2339 1.5	20 SU	0543 3.9	1143 0.8	1826 3.6	
6 SU	0616 3.4	1217 1.3	1908 3.2		21 M	0000 1.3	0652 3.8	1248 0.9	1931 3.6
7 M	0037 1.5	0717 3.4	1311 1.3	2000 3.3	22 TU	0109 1.3	0800 3.8	1351 1.0	2033 3.6
8 TU	0132 1.4	0812 3.4	1400 1.2	2047 3.5	23 W	0216 1.2	0905 3.7	1450 1.0	2130 3.7
9 W	0221 1.3	0901 3.5	1445 1.1	2128 3.6	24 TH	0317 1.1	1003 3.8	1543 1.0	2220 3.8
10 TH	0305 1.1	0946 3.6	1526 1.0	2206 3.7	25 F	0410 1.0	1055 3.8	1628 1.0	2303 3.9
11 F	0347 0.9	1029 3.8	1605 0.9	2245 3.9	26 SA	0456 0.9	1138 3.7	1709 1.0	2338 3.9
12 SA	0429 0.8	1113 3.9	1646 0.8	2325 4.0	27 SU	0538 0.9	1215 3.7	1745 0.9	
13 SU	0512 0.6	1157 3.9	1728 0.7		28 M	0011 3.9	0616 0.8	1248 3.7	1820 1.0
14 M	0008 4.1	0558 0.5	1244 3.9	1812 0.7	29 TU	0046 3.9	0654 0.8	1323 3.6	1856 1.0
15 TU	0055 4.1	0648 0.5	1334 3.9	1900 0.8	30 W	0123 3.9	0732 0.9	1401 3.6	1934 1.0

JULY

Day	Time m	Time m	Time m	Time m	Day	Time m	Time m	Time m	Time m
1 TH	0202 3.9	0812 0.9	1440 3.5	2014 1.1	16 F	0216 4.3	0816 0.4	1455 3.9	2024 0.9
2 F	0244 3.8	0852 1.0	1522 3.4	2057 1.2	17 SA	0310 4.2	0912 0.6	1549 3.8	2121 1.0
3 SA	0328 3.7	0935 1.0	1607 3.4	2144 1.3	18 SU	0409 4.0	1010 0.8	1648 3.7	2222 1.2
4 SU	0416 3.6	1022 1.2	1658 3.3	2237 1.4	19 M	0515 3.8	1111 1.0	1754 3.6	2329 1.3
5 M	0509 3.4	1114 1.3	1757 3.3	2336 1.5	20 TU	0628 3.7	1216 1.2	1903 3.5	
6 TU	0612 3.4	1212 1.4	1901 3.3		21 W	0043 1.4	0741 3.6	1327 1.3	2010 3.6
7 W	0038 1.5	0720 3.4	1312 1.4	2002 3.4	22 TH	0202 1.4	0802 3.6	1434 1.3	2112 3.7
8 TH	0139 1.4	0825 3.4	1409 1.3	2055 3.6	23 F	0311 1.3	0954 3.6	1530 1.3	2206 3.8
9 F	0235 1.2	0921 3.6	1500 1.1	2142 3.8	24 SA	0403 1.1	1046 3.6	1615 1.1	2249 3.9
10 SA	0326 1.0	1011 3.8	1547 1.0	2227 4.0	25 SU	0446 1.0	1127 3.7	1653 1.0	2323 3.9
11 SU	0413 0.7	1058 3.9	1631 0.8	2310 4.1	26 M	0523 0.9	1158 3.7	1727 1.0	2352 4.0
12 M	0459 0.5	1143 4.0	1714 0.7	2353 4.3	27 TU	0557 0.8	1225 3.6	1758 0.9	
13 TU	0545 0.3	1228 4.1	1757 0.6		28 W	0022 4.0	0628 0.8	1254 3.6	1829 0.9
14 W	0037 4.3	0632 0.3	1315 4.0	1842 0.6	29 TH	0055 4.0	0659 0.8	1326 3.6	1900 0.9
15 TH	0126 4.3	0723 0.3	1404 4.0	1931 0.7	30 F	0130 3.9	0729 0.9	1401 3.6	1933 1.0
					31 SA	0208 3.9	0802 0.9	1439 3.6	2010 1.1

AUGUST

Day	Time m	Time m	Time m	Time m	Day	Time m	Time m	Time m	Time m
1 SU	0249 3.8	0839 1.0	1520 3.5	2052 1.2	16 M	0339 3.9	0936 0.9	1611 3.7	2152 1.1
2 M	0334 3.6	0922 1.1	1606 3.4	2140 1.3	17 TU	0446 3.7	1036 1.2	1718 3.5	2300 1.4
3 TU	0424 3.5	1012 1.3	1700 3.3	2237 1.5	18 W	0605 3.5	1143 1.4	1833 3.5	
4 W	0523 3.3	1114 1.4	1806 3.3	2350 1.5	19 TH	0021 1.5	0724 3.4	1302 1.5	1946 3.5
5 TH	0638 3.3	1230 1.5	1922 3.3		20 F	0153 1.4	0841 3.4	1418 1.5	2053 3.6
6 F	0107 1.5	0758 3.4	1342 1.4	2028 3.5	21 SA	0301 1.3	0944 3.5	1514 1.4	2149 3.8
7 SA	0214 1.2	0902 3.5	1442 1.2	2122 3.8	22 SU	0350 1.1	1033 3.6	1557 1.2	2231 3.9
8 SU	0311 0.9	0955 3.8	1532 1.0	2209 4.0	23 M	0428 0.9	1109 3.7	1632 1.0	2303 4.0
9 M	0400 0.6	1042 4.0	1616 0.7	2252 4.3	24 TU	0501 0.8	1136 3.7	1704 0.9	2331 4.0
10 TU	0445 0.3	1126 4.1	1658 0.5	2335 4.4	25 W	0531 0.8	1200 3.7	1733 0.8	2357 4.0
11 W	0528 0.1	1208 4.1	1739 0.4		26 TH	0558 0.8	1225 3.7	1801 0.8	
12 TH	0017 4.5	0612 0.1	1252 4.1	1821 0.4	27 F	0026 4.0	0622 0.8	1253 3.7	1827 0.8
13 F	0102 4.4	0658 0.2	1336 4.1	1906 0.5	28 SA	0059 4.0	0648 0.8	1326 3.7	1858 0.9
14 SA	0150 4.3	0748 0.3	1424 4.0	1956 0.7	29 SU	0136 3.9	0720 0.9	1403 3.7	1934 0.9
15 SU	0242 4.2	0840 0.6	1515 3.8	2051 0.9	30 M	0217 3.8	0757 1.0	1444 3.6	2015 1.1
					31 TU	0301 3.7	0841 1.1	1529 3.5	2103 1.2

Chart Datum: 0·20 metres above Ordnance Datum (Dublin). HAT is 4·5 metres above Chart Datum; see 4.5.

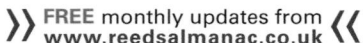

DUBLIN (NORTH WALL) LAT 53°21′N LONG 6°13′W
TIMES AND HEIGHTS OF HIGH AND LOW WATERS

TIME ZONE (UT)
For Summer Time add ONE hour in **non-shaded areas**

Dates in red are **SPRINGS**
Dates in blue are NEAPS

YEAR 2010

S Ireland

SEPTEMBER
Time m | Time m

1 0350 3.5 / 0931 1.3 / W 1622 3.4 / ☽ 2201 1.4
16 0541 3.3 / 1109 1.6 / TH 1801 3.4 / 2356 1.5

2 0450 3.3 / 1035 1.5 / TH 1727 3.3 / 2319 1.5
17 0702 3.3 / 1230 1.7 / F 1916 3.5

3 0609 3.2 / 1200 1.6 / F 1849 3.3
18 0132 1.4 / 0822 3.3 / SA 1352 1.6 / 2025 3.6

4 0045 1.4 / 0737 3.3 / SA 1321 1.5 / 2003 3.5
19 0238 1.2 / 0924 3.5 / SU 1449 1.4 / 2121 3.7

5 0159 1.1 / 0845 3.5 / SU 1426 1.2 / 2101 3.8
20 0325 1.1 / 1008 3.6 / M 1531 1.2 / 2204 3.9

6 0257 0.8 / 0939 3.8 / M 1516 0.9 / 2150 4.1
21 0401 0.9 / 1041 3.7 / TU 1606 1.0 / 2237 3.9

7 0345 0.4 / 1024 4.0 / TU 1559 0.7 / 2233 4.3
22 0433 0.8 / 1108 3.7 / W 1638 0.9 / 2306 4.0

8 0428 0.2 / 1106 4.1 / W 1639 0.4 / ● 2315 4.5
23 0500 0.8 / 1133 3.8 / TH 1706 0.8 / ○ 2332 4.0

9 0509 0.0 / 1146 4.2 / TH 1719 0.3 / 2356 4.5
24 0525 0.8 / 1156 3.8 / F 1733 0.8 / 2359 4.0

10 0551 0.0 / 1226 4.2 / F 1800 0.3
25 0547 0.8 / 1222 3.8 / SA 1759 0.8

11 0040 4.4 / 0633 0.2 / SA 1309 4.1 / 1844 0.4
26 0031 4.0 / 0613 0.8 / SU 1255 3.8 / 1830 0.8

12 0126 4.3 / 0719 0.4 / SU 1354 4.0 / 1932 0.6
27 0109 3.9 / 0646 0.9 / M 1333 3.8 / 1907 0.9

13 0217 4.1 / 0809 0.7 / M 1443 3.9 / 2027 0.9
28 0151 3.8 / 0726 1.0 / TU 1416 3.7 / 1950 1.0

14 0313 3.8 / 0903 1.0 / TU 1537 3.7 / 2128 1.1
29 0236 3.7 / 0811 1.1 / W 1503 3.6 / 2041 1.2

15 0421 3.5 / 1003 1.3 / W 1643 3.5 / ☽ 2236 1.3
30 0329 3.5 / 0905 1.4 / TH 1556 3.5 / 2144 1.3

OCTOBER
Time m | Time m

1 0431 3.4 / 1013 1.5 / F 1701 3.4 / ☽ 2302 1.4
16 0629 3.2 / 1150 1.7 / SA 1838 3.5

2 0551 3.3 / 1138 1.6 / SA 1820 3.4
17 0049 1.4 / 0743 3.3 / SU 1310 1.7 / 1945 3.6

3 0026 1.3 / 0715 3.4 / SU 1259 1.5 / 1934 3.6
18 0159 1.3 / 0844 3.4 / M 1412 1.5 / 2042 3.7

4 0139 1.0 / 0823 3.6 / M 1403 1.2 / 2036 3.9
19 0249 1.1 / 0929 3.6 / TU 1458 1.3 / 2128 3.8

5 0237 0.7 / 0918 3.8 / TU 1455 1.0 / 2128 4.1
20 0327 1.0 / 1004 3.7 / W 1536 1.1 / 2206 3.9

6 0325 0.4 / 1004 4.0 / W 1540 0.7 / 2214 4.3
21 0359 0.9 / 1035 3.8 / TH 1609 1.0 / 2238 3.9

7 0409 0.2 / 1046 4.1 / TH 1621 0.5 / ● 2257 4.4
22 0427 0.9 / 1104 3.8 / F 1639 0.9 / 2307 3.9

8 0450 0.1 / 1125 4.2 / F 1702 0.4 / 2339 4.4
23 0452 0.8 / 1129 3.9 / SA 1706 0.9 / ○ 2336 3.9

9 0531 0.2 / 1205 4.2 / SA 1744 0.4
24 0517 0.8 / 1156 3.9 / SU 1735 0.8

10 0023 4.3 / 0612 0.3 / SU 1246 4.1 / 1827 0.5
25 0009 3.9 / 0546 0.8 / M 1230 3.9 / 1809 0.8

11 0109 4.2 / 0655 0.6 / M 1330 4.1 / 1915 0.6
26 0048 3.9 / 0622 0.9 / TU 1310 3.9 / 1849 0.9

12 0159 4.0 / 0743 0.9 / TU 1417 3.9 / 2008 0.9
27 0132 3.8 / 0703 1.0 / W 1355 3.9 / 1936 1.0

13 0254 3.7 / 0835 1.1 / W 1510 3.8 / 2107 1.1
28 0221 3.7 / 0751 1.2 / TH 1444 3.8 / 2030 1.1

14 0358 3.5 / 0933 1.4 / TH 1612 3.6 / ☽ 2211 1.3
29 0316 3.6 / 0849 1.4 / F 1539 3.7 / 2134 1.1

15 0512 3.3 / 1037 1.6 / F 1725 3.5 / 2324 1.4
30 0420 3.5 / 0957 1.5 / SA 1642 3.6 / ☽ 2247 1.2

31 0533 3.4 / 1114 1.5 / SU 1753 3.7

NOVEMBER
Time m | Time m

1 0002 1.1 / 0648 3.5 / M 1230 1.5 / 1904 3.8
16 0100 1.4 / 0749 3.4 / TU 1321 1.6 / 1954 3.6

2 0111 0.9 / 0755 3.7 / TU 1335 1.3 / 2008 3.9
17 0200 1.3 / 0840 3.5 / W 1416 1.5 / 2045 3.6

3 0211 0.7 / 0852 3.8 / W 1431 1.1 / 2105 4.1
18 0245 1.2 / 0923 3.7 / TH 1500 1.3 / 2129 3.7

4 0303 0.6 / 0942 4.0 / TH 1520 0.8 / 2156 4.2
19 0322 1.1 / 1000 3.8 / F 1537 1.2 / 2208 3.8

5 0350 0.4 / 1027 4.1 / F 1606 0.7 / 2243 4.3
20 0353 1.0 / 1033 3.9 / SA 1610 1.1 / 2242 3.8

6 0433 0.4 / 1108 4.2 / SA 1650 0.6 / ● 2328 4.3
21 0422 1.0 / 1103 3.9 / SU 1642 1.0 / ○ 2315 3.9

7 0514 0.5 / 1148 4.2 / SU 1733 0.6
22 0452 0.9 / 1134 4.0 / M 1716 0.9 / 2352 3.9

8 0012 4.2 / 0554 0.6 / M 1229 4.2 / 1817 0.6
23 0526 0.9 / 1210 4.0 / TU 1754 0.8

9 0057 4.1 / 0636 0.8 / TU 1312 4.1 / 1903 0.7
24 0033 3.9 / 0604 0.9 / W 1252 4.1 / 1837 0.8

10 0145 3.9 / 0721 1.0 / W 1357 4.0 / 1953 0.8
25 0119 3.9 / 0648 1.0 / TH 1338 4.0 / 1926 0.8

11 0236 3.7 / 0810 1.2 / TH 1446 3.9 / 2047 1.0
26 0209 3.8 / 0737 1.1 / F 1429 4.0 / 2020 0.8

12 0333 3.5 / 0904 1.4 / F 1541 3.7 / 2144 1.2
27 0304 3.7 / 0834 1.2 / SA 1523 4.0 / 2120 0.9

13 0437 3.3 / 1003 1.6 / SA 1644 3.6 / ☽ 2245 1.3
28 0404 3.5 / 0937 1.3 / SU 1622 3.9 / ☽ 2224 1.0

14 0544 3.3 / 1107 1.7 / SU 1752 3.5 / 2351 1.4
29 0509 3.6 / 1045 1.4 / M 1726 3.9 / 2332 1.0

15 0650 3.3 / 1215 1.7 / M 1857 3.5
30 0618 3.6 / 1156 1.4 / TU 1833 3.9

DECEMBER
Time m | Time m

1 0039 1.0 / 0724 3.7 / W 1304 1.3 / 1940 3.9
16 0053 1.5 / 0748 3.4 / TH 1323 1.6 / 1957 3.4

2 0144 0.9 / 0826 3.8 / TH 1407 1.2 / 2044 4.0
17 0150 1.4 / 0839 3.5 / F 1417 1.5 / 2050 3.5

3 0242 0.8 / 0921 3.9 / F 1504 1.1 / 2143 4.0
18 0239 1.3 / 0924 3.7 / SA 1503 1.4 / 2136 3.6

4 0333 0.8 / 1012 4.0 / SA 1555 0.9 / 2235 4.0
19 0320 1.2 / 1003 3.8 / SU 1544 1.2 / 2219 3.7

5 0420 0.8 / 1057 4.1 / SU 1643 0.8 / ● 2323 4.0
20 0357 1.1 / 1040 3.9 / M 1622 1.0 / 2258 3.8

6 0502 0.8 / 1137 4.1 / M 1727 0.7
21 0433 1.0 / 1116 4.1 / TU 1701 0.8 / ○ 2338 3.9

7 0006 4.0 / 0542 0.8 / TU 1216 4.2 / 1809 0.7
22 0511 0.9 / 1154 4.2 / W 1741 0.7

8 0047 3.9 / 0621 0.9 / W 1255 4.1 / 1852 0.7
23 0020 4.0 / 0550 0.8 / TH 1236 4.2 / 1825 0.6

9 0129 3.8 / 0701 1.0 / TH 1337 4.1 / 1936 0.8
24 0105 4.0 / 0634 0.8 / F 1322 4.2 / 1912 0.5

10 0213 3.7 / 0744 1.1 / F 1420 4.0 / 2022 0.9
25 0153 4.0 / 0721 0.9 / SA 1411 4.2 / 2003 0.6

11 0300 3.6 / 0832 1.3 / SA 1507 3.9 / 2110 1.1
26 0244 3.9 / 0813 1.0 / SU 1503 4.2 / 2058 0.7

12 0351 3.4 / 0924 1.4 / SU 1557 3.7 / 2201 1.2
27 0339 3.8 / 0911 1.1 / M 1558 4.1 / 2157 0.8

13 0449 3.3 / 1021 1.6 / M 1652 3.6 / ☽ 2256 1.4
28 0439 3.7 / 1013 1.2 / TU 1657 4.0 / ☽ 2259 0.9

14 0551 3.3 / 1121 1.6 / TU 1755 3.5 / 2354 1.4
29 0544 3.7 / 1121 1.3 / W 1804 3.8

15 0652 3.3 / 1222 1.7 / W 1858 3.4
30 0006 1.1 / 0653 3.6 / TH 1234 1.4 / 1917 3.8

31 0116 1.2 / 0800 3.7 / F 1346 1.4 / 2028 3.7

Chart Datum: 0·20 metres above Ordnance Datum (Dublin). HAT is 4·5 metres above Chart Datum; see 4.5.

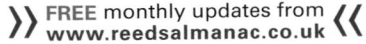

9.12.11 WICKLOW

Wicklow **52°58'·98N 06°02'·70W** ✿✿♨♨♨✿✿

CHARTS AC 1468, 633, 5621; Imray C61.

TIDES –0010 Dover; ML 1·7; Duration 0640

Standard Port DUBLIN (NORTH WALL) (←—)

Times				Height (metres)			
High Water		Low Water		MHWS	MHWN	MLWN	MLWS
0000	0700	0000	0500	4·1	3·4	1·5	0·7
1200	1900	1200	1700				
Differences WICKLOW							
–0019	–0019	–0024	–0026	–1·4	–1·1	–0·4	0·0

SHELTER Very safe, and access H24. Outer hbr is open to NE winds which cause a swell. Moorings in NW of hbr belong to SC and may not be used without permission. 4 berths on E Pier (2·5m) are convenient except in strong winds NW to NE, with fender boards/ladders provided. W pier is not recommended. ⚓ in hbr is restricted by ships' turning circle. Inner hbr (river) gives excellent shelter in 2·5m on N and S Quays, which are used by FVs. Packet Quay is for ships (2·5m), but may be used if none due; fender board needed. Yachts should berth on N or S quays as directed and/or space available.

NAVIGATION WPT 52°59'·20N 06°01'·80W, 220°/0·27M to ent. Appr presents no difficulty; keep in the R sector off the E pier lt to avoid Planet Rk and Pogeen Rk.

LIGHTS AND MARKS No ldg marks/lts; lts are as on the chartlet. W pier head lt, Iso G 4s, is shown H24. ☆ Fl WG 10s on Packet Quay hd is vis 076°-G-256°-W-076°.

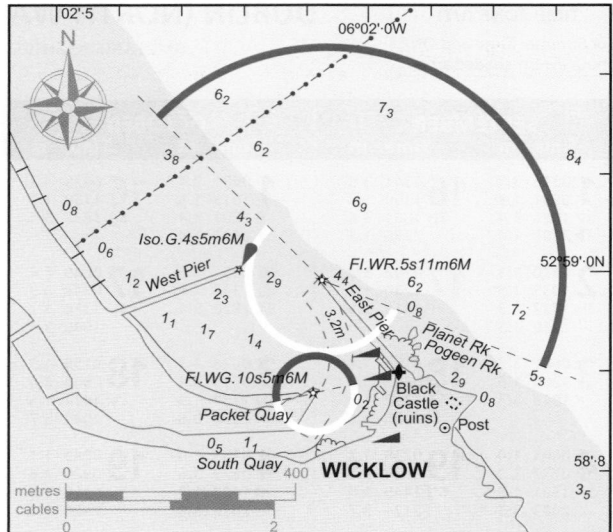

R/T VHF Ch 12, **14**, 16. Wicklow SC Ch M 16 (occas).

TELEPHONE (Code 0404) HM ☎ 67455; MRCC (01) 6620922; Coast/Cliff Rescue Service 69962; ⊖ 67222; Police 67107; Dr 67381.

FACILITIES **East Pier, S and N Quays**, L, FW, AB €14.00/craft, reductions for longer stay, P & D (cans; bulk: see HM); **Wicklow SC** ☎ 67526, Slip (except LWS), M, L, FW, Bar; **Services**: ME, El, C, Kos, Gaz. **Town** CH, ▨, R, Bar, ✉, Ⓑ, ⇌, ✈ (Dublin).

9.12.12 ARKLOW

Wicklow **52°47'·60N 06°08'·20W** ✿✿♨♨♨✿✿

CHARTS AC 1468, 633, 5621; Imray C61.

TIDES –0150 Dover; ML 1·0; Duration 0640

Standard Port DUBLIN (NORTH WALL) (←—)

Times				Height (metres)			
High Water		Low Water		MHWS	MHWN	MLWN	MLWS
0000	0700	0000	0500	4·1	3·4	1·5	0·7
1200	1900	1200	1700				
Differences ARKLOW (Note small Range)							
–0315	–0201	–0140	–0134	–2·7	–2·2	–0·6	–0·1
COURTOWN							
–0328	–0242	–0158	–0138	–2·8	–2·4	–0·5	0·0

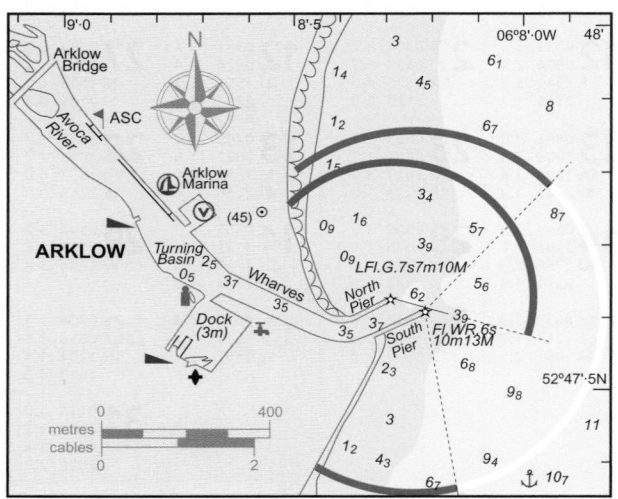

SHELTER Good, access H24.

- Entrance unsafe in strong or prolonged NE to SE winds, when seas break across the bar.

A 60 berth marina lies on NE side of river. Good ⚓ in bay; avoid whelk pots. One AB for ⓥ (1.4m) at ASC quay. AB on SE wall of Dock (ent is 13·5m wide; 3m depth) in perfect shelter, but amidst FVs. **Arklow Roadstone Hbr**, 1M S of Arklow, is not for yachts.

NAVIGATION WPT 52°47'·60N 06°07'·50W, 270°/0·40M to ent. No navigational dangers, but beware ebb setting SE across hbr ent; give S pierhd a wide berth. Ent is difficult without power, due to blanking by piers. 3kn speed limit. Night entry, see below. Caution: Up-river of Dock ent keep to NE side of river.

LIGHTS AND MARKS No ldg lts/marks, see 9.12.4 and chartlet Conspic factory chy 2·5ca NW of piers.

- Beware the Pier Hd lts are very difficult to see due to powerful orange flood lts near the root of both piers shining E/ENE onto them (to assist pilotage of departing shipping).
- Best advice to visitors is to approach from the NE with R sector just showing, or enter by day.

R/T Marina Ch 16 12 (HJ); Arklow SC Ch 10.

TELEPHONE (Code 0402) HM 32466; MRCC (01) 6620922/3; Coast/Cliff Rescue Service 32430; RNLI 32901; ⊖ 32553; Police 32304/5; Dr 32421.

FACILITIES (from seaward) **Dock** €15.00/craft (2nd day free), use showers and toilets in LB Hse, D (Dock ent, HO); **Marina** (60 inc ⓥ €3·35), ☎ 39901/32610. **Arklow SC** (NE bank, 500m up-river from Dock), showers, pontoon €15.00, 1 ⚓. **Services**: FW, P & D (cans ½M), ME, El, ✕, C (20 ton mobile), Kos. **Town** limited CH for yachts, ▨, R, P & D (cans), Bar, ✉, Ⓑ, Wi-fi, @, ⇌, ✈ (Dublin).

MINOR HARBOURS S OF ARKLOW
COURTOWN, Wexford, **52°38'·55N 06°13'·50W**. AC 1787. 9.6M S of Arklow is feasible in settled weather and offshore winds. Caution: 10m wide ent; only 1m (maintained by local YC) at MLWS due to silting. AB on E wall or pick up vacant mooring.

MINOR HARBOURS S OF ARKLOW *continued*

POLDUFF PIER, Wexford, **52°34'·15N 06°11'·97W**. AC 1787. 14M S of Arklow. Pier, 100m long, extends in NE direction from shore. NW side of pier has slipway from shore and 1m depth alongside. Local moorings W of pier. Good shelter for small boats in S to W winds. Swell in winds E of S. Appr in daylight only. Appr is clear from NE to E. Rks extend from shore E'ward 200m N of pier but steering along line of pier will clear them. Pub near pier. Village (Ballygarrett) 1·25M W.

9.12.13 WEXFORD

Wexford **52°20'·10N 06°27'·00W** ✵⚓⚓✿✿

CHARTS AC 1787, 1772, 5621; Imray C61.

TIDES –0450 Dover; ML 1·3; Duration 0630

Standard Port COBH (→)

Times				Height (metres)			
High Water		Low Water		MHWS	MHWN	MLWN	MLWS
0500	1100	0500	1100	4·1	3·2	1·3	0·4
1700	2300	1700	2300				
Differences WEXFORD							
+0126	+0126	+0118	+0108	–2·1	–1·7	–0·3	+0·1

SHELTER 250m of AB available just below bridge. Sheltered ⚓ off town quays in 2·3m, but streams are strong. Some ⚓s are provided by WHBTC, close N of Ballast Bank. There are no commercial users other than FVs. Work continues on new waterfront on W side of river.

NAVIGATION Visitors are strongly advised to obtain up to date local information from the WHBTC. See www.whbtc.ie or ☎ 053 9122039.

- Entry is hazardous in strong winds between SE and NE when the sea breaks on the bar. Entry is also difficult at any time for vessels with a draft >1.3m. For strangers best entry is HW±2.
- From N make good 221° from North Long Buoy for approx 2·4M keeping outside 5m contour to avoid Slaney Wreck and Dogger Bank; from S make good 353° for approx 4M from West Holdens Buoy. PHM Bar Buoy (52°19'·57N 06°19·52W in 2009) on 10m contour marks the entrance.
- The narrow buoyed chan, which constantly shifts, starts approx 245°/8ca from Bar Buoy. Keep close to all PHM buoys. Beware the S training wall (covers) and pass well S of Black Man SHM Bn at end of N training wall.
- Proceed either to the quays or by arrangement (☎ 053 9122039 or Ch 16/69) to club visitor's mooring.

LIGHTS AND MARKS The marks and tracks on chartlet should be treated with great caution as the channel shifts continually. There are no ldg lts. The 2 church spires at Wexford give useful general orientation.

R/T Wexford Hbr BC VHF Ch 16 (best time to try 1000–1200 hrs).

TELEPHONE (Code 053) Wexford Hbr BC 9122039; MRCC (01) 6620922/3; ⊖ 9133116; Police 9122333; Dr 9131154; ⊕ 9142233.

FACILITIES **Wexford Quays**, AB (free), Slip, P, D, FW, ME, El, ⛟, CH; **Wexford Hbr Boat Club**, Slip, C (5 ton), Bar; **Town** ✉, Ⓑ, ⇌, ✈ (Waterford).

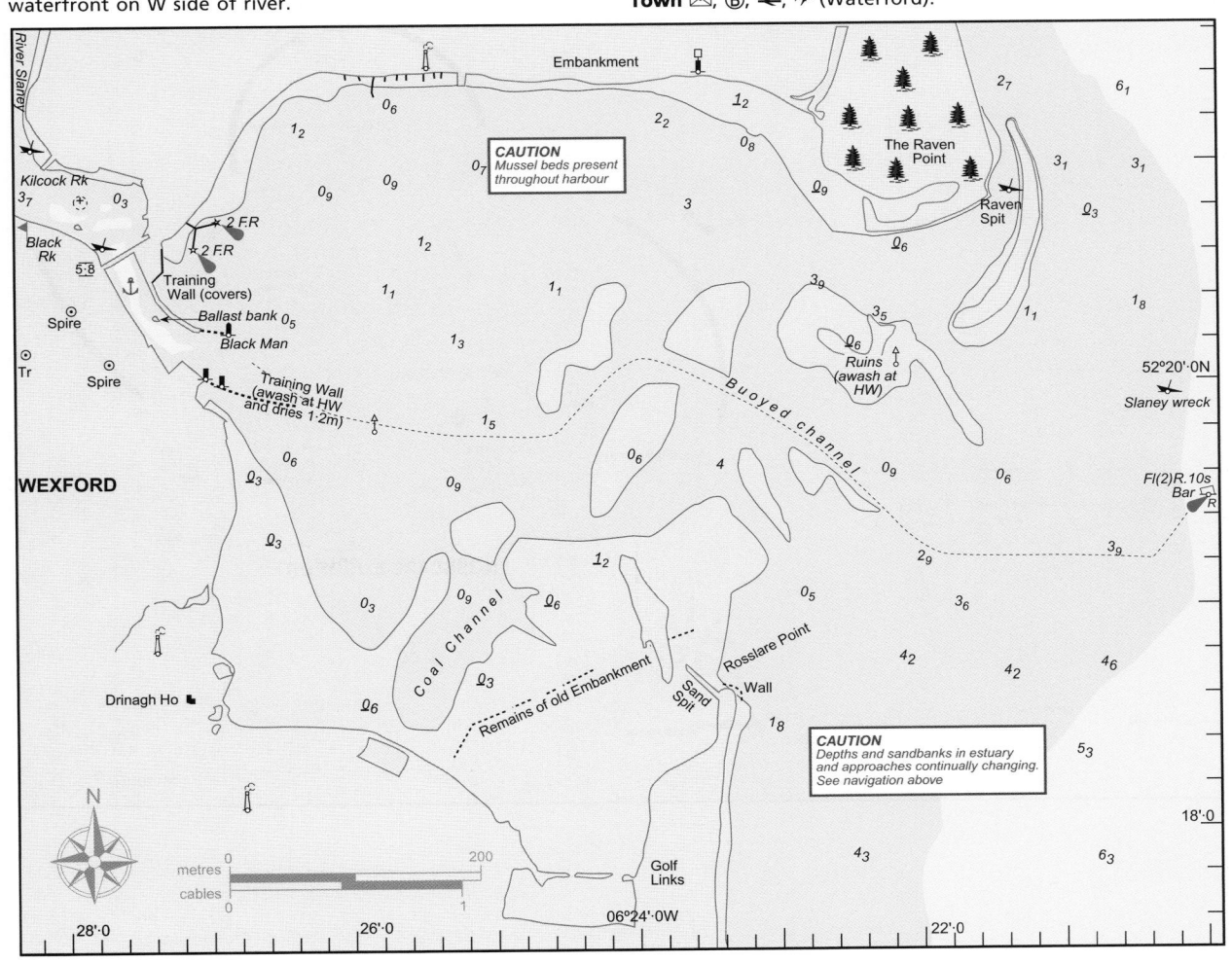

9.12.14 ROSSLARE EUROPORT

Dublin **52°15'·30N 06°20'·90W** ❀❀❀❀⚓❀❀

CHARTS AC 1787, 1772, 5621; Imray C61, C57.

TIDES –0510 Dover; ML 1·1; Duration 0640

Standard Port COBH (➡)

Times				Height (metres)			
High Water		Low Water		MHWS	MHWN	MLWN	MLWS
0500	1100	0500	1100	4·1	3·2	1·3	0·4
1700	2300	1700	2300				
Differences ROSSLARE EUROPORT							
+0045	+0035	+0015	–0005	–2·2	–1·8	–0·5	–0·1

SHELTER Useful passage shelter from SW'lies, but few facilities for yachts which may berth on E wall of marshalling area (⚓ on the chartlet, 3·7m), or ⚓ about 0·5M W of hbr. *Small craft harbour (5ca W) is not recommended. In winds from WNW-NNE it is often uncomfortable and, if these winds freshen, dangerous; leave at once, via S Shear.* Rosslare has 160 ferry/high-speed catamaran (41kn) movements per week.

NAVIGATION WPT 52°14'·82N 06°15·60W (abeam S Long SCM buoy, VQ (6)+L Fl 10s), 285°/2·92M to bkwtr lt. Main appr from E, S and W is via S Shear, buoyed/lit chan to S of Holden's Bed, a shoal of varying depth; the tide sets across the chan. From S, beware rks off Greenore Pt, and overfalls here and over The Baillies. From the N, appr via N Shear. Tuskar TSS is approx 8M ESE of hbr. Yachts, bound N/S, will usually navigate to the W of Tuskar Rk where the 3·5M wide chan lies to seaward of The Bailies. A passage inshore of The Bailies requires local knowledge and should not be attempted at night. In heavy weather or poor vis, passage E of Tuskar Rk is advised.

LIGHTS AND MARKS Tuskar Rk, Q (2) 7·5s 33m 28M, is 5·8M SE of hbr. Water tr (R lt, 35m) is conspic 0·8M SSE of hbr ent. Bkwtr lt, Oc WRG 5s 15m 13/10M, see 9.12.4. Its two W sectors (188°-208° and 283°-286°) cover N and S Shear respectively. Note: Powerful floodlights in the hbr make identification of navigational lights difficult.

R/T VHF Ch **12** (H24) before entering hbr.

TELEPHONE (Code 053) HM 9157921, mobile 087 2320251; MRCC (01) 6620922/3; LB Lookout Stn 9133205; ⊜ 9133116; Police 053 9165200; Dr 9131154; ⊕ 9142233.

FACILITIES Hbr Ops ☎ 9157929, No dues, P&D (cans), L, FW (by hose on Berths 2 and 3), ME, C, Divers, Kos, El. **Village**; 🛒, R, Bar, ✉, Ⓑ, ➾, ✈ (Dublin). **Ferries:** Irish Ferries (www.irish ferries.com): Pembroke Dock, daily, 3¾ Hrs; Cherbourg, 3/week, 18½ hrs; Roscoff, 2/week, 17 hrs. Stena (www.stenaline.co.uk): Fishguard, 2/day, 1¾ Hrs. LD Lines (www.ldlines.co.uk): Le Havre, Sat only, 20 hrs.

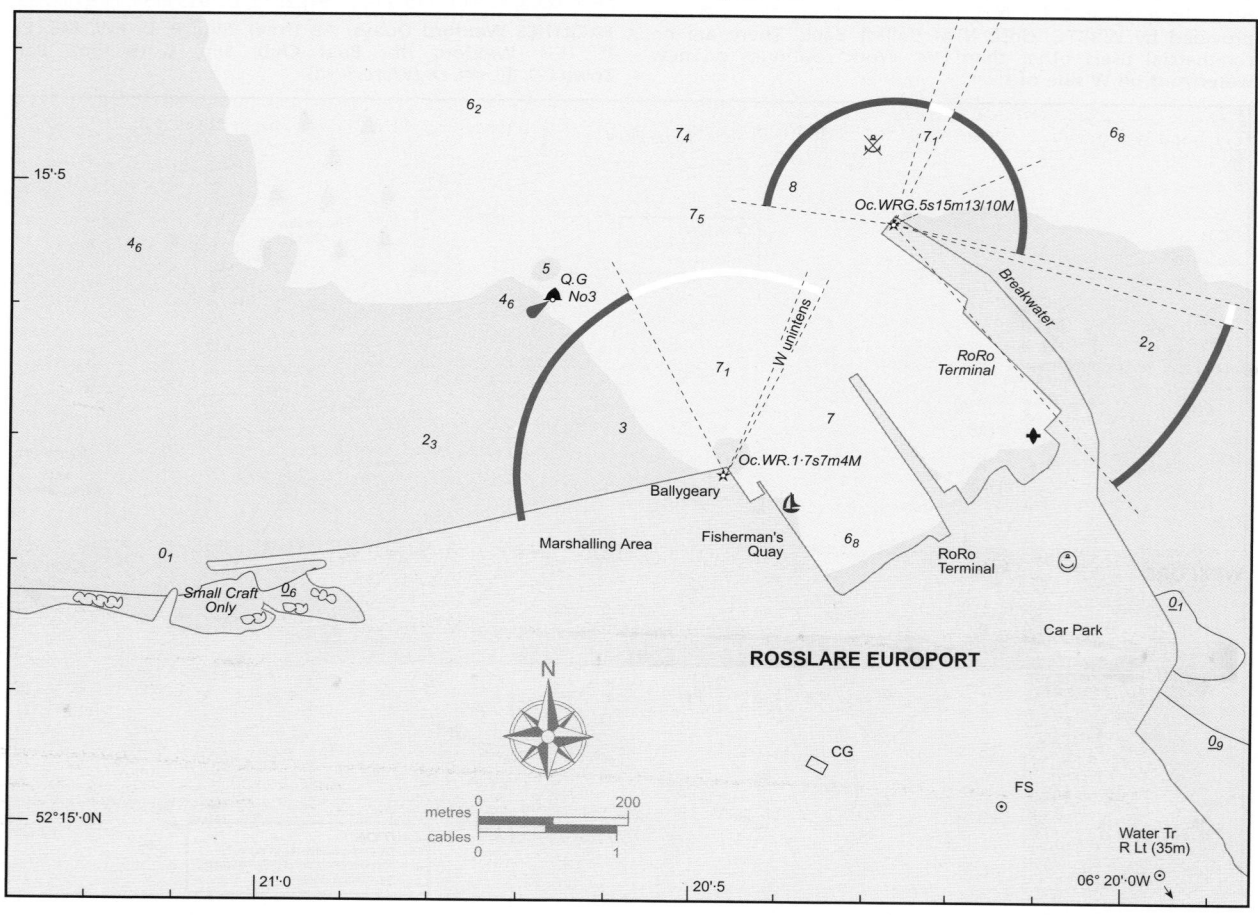

TUSKAR ROCK TO OLD HEAD OF KINSALE

(AC 2049) Dangerous rks lie up to 2ca NW and 6½ca SSW of Tuskar Rk and there can be a dangerous race off Carnsore Pt. In bad weather or poor visibility, use the Inshore Traffic Zone of the Tuskar Rock TSS, passing to seaward of Tuskar Rk (lt), the Barrels ECM lt buoy and Coningbeg buoy.

NOTE: The tide turns on St Patrick's Bridge (e) up to 2 hours earlier than in Saltee Sound

If taking the inshore passage from Greenore Pt, stay inside The Bailies to pass 2ca off Carnsore Pt. Beware of lobster pots in this area. Steer WSW to pass N of Black Rk and the Bohurs, S of which are extensive overfalls. The small hbr of Kilmore Quay has been rebuilt with a new marina, but beware rks and shoals in the approaches.

Saltee Sound (AC 2740) is a safe passage, least width 3ca, between Great and Little Saltee, conspic islands to S and N. ▶ Sebber Bridge extends 7½ca N from the NE point of Great Saltee and Jackeen Rk is 1M NW of the S end of Little Saltee, so care is needed through the sound, where the stream runs 3·5kn at sp. ◀ There are several rks S of the Saltees, but clear passage between many of them. There are no obstructions on a direct course for a point 1M S of Hook Head, to avoid the overfalls and Tower Race, which at times extend about 1M S of the Head.

Dunmore East (AC 2046) is a useful passage port at the mouth of Waterford Hbr. To the W, beware Falskirt, a dangerous rk off Swines Pt. There are few offlying rks from Tramore Bay to Ballinacourty Pt on the N side of Dungarvan Bay (AC 2017). Helvick is a small sheltered hbr approached along the S shore of

the bay, keeping S of Helvick Rk (ECM lt buoy) and other dangers to the N.

Mine Hd (lt) has two dangerous rks, The Rogue about 2½ca E and The Longship 1M SW. To the W is a subm'gd rk 100m SE of Ram Hd. ▶ Here the W-going stream starts at HW Cobh + 0230, and the E-going at HW Cobh −0215, sp rates 1·5kn. ◀ Pass 2ca off Capel Island; the sound between it and Knockadoon Hd is not recommended.

The N side of Ballycotton B is foul up to 5ca offshore. Ballycotton Hbr is small and crowded, but usually there is sheltered anch outside. Sound Rk and Small Is lie between the mainland and Ballycotton Is (lt, fog sig). From Ballycotton to Cork keep at least 5ca off for dangers including The Smiths (PHM lt buoy) 1·5M WSW of Ballycotton Island. Pass between Hawk Rk, close off Power Hd, and Pollock Rk (PHM lt buoy) 1·25M SE.

Near the easy entrance and excellent shelter of Cork Harbour (AC 1777), Ringabella Bay offers temp anch in good weather. 7ca SE of Robert's Hd is Daunt Rk (3·5m) on which seas break in bad weather; marked by PHM lt buoy. Little Sovereign on with Reanies Hd 241° leads inshore of it. The Sovereigns are large rks off Oyster Haven, a good hbr but prone to swell in S'lies. The ent is clear except for Harbour Rk which must be passed on its W side. Bulman Rk (SCM lt buoy) is 4ca S of Preghane Pt at the ent to Kinsale's fine harbour. ▶ The tide on the Cork coast turns to the NE at HW Dover +0045. There is an eddy 5M ESE of Old Head of Kinsale at HW Dover +0400. The ingoing Cork Harbour tide begins at HW Dover +0055.

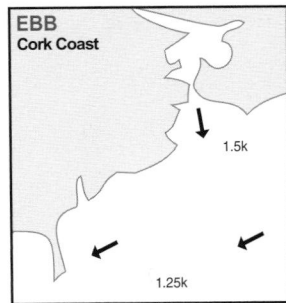

The tide turns SW at HW Dover +0500. The outgoing Cork Harbour tide begins at HW Dover −0540. Old Head of Kinsale (lt, fog sig) is quite steep-to, but a race extends 1M to SW on W-going stream, and to SE on E-going stream. ◀ There is an inshore passage in light weather, but in strong winds keep 2M off.

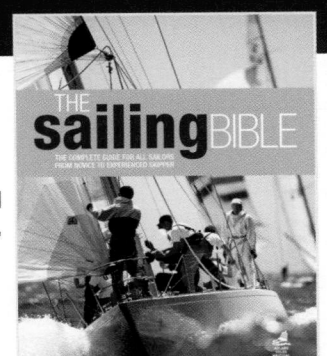

9.12.15 KILMORE QUAY

Wexford 52°10'·25N 06°35'·15W ✿✿✿✿⚓⚓✿✿✿✿

CHARTS AC 2049, 2740, 5621; Imray C61, C57.

TIDES –0535 Dover; ML No data; Duration 0605

Standard Port COBH (→)

Times				Height (metres)			
High Water		Low Water		MHWS	MHWN	MLWN	MLWS
0500	1100	0500	1100	4·1	3·2	1·3	0·4
1700	2300	1700	2300				
Differences BAGINBUN HEAD (5M NE of Hook Hd)							
+0003	+0003	–0008	–0008	–0·2	–0·1	+0·2	+0·2
GREAT SALTEE							
+0019	+0009	–0004	+0006	–0·3	–0·4	No data	
CARNSORE POINT							
+0029	+0019	–0002	+0008	–1·1	–1·0	No data	

SHELTER Excellent in marina (3·0m depth), but hbr ent is exposed to SE'lies. FVs berth on W and E piers, close S of marina.

NAVIGATION WPT 52°09'·22N 06°35'·32W, SWM buoy (Apr-Sep), 007°/1·0M to pier hd lt, on ldg line. Great (57m) and Little (35m) Saltee Islands lie 3M and 1·7M to SSW and S, respectively, of hbr, separated by Saltee Sound. From the E, safest appr initially is via Saltee Sound, then N to WPT. Caution: In bad weather seas break on the Bohurs and The Bore, rks 2M E of

Saltee Islands. Beware Goose Rk (2·6m) close W of Little Saltee and Murroch's Rk (2·1m) 6ca NW of Little Saltee. St Patrick's Bridge, 650m E of the WPT, is a 300m wide E/W chan used by FVs and yachts, but carrying only 2·4m; care needed in strong onshore winds. It is marked by a PHM buoy, Fl R 6s, and a SHM buoy, Fl G 6s, (laid Apr to mid-Sep); general direction of buoyage is E. From the W, appr is clear but keep at least 5ca off Forlorn Pt to avoid Forlorn Rk (1·5m).

LIGHTS AND MARKS See 9.12.4 and chartlet. Ldg lts/marks lead 008° to the hbr.

• From W, ldg lts are obsc'd by piers until S of hbr ent. Turn 90° port into hbr ent, just past ☆ QRG at W Quay Hd; do not overshoot into shoal water ahead. The R sectors of this ☆ QRG warn of Forlorn Rock and The Lings to W of the ldg line and shingle banks drying 0·6m close E of the ldg line.

A white-gabled church is conspic from afar, as are two 20m high flood lt pylons on the E quay. A disused lt ship at the inner end of W quay is a museum of no navigational significance.

R/T VHF Ch 09 (occas).

TELEPHONE (Code 053) HM ☎ 9129955; ⊖ 9133741; MRCC (01) 6620922/3; Emergency/Dr/Police 999.

FACILITIES Marina Ch 09 16 (35+20 Ⓥ) ☎ 9129955, €2.20, Slip, ⚓, D & P, El, ME, LB; **Village** Showers at Stella Maris (10 mins walk), Gaz, CH, ME, El, D & P (cans) is 3M away, R, Bar, 🛒, ✉, Ⓗ (Wexford 15M).

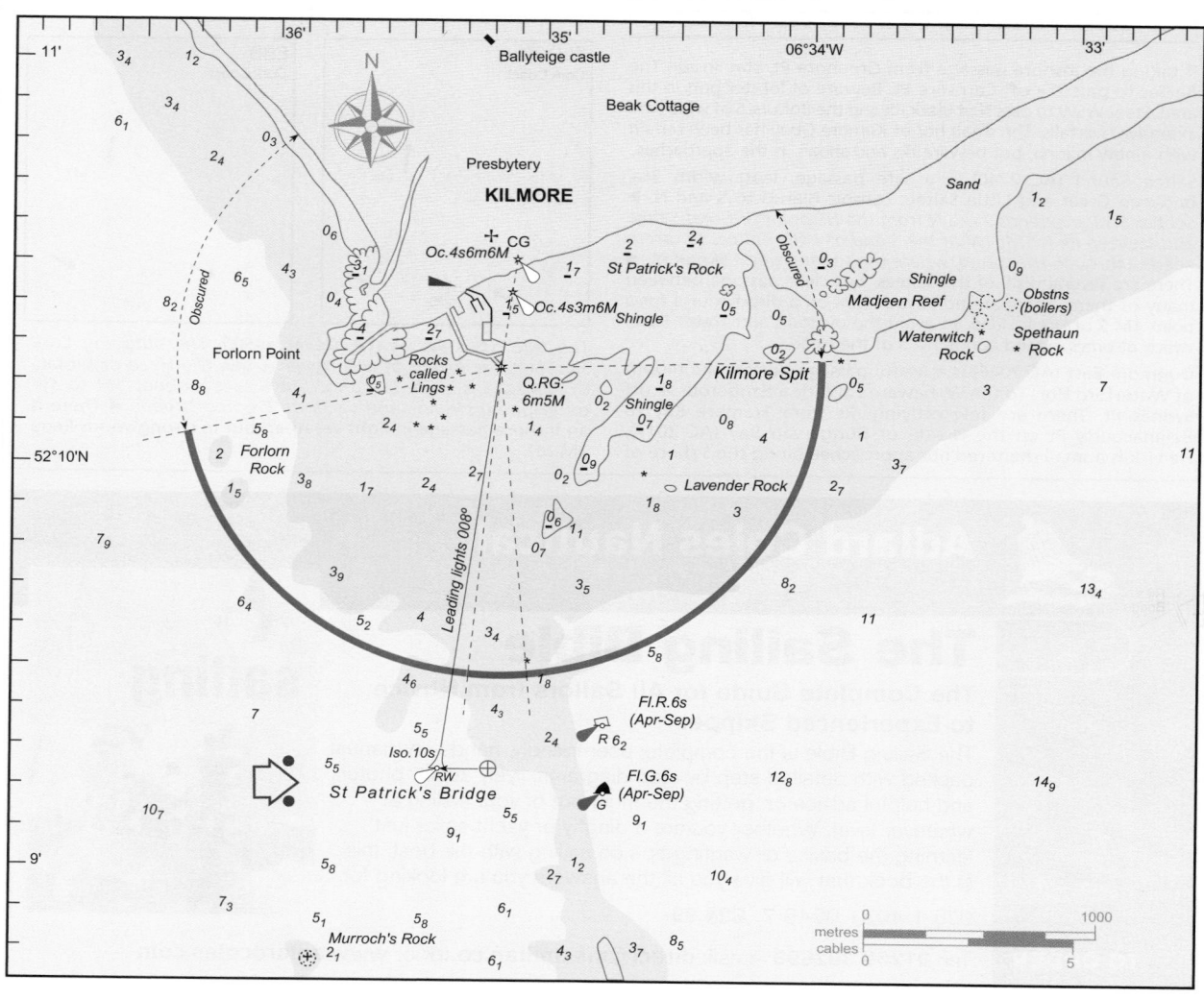

9.12.16 WATERFORD

Waterford 52°15'·50N 07°06'·00W ✿✿✿✿⚓⚓✿✿

CHARTS AC 2049, 2046, 5621, 5622; Imray C57.

TIDES –0520 Dover; ML 2·4; Duration 0605

Standard Port COBH (→)

Times				Height (metres)			
High Water		Low Water		MHWS	MHWN	MLWN	MLWS
0500	1100	0500	1100	4·1	3·2	1·3	0·4
1700	2300	1700	2300				
Differences WATERFORD							
+0057	+0057	+0046	+0046	+0·4	+0·3	–0·1	+0·1
CHEEKPOINT							
+0022	+0020	+0020	+0020	+0·3	+0·2	+0·2	+0·1
KILMOKEA POINT							
+0026	+0022	+0020	+0020	+0·2	+0·1	+0·1	+0·1
NEW ROSS							
+0100	+0030	+0055	+0130	+0·3	+0·4	+0·3	+0·4

SHELTER Very good on 4 long marina pontoons after Nanny pontoon (first one/private) on S bank, abeam cathedral spire. Beware strong tidal stream. Up the estuary are many excellent ⚓s: off S side of R Suir in King's Chan (only to be entered W of Little Is); and up the R Barrow near Marsh Pt (about 2M S of New Ross) and 0·5M S of New Ross fixed bridge.

NAVIGATION WPT 52°06'·50N 06°58'·50W, 002°/6·7M to Dir lt at Duncannon. From the E, keep clear of Brecaun reef (2M NE of Hook Hd). Keep about 1·5M S of Hook Hd to clear Tower Race and overfalls, especially HW Dover ±2. From the W beware Falskirt Rk (3m), 2ca off Swine Head and 2M WSW of Dunmore East (9.12.17). Marine Farms off Creadan Hd and Broomhill Pt; cruise liners and large container ships go up to Waterford; beware ferry between Passage East and Ballyhack.

LIGHTS AND MARKS The estuary and R Suir are very well buoyed/lit all the way to Waterford. The estuary ent is between Dunmore East and Hook Hd. Duncannon dir lt, F WRG, leads 002° into the river. R Barrow is also well lit/marked up to New Ross. The railway swing bridge at the river ent opens at its W end. Call bridge-keeper VHF Ch 14.

R/T Waterford and New Ross VHF Ch **14** 16. No VHF for marina.

TELEPHONE (Code 051) Marina 309900, mobile 087 2384944; HMs Waterford 301400, Mob 08725 98297 or 08722 24961; New Ross 421303; MRCC (01) 6620922; ⊖ 832090; Police 305300; Dr 855411; Ⓗ 848000.

FACILITIES Marina FW, ⫰, AB €2.00. All tides access for 1·5m draft; showers (free) and Ⓒ at HM's office.
Services: ME, El, ✗, C, BY (Ballyhack). **City** P, D (by arrangement with marina or from Dunmore East), Gaz, all facilities, Bus and ⇌ to Rosslare for UK ferries, ✈ (Cork) for UK/Continent, ✈ (Waterford) for Manchester and Luton and summer seasonal to Lorient (9.21.15).

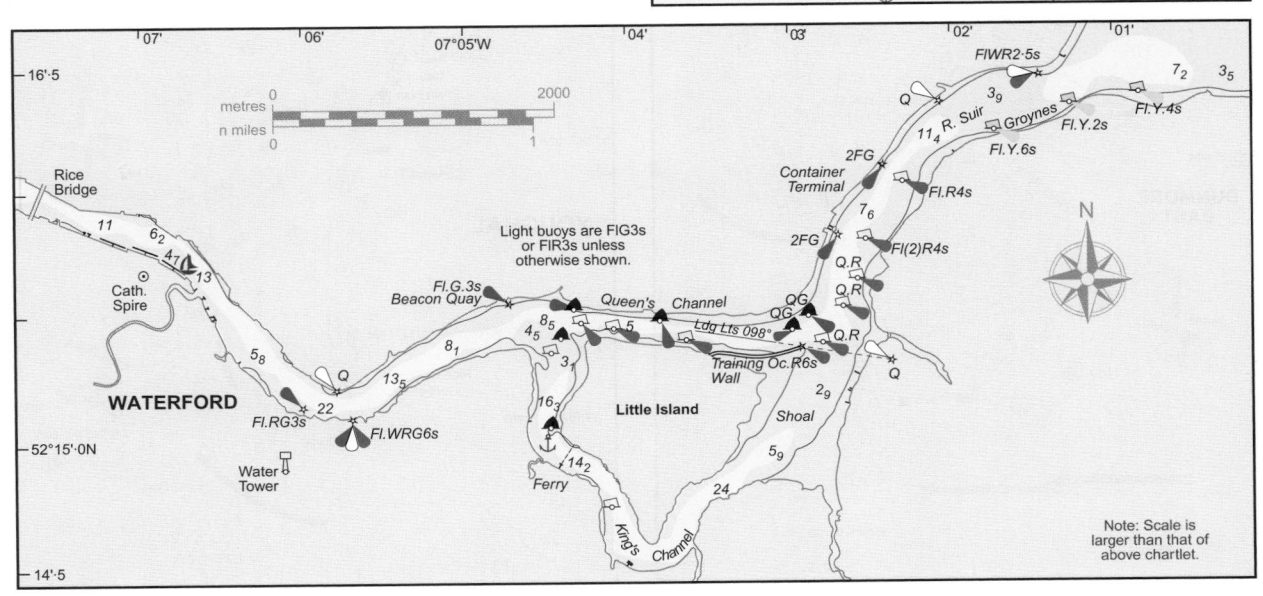

9.12.17 DUNMORE EAST

Waterford **52°08'·95N 06°59'·37W** ✿✿✿✿♦♦✿✿

CHARTS AC 2049, 2046, 5621, 5622; Imray C57, C61.

TIDES −0535 Dover; ML 2·4; Duration 0605

Standard Port COBH (⟶)

Times				Height (metres)			
High Water		Low Water		MHWS	MHWN	MLWN	MLWS
0500	1100	0500	1100	4·1	3·2	1·3	0·4
1700	2300	1700	2300				
Differences DUNMORE EAST							
+0008	+0003	0000	0000	+0·1	0·0	+0·1	+0·2
DUNGARVAN HARBOUR							
+0004	+0012	+0007	−0001	0·0	+0·1	−0·2	0·0

SHELTER Very good in hbr, but moorings exposed in E-ESE'lies >F6. ⚓ N of the hbr. Visitors welcome, moorings administered by Waterford SC (☎ 051 383389). A useful passage port/refuge. Primarily a busy FV hbr and large cruise liners ⚓ off. In bad weather berth alongside FVs at W Wharf, clear of ice plant, in at least 2m or go up R Suir to Waterford (9.12.16).

NAVIGATION WPT (see also 9.12.16) 52°08'·00N, 06°58'·00W, 317°/1·2M to bkwtr lt. Enter under power. From E, stay 1·5M off Hook Hd to clear Tower Race; then steer for hbr in R sector of E pier lt ho. In calm weather Hook Hd can be rounded 1ca off. From W, beware Falskirt Rk (off Swines Hd, 2M WSW) dries 3·0m. By night track E for Hook Hd until in R sector of E pier lt, then alter to N.

LIGHTS AND MARKS Lts as chartlet and see 9.12.4.

R/T VHF Ch 14 16 (Pilot Station).

TELEPHONE (Code 051) HM 383166, mobile 087 7931705; Hbr Foreman 383688; Fuel 087 2503510; Police 383112; ⊖ 832090; MRCC (01) 6620922/3; Duty Coastguard Mob 0868 501764; Health Centre 383347.

FACILITIES Hbr ☎ 383166, D, FW (E pier), Slip, scrubbing grid, Kos, CH, BH (230 ton); **Waterford Hbr SC** ☎ 383230, Bar, showers; **Village** P (cans), Bar, R, 🛒, Ⓑ, ✉, ✈ (Waterford).

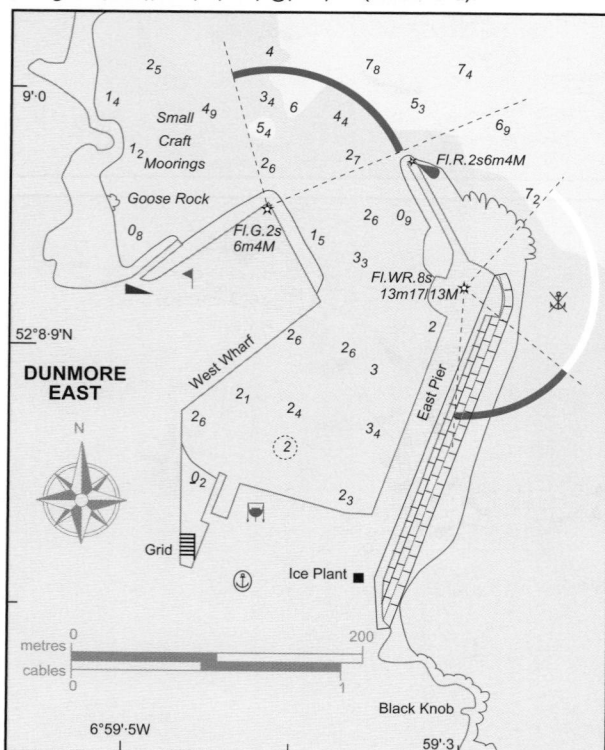

9.12.18 YOUGHAL

Cork **51°56'·54N 07°50'·20W** ✿✿✿✿♦♦✿✿

CHARTS AC 2049, 2071, 5622; Imray C57.

TIDES −0556 Dover; ML 2·1; Duration 0555

Standard Port COBH (⟶)

Times				Height (metres)			
High Water		Low Water		MHWS	MHWN	MLWN	MLWS
0500	1100	0500	1100	4·1	3·2	1·3	0·4
1700	2300	1700	2300				
Differences YOUGHAL							
0000	+0010	+0010	0000	−0·2	−0·1	−0·1	−0·1

SHELTER Good, but strong S'lies cause swell inside the hbr. Possible AB in 1.3m (drying patches just off quay); seasonal short-stay pontoon, with FW, off landing jetty. ⚓ as chartlet; no dues. Strong tidal streams run throughout anchorages.

NAVIGATION WPT, East Bar, 51°55'·62N 07°48'·00W, 302°/1·8M to Fl WR 2·5s lt. Beware Blackball Ledge (ECM lt buoy) and Bar Rks (SCM lt buoy), both outside hbr ent in R sector of lt ho. From W, appr via West Bar (1·7m) is shorter route and E Bar has 2·0m.

- Both Bars in E to SSW'lies >F6 are likely to have dangerous seas.
- Beware salmon nets set during June-July, Mon-Thurs 0400-2100.
- Red Bank is continually changing, obtain local knowledge.

LIGHTS AND MARKS See 9.12.4 and chartlet. Water tr is conspic from seaward; clock tr and ⊕ tr within hbr. Up-river, 175° transit of convent belfry tr/town hall clears W of Red Bank.

R/T VHF Ch 14 16 0900-1700 and when ships expected.

TELEPHONE (Code 024) HM Mobile 0872511143 MRCC (066) 9476109; Coast Guard 93252 or mob 0868 501769; ⊖ (021) 4325000; Police 92200; Dr 92702. Youghal Shipping 92577 (for poss AB).

FACILITIES **Services:** L, FW, Slip, AB (☎Youghal Shipping). **Town** P & D (cans), 🛒, R, Bar, ✉, Ⓑ, Bus (Cork/W'ford), ✈(Cork).

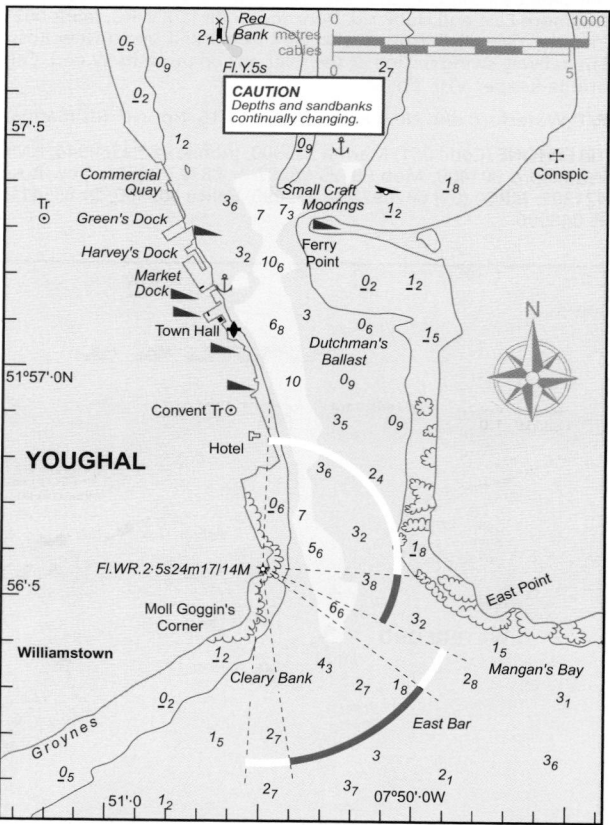

TIME ZONE (UT)
For Summer Time add ONE hour in **non-shaded areas**

COBH   LAT 51°51'N   LONG 8°18'W
TIMES AND HEIGHTS OF HIGH AND LOW WATERS

Dates in red are **SPRINGS**
Dates in blue are NEAPS

YEAR 2010

S Ireland

JANUARY

Time	m		Time	m
1 0529	4.2	**16**	0010	0.7
1202	0.5		0605	4.1
F 1751	4.1	SA 1227	0.8
			1817	3.9
2 0019	0.4	**17**	0040	0.7
0617	4.3		0639	4.1
SA 1249	0.4	SU 1255	0.8
1838	4.2		1847	3.9
3 0105	0.3	**18**	0108	0.7
0704	4.3		0710	4.0
SU 1335	0.4	M 1325	0.9
1924	4.2		1917	3.9
4 0152	0.3	**19**	0138	0.8
0751	4.3		0741	4.0
M 1421	0.4	TU 1357	0.9
2010	4.1		1949	3.9
5 0239	0.4	**20**	0211	0.9
0839	4.1		0813	3.9
TU 1508	0.6	W 1432	1.0
2057	3.9		2023	3.8
6 0328	0.6	**21**	0248	1.0
0927	4.0		0848	3.9
W 1557	0.7	TH 1509	1.1
2146	3.8		2100	3.8
7 0418	0.7	**22**	0328	1.1
1016	3.8		0927	3.8
TH 1648	0.9	F 1550	1.2
☽ 2237	3.7		2142	3.7
8 0513	0.9	**23**	0414	1.2
1110	3.6		1013	3.6
F 1746	1.1	SA 1637	1.3
2334	3.5	☽ 2233	3.5
9 0615	1.1	**24**	0511	1.4
1212	3.5		1108	3.5
SA 1851	1.2	SU 1741	1.4
			2336	3.4
10 0041	3.4	**25**	0624	1.4
0725	1.2		1216	3.4
SU 1322	3.4	M 1900	1.5
2002	1.3			
11 0155	3.4	**26**	0051	3.4
0839	1.2		0743	1.4
M 1431	3.4	TU 1332	3.4
2110	1.2		2018	1.3
12 0303	3.5	**27**	0211	3.5
0945	1.1		0859	1.2
TU 1533	3.5	W 1448	3.8
2210	1.0		2127	1.1
13 0400	3.7	**28**	0324	3.7
1039	1.0		1005	0.9
W 1624	3.7	TH 1555	3.8
2258	0.9		2228	0.7
14 0448	3.9	**29**	0425	4.0
1123	0.9		1101	0.6
TH 1707	3.8	F 1650	4.0
2337	0.8		2319	0.4
15 0529	4.0	**30**	0517	4.2
1157	0.8		1150	0.3
F 1745	3.9	SA 1739	4.2
●		○		
		31	0006	0.2
			0603	4.4
		SU 1235	0.2
			1823	4.3

FEBRUARY

Time	m		Time	m
1 0050	0.1	**16**	0045	0.6
0648	4.4		0646	4.0
M 1318	0.2	TU 1300	0.7
1906	4.3		1855	3.9
2 0134	0.1	**17**	0112	0.7
0731	4.3		0713	4.0
TU 1401	0.2	W 1330	0.7
1949	4.2		1923	3.9
3 0217	0.2	**18**	0143	0.7
0814	4.2		0742	4.0
W 1443	0.4	TH 1402	0.8
2031	4.1		1953	3.9
4 0301	0.4	**19**	0217	0.8
0857	4.0		0814	3.9
TH 1526	0.6	F 1436	0.9
2114	3.9		2026	3.8
5 0345	0.6	**20**	0255	0.9
0940	3.8		0851	3.8
F 1611	0.8	SA 1512	1.0
☽ 2158	3.7		2105	3.7
6 0433	0.9	**21**	0338	1.1
1027	3.5		0934	3.6
SA 1701	1.1	SU 1556	1.2
2249	3.4		2153	3.6
7 0529	1.1	**22**	0432	1.3
1124	3.3		1029	3.4
SU 1803	1.3	M 1657	1.4
2355	3.2	◑ 2257	3.4
8 0639	1.3	**23**	0546	1.4
1240	3.1		1140	3.3
M 1921	1.4	TU 1821	1.4
9 0122	3.2	**24**	0018	3.3
0805	1.4		0713	1.4
TU 1406	3.1	W 1306	3.2
2045	1.3		1949	1.3
10 0242	3.3	**25**	0149	3.4
0928	1.2		0837	1.1
W 1515	3.3	TH 1431	3.4
2155	1.1		2106	1.0
11 0342	3.5	**26**	0309	3.6
1026	1.0		0947	0.8
TH 1608	3.5	F 1540	3.7
2244	0.9		2209	0.6
12 0430	3.8	**27**	0409	4.0
1108	0.8		1043	0.4
F 1651	3.7	SA 1634	4.0
2323	0.7		2301	0.3
13 0510	3.9	**28**	0459	4.2
1141	0.7		1131	0.2
SA 1727	3.9	SU 1721	4.2
2354	0.6	○ 2347	0.1
14 0546	4.0			
1208	0.7			
SU 1800	3.9			
●				
15 0020	0.6			
0617	4.1			
M 1233	0.7			
1828	3.9			

MARCH

Time	m		Time	m
1 0544	4.4	**16**	0550	4.0
1214	0.0		1205	0.6
M 1804	4.3	TU 1802	3.9
2 0030	0.0	**17**	0017	0.5
0626	4.4		0617	4.0
TU 1256	0.0	W 1232	0.6
1844	4.3		1828	3.9
3 0112	0.0	**18**	0045	0.6
0707	4.3		0643	4.0
W 1337	0.1	TH 1303	0.6
1924	4.2		1856	3.9
4 0153	0.1	**19**	0117	0.6
0747	4.2		0713	3.9
TH 1417	0.2	F 1335	0.7
2003	4.1		1927	3.9
5 0234	0.3	**20**	0152	0.7
0826	4.0		0746	3.9
F 1457	0.5	SA 1410	0.8
2043	3.9		2001	3.9
6 0316	0.6	**21**	0232	0.8
0906	3.7		0825	3.8
SA 1539	0.7	SU 1449	0.9
2124	3.7		2042	3.7
7 0401	0.8	**22**	0317	1.0
0949	3.4		0910	3.6
SU 1627	1.0	M 1536	1.1
☽ 2211	3.4		2132	3.6
8 0454	1.1	**23**	0414	1.2
1041	3.2		1007	3.4
M 1726	1.3	TU 1638	1.2
2315	3.1	◑ 2237	3.4
9 0601	1.4	**24**	0526	1.3
1157	2.9		1120	3.2
TU 1844	1.4	W 1800	1.3
			2359	3.3
10 0051	3.0	**25**	0652	1.2
0727	1.4		1247	3.2
W 1338	3.0	TH 1927	1.2
2014	1.3			
11 0217	3.2	**26**	0132	3.4
0858	1.2		0815	1.0
TH 1451	3.2	F 1412	3.4
2128	1.1		2044	0.9
12 0317	3.4	**27**	0248	3.6
0958	1.0		0924	0.7
F 1544	3.4	SA 1519	3.7
2218	0.9		2147	0.5
13 0404	3.7	**28**	0347	3.9
1041	0.8		1020	0.4
SA 1626	3.7	SU 1612	4.0
2257	0.7		2240	0.3
14 0444	3.8	**29**	0437	4.1
1114	0.7		1108	0.1
SU 1702	3.8	M 1659	4.2
2327	0.6		2326	0.1
15 0519	4.0	**30**	0521	4.3
1141	0.6		1152	0.0
M 1734	3.9	TU 1742	4.3
● 2352	0.5	○	
		31	0009	0.0
			0602	4.3
		W 1233	0.0
			1821	4.3

APRIL

Time	m		Time	m
1 0050	0.0	**16**	0021	0.5
0642	4.2		0617	3.9
TH 1313	0.1	F 1240	0.6
1900	4.2		1834	3.9
2 0130	0.2	**17**	0057	0.6
0720	4.1		0651	3.9
F 1353	0.3	SA 1316	0.6
1938	4.0		1909	3.9
3 0210	0.4	**18**	0136	0.6
0758	3.9		0729	3.8
SA 1433	0.5	SU 1356	0.7
2017	3.9		1948	3.9
4 0251	0.6	**19**	0220	0.7
0837	3.6		0812	3.7
SU 1514	0.7	M 1440	0.8
2057	3.6		2033	3.8
5 0335	0.9	**20**	0309	0.9
0918	3.4		0902	3.6
M 1601	1.0	TU 1532	0.9
2143	3.4		2126	3.6
6 0426	1.1	**21**	0408	1.0
1007	3.1		1001	3.4
TU 1658	1.2	W 1634	1.0
☽ 2242	3.1	◑ 2231	3.4
7 0530	1.3	**22**	0517	1.1
1115	2.9		1111	3.3
W 1810	1.3	TH 1748	1.1
			2348	3.4
8 0011	3.0	**23**	0635	1.0
0646	1.4		1230	3.3
TH 1255	2.9	F 1907	1.0
1930	1.3			
9 0138	3.1	**24**	0111	3.5
0805	1.2		0751	0.9
F 1412	3.1	SA 1347	3.4
2040	1.1		2019	0.8
10 0239	3.3	**25**	0222	3.7
0908	1.0		0857	0.6
SA 1506	3.3	SU 1451	3.7
2133	0.9		2122	0.5
11 0327	3.5	**26**	0320	3.9
0955	0.8		0953	0.4
SU 1549	3.5	M 1546	3.9
2215	0.7		2216	0.3
12 0408	3.7	**27**	0411	4.0
1032	0.7		1043	0.3
M 1627	3.7	TU 1635	4.1
2249	0.6		2304	0.2
13 0444	3.8	**28**	0458	4.1
1104	0.6		1129	0.2
TU 1701	3.8	W 1719	4.1
2319	0.6	○ 2348	0.2
14 0516	3.9	**29**	0541	4.1
1134	0.6		1211	0.2
W 1732	3.9	TH 1801	4.1
● 2348	0.5			
15 0546	3.9	**30**	0029	0.2
1206	0.5		0620	4.0
TH 1802	3.9	F 1253	0.3
			1840	4.1

Chart Datum: 0·13 metres above Ordnance Datum (Dublin). HAT is 4·5 metres above Chart Datum; see 4.5.

TIME ZONE (UT)
For Summer Time add ONE hour in **non-shaded areas**

COBH LAT 51°51′N LONG 8°18′W
TIMES AND HEIGHTS OF HIGH AND LOW WATERS

Dates in **red** are **SPRINGS**
Dates in blue are NEAPS

YEAR 2010

MAY

Day	Time m	Day	Time m
1 SA	0110 0.4 / 0658 3.9 / 1332 0.4 / 1918 4.0	**16** SU	0045 0.5 / 0638 3.9 / 1306 0.5 / 1859 4.0
2 SU	0149 0.5 / 0735 3.8 / 1412 0.6 / 1956 3.8	**17** M	0128 0.5 / 0721 3.8 / 1350 0.5 / 1943 3.9
3 M	0229 0.7 / 0813 3.6 / 1454 0.8 / 2036 3.6	**18** TU	0215 0.6 / 0808 3.8 / 1438 0.6 / 2031 3.8
4 TU	0312 0.9 / 0854 3.4 / 1538 1.0 / 2121 3.4	**19**	0306 0.7 / 0900 3.6 / 1530 0.7 / 2126 3.7
5 W	0400 1.1 / 0941 3.2 / 1630 1.1 / 2213 3.2	**20** TH	0403 0.8 / 0957 3.5 / 1628 0.8 / ☽ 2226 3.6
6 TH	0456 1.2 / 1037 3.1 / 1732 1.2 / ☽ 2320 3.1	**21** F	0505 0.9 / 1059 3.5 / 1733 0.9 / 2333 3.5
7 F	0601 1.3 / 1150 3.0 / 1839 1.3	**22** SA	0614 0.9 / 1207 3.4 / 1843 0.8
8 SA	0038 3.1 / 0707 1.2 / 1308 3.1 / 1942 1.2	**23** SU	0044 3.5 / 0723 0.8 / 1316 3.5 / 1951 0.8
9 SU	0144 3.3 / 0806 1.1 / 1409 3.3 / 2036 1.0	**24** M	0151 3.6 / 0827 0.7 / 1455 3.6 / 2054 0.6
10 M	0236 3.4 / 0857 1.0 / 1459 3.4 / 2123 0.9	**25** TU	0251 3.7 / 0925 0.6 / 1517 3.8 / 2152 0.5
11 TU	0321 3.6 / 0943 0.8 / 1542 3.6 / 2205 0.8	**26** W	0346 3.8 / 1019 0.5 / 1610 3.9 / 2243 0.5
12 W	0402 3.7 / 1024 0.7 / 1623 3.7 / 2245 0.7	**27** TH	0436 3.9 / 1108 0.5 / 1659 4.0 / ○ 2330 0.5
13 TH	0441 3.8 / 1105 0.6 / 1701 3.8 / 2324 0.6	**28** F	0521 3.9 / 1153 0.4 / 1743 4.0
14 F	0519 3.9 / 1144 0.6 / 1739 3.9 / ●	**29** SA	0012 0.5 / 0602 3.9 / 1235 0.5 / 1822 4.0
15 SA	0003 0.5 / 0557 3.9 / 1224 0.5 / 1818 4.0	**30** SU	0052 0.6 / 0640 3.8 / 1314 0.6 / 1901 3.9
		31 M	0129 0.7 / 0717 3.7 / 1353 0.7 / 1938 3.8

JUNE

Day	Time m	Day	Time m
1 TU	0207 0.8 / 0754 3.6 / 1432 0.8 / 2017 3.7	**16** W	0208 0.4 / 0803 3.9 / 1431 0.4 / 2027 4.0
2 W	0246 0.9 / 0832 3.5 / 1512 0.9 / 2058 3.6	**17** TH	0258 0.5 / 0853 3.8 / 1521 0.5 / 2117 3.9
3 TH	0329 1.0 / 0915 3.4 / 1556 1.0 / 2143 3.4	**18** F	0350 0.6 / 0944 3.7 / 1613 0.6 / 2211 3.8
4 F	0417 1.1 / 1002 3.3 / 1646 1.1 / ☽ 2233 3.4	**19** SA	0445 0.7 / 1038 3.6 / 1710 0.7 / ☽ 2308 3.6
5 SA	0510 1.2 / 1055 3.3 / 1742 1.2 / 2330 3.3	**20** SU	0545 0.8 / 1137 3.6 / 1813 0.8
6 SU	0609 1.2 / 1156 3.2 / 1842 1.2	**21** M	0011 3.6 / 0649 0.9 / 1241 3.5 / 1919 0.9
7 M	0032 3.3 / 0708 1.2 / 1300 3.3 / 1939 1.1	**22** TU	0117 3.5 / 0755 0.9 / 1347 3.5 / 2026 0.9
8 TU	0133 3.4 / 0804 1.1 / 1400 3.4 / 2034 1.0	**23** W	0222 3.5 / 0859 0.9 / 1451 3.6 / 2130 0.8
9 W	0228 3.5 / 0858 1.0 / 1455 3.5 / 2126 0.9	**24** TH	0322 3.6 / 0959 0.8 / 1550 3.7 / 2227 0.7
10 TH	0320 3.6 / 0950 0.9 / 1546 3.7 / 2216 0.8	**25** F	0417 3.7 / 1052 0.7 / 1642 3.8 / 2316 0.7
11 F	0409 3.7 / 1040 0.7 / 1635 3.8 / 2304 0.6	**26** SA	0505 3.7 / 1138 0.6 / 1727 3.9 / ○ 2358 0.7
12 SA	0457 3.8 / 1127 0.6 / 1721 3.9 / ● 2350 0.5	**27** SU	0547 3.8 / 1218 0.6 / 1808 3.9
13 SU	0543 3.9 / 1212 0.5 / 1807 4.0	**28** M	0034 0.7 / 0624 3.8 / 1256 0.6 / 1844 3.9
14 M	0035 0.4 / 0628 3.9 / 1257 0.4 / 1851 4.0	**29** TU	0108 0.7 / 0659 3.8 / 1330 0.7 / 1920 3.9
15 TU	0121 0.4 / 0715 3.9 / 1343 0.4 / 1938 4.0	**30** W	0141 0.8 / 0733 3.7 / 1404 0.7 / 1955 3.8

JULY

Day	Time m	Day	Time m
1 TH	0216 0.9 / 0808 3.7 / 1439 0.8 / 2031 3.7	**16** F	0240 0.3 / 0834 4.0 / 1501 0.3 / 2058 4.0
2 F	0253 0.9 / 0846 3.6 / 1516 0.9 / 2109 3.6	**17** SA	0327 0.5 / 0921 3.9 / 1549 0.5 / 2145 3.9
3 SA	0334 1.0 / 0926 3.5 / 1556 1.0 / 2150 3.6	**18** SU	0417 0.6 / 1010 3.7 / 1640 0.7 / ☽ 2236 3.7
4 SU	0418 1.1 / 1010 3.5 / 1643 1.1 / ☽ 2236 3.5	**19** M	0510 0.8 / 1103 3.6 / 1737 0.9 / 2334 3.5
5 M	0509 1.2 / 1101 3.4 / 1739 1.2 / 2330 3.4	**20** TU	0612 1.0 / 1205 3.4 / 1843 1.0
6 TU	0610 1.3 / 1200 3.4 / 1843 1.3	**21** W	0042 3.3 / 0722 1.1 / 1318 3.3 / 1958 1.1
7 W	0032 3.4 / 0715 1.3 / 1306 3.4 / 1949 1.2	**22** TH	0156 3.3 / 0836 1.1 / 1431 3.4 / 2113 1.0
8 TH	0139 3.4 / 0819 1.2 / 1413 3.5 / 2053 1.1	**23** F	0304 3.4 / 0944 1.0 / 1534 3.6 / 2216 0.9
9 F	0243 3.5 / 0921 1.0 / 1516 3.6 / 2152 0.9	**24** SA	0402 3.5 / 1040 0.8 / 1627 3.7 / 2305 0.8
10 SA	0344 3.7 / 1018 0.8 / 1614 3.8 / 2247 0.6	**25** SU	0450 3.7 / 1125 0.7 / 1712 3.9 / 2344 0.7
11 SU	0439 3.8 / 1110 0.6 / 1706 4.0 / ● 2336 0.4	**26** M	0530 3.8 / 1202 0.6 / 1750 3.9 / ○
12 M	0529 4.0 / 1157 0.4 / 1754 4.1	**27** TU	0016 0.7 / 0606 3.8 / 1235 0.6 / 1825 4.0
13 TU	0022 0.3 / 0615 4.0 / 1243 0.3 / 1839 4.2	**28** W	0044 0.7 / 0638 3.8 / 1304 0.6 / 1857 3.9
14 W	0108 0.2 / 0702 4.1 / 1329 0.2 / 1925 4.2	**29** TH	0112 0.7 / 0709 3.8 / 1332 0.7 / 1928 3.9
15 TH	0154 0.3 / 0748 4.0 / 1414 0.2 / 2011 4.1	**30** F	0142 0.8 / 0740 3.8 / 1402 0.8 / 1959 3.8
		31 SA	0216 0.9 / 0813 3.7 / 1435 0.9 / 2032 3.8

AUGUST

Day	Time m	Day	Time m
1 SU	0253 1.0 / 0848 3.7 / 1512 1.0 / 2109 3.7	**16** M	0346 0.6 / 0939 3.7 / 1609 0.7 / ☽ 2202 3.6
2 M	0332 1.1 / 0928 3.6 / 1554 1.1 / 2150 3.6	**17** TU	0437 0.9 / 1029 3.5 / 1702 0.9 / 2257 3.3
3 TU	0416 1.2 / 1014 3.5 / 1644 1.2 / ☽ 2241 3.5	**18** W	0537 1.1 / 1132 3.3 / 1808 1.2
4 W	0513 1.3 / 1111 3.4 / 1751 1.3 / 2344 3.3	**19** TH	0009 3.1 / 0652 1.2 / 1255 3.2 / 1932 1.3
5 TH	0627 1.4 / 1222 3.3 / 1909 1.3	**20** F	0136 3.1 / 0818 1.3 / 1416 3.3 / 2100 1.2
6 F	0058 3.3 / 0745 1.3 / 1340 3.4 / 2024 1.2	**21** SA	0249 3.3 / 0932 1.0 / 1519 3.5 / 2203 1.0
7 SA	0216 3.4 / 0855 1.1 / 1454 3.6 / 2131 0.9	**22** SU	0345 3.5 / 1026 0.8 / 1609 3.7 / 2249 0.8
8 SU	0324 3.6 / 0957 0.8 / 1556 3.8 / 2228 0.6	**23** M	0431 3.7 / 1108 0.6 / 1651 3.9 / 2325 0.7
9 M	0421 3.9 / 1051 0.5 / 1648 4.1 / 2319 0.3	**24** TU	0510 3.8 / 1142 0.6 / 1728 4.0 / ○ 2353 0.6
10 TU	0511 4.1 / 1139 0.2 / 1736 4.2 / ●	**25** W	0543 3.9 / 1209 0.6 / 1801 4.0
11 W	0004 0.2 / 0557 4.2 / 1224 0.1 / 1820 4.3	**26** TH	0016 0.7 / 0613 3.9 / 1234 0.6 / 1829 4.0
12 TH	0048 0.1 / 0641 4.2 / 1308 0.1 / 1903 4.3	**27** F	0041 0.7 / 0641 3.9 / 1258 0.7 / 1857 3.9
13 F	0132 0.2 / 0725 4.2 / 1352 0.1 / 1947 4.2	**28** SA	0109 0.7 / 0709 3.8 / 1327 0.7 / 1924 3.9
14 SA	0216 0.2 / 0809 4.1 / 1436 0.2 / 2031 4.1	**29** SU	0142 0.8 / 0738 3.8 / 1359 0.8 / 1955 3.9
15 SU	0300 0.4 / 0853 3.9 / 1521 0.4 / 2115 3.9	**30** M	0216 0.9 / 0812 3.8 / 1436 0.9 / 2030 3.8
		31 TU	0254 1.0 / 0850 3.7 / 1517 1.1 / 2111 3.7

Chart Datum: 0·13 metres above Ordnance Datum (Dublin). HAT is 4·5 metres above Chart Datum; see 4.5.

TIME ZONE (UT)
For Summer Time add ONE hour in **non-shaded areas**

COBH   LAT 51°51'N   LONG 8°18'W
TIMES AND HEIGHTS OF HIGH AND LOW WATERS

Dates in red are **SPRINGS**
Dates in blue are **NEAPS**

YEAR 2010

S Ireland

SEPTEMBER

Time	m		Time	m
1 0337	1.2	**16**	0509	1.2
0935	3.5		1103	3.2
W 1607	1.2	TH	1740	1.3
☽ 2203	3.5		2336	3.0
2 0433	1.3	**17**	0626	1.3
1034	3.4		1233	3.1
TH 1713	1.4	F	1906	1.4
2308	3.3			
3 0551	1.4	**18**	0113	3.0
1149	3.3		0756	1.3
F 1837	1.4	SA	1356	3.2
			2036	1.3
4 0029	3.2	**19**	0228	3.2
0716	1.3		0908	1.1
SA 1316	3.3	SU	1456	3.4
1959	1.2		2137	1.0
5 0154	3.4	**20**	0321	3.5
0832	1.1		0959	0.8
SU 1435	3.6	M	1544	3.7
2109	0.9		2220	0.9
6 0305	3.6	**21**	0405	3.7
0936	0.7		1040	0.7
M 1537	3.9	TU	1624	3.9
2208	0.6		2255	0.7
7 0401	3.9	**22**	0442	3.8
1030	0.4		1112	0.6
TU 1628	4.1	W	1700	4.0
2257	0.3		2322	0.7
8 0450	4.2	**23**	0515	3.9
1117	0.1		1138	0.6
W 1714	4.3	TH	1732	4.0
● 2342	0.1	○	2345	0.7
9 0535	4.3	**24**	0545	3.9
1202	0.0		1202	0.6
TH 1758	4.4	F	1800	4.0
10 0025	0.0	**25**	0010	0.7
0618	4.3		0611	3.9
F 1245	0.0	SA	1228	0.7
1839	4.3		1825	4.0
11 0108	0.1	**26**	0040	0.7
0700	4.3		0639	3.9
SA 1328	0.1	SU	1257	0.7
1921	4.2		1853	4.0
12 0150	0.2	**27**	0113	0.8
0742	4.1		0709	3.9
SU 1411	0.3	M	1332	0.8
2002	4.0		1925	3.9
13 0234	0.4	**28**	0148	0.9
0825	3.9		0743	3.8
M 1455	0.5	TU	1409	0.9
2045	3.8		2002	3.8
14 0319	0.7	**29**	0227	1.0
0909	3.7		0823	3.7
TU 1541	0.8	W	1453	1.1
2129	3.5		2045	3.7
15 0409	0.9	**30**	0314	1.1
0959	3.4		0912	3.6
W 1634	1.1	TH	1546	1.2
☽ 2222	3.3		2139	3.5

OCTOBER

Time	m		Time	m
1 0414	1.3	**16**	0556	1.4
1013	3.4		1158	3.1
F 1653	1.4	SA	1830	1.5
☽ 2247	3.3			
2 0530	1.4	**17**	0032	3.0
1129	3.3		0716	1.3
SA 1815	1.4	SU	1320	3.2
			1950	1.4
3 0008	3.3	**18**	0151	3.2
0653	1.3		0825	1.2
SU 1257	3.4	M	1420	3.4
1937	1.2		2051	1.2
4 0132	3.4	**19**	0245	3.4
0809	1.0		0917	1.0
M 1414	3.6	TU	1508	3.6
2046	0.9		2137	1.0
5 0242	3.7	**20**	0329	3.6
0912	0.7		0959	0.8
TU 1544	3.9	W	1550	3.8
2144	0.6		2214	0.9
6 0338	4.0	**21**	0408	3.8
1007	0.4		1034	0.7
W 1605	4.2	TH	1627	3.9
2234	0.3		2245	0.8
7 0427	4.2	**22**	0443	3.9
1056	0.2		1105	0.7
TH 1652	4.3	F	1700	4.0
● 2320	0.2		2314	0.7
8 0512	4.3	**23**	0515	4.0
1141	0.1		1133	0.7
F 1735	4.4	SA	1730	4.0
		○	2344	0.7
9 0003	0.1	**24**	0545	4.0
0555	4.3		1203	0.7
SA 1225	0.1	SU	1759	4.0
1817	4.3			
10 0046	0.2	**25**	0017	0.7
0637	4.3		0616	4.0
SU 1307	0.2	M	1237	0.8
1857	4.2		1830	4.0
11 0128	0.3	**26**	0053	0.8
0719	4.1		0650	4.0
M 1349	0.4	TU	1314	0.8
1937	4.0		1906	3.9
12 0211	0.5	**27**	0131	0.8
0801	3.9		0726	3.9
TU 1433	0.7	W	1356	0.9
2018	3.8		1946	3.9
13 0257	0.8	**28**	0215	1.0
0845	3.7		0811	3.8
W 1518	0.9	TH	1443	1.0
2101	3.5		2033	3.7
14 0346	1.0	**29**	0305	1.1
0934	3.5		0903	3.7
TH 1610	1.2	F	1537	1.2
☾ 2151	3.3		2128	3.6
15 0445	1.2	**30**	0405	1.2
1036	3.2		1004	3.6
F 1712	1.4	SA	1641	1.3
2258	3.1	☽	2234	3.4
		31	0515	1.2
			1115	3.5
		SU	1756	1.3
			2349	3.4

NOVEMBER

Time	m		Time	m
1 0631	1.2	**16**	0044	3.2
1234	3.5		0727	1.3
M 1913	1.1	TU	1327	3.4
			1951	1.3
2 0106	3.5	**17**	0150	3.4
0744	1.0		0822	1.2
TU 1347	3.7	W	1420	3.5
2021	0.9		2043	1.2
3 0214	3.8	**18**	0242	3.5
0848	0.7		0910	1.1
W 1447	3.9	TH	1507	3.7
2119	0.7		2128	1.0
4 0312	4.0	**19**	0326	3.7
0945	0.5		0953	0.9
TH 1541	4.1	F	1549	3.8
2212	0.5		2208	0.9
5 0404	4.2	**20**	0407	3.9
1036	0.4		1033	0.9
F 1630	4.2	SA	1627	3.9
2300	0.4		2247	0.8
6 0452	4.3	**21**	0446	4.0
1123	0.3		1110	0.8
SA 1715	4.2	SU	1704	4.0
● 2345	0.3		2324	0.8
7 0537	4.3	**22**	0524	4.0
1208	0.4		1148	0.8
SU 1758	4.2	M	1740	4.0
8 0028	0.4	**23**	0002	0.7
0619	4.2		0601	4.1
M 1250	0.4	TU	1226	0.7
1838	4.1		1816	4.0
9 0110	0.5	**24**	0042	0.7
0701	4.1		0640	4.1
TU 1332	0.6	W	1307	0.8
1917	3.9		1856	4.0
10 0152	0.7	**25**	0123	0.8
0742	4.0		0721	4.0
W 1414	0.8	TH	1350	0.8
1956	3.8		1939	3.9
11 0236	0.8	**26**	0209	0.8
0825	3.8		0807	4.0
TH 1457	1.0	F	1438	0.9
2037	3.6		2028	3.8
12 0323	1.0	**27**	0259	0.9
0912	3.6		0858	3.9
F 1545	1.2	SA	1530	1.0
2123	3.4		2121	3.7
13 0415	1.2	**28**	0354	1.0
1004	3.4		0955	3.8
SA 1639	1.4	SU	1627	1.1
☾ 2217	3.2	☾	2220	3.6
14 0516	1.3	**29**	0456	1.1
1108	3.3		1057	3.7
SU 1742	1.5	M	1732	1.1
2326	3.1		2325	3.6
15 0623	1.4	**30**	0604	1.1
1220	3.3		1205	3.7
M 1850	1.4	TU	1843	1.1

DECEMBER

Time	m		Time	m
1 0034	3.6	**16**	0035	3.3
0714	1.0		0722	1.4
W 1314	3.7	TH	1316	3.4
1952	1.0		1947	1.4
2 0142	3.7	**17**	0141	3.4
0821	0.9		0820	1.3
TH 1418	3.8	F	1415	3.5
2054	0.9		2043	1.4
3 0245	3.9	**18**	0241	3.6
0923	0.8		0914	1.2
F 1517	3.9	SA	1509	3.7
2151	0.7		2135	1.1
4 0343	4.0	**19**	0334	3.8
1019	0.7		1005	1.0
SA 1611	4.0	SU	1558	3.8
2243	0.6		2224	0.9
5 0436	4.1	**20**	0422	3.9
1110	0.6		1052	0.9
SU 1700	4.1	M	1643	3.9
● 2330	0.6		2308	0.8
6 0523	4.2	**21**	0507	4.0
1155	0.6		1136	0.7
M 1744	4.1	TU	1726	4.0
		○	2351	0.7
7 0013	0.5	**22**	0550	4.1
0606	4.2		1218	0.6
TU 1237	0.6	W	1808	4.1
1823	4.0			
8 0055	0.6	**23**	0032	0.6
0647	4.1		0632	4.2
W 1316	0.7	TH	1300	0.6
1901	3.9		1849	4.1
9 0134	0.7	**24**	0115	0.6
0726	4.0		0715	4.2
TH 1355	0.9	F	1343	0.6
1937	3.8		1933	4.1
10 0214	0.8	**25**	0200	0.6
0806	3.9		0800	4.1
F 1433	1.0	SA	1428	0.7
2015	3.7		2019	4.0
11 0255	1.0	**26**	0247	0.6
0847	3.8		0848	4.0
SA 1513	1.1	SU	1516	0.8
2055	3.6		2107	3.9
12 0338	1.1	**27**	0337	0.7
0930	3.6		0938	3.9
SU 1558	1.3	M	1606	0.9
2139	3.5		2159	3.8
13 0426	1.3	**28**	0430	0.9
1017	3.5		1032	3.8
M 1648	1.4	TU	1702	1.0
☾ 2230	3.4	☾	2255	3.7
14 0521	1.4	**29**	0530	1.0
1111	3.4		1131	3.7
TU 1745	1.4	W	1806	1.1
2329	3.3		2358	3.6
15 0622	1.4	**30**	0638	1.1
1212	3.4		1238	3.6
W 1847	1.4	TH	1917	1.2
		31	0108	3.6
			0751	1.1
		F	1349	3.6
			2028	1.1

Chart Datum: 0·13 metres above Ordnance Datum (Dublin). HAT is 4·5 metres above Chart Datum; see 4.5.

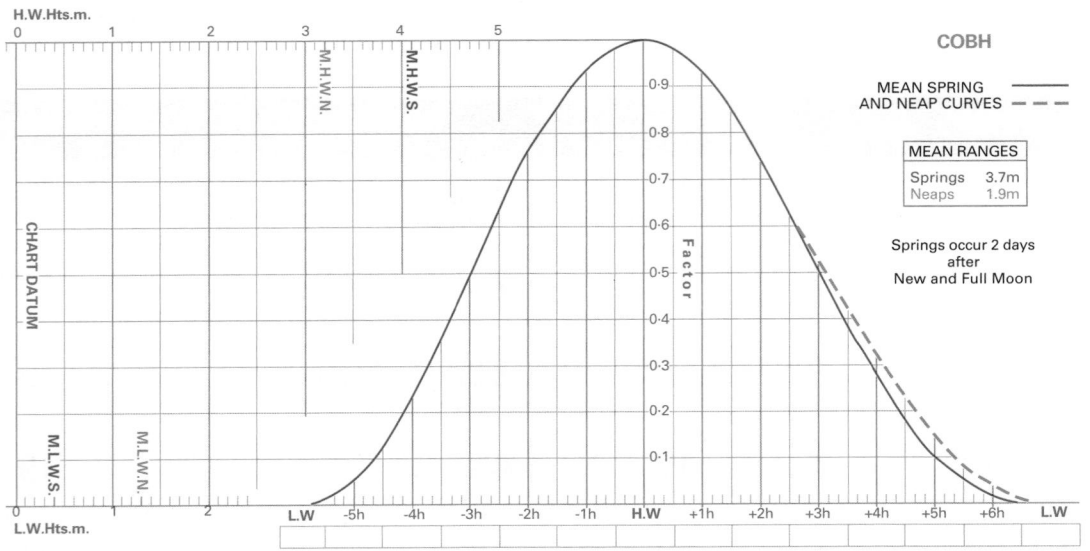

9.12.19   CORK HARBOUR

Cork **51°47'·50N 08°15'·54W** ❀❀❀♺♺♺❀❀❀

CHARTS AC 1765, 1777, 1773, 5622; Imray C57, C56.

TIDES −0523 Dover; ML 2·3; Duration 0555

Standard Port COBH (⟵)

Times				Height (metres)			
High Water		Low Water		MHWS	MHWN	MLWN	MLWS
0500	1100	0500	1100	4·1	3·2	1·3	0·4
1700	2300	1700	2300				
Differences BALLYCOTTON (15M ENE of Roche's Point)							
−0011	+0001	+0003	−0009	0·0	0·0	−0·1	0·0
RINGASKIDDY							
+0005	+0020	+0007	+0013	+0·1	+0·1	+0·1	+0·1
MARINO POINT							
0000	+0010	0000	+0010	+0·1	+0·1	0·0	0·0
CORK CITY							
+0005	+0010	+0020	+0010	+0·4	+0·4	+0·3	+0·2
ROBERTS COVE (approx 4M SW of Roche's Point)							
−0005	−0005	−0005	−0005	−0·1	0·0	0·0	+0·1

SHELTER Very good in all conditions, esp in Crosshaven and East Passage. There are 3 main marinas at Crosshaven (see Facilities), plus a small private marina and several ⚓s up the Owenboy River, in particular at Drake's Pool. There is a marina at E Ferry at the E end of Great Island. Cobh, Ringaskiddy and Cork City are commercial and ferry ports; contact Port Ops for advice on yacht berths.

NAVIGATION WPT 51°46'·57N, 08°15'·39W, 005°/1M to Roche's Pt lt; also on 354°ldg line. Safe hbr with no dangers for yachts; ent is deep and well marked. Sp rate is about 1½kn in ent. Main chan up to Cork and the chan to E Ferry are marked, but shoal outside navigable chan. Ent to Crosshaven/Owenboy River carries at least 3m at LWS, and the chan is buoyed.

LIGHTS AND MARKS See 9.12.4. The 24·5m high hammerhead water tr S of Crosshaven and the R/W power stn chy NE of Corkbeg Is are conspic from seaward. Two set Ldg lts/marks lead through The Sound, either side of Hbr Rk (5·2m), not a hazard for yachts; but do not impede merchant ships. The chan to Crosshaven is marked by C1 SHM lt buoy, C1A SHM lt buoy; C2A PHM lt buoy, C2 PHM lt buoy; and C4 PHM lt buoy.

R/T Call: *Cork Hbr Radio* (Port Ops) VHF Ch 12 14 16 (H24); *Crosshaven BY* Ch **M** (Mon–Fri: 0830–1730LT). *Royal Cork YC Marina* Ch **M** (0900–2359LT) and RCYC water taxi, *Salve Marine* and *East Ferry Marina* both Ch **M** 0830–1730.

TELEPHONE (Code 021) HM 4273125, info@portofcork.ie; Port Ops 4811380; MRSC (066) 9476109; IMES 4831448; ⊖ 4311024; Police 4831222; Dr 4831716; ⊞ 4546400.

FACILITIES   Crosshaven BY Marina (100 + 20Ⓥ) ☎ 4831161, cby@eircom.net, €2.50, BH (40 ton), C (1.5 tons), M, Ⓔ, CH, D, P (cans), El, Gaz, Kos, SM, ME, ✕.

Salve Marine (45 + 12 Ⓥ) ☎ 4831145, AB €2.50, M, BY, El, ME, C, CH, R, D, P (cans), Slip.

Royal Cork YC Marina (170 + 30Ⓥ) ☎ 4831023, www.royalcork.com, €3.00, P , Bar, R, Slip, Ⓛ.

Crosshaven Pier/Pontoon AB €21.00 any size.

East Ferry Marina (85 + 15Ⓥ) ☎ 4811342, €2.50, D, Bar, R, Slip; access all tides, max draft 5·5m.

Crosshaven Village FV pier in 3·5m at Town quay, L, Slip HW±4(for RIBs & small power craft), Grid, SM, Bar, Dr, ✉, R, 🛒 + ATM, Ⓘ.

Cork City All facilities. ⇌, ✈, **Ferries:** Roscoff; weekly; 13 Hrs; Brittany (www.brittany-ferries.co.uk).

MINOR HARBOUR 16M ENE of YOUGHAL
DUNGARVAN BAY, Waterford, **52°05'·15N 07°36'·70W**.❀❀♺♺❀❀.
AC 2017, 5622. HW −0542 on Dover; Duration 0600. See 9.12.17. A large bay, drying to the W, entered between Helvick Hd to the S and Ballynacourty Pt to the N. Appr in W sector (274°-302°) of this lt to clear Carricknamoan islet to the N, and Carrickapane Rk and Helvick Rk (ECM buoy Q (3) 10s) to the S. 5ca W of this buoy are The Gainers, a large unmarked rky patch (dries 0·8m). Beware salmon nets. Off Helvick hbr are 8 Y ⚓s or ⚓ in approx 4m. Dungarvan town hbr is accessible HW+3, via buoyed (FlG/FlR) chan which shifts, the buoys being moved to suit. Appr is difficult in SE'lies >F6. ⚓ in the pool below the town or AB on pontoon (dries to soft mud), S bank below bridge; craft can stay overnight beyond double Y lines. Facilities: D & P (cans), Bar, Ⓑ, ✉, Ⓘ, R, 🛒, Kos.

MINOR HARBOUR 15M ENE of ROCHE'S POINT
BALLYCOTTON, Cork, **51°49'·70N 08°00'·19W**. AC 2424, 5622. HW −0555 on Dover; Duration 0550. See above. Small, NE-facing hbr at W end of bay suffers from scend in strong SE winds; 3m in ent and about 1·5m against piers. Many FVs alongside piers, on which yachts should berth, rather than ⚓ in hbr, which is foul with old ground tackle. 6 Y ⚓s are outside hbr, or good ⚓ in offshore winds in 6m NE of pier, protected by Ballycotton Is. Lt ho Fl WR 10s 59m 21/17M, B tr in W walls; 238°-W-048°-R-238°; Horn (4) 90s. Facilities: FW on pier. **Village** Hotel, R, ✉, 🛒, LB, Kos.

9.12.20 KINSALE

Cork 51°40'·80N 08°30'·00W ✵✵✵♒♒♒♒♒☆☆☆

CHARTS AC 1765, 2053, 5622, 5623; Imray C56.

TIDES –0600 Dover; ML 2·2; Duration 0600

Standard Port COBH (←—)

Times				Height (metres)			
High Water		Low Water		MHWS	MHWN	MLWN	MLWS
0500	1100	0500	1100	4·1	3·2	1·3	0·4
1700	2300	1700	2300				
Differences KINSALE							
–0019	–0005	–0009	–0023	–0·2	0·0	+0·1	+0·2

SHELTER Excellent, except in very strong SE winds. Access H24 in all weathers/tides. Marinas at Kinsale YC and Castlepark; ♥'s berth on outside of pontoons in 10m in both cases; NNW of latter is FV pontoon and no ⚓ area. Possible AB (Sun-Thurs) at Trident Hotel. 2 large ♀s NE of Kinsale Bridge (contact HM). No ⚓ allowed in main channel or within 700m of Town Pier. Contact HM prior to ⚓. All craft have to pay harbour dues as well as berthing/launching fees.

NAVIGATION WPT 51°40'·00N 08°30'·00W, 001°/1·7M to Charles's Fort lt. Beware: Bulman Rk (0·9m; SCM lt buoy) 4ca S of Preghane Pt; and Farmer Rk (0·6m) ¾ca off W bank. Hbr speed limit 6kn.

LIGHTS AND MARKS See 9.12.4 and chartlet. Chan is marked by PHM lt buoys. Marina lts are 2 FG or FR.

R/T KYC VHF Ch M 16. Castlepark marina 06 16 M. HM **14** 16.

TELEPHONE (Code 021) HM 4772503 (HO), 4773047 (OT); MRCC (066) 9476109; Coast/Cliff Rescue Service 4772346; ⊖ 4311044/4315422; Police 4772302; Dr 4772253; Ⓗ 4546400.

FACILITIES Kinsale BY, ☎ 4774774. D, ♥, FW, ME, ✗, El, BH (30 ton). Kinsale YC Marina (170 + 50♥), €3·20, ☎ 4772196, mobile 087 6787377, Slip, D, R, Bar, ⬚; Trident Hotel, D, FW, AB, Sun-Thur try Sail Ireland ☎ 4772927, Mobile 0877 502737. Castlepark Marina (130 inc 20 ♥), €5·50, ☎ 4774959, mob 0877 502737, D (fuel pontoon), Slip, R, Bar, El, ▣. Services: ME, El, Ⓔ, Divers, C (30 ton), D, SM, Gas, Gaz. Town @ & Wi-fi, P (cans), ⬚, R, Bar, ⊠, Ⓑ, (bus to Cork), ⇌, ✈.

ANCHORAGE 2M EAST OF KINSALE

OYSTERHAVEN, Cork, 51°41'·20N 08°26'·90W. ✵✵♒☆☆☆. AC 1765, 2053, 5622. HW –0600 on Dover; ML 2·2m; Duration 0600. Use 9.12.19. Good shelter but ⚓'s subject to swell in S winds. Enter 0·5M N of Big Sovereign, a steep islet divided into two. Keep to S of Little Sovereign on E side of ent. There is foul ground off Ballymacus Pt on W side, and off Kinure Pt on E side. Pass W of Hbr Rk (0·9m) off Ferry Pt, the only danger within hbr. ⚓ NNW of Ferry Pt in 4–6m on soft mud/weed. NW arm shoals suddenly about 5ca NW of Ferry Pt. Also ⚓ up N arm of hbr in 3m off the W shore. Weed in higher reaches may foul ⚓. No lts, marks or VHF radio. Coast/Cliff Rescue Service ☎ (021) 4770711.

Oysterhaven Yacht Harbour (strictly private) 51°42'·10N 08°26'·58W, ☎ (021) 4770878.

OLD HEAD OF KINSALE TO MIZEN HEAD

(AC 2424) From Cork to Mizen Hd there are many natural hbrs. Only the best are mentioned here. ▶ *Offshore the stream seldom exceeds 1·5kn, but it is stronger off headlands causing races and overfalls with wind against tide. Prolonged W winds increase the rate/duration of the E-going stream, and strong E winds have a similar effect on the W-going stream.* ◀

In the middle of Courtmacsherry Bay are several dangers, from E to W: Blueboy Rk, Barrel Rk (with Inner Barrels closer inshore), and Black Tom; Horse Rk is off Barry's Pt at the W side of the bay. These must be avoided going to or from Courtmacsherry, where the bar breaks in strong S/SE winds, but the river carries 2·3m.

Beware Cotton Rk and Shoonta Rk close E of Seven Heads, off which rks extend 50m. Clonakilty B has little to offer. Keep at least 5ca off Galley Hd to clear Dhulic Rk, and further off in fresh winds. ▶ *Offshore the W-going stream makes at HW Cobh +0200, and the E-going at HW Cobh –0420, sp rates 1·5kn.* ◀

Across Glandore Bay there are good anchs off Glandore, or Union Hall. Sailing W from Glandore, pass outside or inside High Is and Low Is; if inside beware Belly Rk (awash) about 3ca S of Rabbit Is. On passage Toe Head has foul ground 100m S, and 7½ca S is a group of rks called the Stags. Castle Haven, a sheltered and attractive hbr, is entered between Reen Pt (lt) and Battery Pt. Baltimore is 10M further W.

Fastnet Rk (lt, fog sig) is nearly 4M WSW of C Clear; 2½ca NE of it is an outlying rk. An E/W TSS lies between 2 and 8M SSE of the Fastnet. Long Island Bay can be entered from C Clear or through Gascanane Sound, between Clear Is and Sherkin Is. Carrigmore Rks lie in the middle of this chan, with Gascanane Rk 1ca W of them. The chan between Carrigmore Rks and Badger Island is best. If bound for Crookhaven, beware Bullig Reef, N of Clear Is.

Schull is N of Long Island, inside which passage can be made W'ward to Crookhaven. This is a well sheltered hbr, accessible at all states of tide, entered between Rock Is lt Ho and Alderman Rks, ENE of Streek Hd. Anch off the village. ▶ *Off Mizen Hd (lt ho) the W-going stream starts at HW Cobh +0120, and the E-going at HW Cobh –0500. The sp rate is 4kn, which with wind against tide forms a dangerous race, sometimes reaching to Brow Hd or Three Castle Hd, with broken water right to the shore.* ◀

9.12.21 COURTMACSHERRY

Cork **51°38'·22N 08°40'·90W** ※※※◊◊✿✿

CHARTS AC 2092, 2081, 5622, 5623; Imray C56.

TIDES HW –0610 on Dover; Duration 0545

Standard Port COBH (←)

Times				Height (metres)			
High Water		Low Water		MHWS	MHWN	MLWN	MLWS
0500	1100	0500	1100	4·1	3·2	1·3	0·4
1700	2300	1700	2300				
Differences COURTMACSHERRY							
–0025	–0008	–0008	–0015	–0·1	–0·1	0·0	+0·1

SHELTER Good shelter up-river, but in strong S/SE winds seas break on the bar (2·3m), when ent must not be attempted. Dry out in small inner hbr or AB afloat on jetty (FVs) or on yacht pontoon (18·5m). ↓ NE of Ferry Pt in about 2·5m or N of pontoon. Weed may foul ↓; best to moor using two ↓s.

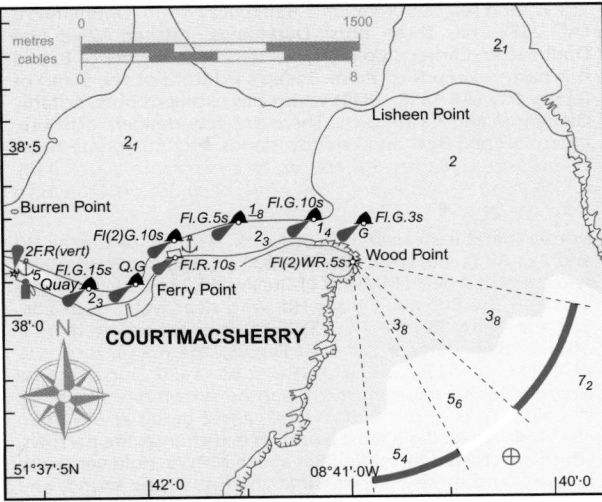

NAVIGATION WPT, 51°37'·50N 08°40'·17W, 324°/0·8M to Wood Pt. Appr in the W sector of Wood Pt lt, between Black Tom and Horse Rk (dries 3·6m); the latter is 3-4½ca E of Barry Pt on the W shore. Black Tom (2·3m), with SHM buoy Fl.G.5s 5ca SSE, is close NE of the appr. Further to NE, in centre of bay, Barrel Rk (dries 2·6m), has unlit perch (ruin). To NNW and E of it are Inner Barrels (0·5m) and Blueboy Rk. Hbr ent is between Wood Pt and SHM buoy 2ca NE, Fl G 3s. Chan (2m but 1·4m close inside ent) is marked by 5 SHM buoys and 1 PHM buoy (off Ferry Point). Keep close N of moorings on S side of harbour.

LIGHTS AND MARKS Wood Pt, Fl (2) WR 5s 15m 5M.

R/T None.

TELEPHONE (023) HM (Mob) 08610 40812; RNLI boathouse 8846600; Dr 8846186 (HN 1850 335999); Police 8846122; Coast Rescue Service (Mob) 08685 01806.

FACILITIES Quay AB (min €15/craft), ⚓, 🚻, FW, 🛒, D (Pier 0930-1800 on request), Slip, LB, R. **Village**, Bar, R, 🍴, (bus to Cork), ⇌, ✈.

9.12.22 GLANDORE/UNIONHALL

Cork, **51°33'·70N 09°07'·20W** ※※※◊◊✿✿✿

CHARTS AC 2092, 5622, 5623; Imray C56.

TIDES Approx as for 9.12.22 Castletownshend

SHELTER Excellent. 12 Y ⚓s or ↓ 1½ca SW of Glandore Pier in 2m or 1ca NE of the New pier at Unionhall in 3m.

NAVIGATION WPT 51°32'·35N 09°05'·10W, 129°/1·2M to Outer Dangers. Approach between Adam Is and Goat's Hd, thence keep E of Eve Is and W of the chain of rocks: Outer, Middle and

Inner Dangers and Sunk Rk. Before altering W for Unionhall, stand on to clear mudbank 1ca off S shore. Speed limit 3kn.

LIGHTS AND MARKS See 9.12.4. Galley Hd, Fl (5) 20s, is 5M E of ent. Outer Dangers are marked by GRG lt buoy, and PHM bn; Middle and Inner Dangers by 2 SHM bns; and Sunk Rk by a NCM lt buoy.

R/T HM Ch 06.

TELEPHONE (Code 028) HM Glandore/Unionhall 34737, mob 0866081944; Police (023) 23088; Dr 23456; Coast Rescue 33115.

FACILITIES Glandore GHYC, ⚓s €14.00/craft (contact Glandore Inn ☎ 33468/33518), FW, 🖂, R, Bar, Kos. **Unionhall** AB (outside of FVs/drying AB Old Quay) €15.00/craft, FW, D(occ quayside) or D & P (by cans from Leap 2M), ME, Gas, showers, 🚻, 🖂, R, Bar, 🍴.

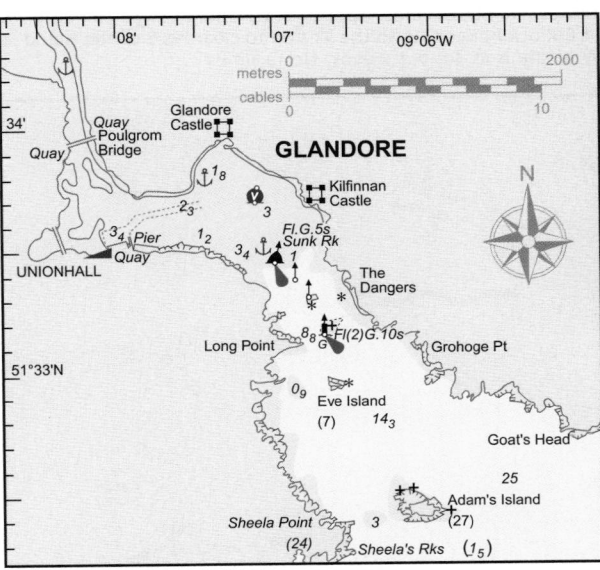

9.12.23 CASTLETOWNSHEND

Cork **51°30'·90N 09°10'·70W** ※※※◊◊✿✿✿

CHARTS AC 2092, 2129, 5623; Imray C56.

TIDES +0605 Dover; ML 2·2; Duration 0605

Standard Port COBH (←)

Times				Height (metres)			
High Water		Low Water		MHWS	MHWN	MLWN	MLWS
0500	1100	0500	1100	4·1	3·2	1·3	0·4
1700	2300	1700	2300				
Differences CASTLETOWNSHEND							
–0020	–0030	–0020	–0050	–0·4	–0·2	+0·1	+0·3
CLONAKILTY BAY (5M NE of Galley Head)							
–0033	–0011	–0019	–0041	–0·3	–0·2	No data	

SHELTER Excellent ↓ in midstream SE of Castletownshend slip, protected from all weathers and available at all tides; but the outer part of hbr is subject to swell in S winds. Or ↓ N of Cat Island, or upstream as depth permits. Caution: An underwater cable runs E/W across the hbr from the slip close N of Reen Pier to the slip at Castletownshend.

NAVIGATION WPT 51°30'·28N, 09°10'·26W, 351°/7ca to Reen Pt lt. Enter between Horse Is (35m) and Skiddy Is (9m) both of which have foul ground all round. Black Rk lies off the SE side of Horse Is and is steep-to along its S side. Flea Sound is a narrow boat chan, obstructed by rks. Colonel's Rk (0·5m) lies close to the E shore, 2ca N of Reen Pt. Beware salmon nets.

Continued overleaf

CASTLETOWNSHEND *continued*

LIGHTS AND MARKS Reen Pt, Fl WRG 10s; a small slender W bn; vis shore-G-338°-W-001°-R-shore. A ruined tr is on Horse Is.

R/T None.

TELEPHONE (Code 028) MRCC (066) 9746109; Coast/Cliff Rescue Service 21039; ⊖ Bantry (027) 50061; Police 36144; Dr 23456; Ⓗ 21677.

FACILITIES Reen Pier L, FW; **Sailing Club** ☎ 36100; **Castletownshend Village** Slip, Bar, R, 🛒, FW, ✉, Ⓑ (Skibbereen), ⇌, ✈ (Cork).

BARLOGE CREEK, Cork, **51°29'·57N 09°17'·58W**. AC 2129. Tides approx as Castletownshend. A narrow creek, well sheltered except from S/SE winds. Appr with Gokane Pt brg 120°. Enter W of Bullock Is, keeping to the W side to clear rks S of the island. ⚓ W of the Is in 3m but weedy. No facilities.

THE WEST COAST

This coast offers wonderful cruising, although exposed to the Atlantic and any swell offshore; but this diminishes mid-summer. In bad weather however the sea breaks dangerously on shoals with quite substantial depths. There is usually a refuge close by, but if caught out in deteriorating weather and poor vis, a stranger may need to make an offing until conditions improve, so a sound yacht and good crew are required. Even in mid-summer at least one gale may be met in a two-week cruise. Fog is less frequent than in the Irish Sea.

▶ *Tidal streams are weak, except round headlands.* ◀ There are few lights, so inshore navigation is unwise after dark, however coastal navigation is feasible at night in good visibility. Keep a good watch for lobster pots in inshore waters. Stores, fuel and water are not readily available.

MIZEN HEAD TO DINGLE BAY

(AC 2423) At S end of Dunmanus Bay Three Castle Hd has rks 1ca W, and sea can break on S Bullig 4ca off Hd. Dunmanus B (AC 2552) has three hbrs: Dunmanus, Kitchen Cove and Dunbeacon. Carbery, Cold and Furze Is lie in middle of B, and it is best to keep N of them. Sheep's Hd (lt) is at the S end of Bantry Bay (AC 1838, 1840) which has excellent hbrs, notably Glengariff and Castletown. There are few dangers offshore, except around Bear and Whiddy Islands. ▶ *Off Blackball Hd at W entrance to Bantry B there can be a nasty race, particularly on W-going stream against the wind. Keep 3ca off Crow Is to clear dangers.* ◀

Dursey Island is steep-to except for rk 7½ca NE of Dursey Hd and Lea Rk (1·4m)1½ca SW. The Bull (lt, fog sig, Racon) and two rks W of it lie 2·5M WNW of Dursey Hd. The Cow is midway between The Bull and Dursey Hd, with clear water each side. Calf and Heifer Rks are 7½ca SW of Dursey Hd, where there is often broken water. ▶ *2M W of The Bull the stream turns NW at HW Cobh +0150, and SE at HW Cobh –0420. Dursey Sound (chart 2495) is a good short cut, but the stream runs 4kn at sp; W-going starts at HW Cobh +0135, and E-going at HW Cobh –0450.* ◀ Flag Rk lies almost awash in mid-chan at the narrows, which are crossed by cables 25m above MHWS. Hold very close to the Island shore. Beware wind changes in the sound, and broken water at N entrance.

Kenmare R. (AC 2495) has attractive hbrs and anchs, but its shores are rky, with no lights. The best places are Sneem, Kilmakilloge and Ardgroom. Off Lamb's Head, Two Headed Island is steep-to; further W is Moylaun Is with a rk 300m SW of it. Little Hog (or Deenish) Island is rky 1·5M to W, followed by Great Hog (or Scariff) Is which has a rk close N, and a reef extending 2ca W.

Darrynane is an attractive, sheltered hbr NNW of Lamb Hd. The entrance has ldg lts and marks, but is narrow and dangerous in bad weather. Ballinskelligs Bay has an anch N of Horse Is, which has two rks close off E end. Centre of bay is a prohib anch (cables reported).

Rough water is met between Bolus Hd and Bray Hd with fresh onshore winds or swell. The SW end of Puffin Island is steep-to, but the sound to the E is rky and not advised. Great Skellig (lit) is 6M, and Little Skellig 5M WSW of Puffin Is. Lemon Rk lies between Puffin Is and Little Skellig. ▶ *Here the stream turns N at HW Cobh +0500, and S at HW Cobh –0110.* ◀ There is a rk 3ca SW of Great Skellig. When very calm it is possible to go alongside at Blind Man's Cove on NE side of Great Skellig, where there are interesting ruins.

9.12.24 BALTIMORE

Cork 51°28'·30N 09°23'·40W ❋❋❋❋👍👍👍

CHARTS AC 2129, 3725, 5623; Imray C56.

TIDES –0605 Dover; ML 2·1; Duration 0610

Standard Port COBH (←—)

Times				Height (metres)			
High Water		Low Water		MHWS	MHWN	MLWN	MLWS
0500	1100	0500	1100	4·1	3·2	1·3	0·4
1700	2300	1700	2300				
Differences BALTIMORE							
–0025	–0005	–0010	–0050	–0·6	–0·3	+0·1	+0·2

SHELTER Excellent. Access H24 from the S. At Baltimore, pontoon (Apr-Sep) on S Pier, AB for up to 20 yachts in 2·4m depth. Inner Hbr, partly drying between N and S piers, mostly used by ferries, local boats and FVs; the latter also berth on N pier. ⚓ about 200m W of S pier, or about 200m N of N Pier. Beware extensive moorings. In strong NW'lies ⚓ in Church Strand Bay. Its are required. Do not ⚓ in dredged chan between Wallis Rk buoy and N Pier, or in chan to Church Strand Bay. In strong W winds ⚓ in lee of Sherkin Is off Castle ruins or berth on pontoon (see Adjacent Anchorages, Sherkin Island).

NAVIGATION WPT 51°27'·93N 09°23'·46W, 000°/5ca to Loo Rk SHM lt buoy. No passage between buoy and mainland. Beware Lousy Rks (SCM bn) and Wallis Rk (PHM lt buoy) in middle of the bay. From/to the N The Sound needs careful pilotage; AC 3725 and ICC SDs essential. R Ilen is navigable on the flood for at least 4M above The Sound. Speed limit 6kn in R Ilen and N/NE of Wallace Rock.

LIGHTS AND MARKS See 9.12.4 and chartlet. Ent easily identified by Barrack Pt lt ho and conspic W tr (Lot's Wife) on Beacon Pt.

R/T VHF (HM) Ch 09, 16.

TELEPHONE (Code 028) HM 087 2351485; MRCC and Coast/Cliff Rescue Service (066) 9476109; ⊖ (027) 53210; Police 20102; Dr 23456/after hrs 1850 335999, Ⓗ 21677.

FACILITIES Berthing: May-Sept from €20/craft, ☎ 22145, 0872 351485 or www.atlanticboat.ie; slip, AB, D (☎ 20106), FW on pontoon; **Baltimore SC,** ☎ 20426, visitors welcome, bar, showers; **Glenans Irish Sailing School** ☎ (01) 6611481, 028 20154; **Sherkin** Pontoon, FW, access to shore in season. Hotel ☎ 20361. **Services:** D (hose), BY (on R Ilen at Old Court), ME, El, CH, 🛒, Gas, Gaz, Kos, ACA; **Village:** Bar, ✉, bus to Cork for ⇌, ✈.

ADJACENT ANCHORAGES

SHERKIN ISLAND on W side of harbour entrance. ⚓s: Horseshoe Harbour (keep well to the W in narrow entrance; unlit); and off Castle ruins, 5ca N, where there are also some AB on pontoons (FW and electricity) belonging to nearby Islander's Rest Hotel.

CLEAR ISLAND, N HARBOUR, 51°26'·60N 09°30'·20W. AC 2129, 5623. Tides approx as Schull, 9.12.24. A tiny, partly drying inlet on N coast of Clear Is, exposed to N'ly swell. Rks either side of outer appr 196°. Inside the narrow (30m), rky ent keep to the E. Lie to 2⚓s on E side in about 1·5m or drying berth in Inner Hbr clear of ferry bad weather berth. **Facilities** D & P (cans), FW, 🛒, ✉,email, R, Bar.

ROARINGWATER BAY, Long Island Bay AC 2129, 5623. Entered between Cape Clear and Mizen Hd and extends NE into Roaringwater Bay, beware extensive marine farms with narrow chans between them. Fastnet Rk/Lt Ho, is 4M to seaward. Safest appr, S of Schull, is via Carthy's Sound (51°30'N 09°30'W). From the SE appr via Gascanane Sound, but beware Toorane Rks, Anima Rk and outlying rks off many of the islands. Shelter in various winds at ⚓s clockwise from Horse Island: 3ca E and 7ca NE of E tip of Horse Is; in Ballydehob B 2m; Poulgorm B 2m; 5ca ENE of Mannin Is in 4m; 2ca SE of Carrigvalish Rks in 6m. Rincolisky Cas (ru) is conspic on S side of bay. The narrow chan E of Hare Is and N of Sherkin Is has two ⚓s; also leads via The Sound into Baltimore hbr. Local advice useful. Temp'y fair weather ⚓s in Carthy's Islands. Rossbrin Cove safe ⚓ 2·5M E of Schull, but many local moorings; no access from E of Horse Is due to drying Horse Ridge. Ballydehob has a good quay for tenders and most facilities.

9.12.25 SCHULL

Cork **51°30'·80N 09°32'·00W** ✿✿✿✿♦♦✿✿✿✿

CHARTS AC 2184, 2129, 5623; Imray C56.

TIDES +0610 Dover; ML 1·8; Duration 0610

Standard Port COBH (←—)

Times				Height (metres)			
High Water		Low Water		MHWS	MHWN	MLWN	MLWS
0500	1100	0500	1100	4·1	3·2	1·3	0·4
1700	2300	1700	2300				
Differences SCHULL							
−0040	−0015	−0015	−0110	−0·9	−0·6	−0·2	0·0

SHELTER Good, except in strong S/SE winds when best shelter is N of Long Island. Schull Hbr access H24. 12 Y ⚓s in NE part of hbr or ⚓ in 3m 1ca SE of pier, usually lit by street lts all night; keep clear of fairway marked by 8 unlit lateral buoys (summer time only).

NAVIGATION WPT 51°29'·60N 09°31'·60W, 346°/2·1M to front ldg lt. In hbr ent, Bull Rk (dries 1·8m), R iron perch, can be passed either side.

LIGHTS AND MARKS See 9.12.4 and chartlet. Ldg lts, lead 346° between Long Is Pt, W conical tr, and Amelia Rk SHM lt buoy; thence E of Bull Rk and toward head of bay. By day in good vis 2 W radomes conspic on Mt Gabriel (2M N of Schull) lead 355° with Long Is Pt lt ho in transit.

R/T None.

TELEPHONE (Code 028) Water Sports Centre 28554; HM 086-1039105; MRCC (066) 9476109; Coast/Cliff Rescue Service 35318;

Inshore Rescue Service 086 236 0206: ⊖ (027) 51562; Police 28111; Dr 28311; ⊞ (027) 50133.

FACILITIES Schull Pier/Hbr Slip (H24 except LWS) FV pier/pontoon for tenders (v.crowded at times), AB tempy, ⚓ €10/night, M, D (large quantities by arrangement), FW, SM; **Sailing Club** ☎ 37352; **Services:** Kos, BY, ✗, CH. **Village** P & D (cans from Ballydehob 5M), ME, El, 🛒, @/Wi-fi, Charts, R, Bar, 🗑, ✉, Ⓑ, bus to Cork for: ⇌, ✈, Ferries.

9.12.26 CROOKHAVEN

Cork **51°28'·50N 09°42'·00W** ✿✿ ✿♦✿✿✿✿

CHARTS AC 2184, 5623; Imray C56.

TIDES +0550 Dover; ML 1·8; Duration 0610

Standard Port COBH (←—)

Times				Height (metres)			
High Water		Low Water		MHWS	MHWN	MLWN	MLWS
0500	1100	0500	1100	4·1	3·2	1·3	0·4
1700	2300	1700	2300				
Differences CROOKHAVEN							
−0057	−0033	−0048	−0112	−0·8	−0·6	−0·4	−0·1
DUNMANUS HARBOUR							
−0107	−0031	−0044	−0120	−0·7	−0·6	−0·2	0·0
DUNBEACON HARBOUR							
−0057	−0025	−0032	−0104	−0·8	−0·7	−0·3	−0·1

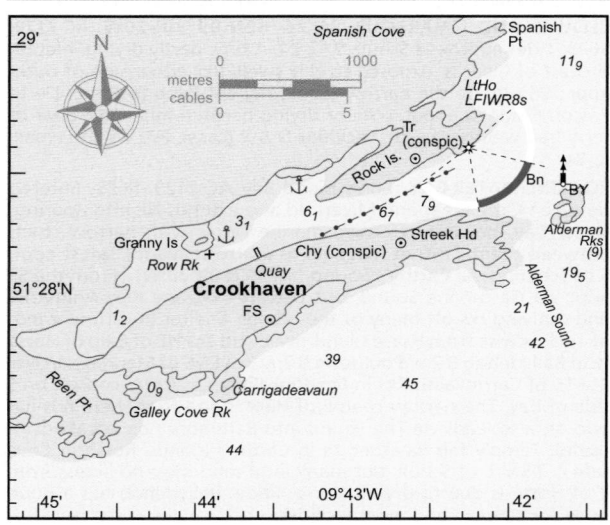

SHELTER Excellent. There are 8 Y ⚓s and 10 dayglow R ⚓s. Short stay pontoon for up to 4 boats (FW/stores/passengers). ⚓s in middle of bay in 3m; off W tip of Rock Is; and E of Granny Is; last two are far from the village. Holding is patchy, especially in strong SW'lies; beware weed, shellfish beds around shoreline and submarine pipeline from Rock Is to Crookhaven.

NAVIGATION WPT 51°28'·50N 09°40'·50W, 274°/1M to Rock Is lt ho. Ent between this lt and NCM bn on Black Horse Rks (3½ca ESE). From S, keep 1ca E of Alderman Rks and ½ca off Black Horse Rks bn. Passage between Streek Hd and Alderman Rks is not advised for strangers. Inside the bay the shores are steep to.

LIGHTS AND MARKS Lt ho on Rock Is (conspic W tr) L Fl WR 8s 20m 13/11M; vis outside hbr: W over Long Is Bay-281°-R-340°; vis inside hbr: 281°-R-348°-W-shore(N).

R/T None.

TELEPHONE (Code 028) HM (O'Sullivan's Bar) 35319; MRCC (066) 9476109; Coast/Cliff Rescue at Goleen 35318; ⊖ (027) 50061; Dr 35148; ✉ 35200.

FACILITIES Village ⚓s €8.00, Bar, R, FW, 🛒, ✉, D (cans), ME, Ⓑ (Schull), taxi to Goleen then bus to Cork, ✈, ⇌.

ADJACENT HARBOURS

GOLEEN (Kireal-coegea), Cork, **51°29'·65N 09°42'·21W**. AC 2184, 5623. Tides as Crookhaven. A narrow inlet 6ca N of Spanish Pt; good shelter in fair weather, except from SE. 2 churches are easily seen, but ent not visible until close. Keep to S side of ent and anchor fore-and-aft just below quay, where AB also possible. Facilities: P, 🛒, Bar.

DUNMANUS BAY, Cork. AC 2552, 5623. Tides see 9.12.25. Appr between Three Castle Hd and Sheep's Hd, Fl (3) WR 15s 83m 18/15M; no other lts. Ent to **Dunmanus Hbr**, 51°32'·70N 09°39'·86W, is 1ca wide; breakers both sides. ⚓ in 4m centre of B. **Kitchen Cove**, 51°35'·50N 09°38'·05W, best of the 3 hbrs; enter W of Owens Is and ⚓ 1ca NNW of it or 2ca further N in 3m. Exposed to S, but good holding. Quay at Ahakista village: AB (drying) FW, ⌁, 🛒, R, Bar. **Dunbeacon Hbr**, 51°36'·35N 09°33'·60W, is shallow and rock-girt. Quay possible AB in 2m (used by FVs), Slip; anchorage E or SE of Mannion Is. Durrus (¾M): Fuel (cans), R, Bar.

9.12.27 BANTRY BAY

Cork 51°34'N 09°57'W ✵✵✵✵⚓⚓✿✿✿

CHARTS AC 2552, 1840, 1838, 5623; Imray C56.

TIDES +0600 Dover; ML 1·8; Duration 0610

Standard Port COBH (←——)

Times				Height (metres)			
High Water		Low Water		MHWS	MHWN	MLWN	MLWS
0500	1100	0500	1100	4·1	3·2	1·3	0·4
1700	2300	1700	2300				
Differences BANTRY							
–0045	–0025	–0040	–0105	–0·7	–0·6	–0·2	+0·1
CASTLETOWN (Bearhaven)							
–0048	–0012	–0025	–0101	–0·9	–0·6	–0·1	0·0
BLACK BALL HARBOUR (51°36N 10°02W)							
–0115	–0035	–0047	–0127	–0·7	–0·6	–0·1	+0·1

SHELTER/NAVIGATION Bantry Bay extends 20M ENE from Sheep's Hd, Fl (3) WR 15s 83m 18/15M. Access is easy, but the Bay is exposed to W'lies. The shore is clear everywhere except off Bear Is and Whiddy Is. Some of the many well sheltered ⚓s on the N shore are detailed on this page. The S shore has few ⚓s.

CASTLETOWNBERE 51°38'·80N 09°54'·45W. AC 1840, 5623. Sheltered ⚓ in 2·4m NW of Dinish Is, to E of 010° ldg line, but never far from FVs; also ⚓ at **Dunboy Bay,** W of Piper Sound (open to E). 4 Y ⚓s are laid Apr-Sep 3ca E of Dinish Is. Lts: At W ent, Ardnakinna Pt, Fl (2) WR 10s 62m 17/14M, H24. At E ent to Bearhaven: Roancarrigmore, Fl WR 3s 18m 18/14M. Appr W of Bear Is on 024° Dir lt, Oc WRG 5s 4m 14/11M (024°-W-024·5°); then inner ldg lts 010°, both Oc 3s 4/7m 1M, vis 005°-015°, via ent chan which narrows to 50m abeam Perch Rk lt bn. Beware Walter Scott Rk (2·7m), SCM lt buoy, and Carrigaglos (0·6m high) S of Dinish Is. VHF Ch 14 16. HM ☎ (027) 70220. Facilities: FW & D on quay; BH on Dinish Is. **Town** El, ME, ✕, P (cans), Bar, Ⓑ, ✉, ☲, R, Kos.

LAWRENCE COVE MARINA 51°38'·28N 09°49'·28W; AC 1840, 5623. *See inset on chartlet below.* Good shelter on N side of Bear Island. Marina on S side of cove has NE/SW pontoon 90m long (40 AB in 3-3·5m). From E keep clear of Palmer Rock and a shoal patch, both 1·8m. ☎ 027 75044; VHF Ch 16 M. AB (€1.52), FW, ⚡, D, BH, Ⓟ. Friendly welcome at the only marina between Kinsale and Dingle. There are 4 yellow ⚓s in 3m close S of Ardagh Point, or ⚓ in 4m to W of Turk Is. At Rerrin village: BY, Slip, Gaz, ☲, R, Bar, ✉, storage facilities. Bus to Cork.

LONEHORT HARBOUR 51°38'·12N 09°47'·80W. AC 1840, 5623. At E tip of Bear Is, good shelter but keep S at ent to clear unmarked rks; then turn ENE to ⚓ in 2·7m at E end of cove. Be aware of Firing Practice Area to east of harbour entrance (full clear range procedure in force).

ADRIGOLE 51°40'·51N 09°43'·22W. AC 1840, 5623. Good shelter, but squally in W/N gales. Beware Doucallia Rk, dries 1·2m, 1M SSW of ent. Beyond the 2ca wide ent, keep E of Orthons Is (rks on W side). 7 Y ⚓s NE of Orthons Is. ⚓s to suit wind direction: off pier on E shore 4m; N or NW of Orthons Is. Drumlave (½M E): Slip, FW, showers (sailing school), D (cans), Gaz, ☲, ✉.

Trafrask Bay, 2M east, has Y ⚓ at 51°40'·8N 09°40'·1W; ☲, Bar/R.

GLENGARRIFF 51°44'·20N 09°31'·90W. AC 1838, 5623. Tides as Bantry. Beautiful ⚓ S of Bark Is in 7-10m; or to NE in 3m, where there are 6 Y ⚓s. Better for yachts than Bantry hbr. Ent between Big Pt and Gun Pt. No lts/marks. Keep 1ca E of rks off Garinish Island (Illnacullen) and Ship Is; beware marine farms. Rky chan W of Garinish, with HT cable 15m clearance, should not be attempted. Facilities: Eccles hotel, showers. **Village** FW (ferry berth 1800-1900), Bar, D & P (cans), ✉, R, ☲, Kos.

BANTRY 51°40'·85N 09°27'·85W. AC 1838, 5623. Beware Gerane Rks ½M W of Whiddy Is. Appr via the buoyed/lit N chan to E of Horse and Chapel Is; keep 2ca off all islands to clear unlit marine farms. The S chan, fair weather only. Appr Relane Pt hdg 063° with HW mark S.Beach (seaward edge of airfield) ⊘ Reenbeg Cliff (distant rounded hill) to clear Cracker Rk, then leave Blue Hill and S Beach to stbd. ⚓'s call Bantry Hbr Ch 14 or ☎ 027 51253; VHF Ch 14 11 16 (H24). HM (027) 53277; ⊖ 50061; Police 50045; Dr 50405; Ⓗ 50133. MRCC (066) 9476109. Facilities: **Pier** AB(drying), L, FW, Gaz; **Bantry Bay SC** ☎ 50081 ⚓s(free),Slip, L, FW, Showers; **Town** @ (Vickery's Inn), P & D (cans), Kos, ME, CH, ☲, R, Bar, ✉, Ⓑ, bus to Cork.

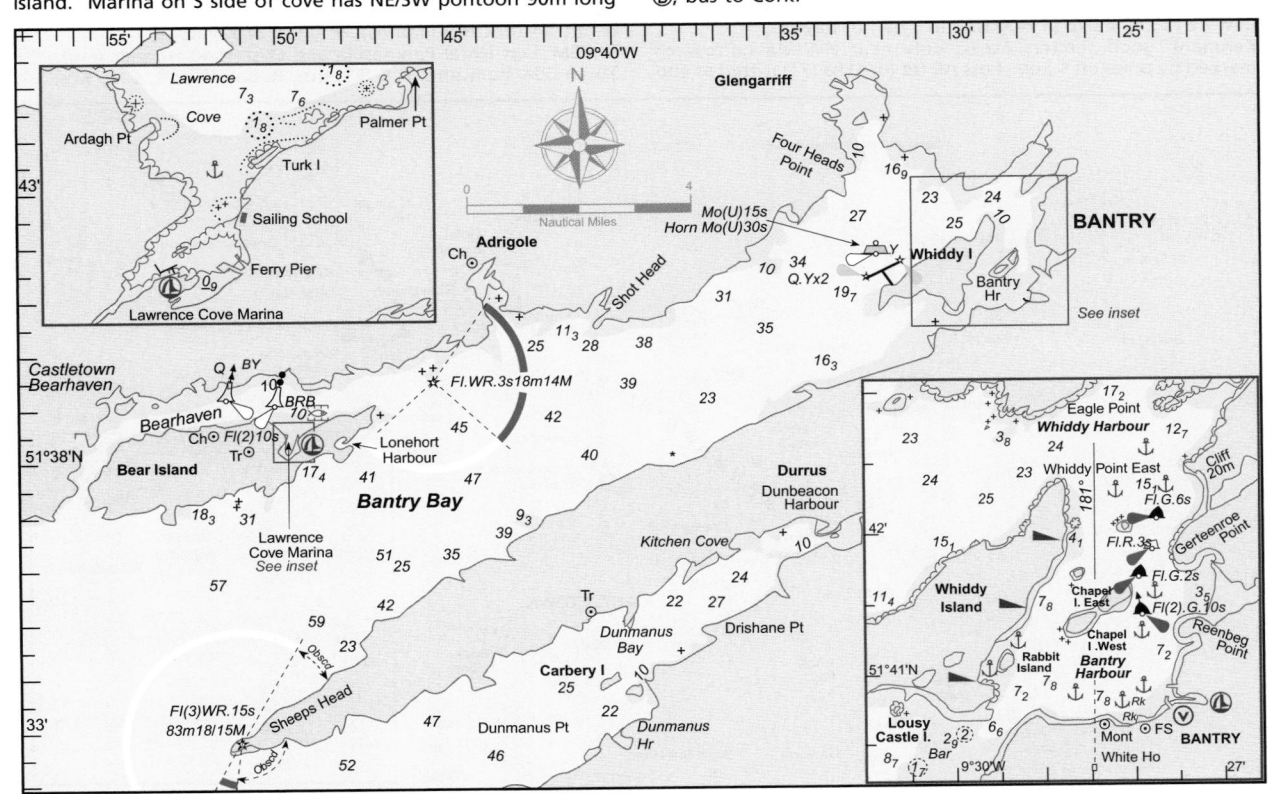

9.12.28 KENMARE RIVER

Kerry 51°45'·00N 10°00'·00W ✿✿✿✿✿✿✿✿

CHARTS AC 2495; Imray C56.

TIDES +0515 Dover; Duration Dunkerron 0620

Standard Port COBH (←—)

Times				Height (metres)			
High Water		Low Water		MHWS	MHWN	MLWN	MLWS
0500	1100	0500	1100	4·1	3·2	1·3	0·4
1700	2300	1700	2300				
Differences BALLYCROVANE HARBOUR (Coulagh Bay)							
−0116	−0036	−0053	−0133	−0·6	−0·5	−0·1	0·0
DUNKERRON HARBOUR							
−0117	−0027	−0050	−0140	−0·2	−0·3	+0·1	0·0
WEST COVE (51°46'N 10°03'W)							
−0113	−0033	−0049	−0129	−0·6	−0·5	−0·1	0·0
BALLINSKELLIGS BAY							
−0119	−0039	−0054	−0134	−0·5	−0·5	−0·1	0·0

SHELTER Garnish Bay (S of Long I): is only good in settled weather and W'ly winds. ⚓ either W or 1ca S of the Carrigduff concrete bn.

Ballycrovane: in NE of Coulagh B is a good ⚓, but open to W'ly swell which breaks on submerged rks in SE. N and E shores are foul 5ca NE of Bird Is.

Cleanderry: ent NE of Illaunbweeheen (Yellow Is) is only 7m wide and rky. ⚓ ENE of inner hbr. Beware marine farms.

Ardgroom: excellent shelter, but intricate ent over rky bar. Appr with B bn brg 135°; then 2 W bns (front on Black Rk, rear ashore) lead 099° through bar. Alter 206° as two bns astern come in transit. When clear, steer WNW to ⚓ 0·5 ca E of Reenavade pier; power needed. Beware marine farms off Ardgroom & Kilmakilloge.

Kilmakilloge: is a safe ⚓ in all winds. Beware mussel beds and rky shoals. On appr keep S side of ent, steer W of Spanish Is, but pass N of it. Bunaw Hbr ldg lts 041°, front Oc R 3s, rear Iso R 2s, (access only near HW; AB for shoal draft). Keep S side of ent; ⚓ 2ca W of Carrigwee bn; S of Eskadawer Pt; or Collorus Hbr W side only.

Ormond's Harbour: good shelter except in SW or W winds, but beware rk 2½ca ENE of Hog Is. ⚓ in S half of bay.

Kenmare: good shelter. Access only near HW via narrow ch marked by poles on S side. Poss AB (☎ (064) 83171) rafted at end

of pier (FW available) at N side of river, just below town. ⚓ in pool (2.5m) just downstream of concrete suspension bridge. Beware very strong ebbs at springs and after heavy rains.

Dunkerron Harbour: ent between Cod Rks and The Boar to ⚓ 1ca NW of Fox Is in 3·2m; land at Templenoe pier. 4ca E of Reen Pt behind pier FW available.

Sneem: enter between Sherky Is and Rossdohan Is. Hotel conspic NE of hbr. 3 Y ⚓s and ⚓ NE of Garinish Is, but uncomfortable if swell enters either side of Sherky Is. Beware of marine farms.

Darrynane: 1½M NW of Lamb's Hd, is appr'd from the S between Deenish and Moylaun Islands, but not with high SW swell. Enter with care on the ldg marks/lts 034°, 2 W bns, both Oc 3s 10/16m 4M. 3 Y ⚓s (beware unmkd drying rk close N) and safe ⚓ (3m) NE of Lamb's Is. Also ⚓s in Lehid Hbr, R Blackwater, Coongar Hbr & W Cove.

NAVIGATION WPT 51°40'·00N 10°17'·20W, 065°/15.6M to 0.5M S of Sherky Island. From SW, keep NW of The Bull and Dursey Is. From SE, Dursey Sound is possible in fair weather but narrow (beware Flag Rk 0·3m) and with cable car, 21m clearance. To clear dangerous rks off Coulagh Bay, keep twr on Dursey Is well open of Cod's Head 220°. From NW, there are 3 deep chans off Lamb's Head: between Scarriff Is and Deenish Is which is clear; between Deenish and Moylaun Is which has rky shoals; and between Moylaun and Two Headed Is which is clear and 4½ca wide. A night appr into the river is possible, but close appr to hbrs or ⚓s is not advised. Up-river from Sneem Hbr, keep N of Maiden Rk, dries 0·5m, and Church Rks; also Lackeen Rks and Carrignarona beg. Beware marine farms, also salmon nets Jun-Sep. See 9.12.5.

LIGHTS AND MARKS On Dursey Is: Old Watch Twr (conspic) 250m. Eagle Hill (Cod's Hd) 216m. Lights are as on chartlet.

R/T None.

TELEPHONE (Code 064) MRCC (066) 9476109; Coast/Cliff Rescue Service (Waterville) (066) 74320; ⊖ Bantry (027) 50061; Ⓗ 4108; Police 41177.

FACILITIES

ARDGROOM Pallas Hbr: D & P (cans), 🛒, R, Bar, Kos, ✉ at Ardgroom village (2M SSW of Reenavade pier).

KILMAKILLOGE: Bunaw Pier, AB, 🛒, Bar/R; 2M to D(cans), Kos, ✉.

KENMARE: AB. Town D & P (cans), Kos, Gaz, R, 🛒, Bar, Ⓗ, ✉ inc @, Ⓑ, ⇌ (bus to Killarney), ✈ (Cork or Killarney).

SNEEM: L at Hotel Parknasilla and Oysterbed Ho pier (FW).

Town (2M from hbr), P & D (cans), R, Bar, ✉, 🛒, Gaz, Kos.

9.12.29 DINGLE BAY

9.12.30 VALENTIA HARBOUR

Kerry 51°55'·7N 10°17'·1W ✿✿❀❀❀❀❀

CHARTS AC 2125; Imray C56.

TIDES +0515 Dover

Standard Port COBH (←)

Times				Height (metres)			
High Water		Low Water		MHWS	MHWN	MLWN	MLWS
0500	1100	0500	1100	4·1	3·2	1·3	0·4
1700	2300	1700	2300				
Differences VALENTIA HARBOUR (Knight's Town)							
–0118	–0038	–0056	–0136	–0·6	–0·4	–0·1	0·0

SHELTER Good ⚓s at: Glanleam B, 6ca S of Fort Pt in 4m; 1ca NW of LB slip in 2·5m, with 6 Y ⚓s (beware The Foot, spit drying 1·2m,

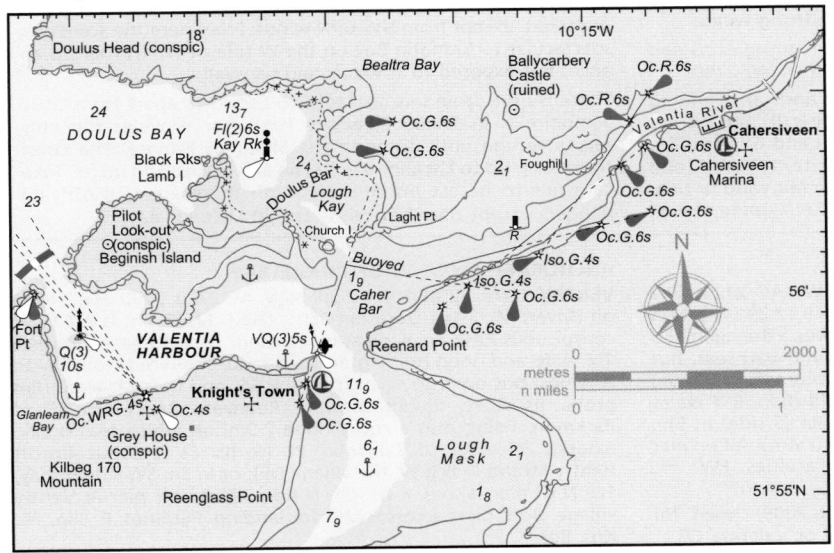

marked by ECM lt buoy; SE of Ferry Pier at Knight's Town (E end of the island) in 4m; in bay on the S side of Beginish Is in 3m.

NAVIGATION Wpt 51°56'·84N 10°20'·15W 147°/1M to Fort Pt lt. Appr the NE end of Valentia Is, either via;

- Doulus Bay, N of Beginish Is (avoid if swell is running). Clear Black Rks by ½ca then head for E end of Beginish Is immediately Reenard Pt opens to port of it. When Lamb Is and the N point of Beginish are about to open astern, alter course to keep them so till Reenard Point opens to the E of Church Is. Then steer to pass 50m E of Church Is to avoid Passage Rk (1$_5$) 1ca E of Is.

- Better ent, between Fort Pt and Beginish Is (easy access except in strong NW'lies). Beware Hbr Rk, 2·6m, 3ca SE of Fort Pt and 100m SW of ldg line and marked by ECM lt Bn.

For **Cahersiveen Marina** from Valentia Is start as early on the tide possible to cross the Caher Bar (buoyed WC, EC ,SH & PHMs), using the ldg lts/lines 019-199°, 100°-280°, 076°-256°, 053°-233°, 035°-215° and then keep to the middle of the river.

For appr S of Island via Portmagee chan see **Portmagee** overleaf for info on availability of the swing bridge across the chan.

LIGHTS AND MARKS See 9.12.4 and chartlet.

R/T Cahersiveen Marina VHF Ch 80.

TELEPHONE Knightstown HM (066) 9476124; CG 9476109; ⊖ 7128540; Dr 9472121; Police 9472111; Ⓗ 9472100; Cahersiveen Marina ☎ 947 2777, www.cahersiveenmarina.ie.

FACILITIES Knight's Town: 6 Y ⚓s; BY, ⚒, ME, Kos, 🛒, R, Bar, ▣. A new marina is under construction and should be available for Summer 2010 (see monthly online updates). Ferry/bus to Cahersiveen (2½M) for usual shops; Bus to ⇌ (Tralee and Killarney), ✈ (Kerry, Shannon, Cork). **Cahersiveen Marina** (2M upriver): (min depth 2.5m in basin, 93 incl Ⓥ) €2.50, BH(14T), ME, El, Ch, Ⓔ, ⚒, P & D, ▣, 🛒, Ⓑ, ✉, R, Bar.

9.12.31 DINGLE

Kerry 52°07'·14N 10°15'·48W ⚓⚓⚓⚓🌊🌊🌊✦✦✦

CHARTS AC 2789, 2790; Imray C55, C56.

TIDES +0540 Dover; ML 2·1m; Duration 0605

Standard Port COBH (←——)

Times				Height (metres)			
High Water		Low Water		MHWS	MHWN	MLWN	MLWS
0500	1100	0500	1100	4·1	3·2	1·3	0·4
1700	2300	1700	2300				
Differences DINGLE							
–0111	–0041	–0049	–0119	–0·1	0·0	+0·3	+0·4
SMERWICK HARBOUR							
–0107	–0041	–0041	–0121	–0·3	–0·4	No data	
FENIT PIER (Tralee Bay)							
–0057	–0017	–0029	–0109	+0·5	+0·2	+0·3	+0·1

SHELTER Excellent at marina (5m depth) in landlocked hbr. *See RMWG.* A busy fishing port. There are 4 Y ⚓s at **Kells Bay** (52°01'·6N 10°06'·3W), 8M SE of Dingle ent.

NAVIGATION WPT 52°06'·20N 10° 15'·48W, 360°/1·06M to lt Fl G 3s. Easy ent H24. Beware Crow Rk (dries 3·7m), 0·8M SW off Reenbeg Pt and rky ledge SW of Black Pt.

- **Castlemaine Hbr**, approx 15M E at the head of Dingle Bay, largely dries and should not be attempted without local knowledge or inspection at LW.

LIGHTS AND MARKS Eask Twr (195m, with fingerpost pointing E) is conspic 0·85M WSW of ent. Lt tr, Fl G 3s 20m 6M, on NE side of ent. Ent chan, dredged 2·6m, is marked by 5 SHM lt buoys and 3 PHM lt buoys, as chartlet. Ldg lts, both Oc 3s, (W ◇s on B poles) lead from astern 182° to hbr bkwtrs. Sectored lt Oc RWG 4s on W side of Main Pier.

R/T Ch **14** 16 M, but no calls required. Valentia Radio (Ch 24 28) will relay urgent messages to Dingle HM.

TELEPHONE (Code 066) HM 9151629; Coastguard (066) 9476109; 🖥 7121480; Dr 9152225; Ⓗ 9151455; Police 9151522. All emergencies: 999 or 112.

FACILITIES Marina (60+20 🅥) ☎ 087 9254115, 1dingle @eircom.net, €2·50, D, Slip (launching €2·00), 🗄, ♿, C (hire). **Town** P (cans), Kos, ME, Ⓔ, Gas, Gaz, SM, ✉, R, Bar, 🛒, Ⓑ, ⇌ Tralee (by bus), ✈ (Kerry 30M).

DINGLE BAY TO LISCANNOR BAY

(AC 2254) Dingle Bay (AC 2789, 2790) is wide and deep, with few dangers around its shores. Cahersiveen and Dingle have small marinas. The best anchs are at Portmagee and Ventry. At the NW ent to the bay, 2·5M SSW of Slea Hd, is Wild Bank (or Three Fathom Pinnacle), a shallow patch with overfalls. 3M SW of Wild Bank is Barrack Rk, which breaks in strong winds.

The Blasket Islands are very exposed, ▶ *with strong tides and overfalls* ◀, but worth a visit in settled weather (AC 2790).

Great Blasket and Inishvickillane each have anch and landing on their NE side. Inishtearaght is the most W'ly Is (lt), but further W lie Tearaght Rks, and 3M S are Little Foze and Gt Foze Rks. Blasket Sound is the most convenient N-S route, 1M wide, and easy in daylight and reasonable weather with fair wind or tide; extensive rks and shoals form its W side. ▶ *The N-going stream* starts at HW Galway + 0430, and the S-going at HW Galway – 0155, with sp rate 3kn. ◀

Between Blasket Sound and Sybil Pt there is a race in W or NW winds with N-going tide, and often a nasty sea. Sybil Pt has steep cliffs, and offlying rks extend 3½ca.

Smerwick hbr, entered between Duncapple Is and the E Sister is sheltered, except from NW or N winds. From here the scenery is spectacular to Brandon Bay on the W side of which there is an anch, but exposed to N winds and to swell.

There is no lt from Inishtearaght to Loop Hd, apart from Little Samphire Is in Tralee B, where Fenit hbr provides the only secure refuge until entering the Shannon Estuary. The coast from Loop Hd to Liscanor Bay has no safe anchs, and no lts. Take care not to be set inshore, although there are few offlying dangers except near Mutton Is and in Liscanor Bay.

ANCHORAGE SW VALENTIA ISLAND

PORTMAGEE, Kerry, **51°53'·20N 10°22'·29W**. AC 2125. HW +0550 on Dover; ML 2·0m; Duration 0610; See 9.12.29. A safe ⚓ 2·5M E of Bray Head in Portmagee Sound between the mainland and Valentia Is. The ent to the Sound often has bad seas, but dangers are visible. Care required E of Reencaheragh Pt (S side) due rks either side. Deepest water is N of mid-chan. 6 Y ⚓s at 51°53'·3N 10°22'·5W (N side), or ⚓ off the pier (S side) in 5m, opposite Skelling Heritage Centre (well worth a visit). AB on pier is not recommended due to strong tides. Facilities: FW, 🛒, showers (at hotel), R, Bar, Kos.

The swing bridge 1ca E of pier is currently (Feb 2009) closed; for further information check with Valentia RNLI or Valentia CG.

ANCHORAGE CLOSE W OF DINGLE BAY

VENTRY Kerry, **52°06'·70N 10°20'·30W**. AC 2789, 2790. HW +0540 on Dover; ML 2·1m; Duration 0605; Use 9.12.30. Ent is 2M W of conspicuous Eask Tr. A pleasant harbour br with easy entrance 1M wide and good holding on hard sand; sheltered from SW to N winds, but open to swell from the SE, and in fresh westerlies prone to sharp squalls. Beware Reenvare Rocks 1ca SE of Parkmore Point; also a rocky ridge 2·9m, on which seas break, extends 2·5ca SSE of Ballymore Pt. No lts. ⚓s in about 4m off Ventry Strand (⊕ brg W, the village NE); or in 3m SW side of bay, 1ca N of pier; also 3 Y ⚓s. On N side 3 Y ⚓s off pier at Ventry village. Both piers access HW±3 for landing. Facilities: P, Slip, 🛒, Kos, Bar, R, ✉.

ANCHORAGES BETWEEN THE BLASKETS AND KERRY HD
SMERWICK HARBOUR, Kerry, **52°13'·00N 10°24'·00W**. AC 2789. Tides 9.12.30. Adequate shelter in 1M wide bay, except from NW'ly when considerable swell runs in. Ent between The Three Sisters (150m hill) and Dunacapple Is to the NE. Beacon Fl.R.3s at pier end at Ballnagall Pt. ⟂s at: the W side close N or S of the Boat Hr in 3-10m; to the S, off Carrigveen Pt in 2·5m; or in N'lies in the bay in NE corner inside 10m line. Facilities at Ballnagall village on SE side: 4 Y ⚓s, pier (0·5m), limited 🛒, Bar, Bus.

BRANDON BAY, Kerry, **52°16'·10N 10°09'·92**W. AC 2739. Tides as Fenit 9.12.30. A 4M wide bay, very exposed to the N, but in moderate SW-W winds there is safe ⟂ in 6m close E of drying Brandon Pier, 2FG (vert). Cloghane Inlet in SW of Bay is not advised. Facilities at Brandon: limited 🛒, P (1M), ✉, R, Bar, bus.

TRALEE BAY, Kerry, **52°18'·00N 09°56'·00W**. AC 2739. HW –0612 on Dover; ML 2·6m; Duration 0605. See 9.12.30. Enter the bay passing 3M N of Magharee Islands. Pick up the W sector (W140°–152°) of Little Samphire Is lt, Fl WRG 5s 17m 16/13M; see 9.12.4 for sectors. Approach between Magharee Is and Mucklaghmore (30m high).

9.12.32 FENIT HARBOUR

Kerry 52°16'·20N 09°51'·61W ⊕⊕⊕⚓⚓🏠🏠

CHARTS AC 2254, 2739; Imray C55.

TIDES –0612 Dover; ML 2·6m; Duration 0605

Standard Port COBH (←—)

Times				Height (metres)			
High Water		Low Water		MHWS	MHWN	MLWN	MLWS
0500	1100	0500	1100	4·1	3·2	1·3	0·4
1700	2300	1700	2300				
Differences FENIT PIER (Tralee Bay)							
–0057	–0017	–0029	–0109	+0·5	+0·2	+0·3	+0·1

SHELTER Good shelter in marina (2.7m depth), but a few berths exposed to SE'ly conditions.

NAVIGATION Appr on 146° to WPT 52°16'·00N 09° 53'·00W, Little Samphire Is, conspic lt ho, Fl WRG 5s 17m 16/13M, thence 7ca E to Samphire Is; lt QR 15m 3M vis 242°–097°. Fenit Pier Hd 2 FR (vert) 12m 3M, vis 148°–058°. Easy ent H24.

LIGHTS AND MARKS See 9.12.4 and chartlet.

R/T Neptune (Tralee SC) VHF Ch 14 16. Port Manager: VHF Ch 16 **14 M** (0900-2100UT).

TELEPHONE (Code 066) Port Manager ☎ 7136231; ⊜ ☎ 7121480.

FACILITIES Marina (130 inc 15 Ⓥ; max LOA 25m, €1.60 min €16.00/craft), FW, ⬦, D, 🅾, ♿; For ⚓s call Neptune (Tralee SC); **Village** Slip, C, P (cans), ME, 🛒, Bar, R, ✉, Ⓑ, ⇌ Tralee (by bus), ✈ (Kerry 30M).

THE SHANNON ESTUARY

(AC 1819, 1547, 1548, 1549) The estuary and lower reaches of the Shannon are tidal for 50M, from its mouth between Loop Hd and Kerry Hd up to Limerick Dock, some 15M beyond the junction with R Fergus. ▶ *The tides and streams are those of a deep-water inlet, with roughly equal durations of rise and fall, and equal rates of flood and ebb streams. In the entrance the flood stream begins at HW Tarbert Is – 0555, and the ebb at HW Tarbert Is + 0015.* ◀

There are several anchorages available for yachts on passage up or down the coast. Kilbaha Bay (AC 1819) is about 3M E of Loop Hd, and is convenient in good weather or in N winds, but exposed to SE and any swell. Carrigaholt B (AC 1547), entered about 1M N of Kilcredaun Pt, is well sheltered from W winds and has little tidal stream. In N winds there is an anchorage SE of Querrin Pt (AC 1547), 4·5M further up-river on N shore. At Kilrush there is a marina and anchorages E of Scattery Is and N of Hog Is. ▶ *Note that there are overfalls 0·75M S of Scattery Is with W winds and ebb tide.* ◀

▶ *Off Kilcredaun Pt the ebb reaches 4kn at sp, and in strong winds between S and NW a bad race forms. This can be mostly avoided by keeping near the N shore, which is free from offlying dangers, thereby cheating the worst of the tide. When leaving the Shannon in strong W winds, aim to pass Kilcredaun Pt at slack water, and again keep near the N shore. Loop Hd (lt) marks the N side of Shannon Est, and should be passed 3ca off. Here the stream runs SW from HW Tarbert Is + 0300, and NE from HW Tarbert Is – 0300.* ◀

▶ *Above the junction with R Fergus (AC 1540) the tidal characteristics become more like those of most rivers, ie the flood stream is stronger than the ebb, but it runs for a shorter time. In the Shannon the stream is much affected by the wind. S and W winds increase the rate and duration of the flood stream, and reduce the ebb. Strong N or E winds have the opposite effect. Prolonged or heavy rain increases the rate and duration of the ebb.* ◀

The Shannon is the longest river in Ireland, rising at Lough Allen 100M above Limerick, thence 50M to the sea.

9.12.33 SHANNON ESTUARY

Clare (N); Kerry and Limerick (S) 52°35'·00N 09°40'·00W

CHARTS AC 1819, 1547, 1548, 1549, 1540; L. Derg 5080; L. Ree 5078. Imray C55. The ICC's *Sailing Directions for S & W Ireland* and/or Admiralty *Irish Coast Pilot* are essential.

TIDES

HW at	HW Tarbert Is	HW Dover
Kilbaha & Carrigaholt	–0030	+0605
Coney Island	+0045	–0500
Foynes	+0030	–0515
Limerick	+0110	–0435

At Limerick strong S-W winds increase the height and delay the times of HW; strong N-E winds do the opposite.

SHELTER The Shannon Estuary is 50M long (Loop Hd to Limerick). For boats on passage N/S the nearest ⟂ is Kilbaha Bay, 3M inside Loop Hd; it has ⚓s sheltered in winds from W to NE, but is exposed to swell and holding is poor. 6M further E, Carrigaholt Bay has ⚓s and good shelter from W'lies; ⟂ just N of the new quay, out of the tide. Kilrush Marina (9.12.34) with all facilities is 7M further E. From Kilcredaun Head in the W to the R Fergus ent (about 25M) there are ⟂s or ⚓s, protected from all but E winds, at Tarbert Is, Glin, Labasheeda, Killadysert (pontoon) and among the islands in the Fergus mouth. There is a pontoon off the YC S of Foynes Is and drying quays at Ballylongford Creek (Saleen), Knock and Clarecastle (S of Ennis, off chartlet). Yachts may enter Limerick Dock, but this is a commercial port with usual problems; major improvements planned.

Continued overleaf

NAVIGATION WPT 52°32'·50N 09°46'·90W, Ballybunnion NCM By VQ, 064°/4·2M to Tail of Beal Bar buoy WCM, Q (9) 15s. For notes on ent and tidal streams see 9.12.5. The ebb can reach 4kn. Ldg lts, Oc. 5s, 046·4° on Corlis Pt. The lower estuary between Kerry and Loop Heads is 9M wide, narrowing to 2M off Kilcredaun Pt.

Here the chan is well buoyed in mid-stream and then follows the Kerry shore, S of Scattery Is. From Tarbert Is to Foynes Is the river narrows to less than 1M in places, before widening where the R Fergus joins from the N, abeam Shannon airport. Above this point the buoyed chan narrows and becomes shallower although there is a minimum of 2m at LWS. AC 1540 is essential for the final 15M stretch to Limerick.

RIVER SHANNON The Shannon, the longest navigable river in the UK or Ireland, is managed by Limerick Hbr Commissioners up to Limerick. Up-stream it effectively becomes an inland waterway; progress is restricted by locks and bridges. Info on navigation and facilities can be obtained from the Waterways Service, Dept of Art, Culture & the Gaeltacht, 51 St Stephen's Green, Dublin 2, ☎ 01-6613111; or from the Inland Waterways Association of Ireland, Kingston House, Ballinteer, Dublin 4, ☎ 01-983392; also from Tourist Offices and inland marinas.

LIGHTS AND MARKS See 9.12.4. There are QW (vert) aero hazard lts on tall chimneys at Money Pt power station 3M ESE of Kilrush. 2 chys at Tarbert Is are conspic (R lts).

R/T Foynes Ch 12 13 16 (occas). *Shannon Estuary Radio* Ch 12 13 16 (HO).

FACILITIES Marine facilities are available at several communities on the Shannon; M, P & D (cans), FW, 🛒, can be found at many villages. ⚓s are being laid at Labasheeda, Glin Pier (pontoon) and Foynes. E of Aughanish Is on S shore, R Deal is navigable 3M to Askeaton. Ent, marked by RW bn, is 8ca SE of Beeves Rk with 1m in buoyed chan. BY at Massey's Pier ☎ 069 73100, ⚓s, FW, C, CH, ⟐, D, Slip. Facilities at Foynes and Limerick include: **Foynes** Slip, L, AB, P & D (cans), FW, ✉, Ⓑ, Dr, 🛒, R, Bar; **Foynes YC** ☎ (069) 65261, AB (pontoon), Bar, R. **Limerick: Hbr Commission** ☎ (061) 315377; ⊖ ☎ 415366. **City** Slip, AB, L, FW, P & D (cans), Kos, Gas, Gaz, ME, El, Dr, Ⓗ, ✉, all usual city amenities, ⇌, ✈ (Shannon).

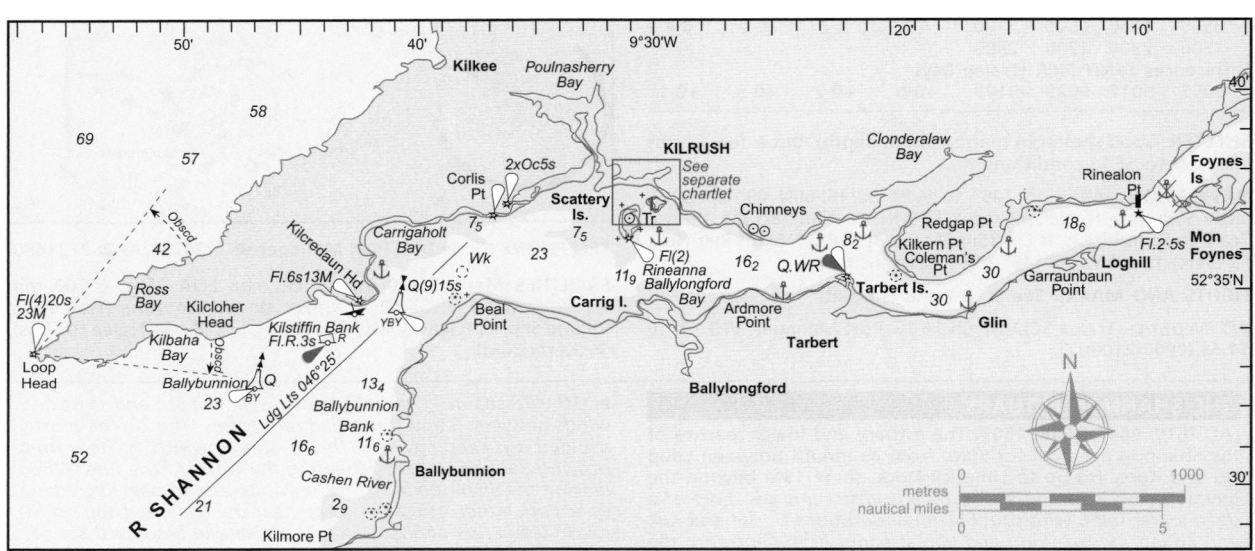

GAELIC							
It helps to understand some of the more common words for navigational features (courtesy of the Irish Cruising Club):							
Ail, alt	cliff, height	*Carrick*	rock	*Inish, illaun*	island	*More, mor*	big
Aird, ard	height, high	*Cladach*	shore	*Inver*	river mouth	*Rannagh*	point
Anna, annagh	marsh	*Cuan, coon*	harbour	*Keal, keel*	narrow place, sound	*Ron, roan*	seal
Ath	ford	*Derg, dearg*	red			*Roe, ruadh*	red
Bal, Bally	town	*Drum*	hill, ridge	*Kill*	church, cell	*Scolt*	split, rky gut
Barra	sandbank	*Duff, dubh*	black	*Kin, ken*	promontory, head	*Scrow*	boggy, grassy sward
Bel, beal	mouth, strait	*Dun, doon*	fort				
Beg	little	*Ennis*	island	*Knock*	hill	*Slieve*	mountain
Ben, binna	hill	*Fad, fadda*	long	*Lag*	hollow	*Slig*	shells
Bo	sunken rock	*Fan*	slope	*Lahan*	broad	*Stag, stac*	high rock
Boy, bwee	yellow	*Fin*	white	*Lea*	grey	*Tawney*	low hill
Bullig	shoal, round rock, breaker	*Freagh, free*	heather	*Lenan*	weed-covered rock	*Tigh, ti*	house
		Gall	stranger			*Togher*	causeway
Bun	end, river mouth	*Glas, glass*	green	*Lis*	ancient fort	*Tra, traw*	strand
		Glinsk	clear water	*Long, luing*	ship	*Turlin*	boulder, beach
Caher	fort	*Gorm*	blue	*Maan*	middle		
Camus	bay, river bend	*Gub*	point of land	*Maol, mwee*	bare	*Vad, bad*	boat
		Hassans	swift current	*Mara*	of the sea		

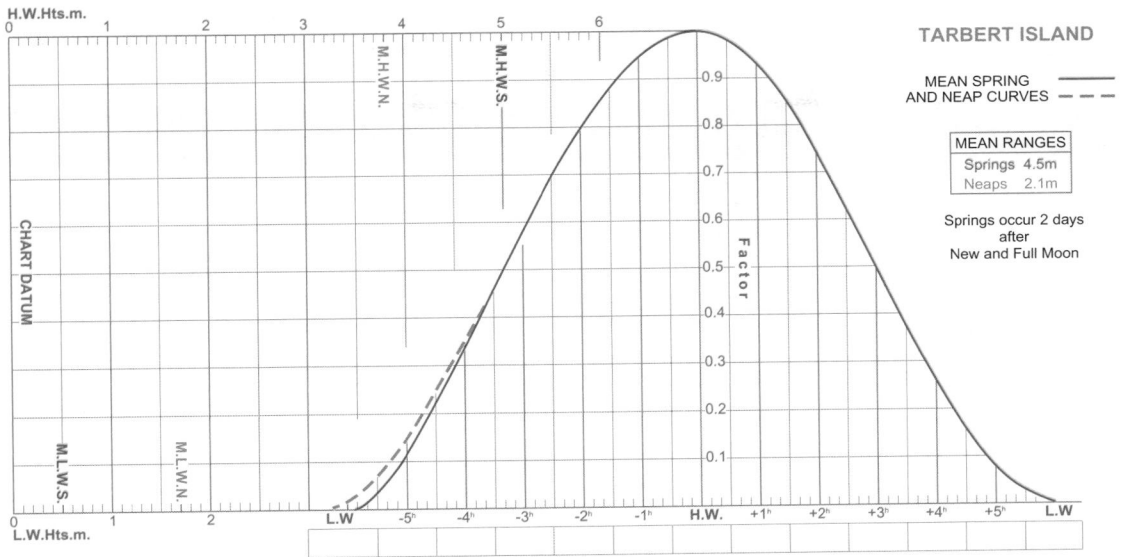

TARBERT ISLAND

MEAN SPRING
AND NEAP CURVES

MEAN RANGES
Springs 4.5m
Neaps 2.1m

Springs occur 2 days
after
New and Full Moon

9.12.34 KILRUSH

Clare 52°37'·90N 09°29'·70W ✿✿⚓⚓✿✿

CHARTS AC 1819, 1547; Imray C55.

TIDES –0555 Dover; ML 2·6; Duration 0610
Standard Port TARBERT ISLAND (→)

Times				Height (metres)			
High Water		Low Water		MHWS	MHWN	MLWN	MLWS
0500	1000	0000	0600	5·0	3·8	1·7	0·5
1700	2200	1200	1800				
Differences KILRUSH							
–0010	–0010	–0005	–0005	0·0	–0·1	0·0	0·0

SHELTER Excellent in Kilrush Marina (2·7m), access via lock (width 9m) H24. Day ⚓ in lee of Scattery Is.

NAVIGATION WPT 52°37'·18N 09°31'·64W, 063°/1M to SWM buoy. From seaward usual appr is N of Scattery Is (conspic Round Twr, 26m); beware Baurnahard Spit and Carrigillaun to the N. Coming down-river between Hog Is and mainland, beware Wolf Rk.

LIGHTS AND MARKS SWM By L Fl 10s marks ent to buoyed chan (dredged 2·5m), with ldg lts 355°, both Oc 3s, to lock. Fl G 3s 2M, S side of lock.

R/T Marina Ch 80. Kilrush Ch 16, 12.

TELEPHONE (Code 06590) Marina 52072 Mobile 086 2313870; Lock 52155; MRCC (066) 9476109; Coast/Cliff Rescue Service 51004; ⊖ (061) 415366; Weather (061) 62677; Police 51017; Dr (065) 51581 also 51470.

FACILITIES Marina (120 inc Ⓥ) ☎ 52072, kcm@shannondev.ie. Lock 52155, €1.90, (minimum €16.00/craft), D, P (cans), Slip, BY, CH, Gas, Gaz, Kos, BH (45 ton), C (26 ton), ME, El, 🔲, 🛒; **Town** El, CH, 🛒, R, Bar, Dr, ✉, Ⓑ, ⇌ (bus to Limerick), ✈ (Shannon).

TIME ZONE (UT)
For Summer Time add ONE hour in **non-shaded areas**

TARBERT ISLAND   LAT 52°35'N   LONG 9°21'W
TIMES AND HEIGHTS OF HIGH AND LOW WATERS

Dates in red are **SPRINGS**
Dates in blue are **NEAPS**

YEAR 2010

JANUARY

Day	Time	m	Day	Time	m
1 F	0537	5.0	16 SA	0000	1.0
	1156	0.4		0615	4.8
	1811	4.9		1226	0.8
				1843	4.6
2 SA	0009	0.5	17 SU	0032	1.0
	0624	5.1		0648	4.9
	1243	0.2		1258	0.8
	1858	5.0		1915	4.6
3 SU	0055	0.5	18 M	0102	1.0
	0710	5.1		0721	4.8
	1327	0.2		1327	0.9
	1945	5.0		1946	4.6
4 M	0139	0.5	19 TU	0132	1.1
	0755	5.1		0753	4.8
	1412	0.3		1356	1.0
	2030	4.8		2018	4.5
5 TU	0224	0.6	20 W	0203	1.2
	0841	4.9		0825	4.7
	1457	0.5		1427	1.1
	2117	4.7		2051	4.4
6 W	0310	0.9	21 TH	0237	1.3
	0929	4.7		0859	4.5
	1546	0.7		1503	1.3
	2207	4.4		2128	4.3
7 TH	0401	1.1	22 F	0316	1.5
	1022	4.4		0939	4.3
	1641	1.1		1544	1.5
	2304	4.2		2213	4.2
8 F	0501	1.4	23 SA	0403	1.7
	1127	4.2		1031	4.1
	1744	1.4		1635	1.7
				2311	4.0
9 SA	0012	4.1	24 SU	0502	1.8
	0610	1.6		1141	4.0
	1249	4.0		1741	1.8
	1852	1.5			
10 SU	0126	4.1	25 M	0023	4.0
	0726	1.6		0619	1.9
	1408	4.0		1301	3.9
	2001	1.6		1859	1.8
11 M	0233	4.2	26 TU	0136	4.1
	0837	1.5		0748	1.7
	1513	4.1		1416	4.1
	2104	1.5		2018	1.6
12 TU	0331	4.3	27 W	0243	4.3
	0939	1.3		0906	1.4
	1608	4.3		1523	4.3
	2158	1.4		2126	1.3
13 W	0420	4.5	28 TH	0343	4.6
	1029	1.1		1007	0.9
	1654	4.4		1621	4.6
	2244	1.2		2222	1.0
14 TH	0503	4.6	29 F	0437	4.9
	1112	1.0		1058	0.5
	1735	4.5		1712	4.9
	2324	1.1		2312	0.6
15 F	0541	4.8	30 SA	0526	5.1
	1151	0.8		1144	0.2
	1811	4.6		1800	5.1
				2357	0.4
			31 SU	0612	5.3
				1228	0.0
				1844	5.2

FEBRUARY

Day	Time	m	Day	Time	m
1 M	0040	0.3	16 TU	0040	0.9
	0655	5.4		0655	5.0
	1310	0.0		1301	0.8
	1926	5.2		1917	4.8
2 TU	0122	0.3	17 W	0108	0.9
	0737	5.3		0724	4.9
	1351	0.1		1328	0.9
	2008	5.1		1946	4.7
3 W	0202	0.4	18 TH	0136	1.0
	0819	5.2		0754	4.9
	1431	0.4		1357	1.0
	2049	4.9		2017	4.7
4 TH	0243	0.7	19 F	0207	1.2
	0903	4.9		0825	4.7
	1514	0.8		1429	1.2
	2132	4.6		2050	4.5
5 F	0327	1.1	20 SA	0243	1.3
	0950	4.5		0902	4.5
	1601	1.2		1506	1.4
	2221	4.3		2129	4.3
6 SA	0418	1.4	21 SU	0326	1.5
	1048	4.1		0950	4.2
	1659	1.6		1553	1.7
	2322	4.1		2221	4.1
7 SU	0525	1.8	22 M	0422	1.8
	1208	3.9		1059	4.0
	1814	1.9		1659	1.9
				2337	3.9
8 M	0043	3.9	23 TU	0543	1.9
	0653	1.9		1230	3.8
	1344	3.8		1830	2.0
	1939	1.9			
9 TU	0207	4.0	24 W	0104	4.0
	0822	1.8		0726	1.8
	1501	4.0		1400	4.0
	2052	1.8		2005	1.7
10 W	0315	4.2	25 TH	0224	4.2
	0929	1.5		0854	1.3
	1557	4.2		1513	4.3
	2147	1.5		2117	1.3
11 TH	0406	4.4	26 F	0330	4.5
	1017	1.2		0954	0.8
	1641	4.4		1610	4.7
	2230	1.3		2211	0.9
12 F	0447	4.6	27 SA	0424	4.9
	1056	1.0		1042	0.4
	1717	4.5		1658	5.0
	2307	1.1		2257	0.5
13 SA	0522	4.8	28 SU	0511	5.2
	1132	0.8		1126	0.1
	1750	4.6		1742	5.2
	2341	1.0		2340	0.2
14 SU	0554	4.9			
	1204	0.7			
	1819	4.7			
15 M	0011	0.9			
	0624	5.0			
	1234	0.7			
	1847	4.8			

MARCH

Day	Time	m	Day	Time	m
1 M	0555	5.4	16 TU	0555	4.9
	1207	-0.1		1203	0.7
	1824	5.4		1817	4.9
2 TU	0020	0.1	17 W	0013	0.8
	0636	5.5		0625	5.0
	1247	-0.1		1232	0.7
	1903	5.4		1846	4.9
3 W	0100	0.2	18 TH	0042	0.8
	0716	5.4		0654	5.0
	1326	0.1		1300	0.8
	1942	5.3		1916	4.9
4 TH	0137	0.3	19 F	0111	0.9
	0756	5.2		0726	4.9
	1403	0.5		1329	0.9
	2020	5.0		1947	4.8
5 F	0215	0.6	20 SA	0142	1.0
	0837	4.9		0800	4.8
	1442	0.9		1401	1.1
	2059	4.7		2021	4.7
6 SA	0256	1.0	21 SU	0218	1.1
	0921	4.5		0840	4.5
	1525	1.3		1439	1.3
	2144	4.4		2102	4.4
7 SU	0342	1.4	22 M	0302	1.3
	1014	4.1		0929	4.2
	1617	1.8		1527	1.6
	2239	4.0		2153	4.2
8 M	0443	1.8	23 TU	0359	1.6
	1133	3.7		1037	3.9
	1734	2.1		1635	1.9
	2359	3.8		2307	3.9
9 TU	0616	2.0	24 W	0523	1.7
	1316	3.6		1210	3.8
	1917	2.1		1814	1.9
10 W	0132	3.8	25 TH	0038	3.9
	0759	1.9		0708	1.6
	1441	3.8		1348	3.9
	2035	1.9		1952	1.7
11 TH	0247	4.1	26 F	0205	4.1
	0906	1.6		0833	1.2
	1535	4.1		1458	4.3
	2126	1.6		2059	1.2
12 F	0340	4.3	27 SA	0311	4.5
	0952	1.3		0930	0.7
	1616	4.3		1551	4.7
	2206	1.3		2151	0.8
13 SA	0419	4.5	28 SU	0404	4.9
	1029	1.0		1018	0.3
	1650	4.5		1637	5.0
	2241	1.1		2237	0.4
14 SU	0453	4.7	29 M	0450	5.2
	1103	0.8		1102	0.1
	1720	4.7		1720	5.3
	2313	0.9		2319	0.2
15 M	0525	4.8	30 TU	0534	5.3
	1134	0.7		1143	0.0
	1748	4.8		1800	5.4
	2344	0.8		2358	0.1
			31 W	0615	5.4
				1222	0.1
				1839	5.3

APRIL

Day	Time	m	Day	Time	m
1 TH	0036	0.2	16 F	0018	0.7
	0655	5.3		0628	4.9
	1300	0.3		1233	0.7
	1916	5.2		1850	4.9
2 F	0114	0.4	17 SA	0051	0.7
	0734	5.1		0704	4.9
	1336	0.6		1306	0.8
	1954	4.8		1925	4.8
3 SA	0151	0.6	18 SU	0126	0.8
	0814	4.7		0744	4.7
	1414	1.0		1342	1.0
	2032	4.7		2004	4.7
4 SU	0230	1.0	19 M	0205	0.9
	0857	4.4		0829	4.5
	1454	1.4		1424	1.2
	2114	4.3		2048	4.5
5 M	0313	1.3	20 TU	0252	1.1
	0946	4.0		0921	4.2
	1542	1.8		1516	1.4
	2204	4.0		2142	4.2
6 TU	0407	1.7	21 W	0351	1.3
	1057	3.7		1028	3.9
	1649	2.1		1627	1.7
	2313	3.8		2250	4.0
7 W	0527	1.9	22 TH	0511	1.4
	1233	3.6		1154	3.8
	1831	2.1		1758	1.7
8 TH	0042	3.7	23 F	0012	4.0
	0705	1.8		0641	1.3
	1355	3.7		1326	4.0
	1953	1.9		1925	1.4
9 F	0158	3.8	24 SA	0138	4.1
	0817	1.6		0758	1.0
	1452	3.9		1433	4.3
	2047	1.7		2031	1.1
10 SA	0254	4.1	25 SU	0245	4.4
	0907	1.3		0857	0.7
	1535	4.1		1526	4.6
	2129	1.4		2124	0.7
11 SU	0338	4.3	26 M	0339	4.7
	0947	1.1		0948	0.4
	1611	4.4		1612	4.9
	2205	1.1		2211	0.5
12 M	0415	4.5	27 TU	0427	4.9
	1023	0.9		1034	0.3
	1643	4.6		1656	5.1
	2240	0.9		2255	0.3
13 TU	0449	4.7	28 W	0511	5.0
	1057	0.8		1117	0.3
	1714	4.7		1737	5.2
	2313	0.8		2336	0.3
14 W	0522	4.8	29 TH	0554	5.1
	1129	0.7		1157	0.4
	1745	4.9		1817	5.1
	2346	0.7			
15 TH	0554	4.9	30 F	0016	0.3
	1201	0.7		0636	5.0
	1817	4.9		1236	0.5
				1855	5.0

Chart Datum: 0·30 metres above Ordnance Datum (Dublin). HAT is 5·5 metres above Chart Datum; see 4.5.

TIME ZONE (UT)
For Summer Time add ONE hour in **non-shaded** areas

TARBERT ISLAND   LAT 52°35'N   LONG 9°21'W
TIMES AND HEIGHTS OF HIGH AND LOW WATERS

Dates in red are SPRINGS
Dates in blue are NEAPS

YEAR 2010

S Ireland

MAY

Day	Time m	Day	Time m
1 SA	0054 0.5 / 0716 4.8 / 1313 0.8 / 1933 4.9	16 SU	0037 0.5 / 0650 4.7 / 1252 0.7 / 1911 4.8
2 SU	0131 0.7 / 0757 4.5 / 1350 1.1 / 2011 4.6	17	0118 0.5 / 0735 4.6 / M 1334 0.8 / 1954 4.7
3 M	0209 0.9 / 0838 4.3 / 1429 1.3 / 2052 4.4	18 TU	0201 0.6 / 0823 4.5 / 1420 1.0 / 2041 4.6
4 TU	0250 1.2 / 0924 4.0 / 1513 1.6 / 2137 4.1	19 W	0250 0.7 / 0916 4.3 / 1513 1.2 / 2134 4.4
5 W	0337 1.4 / 1020 3.7 / 1608 1.8 / 2232 3.9	20 TH	0347 0.9 / 1018 4.1 / 1618 1.3 / 2234 4.2
6 TH	0437 1.6 / 1135 3.6 / 1724 2.0 / 2342 3.7	21 F	0455 1.0 / 1131 4.0 / 1734 1.4 / 2345 4.1
7 F	0554 1.7 / 1252 3.6 / 1847 1.9	22 SA	0608 1.0 / 1252 4.1 / 1850 1.3
8 SA	0055 3.8 / 0708 1.6 / 1354 3.8 / 1949 1.7	23 SU	0102 4.1 / 0718 0.9 / 1401 4.3 / 1956 1.1
9 SU	0157 3.9 / 0806 1.4 / 1443 4.0 / 2039 1.5	24 M	0213 4.3 / 0820 0.8 / 1457 4.5 / 2054 0.9
10 M	0247 4.1 / 0854 1.2 / 1524 4.2 / 2122 1.2	25 TU	0312 4.5 / 0916 0.7 / 1547 4.7 / 2146 0.7
11 TU	0330 4.3 / 0936 1.0 / 1602 4.5 / 2203 1.0	26 W	0404 4.6 / 1006 0.6 / 1633 4.8 / 2234 0.6
12 W	0409 4.5 / 1017 0.9 / 1638 4.6 / 2242 0.8	27 TH	0452 4.7 / 1053 0.6 / 1717 4.9 / 2319 0.5
13 TH	0448 4.6 / 1055 0.8 / 1715 4.8 / 2321 0.7	28 F	0538 4.7 / 1137 0.7 / 1758 4.9
14 F	0527 4.7 / 1134 0.7 / 1752 4.9 / 2359 0.6	29 SA	0000 0.5 / 0621 4.6 / 1218 0.8 / 1838 4.8
15 SA	0607 4.8 / 1212 0.7 / 1831 4.9	30 SU	0040 0.6 / 0702 4.5 / 1256 0.9 / 1916 4.7
		31 M	0117 0.7 / 0742 4.4 / 1332 1.0 / 1954 4.6

JUNE

Day	Time m	Day	Time m
1 TU	0153 0.8 / 0821 4.2 / 1408 1.2 / 2033 4.4	16 W	0157 0.3 / 0816 4.6 / 1415 0.7 / 2032 4.8
2 W	0230 1.0 / 0901 4.1 / 1447 1.4 / 2113 4.3	17 TH	0244 0.4 / 0906 4.5 / 1505 0.8 / 2121 4.6
3 TH	0310 1.2 / 0944 3.9 / 1531 1.6 / 2158 4.1	18 F	0334 0.5 / 1000 4.4 / 1600 1.0 / 2215 4.4
4 F	0355 1.3 / 1036 3.8 / 1624 1.7 / 2249 3.9	19 SA	0431 0.7 / 1102 4.2 / 1704 1.2 / 2316 4.2
5 SA	0448 1.5 / 1139 3.7 / 1730 1.8 / 2349 3.8	20 SU	0534 0.9 / 1213 4.1 / 1814 1.3
6 SU	0552 1.5 / 1245 3.8 / 1842 1.8	21	0027 4.1 / 0640 1.1 / M 1326 4.2 / 1923 1.2
7 M	0052 3.8 / 0657 1.5 / 1344 3.9 / 1944 1.6	22 TU	0142 4.1 / 0746 1.1 / 1429 4.3 / 2028 1.1
8 TU	0151 4.0 / 0756 1.4 / 1435 4.1 / 2038 1.4	23 W	0249 4.2 / 0849 1.1 / 1525 4.4 / 2127 1.0
9 W	0243 4.1 / 0849 1.2 / 1521 4.3 / 2128 1.2	24 TH	0347 4.3 / 0946 1.0 / 1616 4.6 / 2219 0.9
10 TH	0332 4.3 / 0938 1.1 / 1606 4.5 / 2215 0.9	25 F	0439 4.4 / 1038 1.0 / 1702 4.7 / 2307 0.7
11 F	0419 4.5 / 1026 0.9 / 1649 4.7 / 2300 0.7	26 SA	0526 4.4 / 1124 0.9 / 1745 4.7 / 2349 0.7
12 SA	0505 4.6 / 1112 0.7 / 1732 4.8 / 2344 0.5	27 SU	0609 4.5 / 1205 0.9 / 1824 4.8
13 SU	0552 4.7 / 1158 0.6 / 1816 4.9	28 M	0028 0.6 / 0648 4.4 / 1242 0.9 / 1901 4.7
14 M	0028 0.4 / 0639 4.7 / 1243 0.6 / 1900 4.9	29 TU	0104 0.7 / 0724 4.4 / 1316 1.0 / 1936 4.7
15 TU	0112 0.3 / 0727 4.7 / 1328 0.6 / 1945 4.9	30 W	0137 0.8 / 0759 4.3 / 1348 1.1 / 2011 4.6

JULY

Day	Time m	Day	Time m
1 TH	0208 0.9 / 0833 4.3 / 1421 1.2 / 2047 4.4	16 F	0228 0.2 / 0848 4.8 / 1447 0.6 / 2104 4.8
2 F	0241 1.0 / 0909 4.1 / 1457 1.4 / 2124 4.3	17 SA	0314 0.4 / 0936 4.6 / 1536 0.8 / 2153 4.6
3 SA	0317 1.2 / 0949 4.0 / 1539 1.5 / 2205 4.1	18 SU	0403 0.7 / 1030 4.4 / 1632 1.1 / 2249 4.3
4 SU	0400 1.4 / 1038 3.9 / 1628 1.7 / 2255 4.0	19 M	0500 1.1 / 1135 4.1 / 1739 1.4 / 2358 4.0
5 M	0450 1.5 / 1138 3.9 / 1730 1.8 / 2355 3.9	20 TU	0607 1.4 / 1251 4.0 / 1856 1.5
6 TU	0550 1.6 / 1244 3.9 / 1844 1.8	21 W	0119 3.9 / 0720 1.5 / 1407 4.1 / 2011 1.4
7 W	0100 3.9 / 0658 1.6 / 1348 4.0 / 1955 1.6	22 TH	0236 3.9 / 0833 1.5 / 1511 4.2 / 2117 1.2
8 TH	0204 4.0 / 0806 1.5 / 1446 4.2 / 2059 1.4	23 F	0340 4.1 / 0937 1.3 / 1606 4.4 / 2211 1.0
9 F	0303 4.1 / 0908 1.3 / 1540 4.4 / 2155 1.0	24 SA	0433 4.2 / 1028 1.2 / 1652 4.6 / 2256 0.9
10 SA	0358 4.3 / 1005 1.0 / 1630 4.6 / 2246 0.7	25 SU	0517 4.3 / 1112 1.0 / 1732 4.7 / 2337 0.7
11 SU	0451 4.5 / 1058 0.7 / 1718 4.8 / 2333 0.4	26 M	0555 4.4 / 1151 0.9 / 1808 4.8
12 M	0542 4.7 / 1147 0.5 / 1805 5.0	27 TU	0013 0.7 / 0629 4.5 / 1225 0.9 / 1841 4.8
13 TU	0018 0.2 / 0630 4.9 / 1233 0.4 / 1849 5.1	28 W	0046 0.7 / 0700 4.5 / 1255 0.9 / 1913 4.8
14 W	0102 0.0 / 0716 4.9 / 1318 0.3 / 1934 5.1	29 TH	0115 0.7 / 0731 4.5 / 1323 1.0 / 1945 4.7
15 TH	0145 0.0 / 0802 4.9 / 1402 0.4 / 2018 5.0	30 F	0142 0.8 / 0801 4.5 / 1352 1.1 / 2017 4.6
		31 SA	0210 1.0 / 0833 4.4 / 1424 1.2 / 2049 4.5

AUGUST

Day	Time m	Day	Time m
1 SU	0242 1.1 / 0906 4.3 / 1500 1.4 / 2125 4.3	16	0333 0.9 / 0957 4.4 / M 1600 1.2 / 2224 4.2
2 M	0319 1.3 / 0946 4.1 / 1543 1.6 / 2209 4.1	17 TU	0426 1.3 / 1058 4.1 / 1706 1.5 / 2334 3.9
3 TU	0403 1.5 / 1038 4.0 / 1638 1.8 / 2308 3.9	18 W	0535 1.7 / 1220 3.9 / 1834 1.7
4 W	0500 1.7 / 1150 3.9 / 1751 1.9	19 TH	0104 3.7 / 0703 1.8 / 1349 3.9 / 2003 1.6
5 TH	0020 3.8 / 0613 1.8 / 1309 3.9 / 1920 1.8	20 F	0229 3.8 / 0828 1.7 / 1500 4.1 / 2110 1.4
6 F	0136 3.9 / 0736 1.7 / 1420 4.1 / 2040 1.4	21 SA	0333 4.0 / 0930 1.5 / 1554 4.3 / 2159 1.1
7 SA	0245 4.1 / 0851 1.4 / 1522 4.4 / 2141 1.0	22 SU	0421 4.2 / 1016 1.2 / 1637 4.5 / 2240 0.9
8 SU	0347 4.3 / 0954 1.0 / 1617 4.7 / 2233 0.6	23 M	0500 4.4 / 1055 1.0 / 1713 4.7 / 2316 0.7
9 M	0441 4.6 / 1047 0.7 / 1706 5.0 / 2319 0.2	24 TU	0533 4.5 / 1130 0.9 / 1746 4.8 / 2349 0.7
10 TU	0530 4.9 / 1134 0.4 / 1752 5.2	25 W	0603 4.6 / 1201 0.8 / 1816 4.9
11 W	0003 -0.1 / 0616 5.1 / 1219 0.2 / 1835 5.3	26 TH	0019 0.7 / 0630 4.6 / 1229 0.8 / 1845 4.9
12 TH	0045 -0.2 / 0700 5.2 / 1301 0.1 / 1917 5.3	27 F	0047 0.7 / 0659 4.7 / 1256 0.9 / 1915 4.8
13 F	0126 -0.1 / 0742 5.1 / 1342 0.2 / 2000 5.2	28 SA	0113 0.8 / 0728 4.7 / 1324 1.0 / 1945 4.7
14 SA	0207 0.1 / 0825 5.0 / 1424 0.5 / 2043 5.0	29 SU	0140 0.9 / 0757 4.6 / 1354 1.1 / 2016 4.6
15 SU	0248 0.5 / 0909 4.7 / 1509 0.8 / 2130 4.6	30 M	0210 1.1 / 0828 4.5 / 1427 1.3 / 2051 4.4
		31 TU	0244 1.3 / 0905 4.3 / 1508 1.5 / 2135 4.2

Chart Datum: 0·30 metres above Ordnance Datum (Dublin). HAT is 5·5 metres above Chart Datum; see 4.5.

TIME ZONE (UT)
For Summer Time add ONE hour in **non-shaded areas**

TARBERT ISLAND LAT 52°35'N LONG 9°21'W
TIMES AND HEIGHTS OF HIGH AND LOW WATERS

Dates in red are **SPRINGS**
Dates in blue are **NEAPS**

YEAR 2010

SEPTEMBER
Time m   Time m

1 0326 1.5 / 0952 4.1 / W 1601 1.7 / ☽ 2234 3.9	**16** 0503 1.9 / 1147 3.8 / TH 1809 1.8	
2 0423 1.8 / 1103 3.9 / TH 1717 1.9 / 2352 3.8	**17** 0044 3.6 / 0644 2.0 / F 1322 3.8 / 1947 1.7	
3 0544 1.9 / 1235 3.9 / F 1858 1.7	**18** 0212 3.7 / 0813 1.8 / SA 1437 4.0 / 2049 1.4	
4 0118 3.8 / 0719 1.7 / SA 1401 4.1 / 2027 1.4	**19** 0312 3.9 / 0909 1.6 / SU 1529 4.2 / 2134 1.2	
5 0235 4.1 / 0842 1.4 / SU 1508 4.4 / 2127 0.9	**20** 0356 4.1 / 0951 1.3 / M 1610 4.5 / 2212 0.9	
6 0336 4.4 / 0942 0.9 / M 1602 4.8 / 2216 0.4	**21** 0431 4.3 / 1027 1.1 / TU 1644 4.6 / 2246 0.8	
7 0427 4.8 / 1032 0.5 / TU 1650 5.1 / 2300 0.1	**22** 0502 4.5 / 1100 0.9 / W 1716 4.8 / 2318 0.7	
8 0513 5.1 / 1117 0.2 / W 1734 5.3 / ● 2343 -0.1	**23** 0530 4.6 / 1131 0.8 / TH 1746 4.9 / ○ 2348 0.7	
9 0557 5.3 / 1159 0.0 / TH 1817 5.4	**24** 0558 4.7 / 1201 0.8 / F 1816 4.9	
10 0023 -0.2 / 0638 5.3 / F 1240 0.0 / 1858 5.4	**25** 0016 0.7 / 0626 4.8 / SA 1230 0.8 / 1845 4.9	
11 0103 0.0 / 0719 5.2 / SA 1320 0.2 / 1940 5.2	**26** 0044 0.8 / 0656 4.8 / SU 1259 0.9 / 1917 4.8	
12 0142 0.3 / 0759 5.0 / SU 1400 0.5 / 2022 4.9	**27** 0113 0.9 / 0727 4.7 / M 1329 1.0 / 1951 4.6	
13 0222 0.7 / 0841 4.7 / M 1443 0.8 / 2108 4.5	**28** 0144 1.1 / 0801 4.6 / TU 1404 1.1 / 2029 4.4	
14 0304 1.1 / 0926 4.4 / TU 1531 1.2 / 2201 4.1	**29** 0219 1.3 / 0839 4.4 / W 1446 1.3 / 2115 4.2	
15 0354 1.6 / 1024 4.0 / W 1635 1.6 / ☽ 2312 3.7	**30** 0303 1.5 / 0928 4.2 / TH 1540 1.6 / 2215 3.9	

OCTOBER
Time m   Time m

1 0402 1.7 / 1036 3.9 / F 1659 1.7 / ☽ 2334 3.8	**16** 0007 3.6 / 0557 2.0 / SA 1234 3.7 / 1857 1.7
2 0527 1.8 / 1208 3.9 / SA 1839 1.6	**17** 0128 3.6 / 0726 1.9 / SU 1350 3.8 / 2004 1.5
3 0104 3.8 / 0705 1.7 / SU 1341 4.1 / 2004 1.2	**18** 0229 3.8 / 0827 1.6 / M 1446 4.1 / 2052 1.3
4 0221 4.2 / 0825 1.3 / M 1449 4.4 / 2103 0.8	**19** 0314 4.1 / 0911 1.4 / TU 1530 4.3 / 2132 1.1
5 0318 4.5 / 0922 0.8 / TU 1542 4.8 / 2152 0.4	**20** 0352 4.3 / 0950 1.2 / W 1607 4.6 / 2207 0.9
6 0407 4.9 / 1011 0.5 / W 1629 5.1 / 2236 0.1	**21** 0424 4.5 / 1025 1.0 / TH 1641 4.6 / 2241 0.8
7 0452 5.1 / 1055 0.2 / TH 1714 5.3 / ● 2319 0.0	**22** 0455 4.6 / 1059 0.8 / F 1714 4.8 / 2314 0.7
8 0534 5.3 / 1138 0.1 / F 1757 5.3 / 2359 0.0	**23** 0525 4.8 / 1133 0.8 / SA 1746 4.8 / ○ 2346 0.7
9 0616 5.3 / 1218 0.1 / SA 1839 5.3	**24** 0557 4.8 / 1206 0.8 / SU 1820 4.8
10 0039 0.2 / 0655 5.2 / SU 1259 0.3 / 1921 5.1	**25** 0018 0.8 / 0630 4.8 / M 1239 0.8 / 1855 4.8
11 0118 0.5 / 0735 5.0 / M 1339 0.5 / 2004 4.8	**26** 0051 0.9 / 0706 4.8 / TU 1313 0.9 / 1933 4.6
12 0157 0.8 / 0816 4.7 / TU 1420 0.9 / 2049 4.4	**27** 0126 1.0 / 0744 4.7 / W 1351 1.0 / 2016 4.4
13 0237 1.2 / 0900 4.4 / W 1506 1.2 / 2140 4.0	**28** 0205 1.2 / 0826 4.5 / TH 1436 1.1 / 2105 4.2
14 0324 1.6 / 0952 4.0 / TH 1603 1.5 / ☽ 2244 3.7	**29** 0252 1.4 / 0916 4.2 / F 1532 1.3 / 2204 4.0
15 0425 1.9 / 1105 3.8 / F 1726 1.7	**30** 0352 1.6 / 1020 4.0 / SA 1645 1.4 / ☽ 2316 3.9
	31 0511 1.7 / 1141 4.0 / SU 1812 1.3

NOVEMBER
Time m   Time m

1 0042 3.9 / 0639 1.5 / M 1311 4.1 / 1930 1.1	**16** 0129 3.8 / 0724 1.8 / TU 1349 3.9 / 1955 1.5
2 0156 4.2 / 0755 1.2 / TU 1422 4.4 / 2031 0.8	**17** 0221 4.0 / 0819 1.6 / W 1441 4.1 / 2042 1.3
3 0253 4.5 / 0854 0.9 / W 1517 4.7 / 2122 0.5	**18** 0305 4.2 / 0906 1.3 / TH 1525 4.3 / 2125 1.1
4 0343 4.8 / 0946 0.6 / TH 1607 4.9 / 2209 0.3	**19** 0344 4.4 / 0949 1.1 / F 1605 4.5 / 2204 1.0
5 0428 5.0 / 1033 0.4 / F 1653 5.0 / 2254 0.3	**20** 0420 4.6 / 1029 1.0 / SA 1643 4.6 / 2243 0.9
6 0512 5.1 / 1117 0.3 / SA 1738 5.1 / ● 2337 0.3	**21** 0456 4.7 / 1109 0.9 / SU 1720 4.7 / ○ 2321 0.8
7 0554 5.1 / 1200 0.3 / SU 1822 5.0	**22** 0533 4.8 / 1147 0.7 / M 1759 4.7 / 2358 0.8
8 0017 0.5 / 0635 5.0 / M 1241 0.4 / 1905 4.8	**23** 0611 4.9 / 1225 0.7 / TU 1839 4.7
9 0057 0.7 / 0715 4.9 / TU 1321 0.6 / 1948 4.6	**24** 0036 0.8 / 0650 4.8 / W 1305 0.7 / 1921 4.6
10 0135 0.9 / 0756 4.7 / W 1402 0.8 / 2031 4.3	**25** 0116 0.9 / 0732 4.8 / TH 1346 0.7 / 2007 4.5
11 0214 1.2 / 0838 4.4 / TH 1444 1.1 / 2117 4.1	**26** 0158 1.0 / 0817 4.6 / F 1432 0.8 / 2056 4.4
12 0257 1.5 / 0925 4.2 / F 1533 1.4 / 2210 3.8	**27** 0245 1.1 / 0906 4.5 / SA 1524 1.0 / 2150 4.2
13 0347 1.7 / 1020 3.9 / SA 1634 1.6 / ☽ 2314 3.7	**28** 0341 1.3 / 1003 4.3 / SU 1626 1.1 / ☽ 2253 4.1
14 0454 1.9 / 1131 3.8 / SU 1749 1.6	**29** 0448 1.4 / 1111 4.1 / M 1738 1.1
15 0025 3.7 / 0615 1.9 / M 1246 3.8 / 1858 1.6	**30** 0007 4.1 / 0604 1.4 / TU 1232 4.1 / 1849 1.1

DECEMBER
Time m   Time m

1 0121 4.2 / 0718 1.3 / W 1349 4.3 / 1954 1.0	**16** 0120 3.9 / 0722 1.8 / TH 1347 4.0 / 1950 1.6
2 0223 4.4 / 0823 1.1 / TH 1451 4.5 / 2052 0.8	**17** 0215 4.1 / 0822 1.6 / F 1442 4.1 / 2042 1.4
3 0317 4.6 / 0921 0.9 / F 1545 4.6 / 2144 0.7	**18** 0304 4.3 / 0915 1.4 / SA 1530 4.3 / 2131 1.3
4 0407 4.8 / 1013 0.7 / SA 1636 4.7 / 2233 0.7	**19** 0349 4.5 / 1003 1.2 / SU 1616 4.4 / 2216 1.1
5 0453 4.9 / 1101 0.6 / SU 1723 4.8 / ● 2319 0.7	**20** 0432 4.7 / 1049 0.9 / M 1700 4.6 / 2300 0.9
6 0537 4.9 / 1146 0.5 / M 1808 4.8	**21** 0514 4.8 / 1132 0.7 / TU 1743 4.7 / ○ 2343 0.8
7 0001 0.7 / 0619 4.9 / TU 1229 0.5 / 1851 4.7	**22** 0556 4.9 / 1214 0.6 / W 1827 4.8
8 0041 0.8 / 0659 4.9 / W 1308 0.6 / 1932 4.6	**23** 0025 0.7 / 0638 5.0 / TH 1256 0.5 / 1910 4.8
9 0118 1.0 / 0739 4.8 / TH 1346 0.8 / 2012 4.4	**24** 0107 0.7 / 0721 5.0 / F 1338 0.4 / 1955 4.7
10 0154 1.1 / 0818 4.6 / F 1424 1.0 / 2051 4.3	**25** 0149 0.7 / 0805 4.9 / SA 1422 0.5 / 2041 4.7
11 0231 1.3 / 0858 4.4 / SA 1503 1.2 / 2133 4.1	**26** 0234 0.8 / 0851 4.8 / SU 1508 0.6 / 2130 4.5
12 0312 1.5 / 0942 4.2 / SU 1547 1.4 / 2219 3.9	**27** 0323 1.0 / 0942 4.6 / M 1601 0.9 / 2225 4.4
13 0400 1.7 / 1034 4.0 / M 1640 1.6 / ☽ 2315 3.8	**28** 0419 1.2 / 1041 4.3 / TU 1701 1.1 / ☽ 2328 4.2
14 0500 1.8 / 1135 3.9 / TU 1744 1.7	**29** 0525 1.4 / 1152 4.2 / W 1810 1.2
15 0018 3.8 / 0612 1.9 / W 1244 3.9 / 1850 1.7	**30** 0040 4.2 / 0640 1.4 / TH 1315 4.1 / 1920 1.3
	31 0152 4.2 / 0755 1.4 / F 1429 4.2 / 2027 1.3

Chart Datum: 0·30 metres above Ordnance Datum (Dublin). HAT is 5·5 metres above Chart Datum; see 4.5.

ADLARD COLES NAUTICAL
WEATHER FORECASTS
BY FAX & TELEPHONE

Coastal/Inshore	2-day by Fax	5-day by Phone
Caledonia	09065 222 353	09068 969 653
Northern Ireland	09065 222 355	09068 969 655
Clyde	09065 222 352	09068 969 652
North West	09065 222 341	09068 969 641
National (3-5 day)	09065 222 340	09068 969 640

Offshore	2-5 day by Fax	2-5 day by Phone
Irish Sea	09065 222 359	09068 969 659
English Channel	09065 222 357	09068 969 657
Biscay	09065 222 360	09068 969 660
North West Scotland	09065 222 361	09068 969 661

09068 CALLS COST 60P PER MIN. 09065 CALLS COST £1.50 PER MIN.

North Ireland

Lambay Island anti-clockwise to Liscannor Bay

N Ireland

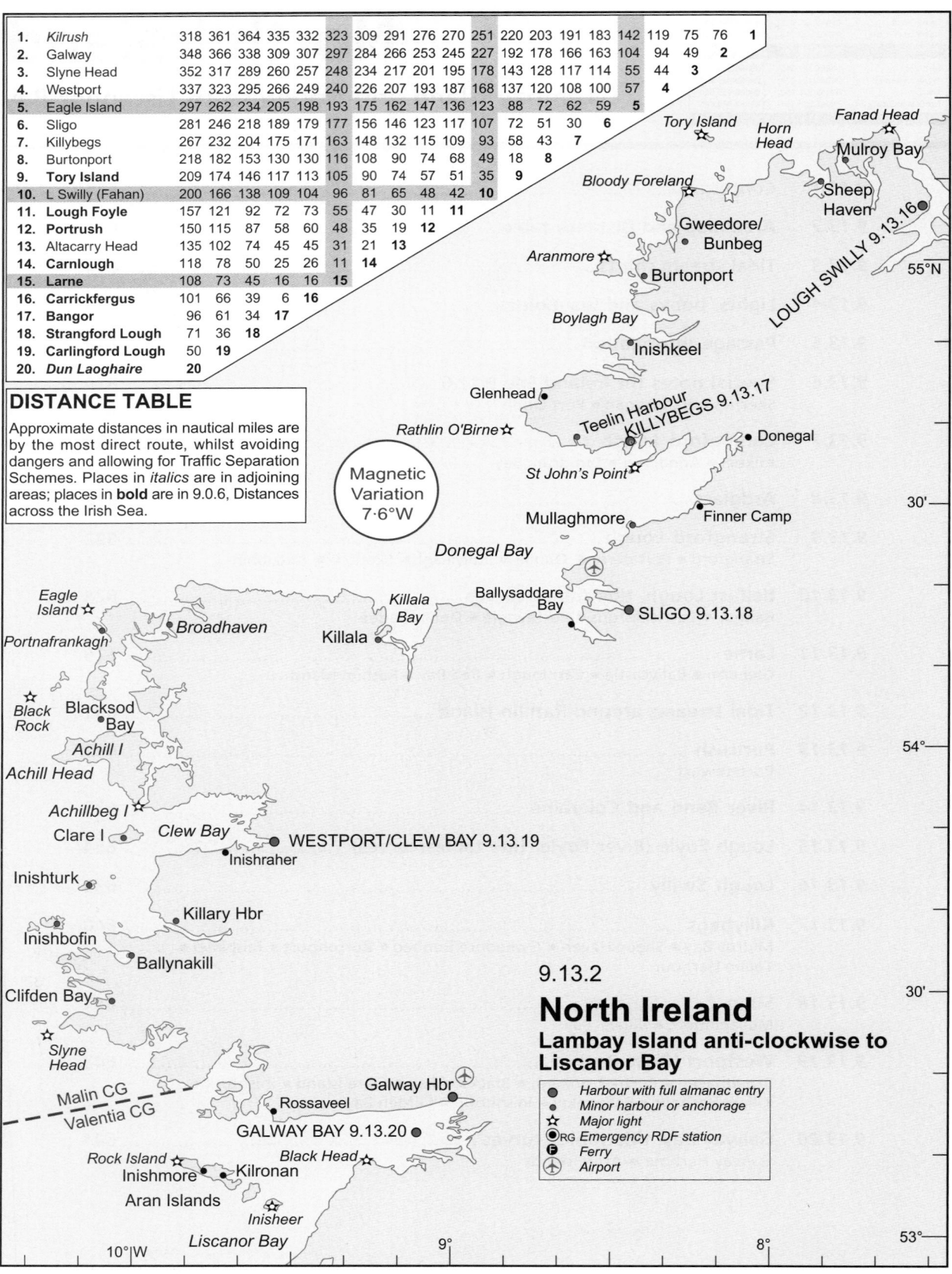

1.	*Kilrush*	318	361	364	335	332	323	309	291	276	270	251	220	203	191	183	142	119	75	76	**1**
2.	*Galway*	348	366	338	309	307	297	284	266	253	245	227	192	178	166	163	104	94	49	**2**	
3.	Slyne Head	352	317	289	260	257	248	234	217	201	195	178	143	128	117	114	55	44	**3**		
4.	Westport	337	323	295	266	249	240	226	207	193	187	168	137	120	108	100	57	**4**			
5.	Eagle Island	297	262	234	205	198	193	175	162	147	136	123	88	72	62	59	**5**				
6.	Sligo	281	246	218	189	179	177	156	146	123	117	107	72	51	30	**6**					
7.	Killybegs	267	232	204	175	171	163	148	132	115	109	93	58	43	**7**						
8.	Burtonport	218	182	153	130	130	116	108	90	74	68	49	18	**8**							
9.	**Tory Island**	209	174	146	117	113	105	90	74	57	51	35	**9**								
10.	**L Swilly (Fahan)**	200	166	138	109	104	96	81	65	48	42	**10**									
11.	**Lough Foyle**	157	121	92	72	73	55	47	30	11	**11**										
12.	**Portrush**	150	115	87	58	60	48	35	19	**12**											
13.	**Altacarry Head**	135	102	74	45	45	31	21	**13**												
14.	**Carnlough**	118	78	50	25	26	11	**14**													
15.	**Larne**	108	73	45	16	16	**15**														
16.	**Carrickfergus**	101	66	39	6	**16**															
17.	**Bangor**	96	61	34	**17**																
18.	**Strangford Lough**	71	36	**18**																	
19.	**Carlingford Lough**	50	**19**																		
20.	*Dun Laoghaire*	**20**																			

DISTANCE TABLE

Approximate distances in nautical miles are by the most direct route, whilst avoiding dangers and allowing for Traffic Separation Schemes. Places in *italics* are in adjoining areas; places in **bold** are in 9.0.6, Distances across the Irish Sea.

Magnetic Variation 7·6°W

9.13.2

North Ireland
Lambay Island anti-clockwise to Liscanor Bay

- ● Harbour with full almanac entry
- • Minor harbour or anchorage
- ☆ Major light
- ⊚RG Emergency RDF station
- Ⓕ Ferry
- ✈ Airport

Fanad Head · Tory Island · Horn Head · Mulroy Bay · Sheep Haven · Bloody Foreland · Gweedore/Bunbeg · LOUGH SWILLY 9.13.16 · 55°N · Aranmore · Burtonport · Boylagh Bay · Inishkeel · Glenhead · Teelin Harbour · KILLYBEGS 9.13.17 · Donegal · Rathlin O'Birne · St John's Point · Mullaghmore · Finner Camp · 30' · Donegal Bay · Killala Bay · Ballysaddare Bay · SLIGO 9.13.18 · Killala · Eagle Island · Broadhaven · Portnafrankagh · Black Rock · Blacksod Bay · Achill I · 54° · Achill Head · Achillbeg I · Clare I · Clew Bay · WESTPORT/CLEW BAY 9.13.19 · Inishraher · Inishturk · Killary Hbr · Inishbofin · Ballynakill · Clifden Bay · Slyne Head · Malin CG · Valentia CG · Galway Hbr · Rossaveel · GALWAY BAY 9.13.20 · Rock Island · Kilronan · Inishmore · Aran Islands · Inisheer · Liscanor Bay · 10°W · 9° · 8° · 53°

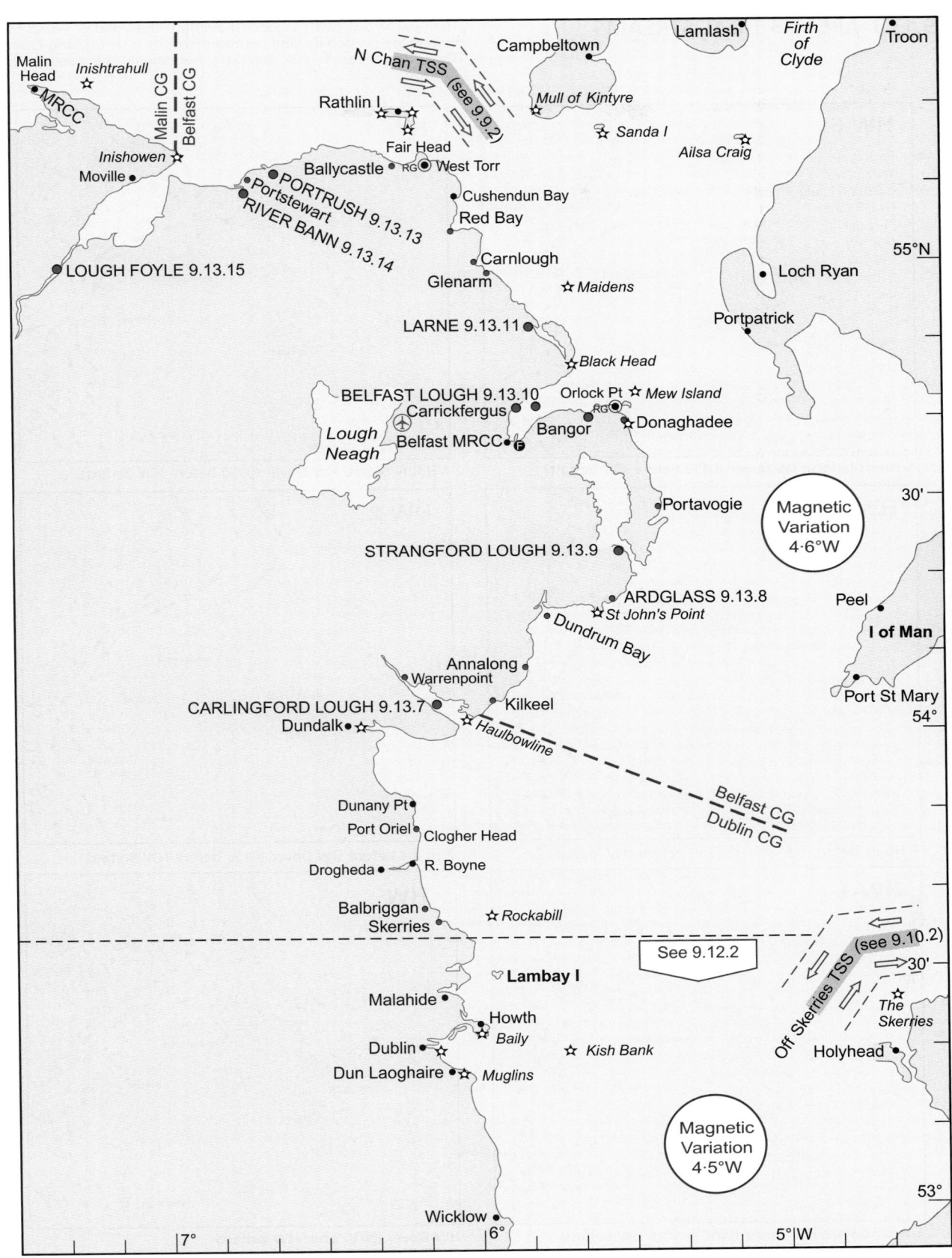

Malin Head
MRCC
Inishtrahull ☆
Malin CG
Belfast CG

N Chan TSS (see 9.9.2)

Campbeltown
Lamlash ☆
Firth of Clyde
Troon

Rathlin I ☆ ☆
Mull of Kintyre ☆
Fair Head
RG West Torr
Ballycastle
☆ *Sanda I*
Ailsa Craig ☆

Inishowen ☆
Moville

PORTRUSH 9.13.13
Portstewart
RIVER BANN 9.13.14

Cushendun Bay
Red Bay

55°N

LOUGH FOYLE 9.13.15

Carnlough
Glenarm
☆ *Maidens*

Loch Ryan

LARNE 9.13.11

Portpatrick

☆ *Black Head*

BELFAST LOUGH 9.13.10
Carrickfergus
Belfast MRCC
Bangor
Orlock Pt ☆ *Mew Island*
RG
Donaghadee

Lough Neagh

Portavogie

30'

STRANGFORD LOUGH 9.13.9

Magnetic Variation 4·6°W

ARDGLASS 9.13.8
☆ *St John's Point*
Dundrum Bay

Peel
I of Man

Annalong
Warrenpoint
CARLINGFORD LOUGH 9.13.7
Dundalk ● ☆
Kilkeel
☆ *Haulbowline*

Port St Mary
54°

Belfast CG
Dublin CG

Dunany Pt
Port Oriel
Clogher Head
Drogheda
R. Boyne

Balbriggan
Skerries
☆ *Rockabill*

See 9.12.2

Off Skerries TSS (see 9.10.2)
30'

♡ **Lambay I**

☆ *The Skerries*

Malahide
Howth
Baily ☆
Dublin ● ☆
Dun Laoghaire ● ☆ *Muglins*
☆ *Kish Bank*

Holyhead

Magnetic Variation 4·5°W

53°

Wicklow

7°   6°   5° W

N Ireland

613

9.13.3 AREA 13 TIDAL STREAMS

The tidal arrows (with no rates shown) off the S and W coasts of Ireland are printed by kind permission of the Irish Cruising Club. They have been found accurate, but should be used with caution.

5 Hours before HW Dover (0450 before HW Belfast)

4 Hours before HW Dover (0350 before HW Belfast)

3 Hours before HW Dover (0250 before HW Belfast)

2 Hours before HW Dover (0150 before HW Belfast)

1 Hour before HW Dover (0050 before HW Belfast)

HW Dover (0010 after HW Belfast)

Rathlin Island 9.13.13   SW Scotland 9.9.3
Mull of Kintyre 9.9.10   South Ireland 9.12.3
North Irish Sea 9.10.3

The tidal arrows (with no rates shown) off the S and W coasts of Ireland are printed by kind permission of the Irish Cruising Club. They have been found accurate, but should be used with caution.

1 Hour after HW Dover (0110 after HW Belfast)

2 Hours after HW Dover (0210 after HW Belfast)

3 Hours after HW Dover (0310 after HW Belfast)

4 Hours after HW Dover (0410 after HW Belfast)

5 Hours after HW Dover (0510 after HW Belfast)

6 Hours after HW Dover (0610 after HW Belfast)

N Ireland

9.13.4 LIGHTS, BUOYS AND WAYPOINTS

Bold print = light with a nominal range of 15M or more. CAPITALS = place or feature. *CAPITAL ITALICS* = light-vessel, light float or Lanby. *Italics* = Fog signal. ***Bold italics*** = Racon. Abbreviations are in Chapter 1.

LAMBAY ISLAND TO DONAGHADEE

Rockabill ☆ 53°35'·82N 06°00'·25W Fl WR 12s 45m **W17M, R13M**; W twr, B band; vis: 178°-W-329°-R-178°.
Skerries Bay Pier Hd ⚓ Oc R 6s 7m 7M; W col; vis: 103°-154°; 53°35'·09N 06°06'·49W.
Balbriggan ⚓ Fl (3) WRG 10s 12m W13M, R10M, G10M; W twr; vis: 159°-G-193°-W-288°-R-305°; 53°36'·76N 06°10'·80W.

DROGHEDA

Port Approach Dir lt 53°43'·30N 06°14'·73W WRG 10m **W19M, R15M**, G15M; vis: 268°-FG-269°-Al WG-269·5°-FW-270·5°-Al WR-271°-FR-272°; H24.

DUNDALK

Dunany ⚓ Fl R 3s; 53°53'·56N 06°09'·47W.
Imogene ⚓ Fl (2) R 10s; 53°57'·41N 06°07'·02W.
Pile Light ☆ 53°58'·56N 06°17'·70W Fl 15s 10m **21M**; W Ho; vis: 124°-W-151°-R-284°-W-313°-R-124°; *Horn (3) 60s*.

CARLINGFORD LOUGH and NEWRY RIVER

Hellyhunter ⚓ Q (6) + L Fl 15s; ***Racon***; 54°00'·35N 06°02'·10W
Haulbowline ☆ 54°01'·19N 06°04'·74W Fl (3) 10s 32m **17M**; Gy twr; reserve lt 15M.
Ldg lts 310·4° Front, Oc 3s 7m 11M; R △ on twr; vis: 295°-325°; 54°01'·80N 06°05'·43W. Rear, 457m from front, Oc 3s 12m 11M; R ▽ on twr; vis: 295°-325°; both H24.
Newry River Ldg lts 310·4°. Front, 54°06'·37N 06°16'·51W. Rear, 274m from front. Both Iso 4s 5/15m 2M; stone cols.

KILKEEL

Pier Hd ⚓ Fl WR 2s 8m 8M; vis: R296°-W313°-017°; 54°03'·46N 05°59'·30W.

ANNALONG

E Bkwtr Hd ⚓ Oc WRG 5s 8m 9M; twr; vis: 204°-G-249°-W-309°-R-024°; 54°06'·51N 05°53'·73W.

DUNDRUM BAY

St John's Point ☆ 54°13'·61N 05°39'·30W Q (2) 7·5s 37m **25M**; B twr, Y bands; H24 when horn is operating. **Auxiliary Light** ☆ Fl WR 3s 14m **W15M**, R11M; same twr, vis: 064°-W-078°-R-shore; Fog Det lt VQ 14m vis: 270°; *Horn (2) 60s*.
DZ East △ 54°13'·51N 05°46'·23W.
DZ Middle △ 54°13'·01N 05°48'·57W.
DZ West △ 54°13'·35N 05°50'·07W.

ARDGLASS

Inner Pier Hd ⚓ Iso WRG 4s 10m W8M, R7M, G5M; twr; vis: shore-G-308°-W-314°-R-shore; 54°15'·79N 05°36'·33W.

STRANGFORD LOUGH

Strangford ⚓ L Fl 10s; 54°18'·61N 05°28'·67W.
Bar Pladdy ⚓ Q (6) + L Fl 15s; 54°19'·34N 05°30'·51W.
Dogtail Pt Ldg lts 341° Front, Oc (4) G 10s 2m 5M; 54°20'·79N 05°31'·83W. Rear, Gowlands Rk, 0·8M from front, Oc (4) G 10s 6m 5M.
Swan Is ⚓ Fl (2) WR 6s 5m; W col; vis: 115°-W-334°-R-115°; 54°22'·38N 05°33'·16W.
Strangford East Ldg lts 256°. Front, Oc WRG 5s 6m W9M, R6M, G6M: vis: 190°-R-244°-G-252°-W- 260°-R-294°; 54°22'·29N 05°33'·27W. Rear, 46m from front, Oc R 5s 10m 6M; vis: 250°-264°.
Portaferry Pier Hd ⚓ Oc WR 10s 9m W9M, R6M; Or mast; vis: W335°- R005°- W017°-128°; 54°22'·82N 05°33'·03W.

SOUTH ROCK

SOUTH ROCK ⚓ 54°24'·49N 05°22'·02W Fl (3) R 30s 9M; *Horn (3) 45s*, ***Racon (T) 13M***.

PORTAVOGIE, BALLYWATER and DONAGHADEE

Plough Rock ⚓ 54°27'·40N 05°25'·12W Fl R 3s.
Outer Bkwtr Hd ⚓ Iso WRG 5s 9m W10M, R8M, G8M; □ twr; vis: shore-G-258°-W-275°-R-348°; 54°27'·44N 05°26'·14W.
Skulmartin ⚓ L Fl 10s; 54°31'·82N 05°24'·80W.
Ballywalter, Bkwtr Hd Fl WRG 1·5s 5m 9M; vis: 240°-G-267°-W-277°-R-314°; 54°32'·68N 05°28'·83W.
Donaghadee ☆, S Pier Hd 54°38'·70N 05°31'·86W Iso WR 4s 17m **W18M**, R14M; W twr; vis: shore-W-326°-R-shore; *Siren 12s*.

BELFAST LOUGH and BANGOR

Mew I ☆ NE end 54°41'·91N 05°30'·79W Fl (4) 30s 37m; B twr, W band; ***Racon (O) 14M***. Fog Det Lt VQ.
Bangor Dir lt 105°. Oc WRG 10s 1M; vis: 093°-G-104·8°-W-105·2°-R-117°; 54°39'·98N 05°40'·15W.
Belfast Fairway ⚓ LFl10s; *Horn (1) 16s*; ***Racon (G)***; 54°41'·71N 05°46'·24W
Cloghan Jetty ⚓ 54°44'·10N 05°41'·58W QG.

CARRICKFERGUS

Marina Ent Appr ⚓ Dir Oc WRG 3s 5m 3M; vis: G308°- W317·5°-R322·5°-332°; 54°42'·58N 05°48'·78W.
Black Hd ☆ 54°45'·99N 05°41'·33W Fl 3s 45m **27M**; W 8-sided twr.

LARNE, CARNLOUGH and RED BAY

N Hunter Rock ⚓ Q; 54°53'·04N 05°45'·13W.
S Hunter Rock ⚓ VQ (6) + L Fl 10s; 54°52'·69N 05°45'·22W.
Larne No. 1 ⚓ QG; 54°51'·68N 05°47'·67W.
Chaine Twr ☆ Iso WR 5s 23m **16M**; Gy twr; vis: 230°-W-240°-240°-R-shore; 54°51'·27N 05°47'·90W.
Ent Ldg lts 184°, No. 11 Front, 54°49'·60N 05°47'·81W Oc 4s 6m 12M; W 2 with R stripe on R pile structure; vis: 179°-189°. No. 12 Rear, 610m from front, Oc 4s 14m 12M; W 2 with R stripe on R □ twr; synch with front; vis: 5° either side of Ldg line.
East Maiden ☆ Fl (3) 20s 29m **24M**; W twr, B band; ***Racon (M) 11-21M***. Auxiliary lt Fl R 5s 15m 8M; 54°55'·74N 05°43'·65W; same twr; vis:142°-182° over Russel and Highland Rks.
Carnlough Hbr N Pier ⚓ Fl G 3s 4m 5M; 54°59'·59N 05°59'·29W.
Red Bay Pier ⚓ Fl 3s 10m 5M; 55°03'·93N 06°03'·21W.

RATHLIN ISLAND TO INISHTRAHULL

RATHLIN ISLAND
Rue Pt ⚓ Fl(2) 5s 16m 14M; W 8-sided twr, B bands; 55°15'·53N 06°11'·47W.
Drake Wreck ⚓ 55°17'·00N 06°12'·48W Q (6) + L Fl 15s.
Altacarry Head Rathlin East ☆ 55°18'·06N 06°10'·30W Fl (4) 20s 74m **26M**; W twr, B band; vis: 110°-006° and 036°-058°; ***Racon (G) 15-27M***.
Rathlin W 0·5M NE of Bull Pt ⚓ 55°18'·05N 06°16'·82W Fl R 5s 62m **22M**; W twr, lantern at base; vis: 015°-225°; H24. Fog Det Lt VQ.
Manor House ⚓ Oc WRG 4s 5M; vis: 020°-G-023°-W-026°-R-029°; 55°17'·52N 06°11'·73W.

PORTRUSH, RIVER BANN and COLERAINE
N Pier Hd ⚓ Fl R 3s 6m 3M; vis: 220°-160°; 55°12'·34N 06°39'·58W.
Portstewart Point ⚓ Oc R 10s 21m 5M; R □ hut; vis: 040°-220°; 55°11'·33N 06°43'·26W.
River Bann Ldg lts 165°. Front, Oc 5s 6m 2M; W twr; 55°09'·96N 06°46'·23W. Rear, 245m from front, Oc 5s 14m 2M; W □ twr.
W Mole ⚓ Fl G 5s 4m 2M; Gy mast; vis: 170°-000°; 56°10'·25N 06°46'·45W.
Foyle ⚓ L Fl 10s; 55°15'·32N 06°52'·60W.
Tuns ⚓ Fl R 3s; 55°14'·00N 06°53'·46W.
Inishowen Dunagree ☆ 55°13'·56N 06°55'·75W Fl (2) WRG 10s 28m **W18M**, R14M, G14M; W twr, 2 B bands; vis: 197°-G-211°-W-249°-R-000°. Fog Det lt VQ 16m vis: 270°.

LOUGH FOYLE

Greencastle S Bkwtr Dir lt 042·5°. Fl (2) WRG 3s 4m W11M, R9M, G9M; vis 307°-G- 040°-W-045°-R-055°; 55°12'·17N 06°59'·13W.
McKinney's ↙ Fl R 5s; 55°10'·9N 07°00'·5W.
Moville ⊥ Fl WR 2·5s 11m 4M; W house on G piles vis: 240°-W-064°-R-240°; 55°10'·98N 07°02'·13W.

INISHTRAHULL TO BLOODY FORELAND

Inishtrahull ☆ 55°25'·86N 07°14'·62W Fl (3) 15s 59m **19M**; W twr; obscd 256°-261° within 3M; *Racon (T) 24M 060°-310°*. Fog Det Lt VQ.

LOUGH SWILLY, BUNCRANA and RATHMULLAN

Fanad Head ☆ 55°16'·57N 07°37'·91W Fl (5) WR 20s 39m **W18M**, R14M; W twr; vis 100°-R-110°-W-313°-R-345°-W-100°.
Swilly More ▲ Fl G 3s; 55°15'·12N 07°35'·79W.
Dunree ⚓ Fl (2) WR 5s 46m W12M, R9M; vis: 320°-R-328°-W-183°-R-196°; 55°11'·88N 07°33'·25W.
Buncrana Pier near Hd ⚓ Iso WR 4s 11m W13M, R10M; R twr, W band; vis: R shore- over Inch spit, 052°-W-139°-R-shore over White Strand Rock; 55°07'·60N 07°27'·86W.
Rathmullan Pier Hd ⚓ Fl G 3s 5M; vis: 206°-345°; 55°05'·70N 07°31'·66W.

MULROY BAY

Limeburner ↙ Q Fl; 55°18'·54N 07°48'·40W.
Ravedy Is ⚓ Fl 3s 9m 3M; twr; vis: 177°-357°; 55°15'·14N 07°46'·90W.

SHEEPHAVEN to BLOODY FORELAND

Portnablahy Ldg lts 125·3°. Front Oc 6s 7m 2M; B col, W bands; 55°10'·79N 07°55'·65W. Rear, 81m from front, Oc 6s 12m 2M; B col, W bands.
Tory Island ☆ 55°16'·36N 08°14'·97W Fl (4) 30s 40m **27M**; B twr, W band; vis: 302°-277°; *Racon (M) 12-23M*; H24.
West Town Ldg lts 001° ⚓ Iso 2s 9m 7M △ on Y structure R stripe; 55°15'·79N 08°13'·50W. Rear Iso 2s 11m 7M ▽ ditto (synchronised)
Ballyness Hbr. Ldg lts 119·5°. Front, Iso 4s 25m 1M; 55°09'·06N 08°06'·98W. Rear, 61m from front, Iso 4s 26m 1M.
Bloody Foreland ⚓ Fl WG 7·5s 14m W6M, G4M; vis: 062°-W-232°-G-062°; 55°09'·51N 08°17'·03W.

BLOODY FORELAND TO RATHLIN O'BIRNE

Glassagh. Ldg lts 137·4°. Front, Oc 8s 12m 3M; 55°06'·83N 08°18'·97W. Rear, 46m from front, Oc 8s 17m 3M; synch.
Inishsirrer, NW end ⚓ Fl 3·7s 20m 4M; W □ twr vis: 083°-263°; 55°07'·40N 08°20'·93W.

BUNBEG, MULLAGHDOO and OWEY SOUND

Gola I s Ldg lts 171·2°. Front, Oc 3s 9m 2M; W Bn, B band; 55°05'·11N 08°21'·07W. Rear, 86m from front, Oc 3s 13m 2M; B Bn, W band; synch with front.
Cruit Is. Owey Sound Ldg lts 068·3°. Front, Oc 10s; 55°03'·06N 08°25'·85W. Rear, 107m from front, Oc 10s.
Rinnalea Point ⚓ 55°02'·59N 08°23'·72W Fl 7·5s 19m 9M; □ twr; vis: 132°-167°.
Aranmore, Rinrawros Pt ☆ 55°00'·90N 08°33'·66W Fl (2) 20s 71m **27M**; W twr; obsc by land about 234°-007° and about 013°. Auxiliary lt Fl R 3s 61m 13M, same twr; vis: 203°-234°.

N SOUND OF ARAN and RUTLAND N CHANNEL

Ldg lts 186°. Front, Oc 8s 8m 3M; B Bn, W band; 54°58'·94N 08°29'·27W. Rear, 395m from front, Oc 8s 17m 3M; B Bn.
Inishcoo Ldg lts 119·3°. Front, Iso 6s 6m 1M; W Bn, B band; 54°59'·43N 08°29'·63W. Rear, 248m from front, Iso 6s 11m 1M.
Rutland I Ldg lts 137·6°. Front, 54°58'·97N 08°27'·68W Oc 6s 8m 1M; W Bn, B band. Rear, 330m from front, Oc 6s 14m 1M.

BURTONPORT

Ldg lts 068·1°. Front , FG 17m 1M; Gy Bn, W band; 54°58'·95N 08°26'·40W. Rear, 355m from front, FG 23m 1M; Gy Bn, Y band.

S SOUND OF ARAN and RUTLAND S CHANNEL

Wyon Point ⚓ Fl (2) WRG 10s 8m W6M, R3M; W □ twr; vis: shore-G-021°-W-042°-R-121°-W-150°-R-shore; 54°56'·51N 08°27'·54W.
Rathlin O'Birne, W side ☆ 54°39'·80N 08°49'·94W Fl WR 15s 35m **W18M**, R14M; W twr; vis: 195°-R-307°-W-195°; *Racon (O) 13M, vis 284°-203°*.

RATHLIN O'BIRNE TO EAGLE ISLAND

DONEGAL BAY, TEELIN and KILLYBEGS

St John's Pt ⚓ Fl 6s 30m 14M; W twr; 54°34'·16N 08°27'·64W.
Bullockmore ↙ Qk Fl (9) 15s; 54°33'·98N 08°30'·14W.
Rotten I ☆ 54°36'·97N 08°26'·41W Fl WR 4s 20m **W15M**, R11M; W twr; vis: W255°- R008°- W039°-208°.
New Landing Dir lt 338°, Oc WRG 6s 17m; vis: 328°-G-334°-Al WG-336°-W-340°-Al WR-342°-R-348°; 54°38'·14N 08°26'·38W.
Killybegs Outer ↙ VQ (6) + L Fl 10s; 54°37'·92N 08°29'·15W.

SLIGO

Wheat Rock ↙ Q (6) + LFl 15s; 54°18'·84N 08°39'·10W.
Black Rock ⚓ Fl WR 5s 24m 10/8M; vis: 130°-W-107°-R-130° (R sector covers Wheat and Seal rks); W twr, B band; 54°18'·45N 08°37'·06W.
Lower Rosses, (N of Cullaun Bwee) ⚓ Fl (2) WRG 10s 8m 13 -10M; W hut on piles; vis: G over Bungar bank-066°-W-070°-R over Drumcliff bar; shown H24; 54°19'·72N 08°34'·41W.
Ldg lts 125°. Front, Metal Man Fl (3) 6s 13m 7M; 54°18'·24N 08°34'·56W. Rear, Oyster I, 365m from front, fL (3) 6s 13m 7M (synchronised); H24.

KILLALA

Inishcrone Pier Root ⚓ Fl WRG 1·5s 8m 2M; vis: 098°-W-116°-G-136°-R-187°; 54°13'·21N 09°05'·79W.
Ldg lts 230°. Rinnaun Point, Front No. 1, Oc 10s 7m 5M; □ twr; 54°13'·21N 09°05'·79W. Rear, 150m from front, No. 2 Oc 10s 12m 5M; □ twr.
Dir lt 215°, Inch I, Fl WRG 2s 6m 3M; □ twr; vis: 205°-G-213°-W-217°-R-225°; 54°13'·29N 09°12'·30W.
Ldg lts 196°. Kilroe, Front, 54°12'·63N 09°12'·33W Oc 4s 5m 2M; □ twr. Rear,120m from front, Oc 4s 10m 2M; □ twr.
Ldg lts 236°. Pier, Front, Iso 2s 5m 2M; W ◇ on twr; 54°13'·02N 09°12'·84W. Rear, 200m from front, Iso 2s 7m 2M; W ◇ on pole.

BROAD HAVEN BAY

Gubacashel Point ⚓ Iso WR 4s 27m **W17M**, R12M; 110°-R-133°-W-355°-R-021° W twr; 54°16'·06N 09°53'·33W.
Rinroe Pt ⚓ Fl (2) 10s 5m 3M; 54°17'·83N 09°50'·59W.

EAGLE ISLAND TO SLYNE HEAD

Eagle Is, W end ☆ 54°17'·02N 10°05'·56W Fl (3) 15s 67m **19M**; W twr.
Black Rock ☆ 54°04'·03N 10°19'·25W Fl WR 12s 86m **W20M**, R16M; W twr; vis: 276°-W-212°-R-276°.

BLACKSOD BAY

Carrigeenmore ↙ VQ(3) 5s 3M; 54°06'·56N 10°03'·4W.
Blacksod ↙ Q (3) 10s; 54°05'·89N 10°03'·01W.
Blacksod Pier Root ⚓ Fl (2) WR 7·5s 13m W12M, R9M; W twr on dwelling; vis: 189°-R-210°-W-018°; 54°05'·91N 10°03'·63W.

ACHILL SOUND

Ldg lts 330°, 53°52'·50N 09°56'·91W Whitestone Point, Front and rear both Oc 4s 5/6m; W ◇, B stripe.
Achill I Ldg lts 310°, Purteen, Oc 8s 5m; 53°57'·83N 10°05'·93W (PA). Rear, 46m from front Oc 8s 6m.

CLEW BAY and WESTPORT
Achillbeg I S Point ☆ 53°51'·51N 09°56'·85W Fl WR 5s 56m **W18M, R18M, R15M**; W☐ twr on ☐ building; vis: 262°-R-281°-W-342°-R-060°-W- 092°-R(intens)-099°-W-118°.

Cloughcormick ⚓ Q (9) 15s; 53°50'·56N 09°43'·20W.

Roonagh Quay Ldg lts 144°. Front 53°45'·75N 09°54'·23W. Rear, 54m from front, both Iso 10s 9/15m.

INISHBOFIN and CLIFDEN BAY
Inishlyon Lyon Head ⚓ Fl WR 7·5s 13m W7M, R4M; W post; vis: 036°-W-058°-R-184°-W-325°-R-036°; 53°36'·74N 10°09'·56W.

Gun Rock ⚓ Fl (2) 6s 8m 4M; W col; vis: 296°-253°; 53°36'·59N 10°13'·23W.

Cleggan Point ⚓ Fl (3) WRG 15s 20m W6M, R3M, G3M; W col on W hut; vis: shore-W-091°-R-124°-G-221°; 53°34'·49N 10°07'·73W.

Carrickrana Rocks Bn, large W Bn; 53°29'·24N 10°09'·48W.

Slyne Head, North twr, Illaunamid ☆ 53°23'·99N 10°14'·06W Fl (2) 15s 35m **19M**; B twr.

SLYNE HEAD TO BLACK HEAD
Inishnee ⚓ Fl (2) WRG 10s 9m W5M, R3M, G3M; W col on W☐ base; vis: 314°-G-017°-W-030°-R-080°-W-194°; 53°22'·75N 09°54'·53W.

Croaghnakeela Is ⚓ Fl 3·7s 7m 5M; W col; vis: 034°-045°, 218°-286°, 311°-325°; 53°19'·40N 09°58'·21W.

GALWAY BAY and INISHMORE
Eeragh, Rock Is ☆ 53°08'·90N 09°51'·40W Fl 15s 35m **18M**; W twr, two B bands; vis: 297°-262°.

Straw Is ☆ 53°07'·06N 09°37'·85W Fl (2) 5s 11m **15M**; W twr.

Killeany Ldg lts 192°. Front, Oc 5s 6m 3M; W col on W☐ base; vis: 142°-197°, 53°06'·25N 09°39'·74W. Rear, 43m from front, Oc 5s 8m 2M; W col on W☐ base; vis: 142°-197°.

Inishmaan, Ldg lts 199°, Oc 6s 8M; 53°06'·08N 09°34'·77W.

KIGGAUL BAY, CASHLA BAY and SPIDDLE
Kiggaul Bay ⚓ Fl WR 3s 5m W5M, R3M; vis: 329°-W-359°-R-059°, part obsc by W shore of bay; 53°14'·02N 09°43'·04W.

Cashla BayEnt, W side ⚓ Fl (3) WR 10s 8m W6M, R3M; W col on concrete structure; vis: 216°-W-000°-R-069°; 53°14'·23N 09°35'·20W.

Lion Pt Dir lt Iso WRG 5s 6m (H24), G6M, W8M, R6M,(night), G2M, W3M, R2M(day); vis: 005°-G- 008·5°-W-011·5°-R-015°; 53°15'·84N 09°33'·95W.

Rossaveel Pier Ldg lts 116° Front, 53°16'·02N 09°33'·38W Oc 3s 7m 3M; W mast. Rear, 90m from front, Oc 3s 8m 3M.

Spiddle Pier Hd ⚓ Fl WRG 3·5s 11m W6M, R4M, G4M; Y col; vis: 102°-G-282°-W-024°-R-066°; 53°14'·42N 09°18'·55W.

GALWAY
Margaretta Shoal ⬆ Fl G 3s; *Whis;* 53°13'·68N 09°05'·99W.

Leverets ⚓ Q WRG 9m 10M; B☐ twr, W bands; vis: 015°-G-058°-W-065°-R-103°-G-143·5°-W-146·5°-R-015°; 53°15'·33N 09°01'·90W.

Rinmore ⚓ Iso WRG 4s 7m 5M; W☐ twr; vis: 359°-G-008°-W-018°-R-027°; 53°16'·12N 09°01'·97W.

Appr Chan Dir lt 325°, WRG 7m 3M; vis: 322·25°-FG-323·75°-AlGW-324·75°-FW-325·25°-AlRW-326·25°-FR-331·25°-FlR-332·25°; 53°16'·12N 09°02'·83W.

Black Hd ⚓ Fl WR 5s 20m W11M, R8M, W ☐ twr; vis: 045°- R268°-276°; 53°09'·26N 09°15'·83W.

Finnis Rock ⚓ Q (3) 10s; 53°02'·82N 09°29'·14W.

Inisheer ☆ 53°02'·78N 09°31'·58W Iso WR 12s 34m **W20M, R16M**; vis: 225°-W(partially vis >7M)-231°, 231°-W-245°-R-269°-W-115°; *Racon (K) 13M.*

9.13.5 PASSAGE INFORMATION

The latest editions of the Irish Cruising Club (www.irish cruisingclub.com) Sailing Directions are strongly recommended for all Irish waters. Particularly useful on the N and W coasts where other information is scarce, they are published in two volumes: *E and N coasts of Ireland* and *S and W coasts of Ireland*. Admiralty Leisure Folio 5612 covers Carlingford Lough to Lough Foyle.

More Passage Information is threaded between the harbours of this Area.

CROSSING THE IRISH SEA
(AC 1123, 1121, 1411) Passages across the Irish Sea can range from the fairly long haul from Land's End to Cork (140M), to the relatively short hop from Mull of Kintyre to Torr Pt (11M). Such distances are deceptive, because the average cruising yacht needs to depart from and arrive at a reasonably secure hbr. ▶ *In the North Chan strong tidal streams can cause heavy overfalls.* ◀ Thus each passage needs to be treated on its merits. See 9.0.6 for distances across the Irish Sea.

Many yachts use the Land's End/Cork route on their way to (and from) the delightful cruising ground along the S coast of Ireland, see 9.12.5. Penzance Bay or one of the Scilly Is ⚓s are convenient places from which to leave, with good lights to assist departure.

▶ *Although the Celtic Sea is exposed to the Atlantic, there are no dangers on passage and the tidal streams are weak.* ◀ A landfall between Ballycotton and Old Hd of Kinsale (both have good lights) presents no offlying dangers, and in poor vis decreasing soundings indicate approach to land. There is a likelihood, outward bound under sail, that the boat will be on the wind – a possible benefit on the return passage. If however the wind serves, and if it is intended to cruise along the southern coast, a

landfall at the Fastnet with arrival at (say) Baltimore will place the yacht more to windward, for little extra distance.

From Land's End the other likely destination is Dun Laoghaire. A stop at Milford Haven enables the skipper to select the best time for passing the Smalls or Bishops (see 9.11.5) and roughly divides the total passage into two equal parts. From S Bishop onwards there are the options of making the short crossing to Tuskar Rk and going N inside the banks (theoretically a good idea in strong W winds), or of keeping to seaward. ▶ *But in bad weather the area off Tuskar is best avoided; apart from the Traffic Separation Scheme, the tide is strong at sp and the sea can be very rough.* ◀

The ferry route Holyhead/Dun Laoghaire is another typical crossing, and is relatively straightforward with easy landfalls either end. ▶ *The tide runs hard round Anglesey at sp, so departure just before slack water minimises the set N or S.* ◀ Beware also the TSS off The Skerries.

The Isle of Man is a good centre for cruising in the Irish Sea, and its hbrs provide convenient staging points whether bound N/S or E/W.

CROSSING TO SCOTLAND
(AC 2198, 2199, 2724) Between Scotland and Northern Ireland there are several possible routes, but much depends on weather and tide. ▶ *Time of departure must take full advantage of the stream, and avoid tide races and overfalls* ◀ (see 9.9.5). **Conditions can change quickly, so a flexible plan is needed.**

▶ *From Belfast Lough ent, the passage distance to Mull of Kintyre is about 35M and, with a departure at local HW (also HW Dover) providing at least 6hrs of N-going tides, fair winds make it possible to get past the Mull or Sanda Is on one tide. But to be more confident of reaching Gigha or the small marina in Port Ellen, a departure from Glenarm Marina or Red Bay at HW makes a shorter passage with better stream advantage. The inshore side of the TSS coincides with the outer limit of the race S and SW off the Mull of Kintyre; this occurs between HW Dover + 0430 and + 0610 when a local S-going stream opposes the main N-going stream.* ◀

For information on submarine exercises/activity see Subfacts.

LAMBAY ISLAND TO FAIR HEAD

(AC 44, 2093, 2198/9) The coast is fairly steep-to except in larger bays, particularly Dundalk. ▶ *Streams offshore run up to 2·5kn as far as Rockabill, but are weaker further N until approaching Belfast Lough.* ◀ Lambay Island is private, and steep-to except on W side, where there can be overfalls. Skerries Islands (Colt, Shenick's and St Patrick's) are 1M E and SE of Red Island, to E of Skerries hbr. Shenick's Island is connected to shore at LW. Pass between Colt and St Patrick's Islands, but the latter has offliers 3ca to S. Rockabill, two steep-to rks with lt ho, is 2·5M E of St Patrick's Island.

NE'wds from Carlingford Lough, after rounding Hellyhunter SCM, there are no offshore dangers until Strangford Lough where ▶ *the tidal cycle is approx 3 hours later than in the N*

FLOOD
St John's Pt **Strangford Lough App**

EBB
St John's Pt **Strangford Lough App**

Channel. Flood runs for 6 hours from HW Belfast –0330 (HW Dover –0345), with a maximum rate of 7.5kn at Rue Point. The strong flow flattens the sea in onshore winds and entrance can be made in strong winds. The ebb runs for 6 hours from HW Belfast +0230 (HW Dover +0215), max rate 7.5kn, E of Angus Rk. If entering against ebb use West Channel with care. Smoothest water near Bar Pladdy Buoy when leaving. ◀

There is a marina at Ardglass. N of Strangford keep 5ca off Ballyquintin Pt. 3M to NE are Butter Pladdy Rks; keep to E of these. 2M further N is South Rk, with disused lt ho, part of group of rks to be avoided in poor vis or bad weather by closing South Rk superbuoy. In good vis pass inshore of South Rk, between it and North Rks (AC 2156), rounding South Ridge PHM buoy.

Three routes lead into Belfast Lough: **a.** E of Mew Is, but beware Ram Race (to the N on the ebb, and the S on the flood). **b.** Copeland Sound, between Mew Is and Copeland Is, is passable but not recommended; **c.** Donaghadee Sound is buoyed and a good short cut for small craft. ▶ *Here the stream runs SSE from HW Belfast + 0530 and NW from HW Belfast – 0030, 4·5kn max. An eddy extends S to Ballyferris Pt, and about 1M offshore.* ◀ For Donaghadee see AC 3709.

(AC 2198) N from Belfast L, Black Hd is steep-to as is Muck Is on its E side. Hunter Rk (0·8m), 2·5M NE of Larne, is marked by N & S cardinals. 2M further N are the Maidens, two dangerous groups of rks extending 2·5M N/S; E Maiden is lit.

Glenarm Marina provides good shelter for small craft and is useful for on passage to the W coasts of Scotland or Ireland. Other ⚓s in offshore winds are at Red Bay 5M further N, and in Cushendun B, 5M NNW of Garron Pt. All provide useful anch on passage to/from the Clyde or Western Is. Fair Hd is a bold 190m headland, steep-to all round, but with extensive overfalls in Rathlin Sound.

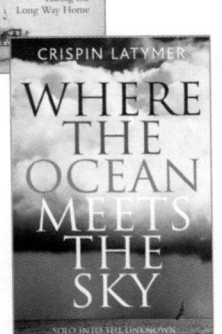

9.13.6 SPECIAL NOTES FOR IRELAND: See 9.12.6

MINOR HARBOURS AND ANCHORAGES BETWEEN LAMBAY ISLAND AND CARLINGFORD LOUGH

SKERRIES, Dublin, **53°35'·09N 06°06'·49W**. AC 633. Tides as Balbriggan, 9.13.7. E & SE of Red Island (a peninsula) lie Colt, Shenick's and St Patrick's Is, the latter foul to S and SW. Inshore passage between Colt and St Patrick's Is uses transit/brg as on chart to clear dangers. Good shelter and holding in 3m at Skerries Bay, W of Red Is. Appr from E or NE outside PHM buoy, Fl R 10s, off Red Is. ‡ WNW of pier, Oc R 6s 7m 7M, vis 103°-154°; clear of moorings. Most facilities; Skerries SC ☎ 1-849 1233, Slip (HW±3). Rockabill Lt, Fl WR 12s 45m 22/18M, is conspic 2·4M ExN of St Patrick's Is.

BALBRIGGAN, Dublin, **53°36'·76N 06°10'·84W**. AC 44, 1468. Tides see 9.13.7. Good shelter in small hbr, dries about 0·9m,

access approx HW ±2. Hbr unattractive, mainly FV's. Appr on SW, to open the outer hbr which is entered on SE; thence to inner hbr and AB on SE quay. Beware shoaling on both sides of outer hbr. Lt, Fl (3) WRG 10s 12m 13/10M, conspic W tr on E bkwtr head, vis 159°-G193°-W-288°-R-305°. Facilities: FW, D (by tanker from Skerries), Gas, Slip (HW±2), R, Bar, 🛒.

PORT ORIEL, Louth, **53°47'·94N 06°13'·37W**. AC 44. Tides see 9.13.7 (Dunany Pt). Good shelter, except in strong NW'lies, in small new fishing harbour. Appr from NE on ldg marks 179°, Fl 3s; Pier Hd Lt Mo(A) R 9s. AB on pier in 4m or dry out in inner hbr. HM ☎ 087 2628777. D by tanker, 🛒 in Clogher Hd village (1·2M).

9.13.7 CARLINGFORD LOUGH

Louth/Down **54°01'·25N 06°04'·30W** ※⊛⚓⚓⚓☆☆☆

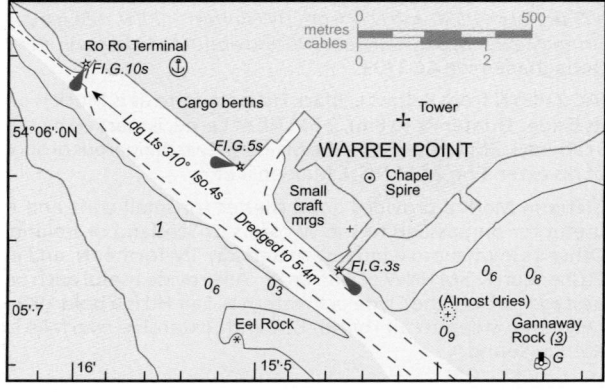

CHARTS AC 44, 2800, 5621, 5612; Imray C62.

TIDES Cranfield Pt +0025 and Warrenpoint +0035 Dover; ML 2·9; Duration Cranfield Pt 0615, Warrenpoint 0540

Standard Port DUBLIN (NORTH WALL) (←—)

Times				Height (metres)			
High Water		Low Water		MHWS	MHWN	MLWN	MLWS
0000	0700	0000	0500	4·1	3·4	1·5	0·7
1200	1900	1200	1700				
Differences CRANFIELD POINT							
−0027	−0011	+0005	−0010	+0·7	+0·9	+0·3	+0·2
WARRENPOINT							
−0020	−0010	+0025	+0035	+1·0	+0·7	+0·2	0·0
NEWRY (VICTORIA LOCK)							
−0005	−0015	+0045	Dries	+1·2	+0·9	+0·1	Dries
DUNDALK (SOLDIERS POINT)							
−0010	−0010	0000	+0045	+1·0	+0·8	+0·1	−0·1
DUNANY POINT							
−0028	−0018	−0008	−0006	+0·7	+0·9	No data	
RIVER BOYNE BAR							
−0005	0000	+0020	+0030	+0·4	+0·3	−0·1	−0·2
BALBRIGGAN							
−0021	−0015	+0010	+0002	+0·3	+0·2	No data	

SHELTER Carlingford Marina is protected on S side by sunken barge; depths 1·4m–3·5m (check with Marina). Appr from N with Nos 18 and 23 buoys in transit astern 012°, to clear the tail of Carlingford Bank (dries) and beware of marine farms in vicinity.

Carlingford Hbr (dries 2·2m), AB at piers.

Warrenpoint has pontoons on NW side of breakwater (Fl G 3s); access dredged 1·1m. ⚓s clockwise from ent include: off Greenore Pt, between SW end of quay and bkwtr, in 3m clear of commercial traffic; off Greer's Quay in 2m; off Rostrevor Quay, Killowen Pt (YC) and off derelict pier at Greencastle Pt (beware rks). Limited space may be available for short-stay visiting craft in the mussel fishing complex (approx £15/night). Call at least 24 hours before arrival.

NAVIGATION WPT 54°00'·09N 06°02'·00W, (2½ ca S of Hellyhunter SCM lt buoy) 311°/1M to first chan buoys. The main chan is Carlingford Cut (6·3m), about 3ca SW of Cranfield Pt, and passing 2ca NE of Haulbowline lt ho. Drying rocks and shoals obstruct most of the entrance. Small craft should at all times keep clear of commercial shipping in the narrow dredged channel. The ent is impassable in strong on-shore winds. The NE bank is **Northern Ireland**, SW bank is **Republic of Ireland**.

The lough becomes choppy in S'ly winds and, due to the funnelling effect of the mountains, NW winds can cause a higher sea state within the lough than outside it.

Tides run up to 5kn off Greenore Pt and entry is impracticable against the ebb. Beware sudden squalls and waterspouts.

Extensive shellfish beds exist along the NE side of the lough; beware fishing vessels on both sides of the channel, and give them a wide berth.

LIGHTS AND MARKS Haulbowline Fl (3) 10s 32m 17M; granite tower. Ldg lts 310°26': both Oc 3s 7/12m 11M, vis 295°–325°; R △ front, ▽ rear, on framework trs. Greenore Pier Fl R 7·5s 10m 5M. Newry R: Ldg lts 310°, both Iso 4s 5/15m 2M, stone columns. Channel from Green Is to Warren Pt marked by lit lateral buoys.

R/T Greenore (*Ferry Greenore*) Ch 12 16 (HJ). Carlingford Marina Ch M 16. Warrenpoint Ch 12 16 (H24); call Ch 12 at By No. 23 to enter dredged chan. Dundalk Ch 14 16 (HW±3).

TELEPHONE (Code Greenore/Carlingford 042; Warrenpoint 028). MRCC (01) 6620922/3 or (02891) 463933; Irish ⊖: Dundalk (042) 34114; Marinecall 09068 969655; Dr (042) 73110; Ⓗ Newry (028) 3026 5511, Dundalk (042) 34701; Police (042) 9373102, (028) 4172 2222.

FACILITIES

Carlingford Marina ☎ 042 9373073, mob 0872 321567. 290 inc ♥, €4.00 (min€20/craft), short stay <5hrs€12.50/craft, D (0900-

2100), C, CH, BH (50T), ME ☎ 0872 301319, Rigger ☎ (048)44 828882, Divers, Slip, ⚡, Bar, R, Wi-fi + @. **Carlingford YC** ☎ (041) 685 1951, Slip, Bar, M, FW.
Village P (cans), 🛒, R, Bar, Ⓑ, ✉. **Hbr** AB, Slip, ME, El, ✗, Kos, Gas. **Warrenpoint** HM ☎ (02841) 752878; AB, M (but no access at LW), FW, P, D, ✉ also at Rostrevor, Ⓑ also Dundalk, ⇌ (Dundalk, Newry), ✈ (Dublin).

MINOR HARBOURS NORTH OF CARLINGFORD LOUGH

KILKEEL, Down, 54°03'·47N 05°59'·26W. AC 44, 2800, 5612. HW +0015 on Dover; ML 2·9m; Duration 0620. See 9.13.8. Inner basin is completely sheltered, but gets crowded by FVs; depth off quays approx 1m. There are drying banks both sides of ent chan and SW gales cause a sandbank right across ent. This is dredged or slowly eroded in E winds. S bkwtr lt Fl WR 2s 8m 8M, 296°-R-313°-W-017°, storm sigs. Meeney's pier (N bkwtr) Fl G 3s 6m 2M. VHF Ch 12 14 16 (Mon-Fri: 0900-2000). HM ☎ (028 417) 62287; Facilities: FW on quay, BY (between fish market and dock), El, ME, ✗, Slip. Town (¾M) Bar, ✉, R, 🛒, Gas, ⚡.

ANNALONG HBR, Down, 54°06'·50N 05°53'·65W. AC 44, 5621, 5612. Tides as Kilkeel, see 9.13.8. Slight silting rep't 2006. Entry HW ±2. Excellent shelter in small drying hbr, dredged to 1·5m 80m beyond pier with 30m pontoon (£12/craft), FW. Appr in W sector of S breakwater light, Oc WRG 5s 8m 9M, vis 204°-G-249°-W-309°-

R-024°. Hug N side of the breakwater to avoid rocky shore to starboard. Surge gate at harbour entrance may be closed in SE winds (3R lts vert shown). IPTS shown at entrance. HM ☎ mob 07739 527036 Facilities: 🛒, Bar, ✉.

DUNDRUM BAY, Down. AC 44, 5612. Tides see 9.13.8. This 8M wide bay to the W of St John's Pt is shoal to 5ca offshore and unsafe in onshore winds. The small drying hbr at **Newcastle** (54°11'·8N 05°53'·0W) is for occas use in fair weather. HM ☎ (02843) 722804, mob 07803 832515. **Dundrum Hbr** (54°14'·2N 05°49'·4W) No longer used by commercial tfc, provides ⚓ in 2m for shoal draft; the bar carries about 0·3m. A steep sea can run at the bar in onshore winds. HW Dundrum is approx that of HW Liverpool; see also 9.13.8 Newcastle. *The Irish Cruising Club's Sailing Directions* are essential for the 1M long, buoyed approach channel. 3 unlit DZ buoys offshore are part of the Ballykinler firing range, 2M E of hbr; R flag/lts indicate range active.

9.13.8 ARDGLASS

Down **54°15´·63N 05°35´·96W** ✿✿✿⚓⚓✿✿

CHARTS AC 2093, 633, 5612; Imray C62.

TIDES HW +0025 Dover; ML 3·0; Duration 0620

Standard Port BELFAST (→)

Times				Height (metres)			
High Water		Low Water		MHWS	MHWN	MLWN	MLWS
0100	0700	0000	0600	3·5	3·0	1·1	0·4
1300	1900	1200	1800				
Differences KILKEEL							
+0040	+0030	+0010	+0010	+1·2	+1·1	+0·4	+0·4
NEWCASTLE							
+0025	+0035	+0020	+0040	+1·6	+1·1	+0·4	+0·1
KILLOUGH HARBOUR							
0000	+0020	No data		+1·8	+1·6	No data	
ARDGLASS							
+0010	+0015	+0005	+0010	+1·7	+1·2	+0·6	+0·3

SHELTER Good, except in strong winds from E to S. It is the only all-weather, all-tide shelter between Howth and Bangor. Phennick Cove marina is on W side of hbr, with depths 1·0m to 2·8m. Visitors should check depth of berth offered by marina against depth drawn. The busy fishing port is in South Hbr, with quays (2·1m) on inside of extended S pier. At NW end of hbr, old drying N Dock is also used by FVs.

NAVIGATION WPT 54°15´·30N 05°35´·32W, 131°/5ca to hbr ent. Appr 311° in W sector of WRG Dir lt. Depth in chan 2·4m. The inner bkwtr is marked by an ECM buoy, VQ (3) 4s. Thence chan 232° into the marina is marked by Nos 2 and 4 PHM buoys, QR and Fl R 4s; and by Nos 3 and 5 SHM buoys, QG and Fl G 4s. (These buoys are not shown on chartlet due to small scale.) Do not cross the drying SW portion of inner bkwtr, marked by two unlit SCM perches.

LIGHTS AND MARKS Dir lt, 311°, conspic W tr at inner hbr, Iso WRG 4s 10m 8/7/5M, 308°-W-314°; reported hard to see against shore lts. S bkwtr Fl R 3s 10m 5M. W roof of shed on S bkwtr is conspic. If entering S Hbr, avoid Churn Rk, unlit SCM bn. Entrance to marina is buoyed. Castle, spire and water tr (off plan) are conspic to W.

R/T Hbr VHF Ch 12 14 16. Marina Ch M, 80.

TELEPHONE (Code 028) HM 4484 1291, mob 07790 648274; MRCC 9046 3933; Marinecall 09068 969655; Police 4461 5011; Dr 9084 1242.

FACILITIES Phennick Cove Marina (55 inc 30🅥 £1.60), ☎ 44842332, www.ardglassmarina.co.uk; Slip(£3.00), D, P (cans), ▢, ⚒. **Town** P (cans), Bar, ✉, R, 🛒, Gas.

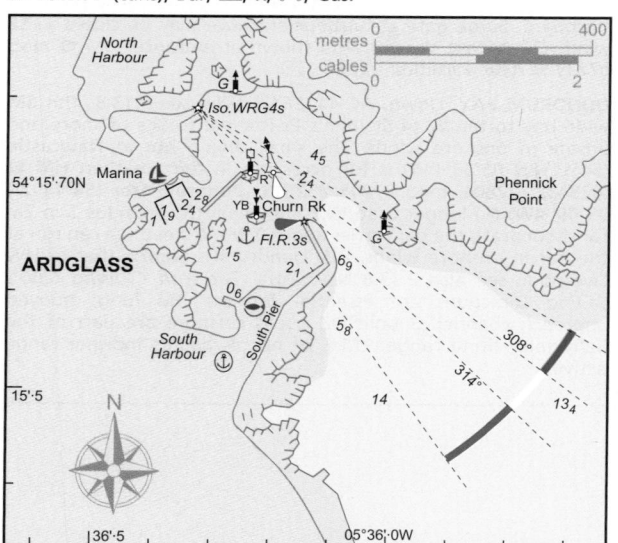

9.13.9 STRANGFORD LOUGH

Down **54°19´·33N 05°30´·85W** (Narrows) ✿✿⚓⚓✿✿✿

CHARTS AC 2156, 2159, 5612; Imray C62.

TIDES Killard Pt 0000, Strangford Quay +0200 Dover; ML 2·0; Duration 0610

Standard Port BELFAST (→)

Times				Height (metres)			
High Water		Low Water		MHWS	MHWN	MLWN	MLWS
0100	0700	0000	0600	3·5	3·0	1·1	0·4
1300	1900	1200	1800				
Differences STRANGFORD (The Narrows)							
+0147	+0157	+0148	+0208	+0·1	+0·1	−0·2	0·0
KILLARD POINT (Entr)							
+0011	+0021	+0005	+0025	+1·0	+0·8	+0·1	+0·1
QUOILE BARRIER							
+0150	+0200	+0150	+0300	+0·2	+0·2	−0·3	−0·1
KILLYLEAGH							
+0157	+0207	+0211	+0231	+0·3	+0·3	No data	
SOUTH ROCK							
+0023	+0023	+0025	+0025	+1·0	+0·8	+0·1	+0·1
PORTAVOGIE							
+0010	+0020	+0010	+0020	+1·2	+0·9	+0·3	+0·2

SHELTER Excellent; largest inlet on E coast. Good ⚓s in the Narrows at Cross Roads; in Strangford Creek (NW of Swan Island, which is marked by 3 lt bns to S, E and N); in Audley Rds and Ballyhenry Bay. 3 ⚓s at Strangford. Portaferry has a small marina with a few visitors' berths. Many good ⚓s and some ⚓s up the lough, by villages and YCs; dues, if applicable, are seldom collected.

NAVIGATION WPT Strangford SWM buoy, L Fl 10s, 54°18´·63N 05°28´·62W, 306°/2·05M to Angus Rk lt tr.

Strangers should use the E Chan. Beware St Patricks Rk, Bar Pladdy and Pladdy Lug; also overfalls in the SE apprs and at the bar, which can be dangerous when ebb is against strong onshore winds.

During flood the bar presents no special problem, preferable to enter on the young flood or at slack water. Strong (up to 7kn at sp) tidal streams flow through the Narrows. The flood starts in the Narrows at HW Belfast –3½ and runs for about 6 hrs; the ebb starts at HW Belfast +2½. Beware car ferry plying from Strangford, S and E of Swan Is, to Portaferry.

Swan Island, seen as a grassy mound at HW, is edged with rks and a reef extends 32m E ending at W bn, Fl (2) WR 6s. Further up the lough, AC 2156 is essential. Pladdies are drying patches, often un-marked.

LIGHTS AND MARKS An IDM, red and black bands, Fl(2) 10s 13m 3M, 54°22´·12N 05°32´·77W (off Strangford) marks a submerged tidal turbine, 3·1m below CD.

R/T HM at Strangford Ferry Terminal Ch 12 14 16 M (Mon-Fri 0900-1700LT). Some YCs Ch **80** M.

TELEPHONE (Code 028) Strangford HM 4488 1637; MRCC 9146 3933; Marinecall 09068 969655; Police 4461 5011; Medical Clinic 4461 3016; Casualty 4461 3311.

FACILITIES Strangford, Portaferry and Killyleagh are easy to access and offer good shops, pubs and restaurants.
STRANGFORD 3 ⚓s SE of Swan Is. **Islander Marine** ☎ 4488 1449: FW, Slip, El, Ⓔ, ⚒, D (cans). Village: 🛒, R, Bar, ✉.
PORTAFERRY: Marina, ☎ 42729598, mobile 07703 209780; barholm.portaferry@virgin.net. AB(limited) £1.50, Gas, Gaz, P & D (cans), 🛒, R, Bar, ✉, Ⓑ, aquarium. **Cook St Pier** (2ca S), limited AB, FW.
QUOILE RIVER: Quoile YC ☎ 4461 2266. AB, M, Slip, FW.
KILLYLEAGH: M, P & D (cans), L, CH, SM (Irish Spars & Rigging ☎ 4482 8882), El, ME, 🛒, Gas, Gaz, Kos, R, Ⓑ, Bar, ✉; **Killyleagh YC** ☎ 4482 8250; N of village, **East Down YC** ☎ 4482 8375, AB (about 1M NE of town).
RINGHADDY QUAY: CC, M, AB drying, FW, Slip.
SKETRICK ISLAND: In White Rk B, **Strangford Lough YC,** ☎ 9754 1883, L, AB, FW, BY, CH, R, Bar. To the NW in the Dorn, **Down CC**, (Old Lightship) FW, D, Bar.
KIRCUBBIN (tidal): Gas, P & D (cans), Ⓑ, R, Bar, 🛒, ✉.

Ballywhite Bay

Ballyhenry
Island

Ballyhenry Point

Bn
QG

59 Ballyhenry
Bay

Chapel Island

57

23'

Walter Rocks

Audleys Point

Audleys
Roads

Audleys
Castle
(Conspic)

2₇
2₃

18
Fl(4)R.10s

PORTAFERRY
(pilots)

See inset

Portaferry House

Tr (conspic)

Strangford
Castleward
Bay

Church Pt

See inset

STRANGFORD

22
Fl(2)10s
Seagen

RBR

Rue
Point

27

Portaferry

metres   0   200
cables   0   1

Ferry
OcWR10s

0₃

2₅

G

4₃

11₃

Iso.WRG.4s

G

0₆

SC

N

Knockinelder
Bay

2₄

4₉

7

Millin
Bay

12₂

17₄

Oc.G(2)10s

Salt
Rock Bn

Fl.R.3s

Gowland
Rks.

22

Cross
Roads

7₃

26

Templecowey Point

South
Bay

Dogtail Point
Oc.G(4)10s

Carstown Point

Carnan
Point

11₆

Guns Is Obelisk and Perch
in line 224° clears Quintin Rock

21'

Bn Q
N.Pladdy

2

Fl(2)WR6s

2

Bn

Swan Is

7₃

Quay

2

S.Pladdy
Bn
Fl(3)10s

6₇

9₁   4₃   256°

20'

Ferry Ramp

OcR5s

OcWRG5s

QR

Grid

metres   100

Strangford

Castle
(conspic)

2₃
Meadows

16

W
Bn

Pladdy
Lug

Ballyquintin Point

Quintin Rocks

**IRISH
SEA**

FlR5s
Twr WR (conspic)

West Channel

Angus
Rock   Bn

0₈
1₄

19₁

East Channel

0₈

Bar Pladdy

Q(6)+LFl15s

YB

11₉

Killard Point

2₄

St. Patrick's
Rock

R

14₃   Overfalls   23

LFl.10s
Strangford SWM Buoy

RW

54°19'N

metres   0   2000
cables   0   10

4

Ballyhornan
Bay

3₄

6₁

18'

10₁

Guns
Island

Obelisk

22

Gowland bn and
Dogtail bn in line,
clears Meadows 341°

36'   05°35'   34'   05°33'W   32'   31'   05°30'   29'   28'

9.13.10 BELFAST LOUGH
County Down and County Antrim 54°42'N 05°45'W
Bangor ✿✿✿⚓⚓⚓✿✿; Carrickfergus ✿✿✿⚓⚓⚓✿✿

CHARTS AC 2198, 1753, 5612; Imray C62, C64

TIDES +0007 Dover; ML Belfast 2·0, Carrickfergus 1·8; Duration 0620

Standard Port BELFAST (→)

Times				Height (metres)			
High Water		Low Water		MHWS	MHWN	MLWN	MLWS
0100	0700	0000	0600	3·5	3·0	1·1	0·4
1300	1900	1200	1800				
Differences CARRICKFERGUS							
+0005	+0005	+0005	+0005	−0·3	−0·3	−0·2	−0·1
DONAGHADEE							
+0020	+0020	+0023	+0023	+0·5	+0·4	0·0	+0·1

SHELTER Main sailing centres, clockwise around Belfast Lough, are at Bangor, Cultra and Carrickfergus.

Donaghadee: small marina at SE ent to the Lough.

Ballyholme Bay: good ⚓ in offshore winds.

Bangor: exposed to N winds, but well sheltered in marina (depths 2·9m to 2·2m). Speed limits: 4kn in marina, 8kn between Luke's Pt and Wilson's Pt.

Cultra: in offshore winds good ⚓ & moorings off RNoIYC.

Belfast Harbour is a major commercial port, but there are pontoons on the NW bank at Donegal Quay (54°36'·16N 05°55'·20W) between Lagan Bridge, 8m clearance, and Lagan Weir. To enter call *Belfast Port Control* VHF Ch **12**.

Carrickfergus: very good in marina, depths 1·8m to 2·3m. The former commercial hbr has 10 yacht berths on the W quay. A stub bkwtr, marked by 2 PHM bns, extends NNE into the hbr from the W pier. The ent and SW part of the hbr are dredged 2·3m; the NE part of the hbr dries 0·7m. Good ⚓ SSE of Carrickfergus Pier, except in E winds.

NAVIGATION WPT Bangor 54°41'·00N 05°40'·00W, 190°/1M to bkwtr lt. Rounding Orlock Pt beware Briggs Rocks extending ¾M offshore. The Lough is well marked. WPT Carrickfergus 54°41'·71N 05°46'·16W, Fairway SWM buoy marks start of the chan to Belfast Hbr. It also bears 121°/301° from/to Carrickfergus Marina, 1.7M. Carrickfergus Bank liable to shift. Deep draft yachts should not enter/leave at LW±2. High speed ferries operate in the area.

LIGHTS AND MARKS Bangor Dir Oc WRG 10s lt; W sector 105° leads into ent. Chan to Belfast Hbr is well marked/lit by buoys and bns. Beyond No 12 PHM bn it is dangerous to leave the chan. Carrickfergus is easily recognised by conspic castle to E of Marina. On Marina Bkwtr, 30m W of the ☆ QR 7m 3M, is a Dir lt 320°, Oc WRG 3s 5m 3M, (H24).

R/T Bangor Marina Ch **80** M (H24); Bangor HM Ch 11 (H24). Royal N of Ireland YC (at Cultra) Ch **16**; 11 (H24) 80. *Belfast Port Control* (at Milewater Basin) Ch **12** 16 (H24); VTS provides info on request to vessels in port area. The greater part of Belfast Lough is under radar surveillance. Carrickfergus Marina Ch M, 80, M2.

TELEPHONE (Codes: Belfast 028) HM Bangor 91453297; HM Belfast 90553012; Belfast VTS 9055 3504; MRCC 91463933; Weather (08494) 22339; Marinecall 09068 969655; Police 90558411, 93362021, 91454444; Dr 91468521.

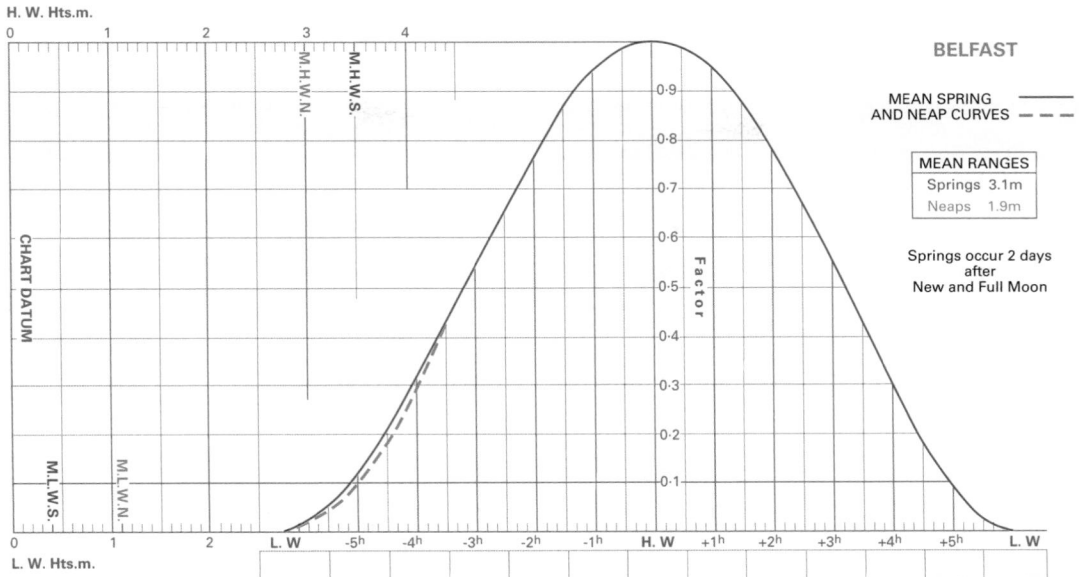

BELFAST

MEAN SPRING
AND NEAP CURVES

MEAN RANGES
Springs 3.1m
Neaps 1.9m

Springs occur 2 days
after
New and Full Moon

BANGOR

CARRICKFERGUS

Carrickfergus
Marina

FACILITIES Clockwise around the Lough:
GROOMSPORT BAY HM ☎ 91278040, M, Slip, FW; **Cockle Island Boat Club**, Slip, M, FW, L, R.
BALLYHOLME BAY Ballyholme YC ☎ 9127 1467, R, Bar; **Royal Ulster YC** ☎ 91270568, M, R, Bar.
BANGOR Bangor Marina (550 + 40❶ inc Ⓖ £2.00) ☎ 91453297, www.quaymarinas.com, Wi-fi, P, D, C, CH, BH (40 ton), ME, El, Ⓔ, ✕, Gas, Gaz, Slip, SM, ☲, ◌; **Todd Chart Agency** ☎ 91466640, ACA, CH. **Services:** BY, Diving, Gas, ME, El, ✕. **Town** ☲, R, Bar, ✉, Ⓑ, ⇌, ✈ (Belfast).
CULTRA Royal North of Ireland YC, ☎ 90428041, M, L, AB, FW, Slip, P (½M), D, R, Bar. **Services:** ME, El, ✕; **Town** P, CH, ☲, R, Bar, ✉, Ⓑ, ⇌, ✈.
BELFAST River Manager ☎ 90328507, AB, P, D, FW, ME, El, ✕, CH, C (200 ton), SM, Gas. **City** EC Wed; all facilities, ⇌, ✈. **Ferries:** Stranraer; 6/week; 2½ Hrs; Stena (www.stenaline.co.uk.). Liverpool; 2/day; 10 Hrs; Norfolk Line (www.norfolkline.com).
CARRICKFERGUS Marina (300 inc ❶) ☎ 93366666, www.carrickfergus.org/site/marina; £2.15 (2nd night free), short stay £0.78 (min £5.88), Wi-fi, El, ✕, Rigging, ME, Ⓔ. **Carrick SC** ☎ 351402, M, L, FW, C, AB. **Hbr:** 10 AB, D, BH (45 ton). **Town:** ☲, R, Ⓑ, ✉, ⇌, ✈ (Belfast).

HARBOURS BETWEEN STRANGFORD AND BELFAST LOUGHS
PORTAVOGIE, Down, **54°27′·45N 05°26′·08W**. ⊛⊛❹⚓⚓. AC 2156, 5612. HW +0016 on Dover; ML 2·6m; Duration 0620. See 9.13.9. Good shelter, but hbr so full of FVs as to risk damage; best only for overnight or emergency. Entrance dangerous in strong onshore winds. Beware Plough Rks to SE marked by PHM buoy, Fl (2) R 10s, and McCammon Rks to NE of ent. Keep in W sector of outer bkwtr lt, Iso WRG 5s 9m 9M, shore-G-258°-W-275°-R-348°. Inner bkwtr 2 FG (vert) 6m 4M. VHF Ch 12 14 16 (Mon-Fri: 0900-1700LT). HM ☎ (028) 4277 1470. Facilities: Slip, FW (on central quay) ✕, ME, El. **Town** CH, D & P (cans), ✉, R, Gas, ☲.

DONAGHADEE, Down, **54°38′·71N 05°31′·85W**. ⊛⊛⚓⚓✿✿✿. AC 1753, 3709, 5612. HW +0025 on Dover; see 9.13.10; ML no data; Duration 0615. Excellent shelter and basic facilities in tiny marina, access HW±4 over sill; covers approx 1.1m at half tide. Appr on about 275° on ldg marks, orange △s to tricky ent with sharp 90° port turn into marina (pilots available). Appr in strong winds or at night not advised. 3ca to the N, the Old Hbr is small and very full; scend often sets in. Beware rocky reef with less than 2m extends 1·5ca ENE from S pier hd. Max depth in hbr is approx 2·5m, dries at SW end; best berth alongside SE quay. S pier lt, Iso WR 4s 17m 18/14M, W shore–326°, R326°–shore. HM ☎ (028) 9188 2377. Police 9188 2526. Facilities: **Copelands Marina** ☎ 9188 2184, mobile 07802 363382; VHF Ch **16** 11 80; AB for 6 ❶, D, C (20 ton). **Old Hbr** AB £4. **Town** Bar, D, P, Gas, ✉, R, ☲, Ⓑ, ⇌ (Bangor), ✈ (Belfast).

TIME ZONE (UT)
For Summer Time add ONE
hour in **non-shaded areas**

BELFAST LAT 54°36'N LONG 5°55'W
TIMES AND HEIGHTS OF HIGH AND LOW WATERS

Dates in red are SPRINGS
Dates in blue are NEAPS

YEAR 2010

JANUARY

Time	m	Time	m
1 0453	0.7	**16** 0523	0.9
1106	3.7	1156	3.6
F 1719	0.4	SA 1758	0.7
2334	3.5		
2 0539	0.7	**17** 0013	3.2
1152	3.8	0555	0.8
SA 1805	0.3	SU 1228	3.5
		1828	0.7
3 0024	3.4	**18** 0045	3.1
0625	0.7	0629	0.8
SU 1241	3.9	M 1256	3.5
1851	0.3	1900	0.7
4 0116	3.4	**19** 0116	3.1
0713	0.7	0703	0.8
M 1330	3.9	TU 1325	3.5
1940	0.3	1933	0.7
5 0209	3.3	**20** 0150	3.1
0803	0.7	0739	0.8
TU 1422	3.8	W 1356	3.5
2031	0.4	2008	0.7
6 0304	3.2	**21** 0228	3.1
0856	0.8	0818	0.8
W 1514	3.8	TH 1432	3.4
2126	0.5	2047	0.7
7 0359	3.2	**22** 0309	3.1
0952	0.9	0900	0.9
TH 1609	3.6	F 1513	3.3
☽ 2225	0.7	2131	0.8
8 0456	3.1	**23** 0356	3.1
1055	1.0	0948	1.0
F 1709	3.4	SA 1601	3.2
2330	0.8	☽ 2223	1.0
9 0558	3.0	**24** 0453	3.0
1204	1.1	1044	1.2
SA 1816	3.3	SU 1703	3.1
		2326	1.1
10 0036	1.0	**25** 0559	2.9
0706	3.0	1154	1.2
SU 1314	1.1	M 1821	3.0
1931	3.2		
11 0141	1.0	**26** 0054	1.1
0812	3.1	0706	3.0
M 1422	1.0	TU 1329	1.2
2038	3.2	1936	3.0
12 0240	1.1	**27** 0211	1.0
0910	3.2	0812	3.1
TU 1524	0.9	W 1440	0.9
2134	3.2	2044	3.1
13 0332	1.0	**28** 0308	0.9
1000	3.4	0911	3.3
W 1614	0.8	TH 1535	0.6
2222	3.2	2143	3.2
14 0414	1.0	**29** 0357	0.7
1043	3.5	1002	3.5
TH 1655	0.7	F 1623	0.4
2303	3.2	2233	3.3
15 0450	0.9	**30** 0442	0.6
1121	3.5	1050	3.7
F 1728	0.7	SA 1708	0.2
● 2340	3.2	○ 2321	3.4
		31 0526	0.5
		1136	3.8
		SU 1751	0.1

FEBRUARY

Time	m	Time	m
1 0008	3.4	**16** 0019	3.1
0609	0.5	0604	0.6
M 1224	3.9	TU 1226	3.4
1835	0.1	1831	0.5
2 0057	3.4	**17** 0042	3.1
0654	0.5	0636	0.6
TU 1313	3.9	W 1249	3.4
1919	0.2	1902	0.5
3 0147	3.3	**18** 0111	3.2
0739	0.5	0709	0.6
W 1402	3.8	TH 1321	3.4
2005	0.3	1934	0.6
4 0235	3.3	**19** 0146	3.2
0827	0.6	0745	0.6
TH 1452	3.7	F 1358	3.4
2053	0.5	2011	0.6
5 0324	3.2	**20** 0226	3.2
0919	0.7	0825	0.7
F 1542	3.6	SA 1439	3.3
☽ 2146	0.7	2053	0.7
6 0413	3.1	**21** 0310	3.1
1019	0.8	0911	0.8
SA 1635	3.3	SU 1527	3.2
2249	0.9	2143	0.9
7 0508	3.0	**22** 0404	3.0
1133	1.0	1007	1.0
SU 1737	3.1	M 1630	3.0
		☽ 2246	1.1
8 0003	1.1	**23** 0516	2.9
0621	2.9	1118	1.1
M 1248	1.1	TU 1754	2.8
1904	2.9		
9 0114	1.2	**24** 0024	1.2
0748	2.9	0634	2.9
TU 1401	1.0	W 1314	1.0
2024	2.9	1916	2.8
10 0220	1.1	**25** 0156	1.0
0852	3.1	0748	3.0
W 1508	0.9	TH 1426	0.8
2121	3.0	2031	3.0
11 0316	1.0	**26** 0254	0.8
0943	3.2	0852	3.3
TH 1600	0.7	F 1520	0.5
2207	3.0	2130	3.1
12 0358	0.9	**27** 0343	0.6
1025	3.4	0944	3.5
F 1637	0.6	SA 1607	0.2
2246	3.1	2218	3.3
13 0431	0.8	**28** 0427	0.5
1103	3.4	1032	3.7
SA 1705	0.5	SU 1651	0.1
2321	3.1	○ 2303	3.3
14 0501	0.7		
1137	3.4		
SU 1732	0.5		
● 2352	3.1		
15 0532	0.7		
1205	3.4		
M 1801	0.5		

MARCH

Time	m	Time	m
1 0509	0.4	**16** 0506	0.6
1118	3.8	1134	3.3
M 1732	0.0	TU 1732	0.5
2348	3.4	2346	3.1
2 0550	0.3	**17** 0538	0.6
1204	3.8	1150	3.3
TU 1813	0.1	W 1802	0.5
3 0034	3.4	**18** 0008	3.2
0631	0.3	0609	0.5
W 1252	3.8	TH 1217	3.4
1854	0.2	1832	0.5
4 0120	3.3	**19** 0039	3.2
0714	0.3	0641	0.5
TH 1340	3.7	F 1252	3.4
1936	0.3	1905	0.5
5 0205	3.3	**20** 0115	3.3
0759	0.4	0718	0.5
F 1427	3.6	SA 1332	3.3
2020	0.5	1942	0.6
6 0250	3.3	**21** 0156	3.3
0848	0.6	0759	0.6
SA 1515	3.4	SU 1416	3.2
2108	0.7	2026	0.8
7 0336	3.1	**22** 0241	3.2
0945	0.7	0847	0.7
SU 1605	3.1	M 1508	3.1
☽ 2205	1.0	2118	0.9
8 0426	3.0	**23** 0336	3.0
1102	0.9	0945	0.9
M 1704	2.9	TU 1617	2.9
2324	1.2	☽ 2223	1.1
9 0529	2.9	**24** 0448	2.9
1220	1.0	1101	1.0
TU 1833	2.7	W 1740	2.8
10 0041	1.3	**25** 0004	1.2
0715	2.8	0609	2.9
W 1333	1.0	TH 1256	0.9
2004	2.7	1903	2.8
11 0150	1.2	**26** 0134	1.0
0827	2.9	0727	3.0
TH 1440	0.8	F 1405	0.6
2059	2.8	2018	2.9
12 0249	1.1	**27** 0233	0.8
0917	3.1	0832	3.3
F 1530	0.7	SA 1459	0.3
2143	2.9	2113	3.1
13 0332	0.9	**28** 0323	0.6
0959	3.2	0925	3.5
SA 1605	0.5	SU 1545	0.2
2220	3.0	2159	3.2
14 0404	0.7	**29** 0408	0.4
1036	3.3	1012	3.6
SU 1633	0.5	M 1628	0.1
2253	3.1	2243	3.3
15 0435	0.7	**30** 0450	0.3
1108	3.3	1058	3.7
M 1701	0.5	TU 1708	0.1
● 2323	3.1	○ 2327	3.4
		31 0530	0.3
		1144	3.7
		W 1748	0.2

APRIL

Time	m	Time	m
1 0010	3.4	**16** 0545	0.5
0611	0.3	1151	3.3
TH 1231	3.7	F 1807	0.6
1828	0.3		
2 0054	3.4	**17** 0015	3.4
0653	0.3	0620	0.5
F 1317	3.6	SA 1231	3.3
1909	0.5	1843	0.6
3 0137	3.4	**18** 0055	3.4
0736	0.4	0659	0.4
SA 1403	3.4	SU 1315	3.3
1951	0.6	1924	0.7
4 0220	3.3	**19** 0138	3.4
0823	0.5	0743	0.5
SU 1450	3.2	M 1405	3.2
2037	0.8	2011	0.8
5 0304	3.2	**20** 0227	3.3
0919	0.7	0834	0.6
M 1539	3.0	TU 1503	3.0
2130	1.1	2107	1.0
6 0353	3.1	**21** 0324	3.2
1032	0.9	0936	0.7
TU 1635	2.8	W 1612	2.9
☽ 2241	1.2	☽ 2214	1.1
7 0450	2.9	**22** 0431	3.1
1147	0.9	1056	0.8
W 1745	2.6	TH 1731	2.8
		2341	1.1
8 0001	1.3	**23** 0548	3.1
0603	2.8	1229	0.7
TH 1254	0.9	F 1851	2.8
1926	2.6		
9 0108	1.2	**24** 0102	1.0
0743	2.9	0705	3.2
F 1355	0.8	SA 1337	0.5
2023	2.8	1957	3.0
10 0206	1.1	**25** 0205	0.8
0839	3.0	0810	3.3
SA 1444	0.7	SU 1432	0.3
2107	2.9	2050	3.1
11 0253	0.9	**26** 0258	0.6
0922	3.1	0904	3.5
SU 1523	0.6	M 1520	0.2
2143	3.0	2138	3.3
12 0331	0.8	**27** 0346	0.5
0959	3.2	0953	3.6
M 1557	0.5	TU 1603	0.2
2216	3.1	2222	3.3
13 0406	0.7	**28** 0430	0.4
1030	3.2	1039	3.6
TU 1629	0.5	W 1645	0.3
2246	3.2	○ 2306	3.4
14 0439	0.6	**29** 0513	0.4
1056	3.3	1125	3.6
W 1701	0.5	TH 1726	0.4
● 2313	3.2	2349	3.4
15 0512	0.6	**30** 0556	0.4
1210	3.3	1210	3.5
TH 1733	0.5	F 1806	0.5
2341	3.3		

Chart Datum: 2·01 metres below Ordnance Datum (Belfast). HAT is 3·8 metres above Chart Datum; see 4.5.

TIME ZONE (UT)
For Summer Time add ONE hour in **non-shaded areas**

BELFAST LAT 54°36'N LONG 5°55'W
TIMES AND HEIGHTS OF HIGH AND LOW WATERS

Dates in red are SPRINGS
Dates in blue are NEAPS

YEAR **2010**

MAY

#	Time	m		#	Time	m
1 SA	0030 / 0638 / 1255 / 1847	3.4 / 0.4 / 3.4 / 0.7		**16** SU	0607 / 1218 / 1829	0.5 / 3.3 / 0.7
2 SU	0112 / 0720 / 1340 / 1928	3.4 / 0.5 / 3.3 / 0.7		**17** M	0041 / 0650 / 1306 / 1914	3.5 / 0.4 / 3.3 / 0.7
3 M	0154 / 0805 / 1425 / 2012	3.4 / 0.6 / 3.1 / 0.9		**18** TU	0128 / 0737 / 1359 / 2005	3.5 / 0.4 / 3.2 / 0.8
4 TU	0237 / 0856 / 1513 / 2101	3.3 / 0.7 / 3.0 / 1.1		**19** W	0218 / 0831 / 1459 / 2102	3.5 / 0.5 / 3.1 / 0.9
5 W	0324 / 0957 / 1606 / 2157	3.2 / 0.8 / 2.8 / 1.2		**20** TH	0313 / 0932 / 1606 / 2206	3.4 / 0.5 / 3.0 / 1.0
6 TH	0416 / 1105 / 1704 / 2307	3.1 / 0.9 / 2.7 / 1.2		**21** F	0415 / 1043 / 1718 / 2316	3.3 / 0.6 / 2.9 / 1.0
7 F	0515 / 1209 / 1809	2.9 / 0.9 / 2.7		**22** SA	0525 / 1158 / 1828	3.3 / 0.6 / 2.9
8 SA	0016 / 0621 / 1307 / 1915	1.2 / 2.9 / 0.8 / 2.8		**23** SU	0026 / 0639 / 1305 / 1930	0.9 / 3.3 / 0.5 / 3.0
9 SU	0116 / 0730 / 1357 / 2008	1.2 / 2.9 / 0.8 / 2.9		**24** M	0132 / 0745 / 1402 / 2025	0.8 / 3.3 / 0.5 / 3.1
10 M	0208 / 0826 / 1440 / 2052	1.1 / 3.0 / 0.7 / 3.0		**25** TU	0231 / 0843 / 1454 / 2116	0.7 / 3.4 / 0.5 / 3.2
11 TU	0253 / 0910 / 1520 / 2132	0.9 / 3.1 / 0.6 / 3.2		**26** W	0325 / 0935 / 1541 / 2203	0.6 / 3.5 / 0.5 / 3.3
12 W	0333 / 0948 / 1556 / 2209	0.8 / 3.2 / 0.6 / 3.3		**27** TH	0415 / 1024 / 1626 / 2248	0.6 / 3.5 / 0.5 / 3.4
13 TH	0411 / 1023 / 1632 / 2244	0.7 / 3.3 / 0.6 / 3.3		**28** F	0501 / 1109 / 1708 / 2331	0.5 / 3.4 / 0.6 / 3.4
14 F	0448 / 1057 / 1709 / 2320	0.6 / 3.3 / 0.6 / 3.4		**29** SA	0544 / 1153 / 1749	0.5 / 3.3 / 0.7
15 SA	0527 / 1135 / 1747 / 2358	0.5 / 3.3 / 0.6 / 3.5		**30** SU	0011 / 0626 / 1235 / 1828	3.5 / 0.5 / 3.3 / 0.8
				31 M	0051 / 0706 / 1317 / 1907	3.5 / 0.5 / 3.2 / 0.9

JUNE

#	Time	m		#	Time	m
1 TU	0131 / 0745 / 1400 / 1947	3.5 / 0.6 / 3.1 / 0.9		**16** W	0117 / 0730 / 1351 / 1956	3.7 / 0.3 / 3.2 / 0.7
2 W	0212 / 0826 / 1446 / 2030	3.4 / 0.7 / 3.0 / 1.0		**17** TH	0207 / 0821 / 1449 / 2050	3.6 / 0.3 / 3.1 / 0.8
3 TH	0256 / 0912 / 1535 / 2117	3.3 / 0.7 / 2.9 / 1.0		**18** F	0300 / 0918 / 1551 / 2147	3.6 / 0.4 / 3.1 / 0.8
4 F	0342 / 1004 / 1627 / 2208	3.2 / 0.8 / 2.9 / 1.1		**19** SA	0357 / 1019 / 1654 / 2249	3.5 / 0.5 / 3.0 / 0.8
5 SA	0433 / 1105 / 1720 / 2305	3.1 / 0.9 / 2.9 / 1.2		**20** SU	0459 / 1126 / 1757 / 2354	3.4 / 0.6 / 3.0 / 0.9
6 SU	0528 / 1208 / 1815	3.0 / 0.9 / 2.9		**21** M	0608 / 1232 / 1900	3.3 / 0.6 / 3.0
7 M	0009 / 0626 / 1306 / 1909	1.2 / 3.0 / 0.9 / 3.0		**22** TU	0102 / 0719 / 1335 / 2000	0.9 / 3.3 / 0.7 / 3.1
8 TU	0113 / 0725 / 1357 / 2001	1.1 / 3.0 / 0.8 / 3.0		**23** W	0208 / 0824 / 1432 / 2056	0.8 / 3.3 / 0.7 / 3.2
9 W	0210 / 0821 / 1443 / 2050	1.0 / 3.1 / 0.8 / 3.2		**24** TH	0309 / 0921 / 1524 / 2148	0.7 / 3.3 / 0.7 / 3.3
10 TH	0301 / 0911 / 1527 / 2136	0.9 / 3.2 / 0.7 / 3.3		**25** F	0404 / 1012 / 1611 / 2235	0.7 / 3.3 / 0.7 / 3.4
11 F	0347 / 0957 / 1609 / 2219	0.8 / 3.2 / 0.7 / 3.4		**26** SA	0451 / 1057 / 1653 / 2317	0.6 / 3.3 / 0.8 / 3.4
12 SA	0430 / 1040 / 1650 / 2301	0.6 / 3.3 / 0.6 / 3.5		**27** SU	0533 / 1139 / 1732 / 2355	0.5 / 3.2 / 0.8 / 3.5
13 SU	0513 / 1123 / 1733 / 2344	0.5 / 3.3 / 0.6 / 3.6		**28** M	0611 / 1217 / 1808	0.5 / 3.1 / 0.8
14 M	0557 / 1208 / 1818	0.4 / 3.3 / 0.7		**29** TU	0032 / 0645 / 1254 / 1843	3.5 / 0.6 / 3.1 / 0.8
15 TU	0028 / 0642 / 1258 / 1905	3.6 / 0.3 / 3.3 / 0.7		**30** W	0108 / 0718 / 1333 / 1919	3.5 / 0.6 / 3.1 / 0.9

JULY

#	Time	m		#	Time	m
1 TH	0145 / 0752 / 1415 / 1957	3.4 / 0.6 / 3.0 / 0.9		**16** F	0151 / 0802 / 1430 / 2027	3.8 / 0.2 / 3.2 / 0.6
2 F	0223 / 0829 / 1459 / 2039	3.4 / 0.7 / 3.0 / 0.9		**17** SA	0242 / 0853 / 1524 / 2120	3.7 / 0.3 / 3.2 / 0.7
3 SA	0303 / 0910 / 1546 / 2123	3.3 / 0.7 / 3.0 / 1.0		**18** SU	0335 / 0949 / 1620 / 2219	3.6 / 0.5 / 3.1 / 0.8
4 SU	0345 / 0956 / 1635 / 2212	3.2 / 0.8 / 3.0 / 1.0		**19** M	0432 / 1052 / 1719 / 2326	3.4 / 0.7 / 3.0 / 0.9
5 M	0433 / 1051 / 1727 / 2307	3.1 / 0.9 / 3.0 / 1.1		**20** TU	0536 / 1202 / 1826	3.2 / 0.8 / 3.0
6 TU	0531 / 1157 / 1822	3.0 / 1.0 / 3.0		**21** W	0038 / 0653 / 1311 / 1937	0.9 / 3.1 / 0.9 / 3.0
7 W	0013 / 0635 / 1312 / 1918	1.2 / 2.9 / 1.0 / 3.0		**22** TH	0151 / 0809 / 1415 / 2040	0.9 / 3.0 / 0.9 / 3.1
8 TH	0130 / 0740 / 1413 / 2014	1.1 / 3.0 / 0.9 / 3.1		**23** F	0259 / 0910 / 1511 / 2134	0.8 / 3.1 / 0.9 / 3.3
9 F	0235 / 0841 / 1505 / 2107	1.0 / 3.1 / 0.8 / 3.3		**24** SA	0356 / 1001 / 1558 / 2221	0.7 / 3.1 / 0.9 / 3.4
10 SA	0329 / 0935 / 1551 / 2155	0.8 / 3.2 / 0.7 / 3.4		**25** SU	0442 / 1045 / 1637 / 2302	0.6 / 3.1 / 0.8 / 3.4
11 SU	0416 / 1023 / 1635 / 2241	0.5 / 3.3 / 0.6 / 3.6		**26** M	0519 / 1123 / 1711 / 2339	0.5 / 3.1 / 0.8 / 3.4
12 M	0501 / 1109 / 1719 / 2326	0.4 / 3.3 / 0.6 / 3.7		**27** TU	0549 / 1158 / 1743	0.5 / 3.1 / 0.8
13 TU	0544 / 1155 / 1803	0.2 / 3.3 / 0.6		**28** W	0012 / 0617 / 1230 / 1815	3.4 / 0.6 / 3.1 / 0.8
14 W	0012 / 0628 / 1244 / 1849	3.7 / 0.2 / 3.3 / 0.6		**29** TH	0042 / 0646 / 1302 / 1848	3.4 / 0.6 / 3.1 / 0.8
15 TH	0101 / 0714 / 1335 / 1937	3.8 / 0.2 / 3.3 / 0.6		**30** F	0112 / 0717 / 1337 / 1923	3.4 / 0.6 / 3.1 / 0.8
				31 SA	0143 / 0750 / 1416 / 2001	3.4 / 0.6 / 3.1 / 0.9

AUGUST

#	Time	m		#	Time	m
1 SU	0217 / 0826 / 1457 / 2043	3.3 / 0.7 / 3.1 / 0.8		**16** M	0312 / 0913 / 1545 / 2148	3.6 / 0.6 / 3.2 / 0.8
2 M	0255 / 0908 / 1543 / 2128	3.3 / 0.8 / 3.1 / 0.9		**17** TU	0406 / 1013 / 1641 / 2300	3.3 / 0.8 / 3.1 / 0.9
3 TU	0339 / 0956 / 1635 / 2220	3.1 / 0.9 / 3.0 / 1.1		**18** W	0507 / 1130 / 1748	3.1 / 1.1 / 3.0
4 W	0437 / 1055 / 1736 / 2324	3.0 / 1.0 / 2.9 / 1.2		**19** TH	0018 / 0628 / 1247 / 1913	1.0 / 2.9 / 1.2 / 3.0
5 TH	0553 / 1221 / 1839	2.9 / 1.1 / 3.0		**20** F	0134 / 0756 / 1357 / 2023	1.0 / 2.9 / 1.1 / 3.1
6 F	0056 / 0708 / 1350 / 1942	1.1 / 2.9 / 1.0 / 3.1		**21** SA	0247 / 0858 / 1457 / 2117	0.8 / 2.9 / 1.0 / 3.2
7 SA	0217 / 0817 / 1447 / 2041	0.9 / 3.0 / 0.9 / 3.2		**22** SU	0344 / 0946 / 1543 / 2202	0.7 / 3.0 / 0.9 / 3.4
8 SU	0313 / 0916 / 1535 / 2133	0.7 / 3.1 / 0.7 / 3.4		**23** M	0426 / 1026 / 1617 / 2241	0.6 / 3.1 / 0.9 / 3.4
9 M	0401 / 1006 / 1619 / 2220	0.4 / 3.3 / 0.6 / 3.6		**24** TU	0456 / 1102 / 1646 / 2316	0.5 / 3.1 / 0.8 / 3.4
10 TU	0444 / 1051 / 1701 / 2306	0.2 / 3.3 / 0.5 / 3.7		**25** W	0520 / 1134 / 1715 / 2347	0.6 / 3.1 / 0.8 / 3.4
11 W	0526 / 1137 / 1743 / 2353	0.1 / 3.4 / 0.5 / 3.8		**26** TH	0546 / 1202 / 1746	0.6 / 3.2 / 0.7
12 TH	0608 / 1224 / 1827	0.1 / 3.4 / 0.4		**27** F	0010 / 0614 / 1227 / 1817	3.4 / 0.6 / 3.2 / 0.7
13 F	0041 / 0650 / 1313 / 1912	3.8 / 0.1 / 3.3 / 0.5		**28** SA	0033 / 0643 / 1256 / 1850	3.4 / 0.6 / 3.2 / 0.7
14 SA	0131 / 0735 / 1404 / 1959	3.7 / 0.2 / 3.3 / 0.5		**29** SU	0103 / 0714 / 1331 / 1926	3.4 / 0.6 / 3.2 / 0.7
15 SU	0221 / 0826 / 1454 / 2050	3.7 / 0.4 / 3.3 / 0.6		**30** M	0138 / 0748 / 1410 / 2006	3.4 / 0.7 / 3.2 / 0.8
				31 TU	0217 / 0829 / 1453 / 2051	3.3 / 0.8 / 3.2 / 0.9

Chart Datum: 2·01 metres below Ordnance Datum (Belfast). HAT is 3·8 metres above Chart Datum; see 4.5.

N Ireland

TIME ZONE (UT)
For Summer Time add ONE hour in **non-shaded areas**

BELFAST LAT 54°36'N LONG 5°55'W
TIMES AND HEIGHTS OF HIGH AND LOW WATERS

Dates in red are SPRINGS
Dates in blue are NEAPS

YEAR 2010

SEPTEMBER

Time	m	Time	m
1 0302	3.2	**16** 0440	3.0
0917	0.9	1054	1.2
W 1546	3.1	TH 1709	3.0
☽ 2144	1.0	2354	1.1
2 0400	3.0	**17** 0602	2.8
1015	1.1	1217	1.3
TH 1654	3.0	F 1841	3.0
2249	1.1		
3 0523	2.8	**18** 0109	1.0
1134	1.2	0737	2.8
F 1806	3.0	SA 1329	1.3
		1958	3.1
4 0029	1.1	**19** 0221	0.9
0643	2.8	0836	2.9
SA 1328	1.2	SU 1431	1.2
1915	3.1	2052	3.2
5 0157	0.9	**20** 0317	0.7
0758	2.9	0922	3.0
SU 1427	0.9	M 1517	1.0
2018	3.3	2136	3.3
6 0253	0.6	**21** 0355	0.7
0859	3.1	1000	3.1
M 1516	0.7	TU 1549	0.9
2112	3.5	2214	3.4
7 0341	0.3	**22** 0421	0.6
0948	3.3	1034	3.2
TU 1559	0.6	W 1618	0.8
2159	3.7	2248	3.4
8 0423	0.2	**23** 0446	0.6
1032	3.4	1105	3.2
W 1640	0.6	TH 1648	0.8
● 2245	3.8	○ 2316	3.4
9 0503	0.1	**24** 0514	0.6
1116	3.4	1131	3.3
TH 1720	0.4	F 1718	0.7
2332	3.9	2335	3.4
10 0543	0.1	**25** 0543	0.7
1202	3.5	1154	3.3
F 1802	0.4	SA 1750	0.7
		2357	3.4
11 0021	3.8	**26** 0612	0.7
0624	0.2	1222	3.4
SA 1249	3.4	SU 1822	0.7
1846	0.4		
12 0110	3.8	**27** 0030	3.4
0707	0.3	0643	0.7
SU 1337	3.4	M 1258	3.4
1932	0.5	1857	0.7
13 0200	3.7	**28** 0109	3.4
0752	0.5	0718	0.8
M 1425	3.4	TU 1337	3.4
2022	0.6	1938	0.8
14 0250	3.5	**29** 0152	3.3
0840	0.8	0800	0.9
TU 1514	3.3	W 1422	3.3
2120	0.8	2024	0.9
15 0342	3.2	**30** 0240	3.2
0936	1.0	0849	1.0
W 1606	3.2	TH 1514	3.2
☽ 2234	0.9	2119	1.0

OCTOBER

Time	m	Time	m
1 0343	3.0	**16** 0524	2.8
0950	1.2	1137	1.4
F 1621	3.1	SA 1745	3.0
☽ 2227	1.1		
2 0504	2.8	**17** 0031	1.1
1109	1.3	0658	2.8
SA 1737	3.1	SU 1247	1.4
		1914	3.1
3 0004	1.0	**18** 0135	1.0
0624	2.9	0800	2.9
SU 1259	1.2	M 1347	1.3
1850	3.2	2015	3.2
4 0131	0.8	**19** 0228	0.9
0740	3.0	0847	3.0
M 1402	1.0	TU 1436	1.2
1956	3.4	2101	3.3
5 0227	0.6	**20** 0309	0.8
0839	3.2	0925	3.2
TU 1452	0.8	W 1514	1.0
2051	3.6	2140	3.3
6 0314	0.4	**21** 0341	0.7
0928	3.4	1000	3.3
W 1536	0.6	TH 1548	0.9
2140	3.7	2215	3.4
7 0357	0.3	**22** 0412	0.7
1012	3.5	1101	3.4
TH 1618	0.5	F 1620	0.9
● 2227	3.8	2244	3.4
8 0437	0.2	**23** 0443	0.7
1056	3.5	1101	3.4
F 1659	0.5	SA 1653	0.8
2314	3.9	○ 2308	3.4
9 0518	0.3	**24** 0515	0.8
1140	3.6	1128	3.5
SA 1741	0.5	SU 1727	0.8
		2334	3.4
10 0001	3.8	**25** 0547	0.8
0559	0.4	1159	3.5
SU 1226	3.6	M 1801	0.7
1825	0.5		
11 0050	3.7	**26** 0009	3.4
0642	0.6	0621	0.9
M 1312	3.6	TU 1236	3.6
1911	0.6	1838	0.7
12 0139	3.6	**27** 0051	3.4
0726	0.8	0659	0.9
TU 1358	3.5	W 1318	3.5
2001	0.7	1920	0.8
13 0228	3.4	**28** 0138	3.3
0814	1.0	0743	1.0
W 1445	3.4	TH 1404	3.5
2057	0.8	2009	0.8
14 0319	3.2	**29** 0230	3.2
0907	1.2	0835	1.1
TH 1536	3.3	F 1457	3.4
☽ 2208	1.0	2105	0.9
15 0415	3.0	**30** 0333	3.1
1015	1.4	0936	1.2
F 1633	3.1	SA 1559	3.3
2323	1.1	☽ 2213	1.0
		31 0447	3.0
		1052	1.3
		SU 1710	3.2
		2336	0.9

NOVEMBER

Time	m	Time	m
1 0606	3.0	**16** 0043	1.1
1218	1.2	0653	2.9
M 1825	3.3	TU 1255	1.4
		1910	3.1
2 0054	0.8	**17** 0136	1.0
0717	3.1	0751	3.0
TU 1327	1.1	W 1349	1.3
1932	3.4	2010	3.2
3 0154	0.6	**18** 0222	1.0
0816	3.2	0838	3.2
W 1423	0.9	TH 1436	1.2
2030	3.6	2057	3.3
4 0245	0.5	**19** 0303	0.9
0907	3.4	0920	3.3
TH 1512	0.7	F 1517	1.0
2122	3.7	2138	3.3
5 0331	0.5	**20** 0340	0.9
0953	3.5	0959	3.4
F 1559	0.6	SA 1555	0.9
2211	3.8	2215	3.4
6 0415	0.5	**21** 0416	0.8
1038	3.6	1035	3.5
SA 1643	0.6	SU 1633	0.9
● 2258	3.8	○ 2248	3.4
7 0458	0.6	**22** 0452	0.8
1122	3.7	1109	3.6
SU 1728	0.6	M 1710	0.9
2345	3.7	2320	3.4
8 0540	0.7	**23** 0529	0.8
1207	3.7	1143	3.7
M 1813	0.6	TU 1749	0.7
		2358	3.4
9 0032	3.6	**24** 0608	0.9
0622	0.8	1221	3.7
TU 1251	3.7	W 1829	0.7
1858	0.6		
10 0119	3.5	**25** 0040	3.4
0706	0.9	0649	0.9
W 1335	3.6	TH 1304	3.7
1945	0.7	1913	0.7
11 0206	3.3	**26** 0128	3.3
0751	1.1	0736	1.0
TH 1420	3.6	F 1351	3.7
2036	0.8	2001	0.7
12 0255	3.2	**27** 0221	3.2
0840	1.2	0827	1.0
F 1508	3.4	SA 1442	3.6
2135	0.9	2056	0.7
13 0347	3.0	**28** 0320	3.1
0936	1.3	0925	1.1
SA 1600	3.3	SU 1539	3.5
☽ 2240	1.0	☽ 2159	0.8
14 0443	2.9	**29** 0428	3.1
1042	1.4	1031	1.2
SU 1657	3.2	M 1644	3.4
2344	1.1	2308	0.8
15 0546	2.9	**30** 0541	3.1
1152	1.4	1142	1.2
M 1802	3.1	TU 1755	3.4

DECEMBER

Time	m	Time	m
1 0018	0.8	**16** 0041	1.1
0650	3.1	0648	3.0
W 1252	1.1	TH 1255	1.3
1906	3.5	1907	3.1
2 0122	0.7	**17** 0137	1.1
0751	3.2	0746	3.1
TH 1355	1.0	F 1355	1.3
2010	3.5	2008	3.1
3 0219	0.7	**18** 0227	1.0
0847	3.4	0840	3.3
F 1452	0.9	SA 1448	1.1
2106	3.6	2103	3.2
4 0311	0.7	**19** 0313	0.9
0937	3.5	0928	3.4
SA 1545	0.7	SU 1534	1.0
2159	3.6	2149	3.3
5 0359	0.7	**20** 0355	0.9
1025	3.6	1011	3.5
SU 1634	0.7	M 1617	0.8
● 2247	3.6	2230	3.4
6 0444	0.8	**21** 0436	0.8
1110	3.7	1050	3.6
M 1720	0.6	TU 1658	0.7
2333	3.5	○ 2309	3.4
7 0527	0.8	**22** 0516	0.8
1153	3.7	1128	3.7
TU 1805	0.6	W 1738	0.6
		2348	3.4
8 0018	3.5	**23** 0557	0.8
0608	0.9	1207	3.8
W 1235	3.7	TH 1820	0.5
1847	0.6		
9 0101	3.4	**24** 0030	3.4
0649	1.0	0640	0.8
TH 1316	3.7	F 1251	3.8
1928	0.7	1904	0.5
10 0144	3.3	**25** 0117	3.3
0729	1.1	0725	0.8
F 1358	3.6	SA 1337	3.8
2010	0.8	1951	0.5
11 0229	3.2	**26** 0208	3.3
0811	1.2	0814	0.8
SA 1441	3.5	SU 1427	3.7
2053	0.9	2041	0.5
12 0316	3.1	**27** 0303	3.2
0856	1.2	0907	0.9
SU 1527	3.4	M 1520	3.7
2142	0.9	2137	0.6
13 0405	3.0	**28** 0402	3.2
0945	1.2	1005	1.0
M 1616	3.3	TU 1619	3.6
☽ 2237	1.0	☽ 2238	0.7
14 0457	3.0	**29** 0507	3.1
1046	1.3	1110	1.0
TU 1710	3.2	W 1724	3.4
2340	1.1	2346	0.8
15 0552	3.0	**30** 0616	3.1
1146	1.4	1222	1.1
W 1807	3.1	TH 1838	3.4
		31 0054	0.9
		0726	3.1
		F 1333	1.0
		1951	3.3

Chart Datum: 2·01 metres below Ordnance Datum (Belfast). HAT is 3·8 metres above Chart Datum; see 4.5.

9.13.11 LARNE

Antrim 54°51'·20N 05°47'·50W ✿✿✿⚓⚓✿✿

CHARTS AC 2198, 1237, 5612; Imray C62, C64.

TIDES +0005 Dover; ML 1·6; Duration 0620

Standard Port BELFAST (◀—)

Times				Height (metres)			
High Water		Low Water		MHWS	MHWN	MLWN	MLWS
0100	0700	0000	0600	3·5	3·0	1·1	0·4
1300	1900	1200	1800				
Differences LARNE							
+0005	0000	+0010	−0005	−0·7	−0·5	−0·3	0·0
RED BAY							
+0022	−0010	+0007	−0017	−1·9	−1·5	−0·8	−0·2
CUSHENDUN BAY							
+0010	−0030	0000	−0025	−1·7	−1·5	−0·6	−0·2

SHELTER Secure shelter in Larne Lough or ⚓ overnight outside hbr in Brown's Bay (E of Barr Pt) in 2-4m. Hbr can be entered H24 in any conditions. Larne is a busy commercial and ferry port; W side is commercial until Curran Pt where there are two YCs with congested moorings. ⚓ S of Ballylumford Power Stn. No AB available for visitors. Yachts should not berth on any commercial quays, inc Castle Quay, without HM's permission. Boat Hbr (0·6m) 2ca S of Ferris Pt only for shoal draft craft.

NAVIGATION WPT 54°51'·70N 05°47'·47W, 184°/2·1M to front ldg lt. Beware Hunter Rk 2M NE of hbr ent. Magnetic anomalies exist near Hunter Rk and between it and the mainland. Inside the narrow ent, the recommended chan is close to the E shore. Tide in the ent runs at up to 3½kn.

LIGHTS AND MARKS No1 SHM Q G 1½ca off chartlet N edge; Ldg lts 184°, Oc 4s 6/14m 12M, synch and vis 179°-189°; W ◇ with R stripes. Chaine Tr and fairway lts as chartlet. Note: Many shore lts on W side of ent may be mistaken for nav lts.

R/T VHF Ch **14** 11 16 *Larne Port Control*. Traffic, weather and tidal info available on Ch 14.

TELEPHONE (Code 02828) HM 872100; MRCC 9146 3933; Pilot 273785; Marinecall 09068 969655; Dr 275331; Police 272266.

FACILITIES **Pier** ☎ 27 9221, M, L, FW, C (33 ton); **E Antrim Boat Club** ☎ 277204, Visitors should pre-contact Sec'y for advice on moorings; Slip, L, 🚻, FW, Bar; **Services:** D, Gas, ⚒, El. **Town** P & D (delivered, tidal), CH, 🛒, R, Bar, ✉, Ⓑ, ⇌, **Ferries:** Cairnryan; 8/day; 1¾ Hrs; P&O (www.poferries.co.uk). Fleetwood; 20/week; 9 Hrs; Stena (www.srenaline.co.uk). Troon; 17/week; 1¾ Hrs; P&O. ✈ (Belfast City and Belfast/Aldergrove).

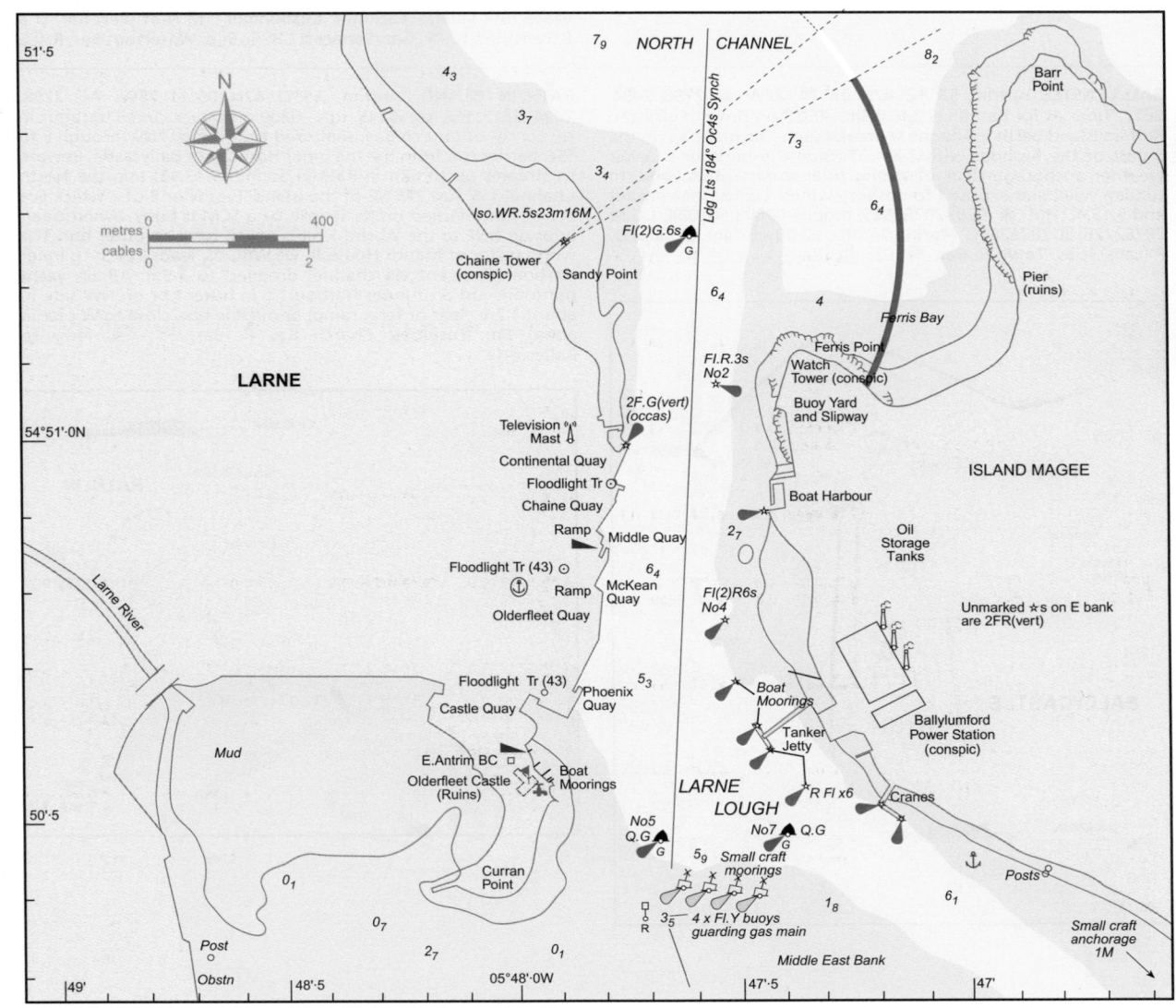

HARBOURS & ANCHORAGES BETWEEN LARNE & PORTRUSH

GLENARM

GLENARM, Antrim, **54°58′N 05°57′W**. AC 2198, 2199, 5612. HW +0006 on Dover, +0005 on Belfast; HW −1·6m on Belfast; ML no data; Duration 0625. Good shelter in marina. Hbr ent lts Q.G.3s3M and Q.R.3s3M. HM and Marina ☎ 028 2884 1285, Mob 07703 606763. **Marina** 40 AB inc Ⓥ in 4-6m, £1.00, FW, D, ⤵. **Village** 🛒, P (cans).

CARNLOUGH HARBOUR, Antrim, **54°59′·87N 05°59′·20W**. AC 2198, 5612. HW +0006 on Dover, +0005 on Belfast; HW −1·6m on Belfast; ML no data; Duration 0625. Good shelter, except in SE gales; do not enter in fresh/strong onshore winds. Entrance shoaling due to build up of kelp, minimum depth 1m (2004). Ldg marks 310°, Y ▽s on B/W posts. N pier lt, Fl G 3s 4m 5M; S pier Fl R 3s 6m 5M, both lts on B/W columns. Beware fish farms in the bay marked by lt buoys (unreliable); and rks which cover at HW on either side of ent. Small harbour used by yachts and small FVs; visitors welcome. HM ☎ (Mobile) 07703 606763. Facilities: **Quay** AB £1, AC (see HM), D (by arrangement), FW, Slip. **Town** P (cans), Gas, Gaz, ✉, R, 🛒, Bar, ♿.

RED BAY, Antrim, **55°03′·91N 06°03′·13W**. AC 2199, 5612. HW +0010 on Dover; ML 1·1m; Duration 0625. See 9.13.11. Good holding, but open to E winds. Beware rks, 2 ruined piers W of Garron Pt and fish farms, marked by lt buoys, on S side of bay, approx ½M from shore. Glenariff pier has lt Fl 3s 10m 5M. In S and E winds ⚓ 2ca off W stone arch near hd of bay in approx 3·5m; in N or W winds ⚓ S of small pier in 2–5m, ½M NE of Waterfoot village. **Facilities: Cushendall** (1M N of pier) Bar, D & P (cans), ✉, R, 🛒, Gas. **Services:** CH, El, Slip. **Waterfoot** Bar, R, ✉.

BALLYCASTLE, Antrim, **55°12′·47N 06°14′·27W**. AC 2798, 2494, 5612. Tides as for Rathlin Is; ML 0·8m; −0320 on Dover. Ferries to Rathlin Island berth inside the N breakwater. The marina is in the S part of the harbour with 2·3m. Outside the harbour is a fair weather anchorage clear of strong tidal streams, but liable to sudden swell and exposed to onshore winds. Lights: see chartlet and 9.13.4. HM ☎ (028) 20768525, mobile 07803 505084; CG ☎ 20762226; Ⓗ 20762666. **Marina** 74 AB , £2·00 <9·14m. El, Slip, D, P (cans), Gas. **Town** R, Bar, 🛒, ✉, Ⓑ, ♿.

RATHLIN ISLAND, Antrim, **55°17′·47N 06°11′·78W**. AC 2798, 2494, 5612. HW sp −0445, nps −0200 on Dover. Small harbour in NE corner of Church Bay, sheltered from winds NW through E to SSE. Ferries run from the the Inner Harbour to Ballycastle. Beware sp streams up to 6kn in Rathlin Sound (9.13.12) and the North Channel TSS, just 2M NE of the island. Pass N or E of a wreck 6ca SW of hbr, marked on its SE side by a SCM lt buoy. When clear, appr on NNE to the W and S piers which form an outer hbr. The white sector of Manor House lt, Oc WRG 4s, leads 024·5° to Inner Harbour (2m) ent via channel dredged to 3·5m. AB on yacht pontoons just S of Inner Harbour. ⚓ in outer hbr on NW side in about 1.2m clear of ferry ramp; or outside hbr, close to W pier in about 5m. **Facilities**: Church Bay R, Bar, 🛒, ✉, ferry to Ballycastle.

BALLYCASTLE

RATHLIN

9.13.12 TIDAL STREAMS AROUND RATHLIN ISLAND

North Ireland 9.13.3   Off Mull of Kintyre 9.9.10   South Ireland 9.12.3
North Irish Sea 9.10.3   SW Scotland 9.9.3

5 Hours before HW Dover (0605 after HW Greenock)

3 Hours before HW Dover (0420 before HW Greenock)

1½ Hours before HW Dover (0250 before HW Greenock)

HW Dover (0120 before HW Greenock)

1 Hour after HW Dover (0020 before HW Greenock)

2 Hours after HW Dover (0040 after HW Greenock)

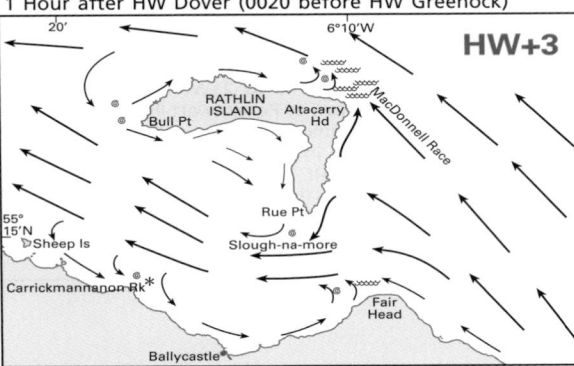

3 Hours after HW Dover (0140 after HW Greenock)

6 Hours after HW Dover (0440 after HW Greenock)

N Ireland

FAIR HEAD TO BLOODY FORELAND

(AC 2723, 5612) This is a good cruising area, under the lee of land in SW'lies, but very exposed to NW or N. Beware fishing boats and nets in many places and the North Channel TSS.

▶ *A fair tide is essential through Rathlin Sound, as sp rates reach 6kn, with dangerous overfalls. The main stream sets W from HW Dover +0030 for 5 hrs, and E from HW Dover −0530 for 5 hrs. The worst overfalls are S of Rue Pt (Slough-na-more) from HW Dover +0130 to +0230, and it is best to enter W-bound at the end of this period, on the last of fair tide. E-bound enter the Sound at HW Dover −0500. Close inshore between Fair Hd and Carrickmannanon Rk a counter eddy runs W from HW Dover −0030, and an E-going eddy runs from HW Dover +0200 to +0300.* ◀ Pass outside Carrickmannanon Rk (0·3m) and Sheep Is. There are small hbrs in Church Bay (Rathlin Is) and at Ballycastle.

Proceeding to Portrush, use Skerries Sound in good weather. ▶ *Enter Lough Foyle by either the North Chan W of The Tuns, or S chan passing 2ca N of Magilligan Pt and allowing for set towards The Tuns on the ebb (up to 3·5kn).* ◀

Tor Rks, Inishtrahull and Garvan Is lie NE and E of Malin Hd. In bad weather it is best to pass at least 3M N of Tor Rks. Inishtrahull is lit and about 1M long; rks extend N about 3ca into Tor Sound. ▶ *Inishtrahull Sound, between Inishtrahull and Garvan Is, is exposed; tidal streams up to 4kn sp can raise a dangerous sea with no warning. Stream also sets hard through Garvan Isles, S of which Garvan Sound can be passed safely in daylight avoiding two sunken rks, one 1½ca NE of Rossnabarton, and*

the other 5ca NW. The main stream runs W for only 3 hrs, from HW Galway −0500 to −0200. W of Malin Hd a W-going eddy starts at HW Galway +0400, and an E-going one at HW Galway −0300. ◀

W of Malin Hd the direction of buoyage changes to E. From Malin Hd SW to Dunaff Hd, at ent to Lough Swilly, keep 5ca offshore. Trawbreaga Lough (AC 2697) gives shelter, but is shallow, and sea can break on bar; only approach when no swell, and at half flood. Ent to L Swilly is clear except for Swilly Rks off the W shore, SSE of Fanad Hd.

W from Lough Swilly the coast is very foul. Beware Limeburner Rk (2m), 6·8M WNW of Fanad Hd. Mulroy Bay has good ⚓s but needs accurate pilotage (see ICC SDs).

Between Mulroy B and Sheephaven there is an inshore passage S of Frenchman's Rk, and between Guill Rks & Carnabollion, safe in good weather; otherwise keep 1M offshore. Sheep Haven B is easy to enter between Rinnafaghla Pt and Horn Hd, and has good ⚓s except in strong NW or N winds. Beware Wherryman Rks, dry 1·5m, 1ca off E shore.

Between Horn Hd and Bloody Foreland (AC 2752) are three low-lying islands: Inishbeg, Inishdooey and Inishbofin. The latter is almost part of the mainland; it has a temp anch on S side and a more sheltered ⚓ on NE side in Toberglassan B. 6M offshore is Tory Is (lt, fog sig, RC) with rks for 5ca off SW side. Temp anch in good weather in Camusmore B. ▶ *In Tory Sound the stream runs W from HW Galway +0230, and E from HW Galway −0530, sp rates 2kn.* ◀

9.13.13 PORTRUSH

Antrim **55°12'·34N 06°39'·49W** ❄❄⚓⚓☆☆☆

CHARTS AC 2798, 2499, 49, 5612; Imray C53, C64.

TIDES −0400 Dover; ML 1·1; Duration 0610

Standard Port BELFAST (◀—)

Times				Height (metres)			
High Water		Low Water		MHWS	MHWN	MLWN	MLWS
0100	0700	0000	0600	3·5	3·0	1·1	0·4
1300	1900	1200	1800				
Differences PORTRUSH							
−0433		−0433		−1·6	−1·6	−0·3	0·0

SHELTER Good in hbr, except in strong NW/N winds. Berth on N pier or on pontoon at NE end of it and see HM. A 🛟 may be available, but very congested in season. ⚓ on E side of Ramore Hd in Skerries Roads 1ca S of Large Skerrie gives good shelter in most conditions, but open to NW sea/swell.

NAVIGATION WPT 55°13'·00N 06°41'·00W, 128° to N pier lt, 1·1M.

Ent with onshore winds >F 4 is difficult. Beware submerged bkwtr projecting 20m SW from N pier. Depth is 2·8m in hbr entrance.

LIGHTS AND MARKS Ldg lts 028° (occas, for LB use) both FR 6/8m 1M; R △ on metal bn and metal mast. N pier Fl R 3s 6m 3M; vis 220°-160°. S pier Fl G 3s 6m 3M; vis 220°-100°.

R/T VHF Ch 12 16 (0900-1700LT, Mon-Fri; extended evening hrs June-Sept; Sat-Sun: 0900-1700, June-Sept only).

TELEPHONE (Code 028) HM 7082 2307; MRCC 9146 3933; Marinecall 09068 969655; Police 7034 4122; Dr 7082 3767; Ⓗ 7034 4177.

FACILITIES Hbr AB £14, D(0900-1800), FW, M, Slip (launching £3), Gas, El, Ⓔ, ⛽; Portrush YC ☎ 7082 3932, Bar; **Town** @ Libray, 🛒, R, Bar, Ⓞ, D & P (cans), ✉, Ⓑ, ⇌, ✈ (Belfast). Giant's Causeway is 10M ENE.

Portstewart, Antrim, **55°11'·21N 06°43'·21W**. AC 49, 5612. Tides as for Portrush. A tiny hbr 1·1ca S of Portstewart Pt lt, Oc R 10s 21m 5M, vis 040°–220°, obscd in final appr. A temp, fair weather berth (£10) at S end of inner basin in 0·8–1·7m; the very narrow ent is open to SW wind and swell. Visitors should obtain fuel at Portrush before proceeding to Portstewart. Beware rocks close to S bkwtr.

Facilities: @ Library, FW, Gas, Slip, Bar, 🛒, R.

9.13.14 RIVER BANN and COLERAINE

Londonderry/Antrim 55°10'·32N 06°46'·35W ✿✿✿♨♨✿✿

CHARTS AC 2723, 2798, 2494, 5612; Imray C64.

TIDES −0345 Dover (Coleraine); ML 1·1; Duration 0540

Standard Port BELFAST (←—)

Times				Height (metres)			
High Water		Low Water		MHWS	MHWN	MLWN	MLWS
0100	0700	0000	0600	3·5	3·0	1·1	0·4
1300	1900	1200	1800				
Differences COLERAINE							
−0403		−0403		−1·3	−1·2	−0·2	0·0

SHELTER Good, once inside the river ent (The Barmouth) between 2 training walls, extending 2ca N from the beaches. Do not try to enter in strong on-shore winds or when swell breaks on the pierheads. If in doubt call Coleraine Hbr Radio or ring HM. ‡ upstream of old CG stn, or berth at Seaton's or Coleraine marinas, 3½M & 4½M from ent, on NE bank.

NAVIGATION WPT 55°11'·00N, 06°46'·65W, 165°/0·72M to ent.

Appr from E of N to bring ldg lts into line at bkwtr ends. The sand bar is constantly moving but ent is dredged to approx 3·5m. Beware commercial traffic.

LIGHTS AND MARKS Ldg lts 165°, both Oc 5s 6/14m 2M, front on W pyramidal metal tr; rear W ☐ tr. Portstewart Pt, Oc R 10s, is 2M ENE.

R/T Coleraine Hbr Radio Ch 12 (Mon-Fri: HO and when vessel due). Coleraine Marina Ch M.

TELEPHONE (Code 028) HM 70342012; MRCC 91463933; Marinecall 09068 969655; Rly Bridge 70325400; Police 70344122; ⊞ 70344177; Dr 70344831.

FACILITIES Seatons Marina ☎ 70832086, mobile 07733100915, BH (14 ton), Slip (£3), D. Coleraine Hbr ☎ 7034 2012, BH (35 ton); Coleraine Marina (90+5♥), ☎ 70344768, £20, ME, ⟊ (by arrangement), ✕, 🛒, Slip, D(H24), R, BH (12.5 ton); Coleraine YC ☎ 70344503, Bar, M; Services: Gas, Kos, El, Ⓔ. Town P & D (cans), 🛒, R, ✉, Ⓑ, ≈, ✈ (Belfast).

9.13.15 LOUGH FOYLE

Londonderry/Donegal 55°14'N 06°54W ❄❄❄❄❄⚓⚓

CHARTS AC 2723, 2798, 2511, 2510, 5612; Imray C53, C64.

TIDES
Warren Point: –0430 Dover
Moville: –0350 Dover
Londonderry: –0255 Dover
ML 1·6; Duration 0615

Standard Port RIVER FOYLE (LISAHALLY) (⟶)

Times				Height (metres)			
High Water		Low Water		MHWS	MHWN	MLWN	MLWS
0100	0800	0200	0700	2·6	1·9	0·9	0·4
1300	2000	1400	1900				
Differences WARREN LIGHTHOUSE							
–0055	–0115	–0155	–0117	–0·3	0·0	No data	
MOVILLE							
–0042	–0057	–0127	–0058	–0·3	0·0	+0·1	0·0
QUIGLEY'S POINT							
–0020	–0027	–0040	–0027	–0·3	–0·1	0·0	–0·1
LONDONDERRY							
+0033	+0035	+0032	+0032	+0·1	+0·2	+0·3	+0·2

SHELTER The SE side of the Lough is low lying and shallow. The NW rises steeply and has several village hbrs between the ent and Londonderry (often referred to as Derry).

White Bay: close N of Dunagree Point is a good ⚓ in settled weather on passage.

Greencastle: a busy fishing hbr, open to swell in winds SW to E. Works in progress (2008). Only advised for yachts in emergency.

Moville: the pier, with 1·5m at the end, is near the village (shops closed all day Wed), but is much used by FVs. ⚓ outside hbr is exposed; inside hbr for shoal draft only. 8 Y ⚓s are about 600m up-stream.

Carrickarory: pier/quay is used entirely by FVs. ⚓ in bay is sheltered in winds from SW to NNW. Plans for possible new marina.

Culmore Bay: good shelter. ⚓ 1½ca W of Culmore Pt in pleasant cove, 4M from Londonderry.

Londonderry, Foyle Pontoon: AB, £12–£17/night, adjacent to the centre of historic city or ⚓ close below Craigavon Bridge clearance 1·7m. Commercial operations are now at Lisahally (55°02'·6N 07°15'·6W).

NAVIGATION WPT Tuns PHM buoy, Fl R 3s, 55°14'·00N 06°53'·49W, 235°/2·5M to Warren Pt lt, 2·5M. The Tuns bank lies 3M NE of Magilligan Pt and may dry. The main or N Chan, ¾M wide, runs NW of The Tuns; a lesser chan, min depth 4m, runs 3ca off shore around NE side of Magilligan Pt. Beware commercial traffic. Foyle Bridge at Rosses Pt has 31m clearance. In June and July the chan is at times obstructed by salmon nets at night. N Chan tides reach 3½kn, and up-river the ebb runs up to 6kn.

LIGHTS AND MARKS Inishowen Fl (2) WRG 10s 28m 18/14M; W tr, 2 B bands; vis G197°–211°, W211°–249°, R249°–000°. Warren Pt Fl 1·5s 9m 10M; W tr, G abutment; vis 232°–061°. Magilligan Pt QR 7m 4M; R structure. The main chan up to Londonderry is very well lit. Foyle Bridge centre FW each side; VQ G on W pier; VQ R on E.

R/T VHF Ch 14 12 16 (H24). Traffic and nav info Ch 14.

TELEPHONE (Code 028) HM (at Lisahally) 7186 0555; MRCC 9146 3933; ☎ 7126 1937 or 9035 8250; Marinecall 09068 969655; Police 7776 6797; Dr 7126 4868; Ⓗ 7034 5171.

FACILITIES Londonderry ☎ 7186 0313 or Ch 14 for Foyle Pontoon, £1·39, M, FW; Prehen Boat Club ☎ 7034 3405. City P & D (cans), ME, El, ⚒, R, Bar, ✉, Ⓑ, ⇌, ✈. Culdaff Bay (10M W of Foyle SWM buoy) 6 Y ⚓s at 55°18'N 07°09'·1W, off Bunnagee Port.

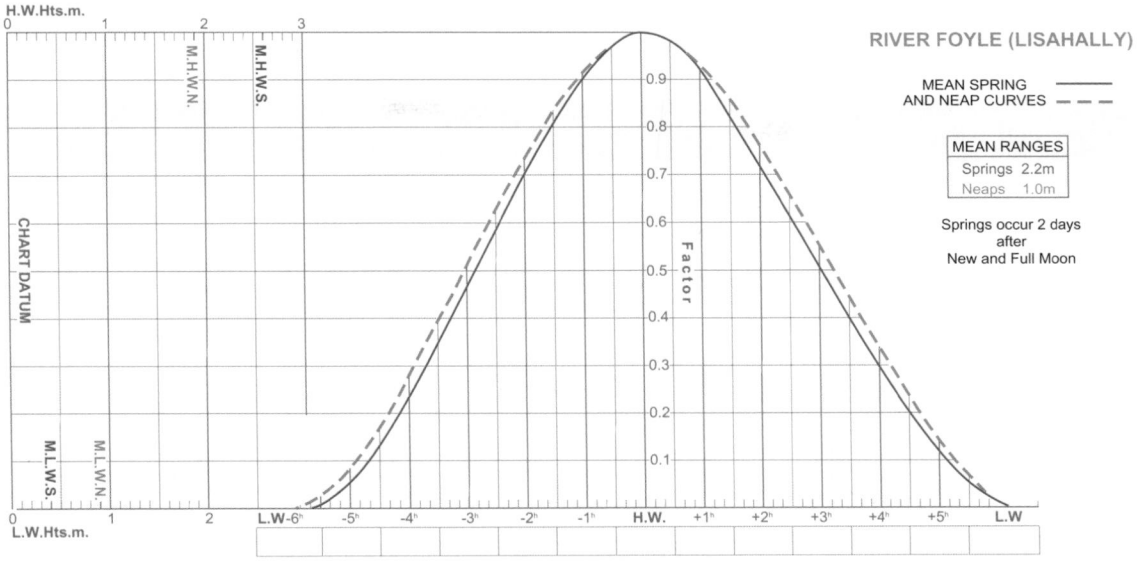

RIVER FOYLE (LISAHALLY)

MEAN SPRING ——
AND NEAP CURVES – – –

MEAN RANGES
Springs 2.2m
Neaps   1.0m

Springs occur 2 days
after
New and Full Moon

N Ireland

TIME ZONE (UT)
For Summer Time add ONE hour in **non-shaded areas**

RIVER FOYLE   LAT 55°03'N   LONG 7°16'W
TIMES AND HEIGHTS OF HIGH AND LOW WATERS

Dates in red are SPRINGS
Dates in blue are NEAPS

YEAR 2010

JANUARY

Time	m	Time	m
1 0140 / 0744 / F 1428 / 2012	0.5 / 2.9 / 0.5 / 2.7	**16** 0220 / 0814 / SA 1440 / 2032	0.5 / 2.7 / 0.7 / 2.3
2 0225 / 0828 / SA 1518 / 2059	0.4 / 3.0 / 0.5 / 2.7	**17** 0252 / 0845 / SU 1511 / 2059	0.5 / 2.7 / 0.7 / 2.3
3 0309 / 0912 / SU 1606 / 2144	0.3 / 3.0 / 0.5 / 2.6	**18** 0322 / 0917 / M 1542 / 2129	0.5 / 2.6 / 0.7 / 2.3
4 0351 / 0958 / M 1652 / 2229	0.3 / 2.9 / 0.5 / 2.5	**19** 0350 / 0951 / TU 1614 / 2202	0.6 / 2.5 / 0.7 / 2.2
5 0433 / 1045 / TU 1740 / 2315	0.4 / 2.8 / 0.6 / 2.3	**20** 0422 / 1027 / W 1651 / 2236	0.6 / 2.4 / 0.7 / 2.1
6 0515 / 1137 / W 1831	0.5 / 2.6 / 0.8	**21** 0457 / 1106 / TH 1732 / 2315	0.7 / 2.3 / 0.7 / 2.0
7 0005 / 0601 / TH 1242 / ◗ 1929	2.2 / 0.7 / 2.4 / 0.9	**22** 0540 / 1154 / F 1821	0.8 / 2.2 / 0.8
8 0110 / 0658 / F 1405 / 2037	2.0 / 0.9 / 2.2 / 1.0	**23** 0002 / 0635 / SA 1258 / ◖ 1919	1.9 / 0.9 / 2.1 / 0.9
9 0229 / 0812 / SA 1530 / 2149	1.9 / 1.0 / 2.2 / 1.0	**24** 0116 / 0746 / SU 1418 / 2022	1.8 / 1.0 / 2.0 / 0.9
10 0349 / 0945 / SU 1648 / 2252	2.0 / 1.0 / 2.2 / 0.9	**25** 0255 / 0904 / M 1534 / 2130	1.9 / 1.0 / 2.1 / 0.9
11 0459 / 1106 / M 1746 / 2343	2.2 / 1.0 / 2.2 / 0.8	**26** 0418 / 1033 / TU 1644 / 2243	2.0 / 0.9 / 2.2 / 0.8
12 0551 / 1202 / TU 1830	2.3 / 0.9 / 2.2	**27** 0520 / 1147 / W 1744 / 2349	2.2 / 0.8 / 2.3 / 0.7
13 0027 / 0632 / W 1248 / 1907	0.7 / 2.5 / 0.8 / 2.3	**28** 0610 / 1244 / TH 1835	2.4 / 0.6 / 2.4
14 0107 / 0708 / TH 1328 / 1939	0.6 / 2.6 / 0.8 / 2.3	**29** 0043 / 0653 / F 1335 / 1921	0.6 / 2.7 / 0.4 / 2.6
15 0145 / 0742 / F 1405 / ● 2006	0.6 / 2.6 / 0.8 / 2.3	**30** 0131 / 0734 / SA 1422 / ○ 2003	0.4 / 2.9 / 0.3 / 2.6
		31 0215 / 0816 / SU 1507 / 2044	0.2 / 3.0 / 0.2 / 2.7

FEBRUARY

Time	m	Time	m
1 0256 / 0856 / M 1549 / 2123	0.2 / 3.0 / 0.3 / 2.6	**16** 0305 / 0851 / TU 1518 / 2103	0.4 / 2.6 / 0.5 / 2.4
2 0336 / 0938 / TU 1629 / 2201	0.2 / 3.0 / 0.4 / 2.6	**17** 0332 / 0923 / W 1546 / 2132	0.4 / 2.5 / 0.5 / 2.3
3 0414 / 1019 / W 1707 / 2240	0.2 / 2.8 / 0.5 / 2.4	**18** 0401 / 0957 / TH 1617 / 2204	0.5 / 2.5 / 0.5 / 2.3
4 0452 / 1104 / TH 1748 / 2322	0.4 / 2.6 / 0.7 / 2.2	**19** 0434 / 1034 / F 1653 / 2238	0.6 / 2.3 / 0.6 / 2.2
5 0534 / 1156 / F 1837	0.6 / 2.3 / 0.9	**20** 0514 / 1117 / SA 1735 / 2318	0.7 / 2.2 / 0.7 / 2.0
6 0015 / 0625 / SA 1323 / 1942	2.0 / 0.8 / 2.0 / 1.1	**21** 0605 / 1213 / SU 1829	0.9 / 2.0 / 0.8
7 0145 / 0737 / SU 1517 / 2111	2.0 / 1.0 / 1.9 / 1.1	**22** 0015 / 0716 / M 1340 / ◗ 1937	1.9 / 1.0 / 1.9 / 0.9
8 0325 / 0936 / M 1646 / 2225	1.9 / 1.1 / 1.9 / 1.0	**23** 0207 / 0846 / TU 1520 / 2054	1.8 / 1.0 / 1.9 / 0.9
9 0444 / 1107 / TU 1742 / 2321	2.1 / 1.0 / 1.9 / 0.9	**24** 0358 / 1039 / W 1639 / 2221	1.9 / 0.8 / 2.0 / 0.8
10 0538 / 1159 / W 1824	2.2 / 0.9 / 2.1	**25** 0506 / 1146 / TH 1739 / 2335	2.2 / 0.6 / 2.1 / 0.7
11 0007 / 0619 / TH 1240 / 1858	0.7 / 2.4 / 0.8 / 2.1	**26** 0555 / 1237 / F 1826	2.4 / 0.4 / 2.3
12 0049 / 0654 / F 1317 / 1928	0.6 / 2.5 / 0.7 / 2.2	**27** 0028 / 0637 / SA 1324 / 1907	0.4 / 2.6 / 0.2 / 2.5
13 0128 / 0725 / SA 1351 / 1952	0.5 / 2.5 / 0.6 / 2.2	**28** 0114 / 0717 / SU 1406 / ○ 1944	0.3 / 2.8 / 0.1 / 2.6
14 0204 / 0754 / SU 1423 / ● 2012	0.4 / 2.6 / 0.6 / 2.3		
15 0237 / 0822 / M 1451 / 2035	0.4 / 2.6 / 0.5 / 2.3		

MARCH

Time	m	Time	m
1 0156 / 0755 / M 1446 / 2020	0.1 / 3.0 / 0.1 / 2.7	**16** 0211 / 0753 / TU 1424 / 2008	0.3 / 2.5 / 0.4 / 2.4
2 0236 / 0834 / TU 1523 / 2056	0.0 / 3.0 / 0.1 / 2.7	**17** 0240 / 0823 / W 1449 / 2034	0.3 / 2.5 / 0.3 / 2.4
3 0314 / 0913 / W 1558 / 2131	0.1 / 2.9 / 0.3 / 2.6	**18** 0308 / 0856 / TH 1516 / 2104	0.4 / 2.5 / 0.3 / 2.4
4 0351 / 0953 / TH 1631 / 2208	0.2 / 2.7 / 0.4 / 2.4	**19** 0339 / 0931 / F 1546 / 2136	0.4 / 2.5 / 0.4 / 2.4
5 0429 / 1034 / F 1706 / 2247	0.3 / 2.4 / 0.6 / 2.2	**20** 0414 / 1009 / SA 1620 / 2211	0.5 / 2.3 / 0.4 / 2.3
6 0511 / 1120 / SA 1748 / 2337	0.6 / 2.1 / 0.8 / 2.0	**21** 0455 / 1053 / SU 1700 / 2252	0.6 / 2.1 / 0.6 / 2.1
7 0602 / 1237 / SU 1846 / ◗	0.8 / 1.8 / 1.0	**22** 0547 / 1149 / M 1749 / 2349	0.8 / 1.9 / 0.7 / 1.9
8 0112 / 0715 / M 1452 / 2022	1.9 / 1.0 / 1.7 / 1.1	**23** 0703 / 1317 / TU 1857 / ◖	0.9 / 1.7 / 0.9
9 0300 / 0928 / TU 1621 / 2151	1.9 / 1.0 / 1.7 / 1.0	**24** 0139 / 0845 / W 1503 / 2023	1.8 / 0.9 / 1.7 / 0.9
10 0414 / 1050 / W 1719 / 2251	2.0 / 0.9 / 1.8 / 0.8	**25** 0333 / 1025 / TH 1621 / 2156	2.0 / 0.7 / 1.9 / 0.8
11 0510 / 1137 / TH 1801 / 2340	2.2 / 0.8 / 1.9 / 0.7	**26** 0439 / 1127 / F 1720 / 2309	2.2 / 0.5 / 2.1 / 0.6
12 0553 / 1216 / F 1836	2.3 / 0.7 / 2.0	**27** 0530 / 1216 / SA 1805	2.4 / 0.3 / 2.2
13 0023 / 0628 / SA 1252 / 1904	0.5 / 2.4 / 0.6 / 2.1	**28** 0002 / 0613 / SU 1301 / 1844	0.4 / 2.6 / 0.1 / 2.4
14 0103 / 0658 / SU 1325 / ● 1926	0.4 / 2.4 / 0.5 / 2.2	**29** 0048 / 0653 / M 1341 / 1920	0.2 / 2.8 / 0.1 / 2.5
15 0139 / 0726 / M 1356 / ● 1945	0.4 / 2.4 / 0.4 / 2.3	**30** 0130 / 0732 / TU 1419 / ○ 1954	0.1 / 2.8 / 0.1 / 2.6
		31 0211 / 0810 / W 1453 / 2029	0.0 / 2.8 / 0.1 / 2.6

APRIL

Time	m	Time	m
1 0249 / 0849 / TH 1526 / 2104	0.1 / 2.7 / 0.2 / 2.6	**16** 0243 / 0832 / F 1450 / 2041	0.4 / 2.5 / 0.3 / 2.5
2 0328 / 0929 / F 1558 / 2142	0.2 / 2.7 / 0.4 / 2.5	**17** 0319 / 0912 / SA 1523 / 2117	0.4 / 2.4 / 0.3 / 2.4
3 0407 / 1011 / SA 1632 / 2223	0.4 / 2.2 / 0.6 / 2.3	**18** 0359 / 0955 / SU 1559 / 2156	0.5 / 2.3 / 0.4 / 2.3
4 0451 / 1056 / SU 1711 / 2314	0.6 / 1.9 / 0.7 / 2.1	**19** 0447 / 1043 / M 1640 / 2243	0.6 / 2.1 / 0.5 / 2.2
5 0545 / 1202 / M 1802	0.8 / 1.7 / 0.9	**20** 0545 / 1142 / TU 1729 / 2346	0.7 / 1.9 / 0.6 / 2.0
6 0048 / 0658 / TU 1403 / ◗ 1923	1.9 / 0.9 / 1.5 / 1.0	**21** 0703 / 1303 / W 1833 / ◖	0.7 / 1.8 / 0.7
7 0226 / 0843 / W 1528 / 2106	1.9 / 0.9 / 1.5 / 0.9	**22** 0130 / 0832 / TH 1433 / 1957	2.0 / 0.7 / 1.8 / 0.8
8 0333 / 0959 / TH 1635 / 2212	2.0 / 0.8 / 1.6 / 0.8	**23** 0301 / 0950 / F 1546 / 2124	2.1 / 0.6 / 1.8 / 0.7
9 0428 / 1052 / F 1724 / 2304	2.1 / 0.7 / 1.7 / 0.6	**24** 0406 / 1052 / SA 1647 / 2235	2.2 / 0.4 / 2.0 / 0.5
10 0514 / 1135 / SA 1801 / 2349	2.1 / 0.6 / 1.8 / 0.5	**25** 0500 / 1145 / SU 1737 / 2331	2.4 / 0.3 / 2.2 / 0.4
11 0551 / 1214 / SU 1830	2.2 / 0.5 / 2.0	**26** 0547 / 1230 / M 1818	2.5 / 0.2 / 2.3
12 0029 / 0622 / M 1250 / 1852	0.4 / 2.3 / 0.4 / 2.1	**27** 0020 / 0630 / TU 1312 / 1855	0.4 / 2.6 / 0.2 / 2.5
13 0106 / 0651 / TU 1322 / 1914	0.4 / 2.3 / 0.3 / 2.2	**28** 0105 / 0710 / W 1350 / ○ 1931	0.2 / 2.6 / 0.2 / 2.5
14 0139 / 0722 / W 1351 / ● 1940	0.4 / 2.4 / 0.3 / 2.4	**29** 0146 / 0750 / TH 1425 / 2007	0.2 / 2.6 / 0.2 / 2.6
15 0210 / 0755 / TH 1420 / 2009	0.4 / 2.5 / 0.3 / 2.5	**30** 0227 / 0831 / F 1459 / 2044	0.2 / 2.5 / 0.3 / 2.6

Chart Datum: 1·37 metres below Ordnance Datum (Belfast). HAT is 3·1 metres above Chart Datum; see 4.5.

RIVER FOYLE LAT 55°03'N LONG 7°16'W
TIMES AND HEIGHTS OF HIGH AND LOW WATERS

TIME ZONE (UT)
For Summer Time add ONE hour in **non-shaded areas**

Dates in red are SPRINGS
Dates in blue are NEAPS

YEAR 2010

MAY

Date	Time	m	Time	m
1 SA	0308 0.3 / 0912 2.3 / 1532 0.4 / 2123 2.5		16 SU 0308 0.4 / 0900 2.4 / 1508 0.3 / 2107 2.5	
2 SU	0350 0.5 / 0954 2.1 / 1606 0.5 / 2206 2.3		17 M 0356 0.4 / 0948 2.3 / 1548 0.3 / 2152 2.4	
3 M	0436 0.6 / 1040 1.9 / 1643 0.6 / 2257 2.1		18 TU 0449 0.5 / 1040 2.2 / 1631 0.4 / 2244 2.3	
4 TU	0529 0.8 / 1133 1.7 / 1727 0.7		19 W 0549 0.5 / 1137 2.0 / 1720 0.5 / 2348 2.2	
5 W	0011 2.0 / 0632 0.8 / 1252 1.5 / 1827 0.8		20 TH 0656 0.6 / 1242 1.9 / 1819 0.6	
6 TH	0139 1.9 / 0745 0.8 / 1415 1.5 / 1956 0.9		21 F 0110 2.1 / 0805 0.6 / 1355 1.8 / 1931 0.6	
7 F	0244 1.9 / 0852 0.8 / 1526 1.5 / 2120 0.8		22 SA 0228 2.2 / 0911 0.6 / 1505 1.8 / 2049 0.6	
8 SA	0338 2.0 / 0949 0.7 / 1627 1.6 / 2220 0.7		23 SU 0333 2.2 / 1013 0.5 / 1610 1.9 / 2201 0.6	
9 SU	0424 2.0 / 1041 0.6 / 1714 1.7 / 2308 0.6		24 M 0432 2.3 / 1111 0.4 / 1708 2.1 / 2303 0.5	
10 M	0505 2.1 / 1127 0.5 / 1748 1.9 / 2350 0.5		25 TU 0525 2.3 / 1201 0.4 / 1755 2.2 / 2356 0.4	
11 TU	0541 2.2 / 1207 0.4 / 1817 2.1		26 W 0613 2.4 / 1245 0.3 / 1836 2.4	
12 W	0028 0.5 / 0616 2.3 / 1845 2.2		27 TH 0044 0.4 / 0657 2.4 / 1326 0.3 / 1914 2.5	
13 TH	0105 0.4 / 0653 2.4 / 1319 0.3 / 1916 2.4		28 F 0129 0.4 / 0739 2.3 / 1404 0.3 / 1952 2.5	
14 F	0143 0.4 / 0733 2.4 / 1354 0.3 / 1950 2.5		29 SA 0212 0.4 / 0820 2.3 / 1440 0.3 / 2030 2.5	
15 SA	0224 0.4 / 0815 2.5 / 1430 0.3 / 2027 2.5		30 SU 0255 0.5 / 0901 2.2 / 1514 0.4 / 2110 2.5	
			31 M 0338 0.6 / 0941 2.0 / 1548 0.4 / 2152 2.4	

JUNE

Date	Time	m	Time	m
1 TU	0423 0.6 / 1022 1.9 / 1623 0.5 / 2238 2.2		16 W 0449 0.4 / 1031 2.3 / 1626 0.3 / 2240 2.5	
2 W	0509 0.7 / 1104 1.8 / 1700 0.6 / 2330 2.1		17 TH 0541 0.4 / 1121 2.2 / 1711 0.3 / 2336 2.4	
3 TH	0559 0.7 / 1150 1.7 / 1745 0.7		18 F 0636 0.6 / 1214 2.0 / 1802 0.5	
4 F	0034 2.0 / 0652 0.7 / 1248 1.6 / 1844 0.8		19 SA 0042 2.3 / 0734 0.5 / 1315 1.9 / 1902 0.6	
5 SA	0142 1.9 / 0747 0.7 / 1358 1.5 / 1957 0.8		20 SU 0155 2.2 / 0835 0.6 / 1424 1.8 / 2014 0.7	
6 SU	0239 1.9 / 0841 0.7 / 1509 1.6 / 2111 0.8		21 M 0305 2.1 / 0938 0.6 / 1535 1.9 / 2131 0.7	
7 M	0329 2.0 / 0936 0.6 / 1613 1.7 / 2215 0.7		22 TU 0413 2.1 / 1041 0.6 / 1644 2.0 / 2243 0.6	
8 TU	0416 2.0 / 1031 0.6 / 1704 1.8 / 2307 0.7		23 W 0516 2.1 / 1137 0.5 / 1741 2.1 / 2344 0.6	
9 W	0502 2.1 / 1123 0.5 / 1745 2.0 / 2354 0.6		24 TH 0610 2.2 / 1226 0.5 / 1827 2.3	
10 TH	0547 2.2 / 1210 0.4 / 1822 2.2		25 F 0035 0.6 / 0656 2.2 / 1310 0.4 / 1906 2.4	
11 F	0040 0.5 / 0632 2.3 / 1254 0.4 / 1859 2.4		26 SA 0122 0.5 / 0737 2.2 / 1350 0.4 / 1944 2.5	
12 SA	0126 0.5 / 0718 2.4 / 1337 0.3 / 1938 2.5		27 SU 0207 0.5 / 0816 2.1 / 1427 0.4 / 2021 2.5	
13 SU	0215 0.4 / 0805 2.4 / 1419 0.3 / 2019 2.6		28 M 0249 0.6 / 0851 2.1 / 1502 0.3 / 2058 2.5	
14 M	0306 0.4 / 0854 2.4 / 1501 0.2 / 2103 2.6		29 TU 0329 0.6 / 0925 2.1 / 1534 0.4 / 2135 2.4	
15 TU	0358 0.4 / 0942 2.4 / 1543 0.2 / 2150 2.6		30 W 0406 0.6 / 0958 2.0 / 1605 0.4 / 2213 2.3	

JULY

Date	Time	m	Time	m
1 TH	0443 0.6 / 1033 1.9 / 1637 0.5 / 2253 2.2		16 F 0521 0.3 / 1054 2.3 / 1655 0.2 / 2312 2.5	
2 F	0523 0.6 / 1110 1.9 / 1714 0.6 / 2339 2.1		17 SA 0608 0.4 / 1140 2.1 / 1739 0.4	
3 SA	0607 0.6 / 1153 1.8 / 1800 0.7		18 SU 0009 2.3 / 0659 0.6 / 1235 2.0 / 1831 0.6	
4 SU	0034 2.0 / 0655 0.6 / 1248 1.7 / 1859 0.8		19 M 0122 2.1 / 0800 0.7 / 1345 1.9 / 1940 0.8	
5 M	0139 1.9 / 0748 0.7 / 1400 1.6 / 2009 0.9		20 TU 0246 2.0 / 0908 0.8 / 1508 1.8 / 2110 0.8	
6 TU	0240 1.9 / 0844 0.7 / 1518 1.7 / 2121 0.8		21 W 0409 2.0 / 1018 0.7 / 1632 1.9 / 2239 0.8	
7 W	0338 2.0 / 0942 0.6 / 1627 1.8 / 2232 0.8		22 TH 0520 2.0 / 1119 0.7 / 1736 2.1 / 2343 0.7	
8 TH	0434 2.0 / 1044 0.6 / 1723 2.0 / 2334 0.7		23 F 0613 2.0 / 1209 0.6 / 1822 2.3	
9 F	0529 2.1 / 1144 0.5 / 1808 2.2		24 SA 0033 0.7 / 0656 2.1 / 1254 0.4 / 1900 2.4	
10 SA	0028 0.6 / 0621 2.2 / 1237 0.4 / 1849 2.4		25 SU 0118 0.6 / 0733 2.1 / 1335 0.4 / 1935 2.5	
11 SU	0121 0.5 / 0710 2.3 / 1325 0.3 / 1930 2.5		26 M 0159 0.6 / 0806 2.1 / 1413 0.3 / 2008 2.5	
12 M	0213 0.4 / 0758 2.4 / 1410 0.2 / 2012 2.7		27 TU 0237 0.5 / 0834 2.1 / 1448 0.3 / 2039 2.5	
13 TU	0303 0.3 / 0844 2.4 / 1453 0.1 / 2055 2.8		28 W 0311 0.5 / 0900 2.1 / 1519 0.3 / 2111 2.5	
14 W	0350 0.2 / 0928 2.4 / 1535 0.1 / 2138 2.8		29 TH 0343 0.5 / 0928 2.1 / 1546 0.3 / 2143 2.4	
15 TH	0436 0.2 / 1011 2.4 / 1615 0.1 / 2223 2.7		30 F 0413 0.5 / 0959 2.1 / 1615 0.4 / 2218 2.3	
			31 SA 0446 0.5 / 1032 2.0 / 1647 0.5 / 2257 2.2	

AUGUST

Date	Time	m	Time	m
1 SU	0524 0.6 / 1109 1.9 / 1726 0.7 / 2343 2.0		16 M 0620 0.7 / 1156 2.1 / 1805 0.6	
2 M	0609 0.6 / 1152 1.8 / 1818 0.8		17 TU 0051 2.0 / 0720 0.8 / 1313 1.9 / 1914 0.9	
3 TU	0044 1.9 / 0701 0.7 / 1256 1.7 / 1927 0.9		18 W 0238 1.9 / 0840 0.9 / 1453 1.9 / 2107 1.0	
4 W	0200 1.9 / 0800 0.7 / 1434 1.7 / 2046 0.9		19 TH 0407 1.9 / 0956 0.8 / 1620 2.0 / 2242 0.9	
5 TH	0312 1.9 / 0903 0.7 / 1602 1.8 / 2215 0.9		20 F 0513 1.9 / 1058 0.7 / 1722 2.2 / 2339 0.8	
6 F	0419 1.9 / 1013 0.7 / 1708 2.0 / 2330 0.7		21 SA 0602 2.0 / 1148 0.6 / 1807 2.3	
7 SA	0521 2.1 / 1125 0.6 / 1757 2.2		22 SU 0023 0.7 / 0641 2.1 / 1234 0.4 / 1843 2.4	
8 SU	0025 0.5 / 0614 2.2 / 1223 0.4 / 1838 2.4		23 M 0103 0.6 / 0715 2.1 / 1315 0.3 / 1916 2.5	
9 M	0116 0.4 / 0701 2.3 / 1312 0.3 / 1917 2.7		24 TU 0140 0.5 / 0744 2.2 / 1352 0.3 / 1945 2.5	
10 TU	0203 0.2 / 0744 2.4 / 1356 0.1 / 1956 2.8		25 W 0214 0.5 / 0807 2.2 / 1427 0.3 / 2013 2.5	
11 W	0249 0.2 / 0825 2.5 / 1438 0.0 / 2036 2.9		26 TH 0245 0.5 / 0829 2.3 / 1457 0.3 / 2041 2.5	
12 TH	0331 0.1 / 0904 2.6 / 1517 0.0 / 2117 2.9		27 F 0312 0.5 / 0855 2.3 / 1523 0.3 / 2111 2.5	
13 F	0412 0.2 / 0943 2.5 / 1555 0.0 / 2159 2.8		28 SA 0338 0.5 / 0924 2.3 / 1549 0.4 / 2144 2.4	
14 SA	0452 0.3 / 1023 2.4 / 1634 0.2 / 2243 2.6		29 SU 0407 0.5 / 0955 2.2 / 1620 0.5 / 2220 2.3	
15 SU	0533 0.5 / 1105 2.3 / 1715 0.4 / 2335 2.3		30 M 0442 0.6 / 1027 2.1 / 1657 0.7 / 2301 2.1	
			31 TU 0523 0.6 / 1104 2.0 / 1744 0.8 / 2356 1.9	

Chart Datum: 1·37 metres below Ordnance Datum (Belfast). HAT is 3·1 metres above Chart Datum; see 4.5.

N Ireland

TIME ZONE (UT)
For Summer Time add ONE hour in **non-shaded areas**

RIVER FOYLE   LAT 55°03′N   LONG 7°16′W
TIMES AND HEIGHTS OF HIGH AND LOW WATERS

Dates in red are **SPRINGS**
Dates in blue are **NEAPS**

YEAR 2010

SEPTEMBER

Time	m		Time	m
1 0613	0.8		**16** 0222	1.8
1155	1.8		0804	1.0
W 1853	1.0		TH 1435	2.0
◐			2105	1.0
2 0122	1.8		**17** 0345	1.8
0715	0.8		0926	0.9
TH 1345	1.7		F 1552	2.1
2023	1.0		2226	0.9
3 0256	1.8		**18** 0448	1.9
0826	0.9		1028	0.8
F 1540	1.8		SA 1652	2.2
2215	0.9		2317	0.8
4 0409	1.9		**19** 0536	2.0
0946	0.8		1120	0.6
SA 1647	2.1		SU 1738	2.4
2322	0.7		2357	0.7
5 0510	2.1		**20** 0615	2.1
1105	0.6		1205	0.5
SU 1735	2.3		M 1816	2.4
6 0013	0.5		**21** 0034	0.6
0559	2.2		0647	2.2
M 1203	0.4		TU 1247	0.4
1816	2.6		1847	2.5
7 0059	0.3		**22** 0109	0.5
0642	2.4		0713	2.2
TU 1250	0.3		W 1325	0.4
1855	2.8		1915	2.5
8 0143	0.2		**23** 0142	0.5
0721	2.5		0734	2.3
W 1333	0.1		TH 1359	0.3
● 1933	2.9		○ 1941	2.6
9 0224	0.1		**24** 0211	0.5
0758	2.6		0756	2.4
TH 1414	0.0		F 1428	0.4
2012	3.0		2009	2.6
10 0303	0.1		**25** 0236	0.4
0836	2.7		0822	2.5
F 1453	0.0		SA 1455	0.4
2051	3.0		2039	2.6
11 0341	0.2		**26** 0302	0.4
0913	2.7		0851	2.5
SA 1532	0.1		SU 1523	0.5
2132	2.8		2113	2.5
12 0417	0.4		**27** 0331	0.5
0952	2.6		0922	2.4
SU 1611	0.3		M 1556	0.6
2216	2.6		2150	2.4
13 0454	0.6		**28** 0405	0.5
1034	2.4		0955	2.3
M 1653	0.5		TU 1634	0.7
2305	2.2		2232	2.2
14 0537	0.8		**29** 0444	0.7
1125	2.2		1033	2.2
TU 1743	0.8		W 1722	0.9
			2326	2.0
15 0023	1.9		**30** 0532	0.8
0635	0.9		1123	2.0
W 1251	2.0		TH 1831	1.0
◐ 1857	1.0			

OCTOBER

Time	m		Time	m
1 0050	1.8		**16** 0301	1.8
0632	0.9		0843	1.0
F 1258	1.9		SA 1513	2.2
◐ 2010	1.0		2144	1.0
2 0233	1.8		**17** 0407	1.8
0749	0.9		0950	0.9
SA 1506	2.0		SU 1611	2.3
2153	0.8		2235	0.9
3 0346	2.0		**18** 0459	1.9
0913	0.8		1045	0.8
SU 1613	2.2		M 1659	2.3
2257	0.6		2318	0.8
4 0445	2.1		**19** 0540	2.0
1032	0.7		1132	0.7
M 1704	2.4		TU 1739	2.4
2348	0.4		2356	0.7
5 0535	2.3		**20** 0612	2.2
1132	0.5		1214	0.6
TU 1749	2.7		W 1812	2.5
6 0033	0.3		**21** 0032	0.6
0616	2.5		0638	2.3
W 1222	0.3		TH 1252	0.5
1829	2.8		1839	2.5
7 0115	0.2		**22** 0105	0.5
0655	2.6		0701	2.4
TH 1306	0.2		F 1325	0.5
● 1908	3.0		1907	2.6
8 0154	0.2		**23** 0134	0.5
0732	2.8		0726	2.5
F 1348	0.1		SA 1356	0.5
1948	3.0		○ 1938	2.6
9 0232	0.2		**24** 0202	0.5
0809	2.8		0754	2.6
SA 1428	0.1		SU 1426	0.5
2028	2.9		2012	2.6
10 0308	0.3		**25** 0231	0.5
0847	2.8		0826	2.6
SU 1509	0.3		M 1500	0.6
2109	2.7		2049	2.6
11 0343	0.5		**26** 0303	0.5
0927	2.7		0900	2.6
M 1550	0.4		TU 1537	0.7
2152	2.5		2130	2.5
12 0419	0.6		**27** 0340	0.5
1010	2.5		0937	2.5
TU 1634	0.7		W 1621	0.8
2241	2.2		2216	2.3
13 0500	0.8		**28** 0420	0.6
1102	2.3		1019	2.4
W 1727	0.9		TH 1714	0.9
2352	1.9		2311	2.1
14 0551	0.9		**29** 0507	0.7
1226	2.1		1113	2.3
TH 1840	1.0		F 1823	0.9
◐				
15 0141	1.8		**30** 0027	2.0
0707	1.0		0603	0.8
F 1403	2.1		SA 1238	2.2
2029	1.1		◑ 1950	0.9
			31 0158	1.9
			0715	0.9
			SU 1425	2.2
			2114	0.8

NOVEMBER

Time	m		Time	m
1 0311	2.0		**16** 0407	1.8
0837	0.9		1000	1.0
M 1535	2.4		TU 1613	2.3
2221	0.7		2227	0.9
2 0413	2.2		**17** 0456	2.0
0954	0.7		1053	0.9
TU 1631	2.5		W 1656	2.3
2315	0.5		2311	0.8
3 0505	2.3		**18** 0534	2.1
1059	0.6		1137	0.8
W 1721	2.7		TH 1732	2.4
			2350	0.7
4 0003	0.4		**19** 0604	2.3
0550	2.5		1216	0.7
TH 1153	0.5		F 1805	2.5
1805	2.9			
5 0046	0.3		**20** 0026	0.6
0631	2.7		0632	2.4
F 1241	0.4		SA 1252	0.7
1847	2.9		1837	2.6
6 0126	0.3		**21** 0101	0.6
0710	2.8		0701	2.5
SA 1325	0.3		SU 1328	0.7
● 1928	2.9		○ 1913	2.6
7 0205	0.4		**22** 0134	0.5
0748	2.9		0734	2.7
SU 1408	0.4		M 1405	0.7
2009	2.8		1952	2.6
8 0241	0.4		**23** 0209	0.5
0827	2.9		0809	2.7
M 1450	0.5		TU 1446	0.7
2051	2.6		2034	2.6
9 0317	0.5		**24** 0246	0.5
0908	2.8		0847	2.7
TU 1533	0.6		W 1530	0.7
2134	2.4		2119	2.5
10 0353	0.6		**25** 0326	0.5
0952	2.6		0929	2.7
W 1618	0.8		TH 1618	0.7
2220	2.2		2207	2.4
11 0431	0.8		**26** 0408	0.6
1042	2.5		1015	2.6
TH 1709	0.9		F 1712	0.8
2314	1.9		2300	2.3
12 0514	0.9		**27** 0454	0.6
1148	2.3		1109	2.5
F 1809	1.0		SA 1813	0.8
13 0033	1.8		**28** 0002	2.1
0607	1.0		0545	0.7
SA 1313	2.2		SU 1218	2.4
◑ 1923	1.1		◐ 1922	0.8
14 0157	1.7		**29** 0115	2.1
0723	1.1		0647	0.8
SU 1424	2.2		M 1344	2.4
2038	1.0		2033	0.8
15 0306	1.7		**30** 0229	2.1
0853	1.0		0800	0.9
M 1523	2.2		TU 1459	2.4
2137	1.0		2141	0.8

DECEMBER

Time	m		Time	m
1 0336	2.1		**16** 0359	1.9
0917	0.8		0954	1.0
W 1603	2.5		TH 1609	2.2
2243	0.7		2214	0.9
2 0436	2.3		**17** 0452	2.0
1029	0.8		1054	1.0
TH 1700	2.6		F 1654	2.3
2336	0.6		2306	0.8
3 0528	2.4		**18** 0533	2.2
1131	0.7		1142	0.9
F 1750	2.6		SA 1736	2.4
			2351	0.7
4 0023	0.5		**19** 0609	2.4
0613	2.6		1226	0.8
SA 1223	0.6		SU 1817	2.5
1835	2.7			
5 0106	0.5		**20** 0034	0.6
0655	2.7		0644	2.5
SU 1311	0.6		M 1310	0.7
● 1918	2.6		1858	2.5
6 0145	0.5		**21** 0115	0.5
0735	2.8		0721	2.7
M 1356	0.6		TU 1355	0.7
1959	2.6		○ 1941	2.6
7 0223	0.5		**22** 0156	0.5
0815	2.9		0759	2.8
TU 1439	0.7		W 1442	0.6
2039	2.5		2025	2.6
8 0259	0.6		**23** 0237	0.4
0855	2.8		0840	2.9
W 1521	0.7		TH 1528	0.6
2119	2.3		2111	2.6
9 0334	0.6		**24** 0319	0.4
0936	2.7		0923	2.9
TH 1603	0.8		F 1615	0.6
2158	2.2		2156	2.5
10 0409	0.7		**25** 0401	0.4
1019	2.6		1008	2.8
F 1645	0.9		SA 1703	0.6
2237	2.1		2243	2.4
11 0444	0.8		**26** 0443	0.5
1106	2.4		1056	2.7
SA 1731	1.0		SU 1753	0.7
2319	1.9		2333	2.3
12 0525	0.9		**27** 0529	0.6
1201	2.3		1152	2.6
SU 1822	1.0		M 1849	0.8
13 0012	1.8		**28** 0031	2.2
0615	1.0		0621	0.7
M 1313	2.2		TU 1302	2.4
◑ 1918	1.0		◑ 1952	0.9
14 0133	1.7		**29** 0142	2.1
0720	1.1		0726	0.8
TU 1421	2.1		W 1425	2.3
2018	1.0		2103	0.9
15 0253	1.8		**30** 0259	2.1
0837	1.1		0843	0.9
W 1519	2.1		TH 1543	2.3
2117	0.9		2214	0.9
			31 0412	2.2
			1008	0.9
			F 1653	2.3
			2316	0.8

Chart Datum: 1·37 metres below Ordnance Datum (Belfast). HAT is 3·1 metres above Chart Datum; see 4.5.

9.13.16 LOUGH SWILLY

Donegal 55°17'N 07°34'W ✿✿✿✿⚓⚓✿✿✿

CHARTS AC 2697; Imray C53

TIDES –0500 Dover; ML 2·3; Duration 0605

Standard Port GALWAY (→)

Times				Height (metres)			
High Water		Low Water		MHWS	MHWN	MLWN	MLWS
0200	0900	0200	0800	5·1	3·9	2·0	0·6
1400	2100	1400	2000				
Differences INISHTRAHULL							
+0100	+0100	+0115	+0200	–1·8	–1·4	–0·4	–0·2
TRAWBREAGA BAY							
+0115	+0059	+0109	+0125	–1·1	–0·8	No data	
FANAD HEAD							
+0115	+0040	+0125	+0120	–1·1	–0·9	–0·5	–0·1
RATHMULLAN							
+0125	+0050	+0126	+0118	–0·8	–0·7	–0·1	–0·1
MULROY BAY (BAR)							
+0108	+0052	+0102	+0118	–1·2	–1·0	No data	
SHEEP HAVEN (DOWNIES BAY)							
+0057	+0043	+0053	+0107	–1·1	–0·9	No data	

SHELTER Good, but beware downdrafts on E side. ⚓s N of 55°05'N may suffer from swell. ⚓s from seaward: Ballymastocher Bay, also 8 Y ⚓s, but exposed to E'lies; inside Macamish Pt, sheltered from SE to N; Rathmullan Roads N of pier, where yacht pontoon lies N/S in 3·6m MLWS; Fahan Creek and marina ent at HW–1.

NAVIGATION WPT 55°17'·50N 07°34'·50W, 172°/5·7M to Dunree Hd lt. Ent is easy and main chan is well lit/buoyed. Beware: off W shore, Swilly More Rks, Kinnegar Spit and Strand; off E shore, Colpagh Rks and Inch Flats. These dangers are buoyed, as is Fahan Creek. There are many marine farms and shellfish beds S from Scraggy Bay (☎ 074 50172/59071 for permission to use pier).

LIGHTS AND MARKS Fanad Hd lt, Fl (5) WR 20s 38m 18/14M, touching Dunree Hd lt, Fl (2) WR 5s 46m 12/9M, leads 151° into the Lough. Thence Ballygreen Pt and Hawk's Nest in line at 202°.

R/T None.

TELEPHONE (Codes: both sides of lough 074) Rathmullan Pontoon 9158131, 9158315 (eves); MRCC 9370243; Police 9153114 (Milford) and 9361555 (Buncrana); Dr 9158416 (Rathmullan), 1850 400911(out of hours), and 9363611 (Buncrana).

FACILITIES **Rathmullan** Pontoon (Easter–October) ☎ 087 2480132 €10/craft/day, €20/craft/overnight, FW, slip, ▣, R, Hotel, Bar, D & P (cans), Kos, ⬛, ✉. **Ramelton** AB (drying),

BY ☎ 9151082, Bar, R, D & P (cans), FW, Kos, ⬛, ✉. **Lough Swilly Marina** ☎ 086 1082111, some Ⓥ, €2/m. **Fahan**, Slip, FW, Bar, R, ✉, **Lough Swilly YC** www.loughswillyyc.com. Services (1M SE): ⬛, D & P (cans), ⇌, ✈ (Londonderry 10M bus/taxi). **Buncrana** AB (congested), Hotel, R, Bar, Ⓑ, ✉, ⬛, ▣, D & P (cans), Kos.

BLOODY FORELAND TO EAGLE ISLAND

(AC 2725) Off low-lying Bloody Foreland (lt) there is often heavy swell. The coast and islands 15M SW to Aran Is give good cruising (AC 1883). An inshore passage avoids offlying dangers: Buniver and Brinlack shoals, which can break; Bullogconnell 1M NW of Gola Is; and Stag Rks 2M NNW of Owey Is. ⚓s include Bunbeg and Gweedore Hbr, and Cruit B which has easier access. Behind Aran Is are several good ⚓s. Use N ent, since S one is shallow (AC 2792). Rutland N Chan is main appr to Burtonport.

Boylagh B has shoals and rks N of Roaninish Is. Connell Rk (0·3m) is 1M N of Church Pool, a good ⚓, best approached from Dawros Hd 4·5M to W. On S side of Glen B a temp ⚓ (but not in W or NW winds) is just E of Rinmeasa Pt. Rathlin O'Birne Is has steps E side; anch SE of them 100m offshore. Sound is 5ca wide; hold Is side to clear rks off Malin Beg Hd.

In Donegal B (AC 2702) beware uncharted rks W of Teelin, a good natural hbr but exposed to S/SW swell. Killybegs has better shelter and is always accessible. Good shelter with fair access in Donegal Hbr (AC 2715). Good ⚓ or ⚓ via YC at Mullaghmore in fair weather; sea state is calm with winds from SE through S to NW. Inishmurray is worth a visit in good weather, anch off S side. There are shoals close E and NE of the Is, and Bomore Rks 1·5M to N. Keep well clear of coast S to Sligo in onshore winds, and beware of lobster pots.

Killala B has temp ⚓ 1M S of Kilcummin Hd, on W side. Proceeding to Killala beware St Patrick's Rks. Ent has ldg lts and marks, but bar is dangerous in strong NE winds.

The coast W to Broadhaven is inhospitable. Only Belderg and Portacloy give a little shelter. Stag Rks are steep-to and high. Broadhaven (AC 2703) is good ⚓ and refuge, but in N/NW gales sea can break in ent. In approaches beware Slugga Rk on E side with offlier, and Monastery Rk (0·3m) on S side.

N Ireland

9.13.17 KILLYBEGS

Donegal 54°36'·90N 08°26'·80W ❄❄❄❄🌢🌢🌢✿✿✿

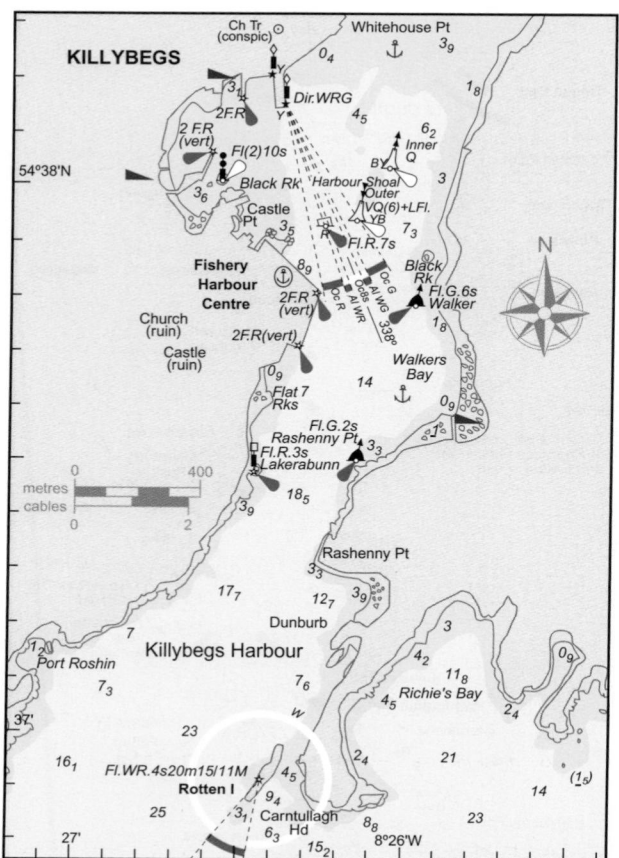

CHARTS AC 2702, 2792; Imray C53

TIDES –0520 Dover; ML 2·2; Duration 0620

Standard Port GALWAY (→)

Times				Height (metres)			
High Water		Low Water		MHWS	MHWN	MLWN	MLWS
0600	1100	0000	0700	5·1	3·9	2·0	0·6
1800	2300	1200	1900				
Differences KILLYBEGS							
+0040	+0050	+0055	+0035	–1·0	–0·9	–0·5	0·0
GWEEDORE HARBOUR							
+0048	+0100	+0055	+0107	–1·3	–1·0	–0·5	–0·1
BURTONPORT							
+0042	+0055	+0115	+0055	–1·2	–1·0	–0·6	–0·1
DONEGAL HARBOUR (SALTHILL QUAY)							
+0038	+0050	+0052	+0104	–1·2	–0·9	No data	

SHELTER Secure natural hbr, but some swell in SSW winds. A busy major FV port, H24 access. ⚓ about 2½ca NE of the Pier, off blue shed (Gallagher Bros) in 3m, clear of FV wash. Or contact HM and berth at pier. **Bruckless Hbr**, about 2M E at the head of McSwyne's Bay, is a pleasant ⚓ in 1·8m but is severely restricted due to fish cages, sheltered from all except SW winds. Ent on 038° between rks; ICC SDs are essential.

NAVIGATION WPT 54°36'·00N 08°27'·00W, 022°/0·94M to Rotten Is lt. From W, beware Manister Rk (covers at HW; dries at LW) off Fintragh B. Keep mid chan until off new Killybegs Fishery Centre, then follow the Dir lt or Y ◇ ldg marks 338° into hbr.

LIGHTS AND MARKS Rotten Is lt, Fl WR 4s 20m 15/11M, W tr, vis W255°-008°, R008°-039°, W039°-208°. Dir lt 338°, Oc WRG 6s 17m; W sector 336°-340° (see 9.13.4). Harbour Shoal (2·3m) is marked by a SCM and NCM lt buoy.

R/T HM Ch **14**; essential to request a berth.

TELEPHONE (Code 07497) HM 31032; MRCC (01) 6620922/3; Bundoran Inshore Rescue ☎ (071) 9841713; ⊜ 31070; Police 31002; Dr 31148 (Surgery).

FACILITIES **Town Pier** ☎ 31032, AB (free), M, D & P (cans), FW, ME, El, CH ⚒, C (12 ton), Kos, Ⓔ, Slip, 🛒, R, Bar. **Black Rock Pier** AB, M, Slip, D.
Town ✉, Ⓑ, ⇌ (bus to Sligo), ✈ (Strandhill).

OTHER HARBOURS AND ANCHORAGES IN DONEGAL

MULROY BAY, Donegal, 55°15'·30N 07°46'·30W. AC 2699; HW (bar) –0455 on Dover. See 9.13.16. Beware Limeburner Rk, (NCM buoy, Q) 3M N of ent & the bar which is dangerous in swell or onshore winds. Obtain local advice on the depths on the bar change considerably. Ent at half flood (not HW); chan lies between Bar Rks and Sessiagh Rks, it is rep'd to run along the alignment of the charted drying spit thence through First, Second and Third Narrows (with strong tides) to Broad Water. HW at the head of the lough is 2¼ hrs later than at the bar. ⚓s: Close SW of Ravedy Is (Fl 3s 9m 3M); Fanny's Bay (2m), excellent; Rosnakill Bay (3·5m) in SE side; Cranford Bay; Milford Port (3 to 4m). Beware power cable 6m, over Moross chan, barring North Water to masted boats. Facilities: **Milford Port** AB, FW, 🛒; **Fanny's Bay** ✉, Shop at Downings village (1M), hotel at Rosepenna (¾M).

SHEEP HAVEN, Donegal, 55°11'·00N 07°51'·00W. AC 2699. HW –0515 on Dover. See 9.13.16. Bay is 2M wide with many ⚓s, easily accessible in daylight, but exposed to N winds. Beware rks off Rinnafaghla Pt, and further S: Black Rk (6m) and Wherryman Rks, which dry, 1ca off E shore. ⚓ or 8 Y ⚓s in Downies Bay to SE of pier; in Pollcormick inlet close W in 3m; in Ards Bay for excellent shelter, but beware the bar in strong winds. Lts: Portnablahy ldg lts 125°, both Oc 6s 7/12m 2M, B col, W bands; Downies pier hd, Fl R 3s 5m 2M, R post. Facilities: (Downies) EC Wed; 🛒, FW, P (cans 300m), R, Bar; (Portnablahy Bay) 🛒, P (cans), R, Bar.

GWEEDORE HBR/BUNBEG, Donegal, 55°03'·75N 08°18'·87W. AC 1883. Tides see 9.13.17. Gweedore hbr, the estuary of the R Gweedore, has sheltered ⚓s or temp AB at Bunbeg Quay, usually full of FVs. Apprs via Gola N or S Sounds are not simple especially in poor visibility. N Sound is easier with ldg lts 171°, both Oc 3s 9/13m 2M, B/W bns, on the SE tip of Gola Is. (There are also ⚓s on the S and E sides of Gola Is.) E of Bo Is the bar 0·4m has a Fl G 3s and the chan, lying E of Inishinny Is and W of Inishcoole, is marked by a QG and 3 QR. A QG marks ent to Bunbeg. Night ent not advised. Facilities: FW, D at quay; 🛒, ✉, Ⓑ, Bar at village ½M.

BURTONPORT, Donegal, 54°58'·93N 08°26'·60W. AC 1879, 2792. HW –0525 on Dover; ML 2·0m; Duration 0605. See 9.13.17. Only appr via N Chan. Ent safe in all weathers except NW gales. Hbr very full, no space to ⚓; berth on local boat at pier or go to Rutland Hbr or Aran Roads: 6 Y ⚓s 250m NE of Black Rks, Fl R 3s. Ldg marks/lts: N Chan ldg lts on Inishcoo 119·3°, both Iso 6s 6/11m 1M; front W bn, B band; rear B bn, Y band. Rutland Is ldg lts 138°, both Oc 6s 8/14m 1M; front W bn, B band; rear B bn, Y band. Burtonport ldg lts 068°, both FG 17/23m 1M; front Gy bn, W band; rear Gy bn, Y band. HM ☎ (075) 42155 (43170 home); VHF Ch 06, 12, **14**, 16. Facilities: D (just inside pier), FW (root of pier), P (½M inland). **Village** Bar, ✉, R, 🛒, Kos.

INISHKEEL, Donegal, 54°50'·82N 08°26'·50W. AC 2792. 6 Y ⚓s in Church Pool, 3ca E of Inishkeel. Open to N/NE'lies.

TEELIN HARBOUR, Donegal, 54°37'·50N 08°37'·87W. AC 2792. Tides as 9.13.17. A possible passage ⚓, mid-way between Rathlin O'Birne and Killybegs. But Hbr is open to S'ly swell and prone to squalls in NW winds. Ent, 1ca wide, is close E of Teelin Pt lt, Fl R 10s, which is hard to see by day. 4 Y ⚓s and ⚓ on E side in 3m to N of pier, or ⚓ on E side near pier. Many moorings and, in the NE, mussel rafts. Facilities: possible FW, D, 🛒 at Carrick, 3M inland.

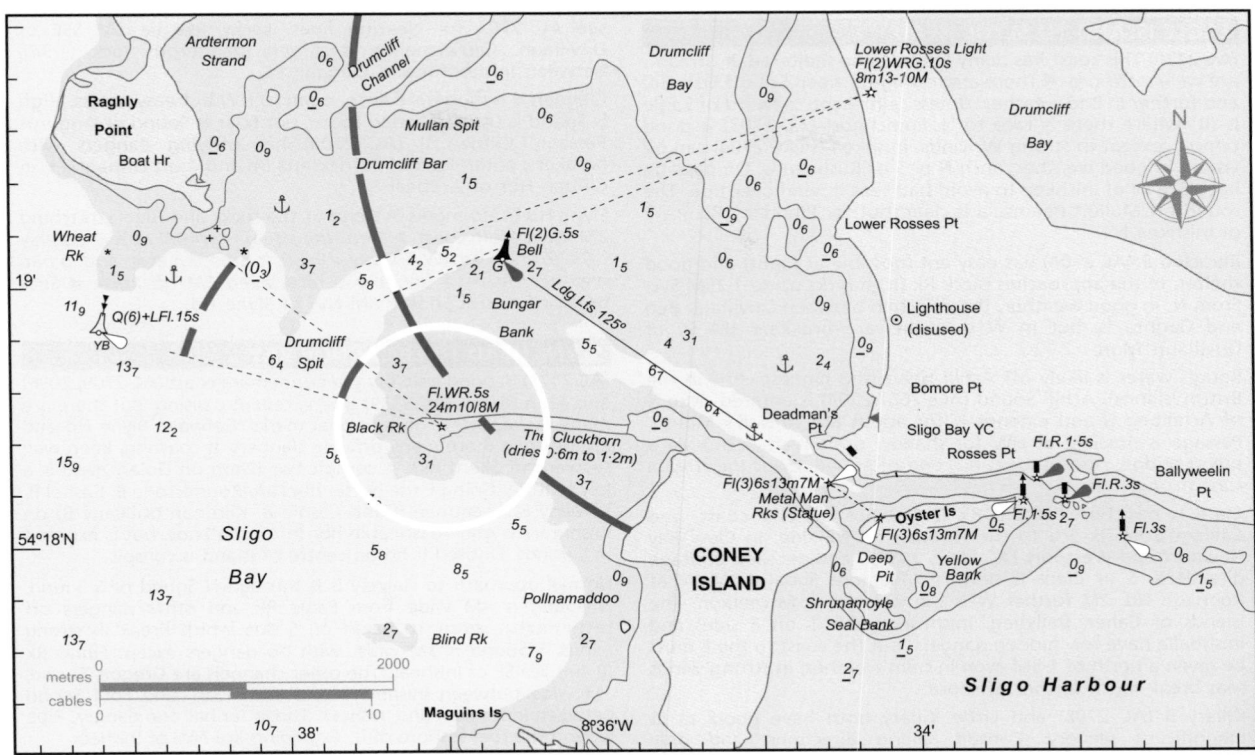

9.13.18 SLIGO

Sligo 54°18'·30N 08°34'·70W ✿✿✿✿✿✿✿

CHARTS AC 2767, 2852; Imray C54.

TIDES –0511 Dover; ML 2·3; Duration 0620

Standard Port GALWAY (→)

Times				Height (metres)			
High Water		Low Water		MHWS	MHWN	MLWN	MLWS
0600	1100	0000	0700	5·1	3·9	2·0	0·6
1800	2300	1200	1900				
Differences SLIGO HARBOUR (Oyster Is)							
+0043	+0055	+0042	+0054	–1·0	–0·9	–0·5	–0·1
MULLAGHMORE							
+0036	+0048	+0047	+0059	–1·4	–1·0	–0·4	–0·2
BALLYSADARE BAY (Culleenamore)							
+0059	+0111	+0111	+0123	–1·2	–0·9	No data	
KILLALA BAY (Inishcrone)							
+0035	+0055	+0030	+0050	–1·3	–1·2	–0·7	–0·2

SHELTER The lower hbr is fairly exposed; ⚓ along N side of Oyster Island, or proceed 4M (not at night) up to the shelter of Sligo town; 2nd berth below bridge for yachts.

NAVIGATION WPT 54°19'·15N 08°36'·77W, 125°/1·6M to front ldg lt.

- The passage between Oyster Island and Coney Island is marked 'Dangerous'.
- Pass N of Oyster Is leaving Blennick Rks to port. Passage up to Sligo town between training walls. Appr quays at HW–3 or higher.
- Some perches are in bad repair. Pilots at Raghly Pt and Rosses Pt. *Tide Tables* (based on Inishraher/Inishgort, published by Westport Hbr Comm.) available locally.

LIGHTS AND MARKS See 9.13.4 and chartlet. Channel to Sligo Deepwater Quay is well marked by lit bcns.

R/T Pilots VHF Ch 12 16. HM Ch 16.

TELEPHONE (Code 071) Hbr Office ☎ 9153819, mob 086 0870767; MRCC (01) 6620922/3; ⊖ 9161064; Police 9157000; Dr 9142886; Ⓗ 9171111.

FACILITIES No 3 berth (next to bridge) AB 20-30ft €19.00, P & D (in cans), FW, ME, EI, ✗, CH, C (15 ton); **Sligo YC** ☎ 9177168, ⚓s, FW, Bar, Slip. **Services:** Slip, D, ME, EI, ✗, SM, Gas; **Town** 🛒, R, Bar, ✉, Ⓑ, ⇌ Irish Rail ☎ 9169888, Bus ☎ 9160066, ✈ (Strandhill) ☎ 9168280.

MINOR HARBOUR ON S SIDE OF DONEGAL BAY

MULLAGHMORE 54°27'·90N 08°26'·80W. AC 2702. Tides see 9.13.18. Pierhead lit Fl G 3s 5m 3M. Fair weather ⚓ in 2-3m off hbr ent, sheltered by Mullaghmore Head, except from N/NE winds. For ⚓s near hbr ent, call Liam Carey at BY, ☎ 071 66106, mobile ☎ 087 2574497. Keep close to N pier to avoid shingle bank drying 1m, ⅔ of the way across the ent toward the S pier. Take the ground or dry out against the piers inside hbr berth on pontoon on bkwtr (min 1m at MLWS). Access approx HW±2 when least depth is 2m. VHF Ch 16, 8, 6. Facilities: FW at S Pier and on bkwtr, BY, ✗, D (cans), 🛒, R, Bar.

MINOR HARBOUR/ANCHORAGE TO THE WEST

KILLALA BAY, Sligo/Mayo, **54°13'·02N 09°12'·80W.** AC 2715. Tides, see 9.13.18. The bay, open to the N-NE, is entered between Lenadoon Pt and Kilcummin Hd, 6M to the W. 1·1M W of Kilcummin Hd are 8 Y ⚓s off Rathlackan pier, well sheltered from W'lies. Carrickpatrick ECM lt buoy, in mid-bay marks St Patrick's Rks to the W. Thence, if bound for Killala hbr, make good Killala SHM lt buoy, 7½ca to the SSW. The Round Tr and cathedral spire at Killala are conspic. Four sets of ldg bns/lts lead via a narrow chan between sand dunes and over the bar (0·3m) as follows:

- 230°, Rinnaun Pt lts Oc 10s 7/12m 5M, ☐ concrete trs.
- 215°, Inch Is, ☐ concrete trs; the rear has Dir lt Fl WRG 2s.
- 196°, Kilroe lts Oc 4s 5/10m 2M, W ☐ trs, which lead to ⚓ in Bartragh Pool, 6ca NE of Killala hbr; thence
- 236°, Pier lts Iso 2s 5/7m 2M, W ◇ daymarks, lead via narrow, dredged chan to pier where AB is possible in about 1·5m.

Facilities: FW, P & D (cans), 🛒 in town ½M.

Other hbrs in the bay: R Moy leading to Ballina should not be attempted without pilot/local knowledge. Inishcrone in the SE has a pier and lt; see 9.13.4.

EAGLE ISLAND TO SLYNE HEAD

(AC 2420) This coast has many inlets, some sheltered. ▶ *Streams are weak offshore.* ◀ There are few lights. Keep 5ca off Erris Hd, and further in bad weather. Unless calm, keep seaward of Eagle Is (lt) where there is race to N. Frenchport (AC 2703) is good temp ⚓ except in strong W winds. Inishkea Is (AC 2704) can be visited in good weather; anch N or S of Rusheen Is. On passage keep 5ca W of Inishkea to avoid bad seas if wind over tide. The sound off Mullett Peninsula is clear, but for Pluddany Rk 6ca E of Inishkea N.

Blacksod B (AC 2704) has easy ent (possible at night) and good shelter. In the approaches Black Rk (lt) has rks up to 1·25M SW. From N, in good weather, there is chan between Duvillaun Beg and Gaghta Is, but in W gales beware breakers 1M SE of Duvillaun More.

Rough water is likely off Achill Head (the highest cliffs in the British Islands). Achill Sound (ACs 2667/2704) is entered close N of Achillbeg Is and extends N for about 8M to Bull's Mouth. Passage is possible at HW for shallow draft craft (<2m) via a swing bridge. Anchorages each end of Sound, ▶*but the stream runs strongly.* ◀

Clare Is has Two Fathom Rk (3·4m) 5ca off NW coast, and Calliaghcrom Rk 5ca to the N; anch on NE side. In Clew Bay Newport and Westport (AC 2667, 2057) need detailed pilotage directions. S of Clare Is beware Meemore Shoal 1·5M W of Roonagh Hd. 2M further W is the isolated rk Mweelaun. The islands of Caher, Ballybeg, Inishturk (with ⚓ on E side) and Inishdalla have few hidden dangers, but the coast to the E must be given a berth of 1·5M even in calm weather; in strong winds seas break much further offshore.

Killary B (AC 2706) and Little Killary both have good ⚓s in magnificent scenery. Consult sailing directions, and only approach in reasonable weather and good vis.

Ballynakill Hbr (AC 2706), easily entered either side of Freaghillaun South, has excellent shelter; Tully mountain is conspic to N. Beware Mullaghadrina and Ship Rk in N chan. ⚓ in Fahy, Derryinver or Barnaderg B. There is ⚓ on S side of Inishbofin (lt), but difficult access/exit in strong SW wind or swell. Rks and breakers exist E of Inishbofin and S of Inishshark;

see AC 2707 for clearing lines. Lecky Rks lie 1M SSE of Davillaun. Carrickmahoy is a very dangerous rock (1·9m) between Inishbofin and Cleggan Pt.

Cleggan B is moderate anch, open to NW but easy access. High Is Sound is usual coasting route, not Friar Is Sound or Aughrus Passage. Clifden B (AC 2708) has offlying dangers with breakers; enter 3ca S of Carrickrana Bn and ⚓ off Drinagh Pt, in Clifden Hbr or Ardbear B.

Slyne Hd Lt Ho marks SW end of the rocks and islets stretching 2M WSW from coast. ▶ *Here the stream turns N at HW Galway – 0320, and S at HW Galway + 0300. It runs 3kn at sp and in bad weather causes a dangerous race; keep 2M offshore.* ◀ Seas break on Barret Shoals, 3M NW of Slyne Hd.

SLYNE HEAD TO LISCANNOR BAY

(AC 2173) In good visibility the Connemara coast (AC 2709, 2096) and Aran Islands (AC 3339) give excellent cruising. But there are many rks, and few navigational marks. Between Slyne Hd and Roundstone B are many offlying dangers. If coasting, keep well seaward of Skerd Rks. A conspic twr (24m) on Golan Head is a key feature. Going E the better hbrs are Roundstone B, Cashel B, Killeany B, Greatman B and Cashla B. Kilronan (Killeany B) on Inishmore is only reasonable hbr in Aran Islands, but is exposed in E winds. Disused lt ho on centre of island is conspic.

Normal approach to Galway B is through N Sound or S Sound. N Sound is 4M wide from Eagle Rk and other dangers off Lettermullan shore, to banks on S side which break in strong winds. S Sound is 3M wide, with no dangers except Finnis Rk (0·4m) 5ca SE of Inisheer. The other channels are Gregory Sound, 1M wide between Inishmore and Inishmaan, and Foul Sound between Inishmaan and Inisheer. The latter has one danger, Pipe Rk and the reef inshore of it, extending 3ca NW of Inisheer.

The N side of Galway Bay is exposed, with no shelter. Galway is a commercial port, with possible marina plans. 3M SE, New Hbr (AC 1984) is a more pleasant anch with moorings off Galway Bay SC. Westward to Black Hd there are many bays and inlets, often poorly marked, but providing shelter and exploration. The coast SW to Liscannor Bay is devoid of shelter. O'Brien's Twr is conspic just N of the 199m high Cliffs of Moher.

9.13.19 WESTPORT (CLEW BAY)

Mayo 53°47'·85N 09°35'·40W ❄❄❄♦♦♻♻♻

CHARTS AC 2667, 2057; Imray C54.

TIDES −0545 Dover; ML 2·5; Duration 0610

Standard Port GALWAY (→)

Times				Height (metres)			
High Water		Low Water		MHWS	MHWN	MLWN	MLWS
0600	1100	0000	0700	5·1	3·9	2·0	0·6
1800	2300	1200	1900				
BROADHAVEN							
+0040	+0050	+0040	+0050	−1·4	−1·1	−0·4	−0·1
BLACKSOD QUAY							
+0025	+0035	+0040	+0040	−1·2	−1·0	−0·6	−0·2
CLARE ISLAND							
+0015	+0021	+0039	+0027	−0·6	−0·4	−0·1	+0·2
INISHGORT/CLEW BAY							
+0035	+0045	+0115	+0100	−0·7	−0·5	−0·2	+0·2
KILLARY HARBOUR							
+0021	+0015	+0035	+0029	−1·0	−0·8	−0·4	−0·1
INISHBOFIN HARBOUR							
+0013	+0009	+0021	+0017	−1·0	−0·8	−0·4	−0·1
CLIFDEN BAY							
+0005	+0005	+0016	+0016	−0·7	−0·5	No data	

SHELTER Secure ⚓s amongst the islands at all times, as follows: E of Inishlyre in 2m; 2ca NE of Dorinish More, good holding in lee of Dorinish Bar (dries); 6 ⚓s in Rosmoney Hbr 53°49'·75N 09°37'·34W; Westport Quay HW±1½, to dry out on S side; Newport Hbr (dries) can be reached above mid-flood with careful pilotage (AC 2667); dry out against N quay or ⚓ at E end of Rabbit Is.

NAVIGATION WPT 53°49'·20N 09°42'·10W, 071°/1·2M to Inishgort lt ho. Contact Tom Gibbons (Inishlyre Is) ☎ (098) 26381 for pilotage advice. Approaches to Westport Channel between Monkellys Rks and Inishmweela are well marked by lit PHMs and SHMs. Beware fish farms E of Clare I and in Newport Bay. Do not anchor or ground in the Carricknacally Shellfish Bed Area.

LIGHTS AND MARKS Westport Bay entered via Inishgort lt, L Fl 10s 11m 10M (H24), and a series of ldg lines, but not advised at night. Final appr line 080° towards lt bn, Fl 3s. but beware of drying patches on this lead inwards from Pigeon PHM. Chan from Westport Bay to Westport Quay, 1½M approx, is marked by bns.

R/T None.

TELEPHONE (Code 098) MRCC (01) 6620922/3; ⊖ (094) 9021131; Police 9025555; Ⓗ (094) 9021733.

FACILITIES Westport Quays M, AB free, Slip, ☷, R, Bar; Services: Kos, El, Ⓔ; Town P & D (cans), ⊠, Ⓑ, ⇌, ✈ (Galway/Knock). Mayo SC Rosmoney ☎ 9026160, Slip, Bar; Glénans Irish SC ☎ 9026046 on Collanmore Is.

OTHER ANCHORAGES FROM EAGLE IS TO SLYNE HEAD

BROAD HAVEN, Mayo, 54°16'·00N 09°53'·20W. AC 2703. A safe refuge except in N'lies. Easy appr across Broad Haven Bay to the ent between Brandy Pt and Gubacashel Pt, Iso WR 4s27m 12/9M, W tr. 7ca S of this lt is Ballyglas Fl G 3s on W side. ⚓ close N or S of Ballyglas which has pier (2m) and 8 Y ⚓s. In E'lies ⚓ 3ca S of Inver Pt out of the tide. Further S off Barrett Pt, the inlet narrows and turns W to Belmullet. Facilities: ☷, ⊠.

PORTNAFRANKAGH Mayo, 54°14'·95N 10°06'·00W. AC 2703. Tides approx as Broad Haven. A safe passage ⚓, close to the coastal route, but swell enters in all winds. Appr toward Port Pt, thence keep to the N side for better water; middle and S side break in onshore winds. ⚓ in 4–5m on S side, close inshore. L and slip at new pier. Unlit, but Eagle Is lt, Fl (3) 10s 67m 26M H24, W tr, is 2M N. No facilities; Belmullet 4M, ☷.

BLACKSOD BAY, Mayo, 54°05'·00N 10°02'·00W. AC 2704. HW − 0525 on Dover; ML 2·2m; Duration 0610. See 9.13.19. Easy appr, accessible by night. Safe ⚓s depending on wind: NW of Blacksod Pt 6 Y ⚓s in 3m; at Elly B in 1·8m; Elly Hbr 6 Y ⚓s; Saleen Bay (ldg lts 319°, both Oc 4s, lead to pier); N of Claggan Pt. Beware drying rk 3·5ca SSE of Ardmore Pt. Lts: Blacksod Pt, Fl (2) WR 7·5s 13m 9M, see 9.13.4. ECM buoy Q (3) 10s. Ldg lts 181°, Oc W 5s, lead to Blacksod pier hd. Few facilities; nearest town is Belmullet.

CLARE ISLAND, Mayo, 53°48'·1N 09°56'·7W. 6 ⚓s on SE side untenable in E winds. Hotel, Bar, some ☷, Wi-fi.

INISHTURK, Mayo, 53°42'·3N 10°05'·2W. 8 Y ⚓s Garranty Hbr. sheltered SW to NNW winds. Slip, quay, Bar, R, ⊠, 6 ⚓s on E side.

KILLARY HARBOUR, Mayo/Galway, 53°37'·83N 09°54'·00W, 4ca W of Doonee Is. AC 2706. Tides 9.13.19. A spectacular 7M long inlet, narrow and deep. Caution fish farms, some with Fl Y lts. Appr in good vis to identify Doonee Is and Inishbarna bns, both LFl G, ldg 099° to ent. ⚓s off Dernasliggaun, Bundorragha and, at head of inlet, Leenaun with 8 Y ⚓s. (Village: L, ☷, Bar, hotel, Wi-fi). Enter Little Killary Bay 4ca S of Doonee Is; drying rks at ent. Good ⚓ in 3m at head of bay.

BALLYNAKILL, Galway, 53°34'·95N 10°03'·00W. AC 2706. Tides as Inishbofin/Killary. Easy appr between Cleggan Pt, Fl (3) WRG 15s and Rinvyle Pt. Then pass N of Freaghillaun South Is, E of which is good passage ⚓ in 7m. Further E, Carrigeen and Ardagh Rks lie in mid-chan. Keep N for ⚓ in Derryinver B. S chan leads to ⚓s: off Ross Pt; S of Roeillaun; in Fahy Bay with 8 Y ⚓s sheltered by bar dries 0·2m. No facilities.

INISHBOFIN, Galway, 53°36'·60N 10°13'·20W. AC 1820, 2707.HW −0555 on Dover; ML 1·9m. Very safe once inside narrow ent. 2 conspic W trs and Dir RWG lt lead 032°. ⚓ between new pier and Port Is. Old pier to the E dries. Gun Rock, Fl (2) 6s 8m 4M, vis 296°-253°. Slip, FW (on both piers), R, Bar, ☷, Wi-fi, Hotel ☎ (095) 45803.

CLIFDEN BAY, Galway, 53°29'·40N 10°05'·90W. AC 1820, 2708. HW −0600 on Dover; Duration 0610. Tides at 9.13.19. Before entering identify the conspic W bn on Carrickrana Rks. To the E keep clear of Coghan's Rks and Doolick Rks. Ldg marks: W bn at Fishing Pt on 080° with Clifden Castle (ruin); caution bar 2·4m off Fishing Pt. 8 Y ⚓s are 3ca S of Castle ruins, or ⚓ NE of Drinagh Pt. In the drying creek to Clifden beware ruined trng wall; dry out against the quay. Or enter Ardbear Bay to ⚓ SE of Yellow Slate Rks in 3·4m. Keep clear of fish farms. Facilities: Town Bar, Ⓑ, CH, D, P, ⊠, R, ☷, Kos, FW, ☷, R, Dr, Ⓗ. Bus to Galway.

9.13.20 GALWAY BAY

Galway 53°12'N 09°08'W ✵✵✵✵≋≋✿✿✿

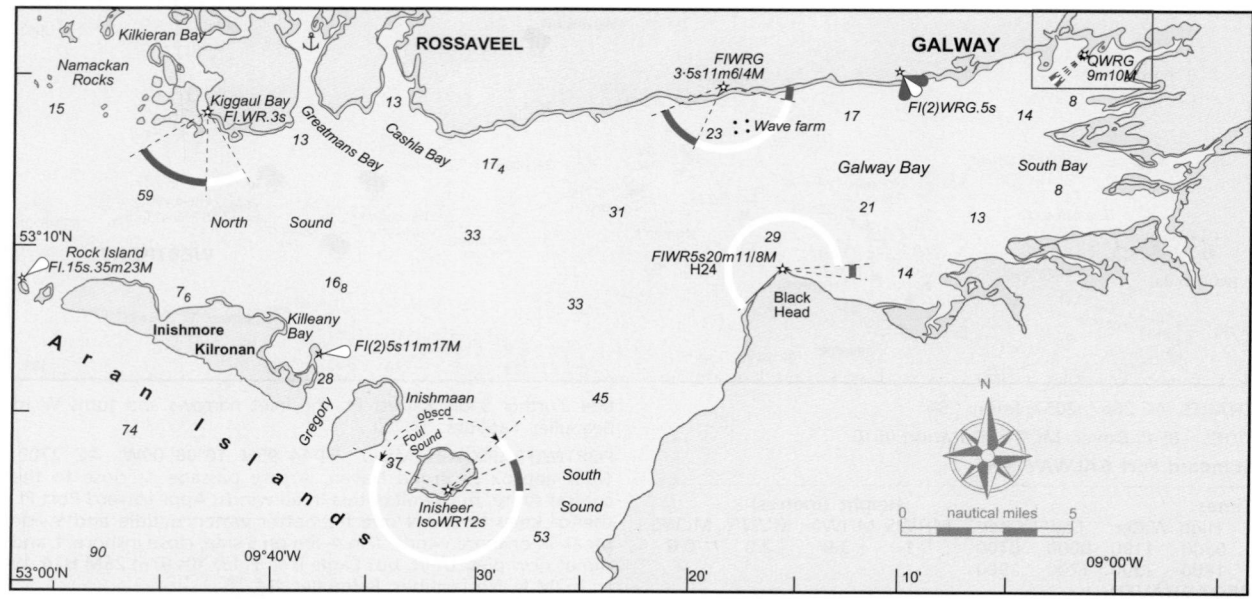

CHARTS AC 2173, 3339, 1984,1904; Imray C55.

TIDES –0555 Dover; ML 2·9; Duration 0620

Standard Port GALWAY (→)

Times				Height (metres)			
High Water		Low Water		MHWS	MHWN	MLWN	MLWS
0600	1100	0000	0700	5·1	3·9	2·0	0·6
1800	2300	1200	1900				
Differences KILKIERAN COVE							
+0005	+0005	+0016	+0016	–0·3	–0·2	–0·1	0·0
ROUNDSTONE BAY							
+0003	+0003	+0008	+0008	–0·7	–0·5	–0·3	–0·1
KILLEANY BAY (Aran Islands)							
–0008	–0008	+0003	+0003	–0·4	–0·3	–0·2	–0·1
LISCANNOR							
–0003	–0007	+0006	+0002	–0·4	–0·3	No data	

SHELTER Galway Bay is sheltered from large swells by Aran Is, but seas get up in the 20M from Aran Is to Galway. Beware salmon drift nets in the apps to many bays. The better ⚓s from Slyne Head and clockwise around Galway Bay are:

Bunowen Bay: (53°24'·6N 10°06'·9W). Sheltered in W-NE winds; unsafe in S'ly. Easy appr with Bunowen House brg 000°, leaving Mullauncarrickscoltia Rk (1·1m) to port. ⚓ in 3-4m below conspic Doon Hill.

Roundstone Bay: AC2709 (Off chartlet at 53°23'N 09°54'·5W). Safe shelter/access, except in SE'ly. 4 Y ⚓s are 5ca SSE of Roundstone, or ⚓ in 2m off N quay. There are other ⚓s E'ward in Bertraghboy and Cashel Bays.

Kilkieran Bay: Easy ent abm Golam Tr (conspic). 12 Y ⚓s off Kilkieran. Many ⚓s in 14M long, sheltered bay.

Kiggaul Bay: Easy ent, H24; ⚓ close W/NW of lt Fl WR 3s 5/3M. Depth 3 to 4m; exposed to S/SE winds.

Greatman Bay: Beware English Rk (dries 1·2m), Keeraun Shoal (breaks in heavy weather), Arkeena Rk, Trabaan Rk, Rin Rks and Chapel Rks. ⚓ off Natawny Quay (E side), or on 4 Y ⚓s off Maumeen Quay (dries), AB possible.

Cashla Bay: Easiest hbr on this coast; ent in all weather. ⚓ and 8 Y ⚓s off Sruthan Quay. Rossaveel, on E side, is a busy fishing and ferry hbr.

Note: There is no safe hbr from Cashla to Galway (20M).

Bays between Black Hd and Galway have rocks and shoals, but give excellent shelter. Kinvarra B, Aughinish B, South B and Ballyvaghan B are the main ones. Enter Kinvarra B with caution on the flood; beware rks. Berth in small drying hbr. Beware fish farm in South B. Ballvaghan B, entered either side of Illaunloo Rk, leads to two piers (both dry) or ⚓ close NE in pool (3m). Best access HW±2.

NAVIGATION Enter the Bay by one of four Sounds:
• North Sound between Inishmore and Golam Tr (conspic), 4½M wide, is easiest but beware Brocklinmore Bank in heavy weather.
• Gregory Sound between Inishmore and Inishmaan, is free of dangers, but give Straw Island a berth of 2-3ca.
• Foul Sound between Inishmaan and Inisheer; only danger is Pipe Rock (dries) at end of reef extending 3ca NW of Inisheer.
• South Sound between Inisheer and mainland. Only danger Finnis Rock (dries 0·4m) 4½ca SE of E point of Inisheer (marked by ECM buoy Q (3) 10s). From S, beware Kilstiffin Rocks off Liscanor Bay.

LIGHTS AND MARKS Roundstone Bay: Croaghnakeela Is Fl 3·7s 7m 5M. Inishnee lt Fl (2) WRG 10s 9m 5/3M, W sector 017°-030°. Kiggaul Bay: Fl WR 3s 5m 5/3M, 329°-W-359°-R-059°.
Cashla Bay: Killeen Pt Fl (3) WR 10s 6/3M; Lion Pt Dir lt 010°, Iso WRG 4s 8/6M, 008·5°-W-011·5°. Rossaveel ldg lts 116°, Oc 3s. Black Head lt Fl WR 5s 20m 11/8M H24, vis 045°-W-268°-R (covers Illanloo Rk)-276°.

FACILITIES
Bunowen Bay: No facilities.
Roundstone Bay: ⚓, FW, Bar, ✉, Bus to Galway.
Kilkieran Bay: Bar, ☎, P, ⚓, Bus to Galway.
Kiggaul Bay: Bar (no ☎), shop at Lettermullen (1M).
Greatman Bay: Maumeen ⚓, P (1M), Bar.
Cashla Bay: Carraroe (1M SW) ⚓, Hotel, ☎; Rossaveel HM ☎ 091 572108, FW, D, ME; Costelloe (1½M E), Hotel, ✉, Gge.

ARAN ISLANDS Beware marine farm activity, only reasonable shelter is off Inishmore in Killeany Bay, but exposed to E/NE winds and crowded with FVs. HM ☎ 099 20946; 8 Y ⚓s available; or ⚓ S of Kilronan pier; or ⚓ E of Killeany Pt; or in good weather ⚓ at Portmurvy. Kilronan, facilities: 8⚓s, ⚓, D, FW, ✉; Ferry to Galway, ✈ to Galway from airstrip on beach. Lights and marks: Inishmore: Eeragh Island (Rk Is) Fl 15s 35m 23M, W tr, B bands. Killeany Bay: Straw Is, Fl (2) 5s 11m 17M. Ldg lts 192° both Oc 5s for Killeany hbr. Inishmaan Ldg lts 199°, both Oc 6s 8M. New harbour being constructed (2009). Inisheer: Iso WR 12s 34m 20/16M, Racon, vis 225°-W-245° (partially obscd 225°-231° beyond 7M), R sector covers Finnis Rk.

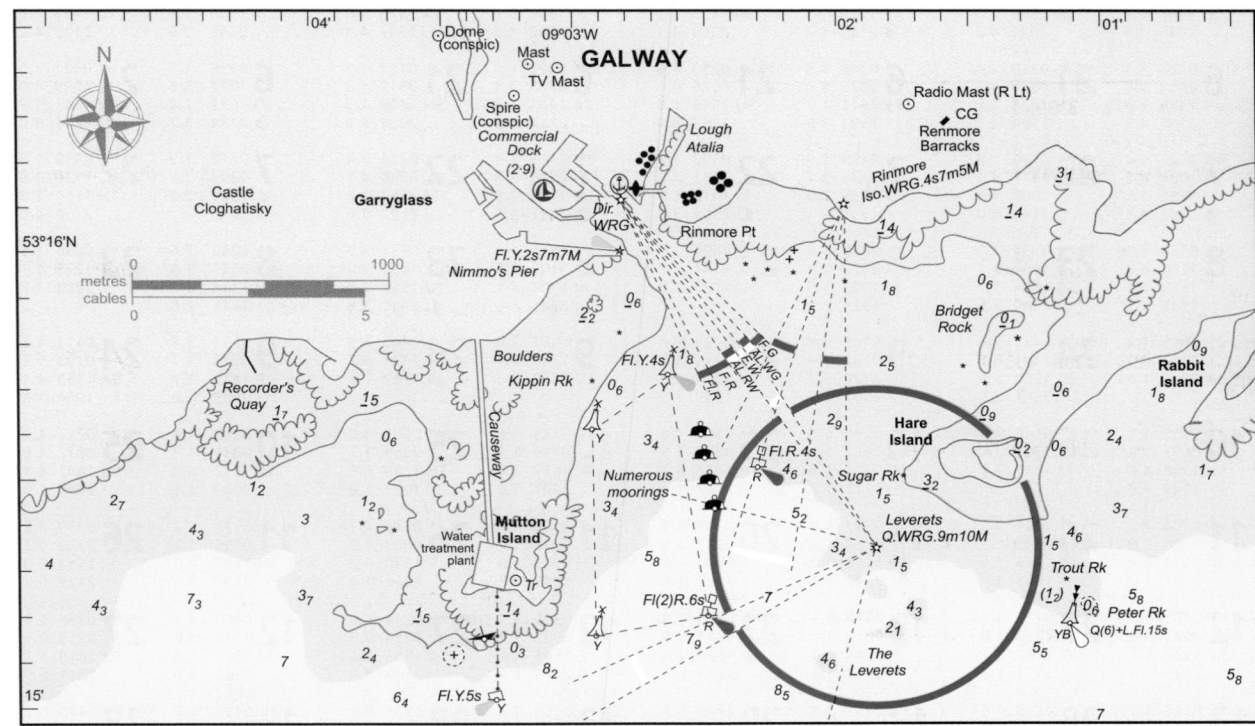

N Ireland

GALWAY HARBOUR 53°16'·07N   09°02'·74W ✤✤✤⚓⚓🛥🏵🏵🏵

SHELTER Very good in Galway hbr, protected from SW'lies by Mutton Island. Dock gates open HW–2 to HW, when min depth is 6m. Enter Galway Dock and secure in SW corner of basin where there is a 25-berth marina, or ask HM for waiting berth on lead-in pier. It is dangerous to lie in the 'Layby' (a dredged cut NE of New pier) when wind is SE or S; if strong from these points, seas sweep round the pierhead. New Harbour (2·5M ESE and home of Galway Bay SC) is nearest safe ⚓ to Galway. 5 Y ⚓s in lee of Mutton Island causeway in 2-4m.

NAVIGATION Galway WPT 53°14'·80N 09°03'·40W, 061°/1·1M to Leverets lt. Tidal information see www.gsmtides.com. Shipping information see www.aislive.com.

LIGHTS AND MARKS See 9.13.4 and chartlet. Leverets Q WRG

9m 10M; B tr, W bands; Rinmore Iso WRG 4s 7m 5M; W □ tr . Appr chan 325° is defined by a Dir lt WRG 7m 3M on New Pier.

R/T Call *Galway Harbour Radio* VHF Ch **12** 16 (HW–2½ to HW+1). Call Galway Pilots on VHF Ch **12** in case ship movements are imminent or under way and follow their instructions on berthing.

TELEPHONE (Code 091) HM 561874; MRCC (066) 9476109; Coast/ Cliff Rescue Service (099) 61107; Police 538000; Dr 562453.

FACILITIES **Dock** AB €15 if space available, FW, D (by r/tanker not small quantities), El, ME, ⚒, C (35 ton), CH, LB, PV, SM, 🛒, R, Bar; **Galway YC** M, Slip, FW, C, CH, Bar; **Galway Bay SC** ☎ 794527, M, CH, Bar; **Town** P, D, ACA, Gas, Gaz, Kos, 🛒, R, Bar, ✉, Ⓑ, ⚞, ✈ Carnmore (6M to the E of Galway City direct flights to UK see www.aerann.com). The nearest D by pump is Rossaveal.

GALWAY LAT 53°16'N LONG 9°03'W

TIMES AND HEIGHTS OF HIGH AND LOW WATERS

TIME ZONE (UT)
For Summer Time add ONE hour in **non-shaded areas**

Dates in red are **SPRINGS**
Dates in blue are **NEAPS**

YEAR **2010**

JANUARY

Time m	Time m
1 0504 5.2 / 1110 0.5 / F 1735 5.1 / 2323 0.7	**16** 0548 4.8 / 1141 0.9 / SA 1813 4.6 / 2354 1.1
2 0553 5.3 / 1155 0.3 / SA 1822 5.2	**17** 0625 4.8 / 1215 0.8 / SU 1848 4.6
3 0009 0.6 / 0639 5.3 / SU 1239 0.2 / 1909 5.1	**18** 0028 1.1 / 0701 4.8 / M 1249 0.8 / 1923 4.6
4 0055 0.6 / 0726 5.3 / M 1323 0.3 / 1956 5.0	**19** 0102 1.1 / 0735 4.8 / TU 1321 0.9 / 1957 4.5
5 0140 0.8 / 0813 5.1 / TU 1408 0.6 / 2046 4.8	**20** 0136 1.2 / 0808 4.6 / W 1354 1.0 / 2030 4.3
6 0228 1.1 / 0904 4.8 / W 1456 1.0 / 2141 4.5	**21** 0210 1.4 / 0840 4.5 / TH 1428 1.2 / 2104 4.2
7 0322 1.4 / 1001 4.5 / TH 1551 1.3 / ☽ 2242 4.3	**22** 0249 1.6 / 0916 4.3 / F 1508 1.5 / 2146 4.0
8 0426 1.7 / 1104 4.2 / F 1659 1.7 / 2346 4.1	**23** 0334 1.9 / 1003 4.1 / SA 1554 1.7 / ☾ 2240 3.9
9 0541 1.9 / 1212 4.0 / SA 1827 1.9	**24** 0431 2.0 / 1101 4.0 / SU 1652 1.9 / 2341 3.9
10 0055 4.1 / 0657 1.9 / SU 1328 4.0 / 1944 1.9	**25** 0546 2.1 / 1207 3.9 / M 1807 2.0
11 0204 4.2 / 0806 1.9 / M 1438 4.0 / 2041 1.8	**26** 0051 3.9 / 0730 1.9 / TU 1327 3.9 / 1949 1.8
12 0301 4.3 / 0901 1.6 / TU 1532 4.2 / 2125 1.6	**27** 0211 4.1 / 0838 1.6 / W 1447 4.2 / 2053 1.5
13 0348 4.5 / 0946 1.4 / W 1617 4.3 / 2205 1.4	**28** 0315 4.5 / 0931 1.1 / TH 1545 4.5 / 2143 1.1
14 0430 4.6 / 1027 1.2 / TH 1658 4.4 / 2242 1.3	**29** 0407 4.8 / 1017 0.6 / F 1636 4.9 / 2228 0.7
15 0510 4.7 / 1105 1.0 / F 1736 4.5 / ● 2319 1.2	**30** 0455 5.1 / 1100 0.3 / SA 1723 5.1 / ○ 2312 0.4
	31 0542 5.4 / 1142 0.0 / SU 1808 5.3 / 2355 0.2

FEBRUARY

Time m	Time m
1 0627 5.4 / 1223 -0.1 / M 1851 5.3	**16** 0005 0.7 / 0639 4.9 / TU 1222 0.6 / 1857 4.7
2 0038 0.2 / 0710 5.4 / TU 1304 0.1 / 1934 5.1	**17** 0037 0.8 / 0711 4.8 / W 1251 0.7 / 1927 4.6
3 0120 0.4 / 0753 5.2 / W 1344 0.3 / 2018 4.9	**18** 0107 0.9 / 0740 4.7 / TH 1322 0.8 / 1953 4.5
4 0204 0.7 / 0838 4.8 / TH 1427 0.8 / 2105 4.5	**19** 0139 1.1 / 0808 4.5 / F 1355 1.0 / 2018 4.3
5 0251 1.1 / 0927 4.4 / F 1514 1.3 / ☽ 2159 4.2	**20** 0216 1.3 / 0840 4.3 / SA 1433 1.3 / 2054 4.1
6 0346 1.5 / 1025 4.0 / SA 1612 1.7 / 2303 3.9	**21** 0259 1.6 / 0926 4.1 / SU 1518 1.6 / 2151 3.9
7 0459 1.9 / 1135 3.7 / SU 1738 2.0	**22** 0353 1.8 / 1031 3.9 / M 1615 1.9 / ☾ 2304 3.8
8 0020 3.8 / 0622 2.0 / M 1303 3.6 / 1915 2.1	**23** 0504 2.0 / 1144 3.7 / TU 1732 2.0
9 0145 3.8 / 0747 1.9 / TU 1428 3.7 / 2027 1.9	**24** 0021 3.8 / 0714 1.9 / W 1310 3.8 / 1939 1.9
10 0249 4.1 / 0852 1.7 / W 1523 3.9 / 2113 1.7	**25** 0156 3.9 / 0826 1.5 / TH 1437 4.1 / 2042 1.4
11 0337 4.2 / 0934 1.4 / TH 1605 4.2 / 2149 1.4	**26** 0304 4.4 / 0917 1.0 / F 1534 4.5 / 2130 1.0
12 0417 4.5 / 1010 1.1 / F 1643 4.4 / 2224 1.1	**27** 0354 4.8 / 1001 0.5 / SA 1620 4.9 / 2213 0.5
13 0455 4.6 / 1044 0.9 / SA 1718 4.5 / 2259 0.9	**28** 0440 5.2 / 1042 0.1 / SU 1704 5.2 / ○ 2255 0.2
14 0531 4.8 / 1118 0.7 / SU 1753 4.6 / ● 2333 0.8	
15 0606 4.8 / 1150 0.6 / M 1826 4.7	

MARCH

Time m	Time m
1 0525 5.4 / 1122 -0.1 / M 1747 5.3 / 2336 0.0	**16** 0541 4.8 / 1121 0.6 / TU 1758 4.8 / 2338 0.6
2 0608 5.5 / 1201 -0.1 / TU 1829 5.3	**17** 0613 4.8 / 1151 0.6 / W 1827 4.8
3 0017 0.0 / 0650 5.4 / W 1240 0.0 / 1909 5.2	**18** 0009 0.7 / 0644 4.8 / TH 1221 0.6 / 1854 4.7
4 0058 0.2 / 0730 5.2 / TH 1319 0.4 / 1949 4.9	**19** 0039 0.8 / 0713 4.7 / F 1252 0.8 / 1920 4.6
5 0139 0.5 / 0812 4.8 / F 1358 0.8 / 2030 4.6	**20** 0113 0.9 / 0744 4.6 / SA 1326 1.0 / 1947 4.4
6 0223 1.0 / 0856 4.4 / SA 1441 1.3 / 2117 4.2	**21** 0151 1.1 / 0819 4.3 / SU 1406 1.3 / 2024 4.2
7 0315 1.4 / 0948 3.9 / SU 1534 1.8 / ☽ 2217 3.8	**22** 0236 1.4 / 0908 4.1 / M 1452 1.6 / 2122 4.0
8 0426 1.8 / 1100 3.6 / M 1703 2.1 / 2343 3.6	**23** 0331 1.7 / 1016 3.8 / TU 1552 1.9 / ☾ 2241 3.8
9 0551 2.0 / 1240 3.4 / TU 1840 2.2	**24** 0445 1.9 / 1131 3.7 / W 1717 2.1
10 0121 3.6 / 0714 1.9 / W 1411 3.6 / 2001 2.0	**25** 0003 3.8 / 0655 1.7 / TH 1258 3.9 / 1921 1.8
11 0228 3.9 / 0828 1.7 / TH 1503 3.9 / 2049 1.7	**26** 0138 4.1 / 0803 1.3 / F 1420 4.2 / 2021 1.4
12 0315 4.1 / 0909 1.4 / F 1543 4.1 / 2125 1.4	**27** 0244 4.5 / 0854 0.9 / SA 1513 4.6 / 2109 0.9
13 0355 4.4 / 0942 1.1 / SA 1619 4.4 / 2159 1.1	**28** 0334 4.9 / 0938 0.5 / SU 1558 5.0 / 2152 0.5
14 0431 4.6 / 1016 0.8 / SU 1653 4.6 / 2233 0.8	**29** 0419 5.2 / 1019 0.2 / M 1641 5.2 / 2233 0.3
15 0507 4.7 / 1049 0.7 / M 1726 4.7 / ● 2306 0.7	**30** 0503 5.3 / 1059 0.1 / TU 1723 5.3 / ○ 2314 0.1
	31 0546 5.4 / 1138 0.1 / W 1803 5.3 / 2355 0.1

APRIL

Time m	Time m
1 0628 5.3 / 1216 0.3 / TH 1843 5.2	**16** 0616 4.8 / 1151 0.7 / F 1824 4.8
2 0036 0.3 / 0708 5.0 / F 1254 0.6 / 1922 5.0	**17** 0015 0.7 / 0651 4.7 / SA 1226 0.8 / 1856 4.7
3 0118 0.6 / 0749 4.7 / SA 1332 1.0 / 2003 4.6	**18** 0053 0.8 / 0728 4.6 / SU 1305 1.0 / 1932 4.6
4 0201 1.0 / 0832 4.3 / SU 1414 1.4 / 2047 4.3	**19** 0135 1.0 / 0810 4.4 / M 1348 1.3 / 2015 4.4
5 0251 1.4 / 0922 3.9 / M 1506 1.9 / 2142 3.9	**20** 0223 1.3 / 0902 4.2 / TU 1438 1.6 / 2115 4.2
6 0359 1.8 / 1027 3.6 / TU 1633 2.2 / ☽ 2258 3.7	**21** 0321 1.5 / 1008 4.0 / W 1541 1.9 / ☾ 2231 4.0
7 0519 1.9 / 1203 3.5 / W 1801 2.2	**22** 0438 1.6 / 1120 3.9 / TH 1711 2.0 / 2350 4.0
8 0040 3.6 / 0630 1.9 / TH 1334 3.6 / 1911 2.0	**23** 0626 1.5 / 1238 4.1 / F 1853 1.7
9 0151 3.8 / 0735 1.7 / F 1431 3.8 / 2008 1.8	**24** 0111 4.2 / 0733 1.3 / SA 1352 4.4 / 1954 1.4
10 0242 4.0 / 0826 1.5 / SA 1512 4.1 / 2050 1.5	**25** 0217 4.5 / 0827 1.0 / SU 1447 4.7 / 2044 1.0
11 0323 4.2 / 0906 1.2 / SU 1547 4.3 / 2127 1.2	**26** 0309 4.8 / 0913 0.7 / M 1533 5.0 / 2129 0.7
12 0400 4.4 / 0942 1.0 / M 1621 4.5 / 2203 0.9	**27** 0356 5.0 / 0955 0.5 / TU 1616 5.2 / 2211 0.5
13 0435 4.6 / 1016 0.8 / TU 1653 4.7 / 2237 0.8	**28** 0440 5.1 / 1035 0.5 / W 1657 5.2 / ○ 2253 0.4
14 0509 4.7 / 1049 0.7 / W 1723 4.8 / ● 2310 0.7	**29** 0524 5.1 / 1117 0.5 / TH 1739 5.2 / 2336 0.5
15 0543 4.8 / 1120 0.7 / TH 1754 4.8 / 2342 0.7	**30** 0607 5.0 / 1154 0.7 / F 1819 5.1

Chart Datum: 0·20 metres above Ordnance Datum (Dublin). HAT is 5·6 metres above Chart Datum; see 4.5.

TIME ZONE (UT)
For Summer Time add ONE hour in **non-shaded areas**

GALWAY LAT 53°16'N LONG 9°03'W
TIMES AND HEIGHTS OF HIGH AND LOW WATERS

Dates in red are **SPRINGS**
Dates in blue are NEAPS

YEAR 2010

N Ireland

MAY

Time	m	Time	m
1 0017	0.6	**16** 0634	4.8
0648	4.8	1209	0.9
SA 1233	0.9	SU 1841	4.9
1900	4.9		
2 0100	0.8	**17** 0041	0.7
0730	4.6	0716	4.7
SU 1312	1.2	M 1252	1.0
1941	4.7	1924	4.8
3 0143	1.1	**18** 0126	0.8
0813	4.3	0802	4.6
M 1353	1.5	TU 1338	1.2
2025	4.4	2012	4.6
4 0232	1.4	**19** 0216	1.0
0900	4.0	0855	4.4
TU 1442	1.8	W 1430	1.4
2116	4.1	2111	4.4
5 0330	1.6	**20** 0313	1.2
0957	3.7	0955	4.2
W 1552	2.1	TH 1531	1.7
2217	3.9	☽ 2219	4.3
6 0438	1.8	**21** 0422	1.4
1106	3.6	1102	4.2
TH 1715	2.2	F 1650	1.8
☽ 2331	3.7	2330	4.3
7 0543	1.8	**22** 0547	1.4
1226	3.6	1210	4.2
F 1821	2.1	SA 1818	1.7
8 0048	3.8	**23** 0041	4.3
0641	1.8	0659	1.3
SA 1336	3.8	SU 1319	4.4
1919	1.9	1925	1.5
9 0150	3.9	**24** 0148	4.5
0736	1.6	0758	1.2
SU 1427	4.0	M 1419	4.6
2009	1.7	2019	1.3
10 0239	4.0	**25** 0244	4.6
0823	1.4	0848	1.1
M 1507	4.2	TU 1508	4.8
2052	1.4	2107	1.0
11 0320	4.2	**26** 0334	4.8
0905	1.2	0933	1.0
TU 1542	4.4	W 1553	4.9
2131	1.2	2152	0.8
12 0358	4.4	**27** 0421	4.8
0942	1.1	1015	0.9
W 1614	4.6	TH 1636	5.0
2208	1.0	○ 2236	0.8
13 0435	4.6	**28** 0506	4.8
1018	0.9	1056	1.0
TH 1647	4.8	F 1718	5.0
2244	0.8	2319	0.8
14 0513	4.7	**29** 0550	4.7
1052	0.9	1136	1.2
F 1723	4.8	SA 1800	4.9
● 2320	0.7		
15 0552	4.8	**30** 0002	0.8
1129	0.8	0632	4.6
SA 1801	4.9	SU 1215	1.1
2359	0.7	1841	4.8
		31 0044	0.9
		0714	4.5
		M 1254	1.3
		1923	4.7

JUNE

Time	m	Time	m
1 0126	1.0	**16** 0118	0.5
0755	4.3	0751	4.8
TU 1334	1.5	W 1330	0.9
2006	4.5	2003	4.8
2 0208	1.2	**17** 0205	0.6
0838	4.2	0840	4.6
W 1417	1.7	TH 1418	1.1
2051	4.3	2058	4.7
3 0254	1.4	**18** 0256	0.6
0925	4.0	0935	4.5
TH 1507	1.9	F 1513	1.3
2141	4.1	2159	4.5
4 0346	1.6	**19** 0355	1.1
1016	3.9	1036	4.3
F 1611	2.0	SA 1619	1.6
☽ 2234	3.9	☽ 2305	4.3
5 0443	1.7	**20** 0504	1.3
1110	3.8	1139	4.2
SA 1722	2.1	SU 1737	1.6
2328	3.8		
6 0542	1.8	**21** 0011	4.2
1208	3.8	0620	1.5
SU 1826	2.0	M 1246	4.2
		1853	1.6
7 0027	3.8	**22** 0120	4.2
0639	1.8	0729	1.5
M 1313	3.9	TU 1351	4.3
1924	1.9	1958	1.5
8 0133	3.9	**23** 0223	4.3
0736	1.7	0827	1.4
TU 1411	4.0	W 1448	4.5
2015	1.6	2051	1.3
9 0231	4.0	**24** 0318	4.4
0826	1.5	0915	1.3
W 1457	4.2	TH 1537	4.6
2100	1.4	2138	1.1
10 0319	4.2	**25** 0408	4.5
0910	1.3	0959	1.3
TH 1537	4.5	F 1621	4.7
2142	1.1	2223	1.0
11 0404	4.4	**26** 0453	4.5
0952	1.1	1040	1.2
F 1617	4.7	SA 1704	4.8
2224	0.9	○ 2306	0.9
12 0449	4.6	**27** 0537	4.5
1033	0.9	1120	1.2
SA 1659	4.9	SU 1746	4.8
● 2306	0.7	2347	0.8
13 0534	4.8	**28** 0618	4.5
1115	0.8	1158	1.1
SU 1744	5.0	M 1826	4.8
2349	0.5		
14 0620	4.9	**29** 0026	0.8
1159	0.8	0657	4.5
M 1829	5.0	TU 1235	1.2
		1906	4.7
15 0033	0.5	**30** 0103	0.9
0704	4.9	0735	4.4
TU 1244	0.8	W 1312	1.2
1915	5.0	1945	4.6

JULY

Time	m	Time	m
1 0140	1.0	**16** 0146	0.3
0814	4.3	0819	4.9
TH 1349	1.4	F 1400	0.7
2024	4.4	2036	4.8
2 0218	1.1	**17** 0232	0.6
0852	4.2	0908	4.6
F 1428	1.5	SA 1448	1.1
2105	4.3	2132	4.5
3 0257	1.3	**18** 0324	1.0
0933	4.1	1003	4.4
SA 1511	1.7	SU 1546	1.4
2149	4.1	☽ 2235	4.2
4 0341	1.5	**19** 0425	1.4
1015	3.9	1105	4.1
SU 1602	1.9	M 1657	1.7
☽ 2236	3.9	2342	4.0
5 0429	1.7	**20** 0541	1.7
1102	3.9	1213	4.0
M 1709	2.0	TU 1822	1.8
2328	3.8		
6 0527	1.8	**21** 0055	3.9
1155	3.8	0701	1.8
TU 1830	2.0	W 1328	4.0
		1941	1.7
7 0027	3.8	**22** 0209	4.0
0637	1.9	0808	1.7
W 1259	3.9	TH 1435	4.2
1940	1.8	2042	1.5
8 0138	3.8	**23** 0309	4.1
0749	1.7	0900	1.6
TH 1410	4.1	F 1527	4.4
2037	1.5	2129	1.2
9 0246	4.0	**24** 0358	4.2
0846	1.5	0944	1.4
F 1507	4.3	SA 1612	4.5
2125	1.2	2210	1.0
10 0341	4.3	**25** 0442	4.4
0935	1.2	1023	1.2
SA 1556	4.6	SU 1652	4.7
2210	0.8	2248	0.9
11 0431	4.6	**26** 0522	4.5
1020	0.9	1101	1.1
SU 1643	4.9	M 1731	4.8
● 2254	0.5	○ 2326	0.7
12 0519	4.8	**27** 0600	4.5
1104	0.7	1137	1.0
M 1730	5.1	TU 1809	4.8
2337	0.2		
13 0605	5.0	**28** 0001	0.7
1148	0.5	0636	4.6
TU 1816	5.2	W 1212	0.9
		1845	4.8
14 0020	0.1	**29** 0035	0.7
0649	5.1	0711	4.6
W 1232	0.4	TH 1245	1.0
1901	5.2	1920	4.7
15 0103	0.1	**30** 0108	0.8
0734	5.0	0746	4.5
TH 1315	0.5	F 1318	1.1
1948	5.1	1955	4.6
		31 0141	0.9
		0818	4.4
		SA 1352	1.3
		2028	4.4

AUGUST

Time	m	Time	m
1 0216	1.1	**16** 0252	1.1
0850	4.2	0927	4.4
SU 1427	1.5	M 1513	1.4
2105	4.2	◐ 2201	4.1
2 0252	1.4	**17** 0349	1.5
0926	4.1	1026	4.0
M 1508	1.7	TU 1622	1.7
2151	4.0	2314	3.8
3 0336	1.6	**18** 0508	1.9
1011	3.9	1141	3.8
TU 1601	2.0	W 1754	1.9
◐ 2247	3.8		
4 0428	1.9	**19** 0036	3.7
1107	3.8	0636	2.0
W 1713	2.1	TH 1310	3.8
2349	3.7	1930	1.8
5 0537	2.0	**20** 0159	3.8
1211	3.8	0749	1.9
TH 1914	1.9	F 1423	4.0
		2040	1.6
6 0102	3.7	**21** 0259	4.0
0721	1.9	0843	1.7
F 1330	3.9	SA 1514	4.3
2021	1.6	2117	1.3
7 0225	3.9	**22** 0343	4.2
0829	1.6	0924	1.4
SA 1448	4.2	SU 1556	4.5
2111	1.1	2151	1.0
8 0326	4.3	**23** 0423	4.4
0920	1.2	1001	1.2
SU 1542	4.6	M 1634	4.7
2155	0.7	2224	0.8
9 0415	4.6	**24** 0500	4.5
1005	0.8	1037	1.0
M 1629	5.0	TU 1711	4.8
2237	0.3	○ 2258	0.7
10 0501	4.9	**25** 0536	4.6
1048	0.5	1112	0.8
TU 1714	5.2	W 1746	4.9
● 2319	0.0	2332	0.6
11 0546	5.2	**26** 0611	4.7
1131	0.2	1145	0.8
W 1759	5.4	TH 1820	4.9
12 0000	-0.1	**27** 0004	0.6
0629	5.2	0643	4.7
TH 1213	0.2	F 1217	0.7
1843	5.4	1853	4.8
13 0041	-0.1	**28** 0035	0.7
0711	5.2	0714	4.6
F 1254	0.2	SA 1247	0.9
1926	5.2	1923	4.6
14 0122	0.2	**29** 0106	0.9
0753	5.0	0743	4.5
SA 1336	0.5	SU 1318	1.1
2011	4.9	1953	4.5
15 0205	0.6	**30** 0138	1.1
0837	4.7	0810	4.3
SU 1421	0.9	M 1352	1.3
2100	4.5	2026	4.3
		31 0214	1.4
		0840	4.2
		TU 1432	1.6
		2112	4.0

Chart Datum: 0·20 metres above Ordnance Datum (Dublin). HAT is 5·6 metres above Chart Datum; see 4.5.

GALWAY LAT 53°16′N LONG 9°03′W
TIMES AND HEIGHTS OF HIGH AND LOW WATERS

TIME ZONE (UT)
For Summer Time add ONE hour in **non-shaded areas**

Dates in red are **SPRINGS**
Dates in blue are NEAPS

YEAR **2010**

SEPTEMBER

Day	Time m	Time m	Time m	Time m
1 W	0257 1.7	0926 4.0	1522 1.9	☽2215 3.8
2 TH	0351 2.0	1031 3.8	1629 2.1	2324 3.7
3 F	0502 2.1	1140 3.8	1856 2.0	
4 SA	0040 3.7	0706 2.0	1303 4.0	2003 1.6
5 SU	0207 4.0	0812 1.6	1431 4.3	2051 1.1
6 M	0307 4.4	0901 1.2	1525 4.7	2134 0.6
7 TU	0354 4.8	0945 0.7	1610 5.1	2215 0.2
8 W	0438 5.1	1027 0.4	1654 5.4	●2255 0.0
9 TH	0521 5.3	1109 0.1	1738 5.5	2336 -0.1
10 F	0604 5.4	1150 0.1	1821 5.5	
11 SA	0016 0.0	0645 5.3	1231 0.2	1903 5.3
12 SU	0057 0.3	0726 5.1	1313 0.5	1945 5.0
13 M	0138 0.7	0807 4.8	1356 0.9	2032 4.5
14 TU	0223 1.3	0853 4.4	1445 1.4	2129 4.1
15 W	0319 1.8	0948 4.1	1553 1.8	☽2246 3.7
16 TH	0443 2.1	1108 3.8	1726 2.0	
17 F	0017 3.6	0611 2.2	1247 3.8	1904 1.9
18 SA	0143 3.8	0722 2.0	1401 4.0	2025 1.7
19 SU	0239 4.0	0816 1.8	1452 4.2	2053 1.4
20 M	0320 4.3	0858 1.5	1533 4.5	2123 1.1
21 TU	0357 4.5	0935 1.2	1610 4.7	2155 0.9
22 W	0432 4.6	1010 1.0	1645 4.8	2228 0.8
23 TH	0507 4.8	1044 0.9	1719 4.9	○2300 0.7
24 F	0540 4.8	1117 0.8	1752 4.9	2331 0.7
25 SA	0611 4.8	1147 0.8	1823 4.8	
26 SU	0001 0.8	0641 4.7	1217 0.9	1853 4.7
27 M	0032 1.0	0709 4.6	1249 1.1	1924 4.6
28 TU	0106 1.2	0737 4.5	1326 1.3	2000 4.4
29 W	0145 1.5	0809 4.3	1408 1.5	2048 4.1
30 TH	0230 1.8	0857 4.1	1458 1.8	2154 3.9

OCTOBER

Day	Time m	Time m	Time m	Time m
1 F	0327 2.1	1006 4.0	1605 2.0	☽2306 3.8
2 SA	0444 2.2	1120 4.0	1828 1.9	
3 SU	0022 3.9	0645 2.0	1242 4.1	1936 1.6
4 M	0143 4.2	0748 1.6	1406 4.5	2026 1.1
5 TU	0242 4.6	0838 1.2	1502 4.9	2110 0.7
6 W	0329 5.0	0922 0.8	1548 5.2	2151 0.4
7 TH	0412 5.3	1004 0.5	1632 5.5	●2231 0.2
8 F	0455 5.5	1046 0.3	1715 5.5	2311 0.2
9 SA	0537 5.5	1128 0.2	1758 5.5	2351 0.4
10 SU	0619 5.4	1209 0.4	1841 5.3	
11 M	0032 0.6	0700 5.2	1252 0.6	1924 4.9
12 TU	0114 1.0	0742 4.9	1335 1.0	2010 4.5
13 W	0159 1.5	0827 4.5	1424 1.4	2103 4.1
14 TH	0254 1.9	0920 4.2	1526 1.8	☽2215 3.8
15 F	0415 2.2	1030 3.9	1650 2.0	2345 3.7
16 SA	0538 2.3	1205 3.8	1812 2.0	
17 SU	0106 3.8	0643 2.2	1322 4.0	1922 1.8
18 M	0206 4.0	0740 1.9	1418 4.2	2011 1.6
19 TU	0249 4.3	0826 1.7	1502 4.4	2048 1.4
20 W	0326 4.5	0905 1.4	1539 4.6	2123 1.2
21 TH	0400 4.7	0942 1.2	1614 4.7	2156 1.0
22 F	0434 4.8	1016 1.0	1648 4.8	2229 1.0
23 SA	0506 4.8	1049 1.0	1720 4.9	○2300 1.0
24 SU	0537 4.9	1121 0.9	1754 4.9	2331 1.0
25 M	0609 4.9	1153 1.0	1829 4.8	
26 TU	0005 1.1	0642 4.8	1229 1.1	1905 4.7
27 W	0044 1.3	0717 4.7	1309 1.2	1946 4.5
28 TH	0126 1.5	0756 4.5	1353 1.4	2037 4.3
29 F	0214 1.8	0845 4.4	1445 1.6	2140 4.1
30 SA	0313 2.0	0951 4.2	1551 1.8	☽2249 4.1
31 SU	0430 2.1	1103 4.2	1733 1.8	

NOVEMBER

Day	Time m	Time m	Time m	Time m
1 M	0001 4.2	0612 2.0	1218 4.3	1902 1.6
2 TU	0113 4.4	0719 1.7	1335 4.6	1957 1.2
3 W	0213 4.8	0812 1.3	1435 4.9	2044 0.9
4 TH	0303 5.1	0859 1.0	1525 5.2	2127 0.7
5 F	0347 5.3	0943 0.7	1610 5.3	2208 0.6
6 SA	0431 5.4	1026 0.6	1655 5.4	●2249 0.6
7 SU	0514 5.4	1109 0.6	1739 5.3	2330 0.8
8 M	0557 5.3	1152 0.6	1823 5.1	
9 TU	0012 1.0	0640 5.2	1235 0.8	1907 4.9
10 W	0055 1.2	0723 4.9	1319 1.1	1952 4.6
11 TH	0139 1.6	0807 4.7	1405 1.4	2042 4.2
12 F	0230 1.9	0856 4.4	1457 1.7	2142 4.0
13 SA	0334 2.2	0953 4.1	1602 1.9	☽2253 3.8
14 SU	0451 2.3	1100 4.0	1714 2.0	
15 M	0005 3.9	0557 2.2	1214 3.9	1819 2.0
16 TU	0111 4.0	0655 2.1	1323 4.0	1917 1.8
17 W	0205 4.1	0747 1.9	1417 4.2	2006 1.7
18 TH	0247 4.3	0832 1.7	1501 4.3	2047 1.5
19 F	0324 4.5	0913 1.5	1540 4.5	2125 1.3
20 SA	0359 4.7	0950 1.3	1616 4.7	2200 1.2
21 SU	0432 4.8	1026 1.1	1652 4.8	○2234 1.1
22 M	0507 4.9	1101 1.0	1730 4.8	2310 1.1
23 TU	0545 5.0	1138 0.9	1810 4.9	2348 1.1
24 W	0624 5.0	1217 0.9	1852 4.8	
25 TH	0030 1.2	0704 4.9	1300 1.0	1936 4.7
26 F	0116 1.3	0748 4.8	1345 1.1	2026 4.6
27 SA	0205 1.5	0837 4.7	1435 1.3	2123 4.4
28 SU	0300 1.8	0936 4.5	1534 1.5	☽2228 4.3
29 M	0408 1.9	1043 4.4	1646 1.6	2334 4.4
30 TU	0529 1.9	1152 4.4	1817 1.6	

DECEMBER

Day	Time m	Time m	Time m	Time m
1 W	0041 4.5	0645 1.7	1304 4.5	1927 1.4
2 TH	0145 4.7	0746 1.5	1410 4.7	2021 1.3
3 F	0239 4.9	0839 1.3	1505 4.9	2108 1.1
4 SA	0327 5.1	0926 1.1	1554 5.0	2151 1.0
5 SU	0413 5.2	1012 0.9	1640 5.0	●2233 1.0
6 M	0457 5.2	1056 0.8	1726 5.0	2315 1.1
7 TU	0542 5.2	1139 0.8	1810 4.9	2357 1.1
8 W	0625 5.1	1222 0.9	1853 4.8	
9 TH	0038 1.3	0707 5.0	1303 1.0	1936 4.6
10 F	0120 1.5	0750 4.8	1344 1.2	2020 4.4
11 SA	0203 1.7	0833 4.6	1426 1.4	2107 4.2
12 SU	0251 1.9	0919 4.3	1513 1.6	2200 4.0
13 M	0348 2.1	1008 4.2	1607 1.8	☽2256 3.9
14 TU	0455 2.2	1059 4.0	1709 2.0	2354 3.9
15 W	0600 2.2	1155 3.9	1814 2.0	
16 TH	0055 3.9	0701 2.1	1304 3.9	1916 1.9
17 F	0156 4.1	0757 2.0	1411 4.0	2011 1.8
18 SA	0245 4.3	0846 1.7	1503 4.2	2057 1.6
19 SU	0326 4.5	0929 1.4	1548 4.4	2138 1.4
20 M	0406 4.7	1010 1.2	1630 4.6	2218 1.2
21 TU	0446 4.9	1050 0.9	1713 4.8	○2259 1.0
22 W	0528 5.0	1130 0.7	1757 4.9	2340 0.9
23 TH	0612 5.1	1210 0.6	1840 5.0	
24 F	0023 0.9	0654 5.1	1252 0.6	1924 4.9
25 SA	0107 0.9	0738 5.1	1335 0.6	2010 4.8
26 SU	0153 1.1	0824 4.9	1421 0.9	2102 4.6
27 M	0243 1.3	0917 4.7	1512 1.1	2200 4.5
28 TU	0341 1.6	1018 4.5	1611 1.4	☽2304 4.3
29 W	0449 1.7	1124 4.4	1725 1.6	
30 TH	0010 4.3	0607 1.8	1235 4.3	1854 1.7
31 F	0118 4.4	0722 1.7	1348 4.3	2003 1.6

Chart Datum: 0·20 metres above Ordnance Datum (Dublin). HAT is 5·6 metres above Chart Datum; see 4.5.

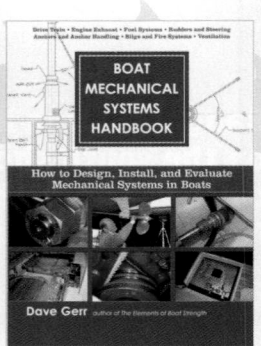

West Denmark

Skagen to Rømø

W Denmark

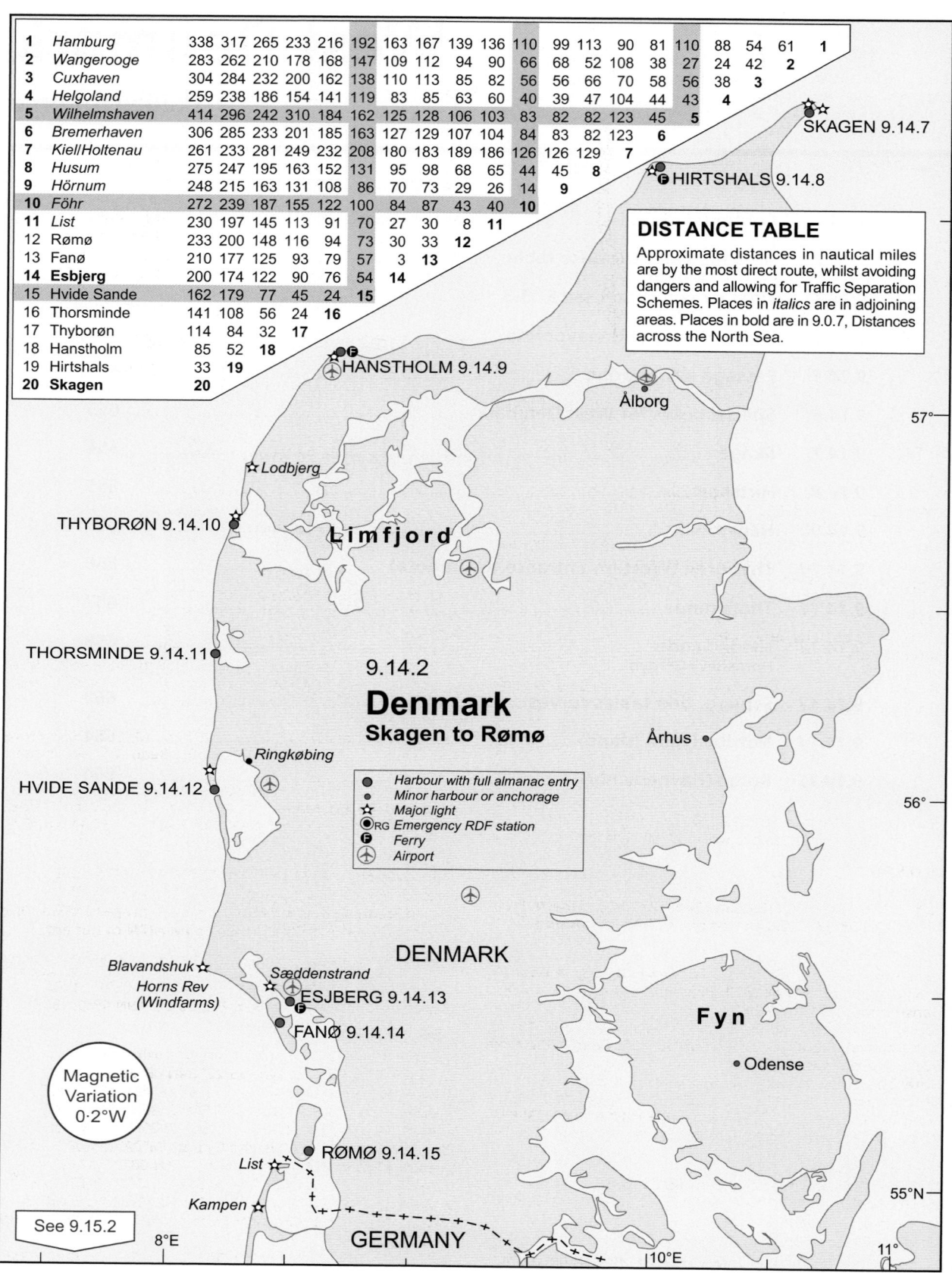

1	*Hamburg*	338	317	265	233	216	192	163	167	139	136	110	99	113	90	81	110	88	54	61	**1**
2	*Wangerooge*	283	262	210	178	168	147	109	112	94	90	66	68	52	108	38	27	24	42	**2**	
3	*Cuxhaven*	304	284	232	200	162	138	110	113	85	82	56	56	66	70	58	56	38	**3**		
4	*Helgoland*	259	238	186	154	141	119	83	85	63	60	40	39	47	104	44	43	**4**			
5	*Wilhelmshaven*	414	296	242	310	184	162	125	128	106	103	83	82	82	123	45	**5**				
6	*Bremerhaven*	306	285	233	201	185	163	127	129	107	104	84	83	82	123	**6**					
7	*Kiel/Holtenau*	261	233	281	249	232	208	180	183	189	186	126	126	129	**7**						
8	*Husum*	275	247	195	163	152	131	95	98	68	65	44	45	**8**							
9	*Hörnum*	248	215	163	131	108	86	70	73	29	26	14	**9**								
10	*Föhr*	272	239	187	155	122	100	84	87	43	40	**10**									
11	*List*	230	197	145	113	91	70	27	30	8	**11**										
12	*Rømø*	233	200	148	116	94	73	30	33	**12**											
13	*Fanø*	210	177	125	93	79	57	3	**13**												
14	**Esbjerg**	200	174	122	90	76	54	**14**													
15	Hvide Sande	162	179	77	45	24	**15**														
16	Thorsminde	141	108	56	24	**16**															
17	Thyborøn	114	84	32	**17**																
18	Hanstholm	85	52	**18**																	
19	Hirtshals	33	**19**																		
20	**Skagen**	**20**																			

SKAGEN 9.14.7

HIRTSHALS 9.14.8

DISTANCE TABLE

Approximate distances in nautical miles are by the most direct route, whilst avoiding dangers and allowing for Traffic Separation Schemes. Places in *italics* are in adjoining areas. Places in **bold** are in 9.0.7, Distances across the North Sea.

57°

HANSTHOLM 9.14.9

Ålborg

Lodbjerg

THYBORØN 9.14.10

Limfjord

THORSMINDE 9.14.11

9.14.2

Denmark
Skagen to Rømø

Århus

Ringkøbing

HVIDE SANDE 9.14.12

56°

●	Harbour with full almanac entry
●	Minor harbour or anchorage
☆	Major light
⊙RG	Emergency RDF station
Ⓕ	Ferry
✈	Airport

DENMARK

F y n

Blavandshuk

Horns Rev
(Windfarms)

Sœddenstrand

ESJBERG 9.14.13

FANØ 9.14.14

• Odense

Magnetic
Variation
0·2°W

RØMØ 9.14.15

55°N

List

Kampen

See 9.15.2

8°E

GERMANY

10°E

11°

Plot waypoints on chart before use

9.14.3 TIDAL STREAM CHARTS see 9.15.3
9.14.4 LIGHTS, BUOYS AND WAYPOINTS

Bold print = light with a nominal range of 15M or more. CAPITALS = place or feature. *CAPITAL ITALICS* = lt-vessel, lt float or Lanby. *Italics* = Fog signal. ***Bold italics*** = Racon. Abbreviations are in Chapter 1.

SKAGEN TO THYBORØN
SKAGEN
Skagen W ☆ Fl(3)WR 10s 31m **W17M**/R12M; 053°-W-248°-R-323°; W ○ twr; 57°44'·94N 10°35·70E.
Skagen ☆ Fl 4s 44m **23M**; Gy ○ twr; ***Racon G, 20M***; 57°44'·14N 10°37'·81E.
Skagen No 1A ⨼ L Fl 10s; ***Racon N***; 57°43'·46N 10°53'·55E. (Route T)
Skagen No. 2 ⨼ L Fl 10s; 57°37'·61N 11°05'·51E. (Route T)
Skagens Rev ⨼ Q; 57°45'·97N 10°43'·74E.
⨼ Q (3) 10s; 57°43'·87N 10°42'·31E.
Skagen Harbour
Ldg lts 334·5°, both Iso R 4s 13/22m 8M. Front, 57°43'·06N 10°35'·45E; mast. Rear, 57°43'·19N 10°35'·34E; twr.
E bkwtr ⚡ Fl G 3s 8m 5M; G twr; *Horn (2) 30s*; 57°42'·88N 10°35'·66E.
W bkwtr ⚡ Fl R 3s 8m 5M; R twr; 57°42'·84N 10°35'·60E.

HIRTSHALS
Hirtshals ☆ F Fl 30s 57m **F 18M**; **Fl 25M**; W ○ twr, approx 1M SSW of hbr ent; 57°35'·10N 09°56'·55E.
Ldg lts 166°, both 156°-176°. Front, Iso R 2s 10m 11M; R △ on twr; 57°35'·69N 09°57'·64E; marina ent is close N of this lt. Rear, Iso R 4s 18m 11M; R ▽ on twr; 330m from front.
Approach chan ◣ Fl (3) G 10s; 57°36'·18N 09°56·94E.
▨ Fl R 3s; 57°36'·44N 09°57'·67E.
◢ Fl (5) Y 20s; 57°36'·43N 09°57'·72E.
◣ Fl G 5s; 57°36'·11N 09°57'·14E.
Outer W mole ⚡ Fl G 3s 14m 6M; G mast; *Horn 15s*; 57°35'·97N 09°57'·37E.
W mole spur ⚡ Fl G 5s 9m 4M; G mast; 57°35'·77N 09°57'·51E.
E mole ⚡ Fl R 5s 9m 6M; G mast; 57°35'·85N 09°57'·61E.

LØKKEN
Lee bkwtr ⚡ Fl 5s 5m 5M; 57°22'·39N 09°42'·11E.

TRANUM STRAND (Firing ranges)
Tranum No. 1 ☆ Al WR 4s 22m W7·5M, R7M; twr; by day Q; shown when firing in progress; 57°12'·43N 09°30'·34E.
Tranum No. 2 ☆ light as per No.1; 57°10'·57N 09°26'·22E.

LILD STRAND
Bragerne ◣ Fl G 5s; 57°10'·67N 08°56'·35E.
Ldg lts 138°, three ⚡: F 12/22m 7/8M; 127°-149°; 3 masts. Front 57°09'·22N 08°57'·75E. Landing place *Siren 30s, fishing.*

HANSTHOLM
Hanstholm ☆ Fl (3) 20s 65m **26M**; shown by day in poor vis; W 8-sided twr; 57°06'·77N 08°35'·92E, approx 1M S of the hbr ent.
Hanstholm ⨼ LFl 10s; 57°08'·06N 08°34'·87E.
Ldg lts 142·6°, both Iso 2s 37/45m 13M; synch; 127·6°-157·6°; R △ on mast. Front, 57°07'·12N 08°36'·15E. Rear, 170m from front, R ▽ on mast.
Note: The 4 outer/inner mole heads are floodlit.
W outer mole ⚡ Fl G 3s 11m 9M; G pillar; 57°07'·56N 08°35'·45E. E outer mole ⚡ Fl R 3s 11m 9M; R pillar; 57°07'·61N 08°35'·57E.
Roshage ⚡ Fl 5s 7m 5M; 57°07'·75N 08°37'·25E (1M E of hbr).

NØRRE VORUPØR
Mole ⚡ Fl G 5s 6m 4M; 57°57'·74N 08°21'·679E.
Ldg lts, both Iso R 4s 20/30m 9M, indicate safest landing place for FVs; vis 22·5° either side of ldg line; synch. Front 57°57'·46N 08°22'·10E. Rear, 80m from front.
Lodbjerg ☆ Fl (2) 20s 48m **23M**; ○ twr; 56°49'·40N 08°15'·76E.

THYBORØN
Landfall ⨼ L Fl 10s; ***Racon T, 10m***; 56°42'·54N 08°08'·69E.
Agger Tange ldg lts 082°: Front, Iso WRG 4s 8m W11M, R/G8M; 074·5°-G-079·5°-W-084·5°-R-089·5°; R △ on bcn; 56°42'·97N 08°14'·14E. Rear, Iso 4s 17m 11M; 075°-089°; synch; R ▽ on Gy twr; 804m from front.
Off Havmolen ▨ 56°43'·25N 08°12'·52E.
Approach ☆ Fl (3) 10s 24m 12M; intens 023·5°-203·5°; also lit by day in poor vis; lattice twr; 56°42'·49N 08°12'·91E (S side of ent).
Langholm ldg lts 120°, both Iso 2s 7/13m 11M; synch; 113°-127°. Front, R △ on R hut, 56°42'·45N 08°14'·54E. Rear, R ▽ on Gy twr.
Thyborøn Havn ⚡ Oc (2) WRG 12s 6m W11M, R/G8M; 122·5°-G-146·5°-W-150°-R-211·3°-G-337·5°-W-340°-R-344°; W twr R band; 56°42'·35N 08°13'·39E (680m N of ent to Yderhavn and Basins).
Yderhavn, N mole ⚡ Fl G 3s 6m 4M; G pedestal; 56°42'·02N 08°13'·52E.
S mole ⚡ Fl R 3s 6m 4M; R pedestal; 56°41'·97N 08°13'·53E.

LIMFJORD (Limited coverage eastward, only to 08°42'E)
Sælhundeholm Løb, into Nissum Bredning ('Broad').
No. 1 ◣ Fl (2) G 5s; 56°41'·14N 08°14'·17E.
No. 3 ◣ Fl G 3s; 56°40'·75N 08°13'·79E.
No. 7 ◣ Fl G 3s; 56°40'·31N 08°13'·52E.
No. 11 ◣ Fl G 3s; 56°39'·83N 08°13'·59E.
No. 16 ▨ Fl R 3s; 56°38'·51N 08°13'·89E.
No. 18 ▨ Fl (2) R 5s; 56°38'·20N 08°14'·34E.
No. 21 ◣ Fl G 3s; 56°38'·98N 08°14'·71E.
No. 26 ▨ Fl R 3s; 56°38'·71N 08°15'·38E.
No. 29 ◣ Fl G 3s; 56°38'·40N 08°15'·94E.
⨼ Q; 56°38'·06N 08°16'·70E.

APPROACHES TO LEMVIG (Marina and Havn)
Toftum Dir ⚡ 120°, Iso WRG 4s 24m, W12M, R/G 8M; 110°-G-120°-W-137°-R-144°; hut; 56°33'·09N 08°18'·33E.
Rønnen ◣ Fl G 3s; 56°34'·71N 08°21'·74E.
Rønnen ⨼ L Fl 10s; 56°35'·58N 08°21'·62E.
Søgard Mark ldg lts 243·5°: both FR 20/30m 5M; vis 90° either side of ldg line. Front, ⨼ R △ on W bcn; 56°34'·39N 08°17'·29E. Rear, R ▽ on W post; 235m from front.
Chan ◣ 56°33'·27N 08°18'·31E.
Ldg lts, W of hbr 177·7°, both FR 8/20m 5M; 153°-203°. Front ⨼ R △ on twr; 56°33'·04N 08°18'·16E. Rear, R ▽ on W post; 184m from front.
Vinkel Hage marina, N mole ⚡ FG 3m 5M; 56°33'·09N 08°18'·33E. S mole, FR 3m 4M. Marina is 9ca N of the Havn on the W side.
Ostre Havn ⨼ 56°33'·17N 08°18'·40E. Havn ent, FG/FR 4m 5M.

THISTED HAVN (Marina)
Outer W mole ⚡ Fl R 3s 4m 2M; 56°57'·10N 08°41'·90E.
Outer E mole ⚡ Fl G 3s 4m 2M; 56°57'·10N 08°41'·95E.
Thisted Bredning ⚡ Aero 3 Fl R 1·5s (vert; 45m apart) 183m 10M; TV mast; 56°58'·52N 08°41'·15E, 1·55M NNW of hbr ent.

THYBORØN TO BLÅVANDS HUK
Bovbjerg ☆ Fl (2) 10s 62m 16M; 56°30'·79N 08°07'·18E.
Wave recorder buoy ◢ Fl (5) Y 20s; 56°28'·49N 08°03'·35E.

THORSMINDE HAVN
(All Lat/Longs for this harbour are approximate)
Lt ho ⚡ F 30m 13M; Gy twr; 56°22'·34N 08°06'·99E.
Groyne, N ⚡ Fl 5s 8m 5M; Gy hut; 56°22'·46N 08°06'·82E.
N mole ⚡ Iso R 2s 9m 4M; R hut; 56°22'·36N 08°06'·62E.
S mole ⚡ Iso G 2s 9m 4M; G hut; 56°22'·26N 08°06'·92E.
West hbr, W mole ⚡ FG 5m 2M; Gy post; 56°22'·36N 08°07'·12E.
E mole ⚡ FR 5m 2M; Gy post; 56°22'·26N 08°07'·18E.
NW dolphin ⚡ FG 5m 4M; Gy post; 56°22'·26N 08°07'·22E.
SE dolphin ⚡ FR 5m 4M; Gy post; 56°22'·26N 08°07'·26E.
Lock, E side ⚡ Iso 4s 12m 4M; Gy mast; 020°-160°; 56°22'·36N 08°07'·22E.
Road bridge ⚡ Iso 4s 5m 4M; 200°-340°; 56°22'·36N 08°07'·26E.

HVIDE SANDE
Lyngvig ☆ Fl 5s 53m **22M**; W ○ twr; 56°02'·95N 08°06'·17E.
N outer bkwtr ⚓ Fl R 3s 7m 8M; R hut; 55°59'·94N 08°06'·55E.
N mole ⚓ Fl R 5s 10m 6·5M; R floodlit edifice; 55°59'·98N 08°06'·84E.
S mole ⚓ Fl G 5s 10m 6M; 55°59'·93N 08°06'·88E.
Lt ho ⚓ F 27m 14M; Gy twr; 56°00'·00N 08°07'·35E.
Nordhavn, E pier ⚓ FG 4m 4M; 56°00'·16N 08°07'·42E.
W pier ⚓ 2 FR 3m 2M; W posts; 060°-035°; 56°00'·07N 08°07'·12E.
Sydhavn, W pier ⚓ FG 4m 2M; 56°00'·06N 08°07'·52E.
E Pier ⚓ FR 4m 2M; Gy post; 56°00'·06N 08°07'·53E.
Lock entrance ldg lts 293·5°: both FR 11/14m 2M; 201·6°-021·6°.
Front, R △ on Gy tr, 56°00'·0N 08°07'·8E. Rear, R ▽ on Gy twr, 72m from front.
Fjordhavn ldg lts 246·6° (both vis 7·5° either side of ldg line):
Front, Iso G 2s 4m 4M; Or △ on mast; 56°00'·5N 08°07'·9E. Rear, Iso G 4s 6m 4M, Or ▽ on mast, 128m from front.

HORNS REV (marks westward from coast)
Oskbøl firing range. Two lights (4M apart), both AlFl WR 4s 35m **16M**, R13M, (by day Q 10M), are shown when firing is in progress:
North ☆ 55°37'·3N 08°07'·1E. South ☆ 55°33'·6N 08°04'·7E.
Range safety buoys: ⚓ Fl Y 5s; 55°42'·32N 08°06'·92E.⚓ Fl Y 3s; 55°38'·63N 07°50'·91E.⚓ Fl Y 3s; 55°37'·35N 07°56'·98E.⚓ 55°36'·02N 08°02'·49E.

Blåvands Huk ☆ Fl (3) 20s 55m **23M**; W □ twr; 55°33'·46N 08°04'·95E.

Horns Rev is encircled by:
Tuxen ⚓ Q; 55°34'·22N 07°41'·92E on the N side.
Vyl ⚓ Q (6) + L Fl 15s; 55°26'·22N 07°49'·99E on the S side.
No. 2 ⚓ L Fl 10s; 55°28'·74N 07°36'·49E on the SW side.
Horns Rev W ⚓ Q (9) 15s; 55°34'·47N 07°26'·05E, off the W end.

Slugen Channel (crosses Horns Rev ESE/WNW)
⚓ L Fl G 10s; 55°33'·99N 07°49'·38E.
⚓ Fl G 3s; 55°32'·26N 07°53'·65E.
⚓ Fl (2) R 5s; 55°31'·46N 07°52'·88E.
⚓ Fl (2) G 5s; 55°30'·52N 07°59'·20E.
⚓ Fl (3) R 10s; 55°29'·42N 08°02'·56E.

Søren Bovbjergs Dyb (unlit N/S side channel off Slugen Chan)
⚓ 55°33'·57N 07°55'·55E.
⚓ 55°32'·80N 07°55'·30E.
⚓ 55°32'·19N 07°56'·29E.
⚓ 55°31'·24N 07°57'·46E.

Wind farm in □ 2·7M x 2·5M, centred on 55°29'·22N 07°50'·21E: 80 turbines all R lts, the 12 perimeter turbines are lit Fl (3) Y 10s.
NE turbine, *Racon (U)*; 55°30'·28N 07°52'·63E & transformer platform, 2 Mo (U) 15s 9m 5M, 55°30'·52N 07°52'·53E.
SW turbine, *Racon (U)*; 55°28'·11N 07°48'·26E.
Met mast (60m) ⚓ 2 Mo (U) 15s 8m 3M; 55°31'·32N 07°47'·33E.
2 Met masts, both 70m, ⚓ 2 Mo (U) 15s 12m 5M and Aero QR: 151B (55°29'·21N 07°54'·72E) and 151C (55°29'·24N 07°58'·52E).

BLÅVANDS HUK TO RØMØ
APPROACHES TO ESBJERG
Grådyb ⚓ L Fl 10s; *Racon G, 10M*; 55°24'·63N 08°11'·59E.
Sædding Strand 053·8° triple ldg lts: valid up to Nos 7/8 buoys.
H24: **Front** Iso 2s 13m **21M**; 052°-056°; R bldg; 55°29'·74N 08°23'·87E.
Middle Iso 4s 26m **21M**; 051°-057°; R twr, W bands; 55°29'·94N 08°24'·33E, 630m from front.
Rear F 37m **18M**; 052°-056°; R twr; 55°30'·18N 08°24'·92E, 0·75M from front.
No. 1 ⚓ Q; 55°25'·49N 08°13'·89E.
No. 2 ⚓ Fl (3) R 10s; 55°25'·62N 08°13'·73E.
No. 3 ⚓ Fl G 3s; 55°25'·93N 08°14'·84E.
No. 4 ⚓ Fl R 3s; 55°26'·02N 08°14'·72E.
Tide Gauge ⚓ Fl (5) Y 20s 8m 4M; 55°26'·05N 08°15'·93E.

No. 5 ⚓ Fl G 5s; 55°26'·32N 08°15'·83E.
No. 6 ⚓ Fl R 5s; 55°26'·44N 08°15'·70E.
No. 7 ⚓ Q; 55°26'·76N 08°16'·91E.
No. 8 ⚓ Fl (2) R 5s; 55°26'·89N 08°16'·81E.
Ldg lts 067°, valid up to Nos 9/10 buoys. Both FG 10/25m **16M**, H24. Front, Gy tripod; rear, Gy twr, 55°28'·76N 08°24'·70E.
No. 9 ⚓ Fl G 10s; 55°27'·04N 08°18'·21E.
No.10 ⚓ Fl (2) R 10s; 55°27'·20N 08°18'·04E.
Ldg lts 049°, valid up to No 16 buoy/Jerg. Both FR 16/27m **16M**, H24. Front, W twr; rear, Gy twr, 55°29'·92N 08°23'·75E.
No. 11 ⚓ Fl G 3s; 55°27'·71N 08°19'·59E.
No. 12 ⚓ Fl R 3s; 55°27'·88N 08°19'·39E.
No. 13 ⚓ Fl G 5s; 55°28'·40N 08°20'·99E.
No. 14 ⚓ Fl R 5s; 55°28'·57N 08°20'·73E.
Jerg ⚓ Fl G 3s 7m 5M; G twr, Y base; 55°28'·88N 08°22'·00E.
No. 16 ⚓ Q (6) + L Fl 15s; 55°29'·04N 08°21'·80E.
No. 15A ⚓ Fl (2) G 5s; 55°29'·01N 08°22'·47E.
No 18 ⚓ Fl (2) R 5s; 55°29'·19N 08°22'·71E.
Fovrfelt N ☆ Oc (2) WRG 6s 7m 5M; 066·5°-G-073°-W-077°-R-085·5°; 327°-G-331°- W-333·5°-R-342°; Y twr; 55°29'·29N 08°23'·79E.
Fovrfelt ⚓ Fl (2) R 10s 11m 6M; R twr; 55°29'·03N 08°23'·75E.
No 15B ⚓ Fl (2) G 10s; 55°28'·83N 08°23'·65E.

ESBJERG HAVN
Strandby, shelter mole, NW corner ⚓ Oc WRG 5s 6m W13M, R/G9M; 101·7°-G-105·5°-W-109·5°-R-111·7°; W bldg, R band; 55°28'·76N 08°24'·63E.
Industrifiskerihavn, W mole ⚓ Fl R 5s 6m 4M; R structure; 55°28'·52N 08°24'·96E.
E mole ⚓ Fl G 5s 6m 4M; G structure; 55°28'·52N 08°25'·03E.
Nordsøkai ⚓ Q (9) 15s 5m; Y twr, B band; 55°28'·45N 08°25'·04E.
Konsumfiskerihavn, W mole ⚓ FlR 3s 6m; 203°-119°; R twr; 55°28'·31N 08°25'·33E. Yacht hbr in SSE part of Basin II.
E mole ⚓ Fl G 3s 6m; 023°-256°; G tr; 55°28'·31N 08°25'·40E.
Trafikhavn, NW corner ⚓ Oc (2) WRG 12s 6m W13M, R/G9M; 118°-G-124·5°-W-129°-R-131°; W bldg, R band; 55°28·22N 08°25·43E.
N mole ⚓ FR 8m 5M; 232°-135°; R bldg; 55°28'·13N 08°25'·46E.
S mole ⚓ FG 8m 4M; 045°-276°; G bldg; 55°28'·08N 08°25'·51E.
No. 22 ⚓ Fl (2) R 5s; 55°27'·62N 08°25'·50E.
Sønderhavn (industrial) W mole ⚓ FR 9m 4M; 55°27'·49N 08°26'·12E. E mole ⚓ FG 9m 4M; 55°27'·43N 08°26'·31E.
Aero ⚓ 3 x Fl 1·5s (vert, 82m apart) 251m 12M, H24; on chimney; 55°27'·27N 08°27'·32E (1200m ESE of Sønderhavn ent).

FANØ
Slunden outer ldg lts 242°, both Iso 2s 5/8m 3M; 227°-257°.
Front, twr; 55°27'·20N 08°24'·53E. Rear, twr, 106m from front.
E shore, reciprocal ldg lts 062°, both FR 10/13m 3M; 047°-077°.
Front, twr; 55°27'·65N 08°26'·01E. Rear, twr, 140m from front.
No. 1 ⚓ Fl (2) G 10s 5m 2M; G pile; 55°27'·45N 08°25'·28E.
No. 2 ⚓ Fl (2+1) Y 5s 5m 2M; Y pile; 55°27'·42N 08°25'·32E.
No. 3 ⚓ Fl G 5s 5m 2M; G pile; 55°27'·39N 08°25'·07E.
No. 4 ⚓ Fl R 3s 5m 2M; R pile; 55°27'·35N 08°25'·10E.
Nordby ldg lts 214°, both FR 7/9m 4M; 123·7°-303·7°. Front , W mast; 55°26'·94N 08°24'·44E. Rear, Gy twr, 84m from front.
Kremer Sand ⚓ FG 5m 3M; G dolphin; 55°27'·3N 08°24'·9E.
Næs Søjord ⚓ FR 5m 3M; R pile; 55°27'·27N 08°24'·86E.
Nordby marina 55°26'·65N 08°24'·53E.

KNUDEDYB
G ⚓ 55°20'·50N 08°24'·28E.
K ⚓ 55°18'·92N 08°20'·06E.
No. 2 ⚓ 55°18'·82N 08°21'·33E.
No. 4 ⚓ 55°18'·81N 08°22'·21E.
No. 6 ⚓ 55°18'·38N 08°24'·63E.
No. 10 ⚓ 55°18'·68N 08°28'·50E.
Knoben ⚓ 55°18'·71N 08°30'·60E.

WGS84 DATUM
Plot waypoints on chart before use

JUVRE DYB
No. 4 ⌕ 55°13'·76N 08°24'·73E.
No. 6 ⌕ 55°13'·41N 08°26'·60E.
No. 8 ⌕ 55°12'·69N 08°26'·83E.
No. 10 ⌕ 55°12'·55N 08°28'·72E.
Rejsby Stjært ⌕ 55°13'·15N 08°30'·55E.

OUTER APPROACH (Lister Tief) TO RØMØ
See also 9.15.4 for details of lights on Sylt.
Rode Klit Sand ⌕ Q (9) 15s, 55°11'·11N 08°04'·88E, (130°/9M to Lister Tief ⌕).
Lister Tief ⌕ Iso 8s, *Whis;* 55°05'·32N 08°16'·80E.
No. 1 ⌕ 55°05'·21N 08°18'·20E.
No. 3 ⌕ Fl G 4s; 55°04'·75E 08°18'·73E.
No. 2 ⌕ Fl (3) R 10s; 55°04'·23N 08°22'·32E.
No. 9 ⌕ Fl (2) G 9s; 55°03'·76N 08°23'·05E.

Lister Landtief No 5 ⌕ 55°03'·68N 08°24'·73E.
No. 4 ⌕ Fl (2) R 5s; 55°03'·84N 08°25'·29E.
G1 ⌕ Fl Y 4s; 55°03'·27N 08°28'·32E.

RØMØ DYB and HAVN
No. 1 ⌕ Fl (2) G 10s; 55°03'·23N 08°30'·30E.
No. 10 ⌕ Fl (2) R 10s 5m 3M; R pole; 55°03'·50N 08°31'·10E.
No. 14 ⌕ Fl R 3s 6m 2M; R pole; 55°03'·85N 08°32'·55E.
No. 20 ⌕ Fl R 5s 5m 2M; R pole; 55°04'·79N 08°34'·13E.
No. 9 ⌕ 55°04'·79N 08°34'·63E.
No. 11 ⌕ 55°05'·17N 08°34'·69E.

Rømø Hbr:
S mole ⌕ Fl R 3s 7m 2M; Gy twr; 55°05'·19N 08°34'·31E.
N mole ⌕ Fl G 3s 7m 2M; Gy twr; 55°05'·23N 08°34'·30E.
Inner S mole ⌕ FR 4m 1M; 55°05'·2N 08°34'·2E.
Inner N mole ⌕ FG 4m 1M; 55°05'·3N 08°34'·2E.

9.14.5 PASSAGE INFORMATION

Reference books include: *North Sea (East) Pilot* (NP 55); *Cruising Guide to Germany and Denmark* (Imray/Navin).

More Passage Information is threaded between successive harbours in this Area.

Jutland's low, sandy W coast is not a notable cruising ground and lacks genuine harbours of refuge in strong onshore winds. Even **Esbjerg** is made difficult by a bar on which seas break heavily in strong W or SW winds. **Thyborøn** should not be approached on the ebb with onshore winds >F5. But in settled weather, these and other ports may break the long passage to the Skagerrak or round **Skagen** (The Skaw) into the Kattegat.

Coastal dangers include: Horns Rev, a reef extending about 22M W of Blåvands Huk, but with a buoyed channel some 5M offshore; and extensive sand ridges lying parallel to and some 5ca off the shore, with depths of 1m to 5.5m. There are many coastal nature reserves, as charted, into which entry is either restricted or prohibited; but they do not deny access to hbrs.

►*Tidal streams are weak as far N as Thyborøn and imperceptible further N, but expect wind-driven currents such as the N-going Stryget.*◄ The general direction of buoyage is northerly. Navigational marks are excellent. There is much fishing activity, including pairs-trawling.

SKAGEN TO HANSTHOLM

(AC 1402) From/to **Skagen** keep outside the cardinal buoys marking Skagen Rev. In Jammerbugt (The Bay of Woe: Hirtshals to Hanstholm) a firing practice area extends 7M off Tranum Strand, 57°10'N 09°25'E.

9.14.6 SPECIAL NOTES for W DENMARK

VOCABULARY A few Danish words which may be useful:

Ashore	Paa Lan	Nautical	
Hello	Goodag	Harbourmaster	Havnefoged
Goodbye	Farvel	Customs	Told
Please	Vaer so gud	Hbr Police	Havnepoliti
Thank you	Tak	Boat name	Bådenavn
Yes	Ja	Length	Længde
No	Nej	Beam	Bredde
Sorry	Undskyld	Draught	Dybgang
How much ..?	Hvor meget koster ..?	Water, fresh	Vand
		Electricity	Electricitet
Where is ..?	Hvor er ..?	Petrol	Benzin
Left	Venstre	Shower	Bruser
Right	Højre	Red	Rød
Doctor	Læge	Green	Grøn
Dentist	Tandlæge	White	Hvid
Hospital	Hospitalet	Anchorage	Ankerplads
Chemist	Apotek	Prohibited	Forbudt
Laundry	Vaskeri	High water	Højvande
Postoffice	Postkontoret	Low water	Lavvande
Bus	Bussen	Chart datum	Kortdatum
Train	Toget	Forecast	Vejrudsigt
Ticket, single	enkeltbillet	Low	Lavtryk
Open	Åben	High	Høj
Closed	Lukket	Gale	Hård kuling
Market	Marked	Squall	Byge
Milk	Mælk	Rough sea	Grov sø
Bread	Brød	Rain	Regn
Meat	Kød	Fog	Tåge

LANGUAGES English and German are widely spoken.

AMTSKOMMUNERS are given in lieu of 'counties' in the UK.

TIME ZONE is –0100 (subtract 1 hour for UT). DST is kept from the last Sunday in March until the last Sunday in October.

CHARTS Danish charts are issued by Kort-og Matrikelstyrelsen, Rentemestervej 8, DK-2400 København. Those prefixed 'DK' are standard Danish nautical charts. Leisure charts for W Jutland are not available. British Admiralty charts are mostly small scale.

LIGHTS Navigational marks, buoys and lights are excellent.

HARBOURS Most yacht hbrs are owned by the state or community and run by a local Yacht Club (as in Germany).

TRAFFIC SEPARATION SCHEMES There are none off West Jutland, but off Skagen heavy traffic between the Skaggerak and Kattegat follows Transit Routes T or B; see chartlet overleaf.

SIGNALS Local port, tidal, distress and traffic signals are given where possible. When motor sailing, always display a motoring ▼.

TELEPHONES To call UK from Denmark: dial 00 44, then the UK area code, minus the initial zero; followed by the number required. To call Denmark, which has no area codes, from the UK: dial 00 (or +) 45, then the required 8 digit number.

EMERGENCIES Police, Fire and Ambulance: dial 112.

PUBLIC HOLIDAYS New Year's Day, Maundy Thurs (Thu before Easter) thru' to Easter Monday, Common Prayer Day (4th Fri after Easter), Ascension Day, Whit Monday, Constitution Day (5 Jun), Christmas Eve to Boxing Day. Local festivals are common.

CURRENCY The Danish krone (Dkr) = 100 øre. Rate of exchange May 2008: £1.00 = approx Dkr 9.11; 1 Dkr = approx £0.11. VAT (MOMS) is 25%, on everything. Banks with ATMs are as common as in the UK. All major credit cards are accepted.

GAS Propane is the norm. Camping Gaz (butane) is available, but Calor gas, whether butane or propane, is not.

USEFUL ADDRESSES Danish Tourist Board, 55 Sloane St, London SW1X 9SY; ☎ 020 7259 5959; dtb.london@dt.dk. The Embassy is at the same address.

Denmark: The main Tourist Office is Vesterbrogade 6D, 1620 København V; ☎ 33 11 14 15; dt@dt.dk; www.dt.dk. There are excellent and very helpful TOs in most fair-sized towns.

British Embassy, Kastelsvej 36-40, DK-2100 København 0; ☎ 33 44 52 00.

British Consulate, Kanalen 1, DK-6700 Esbjerg.
For other addresses see Chapter 1, 1.2.

TRANSPORT DFDS operate the Harwich-Esbjerg ferry. Other ferries run from Hirtshals to Oslo and Kristiansand; and from Hanstholm to Bergen, the Faeroe Is and Iceland.

UK scheduled and low-cost flights go to Billund (35M NE of Esbjerg) and Copenhagen. Internal flights are limited as Denmark is compact and has good trains and buses.

Trains (DSB) are notably reliable and fast, with a broad fare structure. Bicycles are very popular and easy to hire if you do not already have a 'folder'.

SHOPPING Most towns have a market day on either Wed or Sat. Launderettes (*montvaskeri*), coin or token-operated, are to be found in most towns.

9.14.7 SKAGEN (pronounced Skane)

Nordjylland 57°42'·86N 10°35'·63E ✹✹✹◊◊◊✿

TIDAL STREAMS are perceptible only in calm conditions. Wind usually has an over-riding effect such that the current is E-going for 75% of the year.

SHELTER is good, access at all tides/weather. Yachts berth in 4m between Old Pier and Pier 1, NE of the central pontoon. FVs berth either side of Pier 1. There are also yacht pontoons in 3·5m on the N side of Bundgarns Bassin.

NAVIGATION From the W, the WPT is 57°45'·98N 10°43'·74E, a NCM buoy Q, off the NE tip of Skagens Rev. Thence 200°/2·2M to an ECM buoy, Q(3) 10s, at 57°43'·87N 10°42'·35E; thence 258°/3·6M to hbr ent. Routes B and T are buoyed, commercial transit routes.

LIGHTS AND MARKS As chartlet and 9.14.4. The R sector of Skagen West lt ho shows over Skagens Rev. Skagen lt ho is 1·7M NE of the hbr ent, with Racon G, 20M. The peninsula is low-lying, flat and fringed by sand dunes.

R/T Ch 16; 12 13, HX.

CHARTS AC 1402, 2107 with 1:12,500 hbr inset.

TIDES Variations in heights are minimal and largely generated by wind. ATT Vol 2 publishes height differences referred to Bergen and advises the use of harmonic constants for time differences. But for all practical purposes Hirtshals differences are adequate. HW heights are: MHWS 0·2m, MHWN 0·1m.

TELEPHONE HM 98.44.10.60, 98.44.13.46, 98.44.14.66; Coastguard 98.44.12.22; Hospital 99.79.79.79; Police (Emergency) 112; Taxi 98.92.47.00.

FACILITIES AB, FW, ⬨, D, ME, ⚒, SM, WC, Showers. YC Skagen Sejl Klub ☎ 98.45.06.79.

Town: Bar, R, PO, ⇌, ✈ (Aalborg) ☎ 98.17.33.11.

9.14.8 HIRTSHALS ❄✿💧🌿🌸

Nordjylland 57°35'·90N 09°57'·54E

CHARTS AC 1402 with 1:12,500 hbr inset; DK92; D 63

TIDES +0600 Dover, ML 0·0, Duration 0625
Standard Port ESBJERG (→)

Times				Height (metres)			
High Water		Low Water		MHWS	MHWN	MLWN	MLWS
0300	0700	0100	0800	1·9	1·5	0·5	0·1
1500	1900	1300	2000				
Differences HIRTSHALS							
+0055	+0320	+0340	+0100	−1·6	−1·3	−0·4	−0·1

SHELTER Good. Yachts berth in a small marina to stbd and close S of the hbr ent. A further marina in Vestbassin is reported, for details call HM Hirtshals is a commercial and fishing hbr which in theory foreign yachts may use only with HM's prior approval. It is not advisable to attempt entrance in strong onshore winds from N to NW due to heavy seas and strong E-going current. In E gales water levels are lowered by up to 1·0m.

NAVIGATION WPT 57°36'·39N 09°57'·32E, 166°/7ca to marina ent in front of rear 166° ldg lt. The outer PHM and SHM buoys funnel vessels into the entrance. Inbound vessels have precedence over out-bound. Turn to stbd before reaching the Inner Hbr lt FG. Caution: FVs and fast ferries to Norway. Speed limit 3kn.

LIGHTS AND MARKS As chartlet and 9.14.4. 166° ldg bcns: front, R ▲ on frame twr; rear, R ▼ on frame twr. The white lt ho is approx 1M SW of the hbr ent.

R/T VHF Ch 16; 14, HX.

TELEPHONE HM 98.94.14.22; Coastguard 98.92.22.22; Police 96.23.14.48, (emergency 112); Taxi 98.92.47.00; Dr 98.94.11.77; Hospital 70.15.03.00; Hospital (Hjørring) 98.92.72.44.

FACILITIES AB, FW, WC, Showers, SM ☎ 98 94 12 27; **Town**: R, PO, ⇌, ✈ (Aalborg) ☎ 98.17.33.11.

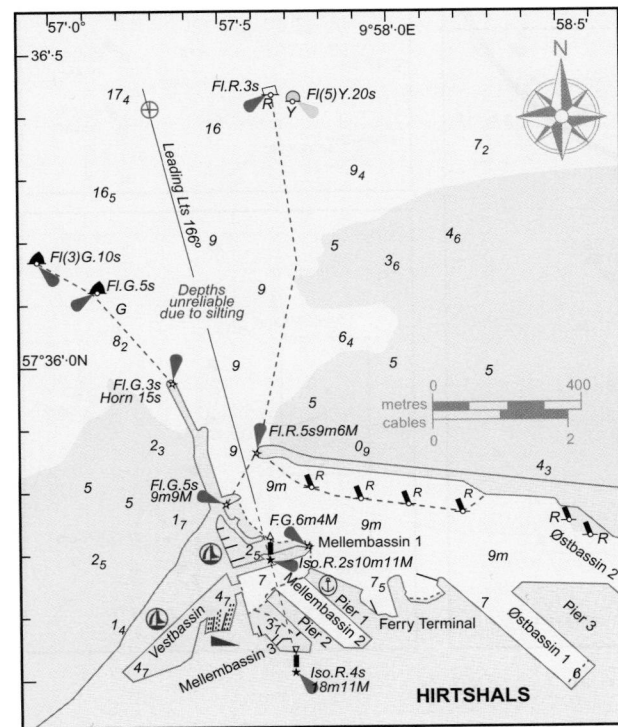

HIRTSHALS

9.14.9 HANSTHOLM ❄✿💧🌿🌸

Viborg 57°07'·57N 08°35'·51

HANSTHOLM

CHARTS AC 1402 with 1:12,500 hbr inset; DK92, 104; D 82

TIDES +0600 Dover, ML 0.0, Duration 0630
Standard Port ESBJERG (→)

Times				Height (metres)			
High Water		Low Water		MHWS	MHWN	MLWN	MLWS
0300	0700	0100	0800	1·9	1·5	0·5	0·1
1500	1900	1300	2000				
Differences HANSTHOLM							
+0100	+0340	+0340	+0130	−1·6	−1·2	−0·4	−0·1

SHELTER Good. The port is a commercial and fishing hbr which in theory foreign yachts may use only with the HM's prior approval. Yachts berth at the SW corner of Bassin 6 or as directed. S of the FG/FR inner mole heads speed limit 3kn.

NAVIGATION WPT 57°08'·10N 08°34'·94E [SWM buoy, L Fl 10s], 142° about 6ca to the hbr entrance. The approach is clear. Ldg marks 142·6° front, R ▲ on mast; rear, R ▼ on mast, lead between the outer moles.

- Charted depths are unreliable due to silting and particularly after E gales when levels may be lowered by up to 1·3m.
- Check on VHF that the entrances are clear of departing ships which may be hidden behind the moles. Inbound vessels have precedence over out-bound.

LIGHTS AND MARKS As chartlet and 9.14.4. Hanstholm lt ho, a W 8-sided twr with R top, is approx 7ca S of the hbr ent and visible by day from seaward, rising above the flat terrain. The outer and inner mole heads are floodlit.

R/T Ch 16; 12 13, HX

TELEPHONE HM 97.96.18.33; Coastguard 97.92.22.22; Hospital (Thisted) 97.92.44.00, (Skagen) 99.79.79.79; Police (Emergency) 112; Taxi 97.96.17.11.

FACILITIES AB, FW, D, ME, Diver ☎ 97.96.27.00.
Town: 🛒, R, ⇌ (Thisted), ✈ (Thisted) ☎ 97.96.51.66.

W Denmark

HANSTHOLM TO THYBORØN

(AC 1404) Off **Hanstholm** S/SW winds may cause currents up to 4kn in rough weather, but tidal streams are imperceptible for 15-20M offshore. It is best to round Hanstholm outside the SWM buoy. Underwater obstructions and the slim possibility of former WW2 mines may make anchoring dangerous.

Thyborøn is the western entrance to the **Limfjord** (*AC 426 to 430*) which gives access to the Baltic via Aalborg and Hals/Egense (91 track miles). It is a large area of sheltered water with many harbours, of which **Lemvig** and Thisted are the most W'ly. Some of the marinas are only suitable for drafts <1·5m, but there are plenty of anchorages and it is a justifiably popular cruising

ground. The Danish word 'Bredning', meaning a Broad (as in Norfolk), aptly describes the stretches of water linked by narrow sounds; least depths are 4m.

THYBORØN TO HVIDE SANDE

(AC 1404) 'Dangerous anchoring' areas fringe the coast to 1M offshore. Bovbjerg lt ho, a red tower on a 38m high sand dune, is conspic. **Thorsminde** is a FV hbr between the sea and Nissum Fjord. S of here coastal dunes are high enough to obscure the houses behind them. ▶*Tidal streams (such as they are) divide off Lyngvig lt ho, ie to the S the in-going stream sets S and the out-going stream sets N; the reverse occurs N of Lyngvig.*◀

9.14.10 THYBORØN

Ringkøbing 56°42'·87N 08°12'·81E ✿✿✿✿✿✿✿

THYBORØN *continued*

CHARTS AC 426 (inc 2 hbr plans); DK 108S; D81

TIDES +0530 Dover; ML 0·0; Duration 0620

Standard Port ESBJERG (→)

Times				Heights (metres)			
High Water		Low Water		MHWS	MHWN	MLWN	MLWS
0300	0700	0100	0800	1·9	1·5	0·5	0·1
1500	1900	1300	2000				
Differences THYBORØN							
+0120	+0230	+0410	+0210	−1·5	−1·2	−0·4	−0·1

SHELTER inside is good. Yachts berth in the N'most basin, Nordre Inderhavn, in 3·5m or as directed. Or at Thyborøn marina 56°41'·25N 08°13'·43E; two 45m long pontoons in 2·5m.

NAVIGATION Entry can be dangerous in near gale force onshore winds which cause breaking seas and violent eddies. Least depth is usually about 6m on appr and 5m-8m within the bar.
WPT 56°42'·55N 08°08'·70E [SWM buoy L Fl 10s, Racon T], 082°/2·5M to abeam unlit SHM buoy at ent. Here turn stbd SSE, past a SHM buoy Fl (2) G 5s, into the main fairway to the Yderhavn ent. Inside the ent turn 90° stbd to Nordre Inderhavn 4 cables N.

LIGHTS AND MARKS As on chartlet and 9.14.4. The Appr lt, Fl (3) 10s, is an all-round lt ho; in poor vis shown by day. The E mole lt, Oc (2) WRG 12s, has a W sector covering a 148·2° approach from the NNW.

Outer 082° ldg marks: front, Agger Tange R ▲ on bn; rear, R ▼ on grey frame twr. Langholm 120° ldg marks: front, R ▲ on R hut; rear, R ▼ on grey frame twr. Caution: light sectors and buoys in the approach chans are moved to reflect changes in depths.

R/T Ch 16; 12 13, H24.

TELEPHONE HM 97.83.10.50; CG 97.82.13.22; Taxi 97.83.25.11; Ⓗ (Thisted) 97.92.44.00.

FACILITIES AB 8.61Dkr/m inc AC, D, WC, showers, ME, ✕ ☎ 97.83.11.26, SM ☎ 97.83.11.25.
Town: R, 🍴, PO, ⇌, ✈ (Thisted) ☎ 97.96.51.66.

> **Limfjord** cuts across Jutland via Aalborg to the E ent at Hals in the Kattegat, approx 91M; saving about 90M over the offshore route via Skagen. Thyborøn is the W ent to Limfjord, a notable cruising ground in its own right.
>
> **Lemvig** (see chartlet opposite) is 10-13M SSE of Thyborøn. A marina at Vinkel Hage, 56°33'·93N 08°17'·86E, is about 9ca N of Lemvig on the W bank.

9.14.11 THORSMINDE (Torsminde)
Ringkøbing **56°22'·32N 08°06'·82E** ✳ ⊛ ◊◊◊◊ ✿

CHARTS AC 1404; DK93; D 82

TIDES +0425 Dover; ML 0·1; Duration 0605

Standard Port ESBJERG (→)

Times				Height (metres)			
High Water		Low Water		MHWS	MHWN	MLWN	MLWS
0300	0700	0100	0800	1·8	1·4	0·4	0·0
1500	1900	1300	2000				
Differences THORSMINDE							
+0045	+0050	+0040	+0010	−1·3	−1·0	−0·4	−0·1

SHELTER Shelter is good inside, but see the notes below. Yachts berth in the Vesthavn between piers 3 & 4. There is no access into Nissum Fjord due to drainage sluices which close off the hbr immediately W of the road bridge.

NAVIGATION WPT 56°22'·34N 08°05'·49E, approx 090°/1M to hbr ent, which is dredged 4m except during onshore gales. Approach directly from seaward and turn stbd into Vesthavn.

Even moderate winds can cause breakers over the bar which normally has less than 2·7m below MSL and the Hbr may have less water than charted due to silting.

WATER LEVEL AND CURRENT

> Strong W'lies can raise the water level by up to 3·0m and E'lies lower it by up to 1·8m. Levels are said to be signalled by a complex array of R & W lts, but before approaching, check conditions with the HM and request a berth.

Sluicing causes currents into and out of the hbr; warning signals, as in 9.14.12, are shown from masts by the sluices.

LIGHTS AND MARKS Lt ho 56°22'·5N 08°07'·2E, F 30m 14M, grey frame tr. Other lts as chartlet and 9.14.4.

R/T VHF Ch **13** 16, 0300-1300 1400-2400 LT.

TELEPHONE HM 97.49.72.44; CG 97.41.22.22; Hospital (Holstebro) 97.41.42.00; Police (Emergency) 112; Taxi 97.82.14.15.

FACILITIES AB 100Dkr all LOA, FW, ⇥, D, ME. **Town:** Bar, R, 🍴, ⇌ (Ramme, Holstebro, Ringkøbing), ✈ (Karup) ☎ 97.10.12.18.

9.14.12 HVIDE SANDE
Ringkøbing 55°59'·93N 08°06'·68E ✿✿♺♺♺♺✿✿

CHARTS AC 1404; DK 93, 99; D82

TIDES +0345 Dover, ML 0·2, Duration 0550. Mean range is about 0·75m.

Standard Port ESBJERG (→)

Times				Height (metres)			
High Water		Low Water		MHWS	MHWN	MLWN	MLWS
0300	0700	0100	0800	1·9	1·5	0·5	0·1
1500	1900	1300	2000				
Differences HVIDE SANDE							
0000	+0010	−0015	−0025	−1·1	−0·8	−0·3	−0·1

SHELTER *Strong W winds can cause breakers over the bar rendering the entrance dangerous.* Good shelter inside, but see notes on Water level and Current. No ⚓ in the hbr channels.

NAVIGATION WPT 55°59'·80N 08°05'·49E, approx 072°/1M Hbr ent. In the approach chan there is usually 2·5m below MSL over two sand ridges, the outer of which is about 3ca offshore. An underwater power cable crosses the ent chan and pipelines cross E of the lock. Hbr speed limit is 3kn.

WATER LEVEL AND CURRENT

• W'lies can raise the water level by up to 3·5m. E'lies lower it by up to 2·0m. Levels are not signalled.

• When drainage sluicing from Ringkøbing Fjord takes place, a strong current runs through the outer hbr. Navigation is prohib within areas 250m W of, and 500m E of the sluices.

• Warning signals are hoisted/shown from a mast on the N side of the sluice:

In-going current: ▲ by day; ● over ○ by night.
Out-going current: ▼ by day; ○ over ● by night.
If in doubt, check with the HM by VHF or telephone.

LIGHTS AND MARKS The lt ho, grey frame twr, is on the stbd side of the fairway. Lyngvig lt ho, W round twr, is 3M N of the hbr ent. Other lts as chartlet and 9.14.4.

R/T Ch 16; 12 13, HX

TELEPHONE HM 97.31.16.33; Lock 97.31.10.93; Customs 97.32.22.22; Hospital (Esbjerg) 75.18.19.00; Police (Emergency) 112; Taxi 97.32.32.32.

FACILITIES The harbour is mainly a fishing port and also gives access to Ringkøbing Fjord, which is drained by sluices at the E end of the Outer Hbr.

Yachts berth on a pontoon in the Sydhavn (first turning to stbd) or as directed by the HM. Or lock through to the Østhavn to enter appr chan (1·8m) and berth in Fjordhavn marina (1·6m). AB, FW, ⟨D⟩, D in fishing hbr, Showers, WC, ME, CH ☎ 97.31.15.22.

Town: Bar, R, 🍴, PO, ⭿ (Ringkøbing), ✈ (Esbjerg).

(AC 1404, 3768, Danish 99) Firing practice areas extend 9M W and 8M NNW from a pos'n 4M N of Blåvands Huk lt ho; and 7-10M to seaward of Nyminde Gab 55°49'N 08°12'E. Charts warn of the dangers of anchoring and fishing due to wrecks and underwater explosives.

Entrance to **Hvide Sande** can be difficult when sluicing causes strong currents in the entrance. Thence Ringkøbing Fjord, a lagoon 15M long by 6M wide, is entered via a lock. There are several attractive hbrs/marinas (Ringkøbing, Bork, Skaven and Stavning) and anchs, but also shallows and conservation areas with prohibited access – see Danish AC 99.

Off Blåvands Huk (AC 3766), Slugen is the well-buoyed/lit and deep inshore channel through the shallow banks of **Horns Rev**. See Fig 14(1). The general direction of buoyage is NW.

Close SW of Slugen a large rectangular wind farm (80 turbines, all marked by R air obstruction lts) is centred on 55°29'·20N 07°50'·30E; there are Racons (U) at the NE and SW corners. 3 meteorological masts (60-70m high) lie close NW and E of the wind farm. Lights, see 9.14.4.

NW of this wind farm a 12M x 3·5M rectangular area is Dangerous for ⚓ing, fishing and seabed ops. It was formerly mined.

Close W a contiguous new wind farm is being built as shown on Fig 14(1). It is marked by 14 SPM buoys, Fl (3) Y 10s, and entry is prohibited.

ESBJERG TO RØMØ

(AC 1404, 3768) Grådyb, the ent channel to **Esbjerg**, is well buoyed. See Fig 14 (2). ▶*In Esbjerg Roads the stream sets ESE from HW Helgoland −0305 and WSW from +0315. Tidal streams in the Fanø Bugt are shown in tables on AC 3768. In the open sea the flood is SE-going and the ebb NW-going; there is no slack water, just a turning of the stream, usually anti-clockwise. The rate is 1½kn at the change; the ebb is often stronger than the flood.*

Abeam Rømø Havn the ingoing stream begins at HW Helgoland −0215 and runs NNE across the hbr entrance; the outgoing stream begins at +0345 and runs SSW across the entrance; max rate in each direction is about 2kn.◀

From Grådyb SWM buoy/Racon to Lister Tief SWM is 171°/ 19·5M. Approach Rømø via the buoyed channel.

A firing practice range extends 12M seaward of Rømø.

CROSSING THE NORTH SEA

(AC 2182A, 2182B, 2182C) Important planning considerations to be taken into account include:

• Distances are considerable, eg Harwich to Esbjerg is 330M and Harwich to Skagen is 483M, so experienced crew, used to night passages, and a well found yacht are essential. See 9.0.7 for distances across the North Sea.

• The many oil/gas rigs must be identified and avoided.

• The extensive Dutch and German TSS south of 54°12'N, and west of Helgoland, must be avoided or carefully negotiated.

From the English S coast it may be prudent to coast-hop via the Netherlands and the Frisian Islands, then make for Helgoland, dependent on weather. A suitable departure point from the Thames estuary is S Galloper SCM, and from Lowestoft, Smiths Knoll SCM. From further N, ie Hartlepool to the Firth of Forth, a track to Esbjerg avoids Dogger Bank and the densest oil/gas rig concentrations. See also 9.15.6 and 9.16.6 for other options.

FIRING
PRACTICE
AREA

Wind farm under
construction 2008
No entry
All buoys
Fl(3)Y.10s

Anchoring,
Fishing and Seabed
Operations
Dangerous

H O R N S   R E V

Q(9)15s

TUXEN

VOVOV

Mast
Mo(U)15s8m3M

Anchoring,
Fishing and
Seabed
Operations
Dangerous

SOREN

BOVBJERGS

Blavands Huk
Fl(3)20s
55m21M

Entry
prohibited

KNOB

Fl.G.3s

LFl.G.10s

MUNK
2Mo(U)
15s15m5M

Fl(2)R.
5s

S L U G E N   C H A N N E L

PSSA

ULVEN

Fl(2)G.5s

Fl(3)R.10s

Mast Mo(U)
15s12m5M

No.2 LFl.10s

Wind Farm
All Its
Fl(3)Y.10s

Mast Mo(U)
15s9m5M &
Aero Q.R

N

Racon (U)

VYL
3₇

Q(6)+LFl.15s

Kilometres 0 ___ 10
Nautical miles 0 ___ 5

30'   07°40'E   50'   08°00'E

Fig 14(1) Horns Rev, wind farm, met masts and Slugen Channel west of Blåvands Huk

Sædding

Sædding Strand N
F.R.28m16M

Sædding Strand
F.37m18M

F.R.17m16M

Iso.4s27m21M

Iso.2s13m21M

Hjerting Løb
Marked by unlit PHMs

PSSA

Skallingen

Langli Sand

CAUTION
up to 1M offshore due
to seabed objects that may
contain explosives.

No.18
Fl(2)R.5s

Fovrfelt N
Oc(2)WRG.6s

Fovrfelt
Fl(2)R.10s

Sædding Strand S
F.G.25m16M

Q(6)+LFl.15s

No.15a
Fl(2)G.5s

F.G.11m16M

A Particularly
Sensitive Sea
Area (PSSA)
extends 3·5M
offshore

55°29'N

No.14
Fl.R.5s

Jerg
Fl.G.3s
7m5M

No.15b
Fl(2)G.10s

ESBJERG

No.13
Fl.G.5s

Fanø Sandende

Gronningen

No.12
Fl.R.3s

No.11
Fl.G.3s

Wk
BRB

049°

Fanø

Wind farm

No.10
Fl(2)R.10s

No.9
Fl(2)G.10s

067°

Søren
Jessens
Sand

Nordby

See separate chartlet

27'

GRÅDYB
Approach channel,
dredged 10m

No.8
Fl(2)R.5s

No.7
Q

No.6
Fl.R.5s

053·8°

No.5
Fl.G.5s

Tidal Gauge
Fl(5)Y.20s

A Particularly
Sensitive Sea
Area (PSSA)
extends 3·5M
offshore

to 1M offshore

No.4
Fl.R.3s

No.2
Fl(3)R.
10s

No.3
Fl.G.3s

N

No.1
Q

SWM buoy, L.Fl.10s, Racon G, is 234°/1·5M

kilometres 0 ___ 3
n miles 0 ___ 2

24'

08°20'E

Fig 14(2) Grådyb: Outer Approach to Esbjerg

W Denmark

659

9.14.13 ESBJERG

Ribe **55°28′·29N 08°25′·36E** (Ent to Konsumfiskerihavn Basin II) ❀❀❀🔱🔱🔱🔱

CHARTS AC 3766, 420; DK 94/5; D83, 109

TIDES ESBJERG is a Standard Port (⟶) +0340 Dover; ML 0·7; Duration 0605; Zone –0100. See differences at 9.14.14.

SHELTER All tide access. Yachts berth on 2 pontoons in the SE part of FV basin No II as shown. Or at Nordby marina on Fanø, 9.14.14.

NAVIGATION Approaching from the N, either pass to seaward of Horns Rev, which extends over 21M W from Blåvands Huk to Horns Rev West WCM buoy, 55°34′·49N 07°26′·08E. See Fig 14(1).

Or take the Slugen chan, 9 to 4M W of Blåvands Huk. This is marked near its N end by Tuxen NCM Q, 55°34′·21N 07°41′·93E, and thence by 2 PHM & 3 SHM lt buoys. The general direction of buoyage through the Slugen is NW. From the E'most PHM buoy, Fl (3) R 10s, to Grådyb SWM is 132°/7·1M.

WPT 55°24′·63N 08°11′·61E, Grådyb SWM buoy L Fl 10s, Racon G. See Fig. 14(2). Thence 3 sets of ldg lts (R, G and White) at Sædding Strand lead through Grådyb (ldg lines on the chartlet are colour-coded R, G, B for clarity). At the Y-junction marked by No 16 SCM buoy, turn E/SE into the Hbr proper:

- Outer triple ldg lts (Iso 2s, Iso 4s and F) lead 053·8°/3·7M (black line) to No 7 and No 8 buoys. There jink stbd 13° onto:
- Middle (Sædding S) ldg lts, both FG, 067°/8ca (green line) to Nos 9 & 10 buoys. Thence jink 16° port onto:
- Inner (Sædding N) ldg lts, both FR, lead 049°/2·8M (red line) to the Y-junction at No 16 SCM buoy.

Here follow the buoyed chan to stbd round onto SSE; this turn is covered by 4 directional lights, should you feel the need. Esbjerg basins lie to port, or deviate stbd at No 21 buoy for Nordby marina.

LIGHTS AND MARKS Blåvands Huk lt ho, W □ twr, is 9·6M NNW of Gradyb SWM buoy.

On SW side of the Slugen chan extensive, well lit windfarms have been built in shoal waters; keep well clear. See 3.14.1 and Fig 14(1) – previous page.

Appr daymarks. Outer 053·8° ldg line: Front, R wooden bldg; Middle, R metal twr W bands; Rear, R framework twr.

Hbr daymark: The conspic power stn chimney (250m high) is 7·5 cables E of No 25 SHM lt buoy; see chartlet. Other light details are on the chartlets or in 9.14.4.

R/T VHF Ch 16: 12 13 14, H24

TELEPHONE HM 75.12.41.44; CG 75.12.82.99; Emergency 112; Taxi 75.12.69.88; Ⓗ 75.18.19.00; ⊖ 75.12.25.00.

FACILITIES Marina, 75Dkr any LOA, D, FW, ME, AC, Showers/WC at Esbjerg Søsport (YC) ☎ 75.14.47.47; ⚒ A-Z Snedkeriet ☎ 75.12.65.99; SM, Vase As ☎ 75.12.33.33; Diver, Bjarnes Dykkerservice ☎ 75.12.04.44. **Town:** 🛒, R, Bar, PO, ⌕, ✈ (8km NE). Ferries to Harwich (see 9.0.4)

TIME ZONE -0100
Subtract 1 hour for UT
For Danish Summer Time add
ONE hour in **non-shaded areas**

ESBJERG   LAT 55°28'N   LONG 8°27'E
TIMES AND HEIGHTS OF HIGH AND LOW WATERS

Dates in red are **SPRINGS**
Dates in blue are **NEAPS**

YEAR 2010

W Denmark

JANUARY

Time	m		Time	m
1 0248	1.7	**16** 0328	1.7
0845	0.0	0934	0.1
F 1521	1.6	SA 1553	1.5
2102	0.1	2137	0.1
2 0336	1.8	**17** 0403	1.7
0934	0.0	1008	0.1
SA 1610	1.6	SU 1624	1.5
2148	0.1	2209	0.1
3 0421	1.8	**18** 0432	1.7
1021	-0.1	1039	0.1
SU 1657	1.6	M 1652	1.4
2233	0.0	2239	0.1
4 0506	1.9	**19** 0457	1.7
1108	-0.1	1107	0.1
M 1742	1.6	TU 1717	1.5
2318	0.0	2309	0.1
5 0551	1.9	**20** 0524	1.7
1154	-0.1	1138	0.1
TU 1827	1.6	W 1745	1.5
		2344	0.0
6 0004	0.0	**21** 0554	1.7
0637	1.9	1213	0.0
W 1242	0.0	TH 1818	1.5
1914	1.5		
7 0053	0.0	**22** 0022	0.0
0728	1.8	0631	1.7
TH 1333	0.0	F 1252	0.0
◑ 2005	1.5	1858	1.5
8 0145	0.1	**23** 0105	0.0
0824	1.8	0716	1.7
F 1427	0.1	SA 1336	0.1
2102	1.5	◐ 1945	1.5
9 0242	0.1	**24** 0154	0.1
0927	1.7	0808	1.6
SA 1528	0.2	SU 1427	0.1
2203	1.5	2041	1.5
10 0348	0.2	**25** 0249	0.1
1034	1.7	0910	1.6
SU 1636	0.4	M 1525	0.2
2309	1.5	2147	1.4
11 0502	0.2	**26** 0355	0.2
1142	1.6	1027	1.5
M 1743	0.2	TU 1634	0.3
		2308	1.4
12 0011	1.6	**27** 0513	0.2
0613	0.2	1154	1.5
TU 1245	1.6	W 1751	0.3
1843	0.2		
13 0109	1.6	**28** 0026	1.5
0715	0.1	0632	0.2
W 1342	1.6	TH 1309	1.5
1936	0.2	1859	0.2
14 0201	1.7	**29** 0133	1.6
0808	0.1	0736	0.0
TH 1432	1.6	F 1412	1.5
2021	0.2	1956	0.1
15 0248	1.7	**30** 0229	1.7
0854	0.1	0831	-0.1
F 1516	1.5	SA 1506	1.6
● 2102	0.1	○ 2045	0.0
		31 0319	1.8
		0919	-0.2
		SU 1554	1.6
		2131	-0.1

FEBRUARY

Time	m		Time	m
1 0406	1.8	**16** 0411	1.6
1005	-0.2	1012	0.0
M 1638	1.6	TU 1629	1.4
2215	-0.1	2215	-0.1
2 0449	1.9	**17** 0436	1.6
1049	-0.2	1039	-0.1
TU 1720	1.6	W 1654	1.4
2259	-0.2	2245	-0.1
3 0532	1.9	**18** 0502	1.6
1133	-0.2	1110	-0.1
W 1800	1.5	TH 1720	1.5
2342	-0.2	2319	-0.1
4 0616	1.8	**19** 0531	1.6
1216	-0.2	1144	-0.1
TH 1842	1.5	F 1750	1.5
		2357	-0.1
5 0027	-0.2	**20** 0606	1.6
0703	1.7	1222	-0.1
F 1302	0.0	SA 1827	1.5
1927	1.5		
6 0116	-0.1	**21** 0039	-0.1
0754	1.7	0649	1.6
SA 1351	0.1	SU 1305	0.0
◑ 2018	1.4	1910	1.5
7 0210	0.0	**22** 0125	-0.1
0853	1.6	0739	1.5
SU 1447	0.2	M 1354	0.0
2120	1.4	◐ 2002	1.4
8 0315	0.1	**23** 0220	0.0
1002	1.5	0842	1.4
M 1556	0.3	TU 1451	0.0
2230	1.4	2107	1.4
9 0436	0.2	**24** 0327	0.1
1114	1.4	1003	1.3
TU 1715	0.3	W 1603	0.2
2339	1.5	2233	1.4
10 0557	0.1	**25** 0452	0.1
1220	1.4	1136	1.3
W 1821	0.2	TH 1727	0.2
11 0042	1.5	**26** 0001	1.4
0700	0.0	0615	0.0
TH 1318	1.4	F 1253	1.2
1915	0.1	1839	0.1
12 0138	1.6	**27** 0111	1.5
0751	0.0	0720	-0.1
F 1409	1.4	SA 1354	1.4
2002	0.1	1936	0.0
13 0226	1.6	**28** 0209	1.6
0835	0.0	0812	-0.2
SA 1454	1.4	SU 1446	1.5
2041	0.0	○ 2025	-0.1
14 0307	1.6		
0912	0.0		
SU 1530	1.4		
● 2115	0.0		
15 0342	1.6		
0944	0.0		
M 1602	1.4		
2145	0.0		

MARCH

Time	m		Time	m
1 0259	1.7	**16** 0314	1.6
0859	-0.3	0913	-0.2
M 1532	1.5	TU 1535	1.4
2110	-0.2	2118	-0.1
2 0345	1.8	**17** 0345	1.5
0942	-0.3	0942	-0.2
TU 1614	1.5	W 1604	1.4
2154	-0.3	2149	-0.2
3 0428	1.8	**18** 0413	1.5
1024	-0.3	1011	-0.2
W 1653	1.5	TH 1630	1.4
2236	-0.3	2221	-0.2
4 0510	1.7	**19** 0442	1.5
1106	-0.3	1042	-0.2
TH 1730	1.5	F 1657	1.4
2318	-0.3	2257	-0.2
5 0551	1.7	**20** 0512	1.5
1147	-0.2	1118	-0.2
F 1809	1.5	SA 1727	1.4
		2335	-0.2
6 0002	-0.3	**21** 0548	1.5
0634	1.6	1157	-0.2
SA 1230	-0.1	SU 1802	1.4
1849	1.4		
7 0048	-0.2	**22** 0018	-0.2
0721	1.5	0630	1.4
SU 1314	0.0	M 1239	-0.1
◑ 1936	1.4	1845	1.4
8 0139	-0.1	**23** 0106	-0.2
0817	1.4	0722	1.4
M 1406	0.2	TU 1329	0.0
2034	1.4	◐ 1937	1.4
9 0242	0.1	**24** 0202	-0.1
0925	1.3	0827	1.3
TU 1511	0.2	W 1428	0.1
2147	1.3	2043	1.3
10 0409	0.1	**25** 0312	0.0
1041	1.2	0954	1.2
W 1638	0.3	TH 1542	0.2
2303	1.4	2212	1.3
11 0534	0.1	**26** 0438	0.0
1149	1.2	1122	1.2
TH 1752	0.2	F 1705	0.1
		2339	1.4
12 0009	1.4	**27** 0557	-0.1
0635	0.0	1233	1.3
F 1248	1.3	SA 1815	0.0
1848	0.1		
13 0106	1.5	**28** 0048	1.5
0724	-0.1	0657	-0.2
SA 1339	1.3	SU 1332	1.4
1934	0.0	1912	-0.1
14 0155	1.5	**29** 0145	1.6
0806	-0.1	0749	-0.3
SU 1424	1.4	M 1422	1.4
2013	0.0	2002	-0.2
15 0238	1.6	**30** 0236	1.7
0842	-0.1	0835	-0.4
M 1502	1.4	TU 1507	1.5
● 2048	-0.1	○ 2048	-0.3
		31 0323	1.7
		0918	-0.4
		W 1548	1.5
		2131	-0.4

APRIL

Time	m		Time	m
1 0406	1.7	**16** 0351	1.5
0959	-0.3	0943	-0.2
TH 1625	1.5	F 1609	1.4
2214	-0.4	2159	-0.2
2 0447	1.6	**17** 0424	1.4
1039	-0.3	1018	-0.2
F 1701	1.5	SA 1639	1.4
2256	-0.4	2237	-0.3
3 0527	1.5	**18** 0459	1.4
1118	-0.2	1056	-0.2
SA 1737	1.4	SU 1711	1.4
2339	-0.3	2318	-0.3
4 0607	1.4	**19** 0538	1.4
1158	-0.1	1136	-0.2
SU 1815	1.4	M 1748	1.4
5 0024	-0.2	**20** 0003	-0.3
0651	1.3	0624	1.3
M 1240	0.0	TU 1222	-0.1
1858	1.4	1832	1.4
6 0112	-0.1	**21** 0054	-0.2
0741	1.2	0718	1.2
TU 1327	0.1	W 1313	0.0
◑ 1950	1.3	◐ 1926	1.4
7 0211	0.0	**22** 0152	-0.1
0844	1.1	0825	1.2
W 1425	0.2	TH 1412	0.1
2058	1.3	2034	1.4
8 0331	0.1	**23** 0302	-0.1
0957	1.1	0945	1.1
TH 1545	0.2	F 1524	0.1
2215	1.3	2157	1.4
9 0456	0.1	**24** 0421	-0.1
1108	1.1	1103	1.2
F 1707	0.2	SA 1640	0.1
2325	1.3	2316	1.4
10 0558	0.0	**25** 0532	-0.2
1208	1.2	1209	1.2
SA 1808	0.1	SU 1748	0.0
11 0024	1.4	**26** 0023	1.5
0648	-0.1	0632	-0.3
SU 1300	1.3	M 1306	1.3
1857	0.0	1846	-0.2
12 0116	1.4	**27** 0121	1.6
0730	-0.1	0724	-0.3
M 1347	1.3	TU 1356	1.4
1938	-0.1	1938	-0.3
13 0201	1.5	**28** 0214	1.6
0806	-0.2	0810	-0.3
TU 1428	1.4	W 1441	1.4
2015	-0.1	○ 2026	-0.4
14 0241	1.5	**29** 0302	1.6
0839	-0.2	0854	-0.3
W 1505	1.4	TH 1523	1.5
● 2049	-0.2	2112	-0.4
15 0317	1.5	**30** 0346	1.5
0911	-0.2	0935	-0.3
TH 1538	1.4	F 1601	1.5
2124	-0.2	2155	-0.4

Chart Datum: 0·69 metres below Dansk Normal Null. HAT is 2·2 metres above Chart Datum; see 4.5

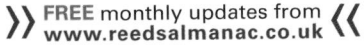

TIME ZONE -0100
Subtract 1 hour for UT
For Danish Summer Time add
ONE hour in **non-shaded areas**

ESBJERG LAT 55°28'N LONG 8°27'E
TIMES AND HEIGHTS OF HIGH AND LOW WATERS

Dates in red are **SPRINGS**
Dates in blue are **NEAPS**

YEAR 2010

MAY

Time m	Time m
1 0427 1.4 / 1015 -0.2 / SA 1637 1.5 / 2237 -0.3	**16** 0411 1.4 / 0958 -0.2 / SU 1625 1.4 / 2223 -0.3
2 0506 1.4 / 1053 -0.1 / SU 1712 1.4 / 2320 -0.2	**17** 0452 1.3 / 1039 -0.2 / M 1702 1.4 / 2307 -0.3
3 0543 1.3 / 1131 -0.1 / M 1748 1.4	**18** 0536 1.3 / 1123 -0.1 / TU 1742 1.5 / 2354 -0.3
4 0003 -0.2 / 0622 1.2 / TU 1211 0.0 / 1827 1.4	**19** 0623 1.3 / 1209 -0.1 / W 1829 1.5
5 0048 -0.1 / 0706 1.1 / W 1254 0.0 / 1912 1.4	**20** 0046 -0.2 / 0717 1.2 / TH 1300 -0.1 / 1923 1.5
6 0139 0.0 / 0759 1.1 / TH 1344 0.1 / ◐ 2009 1.3	**21** 0143 -0.2 / 0819 1.2 / F 1358 0.0 / ◑ 2027 1.4
7 0240 0.1 / 0903 1.1 / F 1445 0.2 / 2115 1.3	**22** 0247 -0.1 / 0927 1.2 / SA 1502 0.0 / 2139 1.4
8 0351 0.1 / 1012 1.1 / SA 1558 0.2 / 2227 1.3	**23** 0355 -0.2 / 1036 1.2 / SU 1612 0.0 / 2251 1.5
9 0500 0.0 / 1116 1.2 / SU 1709 0.1 / 2332 1.4	**24** 0503 -0.2 / 1139 1.3 / M 1719 0.0 / 2357 1.5
10 0555 0.0 / 1214 1.2 / M 1806 0.0	**25** 0603 -0.2 / 1237 1.3 / TU 1821 -0.2
11 0029 1.4 / 0642 -0.1 / TU 1305 1.3 / 1855 0.0	**26** 0058 1.5 / 0658 -0.2 / W 1330 1.4 / 1917 -0.2
12 0120 1.4 / 0724 -0.1 / W 1351 1.4 / 1939 -0.1	**27** 0154 1.5 / 0748 -0.2 / TH 1418 1.4 / 2008 -0.3
13 0206 1.4 / 0803 -0.2 / TH 1433 1.4 / 2020 -0.2	**28** 0244 1.5 / 0833 -0.2 / F 1502 1.5 / ○ 2056 -0.3
14 0250 1.4 / 0841 -0.2 / F 1512 1.4 / ● 2100 -0.2	**29** 0330 1.4 / 0915 -0.2 / SA 1543 1.5 / 2142 -0.3
15 0331 1.4 / 0919 -0.2 / SA 1549 1.4 / 2141 -0.2	**30** 0411 1.4 / 0955 -0.1 / SU 1621 1.5 / 2224 -0.2
	31 0448 1.3 / 1033 -0.1 / M 1655 1.5 / 2305 -0.2

JUNE

Time m	Time m
1 0524 1.2 / 1109 0.0 / TU 1728 1.5 / 2344 -0.1	**16** 0530 1.3 / 1110 -0.2 / W 1738 1.6 / 2345 -0.3
2 0557 1.2 / 1146 0.0 / W 1802 1.4	**17** 0617 1.3 / 1157 -0.1 / TH 1824 1.6
3 0024 0.0 / 0633 1.1 / TH 1225 0.0 / 1840 1.4	**18** 0034 -0.3 / 0706 1.3 / F 1245 -0.1 / 1915 1.6
4 0105 0.0 / 0715 1.1 / F 1308 0.0 / ◑ 1925 1.4	**19** 0127 -0.2 / 0800 1.3 / SA 1339 -0.1 / ◐ 2012 1.6
5 0151 0.0 / 0806 1.1 / SA 1357 0.1 / 2018 1.4	**20** 0223 -0.2 / 0859 1.3 / SU 1436 0.0 / 2116 1.5
6 0243 0.1 / 0905 1.2 / SU 1454 0.1 / 2120 1.4	**21** 0324 -0.1 / 1003 1.3 / M 1541 0.0 / 2225 1.5
7 0342 0.1 / 1011 1.2 / M 1557 0.1 / 2227 1.4	**22** 0430 -0.1 / 1106 1.3 / TU 1650 0.0 / 2333 1.5
8 0445 0.0 / 1117 1.2 / TU 1704 0.1 / 2334 1.4	**23** 0535 0.0 / 1208 1.4 / W 1758 0.0
9 0545 0.0 / 1218 1.3 / W 1807 0.1	**24** 0037 1.5 / 0635 0.0 / TH 1304 1.4 / 1900 -0.1
10 0036 1.4 / 0640 0.0 / TH 1312 1.4 / 1903 0.0	**25** 0136 1.5 / 0728 -0.1 / F 1358 1.5 / 1956 -0.2
11 0133 1.4 / 0729 -0.1 / F 1403 1.4 / 1954 -0.1	**26** 0229 1.4 / 0816 -0.1 / SA 1446 1.5 / ○ 2046 -0.2
12 0226 1.4 / 0815 -0.1 / SA 1449 1.4 / ● 2041 -0.2	**27** 0316 1.4 / 0900 0.0 / SU 1529 1.6 / 2131 -0.2
13 0315 1.4 / 0859 -0.1 / SU 1532 1.5 / 2127 -0.2	**28** 0357 1.3 / 0939 0.0 / M 1607 1.6 / 2212 -0.1
14 0400 1.4 / 0942 -0.1 / M 1614 1.5 / 2212 -0.3	**29** 0433 1.3 / 1016 0.0 / TU 1641 1.5 / 2249 -0.1
15 0446 1.4 / 1026 -0.2 / TU 1655 1.6 / 2258 -0.3	**30** 0505 1.3 / 1050 0.0 / W 1710 1.5 / 2323 0.0

JULY

Time m	Time m
1 0533 1.3 / 1123 0.0 / TH 1739 1.5 / 2356 0.0	**16** 0600 1.4 / 1139 -0.2 / F 1811 1.8
2 0603 1.3 / 1157 0.0 / F 1811 1.5	**17** 0015 -0.2 / 0645 1.4 / SA 1226 -0.2 / 1858 1.7
3 0030 0.0 / 0636 1.3 / SA 1236 0.0 / 1848 1.5	**18** 0103 -0.3 / 0732 1.4 / SU 1315 -0.1 / ◐ 1951 1.7
4 0109 0.0 / 0718 1.3 / SU 1318 0.0 / ◑ 1933 1.5	**19** 0154 -0.1 / 0824 1.4 / M 1409 0.0 / 2050 1.6
5 0153 0.0 / 0807 1.3 / M 1407 0.1 / 2025 1.5	**20** 0251 0.0 / 0925 1.4 / TU 1511 0.0 / 2158 1.5
6 0243 0.1 / 0905 1.3 / TU 1502 0.1 / 2127 1.4	**21** 0355 0.1 / 1032 1.4 / W 1624 0.1 / 2309 1.5
7 0341 0.1 / 1012 1.3 / W 1606 0.1 / 2239 1.4	**22** 0507 0.2 / 1140 1.4 / TH 1741 0.1
8 0447 0.1 / 1124 1.3 / TH 1719 0.1 / 2354 1.4	**23** 0018 1.5 / 0615 0.1 / F 1242 1.5 / 1849 0.0
9 0556 0.1 / 1233 1.4 / F 1830 0.1	**24** 0119 1.5 / 0712 0.1 / SA 1339 1.6 / 1946 0.0
10 0104 1.4 / 0658 0.1 / SA 1333 1.5 / 1931 0.0	**25** 0213 1.5 / 0801 0.1 / SU 1430 1.6 / 2035 -0.1
11 0205 1.4 / 0753 0.0 / SU 1427 1.5 / ● 2024 -0.1	**26** 0300 1.5 / 0845 0.0 / M 1514 1.7 / ○ 2118 -0.1
12 0259 1.5 / 0841 0.0 / M 1515 1.6 / 2113 -0.2	**27** 0341 1.4 / 0923 0.0 / TU 1551 1.7 / 2155 0.0
13 0348 1.5 / 0927 -0.1 / TU 1600 1.7 / 2159 -0.2	**28** 0415 1.4 / 0957 0.0 / W 1624 1.6 / 2227 0.0
14 0433 1.5 / 1011 -0.1 / W 1643 1.7 / 2244 -0.3	**29** 0443 1.4 / 1028 0.0 / TH 1651 1.6 / 2257 0.0
15 0517 1.5 / 1055 -0.2 / TH 1727 1.7 / 2329 -0.3	**30** 0509 1.4 / 1059 0.0 / F 1716 1.6 / 2326 0.0
	31 0533 1.4 / 1130 0.0 / SA 1743 1.6 / 2357 0.0

AUGUST

Time m	Time m
1 0603 1.5 / 1206 0.0 / SU 1816 1.6	**16** 0035 -0.1 / 0700 1.5 / M 1250 -0.1 / ◐ 1926 1.7
2 0033 0.0 / 0639 1.5 / M 1246 0.0 / 1857 1.6	**17** 0122 0.1 / 0748 1.5 / TU 1342 0.0 / 2023 1.6
3 0114 0.0 / 0722 1.5 / TU 1330 0.0 / ◑ 1945 1.6	**18** 0215 0.2 / 0846 1.5 / W 1442 0.1 / 2130 1.5
4 0200 0.1 / 0814 1.5 / W 1422 0.1 / 2042 1.5	**19** 0319 0.3 / 0957 1.5 / TH 1600 0.3 / 2245 1.5
5 0254 0.2 / 0915 1.4 / TH 1524 0.2 / 2154 1.5	**20** 0439 0.4 / 1111 1.5 / F 1727 0.2 / 2356 1.5
6 0400 0.2 / 1032 1.4 / F 1640 0.2 / 2321 1.4	**21** 0554 0.3 / 1218 1.6 / SA 1835 0.1
7 0518 0.3 / 1155 1.5 / SA 1803 0.2	**22** 0058 1.5 / 0653 0.2 / SU 1317 1.7 / 1930 0.1
8 0040 1.4 / 0632 0.2 / SU 1305 1.5 / 1912 0.1	**23** 0151 1.5 / 0742 0.1 / M 1408 1.7 / 2016 0.0
9 0145 1.5 / 0731 0.1 / M 1403 1.7 / 2007 -0.1	**24** 0238 1.6 / 0824 0.1 / TU 1452 1.8 / ○ 2057 0.0
10 0241 1.6 / 0822 0.0 / TU 1455 1.8 / ● 2056 -0.2	**25** 0317 1.6 / 0902 0.1 / W 1530 1.8 / 2130 0.0
11 0330 1.6 / 0908 -0.1 / W 1542 1.8 / 2141 -0.2	**26** 0351 1.6 / 0934 0.1 / TH 1601 1.7 / 2200 0.1
12 0414 1.6 / 0952 -0.1 / TH 1626 1.9 / 2224 -0.2	**27** 0418 1.6 / 1004 0.1 / F 1627 1.7 / 2227 0.1
13 0455 1.6 / 1035 -0.2 / F 1709 1.9 / 2307 -0.2	**28** 0443 1.6 / 1033 0.0 / SA 1652 1.7 / 2255 0.1
14 0536 1.6 / 1118 -0.2 / SA 1751 1.9 / 2351 -0.2	**29** 0507 1.6 / 1104 0.0 / SU 1718 1.7 / 2326 0.1
15 0616 1.6 / 1203 -0.2 / SU 1836 1.8	**30** 0533 1.6 / 1139 0.0 / M 1749 1.7
	31 0001 0.1 / 0606 1.6 / TU 1218 0.0 / 1828 1.7

Chart Datum: 0·69 metres below Dansk Normal Null. HAT is 2·2 metres above Chart Datum; see 4.5

>> **FREE** monthly updates from <<
www.reedsalmanac.co.uk

TIME ZONE -0100
Subtract 1 hour for UT
For Danish Summer Time add
ONE hour in **non-shaded areas**

ESBJERG   LAT 55°28'N   LONG 8°27'E
TIMES AND HEIGHTS OF HIGH AND LOW WATERS

Dates in red are **SPRINGS**
Dates in blue are **NEAPS**

YEAR 2010

SEPTEMBER
Time m	Time m
1 0042 0.1 / 0648 1.6 / W 1303 0.1 / ◑ 1915 1.6	**16** 0142 0.3 / 0809 1.6 / TH 1417 0.2 / 2101 1.5
2 0127 0.2 / 0736 1.6 / TH 1354 0.1 / 2012 1.6	**17** 0243 0.4 / 0919 1.6 / F 1537 0.3 / 2217 1.5
3 0221 0.3 / 0836 1.6 / F 1455 0.2 / 2125 1.5	**18** 0405 0.5 / 1037 1.6 / SA 1705 0.3 / 2327 1.5
4 0327 0.4 / 0951 1.5 / SA 1614 0.3 / 2257 1.5	**19** 0524 0.4 / 1146 1.7 / SU 1812 0.2
5 0448 0.4 / 1122 1.6 / SU 1741 0.2	**20** 0028 1.5 / 0625 0.3 / M 1246 1.7 / 1904 0.2
6 0018 1.5 / 0606 0.3 / M 1238 1.7 / 1850 0.1	**21** 0121 1.6 / 0715 0.3 / TU 1338 1.8 / 1948 0.1
7 0123 1.6 / 0707 0.2 / TU 1339 1.8 / 1945 0.0	**22** 0208 1.7 / 0757 0.2 / W 1423 1.8 / 2027 0.1
8 0218 1.7 / 0759 0.1 / W 1432 1.9 / ● 2033 -0.1	**23** 0248 1.7 / 0834 0.2 / TH 1501 1.8 / ○ 2100 0.1
9 0306 1.7 / 0845 0.0 / TH 1519 1.9 / 2118 -0.2	**24** 0322 1.7 / 0907 0.1 / F 1534 1.8 / 2130 0.1
10 0349 1.7 / 0930 -0.1 / F 1604 2.0 / 2200 -0.2	**25** 0352 1.7 / 0937 0.1 / SA 1603 1.8 / 2157 0.1
11 0429 1.7 / 1013 -0.2 / SA 1647 2.0 / 2242 -0.1	**26** 0418 1.7 / 1008 0.1 / SU 1630 1.8 / 2227 0.1
12 0508 1.7 / 1056 -0.2 / SU 1729 1.9 / 2324 0.0	**27** 0444 1.7 / 1040 0.1 / M 1657 1.8 / 2259 0.1
13 0547 1.7 / 1140 -0.1 / M 1813 1.8	**28** 0511 1.7 / 1116 0.1 / TU 1730 1.7 / 2336 0.1
14 0006 0.1 / 0627 1.7 / TU 1226 0.0 / 1900 1.7	**29** 0543 1.7 / 1157 0.1 / W 1809 1.7
15 0051 0.2 / 0713 1.6 / W 1317 0.1 / ◑ 1954 1.6	**30** 0016 0.2 / 0622 1.7 / TH 1242 0.1 / 1857 1.7

OCTOBER
Time m	Time m
1 0103 0.3 / 0711 1.7 / F 1335 0.2 / ◑ 1955 1.6	**16** 0206 0.5 / 0839 1.7 / SA 1506 0.4 / 2139 1.5
2 0157 0.3 / 0810 1.7 / SA 1438 0.3 / 2109 1.5	**17** 0320 0.5 / 0954 1.7 / SU 1629 0.4 / 2247 1.5
3 0303 0.4 / 0926 1.7 / SU 1556 0.3 / 2238 1.5	**18** 0441 0.5 / 1104 1.7 / M 1735 0.3 / 2348 1.5
4 0422 0.4 / 1054 1.7 / M 1718 0.2 / 2355 1.6	**19** 0546 0.4 / 1206 1.7 / TU 1828 0.2
5 0539 0.4 / 1210 1.8 / TU 1824 0.1	**20** 0042 1.6 / 0639 0.4 / W 1259 1.8 / 1913 0.2
6 0058 1.6 / 0641 0.2 / W 1312 1.9 / 1919 0.0	**21** 0130 1.7 / 0723 0.3 / TH 1346 1.8 / 1952 0.2
7 0151 1.7 / 0733 0.1 / TH 1407 1.9 / ● 2008 0.0	**22** 0213 1.7 / 0803 0.2 / F 1427 1.8 / 2026 0.2
8 0239 1.8 / 0822 0.0 / F 1457 2.0 / 2053 -0.1	**23** 0251 1.8 / 0838 0.2 / SA 1505 1.8 / ○ 2057 0.2
9 0323 1.8 / 0908 -0.1 / SA 1542 2.0 / 2136 0.0	**24** 0325 1.8 / 0911 0.2 / SU 1539 1.8 / 2129 0.2
10 0403 1.8 / 0951 -0.1 / SU 1626 1.9 / 2217 0.0	**25** 0355 1.8 / 0945 0.2 / M 1610 1.8 / 2201 0.2
11 0442 1.8 / 1036 -0.1 / M 1708 1.9 / 2258 0.1	**26** 0424 1.8 / 1021 0.1 / TU 1643 1.7 / 2237 0.2
12 0520 1.8 / 1120 0.0 / TU 1751 1.8 / 2339 0.2	**27** 0454 1.8 / 1100 0.1 / W 1719 1.7 / 2315 0.2
13 0600 1.8 / 1206 0.1 / W 1836 1.7	**28** 0529 1.8 / 1142 0.1 / TH 1800 1.7 / 2359 0.2
14 0023 0.3 / 0643 1.7 / TH 1255 0.2 / ◑ 1927 1.6	**29** 0609 1.8 / 1230 0.1 / F 1849 1.6
15 0110 0.4 / 0735 1.7 / F 1353 0.3 / 2027 1.5	**30** 0047 0.3 / 0657 1.8 / SA 1324 0.2 / ◑ 1948 1.6
	31 0142 0.4 / 0757 1.8 / SU 1426 0.2 / 2100 1.5

NOVEMBER
Time m	Time m
1 0245 0.4 / 0910 1.8 / M 1537 0.2 / 2217 1.5	**16** 0337 0.5 / 1008 1.7 / TU 1639 0.4 / 2256 1.5
2 0357 0.4 / 1030 1.8 / TU 1651 0.2 / 2327 1.6	**17** 0448 0.5 / 1112 1.7 / W 1737 0.4 / 2354 1.6
3 0509 0.3 / 1143 1.8 / W 1755 0.2	**18** 0549 0.4 / 1211 1.7 / TH 1827 0.3
4 0030 1.7 / 0612 0.2 / TH 1247 1.9 / 1852 0.1	**19** 0047 1.7 / 0641 0.4 / F 1303 1.7 / 1910 0.3
5 0124 1.7 / 0709 0.1 / F 1343 1.9 / 1942 0.1	**20** 0135 1.7 / 0727 0.3 / SA 1351 1.8 / 1950 0.2
6 0213 1.8 / 0800 0.0 / SA 1435 1.9 / ● 2029 0.1	**21** 0218 1.8 / 0808 0.2 / SU 1436 1.8 / ○ 2027 0.2
7 0259 1.8 / 0848 0.0 / SU 1523 1.9 / 2112 0.1	**22** 0258 1.8 / 0847 0.2 / M 1516 1.7 / 2103 0.2
8 0341 1.8 / 0934 0.0 / M 1608 1.8 / 2154 0.1	**23** 0335 1.8 / 0926 0.2 / TU 1556 1.7 / 2141 0.2
9 0421 1.8 / 1019 0.0 / TU 1650 1.8 / 2236 0.2	**24** 0409 1.8 / 1006 0.1 / W 1634 1.7 / 2220 0.1
10 0459 1.8 / 1103 0.1 / W 1731 1.7 / 2316 0.3	**25** 0445 1.8 / 1048 0.1 / TH 1715 1.7 / 2302 0.2
11 0537 1.8 / 1148 0.2 / TH 1812 1.6 / 2358 0.3	**26** 0522 1.8 / 1133 0.1 / F 1758 1.6 / 2346 0.2
12 0618 1.8 / 1236 0.2 / F 1857 1.5	**27** 0604 1.8 / 1221 0.1 / SA 1846 1.6
13 0042 0.4 / 0703 1.8 / SA 1327 0.3 / ◑ 1948 1.5	**28** 0034 0.2 / 0653 1.8 / SU 1313 0.1 / ◑ 1941 1.6
14 0131 0.5 / 0757 1.7 / SU 1424 0.4 / 2048 1.5	**29** 0127 0.2 / 0749 1.8 / M 1410 0.1 / 2043 1.5
15 0229 0.5 / 0900 1.7 / M 1531 0.4 / 2153 1.5	**30** 0225 0.3 / 0854 1.8 / TU 1513 0.2 / 2150 1.5

DECEMBER
Time m	Time m
1 0330 0.3 / 1006 1.8 / W 1620 0.2 / 2257 1.6	**16** 0336 0.4 / 1007 1.6 / TH 1623 0.4 / 2254 1.5
2 0439 0.3 / 1117 1.8 / TH 1725 0.2	**17** 0442 0.4 / 1114 1.6 / F 1725 0.3 / 2357 1.6
3 0000 1.6 / 0545 0.2 / F 1223 1.8 / 1825 0.2	**18** 0548 0.4 / 1218 1.6 / SA 1822 0.3
4 0058 1.7 / 0646 0.1 / SA 1324 1.8 / 1919 0.1	**19** 0054 1.6 / 0648 0.3 / SU 1315 1.6 / 1913 0.3
5 0151 1.7 / 0742 0.1 / SU 1418 1.8 / ● 2009 0.1	**20** 0145 1.7 / 0739 0.2 / M 1408 1.7 / 1959 0.2
6 0239 1.8 / 0833 0.0 / M 1509 1.8 / 2054 0.2	**21** 0233 1.7 / 0826 0.2 / TU 1457 1.7 / ○ 2042 0.1
7 0324 1.8 / 0922 0.0 / TU 1554 1.7 / 2137 0.2	**22** 0315 1.8 / 0910 0.1 / W 1542 1.7 / 2124 0.1
8 0406 1.8 / 1007 0.1 / W 1636 1.6 / 2218 0.2	**23** 0356 1.8 / 0954 0.0 / TH 1626 1.6 / 2206 0.1
9 0444 1.8 / 1051 0.1 / TH 1714 1.6 / 2257 0.2	**24** 0436 1.8 / 1037 0.0 / F 1708 1.6 / 2248 0.1
10 0521 1.8 / 1132 0.2 / F 1750 1.5 / 2336 0.3	**25** 0516 1.9 / 1121 0.0 / SA 1751 1.6 / 2333 0.1
11 0556 1.8 / 1213 0.2 / SA 1827 1.5	**26** 0558 1.9 / 1208 0.0 / SU 1836 1.6
12 0015 0.3 / 0633 1.8 / SU 1254 0.3 / 1906 1.5	**27** 0019 0.1 / 0645 1.9 / M 1257 0.0 / 1924 1.5
13 0057 0.3 / 0716 1.7 / M 1338 0.3 / ◑ 1953 1.5	**28** 0109 0.1 / 0736 1.8 / TU 1348 0.0 / ◑ 2018 1.5
14 0143 0.4 / 0805 1.7 / TU 1427 0.3 / 2047 1.5	**29** 0203 0.1 / 0836 1.8 / W 1445 0.1 / 2118 1.5
15 0236 0.4 / 0903 1.6 / W 1521 0.4 / 2149 1.5	**30** 0302 0.2 / 0942 1.7 / TH 1548 0.2 / 2225 1.5
	31 0409 0.2 / 1054 1.7 / F 1656 0.2 / 2332 1.6

Chart Datum: 0·69 metres below Dansk Normal Null. HAT is 2·2 metres above Chart Datum; see 4.5

W Denmark

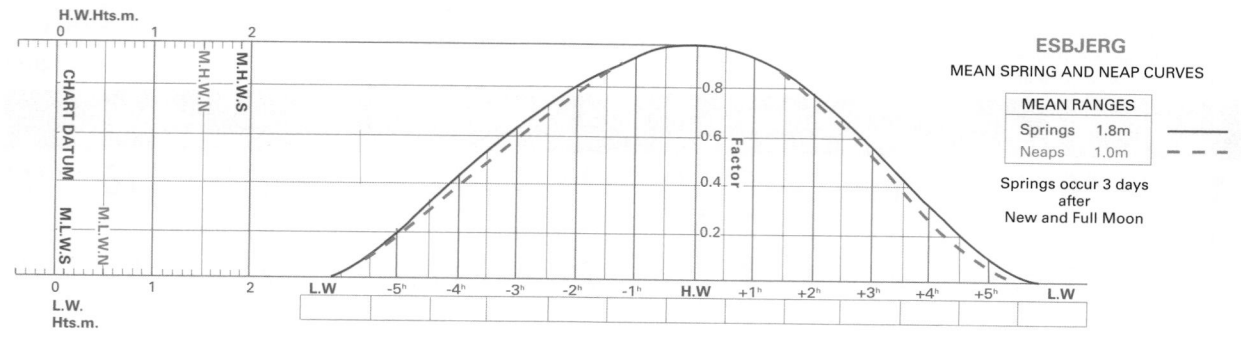

ESBJERG
MEAN SPRING AND NEAP CURVES

MEAN RANGES	
Springs	1.8m
Neaps	1.0m

Springs occur 3 days after New and Full Moon

9.14.14 NORDBY (Fanø Island)

Ribe 55°27'·37N 08°25'·09E ✿✿✿✿✿✿✿

CHARTS AC 3766, 420.

TIDES +0340 Dover; ML 0·7; Duration 0605

Standard Port ESBJERG (⟶)

Times				Height (metres)			
High Water		Low Water		MHWS	MHWN	MLWN	MLWS
0300	0700	0100	0800	1·9	1·5	0·5	0·1
1500	1900	1300	2000				
Differences BLÅVANDS HUK (55°33'·0N 08°05'·0E)							
−0120	−0110	−0050	−0100	−0·1	−0·1	−0·2	−0·1
GRÅDYB BAR (55°26'·0N 08°15'·0E)							
−0130	−0115	No data		−0·4	−0·3	−0·2	−0·1

SHELTER Good at Nordby Marina in 1·8m; access at all tides.

NAVIGATION As for Esbjerg until nearing No 21 buoy; here turn south along the buoyed channel (2·1m) to pass between two lt bcns, FG and FR; thence turn to 214° for FR ldg lts at Nordby. The final appr is on 161·6° transit of two WR bns in the marina. The Slunden chan dredged 2·7m, then 1·4m, is not recommended.

LIGHTS AND MARKS As Esbjerg and see 9.14.4 for lt details.

R/T None

TELEPHONE HM 75.16.31.00; CG 75.16.36.66; Hosp (Esbjerg) 75.18.19.00; Customs (Esbjerg) 75.12.25.00; Police (Emergency) 112.

FACILITIES Pontoons with FW, Showers and WC at SC.
Town: limited 🛒 at Nordby, R, Bar. Full services at Esbjerg via regular ferries.

9.14.15 RØMØ (Havneby) Harbour

Sønderjylland 55°05'·21N 08°34'·31E ✿✿✿✿✿✿✿

CHARTS AC 3766, 3767; DK 94; BSH 3013/2 & 3

TIDES +0315 Dover; ML 0·9; Duration 0620

Standard Port ESBJERG (⟶)

Times				Height (metres)			
High Water		Low Water		MHWS	MHWN	MLWN	MLWS
0300	0700	0100	0800	1·9	1·5	0·5	0·1
1500	1900	1300	2000				
Difference RØMØ HAVN							
−0040	−0005	0000	−0020	0·0	+0·1	−0·2	−0·2
HOJER (54°58'·0N 08°40'·0E)							
−0020	+0015	No data		+0·5	+0·6	−0·1	−0·1

SHELTER Good, access at all tides. Havneby hbr is on the SE tip of Rømø. ⚓ outside the hbr, close N of the entrance.

NAVIGATION WPT 55°05'·33N 08°16'·83E, Lister Tief SWM buoy, 107°/7M via buoyed channel to G1 Pillar buoy Fl Y 4s. Here enter Rømø Dyb (deep water), marked by 3 PHM lt dolphins and by No 1 SHM lt buoy and 5 unlit SHM buoys to the hbr ent.

LIGHTS AND MARKS Rømø has no major lights. On the N end of Sylt: List West (Ellenbogen), Oc WRG 6s, provides a narrow W sector to mark the outer part of Rømø Dyb. The inner part is marked by a narrow W sector from List Land lt Oc WRG 3s, W mast, R band. List Ost, Iso WRG 6s, W twr, R band, R lantern is the 3rd major light. See 9.15.4 for lt sectors. Hbr lts as on chartlet.

R/T VHF Ch 10, 12, 13, 16 HX.

TELEPHONE HM 74.75.55.92; CG 74.75.22.22; Hosp (Esbjerg) 75.18.19.00; Taxi 74.75.11. 00, 74.75.53.94; Police (Emergency) 112.

RØMØ HAVN

FACILITIES Essentially an isolated fishing and ferry port. Yachts berth at 3 pontoons in about 4m on N side of inner hbr. D in FV hbr, FW, ME, ⚒, CH, Showers at SC on N pier.

Havneby town: 🛒. Ferry, every 2 hrs by day, 45 mins to List. Rail at Ribe (mainland, 32km by road). ✈ (Esbjerg).

Germany

Sylt to Emden

Germany

See 9.14.2

DISTANCE TABLE

Approximate distances in nautical miles are by the most direct route, whilst avoiding dangers and allowing for Traffic Separation Schemes. Places in *italics* are in adjoining areas; places in **bold** are in 9.0.7, Distances across the North Sea.

1	*Den Helder*	378	322	187	192	198	229	245	192	175	180	159	150	153	148	130	115	125	115	**1**
2	*Delfzijl*	327	222	155	119	127	159	173	120	105	100	89	83	81	65	56	41	10	22	**2**
3	Borkum	305	200	133	97	105	104	163	110	95	88	80	71	67	55	46	31	32	**3**	
4	Emden	337	232	165	129	137	174	190	137	120	115	106	97	85	80	63	47	**4**		
5	Norderney	291	186	123	77	85	81	137	84	69	62	53	44	44	29	18	**5**			
6	Langeoog	308	204	119	72	77	114	130	77	60	47	43	34	35	21	**6**				
7	Wangerooge	283	178	109	60	52	61	108	55	42	38	27	19	24	**7**					
8	**Helgoland**	259	154	83	38	47	88	104	51	38	44	43	35	**8**						
9	Hooksiel	405	301	116	69	73	101	117	64	47	36	9	**9**							
10	**Wilhelmshaven**	414	310	125	78	82	110	123	70	56	45	**10**								
11	**Bremerhaven**	306	201	127	80	82	81	131	78	58	**11**									
12	Cuxhaven	304	200	110	63	66	54	70	17	**12**										
13	**Brunsbüttel**	301	196	126	75	76	37	53	**13**											
14	Kiel/Holtenau	231	249	179	128	129	90	**14**												
15	Hamburg	338	233	163	112	113	**15**													
16	Husum	268	163	95	48	**16**														
17	**Hörnum Lt (Sylt)**	225	120	47	**17**															
18	*Esbjerg*	195	90	**18**																
19	*Thyborøn*	104	**19**																	
20	*Skagen*	**20**																		

●	Harbour with full almanac entry
•	Minor harbour or anchorage
☆	Major light
RG	Emergency RDF station
⊕	Ferry
✈	Airport

9.15.2
Germany
Danish Border to Emden

Magnetic Variation 0·2°W

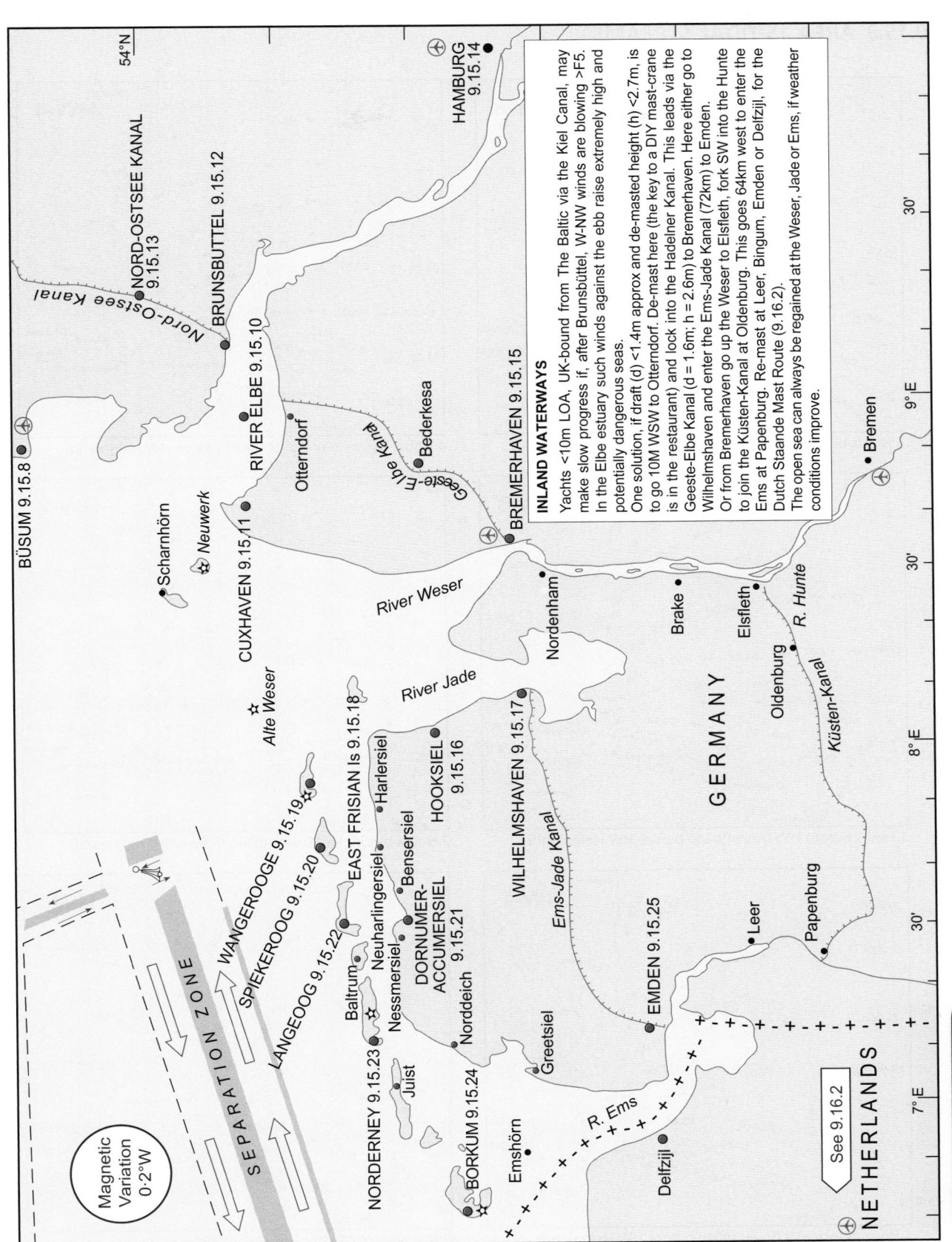

INLAND WATERWAYS

Yachts <10m LOA, UK-bound from The Baltic via the Kiel Canal, may make slow progress if, after Brunsbüttel, W-NW winds are blowing >F5. In the Elbe estuary such winds against the ebb raise extremely high and potentially dangerous seas.

One solution, if draft (d) <1.4m approx and de-masted height (h) <2.7m, is to go 10M WSW to Otterndorf. De-mast here (the key to a DIY mast-crane is in the restaurant) and lock into the Hadeiner Kanal. This leads via the Geeste-Elbe Kanal (d = 1.6m; h = 2.6m) to Bremerhaven. Here either go to Wilhelmshaven and enter the Ems-Jade Kanal (72km) to Emden. Or from Bremerhaven go up the Weser to Elsfleth, fork SW into the Hunte to join the Küsten-Kanal at Oldenburg. This goes 64km west to enter the Ems at Papenburg. Re-mast at Leer, Bingum, Emden or Delfzijl, for the Dutch Staande Mast Route (9.16.2).

The open sea can always be regained at the Weser, Jade or Ems, if weather conditions improve.

9.15.3 AREA 15 TIDAL STREAMS

5 Hours before HW Dover (0440 before HW Helgoland)

4 Hours before HW Dover (0340 before HW Helgoland)

3 Hours before HW Dover (0240 before HW Helgoland)

2 Hours before HW Dover (0140 before HW Helgoland)

1 Hour before HW Dover (0040 before HW Helgoland)

HW Dover (0020 after HW Helgoland)

South-westward 9.16.3

HW+1

1 Hour after HW Dover (0120 after HW Helgoland)

HW+2

2 Hours after HW Dover (0220 after HW Helgoland)

HW+3

3 Hours after HW Dover (0320 after HW Helgoland)

HW+4

4 Hours after HW Dover (0420 after HW Helgoland)

HW+5

5 Hours after HW Dover (0520 after HW Helgoland)

HW+6

6 Hours after HW Dover (0620 after HW Helgoland)

Germany

9.15.4 LIGHTS, BUOYS AND WAYPOINTS

Bold print = light with a nominal range of 15M or more.
CAPITALS = place or feature. *CAPITAL ITALICS* = light-vessel, light float or Lanby. *Italics* = Fog signal. ***Bold italics*** = Racon. Abbreviations are in Chapter 1.

DANISH BORDER TO BUSUM

SYLT
Lister Tief ⚓ Iso 8s; *Whis;* 55°05'·33N 08°16'·79E.
List West (Ellenbogen) ⚡ Oc WRG 6s 19m W14M, R11M, G10M; 040°-R-133°-W-227°-R-266·4°-W-268°-G-285°-W-310°-W(unintens)-040°; W twr, R lantern; 55°03'·15N 08°24'·00E.
List Hafen, S mole ⚡ FR 5m 4M; 218°-353°; R mast; 55°01'·01N 08°26'·51E.
Hörnum ☆ Fl (2) 9s 48m **20M**; 54°45'·23N 08°17'·47E.
Vortrapptief ⚓ Iso 4s; 54°34'·88N 08°12'·97E, toward Hörnum.
S mole ⚡ FR 7m 4M; 54°45'·57N 08°17'·97E.

AMRUM ISLAND
Rütergat ⚓ Iso 8s; 54°30'·08N 08°12'·32E.
Amrum ☆ Fl 7·5s 63m **23M**; R twr, W bands; 54°37'·84N 08°21'·23E.
Wriakhorn Cross ⚡ L Fl (2) WR 15s 26m W9M, R7M; 297·5°-W-319·5°-R-330°-W-005·5°-R-034°; 54°37'·62N 08°21'·22E.
Amrum Hafen ldg lts 272° remain inoperative since at least 2002.

FÖHR ISLAND
Nieblum Dir lt showing over Rütergat. ☆ Oc (2) WRG 10s 11m **W19M, R/G15M**; 028°-G-031°-W-032·5°-R-035·5°; R twr, W band; 54°41'·10N 08°29'·20E.
Ohlörn ⚡ Oc (4) WR 15s 10m 13/10M, 208°-W-237·5°- R-298°-W-353°- R-080°; R twr, Gy lantern; 54°40'·85N 08°34'·00E (SE Föhr).
Wyk Hbr outer ent, FR 54°41'·55N 08°34'·69E; and FG.

DAGEBÜLL
Dagebüll Iso WRG 8s 23m **W18M, R/G15M**; 042°-G-043°-W-044·5°- R-047°; 54°43'·82N 08°41'·43E. FW lts on ent moles.

LANGENESS ISLAND
Nordmarsch ⚡ L Fl (3) WR 20s 13m W14M, R11M; 268°-W-279°-R-306°-W-045°-R-070°-W-218°; dark brown twr; 54°37'·58N 08°31'·85E.

SCHLÜTTSIEL
No. 2/SA 26 ⚓ 54°36'·84N 08°38'·95E. Hbr ent ▲ 54°40'·89N 08°45'·10E.

RIVER HEVER
Hever ⚓ Iso 4s; *Whis;* 54°20'·41N 08°18'·82E.
Westerheversand ☆ Oc (3) WRG 15s 41m **W21M, R17M, G16M**; 012·2°-W-069°-G-079·5°-W-080·5° (ldg sector for Hever)-R-107°-W-233°-R-248°; R twr, W bands; 54°22'·37N 08°38'·36E.
Norderhever No. 1 ⚓ Fl (2+1) R 15s; 54°22'·46N 08°30'·83E.

PELLWORM ISLAND
Pellworm ☆ Oc WRG 5s 38m **20M, R 16M, G 15M**; 037·5°-G-040°-W-042·5°-R-045°; R twr, W band; 54°29'·78N 08°39'·98E.

NORDSTRAND
Suderhafen, S mole ⚓ 54°28'·07N 08°55'·62E.

HUSUM
⚓ Fl G 4s, 54°28'·80N 08°58'·60E, start of access chan.
Ldg lts 090°, both Iso G 8s 7/9m 3M.

RIVER EIDER
Eider ⚓ Iso 4s; 54°14'·54N 08°27'·61E.
St Peter ☆ L Fl (2) WR 15s 23m **W15M**, R12M; 271°-R-280·5°-W-035°-R-055°-W-068°-R-091°-W-120°; 54°17'·24N 08°39'·10E.
Eiderdamm lock, N mole, W end ⚡ Oc (2) R 12s 8m 5M; W twr.

BÜSUM
Süderpiep ⚓ Iso 8s; *Whis;* 54°05'·82N 08°25'·70E.
Büsum ☆ Iso WR 6s 22m **W19M**, R12M; 248°-W-317°-R-024°-W-148°; 54°07'·60N 08°51'·48E.

E mole ⚡ Oc (3) G 12s 10m 4M; vis 260°-168°; G twr; 54°07'·19N 08°51'·65E.

GERMAN BIGHT TO RIVER ELBE

GB Light V ⚓ Iso 8s 12m **17M**; R hull marked G-B; *Horn Mo (R) 30s;* ***Racon T, 8M***; 54°10'·80N 07°27'·60E.

HELGOLAND
Helgoland ☆ Fl 5s 82m **28M**; brown ☐ twr, B lantern, W balcony; 54°10'·91N 07°52'·93E.
Vorhafen. Ostmole, S elbow ⚡ Oc WG 6s 5m W6M, G3M; 203°-W-250°-G-109°; G post; fog det lt; 54°10'·31N 07°53'·94E.

RIVER ELBE (LOWER)

APPROACHES
Nordergründe N ⚓ VQ; 53°57'·06N 08°00'·12E.
Elbe ⚓ Iso 10s; ***Racon T, 8M***; 53°59'·95N 08°06'·49E.
No.1 ⚓ QG; 53°59'·21N 08°13'·20E.
No.25 ⚓ QG; 53°56'·62N 08°38'·25E.
Neuwerk ☆, S side, L Fl (3) WRG 20s 38m **W16M**, R12M, G11M; 165·3°-G-215·3°-W-238·8°-R-321°; 343°-R-100°; 53°54'·92N 08°29'·73E.

CUXHAVEN
No. 31 ⚓ Fl G 4s; 53°53'·93N 08°41'·21E.
Yacht hbr ent, F WR and F WG lts; 53°52'·43N 08°42'·49E.

OTTERNDORF
No. 43 ⚓ Oc (2) G 9s; 53°50'·23N 08°52'·24E.
Medem ⚡ Fl (3) 12s 6m 5M; B △, on B col; 53°50'·15N 08°53'·85E.

BRUNSBÜTTEL
No. 57a ⚓ Fl G 4s; 53°52'·62N 09°07'·93E, 030°/ 8 cables to lock.
Alter Vorhafen ent, mole 1 ⚡ F WG 14m W10M, G6M; 266·3°-W-273·9°-G-088·8°, floodlit; 53°53'·27N 09°08'·59E.

RIVER ELBE (BRUNSBÜTTEL TO HAMBURG)

Some of the more accessible yacht hbrs are listed below , but not the many ldg lts and dir lts which define the main river fairway.

FREIBURG
Reede 1 ⚓ Oc (2) Y 9s; 53°50'·41N 09°19'·45E, off ent.

STÖRLOCH
Stör ldg lts 093·8°, both Fl 3s 7/12m 6M; synch. Front, 53°49'·29N 09°23'·91E; △ on R ○ twr. Rear, 200m east; ▽ on white mast.

GLÜCKSTADT
Glückstadt ldg lts 131·8°, both Iso 8s 15/30m **19/21M**; intens on ldg line; W twrs, R bands. **Front** ☆, 53°48'·31N 09°24'·24E. **Rear** ☆, 0·68M from front.
Rhinplatte Nord ⚡ Oc WRG 6s 11m W6M, R4M, G3M; 122°-G-144°-W-150°-R-177°- W-122°; 53°48'·09N 09°23'·36E.
N mole ⚡ Oc WRG 6s 9m W9M R7M, G6M; 330°-R-343°-W-346°-G-008°; 123°-G-145°-W-150°-R-170°; W twr with gallery; 53°47'·12N 09°24'·53E.
N pier hd ⚡ FR 5m 5M; 53°47'·10N 09°24'·50E. (S mole hd, FG).

KRUCKAU
S mole Oc WRG 6s 8m, W6M, R4M, G3M; 116·3°-W-120·7° (ldg sector)-R-225°-G-315°-R-331·9°-W-335·4° (ldg sector)-335·4°-G-116·3°; B dolphin; 53°42'·85N 09°30'·72E.

PINNAU
Ldg lts 112·7°, both Iso 4s8/13m 6M. Front, 53°40'·08N 09°34'·02E.

STADE
Stadersand ⚡ Iso 8s 20m 14M; 53°37'·69N 09°31'·64E (at ent).

HAMBURG YACHT HARBOUR, WEDEL
Both entrances show FR & FG, May to Oct; 53°34'·25N 09°40'·77E.

CITY SPORTHAFEN
Brandenburger Hafen Ent ⚡ Iso Or 2s; 53°32'·52N 09°58'·81E.

WGS84 DATUM
Plot waypoints on chart before use

WESER ESTUARY
ALTE WESER
Schlüsseltonne ⚓ Iso 8s; 53°56'·25N 07°54'·76E.
Alte Weser ☆ F WRG 33m **W23M, R19M, G18M**; 288°-W-352°-R-003°-W-017° (ldg sector for Alte Weser)- G-045°-W-074°-G-118°- W-123° (ldg sector for Alte Weser)- R-140°-W-175°-W-183°-R-196°-W-238°; R ○ twr, 2 W bands, B base; Fog det lt; *Horn Mo (AL) 60s*; 53°51'·79N 08°07'·65E.
16/A15 ⬟ Fl (2+1) R 15s; 53°49'·66N 08°06'·44E (junction with Neuwe Weser).

NEUE WESER
Tegeler Plate, N end ☆ Oc (3) WRG 12s 21m **W21M, R17M, G16M**; 329°-W-340°-R-014°-W-100°-G-116°- W-119° (ldg sector for Neue Weser)-R-123°-G-144°-W-147° (ldg sector for Alte Weser)-R-264°; R ○ twr, gallery, W lantern, R roof; Fog det lt; 53°47'·87N 08°11'·45E.

BREMERHAVEN
No. 61 ⚓ QG; 53°32'·26N 08°33'·93E (Km 66·0).
Vorhafen N pier ⚓ FR 15m 5M; 245°-166°; F in fog; 53°32'·15N 08°34'·50E.

RIVER JADE
1b/Jade 1: Oc G 4s; 53°52'·40N 07°44'·00E.
Mellumplate ☆ FW 28m **24M**; 116·1°-116·4° (ldg sector for outer part of Wangerooger Fahrwasser); R ☐ twr, W band; 53°46'·28N 08°05'·51E.
No.19 ⚓ QG; 53°47'·10N 08°01'·83E.
No. 31/P-Reede/W Siel 1 ⚓ Oc (3) G 12s; 53°41'·59N 08°04'·51E.

HOOKSIEL
No. 37/Hooksiel 1 ⚓ IQ G 13s; 53°39'·37N 08°06'·58E.
Vorhafen ent ⚓ L Fl R 6s 9m 3M; 53°38'·63N 08°05'·25E.

WILHELMSHAVEN
Fluthafen N mole ⚓ FWG 9m,W6M, G3M; 216°-W-280°-G-010°-W-020°-G-130°; G twr; 53°30'·86N 08°09'·32E.

EAST FRISIAN ISLANDS
NORTH EDGE OF INSHORE TRAFFIC ZONE
TG19/Weser 2 ⚓ Fl (2+1) G 15s; 53°54'·99N 07°44'·52E.
TG13 ⚓ Oc (3) G 12s; 53°50'·85N 07°15'·43E.
TG7 ⚓ Fl (2) G 9s; 53°47'·24N 06°49'·65E.
TG1/Ems ⚓ IQ G 13s; 53°43'·36N 06°22'·24E.

WANGEROOGE
Harle ⚓ Iso 8s; 53°49'·26N 07°48'·92E.
Wangerooge, W end ☆ Fl R 5s 60m **23M**; R ○ twr, 2 W bands; 53°47'·40N 07°51'·37E.
Buhne H ⚓ VQ (9) 10s; 53°46'·86N 07°49'·65E.
D4 ⚓ ; 53°46'·25N 07°51'·89E, off hbr ent.

SPIEKEROOG
Otzumer Balje ⚓ Iso 4s; 53°47'·98N 07°37'·12E (often moved.)
Spiekeroog ⚓ FR 6m 4M; 197°-114°; R mast; 53°45'·0N 07°41'·3E.

LANGEOOG
Accumer Ee ⚓ Iso 8s; 53°46·96N 07°25·91E (frequently moved).
W mole head ⚓ Oc WRG 6s 8m W7M, R5M, G4M; 064°-G-070°-W-074°-R-326°-W-330°-G-335°-R-064°; R basket on R mast; *Horn Mo (L) 30s* (0730-1800LT); 53°43'·42N 07°30'·13E .

BALTRUM
Groyne hd ⚓ Oc WRG 6s 6m; W6M, R4M, G3M; 074·5°-G-090°-W-095°-R-074·5°; 53°43'·3N 07°21'·7E.

NORDERNEY
Norderney ☆ Fl (3) 12s 59m **23M**; unintens 067°-077° and 270°-280°; R 8-sided twr; 53°42'·58N 07°13'·83E.
Dovetief ⚓ Iso 4s; 53°45'·47N 07°12'·70E.

Schluchter ⚓ Iso 8s; 53°44'·48N 07°02'·27E.
W mole head ⚓ Oc (2) R 9s 13m 4M; 53°41'·9N 07°09'·9E.

JUIST
Juist-N ⚓ VQ; 53°43'·82N 06°55'·42E.
Training wall, S end ⚓ Oc (2) R 9s 7m 3M; 53°39'·65N 06°59'·81E.

MAINLAND HARBOURS: RIVER JADE TO RIVER EMS
HARLESIEL
Carolinensieler Balje, Leitdamm ⚓ L Fl 8s 7m 6M; G mast; 53°44'·13N 07°50'·10E.
Ldg lts 138°, both Iso 6s 12/18m 9M, intens on ldg line; Front 53°40'·70N 07°34'·50E. Rear 167m from front.
N mole head ⚓ Iso R 4s 6m 7M; 53°42'·58N 07°48'·64E.

NEUHARLINGERSIEL
Training wall head ⚓ Oc 6s 6m 5M; 53°43'·22N 07°42'·30E.

BENSERSIEL
E training wall head ⚓ Oc WRG 6s 6m W5M, R3M, G2M; 110°-G-119°-W-121°-R-110°; R post & platform; 53° 41'·80N 07°32'·84E.

DORNUMER-ACCUMERSIEL
W bkwtr head, approx 53°41'·04N 07°29'·30E.

NESSMERSIEL
N mole head ⚓ Oc 4s 6m 5M; G mast; 53°41'·9N 07°21'·7E.

NORDDEICH
W trng wall head ⚓ FG 8m 4M, 021°-327°; G framework twr; 53°38'·62N 07°09'·0E.

GREETSIEL
Meßstation lt bcn, Fl Y 4s 15m 3M; 53°32'·94N 07°02'·18E.

RIVER EMS
APPROACHES
GW/EMS ⬤ Iso 8s 12m **17M**; *Horn Mo (R) 30s (H24)*; *Racon T, 8M*; 54°09'·96N 06°20'·72E.
Borkumriff ⚓ Oc 4s; *Racon T, 8M*; 53°47'·44N 06°22'·05E.
Osterems ⚓ Iso 4s; 53°41'·91N 06°36'·17E.
Riffgat ⚓ Iso 8s; 53°38'·96N 06°27'·10E.
Westerems ⚓ Iso 4s; *Racon T, 8M*; 53°36'·93N 06°19'·39E.
H1 ⚓ 53°34'·91N 06°17'·97E.

BORKUM
Borkum Grosser ☆ Fl (2) 12s 63m **24M**; brown ○ twr; 53°35'·32N 06°39'·64E. Same twr, ⚓ F WRG 46m **W19M, R/G15M**; 107·4°-G-109°-W-111·2°- R-112·6°.
Fischerbalje ☆ Oc (2) 16s 15m **3M**; 260°-W-123°. Fog det lt; R/W ○ twr on tripod; 53°33'·18N 06°42'·90E.
Schutzhafen, E mole hd ⚓ FG10m 4M; 53°33'·48N 06°45'·02E.
W mole hd, FR 8m 4M.

RIVER EMS (LOWER)
No. 27 ⚓ Fl G 4s; 53°30'·24N 06°47'·52E.
No. 35 ⚓ Fl G 4s; 53°27'·03N 06°52'·80E.
No. 37 ⚓ QG; 53°26'·01N 06°54'·85E.
No. 41 ⚓ Fl (2) G 9s; 53°24'·25N 06°56'·68E.
No. 49 ⚓ Oc (2) G 9s; 53°19'·95N 06°59'·71E.

KNOCK
Knock ⚓ F WRG 28m W12M,R9M, G8M; 270°-W-299°-R-008·3°-G-023°-W-026·8°-R-039°-W-073°-R-119°-W-154°; fog det lt; Gy twr, white conical radar antenna; 53°20'·32N 07°01'·40E.

EMDEN
No. 59 ⚓ Oc (2) G 9s; 53°19'·41N 07°03'·86E.
No. 65 ⚓ Fl (2) G 9s; 53°19'·82N 07°06'·56E.
Outer hbr, W pier ⚓ FR 10m 4M; R 8-sided twr; *Horn Mo (ED) 30s;* 53°20'·06N 07°10'·49E.
E pier ⚓ FG 7m 5M; G mast on pedestal; 53°20'·05N 07°10'·84E.

Germany

9.15.5 PASSAGE INFORMATION

More Passage Information is threaded between successive harbours in this Area. **Bibliography**: NP 55 *North Sea (East);* 3rd ed 2006 *Cruising Guide to Germany and Denmark* (Imray/Navin). The *Hafenhandbuch, Nord See* (DSV-Verlag) is an invaluable and well illustrated annual guide, detailing major and minor hbrs from Calais to Trondheim and the Lofoten Islands.

NORTH FRISIAN ISLANDS

Lister Tief is the chan between the Danish island of Rømø and the N end of Sylt; it gives access to **List Roads** and hbr as well as to Danish hbrs (AC 1875, 3767). Lister Tief is well buoyed; least depth over the bar is about 4m. Relatively it is the safest chan on this coast (after Süderpiep), available for yachts seeking anch under the lee of Sylt in strong W winds (when however there would be a big swell over the bar on the ebb). Beware buoyed obstructions (ODAS), 18M WSW of List West lt ho.

Sylt is the largest of the N Frisian Islands, almost 20M long from S to N. It has a straight seaward coast, and on its E side is connected by the Hindenburgdamm to the mainland. Vortrapptief is the NNE chan inward between Amrum and Sylt, leading to **Hörnum** Hafen. It has a depth of about 4m (subject to frequent change) and is buoyed and lit. *The area should not be approached in strong W winds.* ▶*The flood (ESE-going) stream begins at HW Helgoland –0350, and the ebb (WNW-going) at HW Helgoland +0110, sp rates 2·5kn.*◀

Rütergat and Schmaltief give access to **Amrum** (Wittdün hbr on SE side), to **Wyk** on the SE corner of **Föhr** and to Dagebüll. The R. Hever consists of several chans on the N side of Eiderstedt Peninsula, and S of the North Frisian Islands of **Süderoogsand** and **Pellworm**. Mittelhever is the most important of the three buoyed chans through the outer grounds, all of which meet SE of Süderoogsand. Here they separate once more into Norderhever, which runs NE between Pellworm and Nordstrand into a number of watt channels; and Heverstrom which leads to Husum.

RIVER EIDER AND SCHLESWIG-HOLSTEIN

Approaching the R. Eider from seaward, find the Eider SWM lt buoy, about 1·2M W of the buoyed ent chan. *The ent can be rough in W winds, and dangerous in onshore gales.* St Peter lt ho is conspic on N shore. Here the estuary winds up to the Eiderdamm, a storm barrage with a lock (H24) and sluices. **Tönning** is about 5M up-river. The upper Eider parallels the Nord-Ostsee Kanal which it joins at Gieselau.

The W coast of Schleswig-Holstein is flat and marshy, with partly-drying banks extending 5–10M offshore. Between the banks and islands, the chans shift frequently. Süderpiep and Norderpiep join S of Blauort and lead to **Büsum** and Meldorfer Hafen (marina). Norderpiep has a bar (depth 3m) and is unlit; Süderpiep is deeper and preferable in W'lies. Landmarks from seaward are Tertius bn and Blauortsand bn, and a conspic silo and tall building at Büsum.

HELGOLAND TO THE RIVER ELBE

Helgoland is a useful staging post for yachts entering the Elbe bound for **Cuxhaven** (38M) or direct **Brunsbüttel** (51M) at the ent to the **Nord-Ostsee Kanal** (AC 2469). From the E end of the TSS the Elbe channel is well marked by buoys and beacon trs. Commercial traffic is very heavy. For further details see River Elbe (9.15.10).

▶*At Elbe SWM buoy the E-going (flood) stream begins at HW Helgoland –0500, and the W-going (ebb) stream at HW Helgoland +0500, sp rates 2kn. The stream runs harder N of Scharhörn, up to 3·5kn on the ebb, when the Elbe estuary is dangerously rough in strong W or NW winds.*◀

At the mouth of the Elbe estuary (AC 3619, 3625, 3267, 3268) Scharhörn and Neuwerk are islets. The latter features in *Riddle of the Sands*, Erskine Childer's classic sailing and spy thriller.

9.15.6 SPECIAL NOTES FOR GERMANY

LANDS are given in lieu of 'counties' in the UK.

TIME ZONE is -0100 (subtract 1 hour for UT). DST is kept from the last Sunday in March to the last Sunday in October

CHARTS: German charts are issued by the Bundesamt für Seeschiffahrt und Hydrographie (BSH), Hamburg. In this Almanac German *seekarten* charts are prefixed 'D'.

The 3000 Series of leisure-craft folios are prefixed BSH. 3010-3015 cover the N Sea coast and 3009 the Kiel Canal. They are a handy size (42 x 59cm), stowed in a large clear polythene envelope; each set has up to 16 sheets at medium/large scale.

All charts are referred to WGS 84 and are corrected by *Nachrichten für Seefahrer* (NfS) = Notices to Mariners. Where possible the AC, Imray and Dutch chart numbers are also quoted.

TIDE TABLES: Admiralty charts of German coastal waters are now referred to LAT (not MLWS), as are German charts. It is therefore no longer necessary to deduct 0·5m from predicted tidal heights (as was previously advised). Nor is it necessary to deduct 0·5m from height differences at German Secondary Ports to get the correct predicted depth.

LIGHTS: In coastal waters considerable use is made of sectored lights. A leading or directional sector (usually W, and often intens) may be flanked by warning sectors to show the side to which the vessel has deviated: If to port, a FR lt or a Fl W lt with an even number of flashes; if to starboard, a FG lt or a Fl W lt with an odd number of flashes. Crossing lts with R, W and G sectors indicate (eg) the limits of roadsteads, bends in chans etc.

SIGNALS: IPTS are widely used in major ports. Local port, tidal, distress and traffic signals are given where possible. Visual storm warning signals are not used. When motoring under sail, always display a black motoring cone (▼). Rule 25e is strictly enforced and non-compliance will incur a fine.

Lights at bridges and locks

Signal		Meaning
●●	=	Passage/entry prohib.
●	=	Prepare to pass or enter; exit from lock prohib.
●	=	Exit from lock permitted.
○ ●●	=	Passage or entry permitted if there is sufficient clearance; beware of oncoming traffic which has right of way.
○○ ●●	=	Lifting bridge is at first lift position; and may be passed by vessels for which the vertical clearance is safe.
●●	=	Passage/entry permitted; oncoming traffic stopped.
○ ●●	=	Passage or entry permitted, but beware oncoming traffic which may have right of way.
● ●	=	Bridge, lock or flood barrage closed to navigation.

Signals hoisted at masts

By day	By night	Meaning
R cylinder	○ ● ○	Reduce speed to minimise wash.
● ● ▼	● ●	Unusual obstruction to navigation.
● ▼ ▲	● ● ○	Long term closure of waterway.

HARBOURS: Most marinas are owned by the state or community and run by a local YC (as in Belgium and the Netherlands).

TRAFFIC SEPARATION SCHEMES: The extensive TSS (off Terschelling, in the German Bight and in the approaches to the Rivers Jade and Elbe) link up with the various Dutch TSS. Information broadcasts by VTS centres and their associated communications are given in Areas 15 and 16.

Caution: Although the TSS may be crossed in accordance with the IRPCS, vessels in the ITZ should not approach the S edge of the E-bound lane of the Terschelling-German Bight TSS (well marked by buoys TG1 to TG17) closer than 1M, unless in emergency or due to stress of weather. The German Marine Police can impose on-the-spot fines or confiscate equipment to the value of €1000 pending payment of the fine.

Navigators are strongly advised to:

- Log positions, times, courses, speeds, wind, weather, seastate, other traffic and use of sail or engine. Such records can be important in any dispute or litigation and also keep the skipper alert to any consequences. In addition, they can demonstrate that the yacht is being responsibly navigated.

- Always monitor the appropriate VTS channel: Ch 80 in E part of Inner German Bight; Ch 79 in W part. If a deviation from the rules is necessary, inform the VTS traffic centre.

- Beware of deep draught vessels S-bound from the German Bight It vessel in the Jade approach TSS and crossing E-bound traffic in the Terschelling-German Bight TSS. The former have right of way over E-bound traffic. Yachts either E- or W-bound must take this into account.

HIGH SPEED CRAFT: High speed craft ply between Emden and Borkum; and from Hamburg to Stadersand, Cuxhaven and Helgoland. Keep a good lookout.

TELEPHONES: To call UK from Germany: dial 00 44; then the UK area code, minus the initial zero; then the number required. To call Germany from UK: dial 00 49; then area code minus initial zero; then desired number. Mobile numbers begin with 015, 016, 017; number of digits varies depending on Service provider.

EMERGENCIES: Police: dial 110. Fire, Ambulance: dial 112.

PUBLIC HOLIDAYS: New Year's Day, Good Friday, Easter Monday, Labour Day (1 May), Ascension Day, Whit Monday, Day of German Unity (3 Oct), Christmas Day and Boxing Day.

NATIONAL WATER PARKS exist in the Wadden Sea areas (tidal mud flats) of Lower Saxony, (excluding the Jade and Weser rivers and the Ems-Dollart estuary), and along the west coast of Schleswig-Holstein to the Germany/Denmark border. *These conservation areas have the status of Particularly Sensitive Sea Areas (PSSA) in or near which vessels should take the utmost care to avoid damaging the marine environment and marine organisms living therein. See 9.0.4 Environmental Guidance.* The Parks (shown on AC & BSH charts) are divided into 3 zones with certain rules:

Zone 1	comprises the most sensitive areas (about 30%) where yachts must keep to buoyed chans, except HW±3. Speed limit 8kn.
Zone 2	is a buffer zone.
Zone 3	is the remainder. No special constraints exist in Zones 2 and 3.

CUSTOMS: Ports of entry are: Borkum, Norderney, Norddeich, Wilhelmshaven, Bremerhaven, Cuxhaven; but not Helgoland.

GAS: Calor gas bottles can sometimes be re-filled. German 'Flussig' gas can be used with Calor regulators.

CURRENCY is the Euro (€). VAT (MWST) is 19%.

TOURISM TAX is used to fund local amenities in tourist areas. It is approx €2–€3 per person per day and may be payable.

9.15.7 SYLT

Schleswig-Holstein **54°45'·51N 08°17'·83E** (Hörnum hbr)
Hörnum ✵✵⟨⟨⟨✿✿✿✿; List ✵✵⟨⟨✿✿✿✿

CHARTS AC 3767; D107, D108; BSH 3013.2/3 List, 3013.4/5 Hörnum

TIDES +0110 Dover; ML 1·8; Duration 0540

Standard Port HELGOLAND (→)

Times				Height (metres)			
High Water		Low Water		MHWS	MHWN	MLWN	MLWS
0100	0600	0100	0800	2·7	2·4	0·5	0·0
1300	1800	1300	2000				
Differences LIST							
+0252	+0240	+0201	+0210	–0·7	–0·6	–0·3	0·0
HÖRNUM							
+0223	+0218	+0131	+0137	–0·4	–0·3	–0·2	0·0
AMRUM-HAFEN							
+0138	+0137	+0128	+0134	+0·2	+0·2	–0·1	0·0
DAGEBÜLL							
+0226	+0217	+0211	+0225	+0·5	+0·5	–0·2	–0·1
SUDEROOGSAND							
+0116	+0102	+0038	+0122	+0·5	+0·4	0·0	0·0
HUSUM							
+0205	+0152	+0118	+0200	+1·2	+1·1	–0·1	0·0

Westerland (the capital) is in the centre of Sylt (about 20M long) where the Hindenburgdamm links it to the mainland. Large areas of Sylt are nature reserves; landing prohib. List is in the N and Hörnum in the S. Two other hbrs which both dry (soft mud) are Munkmarsch and Rantum; access HW ±3.

FACILITIES **WESTERLAND**: CG 85199; Police 70470. ⊕ 04651 840. **Town** 🍴, R, Bar, P & D (cans), Gaz, ⊖ 8356333, ✉, Ⓑ, Wi-fi; ⇌, ✈.

Continued overleaf

LIST

SHELTER The small hbr/marina is sheltered except from NE/E winds.

NAVIGATION WPT 55°05'·32N 08°16'·67E Lister Tief SWM buoy, 111°/7·0M to No 13 SHM buoy. *Strong W/NW winds cause a heavy swell over the bar (depth 3m) on the ebb, which sets on to Salzsand.* Thence 214°/2·0M to the hbr via buoyed chan and W sector of List Land dir lt. Access by day at all tides, but beware strong cross streams. Ent is 25m wide. Enter hbr from SE, keeping List Land lt ho between the mole heads.

LIGHTS AND MARKS Hbr lts as on the chartlet. See 9.15.4 for lts at List West, List Ost, List Land (overlooks List hbr) and Kampen, 5.4M SW. Rømø church, 7M NNE, is conspic.

R/T VHF Ch **11** (0800-1200, 1600-1800).

TELEPHONE (Code 04651 for the whole of Sylt) HM 870374; Police 870510; Marine police 870460; ⊖ 870413, CG 870365; Dr 870350.

FACILITIES Hbr Marina at S end carries 1·1m-2·6m. NE quay is open construction, unsuitable for yachts. AB €1·20+ tax €2·50/day/person, FW, ⊖, Slip, SC. **Village** ☒, R, Bar, P & D (cans). Ferry to Rōmō (Denmark).

HÖRNUM

SHELTER Good in the small hbr, approx 370m x 90m. Yacht haven at the N end. Good ⊥ in Hörnum Reede in W and N winds and in Hörnumtief in E and S winds.

NAVIGATION WPT: 54°34'·87N 08°12'·97E, Vortrapptief SWM buoy, 016°/10M to S tip of Sylt. Hörnum lt bearing 012° leads through buoyed, lit Vortrapptief between drying banks. In strong W winds the sea breaks on off-lying banks and in the chan. Access at all tides but not at night without radar. Beware strong cross-streams.

LIGHTS AND MARKS Hörnum lt is 3½ca SSW of hbr ent. Other lts as chartlet. Conspic radio mast (5 Fl R lts) 3M N of hbr.

R/T VHF Ch 67; Mon-Thu 0700-1600; Fri 0700-1230, all LT.

TELEPHONE (Code 04651) HM 881027; Dr 881016; Police (Westerland) 70470; MRCC (Bremen) 04215 36870, mobile 124124; CG 881256 (volunteer svc).

FACILITIES Sylter YC ☎ 880274, AB €1·20 + tax €2·50/day/person, Bar, ▣. **Town** ☒, R, Bar, ME, ✉, Ⓑ.

OTHER HARBOURS IN THE NORTH FRISIAN ISLANDS

WYK, Island of Föhr, **54°41'·66N 08°34'·72E**. AC 3767; D 107, BSH 3013.6. HW +0107 on Dover (UT); +0137 on Helgoland (zone –0100); ML 2·8. Good yacht hbr (1·2-1·7m) to N of ent, sheltered in all winds; access H24; visitors berth W side of pontoon 1. Also berths on E quay of inner hbr. Ferry hbr (4m). Lts see 9.15.4: Olhörn (SE point of Föhr), R twr. Mole heads, FR, R mast and FG, G mast. Port VHF Ch **11** 16. Yacht hbr HM ☎ (04681) 3030; Commercial HM ☎ 500430; **Marine Police** ☎ 1280; Dr ☎ 8558; ⊖ ☎ 2594; Facilities: **Hbr road** (500m), CH, ▣, P & D (cans); **Yacht Hbr** €1·00, R, ☒; **W Quay** D.

AMRUM-HAFEN, **54°37'·90N 08°23'·04E**. AC 3767; D 107, BSH 3013.6 & 7. HW +0107 on Dover (UT); +0137 on Helgoland (zone –0100); ML 2·7m; Duration 0540. See 9.15.7. Appr via Rütergat and Norderaue. Make good RGR buoy No 26/AH1, Fl(2+1)R 15s, at 54°37'·76N 08°24'·80E where the hbr chan starts; it carries 2·5m and is marked by PHM withies ⌐. Yachts berth S of stone quay, lying bows to pontoon, stern to posts. Good shelter except in E winds. Ferry quay is 800m to the E. The 272° ldg lts have been inoperative since at least 2002. Lt ho Fl 7·5s, R tr, W bands is same location as rear ldg lt. Wriakhörn, Cross lt, is 1M WSW of hbr, see 9.15.4. It is not advisable to enter at night. HM ☎ (04682) 2294; ⊖ 2026; Dr ☎ 531; Facilities: AB €1·20, P & D (cans) at Nebel; **Amrum YC** ☎ 2054.

PELLWORM, 54°31'·27N 08°41'·16E. AC 3767; D 106, BSH 3013.11 & 12C. Tides: see Suderoogsand/Husum, 9.15.7. Outer appr via Norderhever to NH18 RGR buoy, Fl (2+1) R 15s, at the mouth of the ent chan which carries 0·2m (access near HW) and is marked by withies. VHF Ch 11, 0700-1700. Small yacht hbr partly dries to soft mud; 2·8m at MHW. AB €1·00. Village 600m S.

MAINLAND HARBOUR 12 MILES EAST OF PELLWORM

HUSUM, Schleswig-Holstein, **54°28'·74N 08°59'·92E**. AC 3767; D.106, BSH 3013.12. HW + 0036 on Dover (UT); ML 1·9m; Duration 0555. See 9.15.7. SHM bcn, Fl G 4s, 54°28'·80N 08°58'·60E, marks start of access chan; also marked by two PHM bcns, both Fl (2) R 9s. A sluice/lock, 7ca W of rly bridge, is shut when level > 0·3m over MHW, as shown by ●. Beware the canal effect when meeting big ships in the narrow appr chan. In the outer hbr yachts should turn stbd just before rly bridge for pontoons on S bank, or pass through bridge (clnce 5m when shut) to inner hbr by SC Nordsee; both dry. VHF call *Husum Port* Ch 11. Tfc reports broadcast on Ch 11 every H +00 from HW –4 to HW +2. See 9.15.4 for hbr lts. Night entry not advised. HM ☎ (04841) 667218; Sluice ☎ 2565; **Husum YC** ☎ 65670; **SC Nordsee** ☎ 3436; ⊖ ☎ 61759. AB AB €1·00, P, D, at hbr.

MHW), or on river quays. Up river, bridge (clnce 5·6m) opens on request Mon-Sat 0600-SS. HM ☎ (04861) 1400; Dr ☎ 389; Ⓗ ☎ 706; Facilities: **Quay** AB €1·00, FW, P, D, BY, C (5 ton), Slip; **YC** ☎ 754 (all welcome). **Town** Ⓑ, ✉, ≈, Gaz. Tönning is linked to the Kiel Canal (9.15.13) and Rendsburg by the R Eider and the Gieselau Kanal (BSH 3009.7/.6/.5/.2).

MAINLAND HARBOUR 9 MILES NORTH OF BÜSUM
TÖNNING, Schleswig-Holstein, **54°19'·00N 08°57'·00E**. AC 3767 (only appr from Eider SWM buoy); D.104, BSH 3013.14, 3014.8. Eiderdamm lock, 5·5M down-river, opens H24; VHF Ch 14. Lts, see 9.15.4. Above the dam, beware strong currents when sluices are operated HW +3 to HW+½. AB on S side of drying marina (3m at

9.15.8 BÜSUM
Schleswig-Holstein 54°07'·16N 08°51'·52E ✿✿✿♨♨♨✿✿

CHARTS AC 1875, 3767; D.105, BSH 3014.4.

TIDES HW +0036 on Dover (UT); ML 1·9m; Duration 0625

Standard Port HELGOLAND (→)

Times				Height (metres)			
High Water		Low Water		MHWS	MHWN	MLWN	MLWS
0100	0600	0100	0800	2·7	2·4	0·5	0·0
1300	1800	1300	2000				
Differences BÜSUM							
+0054	+0049	−0001	+0027	+0·9	+0·8	−0·1	+0·1
LINNENPLATE 54°13'·0N 08°40'·0E							
+0047	+0046	+0034	+0046	+0·7	+0·6	−0·1	−0·1
SÜDERHÖFT 54°16'·0N 08°41'·8E							
+0103	+0056	+0051	+0112	+0·7	+0·6	−0·2	0·0
EIDERSPERRWERK 54°16'·0N 08°50'·7E							
+0120	+0115	+0130	+0155	+0·7	+0·6	−0·1	0·0

SHELTER Very good. Beware strong cross-tides and sudden winds over moles. A flood barrage closes when level exceeds MHW, but craft < 30m LOA can enter via a lock. For opening (H24), call VHF or sound 1 long blast in appr chan; 2 long blasts at lock if not already open; obey R/G lts. Turn 90° stbd into marina (1·8m LW) Basin IV. Meldorf Marina is 4M ESE with 2-6m and all facilities. Appr via Kronenloch (1·1m); enter via barrage/lock.

NAVIGATION WPT 54°05'·82N 08°25'·70E, Süderpiep SWM buoy Iso 8s, 096°/1·0M to No 1 SHM buoy, Fl G 4s. Chan is lit/well-buoyed. Norderpiep is buoyed, but unlit; beware bar if wind-over-tide. Both are approx 15M long; night appr not advised.

LIGHTS AND MARKS Lt ho, ldg lts 355·1° and hbr lts as chartlet. A 22 storey bldg is conspic 8ca NW of hbr; silo is conspic in hbr.

R/T Call *Büsum Port* Ch 11 16 for lock opening.

TELEPHONE (Code 04834) HM 2183; CG 2246; ⊖ 2376; Dr 2088; YC 2997.

FACILITIES Yacht hbr AB €1.30, M, BY, El, ME, C, P, D, ◎. **Town** CH, ⬒, R, Bar, ✉, Ⓑ, ≈, Ⓗ, ✈ (Hamburg).

9.15.9 HELGOLAND
Schleswig-Holstein 54°10'·28N 07°53'·93E ✿✿✿♨♨♨✿✿

CHARTS AC 1635, 1875; Imray C26; D3, 88; BSH 3014.2/3

TIDES −0030 Dover; ML 1·4; Duration 0540
HELGOLAND is a Standard Port (→).

SHELTER Good in safe artificial hbr (5m); yachts berth on pontoons on the NE side of the Südhafen which gets very crowded, rafting 10 deep. Ostkaie now finished (reports appreciated). Or ⚓ in the SW part of the Vorhafen, sheltered except in SE'lies; ask permission from Port Control Ch 67.

NAVIGATION WPT 54°08'·96N 07°53'·49E, [Helgoland-O ECM buoy, Q (3) 10s, Whis],020°/1·3M to abeam No 3 buoy. Beware: the Hogstean shoal (1m), 4ca S of Sudmole head lt, and other rky shoals either side of chan; lobster pots around Düne and fast ferries using the S appr chan and ent.

- *Between Helgoland and Düne the general direction of buoyage changes at approx 54°11'N; see chartlet overleaf.*
- Entry is prohib at all times into Nature Reserves close to either side of the appr chans from SSW and NW.

These Reserves extend about 2·9M NE and SW of Helgoland; their limits are marked by 7 cardinal buoys. Marine police are active in this respect. A smaller Reserve, lying to the N, E and S of Düne, is a prohib ⚓, with other restrictions. See BSH 3014.2, AC 1635 and 1875 (plan) for limits.

LIGHTS AND MARKS Helgoland is a 60m high red sandstone plateau; in contrast Düne is a low sandy islet. The lt ho is a brown □ twr, B lantern, W balcony. Close S a R/W radio mast and Sig stn are conspic. Düne rear ldg lt is on a red twr with W band.

R/T *Helgoland Port Radio* Ch 67, 16 (**1/5 – 31/8**: Mon-Thur 0700-1200,1300-2000; Fri/Sat 0700-2000; Sun 0700-1200LT. **1/9–30/4**: Mon-Thur 0700-1200, 1300-1600; Fri 0700-1200).

TELEPHONE (Code 04725) HM 81593583, or dial 81593-0 and ask for extension; CG 210; ⊖ 1537 or 304; Met 811007; Police 607; Dr 7345; Ⓗ 8030; Ambulance 7723; SAR 811305; Brit Consul (040) 446071.

FACILITIES *Yachts must not enter the Nordost hafen and Dünen hafen nor land on Düne island.*

NOTE: Helgoland is not a port of entry into Germany. Customs in Helgoland are for passport control. Duty free goods are obtainable; hence many day-trippers by ferry. There is a visitors' tax of €2.75/person/night. useful webcam www.rickmers-online.de/webcam.html.

Vorhafen L, ⚓. **Südhafen** AB €1.32. D, FW on Westkaje, limit 70 litres, €0.50, AC (coins), ME, CH, C (mobile 12 ton), ⬒, R, Bar.

Binnenhafen, closed except for fuel, no FW at fuel station.

Wasser Sport Club ☎ 7422, Berthing <10m with permission; Bar, R, M, C (12 ton), D, P, CH, ME, El, ⚒, FW, ◎, ⬒.

Town Gaz, ⬒, R, Bar, ✉, Ⓑ, ✈ to Bremen, Hamburg, Cuxhaven.

See chartlet overleaf

HELGOLAND

MEAN SPRING ——
AND NEAP CURVES – – –

MEAN RANGES
Springs 2.7m
Neaps 1.9m

Springs occur 3 days
after
New and Full Moon

HELGOLAND *continued*

DÜNE

Airfield

54°11'·0N

10'·5

Nature Reserve
Entry Prohibited

Nature Reserve (restrictions)

Numerous stones

Südreede

Binnenreede

Binnenhafen

Nordkaje

Westkaje

Südkaje

Westmole

Südmole

Südhafen

Vorhafen

Ostkaje

Ostmole

SS(Traffic)

CHURCH

HELGOLAND

Nordosthafen

Pipelines

Dünenhafen Closed

FROM THE GERMAN BIGHT TO THE UK

(AC 2182A, 1423, 1405, 1635) From the Elbe, Weser and Jade estuaries, skirt the E ends of the German Bight western approaches TSS to depart from the vicinity of Helgoland or the GB light vessel. ▶*West of German Bight streams run approx E/W, spring rates <1kn.*◀ Thence parallel the N side of TSS, towards Botney Ground (BG2 buoy) if heading north of Flamborough Head. A WNW track towards the Firth of Forth avoids the areas most densely obstructed by offshore oil and gas installations.

If bound for East Anglia and the Thames Estuary, follow the ITZ westwards until S of Den Helder and Off Texel TSS in about Lat 52° 50'N; thence head west, avoiding areas of offshore industrial activity and the heavy traffic concentrations off the Maas and Westerschelde.

For the English Channel it is best to stay inshore until Cap Gris Nez. For distances across the North Sea, see 9.0.7.

TIME ZONE -0100
Subtract 1 hour for UT
For German Summer Time add
ONE hour in **non-shaded areas**

HELGOLAND LAT 54°11'N LONG 7°53'E
TIMES AND HEIGHTS OF HIGH AND LOW WATERS

Dates in red are **SPRINGS**
Dates in blue are NEAPS

YEAR 2010

JANUARY

Time	m		Time	m
1 0625	0.6	**16** 0024	3.3
1203	3.1	0712	0.7
F 1842	0.7	SA 1248	3.1
		1922	0.7
2 0021	3.3	**17** 0058	3.3
0719	0.5	0748	0.6
SA 1255	3.1	SU 1322	3.0
1933	0.6	1956	0.6
3 0112	3.4	**18** 0131	3.3
0814	0.5	0821	0.6
SU 1347	3.1	M 1353	3.0
2024	0.5	2026	0.6
4 0201	3.4	**19** 0201	3.3
0903	0.4	0850	0.5
M 1435	3.0	TU 1422	3.0
2109	0.5	2052	0.5
5 0246	3.4	**20** 0229	3.2
0946	0.4	0918	0.6
TU 1519	2.9	W 1450	2.9
2152	0.5	2121	0.6
6 0329	3.4	**21** 0300	3.2
1028	0.4	0947	0.6
W 1604	2.9	TH 1521	2.9
2237	0.6	2153	0.6
7 0415	3.3	**22** 0332	3.1
1112	0.5	1017	0.6
TH 1653	2.9	F 1553	2.9
◗ 2325	0.7	2225	0.7
8 0508	3.2	**23** 0405	3.0
1159	0.7	1046	0.7
F 1746	2.8	SA 1628	2.8
		◖ 2301	0.8
9 0019	0.8	**24** 0446	2.9
0607	3.1	1127	0.8
SA 1254	0.8	SU 1716	2.8
1845	2.8	2356	0.9
10 0123	0.9	**25** 0546	2.9
0715	3.0	1231	0.9
SU 1402	1.0	M 1825	2.8
1954	2.9		
11 0238	1.0	**26** 0113	0.9
0829	3.0	0706	2.8
M 1516	1.0	TU 1353	0.9
2104	3.0	1948	2.8
12 0352	1.0	**27** 0241	0.9
0940	3.0	0832	2.9
TU 1622	1.0	W 1518	0.9
2207	3.1	2110	3.0
13 0456	0.9	**28** 0404	0.8
1040	3.1	0951	3.0
W 1717	0.9	TH 1634	0.8
2300	3.2	2220	3.1
14 0549	0.8	**29** 0516	0.6
1129	3.1	1059	3.1
TH 1804	0.9	F 1739	0.7
2345	3.3	2319	3.3
15 0633	0.7	**30** 0617	0.5
1211	3.1	1156	3.1
F 1845	0.8	SA 1834	0.6
●		○	
		31 0011	3.3
		0711	0.4
		SU 1245	3.1
		1925	0.5

FEBRUARY

Time	m		Time	m
1 0100	3.4	**16** 0109	3.2
0803	0.3	0758	0.4
M 1333	3.1	TU 1330	3.1
2014	0.4	2004	0.4
2 0148	3.4	**17** 0137	3.2
0849	0.3	0825	0.4
TU 1418	3.1	W 1356	3.0
2058	0.3	2030	0.4
3 0232	3.4	**18** 0205	3.2
0930	0.3	0852	0.4
W 1500	3.0	TH 1424	2.9
2137	0.3	2059	0.4
4 0312	3.3	**19** 0235	3.1
1006	0.3	0921	0.4
TH 1539	3.0	F 1454	3.0
2215	0.4	2131	0.4
5 0353	3.3	**20** 0308	3.1
1042	0.5	0950	0.5
F 1620	2.9	SA 1524	2.9
2255	0.6	2200	0.5
6 0436	3.2	**21** 0338	3.0
1120	0.7	1014	0.6
SA 1703	2.9	SU 1552	2.9
◗ 2338	0.7	2228	0.6
7 0525	3.0	**22** 0412	2.9
1206	0.8	1046	0.7
SU 1755	2.8	M 1633	2.8
		◖ 2315	0.7
8 0036	0.8	**23** 0507	2.8
0629	2.9	1147	0.9
M 1311	1.0	TU 1740	2.8
1904	2.8		
9 0154	1.0	**24** 0034	0.9
0748	2.8	0631	2.7
TU 1434	1.1	W 1317	1.0
2026	2.9	1912	2.8
10 0322	1.0	**25** 0214	0.8
0913	2.8	0809	2.8
W 1556	1.0	TH 1455	0.9
2143	3.0	2046	2.9
11 0438	0.9	**26** 0348	0.7
1024	2.9	0937	2.9
TH 1700	1.0	F 1620	0.8
2243	3.1	2205	3.1
12 0535	0.8	**27** 0505	0.5
1115	3.0	1048	3.0
F 1749	0.8	SA 1727	0.6
2328	3.2	2305	3.2
13 0618	0.7	**28** 0606	0.4
1155	3.0	1143	3.0
SA 1829	0.7	SU 1823	0.5
		○ 2356	3.3
14 0006	3.2		
0656	0.6		
SU 1229	3.0		
● 1905	0.5		
15 0039	3.2		
0729	0.5		
M 1301	3.0		
1937	0.5		

MARCH

Time	m		Time	m
1 0657	0.2	**16** 0011	3.1
1229	3.1	0659	0.4
M 1911	0.3	TU 1231	3.0
		1909	0.4
2 0043	3.3	**17** 0041	3.1
0742	0.2	0728	0.3
TU 1312	3.1	W 1301	3.0
1956	0.2	1937	0.3
3 0128	3.3	**18** 0110	3.1
0825	0.2	0756	0.4
W 1353	3.1	TH 1328	3.0
2038	0.2	2007	0.3
4 0211	3.3	**19** 0140	3.1
0904	0.2	0824	0.4
TH 1433	3.1	F 1357	3.0
2116	0.2	2038	0.3
5 0251	3.3	**20** 0213	3.1
0938	0.3	0856	0.4
F 1510	3.0	SA 1429	3.0
2151	0.3	2112	0.3
6 0329	3.2	**21** 0247	3.0
1011	0.5	0927	0.4
SA 1546	3.0	SU 1500	3.0
2226	0.4	2143	0.4
7 0407	3.1	**22** 0322	3.0
1044	0.6	0955	0.5
SU 1624	2.9	M 1532	3.0
◗ 2304	0.6	2215	0.5
8 0449	2.9	**23** 0359	2.9
1123	0.8	1029	0.6
M 1711	2.8	TU 1614	2.9
2355	0.7	◖ 2302	0.6
9 0547	2.7	**24** 0453	2.7
1224	1.0	1128	0.8
TU 1817	2.8	W 1721	2.8
10 0112	0.9	**25** 0020	0.7
0707	2.6	0615	2.7
W 1349	1.0	TH 1259	0.9
1943	2.8	1852	2.9
11 0246	0.9	**26** 0200	0.7
0838	2.6	0753	2.7
TH 1521	1.0	F 1439	0.8
2110	2.9	2027	3.0
12 0411	0.8	**27** 0334	0.6
0957	2.7	0921	2.8
F 1635	0.8	SA 1604	0.7
2216	3.0	2146	3.1
13 0511	0.6	**28** 0447	0.4
1051	2.8	1028	2.9
SA 1726	0.7	SU 1708	0.5
2302	3.1	2245	3.2
14 0553	0.5	**29** 0544	0.2
1128	2.9	1120	3.0
SU 1804	0.6	M 1802	0.4
2338	3.1	2335	3.3
15 0627	0.4	**30** 0632	0.2
1200	3.0	1205	3.0
M 1838	0.4	TU 1850	0.3
●		○	
		31 0022	3.3
		0716	0.2
		W 1246	3.1
		1934	0.2

APRIL

Time	m		Time	m
1 0106	3.3	**16** 0042	3.1
0757	0.2	0726	0.4
TH 1325	3.1	F 1300	3.1
2014	0.2	1944	0.3
2 0147	3.2	**17** 0116	3.1
0835	0.3	0759	0.4
F 1404	3.1	SA 1332	3.1
2052	0.2	2020	0.3
3 0227	3.2	**18** 0153	3.0
0910	0.4	0834	0.4
SA 1441	3.1	SU 1408	3.1
2127	0.2	2057	0.3
4 0304	3.0	**19** 0233	3.0
0942	0.4	0910	0.4
SU 1516	3.0	M 1445	3.0
2202	0.3	2135	0.4
5 0341	2.9	**20** 0314	2.9
1013	0.6	0946	0.5
M 1553	2.9	TU 1525	3.0
2238	0.5	2216	0.4
6 0422	2.7	**21** 0359	2.8
1050	0.8	1029	0.6
TU 1637	2.9	W 1613	3.0
◗ 2325	0.6	◖ 2308	0.5
7 0514	2.6	**22** 0456	2.7
1144	0.9	1129	0.7
W 1737	2.8	TH 1718	3.0
8 0033	0.8	**23** 0021	0.6
0626	2.5	0611	2.7
TH 1302	1.0	F 1252	0.8
1857	2.8	1841	3.0
9 0200	0.8	**24** 0150	0.6
0752	2.5	0738	2.7
F 1433	0.9	SA 1423	0.7
2022	2.8	2007	3.0
10 0327	0.7	**25** 0314	0.5
0912	2.6	0858	2.8
SA 1552	0.7	SU 1541	0.6
2133	2.9	2121	3.1
11 0430	0.5	**26** 0420	0.4
1010	2.7	1000	2.9
SU 1646	0.6	M 1641	0.5
2221	3.0	2218	3.2
12 0512	0.4	**27** 0512	0.3
1049	2.8	1050	3.0
M 1725	0.5	TU 1735	0.4
2258	3.0	2310	3.2
13 0547	0.4	**28** 0602	0.3
1123	2.9	1137	3.1
TU 1801	0.4	W 1826	0.3
2334	3.1	○ 2359	3.2
14 0622	0.3	**29** 0648	0.3
1157	3.0	1221	3.1
W 1835	0.4	TH 1911	0.3
●			
15 0009	3.1	**30** 0043	3.2
0654	0.3	0729	0.3
TH 1229	3.0	F 1300	3.1
1909	0.3	1951	0.3

Chart Datum: 1·68 metres below Normal Null (German reference level). HAT is 3·0 metres above Chart Datum; see 4.5

WGS84 DATUM

TIME ZONE –0100
Subtract 1 hour for UT
For German Summer Time add ONE hour in **non-shaded areas**

HELGOLAND   LAT 54°11′N LONG 7°53′E
TIMES AND HEIGHTS OF HIGH AND LOW WATERS

Dates in red are SPRINGS
Dates in blue are NEAPS

YEAR **2010**

MAY

Day	Time m	Time m	Time m	Time m	Day	Time m	Time m	Time m	Time m
1 SA	0124 3.1	0807 0.4	1338 3.1	2029 0.3	16 SU	0056 3.1	0738 0.4	1313 3.1	2007 0.3
2 SU	0202 3.0	0843 0.4	1415 3.1	2106 0.3	17 M	0141 3.0	0820 0.4	1355 3.1	2051 0.3
3 M	0242 2.9	0916 0.4	1453 3.0	2143 0.3	18 TU	0226 3.0	0901 0.4	1438 3.1	2134 0.3
4 TU	0321 2.8	0949 0.5	1531 3.0	2220 0.5	19 W	0311 2.9	0944 0.5	1523 3.1	2222 0.4
5 W	0401 2.7	1026 0.7	1612 3.0	2302 0.6	20 TH	0401 2.8	1033 0.6	1615 3.1	2316 0.4
6 TH	0446 2.6	1112 0.8	1702 2.9	2356 0.7	21 F	0458 2.8	1132 0.6	1717 3.1	
7 F	0544 2.6	1215 0.8	1807 2.8		22 SA	0020 0.5	0605 2.7	1243 0.7	1828 3.1
8 SA	0107 0.7	0655 2.5	1333 0.8	1922 2.8	23 SU	0133 0.5	0718 2.8	1400 0.7	1944 3.1
9 SU	0224 0.6	0809 2.6	1450 0.7	2032 2.8	24 M	0245 0.5	0829 2.9	1511 0.6	2052 3.1
10 M	0330 0.5	0912 2.7	1551 0.6	2128 2.9	25 TU	0347 0.5	0928 3.0	1611 0.5	2151 3.1
11 TU	0418 0.4	1000 2.8	1637 0.5	2212 3.0	26 W	0440 0.4	1020 3.0	1707 0.5	2245 3.1
12 W	0459 0.4	1041 2.9	1720 0.5	2254 3.1	27 TH	0532 0.5	1111 3.1	1802 0.4	2337 3.1
13 TH	0540 0.4	1120 3.0	1802 0.5	2336 3.1	28 F	0622 0.5	1159 3.2	1851 0.4	
14 F	0620 0.4	1157 3.1	1842 0.4		29 SA	0024 3.1	0705 0.4	1240 3.2	1932 0.4
15 SA	0015 3.1	0658 0.4	1234 3.1	1923 0.4	30 SU	0104 3.0	0744 0.5	1318 3.2	2011 0.3
					31 M	0143 3.0	0821 0.5	1356 3.2	2050 0.3

JUNE

Day	Time m	Time m	Time m	Time m	Day	Time m	Time m	Time m	Time m
1 TU	0222 2.9	0856 0.5	1434 3.1	2127 0.4	16 W	0221 3.0	0857 0.4	1432 3.2	2133 0.3
2 W	0301 2.8	0929 0.5	1511 3.1	2203 0.4	17 TH	0307 2.9	0941 0.4	1518 3.2	2220 0.3
3 TH	0339 2.8	1004 0.6	1548 3.1	2239 0.6	18 F	0356 2.9	1031 0.5	1609 3.2	2312 0.4
4 F	0418 2.7	1043 0.7	1629 3.0	2320 0.6	19 SA	0450 2.8	1126 0.5	1706 3.2	
5 SA	0501 2.6	1131 0.7	1717 2.9		20 SU	0006 0.4	0548 2.8	1225 0.5	1808 3.1
6 SU	0011 0.6	0555 2.6	1231 0.8	1817 2.8	21 M	0104 0.5	0649 2.8	1329 0.6	1915 3.1
7 M	0113 0.6	0658 2.6	1339 0.7	1923 2.8	22 TU	0208 0.6	0754 2.9	1438 0.7	2022 3.1
8 TU	0218 0.6	0804 2.7	1446 0.7	2027 2.9	23 W	0313 0.7	0857 3.0	1544 0.7	2126 3.1
9 W	0317 0.5	0904 2.8	1545 0.6	2123 2.9	24 TH	0414 0.7	0955 3.1	1645 0.6	2226 3.1
10 TH	0410 0.5	0956 2.9	1639 0.6	2215 3.0	25 F	0510 0.7	1050 3.1	1743 0.6	2320 3.1
11 F	0501 0.5	1044 3.0	1731 0.6	2306 3.1	26 SA	0601 0.6	1141 3.2	1834 0.5	
12 SA	0551 0.5	1129 3.1	1820 0.5	2355 3.1	27 SU	0008 3.0	0646 0.6	1225 3.2	1917 0.5
13 SU	0637 0.5	1214 3.2	1909 0.4		28 M	0049 3.0	0726 0.5	1303 3.2	1956 0.4
14 M	0043 3.1	0725 0.5	1300 3.2	1959 0.4	29 TU	0128 3.0	0804 0.5	1340 3.2	2034 0.4
15 TU	0132 3.1	0812 0.5	1347 3.3	2047 0.3	30 W	0204 2.9	0839 0.5	1415 3.2	2108 0.4

JULY

Day	Time m	Time m	Time m	Time m	Day	Time m	Time m	Time m	Time m
1 TH	0239 2.9	0909 0.5	1448 3.2	2140 0.5	16 F	0255 3.0	0933 0.3	1506 3.3	2207 0.2
2 F	0312 2.8	0940 0.5	1520 3.1	2212 0.6	17 SA	0340 2.9	1018 0.4	1553 3.2	2252 0.4
3 SA	0346 2.8	1015 0.6	1555 3.1	2245 0.6	18 SU	0428 2.9	1106 0.5	1645 3.2	2338 0.5
4 SU	0421 2.8	1051 0.7	1633 3.0	2320 0.6	19 M	0519 2.9	1156 0.6	1740 3.1	
5 M	0501 2.7	1135 0.7	1718 2.9		20 TU	0027 0.6	0613 2.9	1253 0.7	1842 3.0
6 TU	0006 0.6	0552 2.7	1231 0.8	1817 2.8	21 W	0128 0.7	0717 2.9	1403 0.8	1952 3.0
7 W	0106 0.7	0656 2.7	1341 0.8	1926 2.8	22 TH	0241 0.9	0828 3.0	1520 0.8	2106 3.0
8 TH	0216 0.7	0807 2.8	1454 0.7	2037 2.9	23 F	0353 0.9	0936 3.1	1631 0.7	2213 3.0
9 F	0324 0.6	0914 2.9	1602 0.7	2143 2.9	24 SA	0454 0.8	1035 3.2	1729 0.7	2309 3.0
10 SA	0429 0.6	1015 3.0	1706 0.6	2245 3.0	25 SU	0545 0.8	1126 3.2	1819 0.6	2354 3.0
11 SU	0529 0.6	1109 3.1	1804 0.5	2341 3.1	26 M	0630 0.7	1209 3.3	1901 0.5	
12 M	0624 0.6	1159 3.3	1858 0.4		27 TU	0034 3.0	0711 0.6	1247 3.2	1939 0.5
13 TU	0033 3.1	0715 0.5	1249 3.3	1951 0.3	28 W	0110 3.0	0747 0.5	1321 3.2	2014 0.5
14 W	0123 3.1	0804 0.4	1337 3.3	2040 0.3	29 TH	0142 3.0	0819 0.5	1351 3.2	2044 0.5
15 TH	0211 3.0	0850 0.3	1422 3.3	2124 0.2	30 F	0211 2.9	0845 0.4	1420 3.2	2111 0.5
					31 SA	0240 2.9	0913 0.5	1450 3.1	2140 0.6

AUGUST

Day	Time m	Time m	Time m	Time m	Day	Time m	Time m	Time m	Time m
1 SU	0312 2.9	0945 0.5	1523 3.1	2210 0.6	16 M	0358 3.0	1039 0.5	1618 3.2	2303 0.6
2 M	0344 2.9	1018 0.5	1556 3.0	2238 0.6	17 TU	0443 2.9	1123 0.6	1708 3.0	2348 0.8
3 TU	0417 2.8	1050 0.7	1632 2.9	2311 0.7	18 W	0534 2.9	1216 0.7	1807 2.9	
4 W	0457 2.8	1135 0.8	1722 2.8		19 TH	0047 0.9	0637 2.8	1328 0.9	1922 2.8
5 TH	0005 0.8	0556 2.7	1244 0.8	1835 2.8	20 F	0206 1.0	0757 2.9	1446 0.9	2046 2.8
6 F	0122 0.8	0716 2.7	1410 0.8	2000 2.8	21 SA	0331 1.0	0917 3.0	1617 0.8	2202 2.9
7 SA	0248 0.8	0839 2.8	1534 0.7	2121 2.9	22 SU	0441 0.9	1022 3.1	1717 0.7	2258 2.9
8 SU	0406 0.7	0953 3.0	1648 0.6	2231 3.0	23 M	0531 0.8	1110 3.2	1802 0.6	2338 3.0
9 M	0514 0.7	1054 3.2	1751 0.5	2330 3.1	24 TU	0612 0.7	1148 3.2	1839 0.6	
10 TU	0611 0.6	1146 3.3	1846 0.4		25 W	0013 3.0	0650 0.5	1223 3.2	1914 0.5
11 W	0020 3.1	0702 0.5	1234 3.4	1936 0.3	26 TH	0046 3.0	0723 0.5	1255 3.2	1945 0.4
12 TH	0107 3.1	0750 0.4	1321 3.4	2023 0.2	27 F	0115 3.0	0752 0.4	1324 3.2	2013 0.5
13 F	0152 3.1	0835 0.3	1405 3.3	2105 0.2	28 SA	0142 3.0	0818 0.4	1352 3.2	2038 0.5
14 SA	0235 3.0	0916 0.3	1448 3.3	2144 0.3	29 SU	0208 3.0	0845 0.4	1421 3.1	2107 0.5
15 SU	0316 3.0	0957 0.4	1532 3.2	2223 0.4	30 M	0238 3.0	0917 0.5	1454 3.0	2137 0.6
					31 TU	0310 3.0	0949 0.6	1527 3.0	2203 0.7

Chart Datum: 1·68 metres below Normal Null (German reference level). HAT is 3·0 metres above Chart Datum; see 4.5

TIME ZONE -0100
Subtract 1 hour for UT
For German Summer Time add
ONE hour in **non-shaded areas**

HELGOLAND   LAT 54°11'N LONG 7°53'E
TIMES AND HEIGHTS OF HIGH AND LOW WATERS

Dates in red are **SPRINGS**
Dates in blue are **NEAPS**

YEAR 2010

SEPTEMBER

Time	m		Time	m
1 0341	2.9	**16**	0456	2.9
1018	0.7		1142	0.8
W 1600	2.9	TH 1732	2.7
☽ 2232	0.7			
2 0417	2.8	**17**	0006	1.0
1057	0.8		0559	2.8
TH 1647	2.8	F 1252	0.9
2322	0.9		1848	2.6
3 0515	2.8	**18**	0127	1.1
1205	0.9		0721	2.8
F 1801	2.7	SA 1423	1.0
			2018	2.7
4 0044	1.0	**19**	0259	1.1
0640	2.8		0849	3.0
SA 1339	0.9	SU 1552	0.9
1935	2.7		2140	2.8
5 0221	0.9	**20**	0417	1.0
0813	2.9		1000	3.1
SU 1514	0.8	M 1656	0.7
2105	2.8		2236	2.9
6 0348	0.8	**21**	0509	0.8
0934	3.0		1046	3.1
M 1633	0.6	TU 1735	0.6
2217	2.9		2312	2.9
7 0458	0.7	**22**	0545	0.7
1037	3.2		1119	3.2
TU 1735	0.4	W 1807	0.5
2313	3.0		2342	3.0
8 0554	0.5	**23**	0619	0.6
1128	3.3		1153	3.1
W 1827	0.3	TH 1840	0.5
●		○		
9 0000	3.1	**24**	0014	3.0
0643	0.4		0651	0.5
TH 1215	3.3	F 1225	3.1
1913	0.2		1911	0.5
10 0044	3.1	**25**	0045	3.0
0729	0.3		0722	0.5
F 1300	3.3	SA 1255	3.1
1957	0.3		1939	0.5
11 0126	3.1	**26**	0113	3.0
0813	0.3		0751	0.5
SA 1345	3.3	SU 1325	3.1
2039	0.3		2007	0.5
12 0208	3.1	**27**	0140	3.0
0854	0.3		0821	0.5
SU 1427	3.3	M 1356	3.1
2116	0.4		2037	0.5
13 0248	3.1	**28**	0209	3.0
0933	0.4		0853	0.5
M 1508	3.2	TU 1429	3.0
2152	0.5		2108	0.6
14 0327	3.0	**29**	0242	3.0
1011	0.5		0926	0.5
TU 1550	3.1	W 1505	3.0
2228	0.7		2137	0.7
15 0408	3.0	**30**	0315	3.0
1052	0.6		0958	0.7
W 1636	2.9	TH 1542	2.9
☾ 2310	0.9		2209	0.8

OCTOBER

Time	m		Time	m
1 0355	2.9	**16**	0523	2.9
1039	0.8		1216	0.9
F 1631	2.8	SA 1811	2.6
☽ 2301	1.0			
2 0454	2.9	**17**	0042	1.1
1147	0.9		0639	2.8
SA 1744	2.7	SU 1339	1.0
			1934	2.6
3 0022	1.1	**18**	0211	1.1
0618	2.9		0804	2.9
SU 1320	0.9	M 1506	0.9
1917	2.7		2055	2.7
4 0200	1.0	**19**	0333	1.0
0751	0.8		0917	3.0
M 1456	0.8	TU 1613	0.8
2047	2.8		2155	2.8
5 0328	0.9	**20**	0430	0.8
0913	3.1		1040	3.1
TU 1613	0.6	W 1655	0.6
2157	2.9		2234	2.9
6 0435	0.7	**21**	0507	0.7
1015	3.2		1042	3.1
W 1711	0.4	TH 1726	0.6
2249	3.0		2306	3.0
7 0529	0.5	**22**	0541	0.6
1105	3.3		1117	3.1
TH 1800	0.4	F 1800	0.5
● 2335	3.1		2339	3.0
8 0619	0.4	**23**	0617	0.6
1153	3.3		1153	3.1
F 1846	0.3	SA 1834	0.5
		○		
9 0018	3.1	**24**	0013	3.1
0705	0.4		0651	0.6
SA 1239	3.3	SU 1227	3.1
1929	0.4		1907	0.5
10 0100	3.2	**25**	0045	3.1
0749	0.4		0726	0.5
SU 1323	3.3	M 1300	3.1
2010	0.5		1939	0.6
11 0141	3.2	**26**	0116	3.1
0830	0.4		0801	0.5
M 1405	3.2	TU 1336	3.0
2049	0.5		2013	0.6
12 0221	3.1	**27**	0148	3.1
0910	0.4		0837	0.5
TU 1445	3.1	W 1413	3.0
2124	0.6		2047	0.6
13 0300	3.1	**28**	0223	3.1
0947	0.5		0912	0.6
W 1525	2.9	TH 1452	2.9
2158	0.7		2122	0.7
14 0339	3.0	**29**	0301	3.1
1026	0.6		0950	0.7
TH 1609	2.8	F 1535	2.9
☾ 2237	0.9		2201	0.8
15 0425	2.9	**30**	0346	3.1
1113	0.8		1037	0.8
F 1702	2.6	SA 1626	2.8
2329	1.0	☽ 2254	1.0
		31	0445	3.0
			1142	0.8
		SU 1734	2.7

NOVEMBER

Time	m		Time	m
1 0009	1.0	**16**	0109	1.1
0602	3.0		0701	2.9
M 1305	0.8	TU 1359	0.9
1858	2.8		1948	2.6
2 0138	1.0	**17**	0227	1.0
0728	3.1		0814	2.9
TU 1431	0.8	W 1508	0.8
2021	2.9		2054	2.7
3 0301	0.9	**18**	0332	0.9
0845	3.1		0913	3.0
W 1543	0.6	TH 1559	0.7
2129	3.0		2145	2.9
4 0406	0.7	**19**	0421	0.8
0948	3.2		0959	3.0
TH 1639	0.5	F 1640	0.7
2221	3.0		2226	3.0
5 0501	0.6	**20**	0502	0.7
1041	3.2		1040	3.1
F 1730	0.5	SA 1720	0.7
2308	3.1		2305	3.1
6 0554	0.5	**21**	0544	0.7
1131	3.3		1121	3.1
SA 1819	0.5	SU 1800	0.7
● 2354	3.2	○ 2343	3.1
7 0643	0.5	**22**	0624	0.7
1219	3.2		1201	3.1
SU 1904	0.5	M 1839	0.6
8 0037	3.2	**23**	0020	3.2
0727	0.5		0705	0.6
M 1302	3.2	TU 1241	3.1
1944	0.6		1918	0.7
9 0117	3.2	**24**	0058	3.2
0808	0.5		0747	0.6
TU 1344	3.1	W 1323	3.1
2023	0.6		1958	0.7
10 0158	3.2	**25**	0136	3.2
0849	0.5		0829	0.6
W 1425	3.0	TH 1405	3.0
2100	0.6		2037	0.6
11 0238	3.1	**26**	0215	3.2
0928	0.5		0908	0.6
TH 1505	2.9	F 1446	3.0
2134	0.7		2115	0.7
12 0318	3.1	**27**	0255	3.2
1006	0.6		0950	0.6
F 1547	2.8	SA 1531	2.9
2211	0.8		2159	0.8
13 0359	3.1	**28**	0341	3.2
1048	0.8		1039	0.7
SA 1632	2.7	SU 1622	2.9
☾ 2256	1.1	☽ 2252	0.9
14 0448	3.0	**29**	0437	3.2
1139	0.9		1136	0.7
SU 1728	2.6	M 1723	2.8
2355	1.1		2356	0.9
15 0549	2.9	**30**	0545	3.1
1244	1.0		1243	0.8
M 1835	2.6	TU 1834	2.8

DECEMBER

Time	m		Time	m
1 0111	1.0	**16**	0110	1.0
0700	3.1		0659	2.9
W 1357	0.8	TH 1349	0.9
1948	2.9		1940	2.7
2 0227	0.9	**17**	0222	1.0
0814	3.2		0807	2.9
TH 1507	0.7	F 1453	0.9
2055	3.0		2045	2.8
3 0335	0.8	**18**	0326	0.9
0920	3.2		0909	2.9
F 1608	0.7	SA 1550	0.8
2153	3.1		2142	3.0
4 0435	0.7	**19**	0422	0.8
1018	3.2		1003	3.0
SA 1704	0.7	SU 1642	0.8
2246	3.1		2231	3.1
5 0533	0.7	**20**	0513	0.8
1113	3.2		1053	3.1
SU 1756	0.7	M 1732	0.8
● 2336	3.2		2316	3.2
6 0625	0.6	**21**	0602	0.7
1203	3.2		1141	3.1
M 1843	0.7	TU 1818	0.7
		○		
7 0020	3.2	**22**	0000	3.2
0710	0.6		0649	0.6
TU 1246	3.1	W 1227	3.1
1924	0.7		1904	0.7
8 0100	3.3	**23**	0044	3.3
0751	0.5		0737	0.6
W 1327	3.1	TH 1313	3.1
2003	0.7		1949	0.7
9 0141	3.3	**24**	0128	3.3
0832	0.6		0824	0.5
TH 1408	3.0	F 1359	3.1
2041	0.7		2031	0.6
10 0221	3.2	**25**	0210	3.3
0912	0.6		0906	0.5
F 1448	2.9	SA 1441	3.0
2115	0.7		2111	0.6
11 0258	3.2	**26**	0249	3.3
0948	0.6		0948	0.5
SA 1524	2.9	SU 1524	2.9
2148	0.7		2155	0.6
12 0335	3.2	**27**	0333	3.2
1023	0.8		1033	0.6
SU 1601	2.8	M 1612	2.9
2225	0.9		2244	0.7
13 0413	3.1	**28**	0425	3.3
1100	0.9		1122	0.6
M 1642	2.7	TU 1705	2.9
☾ 2308	1.0	☽ 2338	0.8
14 0458	3.0	**29**	0523	3.2
1145	0.9		1215	0.7
TU 1732	2.7	W 1804	2.9
15 0003	1.0	**30**	0039	0.9
0553	2.9		0628	3.1
W 1242	0.9	TH 1318	0.8
1832	2.7		1910	2.9
		31	0150	0.9
			0740	3.1
		F 1429	0.9
			2021	3.0

Chart Datum: 1·68 metres below Normal Null (German reference level). HAT is 3·0 metres above Chart Datum; see 4.5

9.15.10   RIVER ELBE
Niedersachsen/Schleswig-Holstein

CHARTS AC 3619, 3625, 3267, 3268; D 44, 46, 47, 48; BSH 3010.1-13

TIDES

Standard Port CUXHAVEN (→)

Times				Height (metres)			
High Water		Low Water		MHWS	MHWN	MLWN	MLWS
0200	0800	0200	0900	3·8	3·4	0·9	0·5
1400	2000	1400	2100				
Differences SCHARHÖRN (11M NW of Cuxhaven)							
−0045	−0047	−0101	−0103	0·0	0·0	0·0	−0·1
GROßER VOGELSAND							
−0044	−0046	−0101	−0103	0·0	0·0	+0·1	−0·1
OTTERNDORF							
+0029	+0029	+0027	+0027	−0·1	−0·1	−0·1	0·0
GLÜCKSTADT							
+0205	+0214	+0220	+0213	−0·2	−0·1	−0·1	0·0
STADERSAND							
+0241	+0245	+0300	+0254	−0·1	0·0	−0·2	0·0
SCHULAU							
+0304	+0315	+0337	+0321	+0·1	+0·2	−0·3	−0·1
SEEMANNSHÖFT (53°32'·5N 09°52'·7E)							
+0324	+0332	+0403	+0347	+0·3	+0·3	−0·4	−0·2
HAMBURG							
+0338	+0346	+0422	+0406	+0·4	+0·4	−0·4	−0·3

NAVIGATION Distances: Elbe SWM buoy to Cuxhaven = 24M; Cuxhaven to Wedel Yacht Haven = 45M; Wedel to City Sport Hafen = 11·5M. The river is 13m deep up to Hamburg and tidal to Geesthacht, 24M above Hamburg.

> Strong W winds can raise the level by as much as 4m. Do not try to enter in strong W/NW winds against the ebb. It is a very busy waterway and at night the many lights can be confusing. Yachts should keep to stbd, just outside the marked chan.

SHELTER AND FACILITIES Better hbrs are listed below, with BSH 3010 sheet Nos. It is not a particularly salubrious yachting area:

FREIBURG: 7M above Brunsbüttel on the SW bank. Enter at HW, but mainly commercial at Freiburg Reede; little space for small craft. ML 2·2m. HM ☎ (04779) 8314. Facilities: ME, EI, ✕, C, FW, Slip; Jugendheim & YC Klubheim 🛒, R, Bar. (Sheet 6).

STÖRLOCH/BORSFLETH: Ent approx 600m above locks on E bank. ML 2·8m. HM ☎ (04124) 71437. Facilities: FW, YC. Stör Bridge VHF Ch 09, 16. (Sheet 6).

STÖR/BEIDENFLETH: ML 2·8m. **Langes Rack YC.** (Sheet 6)

GLÜCKSTADT: E bank, mouth of R Rhin (see inset). Good shelter: 1 marina in outer hbr, 5.8m at MHW. Or via entry gate, opens HW –2 to +½, into inner hbr for 3 marinas in 3-5m. VHF Ch 11. HM ☎ (04124) 2087; ⊖ ☎ 2171. YC, FW, C, D, 🛒, R, ⬚, Bar. (Sheet 6).

WISCHHAFEN: HM ☎ (04770) 334; ⊖ 3014 FW, M, Slip, P, D, ML 2·7m. (Sheet 6).

RUTHENSTROM: 197° ldg bns with △ topmarks into hbr. ML 2·6m. HM ☎ (04143) 5282; C, Slip, FW, ME, EI, ✕. (Sheet 7).

KRÜCKAUMÜNDUNG JACHTHAFEN: Entrance via lock gate; ☎ (04125) 1521 Slip, FW. ML 2·7m. ⊖ ☎ 20551. (Sheet 7).

PINNAUMÜNDUNG JACHTHAFEN: Ent via lock gate on N bank after passing through main locks. ML 2·5m. HM ☎ (04101) 22447 Slip, M, FW, YC, C. (Sheets 7/8).

PINNAU-NEUENDEICH: Marina 1½M up the Pinnau from main locks and another at approx 2M. (Sheets 7/8).

ABBENFLETH: Ent marked by two bns in line 221° with △ topmarks. (Sheets 7/8).

HASELDORF Hafen: HM ☎ (04129) 268 Slip, FW, 🛒, YC. (8/9)

R SCHWINGE on SW bank, 12M up-river from Glückstadt: BRUNSHAUSEN (04141) 3085. ML 1·1; Duration 0510. (Sheets 8/9)

HÖRNE/WÖHRDEN ML 2·8m

STADE (04141) 101275 C, YC, 🛒; Access HW ±4. Very good shelter in scenic town. ⊖ ☎ 3014. (Sheets 8/9).

LÜHE: Hafen in town of Lühe (Sheet 8).

RIVER ELBE, VESSEL TRAFFIC SERVICE

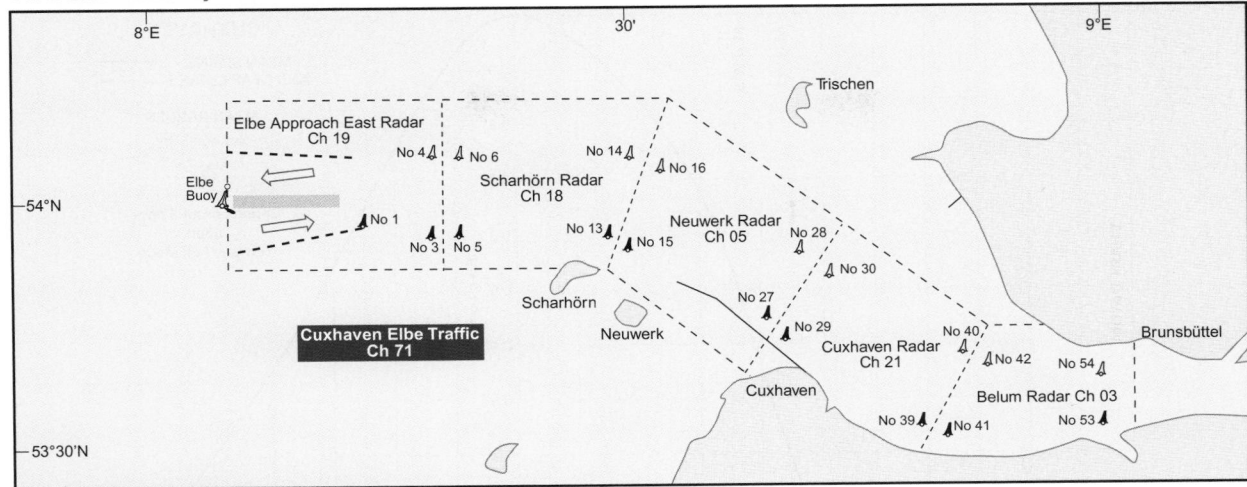

Fig 9.15.10A. Elbe SWM buoy to Brunsbüttel

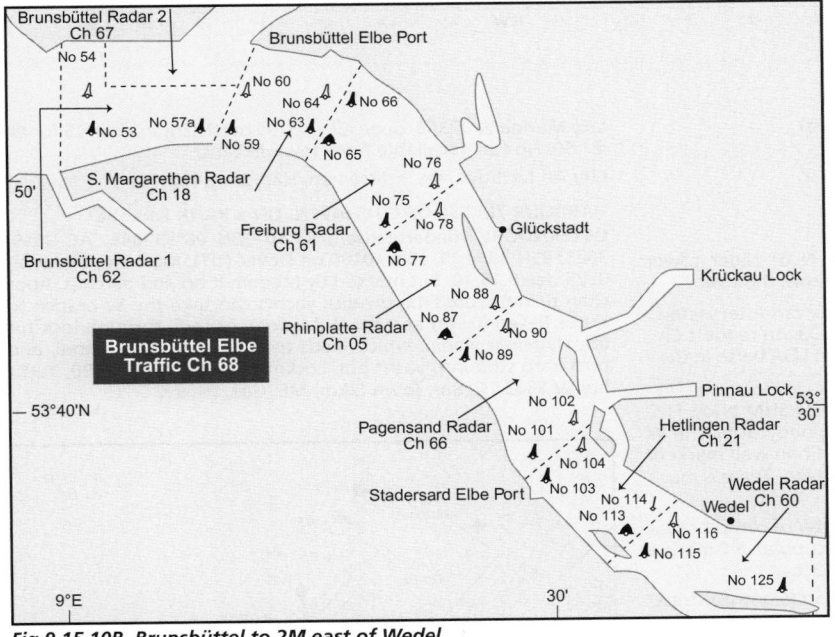

Fig 9.15.10B. Brunsbüttel to 2M east of Wedel

Elbe VTS is not mandatory for yachts, but it is sensible to monitor the 3 Traffic Centres (callsigns and channels below) on your way up-river.

Cuxhaven Elbe Traffic (9.15.11)	Ch 71
Brunsbüttel Elbe Traffic (9.15.12)	Ch 68
Hamburg Port Traffic (9.15.14)	Ch 14/74

Broadcasts of navigational, weather and traffic info are detailed at the references in brackets above.

If radar guidance is required in English, request it from the relevant Traffic Centre.

The radar stations, their areas of coverage and VHF channels are stated for sectors:

Elbe Lt Float-buoy 53	See 9.15.11
Buoys 51-125	See 9.15.12
Then continue with *Hamburg Radar:*	
Buoys 125-129	Ch 19
Buoys 129-Seemanshöft (09°53'E)	Ch 03
Seemanshöft-Vorhafen (09°57'E)	Ch 63
09°57'E-Norderelbe bridges	Ch 05

Fig 9.15.10C. 2M east of Wedel to Hamburg City centre

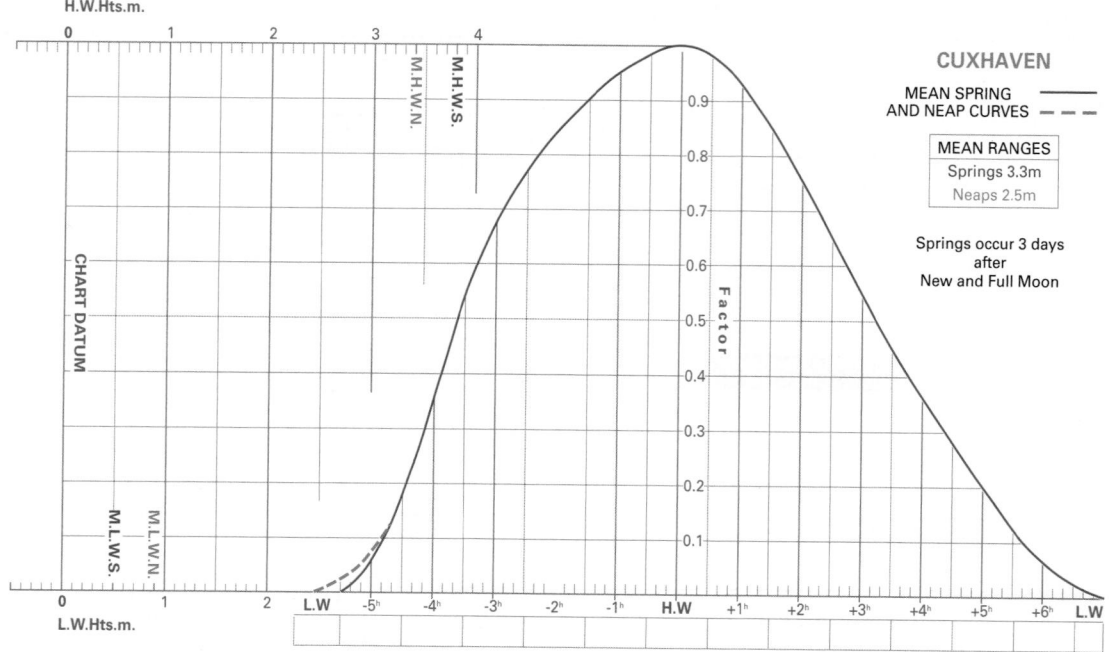

CUXHAVEN

MEAN SPRING — AND NEAP CURVES - - -

MEAN RANGES
Springs 3.3m
Neaps 2.5m

Springs occur 3 days after
New and Full Moon

9.15.11 CUXHAVEN

Niedersachsen 53°52'·43N 08°42'·49E (Marina ent)
❀❀❀❀♤♤♤♧♧♧

CHARTS AC 3619; Imray C26; D44, BSH 3010.1/2

TIDES +0103 Dover; ML 1·7; Duration 0535

CUXHAVEN is a Standard Port (⟶)

SHELTER Good in both marinas: YC marina N of radar tower (2·5–3·5m) is open H24 Apr-Oct, direct access from the river.

City Marina, close S of radio mast, is entered from Alter Hafen via bridge which opens (0600-2100) H and H+30, on request Ch 69, not at night nor in winds > F7. Yachts > 20m LOA berth in the Alter Hafen or Alter Fischereihafen.

NAVIGATION WPT 53°53'·92N 08°41'·20E [No 31 SHM buoy, Fl G 4s], 152°/1·7M to marina ent. From No 27 SHM buoy, appr is in W sector (149°-154°) of Baumrönne ldg lt Iso 4s. Chan well marked/ lit, see 9.15.4. *The ebb runs up to 5kn off Cuxhaven. There is much commercial shipping.*

LIGHTS AND MARKS Ent to YC Marina is close NW of conspic radar tr, and N of disused lt ho (dark R with copper cupola). YC marina ent, N side FWG; S side FWR, shown 1 Apr-31 Oct.

R/T Cuxhaven Port/lock Ch 69. *Cuxhaven Elbe Port* (Sig stn/Distress) Ch **12** 16 (H24). *German Bight Traffic* (VTS) Ch 80; see Fig 9.15.16A. Radar advice for the outer Elbe is provided, in English on request, as follows:

Elbe East Radar	Ch 19	Elbe lt buoy – buoy 5.
Scharhörn Radar	Ch 18	Buoys 3–15.
Neuwerk Radar	Ch 05	Buoys 13–29.
Cuxhaven Radar	Ch 21	Buoys 27–41.
Belum Radar	Ch 03	Buoys 39–53.

Cuxhaven Elbe Traffic (VTS) ☎ 567380, broadcasts nav/tfc/weather info for sector Cuxhaven-Brunsbüttel on Ch 71 in German & English every H + 35. CG & LB: Ch 16. Yachts should monitor Ch **71**.

TELEPHONE (Code 04721) LB 34622; Weather 681757; Port Authority 500150; ⊖ 21085; British Cruising Ass'n and Little Ship Club 57270, or ☎ 51339; Waterway Police 745930; CG 38011/12; Police 110; Dr & Fire 112; Brit Consul (040) 4480320.

FACILITIES **YC Marina (Segler-Vereinigung)** ☎ 34111 (Apr-Oct), €1.50, Slip, P & D in cans from town, C (10 ton), AC (16A/220V / 32A/380V €0.50/kilowatt), BY, ME, El, ✖, CH, SM, Gaz, chart agent, Ⓔ, R ☎ 663650, Bar, ▣, ⊖, Wi-Fi, bikes available foc.

City Marina ☎ 37363, open all year, 90 berths inc approx 45 for Ⓥ, €1.50. No fuel (available from town in cans).

City All facilities, ⇌, ✈ (Bremen, Hamburg, Hanover).

HARBOUR 7M ESE OF CUXHAVEN, ON S BANK OF ELBE
OTTERNDORF, Niedersachsen, **53°50'·10N 08°53'·84E**. AC 3619, 3625; BSH 3014.11. HW +0100 on Dover (UT); ML 2·9m; Duration 0525; see 9.15.10. Ent marked by Medem lt bn and perches. Appr chan (0·8m) from Elbe divides: yachts can take the W branch to Kutterhafen (0·9m) and the R. Medem; or to E, through lock for the Hadelner Kanal, which leads to the Geeste-Elbe Kanal, and turn hard stbd into yacht hbr. Lockmaster ☎ (04751) 2190; Yacht hbr ☎ 13131 C, Bar. **Town** (3km) ME, Gaz, 🛒, ✉.

TIME ZONE -0100
Subtract 1 hour for UT
For German Summer Time add
ONE hour in **non-shaded areas**

CUXHAVEN   LAT 53°52'N   LONG 8°43'E
TIMES AND HEIGHTS OF HIGH AND LOW WATERS

Dates in red are SPRINGS
Dates in blue are NEAPS

YEAR **2010**

JANUARY

Time	m		Time	m
1 0045	3.9	**16**	0133	3.9
0747	0.6		0836	0.6
F 1316	3.8	SA 1401	3.7
2007	0.7		2046	0.7
2 0135	4.0	**17**	0208	3.9
0842	0.6		0911	0.6
SA 1409	3.8	SU 1436	3.6
2059	0.6		2120	0.6
3 0225	4.1	**18**	0241	3.9
0938	0.5		0944	0.6
SU 1502	3.7	M 1508	3.6
2150	0.6		2150	0.6
4 0313	4.1	**19**	0313	3.9
1028	0.4		1012	0.5
M 1550	3.7	TU 1536	3.5
2234	0.5		2215	0.5
5 0357	4.0	**20**	0343	3.8
1111	0.4		1039	0.5
TU 1635	3.5	W 1606	3.5
2315	0.5		2242	0.6
6 0442	4.0	**21**	0414	3.8
1152	0.4		1108	0.6
W 1719	3.5	TH 1637	3.5
2357	0.5		2313	0.7
7 0529	3.9	**22**	0446	3.7
1234	0.5		1137	0.7
TH 1806	3.4	F 1708	3.4
☽			2343	0.7
8 0043	0.7	**23**	0518	3.6
0620	3.8		1204	0.7
F 1320	0.7	SA 1741	3.4
1858	3.4	◖	
9 0134	0.8	**24**	0016	0.8
0717	3.7		0557	3.5
SA 1413	0.8	SU 1242	0.8
1957	3.4		1828	3.3
10 0236	0.9	**25**	0108	0.8
0824	3.6		0657	3.4
SU 1520	1.0	M 1343	0.9
2105	3.5		1936	3.3
11 0352	1.0	**26**	0224	1.0
0939	3.6		0815	3.4
M 1635	1.0	TU 1505	0.9
2215	3.6		2058	3.4
12 0509	1.0	**27**	0354	0.9
1050	3.6		0940	3.5
TU 1744	1.0	W 1633	0.9
2318	3.7		2219	3.5
13 0616	0.9	**28**	0521	0.8
1151	3.6		1100	3.6
W 1841	0.9	TH 1754	0.8
			2331	3.7
14 0010	3.8	**29**	0637	0.7
0712	0.8		1208	3.7
TH 1241	3.7	F 1903	0.7
1928	0.8		
15 0054	3.9	**30**	0031	3.9
0758	0.7		0740	0.5
F 1323	3.7	SA 1307	3.7
● 2009	0.7	○ 2000	0.6
		31	0123	4.0
			0835	0.4
		SU 1400	3.7
			2051	0.5

FEBRUARY

Time	m		Time	m
1 0211	4.1	**16**	0219	3.9
0927	0.3		0920	0.4
M 1448	3.7	TU 1443	3.6
2139	0.4		2129	0.4
2 0258	4.1	**17**	0247	3.9
1015	0.3		0947	0.4
TU 1533	3.7	W 1510	3.6
2222	0.3		2154	0.4
3 0342	4.0	**18**	0316	3.8
1056	0.3		1013	0.4
W 1614	3.6	TH 1538	3.5
2300	0.3		2221	0.4
4 0424	4.0	**19**	0348	3.8
1132	0.3		1042	0.5
TH 1653	3.5	F 1609	3.6
2336	0.4		2252	0.5
5 0506	3.9	**20**	0421	3.7
1206	0.5		1110	0.5
F 1733	3.5	SA 1639	3.6
			2320	0.6
6 0013	0.5	**21**	0450	3.7
0549	3.8		1133	0.6
SA 1240	0.7	SU 1706	3.5
◖ 1815	3.4		2345	0.6
7 0052	0.7	**22**	0524	0.5
0636	3.6		1201	0.7
SU 1322	0.8	M 1745	3.3
1907	3.4	●	
8 0146	0.8	**23**	0026	0.7
0739	3.4		0618	3.3
M 1423	1.0	TU 1257	0.9
2015	3.4		1851	3.3
9 0302	1.0	**24**	0142	0.9
0859	3.4		0740	3.3
TU 1546	1.1	W 1426	1.0
2136	3.5		2022	3.4
10 0433	1.0	**25**	0323	0.8
1023	3.4		0916	3.4
W 1712	1.1	TH 1608	0.9
2253	3.6		2154	3.5
11 0555	0.9	**26**	0503	0.7
1133	3.5		1045	3.5
TH 1821	0.9	F 1739	0.8
2353	3.8		2313	3.7
12 0657	0.8	**27**	0625	0.5
1226	3.6		1158	3.6
F 1911	0.8	SA 1851	0.6
13 0038	3.8	**28**	0016	3.9
0742	0.7		0729	0.4
SA 1307	3.6	SU 1255	3.7
1952	0.7	○ 1948	0.5
14 0115	3.8			
0818	0.5			
SU 1342	3.6			
● 2028	0.6			
15 0148	3.8			
0850	0.5			
M 1414	3.6			
2101	0.5			

MARCH

Time	m		Time	m
1 0107	4.0	**16**	0119	3.8
0820	0.2		0820	0.3
M 1343	3.7	TU 1344	3.6
2036	0.3		2032	0.4
2 0154	4.0	**17**	0150	3.8
0906	0.2		0849	0.3
TU 1427	3.7	W 1413	3.6
2120	0.2		2102	0.3
3 0238	4.0	**18**	0219	3.8
0950	0.2		0917	0.3
W 1508	3.7	TH 1441	3.6
2201	0.2		2130	0.3
4 0321	4.0	**19**	0250	3.8
1030	0.3		0945	0.4
TH 1547	3.7	F 1510	3.6
2238	0.2		2200	0.3
5 0402	3.9	**20**	0324	3.7
1104	0.3		1015	0.4
F 1624	3.6	SA 1543	3.6
2311	0.3		2232	0.3
6 0442	3.8	**21**	0400	3.7
1134	0.5		1046	0.4
SA 1700	3.5	SU 1615	3.6
2344	0.4		2302	0.4
7 0521	3.6	**22**	0434	3.6
1203	0.6		1113	0.5
SU 1737	3.5	M 1646	3.5
☽			2331	0.5
8 0018	0.6	**23**	0511	3.5
0603	3.4		1144	0.6
M 1236	0.8	TU 1727	3.4
1823	3.4	◖	
9 0104	0.7	**24**	0013	0.6
0659	3.2		0605	3.3
TU 1331	0.9	W 1240	0.8
1929	3.3		1833	3.4
10 0217	0.9	**25**	0127	0.7
0818	3.2		0727	3.2
W 1455	1.1	TH 1409	0.9
2054	3.4		2003	3.5
11 0353	1.0	**26**	0308	0.7
0949	3.2		0903	3.3
TH 1632	1.0	F 1553	0.9
2220	3.5		2137	3.6
12 0525	0.8	**27**	0448	0.6
1106	3.3		1032	3.4
F 1752	0.9	SA 1723	0.7
2327	3.7		2254	3.7
13 0631	0.6	**28**	0606	0.4
1201	3.5		1140	3.6
SA 1846	0.7	SU 1831	0.5
			2354	3.8
14 0012	3.7	**29**	0706	0.4
0715	0.5		1233	3.6
SU 1239	3.5	M 1926	0.4
1925	0.6		
15 0047	3.8	**30**	0046	3.9
0749	0.4		0755	0.2
M 1313	3.6	TU 1319	3.7
● 2000	0.5	○ 2014	0.3
		31	0132	3.9
			0839	0.2
		W 1401	3.7
			2056	0.2

APRIL

Time	m		Time	m
1 0217	4.0	**16**	0152	3.8
0920	0.2		0845	0.4
TH 1440	3.7	F 1413	3.7
2136	0.2		2106	0.3
2 0259	3.9	**17**	0227	3.7
0958	0.3		0918	0.4
F 1518	3.7	SA 1446	3.7
2213	0.2		2141	0.3
3 0338	3.8	**18**	0305	3.7
1033	0.4		0953	0.4
SA 1554	3.6	SU 1522	3.7
2246	0.2		2216	0.3
4 0417	3.6	**19**	0346	3.6
1102	0.4		1029	0.4
SU 1630	3.6	M 1600	3.7
2319	0.3		2252	0.3
5 0456	3.5	**20**	0428	3.6
1130	0.6		1105	0.5
M 1707	3.5	TU 1640	3.7
2352	0.5		2332	0.4
6 0536	3.3	**21**	0514	3.4
1202	0.7		1145	0.6
TU 1750	3.4	W 1727	3.6
☽			
7 0034	0.6	**22**	0021	0.5
0627	3.1		0611	3.3
W 1250	0.9	TH 1242	0.7
1849	3.3		1831	3.6
8 0138	0.8	**23**	0131	0.6
0738	3.1		0726	3.2
TH 1406	1.0	F 1404	0.8
2008	3.3		1954	3.6
9 0306	0.8	**24**	0301	0.6
0904	3.1		0853	3.3
F 1540	1.0	SA 1538	0.8
2134	3.4		2119	3.7
10 0438	0.7	**25**	0429	0.5
1022	3.2		1012	3.4
SA 1705	0.8	SU 1659	0.6
2244	3.5		2231	3.8
11 0547	0.5	**26**	0539	0.4
1119	3.3		1114	3.5
SU 1803	0.6	M 1802	0.5
2332	3.6		2328	3.8
12 0632	0.4	**27**	0633	0.3
1200	3.4		1204	3.6
M 1844	0.5	TU 1856	0.4
13 0008	3.7	**28**	0020	3.9
0707	0.3		0724	0.3
TU 1235	3.5	W 1251	3.7
1922	0.4	○ 1947	0.3
14 0043	3.7	**29**	0110	3.9
0741	0.3		0811	0.3
W 1309	3.6	TH 1335	3.8
● 1958	0.4		2033	0.3
15 0118	3.7	**30**	0156	3.9
0814	0.3		0852	0.3
TH 1341	3.7	F 1415	3.8
2033	0.3		2113	0.3

Germany

Chart Datum: 1·66 metres below Normal Null (German reference level). HAT is 3·6 metres above Chart Datum; see 4.5

TIME ZONE -0100
Subtract 1 hour for UT
For German Summer Time add
ONE hour in **non-shaded areas**

CUXHAVEN   LAT 53°52'N   LONG 8°43'E
TIMES AND HEIGHTS OF HIGH AND LOW WATERS

Dates in red are **SPRINGS**
Dates in blue are NEAPS

YEAR 2010

MAY

Time	m	Time	m
1 0237 / 0929 / SA 1451 / 2149	3.8 / 0.4 / 3.8 / 0.3	**16** 0209 / 0858 / SU 1428 / 2126	3.7 / 0.5 / 3.8 / 0.3
2 0317 / 1003 / SU 1528 / 2225	3.7 / 0.4 / 3.7 / 0.3	**17** 0254 / 0940 / M 1510 / 2209	3.7 / 0.4 / 3.8 / 0.3
3 0356 / 1035 / M 1605 / 2259	3.5 / 0.4 / 3.6 / 0.3	**18** 0340 / 1022 / TU 1553 / 2252	3.6 / 0.5 / 3.8 / 0.3
4 0435 / 1106 / TU 1644 / 2335	3.4 / 0.5 / 3.6 / 0.5	**19** 0428 / 1104 / W 1639 / 2338	3.5 / 0.5 / 3.8 / 0.4
5 0515 / 1139 / W 1725	3.3 / 0.7 / 3.6	**20** 0519 / 1152 / TH 1730	3.5 / 0.6 / 3.8
6 0015 / 0601 / TH 1221 / ◑ 1816	0.6 / 3.2 / 0.8 / 3.5	**21** 0032 / 0616 / F 1248 / ◑ 1831	0.5 / 3.4 / 0.7 / 3.7
7 0106 / 0658 / F 1321 / 1920	0.7 / 3.1 / 0.9 / 3.4	**22** 0135 / 0723 / SA 1357 / 1942	0.5 / 3.3 / 0.7 / 3.7
8 0215 / 0809 / SA 1440 / 2035	0.7 / 3.1 / 0.8 / 3.4	**23** 0247 / 0835 / SU 1515 / 2057	0.5 / 3.4 / 0.7 / 3.7
9 0334 / 0922 / SU 1600 / 2144	0.6 / 3.1 / 0.7 / 3.4	**24** 0402 / 0945 / M 1629 / 2204	0.5 / 3.5 / 0.6 / 3.8
10 0444 / 1024 / M 1705 / 2239	0.5 / 3.2 / 0.6 / 3.5	**25** 0506 / 1043 / TU 1730 / 2302	0.5 / 3.6 / 0.6 / 3.8
11 0535 / 1111 / TU 1755 / 2323	0.4 / 3.4 / 0.5 / 3.6	**26** 0601 / 1135 / W 1827 / 2357	0.5 / 3.7 / 0.5 / 3.8
12 0618 / 1152 / W 1840	0.4 / 3.5 / 0.5	**27** 0654 / 1225 / TH 1922	0.5 / 3.8 / 0.5
13 0006 / 0700 / TH 1232 / 1923	3.7 / 0.4 / 3.6 / 0.5	**28** 0050 / 0745 / F 1313 / ○ 2012	3.8 / 0.4 / 3.8 / 0.4
14 0047 / 0739 / F 1310 / ● 2004	3.7 / 0.4 / 3.7 / 0.4	**29** 0138 / 0828 / SA 1354 / 2053	3.7 / 0.4 / 3.8 / 0.4
15 0128 / 0808 / SA 1348 / 2044	3.7 / 0.4 / 3.8 / 0.4	**30** 0220 / 0905 / SU 1431 / 2131	3.7 / 0.4 / 3.8 / 0.4
		31 0259 / 0940 / M 1508 / 2208	3.6 / 0.5 / 3.8 / 0.4

JUNE

Time	m	Time	m
1 0338 / 1015 / TU 1546 / 2244	3.5 / 0.5 / 3.8 / 0.4	**16** 0337 / 1019 / W 1548 / 2253	3.6 / 0.5 / 4.0 / 0.3
2 0416 / 1047 / W 1625 / 2319	3.4 / 0.5 / 3.7 / 0.5	**17** 0425 / 1103 / TH 1634 / 2340	3.5 / 0.5 / 3.9 / 0.4
3 0454 / 1120 / TH 1703 / 2356	3.3 / 0.6 / 3.7 / 0.6	**18** 0515 / 1151 / F 1725	3.5 / 0.5 / 3.9
4 0533 / 1157 / F 1745 / ◐	3.3 / 0.8 / 3.6	**19** 0031 / 0609 / SA 1243 / ◑ 1821	0.4 / 3.4 / 0.6 / 3.8
5 0035 / 0618 / SA 1241 / 1833	0.7 / 3.2 / 0.8 / 3.5	**20** 0125 / 0706 / SU 1340 / 1922	0.5 / 3.4 / 0.6 / 3.8
6 0123 / 0712 / SU 1339 / 1932	0.7 / 3.1 / 0.8 / 3.4	**21** 0223 / 0807 / M 1444 / 2029	0.5 / 3.4 / 0.7 / 3.7
7 0224 / 0815 / M 1448 / 2037	0.6 / 3.1 / 0.7 / 3.4	**22** 0327 / 0911 / TU 1553 / 2136	0.6 / 3.5 / 0.7 / 3.7
8 0330 / 0919 / TU 1559 / 2140	0.6 / 3.2 / 0.7 / 3.5	**23** 0432 / 1013 / W 1701 / 2240	0.7 / 3.6 / 0.7 / 3.7
9 0431 / 1017 / W 1701 / 2237	0.5 / 3.4 / 0.6 / 3.5	**24** 0534 / 1111 / TH 1804 / 2340	0.7 / 3.7 / 0.7 / 3.7
10 0527 / 1109 / TH 1757 / 2330	0.5 / 3.5 / 0.6 / 3.6	**25** 0631 / 1205 / F 1903	0.7 / 3.8 / 0.6
11 0620 / 1158 / F 1850	0.6 / 3.7 / 0.6	**26** 0035 / 0724 / SA 1254 / ○ 1955	3.7 / 0.6 / 3.8 / 0.6
12 0021 / 0710 / SA 1244 / ● 1940	3.7 / 0.6 / 3.8 / 0.5	**27** 0123 / 0809 / SU 1338 / 2039	3.7 / 0.6 / 3.9 / 0.5
13 0109 / 0758 / SU 1329 / 2028	3.7 / 0.6 / 3.9 / 0.4	**28** 0206 / 0849 / M 1416 / 2117	3.6 / 0.5 / 3.9 / 0.5
14 0158 / 0846 / M 1416 / 2119	3.7 / 0.5 / 3.9 / 0.4	**29** 0245 / 0925 / TU 1453 / 2154	3.6 / 0.5 / 3.9 / 0.5
15 0248 / 0934 / TU 1503 / 2208	3.7 / 0.5 / 4.0 / 0.3	**30** 0321 / 0959 / W 1529 / 2228	3.6 / 0.5 / 3.9 / 0.5

JULY

Time	m	Time	m
1 0355 / 1029 / TH 1604 / 2259	3.5 / 0.5 / 3.8 / 0.5	**16** 0414 / 1055 / F 1622 / 2329	3.6 / 0.4 / 4.0 / 0.3
2 0428 / 1059 / F 1638 / 2331	3.4 / 0.6 / 3.8 / 0.6	**17** 0459 / 1138 / SA 1710	3.5 / 0.4 / 3.9
3 0503 / 1131 / SA 1713	3.4 / 0.7 / 3.7	**18** 0014 / 0547 / SU 1225 / ◑ 1801	0.4 / 3.5 / 0.5 / 3.9
4 0003 / 0539 / SU 1206 / ◑ 1750	0.7 / 3.3 / 0.8 / 3.6	**19** 0100 / 0637 / M 1313 / 1854	0.6 / 3.5 / 0.6 / 3.7
5 0037 / 0619 / M 1247 / 1835	0.7 / 3.3 / 0.8 / 3.5	**20** 0148 / 0731 / TU 1408 / 1956	0.7 / 3.4 / 0.7 / 3.6
6 0120 / 0710 / TU 1342 / 1933	0.7 / 3.2 / 0.8 / 3.4	**21** 0246 / 0834 / W 1516 / 2108	0.8 / 3.5 / 0.8 / 3.6
7 0218 / 0814 / W 1452 / 2042	0.7 / 3.3 / 0.8 / 3.4	**22** 0357 / 0944 / TH 1635 / 2223	0.9 / 3.5 / 0.9 / 3.6
8 0328 / 0922 / TH 1607 / 2152	0.7 / 3.3 / 0.8 / 3.4	**23** 0511 / 1052 / F 1749 / 2330	0.9 / 3.7 / 0.8 / 3.6
9 0439 / 1028 / F 1718 / 2259	0.7 / 3.5 / 0.7 / 3.5	**24** 0615 / 1151 / SA 1851	0.8 / 3.8 / 0.7
10 0547 / 1129 / SA 1824	0.7 / 3.6 / 0.7	**25** 0025 / 0708 / SU 1240 / 1942	3.6 / 0.8 / 3.9 / 0.7
11 0000 / 0650 / SU 1225 / ● 1924	3.7 / 0.7 / 3.8 / 0.6	**26** 0111 / 0754 / M 1323 / ○ 2024	3.6 / 0.7 / 3.9 / 0.6
12 0057 / 0746 / M 1316 / 2019	3.7 / 0.6 / 3.9 / 0.4	**27** 0151 / 0834 / TU 1401 / 2102	3.6 / 0.6 / 3.9 / 0.5
13 0150 / 0839 / TU 1405 / 2113	3.7 / 0.6 / 4.0 / 0.4	**28** 0228 / 0910 / W 1436 / 2136	3.6 / 0.5 / 3.9 / 0.5
14 0241 / 0929 / W 1453 / 2203	3.7 / 0.6 / 4.1 / 0.3	**29** 0301 / 0941 / TH 1508 / 2205	3.6 / 0.5 / 3.9 / 0.5
15 0329 / 1014 / TH 1537 / 2247	3.7 / 0.4 / 4.0 / 0.3	**30** 0329 / 1007 / F 1537 / 2231	3.5 / 0.5 / 3.8 / 0.5
		31 0358 / 1033 / SA 1608 / 2300	3.5 / 0.5 / 3.8 / 0.6

AUGUST

Time	m	Time	m
1 0429 / 1104 / SU 1641 / 2330	3.5 / 0.6 / 3.7	**16** 0517 / 1159 / M 1734 / ◐	3.5 / 0.5 / 3.8
2 0502 / 1136 / M 1714 / 2357	3.5 / 0.7 / 3.7 / 0.7	**17** 0026 / 0602 / TU 1241 / 1823	0.7 / 3.5 / 0.6 / 3.6
3 0534 / 1207 / TU 1749	3.4 / 0.8 / 3.5	**18** 0107 / 0652 / W 1330 / 1921	0.8 / 3.4 / 0.8 / 3.4
4 0027 / 0615 / W 1247 / 1840	0.7 / 3.3 / 0.8 / 3.4	**19** 0202 / 0755 / TH 1439 / 2038	0.9 / 3.4 / 0.9 / 3.3
5 0117 / 0715 / TH 1353 / 1952	0.8 / 3.2 / 0.9 / 3.3	**20** 0319 / 0914 / F 1607 / 2204	1.1 / 3.5 / 1.0 / 3.4
6 0233 / 0833 / F 1520 / 2116	0.8 / 3.3 / 0.9 / 3.4	**21** 0446 / 1034 / SA 1734 / 2319	1.1 / 3.6 / 0.9 / 3.4
7 0401 / 0955 / SA 1648 / 2236	0.8 / 3.4 / 0.8 / 3.5	**22** 0600 / 1138 / SU 1840	1.0 / 3.7 / 0.8
8 0524 / 1108 / SU 1807 / 2347	0.8 / 3.6 / 0.7 / 3.6	**23** 0015 / 0654 / M 1226 / 1927	3.5 / 0.8 / 3.8 / 0.7
9 0637 / 1209 / M 1913	0.7 / 3.8 / 0.6	**24** 0055 / 0736 / TU 1304 / ○ 2004	3.6 / 0.7 / 3.8 / 0.6
10 0047 / 0737 / TU 1302 / ● 2009	3.7 / 0.6 / 3.9 / 0.4	**25** 0130 / 0813 / W 1339 / 2038	3.6 / 0.6 / 3.8 / 0.5
11 0139 / 0829 / W 1350 / 2100	3.7 / 0.5 / 4.0 / 0.3	**26** 0203 / 0847 / TH 1411 / 2108	3.6 / 0.6 / 3.8 / 0.5
12 0227 / 0916 / TH 1437 / 2147	3.7 / 0.4 / 4.1 / 0.3	**27** 0233 / 0917 / F 1440 / 2136	3.6 / 0.5 / 3.8 / 0.5
13 0311 / 1000 / F 1521 / 2230	3.7 / 0.3 / 4.0 / 0.3	**28** 0300 / 0942 / SA 1508 / 2200	3.6 / 0.5 / 3.8 / 0.5
14 0353 / 1039 / SA 1604 / 2309	3.6 / 0.3 / 4.0 / 0.3	**29** 0326 / 1007 / SU 1539 / 2228	3.5 / 0.5 / 3.7 / 0.6
15 0434 / 1118 / SU 1648 / 2347	3.6 / 0.4 / 3.9 / 0.5	**30** 0356 / 1038 / M 1611 / 2258	3.6 / 0.5 / 3.7 / 0.6
		31 0428 / 1109 / TU 1643 / 2324	3.5 / 0.6 / 3.6 / 0.7

Chart Datum: 1·66 metres below Normal Null (German reference level). HAT is 3·6 metres above Chart Datum; see 4.5

TIME ZONE -0100
Subtract 1 hour for UT
For German Summer Time add
ONE hour in **non-shaded areas**

CUXHAVEN LAT 53°52'N LONG 8°43'E
TIMES AND HEIGHTS OF HIGH AND LOW WATERS

Dates in red are **SPRINGS**
Dates in blue are **NEAPS**

YEAR 2010

SEPTEMBER

Time	m		Time	m
1 0458	3.5	**16**	0027	0.9
1136	0.7		0613	3.4
W 1716	3.5	TH 1255	0.8
◗ 2350	0.8		1848	3.2
2 0533	3.3	**17**	0118	1.0
1211	0.8		0716	3.3
TH 1803	3.3	F 1402	1.0
			2004	3.1
3 0035	0.9	**18**	0236	1.2
0632	3.3		0838	3.4
F 1314	0.9	SA 1534	1.0
1917	3.3		2134	3.2
4 0155	1.0	**19**	0412	1.2
0757	3.3		1005	3.5
SA 1448	0.9	SU 1708	1.0
2050	3.3		2256	3.3
5 0335	1.0	**20**	0536	1.0
0929	3.4		1115	3.7
SU 1629	0.8	M 1818	0.9
2220	3.4		2353	3.4
6 0508	0.8	**21**	0631	0.8
1049	3.6		1201	3.7
M 1753	0.6	TU 1901	0.6
2334	3.5			
7 0623	0.7	**22**	0029	3.5
1152	3.8		0708	0.7
TU 1859	0.5	W 1234	3.7
			1932	0.5
8 0031	3.6	**23**	0100	3.5
0722	0.6		0747	0.6
W 1244	3.9	TH 1306	3.7
● 1952	0.4	○ 2003	0.5
9 0120	3.7	**24**	0131	3.5
0811	0.4		0816	0.5
TH 1330	4.0	F 1339	3.7
2038	0.3		2034	0.5
10 0204	3.7	**25**	0201	3.6
0856	0.4		0848	0.5
F 1416	4.0	SA 1410	3.7
2122	0.3		2103	0.5
11 0246	3.7	**26**	0229	3.6
0938	0.3		0917	0.5
SA 1500	4.0	SU 1440	3.7
2204	0.3		2130	0.5
12 0327	3.7	**27**	0257	3.6
1018	0.3		0945	0.5
SU 1543	3.9	M 1512	3.7
2243	0.4		2158	0.6
13 0407	3.6	**28**	0327	3.6
1055	0.4		1014	0.5
M 1625	3.8	TU 1546	3.6
2317	0.5		2229	0.6
14 0446	3.6	**29**	0400	3.6
1132	0.5		1045	0.6
TU 1708	3.6	W 1621	3.5
2350	0.7		2258	0.7
15 0527	3.5	**30**	0432	3.5
1210	0.6		1116	0.7
W 1752	3.4	TH 1657	3.5
◗			2329	0.8

OCTOBER

Time	m		Time	m
1 0510	3.4	**16**	0040	1.1
1154	0.8		0638	3.4
F 1746	3.3	SA 1328	1.0
◗			1925	3.0
2 0016	1.0	**17**	0151	1.2
0609	3.4		0754	3.4
SA 1259	0.9	SU 1451	1.0
1900	3.0		2048	3.1
3 0136	1.1	**18**	0322	1.2
0733	3.4		0918	3.4
SU 1432	0.9	M 1621	1.0
2033	3.3		2210	3.2
4 0316	1.1	**19**	0449	1.0
0907	3.5		1031	3.5
M 1612	0.8	TU 1733	0.8
2203	3.4		2310	3.3
5 0450	0.9	**20**	0550	0.8
1028	3.7		1121	3.6
TU 1734	0.6	W 1819	0.6
2314	3.5		2350	3.4
6 0602	0.7	**21**	0630	0.7
1130	3.8		1155	3.6
W 1835	0.5	TH 1851	0.5
7 0007	3.6	**22**	0022	3.5
0657	0.6		0705	0.6
TH 1220	3.9	F 1229	3.6
● 1925	0.4		1924	0.5
8 0053	3.7	**23**	0055	3.5
0747	0.4		0742	0.6
F 1308	3.9	SA 1305	3.7
2011	0.3	○ 1958	0.5
9 0137	3.7	**24**	0128	3.6
0832	0.4		0818	0.6
SA 1353	3.9	SU 1341	3.7
2055	0.4		2030	0.6
10 0219	3.8	**25**	0200	3.6
0914	0.4		0852	0.5
SU 1438	3.9	M 1416	3.7
2136	0.5		2103	0.6
11 0259	3.8	**26**	0232	3.7
0955	0.4		0926	0.5
M 1521	3.8	TU 1451	3.6
2214	0.5		2136	0.6
12 0339	3.7	**27**	0305	3.7
1032	0.4		0958	0.6
TU 1603	3.7	W 1529	3.6
2248	0.6		2209	0.6
13 0417	3.6	**28**	0341	3.7
1108	0.5		1032	0.6
W 1644	3.5	TH 1608	3.5
2319	0.7		2244	0.7
14 0456	3.5	**29**	0419	3.7
1145	0.6		1109	0.7
TH 1726	3.3	F 1650	3.4
◗ 2353	0.9		2322	0.9
15 0540	3.5	**30**	0502	3.6
1228	0.8		1154	0.8
F 1817	3.1	SA 1742	3.3
		◗		
		31	0013	1.0
			0559	3.6
		SU 1257	0.8
			1851	3.2

NOVEMBER

Time	m		Time	m
1 0126	1.1	**16**	0219	1.1
0716	3.6		0814	3.4
M 1420	0.9	TU 1513	1.0
2015	3.3		2102	3.1
2 0256	1.1	**17**	0340	1.0
0842	3.6		0926	3.5
TU 1550	0.8	W 1625	0.8
2138	3.4		2207	3.2
3 0423	0.9	**18**	0449	0.9
0959	3.7		1024	3.5
W 1706	0.7	TH 1720	0.7
2245	3.5		2258	3.4
4 0532	0.8	**19**	0541	0.8
1101	3.8		1110	3.5
TH 1804	0.7	F 1803	0.6
2338	3.6		2340	3.5
5 0628	0.6	**20**	0625	0.7
1155	3.8		1152	3.6
F 1856	0.5	SA 1843	0.6
6 0025	3.7	**21**	0019	3.6
0720	0.6		0708	0.7
SA 1245	3.8	SU 1234	3.6
● 1945	0.5	○ 1923	0.6
7 0111	3.7	**22**	0057	3.7
0809	0.5		0750	0.7
SU 1333	3.8	M 1315	3.6
2030	0.5		2002	0.6
8 0153	3.8	**23**	0134	3.7
0852	0.5		0830	0.6
M 1418	3.8	TU 1355	3.7
2110	0.6		2042	0.7
9 0233	3.8	**24**	0213	3.8
0932	0.5		0911	0.6
TU 1500	3.7	W 1437	3.7
2148	0.6		2122	0.7
10 0313	3.8	**25**	0252	3.8
1011	0.5		0951	0.6
W 1542	3.6	TH 1520	3.6
2223	0.6		2201	0.7
11 0352	3.7	**26**	0332	3.8
1049	0.5		1030	0.6
TH 1623	3.4	F 1602	3.5
2255	0.7		2239	0.7
12 0431	3.6	**27**	0412	3.8
1126	0.6		1113	0.7
F 1704	3.3	SA 1647	3.5
2329	0.8		2321	0.8
13 0513	3.6	**28**	0457	3.8
1206	0.8		1158	0.7
SA 1748	3.2	SU 1738	3.4
◗		◗		
14 0010	1.0	**29**	0012	0.9
0602	3.5		0551	3.8
SU 1254	0.9	M 1255	0.7
1841	3.1		1839	3.3
15 0105	1.1	**30**	0114	0.9
0703	3.4		0657	3.7
M 1358	1.0	TU 1402	0.8
1948	3.1		1949	3.4

DECEMBER

Time	m		Time	m
1 0229	1.0	**16**	0221	1.0
0811	3.7		0810	3.4
W 1518	0.8	TH 1503	0.9
2103	3.5		2052	3.2
2 0347	1.0	**17**	0335	1.0
0925	3.7		0917	3.4
TH 1630	0.8	F 1609	0.9
2210	3.6		2156	3.4
3 0457	0.9	**18**	0444	0.9
1031	3.8		1019	3.5
F 1732	0.7	SA 1709	0.8
2307	3.6		2252	3.5
4 0559	0.8	**19**	0543	0.8
1130	3.8		1114	3.5
SA 1829	0.7	SU 1803	0.8
			2343	3.6
5 0000	3.7	**20**	0636	0.8
0657	0.7		1205	3.6
SU 1226	3.8	M 1854	0.8
● 1923	0.7			
6 0049	3.8	**21**	0030	3.7
0750	0.6		0725	0.7
M 1316	3.7	TU 1253	3.7
2009	0.6	○ 1941	0.7
7 0133	3.8	**22**	0114	3.8
0834	0.6		0812	0.6
TU 1401	3.7	W 1340	3.7
2049	0.6		2028	0.7
8 0212	3.8	**23**	0158	3.9
0915	0.6		0901	0.6
W 1443	3.7	TH 1427	3.7
2128	0.7		2115	0.7
9 0252	3.8	**24**	0242	4.0
0955	0.6		0948	0.6
TH 1524	3.6	F 1513	3.7
2205	0.7		2158	0.6
10 0332	3.8	**25**	0324	4.0
1033	0.6		1030	0.5
F 1603	3.5	SA 1556	3.6
2238	0.7		2236	0.6
11 0410	4.0	**26**	0404	4.0
1108	0.6		1110	0.5
SA 1640	3.4	SU 1640	3.5
2309	0.7		2317	0.6
12 0448	3.7	**27**	0449	3.9
1143	0.7		1154	0.6
SU 1717	3.3	M 1727	3.4
2342	0.9			
13 0527	3.6	**28**	0004	0.7
1219	0.9		0538	3.9
M 1757	3.2	TU 1243	0.7
◗		◗ 1819	3.4
14 0022	1.0	**29**	0056	0.8
0611	3.5		0633	3.8
TU 1302	0.9	W 1337	0.7
1845	3.2		1917	3.4
15 0114	1.0	**30**	0156	0.9
0705	3.4		0737	3.7
W 1357	0.9	TH 1439	0.8
1945	3.2		2023	3.5
		31	0307	1.0
			0849	3.7
		F 1551	0.9
			2133	3.6

Chart Datum: 1·66 metres below Normal Null (German reference level). HAT is 3·6 metres above Chart Datum; see 4.5

Germany

9.15.12 BRUNSBÜTTEL

Schleswig-Holstein 53°53'·27N 09°08'·48E ✵✵✵⚓⚓✿✿

CHARTS AC 2469, 3625; Imray C26; D42; BSH 3010.3/4, 3009.1/2

TIDES +0203 Dover; ML 1·4; Duration 0520

Standard Port CUXHAVEN (→)

Times				Height (metres)			
High Water		Low Water		MHWS	MHWN	MLWN	MLWS
0200	0800	0200	0900	3·8	3·4	0·9	0·5
1400	2000	1400	2100				
Differences BRUNSBÜTTEL							
+0057	+0105	+0121	+0112	−0·3	−0·2	−0·1	0·0

SHELTER Good in the Alter Hafen, a drying yacht hbr, access HW ±3, W of the locks. Waiting area is close E of FWG ☆ at ent to Alter Vorhafen. No smoking in locks area. Once locked through, good shelter, but noisy, in Kanal-Yachthafen, close NW of the larger Neue locks. An alternative Yacht Hbr is 4 cables upstream, same bank.

NAVIGATION WPT 53°53'·01N 09°08'·14E, 039°/6ca to Alte Schleusen (the smaller SE locks, usually for yachts). No navigational dangers in the near apprs, but commercial traffic is heavy. The stream sets strongly across access chan to locks.
Lock Entry Sigs: see 9.15.13; await White signal or loudspeaker.

LIGHTS AND MARKS Lights as chartlet. Ldg lts 065·5° direct large ships from the main fairway to the lock Approach areas.

R/T Request *Kiel Kanal I* on Ch 13 for a locking allocation 15 mins before arrival; see 9.15.13.
Radar cover of the inner Elbe is as follows:

Brunsbüttel Radar I	Ch 62	Buoys 51 - 59;
Brunsbüttel Radar II	Ch 67	Buoys 60 - Elbehafen;
(call if entering locks in dense fog)		
S Margarethen Radar	Ch 18	Buoys 57a - 65;
Freiburg Radar	Ch 61	Buoys 63 - 77;
Rhinplate Radar	Ch 05	Buoys 75 - 89;
Pagensand Radar	Ch 66	Buoys 87 - 89;
Hetlingen Radar	Ch 21	Buoys 101 - 115;
Wedel Radar	Ch 22	Buoys 113 - 125.

VTS, see 9.15.10. *Brunsbüttel Elbe Traffic* broadcasts weather info every H + 05 on Ch 68 in English and German for the inner Elbe. Monitor Ch 68 when underway between buoys 53 and 125.

TELEPHONE (Code 04852) HM Yachthaven 4276; ⊖ 83000; Weather 36400; Police 112; Ⓗ 9800; Brit Consul (040) 446071.

FACILITIES **Alter Hafen** ☎ 0160 697 4729, €0.95, Slip, C (20 ton), R, SC; **Kanal-Yachthafen**, €1.30, ⊖, Bar.

Town P, D (as shown 0800-1800 ☎ 2002), El, ME, ✕, Gaz, 🛒, R, LB, Ⓗ, Bar, ✉, Ⓑ, ⇌, ✈ (Hamburg).

9.15.13 NORD-OSTSEE KANAL (Kiel Canal) Schleswig-Holstein

CHARTS AC 2469; Kieler Förde, inner part 2344, outer part 2341; D42; BSH 3009.1-4

SIGNALS Two sets of Occulting lights must be obeyed: a. Those to move from the Waiting Area (9.15.12) and enter the Approach Area, shown from mast at the lock island; and b. those to enter the lock, shown from a mast at the lock:

● = No entry.   ○
● = Prepare to enter.

○
● = Ships exempt from pilotage enter; secure on central island.

○ Oc = **Yachts should enter outer hbr and lock** (berth on low, narrow pontoons).

In the canal Sidings, the following traffic sigs apply to yachts:

● QR = Entry into a Siding is prohib.

●●● (Oc R, vert) = Exit from a Siding is prohib.

R/T Before entering, yachts should request a lock clearance: at Brunsbüttel from *Kiel Kanal I* on Ch 13. or at Holtenau from *Kiel Kanal IV* on Ch 12.

In the Canal. Maintain listening watch as follows:

Kiel Kanal I	Ch 13	Brunsbüttel approaches and lock area.
Kiel Kanal II	Ch 02	Brunsbüttel to Breiholz.
Kiel Kanal III	Ch 03	Breiholz to Holtenau.
Kiel Kanal IV	Ch 12	Holtenau approaches and lock area.

Info broadcasts by *Kiel Kanal II* on Ch 02 at H+15, H+45; and by *Kiel Kanal III* on Ch 03 at H+20, H+50. Vessels should monitor these broadcasts and avoid calling the station if possible.

NAVIGATION The Canal runs 53·3NM (98·7 km) from Brunsbüttel (9.15.12) to Kiel-Holtenau; it is 103-162m wide and 11m deep. A handbook *Navigation Rules Kiel Canal* in English/German can be downloaded from www.kiel-canal.org/english. Speed limit 8kn. All 8 bridges have 40m clearance. Yachts may only use the Canal and its ents in official daylight hours (next para) and in good visibility (unless going to Brunsbüttel's Alter or Inner Hbrs, or Holtenau's yacht hbr). Motoring or motor-sailing (hoist a B ▼, or a B pennant) is the norm. Pure sailing (no engine) is prohib.

9.15.14 HAMBURG

Schleswig-Holstein 53°32'·52N 09°58'·84E ✲✲✲⚓⚓⚓✿✿

CHARTS AC 3625, 3267, 3268; D48; BSH 3010.9-12 (see below)

TIDES See R Elbe 9.15.10. ML 1·3; Duration 0435.

SHELTER A busy commercial port with several marinas. Visitors berth at Wedel in Hamburger Yachthafen, 12M W of Hamburg, or in the city centre at City Sporthafen, especially for visitors.

HAMBURGER YACHTHAFEN (53°34'·28N 09°40'·53E, N bank). A conspic 50m high radar twr is at SW corner of hbr. Very good shelter, access H24 via 2 ents. 2100 AB, €1.14. D & P (shut Tues), BH (16 ton), BY, C (15 ton), C (masting) CH, El, Ⓔ, ME, SC, ✕, Slip, SM, Gas, Bar, R. HM ☎ (4103) 4438 (office); HM (east) 5632; HM (west) 7751; ✉ ☎ 0172 6423227; www.hamburger-yachthafen.de (Sheets 9/10).

SCHULAU. Good shelter, 7ca E of Wedel. Beware strong tidal streams across ent, marked by FR and FG lts. Depths 0·6m to 1·6m. HM ☎ 2422, Slip, C, P, D, ME, Ⓗ, CH, SC. (Sheets 9/10).

MÜHLENBERG. 53°33'·19N 09°49'·38E, N bank. 250 AB, Slip, FW, SC. Yachts < 9m; 0·6m. (Sheet 10).

TEUFELSBRÜCK. 53°32'·82N 09°52'·06E, N bank, close E of ferry pier. Good shelter in small hbr; 0·9m. Bar, SC. (Sheets 10/11).

RÜSCHKANAL. 53°32'·57N 09°51'·34E, S bank, narrow ent. C, CH, El, ME, Slip, ✕; 4 SCs, pontoons NE side in 3·6m. (Sheet 11).

CITY SPORTHAFEN. 53°32'·52N 09°58'·84E ☎ 364297, mobile 170 805 2004, out of hrs 227 7651. www.city-sporthafen.de info@city-sporthafen-hamburg.de 80-120 AB, €1.30, pay 6 days, 7th free. Berths usually available for <20m LOA; max draft 2·5-4m, max LOA 50m. D & P (cans), Showers €1.00. (Sheet 12).

R/T *Hamburg Port Traffic* and Hbr Control vessel Ch 13 14 **73** (H24). All stns monitor Ch 74.

TELEPHONE (Code 40) Met 3190 8826/7; Auto 0190 116456; Brit Consul 446071.

Daylight hours (LT) in the Kiel Canal are: 1-15 May, 0230-2000; 16-31 May, 0200-2030; 1 Jun-15 Jul, 0130-2100; 16-31 Jul, 0200-2030; 1-15 Aug, 0230-2000; 16-31 Aug, 0300-1930; 1-15 Sep, 0330-1900; 16-30 Sep, 0400-1830. Other months on request.

Canal dues (approx €47), E or W-bound, are paid at Kiel-Holtenau to the Lockmaster if using the Old lock; or at the newspaper stand if using the New lock. Credit cards acceptable.

SHELTER As well as Brunsbüttel and Holtenau, 5 sidings or *weichen* (berthing places, see below) must be reached by yachts during **daylight hours** (see above). Other sidings may not be used; they are likely to be less sheltered and exposed to wash.

- *Dückerswisch siding (km 20·5); W side in turning area.
- *Oldenbüttel siding (km 40·5), off lock to Gieselau Canal (links Kiel Canal to R Eider, thence to Tönning, 9.15.7).
- Rendsburg (ent at km 66). All facilities and 3 marinas in Lake Obereider; the W'most is nearest town centre.
- The Borgstedter See, entrances at km 67.5 and 70;
- *Flemhuder See (km 85·4, E of Grossnordsee siding).
  *Usually for one night only.

KIEL-HOLTENAU (km 98·7) is a major port with two pairs of locks leading into Kieler Förde which is practically tideless and at almost the same level as the canal. Monitor Ch 68 *Kiel Traffic* for VTS info whilst in Kieler Förde. Yachts usually use the smaller Old locks (No smoking); signals and pontoons as at Brunsbüttel.

On the N bank (E of Old locks) is a small Yacht Hbr; no AC, no FW. A BP fuel barge is close E of the locks.

At Wik (S side of locks) **Nautischer Dienst** (Kapt Stegmann & Co) ☎ 0431 331772 are ACA and BSH Agents. Kiel city is S of Wik.

The **British Kiel YC** 54°23'·22N 10°09'·75E is 1·5M NNE of the locks and 5ca NNW of Stickenhörn ECM buoy, Q (3) 10s. It is part of a military training centre with no commercial facilities; but AB (about €15.60) may be available for visitors to whom a friendly welcome is extended. Call *Sailtrain* VHF Ch 6, ☎ (0431) 397921 or www.bkyc.de/.

HAMBURGER YACHTHAFEN, WEDEL

HAMBURG: CITY SPORTHAFEN

9.15.15 BREMERHAVEN

Federal State of Bremen **53°32'·12N 08°34'·50E** ❀❀⛵⛵🏵🏵

CHARTS AC 3617, 3621 plans A & B; Imray C26; D4; BSH 3011.7/8.

TIDES +0051 Dover; ML 2·0; Duration 0600

Standard Port WILHELMSHAVEN (→)

Times				Height (metres)			
High Water		Low Water		MHWS	MHWN	MLWN	MLWS
0200	0800	0200	0900	4·3	3·8	0·6	0·0
1400	2000	1400	2100				

Differences ALTE WESER LT HO (53°51'·8N 08°07'·6E)

−0055	−0048	−0015	−0029	−0·6	−0·5	+0·4	+0·5

DWARSGAT (53°43'·0N 08°18'·0E)

−0015	+0002	−0006	−0001	−0·1	0·0	+0·4	+0·5

ROBBENSUDSTEERT (53°38'·0N 08°27'·0E)

−+0009	+0026	+0015	+0020	−0·4	−0·3	−0·2	0·0

BREMERHAVEN

+0029	+0046	+0033	+0038	−0·2	−0·1	−0·1	−0·1

NORDENHAM

+0051	+0109	+0055	+0058	−0·2	−0·1	−0·4	−0·2

BRAKE

+0120	+0119	+0143	+0155	−0·3	−0·2	−0·4	−0·2

ELSFLETH

+0137	+0137	+0206	+0216	−0·2	−0·1	−0·3	0·0

VEGESACK

+0208	+0204	+0250	+0254	−0·2	−0·2	−0·5	−0·2

BREMEN

+0216	+0211	+0311	+0314	−0·1	−0·1	−0·6	−0·3

SHELTER There are 6 options for visitors. The first three are most suitable and nearest the city centre, on the upper chartlet:

- Berth in R Geeste downstream of Kennedy fixed bridge (clearance 5·5m) on pontoons, but short stay only as it is noisy and exposed to swell/wash. If able to transit the bridge (flood barrage is normally open), berth on quay upstream.

- Lock into the Schleusenhafen via the smaller W lock. Call *Kleine Kammer* Ch 69; opens hourly, H24; ●● (vert) = enter. Floating pontoons in lock. Berth at Fischereihafen West Quay. This gives access to 2 other YC/marinas well to the S.

- The Weser YC marina in Hauptkanal (E of Handelshafen); excellent shelter, central location and close to the lock.

- Bremerhaven Marina, 1·3M S of lock on W side (3m).

- Wulsdorf Marina, 0·5M further south in Luneorthafen.

- Lloyd Marina in Neuer Hafen, 0·6M NNW of the main hbr ent. Access via lock 0600–2200, then turn 90° port.

Up the R Weser (AC 3406/7), Nordenham, Rodenkirchen, Rechtenfleth and Sandstedt have drying yacht hbrs (access HW±2). Other hbrs include Brake on the Weser and Elsfleth and Oldenburg on the R Hunte.

NAVIGATION WPT 53°32'·25N 08°33'·94E [SHM buoy 61, QG], 111°/650m to cross into the Vorhafen. Beware much commercial shipping; also ferries using R Geeste. From buoy 51 to 61 (opp container terminal) sailing yachts may not tack in fairway, where commercial traffic has right of way. The Geeste and Hadelner Kanals (1·5m depth; air draft 2·7m) link Bremerhaven to Otterndorf (32M). For R Weser (very well marked) see 9.15.5.

LIGHTS AND MARKS See upper chartlet and 9.15.4. Ldg lts lead 150.8° up main fairway (R Weser). Vorhafen ent is close SW of conspic 112m radio twr.

R/T Bremerhaven Port Ch 12 (H24); Fischereihafen lock Ch **69** (H24). Weser VTS, see diagram overleaf with radar coverage. Up-river *Bremen-Weser Traffic* broadcasts at H+30 on Ch 19 78 81. *Bremen Port Radio* Ch 03 16 (H24). *Hunte Traffic* broadcasts at H+30 on Ch 63.

TELEPHONE (Code 0471) HM 59613401; HM Neuer Hafen 471 170 1495; Neuer Hafen lock 471 941 2840; Fischereihafen lock 59613440; Police 94667; Ⓗ 2991; Brit Consul (040) 4480320.

FACILITIES R Geeste ☎ 482414. 50 AB + 440 Ⓥ. www.city-port.de
Lloyd Marina ☎ 170 1495. 100 AB, €1.19. P, D, R, VHF Ch 69. www.im-jaich.de
Weser YC ☎ 23531. 150 AB + 20 Ⓥ, €1.29, C, R, Bar. www.weser-yacht-club.de
Fischereihafen II W Quay ☎ 76189. BY, SM, ME.
Bremerhaven Marina ☎ 77555. 280 AB + 30 Ⓥ, P, D, C, Slip.
Wulsdorf Marina ☎ 73268. 150 AB, Ⓥ on request, Slip, C, El.
City all facilities: ACA, Gaz, ≋, ✈.

RIVER WESER

(AC 1875, 3617, 3406, 3407) The R Weser is a major waterway leading to **Bremerhaven, Nordenham, Brake** and **Bremen** which connect with the inland waterways. The upper reaches, *Unterweser*, run from Bremen to Bremerhaven and below Bremerhaven the *Aussenweser* flows into a wide estuary split by two main chans, Neue Weser and Alte Weser. The position and extent of sandbanks vary: on the W side they tend to be steep-to, but on the E side there are extensive drying shoals (eg Tegeler Plate).

The Jade-Weser SWM lt buoy marks the approach from NW to Neue Weser (the main fairway) and Alte Weser which are separated by Roter Sand and Roter Grund, marked by the disused Roter Sand lt tr (conspic). Both chans are well marked and converge about 3M S of Alte Weser lt tr (conspic). From this junction Hohewegrinne (buoyed) leads inward in a SE direction past Tegeler Plate lt tr (conspic) on the NE side and Hohe Weg lt tr (conspic) to the SSE. From Robbenplate to Bremerhaven it is constrained by training walls. ►*In the Aussenweser the stream, which runs over 3kn at sp, often sets towards the banks and the branch chans which traverse them.*◄

The Weser-Elbe Wattfahrwasser is a demanding, but useful inshore passage between R Weser and R Elbe. It leads NNE from the Wurster Arm (E of Hohe Weg), keeping about 3M offshore; SE of Neuwerk and around Cuxhaven training wall. It normally requires two tides, but there are suitable anchorages.

9.15.16 HOOKSIEL ✳❀◊◊✿✿

Niedersachsen 53°38'·61N 08°05'19E

CHARTS AC 3618; Imray C26; D7; BSH 3011.3, 3015.10

TIDES +0034 Dover; ML no data; Duration 0605

Standard Port WILHELMSHAVEN (→)

Times				Height (metres)			
High Water		Low Water		MHWS	MHWN	MLWN	MLWS
0200	0800	0200	0900	4·3	3·8	0·6	0·0
1400	2000	1400	2100				
Differences HOOKSIEL							
–0023	–0022	–0008	–0012	–0.5	–0.4	0.0	0.0
SCHILLIG							
–0031	–0025	–0006	–0014	–0.3	–0.2	+0.4	+0.4

SHELTER Temp AB in the Vorhafen (approx 1m at MLWS) but it is very commercial and uncomfortable in E winds. Beyond the lock there is complete shelter in the Binnentief, 2M long and 2·0-3·5m deep. Best for visitors is Alter Hafen Yacht Hbr in the town; max draft 2m. Larger yachts go to YCs; see lockmaster. Do not enter Watersports Area due to water-ski cables.

NAVIGATION WPT 53°39'·33N 08°06'·52E [No 37/Hooksiel 1 SHM buoy, IQ G 13s], 217°/9ca to H3 SHM buoy, Fl G 4s, approx 350m E of the ent. Caution: aquaculture N of H3, seasonal HS ferry, strong cross tide, transhipment pier and restricted area to SE of ent.

Appr via chan 2·1m deep to Vorhafen, enclosed by two moles. Inner ldg daymarks 276·5°, two RW bcns, lead thru' ent, but are obsc'd when ferry berthed on N pier.

Lock and opening bridge operate Mon-Fri 0800-1900, Sat/Sun 0900-2000 (LT); exact times on noticeboard. Secure well in lock. Dredging may take place at LW.

LIGHTS AND MARKS Ldg lts 164·5°, as chartlet. Conspic chys of chemical works and oil refinery SSE of lock. ✩ L Fl R 6s on dayglo R pile on S mole and street lamp on N mole. R/G tfc lts at lock.

R/T Port VHF Ch 63. See also Jade VTS and Weser VTS below.

TELEPHONE (Code 04425) HM 958050; Lockmaster 430; ⊖ 1302; CG (0421) 5550555; Weather (0190) 116047; Police 269; Ⓗ (04421) 2080; Dr 1080; Brit Consul (040) 446071.

FACILITIES Werft BY ☎ 95850, BH (25 ton), Slip. **Wilhelmshaven YC** ☎ 04421 22983; 50 Ⓥ berths (AB), €0·60, Bar. **Alter Hafen** Ⓥ berth on quays, first night FoC then c. €1·00, www.marinahooksiel. de. **Town** SM, ME, El, CH, P, D, Gaz, 🛒, R, Bar, Ⓑ, ✉, ⇌, ✈ (Wilhelmshaven and Bremen).

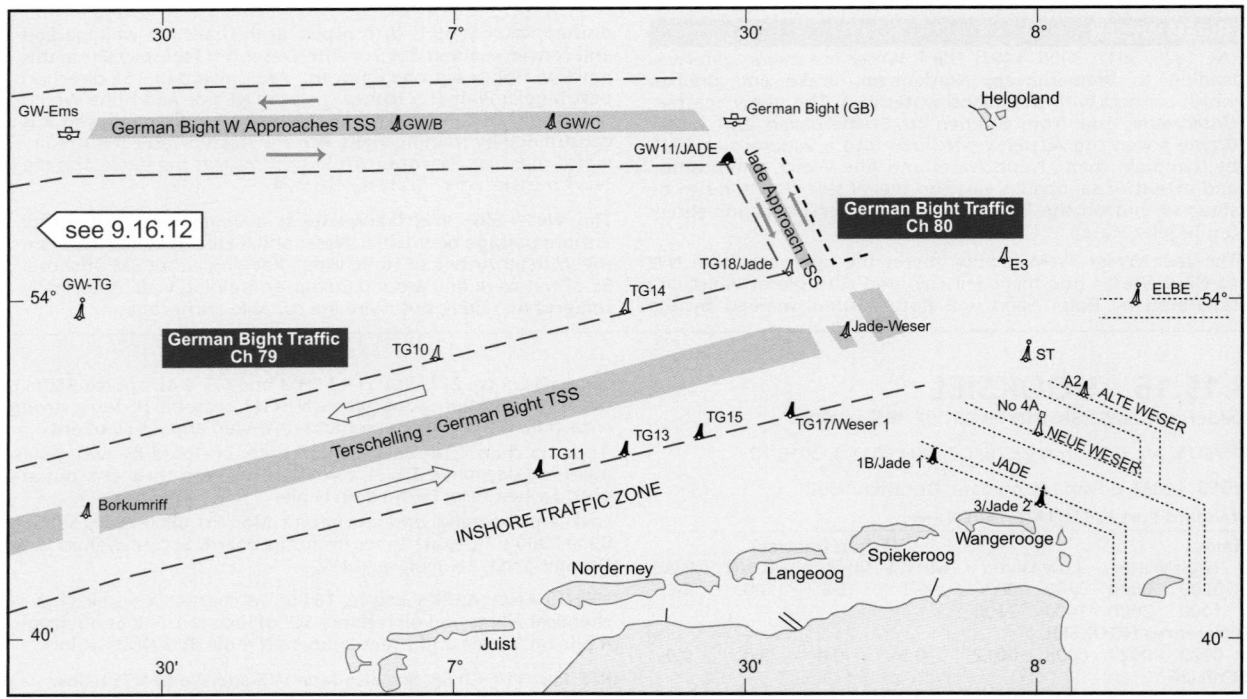

Fig 9.15.15A. Terschelling-German Bight TSS, German Bight Western Approaches TSS and Jade Approach TSS. German Bight VTS: *German Bight Traffic* broadcasts safety and weather info Ch 80 every hour in German/English.

Fig 9.15.15B. Weser and Jade VTS

WESER VTS *Bremerhaven Weser Traffic* broadcasts info in German (English on request) at H+20 on all the chans below. Radar cover in the lower Weser is as Fig. 9.15.15B above.

Alte Weser Radar	Ch 22	Neue Weser: buoys 3a–19H.
ditto	ditto	Alte Weser: buoys A1–16a.
Hohe Weg Radar 1 & 2	Ch 02	Buoys 21–37.
Robbenplate Rdr I & II	Ch 04	Buoys 37–47.
Blexen Radar	Ch 07	Buoys 47–63.

JADE VTS *Jade Traffic* broadcasts info in German on request and every H+10, Ch 20 63. Radar coverage is as follows:

Jade Radar I	Ch 63	Buoys 1–33;
Jade Radar II	Ch 20	Buoys 33–58.

RIVER JADE

(AC 3617, 3618) The estuaries of the River Weser and River Jade flow seaward between Cuxhaven and Wangerooge.

▶*Although not so hazardous as R Elbe, the outer parts of both rivers can become very rough with wind against tide, and are dangerous on the ebb in strong NW winds.*◀

Enter from 1b/Jade 1 buoy via Wangerooger Fahrwasser (buoyed fairway) which initially leads ESE to the N of Wangerooge, then SSE past Minsener Oog and Hooksiel to Wilhelmshaven. S of Wilhelmshaven, the Jadebusen is a large, mostly drying area through which channels run to the small harbours of Dangast and Vareler. Much of it is designated as nature reserves.

Note: Major dredging operations underway for a container term on W bank of the R Jade between Hooksiel and Wilhelmshaven. Pay attention to many Y measuring buoys 1ca outside fairway.

THE EAST FRISIANS, RIVER JADE TO RIVER EMS

(AC 1635. Note: UKHO chart coverage of the East Frisians is too small scale for pilotage. BSH 3015 folio is essential.) Offshore route, passing north of the East Frisian Islands, is about 50 miles long from the E end of Wangerooge to abeam Borkum. This is via the ITZ, south of the Terschellinger-German Bight TSS, whose E-going lane is marked on its S side by SHM buoys TG19/Weser 2 to TG1/Ems. These buoys 5M spacing. *Take care to avoid straying inadvertently into the TSS and incurring possible penalties* – it is far better to stay 1M south of these buoys.

4-5M S of this line of buoys the S side of the ITZ is punctuated by landfall buoys marking the approaches to the eight main seegaten between the East Frisians (9.15.18). There are major lts on Wangerooge, Norderney and Borkum. But the islands are very low lying with bare dunes and are often difficult to identify with any certainty despite the existence of some landmarks. Even radar identification is none too reliable.

▶*Near the TSS the E-going stream begins at HW Helgoland –5, and the W-going at HW Helgoland +1, sp rates 1·2kn. Inshore the stream is influenced by the flow through the seegaten.*◀

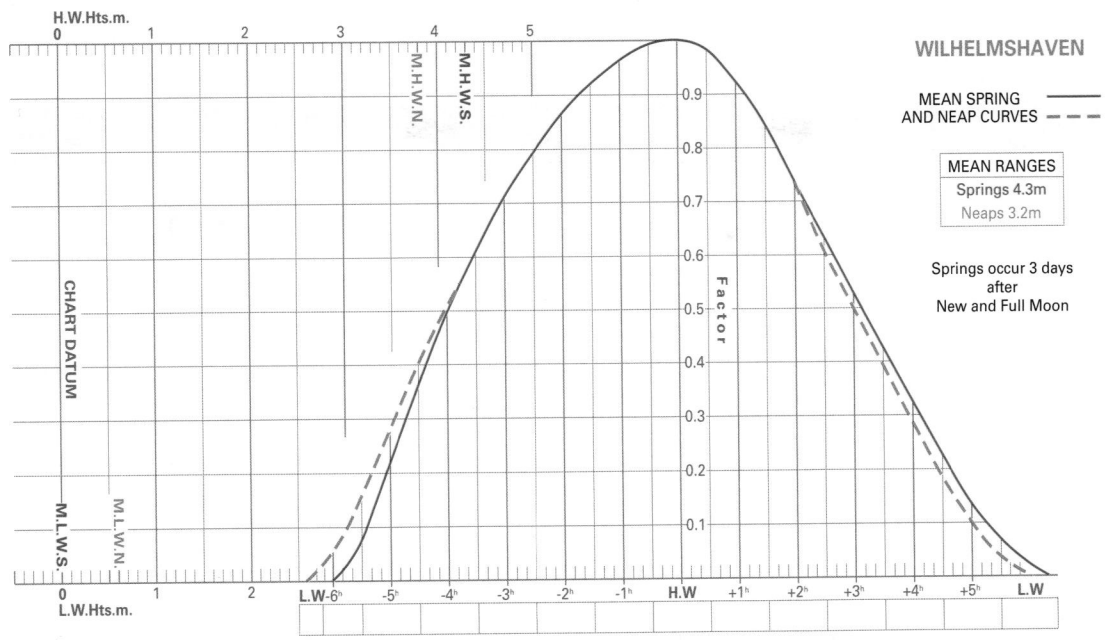

WILHELMSHAVEN

MEAN SPRING ⎯⎯⎯⎯
AND NEAP CURVES ⎯ ⎯ ⎯

MEAN RANGES
Springs 4.3m
Neaps 3.2m

Springs occur 3 days
after
New and Full Moon

9.15.17 WILHELMSHAVEN

Niedersachsen 53°30'·80N 08°09'·17E ✺✺✺⚓⚓⚓✿✿

CHARTS AC 3617, 3618; Imray C26; D7; BSH 3011.3/4, 3015.12

TIDES +0050 Dover; ML 2·3; Duration 0615
WILHELMSHAVEN is a Standard Port. (⟶).

SHELTER Good in yacht hbrs at Nordhafen (rather remote) and Großer Hafen. Access via sea lock which opens H24 at 1 hr's notice. No yacht berths in Neuer Vorhafen (naval port). Nassauhafen in the tidal hbr (*Fluthafen*) has yacht pontoons in about 1·7m, access H24.

NAVIGATION WPT 'A' 53°35'·71N 08°09'·98E (No 45 SHM buoy, QG), 175°/4.4M to WPT 'B' 53°31'·34N 08°10'·57E whence the Fluthafen ent bears 235°/9ca. The fairway is deep, wide and well marked.

Ems-Jade Canal: 39M from Großer Hafen to Emden, can be used by de-masted yachts; max draft 1·7m, min air clearance 3·75m. It has 6 locks. Max speed 4kn.

LIGHTS AND MARKS Principal lts on R Jade, see 9.15.4. Other lts on chartlet.

R/T Port Ch **11** 16 (H24). Sea lock Ch **13**. Bridge opening Ch **11**. See Fig. 9.15.16B above for VTS, broadcast info, radar assistance.

TELEPHONE (Code 04421) HM 154580; Naval base/Port Captain 684923 (operator); Sealock 7557620; VTS 4891281; ⊖ 480723; Weather Bremerhaven 72220; Water Police 942358; Ⓗ 8011; Brit Consul (040) 446071.

FACILITIES Berthing fee at all marinas is €1.70/m. **Nassauhafen Marina** ☎ 41439. 28 + 100 ✔, P, D, BY, Slip, ME, SM, Bar, R. **Wiking Sportsboothafen** ☎ 41301. 30 AB, CH, El, Gaz, ME, SM, ▱, ✕, Bar, R. **Hochsee YC Germania** ☎ 44121. There are 16 YCs in the area. **City** BY, SM, ME, CH, El, Gaz, ▱, ✉, Ⓑ, ⇌, ✈.

Germany

TIME ZONE -0100
Subtract 1 hour for UT
For German Summer Time add
ONE hour in **non-shaded areas**

WILHELMSHAVEN   LAT 53°31'N   LONG 8°09'E
TIMES AND HEIGHTS OF HIGH AND LOW WATERS

Dates in red are **SPRINGS**
Dates in blue are NEAPS

YEAR 2010

JANUARY

Time	m		Time	m
1 0032	4.9	**16** 0119	4.9
0653	0.8	0835	0.8
F 1304	4.7	SA 1349	4.6
1915	0.8	1954	0.8
2 0124	5.0	**17** 0156	4.9
0750	0.7	0818	0.7
SA 1359	4.7	SU 1425	4.6
2009	0.8	2028	0.7
3 0215	5.1	**18** 0230	4.9
0846	0.6	0852	0.6
SU 1452	4.7	M 1456	4.6
2059	0.6	2057	0.7
4 0304	5.1	**19** 0301	4.9
0936	0.5	0921	0.6
M 1541	4.6	TU 1523	4.5
2143	0.6	2122	0.6
5 0349	5.0	**20** 0331	4.8
1017	0.4	0948	0.6
TU 1625	4.5	W 1551	4.4
2222	0.6	2148	0.7
6 0432	5.0	**21** 0401	4.7
1056	0.5	1017	0.7
W 1708	4.4	TH 1620	4.4
2303	0.7	2220	0.8
7 0517	4.9	**22** 0432	4.7
1138	0.6	1046	0.7
TH 1753	4.4	F 1650	4.4
◑ 2347	0.8	2250	0.9
8 0606	4.8	**23** 0502	4.6
1223	0.8	1113	0.8
F 1841	4.3	SA 1723	4.3
		◐ 2321	1.0
9 0037	1.0	**24** 0541	4.4
0701	4.7	1148	0.9
SA 1315	1.0	SU 1809	4.2
1937	4.3		
10 0137	1.1	**25** 0009	1.1
0808	4.6	0639	4.3
SU 1422	1.2	M 1247	1.1
2045	4.4	1917	4.2
11 0251	1.3	**26** 0122	1.2
0922	4.5	0758	4.3
M 1537	1.3	TU 1407	1.2
2156	4.5	2040	4.3
12 0408	1.3	**27** 0250	1.2
1034	4.6	0925	4.4
TU 1647	1.2	W 1534	1.1
2300	4.7	2204	4.5
13 0517	1.1	**28** 0418	1.0
1135	4.6	1046	4.6
W 1746	1.1	TH 1656	1.0
2353	4.8	2318	4.7
14 0614	1.0	**29** 0537	0.8
1226	4.6	1157	4.6
TH 1836	1.0	F 1807	0.9
15 0039	4.9	**30** 0021	4.9
0701	0.9	0644	0.7
F 1310	4.6	SA 1258	4.7
● 1917	0.9	○ 1907	0.8
		31 0115	5.0
		0742	0.5
		SU 1352	4.7
		2000	0.6

FEBRUARY

Time	m		Time	m
1 0205	5.1	**16** 0211	4.9
0835	0.4	0829	0.5
M 1441	4.7	TU 1435	4.6
2049	0.5	2036	0.5
2 0253	5.1	**17** 0239	4.9
0923	0.3	0857	0.5
TU 1527	4.7	W 1501	4.6
2131	0.4	2101	0.5
3 0337	5.1	**18** 0308	4.8
1004	0.3	0923	0.5
W 1607	4.6	TH 1528	4.5
2208	0.4	2128	0.5
4 0418	5.0	**19** 0339	4.7
1038	0.4	0952	0.5
TH 1645	4.5	F 1557	4.5
2243	0.5	2159	0.6
5 0457	4.9	**20** 0410	4.7
1112	0.6	1020	0.6
F 1721	4.5	SA 1624	4.5
2319	0.6	2228	0.6
6 0537	4.8	**21** 0438	4.6
1147	0.8	1043	0.6
SA 1759	4.4	SU 1651	4.4
◑ 2357	0.7	2252	0.7
7 0622	4.6	**22** 0509	4.4
1227	1.0	1110	0.8
SU 1848	4.3	M 1729	4.3
		◐ 2329	0.9
8 0048	1.1	**23** 0602	4.3
0723	4.4	1203	1.1
M 1327	1.2	TU 1835	4.2
1955	4.3		
9 0202	1.3	**24** 0040	1.1
0842	4.3	0725	4.2
TU 1449	1.4	W 1329	1.2
2118	4.4	2006	4.3
10 0331	1.3	**25** 0218	1.1
1007	4.3	0902	4.3
W 1616	1.3	TH 1509	1.2
2236	4.6	2142	4.5
11 0454	1.2	**26** 0358	1.0
1119	4.4	1033	4.4
TH 1726	1.2	F 1640	1.0
2337	4.7	2304	4.7
12 0558	1.0	**27** 0524	0.7
1213	4.5	1147	4.6
F 1818	1.0	SA 1754	0.8
13 0023	4.8	**28** 0009	4.9
0645	0.8	0632	0.5
SA 1255	4.6	SU 1248	4.7
1900	0.8	○ 1854	0.6
14 0103	4.9		
0724	0.7		
SU 1332	4.6		
● 1936	0.7		
15 0139	4.9		
0758	0.6		
M 1406	4.6		
2008	0.6		

MARCH

Time	m		Time	m
1 0102	5.0	**16** 0112	4.8
0727	0.3	0728	0.4
M 1339	4.7	TU 1338	4.6
1945	0.4	1939	0.5
2 0150	5.1	**17** 0144	4.8
0815	0.2	0759	0.4
TU 1424	4.7	W 1408	4.6
2030	0.3	2010	0.4
3 0236	5.1	**18** 0214	4.8
0900	0.2	0827	0.4
W 1505	4.7	TH 1436	4.6
2111	0.2	2039	0.4
4 0318	5.0	**19** 0244	4.8
0940	0.3	0856	0.4
TH 1542	4.7	F 1504	4.6
2147	0.2	2108	0.4
5 0358	4.9	**20** 0318	4.7
1013	0.4	0926	0.4
F 1616	4.6	SA 1534	4.6
2219	0.3	2139	0.4
6 0434	4.8	**21** 0352	4.6
1043	0.5	0956	0.5
SA 1649	4.5	SU 1604	4.6
2251	0.5	2210	0.5
7 0510	4.6	**22** 0424	4.6
1111	0.7	1023	0.6
SU 1723	4.5	M 1633	4.5
◑ 2323	0.7	2238	0.6
8 0549	4.4	**23** 0459	4.4
1143	1.0	1053	0.8
M 1806	4.3	TU 1713	4.4
		◐ 2317	0.7
9 0007	0.9	**24** 0552	4.2
0644	4.2	1146	1.0
TU 1236	1.2	W 1819	4.3
1911	4.2		
10 0118	1.2	**25** 0027	0.9
0802	4.1	0713	4.1
W 1359	1.4	TH 1312	1.2
2037	4.3	1950	4.4
11 0252	1.2	**26** 0206	1.0
0933	4.1	0851	4.2
TH 1536	1.4	F 1454	1.1
2205	4.5	2127	4.5
12 0424	1.1	**27** 0345	0.8
1053	4.3	1021	4.4
F 1656	1.1	SA 1624	0.9
2313	4.6	2247	4.7
13 0532	0.8	**28** 0506	0.6
1150	4.4	1132	4.5
SA 1750	0.9	SU 1735	0.7
2359	4.7	2350	4.9
14 0617	0.7	**29** 0609	0.4
1230	4.5	1228	4.6
SU 1831	0.7	M 1832	0.5
15 0037	4.8	**30** 0043	4.9
0654	0.5	0703	0.2
M 1305	4.6	TU 1317	4.7
● 1906	0.6	○ 1923	0.4
		31 0131	5.0
		0749	0.2
		W 1400	4.7
		2007	0.3

APRIL

Time	m		Time	m
1 0215	5.0	**16** 0147	4.8
0832	0.2	0756	0.4
TH 1438	4.8	F 1409	4.7
2046	0.2	2015	0.4
2 0256	4.9	**17** 0222	4.7
0911	0.3	0829	0.4
F 1513	4.8	SA 1442	4.7
2122	0.2	2049	0.4
3 0335	4.8	**18** 0300	4.7
0944	0.4	0904	0.4
SA 1548	4.7	SU 1516	4.7
2155	0.3	2124	0.4
4 0412	4.6	**19** 0340	4.6
1011	0.5	0939	0.5
SU 1620	4.6	M 1551	4.7
2226	0.4	2201	0.4
5 0446	4.4	**20** 0420	4.5
1038	0.7	1014	0.6
M 1654	4.5	TU 1629	4.6
2258	0.6	2239	0.5
6 0523	4.2	**21** 0503	4.4
1110	0.9	1054	0.7
TU 1735	4.4	W 1715	4.6
◑ 2339	0.8	◐ 2326	0.6
7 0612	4.1	**22** 0558	4.2
1157	1.1	1149	0.9
W 1833	4.3	TH 1819	4.5
8 0042	1.0	**23** 0033	0.7
0721	3.9	0714	4.2
TH 1311	1.3	F 1308	1.0
1953	4.3	1943	4.5
9 0208	1.1	**24** 0200	0.8
0848	4.0	0841	4.2
F 1444	1.3	SA 1440	1.0
2120	4.4	2110	4.6
10 0338	1.0	**25** 0329	0.6
1010	4.1	1003	4.4
SA 1608	1.0	SU 1602	0.8
2232	4.5	2225	4.8
11 0447	0.7	**26** 0440	0.5
1110	4.3	1106	4.5
SU 1706	0.8	M 1707	0.6
2322	4.6	2324	4.8
12 0534	0.5	**27** 0538	0.4
1152	4.4	1159	4.6
M 1749	0.6	TU 1803	0.5
13 0000	4.7	**28** 0018	4.9
0612	0.5	0632	0.3
TU 1228	4.5	W 1249	4.7
1828	0.6	○ 1856	0.4
14 0038	4.7	**29** 0109	4.9
0649	0.4	0722	0.3
W 1303	4.6	TH 1333	4.8
● 1906	0.5	1942	0.3
15 0114	4.7	**30** 0154	4.9
0724	0.4	0804	0.3
TH 1337	4.7	F 1412	4.8
1941	0.4	2022	0.3

Chart Datum: 2·26 metres below Normal Null (German reference level). HAT is 4·5 metres above Chart Datum; see 4.5

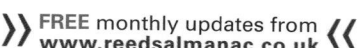

FREE monthly updates from
www.reedsalmanac.co.uk

TIME ZONE –0100
Subtract 1 hour for UT
For German Summer Time add
ONE hour in **non-shaded areas**

WILHELMSHAVEN LAT 53°31'N LONG 8°09'E
TIMES AND HEIGHTS OF HIGH AND LOW WATERS

Dates in **red** are SPRINGS
Dates in blue are NEAPS

YEAR **2010**

MAY

Time	m	Time	m
1 0234	4.8	**16** 0205	4.7
0841	0.4	0809	0.5
SA 1447	4.8	SU 1424	4.8
2057	0.3	2035	0.4
2 0313	4.7	**17** 0250	4.7
0914	0.5	0851	0.5
SU 1522	4.7	M 1505	4.8
2132	0.3	2118	0.4
3 0350	4.5	**18** 0335	4.6
0943	0.5	0932	0.5
M 1558	4.6	TU 1546	4.8
2206	0.4	2201	0.4
4 0426	4.3	**19** 0421	4.5
1013	0.6	1014	0.6
TU 1633	4.6	W 1630	4.8
2241	0.6	2246	0.5
5 0503	4.2	**20** 0510	4.4
1046	0.8	1059	0.7
W 1712	4.5	TH 1720	4.7
2321	0.7	2338	0.5
6 0545	4.1	**21** 0605	4.3
1129	1.0	1154	0.8
TH 1801	4.4	F 1821	4.7
◗			
7 0012	0.9	**22** 0038	0.6
0641	4.0	0711	4.2
F 1227	1.1	SA 1303	0.8
1906	4.3	1932	4.7
8 0119	0.9	**23** 0149	0.6
0753	3.9	0824	4.3
SA 1343	1.1	SU 1419	0.8
2023	4.3	2048	4.7
9 0236	0.8	**24** 0304	0.6
0909	4.0	0934	4.4
SU 1503	1.0	M 1533	0.8
2134	4.4	2156	4.8
10 0344	0.7	**25** 0410	0.6
1013	4.2	1035	4.6
M 1608	0.8	TU 1635	0.7
2230	4.5	2256	4.8
11 0438	0.5	**26** 0507	0.5
1102	4.4	1128	4.6
TU 1659	0.7	W 1733	0.6
2315	4.6	2353	4.8
12 0523	0.5	**27** 0602	0.5
1145	4.5	1219	4.7
W 1746	0.6	TH 1829	0.6
2359	4.7		
13 0607	0.5	**28** 0047	4.8
1226	4.6	0656	0.5
TH 1831	0.6	F 1308	4.8
		○ 1920	0.5
14 0042	4.7	**29** 0135	4.7
0649	0.5	0740	0.5
F 1306	4.7	SA 1349	4.8
● 1912	0.5	2001	0.4
15 0123	4.7	**30** 0216	4.7
0729	0.5	0816	0.5
SA 1344	4.8	SU 1426	4.8
1953	0.4	2038	0.4
		31 0254	4.6
		0851	0.6
		M 1502	4.8
		2115	0.4

JUNE

Time	m	Time	m
1 0331	4.5	**16** 0332	4.6
0923	0.6	0930	0.5
TU 1539	4.8	W 1543	4.9
2152	0.4	2203	0.3
2 0407	4.4	**17** 0419	4.5
0955	0.6	1013	0.5
W 1615	4.7	TH 1628	4.9
2227	0.6	2248	0.4
3 0442	4.3	**18** 0508	4.5
1028	0.7	1058	0.6
TH 1651	4.7	F 1718	4.9
2304	0.7	2337	0.5
4 0518	4.2	**19** 0559	4.4
1105	0.9	1150	0.7
F 1731	4.6	SA 1812	4.8
◗ 2343	0.8	◗	
5 0600	4.1	**20** 0030	0.5
1148	0.9	0654	4.3
SA 1819	4.4	SU 1246	0.7
		1912	4.8
6 0030	0.8	**21** 0127	0.6
0654	4.0	0754	4.4
SU 1244	1.0	M 1349	0.8
1919	4.4	2017	4.7
7 0129	0.8	**22** 0231	0.7
0759	4.1	0858	4.5
M 1352	1.0	TU 1457	0.8
2026	4.4	2126	4.7
8 0233	0.7	**23** 0337	0.7
0905	4.2	1001	4.6
TU 1502	0.9	W 1605	0.8
2130	4.5	2231	4.7
9 0336	0.7	**24** 0440	0.8
1005	4.3	1100	0.7
W 1605	0.8	TH 1709	0.8
2227	4.5	2332	4.7
10 0433	0.7	**25** 0539	0.8
1059	4.5	1155	4.8
TH 1703	0.7	F 1808	0.7
2321	4.6		
11 0528	0.7	**26** 0028	4.7
1150	4.6	0634	0.7
F 1757	0.7	SA 1246	4.8
		○ 1901	0.7
12 0013	4.7	**27** 0118	4.7
0620	0.6	0720	0.6
SA 1238	4.8	SU 1330	4.9
● 1848	0.6	1945	0.6
13 0104	4.7	**28** 0200	4.6
0708	0.6	0759	0.6
SU 1325	4.9	M 1410	4.9
1937	0.5	2025	0.5
14 0154	4.7	**29** 0238	4.6
0757	0.6	0835	0.6
M 1411	5.0	TU 1447	4.9
2029	0.5	2102	0.5
15 0244	4.7	**30** 0314	4.5
0846	0.6	0908	0.6
TU 1458	5.0	W 1522	4.9
2118	0.4	2137	0.5

JULY

Time	m	Time	m
1 0346	4.5	**16** 0409	4.6
0937	0.6	1005	0.4
TH 1555	4.8	F 1618	5.0
2209	0.6	2238	0.3
2 0416	4.4	**17** 0453	4.5
1006	0.6	1047	0.5
F 1627	4.7	SA 1703	4.9
2241	0.7	2322	0.5
3 0448	4.3	**18** 0538	4.5
1040	0.8	1132	0.6
SA 1700	4.7	SU 1751	4.9
2313	0.7	◗	
4 0522	4.3	**19** 0007	0.6
1115	0.8	0624	4.4
SU 1737	4.6	M 1219	0.7
◗ 2346	0.7	1842	4.7
5 0601	4.2	**20** 0054	0.8
1154	0.9	0715	4.4
M 1821	4.5	TU 1312	0.9
		1942	4.6
6 0027	0.8	**21** 0151	0.9
0652	4.2	0817	4.4
TU 1247	1.0	W 1419	1.0
1919	4.4	2054	4.6
7 0124	0.9	**22** 0303	1.1
0756	4.2	0929	4.5
W 1356	1.0	TH 1537	1.0
2029	4.4	2209	4.5
8 0234	0.9	**23** 0417	1.1
0907	4.3	1039	4.6
TH 1510	0.9	F 1651	1.0
2140	4.4	2318	4.6
9 0346	0.8	**24** 0523	1.0
1016	4.4	1139	4.8
F 1621	0.9	SA 1755	0.8
2248	4.5		
10 0455	0.8	**25** 0015	4.6
1120	4.6	0618	0.9
SA 1729	0.8	SU 1249	4.9
2352	4.6	1847	0.8
11 0558	0.8	**26** 0103	4.6
1218	4.8	0705	0.8
SU 1831	0.7	M 1313	4.9
●		○ 1932	0.7
12 0051	4.7	**27** 0144	4.6
0656	0.7	0745	0.7
M 1310	5.0	TU 1353	4.9
1928	0.6	2011	0.6
13 0145	4.7	**28** 0221	4.6
0750	0.6	0820	0.6
TU 1401	5.1	W 1429	4.9
2023	0.4	2046	0.5
14 0237	4.7	**29** 0253	4.6
0840	0.5	0851	0.6
W 1449	5.1	TH 1500	4.9
2114	0.3	2116	0.5
15 0325	4.7	**30** 0320	4.5
0925	0.4	0916	0.6
TH 1534	5.1	F 1529	4.9
2157	0.3	2143	0.5
		31 0347	4.5
		0942	0.6
		SA 1559	4.8
		2211	0.6

AUGUST

Time	m	Time	m
1 0416	4.5	**16** 0507	4.5
1013	0.7	1106	0.6
SU 1630	4.7	M 1724	4.8
2241	0.7	◗ 2335	0.7
2 0447	4.4	**17** 0547	4.5
1046	0.8	1146	0.7
M 1700	4.6	TU 1809	4.6
2308	0.7		
3 0517	4.4	**18** 0015	0.9
1115	0.8	0633	4.4
TU 1733	4.5	W 1233	0.9
◗ 2337	0.8	1906	4.4
4 0556	4.2	**19** 0107	1.1
1154	0.9	0735	4.3
W 1823	4.3	TH 1340	1.1
		2020	4.3
5 0025	1.0	**20** 0224	1.3
0655	4.2	0855	4.4
TH 1257	1.1	F 1507	1.2
1935	4.3	2146	4.3
6 0139	1.1	**21** 0352	1.3
0814	4.2	1017	4.6
F 1421	1.1	SA 1635	1.1
2101	4.3	2303	4.4
7 0306	1.0	**22** 0508	1.1
0939	4.4	1124	4.7
SA 1549	1.0	SU 1743	0.9
2224	4.4		
8 0430	1.0	**23** 0001	4.5
1056	4.6	0604	1.0
SU 1710	0.8	M 1212	4.8
2336	4.6	1832	0.8
9 0543	0.9	**24** 0044	4.6
1201	4.8	0646	0.8
M 1820	0.7	TU 1252	4.9
		○ 1912	0.7
10 0039	4.7	**25** 0121	4.6
0646	0.8	0723	0.7
TU 1256	5.0	W 1329	4.9
● 1919	0.5	1947	0.6
11 0133	4.7	**26** 0155	4.6
0740	0.6	0757	0.6
W 1346	5.1	TH 1403	4.9
2011	0.4	2019	0.5
12 0222	4.7	**27** 0225	4.6
0828	0.4	0827	0.5
TH 1433	5.1	F 1433	4.9
2059	0.3	2047	0.5
13 0308	4.7	**28** 0251	4.6
0911	0.3	0852	0.5
F 1518	5.1	SA 1500	4.8
2141	0.2	2113	0.5
14 0349	4.7	**29** 0316	4.5
0950	0.3	0917	0.5
SA 1600	5.0	SU 1529	4.7
2219	0.3	2140	0.6
15 0428	4.6	**30** 0344	4.5
1027	0.4	0947	0.6
SU 1641	4.9	M 1601	4.7
2257	0.5	2209	0.7
		31 0414	4.5
		1018	0.7
		TU 1630	4.6
		2235	0.8

Chart Datum: 2·26 metres below Normal Null (German reference level). HAT is 4·5 metres above Chart Datum; see 4.5

Germany

TIME ZONE -0100
Subtract 1 hour for UT
For German Summer Time add
ONE hour in **non-shaded areas**

WILHELMSHAVEN LAT 53°31'N LONG 8°09'E
TIMES AND HEIGHTS OF HIGH AND LOW WATERS

Dates in red are **SPRINGS**
Dates in blue are NEAPS

YEAR 2010

SEPTEMBER

Time	m		Time	m
1 0441	4.4	**16**	0554	4.4
1045	0.8		1101	1.0
W 1700	4.5	TH	1830	4.2
◑ 2300	0.9			
2 0515	4.3	**17**	0024	1.3
1117	0.9		0654	4.3
TH 1745	4.3	F	1303	1.2
2344	1.1		1943	4.1
3 0612	4.2	**18**	0141	1.5
1217	1.1		0817	4.3
F 1858	4.2	SA	1433	1.3
			2113	4.1
4 0101	1.2	**19**	0316	1.5
0737	4.2		0947	4.5
SA 1348	1.2	SU	1608	1.2
2033	4.2		2237	4.2
5 0238	1.2	**20**	0441	1.2
0912	4.4		1059	4.6
SU 1528	1.0	M	1720	0.9
2205	4.3		2336	4.4
6 0411	1.1	**21**	0538	1.0
1036	4.6		1146	4.7
M 1655	0.8	TU	1805	0.7
2321	4.5			
7 0528	0.9	**22**	0015	4.5
1143	4.8		0616	0.8
TU 1804	0.6	W	1221	4.8
			1839	0.6
8 0022	4.6	**23**	0048	4.5
0629	0.7		0651	0.7
W 1237	5.0	TH	1256	4.7
● 1901	0.4	○	1912	0.6
9 0114	4.7	**24**	0120	4.5
0722	0.5		0725	0.6
TH 1325	5.0	F	1330	4.7
1949	0.3		1945	0.5
10 0200	4.7	**25**	0152	4.6
0808	0.4		0758	0.6
F 1411	5.1	SA	1401	4.7
2035	0.3		2014	0.5
11 0242	4.8	**26**	0220	4.6
0850	0.3		0827	0.6
SA 1455	5.0	SU	1431	4.7
2118	0.3		2041	0.6
12 0322	4.7	**27**	0247	4.6
0928	0.3		0854	0.6
SU 1537	4.9	M	1502	4.6
2155	0.4		2110	0.6
13 0359	4.7	**28**	0315	4.6
1004	0.4		0923	0.6
M 1617	4.8	TU	1535	4.6
2228	0.6		2140	0.7
14 0434	4.6	**29**	0345	4.6
1039	0.6		0954	0.7
TU 1656	4.6	W	1607	4.5
2300	0.8		2208	0.8
15 0511	4.5	**30**	0415	4.5
1115	0.7		1024	0.8
W 1737	4.4	TH	1641	4.4
◗ 2334	1.0		2238	1.0

OCTOBER

Time	m		Time	m
1 0452	4.4	**16**	0616	4.3
1101	0.9		1229	1.2
F 1727	4.4	SA	1902	3.9
◑ 2324	1.2			
2 0550	4.3	**17**	0055	1.5
1201	1.1		0732	4.3
SA 1839	4.1	SU	1350	1.3
			2025	3.9
3 0040	1.3	**18**	0225	1.5
0714	4.3		0858	4.4
SU 1331	1.2	M	1520	1.2
2013	4.2		2148	4.1
4 0218	1.3	**19**	0351	1.3
0849	4.5		1013	4.5
M 1511	1.0	TU	1633	1.0
2146	4.3		2251	4.3
5 0351	1.1	**20**	0453	1.0
1012	4.6		1105	4.6
TU 1635	0.8	W	1721	0.8
2259	4.5		2333	4.4
6 0505	0.9	**21**	0534	0.8
1117	4.8		1141	4.6
W 1739	0.6	TH	1756	0.7
2356	4.6			
7 0604	0.7	**22**	0006	4.5
1211	4.9		0611	0.8
TH 1834	0.5	F	1216	4.6
●			1831	0.6
8 0046	4.7	**23**	0041	4.5
0656	0.5		0650	0.7
F 1300	4.9	SA	1253	4.6
1923	0.4	○	1907	0.6
9 0132	4.7	**24**	0116	4.6
0743	0.4		0727	0.7
SA 1347	4.9	SU	1329	4.7
2008	0.4		1940	0.6
10 0213	4.8	**25**	0149	4.7
0825	0.4		0801	0.6
SU 1431	4.9	M	1404	4.6
2050	0.4		2013	0.7
11 0251	4.8	**26**	0221	4.7
0904	0.4		0834	0.6
M 1513	4.8	TU	1440	4.6
2127	0.6		2046	0.7
12 0328	4.7	**27**	0253	4.7
0940	0.4		0906	0.6
TU 1553	4.6	W	1517	4.5
2158	0.6		2119	0.7
13 0404	4.6	**28**	0326	4.7
1014	0.5		0940	0.7
W 1630	4.4	TH	1554	4.4
2227	0.8		2153	0.9
14 0440	4.5	**29**	0401	4.6
1049	0.7		1017	0.8
TH 1709	4.2	F	1634	4.4
◗ 2300	1.1		2230	1.0
15 0521	4.4	**30**	0444	4.6
1131	1.0		1101	0.9
F 1757	4.0	SA	1723	4.2
2346	1.3	◑	2319	1.2
		31	0541	4.5
			1200	1.0
		SU	1830	4.1

NOVEMBER

Time	m		Time	m
1 0029	1.3	**16**	0121	1.4
0658	4.5		0754	4.3
M 1319	1.1	TU	1413	1.2
1954	4.2		2038	4.0
2 0158	1.3	**17**	0240	1.3
0824	4.6		0907	4.4
TU 1448	1.0	W	1524	1.1
2118	4.3		2146	4.2
3 0324	1.1	**18**	0350	1.1
0942	4.7		1007	4.5
W 1606	0.8	TH	1620	0.9
2228	4.5		2238	4.3
4 0434	0.9	**19**	0443	1.0
1046	4.8		1053	4.5
TH 1707	0.7	F	1706	0.8
2324	4.6		2321	4.5
5 0532	0.8	**20**	0530	0.9
1141	4.8		1136	4.6
F 1803	0.6	SA	1749	0.8
6 0014	4.7	**21**	0002	4.6
0627	0.7		0615	0.9
SA 1234	4.8	SU	1219	4.6
● 1856	0.6	○	1831	0.8
7 0102	4.7	**22**	0042	4.6
0717	0.6		0657	0.8
SU 1324	4.8	M	1301	4.6
1942	0.6		1911	0.8
8 0144	4.8	**23**	0121	4.7
0801	0.5		0737	0.7
M 1408	4.8	TU	1342	4.6
2022	0.6		1951	0.8
9 0223	4.8	**24**	0200	4.8
0840	0.5		0819	0.7
TU 1450	4.7	W	1425	4.6
2059	0.7		2032	0.8
10 0301	4.8	**25**	0239	4.8
0917	0.5		0900	0.7
W 1530	4.5	TH	1507	4.6
2131	0.7		2111	0.8
11 0339	4.7	**26**	0317	4.8
0954	0.6		0938	0.7
TH 1608	4.4	F	1549	4.5
2201	1.0		2148	0.8
12 0416	4.6	**27**	0356	4.8
1030	0.7		1018	0.7
F 1645	4.2	SA	1632	4.4
2235	1.0		2229	1.0
13 0454	4.5	**28**	0441	4.8
1109	0.9		1104	0.8
SA 1726	4.1	SU	1721	4.3
◗ 2315	1.2	◗	2317	1.1
14 0541	4.4	**29**	0535	4.7
1157	1.1		1158	0.9
SU 1818	4.0	M	1820	4.2
15 0010	1.4	**30**	0018	1.2
0641	4.3		0640	4.7
M 1259	1.2	TU	1303	0.9
1924	3.9		1929	4.2

DECEMBER

Time	m		Time	m
1 0131	1.2	**16**	0123	1.3
0754	4.7		0751	4.3
W 1417	1.0	TH	1404	1.0
2042	4.4		2029	4.2
2 0248	1.2	**17**	0236	1.3
0908	4.7		0859	4.4
TH 1530	0.9	F	1510	1.1
2150	4.5		2135	4.3
3 0358	1.0	**18**	0344	1.1
1014	4.7		1000	4.4
F 1635	0.9	SA	1612	1.0
2250	4.6		2233	4.4
4 0501	0.9	**19**	0444	1.0
1115	4.7		1056	4.5
SA 1734	0.8	SU	1708	1.0
2345	4.7		2325	4.6
5 0601	0.8	**20**	0539	1.0
1212	4.7		1148	4.6
SU 1831	0.8	M	1800	0.9
●				
6 0036	4.8	**21**	0014	4.7
0655	0.7		0630	0.9
M 1304	4.7	TU	1239	4.6
1919	0.7	○	1849	0.9
7 0121	4.8	**22**	0100	4.8
0740	0.7		0719	0.8
TU 1349	4.7	W	1327	4.6
1959	0.7		1937	0.9
8 0200	4.8	**23**	0145	4.9
0820	0.7		0809	0.7
W 1430	4.6	TH	1415	4.7
2036	0.8		2024	0.8
9 0239	4.8	**24**	0230	5.0
0900	0.6		0858	0.7
TH 1510	4.5	F	1501	4.6
2112	0.8		2108	0.7
10 0318	4.8	**25**	0311	5.0
0939	0.6		0939	0.6
F 1548	4.4	SA	1544	4.6
2144	0.8		2146	0.7
11 0355	4.8	**26**	0352	5.0
1014	0.7		1018	0.6
SA 1622	4.3	SU	1627	4.5
2214	0.9		2225	0.8
12 0430	4.7	**27**	0435	4.9
1048	0.9		1100	0.7
SU 1655	4.2	M	1713	4.4
2248	1.0		2310	0.9
13 0507	4.6	**28**	0524	4.9
1125	1.0		1147	0.8
M 1733	4.1	TU	1802	4.4
◗ 2327	1.2	◗		
14 0551	4.5	**29**	0001	1.0
1207	1.1		0619	4.8
TU 1821	4.0	W	1239	0.9
			1857	4.3
15 0017	1.3	**30**	0059	1.1
0645	4.4		0721	4.7
W 1300	1.2	TH	1340	1.0
1922	4.1		2001	4.4
		31	0207	1.2
			0833	4.6
		F	1451	1.1
			2111	4.5

Chart Datum: 2·26 metres below Normal Null (German reference level). HAT is 4·5 metres above Chart Datum; see 4.5

9.15.18   EAST FRISIAN ISLANDS

CHARTS AC 1635, 1875 and 3631 cover the E Frisians at small to medium scales. BSH 3015, sheets 4 to 9, give excellent cover at 1:50,000 with many larger scale insets of the harbours. The *Hafenhandbuch Nordsee* is the most detailed harbour guide with excellent chartlets and aerial shots. It also covers from Calais to Trondheim, Norway.

GEOGRAPHY The East Frisians (*Die Ostfriesischen Inseln*) lie from 3 to 11M off the German coast and were once the N coast of the German mainland. Shoals extend seaward for 2 or more miles in places. Groynes and sea defences are on their W and NW sides. Their bare sand dunes are not easy to identify, so the few conspic landmarks must be carefully selected.

The area between the low-lying islands and the mainland coast is called the *Watten*, ie the watersheds or watts between the islands and the mainland (where the tidal streams meet having swept both ways round the island, usually about ⅓ of the way from the E end). The gaps between the islands are called *Seegats*. They vary in position and depth, and all of them are dangerous on the ebb tide, even in a moderate onshore wind, or in winds >F4 with any N in them.

Cruising between the islands and the mainland is generally only for shoal draft boats able to take the ground. Vessels drawing more than 1·4m are likely to be constrained by their draft. For navigating inside the islands in the shoal or partly drying *wattfahrenwassern* (watt chans), the large scale German leisure charts (BSH) are essential.

TIDES The general strategy, whether E or W-bound, is to leave as early as possible on the flood (dependent on distance) so as to reach your destination or negotiate the shallowest part of the *wattfahrenwassern* near HW. Springs occur around midday and give approx 0·5m more water than neaps.

▶*Streams are very slack over the watts but very strong in the seegats, especially on a sp ebb.*◀

Persistent strong W/NW winds may raise the sea level by > 0·25m (exceptionally by 3m); against the ebb they cause steep dangerous seas over the bars near the entrance to the seegats. Strong E/SE winds can lower sea level by > 0·25m, dangerously reducing clearances.

WITHIES (*pricken*) are used to mark the *wattfahren-wassern*. Unbound withies (⚲, twigs pointing up) are PHMs, and bound withies (⚳, twigs pointing down) are SHMs.

The **conventional direction of buoyage is always Eastward,** even though in places this may conflict with the actual direction of the flood.

NATURE RESERVES inshore of most of the islands must not be entered. Seal and Bird reserves are closed as shown on the charts, but channels are excluded. The Waddenzee Nature Reserve extends from the mainland to the seaward margin of the drying flats.

National Parks are marked on the charts. Within them Zones 1 are closed from HW +3 to HW –3; landing is prohib year round.

PASSAGE INFORMATION *(See also individual entries)*

Alte Mellum, 3015.9, 6M SE of Wangerooge, where the rivers Weser and Jade meet, is part of a drying bird sanctuary; landing is prohibited.

Minsener Oog, 3015.9, 1·2·5M SE of Wangerooge, is two small islets linked by a causeway and with many groynes and a conspic radar twr. Beware overfalls in strong NW'lies. Blau Balje, between Minsener Oog and Wangerooge, is marked by buoys (prefixed 'B' and moved as necessary) but is dangerous in N winds. Seal (RSG) and Bird (VSG) reserves off the E end of Wangerooge are prohib areas (1/5–1/10 and 1/4–1/10 respectively).

Between **Spiekeroog** and **Langeoog**, 3015.8, the Otzumer Balje (buoys OB1-28/AH2) and unmarked Westerbalje chans lead inward. The former is usually deeper (min 3·5m) but both chans may silt up and should be used only in good weather and on a rising tide.

Acummer Ee, 3015.7, leads east of **Baltrum** to **Langeoog** and to **Bensersiel** and **Dornumer-Accumersiel** on the mainland. It is buoyed (A1-A32, moved as required). Shoals extend 2M offshore, depths in the channel vary greatly and it is prone to silting. *In onshore winds the sea breaks on the bar (0·8m) between A1 and A1a.*

Norderneyer Seegat, 3015.6, lies between **Norderney** and **Juist**, but is approached across dangerous offshore shoals (Norder-gründe and Nordwestgründe), via two shallow buoyed channels, Dovetief and Schluchter. Dovetief, from the NNE (buoys D1-44) is the main chan, but Schluchter from the WNW (buoys S1-D5/S8) is better protected in NE'lies. *Depths vary considerably and at times the channels silt up and buoys are lifted. Neither channel should be used in strong winds.* Further inshore, Norderneyer Seegat, now 14–11m deep, hugs the W end of the island and round to Norderney harbour. Beware groynes along the shore.

SW of Norderney, 3015.5, Busetief (buoys B1-24) is deeper than Dovetief and Schluchter. It leads generally S'ward to **Norddeich**, a tidal mainland hbr (2·0m). Norddeich can also be approached with sufficient rise of tide from Osterems via Bantsbalje and the Norddeicher Wattfahrwasser with a depth of about 1·6m at MHWN.

▶*The flood begins at HW Helgoland –0605, and the ebb at HW Helgoland –0040, sp rates 1kn.*◀

Juist, 3015.4, is the last of the chain of similar, long, narrow and low-lying islands. It has a small drying marina in the hbr mid-way along its southern side.

Memmert and **Kachelot**, S of Juist's W tip, and Lütje Horn, an islet E of Borkum, are bird sanctuaries; landing is prohibited.

Borkum (AC 3631 and 3015.3/4) lies between Osterems and Westerems channels, with high dunes each end so that at a distance it looks like two separate islands. Round the W end of Borkum are unmarked groynes, some extending 3ca offshore. Conspic landmarks, all at the W end of the island, include: Grosse and Neue beacons, a water tower, Borkum Grosser lt ho and two disused lt houses.

9.15.19 WANGEROOGE

EAST FRISIAN ISLANDS. See chartlet overleaf
Niedersachsen 53° 46'·46N 07° 52'·10E ❀❀◊◊❀❀

CHARTS AC 1635, 1875, 3617A; Imray C26; D2; BSH 3015.8/9.

TIDES   E Wangerooge, –0009 Dover; ML 1·9. Duration 0600
W Wangerooge, –0014 Dover; ML 1·5

Standard Port WILHELMSHAVEN (←)

Times				Height (metres)			
High Water		Low Water		MHWS	MHWN	MLWN	MLWS
0200	0800	0200	0900	4·3	3·8	0·6	0·0
1400	2000	1400	2100				
Differences MELLUMPLATE (53°46'·0N 08°06'·0E)							
–0046	–0042	–0016	–0024	–0·4	–0·3	+0·4	+0·5
EAST WANGEROOGE							
–0058	–0053	–0024	–0034	–0·5	–0·4	+0·5	+0·4
WEST WANGEROOGE							
–0101	–0058	–0035	–0045	–0·6	–0·5	+0·4	+0·4

SHELTER Good in most winds, but SW gales, and S'lies at HW, cause heavy swell and difficult conditions in hbr when **Harlesiel**, 4M S via Carolinensieler Balje, will be safer. Best access HW±2. Yachts on marina pontoons at E side of hbr have 1·3 to 1·8m depth; rafting no more than two deep. The W jetty is mainly for ferries but yachts >12m may request HM for a berth.

NAVIGATION WPT 53°49'·26N 07°48'·92E Harle SWM buoy, Iso 8s, 122°/8½ca to H2 buoy; 207°/1·4M to H10 buoy; 154°/8ca to Buhne H WCM buoy, VQ (9) 10s; lastly 141°/1M to H7/OB42 buoy and to hbr ent via D4. The Harle chan has least depth 0·4m near H4 buoy; it shifts and buoys are moved accordingly. Beware Buhne H (groyne), extending 7½ca, marked by WCM lt buoy

and in FR sector of Wangerooge lt ho, F WR; outer portion covers at HW.

LIGHTS AND MARKS Wangerooge lt ho, a R twr with two W bands, at the W end of the island has 3 co-located lts with separate characteristics: the main lt, Fl R 5s 60m 23M, with 360° coverage; a F WR sectored lt, showing R over Buhne H; and a F WRG directional light visible from the NW over Harleriff, whose sectors are not shown on the chartlet. See 9.15.4 for details. Conspic daymarks are the 52m high West Tower at the W end and a Sig Stn and disused lt ho in the centre of the island.

R/T HM VHF Ch 17, 0700-1700.

TELEPHONE (Code 04469) HM 630; Yacht Marina 942126 or Mobile (0172) 2622705; ⊖ 519; Weather Bremerhaven (0471) 72220; Police 205; Ambulance 112; Brit Consul (040) 446071; Dr 1700.

FACILITIES Wangerooge YC ☎ (0)172 2622705: €1.20, visitors tax introduced 2009; AC €3.00/day. M, Gaz. **Village** El, 🛒, CH, ▯, Ⓑ, ⇌ (ferry to Harlesiel), ✈ (to Harle and Helgoland). Ferry: Hamburg-Harwich.

MAINLAND HARBOUR 5M SSW OF WANGEROOGE

HARLESIEL, Niedersachsen, **53°42'·60N 07°48'·63E**. AC 1875, 3617; BSH 3015.8. HW –0100 on Dover (UT); HW (zone –0100) –0005 and ht +0·5m on Helgoland. Appr via Carolinensieler Balje which dries S of the training wall lt, L Fl 8s. Excellent shelter S of lock which opens approx HW ±1. 120 pontoon berths to W by village or at BY to E after passing through lock on W side of dyke. Lock, VHF Ch 17, 0700-2100. HM ☎ (04464) 472, berthing fees similar to Wangerooge (9.15.19); ⊖ ☎ (04462) 6154; YC ☎ 1473; Facilities: BY, C, Slip, P, D, FW. **Town** El, ME, Gaz, ✉, 🛒, R, ✈ and ferry to Wangerooge.

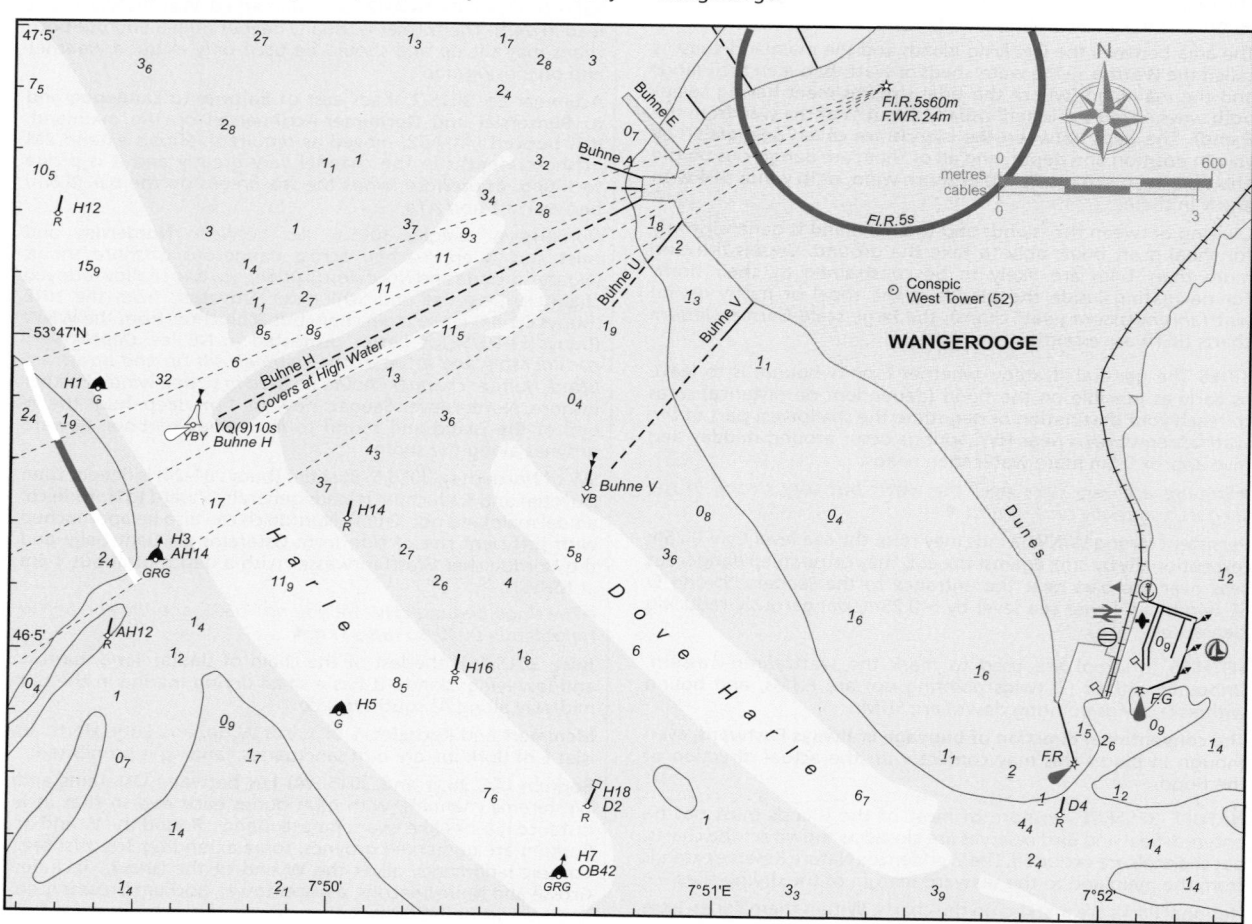

9.15.20 SPIEKEROOG

EAST FRISIAN ISLANDS ✻⚓♦♦✿✿
Niedersachsen **53°45'·00N 07°41'·27E** (ent to inner chan)

CHARTS AC 1635, 1875; Imray C26; D2 89; BSH 3015.8

TIDES HW –0008 on Dover; ML 1·3m; Duration 0555.

Standard Port HELGOLAND (⟵) See differences 9.15.22

SHELTER Good, *but S/SW winds cause heavy swell*. 3 yacht pontoons to the E of ferry berth almost dry to soft mud. Yachts >12m LOA should request a berth on the W jetty.

NAVIGATION WPT 53°48'·11N 07°37'·70E (Otzumer Balje SWM buoy, Iso 4s; often moved), 180°/0·2M to OB1 SHM buoy. Least depth on the bar (between OB2 and OB4) is about 3·5m. Otzumer Balje is well buoyed, but only 4 buoys are lit. The chan skirts the SW end of the island into Schillbalje and to ✫ FR, R mast (lat/long below title) at the ent to inner chan, marked by withies, which leads 020°/1M to small ferry hbr (0.8m).

Westerbalje, a shallow, unbuoyed secondary chan, is not advised.

Spiekeroog can also be approached from E and W via the Harlesieler and Neuharlingersieler Wattfahrwassern respectively.

LIGHTS AND MARKS Sand dunes near the W end of the island are up to 24m high, but the E end is low-lying (3m). Two bcns with spherical topmarks are near the centre and E end of island.

R/T None.

TELEPHONE (Code 04976) HM ☎ 9193 133 (0800-1800); British Consul (040) 446071.

FACILITIES Hbr is run by YC: 130 Ⓥ, €1.30, <4 hrs €5.00, AC €3.00/day; showers €1.00, C (15 ton), R. **Town** ½M from hbr. Neuharlingersiel by ferry.

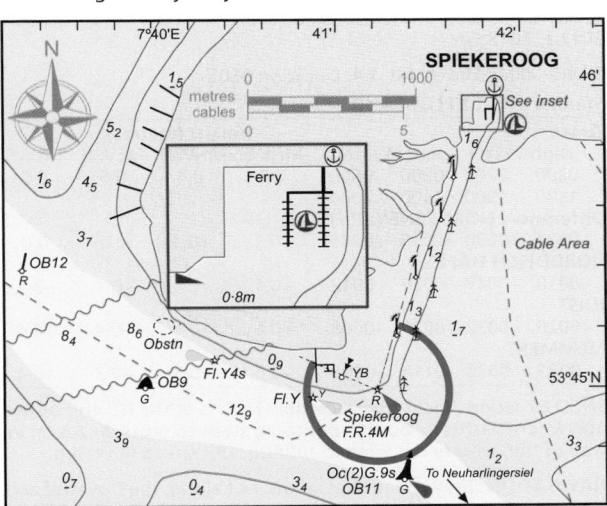

MAINLAND HARBOURS S AND SW OF SPIEKEROOG
NEUHARLINGERSIEL, Niedersachsen, **53°42'·10N 07°42'·29E**. AC 1635, 1875; BSH 3015.8. HW 0000 on Dover (UT); see differences under 9.15.22. Appr via Otzumer Balje and Schillbalje to N end of trng wall, Oc 6s. Training wall, 1M long, covers at HW and is marked by SHM withies ⚲. Beware strong tidal streams across the ent. Yachts lie in NE corner of hbr; very few Ⓥ berths. HM ☎ (04974) 289. Facilities: **Quay** FW, D. **Village** (picturesque) ⛟, R, Bar. Ferry to Spiekeroog (35 mins).

BENSERSIEL, Niedersachsen, **53°40'·81N 07°34'·20E**. AC 1635, 1875; BSH 3015.7E. HW –0024 on Dover (UT); +0005 on Helgoland (zone –0100); HW ht +0·4m on Helgoland. Appr as for Langeoog (9.15.22) thence lit/buoyed Rute chan to training walls with depth of 1·5m, but covering at HW. Very good shelter in the yacht hbr (0·7m) to stbd just before inner hbr ent (2m); also berths on the SW side of main hbr. Lts as 9.15.4. HM VHF Ch 17, ☎ (04971) 2502; Facilities: FW, C (8 ton), D (on E pier), P (cans), El, Slip, ME, ✖. **Town** Ⓑ, Bar, ✉, R, ⇌, ⛟, Gaz. Ferry to Langeoog.

9.15.21 DORNUMER-ACCUMERSIEL

Niedersachsen **53°40'·90N 07°29'·25E** ✻⚓♦♦✿✿

CHARTS AC 1635, 1875; Imray C26; D89; BSH 3015.7

TIDES –0040 Dover; ML 1·4; Duration 0600.

Standard Port HELGOLAND (⟵) Use differences Langeoog (9.15.22)

SHELTER The marina provides complete shelter in all winds; depth 3m, access HW ±4. Ent is narrow; keep to W of chan on entering. Marina is fenced so obtain a key before leaving.

NAVIGATION Appr through Accumer Ee (see 9.15.22) leading into Accumersieler Balje and to AB3 SHM buoy, IQ G 13s, 53°41'·44N 07°29'·27E. From here leave withies ⚲ and posts to stbd. Note warnings on German chart D89.

LIGHTS AND MARKS None.

R/T *German Bight Tfc* (VTS) broadcasts traffic and weather Ch 80 every H in German/English.

TELEPHONE (Code 04933) HM 2510; Deputy HM 441; ⊖ (04971) 7184; Lifeboat (04972) 247; Weather 0190 116048; Police 2218; Ⓗ 04941-940; Brit Consul (040) 446071.

FACILITIES Dornumer Yacht Haven, YC ☎ 2440. All facilities: 250 AB, Slip, C (20 ton), Gaz, D, ME, El, ✖, R; pontoons are lifted out of season. **Town** ⛟, R, Bar, ✉, Ⓑ, ⇌ (Harlesiel), ✈ (Bremen).

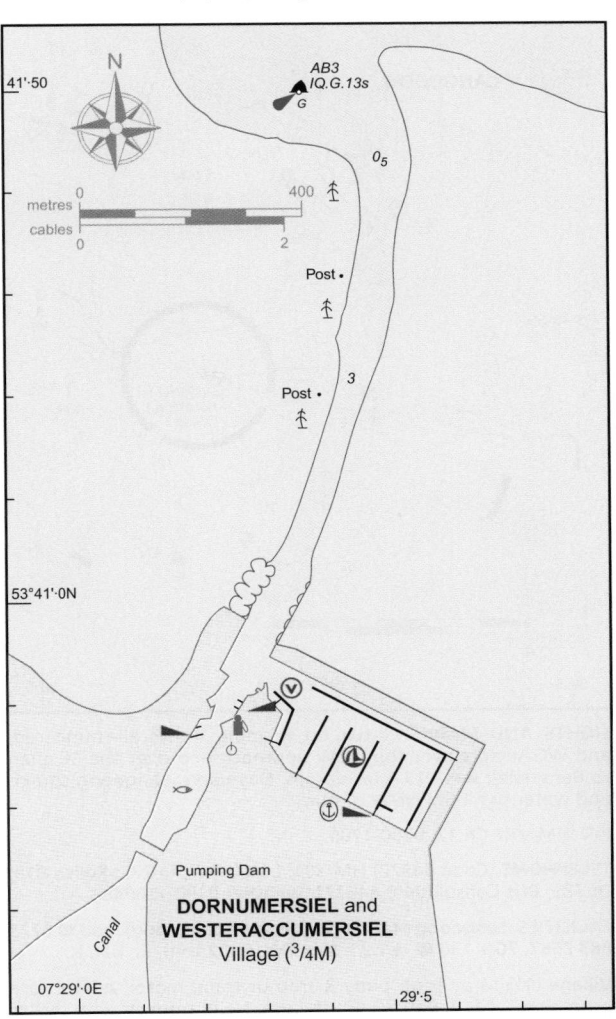

9.15.22 LANGEOOG

EAST FRISIAN ISLANDS
Niedersachsen 53°43'·38N 07°30'·12E ※⊕◊◊✿✿

CHARTS AC 1635, 1875; Imray C26; D89; BSH 3015.7

TIDES –0010 Dover; ML No data; Duration 0600

Standard Port HELGOLAND (←—)

Times				Height (metres)			
High Water		Low Water		MHWS	MHWN	MLWN	MLWS
0200	0700	0200	0800	2·7	2·4	0·5	0·0
1400	1900	1400	2000				
Differences LANGEOOG							
+0003	–0001	–0034	–0018	+0·3	+0·3	0·0	0·0
SPIEKEROOG							
+0003	–0003	–0031	–0012	+0·4	+0·3	–0·1	0·0
NEUHARLINGERSIEL							
+0014	+0008	–0024	–0013	+0·5	+0·4	–0·1	–0·1

SHELTER Hbr is well sheltered by 20m high sand dunes, but is open to the S. Marina dredged 1m; E part of hbr dries 1·5m; chan to ferry pier and marina and is marked by 4 SHM withies ↥.

NAVIGATION WPT 53°46'·96N 07°25'·91E [Accumer Ee SWM buoy, Iso 8s; moved frequently], approx 180°/5ca to A1–2 chan buoys; thence via buoyed chan to A9/B26 GRG buoy, Fl (2+1) G 15s. W sector of W mole lt leads 072°/1·4M to hbr ent. Ice protectors extend about 40m E of E mole, awash at HW, marked by withies. *Buoys shift frequently, call vess Berhard Gruben (Ch 16) for latest info.*

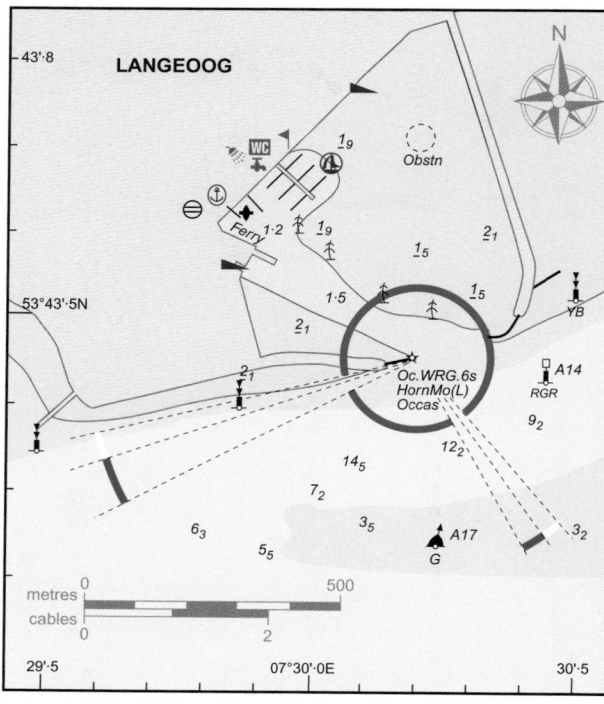

LIGHTS AND MARKS Lt twr on W mole shows all-round red, and WG sectors over the WSW approach and over the SE chan to Bensersiel; see 9.15.4 for details. Daymarks: Langeoog church and water twr 1·5M NNW of hbr.

R/T HM VHF Ch 17, 0700–1700.

TELEPHONE (Code 04972) HM 301; LB/CG 247; ⊖ 275; Police 810; Dr 589; Brit Consul (040) 446071; weather 0190 116048.

FACILITIES Langeoog Marina (Segelverein Langeoog) mob ☎ 0173 883 2567. 70 + 130 ☑, €1.21. Slip, FW, C (12 ton), El, Bar, R.

Village (1½ M by foot, pony & trap or train; motor vehicles are prohibited), 🛒, R, Bar, ✉, Ⓑ. ⇌ Local train connects with ferries to Bensersiel and Norddeich. ✈ Bremen.

ISLAND HARBOUR 3M NORTH OF NESSMERSIEL
BALTRUM, Niedersachsen, **53°43'·26N 07°21'·80E**. AC 1635, 1875; BSH 3015.6/7. HW –0040 on Dover (UT); Use differences Langeoog 9.15.22. The island is about 3 sq miles, 2·5M long, very low in the E and rising in the W to dunes about 15m high. Shelter is good except in strong SW'lies. Approach at HW via the Norderneyer Wattfahrwasser (which also gives access to Neßmersiel) running W-E, S of Norderney. The appr from seaward via the Wichter Ee is not advised without detailed local knowledge and ideal conditions. Tiny hbr partly dries. Yacht pontoons in 1·5m in the Bootshafen at the E end of hbr. HM ☎ (04939) 448; ⊖ ☎ (04939) 668. Facilities: Hbr AB, FW; Baltrumer Bootsclub YC. **Village** (¼M NNE) 🛒, R, Bar. No fuel. Ferry from Nessmersiel.

MAINLAND HARBOUR 5M WEST OF DORNUMER-ACCUMER
NESSMERSIEL, Niedersachsen, **53°41'·14N 07°21'·68E**. AC 1635; D89; BSH 3015.6; HW –0040 on Dover (UT); –0020 on Helgoland (zone –0100); HW ht –0·2m on Helgoland. Appr as for Baltrum above, thence via the buoyed Neßmersieler Balje, then marked by N3–N11 SHM buoys leading to end of trng wall, covers at HW. Here, a lt bn, Oc 4s 5M, and SHM ↥s and PHM ↥s mark the 6 cables long trng wall. Yachthafen with pontoons is on W side, beyond ferry quay. Good shelter in all weathers. Hbr dries (2m at HW). HM ☎ (04933) 1780. Facilities: **Nordsee YC Neßmersiel**; FW, but no supplies. **Village** (1M to S) has only limited facilities. Ferry to Baltrum.

9.15.23 NORDERNEY

EAST FRISIAN ISLANDS
Niedersachsen **53°41'·90N 07°09'·90E** ※⊕◊◊✿✿

CHARTS AC 1635; Imray C26; DYC 1812; Zeekarten 1353; D89; BSH 3012.1, 3015.5/6

TIDES –0042 Dover; ML 1·4; Duration 0605

Standard Port HELGOLAND (←—)

Times				Height (metres)			
High Water		Low Water		MHWS	MHWN	MLWN	MLWS
0200	0700	0200	0800	2·7	2·4	0·5	0·0
1400	1900	1400	2000				
Differences NORDERNEY (RIFFGAT)							
–0024	–0030	–0056	–0045	+0·1	+0·1	0.0	0·0
NORDDEICH HAFEN							
–0018	–0017	–0029	–0012	+0·1	+0·1	–0·1	–0·1
JUIST							
–0026	–0032	–0019	–0008	+0·6	+0·5	+0·4	+0·4
MEMMERT							
–0032	–0038	–0114	–0103	+0·5	+0·5	+0·3	+0·4

SHELTER Good. Yacht hbr, accessible H24, is at the NE end of the hbr, where yachts lie bow to pontoon, stern to posts; or AB on W wall of hbr, as very crowded in Jul/Aug. Hbr speed limit 3kn.

NAVIGATION Tidal streams set across, not along, the Dovetief and Schluchter. **From N/E**, WPT 53°45'·48N 07°12'·70E (Dovetief SWM buoy, Iso 4s), 227°/2·7M to D8 PHM buoy, Oc (2) R 9s. Ent through the Dovetief (see 9.15.5) well buoyed but the bar (3·1m) *can be dangerous in onshore winds & following seas which break on it, esp. on the ebb.*

From W, WPT 53°44'·48N 07°02'·27E (Schluchter SWM buoy, Iso 8s), 121°/2·1M to S1 SHM buoy, Oc (2) G 9s. *Ent at night is dangerous.* Both chans meet at D5/S8 GRG buoy, Fl (2+1) G 15s.

LIGHTS AND MARKS Lts, see 9.15.4. Land marks: lt ho, 8-sided R brick twr, near centre of island. Conspic water twr in town.

R/T Ch 17, Wed–Sun 0700 (0900 Tue)-1200; 1230–1900 (1730 Mon).

TELEPHONE (Code 04932) HM 83545, 0175 2785687; CG 2293; ⊖ 2386; Weather 549; Police 788; Ⓗ 477 and 416; Brit Consul (040) 446071.

FACILITIES Yacht Hbr C (10 ton), CH, SM, Slip, ME, El, ✗, P, D, Gaz, Wi-Fi; **Yacht Club** Bar. **Town** 🛒, R, Bar, ✉, Ⓑ. ⇌ (ferry to Norddeich), ✈ (to Bremen). Ferry: Hamburg-Harwich.

MAINLAND HARBOUR 7M SOUTH OF NORDERNEY

NORDDEICH, Niedersachsen, **53°38'·71N 07°08'·88E**. AC 1635, BSH 3012.1, 3015.5. HW –0030 on Dover (UT); See 9.15.23. Appr as for Norderney (9.15.23), then via buoyed/lit Busetief to two training walls (Lat/Long as above) which cover at HW and are marked by ƚs; see chartlet. The chan is 100m wide, 2·0m deep and 1.2M long. Very good shelter in hbr, divided by central mole. Yacht pontoons and ferry in W hbr; FVs in E hbr. Lts as in 9.15.4. HM VHF Ch 17, ☎ (04931) 81317; ⊖ ☎ (04931) 8435; YC ☎ 3560; Facilities: AB, C (5 ton), D ☎ 2721, FW, Slip, CH, BSH agent. **Town** ⑧, Bar, Dr, ✉, R, ⇌, 🛒, Gaz. Ferry to Juist and Norderney.

ISLAND HARBOUR 8M WEST OF NORDERNEY

JUIST, Niedersachsen, **53°39'·66N 06°59'83E**. AC 3631; D90; BSH 3012.1, 3015.4. HW –0105 on Dover (UT); HW –0035 and +0·1 on Helgoland; or use differences Memmert (see 9.15.23). Off the W end of Juist the unmarked Haaksgat leads into the Juister Balje which runs E for about 6M to Juist hbr.

The easier approach is via Norderney (9.15.23) passing the E tip of Juist and into Memmert and Juister Wattfahrwasseren. Enter hbr via a narrow chan running N into the centre of the S side of island, marked by a red post, Oc (2) R 9s, and by ECM perches to port.

Conspic marks are: West bn, on Haakdünen at W end of island, Juist water twr in centre and East bn, 1M from E end of island. Aero lt Fl 5s at the airfield, see 9.15.4.

There is a small, drying yacht hbr, or yachts can berth in 0.6m alongside quay in ferry hbr. There are extensive No-⚓ areas and underwater power cables, but many drying moorings close E of the hbr. HM ☎ (04935) 724; ⊖ ☎ 1321. Facilities: FW, Slip, C; villages of Ostdorf, Westdorf and Loog in centre of island have limited facilities, 🛒, R, Bar, Gaz. Ferry to Norddeich.

MAINLAND HARBOUR 15M EAST OF BORKUM

GREETSIEL, Niedersachsen, **53°32'·86N 07°02'·07E**. AC 1635, 3631; BSH 89, 3012.1, 3015.2 & .5 (plan). HW –0400 on Dover (UT), –0010 on Helgoland; ML 2·6m. WPT 53°41'·91N 06°36'·17E (Osterems SWM buoy, Iso 4s), 118°/1.2M to chan buoys (O1/O2), passing between Memmert and Borkum. Follow the Osterems chan for 17.5M to O30/L2 buoy; here turn ENE into the Ley chan for 2½M to L8 buoy. Turn 90° stbd to track 165°/7ca, between trng walls to lock which opens HW ±3. Thence 4M chan in 3m depths to Greetsiel, FV hbr and AB on marina pontoons (2m). HM ☎ (04926) 990371; ⊖ ☎ (04931) 2764. **Village** YC, Bar, R, 🛒, ⇌. A canal links Greetsiel to Emden.

9.15.24 BORKUM

EAST FRISIAN ISLANDS

Niedersachsen **53°33'·48N 06°45'·00E** ❀❀❀◊◊✿✿

CHARTS AC 1635, 3631; Imray C26; D90; BSH 3015.2/3/4; DYC 1812.5; ANWB A

TIDES –0105 Dover; ML 1·4; Duration 0610

Standard Port HELGOLAND (←)

Times				Height (metres)			
High Water		Low Water		MHWS	MHWN	MLWN	MLWS
0200	0700	0200	0800	2·7	2·4	0·5	0·0
1400	1900	1400	2000				
Differences BORKUM (FISCHERBALJE)							
–0048	–0052	–0124	–0105	+0·4	+0·4	+0·3	+0·4

SHELTER Good except in strong winds from S; access H24. Berth in Yacht Marina (reported to be silting up), entrance N of F7/F10 buoys, or in Burkana Hafen on steel pontoons wherever space allows. Yachts are not allowed to use the ferry basin (*Fährhafen*).

NAVIGATION From the N, WPT 53°38'·96N 06°27'·10E (Riffgat SWM buoy, Iso 8s), about 122°/11M to Fischerbalje lt. See also 9.16.7. **From the W** appr via the Westerems SWM buoy, Iso 4s, Racon (T) (53°36'·93N 06°19'·39E) to join Riffgat which is covered by the 127° W sector of Campen lt, Dir F. (Hubertgat is still marked (unlit R/W buoys H1-H5), least depths around 9m but prone to silting). Many groynes extend 400m off W end of Borkum. Make for Fischerbalje lt (see 9.15.4 for sectors) at the end of the trng wall which covers at HW. Use the dredged ferry channel and do not cut corners. Beware strong SW'lies and strong currents across the Fischerbalje chan (F1–9 buoys/partly lit). Speed limit in hbrs is 5kn.

LIGHTS AND MARKS Daymarks all WNW of hbr: Water twr, Grosser lt ho (brown brick twr) and disused Kleiner lt ho, R twr with W bands. 3 wind turbines 3ca NNE of Yacht Hbr ent.

R/T *Burkana Hafen* Ch 17. *Borkum Port* Ch 14 (In season: Mon-Fri 0700-2200; Sat 0800-2100; Sun 0700-2000).

TELEPHONE (Code 4922) Port HM 912828; ⊖ 2287; Police 91860; ⊞ 813; Brit Consul (040) 446071.

FACILITIES Yacht Hbr ☎ 7773. 50 + 200 ♥ AB, €1·20, Slip, D (cans), Gas, R, Bar, C (6 ton), 🛒, ◨, ⓖ, P, ME.
Burkana Hafen ☎ 7877. 80 AB (max 12m LOA), €1.30. D (cans via ☎ 7877), ◨.
Town (7km WNW) P, ME, El, Gaz, 🛒, R, Bar, ✉, ⑧. Ferry to Emden ⇌, ✈ (& Bremen). S part of island is a Nature Reserve.

RIVER EMS

(AC 3631, 3632) The Ems forms the Dutch-German border and is a major waterway leading to Eemshaven, Delfzijl, Emden, Leer and Papenburg. Approach via Hubertgat or Westerems, which meet W of Borkum; the former is unlit and sparsely buoyed. ▶*Both can be dangerous with a strong W/NW wind against the ebb. The flood begins at HW Helgoland +0530, and the ebb at HWH −0030, sp rates 1·5kn.*◀

Close SW of Borkum the chan divides: Randzel Gat to the NE side and Alte Ems parallel to it on the SW side – as far as Eemshaven on the S bank; here the stream runs 2-3kn. Keep in Ostfriesisches Gatje, the main chan, for Delfzijl and beyond.

Osterems is the unlit E branch of the Ems estuary, passing between Borkum and Memmert. It is shallower than Westerems and leads to Greetsiel via the Ley channel.

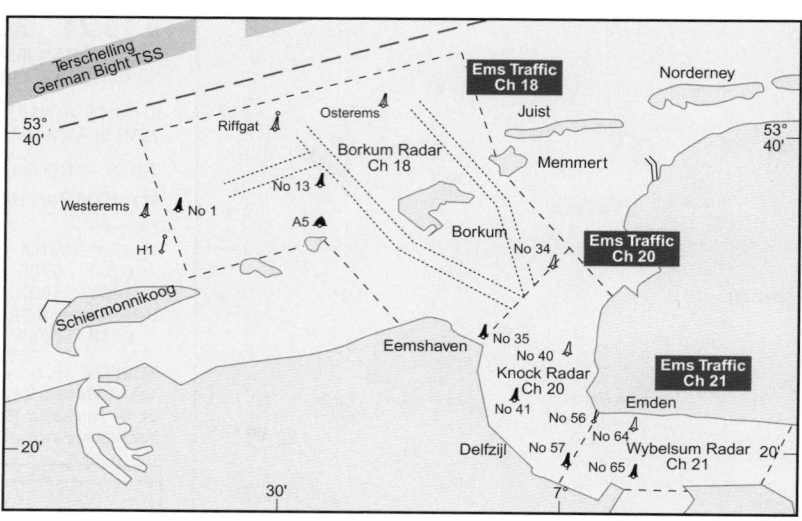

Fig 9.15.24. Ems VTS

9.15.25 EMDEN

Niedersachsen 53°20'·06N 07°10'·69E Hbr ent ✿✿✿✿⚓⚓✿✿

CHARTS AC 3631, 3632; Imray C26; D90, 91; BSH 3012.5/6

TIDES HW +0022 on Dover (UT); ML 1·9m

Standard Port HELGOLAND (◀——)

Times				Height (metres)			
High Water		Low Water		MHWS	MHWN	MLWN	MLWS
0200	0700	0200	0800	2·7	2·4	0·5	0·0
1400	1900	1400	2000				
Differences EMSHÖRN (53°29'·6N 06°50'·5E)							
−0037	−0041	−0108	−0047	+0·6	+0·5	+0·3	+0·4
DUKEGAT (53°26'·0N 06°56'·0E)							
−0019	−0023	−0047	−0028	+0·8	+0·8	+0·4	+0·5
KNOCK (53°19'·6N 07°00'·8E)							
+0018	+0005	−0028	+0004	+1·0	+1·0	+0·4	+0·4
EMDEN							
+0041	+0028	−0011	+0022	+1·3	+1·3	+0·4	+0·4

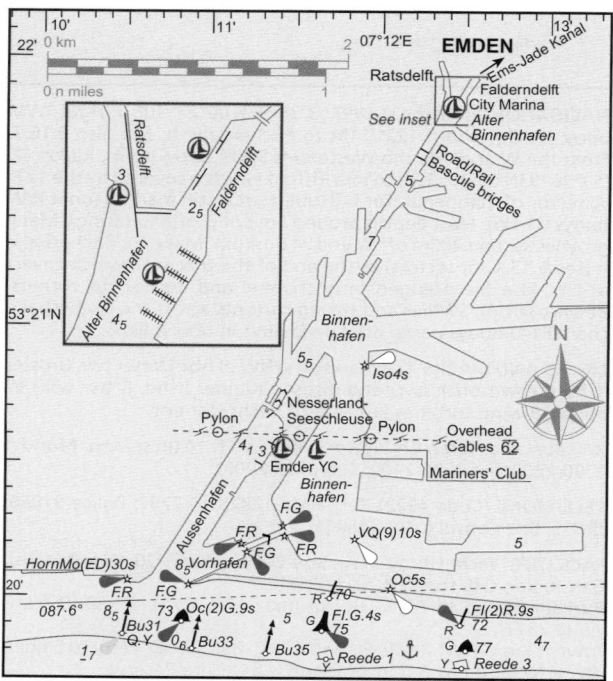

EMS VESSEL TRAFFIC SERVICE *Ems Traffic* broadcasts safety, traffic & weather info in German H+50 on Ch 15, 18, 20 and 21.

Radar advice for the Ems in German, or in English on request, is provided as follows:

Borkum Radar	Ch 18	Buoys 1–35;
Knock Radar	Ch 20	Buoys 35–57;
Wybelsum Radar	Ch 21	Buoy 57–Emden hbr.

SHELTER Good, although the Emder YC marina may be exposed to SSW winds.

NAVIGATION See Borkum and Delfzijl for outer approaches via well buoyed/lit R Ems to No 53 buoy 53°19'·34N 07°01'·15E, south abeam Knock lt ho. Thence 6M east to the hbr ent via Emder Fahrwasser (dredged 8·6m) with drying banks and training walls close outboard of chan buoys. Beware of fast catamaran ferries (*Hochgeschwindigkeitsfahrzeuge*).

Nesserland lock is closed probably until 2010. Enter Binnenhafen via Vorhafen lock ☎ 897265 which opens for small craft near HW, or with commercial traffic, or at other times if sufficient demand.

LIGHTS AND MARKS Fahrwasser outer ldg lts 075°, both Oc (2) 12s 16/28m 12M (at Logum, off chartlet). Inner ldg lts 088°, both Oc 5s 14/30m 12M, lead to hbr ent, marked by FR and FG lts and between Nos 71 and 73 buoys. HT cables on 3 conspic pylons (100m) cross the Außenhafen and Binnenhafen.

R/T Emden Hbr and Locks Ch 13 (H24). No VHF at individual marinas. See Ems VTS above.

TELEPHONE (Code 04921) HM 897260 (H24); Nesserlander lock ☎ 897270; Tourist Info 97400; Police 110; Fire/Ambulance 112; ⊖ 9279-0.

FACILITIES Berthing options from seaward:
Emder YC marina (3m) in the Außenhafen, just before Nesserland sealock. ☎ 997147, €0.77, 3 pontoons, most facilities, C. Through the large Vorhafen sealock for:

Mariners Club, small marina ☎ 0175 7112027, €0.51; no showers.

City Marina, access via two road/rail bridges opening 0650, 0855, 0955, 1140, 1335, 1555, 1735, 1820 and 2140LT on request. For opening sound M (− −). Marina, ☎ 8907211 or 0160 3624744, comprises Alter Binnenhafen (4·5m), Falderndelft (3m), Ratsdelft (3m); all near the city centre. The first two are best for yachts <12m. €0.80, ⬡, ⬡, ⚓. Diesel barge, for location in the hbr call ☎ 0171 324 4337. **City** all amenities. Ferry to Borkum.

CANALS The Ems-Jade canal, 39M to Wilhelmshaven, is usable by yachts with lowering masts and max draft 1·7m. Access at Emden via the Falderndelft. Min bridge clearance 3·75m. It has 6 locks. Speed limit 4kn.

Netherlands & Belgium

Delfzijl to Nieuwpoort

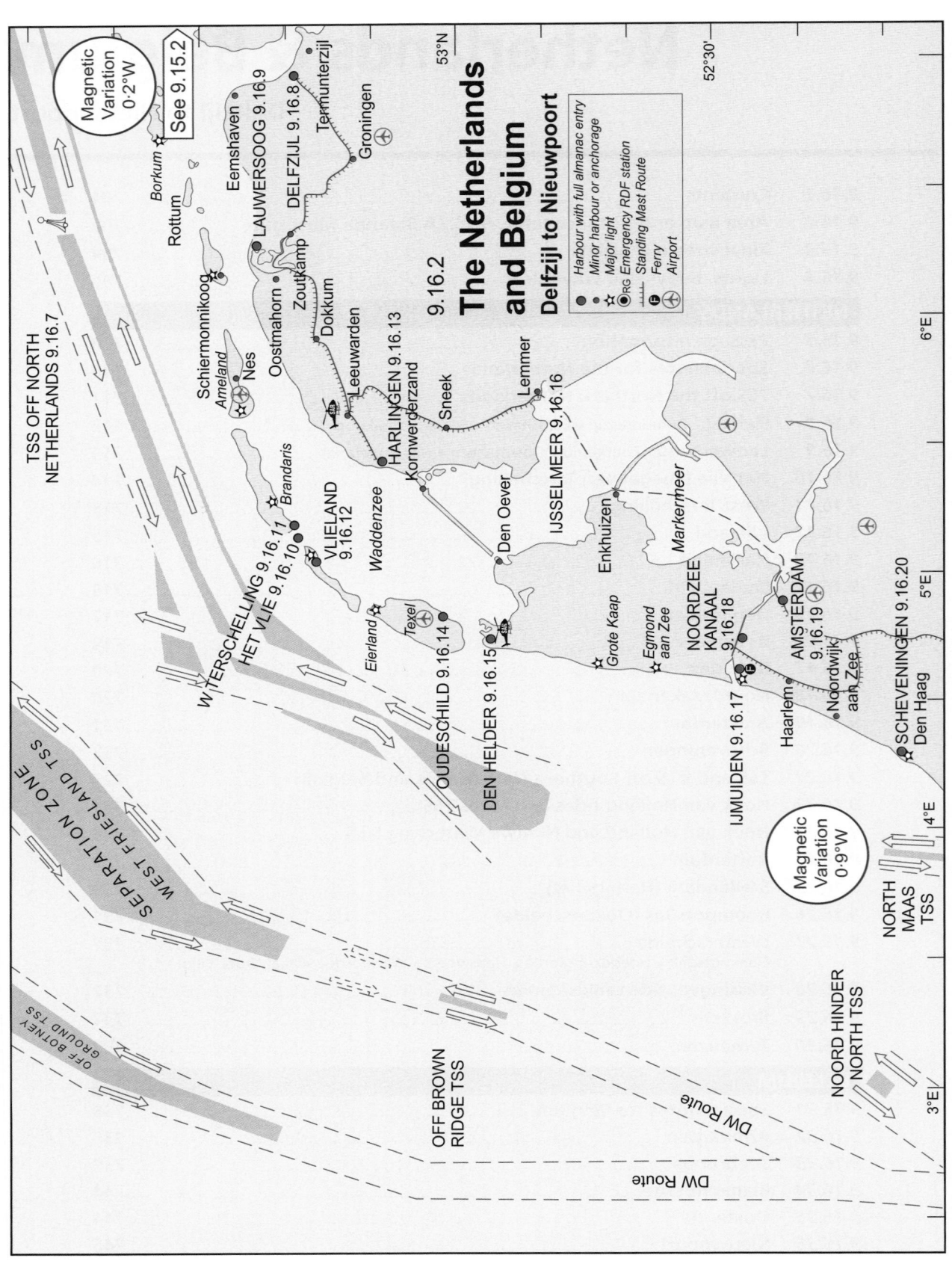

9.16.2
The Netherlands and Belgium
Delfzijl to Nieuwpoort

Harbour with full almanac entry
Minor harbour or anchorage
Major light
RG Emergency RDF station
Standing Mast Route
Ferry
Airport

Magnetic Variation 0·2'W
See 9.15.2

Magnetic Variation 0·9'W

53°N
52°30'
6°E
5°E
4°E
3°E

Borkum
Rottum
Eemshaven
Schiermonnikoog
LAUWERSOOG 9.16.9
DELFZIJL 9.16.8
Termunterzijl
Groningen
Zoutkamp
Oostmahorn
Dokkum
Leeuwarden
Ameland
Nes
HARLINGEN 9.16.13
Kornwerderzand
Sneek
Lemmer
IJSSELMEER 9.16.16
Brandaris
VLIELAND 9.16.12
Waddenzee
Den Oever
Enkhuizen
Markermeer
WITERSCHELLING 9.16.11
HET VLIE 9.16.10
Eierland
Texel
OUDESCHILD 9.16.14
DEN HELDER 9.16.15
Grote Kaap
Egmond aan Zee
NOORDZEE KANAAL 9.16.18
AMSTERDAM 9.16.19
Haarlem
Noordwijk aan Zee
SCHEVENINGEN 9.16.20
Den Haag
IJMUIDEN 9.16.17

TSS OFF NORTH NETHERLANDS 9.16.7
SEPARATION ZONE
WEST FRIESLAND TSS
OFF BOTNEY GROUND TSS
OFF BROWN RIDGE TSS
DW Route
DW Route
NORTH MAAS TSS
NOORD HINDER NORTH TSS

9.16.2A THE STAANDE MASTROUTE

The Standing Mast Route (SMR), which does not require masts to be lowered, can be a useful means of progressing, especially to windward, through the Dutch inland waterways when conditions at sea make this difficult or impossible. Inland the wind may be one or two Forces less and there is usually insufficient fetch to raise a bad sea. The open sea can always be regained at many points. It is a rewarding route and the added interest of progressing through the Dutch countryside and towns is a special bonus.

See also 9.15.2 for the German canals in parts of which masts have to be lowered.

Pre-planning. To minimise delays at bridges and locks and to have a fair idea of your next night-stop, buy the special SMR chart (wire-bound booklet) published by ANWB at €16.95; it contains detailed information in Dutch but the gist is clear. Michelin road maps give a broader 1: 200,000 perspective.

See also 9.16.6 for the ANWB Wateralmanak, Vols 1 and 2 in Dutch.

An International Certificate of Competence (ICC) is required endorsed for Inland Waters, ie CEVNI.

The Route falls broadly into a northern and a southern part, divided by the IJsselmeer/Markermeer. From Delfzijl the Eemskanaal leads to Groningen, thence via the Reitdiep (river) to Zoutkamp and across the Lauwersmeer. Leave via Dokkumer Ee to Leeuwarden where the sea can be regained at Harlingen. If not, continue S past Sneek to enter the IJsselmeer at Lemmer. Cross via Enkhuizen to Amsterdam.

Getting through Amsterdam is complicated by severe restrictions on when bridges may open (due to heavy road/rail traffic). One option is a night convoy through the centre and suburbs. From Het IJ (9.16.19) enter the Westerkanaal near IJ2 buoy. Head SSW past Schiphol airport, Gouda and Rotterdam, thence to Dordrecht.

A simpler daytime option is to detour west via the Noordzeekanaal, turn south at Zijkanaal C through Haarlem and/or Leiden to resume the main route north of Gouda; thence via Rotterdam to Dordrecht.

S of Dordrecht enter Hollandsdiep at which point the SMR has virtually ended. Continue past Willemstad into Volkerak, thence across the Oosterschelde into Veerse Meer and down the Walcheren canal to Vlissingen.

DISTANCE TABLE

Approximate distances in nautical miles are by the most direct route, whilst avoiding dangers and allowing for Traffic Separation Schemes. Places in *italics* are in adjoining areas; places in **bold** are in 9.0.7, Distances across the North Sea.

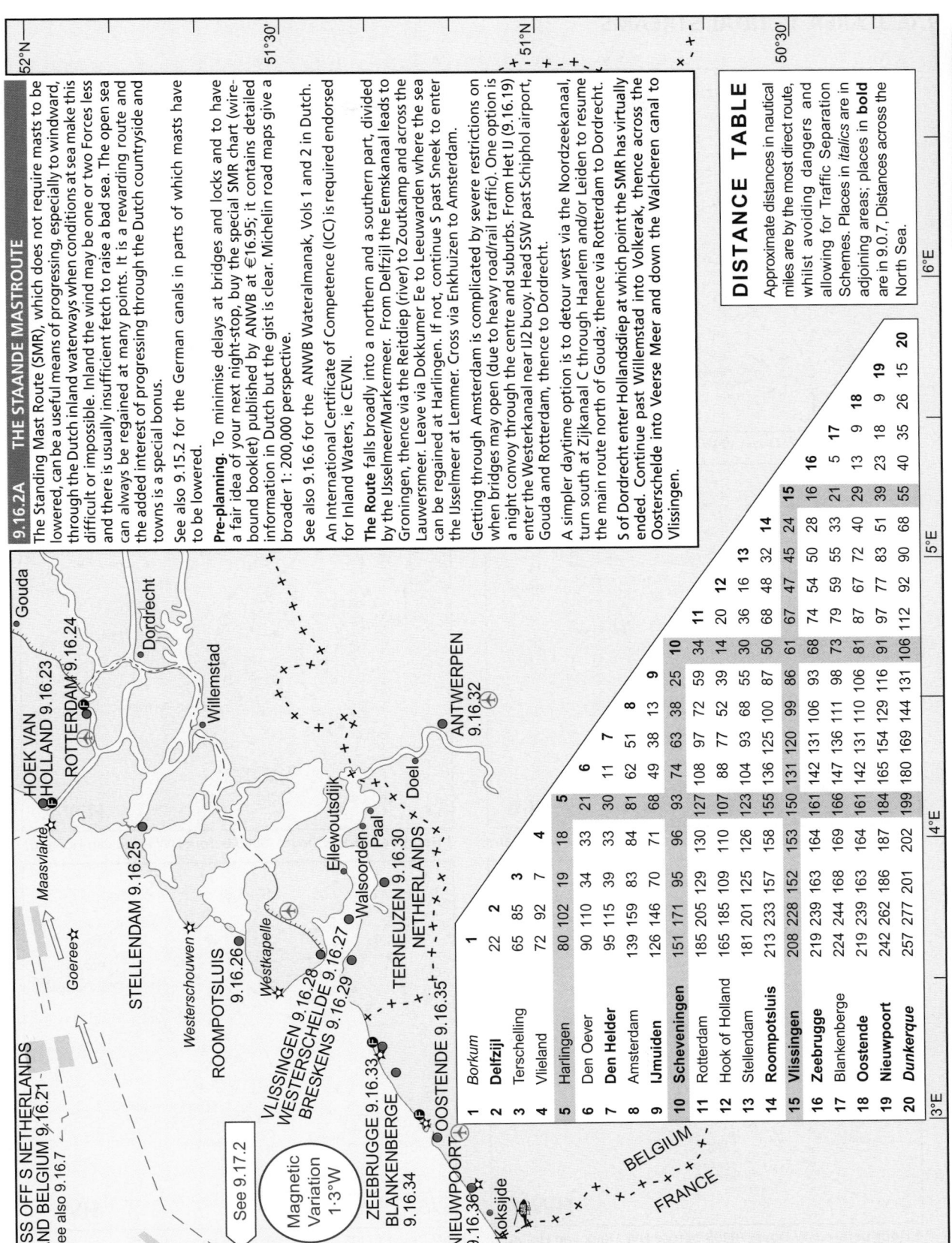

	1	2	3	4	5	6	7	8	9	10	11	12	13	14	15	16	17	18	19	20
1 *Borkum*	1																			
2 **Delfzijl**	22	2																		
3 Terschelling	65	85	3																	
4 Vlieland	72	92	7	4																
5 Harlingen	80	102	19	18	5															
6 Den Oever	90	110	34	33	21	6														
7 **Den Helder**	95	115	39	33	30	11	7													
8 Amsterdam	139	159	83	84	81	62	51	8												
9 IJmuiden	126	146	70	71	68	49	38	13	9											
10 **Scheveningen**	151	171	95	96	93	74	63	38	25	10										
11 Rotterdam	185	205	129	130	127	108	97	72	59	34	11									
12 Hook of Holland	165	185	109	110	107	88	77	52	39	14	20	12								
13 Stellendam	181	201	125	126	123	104	93	68	55	30	36	16	13							
14 **Roompotsluis**	213	233	157	158	155	136	125	100	87	50	68	48	32	14						
15 **Vlissingen**	208	228	152	153	150	131	120	99	86	61	67	47	45	24	15					
16 **Zeebrugge**	219	239	163	164	161	142	131	106	93	68	74	54	50	28	16	16				
17 Blankenberge	224	244	168	169	166	147	136	111	98	73	79	59	55	33	21	5	17			
18 **Oostende**	219	239	163	164	161	142	131	110	106	81	87	67	72	40	29	13	9	18		
19 Nieuwpoort	242	262	186	187	184	165	154	129	116	91	97	77	83	51	39	23	18	9	19	
20 *Dunkerque*	257	277	201	202	199	180	169	144	131	106	112	92	90	68	55	40	35	26	15	20

TSS OFF S NETHERLANDS AND BELGIUM 9.16.21 – See also 9.16.7

See 9.17.2

Magnetic Variation 1·3°W

Gouda
Dordrecht
HOEK VAN HOLLAND 9.16.23
ROTTERDAM 9.16.24
Willemstad
STELLENDAM 9.16.25
ANTWERPEN 9.16.32
Maasvlakte
Goeree
Westerschouwen
ROOMPOTSLUIS 9.16.26
Westkapelle
Ellewoutsdijk
Walsoorden
Paal
Doel
VLISSINGEN 9.16.28
WESTERSCHELDE 9.16.27
BRESKENS 9.16.29
TERNEUZEN 9.16.30
NETHERLANDS
OOSTENDE 9.16.35
ZEEBRUGGE 9.16.33
BLANKENBERGE 9.16.34
NIEUWPOORT 9.16.36
Koksijde
BELGIUM
FRANCE

52°N
51°30'
51°N
50°30'
3°E 4°E 5°E 6°E

9.16.3 AREA 16 TIDAL STREAMS

5 Hours before HW Dover (0420 after HW Hoek van Holland)

4 Hours before HW Dover (0520 after HW Hoek van Holland)

3 Hours before HW Dover (0605 before HW Hoek van Holland)

2 Hours before HW Dover (0505 before HW Hoek van Holland)

1 Hour before HW Dover (0405 before HW Hoek van Holland)

HW Dover (0305 before HW Hoek van Holland)

South-westward 9.17.3   North-westward 9.4.3   North-eastward 9.15.3

1 Hour after HW Dover (0205 before HW Hoek van Holland)

2 Hours after HW Dover (0105 before HW Hoek van Holland)

3 Hours after HW Dover (0005 after HW Hoek van Holland)

4 Hours after HW Dover (0055 after HW Hoek van Holland)

5 Hours after HW Dover (0155 after HW Hoek van Holland)

6 Hours after HW Dover (0255 after HW Hoek van Holland)

9.16.4 LIGHTS, BUOYS AND WAYPOINTS

Bold print = light with a nominal range of 15M or more.
CAPITALS = place or feature. *CAPITAL ITALICS* = light-vessel, light float or Lanby. *Italics* = Fog signal. ***Bold italics*** = Racon. Abbreviations are in Chapter 1.

TSS OFF NORTHERN NETHERLANDS
TERSCHELLING-GERMAN BIGHT TSS
TG1/Ems ⌀ IQ G 13s; 53°43'·33N 06°22'·24E.
TE5 ⬩ Fl (3) G 10s; 53°37'·79N 05°53'·69E.
TE1 ⬩ Fl (3) G 10s; 53°29'·58N 05°11'·31E.

OFF VLIELAND TSS
VL-CENTER ⌷ Fl 5s 12M; ***Racon C, 12-15M;*** 53°26'·93N 04°39'·88E. VL7 ⬩ L Fl G 10s; 53°26'·40N 04°57'·60E.
VL1 ⬩ Fl (2) G 10s; 53°10'·96N 04°35'·31E.

DELFZIJL TO HARLINGEN
DELFZIJL
PS3/BW26 ⬩ Fl (2+1) G 12s; 53°19'·25N 07°00'·32E.
W mole ⌁ FG; 53°19'·01N 07°00'·27E.
Ldg lts 203° both Iso 4s. Front, 53°18'·63N 07°00'·17E.

SCHIERMONNIKOOG AND LAUWERSOOG
WG (Westgat) ⌀ Iso 8s; ***Racon Z;*** 53°32'·00N 05°58'·54E.
WRG ⌀ Q; 53°32'·87N 06°03'·24E.
AM ⌀ VQ; 53°30'·95N 05°44'·72E.
Schiermonnikoog ☆ Fl (4) 20s 43m **28M;** dark R ○ twr. Same twr: F WR 29m **W15M,** R12M; 210°-W-221°-R-230°. 53°29'·20N 06°08'·79E.
Lauwersoog W mole ⌁ FG 3M; *Horn (2) 30s;* 53°24'·68N 06°12'·00E.

ZEEGAT VAN AMELAND
BR ⌀ Q; 53°30'·66N 05°33'·52E.
TS ⌀ VQ; 53°28'·15N 05°21'·53E.
WA ⬩ 53°28'·35N 05°28'·64E. (Westgat buoys are all unlit)
Ameland , W end ☆ Fl (3) 15s 57m **30M;** 53°26'·89N 05°37'·42E.

NES
VA2-R1 ⌀ VQ(6) + L Fl 10s; 53°25'·71N 05°45'·88E.
Reegeul R3 ⬩ Iso G 4s; 53°25'·80N 05°45'·93E.
R7 ⌁ QG; 53°25'·91N 05°46'·21E.

HET VLIE (ZEEGAT VAN TERSCHELLING)
ZS (Zuider Stortemelk) ⌀ Iso 4s; ***Racon T;*** 53°19'·58N 04°55'·77E.
ZS1 ⬩ VQ G; 53°19'·22N 04°57'·58E.
ZS5 ⬩ L Fl G 8s; 53°18'·53N 05°01'·10E.
ZS11-VS2 ⌀ Q (9) 15s; 53°18'·66N 05°05'·95E.

SCHUITENGAT TO WEST TERSCHELLING
VL 4/SG 1 ⌀ 53°19'·17N 05°10'·45E; buoys are frequently moved.
SG 3 ⬩ 53°19'·38N 05°10'·51E.
SG 19 ⬩ L Fl G 5s; 53°20'·89N 05°12'·42E.
SG 23 ⬩ L Fl G 8s; 53°21'·17N 05°13'·28E.

NOORD MEEP/SLENK TO WEST TERSCHELLING
WM3 ⬩ Iso G 2s; 53°17'·45N 05°12'·28E.
NM 4-S 21 ⌀ VQ (3) 5s; 53°19'·02N 05°15'·47E.
SG 15-S 2 ⌀ Q (9) 15s; 53°20'·44N 05°11'·70E.
Brandaris Twr ☆ Fl 5s 54m **29M;** Y □ twr partly obscured by dunes; 53°21'·62N 05°12'·86E.
W Terschelling W hbr mole ⌁ FR 5m 5M; R post, W bands; *Horn 15s;* 53°21'·26N 05°13'·09E. E pier hd ⌁ FG 4m 4M.

VLIELAND
VS3 (Vliesloot) ⬩ VQ G; 53°18'·27N 05°06'·25E.
VS14 ⌿ Iso R 4s; 53°17'·58N 05°05'62E.
VS16-VB1 ⌿ Fl (2+1) R 10s; 53°17'·62N 05°05'·19E.
E/W mole hds ⌁ FG and ⌁ FR; 53°17'·68N 05°05'·51E.

Ldg lts 282° ⌁ Iso 4s 10/16m 1M, synch; 53°17'·75N 05°04'·47W (100m apart); mainly for the ferry terminal at E Vlieland.
E Vlieland (Vuurduin) ☆ Iso 4s 54m **20M;** 53°17'·75N 05°03'·49E.

APPROACHES TO HARLINGEN (selected marks):
VLIESTROOM buoys are frequently moved.
VL1 ⬩ QG; 53°18'·99N 05°08'·82E. VL 2 ⌿ QR; 53°19'·40N 05°09'·19E.
IN 1 ⬩ VQ G; 53°16'·07N 05°09'·70E (Inschot).

BLAUWE SLENK
BS1-IN2 ⌀ VQ (3) 5s; 53°15'·99N 05°10'·32E.
BS13 ⬩ QG; 53°13'·31N 05°17'·13E. BS19 ⬩ VQ G; 53°11'·90N 05°18'·28E.
BS23 ⬩ L Fl G 8s; 53°11'·42N 05°19'·60E.

POLLENDAM
Ldg lts 112°, both Iso 6s 8/19m 13M (H24); B masts, W bands. Front, 53°10'·52N 05°24'·19E. Use only between P2 and P6.
P2 ⌿ Iso R 2s; 53°11'·47N 05°20'·38E on the training wall, as are P4, Iso R 8s; P6, Iso R 4s; P8, Iso R 8s; and P10, Iso R 2s.
Yachts should keep outboard of P1 thru 7 SHM buoys. P1 ⬩ Iso G 2s; 53°11'·39N 05°20'·32E. P7 ⬩ VQ G; 53°10'·68N 05°23'·45E.

HARLINGEN
S mole hd ⌁ FG 9m; *Horn (3) 30s;* 53°10'·56N 05°24'·18E.
N mole hd ⌁ FR 9m 4M; R/W pedestal; 53°10'·59N 05°24'·32E.

TEXEL AND THE WADDENZEE
APPROACHES TO EIERLANDSCHE GAT
Eierland ☆ Fl (2) 10s 52m **29M;** R ○ twr; 53°10'·93N 04°51'·31E.
EG ⌀ VQ (9) 10s; 53°13'·36N 04°47'·08E.

MOLENGAT (from the N)
MG ⌀ Mo (A) 8s; 53°03'·91N 04°39'·37E.
MG1 ⬩ Iso G 4s; 53°02'·89N 04°40'·86E.
MG5 ⬩ Iso G 4s; 53°01'·26N 04°41'·74E.
MG13 ⬩ Iso G 8s; 52°59'·16N 04°42'·35E.
S14-MG17 ⌀ VQ (6) + L Fl 10s; 52°58'·50N 04°43'·60E.

OUDESCHILD
T12 ⌿ Iso R 8s; 53°02'·23N 04°51'·52E.
Oudeschild Dir ⌁ Oc 6s; intens 291°; 53°02'·40N 04°50'·94E; leads 291° into hbr between N mole head FG 6m; and S mole head ⌁ FR 6m; *Horn (2) 30s* (sounded 0600-2300); 53°02'·33N 04°51'·17E.

APPROACHES TO KORNWERDERZAND SEALOCK
DOOVE BALG (From Texelstroom eastward)
T23 ⬩ VQ G; 53°03'·60N 04°55'·85E, 066°/3M from Oudeschild.
T29 ⬩ 53°03'·25N 05°00'·05E.
D1 ⌿ Iso G 4s; 53°02'·18N 05°03'·42E.
D21 ⌿ Iso G 8s; 53°03'·55N 05°15'·71E.
BO2-WG1 ⌀ Q (6) + L Fl 10s; 53°05'·00N 05°17'·91E.

BOONTJES (From Harlingen southward)
BO40 ⌿ Iso R 4s; 53°09'·87N 05°23'·29E.
BO28 ⌿ Iso R 8s; 53°07'·81N 05°22'·49E.
BO9/KZ2 ⌀ Q; 53°04'·95N 05°20'·24E.

KORNWERDERZAND SEALOCK
W mole ⌁ FG 9m 7M; *Horn Mo(N) 30s;* 53°04'·78N 05°20'·03E.
E mole ⌁ FR 9m 7M; 53°04'·70N 05°20'·08E.
W mole elbow ⌁ Iso G 6s 6m 7M; 53°04'·61N 05°19'·90E.

APPROACHES TO DEN OEVER SEALOCK
MALZWIN and VISJAGERSGAATJE CHANS TO DEN OEVER
MH4-M1 ⌀ VQ (9) 10s; 52°58'·09N 04°47'·52E, close N Den Helder.
M15 ⬩ QG; 52°59'·39N 04°55'·48E (hence use DYC 1811.3).
VG1-W2 ⬩ Fl (2+1) G 10s; 52°59'·00N 04°56'·85E.
O9 ⬩ Iso G 8s; 52°56'·63N 05°02'·38E.

DEN OEVER SEALOCK
Ldg lts 131°, both Oc 10s 6m 7M; 127°-137°. Front, 52°56'·32N 05°02'·98E. Rear, 280m from front.
E end of swing bridge, ⚓ Iso WRG 5s 14m 10/7M; 226°-G-231°-W-235°-R-290°-G-327°-W-335°-R-345°; 52°56'·12N 05°02'·52E.

ZEEGAT VAN TEXEL AND DEN HELDER

OFFSHORE MARKS W and SW OF DEN HELDER
NH (Noorderhaaks) ⚲ VQ; 53°00'·24N 04°35'·37E.
MR ⚲ Q (9) 15s; 52°56'·77N 04°33'·82E.
ZH (Zuiderhaaks) ⚲ VQ (6) + L Fl 10s; 52°54'·65N 04°34'·72E.
Vinca G wreck ⚲ Q (9) 15s; *Racon D*; 52°45'·93N 04°12'·31E.

SCHULPENGAT (from the SSW)
Schulpengat Dir ☆ 026·5°, Dir WRG, Al WR, Al WG, **W22M R/G18M**, church spire; 025.1°–FG–025.6°–AlWG–026.3°–FW–026.7°–Al WR–027.4°–F R–027.9°; shown H24.
Schilbolsnol ☆ F WRG 27m **W15M**, R12M, G11M; 338°-W-002°-G-035°-W(ldg sector for Schulpengat)-038°-R-051°-W-068°; post; 53°00'·50N 04°45'·70E (on Texel).
SG ⚲ Mo (A) 8s; *Racon Z*; 52°52'·90N 04°37'·90E.
S1 ⚑ Iso G 4s; 52°53'·53N 04°38'·82E.
S7 ⚑ QG; 52°56'·25N 04°40'·92E. S6A ⚲ QR; 52°56'·52N 04°40'·51E.
S10 ⚲ Iso R 8s; 52°57'·59N 04°41'·57E. S14-MG17 ⚲, see Molengat.
S11 ⚑ Iso G 8s; 52°57'·55N 04°43'·25E.
Huisduinen ⚓ F WR 26m W14M, R11M; 070°-W-113°-R-158°-W-208°; ☐ twr; 52°57'·14N 04°43'·30E (abeam S10 PHM buoy).
Kijkduin ☆ Fl (4) 20s 56m **30M**; vis 360°, except where obsc'd by dunes on Texel; brown twr; 52°57'·33N 04°43'·58E (mainland).

MARSDIEP and DEN HELDER
T1 ⚑ Fl (3) G 10s; 52°57'·99N 04°44'·62E.
T3 ⚑ Iso G 8s; 52°58'·07N 04°46'·42E.
Den Helder ldg lts 191°, both Oc G 5s 15/24m 14M, synch. Front, vis 161°-221°; B ▽ on bldg; 52°57'·37N 04°47'·08E.
Marinehaven, W bkwtr head ⚓ QG 11m 8M; *Horn 20s*; 52°57'·95N 04°47'·07E (Harssens Island).
W side, ⚓ Fl G 5s 9m 4M (H24); 180°-067°; 52°57'·78N 04°47'·08E.
Yacht hbr (KMYC), ent ⚓ FR & FG; 165m SW of ⚓ Fl G 5s, above.
E side, MH6 ⚲ Iso R 4s; 52°57'·99N 04°47'·41E.
Ent E side, ⚓ QR 9m 4M (H24); 52°57'·77N 04°47'·37E.

DEN HELDER TO AMSTERDAM
Zanddijk Grote Kaap ⚓ Oc WRG 10s 30m W11M, R8M, G8M; 041°-G-088°-W-094°-R-131°; brown twr; 52°52'·86N 04°42'·88E.
Petten ⚲ VQ (9) 10s; 52°47'·33N 04°36'·78E (Power stn outfall).
Egmond-aan-Zee ☆ Iso WR 10s 36m **W18M**, R14M; 010°-W-175°-R-188°; W ◯ twr; 52°37'·99N 04°37'·16E.
Wind farm approx 6·4M W of Egmond-aan-Zee is marked by: a Meteomast, Mo (U) 15s 11m 10M; 52°36'·36N 04°23'·41E; and by L Fl Y 15s; Horn Mo (U) 30s on 5 of the peripheral wind turbines.

IJMUIDEN
Baloeran ⚲ Q (9) 15s; 52°29'·21N 04°32'·00E.
IJmuiden ⚲ Mo (A) 8s; *Racon Y, 10M*; 52°28'·45N 04°23'·92E.
Ldg lts 100·5° (FW 5M by day; 090·5°-110·5°). **Front** ☆ F WR 30m **W16M**, R13M; 050°-W-122°-R-145°-W-160°; (Tidal and traffic sigs); dark R ◯ twrs; 52°27'·70N 04°34'·47E. **Rear** ☆ Fl 5s 52m **29M**; 019°-199° (FW 5M by day; 090·5°-110·5°); 560m from front.
S bkwtr hd ⚓ FG 14m 10M (in fog Fl 3s); *Horn (2) 30s;* W twr, G bands; 52°27'·82N 04°31'·93E.
N bkwtr hd ⚓ FR 15m 10M; 52°28'·05N 04°32'·55E.
IJM 1 ⚑ Iso G 4s; 52°27'·75N 04°33'·59E.
S outer chan ⚓ Iso G 6s, 52°27'·75N 04°33'·81E. ⚓ Iso R 6s, 52°27'·84N 04°34'·39E (Forteiland). Kleine Sluis 52°27'·84N 04°35'·43E.

AMSTERDAM
IJ8 ⚲ Iso R 8s (for Sixhaven marina); 52°22'·84N 04°54'·29E.
Oranjesluizen, N lock 52°22'·93N 04°57'·60E (for IJsselmeer).

AMSTERDAM TO ROTTERDAM
Noordwijk-aan-Zee ☆ Oc (3) 20s 32m **18M**; W☐twr; 52°14'·88N 04°26'·02E.

SCHEVENINGEN
Lighthouse ☆ Fl (2) 10s 48m **29M**; 014°-244°; brown twr; 52°06'·23N 04°16'·13E, 5ca E of hbr ent.
Ldg lts 156°, both Iso 4s 18/22m 14M, H24; synch; Gy masts. Front 52°05'·78N 04°15'·60E; rear 100m from front. Intens at night.
SCH ⚲ Iso 4s; 52°07'·76N 04°14'·12E.
KNS ⚲ Q (9)15s; 52°06'·41N 04°15'·32E.
W mole ⚓ FG 12m 9M; G twr, W bands; 52°06'·23N 04°15'·16E.
E mole ⚓, FR 12m 9M; R twr, W bands; 52°06'·24N 04°15'·37E.
Inner ldg lts 131°: both Oc G 5s 8/9m 11M synch; Gy posts. Front 52°05'·81N 04°15'·89E. Rear, 50m from front.

NOORD HINDER N & S TSS and JUNCTION
NHR-N ⚲ L Fl 8s; *Racon K, 10M;* 52°10'·91N 03°04'·76E.
Noord Hinder ⚲ Fl (2) 10s; *Horn (2) 30s; Racon T*, **12-15M**; 52°00'·10N 02° 51'·11E.
NHR-S ⚲ Fl Y 10s; 51°51'·37N 02°28'·72E.
NHR-SE ⚑ Fl G 5s; 51°45'·42N 02°39'·96E.
Birkenfels ⚲ Q (9) 15s; 51°38'·98N 02°31'·75E.
Twin ⚲ Fl (3) Y 9s; 51°32'·00N 02°22'·59E.
Garden City ⚲ Q (9) 15s; 51°29'·20N 02°17'·54E.

APPROACHES TO HOEK VAN HOLLAND
Europlatform ⚓ Mo (U) 15s; W structure, R bands; helicopter platform; *Horn Mo(U) 30s;* 51°59'·89N 03°16'·46E.
Goeree ☆ Fl (4) 20s 32m **28M**; R/W chequered twr on platform; helicopter platform; *Horn (4) 30s; Racon T, 12-15M;* 51°55'·42N 03°40'·03E.
Maasvlakte ☆ Fl (5) 20s 67m **28M**, H24; 340°-267°; W twr, B bands; 51°58'·20N 04°00'·84E, 1·5M SSW of Maas ent.
Maas Center ⚲ Iso 4s; *Racon M, 10M;* 52°00'·92N 03°48'·79E.
SB ⚲ Fl(4)Y 10s; *Racon Z;* 51°59'·8N 3°54·6E
MO ⚲ Mo (A) 8s; 52°00'·95N 03°58'·07E.
MN3 ⚑ Fl (3) G 10s; 52°04'·47N 03°58'·76E.
MN1 ⚑ Fl G 5s; 52°02'·07N 04°00'·83E.

HOEK VAN HOLLAND
Maasmond ldg lts 112° (for deep draught vessels): both Iso 4s 30/46m **21M**; 101°-123°, synch; W twr, B bands. **Front**, 51°58'·88N 04°04'·88E (NW end of Splitsingsdam). Rear, 0·6M from front.
Indusbank N ⚲ VQ; 52°02'·89N 04°03'·57E.
MVN ⚲ VQ; 51°59'·61N 04°00'·20E.
MV ⚲ Q (9) 15s; 51°57'·45N 03°58'·45E.
Maas 1 ⚑ L Fl G 5s; 51°59'·35N 04°01'·68E.
Nieuwe Waterweg ldg lts 107°: both Iso R 6s 29/43m **18M**; 099.5°-114.5°; R twr, W bands. Front, 51°58'·55N 04°07'·52E. Rear, 450m from front.
Nieuwe Noorderdam ⚓ FR 25m 10M (In fog Al Fl WR 6s; 278°-255°); R twr, W bands; 51°59'·67N 04°02'·80E.
Nieuwe Zuiderdam ⚓ FG 25m 10M, 330°-307°; (In fog Al Fl WG 6s); G twr, W bands; 51°59'·14N 04°02'·49E.

ROTTERDAM
Maassluis ⚓ FG 6m; 51°54'·94N 04°14'·81E; and FR.
Vlaardingen ⚓ FG; 51°53'·99N 04°20'·95E; and FR.
Spuihaven, W ent ⚓ FR; 51°53'·98N 04°23'·97E.
Veerhaven, E ent ⚓ FG; 51°54'·42N 04°28'·75E; and FR.
City marina ent, 51°54'·64N 04°29'·76E.

APPROACHES TO HARINGVLIET
Buitenbank , Iso 4s; 51°51'·16N 03°25'·71E.
Hinder ⚲ Q (9) 15s; 51°54'·55N 03°55'·42E.
SH ⚲ VQ (9) 10s; 51°49'·49N 03°45'·79E; also SH-N ⚲ & SH-S ⚲.
Westhoofd ☆ Fl (3) 15s 55m **30M**; R ☐ tr; 51°48'·79N 03°51'·85E.
Ooster ⚲ Q (9) 15s; 51°47'·90N 03°41'·27E.

SLIJKGAT

SG ⌕ Iso 4s; 51°51'·95N 03°51'·42E.
SG 2 ⌕ Iso R 4s; 51°51'·71N 03°53'·45E.
SG 5 ⌅ Iso G 4s; 51°50'·91N 03°55'·44E.
SG 11 ⌅ Iso G 4s; 51°50'·81N 03°58'·52E.
P1 ⌅ Iso G 4s; 51°51'·27N 04°00'·51E.
P3 ⌅ Iso G 8s; 51°51'·12N 04°01'·45E.
P9 ⌅ Iso G 8s; 51°49'·98N 04°02'·15E.

STELLENDAM

N mole ⌁ FG; *Horn (2) 15s;* 51°49'·88N 04°02'·03E.
Buitenhaven ⌁ Oc 6s; 51°49'·73N 04°01'·75E.

APPROACHES TO OOSTERSCHELDE
OUTER APPROACHES

Schouwenbank ⌕ Mo (A) 8s; *Racon O, 10M;* 51°44'·94N 03°14'·32E.
Middelbank ⌕ Iso 8s; 51°40'·86N 03°18'·20E.
MW ⌀ Q (9) 15s; 51°44'·55N 03°24'·04E (Schouwendiep).
MD 3 ⌅ Fl G 5s; 51°42'·70N 03°26'·98E.
TB (Thornton Bank) ⌀ Q; 51°34'·40N 02°59'·11E.
SW Thornton ⌕ Iso 8s; 51°30'·98N 02°50'·90E.
Rabsbank ⌕ Iso 4s; 51°38'·25N 03°09'·93E.
Westpit ⌕ Iso 8s; 51°33'·65N 03°09'·92E.
ZSB ⌀ VQ (9) 10s; 51°36'·57N 03°15'·62E.
OG1 ⌅ QG; 51°36'·14N 03°20'·08E.

WESTGAT, OUDE ROOMPOT and ROOMPOTSLUIS

West Schouwen ☆ Fl (2+1)15s 57m **30M**; Gy twr, R diagonals on upper part; 51°42'·52N 03°41'·50E, 5·8M N of Roompotsluis.
OG-WG ⌀ VQ (9) 10s; 51°37'·18N 03°23'·82E.
WG1 ⌅ Iso G 8s; 51°38'·00N 03°26'·24E.
WG4 ⌁ L Fl R 8s; 51°38'·62N 03°28'·78E.
WG7 ⌅ Iso G 4s 51°39'·40N 03°32'·67E.
WG-GB (Geul van de Banjaard) ⌁ 51°39'·72N 03°32'·69E.
OR1 ⌅ 51°39'·15N 03°33'·59E.
OR5 ⌅ Iso G 8s; 51°38'·71N 03°35'·53E.
OR11 ⌅ Iso G 4s; 51°36'·98N 03°38'·40E.
OR12 ⌕ Iso R 4s; 51°37'·27N 03°39'·25E.
OR-R ⌀ VQ (3) 5s; 51°36'·41N 03°38'·96E.

Roompotsluis ldg lts 073·5°, both Oc G 5s; synch. Front, 51°37'·33N 03°40'·75E. Rear, 280m from front.
N bkwtr ⌁ FR 7m; 51°37'·31N 03°40'·09E.

WESTKAPELLE TO VLISSINGEN
OOSTGAT

Ldg lts 149·5°: Front, Noorderhoofd Oc WRG 10s 20m; W13M, R/G10M; 353°-R-008°-G-029°-W-169°; R ○ twr, W band; 51°32'·40N 03°26'·21E, 0·73M from rear (Westkapelle).
Westkapelle ☆, rear, Fl 3s 49m **28M**; obsc'd by land on certain brgs; □ twr, R top; 51°31'·75N 03°26'·83E.
Kaloo ⌕ Iso 8s; 51°35'·55N 03°23'·24E. Chan is well buoyed/lit.
OG5 ⌅ Iso G 8s; 51°33'·95N 03°25'·92E.
OG-GR ⌀ VQ (3) 5s; 51°32'·74N 03°24'·71E.
Molenhoofd ⌁ Oc WRG 6s 10m; 306°-R-329°-W-349°-R-008°-G-034·5°-W-036·5°-G-144°-W-169°-R-198°; W mast R bands; 51°31'·58N 03°26'·05E.
Zoutelande FR 21m 12M; 321°-352°; R □ twr; 51°30'·28N 03°28'·41E.
Kaapduinen, ldg lts 130°: both Oc 5s 25/34m 13M; synch; Y □ twrs, R bands. Front, 115°-145°; 51°28'·47N 03°30'·99E. Rear, 107·5°-152·5°; 220m from front.
Fort de Nolle ⌁ Oc WRG 9s 11m W6M, R/G4M; 293°-R-309°-W-324·5°-G-336·5°-R-014°-G-064°-R-099·5°-W-110·5°-G-117°-R-130°; W col, R bands; 51°26'·94N 03°33'·12E.
Ldg lts 117°: Front, Leugenaar, Oc R 5s 6m 7M; intens 108°-126°; W&R pile; 51°26'·43N 03°34'·14E.
Rear, Sardijngeul Oc WRG 5s 8m W12M, R9M, G8M; synch;

245°-R-272°-G-282.5°-W-123°-R-147°; R △, W bands on R & W mast; 550m from front; 51°26'·30N 03°34'·56E.

OFFSHORE: W HINDER TSS TO SCHEUR CHANNEL

West Hinder ☆ Fl (4) 30s 23m 13M; *Horn Mo (U) 30s;* **Racon W;** 51°23'·30N 02°26'·27E.
WH Zuid ⌀ Q (6) + L Fl 15s; 51°22'·78N 02°26'·25E.
Oost-Dyck ⌀ Q; 51°21'·38N 02°31'·12E.
Oost-Dyck OD1 ⌀ Q; 51°21'·45N 02°30'·83E.
Bergues N ⌀ Q; 51°19'·96N 02°24'·53E.
Oost-Dyck West ⌀ Q 15s; 51°17'·15N 02°26'·32E.
Oostdyck radar twr; ☆ Mo (U) 15s 15m 12M on 4 corners; *Horn Mo (U) 30s;* **Racon O.** R twr, 3 W bands, with adjacent red twr/helipad; 51°16'·49N 02°26'·83E.
AN ⌕ Fl (4) R 20s; 51°23'·45N 02°36'·92E.
AZ ⌅ Fl (3) G 10s; 51°21'·15N 02°36'·92E.
KB2 ⌀ VQ; 51°21'·04N 02°42'·20E.
KB ⌀ Q; **Racon K;** 51°21'·03N 02°42'·80E.
MBN ⌀ Q; 51°20'·82N 02°46'·19E.
SWA ⌀ Q (9) 15s; 51°22'·28N 02°46'·34E.
VG ⌀ Q ; 51°23'·36N 02°46'·32E, Vaargeul 1.
VG1 ⌅ VQ G; 51°25'·03N 02°49'·04E.
VG2 ⌕ Q (6) + L Fl R 15s; **Racon V;** 51°25'·96N 02°48'·16E.
VG3 ⌅ QG; 51°25'·05N 02°52'·85E.
VG5 ⌅ Fl G 5s; 51°24'·63N 02°57'·90E.
VG7 ⌀ ; 51°24'·53N 02°59'·90E.
Goote Bank ⌀ Q (3) 10s; 51°26'·95N 02°52'·72E.
A1 ⌀ Iso 8s; 51°22'·36N 02°53'·33E.
A1bis ⌀ L Fl 10s; 51°21'·68N 02°58'·02E.

WESTERSCHELDE APPROACHES
SCHEUR CHANNEL

S1 ⌅ Fl G 5s; 51°23'·14N 03°00'·12E.
S3 ⌀ Q; 51°24'·30N 03°02'·92E.
MOW 0 ⊙ Fl (5) Y 20s; **Racon S, 10M;** 51°23'·67N 03°02'·75E.
S5 ⌅ Fl G 5s; 51°23'·69N 03°05'·92E.
S7 ⌅ Fl G 5s; 51°23'·98N 03°10'·42E.
S9 ⌅ QG; 51°24'·42N 03°14'·99E.
S12 ⌕ Fl (4) R 10s; 51°24'·67N 03°18'·22E.
S-W ⌀ Q; 51°24'·13N 03°18'·22E, here Wielingen chan merges.
S14 ⌕ Fl R 5s; 51°24'·58N 03°19'·67E.

WIELINGEN CHANNEL

BVH ⌕ Q (6) + L Fl R 15s; 51°23'·13N 03°12'·04E.
MOW3 tide gauge ⌁ Fl (5) Y 20s; **Racon H, 10M;** 51°23'·38N 03°11'·92E.
W ⌅ Fl (3) G 15s; 51°23'·27N 03°14'·92E.
W1 ⌅ Fl G 5s; 51°23'·48N 03°18'·22E.
Fort Maisonneuve ⌀ VQ (9) 10s; wreck; 51°24'·20N 03°21'·50E.
W3 ⌅ Iso G 8s; 51°23'·96N 03°21'·49E.
W5 ⌅ Iso G 4s; 51°24'·31N 03°24'·50E.
W7 ⌅ Iso G 8s; 51°24'·60N 03°27'·23E.
W9 ⌅ Iso G 4s; 51°24'·96N 03°30'·43E.
Nieuwe Sluis ⌁ Oc WRG 10s 26m W14M, R11M, G10M; 055°-R-089°-W-093°-G-105°-R-134°-W-136·5°- G-156·5°-W-236·5°-G-243° -W-254°-R-292°-W-055°; B 8-sided twr, W bands; 51°24'·41N 03°31'·29E.
Songa ⌅ QG; 51°25'·16N 03°33'·66E.
W10 ⌕ QR; 51°25'·85N 03°33'·28E.

VLISSINGEN

Koopmanshaven, W mole root, ⌁ Iso WRG 3s 15m W12M, R10M, G9M; 253°-R-277°-W-284°-R-297°- W-306·5°-G-013°-W-024°-G-033°-W-035°-G-039°-W-055°-G-084·5°-R-092°-G-111°-W-114°; R pylon; 51°26'·37N 03°34'·52E.
Sardijngeul Oc WRG 5s; 51°26'·30N 03°34'·56E: see OOSTGAT last 3 lines. E mole head, ⌁ FG 7m; W mast; 51°26'·32N 03°34'·67E.
Buitenhaven ent, W side ⌁ FR 10m 5M; also Iso WRG 4s: W073°-

Plot waypoints on chart before use

324°, G324°-352°, W352°-017°, G017°-042°, W042°-056°, R056°-073°; W post, R bands; tfc sigs; 51°26'·38N 03°36'·06E.
Buitenhaven ent, E side ☆ FG 7m 4M; 51°26'·41N 03°36'·38E.

Schone Waardin ☆ Oc WRG 9s 10m W13M, R10M, G9M; 235°-R-271°-W-288°-G-335°-R-341°-G-026°-W-079°-R-091°; R mast, W bands; 51°26'·54N 03°37'·91E (1M E of Buitenhaven ent).

BRESKENS
ARV-VH ₰ Q; 51°24'·71N 03°33'·89E.
VH2 (Vaarwaterlangs Hoofdplaat) ⌐ 51°24'·34N 03°33'·90E.
Yacht hbr, W mole ☆ FG 7m; in fog FY; Gy post; 51°24'·03N 03°34'·06E. E mole ☆ FR 6m; Gy mast; 51°23'·95N 03°34'·09E.

WESTERSCHELDE: TERNEUZEN TO PAAL
TERNEUZEN
Nieuw Neuzenpolder ldg lts 125°, both Oc 5s 6/16m 9/13M; intens 117°-133°; synch. Front, W col, B bands; 51°20'·97N 03°47'·24E. Rear, B & W twr; 365m from front.
Oost Buitenhaven E mole ☆ FR 5M; 51°20'·56N 03°49'·19E.
Former ferry hbr (W part) & marinas (E part), W mole head ☆ FG, Gy mast; 51°20'·57N 03°49'·64E. E mole, FR.
W mole ☆ Oc WRG 5s 15m W9M, R7M, G6M; 090°-R-115°-W-120°-G-130°-W-245°-G-249°-W-279°-R-004°; B & W post; 51°20'·54N 03°49'·58E, close SW of ☆ FG.

HANSWEERT
W mole ☆ Oc WRG 10s 9m W9M, R7M, G6M; (in fog FY); 288°-R-311°-G-320°-W-332·5°-G-348·5°-W-042·5°-R-061·5°-W-078°-G-099°-W-114·5°-R-127·5°-W-288°; R twr, W bands; 51°26'·41N 04°00'·53E.

BELGIUM
ZANDVLIET TO ANTWERPEN
ZANDVLIET
Dir ☆ 118·3°,WRG 20m W4M, R/ G3M; 116·63°-Oc G-117·17°- FG-117·58°-Alt GW-118·63°-F-118·63°-Alt RW-119·18°-FR-119·58°- Oc R-120·13°; 51°20'·61N 04°16'·47E, near Zandvliet locks.

ANTWERPEN
Royerssluis, ldg lts 091°, both FR. Ent FR/FG (for Willemdok ④).
No. 109 ₰ Iso G 8s; 51°13'·88N 04°23'·87E, (off Linkeroever ④).
Linkeroever marina ⚓ F WR 9m W3M, R2M; shore-W-283°- R-shore; B ⊙, R lantern; 51°13'·91N 04°23'·70E. Marina ent, FR/FG.

COASTAL MARKS
SWW ⌐ Fl (4) R 20s; 51°21'·95N 03°00'·94E; Wandelaar.
WBN ◣ QG; 51°21'·50N 03°02'·59E; Wandelaar.
Oostende Bank N ₰ Q; 51°21'·20N 02°52'·93E.
Wenduine Bank E ⌐ QR; 51°18'·83N 03°01'·64E.
Wenduine Bank W ₰ Q (9) 15s; 51°17'·23N 02°52'·76E.
Nautica Ena wreck ₰ Q; 51°18'·08N 02°52'·79E.
Oostendebank E ⌐ Fl (4) R 20s; 51°17'·35N 02°51'·91E.
Oostendebank W ₰ Q (9)15s; 51°16'·20N 02°44'·74E.
LST 420 ₰ Q (9)15s; 51°15'·45N 02°40'·61E.
MBN ₰ Q; 51°20'·82N 02°46'·27E.
Middelkerke Bank ◣ Fl G 5s; 51°18'·19N 02°42'·75E.
Middelkerke Bank S ⌐ Q (9) R 15s; 51°14'·73N 02°41'·89E.
D1 ₰ Q (3) 10s; 51°13'·95N 02°38'·59E.
BT Ratel ⌐ Fl (4) R 15s; 51°11'·63N 02°27'·92E; Buiten Ratel.

ZEEBRUGGE TO THE FRENCH BORDER
ZEEBRUGGE
A2 ₰ Iso 8s; 51°22'·41N 03°07'·05E.
Ldg lts 136°, both Oc 5s 22/45m 8M; 131°-141°; H24, synch; W cols, R bands. Front, 51°20'·71N 03°13'·11E. Rear, 890m SE.
SZ ₰ Q (3) 10s; 51°23'·62N 03°07'·58E (Scheur Channel).
Z ◣ QG; 51°22'·48N 03°09'·95E.
WZ ₰ Q (9) 15s; 51°22'·57N 03°10'·72E.

W outer mole ☆ Oc G 7s 31m 7M; G vert strip lts visible from seaward; 057°-267°; *Horn (3) 30s*; IPTS; 51°21'·74N 03°11'·17E.
E outer mole ☆ Oc R 7s 31m 7M; R vert strip lts visible from seaward; 087°-281°; *Bell 25s*; 51°21'·78N 03°11'·86E.
Ldg lts 154°: Front, Oc WR 6s 20m 3M, 135°-W-160°-R-169°; W pylon, R bands; 51°20'·33N 03°12'·89E. Rear, Oc 6s 38m 3M, H24, synch; 520m from front.
Leopold II mole ☆ Oc WR 15s 22m, **W20M, R18M**; 068°-W-145°-R-212°-W-296°; IPTS; *Horn (3+1) 90s*; 51°20'·85N 03°12'·17E.
Entrance to Marina and FV hbr 51°19'·88N 03°11'·85E.

BLANKENBERGE
Promenade pier Fl (3) Y 20s, 8m 4M; 51°19'·28N 03°08'·18E.
Lt ho ☆ Fl (2) 8s 30m **20M**; 065°-245°; W twr, B top; 51°18'·75N 03°06'·85E.
Ldg lts 134°, both FR 5/9m 3/10M, R cross (X) topmarks on masts; front 51°18'·70N 03°08'·82E; rear 81m from front.
E pier ☆ FR 12m 11M; 290°-245°; W ○ twr; *Bell (2) 15s*; 51°18'·91N 03°06'·55E.
W pier ☆ FG 14m 11M; intens 065°-290°, unintens 290°-335°; W ○ twr; 51°18'·89N 03°06'·42E.
OBST 4 – OBST 14 are eleven ₰s Q approx 3ca offshore, marking Spoil Ground between Blankenberge and Oostende.

OOSTENDE
Oostendebank East ⌐ Fl (4) R 20s; 51°17'·35N 02°51'·91E.
Wenduinebank West ₰ Q (9) 15s; 51°17'·23N 02°52'·76E.
Buitenstroombank ₰ Q; 51°15'·17N 02°51'·71E.
Binnenstroombank ₰ Q (3) 10s; 51°14'·47N 02°53'·65E.
₰ Fl (5) Y 20s, Y beacon; 51°14'·83N 02°55'·33E.
Ldg lts 128°: both Iso 4s (triple vert) 21/32m 4M, 051°-201°; X on framework twrs, R/W bands. Front, 51°14'·13N 02°55'·55E.
Oostende lt ho ☆ Fl (3) 10s 65m **27M**; obsc 069·5°-071°; Gy twr, 2 sinusoidal Bu bands; 51°14'·18N 02°55'·84E.
E pier ☆ and *Horn* have been withdrawn. The E pier has been demolished (2008) and a new pier is being built further east; WIP until 2012 is marked by 1 NCM buoy Q; 2 SPM buoys QY; and 3 PHM buoys QR. IPTS, tidal and storm sigs are shown from sig mast 51°14'·25N 02°55'·44E, plus QY when chan closed for ferry.
W pier ☆ FG 12m 10M, 057°-327°; *Bell 4s*; W ○ twr 51°14'·31N 02°55'·03E.

NIEUWPOORT
Zuidstroombank ⌐ Fl R 5s; 51°12'·28N 02°47'·37E.
Weststroombank ⌐ Fl (4) R 20s; 51°11'·34N 02°43'·03E.
Wreck 4 ₰ Q (6) + L Fl 15s; 51°10'·90N 02°405'·03E.
Nieuwpoort Bank ₰ Q (9) 15s; 51°10'·16N 02°36'·09E.
Oostduinkerke ₰ Q; 51°09'·15N 02°39'·44E.
Lt ho ☆ Fl (2) R 14s 28m **16M**; R/W twr; 51°09'·27N 02°43'·79E.
E pier ☆ FR 11m 10M; vis 025°-250° & 307°-347°; W ○ twr; 51°09'·41N 02°43'·08E.
W pier ☆ FG 11m 9M; vis 025°-250° & 284°-324°; *Bell (2) 10s*; W ○ twr; IPTS from root; 51°09'·35N 02°43'·00E.
☆ QG 51°08'·65N 02°44'·31E marks the Y-junction where the channel forks stbd for KYCN and port for WSKLM and VVW-N.

WESTDIEP and PASSE DE ZUYDCOOTE
Den Oever wreck 2 ₰ Q; 51°08'·11N 02°37'·43E.
Wreck 1 ₰ Q; 51°08'·32N 02°35'·03E (adjacent to ⌐ next line).
Wave recorder ⌐ Fl (5) Y 20s; 51°08'·32N 02°34'·91E.
Trapegeer ◣ Fl G 10s; 51°08'·41N 02°34'·36E.
E12 ₰ VQ (6) + L Fl 10s; 51°07'·89N 02°30'·68E.
French waters, for continuity (see also 9.17.4):
CME ₰ Q (3) 10s; 51°07'·30N 02°30'·00E.
E11 ₰ Fl G 4s; 51°06'·90N 02°30'·90E.
E10 ₰ Fl (2) R 6s; 51°06'·30N 02°30'·47E.
E9 ₰ Fl (2) G 6s; 51°05'·64N 02°29'·68E.
E8 ₰ Fl (3) R 12s; 51°05'·16N 02°28'·67E.

9.16.5 PASSAGE INFORMATION

More Passage Information is threaded between harbours in this Area. **Bibliography** *N France and Belgium CC* (NDL/Featherstone). *N Sea Passage Pilot* (Imray/Navin). NP 55 *N Sea (East) Pilot*. NP 28 *Dover Strait Pilot*. *Hafenhandbuch Nordsee* (DSV-Verlag).

CHARTS, PSSA AND TSS

While AC 2182A, 1405/06/08, 1630/31/32/33, 1872 suffice for coastal passages and entry to the main ports, larger scale **Dutch yacht charts** (1800 series) are essential for exploring the cruising grounds along this coast or entering the smaller hbrs. Inland, the ANWB booklet-style chart (€16.95) of the *Staande-Mast Route* (Fixed Mast Route; see 9.16.2A) is very detailed with copious, but intelligible, notes in Dutch.

From the Ems estuary west to Den Helder a **Particularly Sensitive Sea Area** (PSSA) extends 3M seaward from the West Frisian Islands. Yachts should carefully avoid damaging the maritime environment and marine organisms living in it.

The Terschelling-German Bight TSS, Off Vlieland TSS and Off Texel TSS lie between 5 and 10M to seaward of the West Frisian Islands. Cruising yachts are advised to navigate within this relatively narrow ITZ. Further offshore, and particularly in and near the Off Vlieland TSS, West Friesland TSS and Botney Ground TSS, navigation is further complicated by the many oil and gas fields. For general notes on North Sea oil & gas installations, see Chapter 3 and Area 5.

CROSSING THE NORTH SEA TO THE UK

From ports S of Hoek van Holland make for NHR-SE, where cross the TSS for destinations between Harwich and Great Yarmouth (AC *1406*, *1408*, 1872, *2449*, 3371). From ports N of Hoek van Holland passages can be more problematic. For example, a route from IJmuiden to the Humber crosses two DW routes, N and NW of Brown Ridge, and then runs into extensive offshore Gas Fields. These might cause you to opt for two shorter legs, stopping a night at Great Yarmouth. Similar thinking might apply if coming out of Den Helder, even if a stop at Great Yarmouth might incur some southing. From east of Den Helder, make ground west via the ITZ before taking departure.

9.16.6 SPECIAL NOTES: NETHERLANDS

PROVINCES are given in lieu of UK 'counties'.

CHARTS The following types of chart are available from agents. The Chart catalogue (HP7) is downloadable from www.hydro.nl:

- Zeekaarten (equivalent to AC) are issued by the Royal Netherlands Navy Hydrographer and corrected by Notices to Mariners (*Berichten aan Zeevarenden* or *BaZ*).
- 1800 series *voor Kust-en Binnenwateren* (coastal and inland waters) are yacht charts (DYC) issued annually in March by the Hydrographer in 8 folios (1801-1812, excluding 1802/4/6 & 8); about 9 loose double-sided sheets (54 x 38cm) per folio.

TIME ZONE is –0100, but add 1 hr for DST in the summer months.

TIDES HP 33 *Waterstanden & Stromen* (Tide tables and tidal streams in **English** and Dutch, €18.95) is most useful especially if cruising Dutch waters for any length of time. It contains tide tables for 15 Dutch and 2 Belgian coastal ports; and 8 tidal stream atlases, including Westerschelde, Oosterschelde and the Maas.

REGULATIONS Discharge of toilet waste from recreational boats is forbidden in all Dutch waters, including inland waterways, lakes and the Waddenzee.

MARINAS Most marinas are private YCs or Watersport Associations (WSV or WV): *Gemeentelijke (Gem)* = municipal. Marinas with >50 berths must have a pump-out unit ⚓. Sometimes (in Belgium also) berth-holders show a green tally if a berth is free, or a red tally if returning same day, but check with HM. Duty-free fuel (coloured red) is not available for leisure craft and may only be carried in the tank, NOT in cans. A tourist tax of €0.55–€1.82/head/night is often levied. VAT (BTW) is 19%. A useful website with links to other marinas is www.allejachthavens.nl

CUSTOMS Ports of entry are: Delfzijl, Lauwersoog, W Terschelling, Vlieland*, Harlingen, Kornwerderzand, Den Helder, IJmuiden, Scheveningen, Hoek van Holland, Maassluis, Schiedam, Vlaardingen, Rotterdam, Roompot*, Vlissingen and Breskens. *Summer only. Den Oever and Stellendam are *not* Ports of entry.

FERRIES TO THE UK IJmuiden-Newcastle; Hoek van Holland-Harwich; Rotterdam (Europoort)-Hull.

BUOYAGE Buoys are often named by the abbreviations of the banks or chans which they mark (eg VL = Vliestroom). A division buoy has the abbreviations of both chans meeting there, eg VL2-SG2 = as above, plus Schuitengat.

Some minor, tidal channels are marked by withies: SHM bound ⚲; PHM unbound ⚲. On tidal flats (eg Friesland) where the direction of main flood stream is uncertain, bound withies are on the S side of a chan and unbound on the N side; the banks thus marked are steep-to. In minor chans the buoyage may be moved without notice to accommodate changes.

The SIGNI buoyage system is used in the IJsselmeer, but not in the Eems, Waddenzee and Westerschelde.

SIGNALS When **motor-sailing** yachts must by law hoist a ▼ and when **at anchor** a black ball ●; these laws are rigidly enforced.

IPTS are widely used at coastal ports. Local signals, if any, are given where possible.

Sluicing signals may be shown by day: A blue board, with the word 'SPUIEN' on it; by night 3 ● in a △; sometimes both at once.

Storm warning signals, Its only, are shown by day & night at West Terschelling, Den Helder and IJmuiden; see 6.1.4.

R/T In emergency call *Den Helder Rescue* Ch 16 for Netherlands CG (see 7.19.1); or the working channel of a VTS sector or nearest lock or bridge. Monitor TSS info broadcasts and VTS sector channels. Ch 31 is for Dutch marinas. Note: Do not use Ch M in Dutch waters, where it is a salvage frequency. Ch 13 is for commercial ship-ship calling. English is the second language and widely spoken.

TELEPHONE To call UK from the Netherlands, dial 00-44; then the UK area code minus the prefix 0, followed by the number required. To call the Netherlands from UK dial 00-31 then the area code minus the prefix 0 followed by two or three digits, followed by a 7 or 6 digits subscriber no. Mobile phone Nos start 06.

Emergency: Fire, Police, Ambulance, dial 112 (free); Non-emergency 0900 8844 (local tariff).

PUBLIC HOLIDAYS New Year's Day, Easter Sun and Mon, Queen's Birthday (30 April), Liberation Day (5 May), Ascension Day, Whit Mon, Christmas and Boxing Days

BRITISH CONSULS Contact British Consulate-General, Koningslaan 44, 1075 AE Amsterdam; ☎ 020 676 4343. Or British Embassy, Lange Voorhout 10, 2514 ED The Hague; ☎ 070 427 0427.

INLAND WATERWAYS The sealocks at Kornwerderzand, Den Oever (9.16.16), IJmuiden (9.16.17), Stellendam (9.16.25) and Roompotsluis (9.16.26) are fully covered. The Staandemast (mast-up) route (9.16.2A) and the IJsselmeer (9.16.16) are outlined. Lack of space precludes detailed coverage of other harbours in the very extensive and enjoyable inland seas, waterways and canals.

Regulations. All craft must carry a copy of waterway regulations, *Binnenvaartpolitiereglement (BPR)*, as given in Dutch in the annual ANWB *Wateralmanak Vol 1* or available separately. Vol 2, also in Dutch, is essential reading; it gives pictograph details of marinas and the opening hours of bridges and locks.

Qualifications. Craft >15m LOA or capable of more than 20kph (11kn) must be skippered by the holder of an RYA Coastal Skipper's Certificate or higher qualification; *plus* an International Certificate of Competence (ICC) endorsed for Inland waterways, ie CEVNI.

Bridges and locks mostly work VHF Ch 18, 20 or 22, but CEVNI light signals (shown up/down-stream) largely negate the need for R/T. The most commonly seen signals include:
● = Bridge closed (opens on request).
To request bridges to open, call on VHF low power (1 watt), or sound 'K' (—·—).
● over ● = Bridge about to open.
● = Bridge open.

9.16.7 TSS OFF THE NORTHERN NETHERLANDS

TRAFFIC SEPARATION SCHEMES OFF THE NORTHERN NETHERLANDS

9.16.8 DELFZIJL

Groningen 53°18'·99N 07°00'·45E ✳✳✳⚓⚓✿✿

CHARTS AC 3631, 3632; DYC 1812.6; Zeekaart 1555; Imray C26; ANWB A

TIDES –0025 Dover; ML 2·1; Duration 0605

Standard Port HELGOLAND (←—)

Times				Height (metres)			
High Water		Low Water		MHWS	MHWN	MLWN	MLWS
0200	0700	0200	0800	2·7	2·4	0·5	0·0
1400	1900	1400	2000				
Differences DELFZIJL							
+0020	–0005	–0040	0000	+1·0	+1·0	+0·3	+0·4
EEMSHAVEN							
–0025	–0045	–0115	–0045	+0·5	+0·5	+0·3	+0·4
HUIBERTGAT							
–0150	–0150	–0210	–0210	0·0	0·0	+0·2	+0·3
SCHIERMONNIKOOG							
–0120	–0130	–0240	–0220	+0·2	+0·1	+0·2	+0·3

SHELTER Good in Handelshaven, where at Neptunus Marina a floating jetty acts as a wavebreak.

NAVIGATION From the E or N, WPT 53°38'·96N 06°27'·06E (Riffgat SWM buoy) 121°/4·2M to Nos 11/12 buoys. See also 9.16.7.

From the W, WPT 53°36'·93N 06°19'·39E (Westereems SWM buoy) 091°/8·2M to join Riffgat at Nos 11/12 buoys.

Huibertgat lies parallel to and S of Westereems. It is marked by unlit R/W buoys H1-H5, least depths about 9m but prone to silt.

From Nos 11/12 buoys follow the well marked/lit river channel for approx 25M via Randzelgat or Alte Eems, Dukegat and Ostfriesisches Gatje to enter Zeehavenkanaal abeam Knock lt ho. Beware strong cross tides at the ent (Lat/Long under title).

INLAND ROUTE TO IJSSELMEER See 9.16.2 and 9.16.16.

LIGHTS AND MARKS See chartlet and 9.16.4. From the river, appr ldg lts 203°, both Iso 4s. Hbr ent, FG on W arm and FR on E arm (in fog, FY). Zeehavenkanaal, 2·5M long, has Fl G lts to N and Fl R to S. Entry sign on both piers: 2 ● = No entry, unless cleared by Hbr office on VHF Ch 14.

R/T All vessels, except leisure craft, must call *Delfzijl Radar* VHF Ch 03 (H24) for VTS, co-ordinated with Ems Traffic. *Port Control* is Ch 66. *Eemskanaal lock* Ch 26. Traffic, weather and tidal info is broadcast every even H+10 on Ch 14 in Dutch and English on request. *Ems Traffic* Ch 15, 18, 20 & 21 (H24) broadcasts every H + 50 weather and tidal info in German, and gale warnings for coastal waters between Die Ems and Die Weser. See also 9.15.25.

TELEPHONE (Code 0596) Port HM 640400; HM 't Dok 616560; Eemskanaal Sea locks 613293; CG (Police) 613831; ⊜ 0598 696560; Police 112; ⊞ 644444; Brit Consul (020) 6764343.

FACILITIES Neptunus Yacht Hbr (4·4m, 53°19'·80N 06°55'·86E) ☎ 615004, €0.24 per gross ton, D (not 0900-1700), Bar, M. **Yacht Hbr 't Dok** at N end of the Old Eemskanaal in 4m, AB €0.41, D. Note: Eems (Dutch) = Ems (German). **Ems Canal** L, FW, AB. **Motor Boat Club Abel Tasman** ☎ 616560 Bar, M, D, ▢, ☁. **Services:** CH, ACA, DYC Agent, ME, El, Gaz. **Town** P, D, ☁, R, Bar, Ⓑ, ⊠, ⇌, ✈ (Groningen/Eelde). Ferry: 9.16.22 & .23.

MINOR HARBOUR 1·3M ESE OF DELFZIJL ENTRANCE

TERMUNTERZIJL Groningen, **53°18'·20N 07°02'·21E**. AC 3632; Zeekaart 1555; DYC 1812.6. HW –0025 on Dover (UT); use Differences Delfzijl. Ent (1·3M ESE of Delfzijl ent) is close to BW13 SHM buoy Fl G 5s (53°18'·63N 07°02'·32E); thence chan marked by 7 R and 7 G unlit bns. Yachts berth in Vissershaven (0·9m), stbd of ent, or on pontoons (1m) to port of ent, €0.36. HM ☎ (0596) 601891 (Apr-Sept), VHF Ch 09, FW, ⟨⟩, Bar, R.

COMMERCIAL HARBOUR AT MOUTH OF THE EEMS (EMS)
EEMSHAVEN, Groningen, **53°27'·66N 06°50'·27E**. AC 3631, 3632, Zeekaart 1555; DYC 1812.5/.6. HW –0100 (approx) on Dover. Tides as for Borkum 9.15.24. Eemshaven is a modern commercial port, but

may be used by yachts as a port of refuge. Outer appr via Hubertgat (see 9.16.7) or Westereems; inner appr via Randzelgat or Alte Eems, passing the outer anchorage for merchant ships. From the nearest buoy, A16 PHM Fl R 4s, the hbr ent bears 137°/1·6M. Call *Eemshaven Radar* Ch 01 (H24) for VTS info; and *Eemshaven Port Control* Ch 66 for info and clearance to enter.

There are many wind turbines S, W and NW of the port. A power stn chy (128m high) is conspic 2M ESE of the port; as are white-roofed bldgs at the port. Enter on 175°, ldg lts Iso 4s, between mole hds, FG and FR. Inner ldg lts, both Iso R 4s, leads 195° to S end of port. Here yachts turn 90° stbd into Emmahaven, marked by FG and FR, and berth on floating jetty in SW corner. HM ☎ (Delfzijl Port Authority) (0596) 640400; ⊜ 0598 696560; other ☎ numbers see Delfzijl. No special facilities for yachts, but dues are €0.24 per gross ton.

MINOR HARBOUR IN THE WEST FRISIAN ISLANDS
SCHIERMONNIKOOG, Friesland, **53°28'·07N 06°10'·05E**. AC 3761; Zeekaart 1458; DYC 1812.3. HW –0150 on Dover. See 9.16.8. WPT 53°32'·00N 05°58'·54E, [WG SWM buoy, Iso 8s, Racon Z], 150°/1·1M to WG1 SHM buoy, VQ G, at the ent to Westgat; buoyed/lit, but in bad weather dangerous due to shoals (3·8m) at seaward end. Follow Westgat chan into Zoutkamperlaag; leave at Z4 & Z6-GVS buoys to enter buoyed Gat van Schiermonnikoog (GVS).

From GVS16-R1 buoy a drying chan, marked by perches/withies, runs 1M N to small yacht hbr (1·3-1·5m). Access HW –2 to +1, with 1·5m max depth at HW in apprs. Picturesque, but very full in high season; not cheap, ie €1.27. A ferry pier is 1·26M E of the yacht hbr. HM VHF Ch 31; ☎ (0519) 51544 (May-Sept). Facilities: FW, AC.

Note: Lt ho Fl (4) 20s, R twr, is conspic 1.35M NNW of yacht hbr. The CG at the lt ho gives radar surveillance of the Terschelling/German Bight TSS out to 48M radius and coordinates local SAR operations. It monitors VHF Ch 00, **05**, 16, 67 and 73 (all H24); ☎ 0519 531247.

THE WEST FRISIAN ISLANDS

This chain of islands stretches from the River Ems estuary W and SSW for some 85M along the Dutch coast to Den Helder (AC 1632, 1633). The islands have similar characteristics – being long, low and narrow, with the major axis parallel to the coast. Texel is the largest and, with Vlieland and Terschelling, lies furthest offshore.

Between the islands, narrow channels (*zeegat* in Dutch, *Seegat* in German) give access to/from the North Sea. Most of these channels are shallow for at least part of their length, and in these shoal areas a dangerous sea builds up in a strong onshore wind against the outgoing (ebb) tide. The Westerems and the Zeegaten van Terschelling and van Texel are safe for yachts in SW–NE winds up to force 8. All the others are unsafe in strong onshore winds.

▶*The flood stream along this coast is E-going, so it starts to run in through the zeegaten progressively from W to E. Where the tide meets behind each island, as it flows in first at the W end and a little later at the E end, a bank is formed, called a wad (Dutch) or Watt (German).◀*

These banks between the islands and the coast are major obstacles to E/W progress inside the islands. The chans are narrow and winding, marked by buoys and/or withies (♠ ♣) in the shallower parts, and they mostly dry; so that it is essential to time the tide correctly.

This is an area most suited to shallow-draft yachts, particularly flat bottomed or with bilge keels, centreboards or legs, that can take the ground easily. Whilst the zeegaten are described briefly below, the many channels inside the islands and across the Waddenzee are mentioned only for general orientation.

DELFZIJL TO AMELAND

The Ems estuary (AC 1633, 3631) flows seaward past the SW side of the German island of Borkum. It gives access to **Delfzijl**, **Termunterzijl** and **Emden**. Hubertgat, which runs parallel to and S of the main Westerems chan, is slightly more direct when bound to/from the W, but in both these chans there is a dangerous sea in strong NW winds over the ebb. Hubertgat is now sparsely buoyed and unlit, but is quite acceptable to yachts. ▶*The E-going (flood) stream begins at HW Helgoland +0530, and the W-going (ebb) stream begins at HW Helgoland –0030, sp rates 1·5kn.◀*

Friesche Zeegat (DYC 1812.3 & .9), between Schiermonnikoog and Ameland, contains two channels: Westgat marked by 'WG' buoys and Plaatgat marked by 'PL' buoys. In strong winds the sea breaks across the whole estuary. Westgat trends SE past Wierumergronden and N7-FA-1 platform, the S past Het Rif and Engelsmanplaat (a prominent sandbank) into Zoutkamperlaag, the main channel (buoys prefixed 'Z') to **Lauwersoog**. Here locks give access to the Lauwersmeer and inland waterways. Plaatgat is a buoyed but unlit lesser channel which trends SW passing close NW of **Schiermonnikoog** then merging with Westgat at WG14-PL13.

Zeegat van Ameland (DYC 1811.6), between Ameland and Terschelling, is fronted by the sandbank of Bornrif about 3M offshore. The main entrance is also called Westgat, with buoys prefixed by letters 'WA', all unlit except WA12 QR. The channel runs ESE close N of Terschelling, and divides into Boschgat (BG) at the E end of West Terschelling and Borndiep (BB) the wider, deeper channel. This skirts the W end of Ameland and at WA22-WG1 buoy gives access via the Molengat to the small ferry port and yacht hbr at Nes.

▶*In Westgat the flood stream begins at HW Helgoland +0425, and the ebb stream at HW Helgoland –0150, sp rates 2kn.◀* A dangerous sea develops in strong onshore winds.

9.16.9 LAUWERSOOG

Friesland, **53°24'·68N 06°12'·04E**

CHARTS AC 1632/3; Imray C26; Zeekaart 1458; DYC 1812.3

LAUWERSOOG

TIDES HW –0150 on Dover; ML 1·7m. See 9.16.13

SHELTER Outer hbr suffers swell in bad weather; complete shelter in Noordergat Marina.

NAVIGATION See Schiermonnikoog (9.16.8); continue to Z15 SHM buoy for hbr ent. Await lock on pontoons at W end of FV basin. Lock hrs (LT) **May-Sep**: Mon-Fri 0700-2000 (Sat 1900); Sun 0900-1200, 1400-1830. **Oct-Apr**: Mon-Fri 0700-1800 (Sat 1700); Sun shut. A firing range 1·5m ENE of hbr ent is marked by Fl Y 10s bcns, alternating W/R when the range is active; info broadcasts on Ch 71.

LIGHTS AND MARKS See chartlet and 9.16.4. Four wind turbines on the N bkwtr are conspic.

R/T Hbr VHF Ch 11; Lock Ch 84; Range broadcast Ch 71.

TELEPHONE (Code 0519) Port HM 349023; Lock 349043; ⊜ 0598 696560.

FACILITIES Noordergat Marina, ☎ 349040; (2·4m-2·8m). Ⓥs berth on first pontoon, €1.00. Gaz, BY, D (E end of hbr); P (ferry terminal, W end of hbr), Bar, R, ☳, YC.
The Staande Mastroute (9.16.2A, Delfzijl-Harlingen) can be entered from the Lauwersmeer at Dokkum.

OTHER HARBOURS IN THE LAUWERSMEER

ZOUTKAMP, Groningen, **53°20'·38N 06°17'·55E**. AC 2593, Zeekaarten 1458, DYC 1812·4; non-tidal. Appr down the Zoutkamperril (2·6-4·5m); approx 2ca before lock/bridge, Hunzegat marina (1·5-2·1m) is to port. ☎ (0595) 402875, SC, Slip. Beyond the lock (FR lts) and close to port is Oude Binnenhaven marina (2m), €3.63; C, ME, El, ⚒, C (20 ton), BH.
Town D, P, SM, Gaz, ⊠, R, ☳, Dr.

OOSTMAHORN, Friesland, **53°22'·94N 06°09'·63E**. AC 2593, Zeekaarten 1458, DYC 1812·4. Non-tidal hbr on W side of Lauwersmeer; lock in as for Lauwersoog. Floating bns with Y flags mark fishing areas. Main hbr with FR and FG lts at ent has marina (2·2-3·0m). VHF Ch 10. HM ☎ (0519) 321445; €0.91, D, P, ⊅, Gaz, R, ☳, C, BY, BH (15T). Approx 450m to the SSE, next to the Voorm Veerhaven (ferry hbr), is a tiny marina with 1·5-2m.

AMELAND

NES, Friesland, 53°26'·22N 05°46'·53E. AC 2593, Zeekaart 1458, DYC 1811.10 & .2. HW –0055 on Dover; ML 1·6m; Duration 0625. See 9.16.13. Shelter from all but E/S winds. Appr from WA SWM buoy via Westgat, Borndiep and Molengat to VA2-R1 SCM lt perch, VQ(6) + L Fl 10s. Lts: see 9.16.4. Beware sandbanks.**Yacht hbr** ('t Leije Gat) HM ☎ (0515) 32159. 140 berths, €0.80. L Fl R 8s and L Fl G 8s piles at ent. Yacht pontoons at N end of hbr (0·8m) beyond ferry terminal; W side dries to soft mud. **Facilities:** Gaz, YC.

TERSCHELLING TO TEXEL AND DEN HELDER

Zeegat Het Vlie, aka Zeegat van Terschelling (AC 112 and DYC 1811.4, .5 and .9), between Terschelling and Vlieland, gives access to the hbrs of **Vlieland, West Terschelling and Harlingen**; it is also a northern approach to the sealock at Kornwerder-zand. Shallow banks extend more than 5M seaward narrowing the ITZ to only 4M wide.

▶*The E-going (flood) stream begins at HW Helgoland +0325, while the W-going (ebb) stream begins at HW Helgoland −0230, sp rates 2·5kn.*◀

The main chan (buoyed/lit) through the banks is Zuider Stortemelk (buoys prefixed 'ZS') running ESE close N of Vlieland into Vliesloot (VS) which leads to **Oost Vlieland** hbr. The Stortemelk (SM) forks eastward at SM1-ZS10 buoy towards the deeper wider channel of Vliestroom.

Approach **West Terschelling** via West Meep and Slenk, **not** by the shorter Schuitengat Zuid which is badly silted. From Zuider Stortemelk the Vliestroom, a deep well buoyed chan (buoys prefixed 'VL'), runs S about 4M until its junction with Blauwe Slenk (BS) and Inschot (IN). Blauwe Slenk runs ESE to **Harlingen**; and Inschot SE to the Kornwerderzand locks into the **IJsselmeer**.

Eierlandsche Gat (DYC 1811.7), between Vlieland and Texel, consists of dangerous shoals between which run very shallow and unmarked chans, only used by fishermen.

Zeegat van Texel (AC 1546) lies between Texel and Den Helder, and gives access to the **Waddenzee**, the tidal part of the former Zuider Zee. Haaksgronden shoals extend 5M seaward. The 3 appr channels are: Molengat from the N along the Texel shore; Westgat unmarked through centre of shoals, where the stream

sets across the chan, is only suitable for passage in good weather and in daylight; and from the SSW the well marked/lit main chan Schulpengat, buoys prefixed 'S'; but strong SW winds cause rough seas against ▶*the SW-going (ebb) stream which begins at HW Helgoland −0330, while the NE-going (flood) stream begins at HW Helgoland +0325, sp rates 1·5kn.*◀

Molengat is marked by 'MG' buoys, but strong winds between W and N raise a bad sea. If approaching from the NW or NE the Molengat is always the best route unless the weather is exceptionally bad.

▶*In Molengat the N-going (ebb) stream begins at HW Helgoland −0145, and the S-going (flood) stream at HW Helgoland +0425, sp rates 1·25kn.*◀

From the N the Schulpengat involves a southerly deviation of approx 15M and leads W of the very dangerous Zuider Haaks which should be avoided in bad weather.

E of **Den Helder** and the Marsdiep, the flood makes in three main directions through the SW Waddenzee:

- to E and SE through Malzwin and Wierbalg to **Den Oever** (where the lock into IJsselmeer is only available during daylight hours on working days); thence NE along the Afsluitdijk, and then N towards Harlingen;

- to NE and E through Texelstroom and Doove Balg towards the Pollen flats; and

- from Texelstroom, NE and N through Scheurrak, Omdraai and Oude Vlie, where it meets the flood stream from Zeegat van Terschelling. The ebb runs in reverse. The **Kornwerderzand** locks (available H24), near NE end of Afsluitdijk, also give access to the IJsselmeer.

9.16.10 HET VLIE (ZEEGAT VAN TERSCHELLING)

9.16.11 WEST TERSCHELLING

West Frisian Islands 53°21'·26N 05°13'·13E ❀❀❀♦♦♦♠♠♠

CHARTS AC 1633, 112; Zeekaart 1456; DYC 1811.4/.5; Imray C25

TIDES –0300 Dover; ML 1·4; Duration No data.

Standard Port HELGOLAND (←)

Times				Height (metres)			
High Water		Low Water		MHWS	MHWN	MLWN	MLWS
0200	0700	0200	0800	2·7	2·4	0·5	0·0
1400	1900	1400	2000				
Differences WEST TERSCHELLING							
–0220	–0250	–0335	–0310	–0·3	–0·2	+0·1	+0·3
VLIELAND-HAVEN							
–0250	–0320	–0355	–0330	–0·3	–0·2	+0·1	+0·4

SHELTER Good in the marina; very crowded in season.

NAVIGATION WPT 53°19'·58N 04°55'·77E (ZS buoy) 099°/6·2M to ZS11-VS2 buoy via Zuider Stortemelk which is well marked/lit. In strong W/NW'lies beware dangerous seas from ZS to ZS5/6 buoys. Stortemelk, the deeper N'ly route, is no shorter and is more exposed. From Vlieree (Vlieland Roads) make for the West Meep Channel; approach HW±2. Call *Brandaris* Ch 02 or 04; see R/T.

West Meep/Slenk is long, but wide, safe and 3·2m deep; hence easier for visitors. Route: WM2, 4 & 6 buoys, NM4–S21 buoy to enter Slenk buoyed/lit chan leading NW into the inner Schuitengat (11m) at SG15/S2 WCM buoy. Expect much commercial traffic and ferries in Slenk.

Note: Schuitengat Zuid, a former approach channel, **is no longer an option for the foreseeable future.**

Ameland can be reached if draft <1·5m by the inshore channels across the Waddenzee (Meep, Noorder Balgen and Oosterom; DYC 1811.4 & .6). Leave at HW –3 to arrive at HW.

LIGHTS AND MARKS Hbr lts as chartlet and 9.16.4. The square, yellow Brandaris light tower dominates the town and hbr.

R/T *Brandaris* (VTS) Ch 02, 04 broadcasts weather, visibility, nav info, traffic, tidal data at odd H+30 in Dutch; English on request. Yachts must monitor Ch 02. Port HM Ch 12. Marina Ch 31 HO.

TELEPHONE (Code 0562) Port HM 443337 (H24), mobile 0655 192503; CG 442341; ⊖ 442884.

TERSCHELLING

FACILITIES Marina Stichting Passantenhaven ☎ 443337. info@jachthaventerschelling.nl. Notices on pontoons A-G indicate berths by LOA and type of boat (yacht, motor cruiser or traditional craft). 500 AB, €1.63/metre + €0.80/head + €0.55. D at marina ent, @, Wi-Fi, Slip, C, Gaz, ME, SM, Chart agent, ▣, ♿.

Village is an easy walk: CH, ☴, R, Bar, ✉, P (cans 5km), ⑧. ✈ Amsterdam. Ferry to Harlingen, thence ⇌ for Hook-Harwich.

9.16.12 VLIELAND

WEST FRISIAN ISLANDS
Friesland 53°17'·68N 05°05'·49E ❀❀❀♦♦♠♠

CHARTS AC 1633, 112; Zeekaart 1456; DYC 1811.4/.5; Imray C26

TIDES –0300 Dover; ML 1·4; Duration 0610. See 9.16.11. The Dutch use Harlingen as a Standard Port.

SHELTER Good in yacht hbr. Two ⚓s, both affected by swell in strong SE-SW'lies near HW: (a) in up to 3m ½M S of the hbr or (b) in 4-9m 1M W of the hbr (beyond the ferry pier). Do not ⚓ in buoyed chan from hbr ent to ferry pier (no AB).

NAVIGATION From ZS buoy (WPT) follow 9.16.12 Navigation, lines 1-3. At ZS11-VS2 and VS1 buoys turn S into Vliesloot (narrow and in places only 2·5m MLWS). Keep in mid-chan past VS3-VS7 buoys to hbr ent (strong current across); tight berths difficult in SW wind.

LIGHTS AND MARKS A dark red lt ho (W lantern, R top) stands on Vuurduin, 1·2M W of the hbr. Hbr lts as chartlet. Tfc sigs: R Flag or ●● at ent = hbr closed (full). The 282° ldg lts (9.16.4 & 9.16.11) lead toward the ferry terminal in E Vlieland.

R/T HM Ch 12. All vessels in Zeegat van Terschelling and N Waddenzee must monitor Ch 02 for *Brandaris Traffic Centre VTS*.

TELEPHONE (Code 0562) HM 451729 (mob 06 201 33086); CG 442341; ⊖ 058 2949488 (Leeuwarden); Police 451312; Dr 451307; Brit Consul (020) 6764343.

FACILITIES Yacht Hbr ☎ 451729. 300 inc ♥s; finger berths on all pontoons in 2m. €0.64 per m² + €1.15 per head; dinghy slip, ▣, ♿, P & D (cans, 10 mins); D at Harlingen. Yacht hbr now complete, no details currently.

Village El, Gaz, ☴, R, @, ✉, ⑧, ✈ (Amsterdam). Ferry as 9.16.11.

VLIELAND

9.16.13 HARLINGEN

Friesland 53°10'·58N 05°24'·23E ✲✲✲⟲⟲⟲⟲⟲

CHARTS AC 1633, 112; Zeekaart 1454, 1456; DYC 1811·5; ANWB B; Imray C26

TIDES –0210 Dover; ML 1·2; Duration 0520.

Standard Port HELGOLAND (◄—)

Times				Height (metres)			
High Water		Low Water		MHWS	MHWN	MLWN	MLWS
0200	0700	0200	0800	2·7	2·4	0·5	0·0
1400	1900	1400	2000				
Differences LAUWERSOOG							
–0130	–0145	–0235	–0220	+0·2	+0·2	+0·2	+0·5
HARLINGEN							
–0155	–0245	–0210	–0130	–0·3	–0·3	0·0	+0·4
NES (AMELAND)							
–0135	–0150	–0245	–0225	+0·2	+0·2	+0·2	+0·5

SHELTER Very good in Noorderhaven. Beware strong flood stream across outer hbr ent; it can be rough at HW in W/NW'lies.

NAVIGATION WPT 53°11'·48N 05°19'·63E [abeam BS23 buoy] 110°/2·8M to hbr ent. See 9.16.11 for appr, thence to the WPT via buoyed Vliestroom and Blauwe Slenk chans; the latter is narrow for the last 2½M. A small craft chan, at least 1·8m, lies parallel to Pollendam trng wall and outboard of the main chan SHM buoys; it is marked by SPM buoys A–N in season. Beware ferries passing very close. Caution: When Pollendam is covered, tidal streams sweep across it.

LIGHTS AND MARKS See chartlet and 9.16.4. Ldg lts 112°, both Iso 6s, H24; B masts, W bands. 2 ch spires are conspic almost on ldg line.

R/T VHF Ch 11 (Not on Sun). Harinxma Canal locks Ch 22.

TELEPHONE (Code 0517) HM 492300; CG (Brandaris) (0562)

442341; ⊜ 058 2949444; Police 413333; Ⓗ 499999; Brit Consul (020) 6764343.

FACILITIES Lifting bridges across the Oude Buitenhaven and Noorderhaven open in unison 2 x per hr 0600-2200 in season (on request in winter), but are shut at times of boat trains/ferries and at HW springs.
Noorderhaven Yacht Hbr ☎ 415666, El, CH, ME, D, P, SM, Ⓔ, Gaz, Diving/salvage (by arrangement) 🍴, R, Bar, Ⓒ.
Yacht Hbr Van Harinxma Canal ☎ 416898, Ⓒ, C (6 ton); only relevant if going via the canal to the lakes.
Town 🍴, R, Bar, ✉, Ⓑ, ≈, ✈ (Amsterdam). Ferry: See Hoek van Holland.

9.16.14 OUDESCHILD

Texel, 53°02'·35N 04°51'·18E ✲✲✲⟲⟲⟲⟲⟲

CHARTS AC 1631, 1546; Zeekaart 1546, 1454; DYC 1811·3

TIDES –0355 Dover; ML 1·1m; Duration 0625.

Standard Port HELGOLAND (◄—)

Times				Height (metres)			
High Water		Low Water		MHWS	MHWN	MLWN	MLWS
0200	0700	0200	0800	2·7	2·4	0·5	0·0
1400	1900	1400	2000				
Differences OUDESCHILD							
–0310	–0420	–0445	–0400	–0·8	–0·7	0·0	+0·3

SHELTER Very good in marina (2·4m) in far NE basin. ⚓ prohib. Visitors are always welcome.

NAVIGATION From Waddenzee appr via Doove Balg and Texelstroom. From seaward, app via Schulpengat or Molengat into Marsdiep (9.16.15). Thence NE via Texelstroom for 3·5M to WPT 53°02'·26N 04°51'·55E (abeam T12 PHM buoy), 291°/400m to hbr ent, keeping the dir lt, Oc 6s, midway between FR and FG mole hd lts. Speed limit 5kn.

LIGHTS AND MARKS See chartlet and 9.16.4. Dir lt Oc 6s, on G mast, is vis only on brg 291°. FR/FG lts are on R/G masts with W bands. Horn (2) 30s on S mole may be sounded only 0600-2300.

R/T Marina Ch 31. HM Ch 12, 0800-2000LT. See 9.16.15 for VTS and radar assistance/info on request.

TELEPHONE (Code 0222) Port HM 312710, mobile 06 1502 8380; ⊜ via HM; CG 316270; Police/ambulance 0900 8844 or 112.

FACILITIES Waddenhaven Texel Marina 250 berths ☎ 321227. info@waddenhaventexel.nl €2·00, D & P, Slip, Ⓒ, ⚓, Ⓒ, Bar, R, mini 🛒 in season, bike hire, Gaz, Internet desk, Wi-fi. **YC WSV Texel**, members only. Dry dock (FVs only). **Village** (walking distance), CH, SM, Gaz, 🍴, Ⓑ, ✉, Bar, R. Ferry from 't Horntje to Den Helder. UK ferries from Hook/Rotterdam. ✈ Amsterdam.

9.16.15 DEN HELDER
Noord Holland 52°57'·94N 04°47'·24E

CHARTS AC 1408, 1631, 1546, 126; Zeekaart 1454, 1546; DYC 1811.2, 1801.10; ANWB F; Imray C25; Stanfords 19.

TIDES –0430 Dover; ML 1·1; Duration No data.

Standard Port HELGOLAND (←)

Times				Height (metres)			
High Water		Low Water		MHWS	MHWN	MLWN	MLWS
0200	0700	0200	0800	2·7	2·4	0·5	0·0
1400	1900	1400	2000				

Differences DEN HELDER
–0410	–0520	–0520	–0430	–0·8	–0·7	+0·1	+0·2

K13A PLATFORM (53°13'·0N 03°13'·1E; 58M WNW of Den Helder)
–0420	–0430	–0520	–0530	–0·9	–0·9	+0·2	+0·3

SHELTER Good in all yacht hbrs (see Facilities). Hbr speed limit 5kn. Den Helder is the main base of the Royal Netherlands Navy which manages the Marinehaven Willemsoord and KMYC.

NAVIGATION Caution: fast ferries to/from Texel, many FVs and offshore service vessels, strong tidal streams across the hbr ent.

Two chans lead into Marsdiep for the hbr ent:

- From the N, Molengat is good except in strong NW winds when seas break heavily. WPT 53°03'·90N 04°39'·37E (MG SWM buoy, Mo (A) 8s) 132°/1.34M to first chan buoys, MG 1/2. Thence to join Marsdiep at S14/MG17 SCM lt buoy.

- From S, the Schulpengat is the main chan, well marked/lit. WPT 52°52'·90N 04°37'·90E (SG (SWM) buoy, Mo (A) 8s, Racon Z] 026·5°/6M towards S14/MG17 SCM lt buoy.

LIGHTS AND MARKS See chartlet and 9.16.4. Schulpengat: Ldg lts, both Oc 8s, and spire 026·5° on Texel. Kijkduin lt ho, R twr, is conspic 2·3M WSW of hbr. Hbr 191° ldg lts; front B ▲ on bldg; rear B ▼ on B lattice twr. A 60m radar twr is conspic on E side of hbr.

Entry sigs, from Hbr Control twr (W side of ent): ● ● (vert) = No entry/exit, except for the vessel indicated by Hbr Control.

Bridges: Moorman bridge operates H24 7/7, giving access to Nieuwe Diep, Koopvaarder Lock and N Holland Canal.

Van Kinsbergen bridge is operated by HM, 0500-2300 Mon-Fri; 0700-1400 Sat. All bridges are closed 0715-0810, 1200-1215, 1245-1300, Mon-Fri. Also 0830-0910 Mon and 1545-1645 Fri. All LT.

R/T Monitor Ch 62 *Den Helder Traffic* (VTS) in the Schulpengat, Molengat and Marsdiep; info on request. *Port Control* Ch 14 (H24); also remote control of van Kinsbergen bridge. Moorman bridge Ch 18 (H24). *Koopvaarders Lock* Ch 22 (H24), also remote control of Burgemeester Vissersbrug.

TELEPHONE (Code 0223) VTS 657522; Municipal HM 613955, mobile ☎ 0652 97 94 80; Pilot 0255 564500; Emergency 112; Police 655700; ⊞ 611414; Water Police 616767; Immigration 657515; ⊖ 020 5813614; Brit Consul (020) 6764343.

FACILITIES KMYC is hard to stbd on entering Naval Hbr. ☎ 652645, €1.20 + €0.73/head, D, Bar, R.

In or near Binnenhaven, YCs/marinas (MWV and YC Den Helder) can only be reached via the Rijkshaven, Moorman bridge, Nieuwe Diep and lock:

MWV YC ☎ 624422, €0.54, P (at garage), D, AB.

YC Den Helder ☎ 637444, mobile 0653 78159, €0.73, Ch 31, AB, ME, El, ✕, C, CH, Slip, R, Bar.

YC WSOV ☎ 652173. **YC HWN** ☎ 624422.

Services: CH, SM, Floating dock, Gaz.

Town P, CH, ☳, R, Bar, ✉, Ⓑ, ⇌, ✈ (Amsterdam). Ferry: Hook-Harwich; Rotterdam-Hull.

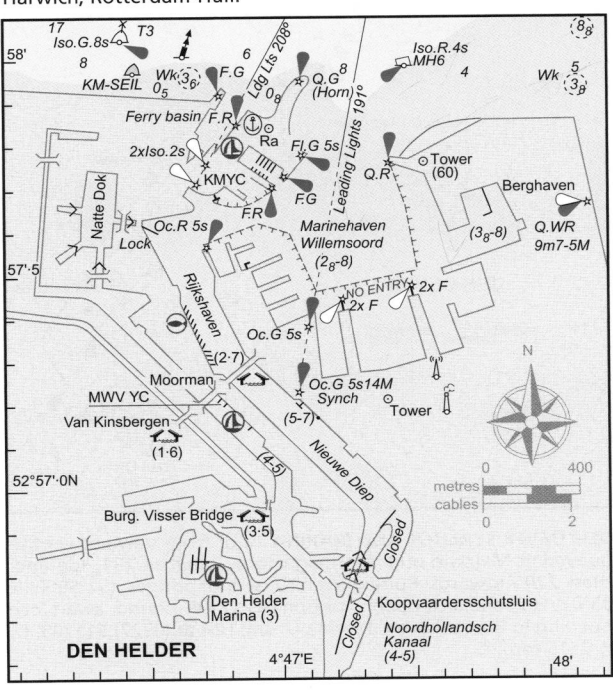

9.16.16 IJSSELMEER

CHARTS Zeekaart 1351, 1454; In-date DYC 1810, sheets 3-5, are essential to avoid live firing ranges, fishing areas and other hazards; 1810 also has many hbr chartlets.

TIDES The IJsselmeer is non-tidal. Tides seaward of Den Oever and Kornwerderzand locks: –0230 Dover; ML 1·2.

Standard Port HELGOLAND (←)

Times				Height (metres)			
High Water		Low Water		MHWS	MHWN	MLWN	MLWS
0200	0700	0200	0800	2·7	2·4	0·5	0·0
1400	1900	1400	2000				
Differences DEN OEVER							
–0245	–0410	–0400	–0305	–0·7	–0·6	–0·1	+0·3
KORNWERDERZAND							
–0210	–0315	–0300	–0215	–0·5	–0·4	0·0	+0·3

SHELTER Excellent in the marinas, but in the IJsselmeer strong winds can get up very quickly and often raise short, steep seas.

NAVIGATION Enter from sea by Den Oever or Kornwerderzand locks; also from IJmuiden via the Noordzeekanaal (9.16.18) and Amsterdam. **Speed limits:** 10·5kn in buoyed chans and <250m from shore. Hbr limits vary; see 9.16.6 for the ANWB *Wateralmanak*.
A firing range, operational Tues to Thurs 1000 - 1900LT, extends S from Breezanddijk (53°01'·0N 05°12'·5E) to 3M NE of Medemblik then NNW to Den Oever (DYC 1811.3 & 1810.3). Call *Schietterrein Breezanddijk* (range control) Ch 71. Firing times are broadcast on VHF Ch 01 by Centrale Meldpost at H +15 on the day of firing, after weather forecasts.

R/T Nav info VHF Ch 01. Sealocks: Kornwerderzand 18; Den Oever 20. Enkhuizen naviduct 22; Lelystad 20; Oranjesluizen 18.

SEALOCKS Standard signals, see 9.16.6.

DEN OEVER SEALOCK AND MARINA Appr from seaward via the buoyed/lit Malzwin and Wierbalg chans. Enter on 131° ldg line, then 220° towards Buitenhaven. 2 swing bridges (52°56'·05N 05°02'·50E) and lock open in unison HO. If NW-bound, await lock opening in Binnenhaven. Marina (2-3m) HM ☎ (0227) 511789, D, P, C (15 ton), ▣.

KORNWERDERZAND SEALOCK From seaward approach from the W via Doove Balg; from NW via shallow Inschot chan; or from N via Boontjes. Entrance to Buitenhaven has FR/G and Iso G 6s lts. When two road bridges (53°04'·44N 05°20'·09E) have opened, yachts enter the smaller Lorentz E lock, operates H24. N-bound, follow 348° ldg lts, Iso 4s, to FR/G at ent. Await lock in Binnenhaven (3·6m). HM ☎ (0517) 578170. ⊜ 058 2949444.

FACILITIES clockwise from Kornwerderzand. Overnight fees range from approx €0.80 - €1.80/metre LOA. Most berths are bows on to a pontoon, stern lines to piles; there are few ⚓s.

IJSSELMEER EAST

MAKKUM: About 1M SE of Kornwerderzand, MA5 SHM buoy, Iso G4s, marks the buoyed chan. FR/FG lts lead 090·5° into Makkum. To stbd, **Marina Makkum** (2·5-2·8m) ☎ (0515) 232828, P, D, SM, Gaz, 🛒, Bar, R, ⬚. 5 other marinas/YCs are further E; BY, ME, C (30 ton), BH (30 ton). **Town** ⬚, Dr, 🛒, R.

WORKUM: 5M S of Makkum; FW ldg lts 081° along buoyed chan to **It Soal Marina** ☎ (0515) 542937, BY, ME, C, D, P (cans), Gaz, BH.

HINDELOOPEN: WV Hylper Haven HM ☎ (0514) 522009, P, D, ME, El, ✕. **Old Hbr** D, P, ME, El, ✕. **Jachthaven Hindeloopen** (500) HM ☎ (0514) 524554, P, D, ⬚, BH (30 ton), CH, R, Bar.

STAVOREN: Ent Buitenhaven 048° on Dir lt Iso 4s between FR/G. Marina, €1·00, E of ent in Oudehaven; ☎ (0514) 681216, VHF Ch 74. Or, 1km S, ent Nieuwe Voorhaven (FR/G & Fl 5s Dir lt) then via lock to **Marina Stavoren** (3m) ☎ (0514) 684684, BY, ME, C, P, D, SM, Gaz, BH (20 ton); **Outer Marina** (3·5m) close S of Nieuwe Voorhaven. Also 3 other marinas. **Town** ⬚, Dr, 🛒, R, ⇌.

LEMMER: Appr on ldg lts 038°, Iso 8s, to KL5/VL2 By; then ldg lts 083°, Iso 8s, through Lemstergeul. Lastly FG and Iso G 4s lead 065° into town and some 14 marinas. **Gem. Jachthaven** HM ☎ (0514) 563343. **Services:** BY, ME, C, P, D, Gaz, SM. **Town** ⬚, Dr, 🛒, R, ⬚.

URK: Hbr ent ½M SE of lt ho. Dir lt Iso G 4s to hbr ent, FR/G. Hbr has 4 basins; keep NNW to berth in Nieuwe Haven, Westhaven or Oosthaven (3·3m). HM ☎ (0527) 689970. **Westhaven** P & D (cans), SM; **Oosthaven** ME, El, ✕, Ⓔ, CH. **Town** EC Tues; ⬚, SM, Dr.

LELYSTAD: Flevo is 2M NNE of lock. (550) ☎ (0320) 279800, BY, ME, C, P, D, Gaz, ⬚, BH (50 ton), R, Bar, 🛒. **Deko Marina** is close N of the lock; ☎ (0320) 269000, SM, C, R. **WV Lelystad, Houtribhaven** (560) HM ☎ (0320) 260198, D, CH, ⬚, 🛒, R, Bar, BH (20 ton). S of lock **Bataviahaven** (150), Ch 14, HM ☎ 06 511 77049. **Marina Lelystadhaven** ☎ (0320) 260326, R.

MARKERMEER is divided from the IJsselmeer by the Houtribdijk 13M long. Access from sea via IJmuiden, Noordzeekanaal, Amsterdam/ Oranjesluizen. Hbrs clockwise from Lelystad to Enkhuizen:

DE BLOCQ VAN KUFFELER: (8·5M SW Lelystad), ☎ 06 2751 2497, R.

MUIDERZAND: Ent 1M N of Hollandsebrug (12·7m cl'nce at SE corner of Markermeer) at buoys IJM5 & IJM7/JH2. **Marina** ☎ (036) 5369151, D, P, C, ME, R, CH.

MUIDEN: Ldg lts Q 181° into **KNZ & RV Marina** (2·6m), W of ent; home of Royal Netherlands YC (150 berths). HM ☎ (0294) 261450, www.knzrv.nl €1·90, D, P (cans), CH, Bar, R. On E bank **Stichting Jachthaven** (70) ☎ (0294) 261223, €1.60, D, P.

DURGERDAM: ½M E of overhead power lines (70m); convenient for Oranjesluizen. Keep strictly in buoyed chan. **WV Durgerdam** Berth to stbd of ent (1·8m). ☎ 06-14750510.

UITDAM: Appr from MIJ5 buoy Fl Y 5s via buoyed chan to FR/FG at ent. C (9 ton), P, D, Gaz, 🛒. HM (020) 4031433.

MARKEN (picturesque show piece): Ent Gouwzee from N, abeam Volendam, thence via buoyed chan; Dir FW lt 116° between FR/G at hbr (2·2m). Lt ho, conspic, Oc 8s 16m 9M, on E end of island. HM ☎ (0299) 601253, free on quay, 🛒, R, ⬚, P & D (cans).

MONNICKENDAM: Appr as for Marken, then W to MO10 Iso R 8s and 236° ldg lts FR. **Hemmeland Marina** ☎ (0299) 655555, (2·0m), C. **Waterland Marina** ☎ 652000, (2·5m), CH, C (15 ton) www.jachthavenwaterland.nl. **Marina Monnickendam** ☎ 652595, (2·0m), C. **Zeilhoek Marina** ☎ 651463, (2·5m), BY.

VOLENDAM: Fork stbd to old hbr (2·4m). Dir lt Fl 5s 313°. FR/FG at ent. ☎ 06 51337494, ME, C, P, D, Gaz, SM. Fork port via unlit buoyed chan to **Marina Volendam** (2·7m) HM(0299) 320262. C (16t), SM, 🛒, B, R.

EDAM: Appr via unlit chan keeping Iso W 8s between FG /R at narrow ent; beware commercial traffic. **Jachthaven WSV De Zeevang** (2·2m) S side of outer hbr. ☎ (0299) 350174, ME, El, ✕. Or lock into the Oorgat and via S canal to Nieuwe Haven. **Town** Bar, ⬚, ⬚, Gaz, ⬚.

HOORN: Radio twr (80m) 1·5M ENE of hbr. Iso 4s 15m 10M and FR/G at W Hbr ent. Four options: To port **Grashaven** (700) HM ☎

(0229) 215208, ⬚, CH, 🛒, ME, El, ✕, C. To stbd ⚓ in **Buitenhaven** (1.6m). Ahead & to stbd **WSV Hoorn**, (100) ☎ 213540. Ahead to **Binnenhaven** (2·5m) via narrow lock (open H24) AB, P. **Town** 🛒, CH, ⬚, R, Dr, P & D (cans), ⬚, Gaz, ⇌.

ENKHUIZEN: 036° ldg lts Iso 4s; 230° ldg lts Iso 8s. Yachts transit the Houtribdijk via a 'Naviduct', ie a twin-chambered lock above the road tunnel below (see chartlet), saving long delays for boat & road traffic; call Ch 22. Krabbersgat lock & bridge, the former bottleneck for both road and sea traffic, can still be used by boats with <6m air clearance.

Compagnieshaven (500) HM ☎ (0228) 313353, P, D, CH, BH (12), Gaz; **Buyshaven** (195) ☎ 315660, FW, AC; **Buitenhaven** ☎ 312444. **Town** EC Mon; Market Wed; C, Slip, CH, SM, ME, El, ✕, ⬚, Bar, P & D (cans), Dr, ⬚, ⇌.

BROEKERHAVEN: Small yacht hbr 1·5M SW of Enkhuizen. Appr from KG15-BR2 buoy. WSV de Broekerhaven ☎ (0228) 518798.

IJSSELMEER WEST

ANDIJK: Visitors use **Stichting Jachthaven Andijk**, the first of 2 marinas; (600) ☎ (0228) 593075, narrow ent with tight turn between FR/G lts. ME, C (20 ton), SM, Gaz, ⬚, D, CH.

MEDEMBLIK: Ent on 232°, Dir lt Oc 5s between FR/G. Thence via Oosterhaven (P & D) into Middenhaven (short stay) and via bridge to Westerhaven. **Pekelharinghaven** (120) HM ☎ (0227) 542175; ent is to port by Castle, CH, Bar, R. **Middenhaven** HM ☎ 541686, FW. **Stichting Jachthaven** HM ☎ 541681 in Westerhaven, ⬚, C. **Town** ⬚, CH, ME, El, SM, ✕, ⬚, Dr, Bar, ⬚, R, 🛒. **Regatta Centre** 0·5M S of hbr entr. HM ☎ (0227) 547781, AB 450, C, Slip, CH, R.

9.16.17   IJMUIDEN

N Holland 52°27'·94N 04°32'·39E (Hbr ent) SPM ✲✿♨♨♨✿✿

CHARTS AC 1631, 124; Zeekaart 1450, 1543, 1035, 1350; DYC 1801.8; Imray C25; Stanfords 19

TIDES +0400 Dover; ML 1·0. Noordzeekanaal level may be above or below sea level

Standard Port VLISSINGEN (→)

Times				Height (metres)			
High Water		Low Water		MHWS	MHWN	MLWN	MLWS
0300	0900	0400	1000	5·0	4·1	1·1	0·5
1500	2100	1600	2200				
Differences IJMUIDEN							
+0145	+0140	+0305	+0325	−2·8	−2·3	−0·7	−0·2
PETTEN (SOUTH) 18M N of IJmuiden							
+0210	+0215	+0345	+0500	−2·9	−2·3	−0·6	−0·2

SHELTER Very good at Seaport (SPM) marina (2·9m-4·8m).

NAVIGATION WPT 52°28'·10N 04°30'·94E, 100°/0·9M to ent. Beware strong tidal streams across hbr ent, scend inside Buitenhaven and commercial tfc – do not impede. Keep a good lookout, especially astern. 3 knots max speed in marina.

Marina access chan is buoyed/lit as per the chartlet.

LOCKS In IJmuiden the 4 locks are North, Middle, South and Small. Yachts normally use the S'most Small lock (Kleine Sluis) which opens H24 on request Ch 22; wait W or E of it.

Lock signals shown W and E from each lock are standard, ie:

- ●
- ● = Lock not in use; no entry.
- ●

- ● = No entry/exit.

- ● = Prepare to enter/exit.

- ● = Enter or exit.

Tidal & sluicing sigs may be shown from or near the conspic Hbr Ops Centre (HOC) bldg, near the front 100·5° ldg lt:

Tidal signals: ● over Ⓦ = rising tide; Ⓦ over ● = falling tide.

Sluicing sigs are a △ of 3 horiz lts and 1 lt at the apex. The sluices are N of the N lock, so unlikely to affect yachts.

LIGHTS AND MARKS Both ldg lt ho's 100·5° for Zuider Buitenkanaal are dark R twrs. The HOC bldg is conspic next to front lt; so are 6 chimneys (138-166m high) 7ca N and ENE of Small lock.

R/T Seaport Marina call *SPM* Ch 74. See also VTS overleaf.

TELEPHONE (Code 0255) Tfc Centre IJmuiden 564500; Hbr Ops 523934; Pilot 564503; ☎ 020 5813614; CG 537644; Police 0900 8844; Ⓗ (023) 5453200; Brit Consul (020) 6764343.

FACILITIES **Seaport Marina** (SPM) ☎ 560300. www.marinaseaport. nl info@ marinaseaport.nl 600 inc Ⓥ, €2.20 inc shwr & AC. Berth as directed, or on M pontoon in a slot with green tally. D & P, El, Ⓔ, BH (70 ton), CH, Gas, Slip, SM, ✕, ME, Wi-fi, R, Bar, ▣, ▦. Buses to Amsterdam and Haarlem in summer.

Town Gaz, ▦, R, Bar, @, ✉, Ⓑ, ⇌ (bus to Beverwijk), ✈ Amsterdam. Ferry: IJmuiden-Newcastle.

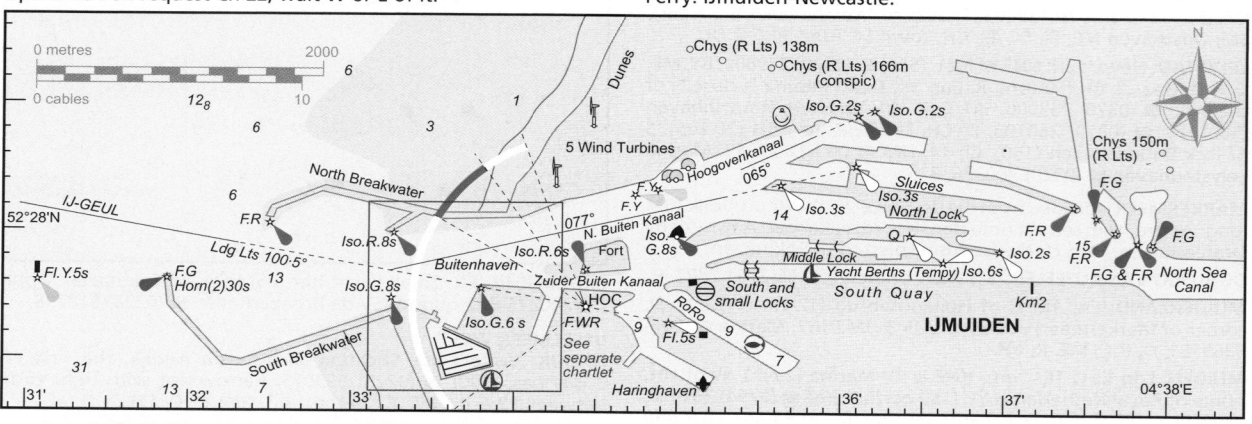

9.16.18   NOORDZEEKANAAL

VTS Monitor the following VTS stns (H24) in sequence to approach, enter and transit the canal (see diagram opposite):

- *Pilot-VTS IJmuiden* — Ch 07 — W of IJM SWM buoy.
- *IJmuiden Port Control* — Ch 61 — IJM buoy to locks.
- *IJmuiden Locks* — Ch 22 — At the locks
- *Sector Noordzeekanaal* — Ch 03 — Locks to km 10·8.
- *Amsterdam Port Control* — Ch 68 — Km 10·8 - Amsterdam City centre (04°55'E)
- *Sector Schellingwoude* — Ch 60 — to Buiten IJ.

Radar surveillance is available on request Ch 07. Visibility reports are broadcast on all VHF chans every H+00 when vis <1000m.

NAVIGATION Canal speed limit is 9 knots. The 13·5M transit is simple, but there is much commercial traffic. Keep as far to stbd as possible. Keep a good lookout for vessels emerging from dock basins and side canals. The banks and ents to basins and side canals are well lit, so night navigation need be no problem apart from the risk of not being seen by other vessels against shore lights.

FACILITIES There are small marinas at IJmond beyond lifting bridge (Ch 18) in Zijkanaal C, km 10 (S bank); and at Nauerna (Zijkanaal D, km 12) (N bank).

WV IJmond ✲✿♨♨✿. Ch 31, HM ☎ (023) 5375003. AB €1.10. AC, D, BY, C (20 ton), ▣, Bar, R.

Fig 9.16.18A Noordzeekanaal VTS

9.16.19 AMSTERDAM ❀❀❀⚓🛥️🌸🌸🌸

Noord Holland 52°22'·97N 04°53'·92E   Marinas

CHARTS AC 124; DYC 1801.8, 1810.2; ANWB G, I

NAVIGATION Het IJ (pronounced eye) is the well lit/buoyed chan through the city centre. From IJ 10/11 to IJ 14/15 buoys yachts must keep out of Het IJ, using a yacht chan between the lateral buoys and RW (N side) or GW (S side) buoys further outboard.

At Oranjesluizen yachts use the most N'ly of 4 locks, marked 'SPORT'; Ch 18, H24. There are waiting piers/jetties either side. The Schellingwoude bridge (9m) opens on the hour and ±20 min, except Mon-Fri 0600-0900 and 1600-1800; VHF Ch 18.

R/T Port Control Ch 68; Info Ch 14. Oranjesluizen Ch 18.

TELEPHONE (Code 020) Port Control (East) 6221515; Port Control (West) 0255 514457; ⊜ 5867511; Emergency 112; Police 0900 8844; Dr 0880 030600; Brit Consul 6764343.

FACILITIES Complete shelter in all yacht hbrs/marinas.

WVDS Sixhaven (52°22'·90N 04°54'·40E, close NE of IJ8 buoy and NE of conspic Central ⇌ Stn) is small and popular, so in season is often full and log-jammed 1800-1100. ☎ 6329429. 100 + Ⓥ, max LOA 15m. €1.50 inc AC, Bar (w/e), ▢, 🛒. www.sixhaven.nl WIP, due to end 2012, on adjacent new Metro N-S line detracts only slightly. Free ferries to N bank (ditto for next entry WV Aeolus).

WV Aeolus 52°22'·91N 04°55'·17E. Few Ⓥ berths and rafting is strictly controlled. ☎ 6360791. Often full in season, no pre-booking, berth as directed. 45 + 8 Ⓥ, €1.10. AC, YC, Bar, 🛒.

Aquadam Twellegea 52°23'·04N 04°56'·63E, ent to Zijkanaal K. ☎ 6320616. €2.50, ⚓, P, C (30 ton). www.aquadam.nl Full BY facilities. Bus to city centre.

WV Zuiderzee 52°22'·95N 04°57'·77E, 140m NE of Oranjesluizen. ☎ 4904222. €1.10, YC.

City All needs; Gaz, Ⓔ, ACA, DYC Agent, Ⓑ, @, Wi-Fi, ✉, ⇌, ✈. Amsterdam gives access to the N Holland and Rijn canals.

9.16.20 SCHEVENINGEN

Zuid Holland 52°06'·24N 04°15'·26E ✦✦✧✧✧✧✧✧

CHARTS AC 1630, 122; Zeekaart 1035, 1349, 1350, 1449; DYC 1801.7; ANWB H/J; Imray C25; Stanfords 19

TIDES +0320 Dover; ML 0·9; Duration 0445.

Standard Port VLISSINGEN (→)

Times				Height (metres)			
High Water		Low Water		MHWS	MHWN	MLWN	MLWS
0300	0900	0400	1000	5·0	4·1	1·1	0·5
1500	2100	1600	2200				
Differences SCHEVENINGEN							
+0105	+0100	+0220	+0245	−2·7	−2·2	−0·7	−0·2

SHELTER Very good in marina. Ent difficult in SW-N F6 winds, and dangerous in NW F6-8 which cause scend in outer hbr.

NAVIGATION WPT 52°07'·75N 04°14'·12E (SCH buoy) 156°/1·6M to ent; access H24. Close west of the 156° leading line and 1M from the hbr ent, outfalls are marked by E and W cardinal light buoys and by 2 SPM buoys (off chartlet). The promenade pier, Iso 5s, is 1·2M NE of the hbr ent. Caution: Strong tidal streams set across the ent. Slack water is about HW Scheveningen −2 and +3. Beware large ships and FVs entering/leaving.

LIGHTS AND MARKS Daymarks include: the reddish-brown lt ho (5ca E of hbr ent); twr bldgs in Scheveningen and Den Haag.

Traffic signals (from signal mast, N side of ent to Voorhaven):

● over ○ = No entry. ○ over ● = No exit.
Fl ● = One or more large vessels are leaving the port.

Tide sigs (same mast): ● over ○ = tide rising. ○ ● = tide falling.

Shown from SE end of narrow chan between 1st and 2nd Hbrs:
● = vessels must not leave the 2nd Hbr. The chan is generally blind, so go slowly and sound horn.

R/T Call *Traffic Centre Scheveningen* Ch 21 (H24) prior to entry/ departure to avoid FVs. Radar (info only) on request Ch 21. When in 2nd Hbr call *Yacht Club Scheveningen* Ch 31 for a berth.

TELEPHONE (Code 070) Port HM 3527701; ⊜ 020 5813614; Police 0900 8844; Dr 3450650; Brit Consul (020) 6764343.

FACILITIES YC Scheveningen ☎ 3520017, mobile 0653 293137. www.jachtclub.com 223 + 100 **Ⓥ**, €1.66 plus tax €1.27 per adult. Visitors *must* turn to berth/raft bows NE, for fire safety reasons. Wi-Fi, ⬚, Bar, R ☎ 3520308.
2nd Harbour Fuel barge GEO (0630-1600), D only. Slip, DYC agent; WIP (2007) on new BY, C, CH, El, ME, ✗, SM.
Town P, ⬚, R, Bar, ✉, Ⓑ, ⇌, ✈ Rotterdam and Amsterdam. The town is effectively merged with Den Haag (The Hague), seat of Dutch government and well worth a visit by bus.

DEN HELDER TO SCHEVENINGEN

South of Den Helder the coast is low, and, like most of the Dutch coast, not readily visible from seaward. Conspic landmarks include: chimneys of nuclear power station 1·5M NNE of Petten; Egmond aan Zee light house; chimneys of steelworks N of IJmuiden; two light houses at IJmuiden; big hotels at Zandvoort; Noordwijk aan Zee light house; and Scheveningen light house and big hotels.

A wind farm centred on 52°36'·2N 04°26'·4E (about 6·7M W of Egmond aan Zee) contains a No Entry area marked by 5 peripheral turbines, each L Fl Y 15s 15m 5M, Horn Mo (U) 30s. A second No Entry wind farm is 8M further W, centred on 52°35'·4N 04°13'·2E and marked by 6 cardinal lt buoys (2W, 2E, 1N, 1S); see AC 1631.

▶*3M W of IJmuiden the N-going stream begins at HW Hoek van Holland –0120, and the S-going at HW Hoek van Holland +0430, sp rates about 1·5kn. Off ent to IJmuiden the stream turns about 1h earlier and is stronger, and in heavy weather there may be a dangerous sea.*◀ From **IJmuiden** the **Noordzeekanaal** leads east to **Amsterdam** and the **IJsselmeer**.

HOEK VAN HOLLAND TO THE WESTERSCHELDE

Off Hoek van Holland at the ent to Europoort and **Rotterdam** shipping is very dense and fast-moving. Yachts must go up-river via the Nieuwe Waterweg which near Vlaardingen becomes the Nieuwe Maas.

The Slijkgat (lit) is the approach chan to **Stellendam** and entry to the Haringvliet. The Schaar, Schouwenbank, Middelbank and Steenbanken lie parallel to the coast off the approaches to Oosterschelde. From the N, Geul van de Banjaard (partly lit) joins

Westgat and leads to Oude Roompot, which with Roompot (unlit) are the main, well marked channels to the **Roompotsluis**, in S half of the barrage. Here the Oosterschelde (AC 192) is entered.

Rounding Walcheren via the Oostgat, close inshore, Westkapelle lt ho is conspic with two smaller lts nearby: Molenhoofd 5ca WSW and Noorderhoofd 7ca NNW. The Oostgat is the inshore link between Oosterschelde and Westerschelde and also the N approach to the latter.

Deurloo and Spleet are unlit secondary channels parallel to Oostgat and a mile or so to seaward. By day they keep yachts clear of commercial traffic in the Oostgat.

All channels converge between **Vlissingen** and **Breskens**. This bottleneck is declared a Precautionary Area in which yachts have no rights of way over other vessels and therefore must keep an above average lookout, staying clear of all traffic. Vessels <20m must give way to larger craft; and yachts <12m should stay just outside the main buoyed chans.

The main approach chan to the Westerschelde from the W is the Scheur, which yachts may follow just outside the fairway. From **Zeebrugge** and the SW use the Wielingen chan, keeping close to S side of estuary until past **Breskens**.

If proceeding to **Vlissingen**, cross between Songa and SS1 buoys, observing the mini-TSS which runs E/W close off Vlissingen. The tide runs hard in the estuary, causing a bad sea in chans and overfalls on some banks in strong winds.

The passage up-river to **Antwerpen** is best made in one leg, starting from Breskens, Vlissingen or **Terneuzen** in order to get the tidal timing right. More detail in *North France and Belgium Cruising Companion*, NDL/Featherstone.

9.16.21   TSS AND VTS OFF S NETHERLANDS AND BELGIUM

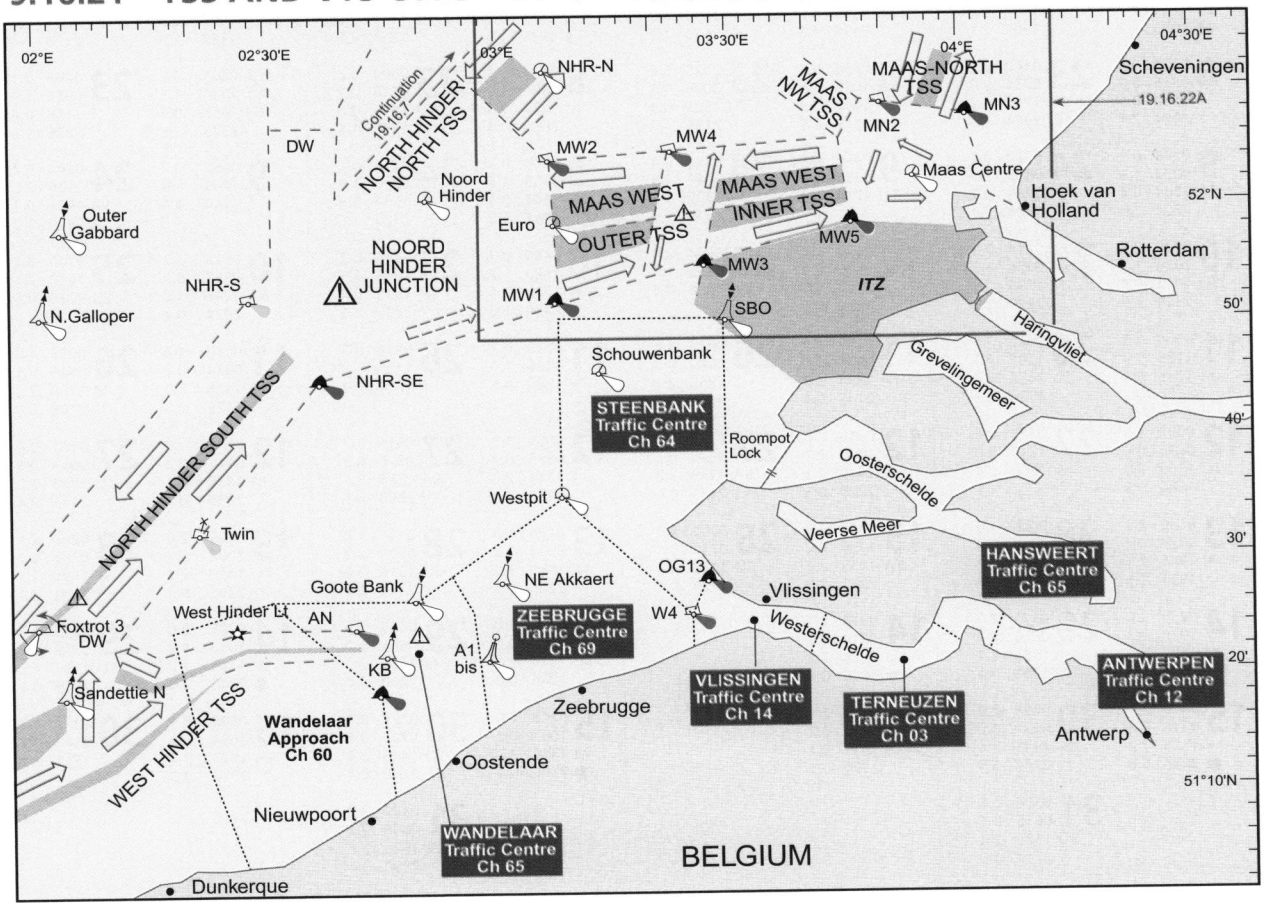

TIME ZONE -0100
Subtract 1 hour for UT
For Dutch Summer Time add
ONE hour in **non-shaded areas**

HOEK VAN HOLLAND   LAT 51°59'N   LONG 4°07'E
TIMES AND HEIGHTS OF HIGH AND LOW WATERS

Dates in red are **SPRINGS**
Dates in blue are **NEAPS**

YEAR 2010

JANUARY

Time	m		Time	m
1 0239	2.1	**16** 0339	2.1
0756	0.3	0851	0.2
F 1457	2.4	SA 1546	2.2
2015	0.5	2104	0.6
2 0325	2.1	**17** 0405	2.1
0836	0.2	0903	0.2
SA 1541	2.4	SU 1619	2.3
2340	0.5	2129	0.6
3 0408	0.2	**18** 0445	2.1
0911	0.2	0934	0.2
SU 1626	2.4	M 1656	2.2
4 0026	0.5	**19** 0000	0.6
0455	2.1	0515	2.1
M 0959	0.1	TU 1016	0.2
1715	2.4	1725	2.2
5 0105	0.5	**20** 0044	0.5
0546	2.1	0545	2.1
TU 1056	0.1	W 1044	0.2
1800	2.4	1800	2.2
6 0150	0.5	**21** 0126	0.5
0635	2.1	0616	2.1
W 1143	0.1	TH 1125	0.1
1859	2.3	1829	2.2
7 0210	0.5	**22** 0140	0.5
0729	2.0	0650	2.0
TH 1254	0.1	F 1204	0.1
☽ 1955	2.2	1905	2.1
8 0205	0.5	**23** 0140	0.5
0825	2.0	0735	2.0
F 1354	0.1	SA 1304	0.2
2054	2.1	☾ 1954	2.1
9 0244	0.5	**24** 0220	0.5
0930	1.9	0836	1.9
SA 1504	0.2	SU 1414	0.2
2204	2.0	2104	2.0
10 0406	0.5	**25** 0315	0.5
1039	1.9	0950	1.9
SU 1615	0.3	M 1524	0.3
2324	1.9	2225	1.9
11 0505	0.5	**26** 0420	0.5
1156	1.9	1105	1.9
M 1735	0.4	TU 1656	0.3
		2334	1.9
12 0033	1.9	**27** 0525	0.4
0825	0.4	1215	2.0
TU 1300	2.0	W 1806	0.4
1840	0.5		
13 0136	2.0	**28** 0045	1.9
0924	0.4	0614	0.4
W 1345	2.1	TH 1305	2.1
1924	0.5	2120	0.4
14 0230	2.0	**29** 0139	0.3
1020	0.3	0656	0.3
TH 1435	2.1	F 1355	2.2
2004	0.5	2155	0.4
15 0310	2.1	**30** 0225	2.0
0810	0.3	0731	0.2
F 1515	2.2	SA 1441	2.4
● 2034	0.6	○ 2246	0.5
		31 0308	2.1
		0815	0.1
		SU 1525	2.4
		2314	0.5

FEBRUARY

Time	m		Time	m
1 0355	2.1	**16** 0416	2.1
0851	0.1	0909	0.2
M 1606	2.5	TU 1626	2.3
		2335	0.5
2 0005	0.5	**17** 0445	2.2
0435	2.2	0934	0.2
TU 0935	0.0	W 1656	2.2
1656	2.4		
3 0044	0.5	**18** 0025	0.4
0521	2.2	0511	2.1
W 1025	0.0	TH 1015	0.2
1737	2.4	1725	2.2
4 0125	0.5	**19** 0105	0.4
0606	2.2	0539	2.1
TH 1119	0.1	F 1045	0.1
1828	2.3	1758	2.2
5 0150	0.5	**20** 0135	0.4
0656	2.1	0616	2.1
F 1234	0.1	SA 1125	0.1
1926	2.1	1836	2.2
6 0127	0.4	**21** 0000	0.3
0750	2.1	0651	2.1
SA 1344	0.1	SU 1209	0.1
☽ 2014	2.0	1915	2.1
7 0226	0.4	**22** 0034	0.3
0850	2.0	0739	2.0
SU 1455	0.2	M 1350	0.2
2129	1.8	☾ 2019	1.9
8 0336	0.4	**23** 0225	0.4
1016	1.8	0906	1.9
M 1605	0.4	TU 1505	0.3
2316	1.7	2155	1.7
9 0456	0.4	**24** 0334	0.4
1135	1.8	1046	1.8
TU 1724	0.4	W 1625	0.4
		2315	1.7
10 0026	1.8	**25** 0444	0.4
0550	0.3	1156	1.9
W 1250	1.8	TH 1950	0.4
1830	0.5		
11 0125	1.9	**26** 0029	1.8
0926	0.3	0544	0.3
TH 1334	2.0	F 1255	2.1
2145	0.4	2106	0.4
12 0216	2.0	**27** 0125	1.9
1010	0.2	0625	0.2
F 1419	2.1	SA 1339	2.2
2225	0.5	2135	0.4
13 0249	2.0	**28** 0205	2.0
1056	0.2	0710	0.1
SA 1455	2.2	SU 1420	2.3
2257	0.5	○ 2225	0.4
14 0314	2.1		
0814	0.2		
SU 1526	2.2		
● 2045	0.5		
15 0345	2.1		
0834	0.2		
M 1555	2.2		
2300	0.5		

MARCH

Time	m		Time	m
1 0251	2.1	**16** 0316	2.1
0745	0.1	0815	0.2
M 1505	2.4	TU 1521	2.2
2254	0.5	2237	0.4
2 0331	2.2	**17** 0339	2.1
0830	0.0	0839	0.2
TU 1547	2.4	W 1556	2.2
2350	0.4	2315	0.4
3 0416	2.2	**18** 0411	2.2
0911	0.0	1155	2.2
W 1633	2.4	TH 1625	2.2
4 0035	0.4	**19** 0016	0.3
0456	2.2	0441	2.2
TH 1005	0.1	F 1235	0.2
1715	2.3	1655	2.2
5 0125	0.4	**20** 0035	0.3
0537	2.2	0515	2.2
F 1055	0.1	SA 1015	0.2
1801	2.1	1729	2.2
6 0210	0.4	**21** 0120	0.3
0625	2.2	0548	2.2
SA 1230	0.2	SU 1059	0.2
1844	2.0	1807	2.1
7 0040	0.3	**22** 0004	0.2
0715	2.1	0625	2.2
SU 1335	0.2	M 1144	0.2
☽ 1935	1.8	1851	2.0
8 0135	0.3	**23** 0004	0.2
0804	1.9	0718	2.1
M 1424	0.3	TU 1416	0.2
2050	1.6	☾ 1956	1.8
9 0300	0.3	**24** 0216	0.2
0935	1.8	0830	1.9
TU 1545	0.4	W 1504	0.3
2235	1.5	2124	1.6
10 0436	0.3	**25** 0315	0.2
1126	1.7	1015	1.8
W 1705	0.4	TH 1615	0.4
2359	1.6	2255	1.6
11 0525	0.2	**26** 0414	0.3
1236	1.9	1131	1.9
TH 1805	0.5	F 1934	0.4
12 0059	1.8	**27** 0015	1.7
0615	0.2	0520	0.2
F 1313	2.0	SA 1235	2.1
2125	0.4	2035	0.3
13 0150	1.9	**28** 0101	1.8
0934	0.2	0559	0.2
SA 1355	2.1	SU 1315	2.2
2205	0.4	2114	0.4
14 0226	2.0	**29** 0145	1.9
1025	0.2	0645	0.1
SU 1426	2.1	M 1401	2.3
2246	0.4	2200	0.4
15 0249	2.0	**30** 0227	2.1
1037	0.2	0725	0.1
M 1456	2.2	TU 1446	2.3
● 2300	0.4	○ 2246	0.4
		31 0307	2.2
		0806	0.1
		W 1525	2.3
		2330	0.4

APRIL

Time	m		Time	m
1 0347	2.2	**16** 0338	2.2
0849	0.1	1125	0.2
TH 1609	2.2	F 1557	2.2
		2355	0.3
2 0026	0.3	**17** 0415	2.2
0431	2.3	1210	0.2
F 1244	0.2	SA 1631	2.1
1652	2.1	2140	0.3
3 0105	0.3	**18** 0448	0.2
0510	2.2	1256	0.2
SA 1325	0.2	SU 1712	2.1
1738	2.0	2226	0.2
4 0156	0.2	**19** 0527	2.2
0555	2.2	1304	0.2
SU 1330	0.3	M 1751	2.0
1822	1.9	2316	0.2
5 0000	0.2	**20** 0612	2.2
0646	2.1	1356	0.3
M 1320	0.3	TU 1839	1.8
1909	1.8		
6 0105	0.2	**21** 0020	0.2
0734	1.9	0705	2.1
TU 1426	0.3	W 1405	0.3
☽ 2004	1.6	☾ 1945	1.7
7 0240	0.2	**22** 0134	0.1
0906	1.7	0819	2.0
W 1525	0.4	TH 1455	0.4
2130	1.5	2115	1.6
8 0405	0.2	**23** 0245	0.1
1034	1.7	0956	1.9
TH 1635	0.4	F 1756	0.4
2325	1.5	2236	1.6
9 0455	0.2	**24** 0344	0.2
1145	1.8	1110	2.0
F 1744	0.4	SA 1905	0.3
		2339	1.7
10 0026	1.7	**25** 0740	0.2
0555	0.2	1210	2.1
SA 1246	1.9	SU 2026	0.3
2024	0.4		
11 0110	1.8	**26** 0035	1.8
0634	0.2	0846	0.1
SU 1325	2.0	M 1258	2.2
2125	0.3	2106	0.3
12 0146	1.9	**27** 0121	2.0
0917	0.2	0619	0.1
M 1356	2.1	TU 1338	2.2
2155	0.3	2135	0.4
13 0209	2.0	**28** 0202	2.1
1006	0.2	0705	0.1
TU 1419	2.1	W 1425	2.2
2246	0.3	○ 2204	0.4
14 0235	2.0	**29** 0245	2.2
1030	0.2	0749	0.2
W 1449	2.2	TH 1507	2.2
● 2240	0.4	2009	0.3
15 0308	2.1	**30** 0327	2.2
1054	0.2	0840	0.2
TH 1525	2.2	F 1551	2.1
2310	0.3		

Chart Datum is 0·84 metres below NAP Datum. HAT is 2·4 metres above Chart Datum; see 4.5.

》》 FREE monthly updates from **《《**
www.reedsalmanac.co.uk

TIME ZONE -0100
Subtract 1 hour for UT
For Dutch Summer Time add
ONE hour in **non-shaded areas**

HOEK VAN HOLLAND   LAT 51°59'N   LONG 4°07'E
TIMES AND HEIGHTS OF HIGH AND LOW WATERS

Dates in **red** are **SPRINGS**
Dates in blue are **NEAPS**

YEAR 2010

Netherlands

MAY

	Time	m		Time	m
1 SA	0005 0411 1215 1636	0.2 2.2 0.3 1.9	**16** SU	0350 1150 1615 2130	2.2 0.3 2.1 0.2
2 SU	0045 0455 1316 1719	0.2 2.2 0.3 1.9	**17** M	0431 1236 1656 2205	2.2 0.3 2.0 0.2
3 M	0135 0535 1350 1759	0.1 2.1 0.3 1.8	**18** TU	0515 1316 1741 2305	2.2 0.3 1.9 0.1
4 TU	0200 0626 1310 1844	0.1 2.1 0.4 1.7	**19** W	0601 1345 1835	2.2 0.3 1.8
5 W	0034 0713 1345 1946	0.1 1.9 0.4 1.7	**20** TH	0004 0659 1440 1956	0.1 2.1 0.3 1.7
6 TH	0150 0820 1500 2035	0.1 1.8 0.4 1.6	**21** F	0120 0815 1600 2106	0.0 2.1 0.4 1.7
7 F	0325 0925 1605 2145	0.1 1.7 0.4 1.5	**22** SA	0225 0929 1730 2206	0.1 2.0 0.4 1.7
8 SA	0445 1055 1710 2330	0.1 1.8 0.4 1.6	**23** SU	0315 1040 1835 2305	0.1 2.1 0.4 1.8
9 SU	0524 1156 1755	0.1 1.9 0.4	**24** M	0420 1139 1950	0.1 2.1 0.3
10 M	0026 0620 1236 2027	1.7 0.2 2.0 0.3	**25** TU	0005 0805 1236 2040	1.9 0.2 2.1 0.3
11 TU	0056 0820 1316 2125	1.8 0.2 2.0 0.3	**26** W	0057 0609 1326 2125	2.0 0.2 2.1 0.4
12 W	0130 0925 1346 2155	1.9 0.2 2.1 0.3	**27** TH	0145 0654 1411 1924	2.0 0.3 2.1 0.3
13 TH	0201 0725 1419 2245	2.0 0.3 2.2 0.3	**28** F	0228 0750 1458 2005	2.1 0.3 2.1 0.3
14 F	0238 0755 1455 2310	2.1 0.3 2.2 0.3	**29** SA	0315 0834 1545 2050	2.2 0.4 2.0 0.2
15 SA	0315 1114 1535 2334	2.2 0.3 2.1 0.3	**30** SU	0357 1205 1625	2.2 0.4 2.0
			31 M	0036 0434 1256 1704	0.1 2.2 0.4 1.9

JUNE

	Time	m		Time	m
1 TU	0110 0521 1336 1745	0.1 2.1 0.4 1.9	**16** W	0506 1300 1739 2245	2.3 0.3 1.9 0.1
2 W	0140 0603 1330 1825	0.1 2.1 0.5 1.8	**17** TH	0555 1356 1829 2345	2.2 0.4 1.9 0.1
3 TH	0000 0656 1330 1916	0.1 2.0 0.5 1.8	**18** F	0648 1425 1924	2.2 0.4 1.8
4 F	0054 0746 1420 2006	0.1 1.9 0.4 1.7	**19** SA	0055 0755 1520 2024	0.0 2.2 0.4 1.8
5 SA	0220 0845 1517 2055	0.1 1.9 0.4 1.7	**20** SU	0154 0905 1650 2135	0.0 2.1 0.4 1.8
6 SU	0400 0940 1615 2155	0.1 1.8 0.4 1.7	**21** M	0306 1005 1757 2240	0.1 2.0 0.4 1.8
7 M	0445 1034 1705 2306	0.2 1.9 0.4 1.7	**22** TU	0405 1111 1855 2339	0.2 2.0 0.4 1.9
8 TU	0540 1133 1745	0.2 1.9 0.4	**23** W	0515 1215 2010	0.2 2.0 0.4
9 W	0006 0617 1230 1830	1.8 0.3 2.0 0.3	**24** TH	0039 0609 1315 1834	2.0 0.3 2.0 0.3
10 TH	0045 0625 1311 1855	1.9 0.3 2.1 0.3	**25** F	0135 0716 1405 1919	2.0 0.4 2.0 0.3
11 F	0129 0655 1355 1930	2.0 0.3 2.1 0.3	**26** SA	0225 0745 1456 2006	2.1 0.4 2.0 0.2
12 SA	0215 0739 1435 2000	2.1 0.3 2.1 0.3	**27** SU	0305 0834 1533 2035	2.1 0.5 2.0 0.2
13 SU	0256 0815 1519 2036	2.2 0.4 2.1 0.2	**28** M	0345 0904 1613 2114	2.2 0.5 2.0 0.1
14 M	0338 1135 1606 2116	2.3 0.5 2.0 0.2	**29** TU	0425 1230 1649 2144	2.2 0.5 2.0 0.1
15 TU	0418 1215 1649 2155	2.3 0.4 2.0 0.1	**30** W	0505 1315 1730 2224	2.2 0.5 2.0 0.1

JULY

	Time	m		Time	m
1 TH	0546 1320 1759 2320	2.1 0.5 1.9 0.1	**16** F	0537 1336 1809 2315	2.3 0.4 1.9 0.0
2 F	0626 1317 1833 2355	2.1 0.5 1.9 0.1	**17** SA	0629 1410 1854	2.3 0.5 2.0
3 SA	0654 1350 1915	2.0 0.5 1.9	**18** SU	0019 0726 1430 1956	0.1 2.2 0.5 2.0
4 SU	0044 0745 1420 2010	0.1 2.0 0.4 1.8	**19** M	0140 0830 1424 2056	0.1 2.1 0.4 1.9
5 M	0144 0835 1445 2105	0.2 1.9 0.4 1.8	**20** TU	0234 0955 1515 2206	0.1 2.0 0.4 1.9
6 TU	0235 0945 1600 2204	0.2 1.9 0.4 1.8	**21** W	0350 1043 1624 2320	0.2 1.9 0.4 1.9
7 W	0344 1046 1710 2316	0.3 1.9 0.4 1.8	**22** TH	0504 1210 1735	0.3 1.9 0.4
8 TH	0520 1145 1800	0.3 1.9 0.4	**23** F	0024 0604 1310 1825	1.9 0.4 1.9 0.3
9 F	0016 0610 1246 1824	1.9 0.3 2.0 0.3	**24** SA	0124 0654 1406 1905	2.0 0.5 1.9 0.3
10 SA	0108 0644 1336 1854	2.0 0.4 2.0 0.3	**25** SU	0213 0734 1445 1950	2.1 0.5 2.0 0.3
11 SU	0152 0724 1418 1935	2.1 0.4 2.0 0.2	**26** M	0254 0805 1523 2014	2.2 0.6 2.0 0.2
12 M	0237 0806 1506 2015	2.2 0.4 2.0 0.2	**27** TU	0328 0840 1554 2044	2.2 0.6 2.1 0.2
13 TU	0321 1120 1548 2056	2.3 0.5 2.0 0.1	**28** W	0405 0904 1629 2126	2.2 0.6 2.1 0.1
14 W	0405 1154 1636 2135	2.4 0.5 2.0 0.1	**29** TH	0446 1220 1659 2200	2.2 0.6 2.1 0.1
15 TH	0447 1245 1721 2221	2.4 0.5 2.0 0.0	**30** F	0515 1237 1729 2236	2.2 0.5 2.1 0.2
31 SA	0545 1307 1759 2309	2.1 0.5 2.0 0.2			

AUGUST

	Time	m		Time	m
1 SU	0615 1829 2349	2.1 2.0 0.2	**16** M	0651 1330 1920	2.2 0.5 2.1
2 M	0649 1330 1904	2.1 0.5 2.0	**17** TU	0115 0749 1354 2013	0.2 2.0 0.4 1.9
3 TU	0035 0729 1400 1953	0.2 2.0 0.4 1.9	**18** W	0225 0855 1444 2136	0.3 1.9 0.4 1.9
4 W	0206 0835 1456 2115	0.2 1.9 0.4 1.8	**19** TH	0325 1024 1614 2306	0.4 1.7 0.4 1.9
5 TH	0254 0955 1600 2236	0.3 1.9 0.4 1.8	**20** F	0444 1155 1714	0.5 1.8 0.4
6 F	0430 1105 1720 2345	0.4 1.8 0.4 1.9	**21** SA	0026 0710 1306 1809	2.0 0.5 1.9 0.3
7 SA	0550 1219 1754	0.4 1.9 0.4	**22** SU	0114 0946 1344 2156	2.1 0.5 2.0 0.3
8 SU	0045 0624 1319 1833	2.0 0.4 1.9 0.3	**23** M	0205 1015 1425 2225	2.2 0.5 2.1 0.3
9 M	0138 0937 1405 1915	2.2 0.5 2.0 0.2	**24** TU	0234 1054 1506 2006	2.2 0.6 2.1 0.3
10 TU	0221 1026 1449 1949	2.3 0.5 2.1 0.2	**25** W	0309 0815 1536 2025	2.2 0.6 2.1 0.2
11 W	0302 1106 1529 2030	2.4 0.5 2.1 0.1	**26** TH	0339 0844 1559 2055	2.3 0.6 2.2 0.2
12 TH	0345 1400 1610 2112	2.5 0.5 2.1 0.1	**27** F	0415 0915 1629 2126	2.3 0.6 2.2 0.2
13 F	0429 1225 1656 2155	2.4 0.5 2.2 0.1	**28** SA	0438 1205 1655 2155	2.3 0.5 2.2 0.3
14 SA	0515 1305 1738 2245	2.4 0.5 2.2 0.1	**29** SU	0509 1250 1726 2230	2.2 0.5 2.1 0.3
15 SU	0601 1347 1825 2349	2.3 0.5 2.2 0.2	**30** M	0537 1050 1755 2305	2.2 0.4 2.2 0.2
			31 TU	0611 1114 1825 2344	2.2 0.4 2.2 0.2

Chart Datum is 0·84 metres below NAP Datum. HAT is 2·4 metres above Chart Datum; see 4.5.

TIME ZONE -0100 **Subtract 1 hour for UT** For Dutch Summer Time add ONE hour in **non-shaded areas**	**HOEK VAN HOLLAND** LAT 51°59'N LONG 4°07'E TIMES AND HEIGHTS OF HIGH AND LOW WATERS

Dates in red are **SPRINGS**
Dates in blue are NEAPS

YEAR 2010

SEPTEMBER

Time	m		Time	m
1 0655	2.1	**16** 0205		0.4
1204	0.4		0814	1.8
W 1909	2.1	TH 1415		0.4
☽			2105	1.9
2 0044	0.3	**17** 0326		0.5
0738	2.0		0955	1.6
TH 1400	0.4	F 1606		0.4
2009	2.0		2256	1.8
3 0235	0.4	**18** 0450		0.6
0916	1.8		1136	1.7
F 1515	0.4	SA 1705		0.4
2206	1.9			
4 0404	0.5	**19** 0006		2.0
1040	1.7		0710	0.6
SA 1624	0.4	SU 1235		1.9
2326	1.9		1745	0.3
5 0610	0.5	**20** 0055		2.1
1154	1.8		0905	0.5
SU 1724	0.4	M 1326		2.0
			2125	0.3
6 0024	2.1	**21** 0134		2.2
0835	0.5		0956	0.5
M 1254	1.9	TU 1405		2.1
1805	0.3		2210	0.3
7 0118	2.3	**22** 0209		2.2
0930	0.5		1036	0.5
TU 1341	2.0	W 1436		2.1
1848	0.2		1945	0.3
8 0159	2.4	**23** 0239		2.3
0955	0.5		1055	0.6
W 1426	2.1	TH 1459		2.1
● 1926	0.2	○ 1954		0.3
9 0241	2.5	**24** 0309		2.3
0749	0.6		0815	0.6
TH 1505	2.2	F 1526		2.2
2002	0.1		2026	0.3
10 0323	2.5	**25** 0339		2.3
0825	0.6		0845	0.5
F 1547	2.3	SA 1556		2.3
2045	0.1		2049	0.3
11 0406	2.5	**26** 0409		2.3
0910	0.6		0929	0.5
SA 1629	2.3	SU 1625		2.3
2129	0.2		2126	0.4
12 0449	2.4	**27** 0439		2.3
0955	0.5		0956	0.5
SU 1712	2.4	M 1656		2.3
2225	0.3		2200	0.3
13 0536	2.2	**28** 0512		2.2
1045	0.5		1013	0.4
M 1756	2.3	TU 1726		2.3
2324	0.3		2240	0.3
14 0621	2.1	**29** 0547		2.2
1144	0.5		1106	0.4
TU 1846	2.2	W 1805		2.3
			2320	0.4
15 0116	0.4	**30** 0625		2.1
0715	1.9		1145	0.3
W 1305	0.4	TH 1848		2.2
◑ 1945	2.1			

OCTOBER

Time	m		Time	m
1 0030	0.4	**16** 0245		0.6
0718	2.0		0904	1.6
F 1257	0.4	SA 1530		0.4
◑ 1946	2.1		2210	1.9
2 0225	0.5	**17** 0430		0.7
0834	1.8		1106	1.7
SA 1434	0.4	SU 1634		0.3
2135	1.9		2336	1.9
3 0350	0.6	**18** 0630		0.6
1015	1.7		1206	1.8
SU 1545	0.4	M 1724		0.3
2300	2.0			
4 0647	0.6	**19** 0019		2.1
1136	1.8		0804	0.5
M 1645	0.4	TU 1250		1.9
			1814	0.3
5 0005	2.2	**20** 0106		2.2
0814	0.5		0854	0.5
TU 1231	1.9	W 1324		2.0
1735	0.3		2110	0.4
6 0055	2.4	**21** 0139		2.2
0916	0.5		0955	0.5
W 1317	2.0	TH 1354		2.1
1820	0.3		2137	0.4
7 0135	2.4	**22** 0210		2.2
0935	0.6		1015	0.5
TH 1358	2.2	F 1425		2.2
● 1859	0.2		1934	0.4
8 0217	2.5	**23** 0235		2.3
0726	0.6		0754	0.5
F 1441	2.3	SA 1455		2.2
1939	0.2	○ 1954		0.4
9 0300	2.5	**24** 0305		2.3
0805	0.5		0825	0.5
SA 1525	2.3	SU 1525		2.3
2025	0.2		2029	0.4
10 0346	2.4	**25** 0338		2.3
0846	0.5		0855	0.5
SU 1605	2.4	M 1557		2.3
2109	0.3		2106	0.4
11 0427	2.3	**26** 0416		2.3
0929	0.5		0925	0.4
M 1647	2.4	TU 1631		2.3
2159	0.4		2139	0.4
12 0516	2.2	**27** 0450		2.2
1026	0.4		0954	0.4
TU 1731	2.3	W 1705		2.3
2305	0.5		2214	0.5
13 0555	2.0	**28** 0530		2.1
1125	0.4		1045	0.3
W 1819	2.2	TH 1748		2.3
			2309	0.5
14 0040	0.5	**29** 0609		2.0
0649	1.9		1134	0.3
TH 1234	0.3	F 1835		2.2
◐ 1915	2.1			
15 0146	0.6	**30** 0150		0.5
0750	1.8		0706	1.9
F 1335	0.3	SA 1250		0.3
2035	1.9	◑ 1935		2.1
		31 0230		0.6
			0824	1.8
		SU 1355		0.3
			2115	2.0

NOVEMBER

Time	m		Time	m
1 0504	0.6	**16** 0440		0.6
0950	1.7		1116	1.7
M 1510	0.3	TU 1704		0.3
2235	2.1		2345	2.0
2 0634	0.6	**17** 0700		0.6
1105	1.8		1206	1.8
TU 1605	0.3	W 1800		0.4
2336	2.2			
3 0745	0.5	**18** 0026		0.5
1206	1.9		0815	0.5
W 2010	0.3	TH 1246		1.9
			1920	0.4
4 0030	2.3	**19** 0055		2.1
0856	0.5		0910	0.5
TH 1255	2.1	F 1315		2.0
1756	0.3		2050	0.4
5 0116	2.3	**20** 0136		2.2
0926	0.6		0944	0.5
F 1338	2.2	SA 1349		2.1
1846	0.3		1914	0.5
6 0157	2.4	**21** 0205		2.2
0705	0.5		0745	0.5
SA 1422	2.3	SU 1426		2.2
● 1928	0.4	○ 1945		0.5
7 0242	2.3	**22** 0241		2.3
0749	0.5		0804	0.5
SU 1506	2.4	M 1500		2.3
2009	0.4		2020	0.5
8 0329	2.3	**23** 0319		2.3
0835	0.4		0850	0.4
M 1547	2.4	TU 1536		2.3
2054	0.5		2049	0.5
9 0415	2.2	**24** 0355		2.2
0920	0.4		0916	0.4
TU 1631	2.4	W 1615		2.4
			2354	0.5
10 0055	0.5	**25** 0438		2.1
0455	2.1		0945	0.3
W 1005	0.3	TH 1655		2.4
1718	2.3			
11 0140	0.6	**26** 0034		0.5
0546	2.0		0517	2.1
TH 1055	0.3	F 1035		0.3
1806	2.2		1736	2.3
12 0007	0.6	**27** 0136		0.5
0624	1.9		0605	2.0
F 1154	0.2	SA 1130		0.2
1900	2.1		1825	2.3
13 0110	0.6	**28** 0205		0.5
0715	1.8		0706	1.9
SA 1304	0.3	SU 1230		0.2
◑ 2006	2.0	◑ 1924		2.2
14 0214	0.7	**29** 0250		0.5
0815	1.7		0815	1.8
SU 1440	0.3	M 1334		0.2
2105	1.9		2045	2.1
15 0325	0.7	**30** 0427		0.6
0925	1.7		0914	1.8
M 1555	0.3	TU 1435		0.2
2224	1.9		2206	2.1

DECEMBER

Time	m		Time	m
1 0610	0.6	**16** 0435		0.6
1036	1.9		1034	1.8
W 1546	0.3	TH 1730		0.4
2306	2.1		2326	1.9
2 0725	0.6	**17** 0540		0.5
1136	1.9		1146	1.8
TH 1646	0.3	F 1820		0.4
3 0006	2.2	**18** 0016		2.0
0826	0.5		0624	0.5
F 1225	2.0	SA 1236		1.9
1739	0.4		1920	0.4
4 0058	2.2	**19** 0059		2.1
0857	0.5		0654	0.5
SA 1318	2.1	SU 1314		2.0
1834	0.4		1905	0.5
5 0148	2.2	**20** 0145		2.1
0705	0.5		0715	0.4
SU 1406	2.2	M 1359		2.2
● 1925	0.4		1934	0.5
6 0236	2.2	**21** 0225		2.2
0745	0.4		0743	0.4
M 1451	2.3	TU 1439		2.3
2004	0.5	○ 2003		0.5
7 0318	2.2	**22** 0300		2.2
0825	0.3		0826	0.3
TU 1535	2.3	W 1518		2.3
2054	0.6		2034	0.5
8 0405	2.1	**23** 0345		2.2
0904	0.3		0855	0.3
W 1618	2.3	TH 1601		2.4
			2334	0.5
9 0036	0.6	**24** 0429		2.1
0444	2.1		0936	0.2
TH 0956	0.2	F 1646		2.4
1705	2.3			
10 0105	0.6	**25** 0030		0.5
0535	2.1		0516	2.1
F 1034	0.2	SA 1020		0.2
1745	2.2		1729	2.4
11 0155	0.6	**26** 0126		0.5
0615	2.0		0554	2.0
SA 1130	0.2	SU 1110		0.1
1836	2.2		1817	2.3
12 0030	0.6	**27** 0206		0.5
0649	2.0		0649	2.0
SU 1215	0.2	M 1159		0.1
1919	2.1		1915	2.3
13 0130	0.6	**28** 0230		0.6
0740	1.9		0745	2.0
M 1320	0.2	TU 1304		0.1
◑ 2015	2.0	◑ 2020		2.2
14 0230	0.6	**29** 0235		0.6
0824	1.8		0844	1.9
TU 1440	0.3	W 1420		0.2
2116	1.9		2126	2.1
15 0340	0.6	**30** 0314		0.6
0924	1.8		0956	1.9
W 1624	0.3	TH 1525		0.2
2216	1.9		2236	2.0
		31 0405		0.6
			1106	1.9
		F 1624		0.3
			2340	2.0

Chart Datum is 0·84 metres below NAP Datum. HAT is 2·4 metres above Chart Datum; see 4.5.

》》 FREE monthly updates from **《《**
www.reedsalmanac.co.uk

HOEK VAN HOLLAND

MEAN SPRING ——
AND NEAP CURVES - - - -

MEAN RANGES
Springs 1.9m
Neaps 1.5m

Springs occur 2 days
after
New and Full Moon

9.16.22 MAAS TSS

Large ships bound up-Channel for Europoort route via the Dover Strait and the Noord Hinder South TSS to Noord Hinder Junction (a large pentagon roughly centred on 52°N 02°51'·1E). Here ships enter the MAAS TRAFFIC SEPARATION SCHEME.

Maas West Outer TSS starts some 33M offshore and funnels large ships 083°/27M via the TSS lanes or Eurogeul (DW route dredged 24·5m) towards a second pentagon 'Maas Precautionary Area' clear of Maas West Inner TSS and 10M offshore. When abeam Maas Centre SWM buoy, ships enter the Maasgeul (Maas narrows) and track inbound 5·5M on the 112° leading lights to the Maasmond (Maas mouth, ie the harbour entrance).

Yachts should avoid the whole complex by using the ITZ and/or crossing the Maasgeul via the recommended track (see 9.16.23). Knowing the above is to be aware of what you are avoiding.

HOEK VAN HOLLAND TO THE SOUTH EAST UK

Yachts out of Rotterdam/Hoek van Holland bound for the southern Thames Estuary should route 254°/52M from MV-N buoy to NHR-SE buoy, passing MW5, Goeree tower, MW3 and MW1 buoys. Cross the Noord Hinder South TSS between NHR-SE and NHR-S buoys. Thence depending on destination, set course 242°/44M to Outer Tongue for the River Thames; or 228°/46M to NE Goodwin for Ramsgate or points south.

If bound for the River Orwell or adjacent rivers, it may be best to pass north (rather than south) of the large and busy Sunk Outer and Inner Precautionary Areas and their associated TSS. From NHR-S buoy route via West Gabbard, North Inner Gabbard, S Shipwash and Rough buoys to pick up the recommended yacht track at Cork Sand Yacht beacon; it is a less direct route than going south via Galloper, but it avoids the worst of the commercial traffic.

9.16.22A MAAS TSS, PRECAUTIONARY AREA AND MAASGEUL

---- Traffic Separation Scheme

Maas Approach
VHF Ch 01
Extends from the limit of radar coverage to the W boundary of the Maas Precautionary Area

NHR-N
Racon K

Noord Hinder North TSS

Maas NW TSS

Maas North TSS

Maas Entrance VHF Ch 03

MWN2   MN2

MN3

MNW3-MW6 Racon O

Pilot Maas VHF Ch 02

Indusbank N

MW2   MW4

Radar Surveillance Maas Approach Ch 01

Maas Precautionary Area

Maasgeul

Hoek van Holland

Maas West Inner TSS

Maas West Outer TSS
Europlatform

EUROGEUL DW ROUTE

Maas Center Racon M   MG

MV-N

Radar Tr

Noord Hinder Racon T

52°N

MAAS JUNCTION

MW5

MV-I

EUROPOORT

Euro

Goeree Radar Racon(T)

Noord Hinder Junction Precautionary Area

MW3

Small craft crossing (9.16.23)

Inshore Traffic Zone

50'

MW1

NHR-SE

Limit of Radar Area

50'   3°E   10'   20'   30'   40'   50'   4°E   10'

9.16.23 HOEK VAN HOLLAND AND NIEUWE WATERWEG VTS

CROSSING THE MAASGEUL To cross the entrance (ie seaward of the bkwtrs), coasting yachts should advise *Maas Ent* Ch 03 of position/course/speed, then monitor Ch 03. Cross on the recommended track, 046° (226°) under power; see chartlet. Beware strong cross tides. Keep a keen lookout for fast moving merchantmen; Rules 18 d (ii) and 28.

HOEK VAN HOLLAND

CHARTS AC 122, 132; Zeekaart 1540, 1349, 1350, 1449; DYC 1801.6, 1801.7; Imray C30, Y5; Stanfords 19

TIDES +0251 Dover; ML 0·9; Duration 0505. HOEK VAN HOLLAND is a Standard Port (←), but has no Secondary ports; see also 9.16.24. Double LWs occur, more obviously at sp; in effect a LW stand. The 1st LW is about 5½ hrs after HW and the 2nd LW about 4¼ hrs before the next HW. Predictions are for the *lower* LW. Prolonged NW gales can raise levels by up to 3m.

SHELTER Entry safe, but in strong on-shore winds heavy seas/swell develop. The first adequate shelter is 6M up river at Maassluis (3m). Complete shelter 10-19M further E at Rotterdam.

NAVIGATION From N, WPT 52°02'·89N 04°03'·57E (Indusbank NCM lt buoy, Q), 190°/3·2M to Noorderdam lt, FR.
From S, WPT 51°59'·61N 04°00'·20E (MV-N buoy), 101°/3·0M to ent to Nieuwe Waterweg. *Yachts must on no account enter the Calandkanaal or Europoort. Stay in the Nieuwe Waterweg.*

LIGHTS AND MARKS See chartlet and 9.16.4 for details. Outer ldg lts 112° to ent; then 107° Red (ie keep to port) ldg lts into Nieuwe Waterweg, both R trs, W bands.

Hbr patrol vessels show a Fl Bu lt; additionally a Fl R lt = 'Stop'.

TELEPHONE (Code 010) Port Authority (HCC) 2522400; ⊜ 2442266; Police 4141414; ⊞ 4112800; Brit Consul (020) 6764343.

FACILITIES Berghaven is currently closed to yachts but a marina is under consideration.
Hoek van Holland ⊠, Ⓑ, ⇌, ⊞, R, Bar, P, D, ✈ (Rotterdam). Ferries: Hook-Harwich; Rotterdam (Vlaardingen)-Hull.

Maassluis Marina ☎ 593 1285. Ent/lock/bridge Ch 80, marina Ch 68. CH, El, FW, BY, ME, ✖. See tidal differences 9.16.24 and chartlet inset above.

NIEUWE WATERWEG VTS

Arrival procedure for yachts First report to *Maas Approach* or *Pilot Maas*, depending on distance offshore (or *Maas Ent* if within 4M of hbr ent), stating name/type of vessel, position and destination. Obey any instructions, monitoring the relevant Radar Ch's (limits as shown by W □ signboards on the river banks; Km signs are similar).

Rules for yachts in Nieuwe Waterweg/Nieuwe Maas:
Monitor VTS channels (see below); transmit only in emergency or if obliged to deviate from the usual traffic flow. Keep to extreme stbd limit of buoyed line, avoiding debris between buoys and bank. No tacking/beating; no ⚓. Engine ready for instant start. Able to motor at 3·24kn (6km/hr). Hoist a radar reflector, esp in poor vis or at night. Cross chan quickly at 90°. All docks are prohib to yachts, except to access a marina. *Keep a good lookout, especially astern.*

The 3 **Traffic Centres (TC)** oversee their Radar surveillance stations and sub-sectors *(italics)*, on dedicated VHF chans below:

- **TC Hoek van Holland (VCH)** Ch 11. (See diagram above)

Maas Approach	Ch 01	38 – 11M W of Hoek;
Pilot Maas	Ch 02	11 – 4M W of Hoek;
Maas Entrance	Ch 03	4M – km 1031.

  English is the primary language on Ch 01, 02 and 03.

Rozenburg	Ch 65	km 1031 – 1028;
Maasluis	Ch 80	km 1028 – 1017.

- **Botlek Information & Tracking system** Ch 14.

Botlek	Ch 61	km 1017 – 1011;
Eemhaven	Ch 63	km 1011 – 1007.

- **TC Rotterdam (VCR)** Ch 11.

Waalhaven	Ch 60	km 1007 – 1003·5;
Maasbruggen	Ch 81	km 1003·5 – 998;
Brienenoord	Ch 21	km 998 – 993.

Harbour Coordination Centre (HCC) administers and controls Rotterdam port, Ch 19 (H24).

MSI broadcasts by TCs Ch 11 and on request by Radar stns.

Nieuwe Waterweg VTS and Nieuwe Maas into central Rotterdam continued

9.16.24 ROTTERDAM

Zuid Holland **51°54'·00N 04°28'·00E** (610m S of Euromast)
❀❀❀❀♋♋♋♋♋

CHARTS AC 122, 132, 133; Zeekaart 1540/1/2; DYC 1809.4, 1809.5; Stanfords 19

TIDES +0414 Dover; ML 0·9; Duration 0440.

Standard Port VLISSINGEN (→)

Times				Height (metres)			
High Water		Low Water		MHWS	MHWN	MLWN	MLWS
0300	0900	0400	1000	5·0	4·1	1·1	0·5
1500	2100	1600	2200				
Differences EUROPLATFORM (30M W of Hoek van Holland)							
+0005	−0005	−0030	−0055	−2·7	−2·2	−0·6	−0·1
MAASSLUIS (Km 1019)							
+0155	+0115	+0100	+0310	−2·9	−2·3	−0·8	−0·2
VLAARDINGEN (Km 1011)							
+0150	+0120	+0130	+0330	−2·9	−2·3	−0·8	−0·2

NOTE: Double LWs occur. Maasluis and Vlaardingen are referenced to Vlissingen, in UK ATT as above. The Dutch HP33 *Tidal heights and streams in Dutch coastal waters* shows the time differences below, relative to HW and the first LW at Hoek van Holland:

HOEK VAN HOLLAND	HW	1st LW
Maasluis	+0102	+0308
Vlaardingen	+0103	+0333
Rotterdam	+0111	+0341

SHELTER Good in the yacht hbrs where visitors are welcome (see Facilities). There is always a considerable chop/swell in the river due to constant heavy traffic to/from Europoort and Rotterdam.

NAVIGATION See 9.16.23 for WPTs (to enter Nieuwe Waterweg) and Yacht Rules. From the hbr ent to the conspic Euromast (51°54'·33N 04°28'·00E) is about 18M (33km). 6M W of the Euromast, the very busy Oude Maas joins at km 1013, giving access to Dordrecht and the Delta network of canals/lakes.

R/T See chartlet above for VTS in central Rotterdam. In emergency call Rotterdam Tfc Centre Ch 11. See Facilities for VHF Chans at locks/bridges. English is the second language.

TELEPHONE (Code 010) Hbr Coordination Centre (HCC) 2522400, also Emergency; ⊖ 2442266; Police 4141414; Ⓗ 4112800; Brit Consul (020) 6764343.

FACILITIES Marinas/yacht harbours from seaward:

Vlaardingen YC, 51°53'·98N 04°20'·93E, 400m E of Delta Hotel. Berth in Buitenhaven (3·6-4·4m) or lock (Ch 20) into Oude Haven (2·7m). HM ☎ 4346786, M, BY, ME, SM, P, D, Gaz, ⇌.

Spuihaven, 51°54'·00N 04°24'·00E, immediately E of the ent to Wilhelmina Haven. No lock/bridge to transit. Schiedam YC ☎ 4267765, AB (1·6-2·8m), D, ME, El, ✗, CH, ⇌.

Coolhaven Yacht Hbr, 51°54'·12N 04°28'·00E; next to Euromast 185m. Access through Parkhaven via lock (Ch 22). ☎ 4738614, AB (2·7m), M, P, D, ME, El, ✗, C, Slip, CH, 🛒, R, Bar.

Veerhaven. 51°54'·39N 04°28'·76E, 5ca E of Euromast. ☎ 4365446. www.veerhavenrotterdam.nl   info@veerhavenrotterdam.nl Centre for traditional sea-going vessels. Ⓥ welcome, €1.50. AB (3·9m), ME, El, SM, CH, 🛒 350m N, Water taxi to S bank. **Royal Maas YC** ☎ 4137681, (clubhouse, members only).

City Marina, 51°54'·64N 04°29'·76E. Go under Erasmus bridge (Ch 18) via lifting section at SE end which only opens 1000, 1100, 1400 & 1500LT or on request Ch 18 1900-0700 (11m clearance under fixed span). Ldg lts 056·7°, both Iso 2s; then 2nd ent to stbd, via lifting bridge. ☎ (0187) 4854096, Mob 0622 215761, www.citymarinarotterdam.nl info@citymarinarotterdam.nl 130 AB +40 Ⓥ in 4m. €1.75/m/night for 2 nights; €1.50 3rd-7th nights; €1.25 7 nights. YC, Water taxi to N bank, @, Wi-Fi, 🛒.

WSV IJsselmonde, 51°54'·24N 04°33'·34E, on S bank at km 994, 800m E of Brienenoordbrug, Ch 20 (off chartlet). ☎ 482833, AB (1·3-2·1m).

City all facilities, ACA, DYC Agent. Ferry: Rotterdam (Vlaardingen)–Hull; Hook–Harwich.

9.16.25 STELLENDAM (for Haringvliet)

Zuid Holland 51°49'·46N 04°02'·29E (Goereesesluis). Stellendam ✿✿♨♨✿

CHARTS AC 1631, 3371, 110; Zeekaart 1447, 1448; DYC 1801.6, 1807.6; Imray C30; Stanfords 19

TIDES +0300 Dover; ML 1·2; Duration 0510.

Standard Port VLISSINGEN (⟶)

Times				Height (metres)			
High Water		Low Water		MHWS	MHWN	MLWN	MLWS
0300	0900	0400	1000	5·0	4·1	1·1	0·5
1500	2100	1600	2200				

Differences HARINGVLIETSLUIZEN

| +0015 | +0015 | +0015 | −0020 | −2·0 | −1·9 | −0·7 | −+0·2 |

NOTE: Double LWs occur. The rise after the 1st LW is called the Agger. Water levels on this coast are much affected by weather. Prolonged NW gales can raise levels by up to 3m.

SHELTER Good in marina. The entrance to the Slijkgat can be rough in strong W/NW winds and with wind against tide.

NAVIGATION WPT 51°51'·95N 03°51'·42E (SG SWM buoy, Iso 4s), 112°/2·6M to SG5/6 chan buoys. Thence 3·3M via the well buoyed/lit Slijkgat chan to SG13 and P1 SHM buoys. Follow P1 to P9 SHM buoys SSE for 2·2M to the Buitenhaven, avoiding the no-entry sluicing area, marked by 4 SPM buoys.

Access is via a lock which operates 24/7 and has recessed bollards. 2 bridges lift in sequence to minimise road tfc delays. Note: the W bridge has 14m vertical clearance when down (with digital clearance gauge outside), the E bridge only 5·4m.

LIGHTS AND MARKS Haringvlietsluizen: 3 ● in △ are shown from pier heads on dam when sluicing in progress.

R/T *Goereese Sluis* Ch 20 for bridges and lock. Marina Ch 31.

TELEPHONE (Code 0187) Lock 497350; Stellendam Port HM 491000; ⊖ Rotterdam (010) 4298088 or Vlissingen (0118) 484600; Emergencies 112; Brit Consul (020) 6764343.

FACILITIES Marina ☎ 493769. www.marinastellendam.nl info@marinastellendam.nl 200 AB inc ♥, €2.00 inc tourist tax & shower. Berth as directed in 3m; all pontoons have fingers. D&P, SM, ME, CH, ▣, C (20 ton), Bar, R ☎ 492344, bike hire.

Town (4½ km) 🛒, R, Bar, ✉. ✈ (Rotterdam). Bus to Vlissingen & Spijkenisse. Ferry: Hoek of Holland-Harwich; Rotterdam-Hull.

9.16.26 ROOMPOTSLUIS (for Oosterschelde)

Zeeland 51°37'·11N 03°41'·08E Roompot Lock

CHARTS AC 1630, 110; Zeekaart 1448; DYCs 1805.8, 1801.5; Imray C30; Stanfords 1, 19

TIDES +0230 Dover.

Standard Port VLISSINGEN (⟶)

Times				Height (metres)			
High Water		Low Water		MHWS	MHWN	MLWN	MLWS
0300	0900	0400	1000	5·0	4·1	1·1	0·5
1500	2100	1600	2200				
Differences ROOMPOT BUITEN							
–0015	+0005	+0005	–0020	–1·3	–1·1	–0·4	–0·1

SHELTER An approach in strong W/NW winds is not advised. The Buitenhaven's inner part is sheltered.

NAVIGATION WPT 51°39'·35N 03°33'·65E (abeam OR1 SHM buoy), 122°/4·2M via Oude Roompot chan to the 073·5° ldg line, both Oc G 5s, into the Buitenhaven. The flood sets E from HW Vlissingen –3 to +1. See 9.16.5 for the several offshore banks.

Alternatively Roompot chan, buoyed but unlit, is further south and closer inshore.

Keep clear of the buoyed areas, W and E of the storm-surge barrier, which are very dangerous due to strong tidal streams and many obstructions.

Roompotsluis lock (☎ 0111 659265). Lock hrs: Mon, Thu 0001-2200; Tue, Sun 0600-2359; Wed 0001-2359; Fri, Sat 0600-2200. Waiting pontoons are W and E of the lock with intercom phones to the lock-keeper. Customs can be cleared at the lock in season.

The fixed bridge has 18·2m least clearance. At LW clearance is approx 21m. Check with tide gauges or lock-keeper if in doubt. Small bollards, fixed at vertical intervals, are recessed into the lock walls. Ent to/exit from the lock is controlled by R/G traffic lights.

LIGHTS AND MARKS See 9.16.4 and chartlet.

R/T Lock *Roompotsluis* Ch 18. Roompot Marina Ch 31. Monitor Ch 68 which broadcasts local forecasts at H+15.

FACILITIES Roompot Marina ✿✿✿✿△△✿✿ Good shelter, 1·5M SE of lock. ☎ (0113) 374125, marina@roompot.nl. 50 + 80 ♥, €2.00, D, P, Slip, Gas, Gaz, ▢, 🛒, Bar, R, Ⓑ. Dr ☎ 372565; ⊖ 0118 484600.

Or follow G3-G17 buoys into **Betonhaven** about 1M NE of the lock. ⚓ in 3-6m, good holding in sticky black mud, or AB on a pontoon (Roompot marina II). €0.85, plus €0.90 tourist tax, for 3 days max stay; no FW, no AC. Easy walk to the Delta Expo.

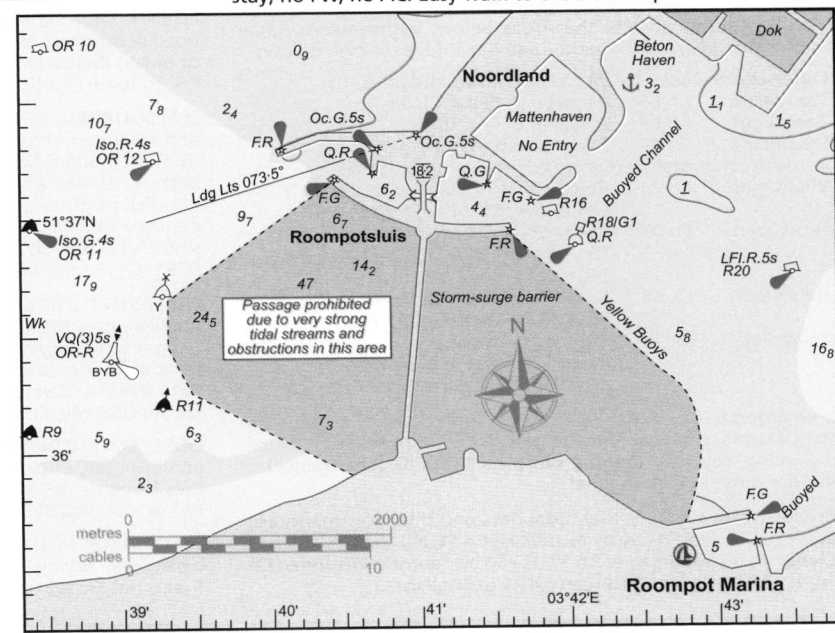

9.16.27 WESTERSCHELDE

Zeeland mostly, but Belgium for the last 12M to Antwerpen

CHARTS AC 1874, 120, 139; Zeekaart 1443; DYC 1803; Imray C30

TIDES +0200 Dover; ML Hansweert 2·7, Westkapelle 2·0, Bath 2·8; Duration 0555.

Standard Port VLISSINGEN (⟶)

Times				Height (metres)			
High Water		Low Water		MHWS	MHWN	MLWN	MLWS
0300	0900	0400	1000	5·0	4·1	1·1	0·5
1500	2100	1600	2200				
Differences WESTKAPELLE (8M NW of Vlissingen)							
–0025	–0015	–0010	–0025	–0·6	–0·6	–0·2	–0·1
HANSWEERT							
+0100	+0050	+0040	+0100	+0·6	+0·7	0·0	0·0
BATH							
+0125	+0115	+0115	+0140	+1·1	+1·0	+0·1	+0·1

SHELTER In strong winds a bad sea can be met in the estuary mouth. Conditions become easier further up-river. See Facilities.

NAVIGATION Westerschelde is the waterway to Antwerpen (and via canal to Gent), very full of ships and barges, especially in the last 15M. The main channel winds through a mass of well marked sand-banks. It is essential to work the tides, which average 2½kn, more at springs. Best timing is most easily achieved by starting from Vlissingen, Breskens or Terneuzen. Yachts should keep to the edge of main chan. Use alternative chans with caution; Vaarwater langs Hoofdplat and de Paulinerploder/Thomaesgeul/

Springergeul are buoyed shortcuts popular with yachtsmen, but note that channels shift regularly.

Commercial Shipping: Yachts should keep just outside the busy shipping chans, ie Wielingen from the SW, Scheur from the W, and Oostgat from the NW.

Be aware of large ship anchorages: Wielingen Noord and Zuid, either side of the fairway, as defined by buoys W6-Trawl-WN6 and W9-Songa. Further E, Flushing Roads anchorage is defined by Songa, SS1, SS5 and ARV-VH buoys. Ocean-going ships often manoeuvre off Vlissingen to transfer pilots.

S of Vlissingen (see Breskens) an E-W TSS (part of a Precautionary area) is best avoided by yachts which should cross the fairway via the recommended N-S track between Buitenhaven and ARV3 SPM lt buoy. Fast ferries, which have right of way, ply half-hourly from Vlissingen Buitenhaven to Breskens. *Keep a sharp lookout.*

Recommended small craft routes: From the SW there are few dangers. After Zeebrugge, keep S of the Wielingen chan buoys (W1-9). Off Breskens avoid fast ferries to/from Vlissingen; continue E to SS1 buoy, then cross to Vlissingen on a N'ly track.

From the W, keep clear of the Scheur chan by crossing to the S of Wielingen as soon as practicable.

From the N, the narrow, busy Oostgat can be used with caution, keeping just outside the SW edge of the buoyed/lit chan.

Three lesser, unlit day-only N'ly routes which avoid Oostgat are:

• From Kaloo or DR1 buoys, follow the Geul van de Rassen, Deurloo and Spleet chans to SP4 buoy. Thence E via WN6 buoy.

- Or continue down the Deurloo from DL5 buoy to join Oostgat at OG19 buoy; thence cross to the Vlissingen shore as and when traffic in Oostgat permits.
- Another route, slightly further offshore, is to skirt the NW side of Kaloo bank to Botkil-W buoy, thence SE via Geul van de Walvischstaart (PHM buoys only) to Trawl SCM buoy.

LIGHTS AND MARKS The apprs are well lit by lighthouses: on the S shore at Nieuwe Sluis, and on the N shore at Westkapelle; see 9.16.4. The main fairways are, for the most part, defined by ldg lts and by the W sectors of the many Dir lts.

SCHELDEMOND VTS covers from the North Sea outer approaches up-river to Antwerpen; see the diagram below and 9.16.21. Yachts should monitor at all times the VHF Ch for the area in which they are, so as to be aware of other shipping and to be contactable if required. Do not transmit, unless called.

7 **Traffic Centres** control the Areas below, within which Radar stations provide radar, weather and hbr info, as shown below:

Outer approaches: (*Traffic Centre* is the callsign prefix)		
Wandelaar	Ch 65	*Zeebrugge Radar* Ch 04.
Zeebrugge	Ch 69	*Radar* as in line above.
Steenbank	Ch 64	*Radar* also on Ch 64.
In the Westerschelde: (*Centrale* is the callsign prefix)		
Vlissingen	Ch 14	*Radar* Ch 21. Vlissingen to E2A/PvN SPR buoys (51°24′N 03°44′E)
Terneuzen	Ch 03	*Radar* Ch 03. Thence to Nos 32/ 35 buoys (51°23′N 03°57′E).
	Ch 11	Terneuzen-Gent Canal.
Hansweert	Ch 65	*Radar* Ch 65. Thence to Nos 46/ 55 buoys (51°24′N 04°02′E).
Zandvliet	Ch 12	Thence to Antwerpen.
		Radar Waarde 19; *Saeftinge* 21; *Zandvliet* 04; *Kruisschans* 66.

In **emergency**, call initially on the working channel in use; state yacht's name, position and the nature of the problem, in Dutch or English. You may then be switched to Ch **67 (Emergency)** or another discrete VHF channel.

Broadcasts of visibility, Met, tidal data and ship movements are made in Dutch at: H +00 by *Terneuzen* Ch 11; H +10 by *Zeebrugge* Ch 69; H +30 by *Zandvliet* Ch 12; H +50 by *Centrale Vlissingen* Ch 14; H +55 by *Radar Vlissingen* Ch 21 in English.

FACILITIES Some minor hbrs from Terneuzen to Antwerpen (38M) are listed below. They may be useful in emergency or offer shelter, but most dry. Yachts usually go non-stop to Antwerpen.

ELLEWOUTSDIJK, 51°23′·10N 03°49′·05E. DYC 1803.2. HW +2 and +0·3m on Vlissingen; ML 2·6m. Small, unlit hbr, 27 AB, voluntary donation. Access HW ±3; 1·5m at MLWS. Strong cross eddy on ebb. HM ☎ (0113) 548431/06 251154766. C (10 ton), Gaz, @, YC.

HOEDEKENSKERKE, 51°25′·11N 03°54′·90E. DYC 1803.3. Disused ferry hbr (dries) abeam MG13 SHM buoy. Access HW–2½ to +3 for 1m draft. €1.00/m (min €8.00/night) inc AC, FW. **YC WV Hoedekenskerke** ☎ (0113) 639278, mob 0653 794069. 33 + 6 ♥, Gaz, FW, SM, Shwrs at campsite 400m. **Town** ⊠, Ⓑ, ⇌ (Goes).

HANSWEERT, 51°26′·37N 04°00′·66E. DYC 1803.3. Tidal differences above. Temporary stop, but it is the busy ent to Zuid Beveland canal. Lt Oc WRG 10s, R lattice tr, W band, at ent. Waiting berths outside lock on E side. ♥ berths in inner hbr, W side; **no smoking or naked flames in, or near lock. Services:** ME, BY, P, D, C (17 ton), CH, R. **Town** ⊠, Ⓑ, ⇌ (Kruiningen-Yerseke).

WALSOORDEN, 51°22′·93N 04°02′·10E. DYC 1803.3. HW is +0110 and +0.7m on Vlissingen; ML 2·6m. Prone to swell. SHM buoy 57, Iso G 8s, is 500m N of ent where 16 silos are conspic. Ldg lts 220° both Oc 3s. Hbr ent FG & FR. Unmarked stone pier just outside E hbr pier, partly dries at LW. Yacht basin dead ahead on ent to hbr, depths 2 to 2·8m. 4/5 AB, €0.30/m, max stay H24. *Zandvliet Radio* VHF Ch 12. WSV d'Ouwe Haven ☎ (0114) 682925, FW, Slip, Gas, P, D, BY, C (16 ton), ME, El, ⬜. **Town** R, Bar, ⊠.

PAAL, 51°21′·25N 04°06′·65E. DYC 1803.3. HW +0120 and +0.8m on Vlissingen; ML 2·7m. Appr HW±2 via No. 63 SHM buoy and tide gauge, across drying Speelmansgat. Unlit, drying yacht hbr on S bank at river mouth, ent marked by withy. HM ☎ (0114) 314974, 0611 028174. *Zandvliet Radio* Ch 12. **Jachthaven** 150 AB, Shwr €0.50, Gaz, ME, El, ⬜, R, @ in YC. P&D (cans) 10 mins walk.

DOEL, 51°18′·67N 04°16′·11E. DYC 1803.5. HW +0100 and +0.7m on Vlissingen. Customs base. Small drying hbr on W bank; no entry LW±2. Ldg lts 185·5°: front Fl WR 3s on N pier hd; rear Fl 3s, synch. HM ☎ (03) 6652585; **YC de Noord** ☎ 7733669, R, Bar, FW.

LILLO, 51°18′·16N 04°17′·30E. DYC 1803.5. 1M SE of Doel on opp bank; small drying hbr for shoal-draft only; HW±3. Customs base. T-jetty has Oc WRG 10s. HM (035) 686456; **YC Scaldis**.

9.16.28 VLISSINGEN (FLUSHING)

Zeeland 51°26′·31N 03°34′·61E Koopmanshaven ✱✱⊛⬦⬦⬦✿✿✿

CHARTS AC 1872, 1874, 120; Zeekaart 1442, 1443, 1533; DYC 1803.8, 1801.3; Imray C30; Stanfords 1, 19.

TIDES +0215 Dover; ML 2·3; Duration 0555. Note: Vlissingen is a Standard Port (→).

SHELTER Very good in both yacht hbrs.

NAVIGATION WPT 51°25′·16N 03°33′·66E (Songa SHM buoy, QG), 027°/1·29M to Koopmanshaven ent. Study 9.16.27.

LIGHTS AND MARKS From NW, Oostgat 117° ldg lts: Front RW pile; rear Sardijngeul, Oc WRG 5s, R/W banded mast, R △. Note: Conspic radar twr (close NW of Koopmanshaven) shows a Fl Y lt to warn when ships are approaching in the blind NW arc from Oostgat-Sardijngeul. A conspic, floodlit R/W metal framework tr (50m) near de Ruyter Marina indicates the appr. Buitenhaven traffic signals from mole W side of ent: R flag or extra ● near FR on W mole hd = No entry.

R/T Michiel de Ruyter and Schelde Marinas: nil VHF; use mobile. Sealock Ch 18, canal bridges Ch 22. See also 9.16.27.

Continued opposite

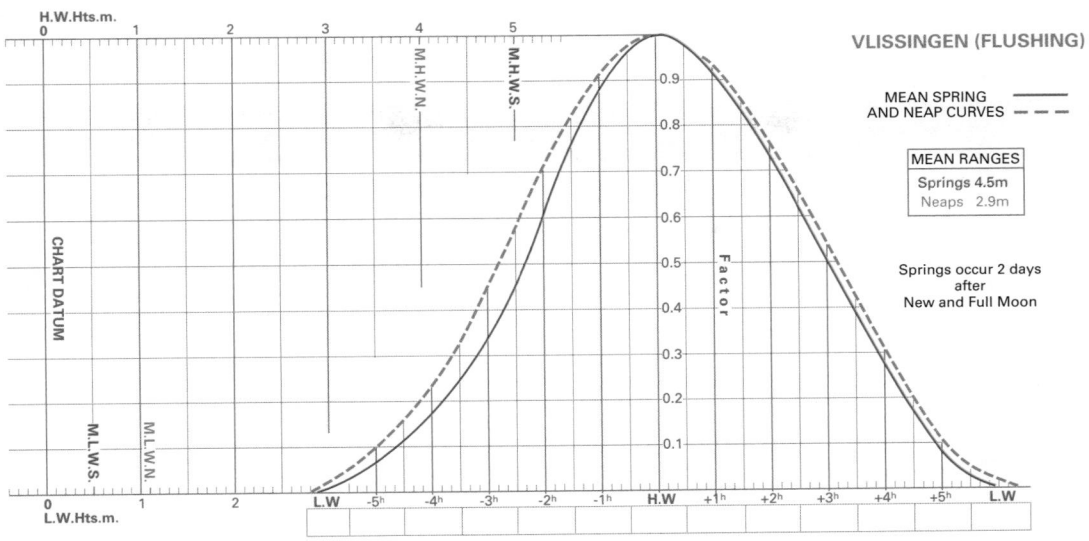

VLISSINGEN (FLUSHING)

MEAN SPRING ——————
AND NEAP CURVES – – – – –

MEAN RANGES
Springs 4.5m
Neaps 2.9m

Springs occur 2 days after New and Full Moon

TELEPHONE (Code 0118) Port HM 0115 647400; Buitenhaven lock 412372; ⊖ 484600; Schelde Traffic Coordination Centre 424790; Police 0900-8844; Dr 412233; Brit Consul (020) 6764343.

FACILITIES

Michiel de Ruyter Marina (2·9m) ☎ 414498, Mob 06 5353 7181, 🖾 4146505. *Pre-booking in season is strongly advised.* 100 + 40 🅥, €2.00. Bar, R, 🖳, Wi-Fi, @. info@montparnasse.nl www.montparnasse.nl

Ent is 6m narrow, over a sill with 1·0m water at MLWS. Access approx HW ±4; check depth gauge on outer wall. 2 small footbridges (R/G tfc lts) are swiftly swung open by HM 0800-2000LT. They stay open 2000–0800LT, but only for yachts to leave;

●● (vert) tfc lts prohibit arrival from sea, because the marina is not lit. Storm barrier is open 1/4-1/11. Pilot boats use the adjacent inlet at high speed with scant regard for safety.

VVW Schelde (3-4·3m) ☎ 465912. www.vvwschelde.nl 90 + 50 🅥, €1.50 + €0.54 tax/head. AC €1.00/4kWh. 500m by road from ferry. D, Bar, R, 🖳, ↗, Slip (12 ton max), @, bike hire, Wi-Fi.

At ent to the Buitenhaven beware ferries; keep to port, pass S of the ferry terminal for the most N'ly and smallest sealock, which operates H24. Waiting possible on piles to SE.

Town D&P (cans), CH, 🛒, R, Bar, ✉, Ⓑ, ⇌, ✈ (Antwerpen). Foot ferry to Breskens; road tunnel to Terneuzen. At Middelburg: BY, ME, �it, SM.

TIME ZONE -0100
Subtract 1 hour for UT
For Dutch Summer Time add
ONE hour in **non-shaded areas**

VLISSINGEN   LAT 51°27'N   LONG 3°36'E
TIMES AND HEIGHTS OF HIGH AND LOW WATERS

Dates in red are **SPRINGS**
Dates in blue are NEAPS

YEAR 2010

JANUARY

Time	m		Time	m
1 F 0152	4.9	**16** SA 0246	4.7
0815	0.6	0902	0.6
1413	5.1	1501	4.8
2036	0.7	2106	1.0
2 SA 0236	5.0	**17** SU 0316	4.8
0905	0.4	0938	0.6
1456	5.2	1535	4.8
2122	0.7	2138	0.9
3 SU 0322	5.0	**18** M 0347	4.8
0955	0.3	1009	0.5
1545	5.2	1606	4.8
2208	0.7	2216	0.9
4 M 0408	5.0	**19** TU 0420	4.8
1046	0.3	1045	0.6
1630	5.2	1637	4.8
2256	0.8	2246	0.9
5 TU 0456	4.9	**20** W 0452	4.8
1136	0.3	1116	0.6
1721	5.1	1710	4.7
2339	0.8	2312	0.9
6 W 0547	4.8	**21** TH 0521	4.7
1220	0.4	1146	0.7
1816	5.0	1739	4.6
		2346	1.0
7 TH 0030	0.9	**22** F 0558	4.6
0639	4.7	1221	0.7
1311	0.5	1820	4.5
◑ 1915	4.7		
8 F 0126	1.0	**23** SA 0026	1.0
0738	4.5	0635	4.5
1405	0.7	1300	0.8
2016	4.5	◐ 1910	4.4
9 SA 0219	1.2	**24** SU 0116	1.1
0840	4.3	0735	4.3
1506	0.9	1356	0.9
2125	4.3	2014	4.2
10 SU 0335	1.2	**25** M 0220	1.2
0956	4.2	0856	4.2
1625	1.0	1510	1.0
2240	4.2	2136	4.1
11 M 0506	1.2	**26** TU 0350	1.2
1110	4.2	1010	4.2
1740	1.1	1625	1.1
2345	4.3	2249	4.2
12 TU 0610	1.1	**27** W 0511	1.1
1215	4.4	1126	4.3
1836	1.1	1746	1.0
		2358	4.4
13 W 0045	4.4	**28** TH 0616	0.9
0706	0.9	1221	4.6
1316	4.5	1839	0.9
1920	1.0		
14 TH 0136	4.5	**29** F 0051	4.6
0750	0.8	0716	0.7
1356	4.7	1310	4.9
1956	1.0	1935	0.7
15 F 0211	4.6	**30** SA 0137	4.8
0826	0.7	0805	0.5
1429	4.7	1356	5.1
● 2029	1.0	○ 2019	0.7
		31 SU 0221	5.0
		0853	0.3
		1442	5.2
		2105	0.6

FEBRUARY

Time	m		Time	m
1 M 0305	5.1	**16** TU 0322	4.9
0940	0.2	0948	0.4
1526	5.3	1537	4.9
2150	0.6	2151	0.8
2 TU 0349	5.1	**17** W 0351	4.9
1027	0.1	1020	0.4
1612	5.3	1607	4.9
2232	0.6	2220	0.8
3 W 0435	5.1	**18** TH 0421	4.9
1110	0.2	1050	0.5
1656	5.1	1637	4.8
2316	0.7	2251	0.8
4 TH 0519	5.0	**19** F 0452	4.8
1151	0.3	1121	0.5
1745	4.9	1707	4.8
		2315	0.9
5 F 0002	0.7	**20** SA 0523	4.8
0607	4.8	1146	0.6
1236	0.5	1742	4.7
1835	4.7	2356	0.8
6 SA 0046	0.9	**21** SU 0559	4.7
0659	4.6	1225	0.7
1325	0.7	1826	4.5
◑ 1938	4.4		
7 SU 0139	1.0	**22** M 0046	0.9
0806	4.3	0649	4.5
1426	1.0	1320	0.9
2046	4.0	● 1930	4.2
8 M 0253	1.2	**23** TU 0146	1.0
0926	4.0	0810	4.2
1535	1.2	1436	1.1
2216	3.9	2055	4.0
9 TU 0424	1.2	**24** W 0316	1.2
1056	4.0	0939	4.1
1716	1.3	1559	1.1
2336	4.0	2228	4.0
10 W 0556	1.1	**25** TH 0446	1.1
1205	4.2	1106	4.2
1815	1.1	1726	1.1
		2339	4.2
11 TH 0029	4.2	**26** F 0605	0.9
0655	0.9	1206	4.6
1255	4.5	1825	0.9
1906	1.1		
12 F 0118	4.3	**27** SA 0035	4.5
0740	0.7	0706	0.6
1339	4.6	1258	4.9
1946	1.0	1915	0.8
13 SA 0156	4.6	**28** SU 0119	4.8
0816	0.7	0749	0.4
1411	4.7	1339	5.1
2016	1.0	○ 2006	0.6
14 SU 0222	4.7		
0845	0.6		
1410	4.8		
● 2045	0.9		
15 M 0251	4.8		
0916	0.5		
1507	4.9		
2116	0.8		

MARCH

Time	m		Time	m
1 M 0201	5.0	**16** TU 0221	4.8
0836	0.2	0846	0.5
1421	5.2	1439	4.9
2048	0.6	2049	0.7
2 TU 0243	5.1	**17** W 0249	4.9
0920	0.1	0918	0.4
1505	5.3	1507	5.0
2129	0.5	2125	0.6
3 W 0326	5.2	**18** TH 0321	5.0
1003	0.1	0952	0.4
1548	5.2	1537	5.0
2212	0.5	2156	0.6
4 TH 0406	5.2	**19** F 0350	5.0
1045	0.2	1026	0.5
1632	5.1	1608	4.9
2256	0.6	2231	0.6
5 F 0450	5.1	**20** SA 0423	4.9
1125	0.3	1052	0.5
1716	4.9	1641	4.8
2336	0.6	2300	0.7
6 SA 0536	4.9	**21** SU 0455	4.9
1205	0.5	1129	0.6
1806	4.6	1717	4.7
		2338	0.7
7 SU 0016	0.8	**22** M 0537	4.8
0625	4.6	1208	0.7
1245	0.8	1806	4.5
◑ 1855	4.2		
8 M 0110	1.0	**23** TU 0026	0.8
0725	4.2	0628	4.5
1356	1.1	1254	0.9
1953	3.9	◐ 1905	4.1
9 TU 0224	1.2	**24** W 0124	0.9
0845	3.9	0745	4.2
1503	1.3	1416	1.1
2146	3.6	2036	3.9
10 W 0355	1.2	**25** TH 0255	1.0
1036	3.8	0922	4.1
1646	1.4	1546	1.2
2305	3.8	2206	3.9
11 TH 0526	1.1	**26** F 0423	1.0
1139	4.1	1045	4.3
1744	1.2	1717	1.1
		2315	4.1
12 F 0008	4.1	**27** SA 0556	0.7
0630	0.9	1148	4.6
1231	4.4	1815	0.9
1846	1.1		
13 SA 0056	4.4	**28** SU 0011	4.5
0712	0.7	0645	0.5
1311	4.6	1235	4.9
1920	1.0	1906	0.8
14 SU 0125	4.5	**29** M 0055	4.7
0745	0.6	0736	0.3
1341	4.7	1316	5.0
1945	0.9	1945	0.6
15 M 0156	4.6	**30** TU 0136	4.9
0816	0.6	0815	0.2
1412	4.8	1400	5.2
● 2015	0.8	○ 2028	0.5
		31 W 0220	5.1
		0858	0.2
		1443	5.2
		2110	0.5

APRIL

Time	m		Time	m
1 TH 0301	5.2	**16** F 0251	5.0
0938	0.2	0919	0.4
1525	5.1	1512	5.0
2152	0.4	2136	0.6
2 F 0346	5.2	**17** SA 0325	5.0
1018	0.3	0955	0.5
1606	5.0	1546	4.9
2232	0.5	2210	0.6
3 SA 0426	5.0	**18** SU 0401	5.0
1055	0.5	1036	0.5
1650	4.7	1623	4.8
2316	0.6	2250	0.6
4 SU 0511	4.8	**19** M 0439	4.9
1136	0.7	1112	0.6
1735	4.5	1702	4.6
2355	0.7	2336	0.6
5 M 0600	4.5	**20** TU 0526	4.8
1216	0.9	1155	0.8
1826	4.2	1751	4.4
6 TU 0046	0.9	**21** W 0026	0.7
0651	4.2	0619	4.5
1305	1.2	1250	0.9
◑ 1920	3.9	◐ 1855	4.1
7 W 0206	1.0	**22** TH 0136	0.8
0805	3.9	0742	4.3
1435	1.4	1359	1.1
2040	3.6	2019	4.0
8 TH 0320	1.1	**23** F 0243	0.8
0956	3.8	0905	4.3
1544	1.4	1535	1.2
2236	3.7	2139	4.0
9 F 0435	1.0	**24** SA 0405	0.8
1106	4.0	1019	4.4
1706	1.3	1656	1.1
2330	4.0	2252	4.2
10 SA 0545	0.9	**25** SU 0525	0.6
1155	4.3	1126	4.6
1805	1.1	1749	0.9
		2345	4.4
11 SU 0016	4.2	**26** M 0626	0.5
0636	0.7	1216	4.8
1235	4.5	1842	0.8
1845	0.9		
12 M 0050	4.4	**27** TU 0032	4.7
0709	0.6	0712	0.4
1306	4.6	1258	4.9
1916	0.8	1925	0.6
13 TU 0120	4.6	**28** W 0116	4.9
0739	0.6	0756	0.3
1342	4.8	1342	5.0
1948	0.7	○ 2008	0.5
14 W 0147	4.8	**29** TH 0159	5.0
0809	0.5	0836	0.3
1405	4.9	1425	5.0
● 2019	0.6	2050	0.4
15 TH 0216	4.9	**30** F 0242	5.1
0846	0.4	0916	0.4
1436	5.0	1507	4.9
2055	0.6	2132	0.4

Chart Datum is 2·32 metres below NAP Datum. HAT is 5·2 metres above Chart Datum; see 4.5.

>> FREE monthly updates from <<
www.reedsalmanac.co.uk

Netherlands

TIME ZONE -0100
Subtract 1 hour for UT
For Dutch Summer Time add
ONE hour in **non-shaded areas**

VLISSINGEN LAT 51°27'N LONG 3°36'E
TIMES AND HEIGHTS OF HIGH AND LOW WATERS

Dates in red are **SPRINGS**
Dates in blue are **NEAPS**

YEAR 2010

MAY

	Time	m		Time	m
1 SA	0325 0956 1551 2215	5.0 0.5 4.8 0.4	**16** SU	0305 0935 1526 2158	5.0 0.5 4.8 0.5
2 SU	0408 1036 1635 2255	4.9 0.7 4.6 0.5	**17** M	0345 1015 1609 2242	5.0 0.6 4.7 0.5
3 M	0455 1110 1715 2335	4.7 0.8 4.4 0.6	**18** TU	0429 1100 1655 2330	4.9 0.7 4.6 0.5
4 TU	0539 1150 1755	4.5 1.0 4.2	**19** W	0517 1145 1749	4.8 0.8 4.4
5 W	0025 0630 1234 1845	0.8 4.2 1.2 4.0	**20** TH	0026 0619 1246 1856	0.5 4.6 0.9 4.2
6 TH ◗	0124 0736 1355 1945	0.9 4.0 1.3 3.8	**21** F ◗	0126 0736 1350 2006	0.6 4.5 1.0 4.2
7 F	0246 0840 1511 2110	1.0 3.9 1.3 3.7	**22** SA	0236 0845 1454 2116	0.6 4.5 1.1 4.2
8 SA	0339 1006 1605 2230	1.0 3.9 1.2 3.9	**23** SU	0346 0955 1604 2220	0.6 4.5 1.1 4.3
9 SU	0445 1106 1705 2322	0.9 4.1 1.1 4.1	**24** M	0500 1056 1726 2317	0.6 4.6 1.0 4.4
10 M	0534 1145 1755	0.8 4.4 1.0	**25** TU	0601 1148 1821	0.5 4.7 0.8
11 TU	0001 0628 1225 1836	4.3 0.7 4.6 0.9	**26** W	0011 0648 1238 1905	4.6 0.5 4.8 0.7
12 W	0037 0700 1259 1916	4.5 0.6 4.7 0.7	**27** TH	0057 0732 1325 1950	4.7 0.5 4.8 0.6
13 TH	0116 0736 1333 1952	4.7 0.6 4.9 0.6	**28** F ○	0146 0816 1410 2036	4.8 0.5 4.8 0.5
14 F ●	0146 0816 1411 2032	4.9 0.5 4.9 0.6	**29** SA	0228 0851 1455 2115	4.9 0.6 4.8 0.4
15 SA	0226 0856 1446 2115	5.0 0.5 4.9 0.5	**30** SU	0315 0936 1537 2158	4.9 0.7 4.7 0.4
			31 M	0357 1010 1620 2240	4.8 0.8 4.6 0.5

JUNE

	Time	m		Time	m
1 TU	0439 1048 1656 2320	4.7 0.9 4.5 0.6	**16** W	0422 1049 1648 2326	5.0 0.7 4.7 0.3
2 W	0525 1126 1738	4.6 1.0 4.4	**17** TH	0512 1140 1741	4.9 0.8 4.6
3 TH	0006 0605 1216 1820	0.7 4.4 1.1 4.2	**18** F	0015 0609 1229 1835	0.3 4.8 0.9 4.4
4 F ◗	0045 0652 1306 1911	0.8 4.2 1.2 4.1	**19** SA ◗	0116 0711 1325 1935	0.4 4.7 0.9 4.4
5 SA	0150 0751 1415 2005	0.8 4.1 1.3 4.0	**20** SU	0210 0816 1425 2039	0.5 4.6 1.0 4.4
6 SU	0256 0845 1516 2104	0.9 4.0 1.2 4.0	**21** M	0316 0926 1535 2146	0.6 4.5 1.0 4.3
7 M	0346 0956 1616 2215	0.9 4.1 1.2 4.0	**22** TU	0420 1031 1655 2256	0.7 4.4 1.0 4.4
8 TU	0434 1056 1705 2316	0.9 4.3 1.1 4.2	**23** W	0530 1131 1755 2356	0.7 4.5 0.9 4.5
9 W	0535 1145 1756 2359	0.8 4.5 0.9 4.4	**24** TH	0626 1225 1850	0.7 4.6 0.8
10 TH	0620 1225 1839	0.7 4.6 0.8	**25** F	0049 0712 1319 1941	4.6 0.7 4.6 0.6
11 F	0045 0706 1307 1928	4.6 0.7 4.8 0.7	**26** SA ○	0138 0756 1405 2022	4.7 0.8 4.7 0.6
12 SA ●	0125 0748 1349 2016	4.8 0.7 4.8 0.6	**27** SU	0225 0836 1445 2106	4.8 0.8 4.7 0.5
13 SU	0206 0832 1432 2100	4.9 0.6 4.9 0.5	**28** M	0306 0909 1526 2146	4.8 0.9 4.7 0.5
14 M	0250 0915 1515 2148	5.0 0.6 4.8 0.4	**29** TU	0345 0948 1558 2226	4.8 0.9 4.7 0.5
15 TU	0335 1001 1601 2238	5.0 0.6 4.8 0.3	**30** W	0418 1025 1636 2254	4.8 0.9 4.7 0.5

JULY

	Time	m		Time	m
1 TH	0458 1059 1712 2340	4.7 1.0 4.6 0.6	**16** F	0456 1122 1721	5.1 0.7 4.9
2 F	0536 1141 1751	4.6 1.0 4.5	**17** SA	0000 0547 1208 1811	0.2 5.0 0.8 4.8
3 SA	0016 0611 1216 1830	0.7 4.4 1.1 4.4	**18** SU ◗	0048 0641 1255 1905	0.3 4.8 0.9 4.6
4 SU ◗	0045 0701 1256 1915	0.8 4.3 1.1 4.2	**19** M	0136 0746 1355 2011	0.5 4.6 1.0 4.5
5 M	0135 0750 1344 2012	0.9 4.2 1.2 4.1	**20** TU	0236 0848 1459 2116	0.7 4.4 1.1 4.3
6 TU	0246 0844 1455 2115	0.9 4.2 1.2 4.1	**21** W	0346 1006 1620 2236	0.9 4.2 1.1 4.2
7 W	0335 0955 1616 2227	1.0 4.2 1.2 4.1	**22** TH	0506 1118 1746 2345	1.0 4.3 1.0 4.4
8 TH	0446 1059 1715 2326	1.0 4.3 1.1 4.3	**23** F	0610 1219 1839	1.0 4.4 0.8
9 F	0546 1200 1816	0.9 4.5 0.9	**24** SA	0045 0700 1311 1929	4.6 1.0 4.6 0.7
10 SA	0022 0640 1249 1905	4.6 0.8 4.6 0.7	**25** SU	0140 0742 1355 2012	4.7 1.0 4.7 0.6
11 SU ●	0109 0725 1335 2001	4.8 0.7 4.8 0.6	**26** M ○	0215 0820 1431 2049	4.8 1.0 4.7 0.6
12 M	0156 0816 1419 2048	5.0 0.7 4.9 0.4	**27** TU	0251 0856 1506 2126	4.8 1.0 4.8 0.5
13 TU	0236 0902 1502 2136	5.1 0.6 4.9 0.3	**28** W	0325 0928 1535 2159	4.9 0.9 4.8 0.5
14 W	0322 0948 1546 2226	5.2 0.7 4.9 0.2	**29** TH	0356 1002 1607 2235	4.9 0.9 4.8 0.5
15 TH	0408 1035 1632 2312	5.2 0.7 4.9 0.2	**30** F	0427 1035 1642 2310	4.8 0.9 4.8 0.6
			31 SA	0459 1106 1711 2338	4.7 1.0 4.7 0.7

AUGUST

	Time	m		Time	m
1 SU	0528 1136 1745	4.6 1.0 4.6	**16** M ◗	0015 0608 1225 1835	0.4 4.8 0.8 4.7
2 M	0006 0606 1206 1819	0.7 4.5 1.0 4.5	**17** TU	0059 0710 1320 1932	0.7 4.5 1.0 4.5
3 TU ◗	0034 0645 1251 1905	0.8 4.4 1.1 4.3	**18** W	0155 0816 1425 2050	0.9 4.2 1.1 4.3
4 W ◗	0130 0750 1344 2026	0.9 4.2 1.2 4.1	**19** TH	0305 0935 1554 2220	1.2 4.0 1.2 4.1
5 TH	0235 0906 1520 2146	1.1 4.1 1.3 4.1	**20** F	0445 1106 1736 2340	1.2 4.1 1.1 4.3
6 F	0406 1026 1639 2300	1.1 4.1 1.2 4.2	**21** SA	0555 1205 1825	1.2 4.3 0.9
7 SA	0526 1135 1755	1.1 4.3 1.0	**22** SU	0041 0644 1300 1914	4.6 1.1 4.5 0.7
8 SU	0001 0626 1231 1852	4.5 0.9 4.5 0.7	**23** M	0125 0730 1335 2000	4.7 1.0 4.7 0.6
9 M	0052 0712 1317 1946	4.8 0.8 4.8 0.5	**24** TU ○	0200 0800 1416 2029	4.8 1.0 4.8 0.6
10 TU ●	0137 0800 1400 2032	5.1 0.7 4.9 0.3	**25** W	0230 0830 1439 2102	4.9 1.0 4.8 0.6
11 W	0220 0845 1443 2118	5.2 0.7 5.1 0.2	**26** TH	0255 0902 1508 2136	4.9 0.9 4.9 0.5
12 TH	0303 0930 1526 2206	5.3 0.6 5.1 0.2	**27** F	0326 0935 1535 2205	4.9 0.9 5.0 0.6
13 F	0346 1016 1608 2248	5.3 0.6 5.1 0.2	**28** SA	0355 1008 1607 2235	4.9 0.9 4.9 0.6
14 SA	0431 1058 1655 2332	5.2 0.7 5.1 0.3	**29** SU	0426 1036 1636 2259	4.8 0.9 4.9 0.7
15 SU	0519 1142 1741	5.0 0.7 4.9	**30** M	0451 1106 1707 2330	4.8 0.9 4.8 0.8
			31 TU	0522 1137 1740	4.7 0.9 4.7

Chart Datum is 2·32 metres below NAP Datum. HAT is 5·2 metres above Chart Datum; see 4.5.

TIME ZONE -0100
Subtract 1 hour for UT
For Dutch Summer Time add ONE hour in **non-shaded areas**

VLISSINGEN   LAT 51°27'N   LONG 3°36'E
TIMES AND HEIGHTS OF HIGH AND LOW WATERS

Dates in red are **SPRINGS**
Dates in blue are **NEAPS**

YEAR 2010

SEPTEMBER

Date	Time	m	Time	m	Time	m	Time	m
1 W	0007	0.8	0601	4.6	1215	1.0	1826 ◑	4.5
2 TH	0056	1.0	0655	4.3	1315	1.1	1926	4.2
3 F	0206	1.2	0814	4.0	1434	1.3	2111	4.1
4 SA	0330	1.3	0949	4.0	1621	1.2	2236	4.2
5 SU	0455	1.2	1112	4.2	1736	1.0	2346	4.5
6 M	0605	1.0	1212	4.5	1841	0.7		
7 TU	0032	4.9	0655	0.9	1256	4.8	1928	0.5
8 W ●	0117	5.1	0740	0.8	1336	5.0	2012	0.3
9 TH	0156	5.3	0825	0.7	1418	5.2	2055	0.2
10 F	0240	5.4	0908	0.6	1500	5.3	2137	0.2
11 SA	0323	5.3	0950	0.6	1543	5.3	2223	0.3
12 SU	0406	5.2	1033	0.7	1626	5.2	2306	0.4
13 M	0452	5.0	1115	0.7	1712	5.0	2341	0.6
14 TU	0541	4.7	1200	0.8	1806	4.7		
15 W ◑	0026	0.9	0636	4.4	1244	1.0	1859	4.4
16 TH	0125	1.2	0736	4.1	1355	1.2	2014	4.1
17 F	0240	1.4	0910	3.8	1536	1.2	2155	4.0
18 SA	0405	1.5	1040	3.9	1706	1.1	2315	4.2
19 SU	0536	1.3	1145	4.2	1810	0.9		
20 M	0015	4.5	0623	1.2	1235	4.5	1855	0.8
21 TU	0055	4.7	0705	1.1	1316	4.7	1936	0.7
22 W	0132	4.8	0735	1.0	1346	4.8	2006	0.7
23 TH ○	0156	4.9	0805	0.9	1407	4.9	2036	0.6
24 F	0226	4.9	0836	0.9	1436	5.0	2106	0.6
25 SA	0256	5.0	0905	0.8	1506	5.0	2132	0.6
26 SU	0326	5.0	0935	0.8	1535	5.0	2206	0.7
27 M	0350	4.9	1018	0.8	1605	5.0	2232	0.7
28 TU	0425	4.9	1041	0.9	1636	4.9	2306	0.8
29 W	0457	4.8	1116	0.9	1713	4.9	2335	0.9
30 TH	0537	4.6	1156	0.9	1800	4.7		

OCTOBER

Date	Time	m	Time	m	Time	m	Time	m
1 F ◑	0028	1.1	0630	4.3	1256	1.1	1906	4.3
2 SA	0136	1.3	0756	4.0	1426	1.2	2046	4.2
3 SU	0305	1.4	0929	4.0	1545	1.2	2205	4.3
4 M	0429	1.3	1054	4.2	1709	1.0	2315	4.6
5 TU	0545	1.1	1145	4.5	1821	0.7		
6 W	0008	4.9	0636	0.9	1229	4.8	1908	0.5
7 TH ●	0056	5.1	0721	0.8	1313	5.0	1950	0.4
8 F	0136	5.3	0803	0.7	1356	5.2	2032	0.3
9 SA	0216	5.3	0846	0.6	1436	5.3	2116	0.4
10 SU	0300	5.2	0928	0.6	1519	5.3	2155	0.5
11 M	0345	5.1	1012	0.6	1605	5.2	2235	0.6
12 TU	0429	4.9	1056	0.7	1649	5.0	2316	0.8
13 W	0516	4.6	1138	0.8	1735	4.7	2356	1.1
14 TH ◐	0605	4.3	1225	1.0	1836	4.4		
15 F	0056	1.3	0659	4.1	1335	1.1	1945	4.1
16 SA	0205	1.5	0826	3.8	1506	1.2	2114	4.0
17 SU	0336	1.6	0954	3.8	1620	1.2	2240	4.1
18 M	0444	1.5	1105	4.1	1736	1.0	2338	4.4
19 TU	0543	1.3	1155	4.3	1819	0.9		
20 W	0019	4.6	0635	1.1	1235	4.5	1900	0.8
21 TH	0052	4.7	0706	1.0	1305	4.7	1925	0.8
22 F	0125	4.8	0736	0.9	1336	4.8	1956	0.7
23 SA ○	0155	4.9	0806	0.9	1402	4.9	2031	0.7
24 SU	0222	5.0	0838	0.8	1436	5.0	2100	0.7
25 M	0256	5.0	0916	0.8	1506	5.1	2136	0.7
26 TU	0325	5.0	0945	0.8	1542	5.0	2211	0.8
27 W	0403	4.9	1026	0.8	1618	5.0	2246	0.9
28 TH	0437	4.7	1106	0.8	1658	4.9	2327	1.0
29 F ◐	0526	4.5	1150	0.9	1747	4.7		
30 SA ◑	0016	1.1	0619	4.3	1256	1.0	1856	4.4
31 SU	0120	1.3	0746	4.1	1406	1.0	2026	4.3

NOVEMBER

Date	Time	m	Time	m	Time	m	Time	m
1 M	0235	1.4	0858	4.1	1525	1.0	2140	4.4
2 TU	0353	1.3	1012	4.2	1646	0.9	2245	4.6
3 W	0516	1.2	1116	4.5	1756	0.7	2345	4.8
4 TH	0610	1.0	1205	4.7	1842	0.6		
5 F	0031	5.0	0658	0.9	1246	4.9	1929	0.5
6 SA ●	0115	5.1	0745	0.7	1335	5.1	2008	0.5
7 SU	0159	5.1	0825	0.6	1418	5.2	2052	0.5
8 M	0243	5.1	0910	0.6	1503	5.2	2132	0.7
9 TU	0328	5.0	0956	0.6	1547	5.1	2212	0.8
10 W	0412	4.8	1035	0.7	1632	4.9	2249	1.0
11 TH	0457	4.6	1115	0.8	1721	4.7	2330	1.2
12 F	0541	4.4	1206	0.9	1812	4.5		
13 SA ◑	0016	1.3	0636	4.2	1305	1.0	1910	4.2
14 SU	0120	1.5	0726	4.0	1417	1.1	2026	4.0
15 M	0246	1.6	0834	3.8	1526	1.2	2140	4.0
16 TU	0346	1.5	1006	3.9	1625	1.1	2245	4.1
17 W	0450	1.4	1101	4.1	1731	1.0	2336	4.3
18 TH	0547	1.3	1148	4.3	1815	1.0		
19 F	0016	4.5	0626	1.1	1225	4.5	1851	0.9
20 SA	0048	4.7	0700	1.0	1258	4.7	1925	0.8
21 SU ○	0121	4.8	0735	0.9	1335	4.8	1958	0.8
22 M	0157	4.8	0812	0.8	1411	5.0	2032	0.7
23 TU	0233	4.9	0852	0.7	1446	5.0	2109	0.8
24 W	0312	4.9	0936	0.7	1526	5.0	2152	0.8
25 TH	0347	4.8	1015	0.7	1606	5.0	2236	0.9
26 F	0431	4.7	1102	0.7	1652	4.9	2321	1.0
27 SA	0517	4.6	1149	0.7	1745	4.8		
28 SU ◑	0008	1.1	0615	4.4	1250	0.7	1850	4.6
29 M	0105	1.2	0722	4.3	1355	0.8	2000	4.4
30 TU	0216	1.3	0830	4.2	1506	0.9	2110	4.5

DECEMBER

Date	Time	m	Time	m	Time	m	Time	m
1 W	0326	1.3	0938	4.3	1604	0.9	2216	4.5
2 TH	0435	1.2	1042	4.4	1720	0.8	2318	4.6
3 F	0546	1.1	1140	4.6	1818	0.8		
4 SA	0011	4.7	0641	0.9	1231	4.8	1906	0.7
5 SU ●	0101	4.8	0728	0.8	1321	4.9	1950	0.7
6 M	0147	4.9	0812	0.7	1406	5.0	2029	0.7
7 TU	0236	4.9	0858	0.6	1452	5.0	2112	0.8
8 W	0317	4.8	0940	0.6	1537	5.0	2152	0.9
9 TH	0359	4.8	1019	0.6	1618	4.9	2228	1.0
10 F	0442	4.7	1106	0.6	1706	4.8	2308	1.1
11 SA	0519	4.6	1146	0.7	1746	4.6	2351	1.2
12 SU	0606	4.4	1225	0.8	1832	4.4		
13 M ◑	0036	1.3	0646	4.3	1315	1.0	1926	4.2
14 TU	0136	1.4	0735	4.1	1416	1.1	2020	4.1
15 W	0246	1.5	0840	4.0	1515	1.1	2126	4.0
16 TH	0346	1.4	0956	4.0	1615	1.2	2230	4.1
17 F	0446	1.3	1052	4.1	1716	1.1	2326	4.3
18 SA	0535	1.2	1146	4.3	1806	1.0		
19 SU	0011	4.5	0628	1.1	1229	4.5	1850	0.9
20 M	0058	4.6	0710	0.9	1312	4.7	1930	0.8
21 TU ○	0138	4.8	0755	0.8	1352	4.9	2016	0.8
22 W	0215	4.9	0841	0.7	1433	5.0	2056	0.8
23 TH	0256	4.9	0923	0.5	1515	5.1	2135	0.8
24 F	0339	4.9	1012	0.5	1556	5.1	2226	0.8
25 SA	0422	4.8	1055	0.4	1646	5.0	2308	0.9
26 SU	0509	4.7	1148	0.4	1735	4.9	2356	0.9
27 M	0602	4.6	1241	0.5	1828	4.8		
28 TU ◑	0048	1.0	0658	4.5	1330	0.6	1931	4.6
29 W	0145	1.1	0801	4.4	1426	0.7	2038	4.5
30 TH	0250	1.2	0906	4.3	1530	0.9	2145	4.4
31 F	0354	1.2	1016	4.3	1656	1.0	2255	4.4

Chart Datum is 2·32 metres below NAP Datum. HAT is 5·2 metres above Chart Datum; see 4.5.

FREE monthly updates from
www.reedsalmanac.co.uk

9.16.29 BRESKENS

Zeeland 51°24'·00N 03°34'·08E ✿✿✿✿✿✿✿✿✿✿

CHARTS AC 1874, 1872, 120; Zeekaart 120, 101; DYC 1801.4, 1803.2; Imray C30; Stanfords 1, 19

TIDES +0210 Dover; ML no data; Duration 0600.

Standard Port VLISSINGEN (←) Use Vlissingen data.

SHELTER Good in all winds except N/NW. In fine weather ⚓ off Plaat van Breskens or in peaceful Vaarwater langs Hoofdplaat; no ⚓ in commercial/fishing hbr.

NAVIGATION WPT 51°24'·71N 03°33'·90E [ARV-VH NCM buoy, Q], 170°/7ca to hbr ent. Beware fast ferries and strong tides across the ent. Do not confuse the ent with the ferry port ent, 0·7M WNW, where yachts are prohib.

LIGHTS AND MARKS Large bldg/silo on centre pier in hbr and three apartment blocks (30m) SE of marina are conspic. See chartlet and 9.16.4 for lights. Nieuwe Sluis lt ho, 28m B/W banded 8-sided twr, is 1·8M W of marina.

R/T Marina Ch 31.

TELEPHONE (Code 0117); ⊖ (0118) 484600; Police 0900 8844; Dr 381566/389284, at night/weekends (0115) 643000; ⊞ (0117) 459000; British Consul (020) 6764343.

FACILITIES Marina jachthavenbreskens@zonnet.nl ☎ 381902, 06 3087873. www.marinabreskens.nl 580 AB inc ❶, €1.70 + €1.05 tourist tax. Enter marina between two wavebreak barges; access H24, 5m at ent. Berth on 1st pontoon where HM assigns a berth via an intercom ☎. ▢, ⛴, SM, CH, D & P (fuel berth in FV hbr), Gaz, ACA, BY, C (30T), BH (70T), El, Ⓔ, ME, ✂, Slip, ▨, Wi-Fi. **YC Breskens** ☎ 383278, Bar, R (book early), @.

Town 🔨, R, Bar, ✉, Ⓑ, Gas, ✈ (Oostende, Antwerp or Brussels). Pedestrian & bike ferry or car tunnel to Vlissingen for ⇌.

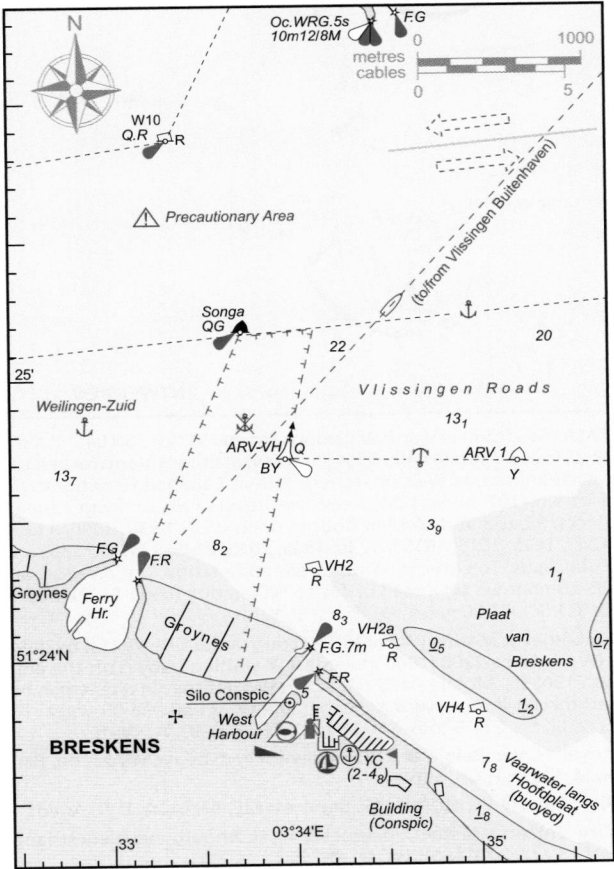

9.16.30 TERNEUZEN

Zeeland 51°20'·58N 03°49'·69E ✿✿✿✿✿✿✿✿✿✿

CHARTS AC 120; Zeekaart 1443; DYC 1803.2; Imray C30

TIDES +0230 Dover; ML 2·5; Duration 0555.

Standard Port VLISSINGEN (←)

Times				Height (metres)			
High Water		Low Water		MHWS	MHWN	MLWN	MLWS
0300	0900	0400	1000	5·0	4·1	1·1	0·5
1500	2100	1600	2200				
Differences TERNEUZEN							
+0020	+0020	+0020	+0030	+0·3	+0·4	0·0	+0·1

SHELTER Very good except in strong N'lies. Exposed ⚓ on N side of fairway between buoys WPT4, WPT6, PvT-ZE & ZE5.

NAVIGATION WPT 51°20'·82N 03°47'·96E [25B SHM buoy], 101°/1M hugging S bank to hbr ent. The fairway is only 500m wide; big ships pass very close; good lookout E/W when leaving. Very busy traffic from/to the locks; call *Centrale-Terneuzen* Ch 03. If S-bound via Gent Canal transit the E lock to berth in Zijkanaal A.

LIGHTS AND MARKS Dow Chemical works and storage tanks are conspic 2M W of hbr. Lt Oc WRG 5s, B/W post, on W mole is a conspic mark for the Veerhaven.

When entry to E Buitenhaven is prohib, a second ● is shown below FR on E mole. For E lock: ● = no entry; ●● (vert) = get ready; ● = go. No yachts in W Buitenhaven, Middle and W locks.

R/T No marina VHF. Call *Port Control* Ch 11 (H24) for locks and Gent canal; also info broadcasts every H+00. East lock Ch 18.

TELEPHONE (Code 0115) Port HM 612161; ⊖ (0118) 484600; Police 0900 8844; ⊞ 688000; Dr 616262; Brit Consul (020) 6764343.

FACILITIES Two marinas in SE corner of former Veerhaven: **WV Honte Marina** where vacant ❶ berths more likely. ☎ 697089, mobile 0651 168987. www.zealand-seaports.com 130 AB €1.40. AC (230v) €1.25, C (6 ton), Wi-Fi, ▢. **WV Neusen Marina** is close ESE (and in Zijkanaal A) ☎ 696331; 100 AB, €0.30/m²; ⛴, Bar, Wi-Fi. Boatyards (full services): **Aricom** www.aricom.nl ☎ 614577, €1.00/m. ME, El, C (50 ton), ✂, Gaz. **Vermeulen's Yachtwerf** ☎ 612716. AB, €0.75, C (50 ton).

Town P, D, CH, 🔨, R, Bar, ✉, Ⓑ, ✈ (Antwerpen). Foot ferry Breskens to Vlissingen. Cars by Schelde tunnel Terneuzen-Ellewoutsdijk.

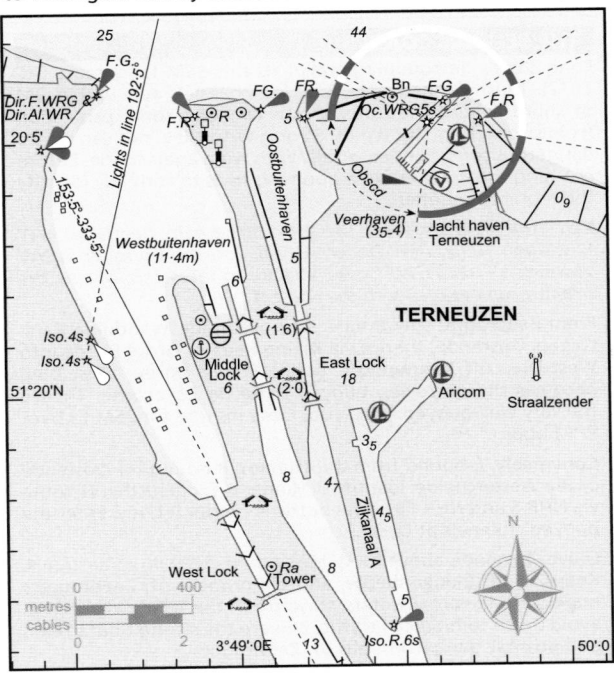

9.16.31 SPECIAL NOTES FOR BELGIUM

PROVINCES are given in lieu of UK 'counties'.

LANGUAGES Flemish, ie Dutch as spoken in Flanders, is the 1st language along the coast and N of Brussels. English is also widely spoken. French, the 2nd language, is spoken in and S of Brussels.

CURRENCY is the Euro €. VAT (BTW/TVA) is 21%.

CHARTS '*Vlaamse Banken*' issued by the Hydrografische Dienst der Kust are most widely used. Dutch yacht charts (DYC 1800 series) cover all Belgian ports. Imray C30 is also popular.

TIME ZONE is –0100, which is allowed for in tidal predictions but no provision is made for daylight saving schemes.

HARBOURS Ports of entry are Nieuwpoort, Oostende and Zeebrugge; plus Blankenberge, early April - late Sep. Berths and moorings are administered by local YCs and municipal authorities. Red diesel fuel, where available, is duty free.

SIGNALS At Nieuwpoort, Oostende and Zeebrugge IPTS are used, and small craft wind warnings (also at Blankenberge). They apply only to craft <6m LOA and indicate onshore wind >F3; offshore wind >F4. Day, 2 ▼s, points together; night, Fl Bu lt.

TELEPHONE To call UK from Belgium, dial 00 44 then the UK area code minus the prefix 0, followed by the number called. To call Belgium from UK, dial 00 32 then the code and 6 digit number.

Emergency: ☎ 101 Police; ☎ 100 Fire, Ambulance and Marine. ☎ 112 (EU emergency number) is also operational.

BRITISH CONSULS Contact British Embassy, Brussels (consular) 02 287 6211 or consularsection.brussels@fco.gov.uk.

MRCC Oostende coordinates SAR operations (7.20). If no contact, call *Oostende Radio* VHF Ch 16 or ☎ 100. For medical advice call *Radiomédical Oostende* on Ch 16.

PUBLIC HOLIDAYS New Year's Day, Easter Mon, Labour Day (1 May), Ascension Day, Whit Mon, National Day (21 July), Feast of the Assumption (15 Aug), All Saints' Day (1 Nov), Armistice Day (11 Nov), King's Birthday (15 Nov), Christmas Day.

RULES A ▼ when motor-sailing and a black ball ● at ⚓ are strictly enforced. Navigation within 200m of shore (MLWS) is prohib.

INLAND WATERWAYS At www.mobilit.fgov.be download CEVNI-based regulations in French or Dutch. Licence plates (*Immatriculatieplaat*) are required on Belgian waterways. Helmsman's Competence criteria are as for the Netherlands.

THE BELGIAN COAST

Long shoals lie roughly parallel to this 36M long coast (AC 1872). Mostly the deeper, buoyed channels run within 3M of shore, where the outer shoals can give some protection from strong W or SW winds. Strong W to NE winds can create dangerous conditions especially with wind against tide. Before reaching shoal water get a good fix, so as to correctly identify the required channel.

▶*Off the Belgian coast the E-going stream begins at HW Vlissingen –0320 (HW Dover –0120), and the W-going at HW Vlissingen +0240 (HW Dover +0440), sp rates 2kn. Mostly the streams run parallel with the coast.*◀

From **Zeebrugge** stay a mile offshore inside Wenduine Bank to pass **Oostende**, thence via Kleine Rede or Grote Reede into West Diep off **Nieuwpoort**. At the French border West Diep becomes the narrower, buoyed Passe de Zuydcoote. Thence the very well buoyed route runs close inshore for 25M to Dyck PHM buoy.

Conversely, E-bound from the Thames, if bound for Oostende or the Westerschelde, identify W Hinder lt. From further N, route via NHR-S and NHR-SE buoys or the N Hinder lt buoy. Enter the buoyed channels at Dyck.

Leave Oostende about ▶*HW Vlissingen –0300 on a fair tide*◀. Keep 2M off **Blankenberge**, and 1M or more off Zeebrugge's huge claw-like breakwaters, staying S of the Scheur channel to avoid much commercial traffic. Beware the strong tidal stream and possibly dangerous seas off Zeebrugge.

9.16.32 ANTWERPEN

Belgium, Antwerpen **51°13'·66N 04°23'·79E** 🏴⚓⚓⚓⚓

CHARTS AC 139; Zeekaart 1443; DYC 1803.5

TIDES +0342 Dover; ML 2·9; Duration 0605.

Standard Port VLISSINGEN (◀—)

Times				Height (metres)			
High Water		Low Water		MHWS	MHWN	MLWN	MLWS
0300	0900	0400	1000	5·0	4·1	1·1	0·5
1500	2100	1600	2200				
Differences ANTWERPEN							
+0128	+0116	+0121	+0144	+1·2	+1·0	+0·1	+0·1

SHELTER Excellent in both marinas. ⚓ in the river is not advised.

NAVIGATION For Westerschelde see 9.16.27. Best to check off the buoys coming up-river. There is a gap of 1·4M between No 116 PHM buoy and No 107 SHM buoy, where the river bends 90° onto S, abeam Royersluis and the waiting pontoon (see above). No 109 SHM buoy is 250m NE of Linkeroever Marina ent.

R/T Royerssluis Ch 22. Access bridges Ch 62. Willemdok Ch 23. Linkeroever Ch 09 (HW±1). Antwerp Port Ops Ch 74 (H24). VTS, Zandvliet Centre Ch 12; Radar Ch 04, 66.

TELEPHONE (Code 03); ⊖ 2292004; Police 5460730; Ⓗ 2852000 (W Bank), 234111 (E Bank).

FACILITIES from seaward: **Willemdok Marina** 51°13'·78N 04°24'·43E. ☎ 2315066, Mobile 0495 535455. www.jachthaven-antwerpen.be jaw@pandora.be Wait on inshore side of T-shaped ferry pontoon S of No. 107 buoy. H24 access via Royerssluis, or from canals/docks. Siberia and Londen bridges open 0630, 0830, 1000, 1130, 1245, 1415, 1515, 1615*, 1730, 1845, 2015, 2145, 2245LT.*Sat/Sun/Public hols. To enter the Dock areas and marina, pre-arrange an FD number via ☎, e-mail or fax to Willemdok (0500-2300). 200 + ⓥ, €1·50, €8·00 week. D, 🛒, 🗑, El, Wi-fi.

Linkeroever Marina (W bank); Lat/Long under title. Access by gate HW ±1, 0800–2200 (1800 in winter). Y waiting buoy is off the ent. ☎ 2190895, Mobile 0475 643957. www.jachthaven-antwerpen.be jachthaven_linkeroever@skynet.be 200+ⓥ, €1·50, €8·00 week. D, Gaz, El, ✄, C (1·5 ton), BH (38 ton), CH, Slip, R, 🗑, Wi-fi.

Royal YC van België ☎ 2195231. www.rycb.be rycb@rycb.be. Bar, R, M, BY, D, P, CH, Slip .

Kon. Liberty YC ☎ 2191147. **Services:** ME, BH, ACA, DYC Agent.

City centre is ¾M from Linkeroever via St. Annatunnel (pedestrian), 51°13'·22N. All facilities, @, ⇌, ✈.

9.16.33 ZEEBRUGGE

Belgium, West Flanders **51°21'·83N 03°11'·39E** ✵✵✵⚓⚓⚓⚑⚑

CHARTS AC *2449*, 3371, 1872, 1874; Zeekaart 1441; DYC 1801.3, 1803; Imray C30; Stanfords 1, 19

TIDES +0110 Dover; ML 2·4; Duration 0535. Note: Zeebrugge is a Standard Port (⟶).

SHELTER Very good in the marina, access H24.

NAVIGATION WPT 51°22'·48N 03°09'·95E [Z SHM buoy, QG], 129°/1·1M to ent (lat/long under title). Lts on outer bkwtr heads show high-vis strip lts to seaward. Beware strong currents in hbr apprs (up to 4kn at HW –1). Caution on ent/dep due to limited vis; give all jetties a wide berth. A busy commercial, naval and fishing port and a ferry terminal. An inner WPT 51°20'·85N 03°12'·29E off Leopold II Dam head is useful to avoid getting 'lost' inside the vast outer hbr, especially in poor vis; see chartlet.

LIGHTS AND MARKS Big ship ldg marks (hard to see by day) & lts (as chartlet) lead in sequence to Vissershaven and the marina:

- 136°: Both W cols, R bands.
- 154°: Front, W pylon, R bands; rear, W bldg, R bands.
- 220°: Both W cols, B bands. • 193°: Both W cols, R bands.

IPTS are shown from W outer bkwtr and Leopold II Dam. Extra sigs: 3 Fl Y lts (vert) + IPTS No 2 or 5 = LNG tanker entering/leaving. No exit/entry without specific permission.

R/T Port Control Ch 71 (H24). Marina, nil VHF. Sealock Ch 68.

TELEPHONE (Code 050) Port HM 543241; Port Control 546867; Lock Mr 543231; CG 545072; Sea Saving Service 544007; ⊜ 54.54.55; Police 544148; Dr 544590; Brit Consul (02) 2179000.

FACILITIES **Marina** ☎ 544903, mob 0496 789053. havenmeester@rbsc.be www.rbsc.be 100 + 100 🅥, €2.19. Slip, ✗, CH, D, ME, El, ⬚.

Royal Belgian SC (VZW) info@rbsc.be Bar, R (Alberta) ☎ 544197.

Town P, D, ✗, Gaz, 🛒, R, Bar, ⊠, Ⓑ. ⇌ 15 mins to Brugge. Tram service to Oostende for ✈. Ferries to Hull and Rosyth (Edinburgh).

BRUGGE Masted yachts can transit Zeebrugge's eastern sealock to go 6M S via the Boudewijnkanaal (Ch 68) & 2 lifting bridges to Brugge docks. Thence unmasted boats can go clockwise on the Oostende-Gent Canal (Ch 18) to Flandria Marina (S of city): ☎ 380866, mob 0477 384456. www.yachtclubflandria.be 10 mins walk to city centre; close to ⇌ (a visit by train is quick and easy).

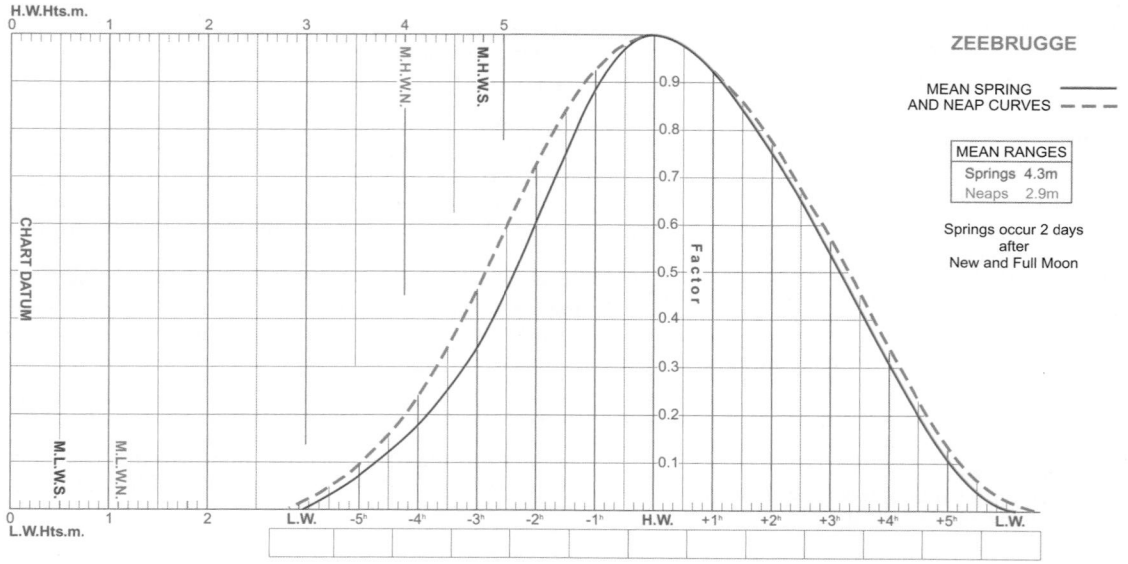

ZEEBRUGGE

MEAN SPRING
AND NEAP CURVES -----

MEAN RANGES
Springs 4.3m
Neaps 2.9m

Springs occur 2 days
after
New and Full Moon

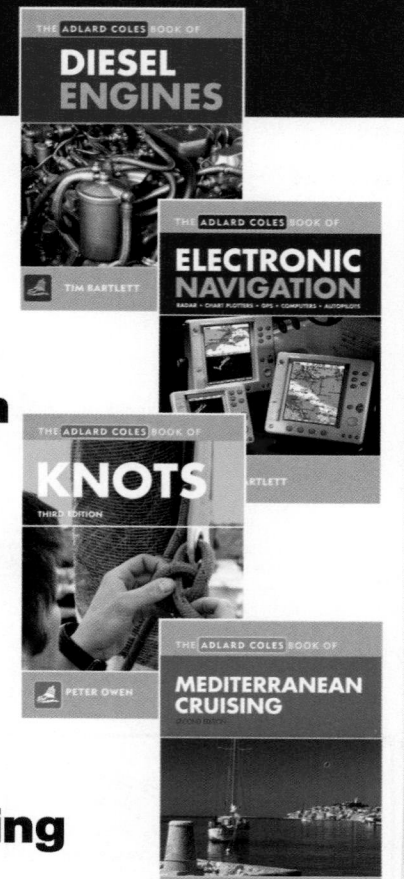

TIME ZONE -0100
Subtract 1 hour for UT
For Dutch Summer Time add
ONE hour in **non-shaded areas**

ZEEBRUGGE   LAT 51°21'N   LONG 3°12'E
TIMES AND HEIGHTS OF HIGH AND LOW WATERS

Dates in red are **SPRINGS**
Dates in blue are **NEAPS**

YEAR 2010

Belgium

JANUARY

Time	m	Time	m
1 0126 0747 F 1346 2005	4.5 0.3 4.7 0.4	**16** 0212 0836 SA 1430 2039	4.3 0.3 4.4 0.7
2 0210 0834 SA 1432 2052	4.5 0.2 4.8 0.4	**17** 0245 0908 SU 1502 2108	4.3 0.3 4.4 0.7
3 0254 0922 SU 1518 2139	4.6 0.1 4.8 0.4	**18** 0315 0938 M 1533 2137	4.3 0.3 4.4 0.7
4 0339 1010 M 1606 2226	4.5 0.0 4.7 0.5	**19** 0345 1008 TU 1603 2208	4.3 0.4 4.3 0.7
5 0426 1059 TU 1656 2314	4.5 0.1 4.6 0.6	**20** 0415 1038 W 1635 2240	4.3 0.4 4.3 0.7
6 0515 1149 W 1749	4.4 0.2 4.4	**21** 0447 1110 TH 1710 2315	4.3 0.5 4.3 0.7
7 0003 0609 TH 1241 ◑ 1847	0.7 4.3 0.3 4.2	**22** 0525 1146 F 1752 2355	4.2 0.6 4.2 0.8
8 0056 0707 F 1338 1949	0.9 4.1 0.5 4.0	**23** 0611 1230 SA 1842 ◐	4.1 0.7 4.1
9 0158 0812 SA 1443 2058	1.0 3.9 0.7 3.8	**24** 0045 0707 SU 1333 1946	1.0 4.0 0.8 3.9
10 0315 0925 SU 1556 2215	1.1 3.8 0.8 3.8	**25** 0200 0819 M 1503 2107	1.1 3.8 0.9 3.7
11 0442 1044 M 1710 2325	1.1 3.8 0.9 3.9	**26** 0341 0941 TU 1615 2226	1.1 3.8 0.9 3.8
12 0551 1150 TU 1811	0.9 4.0 0.8	**27** 0453 1055 W 1717 2332	0.9 3.9 0.8 3.9
13 0019 0642 W 1239 1858	4.0 0.6 4.2 0.7	**28** 0554 1157 TH 1814	0.7 4.2 0.6
14 0101 0725 TH 1320 1937	4.2 0.5 4.3 0.7	**29** 0026 0648 F 1248 1905	4.2 0.4 4.5 0.5
15 0138 0802 F 1356 ● 2010	4.3 0.4 4.4 0.7	**30** 0111 0737 SA 1334 ○ 1952	4.4 0.2 4.7 0.4
		31 0154 0822 SU 1417 2037	4.5 0.0 4.8 0.4

FEBRUARY

Time	m	Time	m
1 0236 0907 M 1501 2121	4.6 -0.1 4.8 0.3	**16** 0247 0910 TU 1505 2111	4.4 0.2 4.4 0.5
2 0319 0952 TU 1546 2205	4.7 -0.1 4.8 0.4	**17** 0315 0939 W 1533 2142	4.4 0.2 4.5 0.5
3 0403 1036 W 1632 2249	4.7 -0.1 4.7 0.4	**18** 0345 1009 TH 1605 2215	4.5 0.3 4.5 0.5
4 0449 1121 TH 1720 2333	4.6 0.0 4.5 0.6	**19** 0418 1041 F 1640 2249	4.5 0.3 4.5 0.5
5 0537 1208 F 1810	4.4 0.3 4.2	**20** 0455 1115 SA 1719 2326	4.5 0.4 4.4 0.6
6 0019 0628 SA 1259 ◑ 1907	0.7 4.2 0.5 3.9	**21** 0538 1156 SU 1805	4.4 0.5 4.2
7 0115 0730 SU 1406 2018	1.0 3.9 0.8 3.6	**22** 0011 0630 M 1251 ◐ 1904	0.7 4.1 0.7 3.8
8 0242 0851 M 1526 2144	1.1 3.6 1.0 3.5	**23** 0116 0741 TU 1426 2032	1.0 3.8 1.0 3.6
9 0414 1023 TU 1645 2303	1.1 3.6 1.0 3.6	**24** 0316 0915 W 1552 2204	1.1 3.7 1.0 3.6
10 0528 1135 W 1753 2359	0.9 3.8 0.9 3.9	**25** 0433 1038 TH 1659 2314	0.9 3.9 0.8 3.8
11 0625 1225 TH 1844	0.6 4.1 0.8	**26** 0538 1142 F 1759	0.6 4.2 0.7
12 0044 0709 F 1305 1922	4.1 0.4 4.2 0.7	**27** 0007 0633 SA 1233 1850	4.1 0.3 4.5 0.5
13 0119 0745 SA 1338 1951	4.2 0.3 4.3 0.7	**28** 0052 0720 SU 1316 ○ 1935	4.4 0.1 4.7 0.4
14 0151 0816 SU 1408 ● 2016	4.3 0.3 4.4 0.6		
15 0220 0843 M 1437 2042	4.3 0.3 4.4 0.6		

MARCH

Time	m	Time	m
1 0133 0804 M 1358 2018	4.6 -0.1 4.8 0.3	**16** 0149 0810 TU 1407 2012	4.3 0.3 4.4 0.5
2 0214 0846 TU 1440 2100	4.7 -0.2 4.8 0.3	**17** 0216 0837 W 1434 2043	4.4 0.2 4.5 0.4
3 0256 0928 W 1522 2141	4.8 -0.2 4.8 0.2	**18** 0245 0908 TH 1504 2117	4.5 0.2 4.5 0.3
4 0339 1011 TH 1606 2223	4.8 -0.1 4.7 0.3	**19** 0317 0942 F 1537 2152	4.6 0.2 4.5 0.3
5 0422 1053 F 1651 2304	4.7 0.0 4.4 0.4	**20** 0352 1016 SA 1614 2228	4.6 0.2 4.5 0.4
6 0507 1136 SA 1737 2346	4.5 0.3 4.2 0.6	**21** 0431 1053 SU 1654 2306	4.6 0.3 4.4 0.5
7 0555 1223 SU 1829 ○	4.2 0.6 3.8	**22** 0515 1135 M 1740 2353	4.4 0.5 4.1 0.6
8 0038 0653 M 1330 1940	0.8 3.8 1.0 3.5	**23** 0607 1231 TU 1840 ◐	4.1 0.8 3.8
9 0216 0833 TU 1457 2110	1.1 3.5 1.2 3.3	**24** 0103 0720 W 1406 2012	0.9 3.8 1.0 3.5
10 0342 0955 W 1613 2232	1.0 3.5 1.2 3.5	**25** 0257 0859 TH 1530 2142	0.9 3.7 1.0 3.6
11 0455 1108 TH 1724 2332	0.9 3.7 1.0 3.7	**26** 0411 1020 F 1638 2250	0.7 3.9 0.9 3.8
12 0556 1200 F 1819	0.6 4.0 0.8	**27** 0515 1122 SA 1739 2344	0.5 4.2 0.7 4.1
13 0017 0642 SA 1239 1857	4.0 0.4 4.2 0.7	**28** 0612 1212 SU 1831	0.2 4.4 0.6
14 0052 0718 SU 1312 1923	4.1 0.3 4.3 0.7	**29** 0029 0659 M 1255 1915	4.3 0.1 4.6 0.4
15 0122 0745 M 1340 ● 1946	4.2 0.3 4.3 0.6	**30** 0110 0741 TU 1336 ○ 1956	4.5 0.0 4.7 0.3
		31 0151 0823 W 1417 2037	4.7 -0.1 4.7 0.2

APRIL

Time	m	Time	m
1 0233 0904 TH 1459 2118	4.8 -0.1 4.7 0.2	**16** 0217 0840 F 1438 2055	4.5 0.1 4.5 0.2
2 0315 0945 F 1542 2158	4.7 0.0 4.5 0.2	**17** 0253 0918 SA 1514 2133	4.6 0.2 4.5 0.2
3 0359 1026 SA 1625 2239	4.6 0.2 4.4 0.3	**18** 0332 0956 SU 1553 2213	4.6 0.2 4.4 0.3
4 0443 1106 SU 1709 2321	4.4 0.4 4.1 0.5	**19** 0413 1037 M 1636 2256	4.6 0.4 4.2 0.4
5 0529 1150 M 1759	4.1 0.7 3.8	**20** 0500 1123 TU 1725 2348	4.4 0.6 4.0 0.6
6 0012 0625 TU 1255 ◑ 1905	0.8 3.8 1.0 3.5	**21** 0556 1224 W 1829 ◐	4.1 0.8 3.7
7 0152 0746 W 1425 2031	1.0 3.5 1.2 3.3	**22** 0108 0713 TH 1350 1957	0.7 3.9 1.0 3.6
8 0307 0914 TH 1534 2148	0.7 3.4 1.2 3.4	**23** 0235 0841 F 1505 2116	0.7 3.8 1.0 3.6
9 0412 1027 F 1639 2250	0.9 3.6 1.1 3.6	**24** 0343 0955 SA 1611 2221	0.6 4.0 0.9 3.8
10 0512 1121 SA 1737 2338	0.7 3.8 0.9 3.8	**25** 0447 1057 SU 1713 2317	0.4 4.2 0.6 4.1
11 0601 1203 SU 1817	0.5 4.0 0.8	**26** 0545 1149 M 1808	0.3 4.3 0.6
12 0015 0637 M 1237 1845	4.0 0.5 4.2 0.7	**27** 0004 0635 TU 1233 1854	4.3 0.3 4.4 0.5
13 0046 0705 TU 1306 1911	4.1 0.4 4.3 0.6	**28** 0048 0718 W 1315 ○ 1936	4.4 0.1 4.5 0.4
14 0115 0733 W 1335 ● 1942	4.3 0.3 4.4 0.4	**29** 0130 0800 TH 1357 2017	4.6 0.1 4.5 0.3
15 0145 0805 TH 1405 2017	4.4 0.2 4.5 0.3	**30** 0213 0841 F 1439 2058	4.6 0.1 4.5 0.2

Chart Datum is 0·23 metres below TAW Datum. HAT is 5·6 metres above Chart Datum; see 4.5.

Zeebrugge tides

TIME ZONE -0100
Subtract 1 hour for UT
For Dutch Summer Time add ONE hour in **non-shaded areas**

ZEEBRUGGE   LAT 51°21'N   LONG 3°12'E
TIMES AND HEIGHTS OF HIGH AND LOW WATERS

YEAR 2010

MAY

Day	Time m	Time m	Time m	Time m
1 SA	0256 4.6	0921 0.2	1521 4.4	2139 0.2
2 SU	0339 4.5	1001 0.4	1604 4.3	2220 0.3
3 M	0423 4.3	1040 0.6	1647 4.1	2303 0.4
4 TU	0509 4.1	1122 0.8	1733 3.8	2356 0.7
5 W	0600 3.8	1215 1.1	1830 3.6	
6 TH	0120 0.8	0707 3.6	1343 1.2	◑ 1943 3.4
7 F	0227 0.9	0824 3.5	1449 1.2	2055 3.4
8 SA	0325 0.9	0932 3.5	1547 1.2	2156 3.5
9 SU	0418 0.8	1029 3.7	1639 1.0	2247 3.6
10 M	0506 0.7	1116 3.9	1724 0.9	2330 3.8
11 TU	0546 0.6	1155 4.0	1801 0.7	
12 W	0007 4.0	0622 0.5	1237 4.2	1837 0.6
13 TH	0041 4.2	0658 0.4	1304 4.2	1915 0.4
14 F	0117 4.4	0736 0.3	1340 4.4	● 1955 0.3
15 SA	0155 4.5	0816 0.2	1418 4.4	2036 0.3
16 SU	0235 4.6	0857 0.2	1458 4.4	2119 0.2
17 M	0317 4.6	0940 0.3	1540 4.3	2204 0.3
18 TU	0402 4.5	1026 0.5	1626 4.2	2253 0.3
19 W	0452 4.3	1116 0.6	1718 4.0	2350 0.4
20 TH	0551 4.2	1217 0.8	1821 3.9	
21 F	0059 0.5	0702 4.0	1326 0.9	◑ 1934 3.8
22 SA	0208 0.5	0817 4.0	1433 0.9	2044 3.8
23 SU	0311 0.4	0925 4.0	1538 0.9	2149 3.9
24 M	0414 0.4	1028 4.1	1644 0.9	2248 4.0
25 TU	0516 0.4	1125 4.2	1745 0.7	2342 4.2
26 W	0611 0.3	1215 4.2	1836 0.6	
27 TH	0030 4.3	0658 0.3	1342 4.3	1920 0.4
28 F	0115 4.4	0741 0.4	1402 4.3	○ 2002 0.3
29 SA	0159 4.5	0821 0.4	1423 4.3	2043 0.3
30 SU	0241 4.5	0901 0.4	1505 4.3	2124 0.2
31 M	0324 4.4	0939 0.5	1545 4.2	2206 0.3

JUNE

Day	Time m	Time m	Time m	Time m
1 TU	0405 4.3	1017 0.7	1626 4.1	2248 0.4
2 W	0447 4.1	1054 0.8	1707 3.9	2334 0.5
3 TH	0531 4.0	1134 1.0	1750 3.8	
4 F	0031 0.7	0620 3.8	1225 1.1	◑ 1842 3.6
5 SA	0134 0.8	0721 3.7	1341 1.2	1946 3.5
6 SU	0230 0.9	0825 3.6	1446 1.2	2049 3.5
7 M	0322 0.9	0925 3.7	1542 1.1	2146 3.6
8 TU	0411 0.8	1020 3.8	1633 1.0	2239 3.7
9 W	0458 0.7	1110 3.9	1721 0.8	2327 3.9
10 TH	0543 0.6	1156 4.1	1807 0.6	
11 F	0012 4.1	0628 0.4	1239 4.2	1852 0.5
12 SA	0055 4.3	0711 0.3	1320 4.3	● 1937 0.3
13 SU	0138 4.5	0756 0.3	1402 4.4	2022 0.2
14 M	0222 4.6	0841 0.3	1445 4.4	2109 0.3
15 TU	0306 4.6	0927 0.4	1529 4.4	2157 0.1
16 W	0353 4.6	1015 0.5	1616 4.3	2247 0.2
17 TH	0444 4.5	1106 0.6	1706 4.2	2341 0.2
18 F	0539 4.4	1159 0.7	1802 4.1	
19 SA	0037 0.3	0640 4.2	1256 0.8	◑ 1904 4.0
20 SU	0136 0.3	0745 4.1	1356 0.9	2008 4.0
21 M	0237 0.4	0850 4.0	1502 0.9	2114 3.9
22 TU	0341 0.5	0958 3.9	1614 0.9	2221 3.9
23 W	0449 0.6	1104 4.0	1726 0.8	2326 4.0
24 TH	0551 0.6	1201 4.1	1823 0.6	
25 F	0020 4.2	0643 0.6	1249 4.2	1910 0.5
26 SA	0107 4.3	0727 0.6	1330 4.2	○ 1952 0.4
27 SU	0148 4.4	0806 0.6	1409 4.3	2032 0.3
28 M	0228 4.4	0843 0.6	1448 4.3	2111 0.2
29 TU	0307 4.4	0919 0.6	1525 4.3	2149 0.3
30 W	0345 4.3	0952 0.7	1601 4.2	2226 0.3

JULY

Day	Time m	Time m	Time m	Time m
1 TH	0421 4.2	1025 0.7	1635 4.1	2301 0.4
2 F	0457 4.2	1058 0.8	1710 4.1	2336 0.6
3 SA	0533 4.1	1134 0.9	1747 4.0	
4 SU	0014 0.7	0615 4.0	1216 1.0	◑ 1832 3.9
5 M	0103 0.8	0706 3.9	1310 1.1	1929 3.8
6 TU	0211 0.9	0811 3.8	1432 1.1	2038 3.7
7 W	0318 0.8	0922 3.8	1547 1.0	2148 3.7
8 TH	0417 0.8	1028 3.8	1648 0.9	2252 3.9
9 F	0512 0.7	1127 4.0	1743 0.7	2348 4.1
10 SA	0603 0.5	1218 4.2	1834 0.5	
11 SU	0038 4.4	0652 0.4	1304 4.3	● 1923 0.3
12 M	0124 4.6	0739 0.4	1347 4.5	2010 0.1
13 TU	0209 4.7	0826 0.4	1430 4.5	2057 0.0
14 W	0253 4.8	0912 0.4	1514 4.6	2144 0.0
15 TH	0339 4.7	1000 0.4	1559 4.5	2232 0.0
16 F	0427 4.7	1047 0.5	1646 4.5	2320 0.0
17 SA	0517 4.5	1134 0.6	1736 4.4	
18 SU	0009 0.1	0611 4.4	1224 0.7	◑ 1831 4.3
19 M	0102 0.3	0710 4.2	1318 0.8	1931 4.1
20 TU	0202 0.5	0814 3.9	1426 1.0	2040 3.9
21 W	0311 0.7	0928 3.8	1549 1.0	2159 3.8
22 TH	0426 0.8	1046 3.8	1710 0.9	2315 4.0
23 F	0535 0.8	1149 4.0	1812 0.6	
24 SA	0013 4.1	0631 0.7	1237 4.1	1900 0.5
25 SU	0057 4.3	0714 0.7	1316 4.3	1941 0.3
26 M	0136 4.4	0751 0.7	1353 4.3	○ 2017 0.3
27 TU	0212 4.4	0824 0.6	1427 4.4	2052 0.2
28 W	0246 4.5	0854 0.6	1500 4.4	2124 0.2
29 TH	0319 4.4	0924 0.6	1531 4.4	2155 0.3
30 F	0351 4.4	0955 0.6	1602 4.4	2225 0.4
31 SA	0422 4.4	1026 0.6	1633 4.4	2255 0.4

AUGUST

Day	Time m	Time m	Time m	Time m
1 SU	0454 4.3	1059 0.7	1707 4.3	2327 0.5
2 M	0531 4.3	1135 0.7	1748 4.3	
3 TU	0006 0.6	0615 4.2	1219 0.8	◑ 1837 4.1
4 W	0057 0.8	0710 4.0	1318 1.0	1942 3.9
5 TH	0221 0.9	0827 3.8	1505 1.1	2105 3.8
6 F	0344 0.9	0953 3.8	1622 0.9	2225 3.9
7 SA	0447 0.8	1103 3.9	1724 0.7	2330 4.2
8 SU	0544 0.6	1159 4.2	1818 0.5	
9 M	0023 4.5	0635 0.5	1246 4.4	1908 0.2
10 TU	0108 4.7	0723 0.4	1328 4.6	● 1954 0.1
11 W	0152 4.8	0809 0.4	1410 4.7	2039 -0.1
12 TH	0235 4.9	0854 0.3	1453 4.8	2124 -0.1
13 F	0319 4.9	0938 0.3	1536 4.8	2209 -0.1
14 SA	0404 4.8	1023 0.4	1622 4.8	2254 0.0
15 SU	0451 4.7	1107 0.4	1709 4.6	2340 0.2
16 M	0540 4.4	1152 0.6	1759 4.4	◐
17 TU	0029 0.4	0634 4.2	1244 0.8	1857 4.1
18 W	0128 0.7	0740 3.9	1357 1.0	2010 3.9
19 TH	0245 0.9	0901 3.7	1529 1.0	2140 3.8
20 F	0404 1.0	1026 3.7	1649 0.9	2302 3.9
21 SA	0517 0.9	1131 3.9	1753 0.6	2359 4.2
22 SU	0615 0.8	1219 4.2	1843 0.4	
23 M	0042 4.4	0658 0.7	1257 4.3	1922 0.3
24 TU	0118 4.5	0732 0.7	1331 4.4	○ 1956 0.3
25 W	0150 4.6	0800 0.6	1402 4.5	2025 0.3
26 TH	0220 4.5	0826 0.6	1431 4.5	2053 0.3
27 F	0250 4.5	0855 0.5	1500 4.5	2122 0.3
28 SA	0319 4.6	0925 0.5	1529 4.6	2152 0.3
29 SU	0348 4.6	0957 0.5	1601 4.6	2222 0.3
30 M	0421 4.6	1030 0.5	1636 4.6	2255 0.4
31 TU	0457 4.5	1106 0.6	1716 4.5	2333 0.5

Chart Datum is 0·23 metres below TAW Datum. HAT is 5·6 metres above Chart Datum; see 4.5.

Belgium

<table>
<tr><td>TIME ZONE -0100
Subtract 1 hour for UT
For Dutch Summer Time add
ONE hour in non-shaded areas</td><td>ZEEBRUGGE   LAT 51°21'N   LONG 3°12'E
TIMES AND HEIGHTS OF HIGH AND LOW WATERS</td><td>Dates in red are SPRINGS
Dates in blue are NEAPS

YEAR 2010</td></tr>
</table>

SEPTEMBER

Time	m		Time	m
1 0540	4.3	**16**	0058	0.9
1147	0.7		0709	3.8
W 1803	4.3	TH 1336		1.0
◑			1945	3.8
2 0020	0.7	**17**	0222	1.1
0632	4.1		0834	3.6
TH 1242	0.9	F 1507		1.0
1905	4.1		2118	3.7
3 0138	1.0	**18**	0339	1.2
0749	3.8		0958	3.6
F 1436	1.1	SA 1620		0.9
2035	3.9		2238	3.9
4 0319	1.0	**19**	0451	1.1
0927	3.7		1104	3.9
SA 1600	0.9	SU 1725		0.7
2204	4.0		2335	4.1
5 0426	0.9	**20**	0551	0.9
1041	3.9		1153	4.1
SU 1704	0.7	M 1817		0.5
2311	4.2			
6 0525	0.7	**21**	0018	4.3
1137	4.2		0635	0.8
M 1800	0.4	TU 1232		4.3
			1856	0.4
7 0004	4.5	**22**	0053	4.5
0618	0.6		0706	0.7
TU 1224	4.5	W 1304		4.4
1849	0.2		1927	0.4
8 0049	4.8	**23**	0123	4.5
0705	0.5		0731	0.6
W 1306	4.7	TH 1333		4.5
● 1934	0.0	○ 1953		0.3
9 0131	4.9	**24**	0152	4.6
0749	0.4		0756	0.6
TH 1348	4.9	F 1401		4.6
2018	-0.1		2020	0.3
10 0213	5.0	**25**	0219	4.6
0832	0.3		0826	0.5
F 1430	5.0	SA 1430		4.6
2101	-0.1		2050	0.3
11 0256	5.0	**26**	0248	4.6
0915	0.3		0859	0.4
SA 1513	5.0	SU 1500		4.7
2145	-0.1		2122	0.3
12 0340	4.9	**27**	0320	4.7
0958	0.3		0933	0.4
SU 1557	4.9	M 1534		4.7
2228	0.1		2156	0.3
13 0425	4.7	**28**	0354	4.6
1041	0.4		1008	0.4
M 1643	4.7	TU 1611		4.7
2312	0.3		2231	0.4
14 0512	4.4	**29**	0431	4.5
1125	0.5		1045	0.5
TU 1732	4.5	W 1652		4.6
2359	0.6		2310	0.6
15 0604	4.1	**30**	0514	4.3
1216	0.8		1128	0.7
W 1828	4.1	TH 1740		4.4
◑				

OCTOBER

Time	m		Time	m
1 0000	0.8	**16**	0155	1.2
0608	4.0		0801	3.6
F 1226	0.9	SA 1438		1.0
◑ 1844	4.1		2045	3.7
2 0119	1.1	**17**	0307	1.3
0727	3.8		0920	3.6
SA 1419	1.0	SU 1545		0.9
2018	3.9		2200	3.8
3 0256	1.1	**18**	0414	1.2
0904	3.7		1026	3.8
SU 1537	0.8	M 1647		0.8
2143	4.0		2259	4.0
4 0403	1.0	**19**	0514	1.0
1015	3.9		1118	4.0
M 1640	0.6	TU 1740		0.6
2248	4.3		2345	4.2
5 0503	0.8	**20**	0601	0.9
1112	4.2		1159	4.2
TU 1737	0.4	W 1821		0.6
2341	4.6			
6 0557	0.6	**21**	0021	4.3
1200	4.5		0633	0.8
W 1827	0.2	TH 1232		4.3
			1851	0.5
7 0027	4.8	**22**	0053	4.5
0645	0.5		0659	0.7
TH 1243	4.7	F 1302		4.4
● 1912	0.1		1918	0.4
8 0109	4.9	**23**	0122	4.5
0729	0.4		0727	0.6
F 1325	4.9	SA 1332		4.5
1955	0.0	○ 1948		0.4
9 0151	4.9	**24**	0151	4.6
0811	0.3		0800	0.4
SA 1408	5.0	SU 1402		4.6
2038	0.0		2021	0.3
10 0234	4.9	**25**	0222	4.6
0854	0.2		0836	0.4
SU 1451	5.0	M 1436		4.7
2121	0.1		2057	0.3
11 0318	4.8	**26**	0256	4.6
0937	0.3		0913	0.4
M 1536	4.9	TU 1513		4.7
2203	0.2		2134	0.4
12 0403	4.6	**27**	0333	4.6
1020	0.3		0952	0.4
TU 1622	4.7	W 1552		4.7
2246	0.5		2213	0.5
13 0449	4.4	**28**	0413	4.4
1104	0.5		1033	0.5
W 1710	4.4	TH 1636		4.6
2332	0.7		2257	0.7
14 0539	4.1	**29**	0459	4.3
1157	0.7		1120	0.6
TH 1806	4.1	F 1727		4.4
◑			2350	0.9
15 0031	1.0	**30**	0555	4.0
0642	3.8		1226	0.8
F 1319	0.9	SA 1834		4.1
1920	3.8	◑		
		31	0106	1.1
			0713	3.8
		SU 1358		0.8
			2000	4.0

NOVEMBER

Time	m		Time	m
1 0229	1.1	**16**	0327	1.3
0837	3.8		0934	3.6
M 1509	0.7	TU 1559		0.9
2117	4.1		2210	3.8
2 0335	1.0	**17**	0424	1.2
0945	4.0		1030	3.8
TU 1611	0.6	W 1651		0.9
2222	4.3		2301	4.0
3 0437	0.9	**18**	0514	1.1
1044	4.2		1117	3.9
W 1710	0.4	TH 1735		0.8
2317	4.5		2344	4.1
4 0535	0.7	**19**	0553	0.9
1135	4.4		1156	4.1
TH 1804	0.3	F 1811		0.7
5 0006	4.6	**20**	0021	4.3
0626	0.6		0627	0.8
F 1222	4.6	SA 1232		4.3
1851	0.2		1845	0.6
6 0050	4.7	**21**	0055	4.4
0711	0.5		0702	0.6
SA 1307	4.8	SU 1306		4.4
● 1935	0.2	○ 1920		0.5
7 0134	4.7	**22**	0128	4.5
0754	0.4		0739	0.4
SU 1351	4.8	M 1341		4.6
2018	0.2		1957	0.4
8 0217	4.7	**23**	0203	4.5
0837	0.3		0819	0.4
M 1435	4.9	TU 1418		4.7
2100	0.3		2037	0.4
9 0301	4.6	**24**	0240	4.5
0920	0.3		0859	0.3
TU 1520	4.8	W 1458		4.7
2142	0.4		2118	0.4
10 0345	4.5	**25**	0319	4.5
1004	0.3		0942	0.4
W 1605	4.6	TH 1541		4.6
2224	0.6		2201	0.6
11 0430	4.3	**26**	0402	4.4
1049	0.4		1028	0.4
TH 1653	4.4	F 1627		4.5
2309	0.8		2248	0.7
12 0518	4.1	**27**	0450	4.2
1142	0.6		1120	0.5
F 1744	4.1	SA 1720		4.4
2359	1.1		2342	0.9
13 0612	3.9	**28**	0545	4.1
1253	0.8		1223	0.6
SA 1847	3.9	SU 1823		4.2
◐		◐		
14 0115	1.3	**29**	0047	1.0
0719	3.7		0653	4.0
SU 1402	0.9	M 1331		0.6
2000	3.7		1936	4.1
15 0226	1.3	**30**	0156	1.0
0830	3.6		0805	3.9
M 1503	0.9	TU 1436		0.6
2109	3.7		2046	4.1

DECEMBER

Time	m		Time	m
1 0302	1.0	**16**	0327	1.3
0912	3.9		0929	3.6
W 1539	0.6	TH 1558		1.0
2152	4.1		2206	3.7
2 0407	1.0	**17**	0423	1.2
1015	4.1		1026	3.7
TH 1643	0.5	F 1647		0.9
2253	4.2		2300	3.9
3 0513	0.9	**18**	0513	1.0
1113	4.2		1117	3.9
F 1743	0.5	SA 1732		0.8
2349	4.3		2348	4.0
4 0611	0.7	**19**	0559	0.8
1207	4.4		1203	4.1
SA 1835	0.5	SU 1815		0.7
5 0038	4.4	**20**	0030	4.2
0700	0.5		0641	0.6
SU 1255	4.5	M 1245		4.3
● 1921	0.4		1857	0.5
6 0122	4.5	**21**	0109	4.4
0744	0.4		0723	0.5
M 1340	4.6	TU 1325		4.5
2003	0.4	○ 1939		0.5
7 0205	4.5	**22**	0148	4.5
0827	0.3		0805	0.3
TU 1424	4.7	W 1405		4.6
2044	0.5		2021	0.4
8 0247	4.5	**23**	0227	4.5
0909	0.3		0849	0.2
W 1507	4.7	TH 1447		4.7
2125	0.6		2105	0.4
9 0329	4.5	**24**	0308	4.5
0952	0.3		0935	0.2
TH 1550	4.6	F 1531		4.7
2205	0.7		2151	0.5
10 0411	4.4	**25**	0351	4.4
1036	0.4		1022	0.2
F 1633	4.4	SA 1617		4.6
2245	0.8		2238	0.6
11 0453	4.2	**26**	0438	4.4
1122	0.5		1112	0.3
SA 1718	4.2	SU 1707		4.5
2326	1.0		2328	0.7
12 0537	4.0	**27**	0529	4.3
1213	0.7		1205	0.3
SU 1806	4.0	M 1803		4.4
13 0012	1.2	**28**	0021	0.8
0626	3.8		0626	4.2
M 1312	0.9	TU 1301		0.4
◐ 1901	3.8	◐ 1906		4.2
14 0116	1.3	**29**	0119	0.9
0724	3.7		0729	4.1
TU 1410	1.0	W 1401		0.5
2004	3.7		2012	4.0
15 0226	1.3	**30**	0224	1.0
0827	3.6		0836	4.0
W 1505	1.0	TH 1506		0.6
2107	3.7		2120	3.9
		31	0338	1.0
			0947	3.9
		F 1617		0.7
			2232	3.9

Chart Datum is 0·23 metres below TAW Datum. HAT is 5·6 metres above Chart Datum; see 4.5.

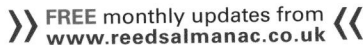

9.16.34   BLANKENBERGE

Belgium, West Flanders **51°18'·90N 03°06'·48E** ✦⊛⊛♦♦♦✿✿

CHARTS AC *2449*, 1872, 1874; DYC 1801.3; Imray C30; Stan 1, 19

TIDES +0130 Dover; ML 2·5; Duration 0535.

Standard Port VLISSINGEN (←)

Times				Height (metres)			
High Water	Low Water			MHWS	MHWN	MLWN	MLWS
All times	All times			5·0	4·1	1·1	0·5
Differences BLANKENBERGE							
–0040	–0040			–0·3	0·0	+0·3	+0·2

SHELTER Good, but entry is dangerous in NW'lies F6 and above.

NAVIGATION WPT 51°19'·60N 03°05'·31E, 134°/1M to pierheads. Caution: 4 unlit Y SPM buoys and one Fl (4) Y 20s lie E and W of hbr ent about 400m offshore. Beware strong tides (& fishing lines) across ent. Access HW ±2 but up to ±4 in season, when it is said to be dredged 2·5m; out of season it silts between piers and dries at LW. Do not try to ent/exit LW±1½, especially at springs. Oct–end May, only ent/exit HW±1, unless depths have been pre-checked. Call dredger Ch 10 for clearance to pass.

LIGHTS AND MARKS Conspic high-rise blocks E of lt ho, W twr B

top. Ldg lts 134°, both FR, (Red X on front mast) show the best water. FG on W pier is more visible than FR (E pier). A water twr is conspic on E side of new Hbr. See also 9.16.4 and chartlet.

R/T VNZ, SYCB and VVW marinas Ch 23. *Blankenberge Rescue* Ch 08; or relay via Zeebrugge Traffic Centre Ch 69. Dredger Ch 10.

TELEPHONE (Code 050) Call VNZ, SYCB or VVW below; ⊖ 544223; Police 429842; Dr 333668; ⊞ 413701; Brit Consul (02) 2179000.

FACILITIES A Port of Entry, with Customs early Apr–late Sept.

Keep to port, past the FV hbr, for the old Yacht Hbr (1·8m); VNZ pontoons are on N side and SYCB to the E. Or turn 90° stbd into new Hbr/marina (2·5m); 12 pontoons, run by VNZ, SYCB & VVW.

Fees (same for all berths): **Beam** <3m €15; <3·5m €22; <4m €29; <4·25m €33; <4·50m €36; <5·00m €45.

VNZ (YC Vrije Noordzeezeilers) ☎ 425292, mobile 0497 565565. www.vnzblankenberge.be vnz@skynet.be Bar, R.

SYCB (Scarphout YC) www.scarphout.be scarphout@skynet.be ☎ 411420, mobile 0476 971692. C (10/2½ ton), Slip, Bar, R, ⚓.

VVW (Marina) www.vvwblankenberge.be ☎ 417536, mobile 0495 527536 info@vvwblankenberge.be. ⚓, Bar, ▣, Slip, P, D (hose, duty free), ME, ✕, Ⓔ, El, SM, CH, C (20 ton).

Town Gaz, R, Bar, ✉, Ⓑ, ⇒, ✈ Ostend.

9.16.35   OOSTENDE

Belgium, West Flanders **51°14'·35N 02°55'·09E** ✦⊛⊛♦♦♦✿✿✿

CHARTS AC *2449*, 1872, 1874, 1873; SHOM 7214; Navi 1010; DYC 1801.2; Imray C30; Stanfords 1, 19, 20

TIDES +0120 Dover; ML 2·79; Duration 0530.

Standard Port ZEEBRUGGE (←)

Times				Height (metres)			
High Water		Low Water		MHWS	MHWN	MLWN	MLWS
0300	0900	0300	0900	4·8	4·0	1·1	0·5
1500	2100	1500	2100				
Differences OOSTENDE							
–0019	–0019	–0008	–0008	+0·4	+0·3	+0·2	+0·1

SHELTER Wash can enter RNSYC (2·2m). Very good in Mercator Marina (5·0m). RYCO (2·7m) may be exposed in strong W/NW'lies. Locals sceptical about the effectiveness of new wavebreaks.

NAVIGATION WPT 51°14'·97N 02°53'·83E, 128°/1M to ent. Avoid the offshore banks esp in bad weather: From the NE stay to seaward of Wenduinebank, except in calm weather. From the NW keep S of W Hinder TSS and approach from MBN buoy. From the SW appr via West Diep and Kleine Rede, inside Stroombank. Major WIP 2008-12: demolish E pier and build new one further E. Note size of Montgomerydok entrance reduced as a result of works.

LIGHTS AND MARKS Europa Centrum bldg (105m; twice as high as other bldgs) is conspic 4ca SSW of ent. W lt ho, 5ca ESE of the ent, is conspic with 2 sinusoidal blue bands. 128° ldg marks are lattice masts with R/W bands and X topmarks. See chartlet and 9.16.4 for lt details.

IPTS from E pier, plus QY = hbr closed, ferry moving. At blind exit from Montgomerydok, QY lts = no exit, ferry/ship moving.

R/T Port Control Ch 09 (H24); Mercator lock/Marina Ch 14 (lock hrs); Weather Ch 27 at 0820 & 1720 UT (English and Dutch). Demey lock (VHF 10) gives access to Oostende-Brugge canal.

TELEPHONE (Code 059) HM 321687; Mercator lock 705762; ⊖ 242070; Police 701111; ⊞ 552000; Brit Consul (02) 2876232.

FACILITIES from seaward: **Royal North Sea YC** (RNSYC), ☎ 430694 HM 505912. www.rnsyc.be robert@rnsyc.be No VHF. 150+50 Ⓥ, much rafting, €1.92 inc AC & shwr (M/Cruisers + 25%). Limited D, Grid, ▣, Wi-fi, ME, CH, ✕, El, SM, R, Bar.

Mercator lock Must pre-call Ch 14 for lock-in time and berth. Waiting pontoon N of lock. No freeflow. R/G tfc lts. Hrs (times in brackets are Fri-Sun & public hols): May/Jun 0800-2000 (2100); Jul/Aug 0700-2200, 7/7; Sep 0800-1800 (2000). Oct–Apr, see web.

Mercator Marina ☎ 705762.www.mercatormarina.be 300+50 Ⓥ, €2.05 inc AC; must pay cash/card before entering lock outbound.

Royal YC Oostende (RYCO) ☎ 321452. ryco@skynet.be www.ryco. be No VHF. 160 + 35 Ⓥ, €2.30 inc AC & shwr. Slip (10 ton), Grid, C (½ ton), Wi-Fi, R, Bar.

Town All needs, ⇒, ✈. Ferry, ☎ 340260 (no foot pax) to Ramsgate.

CROSSING THE NORTH SEA FROM BELGIUM

(AC *1406*, *323*) There are so many permutations that it is better to try to apply just four broad principles:

• Avoid the N Hinder-Maas and W Hinder-Sandettie complexes.

• Cross TSS at their narrowest parts, ie between NHR-SE and Fairy W; and SW of Sandettie.

• Plan to cross the many offshore ridges at their extremities, zigzagging as necessary to achieve this.

• If bound for Dover or down-Channel use the coastal passage W to Dyck, then via MPC to SW Goodwin buoy. Or route via Sandettie to NE Goodwin buoy and into the southern Thames Estuary.

From the Scheur chan off Zeebrugge a fairly direct course via Track Ferry and S Galloper leads into the N Thames Estuary or towards the Suffolk ports. Avoid shoals, particularly in rough weather when the sea-state and under-keel clearance may be crucial problems. See 9.0.7 for distances across the North Sea.

14'·5

Ldg Lts 128°

Q.Y

Q.Y

6   Q.R

WIP 2007

Q

F.G.14m10M
Bell.4s

8

Q.R

Q.R

Q.Y

Fort Napoleon

Radar tower, IPTS,
Storm & Tidal sigs

N

8

3 Iso4s
(vert)

Lt Ho
Fl(3)10s
65m27M

3₇

Royal North Sea YC

2₂

Q.Y

3 Iso4s
(vert)

Conspic
Centrum Bldg
(105m)

Montgomery Dock

5

3₇

14'

Ferry berths

8

F.R

Naval Basin

See inset

Mercator
Lock

Cathedral
(twin spires)

5

F.G

F

Mercator
Marina

5

OOSTENDE

See inset

5

C   B   A   F   E

D

G   RYCO

K   J   I

H

Voorhaven

8

8

5₂

2₇   RYCO

VVW

See inset

0 metres   600

0 cables   4

51°13'·5N

55'

Demey Lock

4₂

Canal to Brugge

02°56'E

Royal
North
Sea YC

Waiting
pontoon

Q.Y

Montgomery Dock

Dredged to 2·7m

Waiting
pontoon

N

MERCATOR MARINA

F   E   D   C   B

Mercator STS

G   A

1–27

40–1

Swing
bridge

49–1

106–102

97–101

96–51

9.16.36 NIEUWPOORT
Belgium, W Flanders **51°09'·38N 02°43'·04** ✳✳✳✳♨♨♨✿✿✿

CHARTS AC *2449*, 1872, 1873; Belgian 101, D11; DYC 1801.2; SHOM 7214; Navicarte 1010; Imray C30; Stanfords 1, 20

TIDES +0105 Dover; ML 2·96; Duration 0515.

Standard Port ZEEBRUGGE (⟵)

Times				Height (metres)			
High Water		Low Water		MHWS	MHWN	MLWN	MLWS
0300	0900	0300	0900	4·8	4·0	1·1	0·5
1500	2100	1500	2100				
Differences NIEUWPOORT							
−0031	−0031	−0010	−0010	+0·7	+0·5	+0·3	+0·1

SHELTER Good except in strong NW'lies. Access H24.

NAVIGATION WPT 51°10'·08N 02°41'·90E, 134°/1M to ent. IPTS, normally Sig 4, are shown from root of W pier. The bar (1·5m) is liable to silt up but there is usually sufficient water for all but the deepest draught yachts. At sp the stream reaches 2kn across the ent. The 1M long access chan to the marinas is marked by white-topped piles and dredged 3·1m, but levels can fall to about 2m. *Speed limit 5kts in hbr.*

LIGHTS AND MARKS The high-rise blocks W of the entrance are in stark contrast to the sand dunes and flatlands to the E. The lt ho is a conspic 28m R twr, W bands; see chartlet and 9.16.4. The central, pyramidal white HM bldg at VVW-N is conspic.

An illuminated red STOP sign near the ents to Novus Portus and KYCN indicates to departing vessels that the fairway is not clear.

R/T Port Ch 09 (H24). *Airforce Yacht Club* (WSKLM): Ch 72. KYCN: Ch 23. VVW-N: Ch 08.

TELEPHONE (Code 058) HM/Pilots 233000; Canal locks 233050; CG/Marine Police 233045; ⊖ 233451; Duty Free Store 233433; Dr 233089; Brit Consul (02) 2876232; Police 234246.

FACILITIES The 3 marinas are: **WSKLM**, N & E sides of Novus Portus. ☎ 233641, www.wsklum.be wsklum@wsklm.be 370 inc ❶ on pontoons A & B, €1.40. H24, CH, BH (16 ton), Slip, ▣, Wi-Fi, Ice, bike hire, R, Bar; Okay 🛒 800m NE at Lombardsijde.

VVW-N, S & W sides of Novus Portus. ☎ 235232, 1000 + ❶, fees not given. El, Ⓔ, BH (50t), Slip, ▣, CH, ⚓, ⚒, SM, R, Bar, free bikes, Wi-Fi. www.vvwnieuwpoort.be info@vvwnieuwpoort.be

KYCN (Royal Nieuwpoort YC). info@kycn.be www.kycn.be ☎ 234413. 420 + 75 ❶, €2.20, often busy. M, C (12 ton), Slip, CH, Gas, ME, El, ⚒, 🛒, D, ▣, R, Bar, Wi-Fi.

Fuel is only available at KYCN and S of VVW-N on the E bank of the river, see inset. The river accesses the N Belgian canals.

Town P, D, Gaz, 🛒, R, Bar, ✉, Ⓑ, ⇌, ✈ (Oostende).

North France

Dunkerque to Cap de la Hague

Contents

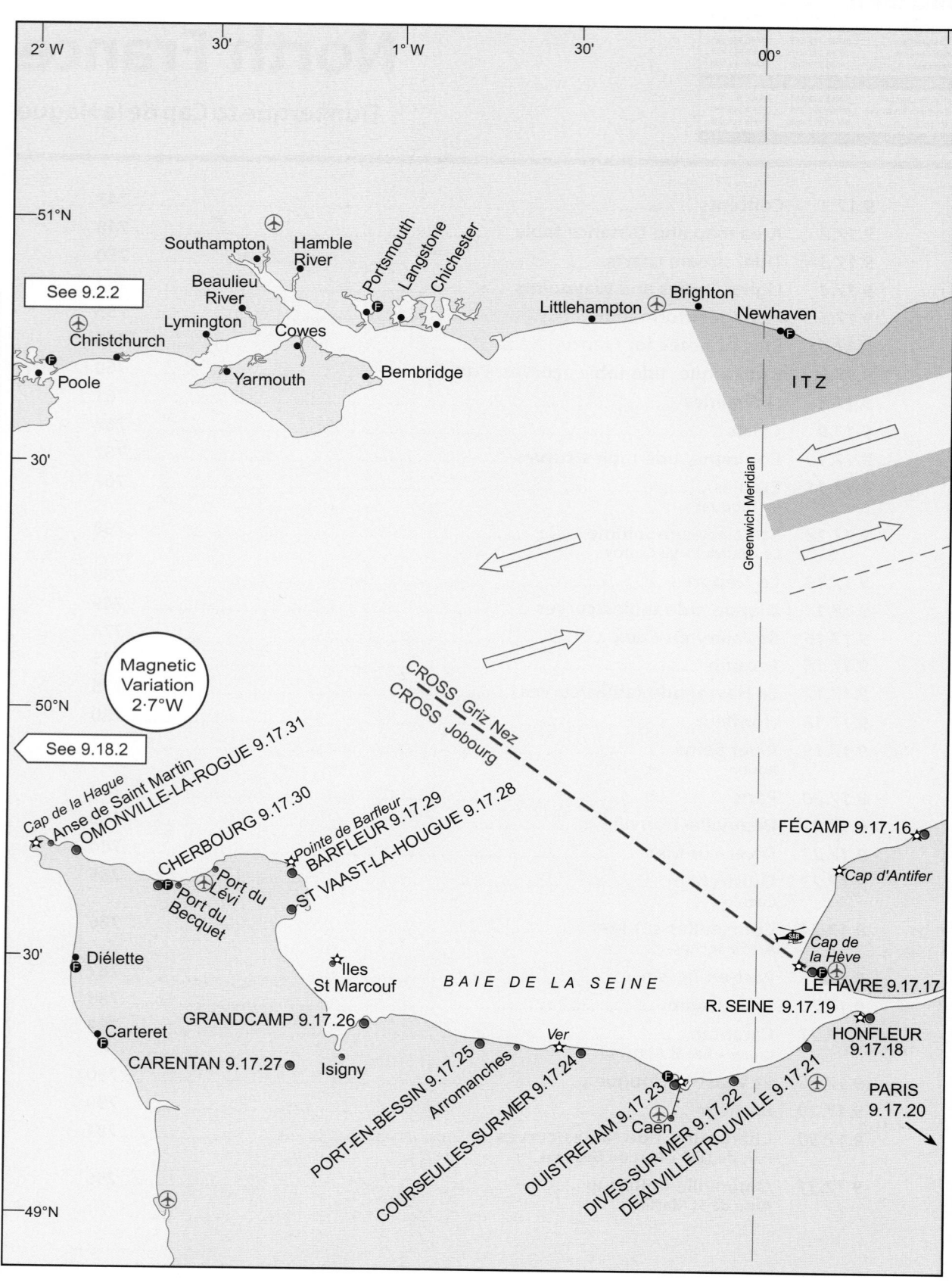

2° W   30'   1° W   30'   00°

51°N

Southampton   Hamble River   Portsmouth   Langstone   Chichester   Littlehampton   Brighton   Newhaven

Beaulieu River

See 9.2.2

Lymington   Cowes

Christchurch

Poole   Yarmouth   Bembridge

ITZ

30'

Greenwich Meridian

50°N

Magnetic Variation 2·7°W

See 9.18.2

CROSS Griz Nez
CROSS Jobourg

Cap de la Hague   Anse de Saint Martin   OMONVILLE-LA-ROGUE 9.17.31

CHERBOURG 9.17.30

Pointe de Barfleur   BARFLEUR 9.17.29

ST VAAST-LA-HOUGUE 9.17.28

FÉCAMP 9.17.16

Cap d'Antifer

Port du Lévi

Port du Becquet

Cap de la Hève

LE HAVRE 9.17.17

30'   Diélette

Iles St Marcouf

BAIE DE LA SEINE

R. SEINE 9.17.19

Carteret

GRANDCAMP 9.17.26

HONFLEUR 9.17.18

CARENTAN 9.17.27   Isigny

Ver

PORT-EN-BESSIN 9.17.25   Arromanches   COURSEULLES-SUR-MER 9.17.24

OUISTREHAM 9.17.23   DIVES-SUR MER 9.17.22   DEAUVILLE/TROUVILLE 9.17.21

Caen

PARIS 9.17.20

49°N

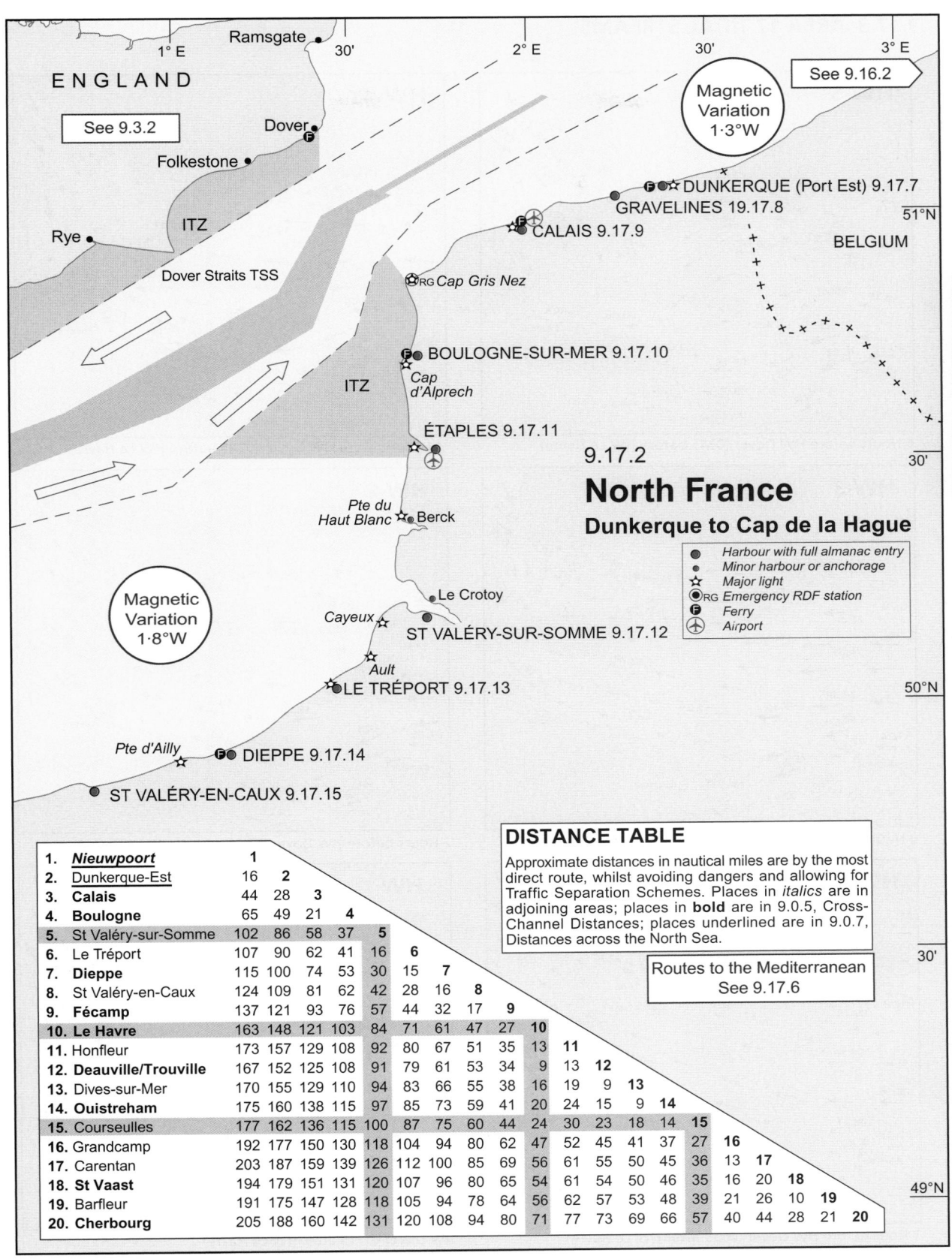

ENGLAND

Ramsgate

Dover

Folkestone

Rye

ITZ

Dover Straits TSS

See 9.3.2

See 9.16.2

Magnetic Variation 1·3°W

DUNKERQUE (Port Est) 9.17.7

GRAVELINES 19.17.8

BELGIUM

CALAIS 9.17.9

Cap Gris Nez

ITZ

BOULOGNE-SUR-MER 9.17.10

Cap d'Alprech

ÉTAPLES 9.17.11

9.17.2

North France

Dunkerque to Cap de la Hague

Pte du Haut Blanc   Berck

Magnetic Variation 1·8°W

Cayeux

Le Crotoy

ST VALÉRY-SUR-SOMME 9.17.12

- ● Harbour with full almanac entry
- • Minor harbour or anchorage
- ☆ Major light
- Ⓡ RG Emergency RDF station
- Ⓕ Ferry
- Ⓐ Airport

Ault

LE TRÉPORT 9.17.13

Pte d'Ailly

DIEPPE 9.17.14

ST VALÉRY-EN-CAUX 9.17.15

DISTANCE TABLE

Approximate distances in nautical miles are by the most direct route, whilst avoiding dangers and allowing for Traffic Separation Schemes. Places in *italics* are in adjoining areas; places in **bold** are in 9.0.5, Cross-Channel Distances; places underlined are in 9.0.7, Distances across the North Sea.

Routes to the Mediterranean
See 9.17.6

1.	*Nieuwpoort*	1																		
2.	Dunkerque-Est	16	2																	
3.	Calais	44	28	3																
4.	Boulogne	65	49	21	4															
5.	St Valéry-sur-Somme	102	86	58	37	5														
6.	Le Tréport	107	90	62	41	16	6													
7.	Dieppe	115	100	74	53	30	15	7												
8.	St Valéry-en-Caux	124	109	81	62	42	28	16	8											
9.	Fécamp	137	121	93	76	57	44	32	17	9										
10.	Le Havre	163	148	121	103	84	71	61	47	27	10									
11.	Honfleur	173	157	129	108	92	80	67	51	35	13	11								
12.	Deauville/Trouville	167	152	125	108	91	79	61	53	34	9	13	12							
13.	Dives-sur-Mer	170	155	129	110	94	83	66	55	38	16	19	9	13						
14.	Ouistreham	175	160	138	115	97	85	73	59	41	20	24	15	9	14					
15.	Courseulles	177	162	136	115	100	87	75	60	44	24	30	23	18	14	15				
16.	Grandcamp	192	177	150	130	118	104	94	80	62	47	52	45	41	37	27	16			
17.	Carentan	203	187	159	139	126	112	100	85	69	56	61	55	50	45	36	13	17		
18.	St Vaast	194	179	151	131	120	107	96	80	65	54	61	54	50	46	35	16	20	18	
19.	Barfleur	191	175	147	128	118	105	94	78	64	56	62	57	53	48	39	21	26	10	19
20.	Cherbourg	205	188	160	142	131	120	108	94	80	71	77	73	69	66	57	40	44	28	21	20

749

9.17.3 AREA 17 TIDAL STREAMS

5 Hours before HW Dover (0345 before HW Le Havre)

4 Hours before HW Dover (0245 before HW Le Havre)

3 Hours before HW Dover (0145 before HW Le Havre)

2 Hours before HW Dover (0045 before HW Le Havre)

1 Hour before HW Dover (0015 after HW Le Havre)

HW Dover (0115 after HW Le Havre)

Westward 9.18.3   Channel Is 9.19.3   Northward 9.2.3   North-eastward 9.3.3   Eastward 9.16.3

1 Hour after HW Dover (0215 after HW Le Havre)

2 Hours after HW Dover (0315 after HW Le Havre)

3 Hours after HW Dover (0415 after HW Le Havre)

4 Hours after HW Dover (0515 after HW Le Havre)

5 Hours after HW Dover (0615 after HW Le Havre)

6 Hours after HW Dover (0510 before HW Le Havre)

N France

9.17.4 LIGHTS, BUOYS AND WAYPOINTS

Bold print = light with a nominal range of 15M or more.
CAPITALS = place or feature. *CAPITAL ITALICS* = light-vessel, light float or Lanby. *Italics* = Fog signal. ***Bold italics*** = Racon. Abbreviations are in Chapter 1.

OFFSHORE MARKS: W Hinder to Dover Strait
Fairy South ⚲ VQ (6) + L Fl 10s; 51°21′·20N 02°17′·31E.
Fairy West ⚲ VQ (9) 10s 6M; 51°23′·86N 02°09′·30E.
Hinder 1 ⚲ Fl (2) 6s; 51°20′·80N 02°10′·93E.
Bergues ⚲ Fl G 4s 7m 4M; 51°17′·14N 02°18′·63E.
Bergues S ⚲ Q (6) + L Fl 15s; 51°15′·09N 02°19′·42E.
Ruytingen E ⚲ VQ; 51°14′·55N 02°17′·93E.
Ruytingen N ⚲ VQ 4M; 51°13′·16N 02°10′·28E.
Ruytingen SE ⚲ VQ (3) 15s; 51°09′·20N 02°08′·94E.
Ruytingen NW ⚲ Fl G 4s 3M; 51°09′·11N 01°57′·30E.
Ruytingen W ⚲ VQ 4M; 51°06′·93N 01°50′·45E.
Ruytingen SW ⚲ Fl (3) G 12s 3M; 51°05′·00N 01°46′·84E.
Sandettié N ⚲ VQ 6M; 51°18′·47N 02°04′·81E.
Sandettié E ⚲ Fl R 4s 7m 3M; 51°14′·88N 02°02′·65E.

DUNKERQUE TO BOULOGNE
PASSE DE ZUYDCOOTE
E12 ⚲ VQ (6) + L Fl 10s; 51°07′·89N 02°30′·68E (Belgium).
CME ⚲ Q (3) 10s; 51°07′·30N 02°30′·00E.
E11 ⚲ Fl G 4s; 51°06′·90N 02°30′·90E.
E10 ⚲ Fl (2) R 6s; 51°06′·30N 02°30′·47E.
E9 ⚲ Fl (2) G 6s; 51°05′·64N 02°29′·68E.
E8 ⚲ Fl (3) R 12s; 51°05′·16N 02°28′·68E. (E7 does not exist)

PASSE DE L'EST
E6 ⚲ QR; 51°04′·90N 02°27′·00E.
E4 ⚲ Fl R 4s; 51°04′·49N 02°24′·54E.
E1 ⚲ Fl (2) G 6s; 51°04′·06N 02°23′·10E.
E2 ⚲ Fl (2) R 6s; 51°04′·35N 02°22′·31E.
⚲ Q (6) + L Fl 15s; 51°04′·28N 02°21′·73E.

DUNKERQUE PORT EST
E jetty ☆ Fl (2) R 6s 12m 10M; R □, W pylon; 51°03′·59N 02°21′·20E.
W jetty ☆ Fl (2) G 6s 35m 11M; W twr, brown top; 51°03′·63N 02°20′·95E.
Ldg lts 137·5°, front Q7m11M 51°02′·98N 02°22′·05E, rear, Q10m11M, 114m from front, both W cols, R tops, synched.
Inner W jetty ⚲ Q 11m 9M; 51°03′·33N 02°21′·43E.
Dunkerque lt ho ☆ Fl (2) 10s 59m **26M**; 51°02′·93N 02°21′·86E.

DUNKERQUE INTERMEDIATE CHANNEL
DW30 ⚲ Fl (3) R 12s; 51°04′·14N 02°20′·16E.
DW29 ⚲ Fl (3) G 12s; 51°03′·83N 02°20′·25E.
DW16 ⚲ Fl (2) R 6s; 51°03′·31N 02°08′·98E.
DKB ⚲ VQ (9) 10s; 51°02′·95N 02°09′·26E.
DW12 ⚲ Fl (3) R 12s; 51°03′·19N 02°05′·57E.
DW11 ⚲ Fl (3) G 12s; 51°02′·88N 02°05′·77E. (DW10-7 omitted)

GRAVELINES
W jetty ⚲ Fl (2) WG 6s 9m W8M, G6M; 317°-W-327°-G-085°-W-244°; Y ○ twr, G top; 51°00′·94N 02°05′·49E.

PASSE DE L'OUEST
DW6 ⚲ VQ R; 51°02′·60N 02°01′·01E.
DW5 ⚲ QG; 51°02′·20N 02°00′·92E.
DKA ⚲ L Fl 10s; 51°02′·55N 01°56′·96E.
RCE (Ridens de Calais East) ⚲ Iso G 4s; 51°02′·44N 01°53′·24E.
Dyck ⚲ Fl 3s; ***Racon B***; 51°02′·99N 01°51′·79E.
RCA (Ridens de Calais Approach) ⚲ Q; 51°00′·90N 01°48′·72E.

CALAIS
E jetty ☆ Fl (2) R 6s 12m **17M**; (in fog two Fl (2) 6s (vert) on request); Gy twr, R top; *Horn (2) 40s;* 50°58′·39N 01°50′·45E.
W jetty ⚲ Iso G 3s 12m 9M; (in fog Fl 5s on request); W twr, G top; *Bell 5s;* 50°58′·24N 01°50′·40E.

Calais ☆ Fl (4) 15s 59m **22M**; vis 073°-260°; W 8-sided twr, B top; 50°57′·68N 01°51′·21E (440m E of marina entry gate).

CALAIS, WESTERN APPROACH
Calais Approach ⚲ VQ (9) 10s 8m 8M; 50°58′·89N 01°45′·11E.
CA2 ⚲ Fl R 4s; 50°58′·15N 01°45′·68E.
CA4 ⚲ Fl (2)R 6s; 50°58′·38N 01°48′·65E.
CA6 ⚲ Fl (3) R 12s; 50°58′·63N 01°49′·92E.
Les Quénocs ⚲ VQ; 50°56′·85N 01°41′·12E.
CA1 ⚲ Fl G 4s; 50°57′·64N 01°46′·14E (0·5M NNW of Sangatte).
Sangatte ⚲ Oc WG 4s 13m W8M, G5M; 065°-G-089°-W-152°-G-245°; W pylon, B top; 50°57′·19N 01°46′·50E.
Abbeville wreck ⚲ VQ (9) 10s; 50°56′·08N 01°37′·58E.
Cap Gris-Nez ☆ Fl 5s 72m **29M**; 005°-232°; W twr, B top; *Horn 60s;* 50°52′·09N 01°34′·96E.

OFFSHORE MARKS: DOVER STRAIT TSS, French side
Colbart N ⚲ Q 6M; 50°57′·46N 01°23′·29E.
Colbart SW ⚲ VQ (6) + L Fl 10s 8m; 50°48′·87N 01°16′·32E.
ZC2 (Zone Cotière) ⚲ Fl (2+1) Y 15s 5M; 50°53′·54N 01°30′·89E.
ZC1 ⚲ Fl (4) Y 15s 4MN; 50°44′·99N 01°27′·21E.
Ridens SE ⚲ VQ (3) 5s 6M; 50°43′·48N 01°18′·87E.
Bassurelle ⚲ Fl (4) R 15s 6M; ***Racon B, 5-8m;*** 50°32′·74N 00°57′·69E.
Vergoyer N ⚲ VQ 5M; ***Racon C, 5-8M;*** 50°39′·67N 01°22′·21E.
Vergoyer NW ⚲ Fl (2) G 6s 4M; 50°37′·16N 01°17′·85E.
Vergoyer E ⚲ VQ (3) 5s 6M; 50°35′·76N 01°19′·70E.
Vergoyer W ⚲ Fl G 4s 4M; 50°34′·66N 01°13′·57E.
Vergoyer SW ⚲ VQ (9) 10s 6M; 50°27′·01N 01°00′·03E.

BOULOGNE TO DIEPPE
BOULOGNE
Bassure de Baas ⚲ VQ; 50°48′·53N 01°33′·05E.
Approches Boulogne ⚲ VQ (6) + L Fl 10s 8m 6M; 50°45′·31N 01°31′·07E.
Digue N (detached) ⚲ Fl (2) R 6s 10m 7M; 50°44′·71N 01°34′·18E.
Digue S (Carnot) ☆ Fl (2+1) 15s 25m **19M**; W twr, G top; 50°44′·44N 01°34′·05E.
Clearing brg 122·4° : Front, FG in a neon ▽ 4m 5M; 50°43′·71N 01°35′·66E. Rear, FR 44m 11M; intens 113°-133°; 560m from front.
Inner NE jetty ⚲ FR 11m 7M; 50°43′·91N 01°35′·24E. Inner SW jetty ⚲ FG 17m 5M; W col, G top; *Horn 30s;* 50°43′·90N 01°35′·11E.
Cap d'Alprech ☆ Fl (3) 15s 62m **23M**; W twr, B top; 50°41′·91N 01°33′·75E, 2·5M S of hbr ent.

LE TOUQUET/ÉTAPLES
Pointe de Lornel ⚲ VQ (9) 10s 6m 3M; 50°33′·24N 01°35′·12E.
Mérida wreck ⚲ 50°32′·85N 01°33′·44E.
Camiers lt ho ⚲ Oc (2) WRG 6s 17m W10M, R/G7M; 015°-G-090°-W-105°-R-141°; R pylon; 50°32′·86N 01°36′·28E.
Canche Est groyne ⚲ Fl R 4s 8m; 50°32′·57N 01°35′·66E.
Le Touquet ☆ Fl (2) 10s 54m **25M**; Or twr, brown band, W&G top; 50°31′·43N 01°35′·52E.

Pointe du Haut-Blanc ☆ Fl 5s 44m **23M**; W twr, R bands, G top; 50°23′·90N 01°33′·67E (Berck).

BAIE DE LA SOMME
ATSO ⚲ Mo (A) 12s; 50°14′·00N 01°28′·08E (shifts frequently).
Pte du Hourdel ⚲ Oc (3) WG 12s 19m, W12M, G9M; 053°-W-248°-G-323°; tidal sigs; *Horn (3) 30s;* W twr, G top; 50°12′·90N 01°33′·98E.
Cayeux-sur-Mer ☆ Fl R 5s 32m **22M**; W twr, R top; 50°11′·65N 01°30′·72E.

Le Crotoy ⚲ Oc (2) R 6s 19m 8M; 285°-135°; W pylon; 50°12′·91N 01°37′·40E. Marina ⚲ Fl R & Fl G 2s 4m 2M; 50°12′·98N 01°38′·20E.

ST VALÉRY-SUR-SOMME
Trng wall head, ⚲ Fl G 2.5s 2m 1M; 50°12′·25N 01°35′·85E,.
Embankment head ⚲ Iso G 4s 9m 9M; 347°-222°; W pylon, G top; 50°12′·25N 01°36′·02E.
La Ferté môle ⚲ Fl R 4s 9m 9M; 000°-250°; W pylon, R top; 50°11′·18N 01°38′·14E (ent to marina inlet).

WGS84 DATUM
Plot waypoints on chart before use

LE TRÉPORT
Ault ☆ Oc (3) WR 12s 95m **W15M**, R11M; 040°-W-175°-R-220°; W twr, R top; 50°06'·28N 01°27'·23E (4M NE of Le Tréport).
W jetty ☆ Fl (2) G 10s 15m **20M**; W twr, G top; *Horn (2) 30s;* 50°03'·88N 01°22'·14E.

DIEPPE
W jetty ⚓ Iso G 4s 11m 8M; W twr, G top; *Horn 30s;* 49°56'·27N 01°04'·97E.
Quai de la Marne ⚓ QR 12m 3M; 49°55'·93N 01°05'·20E, E quay.
Pointe d'Ailly ☆ Fl (3) 20s 95m **31M**; W ☐ twr, G top; *Horn (3) 60s;* 49°54'·96N 00°57'·50E.

DIEPPE TO LE HAVRE
SAINT VALÉRY-EN-CAUX
W jetty ⚓ Fl (2) G 6s 13m 11M; W twr, G top; 49°52'·40N 00°42'·54E. Paluel power station ⚓ Q; 49°52'·22N 00°38'·03E.

FÉCAMP
N jetty ☆ Fl (2) 10s 15m **16M**; Gy twr, R top; 49°45'·94N 00°21'·80E.

PORT D'ANTIFER
Cap d'Antifer ☆ Fl 20s 128m **29M**; 021°-222°; Gy 8-sided twr, G top, on 90m cliffs; 49°41'·01N 00°09'·93E.
A17 ⚓ Iso G 4s; 49°41'·53N 00°01'·75E.
A18 ⚓ QR; 49°42'·02N 00°02'·18E. Cross the chan W of A17/18.
Ldg lts 127·5°, both Dir Oc 4s 113/135m **22M**; 127°-128°; by day F **33M** 126·5°-128·5° occas. **Front** ☆, 49°38'·32N 00°09'·12E.

LE HAVRE, APPROACH CHANNEL
Cap de la Hève ☆ Fl 5s 123m **24M**; 225°-196°; W 8-sided twr, R top; 49°30'·74N 00°04'·16E.
LHA ⌑ Mo (A) 12s 10m 9M; R&W; *Racon, 8-10M* (a series of 8 dots, or 8 groups of dots; distance between each dot or group represents 0·3M); 49°31'·38N 00°09'·86W. Reserve lt Mo (A).
Ldg lts 106·8°, both Dir F 36/78m **25M** (H24); intens 106°-108° ; Gy twrs, G tops. Front, 49°28'·91N 00°06'·50E; rear, 0·73M from front.
LH3 ⚓ QG; 49°30'·84N 00°04'·02W. (LH1 & 2 buoys do not exist).
LH4 ⚓ QR; 49°31'·11N 00°03'·90W.
FVs and yachts <19.8m LOA may cross the appr chan west of LH 7/8 buoys, keeping clear of all other shipping, even if under sail:
LH7 ⚓ Iso G 4s; 49°30'·25N 00°00'·82W.
LH8 ⚓ Fl (2) R 6s; 49°30'·44N 00°00'·70W.
Note the W-E longitude change. (LH9 buoy does not exist).
LH13 ⚓ Fl G 4s; 49°29'·32N 00°03'·62E (Ent to Port 2000).
LH14 ⚓ Fl R 4s; 49°29'·67N 00°03'·43E; 1m shoal depth close W.
LH16 ⚓ Fl (2) R 6s; 49°29'·45N 00°04'·28E.
LH 2000 ⚓ VQ (9) 10s; 49°29'·14N 00°04'·78E (Ent to Port 2000).

LE HAVRE
Digue N ☆ Fl R 5s 15m **21M**; IPTS; W ○ twr, R top; *Horn 15s;* 49°29'·19N 00°05'·44E.
Digue S ⚓ VQ (3) G 2s 15m 11M; W twr, G top; 49°29'·05N 00°05'·38E.
Marina ent, W spur ⚓ Fl (2) R 6s 3M; 49°29'·22N 00°05'·53E.

THE SEINE ESTUARY UP TO HONFLEUR
CHENAL DE ROUEN
Nord du Mouillage ⚓ Fl (4) Y 15s; 49°28'·80N 00°00'·22E.
Rade de la Carosse ⚓ Q (9) 15s; 49°28'·26N 00°00'·69E.
No. 2 ⚓ QR; *Racon T;* 49°27'·40N 00°01'·35E.
No. 4 ⚓ Fl R 2·5s; 49°26'·97N 00°02'·60E. Yachts keep N of chan.
Amfard SW ⚓ Fl (3) R 12s; 49°26'·30N 00°04'·82E.
No. 10 ⚓ QR; 49°26'·10N 00°06'·39E.
Digue du Ratier ⚓ VQ 10m 4M; 49°25'·94N 00°06'·59E.
Falaise des Fonds ☆ Fl (3) WRG 12s 15m, **W17M**, R/G13M; 040°-G-080°-R-084°-G-100°- W-109°-R-162°-G-260°; W twr, G top; 49°25'·47N 00°12'·85E.
No. 20 ⚓ QR; 49°25'·85N 00°13'·71E. (Cross here to Honfleur)

HONFLEUR
Digue Ouest ⚓ QG 10m 6M; 49°25'·67N 00°13'·83E.
Digue Est ⚓ Q 9m 8M; *Horn (5) 40s;* 49°25'·67N 00°13'·95E.
Inner E jetty, Oc (2) R 6s 12m 6M; W twr, R top; 49°25'·38N 00°14'·12E.
No. 22 ⚓ QR; 49°25'·85N 00°15'·38E.

TROUVILLE TO COURSEULLES
CHENAL DE ROUEN TO DEAUVILLE and TROUVILLE
Ratelets ⚓ Q (9) 15s; 49°25'·29N 00°01'·71E.
Semoy ⚓ VQ (3) 5s; 49°24'·15N 00°02'·35E, close to 148° ldg line.
Trouville SW ⚓ VQ (9) 10s; 49°22'·54N 00°02'·56E.

DEAUVILLE and TROUVILLE
Ldg lts 148°, both Oc R 4s 11/17m 12/10M: Front, East inner jetty (*estacade*); 330°-150°; W twr, R top; 49°22'·03N 00°04'·48E.
Rear, Pte de la Cahotte; synch; 120°-170°; 49°21'·93N 00°04'·58E.
W trng wall ⚓ Fl WG 4s 10m W9M, G6M; 005°-W-176°-G-005°; B pylon, G top; 49°22'·37N 00°04'·11E. Also 4 unlit SHM bcns.
E trng wall ⚓ Fl (4) WR 12s 8m W7M, R4M; 131°-W-175°-R-131°; W pylon, R top; 49°22'·22N 00°04'·33E. Also 3 unlit PHM bcns.
W outer bkwtr ⚓ Iso G 4s 9m 5M; 49°22'·11N 00°04'·33E.
West inner jetty (*estacade*) ⚓ QG 11m 9M; 49°22'·03N 00°04'·43E.

DIVES-SUR-MER *Note the E-W longitude change.*
Dir lt 159·5°, Oc (2+1) WRG 12s 6m, W12M, R/G9M, 125°-G-157°-W-162°-R-194°; brown hut; 49°17'·80N 00°05'·22W.
DI ⚓ L Fl 10s; 49°19'·18N 00°05'·85W.
No. 1 ⚓ 49°18'·50N 00°05'·67W. Buoys are moved to mark chan.
No. 2 ⚓ 49°18'·51N 00°05'·56W.
No. 3 ⚓ QG 7m 4M; W pylon, G top; 49°18'·30N 00°05'·55W.
No. 5 ⚓ Fl G 4s 8m 4M; W pylon, G top; 49°18'·09N 00°05'·50W.
Bcns 3 & 5, if damaged, may be temporarily replaced by buoys.
No. 7 ⚓ Fl G 4s; 49°17'·65N 00°05'·31W.

OUISTREHAM and CAEN
Merville ⚓ VQ; 49°19'·65N 00°13'·39W; spoil ground buoy.
Ouistreham ⚓ VQ (3) 5s; wreck buoy; 49°20'·42N 00°14'·81W.
Ldg lts 185°, both Dir Oc (3+1) R 12s 10/30m **17M**; intens 183·5°-186·5°, synch. **Front** ☆, E jetty, W mast, R top, 49°16'·99N 00°14'·81W. **Rear** ☆, 610m from front, tripod, R top.
No. 1 ⚓ QG; 49°19'·19N 00°14'·67W.
No. 2 ⚓ QR; 49°19'·17N 00°14'·43W.
Barnabé ⚓ QG 7m 5M; W pylon, G top; 49°18'·02N 00°14'·76W.
St-Médard ⚓ QR 7m 5M; 49°18'·02N 00°14'·62W.
Riva ⚓ Fl G 4s 9m 3M; W pylon, G top; 49°17'·73N 00°14'·79W.
Quilbé ⚓ Fl R 4s 9m 3M; W pylon, R top; 49°17'·72N 00°14'·67W.
Ouistreham lt ho ☆ Oc WR 4s 37m **W17M**, R13M; 115°-R-151°-W-115°; W twr, R top; 49°16'·79N 00°14'·87W.

COURSEULLES-SUR-MER
Courseulles ⚓ Iso 4s; 49°21'·28N 00°27'·68W.
W jetty ⚓ Iso WG 4s 7m; W9M, G6M; 135°-W-235°-G-135°; brown pylon on dolphin, G top; 49°20'·41N 00°27'·37W.
E jetty ⚓ Oc (2) R 6s 9m 7M; 49°20'·26N 00°27'·39W.

COURSEULLES TO ST VAAST
Ver ☆ Fl (3)15s 42m **26M**; obsc'd by cliffs of St Aubin when brg >275°; conspic lt ho, W twr, Gy top; 49°20'·39N 00°31'·15W.

ARROMANCHES
Ent buoys: ⚓ 49°21'·35N 00°37'·26W; ⚓ 49°21'·25N00°37'·30W.
Bombardons ⚓ wreck buoys; 49°21'·66N 00°38'·97W.

PORT-EN-BESSIN
Ldg lts 204°, both Oc (3) 12s 25/42m 10/11M; synch. Front, 069°-339°, W pylon, G top; 49°20'·96N 00°45'·53W. Rear; 114°-294°, W and Gy ho; 93m from front.
E mole ⚓ Oc R 4s 14m 7M, R pylon; 49°21'·12N 00°45'·38W.
W mole ⚓ Fl WG 4s 14m, W10M, G7M; G065°-114·5°, W114·5°-065°; G pylon; 49°21'·17N 00°45'·43W.

COASTAL MARKS

Omaha Beach, 1M off : *ℓ* 49°22'·66N 00°50'·28W; *ℓ* 49°23'·17N 00°51'·93W; *ℓ* 49°23'·66N 00°53'·74W.
Broadsword *ℓ* Q (3) 10s, wreck buoy; 49°25'·34N 00°52'·96W.
Est du Cardonnet *ℓ* VQ (3) 5s; 49°26'·83N 01°01'·10W.

GRANDCAMP

Les Roches de Grandcamp: No. 1 *ℓ* 49°24'·72N 01°01'·75W;
No. 3 *ℓ* 49°24'·92N 01°03'·70W; No. 5 *ℓ* 49°24'·78N 01°04'·86W.
Ldg lts 146°, both Dir Q 9/12m **15M**, 144·5°-147·5°. **Front** ☆,
49°23'·42N 01°02'·90W. **Rear** ☆,102m from front.
Jetée Est *≼* Oc (2) R 6s 9m 9M; *Horn Mo(N) 30s;* 49°23'·53N
01°02'·96W.
Jetée Ouest *≼* Fl G 4s 9m 6M; 49°23'·47N 01°02'·96W.

ISIGNY-SUR-MER

IS, small B/Y ⚓, no topmark (*ℓ* on AC 2135); 49°24'·28N 01°06'·37W.
Ldg lts 172·5°, both Dir Oc (2+1) 12s 7/19m **18M**; intens 170·5°-
174·5°, synch. **Front** , W mast; 49°19'·55N 01°06·78W. **Rear** , W
pylon, B top; 625m from front.
Training wall heads *⊥* 49°21'·42N 01°07'·24W; *⊥* 49°21'·40N
01°07'·14W, off Pte du Grouin.

CARENTAN

C-I *ℓ* Iso 4s; 49°25'·44N 01°07'·08W; 210°/1·76M to Nos 1 & 2
buoys.
No. 1 *ℓ* Fl G 2·5s; 49°23'·93N 01°08'·52W.
No. 2 *ℓ* Fl R 2·5s; 49°23'·88N 01°08'·37W.
Trng wall *⊥* Fl (4) G 15s; G △ on G bcn;49°21'·96N 01°09'·95W.
Trng wall *⊥* Fl (4) R 15s; R □ on R bcn;49°21'·93N 01°09'·878W.
Ldg lts 209·5°. **Front** ☆ Dir Oc (3) R 12s 6m **18M**; intens 208·2°-
210·7°; W mast, R top; 49°20'·47N 01°11'·17W. Rear, Dir Oc (3) 12s
14m 10M; vis 120°-005°; W gantry, G top; 723m from front.

ÎLES SAINT-MARCOUF

Iles St-Marcouf *≼* VQ (3) 5s 18m 8M; □ Gy twr, G top; 49°29'·86N
01°08'·81W.
Ouest-Saint-Marcouf *ℓ* Q (9) 15s; 49°29'·73N 01°11'·97W.
Saint Floxel *ℓ* 49°30'·64N 01°13'·94W.
Quineville *ℓ* Q (9) 10s, wreck buoy; 49°31'·79N 01°12'·38W.

ST VAAST TO POINTE DE BARFLEUR

ST VAAST-LA-HOUGUE

Ldg lts 267°: Front, La Hougue Oc 4s 9m 10M; W pylon, G top;
49°34'·25N 01°16'·37W. Rear, Morsalines Oc (4) WRG 12s 90m,
W11M, R/G8M; 171°-W-316°-G-321°-R-342°-W-355°; W 8-sided
twr, G top; 49°34'·16N 01°19'·10W, 1·8M from front.
Le Manquet *ℓ* 49°34'·26N 01°15'·56W.
Le Bout du Roc *ℓ* 49°34'·68N 01°15'·27W.
La Dent *ℓ* 49°34'·57N 01°14'·20W.
Le Gavendest *ℓ* Q (6) + L Fl 15s; *Whis;* 49°34'·36N 01°13'·89W.
Jetty *≼* Dir Oc (2) WRG 6s 12m W10M, R/G7M; 219°-R-237°-G-
310°-W-350°-R-040°; W 8-sided twr, R top; *Siren Mo(N) 30s;*
49°35'·17N 01°15'·41W.
Pte de Saire *≼* Oc (2+1) 10s 11m 10M; squat W twr, G top;
49°36'·36N 01°13'·78W.

BARFLEUR

Ldg lts 219·5°, both Oc (3) 12s 7/13m 10M; synch. Front, W □
twr;49°40'·18N 01°15'·61W. Rear, 085°-355°; Gy and W □ twr,
G top; 288m from front.
La Grotte *⚓* 49°41'·06N 01°14'·86W.
Roche-à-l'Anglais *⚓* 49°40'·78N 01°14'·93W.
La Vimberge *⚓* 49°40'·54N 01°15'·25W.
W jetty *≼* Fl G 4s 8m 6M; 49°40'·32N 01°15'·57W.
E jetty *≼* Oc R 4s 5m 6M; 49°40'·31N 01°15'·47W.
La Jamette *⊥* 49°41'·87N 01°15'·59W.

Pte de Barfleur ☆ Fl (2) 10s 72m **29M**; obsc when brg less than
088°; Gy twr, B top; *Horn (2) 60s;* 49°41'·78N 01°15'·96W.

POINTE DE BARFLEUR TO CAP DE LA HAGUE

Les Équets *ℓ* Q 8m 3M; 49°43'·62N 01°18'·36W.
Basse du Rénier *ℓ* VQ 8m 4M; 49°44'·84N 01°22'·09W.
Les Trois Pierres *ℓ* 49°42'·90N 01°21'·80W.
Anse de Vicq, 158° ldg lts; both FR 8/14m 7M; front 49°42'·20N
01°23'·95W.
La Pierre Noire *ℓ* Q (9) 15s 8m 4M;49°43'·54N 01°29'·07W.

PORT DU LÉVI

Cap Lévi ☆ Fl R 5s 36m **22M**; Gy □ twr; 49°41'·75N 01°28'·38W.
Port Lévi *≼* Oc (2) WRG 6s 7m 7M; 055°-G-083°-W-105°-R-163°;
W & Gy hut, W lantern; 49°41'·24N 01°28'·34W.

PORT DU BECQUET

Ldg lts 186·5°, both intens 183°-190°; synch. Front, Oc (2+1) 12s
8m 10M; W 8-sided twr; 49°39'·22N 01°32'·85W. Rear, Oc (2+1)
R 12s 13m 7M. W 8-sided twr, R top; 49m from front.

CHERBOURG, EASTERN ENTRANCES

Passe Collignon *≼* Fl (2) R 6s 5m 4M; 49°39'·59N 01°34'·24W.
Passe de l'Est, Jetée des Flamands ldg lts 189°, both Q 9/16m
13M. Front, 49°39'·33N 01°35'·94W . Rear, 516m from front.
Roches du Nord-Ouest *≼* Fl R 2·5s; 49°40'·64N 01°35'·28W.
La Truite *ℓ* Fl (4) R 15s; 49°40'·33N 01°35'·49W.
Fort d'Île Pelée *≼* Oc (2) WR 6s 19m; W10M, R7M; 055°-W-120°-
R-055°; W & R pedestal; 49°40'·21N 01°35'·08W.
Fort de l'Est *≼* 49°40'·28N 01°35'·92W, Iso G 4s 19m 9M.
Fort Central *≼* VQ (6) + L Fl 10s 5m 4M; 322°-032°; 49°40'·40N
01°37'·04W.

CHERBOURG, PASSE DE L'OUEST

CH1 *ℓ* L Fl 10s 8m 4M; 49°43'·24N 01°42'·09W.
Passe de l'Ouest outer ldg lts 141·2°. **Front,** Dir Q (2 horiz, 63m
apart) 5m **17M**; intens 137·3°-143·3° & 139·2°-145·2°; W △ on
bcn; 49°39'·55N 01°37'·95W. **Rear**, Dir Q 35m **19M**; intens
140°-142·5°; W △ on Gy pylon.
Fort de l'Ouest ☆ Fl (3) WR 15s 19m **W24M, R20M**; 122°-W-355°-
R-122°; Gy twr, R top; *Horn (3) 60s;* 49°40'·45N 01°38'·87W.
Fort de l'Ouest *ℓ* Fl R 4s; 49°40'·39N 01°38'·89W.
ℓ Q (6) + L Fl 15s; 49°40'·34N 01°38'·65W.
Digue de Querqueville *≼* Fl (4) G 15s 8m 4M; W col, G top;
49°40'·30N 01°39'·80W.
Inner ldg lts 124·3°; both intens 114·3°-134·3°: Front, Digue du
Homet head, FG 10m 8M; 49°39'·48N 01°36'·96W. Rear, Dir Iso
G 4s 16m 13M; W col, B bands, 397m from front.
La Ténarde *ℓ* VQ 8m 4M; 49°39'·74N 01°37'·75W.

CHERBOURG, PETITE RADE and MARINA

Entrance, W side, Digue du Homet *≼* FG 10m 8M; intens 114·3°-
134·3°; W pylon, G top; 49°39'·48N 01°36'·96W.
E side, *ℓ* VQ R, off Jetée des Flamands; 49°39'·44N 01°36'·60W.
Marina ent, E side, *≼* Fl (3) R 12s 6m 6M; W col, R lantern;
49°38'·91N 01°37'·08W.
W mole *≼* Fl (3) G 12s 7m 6M; G pylon; 49°38'·87N 01°37'·15W.
E quay*≼* Fl (4) R 15s 3m 3M; R bcn; 49°38'·79N 01°37'·12W.
Wavescreen pontoon, N end *≼* Fl (4) G 15s 4m 2M; W post, G top.
Detached ✪ pontoon, F Vi; 49°38'·77N 01°37'·22W.

CHERBOURG TO CAP DE LA HAGUE

Raz de Bannes *⚓* 49°41'·32N 01°44'·53W.
Omonville Dir lt 257°: Iso WRG 4s13m; W10M, R/G7M; 180°-G-
252°-W-262°-R-287°; W pylon, G top; 49°42'·24N 01°50'·15W.
L'Étonnard *⚓* 49°42'·33N 01°49'·84W.
Basse Bréfort *ℓ* VQ 8m 4M; 49°43'·90N 01°51'·15W.
Jobourg Nuclear plant chimney, R lts; 49°40'·80N 01°52'·91W.
La Plate *ℓ* Fl (2+1) WR 10s 11m; W9M, R6M; 115°-W-272°-R-
115°; Y 8-sided twr, with B top; 49°43'·97N 01°55'·74W.
Cap de la Hague (Gros du Raz) ☆ Fl 5s 48m **23M**; Gy twr, W
top; *Horn 30s;* 49°43'·31N 01° 57'·26W.
La Foraine *ℓ* VQ (9) 10s, 12m 6M; 49°42'·90N 01°58'·31W.

9.17.5 PASSAGE INFORMATION

More Passage Information is threaded between harbours in this Area. **Bibliography**: *The Channel CC* (NDL/Featherstone & Aslett); *North France and Belgium CC* (NDL/Featherstone); *Dover Strait NP28* and *Channel NP27 Pilots. Channel Havens* (ACN/Endean).

The coasts of Picardy and Normandy are hardly more than an overnight passage from harbours on the UK's S coast – eg, Brighton to Fécamp is only 65M. However some of the harbours dry, so that a boat which can take the ground is an advantage. For a chart of the Dover Strait TSS, see 9.3.14. Notes on the English Channel and on cross-Channel passages appear below and in 9.3.5. See 9.0.6 for cross-Channel distances. For a French glossary, see Chapter 1.

DUNKERQUE TO BOULOGNE

Offshore a series of banks lies roughly parallel with the coast (AC *323, 1892, 2451*): Sandettié bank, Outer Ruytingen midway between Sandettié and the coast, and the Dyck banks which extend NE'wards for 30M from a point 5M NE of Calais. There are well-buoyed channels between some of these banks, but great care is needed in poor visibility. In general the banks are steep-to on the inshore side, and slope to seaward. In bad weather the sea breaks on the shallower parts.

Dunkerque Port Est, the old port, has several good yacht marinas and all facilities. Dunkerque Port Ouest is a commercial/ferry port which yachts should not enter. About 3M SW is the drying hbr of **Gravelines**, which should not be entered in strong onshore winds. If E-bound, the Passe de Zuydcoote (4·4m) is a popular inshore link to West Diep and the Belgian ports.

The sea breaks heavily in bad weather on Ridens de Calais, 3M N of **Calais** (AC *1351*), and also on Ridens de la Rade immediately N and NE of the harbour where the least charted depth is 0·1m.

The NE-bound traffic lane of the Dover Strait TSS is only 3M off C Gris Nez. Keep a sharp lookout not only for coastal traffic in the ITZ, but also cross-Channel ferries, particularly very fast catamarans. ▶*1M NW of C Gris Nez the NE-going stream begins at HW Dieppe −0150, and the SW-going at HW Dieppe +0355, sp rates 4kn.*◀ Between C Gris Nez (lt, fog sig) and Boulogne the coastal bank dries about 4ca offshore.

BOULOGNE TO DIEPPE

In the approaches to Pas de Calais a number of shoals lie offshore (AC *2451*): The Ridge (or Le Colbart), Les Ridens, Bassurelle, Vergoyer, Bassure de Baas and Battur. In bad weather, and particularly with wind against tide, the sea breaks heavily on all these shoals.

From **Boulogne** (AC *438*) to Pte de Lornel the coast dries up to 5ca offshore. ▶*Off Boulogne's Digue Carnot the N-going stream begins HW Dieppe −0130, and the S-going at HW Dieppe +0350, sp rates 1·75kn.*◀

Le Touquet and **Étaples** lie in the Embouchure de la Canche, entered between Pte de Lornel and Pte du Touquet, and with a drying bank which extends 1M seaward of a line joining these two points. Le Touquet-Paris-Plage light is shown from a conspic tower, 1M S of Pte du Touquet.

▶*Off the estuary entrance the N-going stream begins about HW Dieppe −0335, sp rate 1·75kn; and the S-going stream begins about HW Dieppe +0240, sp rate 1·75kn.*◀

From Pte du Touquet the coast runs 17M S to Pte de St Quentin, with a shallow coastal bank which dries to about 5ca offshore, except in the approaches to the dangerous and constantly changing Embouchure de l'Authie (Pte du Haut-Blanc, about 10M S), where it dries up to 2M offshore.

Baie de la Somme, between Pte de St Quentin and Pte du Hourdel (lt), is a shallow, drying area of shifting sands. The access channel to **St Valéry-sur-Somme** and **Le Crotoy**, which runs close to Pte du Hourdel, is well buoyed, but the whole estuary dries out 3M to seaward, and should not be approached in strong W/NW winds.

Offshore there are two shoals, Bassurelle de la Somme and Quémer, on parts of which the sea breaks in bad weather. ▶*4·5M NW of Cayeux-sur-Mer (lt) the stream is rotatory anti-clockwise. The E-going stream begins about HW Dieppe −0200, and sets 070° 2·5kn at sp : the W-going stream begins about HW Dieppe +0600, and sets 240° 1·5kn at sp.*◀

S of Ault (lt) the coast changes from low sand dunes to medium-height cliffs. Between **Le Tréport** and Dieppe, 14M SW, rky banks, drying in places, extend 5ca offshore. Banc Franc-Marqué (3·6m) lies 2M offshore, and some 3M N of Le Tréport. About 3M NW of Le Tréport, Ridens du Tréport (5·1m) should be avoided in bad weather. A prohibited area extends 6ca off Penly nuclear power station and is marked by lt buoys.

9.17.6 SPECIAL NOTES FOR FRANCE

Instead of 'County' the 'Département' is given. For details of documentation apply to the French Tourist Office, 178 Piccadilly, London, W1J 9AL; ☎ 0906 824 4123; info@mdlf.co.uk www.franceguide.com.

STANDARD TIME is −0100, to which DST may be added.

VOCABULARY See Chapter 1.

AFFAIRES MARITIMES is a part of the central government Ministry of Transport. It oversees all maritime activities (commercial, fishing, pleasure) and helps them develop harmoniously. Information on navigation and other maritime issues can be supplied by a representative whose ☎ is given under each port; he may be based at the nearest commercial or fishing port. The Head Office is: Ministère des Transports et de la Mer, Bureau de la Navigation de Plaisance, 3 Place de Fontenoy, 75700 Paris, ☎ 01.44.49.80.00. www.mer.gouv.fr

CHARTS Official charts are issued by SHOM (*Service Hydrographique et Oceanographique de la Marine*) the Navy's Hydrographer. (See Chapter 1 for contact details). SHOM charts are excellent for the smaller French ports not covered by UKHO. A free, annual chart catalogue *Le petit catalogue* is downloadable from www.shom.fr. It includes chart agents and mail order specialists. In this Almanac under 'Facilities', SHOM means a chart agent. Any new edition of a SHOM chart receives a new, different chart number.

TIDAL LEVELS SHOM charts refer elevations of lights to MHWS. Heights of other features are referred to Mean Sea Level (*Niveau moyen*), or as indicated on the chart; it is important to check the chart's title block. Clearance under bridges etc is referred to MSL, MHWS or HAT depending on the recency of the chart.

TIDAL COEFFICIENTS See 9.20.26 for coefficients based on Brest, together with explanatory notes and French tidal terms.

PUBLIC HOLIDAYS New Year's Day, Easter Sunday and Monday, Labour Day (1 May), Ascension Day, Armistice Day 1945 (8 May), Whit Sunday and Monday, National (Bastille) Day (14 July), Feast of the Assumption (15 Aug), All Saints' Day (1 Nov), Remembrance Day (11 Nov), Christmas Day.

FACILITIES The cost of a visitor's overnight berth is based on high season rates and is usually quoted as €/metre LOA, although beam may be taken into account at some ports. Low season rates and concessions can be a big saving. The fee usually includes electricity, but rarely showers which range between €1·20 and €2. VAT (TVA) is 19.6%.

Fuel can be obtained/paid for H24 at some marinas by using a smart credit card. The latest British credit cards are now technically able to activate the associated diesel or petrol pumps and make payment. If not in possession of such a card, pre-arrange to pay manually by credit card at the Capitainerie.

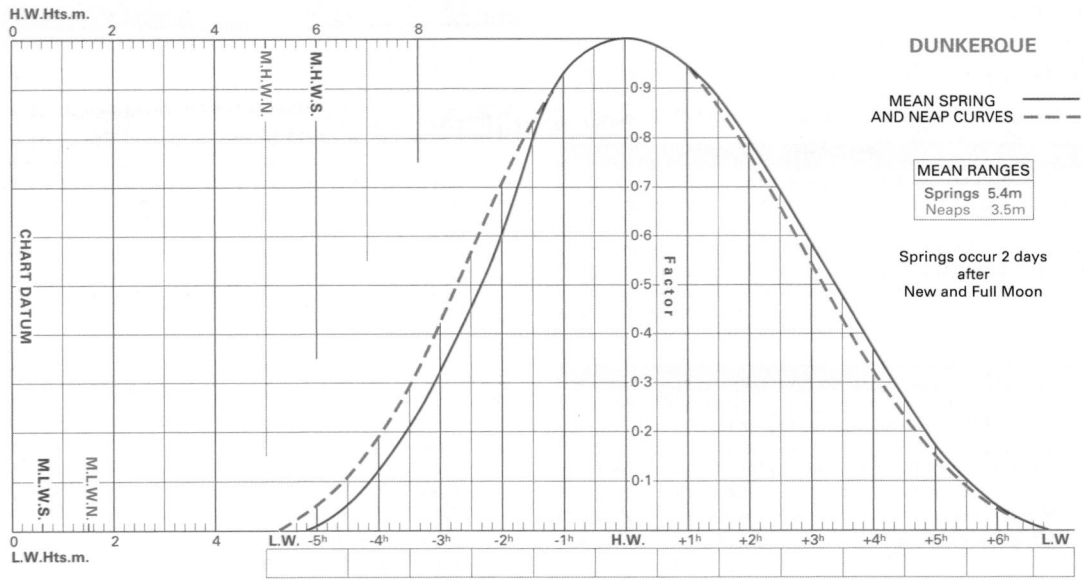

DUNKERQUE

MEAN SPRING ————
AND NEAP CURVES – – –

MEAN RANGES
Springs 5.4m
Neaps 3.5m

Springs occur 2 days
after
New and Full Moon

TELEPHONES ☎ Nos contain 10 digits, the first 2 digits being Zone codes (01 to 05), as appropriate to location. Mobile ☎ Nos are prefixed 06. Info Nos, eg the recorded weather (Auto) are prefixed 08. The ringing tone is long, equal on/off tones (slower than UK engaged tone). Rapid pips mean the call is being connected. Engaged tone is like that in UK.

To call France from UK, dial + (or 00) 33, then the 9 digit number, omitting the 0 from the Zone code prefix. To call UK from France dial + (or 00) 44 followed by the Area Code (omitting the first 0) and the number. Phonecards for public phones may be bought at the PTT, many Hbr offices, cafés and tabacs. Cheap rates are 2130-0800 Mon-Fri 1330-0800 Sat-Mon.

⚠ **Emergencies: Dial 15 Ambulance (SAMU), better than a doctor; 17 Police, better than a gendarmerie; 18 Fire (also divers); or 112 for general emergencies. 1616 for any CROSS.**

BRITISH CONSULS IN FRANCE
The British Consular service assists UK nationals who are travelling abroad and have encountered difficulties or distress ranging from loss of passport or money to the death of or serious injury to a crew member or fellow traveller.

Honorary British consuls at harbours on the Channel and Atlantic coasts are *the first port of call when help is needed*. The relevant Tel No is given under each hbr in Areas 17-22.

SIGNALS International Port Traffic Signals (5.11) and Storm warning signals (6.1.4) are used in many French ports. Tidal signals are now rarely seen in French ports.

INLAND WATERWAYS

TOLLS are due on waterways managed by Voies Navigable de France (VNF). Licence discs (*vignettes*) must be visibly displayed stbd side forward. They are obtainable:

* Online from www.vnf.fr/vignettesVNF/accueil.do in English. Pay on line by Visa, Mastercard or Eurocard.
* By post from VNF offices listed on the website. Allow 2 weeks.
* Over the counter (cash only) from 34 listed VNF offices.

In 2009 licences were valid for one year (1/1-31/12), 4 consecutive months, 30 consecutive days, 16 consecutive days or 1 day. The rates in €s, based on boat area (LOA x Beam (m) = m²), were:

	<12m²	12-25m²	25-40m²	40-60m²	>60m²
1 year	83.60	119.70	240.50	388.50	481.10
4 months	75.30	107.70	216.40	310.80	384.80
30 days	30.50	63.00	93.50	124.00	156.30
16 days	18.00	37.30	55.40	73.40	92.70
1 day	9.20	18.00	27.20	36.20	45.20

CLOSURES
Dates of closures (*chomages*), plus lock hours, water levels and other practicalities, can be obtained from www.vnf.fr or the French National Tourist Office in London (see overleaf).

VNF Head Office, 175 Rue Ludovic Boutleux, BP 820, 62400 Bethune. ☎ 03.21.63.24.54. www.vnf.fr

QUALIFICATIONS
Helmsmen of craft <15m LOA and not capable of >20 kph (11kn) must have an International Certificate of Competence validated for inland waterways, plus a copy of the CEVNI rules. For larger, faster craft the requirements are under review.

INLAND WATERWAYS TO THE MEDITERRANEAN
See 9.17.18 to 9.17.20 for the River Seine, Rouen and Paris.

The quickest route is via Paris to St Mammès – Canal du Loing – Canal de Briare – Canal Latéral à la Loire – Canal du Centre – Saône – Rhône. Approx 1318km (824M), 182 locks; allow 4 weeks. Max dimensions: LOA 38·5m, beam 5m, draft 1·8m, air draft 3·5m.

Alternatives above St Mammès: R Yonne-Laroche, then either Canal de Bourgogne – Saône; or Canal du Nivernais – Canal du Centre – Saône. Both are slowed by many locks.

There are other routes via R Oise/Aisne or R Marne, both continuing via Canal de la Marne à la Saône.

The Saône can also be accessed via the canals of N France, entered at Calais, Dunkerque or Belgian and Dutch ports.

CANALS IN WESTERN FRANCE
See 9.18.14 for inland waterways, especially the Ille et Rance Canal/ Vilaine River from St Malo to Arzal/Camoel in S Brittany.

See 9.22.25 for the R Gironde, Canal Latéral à la Garonne and Canal du Midi. Also the *West France Cruising Companion* (NDL/ Featherstone), new edn 2009, for an outline of this route.

TIME ZONE -0100
Subtract 1 hour for UT
For French Summer Time add
ONE hour in **non-shaded areas**

DUNKERQUE   LAT 51°03'N   LONG 2°22'E
TIMES AND HEIGHTS OF HIGH AND LOW WATERS

Dates in red are SPRINGS
Dates in blue are NEAPS

YEAR 2010

JANUARY
Time m / Time m

1	F	0032 5.9 / 0729 0.7 / 1252 6.1 / 1955 0.7	16	SA	0122 5.6 / 0815 0.8 / 1343 5.7 / 2026 1.0
2	SA	0118 6.0 / 0818 0.5 / 1341 6.2 / 2043 0.7	17	SU	0152 5.7 / 0847 0.8 / 1414 5.8 / 2059 1.0
3	SU	0205 6.1 / 0907 0.4 / 1429 6.2 / 2130 0.7	18	M	0221 5.8 / 0920 0.7 / 1444 5.8 / 2130 1.0
4	M	0253 6.0 / 0955 0.4 / 1518 6.2 / 2217 0.8	19	TU	0251 5.7 / 0950 0.8 / 1512 5.7 / 2201 1.0
5	TU	0339 5.9 / 1043 0.4 / 1607 6.0 / 2304 0.9	20	W	0323 5.7 / 1020 0.8 / 1546 5.6 / 2230 1.1
6	W	0424 5.8 / 1132 0.6 / 1657 5.8 / 2352 1.1	21	TH	0353 5.6 / 1051 0.9 / 1618 5.5 / 2303 1.2
7	TH	0514 5.6 / 1224 0.8 / 1752 5.5 ☽	22	F	0424 5.5 / 1126 1.0 / 1653 5.3 / 2340 1.3
8	F	0045 1.3 / 0613 5.4 / 1321 1.1 / 1856 5.2	23	SA	0503 5.3 / 1207 1.2 / 1741 5.2 ☾
9	SA	0146 1.5 / 0722 5.2 / 1425 1.3 / 2008 5.0	24	SU	0026 1.5 / 0559 5.1 / 1259 1.4 / 1847 5.0
10	SU	0254 1.7 / 0838 5.0 / 1536 1.5 / 2118 4.9	25	M	0127 1.7 / 0712 5.0 / 1413 1.6 / 2000 4.8
11	M	0410 1.6 / 0949 5.0 / 1652 1.5 / 2225 5.0	26	TU	0251 1.7 / 0831 4.9 / 1539 1.5 / 2125 4.9
12	TU	0523 1.5 / 1053 5.2 / 1753 1.3 / 2323 5.2	27	W	0414 1.5 / 0955 5.1 / 1657 1.3 / 2238 5.2
13	W	0618 1.2 / 1148 5.4 / 1840 1.2	28	TH	0527 1.2 / 1104 5.5 / 1802 1.1 / 2335 5.5
14	TH	0010 5.4 / 0702 1.1 / 1232 5.5 / 1919 1.1	29	F	0628 0.9 / 1157 5.8 / 1857 0.8
15	F	0048 5.5 / 0740 1.0 / 1309 5.7 ● 1954 1.0	30	SA	0023 5.8 / 0720 0.5 / 1245 6.1 ○ 1945 0.6
			31	SU	0106 6.0 / 0808 0.3 / 1329 6.3 / 2030 0.5

FEBRUARY
Time m / Time m

1	M	0149 6.1 / 0853 0.2 / 1414 6.3 / 2114 0.5	16	TU	0157 5.8 / 0854 0.6 / 1418 5.8 / 2105 0.8
2	TU	0231 6.2 / 0938 0.1 / 1458 6.2 / 2157 0.6	17	W	0224 5.9 / 0924 0.6 / 1442 5.8 / 2134 0.8
3	W	0315 6.1 / 1022 0.2 / 1543 6.1 / 2239 0.7	18	TH	0251 5.8 / 0953 0.6 / 1512 5.8 / 2202 0.8
4	TH	0356 6.0 / 1106 0.4 / 1627 5.8 / 2321 0.9	19	F	0317 5.8 / 1022 0.7 / 1538 5.7 / 2233 0.9
5	F	0439 5.8 / 1150 0.8 / 1714 5.5	20	SA	0345 5.7 / 1054 0.9 / 1608 5.5 / 2307 1.1
6	SA	0006 1.2 / 0530 5.5 / 1239 1.1 / 1810 5.1 ☽	21	SU	0421 5.6 / 1132 1.1 / 1651 5.3 / 2350 1.3
7	SU	0100 1.4 / 0636 5.1 / 1340 1.5 / 1922 4.8	22	M	0512 5.3 / 1221 1.3 / 1756 5.0 ☾
8	M	0208 1.7 / 0801 4.8 / 1455 1.7 / 2045 4.6	23	TU	0049 1.5 / 0630 5.0 / 1333 1.6 / 1926 4.7
9	TU	0336 1.8 / 0926 4.7 / 1627 1.6 / 2205 4.7	24	W	0214 1.7 / 0804 4.8 / 1509 1.6 / 2104 4.7
10	W	0504 1.6 / 1042 4.9 / 1736 1.5 / 2310 4.9	25	TH	0349 1.5 / 0943 5.0 / 1637 1.4 / 2226 5.1
11	TH	0603 1.3 / 1137 5.2 / 1824 1.3 / 2356 5.2	26	F	0512 1.1 / 1053 5.5 / 1749 1.0 / 2322 5.5
12	F	0647 1.0 / 1218 5.4 / 1902 1.1	27	SA	0615 0.7 / 1145 5.8 / 1842 0.7
13	SA	0032 5.5 / 0723 0.8 / 1253 5.6 / 1934 1.0	28	SU	0007 5.8 / 0705 0.4 / 1230 6.1 ○ 1928 0.6
14	SU	0103 5.6 / 0754 0.8 / 1324 5.7 ● 2004 0.9			
15	M	0131 5.7 / 0824 0.6 / 1351 5.8 / 2034 0.8			

MARCH
Time m / Time m

1	M	0047 6.0 / 0751 0.2 / 1311 6.2 / 2010 0.5	16	TU	0104 5.7 / 0754 0.6 / 1323 5.8 / 2005 0.7
2	TU	0126 6.2 / 0834 0.1 / 1352 6.3 / 2051 0.5	17	W	0128 5.8 / 0825 0.5 / 1349 5.9 / 2036 0.7
3	W	0206 6.2 / 0916 0.1 / 1433 6.2 / 2132 0.5	18	TH	0154 5.9 / 0856 0.5 / 1411 5.9 / 2107 0.7
4	TH	0249 6.2 / 0956 0.2 / 1515 6.0 / 2211 0.6	19	F	0221 5.9 / 0926 0.6 / 1441 5.8 / 2137 0.7
5	F	0328 6.1 / 1036 0.5 / 1556 5.8 / 2250 0.8	20	SA	0249 5.9 / 0957 0.7 / 1509 5.7 / 2209 0.8
6	SA	0409 5.8 / 1116 0.8 / 1639 5.5 / 2331 1.1	21	SU	0320 5.8 / 1030 0.8 / 1543 5.6 / 2245 0.9
7	SU	0457 5.5 / 1200 1.2 / 1730 5.1	22	M	0400 5.6 / 1109 1.0 / 1628 5.3 / 2330 1.2
8	M	0020 1.4 / 0558 5.0 / 1256 1.6 / 1838 4.6	23	TU	0453 5.3 / 1200 1.3 / 1737 4.9 ☾
9	TU	0125 1.7 / 0724 4.6 / 1413 1.9 / 2009 4.4	24	W	0032 1.4 / 0618 5.0 / 1316 1.6 / 1909 4.7
10	W	0257 1.9 / 0900 4.5 / 1552 1.9 / 2136 4.5	25	TH	0158 1.5 / 0753 4.8 / 1452 1.6 / 2050 4.7
11	TH	0433 1.7 / 1017 4.8 / 1707 1.6 / 2242 4.8	26	F	0332 1.4 / 0930 5.1 / 1620 1.3 / 2207 5.1
12	F	0536 1.3 / 1112 5.1 / 1757 1.3 / 2328 5.1	27	SA	0453 1.0 / 1036 5.5 / 1728 1.0 / 2301 5.5
13	SA	0620 1.0 / 1152 5.4 / 1835 1.1	28	SU	0555 0.6 / 1126 5.8 / 1821 0.7 / 2345 5.8
14	SU	0005 5.4 / 0655 0.8 / 1227 5.6 ● 1905 0.9	29	M	0644 0.4 / 1209 6.0 / 1905 0.6
15	M	0036 5.6 / 0724 0.7 / 1257 5.7 ● 1934 0.8	30	TU	0023 6.0 / 0728 0.2 / 1248 6.1 ○ 1947 0.5
			31	W	0101 6.1 / 0810 0.2 / 1327 6.1 / 2027 0.5

APRIL
Time m / Time m

1	TH	0141 6.2 / 0851 0.3 / 1407 6.1 / 2106 0.5	16	F	0125 5.9 / 0828 0.5 / 1342 5.8 / 2043 0.6
2	F	0224 6.1 / 0930 0.4 / 1448 5.9 / 2145 0.6	17	SA	0156 5.9 / 0903 0.5 / 1418 5.8 / 2118 0.7
3	SA	0306 6.0 / 1008 0.6 / 1529 5.7 / 2224 0.8	18	SU	0231 5.9 / 0938 0.7 / 1454 5.7 / 2155 0.7
4	SU	0345 5.7 / 1047 0.9 / 1611 5.4 / 2305 1.0	19	M	0310 5.8 / 1016 0.9 / 1535 5.5 / 2236 0.9
5	M	0433 5.4 / 1129 1.3 / 1700 5.1 / 2350 1.3	20	TU	0358 5.6 / 1100 1.1 / 1630 5.2 / 2325 1.1
6	TU	0530 5.0 / 1220 1.6 / 1801 4.7 ☽	21	W	0503 5.3 / 1156 1.3 / 1743 5.0 ☽
7	W	0049 1.6 / 0646 4.6 / 1330 1.9 / 1922 4.4	22	TH	0029 1.3 / 0619 5.1 / 1312 1.5 / 1859 4.8
8	TH	0212 1.8 / 0819 4.5 / 1503 1.9 / 2052 4.4	23	F	0151 1.3 / 0742 5.0 / 1438 1.5 / 2028 4.9
9	F	0344 1.7 / 0937 4.7 / 1620 1.7 / 2159 4.7	24	SA	0315 1.2 / 0909 5.2 / 1556 1.3 / 2141 5.2
10	SA	0451 1.4 / 1032 5.0 / 1715 1.4 / 2248 5.0	25	SU	0429 0.9 / 1012 5.5 / 1702 1.0 / 2234 5.5
11	SU	0539 1.1 / 1115 5.3 / 1756 1.1 / 2328 5.3	26	M	0529 0.6 / 1102 5.7 / 1755 0.8 / 2319 5.7
12	M	0616 0.9 / 1151 5.5 / 1829 1.0	27	TU	0620 0.5 / 1145 5.9 / 1841 0.7 / 2359 5.9
13	TU	0002 5.5 / 0648 0.8 / 1223 5.6 / 1901 0.8	28	W	0705 0.4 / 1225 5.9 ○ 1923 0.7
14	W	0031 5.7 / 0720 0.7 / 1250 5.7 ● 1934 0.7	29	TH	0039 6.0 / 0747 0.5 / 1304 5.9 / 2004 0.6
15	TH	0057 5.8 / 0754 0.6 / 1318 5.8 / 2008 0.7	30	F	0121 6.0 / 0827 0.5 / 1345 5.9 / 2045 0.6

Chart Datum is 2·69 metres below IGN Datum. HAT is 6·4 metres above Chart Datum; see 4.5.

N France

TIME ZONE -0100
Subtract 1 hour for UT
For French Summer Time add
ONE hour in **non-shaded areas**

DUNKERQUE   LAT 51°03'N   LONG 2°22'E
TIMES AND HEIGHTS OF HIGH AND LOW WATERS

Dates in red are SPRINGS
Dates in blue are NEAPS

YEAR 2010

MAY

Day	Time	m	Day	Time	m
1 SA	0204 / 0907 / 1427 / 2125	6.0 / 0.6 / 5.8 / 0.6	**16** SU	0141 / 0845 / 1404 / 2105	5.9 / 0.7 / 5.8 / 0.6
2 SU	0249 / 0945 / 1509 / 2204	5.9 / 0.8 / 5.6 / 0.8	**17** M	0225 / 0928 / 1450 / 2149	5.9 / 0.8 / 5.7 / 0.6
3 M	0335 / 1024 / 1552 / 2245	5.6 / 1.1 / 5.4 / 1.0	**18** TU	0313 / 1012 / 1541 / 2236	5.8 / 0.9 / 5.6 / 0.7
4 TU	0418 / 1105 / 1637 / 2328	5.4 / 1.3 / 5.1 / 1.2	**19** W	0408 / 1101 / 1636 / 2328	5.7 / 1.0 / 5.4 / 0.9
5 W	0507 / 1151 / 1729	5.1 / 1.6 / 4.8	**20** TH	0507 / 1158 / 1735	5.5 / 1.2 / 5.2
6 TH ☽	0018 / 0605 / 1248 / 1830	1.5 / 4.8 / 1.8 / 4.6	**21** F ☽	0029 / 0609 / 1304 / 1842	1.0 / 5.3 / 1.3 / 5.1
7 F	0122 / 0718 / 1403 / 1945	1.6 / 4.6 / 1.8 / 4.5	**22** SA	0140 / 0722 / 1417 / 1958	1.0 / 5.2 / 1.3 / 5.1
8 SA	0241 / 0837 / 1519 / 2100	1.6 / 4.7 / 1.7 / 4.7	**23** SU	0252 / 0840 / 1527 / 2108	1.0 / 5.3 / 1.3 / 5.2
9 SU	0350 / 0939 / 1619 / 2157	1.4 / 4.9 / 1.5 / 4.9	**24** M	0400 / 0943 / 1632 / 2205	0.9 / 5.4 / 1.1 / 5.4
10 M	0444 / 1027 / 1707 / 2243	1.2 / 5.1 / 1.3 / 5.2	**25** TU	0502 / 1036 / 1729 / 2255	0.8 / 5.6 / 1.0 / 5.6
11 TU	0529 / 1108 / 1748 / 2322	1.0 / 5.4 / 1.1 / 5.4	**26** W	0556 / 1123 / 1820 / 2340	0.7 / 5.6 / 0.9 / 5.7
12 W	0609 / 1144 / 1826 / 2355	0.9 / 5.5 / 1.0 / 5.5	**27** TH	0644 / 1207 / 1905	0.7 / 5.7 / 0.8
13 TH	0647 / 1216 / 1904	0.8 / 5.6 / 0.8	**28** F ○	0025 / 0728 / 1250 / 1948	5.8 / 0.7 / 5.7 / 0.7
14 F ●	0027 / 0725 / 1251 / 1943	5.7 / 0.7 / 5.7 / 0.7	**29** SA	0109 / 0809 / 1332 / 2030	5.8 / 0.8 / 5.7 / 0.7
15 SA	0102 / 0805 / 1323 / 2024	5.8 / 0.7 / 5.8 / 0.6	**30** SU	0154 / 0849 / 1415 / 2110	5.8 / 0.8 / 5.7 / 0.7
			31 M	0238 / 0927 / 1456 / 2149	5.7 / 0.9 / 5.6 / 0.8

JUNE

Day	Time	m	Day	Time	m
1 TU	0320 / 1005 / 1535 / 2227	5.6 / 1.1 / 5.5 / 0.9	**16** W	0311 / 1008 / 1534 / 2233	6.0 / 0.8 / 5.7 / 0.5
2 W	0402 / 1043 / 1614 / 2306	5.4 / 1.2 / 5.3 / 1.1	**17** TH	0402 / 1057 / 1623 / 2323	5.9 / 0.9 / 5.6 / 0.6
3 TH	0443 / 1123 / 1658 / 2347	5.2 / 1.4 / 5.1 / 1.2	**18** F	0454 / 1148 / 1716	5.7 / 1.0 / 5.5
4 F ☽	0528 / 1208 / 1747	5.1 / 1.5 / 5.0	**19** SA ☽	0018 / 0550 / 1245 / 1816	0.7 / 5.5 / 1.2 / 5.4
5 SA	0035 / 0621 / 1301 / 1842	1.3 / 4.9 / 1.6 / 4.8	**20** SU	0119 / 0654 / 1348 / 1921	0.8 / 5.4 / 1.5 / 5.3
6 SU	0134 / 0720 / 1408 / 1944	1.4 / 4.8 / 1.7 / 4.9	**21** M	0223 / 0805 / 1454 / 2033	0.9 / 5.3 / 1.3 / 5.2
7 M	0243 / 0825 / 1516 / 2049	1.4 / 4.9 / 1.6 / 4.9	**22** TU	0330 / 0912 / 1602 / 2139	1.0 / 5.2 / 1.3 / 5.3
8 TU	0346 / 0926 / 1615 / 2148	1.4 / 5.0 / 1.5 / 5.0	**23** W	0437 / 1013 / 1708 / 2238	1.0 / 5.3 / 1.2 / 5.4
9 W	0441 / 1020 / 1706 / 2238	1.2 / 5.2 / 1.3 / 5.2	**24** TH	0539 / 1109 / 1806 / 2332	1.0 / 5.3 / 1.1 / 5.5
10 TH	0531 / 1106 / 1754 / 2323	1.1 / 5.3 / 1.1 / 5.4	**25** F	0631 / 1200 / 1854	1.0 / 5.4 / 0.9
11 F	0617 / 1148 / 1839	1.0 / 5.5 / 0.9	**26** SA ○	0021 / 0716 / 1244 / 1938	5.6 / 1.0 / 5.5 / 0.8
12 SA ●	0005 / 0702 / 1230 / 1924	5.6 / 0.9 / 5.7 / 0.8	**27** SU	0106 / 0815 / 1325 / 2018	5.7 / 0.9 / 5.6 / 0.7
13 SU	0047 / 0747 / 1315 / 2010	5.7 / 0.8 / 5.8 / 0.6	**28** M	0147 / 0834 / 1403 / 2056	5.7 / 0.9 / 5.7 / 0.7
14 M	0133 / 0833 / 1403 / 2057	5.9 / 0.7 / 5.8 / 0.5	**29** TU	0226 / 0910 / 1439 / 2133	5.7 / 1.0 / 5.6 / 0.7
15 TU	0221 / 0920 / 1449 / 2144	6.0 / 0.7 / 5.8 / 0.5	**30** W	0302 / 0945 / 1513 / 2207	5.7 / 1.0 / 5.6 / 0.8

JULY

Day	Time	m	Day	Time	m
1 TH	0338 / 1019 / 1547 / 2241	5.6 / 1.1 / 5.5 / 0.9	**16** F	0344 / 1040 / 1604 / 2307	6.1 / 0.7 / 5.9 / 0.4
2 F	0412 / 1053 / 1624 / 2315	5.5 / 1.2 / 5.4 / 1.0	**17** SA	0432 / 1126 / 1649 / 2356	5.9 / 0.9 / 5.8 / 0.5
3 SA	0450 / 1129 / 1705 / 2353	5.3 / 1.3 / 5.2 / 1.1	**18** SU ◐	0523 / 1216 / 1744	5.7 / 1.1 / 5.6
4 SU ◐	0534 / 1210 / 1752	5.2 / 1.4 / 5.1	**19** M	0050 / 0621 / 1314 / 1846	0.8 / 5.4 / 1.3 / 5.4
5 M	0037 / 0624 / 1259 / 1846	1.3 / 5.0 / 1.6 / 5.0	**20** TU	0151 / 0728 / 1420 / 2001	1.1 / 5.2 / 1.4 / 5.1
6 TU	0133 / 0721 / 1404 / 1946	1.4 / 4.9 / 1.7 / 4.9	**21** W	0300 / 0843 / 1535 / 2118	1.3 / 5.0 / 1.5 / 5.1
7 W	0245 / 0825 / 1519 / 2053	1.5 / 4.9 / 1.6 / 4.9	**22** TH	0417 / 0956 / 1654 / 2228	1.4 / 5.0 / 1.4 / 5.2
8 TH	0355 / 0933 / 1626 / 2200	1.4 / 5.0 / 1.5 / 5.1	**23** F	0527 / 1102 / 1756 / 2329	1.3 / 5.1 / 1.2 / 5.3
9 F	0457 / 1036 / 1726 / 2259	1.3 / 5.2 / 1.2 / 5.3	**24** SA	0620 / 1155 / 1845	1.2 / 5.3 / 1.0
10 SA	0554 / 1129 / 1821 / 2350	1.1 / 5.4 / 1.0 / 5.6	**25** SU	0017 / 0703 / 1236 / 1926	5.5 / 1.1 / 5.5 / 0.8
11 SU ●	0646 / 1216 / 1911	0.9 / 5.7 / 0.7	**26** M ○	0057 / 0741 / 1312 / 2003	5.7 / 1.0 / 5.6 / 0.7
12 M	0037 / 0735 / 1301 / 1959	5.9 / 0.8 / 5.8 / 0.5	**27** TU	0133 / 0815 / 1345 / 2037	5.7 / 0.9 / 5.7 / 0.7
13 TU	0122 / 0822 / 1346 / 2046	6.0 / 0.7 / 5.8 / 0.3	**28** W	0207 / 0848 / 1415 / 2110	5.8 / 0.9 / 5.7 / 0.7
14 W	0209 / 0908 / 1432 / 2133	6.1 / 0.6 / 6.0 / 0.2	**29** TH	0237 / 0920 / 1445 / 2142	5.8 / 0.9 / 5.7 / 0.7
15 TH	0256 / 0954 / 1519 / 2220	6.1 / 0.6 / 6.0 / 0.3	**30** F	0308 / 0951 / 1514 / 2212	5.7 / 1.0 / 5.7 / 0.8
			31 SA	0336 / 1021 / 1546 / 2241	5.6 / 1.0 / 5.6 / 0.9

AUGUST

Day	Time	m	Day	Time	m
1 SU	0410 / 1052 / 1618 / 2314	5.5 / 1.1 / 5.5 / 1.0	**16** M ◐	0452 / 1144 / 1709	5.7 / 1.1 / 5.7
2 M	0444 / 1126 / 1653 / 2351	5.4 / 1.3 / 5.3 / 1.2	**17** TU	0017 / 0546 / 1238 / 1813	1.0 / 5.4 / 1.3 / 5.3
3 TU ◐	0526 / 1208 / 1743	5.2 / 1.5 / 5.1	**18** W	0116 / 0653 / 1346 / 1933	1.3 / 5.0 / 1.6 / 5.0
4 W	0039 / 0626 / 1304 / 1853	1.4 / 4.9 / 1.7 / 4.9	**19** TH	0230 / 0816 / 1511 / 2100	1.6 / 4.7 / 1.7 / 4.9
5 TH	0145 / 0737 / 1424 / 2010	1.6 / 4.8 / 1.8 / 4.8	**20** F	0359 / 0940 / 1639 / 2219	1.7 / 4.8 / 1.5 / 5.0
6 F	0311 / 0858 / 1549 / 2133	1.6 / 4.8 / 1.6 / 5.0	**21** SA	0512 / 1050 / 1741 / 2319	1.5 / 5.0 / 1.2 / 5.3
7 SA	0429 / 1015 / 1703 / 2243	1.5 / 5.1 / 1.3 / 5.3	**22** SU	0604 / 1141 / 1829	1.3 / 5.3 / 0.9
8 SU	0537 / 1114 / 1806 / 2337	1.2 / 5.4 / 0.9 / 5.7	**23** M	0003 / 0645 / 1218 / 1908	5.5 / 1.1 / 5.5 / 0.8
9 M	0633 / 1201 / 1857	0.9 / 5.7 / 0.6	**24** TU ○	0038 / 0720 / 1250 / 1941	5.7 / 1.0 / 5.7 / 0.7
10 TU ●	0023 / 0721 / 1244 / 1944	6.0 / 0.7 / 5.9 / 0.4	**25** W	0110 / 0750 / 1319 / 2011	5.8 / 0.9 / 5.8 / 0.7
11 W	0106 / 0805 / 1325 / 2029	6.2 / 0.6 / 6.1 / 0.2	**26** TH	0140 / 0821 / 1346 / 2042	5.8 / 0.9 / 5.8 / 0.6
12 TH	0150 / 0849 / 1407 / 2114	6.3 / 0.5 / 6.2 / 0.1	**27** F	0206 / 0851 / 1412 / 2112	5.9 / 0.9 / 5.9 / 0.7
13 F	0233 / 0932 / 1452 / 2158	6.3 / 0.6 / 6.2 / 0.2	**28** SA	0235 / 0921 / 1439 / 2141	5.8 / 0.9 / 5.8 / 0.7
14 SA	0318 / 1015 / 1533 / 2242	6.2 / 0.7 / 6.1 / 0.3	**29** SU	0258 / 0949 / 1506 / 2209	5.8 / 1.0 / 5.8 / 0.8
15 SU	0403 / 1059 / 1617 / 2327	6.0 / 0.8 / 5.9 / 0.6	**30** M	0326 / 1018 / 1532 / 2239	5.7 / 1.0 / 5.7 / 1.0
			31 TU	0353 / 1051 / 1604 / 2314	5.5 / 1.2 / 5.5 / 1.2

Chart Datum is 2·69 metres below IGN Datum. HAT is 6·4 metres above Chart Datum; see 4.5.

TIME ZONE -0100
Subtract 1 hour for UT
For French Summer Time add ONE hour in **non-shaded areas**

DUNKERQUE LAT 51°03'N LONG 2°22'E
TIMES AND HEIGHTS OF HIGH AND LOW WATERS

Dates in red are SPRINGS
Dates in blue are NEAPS

YEAR 2010

N France

SEPTEMBER

Time	m		Time	m
1 0429	5.3	**16**	0040	1.6
1131	1.4		0619	4.9
W 1647	5.3		TH 1311	1.7
◑			1905	4.9
2 0000	1.4	**17**	0157	1.9
0525	5.0		0746	4.6
TH 1226	1.6		F 1442	1.8
1803	4.9		2038	4.7
3 0104	1.7	**18**	0332	1.9
0700	4.7		0915	4.7
F 1345	1.8		SA 1613	1.6
1940	4.8		2157	4.9
4 0236	1.8	**19**	0446	1.7
0832	4.7		1023	4.9
SA 1520	1.7		SU 1716	1.3
2113	5.0		2254	5.2
5 0406	1.6	**20**	0539	1.4
0956	5.0		1112	5.3
SU 1643	1.3		M 1803	1.0
2227	5.4		2336	5.5
6 0519	1.2	**21**	0619	1.2
1056	5.5		1149	5.5
M 1748	0.9		TU 1841	0.8
2320	5.8			
7 0615	0.9	**22**	0011	5.7
1142	5.8		0651	1.0
TU 1839	0.5		W 1221	5.7
			1911	0.8
8 0004	6.1	**23**	0042	5.8
0701	0.7		0720	1.0
W 1221	6.1		TH 1249	5.8
● 1925	0.3		○ 1940	0.7
9 0045	6.3	**24**	0109	5.9
0744	0.6		0750	0.9
TH 1300	6.2		F 1315	5.9
2008	0.2		2010	0.7
10 0125	6.4	**25**	0133	5.9
0826	0.6		0820	0.9
F 1340	6.3		SA 1339	5.9
2051	0.2		2040	0.7
11 0206	6.3	**26**	0155	5.9
0907	0.6		0851	0.9
SA 1423	6.3		SU 1406	5.9
2133	0.3		2110	0.8
12 0249	6.2	**27**	0225	5.9
0949	0.7		0921	0.9
SU 1503	6.2		M 1434	5.9
2215	0.5		2140	0.9
13 0333	6.0	**28**	0252	5.8
1031	0.8		0951	1.0
M 1548	6.0		TU 1503	5.8
2257	0.8		2211	1.0
14 0420	5.7	**29**	0323	5.6
1114	1.1		1026	1.2
TU 1640	5.6		W 1538	5.6
2343	1.2		2248	1.2
15 0513	5.3	**30**	0402	5.4
1204	1.4		1108	1.3
W 1744	5.2		TH 1624	5.3
◑			2335	1.5

OCTOBER

Time	m		Time	m
1 0459	5.0	**16**	0115	2.0
1205	1.6		0703	4.6
F 1745	5.0		SA 1400	1.9
◑			2001	4.7
2 0042	1.7	**17**	0245	2.0
0638	4.8		0832	4.6
SA 1323	1.8		SU 1528	1.7
1921	4.9		2118	4.9
3 0213	1.8	**18**	0402	1.8
0808	4.8		0940	4.9
SU 1458	1.6		M 1635	1.5
2053	5.1		2214	5.1
4 0343	1.6	**19**	0459	1.5
0933	5.1		1031	5.2
M 1620	1.2		TU 1725	1.2
2206	5.5		2258	5.4
5 0455	1.2	**20**	0542	1.3
1031	5.5		1112	5.4
TU 1725	0.8		W 1804	1.0
2258	5.9		2336	5.6
6 0551	0.9	**21**	0616	1.1
1117	5.9		1147	5.6
W 1816	0.5		TH 1836	0.9
2341	6.1			
7 0638	0.7	**22**	0008	5.8
1156	6.1		0647	1.0
TH 1902	0.3		F 1217	5.8
●			1906	0.8
8 0020	6.3	**23**	0035	5.8
0720	0.7		0718	1.0
F 1234	6.3		SA 1243	5.8
1944	0.3		○ 1938	0.8
9 0100	6.3	**24**	0101	5.9
0802	0.6		0751	0.9
SA 1315	6.3		SU 1310	5.9
2026	0.4		2011	0.8
10 0140	6.3	**25**	0126	5.9
0843	0.6		0825	0.9
SU 1358	6.3		M 1340	6.0
2108	0.5		2045	0.9
11 0223	6.1	**26**	0159	5.7
0924	0.7		0859	0.9
M 1443	6.2		TU 1413	5.9
2149	0.7		2119	0.9
12 0307	5.9	**27**	0233	5.8
1006	0.9		0934	1.0
TU 1527	5.9		W 1449	5.8
2230	1.0		2154	1.1
13 0353	5.6	**28**	0311	5.6
1049	1.1		1013	1.1
W 1618	5.6		TH 1531	5.6
2314	1.4		2235	1.3
14 0444	5.3	**29**	0356	5.4
1137	1.4		1059	1.3
TH 1718	5.2		F 1627	5.4
◑			2326	1.5
15 0006	1.7	**30**	0502	5.1
0545	4.9		1157	1.4
F 1237	1.7		SA 1743	5.2
1831	4.8		◑	
		31	0031	1.7
			0619	5.0
		SU 1310	1.5
			1901	5.1

NOVEMBER

Time	m		Time	m
1 0153	1.7	**16**	0257	1.9
0740	5.0		0839	4.8
M 1435	1.4		TU 1533	1.6
2026	5.2		2121	5.0
2 0315	1.6	**17**	0400	1.7
0901	5.2		0939	5.0
TU 1552	1.1		W 1630	1.4
2138	5.5		2211	5.2
3 0425	1.3	**18**	0452	1.5
1002	5.5		1027	5.2
W 1657	0.8		TH 1717	1.2
2232	5.8		2254	5.4
4 0524	1.0	**19**	0535	1.3
1050	5.8		1109	5.4
TH 1751	0.6		F 1757	1.1
2317	6.0		2331	5.6
5 0613	0.9	**20**	0613	1.2
1132	6.0		1144	5.6
F 1839	0.5		SA 1834	1.0
2358	6.1			
6 0659	0.8	**21**	0004	5.7
1213	6.2		0649	1.1
SA 1923	0.5		SU 1216	5.7
●			○ 1910	0.9
7 0039	6.1	**22**	0035	5.8
0741	0.7		0727	0.9
SU 1256	6.2		M 1248	5.9
2005	0.6		1948	0.9
8 0121	6.1	**23**	0108	5.9
0824	0.7		0805	0.9
M 1340	6.2		TU 1324	6.0
2047	0.7		2027	0.9
9 0204	6.0	**24**	0143	5.9
0906	0.8		0845	0.8
TU 1427	6.1		W 1404	6.0
2128	0.9		2106	0.9
10 0248	5.8	**25**	0225	5.9
0948	0.9		0927	0.8
W 1515	5.9		TH 1446	5.9
2209	1.2		2148	1.0
11 0333	5.6	**26**	0309	5.7
1030	1.1		1010	0.9
TH 1603	5.6		F 1535	5.8
2250	1.4		2232	1.2
12 0418	5.3	**27**	0358	5.5
1114	1.3		1057	1.0
F 1652	5.3		SA 1629	5.6
2335	1.7		2322	1.3
13 0509	5.1	**28**	0454	5.4
1203	1.6		1151	1.1
SA 1749	5.0		SU 1729	5.5
◑			◑	
14 0029	1.9	**29**	0019	1.5
0608	4.8		0554	5.2
SU 1305	1.7		M 1255	1.2
1859	4.8		1835	5.3
15 0140	2.0	**30**	0128	1.6
0722	4.7		0705	5.2
M 1423	1.8		TU 1409	1.2
2018	4.8		1951	5.3

DECEMBER

Time	m		Time	m
1 0242	1.5	**16**	0250	1.9
0821	5.2		0825	4.8
W 1521	1.1		TH 1526	1.6
2105	5.4		2108	4.9
2 0352	1.4	**17**	0354	1.7
0930	5.4		0931	5.0
TH 1628	1.0		F 1625	1.5
2205	5.6		2206	5.1
3 0456	1.2	**18**	0450	1.6
1026	5.6		1026	5.2
F 1728	0.9		SA 1717	1.3
2257	5.7		2255	5.3
4 0553	1.1	**19**	0539	1.3
1116	5.8		1113	5.4
SA 1821	0.8		SU 1804	1.2
2344	5.8		2337	5.5
5 0643	0.9	**20**	0625	1.1
1203	5.9		1154	5.6
SU 1908	0.8		M 1848	1.0
●				
6 0028	5.9	**21**	0016	5.7
0729	0.8		0708	0.9
M 1248	6.0		TU 1233	5.8
1952	0.8		○ 1930	0.9
7 0110	5.9	**22**	0056	5.8
0812	0.8		0751	0.8
TU 1333	6.0		W 1313	6.0
2033	0.9		2014	0.8
8 0153	5.9	**23**	0138	5.9
0854	0.8		0835	0.6
W 1418	6.0		TH 1356	6.1
2112	1.0		2057	0.8
9 0235	5.8	**24**	0215	5.9
0934	0.8		0920	0.6
TH 1501	5.8		F 1441	6.1
2150	1.1		2141	0.8
10 0315	5.7	**25**	0258	5.9
1013	1.0		1005	0.6
F 1542	5.6		SA 1527	6.0
2228	1.3		2225	0.9
11 0353	5.5	**26**	0344	5.8
1051	1.1		1051	0.7
SA 1624	5.4		SU 1615	5.9
2306	1.5		2311	1.0
12 0434	5.3	**27**	0433	5.7
1130	1.3		1140	0.8
SU 1706	5.2		M 1708	5.7
2347	1.6			
13 0519	5.1	**28**	0001	1.2
1214	1.5		0527	5.5
M 1755	5.0		TU 1235	0.9
◑			◑ 1806	5.5
14 0035	1.8	**29**	0059	1.4
0613	4.9		0628	5.4
TU 1309	1.6		W 1339	1.1
1854	4.9		1914	5.3
15 0138	1.9	**30**	0207	1.5
0715	4.8		0743	5.3
W 1418	1.7		TH 1448	1.2
2001	4.8		2030	5.2
		31	0319	1.5
			0900	5.2
		F 1600	1.2
			2141	5.2

Chart Datum is 2·69 metres below IGN Datum. HAT is 6·4 metres above Chart Datum; see 4.5.

》》 FREE monthly updates from **《《**
www.reedsalmanac.co.uk

9.17.7 DUNKERQUE (PORT EST)
Nord 51°03'·62N 02°21'·09E 🚢🚢🚢🌀🌀🌀🌀🏵🏵

CHARTS AC *323*, 1872, 1350, *5605.11*; SHOM 6651, 7057; Navi 1010; Imray C30; Stanfords 1, 20

TIDES Dunkerque is a Standard Port (⟵). +0050 Dover; ML 3·2; Duration 0530. See 9.17.8 for Dunkerque Port Ouest.

SHELTER Good; access at all tides/weather, but fresh NW–NE winds cause heavy seas at ent and scend in hbr.

NAVIGATION Yachts must not use the W Port. From the east, WPT 51°04'·29N 02°21'·72E (SCM lt buoy), 210°/0·8M to hbr ent. From Nieuwpoort Bank WCM lt buoy, the E1-12 buoys (9.17.4) lead S of Banc Hills but shore lights make navigational and shipping lights hard to see. Keep clear of very large ships manoeuvring into/out of Charles de Gaulle lock.

From the west, WPT 51°03'·83N 02°20'·25E (DW29 lt buoy), 111°/0·6M to hbr ent. Fetch Dyck PHM buoy, 5M N of Calais, thence to DKA SWM buoy, and via DW channel lt buoys past W Port to WPT. Streams reach about 3½kn.

LIGHTS AND MARKS A chimney (116m), 1M WSW of hbr ent and other industrial structures are conspic. The W jetty lt ho is a distinctive, bulky, brown brick twr, green top. The E jetty lt pylon is small, slender and less obvious; the jetty covers at HW but is lit by 9 bright sodiums. The ldg lts, W cols, R tops, and the tall lt ho, W tr with B top, lead 137°/1M toward the marinas. [The F Vi(olet) 179° and 185° ldg lts define big ship turning circles.]

IPTS (full) shown from W jetty head (when big ships under way).

Lock. Enter Trystram lock (5m) for marinas in Bassin du Commerce and Bassin de la Marine via 3 bridges: (a) at S end of the lock; (b) at SE side of Darse No 1; and (c) at ent to Bassin du Commerce. The daily schedule (1 Apr–3 Sep, 7/7, LT), for lock and bridges is:

Outward
Bridges (c) and (b) both open 0815, 1045, 1415, 1615, 1830.
Bridge (a) and lock open 0850, 1105, 1435, 1635, 1900.

Inward
Lock opens 1020, 1530, 1830, 2100. Bridge (a) opens 30 mins later. Bridges (b) and (c) open 20 mins after (a); the 1110 opening is only on Sat/Sun.

Lock/bridge, light and sound signals: ● ● = No entry
2 long blasts = Request open lock or bridge
● + Fl ● = Standby to secure on the side of the Fl ●
● + Fl ● = Enter lock and secure on side of the Fl ●

R/T Monitor *Dunkerque VTS* Ch **73** (H24) for traffic info (English spoken). Locks Ch 73. Marinas Ch 09.

TELEPHONE HM 03.28.28.75.96. www.portdedunkerque.fr Port Control 03.28.28.78.78. ⊖ 03.28.29.25.50. Aff Mar 03.28.26.73.00. CROSS 03.21.87.21.87. Météo 03.28.66.45.25. Auto 08.92.68.08.59. Police 03.28.59.13.22. Ⓗ 03.28.66.70.01. Brit Consul 03.28.66.11.98.

FACILITIES from seaward: The 3 *marinas are municipal and Ⓥ berths are at different rates; all on the same website www.dunkerque-marina.com

***Port du Grand Large** H24 access (3m). ☎ 03.28.63.23.00. 315+25 Ⓥ, €3·80 (discounts for members of Transmanche marinas). D&P (0800-1200, 1400-1830 daily), BH (30 ton), Slip, YC, Bar, R, Ⓒ.

YC Mer du Nord (YCMN) ☎ 03.28.66.79.90. 250+70 Ⓥ, €2·25 plus €0·20 per person per day. H24 access (3m). secreteriat@ ycmn.com www.ycmn.com CH, ME, SM, D&P 0800-1200, 1400-1800 daily, C (7 ton), Ⓒ, Bar, R.

***Bassin de la Marine** 170 inc Ⓥ, €2·40. ☎ 03.28.24.58.80. Access to/from canals via lock at SW end of Darse No 1.

***Bassin du Commerce** 200+30 Ⓥ €1·90. Quai des Hollandais (SE bank pontoon) €1·15. YC de Dunkerque (YCD) marina (5m), ☎ 03.28.21.13.77. D, FW, CH.

Town P, D, 🛒, Gaz, SHOM, ME, El, Ⓔ, ✗, CH, R, Bar, ✉, Ⓑ, ⛽, ✈ (Lille). Vehicle ferry (no foot passengers) to Dover.

9.17.8 GRAVELINES

Nord 51°00'·94N 02°05'·55E ✳✳🌊🌊⚓☆☆

CHARTS AC *323, 5605.11*, 1350; SHOM 6651, 7057; Navi 1010; Stanfords 1, 20.

TIDES HW +0045 on Dover (UT); ML 3·3m; Duration 0520.

Standard Port DUNKERQUE (←)

Times				Height (metres)			
High Water		Low Water		MHWS	MHWN	MLWN	MLWS
0200	0800	0200	0900	6·0	5·0	1·5	0·6
1400	2000	1400	2100				
Differences GRAVELINES (3M SW of Dunkerque Ouest)							
–0010	–0015	–0010	–0005	+0·4	+0·3	+1·0	0·0
DUNKERQUE PORT OUEST (3M ENE of Gravelines)							
–0010	–0015	–0010	–0005	+0·4	+0·3	0·0	0·0

SHELTER Good, but do not enter in strong winds. Appr chan has only 0·5m at LWS. Access approx HW ±3 for shoal draft, ±2 if draft >1·5m; max draft 2·5m. For a first visit HW would be sensible.

In strong NE or SW winds the ancient, manually operated bridge over the entry gate cannot be swung open; ergo the basin cannot be entered or exited.

NAVIGATION WPT 51°01'·30N 02°05'·13E, 142°/0·43M to bkwtr heads; old lt ho (unlit, conspic B/W spiral) in transit with wine-glass shaped water twr 142°. Beware strong E-going stream across ent near HW. Dredger often working at entrance. Do not cut between the E bkwtr head and a NCM lt bcn close N of it.

The approach chan dries to soft mud, all but a trickle; it is about 15m wide and marked by lateral dolphins. Keep to the W on entry and to the E when inside. 650m before the ent to Bassin Vauban the chan turns 60° stbd.

No waiting pontoon, but the 9·8m wide entry gate into the marina stays open approx HW ±3 in season, HW ±1½ out of season. A digital depth gauge shows depth over the sill which dries 0·6m. ♥ berth to stbd.

The River Aa, pronounced Ar-Ar, flows through the Bassin via sluice gates upstream which are usually shut. The river can be accessed by a small lock, No 63bis, which is only 4·3m wide. 48hrs notice required.

LIGHTS AND MARKS Lts as chartlet and 9.17.4. A nuclear power stn with 6 towers (63m) is 1M NE. 1·8M further NE is the ent to Dunkerque Ouest, commercial & ferry port. The disused lt ho, with continuous black and white spiral band, is very distinctive. The G sector (078°-085°) of the W bkwtr lt shines parallel with the coast and just to seaward of the drying line; the white sector (317°-327°) is visible from within the ent chan.

R/T Ch 09 (HO) for entry gate and marina.

TELEPHONE Entry gate ☎ 03.28.23.13.42. Météo 08.92.68.02.59. Aff Mar ☎ 03.28.26.73.00. Police 03.28.23.15.17/03.28.24.56.45. Tourist office 03.28.51.94.00. Brit Consul 03.28.66.11.98.

FACILITIES **Bassin Vauban** ☎ 03.28.65.45.24. 430+20 ♥, €1·85. Bar, R, bike hire. Max LOA 15m, max beam 9·8m for entry gate. port.de.plaisance.gravelines@wanadoo.fr www.plaisance-opale.com Large well equipped BY, C (10 & 3 ton), BH (7 ton), CH, El, ME, ✕.

Berth on ♥ pontoon No 1, first to stbd, or as directed. The marina almost dries, but fin keelers sink upright into soft, glorious mud. It may be advisable to close the engine cooling water seacock after shutting down and to clean the water strainer thereafter.

Town D&P H24 (cans, Super-U 600m), ✉, Ⓑ, Bar, R, ⇌, 🛒, ▣.

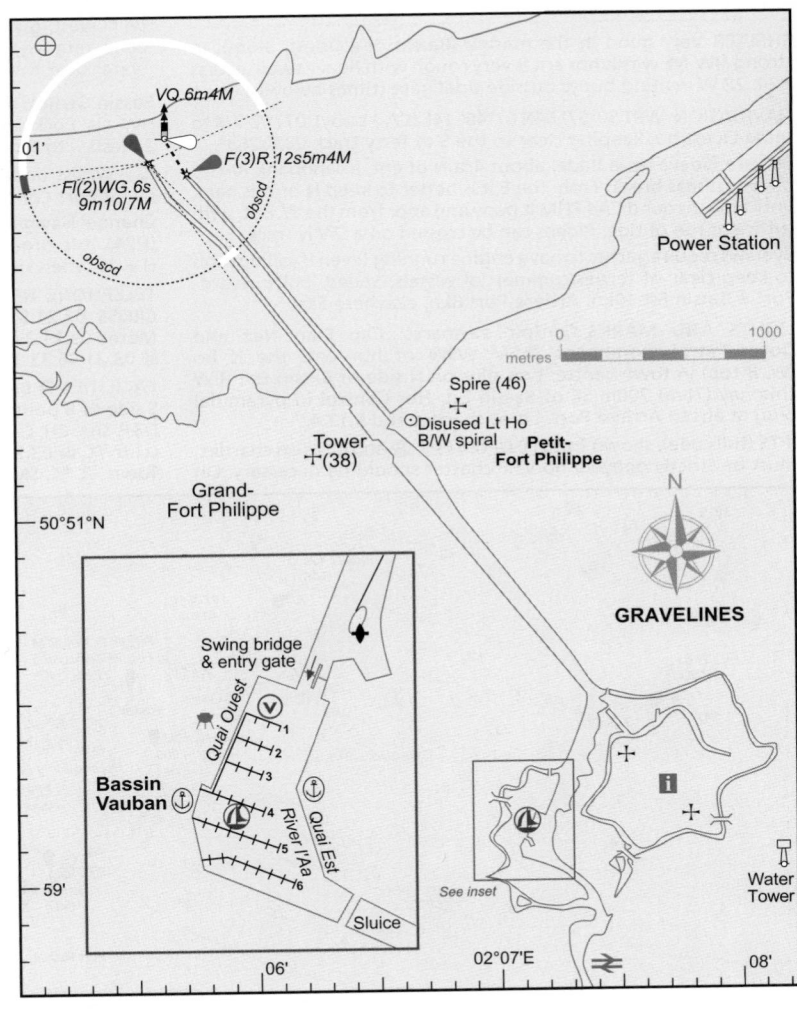

9.17.9 CALAIS

Pas de Calais 50°58'·33N 01°50'·42E ✴✴⚓⚓⚓✿✿

CHARTS AC *1892, 323*, 1351, *5605.10*; SHOM 7323, 6651, 7258; Navi 1010; Imray C8; Stanfords 1, 20

TIDES +0048 Dover; ML 4·0; Duration 0525.

Standard Port DUNKERQUE (←—)

Times				Height (metres)			
High Water		Low Water		MHWS	MHWN	MLWN	MLWS
0200	0800	0200	0900	6·0	5·0	1·5	0·6
1400	2000	1400	2100				
Differences CALAIS							
–0020	–0030	–0015	–0005	+1·2	+0·9	+0·6	+0·3
SANDETTIE BANK (11M N of Calais)							
–0015	–0025	–0020	–0005	+0·1	–0·1	–0·1	–0·1
WISSANT (8M WSW of Calais)							
–0035	–0050	–0030	–0010	+1·9	+1·5	+0·8	+0·4

SHELTER Very good in the marina (Bassin de l'Ouest, 3-6m). In strong NW-NE winds hbr ent is very rough with heavy swell; access H24. 22 W waiting buoys outside tidal gate (times below).

NAVIGATION WPT 50°57'·64N 01°46'·14E (CA 1 buoy), 077°/2·7M to Jetée Ouest hd, keeping clear to the S of ferry track 083°/263°.

Beware Ridens de la Rade, about 4ca N of ent, a sandbank (0·1m) on which seas break. From the E it is better to keep N of this bank until able to round CA4 PHM lt buoy and appr from the W. But, with sufficient rise of tide, Ridens can be crossed on a SW'ly track.

Byelaws require yachts to have engine running (even if sailing) and to keep clear of ferries/commercial vessels. Speed limits: Avant-Port & Bassin Est 10kn; Arrière-Port 8kn; elswhere 5kn.

LIGHTS AND MARKS Conspic daymarks: Cap Blanc-Nez and Dover Patrol monument, 5·5M WSW of hbr ent; the lt ho (W, B top) in town centre; two silos on N side of Bassin Est; R/W chimney (78m) 700m SE of Bassin Est; Hbr Control in pyramidal bldg at ent to Arrière Port. Lts as chartlet and 9.17.4.

IPTS (full code), shown from Ⓐ (Jetée Est), Ⓑ and Ⓒ as on chartlet, must be strictly obeyed; no VHF chatter should be necessary. On arrival, first comply with Ⓐ, then Ⓑ to enter Arrière Port.

If no sigs are shown (ie no ferries under way), yachts may enter/exit. Or follow a ferry entering, keeping to the stbd side of the fairway and not impeding said ferry. Keep a very sharp lookout, especially for ferries closing fast from astern.
One ● (alongside lowest IPTS lt) = dredger working.
On leaving, first comply with Ⓒ, then Ⓑ, Ⓐ for seaward. Yachts are often cleared outward as a convoy; monitor Ch 17.

Bassin de l'Ouest (marina). 17m wide entry gate (sill 2m above CD) stays open HW –2 to +2½. Gate signals:

●	=	All movements prohib.
◐	=	10 mins before gate opens.
●	=	Movement authorised.
4 blasts	=	Request permission to enter.

The co-located Hénon swing bridge opens at HW –2, –1, HW, +1¼, +2½. Times are usually strictly observed. The monthly schedule is posted on www.plaisance-opale.com. The lock gates to Bassin de l'Ouest, giving access to the marina, are reported as having been removed until further notice. A gauge shows depth of water over the sill.

Bassin Carnot: If bound for the canals, lock gates open HW –1½ to HW +¾. Lock sigs are as per the CEVNI code. Call Ch 17 or sound 2 blasts to request permission to enter.

R/T Whilst underway in apprs and hbr, monitor Ch **17** 16 (H24) *Calais Port Control* for VTS, marina and Carnot lock (occas).

Channel Navigation Info Service (CNIS): *Gris Nez Traffic* Ch **13** 79 16 (H24). Info broadcasts in English & French Ch 79, at H + 10, also at H + 25 when vis is < 2M. *CROSS Gris Nez* Ch 15, 67, **68**, 73.

TELEPHONE HM (Port) 03.21.96.31.20; Aff Mar 03.21.34.52.70; CROSS 03.21.87.21.87; SNSM 03.21.96.31.20; ⊖ 03.21.34.75.40; Météo 03.21.33.24.25; Auto 08.92.68.02.62; Police 03.21.34.86.00; Ⓗ 03.21.46.33.33; Brit Consul 03.21.96.33.76.

FACILITIES Ⓥ Berth/raft at 'A' pontoon, 1st to stbd, or on fingers S side of B pontoon. **Marina** ☎ 03.21.34.55.23. 250 + 30 Ⓥ €2·36. D&P, Slip, CH, C (9 ton). www.calais-port.com calais-marina@calais. cci.fr **YC** ☎ 03.21.97.02.34, Bar.
Town ▣, ⚔, SM, CH, ▦, Gaz, R, Bar, ✉, Ⓑ, ⇌, ✈, ferries.

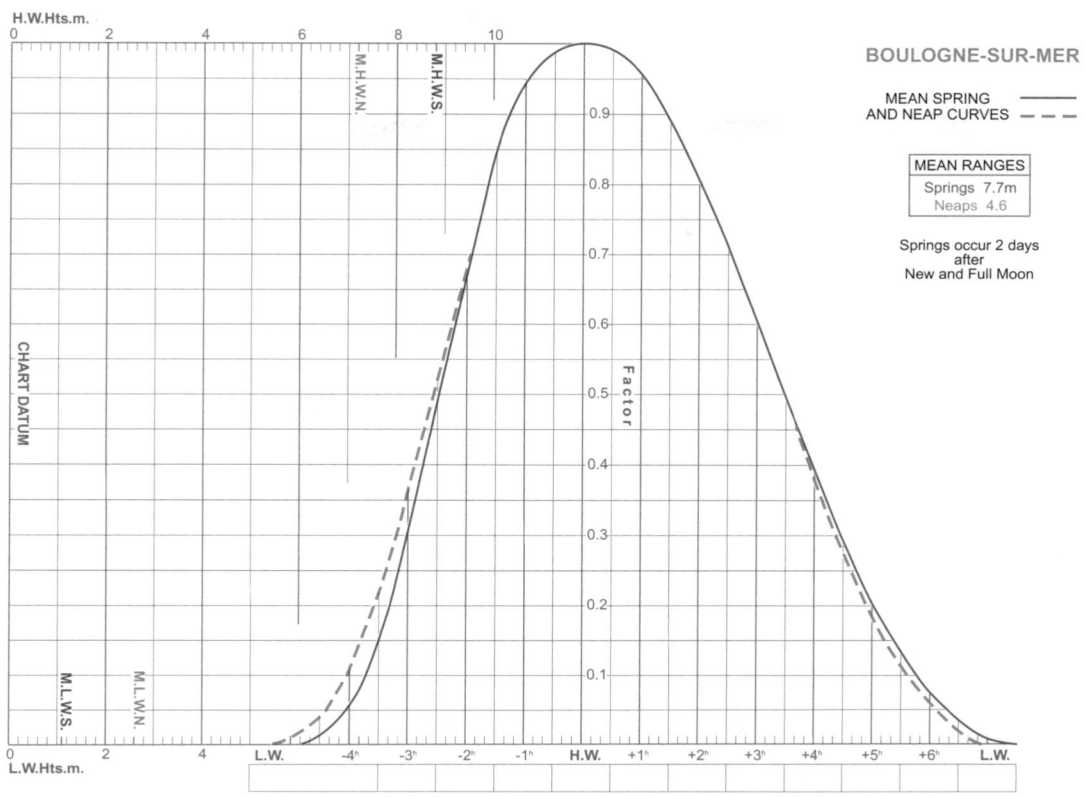

BOULOGNE-SUR-MER

MEAN SPRING ———
AND NEAP CURVES - - -

MEAN RANGES
Springs 7.7m
Neaps 4.6

Springs occur 2 days
after
New and Full Moon

TIME ZONE -0100
Subtract 1 hour for UT
For French Summer Time add
ONE hour in **non-shaded areas**

BOULOGNE-SUR-MER LAT 50°44'N LONG 1°35'E
TIMES AND HEIGHTS OF HIGH AND LOW WATERS

Dates in red are SPRINGS
Dates in blue are NEAPS

YEAR 2010

JANUARY

Day	Time	m	Time	m	Time	m	Time	m
1 F	0700	1.4	1157	8.9	1931	1.1		
16 SA	0030	8.3	0742	1.7	1242	8.4	2001	1.5
2 SA	0029	8.9	0751	1.2	1246	9.1	2022	1.0
17 SU	0103	8.4	0817	1.6	1315	8.5	2035	1.5
3 SU	0118	9.0	0841	1.1	1335	9.1	2112	1.0
18 M	0134	8.5	0847	1.6	1346	8.5	2104	1.5
4 M	0206	9.0	0929	1.1	1424	9.0	2158	1.1
19 TU	0203	8.4	0915	1.7	1416	8.4	2132	1.6
5 TU	0253	8.8	1015	1.3	1512	8.7	2242	1.3
20 W	0233	8.3	0943	1.7	1446	8.2	2200	1.7
6 W	0340	8.6	1100	1.5	1601	8.4	2325	1.7
21 TH	0304	8.2	1012	1.9	1517	8.0	2230	1.9
7 TH	0428	8.3	1147	1.8	1653	8.0		
22 F	0335	8.0	1045	2.1	1552	7.8	2304	2.2
8 F	0012	2.1	0522	7.9	1239	2.2	1752	7.6
23 SA	0413	7.7	1125	2.3	1636	7.5	2348	2.5
9 SA	0106	2.5	0625	7.5	1340	2.5	1903	7.2
24 SU	0505	7.4	1217	2.6	1739	7.1		
10 SU	0212	2.8	0739	7.3	1453	2.7	2020	7.1
25 M	0046	2.7	0613	7.2	1326	2.8	1855	7.0
11 M	0327	2.8	0854	7.3	1606	2.6	2130	7.3
26 TU	0202	2.8	0734	7.2	1449	2.7	2021	7.1
12 TU	0437	2.6	0956	7.6	1708	2.3	2227	7.6
27 W	0330	2.6	0856	7.5	1615	2.3	2137	7.6
13 W	0534	2.3	1047	7.8	1759	2.0	2314	7.9
28 TH	0448	2.1	1002	8.0	1725	1.7	2237	8.1
14 TH	0621	2.1	1130	8.1	1843	1.8	2354	8.1
29 F	0552	1.6	1057	8.5	1826	1.3	2329	8.6
15 F	0703	1.8	1209	8.3	1924	1.6		
30 SA	0650	1.2	1147	8.9	1923	0.9		
31 SU	0017	9.0	0745	1.0	1236	9.2	2016	0.7

FEBRUARY

Day	Time	m	Time	m	Time	m	Time	m
1 M	0105	9.2	0835	0.8	1323	9.3	2103	0.7
16 TU	0110	8.6	0827	1.3	1322	8.6	2043	1.2
2 TU	0151	9.2	0920	0.8	1409	9.2	2144	0.8
17 W	0138	8.6	0854	1.3	1350	8.6	2109	1.3
3 W	0234	9.1	1000	0.9	1451	9.0	2221	1.0
18 TH	0206	8.6	0920	1.4	1418	8.5	2135	1.4
4 TH	0314	8.8	1036	1.2	1533	8.6	2256	1.5
19 F	0232	8.5	0947	1.5	1445	8.3	2201	1.6
5 F	0355	8.4	1114	1.7	1617	8.1	2333	2.0
20 SA	0259	8.2	1016	1.7	1514	8.0	2231	1.9
6 SA	0441	7.9	1157	2.2	1709	7.5		
21 SU	0331	8.0	1051	2.1	1554	7.6	2311	2.3
7 SU	0019	2.5	0539	7.3	1253	2.7	1819	6.9
22 M	0419	7.6	1140	2.4	1655	7.2		
8 M	0122	3.0	0658	6.9	1408	3.0	1951	6.6
23 TU	0008	2.7	0530	7.1	1248	2.7	1821	6.8
9 TU	0249	3.2	0832	6.8	1537	3.0	2115	6.8
24 W	0127	2.9	0705	6.9	1417	2.8	2004	6.9
10 W	0417	2.9	0943	7.1	1652	2.6	2216	7.3
25 TH	0304	2.7	0842	7.3	1555	2.3	2127	7.5
11 TH	0522	2.5	1036	7.6	1748	2.1	2301	7.7
26 F	0431	2.2	0951	7.9	1710	1.7	2225	8.1
12 F	0611	2.0	1117	8.0	1833	1.8	2338	8.1
27 SA	0538	1.6	1045	8.5	1813	1.2	2315	8.7
13 SA	0652	1.7	1152	8.3	1911	1.5		
28 SU	0638	1.1	1134	8.9	1911	0.8		
14 SU	0011	8.4	0727	1.5	1226	8.5	1945	1.3
15 M	0041	8.5	0759	1.4	1253	8.6	2016	1.3

MARCH

Day	Time	m	Time	m	Time	m	Time	m
1 M	0001	9.0	0733	0.8	1220	9.2	2002	0.6
16 TU	0013	8.5	0732	1.3	1227	8.6	1947	1.2
2 TU	0045	9.2	0820	0.6	1305	9.3	2045	0.6
17 W	0041	8.6	0800	1.2	1256	8.7	2015	1.1
3 W	0128	9.3	0901	0.6	1347	9.2	2121	0.7
18 TH	0109	8.7	0829	1.2	1324	8.7	2043	1.2
4 TH	0208	9.1	0936	0.8	1426	9.0	2153	1.0
19 F	0137	8.7	0857	1.2	1354	8.6	2110	1.3
5 F	0245	8.9	1008	1.2	1504	8.6	2223	1.4
20 SA	0205	8.6	0926	1.3	1422	8.4	2138	1.5
6 SA	0323	8.4	1041	1.6	1544	8.0	2256	2.0
21 SU	0234	8.3	0955	1.6	1454	8.1	2209	1.8
7 SU	0405	7.9	1119	2.2	1631	7.4	2338	2.6
22 M	0309	8.0	1032	1.9	1536	7.7	2251	2.2
8 M	0459	7.2	1209	2.8	1739	6.7		
23 TU	0400	7.6	1121	2.3	1640	7.2	2350	2.6
9 TU	0038	3.2	0621	6.6	1323	3.2	1919	6.4
24 W	0514	7.1	1230	2.6	1809	6.8		
10 W	0210	3.4	0806	6.5	1503	3.2	2051	6.6
25 TH	0110	2.8	0653	6.9	1400	2.7	1955	7.0
11 TH	0350	3.1	0921	6.9	1625	2.7	2152	7.1
26 F	0247	2.6	0828	7.3	1538	2.3	2112	7.5
12 F	0458	2.5	1013	7.4	1722	2.2	2236	7.6
27 SA	0413	2.1	0934	7.9	1652	1.7	2209	8.2
13 SA	0546	2.0	1052	7.9	1807	1.8	2311	8.1
28 SU	0520	1.5	1028	8.4	1755	1.2	2258	8.7
14 SU	0626	1.7	1127	8.2	1845	1.5	2344	8.4
29 M	0619	1.1	1115	8.8	1850	0.9	2340	9.0
15 M	0701	1.5	1200	8.5	1918	1.3		
30 TU	0712	0.8	1200	9.1	1938	0.8		
31 W	0021	9.1	0757	0.7	1242	9.1	2018	0.8

APRIL

Day	Time	m	Time	m	Time	m	Time	m
1 TH	0102	9.1	0835	0.8	1323	9.0	2052	0.9
16 F	0040	8.6	0803	1.2	1300	8.6	2018	1.2
2 F	0141	9.0	0909	0.9	1402	8.8	2123	1.1
17 SA	0112	8.7	0836	1.2	1334	8.5	2050	1.3
3 SA	0218	8.7	0940	1.2	1439	8.4	2153	1.5
18 SU	0146	8.6	0910	1.3	1411	8.4	2123	1.5
4 SU	0256	8.3	1012	1.7	1519	7.9	2226	2.0
19 M	0223	8.4	0945	1.5	1451	8.1	2200	1.8
5 M	0337	7.8	1048	2.2	1604	7.3	2306	2.6
20 TU	0307	8.0	1026	1.8	1540	7.7	2247	2.1
6 TU	0428	7.1	1135	2.7	1705	6.7		
21 W	0402	7.6	1119	2.2	1642	7.3	2348	2.4
7 W	0003	3.1	0543	6.6	1242	3.1	1836	6.4
22 TH	0513	7.3	1226	2.4	1803	7.1		
8 TH	0127	3.3	0723	6.4	1414	3.2	2006	6.5
23 F	0104	2.6	0641	7.1	1349	2.4	1936	7.2
9 F	0301	3.1	0838	6.7	1536	2.8	2108	7.0
24 SA	0231	2.4	0806	7.4	1516	2.1	2048	7.7
10 SA	0409	2.6	0932	7.2	1635	2.3	2154	7.5
25 SU	0349	1.9	0911	7.9	1627	1.7	2143	8.2
11 SU	0500	2.1	1014	7.7	1722	1.9	2233	7.9
26 M	0455	1.5	1005	8.3	1728	1.3	2232	8.5
12 M	0543	1.8	1052	8.0	1803	1.6	2308	8.2
27 TU	0553	1.2	1053	8.6	1821	1.2	2317	8.7
13 TU	0621	1.6	1125	8.3	1839	1.4	2340	8.4
28 W	0645	1.1	1138	8.7	1907	1.1	2356	8.8
14 W	0656	1.4	1157	8.4	1913	1.3		
29 TH	0729	1.0	1221	8.7	1947	1.1		
15 TH	0010	8.6	0730	1.3	1228	8.5	1945	1.2
30 F	0038	8.8	0808	1.0	1302	8.7	2023	1.2

Chart Datum is 4·39 metres below IGN Datum. HAT is 9·4 metres above Chart Datum; see 4.5.

BOULOGNE-SUR-MER LAT 50°44'N LONG 1°35'E

TIMES AND HEIGHTS OF HIGH AND LOW WATERS

TIME ZONE -0100
Subtract 1 hour for UT
For French Summer Time add
ONE hour in non-shaded areas

Dates in red are SPRINGS
Dates in blue are NEAPS

YEAR 2010

N France

MAY

Time	m	Time	m
1 0118 / 0843 / SA 1342 / 2057	8.7 / 1.1 / 8.5 / 1.4	**16** 0053 / 0821 / SU 1321 / 2036	8.6 / 1.2 / 8.5 / 1.3
2 0158 / 0917 / SU 1421 / 2130	8.5 / 1.4 / 8.3 / 1.7	**17** 0135 / 0901 / M 1405 / 2117	8.6 / 1.2 / 8.5 / 1.4
3 0237 / 0950 / M 1501 / 2204	8.2 / 1.7 / 7.9 / 2.0	**18** 0220 / 0943 / TU 1451 / 2200	8.5 / 1.4 / 8.3 / 1.6
4 0317 / 1025 / TU 1543 / 2244	7.7 / 2.1 / 7.5 / 2.5	**19** 0308 / 1029 / W 1542 / 2250	8.2 / 1.6 / 8.0 / 1.9
5 0404 / 1108 / W 1634 / 2334	7.3 / 2.5 / 7.0 / 2.8	**20** 0403 / 1121 / TH 1640 / 2348	7.9 / 1.8 / 7.7 / 2.1
6 0502 / 1204 / TH 1741 / ☽	6.8 / 2.8 / 6.7	**21** 0506 / 1223 / F 1748 / ☾	7.6 / 2.1 / 7.5
7 0039 / 0618 / F 1316 / 1859	3.0 / 6.6 / 3.0 / 6.7	**22** 0056 / 0620 / SA 1334 / 1904	2.2 / 7.5 / 2.1 / 7.5
8 0155 / 0735 / SA 1430 / 2007	3.0 / 6.7 / 2.8 / 6.9	**23** 0209 / 0735 / SU 1447 / 2013	2.1 / 7.6 / 2.0 / 7.7
9 0304 / 0837 / SU 1533 / 2101	2.7 / 7.0 / 2.5 / 7.3	**24** 0321 / 0841 / M 1556 / 2114	1.9 / 7.8 / 1.8 / 8.0
10 0401 / 0926 / M 1626 / 2146	2.4 / 7.4 / 2.2 / 7.7	**25** 0426 / 0940 / TU 1657 / 2207	1.7 / 8.0 / 1.7 / 8.2
11 0450 / 1008 / TU 1713 / 2226	2.1 / 7.7 / 1.9 / 8.0	**26** 0525 / 1032 / W 1751 / 2256	1.6 / 8.2 / 1.6 / 8.4
12 0535 / 1047 / W 1756 / 2303	1.8 / 8.0 / 1.7 / 8.2	**27** 0617 / 1124 / TH 1838 / 2340	1.4 / 8.3 / 1.5 / 8.5
13 0618 / 1125 / TH 1837 / 2338	1.6 / 8.2 / 1.5 / 8.4	**28** 0702 / 1205 / F 1920 / ○	1.4 / 8.4 / 1.4
14 0700 / 1201 / F 1917 / ●	1.4 / 8.4 / 1.4	**29** 0021 / 0743 / SA 1247 / 2000	8.5 / 1.3 / 8.4 / 1.4
15 0014 / 0740 / SA 1240 / 1957	8.5 / 1.3 / 8.5 / 1.3	**30** 0102 / 0822 / SU 1328 / 2038	8.5 / 1.3 / 8.3 / 1.5
		31 0143 / 0859 / M 1407 / 2114	8.3 / 1.4 / 8.2 / 1.7

JUNE

Time	m	Time	m
1 0221 / 0934 / TU 1445 / 2149	8.1 / 1.7 / 8.0 / 1.9	**16** 0215 / 0944 / W 1447 / 2202	8.7 / 1.1 / 8.6 / 1.3
2 0300 / 1008 / W 1522 / 2225	7.9 / 1.9 / 7.7 / 2.2	**17** 0304 / 1031 / TH 1536 / 2250	8.5 / 1.2 / 8.4 / 1.4
3 0339 / 1045 / TH 1603 / 2305	7.6 / 2.2 / 7.4 / 2.4	**18** 0355 / 1119 / F 1627 / 2342	8.3 / 1.5 / 8.2 / 1.6
4 0424 / 1129 / F 1651 / ☽ 2354	7.3 / 2.4 / 7.2 / 2.6	**19** 0450 / 1211 / SA 1723 / ☾	8.0 / 1.7 / 7.9
5 0516 / 1221 / SA 1747	7.0 / 2.6 / 7.0	**20** 0038 / 0551 / SU 1309 / 1827	1.8 / 7.8 / 2.0 / 7.7
6 0050 / 0616 / SU 1320 / 1851	2.7 / 6.9 / 2.7 / 7.0	**21** 0141 / 0659 / M 1414 / 1936	2.0 / 7.6 / 2.1 / 7.6
7 0152 / 0721 / M 1423 / 1954	2.7 / 6.9 / 2.6 / 7.1	**22** 0249 / 0811 / TU 1523 / 2046	2.1 / 7.5 / 2.2 / 7.7
8 0255 / 0823 / TU 1525 / 2051	2.6 / 7.1 / 2.4 / 7.4	**23** 0357 / 0918 / W 1628 / 2147	2.0 / 7.6 / 2.1 / 7.8
9 0355 / 0919 / W 1623 / 2142	2.3 / 7.4 / 2.2 / 7.7	**24** 0500 / 1018 / TH 1726 / 2240	1.9 / 7.7 / 1.9 / 8.0
10 0452 / 1009 / TH 1717 / 2228	2.0 / 7.7 / 1.9 / 7.9	**25** 0554 / 1109 / F 1816 / 2328	1.8 / 7.9 / 1.8 / 8.1
11 0544 / 1056 / F 1807 / 2312	1.8 / 8.0 / 1.7 / 8.2	**26** 0642 / 1155 / SA 1902 / ○	1.6 / 8.1 / 1.7
12 0635 / 1141 / SA 1855 / ● 2356	1.5 / 8.2 / 1.5 / 8.5	**27** 0012 / 0726 / SU 1236 / 1944	8.3 / 1.5 / 8.2 / 1.6
13 0723 / 1226 / SU 1942	1.3 / 8.5 / 1.3	**28** 0050 / 0807 / M 1314 / 2024	8.3 / 1.4 / 8.3 / 1.5
14 0041 / 0811 / M 1312 / 2029	8.6 / 1.1 / 8.6 / 1.2	**29** 0128 / 0845 / TU 1351 / 2100	8.3 / 1.4 / 8.3 / 1.6
15 0127 / 0858 / TU 1359 / 2115	8.7 / 1.1 / 8.6 / 1.2	**30** 0204 / 0919 / W 1425 / 2133	8.2 / 1.5 / 8.2 / 1.7

JULY

Time	m	Time	m
1 0238 / 0950 / TH 1457 / 2203	8.1 / 1.7 / 8.1 / 1.8	**16** 0252 / 1022 / F 1520 / 2240	8.8 / 0.9 / 8.7 / 1.1
2 0311 / 1020 / F 1531 / 2235	7.9 / 1.8 / 7.9 / 2.0	**17** 0338 / 1104 / SA 1604 / 2324	8.6 / 1.2 / 8.5 / 1.4
3 0347 / 1054 / SA 1608 / 2312	7.7 / 2.0 / 7.7 / 2.2	**18** 0426 / 1148 / SU 1653 / ☽	8.3 / 1.6 / 8.2
4 0427 / 1133 / SU 1651 / ☾ 2356	7.5 / 2.3 / 7.4 / 2.4	**19** 0012 / 0519 / M 1238 / 1750	1.7 / 7.8 / 2.0 / 7.8
5 0515 / 1221 / M 1744	7.2 / 2.5 / 7.2	**20** 0109 / 0624 / TU 1339 / 1900	2.1 / 7.4 / 2.4 / 7.4
6 0050 / 0612 / TU 1319 / 1845	2.6 / 7.0 / 2.7 / 7.1	**21** 0217 / 0743 / W 1452 / 2023	2.4 / 7.1 / 2.6 / 7.3
7 0153 / 0719 / W 1427 / 1954	2.7 / 6.9 / 2.7 / 7.1	**22** 0332 / 0903 / TH 1607 / 2134	2.4 / 7.2 / 2.5 / 7.4
8 0304 / 0831 / TH 1539 / 2102	2.6 / 7.1 / 2.5 / 7.3	**23** 0441 / 1009 / F 1711 / 2232	2.2 / 7.4 / 2.2 / 7.7
9 0415 / 0937 / F 1646 / 2201	2.3 / 7.4 / 2.1 / 7.7	**24** 0540 / 1102 / SA 1805 / 2319	2.0 / 7.8 / 2.0 / 8.0
10 0518 / 1035 / SA 1744 / 2253	1.9 / 7.8 / 1.8 / 8.1	**25** 0630 / 1145 / SU 1851 / 2359	1.8 / 8.1 / 1.7 / 8.2
11 0616 / 1125 / SU 1839 / ● 2342	1.5 / 8.2 / 1.4 / 8.5	**26** 0713 / 1222 / M 1931 / ○	1.6 / 8.3 / 1.5
12 0711 / 1213 / M 1932	1.2 / 8.6 / 1.2	**27** 0037 / 0753 / TU 1256 / 2009	8.4 / 1.4 / 8.4 / 1.4
13 0029 / 0803 / TU 1301 / 2023	8.8 / 1.0 / 8.8 / 1.0	**28** 0109 / 0828 / W 1329 / 2042	8.4 / 1.4 / 8.4 / 1.4
14 0117 / 0853 / W 1349 / 2112	8.9 / 0.8 / 8.9 / 0.9	**29** 0141 / 0859 / TH 1359 / 2110	8.4 / 1.4 / 8.4 / 1.5
15 0205 / 0940 / TH 1435 / 2157	9.0 / 0.8 / 8.9 / 0.9	**30** 0211 / 0926 / F 1427 / 2137	8.4 / 1.5 / 8.3 / 1.6
		31 0240 / 0952 / SA 1457 / 2204	8.2 / 1.6 / 8.2 / 1.7

AUGUST

Time	m	Time	m
1 0310 / 1020 / SU 1528 / 2235	8.0 / 1.8 / 8.0 / 2.0	**16** 0357 / 1118 / M 1621 / ☽ 2341	8.3 / 1.7 / 8.2 / 1.9
2 0343 / 1051 / M 1602 / 2311	7.7 / 2.1 / 7.7 / 2.2	**17** 0447 / 1203 / TU 1715	7.7 / 2.2 / 7.6
3 0423 / 1131 / TU 1648 / ☾ 2358	7.4 / 2.4 / 7.4 / 2.5	**18** 0035 / 0551 / W 1303 / 1829	2.4 / 7.2 / 2.8 / 7.1
4 0517 / 1224 / W 1750	7.1 / 2.7 / 7.1	**19** 0145 / 0720 / TH 1425 / 2005	2.8 / 6.8 / 3.0 / 6.9
5 0101 / 0628 / TH 1336 / 1907	2.8 / 6.8 / 2.9 / 6.9	**20** 0310 / 0851 / F 1550 / 2124	2.8 / 6.9 / 2.8 / 7.2
6 0220 / 0754 / F 1502 / 2032	2.8 / 6.8 / 2.7 / 7.1	**21** 0427 / 1000 / SA 1659 / 2222	2.5 / 7.3 / 2.4 / 7.6
7 0346 / 0917 / SA 1622 / 2142	2.5 / 7.3 / 2.3 / 7.6	**22** 0528 / 1050 / SU 1752 / 2305	2.1 / 7.8 / 1.9 / 8.0
8 0458 / 1018 / SU 1726 / 2238	1.9 / 7.8 / 1.8 / 8.2	**23** 0616 / 1128 / M 1835 / 2341	1.7 / 8.1 / 1.7 / 8.3
9 0600 / 1109 / M 1824 / 2327	1.4 / 8.3 / 1.3 / 8.6	**24** 0656 / 1201 / TU 1913 / ○	1.5 / 8.4 / 1.5
10 0657 / 1157 / TU 1920 / ●	1.1 / 8.8 / 1.0	**25** 0015 / 0731 / W 1232 / 1946	8.5 / 1.4 / 8.5 / 1.4
11 0015 / 0752 / W 1244 / 2012	9.0 / 0.8 / 9.0 / 0.8	**26** 0044 / 0803 / TH 1301 / 2016	8.6 / 1.3 / 8.6 / 1.4
12 0102 / 0841 / TH 1331 / 2059	9.2 / 0.7 / 9.1 / 0.7	**27** 0113 / 0831 / F 1327 / 2042	8.6 / 1.3 / 8.6 / 1.4
13 0148 / 0925 / F 1414 / 2141	9.2 / 0.7 / 9.1 / 0.8	**28** 0140 / 0857 / SA 1354 / 2108	8.5 / 1.4 / 8.5 / 1.5
14 0232 / 1003 / SA 1455 / 2219	9.0 / 0.8 / 8.9 / 1.0	**29** 0208 / 0921 / SU 1422 / 2134	8.3 / 1.5 / 8.4 / 1.6
15 0314 / 1040 / SU 1536 / 2258	8.7 / 1.2 / 8.6 / 1.4	**30** 0235 / 0947 / M 1448 / 2202	8.2 / 1.7 / 8.3 / 1.8
		31 0303 / 1015 / TU 1517 / 2235	7.9 / 2.0 / 7.9 / 2.2

Chart Datum is 4·39 metres below IGN Datum. HAT is 9·4 metres above Chart Datum; see 4.5.

TIME ZONE -0100
Subtract 1 hour for UT
For French Summer Time add
ONE hour in **non-shaded areas**

BOULOGNE-SUR-MER LAT 50°44'N LONG 1°35'E
TIMES AND HEIGHTS OF HIGH AND LOW WATERS

Dates in red are **SPRINGS**
Dates in blue are **NEAPS**

YEAR 2010

SEPTEMBER

Time	m		Time	m
1 0337	7.5	**16**	0000	2.7
1051	2.4		0521	7.0
W 1559	7.5	TH 1229	3.0
☽ 2318	2.5		1801	6.9
2 0432	7.1	**17**	0112	3.1
1144	2.8		0653	6.6
TH 1706	7.1	F 1356	3.3
			1942	6.7
3 0021	2.8	**18**	0244	3.1
0553	6.8		0828	6.8
F 1259	3.0	SA 1528	3.0
1835	6.8		2102	7.0
4 0146	2.9	**19**	0403	2.7
0730	6.8		0935	7.2
SA 1433	2.9	SU 1635	2.5
2012	7.1		2157	7.5
5 0323	2.6	**20**	0501	2.2
0901	7.3		1021	7.7
SU 1601	2.3	M 1724	2.0
2124	7.7		2238	8.0
6 0439	1.9	**21**	0546	1.8
1000	7.9		1057	8.2
M 1707	1.7	TU 1806	1.7
2220	8.3		2313	8.3
7 0541	1.4	**22**	0625	1.6
1049	8.5		1130	8.4
TU 1806	1.2	W 1842	1.5
2308	8.8		2346	8.5
8 0639	1.0	**23**	0700	1.4
1136	9.0		1200	8.6
W 1902	0.9	TH 1915	1.4
● 2354	9.1	○	
9 0732	0.7	**24**	0013	8.6
1220	9.2		0731	1.4
TH 1953	0.7	F 1228	8.6
			1944	1.4
10 0040	9.3	**25**	0042	8.6
0819	0.7		0759	1.4
F 1305	9.3	SA 1254	8.7
2038	0.7		2012	1.4
11 0124	9.3	**26**	0109	8.6
0900	0.8		0825	1.4
SA 1347	9.2	SU 1321	8.6
2117	0.8		2040	1.5
12 0206	9.1	**27**	0137	8.5
0936	1.0		0852	1.6
SU 1426	9.0	M 1349	8.5
2153	1.1		2108	1.6
13 0247	8.7	**28**	0206	8.3
1009	1.4		0919	1.8
M 1506	8.6	TU 1417	8.3
2228	1.5		2137	1.8
14 0329	8.2	**29**	0236	8.0
1044	1.9		0949	2.0
TU 1550	8.1	W 1449	8.0
2308	2.1		2211	2.1
15 0417	7.6	**30**	0314	7.6
1128	2.5		1027	2.4
W 1645	7.5	TH 1535	7.6
☽			2256	2.5

OCTOBER

Time	m		Time	m
1 0412	7.2	**16**	0033	3.2
1121	2.8		0613	6.7
F 1645	7.1	SA 1317	3.3
☽ 2359	2.8		1900	6.7
2 0534	6.9	**17**	0200	3.2
1237	3.0		0742	6.7
SA 1815	6.9	SU 1444	3.1
			2017	6.9
3 0124	2.9	**18**	0318	2.9
0711	6.9		0848	7.1
SU 1411	2.8	M 1550	2.7
1951	7.2		2113	7.3
4 0301	2.5	**19**	0416	2.4
0838	7.4		0937	7.6
M 1539	2.3	TU 1641	2.2
2102	7.8		2157	7.8
5 0418	1.9	**20**	0503	2.0
0937	8.1		1016	8.0
TU 1645	1.7	W 1724	1.9
2157	8.4		2235	8.1
6 0519	1.4	**21**	0544	1.8
1025	8.6		1052	8.3
W 1743	1.2	TH 1803	1.7
2245	8.9		2311	8.4
7 0615	1.0	**22**	0621	1.6
1110	9.0		1124	8.5
TH 1838	1.0	F 1838	1.6
● 2331	9.1		2340	8.5
8 0706	0.9	**23**	0654	1.6
1153	9.2		1153	8.6
F 1927	0.9	SA 1911	1.5
		○	
9 0015	9.2	**24**	0011	8.6
0751	0.9		0726	1.5
SA 1236	9.3	SU 1222	8.7
2011	0.9		1943	1.5
10 0059	9.2	**25**	0041	8.6
0830	1.0		0757	1.5
SU 1318	9.2	M 1252	8.7
2049	1.0		2015	1.5
11 0141	8.9	**26**	0113	8.5
0905	1.2		0829	1.6
M 1359	8.9	TU 1325	8.6
2125	1.3		2048	1.6
12 0222	8.6	**27**	0149	8.4
0939	1.6		0901	1.8
TU 1440	8.5	W 1401	8.4
2200	1.7		2122	1.8
13 0304	8.1	**28**	0226	8.1
1015	2.1		0936	2.0
W 1524	8.0	TH 1441	8.1
2238	2.2		2200	2.1
14 0352	7.6	**29**	0311	7.8
1057	2.6		1018	2.3
TH 1617	7.4	F 1531	7.7
☽ 2326	2.8		2248	2.4
15 0451	7.0	**30**	0408	7.4
1155	3.1		1114	2.6
F 1728	6.9	SA 1637	7.4
		☽ 2350	2.6
		31	0521	7.2
			1225	2.8
		SU 1757	7.2

NOVEMBER

Time	m		Time	m
1 0107	2.7	**16**	0210	3.0
0647	7.2		0743	7.0
M 1349	2.6	TU 1446	2.9
1922	7.4		2016	7.1
2 0234	2.4	**17**	0315	2.8
0807	7.6		0840	7.3
TU 1512	2.2	W 1545	2.6
2033	7.9		2107	7.4
3 0350	2.0	**18**	0409	2.4
0906	8.1		0927	7.7
W 1619	1.7	TH 1635	2.3
2130	8.4		2152	7.8
4 0452	1.6	**19**	0457	2.2
0957	8.6		1009	8.0
TH 1718	1.4	F 1720	2.0
2220	8.7		2230	8.0
5 0547	1.3	**20**	0540	1.9
1044	8.9		1046	8.3
F 1812	1.2	SA 1802	1.8
2308	8.9		2308	8.3
6 0637	1.2	**21**	0619	1.8
1128	9.1		1121	8.5
SA 1900	1.1	SU 1841	1.7
● 2353	9.0	○ 2344	8.4
7 0722	1.2	**22**	0657	1.7
1212	9.1		1156	8.6
SU 1944	1.1	M 1919	1.6
8 0038	8.9	**23**	0019	8.5
0802	1.3		0735	1.6
M 1256	9.0	TU 1232	8.7
2023	1.2		1958	1.5
9 0121	8.8	**24**	0058	8.6
0839	1.5		0813	1.6
TU 1338	8.8	W 1311	8.7
2101	1.5		2037	1.5
10 0203	8.5	**25**	0139	8.5
0916	1.8		0852	1.7
W 1420	8.4	TH 1353	8.6
2137	1.8		2117	1.6
11 0245	8.1	**26**	0222	8.4
0952	2.1		0933	1.8
TH 1503	8.0	F 1437	8.4
2214	2.2		2200	1.8
12 0329	7.7	**27**	0309	8.1
1032	2.6		1018	2.0
F 1550	7.5	SA 1527	8.1
2256	2.6		2247	2.0
13 0418	7.3	**28**	0402	7.9
1121	2.9		1111	2.3
SA 1647	7.1	SU 1626	7.8
☽ 2350	3.0	☽ 2343	2.3
14 0520	7.0	**29**	0504	7.7
1223	3.2		1213	2.4
SU 1757	6.8	M 1734	7.6
15 0057	3.1	**30**	0048	2.4
0634	6.8		0615	7.6
M 1337	3.2	TU 1324	2.4
1912	6.8		1848	7.6

DECEMBER

Time	m		Time	m
1 0202	2.4	**16**	0156	3.0
0728	7.7		0728	7.1
W 1439	2.2	TH 1432	2.9
2000	7.8		2001	7.0
2 0317	2.2	**17**	0302	2.9
0834	8.0		0830	7.3
TH 1551	2.0	F 1537	2.7
2103	8.1		2102	7.3
3 0423	1.9	**18**	0405	2.6
0932	8.3		0925	7.6
F 1653	1.7	SA 1636	2.4
2200	8.3		2154	7.6
4 0521	1.7	**19**	0501	2.3
1025	8.5		1013	7.9
SA 1748	1.5	SU 1728	2.1
2252	8.5		2240	8.0
5 0612	1.6	**20**	0550	2.0
1112	8.7		1056	8.2
SU 1837	1.4	M 1816	1.8
● 2339	8.7		2323	8.3
6 0658	1.5	**21**	0636	1.7
1157	8.8		1137	8.5
M 1922	1.4	TU 1902	1.5
7 0024	8.6	**22**	0004	8.5
0740	1.5		0720	1.5
TU 1240	8.8	W 1218	8.7
2004	1.4		1947	1.4
8 0107	8.6	**23**	0046	8.7
0821	1.6		0804	1.4
W 1322	8.6	TH 1301	8.8
2043	1.5		2032	1.3
9 0148	8.5	**24**	0130	8.8
0859	1.7		0848	1.4
TH 1403	8.4	F 1345	8.9
2120	1.7		2116	1.3
10 0227	8.3	**25**	0214	8.7
0935	2.0		0932	1.4
F 1442	8.2	SA 1430	8.7
2155	2.0		2200	1.4
11 0304	8.0	**26**	0300	8.6
1010	2.2		1016	1.6
SA 1521	7.8	SU 1518	8.5
2230	2.3		2244	1.6
12 0343	7.7	**27**	0348	8.4
1048	2.5		1103	1.7
SU 1603	7.5	M 1609	8.3
2309	2.5		2331	1.8
13 0427	7.4	**28**	0440	8.1
1131	2.7		1155	2.0
M 1652	7.2	TU 1707	8.0
☽ 2356	2.8	☽	
14 0520	7.2	**29**	0024	2.1
1224	2.9		0540	7.9
TU 1750	7.0	W 1255	2.2
			1813	7.7
15 0052	2.9	**30**	0127	2.4
0622	7.0		0649	7.7
W 1325	3.0	TH 1405	2.4
1856	6.9		1927	7.5
		31	0240	2.5
			0803	7.7
		F 1522	2.3
			2041	7.6

Chart Datum is 4·39 metres below IGN Datum. HAT is 9·4 metres above Chart Datum; see 4.5.

⟫⟫ FREE monthly updates from **⟪⟪**
www.reedsalmanac.co.uk

9.17.10 BOULOGNE-SUR-MER

Pas de Calais 50°44'·58N 01°34'·10E ❀❀⚓⚓✿✿

CHARTS AC *1892, 2451*, 438; SHOM 6824, 7247, 7416,7323; Navi 1010, 1011; Imray C8, C31; Stanfords 1, 9, 20, 30.

TIDES Boulogne is a Standard Port (⟵) 0000 Dover; ML 4·9; Duration 0515.

SHELTER Good, except in strong NW'lies. Entry H24 at all tides and in most weather. Exposed ⚓ in N part of outer hbr; no ⚓ SW of pecked magenta line.

NAVIGATION WPT 50°44'·71N 01°33'·00E, 100°/0·71M to hbr ent (below Title). No navigational dangers, but keep W and S of the free-standing head of Digue Nord, as outer part of bkwtr covers at HW. After rounding Digue Carnot, head S for 325m to a white □ mark (often faded) on bkwtr, thence track 123° to inner ent; caution drying banks on either side. Obey IPTS; keep clear of ferries & FVs.

LIGHTS AND MARKS 'Approches Boulogne' SCM buoy is 295°/2·1M from Digue Carnot lt. Cap d'Alprech lt ho is 2·5M S of hbr ent. Monument is conspic 2M E of hbr ent. Cathedral dome is conspic, 0·62M E of marina. There are no ldg lts/marks.

IPTS are shown from SW jetty hd (FG ☆), and from Quai Gambetta, opposite ☆ 3FG ▽, visible from marina. A Y lt ● by top IPTS = dredger working, but does not prohibit movements.

R/T Control tower, and lock into Bassin Napoléon Ch 12 (H24). Marina Ch 09. Forecasts by CROSS Gris Nez Ch 79 at H+10 (078-1910LT).

TELEPHONE Control twr 03.21.10.35.47; ✆ 03.21.80.89.90; Aff Mar 03.21.30.53.23; CROSS 03.21.87.21.87; Météo 08.92.68.02.62; Auto 08.92.65.08.08; Maritime Police 03.21.30.87.09; Emergency 17; Ⓗ 03.21.99.33.33; Brit Consul 03.21.87.16.80.

FACILITIES Visitors berth in marina (2·7m) on W side of river. FVs berth opposite at Quai Gambetta. Beware turbulence when R Liane is sluicing; indicated at night by 2 Bu lts (hor) S of marina.

Marina www.portboulogne.com/plaisance ☎ 03.21.99.66.50. 114 inc 80 Ⓥ, €2·34 plus €0·20/head holiday tax. D HW ±3, WC (access card), Slip, C (20 ton), Ⓔ, ME, El, ⚒, M, Divers, Wi-Fi. YC Boulonnais ☎ 03.21.31.80.67, C, R, Bar.

Bassin Napoléon pontoons are for locals and long-stay Ⓥ (week or month; 12-25m LOA) by arrangement. Sanson lock (Ch 12) works HW–3¼ to HW+4½ with ent/exits approx every 35 mins, and freeflow HW –2 to +¼. Daily schedules from HM or website.

Town P (cans), 🛒, Gas, Gaz, SHOM, R, Bar, ✉, Ⓑ, ⇌. ✈ Le Touquet. Ferry to Dover.

9.17.11 ÉTAPLES

Pas de Calais 50°31'·00N 01°38'·00E ❀❀⚓⚓✿✿

CHARTS AC *2451*; SHOM 7416; Navi 1011; Imray C31; Stanfords 1.

TIDES –0010 Dover; ML 5·3; Duration 0520.

Standard Port DIEPPE (⟶)

Times				Height (metres)			
High Water		Low Water		MHWS	MHWN	MLWN	MLWS
0100	0600	0100	0700	9·3	7·4	2·5	0·8
1300	1800	1300	1900				
Differences LE TOUQUET (ÉTAPLES)							
+0005	+0015	+0030	+0030	+0·2	+0·3	+0·4	+0·4
BERCK							
+0005	+0015	+0030	+0030	+0·5	+0·5	+0·4	+0·4

SHELTER Good, except in strong W/NW'lies.

NAVIGATION WPT 50°32'·88N 01°32'·36E is on the boundary between W and G sectors of Camiers lt; 090°/0·7M to Mérida unlit WCM buoy (50°32'·88N 01°33'·47E), marking a drying wreck 2M

ÉTAPLES *continued*

NW of Le Touquet lt ho. Best app is at HW –1 to reach Étaples Marina at slack water. Estuary dries 1M offshore; do not attempt entry in even moderate SW/W winds, when seas break heavily a long way out. Careful identification of marks is essential.

The outer part of the buoyed chan constantly shifts, such that the chan ent may lie N or S of the ⊕. Nos 1 & 2 buoys (QG and QR) should be visible from the WPT. Bcn, Fl R 4s, 4ca SW of Camiers lt, marks NE end of covering training wall (also marked by posts).

LIGHTS AND MARKS See 9.17.4. Le Touquet is at the S end of 175m high hills, visible for 25M. Le Touquet lt ho, orange with brown band, is conspic; Camiers' R pylon is hard to see by day.

R/T Ch 09.

TELEPHONE Aff Mar Étaples 03.21.94.61.50; Auto 08.36.68.08.62; ⊖ 03.21.05.01.72; CROSS 03.21.87.21.87; Dr 03.21.05.14.42; Brit Consul 03.21.87.16.80.

FACILITIES **Marina** Access HW±2 to small marina (1·2m) close downriver of low bridge; beware up to 5kn current. Best to berth on first pontoon hammerhead near HW slack. ☎ 03.21.84.54.33. cn.canche@wanadoo.fr 182 + 18 Ⓥ, €2·04. C (8 ton); Quay BH (130 ton), Slip, CH, El, M, ME, ✕. YC ☎ 03.21.94.74.26, Bar, Slip.

Town Ⓑ, Bar, D, P, ✉, R, ⇌, 🛒. ✈ Le Touquet.

Le Touquet Drying moorings to stbd off Le Touquet YC. VHF Ch 09, 77. **Cercle Nautique du Touquet** ☎ 03.21.05.12.77, M, Slip, FW, R, Bar. **Services**: BY, C, CH, ME, ✕, SM. **Town** P, D, 🛒, Gaz, R, Bar, ✉, Ⓑ, ⇌, ✈.

9.17.12 ST VALÉRY-SUR-SOMME

Somme **50°11'·34N 01°38'·90E** ⊛⊛⚓⚓✿✿✿✿

CHARTS AC *2451*; SHOM 7416; Navi 1011; Imray C31; Stanfords 1

TIDES LE HOURDEL –0010 Dover; ML —.

Standard Port DIEPPE (➝)

Times				Height (metres)			
High Water		Low Water		MHWS	MHWN	MLWN	MLWS
0100	0600	0100	0700	9·3	7·4	2·5	0·8
1300	1800	1300	1900				
Differences ST VALÉRY-SUR-SOMME							
+0035	+0035	No data		+0·9	+0·7	No data	
LE HOURDEL							
+0020	+0020	No data		+0·8	+0·6	No data	
CAYEUX							
0000	+0005	+0015	+0010	+0·5	+0·6	+0·4	+0·4

SHELTER The 3 hbrs (Le Hourdel, Le Crotoy and St Valéry-sur-Somme) are well sheltered.

NAVIGATION WPT 50°14'·00N 01°28'·08E ('ATSO' SWM buoy, Mo (A) 12s). The whole estuary dries up to 3M seaward of Le Hourdel. It is open to the W and can be dangerous in onshore winds >F6. Silting is a major problem. The sands build up in ridges offshore, but inside Pte du Hourdel are mostly flat, except where R Somme and minor streams scour their way to the sea. If Dover tidal range >4·4m, there is enough water at HW ±1 for vessels <1·5m draft.

Leave 'ATSO' at HW St Valéry –2. then head SE twds R/W ltho on dunes near Cayeux-sur-Mer to beginning of buoyed chan (S1) Follow chan buoys S1 to S50 (some lit), in strict order (no corner-cutting!) to small unlit WCM BIFurcation buoy, E of Pte du Hourdel. Here fork stbd to St Valéry and its covering training wall with four light beacons; as chartlet & 9.17.4. Continue between the tree-lined promenade to stbd and a covering dyke marked by PHM bns. Bias your track towards the town side, but comply with any

buoys. At W lt bcn on head of Digue du Nord turn stbd past town quay into marina, dredged 2m. Enter St Valéry marina (max draft 2·0m) at HW ±1; usually met and given a berth on pontoons 4-6. If N-bound leave St Valéry HW–2 for a fair tide.

Abbeville Canal (max draft 2·0m) is navigable, by day only, to Abbeville. Lock 03.22.60.80.23; pre-call Amiens ☎ 06.74.83.60.69.

LIGHTS AND MARKS Cayeux-sur-Mer lt ho (W + R top, Fl R 5s) and Le Crotoy water twr are conspic. Pte du Hourdel lt ho is partly obscured by dunes until close to. See also 9.17.4.

R/T Ch 09 (St Valéry HW ±2; Le Crotoy YC Jul/Aug only).

TELEPHONE Aff Mar 03.21.30.87.19 (Boulogne); CROSS 03.21.87.21.87; ⊖ 03.22.24.04.75; Auto 08.92.68.08.80; Police 17 or 03.22.60.82.08; Dr 03.22.26.92.25; Brit Consul 03.21.87.16.80.

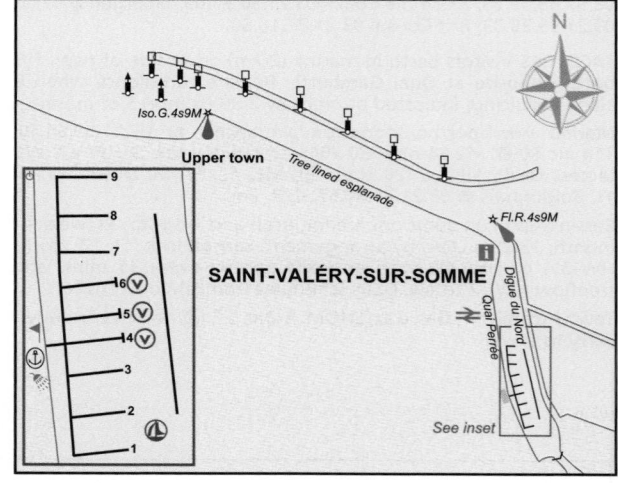

FACILITIES **Marina/YC Sport Nautique Valéricain** ☎ 03.22.60.24.80. snval@wanadoo.fr http://www.portsaintvalery.com/image balisage.htm for latest plan of appr buoys. Access HW ±2. 250 + 30 Ⓥ, AB €2·10. C (10 ton), Slip, ME, El, CH, Ⓔ, Ⓞ, Bar, Wi-Fi. **Town** P, D, CH, 🛒, Gaz, R, Bar, ✉, Ⓑ, ⇌ and ✈ (Abbeville). Ferry: See Dieppe, Boulogne or Calais.

ADJACENT HARBOURS

LE HOURDEL A basic FV hbr. Access HW±1½. After the lt ho, head SW via unmarked side chan to hug the end of shingle spit. Dry out on hard sand. Impossible to leave before HW –2.

LE CROTOY Somme **50°13'·07N 01°37'·99E** ⊛⊛⚓✿✿
From the BIF buoy follow the chan E, marked by buoys C1-C10. Enter hbr very close to FV stages (port-side). The badly silted marina can be entered by max draft 0·8m when tidal range at Dover >4·4m (approx Coeff 85). Secure at last FV stage and ask YC for berth on the two drying pontoons. Departure impossible before HW –2. **Marina** (280) ☎ 03.22.27.83.11 (office in YC bldg), C (6 ton), Slip; **YC Nautique de la Baie de Somme** ☎ 03.22.27.83.11, Bar. **Town** Ⓑ, Bar, D, P, ✉, R, ⇌, 🛒.

9.17.13 LE TRÉPORT

Seine Maritime 50°03'·89N 01°22'·20E ❄️⚓️♨♨☆☆☆

CHARTS AC *2451*, 1354; SHOM 7207, 7416, 7417; Navi 1011; Imray C31; Stanfords 1

TIDES –0025 Dover; ML 5·0; Duration 0530.
Standard Port DIEPPE (→)

Times				Height (metres)			
High Water		Low Water		MHWS	MHWN	MLWN	MLWS
0100	0600	0100	0700	9·3	7·4	2·5	0·8
1300	1800	1300	1900				
Differences LE TRÉPORT							
+0005	0000	+0007	+0007	+0·1	+0·1	0·0	+0·1

SHELTER Good in marina, E of FVs at S side of S Basin (3·7m).

NAVIGATION WPT 50°04'·27N 01°21'·90E, 146°/0·4M to ent. Coast dries to approx 300m off the pier hds. Shingle spit extends NW from E pier hd; keep well to the W. Entry difficult in strong on-shore winds which cause scend in Avant Port. Strong cross-current at entrance; 5kn speed limit. Ent chan and most of Avant Port dry; S chan is dredged 1·5m, but prone to silting; avoid grounding on the triangle between the two channels. Lock opens HW±4; yachts can wait against Quai Francois I with sufficient rise of tide. Berth, if possible, on smooth S wall of lock; vert wires rigged for warps. N wall is corrugated steel shuttering on which fenders can snag. Beware current when leaving.

LIGHTS AND MARKS Le Tréport lies between high chalk cliffs, with crucifix (floodlit) 101m above town and conspic church S of hbr. IPTS at the root of the E Jetty. There are 150° ldg marks, but they are hard to see and not strictly necessary.

Lock sigs shown from head of piled ent chan: 3 ● (vert) = enter; 3 ● (vert) = no entry.

R/T *Capitainerie Le Tréport* Ch 12 (HW ±4) for lock/marina.

TELEPHONE Port HM 06.87.70.30.90; Aff Mar 02.35.06.96.70; SNSM 02.35.86.30.27; Auto 06.70.63.43.40; CROSS 03.21.87.21.87; ⊖ 02.35.86.15.34; Police 02.35.86.12.11; Dr 02.35.86.16.23; Brit Consul 03.21.87.16.80.

FACILITIES Marina/lock ☎ 02.35.50.63.06. www.treport.cci.fr accueilcci@treport.cci.fr 110+15 Ⓥ, €2·13. M, ME, CH, El, Ⓔ, Gaz. **Port de Commerce** is an overflow; access HW –1½ to HW, half-price rates for yachts. C (10 ton). **YC de la Bresle** ☎ 02.35.50.17.60, Bar. **Town** P, D, 🍴, Gaz, R, Bar, ✉, Ⓑ, ⇌, ✈ Dieppe.

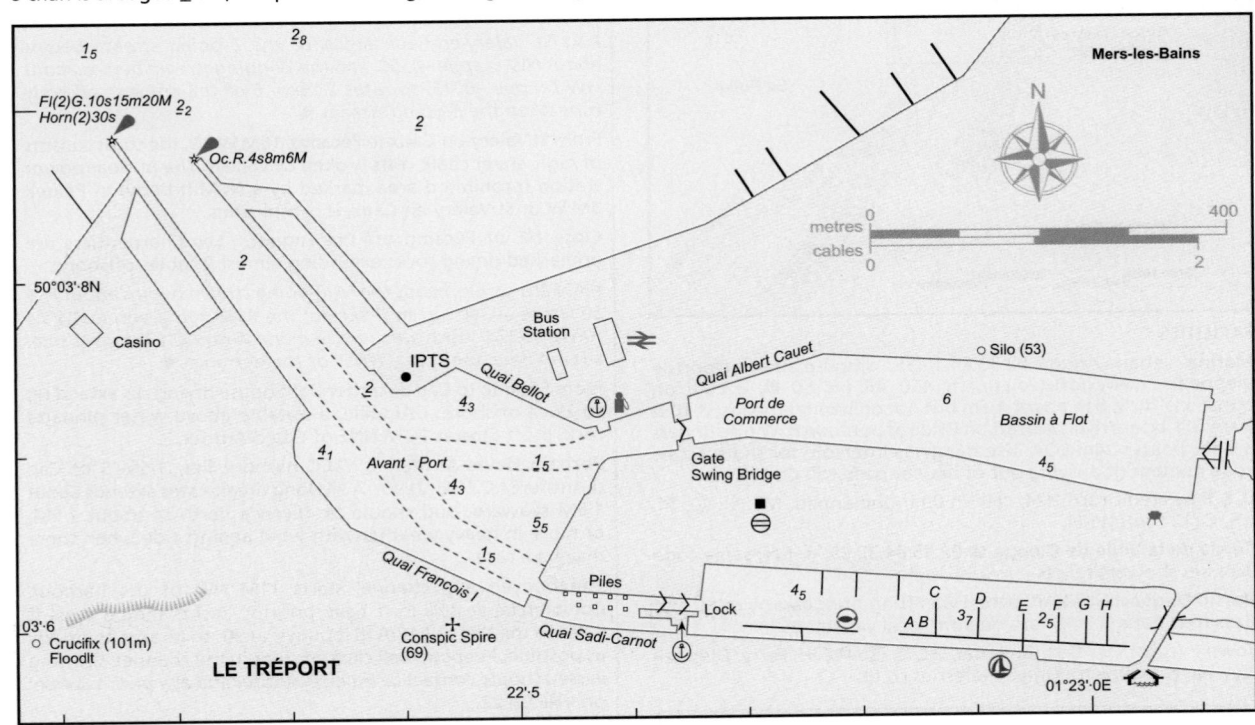

9.17.14 DIEPPE

Seine Maritime 49°56'·31N 01°05'·00E ❄️❄️❄️⚓️♨♨☆☆☆

CHARTS AC *2451*, 2148, 1355; SHOM 7417, 7317; Navi 1011, 1012; Imray C31; Stanfords 1

TIDES –0011 Dover; ML 4·9; Duration 0535; Standard Port (→).

SHELTER Very good. Access all tides, but ent exposed to NW-NE winds, which cause a heavy scend. A fixed wavebreak at the E end of the marina is effective. 3kn max speed in marina.

NAVIGATION WPT 49°56'·66N 01°04'·83E (off chartlet), 167°/4ca to W jetty head. Ent to hbr is simple, but beware strong stream across ent. Ent chan and Avant Port are dredged 4·5m. Be alert for ferry at the outer hbr, and small coasters or FVs in the narrow chan between outer hbr and marina. Due to restricted visibility, monitor Ch 12 during arr/dep. It is vital to comply precisely with IPTS (below), both entering and leaving. Anchoring is prohibited in an inverted triangular area 7ca offshore, as charted.

LIGHTS AND MARKS Dieppe lies in a gap between high chalk cliffs, identified by a castle with pinnacle roofs at the W side and a conspic ch spire on the E cliff. DI, ECM wreck buoy, VQ (3) 5s, bears 288°/2·5M from the hbr ent.

IPTS (full code) shown from root of W jetty and S end of marina wavebreak. Additional sigs may be combined with IPTS:

● ● to right	=	Dredger in chan.
Ⓦ to left	=	Bassin Duquesne entry gate open.

R/T *Dieppe Port* Ch 12 (HO). Marina Ch 09 for a berth. Marina monitors Ch 12 and opens 1/7-24/8 0700-2200.

TELEPHONE Port HM 02.35.84.10.55; Aff Mar 02.35.06.96.70; CROSS 03.21.87.21.87; ⊖ 02.35.82.24.47; SNSM 02.35.84.8.55; Météo 03.21.31.52.23; Auto 08.36.68.08.76; Police 02.35.06.96.74; Ⓗ 02.35.06.76.76; Brit Consul 02.35.19.78.88.

DIEPPE

FACILITIES

Marina Jehan Ango: 02.35.84.10.55. smpd-plaisance@portde dieppe.fr www.portdedieppe.fr 450 AB inc 50 Ⓥ, €3·04, on pontoons 10, 9, 8 in about 4·5m but not on hammerheads. If 10 & 9 are full, late arrivals AB/raft on E side of pontoon 8; W side fingers are for boats >14m LOA. Use gangway intercom for shore access code number (if arriving out of hrs, for code call Ch 12).

D & P by credit card H24, call Ch 09 if unmanned. ME, El, Ⓔ, ✂, CH, C (12 ton), Wi-Fi.

Cercle de la Voile de Dieppe ☎ 02.35.84.32.99, R, Bar; same code accesses showers/toilets.

Bassin Duquesne (70 AB) access via lifting bridge/entry gate, **and Bassin de Paris** (70 AB) are only for local yachts.

Town P (cans), 🍴, Gaz, @, R, Bar, ✉, ▣, Ⓑ, ⇄, ✈. Ferry: Dieppe–Newhaven; www.transmancheferries.co.uk

Port de Plaisance Jehan Ango

DIEPPE TO LE HAVRE

From **Dieppe** to Pte d'Ailly light house the coast (AC 2451) is fringed by a bank, drying in places, up to 4ca offshore.

▶*Off Dieppe the ENE-going stream begins about HW Dieppe –0505, and the WSW-going at about HW Dieppe +0030, sp rates 2kn. E of Pte d'Ailly an eddy runs W close inshore on the first half of the E-going stream.◀*

Drying rks extend 5ca off Pte d'Ailly, including La Galère, a rk which dries 6·8m, about 3ca N of the Pointe (AC 2147). Dangerous wrecks lie between about 1·5M NNW and 1·2M WNW of the light house, the former marked by a NCM light buoy. About 6M N of Pte d'Ailly, Grands and Petits Écamias are banks with depths of 11m, dangerous in a heavy sea.

Between Pte d'Ailly and **St Valéry-en-Caux** (light house) there are drying rks 4ca offshore in places. About 1·5M E of Pte de Sotteville a rocky bank (4·2m) extends about 1M NNW; a strong eddy causes a race, Raz de Saint-Michel, over this bank.

There are rky ledges, extending 4ca offshore in places. Immediately E of St Valéry-en-Caux shallow sandbanks, Les Ridens, with a least depth of 0·6m, extend about 6ca offshore.

▶*At St Valéry-en-Caux entrance the E-going stream begins about HW Dieppe –0550, and the W-going stream begins about HW Dieppe –0015, sp rates 2·75kn. E of the ent a small eddy runs W on the E-going stream.◀*

From St Valéry-en-Caux to **Fécamp**, 15M WSW, the coast consists of high, sheer chalk cliffs broken by valleys. The nuclear power station (prohibited area marked by a NCM lt buoy) at Paluel, 3M W of St Valéry-en-Caux, is conspicuous.

Close NE of Fécamp off Pte Fagnet, Les Charpentiers are unmarked drying rocks extending almost 2 cables offshore.

▶*At Fécamp pierheads the NNE-going stream begins about HW Le Havre –0340, up to 2·9kn sp; the SSW-going about HW Le Havre +0220, much weaker. Diamond A on AC 1354 gives tidal stream data about 9ca WNW of the entrance.◀*

From Fécamp to Cap d'Antifer light house drying rks extend up to 2½ca offshore. L'Aiguille, a notable above water pinnacle rock, is off Étretat 1·7M NNE of Cap d'Antifer.

Port du Havre-Antifer, a VLCC harbour lies, 1·5M S of Cap d'Antifer (AC 2146, 2990). A 2M long breakwater extends about 1·5M seaward, and should be given a berth of about 1·5M, or more in heavy weather with wind against tide when there may be a race.

The buoyed app channel starts 11M NW of the harbour. Commercial vessels in it have priority. Yachts should cross it 3·8M to the NW at A17/A18 lt buoys; at 90° to its axis; as quickly as possible, keeping well clear of ships in the channel. Crossing vessels should contact Le Havre d'Antifer and any priority vessel on VHF Ch 22.

▶*Off Cap d'Antifer the NE-going stream begins about HW Le Havre –0430, and the SW-going at about HW Le Havre +0140. There are eddies close inshore E of Cap d'Antifer on both streams.◀*

Le Havre is a large commercial port, as well as a yachting centre. From the NW, the most useful mark is the Le Havre Lanby 'LHA' 9M W of C de la Hève (lt). The well-buoyed/lit access channel runs 6M ESE from LH 3/4 buoys to the hbr ent.

Strong W'lies cause rough water over shoal patches either side of the channel. Coming from the N or NE, there is deep water close off C de la Hève, but from here steer S to join the main ent chan. Beware Banc de l'Éclat (1·0m), which lies on N side of main channel near LH 14 buoy about 1·5M from harbour entrance.

W and S of Digue Sud yachts should not impede vessels entering/leaving Port 2000, a container terminal. If inbound to the marina it is best to cross early to the N side of the channel.

DIEPPE LAT 49°56'N   LONG 1°05'E
TIMES AND HEIGHTS OF HIGH AND LOW WATERS

YEAR 2010

TIME ZONE -0100
Subtract 1 hour for UT
For French Summer Time add
ONE hour in **non-shaded areas**

Dates in red are **SPRINGS**
Dates in blue are **NEAPS**

N France

JANUARY

Time	m		Time	m
1 F 0623	1.2		**16** SA 0013	8.6
1149	9.2		0701	1.5
1854	0.8		1226	8.8
			1921	1.2
2 SA 0018	9.3		**17** SU 0046	8.7
0716	0.9		0736	1.4
1238	9.5		1259	8.8
1946	0.6		1955	1.2
3 SU 0107	9.4		**18** M 0118	8.8
0807	0.8		0808	1.4
1327	9.6		1331	8.8
2036	0.5		2025	1.2
4 M 0156	9.4		**19** TU 0150	8.7
0855	0.9		0837	1.5
1414	9.5		1403	8.7
2122	0.6		2053	1.3
5 TU 0243	9.3		**20** W 0220	8.6
0941	1.0		0905	1.6
1501	9.2		1433	8.6
2206	0.9		2121	1.5
6 W 0329	9.0		**21** TH 0250	8.5
1025	1.3		0935	1.8
1548	8.8		1504	8.3
2248	1.3		2151	1.7
7 TH 0416	8.6		**22** F 0322	8.2
1110	1.7		1008	2.0
1638	8.3		1539	8.0
◑ 2333	1.8		2225	2.0
8 F 0508	8.1		**23** SA 0359	7.9
1200	2.1		1049	2.3
1734	7.8		1621	7.6
			◖ 2309	2.4
9 SA 0026	2.3		**24** SU 0446	7.6
0609	7.7		1141	2.6
1302	2.4		1716	7.3
1842	7.4			
10 SU 0132	2.6		**25** M 0006	2.7
0723	7.4		0551	7.3
1415	2.6		1248	2.8
2002	7.2		1836	7.1
11 M 0250	2.7		**26** TU 0123	2.8
0840	7.5		0721	7.2
1530	2.4		1414	2.6
2116	7.4		2008	7.3
12 TU 0401	2.5		**27** W 0254	2.6
0944	7.8		0843	7.7
1634	2.1		1539	2.2
2214	7.8		2122	7.8
13 W 0458	2.1		**28** TH 0410	2.0
1034	8.1		0949	8.2
1725	1.8		1647	1.6
2300	8.1		2223	8.4
14 TH 0544	1.9		**29** F 0514	1.5
1115	8.4		1047	8.8
1807	1.5		1749	1.0
2338	8.4		2318	9.0
15 F 0624	1.6		**30** SA 0614	1.0
1152	8.6		1139	9.3
● 1846	1.3		1846	0.6
			○	
			31 SU 0009	9.4
			0709	0.7
			1228	9.7
			1939	0.3

FEBRUARY

Time	m		Time	m
1 M 0056	9.7		**16** TU 0054	9.0
0759	0.5		0747	1.1
1314	9.8		1308	9.0
2025	0.2		2003	1.0
2 TU 0140	9.7		**17** W 0124	9.0
0844	0.5		0815	1.1
1358	9.8		1338	9.0
2107	0.3		2030	1.0
3 W 0222	9.6		**18** TH 0153	9.0
0924	0.6		0842	1.2
1440	9.5		1407	8.9
2145	0.6		2057	1.2
4 TH 0303	9.3		**19** F 0221	8.8
1000	1.0		0910	1.4
1521	9.0		1437	8.7
2219	1.2		2123	1.4
5 F 0343	8.8		**20** SA 0252	8.6
1037	1.5		0940	1.6
1603	8.4		1510	8.3
2254	1.8		2153	1.8
6 SA 0426	8.1		**21** SU 0326	8.2
1118	2.1		1016	2.0
1651	7.7		1549	7.9
◖ 2338	2.4		2233	2.2
7 SU 0519	7.5		**22** M 0408	7.8
1213	2.6		1104	2.4
1756	7.0		1640	7.4
			◑ 2329	2.6
8 M 0041	3.0		**23** TU 0509	7.3
0636	6.9		1210	2.7
1330	2.9		1758	7.0
1930	6.7			
9 TU 0210	3.1		**24** W 0048	2.9
0816	6.9		0646	7.0
1501	2.8		1343	2.7
2101	7.0		1946	7.1
10 W 0340	2.8		**25** TH 0230	2.7
0930	7.4		0823	7.4
1617	2.4		1519	2.2
2201	7.5		2108	7.7
11 TH 0444	2.3		**26** F 0353	2.0
1020	7.9		0936	8.2
1711	1.9		1632	1.5
2245	8.0		2212	8.5
12 F 0531	1.9		**27** SA 0500	1.4
1100	8.3		1034	8.9
1753	1.5		1736	0.9
2321	8.4		2305	9.1
13 SA 0610	1.5		**28** SU 0601	0.8
1134	8.6		1125	9.4
1830	1.3		1833	0.4
2353	8.7		○ 2353	9.6
14 SU 0644	1.3			
1207	8.8			
● 1904	1.1			
15 M 0024	8.9			
0717	1.2			
1238	9.0			
1935	1.0			

MARCH

Time	m		Time	m
1 M 0654	0.5		**16** TU 0650	1.1
1211	9.8		1211	9.0
1922	0.1		1907	0.9
2 TU 0036	9.8		**17** W 0026	9.0
0741	0.3		0720	1.0
1255	9.9		1242	9.1
2006	0.1		1937	0.9
3 W 0117	9.8		**18** TH 0056	9.1
0823	0.3		0750	1.0
1336	9.8		1312	9.1
2044	0.3		2005	0.9
4 TH 0157	9.7		**19** F 0125	9.1
0859	0.5		0819	1.0
1415	9.5		1342	9.0
2117	0.7		2033	1.1
5 F 0234	9.3		**20** SA 0155	9.0
0932	0.9		0849	1.2
1453	9.0		1414	8.8
2147	1.2		2102	1.3
6 SA 0311	8.8		**21** SU 0228	8.7
1004	1.5		0920	1.4
1531	8.4		1449	8.4
2218	1.8		2133	1.7
7 SU 0349	8.1		**22** M 0303	8.3
1041	2.1		0956	1.8
1614	7.6		1530	8.0
◑ 2258	2.5		2214	2.1
8 M 0436	7.3		**23** TU 0348	7.8
1131	2.7		1045	2.2
1714	6.8		1623	7.4
2358	3.1		◖ 2312	2.6
9 TU 0549	6.7		**24** W 0451	7.3
1247	3.1		1152	2.6
1852	6.4		1746	7.0
10 W 0131	3.4		**25** TH 0033	2.8
0744	6.6		0631	7.1
1425	3.0		1327	2.6
2036	6.7		1932	7.2
11 TH 0309	3.0		**26** F 0215	2.5
0904	7.0		0807	7.5
1546	2.5		1503	2.1
2135	7.3		2054	7.9
12 F 0416	2.4		**27** SA 0336	1.9
0954	7.6		0918	8.2
1642	2.0		1615	1.4
2217	7.9		2154	8.6
13 SA 0503	1.9		**28** SU 0442	1.3
1033	8.2		1015	8.9
1725	1.5		1717	0.8
2252	8.4		2245	9.1
14 SU 0542	1.5		**29** M 0541	0.8
1107	8.6		1105	9.4
1802	1.2		1811	0.5
2325	8.7		2330	9.5
15 M 0617	1.3		**30** TU 0632	0.5
1140	8.8		1149	9.6
● 1836	1.0		1858	0.3
● 2356	8.9		○	
			31 W 0012	9.7
			0717	0.4
			1231	9.7
			1939	0.3

APRIL

Time	m		Time	m
1 TH 0051	9.7		**16** F 0027	9.1
0756	0.4		0725	1.0
1311	9.6		1247	9.0
2015	0.5		1940	1.0
2 F 0129	9.5		**17** SA 0100	9.1
0832	0.6		0758	1.0
1349	9.3		1321	9.0
2048	0.9		2013	1.1
3 SA 0206	9.2		**18** SU 0134	9.0
0904	1.0		0833	1.1
1426	8.9		1358	8.8
2117	1.4		2047	1.3
4 SU 0242	8.7		**19** M 0211	8.8
0935	1.5		0909	1.3
1504	8.3		1438	8.5
2149	1.9		2124	1.7
5 M 0319	8.0		**20** TU 0253	8.4
1011	2.0		0950	1.7
1546	7.6		1524	8.0
2229	2.5		2210	2.1
6 TU 0404	7.3		**21** W 0342	7.9
1058	2.6		1041	2.0
1641	6.9		1623	7.6
◑ 2325	3.1		◖ 2310	2.4
7 W 0509	6.7		**22** TH 0451	7.4
1206	3.0		1149	2.3
1805	6.5		1745	7.3
8 TH 0048	3.3		**23** F 0029	2.5
0645	6.5		0620	7.4
1335	3.1		1317	2.3
1942	6.7		1913	7.5
9 F 0218	3.1		**24** SA 0158	2.3
0816	6.8		0744	7.7
1454	2.7		1441	1.9
2049	7.2		2028	8.0
10 SA 0326	2.5		**25** SU 0312	1.8
0911	7.4		0853	8.2
1554	2.2		1550	1.4
2135	7.7		2128	8.6
11 SU 0418	2.0		**26** M 0417	1.3
0954	8.0		0951	8.7
1641	1.7		1650	1.0
2214	8.2		2219	9.0
12 M 0501	1.6		**27** TU 0514	1.0
1032	8.4		1040	9.1
1722	1.4		1743	0.8
2249	8.6		2304	9.2
13 TU 0540	1.4		**28** W 0604	0.8
1107	8.7		1126	9.3
1800	1.2		1828	0.7
2323	8.8		○ 2346	9.3
14 W 0616	1.2		**29** TH 0649	0.7
1141	8.9		1208	9.3
1835	1.0		1909	0.8
● 2356	9.0			
15 TH 0651	1.0		**30** F 0026	9.3
1214	9.0		0729	0.7
1908	1.0		1248	9.2
			1946	0.9

Chart Datum is 4·45 metres below IGN Datum. HAT is 10·1 metres above Chart Datum; see 4.5.

TIME ZONE -0100
Subtract 1 hour for UT
For French Summer Time add
ONE hour in non-shaded areas

DIEPPE LAT 49°56'N LONG 1°05'E
TIMES AND HEIGHTS OF HIGH AND LOW WATERS

Dates in red are SPRINGS
Dates in blue are NEAPS

YEAR 2010

MAY

Time	m	Time	m
1 0104 / 0805 / SA 1326 / 2021	9.2 / 0.9 / 9.0 / 1.2	**16** 0040 / 0742 / SU 1306 / 1958	9.1 / 0.9 / 9.0 / 1.1
2 0141 / 0840 / SU 1405 / 2054	9.0 / 1.1 / 8.7 / 1.5	**17** 0121 / 0822 / M 1349 / 2039	9.0 / 1.0 / 8.9 / 1.3
3 0219 / 0914 / M 1444 / 2128	8.6 / 1.5 / 8.2 / 1.9	**18** 0204 / 0905 / TU 1435 / 2123	8.8 / 1.1 / 8.6 / 1.5
4 0257 / 0949 / TU 1525 / 2206	8.1 / 1.9 / 7.7 / 2.4	**19** 0251 / 0952 / W 1526 / 2213	8.5 / 1.4 / 8.3 / 1.8
5 0341 / 1031 / W 1614 / 2255	7.5 / 2.4 / 7.2 / 2.8	**20** 0345 / 1044 / TH 1625 / 2311	8.2 / 1.7 / 8.0 / 2.0
6 0435 / 1127 / TH 1717 / ◑	7.0 / 2.7 / 6.9	**21** 0449 / 1147 / F 1733 / ◑	7.9 / 1.9 / 7.8
7 0000 / 0546 / F 1237 / 1832	3.0 / 6.8 / 2.9 / 6.8	**22** 0020 / 0601 / SA 1259 / 1845	2.1 / 7.8 / 1.9 / 7.9
8 0114 / 0703 / SA 1349 / 1942	3.0 / 6.8 / 2.7 / 7.1	**23** 0133 / 0713 / SU 1411 / 1955	2.0 / 7.9 / 1.8 / 8.1
9 0222 / 0812 / SU 1453 / 2040	2.7 / 7.2 / 2.4 / 7.5	**24** 0242 / 0822 / M 1518 / 2057	1.8 / 8.1 / 1.6 / 8.4
10 0321 / 0905 / M 1547 / 2127	2.3 / 7.6 / 2.0 / 8.0	**25** 0347 / 0924 / TU 1619 / 2152	1.5 / 8.4 / 1.4 / 8.6
11 0411 / 0949 / TU 1636 / 2209	1.9 / 8.1 / 1.7 / 8.3	**26** 0445 / 1017 / W 1713 / 2241	1.3 / 8.6 / 1.3 / 8.8
12 0457 / 1030 / W 1720 / 2248	1.6 / 8.4 / 1.4 / 8.6	**27** 0537 / 1105 / TH 1800 / 2324	1.2 / 8.8 / 1.2 / 8.9
13 0540 / 1110 / TH 1801 / 2325	1.3 / 8.6 / 1.3 / 8.8	**28** 0622 / 1149 / F 1842 / ○	1.1 / 8.8 / 1.2
14 0622 / 1148 / F 1840 / ●	1.2 / 8.8 / 1.2	**29** 0005 / 0704 / SA 1229 / 1922	8.9 / 1.1 / 8.8 / 1.2
15 0002 / 0702 / SA 1226 / 1919	9.0 / 1.0 / 8.9 / 1.1	**30** 0044 / 0743 / SU 1309 / 1959	8.9 / 1.1 / 8.8 / 1.3
		31 0122 / 0821 / M 1348 / 2036	8.8 / 1.2 / 8.6 / 1.5

JUNE

Time	m	Time	m
1 0201 / 0856 / TU 1426 / 2111	8.5 / 1.4 / 8.3 / 1.8	**16** 0200 / 0906 / W 1432 / 2125	9.1 / 0.8 / 9.0 / 1.1
2 0239 / 0931 / W 1505 / 2146	8.2 / 1.7 / 8.0 / 2.1	**17** 0249 / 0953 / TH 1522 / 2213	8.9 / 1.0 / 8.8 / 1.3
3 0319 / 1007 / TH 1546 / 2225	7.9 / 2.0 / 7.7 / 2.4	**18** 0340 / 1042 / F 1614 / 2304	8.7 / 1.2 / 8.5 / 1.5
4 0402 / 1049 / F 1632 / ◑ 2312	7.5 / 2.3 / 7.4 / 2.6	**19** 0434 / 1134 / SA 1709 / ◑ 2359	8.4 / 1.5 / 8.3 / 1.8
5 0452 / 1140 / SA 1727	7.2 / 2.5 / 7.2	**20** 0533 / 1231 / SU 1811	8.1 / 1.7 / 8.0
6 0008 / 0552 / SU 1239 / 1830	2.7 / 7.1 / 2.6 / 7.2	**21** 0101 / 0639 / M 1336 / 1918	1.9 / 7.8 / 1.9 / 7.9
7 0111 / 0700 / M 1343 / 1936	2.7 / 7.1 / 2.5 / 7.3	**22** 0209 / 0751 / TU 1444 / 2028	2.0 / 7.8 / 2.0 / 8.0
8 0216 / 0806 / TU 1447 / 2036	2.5 / 7.3 / 2.3 / 7.7	**23** 0317 / 0900 / W 1550 / 2129	1.9 / 7.9 / 1.9 / 8.2
9 0318 / 0903 / W 1547 / 2128	2.2 / 7.7 / 2.0 / 8.0	**24** 0420 / 1000 / TH 1648 / 2223	1.7 / 8.1 / 1.8 / 8.4
10 0414 / 0954 / TH 1641 / 2214	1.9 / 8.0 / 1.7 / 8.4	**25** 0515 / 1052 / F 1739 / 2310	1.6 / 8.3 / 1.6 / 8.5
11 0506 / 1041 / F 1730 / 2259	1.5 / 8.4 / 1.5 / 8.6	**26** 0603 / 1137 / SA 1823 / ○ 2352	1.4 / 8.5 / 1.5 / 8.7
12 0555 / 1126 / SA 1817 / ● 2342	1.3 / 8.7 / 1.3 / 8.9	**27** 0646 / 1217 / SU 1904	1.3 / 8.6 / 1.4
13 0643 / 1211 / SU 1904	1.0 / 8.9 / 1.1	**28** 0030 / 0726 / M 1255 / 1943	8.7 / 1.2 / 8.7 / 1.4
14 0027 / 0731 / M 1257 / 1951	9.1 / 0.9 / 9.1 / 1.0	**29** 0107 / 0804 / TU 1331 / 2019	8.7 / 1.2 / 8.7 / 1.5
15 0113 / 0819 / TU 1344 / 2037	9.2 / 0.8 / 9.1 / 1.0	**30** 0143 / 0839 / W 1406 / 2052	8.6 / 1.3 / 8.6 / 1.6

JULY

Time	m	Time	m
1 0218 / 0910 / TH 1441 / 2123	8.5 / 1.5 / 8.4 / 1.8	**16** 0237 / 0945 / F 1506 / 2202	9.4 / 0.6 / 9.2 / 0.9
2 0252 / 0940 / F 1515 / 2154	8.3 / 1.7 / 8.2 / 2.0	**17** 0323 / 1026 / SA 1551 / 2245	9.1 / 0.9 / 8.9 / 1.3
3 0327 / 1013 / SA 1549 / 2231	8.0 / 1.9 / 7.9 / 2.2	**18** 0409 / 1109 / SU 1639 / ◑ 2331	8.7 / 1.3 / 8.5 / 1.7
4 0404 / 1052 / SU 1630 / ◑ 2315	7.7 / 2.2 / 7.6 / 2.4	**19** 0501 / 1157 / M 1734	8.1 / 1.8 / 8.0
5 0449 / 1139 / M 1720	7.4 / 2.4 / 7.4	**20** 0026 / 0604 / TU 1257 / 1842	2.1 / 7.6 / 2.3 / 7.6
6 0008 / 0546 / TU 1236 / 1824	2.6 / 7.1 / 2.6 / 7.2	**21** 0135 / 0722 / W 1412 / 2002	2.3 / 7.3 / 2.5 / 7.5
7 0111 / 0701 / W 1346 / 1940	2.7 / 7.1 / 2.7 / 7.3	**22** 0252 / 0844 / TH 1528 / 2116	2.3 / 7.4 / 2.4 / 7.7
8 0225 / 0818 / TH 1501 / 2048	2.5 / 7.3 / 2.4 / 7.7	**23** 0403 / 0952 / F 1634 / 2214	2.1 / 7.7 / 2.1 / 8.0
9 0336 / 0922 / F 1607 / 2146	2.1 / 7.7 / 2.0 / 8.1	**24** 0503 / 1044 / SA 1727 / 2300	1.8 / 8.1 / 1.8 / 8.4
10 0438 / 1018 / SA 1705 / 2238	1.7 / 8.2 / 1.7 / 8.5	**25** 0553 / 1127 / SU 1811 / 2339	1.5 / 8.4 / 1.6 / 8.6
11 0535 / 1110 / SU 1800 / ● 2328	1.3 / 8.7 / 1.3 / 8.9	**26** 0634 / 1204 / M 1850 / ○	1.3 / 8.6 / 1.4
12 0630 / 1159 / M 1853	1.0 / 9.0 / 1.0	**27** 0016 / 0711 / TU 1237 / 1925	8.7 / 1.2 / 8.8 / 1.3
13 0017 / 0724 / TU 1247 / 1945	9.2 / 0.7 / 9.3 / 0.8	**28** 0048 / 0746 / W 1309 / 1959	8.8 / 1.1 / 8.8 / 1.3
14 0104 / 0815 / W 1335 / 2033	9.4 / 0.5 / 9.4 / 0.7	**29** 0121 / 0817 / TH 1341 / 2029	8.8 / 1.2 / 8.8 / 1.4
15 0151 / 0901 / TH 1420 / 2119	9.5 / 0.4 / 9.4 / 0.7	**30** 0152 / 0845 / F 1412 / 2056	8.8 / 1.2 / 8.7 / 1.5
		31 0223 / 0911 / SA 1441 / 2123	8.6 / 1.4 / 8.5 / 1.7

AUGUST

Time	m	Time	m
1 0252 / 0939 / SU 1511 / 2154	8.4 / 1.6 / 8.3 / 1.9	**16** 0341 / 1038 / M 1606 / ◑ 2259	8.7 / 1.5 / 8.5 / 1.8
2 0324 / 1011 / M 1544 / 2231	8.1 / 2.0 / 8.0 / 2.2	**17** 0428 / 1122 / TU 1657 / 2351	8.0 / 2.1 / 7.8 / 2.3
3 0402 / 1051 / TU 1626 / ◑ 2318	7.7 / 2.3 / 7.6 / 2.5	**18** 0529 / 1221 / W 1807	7.3 / 2.7 / 7.2
4 0452 / 1144 / W 1723	7.3 / 2.7 / 7.2	**19** 0102 / 0656 / TH 1344 / 1941	2.7 / 6.9 / 3.0 / 7.1
5 0019 / 0602 / TH 1255 / 1846	2.8 / 7.0 / 2.9 / 7.1	**20** 0231 / 0834 / F 1512 / 2104	2.7 / 7.1 / 2.7 / 7.4
6 0139 / 0737 / F 1424 / 2015	2.8 / 7.0 / 2.7 / 7.4	**21** 0351 / 0942 / SA 1623 / 2201	2.3 / 7.6 / 2.3 / 7.9
7 0306 / 0857 / SA 1542 / 2124	2.4 / 7.5 / 2.2 / 8.0	**22** 0451 / 1029 / SU 1714 / 2244	1.9 / 8.1 / 1.8 / 8.3
8 0417 / 1000 / SU 1646 / 2222	1.8 / 8.2 / 1.6 / 8.6	**23** 0537 / 1108 / M 1755 / 2320	1.5 / 8.5 / 1.5 / 8.6
9 0519 / 1055 / M 1746 / 2314	1.2 / 8.8 / 1.2 / 9.1	**24** 0615 / 1141 / TU 1830 / ○ 2354	1.3 / 8.7 / 1.3 / 8.8
10 0618 / 1145 / TU 1842 / ●	0.8 / 9.3 / 0.8	**25** 0649 / 1212 / W 1902	1.1 / 8.9 / 1.2
11 0003 / 0713 / W 1232 / 1934	9.5 / 0.4 / 9.6 / 0.5	**26** 0024 / 0721 / TH 1242 / 1933	9.0 / 1.1 / 9.0 / 1.2
12 0049 / 0759 / TH 1317 / 2020	9.7 / 0.2 / 9.8 / 0.4	**27** 0054 / 0750 / F 1312 / 2001	9.0 / 1.1 / 9.0 / 1.2
13 0134 / 0845 / F 1400 / 2102	9.8 / 0.2 / 9.7 / 0.5	**28** 0123 / 0816 / SA 1340 / 2028	8.9 / 1.1 / 8.9 / 1.3
14 0217 / 0925 / SA 1442 / 2141	9.6 / 0.5 / 9.5 / 0.8	**29** 0152 / 0842 / SU 1408 / 2055	8.8 / 1.3 / 8.8 / 1.5
15 0259 / 1001 / SU 1523 / 2218	9.3 / 0.9 / 9.1 / 1.2	**30** 0221 / 0908 / M 1437 / 2123	8.6 / 1.6 / 8.5 / 1.7
		31 0252 / 0937 / TU 1509 / 2156	8.3 / 1.9 / 8.2 / 2.1

Chart Datum is 4·45 metres below IGN Datum. HAT is 10·1 metres above Chart Datum; see 4.5.

TIME ZONE -0100
Subtract 1 hour for UT
For French Summer Time add
ONE hour in **non-shaded areas**

DIEPPE LAT 49°56'N LONG 1°05'E

TIMES AND HEIGHTS OF HIGH AND LOW WATERS

Dates in red are **SPRINGS**
Dates in blue are **NEAPS**

YEAR **2010**

N France

SEPTEMBER

Time	m		Time	m
1 0329	7.9	**16**	0457	7.1
1014	2.3		1148	3.0
W 1549	7.8		TH 1732	7.0
◑ 2240	2.5			
2 0416	7.4	**17**	0029	3.0
1105	2.8		0628	6.7
TH 1644	7.3		F 1315	3.3
2341	2.8		1914	6.8
3 0525	6.9	**18**	0203	3.0
1219	3.0		0812	6.9
F 1809	7.0		SA 1448	3.0
			2041	7.2
4 0106	2.9	**19**	0325	2.5
0710	7.0		0917	7.5
SA 1358	2.9		SU 1557	2.4
1951	7.3		2135	7.8
5 0245	2.5	**20**	0423	2.0
0838	7.6		1002	8.1
SU 1523	2.2		M 1646	1.9
2105	8.0		2217	8.3
6 0359	1.7	**21**	0507	1.6
0943	8.3		1038	8.5
M 1629	1.5		TU 1725	1.5
2204	8.7		2251	8.6
7 0503	1.1	**22**	0544	1.3
1037	9.0		1111	8.8
TU 1729	1.0		W 1800	1.3
2256	9.3		2324	8.9
8 0601	0.6	**23**	0618	1.2
1125	9.5		1142	8.9
W 1824	0.6		TH 1833	1.2
● 2343	9.7		○ 2355	9.0
9 0653	0.3	**24**	0650	1.1
1210	9.8		1212	9.0
TH 1914	0.4		F 1904	1.2
10 0028	9.9	**25**	0025	9.0
0740	0.2		0719	1.1
F 1253	9.9		SA 1241	9.1
1958	0.4		1933	1.2
11 0111	9.9	**26**	0054	9.0
0821	0.3		0747	1.2
SA 1334	9.8		SU 1309	9.0
2038	0.5		2001	1.3
12 0152	9.7	**27**	0124	8.9
0859	0.6		0815	1.3
SU 1414	9.5		M 1338	8.9
2114	0.9		2030	1.4
13 0232	9.2	**28**	0155	8.7
0933	1.1		0843	1.6
M 1454	9.0		TU 1409	8.7
2149	1.3		2100	1.7
14 0313	8.6	**29**	0228	8.4
1007	1.7		0913	1.9
TU 1534	8.4		W 1444	8.3
2227	1.9		2134	2.0
15 0358	7.8	**30**	0307	8.0
1048	2.4		0951	2.3
W 1623	7.6		TH 1525	7.8
◑ 2317	2.6		2218	2.4

OCTOBER

Time	m		Time	m
1 0356	7.5	**16**	0547	6.7
1045	2.8		1236	3.3
F 1622	7.3		SA 1825	6.7
◑ 2319	2.7			
2 0508	7.0	**17**	0118	3.1
1200	3.0		0720	6.8
SA 1751	7.0		SU 1402	3.1
			1954	7.0
3 0046	2.8	**18**	0236	2.8
0652	7.1		0831	7.3
SU 1339	2.8		M 1510	2.6
1929	7.4		2053	7.5
4 0225	2.4	**19**	0336	2.3
0816	7.7		0920	7.8
M 1503	2.0		TU 1602	2.1
2042	8.1		2137	8.0
5 0339	1.7	**20**	0424	1.9
0921	8.5		0959	8.3
TU 1608	1.5		W 1645	1.7
2141	8.8		2215	8.4
6 0441	1.1	**21**	0505	1.5
1014	9.1		1034	8.6
W 1707	1.0		TH 1724	1.5
2233	9.3		2251	8.6
7 0537	0.7	**22**	0542	1.4
1101	9.5		1108	8.9
TH 1800	0.7		F 1800	1.3
● 2320	9.7		2324	8.9
8 0627	0.5	**23**	0616	1.3
1145	9.8		1140	9.0
F 1849	0.5		SA 1833	1.3
			○ 2356	8.9
9 0005	9.8	**24**	0649	1.3
0713	0.5		1211	9.0
SA 1228	9.8		SU 1906	1.2
1932	0.5			
10 0047	9.7	**25**	0028	9.0
0754	0.6		0720	1.3
SU 1308	9.7		M 1242	9.1
2012	0.7		1938	1.2
11 0128	9.5	**26**	0101	9.2
0830	0.9		0752	1.4
M 1348	9.4		TU 1315	9.0
2048	1.0		2011	1.3
12 0208	9.1	**27**	0136	8.8
0905	1.4		0825	1.6
TU 1427	8.9		W 1351	8.8
2123	1.5		2046	1.6
13 0249	8.5	**28**	0214	8.5
0939	2.0		0901	1.9
W 1507	8.3		TH 1430	8.4
2200	2.0		2124	1.9
14 0333	7.8	**29**	0257	8.1
1021	2.6		0944	2.2
TH 1555	7.6		F 1516	8.0
◑ 2247	2.6		2211	2.2
15 0429	7.2	**30**	0350	7.7
1117	3.1		1038	2.6
F 1658	7.0		SA 1616	7.6
2353	3.1		◑ 2311	2.5
		31	0502	7.4
			1150	2.8
			SU 1737	7.4

NOVEMBER

Time	m		Time	m
1 0031	2.6	**16**	0128	2.9
0630	7.5		0721	7.1
M 1318	2.6		TU 1406	2.9
1902	7.6		1952	7.2
2 0200	2.2	**17**	0234	2.7
0747	7.9		0823	7.5
TU 1437	2.1		W 1507	2.5
2014	8.1		2048	7.6
3 0312	1.7	**18**	0331	2.3
0852	8.5		0912	7.9
W 1542	1.5		TH 1559	2.1
2115	8.7		2134	8.0
4 0414	1.3	**19**	0420	1.9
0947	9.0		0955	8.3
TH 1641	1.1		F 1645	1.8
2209	9.1		2215	8.3
5 0510	1.0	**20**	0504	1.7
1036	9.3		1034	8.6
F 1735	0.9		SA 1726	1.5
2257	9.4		2254	8.6
6 0600	0.8	**21**	0544	1.5
1121	9.5		1110	8.8
SA 1823	0.8		SU 1805	1.4
● 2342	9.4		○ 2331	8.8
7 0645	0.9	**22**	0621	1.4
1204	9.5		1146	9.0
SU 1907	0.8		M 1843	1.3
8 0025	9.4	**23**	0008	8.9
0727	1.0		0659	1.4
M 1245	9.4		TU 1222	9.0
1947	0.9		1921	1.2
9 0107	9.2	**24**	0045	9.0
0805	1.2		0737	1.4
TU 1325	9.2		W 1301	9.0
2025	1.1		2000	1.2
10 0148	8.9	**25**	0125	8.9
0842	1.5		0816	1.5
W 1405	8.8		TH 1341	8.9
2101	1.5		2040	1.3
11 0229	8.5	**26**	0208	8.7
0918	2.0		0858	1.7
TH 1446	8.3		F 1426	8.7
2138	2.0		2123	1.5
12 0312	8.0	**27**	0255	8.4
0957	2.4		0944	1.9
F 1531	7.8		SA 1515	8.4
2219	2.4		2211	1.8
13 0400	7.5	**28**	0348	8.1
1045	2.8		1036	2.1
SA 1623	7.3		SU 1611	8.0
◑ 2311	2.8		◑ 2306	2.0
14 0459	7.1	**29**	0450	7.9
1146	3.1		1139	2.3
SU 1727	6.9		M 1718	7.8
15 0017	3.0	**30**	0012	2.2
0609	6.9		0601	7.8
M 1257	3.1		TU 1250	2.3
1841	6.9		1830	7.8

DECEMBER

Time	m		Time	m
1 0127	2.1	**16**	0115	2.9
0713	8.0		0713	7.2
W 1405	2.1		TH 1356	2.9
1942	8.0		1946	7.1
2 0240	1.9	**17**	0226	2.8
0821	8.3		0819	7.4
TH 1514	1.8		F 1505	2.6
2048	8.3		2048	7.5
3 0345	1.7	**18**	0331	2.4
0921	8.6		0914	7.8
F 1616	1.5		SA 1603	2.2
2147	8.6		2140	7.9
4 0444	1.4	**19**	0426	2.1
1014	8.9		1001	8.2
SA 1711	1.2		SU 1654	1.8
2239	8.8		2226	8.3
5 0536	1.3	**20**	0514	1.8
1102	9.1		1045	8.6
SU 1801	1.1		M 1740	1.5
● 2327	9.0		2310	8.6
6 0623	1.2	**21**	0600	1.5
1147	9.2		1127	8.9
M 1846	1.0		TU 1826	1.2
			○ 2352	8.9
7 0011	9.0	**22**	0644	1.3
0705	1.2		1209	9.1
TU 1228	9.2		W 1910	1.0
1928	1.0			
8 0052	9.0	**23**	0035	9.1
0745	1.3		0729	1.2
W 1309	9.1		TH 1252	9.2
2007	1.2		1955	0.9
9 0132	8.9	**24**	0119	9.2
0824	1.5		0813	1.1
TH 1348	8.8		F 1336	9.2
2045	1.4		2040	0.9
10 0211	8.6	**25**	0204	9.1
0900	1.8		0858	1.2
F 1427	8.5		SA 1422	9.1
2119	1.7		2124	1.0
11 0250	8.3	**26**	0250	9.0
0935	2.1		0943	1.3
SA 1506	8.1		SU 1508	8.9
2153	2.0		2208	1.2
12 0329	7.9	**27**	0338	8.7
1011	2.4		1029	1.6
SU 1547	7.7		M 1558	8.6
2230	2.4		2254	1.5
13 0411	7.6	**28**	0429	8.4
1054	2.7		1120	1.8
M 1632	7.4		TU 1652	8.2
◑ 2315	2.6		◑ 2346	1.9
14 0501	7.3	**29**	0527	8.1
1145	2.9		1219	2.1
TU 1727	7.1		W 1756	7.9
15 0010	2.8	**30**	0049	2.1
0602	7.1		0635	7.9
W 1247	3.0		TH 1328	2.2
1834	7.0		1909	7.7
		31	0203	2.3
			0750	7.9
			F 1444	2.1
			2025	7.8

Chart Datum is 4·45 metres below IGN Datum. HAT is 10·1 metres above Chart Datum; see 4.5.

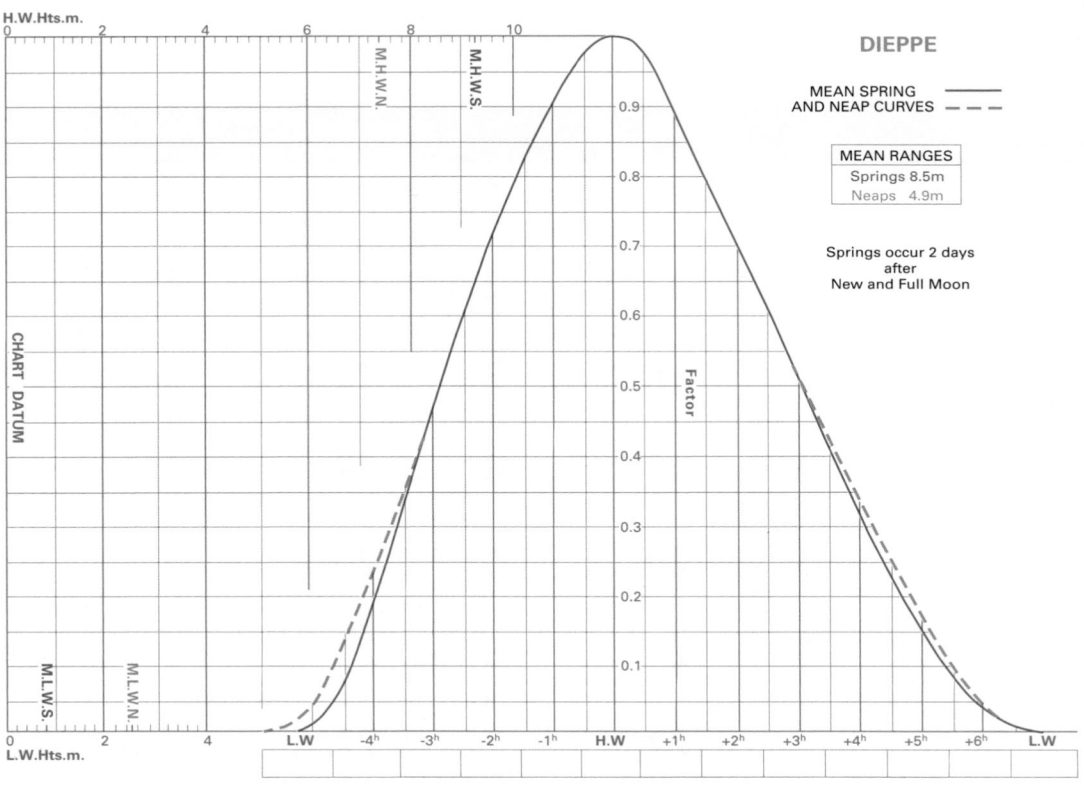

DIEPPE

MEAN SPRING
AND NEAP CURVES

| MEAN RANGES |
| Springs 8.5m |
| Neaps 4.9m |

Springs occur 2 days
after
New and Full Moon

9.17.15   ST VALÉRY-EN-CAUX
Seine Maritime **49°52'·48N 00°42'·64E** ✿✿◊◊◊◊✿✿

CHARTS AC *2451*; SHOM 7417; Navi 1012; Imray C31; Stanfords 1

TIDES –0044 Dover; ML 4·6; Duration 0530.

Standard Port DIEPPE (←—)

Times				Height (metres)			
High Water		Low Water		MHWS	MHWN	MLWN	MLWS
0100	0600	0100	0700	9·3	7·4	2·5	0·8
1300	1800	1300	1900				
Differences ST VALÉRY-EN-CAUX							
–0005	–0005	–0015	–0020	–0·5	–0·4	–0·1	–0·1

SHELTER Good, but confused seas break at entrance in fresh W-NE'lies.

NAVIGATION WPT 49°52'·97N 00°42'·14E, 155°/6ca to W pier. Ent is easy, but tidal streams across ent are strong. Shingle builds up against W wall; hug the E side. Inside the pier hds, wave-breaks (marked by posts) reduce the surge. Avant Port dries 3̲m; access from HW –3. 5 W waiting buoys are in the pool NE of gate.

Gate is open HW ±2¼ by day, 0500-2359; HW±½ at night 0000-0500, (bridge opens H & H+30 in these periods). When entry gate first opens, strong current may complicate berthing on ⓥ pontoon W side; best to wait 15 mins. ⓥ also berth on 'A' pontoon. Traffic sigs at the bridge/gate are coordinated to seaward/inland:
● = ent/exit; ● = no ent/exit; ● + ● = no movements.

LIGHTS AND MARKS From N or W Paluel nuclear power stn is conspic 3M W of ent. From E a TV mast is 1M E of ent. Hbr is hard to see between high chalk cliffs, but lt ho (W twr, G top) on W pierhead is fairly conspic. Lts as on chartlet and 9.17.4.

R/T Ch 09 (French only).

TELEPHONE Aff Mar 02.35.10.34.34; CROSS 03.21.8728.76; Police 02.35.97.00.17; Dr 02.35.97.05.99; Ⓗ 02.35.97.00.11; Brit Consul 02.35.19.78.88.

FACILITIES **Marina** ☎ 02.35.97.01.30, mobile 06.07.31.56.95. www.ville-saint-valery-en-caux.fr 575 + 20 ⓥ €2·20; max LOA 14m. C (5/10 ton), CH, El, Ⓔ, ME, ⚒. **CN Valeriquais** ☎ 02.35.97.25.49, Bar, Shwrs. **Town**: P&D (cans), 🛒, Gaz, R, Bar, ✉, Ⓑ, bus to ⇌ at Yvetot; ✈ & Ferry Dieppe.

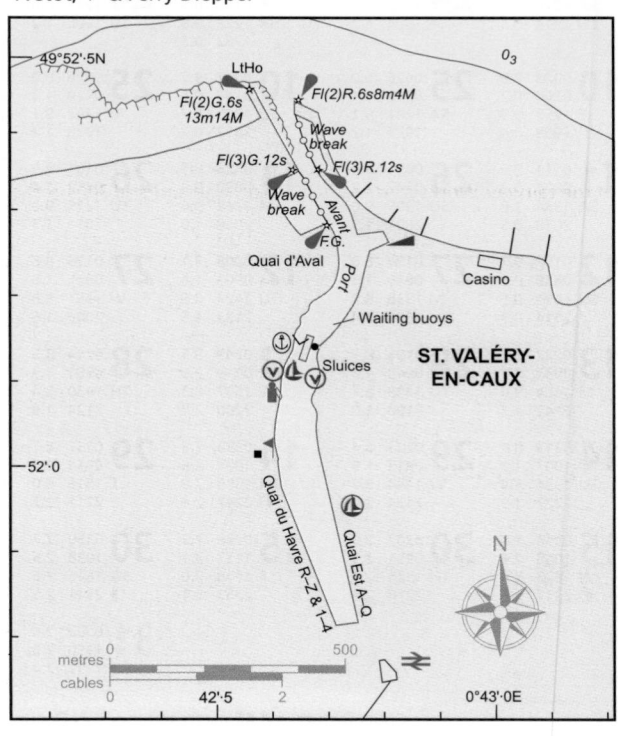

9.17.16 FÉCAMP

Seine Maritime 49°45'·92N 00°21'·80E ❀❀⊕♦♦♦♦❁❁

CHARTS AC *2451, 2148*, 1354; SHOM 6857, 7417, 7207; Navi 1012; Imray C31; Stanfords 1

TIDES –0044 Dover; ML 4·9; Duration 0550.

Standard Port DIEPPE (←)

Times				Height (metres)			
High Water		Low Water		MHWS	MHWN	MLWN	MLWS
0100	0600	0100	0700	9·3	7·4	2·5	0·8
1300	1800	1300	1900				
Differences FÉCAMP							
–0015	–0010	–0030	–0040	–1·0	–0·6	+0·3	+0·4
ETRETAT 49°42'·6N 00°12'·0E							
–0020	–0020	–0045	–0050	–1·2	–0·8	+0·3	+0·4

SHELTER Excellent in basins, but in even moderate W/NW winds a considerable surf runs off the ent and scend can make the Avant Port uncomfortable. Access difficult in onshore winds >F5; do not attempt >F7. Bassin Bérigny for long stay; see HM.

NAVIGATION WPT 49°46'·01N 00°21'·36E, 107°/3ca to hbr ent. Beware the Charpentier Rks off Pte Fagnet and strong cross currents, depending on tides. Ent chan 1·5m is prone to silting; best water is close to N jetty. Access best at HW +1.

LIGHTS AND MARKS Ent lies SW of conspic ⊕, sig stn, TV mast and 5 wind turbines (2 Q) on Pte Fagnet cliff, 142m high. See chartlet and 9.17.4 for lts. Pilots use the QR aligned with QG as a 082° ldg line.

IPTS on column at root of S jetty; a W lt is shown next to top lt when Bassin Bérigny gate is open.

R/T Ch 09 Marina & Écluse Bérigny. Port Ch **12** 16 (HW –3 to +1).

TELEPHONE HM 02.35.28.25.53; CROSS 03.21.87.21.87; SNSM 02.35.28.00.91; ⊖ 02.35.28.19.40; Auto 08.92.68.08.76; Police 02.35.28.16.69; Ⓗ 02.35.28.05.13; British Consul 02.35.19.78.88.

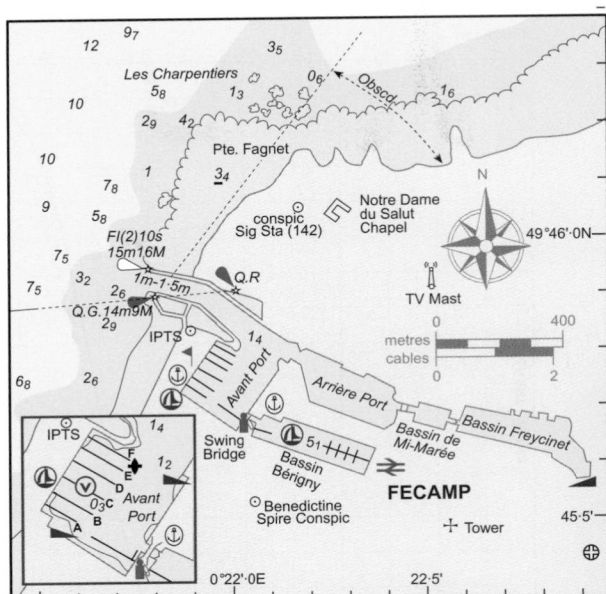

FACILITIES Marina plaisance@fecamp-bolbec.cci.fr www.fecamp-bolbec.cci.fr ☎ 02.35.28.13.58. 725 + 75 Ⓥ at 'C' pontoon fingers, €2·40. D & P (H24 with any credit card), C (mobile 20 ton), 🛟, Slip, ⚓, ME, El, Ⓔ, ✗, CH, Gaz, ▣.

Société des Régates de Fécamp ☎ 02.35.28.08.44; Bar.

Bassin Bérigny is entered via a gate & swing bridge, HW –2½ to HW +¾; pontoons at E end; max LOA for visitors is 45m. ☎ 02.35.28.23.76, FW, Slip, C (30 ton).

Town 🛒, Gaz, R, Bar, ✉, Ⓑ, ⇌. ✈ Le Havre.

9.17.17 LE HAVRE

Seine Maritime 49°29'·12N 00°05·43E ❀❀⊕♦♦♦❁❁

CHARTS AC *2613, 2146*, 2990; SHOM 7418, 6683; Navi 526, 1012; Imray C31; Stanfords 1, 21

TIDES –0103 Dover; ML 4·9; Duration 0543. Le Havre is a Standard Port (←). There is a stand of about 3 hrs at HW.

SHELTER Port of refuge H24. Excellent in marina (see overleaf).

NAVIGATION WPT 49°29'·86N 00°02'·33E (LH12), 108°/2·1M to Digue Nord. Yachts may cross frwy E of buoys LH7/LH8, but not at hbr ent, due to restr vis. Banc de l'Éclat (1m) lies close N of appr chan. Keep clear of vess ent/dept new commercial Port to the SE of the fairway. Works started (2009) to dredge and add 300 berths inside Bassin Vauban, works also at Le Havre Marina, including floating fuel berth and destruction of digue Charles Olsen.

LIGHTS AND MARKS 2 chys, RW conspic, on 106·8° ldg line. Twr of St Joseph's ⊕ is conspic. Obey IPTS at end of Digue Nord.

R/T Port Control & Radar Ch **12**, 20. Marina Ch 09.

TELEPHONE HM 02.35.21.23.95; Aff Mar 02.35.19.29.99; ⊖ 02.35.41.33.51; CROSS 02.33.52.72.23; Météo 02.35.42.21.06; Auto 08.92.68.08.76; Dr 02.35.41.23.61. Brit Consul 02.35.19.78.88.

FACILITIES Marina ☎ 02.35.21.23.95. www.lehavreplaisance.com 973 + 60 Ⓥ, pontoons 'O' or 'A', €2·59. BH (16 ton), de-mast C (6 ton), CH, Slip, P & D, El, Ⓔ, ME, ✗, SHOM, ACA, Gas, Gaz, R, ▣, 🛟, 🛒.

Sport Nautique du Havre (SNH) ☎ 02.35.21.01.41, Bar.

Sté Régates du Havre (SRH) ☎ 02.35.42.41.21, R, Bar (shut Aug).

City. All facilities.

See separate chartlet overleaf

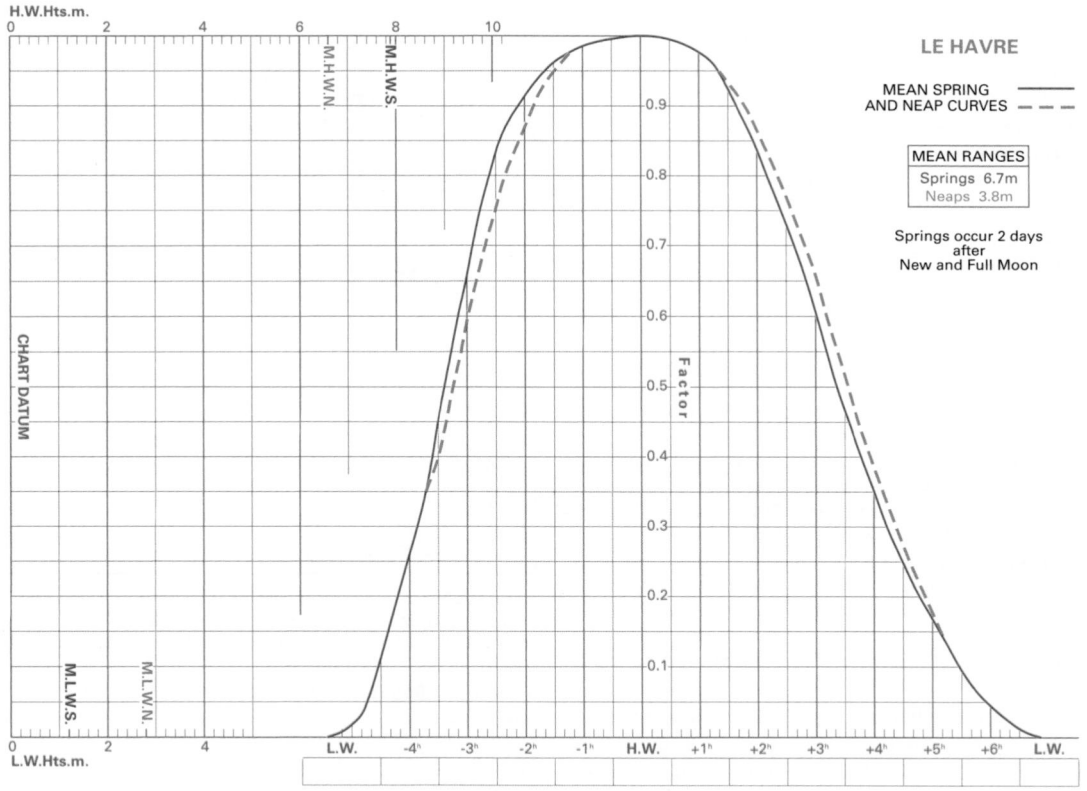

LE HAVRE

MEAN SPRING AND NEAP CURVES

MEAN RANGES
Springs 6.7m
Neaps 3.8m

Springs occur 2 days after New and Full Moon

LE HAVRE MARINA

THE SEINE ESTUARY

The Seine estuary is entered between Le Havre and Deauville, and is encumbered by shallow and shifting banks which extend seawards to Banc de Seine, 15M W of Le Havre. With wind against tide there is a heavy sea on this bank. N and E of it there are 4 big ship waiting anchorages. The estuary is carefully regulated by the port authorities at Le Havre and Rouen. Given the large amount of commercial traffic to/from both these ports, it is sensible for yachtsmen to study AC 2146, 2990 carefully prior to entering the area, so as to gain a sound working knowledge of their routes and the general layout. The Greenwich Meridian lies about 2·7M W of Cap de la Hève and Deauville; check the correct E/W hemisphere is set on your GPS and between your ears.

Yachts leaving **Le Havre** Marina near LW should give the inner spur, Fl (2) R 6s, a wide berth due to shoal ground. If bound for **Honfleur, Rouen** or **Paris**, do not try a short cut east of Rade de la Carosse WCM lt buoy 49°27'·70N 00°01'·17E; to do so risks grounding on Spoil Ground (0·4m). ►*The SW-going stream begins at HW Le Havre +0400, and the NE-going at HW Le Havre –0300, sp rates 1·5kn.*◄ Between Deauville and Le Havre the sea can be rough in W winds.

Chenal du Rouen is the main chan into R. Seine, and carries much commercial tfc. The S side of the chan is defined by Digue du Ratier, a training wall which extends E to Honfleur. Yachts should stay on the N side of the channel, just outside the PHM buoys, whether east or west bound. This rule applies between No 2 buoy and Tancarville bridge.

With 24 hours access/exit, **Honfleur** is a useful starting port when bound up-river. See routes to the Mediterranean (9.17.6), R. Seine, Rouen and Paris.

LE HAVRE   LAT 49°29'N   LONG 0°07'E
TIMES AND HEIGHTS OF HIGH AND LOW WATERS

Dates in red are **SPRINGS**
Dates in blue are **NEAPS**

YEAR 2010

N France

JANUARY

Time	m		Time	m
1 0535	1.5	**16**	0611	1.9
1048	7.9		1125	7.6
F 1807	1.1	SA	1831	1.6
2321	7.9		2348	7.5
2 0629	1.3	**17**	0646	1.8
1136	8.0		1157	7.6
SA 1859	0.9	SU	1905	1.6
3 0010	8.0	**18**	0020	7.5
0720	1.2		0719	1.8
SU 1224	8.1	M	1229	7.6
1948	0.9		1935	1.6
4 0058	8.0	**19**	0051	7.5
0807	1.2		0749	1.9
M 1312	8.0	TU	1300	7.6
2034	1.0		2004	1.7
5 0146	7.8	**20**	0121	7.4
0852	1.4		0817	2.0
TU 1359	7.8	W	1330	7.5
2117	1.2		2031	1.9
6 0233	7.6	**21**	0152	7.3
0935	1.7		0846	2.2
W 1447	7.5	TH	1403	7.3
2158	1.7		2100	2.1
7 0322	7.3	**22**	0225	7.1
1018	2.1		0918	2.4
TH 1537	7.2	F	1439	7.0
☽ 2241	2.1		2132	2.4
8 0415	7.1	**23**	0303	6.9
1106	2.5		0956	2.7
F 1636	6.9	SA	1522	6.8
2332	2.6	☾	2213	2.7
9 0518	6.8	**24**	0350	6.7
1206	2.8		1045	2.9
SA 1748	6.6	SU	1618	6.5
			2310	3.0
10 0039	2.9	**25**	0457	6.5
0632	6.7		1152	3.1
SU 1323	2.9	M	1742	6.4
1913	6.5			
11 0158	3.0	**26**	0027	3.1
0748	6.8		0629	6.5
M 1438	2.8	TU	1322	3.0
2027	6.7		1916	6.5
12 0308	2.8	**27**	0204	2.9
0849	7.0		0748	6.8
TU 1541	2.5	W	1450	2.5
2123	6.9		2029	6.9
13 0405	2.5	**28**	0322	2.4
0937	7.2		0852	7.2
W 1633	2.2	TH	1559	1.9
2207	7.2		2129	7.3
14 0452	2.3	**29**	0427	1.9
1017	7.4		0947	7.6
TH 1716	1.9	F	1702	1.4
2244	7.3		2221	7.7
15 0533	2.1	**30**	0528	1.4
1052	7.5		1037	7.9
F 1755	1.7	SA	1800	0.9
● 2317	7.4	○	2310	8.0
		31	0623	1.0
			1125	8.1
		SU	1852	0.6
			2356	8.1

FEBRUARY

Time	m		Time	m
1 0712	0.8	**16**	0659	1.5
1211	8.2		1205	7.7
M 1937	0.5	TU	1913	1.3
2 0041	8.2	**17**	0024	7.6
0755	0.8		0726	1.5
TU 1255	8.2	W	1235	7.7
2018	0.6		1940	1.4
3 0125	8.0	**18**	0054	7.6
0834	1.0		0754	1.6
W 1338	8.0	TH	1306	7.6
2055	1.0		2007	1.6
4 0206	7.8	**19**	0123	7.5
0910	1.4		0822	1.8
TH 1420	7.7	F	1337	7.4
2130	1.5		2035	1.8
5 0247	7.4	**20**	0154	7.3
0945	1.9		0852	2.0
F 1502	7.3	SA	1411	7.2
2203	2.1		2104	2.2
6 0330	7.1	**21**	0227	7.1
1024	2.4		0925	2.4
SA 1552	6.8	SU	1450	6.9
☽ 2244	2.7		2139	2.5
7 0425	6.7	**22**	0309	6.7
1115	2.9		1009	2.7
SU 1702	6.3	M	1544	6.5
2345	3.2	☾	2232	2.9
8 0546	6.4	**23**	0415	6.5
1233	3.2		1114	3.0
M 1847	6.1	TU	1712	6.3
			2353	3.2
9 0117	3.4	**24**	0600	6.4
0723	6.4		1251	3.0
TU 1406	3.1	W	1859	6.4
2013	6.3			
10 0245	3.2	**25**	0142	3.0
0834	6.6		0730	6.7
W 1523	2.7	TH	1431	2.5
2110	6.8		2015	6.9
11 0353	2.6	**26**	0306	2.4
0922	6.9		0838	7.2
TH 1621	2.3	F	1545	1.9
2151	7.0		2116	7.4
12 0442	2.3	**27**	0415	1.7
1000	7.2		0933	7.6
F 1704	1.9	SA	1650	1.2
2224	7.3		2206	7.8
13 0521	1.9	**28**	0517	1.2
1032	7.4		1022	8.0
SA 1741	1.6	SU	1747	0.8
2254	7.4	○	2252	8.0
14 0557	1.7			
1103	7.6			
SU 1815	1.5			
● 2324	7.5			
15 0629	1.6			
1134	7.7			
M 1845	1.4			
2354	7.6			

MARCH

Time	m		Time	m
1 0609	0.8	**16**	0603	1.5
1107	8.2		1107	7.7
M 1835	0.5	TU	1818	1.3
2336	8.2		2326	7.7
2 0654	0.6	**17**	0632	1.4
1151	8.3		1139	7.8
TU 1917	0.4	W	1846	1.3
			2356	7.7
3 0018	8.2	**18**	0700	1.3
0734	0.6		1210	7.8
W 1233	8.2	TH	1914	1.3
1955	0.6			
4 0058	8.1	**19**	0027	7.7
0810	0.9		0730	1.4
TH 1314	8.0	F	1243	7.7
2028	1.0		1943	1.4
5 0137	7.8	**20**	0058	7.6
0842	1.3		0801	1.5
F 1353	7.6	SA	1317	7.5
2058	1.6		2013	1.7
6 0213	7.4	**21**	0131	7.4
0913	1.8		0833	1.8
SA 1432	7.2	SU	1354	7.2
2127	2.2		2044	2.1
7 0251	7.0	**22**	0207	7.2
0946	2.4		0906	2.2
SU 1517	6.7	M	1437	6.9
☽ 2203	2.8		2121	2.5
8 0341	6.6	**23**	0252	6.8
1032	3.0		0951	2.5
M 1624	6.2	TU	1535	6.5
2301	3.4	☾	2216	2.9
9 0501	6.2	**24**	0401	6.5
1147	3.3		1057	2.9
TU 1812	6.0	W	1706	6.4
			2341	3.1
10 0036	3.6	**25**	0546	6.4
0648	6.1		1237	2.9
W 1327	3.3	TH	1845	6.5
1946	6.2			
11 0214	3.3	**26**	0128	2.9
0807	6.3		0713	6.7
TH 1449	2.9	F	1413	2.4
2044	6.5		1958	7.0
12 0325	2.8	**27**	0249	2.2
0856	6.7		0819	7.2
F 1550	2.4	SA	1525	1.7
2123	6.9		2056	7.4
13 0414	2.3	**28**	0357	1.6
0933	7.1		0913	7.6
SA 1635	1.9	SU	1629	1.2
2155	7.2		2145	7.8
14 0455	1.9	**29**	0456	1.2
1004	7.4		1001	7.9
SU 1714	1.6	M	1724	0.8
2224	7.4		2229	8.0
15 0531	1.6	**30**	0546	0.8
1035	7.6		1045	8.1
M 1748	1.4	TU	1810	0.6
● 2255	7.6	○	2311	8.1
		31	0630	0.7
			1129	8.1
		W	1851	0.7
			2352	8.1

APRIL

Time	m		Time	m
1 0708	0.7	**16**	0635	1.3
1210	8.1		1147	7.7
TH 1927	0.9	F	1849	1.4
2 0031	8.0	**17**	0002	7.7
0743	1.0		0709	1.3
F 1250	7.8	SA	1224	7.6
1959	1.2		1923	1.5
3 0109	7.7	**18**	0038	7.6
0815	1.3		0744	1.4
SA 1329	7.5	SU	1303	7.5
2029	1.7		1957	1.7
4 0145	7.4	**19**	0116	7.4
0845	1.8		0819	1.6
SU 1409	7.1	M	1346	7.3
2058	2.3		2033	2.0
5 0223	7.0	**20**	0159	7.2
0917	2.3		0858	2.0
M 1453	6.6	TU	1434	7.0
2134	2.9		2115	2.4
6 0309	6.6	**21**	0250	6.9
1000	2.9		0946	2.3
TU 1554	6.2	W	1536	6.7
☽ 2229	3.3	☾	2214	2.8
7 0421	6.1	**22**	0359	6.7
1109	3.2		1055	2.6
W 1726	6.0	TH	1702	6.6
2356	3.6		2338	2.9
8 0556	6.0	**23**	0531	6.6
1238	3.2		1225	2.5
TH 1854	6.1	F	1825	6.8
9 0125	3.3	**24**	0109	2.6
0716	6.2		0648	6.9
F 1356	2.9	SA	1348	2.2
1958	6.5		1933	7.1
10 0234	2.9	**25**	0224	2.1
0812	6.6		0753	7.2
SA 1458	2.5	SU	1458	1.7
2041	6.8		2030	7.4
11 0329	2.4	**26**	0329	1.7
0854	6.9		0849	7.5
SU 1550	2.1	M	1600	1.4
2117	7.2		2119	7.7
12 0415	2.0	**27**	0428	1.3
0929	7.3		0938	7.7
M 1634	1.8	TU	1654	1.2
2150	7.4		2204	7.9
13 0455	1.7	**28**	0518	1.1
1004	7.5		1024	7.8
TU 1712	1.6	W	1741	1.1
2223	7.6	○	2247	7.9
14 0530	1.5	**29**	0602	1.0
1038	7.6		1108	7.9
W 1744	1.4	TH	1821	1.1
● 2256	7.6		2328	7.9
15 0602	1.4	**30**	0641	1.0
1112	7.7		1150	7.8
TH 1816	1.4	F	1858	1.3
2328	7.7			

Chart Datum is 4·38 metres below IGN Datum. HAT is 8·4 metres above Chart Datum; see 4.5.

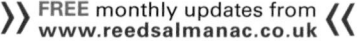

TIME ZONE -0100
Subtract 1 hour for UT
For French Summer Time add
ONE hour in **non-shaded areas**

LE HAVRE LAT 49°29'N LONG 0°07'E
TIMES AND HEIGHTS OF HIGH AND LOW WATERS

Dates in red are SPRINGS
Dates in blue are NEAPS

YEAR 2010

MAY

Day	Time m	Day	Time m
1 SA	0007 7.8 / 0717 1.2 / 1231 7.6 / 1932 1.5	16 SU	0652 1.3 / 1210 7.6 / 1908 1.5
2 SU	0045 7.6 / 0750 1.4 / 1311 7.4 / 2004 1.9	17 M	0023 7.7 / 0733 1.3 / 1254 7.5 / 1949 1.7
3 M	0123 7.4 / 0822 1.8 / 1351 7.1 / 2036 2.3	18 TU	0107 7.6 / 0815 1.5 / 1341 7.4 / 2031 1.9
4 TU	0202 7.0 / 0856 2.2 / 1434 6.7 / 2114 2.7	19 W	0154 7.4 / 0859 1.7 / 1433 7.2 / 2120 2.2
5 W	0245 6.7 / 0937 2.6 / 1525 6.4 / 2204 3.1	20 TH	0248 7.2 / 0950 2.0 / 1533 7.0 / 2219 2.4
6 TH	0342 6.3 / 1034 2.9 / 1634 6.2 / 2312 3.3	21 F	0353 7.0 / 1054 2.2 / 1645 6.9 / 2329 2.5
7 F	0458 6.2 / 1145 3.1 / 1749 6.3	22 SA	0507 6.9 / 1205 2.2 / 1756 7.0
8 SA	0026 3.2 / 0612 6.2 / 1254 2.9 / 1854 6.5	23 SU	0042 2.4 / 0618 7.0 / 1317 2.1 / 1901 7.1
9 SU	0133 3.0 / 0714 6.5 / 1357 2.7 / 1947 6.7	24 M	0152 2.2 / 0724 7.1 / 1425 1.9 / 2001 7.3
10 M	0232 2.6 / 0805 6.8 / 1454 2.3 / 2032 7.0	25 TU	0257 1.9 / 0824 7.3 / 1527 1.8 / 2055 7.5
11 TU	0324 2.3 / 0849 7.0 / 1544 2.1 / 2111 7.3	26 W	0357 1.7 / 0918 7.4 / 1622 1.6 / 2142 7.6
12 W	0410 2.0 / 0930 7.2 / 1628 1.8 / 2149 7.4	27 TH	0449 1.5 / 1007 7.5 / 1711 1.6 / 2227 7.7
13 TH	0452 1.7 / 1009 7.4 / 1709 1.7 / 2226 7.6	28 F	0535 1.4 / 1052 7.6 / 1753 1.6 / 2308 7.7
14 F	0532 1.5 / 1048 7.5 / 1748 1.5 / 2303 7.6	29 SA	0616 1.4 / 1135 7.6 / 1832 1.6 / 2348 7.6
15 SA	0612 1.3 / 1128 7.6 / 1828 1.5 / 2342 7.7	30 SU	0653 1.4 / 1215 7.5 / 1909 1.8
		31 M	0026 7.5 / 0729 1.5 / 1254 7.4 / 1945 1.9

JUNE

Day	Time m	Day	Time m
1 TU	0104 7.4 / 0804 1.7 / 1332 7.2 / 2020 2.2	16 W	0100 7.8 / 0816 1.1 / 1335 7.5 / 2036 1.5
2 W	0142 7.2 / 0839 2.0 / 1411 6.9 / 2056 2.5	17 TH	0149 7.6 / 0903 1.3 / 1426 7.5 / 2123 1.7
3 TH	0221 6.9 / 0915 2.3 / 1452 6.7 / 2137 2.7	18 F	0240 7.5 / 0950 1.5 / 1519 7.3 / 2213 2.0
4 F	0303 6.7 / 0957 2.6 / 1539 6.5 / 2224 2.9	19 SA	0335 7.2 / 1040 1.8 / 1617 7.2 / 2307 2.2
5 SA	0354 6.5 / 1047 2.8 / 1637 6.4 / 2320 3.1	20 SU	0437 7.0 / 1136 2.1 / 1720 7.1
6 SU	0457 6.4 / 1145 2.9 / 1743 6.5	21 M	0009 2.3 / 0544 6.9 / 1241 2.3 / 1826 7.0
7 M	0021 3.0 / 0607 6.4 / 1247 2.8 / 1846 6.6	22 TU	0118 2.4 / 0655 6.9 / 1350 2.3 / 1933 7.1
8 TU	0125 2.9 / 0710 6.6 / 1350 2.7 / 1941 6.8	23 W	0227 2.3 / 0806 7.0 / 1456 2.3 / 2035 7.2
9 W	0227 2.6 / 0808 6.8 / 1451 2.4 / 2031 7.1	24 TH	0329 2.1 / 0906 7.1 / 1555 2.2 / 2127 7.4
10 TH	0325 2.2 / 0856 7.0 / 1546 2.1 / 2116 7.3	25 F	0425 1.9 / 0957 7.3 / 1646 2.0 / 2213 7.5
11 F	0417 1.9 / 0943 7.2 / 1637 1.9 / 2200 7.5	26 SA	0513 1.7 / 1042 7.4 / 1732 1.9 / 2254 7.5
12 SA	0506 1.6 / 1028 7.4 / 1725 1.7 / 2243 7.6	27 SU	0556 1.6 / 1122 7.4 / 1813 1.8 / 2332 7.6
13 SU	0554 1.3 / 1113 7.6 / 1813 1.5 / 2327 7.7	28 M	0635 1.5 / 1159 7.4 / 1852 1.8
14 M	0642 1.2 / 1159 7.7 / 1901 1.4	29 TU	0008 7.6 / 0712 1.5 / 1235 7.4 / 1928 1.8
15 TU	0013 7.8 / 0730 1.1 / 1247 7.7 / 1949 1.4	30 W	0044 7.5 / 0747 1.6 / 1310 7.3 / 2002 2.0

JULY

Day	Time m	Day	Time m
1 TH	0119 7.4 / 0819 1.8 / 1344 7.2 / 2035 2.1	16 F	0136 7.9 / 0855 0.9 / 1408 7.8 / 2112 1.3
2 F	0152 7.2 / 0849 2.0 / 1417 7.0 / 2106 2.3	17 SA	0222 7.7 / 0935 1.3 / 1455 7.6 / 2154 1.7
3 SA	0226 7.0 / 0920 2.2 / 1452 6.9 / 2140 2.6	18 SU	0310 7.4 / 1016 1.7 / 1544 7.3 / 2239 2.1
4 SU	0304 6.8 / 0955 2.5 / 1532 6.8 / 2221 2.8	19 M	0403 7.1 / 1103 2.2 / 1640 7.0 / 2333 2.5
5 M	0350 6.6 / 1040 2.7 / 1623 6.6 / 2313 3.0	20 TU	0509 6.7 / 1202 2.6 / 1750 6.8
6 TU	0449 6.5 / 1137 2.9 / 1730 6.5	21 W	0044 2.7 / 0631 6.6 / 1318 2.8 / 1911 6.8
7 W	0018 3.0 / 0605 6.4 / 1247 2.9 / 1846 6.6	22 TH	0201 2.7 / 0756 6.7 / 1433 2.8 / 2022 6.9
8 TH	0133 2.9 / 0722 6.5 / 1405 2.8 / 1952 6.8	23 F	0309 2.4 / 0900 6.9 / 1537 2.5 / 2117 7.1
9 F	0247 2.5 / 0826 6.8 / 1514 2.4 / 2049 7.1	24 SA	0410 2.2 / 0949 7.1 / 1634 2.3 / 2202 7.3
10 SA	0349 2.0 / 0922 7.1 / 1613 2.0 / 2140 7.4	25 SU	0501 1.9 / 1030 7.3 / 1720 2.0 / 2240 7.5
11 SU	0446 1.6 / 1013 7.4 / 1710 1.7 / 2228 7.7	26 M	0543 1.7 / 1106 7.4 / 1759 1.8 / 2314 7.6
12 M	0542 1.3 / 1101 7.7 / 1805 1.4 / 2315 7.9	27 TU	0620 1.5 / 1138 7.5 / 1836 1.7 / 2346 7.6
13 TU	0636 1.0 / 1148 7.8 / 1857 1.2	28 W	0654 1.5 / 1210 7.5 / 1909 1.7
14 W	0002 8.0 / 0726 0.8 / 1236 7.9 / 1946 1.1	29 TH	0019 7.6 / 0726 1.5 / 1242 7.5 / 1940 1.7
15 TH	0049 8.0 / 0812 0.8 / 1322 7.9 / 2030 1.1	30 F	0051 7.6 / 0754 1.6 / 1313 7.4 / 2008 1.9
		31 SA	0122 7.4 / 0820 1.8 / 1342 7.2 / 2035 2.0

AUGUST

Day	Time m	Day	Time m
1 SU	0152 7.3 / 0847 2.0 / 1413 7.2 / 2104 2.3	16 M	0242 7.4 / 0947 1.8 / 1509 7.3 / 2207 2.1
2 M	0226 7.0 / 0916 2.3 / 1448 7.0 / 2138 2.6	17 TU	0331 7.0 / 1027 2.5 / 1601 6.9 / 2257 2.7
3 TU	0306 6.8 / 0953 2.6 / 1531 6.7 / 2223 2.8	18 W	0437 6.5 / 1124 3.0 / 1715 6.5
4 W	0357 6.5 / 1044 2.9 / 1629 6.5 / 2323 3.1	19 TH	0010 3.0 / 0614 6.3 / 1250 3.3 / 1852 6.4
5 TH	0511 6.3 / 1154 3.2 / 1755 6.4	20 F	0139 3.0 / 0747 6.4 / 1417 3.1 / 2011 6.7
6 F	0048 3.1 / 0648 6.4 / 1330 3.0 / 1922 6.6	21 SA	0256 2.7 / 0850 6.7 / 1528 2.7 / 2105 7.0
7 SA	0220 2.7 / 0805 6.7 / 1452 2.6 / 2028 7.0	22 SU	0400 2.3 / 0934 7.1 / 1624 2.3 / 2145 7.3
8 SU	0329 2.1 / 0905 7.2 / 1557 2.0 / 2123 7.4	23 M	0447 1.9 / 1010 7.3 / 1705 2.0 / 2219 7.5
9 M	0431 1.5 / 0958 7.6 / 1658 1.6 / 2213 7.8	24 TU	0525 1.7 / 1042 7.5 / 1741 1.7 / 2250 7.7
10 TU	0531 1.1 / 1046 7.9 / 1756 1.2 / 2300 8.1	25 W	0559 1.5 / 1111 7.6 / 1814 1.6 / 2320 7.7
11 W	0625 0.7 / 1132 8.1 / 1846 0.9 / 2346 8.2	26 TH	0630 1.4 / 1141 7.6 / 1845 1.6 / 2351 7.7
12 TH	0713 0.5 / 1217 8.2 / 1931 0.8	27 F	0659 1.4 / 1211 7.6 / 1912 1.6
13 F	0031 8.2 / 0755 0.5 / 1301 8.1 / 2013 0.9	28 SA	0022 7.7 / 0725 1.5 / 1240 7.6 / 1939 1.7
14 SA	0115 8.1 / 0834 0.8 / 1344 7.9 / 2051 1.2	29 SU	0051 7.6 / 0751 1.7 / 1309 7.5 / 2006 1.9
15 SU	0159 7.8 / 0911 1.2 / 1426 7.6 / 2128 1.6	30 M	0122 7.4 / 0818 1.9 / 1339 7.3 / 2036 2.1
		31 TU	0155 7.1 / 0847 2.2 / 1412 7.0 / 2107 2.4

Chart Datum is 4·38 metres below IGN Datum. HAT is 8·4 metres above Chart Datum; see 4.5.

》》 **FREE** monthly updates from 《《
www.reedsalmanac.co.uk

TIME ZONE -0100
Subtract 1 hour for UT
For French Summer Time add
ONE hour in **non-shaded areas**

LE HAVRE   LAT 49°29'N   LONG 0°07'E
TIMES AND HEIGHTS OF HIGH AND LOW WATERS

Dates in red are **SPRINGS**
Dates in blue are NEAPS

YEAR 2010

N France

SEPTEMBER

Time	m		Time	m
1 0234	6.8	**16**	0410	6.4
0920	2.6		1050	3.3
W 1453	6.8	TH	1642	6.4
☽ 2148	2.8		2337	3.2
2 0325	6.5	**17**	0551	6.1
1007	3.0		1222	3.5
TH 1551	6.5	F	1824	6.3
2245	3.1			
3 0441	6.3	**18**	0112	3.2
1118	3.3		0725	6.3
F 1723	6.4	SA	1354	3.3
			1949	6.5
4 0015	3.2	**19**	0230	2.8
0628	6.3		0827	6.7
SA 1307	3.2	SU	1503	2.8
1900	6.6		2043	6.8
5 0200	2.7	**20**	0329	2.4
0747	6.8		0908	7.0
SU 1435	2.6	M	1554	2.3
2009	7.1		2118	7.2
6 0312	2.0	**21**	0414	2.0
0847	7.3		0941	7.3
M 1541	1.9	TU	1635	2.0
2105	7.5		2150	7.5
7 0415	1.4	**22**	0453	1.7
0938	7.7		1010	7.5
TU 1642	1.4	W	1712	1.7
2154	7.9		2220	7.7
8 0513	0.9	**23**	0529	1.5
1025	8.0		1039	7.6
W 1737	1.0	TH	1745	1.6
● 2240	8.2	○	2251	7.8
9 0605	0.6	**24**	0600	1.5
1109	8.2		1109	7.7
TH 1826	0.7	F	1815	1.6
2325	8.3		2322	7.8
10 0650	0.5	**25**	0628	1.5
1153	8.3		1139	7.7
F 1910	0.7	SA	1843	1.6
			2353	7.7
11 0009	8.3	**26**	0656	1.5
0731	0.6		1209	7.6
SA 1235	8.2	SU	1912	1.6
1949	0.8			
12 0052	8.1	**27**	0024	7.6
0809	0.9		0724	1.7
SU 1316	8.0	M	1239	7.5
2025	1.2		1942	1.7
13 0134	7.8	**28**	0057	7.4
0843	1.5		0754	1.9
M 1356	7.6	TU	1311	7.4
2100	1.7		2013	2.0
14 0216	7.3	**29**	0134	7.2
0916	2.1		0825	2.3
TU 1437	7.2	W	1347	7.2
2136	2.3		2046	2.3
15 0304	6.8	**30**	0216	6.9
0953	2.7		0900	2.6
W 1527	6.8	TH	1431	6.8
☽ 2222	2.8		2127	2.7

OCTOBER

Time	m		Time	m
1 0310	6.6	**16**	0509	6.2
0948	3.0		1144	3.6
F 1533	6.5	SA	1737	6.2
☽ 2225	3.0			
2 0428	6.4	**17**	0027	3.3
1102	3.3		0637	6.3
SA 1705	6.4	SU	1310	3.4
2357	3.1		1858	6.4
3 0611	6.5	**18**	0142	3.0
1250	3.1		0743	6.6
SU 1839	6.7	M	1417	2.9
			1958	6.7
4 0139	2.6	**19**	0241	2.6
0725	6.9		0828	6.9
M 1415	2.5	TU	1510	2.5
1946	7.1		2041	7.0
5 0251	2.0	**20**	0331	2.2
0824	7.4		0903	7.3
TU 1520	1.9	W	1556	2.1
2042	7.6		2115	7.3
6 0352	1.4	**21**	0415	1.9
0915	7.8		0935	7.5
W 1619	1.4	TH	1636	1.9
2131	8.0		2149	7.5
7 0449	1.0	**22**	0453	1.7
1001	8.1		1006	7.6
TH 1713	1.0	F	1713	1.7
● 2218	8.2		2222	7.7
8 0539	0.8	**23**	0527	1.7
1045	8.2		1038	7.7
F 1801	0.8	SA	1745	1.6
2303	8.3	○	2255	7.7
9 0624	0.7	**24**	0558	1.6
1127	8.2		1110	7.7
SA 1844	0.8	SU	1816	1.6
2347	8.2		2328	7.7
10 0704	0.9	**25**	0629	1.6
1209	8.1		1142	7.7
SU 1923	1.0	M	1849	1.6
11 0030	8.0	**26**	0003	7.6
0741	1.2		0702	1.7
M 1250	7.9	TU	1216	7.6
1959	1.3		1923	1.7
12 0112	7.7	**27**	0041	7.5
0815	1.7		0736	1.9
TU 1330	7.6	W	1253	7.5
2033	1.8		1958	1.9
13 0155	7.3	**28**	0122	7.3
0848	2.3		0811	2.2
W 1411	7.2	TH	1335	7.2
2109	2.3		2035	2.2
14 0242	6.8	**29**	0208	7.0
0926	2.9		0851	2.6
TH 1459	6.7	F	1423	7.0
☽ 2153	2.9		2118	2.5
15 0343	6.4	**30**	0304	6.8
1021	3.3		0943	2.9
F 1607	6.4	SA	1524	6.8
2300	3.2	☽	2218	2.7
		31	0419	6.6
			1056	3.1
		SU	1647	6.7
			2343	2.8

NOVEMBER

Time	m		Time	m
1 0547	6.7	**16**	0036	3.1
1228	2.9		0636	6.5
M 1811	6.8	TU	1316	3.2
			1857	6.5
2 0111	2.5	**17**	0142	2.9
0657	7.1		0732	6.8
TU 1347	2.4	W	1417	2.8
1918	7.2		1951	6.8
3 0222	2.0	**18**	0241	2.6
0756	7.5		0818	7.0
W 1453	1.9	TH	1511	2.5
2016	7.5		2036	7.0
4 0324	1.6	**19**	0331	2.3
0849	7.8		0857	7.3
TH 1553	1.5	F	1557	2.2
2108	7.8		2116	7.3
5 0421	1.3	**20**	0414	2.1
0936	8.0		0934	7.5
F 1647	1.3	SA	1638	1.9
2157	8.0		2154	7.4
6 0512	1.2	**21**	0453	1.9
1021	8.1		1010	7.6
SA 1736	1.1	SU	1716	1.7
● 2243	8.0	○	2232	7.6
7 0557	1.2	**22**	0530	1.8
1105	8.1		1045	7.7
SU 1819	1.1	M	1753	1.6
2328	8.0		2309	7.6
8 0638	1.3	**23**	0608	1.7
1147	8.0		1121	7.7
M 1859	1.2	TU	1832	1.5
			2348	7.6
9 0012	7.8	**24**	0647	1.7
0716	1.6		1200	7.7
TU 1228	7.8	W	1911	1.5
1936	1.5			
10 0054	7.6	**25**	0030	7.6
0752	1.9		0727	1.8
W 1308	7.6	TH	1242	7.6
2011	1.8		1952	1.6
11 0136	7.3	**26**	0114	7.5
0827	2.3		0808	2.0
TH 1349	7.2	F	1327	7.5
2047	2.2		2033	1.8
12 0221	6.9	**27**	0202	7.3
0906	2.8		0852	2.3
F 1433	6.9	SA	1416	7.3
2128	2.7		2120	2.1
13 0312	6.6	**28**	0257	7.1
0953	3.1		0944	2.5
SA 1528	6.5	SU	1513	7.1
☽ 2221	3.0	☽	2215	2.3
14 0416	6.4	**29**	0402	7.0
1055	3.4		1047	2.6
SU 1638	6.3	M	1622	7.0
2326	3.2		2321	2.4
15 0529	6.4	**30**	0515	7.0
1206	3.4		1157	2.6
M 1752	6.3	TU	1737	7.0

DECEMBER

Time	m		Time	m
1 0034	2.4	**16**	0020	3.2
0623	7.1		0626	6.5
W 1312	2.5	TH	1301	3.2
1846	7.1		1852	6.4
2 0148	2.2	**17**	0130	3.1
0726	7.3		0726	6.7
TH 1424	2.2	F	1412	3.0
1951	7.3		1952	6.7
3 0255	1.9	**18**	0238	2.8
0824	7.5		0818	7.0
F 1527	1.9	SA	1513	2.6
2050	7.5		2044	6.9
4 0354	1.8	**19**	0335	2.5
0916	7.7		0903	7.2
SA 1623	1.6	SU	1604	2.2
2143	7.7		2130	7.2
5 0447	1.6	**20**	0423	2.2
1004	7.8		0945	7.4
SU 1713	1.5	M	1651	1.9
● 2231	7.8		2213	7.4
6 0534	1.6	**21**	0509	1.9
1049	7.9		1026	7.6
M 1758	1.4	TU	1736	1.6
2316	7.8	○	2255	7.6
7 0616	1.6	**22**	0554	1.7
1131	7.9		1107	7.8
TU 1839	1.4	W	1821	1.4
2359	7.7		2337	7.7
8 0656	1.7	**23**	0640	1.6
1211	7.8		1150	7.9
W 1917	1.5	TH	1907	1.2
9 0039	7.6	**24**	0021	7.7
0733	1.9		0725	1.5
TH 1249	7.6	F	1234	7.9
1953	1.7		1952	1.2
10 0118	7.4	**25**	0107	7.7
0810	2.1		0810	1.6
F 1328	7.4	SA	1320	7.8
2028	2.0		2036	1.4
11 0156	7.2	**26**	0154	7.6
0846	2.4		0854	1.7
SA 1406	7.1	SU	1407	7.6
2104	2.3		2119	1.6
12 0236	6.9	**27**	0243	7.5
0923	2.7		0939	2.0
SU 1447	6.9	M	1457	7.4
2141	2.6		2203	1.9
13 0320	6.7	**28**	0336	7.3
1005	3.0		1027	2.2
M 1533	6.6	TU	1553	7.2
☽ 2225	2.9	☽	2254	2.2
14 0413	6.5	**29**	0437	7.1
1055	3.2		1124	2.5
TU 1632	6.4	W	1700	7.0
2318	3.1		2355	2.5
15 0518	6.5	**30**	0546	7.0
1154	3.3		1233	2.6
W 1743	6.4	TH	1815	6.9
		31	0111	2.6
			0657	7.0
		F	1353	2.5
			1932	6.9

Chart Datum is 4·38 metres below IGN Datum. HAT is 8·4 metres above Chart Datum; see 4.5.

》》 **FREE** monthly updates from 《《
www.reedsalmanac.co.uk

9.17.18 HONFLEUR
Calvados 49° 25′·69N 00° 13′·90E ✹✹✹✹◊◊◊◊✿✿✿

CHARTS AC *2146*, 2990, 2879, *1349*; SHOM 7418, 6683, 7420; Navi 1012; Imray C31; Stanfords 1, 21

TIDES –0135 Dover; ML 5·0; Duration 0540.

Standard Port LE HAVRE (←)

Times				Height (metres)			
High Water		Low Water		MHWS	MHWN	MLWN	MLWS
0000	0500	0000	0700	7·9	6·6	2·8	1·2
1200	1700	1200	1900				
LE HAVRE-ANTIFER (49°39′·5N 00°06′·8E)							
+0025	+0015	+0005	–0005	+0·1	0·0	0·0	0·0
CHENAL DE ROUEN (49°26′N 00°07′E)							
0000	0000	–0005	+0015	+0·1	0·0	0·0	–0·1
HONFLEUR							
–0135	–0135	+0015	+0040	+0·1	+0·1	+0·1	+0·3

In the Seine a HW stand lasts about 2hrs 50 mins. The HW time differences refer to the beginning of the stand.

SHELTER Excellent in the Vieux Bassin and Bassin de l'Est.

NAVIGATION WPT No 2 PHM buoy, QR, 49°27′·40N 00°01′·35E,

8·7M to Honfleur. From WPT keep N of the Chenal de Rouen between PHM buoys and posts marking Digue basse du Nord; there is no room for E-bound yachts to navigate S of the chan. Beware risk of collision in low vis with W-bound yachts. This rule applies from No 2 buoy to Tancarville bridge.

After No 20 PHM buoy cross to the ent. Caution: strong stream across ent. Rouen is 60M and Paris 192M up-river.

LIGHTS AND MARKS See chartlet and 9.17.4. The radar tower by the lock and the Pont de Normandie 1·6M up-river are highly conspic; slightly less so are the wooded hills SW of Honfleur.

R/T HM Ch **17** 73; Lock **17** (H24); Honfleur Radar Ch **73** (H24).

TELEPHONE Port HM 02.31.14.61.09; CROSS 02.33.52.72.13; Aff Mar 02.31.53.66.50; ⊜ 02.31.14.44.30; SNSM 02.31.89.20.17; Auto (local) 08.92.68.08.14; Auto (regional) 08.92.68.08.76; Auto (offshore) 08.92.68.08.08; Police 02.31.14.44.45; Dr 02.31.89.34.05; Ⓗ 02.31.89.89.89; Brit Consul 02.35.19.78.88.

THE LOCK (☎ 02.31.98.72.82) operates H24 and opens at H, every hour for arrivals; and every H +30 for departures. It is 23m wide and has recessed floating bollards, no pontoons. **IPTS** in force. Freeflow operates from HW Le Havre –1 to HW.

If arriving/departing LW ±2, the pecked line on chartlet indicates best water very close to the E side of the ent; W side is shoal.

Note. Major repairs to the lock began in 2009, and may continue through to the 2010 season. During this time passage will be possible only at HW (freeflow).

THE ROAD BRIDGE at the Vieux Bassin lifts at times (LT) below. Inbound yachts can wait on E side of the jetty immediately outside the Vieux Bassin. Departing yachts take priority over arrivals; be ready 5 mins in advance.

1 May to 31 Aug
Every day: 0830, 0930, 1030, 1130. 1630, 1730, 1830, 1930.

1 Jan to 30 April and 1 Sep to 31 Dec
Every day: 0830, 0930, 1030, 1130. 1430, 1530, 1630, 1730.
Red times must be requested, Mon-Fri.

FACILITIES The Avant Port's W wall, close N of the waiting jetty, can be a temp'y (max 24 hrs) berth, useful for locking out before the Vieux Bassin's 0830 bridge lift or to await the next lock time.

Vieux Bassin ☎ 02.31.98.87.13 (CNH). www.ville-honfleur.fr info@ville-honfleur.fr 120 + 30 Ⓥ, max LOA 20m, €2·30; €2·00 Avant-Port; multihulls and large motor yachts plus 50%. Ⓥ raft on pontoons on NW side; or in a CNH berth as assigned by CNH dory which meets and directs all arrivals.

Cercle Nautique d'Honfleur (CNH) controls all yacht berthing. ☎ 02.31.98.87.13. cnh14@wanadoo.fr M, Bar.

Bassin de l'Est can be used by yachts >20m LOA; see HM. BY, ✖, Ⓔ, C (10 ton and for masting), Slip.

Town P & D (cans), 🛒, R, Bar, ⊚, Gaz, @, ✉, Ⓑ, ⇌, ✈ Deauville.

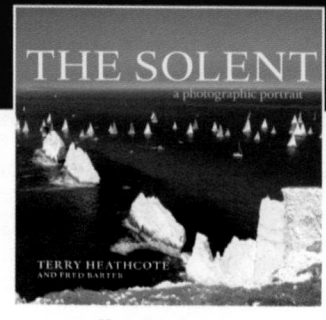

9.17.19 RIVER SEINE

CHARTS AC 2146, 2990, 2879; SHOM 6683, 6796, 6117; Imray C31; Carte-Guide Navicarte No 1.

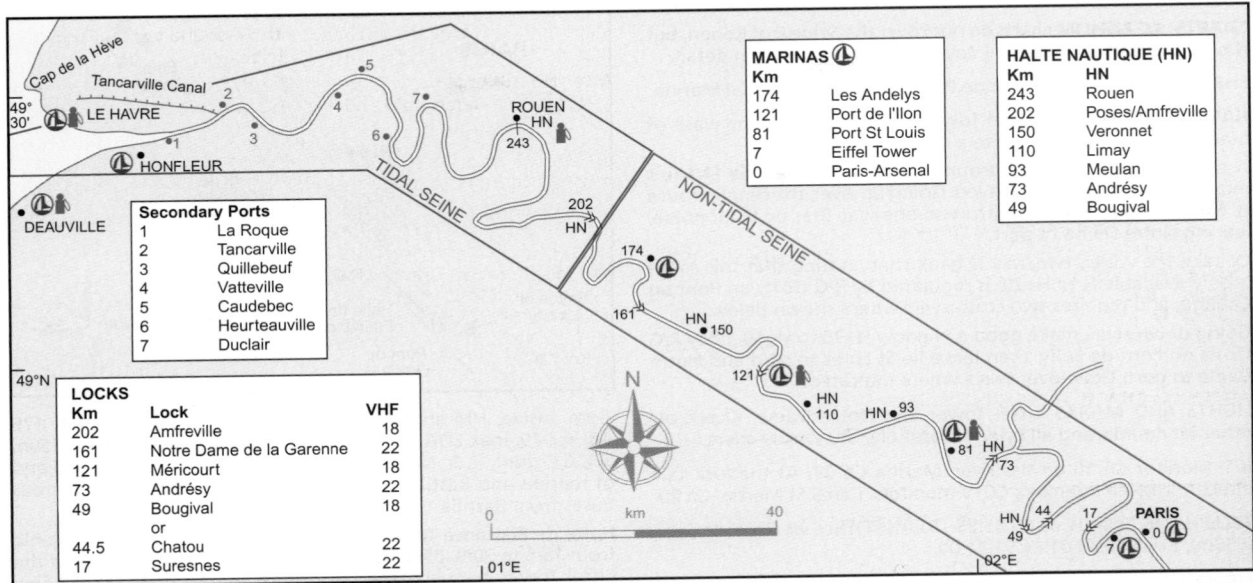

MARINAS ⚓	
Km	
174	Les Andelys
121	Port de l'Ilon
81	Port St Louis
7	Eiffel Tower
0	Paris-Arsenal

HALTE NAUTIQUE (HN)	
Km	HN
243	Rouen
202	Poses/Amfreville
150	Veronnet
110	Limay
93	Meulan
73	Andrésy
49	Bougival

Secondary Ports
1	La Roque
2	Tancarville
3	Quillebeuf
4	Vatteville
5	Caudebec
6	Heurteauville
7	Duclair

LOCKS
Km	Lock	VHF
202	Amfreville	18
161	Notre Dame de la Garenne	22
121	Méricourt	18
73	Andrésy	22
49	Bougival or	18
44.5	Chatou	22
17	Suresnes	22

TIDES Standard Port LE HAVRE (←)

Times				Height (metres)			
High Water		Low Water		MHWS	MHWN	MLWN	MLWS
0000	0500	0000	0700	7·9	6·6	2·8	1·2
1200	1700	1200	1900				

Differences TANCARVILLE* *(Km 338. 49°28'·35N 00°27'·88E)*
−0105	−0100	+0105	+0140	−0.1	−0.1	0.0	+1.0

QUILLEBEUF* *(Km 332. 49°28'·25N 00°32'·00E)*
−0045	−0050	+0120	+0200	0.0	0.0	+0.2	+1.4

VATTEVILLE* *(Km 317. 49°28'·89N 00°40'·01E)*
+0005	−0020	+0225	+0250	0.0	−0.1	+0.8	+2.3

CAUDEBEC* *(Km 309. 49°31'·35N 00°43'·66E)*
+0020	−0015	+0230	+0300	−0.3	−0.2	+0.9	+2.4

HEURTEAUVILLE* *(Km 295. 49°25'·70N 00°48'·17E)*
+0110	+0025	+0310	+0330	−0.5	−0.2	+1.1	+2.7

DUCLAIR* *(Km 278. 49°28'·73N 00°52'·38E)*
+0225	+0150	+0355	+0410	−0.4	−0.3	+1.4	+3.3

ROUEN *(Km 245. 49°26'·50N 01°03'·13E)*
+0440	+0415	+0525	+0525	−0.2	−0.1	+1.6	+3.6

*HW time differences refer to the start of a stand lasting about 2¾ hrs up to Vatteville, decreasing to about 1¾ hrs at Duclair.

SHELTER: Marinas/Haltes Nautiques/fuel, see above. Masts can be lowered at Dives, Deauville, Le Havre, Honfleur and Rouen.

TIDAL STREAMS require careful study; see *N France and Belgium Cruising Companion* (Featherstone/NDL) for tidal stream graphs and a detailed analysis, plus Rouen and Paris. ▶*At Ratier NW SHM buoy the flood starts at LW Le Havre +1 and at La Roque (Km342)* at LW+2, and progressively later further up-river. So even a 5kn boat which left Le Havre at LW (or Honfleur at LW+1) and passed the W end of Digue du Ratier at LW+15, should carry the flood to Rouen. If delayed, try another day rather than stopping en route.

Going down-river on the ebb a boat will meet the flood. In a fast boat it is worth continuing, rather than x for about 4 hrs, because the ebb starts sooner further down-river one gets.◀

NAVIGATION The tidal section to Rouen should be completed in 1 day, because the strong stream and ships' wash make it dangerous to berth alongside and uncomfortable to ⚓. Yacht navigation is prohib at night, and ⚓s are few. A radar reflector, VHF aerial and white ⚓ lt are needed, even with mast down.

Enter the buoyed Chenal de Rouen abm No 2 buoy. Care is needed to avoid the shoal banks N of No 2 buoy, especially in morning fog; keep W of Rade de la Carosse WCM buoy. The approach can be rough in a strong W'ly over ebb tide. From No 2 buoy to Tancarville bridge yachts must keep outboard of the PHM chan buoys, in either direction. Pont de Normandie (52m) is conspic 1·7M E of Honfleur.

Entry via the Canal de Tancarville is possible if sea conditions are bad, but expect delays due to 2 locks and 8 bridges. At Le Havre transit the Bassins Bellot, Vétillart, Despujols and the Canal du Havre, leading via the Canal de Tancarville to the lock (Km338).

From Amfreville lock to Paris current is about 1kn in summer, more after winter floods. 6 of 7 locks must be transited; foc 0700-1900.

R/T Ch 73 (*Rouen Port Control*) gives nav, vis, weather and water level info on request. Monitor Ch 73 for tfc info. Ch 82 broadcasts water levels from Le Havre to Caudebec every 5 mins.

ROUEN, Seine Maritime, **49°26'·07N 01°06'·24E**. AC 2879; SHOM 6796, 6117. Yacht navigation prohib SS+½ to SR−½. AB in the Halte Nautique, NE side of Île Lacroix, Km241 (Lat/Long above). A one-way system in the chan NE of Île Lacroix only allows navigation *against* the stream. For example, if leaving on the young flood to go up-river, you must first go down-river to the NW tip of the island, then turn up-river via the SW chan. *Rouen Port* VHF Ch **73** 68. HM 02.35.52.54.56; Aff Mar 02.35.98.53.98; ⊖ 02.35.98.27.60; Météo 02.35.80.11.44.
Facilities: **Bassin St Gervais** (N bank, Km245). Mast down/up @ pontoon SE side; C (3 to 25 ton) max stay 48 hrs.

Halte Nautique ☎ 02.32.08.31.40, www.rouen.port.fr 50 AB €1·65, FW, ⬦, Slip, C (30 ton), BH (4 ton), ME, El, ✕, CH, Ⓔ, P (cans), D barge at Km239. **Rouen YC** ☎ 02.35.66.52.52.

ROUEN

Pont Corneille
Km 242
■ VNF

One way system: Only against the flood or ebb

Halte Nautique ⚓
⚓
Île Lacroix
N
Pont Mathile
RIVE GAUCHE
0   metres   400

9.17.20   PARIS

Île-de-France, **48°50'·84N 02°22'·02E** (Paris-Arsenal marina).

CHARTS AC & SHOM charts do not cover the Seine E of Rouen, but Navicarte's Carte-Guide No 1 covers Le Havre to Paris in detail.

SHELTER Complete in Halte de Plaisance & Paris-Arsenal Marina.

NAVIGATION Between Eiffel Tower and Notre Dame the wash of many *vedettes* can raise quite a chop.

A traffic system (chartlet) around Île de la Cité and Île St Louis must be understood and obeyed. Going up-river, the simpler route is: Hug the S bank in the narrowish one-way Bras de la Monnaie, leaving Notre Dame to port.

Or take the wider, two-way N bank chan, noting that this route is only available H to H+20; is regulated by R/G tfc lts on Pont au Change; and requires two cross-overs where shown below.

Going down-river, make good a window H+35 to H+50, obey R/G tfc lts on Pont de Sully, then leave Île St Louis to stbd and Notre Dame to port. Cross-over twice where indicated.

LIGHTS AND MARKS Eiffel Tower and Notre Dame. Check off other landmarks and all bridges carefully; obey cross-overs.

R/T Monitor Ch 10 on the river. Marina Ch 09. At the lock talk direct to HM via intercom; CCTV monitors. Canal St Martin, Ch 20.

TELEPHONE Taxi 01.45.85.85.85. Tourist Office at Gare de Lyon (550m); Brit Consul 01.44.51.31.00.

FACILITIES

Paris-Arsenal Marina 11 bld de la Bastille, 75012 Paris. HM Olivier Peresse-Gourbil ☎ 01.43.41.39.32. opg@portparisarsenal.com www.paris-ports.fr No reservations 1/6-30/9, but contact HM several days before arrival. Enter 0800-1900 (2000: w/e, and Jul/Aug) via small lock, with waiting pontoon outside; obey R/G tfc lts signed 'Plaisance'. Air clearance in lock is 5·2m, least depth

1·9m. Inside, HM and office are to stbd; berth as directed. 176 AB, €2·75; max LOA 25m. D & P (by cans & marina trolley, 750m SE), C (7 ton), 🛢, R. Metro stns: Quai de la Rapée (Line 5) at S end of marina and Bastille (Lines 1, 5 & 8) at the N end. Numerous buses from Bastille.

Halte de Plaisance Tour Eiffel (also for larger yachts) is available from 18/5 to 30/9, 0900-1900. It is on the SE bank, 1km SW of the Eiffel Tower, between the rail bridge and Pont de Bir Hakeim; sheltered from wash by Ile aux Cygnes, a long thin islet in mid stream. It can only be accessed in an up-river (NE) direction.

AB €2·27 on 140m long pontoon, with no air clearance limit; book ☎ 01.55.42.79.59. FW, AC, Shwr, D&P (cans). Metro: Bir Hakeim (line 6); Charles Michels (line 10). No 70 bus. RER line C.

City Everything.

9.17.21 DEAUVILLE/TROUVILLE
Calvados **49° 22'·38N 00° 04'·15E** ✿✿✿◊◊◊◊✿✿✿

CHARTS AC *2613, 2146, 1349*; SHOM 7418, 7420; Navi 526; Imray C32; Stanfords 1, 21

TIDES –0130 Dover; ML 5·1; Duration 0510.

Standard Port LE HAVRE (←)

Times				Height (metres)			
High Water		Low Water		MHWS	MHWN	MLWN	MLWS
0000	0500	0000	0700	7·9	6·6	2·8	1·2
1200	1700	1200	1900				
Differences TROUVILLE							
–0100	–0010	0000	+0005	+0·4	+0·3	+0·3	+0·1

NOTE: There is a double HW at Trouville. The HW time differences, when referred to the time of HW Le Havre, give the times of the first HW.

SHELTER Good in Port Deauville (2·8m) & Bassin Morny (3m), but access difficult in NW/N winds >F 5. Only FVs berth at Trouville.

NAVIGATION WPT 49°22'·94N 00°03'·62E, 148°/0·65M to abeam W training wall lt, Fl WG 4s. Semoy ECM lt buoy marks wreck 2·1M from ent, close W of ldg line. Do not appr from E of N due to Les Ratelets drying shoal and Banc de Trouville. Trouville SW WCM buoy is 1M WNW of ent. Chan and river dry 2·4m; no access LW±2½, for 2m draft.

LIGHTS AND MARKS Trouville's Casino and Deauville's Royal Hotel/ Casino (off chartlet to the SW) are conspic. Front 148° ldg lt not visible when brg >150°. Bassin Morny ent gate: **IPTS**, sigs 2-4.

R/T Port Deauville and Bassin Morny: Ch 09.

TELEPHONE Aff Mar 02.31.88.36.21; ⊖ 02.31.88.35.29; SNSM 02.31.88.31.70; CROSS 02.33.52.72.13; Auto (local) 08.92.68.08.14; Auto (regional) 08.92.68.08.76; Auto (offshore) 08.92.68.08.08; Police 02.31.88.13.07; Dr 02.31.88.23.57; Ⓗ 02.31.14.33.33; Brit Consul 02.35.19.78.88. Deauville Tourist office 02.31.14.40.00.

FACILITIES from seaward:
Port Deauville Lock ☎ 02.31.98.30.01 free flow approx HW–2 to +2. Marina ☎ 02.31.98.30.01. port-deauville-sa@wanadoo.fr www. deauville.org 700 + 150 **Ⓥ** €2·70 (Jul, Aug). D, ME, El, ⚒, C (6 ton), BH (45 ton), Slip, CH, SM, R, Bar.

Port Morny Entry gate (☎ 02.31.88.57.89) is open from HW –2 to +2½. Visit www.dyc14.com for actual local times.

Marina ☎ 02.31.98.50.40 (0830-1200, 1330-1800) www.deauville. org 320 AB, no **Ⓥ** (but see Bassin Morny below), Slip, D&P (cans) 1Km. Water taxi to Trouville runs frequently from the LW berth in the river or HW berth when the gate is open.

Bassin Morny ☎ 02.31.98.50.40, 80 **Ⓥ** AB/raft along the eastern quay, €2·92. The footbridge remains open whilst the entry gate is open. Petrol is most easily and cheaply (30% less) obtained by calling *Taupan* ☎ 02.31.79.21.02 who send a bowser to the boat.

Deauville YC ☎ 02.31.88.38.19. deauville.yacht.club@wanadoo.fr www.dyc14.com, Bar. In vicinity: CH, ME, El, ⚒, C (8 ton). Hotel Ibis @.

Both towns 🛒, Gaz, R, Bar, ✉, Ⓑ, BY, CH, Slip, ⚒, ME, El, Ⓔ, ⊡, ⇌, ✈ Deauville. Ferry: See Ouistreham.

DEAUVILLE TO GRANDCAMP

(AC *2146, 2136*). Since access to all the hbrs along this coast is to some extent tidally limited, it is best to cruise this area from W to E, so as to take advantage of the main Channel flood. ▶*Thus you can leave one harbour at the start of the tidal window and reach the next hbr before the window has closed; in the opposite direction this is difficult and may be impossible unless you have a fast boat. Between Le Havre and Ouistreham there is a useful stand at HW of between 2-3hrs.*◀ Le Havre, possibly Ouistreham, and St Vaast (in all but S/SE winds) may be regarded as the only ports of refuge. Strong onshore winds render the approaches to other hbrs difficult or even dangerous.

Deauville, 8M S of Cap de la Hève, is an important yachting hbr. The sands dry more than 5ca offshore; in strong W or N winds the entrance is dangerous and the sea breaks between the jetties. In such conditions it is best attempted within 15 mins of HW, when the stream is slack. To the NE beware Banc de Trouville (1·7m), and Les Ratelets (0·9m) to the N at the mouth of the Seine. 7M SW is **River Dives** with marina. The banks dry for 1M to seaward, and entry is only possible from HW ± 2½, and not in fresh onshore winds when the sea can be rough.

6M W lies **Ouistreham** ferry hbr and marina, the latter accessed by lock. The waiting pontoon N of the locks is for boats intending to transit the locks. It is not for yachts on passage merely pausing to await a fair tide or get some rest. Here a canal leads 7M inland to a marina in the centre of Caen. 2-6M W the drying rocky ledges, Roches de Lion and Les Essarts de Langrune, extend up to 2·25M offshore in places. Roches de Ver (drying rks) lie near the centre of Plateau du Calvados, extending 1M offshore about 2M W of **Courseulles-sur-Mer** which is dangerous to approach in strong onshore winds.

5M W of Courseulles are the remains of the wartime hbr of **Arromanches**, where there is a fair weather anchorage, usually affected by swell. Rochers du Calvados (1·6m) lies close NE of the ruined Mulberry hbr. Beware many wrecks and obstructions.

Between **Port-en-Bessin** and Pte de la Percée a bank lies up to 3ca offshore, with drying ledges and the wrecks and obstructions of Omaha Beach marked by 3 NCM buoys.

▶*A small race forms off Pte de la Percée with wind against tide. Off Port-en-Bessin the E-going stream begins about HW Le Havre –0500, and the W-going at about HW Le Havre +0050, sp rates 1·25kn.*◀

9.17.22 DIVES-SUR-MER

Calvados **49°17'·68N 00°05'·63W** (entry gate) ✱✱✦✧✧✿✿

CHARTS AC *2146, 1349*; SHOM 7418, 7420 (the preferred chart); Navi 526; Imray C32; Stanfords 1, 21

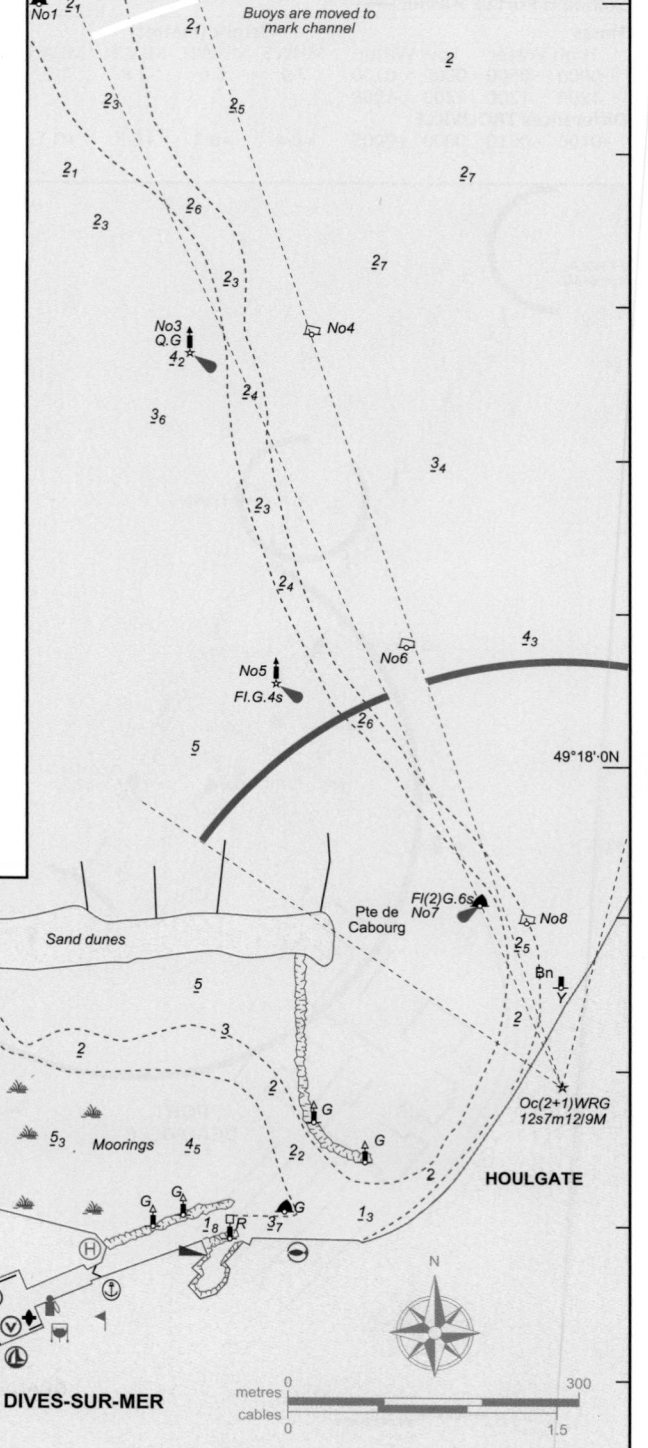

TIDES –0135 Dover; ML 5·1m; Duration.

Standard Port LE HAVRE (←—)

Times				Height (metres)			
High Water		Low Water		MHWS	MHWN	MLWN	MLWS
0000	0500	0000	0700	7·9	6·6	2·8	1·2
1200	1700	1200	1900				
Differences DIVES-SUR-MER							
–0100	–0010	0000	0000	+0·3	+0·2	+0·2	+0·1
OUISTREHAM							
–0045	–0010	–0005	0000	–0·3	–0·3	–0·2	–0·3

NOTE: There is a double HW at Dives. HW time differences, referred to the time of HW Le Havre, give times of the first HW.

SHELTER Excellent inside. Appr can be difficult in NW/NE >F5 when a bad sea can quickly build.

NAVIGATION WPT 49°19'·18N 00°05'·85W, SWM buoy 'DI' (off chartlet), L Fl 10s, 168°/7ca to Nos 1/2 buoys. Appr dries to 1M offshore. See FACILITIES for access times. The W sector of the 159° Dir lt covers the appr as far as Nos 3 & 4 marks; thence follow the buoyed chan between sandbanks (drying 4·2m).

4 PHM and 2 SHM unlit buoys are moved to suit shifting chan; No 7 SHM is the only lit lateral buoy; Nos 3 and 5 SHMs are fixed lt bns which should be given a wide berth. Caution: Buoys/bns may lack numbers.

After last chan buoys, for best water hug the shore to G buoy and 2 G perches marking submerged training wall leading to marina ent. Marina is 400m W of Dir lt, an inconspic R hut.

Or follow drying Dives river to YC's pontoon (2 ♥ berths) E of footbridge.

LIGHTS AND MARKS See 9.17.4 and the chartlet. Wooded hills E of Dives and Houlgate church spire help locate the marina.

R/T Ch 09, H24.

TELEPHONE CROSS/SNSM 02.31.88.11.13; Météo via HM; Auto 08.92.68.08.14; Police 02.31.28.23.00; Dr 02.31.91.60.17; Brit Consul 02.35.19.78.88.

FACILITIES Marina ☎ 02.31.24.48.00. sncport guillaume@cegetel. net www.calvados-nautisme.com Access via entry gate HW±3; HW±2½ for draft >1·5m; HW±1½ in bad conditions. Note: unless recently dredged, craft with draft >1·9m should only attempt entry HW±2. Sill below gate is 2·5m above CD; gate opens when tide 4·5m above CD and at springs may create a 4–5kn current for the first 45 mins. 550+50 ♥ €2·75, max LOA 15m, draft 1·9m. Office hrs: H24 summer; 0900-1200, 1400-1800 winter. P&D H24, ▣, Slip, BH (30 ton), BY, ME, El, CH, ✕, demasting C (1·5 ton). No @ or Wi-Fi.

Cabourg YC ☎ 02.31.91.23.55, Bar. Access HW ±2½ to drying M. Town ☵, R, Bar, Ⓑ, ✉, ▣, ✈ (Deauville). Ferry: Ouistreham.

9.17.23 OUISTREHAM

Calvados 49°16'·82N 00°14'·89W (E lock) ✿✿⚓⚓⚓✿✿

CHARTS AC 2613, 2146, 2136, 1349; SHOM 7418, 7421, 7420; Navi 526; Imray C32; Stanfords 1, 21

TIDES –0118 Dover; ML 4·6; Duration 0525. See 9.17.22.

SHELTER Very good in marina. Access HW–2¼ to +3¼ via lock, where strong N winds may complicate boat handling.

NAVIGATION WPT 49° 19'·18N 00° 14'·54W (abm Nos 1 & 2 buoys) 184·5°/2·1M to front ldg lt. In the outer channel, the harbour and the Canal to Caen ships and ferries have priority over all other craft. Outer chan is marked by lt buoys 1-6 and 3 pairs of lt bns; see half-scale inset on chartlet. Waiting pontoon on E side of Avant Port almost dries. Beware current when securing in lock.

Lock opens 5 times in each direction before/after HW, ie:					
Landward	–2¾	–1¼	+½*	+2¼	+3¾
Seaward	–3¼	–1¾	HW*	+1¾	+3¼
Asterisks = optional, depending on tidal range.					

Times are valid 365/365, inc w/ends and public hols. Detailed timings, which may vary, are posted on the website, waiting pontoon and at Ouistreham marina, or call Ch 12. Yachts usually enter canal via smaller E lock.

LIGHTS AND MARKS See chartlet and 9.17.4. The 184·5° synch ldg lts are easily seen even in poor vis or bright sun. The huge square block of Caen hospital is conspic from afar; ditto the main lt ho, W + R top. IPTS (full code) shown from lock control twr. A Ⓦ port or stbd of lowest main tfc lt, = E or W lock for yachts. Two Iso 4s, two QW and Fl R 4s define the ferry turning area.

R/T Call *Ouistreham Port* Ch **74**, 68; Lock Ch **12**, 68 (HW –2 to +3); Marina Ch 09, 74; Sté des Régates Ch 09 (office hours).

TELEPHONE Port HM & lock 02.31.36.22.00; ⊜ 02.31.96.89.10; Aff Mar 02.31.53.66.50; CROSS 02.33.52.72.13; SNSM 02.31.97.50.49; Ferry terminal 02.31.96.80.80; Météo 02.31.26.68.11; Auto 08.92.68.08.77; Police 02.31.97.13.15; Dr 02.31.97.18.45; Ⓗ (Caen) 02.31.27.27.27; Brit Consul 02.35.19.78.88; Taxi 02.31.97.35.67.

FACILITIES Marina ☎ 02.31.96.91.37. 600 + 65 Ⓥ €2·47. Ⓥ raft on pontoon D in 3·5m. Slip, ME, El, ✕, CH, BH (14 ton), Gas, Gaz, Kos, SM, BY, Ⓔ, SHOM, P&D (fuel available ¾hr before lock opens); www.ouistreham-plaisance.com

Société des Régates de Caen-Ouistreham (SRCO), www.ycf-club. fr ☎ 02.31.97.13.05. Bar. **Town** 🍴, Gaz, R, Bar, ✉, Ⓑ, ⇌ (bus to Caen), ✈ (Caen). Ferry: to Portsmouth.

HARBOUR AT SOUTH END OF OUISTREHAM CANAL

CAEN 49°10'·95N 00°21'·17W. Charts: AC *1349*, SHOM 7420.

NAVIGATION The 8M canal passage is simple and takes approx 1½hrs. Depths 2·5m to 9·8m; max speed 7kn; no overtaking.

The 3 opening bridges are: Bénouville (Pegasus) (2½M S of Ouistreham), Colombelles (5M) and La Fonderie, Caen (8M). Tfc lts are not used; N-bound vessels have right of way at bridges.

Bridges open free† for boats which transit at the scheduled times, 1/4-30/9, ie S-bound: Dep Bénouville bridge* 1010, 1330, 1630. N-bound dep La Fonderie bridge: 0845, 1200, 1500. Times can vary; check with marina or the website below. †At other times fees are due. *Allow ½hr from Ouistreham lock/marina.

R/T Monitor Ch 68 in the canal. *Caen Port* Ch **74**, 68.

Marina ☎ 02.31.95.24.47. www.caen-plaisance.com After La Fonderie bridge turn 90° stbd for marina (4m) at Bassin St Pierre in city centre. Ⓥ berths on pontoon E or as directed. 76 + 16 Ⓥ, €1·90, max LOA 25m, draft 3.8m. ME, ✕, El,SM, CH.

City P&D (cans), Ⓑ, Ⓗ, ✉, Bar, R, @, 🍴, ⇌, ✈ Caen-Carpiquet.

9.17.24 COURSEULLES-SUR-MER

Calvados 49°20'·40N 00°27'·32W ❀❀♓♓✿✿

CHARTS AC *2613, 2136, 1349*; SHOM 7421, 7420; Navi 526; Imray C32; Stanfords 1, 21

TIDES –0145 Dover; ML 4·6; Duration No data. See 9.17.25

SHELTER Good in Bassin Joinville (3m), but appr becomes difficult in strong N to NE winds. Exposed offshore ⚓ (3-5m) at L'Anneau de la Marguerite, 134°/0·4M from SWM buoy.

NAVIGATION WPT 49° 21'·28N 00° 27'·69W (SWM buoy Iso 4s), 134°/5ca, then 198°/5ca, to E jetty hd. Plateau du Calvados extends 2M seaward and banks dry for >0·6M offshore, also beware oyster beds 3·5M W of ent. Outer ldg marks are: front, Bernières ⊕ tower ≠ 134° rear, twin spires of Douvres-La-Délivrande (partly obsc'd by trees and below the skyline when close-in). There are 2 other spires in the vicinity. At night the two bkwtr lts ≠ 186° form a useful ldg line. Beware rks awash at CD either side of ldg line.

Avant Port dries 2·5m; best ent at HW –1, keep to the E side. Entry gate into Bassin Joinville stays open approx HW ±2. The Control Twr opens the swing bridge above it on request Ch 09 or when an arriving yacht is spotted, usually quite quickly. **IPTS** in use. There is space at the SW end of the Bassin to turn a boat round.

LIGHTS AND MARKS See chartlet and 9.17.4. Both drying bkwtrs and their perches are easily seen, as is a conspic crucifix at root of the W bkwtr. A Cross of Lorraine is 4ca, and Pte de Ver lt ho is 2·5M W of the hbr ent.

R/T Ch 09: Control Twr HW±2.

TELEPHONE Control twr 02·31·37·46·03; Aff Mar 02·31·53·66·50; CROSS 02·33·52·72·13; ⊜ 02·31·21·71·09 @ Port-en-Bessin; SNSM 02·31·37·45·47; Météo 08·36·68·08·14; Auto 08·92·68·32·50; Gendarmes 02·31·29·55·20; Dr 02·31·37·45·24; Ⓗ 02·31·27·27·27 (Caen); Fire 18; Ambulance 02·31·44·88·88 or 15; Brit Consul 02·35·19·78·88 (Le Havre).

FACILITIES Bassin Plaisance local shoal draft boats in 1m; no Ⓥ.

Bassin Joinville ☎ 02.31.37.51.69. Marina hours: Apr-Jun, 7/7 0900-1200. Jul/Aug: 7/7 0900-1200 and at tide times (approx HW ±3). Sep-Mar, M-Sat 0900-1200. Other hours exist; 09-1200 is a constant. 730+20 Ⓥ, berth as directed by HM, or if absent, on pontoon 'X' on E Quay. 5m LOA = €8·80; add €4·10 for each additional metre and approx €0·20 holiday tax per head/night, ie a 10m boat is €29·30 + holiday tax. 11m max LOA. Slip, C (25 ton), P & D (cans 600m), BY, ME, El, Ⓔ, ✕, CH, SM.

Société des Régates de Courseulles (SRC) ☎ 02.31.37.47.42, Bar.

Town 🍴, Gaz, R, Bar, Wi-Fi, @, ✉, ⊙, Ⓑ, ⇌ (via bus to Caen), ✈ (Caen-Carpiquet). Taxi ☎ 02.31.37.90.37. Ferry: Ouistreham.

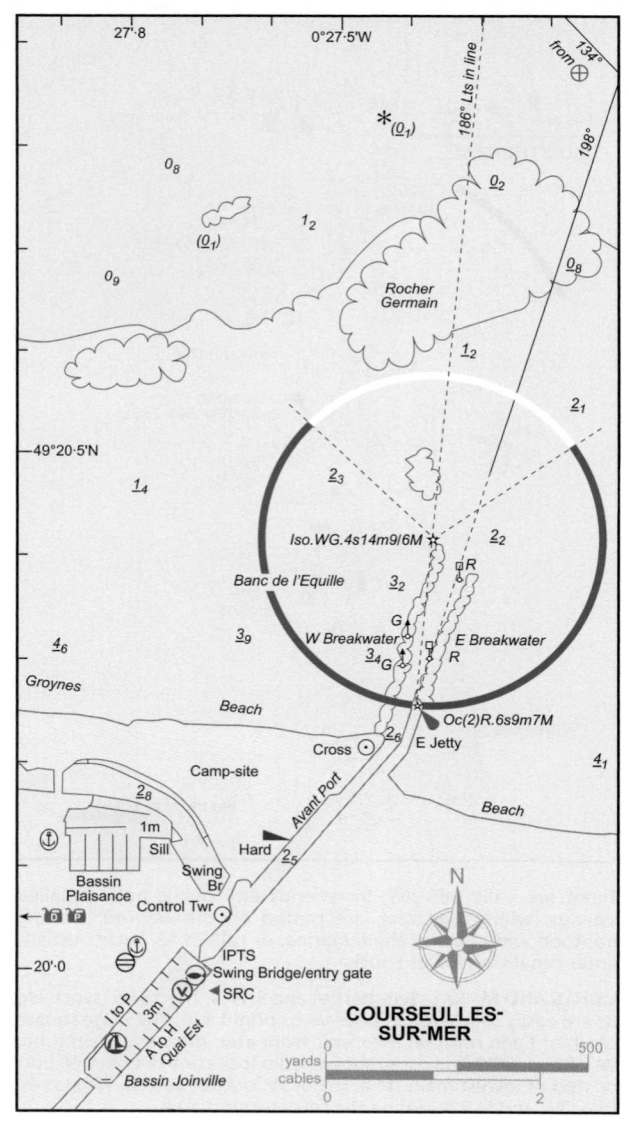

MULBERRY ANCHORAGE 6·5M WEST OF COURSEULLES

ARROMANCHES, Calvados, **49°21'·36N 00°37'·25W**. AC *2613, 2136*; SHOM 7421; Navi 527. Tides, see 9.17.25. Strictly a fair weather anchorage, with limited shelter from the ruined WW II Mulberry caissons which are conspicuous especially at LW. Swell intrudes and can make the anchoring uncomfortable. Rochers du Calvados, 7ca ENE of the entrance, dries 1·6m but can be crossed near HW.

There are many obstructions within the harbour and offshore: 3 to the W and N are marked by a WCM and two ECM buoys. From the more N'ly ECM buoy (Roseberry, 49°23'·10N 00°36'·49W) the entrance (lat/long as line 1) bears approx 196°/1·8M; it is marked by a small unlit SHM and PHM buoy.

Enter on about 245° for charted anchorage in 3-5m to S of the caissons, or sound closer inshore with caution. Entry from E or W is not advised due to uncharted obstructions. Caution: rocky plateau (3·4m) and further obstructions W of the dinghy landing area.

Facilities: YC Port Winston ☎ 02.31.22.31.01, 2 dinghy slips. Worth going ashore for D-Day museums and the panoramic view from the clifftops, but very crowded in season.

9.17.25 PORT-EN-BESSIN

Calvados 49°21'·16N 00°45'·40W (Hbr ent) ⚓♒✿

CHARTS AC *2613, 2136, 1349*; SHOM 7421, 7420; Navi 527; Imray C32; Stanford 1, 21

TIDES −0215 Dover; ML 4·4; Duration 0520.

Standard Port LE HAVRE (←—)

Times				Height (metres)			
High Water		Low Water		MHWS	MHWN	MLWN	MLWS
0000	0500	0000	0700	7·9	6·6	2·8	1·2
1200	1700	1200	1900				
Differences COURSEULLES-SUR-MER							
−0045	−0015	−0020	−0025	−0·5	−0·5	−0·1	−0·1
PORT-EN-BESSIN							
−0055	−0030	−0030	−0035	−0·7	−0·7	−0·2	−0·1
ARROMANCHES							
−0055	−0025	−0025	−0035	−0·6	−0·6	−0·2	−0·2

SHELTER Good. Ent difficult in strong N/NE'lies and dangerous in F8+. No ⚓ in outer hbr nor 1ca either side of 204° ldg line.

NAVIGATION WPT 49°21'·62N 00°45'·09W, 204°/0·5M to hbr ent. Avoid G sector of W mole hd Fl WG 4s which covers the inshore dangers off Omaha Beach, 3 to 6M to the WNW. In the outer hbr beware submerged jetty (marked by R bcn) to E of ent chan. Note 2009 works to sill and gates should be complete by 2010 season.

LIGHTS AND MARKS Conspic marks: a water twr (104m) 1·7M ESE of the hbr; a Sig Stn 7 cables W of hbr. Ldg lts 204°: Front, W pylon, G top, at bottom of hill; rear, W house/grey roof near top of the hillside. See chartlet and 9.17.4 for other lts.

IPTS control entry to the basins. Entry gate opens HW ±2. While gate stays open, swing bridge opens whenever possible to suit yachts and FVs; there is little road traffic. When shut the bridge shows FR in the middle.

R/T Ch 18 (HW ±2) for gate opening H24.

TELEPHONE HM 02.31.21.70.49; Aff Mar 02.31.21.71.52; CROSS 02.33.52.72.13; ⊖ 02.31.21.71.09; Auto 08.92.68.08.14; Sig Stn/SNSM 02.31.21.81.51; Police 02.31.21.70.10; Dr 02.31.21.74.26; Ⓗ 02.31.51.51.51; Brit Consul 02.33.78.01.83.

FACILITIES A major FV port. **Outer Hbr** dries up to 3·7m; Slip, L. Basins accessible HW ±2. Waiting possible on Quai de L'Epi.

Bassin 1: Inside the entry gate, tight turn 90° stbd, berth bows E or W. Space for only 6-8 yachts in NNW corner; usually foc for 1 or 2 nights. Yachts may stay only 24-48 hrs, due to limited space. No berthing on sloping E wall. Call Gate-master ☎ 02.31.21.71.77 (HW ±2) to pre-book gate time if leaving at early hour.

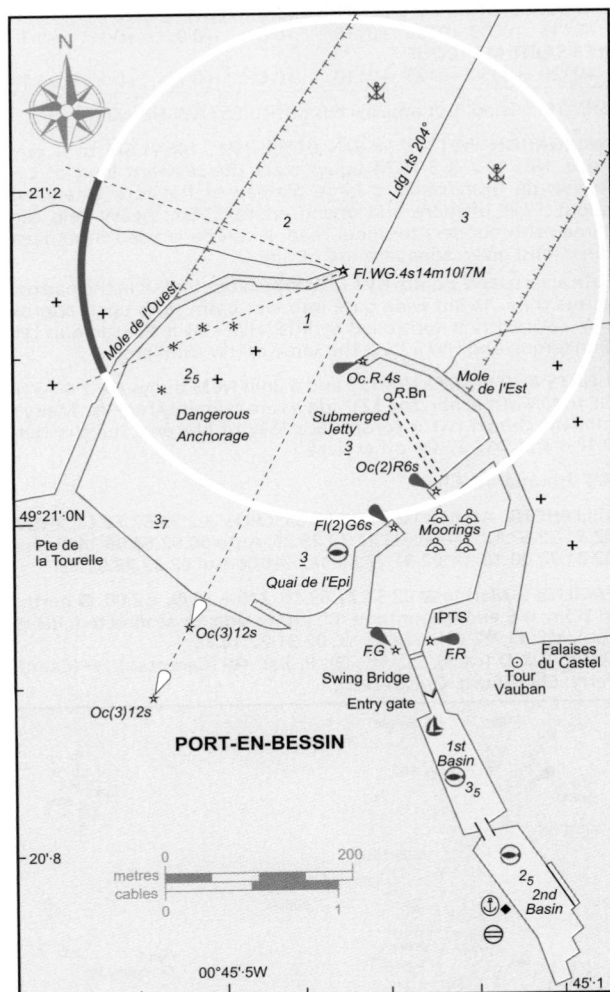

Bassin 2, no entry. **Services:** Slip, M, C (4 ton), CH, El, Ⓔ, ME, ✕.
Town P & D, 🛒, Gaz, R, Bar, ✉, Ⓑ, ⇌ (bus to Bayeux), ✈ (Caen, ☎ 02.31.26.58.00). Ferry: See Ouistreham.

9.17.26 GRANDCAMP

Calvados 49°23'·51N 01°02'·99W (Pierheads) ⚓️🛥🛟🛟⚓️⚓️

CHARTS AC *2613, 2135, 1349*; SHOM 7422, 7420; Navi 527; Imray C32; Stanford 1, 2, 21.

TIDES –0220 Dover; ML Rade de la Capelle 4·4; Duration 0510.
Standard Port CHERBOURG (⟶)

Times				Height (metres)			
High Water		Low Water		MHWS	MHWN	MLWN	MLWS
0300	1000	0400	1000	6·4	5·0	2·5	1·1
1500	2200	1600	2200				
Differences RADE DE LA CAPELLE (3M to NW)							
+0115	+0050	+0130	+0115	+0·8	+0·9	+0·1	+0·1
ILES SAINT MARCOUF							
+0120	+0050	+0125	+0110	+0·6	+0·7	+0·1	+0·1

SHELTER Good, but approach is difficult in NW-NE winds >F6.

NAVIGATION WPT 49°24'·82N 01°04'·33W, 146°/1·6M to E pier head. Nos 1, 3 & 5 NCM buoys mark the seaward limit of Les Roches de Grandcamp, a large plateau of flat rock extending about 1½M offshore and drying approx 1·5m; heavy kelp can cause echosounders to under-read. It can be crossed from most directions, given adequate rise of tide.

Safe appr sp HW ±2, nps HW ±1½. Watch out for FVs in the narrow access chan. 14·3m wide gate into wet basin stays open approx HW ±2½; entry is controlled by IPTS. HW –2½ is the same as LW Dunkerque and HW +2½ is the same as HW Dunkerque.

LIGHTS AND MARKS Nos 1, 3 and 5 unlit NCM buoys are 1·4-1·7M NE to NW of the hbr. The 221° ldg lts are primarily for FVs. Maisy's modern church twr is conspic 6ca SSW of hbr ent. See chartlet, 9.17.4 and 9.17.27 for other data.

R/T Hbr/marina Ch 09.

TELEPHONE Aff Mar 02.31.22.60.65; CROSS 02.33.52.72.13; SNSM 02.31.22.67.12; Météo 02.21.33.25.26; Auto 08.92.68.08.14; Police 02.31.22.00.18; Dr 02.31.22.60.44; Brit Consul 02.33.78.01.83.

FACILITIES Marina ☎ 02.31.22.63.16. 240 + 10 Ⓥ, €2·00. Ⓥ berths in 2·5m at E end of pontoon 'C', either side; or as directed. BH (5 ton), ME, El, ⚒, CH, Gaz, C, YC 02.31.22.14.35.
Town, P & D (cans), ✉, 🛒, Ⓑ, R, Bar, 🚂 (Carentan), ✈ (Caen). Ferry: Cherbourg, Ouistreham.

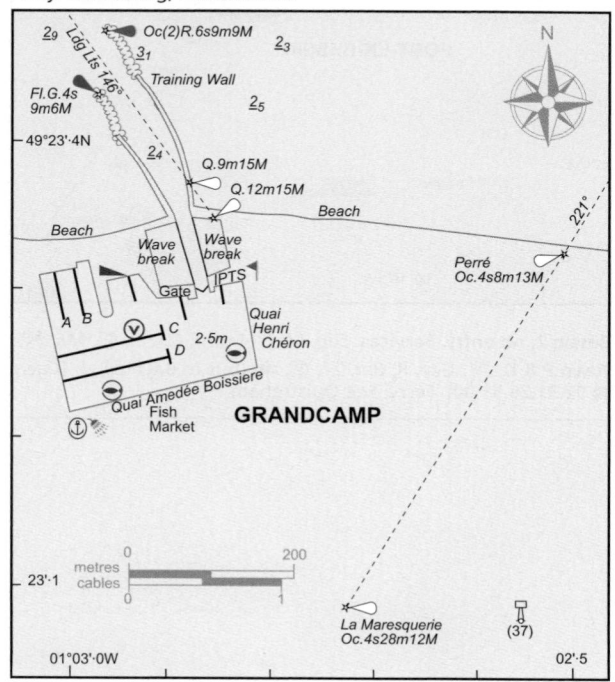

GRANDCAMP TO POINTE DE BARFLEUR

(AC *2135*) On E side of B du Grand Vey, Roches de Grandcamp (dry) extend more than 1M offshore, N and W of **Grandcamp**, but they are flat and can be crossed from the N in normal conditions HW±1½. Three NCM buoys mark the N edge of this ledge. Heavy kelp can give false echo-sounder readings.

At the head of B du Grand Vey, about 10M S of Îles St Marcouf, are the (very) tidal hbrs of Carentan and Isigny; entry is only possible near HW and should not be attempted in strong onshore winds. The **Carentan** chan is well buoyed and adequately lit. It trends SSW across sandbanks for about 4M, beyond which it runs between two training walls leading to a lock, and thence into the canal to Carentan's popular marina. The **Isigny** chan is slightly deeper, but the hbr dries to steepish mudbanks.

Îles St Marcouf lie 7M SE of St Vaast-la-Hougue, about 4M offshore, and consist of Île du Large (lt) and Île de Terre about ¼M apart. The Banc du Cardonnet, with depths of 5·2m and many wks, extends for about 5M ESE from the islands. Banc de St Marcouf, with depths of 2·4m and many wks, extends 4·5M NW from the isles, and the sea breaks on it in strong N/NE winds.

Approach **St Vaast-la-Hougue** S of Île de Tatihou, but beware drying rks: La Tourelle (unmarked), Le Gavendest and La Dent, which lie near the approaches and are buoyed. 2M N is Pte de Saire with rks and shoals up to 1M offshore. From Pte de Saire the coast runs 4M NNW to drying **Barfleur**.

Raz de Barfleur, in which the sea breaks heavily, must be avoided in bad weather, particularly with NW or SE winds against the tide, by passing 5-7M seaward of Pte de Barfleur.

▶*In calmer weather it can be taken at slack water (HW Cherbourg –4½ and +2) via an inshore passage, 3ca NE of La Jamette ECM beacon. Expect some turbulence.*◀

Pte de Barfleur marks the W end of Baie de Seine, 56M west of Cap d'Antifer. There are no obstructions on a direct course across the Bay, but a transhipment area for large tankers is centred about 10M ESE of Pte de Barfleur. Be advised: The W end of the Baie de Seine has at times been affected by floating Sargassum weed; in harbours from Grandcamp to St Vaast propellers may be fouled.

POINTE DE BARFLEUR TO CAP DE LA HAGUE

(AC *1106*) The N coast of the Cotentin peninsula runs E/W for 26M, mostly bordered by rks which extend 2·5M offshore from Pte de Barfleur to C. Lévi, and 1M offshore between Pte de Jardeheu and C. de la Hague. ▶*Tidal streams reach 5kn at sp, and raise a steep, stopping sea with wind against tide.*◀ Between Pte de Barfleur and Cherbourg, yachts commonly route via Les Equets and Basse du Rénier NCM buoys and La Pierre Noire WCM buoy; be alert for opposite direction traffic using the same Wpts.

The inshore passage between Pte de Barfleur and C. Lévi, well S of the above 3 cardinal buoys, is not advised without local knowledge except in fair weather and good visibility when the transits shown on AC *1106* can be positively identified. Port Lévi and Port de Becquet are two small drying hbrs E of Cherbourg.

▶*Tidal streams run strongly with considerable local variations.*

Off C. Lévi a race develops with wind against tide, and extends nearly 2M N. Off Cherbourg the stream is E-going from about HW –0430 and W-going from HW +0230.◀

Cherbourg is a port of refuge, hugely popular with British yachtsmen. A gentle reminder: If not properly catered for, the tidal streams are strong enough to set you down-tide of Cherbourg. Do your sums and bias the approach to be up-tide of the harbour. At night positively identify the leading lights through either entrance, *before* entering.

▶*Close inshore between Cherbourg and C. de la Hague a back eddy runs W.*◀ West of **Omonville** and about 2M E of C. de la Hague there is an anchorage off Port Racine in Anse de St Martin, guarded by at least 3 groups of rocks. It is open to the N, but useful to await a fair tide through the Alderney Race.

9.17.27 CARENTAN

Manche **49°19'·09N 01°13'·53W** ❀❀❀❀❀❀❀ ✿✿✿

CHARTS AC *2613, 2135*; SHOM 7422; Navi 527; Imray C32; Stanford 1, 2, 21.

TIDES –0225 Dover; ML Rade de la Capelle 4·4; Duration 0510.

Standard Port CHERBOURG (→) Use differences **RADE DE LA CAPELLE** 9.17.26. HW Carentan = HW Cherbourg +0110.

SHELTER Complete shelter in the land-locked marina (3kn max), but do not attempt to approach in onshore winds >F5.

NAVIGATION WPT 49°25'·45N 01°07'·07W (C-I SWM buoy), 210°/1·8M to Nos 1/2 buoys. Start from WPT at HW –2 to –1½. Graph inset gives approx availability. In Sept 2008 shallowest water reported was 3·4m between buoys 7-8 and 9-10. Once inside trng walls may be more water.

Appr protected from prevailing S to W winds. Drying out on the hard sands of the estuary is not advised; nor is an early approach, as a bore (*mascaret*) may occur in the river chans between HW –3 and HW –2½ especially at springs. Chan is liable to vary in both depth and direction; buoys are moved accordingly. All buoys have R or G reflective panels; 6 are lit as on chartlet. After about 2·2M the chan lies between 2 training walls, marked by lt bns.

3·8M SW a small pool is formed where R Taute & Douve meet. Ahead, the little lock (room for about 6 boats) opens HW –2 to HW +3. Lock sigs: ● = open, ● = shut (use phone at lock office if lock-keeper absent). Small waiting pontoons are on E side, down- and up-stream of the lock. When crossing the N.13 underpass, electric autopilots may go hard-over due to electro-magnetic field from adjacent pumping station.

LIGHTS AND MARKS See chartlet and 9.17.4. Maisy Ch twr is a good landmark initially. Ldg lts 209·5° are only valid from the training wall bcns to the front lt, ie not in the buoyed chan.

R/T *Écluse de Carentan* Ch 09 (0800-1200, 1400-1600LT & lock opening hrs); sometimes the lockmaster just waves boats in.

TELEPHONE Lockmaster 02.33.71.10.85; Aff Mar 02.33.44.00.13; Auto 08.92.68.08.50; ⊜ 02.31.21.71.09; CROSS 02.33.52.72.13;

Police 02.33.42.00.17; Ⓗ 02.33.42.14.12; Dr 02.33.42.33.21; Brit Consul 02.33.78.01.83.

FACILITIES Marina ☎ 02.33.42.24.44, mob 06.89.13.15.56. port-carentan@wanadoo.fr www.sctel.fr/port-carentan. 310 + 50 Ⓥ, €0·51/m² (L x B). Max/min depths 3·5/3m. Ⓥ berths normally on 'K' pontoon. P & D (7/7: 0900-1000, 1500-1600), Slip, BH (35 ton), C (50 ton), ME, El, ⚒, CH, BY. Additional space for wintering ashore at Top Nautique ☎ 02.33.42.23.87.

YC Croiseurs Côtiers de Carentan ☎ 02.33.42.06.61, Bar. **Town** Ⓑ, @ in ✉, ⇌, Bar, R, 🛒, ✈ and ferry: Cherbourg.

ADJACENT HARBOUR

ISIGNY Calvados **49°19'·31N 01°06'·24W** ❀❀❀❀ ✿

SHELTER Good. Caution: the river bed shelves steeply inwards.

NAVIGATION Leave C-I WPT at HW –2½ tracking 158°/1·25M to IS, a very small unlit NCM buoy at 49°24'·29N 01°06'·37W, near ent to unlit buoyed chan.

From IS buoy track about 204°/0·6M to first chan buoys. Pairs of buoys are spaced at approx 3ca intervals, but between Nos 9/10 and 11/12 the interval is 6ca, with a SHM perch midway. From Pte du Grouin, ldg lts lead 172·5°/1·9M between training walls to a Y-junction. Here turn port into R l'Aure for 4ca to town quays on SW bank.

LIGHTS AND MARKS 172·5° ldg lts as chartlet.

R/T Ch 09 (0900-1200 & 1400-1800LT).

FACILITIES HM ☎ 02.31.51.24.01; **Quay** AB 40+5 Ⓥ. Drying pontoons on SW bank; berth bows-in/stern to buoys. Pay fees at town-hall; P&D (cans), C (8 ton), Slip, BY, ME, El, ⚒. **Town** R, 🛒, Bar, Ⓑ, ✉.

ADJACENT ANCHORAGE

ILES ST MARCOUF, Manche, **49°29'·78N 01°08'·92W**, the charted ⚓. AC *2613, 2135*; SHOM 7422. Tides, 9.17.26. A fair weather ⚓ only, no shelter in S'lies. The two islands, Île du Large and SW of it, Île de Terre, look from afar like ships at ⚓. The former is a fort with a small dinghy hbr on its SW side; the latter is a bird sanctuary, closed to the public. ⚓ SW or SE of Île du Large or SE or NE of Île de Terre. Holding is poor on pebbles and kelp. Île du Large lt, VQ (3) 5s 18m 8M, on top of the fort. Both islands are surrounded by drying rks, uninhabited and have no facilities.

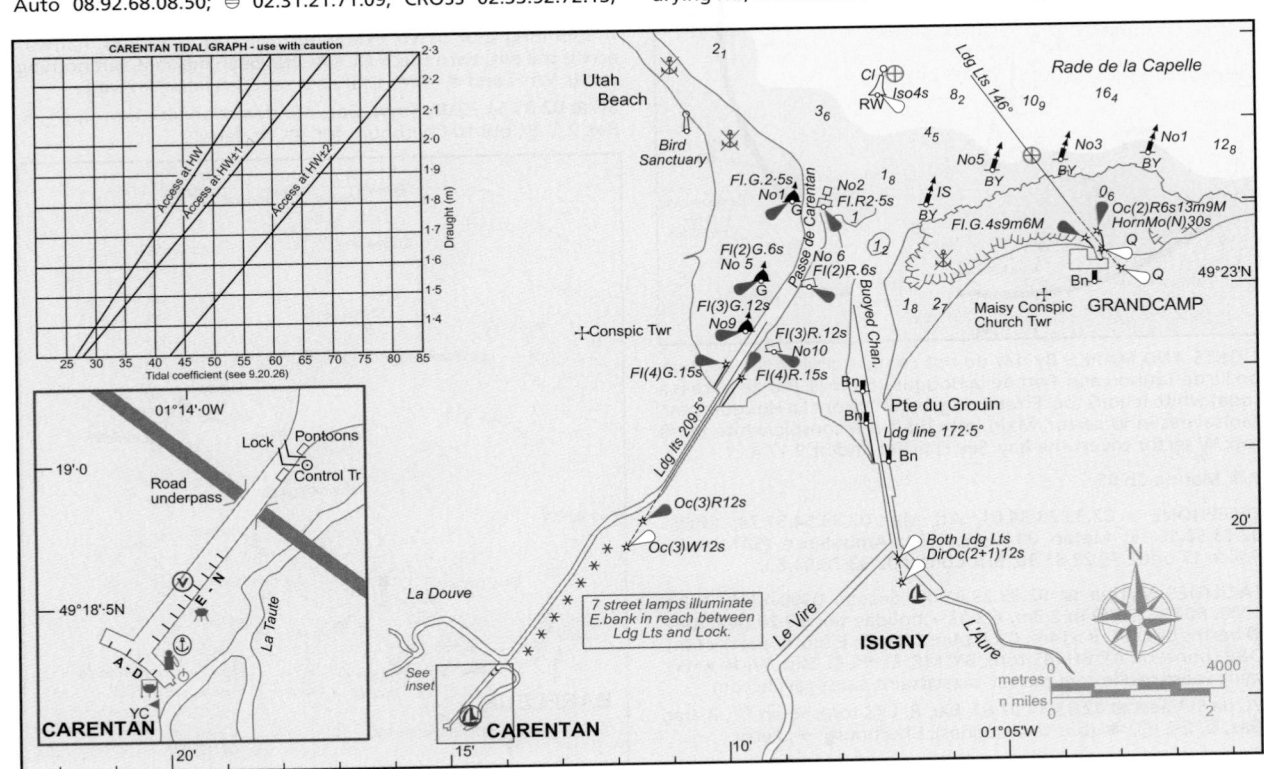

9.17.28   ST VAAST-LA-HOUGUE

Manche 49°35'·17N 01°15'·41W (Jetty head) ⚓⚓♦♦♦☆☆☆

CHARTS AC *2613, 2135*; SHOM 7422, 7120, 7090; Navi 527, 528; Imray C32; Stanfords 1, 2, 7, 21

TIDES −0240 Dover; ML 4·1; Duration 0530.

Standard Port CHERBOURG (➝)

Times				Height (metres)			
High Water		Low Water		MHWS	MHWN	MLWN	MLWS
0300	1000	0400	1000	6·4	5·0	2·5	1·1
1500	2200	1600	2200				
Differences ST VAAST-LA-HOUGUE							
+0120	+0050	+0120	+0115	+0·3	+0·5	0·0	−0·1

SHELTER Excellent in marina especially in W'lies. If full, or awaiting entry, ⚓ off between brgs of 330° and 350° on jetty lt, but this ⚓ becomes untenable in strong E-S winds.

NAVIGATION WPT 49°34'·36N 01°13'·88W (Le Gavendest buoy), 310°/1·3M to main jetty lt, Oc (2) WRG 6s; appr in its wide, well marked W sector. Beware boats at ⚓, cross-currents and oyster beds. 'Le Run' appr is only feasible if draft >1·2m and when the entry gate is open, HW −2¼ to HW +3½. If barometer is high and Coeff 40-50, gate may close 30 mins early; and 1-1¼ hrs early if Coeff <40. Gate and tide times are on the website.

LIGHTS AND MARKS By day do not confuse similar conspic twrs on Ile de Tatihou and Fort de la Hougue. From N, Pte de Saire is a squat white lt ho/G top. From E, ldg lts 267°: front La Hougue; rear, Morsalines in W sector. Main jetty hd lt is a conspic white twr/R top; W sector covers the bay. See chartlet and/or 9.17.4.

R/T Marina Ch 09.

TELEPHONE ⊜ 02.33.23.34.01; Aff Mar 02.33.54.51.74; CROSS 02.33.52.16.16; Météo 08.92.68.02.50; Ambulance (SAMU) 15; Police 17 or 02.33.23.31.90; Brit Consul 02.33.78.01.83.

FACILITIES Marina ☎ 02.33.23.61.00. Season 0900-1200, 1400-1700. 604 + 100 ❶ in 2·3m, €3·03 + holiday tax €0·20 head/day. ❶ berths by LOA: B >14m; C 12-14m; D no ❶; E (outer part) <12m. D&P (pontoon A), BH (45 ton), BY, ME, El, ⚒, ▣, Slip, Wi-fi. www. saint-vaast-reville.com port-st-vaast@saint-vaast-reville.com

YC de St Vaast ☎ 02.33.44.07.87, Bar, R, C (3 ton). Town ▦, R, Bar, Gaz, ▣, ✉, Ⓑ, ➡ (bus to Valognes), Cherbourg: ✈, Ferry.

9.17.29   BARFLEUR

Manche 49°40'·34N 01°15'·48W ⚓⚓♦♦☆☆☆

CHARTS AC *2613, 2135, 1106*; SHOM 7422, 7120, Navi 528; Imray C32; Stanfords 1, 2, 7, 21

TIDES −0208 Dover; ML 3·9; Duration 0550.

Standard Port CHERBOURG (➝)

Times				Height (metres)			
High Water		Low Water		MHWS	MHWN	MLWN	MLWS
0300	1000	0400	1000	6·4	5·0	2·5	1·1
1500	2200	1600	2200				
Differences BARFLEUR							
+0110	+0055	+0050	+0050	+0·1	+0·3	0·0	0·0

SHELTER Excellent, except in fresh NE/E winds when ent is difficult and berths uncomfortable. Hbr dries; access HW ±2½. Rks/shoals in SE of hbr. Safe to ⚓ outside hbr in off-shore winds.

NAVIGATION WPT 49°41'·13N 01°14'·41W, 219·5°/1·0M to hbr ent. Positively identify Roche à l'Anglais SHM and Le Hintar PHM buoys before closing the hbr any further. Beware cross currents.

In rough weather, esp wind against tide, keep 5M off Pte de Barfleur to clear the Race; see 9.17.5. If using the inshore passage, identify La Jamette ECM bn and La Grotte SHM buoy. From the S, keep seaward of Pte Dranguet and Le Moulard, both ECM bns.

LIGHTS AND MARKS Pte de Barfleur lt ho is conspic 1½M NNW of hbr, a 72m high, grey twr/B top. The squat church twr is a conspic daymark. Ldg lts 219·5°: both W ☐ twrs, not easy to see by day. Light details as chartlet and 9.17.4.

R/T None.

TELEPHONE HM 02.33.54.08.29; Aff Mar 02.33.23.36.00; CROSS 02.33.52.72.13; SNSM 02.33.23.10.10; ⊜ 02.33.23.34.01; Météo 02.33.10.16.10; Auto 08.92.68.02.50; Police 17; SAMU 15; Dr 02.33.43.24.00; Brit Consul 02.33.78.01.83.

FACILITIES NW Quay Yachts dry out on firm, level sand/mud at SW end of quay, but space may be restricted by FVs. 20 ❶, rafted; €1·96. 🔌 (long cable needed), M, Slip.

A 55m long spur bkwtr extending from the ☆ Fl G 4s, halfway across the ent, twrd the ☆ Oc R 4s, has been mooted, but nothing so far. Wi-Fi and @ 'due', GPRS but no G3 cellular coverage.

SC ☎ 02.33.54.79.08. **Town** Gaz, ME (Montfarville: 1km S), ▦, R, Bar, ✉, Ⓑ, bus to Cherbourg for ➡, ✈, ferry.

WGS84 DATUM

9.17.30 CHERBOURG
Manche **49°38'·94N 01°37'·11W** (Marina ent) ❋❋❋♤♤♤✿✿

CHARTS AC *2656, 2669, 1106,* 1112; SHOM 7120, 7092, 7086; Navi 528, 1014; Imray C32, C33A; Stanfords 1, 2, 7, 16, 21.

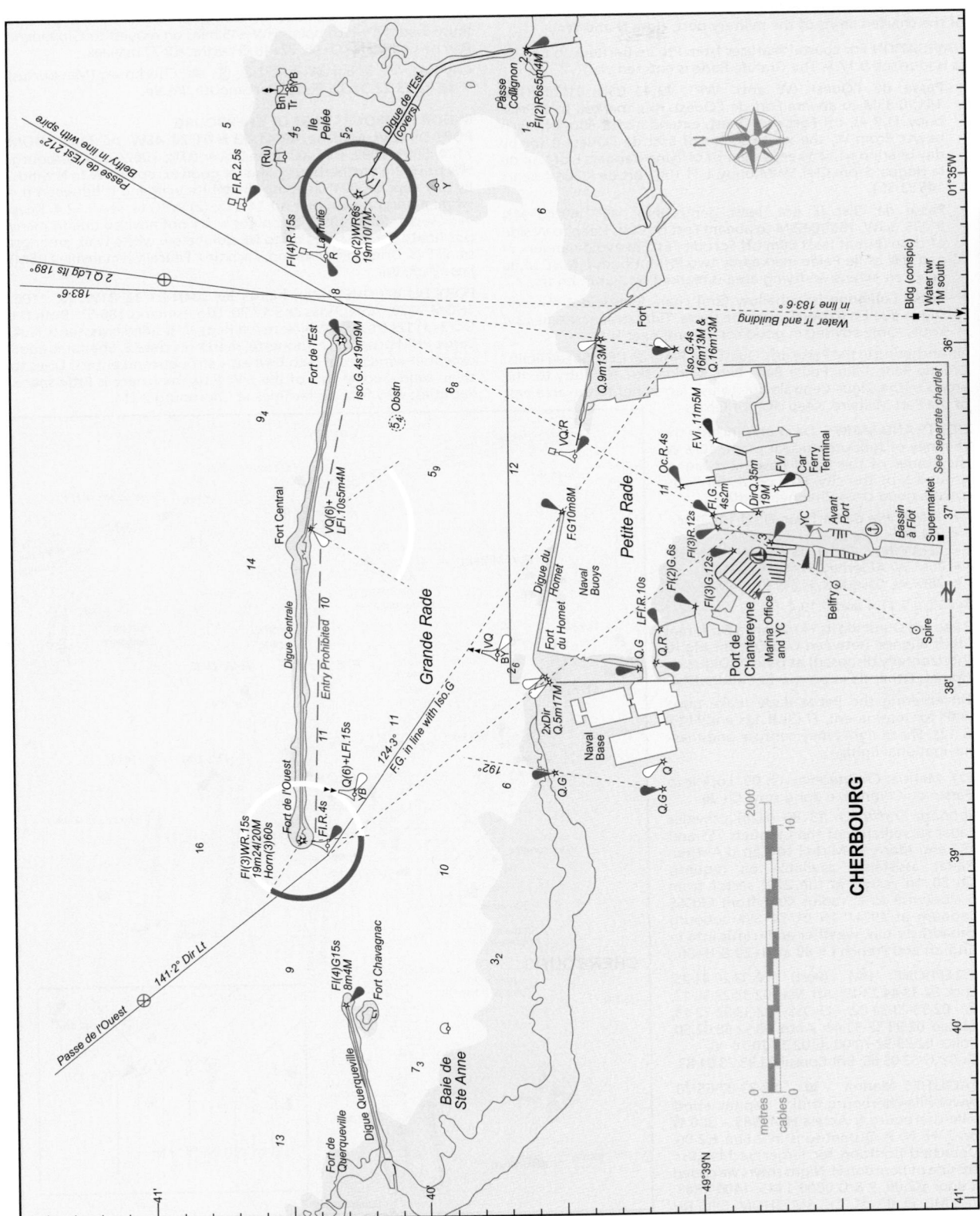

CHERBOURG

TIDES Cherbourg is a Standard Port (⟵). –0308 Dover; ML 3·8; Duration 0535.

SHELTER Excellent; a port of refuge available H24 in all tides and weather. Small craft ⚓ N of marina bkwtr in 2·3m, keeping clear of the charted limits of the military port, close N and W.

NAVIGATION For coastal features from Pte de Barfleur to Cap de la Hague see 9.17.5. The Grande Rade is entered via:

- **Passe de l'Ouest** (W ent). WPT 49°41'·05N 01°39'·81W, 141°/0·85M to abeam Fort de l'Ouest. Rks, marked by a PHM buoy, Fl R 4s, off Fort de l'Ouest, extend about 80m off each bkwtr. From W, the white sector of Fort de l'Ouest lt (or by day bearing >122°) keeps clear of offlying dangers E of Cap de la Hague. From CH1 SWM buoy, L Fl 10s, Fort de l'Ouest bears 145°/3·5M.

- **Passe de l'Est** (E ent, least depth 8m). WPT 49°40'·91N 01°35'·55W, 189°/0·65M to abeam Fort de l'Est. Keep to W side of chan (but at least 80m off Fort de l'Est) to avoid dangers W and NW of Ile Pelée marked by two PHM lt buoys. N/NE of Ile Pelée an extensive drying area is marked by 2 unlit bn trs.

- **Passe Collignon** is a shallow (2m) chan, 93m wide, through Digue de l'Est (covers), near the shore. Tidal stream reaches 3·4 knots. Only advised in good conditions, near HW.

No anchoring in the Passe de L'Ouest and Passe de L'Est. Speed limits: Grande Rade 14kn; Petite Rade 8kn; Marina 3kn. No entry to: the area S of the Digue Centrale due to fish farms, nor to the area east of the Port Militaire. Keep clear of ferries.

LIGHTS AND MARKS Daymarks include the chimney of Jobourg nuclear plant, 10M W; the cranes of the naval base; and higher ground S of the city. Five powerful lights assist a good cross-Channel landfall:

- 13M E, Pte de Barfleur, Fl (2) 10s 29M
- 5M ENE, Cap Lévi, Fl R 5s 22M
- 12M WNW, Cap de la Hague, Fl 5s 23M
- 20M W, Alderney, Fl (4) 15s 23M
- 28M W, Casquets, Fl (5) 30s 24M

See also 9.17.4 and 9.19.4.

Passe de l'Ouest ldg lts 141·2° are a Dir Q rear ldg lt aligned between two Q front ldg lts (horizontally disposed) at base of Digue du Homet. Other lts as on chartlet and 9.17.4.

On entering the Petite Rade make good 200° for marina ent, Fl (3) R 12s and Fl (3) G 12s. Shore lights may confuse and mask navigational lights.

R/T Marina: *Chantereyne* Ch 09. Lock into Bassin du Commerce (long stay) Ch 06.

Jobourg Traffic Ch **13** 80 (H24) provides radar surveillance of the Casquets TSS and ITZ and Mont St Michel to Cap d'Antifer. Radar assistance available on request, Ch 80, to vessels in the 270° sector from S clockwise to E, radius 40M from CROSS Jobourg at 49°41'·1N 01°54'·5W. Jobourg broadcasts nav, weather and traffic info in English and French Ch 80 at H+20 & H+50.

TELEPHONE HM (Port) 02·33·20·41·25; Lock 02·33·44·23·18; Aff Mar 02·33·23·36·12; ⊖ 02·33·23·34·02; CROSS 02·33·52·72·13; Météo 02·33·53·53·44; Auto 08.92.68.02.50; Police 02·33·92·70·00; Ⓗ 02·33·20·70·00; Dr 02·33·53·05·68; Brit Consul 02.33.78.01.83.

FACILITIES Marina ☎ 02.33.87.65.70. www.ville-cherbourg.fr/uk capitainerie@ ville-cherbourg.fr Access H24. 985 + 300 Ⓥ on J, H, N, P, Q pontoons in 2·6m: €2·00. Detached pontoon for larger yachts; also NE side of Pontoon H. Night shwrs use coded S door €2·00. P & D 0800-1145, 1400-1845, 7/7. ME, El, Ⓔ, ✕, CH, SM, SHOM, Slip, BH

(30 ton), @, 🖥, 🗑. Pontoons E,F,G & H are now longer. Extra AB in Avant Port.

YC de Cherbourg ☎ 02·33·53·02·83, R, Bar.

Bassin du Commerce is for longer stay; enter via gate and swing bridge (busy road tfc) which opens HW ±45 mins on request to *Capitanerie Port de Commerce* Ch 06; 22+18 Ⓥ berths. €8·77/m/week.

City Gaz, 🛒, R, Bar, Wi-fi, ✉, 🗑, Ⓑ, ⇌. Cherbourg (Maupertus) ✈ ☎ 02·33·22·91·32. Ferry: Portsmouth, Poole.

MINOR HARBOURS EAST OF CHERBOURG
PORT DE LÉVI, Manche, 49°41'·23 N 01°28'·46W. AC 1106; SHOM 7120, 5609, 7092; HW –0310 on Dover (UT); +0024 on Cherbourg. HW ht +0·2m on Cherbourg. Shelter good except in SW to N winds. By day appr on 094° keeping the white wall and lt between the white marks on each pier hd. Lt is Oc (2) WRG 6s; see 9.17.4. Keep in W sector (083°-105°), but night entry not advised due to many pot floats. Secure bows on to NE side below white wall, amongst small FVs. Dries to clean sand. Facilities: Peace. Fermanville (1·5M) has 🛒, R, Bar.

PORT DU BECQUET, Manche, 49°39'·304N 01°32'·81W. AC 1106; SHOM 7120, 7092. Tides as 9.17.30. Ldg lts/marks 186·5°: Both Dir Oc (2+1) 12s (front lt White; rear lt Red), W 8-sided twrs; see 9.17.4. Large PHM bcn twr, La Tounette, marks rks close E. Shelter is good except in winds from N to E when a strong scend enters. Dries to clean sand. Secure to S of the E/W jetty, but there is little space. Facilities: very few; all facilities at Cherbourg 2·5M.

TIME ZONE -0100
Subtract 1 hour for UT
For French Summer Time add ONE hour in **non-shaded areas**

CHERBOURG   LAT 49°39'N   LONG 1°38'W
TIMES AND HEIGHTS OF HIGH AND LOW WATERS

Dates in red are SPRINGS
Dates in blue are NEAPS

YEAR **2010**

N France

JANUARY

Day	Time	m	Day	Time	m
1 F	0317 / 0851 / 1547 / 2125	1.4 / 6.5 / 1.0 / 6.4	**16** SA	0359 / 0930 / 1618 / 2152	1.7 / 6.1 / 1.4 / 5.9
2 SA	0406 / 0940 / 1635 / 2214	1.2 / 6.6 / 0.8 / 6.5	**17** SU	0432 / 1002 / 1651 / 2223	1.7 / 6.1 / 1.4 / 5.9
3 SU	0455 / 1028 / 1723 / 2302	1.1 / 6.7 / 0.8 / 6.4	**18** M	0504 / 1033 / 1721 / 2252	1.6 / 6.1 / 1.4 / 5.9
4 M	0542 / 1115 / 1810 / 2349	1.2 / 6.6 / 0.9 / 6.3	**19** TU	0534 / 1103 / 1751 / 2322	1.7 / 6.0 / 1.5 / 5.8
5 TU	0629 / 1202 / 1856	1.3 / 6.4 / 1.1	**20** W	0603 / 1133 / 1820 / 2352	1.8 / 5.9 / 1.6 / 5.7
6 W	0036 / 0717 / 1247 / 1944	6.0 / 1.6 / 6.1 / 1.5	**21** TH	0634 / 1204 / 1851	1.9 / 5.7 / 1.8
7 TH	0122 / 0806 / 1336 / 2034	5.7 / 1.9 / 5.7 / 1.9	**22** F	0023 / 0709 / 1238 / 1928	5.5 / 2.1 / 5.5 / 2.0
8 F	0214 / 0902 / 1431 / 2132	5.4 / 2.3 / 5.3 / 2.3	**23** SA	0100 / 0751 / 1319 / 2013	5.3 / 2.4 / 5.2 / 2.3
9 SA	0315 / 1009 / 1541 / 2243	5.2 / 2.5 / 5.1 / 2.5	**24** SU	0148 / 0846 / 1417 / 2114	5.1 / 2.6 / 5.0 / 2.6
10 SU	0428 / 1125 / 1703 / 2359	5.1 / 2.6 / 5.0 / 2.6	**25** M	0256 / 1000 / 1540 / 2235	5.0 / 2.7 / 4.8 / 2.6
11 M	0542 / 1237 / 1820	5.2 / 2.4 / 5.1	**26** TU	0426 / 1128 / 1715	5.0 / 2.5 / 5.0
12 TU	0106 / 0644 / 1337 / 1920	2.4 / 5.4 / 2.2 / 5.3	**27** W	0001 / 0549 / 1246 / 1831	2.5 / 5.3 / 2.2 / 5.3
13 W	0200 / 0735 / 1426 / 2006	2.2 / 5.6 / 1.9 / 5.6	**28** TH	0113 / 0654 / 1349 / 1931	2.1 / 5.7 / 1.7 / 5.8
14 TH	0245 / 0818 / 1507 / 2045	2.0 / 5.9 / 1.7 / 5.8	**29** F	0213 / 0750 / 1445 / 2026	1.7 / 6.1 / 1.2 / 6.2
15 F	0324 / 0855 / 1544 / 2120	1.8 / 6.0 / 1.5 / 5.9	**30** SA	0307 / 0842 / 1536 / 2116	1.3 / 6.5 / 0.8 / 6.5
			31 SU	0357 / 0931 / 1624 / 2204	1.0 / 6.8 / 0.5 / 6.6

FEBRUARY

Day	Time	m	Day	Time	m
1 M	0443 / 1018 / 1709 / 2248	0.8 / 6.9 / 0.5 / 6.7	**16** TU	0441 / 1011 / 1656 / 2227	1.4 / 6.3 / 1.2 / 6.1
2 TU	0527 / 1102 / 1752 / 2330	0.8 / 6.8 / 0.6 / 6.5	**17** W	0510 / 1040 / 1724 / 2255	1.4 / 6.2 / 1.2 / 6.0
3 W	0610 / 1143 / 1833	1.0 / 6.6 / 0.9	**18** TH	0538 / 1108 / 1752 / 2322	1.4 / 6.1 / 1.3 / 5.9
4 TH	0009 / 0650 / 1221 / 1913	6.3 / 1.3 / 6.2 / 1.4	**19** F	0607 / 1137 / 1821 / 2350	1.6 / 5.9 / 1.6 / 5.7
5 F	0047 / 0732 / 1300 / 1954	5.9 / 1.7 / 5.7 / 1.9	**20** SA	0639 / 1206 / 1855	1.8 / 5.6 / 1.8
6 SA	0127 / 0818 / 1346 / 2042	5.5 / 2.2 / 5.2 / 2.4	**21** SU	0020 / 0717 / 1242 / 1936	5.5 / 2.1 / 5.3 / 2.2
7 SU	0219 / 0918 / 1453 / 2150	5.1 / 2.6 / 4.8 / 2.8	**22** M	0102 / 0808 / 1335 / 2034	5.2 / 2.4 / 5.0 / 2.5
8 M	0339 / 1043 / 1635 / 2326	4.8 / 2.8 / 4.6 / 2.9	**23** TU	0207 / 0920 / 1504 / 2159	4.9 / 2.6 / 4.7 / 2.7
9 TU	0515 / 1214 / 1810	4.8 / 2.7 / 4.8	**24** W	0352 / 1058 / 1659 / 2339	4.8 / 2.6 / 4.8 / 2.6
10 W	0049 / 0629 / 1323 / 1910	2.7 / 5.1 / 2.3 / 5.1	**25** TH	0531 / 1227 / 1820	5.1 / 2.2 / 5.3
11 TH	0148 / 0721 / 1412 / 1952	2.4 / 5.4 / 2.0 / 5.4	**26** F	0058 / 0640 / 1335 / 1920	2.1 / 5.6 / 1.6 / 5.8
12 F	0232 / 0802 / 1452 / 2028	2.0 / 5.7 / 1.7 / 5.7	**27** SA	0200 / 0737 / 1430 / 2012	1.6 / 6.1 / 1.1 / 6.2
13 SA	0309 / 0838 / 1527 / 2100	1.8 / 6.0 / 1.5 / 5.9	**28** SU	0253 / 0829 / 1520 / 2100	1.1 / 6.6 / 0.7 / 6.6
14 SU	0342 / 0912 / 1558 / 2131	1.6 / 6.1 / 1.3 / 6.0			
15 M	0412 / 0943 / 1628 / 2200	1.5 / 6.2 / 1.2 / 6.1			

MARCH

Day	Time	m	Day	Time	m
1 M	0341 / 0916 / 1606 / 2145	0.8 / 6.8 / 0.4 / 6.7	**16** TU	0345 / 0917 / 1559 / 2132	1.4 / 6.2 / 1.1 / 6.1
2 TU	0425 / 1000 / 1649 / 2226	0.6 / 7.0 / 0.4 / 6.7	**17** W	0414 / 0946 / 1628 / 2200	1.2 / 6.3 / 1.1 / 6.2
3 W	0506 / 1041 / 1728 / 2304	0.6 / 6.9 / 0.6 / 6.6	**18** TH	0444 / 1016 / 1657 / 2228	1.2 / 6.3 / 1.1 / 6.2
4 TH	0545 / 1118 / 1805 / 2339	0.8 / 6.6 / 0.9 / 6.3	**19** F	0514 / 1045 / 1726 / 2257	1.2 / 6.2 / 1.3 / 6.1
5 F	0622 / 1153 / 1840	1.2 / 6.2 / 1.4	**20** SA	0544 / 1116 / 1757 / 2326	1.4 / 6.0 / 1.5 / 5.9
6 SA	0012 / 0659 / 1228 / 1917	5.9 / 1.6 / 5.7 / 2.0	**21** SU	0617 / 1148 / 1832 / 2359	1.6 / 5.7 / 1.8 / 5.6
7 SU	0047 / 0740 / 1309 / 1959	5.6 / 2.1 / 5.1 / 2.5	**22** M	0657 / 1227 / 1916	1.9 / 5.3 / 2.2
8 M	0132 / 0833 / 1411 / 2102	5.0 / 2.6 / 4.6 / 3.0	**23** TU	0043 / 0749 / 1324 / 2016	5.3 / 2.2 / 5.0 / 2.6
9 TU	0251 / 0956 / 1605 / 2249	4.7 / 2.9 / 4.4 / 3.1	**24** W	0150 / 0903 / 1457 / 2145	5.0 / 2.5 / 4.7 / 2.7
10 W	0442 / 1141 / 1749	4.6 / 2.8 / 4.6	**25** TH	0336 / 1041 / 1650 / 2325	4.9 / 2.4 / 4.9 / 2.5
11 TH	0023 / 0603 / 1254 / 1845	2.9 / 4.9 / 2.4 / 5.0	**26** F	0514 / 1209 / 1805	5.2 / 2.0 / 5.3
12 F	0123 / 0833 / 1345 / 1924	2.4 / 5.3 / 2.1 / 5.4	**27** SA	0041 / 0622 / 1315 / 1902	2.0 / 5.6 / 1.5 / 5.8
13 SA	0206 / 0735 / 1424 / 1959	2.1 / 5.6 / 1.7 / 5.7	**28** SU	0141 / 0718 / 1410 / 1952	1.5 / 6.1 / 1.0 / 6.2
14 SU	0243 / 0812 / 1458 / 2032	1.8 / 5.9 / 1.5 / 5.9	**29** M	0233 / 0809 / 1458 / 2038	1.1 / 6.5 / 0.7 / 6.5
15 M	0315 / 0845 / 1529 / 2103	1.5 / 6.1 / 1.3 / 6.1	**30** TU	0319 / 0855 / 1543 / 2120	0.8 / 6.7 / 0.6 / 6.7
			31 W	0402 / 0937 / 1623 / 2159	0.7 / 6.8 / 0.6 / 6.7

APRIL

Day	Time	m	Day	Time	m
1 TH	0442 / 1017 / 1701 / 2235	0.7 / 6.7 / 0.8 / 6.5	**16** F	0419 / 0953 / 1631 / 2204	1.2 / 6.2 / 1.2 / 6.2
2 F	0519 / 1053 / 1737 / 2309	0.9 / 6.4 / 1.1 / 6.3	**17** SA	0453 / 1027 / 1705 / 2238	1.2 / 6.1 / 1.3 / 6.1
3 SA	0555 / 1128 / 1811 / 2342	1.2 / 6.0 / 1.6 / 5.9	**18** SU	0528 / 1103 / 1740 / 2313	1.3 / 6.0 / 1.5 / 6.0
4 SU	0632 / 1203 / 1847	1.6 / 5.6 / 2.1	**19** M	0606 / 1143 / 1821 / 2354	1.5 / 5.7 / 1.8 / 5.7
5 M	0017 / 0711 / 1244 / 1929	5.5 / 2.1 / 5.1 / 2.6	**20** TU	0650 / 1229 / 1910	1.7 / 5.4 / 2.2
6 TU	0101 / 0800 / 1342 / 2028	5.1 / 2.5 / 4.7 / 2.9	**21** W	0044 / 0746 / 1330 / 2016	5.4 / 2.0 / 5.1 / 2.5
7 W	0211 / 0913 / 1522 / 2203	4.7 / 2.8 / 4.5 / 3.1	**22** TH	0152 / 0859 / 1457 / 2140	5.1 / 2.2 / 4.9 / 2.5
8 TH	0354 / 1049 / 1659 / 2335	4.6 / 2.8 / 4.6 / 2.9	**23** F	0324 / 1026 / 1630 / 2306	5.1 / 2.2 / 5.1 / 2.3
9 F	0516 / 1205 / 1800	4.8 / 2.5 / 4.9	**24** SA	0450 / 1145 / 1740	5.3 / 1.9 / 5.4
10 SA	0039 / 0612 / 1259 / 1843	2.5 / 5.1 / 2.2 / 5.3	**25** SU	0017 / 0556 / 1249 / 1836	2.0 / 5.6 / 1.5 / 5.8
11 SU	0126 / 0656 / 1342 / 1920	2.2 / 5.4 / 1.8 / 5.6	**26** M	0116 / 0653 / 1344 / 1926	1.6 / 6.0 / 1.2 / 6.1
12 M	0205 / 0736 / 1419 / 1956	1.9 / 5.7 / 1.6 / 5.8	**27** TU	0208 / 0744 / 1433 / 2011	1.2 / 6.3 / 1.0 / 6.3
13 TU	0240 / 0812 / 1453 / 2029	1.6 / 5.9 / 1.4 / 6.0	**28** W	0256 / 0831 / 1517 / 2054	1.0 / 6.4 / 0.9 / 6.4
14 W	0313 / 0847 / 1526 / 2101	1.4 / 6.1 / 1.2 / 6.1	**29** TH	0339 / 0915 / 1558 / 2133	0.9 / 6.4 / 1.0 / 6.4
15 TH	0346 / 0920 / 1559 / 2132	1.2 / 6.2 / 1.2 / 6.2	**30** F	0419 / 0955 / 1636 / 2209	1.0 / 6.3 / 1.2 / 6.3

Chart Datum is 3·29 metres below IGN Datum. HAT is 7·0 metres above Chart Datum; see 4.5.

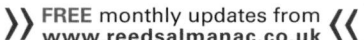

TIME ZONE -0100
Subtract 1 hour for UT
For French Summer Time add ONE hour in **non-shaded areas**

CHERBOURG   LAT 49°39'N   LONG 1°38'W
TIMES AND HEIGHTS OF HIGH AND LOW WATERS

Dates in red are SPRINGS
Dates in blue are NEAPS

YEAR 2010

MAY

Day	Time	m		Day	Time	m
1 SA	0457 / 1032 / 1712 / 2245	1.1 / 6.1 / 1.4 / 6.1		16 SU	0437 / 1014 / 1651 / 2226	1.1 / 6.1 / 1.4 / 6.2
2 SU	0534 / 1109 / 1748 / 2320	1.3 / 5.8 / 1.8 / 5.9		17 M	0518 / 1057 / 1733 / 2308	1.2 / 6.0 / 1.5 / 6.1
3 M	0611 / 1146 / 1826 / 2358	1.6 / 5.5 / 2.1 / 5.6		18 TU	0602 / 1142 / 1820 / 2355	1.3 / 5.8 / 1.7 / 5.9
4 TU	0650 / 1227 / 1908	2.0 / 5.2 / 2.5		19 W	0651 / 1233 / 1913	1.5 / 5.6 / 2.0
5 W	0042 / 0736 / 1318 / 2001	5.2 / 2.3 / 4.9 / 2.7		20 TH	0047 / 0747 / 1332 / 2016	5.6 / 1.7 / 5.4 / 2.2
6 TH	0138 / 0835 / 1429 / 2112	4.9 / 2.5 / 4.7 / 2.9		21 F	0150 / 0852 / 1443 / 2127	5.4 / 1.9 / 5.2 / 2.3
7 F	0254 / 0947 / 1549 / 2231	4.7 / 2.6 / 4.7 / 2.9		22 SA	0303 / 1004 / 1559 / 2240	5.3 / 1.9 / 5.3 / 2.2
8 SA	0410 / 1100 / 1656 / 2338	4.8 / 2.5 / 4.8 / 2.6		23 SU	0418 / 1115 / 1706 / 2348	5.4 / 1.8 / 5.4 / 2.0
9 SU	0513 / 1200 / 1749	4.9 / 2.3 / 5.1		24 M	0525 / 1219 / 1805	5.5 / 1.7 / 5.7
10 M	0032 / 0606 / 1250 / 1834	2.4 / 5.2 / 2.0 / 5.4		25 TU	0049 / 0626 / 1316 / 1858	1.8 / 5.7 / 1.5 / 5.9
11 TU	0118 / 0653 / 1334 / 1915	2.1 / 5.5 / 1.8 / 5.7		26 W	0144 / 0721 / 1408 / 1947	1.5 / 5.9 / 1.4 / 6.1
12 W	0200 / 0736 / 1414 / 1954	1.8 / 5.7 / 1.6 / 5.9		27 TH	0234 / 0812 / 1454 / 2031	1.4 / 6.0 / 1.4 / 6.2
13 TH	0239 / 0816 / 1453 / 2031	1.5 / 5.9 / 1.4 / 6.1		28 F	0319 / 0857 / 1537 / 2112	1.3 / 6.0 / 1.4 / 6.2
14 F	0318 / 0855 / 1532 / 2108	1.3 / 6.0 / 1.3 / 6.2		29 SA	0401 / 0938 / 1617 / 2150	1.3 / 6.0 / 1.5 / 6.1
15 SA	0358 / 0934 / 1611 / 2146	1.2 / 6.1 / 1.3 / 6.2		30 SU	0440 / 1017 / 1655 / 2227	1.3 / 5.9 / 1.6 / 6.0
				31 M	0518 / 1054 / 1732 / 2305	1.4 / 5.8 / 1.8 / 5.9

JUNE

Day	Time	m		Day	Time	m
1 TU	0555 / 1131 / 1809 / 2343	1.6 / 5.6 / 2.0 / 5.7		16 W	0559 / 1139 / 1818 / 2352	1.0 / 6.1 / 1.4 / 6.2
2 W	0632 / 1210 / 1848	1.8 / 5.4 / 2.2		17 TH	0648 / 1228 / 1909	1.1 / 5.9 / 1.6
3 TH	0022 / 0712 / 1251 / 1932	5.4 / 2.0 / 5.1 / 2.4		18 F	0042 / 0739 / 1320 / 2004	6.0 / 1.3 / 5.7 / 1.8
4 F	0106 / 0757 / 1338 / 2022	5.2 / 2.2 / 5.0 / 2.6		19 SA	0135 / 0834 / 1417 / 2103	5.7 / 1.6 / 5.5 / 2.0
5 SA	0157 / 0849 / 1435 / 2123	5.0 / 2.4 / 4.8 / 2.7		20 SU	0235 / 0935 / 1521 / 2209	5.5 / 1.8 / 5.4 / 2.1
6 SU	0257 / 0949 / 1538 / 2229	4.9 / 2.5 / 4.9 / 2.7		21 M	0342 / 1041 / 1629 / 2318	5.3 / 2.0 / 5.3 / 2.1
7 M	0402 / 1053 / 1642 / 2332	4.9 / 2.4 / 5.0 / 2.5		22 TU	0453 / 1149 / 1735	5.2 / 2.0 / 5.4
8 TU	0506 / 1153 / 1740	5.0 / 2.3 / 5.2		23 W	0024 / 0603 / 1252 / 1835	2.0 / 5.4 / 2.0 / 5.6
9 W	0029 / 0606 / 1248 / 1832	2.3 / 5.2 / 2.1 / 5.5		24 TH	0125 / 0706 / 1349 / 1929	1.9 / 5.5 / 1.9 / 5.8
10 TH	0121 / 0659 / 1338 / 1920	2.0 / 5.5 / 1.8 / 5.7		25 F	0218 / 0800 / 1438 / 2016	1.7 / 5.6 / 1.8 / 5.9
11 F	0209 / 0748 / 1425 / 2005	1.7 / 5.7 / 1.6 / 6.0		26 SA	0305 / 0847 / 1522 / 2058	1.5 / 5.7 / 1.7 / 6.0
12 SA	0255 / 0838 / 1511 / 2048	1.4 / 5.9 / 1.5 / 6.1		27 SU	0347 / 0927 / 1603 / 2137	1.4 / 5.8 / 1.7 / 6.0
13 SU	0341 / 0920 / 1557 / 2132	1.2 / 6.1 / 1.3 / 6.2		28 M	0426 / 1004 / 1640 / 2213	1.4 / 5.8 / 1.7 / 6.0
14 M	0427 / 1005 / 1643 / 2218	1.1 / 6.1 / 1.3 / 6.3		29 TU	0503 / 1038 / 1716 / 2249	1.4 / 5.8 / 1.7 / 6.0
15 TU	0513 / 1052 / 1730 / 2304	1.0 / 6.1 / 1.3 / 6.3		30 W	0537 / 1112 / 1750 / 2323	1.4 / 5.7 / 1.8 / 5.9

JULY

Day	Time	m		Day	Time	m
1 TH	0611 / 1145 / 1824 / 2357	1.6 / 5.6 / 2.0 / 5.7		16 F	0634 / 1214 / 1853	0.8 / 6.2 / 1.3
2 F	0644 / 1218 / 1858	1.7 / 5.4 / 2.1		17 SA	0027 / 0719 / 1258 / 1941	6.3 / 1.1 / 6.0 / 1.6
3 SA	0031 / 0718 / 1254 / 1937	5.5 / 1.9 / 5.3 / 2.3		18 SU	0112 / 0807 / 1344 / 2033	5.9 / 1.5 / 5.6 / 1.9
4 SU	0109 / 0758 / 1335 / 2023	5.2 / 2.1 / 5.1 / 2.5		19 M	0202 / 0901 / 1439 / 2135	5.5 / 2.0 / 5.3 / 2.2
5 M	0155 / 0845 / 1426 / 2121	5.0 / 2.4 / 5.0 / 2.6		20 TU	0306 / 1006 / 1549 / 2248	5.2 / 2.3 / 5.1 / 2.4
6 TU	0253 / 0946 / 1530 / 2231	4.9 / 2.5 / 4.9 / 2.7		21 W	0427 / 1122 / 1708	5.0 / 2.5 / 5.1
7 W	0404 / 1057 / 1644 / 2343	4.8 / 2.5 / 5.0 / 2.5		22 TH	0005 / 0551 / 1235 / 1820	2.4 / 5.0 / 2.4 / 5.3
8 TH	0521 / 1206 / 1753	5.0 / 2.3 / 5.2		23 F	0112 / 0701 / 1337 / 1918	2.1 / 5.2 / 2.2 / 5.6
9 F	0047 / 0629 / 1308 / 1852	2.2 / 5.2 / 2.1 / 5.6		24 SA	0208 / 0754 / 1428 / 2005	1.9 / 5.5 / 2.0 / 5.8
10 SA	0144 / 0727 / 1404 / 1944	1.8 / 5.6 / 1.8 / 5.9		25 SU	0254 / 0836 / 1511 / 2046	1.7 / 5.7 / 1.8 / 6.0
11 SU	0237 / 0819 / 1456 / 2034	1.4 / 5.9 / 1.5 / 6.2		26 M	0334 / 0913 / 1549 / 2122	1.5 / 5.8 / 1.7 / 6.1
12 M	0327 / 0908 / 1546 / 2122	1.1 / 6.1 / 1.3 / 6.4		27 TU	0410 / 0946 / 1623 / 2156	1.4 / 5.9 / 1.6 / 6.1
13 TU	0416 / 0956 / 1634 / 2209	0.9 / 6.3 / 1.1 / 6.6		28 W	0443 / 1017 / 1655 / 2227	1.3 / 5.9 / 1.6 / 6.1
14 W	0503 / 1043 / 1721 / 2256	0.7 / 6.4 / 1.0 / 6.6		29 TH	0514 / 1047 / 1725 / 2257	1.3 / 5.9 / 1.6 / 6.0
15 TH	0549 / 1129 / 1807 / 2342	0.7 / 6.4 / 1.1 / 6.5		30 F	0543 / 1115 / 1754 / 2327	1.4 / 5.8 / 1.7 / 5.9
				31 SA	0611 / 1144 / 1824 / 2356	1.5 / 5.7 / 1.9 / 5.7

AUGUST

Day	Time	m		Day	Time	m
1 SU	0640 / 1213 / 1856	1.7 / 5.5 / 2.1		16 M	0044 / 0735 / 1308 / 1959	5.9 / 1.7 / 5.7 / 2.0
2 M	0027 / 0713 / 1246 / 1934	5.4 / 2.0 / 5.3 / 2.3		17 TU	0129 / 0824 / 1357 / 2059	5.4 / 2.2 / 5.3 / 2.4
3 TU	0105 / 0753 / 1328 / 2024	5.2 / 2.3 / 5.1 / 2.6		18 W	0231 / 0929 / 1510 / 2220	4.9 / 2.7 / 4.9 / 2.7
4 W	0156 / 0848 / 1428 / 2134	4.9 / 2.6 / 4.9 / 2.7		19 TH	0408 / 1059 / 1647 / 2349	4.7 / 2.9 / 4.9 / 2.6
5 TH	0311 / 1006 / 1553 / 2302	4.7 / 2.7 / 4.7 / 2.7		20 F	0547 / 1223 / 1808	4.8 / 2.7 / 5.1
6 F	0448 / 1133 / 1723	4.8 / 2.6 / 5.1		21 SA	0100 / 0654 / 1326 / 1905	2.3 / 5.1 / 2.4 / 5.5
7 SA	0021 / 0609 / 1247 / 1832	2.3 / 5.1 / 2.2 / 5.5		22 SU	0153 / 0739 / 1414 / 1948	2.0 / 5.5 / 2.1 / 5.8
8 SU	0125 / 0711 / 1347 / 1928	1.9 / 5.5 / 1.8 / 5.9		23 M	0236 / 0816 / 1453 / 2026	1.7 / 5.7 / 1.8 / 6.0
9 M	0221 / 0804 / 1441 / 2019	1.4 / 6.0 / 1.4 / 6.3		24 TU	0313 / 0849 / 1527 / 2100	1.5 / 5.9 / 1.6 / 6.2
10 TU	0312 / 0854 / 1531 / 2108	0.9 / 6.3 / 1.1 / 6.6		25 W	0346 / 0920 / 1559 / 2131	1.3 / 6.0 / 1.5 / 6.2
11 W	0400 / 0941 / 1618 / 2155	0.6 / 6.5 / 0.8 / 6.8		26 TH	0416 / 0949 / 1628 / 2200	1.3 / 6.1 / 1.5 / 6.2
12 TH	0446 / 1026 / 1703 / 2240	0.5 / 6.6 / 0.8 / 6.9		27 F	0444 / 1016 / 1656 / 2228	1.3 / 6.0 / 1.5 / 6.2
13 F	0530 / 1109 / 1746 / 2323	0.5 / 6.6 / 0.8 / 6.7		28 SA	0511 / 1042 / 1724 / 2255	1.3 / 6.0 / 1.6 / 6.0
14 SA	0611 / 1150 / 1829	0.7 / 6.4 / 1.1		29 SU	0538 / 1108 / 1752 / 2323	1.3 / 5.9 / 1.7 / 5.8
15 SU	0004 / 0653 / 1228 / 1912	6.4 / 1.1 / 6.1 / 1.5		30 M	0606 / 1136 / 1822 / 2352	1.7 / 5.7 / 1.9 / 5.6
				31 TU	0637 / 1205 / 1857	2.0 / 5.5 / 2.2

Chart Datum is 3·29 metres below IGN Datum. HAT is 7·0 metres above Chart Datum; see 4.5.

>> FREE monthly updates from <<
www.reedsalmanac.co.uk

TIME ZONE -0100
Subtract 1 hour for UT
For French Summer Time add
ONE hour in **non-shaded areas**

CHERBOURG LAT 49°39'N LONG 1°38'W
TIMES AND HEIGHTS OF HIGH AND LOW WATERS

Dates in red are SPRINGS
Dates in blue are NEAPS

YEAR 2010

N France

SEPTEMBER

Time	m		Time	m
1 0026	5.3	**16** 0201	4.8
0715	2.3	0853	2.9
W 1243	5.2	TH 1433	4.8
◗ 1944	2.5	2148	2.8
2 0115	4.9	**17** 0348	4.6
0808	2.6	1034	3.1
TH 1342	5.0	F 1621	4.8
2052	2.7	2325	2.8
3 0235	4.7	**18** 0530	4.8
0928	2.8	1202	2.9
F 1516	4.8	SA 1745	5.0
2230	2.7		
4 0429	4.7	**19** 0035	2.4
1109	2.7	0629	5.1
SA 1702	5.0	SU 1302	2.5
		1839	5.4
5 0000	2.3	**20** 0126	2.1
0554	5.1	0710	5.5
SU 1229	2.3	M 1347	2.1
1813	5.5	1920	5.7
6 0106	1.8	**21** 0206	1.8
0654	5.6	0744	5.7
M 1330	1.8	TU 1425	1.8
1909	6.0	1956	6.0
7 0202	1.3	**22** 0242	1.5
0745	6.1	0817	6.0
TU 1423	1.3	W 1458	1.6
2000	6.5	2030	6.2
8 0252	0.8	**23** 0314	1.4
0833	6.5	0848	6.1
W 1512	0.9	TH 1529	1.5
● 2049	6.8	○ 2101	6.2
9 0339	0.5	**24** 0343	1.3
0919	6.7	0917	6.1
TH 1557	0.7	F 1558	1.4
2134	7.0	2130	6.3
10 0423	0.5	**25** 0412	1.3
1002	6.8	0944	6.2
F 1640	0.7	SA 1627	1.4
2218	6.9	2158	6.2
11 0505	0.6	**26** 0440	1.4
1043	6.7	1010	6.1
SA 1722	0.8	SU 1655	1.5
2258	6.7	2226	6.1
12 0544	0.9	**27** 0509	1.5
1120	6.5	1037	6.0
SU 1802	1.1	M 1725	1.6
2337	6.3	2256	5.9
13 0623	1.3	**28** 0538	1.7
1156	6.1	1106	5.9
M 1842	1.6	TU 1756	1.8
		2328	5.7
14 0015	5.8	**29** 0610	2.0
0703	1.9	1138	5.6
TU 1234	5.7	W 1833	2.1
1926	2.1		
15 0059	5.3	**30** 0005	5.3
0748	2.5	0651	2.3
W 1320	5.2	TH 1219	5.3
◗ 2022	2.6	1921	2.4

OCTOBER

Time	m		Time	m
1 0058	5.0	**16** 0307	4.6
0746	2.7	0952	3.1
F 1321	5.0	SA 1534	4.8
◗ 2030	2.6	2239	2.8
2 0222	4.8	**17** 0441	4.7
0909	2.9	1119	3.0
SA 1456	4.9	SU 1657	4.9
2207	2.8	2351	2.6
3 0413	4.9	**18** 0543	5.0
1050	2.7	1221	2.6
SU 1639	5.1	M 1755	5.2
2337	2.3		
4 0533	5.3	**19** 0044	2.3
1208	2.3	0627	5.4
M 1750	5.6	TU 1308	2.3
		1840	5.5
5 0043	1.7	**20** 0127	2.0
0631	5.8	0704	5.7
TU 1308	1.7	W 1348	2.0
1846	6.1	1919	5.8
6 0138	1.3	**21** 0204	1.7
0721	6.2	0739	5.9
W 1400	1.3	TH 1423	1.8
1937	6.5	1955	6.0
7 0228	0.9	**22** 0238	1.6
0808	6.6	0813	6.1
TH 1449	0.9	F 1456	1.6
● 2025	6.8	2029	6.1
8 0314	0.7	**23** 0310	1.5
0852	6.7	0844	6.2
F 1534	0.8	SA 1528	1.5
2110	6.9	○ 2101	6.2
9 0357	0.7	**24** 0341	1.4
0935	6.8	0913	6.2
SA 1616	0.8	SU 1600	1.4
2153	6.8	2132	6.2
10 0438	0.8	**25** 0413	1.5
1014	6.7	0943	6.2
SU 1657	0.9	M 1632	1.4
2233	6.6	2205	6.1
11 0517	1.2	**26** 0445	1.6
1051	6.4	1015	6.2
M 1736	1.2	TU 1706	1.5
2312	6.2	2240	6.0
12 0555	1.6	**27** 0519	1.7
1127	6.1	1050	6.0
TU 1816	1.7	W 1741	1.7
2351	5.7	2318	5.8
13 0634	2.1	**28** 0556	2.0
1205	5.7	1128	5.8
W 1858	2.1	TH 1822	1.9
14 0034	5.3	**29** 0002	5.5
0719	2.6	0642	2.3
TH 1251	5.3	F 1215	5.5
◗ 1950	2.6	1913	2.2
15 0134	4.9	**30** 0058	5.2
0819	3.0	0740	2.6
F 1358	4.9	SA 1317	5.2
2105	2.8	◗ 2021	2.4
		31 0215	5.0
		0858	2.7
		SU 1440	5.1
		2146	2.4

NOVEMBER

Time	m		Time	m
1 0348	5.1	**16** 0436	4.9
1026	2.6	1122	2.8
M 1609	5.3	TU 1654	5.0
2309	2.2	2346	2.5
2 0503	5.4	**17** 0531	5.2
1141	2.2	1218	2.5
TU 1720	5.6	W 1749	5.2
3 0015	1.8	**18** 0037	2.3
0602	5.8	0618	5.4
W 1242	1.8	TH 1305	2.3
1819	6.0	1836	5.5
4 0112	1.4	**19** 0121	2.0
0653	6.2	0659	5.7
TH 1336	1.4	F 1346	2.0
1912	6.3	1919	5.8
5 0203	1.1	**20** 0200	1.8
0741	6.4	0737	5.9
F 1426	1.2	SA 1424	1.7
2001	6.5	1958	6.0
6 0250	1.0	**21** 0238	1.7
0826	6.6	0813	6.1
SA 1512	1.0	SU 1501	1.6
● 2048	6.6	○ 2036	6.1
7 0334	1.1	**22** 0315	1.6
0909	6.6	0848	6.2
SU 1555	1.0	M 1538	1.4
2132	6.5	2113	6.2
8 0415	1.2	**23** 0353	1.5
0948	6.5	0924	6.3
M 1636	1.1	TU 1616	1.4
2212	6.3	2151	6.2
9 0455	1.5	**24** 0431	1.6
1027	6.4	1002	6.3
TU 1716	1.4	W 1655	1.4
2252	6.1	2231	6.1
10 0534	1.8	**25** 0510	1.7
1104	6.1	1042	6.2
W 1755	1.7	TH 1734	1.5
2332	5.7	2314	5.9
11 0613	2.1	**26** 0553	1.8
1144	5.8	1126	6.0
TH 1836	2.0	F 1821	1.6
12 0014	5.4	**27** 0001	5.7
0655	2.5	0641	2.0
F 1228	5.4	SA 1214	5.8
1922	2.4	1911	1.8
13 0105	5.1	**28** 0055	5.5
0746	2.8	0737	2.2
SA 1322	5.1	SU 1310	5.6
◗ 2018	2.6	◗ 2011	2.0
14 0211	4.8	**29** 0159	5.3
0853	3.0	0842	2.4
SU 1433	4.9	M 1417	5.4
2130	2.8	2120	2.1
15 0327	4.8	**30** 0314	5.2
1012	3.0	0956	2.4
M 1548	4.9	TU 1533	5.4
2244	2.7	2234	2.1

DECEMBER

Time	m		Time	m
1 0426	5.4	**16** 0419	4.9
1109	2.2	1112	2.8
W 1646	5.5	TH 1646	4.9
2344	1.9	2336	2.6
2 0530	5.7	**17** 0522	5.1
1215	2.0	1215	2.6
TH 1751	5.8	F 1750	5.1
3 0046	1.7	**18** 0034	2.4
0627	5.9	0617	5.4
F 1314	1.7	SA 1308	2.2
1850		1844	5.4
4 0141	1.6	**19** 0125	2.1
0718	6.2	0704	5.7
SA 1407	1.5	SU 1355	1.9
1944	6.1	1932	5.7
5 0230	1.5	**20** 0211	1.9
0806	6.3	0748	6.0
SU 1455	1.3	M 1439	1.6
● 2033	6.2	2016	5.9
6 0316	1.4	**21** 0255	1.7
0850	6.4	0830	6.2
M 1540	1.3	TU 1522	1.4
2117	6.2	○ 2058	6.1
7 0359	1.5	**22** 0338	1.5
0931	6.4	0911	6.3
TU 1621	1.3	W 1605	1.2
2158	6.1	2141	6.2
8 0439	1.6	**23** 0421	1.4
1010	6.3	0953	6.4
W 1701	1.4	TH 1648	1.1
2237	6.0	2224	6.3
9 0517	1.8	**24** 0505	1.4
1048	6.1	1036	6.4
TH 1739	1.5	F 1731	1.1
2315	5.8	2309	6.2
10 0555	2.0	**25** 0550	1.4
1126	5.9	1121	6.4
F 1816	1.8	SA 1816	1.2
2353	5.6	2355	6.1
11 0633	2.2	**26** 0636	1.6
1205	5.7	1207	6.2
SA 1854	2.0	SU 1903	1.4
12 0032	5.3	**27** 0043	5.9
0713	2.5	0725	1.8
SU 1246	5.4	M 1256	5.9
1936	2.3	1953	1.6
13 0116	5.1	**28** 0135	5.6
0759	2.7	0819	2.0
M 1333	5.1	TU 1350	5.7
◗ 2023	2.5	◗ 2050	1.9
14 0209	4.9	**29** 0235	5.4
0855	2.8	0922	2.2
TU 1430	4.9	W 1455	5.4
2121	2.7	2156	2.1
15 0312	4.9	**30** 0345	5.3
1002	2.9	1034	2.3
W 1537	4.9	TH 1611	5.3
2229	2.7	2311	2.2
		31 0458	5.4
		1149	2.2
		F 1728	5.4

Chart Datum is 3·29 metres below IGN Datum. HAT is 7·0 metres above Chart Datum; see 4.5.

>> FREE monthly updates from <<
www.reedsalmanac.co.uk

CHERBOURG

MEAN SPRING
AND NEAP CURVES

MEAN RANGES
Springs 5.3m
Neaps 2.5m

Springs occur 2 days
after
New and Full Moon

9.17.31 OMONVILLE-LA-ROGUE

Manche 49°42'·29N 01°49'·84W ❀❀☸△△❀❀

CHARTS AC *2669, 1106*; SHOM 7120, 7158, 5636; Navi 528, 1014;
Imray C33A; Stanfords 1, 2, 7, 16, 26.

TIDES −0330 Dover; ML 3·8; Duration 0545.

Standard Port CHERBOURG (⟶)

Times				Height (metres)			
High Water		Low Water		MHWS	MHWN	MLWN	MLWS
0300	1000	0400	1000	6·4	5·0	2·5	1·1
1500	2200	1600	2200				
Differences OMONVILLE							
−0010	−0010	−0015	−0015	−0·1	−0·1	0·0	0·0
GOURY							
−0100	−0040	−0105	−0120	+1·7	+1·6	+1·0	+0·3

OMONVILLE-
LA-ROGUE

SHELTER Good, except in moderate/fresh N to SE winds when it
may become untenable. Swell tends to work in.

NAVIGATION WPT 49°42'·47N 01°48'·66W, 257°/1·0M to Omonville
dir lt. From W or N, keep clear of Basse Brefort (depth 1m, marked
by NCM buoy, VQ) 0·6M N of Pte Jardeheu. Appr on 195° transit
(below), passing 100m E of L'Étonnard and into W sector of lt
before turning stbd 290° for ⚓s.

From E, appr on 257° transit with church spire and in W sector of
lt, until S of L'Étonnard.

Harbour entrance is 100m wide: rocks extend N from Omonville
Fort, and ESE from bkwtr to L'Étonnard, G bcn twr.

LIGHTS AND MARKS Omonville lt, on W framework tr with R
top, Iso WRG 4s 13m 10/7M, vis 180°-G-252°-W-262°-R-287°. Lt in
transit 257° with ✠ steeple (hard to see), 650m beyond, leads S of
L'Étonnard, 200m SE of which is a large unlit mooring buoy. From
N, L'Étonnard in transit 195° with fort just clears Les Tataquets
rocks. Street lights adequately illuminate the hbr area.

R/T None.

TELEPHONE Aff Mar 02.33.23.36.00. CROSS 02.33.52.16.16 or
02.33.52.72.13. Météo 02.33.10.16.10; Auto 08.92.68.02.50.
Police 02.33.01.89.30 or 17. Samu (emergency medical) 15. Fire
(*pompiers*, inc. divers) 18. Doctor 02.33.52.78.07/01.87.00; Brit
Consul 01.44.51.31.02.

FACILITIES **Harbour** There are 6 large W conical ⚓s or ⚓ inside
bkwtr; beware rocks off outer end. L, FW.

Village ☖, Gaz, R, Bar, showers at l'Association du Camping in
village centre; nearest fuel (cans) at Beaumont-Hague 5km, ✉,
Ⓑ, ⇌ (bus to Cherbourg), ✈. Ferry: see Cherbourg.

MINOR HARBOUR 2M EAST OF CAP DE LA HAGUE

ANSE DE ST MARTIN, Manche, **49°42'·72N 01°53'·78W**. AC *1106,
3653*; SHOM 7120, 5636. Tides as 9.17.31. From N, appr with
conspic chy (279m) at Jobourg nuclear plant brg 175°; or from NE
via Basse Brefort NCM buoy, VQ, on with Danneville spire brg 237°.
Both lines clear La Parmentière rks awash in centre of bay and Les
Herbeuses and Le Grun Rk (1·9m) to W and SE respectively. Care
needed, especially in poor visibility.

This bay, 2M E of Cap de la Hague, has ⚓s sheltered from all but
onshore winds. Port Racine (said to be the smallest hbr in France)
is in the SW corner of Anse de St Martin. ⚓ or moor off the hbr
which is obstructed by lines; landing by dinghy.

Central North France

Cap de la Hague to St Quay-Portrieux

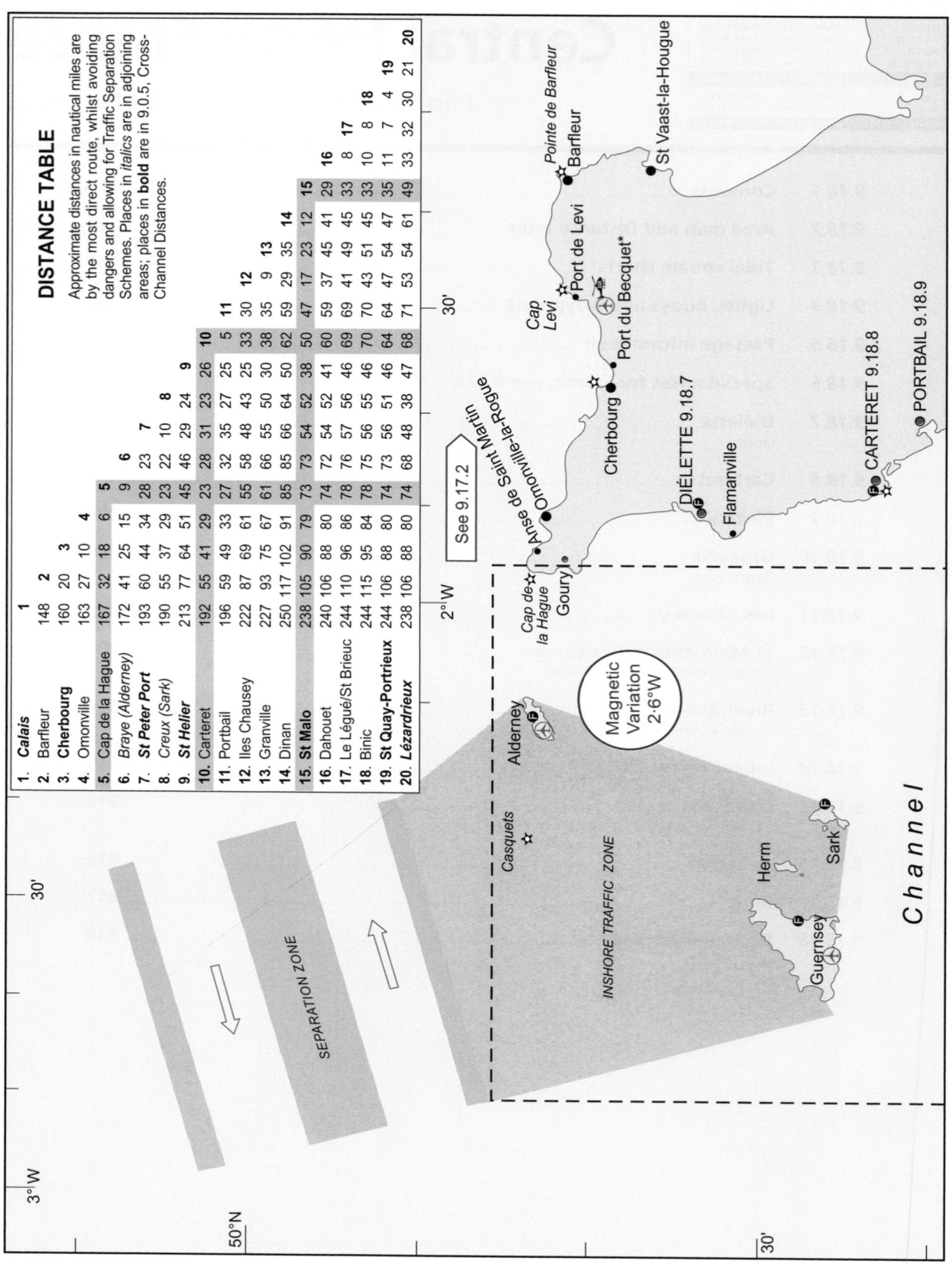

DISTANCE TABLE

Approximate distances in nautical miles are by the most direct route, whilst avoiding dangers and allowing for Traffic Separation Schemes. Places in *italics* are in adjoining areas; places in **bold** are in 9.0.5, Cross-Channel Distances.

	1	2	3	4	5	6	7	8	9	10	11	12	13	14	15	16	17	18	19	20
1. *Calais*	1																			
2. Barfleur	148	2																		
3. **Cherbourg**	160	20	3																	
4. Omonville	163	27	10	4																
5. Cap de la Hague	167	32	18	6	5															
6. *Braye (Alderney)*	172	41	25	15	9	6														
7. **St Peter Port**	193	60	44	34	28	23	7													
8. *Creux (Sark)*	190	55	37	29	23	22	10	8												
9. **St Helier**	213	77	64	51	45	46	29	24	9											
10. Carteret	192	55	41	29	23	28	31	23	26	10										
11. Portbail	196	59	49	33	27	32	35	27	25	5	11									
12. Iles Chausey	222	87	69	61	55	58	48	43	25	33	30	12								
13. Granville	227	93	75	67	61	66	55	50	30	38	35	9	13							
14. Dinan	250	117	102	91	85	85	66	64	50	62	59	29	35	14						
15. **St Malo**	238	105	90	79	73	73	54	52	38	50	47	17	23	12	15					
16. Dahouet	240	106	88	80	74	72	54	52	41	60	59	37	45	41	29	16				
17. Le Légué/St Brieuc	244	110	96	86	78	76	57	56	46	70	69	41	49	45	33	8	17			
18. Binic	244	115	95	84	75	75	56	56	46	70	70	43	51	45	33	10	8	18		
19. St Quay-Portrieux	244	106	88	80	74	73	56	51	46	64	64	47	54	47	35	11	7	4	19	
20. *Lézardrieux*	238	106	88	80	74	68	48	47	47	68	71	53	61	61	49	33	32	30	21	20

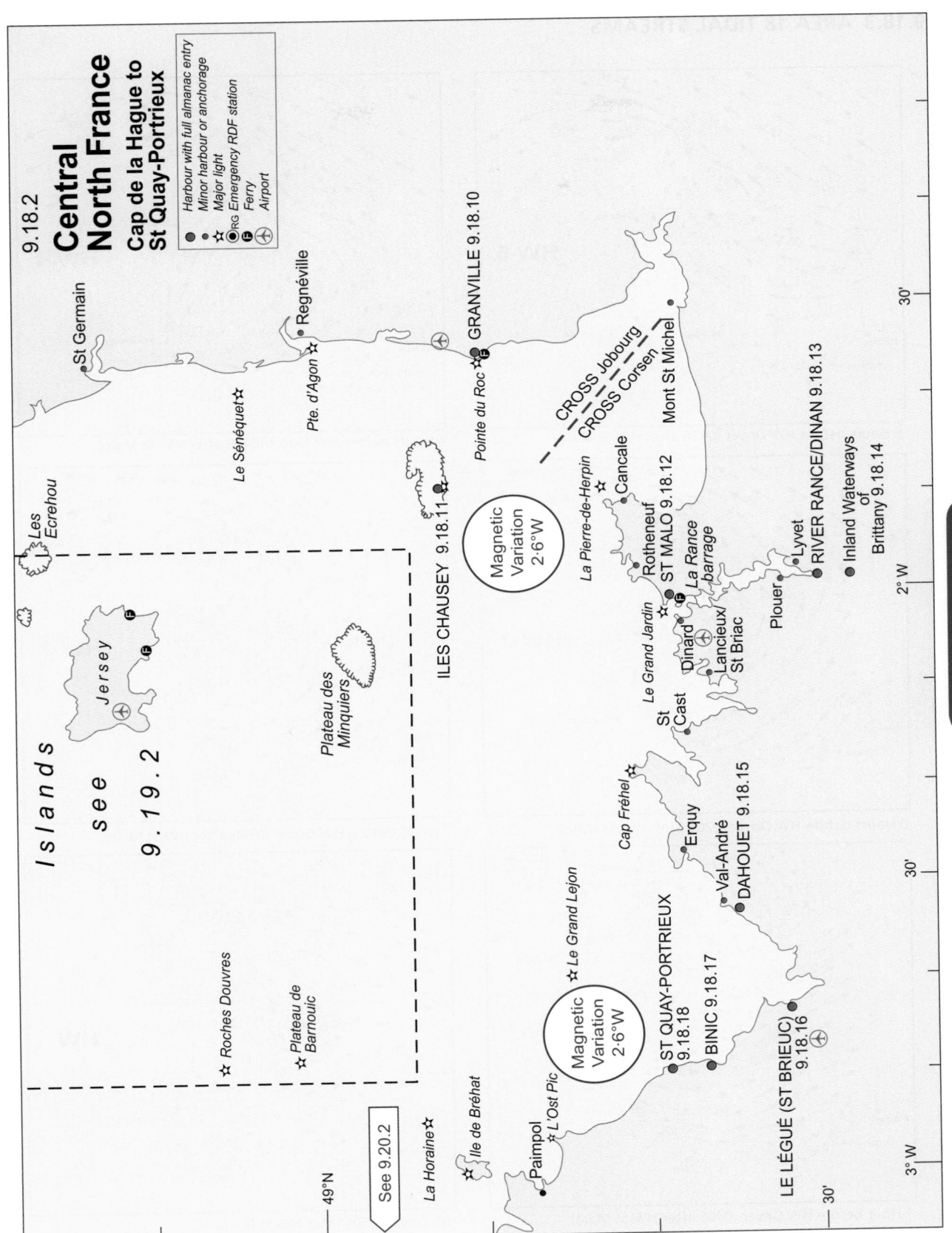

9.18.2

**Central
North France**
Cap de la Hague to
St Quay-Portrieux

Harbour with full almanac entry
Minor harbour or anchorage
Major light
RG Emergency RDF station
Ferry
Airport

St Germain

Les
Ecrehou

Islands

see

9.19.2

Jersey

Plateau des
Minquiers

Roches Douvres

Plateau de
Barnouic

See 9.20.2

La Horaine

Ile de Bréhat

Paimpol

L'Ost Pic

Le Grand Léjon

Magnetic
Variation
2·6°W

ST QUAY-PORTRIEUX
9.18.18

BINIC 9.18.17

Val-André

Erquy

Cap Fréhel

DAHOUET 9.18.15

LE LÉGUÉ (ST BRIEUC)
9.18.16

Le Sénéquet

Regnéville

Pte. d'Agon

Pointe du Roc

ILES CHAUSEY 9.18.11

Magnetic
Variation
2·6°W

GRANVILLE 9.18.10

CROSS Jobourg
CROSS Corsen

Mont St Michel

La Pierre-de-Herpin

Cancale

Rotheneuf

ST MALO 9.18.12

Le Grand Jardin

Dinard

La Rance
barrage

Lancieux
St Briac

St
Cast

Plouer

Lyvet

RIVER RANCE/DINAN 9.18.13

Inland Waterways
of
Brittany 9.18.14

49°N

30'

30'

30'

30'

3°W

2°W

9.18.3 AREA 18 TIDAL STREAMS

5 Hours before HW Dover (0006 after HW St Malo)

4 Hours before HW Dover (0106 after HW St Malo)

3 Hours before HW Dover (0206 after HW St Malo)

2 Hours before HW Dover (0306 after HW St Malo)

1 Hour before HW Dover (0406 after HW St Malo)

HW Dover (0506 after HW St Malo)

Westward 9.20.3   Channel Islands 9.19.3   Eastward 9.17.3   Northward 9.2.3

1 Hour after HW Dover (0554 before HW St Malo)

2 Hours after HW Dover (0454 before HW St Malo)

3 Hours after HW Dover (0354 before HW St Malo)

4 Hours after HW Dover (0254 before HW St Malo)

5 Hours after HW Dover (0154 before HW St Malo)

6 Hours after HW Dover (0054 before HW St Malo)

Central N France

9.18.4 LIGHTS, BUOYS AND WAYPOINTS

Bold print = light with a nominal range of 15M or more.
CAPITALS = place or feature. *CAPITAL ITALICS* = light-vessel,
light float or Lanby. *Italics* = Fog signal. ***Bold italics*** = Racon.
Abbreviations are in Chapter 1.

CAP DE LA HAGUE TO ST MALO

GOURY
La Foraine ⌁ VQ (9) 10s 12m 6M; 49°42'·90 N 01°58'·32W.
Ldg lts 065·2°: Front, QR 5m 7M; R ☐ in W ☐ on pier, 49°42'·89N
01°56'·70W. Rear, 116m from front, Q 11m 7M; intens 056·2°-
074·2°; W pylon on hut.
Hervieu ⌁ 49°42'·77N 01°56'·92W.

DIELETTE
W bkwtr Dir lt 140°, Iso WRG 4s 12m W10M, R/G7M; 070°-G-135°-
W-145°-R-180°; W twr, G top ;49°33'·18N 01°51'·81W.
E bkwtr ⌁ Fl R 4s 6m 2M; 49°33'·21N 01°51'·78W.
Inner N jetty, Fl (2) R 6s. Inner S jetty, Fl (2) G 6s; both 6m
1M.
Banc des Dious ⌁ Q (9) 15s; 49°32'·58N 01°54'·02W.

CARTERET
Cap de Carteret ☆ Fl (2+1) 15s 81m **26M**; Gy twr, G top;
49°22'·40N 01°48'·41W.
W bkwtr ⌁ Oc R 4s 7m 7M; W post, R top; 49°22'·07N
01°47'·32W.
E training wall ⌁ Fl G 2·5s 4m 2M; W post, G top; 49°22'·17N
01°47'·30W.
Channel bend ⌁ Fl (2) R 6s 5m 1M; R pylon; 49°22'·58N
01°47'·23W. Inside the bend: ⌁ Fl (2) G 6s 5m 1M; G pylon;
49°22'·55N 01°47'·20W.
Marina entry sill: ⌁ Fl (3) R 12s and Fl (3) G 12s; R & G pylons.

PORTBAIL
PB ⌁ 49°18'·37N 01°44'·75W.
Ldg lts 042°: Front, Q 14m 10M; W pylon, R top, 49°19'·75N
01°42'·50W. Rear, 870m from front, Oc 4s 20m 10M; stubby
ch spire.
⌁ 49°19'·32N 01°43'·16W.
⌁ 49°19'·20N 01°43'·00W.
Training wall head ⌁ Q (2) R 5s 5m 1M; W mast, R top;
49°19'·43N 01°42'·99W.

REGNÉVILLE
La Catheue ⌁ Q (6) + L Fl 15s, 48°57'·67N 01°42'·23W.
Le Ronquet ⌁ Fl (2) WR 6s, W6M, R4M; 100°-R-293°-W-100°;
49°00'·11N 01°38'·07W.
Pte d'Agon ⌁ Oc (2) WR 6s 12m, W10M, R7M; 063°-R-110°-W-063°;
W twr, R top, W dwelling; 49°00'·18N 01°34'·63W.
Dir lt 028°, Oc WRG 4s 9m, W12M, R/G9M; 024°-G-027°-W-
029°-R-033°; house; 49°00'·63N 01°33'·36W.

PASSAGE DE LA DÉROUTE
Les Trois-Grunes ⌁ Q (9) 15s, 49°21'·84N 01°55'·21W.
Écrévière ⌁ Q (6) + L Fl 15s; *Bell;* 49°15'·27N 01°52'·16W.
Basse Jourdan ⌁ Q (3) 10s; 49°06'·85N 01°43'·96W.
Le Boeuf ⌁ 49°06'·56N 01°47'·17W.
Les Boeuftins ⌁ 49°07'·03N 01°45'·96W.
La Basse du Sénéquet ⌁ 49°05'·96N 01°41'·11W.
Le Sénéquet ⌁ Fl (3) WR 12s 18m W13M, R10M;
083·5°-R-116·5°-W-083·5°; W twr; 49°05'·48N 01°39'·73W.
Les Nattes ⌁ 49°03'·46N 01°41'·81W; *Bell.*
International F ⌁ 49°02'·16N 01°42'·98W.
International E ⌁ 49°02'·08N 01°47'·21W.
Basse le Marié ⌁ Q (9) 15s; 49°01'·79N 01°48'·57W.
NE Minquiers ⌁ VQ (3) 5s; *Bell;* 49°00'·85N 01°55'·30W.
Les Ardentes ⌁ Q (3) 10s; 48°57'·89N 01°51'·53W.
SE Minquiers ⌁ Q (3) 10s; *Bell;* 48°53'·42N 02°00'·09W.
S Minquiers ⌁ Q (6) + L Fl 15s; 48°53'·09N 02°10'·10W.

ÎLES CHAUSEY
La Pointue ⌁ 48°54'·44N 01°50'·92W.
L'Enseigne, W twr, B top; 48°53'·67N 01°50'·37W.
L'Etat, BW ⌁, 48°54'·67N 01°46'·21W.
Anvers wreck ⌁ 48°53'·91N 01°41'·07W.
Le Founet ⌁ Q (3) 10s; 48°53'·25N 01°42'·34W.
Le Pignon ⌁ Fl (2) WR 6s 10m, W9M, R6M; 005°-R-150°-W-005°;
B twr, W band; 48°53'·49N 01°43'·36 W.
La Haute Foraine ⌁ 48°52'·89N 01°43'·66W.

Grande Île ☆ Fl 5s 39m **23M**; Gy ☐ twr, G top; *Horn 30s;*
48°52'·17N 01°49'·34W.
Channel ⌁ Fl G 2s; 48°52'·07N 01°49'·08W.
La Crabière Est ⌁ Dir Oc(3)WRG 12s 5m, W9M, R/G6M;079°-
W-291°-G-329°-W-335°-R-079°; B beacon, Y top; 48°52'·46N
01°49'·39W.
La Cancalaise ⌁ 48°51'·90N 01°51'·11W.

GRANVILLE
Le Videcoq ⌁ VQ (9) 10s; 48°49'·66N 01°42'·06W.
La Fourchie ⌁ 48°50'·15N 01°37'·00W.
Pointe du Roc ☆ Fl (4) 15s 49m **23M**; 48°50'·06N 01°36'·78W.
Le Loup ⌁ Fl (2) 6s 8m 11M; 48°49'·57N 01°36'·24W.
Avant Port, E jetty ⌁ Fl G 2·5s 11m 4M; 48°49'·93N 01°36'·19W.
W jetty ⌁ Fl R 2·5s 12m 4M; 48°49'·86N 01°36'·23W.
Marina S bkwtr ⌁ Fl (2) R 6s 12m 5M; W post, R top; *Horn (2)
40s;* 48°49'·89N 01°35'·90W.
N bkwtr ⌁ Fl (2) G 6s 4m 5M; 48°49'·93N 01°35'·90W.
Sill, E & W sides: Oc (2) G 6s & Oc (2) R 6s, G & R topped pylons.

CANCALE
La Fille ⌁ 48°44'·16N 01°48'·46W.
Pierre-de-Herpin ☆ Oc (2) 6s 20m 13M; W twr, B top and base;
48°43'·77N 01°48'·92W.
Ruet ⌁ *Bell;* 48°43'·44N 01°50'·11W.
Grande Bunouze ⌁ 48°43'·17N 01°50'·95W.
Barbe Brûlée ⌁ 48°42'·11N 01°50'·57W.
Jetty hd ⌁ Oc (3) G 12s 12m 7M; obsc when brg less than 223°;
W pylon, G top, G hut; 48°40'·10N 01°51'·11W.

ST MALO AND RIVER RANCE

CHENAL DE LA BIGNE
Basse Rochefort (aka Basse aux Chiens) ⌁ 48°42'·69N 01°57'·31W.
La Petite Bigne ⌁ 48°41'·66N 01°58'·72W.
La Crolante ⌁; 48°41'·01N 01°59'·51W, off Pte de la Varde.
Les Létruns ⌁; *Bell;* 48°40'·71N 02°00'·61W.
Roches-aux-Anglais ⌁ Fl G 4s; 48°39'·65N 02°02'·27W.
Les Crapauds-du-Bey ⌁ Fl R 4s; 48°39'·37N 02°02'·57W.

CHENAL DES PETITS POINTUS
Dinard ch spire (74m) brg 203° to right of Le Petit Bé rocks.
La Saint-Servantine ⌁ Fl G 2·5s; *Bell;* 48°41'·93N 02°00'·94W.
Les Petits Pontus ⌁ 48°41'·30N 02°00'·86W.

CHENAL DE LA GRANDE CONCHÉE
Villa Brisemoulin 181·5°, on with LH edge of Le Petit Bé rocks.
La Plate ⌁ Q WRG 11m, W10M, R/G7M; 140°-W-203°-R-210°-
W-225°-G-140°; 48°40'·78N 02°01'·91W.
Le Bouton ⌁ 48°40'·59N 02°01'·85W.

CHENAL DU BUNEL
Dinard water twr lt 158·2° on with St Énogat lts.
St Énogat ldg lts 158·2°; both Iso 4s 3/85m 6/8M, synch. Front
48°38'·29N 02°04'·11W, vis 126°-236°. Rear, 1.4M from front,
on water twr; vis 143°-210°.
Bunel ⌁ Q (9) 15s; 48°40'·84N 02°05'·38W.

CHENAL DE LA PETITE PORTE
Outer ldg lts 129·7°: **Front, Le Grand Jardin** ☆ Fl (2) R 10s 24m **15M**,
48°40'·20N 02°04'·97W. Rear, **La Balue** ☆ FG 20m 22M; 3·1M from
front; intens 128°-129·5°; Gy ☐ twr; 48°38'·16N 02°01'·30W.

WGS84 DATUM
Plot waypoints on chart before use

Vieux-Banc E ⚓ Q; 48°42′·38N 02°09′·12W.
Vieux-Banc W ⚓ VQ (9) 10s; 48°41′·84N 02°10′·20W.
St Malo Atterisage (Fairway) ⚓ Iso 4s; 48°41′·39N 02°07′·28W.
Les Courtis ⚓ Fl G 4s 14m 7M; 48°40′·46N 02°05′·80W.

Nearing Le Grand Jardin, jink stbd briefly onto Ch du Bunel
152·8° ldg lts to pick up:
Inner ldg lts 128·6°, both Dir FG 20/69m **22/25M**; H24. Front,
Les Bas Sablons ☆ , intens 127·2°-130·2°; W □ twr, B top;
48°38′·16N 02°01′·30W. Rear, **La Balue** ☆, 0·9M from front;
intens 128°-129·5°; Gy □ twr; 48°37′·60N 02°00′·24W.
Basse du Nord No. 5 ⚓ 48°39′·98N 02°05′·04W.
Les Pierres-Garnier No. 8 ⚓ 48°39′·98N 02°04′·41W.
Les Patouillets ⚓ Fl (3) G 12s, 48°39′·68N 02°04′·30W.
Clef d'Aval No. 10 ⚓ 48°39′·72N 02°03′·91W.
Basse du Buron No. 12 ⚓ Fl (4) R 15s, 48°39′·42N 02°03′·51W.
Le Buron ⚓ Fl (4) G 15s 15m 7M; G twr; 48°39′·32N 02°03′·66W.
Les Grelots ⚓ VQ (6) + L Fl 10s, 48°39′·16N 02°03′·03W.

CHENAL DE LA GRANDE PORTE
Banchenou ⚓ VQ, 48°40′·44N 02°11′·48W.
Outer ldg lts 089·1°: **Front, Le Grand Jardin** ☆ Fl (2) R 10s 24m
15M, 48°40′·20N 02°04′·97W.
Rear, **Rochebonne** ☆ Dir FR 40m **24M**; intens 088·2°-089·7°; Gy
□ twr, R top, 4·2M from front; 48°40′·26N 01°58′·71W.
Buharats W No. 2 ⚓ Fl R 2·5s, 48°40′·22N 02°07′·50W.
Buharats E No. 4 ⚓ *Bell*; 48°40′·24N 02°07′·20W.
Bas du Boujaron No. 1 ⚓ Fl (2) G 6s, 48°40′·17N 02°05′·97W.
Le Sou ⚓ VQ (3) 5s; 48°40′·11N 02°05′·30W.
Continue on inner 128·6° ldg line: see Chenal de la Petite Porte.

RADE DE ST MALO
Plateau Rance Nord ⚓ VQ, 48°38′·64N 02°02′·35W.
Plateau Rance Sud ⚓ Q (6) + L Fl 15s, 48°38′·43N 02°02′·28W.
Crapaud de la Cité ⚓ QG, 48°38′·34N 02°02′·01W.

ST MALO
Môle des Noires hd ⚓ Fl R 5s 11m 13M; W twr, R top; *Horn (2)
20s*; 48°38′·52N 02°01′·91W.
Écluse du Naye ldg lts 070·4°, both FR 7/23m 3/7M. Front,
48°38′·58N 02°01′·48W. Rear, 030°-120°.
Ferry jetty hd, ⚓ VQ G 6M; 48°38′·44N 02°01′·82W (also on
128·6° ldg line).
Ferry jetty, ⚓ Fl R 4s 3m 1M; 260°-080°; 48°38′·44N 02°01′·76W.
Bas-Sablons marina, mole head ⚓ Fl G 4s 7m 5M; Gy mast;
48°38′·42N 02°01′·70W.

LA RANCE BARRAGE
La Jument ⚓ Fl G 4s 6m 4M; G twr, 48°37′·44N 02°01′·76W.
ZI 12 ⚓ Fl R 4s, 48°37′·47N 02°01′·62W.
NE dolphin ⚓ Fl (2) R 6s 6m 5M; 040°-200°, 48°37′·09N 02°01′·71W.
Barrage lock, NW wall ⚓ Fl (2) G 6s 6m 5M,191°-291°; G pylon,
48°37′·06N 02°01′·73W.
Barrage lock, SW wall, ⚓ Fl (3) G 12s, 48°37′·00N 02°01′·70W.
SE dolphin ⚓ Fl (3) R 12s, 48°36′·97N 02°01′·66W.
ZI 24 ⚓ Fl (2) R 6s, 48°36′·63N 02°01′·33W.

ST MALO TO ST QUAY-PORTRIEUX
ST BRIAC
R. Frémur mouth. Dir lt 125° Iso WRG 4s 10m, W13M, R/G
11M; 121·5°-G-124·5°-W-125·5°-R-129·5°; W mast on hut,
48°37′·07N 02°08′·20W.

ST CAST
Les Bourdinots ⚓ 48°39′·01N 02°13′·48W.
St Cast môle ⚓ Iso WG 4s 11m, W11M, G8M; 204°-W-217°-G-233°-
W-245°-G-204°; G & W structure; 48°38′·41N 02°14′·61W.
Laplace ⚓, 48°39′·73N 2°16′·45W; wreck 6m, 5ca SE of Pte de
la Latte.
Cap Fréhel ☆ Fl (2) 10s 85m **29M**; Gy □ twr, G lantern;
48°41′·05N 02°19′·13W. Reserve lt range **15M**

CHENAL and PORT D'ERQUY
Les Justières ⚓ Q (6) + L Fl 15s; 48°40′·56N 02°26′·48W.
Basses du Courant ⚓ VQ (6) + L Fl 10s; 48°39′·21N 02°29′·16W.
L'Evette ⚓ 48°38′·51N 02°31′·45W.
S môle ⚓ Fl (2) WRG 6s 11m W7M, R/G5M; 055°-R-081°-W-094°-
G-111°-W-120°-R-134°; W twr; 48°38′·06N 02°28′·68W.
Inner jetty ⚓ Fl (3) R 12s 10m 3M; R/W twr; 48°38′·09N 02°28′·39W.

DAHOUET
Petit Bignon ⚓ 48°36′·82N 02°35′·06W.
Le Dahouet ⚓ 48°35′·15N 02°35′·43W.
La Petite Muette ⚓ Fl WRG 4s 10m W9M, R/G6M; 055°-G-114°-
W-146°-R-196°; W twr, G band; 48°34′·82N 02°34′·29W.
Entry chan, Fl (2) G 6s 5m 1M; 156°-286°; 48°34′·71N 02°34′·19W.

BAIE DE ST BRIEUC
Grand Léjon ☆ Fl (5) WR 20s 17m **W18M**, R14M; 015°-R-058°-W-
283°-R-350°-W-015°; R twr, W bands; 48°44′·91N 02°39′·87W.
Petit Léjon ⚓ ; 48°41′·80N 02°37′·55W.
Les Landas ⚓ Q, 48°41′·43N 02°31′·29W.
Le Rohein ⚓ Q (9) WRG 15s 13m, W8M, R/G5M; 072°-R-105°-
W-180°-G-193°-W-237°-G-282°-W-301°-G-330°-W-072°; Y twr,
B band; 48°38′·80N 02°37′·77W.

LE LÉGUÉ
Tra-Hillion ⚓ 48°33′·38N 02°38′·50W.
Le Légué ⚓ Mo (A)10s; 48°34′·32N 02°41′·15W.
No. 1 ⚓ Fl G 2·5s; 48°32′·42N 02°42′·51W.
No. 2 ⚓ Fl R 2·5s; 48°32′·37N 02°42′·40W.
No. 3 ⚓ Fl (2) G 6s; 48°32′·27N 02°42′·78W.
No. 4 ⚓ Fl (2) R 6s; 48°32′·23N 02°42′·70W.
No. 5 ⚓ Fl (3) G 12s; 48°32′·18N 02°42′·92W.
No. 6 ⚓ Fl (3) R 12s; 48°32′·14N 02°42′·90W.
NE jetty ⚓ VQ R 4M; 48°32′·12N 02°42′·88W.
Pte à l'Aigle jetty ⚓ VQ G 13m 8M; 160°-070°; W twr, G top;
48°32′·12N 02°43′·11W.
No. 7 ⚓ Fl (4) G 15s; 48°32′·11N 02°43′·08W.
No. 8 ⚓ Fl R 2·5s; 48°32′·01N 02°43′·16W.
No. 9 ⚓ Fl (2) G 6s; 48°31′·96N 02°43′·29W.
No. 10 ⚓ Fl (2) R 6s; 48°31′·91N 02°43′·31W.
Custom House jetty ⚓ Iso G 4s 6m 2M; W cols, G top; 48°31′·90N
02°43′·43W.
No. 11 ⚓ Fl (3) G 12s; 48°31′·90N 02°43′·43W.
No. 13 ⚓ Fl (4) G 15s; 48°31′·76N 02°43′·56W.
No. 14 ⚓ Fl (4) R 15s; 48°31′·70N 02°43′·61W.

BINIC
N môle ⚓ Oc (3) 12s 12m 11M; unintens 020°-110°; W twr, G
lantern; 48°36′·07N 02°48′·92W.

ST QUAY-PORTRIEUX
Les Hors ⚓ 48°39′·60N 02°44′·04W.
Caffa ⚓ Q (3) 10s; 48°37′·82N 02°43′·08W.
La Longue ⚓ 48°37′·88N 02°44′·68W.
La Roselière ⚓ VQ (6) + L Fl 10s; 48°37′·31N 02°46′·19W.
Herflux ⚓ Dir ⚓ 130°, Fl (2) WRG 6s 10m, W 8M, R/G 6M;
115°-G-125°-W-135°-R-145°; 48°39′·07N 02°47′·95W.
Île Harbour (Roches de Saint-Quay) ⚓ Fl WRG 4s 16m, W9M,
R/G 6M; 011°-R-133°-G-270°-R-306°-G-358°-W-011°; W twr &
dwelling, R top; 48°39′·99N 02°48′·49W.
Madeux ⚓ 48°40′·41N 02°48′·81W.
Grandes Moulières de St Quay ⚓ 48°39′·76N 02°49′·91W.
Moulières de Portrieux ⚓ 48°39′·26N 02°49′·21W.
Les Noirs ⚓ 48°39′·09N 02°48·46W.
Marina, **NE mole elbow**, Dir lt 318·2°: Iso WRG 4s 16m **W15M**,
R/G11M; W159°-179°, G179°-316°, W316°-320·5°, R320·5°
-159°; Reserve lt ranges 11/8M; 48°38′·99N 02°49′·09W.
NE môle hd ⚓ Fl (3) G 12s 10m 2M; 48°38′·84N 02°48′·91W.
S môle hd ⚓ Fl (3) R 12s 10m 2M; 48°38′·83N 02°49′·03W.
Old hbr ent: N side, Fl G 2.5s 11m 2M; 48°38′·71N 02°49′·36W.
S side, Fl R 2.5s 8m 2M; 48°38′·67N 02°49′·35W.

9.18.5 Special notes for France: See 9.17.5.

9.18.5 PASSAGE INFORMATION

More Passage Information is threaded between successive harbours in this Area. **Bibliography:** *North Brittany and Channel Islands CC* (Wiley/Cumberlidge); *The Channel CC* (NDL/Featherstone & Aslett); *Channel Pilot* (NP 27). *Channel Havens* (ACN/Endean).

THE WEST COAST OF THE COTENTIN PENINSULA

This coast is exposed and often a lee shore (AC 3653, 3655, 3656, 3659). North of Carteret it is mostly rocky. Southward to Mont St Michel and W to St Malo the coast changes to extensive offshore shoals, sand dunes studded with rocks and a series of drying hbrs; there is little depth of water, so that a nasty sea can build.

▶*The seas around this coast are dominated by powerful tidal streams rotating anti-clockwise; and a very large tidal range. In the Alderney Race the main English Channel tidal streams are rectilinear NE/SW. Tidal streams need to be worked carefully; neaps are best, particularly for a first visit. The Admiralty tidal stream atlas NP 264 covers the French coast and Channel Islands. The equivalent SHOM 562-UJA gives more details.*◀

CAP DE LA HAGUE TO MONT ST MICHEL

Cap de La Hague is low-lying, but the ground rises steeply to the south. Between the coast and Gros du Raz lt ho a difficult and narrow passage leads S to Goury. It is sheltered when the Alderney Race is fully exposed, but is not for the inexperienced.
The high chimneys (279m, R lights) of the Jobourg nuclear plant are conspic 3·7M SE. CROSS Jobourg is adjacent.

5M S of Cap de la Hague beware Les Huquets de Jobourg, an extensive unmarked bank of drying (2·1m) and submerged rks, and Les Huquets de Vauville (5·4m) close SE of them.

The drying hbrs at **Goury, Carteret and Portbail** are more readily accessible if cruising from S to N on the flood. The marinas at **Diélette** and Carteret are non-tidal. The former has H24 access for 1·5m draught if coefficient is <80.

Déroute de Terre and Passage de la Déroute are coastal chans, poorly marked, shallow in places and not advised at night.

Déroute de Terre (not shown on AC 2669 and 3655) passes W of Plateau des Trois Grunes; Basses de Portbail; La Basse du Sénéquet WCM buoy; Les Nattes WCM buoy; Roches d'Agon; E of La Catheue SCM lt buoy; E of Iles Chausey; and W of Pte du Roc (Granville). Between Granville and Îles Chausey it carries <1m in places, but with adequate rise of tide this is not a problem for small craft; the *Channel Pilot* gives directions.

Passage de la Déroute is used by ferries from the UK to St Malo. It passes W of Les Trois Grunes; between Basses de Taillepied and Les Écrehou; Chaussée des Boeufs and Plateau de l'Arconie; E of Les Minquiers and Les Ardentes; thence NW of Îles Chausey via Entrée de la Déroute, a side channel.

Granville has an excellent but very crowded half-tide marina. **Iles Chausey**, 8·3M WNW of Granville, is a popular and attractive archipelago. The Sound can entered from the S or N with careful pilotage and sufficient rise of tide.

The drying expanse of Baie du Mont St Michel should not be entered by sea, but is an enjoyable visit from the mainland.

9.18.6 Special notes for France: see 9.17.6.

MINOR HARBOUR CLOSE SOUTH OF CAP DE LA HAGUE

GOURY, Manche, **49°42'·85N 01°56'·83W**. AC 1106, 3653, 5604.2; SHOM 7158, 5636, 7133 (essential). HW –0410 on Dover (UT); ML 5·1m. See 9.17.31. For visitors, appr at slack water nps with no swell and good vis; a fair weather hbr only, dries to flattish shingle. At tidal diamond M, 1·3M W, the N-S stream reaches 9·7kn at sp, 5·8kn at nps.

Cap de la Hague (Gros du Raz) lt ho is 0·5M NW of hbr; La Foraine WCM lt bn is 1·0M to the W. 065° ldg lts, by day: Front W patch with R ■ at end of bkwtr; rear, W pylon, lead between Diotret to S and Les Grios to N. ⚓ W of the 2 LB slips in 1·7m or dry out on shingle banks SE of the bkwtr.

Facilities: R, Bar at Auderville (0·5M).

9.18.7 DIÉLETTE

Manche, **49°33'·20N 01°51'·79W** ✳✳❄❄❄❄✿✿

CHARTS AC 2669, 3653; SHOM 7158, 7133; Navi 528, 1014; Imray C33A; Stanfords 1, 2, 7, 16.

TIDES HW –0430 on Dover (UT); ML 5·4m.
Standard Port ST MALO (⟶)

Times				Height (metres)			
High Water		Low Water		MHWS	MHWN	MLWN	MLWS
0100	0800	0300	0800	12·2	9·3	4·2	1·5
1300	2000	1500	2000				
Differences DIÉLETTE							
+0045	+0035	+0020	+0035	–2·5	–1·9	–0·7	–0·3

SHELTER Good in marina, but when retaining wall covers boats surge fore and aft; rig good springs. No entry in strong W'lies.

NAVIGATION WPT 49°33'·45N 01°52'·16W, 140°/650m to W bkwtr lt. Appr is exposed to W'ly winds/swell; 2kn cross tide at hbr ent. Caution: drying rks 3ca E of ⊕, marked by unlit WCM buoy. 1·5M WSW, keep seaward of WCM lt buoy off Flamanville power stn. Outer hbr ent dredged CD +0.5m; with Coefficient >55 accessible for 2·5m draft. W side of outer hbr dries approx 5m.

LIGHTS AND MARKS Two power stn chys (69m) are conspic 1·2M to SW. A single conspic house on the skyline is aligned 140° with ent, in 10° W sector of Dir lt 140°, W twr/G top at head of W bkwtr.

R/T Ch 09; summer 08-1300, 14-2000LT; winter 09-1200, 1330-1800LT.

TELEPHONE Aff Mar 02·33.23.36.00; CROSS 02·33.52.72.13; ⊜ 02·33.23.34.00; Météo 08·92.68·12·34; SNSM 02·33.04.93.17; Dr 02·33·52·99·00; YC 02·33·04·14·78; Brit Consul 02·33.78.01.83.

FACILITIES Marina ☎ 02·33.53.68.78; port-dielette@wanadoo.fr www.cg50.fr 350+70 Ⓥ €3·00. Enter about HW±3 for 1·5m draft, over a sill with lifting gate 3·5m above CD; waiting pontoon outside. Ⓥ berths 'A' pontoon and the E ends of 'B' (S side only) and 'C' (N side only). Rig stout springs to minimise surging around HW. D & P, Slip, BH (40 ton); Ferry to CI.

Village, basic foods, mkt Sun AM, Bar, R. **Flamanville** 15 mins walk, 🛒, ✉.

Les Pieux 🛒, R, Bar, ✉, Ⓑ. Tourist office ☎ 02·33.52.81.60. An extra reactor is planned at Flamanville.

9.18.8 CARTERET
Manche 49°22'·08N 01°47'·33W ✳❀♤♤♤♧♧

CHARTS AC 2669, 3655; SHOM 7157, 7158, 7133; Navi 1014; Imray C33A; Stanfords 1, 2, 16, 26.

TIDES –0440 Dover; ML 5·9; Duration 0545.

Standard Port ST MALO (→)

Times				Height (metres)			
High Water		Low Water		MHWS	MHWN	MLWN	MLWS
0100	0800	0300	0800	12·2	9·3	4·2	1·5
1300	2000	1500	2000				
Differences CARTERET							
+0030	+0020	+0015	+0030	–1·6	–1·2	–0·5	–0·2
PORTBAIL							
+0030	+0025	+0025	+0030	–0·8	–0·6	–0·2	–0·1
ST GERMAIN-SUR-AY 49°13'·6N 01°39'·3W							
+0025	+0025	+0035	+0035	–0·7	–0·5	0·0	+0·1
LE SÉNÉQUET 49°05'·9N 01°41'·0W							
+0015	+0015	+0025	+0025	–0·3	–0·3	+0·1	+0·1

SHELTER Good in marina, but very crowded at weekends and in season. No safe ⚓s offshore.

NAVIGATION WPT 49°21'·86N 01°47'·36W, 006°/420m to W bkwtr lt. From N/NW, keep well off shore on appr to avoid rks 1M N of Cap de Carteret extending about 7ca from coast. From W beware Trois Grune Rks (dry 1·6m), about 4M offshore, marked by WCM lt buoy. Appr dries ½M offshore and is exposed to fresh W/SW winds which can make ent rough. Caution: strong cross streams on the flood.

Best appr at HW–1 to avoid max tidal stream, 4½kn sp. The outer end of W bkwtr covers at big springs. Bar, at right angles to W bkwtr, dries 4m; a SHM buoy east of the W bkwtr marks a shifting shoal patch. Best water is to port of a mid-channel course. The

chan dries progressively to firm sand, and is dredged to 4m and 4.5m just W of the marina.

LIGHTS AND MARKS Cap de Carteret, grey lt twr, G top, and conspic Sig stn are 8ca WxN of the ent. Breakwater and channel lts as chartlet. Marina sill is marked by PHM/SHM lt bcns, and Y poles on the retaining wall.

R/T Marina Ch 09. Sig stn 09, 16.

TELEPHONE CROSS/SNSM 02·33·52·72·13; ⊖ 02·33·04·90·08; Météo 02·33·22·91·77; Auto 08.92.68.02.50; Police 02·33·53·80·17; Ⓗ (Valognes) 02·33·40·14·39; Brit Consul 02.33.78.01.83.

FACILITIES Marina Access HW ±2½ for 1·5m draft over sill 5m; lifting flapgate retains 2·3m within. IPTS N side of marina ent control ent/exit (sigs 2 & 4). Cross the sill squarely, ie heading NE, to clear the concrete bases each side. ❶ AB/rafted on E side only of 'F' pontoon (no need to stop at accueil pontoon).

☎ 02·33·04·70·84. www.barneville-carteret.net barneville-carteret@wanadoo.fr 311 + 60 ❶, €2·95 (Apr-Sep; discounts possible Mon-Thu). D & P at accueil pontoon (limited hrs, as posted on the pumps), BH (35 ton), C (24 ton), CH, ME. **YC** ☎ 02·33·52·60·73, Shwrs, Slip, M, Bar.

West quay Possible waiting berth clear of ferry, if too late for the marina. A 1·5m draft boat can stay afloat for 6 hrs np, 9 hrs sp. AB free for 6 hrs then at 50% of marina rates. FW, Slip.

Other options: Dry out in the tiny Port des Américains and basin close W of marina (up to 5m at HW); or on fine sand SW of marina.

Town ME, P & D (cans), 🛒, Gaz, R, Bar, ✉, Ⓑ, ⇌ (Valognes), ✈ (Cherbourg). Ferry: Cherbourg, Jersey.

9.18.9 PORTBAIL

Manche 49°19'·72N 01°42'·42W (Basin ent) ❄❄❄💧💧🌸🌸

CHARTS AC 2669, 3655; SHOM 7157, 7133; Navi 1014; Imray C33A; Stanfords 1, 2, 16, 26.

TIDES See 9.18.8. HW –0440 on Dover; ML 6·3m; Duration 0545.

SHELTER Good in all winds. Occasional swell after SW gales.

NAVIGATION WPT 49°18'·25N 01°44'·58W (off chartlet, abeam unlit 'PB' SWM buoy), 042°/1·5M to training wall lt bcn. 7ca offshore the 042° ldg line crosses banks drying 5.3m, thence between a pair of unlit PHM/SHM buoys, least depth 8.1m. Beware very strong tidal stream, esp during flood. When base of training wall bcn is covered, there is at least 2·5m in the chan, dredged 5·2m, however note frequent inundations of sand reported.

LIGHTS AND MARKS A water twr (38m) is conspic 6ca NNW of ent. Ldg marks/lts 042°: Front (La Caillourie), W pylon, R top; rear, church belfry in town. Trng wall, which covers near HW, head: W mast/R top, followed by 2 R perches. See chartlet and 9.18.4 for lts.

R/T Port/marina Ch 09.

TELEPHONE CROSS 02·33·52·72·13; ⊖ 02·33·04·90·08 (Carteret); Brit Consul 02.33.78.01.83.

FACILITIES Yacht basin dries 7·0m, frequent dredging needed. Enlarged Ⓥ pontoon parallel to road on NW side of basin; also Ⓥ on the E side of adjacent stone FV jetty; or as directed. At NE side of basin pontoon with fingers is for locals <7.5m LOA.
HM ☎ 02·33·04·83·48 (15 Jun-31 Aug, tide times; 0830-1200 & 1400-1700). portbail@wanadoo.fr www.portbail.com 160 + 30 Ⓥ, €1·41. Slip, C (5 ton), ✗, ME, El. **YC** ☎ 02·33·04·86·15 Shwr, Bar, R.
Town (½M by causeway) Bar, R, Ⓑ, ✉, 🛒, D, P, ≈ (Valognes).

9.18.10 GRANVILLE Manche 48°49'·94N 01°35'·93W (Marina ent) ❄❄❄💧💧🌸🌸

GRANVILLE *continued*

CHARTS AC 3656, 3659, 3672; SHOM 7156, 7341; Navi 534, 535; Imray C33B; Stanfords 1, 2, 16, 26

TIDES −0510 Dover; ML 7·1; Duration 0525.

Standard Port ST MALO (→)

Times				Height (metres)			
High Water		Low Water		MHWS	MHWN	MLWN	MLWS
0100	0800	0300	0800	12·2	9·3	4·2	1·5
1300	2000	1500	2000				
Differences REGNÉVILLE-SUR-MER							
+0010	+0010	+0030	+0020	+0·5	+0·4	+0·2	0·0
GRANVILLE							
+0005	+0005	+0020	+0010	+0·7	+0·5	+0·3	+0·1
CANCALE							
0000	0000	+0010	+0010	+0·8	+0·6	+0·3	+0·1

SHELTER Good in the marina. Appr is rough in strong W winds. ⚓ in 2m about 4ca WSW of Le Loup to await the tide.

NAVIGATION WPT 48°49'·60N 01°36'·30W (abm Le Loup IDM), 042°/0·40M to S bkwtr lt. Beware rks seaward of La Fourchie WCM bcn twr, pot markers off Pte du Roc and 0·4m patches on Banc de Tombelaine, 1M SSW of Le Loup lt. At night best to keep at least 8ca W of Pte du Roc to avoid the worst of these dangers.

At bkwtr hd turn port wide into marina ent to avoid yachts leaving; cross the sill between R/G piles. The 5 R piles, Fl Bu 4s, mark the covering wall of a windsurfing/dinghy area to stbd. Ent/exit under power; speed limit 5kn in the near approach, 3kn in hbr.

LIGHTS AND MARKS Pte du Roc is a conspic headland with large old bldgs and lt ho, grey twr, R top; the Sig stn and church spire are also obvious. The twin domes of St Paul's church in transit 034° with Le Loup lead towards the marina ent. No ldg lts, but S bkwtr hd on with TV mast leads 057° to ent; hbr lts are hard to see against town lts. 3·5M W of Pte du Roc, Le Videcoq rock drying 0·8m, is marked by a WCM lt buoy. See chartlet and 9.18.4 for lt details.

R/T Port Ch 12, 16 (HW±1½). Marina Ch 09, H24 in season.

TELEPHONE Port HM 02·33·50·17·75; Aff Mar 02·33·91·31·40; CROSS 02·33·52·16·16; SNSM 02·33·61·26·51; ⊖ 02·33·50·19·90; Météo 02·33·22·91·77; Auto 08.92.68.08.50; Police 02·33·91·22·50; Dr 02·33·50·00·07; 🏥 02·33·91·51·51; Brit Consul 02.23.18.30.30.

FACILITIES Hérel Marina Access over sill HW −2½ to +3½. Depth over sill shown on digital display atop S bkwtr: eg 76 = 7·6m; 00 = no entry; hard to read in bright sun. Speed limit 2kn.

HM ☎ 02·33·50·20·06. www.granville.cci.fr/herel cci@granville.cci.fr 850+150 Ⓥ pontoon G, 1·5–2·5m. Up to 20m² (L x B) = €16·51, plus €0·61 each additional m². Slip, P, D, ME, BH (12 ton), C (1·5 ton), CH, Gaz, ⚙, 🛒, SM, El, 🔧, 🅰, Ⓔ, SHOM.

YC de Granville ☎ 02·33·50·04·25, Bar, R.

Town P, D, ME, 🛒, Gaz, R, Bar, ✉, Ⓑ, ⇄, ✈ (Dinard). Ferry: UK via Jersey or Cherbourg.

MINOR HARBOUR 10M NORTH OF GRANVILLE

REGNÉVILLE, Manche, **48°59'·72N 01°34'·05W** (SHM buoy abm Pte d'Agon). AC 2669, 3656; SHOM 7156, 7133. HW −0500 on Dover (UT); ML 7·0m; Duration 0535. See 9.18.10. A seriously drying hbr on the estuary of R. La Sienne; few yachts visit, a magnet for hardy adventurers seeking sand and solitude.

From 48°57'·65N 01°38'·86W (2·2M E of La Catheue SCM buoy) identify Pte d'Agon lt ho, W twr/R top, and Regnéville's 028° dir lt, both 4M NE at the river mouth (see 9.18.4). Thence track 056°/3·8M across the drying estuary to the SHM buoy (Lat/Long in line 1) marking a drying mole extending SW from the sandspit to stbd. Here there are landing stages; a small pontoon at Regnéville is 1·2M NNE. Drying heights are around 9m and 12·7m off Pte d'Agon.

Access HW −1 to +2 for 1·3m draft. Approx 80 moorings inc ⚓s. YC ☎ 02·33·46·36·76. **Facilities**: Quay, CH, BY, C (25 ton).

Town: D&P (cans), Ⓑ, ✉, Bar, R, 🛒. Tourism ☎ 02·33·45·88·71.

9.18.11 ÎLES CHAUSEY

Manche 48°52'·08N 01°49'·08W SHM By, S ent ❀❀⌑✿✿✿

CHARTS AC 3656, 3659; SHOM 7156, 7155, 7161, 7134; Navi 534, 535; Imray C33B; Stanfords 1, 2, 16, 26.

TIDES −0500 Dover; ML 7·4; Duration 0530.

Standard Port ST MALO (→)

Times				Height (metres)			
High Water		Low Water		MHWS	MHWN	MLWN	MLWS
0100	0800	0300	0800	12·2	9·3	4·2	1·5
1300	2000	1500	2000				
Differences ÎLES CHAUSEY (Grande Île)							
+0005	+0005	+0015	+0015	+0·8	+0·7	+0·6	+0·4
LES ARDENTES (48°58'N 01°52'W, 6M NNW of Grande Île)							
+0010	+0010	+0020	+0010	0·0	−0·1	0·0	−0·1

SHELTER Good except in strong NW or SE winds. Grande Île is privately owned, but may be visited; it is not a Port of Entry.

NAVIGATION WPT 48°51'·43N 01°48'·55W, 332°/1·1M to Crabière lt. In transit with L'Enseigne, W bn tr, B top, leads 332° to Sound. 1 SHM lt buoy, 2 unlit ECM buoys, 1 ECM & 2 WCM unlit bns mark the S chan.

The N chan needs adequate ht of tide (max drying ht 5·3m), SHOM 7134, a good Pilot and/or local knowledge, plus careful pilotage. L'Enseigne ≠ Grande Île lt ho leads 156° to the N ent; thence follow 4 ECM, 3 WCM, 1 SCM & 1 NCM unlit bcns.

No access 1/4 - 30/6 to a bird sanctuary, ie all E of line from Grande Île lt ho to L'Enseigne bcn twr (except Aneret).

LIGHTS AND MARKS Grande Île lt ho is conspic. La Crabière lt is on blackish stilts with Y top. See chartlet and 9.18.4 for lts.

R/T None. **TELEPHONE** Police 02·33·52·72·02; CROSS 02·33·52·72·13; Auto 08.92.68.08.50; SNSM 02.33.50.28.33.

FACILITIES Moor fore-and-aft to W ⚓s, free, in about 1·3m; some dry at sp. Very crowded w/ends in season, especially as drying out in Port Homard (W side of Grande Île) is discouraged. Tidal streams are moderate. **Village** FW & 🛒 (limited), Gaz, R, Bar, 🗋.

MONT ST MICHEL TO ST MALO

West from Mont St Michel (AC 3659), the drying harbour of **Cancale** lies 4M S of Pte du Grouin. There are many oyster beds and a fair weather anchorage SE of Île des Rimains, N of which the many dangers are marked by La Pierre-de-Herpin (lt, fog sig). The large drying inlet of **Rothéneuf**, with a fair weather anchorage outside, is 4M NE of St Malo.

St Malo approaches (AC 2700) include 6 channels between the many islets, rocks and shoals across which tidal streams set at up to 4kn sp. Approaching from E or N, with sufficient rise of tide, Chenal de la Bigne, Chenal des Petits Pointus or Chenal de la Grande Conchée can be used in good visibility, but they all pass over or near to shoal and drying patches.

From the W and NW, Chenal de la Grande Porte and Chenal de la Petite Porte are the principal routes and are well marked/lit. Chenal du Décollé is a shallow, ill-marked inshore route from the W, and no shorter than Chenal de la Grande Porte.

▶*Here the E-going stream begins at HW St Helier –0510, and the W-going at HW St Helier +0030, max sp rates 3.75kn. The streams set across the Chenal between Grand Jardin and Buron.*◀

Both marinas at St Malo have tidal restrictions due to either a lock or a sill. **Dinard** has a small basin 2.0m which is usually full of local boats, but it is pleasant to visit by ferry.

The **River Rance** barrage (SHOM 4233) gives access via a lock to many delightful anchorages and marinas at Plouër and Lyvet. It helps to know how the barrage affects water levels up-river. Continue to the lock at Châtelier, thence on to Dinan – subject to draught. Here enter the Canal d'Ille et Rance (9.18.14) which leads to the S Brittany coast and provides a fascinating alternative to the offshore passage around NW Brittany.

ST MALO TO L'OST PIC AND BEYOND

From **St Malo to St Quay-Portrieux** (AC 2028, 2029) the coast has deep bays (often drying), a few rugged headlands and many offlying rocks. 6M NW of St Malo beware Le Vieux-Banc (1.2m), buoyed.

▶*Here the ESE-going stream begins at HW St Helier –0555, and the NW-going at HW St Helier –0015, sp rates 2.5kn. There are W-going eddies very close inshore on the E-going stream.*◀

Between St Malo and Cap Fréhel there are anchorages S of Île Agot in the apprs to the drying hbr of St Briac and in Baie de l'Arguenon, SE of St Cast hbr. More anchorages may be found in Baie de la Fresnaye and off Pte de la Latte. From Cap Fréhel, a bold steep headland, to Cap d'Erquy there are plenty of inshore rocks but no worthwhile hbrs.

Between Cap d'Erquy and the various rocky patches close to seaward, Chenal d'Erquy runs WSW/ENE into the E side of the Baie de St Brieuc. **Erquy** is a pleasant, drying hbr much used by fishing boats. There are several rocky shoals within the Baie itself, some extending nearly 2M offshore.

Baie de St Brieuc is a 20M wide bight between Cap d'Erquy and L'Ost Pic. Principal features are: to the N, Grand Léjon a rocky shoal extending 2½ca W and 8ca NNE of its lt ho. Petit Léjon (3.1m) lies 3.5M SSE. Roheinlt bcn, 3M further S, is in the centre with rocky plateaux to E and W. A 3M wide chan leads W of these features and S into the shallow, partly-drying S end of the Bay and the interesting hbrs of **Dahouet, Le Légué and Binic**.

On the W side of Bay de St Brieuc, Roches de St Quay and offlying rocky patches extend 4M east from **St Quay-Portrieux** which can only be approached from NNW or SE. St Quay Marina is a good all-tide base from which to explore the drying hbrs around Baie de St Brieuc.

The next 2 paragraphs are covered in greater detail in 9.20.5:

To the N and NE of L'Ost-Pic lt ho extensive offshore shoals guard the approaches to Paimpol, Ile de Bréhat and the Trieux river. Further N, the Plateau de Barnouic and Plateau des Roches Douvres (lt, fog sig) must be given a wide berth.

▶*Here the E-going stream begins at about HW St Malo –0400 and the W-going at about HW St Malo +0100 with Spring rates exceeding 4kn.*◀

MINOR HARBOURS EAST OF ST MALO

CANCALE, Ille-et-Vilaine, **48°40′.10N 01°51′.11W**. AC 3659; SHOM 7155, 7131. HW –0510 on Dover (UT); ML 7.2m; Duration 0535; see 9.18.10. La Houle is the drying hbr of Cancale just inside Bay of Mont St Michel, 2.6M S of Pte du Grouin; exposed to winds SW to SE. Drying berths may be available. Pier hd lt, obsc'd from the N, is on a W twr, G top. Avoid oyster beds at all costs. Area dries to about 1M off-shore. ⚓ in 4m SE of Île des Rimains or further N off Pte Chatry. Facilities: **Quay** C (1.5 ton). **Services:** El, M, ME, ✕; **CN de Cancale** ☎ 02.99.89.90.22. **Town** (famous for oysters), ⒷＢ, 🛒, ✉, Bar, R, D&P (cans).

ROTHENEUF, Ille-et-Vilaine, **48°41′.38N 01°57′.64W**. AC 3659; SHOM 7155, 7131. HW –0510 on Dover (UT); Tides as for St Malo; ML 7.0m; Duration 0540. Complete shelter in hbr which dries up to 8.6m. ⚓ outside in 4m just N of SHM bn marking ent. Rks on both sides of ent which is barely 230m wide. Safest to enter when rks uncovered. Ldg line at 163°, W side of Pte Benard and old windmill (white twr). There are no lts. Facilities: FW, Slip. **Village** D&P (cans), Bar, R, 🛒.

9.18.12   ST MALO

Ille et Vilaine 48°38′.48N 02°01′.91W
Bassin Vauban and Bas Sablons Marinas ✿✿♦♦✿✿✿

CHARTS AC 2669, 3659, 2700; SHOM 7155, 7156, 7130; Navi 535; Imray C33B; Stanfords 2, 16, 26.

TIDES –0506 Dover; ML 6.8; Duration 0535.

SHELTER Good at Bas Sablons Marina, but in fresh W/NW'lies ❶ berths at outer ends of A & B pontoons are very uncomfortable. Excellent shelter in Bassin Vauban near the walled city.

NAVIGATION Care is needed due to strong tidal streams and many dangerous rocks close to the appr Chans, which from W to E (see chartlet and 9.18.4) are:

1. Grande Porte, from the W, lit. WPT 48°40′.17N 02°08′.49W.
2. Petite Porte, the main lit chan from NW. WPT 48°42′.44N 02°09′.04W (abm Vieux-Banc Est NCM buoy, Q).
3. Bunel, from NNW, lit. WPT 48°42′.29N 02°06′.51W.

The above chans converge at or near Le Grand Jardin lt ho, 48°40′.20N 02°04′.97W. Thence continue in the main fairway 129°/2.8M to Môle des Noires.

4. Grande Conchée, from N, unlit. WPT 48°42′.15N 02°02′.12W.
5. Petits Pointus, from NNE, unlit. WPT 48°42′.34N 02°00′.38W.
6. La Bigne, from NE, unlit. WPT 48°42′.67N 01°57′.25W.

The above chans converge at or near Roches aux Anglais SHM buoy, 48°39′.66N 02°02′.22W. Thence continue 221°/8ca to enter the main 129° fairway.

NOTE
Some buoys and marks have been omitted for clarity

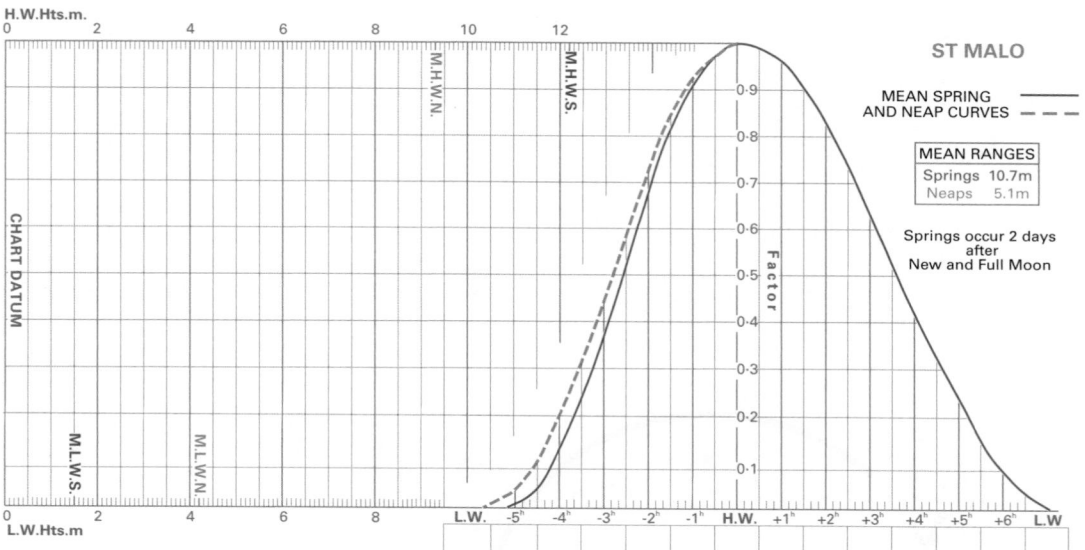

St Malo tidal curve:
- ST MALO
- MEAN SPRING AND NEAP CURVES
- MEAN RANGES: Springs 10.7m, Neaps 5.1m
- Springs occur 2 days after New and Full Moon

LIGHTS AND MARKS See chartlets/9.18.4 for ldg lts/buoys. Conspic daymarks: Île de Cézembre, Le Grand Jardin lt ho, Le Buron SHM twr, Petit and Grand Bé islets, the W lt twr/R top on Mole des Noires head and St Malo cathedral spire.

R/T Marinas Ch 09. *St Malo Port* Ch **12**.

TELEPHONE Port HM 02·99·20·63·01; Aff Mar 02·99·56·87·00; ⊖ 02·99·81·65·90; CROSS 02·98·89·31·31; Météo 02·99·46·10·46; Auto 08.92.68.08.35; Police 02·99·81·52·30; Ⓗ 02·99·56·56·19; Brit Consul 02.23.18.30.30.

FACILITIES Les Bas-Sablons Marina is entered over sill 2m. Access for 1·5m draft approx HW −3½ to +4½ sp; H24 at nps. 2 W waiting buoys outside. A conventional gauge on S bkwtr head shows depths <3m over sill. A large digital gauge on N side of marina is visible from all berths.
☎ 02·99·81·71·34. port.plaisance@ville-saint-malo.fr www.ville-saint-malo.fr 1216 + 64 Ⓥ, €3·05. Ⓥ berths on A pontoon: 32-66 (E side) and 43-75 (W side), and on B pontoon: 92-102 and 91-101. Slip, C (2·5 ton), BH (20 ton), Gaz, El, Ⓔ, ME, CH, ⚒, 🛠, SM, SHOM, R, YC, Bar, P & D pontoon 'I'; use French credit card or pay at office. **St Malo/St Servan**: Gaz, 🛒, R, Bar, ✉, Ⓑ, 🚆. Ferry: Portsmouth, Poole, Weymouth.

Bassin Vauban (6m) is entered by lock; help given with warps. Outside the lock 3 waiting buoys are N of appr chan; keep clear of vedette and ferry berths.
Lock times may vary with traffic & tides. Lock is scheduled to operate 5 or 6 times in each direction, ie:

Inward	−2½	−1½	−½	+½	+1½	+2½
Outward		−2	−1	HW	+1	+2

Lock sigs are IPTS Nos 2, 3 and 5. In addition:
⬤ next to the top lt = both lock gates are open, ie freeflow, beware current initially. Main message is the same. Freeflow is rare due to busy road traffic over retracting roller bridges.
⬤ ⬤ over ⬤ = all movements prohib, big ship is outbound.

Port Vauban ☎ 02·99·56·51·91 www.saint-malo.cci.fr

portplaisancevauban@saint-malo.cci.fr. 175 + 50 Ⓥ, €3·13. Ⓥ AB E side of pontoon No 3 or larger yachts on wall in front of YC; no fingers; no turning room between pontoons 1-3. No ⚓ in basins; 3kn speed limit. C (1 ton). **YC** ☎ 02·99·40·84·42, Bar (Ⓥ welcome). Bassin Duguay-Trouin is better for long stay.

DINARD Access by 1m marked chan to yacht basin 2m; see inset overleaf (many local boats; best to pre-arrange). **HM** ☎ 02·99·46·65·55. ⚓, M €2·30 (afloat), €1·56 (drying). Slip, P&D, ME, El, Ⓔ, ⚒, SM. **YC** ☎ 02·99·46·14·32, R, Bar. **Town** CH, 🛒, Gaz, R, Bar, ✉, Ⓑ, 🚆, ✈. Ⓗ 02·99·46·18·68. Ferries to St Malo.

ST MALO LAT 48°38'N LONG 2°02'W

TIMES AND HEIGHTS OF HIGH AND LOW WATERS

TIME ZONE -0100
Subtract 1 hour for UT
For French Summer Time add
ONE hour in **non-shaded areas**

Dates in red are SPRINGS
Dates in blue are NEAPS

YEAR **2010**

JANUARY

Time m	Time m
1 0142 1.9 / 0711 12.1 / F 1413 1.5 / 1943 11.9	**16** 0218 2.5 / 0748 11.4 / SA 1438 2.2 / 2008 11.1
2 0235 1.5 / 0800 12.5 / SA 1505 1.2 / 2031 12.3	**17** 0252 2.4 / 0820 11.5 / SU 1512 2.1 / 2039 11.2
3 0325 1.3 / 0847 12.6 / SU 1555 1.1 / 2118 12.2	**18** 0324 2.3 / 0851 11.4 / M 1544 2.1 / 2109 11.1
4 0412 1.4 / 0933 12.5 / M 1641 1.3 / 2203 11.9	**19** 0354 2.4 / 0921 11.3 / TU 1613 2.3 / 2138 11.0
5 0458 1.7 / 1019 12.1 / TU 1726 1.7 / 2247 11.4	**20** 0422 2.6 / 0949 11.0 / W 1642 2.5 / 2206 10.7
6 0541 2.2 / 1103 11.5 / W 1809 2.4 / 2331 10.8	**21** 0450 2.9 / 1018 10.7 / TH 1710 2.9 / 2236 10.3
7 0625 2.9 / 1150 10.7 / TH 1853 3.1 / ◑	**22** 0520 3.3 / 1048 10.2 / F 1743 3.4 / 2308 9.8
8 0019 10.1 / 0713 3.5 / F 1242 10.0 / 1943 3.8	**23** 0556 3.8 / 1125 9.7 / SA 1821 3.8 / ◑ 2350 9.4
9 0118 9.5 / 0812 4.0 / SA 1350 9.4 / 2046 4.2	**24** 0643 4.2 / 1216 9.2 / SU 1916 4.3
10 0235 9.2 / 0924 4.2 / SU 1512 9.2 / 2201 4.3	**25** 0054 9.0 / 0751 4.5 / M 1338 8.8 / 2035 4.4
11 0356 9.4 / 1038 4.0 / M 1630 9.4 / 2312 4.0	**26** 0229 8.9 / 0922 4.4 / TU 1520 9.0 / 2207 4.1
12 0501 9.8 / 1143 3.6 / TU 1731 9.8	**27** 0400 9.5 / 1050 3.7 / W 1642 9.7 / 2326 3.4
13 0011 3.6 / 0553 10.4 / W 1236 3.1 / 1819 10.3	**28** 0511 10.4 / 1203 2.8 / TH 1748 10.6
14 0059 3.1 / 0636 10.8 / TH 1321 2.7 / 1859 10.7	**29** 0033 2.5 / 0610 11.3 / F 1307 1.9 / 1844 11.4
15 0140 2.8 / 0713 11.1 / F 1401 2.4 / ● 1935 11.0	**30** 0134 1.7 / 0703 12.1 / SA 1406 1.2 / ○ 1935 12.1
	31 0228 1.0 / 0752 12.8 / SU 1458 0.6 / 2022 12.6

FEBRUARY

Time m	Time m
1 0318 0.7 / 0837 13.1 / M 1546 0.4 / 2105 12.7	**16** 0306 1.9 / 0830 11.8 / TU 1523 1.7 / 2047 11.6
2 0402 0.6 / 0920 13.0 / TU 1628 0.6 / 2145 12.4	**17** 0334 1.9 / 0859 11.7 / W 1551 1.9 / 2114 11.5
3 0443 1.0 / 1000 12.6 / W 1707 1.2 / 2224 11.9	**18** 0401 2.0 / 0925 11.5 / TH 1618 2.0 / 2140 11.2
4 0520 1.6 / 1038 11.8 / TH 1742 2.0 / 2300 11.2	**19** 0428 2.3 / 0952 11.2 / F 1644 2.4 / 2207 10.9
5 0555 2.5 / 1116 10.9 / F 1816 3.0 / 2338 10.3	**20** 0455 2.8 / 1020 10.7 / SA 1712 3.0 / 2236 10.4
6 0632 3.4 / 1158 9.9 / SA 1854 3.9 / ◑	**21** 0526 3.3 / 1052 10.1 / SU 1747 3.6 / 2312 9.8
7 0025 9.5 / 0721 4.2 / SU 1255 9.0 / 1949 4.6	**22** 0607 3.9 / 1136 9.4 / M 1836 4.2 / ◐
8 0137 8.8 / 0835 4.7 / M 1431 8.5 / 2116 5.0	**23** 0007 9.0 / 0710 4.4 / TU 1252 8.7 / 1953 4.6
9 0325 8.7 / 1007 4.6 / TU 1613 8.7 / 2248 4.6	**24** 0148 8.8 / 0847 4.5 / W 1459 8.7 / 2140 4.4
10 0445 9.2 / 1123 4.0 / W 1718 9.4 / 2355 3.9	**25** 0341 9.2 / 1031 3.8 / TH 1631 9.4 / 2310 3.5
11 0538 9.9 / 1220 3.4 / TH 1804 10.0	**26** 0458 10.3 / 1150 2.8 / F 1737 10.6
12 0044 3.3 / 0619 10.6 / F 1305 2.8 / 1841 10.6	**27** 0021 2.4 / 0557 11.4 / SA 1255 1.8 / 1831 11.6
13 0125 2.7 / 0655 11.1 / SA 1345 2.3 / 1915 11.0	**28** 0121 1.5 / 0649 12.3 / SU 1352 0.9 / ○ 1919 12.4
14 0202 2.3 / 0729 11.4 / SU 1420 2.0 / ● 1947 11.3	
15 0235 2.1 / 0800 11.7 / M 1453 1.8 / 2018 11.5	

MARCH

Time m	Time m
1 0214 0.7 / 0735 13.0 / M 1442 0.4 / 2003 12.8	**16** 0208 2.0 / 0734 11.7 / TU 1425 1.7 / 1950 11.7
2 0301 0.3 / 0819 13.2 / TU 1526 0.2 / 2043 12.9	**17** 0239 1.8 / 0805 11.9 / W 1456 1.5 / 2020 11.8
3 0342 0.4 / 0858 13.1 / W 1605 0.5 / 2121 12.7	**18** 0309 1.7 / 0834 11.9 / TH 1525 1.6 / 2047 11.8
4 0419 0.8 / 0936 12.6 / TH 1639 1.1 / 2156 12.1	**19** 0338 1.8 / 0901 11.8 / F 1553 1.8 / 2115 11.6
5 0452 1.5 / 1010 11.9 / F 1709 1.9 / 2229 11.4	**20** 0407 2.1 / 0930 11.4 / SA 1621 2.2 / 2143 11.3
6 0523 2.4 / 1044 10.9 / SA 1737 3.0 / 2302 10.5	**21** 0436 2.5 / 1000 10.9 / SU 1651 2.8 / 2214 10.7
7 0553 3.4 / 1120 9.8 / SU 1807 4.0 / ◐ 2341 9.5	**22** 0508 3.1 / 1035 10.2 / M 1725 3.5 / 2254 10.1
8 0635 4.3 / 1209 8.8 / M 1856 4.9	**23** 0550 3.7 / 1122 9.5 / TU 1816 4.2 / ◐ 2352 9.3
9 0045 8.6 / 0744 4.9 / TU 1347 8.1 / 2028 5.4	**24** 0653 4.3 / 1245 8.8 / W 1937 4.6
10 0248 8.3 / 0930 5.0 / W 1547 8.4 / 2219 5.0	**25** 0138 8.9 / 0831 4.4 / TH 1449 8.9 / 2126 4.4
11 0418 8.9 / 1056 4.3 / TH 1652 9.1 / 2329 4.2	**26** 0325 9.4 / 1016 3.7 / F 1615 9.7 / 2254 3.4
12 0511 9.6 / 1152 3.6 / F 1736 9.9	**27** 0439 10.4 / 1133 2.7 / SA 1718 10.7
13 0017 3.4 / 0551 10.4 / SA 1236 2.9 / 1812 10.5	**28** 0002 2.4 / 0537 11.4 / SU 1235 1.8 / 1809 11.7
14 0057 2.8 / 0627 11.0 / SU 1316 2.3 / 1846 11.1	**29** 0059 1.5 / 0627 12.3 / M 1330 1.0 / 1855 12.3
15 0134 2.3 / 0701 11.4 / M 1352 1.9 / ● 1919 11.5	**30** 0151 0.9 / 0713 12.8 / TU 1417 0.6 / ○ 1938 12.7
	31 0236 0.6 / 0755 13.0 / W 1459 0.6 / 2017 12.8

APRIL

Time m	Time m
1 0316 0.7 / 0833 12.8 / TH 1536 0.9 / 2053 12.6	**16** 0243 1.7 / 0808 11.9 / F 1459 1.7 / 2021 12.0
2 0351 1.0 / 0909 12.3 / F 1608 1.5 / 2127 12.1	**17** 0316 1.8 / 0840 11.8 / SA 1532 1.9 / 2053 11.9
3 0423 1.7 / 0943 11.6 / SA 1636 2.3 / 2159 11.4	**18** 0350 2.0 / 0914 11.5 / SU 1605 2.3 / 2128 11.5
4 0452 2.5 / 1017 10.8 / SU 1702 3.2 / 2232 10.5	**19** 0424 2.4 / 0950 11.0 / M 1637 2.8 / 2206 11.0
5 0522 3.4 / 1052 9.8 / M 1733 4.1 / 2310 9.6	**20** 0502 2.9 / 1034 10.4 / TU 1720 3.4 / 2254 10.3
6 0601 4.2 / 1138 8.9 / TU 1818 4.9 / ◐	**21** 0549 3.5 / 1130 9.7 / W 1815 4.0 / ◐
7 0007 8.8 / 0701 4.9 / W 1301 8.3 / 1939 5.4	**22** 0001 9.7 / 0655 4.0 / TH 1255 9.2 / 1937 4.4
8 0155 8.4 / 0837 5.0 / TH 1455 8.3 / 2129 5.2	**23** 0133 9.4 / 0825 4.0 / F 1431 9.3 / 2111 4.1
9 0328 8.7 / 1007 4.6 / F 1606 8.9 / 2242 4.5	**24** 0301 9.8 / 0955 3.5 / SA 1549 10.0 / 2229 3.3
10 0427 9.4 / 1107 3.9 / SA 1654 9.7 / 2333 3.7	**25** 0412 10.5 / 1107 2.8 / SU 1650 10.8 / 2335 2.5
11 0511 10.1 / 1154 3.2 / SU 1733 10.4	**26** 0510 11.3 / 1208 2.1 / M 1742 11.5
12 0016 3.1 / 0550 10.7 / M 1236 2.6 / 1810 11.0	**27** 0032 1.9 / 0601 11.9 / TU 1301 1.6 / 1828 12.0
13 0056 2.5 / 0627 11.2 / TU 1315 2.2 / 1845 11.4	**28** 0123 1.4 / 0647 12.2 / W 1348 1.3 / ○ 1911 12.3
14 0133 2.1 / 0702 11.6 / W 1351 1.9 / ● 1919 11.7	**29** 0208 1.2 / 0729 12.3 / TH 1431 1.3 / 1950 12.4
15 0209 1.9 / 0736 11.8 / TH 1426 1.7 / 1950 11.9	**30** 0247 1.3 / 0809 12.2 / F 1505 1.6 / 2026 12.2

Chart Datum is 6·29 metres below IGN Datum. HAT is 13·6 metres above Chart Datum; see 4.5.

Central N France

ST MALO LAT 48°38'N LONG 2°02'W
TIMES AND HEIGHTS OF HIGH AND LOW WATERS

TIME ZONE -0100
Subtract 1 hour for UT
For French Summer Time add
ONE hour in **non-shaded areas**

Dates in **red** are **SPRINGS**
Dates in **blue** are **NEAPS**

YEAR **2010**

MAY

Day	Time m			Day	Time m		
1 SA	0323 1.5	0846 11.8	1537 2.0 / 2101 11.9	**16** SU	0259 1.8	0825 11.8	1516 2.0 / 2040 12.0
2 SU	0356 2.0	0921 11.3	1608 2.6 / 2136 11.3	**17** M	0339 1.9	0906 11.6	1556 2.2 / 2122 11.8
3 M	0427 2.6	0956 10.7	1638 3.2 / 2211 10.6	**18** TU	0421 2.2	0951 11.2	1639 2.6 / 2208 11.4
4 TU	0500 3.3	1034 10.0	1711 3.9 / 2250 9.9	**19** W	0506 2.6	1040 10.7	1726 3.1 / 2301 10.8
5 W	0538 3.9	1118 9.3	1754 4.6 / 2341 9.2	**20** TH	0557 3.1	1138 10.2	1823 3.6
6 TH ☽	0629 4.5	1218 8.8	1856 5.0	**21** F ☽	0003 10.3	0658 3.4	1246 9.8 / 1932 3.8
7 F	0053 8.8	0739 4.8	1341 8.6 / 2019 5.1	**22** SA	0114 10.1	0811 3.6	1402 9.8 / 2047 3.7
8 SA	0217 8.8	0858 4.6	1458 8.9 / 2136 4.7	**23** SU	0229 10.1	0925 3.4	1515 10.1 / 2158 3.3
9 SU	0325 9.2	1005 4.1	1557 9.4 / 2236 4.1	**24** M	0339 10.4	1034 3.0	1619 10.6 / 2303 2.9
10 M	0418 9.7	1100 3.6	1645 10.0 / 2326 3.5	**25** TU	0440 10.8	1136 2.6	1714 11.1
11 TU	0505 10.3	1149 3.0	1727 10.6	**26** W	0001 2.5	0535 11.2	1230 2.3 / 1803 11.5
12 W	0012 2.9	0548 10.8	1234 2.6 / 1808 11.2	**27** TH	0054 2.1	0624 11.4	1318 2.2 / 1847 11.7
13 TH	0056 2.5	0629 11.3	1317 2.1 / 1846 11.6	**28** F ○	0140 2.0	0709 11.5	1400 2.1 / 1928 11.8
14 F ●	0138 2.1	0708 11.6	1357 2.0 / 1923 11.9	**29** SA	0221 1.9	0750 11.5	1438 2.2 / 2006 11.8
15 SA	0219 1.9	0746 11.7	1437 1.9 / 2001 12.0	**30** SU	0259 2.0	0828 11.4	1514 2.4 / 2043 11.6
				31 M	0335 2.2	0905 11.1	1548 2.7 / 2119 11.3

JUNE

Day	Time m			Day	Time m		
1 TU	0409 2.6	0941 10.7	1621 3.1 / 2155 10.8	**16** W	0423 1.7	0951 11.7	1641 2.1 / 2207 11.9
2 W	0443 3.0	1018 10.3	1655 3.5 / 2232 10.3	**17** TH	0510 2.0	1039 11.4	1729 2.4 / 2257 11.5
3 TH	0519 3.5	1056 9.8	1733 4.0 / 2313 9.8	**18** F	0558 2.4	1129 10.9	1819 2.8 / 2349 11.0
4 F	0600 3.9	1139 9.4	1818 4.4	**19** SA ○	0650 2.8	1224 10.4	1914 3.3
5 SA	0001 9.3	0649 4.2	1233 9.1 / 1915 4.7	**20** SU	0047 10.5	0746 3.3	1325 10.1 / 2016 3.5
6 SU	0101 9.1	0748 4.4	1339 9.0 / 2022 4.7	**21** M	0152 10.2	0850 3.5	1435 9.9 / 2124 3.6
7 M	0211 9.1	0855 4.3	1448 9.2 / 2131 4.4	**22** TU	0304 10.0	0958 3.5	1546 10.1 / 2232 3.4
8 TU	0317 9.3	1001 4.0	1550 9.6 / 2233 3.9	**23** W	0413 10.1	1104 3.4	1650 10.4 / 2335 3.1
9 W	0415 9.8	1101 3.5	1643 10.2 / 2329 3.4	**24** TH	0516 10.4	1204 3.1	1744 10.8
10 TH	0508 10.3	1155 3.0	1732 10.8	**25** F	0030 2.8	0610 10.7	1255 2.9 / 1832 11.2
11 F	0021 2.8	0558 10.8	1245 2.6 / 1819 11.3	**26** SA ○	0119 2.5	0656 10.9	1340 2.7 / 1914 11.4
12 SA ●	0111 2.4	0645 11.3	1334 2.2 / 1903 11.7	**27** SU	0203 2.3	0738 11.1	1421 2.6 / 1953 11.5
13 SU	0200 2.0	0731 11.6	1421 2.0 / 1948 12.1	**28** M	0243 2.2	0815 11.1	1458 2.5 / 2029 11.5
14 M	0248 1.7	0817 11.8	1508 1.9 / 2033 12.2	**29** TU	0319 2.2	0850 11.1	1533 2.6 / 2103 11.4
15 TU	0336 1.6	0903 11.8	1554 1.9 / 2120 12.2	**30** W	0354 2.4	0924 11.0	1606 2.7 / 2137 11.1

JULY

Day	Time m			Day	Time m		
1 TH	0427 2.6	0957 10.7	1638 3.0 / 2209 10.8	**16** F	0504 1.3	1025 11.9	1720 1.7 / 2241 12.1
2 F	0458 2.9	1029 10.4	1709 3.4 / 2242 10.3	**17** SA	0546 1.8	1109 11.4	1803 2.3 / 2326 11.4
3 SA	0530 3.3	1102 10.0	1743 3.8 / 2317 9.9	**18** SU ◐	0628 2.5	1154 10.8	1848 3.0
4 SU ○	0606 3.7	1141 9.6	1823 4.2	**19** M	0014 10.6	0714 3.3	1246 10.1 / 1942 3.7
5 M	0000 9.5	0649 4.0	1230 9.3 / 1915 4.5	**20** TU	0113 9.9	0811 3.9	1353 9.6 / 2049 4.0
6 TU	0057 9.1	0746 4.3	1336 9.1 / 2022 4.6	**21** W	0230 9.4	0923 4.2	1517 9.5 / 2205 4.0
7 W	0212 9.0	0858 4.2	1453 9.2 / 2140 4.3	**22** TH	0355 9.4	1039 4.1	1634 9.8 / 2316 3.7
8 TH	0328 9.3	1014 4.0	1603 9.7 / 2251 3.8	**23** F	0506 9.8	1146 3.7	1733 10.4
9 F	0435 9.8	1121 3.5	1704 10.4 / 2354 3.1	**24** SA	0016 3.2	0600 10.3	1241 3.2 / 1821 10.9
10 SA	0535 10.4	1221 2.9	1759 11.1	**25** SU	0106 2.8	0645 10.7	1327 2.8 / 1901 11.2
11 SU ●	0052 2.5	0630 11.1	1318 2.3 / 1850 11.7	**26** M ○	0149 2.4	0723 11.0	1408 2.6 / 1938 11.5
12 M	0148 1.9	0721 11.6	1412 1.8 / 1939 12.3	**27** TU	0228 2.2	0758 11.2	1444 2.4 / 2011 11.6
13 TU	0242 1.4	0810 12.1	1503 1.4 / 2026 12.6	**28** W	0303 2.1	0830 11.3	1517 2.3 / 2043 11.6
14 W	0332 1.1	0857 12.3	1551 1.3 / 2112 12.7	**29** TH	0335 2.1	0901 11.3	1547 2.4 / 2113 11.5
15 TH	0419 1.1	0942 12.2	1637 1.4 / 2157 12.5	**30** F	0404 2.2	0930 11.2	1614 2.6 / 2142 11.2
				31 SA	0431 2.5	0958 10.9	1641 2.9 / 2209 10.8

AUGUST

Day	Time m			Day	Time m		
1 SU	0459 2.8	1026 10.5	1709 3.3 / 2238 10.4	**16** M ◑	0558 2.6	1120 10.9	1816 3.1 / 2340 10.4
2 M	0528 3.3	1056 10.0	1741 3.8 / 2311 9.8	**17** TU	0636 3.6	1206 10.0	1904 4.0
3 TU ◑	0602 3.7	1133 9.6	1823 4.3 / 2355 9.3	**18** W	0034 9.5	0728 4.4	1312 9.2 / 2012 4.6
4 W	0650 4.3	1228 9.1	1923 4.6	**19** TH	0159 8.8	0849 4.9	1453 9.0 / 2142 4.6
5 TH	0107 8.8	0800 4.6	1357 8.9 / 2050 4.7	**20** F	0343 8.9	1022 4.7	1621 9.4 / 2302 4.1
6 F	0249 8.8	0933 4.5	1531 9.3 / 2222 4.1	**21** SA	0455 9.5	1134 4.0	1719 10.1
7 SA	0413 9.4	1056 3.8	1644 10.1 / 2334 3.3	**22** SU	0002 3.4	0545 10.2	1226 3.3 / 1804 10.8
8 SU	0520 10.3	1204 3.0	1744 11.1	**23** M	0049 2.8	0625 10.7	1310 2.8 / 1841 11.3
9 M	0038 2.4	0618 11.2	1305 2.1 / 1838 11.9	**24** TU ○	0129 2.4	0700 11.1	1348 2.4 / 1915 11.6
10 TU ●	0137 1.6	0709 11.9	1401 1.4 / 1927 12.6	**25** W	0206 2.1	0733 11.4	1422 2.2 / 1947 11.8
11 W	0231 1.0	0756 12.5	1452 0.9 / 2013 13.1	**26** TH	0239 2.0	0804 11.6	1453 2.1 / 2017 11.8
12 TH	0321 0.6	0841 12.7	1539 0.7 / 2057 13.2	**27** F	0309 1.9	0833 11.6	1521 2.1 / 2045 11.8
13 F	0405 0.6	0923 12.7	1621 0.9 / 2138 12.9	**28** SA	0336 2.0	0900 11.5	1547 2.3 / 2112 11.5
14 SA	0445 1.0	1003 12.3	1700 1.4 / 2218 12.3	**29** SU	0402 2.4	0925 11.3	1613 2.6 / 2137 11.2
15 SU	0523 1.7	1041 11.7	1738 2.2 / 2257 11.5	**30** M	0428 2.6	0951 10.9	1639 3.0 / 2203 10.7
				31 TU	0455 3.1	1018 10.5	1708 3.5 / 2233 10.1

Chart Datum is 6·29 metres below IGN Datum. HAT is 13·6 metres above Chart Datum; see 4.5.

ST MALO LAT 48°38'N LONG 2°02'W
TIMES AND HEIGHTS OF HIGH AND LOW WATERS

YEAR 2010

TIME ZONE -0100
Subtract 1 hour for UT
For French Summer Time add ONE hour in **non-shaded areas**

Dates in red are SPRINGS
Dates in blue are NEAPS

SEPTEMBER

Day	Time	m	Day	Time	m
1 W	0526 / 1052 / 1746 / 2313 ◗	3.7 / 9.9 / 4.1 / 9.4	16 TH	0645 / 1233 / 1932	4.8 / 9.0 / 4.9
2 TH	0611 / 1141 / 1842	4.3 / 9.3 / 4.6	17 F	0129 / 0811 / 1426 / 2114	8.5 / 5.4 / 8.7 / 5.0
3 F	0020 / 0718 / 1313 / 2011	8.8 / 4.8 / 8.8 / 4.8	18 SA	0323 / 1000 / 1557 / 2240	8.6 / 5.1 / 9.2 / 4.4
4 SA	0224 / 0903 / 1509 / 2159	8.7 / 4.8 / 9.2 / 4.3	19 SU	0432 / 1111 / 1654 / 2336	9.3 / 4.3 / 9.9 / 3.6
5 SU	0358 / 1038 / 1627 / 2318	9.4 / 4.0 / 10.1 / 3.3	20 M	0518 / 1200 / 1736	10.1 / 3.5 / 10.6
6 M	0505 / 1148 / 1727	10.4 / 2.9 / 11.2	21 TU	0020 / 0556 / 1241 / 1812	3.0 / 10.7 / 2.9 / 11.2
7 TU	0022 / 0600 / 1249 / 1820	2.2 / 11.4 / 1.9 / 12.2	22 W	0059 / 0629 / 1318 / 1845	2.5 / 11.2 / 2.5 / 11.6
8 W ●	0120 / 0649 / 1343 / 1908	1.3 / 12.2 / 1.1 / 12.9	23 TH ○	0135 / 0702 / 1352 / 1917	2.2 / 11.5 / 2.2 / 11.8
9 TH	0213 / 0735 / 1433 / 1952	0.7 / 12.8 / 0.7 / 13.3	24 F	0208 / 0732 / 1423 / 1948	2.0 / 11.7 / 2.1 / 11.9
10 F	0300 / 0818 / 1518 / 2034	0.5 / 13.0 / 0.5 / 13.3	25 SA	0238 / 0801 / 1452 / 2016	1.9 / 11.8 / 2.1 / 11.9
11 SA	0342 / 0858 / 1558 / 2114	0.6 / 12.9 / 0.8 / 13.0	26 SU	0306 / 0829 / 1519 / 2043	2.0 / 11.8 / 2.2 / 11.7
12 SU	0419 / 0935 / 1635 / 2151	1.1 / 12.5 / 1.4 / 12.2	27 M	0333 / 0855 / 1547 / 2110	2.2 / 11.6 / 2.4 / 11.4
13 M	0453 / 1011 / 1708 / 2228	1.9 / 11.8 / 2.3 / 11.3	28 TU	0400 / 0922 / 1615 / 2138	2.6 / 11.3 / 2.9 / 10.9
14 TU	0524 / 1047 / 1742 / 2307	2.9 / 10.9 / 3.3 / 10.2	29 W	0429 / 0952 / 1646 / 2211	3.1 / 10.8 / 3.4 / 10.3
15 W ◗	0557 / 1129 / 1825 / 2358	4.0 / 9.9 / 4.2 / 9.2	30 TH	0502 / 1028 / 1725 / 2253	3.7 / 10.2 / 4.0 / 9.6

OCTOBER

Day	Time	m	Day	Time	m
1 F ◗	0548 / 1120 / 1822	4.4 / 9.5 / 4.5	16 SA	0047 / 0725 / 1338 / 2024	8.5 / 5.4 / 8.6 / 5.2
2 SA	0005 / 0658 / 1256 / 1950	8.9 / 4.8 / 9.0 / 4.7	17 SU	0236 / 0913 / 1512 / 2153	8.5 / 5.3 / 8.9 / 4.7
3 SU	0209 / 0844 / 1448 / 2139	8.8 / 4.7 / 9.3 / 4.2	18 M	0349 / 1027 / 1612 / 2253	9.1 / 4.6 / 9.5 / 4.0
4 M	0339 / 1018 / 1605 / 2258	9.5 / 3.9 / 10.3 / 3.2	19 TU	0438 / 1118 / 1657 / 2339	9.8 / 3.9 / 10.2 / 3.4
5 TU	0443 / 1126 / 1704	10.6 / 2.8 / 11.3	20 W	0517 / 1201 / 1735	10.5 / 3.2 / 10.8
6 W	0001 / 0537 / 1226 / 1756	2.2 / 11.5 / 1.9 / 12.2	21 TH	0020 / 0553 / 1239 / 1811	2.8 / 11.0 / 2.8 / 11.3
7 TH ●	0057 / 0625 / 1320 / 1844	1.4 / 12.3 / 1.2 / 12.8	22 F	0058 / 0627 / 1316 / 1845	2.4 / 11.4 / 2.4 / 11.6
8 F	0147 / 0710 / 1408 / 1928	0.9 / 12.8 / 0.8 / 13.1	23 SA ○	0133 / 0700 / 1350 / 1918	2.2 / 11.7 / 2.2 / 11.8
9 SA	0233 / 0751 / 1452 / 2010	0.8 / 12.9 / 0.8 / 13.0	24 SU	0206 / 0731 / 1423 / 1949	2.1 / 11.9 / 2.1 / 11.8
10 SU	0313 / 0830 / 1531 / 2048	1.0 / 12.8 / 1.1 / 12.6	25 M	0238 / 0801 / 1455 / 2019	2.1 / 11.9 / 2.2 / 11.7
11 M	0349 / 0907 / 1607 / 2125	1.5 / 12.4 / 1.7 / 11.9	26 TU	0309 / 0831 / 1528 / 2051	2.3 / 11.8 / 2.4 / 11.5
12 TU	0421 / 0942 / 1640 / 2202	2.3 / 11.7 / 2.5 / 11.1	27 W	0341 / 0903 / 1601 / 2125	2.6 / 11.6 / 2.7 / 11.1
13 W	0451 / 1018 / 1713 / 2240	3.2 / 10.8 / 3.4 / 10.1	28 TH	0413 / 0940 / 1637 / 2205	3.0 / 11.1 / 3.2 / 10.5
14 TH ◗	0524 / 1059 / 1752 / 2328	4.1 / 9.9 / 4.3 / 9.2	29 F	0454 / 1023 / 1721 / 2255	3.6 / 10.5 / 3.7 / 9.8
15 F	0608 / 1157 / 1851	4.9 / 9.1 / 4.9	30 SA ◗	0544 / 1122 / 1819	4.1 / 9.8 / 4.2
			31 SU	0009 / 0654 / 1247 / 1940	9.3 / 4.5 / 9.5 / 4.4

NOVEMBER

Day	Time	m	Day	Time	m
1 M	0146 / 0826 / 1419 / 2114	9.2 / 4.4 / 9.7 / 4.0	16 TU	0240 / 0917 / 1511 / 2150	8.8 / 4.9 / 9.1 / 4.4
2 TU	0310 / 0950 / 1535 / 2230	9.7 / 3.9 / 10.3 / 3.2	17 W	0342 / 1021 / 1606 / 2246	9.3 / 4.4 / 9.6 / 3.9
3 W	0415 / 1059 / 1637 / 2333	10.6 / 2.9 / 11.1 / 2.4	18 TH	0430 / 1112 / 1652 / 2334	9.9 / 3.8 / 10.2 / 3.3
4 TH	0510 / 1159 / 1731	11.4 / 2.2 / 11.8	19 F	0512 / 1157 / 1733	10.5 / 3.2 / 10.7
5 F	0030 / 0559 / 1253 / 1820	1.8 / 12.0 / 1.6 / 12.3	20 SA	0018 / 0551 / 1239 / 1813	2.9 / 11.1 / 2.8 / 11.1
6 SA ●	0120 / 0644 / 1342 / 1905	1.5 / 12.4 / 1.3 / 12.5	21 SU ○	0059 / 0629 / 1320 / 1851	2.5 / 11.5 / 2.4 / 11.4
7 SU	0205 / 0726 / 1426 / 1947	1.4 / 12.5 / 1.3 / 12.4	22 M	0138 / 0705 / 1359 / 1928	2.3 / 11.7 / 2.2 / 11.6
8 M	0245 / 0806 / 1506 / 2027	1.6 / 12.4 / 1.5 / 12.1	23 TU	0216 / 0740 / 1438 / 2004	2.2 / 11.9 / 2.1 / 11.7
9 TU	0322 / 0845 / 1542 / 2105	2.0 / 12.1 / 2.0 / 11.6	24 W	0254 / 0817 / 1517 / 2042	2.2 / 11.9 / 2.2 / 11.6
10 W	0355 / 0920 / 1617 / 2143	2.5 / 11.6 / 2.6 / 10.9	25 TH	0333 / 0856 / 1557 / 2123	2.4 / 11.8 / 2.3 / 11.3
11 TH	0428 / 0958 / 1651 / 2221	3.2 / 10.9 / 3.2 / 10.2	26 F	0413 / 0939 / 1639 / 2209	2.7 / 11.5 / 2.7 / 10.9
12 F	0502 / 1037 / 1729 / 2304	3.9 / 10.1 / 3.9 / 9.5	27 SA	0457 / 1027 / 1726 / 2300	3.1 / 11.0 / 3.1 / 10.4
13 SA ◑	0542 / 1126 / 1816	4.6 / 9.4 / 4.5	28 SU ◑	0548 / 1123 / 1821	3.5 / 10.5 / 3.5
14 SU	0000 / 0639 / 1233 / 1921	8.9 / 5.0 / 8.9 / 4.4	29 M	0002 / 0649 / 1229 / 1927	9.9 / 3.9 / 10.1 / 3.8
15 M	0118 / 0757 / 1358 / 2039	8.6 / 5.2 / 8.8 / 4.8	30 TU	0115 / 0801 / 1344 / 2042	9.7 / 4.0 / 10.0 / 3.7

DECEMBER

Day	Time	m	Day	Time	m
1 W	0232 / 0917 / 1500 / 2156	9.8 / 3.7 / 10.2 / 3.4	16 TH	0225 / 0905 / 1459 / 2141	8.9 / 4.7 / 9.0 / 4.4
2 TH	0343 / 1027 / 1607 / 2303	10.3 / 3.2 / 10.6 / 2.9	17 F	0333 / 1015 / 1602 / 2245	9.2 / 4.3 / 9.4 / 3.9
3 F	0443 / 1131 / 1707	10.8 / 2.7 / 11.1	18 SA	0429 / 1114 / 1656 / 2340	9.8 / 3.8 / 10.0 / 3.4
4 SA	0002 / 0537 / 1228 / 1801	2.5 / 11.4 / 2.2 / 11.5	19 SU	0518 / 1206 / 1745	10.4 / 3.2 / 10.5
5 SU ●	0055 / 0625 / 1319 / 1849	2.2 / 11.8 / 1.9 / 11.7	20 M	0029 / 0604 / 1254 / 1830	2.9 / 11.0 / 2.6 / 11.0
6 M	0142 / 0709 / 1405 / 1933	2.0 / 12.0 / 1.8 / 11.7	21 TU ○	0116 / 0646 / 1341 / 1914	2.5 / 11.5 / 2.2 / 11.4
7 TU	0224 / 0750 / 1446 / 2013	2.1 / 12.0 / 1.8 / 11.6	22 W	0201 / 0728 / 1427 / 1956	2.1 / 11.9 / 1.9 / 11.7
8 W	0302 / 0828 / 1524 / 2051	2.2 / 11.8 / 2.0 / 11.4	23 TH	0246 / 0811 / 1513 / 2039	1.9 / 12.1 / 1.7 / 11.8
9 TH	0338 / 0906 / 1600 / 2128	2.5 / 11.5 / 2.4 / 11.0	24 F	0331 / 0854 / 1558 / 2123	1.8 / 12.2 / 1.7 / 11.8
10 F	0412 / 0942 / 1635 / 2204	2.9 / 11.1 / 2.8 / 10.5	25 SA	0415 / 0938 / 1643 / 2207	1.9 / 12.1 / 1.9 / 11.5
11 SA	0445 / 1018 / 1709 / 2240	3.4 / 10.5 / 3.3 / 10.0	26 SU	0500 / 1024 / 1728 / 2254	2.2 / 11.7 / 2.2 / 11.1
12 SU	0520 / 1055 / 1745 / 2318	3.9 / 10.0 / 3.8 / 9.5	27 M	0546 / 1112 / 1815 / 2343	2.6 / 11.2 / 2.7 / 10.5
13 M ◑	0559 / 1137 / 1828	4.3 / 9.4 / 4.3	28 TU ◑	0635 / 1205 / 1906	3.1 / 10.6 / 3.2
14 TU	0005 / 0648 / 1231 / 1923	9.1 / 4.7 / 9.0 / 4.6	29 W	0040 / 0733 / 1307 / 2007	10.0 / 3.6 / 10.1 / 3.6
15 W	0109 / 0752 / 1343 / 2029	8.8 / 4.9 / 8.8 / 4.6	30 TH	0149 / 0841 / 1421 / 2119	9.7 / 3.8 / 9.8 / 3.8
			31 F	0307 / 0955 / 1540 / 2233	9.7 / 3.7 / 9.9 / 3.6

Central N France

Chart Datum is 6·29 metres below IGN Datum. HAT is 13·6 metres above Chart Datum; see 4.5.

9.18.13 RIVER RANCE

Ille-et-Vilaine 48°37'·04N 02°01'·71W (Barrage) ❀❀⛴⛴❀❀❀

CHARTS AC 3659, 2700; SHOM 7130, 4233; Imray C33B; Stanfords 26

TIDES Standard Port ST MALO (←)
Water levels up-river of the Rance hydro-electric tidal barrage are strongly affected by the operation of the sluice gates and occasional use of the turbines as pumps. On most days from 0700–2100LT, 4m above CD is maintained. There is generally 8·5m above CD for a period of 4 hours from 0700–2000LT. A French language pamphlet, issued by Électricité de France (EDF), should be obtained from HMs at St Malo or Bas Sablons, or from the office at the barrage lock. It gives forecasts for the summer months of when heights of 4m and 8·5m above CD will occur in the period 0700–2000LT. The local daily paper *Ouest-France* gives a forecast for the next day of HW and LW up-stream of the barrage, under the heading *Usine Marémotrice de la Rance*.

SHELTER Good shelter up-river dependent on wind direction. The principal ⚓s/moorings on the E bank are at St Suliac and Mordreuc, and at La Richardais, La Jouvente, Le Minihic and La Pommeraie on the W bank. Marinas at Plouër, Lyvet (E bank, beyond Chatelier lock) and Dinan: see next column.

NAVIGATION From St Malo/Dinard, appr the lock (at the W end of the barrage) between Pte de la Jument to stbd and a prohib sluicing zone to port, marked by PHM buoys linked by wire cables. 3 white waiting buoys are on the E side of the appr chan, close to the prohibited zone; a similar buoy is upstream.

Barrage lock opens day/night (on request 2030–0430) on the hour, every hour provided the level is at least 4m above CD on both sides of the barrage. Yachts should arrive at H –20 mins. An illuminated display board gives access times in French/English. Lock entry sigs are **IPTS** sigs 2, 3 and 5. Masted boats entering from sea should berth at the S end of the lock so that the bridge can close astern of them. Vertical wires assist berthing/warp-handling. The lifting road-bridge across the lock opens only between H and H +15. Up-stream of the lock a further prohib area to port is marked as above.

The chan up-river is marked by perches; binos needed. The 3M chan to St Suliac has min depth of 2m. The next 6M to the Chatelier lock partially dries and is buoyed; keep to the outside of bends. The suspension bridge and road bridge at Port St. Hubert have 23m clearance. A viaduct 1M beyond Mordreuc has 19m clearance. Allow 2-3 hours from the barrage to Chatelier.

Chatelier lock and swing bridge operate 0600-2100LT, provided there is at least 8·5m rise of tide. HW Chatelier is 2-3 hours after HW St Malo depending on the barrage. Entry is controlled by CEVNI sigs (variations on a R and G theme).

The final 3M to Dinan has a published min depth in the marked chan of 1·4m; check with lock-keeper. Dinan gives access to Ille et Rance Canal and River Vilaine to Biscay (see 9.18.14).

LIGHTS AND MARKS Approaching the barrage from seaward: Pte de la Jument bn tr, Fl G 4s 6m 4M; PHM buoy opposite, Fl R 4s (prohib zone). The lock control twr is conspic. NW side of lock, Fl (2) G 6s, with G ▲ on W □. First dolphin, Fl (2) R 6s, with R ■ on W □.

Approaching from Dinan: PHM buoy, Fl (2) R 6s, at S end of prohib zone; leave to stbd. First dolphin, Fl (3) R 12s, with R ■ on W □. SW side of lock, Fl (3) G 12s, G ▲ on W □.

R/T *Barrage de la Rance* (lock) Ch 13. Chatelier lock Ch 14.

TELEPHONE Water levels/navigation 02·99·46·14·46; Barrage/lock info 02·99·46·21·87; Chatelier lock 02·96·39·55·66; Météo 02·99·46·10·46; Auto 08.92.68.08.35; Aff Mar 02·96· 39·56·44; Police 02·99·81·52·30; Brit Consul 02.23.18.30.30.

FACILITIES St Suliac Slip, M, Bar, R, 🛒, Divers (Convoimer).
Mordreuc Slip, L, M, Bar, R.
La Richardais HM 02·99·46·24·20; El, ME, ✕, Bar, D, P, ✉, R, 🛒, ⑧. **La Jouvente** AB, Bar, R.
Le Minihic M, L, Slip, ME, El, ✕.
La Cale de Plouër M, L, SC, R.

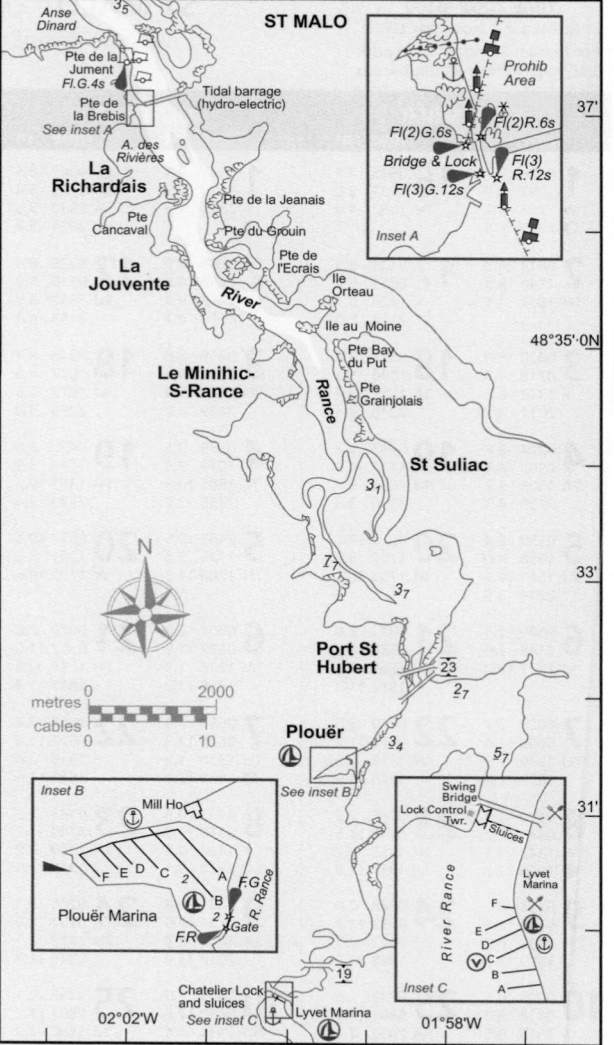

MARINAS ON THE RIVER RANCE

PLOUËR, Côtes d'Armor, **48°31'·54N 01°58'·95W**. ❀❀⛴⛴❀❀.
On W bank of R Rance, 6M S of the barrage and 2M N of the Chatelier lock. Access approx HW±3, when tide is 8m above CD, giving at least 1·5m water above rising gate. Appr with Plouër ✠ spire brg 285°. Unlit PHM and SHM perches are 30m from ent at S end of bkwtr. Accessible when FR and FG lts marking the sill are lit, day/night. Depth gauge (hard to read) is floodlit. **Marina** plouer.portplaisance@wanadoo.fr www.rance-fremur.com/plouer ☎ 02·96·86·83·15; 📠 02·96·89·11·00. Ch 09. HM, Mlle Liliane Faustin, is most helpful. 230 AB, +10 ♥ pontoon B, €1·65. Slip, CH, BY, C, ME, BH (10-14 ton), R, Bar. 🛒 in village 1M.

LYVET, 48°29'·40N 02°00'·00W, on the E bank just S of Chatelier lock. ❀❀⛴⛴❀. **Marina** ☎ 02·96·83·35·57. 210+25 ♥, €1·50. Berth in 2m on D pontoon or as directed. R, Bar, limited 🛒.

DINAN ❀❀⛴⛴❀❀❀. **Marina** ☎ 02·96·39·56·44. Alongside berths line the W bank of the river, with fingers (€1·50) near to the Port in about 1·5m. P, D, C for de-masting, R, Bar. Low bridge beyond Port has 2·5m headroom, giving access to the Ille et Rance canal. **Town** (75m above river) 🛒, R, ✉, ⑧, ⇌, ✈ (Dinard).

Ille et Rance Canal (see opposite): On the Breton canals the tolls charged elsewhere in France (see 9.17.6) are not levied nor envisaged. A certificate of competence is required, unless vessel is <5m LOA *and* not capable of more than 20kph/11kn.

9.18.14 INLAND WATERWAYS OF BRITTANY

NAVIGATION Canals and rivers across and within Brittany enable boats of limited water and air draughts to go from the English Channel to the Bay of Biscay avoiding the passage around Finistère. Distances, number of locks, boat size and speed limits are summarised below. Dinan-Arzal takes about 5 days. Despite the many locks it can be a thoroughly enjoyable trip through unspoiled countryside and some interesting towns. Most overnight stops are free or at nominal cost.

LOCKS From Apr to Sept locks are worked 7 days a week 0800–1930LT, closing for lunch 1230-1330 approx. All locks are attended, but a fair measure of self-help is the order of the day. In Jul/Aug, in order to conserve water, locks may open on the hour only (and at H+30 if traffic demands).

ACCESS For prior estimate of max possible draught, contact: Equipement, Ille et Vilaine, 1 Avenue de Mail, 35000 Rennes. (☎ 02·99·59·20·60; or obtain recorded information update on ☎ 02·99·59·11·12. For latest info on the Ille et Rance Canal/R Vilaine, contact: Rennes ☎ 02·99·59·20·60 or Redon ☎ 02·99·71·03·78. For the Lorient-Nantes Canal, contact: Lorient ☎ 02·97·21·21·54; Hennebont ☎ 02·97·85·15·15; Pontivy ☎ 02·97·25·55·21; Nantes ☎ 02·40·71·02·00. Closures (Chômages) for maintenance are scheduled every Wednesday from approx first week in November to last week in March.

INFORMATION *Cruising French Waterways:* (McKnight/ACN), *Through the French Canals* (Jefferson/ACN) and *Navicarte Guide No 12* (Bretagne).

TOLLS may be due on the R Loire only; see 9.17.6 for rates.

SUMMARY	Length km	No of locks	Max draft m	Max air draft m	Max LOA m	Max beam m	Speed limit kn
St MALO-ARZAL (Ille et Rance Canal and La Vilaine river)							
R Rance-Dinan	29·0	1	1·3	19	25	–	5·4
Ille et Rance Canal							
Dinan-Rennes	79·0	48	1·2	2·5	25	4·5	4·3
Rennes-Redon	89·0	13	1·2	3·2/2·6*	25	4·5	4·3
Redon-Arzal	42·0	1	1·3	–			
*Depending on water level							
LORIENT - NANTES							
Canal du Blavet (See 9.21.14)							
Lorient-Pontivy	70	28	1·4	2·6	25	4·6	4·3
Nantes-Brest Canal							
	184·3	106	–	3	25	4·6	4·3
Pontivy-Rohan			0·8 (possible closure)				
Rohan-Josselin			1·0				
Josselin-Redon			1·4				
Redon-Quiheix			1·1				
L'Erdre River	27·6	1	1·4	3·8	400	6·2	13·5
R Loire, above Nantes (9.21.31), may be navigable to Angers.							
R L'AULNE (See 9.20.27)							
Brest-Chateaulin	42	1	3·0	N/A	25	–	–
Chateaulin-Carhaix							
	72	33	1·1	2·5	25	4·6	4·3

MINOR HARBOURS BETWEEN ST MALO AND DAHOUET
ST BRIAC 48°37´·31N 02°08´·71W. AC 3659, 2700; SHOM 7155, 7130, 7129. HW –0515 on Dover (UT); ML 6·8m;–Duration 0550. Tides as 9.18.15; use Ile des Hébihens. Drying hbr open to SW-NW; access HW±2½. A Dir Iso WRG 4s lt leads 125° between offlying drying and beaconed rocks/islets. The last 6ca are marked by 4 PHM and 3 SHM perches. 10 ⚓s in Le Bechet cove or ⚓ on sand SW of Ile du Perron in 3-5m. HM ☎ 02·99·88·01·75, FW, Slip. **YC de St Briac** ☎ 02·99·88·31·45. **Town** Bar, R, ⬚.

ST CAST 48°38´·39N 02°14´·60W. AC 2669, 3659; SHOM 71; see 9.18.15. Good shelter from SW to N winds; ⚓s available in 1·8m. Beware Les Bourdinots (dry 2m) with ECM ¾M NE of Pte de St Cast, and La Feuillade (IDM bn) and Bec Rond (R bn) off hbr. Mole hd, Iso WG 4s 11m 11/8M; appr in either W

9.18.15 DAHOUET

Côtes d'Armor **48°34´·79N 02°34´·39W** ❀❀⚓⚓✿

CHARTS AC 2669, 2029; SHOM 7154, 7310; Navi 536; Imray C33B, C34; Stanfords 2, 16

TIDES –0520 Dover; ML 6·3; Duration 0550.

Standard Port ST MALO (◀—)

Times				Height (metres)			
High Water		Low Water		MHWS	MHWN	MLWN	MLWS
0100	0800	0300	0800	12·2	9·3	4·2	1·5
1300	2000	1500	2000				
Differences ÎLE DES HÉBIHENS (7M W of St Malo)							
0000	0000	–0005	–0005	–0·2	–0·2	–0·1	–0·1
SAINT CAST							
0000	0000	–0005	–0005	–0·2	–0·2	–0·1	–0·1
ERQUY							
–0010	–0005	–0025	–0015	–0·6	–0·5	0·0	0·0
DAHOUET							
–0010	–0010	–0025	–0020	–0·9	–0·7	–0·2	–0·2

SHELTER Good, but ent (dries 4m) has strong currents and is unsafe in fresh/strong NW'lies, when a bar may form.

NAVIGATION WPT 48°35´·15N 02°35´·44W, unlit NCM buoy, 117°/0·8M to La Petite Muette (LPM) lt tr. Appr in W sector, crossing into the R until LPM bears 160°. Enter the narrow break in the cliffs on that track leaving LPM to stbd and 2 W poles to port (they are not ldg marks). It is dangerous to enter S of LPM, due to rocks. At SHM bcn the chan turns E, then SE to the marina sill marked by PHM/SHM perches. Night entry not advised without prior day experience.

LIGHTS AND MARKS La Petite Muette (see 9.18.4) is the key feature. Conspic daymarks: the wide beach NE at Val André and, in the hbr ent, a pagoda-like shrine. See also 9.18.16.

9.18.16 LE LÉGUÉ

Côtes d'Armor **48°31´·68N 02°43´·97W (lock)** ❀❀⚓⚓✿

CHARTS AC 2669, 2029; SHOM 7154, 7128; Navi 536; Imray C34, C33B; Stanfords 2, 16

TIDES –0520 Dover; ML 6·5; Duration 0550.

Standard Port ST MALO (◀—)

Times				Height (metres)			
High Water		Low Water		MHWS	MHWN	MLWN	MLWS
0100	0800	0300	0800	12·2	9·3	4·2	1·5
1300	2000	1500	2000				
Differences LE LÉGUÉ (SWM buoy)							
–0010	–0005	–0020	–0015	–0·8	–0·5	–0·2	–0·1

SHELTER Very good in the marina (Bassin No 2, min 3·2m) near the viaduct. Le Légué is also the commercial port for St Brieuc.

NAVIGATION WPT 48°34´·33N 02°41´·15W, Le Légué SWM buoy, Fl Mo (A) 10s, 210°/2·6M to abm Pte à l'Aigle lt. The bay dries E/SE of conspic Pte du Roselier. Access via well buoyed/lit chan, dredged 5m above CD; but not advised in strong N/NE winds. The outer hbr is entered between Pte à l'Aigle on the NW bank of Le Gouet river and the SE jetty head.

sector (see 9.18.4). HM ☎ 02·96·70·88·30; Facilities: **❶** €1·94, D, P, C. **YC** ☎ 02·96·41·71·71. **Port d'Armor Marina (700+40❶)** ☎ 02·96·81·04·43 stcast.plaisance@cotesdarmor.cci.fr. Opened July 2009. **Town** CH, El, ME, ✗, Ⓑ, Bar, R, ⬚.

ERQUY (pronounced Erky) **48°38´·04N 02°28´·69W.** AC 2669, 2029, 3672; SHOM 7154, 7310; HW –0515 on Dover (UT); ML 6·5m; Duration 0550; see 9.18.15. Sheltered from E, but open to SW/W'lies. An active FV hbr, but yachts can dry out E of the inner jetty hd Fl (3) R 12s; or ⚓ on sand 3ca SW of the outer mole. Beware Plateau des Portes d'Erquy (dry) about 2M to W. Beware rks off Pte de Lahoussaye. Mole hd lt Fl (2) WRG 6s 11m W7M, R/G5M; approach in either W sector (see 9.18.4). HM & ⊖ 02·96·72·19·32. **YC** ☎ 02·96·72·32·40. Facilities: **❶** (drying) €0·56, **Quay** C (3·5 ton), D, FW, P. **Town** CH, El, ME, ✗, R, ⬚, Bar.

R/T Ch 09, 16. **TELEPHONE** Aff Mar 02·96·72·31·42; CROSS 02·96·70·42·18; ⊖ 02·96·74·75·32; Météo 02·36·65·02·22; Auto 08.92.68.02.22; Ⓗ 02·96·45·23·28; Police 02·96·72·22·18; Brit Consul 02.23.18.30.30.

FACILITIES Outer hbr (FVs) dries 5·5m. **Marina**, min depth 2m, is entered HW±2 over sill 5·5m, with depth gauge. Very crowded in season. ☎ 02·96·72·82·85. 318+25 **❶** berths on 'O' pontoon in about 1·6-2·0m, €2·25. Slip, P&D (cans), C (8 ton mobile), CH, El, ME, ✗. **YC du Val-André** ☎ 02·96·72·21·68, showers. **Town**, ⬚, R, Bar, ⇆ (Lamballe), ✈ (St. Brieuc). Ferry: St Malo.

Lock opens, relative to height of tide at St Malo, *at local HW*:

(MHWN 9·3m)	<9·4m	±1
	9·4-10·3m	±1¼
	10·3-10·8m	±1½
(MHWS 12·2m)	>10·8m	–2 to +1½

The lock is 85m x 14m; sill dries 5·0m. Lock staff help with warps. Commercial ships take priority. A low swing bridge at the ent to Bassin No 2 opens when the lock is in use.

LIGHTS AND MARKS Conspic marks: Le Verdelet Is (42m) from E; Rohein twr, from N; Pte du Roselier in near appr; St Brieuc.

R/T *Le Légué Port* Ch 12, 16 (approx HW–2 to +1½).

TELEPHONE Port HM 02·96·33·35·41; Aff Mar 02·96·68·30·70; CROSS 02·98·89·31·31; Météo 02·99·46·10·46; Auto 08·92·68·08·22; SNSM 02·96·88·35·47; ⊖ 02·96·74·75·32; Police 02·96·61·22·61; Dr 02·96·61·49·07; Brit Consul 02.23.18.30.30.

FACILITIES Marina ☎ 02·96·77·49·85, mobile ☎ 06·86·49·09·13. 100 + 20 **❶**, €2·10. Berth in front of HM's office on N quay; then as directed. P & D (cans), C (2 ton de-masting), BH (20 & 350 ton), ✗, ME, El, CH, SM, ⚓, Ⓔ, CH, Shwrs, YC, R, Bar. legue.plaisance@ cotesdarmor.cci.fr/ www.cotesdarmor.cci.fr

Town Gaz, ⬚, @, ✉, Ⓑ, ⇆, ✈. Ferry: St Malo.

LE LÉGUÉ *continued*

[Chart showing Le Légué / St Brieuc area with depths, lights and marks:]

Le Légué Mo(A)10s 6

(0₃) Petit Gripet

Obstn (1₈)

Greve des Rosaires

Rocher des Tablettes

Rocher Martin (whitened)

Pointe du Roselier

Pointe de Châtel Renault

Fl.G.2·5s 1

Fl.R.2·5s

Pte á l'Aigle VQ.G.13m8M

Fl(2)G.6s 3 4
Fl(2)R.6s 5

Iso.G4s.6m2M

VQ.R.4M

Buoyed chan

Tour de Cesson (ruined)

Pte de Cesson

LE LÉGUÉ

Bassin No 1

Swing bridge

Cesson

See upper inset

See lower inset

ST BRIEUC

[Upper inset — Port Seberg / Le Gouet:]

Pte á l'Aigle VQ.G.13m8M

Fl(3)G.12s
Fl(3)R.12s 5 6
VQ.R.4M

Fl(4)G.15s 7

Dredged 5m above CD

Rubble training wall

Port Seberg

Fl(2)G.6s 9
Iso.G.4s.6m2M
Sous la Tour
Fl(2)R.6s 10

La Ville Gilette
Fl(4)G.15s 11
12
Le Gouet 13
Quai
5·8m 16 14
Fl(4)R.15s

Tour de Cesson (ruined)

Pointe de Cesson

[Lower inset — LE LÉGUÉ bassins:]

LE LÉGUÉ

5·4m Fl.R.2·5s

Conspic viaduct

Bassin No2 4·2m Swing bridge Bassin No1

9.18.17 BINIC

Côtes d'Armor **48°36′·06N 02°48′·99W**

CHARTS AC 2668/9, 2029; SHOM 7154, 7128; Navi 536; Imray C33B, C34; Stanfords 2, 16

TIDES –0525 Dover; ML 6·3; Duration 0550.

Standard Port ST MALO (←)

Times				Height (metres)			
High Water		Low Water		MHWS	MHWN	MLWN	MLWS
0100	0800	0300	0800	12·2	9·3	4·2	1·5
1300	2000	1500	2000				
Differences BINIC							
–0010	–0010	–0030	–0015	–0·8	–0·7	–0·2	–0·2

SHELTER Good in marina. Appr not advised in strong E/NE'lies.

NAVIGATION WPT 48°35′·86N 02°46′·68W, 276·5°/1·5M to ent. 2M E of hbr beware oyster beds marked by unlit W ⌀s. Appr dries 7ca offshore. From E, appr via Caffa ECM buoy, whence ent bears 246°/4·2M; or from N through Rade de St Quay-Portrieux.

Access HW±3 to Avant Port, dries 5·5m, is easy day/night, except in E'lies. IPTS, sigs 2 & 3, control entry H24 to the marina via gate and retracting bridge. Gate opens when height of tide >8·5m. Times vary (see www.ville-binic.fr) with coefficient/barometer:

Coeff 40	<8·5m	=	No entry; no exit, ie neaped
40-50	8·5m	=	HW –1 to HW
50-60	9·15m	=	HW –1½ to HW +10 mins
60-80	9·5m	=	HW –2 to HW +10 mins
>80	10·6m	=	HW –2¼ to HW +¼

Outbound vessels have priority. Beware strong current (up to 5kn) in the ent for 20 mins after the gate first opens.

LIGHTS AND MARKS Ldg line 276·5°: N mole lt, W twr, G gallery, ≠ church spire. A water twr is conspic 8ca N of hbr.

R/T Call Port/marina Ch 09 with size of boat and length of stay.

TELEPHONE Aff Mar 02·96·70·42·27; CROSS 02·98·89·31·31; ⊖ 02·96·74·75·32; Météo 02·99·46·10·46; SAMU 16; Ⓗ 02·96·94·31·71.

FACILITIES Marina ☎ 02·96·73·61·86. English spoken. port-de-binic@wanadoo.fr www.ville-binic.fr 350 + 50 Ⓥ, €2·05. Ⓥ berth/raft on 'K' pontoon, to stbd on entry (1·5-3m). CH, C (20 ton mobile), Slip, ⚓, Ⓔ, ✕, SHOM, SC. From St Quay-Portrieux or nearby: SM, ME, El, Wi-Fi, hire car available.

Town ☷, Gaz, ▣, R, Bar, @, ✉, Ⓑ. Bus to St Brieuc ⇌, ✈. Ferry: St Malo.

[Chart of BINIC harbour with pontoons A–K, Quai Surcouf, Quai Jean Bart, Port de Penthièvre, IPTS, Gate, Oc(3)12s 12m12M, Ldg line 276·5°, Plage de la Barche]

9.18.18 ST QUAY-PORTRIEUX

Côtes d'Armor 48°38´·84N 02°48´·97W ⚓⚓⚓🌊🌊🌊🏳🏳

CHARTS AC 2668, 2669, 3674, 3672; SHOM 7154, 7128; Navi 536, 537; Imray C33B, C34; Stanfords 2, 16.

TIDES –0520 Dover; ML 6·3; Duration 0550.

Standard Port ST MALO (←)

Times				Height (metres)			
High Water		Low Water		MHWS	MHWN	MLWN	MLWS
0100	0800	0300	0800	12·2	9·3	4·2	1·5
1300	2000	1500	2000				
Differences ST QUAY-PORTRIEUX							
–0010	–0005	–0025	–0020	–0·9	–0·7	–0·2	–0·1

SHELTER Excellent in marina. ⚓ in the Rade de St Quay-Portrieux, sheltered by Roches de St Quay, but open to NW & SE winds.

NAVIGATION From E and SE appr via Caffa ECM lt buoy to WPT 48°37´·08N 02°46´·18W (2ca S of La Roselière SCM buoy VQ (6) + L Fl 10s); thence 314°/2·5M to NE mole head.

From the N, WPT 48°40´·94N 02°49´·69W, 169°/2·0M to NE mole elbow. At night , to avoid rocks/shoals, follow the white sectors of 4 Dir lts (see chartlet and below), tracking 169°, 130°, 185° (astern) and 318° in sequence to the marina ent:

- NE mole elbow lt, **W159°-179°**. White concrete twr.
- Herflux lt, **W125°-135°**. A white bcn twr on drying rock.
- Ile Harbour lt, **W358°-011°**. Short W twr/R top on an islet.
- NE mole elbow lt (as first ● above), **W316°-320·5°**.

LIGHTS AND MARKS For lt details see chartlet and 9.18.4. Signal stn at Pointe de St Quay, NNW of the marina, is conspic. N of the marina Moulières de Portrieux, ECM bcn twr is unlit. E of the marina an unlit WCM buoy marks Les Noirs rks (2·4m).

R/T Marina Ch 09 H24.

TELEPHONE HM (Old Hbr) 02·96·70·95·31; ⊖ 02·96·33·33·03; Aff Mar 02·96·70·42·27; CROSS 02·98·89·31·31; Météo 02·96·76·76·80; Auto 08.92.68.08.22; Police 02·96·70·61·24; Dr 02·96·70·41·31; Brit Consul 02.23.18.30.30.

FACILITIES Marina ☎ 02·96·70·81·30. welcome@port-armor.com www.port-armor.com 900+100 **Ⓥ**, €2·60. **Ⓥ** berths on No 7 pontoon (no fingers NW side). Jul/Aug pre-call for a berth if LOA >12m. D&P, BH (40 ton), C (20 ton), mobile C (5 ton) ME, El, Ⓔ, ⚒, CH, Wi-Fi, R, Bar.

SN de St Quay-Portrieux ☎ 02·96·70·93·34.

Cercle de la Voile de Portrieux ☎ 02·96·70·41·76.

Old Hbr ☎ 02·96·70·95·31, dries approx 5·3m. 500+8 ⚓, €1·50. M, Slip, C (1·5 ton).

Town 🛒, Gaz, R, Bar, ✉, Ⓑ. Bus to St Brieuc ⇌, ✈. Ferry: St Malo –Poole, Portsmouth.

On an island paradise...

BEAUCETTE
M A R I N A

... one gem shines above all else

Accesible 3 hours either side of high water at St Peter Port, Beaucette Marina, situated on the North East of Guernsey, is the perfect base to discover the island.

All the services you would expect from a modern facility are on-hand to make your stay easy and ejoyable. Our staff are highly experienced and ready to help, so you can feel safe in the knowledge that your boat and your crew are in good hands.

Contact us by using the details below or call us on VHF 80 - call sign 'Beaucette Marina'. If you are unsure of the buoyed channel or the entrance to Beaucette, please call on VHF 80 and we will send a boat out to assist you.

For more information, please visit our website at: www.beaucettemarina.com

We look forward to welcoming you.

BEAUCETTE MARINA LTD,
VALE, GUERNSEY,
CHANNEL ISLANDS GY3 5BQ
T: +44 (0)1481 245000
F: +44 (0)1481 247071
E: INFO@BEAUCETTEMARINA.COM
M: +44 (0)7781 102302
W: WWW.BEAUCETTEMARINA.COM
VHF CHANNEL 80

VISITING & ANNUAL BERTHS | WATER & ELECTRICITY ON ALL BERTHS | FUEL & GAS | LAUNDERETTE RESTAURANT | SHOWERS & TOILETS | WEATHER FORECAST | FREE WIFI ACCESS | CAR HIRE

2010/MA67/e

ADLARD COLES NAUTICAL
WEATHER FORECASTS
BY FAX & TELEPHONE

Coastal/Inshore	2-day by Fax	5-day by Phone
N France	09065 501 612	09064 700 422
South West	09065 222 348	09068 969 648
Mid Channel	09065 222 347	09068 969 647
N Brittany	09065 501 613	09064 969 423
National (3-5 day)	09065 222 340	09068 969 640

Offshore	2-5 day by Fax	2-5 day by Phone
English Channel	09065 222 357	09068 969 657
Southern North Sea	09065 222 358	09068 969 658
Irish Sea	09065 222 359	09068 969 659
Biscay	09065 222 360	09068 969 660

09064/68 CALLS COST 60P PER MIN. 09065 CALLS COST £1.50 PER MIN.

Channel Islands

Alderney to Jersey

Channel Islands

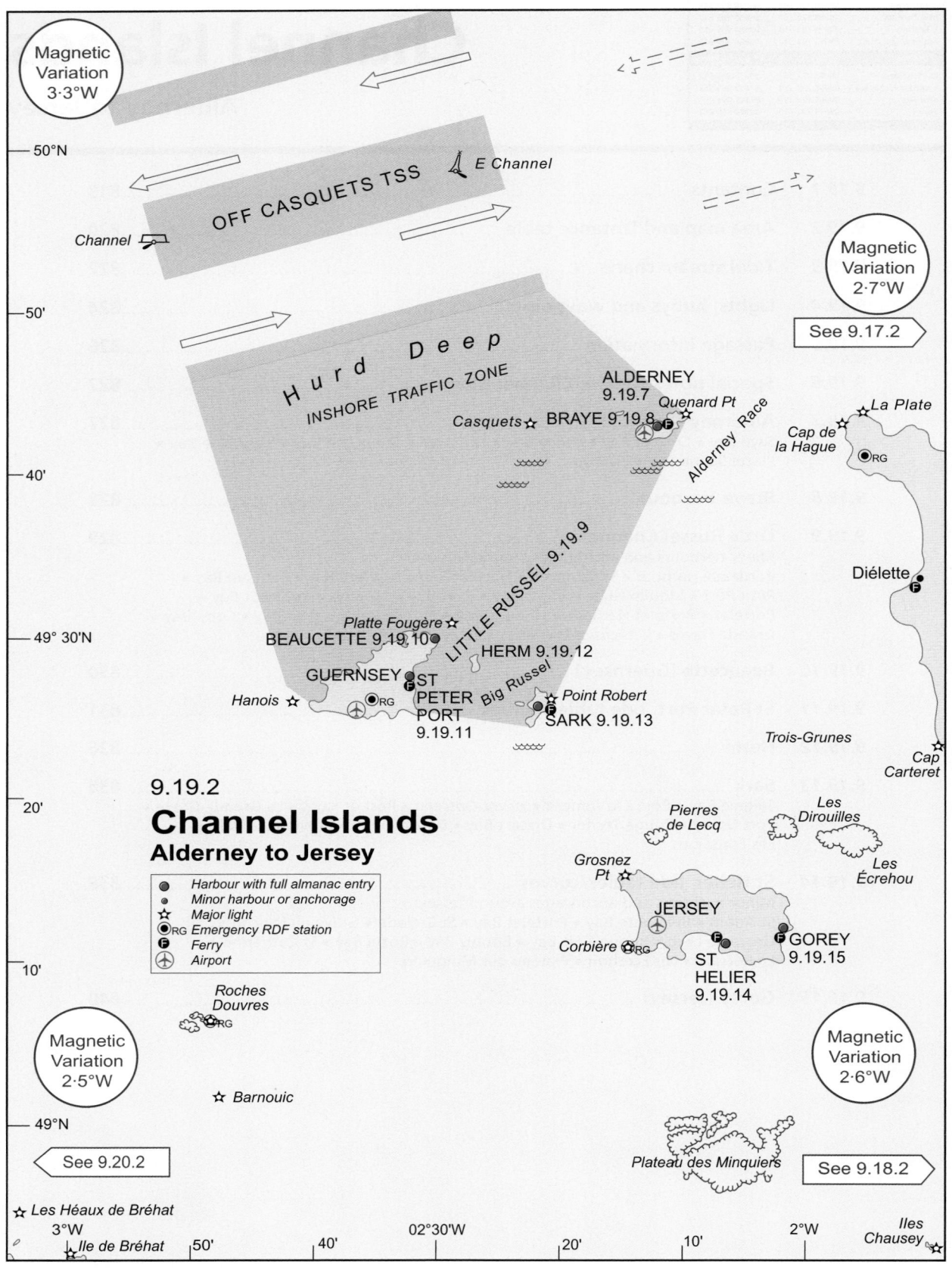

Magnetic
Variation
3·3'W

50°N

OFF CASQUETS TSS

Channel

E Channel

Magnetic
Variation
2·7'W

See 9.17.2

50'

H u r d   D e e p

INSHORE TRAFFIC ZONE

ALDERNEY
9.19.7

Quenard Pt

Casquets ☆ BRAYE 9.19.8

La Plate

Cap de
la Hague ●RG

40'

Alderney Race

Diélette ●F

LITTLE RUSSEL 9.19.9

Platte Fougère ☆

49° 30'N   BEAUCETTE 9.19.10 ●

HERM 9.19.12

GUERNSEY ●F ST
PETER
PORT
9.19.11

Big Russel

●F Point Robert
SARK 9.19.13

Hanois ☆ ●RG

Trois-Grunes

Cap
Carteret ☆

20'

9.19.2

Channel Islands
Alderney to Jersey

●	Harbour with full almanac entry
•	Minor harbour or anchorage
☆	Major light
●RG	Emergency RDF station
F	Ferry
✈	Airport

Pierres
de Lecq

Les
Dirouilles

Grosnez
Pt ☆

Les
Écrehou

JERSEY ✈

Corbière ●RG

●F
ST
HELIER
9.19.14

●F GOREY
9.19.15

10'

Roches
Douvres
●RG

Magnetic
Variation
2·5'W

☆ Barnouic

49°N

See 9.20.2

Magnetic
Variation
2·6'W

See 9.18.2

☆ Les Héaux de Bréhat

Plateau des Minquiers

Iles
Chausey ☆

3'W   ☆ Ile de Bréhat   50'   40'   02°30'W   20'   10'   2°W

1.	*L'Aberwrac'h*	145	131	126	128	116	115	122	107	103	93	109	110	123	103	91	88	84	72	32	**1**
2.	*Roscoff*	117	103	95	96	84	87	94	77	73	63	79	80	93	71	59	58	54	41	**2**	
3.	*Tréguier*	94	80	72	72	60	66	72	56	52	42	58	53	63	58	46	29	22	**3**		
4.	*Lézardrieux*	88	74	68	54	49	65	68	52	48	42	38	47	55	33	21	14	**4**			
5.	*Paimpol*	91	77	65	56	42	67	70	54	50	45	50	45	53	24	24	**5**				
6.	*St Quay-Portrieux*	88	74	64	54	35	71	73	55	56	48	51	46	52	12	**6**					
7.	*Dahouet*	88	74	62	44	28	70	72	62	58	57	53	41	47	**7**						
8.	*Gorey (Jersey)*	47	33	16	29	38	36	35	32	29	35	20	13	**8**							
9.	*St Helier*	59	45	28	30	38	43	46	33	29	32	24	**9**								
10.	Creux (Sark)	37	23	23	50	52	18	22	11	10	16	**10**									
11.	Les Hanois	49	35	37	58	56	23	29	14	10	**11**										
12.	**St Peter Port**	42	28	31	55	54	18	23	4	**12**											
13.	Beaucette	39	25	34	59	58	15	19	**13**												
14.	**Braye (Alderney)**	23	9	26	66	73	8	**14**													
15.	Casquets	31	17	32	63	70	**15**														
16.	*St Malo*	87	73	49	23	**16**															
17.	*Granville*	75	61	38	**17**																
18.	*Carteret*	41	23	**18**																	
19.	*Cap de la Hague*	14	**19**																		
20.	***Cherbourg***	**20**																			

DISTANCE TABLE

Approximate distances in nautical miles are by the most direct route, whilst avoiding dangers and allowing for Traffic Separation Schemes. Places in *italics* are in adjoining areas; places in **bold** are in 9.0.5, Cross-Channel Distances.

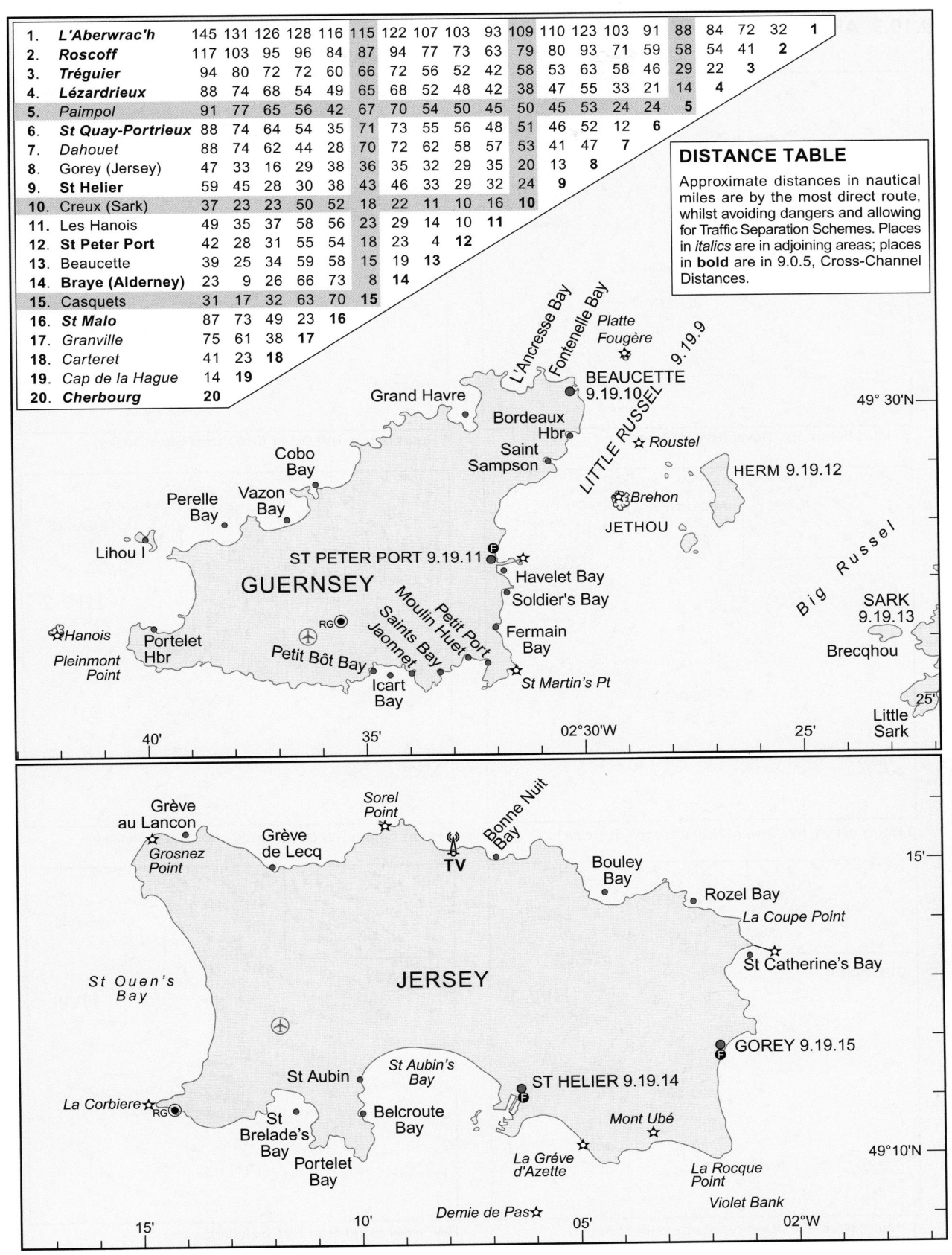

9.19.3 AREA 19 TIDAL STREAMS

5 Hours before HW Dover (HW St Helier)

4 Hours before HW Dover (0100 after HW St Helier)

3 Hours before HW Dover (0200 after HW St Helier)

2 Hours before HW Dover (0300 after HW St Helier)

1 Hour before HW Dover (0400 after HW St Helier)

HW Dover (0500 after HW St Helier)

Westward 9.20.3   Southward 9.18.3   Northward 9.2.3   Eastward 9.17.3

1 Hour after HW Dover (0600 after HW St Helier)

2 Hours after HW Dover (0530 before HW St Helier)

3 Hours after HW Dover (0430 before HW St Helier)

4 Hours after HW Dover (0330 before HW St Helier)

5 Hours after HW Dover (0230 before HW St Helier)

6 Hours after HW Dover (0130 before HW St Helier)

9.19.4 LIGHTS, BUOYS AND WAYPOINTS

Bold print = light with a nominal range of 15M or more. CAPITALS = place or feature. *CAPITAL ITALICS* = light-vessel, light float or Lanby. *Italics* = Fog signal. ***Bold italics*** = Racon. Abbreviations are Chapter 1.

MID-CHANNEL MARKS

CHANNEL LT VESSEL ⌁ Fl 15s 12m **15M**; R hull with lt twr amidships; *Horn (20s)*; ***Racon O, 15M***; 49°54'·46N 02°53'·74W. E Channel ⌁ Fl Y 5s 6M; ***Racon T, 10M***; 49°58'·67N 02°29'·01W.

COTENTIN PENINSULA (NW COAST)

La Plate ⌁ Fl (2+1) WR 10s 11m; W9M, R6M; 115°-W-272°-R-115°; Y 8-sided twr, with B top; 49°43'·98N 01°55'·76W.
Cap de la Hague (Gros du Raz) ☆ Fl 5s 48m **23M**; Gy twr, W top; *Horn 30s*; 49°43'·31N 01° 57'·27W.
La Foraine ⌁ VQ (9) 10s 12m 6M; 49°42'·90 N 01°58'·32W.
Cap de Carteret ☆ Fl (2+1) 15s 81m **26M**; Gy twr, G top; 49°22'·41N 01°48'·41W.

THE CASQUETS AND ALDERNEY

Casquets ☆ Fl (5) 30s 37m **24M**, H24; W twr, 2 R bands; NW'most of three; *Horn (2) 60s*; ***Racon T, 25M***; 49°43'·32N 02°22'·63W.
Ortac rock, unlit; 49°43'·40N 02°17'·44W.
Pierre au Vraic, unmarked rk 1·2m ⊛; 49°41'·61N 02°16'·94W.
Quenard Pt (Alderney) ☆ Fl (4) 15s 37m **23M**, H24; 085°-027°; W ○ twr, B band; *Horn 30s*; 49°43'·75N 02°09'·86W.
Château à L'Étoc Pt ⌁ Iso WR 4s 20m W10M, R7M; 071·1°-R-111·1°-W-151·1°; 49°43'·94N 02°10'·63W.

BRAYE

Ldg bns 142° (to clear the submerged Adm'ty bkwtr). Front, W ⌁, 49°43'·90N 02°10'·97W. Rear, BW ⌁; 720m from front.
Ldg lts 215°: both Q 8/17m 9/12M, synch; 210°-220°; orange △s. Front, old pier elbow, 49°43'·40N 02°11'·91W. Rear, 215°/335m.
Admiralty bkwtr head ⌁ L Fl 10s 7m 5M; 49°43'·82N 02°11'·67W.
FairwayNo. 1 ▲ QG; 49°43'·72N 02°11'·72W.
No. 2 ⬳ QR; 49°43'·60N 02°11'·75W.
Inner fairway ▲ Q (2) G 5s; 49°43'·58N 02°11'·98W.
Braye quay ⌁ 2 FR (vert) 8m 5M; 49°43'·53N 02°12'·00W.
Little Crabby hbr ent ⌁ FG & FR 5m 2M; 49°43'·45N 02°12'·12W.

GUERNSEY, NORTHERN APPROACHES

LITTLE RUSSEL CHANNEL

Grande Amfroque, two unlit bcn twrs: larger, BW-banded; smaller, white; 49°30'·57N 02°24'·62W.
Tautenay ⌁ Q (3) WR 6s 7m W7M, R6M; 050°-W-215°- R-050°; B & W striped bcn 49°30'·11N 02°26'·84W.
Platte Fougère ☆ Fl WR 10s 15m 16M; 155°-W-085°-R-155°; W 8-sided twr, B band; *Horn 45s*; ***Racon P***; 49°30'·83N 02°29'·14W.
Corbette d'Amont ⌁ Y bcn twr, topmark; 49°29'·64N 02°29'·38W.
Roustel ⌁ Q 8m 7M; BW chequered base, W framework col; 49°29'·23N 02°28'·79W.
Rousse, Y bcn twr, topmark ⊞; 49°28'·98N 02°28'·36W.
Platte ⌁, Fl WR 3s 6m, W7M, R5M; 024°-R-219°-W-024°; G conical twr; 49°29'·08N 02°29'·57W.
Vivian bcn twr, BW bands, 49°28'·45N 02°30'·66W.
Brehon ⌁ Iso 4s 19m 9M; bcn on ○ twr, 49°28'·28N 02°29'·28W.
Demie Flieroque, Y bcn twr, topmark F; 49°28'·13N 02°31'·38W.

BIG RUSSEL

Noire Pute ⌁ Fl (2) WR 15s 8m 6M; 220°-W-040°-R-220°; on 2m high rock; 49°28'·21N 02°25'·02W.
Fourquies ⌁ Q; 49°27'·34N 02°26'·47W.
Lower Heads ⌁ Q (6) + L Fl 15s; *Bell*; 49°25'·85N 02°28'·55W.

GUERNSEY, HERM AND SARK

BEAUCETTE MARINA

Petite Canupe ⌁ Q (6) + L Fl 15s; 49°30'·20N 02°29'·14W.
Ldg lts 277°: Both FR. Front, W □, R stripe; 49°30'·19N 02°30'·23W. Rear, R □, W stripe; 185m from front.
Appr chan buoys: SWM L Fl 10s 49°30'·15N 02°29'·66W. SHM Fl G 5s, PHM Fl R 5s & Fl (3) R 5s. NCM perch Q 49°30'·165N 02°30'·06W. SHM perch Q (3) G 5s at ent; 49°30'·18N 02°30'·24W.

ST SAMPSON

Ldg lts 286°: Front, FR 3m 5M; 230°-340°; tfc sigs; 49°28'·90N 02°30'·74W. Rear, FG 13m; clock twr, 390m from front.
N Pier ⌁ FG 3m 5M; 230°-340°; 49°28'·92N 02°30'·71W.
Crocq pier ⌁ FR 11m 5M; 250°-340°; 49°28'·98N 02°31'·00W.

ST PETER PORT

Outer ldg lts 220°: **Front**, Castle bkwtr, Al WR 10s 14m **16M**; 187°-007°; dark ○ twr, W on NE side; *Horn 15s*; 49°27'·31N 02°30'·45W.
GY RDF beacon 304·5kHz is synchronised with the co-located horn (15s) to give distance finding. After the 4 GY ident signals (— — · — · —), a 27 sec long dash begins at the same time as the horn blast. Time the number of seconds from the start of the long dash until the horn is next heard, multiply by 0·18 = distance in M from the horn; several counts are advised.
Rear 220° ldg lt, Belvedere, Oc 10s 61m 14M; 179°-269°; intens 217°-223°; W □ on W twr; 980m from front.
Queen Elizabeth II marina, 270° Dir Oc ⌁ WRG 3s 5m 6M; 258°-G-268°-W-272°-R-282°; 49°27'·73N 02°31'·87W.
Reffée ⌁ VQ (6) + L Fl 15s; 49°27'·74N 02°31'·27W.
Appr buoys: outer pair ▲ QG; 49°27'·83N 02°31'·54W. ⬳ QR; 49°27'·71N 02°31'·52W. Inner pair: ▲ QG; 49°27'·76N 02°31'·74W. ⬳ QR; 49°27'·72N 02°31'·74W.
The Pool ldg lts 265° (*not* into moorings): Front, Victoria marina, S Pier, ⌁ Oc R 5s 10m 14M; 49°27'·32N 02°32'·03W. Rear, ⌁ Iso R 2s 23m 3M; 260°-270°; on Woolworth's bldg, 160m from front.
White Rock pier ⌁ Oc G 5s 11m 14M; intens 174°-354°; ○ twr; tfc sigs; 49°27'·38N 02°31'·59W.
S Fairway ▲ QG; 49°27'·30N 02°31'·76W; pontoon W of buoy. ⬳ Fl R; 49°27'·28N 02°31'·74W. 49°27'·27N 02°31'·80W. 49°27'·27N 02°31'·86W.

HAVELET BAY

Oyster Rock ⌁ Y bcn, topmark 'O'; 49°27'·09N 02°31'·46W.
Oyster Rock ▲ QG; 49°27'·04N 02°31'·47W.
Moulinet ⬳ QR; 49°26'·97N 02°31'·54W.
Moulinet ⌁ Y bcn, topmark 'M'; 49°26'·95N 02°31'·58W.

GUERNSEY, SOUTH-EAST and SOUTH COASTS

Anfré, Y bcn, topmark 'A'; 49°26'·45N 02°31'·48W.
Longue Pierre, Y bcn, topmark 'LP'; 49°25'·36N 02°31'·48W.
St Martin's Pt ☆ Fl (3) WR 10s 15m 14M; 185°-R-191°-W-011°-R-061·5°; flat-topped, W bldg. *Horn (3) 30s*; 49°25'·30N 02°31'·70W.

GUERNSEY, NORTH-WEST COAST

Les Hanois ☆ Fl (2) 13s 33m **20M**; 294°-237°; Gy ○ twr, B lantern, helicopter platform; *Horn (2) 60s*. 49°26'·10N 02°42'·15W.
4 FR on mast 1·3M ESE of Les Hanois lt ho.
Portelet Hbr, bkwtr bcn, 49°26'·16N 02°39'·84W.
Cobo Bay, Grosse Rock, B bcn 11m; 49°29'·02N 02°36'·19W.
Grand Havre, Rousse Point bkwtr, B bcn; 49°29'·92N 02°33'·05W.

HERM

Corbette de la Mare, white disc on Y pole, 49°28'·48N 02°28'·72W.
Petit Creux ⌁ QR; red 'C' on red pole; 49°28'·09N 02°28'·72W.
Alligande ⌁ Fl (3) G 5s; B pole, Or 'A'; 49°27'·86N 02°28'·78W.
Épec ⌁ Fl G 3s; black 'E' on G mast; 49°27'·98N 02°27'·89W.
Vermerette ⌁ Fl (2) Y 5s; Or 'V' on bcn; 49°28'·12N 02°27'·75W.
Gate Rock (Percée Pass) ⌁ Q (9) 15s; 49°27'·88N 02°27'·54W.
Hbr ldg lts 078°: White drums. ⌁ 2F occas; 49°28'·25N 02°27'·11W.
Hbr pier, N end ⌁ 2 FG; G □ on G bcn; 49°28'·21N 02°27'·26W.

SARK
Corbée du Nez ⚡ Fl (4) WR 15s 14m 8M; 057°-W-230°-R-057°; W structure on rock; 49°27'·09N 02°22'·17W.
Point Robert ☆ Fl 15s 65m **20M**; vis 138°-353°; W 8-sided twr; *Horn (2) 30s;* 49°26'·19N 02°20'·75W.
Founiais ⚓, topmark 'F'; 49°26'·02N 02°20'·36W.
Blanchard ⚡ Q (3) 10s; *Bell;* 49°25'·36N 02°17'·42W.
Pilcher monument (070° appr brg); 49°25'·71N 02°22'·44W.

JERSEY, WEST AND SOUTH COASTS
Desormes ⚡ Q (9) 15s; 49°18'·94N 02°17'·98W.
Grosnez Point ☆ Fl (2) WR 15s 50m **W19M, R17M**; 081°-W-188°-R-241°; W hut; 49°15'·50N 02°14'·80W.
L a Rocco twr (conspic) 15m; 49°11'·90N 02°14'·05W.
La Frouquie ⚓ (seasonal); 49°11'·30N 02°15'·38W.
La Corbière ☆ Iso WR 10s 36m **W18M, R16M**; shore-W-294°-R-328°-W-148°-R-shore; W ○ twr; *Horn Mo (C) 60s;* 49°10'·79N 02°15'·01W.
Pt Corbière ⚡ FR; R □, W stripe; 49°10'·87N 02°14'·38W.

WESTERN PASSAGE
Ldg lts 082°. Front, La Gréve d'Azette Oc 5s 23m 14M; 034°-129'; 49°10'·16N 02°05'·09W. Rear, Mont Ubé, Oc R 5s 46m 12M; 250°-095'; 1M from front.
Passage Rock ⚡ VQ; 49°09'·54N 02°12'·26W.
Les Fours ⚡ Q; 49°09'·59N 02°10'·16W.
Noirmont Pt ⚡ Fl (4) 12s 18m 10M; B twr, W band; 49°09'·91N 02°10'·08W.
Pignonet ⚓ 49°09'·88N 02°09'·70W.
Ruaudière Rock ⚓ Fl G 3s; *Bell;* 49°09'·74N 02°08'·62W.

ST AUBIN'S BAY and HARBOUR
Les Grunes du Port ⚓ 49°10'·02N 02°09'·14W.
Diamond Rock ⚓ Fl (2) R 6s; 49°10'·12N 02°08'·64W.
Castle pier ⚡ Fl R 4s 8m 1M; 49°11'·13N 02°09'·634W.
North pier, Dir lt 254° ⚡ F WRG 5m, 248°-G-253°-W-255°-R-260°; 49°11'·22N 02°10'·03W. Same col, Iso R 4s 12m 10M.
Beach Rock ⚓ 49°11'·29N 02°08'·42W, (Apr-Oct).
Rocquemin ⚓ 49°10'·64N 02°07'·95W.
Baleine ⚓ 49°10'·41N 02°08'·23W.

ST HELIER
Elizabeth marina, west appr: Dir ⚡ 106°: F WRG 4m 1M; 096°-G-104°-W-108°-R-119°; R dayglo □, B stripe; 49°10'·76N 02°07'·12W.
La Vrachiére ⚓ 49°10'·90N 02°07'·59W, Fl (2) 5s 1M.
Fort Charles North ⚓ 49°10'·81N 02°07'·50W.
Marina ent ⚡ Oc G & Oc R, both 4s 2M; 49°10'·83N 02°07'·13W.
Red & Green Passage, ldg lts 022·7° on dayglo R dolphins: Front, Elizabeth E berth Dn ⚡ Oc G 5s 10m 11M; 49°10'·63N 02°06'·94W. Rear, Albert Pier root ⚡ Oc R 5s 18m 12M; synch; 230m SSW.
East Rock ⚓ QG; 49°09'·96N 02°07'·28W.
Oyster Rocks, R/W bcn, topmark 'O'; 49°10'·10N 02°07'·49W.
Platte Rock ⚓ Fl R 1·5s 6m 5M; R col; 49°10'·16N 02°07'·34W.
Small Road No. 2 ⚓ QR; 49°10'·39N 02°07'·24W.
No. 4 ⚓ QR; 49°10'·53N 02°07'·12W.
Elizabeth marina, S appr: E1 ⚓ Fl G 3s; 49°10'·59N 02°07'·09W.
E2 ⚓ Fl R 2s; 49°10'·58N 02°07'·13W.
E5 ⚓ Fl G 5s; 49°10'·70N 02°07'·17W.
E6 ⚓ Fl R 2s; 49°10'·69N 02°07'·21W.
Fort Charles East ⚓ Q (3) 5s 2m 1M; 49°10'·74N 02°07'·26W.
La Collette basin
    ⚓ QR; 49°10'·54N 02°06'·91W. ⚓ 49°10'·52N 02°06'·90W.
St Helier Hbr, ldg lts 078°, both FG on W cols. Front, 49°10'·62N 02°06'·66W. Rear, 80m from front.
Victoria pier hd, Port control twr; IPTS; 49°10'·57N 02°06'·88W.

JERSEY, SOUTH-EAST AND EAST COASTS
Hinguette ⚓ QR; 49°09'·33N 02°07'·32W.
Hettich ⚡ Fl Y 5s; 49°08'·10N 02°09'·00W.
South Pier Marine ⚡ Fl Y 5s; 49°09'·10N 02°06'·30W.

Demie de Pas ⚓ Mo (D) WR 12s 11m, W14M, R10M; 130°-R-303°-W-130°; *Horn (3) 60s;* **Racon T, 10M**; B bn twr, Y top; 49°09'·01N 02°06'·15W. Icho Tower (conspic, 14m) 49°08'·89N 02°02'·90W.
Canger Rock ⚡ Q (9) 15s; 49°07'·35N 02°00'·38W.
La Conchière ⚓ 49°08'·22N 02°00'·17W.
Frouquier Aubert ⚡ Q (6) + L Fl 15s; 49°06'·08N 01°58'·84W.
Violet ⚡ L Fl 10s; 49°07'·81N 01°57'·14W.
Petite Anquette, W bcn, topmark 'PA'; 49°08'·46N 01°56'·30W.
Grande Anquette, W bcn ⚡ 49°08'·32N 01°55'·20W.
Le Cochon ⚓ 49°09'·77N 01°58'·80W.
La Noire ⚓ 49°10'·13N 01°59'·23W. Le Giffard ⚓ 49°10'·59N 01°59'·00W.

GOREY
Pier Hd Dir lt 298°, ⚡ WRG, 6m 8M; 293·5°-G-296·5°-W-299·5°-R-302·5°; ⚡ Oc RG 5s 8m 12M; 304°-R-353°-G-304°; W twr on pierhead; 49°11'·80N 02°01'·34W.
Horn Rock ⚓, topmark 'H'; 49°10'·96N 01°59'·85W.
Les Burons, RW bcn, topmark 'B'; 49°11'·33N 02°00'·81W.
Fairway ⚓ QG; 49°11'·50N 02°00'·34W.
Écureuil Rock ⚓ 49°11'·67N 02°00'·78W.
Equerrière Rk, bcn 'fishtail' topmark; 49°11'·80N 02°00'·67W.
Les Arch ⚓, BW bcn, 'A' topmark; 49°12'·02N 02°00'·60W.

ST CATHERINE BAY
St Catherine Bay, Le Fara ⚓ 49°12'·85N 02°00'·48W.
Archirondel Tower (conspic, 16m) 49°12'·72N 02°01'·42W.
Verclut bkwtr ⚡ Fl 1·5s 18m 13M; 49°13'·34N 02°00'·64W. In line 315° with unlit turret, 49°13'·96N 02°01'·57W, on La Coupe Pt.

JERSEY, NORTH COAST
Rozel Bay Dir lt 245°, F WRG 11m 5M; 240°-G-244°-W-246°-R-250°; W col; 49°14'·21N 02°02'·76W.
Bonne Nuit Bay ldg lts 223°: both FG 7/34m 6M. Front, Pier 49°15'·10N 02°07'·17W. Rear, 170m from front.
Demie Rock ⚓ 49°15'·56N 02°07'·36W.
Sorel Point ☆ L Fl WR 7·5s 50m **15M**; 095°-W-112°-R-173°-W-230°-R-269°-W-273°; B&W chequered ○ twr, only 3m high; 49°15'·60N 02°09'·54W.

OFFLYING ISLANDS
LES ÉCREHOU
Écrevière ⚡ Q (6) + L Fl 15s; 49°15'·26N 01°52'·15W.
Mâitre Ile ⚓ 49°17'·08N 01°55'·60W.

PLATEAU DES MINQUIERS
N Minquiers ⚡ Q; 49°01'·64N 02°00'·58W.
NE Minquiers ⚡ VQ (3) 5s; *Bell;* 49°00'·85N 01°55'·30W.
SE Minquiers ⚡ Q (3) 10s; *Bell;* 48°53'·42N 02°00'·09W.
S Minquiers ⚡ Q (6) + L Fl 15s; 48°53'·09N 02°10'·10W.
SW Minquiers ⚡ Q (9) 15s 5M; *Bell;* 48°54'·35N 02°19'·41W.
NW Minquiers ⚡ Q 5M; *Bell;* 48°59'·63N 02°20'·59W.
Refuge ⚓; B/W bcn; 49°00'·13N 02°10'·16W.
Demie de Vascelin ⚓ 49°00'·81N 02°05'·17W.
Grand Vascelin, BW bcn ⚓ 48°59'·97N 02°07'·26W.
Maitresse Ile, Puffin B&W bcn twr ⚓ 48°58'·33N 02°03'·65W.
Récif Le Coq, RW bcn ⚓ 48°57'·88N 02°01'·29W.

FRENCH MARKS NORTH OF ILE DE BRÉHAT
Roches Douvres ☆ Fl 5s 60m **24M**; pink twr on dwelling with G roof; *Siren 60s;* 49°06'·30N 02°48'·87W (16M NNE of Ile de Bréhat).
Barnouic ⚡ VQ (3) 5s 15m 7M; 49°01'·64N 02°48'·41W.
Roche Gautier ⚡ VQ (9) 10s; *Whis;* 49°02'·013N 02°54'·36W.
Les Héaux de Bréhat ☆ Oc (3) WRG 12s 48m, **W15M**, R/G11M; 227°-R-247°-W-270°-G-302°-W-227°; Gy ○ twr; 48°54'·50N 03°05'·18W (4·7M WNW of Ile de Bréhat).

9.19.5 PASSAGE INFORMATION

More Passage Information is threaded between successive harbours in this Area. **Bibliography:** *N Brittany & Channel Islands CC* (Cumberlidge/Wiley); *The Channel CC* (Featherstone & Aslett/NDL); *Channel Pilot* (NP27). *Channel Havens* (ACN/Endean).

THE CHANNEL ISLANDS

In an otherwise delightful cruising area (AC 2669), the main problems include fog and poor visibility, the very big tidal range, strong tidal streams, overfalls and steep seas which get up very quickly. The shoreline is generally rugged with sandy bays and many offlying rks. It is important to use large scale AC, and recognised leading marks (of which there are plenty) when entering or leaving many of the harbours and anchs. Several passages are marked by beacons and perches identified by an alphabetical letter(s) in lieu of topmark. Beware high speed ferries.

From the N, note the Casquets TSS and ITZ. Soundings of Hurd Deep can help navigation. The powerful lights at the Casquets, Alderney, Cap de la Hague, Cap Levi and Barfleur greatly assist a night or dawn landfall. By day Alderney is relatively high and conspicuous. Sark is often seen before Guernsey which slopes down from S to N. Jersey is low-lying in the SE. The islands are fringed by many rky dangers. In poor visibility stay in harbour.

▶*Over a 12 hour period tidal streams broadly rotate anti-clockwise around the Islands, particularly in open water and in wider chans. The E-going (flood) stream is of less duration than the W-going, but is stronger. The islands lie across the main direction of the streams, so eddies are common along the shores. The range of tide is greatest in Jersey (9·6m sp, 4·1m np), and least in Alderney (5·3m sp, 2·2m np). Streams run hard through the chans and around headlands and need to be worked carefully; neaps are easier, particularly for a first visit. Strong W'lies cause a heavy sea, usually worst HW ±3.◀*

As well as the main harbours, described in some detail, there are also many attractive minor harbours and anchorages. In the very nature of islands a lee can usually be found somewhere. Boats which can take the ground can better explore the quieter hbrs. Avoid lobster pots and oyster beds.

THE CASQUETS AND ORTAC ROCK

Casquets It ho (fog sig) is conspic on the largest island of this group of rks 5·5M W of Alderney (AC 60). Off-lying dangers extend 4ca W and WSW (The Ledge and Noire Roque) and 4ca E (Pt Colote). The tide runs very hard around and between these obstructions. A shallow bank, on which are situated Fourquie and l'Equêt rks (dry), lies from 5ca to 1M E of Casquets, and should not be approached. Ortac Rk (24m) is 3·5M E of Casquets. Ortac Chan runs NNW/SSE 5ca W of Ortac.

▶*Here the stream starts to run NE at HW St Helier – 2½ and SW at HW St Helier +0355; sp rates up to 5½kn (7kn reported).◀*

Ortac Channel should not be used in bad weather due to tremendous overfalls; these and violent eddies also occur over Eight Fathom Ledge (8½ca W of Casquets) and over the SW, SSW and SSE Casquet Banks where least depths of 7·3m occur.

ALDERNEY AND THE SWINGE

Braye Harbour (AC 2845), together with pleasant bays and anchs around the island, offer shelter from different wind/sea directions. The sunken NE extremity of Admiralty Breakwater should only be crossed in calm conditions, outside LW±2 and about 50m off the head of the Breakwater where there is 2·3m.

The **Swinge** lies between Burhou with its bordering rks, and the NW coast of Alderney. It can be a dangerous chan, and should only be used in reasonable vis and fair weather. On the N side of the

Swinge the main dangers are Boues des Kaines, almost awash at LW about 7½ca ESE of Ortac, and North Rk 2½ca SE of Burhou. On S side of the Swinge beware Corbet Rk (0·5m high), with drying outliers, 5ca N of Fort Clonque, and Barsier Rk (0·9m) 3½ca NNW of Fort Clonque.

▶*The SW-going stream begins at HW St Helier +0340, and the NE stream at HW St Helier –0245, sp rates 7-8kn. On the NE-going stream, beware the very strong northerly set in vicinity of Ortac.◀*

The tide runs very hard, and in strong or gale force winds from S or W there are very heavy overfalls on the SW-going stream between Ortac and Les Etacs (off W end of Alderney).

In strong E winds, on the NE-going stream, overfalls occur between **Burhou** and Braye breakwater. These overfalls can mostly be avoided by choosing the best time and route (see below), but due to the uneven bottom and strong tides broken water may be met even in calm conditions.

▶*It is best to pass SW through the Swinge is about HW St Helier +4, when the SW-going stream starts; hold to the SE side of the chan since the stronger stream runs on the Burhou side. But after HW St Helier +5, to clear the worst of the overfalls keep close to Burhou and Ortac, avoiding North Rk and Boues des Kaines◀*

Pierre au Vraic (dries 1·2m) is an unmarked pinnacle rock at 49°41'·61N 02°16'·94W, 1·8M S of Ortac and 1·8M WSW of Les Étacs, almost in the fairway to/from the Swinge. Arriving on a fair tide from Guernsey it will be well covered, but it is a serious hazard if leaving the Swinge on a SW-going Spring tide close to local LW. AC 60 gives clearing bearings.

Heading NE at about HW St Helier –2, Great Nannel in transit with E end of Burhou clears Pierre au Vraic to the E, but passes close W of Les Etacs. On this transit, when Roque Tourgis fort is abeam, alter slightly to stbd to pass 1ca NW of Corbet Rk; keep near SE side of the channel.

THE ALDERNEY RACE

This race, characterised by very strong tidal streams, runs SW/NE between Cap de la Hague and Alderney, but its influence extends at least as far SW as 02° 20'W (AC 3653). The fairway, approx 4M wide, is bounded by Race Rk and Alderney S Banks to the NW, and to the SE by rky banks 3M E of Race Rk, and by Milieu and Banc de la Schôle (least depth 2·7m). These dangers which cause breaking seas and heavy overfalls should be carefully avoided. In bad weather and strong wind-against-tide the seas break in all parts of the Race and passage is not advised. Conditions are worst at sps.

▶*In mid-chan the SW-going stream starts at HW St Helier +4½ (HW Dover) and the NE-going stream at HW St Helier –2¼ (HW Dover +5½), sp rates both 5·5kn. The times at which the stream turns do not vary much in various places, but the rates do; for example, 1M W of Cap de la Hague sp rates reach 7-8kn.◀*

For optimum conditions, timing is of the essence. As a rule of thumb the Race should be entered on the first of the fair tide so as to avoid peak tidal streams with attendant overfalls/seas.

▶*Thus SW-bound, arrrive off Cap de la Hague at around HW St Helier +4½ (HW Dover) when the stream will be slack, whilst just starting to run SW off Alderney. A yacht leaving Cherbourg at HW Dover –3 will achieve the above timing by utilising the inshore W-going tidal eddy.*

Conversely, NE-bound, leave St Peter Port, say, at approx local HW St Helier –4½ (HWD+3) with a foul tide so as to pass Banc de la Schôle as the fair tide starts to make.◀ A later departure should achieve a faster passage, but with potentially less favourable conditions in the Race. On the NE-going stream the worst overfalls are on the French side.

9.19.6 SPECIAL NOTES: CHANNEL ISLANDS

The Channel Islands (Alderney, Guernsey, Sark, Jersey and other smaller islands) lie, not in the Channel, but in the Bay of St Malo. Alderney, Herm, Jethou, Sark and Brecqhou are all part of the Bailiwick of Guernsey and the States (Parliament) of Alderney have seats in the States of Guernsey.

The Islands are self-governing with their own laws, judiciary and Customs, but conduct their foreign affairs mostly through the English crown. They are not part of either the UK or the EU. The French call the CI Les Îles Anglo-Normandes (Aurigny, Guernsey, Sercq et Jersey). Standard Time is UT (Zone 0).

Charts Admiralty Leisure folio SC5604 (£44·30, 6th ed. published May 2009) contains 17 sheets of the CIs These and other leisure charts are listed under individual ports.

Ports of Entry: Braye, Beaucette, St Sampson, St Peter Port, St Helier and Gorey.

Customs British yachts entering the CI, except Jersey, must complete the local Customs declaration form and may have to show the vessel's registration documents; they will also be subject to customs formalities on return to UK. Yachts going to France need the usual documents (passports etc). British yachts returning to the CI from France, must, like French yachts, wear the Q flag. (It is advisable, but not mandatory, to do so when arriving from UK except in Alderney.)

Medical The CI do not have reciprocal medical arrangements with UK and visitors will have to pay for both inpatient and outpatient care. Medical insurance is recommended as costs are high.

Weather forecasts prepared by Jersey Met Office for the CI area and adjacent coasts of Normandy and Brittany are available ☎ 0900 665 0022 (premium rate). This number is available throughout the Channel Is, UK and France (from the latter replace the first 0 by 00 44).

SAR operations are directed by the HMs of St Peter Port (for the N area) and St Helier (for the S area), via St Peter Port and Jersey Coastguard respectively. Major incidents are co-ordinated with CROSS Jobourg and Falmouth MRCC. Unlike the UK there are no CGs, but there are LBs at Braye, St Peter Port, St Helier and St Catherines (Jersey).

Telephones CI phones are integrated with the UK, but charges, especially on mobiles, may vary. For an on-line Tel directory visit www.theguernseydirectory.com

Courtesy flags Many yachts fly a courtesy flag in CI ports as a mark of politeness but it is not essential. The local flags are:

Jersey W flag with R diagonal cross, with the Jersey Royal Arms (three lions passant with gold crown above) in the canton.

Guernsey R ensign with Duke William's cross in the fly. Vessels owned by Guernsey residents may wear this ensign; see Fig 5(6).

Sark The English (St George's) flag with the Normandy arms in the canton.

Alderney The English (St George's) flag and in the centre a green disc charged with a gold lion.

Herm The English (St George's) flag, and in the canton the Arms of Herm (three cowled monks on a gold diagonal stripe between blue triangles containing a silver dolphin).

Cars can be hired in Jersey, Guernsey & Alderney. In Sark cars are prohib, but bikes and horse-drawn carriages can be hired.

Animals may only be landed from boats from the UK, Ireland, Isle of Man or other CI, but not if the boat has visited France. Unless expressly permitted by a Revenue Officer, no vessel may lie alongside a pontoon or quay with an animal on board.

UK currency can be used in the Islands but not vice versa. Postage stamps, issued by Jersey, Guernsey and Alderney must be used in the appropriate Bailiwick; Guernsey and Alderney stamps are interchangeable. There is only one class of post.

9.19.7 ALDERNEY

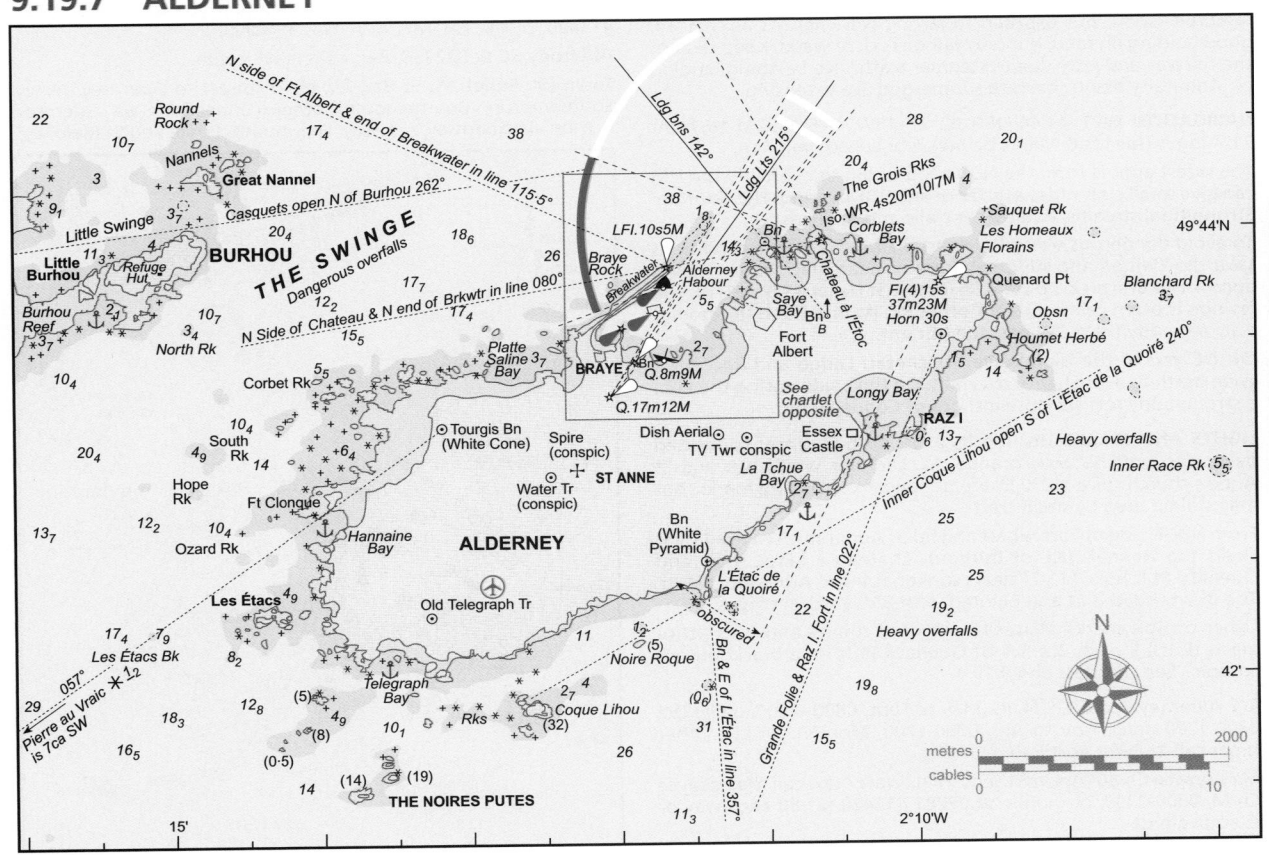

ANCHORAGES AROUND ALDERNEY There are several ⚓s, all picturesque but only safe in settled weather and off-shore winds; most are very small and many have offlying rocks. Entry to these anchorages is not advised without local knowledge, advice from the HM, a good Pilot book plus AC 60 and/or preferably 2845. None provide any facilities. Clockwise from Braye they are:

Saye Bay 49°43′·85N 02°10′·87W. Small sandy bay 4ca E of ent to Braye Hbr. Appr on transit 142° of ldg bns; move E to open up the ent. Ent is 100m wide between Homet des Pies and Homet des Agneaux. Exposed to N'lies. Château à l'Étoc ✶ is 300m ENE. Speed limit 4kn.

Longy Bay 49°43′·06N 02°10′·29W. Wide drying bay with good holding on sand. Speed limit 4kn. Appr on N between Queslingue (a 14m high stack) and a rk 0·6m to stbd. ⚓ in 3·5m closer to Essex Castle than to Raz Island to await fair tide in the Race. Whilst the stream is setting SW offshore, a NE-going eddy develops along the island's southern shore and this would assist a straightforward arrival.

La Tchue 49°42′·78N 02°10′·75W. Good holding in small bay surrounded by cliffs. La Rocque Pendante to the E and smoking rubbish tip to the NW are both conspic.

Telegraph Bay 49°42′·01N 02°13′·51W. Pleasant sandy bay on SW tip of the island but ringed by rks. Appr 035° between Noires Putes and Coupé. Old Telegraph Twr (93m) is conspic until obsc'd close inshore, when a pillar on the cliff edge offers brgs, as does the astern transit of Coupé (7m) and and Orbouée (0.5m).

Hannaine Bay 49°42′·73N 02°13′·98W. A good place to await the flood tide. Appr Tourgis Bn △ ≠ 057° SE side of Fort Clonque. Beware rks either side. ⚓ on sand in 3m, 100m S of Fort.

Platte Saline Bay 49°43′·37N 02°12′·65W. Good shelter from E'lies. Les Jumelles and Outer Fourchie guard the ent. Beach is unsafe for swimming.

Burhou 49°43′·64N 02°15′·49W. Temp'y ⚓ in bay SW of Burhou, only on SW stream; exposed at HW on the NE-going stream. Appr on 010° for the gap between Burhou and Little Burhou.

9.19.8 BRAYE HARBOUR
Alderney 49°43′·77N 02°11′·51W ✿✿✿✿⚓⚓⚓✿✿✿

CHARTS AC 2669, 3653, 60, 2845, 5604.7/.8; SHOM 7158, 6934; Navi 1014; Imray C33A; Stanfords 2, 7, 16, 26, 2500.2

TIDES –0400 Dover; ML 3·5; Duration 0545

Standard Port ST HELIER (⟶)

Times				Height (metres)			
High Water		Low Water		MHWS	MHWN	MLWN	MLWS
0300	0900	0200	0900	11·0	8·1	4·0	1·4
1500	2100	1400	2100				
Differences BRAYE							
+0050	+0040	+0025	+0105	–4·8	–3·4	–1·5	–0·5

SHELTER Good, but exposed to strong N/NE'lies. ⚓s as charted; good holding on sand, but only fair on rock or weed. Keep clear of the fairway and jetty due to steamer traffic. No berthing/landing on Admiralty bkwtr; beware submerged 3ca extension.

NAVIGATION WPT 49°44′·08N 02°11′·18W, 215°/0.82M to front 215° ldg lt (see Lts & Marks below). Hbr speed limit 4kn.

The safest appr is from the NE. In fog or limited visibility the HM can give small craft radar assistance and RDF bearings HO. Caution: Strong tidal streams, eddies, overfalls and many rocks.

To avoid dangerous overfalls in certain wind and tide conditions take the Swinge and Alderney Race at/near slack water; this is approx HW Braye +2½ & LW +2½ (or HW St Helier +3½ and –3). The Swinge is often calmest near Corbet Rk. At mid-flood (NE-going) a strong eddy flows SW past the hbr ent.

Off NE end of the island give Brinchetais Ledge and Race Rk a wide berth to avoid heavy overfalls. On the S side during the ebb, a strong eddy sets NE close inshore of Coque Lihou.

LIGHTS AND MARKS Hbr ldg lts 215°, both Q synch; co-located daymarks, both W cols, orange △s. Old Hbr white bcn and St Anne's church spire ≠ 210·5° are no longer official ldg marks, but may still be used by small craft.

From NW, N side of Fort Albert and hd of Admiralty Bkwtr ≠ 115·5° clears the Nannels (NE of Burhou). Château à l'Etoc lt ho and Quenard Pt lt ho ≠ 111·1° clears sunken ruins of Admiralty Bkwtr. The Bkwtr head is lit and painted with B/W vertical stripes.

Other conspic marks: Water twr W of St Anne's and two lattice masts (R lts) E of it. 2ca SW of Quenard Pt lt ho a blockhouse is conspic. See chartlets and 9.19.4.

R/T Alderney Radio Ch 74 16 (May to Sept, 0800 -2000, daily; Oct 0800-1700 daily; Nov to Apr, 0800-1700, Mon-Fri: all LT). Other times call St Peter Port Radio Ch 20.

Mainbrayce Ch 80 (Apr-mid Sept: HO). Water taxi call Mainbrayce Ch M, 0800-2359; or mobile ☎ 07781 415420 (£1·80 each way or € equivalent).

TELEPHONE (Code 01481) Marinecall 09068 969656; Recorded forecasts see Chapter 5, 5.11; Police 822731; Dr 822077; Ⓗ 822822; Ⓥ Info 822994 (H24); Tourist office 822811.

FACILITIES 70 Y ⚓s (£12) with pick-up lines lie parallel to the Admiralty bkwtr and in blocks E of Braye Jetty and SW of Toulouse Rock. Orange buoys are for locals only. Moor with chain to avoid chafe in persistent swell. If >12m LOA, check adequacy of ⚓ with HM. ⚓s (£3·00 inc shwr) as on chartlet.

HM (aka CG & ☺): ☎ 822620. steve.shaw@gov.gg www.sailalderney.com/harbour.html www.alderney.gov.gg

Braye Jetty, FW, Shwrs, C (25 ton), ⬛, Slip, El, Ⓔ, ✕. WIP to widen and lengthen this jetty should now be complete. **Alderney Small Boat Services** ☎ 823060, CH, ME, El.

Little Crabby Hbr Access HW±2 for **Mainbrayce**, ☎ 822722, 07781 415420: D, FW, CH, ME, ACA, Gas, P (cans).

Alderney SC ☎ 822758, Bar, visitors welcome.

Town (St Anne) 🍴, R, Bar, ✉, Ⓑ. ✈ direct to Guernsey, Jersey, Southampton, Bournemouth; other connections via Guernsey. Ferries: via Guernsey to Jersey, Weymouth, Poole and St Malo.

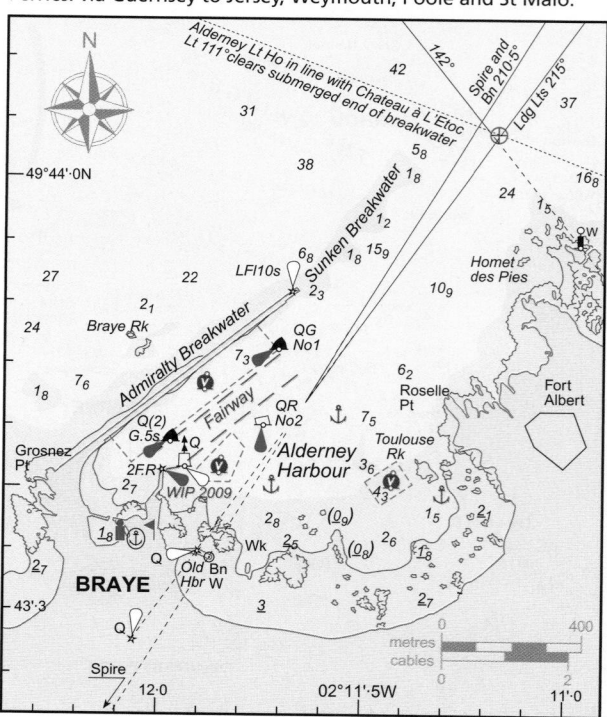

APPROACHES TO GUERNSEY

From the N/NE, The Little Russel Channel (AC 3654, 808) gives the most convenient access to Beaucette marina and St Peter Port (AC 3140). But it needs care, due to rks which fringe the chan and appr, and the strong tide which sets across the ent.

▶*In mid chan, S of Platte and NW of Bréhon, the NE-going stream begins at HW St Peter Port –0245, and the SW stream at HW St Peter Port +0330, sp rates both 5·25kn which can raise a very steep sea with wind against tide.*◀

With lts on Platte Fougère, Tautenay, Roustel, Platte and Bréhon, plus the 220° ldg lts for St Peter Port, the Little Russel can be navigated day or night in reasonable vis, even at LW.

The Big Russel is wider and easier. In bad weather or poor vis it may be a better approach to St Peter Port, via Lower Heads SCM lt buoy, though may be lumpy on a rising sp tide. From the NW, Doyle Passage, which is aligned 146°/326° off Beaucette, can be used but only by day with local knowledge. From the S or W, the natural route is around St Martin's Pt, keeping 1·5ca ENE of Longue Pierre bcn (LP) and a similar distance off Anfré bcn (A).

In onshore winds keep well clear of the W coast, where in bad weather the sea breaks on dangers up to 4M offshore. But in settled weather it is worth exploring the rock strewn bays.

9.19.9   LITTLE RUSSEL CHANNEL

See notes above and AC 5604.9/10, 807, 808

MINOR HARBOURS AND ANCHORAGES AROUND GUERNSEY

Hbrs and ‡ages are listed clockwise from the north. All have buses to St Peter Port (from cliff-top level on the E and S coasts).

EAST COAST

Bordeaux Hbr 49°29'·31N 02°30'·37W. Small drying hbr full of moorings. Rky appr and strong cross tide. Open to E. Café.

St Sampson's Hbr 49°28'·91N 02°30'·73W. Dries 3·6m. Port of entry. Good shelter but also a commercial and FV hbr. Visitors can only enter for commercial services or by prior arrangement. Marina only for locals; entry over lifting flapgate. Marina tfc sigs shown from Abraham's Bosom: steady ● = ent/exit; Fl ◐ or steady ● = No ent/exit.

Channel Islands

WPT 49°28'·70N 02°29'·65W (intersection of St Peter Port and St Sampson ldg lts). 2 chimneys NW of hbr are conspic. Ldg lts 286°: Front on S Pier, FR; rear on clocktower, FG. Other lts as chartlet & 9.19.4. On S Pier a 360° Fl R above FR (shown landward) = large commercial vessel under way in the hbr; no ent/exit for other craft without Dockmaster's approval on Ch 12 (H24) or ☎ 720229. Speed limit 6kn. No ⚓ in hbr. **Services:** BY, BH (70 ton), ME, El, ✹, C, @. Low cost diesel by bowser at E side of Abraham's Bosom, only if pre-booked ☎ 200800.

Havelet Bay 49°27'·06N 02°31'·68W. Enter between SHM buoy QG and PHM buoy QR, marking Oyster Rk, bn 'O', and Moulinet Rk, bn 'M'. SHM and PHM lt buoys about 100m closer inshore. Crowded in summer but sheltered in SW gales; no ⚓s. Landing slip close W of Castle Cornet. Power cables on chartlet overleaf are normally buried to 1m but should be avoided.

Soldier's Bay 49°27'·06N 02°31'·68W. Good holding on sand; open to E. Beware Boue Sablon and rks off Les Terres Point. Anfré Rk (3$_3$), bn 'A', is 4ca offshore. Steps to cliff path.

Fermain Bay 49°26'·05N 02°31'·95W. Good holding on sand; open to E. Beware Gold Fisher Rk (3$_6$) and Gabrielle Rk (2$_1$). Popular tourist beach. R, hotel, Bar.

SOUTH COAST
In centre of first bay W of St Martin's Pt, beware Mouillière (8$_5$) 49°25'·28N 02°32'·86W. S'lies can bring swell above half tide. In this bay are:

Petit Port Good holding on sand. Steep steps to cliff-top pub/restaurant The Auberge, make it attractive to yachtsmen.

Moulin Huet Good holding on sand. Tea garden and hotel.

Saints Bay Good holding on sand. Below half tide beware uncharted rock in middle and unburied telephone cable on E side. ⚓ outside moorings with trip line. Café, hotel, bar.

Icart Bay Beware Fourquie de la Moye (3$_1$) 49°25'·28N 02°32'·86W between Icart Pt and Pte de la Moye. Within Icart Bay are:

Jaonnet. Good holding on sand off small beach or further E off rky shore. Exposed to S. No facilities. Cliff path inland.

Petit Bôt Bay Beware drying reef on E side. A short swell often works in. Café; up hill to hotel, bar, airport, ✉, 🛒. Better ⚓ close W at:

Portelet 49°25'·11N 02°35'·28W. Good holding on sand. Sheltered from N and W. No access inland. Facilities via dinghy/Petit Bôt.

WEST COAST
Good visibility and AC 807 essential; an E'ly wind is desirable. Pass outside Les Hanois, unless bound for:

Portelet Harbour ⚓ at 49°26'·40N 02°40'·26W, outside moorings. Good holding on sand. Exposed to W. Rky appr; local knowledge advised. Avoid small drying stone quay. Hotel, bar, café.

Lihou Island ⚓ 49°27'·88N 02°39'·46W, off NE corner. Sheltered from E. Between Lihou and Guernsey is a drying causeway. Tide runs fast. Avoid bird sanctuaries on off-lying islets. No facilities.

Perelle Bay 49°28'·23N 02°38'·89W. Good holding on sand. Exposed to W; rky appr. Beware Colombelle Rk (1$_5$) NE of brg 128° on cement mill. ⚓ outside moorings. Bar, hotel, D & P (cans).

Vazon Bay 49°28'·29N 02°37'·09W. Wide sandy beach for settled conditions, but open to the W. Beware Boue Vazon (3) in appr, many lobster pots, surfers and bathers. Long surf line. Hotel, R.

Cobo Bay 49°28'·66N 02°36'·33W. Beware lobster pots and Boue Vazon (3) in appr. Rky appr from S of Moulière. Good holding on sand; ⚓ outside moorings. Hotel, Bar, R, B, ✉, 🛒, D & P.

Grande Havre 49°30'·11N 02°33'·09W. Very popular, many local moorings. Rky appr 171° as charted; exposed to NW, sheltered from S'lies. ⚓ to W of Hommet de Grève. Stone slip, busy in summer; lying alongside not advised. Facilities: Hotel, Bar.

L'Ancresse Bay 49°30'·45N 02°31'·38W. Good holding on sand. Exposed to the N, but good shelter from S/SW. Hotel, Bar, Café.

Fontenelle Bay 49°30'·48N 02°30'·69W. Good holding on sand. Exposed to the N. Beware drying rks on E of ent. No facilities.

9.19.10 BEAUCETTE

Guernsey 49°30'·19N 02°30'·20W ❀❀❀❀❀❀❀❀

CHARTS AC 3654, 807, 808, 5604.9; SHOM 7159, 6904, 6903; Navi 1014; Imray C33A; Stanfords 2, 16, 26, 2500.2 & .3

TIDES –0450 Dover; ML 5·0; Duration 0550. See Facilities and 9.19.11 for access times.

SHELTER Excellent in marina. Entry not advised in strong N – SE onshore winds.

NAVIGATION WPT 49°30'·15N 02°28'·85W, 277°/8½ ca to ent. Appr from Little Russel to mid-way between Platte Fougère lt tr (W with B band, 25m) and Roustel lt tr. Pick up the ldg marks/lts, SWM L Fl 10s, a SHM Fl G 5s, 2 PHM buoys Fl R 5s & Fl (3) R 5s, a NCM perch Q and a SHM perch Q (3) G 5s at the ent. Beware stream setting across the appr chan and drying rocks either side.

LIGHTS AND MARKS See chartlet and 9.19.4. Petite Canupe is a very spindly SCM lt bcn. 277° ldg lts: Both FR. Front, R arrow on W background, stbd side of ent; rear, W arrow on R background, on roof of W bldg, with windsock.

R/T Ch 80 (0700-2200) for HM & water taxi.

TELEPHONE (Code 01481); Marinecall 09068 969656; Police 725111; ⊖ 245000; St John Ambulance 725211.

FACILITIES Marina sill dries 2·37m; access HW St Peter

Port ±3½. 6 Y waiting buoys lie outside and a tide gauge is inside the 8m wide ent channel. For entry sequence and a berth it is essential to pre-call HM with boat details: ☎ 245000, mobile 07781 102302. www.beaucettemarina.com info@ beaucettemarina.com

115 inc ±45 ✔, £2·25, min charge £15·75/boat; £0·75 for <4 hrs. D on 'B' pontoon, Gas, Gaz, Slip, ME, El, C (12 ton), BH (16 ton), Bar, R ☎ 247066, 🛒, 🅿, bike hire, ♿ access ramp is steep @ LW.

Village Basic food shop. Good coastal walks. For further information see St Peter Port (9.19.11); 20 mins by bus 6/6A (but bus stop is nearly a mile away).

9.19.11 ST PETER PORT
Guernsey ❄❄❄❄❄💧💧❄❄❄

N appr: 49°30'·23N 02°27'·68W (Little Russel)
S appr: 49°25'·00N 02°31'·17W (St Martin's Point)

metres 0 200
cables 0 1

ST PETER PORT

Q.G
Dir.Oc.WRG.3s5m6M
Q.R
Q.R
YB
Reffée
Q(6)+LFl.15s
6₄
8₉
9₂

North Quay
Sill
La Demie de Goubeau
G
Y
Goubeau
0₆
1₂
9₂

2₂
2₇
Queen Elizabeth II Marina
A B C D
E
R
V
EC
EB
EA
EX
2₇
2₇
8₉
Sardrette
S
Y
L K J I H G F
2
2₂
South Quay

East Breakwater
4
Boue Gosselin
4₃

49°27'·5N
St Julians Pier
Careening Hard
2₇
Ro Ro
Tfc sig
Inter-Island Quay
New Jetty
1₃
6₇
Within circular area
Ldg Lts 220°

Royal Channel Is. YC
2₂
North Pier
5
4
3
2 1₆
2
1
0₆
Local small craft moorings
6₄
Tfc sig
4₈
4₂
White Rock Pier
OcG5s11m14M
Port Control
Tfc sig
5₅
4₂
Ldg Lts 265°
13₄

Victoria Pier
Grids
C B A
D E F G
Iso.R.2s 22m3M
Victoria Marina
V
Sill
Oc.R.5s.10m14M
South Pier
Waiting Pontoon
Speed limit 4kn
5₅
Speed limit 6kn
The Pool
8
Yacht track
15₆
AlWR.10s14m16M
Lt Ho Horn15s
Tremies
Ldg Lts 265°

V W X Y U Z
Sill
Albert Marina
1₁
Fish Quay
F.R
F.R
2₄
2₈
Q.G
GRG
Fl.R Fl.R Fl.R
Cow Bay
Castle Breakwater
W patch in line with Belvedere Ho 223°
11

1₆
Albert Dock
F.R
2
Fuel pontoon
Model Yacht pond
Guernsey YC Viaduct
0₉ Ferico

2
Castle Pier
2₄
0₃
Castle Cornet
White Patch
0₉ Ferico

Obstn (3)
2₁
3₇
4₆ Oyster Rock
13₁

South Beach
0₆
0₆
Moorings
2₅
2₅
4₃
Havelet Bay
6₁
Q.G
6₇
Q.G
10₇

2₇
0₉
2₇
Q.R
7
Q.R
Moulinet
M
4₃
0₃

Bathing Pool
Belvedere
Oc10s61m14M
Belvedere House
Conspic white bldg
02°32'·0W
4₆
Bathing Pool
3₄
31'·5
26

49°27'·0N

Channel Islands

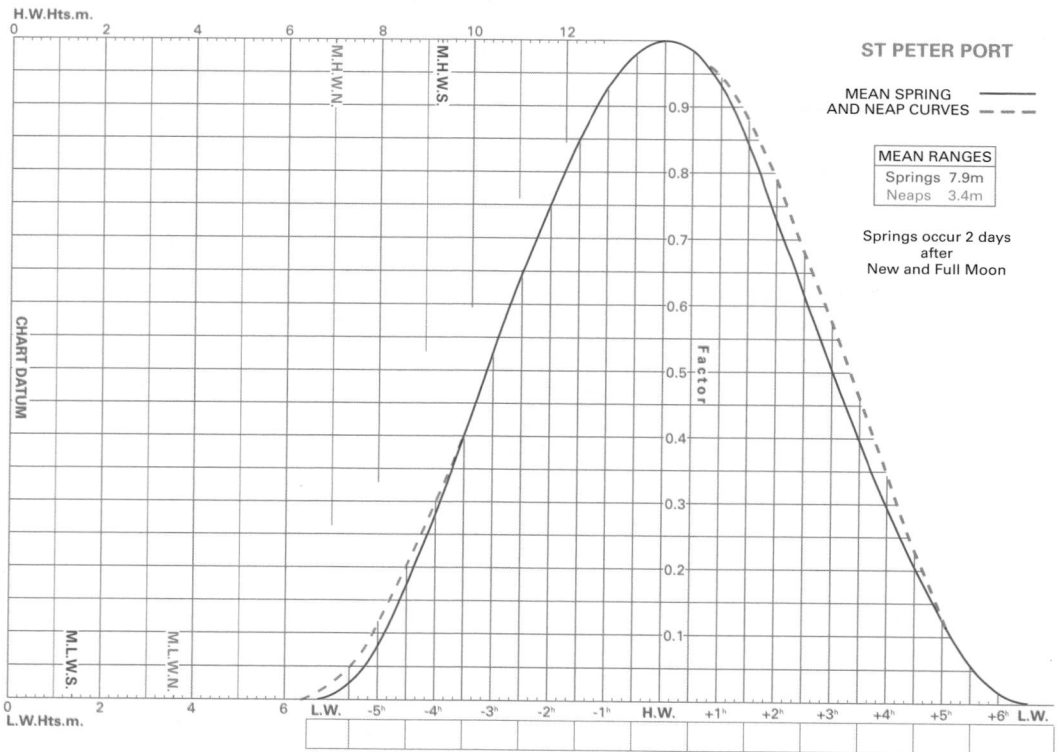

ST PETER PORT

MEAN SPRING ——————
AND NEAP CURVES – – – –

MEAN RANGES
Springs 7.9m
Neaps 3.4m

Springs occur 2 days
after
New and Full Moon

CHARTS AC 3654, 808, 807, 3140, 5604.10/11; SHOM 7159, 6903, 6904; Navi 1014; Imray C33A; Stanfords 2, 16, 26, 2500.2, .3, .4

TIDES −0439 Dover; ML 5·2; Duration 0550.
NOTE: St Peter Port is a Standard Port (⟶).
To find depth of water over the sill into Victoria Marina:
1. Look up predicted time and height of HW St Peter Port.
2. Enter table below on the line for height of HW.
3. Extract depth (m) of water for time before/after HW.

Ht (m) of HW St Peter Port	Depth of water in metres over the sill (dries 4·2 m)						
	HW	±1hr	±2hrs	±2½hrs	±3hrs	±3½hrs	±4hrs
6·20	1·85	1·67	1·30	1·03	0·75	0·47	0·20
·60	2·25	2·00	1·50	1·13	0·75	0·37	–
7·00	2·65	2·34	1·70	1·23	0·75	0·27	–
·40	3·05	2·67	1·90	1·33	0·75	0·27	–
·80	3·45	3·00	2·10	1·43	0·75	0·07	–
8·20	3·85	3·34	2·30	1·53	0·75	–	–
·60	4·25	3·67	2·50	1·63	0·75	–	–
9·00	4·65	4·00	2·70	1·73	0·75	–	–
·40	5·05	4·34	2·90	1·83	0·75	–	–
·80	5·45	4·67	3·10	1·93	0·75	–	–

SHELTER Good, but Victoria Marina is exposed to strong E'lies.

NAVIGATION WPT 49°27'·82N 02°30'·78W, 227°/0·68M to hbr ent. Offlying dangers, big tidal range and strong tidal streams demand careful navigation. From N the Little Russel is most direct appr, but needs care especially in poor visibility; see 9.19.5 and 9.19.9 chartlet. Big Russel between Herm and Sark, passing S of Lower Hds SCM lt buoy, is an easier appr. From W and S of Guernsey, give Les Hanois a wide berth. Beware ferries and shipping. Hbr speed limits: 6kn from outer pier hds to line S from New Jetty to Castle pier; 4kn W of that line (see chartlet).

Access via buoyed/lit chan along S side of hbr. Marina boat will direct yachts to marina, waiting pontoon or ♥ pontoons (nos 1–5, with FW) N of the waiting pontoon. Pontoons for tenders are each side of marina ent. Local moorings are in centre of hbr, with a secondary fairway N of them. ⚓ prohib. ♥ berths in Queen

Elizabeth II and Albert Marinas only by prior arrangement.
GY RDF beacon, 304·50kHz, on Castle Bkwtr is synchronised with the co-located horn (15s) to give distance finding; see 9.19.4.

LIGHTS AND MARKS See chartlet and 9.19.4. Outer ldg lts 220°: Front, Castle bkwtr hd; rear, Belvedere. By day, white patch at Castle Cornet in line 223° with Belvedere Ho (conspic). Inner ldg lts 265° are for ferries berthing at New Jetty. The ldg line stops short of moorings in The Pool. Yachts should appr Victoria marina via the buoyed/lit S channel (dashed line).

Traffic Signals When a large vessel is under way a single FR ● is shown from: White Rock pier hd, facing landward and/or seaward; S ends of New Jetty* and the Inter-Island Quay*. It means 'No vessel may enter or leave hbr', but boats <15m LOA under power are exempt and may proceed, keeping well clear of access to commercial vessel berths. *with an attention-getter ☆ Fl Y above.

R/T Monitor *St Peter Port Control* Ch **12** (H24); only calling, if necessary, when within the pilotage area. *St Peter Port Marinas* Ch M, 80 (office hrs). *Water taxi* Ch 10 (0800-2359LT). *St Peter Port Radio* CRS Ch 20 for safety traffic; Ch 16/67 for emergency DF brgs; Ch 62 for link calls. *St Sampson* Ch 12 (H24).

TELEPHONE (Code 01481) HM 720229; ⊖ 729535; Port Control 720672; Marinecall 09068 969656; Dr 711237 (H24), Pier Steps at Boots; St John Ambulance 725211; Police 725111; Water taxi 424042. Guernsey Met office 0906 713 0111 (from Guernsey only, at lowest premium rate) for local weather.

FACILITIES Victoria Marina has a sill 4·2m; a gauge shows depth over sill. Access approx HW±2½ iaw tide & draft; see Table above. Marina staff and/or R/G tfc lts control ent/exit. ☎ 725987. guernsey. harbour@gov.gg www.guernseyharbours.gov.gg 400, all ♥, £2·10, special deals outside Jul/Aug. Max LOA/draft = 16m/1·8m; max stay 14 days, longer if arranged. Slip,Wi-fi, ♿, ▣.
Castle Pier FW, P, D approx HW±3 (risk of grounding outside these hours), 0730-1730 Mon-Sat, 0730-1200 Sun; (also fuel pontoon at QE II marina). CH, Gas, Gaz, ACA, ME, El, SM, BY, Ⓔ.
Royal Channel Islands YC ☎ 723154 Bar. **Guernsey YC** ☎ 722838.
Town 🛒, CH, ▣, Bar, @, R, ✉, Ⓑ. Fast ferry to Weymouth, Poole, Jersey, St Malo. Ferry to Portsmouth, Diélette, Sark, Herm; ✈.

TIME ZONE (UT)
For Summer Time add ONE hour in **non-shaded areas**

ST PETER PORT LAT 49°27'N LONG 2°32'W
TIMES AND HEIGHTS OF HIGH AND LOW WATERS

Dates in red are **SPRINGS**
Dates in blue are NEAPS

YEAR 2010

JANUARY

Time	m		Time	m
1 F 0036 / 0634 / 1307 / 1906	1.7 / 9.3 / 1.3 / 9.2		**16** SA 0114 / 0709 / 1337 / 1931	2.2 / 8.8 / 1.9 / 8.5
2 SA 0125 / 0723 / 1356 / 1954	1.3 / 9.6 / 1.0 / 9.4		**17** SU 0147 / 0744 / 1410 / 2004	2.0 / 8.9 / 1.9 / 8.6
3 SU 0213 / 0810 / 1443 / 2040	1.1 / 9.8 / 0.9 / 9.4		**18** M 0218 / 0816 / 1440 / 2034	2.0 / 8.8 / 1.9 / 8.5
4 M 0258 / 0855 / 1528 / 2124	1.1 / 9.8 / 1.0 / 9.2		**19** TU 0247 / 0846 / 1509 / 2103	2.1 / 8.6 / 2.1 / 8.3
5 TU 0343 / 0940 / 1612 / 2208	1.4 / 9.4 / 1.3 / 8.9		**20** W 0315 / 0915 / 1536 / 2131	2.3 / 8.4 / 2.3 / 8.1
6 W 0427 / 1025 / 1656 / 2253	1.8 / 8.9 / 1.9 / 8.4		**21** TH 0343 / 0944 / 1605 / 2201	2.6 / 8.1 / 2.6 / 7.8
7 TH 0513 / 1113 / 1743 / ☽2343	2.4 / 8.3 / 2.5 / 7.8		**22** F 0413 / 1018 / 1638 / 2237	2.9 / 7.8 / 2.9 / 7.6
8 F 0605 / 1207 / 1838	2.9 / 7.7 / 3.1		**23** SA 0451 / 1100 / 1721 / ☽2323	3.2 / 7.5 / 3.3 / 7.3
9 SA 0043 / 0709 / 1316 / 1946	7.3 / 3.4 / 7.2 / 3.5		**24** SU 0543 / 1157 / 1820	3.5 / 7.1 / 3.5
10 SU 0200 / 0831 / 1436 / 2108	7.1 / 3.6 / 7.0 / 3.6		**25** M 0028 / 0659 / 1315 / 1943	7.0 / 3.7 / 6.9 / 3.6
11 M 0318 / 0948 / 1550 / 2217	7.2 / 3.5 / 7.2 / 3.4		**26** TU 0156 / 0838 / 1448 / 2114	7.0 / 3.6 / 7.1 / 3.4
12 TU 0420 / 1049 / 1648 / 2311	7.5 / 3.1 / 7.5 / 3.1		**27** W 0325 / 1001 / 1608 / 2229	7.4 / 3.0 / 7.5 / 2.8
13 W 0510 / 1138 / 1735 / 2357	7.9 / 2.7 / 7.8 / 2.7		**28** TH 0435 / 1108 / 1712 / 2331	8.1 / 2.3 / 8.2 / 2.1
14 TH 0553 / 1221 / 1817	8.3 / 2.4 / 8.1		**29** F 0533 / 1205 / 1807	8.8 / 1.6 / 8.8
15 F 0037 / 0632 / 1301 / ●1855	2.4 / 8.6 / 2.1 / 8.4		**30** SA 0026 / 0624 / 1258 / ○1856	1.5 / 9.4 / 0.9 / 9.4
			31 SU 0116 / 0713 / 1345 / 1942	0.9 / 9.9 / 0.5 / 9.7

FEBRUARY

Time	m		Time	m
1 M 0202 / 0757 / 1429 / 2025	0.6 / 10.1 / 0.3 / 9.8		**16** TU 0158 / 0755 / 1417 / 2011	1.6 / 9.0 / 1.5 / 8.8
2 TU 0244 / 0840 / 1510 / 2105	0.5 / 10.1 / 0.4 / 9.7		**17** W 0226 / 0824 / 1444 / 2038	1.7 / 8.9 / 1.7 / 8.7
3 W 0324 / 0920 / 1549 / 2143	0.8 / 9.8 / 0.9 / 9.3		**18** TH 0252 / 0850 / 1509 / 2103	1.9 / 8.7 / 1.9 / 8.5
4 TH 0402 / 0959 / 1626 / 2220	1.3 / 9.2 / 1.6 / 8.6		**19** F 0317 / 0917 / 1536 / 2131	2.1 / 8.4 / 2.2 / 8.2
5 F 0440 / 1038 / 1703 / ☽2259	2.0 / 8.4 / 2.4 / 7.9		**20** SA 0345 / 0948 / 1606 / 2203	2.5 / 8.1 / 2.6 / 7.9
6 SA 0522 / 1121 / 1746 / 2347	2.8 / 7.6 / 3.2 / 7.2		**21** SU 0418 / 1026 / 1644 / 2245	2.9 / 7.6 / 3.1 / 7.5
7 SU 0615 / 1220 / 1846	3.5 / 6.8 / 3.8		**22** M 0505 / 1120 / 1739 / ☽2347	3.4 / 7.1 / 3.5 / 7.1
8 M 0100 / 0736 / 1357 / 2022	6.7 / 4.0 / 6.4 / 4.1		**23** TU 0618 / 1240 / 1905	3.7 / 6.8 / 3.8
9 TU 0249 / 0926 / 1535 / 2200	6.6 / 3.9 / 6.6 / 3.9		**24** W 0121 / 0812 / 1429 / 2055	6.9 / 3.6 / 6.9 / 3.5
10 W 0404 / 1036 / 1636 / 2258	7.1 / 3.4 / 7.1 / 3.4		**25** TH 0307 / 0948 / 1559 / 2217	7.3 / 3.0 / 7.4 / 2.9
11 TH 0455 / 1124 / 1721 / 2342	7.6 / 2.9 / 7.6 / 2.8		**26** F 0423 / 1056 / 1701 / 2319	8.0 / 2.2 / 8.2 / 2.0
12 F 0537 / 1205 / 1800	8.1 / 2.4 / 8.1		**27** SA 0520 / 1151 / 1753	8.8 / 1.3 / 9.0
13 SA 0021 / 0615 / 1242 / 1836	2.3 / 8.6 / 2.0 / 8.5		**28** SU 0011 / 0609 / 1241 / ○1839	1.2 / 9.5 / 0.7 / 9.6
14 SU 0056 / 0651 / 1317 / ●1911	2.0 / 8.9 / 1.7 / 8.7			
15 M 0128 / 0724 / 1348 / 1942	1.7 / 9.0 / 1.5 / 8.8			

MARCH

Time	m		Time	m
1 M 0059 / 0655 / 1326 / 1922	0.6 / 10.0 / 0.2 / 9.9		**16** TU 0101 / 0658 / 1320 / 1915	1.6 / 9.0 / 1.4 / 9.0
2 TU 0143 / 0738 / 1408 / 2002	0.3 / 10.3 / 0.1 / 10.0		**17** W 0132 / 0729 / 1349 / 1944	1.4 / 9.1 / 1.4 / 9.0
3 W 0223 / 0818 / 1446 / 2040	0.2 / 10.2 / 0.3 / 9.8		**18** TH 0200 / 0758 / 1417 / 2011	1.5 / 9.0 / 1.5 / 8.9
4 TH 0301 / 0856 / 1522 / 2115	0.5 / 9.8 / 0.8 / 9.4		**19** F 0228 / 0826 / 1443 / 2038	1.6 / 8.9 / 1.7 / 8.7
5 F 0336 / 0931 / 1555 / 2148	1.1 / 9.1 / 1.6 / 8.7		**20** SA 0254 / 0854 / 1511 / 2107	1.9 / 8.6 / 2.1 / 8.4
6 SA 0409 / 1005 / 1627 / 2221	1.9 / 8.3 / 2.4 / 7.9		**21** SU 0323 / 0927 / 1542 / 2141	2.2 / 8.2 / 2.5 / 8.1
7 SU 0445 / 1042 / 1703 / ☽2300	2.7 / 7.4 / 3.3 / 7.2		**22** M 0359 / 1007 / 1622 / 2225	2.7 / 7.7 / 3.0 / 7.6
8 M 0531 / 1132 / 1755	3.5 / 6.7 / 4.0		**23** TU 0448 / 1103 / 1720 / ☽2329	3.2 / 7.1 / 3.5 / 7.1
9 TU 0002 / 0648 / 1308 / 1928	6.6 / 4.1 / 6.2 / 4.4		**24** W 0604 / 1227 / 1850	3.5 / 6.8 / 3.8
10 W 0208 / 0852 / 1512 / 2134	6.4 / 4.1 / 6.4 / 4.1		**25** TH 0104 / 0800 / 1418 / 2041	7.0 / 3.5 / 6.9 / 3.5
11 TH 0338 / 1011 / 1612 / 2234	6.8 / 3.6 / 6.9 / 3.5		**26** F 0250 / 0932 / 1542 / 2200	7.3 / 2.8 / 7.6 / 2.7
12 F 0430 / 1058 / 1656 / 2316	7.4 / 3.0 / 7.5 / 2.9		**27** SA 0403 / 1036 / 1641 / 2259	8.1 / 2.0 / 8.3 / 1.9
13 SA 0511 / 1137 / 1733 / 2354	8.0 / 2.4 / 8.0 / 2.3		**28** SU 0459 / 1129 / 1730 / 2349	8.8 / 1.3 / 9.0 / 1.2
14 SU 0549 / 1213 / 1809	8.5 / 1.9 / 8.5		**29** M 0547 / 1216 / 1815	9.5 / 0.7 / 9.5
15 M 0028 / 0624 / 1248 / ●1843	1.9 / 8.8 / 1.6 / 8.8		**30** TU 0036 / 0632 / 1301 / ○1857	0.7 / 9.9 / 0.4 / 9.8
			31 W 0119 / 0714 / 1342 / 1936	0.4 / 10.0 / 0.3 / 9.9

APRIL

Time	m		Time	m
1 TH 0159 / 0754 / 1420 / 2013	0.4 / 9.9 / 0.6 / 9.7		**16** F 0134 / 0732 / 1350 / 1945	1.5 / 9.0 / 1.5 / 9.0
2 F 0236 / 0831 / 1454 / 2048	0.7 / 9.5 / 1.1 / 9.2		**17** SA 0206 / 0804 / 1421 / 2017	1.5 / 8.9 / 1.7 / 8.9
3 SA 0311 / 0905 / 1526 / 2120	1.3 / 8.8 / 1.8 / 8.6		**18** SU 0238 / 0838 / 1454 / 2051	1.7 / 8.6 / 2.0 / 8.6
4 SU 0344 / 0939 / 1557 / 2152	2.0 / 8.1 / 2.6 / 8.0		**19** M 0312 / 0917 / 1531 / 2131	2.1 / 8.2 / 2.4 / 8.2
5 M 0418 / 1015 / 1631 / 2230	2.7 / 7.4 / 3.3 / 7.3		**20** TU 0354 / 1003 / 1616 / 2221	2.5 / 7.8 / 2.9 / 7.8
6 TU 0503 / 1103 / 1719 / ☽2325	3.5 / 6.7 / 4.0 / 6.7		**21** W 0448 / 1103 / 1717 / ☽2327	2.9 / 7.3 / 3.3 / 7.4
7 W 0613 / 1222 / 1844	4.0 / 6.2 / 4.3		**22** TH 0607 / 1222 / 1845	3.2 / 7.0 / 3.5
8 TH 0104 / 0750 / 1420 / 2032	6.4 / 4.0 / 6.3 / 4.2		**23** F 0052 / 0744 / 1357 / 2018	7.3 / 3.1 / 7.2 / 3.2
9 F 0250 / 0920 / 1529 / 2148	6.7 / 3.7 / 6.8 / 3.7		**24** SA 0223 / 0920 / 1513 / 2133	7.6 / 2.6 / 7.7 / 2.6
10 SA 0349 / 1015 / 1616 / 2236	7.2 / 3.1 / 7.4 / 3.1		**25** SU 0334 / 1008 / 1611 / 2231	8.1 / 2.0 / 8.3 / 2.0
11 SU 0433 / 1057 / 1656 / 2315	7.7 / 2.6 / 7.9 / 2.5		**26** M 0431 / 1101 / 1702 / 2323	8.7 / 1.5 / 8.9 / 1.4
12 M 0513 / 1135 / 1733 / 2352	8.2 / 2.1 / 8.3 / 2.1		**27** TU 0521 / 1149 / 1747	9.1 / 1.1 / 9.3
13 TU 0550 / 1211 / 1809	8.6 / 1.7 / 8.7		**28** W 0010 / 0607 / 1234 / ○1830	1.1 / 9.4 / 0.9 / 9.5
14 W 0027 / 0626 / 1245 / ●1842	1.7 / 8.8 / 1.5 / 8.9		**29** TH 0054 / 0650 / 1316 / 1911	0.9 / 9.4 / 1.0 / 9.5
15 TH 0101 / 0700 / 1318 / 1914	1.5 / 9.0 / 1.4 / 9.0		**30** F 0135 / 0731 / 1355 / 1949	0.9 / 9.2 / 1.2 / 9.3

Channel Islands

Chart Datum is 5·06 metres below Ordnance Datum (Local). HAT is 10·3 metres above Chart Datum; see 4.5.

ST PETER PORT LAT 49°27'N LONG 2°32'W

TIMES AND HEIGHTS OF HIGH AND LOW WATERS

TIME ZONE (UT)
For Summer Time add ONE hour in **non-shaded areas**

Dates in **red** are **SPRINGS**
Dates in **blue** are **NEAPS**

YEAR 2010

MAY

Time	m	Time	m
1 0214 / 0809 / SA 1430 / 2024	1.2 / 9.0 / 1.6 / 9.0	**16** 0149 / 0749 / SU 1407 / 2003	1.5 / 8.8 / 1.7 / 9.0
2 0250 / 0845 / SU 1504 / 2058	1.6 / 8.5 / 2.1 / 8.5	**17** 0229 / 0831 / M 1447 / 2045	1.6 / 8.7 / 1.9 / 8.8
3 0324 / 0920 / M 1536 / 2132	2.1 / 8.0 / 2.7 / 8.0	**18** 0312 / 0915 / TU 1530 / 2130	1.8 / 8.4 / 2.2 / 8.5
4 0401 / 0958 / TU 1611 / 2211	2.7 / 7.4 / 3.2 / 7.5	**19** 0359 / 1006 / W 1619 / 2222	2.1 / 8.1 / 2.5 / 8.2
5 0443 / 1043 / W 1656 / 2300	3.2 / 6.9 / 3.7 / 7.0	**20** 0455 / 1102 / TH 1719 / 2322	2.5 / 7.7 / 2.9 / 7.7
6 0541 / 1143 / TH 1801 / ◑	3.6 / 6.6 / 4.0	**21** 0602 / 1210 / F 1830	2.7 / 7.5 / 3.0
7 0008 / 0653 / F 1304 / 1920	6.7 / 3.8 / 6.5 / 4.1	**22** 0033 / 0716 / SA 1325 / 1947	7.7 / 2.8 / 7.5 / 3.0
8 0133 / 0807 / SA 1421 / 2035	6.7 / 3.7 / 6.7 / 3.8	**23** 0149 / 0830 / SU 1436 / 2059	7.7 / 2.6 / 7.8 / 2.7
9 0246 / 0911 / SU 1520 / 2136	7.0 / 3.3 / 7.1 / 3.3	**24** 0300 / 0935 / M 1538 / 2202	8.0 / 2.3 / 8.1 / 2.3
10 0341 / 1003 / M 1608 / 2225	7.4 / 2.9 / 7.6 / 2.8	**25** 0401 / 1031 / TU 1632 / 2256	8.2 / 2.0 / 8.4 / 2.0
11 0428 / 1048 / TU 1651 / 2309	7.8 / 2.5 / 8.0 / 2.4	**26** 0455 / 1122 / W 1721 / 2346	8.5 / 1.8 / 8.7 / 1.7
12 0510 / 1130 / W 1731 / 2350	8.2 / 2.1 / 8.4 / 2.0	**27** 0544 / 1209 / TH 1807 / ○	8.7 / 1.7 / 8.9
13 0551 / 1210 / TH 1809	8.5 / 1.8 / 8.7	**28** 0032 / 0630 / F 1254 / 1849	1.5 / 8.8 / 1.7 / 9.0
14 0030 / 0630 / F 1249 / ● 1847	1.7 / 8.7 / 1.7 / 8.9	**29** 0116 / 0713 / SA 1334 / 1929	1.5 / 8.7 / 1.7 / 9.0
15 0110 / 0710 / SA 1328 / 1924	1.6 / 8.8 / 1.6 / 9.0	**30** 0156 / 0753 / SU 1412 / 2006	1.6 / 8.6 / 1.9 / 8.8
		31 0233 / 0830 / M 1447 / 2041	1.8 / 8.4 / 2.2 / 8.5

JUNE

Time	m	Time	m
1 0309 / 0906 / TU 1520 / 2116	2.1 / 8.0 / 2.6 / 8.1	**16** 0312 / 0913 / W 1530 / 2127	1.3 / 8.8 / 1.7 / 9.0
2 0345 / 0942 / W 1554 / 2153	2.5 / 7.7 / 3.0 / 7.8	**17** 0359 / 1000 / TH 1617 / 2216	1.5 / 8.6 / 1.9 / 8.7
3 0422 / 1021 / TH 1632 / 2233	2.9 / 7.3 / 3.3 / 7.4	**18** 0449 / 1051 / F 1708 / 2308	1.9 / 8.3 / 2.3 / 8.4
4 0505 / 1106 / F 1719 / ◑ 2322	3.2 / 7.1 / 3.6 / 7.1	**19** 0543 / 1146 / SA 1805 / ◐	2.2 / 8.0 / 2.6
5 0558 / 1200 / SA 1818	3.4 / 6.9 / 3.8	**20** 0006 / 0643 / SU 1249 / 1910	8.0 / 2.6 / 7.7 / 2.9
6 0021 / 0659 / SU 1304 / 1924	6.9 / 3.5 / 6.8 / 3.8	**21** 0114 / 0751 / M 1358 / 2023	7.7 / 2.8 / 7.6 / 3.0
7 0130 / 0802 / M 1411 / 2030	6.9 / 3.4 / 7.0 / 3.5	**22** 0226 / 0901 / TU 1507 / 2133	7.6 / 2.9 / 7.7 / 2.9
8 0237 / 0903 / TU 1511 / 2131	7.1 / 3.2 / 7.3 / 3.2	**23** 0335 / 1006 / W 1608 / 2235	7.6 / 2.7 / 7.9 / 2.6
9 0337 / 0959 / W 1604 / 2226	7.4 / 2.9 / 7.7 / 2.8	**24** 0436 / 1102 / TH 1701 / 2328	7.8 / 2.5 / 8.2 / 2.3
10 0430 / 1050 / TH 1653 / 2316	7.8 / 2.5 / 8.1 / 2.3	**25** 0529 / 1152 / F 1749	8.1 / 2.3 / 8.5
11 0520 / 1139 / F 1740	8.2 / 2.2 / 8.5	**26** 0016 / 0616 / SA 1238 / ○ 1833	2.1 / 8.3 / 2.2 / 8.7
12 0005 / 0607 / SA 1225 / ● 1825	1.9 / 8.5 / 1.9 / 8.9	**27** 0101 / 0659 / SU 1319 / 1913	1.9 / 8.4 / 2.1 / 8.8
13 0053 / 0654 / SU 1313 / 1910	1.6 / 8.8 / 1.6 / 9.1	**28** 0141 / 0739 / M 1357 / 1951	1.8 / 8.5 / 2.1 / 8.7
14 0140 / 0741 / M 1359 / 1956	1.4 / 8.9 / 1.5 / 9.2	**29** 0218 / 0815 / TU 1431 / 2026	1.8 / 8.4 / 2.1 / 8.6
15 0226 / 0827 / TU 1444 / 2041	1.3 / 8.9 / 1.5 / 9.2	**30** 0252 / 0849 / W 1503 / 2059	2.0 / 8.3 / 2.3 / 8.4

JULY

Time	m	Time	m
1 0324 / 0921 / TH 1533 / 2131	2.2 / 8.1 / 2.6 / 8.1	**16** 0347 / 0945 / F 1603 / 2200	1.0 / 9.2 / 1.4 / 9.2
2 0356 / 0953 / F 1604 / 2203	2.5 / 7.8 / 2.8 / 7.8	**17** 0430 / 1029 / SA 1647 / 2245	1.4 / 8.7 / 1.9 / 8.7
3 0428 / 1027 / SA 1638 / 2240	2.8 / 7.5 / 3.1 / 7.5	**18** 0515 / 1116 / SU 1735 / ◑ 2334	2.0 / 8.2 / 2.5 / 8.0
4 0505 / 1106 / SU 1719 / ◑ 2323	3.1 / 7.3 / 3.4 / 7.2	**19** 0606 / 1210 / M 1832	2.7 / 7.6 / 3.0
5 0551 / 1154 / M 1814	3.4 / 7.1 / 3.6	**20** 0035 / 0709 / TU 1319 / 1945	7.4 / 3.2 / 7.3 / 3.4
6 0019 / 0652 / TU 1257 / 1925	7.0 / 3.5 / 7.0 / 3.7	**21** 0155 / 0830 / W 1440 / 2112	7.0 / 3.5 / 7.2 / 3.4
7 0131 / 0804 / W 1411 / 2040	7.1 / 3.5 / 7.1 / 3.5	**22** 0319 / 0949 / TH 1552 / 2223	7.1 / 3.4 / 7.4 / 3.1
8 0248 / 0915 / TH 1522 / 2149	7.1 / 3.3 / 7.4 / 3.1	**23** 0426 / 1051 / F 1649 / 2318	7.4 / 3.1 / 7.8 / 2.7
9 0357 / 1019 / F 1623 / 2251	7.5 / 2.9 / 7.9 / 2.5	**24** 0519 / 1141 / SA 1736	7.7 / 2.7 / 8.2
10 0457 / 1117 / SA 1719 / 2348	8.0 / 2.4 / 8.4 / 2.0	**25** 0005 / 0603 / SU 1225 / 1818	2.4 / 8.1 / 2.4 / 8.5
11 0552 / 1211 / SU 1811 / ●	8.4 / 1.9 / 8.9	**26** 0047 / 0644 / M 1304 / ○ 1857	2.0 / 8.4 / 2.1 / 8.8
12 0041 / 0643 / M 1304 / 1900	1.5 / 8.9 / 1.4 / 9.3	**27** 0125 / 0721 / TU 1340 / 1933	1.8 / 8.6 / 1.9 / 8.9
13 0132 / 0732 / TU 1351 / 1947	1.0 / 9.2 / 1.1 / 9.6	**28** 0159 / 0754 / W 1412 / 2006	1.7 / 8.7 / 1.9 / 8.9
14 0219 / 0818 / W 1437 / 2032	0.8 / 9.4 / 1.0 / 9.7	**29** 0230 / 0826 / TH 1441 / 2036	1.7 / 8.6 / 2.0 / 8.7
15 0304 / 0902 / TH 1521 / 2116	0.8 / 9.4 / 1.1 / 9.6	**30** 0258 / 0854 / F 1508 / 2104	1.9 / 8.4 / 2.2 / 8.5
		31 0325 / 0922 / SA 1534 / 2132	2.2 / 8.2 / 2.5 / 8.2

AUGUST

Time	m	Time	m
1 0351 / 0949 / SU 1601 / 2202	2.5 / 7.9 / 2.8 / 7.8	**16** 0443 / 1042 / M 1702 / ◐ 2300	2.1 / 8.3 / 2.5 / 7.9
2 0420 / 1021 / M 1634 / 2238	2.9 / 7.6 / 3.1 / 7.5	**17** 0527 / 1130 / TU 1754 / 2356	2.9 / 7.5 / 3.3 / 7.1
3 0457 / 1102 / TU 1718 / 2327	3.2 / 7.3 / 3.5 / 7.1	**18** 0627 / 1239 / W 1910	3.7 / 6.9 / 3.8
4 0550 / 1159 / W 1823	3.6 / 7.0 / 3.7	**19** 0127 / 0802 / TH 1420 / 2058	6.6 / 4.1 / 6.8 / 3.9
5 0036 / 0709 / TH 1319 / 1957	6.9 / 3.8 / 6.9 / 3.7	**20** 0313 / 0939 / F 1541 / 2215	6.7 / 3.9 / 7.1 / 3.5
6 0210 / 0842 / F 1450 / 2126	6.9 / 3.6 / 7.2 / 3.3	**21** 0418 / 1040 / SA 1635 / 2306	7.1 / 3.4 / 7.6 / 2.9
7 0337 / 0959 / SA 1604 / 2236	7.3 / 3.1 / 7.8 / 2.6	**22** 0505 / 1126 / SU 1720 / 2348	7.7 / 2.8 / 8.2 / 2.4
8 0444 / 1103 / SU 1705 / 2336	7.9 / 2.4 / 8.5 / 1.9	**23** 0545 / 1206 / M 1759	8.1 / 2.4 / 8.6
9 0540 / 1159 / M 1758	8.6 / 1.7 / 9.1	**24** 0025 / 0621 / TU 1242 / ○ 1835	2.0 / 8.5 / 2.0 / 8.9
10 0029 / 0631 / TU 1250 / ● 1847	1.2 / 9.2 / 1.1 / 9.7	**25** 0101 / 0655 / W 1316 / 1909	1.7 / 8.8 / 1.8 / 9.1
11 0118 / 0717 / W 1337 / 1933	0.7 / 9.6 / 0.7 / 10.1	**26** 0133 / 0728 / TH 1346 / 1941	1.6 / 8.9 / 1.7 / 9.1
12 0203 / 0801 / TH 1421 / 2016	0.4 / 9.9 / 0.6 / 10.2	**27** 0202 / 0757 / F 1414 / 2009	1.6 / 8.9 / 1.8 / 9.0
13 0245 / 0842 / F 1503 / 2057	0.4 / 9.8 / 0.6 / 10.0	**28** 0229 / 0824 / SA 1439 / 2036	1.7 / 8.7 / 1.9 / 8.8
14 0325 / 0922 / SA 1542 / 2137	0.7 / 9.5 / 1.0 / 9.4	**29** 0253 / 0849 / SU 1504 / 2101	2.0 / 8.5 / 2.2 / 8.5
15 0404 / 1001 / SU 1621 / 2217	1.3 / 9.0 / 1.7 / 8.7	**30** 0318 / 0915 / M 1529 / 2129	2.4 / 8.2 / 2.6 / 8.1
		31 0345 / 0944 / TU 1559 / 2203	2.8 / 7.9 / 3.0 / 7.7

Chart Datum is 5·06 metres below Ordnance Datum (Local). HAT is 10·3 metres above Chart Datum; see 4.5.

TIME ZONE (UT)
For Summer Time add ONE hour in **non-shaded areas**

ST PETER PORT
LAT 49°27'N   LONG 2°32'W
TIMES AND HEIGHTS OF HIGH AND LOW WATERS

Dates in red are **SPRINGS**
Dates in blue are **NEAPS**

YEAR 2010

SEPTEMBER

	Time	m		Time	m
1	0420	3.2	**16**	0549	4.0
	1023	7.5		1200	6.8
W	1640	3.4	TH	1837	4.1
	☾ 2250	7.2			
2	0509	3.6	**17**	0056	6.4
	1120	7.1		0730	4.4
TH	1744	3.8	F	1356	6.6
				2035	4.1
3	0002	6.8	**18**	0255	6.5
	0629	4.0		0920	4.1
F	1246	6.9	SA	1518	7.0
	1929	3.9		2153	3.7
4	0148	6.8	**19**	0356	7.1
	0822	3.8		1018	3.5
SA	1430	7.2	SU	1611	7.6
	2112	3.4		2241	3.1
5	0325	7.3	**20**	0439	7.6
	0946	3.2		1100	2.9
SU	1550	7.9	M	1653	8.1
	2223	2.6		2320	2.5
6	0431	8.1	**21**	0516	8.2
	1049	2.3		1138	2.4
M	1649	8.6	TU	1731	8.6
	2320	1.7		2356	2.1
7	0524	8.8	**22**	0551	8.6
	1142	1.6		1213	2.0
TU	1741	9.4	W	1806	8.9
8	0010	1.0	**23**	0029	1.8
	0611	9.5		0625	8.9
W	1232	0.9	TH	1246	1.8
	● 1827	9.9		○ 1840	9.1
9	0057	0.5	**24**	0101	1.6
	0655	9.9		0657	9.0
TH	1317	0.5	F	1316	1.7
	1912	10.3		1911	9.2
10	0141	0.3	**25**	0131	1.6
	0738	10.1		0727	9.0
F	1400	0.3	SA	1345	1.7
	1954	10.3		1941	9.1
11	0222	0.4	**26**	0158	1.7
	0818	10.0		0754	8.9
SA	1440	0.5	SU	1412	1.9
	2034	10.0		2008	8.9
12	0300	0.8	**27**	0224	2.0
	0856	9.6		0820	8.7
SU	1518	1.0	M	1438	2.1
	2112	9.4		2035	8.6
13	0336	1.5	**28**	0251	2.3
	0932	9.0		0847	8.4
M	1555	1.8	TU	1505	2.5
	2149	8.6		2105	8.2
14	0412	2.3	**29**	0320	2.7
	1010	8.2		0919	8.1
TU	1633	2.6	W	1538	2.9
	2228	7.7		2141	7.8
15	0452	3.2	**30**	0356	3.2
	1053	7.4		1000	7.7
W	1721	3.5	TH	1621	3.3
	☾ 2320	6.9		2231	7.3

OCTOBER

	Time	m		Time	m
1	0448	3.7	**16**	0012	6.5
	1100	7.2		0642	4.4
F	1727	3.7	SA	1304	6.6
	☾ 2347	6.9		1939	4.2
2	0611	4.0	**17**	0207	6.5
	1228	7.0		0832	4.3
SA	1916	3.8	SU	1435	6.9
				2106	3.8
3	0133	6.9	**18**	0315	7.0
	0805	3.8		0938	3.8
SU	1411	7.3	M	1532	7.4
	2054	3.3		2200	3.3
4	0307	7.5	**19**	0401	7.5
	0927	3.1		1023	3.2
M	1529	8.0	TU	1616	7.9
	2203	2.5		2241	2.8
5	0409	8.3	**20**	0440	8.0
	1028	2.3		1101	2.7
TU	1627	8.8	W	1655	8.3
	2258	1.7		2318	2.4
6	0500	9.0	**21**	0516	8.5
	1120	1.5		1137	2.3
W	1717	9.4	TH	1732	8.7
	2346	1.1		2353	2.1
7	0546	9.5	**22**	0550	8.8
	1208	1.0		1211	2.0
TH	1804	9.9	F	1808	8.9
●					
8	0032	0.7	**23**	0026	1.8
	0630	9.9		0624	9.0
F	1254	0.6	SA	1245	1.8
	1848	10.1		○ 1841	9.0
9	0116	0.6	**24**	0059	1.8
	0712	10.0		0656	9.1
SA	1336	0.6	SU	1317	1.8
	1931	10.0		1914	9.0
10	0157	0.7	**25**	0130	1.8
	0752	9.9		0726	9.0
SU	1417	0.8	M	1348	1.9
	2011	9.7		1945	8.9
11	0235	1.2	**26**	0201	2.0
	0830	9.5		0757	8.9
M	1455	1.3	TU	1419	2.1
	2048	9.1		2017	8.7
12	0311	1.8	**27**	0232	2.3
	0906	8.9		0830	8.6
TU	1532	2.0	W	1452	2.4
	2125	8.4		2053	8.3
13	0346	2.6	**28**	0307	2.6
	0943	8.2		0907	8.3
W	1611	2.8	TH	1530	2.7
	2204	7.6		2135	7.9
14	0424	3.4	**29**	0348	3.1
	1025	7.5		0954	7.9
TH	1657	3.5	F	1619	3.1
	☾ 2253	6.9		2228	7.5
15	0516	4.0	**30**	0443	3.5
	1125	6.9		1055	7.5
F	1805	4.0	SA	1726	3.4
				☾ 2340	7.2
31	0603	3.7			
	1214	7.4			
SU	1858	3.5			

NOVEMBER

	Time	m		Time	m
1	0111	7.2	**16**	0204	6.8
	0740	3.6		0826	4.0
M	1343	7.6	TU	1431	7.1
	2025	3.1		2055	3.6
2	0236	7.7	**17**	0305	7.2
	0859	3.0		0927	3.6
TU	1458	8.1	W	1526	7.4
	2134	2.5		2148	3.2
3	0339	8.3	**18**	0353	7.6
	1001	2.4		1014	3.1
W	1559	8.6	TH	1612	7.8
	2230	1.9		2233	2.8
4	0432	8.8	**19**	0435	8.1
	1055	1.8		1056	2.7
TH	1652	9.1	F	1654	8.2
	2321	1.5		2313	2.5
5	0520	9.3	**20**	0514	8.5
	1144	1.3		1136	2.4
F	1740	9.4	SA	1735	8.5
				2352	2.2
6	0008	1.2	**21**	0552	8.8
	0605	9.6		1215	2.1
SA	1231	1.1	SU	1814	8.7
	● 1826	9.6		○	
7	0053	1.1	**22**	0030	2.0
	0648	9.7		0629	8.9
SU	1315	1.1	M	1253	1.9
	1910	9.5		1851	8.8
8	0134	1.3	**23**	0108	1.9
	0730	9.6		0705	9.0
M	1357	1.2	TU	1331	1.9
	1951	9.3		1929	8.8
9	0214	1.6	**24**	0145	1.9
	0809	9.3		0743	9.0
TU	1437	1.6	W	1410	1.9
	2030	8.8		2008	8.7
10	0251	2.1	**25**	0224	2.1
	0846	8.9		0822	8.9
W	1515	2.1	TH	1450	2.1
	2108	8.3		2049	8.5
11	0326	2.7	**26**	0304	2.3
	0924	8.3		0905	8.7
TH	1554	2.7	F	1533	2.3
	2146	7.8		2135	8.3
12	0403	3.3	**27**	0349	2.6
	1004	7.7		0953	8.4
F	1636	3.2	SA	1622	2.6
	2230	7.2		2226	7.9
13	0448	3.8	**28**	0442	3.0
	1053	7.2		1049	8.1
SA	1729	3.7	SU	1721	2.9
	☾ 2326	6.8		☾ 2327	7.7
14	0550	4.2	**29**	0548	3.2
	1159	6.9		1154	7.8
SU	1835	3.9	M	1831	3.0
15	0043	6.6	**30**	0039	7.6
	0707	4.2		0705	3.3
M	1320	6.8	TU	1309	7.8
	1948	3.9		1947	3.0

DECEMBER

	Time	m		Time	m
1	0157	7.7	**16**	0148	6.9
	0823	3.1		0812	3.9
W	1423	7.9	TH	1421	7.0
	2059	2.7		2042	3.6
2	0306	8.0	**17**	0255	7.2
	0932	2.7		0917	3.6
TH	1530	8.2	F	1523	7.3
	2202	2.4		2141	3.3
3	0405	8.4	**18**	0351	7.6
	1031	2.3		1013	3.2
F	1628	8.5	SA	1616	7.7
	2257	2.1		2234	2.9
4	0457	8.8	**19**	0439	8.0
	1124	1.9		1103	2.7
SA	1721	8.8	SU	1705	8.1
	2347	1.9		2322	2.5
5	0545	9.1	**20**	0525	8.4
	1213	1.7		1150	2.3
SU	1810	8.9	M	1751	8.4
●					
6	0034	1.7	**21**	0008	2.2
	0630	9.2		0608	8.8
M	1300	1.5	TU	1237	1.9
	1855	9.0		○ 1836	8.7
7	0118	1.7	**22**	0053	1.9
	0713	9.3		0651	9.1
TU	1343	1.6	W	1322	1.6
	1937	8.9		1920	8.9
8	0158	1.9	**23**	0137	1.7
	0753	9.1		0735	9.3
W	1423	1.7	TH	1406	1.5
	2017	8.7		2003	9.0
9	0235	2.1	**24**	0220	1.6
	0831	8.9		0818	9.3
TH	1501	2.0	F	1449	1.4
	2053	8.4		2046	9.0
10	0310	2.5	**25**	0303	1.7
	0907	8.5		0901	9.2
F	1537	2.4	SA	1532	1.6
	2129	8.0		2130	8.8
11	0344	2.9	**26**	0347	1.9
	0943	8.1		0947	9.0
SA	1612	2.8	SU	1617	1.8
	2205	7.7		2216	8.5
12	0419	3.3	**27**	0433	2.3
	1021	7.7		1035	8.6
SU	1651	3.2	M	1705	2.2
	2245	7.3		2305	8.1
13	0501	3.6	**28**	0525	2.7
	1106	7.3		1129	8.2
M	1736	3.5	TU	1759	2.6
	☾ 2334	7.0		☾	
14	0555	3.9	**29**	0004	7.8
	1201	7.0		0627	3.0
TU	1832	3.7	W	1233	7.8
				1904	3.0
15	0035	6.8	**30**	0114	7.5
	0701	4.0		0742	3.2
W	1310	6.9	TH	1347	7.5
	1936	3.8		2021	3.1
			31	0233	7.5
				0903	3.1
			F	1505	7.6
				2137	3.0

Chart Datum is 5·06 metres below Ordnance Datum (Local). HAT is 10·3 metres above Chart Datum; see 4.5.

Channel Islands

9.19.12 HERM
49°28´·22N 02°27´·26W ✦✦✦✧✧✧

SHELTER Good shelter E or W of island depending on winds.

NAVIGATION Access is not difficult, if properly planned. Herm is reached from the Little Russel Channel via any of 7 passages all of which require reasonable visibility and care with tidal streams. AC 807 & 808 list the marks and bearings of all the passages.

The Alligande Passage is the simplest and most direct from St Peter Port. Approach with the Vermerette bcn (topmark 'V') in transit 074° with W patch on Hbr quay. Leave Alligande 'A', Godfrey 'GB' and Epec 'E' bcns to starboard; skirt close N of Vermerette. When its base is awash, there is 1m at hbr ent. The tide will be setting N. Sand build-up W of Vermerette affects craft NW-bound in the Percée Passage. Hbr access HW±2½.

The appr from the Big Russel is more open and leads easily to pleasant ⚓s at Belvoir Bay and Shell Bay.

LIGHTS AND MARKS Ldg lts, both FW (occas) and W drums at 078°. 2FG (vert) on quay hd. Night appr not advised for visitors.

TELEPHONE Island Admin ☎ 722377 for overnight stay in hbr.

FACILITIES
Herm Harbour, options:
- Lie to mooring lines secured to N and S walls inside hbr.
- Dry out on the beach to the E, moored fore/aft to chains.
- 5 ⚓s to N and 6 to W of hbr dry out; 6 more to NW: rky bottom to the N; isolated boulders/sand to W.

www.herm-island.com for navigation details and webcams of hbr & buoys. No fees; donations welcome. Showers, FW, Bar, R, limited 🛒. Can be busy at summer weekends, better mid-week.

HERM HARBOUR
Sketch not to scale
Consult Admiralty chart 808

Rosière Steps ⚓ 49°28´·22N 02°27´·22W NW of Rosière steps; good holding on sand, but exposed to S and SW. Access for landing only; do not linger alongside. Buoys are for ferries and Herm-owned boats only; hourly ferries by day. The bottom step is about 1.5m above the seabed which may be inconvenient at LWS. Caution: From just before HW to HW+2 tide sets hard onto the steps. Easiest appr is from the Big Russel via Percée passage; avoid Fourquies (2₃, NCM lt buoy), Meulettes (1₇) and Tinker (2₇).

Belvoir Bay 49°28´·40N 02°26´·34W and **Shell Bay** are good ⚓s on sand, sheltered from W. Easy access from E; from S keep 400m offshore. Beach café or walk 800m to Harbour village. Note: Jethou, Crevichon and Grande Fauconnière are private. No landing.

9.19.13 SARK
Sark **49°25´·81N 02°20´·45W** Creux ✦✦✦✧✧✧

CHARTS AC 808, 5604.12; SHOM 7159, 6904; Navi 1014; Imray C33A; Stanfords 2, 16, 26, 2500.3

TIDES –0450 Dover; ML 5·3; Duration 0550
Standard Port ST HELIER (→)

Times				Height (metres)			
High Water		Low Water		MHWS	MHWN	MLWN	MLWS
0300	0900	0200	0900	11·0	8·1	4·0	1·4
1500	2100	1400	2100				
Differences SARK (MASELINE PIER)							
+0005	+0015	+0005	+0010	–2·1	–1·5	–0·6	–0·3

Tidal streams Beware large tidal range, strong streams and many lobster pots. In Gouliot (W coast) and Goulet Passages the streams reach 6-7kn at springs. Note that at about half-tide the streams are slack around Sark. At HW the stream sets hard to the N, ie onto Little Sark. At LW the stream sets hard to the S, ie onto Bec du Nez (N tip). If bound from Guernsey to Sark's E coast, go N-about at HW and S-about at LW; conversely on the return.

SHELTER Sark is fringed by rocks, but the centres of the bays are mainly clear of dangers. A safe ⚓age or ⚓s can usually be found sheltered from offshore winds. But, depending on wind and tide, they may be uncomfortable, except in settled weather; see also Facilities.

NAVIGATION From the West, WPT 49°25´·27N 02°24´·30W, 070°/1·29M towards the Pilcher monument (Sark mill is obsc'd by trees) for Havre Gosselin or La Grande Grève.
From the N or after rounding Bec du Nez, the WPT is 49°27´·30N 02°21´·42W, on the 153° charted transit (aka the outside passage) towards Grève de la Ville and Maseline. The inside passage, W of drying Pécheresse, is used by locals but ill advised for visitors.

LIGHTS AND MARKS Point Robert lt ho and Courbée du Nez are the only navigational lights on Sark; see chartlet and 9.19.4.

R/T Maseline Hbr Ch 13, season only. Water taxi Ch 10 from ⚓s.

TELEPHONE (Code 01481) HM 832323; ⊖ (Guernsey) 726911; Marinecall 09068 969656; Police (Guernsey) 725111; Dr 832045.

ANCHORAGES, ⚓s, HARBOURS AND FACILITIES
Anti-clockwise from Bec du Nez, the ⚓s below (all unlit) are safe in off-shore winds; in other conditions they can be exposed and sometimes dangerous. Some are only suitable around LW.

For ⚓s at Havre Gosselin, Port Gorey and Grève de la Ville call ☎ 832260, mobile 07781 106065: £14/night. Water taxi Ch 10. All other moorings are private; use only in emergency.

WEST COAST (all ⚓s are exposed to W'lies)
Saignie Bay 49°26´·53N 02°22´·10W. Sand and shingle with fair holding. Picturesque rock formations.

Port à la Jument 49°26´·17N 02°22´·42W. Sand and shingle with fair holding. Difficult shore access.

Brecqhou Island is strictly private; landing prohibited.

Havre Gosselin 49°25´·77N 02°22´·68W. Popular deep (4-9m) ⚓. 20 Y ⚓'s (see above). Beware of drying rk at extreme NW of bay. Crowded in summer. 299 steps to cliff top and panoramic views.

Port és Saies 49°25´·41N 02°22´·28W. Sandy inlet, steep cliff path.

La Grande Grève 49°25´·38N 02°22´·59W. Wide sandy bay, subject to swell, but popular day ⚓. Beware two rks (drying 0·3m and ⊛) in the appr. Many steps to cliff-top and panoramic views.

LITTLE SARK
Port Gorey 49°24´·60N 02°22´·72W. ⚓ or pick up Y ⚓ in centre of deep, weedy bay over LW only; heavy swell begins near half-flood. Rocky appr from just NW of Grande Bretagne (18m high) then 045° into bay. Rocks must be positively identified. Remains of quay with ladder. Cliff walk past silver mine ruins to hotel.

Rouge Terrier 49°24´·78N 02°21´·87W. Sandy with some local moorings under high cliffs. Exposed to E. Landing with cliff path to hotel. Also ⚓ 49°25´·09N 02°21´·70W, 4ca NNE in Baleine Bay.

EAST COAST

Dixcart Bay 49°25′·33N 02°21′·48W. Popular sandy bay with good holding, but open to S'lies. Drying rocks either side of the bay but not in the centre. Cliff path and walk to hotels.

Derrible Bay 49°25′·41N 02°21′·07W. Sandy bay with good holding. Open to the S. No dangers in the bay, but keep off SW tip of Derrible Pt. Picturesque caves and steep climb ashore.

Creux Harbour 49°25′·80N 02°20′·61W dries completely, prone to surge/swell. In fair weather access approx HW ±2. Local transits: Pinnacle Rk on with E edge of Grand Moie 001°; or Creux tunnel (white arch) on with Pt Robert lt ho 344°. The lt ho dips behind the cliffs when close inshore. In the Goulet Passage (E of Creux) S-bound navigation is prohibited to commercial vessels (except with HM's permission), but not to yachts in either direction.

Dry out bow to NE wall, stern to ⚓. AB possible only at inner part of the S pier, clear of steps and cargo berth at outer end. ☎ 832025

(kiosk), Slip, M (free), L, FW, P & D (cans) via HM; walk or tractor up steep hill to **Village**: P & D (cans), Gas, Gaz, Kos, 🛒, R, Bar, ✉, Ⓑ. Bikes and horse-drawn carriages for hire.

Maseline Harbour 49°25′·96N 02°20′·60W is prone to surge/swell. Busy ferry hbr with no yacht berths (except to land people). Call HM Ch 13 for approval to ⚓. Moorings are private. ☎ 832070 (kiosk), M (free), C (3 ton). Condor catamaran to Jersey/St Malo.

Grève de la Ville 49°26′·35N 02°21′·06W. ⚓ close in out of tide. Fair holding sand/shingle. Open to E. 20 Y ⚓'s (see above). Easy walk ashore.

Les Fontaines 49°26′·78N 02°21′·62W. Sand and shingle with fair holding. Reef drying 4·5m extends 1ca N from shore. ⚓ between reef and Eperquerie headland. Exposed to the E.

With grateful acknowledgements to John Frankland, author of *Sark, a Yachtsman's Guide* (2005 edition).

JERSEY

▶*The rotary pattern of tidal streams affecting the Channel Islands as a whole dictates that when streams are slack on the N and S coasts of Jersey, they are running strongly on the E and W coasts; and vice versa. If approaching Jersey from Guernsey/Alderney at HW St Helier +4, a fair tide can be carried for at least 6 hrs down the W coast and along the S coast to St Helier. From the S, leave St Malo at about HW, keeping E of the Minquiers, in order to carry a fair tide for 6 hrs to St Helier. Follow similar tidal tactics when coasting around the island.*◀

To N and NE of Jersey, Les Pierres de Lecq (Paternosters), Les Dirouilles and Les Écrehou are groups of islets and drying rks, 2–4M offshore (AC *3655*, 1136, *1137*, 1138).

From the N, a convenient landfall is Desormes WCM buoy, 4M NNW of Grosnez Pt (conspic lookout tr). On the N coast several bays offer anchs sheltered in offshore winds.

In St Ouen Bay on the W coast, which has drying rks almost 1M offshore, there are no good anchorages except NW of La Rocco tower which is sheltered in offshore winds.

Rounding the SW tip, to clear offlying dangers by 1M, keep the top of La Corbière lt ho (conspic) level with or below the FR lt on the clifftops behind. The inshore Boat Passage over the drying causeway between Jersey and Corbière lt ho is not advised. La Frouquie rock (9.8m) is marked by a WCM buoy.

Along the S coast the **NW and W Passages** (buoyed) lead E past Noirmont Pt towards St Helier. St Brelade and St Aubin Bays provide some shelter from W'lies.

From the SW and S St Helier can be approached via **Danger Rock Passage** or **Red & Green Passage**. Both require good visibility to identify the transit marks and care to maintain the transits exactly. Only the Red & Green Passage is lit, but it needs sufficient water to pass over Fairway Rk (1.2m). Although charted, the marks for the South Passage 341° are hard to see.

Elizabeth marina at St Helier can be entered either from the R & G Passage or, with sufficient rise of tide, from St Aubin Bay. The latter appr on 106° passes N of Elizabeth Castle, crossing the causeway which dries approx 5.3m. It is well marked/lit and is the preferred option (to keep Small Road clear).

SE of St Helier the drying, rocky Violet Bank extends 1M S to Demie de Pas lt bcn, thence E past Icho Twr (conspic). It extends 1.7M S and 2M SE of La Rocque Pt. Further rky plateaux extend 1M offshore. The **Violet Channel** (AC 1138), although buoyed, is best avoided in bad weather, wind-over-tide or poor vis. From St Helier make good Canger Rk WCM lt buoy, thence track 078° for 2.2M to Violet SWM lt buoy.

Turn N to pick up the charted ldg lines towards Gorey (dries) or to St Catherine Bay, both popular hbrs. The safe width of Violet Chan is only 5ca in places. The E coast of Jersey is well sheltered from W'lies, but requires careful pilotage.

If bound for the adjacent French coast, proceed NE from Violet buoy via the **Anquette Channel**, between Petite and Grande Anquette bcns. See Area 18 for Passage de la Déroute.

Les Minquiers, an extensive rocky plateau 10–18M S of St Helier, can be left to port, ie via NW and SW Minquiers buoys, if making for St Malo; or to stbd via NE and SE Minquiers buoys. A more direct route via N and SE Minquiers buoys requires sufficient height of tide to clear rocks drying 2m in the northern part. For a first visit the plateau should only be entered in settled weather, with exquisite care and a good Pilot book – not to mention *The Wreck of the Mary Deare* by Hammond Innes. The anchorage off Maîtresse Île is the principal attraction. From Jersey approach via the Demie de Vascelin SHM buoy with bcns in transit 167°. See 9.19.14.

9.19.14 ST HELIER

Jersey 49°10'·57N 02°06'·98W ✿✿✿✿◊◊◊✿✿

CHARTS AC 3655, 1137, 3278, 5604.14/15; SHOM 7160, 7161, 6938; Navi 534, 1014; Imray C33B; Stanfords 2, 16, 26, 2500.4, .5

TIDES –0455 Dover; ML 6·1; Duration 0545. St Helier is a Standard Port (⟶). The tidal range is very large, 9·6m at springs.

SHELTER Excellent in 2 marinas and La Collette basin (no ⊗).

NAVIGATION WPT (where all apprs converge) 49°09'·95N 02°07'·38W, 023°/0·74M to front 023° ldg lt. WPT is near the centre of a Precautionary Area extending up-hbr to the ferry terminal. Caution: Rule 9 (narrow channels) applies. ⚓ in Small Road is not encouraged. Speed limit 5kn N of La Collette Yacht Basin. Approach channels:

- **W Passage** 082° ldg lts and Dog's Nest Rock bcn (unlit W bcn with globe topmark) lead N of Les Fours and Ruaudière Rock SHM lt buoys, to WPT. Beware race off Noirmont Pt.
- **NW Passage** (095°/110°, much used by yachts) passes 6ca S of La Corbière lt ho to join W Passage abeam Noirmont Pt.
- **Danger Rock Passage** (044°) unlit; leads past rky, drying shoals; needs precision and good visibility.
- **Red & Green Passage** Ldg line 022·7° passes over Fairway Rk 1·2m, 8ca SSW of the WPT, with drying rocks either side; thence via Small Road to the ferry terminal, where daymarks are red dayglow patches on front dolphin and rear lt twr. The fairway's W side is beaconed and buoyed. Outer pier hds and dolphin are painted white and floodlit.
- **S Passage** (341°), unlit marks are hard to see. Demie de Pas in transit 350° with floodlit power stn chy is easier to see D/N.
- **E Passage** 290° from Canger Rock WCM lt buoy passes close SW of Demie de Pas, B tr/Y top (at night stay in W sector); thence 314° past Hinguette buoy and 341° to the WPT.

Other Passages Middle Passage, unlit, leads 339° towards St Aubin Hbr. Violet Channel skirts round SE tip of Jersey to/from the N and would normally link to the E Passage to/from St Helier. Caution: many offlying reefs.

LIGHTS AND MARKS See chartlet and 9.19.4 for lights. Power station chy (95m, floodlit), Sig mast, W concave roofs of Fort Regent and Elizabeth Castle are conspic in the harbour area.

IPTS Sigs 1-4 are shown from the Port Control tower and are easily seen from Small Road and the Main Hbr. An Oc Y 4s, shown above Sigs 1-4, exempts power-driven craft <25m LOA from the main signals. All leisure craft should: *Keep to starboard, well clear of shipping; maintain a sharp all-round lookout and monitor VHF Ch 14 during arrival/departure.*
Sig 2 is also shown when vessels depart the Tanker Basin. Departing tankers, which can be hidden at LW, sound a long blast if small craft are approaching.

R/T Monitor *St Helier Port Control* Ch 14 (H24) for ferry/shipping movements. No marina VHF, but call *Port Control* if essential. Do not use Ch M. If unable to pass messages to *Port Control*, these can be relayed via *Jersey Coastguard*, Ch 82, 25[1], 16 (H24) or ☎ 885505, [1]available for link calls by charge card.

St Helier Pierheads on Ch 18 broadcasts recorded wind direction, speed and gusts meaned over the last 2 minutes.

TELEPHONE (Code 01534) Port HM 447788; ⊖ 448000; Marine leisure centre (enquiries) 447708; Jersey Coastguard 447705; Marinecall 09068 969656; Police 612612; Dr 835742 and 853178; Ⓗ 622000.

FACILITIES Hbrs Dept ☎ 447708 or 447788. FW, C (32 ton), Slip, Grids. www.jersey-harbours.com jerseyharbours@gov.je

Fuel (D & P) by hose from: the ent (HW ±4; 07797 718310) to La Collette; a fuel barge (H24; 711000) by ent to Old Hbr; Elizabeth marina (HW ±3; 888100). (The fuel berth at S Pier is no more.)

La Collette Basin, good shelter in 1·8m. Access H24. Caution: Ent narrow at LWS; keep close to W side; PHM buoys mark shoal on E side. 130 AB only for locals and FVs, ie no ⊗ berths. ☎ 447729; access H24. P&D HW ±4, BH (65, 15 ton, ☎ 447773), Slip.

St Helier YC ☎ 721307, R, Bar.
Continued overleaf

St Helier Marina ☎ 447708. Access HW±3 over sill drying 3·6m; hinged gate rises 1·4m above sill to retain 5m. Digital gauge shows depth when more than 2·2m over sill. Adjacent IPTS then control ent/exit. A 150m long waiting pontoon is SW of marina ent, with FW & AC; rafting and overnight stays are permitted.

Ⓥ berths: yachts >12m LOA or >2·1m draft, use pontoon A. Smaller craft on fingers N side of D and on E in 2m; or rafted alongside F & G pontoons in 2m; or as directed, £2·13. CH, ME, El, Ⓔ, ✗, SM, Grid, Gas, Gaz, ▨, ⬚. s.marina@gov.je

Elizabeth Marina. Preferred appr, when height of tide >7m, is from the W on 106°. Ldg marks, just S of ent, are orange ☐s with B vert line; at night stay in the W sector of Dir lt at front daymark. Pass S of La Vrachère IDM lt bn, cross the causeway 5·3m, turn ENE then NNE into the ent.

The secondary appr chan 338° from Small Road (ie N of No 4 PHM buoy) is marked by 3 pairs of PHM and SHM buoys, 1st and 3rd pairs are lit. 5 Y can waiting buoys in about 1·0m are outboard of the lateral buoys (3 to the W, 2 to the E).

The marina is mainly for local boats, also large visiting yachts by prior arrangement. Access HW±3 over sill/flapgate; max LOA 20m, drafts 2·1–3·5m. At ent a digital gauge reads depth over sill. IPTS (sigs 2 & 3) control one-way ent/exit, usually 10 mins in each direction. ☎ 447730. 564 AB; D & P (H24), ⛽.

Town CH, ⬚, R, Bar, ✉, Ⓑ, ✈. Fast ferries (Mar-Nov): Portsmouth, Poole, Weymouth, St Malo, Granville, Sark, Guernsey. Ro Ro Ferry: Portsmouth.

OTHER HARBOURS AND ANCHORAGES AROUND JERSEY
The main hbrs and ⚓s, clockwise from St Helier, are:
SOUTH COAST
St Aubin 49°11'·21N 02°10'·02W. Access HW ±1. From seaward Middle Passage (339°, Mon Plaisir Ho ≠ twr on St Aubin Fort) leads towards St Aubin Fort. Final appr with N pier head bearing 254° lies N of St Aubin Fort; at night in W sector of the pier head lt – see chartlet and 9.19.4. Castle pier head is also lit. Beware very strong tidal streams in ent during full flood. Dry out alongside N pier or on wide grid. With offshore winds, quiet ⚓ in bay (partly dries). Hbr is administered by St Helier. Facilities: AB, FW, Slip, C (1 and 5 ton), Grid. **Royal Channel Islands YC** ☎ 741023, Bar, R, M, Slip. **Town** Bar, ▨, P, R, ⬚, bus to St Helier.

Belcroute Bay 49°10'·43N 02°09'·60W. Excellent shelter from W/

SW'lies, but dries 3·5m and many moorings; ⚓ off Pt de Bût in 2·7m. Platte and Grosse Rks are marked by poles.

Portelet Bay 49°10'·13N 02°10'·61W. W of Noirmont Pt. Good ⚓ in N'lies, either side of Janvrin Twr.

St Brelade Bay 49°10'·64N 02°11'·84W. Good shelter from N and W, but open to SW'ly swell. Beware many drying rks, especially Fournier Rk (0·9m) and Fourché (3·4m) in centre. A quiet ⚓ is in Beau Port. Bouilly Port in NW corner has local moorings and a small stone jetty. Very popular sandy tourist beach with hotels.

NORTH COAST
Grève au Lancon 49°15'·50N 02°14'·07W. Between Grosnez Pt's squat lt ho and Plemont Pt (conspic hotel), a wide, part-drying sandy bay, suitable for short stay on calm days. Open to swell.
Grève de Lecq 49°14'·98N 02°12'·12W. Ldg line 202°: W Martello

tr on with W hotel with grey roof. ⚓ in 5m N of pier and W of submarine cables. Exposed to swell. Pub, and bus to St Helier.
Bonne Nuit Bay 49°15'·19N 02°07'·09W. To the NNW beware Demie Rk (5·2m; SHM buoy); and to the E Les Sambues 5·5m. Conspic TV mast (232m) is ½M W of the bay. Ldg lts 223°. ⚓ in 5m NNE of pier and W of Chevel Rk. Hbr dries to sand/shingle. Many local moorings. Hotel.
Bouley Bay 49°14'·50N 02°04'·70W. Good ⚓ on sand in 2·5m SE of pier (rocky footings). Exposed to NE. Local moorings. Hotel.
Rozel Bay 49°14'·25N 02°02'·43W. Appr with pierhead brg 245°, in W sector of Dir lt on shore. Conspic bldg close N on Nez du Guet. Pass between pierhead and WCM bn. Hbr, dries 1·5m to sand/shingle, and is full of moorings; ⚓ outside in 4-5m S of appr. Shops and pubs, bus to St Helier.

EAST COAST
St Catherine Bay 49°13'·30N 02°00'·90W. Local moorings off W end of Verclut bkwtr. Clear the bkwtr hd by at least 50m due to strong tidal streams and the new rock armour extending 15m seaward. ⚓ S of bkwtr in 3–7m, but not in S/SE winds. Land on slip at root of bkwtr. Beware rocky St Catherine Bank, 3·1m (ECM bcn) and submarine cables to the S. Dinghy SC, RNLI ILB, café.

Gorey. See 9.19.15 below.

La Rocque 49°09'·80N 02°01'·88W. Small hbr dries 6·5m–9·6m; bkwtr, local moorings, sandy beach, slip. Appr 330° across Violet Bank requires detailed local knowledge. No facilities.

OFFLYING ISLANDS
Les Écrehou 49°17'·39N 01°55'·58W (States 🏴). AC 3655, 5604.15; SHOM 6937 (1:25,000). 5M NE of Rozel Bay, has about 12 cottages. ML 6·2m. Arrive at about ½ tide ebbing; see 9.19.15. Appr with Bigorne Rk on 022°; when SE of Maître Ile alter to 330° for FS on Marmotière Is. Beware of strong and eddying tidal streams 4–8kn. No lts. Pick up 🏴 close SE of Marmotière or ⚓ in a pool 3ca WSW of Marmotière (with houses); other islands are Maître Ile (one house), Blanche and 5 other small islets. Local knowledge or a detailed pilotage book is essential.

Plateau des Minquiers 48°58'·04N 02°03'·74W. AC 5604.17 (1:25,000); 3656 and SHOM 7161 are both 1:50,000. About 12M S of Jersey, encircled by six cardinal light buoys. See 9.19.15 for tides. ML 6·4m. Beware of strong and eddying tidal streams. Appr by day in good vis from Demie de Vascelin SHM buoy, 49°00'·81N 02°05'·15W, on 161°: Jetée des Fontaines RW bn in transit with FS on Maîtresse Ile. Further transits skirt the W side of the islet to ⚓ due S of it; safe only in settled weather and light winds. Maîtresse Ile has about a dozen cottages. Land at the slipway NW of the States of Jersey 🏴. Without local knowledge a detailed pilotage book is essential.

9.19.15 GOREY
Jersey 49°11'·78N 02°01'·37W ✿✿◊◊✿✿✿

CHARTS AC 3655, 5604./16, 1138; SHOM 7157, 7160, 6939; Navi 534, 1014; Imray C33B; Stanfords 2, 16, 26, 2500.4, .5

TIDES –0454 Dover; ML 6·0; Duration 0545 Note the very large tidal range.

Standard Port ST HELIER (→)

Times				Height (metres)			
High Water		Low Water		MHWS	MHWN	MLWN	MLWS
0300	0900	0200	0900	11·0	8·1	4·0	1·4
1500	2100	1400	2100				
Differences ST CATHERINE BAY							
0000	+0010	+0010	+0010	0·0	–0·1	0·0	+0·1
BOULEY BAY							
+0002	+0002	+0004	+0004	–0·3	–0·3	–0·1	–0·1
LES ECREHOU							
+0005	+0009	+0011	+0009	–0·2	+0·1	–0·2	0·0
LES MINQUIERS							
–0014	–0018	–0001	–0008	+0·5	+0·6	+0·1	+0·1

SHELTER Good in the hbr, except in S/SE winds. ⚓ about 2ca E of pier hd or in deeper water in the Roads.

ST HELIER

MEAN SPRING ——————
AND NEAP CURVES – – – – –

MEAN RANGES
Springs 9.6m
Neaps 4.1m

Springs occur 2 days
after
New and Full Moon

CHART DATUM

Factor

H.W.Hts.m.

M.H.W.N.

M.H.W.S.

M.L.W.N.

M.L.W.S.

L.W.Hts.m.

1935 2055 2135 2235 2335 0035

NAVIGATION WPT 49°11'·18N 01°59'·59W, 298°/1·3M to pier hd/front ldg lt. On appr, keep well outside all local bcns until the ldg marks are identified, but beware Banc du Chateau (0·4m least depth), 1M offshore NE of 298° ldg line; and Azicot Rk (dries 2·2m) just S of 298° ldg line, 2ca from ent. There are at least 3 approaches:

- Dir lt 298°: Gorey pierhead, W framework twr; rear ldg mark House (west gable end). Best for visitors.
- Pierhead ≠ ⊞ spire 304° (line between R & G sectors) leads close to Road Rk (3·3m) and over Azicot Rk (2·2m).
- Pierhead ≠ white house/R roof 250° leads close to Les Arch bn (B/W with A topmark) and Pacquet Rk (0·3m).

See 9.19.5 for the Violet Chan to St Helier. The Gutters and Boat Passage across Violet Bank are not advised.

LIGHTS AND MARKS See chartlet and 9.19.4. Mont Orgueil Castle (67m) is highly conspic.

R/T *Gorey Hbr* Ch 74; not permanently manned. Call *Jersey Radio* Ch 82 for info.

TELEPHONE (Code 01534) ⊖ 833833; Marinecall 09068 969656; for Dr contact HM St Helier 447788.

FACILITIES Hbr dries completely to 6·9m. Access HW±3. 12 drying ⚓s are 150m W of pier hd. 4 drying berths against pierhead. HM☎ 447788 (Jersey Harbours) or 447708. M, AB free. P & D HW ±3 by hose at pierhead. FW, C (7 ton), ME, El, Gas. **Town** CH, ⛽, ▯, R, Bar, ⊠, Ⓑ, bus to St Helier. Ferry (Mar-Nov) to Portbail, Carteret.

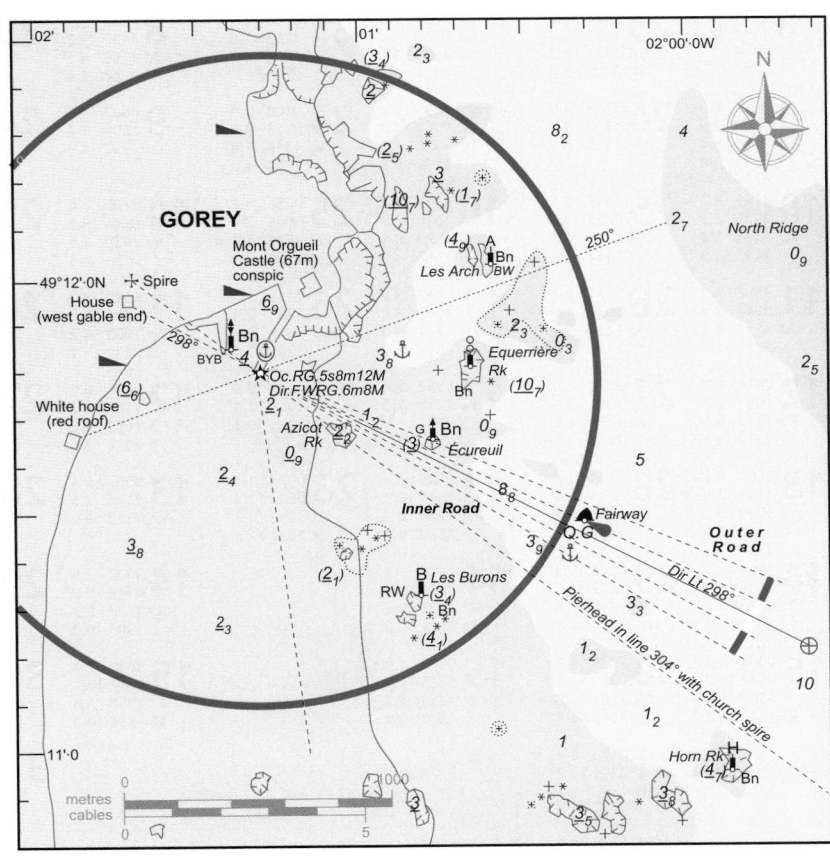

GOREY

Mont Orgueil
Castle (67m)
conspic

House ▯
(west gable end)

White house
(red roof)

Azicot
Rk

Les Arch

North Ridge

Equerrière
Rk

Inner Road

Les Burons

Fairway

Outer
Road

Dir LL 298°

Pierhead in line 304° with church spire

Horn Rk

Oc.RG.5s8m12M
Dir.F.WRG.6m8M

ST HELIER LAT 49°11′N LONG 2°07′W

TIMES AND HEIGHTS OF HIGH AND LOW WATERS

Dates in red are **SPRINGS**
Dates in blue are **NEAPS**

YEAR 2010

JANUARY

Time	m		Time	m
1 0046	1.7	**16** 0121	2.3
0626	11.0	0751	10.2
F 1316	1.3	SA 1342	2.1
1858	10.9	1922	10.0
2 0137	1.4	**17** 0154	2.2
0715	11.3	0734	10.3
SA 1406	1.0	SU 1414	2.0
1947	11.1	1953	10.1
3 0225	1.2	**18** 0224	2.2
0803	11.5	0805	10.3
SU 1454	0.9	M 1444	2.0
2033	11.1	2022	10.0
4 0311	1.2	**19** 0253	2.2
0849	11.4	0835	10.2
M 1540	1.0	TU 1513	2.1
2118	10.9	2051	9.9
5 0356	1.4	**20** 0321	2.4
0933	11.1	0904	10.0
TU 1623	1.4	W 1541	2.4
2201	10.4	2120	9.7
6 0439	1.9	**21** 0350	2.7
1016	10.5	0932	9.6
W 1706	2.0	TH 1611	2.7
2244	9.8	2150	9.3
7 0522	2.5	**22** 0420	3.1
1100	9.8	1003	9.2
TH 1750	2.7	F 1642	3.2
◗ 2331	9.2	2223	8.9
8 0611	3.1	**23** 0455	3.6
1151	9.0	1041	8.7
F 1841	3.3	SA 1721	3.7
		◖ 2307	8.4
9 0027	8.6	**24** 0543	4.0
0710	3.6	1135	8.2
SA 1256	8.4	SU 1818	4.1
1947	3.8		
10 0141	8.3	**25** 0013	8.1
0826	3.9	0657	4.2
SU 1417	8.2	M 1257	7.9
2105	3.9	1944	4.0
11 0302	8.4	**26** 0144	8.1
0944	3.7	0835	4.0
M 1537	8.3	TU 1434	8.2
2218	3.7	2119	3.8
12 0410	8.8	**27** 0312	8.6
1051	3.3	1001	3.4
TU 1641	8.8	W 1557	8.9
2317	3.3	2235	3.0
13 0504	9.3	**28** 0424	9.5
1144	2.9	1111	2.5
W 1730	9.2	TH 1703	9.7
		2339	2.2
14 0005	2.9	**29** 0524	10.3
0548	9.7	1212	1.7
TH 1229	2.5	F 1759	10.5
1812	9.6		
15 0045	2.6	**30** 0035	1.5
0627	10.0	0617	11.1
F 1307	2.2	SA 1307	1.0
● 1848	9.8	○ 1849	11.1
		31 0128	0.9
		0706	11.7
		SU 1358	0.5
		1935	11.5

FEBRUARY

Time	m		Time	m
1 0215	0.6	**16** 0206	1.8
0751	12.0	0744	10.6
M 1443	0.3	TU 1424	1.6
2018	11.6	1959	10.4
2 0259	0.5	**17** 0234	1.8
0833	11.9	0812	10.6
TU 1524	0.5	W 1451	1.7
2058	11.4	2026	10.4
3 0339	0.8	**18** 0301	1.9
0913	11.5	0840	10.4
W 1602	1.0	TH 1518	1.9
2136	10.9	2053	10.2
4 0416	1.4	**19** 0328	2.2
0950	10.8	0906	10.1
TH 1637	1.7	F 1544	2.3
2212	10.1	2120	9.8
5 0451	2.2	**20** 0355	2.6
1027	9.9	0934	9.6
F 1710	2.6	SA 1612	2.8
◗ 2249	9.3	2149	9.3
6 0528	3.1	**21** 0425	3.2
1107	8.9	1007	9.0
SA 1749	3.5	SU 1646	3.4
2335	8.5	2228	8.7
7 0617	3.9	**22** 0507	3.7
1203	8.0	1055	8.3
SU 1847	4.3	M 1736	4.0
		◗ 2328	8.2
8 0047	7.8	**23** 0616	4.1
0736	4.4	1218	7.8
M 1336	7.5	TU 1904	4.3
2024	4.6		
9 0231	7.8	**24** 0108	7.9
0917	4.3	0805	4.1
TU 1520	7.7	W 1416	7.9
2159	4.2	2056	4.0
10 0354	8.3	**25** 0256	8.4
1036	3.7	0945	3.4
W 1629	8.4	TH 1548	8.7
2304	3.5	2220	3.1
11 0449	8.9	**26** 0413	9.4
1130	3.0	1058	2.4
TH 1717	9.0	F 1652	9.7
2350	2.9	2325	2.1
12 0533	9.6	**27** 0512	10.4
1212	2.5	1158	1.4
F 1756	9.5	SA 1745	10.7
13 0029	2.5	**28** 0021	1.3
0610	10.0	0603	11.3
SA 1250	2.1	SU 1252	0.7
1830	9.9	○ 1832	11.3
14 0105	2.1		
0644	10.3		
SU 1324	1.8		
● 1902	10.2		
15 0137	1.9		
0715	10.5		
M 1355	1.7		
1931	10.4		

MARCH

Time	m		Time	m
1 0111	0.6	**16** 0111	1.8
0649	11.9	0648	10.5
M 1339	0.3	TU 1329	1.6
1915	11.7	1903	10.5
2 0157	0.3	**17** 0142	1.6
0732	12.1	0718	10.7
TU 1422	0.1	W 1359	1.5
1956	11.8	1932	10.6
3 0238	0.3	**18** 0211	1.6
0811	12.0	0747	10.7
W 1500	0.4	TH 1427	1.5
2033	11.6	2000	10.6
4 0315	0.6	**19** 0239	1.7
0848	11.5	0816	10.6
TH 1535	1.0	F 1454	1.7
2107	11.0	2028	10.4
5 0348	1.3	**20** 0307	1.9
0923	10.7	0844	10.2
F 1605	1.8	SA 1522	2.1
2140	10.2	2056	10.1
6 0420	2.2	**21** 0336	2.4
0955	9.7	0914	9.7
SA 1633	2.8	SU 1552	2.7
2212	9.3	2127	9.5
7 0451	3.1	**22** 0409	2.9
1031	8.7	0950	9.0
SU 1704	3.7	M 1628	3.3
◗ 2251	8.4	2208	8.9
8 0533	3.9	**23** 0453	3.5
1120	7.8	1041	8.3
M 1753	4.5	TU 1721	3.9
2358	7.6	◗ 2311	8.3
9 0647	4.6	**24** 0604	3.9
1259	7.2	1210	7.8
TU 1937	4.9	W 1851	4.2
10 0200	7.4	**25** 0055	8.0
0844	4.5	0751	3.9
W 1458	7.5	TH 1407	8.0
2133	4.4	2040	3.8
11 0329	8.0	**26** 0241	8.5
1009	3.9	0927	3.2
TH 1605	8.2	F 1532	8.9
2239	3.7	2201	2.9
12 0425	8.7	**27** 0355	9.5
1102	3.2	1038	2.2
F 1651	8.9	SA 1633	9.8
2324	3.0	2304	2.0
13 0507	9.4	**28** 0452	10.4
1144	2.5	1136	1.4
SA 1729	9.5	SU 1724	10.7
		2358	1.2
14 0002	2.5	**29** 0541	11.2
0543	9.9	1227	0.8
SU 1222	2.1	M 1809	11.3
1803	10.0		
15 0038	2.1	**30** 0047	0.7
0617	10.3	0626	11.6
M 1256	1.8	TU 1314	0.5
● 1834	10.3	○ 1851	11.6
		31 0132	0.5
		0708	11.8
		W 1355	0.5
		1930	11.6

APRIL

Time	m		Time	m
1 0212	0.6	**16** 0147	1.6
0747	11.6	0722	10.6
TH 1432	0.8	F 1402	1.6
2006	11.4	1935	10.7
2 0248	0.9	**17** 0218	1.6
0823	11.1	0755	10.5
F 1505	1.3	SA 1433	1.7
2039	10.8	2007	10.6
3 0321	1.5	**18** 0250	1.8
0857	10.4	0829	10.2
SA 1535	2.1	SU 1506	2.1
2111	10.1	2042	10.2
4 0352	2.3	**19** 0325	2.2
0929	9.5	0906	9.7
SU 1603	2.9	M 1541	2.6
2143	9.3	2120	9.7
5 0424	3.1	**20** 0404	2.7
1004	8.6	0950	9.1
M 1634	3.7	TU 1624	3.1
2221	8.4	2208	9.1
6 0504	3.9	**21** 0455	3.2
1052	7.8	1050	8.5
TU 1720	4.4	W 1723	3.6
◗ 2322	7.7	◗ 2316	8.6
7 0608	4.4	**22** 0607	3.5
1220	7.3	1213	8.2
W 1845	4.9	TH 1846	3.8
8 0113	7.4	**23** 0046	8.5
0750	4.5	0738	3.5
TH 1411	7.4	F 1348	8.4
2039	4.6	2018	3.5
9 0245	7.8	**24** 0216	8.8
0919	4.0	0901	2.9
F 1522	8.0	SA 1504	9.1
2152	4.0	2133	2.8
10 0344	8.5	**25** 0326	9.5
1016	3.4	1008	2.2
SA 1610	8.7	SU 1604	9.8
2241	3.3	2235	2.1
11 0428	9.1	**26** 0424	10.2
1101	2.8	1106	1.7
SU 1650	9.3	M 1656	10.4
2323	2.7	2330	1.6
12 0507	9.6	**27** 0515	10.7
1142	2.3	1158	1.3
M 1726	9.8	TU 1742	10.9
13 0002	2.2	**28** 0020	1.2
0542	10.1	0600	11.0
TU 1214	1.9	W 1245	1.2
1759	10.2	○ 1824	11.1
14 0039	1.9	**29** 0106	1.1
0616	10.4	0643	11.1
W 1257	1.7	TH 1327	1.2
● 1831	10.5	1903	11.1
15 0114	1.7	**30** 0146	1.2
0649	10.6	0723	10.9
TH 1330	1.6	F 1405	1.4
1903	10.7	1940	10.9

Chart Datum is 5·88 metres below Ordnance Datum (Local). HAT is 12·2 metres above Chart Datum; see 4.5.

》》 FREE monthly updates from **《《**
www.reedsalmanac.co.uk

TIME ZONE (UT)
For Summer Time add ONE hour in **non-shaded areas**

ST HELIER LAT 49°11'N LONG 2°07'W
TIMES AND HEIGHTS OF HIGH AND LOW WATERS

Dates in red are SPRINGS
Dates in blue are NEAPS

YEAR 2010

MAY

Day	Time m	Time m	Time m	Time m
1 SA	0224 1.4	0800 10.5	1439 1.8	2015 10.5
2 SU	0258 1.8	0836 10.0	1516 2.4	2049 10.0
3 M	0331 2.4	0910 9.4	1541 3.0	2123 9.3
4 TU	0404 3.0	0947 8.7	1615 3.6	2202 8.7
5 W	0444 3.6	1033 8.1	1658 4.1	2254 8.1
6 TH	0536 4.1	1137 7.7	1800 4.5	◗
7 F	0012 7.7	0646 4.3	1302 7.6	1922 4.5
8 SA	0139 7.8	0806 4.1	1418 7.9	2043 4.2
9 SU	0246 8.2	0914 3.7	1515 8.4	2144 3.7
10 M	0337 8.7	1008 3.2	1601 9.0	2234 3.1
11 TU	0422 9.2	1056 2.7	1642 9.5	2319 2.6
12 W	0503 9.7	1140 2.3	1721 9.9	
13 TH	0002 2.2	0542 10.0	1223 2.0	1759 10.3
14 F	0044 1.9	0621 10.3	1302 1.8	● 1837 10.6
15 SA	0123 1.7	0700 10.5	1341 1.7	1915 10.7
16 SU	0202 1.6	0741 10.5	1419 1.8	1955 10.7
17 M	0241 1.7	0823 10.3	1458 2.0	2037 10.4
18 TU	0322 1.9	0908 9.9	1540 2.3	2123 10.1
19 W	0408 2.3	0958 9.5	1629 2.7	2215 9.6
20 TH	0502 2.6	1055 9.1	1726 3.1	◐ 2315 9.2
21 F	0604 2.9	1201 8.8	1834 3.2	
22 SA	0026 9.0	0715 3.0	1315 8.8	1948 3.2
23 SU	0141 9.1	0827 2.9	1426 9.1	2059 2.9
24 M	0251 9.3	0934 2.6	1530 9.5	2203 2.5
25 TU	0353 9.7	1034 2.3	1625 9.9	2301 2.2
26 W	0448 10.0	1129 2.1	1715 10.2	2354 1.9
27 TH	0537 10.2	1218 1.9	1800 10.5	○
28 F	0042 1.8	0622 10.3	1303 1.9	1841 10.5
29 SA	0125 1.8	0704 10.3	1342 2.0	1920 10.5
30 SU	0204 1.9	0743 10.1	1418 2.2	1957 10.3
31 M	0240 2.1	0820 9.8	1452 2.5	2033 10.0

JUNE

Day	Time m	Time m	Time m	Time m
1 TU	0314 2.4	0855 9.4	1525 2.8	2108 9.5
2 W	0348 2.8	0930 9.0	1558 3.2	2144 9.1
3 TH	0423 3.2	1009 8.6	1635 3.6	2225 8.6
4 F	0504 3.5	1054 8.3	1720 4.0	◗ 2315 8.3
5 SA	0554 3.8	1150 8.0	1817 4.2	
6 SU	0019 8.0	0653 4.0	1258 7.9	1925 4.2
7 M	0131 8.0	0801 3.9	1405 8.1	2036 4.0
8 TU	0235 8.3	0908 3.6	1504 8.6	2140 3.6
9 W	0331 8.7	1007 3.2	1556 9.1	2236 3.0
10 TH	0422 9.2	1100 2.7	1644 9.6	2328 2.5
11 F	0511 9.7	1150 2.3	1730 10.1	
12 SA	0017 2.1	0558 10.1	1239 2.0	● 1816 10.5
13 SU	0105 1.7	0646 10.4	1325 1.7	1902 10.8
14 M	0152 1.5	0733 10.6	1410 1.6	1949 10.9
15 TU	0238 1.4	0820 10.6	1456 1.6	2035 10.9
16 W	0324 1.4	0907 10.5	1541 1.7	2122 10.7
17 TH	0410 1.6	0954 10.2	1628 2.0	2210 10.3
18 F	0458 2.0	1043 9.8	1718 2.4	2301 9.9
19 SA	0549 2.5	1136 9.4	1812 2.8	◐ 2356 9.4
20 SU	0645 2.8	1236 9.0	1914 3.1	
21 M	0101 9.0	0748 3.1	1344 8.9	2022 3.2
22 TU	0212 8.9	0857 3.1	1454 9.0	2131 3.1
23 W	0323 8.9	1005 3.0	1558 9.2	2237 2.8
24 TH	0427 9.2	1106 2.8	1654 9.6	2335 2.5
25 F	0521 9.5	1159 2.6	1743 9.9	
26 SA	0025 2.3	0608 9.7	1246 2.4	○ 1826 10.1
27 SU	0110 2.1	0650 9.9	1327 2.3	1905 10.3
28 M	0149 2.1	0728 9.9	1403 2.4	1942 10.2
29 TU	0224 2.1	0803 9.9	1436 2.4	2016 10.1
30 W	0257 2.2	0836 9.8	1507 2.5	2049 9.9

JULY

Day	Time m	Time m	Time m	Time m
1 TH	0328 2.4	0908 9.5	1538 2.7	2121 9.6
2 F	0359 2.6	0940 9.3	1609 3.0	2153 9.3
3 SA	0432 3.0	1014 8.9	1644 3.4	2229 8.8
4 SU	0509 3.4	1053 8.5	1725 3.8	◗ 2313 8.4
5 M	0553 3.7	1143 8.2	1818 4.1	
6 TU	0011 8.1	0651 4.0	1248 8.1	1927 4.2
7 W	0125 8.0	0804 4.0	1403 8.2	2045 3.9
8 TH	0241 8.3	0920 3.7	1513 8.7	2157 3.4
9 F	0348 8.8	1027 3.1	1614 9.3	2300 2.7
10 SA	0448 9.5	1126 2.5	1710 10.0	2357 2.1
11 SU	0544 10.1	1221 2.0	1803 10.6	●
12 M	0052 1.5	0635 10.6	1314 1.5	1853 11.1
13 TU	0144 1.1	0724 11.0	1403 1.2	1940 11.4
14 W	0232 0.9	0811 11.2	1450 1.0	2026 11.5
15 TH	0318 0.8	0855 11.1	1534 1.1	2111 11.3
16 F	0401 1.0	0938 10.8	1617 1.4	2154 10.9
17 SA	0442 1.5	1021 10.3	1659 1.9	2237 10.2
18 SU	0524 2.1	1104 9.7	1744 2.6	◐ 2323 9.5
19 M	0610 2.9	1155 9.0	1837 3.2	
20 TU	0020 8.7	0707 3.5	1301 8.5	1945 3.7
21 W	0136 8.2	0823 3.8	1423 8.4	2106 3.7
22 TH	0302 8.2	0944 3.7	1540 8.7	2222 3.4
23 F	0415 8.6	1053 3.3	1641 9.2	2324 2.9
24 SA	0511 9.1	1147 2.9	1730 9.7	
25 SU	0014 2.5	0556 9.5	1233 2.5	1812 10.0
26 M	0056 2.2	0636 9.9	1312 2.3	○ 1850 10.3
27 TU	0133 2.0	0711 10.0	1346 2.2	1924 10.4
28 W	0206 1.9	0742 10.1	1416 2.1	1955 10.4
29 TH	0236 1.9	0812 10.1	1445 2.1	2025 10.3
30 F	0304 2.0	0841 10.0	1513 2.3	2053 10.1
31 SA	0332 2.2	0909 9.8	1541 2.6	2121 9.7

AUGUST

Day	Time m	Time m	Time m	Time m
1 SU	0400 2.6	0937 9.4	1610 3.0	2150 9.3
2 M	0430 3.1	1007 9.0	1643 3.5	2223 8.7
3 TU	0505 3.6	1046 8.5	1722 3.9	◗ 2309 8.2
4 W	0553 4.0	1143 8.1	1829 4.3	
5 TH	0023 7.9	0708 4.3	1309 8.0	1959 4.2
6 F	0202 7.9	0843 4.1	1441 8.4	2129 3.6
7 SA	0328 8.5	1003 3.4	1555 9.2	2240 2.8
8 SU	0435 9.4	1109 2.5	1656 10.1	2342 2.0
9 M	0532 10.2	1207 1.8	1750 10.9	
10 TU	0039 1.2	0622 10.9	1301 1.2	● 1840 11.5
11 W	0131 0.7	0709 11.4	1350 0.7	1926 11.9
12 TH	0218 0.4	0754 11.7	1435 0.6	2010 12.0
13 F	0301 0.4	0835 11.6	1517 0.7	2051 11.7
14 SA	0341 0.7	0915 11.2	1556 1.1	2130 11.1
15 SU	0418 1.4	0952 10.5	1634 1.8	2208 10.2
16 M	0454 2.3	1030 9.7	1713 2.7	◐ 2249 9.3
17 TU	0533 3.2	1115 8.8	1800 3.6	2341 8.3
18 W	0627 4.0	1220 8.1	1912 4.2	
19 TH	0105 7.7	0754 4.5	1401 7.9	2049 4.2
20 F	0253 7.8	0931 4.2	1529 8.3	2212 3.7
21 SA	0407 8.4	1042 3.6	1629 9.0	2310 3.1
22 SU	0458 9.0	1132 3.0	1714 9.6	2355 2.5
23 M	0539 9.6	1213 2.5	1753 10.1	
24 TU	0034 2.1	0614 10.0	1250 2.2	○ 1828 10.4
25 W	0109 1.9	0646 10.3	1322 2.0	1900 10.6
26 TH	0140 1.8	0716 10.4	1352 1.9	1929 10.6
27 F	0209 1.7	0744 10.5	1420 1.9	1958 10.6
28 SA	0237 1.8	0811 10.4	1447 2.0	2025 10.4
29 SU	0303 2.0	0838 10.2	1514 2.3	2051 10.1
30 M	0330 2.4	0903 9.8	1541 2.7	2117 9.5
31 TU	0357 2.9	0931 9.3	1611 3.3	2147 9.0

Channel Islands

Chart Datum is 5·88 metres below Ordnance Datum (Local). HAT is 12·2 metres above Chart Datum; see 4.5.

TIME ZONE (UT)
For Summer Time add ONE hour in **non-shaded areas**

ST HELIER   LAT 49°11'N   LONG 2°07'W
TIMES AND HEIGHTS OF HIGH AND LOW WATERS

Dates in red are **SPRINGS**
Dates in blue are **NEAPS**

YEAR 2010

SEPTEMBER

Time	m		Time	m
1 0429	3.5	**16**	0549	4.4
1005	8.8		1143	7.9
W 1649	3.8		TH 1840	4.5
◑ 2228	8.3			
2 0514	4.1	**17**	0040	7.4
1057	8.2		0725	4.8
TH 1750	4.3		F 1339	7.6
2342	7.8		2027	4.5
3 0632	4.4	**18**	0237	7.6
1231	7.9		0912	4.5
F 1930	4.3		SA 1510	8.1
			2150	3.9
4 0140	7.8	**19**	0346	8.3
0819	4.2		1019	3.8
SA 1423	8.3		SU 1606	8.9
2110	3.7		2243	3.2
5 0316	8.5	**20**	0433	9.0
0946	3.4		1105	3.1
SU 1542	9.2		M 1649	9.6
2224	2.7		2325	2.6
6 0422	9.5	**21**	0511	9.6
1052	2.4		1144	2.5
M 1642	10.2		TU 1726	10.1
2325	1.8			
7 0516	10.5	**22**	0002	2.2
1149	1.6		0545	10.1
TU 1734	11.1		W 1219	2.2
			1759	10.4
8 0020	1.0	**23**	0037	1.9
0604	11.2		0616	10.4
W 1241	0.9		TH 1252	2.0
● 1821	11.8		○ 1831	10.6
9 0110	0.5	**24**	0109	1.8
0648	11.7		0646	10.5
TH 1329	0.5		F 1323	1.8
1905	12.1		1901	10.7
10 0156	0.3	**25**	0139	1.7
0731	11.9		0714	10.6
F 1413	0.4		SA 1352	1.8
1947	12.1		1929	10.7
11 0237	0.4	**26**	0208	1.8
0810	11.7		0742	10.6
SA 1453	0.7		SU 1421	1.9
2027	11.7		1957	10.5
12 0315	0.9	**27**	0236	2.2
0848	11.3		0809	10.4
SU 1531	1.2		M 1449	2.2
2104	11.0		2025	10.2
13 0350	1.7	**28**	0304	2.4
0923	10.5		0836	10.1
M 1606	2.0		TU 1517	2.6
2140	10.0		2053	9.7
14 0423	2.6	**29**	0333	2.9
0958	9.6		0906	9.6
TU 1642	3.0		W 1549	3.1
2218	9.0		2126	9.1
15 0458	3.6	**30**	0407	3.5
1039	8.7		0942	9.0
W 1727	3.9		TH 1630	3.7
◑ 2308	8.0		2211	8.4

OCTOBER

Time	m		Time	m
1 0456	4.0	**16**	0004	7.5
1038	8.4		0641	4.9
F 1735	4.1		SA 1255	7.6
◑ 2330	7.9		1941	4.6
2 0616	4.4	**17**	0152	7.6
1214	8.0		0825	4.7
SA 1914	4.2		SU 1427	8.0
			2104	4.1
3 0128	7.9	**18**	0304	8.2
0801	4.2		0936	4.1
SU 1405	8.4		M 1527	8.6
2051	3.6		2200	3.5
4 0258	8.7	**19**	0354	8.8
0926	3.3		1024	3.4
M 1522	9.3		TU 1612	9.2
2203	2.6		2244	2.9
5 0401	9.7	**20**	0434	9.4
1030	2.4		1105	2.8
TU 1620	10.3		W 1651	9.8
2302	1.7		2323	2.5
6 0453	10.6	**21**	0509	9.9
1125	1.6		1142	2.4
W 1711	11.1		TH 1726	10.1
2355	1.1			
7 0540	11.2	**22**	0000	2.1
1216	1.0		0542	10.2
TH 1758	11.6		F 1219	2.1
●			1759	10.4
8 0043	0.7	**23**	0036	1.9
0623	11.6		0614	10.5
F 1304	0.7		SA 1253	1.9
1842	11.9		○ 1831	10.5
9 0129	0.7	**24**	0110	1.9
0705	11.8		0644	10.6
SA 1347	0.7		SU 1326	1.9
1923	11.8		1903	10.6
10 0210	0.9	**25**	0142	1.9
0744	11.6		0715	10.7
SU 1428	1.0		M 1358	1.9
2003	11.4		1935	10.5
11 0247	1.4	**26**	0213	2.0
0821	11.1		0747	10.6
M 1505	1.5		TU 1429	2.1
2040	10.7		2007	10.2
12 0322	2.1	**27**	0244	2.3
0856	10.4		0819	10.3
TU 1541	2.3		W 1502	2.4
2116	9.8		2043	9.8
13 0355	2.9	**28**	0318	2.8
0931	9.5		0855	9.8
W 1617	3.1		TH 1540	2.9
2154	8.9		2123	9.3
14 0430	3.8	**29**	0359	3.3
1011	8.7		0939	9.3
TH 1700	3.9		F 1627	3.4
◑ 2242	8.0		2216	8.7
15 0518	4.5	**30**	0452	3.7
1111	7.9		1039	8.7
F 1806	4.5		SA 1732	3.7
			◑ 2331	8.3
		31	0608	4.0
			1203	8.5
			SU 1858	3.8

NOVEMBER

Time	m		Time	m
1 0104	8.3	**16**	0158	7.9
0738	3.9		0828	4.4
M 1335	8.7		TU 1429	8.2
2023	3.4		2059	3.9
2 0227	8.9	**17**	0259	8.4
0857	3.2		0930	3.9
TU 1451	9.4		W 1524	8.7
2134	2.7		2153	3.5
3 0331	9.6	**18**	0347	8.9
1001	2.5		1019	3.4
W 1552	10.1		TH 1609	9.2
2233	2.0		2240	3.0
4 0425	10.3	**19**	0429	9.4
1058	1.9		1103	2.9
TH 1646	10.7		F 1649	9.6
2327	1.6		2323	2.6
5 0514	10.9	**20**	0507	9.9
1150	1.4		1145	2.5
F 1734	11.1		SA 1727	10.0
6 0016	1.3	**21**	0004	2.3
0559	11.2		0543	10.2
SA 1239	1.2		SU 1225	2.2
● 1819	11.2		○ 1804	10.2
7 0103	1.1	**22**	0043	2.1
0641	11.3		0619	10.5
SU 1324	1.2		M 1303	2.0
1902	11.2		1842	10.4
8 0144	1.5	**23**	0120	2.0
0721	11.2		0655	10.7
M 1405	1.4		TU 1341	1.9
1942	10.9		1920	10.5
9 0223	1.8	**24**	0157	2.0
0759	10.8		0733	10.7
TU 1444	1.7		W 1418	2.0
2021	10.3		2000	10.3
10 0259	2.3	**25**	0234	2.1
0836	10.3		0813	10.5
W 1521	2.4		TH 1457	2.1
2058	9.7		2042	10.1
11 0334	3.0	**26**	0314	2.4
0912	9.6		0856	10.2
TH 1557	3.0		F 1540	2.4
2136	9.0		2128	9.7
12 0409	3.6	**27**	0359	2.7
0952	9.0		0944	9.8
F 1637	3.6		SA 1629	2.7
2220	8.4		2219	9.3
13 0451	4.2	**28**	0451	3.1
1040	8.3		1038	9.4
SA 1727	4.1		SU 1726	3.1
◑ 2318	7.9		◑ 2320	8.9
14 0549	4.6	**29**	0554	3.4
1150	7.9		1143	9.1
SU 1834	4.4		M 1834	3.3
15 0037	7.7	**30**	0030	8.8
0708	4.7		0706	3.5
M 1317	7.9		TU 1257	9.0
1952	4.3		1947	3.2

DECEMBER

Time	m		Time	m
1 0145	8.9	**16**	0144	8.0
0821	3.3		0817	4.4
W 1412	9.2		TH 1419	8.0
2058	3.0		2051	4.0
2 0255	9.3	**17**	0250	8.3
0930	2.9		0925	4.0
TH 1521	9.5		F 1519	8.4
2203	2.6		2153	3.6
3 0356	9.7	**18**	0344	8.6
1031	2.4		1022	3.4
F 1621	9.9		SA 1611	8.9
2301	2.3		2246	3.1
4 0450	10.2	**19**	0431	9.4
1128	2.1		1113	2.9
SA 1714	10.3		SU 1658	9.5
2355	2.0		2335	2.6
5 0539	10.6	**20**	0516	9.9
1220	1.8		1200	2.4
SU 1803	10.5		M 1743	9.9
●				
6 0043	1.9	**21**	0021	2.2
0623	10.8		0559	10.4
M 1307	1.7		TU 1246	2.0
1847	10.5		○ 1827	10.3
7 0127	1.9	**22**	0105	1.9
0705	10.8		0643	10.7
TU 1350	1.7		W 1331	1.7
1928	10.4		1911	10.6
8 0207	2.1	**23**	0148	1.7
0744	10.7		0726	10.9
W 1429	1.9		TH 1414	1.5
2007	10.2		1955	10.7
9 0243	2.3	**24**	0231	1.7
0821	10.4		0810	11.0
TH 1505	2.2		F 1457	1.5
2043	9.8		2040	10.6
10 0317	2.7	**25**	0314	1.7
0857	9.9		0855	10.9
F 1539	2.7		SA 1541	1.6
2118	9.4		2124	10.4
11 0349	3.1	**26**	0357	1.9
0932	9.4		0939	10.6
SA 1613	3.1		SU 1625	1.9
2154	8.9		2210	10.1
12 0423	3.5	**27**	0443	2.3
1009	8.9		1026	10.2
SU 1650	3.5		M 1712	2.3
2234	8.5		2258	9.6
13 0503	3.9	**28**	0533	2.7
1054	8.5		1117	9.6
M 1734	3.9		TU 1804	2.8
◑ 2324	8.1		◑ 2353	9.1
14 0554	4.3	**29**	0631	3.2
1151	8.1		1217	9.1
TU 1830	4.2		W 1907	3.2
15 0029	7.9	**30**	0059	8.8
0700	4.5		0741	3.4
W 1306	7.9		TH 1330	8.8
1939	4.2		2020	3.4
		31	0216	8.7
			0857	3.4
			F 1449	8.8
			2135	3.3

Chart Datum is 5·88 metres below Ordnance Datum (Local). HAT is 12·2 metres above Chart Datum; see 4.5.

North Brittany

Paimpol to Pointe de Penmarc'h

OFF USHANT (OUESSANT) TSS
See facing page

Ouessant NE
L.Fl.10s
Racon B

Inshore

Traffic

Zone

île d'Ouessant

Fl(2)R.20s.24M

VQ(3)WR.5s8M

Oc(2+1)WR.17/7M

RW
Ouessant SW Lanby
Fl.4s Racon M AIS

Fl(2)10s.32M

Fl(3)R.15s.22M

VQ(9)10s

SEPARATION ZONE

Brignogan

île Vierge

L'ABERWRAC'H 9.20.20

L'ABERBENOIT 9.20.21

Portsall

Le Four

Argenton

L'ABERILDUT 9.20.22

ITZ

Baie du Stiff

BREST
9.20.28

îLE D'OUESSANT
9.20.25

Trézien

Île de Molène

Anse de
Bertheaume

RADE DE

LE CONQUET 9.20.23

BREST 9.20.27

Les Pierres
Noires

CAMARET 9.20.29

L'IROISE

MORGAT 9.20.30

Magnetic
Variation
3·4°W

RAZ DE SEIN 9.20.32

DOUARNENEZ 9.20.31

îLE DE SEIN 9.20.33

Ar-Men

Île de Sein

See 9.21.2

CROSS Corsen
CROSS Etel

AUDIERNE 9.20.34

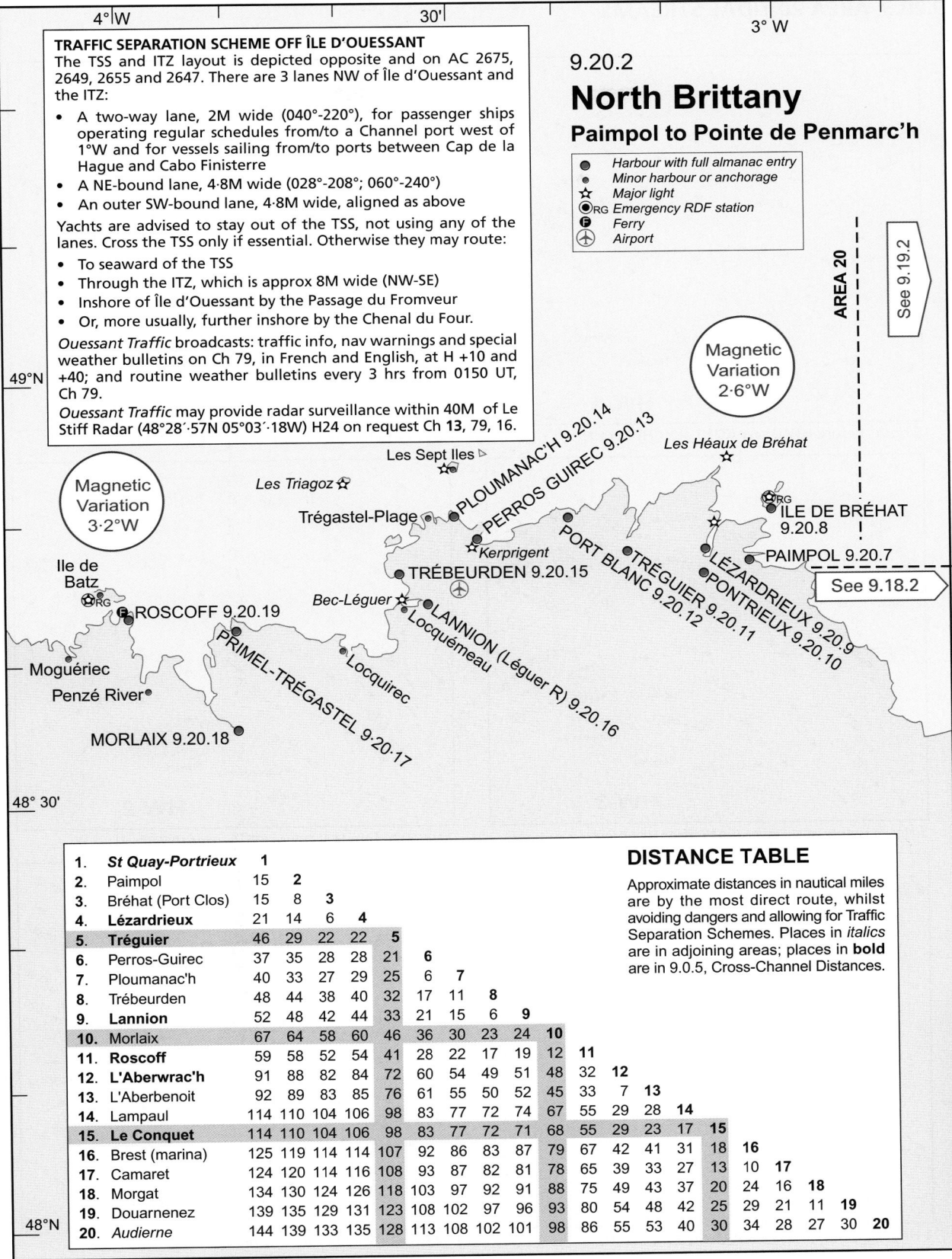

TRAFFIC SEPARATION SCHEME OFF ÎLE D'OUESSANT

The TSS and ITZ layout is depicted opposite and on AC 2675, 2649, 2655 and 2647. There are 3 lanes NW of Île d'Ouessant and the ITZ:

- A two-way lane, 2M wide (040°-220°), for passenger ships operating regular schedules from/to a Channel port west of 1°W and for vessels sailing from/to ports between Cap de la Hague and Cabo Finisterre
- A NE-bound lane, 4·8M wide (028°-208°; 060°-240°)
- An outer SW-bound lane, 4·8M wide, aligned as above

Yachts are advised to stay out of the TSS, not using any of the lanes. Cross the TSS only if essential. Otherwise they may route:

- To seaward of the TSS
- Through the ITZ, which is approx 8M wide (NW-SE)
- Inshore of Île d'Ouessant by the Passage du Fromveur
- Or, more usually, further inshore by the Chenal du Four.

Ouessant Traffic broadcasts: traffic info, nav warnings and special weather bulletins on Ch 79, in French and English, at H +10 and +40; and routine weather bulletins every 3 hrs from 0150 UT, Ch 79.

Ouessant Traffic may provide radar surveillance within 40M of Le Stiff Radar (48°28'·57N 05°03'·18W) H24 on request Ch 13, 79, 16.

9.20.2
North Brittany
Paimpol to Pointe de Penmarc'h

- Harbour with full almanac entry
- Minor harbour or anchorage
- ☆ Major light
- Ⓡ RG Emergency RDF station
- Ⓕ Ferry
- ✈ Airport

Magnetic Variation 2·6°W

Magnetic Variation 3·2°W

AREA 20

See 9.19.2

See 9.18.2

Les Héaux de Bréhat ☆

Les Sept Iles ▷

Les Triagoz ☆

PLOUMANAC'H 9.20.14

PERROS GUIREC 9.20.13

Trégastel-Plage

Kerprigent ☆

TRÉBEURDEN 9.20.15

Bec-Léguer ☆

LANNION (Léguer R) 9.20.16

Locquémeau

PORT BLANC 9.20.12

TRÉGUIER 9.20.11

PONTRIEUX 9.20.10

LÉZARDRIEUX 9.20.9

ÎLE DE BRÉHAT 9.20.8

PAIMPOL 9.20.7

Ile de Batz

ROSCOFF 9.20.19

Moguériec

Penzé River

PRIMEL-TRÉGASTEL 9.20·17

Locquirec

MORLAIX 9.20.18

49°N

48° 30'

48°N

DISTANCE TABLE

Approximate distances in nautical miles are by the most direct route, whilst avoiding dangers and allowing for Traffic Separation Schemes. Places in *italics* are in adjoining areas; places in **bold** are in 9.0.5, Cross-Channel Distances.

		1	2	3	4	5	6	7	8	9	10	11	12	13	14	15	16	17	18	19	20
1.	*St Quay-Portrieux*	**1**																			
2.	Paimpol	15	**2**																		
3.	Bréhat (Port Clos)	15	8	**3**																	
4.	**Lézardrieux**	21	14	6	**4**																
5.	**Tréguier**	46	29	22	22	**5**															
6.	Perros-Guirec	37	35	28	28	21	**6**														
7.	Ploumanac'h	40	33	27	29	25	6	**7**													
8.	Trébeurden	48	44	38	40	32	17	11	**8**												
9.	**Lannion**	52	48	42	44	33	21	15	6	**9**											
10.	Morlaix	67	64	58	60	46	36	30	23	24	**10**										
11.	**Roscoff**	59	58	52	54	41	28	22	17	19	12	**11**									
12.	**L'Aberwrac'h**	91	88	82	84	72	60	54	49	51	48	32	**12**								
13.	L'Aberbenoit	92	89	83	85	76	61	55	50	52	45	33	7	**13**							
14.	Lampaul	114	110	104	106	98	83	77	72	74	67	55	29	28	**14**						
15.	**Le Conquet**	114	110	104	106	98	83	77	72	71	68	55	29	23	17	**15**					
16.	Brest (marina)	125	119	114	114	107	92	86	83	87	79	67	42	41	31	18	**16**				
17.	Camaret	124	120	114	116	108	93	87	82	81	78	65	39	33	27	13	10	**17**			
18.	Morgat	134	130	124	126	118	103	97	92	91	88	75	49	43	37	20	24	16	**18**		
19.	Douarnenez	139	135	129	131	123	108	102	97	96	93	80	54	48	42	25	29	21	11	**19**	
20.	*Audierne*	144	139	133	135	128	113	108	102	101	98	86	55	53	40	30	34	28	27	30	**20**

N Brittany

9.20.3 AREA 20 TIDAL STREAMS

5 Hours before HW Dover (0215 after HW Brest)

4 Hours before HW Dover (0315 after HW Brest)

3 Hours before HW Dover (0415 after HW Brest)

2 Hours before HW Dover (0515 after HW Brest)

1 Hour before HW Dover (0615 after HW Brest)

HW Dover (0510 before HW Brest)

Southward 9.21.3   Eastward 9.18.3   Northward 9.1.3

1 Hour after HW Dover (0410 before HW Brest)

2 Hours after HW Dover (0310 before HW Brest)

3 Hours after HW Dover (0210 before HW Brest)

4 Hours after HW Dover (0110 before HW Brest)

5 Hours after HW Dover (0010 before HW Brest)

6 Hours after HW Dover (0050 after HW Brest)

N Brittany

9.20.4 LIGHTS, BUOYS AND WAYPOINTS

Bold print = light with a nominal range of 15M or more. CAPITALS = place or feature. *CAPITAL ITALICS* = light-vessel, light float or Lanby. *Italics* = Fog signal. ***Bold italics*** = Racon. Abbreviations are in Chapter 1.

OFFSHORE MARKS

Roches Douvres ☆ Fl 5s 60m **24M**; pink twr on dwelling with G roof; 49°06'·30N 02°48'·87W.
Barnouic ↓ VQ (3) 5s 15m 7M; 49°01'·63N 02°48'·41W.
Roche Gautier ↙ VQ (9) 10s; 49°02'·013N 02°54'·36W.

PAIMPOL TO ÎLE DE BRÉHAT

PAIMPOL

Les Calemarguiers ↙ 48°46'·98N 02°54'·84W.
L'Ost Pic ↙ Fl(4)WR 15s 20m, W9M, R6M; 105°-W-116°-R-221°-W-253°- R-291°-W-329°; obsc by islets near Bréhat when brg < 162°; W twr/turret, R top; 48°46'·77N 02°56'·42W.
Les Charpentiers ↓ 48°47'·89N 02°56'·01W.
Pte de Porz-Don ☆ Oc (2) WR 6s 13m **W15M**, R11M; 269°-W-272°-R-279°; W house; 48°47'·48N 03°01'·55W.
El Bras ◢ Fl G 2·5s; 48°47'·21N 03°01'·50W.
♦ Fl R 2·5s; 48°47'·17N 03°01'·49W.
Ldg lts 262·2°, both QR 5/12m 7/14M. Front, Kernoa jetty; W & R hut; 48°47'·09N 03°02'·44W. Rear, Dir QR, intens 260·2°-264·2°; W pylon, R top; 360m from front. ↙ QG 48°47'·12N 03°02'·47W.

CHENAL DU FERLAS (277°-257°-271°)

Lel Ar Serive ↙ 48°49'·98N 02°58'·76W.
Loguivy Dir lt 257°: Q WRG 12m 10/8M; 254°-G-257°-W-257·7°-R-260·7°; Gy twr; 48°49'·37N 03°03'·67W.
Les Piliers ↓ 48°49'·77N 02°59'·99W.
Kermouster Dir ↙ 271°: Fl WRG 2s 16m, W 10M, R/G 8M; 267°-G-270°-W-272°- R-274°; W col; 48°49'·55N 03°05'·19W (R. Trieux).

ÎLE DE BRÉHAT

Le Paon ↙ Oc WRG 4s 22m W11M, R/G8M; 033°-W-078°-G-181°-W-196°- R-307°-W-316°-R-348°; Y twr; 48°51'·92N 02°59'·15W.
Roche Guarine ↙ 48°51'·63N 02°57'·63W, Chenal de Bréhat.
Rosédo ☆ Fl 5s 29m **20M**; W twr; 48°51'·45N 03°00'·29W.
La Chambre ↓ 48°50'·16N 02°59'·58W.
Men-Joliguet ↓ Iso WRG 4s 6m W13M, R/G10M; 255°-R-279°-W-283°-G-175°; 48°50'·12N 03°00'·20W.

LÉZARDRIEUX TO TRÉGUIER

LE TRIEUX RIVER to LÉZARDRIEUX

Nord Horaine ↙ 48°54'·54N 02°55'·23W.
La Horaine ◣ Fl (3) 12s 13m 7M; Gy 8-sided twr on B hut; 48°53'·50N 02°55'·22W.
Men-Marc'h ↙ 48°53'·17N 02°51'·82W.
Ldg lts 224·7°: Front, **La Croix** ☆ Q 15m **18M**; intens 215°-235°; two Gy ○ twrs joined, W on NE side, R tops; 48°50'·23N 03°03'·25W. Rear **Bodic** ☆ Dir Q 55m **22M**; intens 221°-229°; W ho with G gable; 2·1M from front.
Les Sirlots ◢ *Whis;* 48°52'·95N 02°59'·58W.
Men-Grenn ↓ Q (9) 15s 7m 7M; 48°51'·22N 03°03'·89W.
Coatmer ldg lts 218·7°. Front, Q RG 16m R/G7M; 200°-R-250°-G-053°; W gable; 48°48'·26N 03°05'·75W. Rear, QR 50m 7M; vis 197°-242°; W gable; 660m from front.
Les Perdrix ◣ Fl (2) WG 6s 5m, W6M, G3M; 165°-G-197°-W-202·5°-G-040°; G twr; 48°47'·74N 03°05'·79W.

CHENAL DE LA MOISIE (339·4°); PASSE DE LA GAINE (241·5°)

La Vieille du Tréou ◢ 48°52'·00N 03°01'·09W.
An Ogejou Bihan ↓ 48°53'·37N 03°01'·91W.
La Moisie ↓ 48°53'·83N 03°02'·22W.
Les Héaux de Bréhat ☆ Oc (3) WRG 12s 48m, **W15M**, R/G11M; 227°-R-247°-W-270°-G-302°-W-227°; Gy ○ twr; 48°54'·50N 03°05'·17W.

Basse des Héaux ↓ 48°54'·07N 03°05'·28W.
Pont de la Gaine ↓ 48°53'·12N 03°07'·40W.

JAUDY RIVER TO TRÉGUIER

La Jument des Héaux ↙ VQ; 48°55'·36N 03°08'·04W.
Grande Passe ldg lts 137°. Front, Port de la Chaine, Oc 4s 12m 11M; 042°-232°; W house; 48°51'·55N 03°07'·89W. Rear, **St Antoine** ☆ Dir Oc R 4s 34m **15M**; intens 134°-140°; R & W house; 0·75M from front. (Both marks are hard to see by day.)
Basse Crublent ↙ QR; *Whis;* 48°54'·29N 03°11'·16W.
Le Corbeau ◢ Fl R 4s; 48°53'·35N 03°10'·26W.
Pierre à l'Anglais ◣ Fl G 4s; 48°53'·21N 03°10'·46W.
Petit Pen ar Guézec ◣ Fl (2) G 6s; 48°52'·52N 03°09'·44W.
La Corne ↙ Fl (3) WRG 12s 14m W8M, R/G6M; 052°-W-059°-R-173°-G-213°-W-220°-R-052°; W twr, R base; 48°51'·35N 03°10'·62W.

TRÉGUIER TO TRÉBEURDEN

PORT BLANC

Le Voleur Dir ↙ 150·4°: Fl WRG 4s 17m, W14M, R/G 11M; 140°-G-148°-W-152°-R-160°; W twr; 48°50'·20N 03°18'·52W.
Basse Guazer ◢; 48°51'·58N 03°20'·96W.

PERROS-GUIREC

Passe de l'Est, ldg lts 224·5°. Front, **Le Colombier** ☆ Dir Oc (4) 12s 28m **15M**; intens 214·5°-234·5°; W house; 48°47'·87N 03°26'·66W. Rear, **Kerprigent** ☆, Dir Q 79m **21M**; intens 221°-228°; W twr, 1·5M from front.
Pierre du Chenal ↓ 48°49'·29N 03°24'·67W.

Passe de l'Ouest. Kerjean ☆ Dir lt 143·6°, Oc (2+1) WRG 12s 78m, **W15M**, R/G12M; 133·7°-G-143·2°-W-144·8°- R-154·3°; W twr, B top; 48°47'·79N 03°23'·39W.
Les Couillons de Tomé ↙ 48°50'·88N 03°25'·68W.
La Horaine ↓ 48°49'·89N 03°27'·26W.
Roche Bernard ◣ 48°49'·43N 03°25'·46W.
Gommonénou ↓ VQ R 1M; 48°48'·27N 03°25'·83W.
Jetée du Linkin ↙ Fl (2) G 6s 4m 7M; W pile, G top; 48°48'·20N 03°26'·31W.

PLOUMANAC'H

Mean-Ruz ↙ Oc WR 4s 26m W12M, R9M; 226°-W-242°-R-226°; obsc by Pte de Trégastel when brg <080°; partly obsc by Les Sept-Îles 156°-207° and partly by Île Tomé 264°-278°; pink □ twr; 48°50'·26N 03°29'·01W.

LES SEPT ÎLES

Île-aux-Moines ☆ Fl (3) 15s 59m **24M**; obsc by Îliot Rouzic and E end of Île Bono 237°-241°, and in Baie de Lannion when brg <039°; Gy twr and dwelling; 48°52'·72N 03°29'·40W.
Les Dervinis ↓ 48°52'·35N 03°27'·32W.

TRÉGASTEL-PLAGE

Île Dhu ↙ 48°50'·37N 03°31'·24W.

Les Triagoz ↙ Oc(2)WR6s31mW14M, R11M; 010°-W-339°-R-010°; obsc in places 258°-268° by Les Sept-Îles; Gy □ twr, R lantern; 48°52'·28N 03°38'·80W.
Bar-ar-Gall ↙ VQ (9) 10s; 48°49'·79N 03°36'·22W.
Le Crapaud ↙ Q (9) 15s; 48°46'·67N 03°40'·59W.

TRÉBEURDEN

Pte de Lan Kerellec ↙ Iso WRG 4s; W8M, R/G5M; 058°-G-064°-W-069°-R-130°; Gy twr; 48°46'·74N 03°35'·06W.
Ar Gouredec ↓ VQ (6) + L Fl 10s; 48°46'·41N 03°36'·59W.
An Ervennou ◢ Fl (2) R 6s; 48°46'·48N 03°35'·96W.
NW bkwtr ↙ Fl G 2·5s 8m 2M; IPTS; 48°46'·33N 03°35'·21W.

TRÉBEURDEN TO MORLAIX

LÉGUER RIVER

Beg-Léguer ↙ Oc (4) WRG 12s 60m W12M, R/G9M; 007°-G-084°-W-098°-R-129°; west face of W house, R lantern; 48°44'·31N 03°32'·91W.
Kinierbel ◣ *Bell;* 48°44'·15N 03°35'·18W.

WGS84 DATUM
Plot waypoints on chart before use

LOCQUÉMEAU
Ldg lts 121°: Front, ⚡ QR 19m 6M; 068°-228°; W pylon, R top; 48°43'·41N 03°34'·44W. Rear, ⚡ QR 39m 7M; 016°-232°; W gabled house; 484m from front.
Locquémeau ⚓ *Whis;* 48°43'·86N 03°35'·93W.

LOCQUIREC
Gouliat ⌁ 48°42'·57N 03°38'·97W.

PRIMEL-TRÉGASTEL
Méloine ⌁ 48°45'·56N 03°50'·68W.
Ldg lts 152°, both ⚡ QR 35/56m 7M. Front, 134°-168°; W ▢, R stripe, on pylon; 48°42'·45N 03°49'·19W. Rear, R vert stripe on W wall; 172m from front.
W bkwtr ⚡ Fl G 4s 6m 7M; 48°42'·77N 03°49'·52W.

BAIE DE MORLAIX
Chenal de Tréguier ldg lts 190·5°: Front, ⚡ Île Noire Oc (2) WRG 6s 15m, W11M, R/G8M; 051°-G-135°-R-211°-W-051°; obsc in places; W ▢ twr, R top; 48°40'·35N 03°52'·54W. Common Rear, **La Lande** ☆ Fl 5s 85m **23M**; obsc by Pte Annelouesten when brg >204°; W ▢ twr, B top; 48°38'·20N 03°53'·14W.
La Pierre Noire ⌁ 48°42'·56N 03°52'·20W.
La Chambre ⚓ 48°40'·74N 03°52'·51W.

Grande Chenal ldg lts 176·4°: Front, **Île Louet** ☆ Oc (3) WG 12s 17m **W15M**,G10M; 305°-W (except where obsc by islands)-244°-G-305°; W ▢ twr, B top; 48°40'·41N 03°53'·34W. Common Rear, **La Lande** as above.
Pot de Fer ⌁ *Bell;* 48°44'·23N 03°54'·02W.
Stolvezen ⌁ 48°42'·64N 03°53'·41W.
Ricard ⚓ 48°41'·54N 03°53'·51W.
Vieille ⚓ 48°42'·60N 03°54'·11W. (Chenal Ouest de Ricard 188·8°)
La Noire ⌁ 48°41'·65N 03°54'·06W.
Corbeau ⚓ 48°40'·63N 03°53'·33W.

MORLAIX RIVER
Barre de-Flot No. 1 ⚓ 48°40'·18N 03°52'·95W.
No. 2 ⚑ Fl R 2s; 48°39'·88N 03°52'·53W.
No. 3 ⌁ Fl G 2s; 48°39'·25N 03°52'·32W.
No. 4 ⚑ Fl R 2s; 48°38'·62N 03°51'·62W.
No. 5 ⚑ Fl G 2s; 48°38'·04N 03°51'·34W.
No. 7 ⚓ 48°37'·68N 03°51'·03W.

PENZÉ RIVER
Cordonnier ⌁ 48°42'·93N 03°56'·59W.
Guerhéon ⚓ 48°42'·73N 03°57'·18W.
Trousken ⚓ 48°42'·26N 03°56'·54W.
Pte Fourche ⚓ 48°42'·14N 03°56'·76W.
Ar Tourtu ⌁ 48°41'·99N 03°56'·57W.
An Nehou (Caspari) ⌁ 48°41'·56N 03°56'·45W.
Le Figuier ⌁ 48°40'·46N 03°56'·16W.

ROSCOFF TO ÎLE VIERGE

BLOSCON/ROSCOFF
Astan ⌁ VQ (3) 5s 9m 6M; 48°44'·91N 03°57'·66W.
Le Menk ⌁ Q (9) WR 15s 6m W5M, R3M; 160°-W-188°-R-160°; 48°43'·28N 03°56'·71W.
Basse de Bloscon ⌁ VQ; 48°43'·71N 03°57'·55W.
Bloscon pier ⚡ Fl WG 4s 9m W10M, G7M (in fog Fl 2s); 200°-W-210°-G-200°; W twr, G top; 48°43'·21N 03°57'·69W.
⚑ Fl (2) R 6s, 48°43'·11N 03°57'·92W.
Ar Pourven ⌁ Q; 48°43'·04N 03°57'·70W.

Ar-Chaden ⌁ Q (6) + L Fl WR 15s 14m, W8M, R6M; 262°-R-289·5°-W-293°-R-326°- W-110°; YB twr; 48°43'·94N 03°58'·26W.
Men-Guen-Bras ⌁ Q WRG 14m, W9M, R/ G6M; 068°-W-073°-R-197°-W-257°-G-068°; BY twr; 48°43'·76N 03°58'·07W.
Roscoff ldg lts 209°: Front, N môle ⚡ Oc (3) G 12s 7m 7M; synch; 078°-318°; W col, G top; 48°43'·56N 03°58'·67W. **Rear** ☆ Oc (3) 12s 24m **15M**; 062°-242°; Gy ▢ twr, W on NE side; 430m from front.

CANAL DE L'ÎLE DE BATZ
Roc'h Zu ⌁ 48°43'·88N 03°58'·59W.
Jetty hd (LW landing) ⚡ Q 5m 1M; BY col; 48°43'·92N 03°58'·97W.
Run Oan ⌁ 48°44'·10N 03°59'·30W.
Perroch ⚓ 48°44'·10N 03°59'·71W.
Tec'hit Bihan ⌁ 48°44'·02N 04°00'·88W.
La Croix ⌁ 48°44'·19N 04°01'·30W.
L'Oignon ⌁ 48°44'·04N 04°01'·35W.
Basse Plate ⚓ 48°44'·25N 04°02'·53W.

ÎLE DE BATZ
Île aux Moutons ⌁ VQ (6)+ L Fl 10s 3m 7M; 48°44'·25N 04°00'·52W; landing stage, S end and ent to hbr.
Malvoch⌁ 48°44'·26N 04°00'·67W, W side of ent.
Lt ho ☆ Fl (4) 25s 69m **23M**; Gy twr; 48°44'·71N 04°01'·62W.
Same twr, auxiliary lt, FR 65m 7M; 024°-059°.

MOGUÉRIEC
Ldg lts 162°: Front ⚡ Iso WG 4s 9m W11M, G6M; 158°-W-166°-G-158°; W twr, G top; jetty 48°41'·34N 04°04'·47W.
Rear ⚡ Iso G 4s 22m 7M, synch; 142°-182°; W col, G top; 440m from front.

PONTUSVAL
Pointe de Pontusval ⌁ 48°41'·42N 04°19'·32W.
Ar Peich ⚓ 48°40'·90N 04°19'·16W.
Pte de Beg-Pol ⚡ Oc (3) WR 12s 16m W10M, R7M; Shore-W-056°-R-096°-W-shore; W twr, B top, W dwelling; 48°40'·67N 04°20'·76W. QY and FR lts on towers 2·4M S.
Aman-ar-Ross ⌁ Q 7M; 48°41'·88N 04°27'·03W.
Lizen Ven Ouest ⌁ VQ (9) 10s 5M; 48°40'·53N 04°33'·63W.
Île-Vierge ☆ Fl 5s 77m **27M**; 337°-325°; Gy twr; *Horn 60s;* 48°38'·33N 04°34'·05W.

ÎLE VIERGE TO L'ABER-ILDUT

L'ABER WRAC'H
Libenter ⌁ Q (9) 15s 6M; 48°37'·50N 04°38'·45W.
Outer ldg lts 100·1°: Front, Île Wrac'h ⚡ QR 20m 7M; W ▢ twr, Or top; 48°36'·88N 04°34'·56W. Rear, Lanvaon ⚡ Q 55m 12M; intens 090°-110°; W ▢ twr, Or △ on top; 1·63M from front.
Grand Pot de Beurre ⌁ 48°37'·21N 04°36'·48W.
Petit Pot de Beurre ⚓ 48°37'·12N 04°36'·23W.
Basse de la Croix ⚑ Fl G 2·5s; 48°36'·92N 04°35'·99W.
Breac'h Ver ⚓ Fl (2) G 6s 6m 3M; △ on twr; 48°36'·63N 04°35'·38W.
Dir ⚡ 128°, Oc (2) WRG 6s 5m W13M, R/G11M; 125·7°-G-127·2°-W-128·7°-R-130·2°; 48°35'·89N 04°33'·82W, root of W bkwtr . Marina ent: QG 3m 2M; vis 186°-167° (341°); 48°36'·04N 04°33'·55W. QR 3m 2M; vis 244°-226° (342°).

L'ABER BENOÎT
Petite Fourche ⌁ 48°36'·99N 04°38'·75W.
Rusven Est ⚓ 48°36'·30N 04°38'·63W.
Rusven Ouest ⌁ *Bell;* 48°36'·07N 04°39'·43W.
Basse du Chenal ⌁ 48°35'·81N 04°38'·53W.
Poul Orvil ⌁ 48°35'·52N 04°38'·29W.
La Jument ⌁ 48°35'·10N 04°37'·41W.
Ar Gazel ⚓ 48°34'·90N 04°37'·27W.
Le Chien ⚓ 48°34'·67N 04°36'·88W.

ROCHES DE PORTSALL
Le Relec ⌁ 48°35'·99N 04°40'·84W.
Corn-Carhai ⚡ Fl (3) 12s 19m 9M; W 8-sided twr, B top; 48°35'·19N 04°43'·94W.
Grande Basse de Portsall ⌁ VQ (9) 10s 9m 4M; 48°36'·70N 04°46'·13W.
Basse Paupian ⌁ 48°35'·31N 04°46'·27W.
Bosven Aval ⚓ 48°33'·82N 04°44'·27W.
Men ar Pic ⚓ 48°33'·65N 04°44'·03W.
Portsall ⚡ Oc (4) WRG 12s 9m W13M, R/G10M; 058°-G-084°-W-088°-R-058°; W col, R top; 48°33'·84N 04°42'·26W.

ARGENTON to L'ABER-ILDUT

Le Taureau ⚓ 48°31'·46N 04°47'·34W.
Argenton, Île Dolvez, front ldg bcn 086° ⚓ 48°31'·25N 04°46'·23W.
Le Four ☆ Fl (5) 15s 28m **18M**; Gy ○ twr; *Horn (3+2) 60s*; 48°31'·38N 04°48'·32W.
L'Aber-Ildut ☆ Dir Oc (2) WR 6s 12m **W25M, R20M**; 081°-W-085°-R-087°; W bldg; 48°28'·26N 04°45'·56W.

CHENAL DU FOUR AND CHENAL DE LA HELLE

Ldg lts 158·5°. Front, **Kermorvan** ☆ Fl 5s 20m **22M**; obsc'd by Pte de St Mathieu when brg <341°; W □ twr; *Horn 60s*; 48°21'·72N 04°47'·40W.
Rear, **Pte de St Mathieu** ☆ Fl 15s 56m **29M**; W twr, R top; 48°19'·79N 04°46'·26W. Same twr: Dir F 54m **28M**; intens 157·5°-159·5°.
⚓ Q WRG 26m, W14M, R/G11M; 085°-G-107°-W-116°-R-134°; W twr 54 m WNW of previous entry; 48°19'·80N 04°46'·30W.
Plâtresses N ⚓ Fl G 2·5s; 48°26'·61N 04°50'·73W.
Valbelle ⚓ Fl (2) R 6s 8m 5M; 48°26'·42N 04°50'·03W.
Plâtresses SE ⚓ Fl (2) G 6s; 48°25'·96N 04°50'·52W.
Tendoc ⚓ 48°25'·67N 04°49'·44W.
Saint Paul ⚓ Oc (2) R 6s; 48°24'·82N 04°49'·16W.
Pte de Corsen ⚓ Dir Q WRG 33m W12M, R/G8M; 008°-R-012°-W-015° (ldg sector)- G-021°; W hut; 48°24'·89N 04°47'·61W.
Taboga ⚓ 48°23'·77N 04°48'·08W.

CHENAL DE LA HELLE

Ldg lts 137·9°: Front, **Kermorvan** ☆ see above. Rear, **Lochrist** ☆ Dir Oc (3) 12s 49m **22M**; intens 135°-140°; W 8-sided twr, R top; 48°20'·55N 04°45'·82W.
Luronne ⚓ Bell; 48°26'·61N 04°53'·78W.
Ldg lts 293·5° astern (to join Ch du Four S of St Paul ⚓): Front, Le Faix ⚓ VQ 16m 8M; 48°25'·73N 04°53'·91W. Rear, **Le Stiff** ☆ (below at Ouessant); 6·9M from front.
Ldg line 142·5°, optional day only (to join Ch du Four SE of St Pierre ⚓): Front, **Kermorvan** ☆ see above. Rear, two W gables (Les Pignons de Kéravel, 48m) 48°20'·10N 04°45'·55W.
Pourceaux ⚓ Q; 48°24'·00N 04°51'·31W.
Saint-Pierre ⚓ 48°23'·09N 04°49'·09W.

Rouget ⚓ Fl G 4s; 48°22'·04N 04°48'·88W (Ch du Four).
Grande Vinotière ⚓ L Fl R 10s 15m 5M; R 8-sided twr; 48°21'·93N 04°48'·42W.
Le Conquet, Môle Ste Barbe ⚓ Oc G 4s 5m 6M; 48°21'·58N 04°46'·98W.
Les Renards ⚓ 48°21'·00N 04°47'·48W.
Tournant et Lochrist ⚓ 48°20'·64N 04°48'·12W, Iso R 4s.
Ar Christian Braz ⚓ 48°20'·68N 04°50'·14W, E of Ile de Béniguet.
Ldg line 325°: Front, Grand Courleau ⚓; rear, La Faix (above).
Ldg lts 007°: Front, **Kermorvan** ☆ above. Rear, **Trézien** ☆ Dir Oc (2) 6s 84m **20M**; intens 003°-011°; Gy twr, W on S side; 48°25'·41N 04°46'·74W.
Les Vieux-Moines ⚓ Fl R 4s 16m 5M; 280°-133°; R 8-sided twr; 48°19'·33N 04°46'·63W, 5ca SSW of Pte de St Mathieu.
La Fourmi ⚓ 48°19'·25N 04°47'·97W.

OUESSANT AND ILE MOLENE

OFF USHANT TSS

Ouessant NE ⚓ L Fl 10s; *Whis*; *Racon B, 20M*; 48°59'·51N 05°24'·00W.
Ouessant SW ⚓ Fl 4s 10m 7M; *Racon M, 10M*; AIS MMSI 992271303; 48°30'·00N 05°45'·00W.

ÎLE D'OUESSANT

Le Stiff ☆ Fl (2) R 20s 85m **24M**; two adjoining W twrs; 48°28'·47N 05°03'·41W. Radar twr, conspic, 340m NE, ⚓ Q (day); ⚓ FR (night).
Port du Stiff, E môle ⚓ Dir Q WRG 11m W10M, R/G7M; 251°-G-254°-W-264°-R-267°; W twr, G top; 48°28'·12N 05°03'·25W.

Baie du Stiff: Gorle Vihan ⚓ 48°28'·32N 05°02'·60W.
Men-Korn ⚓ VQ (3) WR 5s 21m 8M; 145°-W-040°-R-145°; BYB twr; 48°27'·96N 05°01'·32W.
Men ar Froud ⚓ 48°26'·62N 05°03'·67W.
La Jument ☆ Fl (3) R 15s 36m **22M**; 241°-199°; *Horn (3) 60s*; Gy 8-sided twr, R top; 48°25'·33N 05°08'·03W.
Nividic ⚓ VQ (9) 10s 28m 10M; 290°-225°; Gy 8-sided twr, helicopter platform; 48°26'·74N 05°09'·06W.
Créac'h ☆ Fl (2) 10s 70m **32M**; obsc 247°-255°; *Horn (2) 120s*; *Racon C (3cm), 20M, 030°-248°*; W twr, B bands; 48°27'·55N 05°07'·76W.

ÎLE MOLÈNE and ARCHIPELAGO

Kéréon ☆ Oc (2+1) WR 24s 38m **W17M**, R7M; 019°-W-248°-R-019°; Gy twr; *Horn (2+1) 120s*; 48°26'·24N 05°01'·55W.
Les Trois-Pierres ⚓ Iso WRG 4s 15m W9M, R/G6M; 070°-G-147°-W-185°-R-191°-G-197°-W-213°-R-070°; W col; 48°24'·70N 04°56'·84W.
Molène, Old môle Dir ⚓ 191°, Fl (3) WRG 12s 6m W9M, R/G7M; 183°-G-190°-W-192°-R-203°; 48°23'·85N 04°57'·29W.
Same structure: Chenal des Laz, Dir ⚓ 261°: Fl (2) WRG 6s 9m W9M, R/G7M; 252·5°-G-259·5°-W-262·5°-R-269·5°.
Pierres-Vertes ⚓ VQ (9) 10s 9m 5M; 48°22'·19N 05°04'·76W.
Pierres Noires ⚓ Bell; 48°18'·47N 04°58'·15W.
Les Pierres Noires ☆ Fl R 5s 27m **19M**; W twr, R top; *Horn (2) 60s*; 48°18'·67N 04°54'·88W.

BREST AND APPROACHES

Basse Royale ⚓ Q (6) + L Fl 15s; 48°17'·45N 04°49'·61W.
Vandrée ⚓ VQ (9) 10s; *Whis*; 48°15'·21N 04°48'·24W.
Goëmant ⚓; 48°15'·12N 04°46'·34W.
La Parquette ⚓ Fl RG 4s 17m R6M, G6M; 244°-R-285°-G-244°; W 8-sided twr, B diagonal stripes; 48°15'·90N 04°44'·29W.
Coq Iroise ⚓ 48°19'·07N 04°43'·99W.
Charles Martel ⚓ Fl (4) R 15s; 48°18'·84N 04°42'·18W.
Trépied ⚓ 48°16'·73N 04°41'·50W.
Swansea Vale ⚓ Fl (2) 6s; *Whis*; 48°18'·27N 04°38'·85W.

GOULET DE BREST

Le Chat ⚓ 48°20'·29N 04°41'·72W (Anse de Bertheaume).
Le Trez Hir ⚓ 48°20'·78N 04°41'·96W.
Pen-Hir ⚓ 48°20'·02N 04°39'·55W.
Pte du Petit-Minou ☆ Fl (2) WR 6s 32m **W19M, R15M**; Shore-R-252°-W-260°-R-307°-W(unintens)-015°-W-065·5°; 70·5°-W-shore; Gy twr, R top; *Horn 60s*; 48°20'·19N 04°36'·86W.
Ldg lts 068°, both Dir Q 30/54m **23/22M**. Front, **Pte du Petit-Minou**, intens 067·3°-068·8°. Rear, **Pte du Portzic** ☆, Aux Dir Q 54m **22M**; intens 065°-071° (see below).
Fillettes ⚓ VQ (9) 10s; 48°19'·75N 04°35'·66W.
Kerviniou ⚓ Fl (2) R 6s; 48°19'·77N 04°35'·25W.
Basse Goudron ⚓ QR; 48°20'·03N 04°34'·86W.
Mengam ⚓ Fl (3) WR 12s 10m W11M, R8M; 034°-R-054°-W-034°; R twr, B bands; 48°20'·19N 04°34'·56W.
Pte du Portzic ☆ Oc (2) WR 12s 56m **W19M, R15M**; 219°-R-259°-W-338°-R-000°-W-065·5° (vis 041°-069° when west of Goulet)-W-219°; Gy twr; 48°21'·49N 04°32'·05W. Same lt ho, Aux Dir Q, rear 068° ldg lt. Aux ⚓ Dir Q (6) + L Fl 15s 54m **23M**; intens 045°-050°.

BREST

Pénoupèle ⚓ Fl (3) R 12s; 48°21'·45N 04°30'·53W.
S jetty ⚓ QR 10m 5M; 094°-048°; W/R twr; 48°22'·10N 04°29'·46W.
E jetty ⚓ QG 10m 7M; 299°-163°; W/G twr; 48°22'·15N 04°29'·22W.
Ldg lts 344°: Front ⚓ VQ WRG 24m W10M, R/G5M; 334°-G-342°-W-346°-R-024°; 48°22'·79N 04°29'·63W. Rear ⚓ Dir VQ 32m 10M; intens 342°-346°; 115m from front.
Le Château Marina, S Jetty hd, ⚓ Fl G 2·5s 8m 4M; 48°22'·66N 04°29'·49W.
Le Château Marina, N Jetty hd, ⚓ Fl R 2·5s 8m 4M; 48°22'·67N 04°29'·45W.

Plot waypoints on chart before use

Port de Commerce, E ent: N jetty ⚓ Oc (2) G 6s 8m 7M; W/G pylon; 48°22'·76N 04°28'·53W. S jetty ⚓ Oc (2) R 6s 8m 5M; 018°-301°; W pylon, R top; 48°22'·69N 04°28'·48W.
R2 ⚓ Fl (2) R 6s; 48°22'·01N 04°28'·75W.
R1 ⚓ Fl G 4s; 48°21'·83N 04°28'·29W.
R4 ⚓ L Fl R 10s; 48°22'·22N 04°28'·06W.
R3 ⚓ Q (6) + L Fl 15s; 48°22'·48N 04°27'·36W.

LE MOULIN BLANC MARINA
Moulin Blanc ⚓ Fl (3) R 12s; 48°22'·79N 04°25'·99W.
MBA ⚓ Q(3) 10s 3m 2M; pontoon elbow; 48°23'·54N 04°25'·74W.

CAMARET
N môle ⚓ Iso WG 4s 7m W12M, G9M; 135°-W-182°-G-027°; W pylon, G top; 48°16'·85N 04°35'·31W.
Port Vauban wavebreak, S end, ⚓ Fl (2) G 6s 2m 2M; 48°16'·74N 04° 35'·33W.
S môle ⚓ Fl (2) R 6s 9m 5M; R pylon; 48°16'·63N 04°35'·33W.
Fish farm: ⚓ Q; 48°17'·13N 04°34'·83W. ⚓ VQ (9) 10s; 48°16'·90N 04°34'·86W. ⚓ 48°17'·07N 04°34'·68W. ⚓ 48°16'·81N 04°34'·75W.

POINTE DU TOULINGUET TO RAZ DE SEIN
Pte du Toulinguet ☆ Oc (3) WR 12s 49m **W15M**, R11M; Shore-W-028°-R-090°-W-shore; W □ twr; 48°16'·81N 04°37'·72W.
La Louve ⚓ 48°16'·76N 04°38'·03W.
Mendufa ⚓ 48°16'·05N 04°39'·43W.
Basse du Lis ⚓ Q (6) + L Fl 15s 9m 6M; 48°12'·99N 04°44'·53W.
Le Chevreau △ 48°13'·30N 04°36'·98W.
Le Bouc ⚓ Q (9) 15s; *Bell;* 48°11'·51N 04°37'·37W.
Basse Vieille ⚓ Fl (2) 6s 8m 7M; 48°08'·22N 04°35'·75W.

MORGAT
Pointe de Morgat ☆ Oc (4) WRG 12s 77m **W15M**, R11M, G10M; Shore-W-281°-G-301°-W-021°-R-043°; W □ twr, R top, W dwelling; 48°13'·17N 04°29'·80W. ⚓ Fl R 4s; 48°13'·60N 04°29'·55W.

DOUARNENEZ to RAZ DE SEIN
Île Tristan ⚓ Oc (3) WR 12s 35m, W13M, R10M; Shore-W-138°-R-153°-W-shore; Gy twr, W band, B top; 48°06'·14N 04°20'·24W.
Port Rhu, Dir ⚓ 157°: Fl(5)WRG 20s16m, W5M, R/G4M; 154°-G-156°-W-158°-R-160°; lt on bridge; 48°05'·40N 04°19'·98W.

Pointe du Millier ☆ Oc (2) WRG 6s 34m **W16M**, R12M, G11M; 080°-G-087°-W-113°-R-120°-W-129°-G-148°-W-251°-R-258°; W house; 48°05'·92N 04°27'·93W.
Basse Jaune ⚓ 48°04'·70N 04°42'·45W.

RAZ DE SEIN
Tévennec ⚓ Q WR 28m W9M R6M; 090°-W-345°-R-090°; W □ twr and dwelling; 48°04'·28N 04°47'·73W. Same twr, Dir ⚓ Fl 4s 24m 12M; intens 324°-332° (through Raz de Sein).

La Vieille ☆ Oc (2+1) WRG 12s 33m **W18M**, R13M, G14M; 290°-W-298°-R-325°-W-355°-G-017°-W-035°-G-105°-W-123°-R-158°-W-205°; Gy □ twr; *Horn (2+1) 60s;* 48°02'·44N 04°45'·40W.
La Plate ⚓ VQ (9) 10s 19m 8M; 48°02'·37N 04°45'·58W.
Le Chat ⚓ Fl (2) WRG 6s 27m, W9M, R/ G6M; 096°-G-215°-W-230°-R-271°-G-286°-R-096°; YB twr; 48°01'·43N 04°48'·86W.

CHAUSSÉE DE SEIN and ÎLE DE SEIN
Men-Brial ⚓ Oc (2) WRG 6s 16m, W12M, R9M, G7M; 149°-G-186°-W-192°-R-221°-W-227°-G-254°; G&W twr; 48°02'·28N 04°50'·97W.
Île de Sein Fl (4) 25s 49m **29M**; W twr, B top; 48°02'·62N 04°52'·02W.
Same twr, Dir Q WRG, W8M, R/G 6M; 267°-G-269°-W-271°-R-275°.
Ar-Men Fl (3) 20s 29m **23M**; W twr, B top; 48°03'·01N 04°59'·87W.
Chaussée de Sein ⚓ VQ (9) 10s 9m 6M; *Whis;* **Racon O (3cm), 10M;** 48°03'·74N 05°07'·75W.

AUDIERNE
Pointe de Lervily ⚓ Fl (3) WR 12s 20m W14M, R11M; 236°-W-269°-R-294°-W-087°-R-109°; W twr, R top; 48°00'·04N 04°33'·94W.
Gamelle W ⚓, VQ (9) 10s; 47°59'·46N 04°32'·85W.
Jetée de Ste-Évette ⚓ Oc (2) R 6s 2m 7M; R lantern; 090°-270°; 48°00'·31N 04°33'·07W.
Passe de l'Est ldg lts 331°: Front, Jetée de Raoulic ⚓ Fl (3) WG 12s 11m, W14M, G9M; Shore-W-034°-G-shore; 48°00'·55N 04°32'·46W.
Rear, Kergadec ⚓ FR 44m 9M; intens 321°-341°; 0·5M from front.
Same twr Dir ⚓ 006°: Q WRG 43m W12M, R/G9M; 000°-G-005·3°-W-006·7°-R-017°; W 8-sided twr, R top; 48°00'·95N 04°32'·79W.
Gamelle E ⚓; 47°59'·46N 04°32'·05W.

POINTE DE PENMARC'H
Eckmühl ☆ Fl 5s 60m **23M**; Gy 8-sided twr; *Horn 60s;* 47°47'·89N 04°22'·36W.
Men-Hir ⚓ Fl (2) WG 6s 19m, W7M, G4M; G135°-315°, W315°-135°; W twr, B band; 47°47'·74N 04°23'·99W.
Cap Caval ⚓ Q (9) 15s; 47°46'·47N 04°22'·68W.
Locarec ⚓ Iso WRG 4s 11m, W9M, R/G6M; 063°-G-068°-R-271°-W-285°-R-298°-G-340°-R-063°; iron col on rk; 47°47'·29N 04°20'·31W.-

LE GUILVINEC
Névez ⚓ Fl G 2·5s; 47°45'·84N 04°20'·08W.
Ldg lts (triple Q) 053°, all synch: Front, ⚓ Q 7m 8M; 233°-066°; W pylon; Môle de Léchiagat, spur; 47°47'·43N 04°17'·07W.
Middle, ⚓ WG 12m W14M, G11M; 006°-W-293°-G-006°; synch; R □ on R col; Rocher Le Faoutés, 210m from front.   **Rear,** ⚓ Q 26m 8M; 051·5°-054·5°, R □ on W twr; 0·58M from front.
Spineg ⚓ Q (6) + L Fl 15s; 47°45'·19N 04°18'·90W.

LESCONIL
Karek Greis ⚓ Q (3) 10s; 47°46'·03N 04°11'·36W.
Men-ar-Groas ⚓ Fl (3) WRG 12s 14m, W10M, R/G7M; 268°-G-313°-W-333°-R-050°; W lt ho, G top; 47°47'·79N 04°12'·68W.

9.20.5 PASSAGE INFORMATION
More Passage Information is threaded between successive harbours in this Area. **Bibliography**: *North Brittany and Channel Islands CC* (Wiley/Cumberlidge); *The Channel CC* (NDL/Featherstone & Aslett); *Channel Pilot* (NP 27); *Channel Havens* (ACN/Endean).

NORTH BRITTANY
This ever-popular cruising ground (AC 2668, 2647, 2643, 2028) is not one to trifle with, but conversely it is rewarding to navigate into a remote anchorage or small fishing harbour. Here the unique character and appeal of N Brittany is all around you.

Good landfall marks must be carefully identified, as a back-up to GPS, before closing the rock-strewn coast. In rough weather, poor visibility (fog and summer haze are frequent) or if uncertain of position, it may be prudent to lie off and wait for conditions

to improve; there are few safe havens. Closer inshore the tidal streams are variable with associated overfalls. Thorough careful planning remains the key to safe pilotage.

In the E of the area the outer approaches to **Paimpol, Île de Bréhat, Lézardrieux** and **Tréguier** may be complicated by strong tidal streams. At times there may be a proliferation of landmarks which must be selectively identified. Concentrate on those which affect your pilotage and discard those which are non-essential and may even distract you from the task.

Once W of **Roscoff** there are few safe hbrs and anchorages until **L'Aberwrac'h** where many British yachts tend to pause and await good conditions for negotiating the Chenal du Four. This is rarely as difficult as it is imagined to be. The Atlantic swell can be a new experience for some, but in moderate winds it is rarely a hazard. It can however much reduce the range at which objects, especially floating marks and other small craft, are seen.

PAIMPOL TO PLOUMANAC'H

In the offing, 11-18M NNE of Île de Bréhat and on a direct track from/to Guernsey, are Plateau de Barnouic (lit) and **Plateau des Roches Douvres** (light house); both with drying and sub-merged rks, to be given a wide berth in poor vis (AC 2027, 2028, 3673, 3672).

Approaching L'Ost-Pic from the SE, keep to seaward of the three ECM marks E of it or enter Baie de **Paimpol** from a point about 1M E of the most N'ly ECM (Les Charpentiers); but it is safe to pass about 300m east of L'Ost Pic in moderate weather.

The Ferlas channel (AC 3673) lies E-W south of Ile de Bréhat, and is useful if entering/leaving R. Trieux from/to the E. It is easiest to beacon-hop past the 5 SCM bcns and 1 IDM bcn marking the N side of the chan; the S side is less well marked.

For the many yachts approaching from Guernsey, Les Héaux-de-Bréhat light house is a conspic landfall day/night for either Tréguier or Lézardrieux. Closer in or from the E, La Horaine (lt beacon) is a better landfall for the latter. It marks the Plateaux de la Horaine and des Échaudés and other rocks to the SE. In poor visibility it should be closed with caution and left at least 7ca to the SE, as the flood stream sets strongly onto it.

The Grand Chenal 224·7° is the main, lit channel into the R. de Trieux for **Lézardrieux** and further up-river to **Pontrieux**. From NW the unlit Chenal de La Moisie leads 159° to join the Grand Chenal off Ile de Bréhat.

The **Passe de la Gaine** 241·5° is a useful inshore route between Lézardrieux and Tréguier, avoiding a detour round Les Héaux. If taken at above half tide, it presents no problem in fair weather. But it is unlit and from the NE the distant ldg marks are hard to see in poor visibility or against a low sun. However two SHM beacons to the S and SW of Les Héaux-de-Bréhat light house can be used as a handrail towards Pont de la Gaine.

The Grande Passe 137·3° into **Rivière de Tréguier** is well lit, but ldg marks are hard to see by day. Use the NE Passage with caution.

Between Basse Crublent lt buoy and Port Blanc unmarked rocks extend 2M offshore. **Port Blanc** (AC 3672) can be difficult to identify by day until it opens on 150°. **Perros-Guirec** is approached either side of Ile Tomé from NE or NW via well lit/marked channels; take care not to be neaped. **Ploumanac'h** can only be entered by day. It boasts some of the most spectacular pink granite along the North Brittany coast.

LES SEPT ÎLES TO BAIE DE MORLAIX

(AC 2026). **Les Sept Îles** (AC 2027) consist of five main islands and several islets, through which the tide runs strongly. Île aux Moines is lit, and all the islands are bird sanctuaries. Further W, Plateau des Triagoz has offlying dangers WSW and NE of the lt, where the sea breaks heavily.

▶*Here the stream turns ENE at HW Brest −0325, and WSW at HW Brest +0245, sp rates both 3·8kn.*◀

Trégastel-Plage is a small anchorage W of Ploumanac'h. To the SW the coast as far as **Trébeurden** is not easily approached due to many offlying rks. The radome NE of Trébeurden is conspic. Further S in the Baie de Lannion is Locquémeau and anchorages near the mouth of the drying R. Léguer up to **Lannion**. Locquemeau is a pleasant drying harbour 3·5M SW of Locquemeau. **Primel-Trégastel**, at the E ent to Baie de Morlaix, is a useful inlet to await the tide up to Morlaix. To the N Plateau de la Méloine dries.

The B de Morlaix (AC 2745) is bestrewn with drying rks and shoals, all marked. Careful pilotage and adequate visibility are needed to negotiate any of the chans which are narrow in parts. Chenal de Tréguier 190·5° and the Grand Chenal 176·4° are both lit. The former should only be used HW ±3 due to shoals at the S end. Grand Chenal passes close E of Île Ricard with Île Louet and La Lande lights in transit; abeam Calhic bn tr alter to port to pass between Château du Taureau (conspic) and Île Louet. Continue SSE and up-river to lock into **Morlaix** Marina in complete shelter. The ⚓age NE of Carantec is reached from Chenal Ouest de Ricard.

ÎLE DE BATZ TO LE FOUR

▶*2M N of Île de Batz the E-going stream begins at HW Brest −0400, and the W-going stream at HW Brest +0200, sp rates 3·8kn. The flood and ebb streams deflected N of Ile de Batz may be >5kn, in opposition and violent. Against any existing sea state, the resultant breaking seas can endanger small craft which are therefore strongly advised to pass at least 2-2½M north of Batz. See the French tidal stream atlas 563-UJA.*◀

Approaching **Roscoff** from the NE, leave Astan ECM lt buoy to stbd tracking with Men Guen Bras lt bcn in transit 213° with Chapelle St Barbe, to round Ar Chaden lt bcn for Roscoff's drying harbour (AC 2026, 2025).

S of the island **Canal de L'Île de Batz**, day only and above half tide, requires careful pilotage at its narrower eastern end. From near Ar Chaden steer 275° for the Q bn at end of the conspic LW ferry pier. Pass 30m N of this bn, then alter to 300° for Run Oan SCM. Thence steer 283°, leaving Perroch NCM bcn twr 100m to port. When clear of this rky, drying shoal alter to 270°, leaving Porz Kernok hbr bkwtrs well to stbd and aiming midway between L'Oignon NCM and La Croix SCM bcns. With these abeam steer 281° for Basse Plate NCM bn; thence West into open waters.

Proceeding W from Île de Batz towards Le Four there are many off-lying dangers, in places 3M offshore. Swell may break on shoals even further to seaward. The tide runs strongly, and in poor vis or bad weather it is a coast to avoid. But in good conditions this is an admirable cruising ground with delightful harbours such as Moguériec, Brignogan, L'Aberwrac'h, L'Aberbenoit, Portsall and Argenton. N of L'Aberwrac'h is the conspic Île Vierge lt ho, reputedly the tallest in the world.

▶*N of Le Libenter buoy, off L'Aberwrac'h, the NE-going stream starts at HW Brest −0500, sp rate 3·8kn, and the WSW-going stream at HW Brest +0100.*◀

L'Aberwrac'h is accessible at all tides and makes a useful staging post to catch the tide S through Chenal du Four. Its appeal is enhanced by the marina's protection from NW'lies.

W of L'Aberwrac'h a chan leads inshore of Roches de Portsall to Le Four lt ho. To identify positively the distant marks it needs care, by day only, in good vis without the sun in your eyes. It saves only 1M against the outer route via Basse Paupian WCM buoy. Use AC 1432 or SHOM 7094 and a detailed pilot book.

OUESSANT (USHANT)

(AC 2356) Île d'Ouessant lies 10M off NW Brittany, surrounded by five lt ho's. It is a rky island, with dangers extending 5ca to NE, 7½ca to SE, 1·5M to SW and 1M to NW; here Chaussée de Keller is a dangerous chain of unmarked drying and submerged rks running 1M W of Île de Keller and into the ITZ. There are anchorages and moorings at **Lampaul** and **Baie du Stiff**, the former exposed to the SW and the latter to the NE.

Ouessant is an important landfall, but in thick weather it is an unhealthy area, and it is prudent to stay in harbour until the vis improves. In fair weather and reasonable visibility the pilotage in the well marked chans between it and the mainland is not too demanding. But the tide runs hard in places, causing overfalls when against wind >F5.

▶*Tidal streams are strong around the island, and in the chans between it and mainland. Off Baie du Stiff (lt, radar twr) the stream turns NW at HW Brest +0400, and SE at HW Brest −0200, max rates 2¾kn.*◀

The routes outside Ouessant TSS or via the ITZ add much to the distance and are exposed to sea, swell and shipping. Yachts usually take the inshore chans, ie: Chenal du Four, most direct and popular; Chenal de la Helle, an alternative to N part of Chenal du Four (also gives access to Île Molène), is less direct but better in bad weather. Passage du Fromveur, SE of Ouessant, is easiest but longer and can be extremely rough. ▶*The NE-going stream starts HW Brest −0515, max rates 8-9kn; the SW-going stream starts HW Brest +0045, max rates 7-8kn.*◀

9.20.6 Special Notes for France: See 9.17.6.

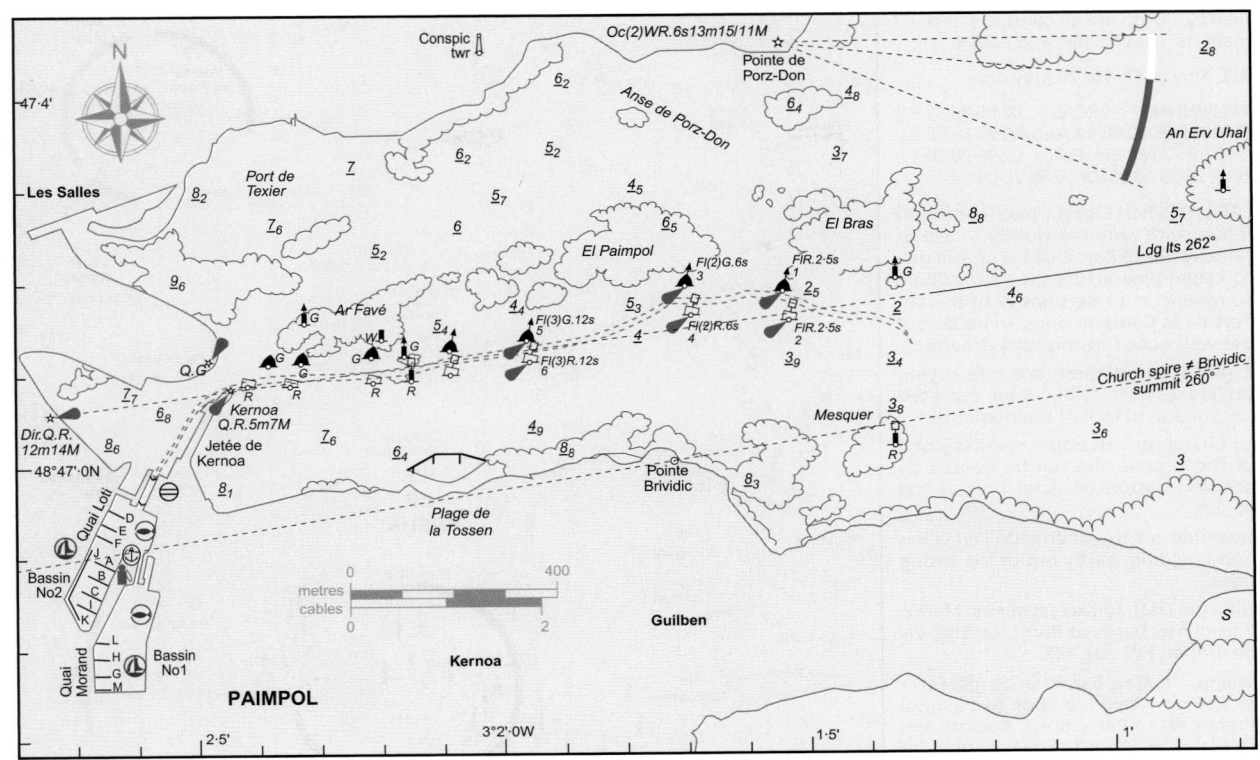

9.20.7 PAIMPOL

Côtes d'Armor **48°47´·00N 03°02´·56W** ❄❄⚓♦♦♦♦✿✿

CHARTS AC 2668, 2027, 2028, 3673; SHOM 7152, 7154, 7127; Navi 537; Imray C34; Stanfords 2, 17.

TIDES Dover −0525; ML 6·1; Duration 0600.

Standard Port ST MALO (←—)

Times				Height (metres)			
High Water		Low Water		MHWS	MHWN	MLWN	MLWS
0100	0800	0300	0800	12·2	9·3	4·2	1·5
1300	2000	1500	2000				
Differences PAIMPOL							
−0010	−0005	−0035	−0025	−1·4	−1·0	−0·4	−0·2

SHELTER Good shelter from all winds in hbr, but few ⚓s as most of the Anse de Paimpol dries, including the appr chan to hbr.

NAVIGATION Bearing in mind the very large tidal range, there is enough water in the bay for most craft from half-flood.

WPT 48°47´·82N 02°54´·58W, 262°/5·2M to Kernoa jetty hd. Chenal de la Jument 260° is the outer appr. After La Jument PHM bn tr, alter onto 262·2° inner ldg line; or ⚓ in 5m to await the tide. Small buoys/bns in final 1M of chan (dries 6–7m) may be hard to see against a low evening sun. The drying rks (El Paimpol, El Bras and Ar Fav) are close N of the ldg line.

An alternative appr from Île de Bréhat at HW±4 lies E of Les Piliers NCM bn tr, thence S past Pte de la Trinité. Or appr via Cadenenou NCM and Chenal du Denou 193°. SHOM 7127 is essential for these and other inshore passages.

LIGHTS AND MARKS From the S L'Ost-Pic lt is a conspic □ W tr 4M E of Paimpol. Pte de Porz-Don, lt ho on a white house, is 7ca ENE of hbr ent; its W sector leads 270° to intercept the inner 262·2° ldg lts at La Jument bcn twr. A conspic twr (52m) is 3ca W of Porz-Don.

Chenal de la Jument, outer ldg marks 260°: Paimpol ✠ spire (the N'ly of two) on with the ill-defined summit of Pte Brividic. Inner ldg lts, both QR, 262·2°: front, Jetée de Kernoa.

R/T HM and Lock Ch 09 (0800-1200LT and lock opening hrs).

TELEPHONE Port Mgr 02·96·20·80·77; ⊖ 02·96·20·81·87; Aff Mar 02·96·55·35·00; CROSS 02·98·89·31·31; Auto 08·92·68·08·22; Police 02·96·20·80·17; Ⓗ 02·96·55·60·00; Dr 02·96·55·15·15; Brit Consul 02.23.18.30.30.

FACILITIES Lock opens HW ±2½, 60m x 12m, ☎ 02·96·20·90·02. **Marina** ☎ 02·96·20·47·65. port-plaisance.paimpol@wanadoo.fr www.ville-paimpol.fr **Basin No 2** 306+24 Ⓥ, €2·25; Ⓥ berths at pontoon A, min depth 3·8m. D (hose), Slip, Wi-Fi, @, ♿. **Basin No 1** Yachts up to 40m LOA. C (25, 6 and 4 ton). **E Quays**, ⚒, ME, El, CH, SHOM, Ⓔ. **Town** 🛒, Ⓗ, R, Bar, Gaz, P (cans), 🔲, ✉, Ⓑ, ≠, ✈ Dinard, Brest, Rennes. Ferry: Roscoff, St Malo.

9.20.8 ÎLE DE BRÉHAT

Côtes d'Armor **48°51´·00N 03°00´·00W** ❄❄❄⚓♦♦✿✿✿

CHARTS AC 2668, 2027, 2028, 3673; SHOM 7152, 7154; Navi 537; Imray C34; Stanfords 2, 17.

TIDES −0525 Dover; ML 5·8; Duration 0605.

Standard Port ST MALO (←—)

Times				Height (metres)			
High Water		Low Water		MHWS	MHWN	MLWN	MLWS
0100	0800	0300	0800	12·2	9·3	4·2	1·5
1300	2000	1500	2000				
Differences LES HEAUX DE BRÉHAT							
−0020	−0020	−0055	−0045	−2·4	−1·7	−0·7	−0·3
ÎLE DE BRÉHAT							
−0015	−0015	−0045	−0035	−1·9	−1·4	−0·6	−0·3

SHELTER Good in Port Clos and at Port de la Corderie, except in W-NW'lies. See Facilities for other ⚓s depending on wind direction.

NAVIGATION From the NE use R. Trieux WPT (9.20.9) and 224·7° ldg line. From the N use Ch de Bréhat 167·4° (distant ldg marks), then enter Ferlas Chan from the E via WPT 48°49´·39N 02°55´·08W, 277°/3·4M to abm Port Clos. For the R Trieux, follow Ferlas Chan transits Ⓒ – Ⓕ, as shown on AC 3673.

LIGHTS AND MARKS Chapelle St Michel, Amer du Rosedo and the nearby Sig stn are all conspic. For the 3 main lts, see chartlet and 9.20.4.

R/T Sig stn Ch 16, 10, day only.

TELEPHONE CROSS 02·98·89·31·31; SNSM 02·96·20·00·14; Auto 08·92·68·08·22; ⊖ 02·96·20·81·87; Police 02·96·20·80·17; Ⓗ 02·96·55·60·00; Dr 02·96·20·09·51.

FACILITIES Port Clos the main hbr (dries) is busy with vedettes. No AB; ⌕ clear of fairway. SW of Port Clos ⌕ is prohib due to cables/pipe across the Ferlas Chan. So moor/⌕ in **Le Kerpont** W of Bréhat.
Port de la Corderie dries; some ⚓s but get well out of strong tidal streams.

E of Le Bourg there are free drying private ⚓s near ⌕, but some reported unsafe due to lack of maintenance.

La Chambre: ⌕ in upper reaches just S of the ⚓ area. Slip can be floodlit by pressing button on lamp post at top of slip.

Guerzido off the Chenal de Ferlas has good holding, partly out of the strong tides.

Hbrs (no HM), full access at HW, M, FW, P from fuel barge at Port Clos, Slip; CN de Bréhat, FW, Bar, ME.

Village 🛒, Gaz, Bar, R, 🗊, ✉, Ⓑ. Ferry to Pte de l'Arcouest, bus to Paimpol thence ⇌ to Paris, Brest, Roscoff and St Malo. ✈ Dinard, Brest, Rennes to London. No cars on island.

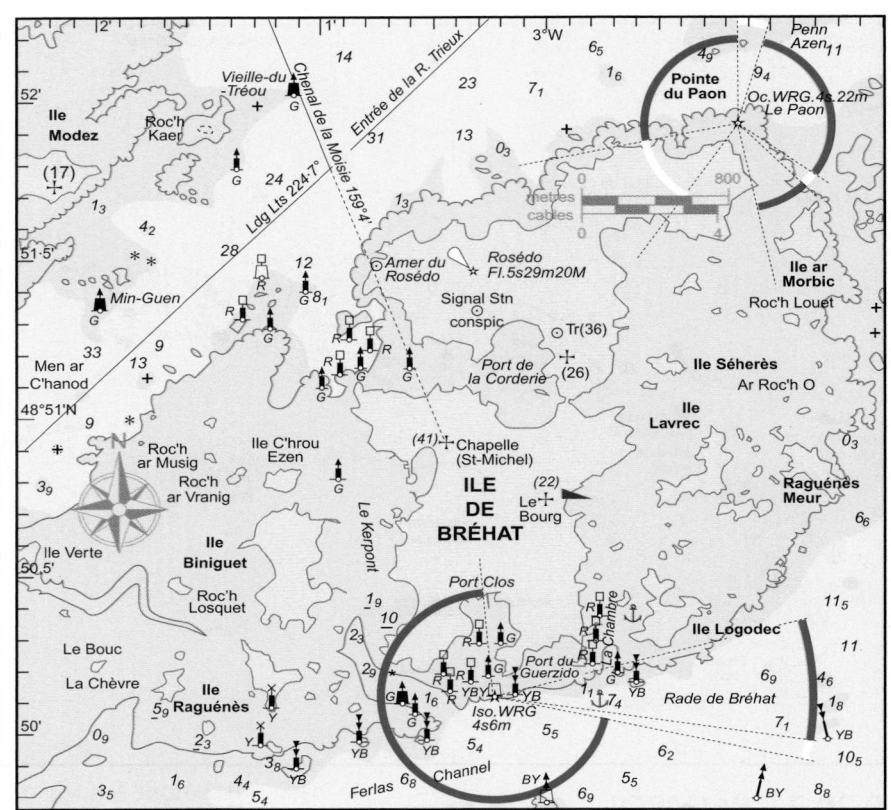

OUTER APPROACHES TO LÉZARDRIEUX AND TRÉGUIER WITH PASSE DE LA GAINE BETWEEN

9.20.9 LÉZARDRIEUX

Côtes d'Armor 48°47´·34N 03°05´·89W ✵✵✵⚓⚓⚓🏵🏵

CHARTS AC 2668, 2027, 2028, 3673; SHOM 7152/3, 7126/7; Navi 537; Imray C34; Stanfords 2, 17.

TIDES –0510 Dover; ML 5·9; Duration 0610.

Standard Port ST MALO (←)

Times				Height (metres)			
High Water		Low Water		MHWS	MHWN	MLWN	MLWS
0100	0800	0300	0800	12·2	9·3	4·2	1·5
1300	2000	1500	2000				
Differences LÉZARDRIEUX							
–0020	–0015	–0055	–0045	–1·7	–1·3	–0·5	–0·2

SHELTER Very good in all weathers. Strong stream at half tide.

NAVIGATION WPT 48°54´·98N 02°56´·07W, 224·7°/6·7M to La Croix, front 224·7° ldg lt. Offshore dangers include Roches Douvres, Barnouic, Plateau de la Horaine and rky shoals to the W in the outer apps. Off the river ent allow for strong cross streams.

The 3 well-marked approach channels are:
- **Grand Chenal**, main lit chan from NE, best for strangers. Ldg lts 224·7°: Front, La Croix, two double-barrelled trs, W on NE side with R tops. Rear, Bodic (2·1M from front) high up amongst the trees.
- **Ch de la Moisie**, unlit from the NW: Amer du Rosédo, W obelisk on 159·4° with St Michael's chapel (both conspic on Île de Bréhat). It also connects with Passe de la Gaine, short cut from/to Tréguier (9.20.11); see chartlet on previous page.
- **Ferlas Chan** (lit) from E or W, passing S of Île de Bréhat. By day follow the 5 SCM bcns on the N side of the chan. At night: W sector (281°) of Men Joliguet, WCM bcn twr. W sector (257°) of Roche Quinonec at Loguivy. W sector (271°) of Kermouster joins Coatmer 218·7° ldg line.

Within the Trieux river:
- Coatmer ldg lts 218·7°: front, low down amongst trees; rear, 660m from front, high up almost obsc'd by trees.
- W sector (200°) of Les Perdrix, a stout green bcn twr. Speed limit 5kn from Perdrix to the bridge.

LIGHTS AND MARKS See 9.20.4 for offshore lts at Roches Douvres lt ho, Barnouic ECM bn tr, Les Héaux de Bréhat lt ho and, on Île de Bréhat, Pte du Paon and Rosédo. Outer and inner approach marks are described above. There are no navigational lights S of Perdrix.

Beware, at night, the unlit, 16m high Roc'h Donan 400m S of Perdrix. At the tidal marina floodlights on shore may dazzle yachts arriving.

R/T Marina Ch 09 (0730-2200 Jul/Aug. 0800-1200 and 1400-1800 rest of year).

TELEPHONE Aff Mar (Paimpol) 02·96·55·35·00; ⊖ at Paimpol 02·96·20·81·87; CROSS 02·98·89·31·31; Auto 08·92·68·08·22; Police 02·96·20·18·17; Dr 02·96·20·18·30; Brit Consul 02.23.18.30.30.

FACILITIES Tidal marina ☎ 02·96·20·14·22. http://port.3douest. com/lezardrieux/ port-lezardrieux@wanadoo.fr Access H24. 380 + 50 Ⓥ. Berth on the first pontoon (No 1) or as directed by HM. AB €2·39. Multihulls and boats >12·5m LOA should moor on ⚓s €1·67 or Ⓥ pontoon. Slip, P, D, ME, El, CH, SM, ✕, C (50 ton), Divers, Ⓔ, Gaz, 🗑, R, Bar, Shwrs €2·00.

YC de Trieux ☎ 02·96·20·10·39.

Non-tidal marina (247 AB) has some Ⓥ berths (2·4m inside). The retaining wall is marked by 5 unlit Y SPM perches, the sill by PHM/SHM perches. Access over sill 4·9m with automatic flap. As sill covers on the flood, @ CD +6·15m, flap drops to give 1·1m clearance. A depth gauge shows water over sill. The waiting pontoon is as on chartlet. IPTS sigs 2 & 4 control entry/exit.

Town 🛒, Gaz, R, Bar, ✉, Ⓑ, ⇌ (occas bus to Paimpol & Lannion), ✈ Lannion. Ferry: Roscoff.

Yachts can continue about 12km up river (via bridge, clearance 17m) to lock in at Pontrieux (9.20.10) in complete shelter.

9.20.10 PONTRIEUX

Côtes d'Armor 48°42'·74N 03°08'·98W ✤✤✤⚓⚓⚓✿✿✿

CHARTS Navi 537; AC 3673 & SHOM 7126 end S of Lézardrieux. A useful river guide/map is available from HM Pontrieux.

TIDES HW at Pontrieux lock is also HW St Malo (9.18.12).

SHELTER Complete.

NAVIGATION See 9.20.9 for the river up to Lézardrieux. Not before HW –3, proceed via suspension bridge (17m clearance at MHWS) for 6M up-river, keeping to high, rky bank on bends. Between river bends the best water is indicated by the alignment of reflective posts (1-2m high) near the bends. Allow 1½ hrs for the passage aiming to reach the lock at HW –1, to de-conflict from sand coasters *(sabliers)* which use the lock occas at HW. Below Château de la Roche Jagu a waiting buoy is accessible HW±3.

Lock (48°42'·78N 03°08'·31W) ☎ 02·96·95·60·70; opens HW –2¼ to +2¼ Jun-Sep; –2 to +1¼ Oct-May. 2 half-tide waiting buoys.

LIGHTS AND MARKS River is unlit; few marks.

R/T Lock and port Ch 12, at lock hrs. ☎ link to HM Pontrieux.

TELEPHONE Auto 08·36·68·08·22. Public ☎ at Ch Roche Jagu.

FACILITIES Berth in 1·5-3m at quay (SE bank), about 1km WSW of lock. HM ☎ 02·96·95·34·87, 06.73.87.07.95. www.letrieux.com 80+40 ♥, AB €1·88, FW, AC, C (6 & 20 ton), ▯, R, Bar, &.
Town Bar, R, Slip, 🛒, Gaz, P, D, @, ⒷⒸ, ✉, ⇌ Paimpol/Guingamp, ✈ Brest, Rennes, Dinard & Paris. Taxi 02·96·95·60·43.

9.20.11 TRÉGUIER

Côtes d'Armor 48°47'·21N 03°13'·27W ✤✤✤⚓⚓⚓✿✿✿

CHARTS AC 2668, 2027, 2028, 3672; SHOM 7152, 7126; Navi 537; Imray C34; Stanfords 2, 17.

TIDES –0540 Dover; ML 5·7; Duration 0600.

Standard Port ST MALO (←)

Times				Height (metres)			
High Water		Low Water		MHWS	MHWN	MLWN	MLWS
0100	0800	0300	0800	12·2	9·3	4·2	1·5
1300	2000	1500	2000				
Differences TRÉGUIER							
–0020	–0020	–0100	–0045	–2·3	–1·6	–0·6	–0·2
PORT-BÉNI (5ca SSE of La Corne lt twr)							
–0025	–0025	–0105	–0050	–2·4	–1·7	–0·6	–0·2

SHELTER Good. Possible ⚓s, keeping clear of fairway and fish farms, as shown on AC 3672: 7ca SW of La Corne lt tr, but exposed to N'lies; N and S of La Roche Jaune village; and in well sheltered pool (6m) 1ca NE of No 10 buoy (8ca N of marina).

NAVIGATION WPT 48°54'·13N 03°11'·50W (abeam Basse Crublent PHM buoy), 137°/2·1M to Pen ar Guézec SHM light buoy, a key turning point. Caution: strong tidal streams across the well lit chan. The three approach channels, with marks, are:

- **Grande Passe** 137·3°. Ldg marks (hard to see by day): Front, Port de la Chaine, white ho; rear, St Antoine, RW ho. At Pen ar Guézec SHM buoy alter 216° in La Corne's W sector. A clearer transit from Basse Crublent is: Pleubian spire (charted) and adjacent water tower (on the skyline), ≠ 154° to pass between Pierre à l'Anglais and Le Corbeau buoys (both lit).

- **Passe de la Gaine** Unlit short cut to/from Lézardrieux. See chartlet below 9.20.8. Adequately marked, navigable by day with care, sufficient rise of tide, good vis; but marks hard to see from afar, especially against a low sun or in poor vis. 241·5° ldg marks: Front, Men Noblance bcn twr, W with B band, ≠ rear mark (W wall with B vert stripe) below the skyline and just right of conspic Plougrescant ✠ spire. Stay exactly on transit to keep in narrow chan. See 9.20.5.

- **Passe du Nord-Est** 205°/207°: unlit, dangerous with W-NW winds as sea breaks across the shallowest part of chan. On 205° keep W of La Jument NCM buoy and adjacent rky shoals; jink port onto 207° transit of Tréguier spire and Skeiviec bcn twr, for direct appr to La Corne.

Within the river heed lateral buoys and bns, eg keep E of Taureau SHM light buoy, 300m SW of La Corne lt ho, to clear the adjacent drying mudbank. Speed limit is 6kn south of No 3 SHM lt buoy.

LIGHTS AND MARKS See 9.20.4 and chartlet. Important marks: La Corne, a stumpy WR lt tr; 6ca to the N is Men Noblance black/white bcn tr (for Passe de la Gaine); and 4ca SW is Skeiviec W bn tr. The spire of Tréguier cathedral is 4·6M SSW of La Corne and may be obscured by high wooded banks on first entering the estuary.

R/T Marina Ch 09. Office hrs in season, 7/7: 0700-2145 All LT. Winter, M-F 0800-1200 & 1330-1730 (Sat 1630); Sun shut.

TELEPHONE Aff Mar 02·96·92·30·38 (Paimpol); ⊖ 02·96·20·81·37; CROSS 02·96·89·31·31; Auto 08·92·68·08·22; Police 02·96·20·84·30; Dr 02·96·92·32·14; Ⓗ 02·96·05·71·11; Brit Consul 02.23.18.30.30.

FACILITIES A 30m waiting pontoon, least depth 1·2m LWS, is 500m N of marina. Boats >15m LOA & multihulls may use it overnight. **Marina** *Arr/dep at slack water* as the tide sets hard N/S diagonally through the pontoons. Berth bows into tide on outer part of E, D or C pontoons. HM portplaisance.treguier@wanadoo.fr ☎ 02·96·92·42·37, mobile 06.72.70.70.20 www.ville-treguier.fr/ port.php 260 + 70 ♥, €2·20. D (E pontoon), Slip, @, Wi-Fi, ME, C (40 ton) CH, El, ✕, Gaz, ▯, BY ☎ 02·96·92·15·15.

Bar des Plaisanciers ☎ 02·96·92·49·69, 365/365. **CN de Tréguier** ☎ 02.96.92.37.49, opposite marina, Bar open Sat evenings only.

Town P & D (cans), 🛒 (small s/market near cathedral delivers), R, Bar, ✉, Ⓑ. Market Wed. ⇌ via bus to Paimpol, Guingamp, Lannion. ✈ Brest, Rennes, Dinard. Ferry: Roscoff, St Malo.

150·4° towards Le Voleur Dir lt; the rear ldg mark is hard to see amongst trees. From the SW approach via Basse Guazer PHM buoy, 7ca SW of the WPT. Beware ebb tide initially setting hard toward drying Plateau du Four.

LIGHTS AND MARKS 150·4° ldg marks: Front, Le Voleur Dir lt, low down amongst trees (between white cottage and Grand Hotel, conspic white block); rear, 5ca from front, La Comtesse Mill, unlit and obscured by trees on skyline. A white obelisk (16m) on Île du Château Neuf is conspic to stbd of the fairway. A smaller obelisk to port on Île St Gildas is less obvious.

R/T *Port Blanc* Ch 09, 16.

TELEPHONE Aff Mar 02.96.92.30.38; ⊖ 02.96.20.81.87; CROSS 02.33.52.72.13; Auto 08.92.68.02.22; Brit Consul 02.23.18.30.30.

FACILITIES 5 Y ⚓s, marked VISIT (A-E) in approx 5m. Safe ⚓ and good holding, where charted in 7m. Or dry out alongside quays, 1·3m; pre-recce advised. HM ☎ 02.96.92.89.11 in sailing school. AB or ⚓ €7.00 all LOA, FW, P&D (cans), C (16 ton), Slip, CH, El, ME, ⚒.

Town 🛒 (basic), R, Bar; Taxi 02.96.92.64.00, ⇌ Lannion. ✈ Brest, Rennes, Dinard. Ferry: Roscoff.

9.20.13 PERROS-GUIREC

Côtes d'Armor **48° 48'·17N 03° 26'·21W** (Jetty hd)
❄❄⚓⚓⚓✿✿

CHARTS AC 2668, 2027, 3672; SHOM 7152, 7125; Navi 537, 538; Imray C34; Stanfords 2, 17.

TIDES –0550 Dover; ML 5·4; Duration 0605.

Standard Port ST MALO (←)

Times				Height (metres)			
High Water		Low Water		MHWS	MHWN	MLWN	MLWS
0100	0800	0300	0800	12·2	9·3	4·2	1·5
1300	2000	1500	2000				
Differences PERROS-GUIREC							
–0040	–0045	–0120	–0105	–2·9	–2·0	–0·8	–0·3

SHELTER Very good in marina. Off Pointe du Chateau safe ⚓, except in NE'lies, in approx 3m good holding; plus 5 small W ⚓s.

NAVIGATION From the E, WPT 48°49'·86N 03°23'·66W, 224·5°/2·4M to Jetée Linkin. From the W, WPT 48°50'·53N 03°26'·45W, 143·5°/1·8M to join 224·5° ldg line. Caution: Rocks extend 7ca W and 6ca NE of Île Tomé. Local moorings E of Jetée du Linkin are marked by 2 SHM buoys.

9.20.12 PORT BLANC

Côtes d'Armor **48°50'·54N 03°18'·89W** ❄❄⚓⚓⚓✿✿

CHARTS AC 2668, 2027, 3672; SHOM 7152, 7125/6; Navi 537, 538; Imray C34; Stanfords 2, 17.

TIDES –0545 Dover; ML 5·3; Duration 0600. Interpolate between Les Héaux de Bréhat and Perros-Guirec. HW–0040 and ht –2·0m on St Malo. MHWS 9·0m; MHWN 6·8m.

SHELTER Good in natural hbr (aka as Port Bago), but very uncomfortable in winds with any N in them.

NAVIGATION WPT 48°52'·24N 03°20'·16W, 150°/1·9M to first ⚓. The fairway does not open up until at the WPT. Appr on ldg line

LIGHTS AND MARKS See chartlet and 9.20.4. 225° ldg marks are distant and hard to see by day, but bcns/buoys in the appr are adequate. Passe de l'Ouest: Kerjean Dir lt 143·5° is also hard to see, but the old lt ho (gable end) on the foreshore is clearer.

R/T Marina Ch 09, 16.

TELEPHONE Entry gate 02·96.23.19.03; Aff Mar 02·96.91.21.28; ⊖ 02·96.20.81·87; Auto 08·92.68·08·22; CROSS 02·98·89.31.31; SNSM 02·96.91.40.10; Dr 02·96.23.20.01; Police 02·96.23.20.17; Brit Consul 02.23.18.30.30.

FACILITIES Access: 6m narrow gate (no lock) opens when rise of tide reaches 7m. Sill under gate dries 3·5m, giving 3·5m water inside gateway on first opening. Caution: strong current initially. Gate sigs: IPTS. No ⚓ in basin. R & W poles mark retaining wall; do not try to cross it near HW.

Gate opens depending on tidal Coefficient:

Coeff		
<40	=	Shut, 4 days max
40-50	=	HW −½ to HW
50-60	=	HW −1 to +½
60-70	=	HW ±1
>70	=	approx HW ±1½

Gate may open up to 30 mins before the published times, but does not close early.

Marina ☎ 02·96.49.80.50. www.port-perros-guirec.com 720+80 Ⓥ, €2·83. Ⓥ berth on N'most 2 pontoons in 2·5m. P, D, El, ME, ⚒, C (7 ton), CH, Ⓔ, SHOM, SM, Gas, Gaz, Kos, @, ⊡. **YC** ☎ 02·96·91·12·65. **Town** 🛒, R, Bar, Wi-Fi, ✉, Ⓑ. ⇌ Lannion. ✈ Brest. Ferry: Roscoff.

LES SEPT ÎLES *See notes on facing page*

OFFSHORE ISLANDS

LES SEPT ÎLES, Côte d'Armor, **48° 52´·72N 03°29´·16W**. AC 2026, 2027; SHOM 7152 (large scale 1:20,000). See chartlet on previous page. HW–0550 on Dover (UT); +0005 on Brest. HW ht –1·8m on Brest. ML 5·2m. Use 9.20.14 differences.

The whole archipelago, outlined in magenta, is a no-entry bird sanctuary. Île aux Moines is the only one of the 7 islands/islets on which landing is permitted; no shore facilities. It is safe to sail NW of Les Dervinis (SCM buoy) and Les Noires de Rouzic (always visible), a steep-to rocky chain SE of the main group.

Straightforward approach to Île aux Moines, allowing for strong stream. Avoid a rock (0·6m) 300m SE of the island. Best ⚓ (Lat/Long as on line 1) is due E of jetty at E end of Île aux Moines and S of W end of Île Bono; overnight only in calm settled weather. Vedettes use a mooring buoy here. More exposed ⚓s are S of the Old Fort (W end of island), or close S of Île Bono; both require care due to rocks, clearly shown on SHOM 7152. The most dangerous is at 48° 52´·45N 03°28´·68W; it dries 0·1, is rarely seen but often encountered. Only slightly less dangerous is the rock drying 1·4 at 48° 52´·64N 03°28´·28W.

Île aux Moines lt ho is a very conspic grey twr whose 24M beam is obscured by Bono and Rouzic in a 4° arc (237°–241°) and when brg < 039°, ie if tucked into the Baie de Lannion.

9.20.14 PLOUMANAC'H

Côtes d'Armor 48° 49´·78N 03° 29´·51W (Sill) ✦✦⚓⚓✦✦✦

CHARTS AC 2668, 2026, 2027 (limited scale 1:48,700); SHOM 7125 (1:10,000 inset); Navi 537, 538; Imray C34; Stanfords 2, 17.

TIDES –0550 Dover; ML 5·5; Duration 0605.

Standard Port ST MALO (←)

Times				Height (metres)			
High Water		Low Water		MHWS	MHWN	MLWN	MLWS
0100	0800	0300	0800	12·2	9·3	4·2	1·5
1300	2000	1500	2000				
Differences PLOUMANAC'H							
–0035	–0040	–0120	–0100	–2·9	–2·0	–0·7	–0·2

SHELTER Good inside, but appr is difficult in strong N'lies against the ebb. No ⚓ from abeam Mean Ruz lt ho to the hbr sill.

NAVIGATION WPT 48°51´·44N 03°29´·09W, 188°/1·2M to ent between Mean Ruz lt ho and Château Costaérès (conspic). At the entrance beware An Dreuzinier, unmarked rocks (drying 1·4m), 100m N and NE of No 1 SHM perch; not a problem with sufficient rise of tide, but near LW keep very close W of a line 225° through the Nos 2 and 4 PHM perches. 11 unlit perches mark the chan.

Access approx HW ±4¼ at nps, ±3½ at sp. Enter over a sill, drying 2·55m, which retains 1·2m to 2·3m within. Depth gauges are on No 4 (unreliable) and No 12 PHM perches. If the concrete base of No 5 perch (the 3rd SHM) is covered, depth over sill is >1·4m.

LIGHTS AND MARKS See chartlet and 9.20.4. Mean Ruz lt ho is a reddish square twr. Signal stn, 8ca SSE, is conspic from the E. Night entry not advised.

R/T VHF Ch 09.

TELEPHONE Auto 08.92.68.08.22; Dr 02.96.91.42.00; SNSM 02.96.20.00.45; Brit Consul 02.23.18.30.30.

FACILITIES Between Nos 8 and 8bis perches on the E side of chan are 3 waiting buoys marked VPG in 1·5m least depth.

Port de Plaisance Inside the sill, are moorings for FVs and yachts >12m in a trot to stbd of ent in 3m, with 2 drying trots of small craft outboard. For best water keep to port and approach the yacht moorings from NW. ⚓s are 1st trot (A) of dumbell buoys; max LOA 12m. SE & SW sides of hbr are very shallow.

HM (part time) ☎ 02.96.91.44.31 or 02.96.49.80.50 (Perros-Guirec). www.port-perros-guirec.com 230 + 20 ⚓s, €2·37. The full time Perros HM also oversees Ploumanac'h and Anse de Trestraou, a pleasant anchorage on N side of Perros town, well sheltered from S and W winds; exposed to NE'lies.

Quai Bellevue L, Slip, P & D cans. ME ☎ 02.96.23.05.89. **YC de Perros-Guirec** Bus to Lannion & Perros. Ferry: See Roscoff.

ANCHORAGE 1M WEST OF PLOUMANAC'H

TRÉGASTEL-PLAGE, Côtes d'Armor, **48°50´·04N 03°31´·29W**, AC 2026, 2027; SHOM 7152, 7125. HW –0550 on Dover (UT); +0005 and –1·8m on Brest HW; ML 5·1m; Duration 0605. Use 9.20.14 differences.

A large W radome, conspic 3·2M S of the ent, gives general orientation. Enter between PHM bcn on Île Dhu (just W of Île Dé, with dice-shaped Pierre Pendue) and SHM bcn off Le Taureau, rk drying 4·5m (if destroyed the bcn is replaced by a buoy). A conspic house with □ turret, brg approx 165° leads between Île Dhu and Le Taureau. But it is easier to track 183° leaving the 3 PHM bcns about 60m to port. SHOM 7125 (1: 20,000) is strongly advised.

Thence after a SHM bcn, ⚓ or pick up orange ⚓s S of Île Ronde. Good ⚓ in 2m, but exposed to winds from W to N and very uncomfortable near HW springs when swell gets in; quite pleasant at neaps.

Facilities: Slip in E part of hbr. **CN de Trégastel** ☎ 02.96·23·45·05.

Town (Ste Anne, 0·5M inland) CH, ⒷÂⒷ, ✉, ▢, Bar, R, ▦; Dr 02.96·23·88·08; 02.96·15·96·49.

9.20.15 TRÉBEURDEN

Côtes d'Armor **48°46′·29N 03°35′·15W** 🕈 ⚓ ⚓ ⚓ ⚓ 🌸 🌸

TIDES –0605 Dover; ML 5·5; Duration 0605.

Standard Port BREST (→)

Times				Height (metres)			
High Water		Low Water		MHWS	MHWN	MLWN	MLWS
0000	0600	0000	0600	7·0	5·5	2·7	1·1
1200	1800	1200	1800				
Differences TRÉBEURDEN							
+0100	+0110	+0120	+0100	+2·2	+1·8	+0·8	+0·3

CHARTS AC 2026; SHOM 7151/2, 7125, 7124; Navi 537, 538; Imray C34; Stanfords 2, 17.

SHELTER Good in marina (2 - 2·6m). ⚓ off NE side of Île Milliau is exposed to W'lies.

NAVIGATION WPT 48°45′·34N 03°40′·00W, 067°/3M to first PHM buoy in white sector of Lan Kerellec Dir lt. From WSW, go direct to ⊕; thence enter the buoyed chan (105°/088°) to marina.
From E and N, round Bar-ar-Gall and Le Crapaud WCM buoys; continue S for 1·4M, before altering 067° towards the ⊕. If properly planned, the short-cut 183° between Le Crapaud reef and reefs N and S of Île Losket is safe in offshore winds.

LIGHTS AND MARKS See chartlet and 9.20.4. Lan Kerellec Dir lt leads 067° to the start of buoyed chan, aligned approx 100° with ✠ spire (conspic, 115m).

R/T *Port Trébeurden* Ch 09, 16.

TELEPHONE Aff Mar 02·96·91·21·28; ⊖ 02·96·48·45·32; CROSS 02·98·89·31·31; Police 02·96·23·51·96 (Jul/Aug); Brit Consul 02.23.18.30.30.

FACILITIES 10 Y waiting buoys lie S of the fairway and some 600m W of marina ent. Access times based on Coefficients are:

95 (sp)	HW –3½ to +4
70	HW –3¾ to +4¼
45 (np)	HW –4¾ to +5¼

An automatic flap (2·5m) above the sill starts to open when ht of tide is 4·0m and is fully open at 4·3m (conversely on the ebb). Best to calculate tidal heights.
IPTS (sigs 2 and 4) on bkwtr and at gate show when access is possible. Do not ent/exit within 20 mins of the flap moving, due to fast, turbulent water in the entrance.
Enter between gate posts in retaining wall, which dries 3·5m and is marked by 4 Y SPM bns. A floodlit tide gauge is port side of the 15m wide gate.
Marina ☎ 02·96·23·64·00. portrebeurden@ wanadoo.fr www.port-trebeurden.com 625 + 80 Ⓥ on pontoons F & G, €3·17, inc AC. Wi-Fi, @.
D&P, BY, ME, El, ⚒, CH, ▣, C (16 ton mobile).
YC ☎ 02·96·15·45·97 (July-Aug).
Town 🛒, R, Bar, ✉, Ⓑ. ✈ Brest, Rennes, Dinard. Ferry: Roscoff or St Malo.

9.20.16 LANNION (Léguer River)

Côtes d'Armor **48°43′·76N 03°33′·28W (2nd G bcn)** 🕈 ⚓ ⚓ 🌸 🌸 🌸

CHARTS AC 2668, 2026; SHOM 7124; Navi 537, 538; Imray C34; Stanfords 2, 17.

TIDES –0605 Dover; ML 5·4; Duration: no data.

Standard Port BREST (⟶)

Times				Height (metres)			
High Water		Low Water		MHWS	MHWN	MLWN	MLWS
0000	0600	0000	0600	7·0	5·5	2·7	1·1
1200	1800	1200	1800				
Differences LOCQUIREC							
+0100	+0110	+0120	+0100	+2·1	+1·7	+0·7	+0·2

SHELTER Good, except in strong W/NW winds. No access at LW sp, esp in strong NW'lies when seas break on the drying bar. ⚓ in non-drying pools off Le Yaudet and up to the 2nd Y perch, but very little space due to silting and many local moorings; a vacant mooring is possible or ⚓ outside and recce by dinghy.

NAVIGATION WPT 48°44'·38N 03°36'·87W, 091°/2·6M to Pte Beg-Léguer lt (also on Locquémeau ldg lts 121°). Leave Kinierbel SHM buoy close to stbd; stand on until Trébeurden spire bears 004° (to clear a drying patch), then alter 135° for the ent, passing close to two G bcn twrs. Le Yaudet pool is 8ca further E.

Chan up-river to Lannion is narrow, steep-to, dries and is unmarked by bcns; best seen at LW before attempting. Just below Lannion town, opp Quai de Loguivy, drying out on the N bank may be feasible; a recce by dinghy or on foot is advised.

LIGHTS AND MARKS See chartlet and 9.20.4. Pte de Beg-Léguer lt ho is a squat twr, R top, built onto a house and on high cliffs. Le Yaudet spire helps to pinpoint the river ent.

R/T None. **TELEPHONE** Aff Mar 02·96·55·35·00; CROSS 02·98·89·31·31; ⊖ 02·96·48·45·32; Auto 08·92·68·08·22; Police 02·96·46·69·50; Dr 02·96·47·23·15; Brit Embassy 01·44·51·31·00.

FACILITIES HM 02·96·37·65·15. Slip (dries), FW, C (1 ton), M, AB only in emergency. Bar, R in Le Yaudet, but few supplies.

Lannion, ME, El, ⚒, SHOM, Ⓔ, CH, 🛒, Gaz, R, Bar, ⊠, Ⓑ.

ADJACENT HARBOURS IN BAIE DE LANNION

LOCQUÉMEAU, Côtes d'Armor, **48°43'·60N 03°34'·96W** (1st SHM perch). AC 2668, 3669; SHOM 7124. HW –0600 on Dover (UT); +0110 on Brest; HW ht +1·5m on Brest; ML 5·3m. SHOM 7124 is desirable as it shows the various perches. A small drying hbr by ent to Lannion River (9.20.16); use the same WPT. Approach leaving Locquémeau SHM buoy close to stbd. There are two quays: the outer is accessible at LW, but open to W winds. Yachts can dry out at inner quay, on S side. Ldg lts 121° to outer quay: front, W pylon + R top; rear, hard-to-see W gable and R gallery. **Facilities:** ME, El, ⚒. **Town** Bar, R.

LOCQUIREC, Finistère, **48°41'·41N 03°38'·79W**. AC 3669, 2668; SHOM 7124. Tidal data see 9.20.16. Small drying hbr at mouth of Le Douron R, with good shelter from W'lies. The whole estuary dries to extensive, shifting sandbanks (2·9m to 6·1m). Access HW±3. No lights, but Gouliat NCM buoy is 7ca N of Pte du Château and a SHM bcn twr (6ca S of the hbr, marking Roche Rouge) is conspic as the bay opens up. 27 white moorings, inc 10 🅐s in up to 4m @ €6·10/ night, lie NNE of the hbr. Pleasant temp ⚓, or overnight if able to take the ground. Land at slip. Facilities of a small, laid-back resort, inc some fine traditional hotel-restaurants and ATM. Mairie (Port authority) ☎ 02·98·67·42·20.

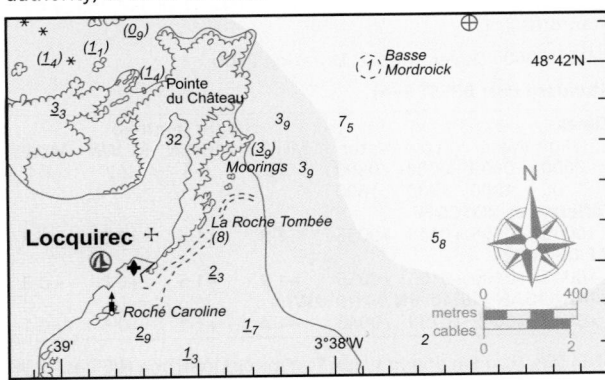

9.20.17 PRIMEL-TRÉGASTEL

Finistère 48°42'·79N 03°49'·46W ❀❀⚓⚓⚓✿✿

CHARTS AC 2026, 2745; SHOM 7151, 7124, 7095; Navi 538; Imray C34, C35; Stanfords 2, 17.

TIDES See 9.20.18 for differences ANSE DE PRIMEL. –0610 Dover; ML 5·3; Duration 0600.

SHELTER Access at all tides, but exposed to N/NW'lies; if strong, seas break across ent. Drying upper reaches are well sheltered.

NAVIGATION WPT 48°43'·59N 03°50'·10W, 152°/0·9M to the hbr bkwtr. Beware drying rks NE of Pte de Primel. Enter exactly on 152° ldg marks, past a SHM bcn marking Ar Zammeguez (3m high). The ent, between a PHM and 2nd SHM bcns, is narrow. A useful hbr to await the tide up to Morlaix.

LIGHTS AND MARKS Pte de Primel is a conspic 42m high rky islet NNE of the hbr. 152° ldg marks/lights are very clear: three whited walls with R vert stripe in serried ranks up the hillside; ldg lts, both QR, are on the front and rear marks.

R/T Port Ch 09, 16 (season).

TELEPHONE HM ☎ 02·98·62·28·40; Brit Consul 02.23.18.30.30.

FACILITIES Le Diben on W side is a FV hbr. FVs occupy most of the bkwtr; rafting possible. A small ⚓age and 15 W 🅐s in about 1m (10 in 'deep' water) are SE of the bkwtr head. Or ⚓ to SE or SW of bkwtr hd in 2·9m. C (25 ton), Slip, CH, El, ME, ⚒, Ⓔ.
Primel-Trégastel P, D, 🛒, Gaz, R, Bar, ⊠, Ⓑ, ⊡. Ferry: Roscoff.

9.20.18 MORLAIX

Finistère 48°35′·31N 03°50′·30W (Lock) ✿✿✿❀❀❀✿✿✿

CHARTS AC 2026, 2745; SHOM 7151, 7095; Navi 538; Imray C34, C35; Stanfords 2, 17.

TIDES −0610 Dover; ML 5·3; Duration 0610.

Standard Port BREST (→)

Times				Height (metres)			
High Water		Low Water		MHWS	MHWN	MLWN	MLWS
0000	0600	0000	0600	7·0	5·5	2·7	1·1
1200	1800	1200	1800				

Differences MORLAIX (CHÂTEAU DU TAUREAU)
| +0055 | +0105 | +0115 | +0055 | +1·9 | +1·6 | +0·7 | +0·2 |

ANSE DE PRIMEL
| +0100 | +0110 | +0120 | +0100 | +2·0 | +1·6 | +0·7 | +0·2 |

SHELTER Good in the bay, except in onshore winds. Strong N'lies can raise a steep sea even in the estuary. ↓ NE of Carantec is exposed, especially to NW; landing stage dries about 4·6m. Complete shelter in the marina.

NAVIGATION The three appr channels have rocky dangers and require careful pilotage; they converge near No 1 buoy, Barre de Flot. La Lande is the rear ldg lt/mark for the first two channels.

Chenal de Tréguier is best at night, but almost dries: WPT 48°42′·55N 03°51′·93W (abm La Pierre Noire SHM bcn) 190·5°/1·84M to La Chambre bcn twr. Ldg lts 190·5°: Front mark, Île Noire lt bcn.

Grand Chenal is shallower but lit: WPT 48°42′·65N 03°53′·53W, (abm Stolvezen PHM buoy) 176°/2·23M to Île Louet lt, passing E of Ile Ricard. Ldg lts 176·4°: Front mark, Île Louet lt ho.

Chenal Ouest de Ricard is the deepest, but unlit. It deviates 188·8° from Grand Chenal, passing W of Ile Ricard. 188·8° ldg marks: Pierres de Carantec and Kergrist, both painted white.

The Morlaix River is buoyed/bcn'd but unlit and prone to silting. ↓ off Pen al Lann and Dourduff (dries), clear of extensive oyster beds marked by small orange buoys/stakes. Morlaix lock, marina and town are 5·5M up-river from No 1 SHM buoy.

LIGHTS AND MARKS See 9.20.4 and chartlet. Château du Taureau fort is conspic 4ca N of No 1 buoy. Some marks omitted for clarity.

R/T Port and marina Ch 09.

TELEPHONE Aff Mar 02·98·62·10·47; CROSS 02·98·89·31·31; SNSM 02·98·72·35·10; ⊖ 02·98·88·06·31; Auto 08·92·68·02·29; Police 02·98·88·58·13; Ⓗ 02·98·62·61·60; Brit Consul 02.23.18.30.30.

FACILITIES Morlaix lock ☎ 02·98·88·15·10 opens by day only (SR-SS) at HW −1½, HW and HW+1; wait alongside W quay.

Marina ☎ 02·98·62·13·14 www.morlaix.cci.fr 150+32 Ⓥ, €2·40. Ⓥ pontoon (fingers) on E bank, parallel to road. In lock hours a movable footbridge across the marina is usually open. D, C (8 ton), Slip, ME, El, ⚒, CH, Wi-Fi. plaisance@morlaix.cci.fr

YC de Morlaix ☎ 02·98·88·38·00.

Town P, D, SM, Ⓔ, SHOM, 🛒, Gaz, R, Bar, ✉, Ⓑ, ▣. Ferry: Roscoff.

ANCHORAGES W AND NW OF MORLAIX
PENZÉ RIVER, Finistère, Ent 48°42′·24N 03°56′·66W, AC 2745; SHOM 7095. HW −0610 on Dover (UT), +0105 on Brest; HW ht +1·2m Brest; ML 5·0m; Duration 0605.

The Penzé river lies W of Île Callot. From NNW, appr between Cordonnier and Guerhéon bcn twrs at mid-flood. Or, for deeper water, from the ENE pass between Les Bizeyer reef and Le Paradis bcn twr; thence S via beaconed channel.

Passe aux Moutons, between Carantec and Île Callot, is a drying (6·2m) short cut from the E into the Penzé, with adequate rise.

S of Le Figuier IDM bcn the chan narrows and is scantily marked by small oyster withies, then by mooring trots. Best shelter is SW of Pte de Lingos: moor in 1·2m off St Yves where the old ferry slips provide landing places.

S of Pont de la Corde (10m clearance) the river is buoyed and navigable on the tide for 3M to Penzé. No access 1 Mar–31 Aug to a Nature Reserve at the head of the river.

Facilities at Carantec: El, ME, ⚒, M, CH, P, D, Ⓔ. **Town** Ⓑ, ✉, R, Bar, 🛒. **Penzé** AB (drying), limited 🛒, R, Bar.

9.20.19 ROSCOFF

Finistère 48°43′·54N 03°58′·59W ✿✿❀❀✿✿✿

CHARTS AC 2026, 2745; SHOM 7151, 7095; Navi 538; Imray C35; Stanfords 2, 17.

TIDES −0605 Dover; ML 5·2; Duration 0600.

Standard Port BREST (→)

Times				Height (metres)			
High Water		Low Water		MHWS	MHWN	MLWN	MLWS
0000	0600	0000	0600	7·0	5·5	2·7	1·1
1200	1800	1200	1800				

Differences ROSCOFF
| +0055 | +0105 | +0115 | +0055 | +1·8 | +1·5 | +0·7 | +0·2 |

ÎLE DE BATZ
| +0045 | +0100 | +0105 | +0055 | +1·9 | +1·5 | +0·8 | +0·3 |

BRIGNOGAN (48°40′·6N 04°19′·2W)
| +0040 | +0045 | +0100 | +0040 | +1·4 | +1·1 | +0·5 | +0·1 |

SHELTER Good in drying Vieux Port except in strong N/E'lies. 12 W ⚓s, €8·20 all LOA, in 4-5m close W of Ar Chaden are exposed.

WGS84 DATUM

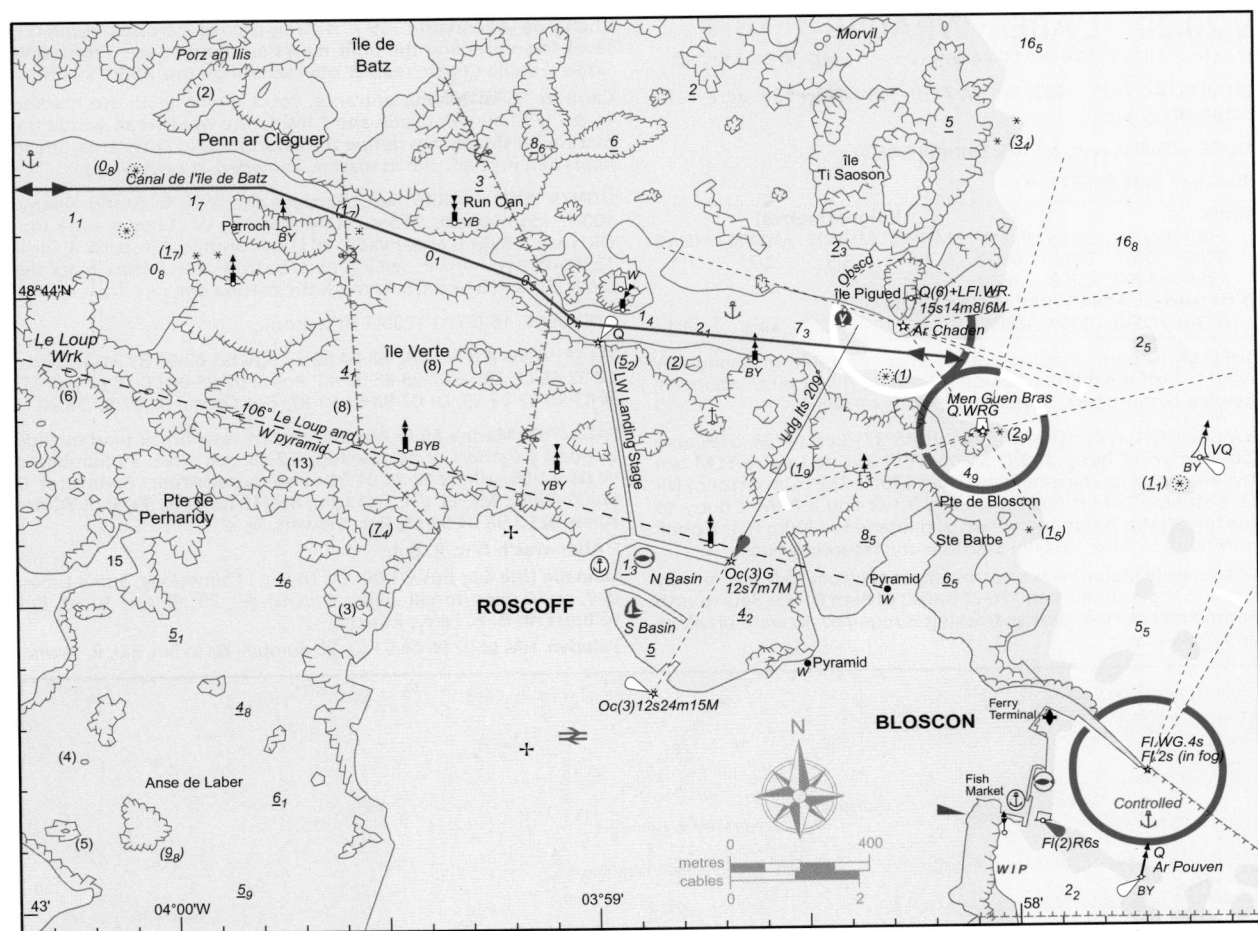

NAVIGATION From the N, WPT 48°45´·88N 03°56´·00W, 213°/2·5M to Men Guen Bras lt. From the E approach between Plateau de la Méloine and Plateau des Duons; or pass S of the latter and N of Le Menk bcn lt twr in Ar Chaden's W sector (289·5°–293°).

From the W, WPT 48°44´·27N 04°04´·06W, 090°/1M to Basse Plate bcn twr; thence via well-marked Canal de l'Île de Batz; see 9.20.5.

Vieux Port Approach near HW over many large drying rks on 209° ldg line: see 9.20.4. N mole hd has B/W vert stripes.

Bloscon Appr H24 on 205° in W sector of mole hd lt. Avoid ferries.

LIGHTS AND MARKS See chartlet and 9.20.4. Île de Batz lt ho is conspic through 360°. E ent to Canal de l'Île de Batz is marked by conspic bcn twrs: Ar Chaden YB and Men-Guen-Bras BY.

R/T Roscoff Ch 09. *Bloscon* Ch 12, 16; 1 hr before/after ferry sailings.

TELEPHONE ⊖ (Bloscon) 02·98·69·70·84; ⊖ (Roscoff) 02·98·69·70·15; Aff Mar 02·98·69·70·15; CROSS 02·98·89·31·31; SNSM 06·82·18·01·34; Auto 08·92·68·08·29; Police 02·98·69·00·48; ℍ 02·98·88·40·22; Dr 02·98·69·71·18; Brit Consul 02.23.18.30.30.

FACILITIES Roscoff HM ☎ 02·98·69·76·37; mob 06·70·50·96·68.

Vieux Port, S Basin 5m. Access HW±2. Dry out with fender board against rough inner jetty or quay. 280+20 Ⓥ, €0·73. BY, ME, El, ✖, CH. N Basin for FVs, C (5 ton). **CN de Roscoff** ☎ 02·98·69·72·79, Bar.

Bloscon ferry terminal. HM ☎ 02·98·61·27·84. www.roscoff.fr Work on a **new 600 berth marina** S of the FV quay began Sep 2009; keep clear. Adjacent controlled ⚓age may be used only with HM's approval; L, Slip. Beware Ar Pouven shoal drying 2·3m (NCM buoy, Q); possibly foul ground inshore.

Roscoff town is rather pleasant. P, D, ME, El, ✖, CH, Gaz, ▤, R, Bar, ⊠, Ⓑ, ⇌, ✈ Brest, Morlaix. Ferry to Plymouth, Rosslare, Cork.

ÎLE DE BATZ, HARBOUR/ANCHORAGE

ÎLE DE BATZ, Finistère, **48°44´·26N 04°00´·60W** (Porz-Kernok ent). AC 2026, 2745; SHOM 7151, 7095; HW +0610 Dover (UT); ML 5·2m. See 9.20.19. Good shelter but hbr dries up to 5m; ⚓ where space permits. E landing stage is for ferries only. Charted ⚓ in the chan E of hbr ent, but poor holding and may be exposed. ⚓ prohib between SE tip of Batz and Roscoff LW landing jetty, due to cables. Île de Batz lt ho (gy twr, B top), the CG Stn and church spire are all conspic. Facilities: R, basic shops, bike hire.

OTHER HARBOURS WEST OF ROSCOFF

MOGUÉRIEC, Finistère, **48°41´·35N 04°04´·41W**, AC 2668, 2026; SHOM 7151. Tides approx as Île de Batz. A small drying fishing hbr, 3M SSW of W ent to Canal de l'Île de Batz, open to NW swell. Ldg lts 162°, both W trs/G tops: Front on jetty, Iso WG 4s 9m, W158°–166°; rear Iso G 4s 22m. Beware Méan Névez rk, dries 3·3m, to W of appr. ⚓ close SW of Île de Siec, or 3ca WSW of Ar Skeul WCM bn tr in 4m, or 2ca NNE of Moguériec's drying jetty. AB against jetty, but clear of FVs. AB also possible against jetty at Île de Siec's drying hbr, but rky bottom. Facilities: ▤, R, Bar.

BRIGNOGAN (Pontusval), Finistère, **48°40´·59N 04°19´·17W**, about 10M ENE of Île Vierge lt ho. AC 2025; SHOM 7150. HW +0605 on Dover (UT); ML 4·7m; Duration 0600; see 9.20.19.

Pontusval is the port, Brignogan a small resort. App from ECM buoy (48°41´·42N 04°19´·33W) via 178° ldg marks, W bn on with Plounéour ch spire 1M S. Ent between Ar Neudenn R bn tr to E and 3 white-topped rks to W. ⚓ here in approx 4m or dry out closer in. Hbr is open to N winds and often full of FVs. Entry at night prohib as it is unlit. Pte de Beg Pol, Oc (3) WR 12s, 1M to the west. Facilities: Bar, FW, R, ▤, 5 ⚓'s (free).

9.20.20 L'ABER WRAC'H

Finistère 48°35'·94N 04°33'·64W (pontoon end) ✸✸✿✿✿✿✿✿

CHARTS AC 2025, 1432; SHOM 7150, 7094; Navi 539; Imray C35; Stanfords 2, 17.

TIDES +0547 Dover; ML 4·5; Duration 0600.

Standard Port BREST (→)

Times				Height (metres)			
High Water		Low Water		MHWS	MHWN	MLWN	MLWS
0000	0600	0000	0600	7·0	5·5	2·7	1·1
1200	1800	1200	1800				
Differences L'ABER WRAC'H, ÎLE CÉZON							
+0030	+0030	+0040	+0035	+0·7	+0·6	+0·1	−0·1

SHELTER Good in marina, but ⚓s uncomfortable in strong NW wind N ⚓ off the marina. Paluden, 1·5M up-river (unlit/unbuoyed; beware oyster beds), is well sheltered in all winds.

NAVIGATION WPT (Grand Chenal) 48°37'·35N 04°38'·51W, abm Libenter WCM buoy, 100°/1·5M to Petit Pot de Beurre ECM bcn twr. Here pick up the inner appr chan 128°/1·7M, in W sector of Dir Lt, passing a SHM lt buoy, SHM bcn lt twr and a PHM lt buoy, to the last SHM bcn twr; thence visual pilotage for 700m to the pool/pontoon at L'Aber Wrac'h. Caution: unlit mooring buoys.

Chenal de la Malouine is a narrow short cut from/to N & E, only by day and in good weather: 176·2° transit of Petit Pot de Beurre with Petite Île W obelisk; precise tracking is required. Beware breakers and cross-tides.

Chenal de la Pendante 135·7° is rarely used as it crosses drying rks, saves few miles and the unlit marks are hard to see. Front, B/W 'smiley' on Île Cézon; rear, W obelisk/orange top, 650m S of hbr.

Caution: SE of marina entrance, rocks drying 0·5m are marked by 3 Y SPM buoys outside and 1 inside the wavebreak. Inside the marina 2 PHM perches define the associated No Entry area. Speed limits 5kn in chan, 3kn in marina. Crowded at peak times.

LIGHTS AND MARKS See chartlets and 9.20.4. Grand Chenal 100·1° ldg marks/lts: front on Île Wrac'h, W ☐ twr orange top, QR; rear, 1·63M E at Lanvaon, W ☐ twr orange top, Q. A Dir lt 128° and two hard-to-see ldg twrs, both W with R tops, mark the inner chan. QG and QR lts mark the marina ent.

R/T Ch 09, 16 (0700-2200LT in season).

TELEPHONE Aff Mar 02·98·04·90·13; CROSS 02·98·89·31·31; Auto 08·92·68·02·29; ⊖ 02·98·85·07·40; Police 02·98·04·00·18 or just 17; Ⓗ 02·98·22·33·33; Dr 02·98·04·91·87; Brit Consul 02·97·87·36·20.

FACILITIES Marina 80 Ⓥ AB on inside of wavebreak (and outside in good weather) or as directed, €2·45; see inset. 30 numbered W ⚓s €1·96. HM ☎ 02·98·04·91·62 aberwrach@port.cci-brest.fr. D (0800-2000), ME, El, CH, C (1 ton), BH (15 ton), ✕, Ⓔ, Slip. **YC des Abers** ☎ 02·98·04·92·60, Bar, showers, &, ▣.

L'Aberwrac'h Gaz, R, Bar.

Landéda (Jul/Aug bus €1·00 rtn: M-Sat 11 times/day; Sun 3 times/ day; or 20 mins up-hill walk): P (cans), ⊠, 🛒, Ⓑ a.m. Tu-Fri. Bus to Brest ⇌ & ✈. Ferry: Roscoff.

Paluden. HM ☎ 02·98·04·63·12. 20 dumbell ⚓s in 5m. Bar, R, shwrs.

9.20.21 L'ABER BENOIT

Finistère **48°34'·64N 04°36'·89W** ✳❀♨⚓☆☆☆ ⚓

CHARTS AC 2025, 1432; SHOM 7150, 7094; Navi 539, 540; Imray C35; Stanfords 2.

TIDES +0535 Dover; ML 4·7; Duration 0555.

Standard Port BREST (→)

Times				Height (metres)			
High Water		Low Water		MHWS	MHWN	MLWN	MLWS
0000	0600	0000	0600	7·0	5·5	2·7	1·1
1200	1800	1200	1800				
Differences L'ABER BENOIT							
+0022	+0025	+0035	+0020	+0·9	+0·8	+0·3	+0·1
PORTSALL							
+0015	+0020	+0025	+0015	+0·5	+0·4	0·0	−0·1

SHELTER Excellent, but do not enter at night, in poor vis nor in strong WNW winds; best near LW when dangers can be seen.

NAVIGATION WPT 48°37'·00N 04°38'·84W, close W of Petite Fourche WCM buoy; thence follow the tracks shown on chartlet. Beware oyster beds. Tidal streams up to 3kn at half-tide. River is navigable on the tide to Tréglonou bridge 3M upstream.

LIGHTS AND MARKS Unlit. Vital to identify correctly buoys and beacons in the approach chan.

R/T None. No HM.

TELEPHONE CROSS/SNSM 02·98·89·31·31; Auto 08·92·68·08·29; ⊖ 02·98·85·07·40; Police 02·98·48·10·10 or 17; Brit Consul 02.23.18.30.30.

FACILITIES 6 free ⚓s and ⚓ as shown or further up-river. Slip, M, L, FW, ✗ (☎ 02·98·89·86·55), ME, El. **Village** P&D (cans, ☎ 02·98·89·87·06), Gaz, ✉, Ⓑ. Bus to Brest ⇌, ✈. Ferry: Roscoff.

THE PASSAGE INSHORE OF ROCHES DE PORTSALL AND ROCHES D'ARGENTON
This 8·5M passage is only 1M shorter than the offshore passage from L'Aberwrac'h towards Le Four lt ho. It requires about 6M visibility in daylight (to see the more distant marks) and is navigationally challenging because of strongish tidal streams and the risk of mis-identifying the marks. A well illustrated Pilot and detailed study of AC 1432, or SHOM 7094, are essential.

The passage from NE to SW is summarised in 3 main sections:

- 7 ca SW of Libenter WCM buoy (see 9.20.20), enter Ch du Relec 218·5°: Pte de Landunvez W bcn twr, R top (rear mark, 6M distant) just open left of Petit Men Louet, W bcn twr 4M distant. Leave Le Relec ECM buoy (1.5M distant) close to stbd.
- With Corn Carhai lt ho almost abeam to stbd, alter stbd into Ch du Raous: Bosven Kreiz W bcn twr in transit 249° with rks S of Le Gremm, a 12m high rk. Hold this for 7 ca then alter port 228°: Le Four lt ho open left of Bosven Aval W bcn twr. 7ca later jink 7° to port to clear Bosven Aval; then pick up:
- The astern transit 036° of Bosven Aval with Bosven Kreiz. After 1·5M (Pte de Landunvez to port) intercept Chenal Méridional de Portsall, another astern transit 049°: the saddle of Le Yurc'h (7m high rk) on with Grand Men Louet W bcn twr. After 2·2M pass SE of Le Four lt ho into the Ch du Four.

HARBOURS ADJACENT TO THE INSHORE PASSAGE
PORTSALL, Finistère, **48°33'·79N 04°43'·04W**. AC 3688, 1432; SHOM 7150, 7094. HW +0535 on Dover (UT); ML 4.4m; Duration 0600. See 9.20.21.

Small drying hbr at head of bay. Access HW±3. Good shelter except in strong NW'lies. Outer 109° ldg marks: Le Yurc'h rk (7m) on with Ploudalmézeau spire. Inner 085° ldg marks (W cols; rear with R top). Front col has Oc (4) WRG 12s, W sector 084°-088°. Appr marked by 3 W bn trs to port, 1 SHM and 1 NCM bcn twr. ⚓ in >10m to W of ent, or enter inner hbr to berth on quay. **Tel/Facilities:** Aff Mar ☎ 02·98·48·66·54; SNSM ☎ 02·98·48·69·17; Dr ☎ 02·98·48·75·52; Police 02·98·48·10·10; Taxi 02·98·48·68·48. **Quay** C (0·5 ton), D & P, FW, Slip; **CN Portsall Kersaint** ☎ 02·98·48·77·49; **Ancre an Eor** ☎ 02·98·48·73·19, CH. **Town** Bar, ✉, R, 🛒.

ARGENTON, Finistère, **48°31'·26N 04°46'·34W**. AC 1432, 3345; SHOM 7150, 7122. HW +0535 on Dover (UT); ML 4·6m; Duration 0600; use PORTSALL diffs 9.20.21.

Small hbr drying approx 5·5m; good shelter except in W winds when swell enters. Access HW±3. WPT 48°31'·14N 04°48'·29W (2½ca S of Le Four lt ho), 084·6°/1·4M to first of 2 W bcn twrs and a white wall with R vert stripe, all on Île Dolvez and in transit. A conspic water twr is slightly S of this ldg line and 1M inland. The N side of chan is marked by 3 PHM bcn twrs. Beware strong NE-SW tidal streams in the approach.

⚓ W of Île Dolvez in about 2m; or skirt round its N side to enter the inner hbr and dry out against the stone quay/slip on N side. 10 s reported but not seen. Facilities: FW, P on quay. **Nautisme en Pays d'Iroise** ☎ 02·98·89·54·04 shwrs. **Village** Bar, R, 🛒.

9.20.22 L'ABERILDUT

Finistère **48°28'·24N 04°45'·75W** (1st PHM bcn) ✳❀♨⚓☆☆☆

CHARTS AC 2647, 2356, 3345; SHOM 7149, 7122; Navi 540; Imray C36; Stanfords 2.

TIDES +0520 on Dover (UT); ML 4·2m.

Standard Port BREST (→)

Times				Height (metres)			
High Water		Low Water		MHWS	MHWN	MLWN	MLWS
0000	0600	0000	0600	7·0	5·5	2·7	1·1
1200	1800	1200	1800				
Differences L'ABERILDUT							
+0010	+0010	+0023	+0010	+0·3	+0·2	−0·1	−0·1

SHELTER Good, but in the appr a high swell runs in strong W'lies; strong river current inside. In fair weather ⚓ outside, as chartlet.

NAVIGATION WPT 48°28'·07N 04°47'·95W, 083°/1·6M to Dir lt which is on conspic white gable end of house. Beware: Les Liniou rks 1·5M NNW of the WPT, Plateau des Fourches 1·2M S and strong cross tides in the approach. Drying rks are marked by Pierre de l'Aber SHM bcn and Le Lieu PHM bcn twr 5m; the latter is easier to see. At the narrow ent (2m) leave Men Tassin PHM bn and Rocher du Crapaud, a large rounded rock, 30m to port to clear drying spit on S side, marked by SHM buoy. Care needed at LWS (max draft 2m) and at night (not advised for a first visit). A good hbr to await the tide in the Ch du Four, 9.20.5 & 9.20.24.

LIGHTS AND MARKS See chartlet and 9.20.4. Glizit water twr is conspic 6·5ca N of the ent. Dir lt 083° is a good daymark (see above); its 2° R sector marks dangers on N side of chan, but do not take liberties with the S side. An inland uncharted water twr is almost on 083°. Lanildut and Brélès spires, in transit 078·5°, are small, very hard to see and obsc'd by trees when close in.

R/T Ch 09, Jun-Sep in office hours.

TELEPHONE Aff Mar 02·98·48·66·54; Auto 08·36·68·08·08; ⊖ 02·98·44·35·20; CROSS 02·98·89·31·31; Dr 02·98·04·33·08; SNSM 02·98·89·30·31; Police 02·98·48·10·10 (or emergency 17).

FACILITIES HM 02.98.04.36.40 (season), mob 06.11.66.31.64. www.lanildut.fr syndicat-port-aber-ildut@nordnet.fr **Hbr:** 410 M, inc 16 🛥s; €1·75 (average), multihull +50%; max LOA 13m, draft 2m. Raft on dumbells ('V' trot), just before 2nd PHM bcn or beyond FV quay (landing) on outer dumbells ('G' trot). No ⚓ inside hbr. P&D ask at ✕, Shwrs, Gas, Ice, no CH, 🛠, Slips, BY, ✕, ME, El. AC, FW at short stay (1hr max) yacht pontoon close N of FV jetty. **Village** 🛒, R, Bar, ✉. Bus to Brest 25km. Ferries: Ouessant, Molène.

9.20.23 LE CONQUET
Finistère 48°21'·60N 04°47'·00W (Hbr ent) ※※♦♦✿✿

CHARTS AC 2356, 3345 with 1:10,000 inset; SHOM 7149, 7148, 7122; Navi 540; Imray C36; Stanfords 2.

TIDES +0535 Dover; ML 3·9; Duration 0600.

Standard Port BREST (→)

Times				Height (metres)			
High Water		Low Water		MHWS	MHWN	MLWN	MLWS
0000	0600	0000	0600	7·0	5·5	2·7	1·1
1200	1800	1200	1800				
Differences LE CONQUET							
0000	0000	+0005	+0005	–0·2	–0·2	–0·1	0·0
LE TREZ HIR (Anse de Bertheaume)							
–0005	–0005	–0015	–0010	–0·4	–0·4	–0·2	–0·1

SHELTER Good except in strong W'lies. Nearest ⚓ is in Anse des Blancs Sablons, sheltered from W/SW but fair weather only.

NAVIGATION WPT 48°21'·68N 04°48'·50W, 096°/1M to Mole Ste Barbe lt. From the NW, beware Grande and Petite Vinotière rks. From the SSW keep seaward of Les Renards IDM buoy and R bcn twr closer inshore. In hbr ent keep closer to Mole Ste Barbe lt, to avoid La Basse du Filet (1·4m) on N side.

LIGHTS AND MARKS See chartlet and 9.20.4. Mole Ste-Barbe lt in line 096° with church spire leads to hbr ent. 079° transit of La Louve R bn tr and end of Mole St Christophe (inner mole) is only valid outside the hbr.

R/T Le Conquet Port (HM) VHF 08 16.

TELEPHONE Aff Mar 02·98·89·00·05; Météo 02·98·84·60·64; Auto 08·92·68·08·29; CROSS 02·98·89·31·31 and 1616; Police 02·98·89·00·13; Dr 02·98·89·01·86; Brit Consul 02.23.18.30.30.

FACILITIES The Avant Port is reserved for FVs & workboats; ferries use Mole Ste Barbe; ⚓ prohib. Call the HM for a vacant mooring or dry out further ENE on one of 12 🛥s; all LOA €7·00 per day. **HM** yann.lagadec@leconquet.fr 02·98·89·18·58, mobile 06·71·11·67·41. ME, El, CH, Slip. **Town** R, Bar, P&D (cans), 🛒, Gaz, ✉, Ⓑ. Bus to Brest. Ferries to: Molène, Brest and Ouessant.

ANCHORAGE EAST OF PTE DE ST MATHIEU
ANSE DE BERTHEAUME, 48°20'·44N 04°41'·84W. AC 2350, 3427. SHOM 7401. A useful passage ⚓ to await the tide E to Brest, N into Ch du Four, or S toward Raz de Sein. ⚓ in 3-5m between slip NNW of the Fort and an ECM bcn 3ca further N. Good shelter in W'lies. 1ca NE of Fort de Bertheaume (32m, conspic), Le Chat rk (6·8m) is marked by an ECM bcn. No lights.

CHENAL DU FOUR

The Chenal du Four (and de la Helle; AC 3345, *2356*) are unhappily split between the small scale Admiralty tidal stream atlases for the English Channel (NP 250) and W France (NP 265). Both channels and the Raz de Sein are better covered at large scale by the French atlas (560-UJA: NW Brittany, Brignogan to Penmarc'h).

If the tides are worked to advantage it is perfectly possible for a 5½kn boat to pass through the Chenal du Four and Raz de Sein in one leg from L'Aberwrac'h to Audierne or vice versa. Anse de Bertheaume (anchorage 4M east of Pte de Ste Mathieu), Camaret or Brest are alternative interim stops.

▶*1M W of Le Four the S-going stream begins at HW Brest +1½; the N-going stream at HW Brest – 5¾, sp rates 3·6kn. Further S, off Pte de Corsen, the stream is weaker, max 2·3kn at springs.*

The tide runs strongest at S end of Chenal du Four, off Le Conquet. Here the S-going stream starts at HW Brest +¼, max 5kn; the N-going stream begins at HW Brest – 5¾, 5·2kn max at sp. Wind-over-tide may raise many short, steep seas.◀

Pilotage. On the mainland coast are 6 major lights, either directional or leading. The charted transits are: St Mathieu directional lt and Kermorvan ≠ 158·5°; Pte de Corsen directional light bearing 012° (in its white sector and on your port quarter). Thence pass between Rouget SHM lt buoy and Grande Vinotière lt bn. Maintain the 325·5° astern transit of Grand Courleau unlit NCM bcn twr ≠ Le Faix NCM lt bcn twr. Track 145·5° to pass midway between La Fourmi SHM lt buoy and Vieux-Moines lt bcn twr.

Alternatively a simple buoy-hopping sequence (below) can be used day or night, assuming you have confidence in tracking accurately on GPS. The word 'tracking', as opposed to heading or steering, implies that the rhumb-line track is accurately maintained with little or no lateral deviation.

The 3 legs are short and swift given the higher than average Speed over the Ground (SOG). Other buoys in between waypoints enable you to verify your progress and any lateral deviation from track.

Leg 1:	From ⊕ 48°31′·5N 04°49′·0W (5ca W of Le Four), track 188°/5M (leaving Les Liniou well to port) to Valbelle PHM buoy.
Leg 2:	Thence track 168°/4·6M to abeam Grande Vinotière lt bn.
Leg 3:	Finally track 172°/2·7M to La Fourmi SHM lt buoy (for Raz de Sein); or
Leg 3A:	156°/2·9M to Vieux-Moines lt bcn (for Brest/Camaret).

Homeward-bound, or along the N Brittany coast, enter the S end of Chenal du Four at LW Brest; a fair tide can then be carried through the channel and NE past Île Vierge. The reverse sequence of pilotage is followed. Two hours is par for the 12M passage.

L'Aberildut, 3·5M SSE of Le Four lt ho, and **Le Conquet**, 3ca SE of Pte de Kermorvan, are the only ports on the mainland coast: the former is safe if there is no swell or W'lies; the latter has limited facilities for yachts but in offshore winds there are anchorages in Anse de Porsmoguer and Anse des Blancs-Sablons, both between Corsen and Kermorvan.

CHENAL DE LA HELLE

▶*At N end of Chenal de la Helle the ENE-going stream starts at HW Brest –0520 (sp rate 2·8kn), and the SW-going stream at HW Brest –0045 (sp rate 3·8kn).*◀

The Chenal de la Helle converges at a 20° angle with the Chenal du Four and the two meet WSW of Pte de Corsen or just N of Grande Vinotière, depending on which of two track variants you take (AC 3345, *2356*).

A simple GPS-based buoy-hopping sequence is as follows:

From close abeam Luronne WCM buoy track 137°/4·7M to St Pierre SHM buoy, passing Le Faix lt twr and Le Pourceau NCM lt buoy. Thence 169°/3·9M to La Fourmi SHM buoy, passing Rouget SHM lt buoy, Grande Vinotière and Tournant et Lochrist PHM lt buoy en route.

APPROACHES TO BREST

The outer approaches lie between Chaussée des Pierres Noires and Pte St Mathieu to the N and Pte du Toulinguet to the S (AC 2350, 3427, 3428). From the W maintain the 068° transit of Petit-Minou and Portzic ldg lts on the N shore; or keep slightly north of this transit to avoid large ships. From the S steer NNE towards Pte du Petit-Minou to pick up the transit, but beware rks 7M W and SW of Pte du Toulinguet. Yachts <25m LOA are exempt from VTS, but should monitor VHF Ch 08 or 16.

Abeam Petit-Minou lt ho the Goulet (Straits) de Brest narrows to 1M. Drying rocks almost in mid-stream may be left to port or starboard; they are marked by a WCM lt buoy, 2 PHM lt buoys and Roche Mengam IDM lt bn. A course of 075° through the Passe Nord leaves the latter 2ca to stbd.

▶*In Passe Sud a useful back-eddy close inshore sets ENE during the ebb. Tidal streams reach 4·5kn in the Goulet.*◀

Beyond Pte du Portzic a buoyed chan leads ENE to **Brest** and the marinas at Le Château and Moulin Blanc. In the **Rade de Brest** (AC 3429) around Île Longue (a peninsula) are DG ranges, no-anchoring and no-entry areas, but there is room to anchor off Roscanvel in the lee of the Quélern peninsula. Further east the beautiful River Aulne can be explored well inland to Port Launay and as far as **Chateaulin**.

L'IROISE AND BAIE DE DOUARNENEZ

L'Iroise is the sea area SW of Chaussée des Pierres Noires and N of Chaussée de Sein (AC 2350, 2349). On the NE side of L'Iroise (AC 3427) a chain of rks extends 7M W from Pte du Toulinguet. There are several chans through these rocks, of which the simplest for Brest and Camaret is the 3ca wide **Chenal du Toulinguet** which runs NNW/SSE between La Louve WCM bcn twr (1ca W of Pte du Toulinguet) on E side and Le Pohen rk on the W side.

▶*Here the N-going stream begins at HW Brest –0550, and the S-going at HW Brest +0015, sp rates 2·75kn.*◀

3·5M SSE of Pte du Toulinguet is Le Chevreau (WCM bcn; dries 5·9m) with La Chèvre 5ca NE of it. 1·9M S of Le Chevreau is Le Bouc (WCM lt buoy; dries 7·4m). 5·7M SW of Pte du Toulinguet lies Basse du Lis, rky shoals with depth of 2·7m and WCM lt buoy, and the last of a string of underwater rocks extending seaward from Les Tas de Pois (Pile of Peas). Close E of Les Tas de Pois, the Anse de Pen-Hir is a useful anch in NE'lies.

The Baie de Douarnenez is entered between C. de la Chèvre and Pte du Van. Off C. de la Chèvre various dangers, on which the sea breaks, extend SW for 2·25M to Basse Vieille (dries 0·8m), lt buoy. Basse Laye (dries 0·7m) is unmarked 7ca SSE of the CG stn on C. de la Chèvre and a hazard if rounding the headland close inshore. **Morgat** lies 4M NNE of C. de la Chèvre. 2·5M ESE of Morgat beware Les Verrès (12m high rk) and a group of drying rks, including La Pierre-Profonde and Le Taureau.

Approaching **Douarnenez** beware Basse Veur and Basse Neuve (2·2m). The S shore of the B is clear of dangers more than 2ca offshore, except for Duellou Rk (7m high) 5ca offshore, and other rks 1M eastward. Further W Basse Jaune is an isolated rk (dries 1·4m; IDM buoy) about 1M N of Pte du Van. This rocky headland with offliers is 2·25M NE of Pte du Raz and La Vieille lt twr and is the NE corner of the Raz de Sein.

RAZ DE SEIN TO POINTE DE PENMARC'H

Chaussée de Sein (AC 2350, 2819, 2348) is a chain of islands, rks and shoals extending 15M W of the Pointe du Raz. A WCM lt buoy marks the seaward end. See 9.20.32 for directions through the **Raz de Sein**. **Audierne** is 10M ESE where **Ste Evette** is a good passage ⚓ before or after tackling the Raz.

Off Pte de Penmarc'h (light house, fog signal) depths shoal very rapidly from >60m to <5m in the space of 7ca; dangers extend 1M to NW, W and S, and 3M to SE, and breaking seas occur in strong winds. In onshore winds it is best to keep at least 3M off the light house. The fishing harbours of Le Guilvinec and Lesconil are well sheltered, but have difficult entrances and limited yacht facilities; feasible in emergency.

9.20.24 CHENAL DU FOUR

AC 3345. Simple buoy-hopping/GPS track: — — — — *See overleaf for notes on this passage and the Chenal de la Helle.*

9.20.25 ÎLE D'OUESSANT

Finistère 48°26'·64N 05°07'·49W (B de Lampaul) ❄🐚⚓🏴🏴🏴

CHARTS AC 2356; SHOM 7149, 7123; Navi 540; Imray C36; Stan 2.

TIDES +0522 Dover; ML 3·9; Duration 0555.
Standard Port BREST (→)

Times				Height (metres)			
High Water		Low Water		MHWS	MHWN	MLWN	MLWS
0000	0600	0000	0600	7·0	5·5	2·7	1·1
1200	1800	1200	1800				
Differences BAIE DE LAMPAUL							
+0010	+0010	0000	+0005	–0·1	–0·1	–0·1	–0·1
ÎLE DE MOLENE							
+0015	+0010	+0020	+0020	+0·3	+0·3	+0·1	+0·1

SHELTER Good in Baie de Lampaul in N-E winds, and in Baie du Stiff in S-NW winds; fresh/strong winds from the opposite directions render the bays untenable. For a first visit settled weather, no swell and good vis (often poor in July) are ideal.

NAVIGATION See 9.20.2 for notes on Ouessant TSS.

Lampaul WPT 48°25'·38N 05°09'·96W, 054·4°/2·4M to LH edge of Youc'h Korz (a 28m high rock which may be passed on either side) in transit with Le Stiff lt ho. Do not attempt Chenal de la Fourche, a short cut inside La Jument lt ho.

Baie du Stiff WPT 48°28'·38N 05°01'·32W, 259°/1·3M to Dir lt.-

LIGHTS AND MARKS The radar twr (129m) at Le Stiff is highly conspic. See 9.20.4 for La Jument, Nividic, Creac'h and Le Stiff lt ho's; also Gorle Vihan IDM bcn twr in Baie du Stiff, where a Dir lt Q WRG marks the 259° appr for ferries; Men-Korn bcn twr (lit) is 1.3M E. Kéréon lt ho marks the S side of Passage du Fromveur.

R/T None.

TELEPHONE HM 02·98·48·80·06; Aff Mar 02·98·89·00·05; CROSS 02·98·89·31·31 & 1616; Auto 08·92·68·08·29; SNSM 02·98·48·84·33; Dr 02·98·48·83·22; Police (summer only) 02·98·48·81·61; Tourist Office 02·98·48·85·83; Brit Consul 02.23.18.30.30.

FACILITIES Lampaul has room to ⚓ in 6-10m and 29 free ⚓s SE of the PHM/SHM bcn twrs off the narrow drying hbr (not usually accessible to visitors). Ferries no longer use Lampaul. FW, Slip.
Village P & D (cans), R, Gaz, ✉, Ⓑ, @, bike hire, ✈.

Baie du Stiff has 4 W ⚓s (free) in 5m on S side at 48°28'·03N 05°03'·11W, but there is little space to ⚓ and holding is poor. S of the lt ho, Porz Liboudou is for ferries to Le Conquet and Brest, berthing on either jetty; keep clear.

ADJACENT ISLAND HARBOUR
ÎLE MOLÈNE, Finistère, **48°24'·07N 04°57'·30W** (LB mooring).

CHARTS AC 2356, 3345; SHOM 7149, 7148, 7122, 7123; Navi 540; Imray C36; Stanford 17.

TIDES See 9.20.25; +0520 Dover; ML 4·6.

SHELTER Good, except in strong N/NE'lies; streams are strong. ⚓ near LB in about 1·2m. Appr is easier in settled weather, good vis and nps.

NAVIGATION The simpler appr is from the NE, near Luronne WCM buoy, to WPT 48°25'·00N 04°56'·97W; thence 191°/8·5ca to the LB mooring (a good ref point in the hbr), passing between ECM bcn twr and WCM lt buoy, VQ (9) 10s; see inset on 9.20.24.

From the E (Chenal des Laz), WPT 48°24'·35N 04°51'·30W (650m N of Pourceaux NCM lt buoy), 264°/2·7M to 48°24'·07N 04°55'·41W. Here make good 315°/1·1M to skirt round Les Trois Pierres lt twr and continue via the N ⊕. This appr is used by mainland ferries.

Day transits define both appr chans: from the N, Moulin Sud and white mark on N jetty ≠ 190°. From the E, Moulin Nord (W bcn, orange top) and white twr ≠ 264°.

LIGHTS AND MARKS The church spire and old CG twr are both conspic from afar. At old S pier the two lts (on same column) are: Fl (3) WRG 12s whose W sector covers the 191° appr; and Fl (2) WRG 6s whose W sector covers the Chenal des Laz 261°.

R/T None. **TELEPHONE** HM, via Mairie 02·98·07·39·05.

FACILITIES 12 white ⚓s, €8·00 all LOA. Ferries berth on N jetty. FW, 🛒, CH, R, Bar, ✉; Shwrs near museum. www.iledemolene.fr

TIME ZONE -0100
Subtract 1 hour for UT
For French Summer Time add
ONE hour in **non-shaded areas**

BREST LAT 48°23'N LONG 4°30'W
TIMES AND HEIGHTS OF HIGH AND LOW WATERS

Dates in red are **SPRINGS**
Dates in blue are **NEAPS**

YEAR 2010

JANUARY

Day	Time	m	Day	Time	m
1 F	0500 / 1125 / 1728 / 2344	7.2 / 1.1 / 7.1 / 1.1	**16** SA	0537 / 1158 / 1753	6.7 / 1.6 / 6.5
2 SA	0548 / 1213 / 1816	7.4 / 0.9 / 7.2	**17** SU	0011 / 0609 / 1230 / 1824	1.7 / 6.8 / 1.5 / 6.5
3 SU	0032 / 0636 / 1301 / 1903	1.0 / 7.5 / 0.8 / 7.2	**18** M	0043 / 0641 / 1301 / 1854	1.7 / 6.8 / 1.6 / 6.5
4 M	0120 / 0723 / 1349 / 1950	1.0 / 7.4 / 0.9 / 7.0	**19** TU	0115 / 0711 / 1332 / 1924	1.7 / 6.7 / 1.7 / 6.4
5 TU	0207 / 0810 / 1438 / 2038	1.2 / 7.1 / 1.2 / 6.7	**20** W	0146 / 0742 / 1404 / 1955	1.9 / 6.5 / 1.9 / 6.2
6 W	0256 / 0858 / 1528 / 2128	1.5 / 6.8 / 1.6 / 6.4	**21** TH	0219 / 0815 / 1438 / 2029	2.1 / 6.3 / 2.1 / 6.0
7 TH	0348 / 0949 / 1621 / 2222	1.9 / 6.3 / 2.1 / 6.0	**22** F	0255 / 0851 / 1516 / 2111	2.3 / 6.0 / 2.3 / 5.8
8 F	0444 / 1048 / 1721 / 2325	2.3 / 5.9 / 2.4 / 5.7	**23** SA	0338 / 0936 / 1604 / 2204	2.5 / 5.7 / 2.6 / 5.5
9 SA	0548 / 1158 / 1829	2.6 / 5.6 / 2.7	**24** SU	0432 / 1037 / 1705 / 2314	2.8 / 5.5 / 2.8 / 5.4
10 SU	0037 / 0701 / 1315 / 1941	5.6 / 2.7 / 5.5 / 2.7	**25** M	0542 / 1156 / 1821	2.9 / 5.4 / 2.8
11 M	0150 / 0817 / 1426 / 2046	5.7 / 2.6 / 5.6 / 2.5	**26** TU	0035 / 0704 / 1321 / 1941	5.5 / 2.8 / 5.5 / 2.6
12 TU	0252 / 0918 / 1522 / 2139	5.9 / 2.4 / 5.9 / 2.3	**27** W	0155 / 0824 / 1436 / 2051	5.8 / 2.4 / 5.9 / 2.2
13 W	0343 / 1007 / 1608 / 2224	6.2 / 2.1 / 6.1 / 2.1	**28** TH	0302 / 0928 / 1537 / 2150	6.3 / 1.8 / 6.4 / 1.7
14 TH	0426 / 1049 / 1646 / 2303	6.4 / 1.9 / 6.3 / 1.9	**29** F	0359 / 1023 / 1629 / 2243	6.8 / 1.3 / 6.9 / 1.2
15 F	0503 / 1124 / 1721 / 2338	6.6 / 1.7 / 6.4 / 1.8	**30** SA	0450 / 1114 / 1717 / 2332	7.3 / 0.8 / 7.2 / 0.8
			31 SU	0537 / 1201 / 1803	7.6 / 0.5 / 7.4

FEBRUARY

Day	Time	m	Day	Time	m
1 M	0019 / 0623 / 1247 / 1846	0.6 / 7.7 / 0.5 / 7.5	**16** TU	0020 / 0617 / 1236 / 1828	1.4 / 6.9 / 1.3 / 6.7
2 TU	0104 / 0706 / 1331 / 1929	0.6 / 7.7 / 0.6 / 7.3	**17** W	0049 / 0646 / 1305 / 1856	1.5 / 6.9 / 1.4 / 6.6
3 W	0148 / 0748 / 1414 / 2011	0.8 / 7.4 / 1.0 / 6.9	**18** TH	0119 / 0715 / 1334 / 1925	1.6 / 6.7 / 1.6 / 6.5
4 TH	0232 / 0830 / 1458 / 2053	1.2 / 6.9 / 1.5 / 6.5	**19** F	0150 / 0745 / 1406 / 1957	1.7 / 6.5 / 1.8 / 6.3
5 F	0317 / 0913 / 1544 / 2140	1.7 / 6.3 / 2.1 / 6.0	**20** SA	0225 / 0819 / 1443 / 2035	2.0 / 6.2 / 2.1 / 6.0
6 SA	0407 / 1004 / 1638 / 2238	2.2 / 5.8 / 2.6 / 5.6	**21** SU	0306 / 0900 / 1528 / 2124	2.3 / 5.9 / 2.5 / 5.7
7 SU	0507 / 1112 / 1746 / 2356	2.7 / 5.3 / 3.0 / 5.3	**22** M	0358 / 0958 / 1627 / 2234	2.6 / 5.5 / 2.8 / 5.4
8 M	0625 / 1245 / 1912	3.0 / 5.1 / 3.0	**23** TU	0506 / 1121 / 1746	2.8 / 5.2 / 2.9
9 TU	0126 / 0757 / 1414 / 2030	5.3 / 2.9 / 5.3 / 2.8	**24** W	0004 / 0636 / 1300 / 1918	5.4 / 2.8 / 5.4 / 2.7
10 W	0238 / 0905 / 1512 / 2126	5.6 / 2.5 / 5.6 / 2.5	**25** TH	0136 / 0807 / 1424 / 2036	5.7 / 2.4 / 5.8 / 2.2
11 TH	0330 / 0953 / 1555 / 2209	6.0 / 2.2 / 6.0 / 2.1	**26** F	0248 / 0915 / 1524 / 2136	6.2 / 1.8 / 6.4 / 1.6
12 F	0410 / 1032 / 1630 / 2245	6.3 / 1.9 / 6.2 / 1.8	**27** SA	0345 / 1009 / 1614 / 2227	6.8 / 1.2 / 7.0 / 1.1
13 SA	0445 / 1105 / 1702 / 2318	6.6 / 1.6 / 6.5 / 1.6	**28** SU	0434 / 1057 / 1700 / 2315	7.4 / 0.7 / 7.4 / 0.7
14 SU	0517 / 1136 / 1731 / 2349	6.8 / 1.5 / 6.6 / 1.5			
15 M	0547 / 1206 / 1800	6.9 / 1.4 / 6.7			

MARCH

Day	Time	m	Day	Time	m
1 M	0520 / 1143 / 1743	7.7 / 0.4 / 7.6	**16** TU	0520 / 1138 / 1732 / 2352	6.9 / 1.3 / 6.8 / 1.3
2 TU	0000 / 0603 / 1226 / 1824	0.5 / 7.8 / 0.4 / 7.6	**17** W	0550 / 1208 / 1801	7.0 / 1.3 / 6.8
3 W	0043 / 0644 / 1307 / 1903	0.5 / 7.7 / 0.6 / 7.4	**18** TH	0023 / 0619 / 1237 / 1829	1.3 / 6.9 / 1.3 / 6.8
4 TH	0124 / 0722 / 1347 / 1941	0.7 / 7.3 / 1.0 / 7.0	**19** F	0053 / 0649 / 1308 / 1859	1.4 / 6.8 / 1.5 / 6.6
5 F	0206 / 0800 / 1427 / 2019	1.2 / 6.8 / 1.5 / 6.5	**20** SA	0126 / 0721 / 1342 / 1933	1.6 / 6.6 / 1.7 / 6.4
6 SA	0248 / 0840 / 1509 / 2102	1.7 / 6.2 / 2.1 / 6.0	**21** SU	0203 / 0757 / 1420 / 2012	1.8 / 6.3 / 2.0 / 6.1
7 SU	0334 / 0925 / 1558 / 2157	2.3 / 5.6 / 2.7 / 5.5	**22** M	0246 / 0841 / 1506 / 2103	2.2 / 5.9 / 2.4 / 5.8
8 M	0431 / 1030 / 1705 / 2317	2.8 / 5.1 / 3.1 / 5.2	**23** TU	0340 / 0941 / 1607 / 2216	2.5 / 5.5 / 2.7 / 5.5
9 TU	0548 / 1210 / 1838	3.1 / 4.9 / 3.2	**24** W	0450 / 1107 / 1728 / 2349	2.7 / 5.2 / 2.9 / 5.4
10 W	0056 / 0728 / 1352 / 2006	5.2 / 3.0 / 5.1 / 3.0	**25** TH	0621 / 1247 / 1902	2.7 / 5.4 / 2.7
11 TH	0213 / 0840 / 1450 / 2102	5.5 / 2.7 / 5.5 / 2.6	**26** F	0120 / 0750 / 1407 / 2019	5.8 / 2.3 / 5.9 / 2.2
12 F	0304 / 0926 / 1530 / 2143	5.8 / 2.3 / 5.9 / 2.2	**27** SA	0230 / 0856 / 1504 / 2117	6.3 / 1.7 / 6.5 / 1.6
13 SA	0343 / 1004 / 1604 / 2218	6.2 / 1.9 / 6.2 / 1.9	**28** SU	0325 / 0948 / 1553 / 2207	6.9 / 1.1 / 7.0 / 1.1
14 SU	0418 / 1037 / 1634 / 2251	6.5 / 1.6 / 6.5 / 1.6	**29** M	0413 / 1036 / 1637 / 2254	7.3 / 0.7 / 7.3 / 0.7
15 M	0449 / 1108 / 1704 / 2322	6.7 / 1.4 / 6.7 / 1.4	**30** TU	0457 / 1120 / 1719 / 2337	7.5 / 0.6 / 7.5 / 0.6
			31 W	0539 / 1202 / 1758	7.6 / 0.6 / 7.5

APRIL

Day	Time	m	Day	Time	m
1 TH	0019 / 0619 / 1241 / 1836	0.7 / 7.4 / 0.8 / 7.3	**16** F	0554 / 1212 / 1806	6.9 / 1.4 / 6.9
2 F	0100 / 0657 / 1320 / 1913	0.9 / 7.1 / 1.2 / 6.9	**17** SA	0031 / 0628 / 1246 / 1840	1.4 / 6.8 / 1.5 / 6.8
3 SA	0140 / 0734 / 1358 / 1951	1.3 / 6.6 / 1.7 / 6.5	**18** SU	0108 / 0704 / 1324 / 1918	1.5 / 6.6 / 1.7 / 6.5
4 SU	0222 / 0812 / 1439 / 2032	1.8 / 6.1 / 2.2 / 6.0	**19** M	0150 / 0746 / 1407 / 2003	1.7 / 6.3 / 2.0 / 6.2
5 M	0307 / 0856 / 1526 / 2124	2.3 / 5.6 / 2.7 / 5.5	**20** TU	0237 / 0836 / 1457 / 2059	2.0 / 5.9 / 2.3 / 5.9
6 TU	0400 / 0956 / 1627 / 2238	2.7 / 5.1 / 3.1 / 5.2	**21** W	0334 / 0941 / 1600 / 2212	2.3 / 5.6 / 2.6 / 5.7
7 W	0509 / 1123 / 1751	3.0 / 4.9 / 3.2	**22** TH	0445 / 1101 / 1718 / 2336	2.5 / 5.4 / 2.7 / 5.7
8 TH	0008 / 0634 / 1259 / 1919	5.1 / 3.0 / 5.0 / 3.1	**23** F	0608 / 1228 / 1843	2.4 / 5.6 / 2.5
9 F	0126 / 0752 / 1406 / 2020	5.3 / 2.8 / 5.3 / 2.7	**24** SA	0057 / 0726 / 1341 / 1954	5.9 / 2.1 / 6.0 / 2.1
10 SA	0221 / 0844 / 1450 / 2104	5.7 / 2.4 / 5.7 / 2.3	**25** SU	0204 / 0830 / 1438 / 2052	6.3 / 1.7 / 6.4 / 1.6
11 SU	0303 / 0924 / 1526 / 2141	6.0 / 2.1 / 6.1 / 2.0	**26** M	0259 / 0923 / 1527 / 2144	6.7 / 1.3 / 6.8 / 1.3
12 M	0340 / 0959 / 1559 / 2216	6.3 / 1.8 / 6.4 / 1.7	**27** TU	0348 / 1011 / 1612 / 2231	7.0 / 1.1 / 7.1 / 1.0
13 TU	0415 / 1033 / 1631 / 2250	6.6 / 1.6 / 6.6 / 1.5	**28** W	0433 / 1056 / 1654 / 2315	7.1 / 1.0 / 7.2 / 1.0
14 W	0448 / 1106 / 1702 / 2323	6.7 / 1.4 / 6.8 / 1.4	**29** TH	0516 / 1137 / 1734 / 2357	7.1 / 1.1 / 7.2 / 1.0
15 TH	0521 / 1139 / 1734 / 2357	6.8 / 1.3 / 6.9 / 1.3	**30** F	0556 / 1217 / 1812	7.0 / 1.2 / 7.0

Chart Datum is 3·64 metres below IGN Datum. HAT is 7·8 metres above Chart Datum; see 4.5.

TIME ZONE -0100
Subtract 1 hour for UT
For French Summer Time add
ONE hour in **non-shaded areas**

BREST LAT 48°23'N LONG 4°30'W
TIMES AND HEIGHTS OF HIGH AND LOW WATERS

Dates in **red** are **SPRINGS**
Dates in **blue** are **NEAPS**

YEAR 2010

MAY

Time	m	Time	m
1 0038	1.2	**16** 0014	1.4
0634	6.7	0613	6.7
SA 1256	1.5	SU 1231	1.5
1850	6.8	1828	6.8
2 0118	1.5	**17** 0057	1.4
0712	6.4	0656	6.6
SU 1334	1.9	M 1314	1.6
1928	6.4	1913	6.7
3 0159	1.9	**18** 0143	1.5
0751	6.0	0744	6.4
M 1414	2.2	TU 1401	1.8
2010	6.1	2002	6.5
4 0242	2.2	**19** 0234	1.7
0833	5.6	0837	6.1
TU 1458	2.6	W 1454	2.0
2058	5.7	2059	6.2
5 0330	2.6	**20** 0330	2.0
0925	5.3	0938	5.9
W 1551	2.9	TH 1554	2.3
2157	5.4	2204	6.0
6 0427	2.8	**21** 0435	2.1
1031	5.1	1046	5.7
TH 1657	3.1	F 1703	2.4
☽ 2308	5.2	☽ 2315	5.9
7 0533	2.9	**22** 0546	2.1
1147	5.1	1158	5.8
F 1811	3.1	SA 1815	2.3
8 0019	5.3	**23** 0027	6.0
0641	2.8	0656	2.1
SA 1256	5.2	SU 1307	5.9
1918	2.9	1924	2.1
9 0120	5.5	**24** 0133	6.2
0741	2.6	0759	1.9
SU 1353	5.5	M 1407	6.2
2011	2.6	2025	1.9
10 0211	5.8	**25** 0232	6.3
0831	2.3	0856	1.7
M 1438	5.8	TU 1501	6.5
2057	2.2	2120	1.6
11 0256	6.1	**26** 0325	6.5
0915	2.0	0947	1.6
TU 1519	6.2	W 1549	6.7
2138	1.9	2210	1.5
12 0337	6.3	**27** 0412	6.6
0955	1.8	1033	1.5
W 1556	6.4	TH 1633	6.8
2217	1.7	2256	1.4
13 0416	6.5	**28** 0456	6.6
1034	1.6	1116	1.5
TH 1633	6.7	F 1715	6.8
2255	1.5	○ 2338	1.4
14 0454	6.7	**29** 0537	6.6
1112	1.5	1157	1.6
F 1710	6.8	SA 1754	6.8
● 2334	1.4		
15 0533	6.7	**30** 0019	1.5
1150	1.4	0616	6.4
SA 1748	6.9	SU 1235	1.7
		1832	6.6
		31 0059	1.6
		0653	6.3
		M 1314	1.9
		1910	6.4

JUNE

Time	m	Time	m
1 0138	1.8	**16** 0136	1.2
0731	6.1	0739	6.7
TU 1352	2.1	W 1354	1.4
1949	6.2	1958	6.8
2 0217	2.1	**17** 0226	1.3
0809	5.8	0829	6.5
W 1432	2.4	TH 1445	1.6
2030	5.9	2050	6.6
3 0258	2.3	**18** 0319	1.6
0851	5.6	0923	6.2
TH 1515	2.6	F 1540	1.8
2116	5.7	2145	6.3
4 0343	2.5	**19** 0415	1.8
0940	5.4	1020	6.0
F 1604	2.8	SA 1639	2.1
☽ 2209	5.5	☽ 2246	6.1
5 0434	2.7	**20** 0517	2.1
1038	5.2	1123	5.9
SA 1703	2.9	SU 1744	2.2
2310	5.4	2352	5.9
6 0533	2.8	**21** 0622	2.2
1142	5.2	1230	5.8
SU 1807	2.9	M 1852	2.3
7 0013	5.4	**22** 0101	5.8
0634	2.7	0728	2.2
M 1245	5.4	TU 1337	5.9
1910	2.7	1959	2.2
8 0113	5.5	**23** 0208	5.9
0734	2.5	0831	2.2
TU 1343	5.6	W 1438	6.1
2007	2.5	2101	2.0
9 0208	5.8	**24** 0306	6.0
0828	2.3	0927	2.0
W 1435	5.9	TH 1531	6.3
2058	2.2	2155	1.9
10 0259	6.0	**25** 0357	6.2
0918	2.1	1017	1.9
TH 1522	6.2	F 1619	6.5
2146	1.9	2242	1.7
11 0347	6.3	**26** 0442	6.3
1004	1.8	1101	1.8
F 1607	6.5	SA 1701	6.6
2231	1.6	○ 2324	1.6
12 0432	6.5	**27** 0522	6.3
1049	1.6	1140	1.7
SA 1651	6.7	SU 1740	6.6
● 2316	1.4		
13 0518	6.7	**28** 0003	1.6
1134	1.4	0559	6.3
SU 1735	6.9	M 1218	1.7
		1816	6.6
14 0002	1.2	**29** 0039	1.6
0603	6.8	0634	6.3
M 1219	1.3	TU 1253	1.8
1821	7.0	1851	6.5
15 0048	1.2	**30** 0114	1.7
0650	6.8	0708	6.2
TU 1306	1.3	W 1328	1.9
1908	7.0	1925	6.4

JULY

Time	m	Time	m
1 0149	1.8	**16** 0210	1.0
0741	6.1	0810	6.8
TH 1403	2.1	F 1428	1.2
1959	6.2	2030	6.9
2 0224	2.0	**17** 0258	1.3
0815	5.9	0857	6.5
F 1438	2.3	SA 1518	1.6
2036	6.0	2119	6.5
3 0300	2.2	**18** 0348	1.7
0853	5.7	0948	6.2
SA 1517	2.5	SU 1611	1.9
2116	5.8	☽ 2213	6.1
4 0341	2.4	**19** 0444	2.1
0937	5.5	1046	5.8
SU 1603	2.7	M 1711	2.3
☽ 2205	5.5	2316	5.7
5 0429	2.6	**20** 0547	2.5
1032	5.4	1155	5.6
M 1659	2.8	TU 1821	2.5
2305	5.4		
6 0528	2.7	**21** 0032	5.5
1138	5.3	0659	2.6
TU 1806	2.9	W 1311	5.6
		1938	2.5
7 0014	5.4	**22** 0150	5.5
0636	2.7	0812	2.5
W 1248	5.4	TH 1422	5.8
1916	2.7	2049	2.3
8 0123	5.5	**23** 0256	5.7
0743	2.6	0914	2.3
TH 1354	5.7	F 1520	6.1
2021	2.4	2145	2.1
9 0227	5.8	**24** 0347	5.9
0845	2.3	1004	2.1
F 1453	6.0	SA 1607	6.3
2119	2.0	2231	1.8
10 0324	6.1	**25** 0430	6.2
0940	1.9	1047	1.9
SA 1547	6.4	SU 1647	6.5
2212	1.6	2309	1.7
11 0416	6.5	**26** 0507	6.3
1031	1.6	1124	1.7
SU 1636	6.8	M 1723	6.6
● 2302	1.2	○ 2344	1.5
12 0505	6.8	**27** 0540	6.4
1120	1.3	1158	1.7
M 1724	7.1	TU 1755	6.7
2349	0.9		
13 0552	7.0	**28** 0017	1.5
1207	1.0	0611	6.5
TU 1811	7.3	W 1230	1.7
		1827	6.7
14 0036	0.8	**29** 0048	1.5
0638	7.1	0640	6.4
W 1254	0.9	TH 1301	1.7
1857	7.3	1857	6.6
15 0123	0.8	**30** 0119	1.6
0724	7.0	0710	6.3
TH 1341	1.0	F 1332	1.8
1943	7.2	1927	6.5
		31 0149	1.8
		0740	6.2
		SA 1403	2.0
		1958	6.3

AUGUST

Time	m	Time	m
1 0221	2.0	**16** 0318	1.8
0812	6.0	0914	6.2
SU 1437	2.2	M 1542	2.0
2032	6.0	☽ 2139	6.0
2 0256	2.2	**17** 0410	2.3
0849	5.8	1010	5.8
M 1517	2.5	TU 1640	2.5
2113	5.7	2242	5.5
3 0339	2.5	**18** 0514	2.8
0937	5.5	1123	5.4
TU 1606	2.7	W 1754	2.8
☽ 2208	5.4		
4 0434	2.7	**19** 0008	5.2
1041	5.4	0635	2.9
W 1711	2.9	TH 1251	5.4
2322	5.3	1922	2.8
5 0545	2.9	**20** 0139	5.3
1201	5.3	0758	2.8
TH 1831	2.9	F 1409	5.6
		2037	2.5
6 0046	5.3	**21** 0246	5.6
0706	2.7	0901	2.5
F 1321	5.6	SA 1506	6.0
1952	2.6	2130	2.2
7 0204	5.6	**22** 0333	5.9
0820	2.4	0948	2.1
SA 1432	6.0	SU 1550	6.3
2059	2.1	2212	1.9
8 0308	6.1	**23** 0412	6.2
0922	1.9	1027	1.9
SU 1530	6.5	M 1627	6.5
2156	1.5	2248	1.6
9 0401	6.6	**24** 0445	6.4
1015	1.4	1102	1.7
M 1621	7.0	TU 1659	6.7
2246	1.0	○ 2320	1.5
10 0450	7.0	**25** 0515	6.6
1104	1.0	1133	1.6
TU 1709	7.4	W 1730	6.8
● 2334	0.7	2350	1.4
11 0536	7.3	**26** 0543	6.6
1151	0.7	1203	1.5
W 1755	7.6	TH 1759	6.9
12 0019	0.5	**27** 0019	1.4
0620	7.4	0611	6.6
TH 1237	0.6	F 1232	1.5
1839	7.7	1828	6.8
13 0104	0.5	**28** 0048	1.5
0702	7.3	0639	6.6
F 1321	0.7	SA 1302	1.6
1922	7.5	1856	6.7
14 0148	0.8	**29** 0117	1.6
0745	7.1	0707	6.5
SA 1406	1.0	SU 1332	1.8
2005	7.1	1925	6.5
15 0232	1.2	**30** 0147	1.8
0828	6.7	0737	6.3
SU 1452	1.5	M 1404	2.1
2049	6.5	1958	6.2
		31 0222	2.1
		0813	6.0
		TU 1443	2.3
		2037	5.8

Chart Datum is 3·64 metres below IGN Datum. HAT is 7·8 metres above Chart Datum; see 4.5.

N Brittany

TIME ZONE -0100
Subtract 1 hour for UT
For French Summer Time add
ONE hour in **non-shaded areas**

BREST LAT 48°23'N LONG 4°30'W

TIMES AND HEIGHTS OF HIGH AND LOW WATERS

Dates in red are **SPRINGS**
Dates in blue are NEAPS

YEAR 2010

SEPTEMBER

Time	m		Time	m
1 0304	2.5	**16**	0443	3.0
0858	5.7		1055	5.3
W 1532	2.7	TH 1727	2.7
☽ 2130	5.5		2343	5.0
2 0358	2.8	**17**	0609	3.1
1002	5.4		1228	5.3
TH 1636	2.9	F 1900	3.0
2247	5.2			
3 0510	3.0	**18**	0119	5.2
1129	5.3		0736	2.9
F 1801	2.9	SA 1347	5.6
			2014	2.6
4 0022	5.3	**19**	0223	5.5
0640	2.9		0837	2.6
SA 1300	5.6	SU 1441	5.9
1931	2.6		2104	2.3
5 0147	5.7	**20**	0308	5.9
0801	2.4		0922	2.2
SU 1414	6.1	M 1523	6.3
2042	2.0		2144	1.9
6 0251	6.2	**21**	0344	6.2
0904	1.8		1000	1.9
M 1512	6.7	TU 1558	6.5
2137	1.4		2218	1.7
7 0343	6.8	**22**	0416	6.5
0956	1.3		1033	1.7
TU 1603	7.2	W 1630	6.7
2227	0.8		2250	1.5
8 0430	7.2	**23**	0446	6.6
1045	0.8		1104	1.6
W 1650	7.6	TH 1700	6.9
● 2313	0.5	○ 2320	1.4
9 0514	7.5	**24**	0514	6.8
1131	0.6		1134	1.5
TH 1734	7.8	F 1730	6.9
2358	0.4		2349	1.4
10 0556	7.6	**25**	0542	6.8
1215	0.5		1204	1.5
F 1816	7.7	SA 1759	6.9
11 0040	0.5	**26**	0019	1.5
0637	7.5		0610	6.8
SA 1258	0.7	SU 1234	1.6
1857	7.5		1828	6.8
12 0122	0.9	**27**	0048	1.6
0718	7.2		0639	6.6
SU 1342	1.1	M 1306	1.7
1938	7.0		1859	6.5
13 0204	1.4	**28**	0120	1.8
0758	6.7		0711	6.4
M 1426	1.6	TU 1341	2.0
2020	6.4		1933	6.3
14 0248	2.0	**29**	0157	2.1
0843	6.2		0748	6.2
TU 1514	2.1	W 1422	2.3
2108	5.8		2015	5.9
15 0338	2.5	**30**	0241	2.4
0938	5.7		0835	5.8
W 1612	2.7	TH 1512	2.6
☽ 2212	5.3		2111	5.5

OCTOBER

Time	m		Time	m
1 0337	2.8	**16**	0530	3.2
0942	5.5		1148	5.3
F 1618	2.8	SA 1815	3.0
☽ 2231	5.3			
2 0451	2.9	**17**	0035	5.1
1111	5.4		0654	3.1
SA 1743	2.8	SU 1304	5.5
			1931	3.0
3 0006	5.4	**18**	0142	5.4
0621	2.8		0758	2.8
SU 1241	5.7	M 1401	5.8
1912	2.5		2024	2.5
4 0128	5.8	**19**	0230	5.8
0741	2.4		0845	2.4
M 1354	6.1	TU 1445	6.1
2020	1.9		2106	2.2
5 0230	6.4	**20**	0308	6.1
0843	1.8		0924	2.1
TU 1451	6.8	W 1523	6.4
2115	1.3		2142	1.9
6 0321	6.9	**21**	0342	6.4
0935	1.2		1000	1.9
W 1541	7.3	TH 1557	6.6
2204	0.9		2216	1.7
7 0407	7.3	**22**	0414	6.6
1023	0.8		1034	1.7
TH 1627	7.6	F 1630	6.8
● 2250	0.6		2249	1.6
8 0451	7.5	**23**	0445	6.8
1109	0.6		1106	1.6
F 1711	7.7	SA 1703	6.8
2334	0.6	○ 2321	1.5
9 0533	7.6	**24**	0516	6.8
1153	0.7		1139	1.6
SA 1753	7.6	SU 1735	6.8
			2353	1.6
10 0017	0.8	**25**	0547	6.8
0613	7.4		1212	1.6
SU 1236	0.9	M 1807	6.7
1834	7.3			
11 0058	1.1	**26**	0027	1.7
0653	7.1		0620	6.8
M 1319	1.2	TU 1247	1.7
1914	6.8		1842	6.6
12 0139	1.6	**27**	0103	1.8
0733	6.7		0656	6.6
TU 1403	1.7	W 1326	1.9
1956	6.3		1921	6.3
13 0222	2.1	**28**	0143	2.1
0817	6.2		0737	6.3
W 1450	2.2	TH 1411	2.1
2043	5.8		2008	6.0
14 0311	2.6	**29**	0230	2.4
0910	5.8		0828	6.0
TH 1545	2.7	F 1504	2.4
☽ 2143	5.3		2107	5.7
15 0411	3.0	**30**	0327	2.6
1022	5.4		0934	5.8
F 1654	3.0	SA 1608	2.6
2306	5.1	☽ 2222	5.5
		31	0438	2.8
			1055	5.7
		SU 1727	2.6
			2345	5.6

NOVEMBER

Time	m		Time	m
1 0559	2.7	**16**	0038	5.3
1216	5.9		0659	3.0
M 1847	2.3	TU 1304	5.6
			1926	2.7
2 0101	5.9	**17**	0136	5.6
0715	2.3		0756	2.7
TU 1327	6.3	W 1357	5.8
1954	1.9		2017	2.5
3 0203	6.4	**18**	0224	5.9
0818	1.9		0843	2.4
W 1426	6.7	TH 1442	6.1
2050	1.5		2101	2.2
4 0256	6.8	**19**	0305	6.2
0912	1.4		0925	2.1
TH 1518	7.1	F 1523	6.3
2141	1.2		2141	2.0
5 0344	7.1	**20**	0343	6.4
1002	1.1		1004	1.9
F 1606	7.3	SA 1602	6.5
2228	1.0		2219	1.8
6 0429	7.3	**21**	0419	6.7
1049	1.0		1041	1.7
SA 1651	7.3	SU 1639	6.7
● 2313	1.0	○ 2256	1.7
7 0512	7.4	**22**	0455	6.8
1134	1.0		1119	1.6
SU 1734	7.2	M 1716	6.7
2355	1.2		2333	1.6
8 0553	7.3	**23**	0531	6.9
1217	1.1		1157	1.7
M 1815	7.0	TU 1754	6.7
9 0037	1.4	**24**	0012	1.6
0634	7.0		0609	6.9
TU 1300	1.4	W 1236	1.6
1856	6.6		1834	6.6
10 0118	1.8	**25**	0052	1.7
0714	6.7		0650	6.8
W 1343	1.8	TH 1319	1.7
1937	6.2		1918	6.5
11 0200	2.1	**26**	0136	1.8
0757	6.3		0735	6.6
TH 1428	2.2	F 1406	1.8
2021	5.8		2007	6.3
12 0245	2.5	**27**	0225	2.0
0844	5.9		0824	6.4
F 1516	2.5	SA 1458	2.0
2111	5.5		2102	6.0
13 0337	2.9	**28**	0319	2.3
0941	5.6		0925	6.2
SA 1612	2.8	SU 1557	2.2
☽ 2215	5.2	☽ 2206	5.9
14 0439	3.1	**29**	0422	2.4
1049	5.4		1032	6.0
SU 1717	3.0	M 1705	2.3
2328	5.2		2316	5.8
15 0551	3.1	**30**	0532	2.5
1200	5.4		1145	6.0
M 1825	2.9	TU 1816	2.3

DECEMBER

Time	m		Time	m
1 0027	5.9	**16**	0028	5.3
0644	2.3		0652	3.0
W 1256	6.1	TH 1258	5.5
1924	2.1		1920	2.8
2 0133	6.2	**17**	0130	5.5
0751	2.1		0754	2.8
TH 1401	6.4	F 1358	5.7
2025	1.9		2017	2.6
3 0231	6.5	**18**	0224	5.8
0851	1.8		0848	2.5
F 1458	6.6	SA 1450	6.0
2119	1.6		2107	2.3
4 0324	6.8	**19**	0312	6.2
0945	1.5		0935	2.1
SA 1549	6.8	SU 1536	6.2
2210	1.5		2152	2.0
5 0412	7.0	**20**	0356	6.5
1034	1.4		1019	1.8
SU 1636	6.9	M 1620	6.5
● 2256	1.4		2235	1.8
6 0457	7.1	**21**	0438	6.7
1120	1.3		1102	1.6
M 1720	6.8	TU 1702	6.7
2339	1.5	○ 2318	1.6
7 0539	7.1	**22**	0520	7.0
1203	1.3		1144	1.4
TU 1801	6.7	W 1744	6.8
8 0021	1.6	**23**	0000	1.4
0620	7.0		0602	7.1
W 1244	1.5	TH 1227	1.2
1840	6.6		1828	6.9
9 0101	1.7	**24**	0044	1.4
0659	6.8		0645	7.1
TH 1324	1.7	F 1311	1.2
1918	6.3		1912	6.8
10 0140	2.0	**25**	0129	1.4
0737	6.5		0730	7.0
F 1404	2.0	SA 1357	1.3
1956	6.1		1959	6.7
11 0219	2.3	**26**	0216	1.5
0816	6.2		0818	6.8
SA 1444	2.2	SU 1446	1.5
2036	5.8		2048	6.5
12 0301	2.5	**27**	0306	1.8
0906	5.9		0908	6.6
SU 1527	2.5	M 1538	1.8
2122	5.5		2142	6.2
13 0347	2.8	**28**	0400	2.0
0948	5.6		1005	6.3
M 1616	2.8	TU 1637	2.1
☽ 2216	5.3	☽ 2242	6.0
14 0442	3.0	**29**	0502	2.3
1047	5.4		1110	6.0
TU 1713	2.9	W 1742	2.3
2321	5.3		2350	5.8
15 0545	3.1	**30**	0611	2.4
1153	5.4		1224	5.9
W 1817	2.9	TH 1853	2.4
		31	0103	5.9
			0725	2.4
		F 1339	5.9
			2002	2.3

Chart Datum is 3·64 metres below IGN Datum. HAT is 7·8 metres above Chart Datum; see 4.5.

9.20.26 TIDAL COEFFICIENTS (See also overleaf)

YEAR **2010**

Date	Jan am	Jan pm	Feb am	Feb pm	Mar am	Mar pm	Apr am	Apr pm	May am	May pm	June am	June pm	July am	July pm	Aug am	Aug pm	Sept am	Sept pm	Oct am	Oct pm	Nov am	Nov pm	Dec am	Dec pm
1	93	97	112	112	113	115	107	103	88	83	68	65	69	66	64	60	48	43	41	38	53		59	62
2	99	101	110	106	116	115	97	90	78	72	61	57	63	59	55	51	39	36	38		58	65	66	70
3	101	101	101	94	113	108	83	75	66	60	53	49	56	52	46	42	35		41	47	72	79	74	78
4	99	96	87	79	102	95	67	59	54	48	46	43	48	45	39	37	38	44	55	64	85	91	82	85
5	91	86	70	61	87	78	51	43	43	39	41	40	43	41	38		51	61	73	82	95	99	87	89
6	80	74	53	45	69	60	37	32	36	35	40		40		40	45	70	79	90	97	101	101	89	89
7	67	61	39	35	51	43	30		35		41	44	41	43	52	59	88	97	103	108	101	99	88	87
8	55	50	34		35	30	30	33	37	41	47	51	47	51	67	76	103	109	111	112	96	92	84	81
9	47		36	40	29		38	44	44	49	55	59	56	62	83	91	113	115	111	109	88	82	78	74
10	45	45	45	51	30	35	49	55	54	59	64	69	68	74	98	103	116	114	106	100	76	70	70	66
11	47	50	56	62	41	47	60	66	63	68	73	77	80	86	108	111	111	106	94	87	64	57	61	57
12	53	58	67	71	53	59	71	75	72	76	81	85	91	95	112	111	99	92	79	70	52	46	52	48
13	62	66	75	79	65	70	79	83	80	83	87	89	98	101	109	105	83	74	62	54	42	38	44	41
14	69	72	81	84	75	79	85	88	85	87	90	91	102	102	100	93	65	55	46	40	36	35	38	37
15	75	77	85	86	82	85	89	90	88	88	91	89	100	98	86	77	47	40	35	33	36		37	
16	78	79	87	87	88	89	90	89	87	86	88	85	94	89	69	60	35	32	33		39	42	38	41
17	80	80	86	84	90	90	87	85	84	81	82	79	84	77	52	45	33		35	39	46	51	44	48
18	80	79	82	79	90	89	81	77	77	74	75	71	71	64	40		37	43	44	49	55	59	53	58
19	77	75	75	71	87	84	73	67	70	66	67	64	58	53	38	38	49	54	55	60	64	68	63	67
20	73	69	67	61	80	75	62	57	63	60	61	59	49		41	46	60	65	65	69	72	75	72	76
21	66	62	56	50	71	65	52	49	58	58	58		47	47	51	57	70	74	73	76	78	81	81	84
22	58	54	45	40	59	53	47	48	58		58	59	49	52	62	67	78	81	79	82	82	84	87	89
23	50	46	38		47	42	52		60	63	61	63	56	60	72	75	83	85	83	85	84	84	90	91
24	42	40	38	42	40	40	57	63	67	70	66	69	64	68	79	81	86	86	85	85	83	82	91	90
25	39		48	57	45		70	77	74	77	72	74	72	75	83	84	86	86	84	83	80	77	88	86
26	41	45	66	76	52	60	83	89	80	83	76	77	77	79	85	85	84	82	81	78	74	71	82	79
27	51	58	86	94	69	78	93	97	84	86	78	79	81	81	85	84	79	76	74	70	67	64	74	70
28	66	74	102	108	87	94	99	100	86	86	79	78	81	81	82	80	72	67	65	61	60	58	65	61
29	83	90			101	106	100	99	85	83	77	76	80	79	76	73	62	56	56	51	56	56	58	56
30	97	103			110	112	96	93	81	79	74	72	76	74	69	64	51	45	48	46	57		55	
31	108	111			112	110			75	72			71	68	59	54			46	48			55	57

French translations/abbreviations of common tidal terms are as follows:

HW	Pleine mer (PM)	LAT	Plus basse mer astronomique (PBMA)
LW	Basse mer (BM)	MHWS	Pleine mer moyenne de VE (PMVE)
Springs	Vive eau (VE)	MHWN	Pleine mer moyenne de ME (PMME)
Neaps	Morte eau (ME)	MLWN	Basse mer moyenne de ME (BMME)
CD	Zero des cartes (Chart Datum)	MLWS	Basse mer moyenne de VE (BMVE)
HAT	Plus haute mer astronomique (PHMA)	ML/MSL	Niveau moyen (NM)

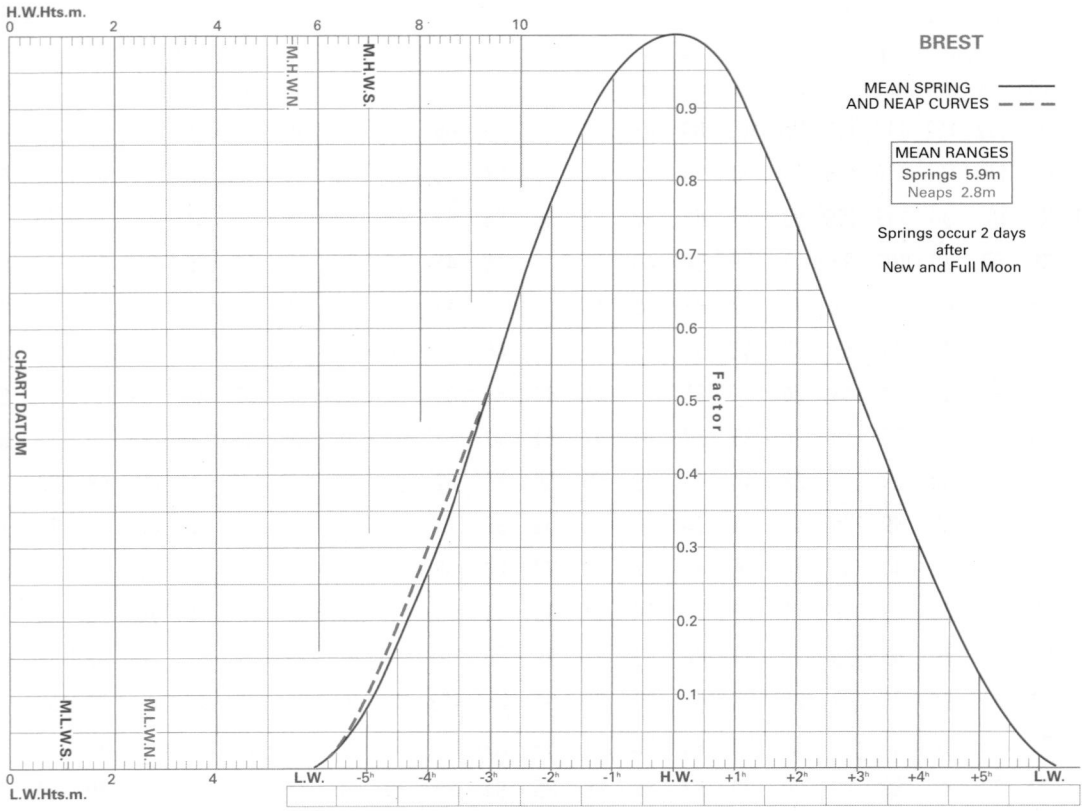

BREST

MEAN SPRING ——————
AND NEAP CURVES – – – –

MEAN RANGES
Springs 5.9m
Neaps 2.8m

Springs occur 2 days
after
New and Full Moon

TIDAL COEFFICIENTS

The magnitude, ie range, of the tide on any given day, a.m and p.m, can be expressed by a non-dimensional coefficient. With a working knowledge of coefficients the reader can see instantly whether it is neaps, springs or in between. There is no need to look up or try to recall the range in metres at the nearest Standard Port. Just remember the magic numbers 45, 70 and 95.

The salient coefficients, as tabulated overleaf for Brest, are:

120	=	A very big spring tide
95	=	Mean springs (vive eau)
70	=	An average tide
45	=	Mean neaps (morte eau)
20	=	A very small neap tide

Brest coefficients are valid along the Channel and Atlantic coasts of France and around the UK. Access times to French ports (eg Binic 9.18.17) may be given with reference to coefficients.

French tide tables, like Admiralty tide tables, show secondary ports' time and height differences against the appropriate standard port at springs and neaps. The coefficient for the day may also be used to decide which correction(s) to apply. Use vive eau corrections for coefficients >70 and morte eau corrections for <70. Where (eg in estuaries) more accurate corrections are required, interpolate or extrapolate.

Tidal stream rates may also be calculated from a graph like Fig 4(9), modified as follows: On the vertical axis, replace range with coefficients from 20 at the bottom to 120 at the top. The horizontal axis is unchanged, ie rates in kn. From a tidal stream atlas or chartlet, plot np and sp rates against coefficients 45 and 95 respectively; join these two points. Enter with the coefficient for the day; go horizontally to the sloping line, then vertically to the horizontal axis; read off the required rate in knots.

9.20.27 RADE DE BREST

Finistère **48°20´·75N 04°32·10W** (Goulet de Brest, E end)

CHARTS AC 3427, 3428, 3429; SHOM 7401, 7400, 7397, 7398, 7399; Navi 542; Imray C36; Stanfords 2. Beyond the N and E edges of AC 3429 & SHOM 7400, the Rivers Elorn and Aulne are usefully covered on IGN land maps 0516, 0517 & 0518 (1:25,000). These maps show some depths, Lat/Long values, much valuable topographical data and are readily available.

TIDES
Standard Port BREST (⟶)

Times				Height (metres)			
High Water		Low Water		MHWS	MHWN	MLWN	MLWS
0000	0600	0000	0600	7·0	5·5	2·7	1·1
1200	1800	1200	1800				
Differences TINDUFF (48°20´·2N 04°21´·9W)							
+0005	+0005	+0005	+0005	+0·3	+0·2	+0·1	+0·1
PONT DE TERENEZ (48°16´·1N 04°15´·7W)							
+0005	+0005	+0010	+0005	+0·4	+0·3	+0·2	+0·2

In most of the bays in the Rade de Brest tidal streams are weak, but in the main rivers they can exceed 2kn at sp.

SHELTER The Rade (50 sq miles) is a sheltered cruising ground when the weather offshore is bad. There are attractive ⚓s in the SE part of the Rade and up the Rivers Elorn and Aulne.

NAVIGATION WPT 48°18´·20N 04°44´·26W, 068°/5·3M to front ldg lt (Pte du Petit Minou); thence through the Goulet de Brest. See 9.20.4 for light details. Tidal streams run hard, max 4·6kn on the spring ebb and 3·5kn on the flood.

Pass either side of Plateau des Fillettes, rks well marked by 3 lt buoys and Mengam IDM lt bcn twr. Keep well inshore to avoid warships and commercial vessels and to cheat any foul tide.

The area S and SW from the Moulin Blanc Marina is very shoal, and yachts should head WSW from the marina to R1 buoy and Basse du Renard WCM buoy or Pte de l'Armorique.

In the SW part of Rade de Brest are various naval sites with no ⚓, prohib zones and DG ranges around Île Longue. There are however ⚓s at Le Fret (SE of Île Longue) whence a ferry runs to Brest; and off Roscanvel in the lee of the Quélern Peninsula.

E of Pte de l'Armorique there are ⚓s and W ⚓s in 3m in Anse de L'Auberlac'h, Baie de Daoulas and its inlets/creeks (very shoal), at the mouth of the River de l'Hôpital and up the drying/buoyed River de Faou.

S of here the much larger River Aulne (see below) can easily be explored 18M up-river from Landévennec to Châteaulin.

RIVERS FLOWING INTO THE RADE DE BREST

RIVER ÉLORN, entered 1·2M E of Moulin Blanc Marina, is navigable to Landerneau, 6M up-river. From Pont Albert-Louppe (29m) and Pont de l'Iroise (25m clearance) the river is buoyed/lit for 2M. But further up it is marked by smaller unlit buoys and perches, some of which may well be some distance outboard of navigable water. Good ⚓s are at Le Passage, 8ca above the bridges, or further NE in Anse St Nicolas.

The drying port of Landerneau can be reached on the tide via a lifting bridge, ☎ 06·11·03·31·20. Dry out against the N quay. Few nautical facilities, but a pleasant town.

RIVER AULNE To the SE of Rade de Brest, L'Aulne is a lovely river with steep wooded banks. There are ⚓s off Landévennec, below Térénez bridge (27m), and also ⚓s 1½M above that bridge. Charted depths are optimistic.

At Guily-Glaz, 14M above Landévennec, a lock (operating HW Brest −2 to +1½, but not between 2100 and 0700; ☎ 02.98.86.03.21) gives access to the canalised river (2·7m) and Port Launay on a U-bend. Port Launay is a popular place to winter against the attractive stone quays in complete shelter. Facilities: AB on quay, AC, FW, R; easy access to the N165 motorway.

3M further on is Châteaulin, a charming country town and head of the navigable river. Facilities: ❷ pontoon, AC, FW, 🛒 100m from quay.

9.20.28 BREST

Finistère **48°22'·00N 04°28'·28W** (Port centre) ❀❀❀❀⚓⚓⚓❀❀

CHARTS See under 9.20.27.

TIDES +0520 Dover; ML 4·0; Duration 0605. Note: Brest is a Standard Port (⟵). Tidal coefficients are in 9.20.26.

SHELTER Excellent in Moulin Blanc Marina and probably also in the new Marina du Château. Access all tides H24. Brest is a busy naval, commercial and fishing port.

NAVIGATION See 9.20.27 for the outer approaches. Ldg lts 068° at Pte du Petit Minou and Pte du Portzic.

WPT 48°21'·75N 04°29'·18W, 347°/1M to the new marina via the Passe Sud, leaving the Naval Base (a restricted area) to port; or S of the Port de Commerce via the E and W Passes. Le Château and the American Monument are conspic. Keep clear of all warships.

WPT 48°22'·80N 04°25'·88W, thence 007°/7ca via MB1/MB2 chan buoys to Q (3) 10s in centre of Moulin Blanc Marina. The Océanopolis bldg, W roof, is conspic except near LW.

R/T Monitor *Brest Port* (at Pte du Portzic) Ch **08** (controls apprs to Brest). Marinas Ch 09 (HO).

TELEPHONE HM Brest 02·98·33·41·41; Aff Mar 02·98·80·62·25; CROSS 02·98·89·31·31; ⊖ 02·98·44·35·20; Auto 08·92·68·08·29; Météo 02·98·32·55·55; Police 02·98·43·77·77; Dr 02·98·44·38·70; Ⓗ 02·98·22·33·33; Brit Consul 02.23.18.30.30.

FACILITIES Moulin Blanc Marina, see overleaf. **Sté des Régates de Brest** ☎ 02·98·02·53·36, R. **YC Rade de Brest** ☎ 02·98·44·63·32. **CN Municipal** ☎ 02·98·34·64·64.

Marina du Château in central Brest opened 2009. See overleaf for chartlet and further details. Navigation within the Naval Port and the River Penfeld is strictly prohibited; see AC 3428 and chartlet. The marina is within easy (uphill) walking distance of central Brest. Regeneration of the adjacent shore areas is well under way; some villagey cafés and bars already exist.

City all facilities: ✉, Ⓑ, ⇌, Guipavas ✈. Ferry: Roscoff. Brest Festival of the sea is held every 4 years, usually 2nd week in July.

Marina du Château, ent 48°22´·68N 04°29´·48W, in central Brest between Port Militaire and Port de Commerce, opened fully 2009. 575 AB and 47 ▼. It is run by SOPAB which also manages Moulin Blanc Marina. HM ☎ 02·98·02·20·02 port-de-plaisance@sopab.fr D&P, BH (20t), ⚓, Wi-Fi, CH. Reports on this new marina welcome, see www.reedsalmanac.co.uk for updates.

Moulin Blanc Marina, ☎ 02·98·02·20·02. www.portmoulinblanc. com port-de-plaisance@sopab.fr Excellent facilities and very helpful bi-lingual staff. 1340+120 ▼, €2·10. P & D H24 (French credit card or pre-arrange with HM), Slip, ME, El, ⓔ, ✕, ⚓, C (18 ton), BH (14 & 35 ton), SM, CH, SHOM, Gaz, Wi-Fi, ▣, &, 🛒, Bar, R. No 7 bus, 20 mins to city centre.

9.20.29   CAMARET

Finistère **48°16'·85N 04°35'·31W** ✿✿✿✿✿✿✿✿

CHARTS AC 2350, 3427 ; SHOM 7149, 7148, 7401; Imray C36; Navi 540, 542; Stanfords 17

TIDES +0500 Dover; ML 3·8; Duration 0610.

Standard Port BREST (◄——)

Times				Height (metres)			
High Water		Low Water		MHWS	MHWN	MLWN	MLWS
0000	0600	0000	0600	7·0	5·5	2·7	1·1
1200	1800	1200	1800				
Differences CAMARET							
–0010	–0010	–0015	–0010	–0·4	–0·4	–0·3	–0·1

SHELTER Good, except in strong E'lies. Access H24. Good ⚓ and ⚓s SE of Port Vauban. No ⚓ within fairway and hbr.

NAVIGATION WPT 48°17'·44N 04°36'·09W, 139°/0·8M to N mole lt and in its W sector. Beware rks W & N of Pte du Grand Gouin.

LIGHTS AND MARKS The G SHM bcn twr at the W end of the N mole is very conspic; ditto Tour Vauban and chapel. A fish farm, 3ca ENE of Port Vauban, is marked by a NCM buoy Q, a WCM bcn VQ (9) 10s (destroyed) and unlit ECM and SCM buoys; see 9.20.4.

R/T Ch 09.

TELEPHONE Aff Mar 02·98·27·93·28; CROSS 02·98·89·31·31; ⊖ 02·98·33·97·11 (Brest); Auto 08·92·68·08·29; Police 02·98·27·84·94 (Jul/Aug); SAMU 15; Brit Consul 02.23.18.30.30.

FACILITIES Port Vauban (5m), inside the N mole; enter via the S end of wavebreak. Especially for ♥, AB/rafted, plus a few fingers. ☎ 02·98·27·95·99, mob ☎ 06·79·19·55·68 in emergency. 250 ♥, €2·20. D, C (mobile, 20 ton), Shwrs (underground!), Ice, bread. ⚓s SE of the marina.
Port du Notic, in town, has 200 AB and 50 ♥ berths €2·20 on outside (only) of E and A pontoons in 1·5m for yachts <11m LOA. HM ☎ 02·98·27·89·31. www.camaret-sur-mer.com ♿, @, ▢, ME, El, ⒺⒻ, ✕, CH, C (5 ton), SM, SHOM.
Port du Styvel, N of Port du Notic, is strictly for local boats; no ♥.
Town P, 🛒, Gaz, R, Bar, ✉, Ⓑ. ⇌ (Brest), ✈ (Brest or Quimper).

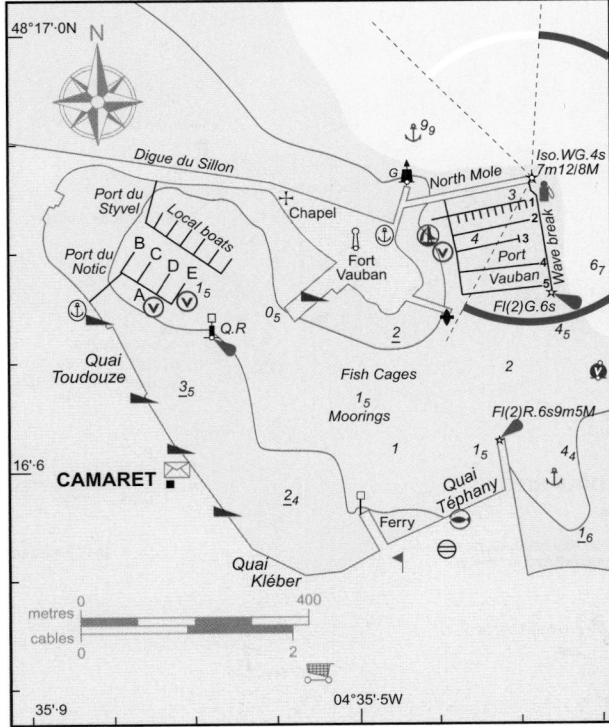

9.20.30   MORGAT

Finistère **48°13'·56N 04°29'·76W** ✿✿✿✿✿✿✿✿

CHARTS AC 2350, 2349; SHOM 7172, 7121; Imray C36; Navi 541, 542; Stanfords 17

TIDES +0500 Dover; ML 3·8; Duration No data.

Standard Port BREST (◄——)

Times				Height (metres)			
High Water		Low Water		MHWS	MHWN	MLWN	MLWS
0000	0600	0000	0600	7·0	5·5	2·7	1·1
1200	1800	1200	1800				
Differences MORGAT							
–0005	–0010	–0020	–0005	–0·5	–0·4	–0·2	0·0
DOUARNENEZ							
–0010	–0010	–0020	–0010	–0·4	–0·4	–0·2	–0·1

SHELTER Good, except in W-N winds. Access H24. ⚓ in the bay in 2m on sand. Pleasant day ⚓s, sheltered from the W, are S of Morgat in the bays of St Hernot, St Norgard and St Nicolas.

NAVIGATION WPT 48°13'·60N 04°29'·15W, 270°/500m to first PHM buoy. Chan is nominally dredged 1·5m, but may have only 0.5m due silting; it shoals abruptly on its unmarked N edge. Rocks lurk close under the cliffs S of Pte de Morgat. Les Verrès, 2–2·5M ESE of ent, are in the G sector of Pte de Morgat lt. See 9.20.5 for dangers off Cap de la Chèvre.

LIGHTS AND MARKS Pte de Morgat lt is on the clifftop among trees. See chartlet and 9.20.4.

R/T Marina Ch 09.

TELEPHONE Aff Mar 02·98·27·09·95; CROSS 02·98·89·31·31; Auto 08·92·68·08·29; SNSM 02·98·10·51·41; ⊖ 02·98·33·97·11 (Brest); Police 02·98·27·00·22; Ⓗ 02·98·27·05·33; Brit Consul 02.23.18.30.30; tourist office 02·98·27·29·49 (Crozon).

FACILITIES Marina ☎ 02·98·27·01·97. port-de-morgat@crozon. fr www.crozon.com 646 + 35 ♥, €1·59. ♥ on small H pontoon: fingers on E side or AB on W side for larger yachts. 40 unmarked ⚓s, €0·79. Slip, CH, D, P, ME, M, C (6 ton), El, ✕, Ⓔ, ▢, ♿.
YC ☎ 02·98·16·00·01. **Town** (Crozon), 🛒, Gaz, R, Bar, ✉, Ⓑ, ⇌, ✈ (Brest or Quimper). Ferry: Roscoff.

9.20.31 DOUARNENEZ

Finistère **48°05'·98N 04°20'·35W** ✳❋❋♨♨♨♨❀❀

CHARTS AC 2349; SHOM 7121; Imray C36; Navi 542; Stanfords 17

TIDES Differences 9.20.30. +0500 Dover; ML 3·7; Duration 0615.

SHELTER In strong NW'lies due to seas/swell the outer Grande Passe ♥ pontoons can be uncomfortable. Rade de Guet ⚓ areas in 1·5-3m are exposed to N/NE'lies. Good shelter in Port Rhu.

NAVIGATION WPT 48°06'·71N 04°20'·83W, 157°/0·8M to abeam outer ♥ pontoon. Basse Veur (4·8m) and Basse Neuve (2·2m) are 8 and 4ca NNW of Île Tristan lt and in its R sector. 5ca NW of Tréboul jetty, QG, keep well NE of Rochers le Coulinec and La Tête de Pierre, a rocky ledge, both off chartlet.

LIGHTS AND MARKS Daymarks: Two conspic spires and Île Tristan lt twr are in transit 147°. Île Tristan is a cliffy, wooded island. Dir lt 157°, on the 16m high bridge at S end of Port Rhu, covers the inner appr, Grande Passe. See chartlet and 9.20.4 for light details.

R/T Marina and Port Rhu Ch 09. FV Port Ch 12.

TELEPHONE Port HM 02·98·92·14·85; Aff Mar 02·98·75·31·30; CROSS 02·98·89·31·31; Météo 02·98·84·60·64; ⊖ 02·98·33·97·11 (Brest); Auto 08·92·68·08·29; Ⓗ 02·98·92·25·00; Brit Consul 02.23.18.30.30.

FACILITIES from seaward: Grande Passe 60 ♥; the southerly pontoons project slightly into the fairway. AC, FW, access H24. Other facilities as per Tréboul.

Tréboul Marina (1·5m) is full of local boats. ☎ 02·98·74·02·56. www.inet-bretagne.fr 463 AB, €2·06. Shwrs, Ⓘ N of D & P berth, Slip, C (6 ton), ME, CH, BH (12 ton), SM, Ⓔ, El, ✖, Wi-Fi. **YC** ☎ 02·98·92·02·03.

Port Rhu ☎ 02·98·92·00·67. 30 ♥, €1·74. If conditions are bad in Grande Passe pre-arrange a berth at Port Rhu's non-tidal basin (3·2m); or at pontoons S of the bridge (16·5m clnce at HW, coeff 80) in 2·2m. Enter over a sill (1·1m) via 10m wide gate which opens approx HW ±2 when Coeff >70.

Port Neuf is for FVs only. **Port de Rosmeur** is full of moorings, but ⚓ S of it, as charted, in about 1·5m; convenient for town.

Town Gaz, 🛒, R, Bar, @, ✉, Ⓑ, ⇌ & ✈ (Quimper). Ferry: Roscoff.

9.20.32 THE RAZ DE SEIN

GEOGRAPHY The Raz (pronounced *Raah*) is bounded by Le Chat bcn twr to the W (at E end of Chaussée de Sein) and to the E by La Vieille lt ho which with La Plate lt tr marks the dangers extending 8ca off Pte du Raz. Plateau de Tévennec, 2·9M NNE of Le Chat, consists of islets, drying rks and shoals which extend 5ca in all directions from the lt ho thereon. Other dangers on the N side of the Raz are rks and shoals extending nearly 1M W and WSW from Pte du Van, and Basse Jaune (1·4m) 1M to N.

On the S side the main dangers, all 1·5M off La Vieille, are: to the SW, Kornog Bras, a 3·7m deep rk; to the S, Masklou Greiz, rky shoals (7·6m) on which sea can break heavily; and to the SE, Roche Moulleg (5·2m).

TIDAL STREAMS ▶*In the middle (48°02'·88N 04°46'·76W) of the Raz the NE-going (flood) stream begins at HW Brest +0550, sp rate 6·5kn; the SW-going (ebb) stream begins at HW Brest –½, sp rate 5·5kn. Slack water, as the N-going flood expires, occurs between about HW Brest –1 and –½; if S-bound aim for the middle of that window, ±15 mins. If N-bound, slack water is about HW Brest +5½. Study tidal diamond 'D' on chart 2348. There are eddies near La Vieille on both streams.*

As a rule the Raz should always be taken at slack water to ensure the least uncomfortable conditions. Precise timing is vital: even an hour early or late on slack water can greatly affect the sea state. In good weather, near nps, wind and tide together, it is not difficult. But in moderate to strong winds it **must** *be taken at slack water. In strong winds-against-tide which raise steep breaking seas and overfalls, the chan* **must not** *be used.*◀

NAVIGATION By day, WPT 'D' 48°02'·37N 04°45'·88W, 2ca W of La Plate, allows visual pilotage in normal sea states. By night use WPT 'N' 48°02'·91N 04°46'·61W, 308°/9ca from La Plate, and at the intersection of the white sectors of Tévennec, La Vieille and Le Chat. Take care to correct minor track deviations before they become major. Ensure accurate timing. Take all the usual safety precautions. Sig stn at Pte du Raz monitors Ch 16. Bon passage!

MARKS Tévennec lt ho is a white twr perched on a house, atop a substantial and distinctive rock. La Vieille is a stone twr, B top, with a derrick on its E side. La Plate is a smaller YBY bcn twr. Le Chat is a B twr, Y top marking rocks on its W, N and E sides; keep at least 0·5M E of it. See chartlet and 9.20.4 for lt details.

9.20.33 ÎLE DE SEIN

Finistere 48°02'·34N 04°50'·89W ❀⚓✿

CHARTS AC 2348*; SHOM 7147, 7148, 7423*; Imray C36, C37; Navi 541. *Both have 1:10,000 insets of the island.

TIDES ML 3·6.

Standard Port BREST (←—)

Times				Height (metres)			
High Water		Low Water		MHWS	MHWN	MLWN	MLWS
0000	0600	0000	0600	7·0	5·5	2·7	1·1
1200	1800	1200	1800				
Differences ÎLE DE SEIN							
–0005	–0005	–0015	–0010	–0·9	–0·8	–0·4	–0·2

SHELTER The non-drying N part of the hbr is open to N and E winds; the drying S part of the hbr is protected from E and S by two large bkwtrs. The island itself affords some shelter from W'lies. ⚓ near the LB, but clear of 3 pairs of small lateral buoys (Apr-Oct) marking the fairway between N mole and S quay, which is used at HW by ferries. Île de Sein is worth visiting in fair weather, good visibility and preferably near nps.

NAVIGATION WPT 48°03'·67N 04°50'·71W, 187°/1·4M to Men-Brial lt ho ≠ B vert stripe on W house. (3rd from left, close S of lt ho and within its W sector (186°-192°)). This N appr is advised except in strong N'lies. Cornoc-An-Ar-Braden SHM lt buoy, where the tide sets across the chan, is 4ca S of the ⊕.

Chenal d'Ar Vas Du is aligned 224°: bcn on An Nerroth ≠ Men-Brial lt ho W sector (221°-227°). Chenal Oriental is aligned 270° on Sein lt ho and in the W sector (269°-271°) of its Dir Q WRG lt. By day appr with front bcn (close N of An Nerroth) ≠ 265° bcn close SSW of Sein lt ho. All bcns are reported hard-to-identify.

LIGHTS AND MARKS Men-Brial lt ho, G/W bands, has two white sectors leading towards the hbr. Cornoc-an-ar-Braden SHM lt buoy marks a rock on the W side of the N'ly white sector. Sein lt ho, W twr/B top, and two lattice masts are conspic at the W end of Île de Sein (which first appears as a low rounded hummock). See 9.20.4 for lts further W on Chaussée de Sein.

R/T None. Sig stn at Pte du Raz Ch 16. **TEL** Mairie 02·98·70.90.35.

FACILITIES Limited 🛒, ✉, R, Bar, CH, ✕. www.enezsun.com

9.20.34 AUDIERNE

Finistere 48°00'·55N 04°32'·42W ✿✿⚓⚓⚓✿✿✿✿

CHARTS AC 2819 inc inset; SHOM 7147, 7148; Imray C36, C37; Navi 541

TIDES +0440 Dover; ML 3·1; Duration 0605.

Standard Port BREST (←—)

Times				Height (metres)			
High Water		Low Water		MHWS	MHWN	MLWN	MLWS
0000	0600	0000	0600	7·0	5·5	2·7	1·1
1200	1800	1200	1800				
Differences AUDIERNE							
−0035	−0035	−0030	−0030	−1·8	−1·4	−0·7	−0·3
ANSE DE FEUNTEUN AOD (6M WNW Audierne)							
−0030	−0040	−0035	−0025	−1·4	−1·2	−0·6	−0·2
LE GUILVINEC							
−0010	−0025	−0025	−0015	−1·9	−1·5	−0·7	−0·2
LESCONIL							
−0010	−0030	−0030	−0020	−2·0	−1·5	−0·7	−0·2

SHELTER Good in marina; see also Ste Evette below. There is limited room to ⚓ in the bight N of La Petite Gamelle SCM bcn.

NAVIGATION From the W, WPT 47°59'·47N 04°33'·01W (abeam Gamelle Ouest WCM buoy), 006°/1·5M to Kergadec Dir lt. Appr between La Gamelle, rks drying 0·9m in the middle of the bay, and Le Sillon de Galets rks to the W. Appr is difficult in strong S'lies, when seas break at the ent.

From the SE, WPT 47°59'·46N 04°31'·56W (3ca E of Gamelle Est SCM buoy), 331°/1·2M to bkwtr lt. This track leaves La Gamelle reef 300m to port. If bound for Ste Evette, do not turn WNW until well clear N of La Gamelle and Pte de Lervily's R sector.

Bar at ent; inside, dredged chan initially lies about 25m off the bkwtr. Pick up the 359° ldg marks, vert R/W chevrons, to avoid rocks at foot of bkwtr and banks to stbd drying 1·1m to 2·1m.

At root of bkwtr pick up 2nd set of R/W chevrons on corner of fish market bldg ≠ 045°; leave the fish market close (15m) to stbd, then alter 90° port towards the marina.

Leave the FV quays and yacht pontoons close to port to clear the bank to stbd, drying 1·9m and more. On departure there are 225° ldg chevrons by the roadside at root of W bkwtr.

LIGHTS AND MARKS See chartlet and 9.21.4. By day from the W WPT, Kergadec, W 8-sided lt tr, R top, ≠ old lt ho (hard to see) leads 006°. At night stay in the W sector (005°-007°) of Kergadec. From SE WPT, 331° ldg marks are: Front, conspic white twr on Jetée du Raoulic (long W bkwtr); rear Kergadec. Fish market is a conspic B/W bldg.

R/T None.

TELEPHONE Aff Mar 02·98·70·03·33; CROSS 02·98·89·31·31; SNSM 02·98·70·07·54; Police 02·98·70·04·38; ⊖02·98·33·97·11 (Brest); Auto 08·92·68·08·29; Ⓗ 02·98·75·10·10; Brit Consul 06·17·32·63·10.

FACILITIES Marina Access HW −2 to +1 for 2m draft. Quays reserved for FVs. Berth initially on any hammerhead. Pontoons A-C are dredged 2m at the outer end, but 1·6m will be found between dredgings. Pontoons D-G are dredged 2m; avoid F & G as the flood

sets strongly towards the bridge. HM ☎ 02·98·75·04·93, mob 06·72·91·70·52. www.audierne.info 100 + 30 **Ⓥ**, €1·69 plus €0·15 per person. **Poulgoazec** C (15 ton), Slips.

Town P & D (cans), CH, ME, El, ⚒, Ⓔ, Gaz, 🛒, R, Bar, ✉, Ⓑ. Bus to Quimper for ⇌, ✈. Ferry: Roscoff.

SAINTE EVETTE The long bkwtr gives good shelter, but in strong SE-SW winds it is very uncomfortable and swell intrudes. Access H24. 30 W 🛟s (€1·29) in 1-2m, some very close together. Or ⚓ free in 3-4m close to seaward of 🛟s in moderate holding on sand. Avoid the S side of N pier/slip used by vedettes.

HM ☎ 02·98·70.00.28. D by hose from N side of N jetty (approx HW ±3), P (cans), 🅿, Showers, R, Bar, limited victuals.

Three 053° ldg lts, all Q synch (see 9.21.4): front, W pylon; middle, 210m from front, R ☐ on W pylon; rear, 0·58M from front, R ☐ on W pylon with R stripe. VHF Ch 12. HM (Plaisance) ☎ 02·98·58·14·47; www.leguilvinec.com Facilities: 4 🛟s, 4 AB at NE end of hbr, €1·56, ⊖, C, D, P, El, ME, ⚒, CH, Ⓔ.

LESCONIL, Finistere, **47°47'·70N 04°12'·64W**. AC 2820, 3640; SHOM 7146, 6646; Navi 543. Tides, see 9.21.8; ML 3m. Fishing port 3M SW of Loctudy; yachts only in emergency. Do not enter/leave 1630-1830LT due to FV inrush.

Appr from Karek Greis ECM buoy, on ldg line 325°, church spire just open W of Men ar Groas lt ho, W twr/G top; at night in W sector 313°-333°. Bkwtr lts are QG and Oc R 4s. Possible drying mooring inside S bkwtr; no 🛟s, no AB on quays. HM ☎ 02·98·82.22.97. Facilities of a fishing port.

FISHING HARBOURS N AND E OF THE POINTE DE PENMARC'H

ST GUÉNOLÉ, Finistere, **47°48'·68N 04°22'·93W**. AC 2819, 2820; SHOM 7146/7, 6645; Navi 543. Strictly a fishing port; yachts only in emergency/force majeure. Access difficult in fresh W'lies, impossible in heavy weather. 3 sets of ldg marks/lts. Lts as 9.21.4. Pilot book & SHOM 6645 essential. HM ☎ 02.98.58.60.43.

LE GUILVINEC, Finistere, **47°47'·46N 04°17'·17W**. AC 2819, 2820, 3640; SHOM 7146/7, 6646. HW + 0447 on Dover (UT); ML 3·0m. See 9.21.8. Good shelter and useful passage port (3m), but total priority to FVs; no ent/exit 1600-1830. Access H24 for <2·5m draft. Start from Névez SHM buoy. Appr is easy if able to see 053° triple ldg lts or the large, conspic dayglo red daymarks. Close in, beware Lost Moan rocks, SE of ent, marked by RW bcn lt twr. Good ⚓ SE of hbr ent in 7·7m staying clear of fairway.

South Brittany

Loctudy to St Nazaire

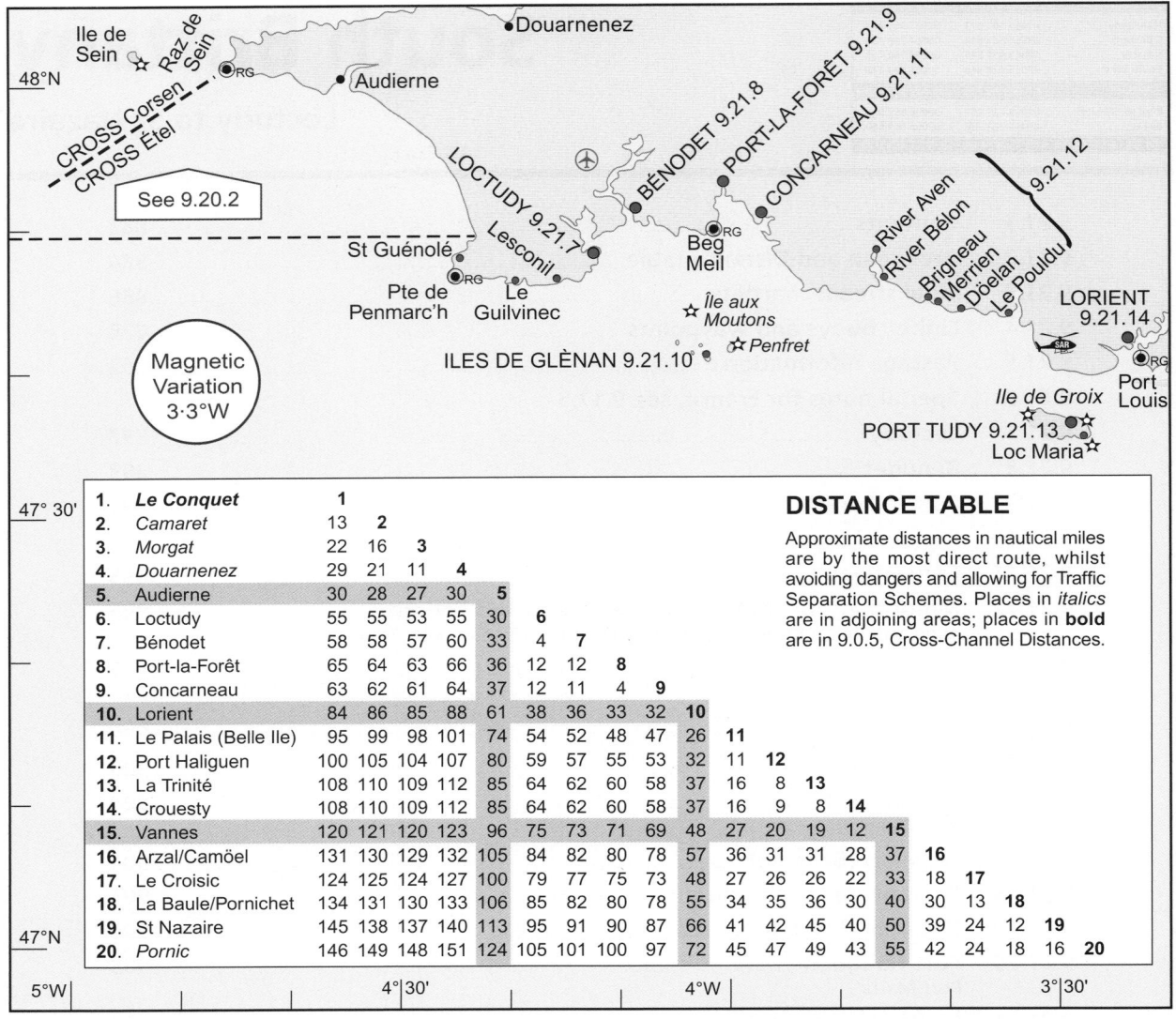

DISTANCE TABLE

Approximate distances in nautical miles are by the most direct route, whilst avoiding dangers and allowing for Traffic Separation Schemes. Places in *italics* are in adjoining areas; places in **bold** are in 9.0.5, Cross-Channel Distances.

1.	*Le Conquet*	**1**																		
2.	*Camaret*	13	**2**																	
3.	*Morgat*	22	16	**3**																
4.	*Douarnenez*	29	21	11	**4**															
5.	Audierne	30	28	27	30	**5**														
6.	Loctudy	55	55	53	55	30	**6**													
7.	Bénodet	58	58	57	60	33	4	**7**												
8.	Port-la-Forêt	65	64	63	66	36	12	12	**8**											
9.	Concarneau	63	62	61	64	37	12	11	4	**9**										
10.	Lorient	84	86	85	88	61	38	36	33	32	**10**									
11.	Le Palais (Belle Ile)	95	99	98	101	74	54	52	48	47	26	**11**								
12.	Port Haliguen	100	105	104	107	80	59	57	55	53	32	11	**12**							
13.	La Trinité	108	110	109	112	85	64	62	60	58	37	16	8	**13**						
14.	Crouesty	108	110	109	112	85	64	62	60	58	37	16	9	8	**14**					
15.	Vannes	120	121	120	123	96	75	73	71	69	48	27	20	19	12	**15**				
16.	Arzal/Camöel	131	130	129	132	105	84	82	80	78	57	36	31	31	28	37	**16**			
17.	Le Croisic	124	125	124	127	100	79	77	75	73	48	27	26	26	22	33	18	**17**		
18.	La Baule/Pornichet	134	131	130	133	106	85	82	80	78	55	34	35	36	30	40	30	13	**18**	
19.	St Nazaire	145	138	137	140	113	95	91	90	87	66	41	42	45	40	50	39	24	12	**19**
20.	*Pornic*	146	149	148	151	124	105	101	100	97	72	45	47	49	43	55	42	24	18	16	**20**

TABLE OF BUDGET AIRLINE ROUTES

The table below shows direct flights by 7 budget airlines from 6 coastal airports (Nantes and Bordeaux are only 45 minutes by train to/from the coast) to no less than 11 UK regional and 3 London airports.

UK: A – Z / FRANCE: N – S	Birmingham	Bristol	Cardiff	East Midlands	Edinburgh	Exeter	Gatwick	Glasgow	Leeds/Bradford	Liverpool	Luton	Manchester	Southampton	Stansted
Brest	FB					FB					RY	FB	FB	
Lorient			Only by Aer Arann from/to Waterford, Cork, Kerry and Galway											
Nantes			AA	RY						RY				RY
La Rochelle	FB	EJ			J2		EJ	FB	J2			FB	FB	RY
Bordeaux	BY	EJ					BA				EJ	BY	FB	
Biarritz														RY

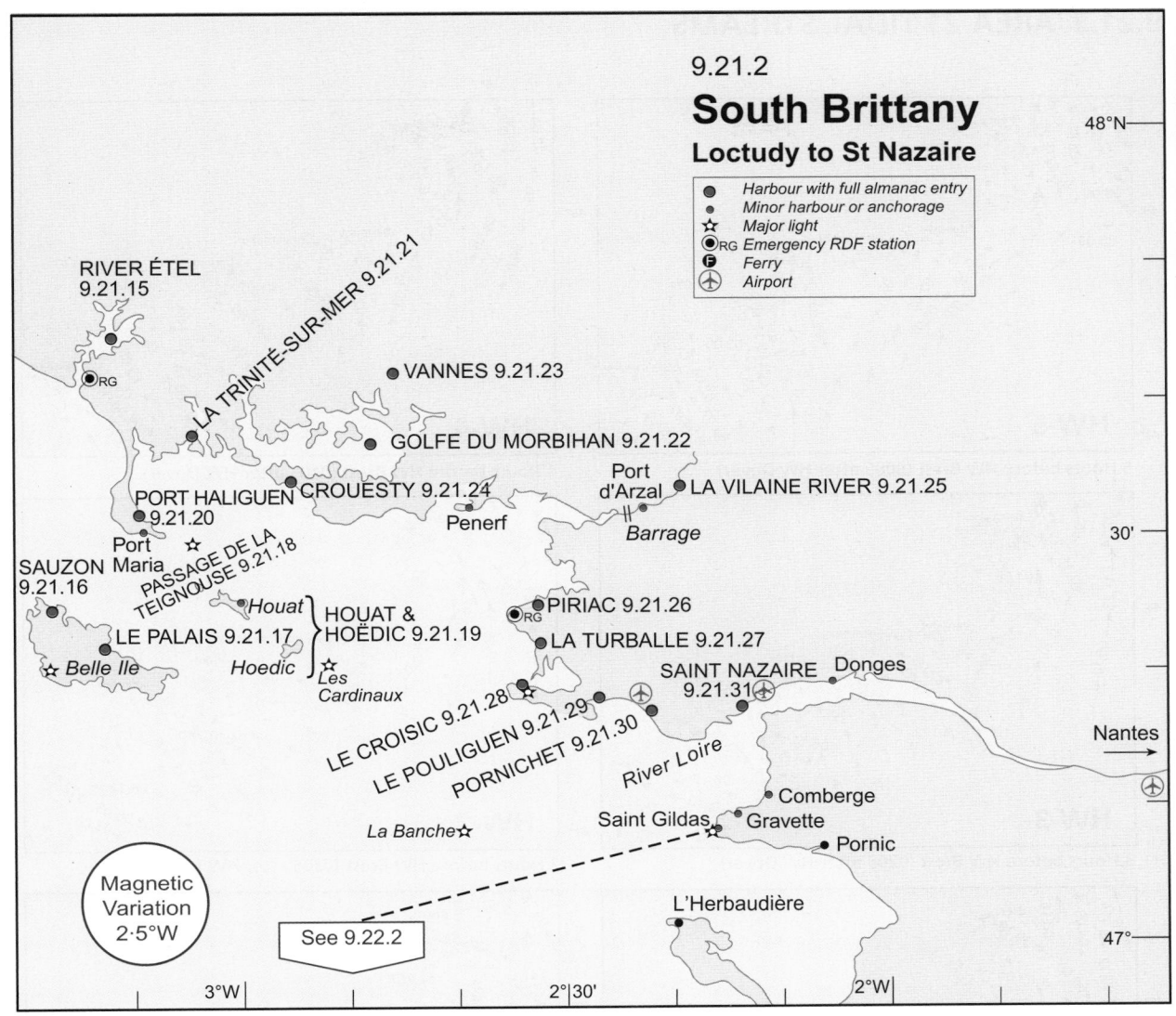

9.21.2
South Brittany
Loctudy to St Nazaire

48°N

●		Harbour with full almanac entry
·		Minor harbour or anchorage
☆		Major light
⊙RG		Emergency RDF station
Ⓕ		Ferry
⊕		Airport

RIVER ÉTEL
9.21.15

LA TRINITÉ-SUR-MER 9.21.21

●VANNES 9.21.23

●GOLFE DU MORBIHAN 9.21.22

Port d'Arzal

CROUESTY 9.21.24

●LA VILAINE RIVER 9.21.25

PORT HALIGUEN
9.21.20

Penerf

Barrage

30'

Port Maria

PASSAGE DE LA TEIGNOUSE 9.21.18

SAUZON
9.21.16

☆Houat

HOUAT & HOËDIC 9.21.19

PIRIAC 9.21.26

LE PALAIS 9.21.17

☆ Belle Ile

Hoedic

LA TURBALLE 9.21.27

SAINT NAZAIRE
9.21.31

Donges

Les Cardinaux

LE CROISIC 9.21.28

LE POULIGUEN 9.21.29

PORNICHET 9.21.30

River Loire

Nantes →

Magnetic Variation 2·5°W

La Banche ☆

See 9.22.2

Saint Gildas

Comberge
Gravette

Pornic

L'Herbaudière

47°

3°W   2°|30'   2°W

9.21.3 AREA 21 TIDAL STREAMS

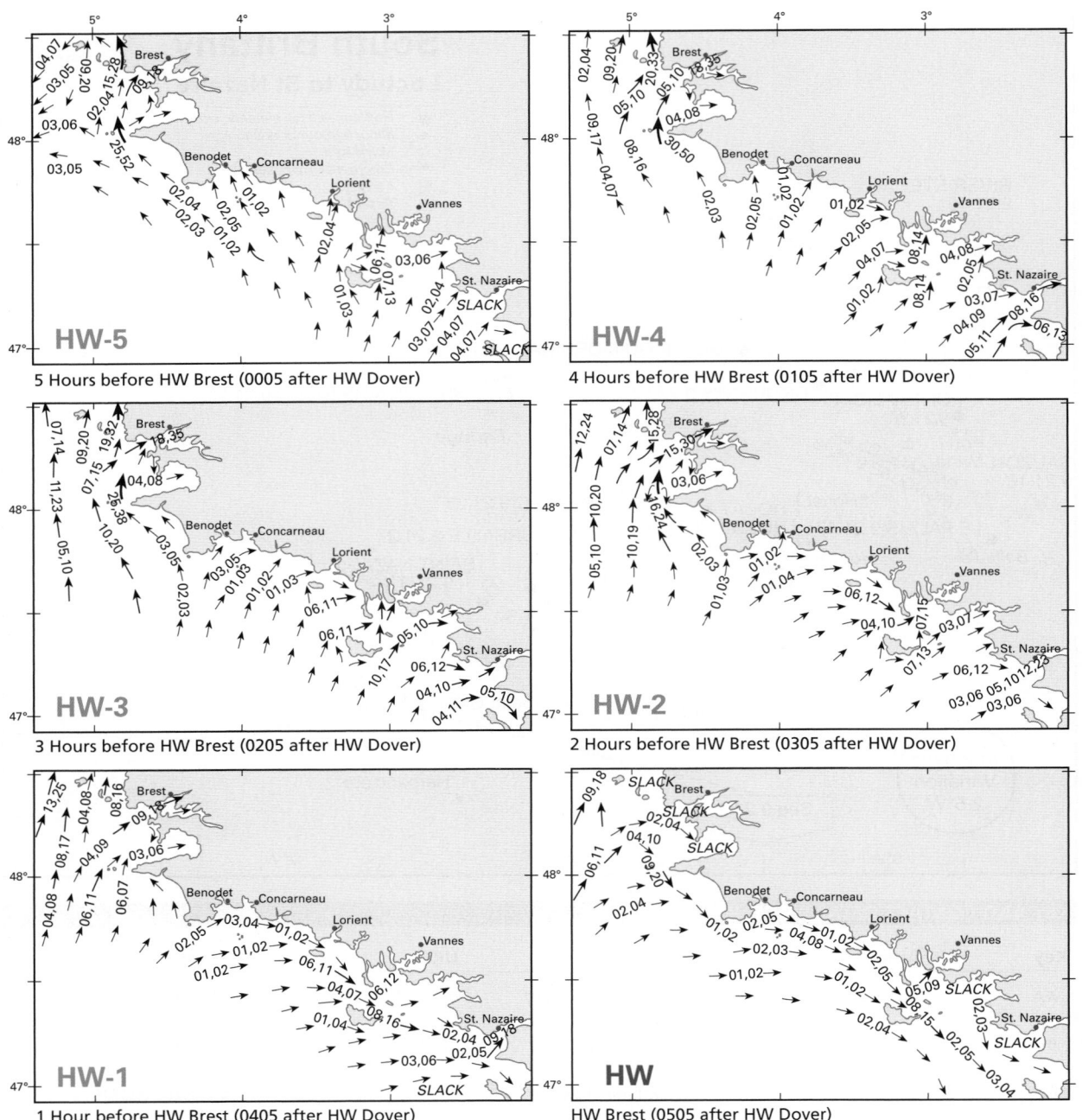

HW-5
5 Hours before HW Brest (0005 after HW Dover)

HW-4
4 Hours before HW Brest (0105 after HW Dover)

HW-3
3 Hours before HW Brest (0205 after HW Dover)

HW-2
2 Hours before HW Brest (0305 after HW Dover)

HW-1
1 Hour before HW Brest (0405 after HW Dover)

HW
HW Brest (0505 after HW Dover)

CAUTION: Due to the very strong rates of the tidal streams in some of the areas covered by these chartlets, many eddies and overfalls may occur. Where possible some indication of these eddies has been included. In many areas there is either insufficient information or the eddies are unstable. Tidal streams are generally weak offshore.

Strong winds may also have a great effect on the rate and direction of the tidal streams in all these chartlets.

Note: These chartlets are based on the Admiralty tidal stream atlas for France, W coast (NP 265, 2nd edition 2005) which uses data from actual observations out to 20-35M offshore.

The comparable French atlas (558-UJA; 2005) gives data for further offshore, based on computer predictions. It covers from Audierne to Le Croisic and contains large scale chartlets of the areas from Loctudy to Concarneau inc Iles de Glénan; Lorient and Ile de Groix; Belle Ile and the west part of Quiberon Bay.
560-UJA (1994) is recommended for large scale coverage of the Chenal du Four and Raz de Sein.

Northward 9.20.3   Southward 9.22.3

HW+1
1 Hour after HW Brest (0605 after HW Dover)

HW+2
2 Hours after HW Brest (0515 before HW Dover)

HW+3
3 Hours after HW Brest (0415 before HW Dover)

HW+4
4 Hours after HW Brest (0315 before HW Dover)

HW+5
5 Hours after HW Brest (0215 before HW Dover)

HW+6
6 Hours after HW Brest (0115 before HW Dover)

CAUTION: Due to the very strong rates of the tidal streams in some of the areas covered by these chartlets, many eddies and overfalls may occur. Where possible some indication of these eddies has been included. In many areas there is either insufficient information or the eddies are unstable. Tidal streams are generally weak offshore.

Strong winds may also have a great effect on the rate and direction of the tidal streams in all these chartlets.

Note: These chartlets are based on the Admiralty tidal stream atlas for France, W coast (NP 265, 2nd edition 2005) which uses data from actual observations out to 20-35M offshore.

The comparable French atlas (558-UJA; 2005) gives data for further offshore, based on computer predictions. It covers from Audierne to Le Croisic and contains large scale chartlets of the areas from Loctudy to Concarneau inc Iles de Glénan; Lorient and Ile de Groix; Belle Ile and the west part of Quiberon Bay.
560-UJA (1994) is recommended for large scale coverage of the Chenal du Four and Raz de Sein.

9.21.4 LIGHTS, BUOYS AND WAYPOINTS

Bold print = light with a nominal range of 15M or more. CAPITALS = place or feature. *CAPITAL ITALICS* = light-vessel, light float or Lanby. *Italics* = Fog signal. ***Bold italics*** = Racon. Abbreviations are in Chapter 1.

LOCTUDY TO CONCARNEAU

Rostolou ⚓ 47°46'·64N 04°07'·29W.
Boulanger ⚓ VQ (6) + L Fl 10s;47°47'·38N 04°09'·13W.
Chenal de Bénodet ⚓ 47°48'·53N 04°07'·04W.
Bilien ⚓ VQ (3) 5s; 47°49'·10N 04°08'·09W.

LOCTUDY

Pte de Langoz ☆ Fl (4) WRG 12s 12m, **W15M**, R/G11M; 115°-W-257°-G-284°-W-295°-R-318°-W-328°-W-025°; W twr, R top; 47°49'·88N 04°09'·55W.
Karek-Saoz ⚓ Fl R 2·5s 3m 1M; R twr; 47°50'·02N 04°09'·38W.
Men Audierne ⚓ 47°50'·31N 04°09'·06W.
No. 2 (Karek-Croisic) ⚓ Fl (2) R 6s; 47°50'·19N 04°09'·49W.
No. 1 ⚓ Fl (2) G 6s; 47°50'·22N 04°09'·73W.
No. 3 ⚓ Fl (3) G 12s; 47°50'·22N 04°09'·99W.
Groyne head ⚓ Q 3m 10M; 47°50'·21N 04°10'·34W.
Le Blas ⚓ Fl (4) G 15s 5m 1M; truncated col; 47°50'·28N 04°10'·23W.

BENODET

Ldg lts 345·5°: Front, **Pte du Coq** ☆ Dir Oc (2+1) G 12s 11m **17M**; intens 345°-347°; W ○ twr, G stripe; 47°52'·31N 04°06'·70W.
Pyramide ⚓ Oc (2+1) 12s 48m 11M; 338°-016°, synch; W twr, G top; common rear, 336m from front.
Lts in line 000·5°: Front, Pte de Combrit ⚓ Oc (3+1) WR 12s 19m, W12M, R9M; 325°-W-017°-R-325°; W □ twr, Gy corners 47°51'·86N 04°06'·78W. Common rear, Pyramide; see above.
Rousse ⚓ 47°51'·55N 04°06'·47W. La Potée ⚓ 47°51'·78N 04°06'·55W.
Pte du Toulgoët ⚓ Fl R 2·5s 2m 1M; 47°52'·30N 04°06'·86W.
Le Taro ⚓ 47°50'·51N 04°04'·83W.
La Voleuse ⚓ Q (6) + L Fl 15s; 47°48'·76N 04°02'·49W.

ILE AUX MOUTONS and LES POURCEAUX

Île-aux-Moutons ☆ Iso WRG 2s 18m, **W15M**, R/G11M; 035°-W-050°-G-063°-W-081°-R-141°-W-292°-R-035°; W □ twr and dwelling; 47°46'·48N 04°01'·66W.
Rouge de Glénan ⚓ VQ (9) 10s 8m 8M; 47°45'·48N 04°03'·95W.
Grand Pourceaux ⚓ Q; 47°45'·98N 04°00'·80W.

ÎLES DE GLÉNAN

Penfret ☆ Fl R 5s 36m **21M**; W □ twr, R top; 47°43'·26N 03°57'·18W. Same twr: auxiliary ⚓ Dir Q 34m 12M; 295°-315°.
La Pie ⚓ Fl (2) 6s 9m 3M; 47°43'·75N 03°59'·76W.
Pte de la Baleine ⚓ VQ (3) 5s 2M; 47°43'·26N 03°59'·20W.
Les Bluiniers ⚓ 47°43'·35N 04°03'·81W.
Offlying marks, anticlockwise from the west:
Basse Pérennès ⚓ Q (9) 15s 8m 5M; 47°41'·06N 04°06'·14W.
Jument de Glénan ⚓ Q (6) + L Fl 15s 10m 4M; 47°38'·76N 04°01'·41W.
Laoennou ⚓ 47°39'·65N 03°54'·70W.
Jaune de Glénan ⚓ Q (3) 10s; 47°42'·56N 03°49'·83W.

PORT-LA-FORÊT

Linuen ⚓ Q (3) 10s; 47°50'·76N 03°57'·31W.
Laouen Pod ⚓ 47°51'·23N 03°58'·00W.
Cap Coz mole ⚓ Fl(2) WRG 6s 5m, W7M, R/G5M; Shore-R-335°-G-340°-W-346°-R-shore; 47°53'·49N 03°58'·28W.
Le Scoré ⚓ 47°52'·75N 03°57'·56W.
Les Ormeaux ⚓ 47°53'·27N 03°58'·34W.
Entry channel ⚓ Fl G 2·5s; 47°53'·39N 03°58'·12W.
⚓ Fl R 2·5s; 47°53'·39N 03°58'·22W.
Kerleven mole ⚓ Fl G 4s 8m 6M; 47°53'·60N 03°58'·37W.

CONCARNEAU

Ldg lts 028·5°: Front, La Croix ⚓ Q 14m 13M; 006·5°-093°; R&W

twr; 47°52'·16N 03°55'·08W. **Rear, Beuzec** ☆ Dir Q 87m **23M**; synch, intens 026·5°-030·5°; spire, 1·34M from front.
⚓ QR; 47°51'·40N 03°55'·75W.
Le Cochon ⚓ Fl (3) WRG 12s 5m W9M, R/G6M; 230°-R-352°-W-048°-G-207°-Obsc'd-230°; G twr; 47°51'·47N 03°55'·54W.
Basse du Chenal ⚓ Fl R 4s; 47°51'·54N 03°55'·66W.
Men Fall ⚓ Fl (2) G 6s; 47°51'·76N 03°55'·28W.
Kersos ⚓ 47°51'·80N 03°54'·93W (Anse de Kersos).
Lanriec ⚓ QG 13m 8M; 063°-078°; G window on W gable end; 47°52'·01N 03°54'·64W.
La Medée ⚓ Fl (3) R 12s 9m 4M; 47°52'·07N 03°54'·80W.
Ville-Close ⚓ Q WR, W9M, R6M; 209°-R-354°-W-007°-R-018°; R turret; 47°52'·27N 03°54'·76W.
No. 1 ⚓ Fl (4) G 15s 4m 5M; G turret; 47°52'·16N 03°54'·72W.
Marina wavescreen ⚓ Fl(4) R 15s 3m 1M; 47°52'·23N 03°54'·79W.
No. 2 ⚓ Fl R 4s 4m 5M; G turret; 47°52'·31N 03°54'·71W.
Ville-Close (NE end) ⚓ Fl (2) R 6s; R twr; 47°52'·37N 03°54'·68W.
Ent to FV basin ⚓ Fl (2) G 6s; G twr; 47°52'·36N 03°54'·63W.
Pouldohan ⚓ Fl G 4s 6m 8M; 053°-065°; W □ twr, G top; 47°50'·97N 03°53'·69W.
Roché Tudy ⚓ 47°50'·52N 03°54'·49W.

CONCARNEAU TO ÎLE DE GROIX

PTE DE TRÉVIGNON TO PORT MANEC'H

Les Soldats ⚓ VQ (9) 10s; 47°47'·86N 03°53'·42W.
Trévignon mole ⚓ Fl G 4s 5m 8M; 47°47'·70N 03°51'·30W.
Trévignon bkwtr root ⚓ Oc (3+1) WRG 12s 11m, W14M, R/G11M; 004°-W-051°-G-085°-W-092°-R-127°; 322°-R-351°; W □ twr, G top; 47°47'·59N 03°51'·32W.
Men Du ⚓ 47°46'·41N 03°50'·50W.
Men an Tréas ⚓ 47°45'·77N 03°49'·66W.

PORT MANEC'H (Aven and Bélon rivers)

Port Manech ⚓ Oc (4) WRG 12s 38m, W10M, R/G7M; obscd by Pte de Beg-Morg when brg < 299°; 050°-W (unintens)-140°-W-296°-G-303°-W-311°-R (over Les Verrès)-328°-W-050°; W & R twr; 47°47'·99N 03°44'·34W.
Les Verrès ⚓ 47°46'·65N 03°42'·71W.

BRIGNEAU

Brigneau ⚓ 47°46'·11N 03°40'·10W.
W mole ⚓ Oc (2) WRG 6s 7m, W12M, R/G9M; R col, W top; 280°-G-329°-W-339°-R-034°; 47°46'·86N 03°40'·18W. In line 331° with W □ daymark behind, Hard to see, rear beacon unlit.

MERRIEN

⚓ Dir QR 26m 7M; 004°-009°; W □ twr, R top; 47°47'·04N 03°38'·97W.
Ent, W side ⚓. E side ⚓ 47°46'·45N 03°38'·89W.

DOËLAN

Ldg lts 013·8°: Front ⚓ Oc (3) WG 12s 20m, W13M, G10M; W shore-305°, G305°-314°, W314°-shore; W lt ho, G band and top; 47°46'·32N 03°36'·51W. Rear ⚓ Oc (3)R 12s 27m 9M; W lt ho, R band & top; 326m from front.

LE POULDU

Ent ⚓ 47°45'·74N 03°32'·25W.
Grand Cochon ⚓ 47°43'·03N 03°30'·81W.
Pte de Kerroc'h ⚓ Oc (2) WRG 6s 22m W11M, R/G8M; 096·5°-R-112°·5-G-132°-R-302°-W-096·5°; W twr, R top; 47°41'·97N 03°27'·66W.

ÎLE DE GROIX

Pen Men ☆ Fl (4) 25s 60m **29M**; 309°-275°; W □ twr, B top; 47°38'·84N 03°30'·56W.
Speerbrecker, ⚓ 47°39'·10N 03°26'·33W.
Port Tudy, N môle ⚓ Iso G 4s 12m 6M; W twr, G top; 47°38'·72N 03°26'·74W.

WGS84 DATUM
Plot waypoints on chart before use

E môle ⚶ Fl (2) R 6s 11m 6M; 112°-226°; W twr R top; 47°38'·68N 03°26'·78W.

Basse Melité ↯ 47°38'·84N 03°25'·54W.

Pte de la Croix ⚶ Oc WR 4s 16m, W12M, R9M; 169°-W-336°-R-345°-W-353°; W pedestal, R lantern; 47°38'·05N 03°25'·02W.

Edouard de Cougy ↯ 47°37'·93N 03°23'·90W.

Pointe des Chats ☆ Fl R 5s 16m **19M**; W □ twr and dwelling; 47°37'·24N 03°25'·30W.

Les Chats ↯ Q (6) + L Fl 15s; 47°35'·70N 03°23'·57W.

LORIENT AND RIVER ÉTEL
LORIENT, PASSE DE L'OUEST

Passe de l'Ouest ldg lts 057°: both Dir Q 11/22m 13/**18M**. Front, Les Sœurs; intens 042·5°-058·5°, 058·5°-042·5°, 4M range only; R twr, W bands; 47°42'·13N 03°21'·84W. Rear **Port Louis** ☆, 740m from front (see below).

Banc des Truies ↯ Q (9) 15s; 47°40'·76N 03°24'·48W.

Loméner, Anse de Stole, Dir ⚶ 357·2°: Q WRG 13m, W10M, R/G8M; 349·2°-G-355·2°-W-359·2°-R-005·2°; W twr, R top; 47°42'·30N 03°25'·54W.

A2 ↯ Fl R 2·5s; 47°40'·94N 03°24'·98W.

Les Trois Pierres ↯ Q RG 11m R/G6M; 060°-G-196°-R-002°; B twr, W bands; 47°41'·53N 03°22'·47W.

A8 ↯ Fl R 2·5s; 47°41'·90N 03°22'·52W.

PASSE DU SUD

Bastresses Sud ↯ QG; 47°40'·77N 03°22'·09W.

Les Errants ↯ Fl (2) R 6s; 47°41'·10N 03°22'·38W.

Bastresses Nord ↯ Fl (2) G 6s; 47°41'·11N 03°22'·20W.

Locmalo ↯ Fl (3) G 12s; 47°41'·67N 03°22'·13W.

SOUTH OF PORT LOUIS

La Paix ↯ Fl G 2·5s; 47°41'·84N 03°21'·92W.

Île aux Souris ☆ Dir Q WG 6m, W3M, G2M; 041·5°-W-043·5°-G-041·5°; G twr; 47°42'·15N 03°21'·52W.

↯ Fl G 2·5s; 47°42'·13N 03°21'·21W.

Ban-Gâvres FV/yacht hbr, W jetty ☆ Fl (2) G 6s 3M; 47°42'·06N 03°21'·11W. E jetty ☆ Fl (2) R 6s 3M; 47°42'·06N 03°21'·06W.

ENTRANCE CHANNEL

Ldg lts 016·5°, both Dir QG 8/14m 13M; intens 014·5°-017·5°; synch; W twrs, G tops. Front ☆, 47°43'·47N 03°21'·63W (Île St Michel). Rear ☆, 306m from front.

La Citadelle ↯ Oc WG 6s 6m 6M; 012°-192°; 47°42'·59N 03°21'·94W.

Secondary yacht chan, ▪ RGR, 47°42'·49N 03°22'·12W.

La Petite Jument ↯ Oc R 4s 5m 6M; 182°-024°; R twr; 47°42'·58N 03°22'·07W.

Le Cochon ↯ Fl R 4s 5m 5M; RGR twr; 47°42'·80N 03°22'·00W.

No. 1 ↯ 47°42'·80N 03°21'·84W.

PORT LOUIS (Port de la Pointe)

D 1 ↯ 47°42'·76N 03°21'·52W.

Jetty ⚶ Iso G 4s 7m 6M; W twr, G top; 47°42'·71N 03°21'·37W.

KERNEVEL

Kéroman ldg lts 350°, both Dir Oc (2) R 6s 25/31m **15M**; synch; intens 349°-351°: **Front** ☆, 47°43'·60N 03°22'·02W, R ho, W bands. **Rear** ☆ R&W topmark on Gy pylon, R top; 91m from front.

Banc du Turc ↯ Fl G 2·5s; 47°43'·33N 03°21'·85W.

Kernével marina, entrance: ⚶ QR 1M; 47°43'·39N 03°22'·10W.

Ldg lts 217°, both Dir QR 10/18m **15M**; intens 215°-219°; synch: **Front, Kernével** ☆ R&W twr; 47°43'·02N 03°22'·32W. **Rear** ☆ W □ twr, R top; 290m from front.

↯ Q (3) 10s; marks wreck; 47°43'·49N 03°22'·05W.

NORTHERN PART OF LORIENT HARBOUR

Grand Bassin (FV hbr), E side of ent, ⚶ Fl RG 4s 7m 6M; 000°-G-235°-R-000°; W twr, G top; 47°43'·63N 03°21'·87W.

Ste Catherine marina ent ⚶ QG 5m 3M; 47°43'·52N 03°21'·12W.

N side of marina ent ⚶ QR 2m 2M 47°43'·53N 03°21'·10W.

Pengarne ↯ Fl G 2·5s 3m 3M; G twr; 47°43'·88N 03°21'·23W.

No. 9 ↯ Fl (2) G 6s; 47°43'·95N 03°21'·16W.

No. 11 ↯ Fl (3) G 12s; 47°44'·04N 03°21'·01W.

Pen-Mané marina, bkwtr elbow ⚶ Fl (2) G 6s 4M; 47°44'·11N 03°20'·86W.

Blavet River, No. 1 ↯ Fl (2+1)G 10s; 47°44'·20N 03°20'·78W.

No. 2 ↯ Fl R 2·5s; 47°44'·26N 03°20'·74W.

Pointe de l'Espérance, Dir ⚶ 037°, Q WRG 8m W10M, R/G8M; 034·2°-G-036·7°-W-037·2°-R-047·2°; W twr, G top; 47°44'·51N 03°20'·66W.

Ro-Ro jetty ⚶ QR 7m 2M; 47°44'·42N 03°20'·96W.

No. 8 ↯ Fl R 2·5s; 47°44'·56N 03°20'·98W, ent to Lorient marina.

RIVIÈRE D'ÉTEL

Roheu ↯ 47°38'·54N 03°14'·70W.

Épi de Plouhinec ⚶ Fl R 2·5s 7m 2M; 47°38'·59N 03°12'·86W.

W side ent ⚶ Oc (2) WRG 6s 13m W9M, R/G6M; 022°-W-064°-R-123°-W-330°-G-022°; R twr; 47°38'·69N 03°12'·83W.

Conspic R/W radio mast (CROSS Étel), 47°39'·73N 03°12'·11W.

Les Pierres Noires ↯ 47°35'·53N 03°13'·29W.

BELLE ÎLE AND QUIBERON BAY (W OF 2° 50'W)
PLATEAU DES BIRVIDEAUX (6M NNW of Belle Île)

↯ Fl (2) 6s 24m 10M; BRB twr; 47°29'·15N 03°17'·46W.

BELLE ÎLE

Pte des Poulains ☆ Fl 5s 34m **23M**; 023°-291°; W □ twr and dwelling; 47°23'·31N 03°15'·11W.

Les Poulains ↯ 47°23'·44N 03°16'·68W.

N Poulains ↯ 47°23'·68N 03°14'·88W.

Sauzon, NW jetty ⚶ Fl G 4s 8m 8M; 47°22'·49N 03°13'·04W.

SE jetty ⚶ Fl R 4s 8m 8M; 315°-272°; W twr, R top; 47°22'·45N 03°13'·00W. Inner hbr, W jetty ↯, QG 9m 5M; 194°-045°; W twr, G top; 47°22'·37N 03°13'·13W.

Le Palais, N jetty ⚶ QG 11m 7M; obsc 298°-170° by Ptes de Kerdonis and Taillefer; W twr, G top; 47°20'·84N 03°09'·04W.

No 1 ↯ Fl (2) G 6s; 47°20'·82N 03°08'·96W;

No 2 ↯ Fl R 4s; 47°20'·71N 03°08'·89W;

No 4 ↯ Fl (2) R 6s; 47°20'·78N 03°09'·01W.

S jetty ⚶ QR 11m 7M; obsc'd 298°-170° (see N jetty); W twr, R lantern; 47°20'·82N 03°09'·07W.

Pointe de Kerdonis ☆ Fl (3) R 15s 35m **15M**; obsc'd 025°-129° by Pointes d'Arzic and de Taillefer; W □ twr, R top and W dwelling; 47°18'·60N 03°03'·58W.

Les Galères ↯ 47°18'·77N 03°02'·76W.

SW coast of Belle Île: La Truie ↯ 47°17'·11N 03°11'·79W.

Goulphar ☆ Fl (2) 10s 87m **27M**; Gy twr; 47°18'·65N 03°13'·63W.

PORT MARIA (Quiberon ferry port)

Light ho ⚶ Q WRG 28m W14M, R/ G10M; 246°-W-252°-W-297°-G-340°-W-017°-R-051°-W-081°-G-098°-W-143°; W twr, G lantern; 47°28'·78N 03°07'·45W.

Le Pouilloux ↯ 47°27'·88N 03°08'·01W.

Ldg lts 006·5°, both Dir QG 5/13m **16/17M**; intens 005°-008°; W twrs, B bands: **Front**, 47°28'·63N 03°07'·18W. **Rear**, 230m north.

Les Deux Frères ↯ Fl R 2·5s; 175°-047°; 47°28'·34N 03°07'·29W.

S bkwtr ⚶ Oc (2) R 6s 9m 7M; W twr, R top; 47°28'·54N 03°07'·31W.

CHAUSSÉE and PASSAGE DE LA TEIGNOUSE

Le Four ↯ 47°27'·78N 03°06'·54W.

Les Trois Pierres ↯ 47°27'·46N 03°05'·24W.

Roc er Vy ↯ 47°27'·70N 03°04'·40W; Chenal en Toull Bras.

Roc er Vy ↯ 47°27'·86N 03°04'·35W.

Basse Cariou ↯ 47°26'·94N 03°06'·38W.

Basse du Chenal ↯ 47°26'·66N 03°05'·77W.

Goué Vaz S ↯ Q (6) + L Fl 15s; 47°25'·76N 03°04'·93W.

La Teignouse ☆ Fl WR 4s 20m **W15M**, R11M; 033°-W-039°-R-033°; W ○ twr, R top; 47°27'·44N 03°02'·75W.

Basse du Milieu ↯ Fl (2) G 6s 9m 2M; 47°25'·91N 03°04'·12W.

Goué Vaz E ↯ Fl (3) R 12s; 47°26'·23N 03°04'·28W.

NE Teignouse ≴ Fl (3) G 12s; 47°26'·55N 03°01'·87W.
Basse Nouvelle ≴ Fl R 2·5s; 47°26'·98N 03°01'·99W.
CHAUSSÉE and PASSAGE DU BÉNIGUET
Les Esclassiers ≜ 47°25'·68N 03°03'·05W.
Le Grand Coin ≜ 47°24'·45N 03°00'·26W.
Bonen Bras ≜ 47°24'·26N 02°59'·88W.
ÎLE DE HOUAT
Le Rouleau ≜ 47°23'·67N 03°00'·31W.
Port St-Gildas N môle ≴ Fl (2) WG 6s 8m W9M, G6M; 168°-W-198°-G-210°-W-240°-G-168°; W twr, G top; 47°23'·57N 02°57'·34W.
Mussel beds, 1 -1.5M NNE of above ≴ and in its G sector (198°-210°), marked by 2 ∠ at S end, and ∠ VQ (3) 5s & ∠ VQ at N end.
Bcns SE and S of Houat: Men Groise ∤ 47°22'·77N 02°55'·00W.
Er Spernec Bras ≜ 47°22'·09N 02°55'·23W.
Men er Houteliguet ≜ 47°22'·54N 02°56'·38W.

ÎLE DE HOËDIC
Les Sœurs ≜ 47°21'·14N 02°54'·74W.
La Chèvre ∤ 47°21'·08N 02°52'·55W.
Port de l'Argol bkwtr ≴ Fl WG 4s 10m W9M, G6M; 143°-W-163°-G-183°-W-194°-G-143°; W twr, G top; 47°20'·66N 02°52'·48W.
Er Gurranic'h ≜ 47°20'·51N 02°50'·44W.
Cohfournik ≜ 47°19'·49N 02°49'·69W.
Grands Cardinaux ≴ Fl (4) 15s 28m 13M; R and W twr; 47°19'·27N 02°50'·10W, 2·1M SE of Argol.
Le Chariot ∤ 47°18'·87N 02°52'·95W.
Er Palaire ≜ 47°20'·16N 02°55'·01W.

PORT HALIGUEN
Banc de Quiberon S ∤ Q (6) + L Fl 15s; 47°28'·04N 03°02'·34W.
Banc de Quiberon N ∤ 47°29'·65N 03°02'·58W.
E bkwtr hd ≴ Oc (2) WR 6s 10m, W11M, R8M; 233°-W-240·5°-R-299°-W-306°-R-233°; W twr, R top; 47°29'·36N 03°05'·94W.
Port Haliguen ∤ 47°29'·38N 03°05'·55W; marks 1·7m patch.
NW bkwtr hd ≴ Fl G 2·5s 9m 6M; 47°29'·34N 03°06'·02W.
Bugalet wreck ∤ 47°31'·19N 03°05'·45W.
Men er Roué ∤ 47°32'·25N 03°06'·06W.

LA TRINITÉ-SUR-MER
Ldg lts 347°, both W twrs, G tops: Front, ≴ Q WRG 11m W10M, R/G7M; 321°-G-345°-W-013·5°-R-080°; 47°34'·09N 03°00'·37W.
Rear ☆ Dir Q 21m **15M**, intens 337°-357°; synch; 540m NNW.
Buissons de Méaban ∤ 47°31'·66N 02°58'·49W.
Le Petit Buisson ∤ 47°32'·14N 02°58'·57W.
Roche Révision ∤ 47°32'·63N 02°59'·36W.
Petit Trého ∤ Fl (4) R 15s; 47°33'·47N 03°00'·71W.
R. de Crac'h Dir ≴ 347°: Oc WRG 4s 9m W13M, R/G 11M; 345°-G-346°-W-348°-R-349°; W twr; 47°35'·03N 03°00'·98W.
S pier ≴ Oc (2) WR 6s 6m, W9M, R6M; 090°-R-293·5°-W-300·5°-R-329°; W twr, R top; 47°35'·09N 03°01'·50W.
Marina wavebreak/pier ≴ Iso R 4s 8m 5M; 47°35'·28N 03°01'·46W.

GOLFE DU MORBIHAN
Méaban ∤ 47°30'·77N 02°56'·23W.
Outer ldg marks 001°: Front, Petit Vezid ⌂; W obelisk; 47°34'·17N 02°55'·23W. Rear, Baden ch spire (83m); 47°37'·20N 02°55'·14W.
Pointe de Port-Navalo ☆ Oc (3) WRG 12s 32m, **W15M**, R/G11M; 155°-W-220°; 317°-G-359°-W-015°-R-105°; W twr and dwelling; 47°32'·87N 02°55'·11W.
Ldg marks 359°: Front, Grégan ∤ Q (6) + L Fl 15s 3m 8M; 47°33'·91N 02°55'·05W. Rear, Baden ch spire (5 lines above).
Auray river: Catis ∤ 47°36'·14N 02°57'·23W.
César ⌂ 47°38'·36N 02°58'·22W.
No. 13 ∤ 47°39'·48N 02°58'·64W (last bcn before 14m bridge).
Morbihan: Grand Mouton ∤ QG; 47°33'·71N 02°54'·85W.
Gavrinis ⌂ 47°34'·21N 02°54'·05W.
Jument ∤ 47°34'·29N 02°53'·43W.
Creizic S ∤ 47°34'·63N 02°52'·84W.

Creizic N ∤ 47°34'·93N 02°52'·20W.
Les Rechauds, two ∤ 47°36'·18N 02°51'·30W.
Truie d'Arradon ⌂ 47°36'·58N 02°50'·27W.
Logoden ∤ 47°36'·70N 02°49'·91W.
Drenec ∤ 47°36'·84N 02°48'·39W.
Bœdic ∤ 47°36'·85N 02°47'·59W.
Roguédas ∤ Fl G 2·5s 4m 4M; G twr; 47°37'·12N 02°47'·28W.

CROUESTY
Ldg lts 058°, both Dir Q 10/27m **19M**; intens 056·5°-059·5°:
Front ☆ R panel, W stripe; 47°32'·53N 02°53'·95W. **Rear** ☆, grey lt ho; 315m from front.
No. 1 ∤ QG; 47°32'·26N 02°54'·76W.
No. 2 ⌂ 47°32'·26N 02°54'·76W.
N jetty ≴ Fl R 4s 9m 7M; R&W □ twr; 47°32'·47N 02°54'·14W.
S jetty ≴ Fl G 4s 9m 7M; G&W □ twr; 47°32'·45N 02°54'·10W.

PLATEAU DU GRAND MONT
Chimère ∤ 47°28'·83N 02°53'·98W.
L'Epieu ∤ 47°29'·51N 02°52'·91W.
St Gildas ∤ 47°29'·78N 02°52'·87W.
Grand Mont ∤ 47°28'·98N 02°51'·12W.

QUIBERON BAY (E OF 2° 50'W) TO PTE DU CROISIC
PLATEAU DE SAINT JACQUES
Le Bauzec ≜ 47°28'·89N 02°49'·40W.
St Jacques ∤ 47°28'·17N 02°47'·52W.
Port St Jacques, jetty ≴ Oc (2) R 6s 5m 6M; W 8-sided twr, R top; 47°29'·24N 02°47'·41W.

PLATEAU DE LA RECHERCHE
Recherche ∤ Q (9) 15s; 47°25'·56N 02°50'·39W.
Locmariaquer ∤ 47°25'·82N 02°47'·36W.

PÉNERF
∤ Fl (5) Y 20s; 47°27'·58N 02°39'·56W.
Penvins ∤ 47°28'·93N 02°40'·09W. Borenis ∤ 47°29'·21N 02°38'·35W.
Tour des Anglais ⌂ W bcn; 47°30'·21N 02°37'·94W; appr brg 031·4°.
Pignon ∤ Fl (3) WR 12s 6m W9M, R6M; 028·5°-R-167°-W-175°-R-349·5°-W-028·5°; R twr; 47°30'·03N 02°38'·89W.

VILAINE RIVER
Pte de Penlan ☆ Oc (2) WRG 6s 26m, **W15M**, R/G11M; 292·5°-R-025°-G-052°-W-060°-R-138°-G-180°; W sector defines Passe de la Grande Accroche; W twr, R bands; 47°30'·97N 02°30'·11W.
Bertrand ∤ Iso WG 4s 6m, W9M, G6M; 040°-W-054°-G-227°-W-234°-G-040°; G twr; 47°31'·06N 02°30'·72W.
Basse de Kervoyal ∤ Dir Q WR W8M, R5M; 269°-W-271°-R-269°; W sector leads to/from Nos 1 & 2 buoys; 47°30'·37N 02°32'·62W.
No. 1 ∤ Fl G 2·5s; 47°30'·32N 02°28'·73W.
No. 2 ⌂ Fl R 2·5s; 47°30'·41N 02°28'·71W.
Pointe du Scal ≴ QG 8m 4M; 47°29'·67N 02°26'·87W.

ÎLE DUMET
Fort ≴ Fl (3) WRG 15s 14m, W7M, R/G4M; 090°-G-272°-W-285°-R-335°-W-090°; W col, G top; 47°24'·69N 02°37'·21W.
Basse-Est Île Dumet ∤ Q (3) 10s; 47°25'·20N 02°34'·93W.

MESQUER
Laronesse ∤ 47°25'·96N 02°29'·50W.
Basse Normande ∤ 47°25'·47N 02°29'·80W.
Jetty ≴ Oc WRG 4s 7m W10M, R/G7M; 067°-W-072°-R-102°-W-118°-R-293°-W-325°-G-067°; W col & bldg; 47°25'·31N 02°28'·05W.

PIRIAC-SUR-MER
Grand Norven ∤ Q; 47°23'·55N 02°32'·89W.
Inner mole ≴ Oc (2) WRG 6s 8m, W10M, R/G7M; 066°-R-148°-G-194°-W-201°-R-221°; W col; 47°22'·93N 02°32'·71W. *Siren 120s (occas), 35m SW.* E bkwtr ≴ Fl R 4s 4m 5M; W pylon, R top; 47°23'·00N 02°32'·67W.
Les Bayonnelles ∤ Q (9) 15s; 47°22'·56N 02°35'·23W.

Plot waypoints on chart before use

LA TURBALLE
Ldg lts 006·5°, both Dir Iso R 4s 11/19m 3M; intens 004°-009°: Front, 47°20'·70N 02°30'·87W. Rear, 275m N of the front lt.
Ouest Jetée de Garlahy ⚐ Fl (4) WR 12s 13m, W10M, R7M; 060°-R-315°-W-060°; W pylon, R top; 47°20'·70N 02°30'·93W.
Digue Tourlandroux ⚐ Fl G 4s 4m 2M; G post, E side of access chan; 47°20'·75N 02°30'·88W.

LE CROISIC
Basse Hergo ⚑ Fl G 2·5s 5m 3M; 47°18'·62N 02°31'·69W.
Jetée du Tréhic ⚐ Iso WG 4s 12m W14M, G11M; 042°-G-093°-W-137°-G-345°; Gy twr, G top; 47°18'·49N 02°31'·42W. F Bu fog det lt, 100m SE.
Outer ldg lts 155·5°, both Dir Q 10/14m 13M; intens 154°-158°: Front ☆ 47°17'·96N 02°30'·99W . Rear ☆, 116m from front.
Middle ldg lts 174°, both QG 5/8m 11M; 170·5°-177·5°: Front 47°18'·06N 02°31'·07W. Rear, 48m from front.
Le Grand Mabon ⚑ Fl (3) R 12s 6m 2M; 47°18'·05N 02°31'·03W.
Inner ldg lts 134·7°, both QR 6/10m 8M; intens 132·5°-143·5°; synch.
Basse Castouillet ⚑ Q (9) 15s; 47°18'·12N 02°34'·37W.
Basse Lovre ⚑ 47°15'·87N 02°29'·58W, Chenal du Nord.

PLATEAU DU FOUR/BANC DE GUÉRANDE
Bonen du Four ⚑ Q; 47°18'·53N 02°39'·29W.
Le Four ☆ Fl 5s 23m **18M**; W twr, B diagonal stripes; 47°17'·87N 02°38'·05W.
Ouest Basse Capella ⚑ Q (9) 15s; *Whis;* 47°15'·66N 02°42'·78W.
Goué-Vas-du-Four ⚑ Q (6) + L Fl 15s; 47°14'·91N 02°38'·20W.
Sud Banc Guérande ⚑ VQ (6) + L Fl 10s; 47°08'·80N 02°42'·81W.

POINTE DU CROISIC TO POINTE DE ST GILDAS
PLATEAU DE LA BANCHE
NW Banche ⚑ Q 8m 4M; 47°12'·86N 02°31'·02W.
W Banche ⚑ VQ (9) 10s; 47°11'·64N 02°32'·41W.
La Banche ☆ Fl (2) WR 6s 22m **W15M**, R11M; 266°-R-280°-W-266°; B twr, W bands; 47°10'·62N 02°28'·08W.
SE Banche ⚑ 47°10'·40N 02°26'·10W.

PLATEAU DE LA LAMBARDE
NW Lambarde ⚑ 47°10'·84N 02°22'·93W.
SE Lambarde ⚑ Q (6) + L Fl 15s; 47°10'·04N 02°20·80W.

BAIE DU POULIGUEN (or Baie de la Baule)
Penchateau ⚑ Fl R 2·5s; 47°15'·24N 02°24'·35W.
Les Guérandaises ⚑ Fl G 2·5s; 47°15'·03N 02°24'·29W.
⚓ 47°15'·24N 02°23'·50W.
Les Evens ⚑ Q (9) 15s; 47°14'·32N 02°22'·55W.
Les Troves ⚑ 47°14'·23N 02°22'·41W.
NNW Pierre Percée ⚑ 47°13'·63N 02°20'·63W.
La Vieille ⚑ 47°14'·03N 02°19'·51W.
Sud de la Vieille ⚑ 47°13'·75N 02°19'·54W.
Le Caillou ⚑ 47°13'·65N 02°19'·18W.
Le Petit Charpentier ⚑ 47°13'·34N 02°18'·95W.
Le Grand Charpentier ⚐ Q WRG 22m W14M, R/G10M; 020°-G-049°-W-111°-R-310°-W-020°; Gy lt ho, G lantern; 47°12'·83N 02°19'·13W.

LE POULIGUEN
Basse Martineau ⚐ 47°15'·54N 02°24'·34W.
Petits Impairs ⚑ Fl (2) G 6s 6m 2M; 47°15'·99N 02°24'·61W.
SW jetty ⚐ QR 13m 9M; 171°-081°; W col; 47°16'·39N 02°25'·39W.

PORNICHET (La Baule)
S bkwtr ⚐ Iso WRG 4s 11m, W10M, R/G7M; 303°-G-081°-W-084°-R-180°; W twr, G top; 47°15'·49N 02°21'·14W.
Ent, W side ⚐ QG 3m 1M; B perch, G top; 47°15'·51N 02°21'·12W.
E side ⚐ QR 4m 1M; B perch, R top; 47°15'·50N 02°21'·10W.

ST NAZAIRE APPROACH (Chenal du Sud)
S-N1 ⚑ L Fl 10s 8m 5M; *Racon Z (3cm), 3-8M;* 47°00'·07N 02°39'·84W.

S-N2 ⚑ Iso 4s 8m 5M; 47°02'·08N 02°33'·47W.
Les Chevaux ⚑ Fl G 2·5s; 47°03'·53N 02°26'·37W.
Thérèsia ⚑ Fl R 2·5s; 47°04'·84N 02°27'·27W.
La Couronnée ⚑ Fl (2) G 6s; *Racon T, 3-5M;* 47°07'·60N 02°20'·05W.
Lancastria ⚑ Fl (2) R 6s; 47°08'·88N 02°20'·37W.

PASSE DES CHARPENTIERS
Portcé ☆ ldg lts 025·5°, both Dir Q 6/36m **22/24M: Front**, intens 024·7°-026·2°; synch; W col; 47°14'·57N 02°15'·44W. **Rear** ☆ (H24); intens 024°-027°; W □ twr, W stripe; 0·75M from front.
Wreck (anon) ⚑ Fl R 12s; 47°09'·87N 02°19'·46W.
No. 1 ⚑ VQ G; 47°09'·94N 02°18'·40W.
No. 2 ⚑ VQ R; 47°10'·06N 02°18'·72W.
No. 6 ⚑ Fl (3) R 12s; 47°12'·05N 02°17'·31W.
No. 5 ⚑ Fl (4) G 15s; 47°12'·65N 02°16'·57W.
No. 8 ⚑ Fl (4) R 15s; 47°12'·75N 02°16'·86W.
No. 7 ⚑ VQ G; 47°13'·30N 02°16'·11W.
No. 10 ⚑ VQ R; 47°13'·62N 02°16'·16W. (Buoys 9 - 18 not listed).
Pointe d'Aiguillon ☆ Oc (3) WR 12s 27m, W13M, R10M; 207°-R-233°-W-293°; 297°-W-300°-R-327°-W-023°; 027°-R-089°; W lt ho, conspic; 47°14'·54N 02°15'·79W.
Ville-ès-Martin jetty ⚐ Fl (2) 6s 10m 10M; W twr, R top; 47°15'·33N 02°13'·65W.
Morées ⚓ Fl (3) WR 12s 12m, W6M, R4M; W058°-224°, R300°-058°; G twr; 47°15'·00N 02°13'·02W.

SAINT NAZAIRE
W jetty ⚐ Oc (4) R 12s 11m 8M; W twr, R top; 47°15'·97N 02°12'·25W.
E jetty ⚐ Oc (4) G 12s 11m 11M; W twr, G top; 47°15'·99N 02°12'·14W. (Ent for big ships locking into Bassin St Nazaire)
No. 20 ⚑ QR; 47°16'·19N 02°11'·37W.
Sud Villès Martin ⚑ Q (6) + L Fl 15s; 47°16'·21N 02°11'·51W.
Basse Nazaire ⚑ Fl G 2·5s; 47°16'·24N 02°11'·63W.
SE Old mole ⚐ Fl R 2·5s; 47°16'·24N 02°11'·73W.
Old Môle ⚐ Q (3) 10s 18m 11M; 153·5°-063·5°; W twr, R top; weather signals; 47°16'·27N 02°11'·82W.
⚑ Fl (2) R 6s 5m 1M; R dolphin ; 47°16'·37N 02°11'·80W.
⚐ Fl (3) R 12s 9m 9M; R pylon; 47°16'·47N 02°11'·85W.
Ldg lts 280° (into E lock) 2 VQ Vi; front 47°16'·49N 02°11'·92W.

EAST SIDE OF RIVER, SOUTH TO PTE DE ST GILDAS
Le Pointeau, Digue S ⚐ Fl WG 4s 4m, W10M, G7M; 050°-G-074°-W-149°-G-345°-W-050°; G&W ○ hut; 47°14'·02N 02°10'·96W.
Port de Comberge La Truie ⚑ 47°12'·06N 00°13'·36W.
S jetty ⚐ Fl (2) WG 6s 7m W9M, G6M; 123°-W-140°-G-123°; W twr, G top; 47°10'·53N 02°10'·01W.
Port de la Gravette La Gravette ⚑ 47°09'·81N 02°13'·06W.
Bkwtr hd ⚐ Fl (3) WG 12s 7m, W8M, G5M; 183°-W-188°-G-124°-W-138°-G-183°; W structure, G top; 47°09'·64N 02°12'·70W.
Anse du **Boucau** bkwtr ⚐ Fl (2) G 6s 3M; 47°08'·41N 02°14'·80W.
Pte de Saint Gildas ⚐ Q WRG 20m, W14M, R/G10M; 264°-R-308°-G-078°-W-088°-R-174°-W-180°-G-264°; col on W house, G top; 47°08'·02N 02°14'·74W.
Nord Couronnée ⚑ Q; 47°07'·34N 02°17'·78W.

RIVER LOIRE TO NANTES
Well buoyed/lit to Île de Bois, thence G lts, S side; R lts N side.
No. 21 ⚑ VQ G; 47°16'·96N 02°10'·25W.
Suspension bridge, mid-span ⚐ Iso 4s 55m, vis up/down stream; 47°17'·10N 02°10'·24W; between 2 conspic R/W twrs.
MA ⚑ Fl (2) G 6s; 47°17'·50N 02°09'·22W.
MB ⚑ Fl (3) G 12s; 47°17'·95N 02°07'·53W.
Fernais-25 ⚑ Fl (4) G 15s; 47°18'·10N 02°06'·60W.
Paimboeuf, môle root ⚐ Oc (3) WG 12s 9m, W10M, G7M; Shore-G-123°-W-shore; W twr, G top; 47°17'·42N 02°01'·95W.
Île de Bois (upstream) Fl (2) G 6s; 47°12'·79N 01°48'·27W.
Ldg lts 064° Rear Dir VQ R; 47°12'·00N 01°34'·35W, Y-junction with Bras de la Madeleine.

9.21.5   PASSAGE INFORMATION

More Passage information is threaded between successive ports. *West France Cruising Companion* (Wiley/Featherstone); NP 22 *Bay of Biscay Pilot.*

SOUTH BRITTANY

▶*Tidal streams are weak offshore, but can be strong in estuaries, channels and around headlands, especially in the north of the Area. The Admiralty tidal stream atlas for W France uses data from actual observations. The French equivalent gives much more computer-based data.*◀

Mist and haze are quite common in the summer, fog less so. Winds are predominantly from SW to NW, often light and variable in summer, but in early and late season N or NE winds are common. Summer gales are rare and usually related to passing fronts; the sea is often calm or slight, but swell, usually from W or NW, can severely affect exposed anchorages.

In summer the sea/land breeze cycle, known locally as the *vent solaire*, can disrupt moorings and anchorages open to the NE: After a quiet forenoon, a W'ly sea breeze sets in about midday, blowing onshore. It slowly veers to the NW, almost parallel to the coast, reaching Force 4 by late afternoon; it then veers further to the N, expiring at dusk. Around midnight a land breeze may pipe up from the NE and freshen sufficiently to kick up rough seas. By morning the wind has abated.

The following Breton words have navigational significance:

Aber: estuary. *Aven*: river, stream. *Bann*: hill. *Bian*: small. *Bras*: great. *Du*: black. *Enez, Inis*: island. *Garo*: rough, hard. *Glas*: green. *Goban*: shoal. *Gwenn*: white. *Karreg*: rock. *Ker*: house. *Men, mein*: rock, stone. *Morlenn*: creek. *Penn*: strait. *Porz*: harbour. *Raz*: tide race. *Ruz*: red. *Trez*: sand.

LOCTUDY TO CONCARNEAU

Loctudy is well sheltered from W/SW, but be wary of shallow patches in the outer approaches (AC 2646, 2820). Further east the larger ports are **Bénodet, Port-la-Forêt** and **Concarneau**, all with marinas. Anse de Bénodet has rocky shoals on both sides but is clear in the middle. The coast from Pte de Mousterlin to Beg Meil is fringed by rocks, many of which dry, extending 1M offshore. Chaussée de Beg Meil extends 8½ca SE, where Linuen rock (dries) is marked by bn. From Concarneau to Pte de Trévignon rocks extend nearly 1·5M offshore in places.

Îles de Glénan lie to seaward of Loctudy and Concarneau. With offlying dangers they stretch 5M from W to E and 4M from N to S. The islands are interesting to explore, but anchorages are rather exposed. Between Îles de Glénan and Bénodet lie Les Pourceaux, reefs which dry, and Île aux Moutons which has dangers extending SW and NW.

9.21.6 Special Notes for France: See 9.17.6.

9.21.7   LOCTUDY

Finistere **47°50´·34N 04°10´·55W** ✲✲⊛♤♤♤♤✿✿

CHARTS   AC 2820, 3641; SHOM 7146, 6649; Navi 543; Imray C37, 38

TIDES   +0505 Dover (UT); ML 3·0; Duration 0615. See 9.21.8

SHELTER   Excellent in marina and hbr, except in strong ESE'lies. Little space to ⚓ due many ♤s/moorings in the river.

NAVIGATION   WPT 47°50´·21N 04°09´·06W, 270°/0·8M to abeam the SHM bcn Fl (4) G 15s; thence alter stbd 305° to marina. Stay on the N side of buoyed chan (2 SHM lt buoys). Karek Croisic PHM lt buoy marks a 1·1m rock. Beware shoals and drying patches from W to ENE of Men Audierne SHM unlit spar buoy. From S and W, appr via Bilien ECM buoy to WPT. Sp ebb runs at 3½kn.

Yachts must enter/leave hbr under power. Keep clear of FVs, esp 1630-1830LT daily when yachts should NOT enter/exit hbr.

Pont l'Abbé (3M up-river; 2m) is accessible to shoal draft boats on the flood; chan marked by perches.

LIGHTS AND MARKS   See chartlet and 9.21.4. Perdrix twr, N of appr chan, has conspic B/W chequers.

R/T   Marina Ch 09 (Office hrs); Port Ch 12.

TELEPHONE   Météo ☎ 08·36·68·08·29, Aff Mar 02·98·87·41·79; CROSS 02·97·55·35·35; SNSM 02·98·87·41·12; ⊖ 02·98·58·28·80; Auto 08·92·68·08·29; Dr 02·98·87·41·80; Ⓗ (6km) 02·98·82·40·40.

FACILITIES   Marina☎02·98·87·51·36. www.loctudy.fr portplaisance. loctudy@wanadoo.fr 592 + 65 Ⓥ AB 'A' pontoon, €2·52; 50 ♤s €1·90. Slip, D&P, C (9 tons), CH, ✖, ME, El, ⚫, ⚓. **Town** 🛒, Bar, R, Ⓑ.

9.21.8 BÉNODET

Finistere 47°51′·56N 04°06′·42W ✿✿✿✿✦✦✦✿✿✿

CHARTS AC 2820, 3641; SHOM 6649, 6679; Navi 543; Imray C37

TIDES +0450 Dover; ML 3·1; Duration 0610.

Standard Port BREST (←)

Times				Height (metres)			
High Water		Low Water		MHWS	MHWN	MLWN	MLWS
0000	0600	0000	0600	7·0	5·5	2·7	1·1
1200	1800	1200	1800				
Differences BÉNODET							
0000	–0020	–0025	–0015	–1·8	–1·4	–0·6	–0·2
PORT DU CORNIGUEL							
+0015	+0010	–0015	–0010	–2·1	–1·7	–1·1	–0·8
LOCTUDY							
–0010	–0030	–0030	–0020	–2·1	–1·7	–0·8	–0·4

SHELTER Good in Ste-Marine (W bank) and Penfoul (E bank) marinas; see Facilities for note about strong tidal streams. ⚓ in Anse du Trez in offshore winds or N of Cornouaille bridge. Between these two points ⚓ in the fairway is prohib.

NAVIGATION WPT 47°51′·25N 04°06′·30W, 345·5°/1·1M to front ldg lt. The centre of the bay is clear for small craft, but beware Roches de Mousterlin at the SE end of the bay (La Voleuse SCM lt buoy) and various rks off Loctudy to the SW.

The 000° ldg line has no special merit and must be vacated early to avoid grounding on Pte de Combrit. Beware drying ledges around Les Verrès, La Rousse and Le Four unlit bcn twrs. Speed limit 3kn in hbr.

LIGHTS AND MARKS 345·5° ldg lts, synch/daymarks: Front, W ○ tr, G vert stripe, G top (hard to see until close); rear, conspic W tr, G top. See chartlet for details. New W lt La Poule expected 2010.

R/T Marinas Ch 09 (0800-2000LT in season).

TELEPHONE Aff Mar 02·98·58·13·13; CROSS 02·97·55·35·35; SNSM 02·98·57·02·00; ⊖02·98·55·04·19 (Quimper); Météo 02·98·94·03·43; Dr 02·98·57·22·21; Brit Consul 06·17·32·63·10.

FACILITIES Both marinas accessible H24 at any tide, but it is best to arr/dep near slack water to avoid the strong stream, esp 4kn ebb, through the pontoons with risk of damage. At Ste-Marine the hammerheads and at Penfoul berths on both inside and outside of the wavebreak are best avoided except by larger vessels.

SAINTE-MARINE: Marina ☎ 02·98·56·38·72. port.plaisance@combrit-saintemarine.fr www.combrit-saintemarine.fr 670+100 Ⓥ, €2·46; or €1·56 for ⚓, CH. Town 🛒, R, Bar, ☐, Ⓔ, ✉, Ⓑ, Wi-Fi. Pedestrian ferry to Bénodet, only in July and August.

BÉNODET: Penfoul Marina ☎ 02·98·57·05·78. www.benodet.fr 510+40 Ⓥ, AB €2·47; also 175 buoys +15 ⚓. ☐, R, CH, ME, 🛒, P, D, M, El, Ⓔ, ✕, SM, Divers, C (10 ton).

Town All facilities, Gaz, ✉, Ⓑ. Bus to Quimper for ≥, ✈.

> Above the Cornouaille Bridge (28m) the charming R Odet is navigable on the tide for some 7M. Beware vedettes. There are pleasant ⚓s at Anse de Combrit, Anse de Kérautren, Porz Keraign, Porz Meilou, Anse de Toulven (a hidden creek) and SW of Lanroz. SHOM 6679 is advised.
>
> N of Lanroz the river shoals progressively to 0·5m in places and is less interesting. Quimper is the limit of navigation for Bridge (5·8m clearance), 0·5M below the city.

9.21.9 PORT-LA-FORÊT

Finistere 47°53′·49N 03°58′·24W ✿✿✿✿✦✦✦✿✿

CHARTS AC 2820, 3641; SHOM 7146, 6650; Navi 543, 544; Imray C38

TIDES +0450 Dover; ML 2·9; Duration 0615.

Use Differences CONCARNEAU 9.21.11

SHELTER Very good in marina (2m). Restricted ⚓ inside Cap Coz; or to seaward on the W side of the Bay N'ward from Beg-Meil.

NAVIGATION WPT 47°52′·53N 03°57′·85W, 343°/1·0M to Cap Coz lt. Beware: Basse Rouge 0·8m, 6·5ca S of Cap Coz; Le Scoré (unlit SCM perch) and buoyed oyster farms in apprs. At sp a shoal patch 0·8m just S of the ent denies access LW±1½; but there are 3 W waiting buoys close SSW of ent. Shoaling reported in the inner chan, dredged 1·2m, to marina.

LIGHTS AND MARKS Cap Coz, Dir lt (see chartlet and 9.21.4), leads 343° into chan marked with buoys and bns; the first pair of chan buoys are lit, Fl R 2·5s and Fl G 2·5s. The only conspic landmarks are Beg-Meil sig stn, 2·2M S of Cap Coz; the bldgs of Concarneau to the E and a forest of masts at PLF marina.

R/T Ch 09.

TELEPHONE Aff Mar 02·98·60·51·42; CROSS-Etel 02·97·55·35·35; Auto 08·92·68·08·29; SNSM 02·98·94·99·91 (Beg Meil); ⊖ and Ⓗ see Concarneau; Police 02·98·50·15·00 (Concarneau); Brit Consul 06·17·32·63·10.

FACILITIES Marina ☎ 02·98·56·98·45. port-la-foret@wanadoo.fr (No website). 1069 inc Ⓥ (€2·50), plus 61 ⚓. Ⓥ pontoon between C & D. D, P, ME, El, ✕, CH, Gaz, ☐, SM, 🛒 (delivers ☎ 02·98·56·97·44) BH (30 ton), C (4 ton), Slip (multihull), ATM, Bar, R, Wi-Fi. YC ANPLF ☎ 02·98·56·84·13.

Town Bar, R, 🛒, Gaz, ✉, Ⓑ. ≥, ✈ Quimper. Ferry: Roscoff.

See chartlet overleaf

PORT LA FORÊT

Vieux Port

Dns

Kerléven

Plage de Kerléven

Fl.G.4s
8m1M

Carrec Zu

Oyster Beds

Anse de Penfoulic

Cap-Coz
Fl(2)WRG.6s
5m5/7M

Plage du Cap-Coz

Fl.R.2·5s

Fl.G.
2·5s

Les Ormeaux

Waiting buoys

03°58'·5W

58.1'

59.9'

9.21.10   ÎLES DE GLÉNAN

Finistere **47°42'·98N 03°59'·60W** (Île Cignone) ✿✿◊✿✿✿

CHARTS AC 2820, 3640; SHOM 7146, 6648; Navi 243; Imray C38

TIDES ML 3·0. See 9.21.11 for differences.

SHELTER Visit in settled weather as ⚓s can be exposed, especially near HW. The more popular are close W of N tip of Île de Penfret and on its E side; in La Chambre; close E of Île Cigogne; N of Île du Loc'h; and NW of Île de Bananec. Other ⚓s can be found.

NAVIGATION Cardinal buoys mark the S and SW limits of the islands; and Basse Jaune, a large, offlying shoal to the SE. Les Pourceaux (rocks) and Île aux Moutons are close N.

WPT 47°44'·15N 03°57'·04W, 186°/0·9M to Penfret lt ho, is the easiest entry point to Glénan. There is enough water HW±3 for most boats, but below half-tide careful pilotage is needed and a constant awareness of the state of the tide. Boats of the Glénan Sailing School abound and are best avoided. Speed limit is 8kn mid-Jun to mid-Sept.

Other approaches: Also from N, Cigogne twr in transit 182° with chimney on Île du Loc'h leads close E of La Pie IDM lt bcn; avoiding the drying Pierres-Noires further E.

From the W, Chenal des Bluiniers 095°/088° dries 0·7m between Îles Drénec and St Nicolas. S apprs and night navigation are not advised.

LIGHTS AND MARKS See chartlet and 9.21.4. Conspic marks: Penfret, highest (17m) island with W lt ho/R top; the tower (W with B top on E side only) on Île Cigogne; fish tank and a wind turbine (5 FR) at SW end of Île Saint-Nicolas.

FACILITIES There is no Capitainerie. www.glenans.fr ⚓s are laid in La Chambre and in the bay S of La Pie; fees €9·00/boat. R, Bar, Shwrs in Saint-Nicolas. Frequent ferries shuttle to/from Bénodet and Concarneau, berthing on a small jetty at the SW end of Île Saint-Nicolas.

If visiting for more than a day or two come fully victualled, watered and self-sufficient. Repairs are not easily effected, although the Sailing School may assist in extremis; they have bases on Îles Cignone, Penfret, St-Nicolas, Bananec and Drénec and monitor VHF Ch 16.

Les Pierres Noires
Ile de Brunec
La Pie
Fl(2)6s
Basse Krenn

Ile Saint-Nicolas
Ile de Guiriden
Fish tank
Ile de Bananec
Pen-a-Men
PENFRET
Fl.R5s36m21M&
DirQ.34m12M
VQ(3)5s
BYB
Ile de Drénec
Ile Cigogne
Ile Guéotec
Ile de Penfret
La Bombe
BW
Ile Quignenec
La Pie
Ile du Loc'h
Ile de Brilimec

metres
cables

9.21.11 CONCARNEAU

Finistere 47°52′·15N 03°54′·77W ✹✹✹✹✦✦✦✿✿✿

CHARTS AC 2820, 3641; SHOM 7146, 6650; Navi 543/4; Imray C38

TIDES +0455 Dover; ML 3·0; Duration 0615.

Standard Port BREST (←—)

Times				Height (metres)			
High Water		Low Water		MHWS	MHWN	MLWN	MLWS
0000	0600	0000	0600	7·0	5·5	2·7	1·1
1200	1800	1200	1800				
Differences CONCARNEAU							
−0010	−0030	−0030	−0020	−2·0	−1·6	−0·8	−0·3
ÎLE DE PENFRET (Îles de Glénan)							
−0005	−0030	−0030	−0020	−2·0	−1·6	−0·8	−0·3

SHELTER Good, except in strong S'lies; not ideal for wintering.

NAVIGATION WPT 47°50′·62N 03°56′·33W, 028·5°/1·0M to abm le Cochon SHM bcn twr. Beware large FVs and rks around Men Cren and Le Cochon. Speed limits: 5kn between le Cochon and Men Fall; 4kn inshore of Men Fall SHM lt buoy.

LIGHTS AND MARKS See chartlet and 9.21.4. Ldg lts 028·5°: front, small RW twr, very hard to see against bldgs behind; rear, Beuzec spire on skyline, 1·34M from front. Pass between Le Cochon G bcn twr (easier to see than the ldg marks) and Basse du Chenal PHM

buoy, QR. After Men Fall SHM buoy, track 070° toward Lanriec lt, in a G window on W gable end. It is better to lower sail here as there is little room to do so further up-chan. Note the 0·5m depth close SSW of La Médée PHM bcn twr.

R/T Marina Ch 09 (0700-2100LT in season). Port Ch **12** (H24).

TELEPHONE HM (Port) 02·98·97·57·96; Aff Mar 02·98·60·55·56; CROSS 02·97·55·35·35; ⊖ 02·98·97·01·73; Police 17; Fire 18; ⊞ 02·98·52·60·60; Dr 02·98·97·85·95; Brit Consul 06·17·32·63·10.

FACILITIES **Marina** is very crowded in high season. 290 52 **Ⓥ**, €2.96, on both sides of pontoon 'D' (2m). Avoid arriving Fridays when D and E pontoons are usually cluttered by Glénans sailing school boats changing crews etc. Yachts can also berth on the inside of the anti-wash barrier. port-de-plaisance@concarneau.fr ☎ 02·98·97·57·96. M, Slip, C (17 ton), ✗, ME, El, CH, SHOM, ACA, SM, Ⓐ. P&D berth in about 1m is only accessible near HW, depending on draft.

Yacht pontoon on NE corner of La Ville Close is only for locals. The Arrière Port is solely for FVs. It has good heavy maintenance/repair facilities; or go to Port-la-Forêt or Bénodet.

Town Ⓔ, Gaz, 🛒, R, Bar, ✉, Ⓑ, bus to Quimper ⇌ and ✈. Ferry: Roscoff.

CONCARNEAU TO LORIENT

Between Pte de Trévignon and Lorient are rocky cliffs and several interesting minor hbrs and anchs, delightful in fair weather; but most dry and are dangerous to approach in strong onshore winds. The Aven and Bélon rivers, Brigneau, Merrien, Doëlan and Le Pouldu (Rivière de Quimperlé), are described below.

Hazards SE and E of Pte de Trévignon include: Men Du, a rk 0·3m

high, marked by IDM bn, about 1·25M SE of the same Pte. Corn Vas, depth 1·8m, and Men ar Tréas, a rk which dries, are close S, both buoyed. Île Verte lies 6ca S of Île de Raguénès, with foul ground another 2ca to S. The approaches to Aven and Bélon Rivers are clear, except for Le Cochon and Les Verrés (IDM bn) to the SE. Between Le Pouldu and Lorient, Grand Cochon (SCM buoy) and Petit Cochon lie about 1M offshore.

9.21.12 MINOR HARBOURS BETWEEN CONCARNEAU AND LORIENT

The six places listed below are all in Finistere and share the same charts: AC 2821, SHOM 7138 (essential) and Navi 544.

AVEN and BELON RIVERS, 47°47′·94N 03°43′·87W, HW +0450 on Dover (UT), –0030 on Brest. HW ht –1·9m on Brest; ML 2·8m; Duration 0608.

1·6M SW of ent beware Les Cochons de Rospico (0·5m) and 1·6M to SE Le Cochon (0·8m) and Les Verrès (IDM bcn). The latter are in the R sector of Port Manec'h's lt ho, Oc (4) WRG 12s; see 9.21.4 for details. Night entry not advised to either river. Both rivers have bars and are shallow/dry in their upper reaches. Seas rarely break on the Aven bar, but the Belon bar is impassable in bad weather. SHOM 7138 and a good pilot book are essential.

The Aven: Port Manec'h has ⌀s and a good ⚓ in 2·5m outside the bar which is crossed by a buoyed chan dredged 0·6m; best to arr/dep HW ±3. Beyond, the river has patches drying up to 1·6m. Very good shelter at Rosbras in a crowded pool with up to 1·6m depth but no ⌀s. Pont-Aven, 3·6M up-river, is only accessible for shoal craft or a dinghy exped. Moorings in 2·5m; or AB at the quay dries 2·5m.

Facilities: HM ☎ 02·98·71·08·65; **YC de l'Aven** (Port Manec'h). **Town** ME, Slip, C, FW, P & D (cans), R, Bar.

The Belon: Cross the unmarked bar (0·6m) HW –1 in mid-river. After about 700m the chan S-bends; take care to avoid drying banks. 1M up-river off NW bank raft F&A on 3 large W ⌀s (€1·10/m) or ⚓ in pool up to 12·4m deep; ⌀s trots higher up. Beware 3kn streams. Slip, C, R (Chez Jacky), Bar.

BRIGNEAU, 47°46′·87N 03°40′·13W. HW –0020 on Brest; ML 2·8m. Small drying, fair weather hbr. In strong onshore winds ent is dangerous and the hbr untenable due to swell. WPT 47°46′·11N 03°40′·08W, unlit SWM buoy, 358°/7ca to ent. 331° ldg line: bkwtr Dir lt, W twr/R top, ≠ rear W panel (hard to see); at night the white sector (329°-339°) leads to ent; see 9.21.4 for details. Some ⌀s (€1·10/m) or ⚓ E side of ent or AB on drying W quay. HM ☎ 02·98·71·08·65 Belon), FW, ⏚, 🛒, R, Bar.

MERRIEN, 47°46′·77N 03°39′·02W. Tides as Brigneau. Small drying inlet, rky ledges either side of appr; sandbar 0·1m. Appr with W ☐ lt twr/R top (on skyline above trees) brg 005°; at night (not advised) QR, vis 004°-009°. ⚓ or moor to 2 W ⌀s outside ent (€1·10/m) or AB on drying quay SE side; keep clear of oyster beds beyond. HM ☎ 02·98·71·08·65 (@ Belon), FW, Bar, R.

DOËLAN, 47°46´·21N 03°36´·55W. HW +0450 on Dover (UT), –0035 on Brest; HW ht –2·2m on Brest; ML 3·1m; Duration 0607. Fair weather only, open to onshore winds. 2 large W round buoys just N and S of bkwtr are for temp/short stay. 4 small dayglo red Øs (€1·10/m) afloat in outer hbr. Drying AB at W quay or raft on FV up-river. Daymarks: Two outsize lt ho's in transit 013·8°: front (*aval*), W twr/G band & top; rear (*amont*), W twr/R band & top. See 9.21.4 for lt details. Conspic factory chy E of front ldg lt. Facilities: HM ☎ 02·98·71·53·98. CH, El, Ⓔ, ME, ✕. **Village** D, P (cans), FW, Dr, ✉, R, 🛒, Bar.

LE POULDU, 47°45´·70N 03°32´·23W. Tides as Brigneau. Strictly fair weather appr HW ±1, close to W side of the wide Quimperlé estuary, marked by low cliffs and 2 unlit PHM bcns; chan shifts. In onshore winds the bar is dangerous on the ebb, up to 6kn sp. Guidel marina (E bank): adequate shelter for boats <9·5m/1·5m draft, €1·70. HM ☎ 02·97·05·99·92/06·07·18·11·54. Ch 09. www. sellor.com Slip, FW, 🛒, R, Bar, Bus. ⚓ 300m NW in 2·8m pool.

9.21.13 PORT TUDY, Île de Groix

Morbihan 47°38´·72N 03°26´·73W ✽✽✽✽⚓⚓✿✿

CHARTS AC 2821, 2822; SHOM 7031, 7032, 7139; Navi 544; Imray C38

TIDES +0505 Dover; ML 3·1; Duration 0610.

Standard Port BREST (←)

Times				Height (metres)			
High Water		Low Water		MHWS	MHWN	MLWN	MLWS
0000	0600	0000	0600	7·0	5·5	2·7	1·1
1200	1800	1200	1800				
Differences PORT TUDY (Île de Groix)							
0000	–0025	–0025	–0015	–1·9	–1·5	–0·7	–0·2

SHELTER Good, but in strong N/NE'lies swell enters outer hbr.

NAVIGATION WPT 47°39´·11N 03°26´·29W (100m E of Speerbrecker ECM buoy), 218°/0·5M to N mole hd lt, just in R sector of E mole hd lt. Beware large unlit mooring buoy 0·6M NW of ent, rks SE of appr, and ferries. From E or SE pass N of Basse Mélite NCM buoy.

Use SHOM 7139 (1:20,000) for exploring the island, including Locmaria (below), Port St Nicolas and Port Lay.

LIGHTS AND MARKS See chartlet and 9.21.4. The three principal lts on Groix are: Pen-Men lt ho at NW end of island, W □ tr, B top; Pte de la Croix lt at NE end; and Pte des Chats at SE end. There are no ldg lts, although the mole head lts in transit 219° clear offlying rks to the E. By day the N mole lt ho and conspic water twr (1M SW of hbr) ≠ 220° lead close W of Speerbrecker to ent.

R/T Ch 09 during opening hours for gate into wet basin.

TELEPHONE Aff Mar 02·97·37·16·22; CROSS 02·97·55·35·35; ⊜ 02·97·86·80·93; Auto 08·92·68·08·56; Police 02·97·86·81·17; Ⓗ (Lorient) 02·97·83·04·02; Brit Consul 06·17·32·63·10.

FACILITIES HM ☎ 02·97·86·54·62. Access H24.

Outer hbr, moor fore & aft; 120 Øs in 2-4m, <10M €6·00, >10M €8·00. No ⚓ in hbr, often full in season. Caution: Ferry wash/noise.
Marina 43 Ⓥ AB, €2·53, on first 2 pontoons inside E mole, dredged 2·0-2·5m.
Wet basin (104 AB, mostly locals), access via gate HW±2 (0630–2200), but less at small neaps. No opening if swell/backwash.
Quay P & D (cans, 0800–1200 & 1400–1900, ☎ 02·97·86·80·96), ME, El, ✕, C (3 ton), CH. **Town** 🛒, R, 🏧, ✉, Bar. Ferry to Lorient.

DRYING HARBOUR NEAR SE END OF ÎLE DE GROIX

LOCMARIA, Morbihan, **47°37'·40N 03°26'·42W**. AC 2820/1, SHOM 7139; –0020 Brest; ML 2·8m. Appr is open to the S, but in offshore winds tiny drying hbr gives shelter. Steer N initially for G bcn twr; then pick up 350° ldg line, W bcn ≠ conspic Ho. Enter between PHM/SHM bcns; a SCM and NCM bcn drying reef. Limited space inside to dry out; or ⚓ outside the hbr either side of the ldg line. Facilities in village, 🍴, R. Le Bourg is approx 1M walk.

ÎLE DE GROIX, LORIENT AND BELLE ÎLE

(AC 2352, 2353) Île de Groix lies 4M SW of Lorient. Its main offlying dangers are to the E and SE: shoals off Pte de la Croix; Les Chats which extend 1M SE from Pte des Chats; and shoals extending 7½ca S of Loc Maria. **Port Tudy** is the main hbr with easy access and good shelter except from NE'lies.

Lorient is a port of refuge with sheltered apprs and 5 marinas.

7M SE of Lorient, **River Étel** has a pleasant marina but access is via a potentially difficult ent, shifting bar; only approach in good weather and on the last of the flood. Further S do not approach the isthmus of the Quiberon peninsula closely due to rky shoals. 6M W of Quiberon lies Plateau des Birvideaux (lt), a rky bank (depth 4·6m) on which the sea breaks in bad weather.

Belle Île has no dangers more than 2½ca offshore, apart from buoyed rks which extend 7½ca W of Pte des Poulains, and La Truie rk marked by IDM bn tr 5ca off the S coast. The S coast is much indented and exposed to swell from W. In good settled weather (only) and in absence of swell there is an attractive anch in Port du Vieux Château (Ster Wenn), 1M S of Pte des Poulains; see *North Biscay Pilot*. On the NE coast lie **Sauzon**, which partly dries but has good anch off and is sheltered from S and W, and **Le Palais**.

9.21.14 LORIENT

Morbihan **47°42'·60N 03°22'·00W** ❀❀❀❀🌙🌙🌙✿✿

CHARTS AC 2821, 304; SHOM 7031, 7032, 7139, 7140; Navi 544, 545; Imray C38

TIDES +0455 Dover; ML 3·1; Duration 0620.

Standard Port BREST (◀—)

Times				Height (metres)			
High Water		Low Water		MHWS	MHWN	MLWN	MLWS
0000	0600	0000	0600	7·0	5·5	2·7	1·1
1200	1800	1200	1800				
Differences LORIENT and PORT LOUIS							
+0005	–0020	–0020	–0010	–1·9	–1·5	–0·7	–0·3
HENNEBONT (Blavet River)							
+0015	–0015	+0005	+0005	–2·0	–1·6	–0·9	–0·3
PORT D'ETEL (9.21.15)							
+0020	–0010	+0030	+0010	–2·1	–1·4	–0·5	+0·4

SHELTER Very good, a port of refuge. Île de Groix shelters the ent from SW'lies. Access H24 all tides/weather to all 5 marinas. No ⚓ in Lorient hbr/chans, but moorings ENE of La Citadelle and ⚓ for shoal draft in Petite Mer de Gâvres (E of Port Louis).

NAVIGATION WPT Passe de l'Ouest, 47°40'·80N 03°24'·85W, 057°/2·0M to 016·5° ldg line. WPT Passe du Sud 47°40'·47N 03°22'·46W, 008·5°/2·15M to abm La Citadelle.

Here a secondary yacht chan passes W of La Jument. It is marked by a RGR buoy to the S and by Le Cochon RGR bcn twr to the N. Ldg/dir lts (see 9.21.4) for the Passe de l'Ouest is shown below:

- **Passe de l'Ouest**: ldg lts 057°, both Dir Q near Port Louis. Front, R twr, W bands. Rear, W daymark, R bands on bldg.
- **Passe du Sud** no longer has leading lights.

Within the hbr there are few navigational dangers and chans are well marked/lit. Yachts do not usually need the inner ldg lines.

LIGHTS AND MARKS Conspic daymarks: Water twr 8ca W of Kernével; La Citadelle stbd of ent; Port-Louis spire further E,

submarine pens at Pointe de Kéroman and 2 silos N of Île St Michel.

R/T *Vigie Port Louis* Ch 11 (H24). Marinas Ch 09 (In season: 0800-1230, 1330-2000. Out of season 0830-1200, 1400-1800).

TELEPHONE Port HM 02·97·37·11·86; Aff Mar 02·97·37·16·22; CROSS 02·97·55·35·35; SNSM 02·97·86·29·62; ⊖02·97·37·34·66; Auto 08.92.68.08.56; Police 02·97·64·27·17; Sea Police 02·97·12·12·12; Ⓗ 02·97·64·81·58; Brit Consul 06·17·32·63·10.

FACILITIES **Lorient Marina** is inset on the main chartlet. ☎ 02·97·21·10·14. www.sellor.com port-lorient@sellor.com €2·65. The only fuel (P & D) in Lorient is at S end of Kernével Marina; call Ch 09. Water bus runs regularly from first 3 marinas to city.

Kernével ☎ 02·97·65·48·25. www.sellor.com port-kernevel@sellor. com. Enter at N end of wave-break, ❶ berths at S end, 3m. 580+100 ❶, €2·65. P & D, ▣, Slip, YC.

Ban-Gâvres ☎ 02·97·65·48·25. Tiny, part-drying harbour. Strong tides need care on the approach which is from the SW, passing W and N of Île aux Souris; pre-recce by foot ferry from/ to Port Louis. 81+2 ❶ berths (2m) on W end of yacht pontoon, €1·75.

Port Louis ☎ 02·97·82·59·55. port-portlouis@sellor.com 220+15 ❶, €2·10, dredged 2m, C (50 ton). Exposed to strong N'lies. A few FVs; basic facilities; but friendly; interesting town.

Locmiquélic 02·97·33·59·51. www.locmiquelic.com locmiquelic@ sagemor.fr 607+15 ❶, €2·20, in 1·5-3m. No ❶ pontoon: pre-call Ch 09 or berth as available and check in. The town is 500m walk. C, ▣. **Pen Mané Marina** has no ❶ AB.

River Blavet is navigable on the flood for 6·3M to Hennebont. Use AC 304 plan Ⓐ. Leave Lorient at about HW–2. The river is attractive once clear of industrial areas in the buoyed lower reaches. The 3 bridges have least clearance of 21m. 0·3m patches occur beyond the 1st bridge and before and after the 2nd.

At Hennebont the sheltered 14m ❶ pontoon is first to stbd; the 2nd is for vedettes only. No AC, FW; 12 hrs max stay. Good facilities in town. See also 9.18.14 for the Canal du Blavet to Pontivy.

Lorient ☎ 02·97·21·10·14. port-lorient@sellor.com   AB in Avant Port 2·5-3m, crowded in season. 320+50 Ⓥ, €2·77. Wet Basin 2·5m, long stay by prior arrangement; access by day via entry gate HW±1 sp, ±15 mins nps. Ⓞ, Slip, BH (25 ton), C (1½ ton), ME, El, Ⓔ, ⚒, CH, SHOM, ACA, SM. **YC de Lorient**, Bar.
City All facilities, ✉, Ⓑ, ≷, ✈. Water bus, marinas to/from city.

9.21.15 RIVER ÉTEL

Morbihan 47°38′·65N 03°12′·69W (Hbr ent) 🌊🌊⚓⚓✿✿

CHARTS AC 2822; SHOM 7032, 7138; Navi 545; Imray C38

TIDES +0505 Dover (UT); ML 3·2m; Duration 0617. See 9.21.14.

SHELTER Excellent in marina inside the town quay. Possible ⚓s S of conspic LB ho, off Le Magouër on the W bank or N of marina.

NAVIGATION WPT 47°37′·31N 03°13′·44W, 020°/1·4M to hbr ent, aligned 020° with a R/W radiomast (off chartlet). Appr HW −3 to +2 only by day, in good vis and settled weather; best at about HW −1½ on the last of the flood. The chan is well buoyed/lit but shifts radically; bar dries approx 0·4m. Call *Semaphore d'Etel* Ch 13 or ☎ (below) for clearance to enter, and directions in simple French.

If no VHF radio, pre-notify ETA by ☎, so that entry/pilotage signals can be shown by movable red arrow on Fenoux mast:

> Arrow vertical (also stowed position) = Enter, maintain track.
> Arrow deflected L/R = turn in direction indicated.
> Arrow horiz = no vessels to ent/exit, conditions dangerous.
> R flag = no ent/exit, insufficient depth over bar.
> ● = no ent/exit for undecked boats and craft <8m LOA.

LIGHTS AND MARKS Dir lt W side of ent, Oc (2) WRG 6s; no ⚓ within 5ca of it. Épi de Plouhinic bn, Fl R 2·5s 7m 2M, marks groyne at ent. Other lts & marks as chartlet and 9.21.4.

R/T Marina Ch 9, 13, 16 (in season 7/7 0800-1900 and at tide times).

TELEPHONE Pilotage Stn 02·97·55·35·59; Aff Mar 02·97·55·30·32; ⊜ 02·97·36·20·76; Auto 08·92·65·02·56; CROSS 02·97·55·35·35; Police 02·97·55·32·11; Brit Consul 06·17·32·63·10.

FACILITIES Marina ☎ 02·97·55·46·62. www.ria-etel.com etel@sagemor.fr 380 + 20 Ⓥ in 1·5-2m, €2.40. **Quay** P & D (cans), CH, El, ME, 🔧, C (6 ton), Slip.
Town Bar, R, 🍴, 🅿. Bus to 🚉 (Auray 15km) & ✈ (Lorient 32km).

9.21.16 SAUZON, Belle Île

Morbihan 47°22′·47N 03°13′·01W 🌊⚓⚓⚓✿✿✿

CHARTS AC 2822; SHOM 7032, 7142 (1:7,500 plan); Navi 545

TIDES +0450 Dover; ML 3·0; Duration 0615. Use differences for Le Palais (9.21.17).

SHELTER Good except in NE'lies. Drying creek extends 0·5M S.

NAVIGATION WPT 47°22′·88N 03°12′·73W, 205°/685m to NW Jetée lt. Main lt, QG, and NW Jetée, Fl G 4s, form a 205° transit. No navigational dangers. No ⚓ between Sauzon and Le Palais.

LIGHTS AND MARKS See chartlet and 9.21.4. Le Gareau SHM bcn is conspic 0·9M N of hbr; ditto Pte des Poulains lt ho 1·6M NW.

R/T Ch 09, Jul/Aug: 0900-1230, 1700-2000; closed Sun.

TELEPHONE HM 02·97·31·63·40; see also 9.21.17.

FACILITIES www.sauzon.fr/Leport.htm Yachts may:

> • ⚓ ENE of hbr ent • Pick up one of 21 W ⚓s N of the N jetty • Raft up between 9 W ⚓s in about 1·5m on W side of Avant Port. (FVs moor E side of Avant Port) • Dry out on the E side of the inner hbr on 41 R ⚓s, fore and aft; firm, level mud/sand. Inner hbr dries about 1·6 – 2m; access approx HW ±1½.

Note: ⚓s are R; locals' buoys are G. ⚓s €1·18, ⚓ €0·70. FW on quay.
Village 🍴, 🅿, R, Bar, ✉, Ⓑ, ATM; market Thurs. Bus to Le Palais. Repairs best done at Port Haliguen, La Trinité or Crouesty.

STER WENN, Morbihan, **47°22′·30N 03°15′·24W**. AC 2822; SHOM 7032, 7142. Tides as 9.21.18. A very popular W coast anchorage 1·1M S of the N tip of Belle Île (recce from Sauzon, 3km by bike). From the NW enter Ster-Vraz, the outer inlet. When abeam the 5th hole of the golf course to the N, Ster Wenn opens to stbd. ⚓ where space permits, stern line ashore. Shelter is good in all winds. Facilities: None, other than relative peace.

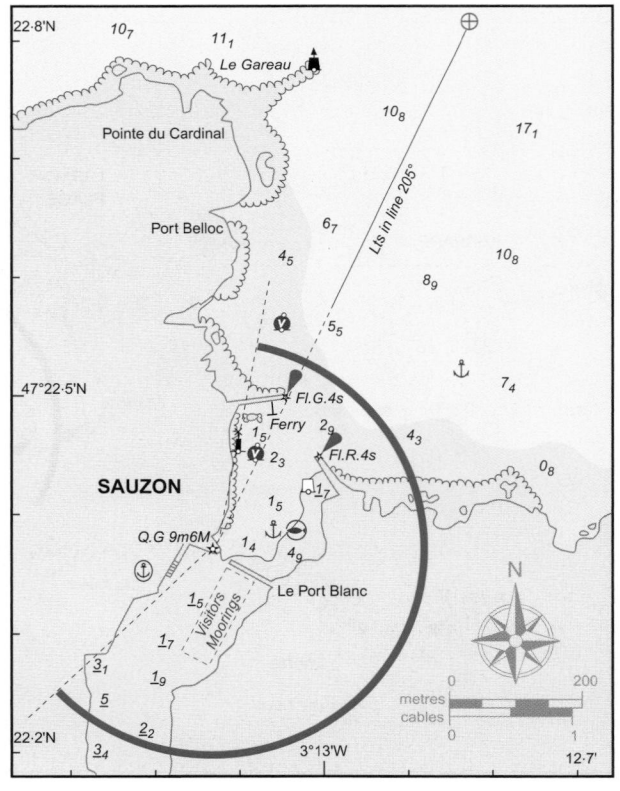

9.21.17   LE PALAIS, Belle Île

Morbihan 47°20'·84N 03°08'·98W ❀❀❀⚓⚓♜♜♜

CHARTS AC 2822, 2823; Imray C39; SHOM 7032, 7142; Navi 545

TIDES +0458 Dover; ML 3·1; Duration 0615.

Standard Port BREST (←—)

Times				Height (metres)			
High Water		Low Water		MHWS	MHWN	MLWN	MLWS
0000	0600	0000	0600	7·0	5·5	2·7	1·1
1200	1800	1200	1800				
Differences LE PALAIS							
−0005	−0025	−0025	−0010	−1·9	−1·4	−0·8	−0·3

SHELTER Good, but strong E'lies cause heavy swell in Avant Port. No ⚓ between Le Palais and Sauzon, nor in hbr.

NAVIGATION WPT 47°21'·20N 03°08'·39W, 231°/6ca to N Pier lt. Obey 3 lateral lt buoys off hbr ent; give way to fast ferries.

LIGHTS AND MARKS Lts as chartlet. La Citadelle is conspic.

R/T Ch 09 (Season: 0800-1200, 1400-2000. Out of season 0800-1200, 1500-1800).

TELEPHONE Aff Mar 02·97·31·47·08; CROSS 02·97·55·35·35; ⊖ 02·97·31·85·95; Police 02·97·31·80·22; Auto 08.92.68.08.56; Dr 02·97·31·40·90; Ⓗ 02·97·31·48·48; Brit Consul 06·17·32·63·10.

FACILITIES HM 02·97·31·42·90. www.belle-ile.com **Avant Port** 80 ⚓s (€1·33) in 3 trots inside Mole Bourdelle for yachts <18m LOA; shallow draft on ⚓s to port. P, D, Slip, FW, C (10 & 5 ton). Packed in season. **Inner hbr** mostly dries.

Bassin á Flot Enter via a gate/small lifting bridge open HW −1½ to +1 (0600-2200LT), for rafted berthing on either side in 2·5m. AB (90) €1·98; max LOA 30m. ME, El, ✖.

Marina (Bassin de la Saline, 1·7–2m) Continue WSW via lifting bridge into marina by prior arrangement, if finger berths vacant; max LOA 13m. 8 **Ⓥ** €2·46. **YC** ☎ 02·97·31·55·85.

Town 🛒, Gaz, CH, R, Bar, 🔧, ✉, Ⓑ. Ferry to Quiberon ⇌, ✈. UK ferry: Roscoff.

9.21.18   PASSAGE DE LA TEIGNOUSE *See upper chartlet overleaf*

This is the easiest route through the Chaussée de La Teignouse being deep, wide, well buoyed and lit. See AC 2357; SHOM 7141. From WPT 47°25'·35N 03°05'·00W appr with La Teignouse lt ho brg 036° (by night in its W sector 033°-039°). The chan is marked by Goué Vas Sud SCM, Basse du Milieu SHM and Goué Vas Est PHM lt buoys. Abeam Goué Vas Est, turn stbd 068°, passing between Basse Nouvelle PHM and NE Teignouse SHM lt buoys, into open waters. Minor variations on this route can be used.   Further SE, **Passage**

du Béniguet 044° lies NW of Houat and **Passage des Soeurs** 016° between Houat and Hoëdic, both unlit.

The **shortest passage**, saving 3M if to/from Port Haliguen, lies between Le Four SCM and Les Trois Pierres NCM bcn twrs with La Teignouse lt ho brg 094°. Turn N as the rocky chan opens between Iniz en Toull Bras to stbd and a SCM and 2 ECM perches to port; see pecked line. Only for experienced navigators by day; pre-study SHOM 7141 carefully; expect strong cross-streams.

9.21.19   HOUAT and HOËDIC ❀❀⚓♜♜♜

CHARTS AC 2823, 2835; Imray C39; SHOM 7033, 7143; Navi 545

TIDES +0505 Dover; ML 3·1; Duration 0605.

Standard Port BREST (←—)

Times				Height (metres)			
High Water		Low Water		MHWS	MHWN	MLWN	MLWS
0000	0600	0000	0600	7·0	5·5	2·7	1·1
1200	1800	1200	1800				
Differences HOUAT							
+0005	−0025	−0025	−0010	−1·8	−1·4	−0·7	−0·4
HOËDIC							
+0010	−0035	−0025	−0020	−1·9	−1·5	−0·8	−0·4

HOUAT, 47°23'·57N 02°57'·34W (Port St Gildas). Appr from N or NE passing abeam La Vieille rk (conspic 17m), NNE of which mussel beds are marked by 4 buoys: NCM VQ, ECM VQ(3) 5s and 2 unlit SPM. The only lt on the island is on the hbr bkwtr head, Fl (2) WG 6s; the G sector covers La Vieille and buoyed mussel beds. At night appr in W sectors on either side; details in 9.21.4.

Good shelter, except from N/NE'lies, at Port St Gildas, near E end

of the N coast. Moor on double trots; no ⚓ in hbr. S part of hbr dries. Keep clear of ferries on W quay and FVs on N quay. E of the hbr are 15 W ⚓s and space to ⚓.

Tréach er Gourhed, aka Rade de Houat, is a 7 cables wide, crab-shaped bay at the ESE end of Houat, designated a No-anch area due to cables. Other ⚓s at Tréach er Béniguet, Portz Ler and Portz Navallo, all at NW end of Houat. No ent (15/4-31/8) to Nature reserves at Er Yoc'h and Ile Guric and Séniz at NW end. Facilities: Mairie 02·97·30·68·04. Bar, R, 🛒, Gaz, CH, 🔧, ✉, Dr. Ferries to Quiberon, Lorient, La Turballe, Le Croisic.

HOËDIC, 47°20'·67N 02°52'·45W (Port de L'Argol). Appr from NNW or NNE passing abeam La Chèvre rk (unlit IDM bcn) and in either W sector of the bkwtr lt, Fl WG 4s; its G sector (163°-183°) covers La Chèvre; see 9.21.4 for lt details.

Good shelter, except from N/NE'lies, at Port de L'Argol, in the centre of the N coast. Ferries berth at the W end; there is just room to ⚓ at the E end or outside to the NNE. On the S of island the old hbr, Port de la Croix, dries but ⚓ outside in 2-4m. Other ⚓s may be found in the island's lee. 1·5M SE of Hoëdic, Grands Cardinaux lt ho, R twr/W band Fl (4) 15s, marks the eponymous reefs. Facilities: Bar, R, limited victuals. Ferries as for Houat.

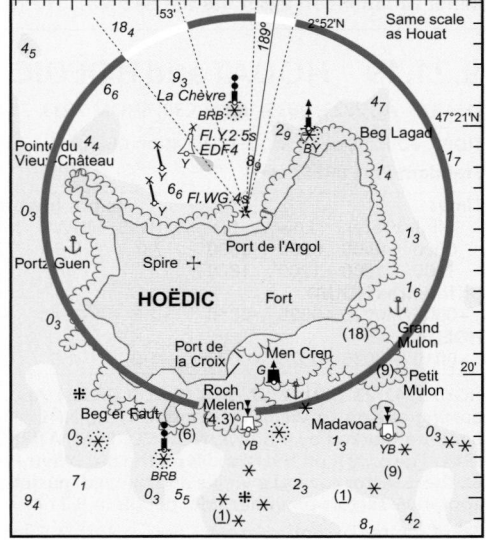

9.21.20 PORT HALIGUEN

Morbihan 47°29'·35N 03°05'·97W ※※※※♦♦♦✿✿

CHARTS AC 2357; Imray C38, 39; SHOM 7141, 7032, 7033; Navi 545

TIDES +0500 Dover; ML 3·1; Duration 0615.

Standard Port BREST (◄──)

Times				Height (metres)			
High Water		Low Water		MHWS	MHWN	MLWN	MLWS
0000	0600	0000	0600	7·0	5·5	2·7	1·1
1200	1800	1200	1800				
Differences PORT HALIGUEN							
+0010	−0020	−0015	−0010	−1·7	−1·3	−0·7	−0·3
PORT MARIA							
+0010	−0025	−0025	−0015	−1·7	−1·4	−0·7	−0·2
LA TRINITÉ							
+0025	−0020	−0015	−0010	−1·7	−1·2	−0·6	−0·3

SHELTER Good, but uncomfortable in strong NW to NE winds.

NAVIGATION WPT 47°29'·80N 03°05'·00W, 237°/7ca to bkwtr lt. From W or S, appr via Passage de la Teignouse (9.21.18).

LIGHTS AND MARKS Hazards: Banc de Quiberon (2·7m at S end), marked by an unlit NCM and a lit SCM buoy. The W sector (299°-306°) of bkwtr lt, Oc (2) WR 6s, clears its S end. A 1·7m shoal marked by an unlit SCM buoy 'Port Haliguen', is avoided by approaching in the other W sector (233°-240·5°) of the bkwtr lt.

R/T Marina Ch 09.

TELEPHONE CROSS 02·97·55· 35·35; Météo 02·97·64·34·86; Auto 08.92.68.08.56; Police 02·97·50·07·39; Dr 02·97·50·13·94.

FACILITIES Marina Access H24. ☎ 02·97·50·20·56. www.baie-de-quiberon.com port-haliguen@sagemor.fr 970 + 100 Ⓥ, €2·80. Ⓥ berths alongside/rafted both sides of 'V' pontoon, with 10 finger berths on the NW end arm. Slip, P, D, C (2 ton), BH (13 ton), ME, El, ✕, CH, ▢, SM, Ice, Bar, R, ▨.

Town (Quiberon) ▨, Gaz, R, Bar, ⊠, Ⓑ, ⇌, ✈.

PORT MARIA, Morbihan, **47°28'·54N 03°07'·31W**. AC 2357; SHOM 7032, 7141. See 9.21.20. Shelter good in all winds, but access dangerous in strong SE–SW winds. It is a very busy ferry/FV port, only feasible for yachts in emergency. ⚓ in SW of hbr in approx 2m. HM ☎ 02·97·50·08·71. Facilities: C (6 ton), FW at E quay, El, ME, ✕, SHOM.

9.21.21 LA TRINITÉ-SUR-MER

Morbihan 47°35'·28N 03°01'·46W ※※※※♦♦♦✿✿

CHARTS AC 2358, 2357; Imray C39; SHOM 7033, 7141,7034; Navi 545, 546

TIDES +0455 Dover; ML 3·2; Duration 0610.
Standard Port BREST (◄──). Differences see 9.21.20.

SHELTER Very good, except in strong SE/S winds near HW when La Vaneresse sandbank is covered. No ⚓/fishing in river.

NAVIGATION WPT 47°33'·38N 03°00'·42W, 347°/1·0M to No 2 PHM buoy. No navigational dangers; the Rivière de Crac'h is well marked by buoys and perches. Best water close to E bank. Beware many oyster beds, marked with perches. The channel is buoyed on both W sectors. Speed limit 5kn.

LIGHTS AND MARKS Daymarks include: Mousker, a 4.5m rk, off-white paint; and ⊞ spire at La Trinité. Ldg marks are hard to see by day. Lts, see chartlet and 9.21.4. Pte de Kernevest ldg lts 347°, both W twrs/G tops, but amid trees. 1M up-river: Dir lt 347°, Oc WRG 4s, W twr. S Pier, Oc (2) WR 6s, W twr/R top, W 293·5°-300·5°.

R/T Marina Ch 09.

TELEPHONE Aff Mar 02·97·24·01·43; CROSS 02·97·55·35·35; SNSM 02·97·55·01·15; Police 02·97·55·71·62; ⊖ 02·97·55·73·46; Météo 02·97·64·34·86; Auto 08.92.68.08.56; Dr 02·97·55·74·03; Brit Consul 06·17·32·63·10.

FACILITIES Marina Access H24 at all tides. Marina boat will meet. Ⓥ pontoon (fingers) is first N of ☆ Iso R 4s. ☎ 02·97·55·71·49. www.baie-de-quiberon.com 1030 +120 Ⓥ, €2·80. P, D, BH (36 ton), Grid, ME, El, CH, SHOM, Ⓔ, SM, ✕, Ice.

CN ☎ 02·97·55·73·48.

Town ▨, Gaz, R, Bar, ⊠, Ⓑ. ⇌ Auray. ✈ Lorient, Rennes. Ferry: Roscoff, St Malo.

9.21.22   GOLFE DU MORBIHAN
Morbihan **47°32'·87N 02°55'·28W** (Ent) ✿✿♦♦♦✿✿✿

CHARTS AC 2823, 2358; SHOM 7033, 6992, 7034; Imray C39; Navi 546. Road map N° 0921 (IGN TOP 25 series, 1:25,000) is most useful in the Morbihan as a shoreside complement to charts.

WGS84 DATUM

TIDES +0515 Dover; ML 3·0.
Standard Port BREST (←——)

Times				Height (metres)			
High Water		Low Water		MHWS	MHWN	MLWN	MLWS
0000	0600	0000	0600	7·0	5·5	2·7	1·1
1200	1800	1200	1800				
Differences PORT NAVALO							
+0030	−0005	−0010	−0005	−2·1	−1·6	−0·9	−0·4
AURAY							
+0035	0000	+0015	−0005	−2·3	−1·9	−1·2	−0·5
ARRADON							
+0135	+0145	+0140	+0115	−3·9	−3·1	−1·9	−0·8
VANNES							
+0200	+0150	+0140	+0120	−3·8	−3·0	−2·1	−0·9
LE PASSAGE (47°35'·4N 02°43'·1W)							
+0200	+0200	+0210	+0135	−3·8	−3·0	−2·0	−0·9
LE LOGEO							
+0140	+0140	+0145	+0115	−4·1	−3·2	−2·1	−0·9

SHELTER The Golfe du Morbihan is a large, inland tidal sea with deep apprs and entrance. A significant sea state is rare, except for tide rips in the ent. Shelter can usually be found from all winds, but the many ⚓s (see chartlet and Facilities) are increasingly restricted by extensive local moorings. It is essential to use chain when ⚓ing, unless well out of the tide. Île aux Moines and Île d'Arz are the only public islands. Vannes is the only marina.

NAVIGATION WPT 47°31'·97N 02°55'·29W (as for Crouesty), 001°/1·7M to abeam Grand Mouton lt bcn. Pilotage is not difficult and the strong streams are not inherently dangerous, but due to higher than usual speeds over the ground, it helps to pre-plot the desired tracks/distances within the channels. Marks can then be more readily identified and track adjusted with ease, especially if beating. Night navigation is not advised.

Caution: Many vedettes in season. Frequent ferries cross from Port Blanc to Île aux Moines, at times with scant regard for IRPCS; keep well clear of them. Avoid numerous bird sanctuaries in SE, and oyster beds marked by withies. Much of the E & SE dries.

TIDAL STREAMS *The very strong tidal streams which reach 9·1kn between Île Berder and Île de la Jument dictate ent/exit times.*

On AC 2358 study tidal diamonds ◇ C (off Port Navalo lt ho), ◇ D at Grand/Petit Mouton and ◇ G at the S tip of Ile Berder. These give a good idea of when the flood and ebb should start, hence earliest times to ent/exit. At ◇ C the flood starts at about HW Brest −4½. At ◇ G the ebb starts at about HWB +2¼. Their rates however may be conservative. At ◇ D for example the max rate is 5·2kn whereas the tidal vectors here show 6·9 to 8kn.

For a first visit avoid springs; entry at night with a tide running is hazardous. Off Grand Mouton sp rates reach 8kn and in the ent can exceed 4kn. Flood starts HW Brest − 0400 and turns at HW Brest + 0200. Here the flood divides: the weaker flow enters the R. Auray; whilst the major stream sets strongly toward Petit & Grand Mouton rks before setting into the main chan. Maintain 001° until Grand Mouton lt bcn is abaft the beam, but beware shoals E of Goémorent R bcn twr.

The streams ease in the upper reaches except between Pte de Toulindag and Port Blanc where ◇ K indicates >5kn. HW times become later further E, eg HW Vannes is 2 hrs after HW Pt Navalo. HW Auray is only 25 mins after HW Port Navalo.

LIGHTS AND MARKS The 001° appr ldg daymarks are: front, Petit Vézid W obelisk (from afar looks like a yacht sail); rear, Baden ✠ spire (3·3M). Chans and dangers are well marked. The only lts are: Port Navalo lt ho at the ent. Inside ent: Grand Mouton SHM bcn and Le Grégan, a squat SCM bcn. Roguédas, a large SHM bcn is near the appr chan to Vannes.

FACILITIES, clockwise from **AURAY RIVER**
LOCMARIAQUER 47°34'·19N 02°55'·81W. Two drying quays 500m apart: To S, ferries use the buoyed chan to Cale du Guilvin, AB (S side only, max 30 mins), slip, fuel 06.03.09.15.06; drying ⚓ to the W. To N, Cale de Locmariaquer (used by vedettes), slip. **Village:** Bar, R, shop, ATM, ✉, bike hire, buses.

SEPT ÎLES 47°35'·09N 02°56'·18W: Small, quiet ⚓. Enter Anse de

Baden, mostly dries, between mainland and W end of island.
PORT DU PARUN 47°36'·76N 02°56'·96W: Drying inlet: no moorings but BY with quay, slip & all facilities. ☎ 02·97·57·00·15.
LE ROCHER 47°38'·17N 02°57'·75W: Sheltered, but full of moorings.
LE BONO 47°38'·43N 02°57'·21W: Moor or ⚓ (rky bottom) off Banc de la Sarcelle. AB in drying basin, ☎ 02·97·57·88·98. **Village**, ATM, ME, R, ⛽, Gaz, ✉.
AURAY 47°39'·84N 02°58'·73W: The river shoals to 0·2m, but St Goustan is accessible at mid-flood via a bridge with 14m MSL and 0·4m depth; gauge shows air clearance. Calculate tides carefully for a safe passage. 12 dumbell ⚓s in a pool up-river; drying AB at St Goustan; or ⚓s S of 14m bridge. HM ☎ 02.97.56.29.08. Slip, ME, El, ⚒. **Town** R, ⛽, Bar, ATM, ✉, ⇌.

NW AND CENTRAL AREAS
ÎLE LONGUE 47°34'·17N 02°54'·44W: ⚓ out of the stream. No landing.
LARMOR BADEN 47°34'·82N 02°53'·62W: good ⚓s to S and further W, but many moorings, HM ☎ 02.97.57.20.86; 06.14.19.12.76. **Village:** Slip, C (4 ton), ⛽, R, Bar, ✉. Ferry to Île Gavrinis all year.
ÎLE BERDER 47°34'·81N 02°53'·05W: pleasant ⚓ E of the island.
PORT BLANC 47°36'·32N 02°51'·66W: HM ☎ 02·97·26·30·57, mob 06.11.07.56.89. Ch 09, 0845-1230; many moorings €2·40. Quay, slip, AC, FW, ATM, Bar, R, ✉, water taxi. Ferry ½hrly to Île aux Moines.
ÎLE AUX MOINES: a much-frequented, public island. The narrows between Pte de Toulindag and Port Blanc can be rough; beware Les Réchauds drying rks. ⚓ 47°36'·22N 02°51'·11W; or ♥ pontoon (AC, FW), the W'ly of two; land at small marina. Ch 09 or sound horn for water taxi. HM ☎ 02·97·26·30·57, 0845-1230; FW, M. Quieter ⚓s S of PdT, E of Pte du Trec'h and off SE tip of island.
ARRADON: limited ⚓ 47°36'·84N 02°50'·24W, exposed to S'lies. HM ☎ 02·97·44·01·23. Ch 09. Apr-Sep 1400-1700. Many local moorings, €2·40. Slip, FW. Pier with depth gauge and disabled access, 15 mins waiting time on W side only.
ÎLE PIRENN: exposed ⚓ 47°35'·79N 02°49'·42W in tidal stream.
ÎLE D'ARZ, a public island. ⚓ 47°36'·45N 02°47'·43W NE of Pte du Béluré (ferry landing); E of Le Bourg (good shelter); or to the W, depending on winds. Rudevent village: ME, El, ⚒.
ÎLE DE BOËDIG: sheltered ⚓ 47°37'·00N 02°46'·53W, if moorings permit, in Chenal de Badel N of the island.
ÎLE DE CONLEAU 47°37'·62N 02°46'·73W: ⚓ or moor in bight just S of village, as space permits. ME, El, ⚒, R in village.

EAST AND SOUTH AREAS
SÉNÉ 47°37'·19N 02°44'·49W: dry out in traditional hbr at head of inlet; ME. Easy bike recce 2M SSE from Vannes.
LE PASSAGE: ⚓ 47°35'·43N 02°42'·93W off Pte du Passage (depths up-river not charted). Village (St Armel): ⛽, Bar. Seasonal ferry.
KERNERS: ⚓ 47°33'·65N 02°52'·44W in 3-6m off Anse de Kerners or further SE off Anse de Pen Castel. Ferry to Île aux Moines.
ÎLE DE LA JUMENT 47°34'·20N 02°53'·15W: good shelter E of island out of the tide; handy for leaving the gulf on the tide.
PORT NAVALO 47°33'·00N 02°54'·86W: ⚓ in bay, but full of moorings, and open to W/NW winds. Convenient to await the tide. HM ☎ 02·97·53·82·12. All facilities at Crouesty (½M by road).

BAIE DE QUIBERON

This is an important and attractive cruising area with centres at **Port Haliguen, La Trinité,** the **Morbihan** and **Crouesty** (AC 2823). The S side of the bay is enclosed by a long chain of islands, islets, rocks and shoals from Presqu'île de Quiberon to Les Grands Cardinaux 13M SE. This chain includes the remote but appealing islands of **Houat** and **Hoëdic**, well worth visiting, preferably mid-week. The Bay is open to the E and SE.
From W or S, enter the Bay via Passage de la Teignouse in W sector (033°-039°) of La Teignouse lt ho; thence 068° between Basse Nouvelle lt buoy and NE Teignouse lt buoy.
▶*In this channel the NE-going flood starts at HW Brest −6¼, and the SW-going at HW Brest, sp rates 3·75kn; in strong winds it is best to pass at slack water.*◀
Passage du Béniguet and Passage des Soeurs are alternatives.

9.21.23 VANNES

Morbihan 47°38'·45N 02°45'·62W ❀❀❀♠♠♠❀❀❀

CHARTS AC 2823, 2358; Imray C39; SHOM 7034; Navi 546

TIDES See GOLFE DU MORBIHAN 9.21.22. ML 2·0m.

SHELTER Excellent in all winds.

ACCESS by day only. Whilst the entry gate stays open (HW±2½), Kérino **swing bridge** (road tfc) opens at H and H+30 in season (15 Jun–15 Sep) and at weekends; but only at H out of season. During the first and final ½ hour periods when the entry gate is open, the bridge will open on request VHF Ch 09. Outbound craft have priority over arrivals. Waiting pontoons (partly drying) are up/downstream; intercom to HM on downstream pontoon. Bridgemaster may occasionally speak by loudhailer.

> Traffic signals (3 vert lts) on the bridge's western pier are:
> F ●●● = no passage; F ●●● = proceed;
> Oc ●●● = No passage unless committed, but unmasted boats may transit.

An **entry gate** (not a lock), approx 250m N of the bridge and remotely-controlled by the HM, stays open HW±2½. HW Vannes –2½, when the gate opens, is the same as HW Port Tudy (a French Standard Port for which a freebie may be issued). The sill, 0·4m, retains 2·1m in the wet basin. F ●●●●● = NO GO; F ●●● = GO.

Guide pratique du Port (a free annual schedule of gate hrs etc) is available from Port de Plaisance, La Rabine, 56019 Vannes or download from www.mairie-vannes.fr.

NAVIGATION WPT: see 9.21.22. After Roguédas SHM lt bcn do not cut the shallow corner to port; if anything head ESE until the chan opens up. Turn N'wards when a pink house on its E bank bears 020°. Passage upstream past Île de Conleau is easy and well marked. Beacon'd appr chan to Vannes is narrow, least charted depth 0·7m, but dredged 2·1m from No 6 bcn to the bridge.

LIGHTS AND MARKS No navigation lts N of Roguédas, Fl G 2.5s.

R/T VHF Ch 09.

TELEPHONE Aff Mar 02·97·63·40·95; CROSS 02·97·55·35·35; ⊖ 02·97·01·36·00; Météo 02·97·42·49·49; Police 02·97·47·19·20; Ⓗ 02·97·01·41·41; Brit Consul 06·17·32·63·10.

FACILITIES Marina. ☎ 02·97·54·16·08. www.mairie-vannes.fr contact@mairie-vannes.fr 214+70 Ⓥ, €2·45. Dory may allot a finger berth. If not, visitors berth/raft N/S on pontoons D and G, just S of mobile foot-bridge (*passerelle*).

Slip, ▣, ATM, ✕, ME, C (10 ton), CH, El, Ⓔ, SM. P & D (cans only); nearest fuel by hose is at Crouesty. New works: ⊕ on E bank; underground car park; landscaping continues.

City R, 🍴, Bar, SHOM, ✉, Ⓑ, ⇌, ✈.

CROUESTY TO LE CROISIC

East of the Morbihan entrance, dangers extend 1M seaward of Pte de St Jacques (where a small hbr dries). 3M offshore Plateau de la Recherche has depths of 1·8m (AC 2823). SE of **Pénerf**, which provides good anchorage, Plateau des Mats is a rocky bank, drying in places, extending up to 1·75M offshore.

Across the ent to the **Vilaine River** beware La Grande Accroche, a large shoal with least depth 1m. The main lit chan leads NW of La Grande Accroche, to the bar on N side.

▶ *Here the flood begins at HW Brest –0515, and the ebb at HW Brest +0035, sp rates 2·5kn.*◀

In SW winds against tide the sea breaks heavily; the Passe de la Varlingue, 5ca W of Pte du Halguen, is then better, but beware La Varlingue (dries 0·3). At **Arzal/Camoël** yachts can lock into the non-tidal Vilaine River for **La Roche Bernard** and the **Canal de l'Ille et Rance** to Dinan/St Malo.

South of Pte du Halguen in a little frequented corner of Quiberon Bay, other dangers include the rocky shoals, both 0·6m, of Basse de Loscolo and Basse du Bile, close inshore. Off Pte du Castelli, the Plateau de Piriac extends about 1·75M NW with depths of 2·3m and drying rocks closer inshore. The small hbr and marina at **Piriac** lies on the N side of Pointe du Castelli and Les Bayonelles (dry) extend 5ca W. A chan runs between Plateau de Piriac and Île Dumet (lt), which is fringed by drying rocks and shoals particularly on N and E sides.

In the Rade du Croisic are the fishing hbrs of **La Turballe** and **Le Croisic**, the former with a marina. Off Pte du Croisic dangers extend 1M to N and W. Plateau du Four, a dangerous drying bank of rocks, lies about 4M W and WSW of Pte du Croisic, marked by buoys and lt ho near N end. 2·8M ESE of Pte du Croisic, Basse Lovre is a rocky shoal with depths of 0.7m, 5ca offshore, marked by a SCM buoy.

9.21.24 CROUESTY

Morbihan **47°32'·46N 02°54'·13W** ✿✿✿❀❀❀❀❀❀

CHARTS AC 2823, 2358; Imray C39; SHOM 6992, 7034, 7033; Navi 546

TIDES +0505 Dover; ML 3·0; Duration 0555.

Standard Port BREST (◀—)

Times				Height (metres)			
High Water		Low Water		MHWS	MHWN	MLWN	MLWS
0000	0600	0000	0600	7·0	5·5	2·7	1·1
1200	1800	1200	1800				
Differences CROUESTY							
+0010	–0025	–0025	–0030	–1·7	–1·3	–0·7	–0·4

SHELTER Very good, but strong onshore winds can raise dangerous seas in the ent. Quiberon peninsula gives some shelter from W'lies.

NAVIGATION WPT 47°31'·97N 02°55'·30W, 058°/0·9M to hbr ent. Access chan is dredged 1·8m and buoyed. Caution: drying shoal close NW of ldg line between Nos 6 and 8 buoys; stay in the chan especially near LW.

LIGHTS AND MARKS Ldg marks/lts 058°: Front W vert stripe on R panel; rear the tall grey lt ho. Only No.1 SHM lead-in buoy is lit, QG. See chartlet and 9.21.4 for light details.

R/T Ch 09.

TELEPHONE Aff Mar 02·97·41·84·10; ⊜ 02·97·01·36·00; CROSS 02·97·55·35·35; Auto 08·92·68·08·56; SNSM 02·97·41·35·35; Police 02·97·53·71·65; Dr 02·97·53·71·61; Brit Consul 06·17·32·63·10.

FACILITIES The enormous marina has 6 large separate basins; see large scale chartlet below. V1, 2 & 3 pontoons are part of Ⓥ basin on S side of fairway; boats >12m LOA can berth on the wall between V1 and V2. HM ☎ 02·97·53·73.33. www.baie-de-quiberon.com 1432+130 Ⓥ, €2·80. P, D, ME, El, ✕, Slip, BH (45 ton), C (10 ton), CH, Ⓔ, SM.

Town (Arzon) ⛴, Gaz, R, Bar, ✉, Ⓑ. ⇌ Vannes. ✈ Vannes, Lorient, St Nazaire, Rennes.

MINOR HARBOUR, approx 13 track miles east of Crouesty

PÉNERF RIVER, Morbihan, **47°30'·03N 02°38'·89W**, AC 2823; SHOM 7033, 7135 (advised, plus good Pilot). HW +0515 on Dover (UT); Duration 0610; ML 3·3m. See 9.21.25. Shelter good, except in fresh W'lies. The 3 ents require careful planning & pilotage:

Passe de l'Ouest is shoal and ill marked. **Passe du Centre** is the widest and easiest, least depth 0·7m. Appr on 359° ldg line, Le Pignon red lt bcn ≠ Le Tour du Parc spire, passing between Penvins PHM buoy and Borénis SHM buoy. Leave a SHM bcn (marking a drying reef) 150m to the E; thence pass 40m E of Le Pignon, whose white sector (see 9.21.4) covers the appr, but night entry is not advised for a first visit.

Passe de l'Est has 4m, but is narrower and rks are close to stbd. It joins Passe du Centre E of Le Pignon bcn. Once in the river, head ENE for 1M to ⚓ off Pénerf quay. Beware oyster beds. Facilities: P & D (on quay), Slip, CH, El, ME, ✕. **Village** R, Bar, ⛴.

9.21.25 VILAINE RIVER

Morbihan **47°30'·38N 02°28'·71W** (1st lt buoys) ❀❀⚓♨♨✿✿

CHARTS AC 2823; SHOM 7033, 7144; Navi 546; Imray C39. Note: 2823 ends at the river mouth. 7144 continues to La Roche-Bernard.

TIDES +0500 Dover; ML (Pénerf) 3·3; Duration 0610.

Standard Port BREST (←—)

Times				Height (metres)			
High Water		Low Water		MHWS	MHWN	MLWN	MLWS
0000	0600	0000	0600	7·0	5·5	2·7	1·1
1200	1800	1200	1800				
Differences TRÉHIGUIER							
+0035	−0020	−0005	−0010	−1·5	−1·1	−0·6	−0·4
PÉNERF RIVER							
+0015	−0025	−0015	−0015	−1·6	−1·2	−0·7	−0·4

SHELTER Some shelter on 4 blue ⚓s to S of Tréhiguier. Total shelter in marinas at Arzal, Camoël, La Roche Bernard and Foleux.

NAVIGATION WPT 47°28'·95N 02°33'·96W, 052°/3·3M to Penlan lt ho; see chartlet. The 3 appr's to the river mouth are:

- Passe de la Grande Accroche: Penlan lt ho ≠ Abbey de Prières 052°. Marks are reportedly conspic by day.
- Penlan lt ≠ Billiers ch tr 025·5°, leaving La Varlingue Rk (0·3m) close to stbd.
- Passe de la Varlingue (unlit): W wall ≠ Abbey Tr 023°, passing close to WCM bcn and oyster poles off Le Logui.

In strong onshore winds, especially at sp ebb, seas break on La Vilaine bar (min 0·5m). Best to enter/leave on last of the flood. River is well buoyed up to Tréhiguier and adequately so beyond; keep strictly to buoyed chan as river silts.

Arzal lock opens in theory at H, up to 9 times per day, 0700–2200 (LT) in Jul/ Aug; in other months 0800, 0900, 1100, 1400, 1600, 1800, 1900, 2000LT. But times vary daily: call Ch 09, HM ☎ or ☎ 08·25·00·01·99 for recorded info. Keep strictly to the buoyed chan to avoid the prohib areas (Y buoys) below/above the barrage. There are waiting ⚓s and room to ⚓ downstream.

LIGHTS AND MARKS See chartlet and 9.21.4. Two Dir lts are visible in the approaches:

- Basse Bertrand, 14m G twr. The W sector (040°-054°) overlaps the W sector of Penlan in Passe de la Grande Accroche.
- Pte de Penlan, 18m W twr, R bands; W sector 052°-060°.

At river ent Petit Sécé W bcn twr is easier to see than Nos 1 & 2 buoys. On S side of lock the red control twr is conspic.

R/T Ch 09: Arzal-Camoël, La Roche Bernard, Foleux and Redon marinas. Ch 10: Pont de Cran and R. Vilaine/canal.

TELEPHONE Pont de Cran 02·99·90·11·31; Aff Mar 02·99·90·32·62; CROSS 02·97·55·35·35; ⊖02·97·63·18·71 Vannes; Auto 08·92·68·08·56; Dr 02·97·45.01.21; Ⓗ 02·99.90.61.20; Brit Consul 02·51·72·72·60.

FACILITIES ARZAL: HM ☎ 02·97·45·02·97. arzal-camoel@sagemor. fr www.baie-de-quiberon.com 905 + 20 Ⓥ, €2·10. D & P H24. BH (35 ton), Gaz, SM, ME, El, ⚒, CH, Ⓔ, ▣, R, Bar, @, Wi-Fi.

CAMOËL has 20 Ⓥ, showers. Check in first at Arzal.

Towns (both 3km) ▤, R, Bar, Ⓑ, ✉.

LA ROCHE BERNARD: HM ☎ 02·99·90·62·17, roche-bernard@ wanadoo.fr **Old Port** (95), C, CH, Slip.

Ⓥ AB possible on pontoon A, €1·90. **New Port** (230), M, ME, El, Ⓔ, ⚒, CH, C (13T). **Town** P & D (cans), ▤, Gaz, ▣, R, Bar, Ice, ✉, Ⓑ. Wi-Fi. ⇌ Pontchateau. ✈ Nantes or Rennes.

Foleux: ☎ 02·99·91·80·87. foleux@sagemor.fr; 321 AB inc 30 Ⓥ at pontoon N bank; buoys off both banks. C (15 ton), R.

To reach Redon masted yachts must transit Cran swing bridge which opens(1/4-31/102): 0900, 1000, 1100, 1430, 1630, 1830, 1930. Clearance under the closed bridge is quoted as 5·5m.

Redon is a pleasant, fair sized country town. The marina (☎ 02·99·71·35·28) is part of a larger basin at the south end of town. It has D, mast crane (500kg) and gives access to the Brittany canals (9.18.14) including the Ille et Rance (9.18.13).

9.21.26 PIRIAC

Loire Atlantique **47°23′·02N 02°32′·67W** ✵✵♦♦♦✿✿

CHARTS AC 2823; Imray C39, 40; SHOM 7033, 7136; Navi 546

TIDES Interpolate between 9.21.25 (Penerf) and 9.21.28. HW +0505 on Dover (UT); ML 3·3m; Duration 0605.

SHELTER Good in marina, but near HW may be exposed to N'lies.

NAVIGATION WPT 47°23′·69N 02°32′·38W, 197°/7ca to hbr ent in the W sector (194°-201°) of Piriac lt, Oc (2) WRG 6s.

Plateau de Piriac extends about 1M W and N from the hbr; to the SW it is marked by a WCM buoy, Q (9) 15s, and to the NNW by Le Rohtrès NCM bcn twr and by Grand Norven NCM lt bcn, Q. Due to shoals and drying patches do not attempt to pass S of these bcns even near HW.

At night the W sectors of Île Dumet lt (272°-285°) and of Pte de Mesquer lt (067°-072°) help to position within the W sector of Piriac lt; care is required.

LIGHTS AND MARKS See 9.21.4 and the chartlet for details of the lights. Piriac church belfry is a conspic daymark, aligned approx 197° with chan. The Sig stn at Pte de Castelli, 8ca SW of the hbr, is a conspic white, prow-shaped structure.

R/T Ch 09.

TELEPHONE Aff Mar 02·40·23·33·35; ⊖ 02·40·23·32·51 Turballe; CROSS 02·97·55·35·35; Auto 08·92·68·08·44; SNSM 02·40·23·55·74 (Jul-Aug only); Brit Consul 02·51·72·72·60.

FACILITIES **Marina** Access HW±3 over sill 2·2m; HW±4 for draft <1.5m, more at nps. The retaining wall is marked by Y SPM perches, and the flap gate by a PHM & SHM perch. IPTS, sigs 2 or 4; the latter shows when depth over sill is >1·5m. ☎ 02·40·23·52·32. 480 + 20 ⓥ, €3·40. www.ports-plaisance.loire-atlantique.fr D (hose), P (cans) on quay, Slip, C (12 ton), CH, Ⓔ, El, ME, ✕.

Town The attractive small town has R, Bar, 🛒, Ⓑ, ✉, market.

PIRIAC-SUR-MER

9.21.27 LA TURBALLE

Loire Atlantique **47°20′·70N 02°30′·89W** ✵✵♦♦♦✿✿

CHARTS AC 2823; Imray C39, 40; SHOM 6826, 7033; Navi 546

TIDES Approx as for Le Croisic 9.21.28.

SHELTER Good in all winds, but in strong SSW'lies heavy swell can close the hbr. In N to E winds it is possible to ⚓ S of the hbr.

NAVIGATION WPT 47°20′·19N 02°30′·99W, 006·5°/5ca to W bkwtr lt. The ent is not easily seen until S of the hbr. Appr in W sector (315°-060°) of W bkwtr lt to pick up the 006·5° ldg lts. Jun-Sep a buoyed No ⚓ area lies between 060° and 090° 8 cables to the west bkwtr lt. From the SW avoid Plateau du Four and shoals off Le Croisic.

LIGHTS AND MARKS By day Trescalan ✠ and water tr (conspic), 1M ENE of hbr, lead 070° to just S of ent. R bcn twr is 80m off W bkwtr. See chartlet and 9.21.4 for light details.

R/T Call Ch 09 before entering. If in Jul/Aug the marina is full and closed to new arrivals, it is announced Ch 09. There is an active fleet of 80 FVs.

TELEPHONE Aff Mar 02·40·23·33·35; ⊖ 02·40·23·37·51; Auto 08·92·68·08·44; CROSS 02·97·55·35·35.

FACILITIES Access H24. Inside ent, turn 110° stbd round a blind corner into the marina (1·5-2m). Due to shoal patches (lack of dredging) between A–G and B–F pontoons craft >1·5m draught should not enter LW springs ±2 to avoid grounding.

Visitors are rafted tight into the rectangular box off B pontoon; if staying a few days a vacant finger berth may be allotted on request. Call before entering; see R/T.

Marina ☎ 02·40·23·41·65. www.port-peche-turballe.fr plaisance. turballe@wanadoo.fr 315+30 ⓥ, €2·10. D (min 10 ltrs); pay by French credit card or at Coopérative Maritime ☎ 02·40·62·80·05 (facing hbr); P&D at garage 500m. Slip, BH (32 ton) ☎ 02·40·62·80·40, ME, El, Ⓔ, ✕, CH, ◙, 🅿 in Capitainerie, Gaz, SM, YC, SHOM, Ice, Internet in Capitainerie and the Municipal library.

Town 🛒, Bar, R, Ⓑ, ✉, Dr. Buses to St Nazaire and Nantes.

LA TURBALLE

9.21.28 LE CROISIC

Loire Atlantique **47°18'·52N 02°31'·35W** ✵✵♁♁♁♁♁✿✿✿

CHARTS AC 2646, 2986, 2823; Imray C39; SHOM 7033, 7395, 7145 (the preferred large scale chart); Navi 546, 547

TIDES +0450 Dover; ML 3·3; Duration 0605.

Standard Port BREST (←——)

Times				Height (metres)			
High Water		Low Water		MHWS	MHWN	MLWN	MLWS
0000	0600	0000	0600	7·0	5·5	2·7	1·1
1200	1800	1200	1800				
Differences LE CROISIC							
+0015	−0040	−0020	−0015	−1·6	−1·2	−0·7	−0·4

SHELTER Good. No ⚓ in Le Poul; full of moorings, very strong ebb.

NAVIGATION WPT 47°18'·97N 02°31'·65W, 155·5°/5ca to Tréhic bkwtr hd. Safest ent is HW±1 sp, HW±2 np or around LW with care and shoal draft. Beware rks and shoals close in to Hergo SHM bcn twr in Tréhic's W sector (093°-137°). In its SW G sector dangers extend 2M W to Basse Castouillet WCM buoy. Keep strictly on the ldg lines as appr and hbr dry extensively; chan is dredged 2m at first, then 1·6m and 1·2m. Sp tides reach 4kn. 4 drying basins (*Chambres*) are formed by islets (*Jonchères*).

LIGHTS AND MARKS A ✠ dome, almost on the 155·5° ldg line, and hospital at Pte de Pen Bron are conspic. 3 sets of ldg lines:

> **Outer** 155·5°: both Dir Q; R ☐s on W pylons, rear has G top.
> **Middle** 173·4°: both Dir QG; Y ☐s with G stripe on G & W pylons, almost obsc'd by trees.
> **Inner** 134·7°: both Dir QR; R/W chequered ☐s on fish market roof. At the marina the BY is a large, white conspic shed.

R/T Marina Ch 09 (0800-1200; 1330-2000 in season).

TELEPHONE Aff Mar 02·40·23·06·56; CROSS 02·97·55·35·35; ⊜ 02·40·23·05·38; Météo 08·92·68·02·44; Police 02·40·23·00·19; Dr 02·40·23·01·70; Ⓗ 02·40·23·01·12; Brit Consul 02·51·72·72·60.

FACILITIES **Marina** (*Chambre 4*). ☎ 02·40·23·10·95, 06·88·99·05·01. www.ports-plaisance.loire-atlantique.fr Access HW±1. Visitors dry out against the marina's outer wall. 360+27 ✓, €1·35, plus €0·20 holiday tax per head. Slip, C (8 ton), BH (180 ton), ME, El, ✕, CH, Ⓔ, YC, Divers, ♿.

Town P & D (cans), 🛒, Gaz, R, Bar, ✉, Ⓑ, ⇌, ✈ (St Nazaire).

From Chenal du Nord, the **Baie du Pouliguen** is entered between Pte de Penchâteau and Pte du Bec, 3M to E (AC 2986). **Pornichet** marina is in the SE corner of the bay which is partly sheltered from the S by reefs extending SE from Pte de Penchâteau to Le Grand Charpentier, but a heavy sea develops in strong S-SW winds. The W approach chan through these reefs lies between Penchâteau and Les Guérandaises lateral buoys. From the south the easiest channel through the reefs, especially if bound for Pornichet, is between Les Evens and Les Troves, buoyed but unlit.

The **River Loire** is France's longest river (1000km), rising in the Massif Central a mere 160km north of the Med. It flows north towards Never and Orleans and then west past Tours, Angers and Nantes to the Atlantic at St Nazaire.

Its estuary (AC 2986, 2989), with much commercial traffic, is entered from seaward via either the Chenal du Nord or the Chenal du Sud. The former, used by yachts and coastal traffic, runs ESE between the mainland and two shoals, Plateau de la Banche and Plateau de la Lambarde.

Chenal du Sud, the main DW chan, leads NE between Plateau de la Lambarde and Pte de St Gildas.

A secondary chan, which yachts should use to avoid large ships in the main chan, lies close NW of and parallel to the main chan. It extends 4·5M NE from abeam Pte d'Aiguillon to St Nazaire suspension bridge and is marked by seven SCM lt buoys, ZD1-7, all Q(6) + L Fl 15s; stay between these and the main channel PHM buoys.

▶ *Here the in-going stream begins at HW Brest −0500, and the out-going at HW Brest +0050, sp rates about 2·75kn.* ◀

On the E side of the Loire estuary, up to 4M NE of Pte de St Gildas, are the small drying hbrs of St Gildas, La Gravette and Comberge. Beware Les Jardinets and La Truie (both drying) close E of the chan and 4·5M SSW of St Nazaire.

The 28M passage from St Nazaire to Nantes (AC 2985) is well marked. Carry the flood so as to reach Nantes around local HW, monitoring VHF Ch 14 *Loire Port Control*. See 9. 21.31 for a yacht pontoon in central Nantes (Bras de la Madeleine). Trentemoult Marina no longer accepts visitors due to silting.

9.21.29 LE POULIGUEN

Loire Atlantique **47°16'·42N 02°25'·33W** ✵✵♁♁✿✿✿

CHARTS AC 2646, 2986; Imray C39; SHOM 7395, 7145; Navi 547

WGS84 DATUM

TIDES Sp +0435 Dover, Nps +0530 Dover; ML 3·3; Duration Sp 0530, Nps 0645.

Standard Port BREST (←——)

Times				Height (metres)			
High Water		Low Water		MHWS	MHWN	MLWN	MLWS
0000	0600	0000	0600	7·0	5·5	2·7	1·1
1200	1800	1200	1800				
Differences LE POULIGUEN							
+0020	−0025	−0020	−0025	−1·6	−1·2	−0·7	−0·4

SHELTER Very good, except in SE winds. In strong S'lies, beware swell and breakers in the approach chan. Pornichet, 3M to the E, has a much easier approach and ent.

NAVIGATION WPT 47°15'·54N 02°24'·34W, Basse Martineau unlit PHM buoy, 321°/1.1M to hbr ent. Reefs running 4M ESE towards Grand Charpentier lt ho, Q WRG, form a barrier across the Baie du Pouliguen which may be entered via any of 4 passes; see AC 2986 or the larger scale SHOM 7145.

Best appr at HW −1 from W/SW between Pte de Penchâteau and Les Evens (drying reef). From Basse Martineau, leave La Vieille SHM perch and Petits Impairs bcn twr, Fl (2) G 6s, well to stbd, and 3 PHM bns closer to port. The inner access chan shifts, dries approx 1·5m and is marked by one PHM and 5 SHM poles.

LIGHTS AND MARKS See chartlet and 9.21.4 for light details. W jetty, QR, is a slim, conspic white column, R top. The final SHM pole marks the narrowing chan and E training wall which covers. Navigational lights are very hard to see against shore lts of La Baule and night appr is not advised without a prior day visit.

R/T Pouliguen Ch 09, 0900-2000 in season.

TELEPHONE ⊖ 02·40·61·32·04; Aff Mar 02·40·23·06·56; SNSM 02·40·61·03·20; CROSS 02·97·55·35·35; Auto 08.92.68.08.44; Police 02·40·24·48·17; Dr 08·36·69·12·34; Brit Consul 02·51·72·72·60.

FACILITIES 30 ♥ berths on pontoon A, to stbd at ent. Here yachts up to 2m draft can stay afloat but further N will be aground. First fixed bridge has 2·5m clearance. Beware strong ebb tide.

HM (E Quay) ☎ 02·40·11·97·97. capitaine-la-baule@wanadoo.fr www.lepouliguen.fr 720+30 ♥, max LOA 11·5m, €3.25. Slip, P, D, C (17 ton), C (Mast 500kg), M, ME, ⚓, CH, Ⓔ, El, Divers, SM, YC ☎ 02·40·60·57·87.

Town (W bank) 🍴, Gaz, R, Bar, ✉, Ⓑ, ⇌. ✈ St Nazaire.

9.21.30 PORNICHET ✳✳✳❄❄❄

Loire Atlantique 47°15'·51N 02°21'·11W ✳✳✳❄❄❄❄✿✿✿

CHARTS AC 2986, 2989; Imray C39; SHOM 7395, 6797, 7145; Navi 547

TIDES Sp +0435 Dover, Nps +0530 Dover; ML 3·3; Duration Sp 0530, Nps 0645.

Standard Port BREST (←——)

Times				Height (metres)			
High Water		Low Water		MHWS	MHWN	MLWN	MLWS
0000	0600	0000	0600	7·0	5·5	2·7	1·1
1200	1800	1200	1800				
Differences PORNICHET							
+0020	−0045	−0022	−0022	−1·5	−1·1	−0·6	−0·3
LE GRAND CHARPENTIER							
+0015	−0045	−0025	−0020	−1·6	−1·2	−0·7	−0·4

SHELTER Very good in large man-made marina; full facilities.

NAVIGATION WPT 47°15'·41N 02°22'·15W, 082·5°/0·7M to N-facing ent in W sector (081°-084°) of bkwtr lt. From SW, track 037°/1·5M between Les Evens PHM and Les Troves SHM unlit buoys. From SSE track 333°/3M from Le Grand Charpentier lt ho.

LIGHTS AND MARKS Navigational lts are very hard to see against shore lts of La Baule. Masts in the marina are conspicuous.

R/T Ch 09.

TELEPHONE Aff Mar 02·40·23·06·56; CROSS 02·97·55·35·35; ⊖ 02·40·45·88·78; Météo 02·40·90·08·80; Auto 08·92·68·08·44; Ⓗ 02·40·90·60·60; Dr 02·40·60·17·20; Brit Consul 02·51·72·72·60.

FACILITIES Marina ☎ 02·40·61·03·20. Access H24 for <2·5m draft. Best to pre-call, or tempy berth on hammerheads A, B, D, F, G, L, M and N. 1000+150 ♥, €2.75. Slip, P, D, Ⓔ, El, ME, BH (25 ton), ⚓, CH, SHOM, R, Bar. portdepornichet@wanadoo.fr www.ports-plaisance.loire-atlantique.fr

Town Bar, R, 🍴, ⊚, Dr, Ⓑ, ✉, ⇌. ✈ St Nazaire (Montoir).

9.21.31 SAINT NAZAIRE

Loire Atlantique **East lock 47°16′·51N 02°11′·93W** ※※◊♤.

CHARTS AC 2986, 2989, 2985; Imray C40; SHOM 7395, 6797, 7396; Navi 248, 547

TIDES St Nazaire: Sp +0445 Dover, Nps −0540 Dover; ML 3·6; Duration Sp 0640, Nps 0445.

Standard Port BREST (←)

Times				Height (metres)			
High Water		Low Water		MHWS	MHWN	MLWN	MLWS
0000	0600	0000	0600	7·0	5·5	2·7	1·1
1200	1800	1200	1800				
Differences ST NAZAIRE							
+0030	−0040	−0010	−0010	−1·2	−0·9	−0·5	−0·3
NANTES							
+0135	+0055	+0215	+0125	−0·7	−0·4	−0·9	−0·2

SHELTER Complete in Bassin de St Nazaire or at S end of Bassin Penhoët. Nearest ⚓ is close inshore 5ca NNE of Pte d'Aiguillon.

NAVIGATION From all directions make good a WPT 47°13′·94N 02°16′·01W: ZD1 SCM buoy, the first of 7 SCM lt buoys (ZD1-7, all Q (6) + L Fl 15s) marking a secondary channel parallel to and NW of the PHM buoys of the main chan (Chenal de Bonne-Anse). Track 053°/3·7M until 1 ca before ZD6 buoy; thence alter 344° between two lateral buoys, Fl R and G 2·5s, for the small E lock & swing bridge which open (H24, all tides) at even H for departures and even H+10 for arrivals. Waiting on the seaward side is possible against the piled quay.

LIGHTS AND MARKS Ldg lts VQ Vi 280° into E lock. The Loire suspension bridge (R/W twrs, R lts) is conspic.

R/T Pre-call lock VHF Ch 14 or ☎ 02.40.00.45.17 for entry into lock/Bassins. Monitor *Loire Ports Control* Ch 06, **14**, 16, 67, 69 (H24). Tidal info is broadcast Ch 23 at H, +15, +30, +45.

TELEPHONE Port HM 02·40·45·39·00; Aff Mar 02·40·22·46·32; CROSS 02·97·55·35·35; ⊜ 02·40·45·88·71; Météo 02·40·90·00·80; Auto 08.92.68.08.44; Police 17; SAMU 15; Fire 18; Dr 02·40·22·15·32; Ⓗ 02·40·90·60·60; Brit Consul 02·51·72·72·60; Taxi 02·51·76·04·04.

FACILITIES HM Plaisance ☎ 02.40.00.45.24 at E lock control twr. Berth/raft on quays or yacht pontoons W side of Bassin de St Nazaire, despite the negative signs; €8·25/m/week. C, ME, El, ✖, CH, Ⓔ, SHOM. www.mairie-saintnazaire.fr

City All facilities; ⇌, ✈. Re-generation of the disused WW2 submarine pens and surroundings is in hand.

NANTES AC 2985 Ⓓ, SHOM 7396. Ponton des Chantiers (two pontoons, 48m x 9m, 1 for vedettes 15/6-30/8, the other for 20 yachts in >2m) is on the SE bank of Bras de la Madeleine, at 47°12′·37N 01°34′·18W, close NE of a huge, conspic yellow crane; see Nantes inset opposite. Call NGE ☎ 02.40.37.04.62 for a berth €1·80. FW, AC. Trentemoult marina is badly silted; no visitors.

MINOR HARBOURS FROM PTE ST GILDAS TO ST NAZAIRE
Three small hbrs (below, from N to S) are NE of Pte de St-Gildas, on the E side of the R. Loire. They are flanked by shellfish beds on rky ledges drying to about 4ca offshore, and sheltered from W'lies by bkwtrs but open to N/NE'lies.
Charts: AC 2986, 2981, 2989; SHOM 7395, 6797; Navi 547.
Tides: Interpolate between Le Grand Charpentier, St-Nazaire and Pornic. **Lights**: see 9.21.4.

PORT DE COMBERGE, Loire Atlantique, **47°10′·52N 02°09′·96W** . 2·7M NW is La Truie rk, 3m and marked by unlit IDM bn; 1·5M W of it are rocks drying 1·2m.- Appr on 136° in the W sector or by day with the bkwtr lt in transit with the disused lt ho beyond. Beware Les Moutons, rk drying 0·7m, 7½ca NW of the bkwtr lt, close to the approach track. The ent is narrow; tiny hbr dries about 2m, access from half-flood. HM ☎ 02.40.27.82.85. Facilities: M, FW, YC, Slip, C (6 ton), L; and at St Michel-Chef-Chef.

PORT DE LA GRAVETTE, Loire Atlantique, **47°09′·64N 02°12′·71W**, 2·2M NE of Pte de St Gildas. Daymarks are bkwtr lt in transit 130° with La Treille water tr, 2M inland. Shellfish beds are marked by unlit NCM bns. On rounding the 600m long bkwtr, turn stbd between lateral buoys; there is about 1·2m water in the N part of the hbr which dries closer in. Many local moorings, few facilities.

ST GILDAS (Anse du Boucau), Loire Atlantique, **47°08′·47N 02°14′·74W**. The hbr is 5ca N of Pte de St Gildas lt ho, Q WRG. The hbr bkwtr extends 3ca N, with a large automatic tide gauge and ☆ at its N end. An unlit SHM bn, and a SHM buoy, Fl G 2·5s (May-Sept), lie 150m and 300m NNW of bkwtr hd. Appr from about 1M N of Pte de St Gildas on a brg of 177° or at night in the W sector 174°-180° of St Gildas lt ho. L'Ilot rky ledge is marked by a PHM bn. Pick up a mooring in 1·5m in the N part of the hbr or dry out further S. HM ☎ 02.40.21.60.07. VHF Ch 09. Facilities: Slips, YC, FW, C (5 ton), 🛒 at Préfailles 1M to E.

South Biscay

River Loire to the Spanish border

S Biscay

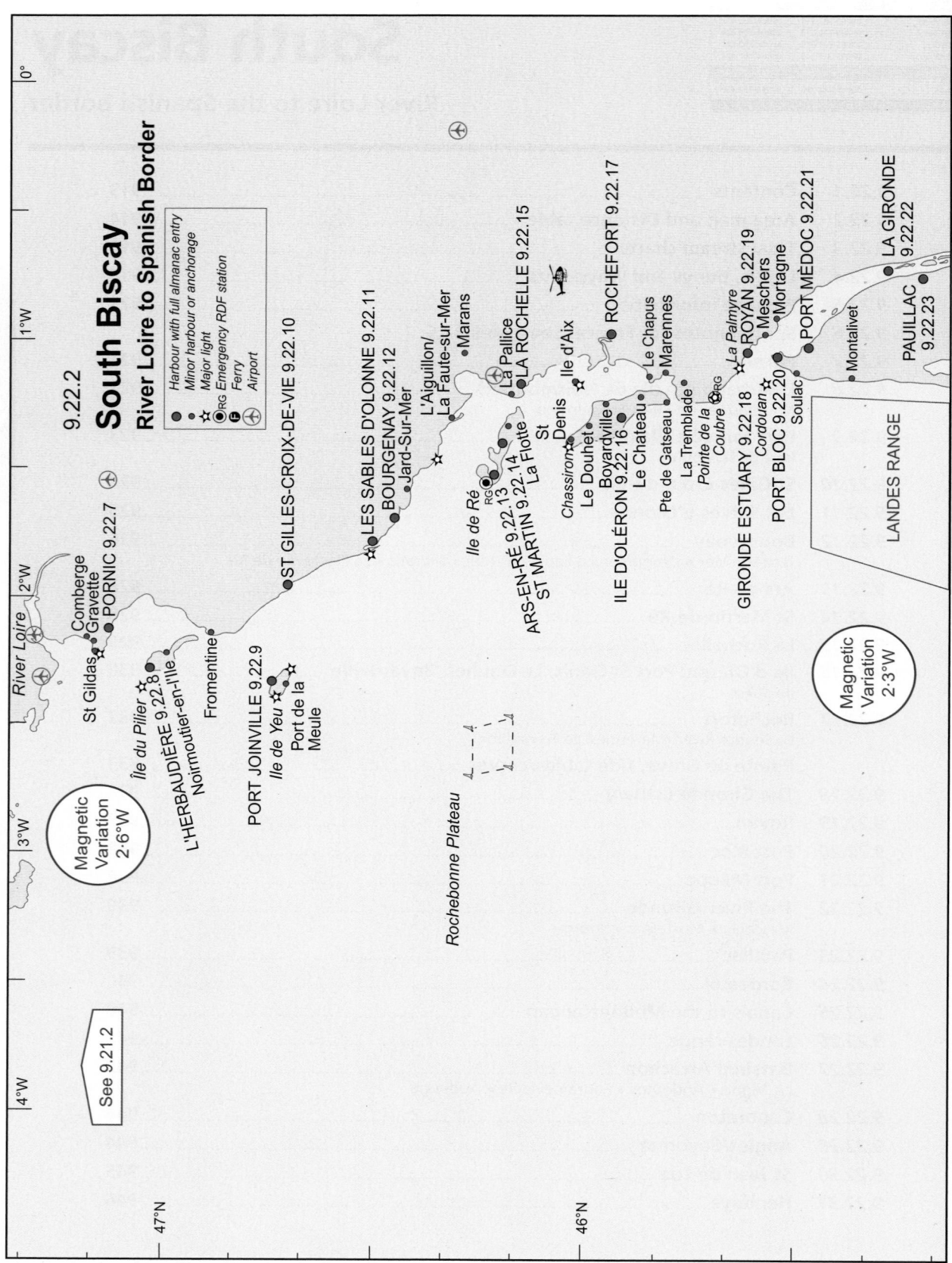

9.22.2

South Biscay

River Loire to Spanish Border

Harbour with full almanac entry
Minor harbour or anchorage
Major light
RG Emergency RDF station
Ferry
Airport

River Loire

Comberge
Gravette
St Gildas
PORNIC 9.22.7

Île du Pilier
L'HERBAUDIÈRE 9.22.8
Noirmoutier-en-l'Île
Fromentine

PORT JOINVILLE 9.22.9
Île de Yeu
Port de la
Meule

Rochebonne Plateau

ST GILLES-CROIX-DE-VIE 9.22.10

LES SABLES D'OLONNE 9.22.11
BOURGENAY 9.22.12
Jard-Sur-Mer

L'Aiguillon/
La Faute-sur-Mer
Marans

Île de Ré
RG
ARS-EN-RÉ 9.22.13
ST MARTIN 9.22.14
La Flotte

La Pallice
LA ROCHELLE 9.22.15
Île d'Aix

St
Denis
Chassiron
Le Douhet
Boyardville
ILE D'OLÉRON 9.22.16
Le Chateau
Pte de Gateau

ROCHEFORT 9.22.17

Le Chapus
Marennes
La Tremblade
Pointe de la
Coubre
RG

GIRONDE ESTUARY 9.22.18
Cordouan
PORT BLOC 9.22.20
Soulac

La Palmyre
ROYAN 9.22.19
Meschers
Mortagne

PORT MÉDOC 9.22.21
Montalivet

LA GIRONDE
9.22.22

PAUILLAC
9.22.23

LANDES RANGE

Magnetic
Variation
2·6°W

Magnetic
Variation
2·3°W

See 9.21.2

4°W 3°W 2°W 1°W 0°

47°N

46°N

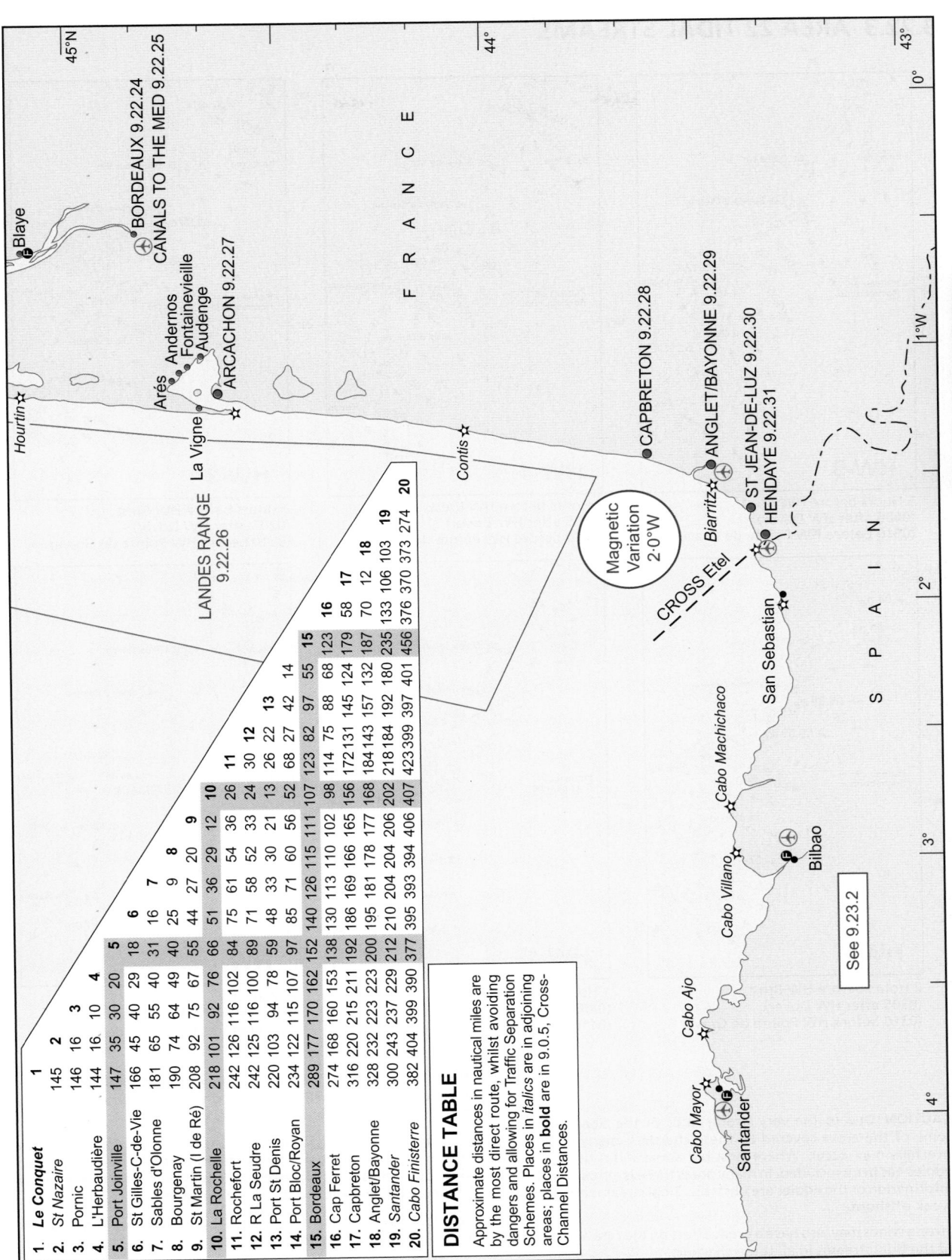

Map labels: 45°N · 44° · 43° · 0° · 1°W · 2° · 3° · 4°

Blaye · BORDEAUX 9.22.24 · CANALS TO THE MED 9.22.25 · Andernos · Fontainevieille · Audenge · Arès · ARCACHON 9.22.27 · La Vigne · Hourtin · LANDES RANGE 9.22.26 · Contis · F R A N C E

CAPBRETON 9.22.28 · ANGLET/BAYONNE 9.22.29 · ST JEAN-DE-LUZ 9.22.30 · HENDAYE 9.22.31 · Biarritz · CROSS Etel

Magnetic Variation 2·0°W

San Sebastian · Cabo Machichaco · Bilbao · Cabo Villano · Cabo Ajo · Cabo Mayor · Santander · S P A I N

See 9.23.2

DISTANCE TABLE

	1	2	3	4	5	6	7	8	9	10	11	12	13	14	15	16	17	18	19	20
1. *Le Conquet*	1																			
2. *St Nazaire*	145	2																		
3. Pornic	146	16	3																	
4. L'Herbaudière	144	16.	10	4																
5. Port Joinville	147	35	30	20	**5**															
6. St Gilles-C-de-Vie	166	45	40	29	18	6														
7. Sables d'Olonne	181	65	55	40	31	16	7													
8. Bourgenay	190	74	64	49	40	25	9	8												
9. St Martin (I de Ré)	208	92	75	67	55	44	27	20	9											
10. La Rochelle	218	101	92	76	66	51	36	29	12	**10**										
11. Rochefort	242	126	116	102	84	75	61	54	36	26	**11**									
12. R La Seudre	242	125	116	100	89	71	58	52	33	24	30	**12**								
13. Port St Denis	220	103	94	78	59	48	33	30	21	13	26	22	**13**							
14. Port Bloc/Royan	234	122	115	107	97	85	71	60	56	52	68	27	42	14						
15. Bordeaux	289	177	170	162	152	140	126	115	111	107	123	82	97	55	**15**					
16. Cap Ferret	274	168	160	153	138	130	113	110	102	98	114	75	88	68	123	**16**				
17. Capbreton	316	220	215	211	192	186	169	166	165	156	172	131	145	124	179	58	**17**			
18. Anglet/Bayonne	328	232	223	223	200	195	181	178	177	168	184	143	157	132	187	70	12	**18**		
19. *Santander*	300	243	237	229	212	210	204	206	202		218	184	192	180	235	133	106	103	**19**	
20. *Cabo Finisterre*	382	404	399	390	377	395	393	394	406	407	423	399	397	401	456	376	370	373	274	**20**

Approximate distances in nautical miles are by the most direct route, whilst avoiding dangers and allowing for Traffic Separation Schemes. Places in *italics* are in adjoining areas; places in **bold** are in 9.0.5, Cross-Channel Distances.

9.22.3 AREA 22 TIDAL STREAMS

HW-5
5 Hours before HW Brest
(0005 after HW Dover)
(0510 before HW Pointe de Grave)

HW-4
4 Hours before HW Brest
(0105 after HW Dover)
(0410 before HW Pointe de Grave)

HW-3
3 Hours before HW Brest
(0205 after HW Dover)
(0310 before HW Pointe de Grave)

HW-2
2 Hours before HW Brest
(0305 after HW Dover)
(0310 before HW Pointe de Grave)

HW-1
1 Hour before HW Brest
(0405 after HW Dover)
(0110 before HW Pointe de Grave)

HW
HW Brest
(0505 after HW Dover)
(0010 before HW Pointe de Grave)

CAUTION: Due to the very strong rates of the tidal streams in some of the areas covered by these chartlets, many eddies and overfalls may occur. Where possible some indication of these eddies has been included. In many areas there is either insufficient information or the eddies are unstable. Tidal streams are generally weak offshore.

Strong winds may also have a great effect on the rate and direction of the tidal streams in all these chartlets.

Note: These chartlets are based on the Admiralty tidal stream atlas for France, W coast (NP 265, 2nd edition 2005) which uses data from actual observations out to 20-35M offshore.

The comparable French atlas (559-UJA; 2001) gives data for further offshore, based on computer predictions. It covers at large scale the approaches to St Nazaire; Les Sables d'Olonne to Pertuis de Maumusson; and the mouth of the Gironde.

No tidal stream atlas is published by either the French or UK Hydrographic Offices for the waters southward to the Spanish border.

Northward 9.21.3

HW+1

1 Hour after HW Brest
(0605 after HW Dover)
(0050 after HW Pointe de Grave)

HW+2

2 Hours after HW Brest
(0515 before HW Dover)
(0150 after HW Pointe de Grave)

HW+3

3 Hours after HW Brest
(0415 before HW Dover)
(0250 after HW Pointe de Grave)

HW+4

4 Hours after HW Brest
(0315 before HW Dover)
(0350 after HW Pointe de Grave)

HW+5

5 Hours after HW Brest
(0215 before HW Dover)
(0450 after HW Pointe de Grave)

HW+6

6 Hours after HW Brest
(0115 before HW Dover)
(0550 after HW Pointe de Grave)

Note: These chartlets are based on the Admiralty tidal stream atlas for France, W coast (NP 265, 2nd edition 2005) which uses data from actual observations out to 20-35M offshore.

The comparable French atlas (559-UJA; 2001) gives data for further offshore, based on computer predictions. It covers at large scale the approaches to St Nazaire; Les Sables d'Olonne to Pertuis de Maumusson; and the mouth of the Gironde.

No tidal stream atlas is published by either the French or UK Hydrographic Offices for the waters southward to the Spanish border.

CAUTION: Due to the very strong rates of the tidal streams in some of the areas covered by these chartlets, many eddies and overfalls may occur. Where possible some indication of these eddies has been included. In many areas there is either insufficient information or the eddies are unstable. Tidal streams are generally weak offshore.

Strong winds may also have a great effect on the rate and direction of the tidal streams in all these chartlets.

9.22.4 LIGHTS, BUOYS AND WAYPOINTS

Bold print = light with a nominal range of 15M or more.
CAPITALS = place or feature. *CAPITAL ITALICS* = light-vessel,
light float or Lanby. *Italics* = Fog signal. ***Bold italics*** = Racon.
Abbreviations are in Chapter 1.

POINTE DE SAINT GILDAS TO FROMENTINE

Pte de Saint Gildas ° Q WRG 20m, W14M, R/G10M; 264°-R-308°-
G-078°-W-088°-R-174°-W-180°-G-264°; 47°08'·02N 02°14'·75W.
Notre Dame ↓ VQ (9) 10s 7m 3M; 47°05'·42N 02°08'·26W.

PORNIC

Entrance buoy ⌀ L Fl 10s; 47°06'·45N 02°06'·63W.
Marina ent, S side ⚓ Fl (2) R 6s 4m 2M; 47°06'·47N 02°06'·67W.
Pte de Noëveillard ⚓ Oc (4) WRG 12s 22m W13M, R/G9M;
Shore-G-051°-W-079°-R-shore; W □ twr, G top, W dwelling;
47°06'·62N 02°06'·92W.

ÎLE DE NOIRMOUTIER anti-clockwise from the East

Pte des Dames ☆ Oc(3) WRG 12s 34m, **W19M, R/G15M**; 016·5°-G-057°-
R-124°-G-165°-W-191°, R191°-267°-W-357°-R-016·5°; W □ twr;
47°00'·67N 02°13'·26W. La Chaise ↓ 47°01'·21N 02°12'·64W.
L'Herbaudière, ldg lts 187·5°, both Q 5/21m 7M, Gy masts.
Front, 47°01'·59N 02°17'·84W. Rear, 310m from front.
Martroger ↓, Q WRG 11m W9M, R/G6M; 033°-G-055°-W-060°-R-095°-
G-124°-W-153°-R-201°-W-240°-R-033°; 47°02'·61N 02°17'·11W.
W jetty ⚓ Oc(2+1) WG 12s 9m W10M, G7M; 187·5°-W-190°-G-187·5°;
W col and hut, G top; 47°01'·63N 02°17'·84W.
E jetty ⚓ Fl (2) R 6s 8m 4M; 47°01'·61N 02°17'·81W.
Île du Pilier ☆ Fl (3) 20s 33m **29M**; Gy twr; 47°02'·55N
02°21'·60W. Same twr, auxiliary ⚓ QR 10m 11M, 321°-034°.
Passe de la Grise ↓ Q (6) + L Fl 15s; 47°01'·66N 02°19'·97W.
Les Boeufs ↓ VQ (9) 10s; 46°55'·04N 02°27'·99W.
Réaumur ↓ Q (9) 15s; 46°57'·46N 02°24'·22W.
Le Bavard ↓ VQ (6) + L Fl 10s; 46°56'·79N 02°23'·34W.
Pte du Devin (Morin) ⚓ Oc(4) WRG 12s 10m W11M, R/G8M; 314°-G-028°-
W-035°-R-134°; W col & hut, G top; 46°59'·15N 02°17'·60W.

GOULET DE FROMENTINE

Fromentine ⌀ L Fl 10s; 46°53'·07N 02°11'·63W (buoyed chan).
Milieu ↓ Fl (4) R 12s 6m 5M; 46°53'·59N 02°09'·63W.
Pte de Notre Dame-de-Monts ⚓ Dir Oc (2) WRG 6s 21m, W13M,
R/G10M; 000°-G-043°-W-063°-R-073°-W-094°-G-113°-W-116°-
R-175°-G-196°-R-230°; W twr, B top; 46°53'·33N 02°08'·54W.

ÎLE D'YEU TO BOURGENAY

ÎLE D'YEU

Petite Foule (main lt) ☆ Fl 5s 56m **24M**; W □ twr, G lantern;
46°43'·04N 02°22'·91W.
Les Chiens Perrins ↓ Q (9) WG 15s 16m W7M, G4M;
330°-G-350°-W-330°; 46°43'·60N 02°24'·58W.
Pont d'Yeu ↓ 46°45'·81N 02°13'·81W.
La Sablaire ↓ Q (6) + L Fl 15s; 46°43'·62N 02°19'·49W.
Port Joinville ldg lts 219°, both QR 11/16m 6M, 169°-269°: Front,
Quai du Canada 46°43'·61N 02°20'·94W. Rear, 85m from front.
NW jetty ⚓ Oc (3) WG 12s 7m, W11M, G8M; Shore-G-150°-W-
232°-G-279°-W-285°-G-shore; W 8-sided twr, G top; 46°43'·77N
02°20'·82W. La Galiote ⚓ 46°43'·73N 02°20'·71W.
Pte des Corbeaux ☆ Fl (2+1) R 15s 25m **20M**; 083°-143° obsc by
Île de Yeu; W □ twr, R top; 46°41'·41N 02°17'·08W.
Port de la Meule ⚓ Oc WRG 4s 9m, W9M, R/G6M; 007·5°-G-018°-
W-027·5°-R-041·5°; Gy twr, R top; 46°41'·62N 02°20'·72W.

SAINT GILLES-CROIX-DE-VIE

Pte de Grosse Terre ☆ Fl (4) WR 12s 25m, **W18M, R15M**; 290°-
R-339°-W-125°-R-145°; W truncated twr; 46°41'·54N 01°57'·92W.
Ldg lts 043·7°, both Q 7/28m **15M**; 033·5°-053·5°; synch; W □
twrs, R tops: Front, 46°41'·86N 01°56'·75W. Rear, 260m NE.

Pilours ↓ Q (6) + L Fl 15s; *Bell*; 46°40'·99N 01°58'·09W.
Jetée de la Garenne ⚓ Fl G 4s 8m 6M; 46°41'·46N 01°57'·25W.
Jetée de Boisvinet ⚓ Fl R 4s 8m 6M; 46°41'·62N 01°57'·16W.

LES SABLES D'OLONNE

Les Barges ⚓ Fl (2) R 10s 25m 13M; Gy twr; 46°29'·70N 01°50'·50W.
Petite Barge ↓ Q (6) + L Fl 15s 3M; *Whis*; 46°28'·90N 01°50'·61W.
L'Armandèche ☆ Fl (2+1) 15s 42m **24M**; 295°-130°; W 6-sided
twr, R top; 46°29'·39N 01°48'·29W.
Nouch Sud ↓ Q (6) + L Fl 15s; 46°28'·55N 01°47'·41W.
Nouch Nord ↓ 46°28'·88N 01°47'·36W.
SW Pass, ldg lts 032·5°, both Iso 4s 12/33m **16M**, H24: **Front** ☆,
46°29'·42N 01°46'·37W; mast. **Rear** ☆, La Potence, W □ twr.
SE Pass, ldg lts 320°: Front, E jetty ⚓ QG 11m 8M; W twr, G top;
46°29'·44N 01°47'·51W. Rear, Tour d'Arundel ⚓ Q 33m 13M,
synch; large Gy □ twr; 46°29'·63N 01°47'·74W.
Jetée St Nicolas (W jetty) ⚓ QR 16m 8M; 143°-094°; W twr, R
top; 46°29'·23N 01°47'·52W.

BOURGENAY

Ldg lts 040°, both QG 9/19m 7M. Front, 020°-060°; on S bkwtr;
46°26'·34N 01°40'·62W. Rear, 010°-070°; 162m from front.
Landfall ↓ L Fl 10s; 46°25'·26N 01°41'·93W.
Ent ⚓ Fl R 4s 8m 9M & ⚓ Iso G 4s 6m 5M; 46°26'·29N 01°40'·75W.

PLATEAU DE ROCHEBONNE (Shoal 32M offshore)

NW ↓ Q (9) 15s; *Whis*; 46°12'·92N 02°31'·58W.
NE ↓ Iso G 4s; 46°12'·73N 02°24'·83W.
SE ↓ Q (3) 10s; *Bell*; 46°09'·20N 02°21'·13W.
SW ↓ Fl (2) R 6s; 46°10'·11N 02°27'·04W.

PERTUIS BRETON

JARD-SUR-MER and LA TRANCHE-SUR-MER

Ldg marks 036°, two unlit W bcns; 46°24'·47N 01°34'·16W.
Pte du Grouin du Cou ☆ Fl WRG 5s 29m, **W20M, R/G16M**;
034°-R-061°-W-117°-G-138°-W-034°; W 8-sided twr, B top;
46°20'·67N 01°27'·83W.
La Tranche pier ⚓ Fl (2) R 6s 6m 6M; R col; 46°20'·55N 01°25'·63W.
Mussel farm, No entry, marked by: ↓ Q, 46°17'·17N 01°22'·19W.
↓ Q (3) 10s, 46°15'·84N 01°18'·60W. ↓ Q (6) + L Fl 15s, 46°14'·92N
01°19'·32W. ↓ Q (9) 15s, 46°16'·28N 01°22'·88W.

L'AIGUILLON and LA FAUTE-SUR-MER

Le Lay ↓ Q (6) + L Fl 15s; 46°16'·10N 01°16'·53W.
No. 1 ▲ 46°16'·65N 01°16'·25W. Many mussel beds.

ANSE DE L'AIGUILLON (for La Sèvre Niortaise & Marans)

ATT de L'Aiguillon ↓ L Fl 10s; 46°15'·33N 01°11'·50W.
Inner fairway ↓ 46°17'·19N 01°09'·65W.
Port du Pavé ⚓ Fl G 4s 9m 7M; W col, G top; 46°18'·15N 01°08'·01W.

ÎLE DE RÉ

Les Baleineaux ⚓ VQ 23m 7M; pink twr, R top; 46°15'·81N
01°35'·22W.
Les Baleines ☆ Fl (4) 15s 53m **27M**; conspic Gy 8-sided twr, R
lantern; 46°14'·64N 01°33'·69W.

ARS-EN-RÉ

Dir ⚓ 268° Oc WRG 4s, W10M, R/G 7M, 275·5°-G-267·5°-W-
268·5°-R-274·5°; W hut with W □ topmark; 46°14'·05N 01°28'·60W.
Les Islattes ↓ Q 13m 8M; NCM bcn twr 46°14'·03N 01°23'·32W.
Bûcheron No 1 ▲ Fl G 2·5s; 46°14'·21N 01°25'·98W.
Bûcheron No 3 ▲ Fl (2) G 6s; 46°14'·14N 01°26'·94W.
Le Fier d'Ars, inner ldg lts 232·5°, both Q 5/13m 9/11M: Front ⚓
R/W frame on W col; 46°12'·75N 01°30'·59W. Rear ⚓ 142°-322°;
B vert rectangle on W mast, 370m from front.

ST MARTIN DE RÉ

Lt ho, E of ent ⚓ Oc (2) WR 6s 18m W10M, R7M; Shore-W-245°-
R-281°-W-shore; W twr, R top; 46°12'·44N 01°21'·89W.

Plot waypoints on chart before use

W mole ⚓ Fl G 2·5s 10m 5M; obsc'd by Pte du Grouin when brg <124°; W post, G top; 46°12'·49N 01°21'·91W.

LA FLOTTE
N bkwtr ⚓ Fl WG 4s 10m W12M, G9M; 130°-G-205°-W-220°-G-257°; W ○ twr, G top; 46°11'·33N 01°19'·30W.
Dir lt 212·5°, Moiré effect, is next to the main lt twr.
ÎLE DE RÉ (South coast, from the W, inc bridge)
Chanchardon ⚓ Fl WR 4s 15m W11M, R8M; 118°-R-290°-W-118°; B 8-sided twr, W base; 46°09'·71N 01°28'·41W.
Chauveau ☆ Oc (3) WR 12s 27m **W15M**, R11M; 057°-W-094°-R-104°-W-342°-R-057°; W ○ twr, R top; 46°08'·03N 01°16'·42W.
Bridge span (30m cl'nce) for SE-bound vessels, ⚓ Iso 4s 34m 8M; 46°10'·18N 01°14'·75W . Span (30m cl'nce) for NW-bound vessels, ⚓ Iso 4s 34m 8M; 46°10'·26N 01°14'·52W.
La Pallice, W mole, ⚓ Fl G 4s 5m 6M; 46°09'·78N 01°14'·45W.
S end, ⚓ Q (6) + L Fl 15s 6m 9M; 46°09'·36N 01°14'·52W.

LA ROCHELLE AND LA CHARENTE TO ROCHEFORT
LA ROCHELLE
PA ⚓ Iso 4s 8m 7M; *Whis*; 46°05'·62N 01°42'·45W.
Chauveau ⚓ VQ (6) + L Fl 10s; 46°06'·56N 01°16'·06W.
Roche du Sud ⚓ Q (9) 15s; 46°06'·37N 01°15'·22W.

La Rochelle ldg lts 059°, both Dir Q 15/25m 13/14M; synch; by day Fl 4s. Front; intens 056°-062°; R ○ twr, W bands; 46°09'·35N 01°09'·16W. Rear, 044°-074°, obsc'd 061°-065°; W 8-sided twr, G top, 235m from front.

Lavardin ⚓ Fl (2) 6s 14m 7M; BRB IDM twr; 46°08'·09N 01°14'·52W.
Les Minimes ⚓ Q (9) 15s; 46°08'·01N 01°11'·60W.
Pte des Minimes ⚓ Fl (3) WG 12s 8m; W8M, G5M; 059°-W-213°; 313°-G-059°; 8-sided twr on piles; 46°08'·27N 01°10'·76W.
Chan buoy ⚓ QG; 46°08'·53N 01°10'·87W; marking hbr limit.
Tour Richelieu ⚓ Fl R 4s 10m 9M; R twr; 46°08'·90N 01°10'·34W.
Port des Minimes, W bkwtr ⚓ Fl (2) G 6s 9m 7M; 46°08'·82N 01°10'·15W.

LA CHARENTE
Fort Boyard twr ⚓ Q (9) 15s; 45°59'·96N 01°12'·85W.
Ldg lts 115°, both Dir QR 8/21m **19/20M**; intens 113°-117°; W □ twr, R top: Front ☆, 45°57'·96N 01°04'·38W. **Rear, Soumard** ☆, 600m from front. Same twr: ⚓ QR 21m 8M; vis 322°-067°.
Île d'Aix ☆ Fl WR 5s 24m **W24M, R20M**; 103°-R-118°-W-103°; two conspic W ○ twrs, R top; 46°00'·60N 01°10'·67W.
Pte Ste Catherine, jetty hd ⚓ Q (6) + L Fl 15s 5m 4M; 45°59'·05N 01°07'·85W. Les Palles ⚓ Q; 45°59'·54N 01°09'·56W.

Fouras, Port Sud bkwtr ⚓ Fl WR 4s 6m 9/6M; 115°-R-177°-W-115°; 45°58'·97N 01°05'·72W. Rear 75m from front.

ROCHEFORT Night passage by yachts is not advised.
⚓ Fl (2) G 6s; bcn 45°55'·21N 00°56'·98W, 1·4M S of Rochefort.

ÎLE D'OLÉRON
Pte de Chassiron ☆ Fl 10s 50m, **28M**; conspic W twr, B bands; 46°02'·80N 01°24'·62W, NW tip of island.
Antioche ⚓ Q 20m 11M; 46°03'·94N 01°23'·71W.

ST DENIS
Dir ⚓ 205°, Iso WRG 4s 14m, W11M, R/G8M; 190°-G-204°-W-206°-R-220°; 46°01'·61N 01°21'·92W.
E jetty ⚓ Fl (2) WG 6s 6m, W9M, G6M; 205°-W-277°-G-292°-G-165°; □ hut; 46°02'·10N 01°22'·06W.

PORT DU DOUHET and PASSAGE DE L'OUEST
Seaweed farm ⚓ VQ; 46°00'·65N 01°17'·38W.
N ent ⚓ 46°00'·10N 01°19'·20W.
Fishfarm ⚓ Q; 46°00'·24N 01°15'·34W. ⚓ Q (3) 10s; 45°59'·84N 01°14'·79W. (Fort Boyard see previous page under La Charente).

BOYARDVILLE
Mole ⚓ Fl (2) R 6s 8m 5M; obsc'd by Pte des Saumonards when brg <150°; W twr, R top; 45°58'·24N 01°13'·83W.

COUREAU D'OLÉRON and LE CHÂTEAU D'OLÉRON
Juliar ⚓ Q (3) WG 10s 12m, W11M; G8M; 147°-W-336°-G-147°; 45°54'·11N 01°09'·48W.
Chateau d'Oléron, ldg lts 318·5°, both QR 11/24m 7M; synch. Front, 191°-087°; R line on W twr; 45°53'·03N 01°11'·45W. Rear, W twr, R top; 240m from front.

LA SEUDRE RIVER
Pte du Mus de Loup ⚓ Oc G 4s 8m 6M; 118°-147°; 45°47'·70N 01°08'·60W.
Pertuis de Maumusson. Depths & buoys subject to change.
ATT Maumusson ⚓ L Fl 10s; 45°46'·86N 01°18'·29W.
La Barre ⚓ 45°46'·36N 01°16'·02W.
Tabouret ⚓ 45°46'·56N 01°16'·02W.
Mattes ⚓ 45°46'·93N 01°15'·29W.
Gatseau ⚓ 45°47'·36N 01°14'·70W.

LA COTINIÈRE (SW side of island)
Ent ldg lts 339°, both ⚓ Dir Oc (2) 6s 6/14m 13/12M; synch: Front, 329°-349°; W twr, R top; 45°54'·72N 01°19'·79W. Rear, intens 329°-349°; W twr, R bands; 425m from front on W bkwtr.
W bkwtr head, Fl R 4s 10m; 45°54'·63N 01°19'·70W.

GRANDE PASSE DE L'OUEST
Pte de la Coubre ☆ Fl (2) 10s 64m **28M**; W twr, R top; 45°41'·78N 01°13'·99W. Same twr, F RG 42m10M; 030°-R-043°-G-060°-R-110°.
BXA ⚓ Iso 4s 8m 7M; *Racon B*; 45°37'·53N 01°28'·69W.
Ldg lts 081·5°. **Front** ☆, Dir Iso 4s 21m **20M**; intens 080·5°-082·5°; W pylon on dolphin; 45°39'·56N 01°08'·78W, 1·1M from rear. Same structure, Q (2) 5s 10m 3M.
La Palmyre, common rear ☆ Dir Q 57m **27M**; intens 080·5°-082·5°; W radar twr; 45°39'·71N 01°07'·25W.
Same twr, Dir FR 57m **17M**; intens 325·5°-328·5°.
No. 1 ⚓ QG; 45°38'·03N 01°22'·69W
No. 6 ⚓ VQ (6) + L Fl 10s; 45°38'·28N 01°18'·68W.
No. 7a ⚓ Fl G 4s; 45°38'·96N 01°14'·85W.
No. 9 ⚓ Q; 45°39'·43N 01°12'·79W.
No. 11 ⚓ Iso G 4s; 45°39'·06N 01°10'·60W.
No. 11A ⚓ Fl G 2·5s; 45°38'·37N 01°07'·90W.
No. 13 ⚓ Fl (2) G 6s; 45°37'·33N 01°06'·41W.
No. 13A ⚓ Fl (3) G 12s; 45°35'·68N 01°04'·19W.
No. 13B ⚓ QG; 45°34'·67N 01°02'·98W.
Ldg lts 327° (down-river): Front, **Terre-Nègre** ☆, Oc (3) WRG 12s 39m **W18M**, R/G14M; 304°-R-319°-W-327°-G-000°-W-004°-G-097°-W-104°-R-116°; W twr, R top on W side; 45°38'·77N 01°06'·39W, 1·1M from rear (La Palmyre above).

Cordouan ☆ Oc (2+1) WRG 12s 60m, **W22M, R/G18M**; 014°-W-126°-G-178·5°-W-250°-W (unintens) -267°-R (unintens)-294·5°-R-014°; obsc'd in estuary when brg >285°; W twr, Gy band; 45°35'·18N 01°10'·40W.

PASSE SUD (or DE GRAVE)
Ldg lts 063°: **Front, St Nicolas** ☆ Dir QG 22m **16M**; intens 061·5°-064·5°; W □ twr; 45°33'·73N 01°05'·01W.
Rear, Pte de Grave ☆ Oc WRG 4s 26m, **W19M, R/G15M**; 033°-W(unintens)-054°-W-233·5°-R-303°-W-312°-G-330°-W-341°-W(unintens)-025°; W □ twr, B corners and top, 0·84M from front. G ⚓ 45°30'·33N 01°15'·55W. G3 ⚓ 45°32'·79N 01°07'·72W.
Ldg lts 041°, both Dir QR 33/61m **18M. Front, Le Chay** ☆ 45°37'·31N 01°02'·43W. **Rear, St Pierre** ☆, 0·97M from front. G4 ⚓ 45°34'·70N 01°05'·80W. G6 ⚓ 45°34'·88N 01°04'·80W.

ROYAN
R1 ⚓ Iso G 4s; 45°36'·56N 01°01'·96W.

S jetty ⚡ Fl (2) R 10s 11m 12M; 199°-116°; 45°37'·00N 01°01'·81W.
Hbr ent, W jetty ⚡ Fl (3) R 12s 8m 6M; 45°37'·12N 01°01'·53W.

PORT BLOC and PORT-MÉDOC
Pte de Grave, jetty ⚓ Q 6m 2M; 45°34'·42N 01°03'·68W.
Port Bloc, ent N side ⚡ Fl G 4s 9m 3M; 45°34'·14N 01°03'·74W.
Port-Médoc, N bkwtr head ⚡ QG 4M; 45°33'·40N 01°03'·39W.

MESCHERS, MORTAGNE, PORT MAUBERT, PAUILLAC and BLAYE
Meschers ldg lts 349·5°: 2 FW (privately maintained). Front 45°33'·20N 00°56'·62W, on E bkwtr head. Rear, 130m from front.
Mortagne ent ⚓ VQ (9) 10s; 45°28'·24N 00°49'·02W.
Port Maubert, ldg lts 024·5°, both QR 5/9m 5M; 45°25'·56N 00°45'·47W.
Pauillac, No. 43 ⚓ Fl (2) G 6s; 45°12'·44N 00°44'·27W.
NE elbow ⚡ Fl G 4s 7m 5M; 45°11'·95N 00°44'·59W.
Ent E side ⚡ QG 7m 4M; 45°11'·83N 00°44'·59W.
Blaye, No. S9 ▲ 45°09'·35N 00°40'·27W; 1·8M N of Blaye.
N quay ⚡ Q (3) R 5s 6m 3M; 45°07'·49N 00°39'·99W.
D6 ⚓ Fl (2) R 6s; 45°06'·91N 00°39'·93W, 0.6M S of Blaye.
Bec d'Ambés ⚓ QG 5m 5M; 45°02'·53N 00°36'·47W (here Rivers Dordogne and Garonne flow into River Gironde).

BORDEAUX
Pont d'Aquitaine ⚡ 4 F Vi; 44°52'·82N 00°32'·28W.
No 73 ⚓ Iso G 4s; 44°52'·72N 00°32'·24W.
Lormont Iso R 4s, S end of ⓥ pontoon; 44°52'·62N 00°32'·12W.
Lock ent to Bassins Nos 1 and 2, 44°51'·72N 00°33'·07W.
Pont de Pierre, 44°50'·30N 00°33'·78W, Km 0.

POINTE DE GRAVE TO THE SPANISH BORDER
Hourtin ☆ Fl 5s 55m **23M**; R ☐ twr; 45°08'·51N 01°09'·63W.
Cap Ferret ☆ Fl R 5s 53m **27M**; W ◯ twr, R top; 44°38'·72N 01°14'·90W. Same twr, ⚡ Oc (3) 12s 46m 14M; 045°-135°.

ARCACHON, PASSE NORD
Note: Buoys may be moved as the chan shifts. ATT-ARC–2NA were validated June 2009. Positions marked † were not validated and should be used with caution.
ATT-ARC ⚓ L Fl 10s 8m 5M; 44°34'·51N 01°18'·74W.

Buoy	Mark	Position
1N	⚓	44°34'·46N 01°17'·86W.
2N	⚓	44°34'·62N 01°17'·87W.
2NA	⚓	44°34'·64N 01°16'·93W.
3N †	⚓	44°34'·49N 01°16'·43W.
4N †	⚓	44°34'·61N 01°16'·57W.
5N †	⚓	44°34'·78N 01°15'·92W.
7N †	⚓	44°35'·12N 01°15'·33W.
7NA †	⚓	44°35'·44N 01°14'·76W.
6N †	⚓	44°35'·87N 01°14'·66W.
8N †	⚓	44°36'·53N 01°14'·39W.
9N †	⚓	44°36'·96N 01°14'·34W.
11 †	⚓	44°37'·35N 01°14'·10W.
13 †	⚓	44°38'·16N 01°14'·04W.
14 †	⚓	44°39'·60N 01°13'·06W.
15 †	▲	44°39'·85N 01°12'·04W.

Marina W bkwtr ⚡ QG 6m 6M; 44°39'·77N 01°09'·14W.
E bkwtr ⚡ QR 6m 6M; 44°39'·76N 01°09'·07W.
Port de La Vigne ⚡ Iso R 4s 7m 5M, occas; 44°40'·43N 01°14'·36W.

PASSE SUD (Closed to navigation; the ent is dangerous.)
La Salie ⚓ Fl (2) 6s; 44°30'·43N 01°17'·75W.
La Salie wharf hd ⚓ Q (9) 15s 18m 4M; 44°30'·89N 01°15'·67W.
La Lagune (B) ⚓ 44°32'·81N 01°15'·48W.
SM ⚓ Fl (3) Y 12s; 44°20'·36N 01°28'·69W.
Contis ☆ Fl (4) 25s 50m **23M**; W ◯ twr, B diagonal stripes; 44°05'·59N 01°18'·99W.

CAPBRETON
Digue Nord ⚡ Fl (2) R 6s 13m 12M; W ◯ twr, R top; *Horn 30s*; 43°39'·38N 01°26'·95W.

Estacade Sud ⚡ Fl (2) G 6s 9m 8M; 43°39'·27N 01°26'·83W.

ANGLET and BAYONNE
BA ⚓ L Fl 10s; 43°32'·59N 01°32'·76W, 144°/0.93M to hbr ent.
Outer ldg lts 090°, both Dir Q 9/15m **19M**; intens 086·5°-093·5°; synch; W twrs, R tops. Front, **Boucau** ☆ 43°31'·81N 01°31'·23W. Rear, 250m from front.
Outer N bkwtr ⚓ QR 11m 8M; W/R twr; 43°31'·88N 01°31'·99W.
Outer S bkwtr ⚓ Q (9) 15s 15m 6M; 43°31'·53N 01°31'·76W.
Inner ldg lts 111·5°, both Dir QG 6/10m 14M; intens 109°-114° (moved as necessary and lit when chan is practicable). Front, W hut, G band; 43°31'·63N 01°30'·94W. Rear, 149m from front.
Inner N jetty ⚡ Iso R 4s 12m 8M; 43°31'·82N 01°31'·42W.
Inner S jetty ⚡ Iso G 4s 9m 10M; W ☐ twr, G top; 43°31'·73N 01°31'·48W. IPTS from twr 260m ESE.
N training wall ⚡ Fl (2) R 6s 9m 8M; 43°31'·76N 01°31'·25W.
N training wall ⚡ Fl (3) R 12s 9m 3M, 43°31'·75N 01°31'·18W.
N training wall ⚡ Fl (4) R 15s 9m 3M, 43°31'·73N 01°30'·97W.
S training wall ⚡ Fl (3) G 12s 9m 3M; 43°31'·67N 01°31'·21W.
S training wall ⚡ Fl (4) G 15s 9m 3M, 43°31'·64N 01°30'·96W.
S training wall ⚡ QG 7m 8M; 43°31'·63N 01°30'·90W.
Anglet marina ent ⚡Fl G 2·5s 6m 2M; 43°31'·57N 01°30'·51W.

Up-river toward Bayonne fixed bridge, 5·2m clearance:
Digue Basse ⚡ Fl G 4s 3m 4M, 43°31'·54N 01°30'·08W.
Ldg lts 322·4°: Front, Forges QR 14m 8M; vis 188°-098°; 43°31'·61N 01°29'·92W. Rear, Dir Iso R 4s 18m 13M; intens 312·4°-332·4°.
No. 1 ⚓ Iso G 4s; 43°31'·34N 01°29'·72W.
No. 2 ⚓ QR; 43°30'·89N 01°29'·46W.
Pte de Blanc-Pignon ⚡ Fl (2) G 6s 8m 9M; 43°30'·92N 01°29'·61W.
No. 10 ⚓ VQR; 43°30'·11N 01°29'·39W.
Pont de l'Aveugle ⚡ Dir Q WRG W10M, R/G7M; 165°-G-170°-W-175°-R-195°; 43°30'·05N 01°29'·53W.

BIARRITZ
Pointe Saint-Martin ☆ Fl (2) 10s 73m **27M**; W twr, B top; 43°29'·62N 01°33'·24W.

ST JEAN DE LUZ
Outer ldg lts 138·5° (Passe d'Illarguita): Front, Socoa ⚡ Q WR 36m W12M, R8M; shore-W-264°-R-282°-W-shore; W ☐ twr, B stripe; 43°23'·70N 01°41'·20W.

Rear, Bordagain, Dir Q 67m **20M**; intens 134·5°-141·5°; B/W panel, B/W pylon; 43°23'·12N 01°40'·50W.

Middle ldg lts 101°, both Oc (4) R 12s 30/47m **18M**; intens 095°-107°; synch. **Front, Ste Barbe** ☆, W △ on W hut; 43°23'·96N 01°39'·88W. **Rear** ☆, B △ on W ☐ twr, 340m from front.

Inner ldg lts 150·7°, both Dir QG 18/27m **16M**; intens 149·5°-152·2°. **Front, E jetty** ☆ W ☐ twr, R stripe; 43°23'·25N 01°40'·15W. **Rear** ☆, W ☐ twr, G stripe; 410m from front, at S corner of marina.
Digue des Criquas (W bkwtr) ⚡ Iso G 4s 11m 6M; G ☐ twr; 43°23'·84N 01°40'·67W.
East Groyne ⚡ Fl R 4s 7m 2M; 43°23'·29N 01°40'·18W.

HENDAYE
Cabo Higuer ☆ Fl (2) 10s 63m **23M**; 072°-340°; ☐ twr, R cupola; 43°23'·52N 01°47'·52W (in Spain).
Refuge port ent, Fl (2) G 7s 7m 5M; 43°23'·13N 01°47'·35W.
W training wall ⚡ Fl (3) G 9s 9m 5M; 43°22'·82N 01°47'·34W.
E training wall hd ⚡ L Fl R 10s 8m 5M; 43°22'·67N 01°47'·22W.
E training wall root, Pte des Dunes ⚡Fl R 2·5s 6m 4M; 43°22'·38N 01°47'·34W.
▲ Fl G 5s; 43°22'·33N 01°47'·48W.
⚓ VQ (3) G 5s 3m 3M; G bent mast; 43°22'·10N 01°47'·27W.
Marina, W bkwtr, elbow ⚡ Fl (2) R 6s 6m 2M; 294°-114°; 43°22'·08N 01°47'·16W.
S jetty ⚡ Fl Y 4s 5m 4M; Y col; 43°22'·05N 01°47'·05W.
⚓ L Fl G 10s 3m 4M; G mast; 43°21'·99N 01°47'·07W.

9.22.5 PASSAGE INFORMATION

More Passage Information is threaded between successive harbours in this Area. **Bibliography:** *West France CC* (NDL/Featherstone). The *Bay of Biscay Pilot* NP22. AC 1104, 20, 2664, 1102; carry also large scale French charts for inshore waters.

THE BAY OF BISCAY AND WEST COAST OF FRANCE

Despite its reputation, weather in the southern part of the Bay is often warm and settled in summer when the Azores high and Spanish heat low are the dominant weather features.

NE'lies prevail in sea area Fitzroy in summer and gales may occur twice monthly, although forecast more frequently. Atlantic lows can bring W'ly spells at any time together with long swells which are dangerous inshore. SE or S winds are rare, but wind direction and speed often vary from day to day. Sea and land breezes can be well developed in the summer. Off N Spain *Galernas* are dangerous squally NW winds which blow with little warning. Visit www.franksingleton.clara.net/biscay.html for useful Met and routeing information.

Rainfall is moderate, increasing in the SE, where thunder is more frequent. Sea fog occurs May-Oct, but is less common in winter. Japanese seaweed has been reported as a nuisance.

▶ *Tidal streams are weak offshore, but can be strong in estuaries and channels, and around headlands. The tidal stream chartlets at 9.22.3 are based on NP 265 (Admiralty tidal stream atlas for France, W Coast) which uses data from actual observations out to 15-25M offshore. The equivalent French Atlas gives more data, based on computer predictions.◀*

The general direction and rate of the surface current much depends on wind: in summer it is SE, towards the SE corner of B of Biscay, where it swings W along the N coast of Spain. In winter with W gales, the current runs E along N coast of Spain, sometimes at 3kn or more. When crossing the Bay of Biscay, allow for a likely set to the E, particularly after strong W winds.

The Continental Shelf with mean depths of 130m is a major feature of the Bay of Biscay. From 75M SW of Pointe du Raz it closes the French coast near Capbreton. AC 1104 shows depths plummeting to 4000m in the space of 20M. This steep slope allied to Atlantic swell can cause severe sea states.

9.22.6 Special notes for France: See 9.17.6.

9.22.7 PORNIC

Loire Atlantique 47°06′·54N 02°06′·59W ✹✹✹☆⚓⚓☆☆☆

CHARTS AC 2646, 2986, 2981; Imray C40; SHOM 7395, 7394; Navi 547, 549

TIDES +0515 Dover; ML 3·6; Duration 0540.

Standard Port BREST (←)

Times				Height (metres)			
High Water		Low Water		MHWS	MHWN	MLWN	MLWS
0500	1100	0500	1100	7·0	5·5	2·7	1·1
1700	2300	1700	2300				
Differences PORNIC							
−0050	+0030	−0010	−0010	−1·2	−0·9	−0·5	−0·3
POINTE DE SAINT GILDAS							
−0045	+0025	−0020	−0020	−1·4	−1·1	−0·6	−0·3

SHELTER Very good in the large marina.

NAVIGATION WPT 47°05′·98N 02°08′·86W, 073°/1·6M to hbr ent, is in the W sector of Pte de Noëveillard lt ho. A SPM buoy, FlY 2·5s, at 47°06′·17N 02°07′·40W marks the seaward end of an outfall.

Beware Banc de Kerouars 4-6M WSW of harbour, least depth 0·7m, on which seas break; it is unmarked, but the W sector of Pte de Noëveillard lt clears it by night. From the NW pass between this bank and the mainland. All other hazards are well marked. The S end of B de Bourgneuf is full of oyster beds, and many obstructions.

In the near appr leave the small SWM buoy to stbd, especially near LWS. Do not cut the corner round the S bkwtr head due to rocky spur. Enter between the SHM and PHM piles, on which the ☆s are mounted. A rky spur also extends SW from the head of the E jetty.

LIGHTS AND MARKS See chartlet and 9.22.4. The W sector (051°-079°) of Pte de Noëveillard lt ho lies between Notre-Dame WCM bcn twr VQ (9) 10s, and the E end of Banc de Kerouars 0·7m. The lt ho and trees behind are easily seen.

R/T Ch 09 (H24).

TELEPHONE CROSS 02·97·55·35·35; SNSM 1616/02·28·53·01·46; Auto 08·92·68·08·44; Police 02·40·82·00·29; Dr 02·40·82·01·80; Brit Consul 02·51·72·72·60.

FACILITIES Marina (2m). Access HW±4. No access LW±2 for draft >1·5m when Coeff >75, nor in SE-SW winds >F7. ⓥ berths are at S ends of pontoons P3 (1st to stbd, LOA <8m); P2 (<10m); and P1 (>12m). PA for yet larger boats. ☎ 02·40·82·05·40. 754+165 ⓥ, €2·60. www.port-pornic.com contact@ port-pornic.com P&D on small pontoon with drying ledge inshore of it, ME, El, ✗, BH (50 ton), CH, Ⓔ, SM, ▣.

CN de Pornic ☎ 02·40·82·34·72.

Old hbr dries 2·5m; access HW ±2½ via marked, lit drying channel. Locals only, C (6 ton).

Town Market Thurs & Sun am. ⌸, Gaz, R, Bar, ✉, Ⓑ, ⇌, ✈ (Nantes). Ferry: Roscoff/ St Malo.

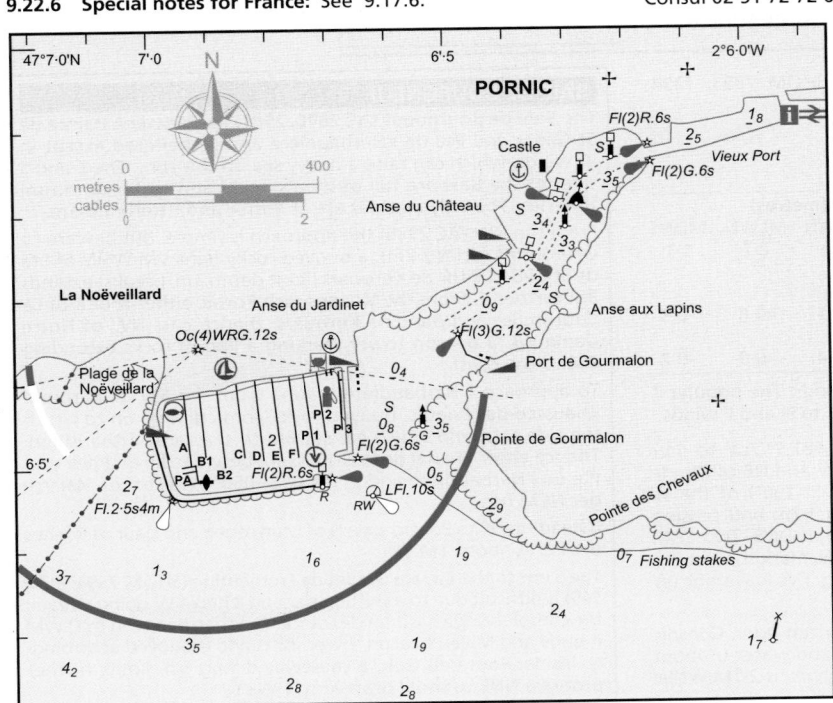

9.22.8 L'HERBAUDIÈRE Loire Atlantique 47°06'·54N 02°06'·59W ✿✿✿⚓⚓⚓✿✿

At night initial positioning is assisted by any of the 3 W sectors (see 9.22.4) of Basse de Martroger, NCM bcn twr. Ldg lts 187·5°, both hard-to-see-by-day grey masts, Q, lead over Banc de la Blanche (1·5m) approx 2M N of hbr.

R/T HM Ch 09 (HO).

TELEPHONE
Aff Mar 02·51·39·94·03;
SNSM 02·51·39·33·90;
CROSS 02·97·55·35·35;
Météo 02·40·84·80·19;
Auto 08·92·68·08·85;
⊖ 02·51·39·06·80;
Police 02·51·39·04·36;
Dr 02·51·39·05·64;
British Consul 02·51·72·72·60.

FACILITIES Marina, dredged 1·5m. Ⓥs berth on pontoon F or as directed. ☎ 02·51.39.05.05, herbaudiere.port@wanadoo.fr www.portdeplaisance-herbaudiere.com. 572 + 50 Ⓥ, €3·06. P&D, C (30 ton), Slip, ME, SM, El, Ⓔ, CH, Ⓧ, Gas, Gaz, Bar (JulAug), ✗, SC.

Town 🛒, Bar, R, ✉, Ⓑ, ⇌, ✈ (Nantes). Ferry: Roscoff/St Malo.

CHARTS AC 2646, 2986, 2981; Imray C40; SHOM 7395, 7394; Navi 547, 549

TIDES +0500 Dover; ML 3·4.

Standard Port BREST (←)

Times				Height (metres)			
High Water		Low Water		MHWS	MHWN	MLWN	MLWS
0500	1100	0500	1100	7·0	5·5	2·7	1·1
1700	2300	1700	2300				
Differences L'HERBAUDIÈRE							
−0045	+0025	−0020	−0020	−1·5	−1·1	−0·6	−0·3
FROMENTINE							
−0045	+0020	−0015	+0005	−1·8	−1·4	−0·9	−0·2

SHELTER Good in marina, except in N to E winds. The popular ⚓ off Pte des Dames lt, 4+M to the E, is exposed to N and E winds.

NAVIGATION WPT 47°02'·32N 02°17'·70W, 187·5°/7ca to hbr ent. There are rocks and banks to the SW, NW and NE of Pte de l'Herbaudière. Ldg lts and white sector (187·5°-190°) of the W jetty lt both lead into ent chan, dredged to 1·2m and passing close W of two 0·3m patches; care is needed at LWS. Two SHM buoys, both Fl G 2·5s, and a PHM buoy, Fl R 2·5s, mark the last 2ca of the chan. W bkwtr obscures vessels leaving. FVs leave hbr (W side) early morning.

LIGHTS AND MARKS Visibility in summer is often poor. Conspic daymarks are R/W radio mast 500m W of hbr and water tr about 1M SE. Ile du Pilier lt ho, with two distinctive twrs, is 2·7M WNW of hbr. Other lts/marks as chartlet and 9.22.4.

BAIE DE BOURGNEUF

The Baie de Bourgneuf (AC 2646, 2981) lies between Pointe de St Gildas and Pte de l'Herbaudière and is sheltered except in W winds, which can raise a heavy sea on the ebb. The E and S sides of the Baie are full of shoals, rocks and oyster or mussel fisheries. The only marinas are at Pornic and L'Herbaudière.

From the NW (AC 2986) the approach is simple, but beware La Couronnée (dries 2·2m), a buoyed rocky bank 2M WSW of Pte de St Gildas. Banc de Kerouars (least depth 1m; breaks) extends 3M further E. From the W approach **Pornic** either N or S of La Couronnée and Banc de Kerouars; thence pass NW of Notre Dame WCM beacon tower marking a line of rocks extending ESE to the coast.

To approach **L'Herbaudière** marina from the SW, skirt round Chaussée des Boeufs, buoyed rocks, some drying, on to which the tide sets; and which extend 6M to seaward of the island. Thence enter Chenal de la Grise (3m), between Île du Pilier and Pte de l'Herbaudière and in the 055°-060° W sector of Martroger NCM bcn.

If heading NE to Pornic, pass N of Martroger, and clear of Roches des Pères about 1M ENE.

The S ent to the Bay via Goulet de Fromentine (SHOM 7394; ECM 549) is difficult due to a shifting bar and 8 hrs of W-going stream; the conspic bridge has 24m clearance. The chan between the SWM lt buoy and Milieu beacon tower shifts and is buoyed accordingly. Inside, Route du Gois, a causeway drying 3m, limits further progress NNE to shoal draft at sp HW±1.

MINOR HARBOUR ON NE CORNER OF ÎLE DE NOIRMOUTIER
NOIRMOUTIER-EN-L'ÎLE 46°59'·33N 02°13'·17W. AC 2981; SHOM 7394. Tides as opposite. Good shelter and AB, 4M SE of

L'Herbaudière, but this FV hbr dries up to 3·6m on mud/gravel. Appr HW±1 across extensive drying rock ledges to the N and E of ent. The E'ly of 2 chans runs SSW from approx 47°00'·70N 02°11'·10W, then doglegs WNW to the ent. It is marked by 5 unlit PHM bns. An inshore chan runs S from off Pte des Dames lt ho, Oc (3) WRG12s. It is more easily followed, keeping about 400m off 5 unlit SHM bns along the shore. Both chans meet at the ent where the flood tide sets S. S jetty hd has ☆ Oc (2) R 6s. Follow the jetty on N side for about 1M to hbr. A prior recce is advised (3M overland from L'Herbaudière).

HM ☎ 02.51.39.08.39. **Quay** AB, FW, C (4 ton), ME, El, Ⓔ, ✕, CH, SM. **Town** P, D, ▣, Gaz, R, Bar, ▣, ✉, Ⓑ, ⇌ ✈ at Nantes, via ferry to Pornic and bus. Ferry: Roscoff or St Malo.

MINOR HARBOUR AT SOUTH END OF ÎLE DE NOIRMOUTIER
FROMENTINE, Vendée, 46°53'·60N 02°08'·60W. AC 2981, SHOM 7394. HW +0550 on Dover (UT); ML 3·2m; Duration 0540. Tides 9.22.8. Do not appr from Baie de Bourgneuf as there is a road causeway (Le Gois), dries 3m, from Île de Noirmoutier to the mainland.

From Fromentine SWM lt buoy, L Fl 10s, 46°53'·07N 02°11'·63W, track 072°/1·4M via Goulet de Fromentine to Tourelle Milieu, Fl (4) R 12s, R twr, and Boisvinet W bcn twr. The chan is buoyed, moved as necessary, but is very shallow, so dangerous in bad weather. At sp the ebb can reach 8kn, the flood 5kn. Do not attempt night entry. Pass under the bridge (clearance 24m, two x Iso 4s 32m 18M). ⚓ W of pier near PHM buoy Fl R 2s. At Pte du Notre Dames-de-Monts, there is a Dir lt, Oc (2) WRG 6s; see chartlet and 9.22.4 for sector details.

Facilities: Quay Slip, C (3 ton), FW, ME, El, ✕, CH.

9.22.9 PORT JOINVILLE, Île d'Yeu
Vendée 46°43'·75N 02°20'·77W

Continued overleaf

PORT JOINVILLE *continued*

CHARTS AC 2663, 2997, 3640; Imray C40; SHOM 7402, 7410; Navi 549

TIDES +0550 Dover; ML 3·1; Duration 0600.

Standard Port BREST (←—)

Times				Height (metres)			
High Water		Low Water		MHWS	MHWN	MLWN	MLWS
0500	1100	0500	1100	7·0	5·5	2·7	1·1
1700	2300	1700	2300				
Differences *PORT JOINVILLE							
−0040	+0015	−0030	−0035	−2·0	−1·5	−0·8	−0·4

*Local information gives a little more water at all states.

SHELTER Good in marina, but swell enters outer hbr in N/NE winds. Visitors' dedicated ⚓age is E of the marina as per chartlet; 4-5m on sand, but only in suitable conditions. No ⚓ in outer hbr.

NAVIGATION WPT 46°44'·30N 02°20'·13W (7ca SW of Basse Mayence NCM buoy), 219°/7ca to abeam bkwtr lt. Approach with caution in strong N-E winds; if F8 do not attempt entry. Beware Basse du Bouet (dries 0·6m) 3ca NW, La Sablaire shoal to the E and rks along the coast both sides of hbr ent. Outer chan dredged 1·2m; appr with care at LW, avoiding bank (dries 2·3m) filling the W half of outer hbr. Keep clear of ferries.

LIGHTS AND MARKS Daymarks: Very conspic water twr leads 224° to hbr. Two green-topped white twrs (front, Quai du Canada Iso G 4s; rear, Old lt ho) ≠ 203° also lead into hbr. Conspic chimney W of hbr ent. Ldg lts 219°, both QR. Other lts: 9.22.4.

R/T Marina Ch 09, 16 (HO).

TELEPHONE Aff Mar 02·51·59·42·60; ⊖ 02·51·39·06·80; CROSS

02·97·55·35·35; Météo 02·51·36·10·78; Auto 08·92·68·08·85; SNSM 02·51·58·32·01; Police 02·51·58·30·05; Ⓗ 02·51·68·30·23; Dr 02·51·59·30·00/02·51·58·30·58; Brit Consul 02·51·72·72·60.

FACILITIES Marina Very crowded in season; best to pre-book as it is the only secure hbr on Yeu. Ⓥ pontoon is at E end of A & B. ☎ 02·51·58·38·11. plaisance.iledyeu@vendee.cci.fr 330 + 170 Ⓥ, €3·23. P&D, Ⓞ, El, ME, ✗, CH, Ⓔ, Slip, C (15 ton). **CN Ile d'Yeu** ☎ 02·51·58·31·50.

The wet basin (3·7m), access HW±1½ via entry gate 02·51·58·37·01, is mainly for FVs, but possible overflow for yachts in high season; no pontoons; R/G tfc lts at the gate.

Town ⛟, Gaz, R, Bar, ⊠, Ⓑ, ⇌ (St Gilles-Croix-de-Vie), ✈ (Nantes). Helo from hbr to La Barre de Monts. Flights from airfield 2M west of hbr to Nantes and (summers only) to Les Sables d'Olonne. Ferry: Roscoff or St Malo. Ferries to Fromentine, St Gilles and Les Sables d'Olonne.

ANCHORAGES ON S COAST OF ILE D'YEU

PORT DE LA MEULE, 46°41'·68N 02°20'·75W. AC 2663; SHOM 7410. −0050 sp and −0020 nps on Brest; ML 3·0m. Small, drying fishing hbr on S side of Ile d'Yeu, only safe in settled offshore weather; untenable in S winds. Many little FVs inside hbr; best to ⚓ outside and W of the ent.

Between Pte de la Père to the W and Pte de la Tranche to the SE, appr on 023° towards W square patch on Gy □ lt tr, R top, Oc WRG 4s; at night in W sector (018°-027·5°), but night ent not advised. Within 1ca of ent beware rks, first to port, then to stbd. Few facilities: Slips, R, Bar; ⛟ 1½ miles.

ANSE DES VIEILLES, 46°41'·53N 02°18'·70W; 1M W of Pte des Corbeaux. Use SHOM 7410. Good shelter from N'lies. ⚓ clear of bathing area in 8-9m N or NE of Ours des Vieilles rks drying 3·5m.

9.22.10 ST GILLES-CROIX-DE-VIE

Vendée **46°41'·47N 01°57'·29W** (abm bkwtr hd) ❀❀❀⚓⚓⚓❀❀

CHARTS AC 2663, 2997; Imray C40; SHOM 7402; Navi 1022, 549

TIDES +0500 Dover; ML 3·2; Duration 0600.

Standard Port BREST (←)

Times				Height (metres)			
High Water		Low Water		MHWS	MHWN	MLWN	MLWS
0500	1100	0500	1100	7·0	5·5	2·7	1·1
1700	2300	1700	2300				
Differences ST GILLES-CROIX-DE-VIE							
−0030	+0015	−0030	−0030	−1·9	−1·4	−0·7	−0·4

SHELTER Good in marina and easy access except in strong SW'lies or swell when breakers form off ent. Waiting ⚓ off ent, NW or SE of ldg line in 2·0–3·5m.

NAVIGATION WPT 46°40'·94N 01°58'·02W, on the 043·7° ldg line and abeam Pilours SCM lt buoy, 043·7°/0·72M to Jetée de la Garenne lt. From W & NW, beware Rocher Pill'Hours (2·8m) and drying reefs extending 1ca SE.

Ent chan (⚓ prohib) is dredged 1·0m, but narrow and very shallow near bkwtr hds due to silting which persists despite dredging; depths may be further reduced. Keep well off the first two chan buoys which are laid outboard of drying rks; and, tfc permitting, keep slightly W of 043·7° ldg line.

Best arr/dep HW –2 to HW to avoid strong ebb, up to 6kn in ent at springs which may complicate berthing on outer ends of pontoons. Do not arr/dep LW±2 if >1·5m draft.

LIGHTS AND MARKS Daymarks are Pte de Grosse-Terre (rky hdland) with lt ho, W truncated conical tr; and two spires NE of the marina. The front ldg mark is initially hard to see against bldgs behind. Lights as per chartlet and 9.22.4.

R/T Ch 09 (season 0600-2200; out of season 0800-1200, 1400-1800LT).

TELEPHONE Aff Mar 02·51·55·10·58; ⊖ 02·51·55·10·18; CROSS 02·97·55·35·35; SNSM 02·51·55·01·19; Météo 02·51·36·10·78; Auto 08·92·68·08·85; Police 02·51·55·01·19; Dr 02·51·55·11·93; Brit Consul 02·51·72·72·60.

FACILITIES Marina nominally dredged 1·3–1·5m. Berth/raft on No. 8 ❾ pontoon or as directed. Or pick up ⚓ S of marina. ☎ 02·51·55·30·83. port.la.vie@wanadoo.fr www.semvie.com 900+100 ❾, €2·67. P&D, ME, El, CH, Gaz, SM, BH (35 ton), ✕, Ⓔ, C (2·2 ton), SHOM, Slip, ▢, R, 🍽, Bar. **CN** ☎ 02·51·54·09·31.

Town 🍽, Gaz, R, Bar, ✉, Ⓑ, ≥. A ferry runs to Ile d'Yeu. Ferry: Roscoff or St Malo.

9.22.11 LES SABLES D'OLONNE

Vendée 46°29'·42N 01°47'·54W ✱✱⚓⚓⚓✿✿

CHARTS AC 2663, 2998, 3638; Imray C40, C41; SHOM 7402, 7403, 7411; Navi 1022

TIDES +0530 Dover; ML 3·2; Duration 0640.

Standard Port BREST (←)

Times				Height (metres)			
High Water		Low Water		MHWS	MHWN	MLWN	MLWS
0500	1100	0500	1100	7·0	5·5	2·7	1·1
1700	2300	1700	2300				
Differences LES SABLES D'OLONNE							
−0030	+0015	−0035	−0035	−1·8	−1·4	−0·7	−0·4

SHELTER Very good in Quai Garnier and Port Olona marinas.

NAVIGATION WPT 46°28'·49N 01°47'·23W (abeam Nouch Sud SCM buoy, Q (6)+L Fl 15s), 032·5°/5ca to intersection with 320° ldg line; thence 7ca to the hbr ent. To the W, beware Les Barges d'Olonne, extending 1·3M W of Pte de Aiguille.

The 2 appr chans are: the SW chan with La Potence ldg lts 032·5°, which lead into SE chan on ldg line 320°. In bad weather use the SE chan. Le Noura (1·3m) and Le Nouch (0·7m) are isolated rks on shoals S of Jetée St Nicolas. Further SE, Barre Marine breaks, even in moderate weather. A buoyed wk (dries) lies off hbr ent, to E of 320° ldg line.

Access at all tides; entry is easy except in strong winds from SE to SW when apprs get rough. Sailing is prohib in the narrow dredged chan (2m). Best water initially is on the E side, then mid-chan. Caution: oncoming vessels passing very close.

LIGHTS AND MARKS See 9.22.4 and chartlet for lt details. Les Barges lt ho, 2M W of ent. L'Armandèche lt ho, conspic 6ca W of ent. SW Chan ldg lts 032·5°: both Iso 4s H24. SE Chan ldg lts 320°: front QG on E bkwtr; rear, Q on Tour d'Arundel a large grey twr. St Nicolas jetty hd, QR. Inner ldg lts 328·1°, both Iso R 4s; R/W vert stripes, hard to see by day but not essential for yachts.

R/T Marinas Ch 09 *Plaisance Quai Garnier* or *Port Olona* (0600-2400LT in season). Port Ch 12 (0800-1800).

TELEPHONE Port HM 02·51·95·11·79; Aff Mar 02·51·28·81·91; CROSS 02·97·55·35·35; Météo 02·51·36·10·78; Auto 08·92·68·08·85; ⊖ 02·51·23·58·00; Police 02·51·33·69·91; Dr 02·51·95·14·47; Ⓗ 02·51·21·06·33; Brit Consul 02·51·72·72·60.

Continued overleaf

LES SABLES D'OLONNE *continued*

FACILITIES Marina Quai Garnier 119 AB inc ⊕ on 10 pontoons (J-A); €3·00; ☎ 06·78·07·15·15. www.vendee.cci.fr Occas wash from FVs. N of pontoon J at the gate into the Commercial basin an Oc Y lt shows when a vessel is entering/leaving (HW ±2); keep clear. Improvements were made in 2008/9, but mixed reports received, so further feedback welcome. Very close to town centre, shops and many restaurants.

Port Olona Marina (1·5–3·5m). Access H24. Visitors check in at accueil/fuel pontoon port side, by Capitainerie. Distant pontoon L, at NE end, is for ⊕ and multihulls, but on request a berth may be found in pontoons A–C. ☎ 02·51·32·51·16. www.lessablesdolonne.fr portolona@wanadoo.fr 990+110 ⊕, €2·95. Slip, P & D (0800-2000), ME, El, ✕, ☐, CH, BH (28 ton), ⓔ, SHOM, SM, Divers.

Town 🛒, Gaz, R, Bar, ✉, Ⓑ, ➾, ✈. Ferry: Roscoff or St Malo.

9.22.12 BOURGENAY

Vendée 46° 26'·27N 01° 40'·70W ❀❀❀♦♦♦✿✿

CHARTS AC 2663, 2998; Imray C41; SHOM 7069, 7403; Navi 1022

TIDES +0600 Dover; ML 3·1; Duration 0640. Use Differences LES SABLES D'OLONNE (9.22.11), 5·5M NW.

SHELTER Good in marina (2m). Even in moderate weather, and especially with SW'lies, a big swell can break at the ent; care needed and/or divert to Les Sables d'Olonne.

NAVIGATION WPT 46°25'·27N 01°41'·93W (SWM buoy, L Fl 10s) 040°/1·32M to pier head. 600m ENE of WPT, beware Roches du Joanne (2·9m; dangerous in bad weather) and shoal/drying patches to E of ent, marked by unlit SHM buoy and bcn.

West pierhead is painted white. Ent chan, dredged 1·0m, makes a pronounced, blind S-bend marked by reflective chevrons; 3kn speed limit. May be less water than charted.

LIGHTS AND MARKS Ldg lts 040° QG; front W hut; rear W pylon, both with G ☐ & W border. Large white bldg is conspic near ldg lts. The Iso G 4s and Fl (2) R 6s are obsc'd until inside hbr ent.

R/T Ch 09 16 (office hrs; in season 0800-2100LT, out of season 0900-1200, 1400-1800).

TELEPHONE Aff Mar 02·51·21·81·81; CROSS 02·97·55·35·35; Auto 08·92·68·08·85; ⊖02·51·95·11·33; Dr02·51·90·62·68; ℍ02·51·21·85·85; Police 02·51·90·60·07; Brit Consul 02·51·72·72·60.

FACILITIES Marina ☎ 02·51·22·20·36. 610+50 ⊕, €2·67. ⊕ AB/raft on long pontoon (no fingers) N side of E bkwtr; or as directed. portbourgenay@wanadoo.fr P&D, ☐, Slip, CH, C (20 ton), Gaz. **YC** ☎ 08.74.50.57.57.

Town R, 🛒, Bar, ✉, Ⓑ. ➾ (Les Sables d'Olonne). ✈ (La Lande, Chateau d'Olonne). Ferry: Roscoff or St Malo.

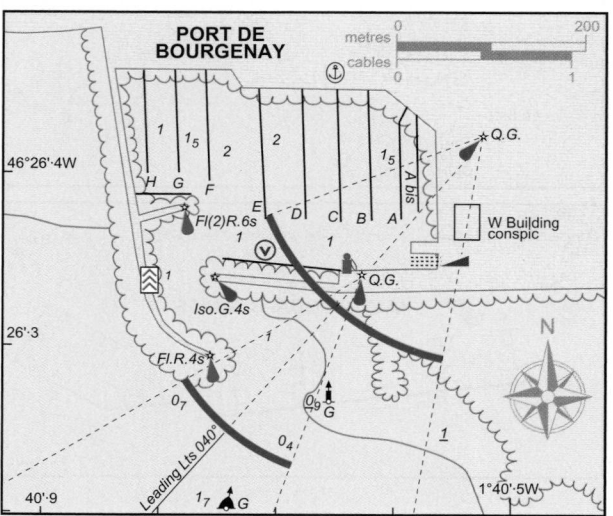

PORT DE BOURGENAY

ILE D'YEU TO PERTUIS BRETON

Île d'Yeu, 30m high, has its main lt ho near the NW end where Les Chiens Perrins lt bcn marks offliers. On the NE coast a very conspicuous water twr gives a good lead into **Port Joinville**, crowded in season. The passage along the NE of the island carries 6-7m nearer to the island. Pte des Courbeaux lt ho is at the low SE end of the island. The passage along the NE of the island carries 6-7m nearer to the island. ▶*Here the E-going stream starts at HW Brest −5¾ and the W-going at HWB −¼.*◀ The SW coast is steep-to and rky, with a tiny drying hbr at Port de la Meule (best to anch outside) and, further E, anch at Anse des Vieilles, both only tenable in settled conditions.

Les Marguerites, rky shoals, lie SSW of Goulet de Fromentine, with the part-drying reef, Pont d'Yeu (SCM buoy), extending midway between the mainland and the Île d'Yeu; here anch is prohibited in a 2·2M wide strip due to underwater cables (AC 2663, 2997, 2998).

The low-lying, wooded Côte de la Vendée continues 40M SE to Pte du Grouin-du-Cou with few dangers more than 1·5M offshore, except near Les Sables d'Olonne. 17M E of Port Joinville is **St Gilles-Croix-de-Vie**. Thence 17M SSE is **Les Sables d'Olonne**, with Les Barges drying reef (lt) extending 2·5M W of the entrance. **Bourgenay** is 6M further SE. The approaches to these secure hbrs, all with marinas, are exposed to onshore winds from SE to NW, and susceptible to swell. **Jard-sur-Mer** is a small drying harbour midway between Bourgenay and Pte du Grouin-du-Cou.

PERTUIS BRETON

Pertuis Breton is entered between Pte du Grouin-du-Cou and Pointe des Baleines (both lit) on **Île de Ré**, which is surrounded by shallows and drying areas (AC 2999). Beware rocky ledges (dry) extending 2·5M NW from Les Baleines. Pertuis Breton gives access to the harbours of **Ars-en-Ré**, **St Martin** and **La Flotte** on the N shore of Île de Ré. From St Martin to Pte de Sablanceaux (SE tip) there are extensive oyster beds.

On the mainland side, in fresh NW winds against tide a bad sea builds on the bank which extends 8M W of Pointe du Grouin du Cou. 1M SSE of the Pointe is the unmarked Roche de l'Aunis (depth 0·8m). SE of the Pte the coast is fronted by sand dunes and mussel beds, whose seaward limits are marked by unlit buoys. 8M ESE is the drying ent to Rivière Le Lay, with a bar (dries 1m), dangerous in bad weather. Thence the channel to L'Aiguillon and La Faute-sur-Mer is marked by bcns and buoys. Offshore a large mussel farm (2·8M x 1M) is marked by 4 cardinal and 2 SPM light buoys.

5M further E is the entrance to Anse de l'Aiguillon, in which there are extensive mussel beds. Here the Sèvre Niortaise estuary, after 3·5M, leads via a canal into the port of **Marans**. Further S the main route continues SE and E, passing under the fine road bridge (30m clearance) between the mainland and Île de Ré and into Rade de la Pallice; thence to La Rochelle or the Pertuis d'Antioche.

PERTUIS D'ANTIOCHE

'PA' SWM lt buoy, 22M WSW of La Rochelle, marks the western approach into Pertuis d'Antioche (AC 2999). Its low-lying shores converge eastwards to **La Rochelle, Ile d'Aix**, La Charente river and **Rochefort**. Île de Ré forms the N side, fringed by rocky ledges extending 2·5M SE from Pte de Chanchardon (lt) and nearly 1M from Pte de Chauveau (marked by lt twr and two bcns).

Île d'Oléron lies SE of Pertuis d'Antioche. At its N tip, off Pte de Chassiron (light house and signal station), reefs extend 5ca W, 1·5M N to Rocher d'Antioche (lit), and 1·5M E; here there is often a nasty sea.

Well offshore, 43M WNW of Pointe de Chassiron, The Plateau de Rochebonne is a chain of rocks on which the sea breaks dangerously. It has least depth 3·3m, is marked by 2 cardinal and 2 lateral light buoys and is enclosed by a circular 'Area to be avoided', radius 7M centred on 46°10'·00N 02°25'·60W – although the rocks only occupy the NNE half of the circle.

MINOR HARBOURS ON THE N SHORE OF PERTUIS BRETON

JARD-SUR-MER, Vendée, **46°24´·43N 01°34´·78W**. ✪✪✪⚓⚓. AC 2663, 2998 (1:10,000 inset); SHOM 7403. HW +0600 on Dover (UT); HW–0010 & ht –2·0m on Brest; ML 3·1m; Duration 0640. 2 W bcns 4ca E of hbr ent lead 036° between the drying Roches de l'Islatte and Roches de la Brunette, marked by buoys (May-Sep). Inner RW bcns at W end of hbr lead 293° into small drying unlit hbr, access HW±2, 4·5m max at HW.

Moorings inside bkwtr, inc 7 Y ⚓s. HM's office with blue roof and adjacent bldgs are conspic. HM (occas) ☎ 02·51·33·90·61; ⊖ ☎ 02·51·95·11·33. Facilities: **Jetty** FW, C (5 ton), CH, Divers.

L'AIGUILLON/LA-FAUTE-SUR-MER, Vendée, **46°19´·95N 01°18´·78W**. ✪✪✪⚓⚓ ✿✿. AC 2663, 2999; SHOM 7404. HW +0535 on Dover (UT), HW –0030, ht +0·6m on Pte de Grave (Zone –0100); ML 3·4m. The bar dries and is dangerous in bad weather; avoid in strong S or W winds. The ent is only safe in fine weather with offshore winds. A transformer at 46°18´·20N 01°14´·90W is conspic on a hill NE of Pte d'Arcay. Beware mussel beds with steel piles which cover at HW; also oyster beds.

Access HW±3, max 1·5m draft; not suitable for keel boats. Appr from Le Lay SCM buoy, 46°16´·15N 01°16´·49W, with transformer brg 033°. The drying berths at both hbrs are small enclosures made of rough timber framing; no facilities for visitors. Up-river the low bridge has 3m clearance. HM L'Aiguillon ☎ 05·51·97·06·57; HM La Faute ☎ 05·51·56·45·02; ME, CH.

MARANS, Vendée, approx **46°18´·70N 01°00´·00W**. ✪✪⚓⚓ ✿✿. AC 2663, 2999; SHOM 7404; Navi 551. Tides: see L'Aiguillon above; HW at Brault lock = HW La Rochelle + 0020. From SWM buoy, L Fl 10s, (46° 15´·33N 01°11´·50W) the buoyed chan, dries 1·0m, leads NE past Pavé jetty, Fl G 4s. In the estuary and lower chan beware mussel beds with many posts which cover at HW.

Waiting buoys below Brault bridge, which lifts at between HW±1 when the lock opens, day only. Pre-check times ☎ 05.46.01.53.77 before entering the river. The vast lock (104 x 45m wide, with sloping sides) contains a waiting pontoon and small swing bridge at the far end.

A straight 3M long canal (4·7m) leads to good shelter in non-tidal hbr, max LOA 16m. Beyond new finger pontoons raft on other yachts. HM ☎ 05.46.01.02.99, AB (40+10 Ⓥ), €0·59, FW, C (3 tons); BY, ME, ⚒ (wood), SM. **Town** 🛒, R, Bar. A new BY ☎ 05.46.01.53.33, 0·5M below Brault bridge, has BH for larger yachts.

MINOR HARBOUR ON ÎLE DE RÉ

LA FLOTTE, Charente Maritime, **46°11´·34N 01°19´·30W**. ✪✪⚓⚓⚓ ✿✿. AC 2999; SHOM 7404, 7412. HW +0535 on Dover (UT). From NW keep clear of Le Couronneau; from E, keep N of bcn off Pte des Barres. Appr on 212·5° in W sector (205°-220°) of La Flotte lt ho, W tr + G top, Fl WG 4s. Alongside it a Moiré indicator shows vert B line when on track 212·5°, or chevrons pointing in the direction to regain track. 5 waiting buoys outside; or ⚓ off in 3m, sheltered from S & W.

Outer hbr is sheltered by mole and dries 2·0m; access HW±3. 3 pontoons (6 Ⓥ berths, max LOA 10m, on mole, €2·50) in outer hbr: the hammerhead of E pontoon (3rd to stbd) is dredged 2m for deep draft yachts; pre-booking advised. Inner hbr dries 2·8m. HM ☎ 05.46.09.67.66. **Quay**, Slip, FW, Grid, P & D (cans), CH, ME, SM, 🅘. **CN de la Flotte-en-Ré** ☎ 05.46.09.97.34; (Jul-15 Sep), Bar.

ILE DE RÉ (9.22.13 and 9.22.14). *See overleaf*

9.22.13 ARS-EN-RÉ

Charente Maritime 46°12'·64N 01°30'·71W ❀❀❀❄❄❄❄❄

CHARTS AC 2998, 2999; Imray C41; SHOM 7404, 7412; Navi 1022

TIDES +0540 Dover; ML 3·7m; See 9.22.14

SHELTER ⚓ clear of channel in a pool (2m) close S of Pte du Fier. Both small marinas are sheltered, but in the confined space with strong NE'lies manoeuvring may be difficult for LOA >13m.

NAVIGATION WPT 46°14'·18N 01°23'·25W, 268°/1·8M to first SHM chan buoy, Bûcheron 1. Beware shoal ground 0·8m to 2·5m both sides of the outer appr chan. Continue to the inner, buoyed and beaconed 232·5° ldg line, where buoys are moved to mark new sand/mudbanks. Port d'Ars is at the head of a dog-legged chan in the SW corner of the bay, Le Fier d'Ars, which dries to salt pans & oyster beds. Night appr not advised without prior day visit. *HW –1 is best time to arr/dep the basins. Times vary with draft (max 1·8m), coefficient, wind and barometer.

LIGHTS AND MARKS Les Islattes NCM bcn lt twr is conspic S of the ⊕. Loix water twr is conspic S of the 268° appr chan.

Dir ✲, Oc WRG 4s (hard to see by day), covers the 268° outer appr chan. To the right of it and 3M west, Les Baleines lt ho may be seen.

Inner 232·5° ldg lts, hard to see by day, lead across Fiers d'Ars into Port d'Ars: front, W □ with R lantern; rear, B □ on W framework tr, G top. See chartlet and 9.22.4 for light details. In the town the ✠ spire, white with black top, is conspic about 330m SSW of the rear 232·5° ldg lt.

R/T Marinas Ch 09.

TELEPHONE Aff Mar 05·46·09·68·89 (at La Flotte); CROSS 02·97·55·35·35; ⊖ 05·46·41·11·73; Auto 08·92·68·08·17; Police 05·46·84·32·67; Dr 05·46·29·44·19; Brit Consul 02·51·72·72·60.

FACILITIES Marinas (depth gauges at both entrances):

- Bassin de la Criée (2m) on NW side of chan approx 600m NE of town. Access HW±2* over sill 2·5m. ♥ berths on pontoon H, first to port, fingers only. ☎ 05·46·29·25·10.
- Bassin de la Prée at head of chan. Access HW ±2* over sill 2·9m. ♥ berth/raft immediately to stbd on D pontoon in 1·8m. Rafted up to 5 deep in season; manoeuvring & berthing may be tight for LOA >13m. ☎ 05·46·29·08·52. AB outside marina against NW stone quay, drying to mud.

€3·00, Slip, C (6 ton), ME, El, ✖. portarsenre@mairie17.com

CN d'Ars-en-Ré ☎ 05·46·29·23·04 (Apr to Nov).

9.22.14 ST MARTIN-DE-RÉ

Charente Maritime 46°12'·50N 01°21'·93W ❀❀❀❄❄❄❄

CHARTS AC 2998, 2999; Imray C41; SHOM 7404, 7412; Navi 551, 1022

TIDES +0535 Dover; ML 3·7.

Standard Port POINTE DE GRAVE (→)

Times				Height (metres)			
High Water		Low Water		MHWS	MHWN	MLWN	MLWS
0000	0600	0000	0500	5·4	4·4	2·1	1·0
1200	1800	1200	1700				
Differences ST MARTIN, Ile de Ré							
+0005	–0030	–0025	–0030	+0·5	+0·3	+0·2	–0·1

SHELTER 4 W waiting buoys or ⚓ off ent which is difficult in strong NW-NE winds. These winds also render untenable a waiting pontoon (in season; only partially dredged) inside NW mole. Complete shelter in marina (depth 3m).

NAVIGATION WPT 46°14'·68N 01°20'·74W, 200°/2·3M to St Martin mole hd. From the NW, keep N and E of Banc du Rocha (1·2m) extending 2½M ENE from Pte du Grouin. From SE, pass well N of unlit NCM bcn, about ¾M NE of ent, marking Le Couronneau drying ledge in R sector (245°-281°) of St Martin lt ho. By day appr 210·5° lt ho ≠ □ ✠ tr; or 202° mole hd ≠ ✠ tr; the lt ho is far easier to see than the mole head.

LIGHTS AND MARKS Conspic daymarks: La Citadelle 3ca E of hbr ent; Lt ho, Oc (2) WR 6s, W twr/R top, on ramparts SE of ent; and the □ ✠ tr and nearby ruins. Mole hd, Fl G 2·5s, is obsc'd by Pte du Grouin when brg <124°. See chartlet and 9.22.4 for details.

R/T Ch 09 (0700-1900LT in summer).

TELEPHONE Aff Mar 05·46·09·68·89; ⊖ 05·46·09·21·78; Météo 05·46·41·29·14; Auto 08·92·68·08·17; CROSS 02·97·55·35·35; Police 05·46·09·21·17; Dr 05·46·09·20·08; Ⓗ 05·46·09·20·01; Brit Consul 02·51·72·72·60.

FACILITIES Marina gate (sill 0·8m) opens 0630-2200 in May, Jun, Sep and 0500-2300 Jul/Aug; approx HW–2 to +2½, depending on coefficient. Often very crowded so best to pre-book. Get heads key code by 1900. ♥ berth/raft W of gate or on a pre-booked finger.

☎ 05·46·09·26·69. portstmartindere@wanadoo.fr 170 + 50 ♥, €3·53; max LOA 16m. ME, Ⓔ, El, ✖, C (10 ton). P & D as shown on chartlet; 7/7, 0800-1200 & 1400-1800. D also in FV basin (1·5m); access HW –3 to +2. **YC St Martin** ☎ 05·46·09·22·07.

Town CH, SHOM, 🗑, Gaz, R, Bar, ✉, Ⓑ. La Rochelle ⇌, ✈. Ferry: Roscoff or St Malo.

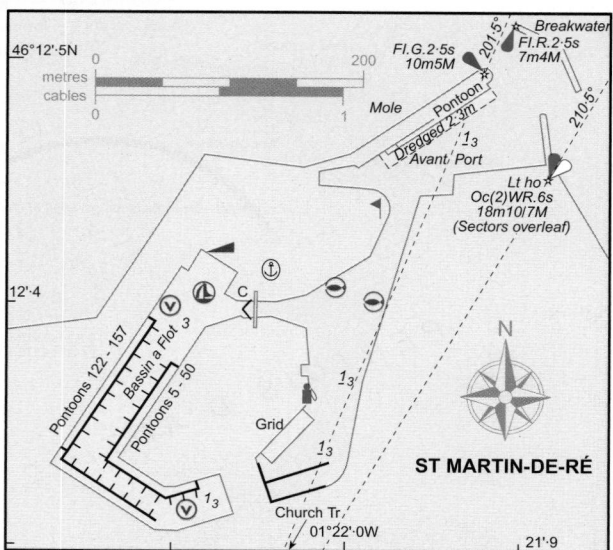

9.22.15 LA ROCHELLE

Charente Maritime 46°08′·83N 01°10′·11W ❄❄❄☆☆☆☆🏛🏛🏛

CHARTS AC 2999, 3000, 2743; Imray C41; SHOM 7404, 7413; Navi 551, 1022

TIDES +0515 Dover; ML 3·8.

Standard Port POINTE DE GRAVE (→)

Times				Height (metres)			
High Water		Low Water		MHWS	MHWN	MLWN	MLWS
0000	0600	0000	0500	5·4	4·4	2·1	1·0
1200	1800	1200	1700				
Differences LA ROCHELLE and LA PALLICE							
+0015	–0030	–0020	–0025	+0·6	+0·5	+0·3	–0·1

SHELTER Very good in Port des Minimes, excellent in Vieux Port.

NAVIGATION WPT 46°08′·41N 01°11′·40W, 059°/0·9M to abm Tour Richelieu (with tide gauge) marking a drying rky spit N of the chan. Appr from N or S of Plateau du Lavardin to pick up 059° ldg line. Pte des Minimes lt bcn (aka Bout du Monde) and a WCM lt buoy mark drying rks extending 4ca SW of the marina.

Shallow (0·5m) appr chan needs care at MLWS; speed limit 5kn. Ent to Port des Minimes, 1ca past Tour Richelieu, is marked by unlit WCM and 2 PHM buoys. Speed limit 3kn in all basins.

For Vieux Port stay on 059° ldg line in chan (35m narrow), leaving 4 small PHM buoys well to port. Caution: Vedettes run at all hours. The unlit chan is not advised at night.

LIGHTS AND MARKS See chartlet and 9.22.4. The rear 059° ldg lt, Q, is briefly obscured by Tour St Nicolas between 061°-065°, ie when approaching between La Pallice and Lavardin plateau. Tour St Nicolas, Tour de la Chaine and Tour de la Lanterne, near the Vieux Port, are conspic by day and floodlit at night.

R/T Port des Minimes Ch 09 (H24); Vieux Port Ch 09.

TELEPHONE Aff Mar 05·46·28·07·28; CROSS 02·97·55·35·35; ✉ 05·46·41·11·73; Météo 05·46·50·86·00; Auto 08·92·68·08·17; Dr 05·46·42·19·22; Police 05·46·00·50·99; 🏥 05·46·27·33·33; Brit Consul 02·51·72·72·60.

FACILITIES Port des Minimes Marina 05·46·44·41·20. 3,000 + Ⓥ on pontoon extending S from the accueil pontoon to the Capitainerie, max LOA 25m. €2·40 (pay 2 nites, 3rd free). Slip, C (10 ton), P & D (Jul/Aug 0800-2000), BH (50 ton), R, Ice, Bar, Ⓑ, ✉, Ⓛ, ME, ✕, CH, Ⓔ, El, SHOM. Water bus to the town (Bassin d'Echouage) every H, 1000-2000, except 1300; Jul/Aug H and H+30, 0900-2330, except 1300. Work to extend the marina NW'ward to the fairway, with ±1000 extra berths, began in 2009 and is due to finish by 2010. www.port larochelle.com capitainerie@portlarochelle.com.

VIEUX PORT comprises 3 separate basins, call ☎ 05·46·41·32·05, mobile ☎ 06·03·54·00·57. From S to N:

Bassin des Chalutiers (5m). Access HW –2 to +½ by prior arrangement. Entry gate ☎ 05·46·52·14·56, mob 06·16·46·60·26. Mainly used for events and by long-stay and mega-yachts.

Bassin d'Echouage (part-dredged 1·3m) is entered between the twin twrs of St Nicolas and La Chaine. It is an atmospheric tidal basin, but can be noisy at night. vieuxport@portlarochelle.com 75 + 40 Ⓥ, €2·40. First 2 pontoons for Ⓥ.

Bassin des Yachts (3m). Access HW –2 to +½ via entry gate with sill 1·2m; gate ☎ 05·46·52·14·56, mobile 06·16·46·60·26. Night ent by prior arrangement. 100 AB, €2·40; 15m max LOA. C (10 ton), BH (150 ton), SM, ME, ✕, CH.

Town 🛒, Gaz,@, R, Bar, ✉, Ⓑ, ⇌, Laleu ✈ direct flts to London, Birmingham, So'ton etc; see 9.21.2A & B. Ferry: Roscoff, St Malo.

La Pallice, 3M W, is a commercial/FV port with no yacht facilities.

Note: The adjacent bridge to Ile de Ré is lit and buoyed for big ships: N-bound between piers Nos 13 and 14; S-bound between piers Nos 10 and 11; 30m air clearance. Yachts may transit other spans, subject to air and water clearances.

ÎLE D'OLÉRON

On the NE coast of Ile d'Oléron (AC 2663, 2999, 3000) there are marinas at **Port St Denis** and **Le Douhet** at the N end; further S is a yacht basin at **Boyardville** and a fishing harbour at Le Château. All are sheltered from the prevailing W'lies.

From Pertuis d'Antioche, Grande Rade des Trousses is entered via either Passage de l'Est close to Île d'Aix or Passage de l'Ouest, which run each side of La Longe and Le Boyard, an extensive sandbank on which stands Fort Boyard with light tower. From Grande Rade, where good anch is found except in fresh NW winds, the narrow and shallow Coureau d'Oléron runs between ledges, oyster beds and constantly shifting shoals, with buoys moved to conform. About 2M SE of Le Chateau it is crossed by a bridge, clearance 18m; the bridge arch for the navigable chan is marked at road level by W □ boards, with ▲ or ■ superimposed, illuminated at night. Just N of bridge is Fort-Louvois (32m), connected to mainland by causeway. SHOM 7414 is needed.

▶S-going stream starts at HW Pte de Grave –2½; N-going at HW Pte de Grave +5, sp rates 2kn.◀ Up the Seudre River there are anchs and yacht facilities at **Marennes** and **La Tremblade**.

The W coast, from Pointe de Chassiron 15M SSE to Pte de Gatseau, is bounded by drying rks and shoals. In bad weather the sea breaks 4 or 5M offshore. La Cotinière, the only hbr, is almost exclusively a fishing port, exposed to the Atlantic.

▶Tidal streams are weak, sp rate 1kn, starting NW at HW Pte de Grave +0300 and SE at HW Pte de Grave –0505, but often overcome by current due to prevailing wind. The rate, however, increases towards Pte de Gatseau.◀

Here **Pertuis de Maumusson** separates the island from the mainland. A SWM lt buoy 'ATT Maumusson' about 3M WSW of Pointe de Gatseau marks the approach. Banc de Gatseau and Banc des Mattes, both of which dry up to 3.9m, lie N and S of the chan; the sand bar usually has a depth of about 1·5m. Depth and position vary, and unlit lateral buoys are moved accordingly. Any swell speedily forms breakers, and the chan is very dangerous then or in any onshore winds, especially on the ebb (sp rate 4kn). In calm weather with no swell, a stout craft and reliable engine, and having gained local knowledge, consider entering about HW –1; ideally following a local FV with deeper draught. But recent research suggests that local advice is likely to be emphatically negative.

9.22.16 ILE D'OLÉRON

CHARTS AC 2999, 3000; Imray C41; SHOM 7404, 7405, 7414, 7415; Navi 552

TIDES +0545 Dover; ML 3·9; Duration 0540.

Standard Port POINTE DE GRAVE (→)

Times				Height (metres)			
High Water		Low Water		MHWS	MHWN	MLWN	MLWS
0000	0600	0000	0500	5·4	4·4	2·1	1·0
1200	1800	1200	1700				
Differences ILE D'AIX							
+0015	–0040	–0025	–0030	+0·7	+0·5	+0·3	–0·1
LE CHAPUS (Bridge to mainland)							
+0015	–0040	–0015	–0025	+0·6	+0·6	+0·4	+0·2
POINTE DE GATSEAU (S tip of Île d'Oléron)							
+0005	0000	–0020	–0015	–0·1	–0·1	+0·2	+0·1

OVERVIEW Marinas at St Denis, Le Douhet and Boyardville. La Cotinière is a FV hbr prone to frequent swell; yachts only in emergency.

ST DENIS D'OLÉRON 46°02'·07N 01°22'·06W ✸✸⚓⚓✿✿

SHELTER Very good in marina. www.st-denis-oleron.com

NAVIGATION WPT 46°03'·26N 01°20'·82W, 205°/1·35M to chan ent. Appr chan (about 1·1m) is buoyed. Daymarks: SHM perch ≠ ✳ twr leads 257° to ent. By night 2 Dir lts lead 205° and 284° in sequence. Beware fishing nets with very small floats.

LIGHTS AND MARKS Pte de Chassiron, W lt ho + B bands, is conspic 1·9M WNW at N tip of island. Antioche lt bcn marks dangerous reef 2·2M NNW. Dir lt, ½M S of hbr ent, leads 205° in W sector

(204°-206°), to intercept W sector (277°-292°) of second Dir lt on N pier; or use this sector if coming from the SE.

R/T Ch 09. **TELEPHONE** Aff Mar 05·46·85·14·33; Ⓗ (12km) 05·46·47·00·86; Auto 08·92·68·08·17; CROSS 02·97·55·35·35.

FACILITIES Marina 3 W waiting buoys about 700m E of ent in 0·7–1m. Access over sill 1·5m is approx HW±2½ for 2m draft. Depth gauge on S bkwtr. port.stdenis@wanadoo.fr ☎ 05·46·47·97·97. 600+70 Ⓥ, €2·05. Ⓥ A pontoon, max depth 2·5m: N side if <10m, S side >10m LOA, dredged 2009. P&D, Slip, BH (10 ton), ♿.

LE DOUHET 46°00′·09N 01°19′·20W ❀❀❀♦♦❀❀

SHELTER Very good in marina, SE part of hbr; FVs use NW part.

NAVIGATION WPT 46°00′·65N 01°17′·38W, NCM buoy VQ, 246°/1·4M to ent. Unlit, buoyed appr chan dries about 1·6m to approx 0·35M offshore. Ent difficult in fresh NE'lies against ebb; beware swell and overfalls.

LIGHTS AND MARKS The WPT buoy is 1·4M W of another NCM lt buoy Q; the latter plus an ECM buoy, Q (3) 10s, mark a fish farm in Passage de l'Ouest (toward Boyardville). La Longe and Le Boyard, rocky/sandy shoals, are marked by an unlit WCM buoy and by Fort Boyard, conspic twr 29m, Q (9) 15s. The Capitainerie and yacht masts are the only conspic features; no lts at marina.

R/T Ch 09. port-plaisancedudouhet@wanadoo.fr

FACILITIES Marina Access HW±2 for 1·5m draft, over sill 1·8m CD. Sill is marked by tide gauge. Caution: sandbanks encroach on appr chan, reduce access times and need frequent dredging, sometimes closing hbr completely. Not advised for draft >1.5m. ☎ 05·46·76·71·13. 326 + 30 Ⓥ, €1·96; max LOA 15m. 🛁, 🛒 at St Georges d'Oléron and La Brée.

BOYARDVILLE 45°58′·25N 01°13′·83W ❀❀❀♦♦❀❀

TIDES HW +0545 on Dover (UT); use Ile d'Aix (9.22.17).

SHELTER Very good in non-tidal marina (2·2m). 3 W waiting buoys are 7ca N of bkwtr hd, or ⚓ there in 3m.

NAVIGATION WPT 45°58′·44N 01°13′·36W, La Perrotine SHM buoy, 240°/4ca between sandbanks to S bkwtr head; in the ent chan hug the S bkwtr for best water. Strong river current, 2kn @ sp. Stand on beyond the ent to avoid a bank to stbd, then turn stbd onto about 350° for the gate; allow departures to leave first.

LIGHTS AND MARKS Le Boyard, a sandy shoal, is marked by Fort Boyard, conspic twr 29m, Q (9) 15s. A fish farm in the Passage de l'Ouest is marked by an ECM buoy, Q (3) 10s and NCM buoy Q.

R/T Ch 09. **TELEPHONE** Gatemaster 05·46·47·23·71; Aff Mar 05·46·47·00·18; Auto 08·92·68·08·17; Brit Consul 05.57.22.21.10.

FACILITIES Marina Access HW±2 to drying appr chan. Waiting pontoon on NW bank is 50m SW of automatic gate which opens H24, approx HW±1½ nps and HW±3 sp. ● = ent gate is shut. Ⓥ berths/rafting against NE quay to stbd. ☎ 05·46·76·48·56. port-plaisance.boyardville@wanadoo.fr 190+60 Ⓥ, €1·96. Slip, C (14 ton), ME, EI, 🔧, CH, 🛁, P & D on SE bank ☎ 05·46·47·01·36; 0800-1230, 1400-1830. YCB ☎ 05·46·47·10·28.

LA CHARENTE RIVER

MINOR HARBOURS & ANCHORAGES

CHARTS AC 3000, 2747; SHOM 7414, 7415.

TIDES see 9.22.16/17; interpolate between Ile d'Aix and Rochefort. Ile d'Aix, HW + 0545 (UT) on Dover; ML 3.9m.

NAVIGATION See notes under 9.22.17. Fort Boyard, 1·6M WSW of Pte St Catherine's, is conspic and lit Q (9) 15s 29m; ringed by a No entry area, radius 200m. Up-river expect to meet sea-going cargo ships which have priority. Night navigation by yachts is prohibited because the banks cannot be seen.

ILE D'AIX Charente Maritime, **46°00′·60N 01°10′·45W.** Fair weather ⚓s are charted SW, S and NE of the island. On W side of island, near LW keep 3ca off the two WCM perches. St Catherine's Pt (S tip of d'Aix), Fl WR 5s, two conspic white lt twrs, R tops; 103°-R-118°-W-103° (345°). R sector (15°) covers rks off NW tip of Ile d'Oléron.

Off Pte St Catherine are 25 drying ⚓s (W with dayglo G band, €10); buoys with R band = locals only; Blu band = with HM's approval. HM 06·17·80·38·07.

Facilities: FW, ⚡, Slip, Shwrs, 🛒, R, ferry to Fouras. CNIA 05·46·84·69·89.

Continued overleaf

FOURAS 45°58'·99N 01°05'·69W (S Hbr). A small town on N bank of the Charente from which ferries cross to Ile d'Aix; good beaches and many mussel/oyster beds. The 3 drying hbrs are: South, North and Port de la Fumée. A chequered twr near S Hbr and the ch spire are both conspic.

South Harbour Access HW ±2 for max draft 1·5m. 55 + 20 Ⓥ on drying pontoons. Facilities: FW, ⍰🄳, Slip, C (3 ton), Shwrs. Lights: Fouras Sud ✠ Fl WR 4s. Ldg lts 042·5°, both ✠ Oc (2) R 6s; see 9.22.4 for details. HM 05·46·84·23·10 (1 Jun-30 Sep); other months, Mairie 05·46·84·66·09. YC: Cercle Nautique de Fouras.

North Harbour Access HW ±3; No 3 🄰 is free but dries. FW, ⍰🄳, Slip. Fouras Nord ✠ Oc (3+1) WG 12s, see 9.22.4. Mairie 05·46·84·60·11.

Port de la Fumée Mairie 05·46·84·60·11. Access H24, except near LWS. Jetty is for ferries. No 53 🄰 is free but dries, Slip. SHM bcn, ✠ QG.

PORT DES BARQUE approx **45°57'N 01°04'W**. 2 free 🄰s (afloat) Apr-Oct; shift to afloat pontoon overnight (when ferry stops running). HM 05·46·84·51·24/ 06·78·90·45·10. FW, ⍰🄳, Slip, P & D.

PORT NEUF 45°57'·02N 00°59'·80W. 2 free 🄰s (afloat); also a 64m long pontoon at the drying line. **CN Rochefortais** 05·46·87·34·61 (on site); Slip, FW.

SOUBISE 45°55'·75N 01°00'·32W, 8 berths (€6, pay at camp site) on a 48m afloat pontoon, SW bank. Beware big ship wash. Mairie 05·46·84·92·04. Facilities: Showers; village shops.

MARTROU (Echillais), 45°54'·95N 00°57'·85W approx; 10·5M from Fouras S. 2 free buoys, access HW ±3, are off the S bank and down-stream of the abutments (☆ QG) to the old dismantled road bridge, 200m East of the new viaduct (32m). 2 other free buoys are off the N bank up-stream of ☆ QR. This is a No ⚓ Area. Mairie 05·46·83·03·74. Village shops at Martrou.

9.22.17 ROCHEFORT

Charente Maritime **45°56'·55N 00°57'·29W** ❄❅⚓⚓⚓✿✿✿

CHARTS AC 3000, 2747; Imray C41; SHOM 7414, 7415; Navi 552

TIDES +0610 Dover.

Standard Port POINTE DE GRAVE (→)

Times				Height (metres)			
High Water		Low Water		MHWS	MHWN	MLWN	MLWS
0000	0600	0000	0500	5·4	4·4	2·1	1·0
1200	1800	1200	1700				
Differences ROCHEFORT							
+0035	−0010	+0125	+0030	+1·1	+0·9	+0·1	−0·2
LA CAYENNE (R. Seudre)							
+0030	−0015	−0005	−0010	+0·2	+0·2	+0·3	0·0

SHELTER Excellent in the marina, popular for over-wintering.

NAVIGATION WPT 45°59'·63N 01°09'·51W (N-abeam Les Palles NCM buoy, Q), 115°/2·1M to next ldg line 134·5°. Beware drying wreck just S of WPT. The bar, 1M S of Fouras, carries least depth 0·9m. Beware very strong currents here, except at HW or LW. Stream in river runs about 2kn (4kn in narrows), and at sp there is a small bore. Leave Fort Boyard/Ile d'Aix approx HW −3 to reach Rochefort (about 13M from the WPT) near HW while the ent gate is open. The river is navigable 3·5M on to Tonnay-Charente.

Progress is straightforward and swift on the flood. An elegant viaduct, 32m cl'nce, and 400m east an aerial transporter bridge (to which yachts should give way if it is operating) are 2M downstream of Rochefort.

LIGHTS AND MARKS Ldg lts at river mouth (for big ships): First 115°, both QR, W ☐ trs/R tops; Soumard lt ho is the conspic rear mark. Second, abeam Fontenelles ⚓: Port-des-Barques ldg lts 134·5°, both Iso G 4s, W ☐ trs; rear has a B band on its west side. 19 pairs of unlit white ldg bcns (lettered TT to AA; no S) are mainly for big ships; ditto 10 Y SPM buoys, Fl Y 4s.

R/T Marina Ch 09 (HW±1). Commercial port Ch 12.

TELEPHONE Aff Mar 05·46·84·22·67; CROSS 02·97·55·35·35; Météo 05·46·41·11·11; Auto 08.92.68.08.17; ⊖ 05·46·99·03·90; Dr 05·46·99·61·11; Police 05·46·87·26·12; Brit Consul 05·57·22·21·10.

FACILITIES Marina Entry gate opens on average HW La Rochelle −¾ to +1¼ 0530-2230 in season; pre-check with HM or website.

A 36m pontoon, 120m S of ent to Bassin 1, is short stay foc + ⍰🄳, FW. A waiting pontoon, just outside gate, dries to soft mud. Road bridge between Bassins Nos 1 and 2 lifts when gate open.

HM ☎ 05.46.83.99.96, mobile 06.86.01.64.29. port.plaisance@ ville-rochefort.fr www.ville-rochefort.fr 300+40 Ⓥ in Bassins 1 & 2, €1.98, plus holiday tax €0·20 per head/day. Berth as directed by HM. ME, El, ✖, Ⓔ, CH, C (7 & 16 ton), 🄰, ♻.
Town P & D (cans), 🛒, Gaz, R, Bar, ✉, Ⓑ, ⇌, ✈ (Rochefort, winter only, and La Rochelle). Ferry: Roscoff or St Malo.

MINOR HARBOURS ON THE RIVER SEUDRE
AC 3000; SHOM 7405, 7414 (essential). Tides, see 9.22.17. +0545 Dover; Duration Sp 0545, Np 0700. Good shelter in both hbrs.

NAVIGATION Warning: Passage through Pertuis de Maumusson (S of Ile d'Oléron) is not advised even in good weather.
The N appr applies to both hbrs. WPT 45°56'·00N 01°08'·56W, Chenal Est-Nord *i*, thence Chenal Est, Coureau d'Oléron, Viaduc d'Oléron (18m) and Ch de la Soumaille (dries initially about 0·7m). Power cables (16m cl'nce) cross Canal de Marennes and de la Tremblade. Marennes spire (88m) is conspic. Lts see 9.22.4.

FACILITIES There are ⚓s off La Cayenne village (very crowded), La Grève (½M upstream), and at the ent to Chenal de la Tremblade.
MARENNES, 45°49'·17N 01°06'·67W. Yacht basin (2·5m). Access via automatic ent gate, opens about HW±2 sp, HW±1 np. ☎ 05·46·85·02·68. Slip, M, C (6 ton), ME, CH, ✈.
Town P & D (cans), 🛒, R, Bar, ✈ (La Rochelle).

LA TREMBLADE 45°46'·07N 01°08'·17W. Small hbr (3m) in the town centre; yachts dry on soft mud against stone quay. HM ☎ 05·46·76·47·97. Ch 09. Slip, C (5 ton), ME, ✖, SM, CH.
Town Slip, P & D (cans), Gaz, 🛒, R, Bar, ✉, Ⓑ, ⇌.

POINTE DE GRAVE LAT 45°34'N LONG 1°04'W

TIMES AND HEIGHTS OF HIGH AND LOW WATERS

TIME ZONE -0100
Subtract 1 hour for UT
For French Summer Time add
ONE hour in **non-shaded areas**

Dates in **red** are SPRINGS
Dates in blue are NEAPS

YEAR 2010

S Biscay

JANUARY

Day	Time	m	Time	m	Time	m	Time	m
1 F	0508	5.6	1115	1.1	1739	5.5	2332	1.2
16 SA	0539	5.3	1148	1.4	1801	5.0	2358	1.5
2 SA	0557	5.7	1205	1.0	1828	5.5		
17 SU	0611	5.3	1220	1.4	1829	5.0		
3 SU	0021	1.1	0646	5.8	1253	0.9	1916	5.5
18 M	0030	1.5	0642	5.3	1251	1.4	1856	5.0
4 M	0108	1.1	0734	5.7	1340	1.0	2005	5.3
19 TU	0102	1.5	0712	5.2	1323	1.4	1925	4.9
5 TU	0155	1.2	0823	5.5	1427	1.2	2054	5.1
20 W	0133	1.6	0744	5.1	1354	1.5	1956	4.8
6 W	0243	1.4	0913	5.2	1515	1.4	2147	4.9
21 TH	0206	1.7	0819	4.9	1427	1.7	2031	4.6
7 TH	0334	1.6	1009	4.9	1608	1.7	2249 ◐	4.6
22 F	0243	1.8	0859	4.7	1505	1.8	2116	4.5
8 F	0431	1.8	1116	4.7	1709	2.0		
23 SA	0327	2.0	0950	4.5	1552	2.0	2218 ◐	4.3
9 SA	0000	4.5	0537	2.0	1235	4.5	1820	2.1
24 SU	0424	2.1	1058	4.4	1654	2.2	2342	4.3
10 SU	0112	4.5	0650	2.1	1352	4.5	1932	2.1
25 M	0537	2.2	1223	4.3	1812	2.2		
11 M	0216	4.6	0802	2.1	1456	4.6	2035	2.0
26 TU	0107	4.4	0657	2.1	1345	4.5	1929	2.1
12 TU	0310	4.8	0903	1.9	1546	4.7	2127	1.8
27 W	0218	4.7	0810	1.9	1453	4.8	2038	1.8
13 W	0354	4.9	0954	1.7	1626	4.8	2211	1.7
28 TH	0317	5.0	0915	1.5	1550	5.1	2138	1.5
14 TH	0431	5.1	1036	1.6	1700	4.9	2250	1.6
29 F	0409	5.4	1013	1.2	1641	5.4	2232	1.2
15 F	0506	5.2	1114	1.5	1731	5.0	2325 ●	1.5
30 SA	0458	5.7	1105	0.9	1729	5.6	2322 ○	1.0
31 SU	0546	5.9	1153	0.7	1814	5.7		

FEBRUARY

Day	Time	m	Time	m	Time	m	Time	m
1 M	0009	0.8	0631	5.9	1239	0.7	1858	5.7
16 TU	0008	1.3	0617	5.4	1226	1.2	1829	5.1
2 TU	0053	0.8	0716	5.9	1322	0.8	1941	5.5
17 W	0038	1.3	0646	5.3	1255	1.3	1856	5.1
3 W	0136	0.9	0759	5.6	1403	1.0	2022	5.2
18 TH	0107	1.3	0715	5.2	1324	1.3	1924	5.0
4 TH	0219	1.1	0841	5.3	1446	1.3	2104	4.9
19 F	0137	1.4	0747	5.0	1354	1.4	1956	4.8
5 F	0304	1.4	0926	4.9	1532	1.7	2154	4.6
20 SA	0211	1.5	0824	4.8	1430	1.6	2035	4.6
6 SA	0355	1.8	1026	4.5	1628	2.0	2306 ◐	4.4
21 SU	0252	1.7	0911	4.6	1513	1.9	2131	4.4
7 SU	0458	2.1	1157	4.2	1740	2.3		
22 M	0344	2.0	1019	4.3	1611	2.1	2257 ◐	4.3
8 M	0037	4.3	0619	2.3	1332	4.2	1905	2.4
23 TU	0458	2.2	1155	4.2	1734	2.3		
9 TU	0156	4.4	0744	2.2	1444	4.3	2018	2.2
24 W	0040	4.3	0630	2.1	1329	4.4	1906	2.2
10 W	0256	4.6	0850	2.0	1534	4.6	2112	2.0
25 TH	0200	4.7	0754	1.9	1440	4.8	2023	1.8
11 TH	0341	4.8	0939	1.8	1612	4.7	2156	1.7
26 F	0302	5.1	0902	1.5	1537	5.1	2124	1.4
12 F	0417	5.0	1019	1.6	1643	4.9	2233	1.6
27 SA	0355	5.4	0958	1.2	1626	5.4	2217	1.1
13 SA	0449	5.2	1054	1.4	1711	5.0	2306	1.4
28 SU	0443	5.7	1048	0.8	1711	5.7	2305 ○	0.8
14 SU	0520	5.3	1126	1.3	1738	5.1	2338 ●	1.3
15 M	0549	5.3	1157	1.3	1804	5.1		

MARCH

Day	Time	m	Time	m	Time	m	Time	m
1 M	0528	5.9	1134	0.6	1753	5.8	2349	0.7
16 TU	0522	5.4	1128	1.2	1735	5.2	2342	1.2
2 TU	0610	6.0	1217	0.6	1834	5.7		
17 W	0550	5.4	1158	1.2	1802	5.2		
3 W	0032	0.7	0652	5.8	1257	0.8	1912	5.6
18 TH	0013	1.2	0620	5.4	1227	1.2	1830	5.2
4 TH	0112	0.8	0731	5.6	1336	1.0	1949	5.3
19 F	0043	1.2	0650	5.3	1256	1.2	1900	5.1
5 F	0152	1.0	0808	5.2	1415	1.3	2025	5.0
20 SA	0114	1.3	0723	5.1	1328	1.4	1933	5.0
6 SA	0234	1.4	0847	4.8	1457	1.7	2107	4.7
21 SU	0148	1.4	0802	4.9	1405	1.6	2014	4.8
7 SU	0321	1.8	0939	4.4	1549	2.1	2209 ◐	4.4
22 M	0230	1.6	0852	4.6	1449	1.8	2112	4.5
8 M	0421	2.2	1112	4.1	1659	2.4	2351	4.2
23 TU	0323	1.9	1004	4.4	1549	2.1	2238 ◐	4.4
9 TU	0544	2.4	1302	4.1	1831	2.5		
24 W	0438	2.1	1143	4.3	1715	2.2		
10 W	0123	4.3	0716	2.3	1417	4.2	1950	2.3
25 TH	0019	4.4	0613	2.0	1313	4.5	1848	2.1
11 TH	0228	4.5	0824	2.1	1507	4.5	2046	2.1
26 F	0140	4.7	0738	1.8	1422	4.8	2004	1.8
12 F	0315	4.7	0912	1.8	1544	4.7	2129	1.8
27 SA	0243	5.1	0843	1.4	1517	5.2	2104	1.4
13 SA	0351	5.0	0950	1.6	1614	4.9	2206	1.6
28 SU	0335	5.4	0937	1.1	1604	5.4	2155	1.1
14 SU	0423	5.1	1025	1.4	1642	5.1	2239	1.4
29 M	0422	5.7	1025	0.8	1648	5.6	2243	0.8
15 M	0453	5.3	1057	1.3	1709	5.2	2311 ●	1.3
30 TU	0506	5.8	1109	0.7	1728	5.7	2327 ○	0.7
31 W	0547	5.8	1151	0.8	1807	5.7		

APRIL

Day	Time	m	Time	m	Time	m	Time	m
1 TH	0008	0.7	0627	5.7	1230	0.9	1844	5.5
16 F	0557	5.3	1200	1.2	1810	5.3		
2 F	0048	0.9	0705	5.4	1308	1.1	1920	5.3
17 SA	0021	1.2	0632	5.3	1234	1.2	1844	5.2
3 SA	0127	1.1	0741	5.1	1346	1.4	1956	5.0
18 SU	0057	1.2	0711	5.1	1310	1.4	1924	5.1
4 SU	0207	1.4	0819	4.7	1426	1.8	2036	4.7
19 M	0135	1.3	0755	4.9	1350	1.6	2011	4.9
5 M	0251	1.8	0907	4.4	1515	2.1	2132	4.4
20 TU	0220	1.5	0851	4.7	1440	1.8	2113	4.7
6 TU	0346	2.1	1025	4.1	1619	2.4	2257 ◐	4.2
21 W	0317	1.8	1004	4.5	1543	2.0	2231 ◐	4.6
7 W	0501	2.3	1211	4.0	1744	2.5		
22 TH	0431	1.9	1132	4.4	1704	2.1	2359	4.6
8 TH	0031	4.2	0628	2.3	1329	4.2	1904	2.4
23 F	0556	1.9	1252	4.6	1826	2.0		
9 F	0141	4.4	0739	2.2	1423	4.4	2004	2.2
24 SA	0115	4.8	0714	1.7	1357	4.9	1937	1.7
10 SA	0233	4.6	0830	1.9	1503	4.6	2050	1.9
25 SU	0218	5.1	0817	1.4	1452	5.1	2038	1.4
11 SU	0313	4.8	0911	1.7	1536	4.8	2129	1.7
26 M	0312	5.3	0911	1.2	1539	5.3	2130	1.1
12 M	0348	5.0	0947	1.5	1607	5.0	2205	1.5
27 TU	0400	5.5	0959	1.0	1622	5.5	2219	1.0
13 TU	0421	5.2	1022	1.3	1637	5.2	2240	1.3
28 W	0444	5.5	1044	0.9	1703	5.5	2304 ○	0.9
14 W	0452	5.3	1055	1.2	1706	5.2	2314 ●	1.2
29 TH	0526	5.5	1125	1.0	1742	5.5	2346	0.9
15 TH	0524	5.3	1128	1.2	1737	5.3	2348	1.2
30 F	0606	5.4	1205	1.1	1820	5.4		

Chart Datum is 2·83 metres below IGN Datum. HAT is 6·1 metres above Chart Datum; see 4.5.

POINTE DE GRAVE LAT 45°34'N LONG 1°04'W
TIMES AND HEIGHTS OF HIGH AND LOW WATERS

TIME ZONE -0100
Subtract 1 hour for UT
For French Summer Time add ONE hour in **non-shaded areas**

Dates in red are **SPRINGS**
Dates in blue are **NEAPS**

YEAR 2010

MAY

Day	Time	m	Day	Time	m
1 SA	0025 / 0644 / 1242 / 1858	1.0 / 5.2 / 1.3 / 5.3	16 SU	0005 / 0622 / 1218 / 1838	1.1 / 5.2 / 1.3 / 5.3
2 SU	0104 / 0721 / 1320 / 1936	1.2 / 5.0 / 1.5 / 5.1	17 M	0047 / 0706 / 1300 / 1923	1.2 / 5.1 / 1.3 / 5.2
3 M	0144 / 0800 / 1401 / 2017	1.5 / 4.7 / 1.7 / 4.8	18 TU	0131 / 0756 / 1346 / 2015	1.3 / 5.0 / 1.5 / 5.1
4 TU	0226 / 0845 / 1446 / 2106	1.7 / 4.4 / 2.0 / 4.6	19 W	0219 / 0852 / 1439 / 2113	1.4 / 4.8 / 1.6 / 4.9
5 W	0316 / 0944 / 1542 / 2209	2.0 / 4.2 / 2.2 / 4.4	20 TH	0316 / 0958 / 1540 / 2221	1.5 / 4.7 / 1.8 / 4.8
6 TH	0416 / 1102 / 1650 / 2324	2.2 / 4.1 / 2.4 / 4.3	21 F	0421 / 1112 / 1649 / 2335	1.7 / 4.6 / 1.8 / 4.8
7 F	0527 / 1221 / 1802	2.2 / 4.2 / 2.4	22 SA	0532 / 1224 / 1800	1.7 / 4.7 / 1.8
8 SA	0037 / 0636 / 1323 / 1906	4.4 / 2.2 / 4.3 / 2.2	23 SU	0046 / 0643 / 1328 / 1908	4.8 / 1.6 / 4.8 / 1.7
9 SU	0137 / 0734 / 1412 / 1959	4.5 / 2.0 / 4.5 / 2.0	24 M	0152 / 0748 / 1425 / 2010	4.9 / 1.5 / 5.0 / 1.5
10 M	0226 / 0822 / 1452 / 2045	4.7 / 1.8 / 4.7 / 1.8	25 TU	0250 / 0844 / 1515 / 2106	5.0 / 1.4 / 5.1 / 1.3
11 TU	0308 / 0904 / 1529 / 2127	4.9 / 1.6 / 4.9 / 1.6	26 W	0341 / 0935 / 1600 / 2157	5.1 / 1.3 / 5.2 / 1.2
12 W	0346 / 0944 / 1604 / 2207	5.0 / 1.5 / 5.1 / 1.4	27 TH	0427 / 1021 / 1642 / 2244	5.2 / 1.2 / 5.3 / 1.2
13 TH	0424 / 1022 / 1640 / 2246	5.2 / 1.3 / 5.2 / 1.3	28 F	0510 / 1104 / 1723 / 2327	5.2 / 1.2 / 5.3 / 1.2
14 F	0501 / 1100 / 1717 / 2326	5.2 / 1.2 / 5.3 / 1.2	29 SA	0550 / 1144 / 1802	5.1 / 1.3 / 5.3
15 SA	0541 / 1139 / 1756	5.3 / 1.2 / 5.3	30 SU	0008 / 0628 / 1222 / 1841	1.2 / 5.0 / 1.4 / 5.2
			31 M	0046 / 0705 / 1300 / 1918	1.3 / 4.9 / 1.5 / 5.1

JUNE

Day	Time	m	Day	Time	m
1 TU	0124 / 0741 / 1338 / 1957	1.4 / 4.7 / 1.7 / 4.9	16 W	0127 / 0752 / 1343 / 2011	1.0 / 5.2 / 1.3 / 5.3
2 W	0204 / 0819 / 1420 / 2039	1.6 / 4.6 / 1.8 / 4.7	17 TH	0215 / 0844 / 1433 / 2104	1.1 / 5.0 / 1.4 / 5.2
3 TH	0246 / 0904 / 1506 / 2127	1.8 / 4.4 / 2.0 / 4.6	18 F	0306 / 0941 / 1527 / 2202	1.3 / 4.8 / 1.5 / 5.0
4 F	0334 / 0958 / 1558 / 2223	1.9 / 4.3 / 2.1 / 4.4	19 SA	0402 / 1043 / 1626 / 2306	1.4 / 4.7 / 1.6 / 4.8
5 SA	0428 / 1102 / 1658 / 2326	2.0 / 4.2 / 2.2 / 4.4	20 SU	0503 / 1151 / 1730	1.6 / 4.6 / 1.7
6 SU	0529 / 1210 / 1802	2.1 / 4.2 / 2.2	21 M	0016 / 0610 / 1258 / 1839	4.7 / 1.7 / 4.7 / 1.7
7 M	0031 / 0631 / 1311 / 1902	4.4 / 2.0 / 4.3 / 2.1	22 TU	0127 / 0718 / 1401 / 1946	4.7 / 1.7 / 4.7 / 1.7
8 TU	0130 / 0728 / 1404 / 1957	4.5 / 1.9 / 4.5 / 1.9	23 W	0232 / 0821 / 1456 / 2047	4.7 / 1.6 / 4.9 / 1.6
9 W	0224 / 0820 / 1451 / 2048	4.6 / 1.8 / 4.7 / 1.7	24 TH	0328 / 0916 / 1545 / 2142	4.8 / 1.5 / 5.0 / 1.5
10 TH	0312 / 0907 / 1534 / 2135	4.8 / 1.6 / 4.9 / 1.5	25 F	0417 / 1005 / 1628 / 2230	4.8 / 1.4 / 5.1 / 1.4
11 F	0358 / 0953 / 1617 / 2222	5.0 / 1.4 / 5.1 / 1.3	26 SA	0459 / 1049 / 1709 / 2314	4.9 / 1.4 / 5.2 / 1.3
12 SA	0443 / 1038 / 1701 / 2308	5.1 / 1.2 / 5.3 / 1.2	27 SU	0537 / 1129 / 1747 / 2353	4.9 / 1.4 / 5.2 / 1.3
13 SU	0529 / 1124 / 1746 / 2354	5.2 / 1.2 / 5.4 / 1.1	28 M	0612 / 1206 / 1823	4.9 / 1.4 / 5.2
14 M	0615 / 1209 / 1832	5.3 / 1.2 / 5.4	29 TU	0029 / 0645 / 1241 / 1857	1.3 / 4.9 / 1.4 / 5.1
15 TU	0040 / 0703 / 1255 / 1921	1.0 / 5.2 / 1.2 / 5.4	30 W	0104 / 0716 / 1316 / 1931	1.4 / 4.8 / 1.5 / 5.0

JULY

Day	Time	m	Day	Time	m
1 TH	0139 / 0748 / 1352 / 2007	1.4 / 4.7 / 1.6 / 4.9	16 F	0201 / 0825 / 1417 / 2044	0.9 / 5.2 / 1.1 / 5.3
2 F	0215 / 0824 / 1429 / 2046	1.5 / 4.6 / 1.7 / 4.7	17 SA	0246 / 0914 / 1505 / 2135	1.1 / 5.0 / 1.3 / 5.0
3 SA	0252 / 0904 / 1511 / 2131	1.7 / 4.4 / 1.9 / 4.5	18 SU	0335 / 1008 / 1558 / 2235	1.4 / 4.7 / 1.5 / 4.7
4 SU	0334 / 0953 / 1559 / 2223	1.8 / 4.3 / 2.0 / 4.4	19 M	0431 / 1114 / 1700 / 2347	1.6 / 4.5 / 1.7 / 4.5
5 M	0424 / 1055 / 1657 / 2325	2.0 / 4.2 / 2.1 / 4.3	20 TU	0537 / 1229 / 1812	1.9 / 4.5 / 1.9
6 TU	0524 / 1206 / 1805	2.0 / 4.2 / 2.1	21 W	0108 / 0652 / 1342 / 1928	4.4 / 2.0 / 4.5 / 1.9
7 W	0034 / 0632 / 1316 / 1911	4.3 / 2.0 / 4.3 / 2.0	22 TH	0222 / 0803 / 1444 / 2035	4.4 / 1.9 / 4.6 / 1.8
8 TH	0142 / 0736 / 1416 / 2012	4.4 / 1.9 / 4.6 / 1.8	23 F	0322 / 0903 / 1535 / 2132	4.5 / 1.7 / 4.8 / 1.6
9 F	0243 / 0835 / 1510 / 2109	4.6 / 1.7 / 4.8 / 1.6	24 SA	0409 / 0952 / 1617 / 2218	4.7 / 1.6 / 5.0 / 1.5
10 SA	0338 / 0929 / 1559 / 2202	4.8 / 1.5 / 5.1 / 1.3	25 SU	0447 / 1035 / 1654 / 2259	4.8 / 1.5 / 5.1 / 1.4
11 SU	0429 / 1021 / 1647 / 2253	5.1 / 1.3 / 5.3 / 1.1	26 M	0520 / 1113 / 1728 / 2335	4.9 / 1.4 / 5.2 / 1.3
12 M	0517 / 1111 / 1735 / 2343	5.3 / 1.1 / 5.5 / 0.9	27 TU	0550 / 1147 / 1800	4.9 / 1.3 / 5.2
13 TU	0605 / 1159 / 1822	5.4 / 1.0 / 5.6	28 W	0008 / 0619 / 1219 / 1831	1.3 / 4.9 / 1.3 / 5.2
14 W	0030 / 0652 / 1245 / 1909	0.8 / 5.4 / 0.9 / 5.6	29 TH	0040 / 0646 / 1250 / 1901	1.3 / 4.9 / 1.4 / 5.1
15 TH	0116 / 0738 / 1331 / 1956	0.8 / 5.3 / 1.0 / 5.5	30 F	0110 / 0714 / 1322 / 1932	1.3 / 4.8 / 1.4 / 5.0
			31 SA	0141 / 0744 / 1353 / 2005	1.4 / 4.7 / 1.5 / 4.8

AUGUST

Day	Time	m	Day	Time	m
1 SU	0212 / 0817 / 1428 / 2043	1.5 / 4.6 / 1.7 / 4.6	16 M	0306 / 0931 / 1529 / 2202	1.4 / 4.7 / 1.5 / 4.5
2 M	0247 / 0857 / 1508 / 2129	1.7 / 4.4 / 1.8 / 4.4	17 TU	0358 / 1035 / 1629 / 2322	1.8 / 4.4 / 1.9 / 4.2
3 TU	0329 / 0951 / 1559 / 2230	1.8 / 4.2 / 2.0 / 4.2	18 W	0504 / 1202 / 1747	2.1 / 4.3 / 2.1
4 W	0424 / 1106 / 1709 / 2347	2.0 / 4.1 / 2.2 / 4.2	19 TH	0055 / 0627 / 1327 / 1913	4.1 / 2.2 / 4.4 / 2.1
5 TH	0538 / 1233 / 1830	2.1 / 4.2 / 2.1	20 F	0214 / 0747 / 1433 / 2025	4.3 / 2.1 / 4.5 / 1.9
6 F	0110 / 0658 / 1348 / 1944	4.3 / 2.1 / 4.5 / 1.9	21 SA	0311 / 0847 / 1522 / 2117	4.4 / 1.9 / 4.8 / 1.7
7 SA	0221 / 0809 / 1449 / 2048	4.5 / 1.8 / 4.8 / 1.6	22 SU	0353 / 0935 / 1601 / 2200	4.6 / 1.7 / 4.9 / 1.5
8 SU	0321 / 0910 / 1542 / 2145	4.8 / 1.6 / 5.1 / 1.2	23 M	0426 / 1015 / 1633 / 2237	4.8 / 1.5 / 5.1 / 1.4
9 M	0413 / 1005 / 1631 / 2237	5.1 / 1.2 / 5.5 / 0.9	24 TU	0454 / 1050 / 1703 / 2310	4.9 / 1.4 / 5.2 / 1.3
10 TU	0501 / 1055 / 1718 / 2326	5.4 / 0.9 / 5.7 / 0.7	25 W	0521 / 1123 / 1732 / 2341	5.0 / 1.3 / 5.2 / 1.2
11 W	0547 / 1143 / 1804	5.5 / 0.8 / 5.8	26 TH	0547 / 1153 / 1801	5.0 / 1.3 / 5.2
12 TH	0012 / 0632 / 1228 / 1849	0.6 / 5.6 / 0.7 / 5.8	27 F	0010 / 0613 / 1223 / 1829	1.2 / 5.0 / 1.3 / 5.2
13 F	0056 / 0715 / 1311 / 1934	0.7 / 5.5 / 0.8 / 5.6	28 SA	0039 / 0639 / 1251 / 1857	1.3 / 5.0 / 1.3 / 5.1
14 SA	0139 / 0758 / 1354 / 2018	0.8 / 5.3 / 0.9 / 5.3	29 SU	0107 / 0707 / 1321 / 1928	1.3 / 4.9 / 1.4 / 4.9
15 SU	0221 / 0842 / 1439 / 2105	1.1 / 5.1 / 1.2 / 4.9	30 M	0136 / 0737 / 1352 / 2002	1.4 / 4.7 / 1.6 / 4.7
			31 TU	0209 / 0813 / 1430 / 2046	1.6 / 4.6 / 1.7 / 4.5

Chart Datum is 2·83 metres below IGN Datum. HAT is 6·1 metres above Chart Datum; see 4.5.

TIME ZONE -0100
Subtract 1 hour for UT
For French Summer Time add ONE hour in **non-shaded areas**

POINTE DE GRAVE   LAT 45°34'N   LONG 1°04'W

TIMES AND HEIGHTS OF HIGH AND LOW WATERS

Dates in **red** are **SPRINGS**
Dates in blue are NEAPS

YEAR 2010

S Biscay

SEPTEMBER

Day	Time	m	Day	Time	m
1 W	0249 / 0904 / 1518 / ☽ 2150	1.8 / 4.4 / 2.0 / 4.2	16 TH	0432 / 1131 / 1719	2.3 / 4.3 / 2.3
2 TH	0342 / 1023 / 1625 / 2317	2.0 / 4.2 / 2.2 / 4.1	17 F	0036 / 0559 / 1302 / 1851	4.1 / 2.4 / 4.3 / 2.3
3 F	0457 / 1201 / 1757	2.2 / 4.2 / 2.2	18 SA	0152 / 0722 / 1409 / 2002	4.2 / 2.3 / 4.5 / 2.1
4 SA	0049 / 0629 / 1325 / 1921	4.3 / 2.2 / 4.5 / 1.9	19 SU	0246 / 0822 / 1457 / 2052	4.4 / 2.0 / 4.7 / 1.8
5 SU	0203 / 0747 / 1429 / 2029	4.6 / 1.9 / 4.9 / 1.6	20 M	0324 / 0908 / 1534 / 2132	4.6 / 1.8 / 4.9 / 1.6
6 M	0302 / 0850 / 1523 / 2126	4.9 / 1.5 / 5.3 / 1.2	21 TU	0354 / 0947 / 1605 / 2206	4.8 / 1.6 / 5.1 / 1.4
7 TU	0353 / 0945 / 1611 / 2217	5.2 / 1.1 / 5.6 / 0.9	22 W	0422 / 1021 / 1634 / 2239	4.9 / 1.4 / 5.2 / 1.3
8 W	0440 / 1034 / 1657 / ● 2304	5.5 / 0.9 / 5.8 / 0.7	23 TH	0448 / 1053 / 1702 / ○ 2309	5.0 / 1.3 / 5.3 / 1.3
9 TH	0524 / 1121 / 1742 / 2349	5.6 / 0.7 / 5.9 / 0.6	24 F	0515 / 1124 / 1731 / 2339	5.1 / 1.3 / 5.3 / 1.3
10 F	0606 / 1205 / 1825	5.7 / 0.6 / 5.8	25 SA	0541 / 1154 / 1759	5.1 / 1.3 / 5.2
11 SA	0031 / 0648 / 1248 / 1908	0.7 / 5.6 / 0.7 / 5.6	26 SU	0008 / 0608 / 1224 / 1828	1.3 / 5.1 / 1.3 / 5.1
12 SU	0112 / 0728 / 1330 / 1950	0.9 / 5.3 / 1.0 / 5.2	27 M	0036 / 0637 / 1254 / 1859	1.4 / 5.0 / 1.4 / 5.0
13 M	0153 / 0809 / 1413 / 2035	1.2 / 5.1 / 1.3 / 4.8	28 TU	0107 / 0709 / 1327 / 1935	1.5 / 4.9 / 1.5 / 4.8
14 TU	0236 / 0855 / 1500 / 2130	1.6 / 4.4 / 1.7 / 4.4	29 W	0142 / 0747 / 1405 / 2022	1.6 / 4.7 / 1.7 / 4.5
15 W	0326 / 0958 / 1559 / ☽ 2257	2.0 / 4.4 / 2.1 / 4.1	30 TH	0224 / 0841 / 1454 / 2130	1.8 / 4.5 / 2.0 / 4.3

OCTOBER

Day	Time	m	Day	Time	m
1 F	0318 / 1001 / 1602 / ☽ 2302	2.1 / 4.3 / 2.2 / 4.2	16 SA	0518 / 1216 / 1808	2.5 / 4.3 / 2.4
2 SA	0434 / 1139 / 1734	2.2 / 4.4 / 2.2	17 SU	0110 / 0639 / 1326 / 1922	4.2 / 2.4 / 4.5 / 2.2
3 SU	0033 / 0606 / 1302 / 1900	4.4 / 2.2 / 4.6 / 1.9	18 M	0204 / 0742 / 1417 / 2013	4.4 / 2.2 / 4.7 / 2.0
4 M	0143 / 0723 / 1407 / 2007	4.7 / 1.9 / 5.0 / 1.6	19 TU	0244 / 0830 / 1457 / 2053	4.6 / 2.0 / 4.9 / 1.8
5 TU	0240 / 0826 / 1501 / 2103	5.0 / 1.5 / 5.4 / 1.2	20 W	0317 / 0911 / 1531 / 2130	4.8 / 1.8 / 5.0 / 1.6
6 W	0330 / 0921 / 1550 / 2153	5.3 / 1.2 / 5.6 / 0.9	21 TH	0347 / 0947 / 1602 / 2203	5.0 / 1.6 / 5.2 / 1.5
7 TH	0415 / 1011 / 1635 / ● 2239	5.5 / 0.9 / 5.8 / 0.8	22 F	0416 / 1022 / 1633 / 2236	5.1 / 1.5 / 5.2 / 1.4
8 F	0458 / 1058 / 1719 / 2323	5.7 / 0.8 / 5.8 / 0.8	23 SA	0445 / 1055 / 1704 / ○ 2308	5.2 / 1.4 / 5.3 / 1.4
9 SA	0540 / 1142 / 1802	5.7 / 0.8 / 5.7	24 SU	0515 / 1128 / 1735 / 2340	5.2 / 1.3 / 5.3 / 1.4
10 SU	0005 / 0621 / 1225 / 1844	0.9 / 5.6 / 0.9 / 5.5	25 M	0546 / 1202 / 1808	5.2 / 1.4 / 5.2
11 M	0046 / 0701 / 1306 / 1926	1.1 / 5.4 / 1.1 / 5.1	26 TU	0013 / 0619 / 1235 / 1844	1.4 / 5.1 / 1.4 / 5.0
12 TU	0126 / 0742 / 1348 / 2009	1.4 / 5.1 / 1.4 / 4.8	27 W	0047 / 0656 / 1312 / 1925	1.5 / 5.0 / 1.5 / 4.8
13 W	0208 / 0827 / 1434 / 2102	1.7 / 4.8 / 1.8 / 4.4	28 TH	0126 / 0741 / 1354 / 2017	1.7 / 4.9 / 1.7 / 4.6
14 TH	0257 / 0924 / 1529 / ☽ 2221	2.1 / 4.5 / 2.1 / 4.1	29 F	0211 / 0838 / 1445 / 2125	1.9 / 4.7 / 1.9 / 4.4
15 F	0359 / 1047 / 1642 / 2355	2.4 / 4.3 / 2.4 / 4.1	30 SA	0308 / 0952 / 1552 / ☽ 2250	2.1 / 4.6 / 2.0 / 4.4
			31 SU	0422 / 1117 / 1714	2.2 / 4.6 / 2.0

NOVEMBER

Day	Time	m	Day	Time	m
1 M	0012 / 0543 / 1236 / 1833	4.5 / 2.1 / 4.8 / 1.9	16 TU	0106 / 0646 / 1323 / 1918	4.3 / 2.4 / 4.5 / 2.2
2 TU	0119 / 0656 / 1341 / 1940	4.8 / 1.9 / 5.1 / 1.6	17 W	0155 / 0742 / 1412 / 2007	4.5 / 2.2 / 4.7 / 2.0
3 W	0215 / 0759 / 1438 / 2037	5.1 / 1.6 / 5.3 / 1.3	18 TH	0236 / 0829 / 1454 / 2049	4.7 / 2.0 / 4.9 / 1.8
4 TH	0305 / 0856 / 1529 / 2128	5.3 / 1.3 / 5.5 / 1.1	19 F	0312 / 0911 / 1531 / 2128	4.9 / 1.8 / 5.0 / 1.7
5 F	0351 / 0948 / 1616 / 2215	5.5 / 1.1 / 5.6 / 1.0	20 SA	0347 / 0950 / 1607 / 2205	5.0 / 1.6 / 5.1 / 1.5
6 SA	0435 / 1036 / 1701 / ● 2300	5.6 / 1.0 / 5.6 / 1.0	21 SU	0421 / 1029 / 1643 / ○ 2242	5.2 / 1.5 / 5.2 / 1.5
7 SU	0518 / 1122 / 1744 / 2342	5.6 / 1.0 / 5.5 / 1.1	22 M	0456 / 1107 / 1719 / 2319	5.3 / 1.4 / 5.2 / 1.4
8 M	0600 / 1205 / 1826	5.5 / 1.1 / 5.3	23 TU	0533 / 1146 / 1758 / 2357	5.3 / 1.4 / 5.2 / 1.4
9 TU	0023 / 0641 / 1246 / 1907	1.3 / 5.4 / 1.3 / 5.1	24 W	0612 / 1225 / 1839	5.3 / 1.4 / 5.1
10 W	0103 / 0722 / 1328 / 1949	1.5 / 5.2 / 1.5 / 4.8	25 TH	0037 / 0655 / 1306 / 1925	1.5 / 5.2 / 1.4 / 5.0
11 TH	0145 / 0805 / 1412 / 2034	1.8 / 4.9 / 1.8 / 4.5	26 F	0120 / 0742 / 1351 / 2017	1.6 / 5.1 / 1.5 / 4.8
12 F	0231 / 0853 / 1501 / 2132	2.0 / 4.7 / 2.0 / 4.3	27 SA	0208 / 0836 / 1442 / 2118	1.7 / 5.0 / 1.7 / 4.7
13 SA	0324 / 0955 / 1559 / ◑ 2247	2.3 / 4.5 / 2.3 / 4.2	28 SU	0303 / 0940 / 1542 / ◑ 2229	1.9 / 4.9 / 1.8 / 4.6
14 SU	0428 / 1109 / 1708	2.4 / 4.4 / 2.4	29 M	0407 / 1052 / 1650 / 2343	1.9 / 4.8 / 1.9 / 4.7
15 M	0003 / 0539 / 1222 / 1818	4.2 / 2.5 / 4.4 / 2.3	30 TU	0516 / 1206 / 1802	1.9 / 4.9 / 1.8

DECEMBER

Day	Time	m	Day	Time	m
1 W	0051 / 0626 / 1316 / 1910	4.8 / 1.8 / 5.0 / 1.7	16 TH	0058 / 0644 / 1319 / 1913	4.3 / 2.3 / 4.5 / 2.2
2 TH	0151 / 0733 / 1418 / 2012	5.0 / 1.7 / 5.1 / 1.6	17 F	0153 / 0743 / 1414 / 2007	4.5 / 2.2 / 4.6 / 2.1
3 F	0244 / 0834 / 1514 / 2107	5.1 / 1.5 / 5.2 / 1.4	18 SA	0239 / 0834 / 1502 / 2054	4.7 / 2.0 / 4.8 / 1.9
4 SA	0334 / 0930 / 1604 / 2156	5.3 / 1.4 / 5.3 / 1.3	19 SU	0322 / 0921 / 1545 / 2138	4.9 / 1.8 / 5.0 / 1.7
5 SU	0419 / 1020 / 1650 / ● 2243	5.4 / 1.3 / 5.3 / 1.3	20 M	0402 / 1006 / 1627 / 2222	5.1 / 1.6 / 5.1 / 1.5
6 M	0503 / 1107 / 1733 / 2326	5.5 / 1.2 / 5.3 / 1.3	21 TU	0443 / 1051 / 1709 / ○ 2305	5.3 / 1.4 / 5.2 / 1.4
7 TU	0545 / 1151 / 1813	5.5 / 1.3 / 5.2	22 W	0524 / 1135 / 1752 / 2348	5.4 / 1.3 / 5.3 / 1.3
8 W	0006 / 0626 / 1232 / 1852	1.4 / 5.4 / 1.3 / 5.1	23 TH	0607 / 1219 / 1835	5.5 / 1.2 / 5.3
9 TH	0046 / 0704 / 1311 / 1928	1.5 / 5.3 / 1.5 / 4.9	24 F	0032 / 0651 / 1303 / 1921	1.3 / 5.5 / 1.2 / 5.3
10 F	0125 / 0742 / 1350 / 2004	1.7 / 5.1 / 1.7 / 4.7	25 SA	0116 / 0738 / 1347 / 2009	1.3 / 5.5 / 1.2 / 5.1
11 SA	0205 / 0822 / 1431 / 2045	1.9 / 4.9 / 1.8 / 4.5	26 SU	0203 / 0827 / 1434 / 2102	1.4 / 5.3 / 1.4 / 5.0
12 SU	0249 / 0907 / 1516 / 2135	2.0 / 4.7 / 2.0 / 4.4	27 M	0252 / 0921 / 1525 / 2201	1.5 / 5.1 / 1.5 / 4.8
13 M	0338 / 1001 / 1607 / ◑ 2239	2.2 / 4.5 / 2.2 / 4.2	28 TU	0347 / 1023 / 1623 / ◑ 2309	1.7 / 4.9 / 1.7 / 4.7
14 TU	0435 / 1105 / 1707 / 2351	2.3 / 4.4 / 2.3 / 4.2	29 W	0448 / 1135 / 1729	1.8 / 4.8 / 1.9
15 W	0539 / 1215 / 1812	2.4 / 4.4 / 2.3	30 TH	0021 / 0557 / 1252 / 1841	4.7 / 1.9 / 4.7 / 1.9
			31 F	0129 / 0710 / 1404 / 1951	4.8 / 1.9 / 4.8 / 1.9

Chart Datum is 2·83 metres below IGN Datum. HAT is 6·1 metres above Chart Datum; see 4.5.

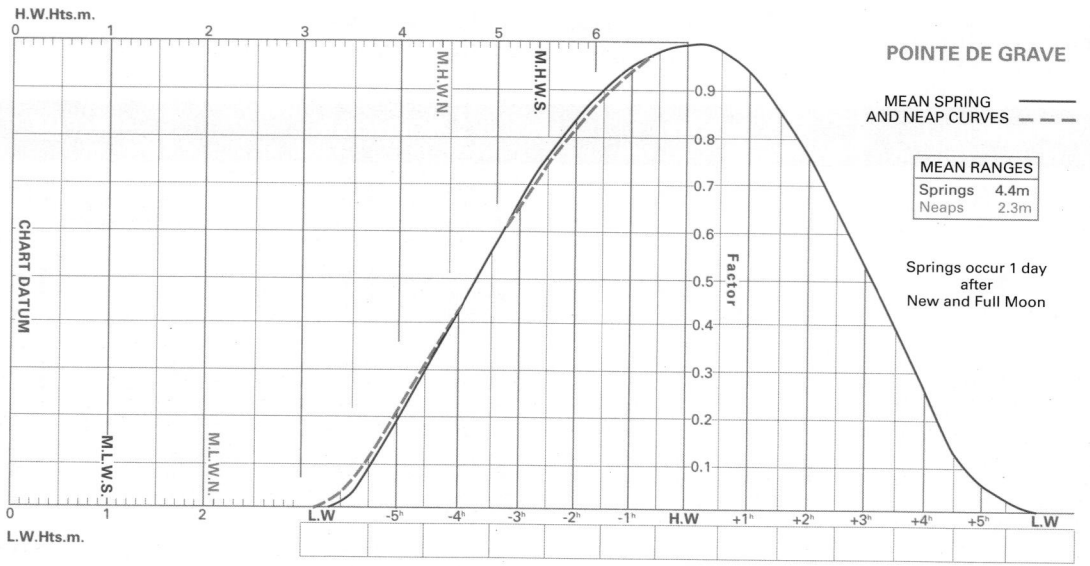

9.22.18 THE GIRONDE ESTUARY

CHARTS AC 3057/8, 3068; SHOM 7425/6/7: all these are essential.

TIDES
Standard Port POINTE DE GRAVE (⟵)

Times				Height (metres)			
High Water		Low Water		MHWS	MHWN	MLWN	MLWS
0000	0600	0000	0500	5·4	4·4	2·1	1·0
1200	1800	1200	1700				
Differences CORDOUAN							
−0010	−0010	−0025	−0015	−0·5	−0·4	−0·1	−0·2
RICHARD							
+0020	+0020	+0035	+0030	−0·1	−0·1	−0·4	−0·5
LAMENA							
+0035	+0045	+0125	+0100	+0·2	+0·1	−0·5	−0·3
LA REUILLE							
+0135	+0145	+0305	+0230	−0·2	−0·3	−1·3	−0·7
LE MARQUIS							
+0145	+0150	+0320	+0245	−0·3	−0·4	−1·5	−0·9
LIBOURNE (La Dordogne)							
+0250	+0305	+0540	+0525	−0·7	−0·9	−2·0	−0·4

In the Gironde and the R Dordogne the sp flood reaches 3kn and the ebb 4kn, continuing for 1½hrs after predicted LW time. In the Garonne the sp flood starts with a small bore and runs at 3kn, ebb reaches 5kn. *The Annuaire des Marées Estuaire de la Gironde*, downloadable from www.bordeaux-port.fr, is full of useful tidal information for the Gironde and also Arcachon.

▶*Off Terre-Nègre lt the SE-going stream begins at HW −0500 (sp 1·5kn), and the NW-going at HW+0130 (sp 2·5kn).*◀

Between Pte de Grave and Bordeaux the height of water at Verdon, Richard, Lamena, Pauillac, Fort Médoc, Bec d'Ambes, Le Marquis and Bordeaux (see 9.22.22 chartlet) is automatically broadcast H24 on Ch 17 every 5 mins. From these read-outs it is possible to deduce, for example, when the flood starts to make.

SHELTER See 9.22.19 to 9.22.24.

NAVIGATION La Gironde is a substantial waterway. The mouth of the estuary is 9M wide between Pte de la Coubre and Pte de Grave and narrows from 6M wide off Royan to 2.5M at Pauillac. The Garonne and Dordogne flow into the Gironde at Bec d'Ambes (45°02′N). Be alert for ferries and shipping.

The outer apprs can be dangerous due to Atlantic swell, very strong tidal streams and currents, extensive shoals and shifting sandbanks. Swell, strong W'lies and an ebb tide raise dangerous, breaking seas some 5m high; in such conditions do not attempt entry. Nevertheless at the right time and in the right weather both entrances are straightforward by day and night.

The two approach channels are:

- **Grande Passe de l'Ouest**. WPT BXA SWM buoy, Iso 4s, 45°37′·53N 01°28′·68W, 081·5°/4·8M to Nos 1 & 2 buoys. The chan is deep and well marked/lit. Keep well clear of La Mauvaise bank and the drying Banc de la Coubre and Plateau de Cordouan.
  Leave No 1 buoy at LW on La Palmyre 081° ldg lts (Front, Iso 4s; rear, Q), only valid to Nos 4/5 buoys. Thereafter follow the buoys (do not cut corners) to Nos 8/9 buoys. Thence use W sector (097°- 104°) of Terre-Nègre lt. Enter the river on astern transit 327° of Terre-Nègre lt with La Palmyre, FR. Pass between Nos 12 & 13a buoys into R Gironde.

- **Passe du Sud** is a useful short cut if arriving from the S. It carries approx 5m through shoals, but Platin de Grave, N of G4 and G6 buoys, has only 1·4m or less. Not advised in poor vis or heavy swell. The six lateral buoys are unlit. WPT 45°30′·00N 01°15′·33W, abeam 'G' unlit SWM buoy, 063°/5·5M (063° ldg lts: Front, QG; rear, Oc WRG 4s) to G3 buoy. Here pick up the 041° ldg lts (both QR) to G4 buoy where alter stbd to G6 buoy passing S of Platin de Grave. Thence track direct to Royan or via No 13b buoy to Port-Médoc.

LIGHTS AND MARKS See chartlet and 9.22.4 for details of lights mentioned above. **Other major lts in estuary**: La Coubre lt ho, W twr, top third R. 2M NNE is a R/W CG twr. Cordouan lt ho is an elegant, W sculpted twr on a drying plateau in mid-estuary.

R/T *Bordeaux Port Control* Ch 12 (H24) provides radar surveillance from BXA buoy to Bordeaux, plus MSI on request.

9.22.19 ROYAN

Charente Maritime 45°37′·12N 01°01′·50W ✿✿✪♦♦♦✿✿✿

CHARTS AC 3057, 3058; Imray C42; SHOM 7426, 7425; Navi 553, 554.

TIDES +0530 Dover; ML 3·2; Duration Sp 0615, Np 0655.

Standard Port POINTE DE GRAVE (⟵)

Times				Height (metres)			
High Water		Low Water		MHWS	MHWN	MLWN	MLWS
0000	0600	0000	0500	5·4	4·4	2·1	1·0
1200	1800	1200	1700				
Differences ROYAN							
0000	−0005	0000	0000	−0·2	−0·1	0·0	0·0

SHELTER Good in marina. Access difficult in strong W/NW'lies.

NAVIGATION WPT 45°36′·56N 01°01′·96W (R1 SHM buoy, Iso G 4s; marks wk (3m) 260m E), 030°/0·64M to hbr ent. The Gironde apprs can be dangerous; see 9.22.5 and 9.22.18 for details; allow about 2 hrs from Pte de la Coubre to Royan. Beware Banc de St Georges (0·4m), 1M S of WPT. Off hbr ent, there is an eddy, running S at about 1kn on the flood and 3kn on the ebb. Caution: FVs and fast ferries.

LIGHTS AND MARKS Cathedral spire is conspic modern 'spike'. See chartlet and 9.22.4 for lt details.

R/T Ch 09 16 (season 0800-2000; otherwise 0900-1800LT).

TELEPHONE Aff Mar 05·46·39·26·30; CROSS 02·97·55·35·35; ⊜ 05·46·23·10·24; Auto 08.92.68.08.17; Météo 05·56·34·20·11; Ⓗ 05·46·38·01·77; Police 05·46·38·34·22; Brit Consul 05·57·22·21·10.

FACILITIES Marina Best access HW±3; care needed near LW sp. Ent chan, least depth 0·1m, silts but is regularly dredged to at least 0·8m; it narrows markedly off New Jetty hd. Accueil pontoon is dead ahead, W of the ent.

☎ 05·46·38·72·22; HM hrs, Jul/Aug 7/7 0800-2000. www.port-royan.com port.royan@wanadoo.fr 900 + 100 Ⓥ, €2·12. Slip, P & D (☎ 05·46·38·53·39. 0830-1200, 1430-1830, 7/7 in season), de-mast C (1·5 ton), BH (26 ton), ME, El, ✖, Grid, Ice, CH, Ⓔ, SM, SHOM. **Base Nautique (YC)** ☎ 05·46·05·44·13.

Town ☷, R, Bar, Gaz, ☺, ✉, Ⓑ, ⇌, ✈ (Bordeaux). Ferry: Roscoff or St Malo; fast ferries to Port Bloc.

9.22.20 PORT BLOC

Gironde **45°34'·12N 01°03'·72W** ✿✿♦♦♦✿

CHARTS AC 3057, 3058; Imray C42; Navi 553, 554; SHOM 7426, 7425.

TIDES Use predictions for Pointe de Grave (←); 4ca N. Caution strong tidal streams.

SHELTER Good, but primarily a ferry harbour (caution: wash) and Service station for Bordeaux port authority and pilot boats, plus some fishing vessels. Swell enters in bad weather.

NAVIGATION WPT 45°34'·66N 01°02'·98W (13b SHM buoy, QG), 224°/7ca to harbour ent. Ent is 30m wide and is effectively fully used by ferries which have priority. Pauillac 25M; Bordeaux 53M.

LIGHTS AND MARKS Pte de Grave lt ho, W □ twr, B corners and top. Woods behind the hbr. See chartlet and 9.22.4.

R/T Radar Verdon Ch **12** 11 (H24).

TELEPHONE Aff Mar 05·56·09·60·23; CROSS 02·97·55·35·35; Météo 05·56·34·20·11; Auto 08.92.68.08.17; ⊖ 05·56·09·65·14; Police 05·56·09·80·29; Dr 05·56·09·60·37; Brit Consul 05·57·22·21·10.

FACILITIES Space for yachts is limited; possible AB on pontoons W side of the hbr dredged 3m. Berthing for visitors requires prior approval from AUPB (Port Bloc Users' Association). Royan (3·4M NNE) or Port-Médoc 7ca S are far better options.

HM ☎ 05·56·09·63·91; **AUPB** ☎ 05.56.09.72.64. **Moto YC de la Pte de Grave** ☎ 05.56.09.84.02, D, C (10 ton), ME, El, ✕, CH.

Town P, Gaz, 🛒, R, ✉ & Ⓑ (Verdon), ⇌, ✈ Bordeaux. Fast local ferries to Royan every 45 mins.

9.22.21 PORT MÉDOC

Gironde **45°33'·40N 01°03'·46W** ✿✿♦♦♦✿✿

CHARTS AC 3057, 3058; SHOM 7426, 7425; Imray C42; Navi 553, 554.

TIDES Pointe de Grave is a Standard Port whose predictions (←) apply to Port Bloc and Port-Médoc; no tidal constraints.

SHELTER Good, in depths 2-3m. Shoreside infrastructure work continues. It is approx 1M S of Pte de Grave and 0·7ca S of Port Bloc on the W bank of the R Gironde.

NAVIGATION WPT 45°34'·66N 01°02'·97W (13b SHM buoy, QG), about 195°/1·3M to hbr ent, dredged 3m. Access H24 at all states of the tide. Le Verdon oil jetty, about 8ca SE, is dangerous and in a prohib area; no landing. Caution strong tidal streams.

LIGHTS AND MARKS Marina's N and S bkwtr heads are lit QG and QR respectively. Pte de Grave lt ho (see 9.22.4) is 8ca NNW of the marina ent. Just N of the lt ho a 51m high red radio mast is marked by R lts. At Le Verdon oil tanks are conspic. The oil jetty is marked by: Fl (3) G 12s at its N end and Fl G 2·5s at the S end. 9 ca further S is a Dir lt 171·5°, Iso WRG 4s.

R/T Marina Ch 09. *Radar de Bordeaux* (VTS) Ch 12 (H24).

TELEPHONE Aff Mar 05·56·09·60·23; CROSS 02·97·55·35·35; Auto 08.92.68.02.17; ⊖ 05·56·09·65·14; Police 05·56·09·80·29; Dr 05·56·09·60·37; Brit Consul 05·57·22·21·10.

FACILITIES HM ☎ 05·56·09·69·75. www.port-medoc.com capitainerie@port-medoc.com 740 + 60 🅥, max LOA 25m, €2·42. The accueil pontoon is at the N end of marina. D & P, BH (70 ton), ME, El, ✕, CH, Bar, R, some shops, bike/car hire.

Le Verdon (1·3km S): 🛒, R, ✉, Ⓑ. ⇌, ✈ (Bordeaux). Fast ferry Port Bloc to Royan every 45 mins €3·00; info ☎ 05·56·73·37·73.

Soulac-sur-Mer is 7·5km SW.

9.22.22 THE RIVER GIRONDE

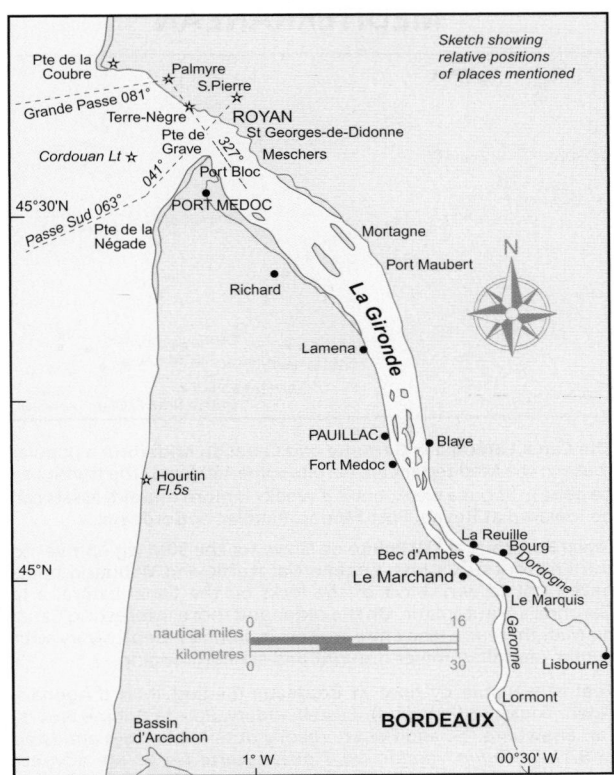

Sketch showing relative positions of places mentioned

MINOR HARBOURS ON THE GIRONDE

MESCHERS-sur-GIRONDE, Charente Maritime, **45°33'·20N 00°56'·63W**. AC 3058, 3057 (with 1:10,000 inset); SHOM 7426; Navi 554. Tides as for ROYAN. Talmont church is conspic 1·8M up-river. Appr close to Pte de Meschers between PHM and SHM unlit perches. Access HW–3 to HW via narrow, drying chan perched to port and mudbank close to stbd. Ldg marks/lts 349·5° are 2 W posts with fixed white lts (private); just before the front ldg mark turn port 330° to enter hbr.

To stbd drying marina basin has access HW±3, pontoons A-C. Dead ahead an automatic entry gate gives access HW±2½ over sill 2m above CD to a wet basin in 2·5m on pontoons D-F; H24 in season, otherwise 0730-1930; waiting pontoons. Good shelter in all weathers. Both basins are small; max LOA 9m.

HM (M. Jean-Luc Rat, available around HW) ☎ 05.46.02.56.89; Auto 05.36.68.08.17. **Marinas** 125 AB in drying basin, 123 in wet basin: 18 ♥ €1·80. **Town** P & D (cans), R, Bar, 🛒.

MORTAGNE-sur-GIRONDE, Charente Maritime, **45°28'·21N 00°48'·81W**. AC 3058, 3057; SHOM 7426. Tides, use RICHARD differences (9.22.18). Good shelter in marina on E bank of river, 14M from Royan/40M from Bordeaux (near the 75km mark). Leave the main Gironde chan at No 18 PHM buoy, Fl (2) R 6s; track 094°/4·6M to Mortagne access chan.

Ent is marked by a WCM buoy, VQ (9) 10s, an unlit PHM buoy, PHM and SHM perches and the ruins of a bcn twr. Buoyed chan, 2·5m at half tide, trends 063°/0·9M across drying mudbanks to entry gate which opens HW–1 to HW (give 48 hrs notice out of season). VHF Ch 09. HM ☎ 05.46.90.63.15. Facilities: **Marina** (130+20 ♥ in 4·5m) €1·65, Slip, ME, BY, BH (10 ton), 🛒, Ice; Fuel, Aff Mar, ⊖, and SNSM at Royan; Auto 05.36.68.08.17.

BOURG-sur-GIRONDE, (it's actually on the Dordogne) **45°02'·28N 00°33'·61W**. AC 3068, 3069; SHOM 7030. Tides, use LA REUILLE (9.22.18). 18 AB + 2 ♥ <12m LOA, no rafting, on the W'ly of 2 long pontoons (parallel to shore); in strong W'lies very choppy against the ebb. HM ☎ 05.57.68.40.06. FW, AC, C (9T), Slip, BY.

9.22.23 PAUILLAC

Gironde, 45°11'·83N 00°44'·59W ❄❄🌊🌊🌸🌸🌸.

CHARTS AC 3058, 3068 (Inset D; 1: 20,000); SHOM 7427.

TIDES HW +0620 on Dover (UT); ML 3·0m.

Standard Port POINTE DE GRAVE (◄—)

Times				Height (metres)			
High Water		Low Water		MHWS	MHWN	MLWN	MLWS
0000	0600	0000	0500	5·4	4·4	2·1	1·0
1200	1800	1200	1700				
Differences PAUILLAC							
+0100	+0100	+0205	+0135	+0·1	0·0	–1·0	–0·5
BORDEAUX							
+0200	+0225	+0405	+0330	–0·1	–0·2	–1·7	–1·0

SHELTER Excellent in marina. ⚓ possible close E of marina; or 500m further S clear of a 250m wide No-anch area (due to underwater cables).

NAVIGATION WPT 45°12'·45N 00°44'·27W [No. 43 SHM buoy, Fl (2) G 6s], 196°/0·65M to hbr ent. Access HW±5 (depths 2·0-4·5m); at LW hug the E side of offset entrance, due to silting. Do NOT arrive on the ebb; only manoeuvre at slack water, approx HW Pte de Grave –3 and +2; see tidal diamond 'C' (45°13'·80N, 2M N). Beware current in the river on ent/dep. Keep clear of the oil refinery quays, 1·2-1·7M north.

LIGHTS AND MARKS See chartlet and 9.22.4 for lt details. The church twr, NW of the marina ent is conspic. So too is a large bottle of Pauillac marking the W side of the ent.

R/T Ch 09 (0800–1200 & 1400-1800LT).

TELEPHONE Aff Mar 05.56.59.01.58; CROSS 02.97.55.35.35; ⊖ 05.56.59.04.01; Météo 05.36.68.08.33; Brit Consul 05.57.22.21.10.

FACILITIES Marina ☎ 05.56.59.12.16. 130+20 ♥, €2·45; max LOA 15m. ♥ berth on W end of A or B pontoons or any hammerhead; see HM for vacant berth. Slip, ME, El, 🔧, C (15 ton), de-masting C (1 ton), CH, D (0700-2000).

CN de Pauillac ☎ 05.56.59.12.58.

Town: R, Bar, 🛒, ⊚, ✉, Ⓑ. mtvp@wanadoo.fr www.pauillac-medoc.com

9.22.24 BORDEAUX

Gironde, **44°52′·79N 00°32′·18W** (Pont d'Aquitaine) ✿✿✿✿🌧🌧🌸🌸🌸

CHARTS AC 3068, 3069; SHOM 7030.

TIDES HW +0715 on Dover (UT); ML 2·4m. Slack water is at approx HW Pte de Grave –2 and +2½; see tidal ◊s C and D.

SHELTER Good. Both Lormont and the Halte Nautique may be exposed to wash and flotsam. Do not berth on city quays.

NAVIGATION The chan is well marked/lit. Beware big ships, strong currents (up to 5kn if river in spate) and possibly large bits of flotsam. At No 62 WCM buoy (close NW of Bec d'Ambès) keep to stbd into the R. Garonne, with 12M to run to Bordeaux. De-mast before the Pont de Pierre (4·2m).

LIGHTS AND MARKS Pont d'Aquitaine (51m) is an unmistakable suspension bridge, gateway to Bordeaux. Lts as on chartlet.

R/T *Bordeaux Traffic* Ch 12. Bègles marina Ch 09.

TELEPHONE Bordeaux Port (PAB) ☎ 05·56·90·59·57; postoffice@bordeaux-port.fr www.bordeaux-port.fr; Aff Mar 05·56·00·83·00; ⊜ 05·57·81·03·60; Brit Consul 05.57.22.21.10.

FACILITIES from seaward: **Lormont YC** ☎ 05·56·31·50·10 is almost under Pont d'Aquitaine on E bank: limited space on S pontoon; de-masting crane; Clubhouse. FVs/ferries use the N pontoon. (The marina on the opposite bank is private, no ⓥ).
Bassin No 2, (1·5M S of bridge). Pre-arrange with HM ☎ mob 06·13·79·10·75, ☎ 05·56·90·59·57 or Ch 12. Enter lock HW –1; exit HW –½. A waiting pontoon is just S of the lock; 05·56·90·59·85 for latest info. No ⧇ or security. Facilities await development. Slip, C (mobile, 5 ton masting), ME, El, ✕, CH, Ⓔ, SHOM.
Halte Nautique, E bank close SE of Pont de Pierre. ⧇.
Bègles marina (Port Garonne), W bank, Km66. 4km S of Pont de Pierre. ☎ 05·56·85·76·04. 60+ 20 ⓥ at N end of the wave-break.

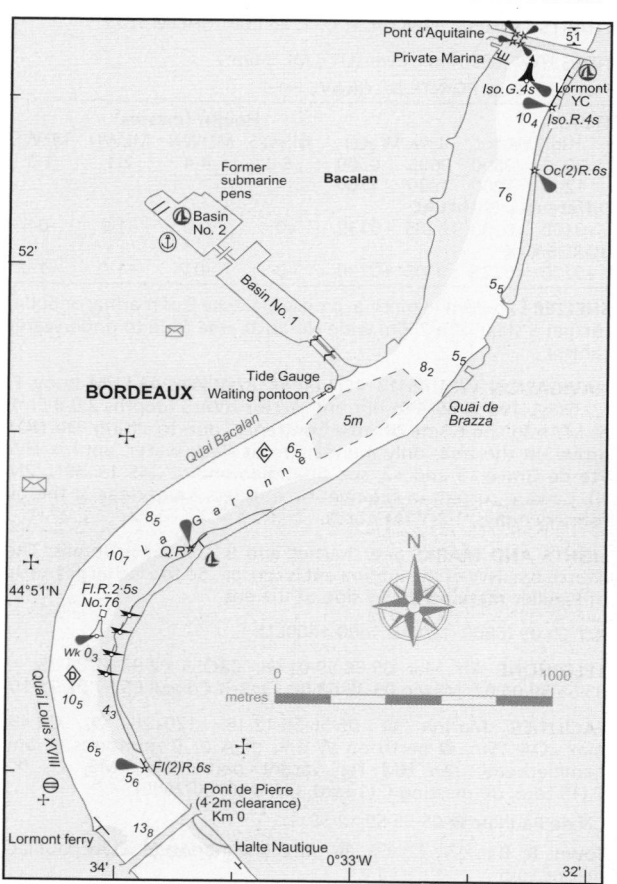

9.22.25 CANALS TO THE MEDITERRANEAN

The **Canal Latéral à la Garonne** and **Canal du Midi** form a popular route to the Mediterranean, despite some 120 locks. The transit can be done in about a week, but 2-3 weeks is more relaxed. Masts can be lowered at Royan, Port-Médoc, Pauillac or Bordeaux.

Leave Bordeaux at LW Pointe de Grave for the 30M leg up-river to the first lock at Castets. Commercial traffic and W-bound boats have right of way. Most of the locks on the Canal Latéral à la Garonne are automatic. On the older and more interesting Canal du Midi there are many hire cruisers in summer. Depths vary with winter rainfall, summer drought and silting/dredging.

Fuel is available by hose at Bordeaux (Bègles), Mas d'Agenais, Agen, Toulouse (Port Sud), Castelnaudary, Port la Robine and by can elsewhere. ▨ and FW are readily obtainable. Tolls are listed in 9.17.6. *Guide Vagnon No 7* or *Navicarte No 11* are advised. Further info from: Service de la Navigation de Toulouse, 8 Port St Etienne, 31079 Toulouse Cedex, ☎ 05·61·80·07·18.

SUMMARY Canal	From	To	Km/ Locks	Min Depth(m)	Min Ht(m)
Canal Latéral à la Garonne	Castets	Toulouse	193/53	2·2	3·5
Canal du Midi	Toulouse	Sète	240/65	1·6	3·0
Canal de la Nouvelle	Salleles	Port la Nouvelle	37/14	1·5	3·1

Dimensions: Max LOA 30m; draft 1·5m (varies with season); max beam 5·5m. Headroom of 3·3m is to centre of arch; over a width of 4m, clearance is about 2·4m.

Speed limits: 8km/hr (about 4½kn), but 3km/hr under bridges and over aqueducts.

S Biscay

POINTE DE GRAVE TO ARCACHON

(AC 2664, 1102) From Pte de la Négade to Capbreton, the coast is a featureless stretch of 107M broken only by the estuary which gives access to Arcachon. It is bordered by sand dunes and pine trees, and is often a lee shore with no shelter from W winds. 5M offshore a current usually sets N at about 0·5kn, particularly with a S wind; in winter this may be stronger after W winds. Within 1M of the coast there may be a S'ly counter-current.

A missile range, operated by Centre d'Essais des Landes, lies between Pointe de la Négade and Capbreton and extends up to 45M offshore. For details of boundaries, activity and sources of information, see below. Make every effort to obtain the latest information about range activity.

9.22.26   LANDES RANGE

Centre d'Essais des Landes (CEL: Landes Test Centre) firing range extends from Pointe de la Negade to Capbreton and up to 45M offshore. It is bounded by 45°27'N 01°13'W (inshore N), 45°12'N 02°00'W (NW corner), 44°00'N 02°25'W (SW corner) and 43°41'N 01°30'W (inshore S). The inshore boundary lies parallel to and about 3M off the coast. See chartlet, AC 1104 & 2664. CEL Range Control is at 44°26'N 01°15'W.

Sectors: The range is in two blocks, N and S of an 8M wide, 39M long, safe access corridor to Arcachon, orientated E-W from ATT-ARC buoy to the range boundary at 44°34'·05N 02°12'·91W.
Within the two blocks those sectors which are active, or are planned to be, are referred to by their Lat/Long coordinates in all radio broadcasts, telephone recordings and enquiries.

Range activity: Sectors may be active Mon-Fri from 0800 LT, but are usually inactive Sat/Sun, at night and in August. **However there can be exceptions to the above.** Navigation may be prohibited in active sectors inside the 12M territorial limit. Beyond 12M it *'is strongly discouraged due to the particularly dangerous tests carried out'*. A No-entry box (1·6M x 1M) is centred on 44°22'·70N 01°25'·50W, 13M SSW of ATT-ARC buoy. **You must check range activity before entering the range.**

Information on Range activity is available from:
- ☎ +33 (0)5.58.82.22.42 & 43 recorded info H24, inc daily activity.
- Semaphore stations at Chassiron (Île d'Oléron), Pte de Grave, Cap Ferret, Messanges and Socoa (St Jean-de-Luz): on request Ch 16 for advance notice of activity. See also 7.21.3 for ☎ Nos. Some English spoken.
- CROSS Etel broadcasts 0703, 0715, 0733, 0745 and 0803LT.
- CEL, after announcement on Ch 16, broadcasts Ch 06, 10: Mon-Thu, 0815 & 1615, and Fri 0815 & 1030; all LT.
- CEL on request Ch 06, Mon-Thu 0800-1700 (1100 Fri).
- CEL ☎ +33 (0)5.58.78.18.00; same hrs as previous line.
- Local NMs (AvUrNavs) at HMs' offices and Affaires Maritimes in Arcachon.

Options:
- Keep clear to seaward of the range. For example, a rhumb line track 200°/173M from PA buoy (22M W of La Rochelle) to Bilbao clears the range by at least 6M.

Subject to notified range activity and monitoring Ch 16:
- Navigate within the 3M wide coastal strip.
- Cross the range when it is usually inactive, ie at night, at weekends and in August.

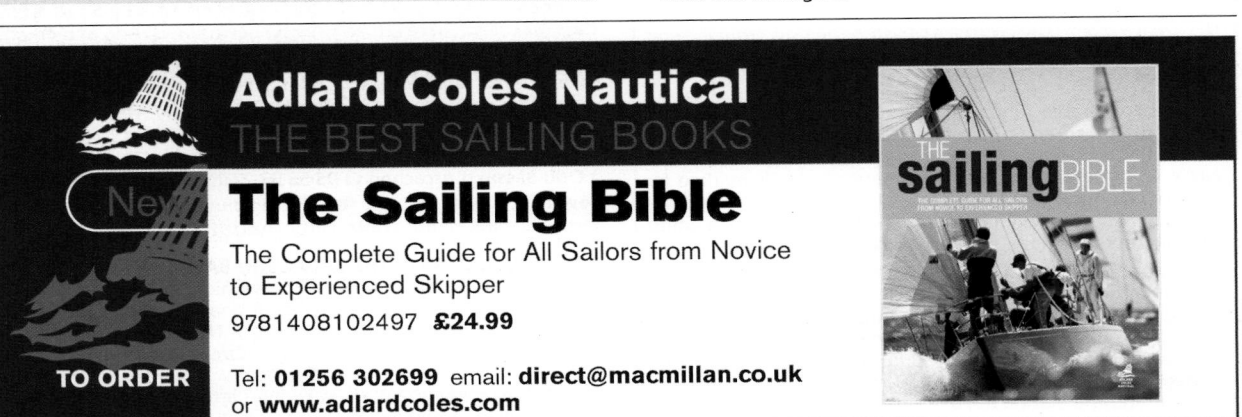

ARCACHON TO THE SPANISH BORDER

Arcachon is accessible from offshore via an E-W corridor (not normally active) through the Landes range. The entrance to Bassin d'Arcachon and the marina is via the well buoyed, but unlit, Passe Nord between extensive, shifting sandbanks on which the sea breaks even in calm conditions. Study the text for optimum timing, swell and weather conditions before attempting entry (AC 1102, 1343).

▶ *On AC 2750 the only tidal stream diamond relevant to the entrance to the Passe du Nord is f B. Diamonds f D to H are in the Rade d'Eyrac, the roadstead lying north of the town of Arcachon. The times of HW and LW occur progressively later from the seaward to the inner ends of the access channel. For example HW at a position 8 cables N off A occurs ¾ hour earlier than at Cap Ferret. In the same position, the ingoing stream starts at HW Pointe de Grave (PdG) −5¼, max sp rate 2kn. The ebb starts at HW PdG +½, sp rate 3·5kn.* ◀

It is worth inserting in your GPS the Lat/Long of the key buoys as waypoints; see 9.22.4 and also get the latest update from Cap Ferret sig station on Ch 13 or ☎ 05·56·60·60·03. Positively identify each buoy as you pass it; do not cut corners. Passe Sud is closed to navigation and most of the buoys have been lifted.

Strong N or W winds and swell make the narrow approach chan to the large marina at **Capbreton** impassable. Anglet/Bayonne may then be a safer option; or stay at sea. The Fosse (or Gouf) de Capbreton, a submarine canyon, lies at right angles to the coast. The 50m depth contour is 3ca W of Capbreton hbr bkwtr and the 100m line is 4ca further W. In strong W winds a dangerous sea breaks along the N and S edges of it, but within the very deep waters of the Fosse the sea is relatively calm.

Anglet has a marina, but there are few if any facilities for yachts further up the R. Adour at Bayonne.

▶ *At L'Adour entrance the flood runs E and SE from HW Pointe de Grave (PdG) −6½, sp rate 2-4kn. The ebb runs W from HW PdG −½, sp rate 3-5kn. Slack water lasts for a mere 15 minutes, after which the rate increases rapidly.* ◀

S of Pte St Martin the coast has mostly sandy beaches and rocky cliffs, with offlying rocky shoals and the Pyrenees visible as a backdrop.

St Jean-de-Luz (AC 1343) is best approached for the first time or in bad weather through Passe d'Illarguita (between Illarguita and Belhara Perdun shoals): follow the 138° transit (Le Socoa lt on with Bordagain lt) until the Ste Barbe ldg lts (101°) are in transit; thence enter by Passe de l'Ouest on the 151° transit of the inner hbr ldg lts. In strong W winds the sea breaks on Plateau de St Jean-de-Luz, a chain of rky shoals lying 1-4M offshore.

▶ *On the rising tide the incoming stream sets more strongly through the East entrance, then follows the E shore of the Bay to where the River Nivelle enters. In the yacht anchorages in the NW part of the Bay an eddy sets N at about 0·5kn.*

During the falling tide the out-going flow from La Nivelle sets through the West entrance; the rate in the yacht anchorages is 1kn. Heavy seas in the entrance can stop the flow from leaving the Bay and it continues clockwise around the eastern part of the Bay. ◀

Baie de Fontarabie (Rada de Higuer in Spanish) lies on the border of France and Spain and is entered between Pte Ste Anne and Cabo Higuer (a bare, rugged cape with lt ho) 1·75M WNW. In the middle of the bay a neutral area is marked by beacons as shown on AC 1171. To seaward of this area the boundary line (approximately 01°46'·2W) runs N from a white pyramid on the S shore, about 1M SW of Pte Ste Anne.

Les Briquets (dry) lie 1M N of Pte Ste Anne. Keep to W of Banc Chicharvel and Bajo Iruarri in ent to B. Entry should not be attempted with strong onshore winds or heavy swell. R La Bidassoa (Ría de Fuenterrabía in Spanish) is entered between breakwaters in SW corner of the B, giving access to the marina at **Hendaye-Plage**. See Area 23 for the Spanish part of the harbour and the marina at Fuenterrabía.

9.22.27 BASSIN D'ARCACHON

Gironde **44°39'·77N 01°09'·11W** (marina ent) ❀&&&&✿✿✿

CHARTS AC 2664, 2750; Imray C42; SHOM 6766; Navi 255, 1024

TIDES +0620 Dover; ML 2·5.

Standard Port POINTE DE GRAVE (◀—)

Times				Height (metres)			
High Water		Low Water		MHWS	MHWN	MLWN	MLWS
0000	0600	0000	0500	5·4	4·4	2·1	1·0
1200	1800	1200	1700				
Differences ARCACHON (7 cables WNW of marina)							
+0010	+0020	+0030	+0005	−1·1	−1·0	−0·8	−0·6
CAP FERRET							
−0015	+0005	+0020	−0005	−1·4	−1·2	−0·8	−0·6

SHELTER Good in marina. If full, ⚓ N of it, except in strong N'lies. No access to Bassin d'Arcachon in strong SW-N winds or at night.

NAVIGATION WPT 44°33'·80N 01°18'·69W (ATT-ARC SWM buoy), 088°/0·64M to 1N & 2N buoys in the well buoyed, unlit N Passe.

Before approaching, visitors should make every effort to contact the English-speaking *Cap Ferret Semaphore* Ch 16, 13 (HJ), ☎ 05·56·60·60·03 for a buoyage/navigational update.

Buoys may at times be off station or missing and are only relaid annually. Most recent positions in 9.22.4 were valid June 2009.

N Passe trends NE then N between Banc d'Arguin and Banc du Toulinguet towards Cap Ferret. The longer S Passe is un-marked and closed to navigation, although some local FVs may still use it. In any wind the sea breaks on the shifting sand banks between Cap Ferret and Wharf de la Salie, but the chan buoys can be seen between the breakers (not as fearsome as it sounds).

Start appr ideally at HW−1 and no later than HW+1. Due to the very strong ebb (6kn sp) the chan bar (mean depth 3·7-4·5m) is impassable from HW+1 until LW, better to wait until LW+3. Best to leave on the last of the flood. When swell is higher than 1m, bar may be dangerous. If in doubt, stay out.

Be aware of any activity in firing ranges between Pte de la Negade and Capbreton, out to 40M offshore; see 9.22.26.

LIGHTS AND MARKS ATT-ARC (SWM lt buoy) is moved to show approach to N Passe. See 9.22.4 and website Updates for the most recent positions of appr buoys for use as waypoints.

Cap Ferret is low-lying but its white/red lt ho is conspic, as are a water twr close N and the white Sig stn close S. The Dune de Pyla (103m high) on the E shore is very conspic, unless hidden in haze.

R/T Ch 09 16 (H24).

TELEPHONE Sig Stn 05·56·60·60·03; ⊖ 05·56·72·29·24; Aff Mar 05·57·52·57·07; SNSM 05·56·22·36·75; CROSS 02·97·55·35·35; Auto 08·92·68·08·33; Police 05·56·83·04·63; Dr 05·56·83·04·72; Ⓗ 05·56·83·39·50; Brit Consul 05·57·22·21·10.

FACILITIES Marina ☎ 05·56·22·36·75. plaisance@port-arcachon.com www.arcachon.com 2350+250 Ⓥ; €4·22. Access HW±3, very crowded in season. Berth/raft on accueil pontoon (35m long); 2 days max stay. There are *very few* Ⓥ berths in Jul/Aug and on any public Hol in summer. Waiting list: 9,645 applicants and 26 years.

Extensive moorings (Areas U-Z) along the S shore west of the marina are not for daily use. They are patrolled by police launches.

D&P ☎ 05·56·22·36·74 (0800-1845 Aug; OT 0815-1845), Slip, C (20 ton), BH (45 ton), ⚓, ME, El, Ⓔ, SHOM, ✕, CH, SM, ▣. **YC du Bassin d'Arcachon** ☎ 05·56·83·22·11, Slip, R, Bar.

Town ☶, R, Gaz, ✉, Ⓑ, ⛽. Electric minibus into town approx every 20 mins. ✈ Bordeaux. Ferry: Roscoff/St Malo.

MINOR HARBOURS IN THE ARCACHON BASIN

Around the Basin are many small hbrs which dry LW ±2 or 3 hours, but are worth exploring by shoal draft boats: To the W, La Vigne*, Le Canon, Piquey and Claouey; to the NE, Port de Lège, Arès, Andernos*, Fontanevieille*, Lanton (Cassy) and Audenge*; and to the S, La Teste and Gujan. *See below. Secondary chans in the Bassin d'Arcachon are marked by piles lettered A to K, clockwise from the N, plus pile number.

LA VIGNE, 44°40´·44N 01°14´·35W. HW time & ht approx as Cap Ferret above; ML 2·4m. Access HW±2. See 9.22.27. Good shelter, but crowded; beware strong currents across hbr ent. 2 perches mark the ent and on the SW point, a It Iso R 4s 7m 5M. A small bkwtr (unlit) protrudes into the ent from the NE side. Aff Mar ☎ 05.56.60.52.76. Facilities: **Marina** ☎ 05·56·60·54·36. 268 + 2, max LOA 8·5m. Slip, CH, C (2 ton), P, D.

ANDERNOS, 44°44´·53N 01°06´·54W. HW time & ht approx as Arcachon 9.22.27; access about HW±2. Dredged chan to Bétey is marked by lateral poles D0 to D14; thence side chan to Andernos. Ent Fl G 4s and Fl R 4s. Jetty + pontoon for yachts able to dry out, max LOA 12m. Bad silting may occur despite dredging. Also ⚓ on flat drying foreshore. HM ☎ 05.56.82.00.12. Few facilities.

FONTAINEVIEILLE, 44°43´·30N 01°04´·63W. Tides as 9.22.27. Drying marina on NE side of Bassin d'Arcachon, access HW±3 via Chenal de Mouchtalette. Proceed from E0 PHM pile to E8, where fork left onto NNE for 7ca to hbr ent. No Its. Boats dry out on pontoons. Auto 05.36.65.08.33.
Facilities: **Marina** ☎ 05.56.82.17.31. 178+ 2, Fuel, Slip, ME.

AUDENGE, 44°40´·58N 01°01´·57W. Tides as 9.22.27. Drying marina and oyster port 5·5M E of Arcachon, access sp HW–2 to HW, nps HW–1 to HW. Appr from G0 PHM pile via drying Chenal d'Audenge to G8 pile, 5ca short of the ent. Mairie ☎ 05.56.03.81.50. The Old Port (84 berths) is to the N; the New Port has 130 pontoon berths, Slip, YC, P&D (cans).

Other drying hbrs: to the NE, Port du Bétey & de Cassy; and E of Arcachon, Ports de La Teste & de La Hume and Port du Teich.

9.22.28 CAPBRETON

Landes 43°39'·34N 01°27'·00W ✳✲⚓⚓⚓🏵🏵

CHARTS AC 1102; SHOM 6786, 6557, 6586; Navi 555, 1024

TIDES +0450 Dover; ML 2·3. Use differences 9.22.29.

SHELTER Good, but the narrow canalised ent (Canal du Boucarot) is dangerous in strong winds from W to N. Do not enter if swell or seas are seen to be breaking in mid-chan, although they often break either side. No ⚓ outside the entrance.

NAVIGATION WPT 43°39'·63N 01°27'·49W, 123°/5ca to N pier lt. Bkwtr lts in line 123° lead to hbr ent. Gouf de Capbreton is a submarine canyon off the hbr ent where in last 3ca depths shoal rapidly from 50m to 3m; see 9.22.5. Silting occurs around head of S jetty, a wooden *estacade* which should be given a wide berth. An obstn 255° S jetty lt 300m is dangerous at LW; take great care.

Best appr at HW or HW–3 to +1; but not LW ±2½. Inside Canal du B best water is close to N jetty initially; from abeam small statue of Virgin Mary, move to mid-chan or just S of mid-chan. Marina entrance is via the obvious gap in training wall on SE side of chan, abeam conspic Capitainerie.

LIGHTS AND MARKS A casino and red-roofed sanatorium are conspic S of ent and a water twr 1M ENE. Lts as chartlet and 9.22.4. S jetty is on an extension close W of the former lt bcn.

R/T Ch 09 (0700-2100 in season).

TELEPHONE Aff Mar 05·58·72·10·43; CROSS 02·97·55·35·35; ⊖ 05·59·46·68·80; Auto 08.92.68.08.40; Ⓗ (Bayonne) 05·59·44·35·35; Police 05·59·50·31·52; Brit Consul 05.57.22.21.10.

FACILITIES Marina The 3 basins are in an inverted Y-shape. Chan and basins dredged 1·5m. ☎ 05·58·72·21·23. www.port-capbreton.com info@port-capbreton.com

890+60 Ⓥ, €2·47. Ⓥ pontoon 'B' (2nd to stbd of marina ent). P&D (☎ 05.58.72.15.66, 0830-1300, 1400-2000), Slip, BH (30 ton), C (1·5 ton), ME, El, ⚒, CH, SM, Ⓔ, ▣. **CNCP** ☎ 05·58·72·67·09.

Town: Bar, R, 🛒, ✉, Ⓑ. ⇌ Bayonne (17km); ✈ Biarritz (25km).

9.22.29 ANGLET/BAYONNE

Pyrénées Atlantique 43°31'·81N 01°31'·95W ✳⚓⚓⚓🏵

CHARTS AC 1102, 1175; SHOM 6786, 6558/7, 6536; Navi 555

TIDES +0450 Dover (UT); ML 2·5.

Standard Port POINTE DE GRAVE (⟵)

Times				Height (metres)			
High Water		Low Water		MHWS	MHWN	MLWN	MLWS
0000	0600	0000	0500	5·4	4·4	2·1	1·0
1200	1800	1200	1700				
Differences L'ADOUR (BOUCAU)							
–0030	–0035	–0040	–0025	–1·2	–1·1	–0·4	–0·3

SHELTER Very good in Anglet Marina, 7ca E of ent on S bank of R Adour, but in NE winds cement dust from the industrial N bank may be a problem. No ⚓ due to commercial ships to which yachts must give way.

NAVIGATION WPT 43°32'·59N 01°32'·76W (BA SWM buoy, L Fl 10s), 142°/0·9M to N bkwtr lt. Easy access except in strong W winds. Strong tidal streams: 1·5-4kn flood, 2·4-5kn at sp ebb.

At Bayonne no passage for masted craft beyond bridge (9·5m clearance); interesting old quarter, 3M up river on S bank.

LIGHTS AND MARKS Outer ldg lts 090°, both Q, W pylons/R tops. Inner ldg lts 111°, both QG, lit when chan is practicable. 3 more sets of ldg lts upriver to Bayonne. Other lts as chartlet and 9.22.4. Pte St Martin lt ho is 2·45M SSW of hbr.

IPTS (full code) from conspic Sig twr (W, B stripe) S side of ent.

R/T Marina Ch 09. Port/pilots 12, 16 (0800-1200, 1400-1800LT).

TELEPHONE HM Port 05·59·63·11·57; CROSS 02·97·55·35·35; ⊖ 05·59·59·08·29; Aff Mar 05·59·55·06·68; Météo 05·59·23·84·15; Auto 08·92·65·08·64; Ⓗ 05·59·44·35·35; Brit Consul 05.57.22.21.10.

FACILITIES Marina (Port du Brise-Lames; 1·7-3·5m). ☎ 05·59·63·05·45, 🖷 05·59·63·22·12. portdeplaisance@agglo-bab.fr www.agglo-bab.fr 367+58 Ⓥ, €2·38. P&D, ME, El, C (1·3 ton), ▣, BH (25 ton), Slip, ⚒, CH, Ⓔ, SHOM. **YC Adour Atlantique** ☎ 05·59·63·16·22.

Bayonne Bar, R, 🛒, ✉, Ⓑ, ⇌, ✈ (Biarritz). Ferry: Bilbao.

9.22.30 ST JEAN DE LUZ
(Basque name: Donibane Lohizune)
Pyrénées Atlantique, 43°23'·85N 01°40'·61W ✷✷♁♁♁✿✿✿

CHARTS AC 1102, 1170; SHOM 6786, 6558, 6526; Navi 555

TIDES HW +0435 on Dover (UT); ML 2·5m.
Standard Port POINTE DE GRAVE (←)

Times				Height (metres)			
High Water		Low Water		MHWS	MHWN	MLWN	MLWS
0000	0600	0000	0500	5·4	4·4	2·1	1·0
1200	1800	1200	1700				
Differences ST JEAN DE LUZ (SOCOA)							
−0040	−0045	−0045	−0030	−1·1	−1·1	−0·6	−0·4

SHELTER Except in strong NW winds, the bay can be entered H24. The 3 designated yacht anchorages (see chartlet) offer safe holding in 2-4m; the SE is less prone to swell. See Facilities for the marina and Socoa harbour.

NAVIGATION WPT 43°24'·09N 01°40'·79W (at the intersection of the 101° and 150·7° ldg lines), 150·7°/500m to W ent. In good weather yachts can approach within the N quadrant direct to hbr ent, but in heavy W'ly weather seas break on various shoals on the Plateau de St Jean-de-Luz, extending SW from Biarritz almost to Hendaye. 3M W of hbr ent and 2M NE of Hendaye, beware Les Briquets rks, drying 0·4m.

The 3 appr chans (outer, middle, inner) are for big ships or smaller craft in bad weather and should be taken in sequence:

Outer chan leads 138° between Illarguita and Belhara Perdun banks. It is the main and only safe approach at night and in bad weather. Ldg lts: Front, Socoa QWR, 12m; W □ twr, B stripes; (R sector covers Socoa hbr ent). Rear Q; B ■/W bands on W pylon/B bands, hard to see by day, but the nearby Bordagain twr, 100m, is more readily visible.

Middle chan 101° is intercepted at 43°24'·23N 01°41'·90W. Thence, or if arriving direct from the W, it leads past the hbr's W bkwtr, to the WPT. Ldg lts at Ste Barbe: Both Oc (4) R 12s; front, W △ on W bldg; rear, B ▲ on W twr.

Inner chan leads 150·7° from the WPT through the W ent into the bay and via a buoyed chan to St Jean de Luz hbr. Ldg lts: Both Dir QG, conspic white twrs: front has a R vert stripe; rear, a G vert stripe.

The unmarked E ent to the bay is used by locals, but is not recommended. Beware: a large unlit mooring buoy S of Digue d'Artha, antipollution booms off the SW and SE beaches and an unmarked submerged jetty in the SE corner of bay.

Speed limits: in the bay 7kn; port area 5kn. Ent/exit the port only under power. FVs tend to ent/exit the FV hbr at speed and with much wash in the narrow access channel.

LIGHTS AND MARKS La Rhune, an 898m high conical mountain bears 160°/5·5M from the W ent; conspic in good visibility. Digue des Criquas (the W bkwtr) is lit, Iso G 4s. Digue d'Artha is a detached unlit bkwtr across the middle of the bay. See chartlet and 9.22.4 for light details.

R/T Marina Ch 09, 16; 0700-1230 & 1400-2000 in season.

TELEPHONE Aff Mar 05·59·47·14·55; ⊜ 05·59·47·18·61; CROSS 02·97·55·35·35; Météo 05·59·22·03·30; Auto 08·92·68·08·64; SNSM 05·59·47·22·98; Police 05·59·26·01·55; Brit Consul 05·57·22·21·10.⁻

FACILITIES
ST JEAN DE LUZ has a small marina (2·5m) at Ciboure, in Bassin de Larraldénia, close to rear 150·7° ldg lt and W and SW of the FV hbr.

Berth/raft on hammerheads of the first 2 pontoons, or as directed. East of the pontoons beware the long slipway marked by 2 PHM bcns.**Marina** ☎ 05·59·47·26·81, ▦ 05·59·47·86·11. 73+8 ✔, max LOA 16m; €3·03. D by tanker, C (6 ton), Slip, Ⓔ, ME, El, ✕, CH.

Town 🛒, R, Bar, ⊚, ✉, Ⓑ, ⇌.

SOCOA hbr in the NW corner of the bay is close S of conspic fort. It dries about 0·5m; tide gauge at ent. Here small craft can dry out, but it is little more than a landing place for yachts anchored E & SE of it in designated anchorages. It is over 2km walk to the town centre.
Jetty C (1 ton), D by tanker, Slip, BY, ME, CH, El, ✕. **YC Basque** ☎ 05·59·47·18·31.

9.22.31 HENDAYE

Pyrénées Atlantique **43°22´·75N 01°47´·28W** ✲✲✲✿✿✿✿✿✿

CHARTS AC 1102, 1170, 1171; SHOM 6786, 6558, 6556; Navi 555

TIDES HW +0450 on Dover (UT); ML 2·3m.
Use differences ST JEAN DE LUZ (SOCOA) 9.22.30

SHELTER Excellent in marina. Access H24, but exposed to N/NE and S/SW gales. Possible ⚓ in river or the Baie de Chingoudy but both are overcrowded. A Spanish port of refuge (2-3m) lies S of C Higuer, for FVs rather than for yachts. Note: Fuenterrabía (Hondarrabia, 9.23.6) is Spanish. See chartlet for neutral zone.

NAVIGATION WPT 43°23´·81N 01°46´·51W, 212°/1·15M to W bkwtr hd. Beware Les Briquets 8ca N of Pte Ste Anne at E end of the Baie; near centre of B, keep clear of Bajo Iruarri. River ent 6·5-1·3m is easy except in heavy N'ly swell; sp ebb is very strong. Inshore of Pte des Dunes, Fl R 2·5s, hug the E training wall for best water. A spit drying 1·3m (SHM bn, VQ (3) G 5s) off Fuenterrabía narrows the chan to about 100m wide before the marina ent opens.

LIGHTS AND MARKS La Rhune, a 900m high conical mountain, is conspic in good vis 8M ESE of hbr. Cabo Higuer lt ho is conspic at W side of bay on a rugged headland.

R/T Marina Ch 09 (H24).

TELEPHONE Aff Mar 05·59·47·14·55; ⊖ 05·59·48·10·68; CROSS 02·97·55·35·35; Météo 05·59·24·58·80; Auto 08.92.68.08.64; Police 05·59·50·31·52; 🄷 05·59·20·08·22; Brit Consul 05.57.22.21.10.

FACILITIES Marina (2·5-3m) is entered close W of a Fl Y 4s and a conspic RW TV relay mast (40m). Accueil pontoon 'A' in NW corner. ☎ 05·59·48·06·10. 803 + 50 Ⓥ, €3·10 (3rd night free). P&D (H24), BH (30 ton), Slip, CH, ⚒, El, Ⓔ, ME, ☐, @, Wi-Fi. www.hendaye-tourisme.fr station.littorale@hendaye.com

YC ☎ 05·59·20·03·02, Bar.

Town 🍴, R, Bar, Gaz, ⊠, Ⓑ, ⇌ (TGV Paris-Madrid), ✈ Fuenterrabía, or for UK flights Biarritz (☎ 05·59·43·83·83). Local ferry from Hendaye to Fuenterrabía every 15 mins. UK ferry from Bilbao or Santander.

Fuenterrabía Marina, see 9.23.6.

N & NW Spain

Fuenterrabía to Bayona

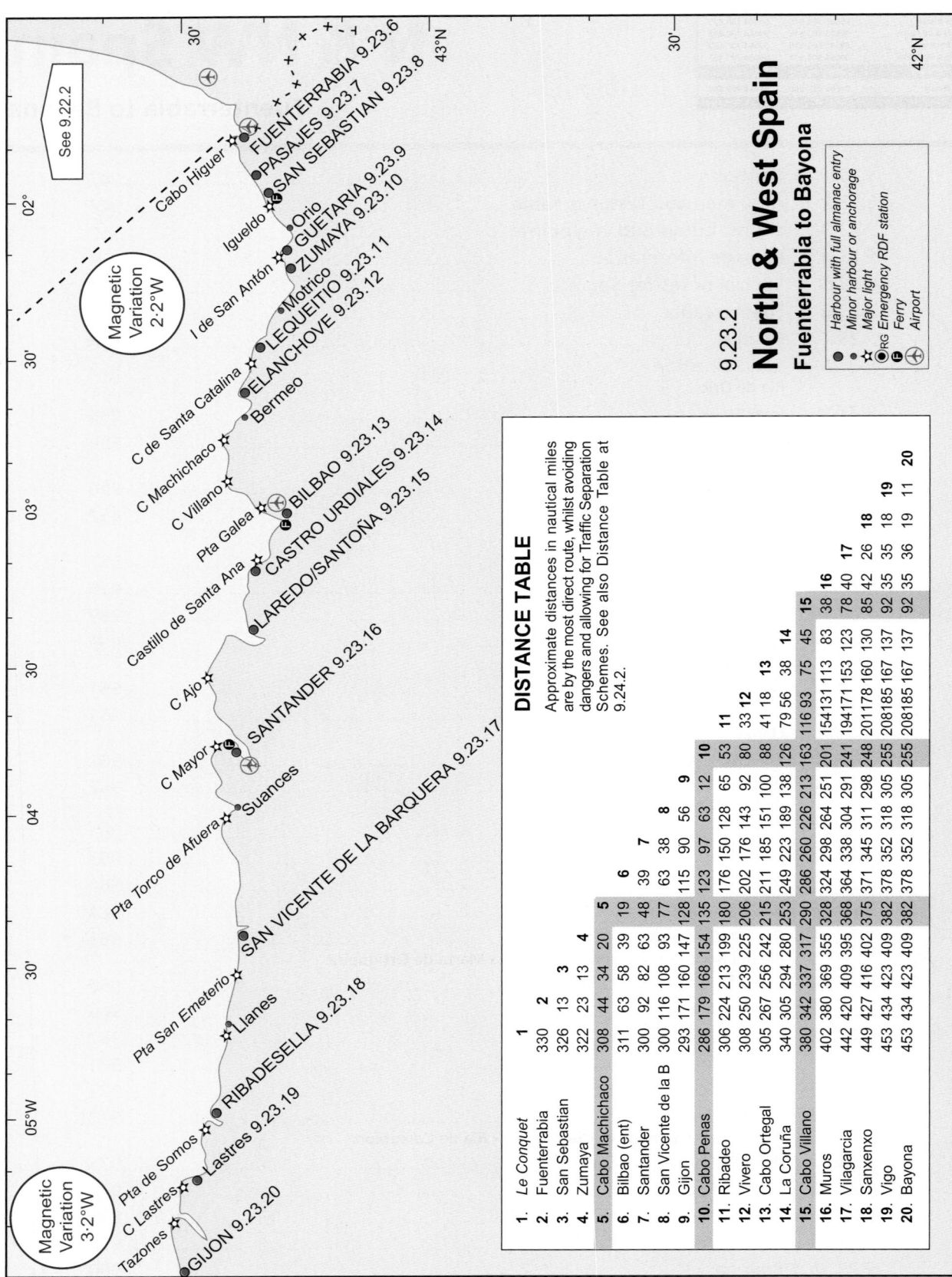

9.23.2
North & West Spain
Fuenterrabia to Bayona

Legend:
- Harbour with full almanac entry
- Minor harbour or anchorage
- ☆ Major light
- ◉RG Emergency RDF station
- Ⓛ Ferry
- ✈ Airport

Magnetic Variation 2·2'W

Magnetic Variation 3·2'W

See 9.22.2

Map labels

- Cabo Higuer
- FUENTERRABIA 9.23.6
- PASAJES 9.23.7
- SAN SEBASTIAN 9.23.8
- Igueldo
- Orio
- GUETARIA 9.23.9
- ZUMAYA 9.23.11
- I de San Antón
- Motrico
- LEQUEITIO 9.23.11
- ELANCHOVE 9.23.12
- C de Santa Catalina
- Bermeo
- C Machichaco
- C Villano
- Pta Galea
- BILBAO 9.23.13
- CASTRO URDIALES 9.23.14
- Castillo de Santa Ana
- LAREDO/SANTOÑA 9.23.15
- C Ajo
- SANTANDER 9.23.16
- C Mayor
- Suances
- Pta Torco de Afuera
- SAN VICENTE DE LA BARQUERA 9.23.17
- Pta San Emeterio
- Llanes
- RIBADESELLA 9.23.19
- Pta de Somos
- C Lastres
- Lastres 9.23.19
- Tazones
- GIJON 9.23.20

DISTANCE TABLE

Approximate distances in nautical miles are by the most direct route, whilst avoiding dangers and allowing for Traffic Separation Schemes. See also Distance Table at 9.24.2.

	1	2	3	4	5	6	7	8	9	10	11	12	13	14	15	16	17	18	19	20
1. Le Conquet	1
2. Fuenterrabia	330	2
3. San Sebastian	326	13	3
4. Zumaya	322	23	13	4
5. Cabo Machichaco	308	44	34	20	5
6. Bilbao (ent)	311	63	58	39	19	6
7. Santander	300	92	82	63	48	39	7
8. San Vicente de la B	300	116	108	93	77	63	38	8
9. Gijon	293	171	160	147	128	115	90	56	9
10. Cabo Penas	286	179	168	154	135	123	97	63	12	10
11. Ribadeo	306	224	213	199	180	176	150	128	65	53	11
12. Vivero	308	250	239	225	206	202	176	143	92	80	33	12
13. Cabo Ortegal	305	267	256	242	215	211	185	151	100	88	41	18	13
14. La Coruña	340	305	294	280	253	249	223	189	138	126	79	56	38	14
15. Cabo Villano	380	342	337	317	290	286	260	226	213	163	116	93	75	45	15
16. Muros	402	380	369	355	328	324	298	264	251	201	154	131	113	83	38	16
17. Vilagarcia	442	420	409	395	368	364	338	304	291	241	194	171	153	123	78	40	17
18. Sanxenxo	449	427	416	402	375	371	345	311	298	248	201	178	160	130	85	42	26	18
19. Vigo	453	434	423	409	382	378	352	318	305	255	208	185	167	137	92	35	35	18	19
20. Bayona	453	434	423	409	382	378	352	318	305	255	208	185	167	137	92	35	36	19	11	20

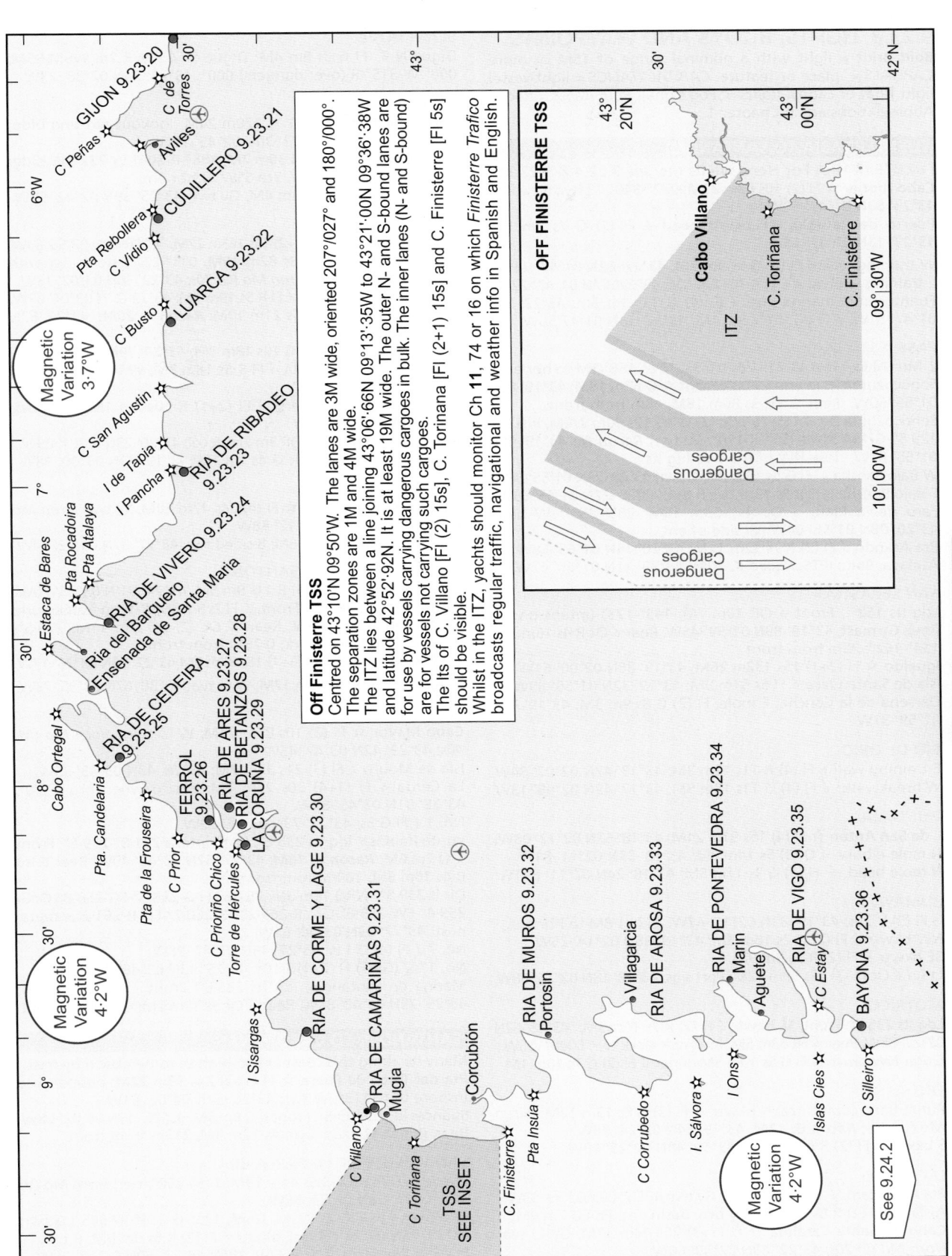

Off Finisterre TSS

Centred on 43°10'N 09°50'W. The lanes are 3M wide, oriented 207°/027° and 180°/000°.
The separation zones are 1M and 4M wide.
The ITZ lies between a line joining 43°06'·66N 09°13'·35W to 43°21'·00N 09°36'·38W and latitude 42°52'·92N. It is at least 19M wide. The outer N- and S-bound lanes are for use by vessels carrying dangerous cargoes in bulk. The inner lanes (N- and S-bound) are for vessels not carrying such cargoes.
The lts of C. Villano [Fl (2) 15s], C. Torinana [Fl (2+1) 15s] and C. Finisterre [Fl 5s] should be visible.
Whilst in the ITZ, yachts should monitor Ch **11**, 74 or 16 on which *Finisterre Trafico* broadcasts regular traffic, navigational and weather info in Spanish and English.

OFF FINISTERRE TSS

GIJON 9.23.20
CUDILLERO 9.23.21
LUARCA 9.23.22
RIA DE RIBADEO 9.23.23
RIA DE VIVERO 9.23.24
RIA DE CEDEIRA 9.23.25
FERROL 9.23.26
RIA DE ARES 9.23.27
RIA DE BETANZOS 9.23.28
LA CORUÑA 9.23.29
RIA DE CORME Y LAGE 9.23.30
RIA DE CAMARIÑAS 9.23.31
RIA DE MUROS 9.23.32
RIA DE AROSA 9.23.33
RIA DE PONTEVEDRA 9.23.34
RIA DE VIGO 9.23.35
BAYONA 9.23.36

Magnetic Variation 3·7°W

Magnetic Variation 4·2°W

Magnetic Variation 4·2°W

TSS SEE INSET

See 9.24.2

C de Torres
C Peñas
Aviles
Pta Rebollera
C Vidio
C Busto
C San Agustin
I de Tapia
I Pancha
Pta Rocadoira
Pta Atalaya
Estaca de Bares
Ria del Barquero
Ensenada de Santa Maria
Cabo Ortegal
Pta. Candelaria
Pta de la Frouseira
C Prior
C Prioriño Chico
Torre de Hércules
I Sisargas
C Villano
Mugia
C Toriñana
C. Finisterre
Pta Insúa
Corcubión
Portosin
Villagarcia
I. Sálvora
I Ons
Marin
Aguete
C Estay
Islas Cies
C Silleiro
C Corrubedo

Cabo Villano
ITZ
C. Toriñana
C. Finisterre
Dangerous Cargoes
Dangerous Cargoes

43°20'N
43°00'N
09°30'W
10°00'W

43°
42°N
30'
30'
30'
30'

6°W
7°
8°
9°

9.23.3 LIGHTS, BUOYS AND WAYPOINTS

Bold print = light with a nominal range of 15M or more.
CAPITALS = place or feature. *CAPITAL ITALICS* = light-vessel, light float or Lanby. *Italics* = Fog signal. ***Bold italics*** = Racon. Abbreviations are in Chapter 1.

FUENTERRABÍA TO SANTANDER

FUENTERRABÍA For Hendaye lts etc, see 9.22.4 & 9.22.31.
Cabo Higuer ☆ Fl (2) 10s 63m **23M**; 072°-340°; □ twr, R cupola; 43°23'·52N 01°47'·52W.
Puerto de Refugio, NE bkwtr head ⚡ Fl (2) G 7s 7m 5M; 43°23'·13N 01°47'·35W.

W training wall ⚡ Fl (3) G 9s 9m 5M; 43°22'·82N 01°47'·34W.
E training wall hd ⚡ L Fl R 10s 8m 5M; 43°22'·67N 01°47'·22W.
Fuenterrabía marina ent, ⚡ Fl (4) G 11s 9m 3m; 43°22'·59N 01°47'·51W. ⚡ Fl (4) R 11s 9m 1M; 43°22'·56N 01°47'56W.

PASAJES

⚓ Mo (A) 6s 11M; 43°21'·19N 01°56'·12W; 166°/1M to hbr ent.
Senocozulúa lts in line 154·8°: **Front** ☆ Q 67m **18M**; 43°19'·89N 01°55'·60W. **Rear** ☆ Oc 3s 86m **18M**, 40m from front.
Senocozulúa Dir ⚡ 155·75°: Oc (2) WRG 12s 50m W6M, R/G3M; 129·5°-G-154·5°-W-157°-R-190°; W twr; *Racon M*; 43°19'·90N 01°55'·61W, close NW of the two ldg lts.
W Bajo Bancha ◤ Fl G 5s 18m 7M; G twr; 43°20'·23N 01°55'·88W.
E Bajo Bancha ◢ Fl R 5s 18m 7M; R twr; 43°20'·22N 01°55'·65W.
Faro de la Plata ⚡ Oc 4s 153m 13M; 285°-250°; W bldg; 43°20'·08N 01°56'·04W (W side of ent).
Pta Arando ⚡ Fl (2) R 7s 12m 11M; 43°20'·14N 01°55'·68W
Atalaya, 96m; IPTS; *Racon K, 20M*; 43°20'·11N 01°55'·47W.

SAN SEBASTIÁN

Ldg lts 158°: Front ⚡ QR 10m 7M; 143°-173° (intens on ldg line); Gy mast; 43°18'·89N 01°59'·45W. Rear ⚡ Oc R 4s 16m 7M; 154°-162°; 25m from front.
Igueldo ☆ Fl (2+1) 15s 132m **26M**; 43°19'·36N 02°00'·61W.
Isla de Santa Clara ⚡ Fl 5s 51m 9M; 43°19'·32N 01°59'·89W.
Dársena de la Concha, E mole, Fl (2) G 8s 9m 3M; 43°19'·34N 01°59'·37W.

RÍO DE ORIO

E training wall ⚡ Fl (4) R 11s 12m 3M; 43°17'·47N 02°07'·84W.
W breakwater ⚡ Fl (4) G 11s 18m 5M; 43°17'·49N 02°08'·13W.

GUETARIA

I. de San Antón ☆ Fl (4) 15s 91m **21M**; 43°18'·62N 02°12'·08W.
N mole elbow ⚡ Q (3) 5s 14m 3M; 43°18'·33N 02°11'·81W.
N mole head ⚡ Fl (3) G 9s 11m 5M; 43°18'·24N 02°11'·891W.

ZUMAYA

⚓ Fl (5) Y 20s; 43°19'·83N 02°13'·47W, 213°/1·8M to hbr ent.
NW bkwtr ⚡ Fl (2) G 7s 18m 5M; 43°18'·38N 02°14'·75W.
SE bkwtr ⚡ Fl (2) R 7s 8m 3M.
Lt ho ⚡ Oc (1+3) 12s 39m 12M; Port sigs; 43°18'·18N 02°15'·08W.

MOTRICO

Ldg lts 236·5°: Front, SE bkwtr ⚡ Fl (2) R 7s 10m 3M; 43°18'·52N 02°22'·85W. Rear ⚡ FR 63m 5M; inconspic clock twr; 600m WSW.
Outer NW bkwtr ⚡ Fl G 5s 10m 5M. Inner ⚡ Fl (2) G 7s 10m 1M.

ONDÁRROA

Punta Barracomuturra, N bkwtr ⚡ Fl (3) G 8s 13m 12M; *Siren Mo (O) 20s*; *Racon G, 12M*; 43°19'·54N 02°24'·94W.
S bkwtr ⚡ Fl (2) R 6s 7m 6M; 43°19'·49N 02°25'·10W.

LEQUEITIO

Pta Amandarri ⚡ Fl G 4s 8m 5M; Gy twr; 43°22'·00N 02°29'·93W.
Aislado, Fl (2) R 8s 5m 4M; Gy bcn. Basin ent: FR/FG 7m 4M.
Cabo de Santa Catalina ☆ Fl (1+3) 20s 44m **17M**; Gy ○ twr; *Horn Mo (L) 20s*; 43°22'·63N 02°30'·60W.

ELANCHOVE

Digue N ⚡ Fl G 3s 8m 4M. Digue S ⚡ F WR 7m W8M,R5M; 000°-W-315°-R (over dangers)-000°; 43°24'·24N 02°38'·23W.

BERMEO

Cabo Machichaco ☆ Fl 7s 120m **24M**; lookout twr and bldg; *Siren Mo (M) 60s*; 43°27'·30N 02°45'·19W.
Rosape ⚡ Fl (2) WR 10s 36m 7M; 108°-R-204°-W-232°; W bldg; 43°25'·07N 02°42'·76W, 3ca SSW of hbr ent.
N bkwtr ⚡ Fl G 4·5s 16m 4M; Gy twr; 43°25'·39N 02°42'·59W.

BILBAO

C. Villano (Gorliz) ☆ Fl (1+2) 16s 163m **22M**; 43°26'·03N 02°56'·63W.
Punta Galea ☆ Fl (3) 8s 82m **19M**; 011°-227°; stone twr with dwelling, Gy cupola; *Siren Mo (G) 30s*; 43°22'·30N 03°02'·13W.
E bkwtr hd (detached) ⚡ Fl R 5s 19m 7M; 43°22'·77N 03°04'·67W.
W bkwtr head ⚡ Fl G 5s 21m 10M; *Racon X, 20M*; 43°22'·67N 03°05'·04W.
Santurce Quay ⚡ Fl (3) G 10s 18m 3M; 43°20'·79N 03°01'·91W.
Contradique de Algorta ⚡ Fl R 5s 18m 3M, W twr; 43°20'·51N 03°01'·67W.
Mole head (cruise liners) ⚡ Fl (2+1) R 10s 7m 1M; R/G post; 43°20'·34N 03°01'·57W.
Getxo marina bkwtr ⚡ QR 3m 2M, R col; 43°20'·23N 03°01'·03W.
Las Arenas marina ⚡ Oc G 4s 1m 1M; 43°19'·83N 03°00'·98W.

CASTRO URDIALES

Castillo de Santa Ana ☆ Fl (4) 24s 47m **20M**; W twr; *Siren Mo (C) 60s*; 43°23'·07N 03°12'·88W.
N bkwtr ⚡ Fl G 3s 12m 6M; 8-sided twr; 43°22'·87N 03°12'·54W.

LAREDO and RIA DE SANTOÑA

Laredo N bkwtr ⚡ Fl (4) R 11s 9m 5M; 43°24'·91'N 03°25'·20W.
Santoña ldg lts 283·5°: Front, ⚡ Fl 2s 5m 8M; B ▼ on framework; 43°26'·34N 03°27'·60W. Rear, ⚡ Oc (2) 5s 12m 11M; 279·5°-287·5°; ○ on framework; 0·75M from front.
Pta Pescador lt ho ⚡ Fl (3+1) 18s 37m 9M; 43°27'·90N 03°26'·17W.
C. Ajo ☆ Oc (3) 16s 69m **17M**; W ○ twr; 43°30'·67N 03°35'·73W.

SANTANDER

Cabo Mayor ☆ Fl (2) 10s 89m **21M**; W ○ twr; *Horn Mo (M) 40s*; 43°29'·42N 03°47'·45W.
Isla de Mouro ⚡ Fl (3) 21s 37m 7M; 43°28'·40N 03°45'·35W.
La Cerda ⚡ Fl (1+4) 20s 22m 7M; obsc'd when brg <160°; 43°28'·01N 03°45'·83W.
No. 1 ⚓ Fl G 5s; 43°27'·73N 03°46'·22W.
Punta Rabiosa ldg lts 235·8°, both intens 231·8°-239·8°: Front ⚡ Q 7m 6M; *Racon K, 10M*; 43°27'·52N 03°46'·43W. Rear ⚡ Iso R 4s 10m 6M, 100m from front.
Dir lt 259·5°, WRG 18m 6M; 257·8°-Fl G-258·3°-FG-258·8°-OcG-259·4°-FW-259·6°-Oc R-260·2°-FR-260·7°-Fl R-261·2°; metal post; 43°27'·33N 03°48'·61W.
No. 7 ⚡ Fl (4) G 11s; 43°27'·46N 03°47'·98W.
No. 17 ◢ (GRG) Fl (2+1)G 10s; 43°25'·93N 03°48'·25W.
Marina de Santander, ldg lts 235·6°: Front ⚡ Iso 2s 9m 2M; 43°25'·75N 03°48'·84W. Rear ⚡ Oc 5s 10m 2M; 46m from front.

SANTANDER TO CABO PEÑAS

Many lts along this coast are so high as to be obsc'd by mist.
Pta del Torco de Fuera ☆ Fl (1+2) 24s 33m **22M**; obsc'd close inshore 091°-113°; W twr; 43°26'·51N 04°02'·61W.
Suances ldg lts 149·5°: Front ⚡ Q 8m 5M; 43°26'·19N 04°02'·08W. Rear, Punta Marzán ⚡ Iso 4s 12m 5M; 212m from front.

SAN VICENTE DE LA BARQUERA

Pta de la Silla ⚡ Oc 3·5s 41m 13M; 115°-250°; twr; *Horn Mo (V) 30s*; 43°23'·58N 04°23'·56W.
W bkwtr ⚡ Fl WG 2s W7M, G6M; 175°-G-235°-W-045°; G twr; 43°23'·73N 04°23'·11W. E bkwtr ⚡ Fl (2) R 8s 6m 5M; R twr.
Pta San Emeterio ☆ Fl 5s 66m **20M**; 43°23'·90N 04°32'·20W.

Plot waypoints on chart before use

LLANES
Pta de San Antón ☆ Fl (4) 15s 16m **15M**; W 8-sided twr; 43°25'·09N 04°44'·93W, 150m S of hbr ent.
N bkwtr (Osa) ⚡ Fl G 5s 13m 5M; 43°25'·18N 04°44'·90W.
Dock hd ⚡ Fl (3) G 9s 6m 1M.

RIBADESELLA
Pta del Caballo ⚡ Fl (4) R 11s 10m 5M; 278·4°-212·9°; 43°28'·08N 05°03'·98W. Fl R 5s 7m 3M; R post; 43° 28'·06N 05°03'·92W.
Somos ☆ Fl (2+1) 12s 113m **25M**; twr; 43°28'·36N 05°04'·97W.

LASTRES
E bkwtr ⚡ Fl (3) G 9s 13m 4M; 43°30'·89N 05°15'·90W.
C. Lastres ☆ Fl (5) 25s 116m **23M**. W ○ twr; 43°32'·04N 05°18'·02W.
Tazones ☆ Fl 7·5s 127m **20M**; W 8-sided twr; *Horn Mo (V) 30s;* 43°32'·87N 05°23'·94W. Bkwtr head, ⚡ Fl (2) G 7s 10m 5M.

GIJÓN
El Musel, NE mole ⚡ Fl G 4s 22m 7M; 43°34'·26N 05°40'·58W.
Piedra Sacramento ⚓ Fl (2) G 6s 9m 5M; 8-sided twr; 43°32'·83N 05°40'·30W. Marina ent ⚡ Fl (2) R 6s 7m 3M; 43°32'·79N 05°40'·21W.
Cabo de Torres ☆ Fl (2) 10s 80m **18M**; 43°34'·31N 05°41'·96W.
Punta del Cuerno ☆ Oc (2)10s 38m **15M**; R twr, W ho; *Horn Mo (C) 60s;* 43°35'·66N 05°45'·65W.
Candás, ldg lts290°: Front QR 22m 5M, W col; 43°35'·87N 05°46'·28W. Rear, Iso R 4s 55m 5M. N bkwtr hd ⚡ Fl (3) G 9s 11m 3M.
Luanco ldg lts 255°: Front, inner bkwtr ⚡ FlWG 5s 3m 5M; 43°36'·91N 05°47'·36W. Rear ⚡ Oc G 4s 6m 5M, 200m from front.
Cabo Peñas ☆ Fl (3) 15s 115m **35M**; Gy 8-sided twr; *Siren Mo (P) 60s;* 43°39'·33N 05°50'·92W.

CABO PEÑAS TO PUNTA DE LA ESTACA DE BARES
Avilés, Pta de la Forcada ⚡ Fl R 5s 25m **17M**; R mast on W truncated twr; 43°35'·82N 05°56'·84W. 80m E: *Siren Mo (A) 30s.*
Pta del Castillo ☆ Oc WR 5s 38m **W20, R17M**; 091·5°-R-113°-W-091·5°; W ☐ twr; 43°35'·72N 05°56'·72W. ⚡ Fl (2) R 7s is 30m SW.
Ent chan, S side ⚡ Fl (2) G 7s 12m 5M; 106°-280°; W ○ twr, G band; 43°35'·57N 05°56'·49W. ⚡ Fl G 5s 15m 5M is 390m west.
San Estaban de Pravia, W bkwtr ☆ Fl (2) 12s 19m **15M**; W ○ twr, B bands; *Siren Mo (N) 30s;* 43°34'·21N 06°04'·64W.
Ldg lts 206·2°: Front, Q 7m 1M; W twr, R bands; 43°34'·05N 06°04'·71W. Rear, Iso 4s 28m 1M; W pylon, R bands; 206·2°/360m.
Cudillero, Pta Rebollera ☆ Oc (4) 16s 42m **16M**; W 8-sided twr; *Siren Mo (D) 30s;* 43°33'·96N 06°08'·68W. N bkwtr ⚡ Fl (3) G 9s.
Cabo Vidio ☆ Fl 5s 99m **25M**; ○ twr; *Siren Mo (V) 60s;* 43°35'·62N 06°14'·76W.
Cabo Busto ☆ Fl (4) 20s 84m **25M**; 43°34'·15N 06°28'·17W.

LUARCA
Punta Altaya ⚡ Oc (3) 15s 63m 14M; W ☐ twr; *Siren Mo (L) 30s;* 43°32'·98N 06°31'·95W.
Ldg lts 170°, both W cols, R bands: Front ⚡ Fl 5s 19m 3M; 43°32'·78N 06°32'·11W. Rear ⚡ Oc 4s 26m 3M; 41m from front.
W Dique ⚡ Fl (2) G 7s 6m 3M; 43°32'·96N 06°32'·24W.
Cabo de San Agustín ☆ Oc (2) 12s 70m **25M**; W ○ twr, B bands; 43°33'·81N 06°44'·05W.
C. San Sebastián ☆ Fl (2+1) 19s 22m **18M**; 43°34'·43N 06°56'·75W.

RÍA DE RIBADEO
Punta de la Cruz ⚡ Fl (4) R 11s 16m 7M; 43°33'·39N 07°01'·74W.
Isla Pancha ☆ Fl (3+1) 20s 26m **21M**; W ○ twr, B bands; *Siren Mo (R) 30s;* 43°33'·39N 07°02'·52W, W side of entrance.
1st ldg lts 140°, both R ◇s, W twrs. Front, Pta Arroxo ⚡ Iso R 18m 5M; 43°32'·81N 07°01'·52W. Rear ⚡ Oc R 4s 24m 5M; 228m SE.
2nd ldg lts 205°. Front, Muelle de García ⚡ VQ R 8m 3M; R ◇, W twr; 43°32'·49N 07°02'·23W. Rear ⚡ Oc R 2s 18m 3M.
Marina, ⚡ Fl G 5s 9m 3M; 43°32'·45N 07°02'·16W. ⚡ Fl R 5s 9m 1M.
Punta Atalya (San Ciprian) ☆ Fl (5) 20s 39m **20M**; W ○ twr, B band;

43°42'·03N 07°26'·20W. Alúmina Port, N bkwtr Fl (2) WG 8s 17m 4M; 110°-W-180°-G-110°; 43°42'·98N 07°27'·58W.

RÍA DE VIVERO
Pta Roncadoira ☆ Fl 7·5s 92m **21M**; W twr; 43°44'·15N 07°31'·58W.
Pta de Faro ⚡ Fl R 5s 18m 7M; W twr; 43°42'·74N 07°35'·03W.
Pta Socastro ⚡ Fl G 5s 18m 7M; G twr; 43°43'·08N 07°36'·42W.
Cillero, outer bkwtr ⚡ Fl (2) R 7s 8m 5M; 43°40'·93N 07°36'·16W.
Marina ent ⚡ Fl (3) G 9s 7m 1M; 43°40'·15N 07°35'·71W.

RÍA DEL BARQUERO
Isla Coelleira ⚡ Fl (4) 24s 87m 7M; 43°45'·52N 07°37'·77W.
Pta de la Barra ⚡ Fl WRG 3s 15m 5M; 198°-G-213°-W-240°-R-255°-G-213°; W twr; 43°44'·51N 07°41'·31W.
Pta del Castro ⚡ Fl (2) 7s 14m 5M; 43°44'·46N 07°40'·48W.

PTA DE LA ESTACA DE BARES TO CABO VILLANO
Pta de la Estaca de Bares ☆ Fl (2) 7·5s 99m **25M**; obsc'd when brg >291°; 8-sided twr; *Siren Mo (B) 60s;* 43°47'·21N 07°41'·08W.
Espasante, W bkwtr ⚡ Fl R 5s 11m 3M; 43°43'·36N 07°48'·88W.
Carino bkwtr ⚡ Fl (3) G 9s 12m 5M; 43°44'·05N 07°51'·73W.
Cabo Ortegal (Pta de los Aguillones) ☆ Oc 8s 122m **18M**; W ○ twr, R band; 43°46'·22N 07°52'·27W. **Note:** Fl 5s 10M (T) 2009
Punta Candelaria ☆ Fl (3+1) 24s 87m **21M**; 43°42'·63N 08°02'·88W.

RÍA DE CEDEIRA
Punta del Sarridal ⚡ Oc WR 6s 39m 11M; Shore-R-145°-W-172°-R-145°; R ○ twr; 43°39'·65N 08°04'·53W.
Pta Promontorio ⚡ Oc (4) 10s 24m 11M; 43°39'·05N 08°04'·20W.
Piedras de Media Mar ⚓ Fl (2) 5s 13m 4M; BRB twr; 43°39'·37N 08°04'·79W.
Bkwtr hd ⚡ Fl (2) R 7s 10m 5M; R post; 43°39'·30N 08°04'·20W.
Punta Frouxeira ☆ Fl (5) 15s 73m **20M**; 43°37'·05N 08°11'·25W.
Cabo Prior ☆ Fl (1+2) 15s 105m **22M**; 055·5°-310°; 6-sided twr; 43°34'·06N 08°18'·86W. ODAS buoy Fl (5) Y 20s at 43°35'·41N 08°19'·45W, 1·4M NNW of Cabo Prior.
Punta del Castro ⚡ Fl (2) 7s 42m 8M; 6-sided twr; 43°30'·47N 08°19'·73W.

RÍA DE FERROL
Cabo Prioriño Chico ☆ Fl 5s 35m **23M**; 225°-129·5°; W 8-sided twr; 43°27'·53N 08°20'·40W.
Ent bkwtr head ⚡ Fl R 5s 21m 7M; *Racon N 12M;* 43°27'·23N 08°19'·80W. Bkwtr spur on NE side Fl (2) R 7s 12m 3M.
Batería de San Cristóbal ⚡ 042° Dir WRG 33m 5M, 038·2°-FG-040°-AlWG-041·5°-W-042·5°-AlWR-044°-FR-045·7°; white ☐ twr; 43°27'·93N 08°18'·25W.
Ldg lts 085·2°: Front, Pta de San Martín ⚡ Fl 1·5s 10m 5M; 43°27'·58N 08°17'·06W. Rear ⚡ Oc 4s 5M; 701m from front.
Dársena de Curuxeiras ⚡ Fl (4) R 11s 5m 3M; 43°28'·54N 08°14'·67W.

RÍA DE ARES and RÍA DE BETANZOS
Ares bkwtr ⚡ Fl (4) R 11s 10m 5M; R twr; 43°25'·35N 08°14'·27W.
Sada N pier ⚡ Fl (4) G 11s 11m 5M; G twr; 43°21'·77N 08°14'·52W.

LA CORUÑA
Torre de Hércules ☆ Fl (4) 20s 104m **23M**; ☐ twr, 8-sided top; *Siren Mo (L) 30s;* 43°23'·15N 08°24'·39W.
Canal del Oeste ldg lts 108·5°, both W 8-sided twrs: Front, Pta de Mera ⚡ Oc WR 4s 54m, W8M R3M; 000°-R-023°; 100·5°-R-105·5°-W-114·5°-R-153°; *Racon M, 18M; 020°-196°;* 43°23'·00N 08°21'·27W. Rear ⚡ Fl 4s 79m 8M; 357·5°-177·5°; 300m from front.
Canal del Este ldg lts 182°, both R/W chequered ☐ twrs: Front, Pta Fiaiteira ⚡ Iso WRG 2s 27m, W10M, R/G7M; 146·4°-G-180°-W-184°-R-217·6°; *Racon X, 11-21M;* 43°20'·59N 08°22'·25W. Rear ⚡ Oc 4s 52m 3M; 380m from front.
Dique d'Abrigo ⚡ Fl G 3s 16m 6M; 43°21'·90N 08°22'·48W.
Dársena de la Marina ⚡ Fl (3) G 9s 8m 2M; 43°22'·01N 08°23'·66W.
Islas Sisargas ☆ Fl (3) 15s 108m **23M**; W 8-sided twr and W bldg; *Siren Mo (S) 30s;* 43°21'·51N 08°50'·72W.
Punta Nariga ☆ Fl (3+1) 20s 53m **22M**; W ○ twr; 43°19'·24N 08°54'·69W.

RÍA DE CORME Y LAXE
Pta del Roncudo ⚓ Fl 6s 36m10M; 43°16′·50N 08°59′·47W.
Pta de Laxe ☆ Fl (5) 20s 64m **20M**; W twr; 43°13′·84N 09°00′·65W.
Corme, mole ⚓ Fl (2) R 5s 12m 3M; 43°15′·64N 08°57′·83W.
Laxe, N mole ⚓ Fl G 3s 15m 4M; G ○ twr; 43°13′·35N 08°59′·95W.

CABO VILLANO TO THE PORTUGUESE BORDER
RÍA DE CAMARIÑAS and to PUNTA INSUA
C. Villano ☆ Fl (2) 15s 102m **28M**; 031·5°-228·5°; 8-sided twr, Gy cupola; *Siren Mo (V) 60s; Racon M, 35M;* 43°09′·61N 09°12′·69W.
Camariñas ldg lts 081°: Front, Pta Villueira ⚓ Fl 5s 13m 9M; W ○ twr; 43°07′·38N 09°11′·56W. Rear, Pta del Castillo, ⚓ Iso 4s 26m 11M; 079·5°-082·5° (3°); W twr, 612m from front.
Camariñas, outer bkwtr ⚓ Fl R 5s 7m 3M; 43°07′·45N 09°10′·69W.
Pta de la Barca ⚓ Oc 4s 11m 6M; 43°06′·79N 09°13′·19W.
Muxia bkwtr ⚓ Fl (2) G 10s 11m 4M; 43°06′·35N 09°12′·75W.
Pta de Lago ⚓ Oc (2) WRG 6s 13m, W6M, R/G4M; 029·5°-W-093°-G-107·8°-W-109·1°-R-139·3°-W-213·5°; W twr; 43°06′·60N 09°10′·01W.
Cabo Toriñana ☆ Fl (2+1) 15s 63m **24M**; 340·5°-235·5°; *Racon T, 35M (1·7M SE of ☆);* 43°03′·19N 09°17′·84W.
Cabo Finisterre ☆ Fl 5s 141m **23M**; 8-sided twr; obscd when brg >149°; *Racon O, 35M;* 42°52′·94N 09°16′·31W.

Seno de Corcubión
Lobeira Grande ⚓ Fl (3) 15s 16m 9M; 42°52′·84N 09°11′·12W.
Carrumeiro Chico ⚓ Fl (2) 7s 6m 6M; 42°54′·37N 09°10′·76W.
Cabo Cée ⚓ Fl (5) 13s 25m 7M; Gy twr; 42°54′·98N 09°11′·02W.
Corcubión bkwtr ⚓ Fl (2) R 8s 9m 4M; 42°56′·70N 09°11′·39W.
Pta Insúa ☆ Fl (3) WR 9s 25m; **W15M**, R14M; 020°-R-045°-W-070°-R-090°-W-125°-R-152°-W-020°; 42°46′·29N 09°07′·55W.

RÍA DE MUROS
Pta Queixal ⚓ Fl (2+1) 12s 25m 9M; 42°44′·36N 09°04′·73W.
Cabo Rebordiño ⚓ Fl (2) R 7s 16m 7M; 42°46′·20N 09°02′·90W.
Muros Fl R 5s 9m 3M; R/W bcn; 42°46′·67N 09°03′·28W.
Portosin bkwtr ⚓ Fl (3) G 9s 8m 5M; 42°45′·94N 08°56′·93W.
Pta Cabeiro ⚓ Oc WR 3s 35m W9M, R6M; 050°-R-054·5°-W-058·5°-R-099·5°-W-189·5°; Gy twr; 42°44′·36N 08°59′·44W.
O Son outer bkwtr ⚓ Fl G 5s 4m 5M; 42°43′·73N 08°00′·05W.
Pta Focha ⚓ Fl 5s 27m 4M; ○ twr; 42°41′·98N 09°01′·59W.

RÍA DE AROUSA (Selected lights only)
C. Corrubedo ☆ Fl (2+3) WR 20s 30m **15M**; dangerous sector 347°-R-040°; *Siren Mo (O) 60s; Racon K;* 42°34′·57N 09°05′·39W.
Isla Sálvora ☆ Fl (3+1) 20s 38m **21M**; vis 217°-126°; 42°27′·97N 09°00′·80W. Same twr, ⚓ Fl (3) 20s; 126°-160° danger sector.
Santa Uxia marina bkwtr knuckle ⚓ Fl (2+1) G 15s 8m 3M; G ○ twr +R band; 42°33′·76N 08°59′·27W. 1ca NW ⚓ Fl (2) R 7s 8m 3M.
Isla Rúa ⚓ Fl (2) WR 7s 25m 12M; 121·5°-R-211·5°-W-121·5°; *Racon K, 211°-121°, 10-20M;* 42°32′·96N 08°56′·38W.
Pobra do Caramiñal Marina bkwtr ⚓ Fl (2+1) R 15s 3M; R post, G band; 42°36′·33N 08°56′·04W.
Rianxo NW bkwtr hd ⚓ Fl (3) G 9s 3M; 42°39′·00N 08°49′·54W.
Vilagarcia, N mole ⚓ Iso 2s 2m 10M; ○ twr; 42°36′·14N 08°46′·37W. **I Arousa** Pta Caballo ⚓ Fl (4) 11s 12m 10M; 42°34′·34N 08°53′·04W.

Peninsula del Grove
Roca Pombeiriño ⚓ Fl (2) G 12s 13m 8M; WGW bcn twr; 42°28′·93N 08°56′·83W.
Piedras Negras marina, bkwtr hd ⚓ Fl (4) WR 11s 5m, W4M R3M; 305°-W-315°-R-305°; R post; 42°27′·49N 08°55′·11W.
Bajo Piedra Seca ⚓ Fl (3) R 9s 4m 5M; 42°27′·00N 08°54′·62W.

RÍA DE PONTEVEDRA
Bajo Fagilda ⚓ QR 1s 16M; 42°24′·76N 08°53′·77W.
Bajo Picamillo ⚓ Fl G 5s 10m 8M; twr; 42°24′·25N 08°53′·46W.
Bajo Los Camoucos ⚓ Fl (3) R 18s 10m 8M; 42°23′·70N 08°54′·71W.
Isla Ons ☆ Fl (4) 24s 125m **25M**; 8-sided twr; 42°22′·95N 08°56′·19W.
Almacén pier ⚓ Fl R 4s 7m 2M; R ○ twr; 42°22′·63N 08°55′·77W.

Portonovo mole ⚓ Fl (3) R 6s 9m 4M; 42°23′·65N 08°49′·13W.
Sangenjo marina, mole ⚓ QR 5m 4M; 42°23′·81N 08°48′·06W.
NE side ⚓ Fl (3) G 9s 6m 2M; 42°23′·83N 08°48′·03W.
Cabezo de Morranzán ⚓ Iso R 5s; 42°22′·37N 08°47′·04W.
Rajó mole ⚓ Fl (2) R 8s 9m 3M; R ○ twr; 42°24′·10N 08°45′·26W.
Isla Tambo ⚓ Fl (3) 8s 35m 11M; W ○ twr; 42°24′·48N 08°42′·47W.
Combarro N mole ⚓ Fl (2) R 8s 7m 3M; 42°25′·78N 08°42′·23W.
S jetty head ⚓ Oc (2) R 6s 3M; 42°25′·62N 08°42′·22W.
Rio Lérez mouth ⚓ Fl R 5s; ⚓ Fl G 5s; 42°24′·84N 08°41′·22W.
Aguete ⚓ Fl (4) G 11s 3M; 42°22′·66N 08°44′·20W.
Marina, wavebreak, E end ⚓ Fl (2) G 7s 1M; 42°22′·55N 08°44′·16W.
Bueu N bkwtr ⚓ Fl G 3s 7m 4M; twr; 42°19′·79N 08°47′·02W.
Beluso N bkwtr ⚓ Fl (3) G 9s; 42°20′·02N 08°47′·90W.
S bkwtr ⚓ Fl (3) R 9s; 42°20′·00N 08°47′·97W.
Cabeza de la Mourisca ⚓ Fl (2) G 7s 10m 5M; 42°20′·90N 08°49′·17W.
Aldán jetty head ⚓ Fl (2) R 10s 5m 5M; 42°16′·95N 08°49′·38W.
Punta Couso ⚓ Fl (3) WG 10·5s 18m, W10M, G8M; 060°-G-096°-W-190°-G-000°; 42°18′·56N 08°51′·33W.

ISLAS CÍES
Isla del Norte, Pta de Monte Agudo ⚓ Fl G 5s 24m 10M; 42°14′·60N 08°54′·19W.
Piedra Borron ⚓ Fl (2) 10s 3M; 42°13′·49N 08°54′·00W.
Monte Faro ⚓ Fl (2) 8s 186m **22M**; obsc'd 315°-016·5° over Bajos de Los Castros and Forcados; ○ twr; 42°12′·85N 08°54′·90W.
Isla del Faro, Pta Canabal ⚓ Fl (3) 20s 63m 9M; W twr; 42°12′·73N 08°54′·77W.
Isla de San Martin, Cabo Vicos ⚓ Fl (3) R 9s 93m 10M; obsc'd 108°-210·5°; W twr; 42°11′·51N 08°53′·48W.
Islote Boeiro ⚓ Fl (2) R 8s 22m 5M; W twr; 42°10′·75N 08°54′·61W.

RÍA DE VIGO
N Chan, outer ldg lts 129°, both 090°-180°; W ○ twrs: Front, Cabo del Home ⚓ Fl 3s 36m 9M; 42°15′·15N 08°52′·37W. Rear, Pta Subrido ⚓ Oc 6s 53m 11M; 815m from front,.
Punta Robaleira ⚓ Fl (2) WR 7·5s 25m, W11M, R9M; 300·5°-W-321·5°-R-090°; 115·5°-R-170·5°; R twr; *Racon C;* 42°15′·00N 08°52′·38W (285m S of Cabo del Home ldg lt).
Cangas NE mole ⚓ Fl R 5s 8m 5M; R ○ twr; 42°15′·61N 08°46′·83W.
S Chan ldg lts 069·3°, both R twrs, W bands; vis 066·3°-072·3°. **Front** ☆ Iso 2s 16m **18M**; *Horn Mo (V) 60s; Racon B, 22M;* 42°11′·11N 08°48′·88W. **Rear** Oc 4s 48m **18M**, 660m from front.
No. 1 ⚓ Fl (3) G 9s 5M; 42°12′·31N 08°48′·62W.
No. 3 ⚓ Fl (4) G 14s 11m 5M; GW twr; 42°13′·71N 08°46′·73W.
Bouzas, NE head ⚓ Fl (2+1) G 15s 9m 5M; 42°14′·07N 08°44′·67W.
Marina Dávila Sport ⚓ Fl (2) G 7s 10m 5M; 42°13′·99N 08°44′·42W.
Muelle del Berbés, N head ⚓ Fl (3) G 9s 9m 5M; G twr; 42°14′·43N 08°44′·01W.
Muelle de Transatlánticos, NE head ⚓ Fl (4) G 11s 9m 5M; col; 42°14′·59N 08°43′·56W.
Vigo marina ent, QG and QR 9m 5M; 42°14′·57N 08°43′·41W.
Bajo Lagao, ⚓ Fl (2) 6s; 42°15′·28N 08°42′·73W.
Pta Lagoa marina, bkwtr hd, ⚓ QG 3m 2M, 42°15′·51N 08°42′·46W.
La Guia ☆ Oc (2+1) 20s 37m **15M**; W twr; 42°15′·57N 08°42′·14W.

BAYONA to the PORTUGUESE BORDER
Las Serralleiras ⚓ Q (9) 15s 4M; 42°09′·23N 08°53′·35W.
Las Serralleiras ⚓ Fl G 4s 9m 6M; 42°08′·78N 08°52′·66W.
Pta Lameda ⚓ Fl (2) 8s 27m 5M; W twr; 42°09′·39N 08°50′·98W.
Ldg/Dir lts 084°, both W twrs: Front, Cabezo de San Juan ⚓ Fl 6s 8m 10M; 42°08′·13N 08°50′·10W. Rear, **Panjón Dir** ⚓ 084°, Oc WRG 4s **W18M, R15M**, G14M; 079°-G-083°-W-085°-R-088°; 42°08′·34N 08°48′·84W.
Dique de Abrigo ⚓ QG 10m 5M; G/W twr; 42°07′·49N 08°50′·58W.
C. Silleiro ☆ Fl (2+1) 15s 84m **24M**; W 8-sided twr, R bands; 42°06′·17N 08°53′·78W. ⚓ Q; 42°07′·29N 08°54′·73W
La Guardia N bkwtr ⚓ Fl (2) R 7s 11m 5M; R twr; *Siren Mo (L) 30s;* 41°54′·01N 08°52′·94W. S bkwtr ⚓ Fl (2) G 7s 11m 5M; G twr.

9.23.4 PASSAGE INFORMATION

More Passage information is threaded between successive hbrs in this Area. **Bibliography:** *see the foot of the next column.*

BAY OF BISCAY: WIND, WEATHER AND SEA

NE'lies prevail in sea area Finisterre in summer and gales may occur twice monthly, although forecast more frequently. Atlantic lows can bring W'ly spells at any time. Wind direction and speed often vary from day to day, but SE or S winds are rare. Sea and land breezes can be well developed in the summer. Off N Spain *Galernas* are dangerous squally NW winds which blow with little warning. Coastal winds are intensified by the Cordillera Cantábrica (2615m mountains).

Despite its reputation, the S part of the Bay is often warm and settled in summer when the Azores high and Spanish heat low are the dominant weather features. Rainfall is moderate, increasing in the SE, where thunder is more frequent. Sea fog, which may mean strong winds are imminent, occurs May-Oct, but is less common in winter.

▶*There are no tidal stream atlases. Streams are weak offshore, but can be strong in narrow channels and off headlands.*◀

Surface current much depends on wind: in summer it sets SE ½–¾kn, towards the SE corner of Bay of Biscay, thence W along N coast of Spain. When crossing the Bay, allow for some set to the E, particularly after strong west winds.

CROSSING THE BAY OF BISCAY

Distances across the Bay are tabulated at 9.0.8. Leaving the English Channel, the track (208°/362M) from Ushant ITZ to Cabo Villano (AC 1104) lies undesirably close to busy shipping lanes, but a track (213°/287M) from, say, harbours between **Loctudy** and **Concarneau**, to Cabo Ortegal is substantially offset to the SE of the shipping route. Cabo Ortegal as a landfall permits onward passage to **La Coruña**. Or, if conditions for rounding Ortegal are bad (as is not unknown), **Ría de Vivero** is a safe refuge. From Scilly or Ireland the direct track lies in about 7°-8°W.

Within the Bay itself, sailing down the French coast is attractive and allows a 200M passage from, say, **La Rochelle** to **Santander**. Landes missile range between Pointe de Grave and Capbreton extends up to 45M offshore. It may inhibit coastal passages, but is usually inactive at night, w/ends and August.

The Continental Shelf, where depths plummet from 150m to over 4000m in only 30M, can cause dangerous seas in swell and bad weather. From a position about 60M SW of Ile de Sein it trends SE to the Franco/Spanish border as shown on AC 1104.

Atlantic swell runs in mainly from W or NW; see 6.1.1. It is not a problem well offshore, except over the Continental Shelf in bad weather. Considerable rolling is probable and other yachts or even small ships may be lost to view in the troughs. Closer inshore swell will exacerbate the sea state and render entry to, and exit from, lee shore harbours dangerous. For example, with a 2m swell running, crossing a bar with 4m depth over it and breaking seas would be foolhardy. In winter some harbours may be closed for long periods.

FRENCH BORDER TO SANTANDER

The N coast of Spain is bold and rocky (AC 1102, 1105, 1108). In clear visibility the peaks of the **Cordillera Cantábrica** may be seen from well offshore. Although the coast is mostly steep-to, it is best to keep 2-3M offshore (beyond the 50m contour) to avoid short, steep seas breaking on isolated shoals. Many major lights are sited so high as to be obscured by low cloud/mist in onshore weather. Of the many small rivers, most are obstructed by bars and none are navigable far inland.

From Hendaye to Santander harbours are closely spaced compared with further west. Ports of refuge in NW gales are: **Pasajes** (no yacht facilities), **Guetaria, Bermeo, Bilbao, Castro Urdiales** and **Santander**. San Sebastián is an attractive ⚓ but exposed to the NW. **Bilbao** and **Santander** are ferry ports and major cities with marinas. Fishing hbrs with AB or ⚓ include: **Guetaria, Motrico, Bermeo, Lequeitio, Elanchove** and **Laredo**.

9.23.5 SPECIAL NOTES FOR SPAIN

Regions/Provinces: Spain is divided into 17 autonomous regions, ie in Area 23, Guipuzcoa (Basque Country), Cantabrica, Asturias and Galicia. Most regions are sub-divided into provinces, eg in Galicia: Lugo, La Coruña, Pontevedra and Orense (inland). The province is shown below the name of each main port.

Language: This Almanac recognises regional differences (eg Basque, Gallego), but in the interests of standardisation uses the spelling of Castilian Spanish where practicable.

Spanish Charts (SC). Contact Instituto Hidrográfico de la Marina, Plaza San Severiano 3, 11007 Cádiz, ☎ (956) 599 414; www. armada.mde.es/ihm or order from chart agents in Madrid, Bilbao, Santander, Gijon, La Coruña, Villagarcia de Arousa and Vigo.

Currency is the Euro €. VAT (IVA) 16%.

Courtesy Ensign: E of Bilbao it may be politic to fly the Basque flag, Fig 5 (6), or none at all. The Spanish ensign may give offence, especially if flown above the autonomous Basque flag.

Fuel: Diesel (*Gasoleo*) is of two types: *Gasoleo A* is taxed and supplied to yachts from marina pumps or by cans from a filling station ashore. *Gasoleo B* is untaxed and usually only available to FVs from a pump on the fish quay.

Standard Time in Spain is UT –1, but in Portugal it is UT.

Spanish secondary ports referenced to Lisboa. Time differences for those Spanish ports which are referenced to Lisboa (all south of Ría de Muros), when applied to the printed times of HW and LW for Lisboa, give HW and LW times in Spanish Standard Time. DST is the only correction required.

Telephone: To call Spain from UK dial 00 34, then the area code, followed by the 6 digit ☎ number. Internally dial the area code plus the ☎ number. To call UK from Spain, dial 07 44, then area code less the initial 0, plus the ☎ number.

Emergencies: ☎ 900 202 202 for Fire, Police and Ambulance. *Rioja Cruz* (Red Cross) operate LBs.

Public Holidays: Jan 1, 6; Apr 10 (Good Friday); 1 May (Labour Day); June 11 (Corpus Christi); Aug 15 (Assumption); Oct 12 (National Day); Nov 1 (All Saints Day); Dec 6, 8 (Immaculate Conception), 25.

Representation: Spanish Tourist Office, 22-23 Manchester Square, London W1U 3PX; ☎ 020 7486 8077. londres@tourspain.es www. tourspain.uk

British Embassy, Calle de Fernando el Santo 16, 28010 Madrid; ☎ (91) 700 8200. Consuls: Bilbao ☎ (944) 157600; Santander ☎ (942) 220000; Vigo ☎ (986) 437133.

Buoyage: Preferred channel buoys [RGR, Fl (2+1) R and GRG, Fl (2+1) G] are quite widely used; see Chapter 3.

Documents: Spain, although an EU member, still checks papers. This can be a time-consuming, repetitive and inescapable process. The only palliatives are courtesy, patience and good humour. Organise your documents to include:

Personal – Passports; crew list, ideally on headed paper with the yacht's rubber stamp, giving DoB, passport nos, where joined/ intended departure. Certificate of Competence (Yachtmaster Offshore, ICC/HOCC etc). Radio Operator's certificate. EHIC is advised for medical treatment.

Yacht – Registration certificate, Part 1 or SSR. Proof of VAT status. Marine insurance. Ship's Radio licence. Itinerary and ship's log.

Access: Ferries from UK to Santander and Bilbao. Flights from UK to Bilbao, Santiago de Compostela and Madrid. Internal flights via Madrid to Asturias, La Coruña and Vigo. Buses are mostly good and trains adequate, except in more remote regions.

Bibliography: *NW Spain CC* (NDL/Jens, 2002) French border to Bayona. *S Biscay Pilot* (Imray/RCC, 6th ed'n 2006) Gironde to La Coruña. *Atlantic Spain and Portugal* (Imray/RCC, 5th ed'n 2006) El Ferrol to Gibraltar. *Bay of Biscay Pilot* (NP 22, 10th ed'n 2007) Pte de Penmarc'h to Cabo Ortegal. *W Coasts of Spain and Portugal Pilot* (NP 67, 9th ed'n 2005) Cabo Ortegal to Gibraltar.-

9.23.6 FUENTERRABÍA (Hondarribia)

Guipúzcoa 43°22'·56N 01°47'·52W ✴✴✴✴🌢🌢🌣🌣🌣

CHARTS AC 1102, 1170, 1171; SC 391, 3910; SHOM 6556, 6558, 6786; Navi 555. *Spanish* and French names for the same feature: *Rada de Higuer* = Baie de Fontarabie or de Figuier; *Ría de Fuenterrabía* = La Bidassoa (river).

TIDES HW +0450 on Dover (UT); ML 2·3m.
Interpolate between SOCOA 9.22.30 and PASAJES 9.23.7.

SHELTER Excellent in marina, access H24. S of Cabo Higuer, a FV hbr, 2-3m, is a port of refuge. Good ⚓ in river off Pta Roca.

NAVIGATION WPT 43°23'·87N 01°46'·44W, 212°/1·15M to W bkwtr hd. Beware Les Briquets 8ca N of Pte Ste Anne at E end of the Baie. Near centre of B, keep clear of Bajo Iruarri. River ent (6·5-1·3m) is easy except in heavy N'ly swell; sp ebb is very strong.
The neutral zone between France and Spain is delineated by the alignment of 4 pairs of beacons; see 9.22.31.

LIGHTS AND MARKS Cabo Higuer lt ho, a square stone twr with R top, is conspic at W side of bay, as is the high dorsal ridge which runs down to the headland. A red-roofed castle is prominent 2 cables SSE of Cabo Higuer lt ho. La Rhune, an 898m high conical peak, bears 120°/8M from the marina.

R/T Marina Ch 09 (H24).

TELEPHONE (Code 943) MRSC Santander (942) 213030.

FACILITIES Marina (3m). ☎ 641711. 595 + 25 🆅; berth on pontoon G (1st to port). Pontoons A-E are NW of the central pontoon F; G-J are to the SE. €0.5189 x LOA x beam (m)/per day (30 days pa max); max LOA 16m. Boats > 16m LOA should ⚓ in the Bay or in Baie de Chingoudy. D & P (UK cards), ME, BH (35 ton), C (3 ton), Wi-Fi free. Club Nautico ☎ 642788.
Town 🛒, R, Bar, Gaz, ⊠, Ⓑ, ⇌, ✈ (Fuenterrabía or Biarritz). Ferries, local: Fuenterrabía to Hendaye. UK: Santander, Bilbao.

9.23.7 PASAJES (Pasaia)

Guipúzcoa 43°20'·23N 01°55'·82W ✴✴✴✴🌢🌢🌣

CHARTS AC 1102, 1171, 1157; SC 391/2, 3911; SHOM 6375, 6558

TIDES See 9.23.8.

SHELTER A port of refuge (3·5M E of San Sebastián, 7M from France). Yachts may ⚓ as shown on the chartlet: the bay NE of Dir lt is fair weather only; the other two ⚓s are outside local small craft moorings, as space allows; the N'ly is subject to wash.

NAVIGATION WPT 43°21'·15N 01°56'·12W, SWM buoy [Mo (A) 6s], 161°/1·0M to hbr ent, a 200m wide cleft in spectacular cliffs. Appr on 154·8° transit of Dir lt, Oc (2) WRG 12s (Racon M), with ldg lts: front Q, rear Oc 3s; all on the W cliff.

Banks, 3·4 and 1·5m W and E of ent, are marked by conspic R and G 18m high lt twrs. Inner chan, dredged 10m, is only 100m wide, but well marked/lit; do not impede large vessels/FVs; be alert for departing ships.

LIGHTS AND MARKS Observe and obey IPTS located high on the E cliff at Atalya de Pasajes (Racon K). Sigs 1, 2 and 3 are shown to seaward and inwards; the ent is blind and narrow for big ships.

R/T Port Ch 09 (H24).

TELEPHONE (Code 943) HM ppasajes@sarenet.es ☎ 351816. MRSC Santander (942) 213030; Brit Consul 944 157600.

FACILITIES Pasajes is a busy FV and commercial hbr with no yacht facilities. Big ship ✕, El, Ⓔ, ME. Town 🛒, R, Bar, ⊠, Ⓑ.

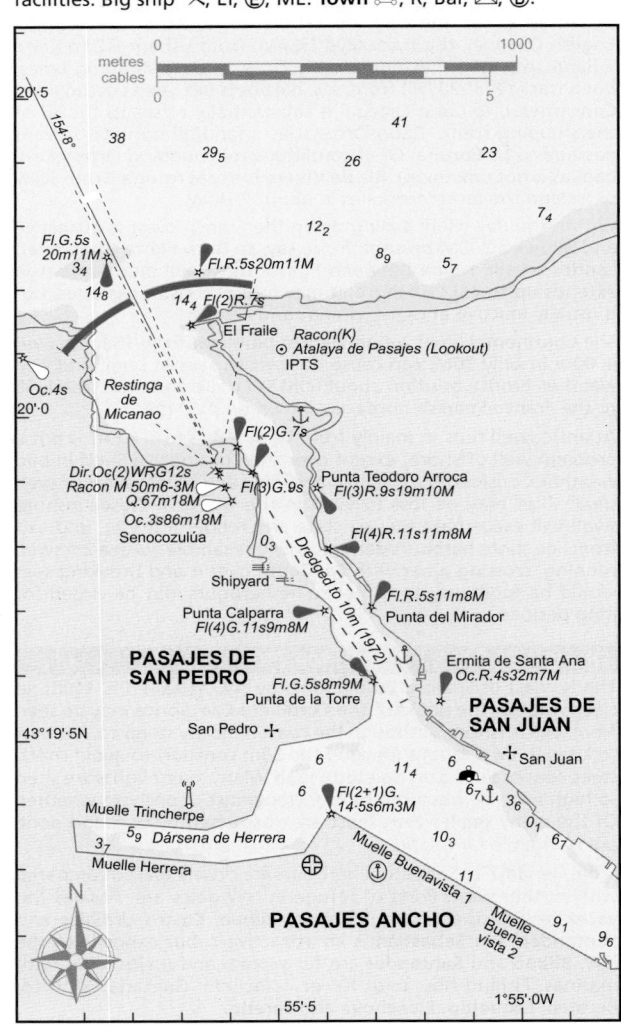

9.23.8 SAN SEBASTIÁN (Donostia)

Guipúzcoa **43°19'·48N 01°59'·79W** ✸✸✸✸🌢🌢✿✿✿

CHARTS AC 1102, 1171; SC 391, 392, 3910; SHOM 6558, 6786

TIDES

Standard Port POINTE DE GRAVE (←—)

Times				Height (metres)			
High Water		Low Water		MHWS	MHWN	MLWN	MLWS
0000	0600	0000	0500	5·4	4·4	2·1	1·0
1200	1800	1200	1700				
Differences SAN SEBASTIÁN							
–0110	–0030	–0040	–0020	–1·2	–1·2	–0·5	–0·4
PASAJES							
–0050	–0030	–0045	–0015	–1·2	–1·3	–0·5	–0·5

SHELTER Fair; the ⚓ becomes lively or dangerous in any NW/N'lies when heavy swell enters. ⚓ S of Isla Santa Clara or SW of YC, in both cases clear of moorings and with ⚓ buoyed.

NAVIGATION WPT 43°19'·85N 02°00'·00W, 158°/0·4M to hbr ent (between Isla de Santa Clara and Monte Urgull). Avoid La Bancha on which the sea breaks in swell and heavy weather. Open up the bay before standing in.

LIGHTS AND MARKS Monte Urgull (huge statue of Virgin Mary) is prominent from all directions; from E it looks like an island. Monte Igueldo on W side of ent is only slightly less obvious. Isla de Santa Clara is lower and inconspicuous; not seen until the nearer appr. Ldg marks (grey masts) are hard to see, but a large R and W Palladian-styled villa is conspic on 158°. Ldg lts, although intense, may be masked by shore lts. See chartlet and 9.23.3.

R/T Real Club Nautico Ch 09 (H24).

TELEPHONE (Code 943) MRSC Santander (942) 213030; Met 274030; Auto 906 365320; Ⓗ 945 454000; Brit Consul 944 157600.

FACILITIES for visiting boats do not match the city's elegance. **Real Club Náutico** ☎ 423574, M (best to pre-arrange), R, Bar, Ice. YC launch will meet and direct (Ch 09) to a vacant ⚓.

Dársena de la Concha is over-crowded, with limited space on ⓥ pontoon dead ahead of ent; inner basins are locals/FVs only.

City Gaz, 🛒, R, Bar, Ⓑ, ✉, Ⓗ. ⚒ & ✈ Fuenterrabia (25km). ✈ also at Bilbao (92km) and ferry to UK.

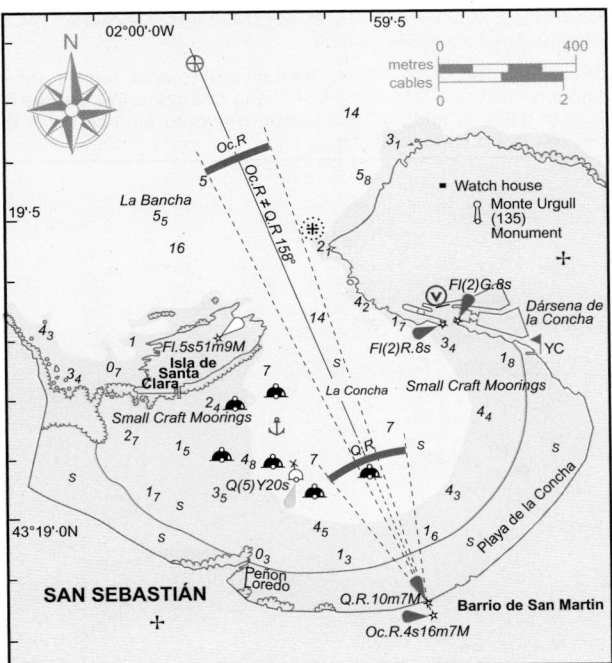

MINOR HARBOUR 3M ESE OF GUETARIA

RÍA DE ORIO Guipúzcoa **43°17'·49N 02°07'·98W**. AC 1102; SC 944, 303A; SHOM 6786, 6379. Tides: MHWS 4·1m, MLWS 0·5m; MHWN 3·2m, MLWN 1·4m. Interpolate between San Sebastian & Guetaria. WPT 43°17'·97N 02°07'·95W, 180°/5ca to W bkwtr between Mte Talai (360m) to the E and Mte Amesti (188m) to the W. Small marina (2-3m) 5ca up-river from the ent, on the east bank and just N of the road bridge, 17·5m clearance. Best water to the E. Good shelter, but exposed to N'lies when swell may work in. Fair weather tempy ⚓ outside to the E off San Juan beach in 5m.

Appr at HW –1. See 9.23.3 for the two entrance lts. A first visit at night is not advised despite a total of 17 nav lts.

HM ☎ (943) 249400. www.ekpsa.com VHF 09. kirolportua@ekpsa.com 300 AB, €0.71303 x LOA x beam (m)/per day (30 days max); max LOA 12m. **Facilities:** FW, AC, Slip, P&D (H24), BH (35 ton). **Town** 800m south. Bar, R, 🛒.

9.23.9 GUETARIA (Getaria)

Guipúzcoa **43°18'·23N 02°11'·93W** ✸✸✸✸🌢🌢✿✿✿

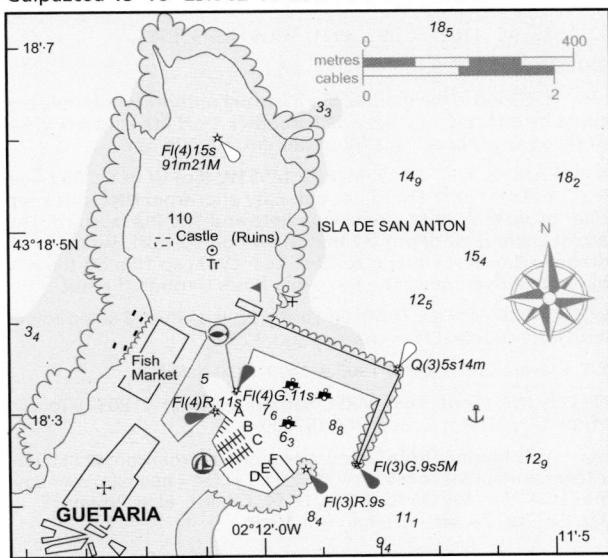

CHARTS AC 1102, 1171; SC 392, 3921; SHOM 6379, 6786

TIDES

Standard Port POINTE DE GRAVE (←—)

Times				Height (metres)			
High Water		Low Water		MHWS	MHWN	MLWN	MLWS
0000	0600	0000	0500	5·4	4·4	2·1	1·0
1200	1800	1200	1700				
Differences GUETARIA							
–0110	–0030	–0040	–0020	–1·0	–1·0	–0·5	–0·4

SHELTER The only good shelter in S-NW winds between Pasajes and Bilbao. No ⚓ in hbr which is generally foul. In fair weather ⚓ on sand or pick up a buoy close S of hbr ent, but exposed to E'lies.

NAVIGATION WPT 43°18'·90N 02°11'·00W, 225°/9½ca to hbr ent. Appr is straightforward day/night in fair visibility.

LIGHTS AND MARKS Lts as chartlet & 9.23.3. The mouse-like profile of Isla de San Anton is distinctive; lt ho on its N side.

R/T Ch 09 H24.

TELEPHONE (Code 943) ⊜ via Marina; Met 906 365 320; Auto 906 365365; MRSC Santander (942) 213030; Brit Consul 944 157600.

FACILITIES **Marina** pontoons A-F to port on entry. ☎ 580959, thage@infonegocio.com. 300 AB, ; max LOA 14m. BH (30 ton). Slip, D, ✖, CH, SM, ME, El, C (5 ton). **Club Náutico y Pesca** ☎ 140201, R, Bar. FVs use N side of outer hbr and all the inner hbr.

Town 🛒, R, Bar, Gaz, ☎, ✉, ⇌; ✈ Bilbao (UK ferry).

MINOR HARBOUR 6M W OF ZUMAYA

MOTRICO (Mutriku) Guipúzcoa **43°18'·80N 02°22'·80W.** Tides: interpolate between Guetaria & Lequeitio. AC 1102; SC 392, 3922; SHOM 6379. Small FV hbr (4m) in rky inlet. Good shelter from NE winds thanks to a large new outer bkwtr (completed 2009), but swell may still work in. Yacht berths/facilities were due to be finished summer 2007, but still incomplete 2009. Please send reports and/or photos to the address in 0.4.1.

WPT 43°19'·73N 02°21'·68W, on the 236·5° ldg line, 7ca to outer bkwtr which must be left to stbd. Beware: the ldg line crosses the new outer bkwtr. The ent is easily seen from E, but from W open hbr & town before approaching. 236·5° ldg lts/marks: front on S bkwtr; rear, on clock twr (hard to see by day). Lts as chartlet.

⚓ inside the new bkwtr in 5m; or possible AB at inner end of SE quay if FVs are away. HM ☎ (943) 603204. www.mutriku.net udala@mutriku.net **Facilities** (FV quay): FW, ⟨D⟩, D, P, C (5 ton), Ice, Slip. **Town** Bar, R, 🛒.

9.23.10 ZUMAYA (Zumaia)

Guipúzcoa **43°18'·36N 02°14'·92W** (Hbr ent) ❀❀❀⬧⬧⬧✿✿✿

CHARTS AC 1102; SC 392, 3921; SHOM 6379, 6786.

TIDES As for 9.23.9.

SHELTER Good in the marina, but in strong onshore winds the appr could be difficult. In E'lies a fair weather ⚓ off Pta Izustarri, clear of rks at sandy beach 3ca NE of hbr ent. No ⚓ in hbr.

NAVIGATION WPT 43°19'·85N 02°14'·51W (8ca W of ODAS buoy, Fl (5) Y 20s), 190°/1·5M to hbr ent. Easy appr from NNE, but keep clear of rocks W of Pta Iruarriaundieta and S of Pta Izustarri. The access chan, least depth 0·1m as shown on SC 3921, is said to be dredged 3m. Best water is to stbd; near LW keep 10m off the NW bkwtr and river bank. The Rio Urola flows through the hbr.

LIGHTS AND MARKS Lt ho, Oc (1+3) 12s, is a white 8-sided tower with blue cupola. Lts as chartlet and 9.23.3.

R/T Marina Ch 09 (0900-1300 & 1400-1930 daily).

TELEPHONE (Code 943) MRSC Santander (942) 213030. Tourist office 143396; Brit Consul 944 157600.

FACILITIES Marina Urola (2·5m) www.marinaurola.com ☎ 860938. info@marinaurola.com 515 inc Ⓥ, €0.55 x LOA x beam (m)/per day; max LOA 15m. BH (35 ton), Slip, D, 🔧, CH, ME, El, R. **Town:** 🛒, R, Bar, Gaz, ☎, ✉, ⇌. ✈ Bilbao (UK ferry).

ZUMAYA

9.23.11 LEQUEITIO (Lekeitio)

Vizcaya **43°22'·00N 02°29'·91W** ❀❀❀⬧⬧⬧✿✿

CHARTS AC 1102, 1171; SC 392, 393; SHOM 6379, 5009.

TIDES
Standard Port POINTE DE GRAVE (←)

Times				Height (metres)			
High Water		Low Water		MHWS	MHWN	MLWN	MLWS
0000	0600	0000	0500	5·4	4·4	2·1	1·0
1200	1800	1200	1700				
Differences LEQUEITIO							
−0115	−0035	−0045	−0025	−1·2	−1·2	−0·5	−0·4

SHELTER Good. ⚓ in about 3m or pick up a vacant buoy at the S end of basin where there are extensive small craft trots. In settled weather ⚓ further out, to E or W of Isla de San Nicolas.

NAVIGATION WPT 43°22'·25N 02°29'·68W, 214°/3ca to abeam Pta Amandarri lt. Avoid rky shoals close E of 213·8° ldg line and ruins of old bkwtr (Fl (2) R 8s) further S.

LIGHTS AND MARKS Conspic daymarks: Cabo de Santa Catalina 0·8M to the NW. Isla de San Nicolas is rky, steep-sided, wooded and linked to mainland by a part-drying causeway. Church dome SSW of hbr. Palacio Uribarren, the rear 213·8° ldg mark.

R/T Ch 09.

TELEPHONE (Code 946) HM ☎ 243324. MRSC Santander (942) 213030; Brit Consul 944 157600.

FACILITIES Busy with FVs so limited space, poss temp'y (few minutes) berthing on pontoon at N end of E quay. FVs use the N part of basin. Friendly YC but can be crowded. Club de Pesca ☎ 840500. D, P, CH, Slip, ME, 🛒.

LEQUEITIO

9.23.12 ELANCHOVE (Elantxobe)

Vizcaya 43°24'·23N 02°38'·21W ❀❀◈◊❀❀❀

CHARTS AC 1102, 1171; SC 393; SHOM 6380, 6991

TIDES Interpolate between Lequeitio and Bermeo.
Standard Port POINTE DE GRAVE (◄—)

Times				Height (metres)			
High Water		Low Water		MHWS	MHWN	MLWN	MLWS
0000	0600	0000	0500	5·4	4·4	2·1	1·0
1200	1800	1200	1700				
Differences BERMEO							
–0055	–0015	–0025	–0005	–0·8	–0·7	–0·5	–0·4

SHELTER Sheltered from W in lee of Cabo Ogoño, but exposed to N/E. In calm weather temporary ⚓ to E of hbr ent in 5m.

NAVIGATION WPT 43°24'·67N 02°37'·61W, 225°/6ca to N mole hd. From the W, hbr is not visible until bearing >205°.

LIGHTS AND MARKS See chartlet and 9.23.3. The S Mole, F WR lt shows Red (315°-000°) over inshore dangers to the SE. Cabo Machichaco, Fl 7s, is 6M WNW.

R/T Nil   TELEPHONE (Code 944) HM ☎ 881323.

HARBOUR 2·7M SE OF CABO MACHICHACO

BERMEO 43°25'·35N 02°42'·57W. Tides: see 9.23.12. AC 1102, 1172; SC 393, 3931; SHOM 6380, 6991. A busy commercial & FV port, well sheltered from the N, but swell enters in E'lies.

Hbr is between the wide drying estuary of Rio Mundaca and conspic Cabo Machichaco to NW. Appr on 218° in W sector (204°-232°) of Rosape Dir lt to clear unlit Isla de Izaro, 1M ENE of hbr and the N mole. See 9.23.3 for lights.

❶ limited, poss AB as on chartlet in 2m or in the round inner hbr (2m) amid local small craft. Piling reported in outer hbr, but (2009) no pontoons to go with them.

VHF Ch 09,16. HM ☎ (946) 18 64 45 or mobile ☎ 908 87 33 30. www.euskadi.net/portuak/ AB, FW, D, Slip, C (12 ton), ME, ✖, Ice.
Town: ⧈, R, P, Gaz, El, Ⓔ, Ⓑ, ✉, ≥ to Guernica.

9.23.13 BILBAO (Bilbo)

Vizcaya 43°22'·73N 03°04'·87W (outer ent) ❀❀❀◊◊◊❀❀❀

CHARTS AC 1102, 1174, 1173; SC 394, 394A, 3941; SHOM 6774, 6991

TIDES

Standard Port POINTE DE GRAVE (◄—); ML 2·4.

Times				Height (metres)			
High Water		Low Water		MHWS	MHWN	MLWN	MLWS
0000	0600	0000	0500	5·4	4·4	2·1	1·0
1200	1800	1200	1700				
Differences ABRA DE BILBAO							
–0125	–0045	–0055	–0035	–1·2	–1·2	–0·5	–0·4
PORTUGALETE (INNER HARBOUR)							
–0100	–0020	–0030	–0010	–0·7	–1·2	–0·2	–0·6

SHELTER Excellent in both marinas. ⚓ in 3-5m between these two havens which are adjacent to a pleasant suburb.

NAVIGATION WPT 43°23'·17N 03°05'·21W, 150°/5ca to outer hbr ent. This is formed by a W bkwtr extending 1·25M NE from Punta Lucero, a 308m high unlit headland on the W side. The submerged E bkwtr extends WNW for almost 2M from Punta Galea, Fl (3) 8s, on the E side of El Abra. It is marked by 3 SPM lt buoys, but can be crossed with caution; approx 7m depth was found close off Pta Galea. A mini-TSS is aligned 150°/330° 1·6M toward the outer hbr ent.

From the outer ent follow the buoyed fairway/TSS 120°/2M and 143°/1M across El Abra (= outer hbr/roads) to Dique de Santurtzi. thence 195°/3 cables to the inner hbr. Yachts should stay just outside the fairway buoys and keep clear of ships using the TSS.

After passing Contradique de Algorta, Fl R 5s, round the head, Fl (2+1) R 10s, of a new jetty (for cruise liners) extending W from

MRSC Santander (942) 213030; Brit Consul 157600.

FACILITIES Tiny hbr in spectacular setting at foot of steep 100m cliffs. The N part of outer hbr and all the inner hbr dry. At ent turn hard port into S part of outer hbr to pick up buoy in about 3m or ⚓ with tripping line as the bottom may well be foul. AB on S mole is feasible, but a 1m wide underwater ledge requires a holding-off line to kedge ⚓.

Village: FW, Basic ⧈, R, Bar; Bus to Bilbao for ≥, ✈. 15km south by road is Guernica, the ancient sacred city of the Basques.

Getxo bkwtr. When clear turn SE for Getxo Marina and SSE across the inner hbr to Las Arenas yacht hbr.

LIGHTS AND MARKS See chartlet and 9.23.3 for lt details. 5 wind turbines (inc 3 lit) near the head of W bkwtr are prominent. The Port Control bldg/twr is conspic at the SE end of Dique de Santurtzi. 2 power stn chimneys (200m high) with R/W bands are conspic 1M SW of Port Control. Glare from industrial plants may be seen from afar at night. Caution: Flood lights for WIP on the beach at Algorta (43°21'·34N 03°01'·08W) shine seaward and are very distracting when inbound at night, up to 0100LT.

R/T Port Control Ch 05, 12, 16. Marinas Ch 09.

TELEPHONE (Code 944) Port HM 241416; ⊖ 234700; Met via YC; Police 246445; Ⓗ 903100; Brit Consul 157600; MRCC 839411.

FACILITIES Getxo marina (1·9-2·9m) on S side of Contramuelle de Algorta. www.getxokaia.com getxokaia@getxokaia.com ☎ 912367. 827 AB inc ❶; €3.25; max LOA 18m. D&P, ME, El, Ⓔ, ✖, CH, SM, C (5 ton), BH (45 ton). Metro line 1 for downtown, board at Arreta station.

Las Arenas Yacht hbr, near the mouth of R. Bilbao in 1-3m, is run jointly by Real Club Maritimo del Abra and Real Sporting Club. ☎ 637600; www.rcmarsc.es puerto@rcmarsc.es 250 + 50 ❶, €3.00 plus AC €3.44/day. M, D&P, Slip, ME, ✖, CH, SM, El, Ⓔ, BH (35 ton), C (5 ton), Bar, R. Metro line 1 for downtown, board at Neguri station.

City centre is 10km SE of marinas. There are no yacht berths up-river. Bilbao is a major industrial city, but also a leading cultural and commercial centre. The Guggenheim museum is close to the Old Quarter. Main tourist office ☎ 910800.

All facilities; ≥, Sondika ✈ is 10km NE of the city centre. P & O ferry to/from Portsmouth, approx 33 hrs, every 3 days.

BILBAO *continued*

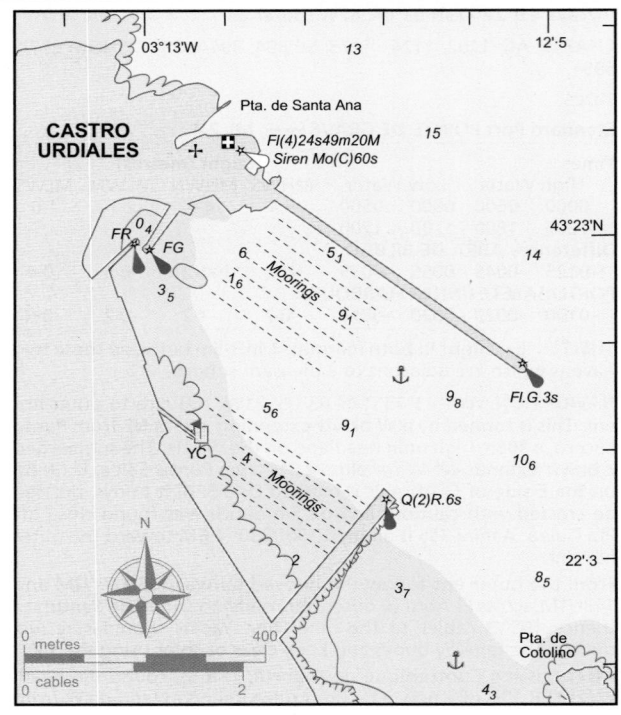

9.23.14 CASTRO URDIALES

Cantabria **43°22'·80N 03°12'·60W** ❀❀❀♘♘♕♕♕

CHARTS AC 1102, 1174; SC 394, 394A; SHOM 3542, 6991

TIDES Differences, see 9.23.15 facing page.

SHELTER Good, except in N-E winds when swell enters. A few ⚓s or ⚓ in 9m on mud to seaward of the 6 lines of mooring trots which fill the NE part of hbr.

NAVIGATION WPT 43°23'·55N 03°11'·69W, 222°/1·0M to hbr ent, as under title. N mole lt ≠ S mole lt form an approx 222° ldg line. The approach is straightforward with no hazards. In the hbr use the fairway to avoid extensive mooring trots.

LIGHTS AND MARKS From the NW, town and hbr are obsc'd until rounding Pta del Rabanal with its conspic cemetery. The ⚓, lt ho and castle are easily identified on Santa Ana which dominates the hbr. Lts as chartlet and 9.23.3.

R/T Use free YC launch *Blancona* Ch 09, **not** your own tender, as there is insufficient room for berthing tenders at YC.

TELEPHONE (Code 942) Met via HM (below); ⊖ 861146; CG/LB 900 202 202; Dr 861640 (Red Cross); Police 092; MRCC (944) 839411; Brit Consul 944 157600.

FACILITIES Many private moorings off the YC; FVs fill inner hbr. AB on N mole possible if calm and no swell. HM/Club ☎ 861585. www. cncu.es 150 + 40 ⚓s; ⚓ €15.00 includes launch service & shwr; Slip, BY, ME. **YC** Bar, R ☎ 861234 to reserve a table.

Town 🛒, R, Bar, Ⓑ, ✉, D & P (cans); ✈ Bilbao.

9.23.15 LAREDO and SANTOÑA

Cantabria **43°26'·24N 03°27'·00W (abm Pta Pasaje)** ❀❀◍◍◍✿✿

CHARTS AC 1102, 1171; SC 394, 3942; SHOM 3542.

TIDES Standard Port POINTE DE GRAVE (←—)

Times				Height (metres)			
High Water		Low Water		MHWS	MHWN	MLWN	MLWS
0000	0600	0000	0500	5·4	4·4	2·1	1·0
1200	1800	1200	1700				
Differences CASTRO URDIALES							
−0040	−0120	−0110	−0020	−1·4	−1·5	−0·6	−0·6
RIA DE SANTOÑA (03°28'W)							
−0005	−0045	−0035	+0015	−0·7	−1·2	−0·3	0·7

SHELTER Good W of Pta del Pasaje where the CN de Laredo has ⚓ sheltered from E'lies. Wash from FVs can be a problem.

9.23.16 SANTANDER

Cantabria **43°27'·66N 03°46'·13W (between Nos 1 & 2 chan buoys)** ❀❀◍◍◍✿✿

CHARTS AC 1102/5, 1145; SC 401, 4011; SHOM 7365, 6991.

TIDES Standard Port POINTE DE GRAVE (←—); ML 2·5

Times				Height (metres)			
High Water		Low Water		MHWS	MHWN	MLWN	MLWS
0000	0600	0000	0500	5·4	4·4	2·1	1·0
1200	1800	1200	1700				
Differences SANTANDER							
−0020	−0100	−0050	0000	−0·7	−1·2	−0·3	−0·7
RÍA DE SUANCES (04°03'W)							
0000	−0030	−0020	+0020	−1·5	−1·5	−0·6	−0·6

SHELTER Access H24, all weather/tides. Fair shelter off the city but subject to wash; very good shelter up-river at marina.

NAVIGATION From the E, WPT 43°28'·45N 03°44'·54W (E of Isla de Mouro), 236°/1·4M to Nos 1/2 buoys.

From the W, WPT 43°29'·49N 03°46'·57W (4ca E of Cabo Mayor). Thence in fair weather head SE between Isla de Mouro and Peninsula de la Mágdalena (min depth 7·3m). In heavy weather keep NE of Isla de Mouro. Punta Rabiosa ldg lts lead 235·8° into the well-buoyed/lit DW chan, defined by a Dir WRG lt 259·5°.

For Marina Santander (see chartlet inset) follow the buoyed chan

NAVIGATION WPT 43°25'·88N 03°25'·00W, 283·5°/1·5M to the Lat/Long given under the title. This is in the narrows N abeam of Pta del Pasaje, the N tip of the long sandy spit extending 2M NW from Laredo. The least charted depth on the ldg line is 3·5m, but expect less due to silting. The sandy estuary is exposed to E and S. A shallow chan runs 2·3M S to Colindres.

LIGHTS AND MARKS 283·5° ldg marks are hard to see. Monte Ganzo, 374m conspic mountain on N side is 1.5M NW of the Wpt. Pta del Pescador lt ho is 1M N of Monte Ganzo. See chartlet and 9.23.3 for lights.

R/T None. TELEPHONE (Code 942) MRCC (944) 839411; Brit Consul 944 157600.

FACILITIES **Santoña** has 2 basins; the S'ly (2-3m) has small craft pontoons or AB on N or NE walls. D, FW at the SE corner; 🛒, R, Bar.

Laredo YC, W of Pta del Pasaje, has a few ⚓s and ⚓ in about 2m inside an area marked by 4 Y buoys, Fl Y 2s. A jetty and pontoons extend to the drying line. ☎ 605812/16, www.rcnlaredo.es info@rcnlaredo.es M, Slip, C (6 ton), R, Bar.

Laredo's part-drying FV hbr has little space for yachts. Village: Small 🛒, R, Bar, ⑧, ✉, ✈ Bilbao. Taxi to Colindres for large 🛒.

to No 17 small GRG buoy, Fl (2+1) G 10s; here turn WSW for marina ent. Caution: the hard-to-see 235·6° ldg marks to marina lead close to or over a shifting, drying sandbank. Night entry not advised unless already visited by day.

LIGHTS AND MARKS The university, formerly a Royal Palace, is conspic on Peninsula de la Mágdalena. City buildings are prominent. Long oil jetty is conspic N of Marina Santander; 400m westward a glazed pyramid-shaped building is a good daymark.

R/T Port Authority *Santander Prácticos* Ch **14**, 16. Marinas Ch 09. Local weather broadcast Ch 11 every 4 hrs, 0245-2245.

TELEPHONE (Code 942) Port HM 223900; ⊖ and Met via HM; MRSC 213030; Airport 202120; Brit Consul 220000.

FACILITIES Four options, from seaward:

- **Club Nautico de La Horadada** (CNH), ☎ 280402, ⚓. ⚓ for 7–10m LOA craft NW of Nos 1 & 3 buoys, in 5m on rock; bay is almost full of local moorings.

- **Pedreña Marina**, 8ca SSE of Pta Rabiosa and the main channel. Access from No 4 buoy via buoyed/lit chan with least depth 0·4m. No details, so reports would be welcomed.

- **Darsena de Molnedo**: Real Club Marítimo de Santander (RCMS; near city), www.rcmsantander.com ☎ 214050. 108 AB, max LOA 12m in 1·7m but few if any ❶. RCMS berths S side, misc N side. Slip, D, BH (27 ton), C (1·5 ton). ⚓s and ⚓ S of the dock are exposed to wash.

- **Marina de Santander** is approx 2·7M further upriver, but 20 mins bus/taxi ride to the city. ☎ 369298; 1400 AB inc Ⓥ in 2·2-3·1m, max LOA 23m, €3.16, max 15 days. C, D&P, Slip, BH (27 ton), CH, ME, 🔧, El, Ⓔ, Gaz, R, Bar. Security adequate to leave a yacht. Little noise from adjacent Parayas airport. marinasantander@marinasantander.com www.marinasantander.com

City: www.puertosantander.com All amenities; ⇌ & bus; Brittany ferry terminal ☎ 360611 is 6ca W of Darsena de Molnedo; ✈.

SUANCES, Cantabria. **43°25'·78N 04°02'·08W** (marina). AC 1105, 1150; SC 4012; SHOM 2042. Tidal differences overleaf. No access in N'lies or when swell breaking over bar, 1m; not advised at night. HW −1 from ⊕ 43°25'·78N 04°02'·08W track 149·5°/8ca on ldg bcns (Q & Iso 4s) to Fl(4)R 11s bcn at hd of trng wall. Best water E side of chan. Marina (Fl (4) R & G 11s) has small craft pontoon. If >8m LOA, AB on piled N or W walls. Basics in village, Bar, R.

SANTANDER TO CABO ORTEGAL

Harbours west of Santander (AC 1105, 1108) are increasingly far apart compared with those to the east. 60M west of Santander, **Ribadesella**'s marina is for local boats <10m LOA, but there is AB against the quays which front the interesting town. Here the **Picos de Europa** (2648m) form a magnificent backdrop often being visible from 15M offshore whilst cloud obscures their lower slopes.

Further west a heavy NW swell, known as a *Vaga de Mar*, breaks over banks and closes any ports which have bars. It can occur quite suddenly in calm weather, but is usually associated with strong NW'lies. In summer NE winds predominate and fog occurs fairly often especially in late June to early July.

Gijón with a modern marina offers refuge; it lies close SE of, but quite distinct from, El Musel the very large commercial harbour whose northerly extension, under construction, may be a trap for unwary yachts cruising close inshore.

Cudillero and **Luarca** are small fishing hbrs worth visiting, but beware swell especially off Cudillero. **Ría de Ribadeo** (with a much improved marina) is the first of the *Rías altas* (ie upper or northern), sunken estuaries not unlike a Scottish sea loch. **San Ciprian**'s aluminium port (AC 1122) offers within its long bkwtrs a sheltered ⚓ of refuge close to its W shore.

Ría de Vivero has a well sheltered marina and several anchorages to await fair winds around Cabo Ortegal. **Ría del Barquero** and the **Ensenada de Santa Marta**, to E and W of Pta de la Estaca de Bares, offer many attractive ⚓s exposed only to N/NE winds; but beware S/SW winds off the mountains being accelerated through the valleys. This stretch of steep, rocky coast is deeply indented and rises to over 500m a few miles inland.

▶From Pta de la Estaca de Bares to Cabo Ortegal (8M) the tidal stream sets E or NE on a rising tide and W or SW when falling, rates up to 2kn inshore and perceptible for a considerable distance offshore.◀

9.23.17
SAN VICENTE DE LA BARQUERA
Cantabria. 43°23'·69N 04°23'·06W ✳✳⚓♨♨♨🏳🏳🏳

CHARTS AC 1105; SC 402, 4021; SHOM 6381, 6991

TIDES
Standard Port POINTE DE GRAVE (←—)

Times				Height (metres)			
High Water		Low Water		MHWS	MHWN	MLWN	MLWS
0000	0600	0000	0500	5·4	4·4	2·1	1·0
1200	1800	1200	1700				
Differences SAN VICENTE DE LA BARQUERA							
−0020	−0100	−0050	0000	−1·5	−1·5	−0·6	−0·6
RÍA DE TINA MAYOR (04°31'W, 6M W of San Vicente)							
−0020	−0100	−0050	0000	−1·4	−1·5	−0·6	−0·6

SHELTER Good in large shallow estuary, access HW±3; but HW±1 is advised if there is any swell. This is an active FV hbr with virtually no berth availability for yachts, a yacht marina at S end of Puenta Noeva was reported to be under construction but has not materialised, though FVs occupy newly-built pontoons nearby. Reports welcome.

NAVIGATION WPT 43°24'·39N 04°22'·16W, 223°/1M to hbr ent (abeam Isla Peña Menor). Beware shallow bar and tidal streams 3-4kn. Depths are as per SC 4021 but more water is likely.

LIGHTS AND MARKS Pta de la Silla lt ho and hbr lts: see chartlet and 9.23.3. Beach E of ent, castle & church up-river are conspic.

R/T None.

TELEPHONE (Code 942) Port HM ☎ 710004; MRCC 326050; Dr 712450; Police 710007; Brit Consul (942) 220000.

FACILITIES Town: About 41km NExE of the Picos de Europa. ⬜, R, Bar, ⒷÝ, ✉; ✈ (Santander). www.sanvicentedelabarquera.org

HARBOUR 16M WEST OF SAN VICENTE DE LA BARQUERA
LLANES, Asturias. 43°25'·15N 04°44'·92W. AC 1105; SC 403; SHOM 5009. Tides: Interpolate between 9.23.17 and 9.23.18. The small FV hbr faces E; best access HW −1 to HW. Do not enter in strong N to E winds or heavy swell.

The N pierhead, ⚡ Fl G 5s, is conspic due to brilliantly coloured concrete rock armour. The S side of the ent is marked by ⚡ Fl R 5s and San Anton lt ho (see 9.23.3), easily seen from the E. Approx 150m further W a ⚡ Fl (3) G 9s marks a small basin to stbd; berth/raft in 2m where space permits on smooth N or E walls or as directed. No room to ⚓. An inner basin, entered over a sill, is full of small local craft. FW, Slip, C, D&P (cans), good shops, Bar, R, ⇌. turismo@ayuntiamentodellanes.com www.llanes.com

9.23.18   RIBADESELLA
Asturias 43°28'·06N 05°03'·99W ✳✳⚓♨♨🏳🏳🏳

CHARTS AC 1105, 1150; SC 403, 4031; SHOM 6381, 6691

TIDES
Standard Port POINTE DE GRAVE (←—)

Times				Height (metres)			
High Water		Low Water		MHWS	MHWN	MLWN	MLWS
0000	0600	0000	0500	5·4	4·4	2·1	1·0
1200	1800	1200	1700				
Differences RIBADESELLA							
+0005	−0020	−0020	+0020	−1·4	−1·3	−0·6	−0·4

SHELTER Good. No space within the hbr to ⚓.

NAVIGATION WPT 43°28'·59N 05°04'·02W, 180°/5ca to Pta del Caballo. Bajo Serropio, 7ca NNE of ent, breaks in heavy seas. Easy appr from about HW−1 to HW, but do not attempt in strong onshore winds when seas and swell break on the bar, reported as 2m, but less after NW gales. Hug the N bank 25m off the promenade to clear drying, buoyed sandbanks to stbd.

LIGHTS AND MARKS E of hbr ent smooth, dark cliffs and a chapel are distinctive. To the W a white beach is obvious. The channel upriver is now well lit and buoyed; see chartlet.

R/T Ch 09 occas.

TELEPHONE (Code 985) HM 860038. MRCC 326050; Tourist office 860255; Brit Consul (942) 220000.

FACILITIES Berth/raft on the NE/E quays in 2-3m, clear of FVs and well N of the 2m high bridge; pre-rig a fender board. Slip, ME, CH, El, ✗, Ⓔ, YC. A small marina off the W bank in 3m, ent dredged 2·5m, is full of small local boats; no Ⓥ; locked gate.

Town: R, Bar, ✉, ⒷÝ, D & P (cans), ⬜, 🗓, ⇌; ✈ Oviedo (78 km).

9.23.19 LASTRES

Asturias 43°30'·90N 05°15'·93W ※※◐♭♭♤♤

CHARTS AC 1105, 1153, 1150; SC 403, 4041; SHOM 6991, 5009

TIDES Interpolate between Ribadesella and Gijon.

SHELTER Well protected from W'lies by steep hillside, but in strong E'lies it becomes uncomfortable despite a substantial E bkwtr. ⌕ about 1ca S of the hbr in 5m on sand, clear of a fish farm marked by ⌓ Fl Y 2·5s.

NAVIGATION WPT 43°31'·16N 05°15'·35W, 235°/5ca to hbr ent. Access H24. Easy approach in all but strong E'lies, avoiding Bajo de la Plancha (5·7m), 3ca NNE of ent, breaks in heavy seas; also a pinnacle rk (0·3m) close NNE of the E bkwtr.

LIGHTS AND MARKS A 118m high, R/W TV mast (R lts) is conspic close W of the hbr. Cabo Lastres lt ho is 1·9M NW, see 9.23.3.

TELEPHONE (Code 985) HM 850003. FV President 850075. MRCC 326050. Tourist office (Colunga) 852200. Brit Consul (942) 220000.

FACILITIES Berth/raft at the S end of the E bkwtr in 4-7m. FVs berth on W quays or moor in E-W trots across the centre of the hbr. At the N end of the hbr a pontoon with fingers is for local boats only, ditto the inlet in SW corner. Slip, D (FV quay), C (4 t).

Village: Basic shops, R, Bar. ⇌ Oviedo (62 km). Asturias ✈ is 5M E of Cudillero. www.infoasturias.com

9.23.20 GIJÓN

Asturias 43°32'·78N 05°40'·26W ※※◐♭♭♤♤♤

CHARTS AC 1105, 1108, 1153, 1154; SC 404, 404A, 4042; SHOM 6381, 5009

TIDES

Standard Port POINTE DE GRAVE (←); ML 2·3

Times				Height (metres)			
High Water		Low Water		MHWS	MHWN	MLWN	MLWS
0000	0600	0000	0500	5·4	4·4	2·1	1·0
1200	1800	1200	1700				
Differences GIJON							
–0005	–0030	–0030	+0010	–1·0	–1·4	–0·4	–0·7
LUANCO (05°47'W)							
–0010	–0035	–0035	+0005	–1·4	–1·3	–0·6	–0·4
AVILÉS (05°56'W)							
–0100	–0040	–0050	–0015	–1·2	–1·6	–0·5	–0·7
SAN ESTABAN DE PRAVIA (06°05'W)							
–0005	–0030	–0030	+0010	–1·4	–1·3	–0·6	–0·4

SHELTER Excellent in marina; care needed in strong N'lies.

NAVIGATION WPT 43°33'·78N 05°40'·26W, 180°/1·3M to marina ent, 1M SE of Puerto de El Musel, the vast conspic industrial port. The WPT is at the Y-junction of two mini-TSS chans, which lead in from NE and NNW, primarily for big ships. Banco Las Amosucas, marked by 4 cardinal lt buoys, lies within the Y. From the E yachts can approach more directly, passing N of Peninsula de Sta Catalina. In the near appr leave Sacramento G twr (marks drying reef) close to stbd.

LIGHTS AND MARKS NW of the marina are conspic W tanks in El Musel, many nav/shore lts and Cabo de Torres, Fl (2) 10s.

R/T Marina Ch 09. Puerto de El Musel Ch 10, 11, 12, **14**, 16.

TELEPHONE (Code 985) ⊖ & Met via marina. MRCC 326050.

FACILITIES **Marina** (aka Puerto Local), access H24, (1·2–2·5m) in 4 basins. Berth initially dead ahead for check-in/fuel, then shift to Ⓥ finger berths in N Basin (Antepuerto). ☎ 344543. www.puertodeportivogijon.es info@puertodeportivogijon.es 658+88 Ⓥ, €0.6428/m², inc AC & shwrs. P, D, Slip, BH (30 ton),YC, ME, El, ✕, CH, SM, Ⓔ, Wi-Fi, ▣.

Town 🛒, R, Bar, @, ✉, Ⓑ, ⇌. ✈ Oviedo (42 km).

HARBOUR 6M SOUTH WEST OF CABO PEÑAS
AVILÉS, Asturias. **43°35'·65N 05°56'·77W**. AC 1108, 1142; SC 405A, 4052; SHOM 5009, 7361. Tides: 9.23.20. A port of refuge, except in W/NW'lies >F9, but also heavily industrialised and a FV hbr. The ent, S of Pta del Castillo lt ho and N of conspic white beach, is open to W/NW but well sheltered from N'lies. The well marked/lit ent chan runs ExS for 7ca then turns S for 2M to club pontoons at 43°33'·66N 05°55'·28W, W side of chan; max LOA about 12m. FV supplies only. Caution FV wash.
Port VHF Ch **12** 16. HM ☎ (985) 541 111, paviles@paviles.com. YC at Salinas, 2M NW. Old town is close SW. Usual domestics.

HARBOUR 3M EAST OF CUDILLERO
SAN ESTEBAN DE PRAVIA, Asturias. **43°34'·21N 06°04'·54W**. AC 1108, 1133; SC 405, 405A, 4041; SHOM 5009. Tides: 9.23.20. A former coaling port, now only a few FVs berth on E bank at San Juan de la Arena quay, 90m long. The 206·2° ldg lts lead very close to the W bkwtr hd; see 9.23.3 for lts. Appr near HW due to silting in the ent. Possible AB on FV quay or on facing quays on W bank. Or ⚓ in river on sand in 2·2m just S of ent to town quays.

9.23.21 CUDILLERO

Asturias **43°33'·96N 06°08'·80W** (W bkwtr hd) ❀❀⚓⚓✿✿✿

CHARTS AC 1108; SC 934, 405, 405A; SHOM 5009.

TIDES Use San Estaban de Pravia, 3M W; see 9.23.20.

SHELTER Good in large modern basin, NW of hbr ent, but N'ly swell can make entry/exit difficult and may work into the basin.

NAVIGATION WPT 43°34'·33N 06°08'·71W, 190°/3½ca to W bkwtr hd. From the W keep at least 5ca offshore until clear of Piedras las Colinas, tall islets/reefs NW of ent. From the E appr with Pta Rebollera lt ho on initial bearing of 200°. The rocky ent opens up only when close to. Narrow chan skirts the W bkwtr into basin. Before leaving look over the bkwtr to assess swell.

LIGHTS AND MARKS Pta Rebollera lt ho is conspic W 8-sided twr.

R/T HM Ch 27.

TELEPHONE (Code 985) MRCC 326050; Brit Consul (942) 220000.

FACILITIES Limited AB on pontoons or ⚓ off them in 8-9m. FVs moor/berth at NW end of the basin. The old drying hbr, S of ent, is exposed to swell, but convenient for dinghies; yachts can dry out on slip. HM ☎ 591114. FW, D (gasoleo B) from FV quay, P (cans), ME, Slip, small commercial shipyard.

Village: 5 mins by dinghy, 25 mins on foot. 🛒, R, Bar, ⊠.

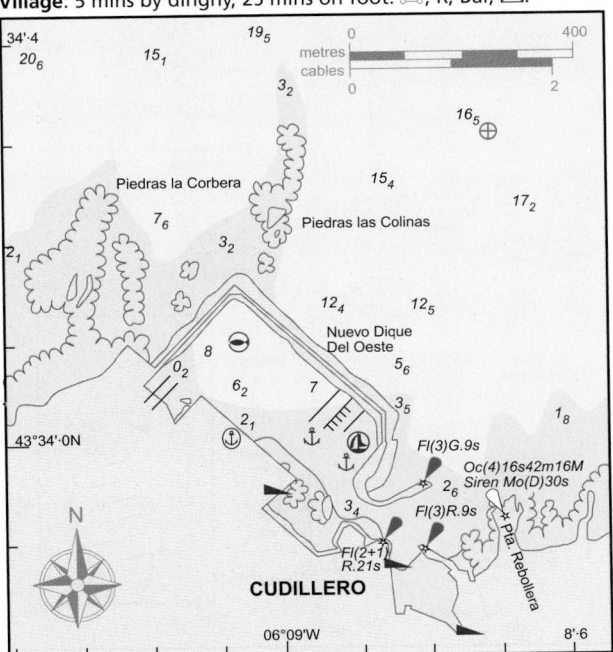

9.23.22 LUARCA

Asturias **43°32'·95N 06°32'·20W** ❀❀❀⚓⚓✿✿✿

CHARTS AC 1108, 1133; SC 933, 934, 4061; SHOM 6381, 5009

TIDES
Standard Port POINTE DE GRAVE (←)

Times				Height (metres)			
High Water		Low Water		MHWS	MHWN	MLWN	MLWS
0000	0600	0000	0500	5·4	4·4	2·1	1·0
1200	1800	1200	1700				
Differences LUARCA							
+0010	−0015	−0015	+0025	−1·2	−1·1	−0·5	−0·3

SHELTER The outer hbr is protected from all but N'lies, but swell can intrude. No room to ⚓ inside the hbr.

NAVIGATION WPT 43°33'·51N 06°32'·29W, 170°/6ca to E bkwtr hd lt ho which is conspic and almost in transit with the ldg marks. Appr on the ldg lts/marks 170° to clear rky shoals either side.

LIGHTS AND MARKS See chartlet and 9.23.3. Cabo Busto is 3M ENE of hbr ent. Pta Blanca (or Focicón) lt ho is W ☐ tr and house on prominent headland 300m ENE of hbr ent; conspic ✠ close by. 170° ldg lts are on thin W lattice pylons, R bands; not easy to see until close in.

R/T None. **TELEPHONE** (Code 985) HM 640176/640083; MRCC 326050; Brit Consul (942) 220000.

FACILITIES Moor fore and aft to the E bkwtr, stern to steel 🅜s which are close together. Underwater obst'ns are said to lie up to 2m from bkwtr but in calm conditions it is possible to lie alongside the bkwtr.

Narrow chan leads SE to inner hbr dredged 2m (prone to silting). Pontoons in SE corner are full of local craft, little chance of a berth. Temp'y AB on NW side may be possible. D from FV quay, P (cans), ME, CH, Slip, C (8 ton).

Town: Friendly YC next to front ldg lt, 🛒, R, Bar, Ⓑ, ⊠, ⇌.

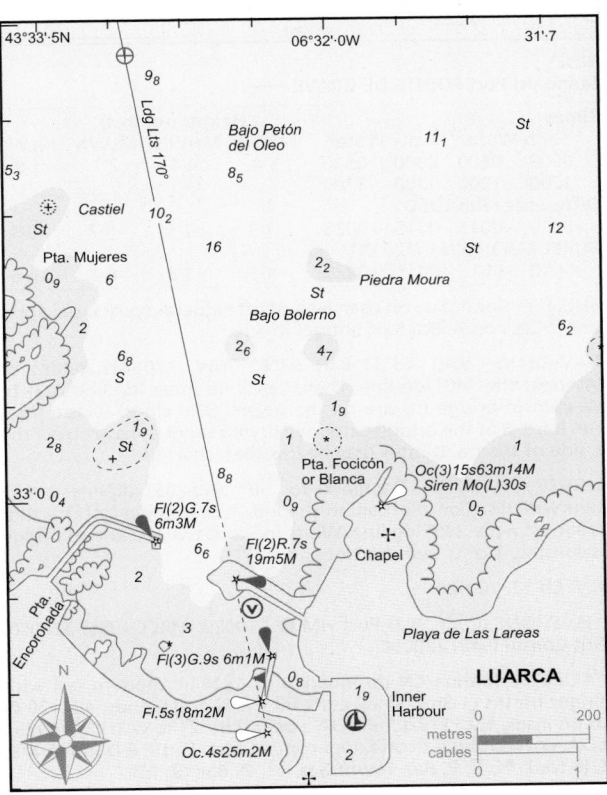

9.23.23   RÍA DE RIBADEO

Lugo **43°32'·44N 07°02'·16W** (Marina ent) ✻✻❀⬧⬧❀❀❀

CHARTS AC 1108, 1096; SC 932, 4071; SHOM 5009

TIDES
Standard Port POINTE DE GRAVE (⟵)

Times				Height (metres)			
High Water		Low Water		MHWS	MHWN	MLWN	MLWS
0000	0600	0000	0500	5·4	4·4	2·1	1·0
1200	1800	1200	1700				
Differences RIBADEO							
+0010	−0015	−0015	+0025	−1·3	−1·5	−0·7	−0·8
BURELA (43°40'N 07°20'W)							
+0010	−0015	−0015	+0025	−1·5	−1·5	−0·7	−0·6

SHELTER Good. ⚓ as on chartlet and off Figueras (very shoal appr) or off Castropol (8ca S of bridge) in 4m.

NAVIGATION WPT 43°33'·84N 07°02'·30W, 170°/4½ cables to intersect the 140° ldg line. Thence pick-up inner ldg line 205° to W span of bridge (lts are on the pillars; 32m clnce) where tides run hard. S of the bridge extensive drying sandbanks obstruct the E side of the ría. Depths may be less than charted.

LIGHTS AND MARKS Daymarks for 140° and 205° ldg lines are W twrs with R ◊. Conspic R onion-shaped ✠ twr in town (off chartlet) is almost ≠ the 205° ldg line. White lookout twr at E end of bridge is conspic. Lights: see chartlet and 9.23.3.

R/T Ch 12, 16 H24.

TELEPHONE (Code 982) Port HM ☎ 110020; MRCC (985) 326050; Brit Consul (942) 220000.

FACILITIES **Marina/CN de Ribadeo** ☎ 131444; modernised with finger berths (1-3m). Small craft fill the N and S ends. 484+20 Ⓥ as on inset, €0.111370/m² (LOA x beam) inc 21% VAT; 13·7m max LOA. www.clubnauticoribadeo.com/ ⊖, Met, Slip, P & D (cans), ME, C (8 ton), ✕, ▣, R, Bar. **Town:** Gas, 🛒, R, Bar, Ⓑ, ✉.

9.23.24   RÍA DE VIVERO

Lugo **43°40'·93N 07°36'·16W** (Cillero bkwtr hd) ✻✻❀⬧⬧❀❀

CHARTS AC 1108, 1122; SC 931, 4082; SHOM 5009

TIDES
Standard Port POINTE DE GRAVE (⟵)

Times				Height (metres)			
High Water		Low Water		MHWS	MHWN	MLWN	MLWS
0000	0600	0000	0500	5·4	4·4	2·1	1·0
1200	1800	1200	1700				
Differences RÍA DE VIVERO							
+0010	−0015	−0015	+0025	−1·4	−1·3	−0·6	−0·4

SHELTER Good, except in N'lies. ⚓ in E'lies inside Isla Insua d'Area, 1·3M NE of Cillero. In S-W winds ⚓ at the head of the ria off Playa de Covas in 6-7m.

NAVIGATION Easy ent, 7ca wide, between Isla Gabeira and Pta de Faro. WPT 43°43'·25N 07°35'·30W (mouth of the ria), 195°/2·4M to round Cillero bkwtr hd. Keep clear of this major FV hbr.

LIGHTS AND MARKS See chartlet and 9.23.3. Mte Faro Juances is a distinctive conical peak (193m) close SE of Pta de Faro.

R/T Marina Ch 09. Cillero Port Ch 16.

TELEPHONE (Code 982) Cillero HM ☎ 560074; Ⓗ ☎ 589900 (Burela, 20km); Police 562922; MRCC (985) 326050; Brit Consul (942) 220000.

FACILITIES **Marina** (2-3·5m) ☎ 570610, 657 152214, 609 763606. www.miclubnautico.com pdviveiro@pdviveiro.com. 208 + Ⓥ, €2.10. D & P, C (8 ton), BH (35 ton), CH.

Town: 🛒, R, Bar, Ⓑ, ✉, 🚄.

MINOR HARBOUR SOUTH OF PUNTA DE LA ESTACA DE BARES

RÍA DEL BARQUERO. 43°45'·00N 07°40'·70W. AC 1108, 1122; SC 931, 4082; SHOM 6383. Tides: 9.23.24. A delightful ría, exposed only to NE'lies. There is an ⚓ at Bares below the steep, high W bank and 2·5M SSW a shallow access channel leads to a tiny hbr at El Barquero (☎ 981 414002) in depths 1·5-2·5m.

On the E side of the ría, yachts may ⚓ N of Pta del Castro, clear of an outfall; or a berth may be found in the modern FV port at Vicedo on the S or W quays.

See 9.23.3 for lts at: Isla Coelleira (an islet between this ría and Ría de Vivero); Pta de la Estaca de Barra; Pta de la Barra; Pta del Castro; and Vicedo.

MINOR HARBOURS SOUTH OF CABO ORTEGAL

CARIÑO. 43°44'·21N 07°52'·14W is 2M S of Cabo Ortegal (AC 1122) and well sheltered from all W'lies. After rounding the outer commercial jetty yachts may berth on an extended pontoon in the NW corner of the hbr; or ⚓ in 6m on sand within the bay. See 9.23.3 for lts. Ashore: shops, Bar, R, CH, D&P cans. In E'lies, ⚓ off **Espasante** FV hbr, 2·3M ESE of Cariño (AC 1111).

RÍA DE SANTA MARTA DE ORTIGUEIRA. 43°42'·78N 07°50'·60W. Tides: +0050 La Coruña (→); MHWS −0·1; MHWN +0·4; MLWN −0·1; MLWS +0·3; streams reach 5kn sp. SC 4083 (1:20,000) is essential for pilotage. WPT 43°45'·00N 07°50'·60W, 180°/2·4M to the Ría ent (L/L above) at HW −2. ⚓s in 3 pools off Pta Postina (11·4m), Pta Sismundi (11·1m) and Pta Redonda (5·2m).

The access chan crosses the 0·4m bar on a S'ly track with Isla de San Vicente 50m to port. It then turns W, SW and S in three legs each about 1M long and is marked by small lateral buoys and occas perches/withies. The eponymous town will be seen when 7 ca WNW of it. In sequence pass first a quay with blue crane, then a small private jetty, finally the marina ent. Rewarding pilotage to an elegant town.

Facilities: ♥ welcome; 3 YC pontoons (2m max), max LOA 12m. D & P (cans), 🛢, R, Bar, Ⓑ, ✉; coast road & ⇌ to La Coruña ✈.

CABO ORTEGAL TO CABO FINISTERRE

Cabo Ortegal should be rounded at least 2M off due to the offlying needle rocks, Los Aguillones. Most of the major headlands should be given a good offing to avoid fluky winds and, in some cases, pinnacle rocks. The deeply indented coast (AC 1111, 3633, 3764) begins to trend WSW, with 600m high mountains rising only 5M inland. Coastal features are often hard to identify against this background. Here many major lights are sited so high as to be obscured by low cloud/mist in onshore weather.

▶ *Tidal streams set SW on the ebb and NE on the flood. Any current tends to run SW, then S.*◀

The **Ría de Cedeira** is entered 3M SSW of Pta Candelaria lt ho. This small attractively wooded ría offers refuge by day/night to yachts unable to round Cabo Ortegal in strong NE'lies. Several banks along this stretch break in heavy weather when they should be passed well to seaward.

About 20M further SW, having passed Pta de la Frouxeira, Cabo Prior, Pta de Castro and Cabo Prioriño Chico, all lit, is the entrance to **Ría de Ferrol**, a well sheltered commercial and naval port, but with limited yacht facilities. The adjacent **Ría de Ares** and **Ría de Betanzos** are attractive alternatives, both with easy access to their marinas.

La Coruña is a port of refuge, accessible in all weathers and has excellent yacht facilities with two marinas near the city centre and another to the south.

W of the conspicuous Torre de Hércules lt ho a 19M wide bight is generally foul as far as Islas Sisargas, three islets 2M offshore; here the inshore passage is not advised. 8M SW of Pta Nariga, between Pta del Roncudo and Pta de Lage, is the unspoiled **Ría de Corme y Laxe** with two small fishing hbrs in the NNE and SSW corners of the bay and some yacht pontoons.

Cabo Villano, a rocky headland with light house, siren and conspicuous wind turbines, is a possible landfall after crossing Biscay. 4ca NW of it El Bufardo (43°10'·00N 09°13'·28W) is a dangerous pinnacle rock awash at CD.

20M NW of Cabo Villano and 22M NW of Punta de la Barca is the **Off Finisterre TSS**; see 9.23.2. Yachts have more than adequate searoom within the ITZ whose southern boundary lies due west of Cabo Finisterre. *Finisterre Tráfico* (VTS) on VHF **11**, 16 broadcasts regular information about Navwarnings, weather and traffic in Spanish and English. On request it can also provide the vessel's position, course and speed and the identity of other vessels in the vicinity.

The entrance to **Ría de Camariñas**, the last of the rías altas and a safe refuge, is 2·4M S of Cabo Villano. There is a small, friendly marina and on the SW side of the ria Muxia offers a sheltered ⚓.

Cabo Toriñana and **Cabo Finisterre** both have charted dangers, mostly pinnacle rocks, lying up to 1M offshore; hence the popular name *Costa del Morte* for this wild, magnificent and sometimes forbidding coast.

9.23.25 RÍA DE CEDEIRA

La Coruña **43°39'·38N 08°03'·86W** (⚓) ❀❀❀⚓⚓✿✿✿

CHARTS AC 1108, 1111, 1122; SC 411; SHOM 5009, 3007

TIDES Interpolate between Santa Marta de Ortigueira (9.23.24) and Ferrol (9.23.26). ML No data.

SHELTER Very good; a pleasant refuge for yachts awaiting a fair wind to round Cabo Ortegal. ⚓ in 3-4m about 500m E of the modern FV port, excellent holding on sand.

NAVIGATION WPT 43°41'·00N 08°05'·41W (off chartlet), 155°/1·7M to Pta del Sarridal. From N keep at least 1M off Pta Candelaria until the ría opens. From the S a similar offing clears rks N/NW of Pta Chirlateira.

155° ldg line Pta Promontorio lt ho ≠ Pta del Sarridal. Abeam Pta Chirlateira with Pta Xian brg 161°, track midway between Pta del Sarridal and Piedras de Media Mar. When the bkwtr hd bears 060° turn toward the anchorage. The E end of the bay shoals rapidly toward the drying mouth of Rio de Cedeira.

LIGHTS AND MARKS Piedras de Media Mar, BRB lt twr conspic in centre of ría, can be passed on either side. A chapel is conspic 4ca N of the hbr. Lts as chartlet and 9.23.3.

R/T No VHF. MF *Cedeira Cofradia* 1800kHz, 2182.

TELEPHONE (Code 981) HM 480389; MRSC 209541; Brit Consul (986) 437133.

FACILITIES Hbr: ⊖, Met Slip, ME, El, ✗, L just N of ⚓ symbol. **Town:** Ⓔ, D & P (cans), 🛢, R, Bar, Ⓑ, ✉, ▣; ⇌ & ✈ La Coruña.

9.23.26 FERROL

La Coruña 43°28'·56N 08°14'·61W (Curuxeiras dock) ⊛⊛⊛♨☆☆

CHARTS AC 1111, 1094, 1118, 1117; SC 412, 412A, 4122, 4123; SHOM 3007

TIDES
Standard Port LA CORUÑA (→); ML 2·2.

Times				Height (metres)			
High Water		Low Water		MHWS	MHWN	MLWN	MLWS
0000	0600	0000	0500	4·2	2·8	1·6	0·3
1200	1800	1200	1700				
Differences FERROL (La Grana)							
−0002	−0002	+0001	+0001	0·0	0·0	0·0	0·0

SHELTER Very good inside ría, but be aware of strong tides and occasional squalls in the narrows.

‡s, from seaward, N shore of appr chan: Ensenada de Cariño (poor holding, good shelter except in S'lies); inshore of Pereiro PHM buoy in 5-6m. Inside the ría (see chartlet), S shore: Ensenada de el Baño and off Mugardos; on N shore off Pta de Caranza, ESE of chapel and near No 2 PHM buoy (off chartlet).

NAVIGATION WPT 43°26'·55N 08°19'·97W (close to WCM lt buoy and in the white sector (041·5°-042·5°) of Batería de San Cristóbal Dir lt) 042°/1·3M to pick up the 085·2° ldg line. Caution: From near Cabo Prioriño Chico lt ho a substantial bkwtr extends 145°/0·5M, halfway across the ent to the Ria. Chan is deep and adequately buoyed/lit. In bad weather avoid the outer banks (Tarracidos, Cabaleiro and Leixiñas) to the N and W.

LIGHTS AND MARKS C. Prioriño Chico bkwtr head, Fl R 5s 21m 7M; adjacent T-jetty Fl (2) R 7s 10m 3M. Ldg lts 085·2° through the narrows; see 9.23.3.

R/T Port Control *Ferrol Prácticos* Ch **14** (H24).

TELEPHONE (Code 981) HM 352945. MRSC 209541; Brit Consul (986) 437133.

FACILITIES Limited yacht facilities in this naval, commercial and ship-building port. **Marina Terramar** at La Graña: approx 50 AB, a few ⚓s or ‡. ⊖, Met, Slip, ME, P & D (cans), El, C (1·5 ton), YC, ✖. Bus every ½hr to the city (20 mins).

Dársena de Curuxeiras is central, but AB in 2m on NE side is against stone walls and prone to ferry wash. The 3 pontoons at the head of this inlet are not available to visitors. ☎ 321594; Slip, FW, P & D (cans), ME, El, C (8 ton).

Other options: Ría de Ares (9.23.27) has yacht pontoons in the small FV hbr. Marina Sada (9.23.28) has good bus links to La Coruña (9.23.29), but here Darsena de la Marina is very crowded.

City all facilities.

9.23.27 RÍA DE ARES

Marina 43°25'·34N 08°14'·38W ⊛⊛⊛♨☆☆☆

CHARTS AC 1111, 1094; SC 412, 412A; SHOM 3007, 7598, 6665

TIDES Differences for La Coruña are satisfactory.

SHELTER Good in the marina/fishing hbr at the W end of the 1M wide, sheltered bay (Ensenada de Ares), but the ría is exposed to strong NW'lies and swell. ‡ NE of the hbr in 3-5m, good holding on muddy sand. The ambience is peaceful and relaxed. The ría extends E past Redes toward Puentedeume, where there is day ‡ in shoaling waters, clear of mussel beds.

NAVIGATION WPT 43°24'·88N 08°14'·03W, 340°/0·5M to hbr's Emole hd. The appr is simple, but keep clear of Bajo La Miranda (3·7m; 1·5M WSW of the hbr) and adjacent islets off Pta Miranda. In the near approach avoid Bajo Cagarroso (2·1m), 5 cables SSW of the E mole head. To the W of Ares there are two Measured miles with transit bcns, should you need to check your speedo.

LIGHTS AND MARKS As on the chartlet. Cabo Prioriño Chico is 5M WNW. Sada/Fontan marina/hbr is 4M S; see 9.23.28. A conspic rounded hill (Monte de San Miguel de Breamo) with chapel on top is 2·7M ESE of the hbr.

R/T Ch 09.

TELEPHONE (Code 981) English spoken, ask for Marco. ⊖ & Met via Club (below), which is welcoming. MRSC 209541; Brit Consul (986) 437133.

FACILITIES **Marina/CN Ría de Ares** ☎ 468787. mob 610 737344. secretaria@nauticoares.com www.nauticoares.com 4 pontoons in 2m for yachts; FVs berth inside E mole. 325 + 16 Ⓥ, €2·65 max LOA 20m on fingers, mostly on outer end of pontoon No 1. D & P, C (8 ton), BH (35 ton), El, ME, Slip, R, Bar. **Town** 🛒, 🏧, Ⓑ, ✉, R, Bar. Bus to Ferrol.

LA CORUNA

MEAN SPRING —
AND NEAP CURVES - - - -

MEAN RANGES
Springs 3.9m
Neaps 1.2m

Springs occur 1 day
after
New and Full Moon

9.23.28   RÍA DE BETANZOS

La Coruña 43°21'·73N 08°14'·45W ✿✿✿✿◊◊◊✿✿✿

CHARTS AC 1111, 1094; SC 412, 412A; SHOM 3007, 7598, 6665

TIDES Differences for La Coruña are satisfactory. **SHELTER** Very good in Sada Marina which is actually at Fontan, and an attractive alternative to La Coruña if the latter is full. It is a safe haven for long stay or winter lay-up; visitors are welcome at this well-run and fully-equipped marina. Pulgueira rock near the middle of the marina has been demolished, but keep close to the eastern hammerheads on arrival. ⚓ N or E of the hbr in 4-7m, but the bottom is weedy.

The little drying marina at Miño, 1·3M ESE of Sada, may be worth visiting; any reports on it would be gratefully received.

NAVIGATION WPT 43°24'·34N 08°15'·07W, 171°/2·6M to Fontan hbr's N mole hd. Appr the WPT on an ESE track midway between Pta Miranda to the NE and Pta Redonda* to the SW; Bajo La Miranda (3·7m) lies 6ca SW of the former. The Ria is wide and easy to enter, but shoals steadily S of the hbr.

*Note: a second Pta Redonda is 4M ESE of the first mentioned, opposite Fontan.

LIGHTS AND MARKS Hbr lts proliferate, as on the chartlet, mostly marking FV quays on the N and W side of the hbr. 1·4M NE of the hbr Pta de San Pedro lt (off chartlet) is listed as Perbes pierhd, Fl (2) WR 7s; see 9.23.4. At the head of the ría a bridge across the Río Mandeo is clearly visible.

R/T Ch 09.

TELEPHONE (Code 981) MRSC 209541; Brit Consul (986) 437133.

FACILITIES Marina ☎ 619015 (1000-1400, 1600-1900). Manager Santiago Ferreiro. marinasada@marinasada.com www.marinasada.com 630 + ♥ on fingers, approx €2.38; max LOA 20m; max stay 7 days. ⊖, Met, Slip, BH (32 ton), P & D (1000-2000), ME, SM, El, Ⓔ, CH, ⚒, ⛽, ♿, 🛒, ▣, R, Bar. Safe over-wintering.

Town: Facilities at Sada (10 mins walk) are better than Fontan: R, Bar, Ⓑ, ✉, Ⓗ. La Coruña by taxi 20 mins, by hourly bus 30 mins.

TIME ZONE −0100
Subtract 1 hour for UT
For French Summer Time add
ONE hour in **non-shaded areas**

LA CORUÑA   LAT 43°22′N   LONG 8°24′W
TIMES AND HEIGHTS OF HIGH AND LOW WATERS

Dates in red are **SPRINGS**
Dates in blue are NEAPS

YEAR 2010

JANUARY

Time	m	Time	m
1 0410 F 1640	4.1 0.5 1027 3.9 2239 0.5	**16** 0449 SA 1708	3.8 1102 0.8 2307 0.8
2 0458 SA 1728	4.3 0.3 1115 4.0 2326 0.5	**17** 0521 SU 1738	3.8 1133 0.8 2339 0.9
3 0546 SU 1815	4.3 0.3 1203 3.9	**18** 0552 M 1808	3.8 1204 0.8 3.5
4 0013 M 1251 1904	0.5 4.3 0634 0.4 1251 3.8	**19** 0010 TU 1235 1840	0.9 3.7 0624 0.9 3.4
5 0101 TU 1340 1953	0.6 4.1 0724 0.6 3.6	**20** 0042 W 1307 1913	1.0 3.6 0657 1.0 3.3
6 0151 W 1432 2046	0.8 3.9 0816 0.9 3.4	**21** 0116 TH 1342 1951	1.1 3.5 0733 1.1 3.2
7 0245 TH 1528 ☽ 2146	1.0 3.6 0912 1.1 3.2	**22** 0154 F 1422 2035	1.2 3.3 0812 1.2 3.1
8 0347 F 1633 2255	1.3 3.3 1015 1.3 3.1	**23** 0240 SA 1512 ☽ 2131	1.4 3.2 0859 1.4 3.0
9 0500 SA 1744	1.4 3.1 1128 1.4	**24** 0341 SU 1616 2244	1.5 3.0 1000 1.5 3.0
10 0010 SU 1244 1854	3.1 3.0 0619 1.5 1.4	**25** 0500 M 1734	1.6 2.9 1120 1.5
11 0118 M 1351 1953	3.2 3.1 0731 1.4 1.3	**26** 0006 TU 1244 1851	3.0 3.0 0625 1.5 1.3
12 0214 TU 1444 2042	3.3 3.2 0829 1.3 1.2	**27** 0119 W 1354 1957	3.3 3.2 0738 1.2 1.1
13 0300 W 1526 2124	3.5 3.3 0915 1.1 1.1	**28** 0219 TH 1451 2052	3.6 3.5 0837 0.9 0.8
14 0340 TH 1603 2201	3.6 3.4 0954 1.0 1.0	**29** 0311 F 1541 2141	3.9 3.8 0929 0.6 0.6
15 0415 F 1636 ● 2235	3.7 3.4 1029 0.9 0.9	**30** 0359 SA 1628 ○ 2227	4.2 4.0 1016 0.3 0.4
		31 0445 SU 1713 2311	4.4 4.1 1102 0.1 0.2

FEBRUARY

Time	m	Time	m
1 0531 M 1756 2355	4.4 4.1 1145 0.1 0.3	**16** 0527 TU 1741 2344	3.8 3.6 1135 0.6 0.7
2 0615 TU 1840	4.4 3.9 1228 0.2	**17** 0557 W 1810	3.8 3.6 1204 0.7
3 0039 W 1312 1924	0.4 4.2 0700 0.5 3.7	**18** 0014 TH 1234 1842	0.8 3.7 0628 0.8 3.5
4 0123 TH 1356 2010	0.6 3.8 0742 0.8 3.5	**19** 0046 F 1306 1916	0.9 3.6 0701 0.9 3.4
5 0212 F 1445 2102	0.9 3.5 0835 1.1 3.2	**20** 0122 SA 1342 1956	1.0 3.4 0737 1.1 3.2
6 0307 SA 1543 ☽ 2209	1.2 3.1 0931 1.4 3.0	**21** 0205 SU 1427 2047	1.2 3.2 0821 1.3 3.1
7 0420 SU 1700 2333	1.5 2.9 1047 1.6 2.9	**22** 0302 M 1530 ☽ 2200	1.4 3.0 0921 1.4 3.0
8 0553 M 1827	1.6 2.8 1221 1.6	**23** 0424 TU 1659 2335	1.5 2.8 1048 1.5 3.0
9 0056 TU 1340 1938	3.0 2.8 0719 1.5 1.4	**24** 0604 W 1832	1.4 2.9 1228 1.4
10 0159 W 1433 2029	3.2 3.0 0819 1.3 1.3	**25** 0101 TH 1342 1943	3.2 3.2 0724 1.1 1.1
11 0245 TH 1513 2110	3.5 3.2 0903 1.1 1.1	**26** 0204 F 1438 2038	3.5 3.5 0824 0.8 0.8
12 0323 F 1546 2144	3.5 3.3 0938 0.9 0.9	**27** 0256 SA 1526 2125	3.9 3.8 0914 0.4 0.5
13 0357 SA 1616 2216	3.6 3.4 1009 0.8 0.8	**28** 0343 SU 1609 ○ 2209	4.2 4.0 0958 0.2 0.2
14 0428 SU 1645 ● 2246	3.7 3.5 1039 0.7 0.7		
15 0458 M 1713 2315	3.8 3.6 1107 0.6 0.7		

MARCH

Time	m	Time	m
1 0427 M 1651 2251	4.4 4.1 1041 0.0 0.1	**16** 0430 TU 1644 2248	3.8 3.7 1037 0.6 0.6
2 0510 TU 1732 2333	4.4 4.1 1122 0.0 0.2	**17** 0459 W 1713 2317	3.8 3.7 1105 0.6 0.6
3 0552 W 1813	4.3 4.0 1202 0.2	**18** 0529 TH 1743 2348	3.8 3.7 1134 0.6 0.7
4 0015 TH 1241 1853	0.3 4.1 0634 0.5 3.8	**19** 0601 F 1815	3.7 3.6 1204 0.7
5 0057 F 1322 1936	0.6 3.7 0717 0.8 3.5	**20** 0022 SA 1237 1851	0.8 3.6 0636 0.8 3.5
6 0142 SA 1405 2024	0.9 3.3 0801 1.1 3.2	**21** 0100 SU 1316 1932	0.9 3.4 0715 1.0 3.4
7 0235 SU 1459 ☽ 2126	1.2 3.0 0853 1.4 3.0	**22** 0146 M 1403 2026	1.1 3.2 0802 1.3 3.2
8 0345 M 1616 2252	1.5 2.7 1007 1.6 2.9	**23** 0246 TU 1510 ☽ 2142	1.3 3.0 0906 1.4 3.1
9 0521 TU 1754	1.6 2.6 1152 1.7	**24** 0412 W 1643 2318	1.4 2.8 1038 1.5 3.1
10 0023 W 1317 1912	2.9 2.7 0652 1.5 1.5	**25** 0550 TH 1815	1.3 3.0 1215 1.4
11 0131 TH 1409 2005	3.0 2.9 0753 1.4 1.3	**26** 0041 F 1325 1923	3.3 3.2 0706 1.0 1.1
12 0219 F 1447 2045	3.2 3.1 0835 1.1 1.1	**27** 0144 SA 1418 2017	3.6 3.5 0803 0.7 0.7
13 0257 SA 1519 2119	3.4 3.3 0910 0.9 0.9	**28** 0235 SU 1504 2104	3.9 3.8 0852 0.4 0.5
14 0330 SU 1548 2150	3.6 3.5 0941 0.8 0.8	**29** 0322 M 1547 2148	4.1 4.0 0935 0.2 0.3
15 0400 M 1616 ● 2219	3.7 3.6 1009 0.7 0.7	**30** 0405 TU 1627 ○ 2230	4.3 4.1 1017 0.1 0.2
		31 0448 W 1707 2311	4.2 4.1 1056 0.2 0.2

APRIL

Time	m	Time	m
1 0529 TH 1747 2352	4.1 4.0 1135 0.4 0.4	**16** 0505 F 1719 2328	3.8 3.8 1107 0.6 0.7
2 0610 F 1827	3.9 3.8 1213 0.6	**17** 0541 SA 1755	3.7 3.8 1141 0.7
3 0034 SA 1252 1908	0.7 3.6 0651 0.9 3.6	**18** 0007 SU 1219 1836	0.7 3.6 0620 0.9 3.7
4 0119 SU 1334 1954	0.9 3.2 0734 1.2 3.3	**19** 0050 M 1303 1923	0.9 3.4 0705 1.2 3.5
5 0210 M 1425 2051	1.2 3.0 0824 1.4 3.1	**20** 0141 TU 1356 2022	1.1 3.2 0759 1.2 3.3
6 0314 TU 1536 ☽ 2207	1.5 2.7 0931 1.6 2.9	**21** 0246 W 1506 ☽ 2137	1.2 3.0 0907 1.4 3.2
7 0438 W 1708 2334	1.6 2.6 1105 1.7 2.9	**22** 0407 TH 1631 2301	1.3 2.9 1031 1.4 3.2
8 0603 TH 1829	1.5 2.7 1231 1.6	**23** 0530 F 1752	1.2 3.1 1153 1.3
9 0046 F 1328 1926	3.0 2.9 0707 1.4 1.4	**24** 0017 SA 1259 1858	3.4 3.3 0640 1.0 1.0
10 0138 SA 1409 2009	3.1 3.1 0754 1.2 1.2	**25** 0119 SU 1353 1953	3.6 3.5 0737 0.6 0.8
11 0219 SU 1443 2045	3.3 3.3 0831 1.0 1.0	**26** 0212 M 1440 2041	3.8 3.7 0826 0.6 0.6
12 0255 M 1514 2118	3.5 3.4 0904 0.9 0.9	**27** 0300 TU 1523 2126	3.9 3.9 0910 0.5 0.5
13 0327 TU 1544 2149	3.6 3.6 0935 0.7 0.7	**28** 0344 W 1604 ○ 2210	4.0 4.0 0952 0.4 0.4
14 0359 W 1614 ● 2221	3.7 3.7 1005 0.7 0.7	**29** 0427 TH 1645 2252	4.0 4.0 1032 0.5 0.5
15 0431 TH 1646 2253	3.8 3.8 1035 0.6 0.6	**30** 0508 F 1725 2335	3.8 3.9 1111 0.6 0.6

Chart Datum is 1·86 metres below NMMA Datum. HAT is 4·5 metres above Chart Datum; see 4.5.

》》 **FREE** monthly updates from 《《
www.reedsalmanac.co.uk

TIME ZONE -0100
Subtract 1 hour for UT
For French Summer Time add ONE hour in **non-shaded areas**

LA CORUÑA LAT 43°22'N LONG 8°24'W
TIMES AND HEIGHTS OF HIGH AND LOW WATERS

Dates in red are **SPRINGS**
Dates in blue are **NEAPS**

YEAR 2010

N & NW Spain

MAY

Time	m		Time	m
1 0549	3.7		**16** 0527	3.7
1149	0.8		1126	0.7
SA 1805	3.8		SU 1743	3.9
			2359	0.7
2 0017	0.8		**17** 0612	3.6
0630	3.4		1210	0.8
SU 1229	1.0		M 1830	3.8
1847	3.6			
3 0101			**18** 0047	0.8
0713	3.2		0702	3.5
M 1311	1.2		TU 1259	1.0
1931	3.4		1921	3.7
4 0149	1.2		**19** 0141	0.9
0800	3.0		0758	3.4
TU 1359	1.4		W 1355	1.1
2022	3.2		2020	3.6
5 0243	1.4		**20** 0243	1.0
0856	2.8		0901	3.2
W 1500	1.6		TH 1459	1.2
2123	3.0		2127	3.5
6 0348	1.5		**21** 0352	1.1
1007	2.7		1012	3.2
TH 1613	1.6		F 1611	1.2
◑ 2234	3.0		◑ 2238	3.4
7 0500	1.5		**22** 0503	1.1
1125	2.8		1124	3.2
F 1729	1.6		SA 1723	1.2
2344	3.0		2348	3.4
8 0607	1.4		**23** 0610	1.0
1229	2.9		1229	3.3
SA 1832	1.5		SU 1830	1.1
9 0044	3.1		**24** 0052	3.5
0700	1.3		0709	0.9
SU 1319	3.0		M 1326	3.4
1922	1.3		1928	1.0
10 0132	3.2		**25** 0149	3.6
0744	1.2		0801	0.8
M 1400	3.2		TU 1417	3.6
2004	1.2		2021	0.8
11 0213	3.3		**26** 0240	3.6
0822	1.0		0848	0.8
TU 1436	3.4		W 1503	3.7
2042	1.0		2110	0.7
12 0251	3.5		**27** 0327	3.7
0858	0.9		0931	0.7
W 1511	3.6		TH 1546	3.8
2119	0.9		2156	0.7
13 0328	3.6		**28** 0411	3.7
0932	0.8		1013	0.7
TH 1546	3.7		F 1628	3.8
2156	0.7		○ 2240	0.7
14 0406	3.7		**29** 0453	3.6
1008	0.7		1052	0.8
F 1622	3.8		SA 1708	3.8
● 2234	0.7		2322	0.7
15 0445	3.7		**30** 0533	3.5
1046	0.7		1131	0.9
SA 1701	3.9		SU 1748	3.8
2315	0.6			
			31 0002	0.8
			0613	3.4
			M 1210	1.0
			1828	3.6

JUNE

Time	m		Time	m
1 0043	0.9		**16** 0041	0.5
0652	3.3		0655	3.7
TU 1251	1.1		W 1252	0.7
1909	3.5		1914	3.9
2 0124	1.1		**17** 0132	0.6
0734	3.1		0747	3.5
W 1334	1.2		TH 1344	0.8
1952	3.3		2009	3.8
3 0209	1.2		**18** 0227	0.8
0819	3.0		0843	3.4
TH 1422	1.4		F 1441	1.0
2040	3.2		2107	3.6
4 0258	1.3		**19** 0326	0.9
0911	2.9		0944	3.3
F 1517	1.5		SA 1544	1.1
◑ 2135	3.1		◑ 2210	3.5
5 0355	1.4		**20** 0430	1.0
1013	2.8		1051	3.2
SA 1620	1.5		SU 1652	1.2
2236	3.0		2318	3.3
6 0457	1.4		**21** 0537	1.1
1119	2.9		1158	3.2
SU 1726	1.5		M 1802	1.2
2339	3.0			
7 0557	1.4		**22** 0027	3.3
1219	3.0		0641	1.1
M 1826	1.4		TU 1302	3.3
			1909	1.1
8 0038	3.1		**23** 0131	3.3
0651	1.3		0740	1.1
TU 1311	3.1		W 1359	3.4
1919	1.3		2009	1.0
9 0130	3.2		**24** 0228	3.3
0738	1.2		0831	1.0
W 1357	3.3		TH 1449	3.5
2007	1.1		2101	0.9
10 0217	3.3		**25** 0317	3.4
0822	1.0		0917	0.9
TH 1440	3.5		F 1534	3.7
2052	1.0		2148	0.8
11 0302	3.5		**26** 0401	3.4
0905	0.9		0959	0.9
F 1522	3.7		SA 1615	3.7
2135	0.8		○ 2229	0.8
12 0346	3.6		**27** 0440	3.4
0948	0.8		1041	0.8
SA 1604	3.8		SU 1654	3.8
● 2220	0.6		2308	0.7
13 0431	3.7		**28** 0517	3.4
1031	0.7		1115	0.8
SU 1649	4.0		M 1731	3.7
2305	0.5		2345	0.8
14 0518	3.7		**29** 0553	3.4
1116	0.6		1152	0.9
M 1735	4.0		TU 1807	3.7
2352	0.5			
15 0605	3.7		**30** 0020	0.8
1203	0.7		0627	3.4
TU 1823	4.0		W 1228	1.0
			1843	3.6

JULY

Time	m		Time	m
1 0055	0.9		**16** 0112	0.4
0703	3.3		0726	3.7
TH 1304	1.1		F 1324	0.6
1920	3.5		1948	3.9
2 0132	1.0		**17** 0201	0.6
0740	3.1		0816	3.5
F 1342	1.2		SA 1416	0.8
1959	3.3		2041	3.7
3 0211	1.2		**18** 0255	0.9
0821	3.0		0912	3.3
SA 1425	1.3		SU 1514	1.0
2043	3.2		◑ 2140	3.4
4 0256	1.3		**19** 0355	1.1
0909	2.9		1016	3.2
SU 1516	1.4		M 1622	1.2
◑ 2133	3.1		2249	3.2
5 0349	1.4		**20** 0504	1.3
1008	2.9		1130	3.1
M 1617	1.5		TU 1740	1.3
2233	3.0			
6 0450	1.4		**21** 0007	3.0
1115	2.9		0618	1.3
TU 1727	1.5		W 1244	3.1
2341	2.9		1858	1.3
7 0555	1.4		**22** 0122	3.0
1222	3.0		0725	1.3
W 1835	1.4		TH 1348	3.3
			2004	1.2
8 0049	3.0		**23** 0222	3.1
0657	1.3		0821	1.2
TH 1321	3.2		F 1439	3.4
1936	1.2		2056	1.0
9 0149	3.2		**24** 0309	3.2
0753	1.1		0906	1.0
F 1414	3.4		SA 1523	3.6
2030	1.0		2138	0.9
10 0242	3.4		**25** 0349	3.3
0844	0.9		0946	0.9
SA 1503	3.7		SU 1601	3.7
2120	0.8		2215	0.8
11 0331	3.6		**26** 0424	3.4
0932	0.7		1022	0.8
SU 1550	3.9		M 1636	3.7
● 2207	0.5		○ 2249	0.7
12 0419	3.8		**27** 0456	3.5
1018	0.6		1056	0.8
M 1636	4.1		TU 1709	3.8
2253	0.3		2321	0.7
13 0505	3.9		**28** 0527	3.5
1104	0.4		1128	0.8
TU 1723	4.2		W 1742	3.7
2339	0.2		2352	0.7
14 0551	3.9		**29** 0558	3.4
1150	0.4		1200	0.8
W 1810	4.2		TH 1813	3.7
15 0025	0.3		**30** 0023	0.8
0638	3.9		0629	3.4
TH 1236	0.4		F 1231	0.9
1858	4.1		1846	3.6
			31 0054	0.9
			0701	3.3
			SA 1304	1.0
			1920	3.4

AUGUST

Time	m		Time	m
1 0128	1.0		**16** 0220	0.9
0737	3.2		0839	3.4
SU 1341	1.2		M 1444	1.1
1957	3.3		◑ 2109	3.3
2 0205	1.2		**17** 0318	1.3
0818	3.1		0943	3.1
M 1424	1.3		TU 1554	1.3
2042	3.1		2222	3.0
3 0251	1.3		**18** 0433	1.5
0909	3.0		1104	3.0
TU 1520	1.5		W 1723	1.5
◑ 2138	2.9		2352	2.8
4 0349	1.4		**19** 0559	1.5
1016	2.9		1228	3.0
W 1634	1.5		TH 1851	1.4
2253	2.9			
5 0505	1.5		**20** 0114	2.9
1138	3.0		0713	1.4
TH 1759	1.5		F 1335	3.2
			1956	1.3
6 0018	2.9		**21** 0212	3.0
0624	1.4		0808	1.3
F 1253	3.1		SA 1425	3.4
1914	1.3		2042	1.1
7 0130	3.1		**22** 0255	3.2
0732	1.2		0851	1.1
SA 1354	3.4		SU 1505	3.5
2013	1.0		2120	0.9
8 0227	3.4		**23** 0329	3.3
0827	0.9		0927	0.9
SU 1446	3.7		M 1540	3.6
2104	0.7		2152	0.8
9 0316	3.6		**24** 0401	3.5
0916	0.6		1000	0.8
M 1534	4.0		TU 1613	3.7
2151	0.4		○ 2223	0.7
10 0402	3.9		**25** 0430	3.5
1002	0.4		1031	0.7
TU 1619	4.2		W 1643	3.8
● 2235	0.1		2252	0.7
11 0446	4.0		**26** 0458	3.6
1046	0.2		1101	0.7
W 1704	4.4		TH 1712	3.8
2319	0.1		2320	0.7
12 0530	4.1		**27** 0526	3.6
1130	0.2		1130	0.7
TH 1750	4.4		F 1742	3.7
			2349	0.7
13 0002	0.1		**28** 0555	3.6
0614	4.0		1200	0.8
F 1214	0.3		SA 1812	3.7
1835	4.2			
14 0046	0.3		**29** 0018	0.8
0659	3.9		0626	3.5
SA 1300	0.5		SU 1231	0.9
1922	4.0		1845	3.5
15 0131	0.6		**30** 0049	1.0
0746	3.6		0659	3.4
SU 1349	0.8		M 1306	1.1
2012	3.6		1920	3.4
			31 0124	1.1
			0738	3.2
			TU 1347	1.3
			2003	3.2

Chart Datum is 1·86 metres below NMMA Datum. HAT is 4·5 metres above Chart Datum; see 4.5.

TIME ZONE –0100
Subtract 1 hour for UT
For French Summer Time add
ONE hour in **non-shaded areas**

LA CORUÑA LAT 43°22'N LONG 8°24'W
TIMES AND HEIGHTS OF HIGH AND LOW WATERS

Dates in red are **SPRINGS**
Dates in blue are **NEAPS**

YEAR 2010

SEPTEMBER

Day	Time m	Day	Time m
1 W ◐	0206 1.3 / 0827 3.1 / 1441 1.4 / 2100 3.0	**16** TH	0400 1.6 / 1034 3.0 / 1703 1.6 / 2333 2.8
2 TH	0305 1.5 / 0935 3.0 / 1559 1.6 / 2222 2.8	**17** F	0534 1.7 / 1202 3.0 / 1830 1.5
3 F	0430 1.6 / 1105 3.0 / 1735 1.5 / 2358 2.9	**18** SA	0055 2.9 / 0651 1.5 / 1310 3.2 / 1932 1.3
4 SA	0602 1.5 / 1231 3.2 / 1855 1.3	**19** SU	0149 3.0 / 0745 1.3 / 1400 3.3 / 2016 1.2
5 SU	0113 3.1 / 0714 1.2 / 1335 3.5 / 1955 0.9	**20** M	0229 3.2 / 0827 1.1 / 1439 3.5 / 2051 1.0
6 M	0209 3.5 / 0809 0.9 / 1427 3.8 / 2044 0.6	**21** TU	0302 3.4 / 0902 1.0 / 1513 3.6 / 2123 0.8
7 TU	0257 3.8 / 0857 0.6 / 1514 4.1 / 2129 0.3	**22** W	0332 3.5 / 0933 0.8 / 1544 3.7 / 2152 0.8
8 W ●	0341 4.0 / 0941 0.3 / 1558 4.4 / 2213 0.1	**23** TH ○	0400 3.6 / 1003 0.8 / 1613 3.8 / 2220 0.7
9 TH	0423 4.2 / 1024 0.2 / 1642 4.4 / 2255 0.1	**24** F	0428 3.7 / 1032 0.7 / 1704 3.8 / 2248 0.7
10 F	0506 4.2 / 1107 0.1 / 1726 4.4 / 2336 0.2	**25** SA	0456 3.7 / 1101 0.7 / 1712 3.8 / 2316 0.7
11 SA	0548 4.1 / 1151 0.3 / 1810 4.2	**26** SU	0525 3.7 / 1132 0.8 / 1743 3.7 / 2346 0.8
12 SU	0018 0.4 / 0631 3.9 / 1235 0.5 / 1856 3.9	**27** M	0556 3.7 / 1204 0.9 / 1816 3.6
13 M	0101 0.7 / 0716 3.7 / 1323 0.8 / 1944 3.5	**28** TU	0018 1.0 / 0631 3.6 / 1241 1.1 / 1854 3.4
14 TU	0147 1.1 / 0807 3.4 / 1419 1.2 / 2040 3.1	**29** W	0054 1.2 / 0711 3.4 / 1325 1.3 / 1940 3.2
15 W ◐	0243 1.4 / 0911 3.2 / 1530 1.5 / 2155 2.9	**30** TH	0139 1.4 / 0802 3.2 / 1422 1.4 / 2040 3.0

OCTOBER

Day	Time m	Day	Time m
1 F ◐	0241 1.5 / 0913 3.1 / 1542 1.5 / 2206 2.9	**16** SA	0452 1.7 / 1119 3.1 / 1747 1.6
2 SA	0409 1.6 / 1044 3.1 / 1717 1.4 / 2340 3.0	**17** SU	0014 2.9 / 0611 1.6 / 1229 3.1 / 1850 1.4
3 SU	0541 1.6 / 1208 3.3 / 1833 1.2	**18** M	0111 3.0 / 0708 1.5 / 1322 3.3 / 1937 1.3
4 M	0053 3.2 / 0651 1.2 / 1312 3.6 / 1932 0.9	**19** TU	0153 3.2 / 0753 1.3 / 1404 3.4 / 2015 1.1
5 TU	0147 3.6 / 0746 0.9 / 1404 3.9 / 2021 0.6	**20** W	0228 3.4 / 0830 1.1 / 1439 3.6 / 2048 1.0
6 W	0234 3.9 / 0834 0.6 / 1452 4.2 / 2106 0.3	**21** TH	0259 3.5 / 0903 1.0 / 1512 3.7 / 2119 0.9
7 TH ●	0318 4.1 / 0919 0.4 / 1536 4.3 / 2148 0.2	**22** F	0329 3.7 / 0934 0.9 / 1543 3.8 / 2148 0.8
8 F	0400 4.2 / 1003 0.3 / 1620 4.4 / 2230 0.2	**23** SA ○	0358 3.8 / 1005 0.8 / 1614 3.8 / 2218 0.8
9 SA	0442 4.2 / 1046 0.3 / 1704 4.3 / 2311 0.4	**24** SU	0429 3.8 / 1037 0.8 / 1646 3.8 / 2248 0.8
10 SU	0524 4.2 / 1130 0.4 / 1748 4.0 / 2352 0.6	**25** M	0501 3.9 / 1111 0.8 / 1721 3.7 / 2321 0.9
11 M	0606 4.0 / 1215 0.7 / 1832 3.7	**26** TU	0535 3.8 / 1147 0.9 / 1758 3.6 / 2357 1.0
12 TU	0033 0.9 / 0651 3.8 / 1303 0.9 / 1919 3.4	**27** W	0613 3.7 / 1228 1.0 / 1840 3.5
13 W	0118 1.2 / 0741 3.5 / 1356 1.2 / 2013 3.1	**28** TH	0038 1.2 / 0658 3.6 / 1316 1.2 / 1931 3.3
14 TH ◐	0212 1.5 / 0840 3.3 / 1502 1.5 / 2123 2.9	**29** F ◐	0127 1.3 / 0752 3.4 / 1415 1.3 / 2033 3.1
15 F	0324 1.7 / 0955 3.1 / 1625 1.6 / 2252 2.8	**30** SA	0231 1.5 / 0901 3.3 / 1530 1.4 / 2152 3.1
		31 SU	0351 1.5 / 1022 3.3 / 1652 1.5 / 2315 3.1

NOVEMBER

Day	Time m	Day	Time m
1 M	0514 1.4 / 1139 3.4 / 1805 1.2	**16** TU	0015 3.0 / 0616 1.6 / 1229 3.2 / 1846 1.4
2 TU	0025 3.3 / 0623 1.2 / 1245 3.6 / 1904 0.9	**17** W	0107 3.1 / 0708 1.5 / 1319 3.3 / 1931 1.3
3 W	0122 3.6 / 0721 1.0 / 1340 3.9 / 1956 0.7	**18** TH	0148 3.3 / 0752 1.3 / 1401 3.4 / 2010 1.2
4 TH	0211 3.8 / 0812 0.8 / 1430 4.0 / 2042 0.6	**19** F	0225 3.5 / 0846 1.2 / 1438 3.5 / 2045 1.0
5 F	0256 4.0 / 0900 0.6 / 1517 4.1 / 2126 0.5	**20** SA	0259 3.6 / 0907 1.0 / 1514 3.6 / 2118 0.9
6 SA ●	0340 4.1 / 0945 0.5 / 1602 4.1 / 2208 0.5	**21** SU ○	0332 3.8 / 0942 0.9 / 1550 3.7 / 2152 0.9
7 SU	0422 4.2 / 1030 0.5 / 1646 4.0 / 2249 0.6	**22** M	0407 3.9 / 1018 0.9 / 1627 3.7 / 2228 0.8
8 M	0504 4.1 / 1115 0.6 / 1730 3.9 / 2330 0.8	**23** TU	0443 3.9 / 1056 0.8 / 1706 3.7 / 2305 0.9
9 TU	0547 4.0 / 1159 0.8 / 1813 3.6	**24** W	0522 3.9 / 1137 0.8 / 1748 3.7 / 2346 0.9
10 W	0012 1.0 / 0631 3.8 / 1245 1.0 / 1858 3.4	**25** TH	0605 3.9 / 1222 0.9 / 1834 3.6
11 TH	0055 1.2 / 0717 3.6 / 1334 1.2 / 1946 3.2	**26** F	0031 1.0 / 0652 3.8 / 1311 1.0 / 1925 3.5
12 F	0144 1.4 / 0808 3.4 / 1428 1.4 / 2043 3.0	**27** SA	0121 1.1 / 0746 3.7 / 1407 1.1 / 2023 3.3
13 SA ◐	0243 1.6 / 0908 3.2 / 1532 1.5 / 2152 2.9	**28** SU ◑	0220 1.3 / 0847 3.6 / 1511 1.2 / 2130 3.3
14 SU	0355 1.7 / 1018 3.1 / 1644 1.6 / 2309 2.9	**29** M	0328 1.3 / 0955 3.5 / 1621 1.2 / 2242 3.2
15 M	0511 1.7 / 1128 3.1 / 1751 1.5	**30** TU	0441 1.3 / 1107 3.5 / 1731 1.2 / 2353 3.3

DECEMBER

Day	Time m	Day	Time m
1 W	0552 1.3 / 1216 3.5 / 1835 1.1	**16** TH	0005 3.0 / 0612 1.6 / 1223 3.1 / 1838 1.5
2 TH	0055 3.5 / 0657 1.1 / 1318 3.6 / 1932 1.0	**17** F	0101 3.1 / 0709 1.5 / 1318 3.2 / 1928 1.3
3 F	0150 3.7 / 0754 1.0 / 1413 3.7 / 2023 0.8	**18** SA	0148 3.3 / 0758 1.3 / 1406 3.3 / 2012 1.2
4 SA	0239 3.8 / 0846 0.8 / 1504 3.8 / 2109 0.8	**19** SU	0230 3.5 / 0842 1.2 / 1450 3.4 / 2053 1.1
5 SU ●	0325 4.0 / 0935 0.7 / 1550 3.8 / 2153 0.7	**20** M	0310 3.7 / 0924 1.0 / 1532 3.6 / 2133 0.9
6 M	0409 4.0 / 1021 0.7 / 1634 3.8 / 2234 0.8	**21** TU ○	0350 3.9 / 1005 0.9 / 1614 3.7 / 2213 0.8
7 TU	0451 4.0 / 1104 0.7 / 1716 3.7 / 2314 0.8	**22** W	0430 4.0 / 1046 0.7 / 1656 3.8 / 2255 0.7
8 W	0532 4.0 / 1146 0.8 / 1757 3.6 / 2354 0.9	**23** TH	0513 4.1 / 1129 0.6 / 1739 3.8 / 2337 0.7
9 TH	0612 3.9 / 1227 0.9 / 1836 3.4	**24** F	0557 4.1 / 1213 0.6 / 1825 3.8
10 F	0034 1.1 / 0653 3.7 / 1308 1.1 / 1917 3.3	**25** SA	0022 0.7 / 0643 4.1 / 1300 0.7 / 1913 3.7
11 SA	0116 1.2 / 0735 3.5 / 1351 1.2 / 2000 3.1	**26** SU	0110 0.8 / 0733 3.9 / 1350 0.9 / 2004 3.5
12 SU	0201 1.4 / 0821 3.3 / 1438 1.4 / 2049 3.0	**27** M	0202 1.0 / 0826 3.8 / 1444 0.9 / 2101 3.4
13 M ◑	0254 1.5 / 0913 3.2 / 1533 1.5 / 2149 2.9	**28** TU ◑	0300 1.1 / 0926 3.6 / 1546 1.1 / 2206 3.3
14 TU	0356 1.6 / 1014 3.1 / 1636 1.6 / 2258 2.9	**29** W	0407 1.3 / 1034 3.4 / 1655 1.2 / 2318 3.2
15 W	0505 1.7 / 1119 3.0 / 1740 1.5	**30** TH	0522 1.3 / 1148 3.3 / 1806 1.2
		31 F	0030 3.3 / 0637 1.3 / 1301 3.3 / 1913 1.2

Chart Datum is 1·86 metres below NMMA Datum. HAT is 4·5 metres above Chart Datum; see 4.5.

>> **FREE** monthly updates from <<
www.reedsalmanac.co.uk

9.23.29 LA CORUÑA (A Coruña)

La Coruña **43°22'·01N 08°23'·69W** (Marina) ❁❁❁◊◊◊✿✿✿

CHARTS AC 1111, 1094, 1110; SC 412, 412A, 4126; SHOM 3007, 7598, 6665

TIDES ML 2·2. Note: La Coruña is a Standard Port (⟵).

SHELTER from seaward: Marina Coruña, close N of Castillo de San Antón, is sheltered from wash/swell by two new wavebreaks. ⚓ further ESE on possible foul ground; no 🛟s. Dársena de la Marina in 3-4m is well sheltered.

NAVIGATION WPT 43°23'·21N 08°22'·12W, 189°/1·3M to head of Dique de Abrigo; thence 6-9ca west to marina. The WPT is where the 108·5° & 182° ldg lines intersect. Avoid Banco Yacentes, about 1M NW of WPT (off chartlet). Speed limit 3kn in hbr.

LIGHTS AND MARKS Conspic marks: Torre de Hércules lt ho; 5·3M SW of which is power stn chy (218m); twin white twrs (85m, R lts) of Hbr Control on Dique Barrié de la Maza. Storm signals are displayed from Castillo de San Antón. See chartlet and 9.23.3.

R/T Marinas Ch 09. Port Control Ch 12. VTS Ch 13.

TELEPHONE (Code 981) Port HM 226001; ⊖ & Met via YCs; Dr 287477; Ⓗ 277905; MRSC 209541; Brit Consul (986) 437133.

FACILITIES **Marina Coruña** ☎ 920428, www.marinacoruna.es jesusga@marinacoruna.es Extensive new pontoons and other facilities opened in 2009. 700 AB inc 100 🅥 (max LOA 50m), €2.40. Ⓡ, CH, C (50t), P & D (sole source in hbr), 🍴, Bar, R, @, Wi-Fi. Repairs go to **Marina Seca** 1·5M S at 43°20'·92N 08°22'·97W; ☎ as above.

Dársena de la Marina ☎ 914142, 350 inc 40 🅥, €2.45, AB (max LOA 30m). Ⓡ, BH (32 ton), ME, El, ⚒, Ⓔ, CH, SM. www.darsenacoruna.com info@darsenacoruna.com

Real Club Náutico ☎ 203265. The clubhouse (in the marina) welcomes visitors but requires jacket/tie, esp evenings.

Nauta Coruña ☎ 217678, www.nautacoruna.com administracion@nautacoruna.com. 132 inc 🅥, €2.20. Bar, slip, CH, @.

City: All amenities. Bus, ⇌, ✈ Santiago de Compostela (72km).

9.23.30 RÍA DE CORME Y LAXE

La Coruña. Corme It **43°15'·63N 08°57'·83W** ❋❋❋⚓✿✿
Laxe, E It **43°13'·35N 08°59'·95W** ❋❋❋⚓✿✿

CHARTS AC 3633, 1111, 1113; SC 928; SHOM 3007

TIDES
Standard Port LA CORUÑA (←—)

Times				Height (metres)			
High Water		Low Water		MHWS	MHWN	MLWN	MLWS
0000	0600	0000	0500	4·2	2·8	1·6	0·3
1200	1800	1200	1700				
Differences RÍA DE CORME							
−0005	−0005	−0004	−0004	−0·3	−0·2	−0·1	0·0

SHELTER Corme is well sheltered from N and E winds. Its pier has been extended to enlarge the crowded ⚓age. **Laxe** (Lage) is well sheltered from W and S. Both hbrs may be affected by swell.

NAVIGATION WPT 43°15'·31N 09°00'·63W: 081°/2·1M to Corme pierhd; 166°/2·0M to Lage pierhd. The ría is over 2M wide and the appr is straightforward, but beware rocks off Pta del Roncudo and Pta de Laxe. In bad weather follow the ldg lines to Corme to avoid Bajo de La Averia (5·6m). On SC 4131 many depths in apprs and in the ría may be less than charted on AC 1113.

LIGHTS AND MARKS All lts and ldg lines as on the chartlet.

R/T Ch 09. See 9.23.2 and 9.23.4 for the TSS/ITZ off Finisterre.

TELEPHONE (Code 981). MRSC 209541; Brit Consul (986) 437133.

FACILITIES Corme ☎ 738043: C (4 ton), Slip. **Laxe** ☎ 728255: C (16 ton), ME. **CN de Laxe** www.nauticodelaxe.com nauticolaxe@ hotmail.com A 50m yacht pontoon, 45 AB bows-in, extends ESE from the S mole hd. Space may be available on the piers, or raft up on FVs; or ⚓ close in to the piers, good holding on sand. Both hbrs; €1.25/m, AC, FW. **Both villages** are small: 🛒, R, Bar, ✉, Ⓑ, D & P (cans). Bus to La Coruña, ✈ Santiago.

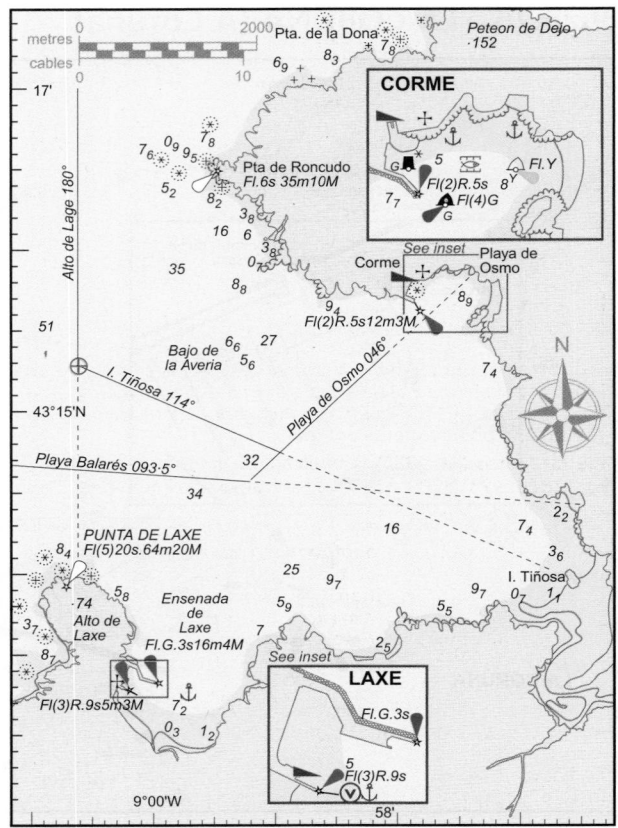

9.23.31 RÍA DE CAMARIÑAS

La Coruña **43°07'·58N 09°10'·94W** (CNC) ❋❋❋⚓⚓✿✿✿

CHARTS AC 1111, 3633, 1113; SC 928, 927; SHOM 3007

TIDES
Standard Port LA CORUÑA (←—)

Times				Height (metres)			
High Water		Low Water		MHWS	MHWN	MLWN	MLWS
0000	0600	0000	0500	4·2	2·8	1·6	0·3
1200	1800	1200	1700				
Differences RÍA DE CAMARIÑAS							
−0005	−0005	0005	−0005	−0·2	−0·2	−0·1	0·0

SHELTER Good at **Camariñas**, except in E/NE'lies; or ⚓ to S, inside bkwtr. **Mugia** (43°06'·36N 09°12'·73W) is solely a FV hbr, sheltered from all but E/SE'lies; ⚓ outside or in lee of bkwtr.

NAVIGATION El Bufardo (43°10'·00N 09°13'·28W, 4ca NW of C. Villano) is a dangerous pinnacle rk awash at CD. From the N follow the coast to pass E of Las Quebrantas shoal (0·6m). From the S appr on the 081° ldg lts.
WPT 43°07'·27N 09°12'·65W (intersection of the 108° and 081° ldg lines). Thence track 108°/1·1M, then 039°/0·7M to Camariñas bkwtr hd. For Mugia bkwtr 180°/0·9M.

LIGHTS AND MARKS C. Villano, with 23 conspic wind turbines close SE, is 2·2M N of ent to ría. Pta de la Barca lt ho marks the SW side of the ría ent. Pta de Lago dir lt ≠ bcn leads 108° into the ría. See chartlet and 9.23.3 for lights.

R/T Camariñas YC Ch 09. Mugia no VHF.

TELEPHONE (Code 981) Brit Consul (986) 437133.

FACILITIES **CN Camariñas** (CNC) http://nauticam.tripod.com ☎ 737130; xlblanco@mundo-r.com F&A, 60 + ⓥ €6.97 on 3 YC pontoons. ⊖ & Met; Slip, D & P (cans), ME, C, 🔧. **Mugia**, HM ☎

742030. Possible temp'y AB with fender board. **Villages**: 🛒, R, Bar, ✉, Ⓑ; Bus to La Coruña, ✈ Santiago de Compostela.

CABO FINISTERRE TO THE PORTUGUESE BORDER

NE of Cabo Finisterre (AC 3674) the Ensenada del Sardineiro and Ría de Corcubión are sheltered ⚓s except in S'lies and despite fish farms. From 5 to 11M south, beware various islets, reefs and shoals N and NW of Pta Insua, notably the unmarked Las Arrosas and Bajo de los Meixidos; the latter is in the red sector (070°-090°) of Pta Insua and can be passed inshore if bound to/ from Ría de Muros.

The 40M stretch (AC 3633) from Pta Queixal to Cabo Silleiro makes an impressive cruising ground, encompassing the four major rías bajas (lower or southern), from N to S: Muros, Arousa, Pontevedra and Vigo. All resemble large and scenic Scottish sea lochs with interesting pilotage to fishing hbrs and the many sheltered anchorages. In summer NE winds can blow strongly down all rías, usually without raising any significant sea. The last three rías are sheltered from onshore winds by the coastal islands at their mouth. These Galician islands are now protected by the status of National Park which imposes restrictions on fishing and underwater activities.

Ría de Muros (AC 1756) is the smallest and easiest to enter. Monte Louro at the N side of the entrance is a distinctive, 239m high, conical hill. The ancient town of Muros itself is worth visiting but holding in the anchorage is notoriously patchy, whilst the 2 small yacht pontoons are almost always crowded with local boats. Most of the bays and inlets are occupied by fish farms, often unlit and unmarked, so night pilotage is not advised. On the eastern shore **Portosin** is a very well run, modern marina with every facility.

Ría de Arousa (AC 1764), the largest ría, runs 14M inland and is up to 6M wide. Isla Sagres and Isla Salvora at the western side of the entrance provide shelter from SW'lies and are within the National Park. **Villagarcia** is the principal hbr and marina, but there are other marinas at **Santa Uxia de Ribeira, Caraminal, Rianxo, Vilanova** and **Piedras Negras**. There are many anchorages, mostly good holding on mud, several active fishing fleets and numerous fish farms and nets. Isla de Arousa and Peninsula del Grove, both in the SE part of the Ria, provide intricate pilotage and secluded anchorages.

Ría de Pontevedra (AC 1732) can be entered from the NW by one of two minor channels (Canals de la Fagilda and de Los Camoucos) between the mainland and Isla Ons. The main entrance, Boca del Sudoeste, is from the SW where the channel is unobstructed and 3·5M wide. On the N shore **Sanxenxo** is a modern marina whilst near the N end (AC 1733) **Combarro** is a sheltered anchorage and popular tourist spot. The naval base at Marin has nothing for yachts, but **Aguete** has a small marina and **Beluso** caters for yachts and FVs. Isla Ons and Isla Onzas are protected by National Park rules.

Ría de Vigo (AC 1730) is notable for the large busy port of **Vigo** and, to the S, Bayona's pleasant hbr with 2 marinas. The beautiful Islas Cies, comprising Isla del Norte and the smaller Isla de San Martin, are within the National Park and also provide considerable shelter to the ría against onshore winds. The two approach channels, from NW and SW, have been formalised into 2 mini-TSS which meet in a Precautionary area where the ría narrows down and the docks begin. **Davila Sport** is a new marina with first class BY in the Bouzas area, 1M SW of the long-established but rather small marina near central Vigo. 1M NE **Punta Lagao** Marina is on the W side of Monte de la Guia which is topped by a conspic chapel. Several lesser marinas are on the N bank and within the Ensenada de San Simón beyond the Rande bridge (38·8m clearance).

Bayona AC 3633 is too small a scale, 1:200,000, for pilotage. AC 1730, 1:25,000, subject to bilateral agreement with Spain, will hopefully include Bayona which is usually approached from seaward on the 084° leading line, passing between Las Serralleiras, rky islets to the N, and to the S Cabo Silleiro and its offshore reefs marked by a NCM buoy. The long-established Monte Real YC marina has been supplemented by Bayona marina close S; there is still space to anchor.

The Río Miño, 15M S of Cabo Silleiro, is the Spanish/Portuguese border. The river ent is difficult and best not attempted.

SENO DE CORCUBIÓN

MINOR HARBOURS IN SENO DE CORCUBIÓN

FINISTERRE. 42°54'·59N 09°15'·36W (hbr ent). AC 1111, 3764; SC 927, 9270. Tides: 9.23.32, Corcubión. Finisterre (or Fisterra, the end of the Ancient World) is famous and imposingly massive. The touristy town has no yacht facilities. But it is worth walking 1·5M from the hbr to the granite lt ho for the views and ambience.

Dense fog, which sometimes forms very quickly, is frequent on this coast. From the N, Centolo de Finisterre is a 23m high pinnacle rock 9 cables WNW of the lt ho. Beware La Carraca with 2·1m over it (42°53'·93N 09°18'·53W), less obvious therefore more dangerous. El Turdeiro (1·9m) is 300m due S of the cape, with a sprinkling of lesser rocks closer inshore where small FVs cluster; keep well clear. The E side is mostly steep-to.

The hbr (see chartlet) is usually full of small FVs, but in settled weather it is safe to ⚓ outside in 5-10m, either close S of the bkwtr or to the N off the Playa de Llagosteira.

ENSENADA DEL SARDIÑEIRO 42°56'·36N 09°13'·82W, ⚓ off the village of Sardineiro at the NW corner. Charts and Tides as for 9.23.32. This S-facing inlet is about 6ca wide and lies between Playa de Lagosteira to the W and to the E the peninsula which forms the W bank of Ría de Corcubión. There are no lights.

Most of the E half of the inlet is taken up by shellfish beds as charted. Approach along the W bank sounding carefully to avoid a 0·7m patch which lies just outside the W edge of the shellfish beds. ⚓ in 4-5m off the sandy beach which fronts the village of Sardineiro. Only basic facilities ashore.

RÍA DE CORCUBIÓN 42°56'·77N 09°11'·28W (⚓ at head of ria). AC 1111, 3764; SC 927, 9270. Tides: 9.23.32. A pleasant ría, well sheltered from the summer NE'lies, open only to S'lies. Three features south of the ría which are seen on the approach are: Lobeira Grande, a group of yellowish rocky islets with lt; Carrumeiro Grande, a single flat island with ldg bcn; and Carrumeiro Chico, a small rock with IDM bcn twr and lt. It bears 162°/6ca from Cabo Cée lt ho at the SW side of the ent to ría. See chartlet and 9.23.3 for light details.

The simplest approach for yachts is to pass between Cabo Cée and Carrumeiro Chico on a NE'ly heading, thence straight up the ría on 342° for 1·5M, with Carrumeiro Grande bearing 162° astern, if this is found necessary. A night appr presents no great difficulties: the ría is 0·5M wide and of the 3 lts at its head, as on the chartlet, keep midway between ✦ Fl (2) R 8s on the W bank and ✦ Fl (4) G 11s on the E bank.

⚓ NE of the ✦ Fl (2) R 8s in 6-7m, clear of the commercial quays and mussel beds. Holding is variable. Corcubión is nearer and more attractive than Cée; both towns have the usual facilities and shops.

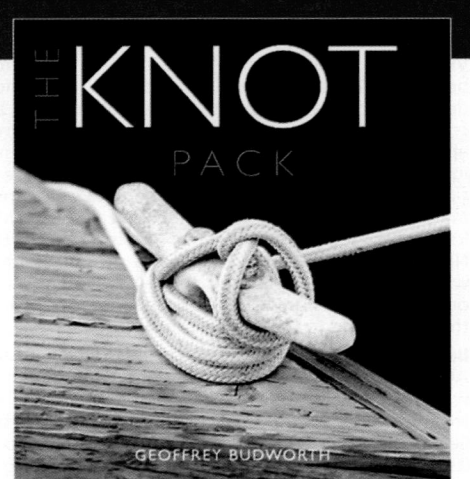

9.23.32 RÍA DE MUROS

La Coruña **42°46'·56N 09°03'·41W** (Muros) ⚓⚓⚓🏴🏳🏳🏵🏵🏵

CHARTS AC 1756; SC 415, 415A; SHOM 3007

TIDES

Standard Port LISBOA (⟶)

Times				Height (metres)			
High Water		Low Water		MHWS	MHWN	MLWN	MLWS
0500	1000	0300	0800	3·8	2·9	1·5	0·6
1700	2200	1500	2000				
Differences CORCUBION							
+0055	+0110	+0120	+0135	–0·5	–0·3	–0·3	–0·1
MUROS							
+0050	+0105	+0115	+0130	–0·3	–0·2	–0·2	–0·1

SHELTER Good at Muros. ⚓ off on weedy holding (2 or 3 shots may be needed) or at Ensenada de San Francisco to the SSW. Noya, at the head of the ría, is only accessible to shoal draft. CN Portosín on the E shore is sheltered, efficient and welcoming – a real pleasure; see Facilities.

NAVIGATION WPT 42°43'·60N 09°03'·36W, 1·25M SE of Punta Queixal lt and 2·0M NW of Punta Focha lt (off chartlet). From the N, the Canal de los Meixidos (between the mainland and Bajo de los Meixidos and Los Bruyos, where its least width is 1.1M) is usable with care. From the S avoid Bajos la Baya. The ría is mostly deep and clear, but beware mussel rafts off the N shore.

LIGHTS AND MARKS Mte Louro is a conspic conical hill (239m) N of Pta Queixal. Isla Creba is a good mark NW of Portosin. Principal lts: Pta Queixal, C. Reburdino, Pta Cabeiro, Pta Focha.

R/T Club Náutico Portosín Ch 09.

TELEPHONE (Code 981) MRSC 767320; Brit Consul (986) 437133.

FACILITIES **Muros** HM 826005; no VHF. The 2 pontoons in the inner hbr are usually full of locals. D (not near LW), P (cans), 🛒, R, Bar, ⓑ, ✉; ⚓ and ✈ Santiago de Compostela (40 km by bus). **CN Portosín** 42°45'·94N 08°56'·92W. ☎ 766598 info@cnportosin. com www.cnportosin.com 220 inc ✅, F&A, plus fingers in 3·5-8m; €2.52. Slip, BH (32 ton), D, ME, El, C (3 ton), ⚒, @, Wi-Fi, R, Bar, 🅿, CH. **Village** 2km: 🛒, R, Bar, ⓑ, ✉, car hire. ✈ Santiago de Compostela, 1 hr's drive.

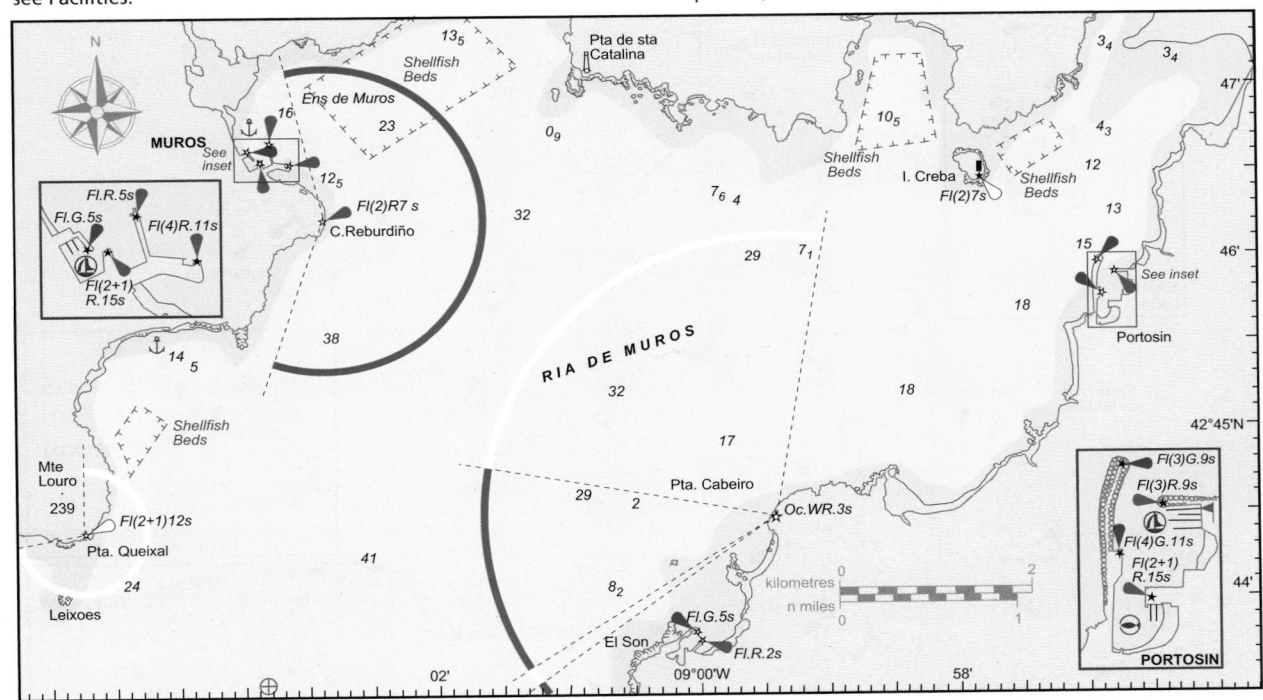

9.23.33 RÍA DE AROUSA

La Coruña (NW shore), Pontevedra (SE shore).
42°34'·58N 08°54'·15W (mid-Ría) ⚓⚓⚓🏴🏳🏳🏵🏵🏵

CHARTS AC 1734, 1764, 1762, 1755; SC 415, 415B/C.

TIDES

Standard Port LISBOA (⟶); ML 2·05

Times				Height (metres)			
High Water		Low Water		MHWS	MHWN	MLWN	MLWS
0500	1000	0300	0800	3·8	2·9	1·5	0·6
1700	2200	1500	2000				
Differences VILAGARCIA							
+0040	+0100	+0110	+0120	–0·3	–0·1	–0·2	–0·1

SHELTER Shelter can be found from most winds. Many ⚓ages are waiting to be explored with large scale charts and a good Pilot.

NAVIGATION WPT 42°27'·00N 08°59'·50W, 025°/6·6M to 5ca E of Is Rua (lt) 42°32'·96N 08°56'·38W. Leave Isla Sálvora (lt) to port; the

rocky chans between it and the mainland are best not attempted by strangers.

Ría de Arousa, the largest ría (approx 14M x 7M), is a not so mini-cruising ground with interesting pilotage. Its coast is heavily indented and labyrinthine. AC 1734 or SC 4152/3 are essential. The fairway up to Vilagarcia is buoyed/lit, but to either side are many mussel rafts (*viveros*), often unmarked/unlit. Some minor chans need careful pilotage to clear shoals/rocks. The low bridge from Isla de Arousa east to the mainland prevents passage.

LIGHTS AND MARKS Principal lts/marks are on the chartlet as scale permits. Isla Rúa, a prominent rky islet with lt ho, is a key feature. The many Y lt buoys usually mark fish farms.

R/T Santa Uxia, Caramiñal, Rianxo and Vilagarcia Ch 09, 16.

TEL (Codes: 981 La Coruna, NW shore. 986 Pontevedra, SE shore). MRSC (981) 767320; Brit Consul (986) 437133.

FACILITIES Marinas (see insets) are listed clockwise from the west. **Santa Uxia** 42°33'·80N 08°59'·34W. ☎ (981) 873801. 70 F & A on 4 pontoons in 4m. **Town**: all facilities.

Caramiñal 42°36'·27N 08°56'·10W. ☎ (981) 832504. cncaraminal@ hotmail.com VHF 09. 281 AB in 3·5m. P & D, C; **YC** ☎ (981) 877317. (see inset).

Rianxo 42°39'·00N 08°49'·51W. 2 pontoons at SE corner in 1·4m; 80 AB; ☎ 866107 (see inset).

Vilagarcia 42°36'·04N 08°46'·21W. ☎ (986) 511175. marinavilagarcia@marinavilagarcia.com 450 AB; ❶ as directed or on 1st pontoon to stbd in 3-5m; €0.46/m². Slip, C (50 ton), P, D, ME, El, ⚒, BH (70 ton), SM, Ⓔ, YC. **Town** CH, 🛒, R, Bar, Ⓑ, ✉, 🖂, ⇌. ✈ Santiago.

Vilanova Marina 42°33'·98N 08°50'·05W. ☎ (986) 554113. Due to extensive *viveros* the only appr is from the N: WPT at 42°35'·09N 08°50'·87W (↓ Fl (3) G 10s); thence 179°/1·2M to 0·5M abm Vilanova. D, BH, Slip in FV basin to the S.

Piedras Negras 42°27'·50N 08°55'·09W. ☎ (986) 738430. www.cnsvicente.com club.nautico.s.v.@wanadoo.es ⊕ 42°26'·97N 08°54'·28W, 310°/8ca to ent in W sector (305°-315°) of Fl (4) WR 11s. 134 AB, €1.55; 2 pontoons + fingers, 12m max LOA; depths 4-6m. P & D, BH (35t), CH. CN ☎ 738325, Bar, R ☎ 738435.

FV harbours with yacht facilities or ⚓s include:

San Xulian (Isla Arousa, N Bay) 42°33'·94N 08°52'·14W; ⚓ 1ca NW of the pier, on the W side of which are 4 pontoons for small craft. ⚓ in S Bay at 42°33'·36N 08°52'·57W in 5-8m; restricted by many moorings. Slip at head of the bay.

Cambados 42°30'·69N 08°49'·11W, S of Tragove FV hbr. Very shallow, 0·3m; only advised for multihulls and bilge-keelers. D.

9.23.34 RÍA DE PONTEVEDRA

Pontevedra 42°22'·00N 08°50'·00W (mid-Ría) ❁❁❁⚓⚓⚓⚓✿✿✿

CHARTS AC 3633, 1732/3; SC 416A/B; SHOM 3007

N & NW Spain

TIDES

Standard Port LISBOA (⟶); ML 1·9

Times				Height (metres)			
High Water		Low Water		MHWS	MHWN	MLWN	MLWS
0500	1000	0300	0800	3·8	2·9	1·5	0·6
1700	2200	1500	2000				
Differences MARIN (42°24'N 08°42'W)							
+0050	+0110	+0120	+0130	–0·5	–0·3	–0·3	–0·1

SHELTER Good shelter can be found from any wind. Islas Ons and Onza across the mouth of the ría offer a barrier to wind and swell. Marinas, hbrs and ⚓s are listed under Facilities.

NAVIGATION From WPT 42°18'·00N 08°57'·16W, (which also lies on the 129° ldg lts for Ria de Vigo) track 053° to enter via the main chan, Boca del Sudoeste, into centre of ria between Cabo de Udra and Pta Cabicastro. From NW, transit Canal de la Fagilda on 125°, or Canal de Los Camoucos on 180°; both are about 3 cables wide and need care.

LIGHTS AND MARKS As chartlet. Isla Ons is a steep, cliffy, rocky island with conspic octagonal lt ho.

R/T Marinas Ch 09. Marin Ch 12, 16.

TELEPHONE (Code 986). MRSC (981) 767320; Brit Consul 437133.

FACILITIES (Clockwise from NW)

Porto Novo 42°23'·71N 08°49'·28W. FV hbr with marina (100+ berths) and Real Club Nautico. ☎ 720802. Ferry to Isla Ons.

Off **Playa de Silgar** (between Porto Novo and Sanxenxo) there is a pleasant ⚓ on sand in 3-5m, exposed only to S'lies.

Sanxenxo Marina 42°23'·83N 08°48'·04W. Track N to the ent where a SHM lt bcn marks drying rocks on N side. CN ☎ 720517. nauta@sanxenxo.org www.rcnsanxenxo.com 500 AB, D, BH, C (5 ton), ME, ⎖, R, Bar, Ⓑ, ✉.

Raxó 42°24'·06N 08°45'·34W. Temp'y ⚓ in about 5m off bkwtr hd.

Combarro 42°25'·70N 08°42'·24W. AC 1733. ⚓ in about 2m to S of N bkwtr hd Fl (2) R 8s. The FV jetty, 300m S, gives added shelter. The bay is generally shallow. The village is noted for *horreos* and tourists. Possible security risk to unattended boats.

Pontevedra 42°24'·86N 08°41'·35W, mouth of Rio Lérez. Near LW a dinghy recce of shoals in shallow chan between training walls is advised; least depth 1·3m. Access is restricted by overhead cables (19m clearance) and motorway bridge (12m clearance). A small private marina is beyond a 2nd bridge. Town: the provincial capital has all domestic facilities and good road links.

Marin 42°23'·94N 08°42'·21W, a naval, commercial and FV port has no yacht facilities (tiny private marina in W basin). Isla Tambo, close NW, is a restricted military area; landing prohib.

Continued overleaf

Aguete 42°22'·55N 08°44'·16W. YC marina in pleasant bay; many ⚓s. To clear offlying rks, round the SHM buoy before turning S. **Marina** ☎ 702373. Approx 100 AB, inc ♥. N'most pontoon is a wavebreak. Slip, BH (28 ton), P, D, ME, M, El, C (8 ton), ✖. **Real Club de Mar** bldg resembles a liner's superstructure. R, Bar. Village: few shops.

Bueu 42°19'·79N 08°47'·02W. A FV hbr, yacht berths unlikely; ⚓ to W of hbr in about 5m. Caution: mussel rafts to NNW and NNE. Hbr ent is lit as chartlet. HM ☎ 320042. P & D (cans), CH, ▦, R, Bar. Ferry to Isla Ons. Good shops.

Beluso 42°20'·01N 08°47'·90W. Mussel rafts are E/NE of the hbr.

9.23.35 RÍA DE VIGO

Pontevedra **42°13'·85N 08°48'·26W** (centre of precautionary area) ✿✿✿⚓⚓⚓✿✿✿

CHARTS AC 3633, 1730, 1731; SC 416, 416B; SHOM 7595.

TIDES
Standard Port LISBOA (⟶); ML 1·96

Times				Height (metres)			
High Water		Low Water		MHWS	MHWN	MLWN	MLWS
0500	1000	0300	0800	3·8	2·9	1·5	0·6
1700	2200	1500	2000				
Differences VIGO							
+0040	+0100	+0105	+0125	+0·1	−0·3	0·0	−0·3

2nd pontoon to stbd is for yachts, F & A berths. HM ☎ 400870 if he can be found; if not, no fees! Excellent R. 20 mins walk to Bueu.

Ria de Aldán Punta del Con at 42°20'·01N 08°47'·90W, head of Ria. Worth exploring in settled weather; beware mussel rafts on W side. Temp'y ⚓s may be found on E side and at head of ría; uncomfortable in fresh N'lies.

Isla Ons Almost uninhabited, but tourist trap in season. At Almacen jetty (Fl R 4s) frequent ferries detract from the ⚓ or possible ⚓s; Bar, R. Fair weather ⚓ in 5m off Melide beach 42°23'·37N 08°55'·50W, but within National Park. No landing on Isla Onza (bird sanctuary).

SHELTER The ría is sheltered by Islas Cies, which have attractive ⚓s on E side; also sheltered ⚓s in Ens de San Simon. 3 marinas near Vigo centre are well sheltered, unless a NW'ly scend enters.

NAVIGATION N Chan (129° ldg lts) WPT 42°16'·09N 08°53'·94W, thence 160°/2M via a northern TSS to intersect the 095° ldg line.

S Chan (069° ldg lts) WPT 42°09'·42N 08°54'·86W, thence via a southern TSS to intersect the 041° ldg line.

A precautionary area is centred on the intersection (see L/L under title) of the 095° and 041° ldg lines. Small craft should not impede big ships in the TSS and/or the Precautionary area.

The buoyed inner fairway is defined by brgs of 068° and 074°

on the conspic Hermitage (chapel) tower on Monte de la Guía. Beware extensive unlit mussel rafts along the N shore.

LIGHTS AND MARKS Islas Cies are easily identified by their high, rugged bare slopes and white beaches on the E side. Ldg lts/marks for the appr chans are as per the chartlet and 9.23.3.

R/T Port Control *Vigo Prácticos* Ch 14, 16. Marinas Ch 09.

TELEPHONE (Code 986); ⊖ & Met at marinas; MRCC 431350; ≋269414; ✈ 268200; Turismo 224757; Brit Consul 437133.

FACILITIES heading NE up the Ria:
NW shore
Cangas 42°15'·66N 08°46'·97W. Rodeira is a small friendly YC marina in the NW corner of Ensenada de Cangas. AB on fingers as directed; approx €1.15. ☎ 300165. D, BH (64 ton), C (8 ton), **YC** (English spoken) Bar. Good security, 24 hrs guard. If full, ⚓ ESE of marina clear of ferries and FVs. **Town**, usual facilities, P (cans). Ferry to Vigo ½ hourly.

Moaña Marina 42°16'·66N 08°44'·00W. Appr from S, passing El Con hbr. Avoid *viveros* to NE and E. ☎ 310309. Possible AB on fingers at N end of 1st pontoon (other fingers are too short), Slip.

Domaya Marina 42°17'·26N 08°40'·60W, 7ca W of suspension bridge between Domayo hbr Fl R 5s and conspic factory quay to NE. Best approach from the SW, close inshore of fish farms (*viveros*).

NE of Rande suspension bridge (38.8m clearance)
Ensenada de San Simón, 42°17'·29N 08°39'·63W (AC 1730) has peaceful ⚓s in 3-4m mud off W, E and S sides, clear of *viveros*.

San Adrián de Cobres marina 42°18'·08N 08°39'·20W. Skirt a large *vivero* S and E of the marina to appr from the NE. Pierhead lt Fl (4) R 11s is the only lt, close NW of the marina. 204 AB on fingers inc ⓥ, max LOA 18m, €1.25. ☎ 874007. R, Wi-Fi, @. contacto@acimutnorte.com www.acimutnorte.com

SE shore (Vigo city)
Marina Dávila Sport 42°13'·97N 08°44'·42W, Darsena de Bouzas. www.davilasport.es info@davilasport.es ☎ 244612. Dutch manager (good English). €2.25. D&P, BH (70 ton), Wi-Fi, CH, modern repair facilities for all yacht sizes. **CN** ☎ 232442.

Vigo Marina 42°14'·56N 08°43'·42W. Narrow ent, between PHM/SHM lt twrs. ☎ 449694. www.rcnauticovigo.com puertodeportivo@rcnauticovigo.com 436 F&A + few ⓥ, €1.16. P & D, Slip, BH (32 ton), C (3 ton), ME, El, Ⓔ, CH, ✎, ▣. RCN clubhouse ☎ 433588, R, Bar.

Pta Lagoa Marina 42°15'·51N 08°42'·46W. ☎ 410096. www.yatesport.es lagoa@yatesport.es VHF 09. 250 + 100 ⓥ, €3.40, max LOA 24m, draft 3·5m. P & D, BH (70 ton), ME, El, Ⓔ, CH, ⚓, ▣; 2½km N of city.

City of Vigo: all amenities, ≋, ✈ (internal flights).

9.23.36 BAYONA

Pontevedra **42°07'·45N 08°50'·55W** (MRCY) ✿✿✿✿♤♤♤♧♧♧

CHARTS AC 3633, 1730; SC 417, 416B; SHOM 7596, 7595

TIDES
Standard Port LISBOA (→)

Times				Height (metres)			
High Water		Low Water		MHWS	MHWN	MLWN	MLWS
0500	1000	0300	0800	3·8	2·9	1·5	0·6
1700	2200	1500	2000				
Differences BAYONA							
+0035	+0050	+0100	+0115	−0·3	−0·2	−0·2	−0·1
LA GUARDIA (41°54'N 08°53'W)							
+0040	+0055	+0105	+0120	−0·5	−0·3	−0·3	−0·2

SHELTER Excellent in both marinas; possibly no wavebreak at Bayona Marina. ⚓ E/NE of marinas, clear of fairway to FV jetty.

NAVIGATION WPT 42°07'·78N 08°55'·06W (see 9.23.35 chartlet), 084°/2·8M to SPM buoy QY. From S keep 1M off Cabo Silleiro to clear reefs marked by NCM buoy, Q. Las Serralleiras, rks/islets N of ldg line, are marked by SCM & WCM lt buoys and by a lt bcn. The Canal de la Porta, between Monte Ferro and Las Estelas is a useful shortcut to/from Ría de Vigo, but avoid a 0·9m patch and a rock which covers/uncovers close W of mid-channel.

LIGHTS AND MARKS Ldg/Dir lts 084° as chartlet and 9.23.5, hard-to-see white conical twrs, the front on a tiny rky islet. N of the bay, a prominent white monument is on Monte Ferro. Dique de Abrigo (white wall) has a G/W tower QG. Other conspic daymarks: castle walls (parador), and MRCY flag-mast. FV jetty has white crane.

R/T *Monte Real Club de Yates* Ch 06. *Puerto Deportivo de Bayona* Ch 09.

TELEPHONE (Code 986) ⊜ & Met via YC/marina; Ⓗ 352011; Police 355027; Brit Consul 437133.

FACILITIES **Monte Real Club de Yates (MRCY)** is usually full. ☎ 385000. mrycb@mrcyb.com www.mrcyb.com 200 F&A, €2.75, + some ⚓s in 6m. P & D, Slip, BH (20 ton), C (1·5 ton), Bar, Ice, R, ◎. Clubhouse is very well appointed.

Bayona Marina, ☎ 385107, Mobile 626 299 162. puertobaiona@ puertobaiona.com www.puertobaiona.com 297 + 19 Ⓥ, €2.41. P & D, BH (35 ton), C (6 ton), Slip, Bar, Ice, R.

Town: ME, El, Ⓔ, CH, SM, ✕; most domestic needs inc 🛒, ◎, ⇶ and ✈ Vigo (21 km).

Portugal & the Azores

Viana do Castelo to Vila Real de Santo António.
Azores: Flores, Faial, Terceira and São Miguel

Portugal & Azores

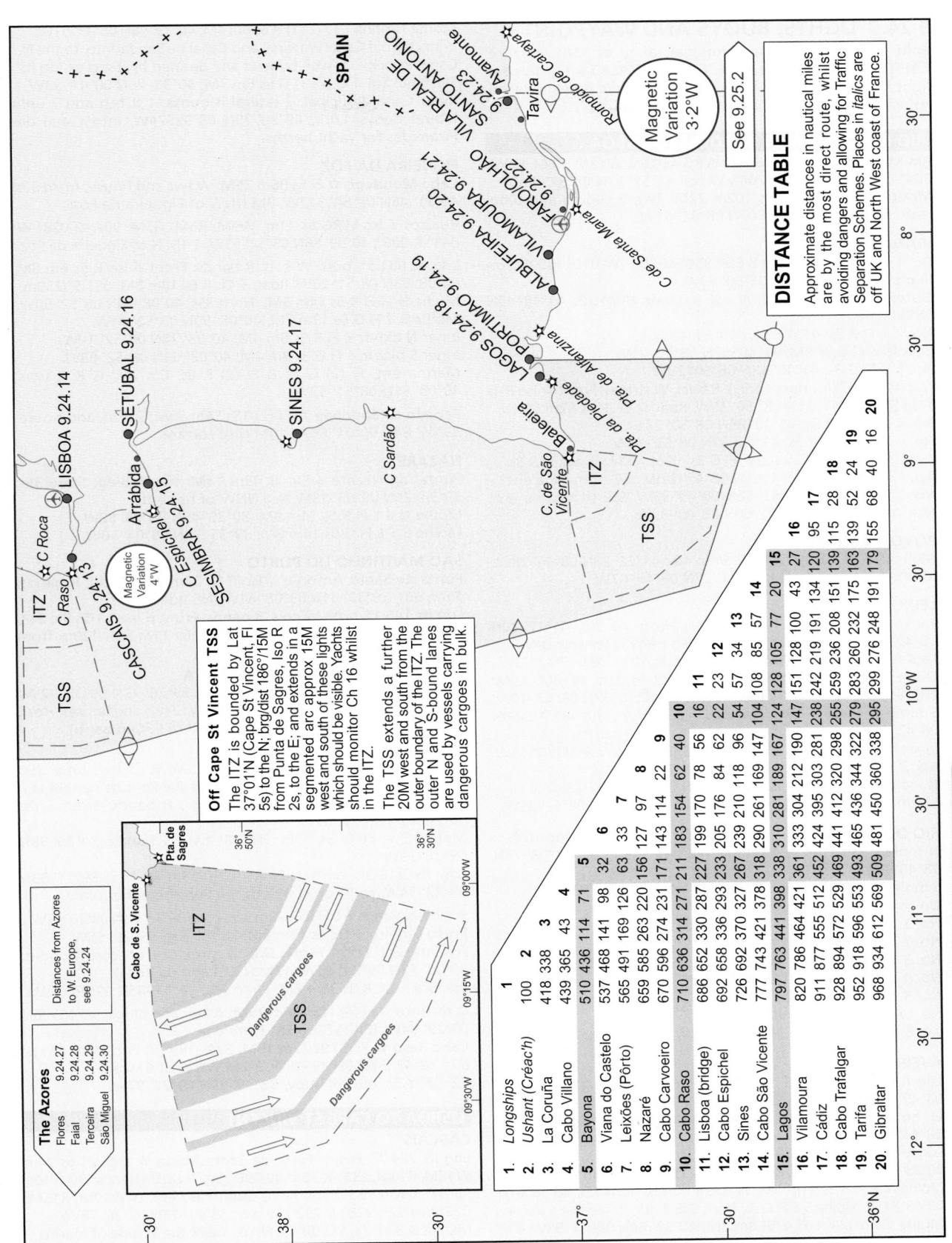

SPAIN

RIBEIRA DE CARAYA
VILA REAL DE SANTO ANTÓNIO 9.24.23
FARO/OLHÃO 9.24.20
VILAMOURA 9.24.20
ALBUFEIRA 9.24.21
PORTIMÃO 9.24.19
LAGOS 9.24.18
SINES 9.24.17
SETÚBAL 9.24.16
LISBOA 9.24.14
CASCAIS 9.24.13
SESIMBRA 9.24.15
C Espichel 9.24.15
Arrábida · SETÚBAL 9.24.16

Tavira
C de Santa Maria
Pta. de Alfanzina
Baleeira
C. de São Vicente
C Sardão
C Roca
C Raso

Magnetic Variation 3·2W
See 9.25.2

Magnetic Variation 4°W

ITZ · TSS

The Azores
Flores 9.24.27
Faial 9.24.28
Terceira 9.24.29
São Miguel 9.24.30

Distances from Azores to W. Europe, see 9.24.24

Off Cape St Vincent TSS
The ITZ is bounded by Lat 37°01'N (Cape St Vincent, Fl 5s) to the N; brg/dist 186°/15M from Punta de Sagres, Iso R 2s, to the E; and extends in a segmented arc approx 15M west and south of these lights which should be visible. Yachts should monitor Ch 16 whilst in the ITZ.

The TSS extends a further 20M west and south from the outer boundary of the ITZ. The outer N and S-bound lanes are used by vessels carrying dangerous cargoes in bulk.

Cabo de S. Vicente
Pta. de Sagres
ITZ
TSS
Dangerous cargoes

DISTANCE TABLE

Approximate distances in nautical miles are by the most direct route, whilst avoiding dangers and allowing for Traffic Separation Schemes. Places in *italics* are off UK and North West coast of France.

	1	2	3	4	5	6	7	8	9	10	11	12	13	14	15	16	17	18	19
1. *Longships*																			
2. *Ushant (Créac'h)*	100																		
3. La Coruña	418	338																	
4. Cabo Villano	439	365	43																
5. Bayona	510	436	114	71															
6. Viana do Castelo	537	468	141	98	32														
7. Leixões (Pórto)	565	491	169	126	63	33													
8. Nazaré	659	585	263	220	156	127	97												
9. Cabo Carvoeiro	670	596	274	231	171	143	114	22											
10. Cabo Raso	710	636	314	271	211	183	154	62	40										
11. Lisboa (bridge)	686	652	330	287	227	199	170	78	56	16									
12. Cabo Espichel	692	658	336	293	233	205	176	84	62	22	23								
13. Sines	726	692	370	327	267	239	210	118	96	54	57	34							
14. Cabo São Vicente	777	743	421	378	318	290	261	169	147	104	108	85	57						
15. Lagos	797	763	441	398	338	310	281	189	167	124	128	105	77	20					
16. Vilamoura	820	786	464	421	361	333	304	212	190	147	151	128	100	43	27				
17. Cádiz	911	877	555	512	452	424	395	303	281	238	242	219	191	134	120	95			
18. Cabo Trafalgar	928	894	572	529	469	441	412	320	298	255	259	236	208	151	139	115	28		
19. Tarifa	952	918	596	553	493	465	436	344	322	279	283	260	232	175	163	139	52	24	
20. Gibraltar	968	934	612	569	509	481	450	360	338	295	299	276	248	191	179	155	68	40	16

Portugal & Azores

9.24.3 LIGHTS, BUOYS AND WAYPOINTS

Bold print = light with a nominal range of 15M or more.
CAPITALS = place or feature. *CAPITAL ITALICS* = light-vessel,
light float or Lanby. *Italics* = Fog signal. **Bold italics** = Racon.
Abbreviations are in Chapter 1.

RIO MIÑO (SPANISH BORDER) TO LISBOA

Río Miño ent, Fort Ínsua ⚡ Fl WRG 4s 16m W12M, R8M, G9M;
204°-G-270°-R-357°-W-204°; W col; 41°51'·57N 08°52'·48W.
Montedor ☆ Fl (2) 9·5s 102m **22M**; Twr, R cupola and bldg;
Horn Mo (S) 25s; 41°45'·07N 08°52'·41W.

VIANA DO CASTELO

Dir lt ⚡ Oc WRG 4s 15m 8/6M; 350°-G-005°-W-010°-R-025°; on
Pilots' twr; 41°41'·05N 08°50'·30W.
Outer mole ⚡ Fl R 3s 9M; W col, R bands; *Horn 30s*; 41°40'·46N
08°50'·66W.
No. 2 ⚡ Fl R 3s; 41°40'·53N 08°50'·48W.
E mole ⚡ Fl G 3s 9M; 41°40'·67N 08°50'·25W.
No. 1 ⚡ Fl G 3s; 41°40'·68N 08°50'·29W.
Ldg lts 012·5° (for docks only); R twrs, W stripes: **Front** ☆ Iso R 4s
14m 5M; 41°41'·33N 08°50'·35W. **Rear** ☆ Oc R 6s 32m 5M.
No. 3 ⚡ Fl (2) G 3s; 41°40'·86N 08°50'·24W.
No. 4 ⚡ Fl (2+1) R 5s; 41°40'·89N 08°50'·36W.
Rio Lima: Nos. 5-13 ⚡s are Fl G 3s. Nos. 6-14 ⚡s are Fl R 3s.
No. 13 ⚡ Fl G 3s; 41°41'·49N 08°49'·27W, SSE of marina ent.
No. 14 ⚡ Fl R 3s; 41°41'·56N 08°49'·33W, SSE of marina ent.
Marina ent, unlit; 41°41'·60N 08°49'·33W.

PÓVOA DE VARZIM

Molhe N ⚡ Fl R 3s 14m 12M; *Siren 40s*; 41°22'·23N 08°46'·28W.
Molhe S ⚡ L Fl G 6s 4M; 41°22'·27N 08°46'·07W.

LEIXÕES

Tanker mooring ⚡ Fl (3) 15s 6M; *Horn (U) 30s*; 41°12'·10N
08°45'·06W. Oil refinery 2M E of this buoy is conspic D/N.
Leça ☆ Fl (3) 14s 56m **28M**; W twr, B bands; 41°12'·08N 08°42'·73W.
Outer N mole, Quebra-Mar ⚡ Fl WR 5s 23m W12M, R9M;
001°-R-180°-W-001°; Gy twr; *Horn 20s*; 41°10'·37N 08°42'·49W.
S mole ⚡ Fl G 4s 16m 7M; 328°-285°; *Horn 30s*; 41°10'·68N
08°42'·34W.
Inner N mole ⚡ Fl R 4s 8m 6M; 173°-353°; 41°10'·70N 08°42'·51W.
No. 2 buoy ⚡ Fl (3) R 8s; 41°10'·82N 08°42'·51W.
No. 4 buoy ⚡ Fl (2) R 5s; 41°10'·87N 08°42'·60W.
Marina bkwtr ⚡ L Fl (2) R 12s 4m 2M; 41°11'·08N 08°42'·25W.

RIO DOURO/PORTO (See 9.24.8 for WIP at river mouth)

N mole head Fl R 5s 16m 9M; W twr, R stripes; 41°08'·73N
08°40'·72W.
S mole head Fl G 3s 8m 3M; 41°08'·67N 08°40'·53W.
Up-river buoys in sequence:
No. 1 ⚡ Fl G 3s; 41°08'·74N 08°40'·29W.
No. 2 ⚡ Fl R 3s; 41°08'·72N 08°39'·77W.
No. 3 ⚡ Fl (2) G 5s; 41°08'·65N 08°39'·52W.
No. 4 ⚡ Fl (2) R 5s; 41°08'·80N 08°39'·12W.
No. 5 ⚡ ; 41°08'·79N 08°38'·85W.
No. 6A ⚡ 41°08'·45N 08°37'·26W.
No. 8 ⚡ Fl R 4s; 41°08'·39N 08°37'·12W; 4 ca W of bridge, 8·8m.

AVEIRO

Ldg lt 085·4°: Front, S mole hd ⚡ Fl G 3s 16m 9M; 40°38'·54N
08°45'·48W. Rear ⚡ Fl G 4s 53m 9M; 065·4°-105·4°.
Lt ho Aero ☆ Fl (4) 13s 65m **23M**; R/W twr; 40°38'·57N
08°44'·88W; same twr as rear ldg lt Fl G 4s as above.
Ldg lts 065·6°; 060·6°-070·6°; both R ○ cols: Front ⚡ Oc R 3s 7m 9M;
40°38'·81N 08°44'·99W. Rear ⚡Oc R 6s 15m, 8M, 440m from front.
Molhe N ⚡ Fl R 3s 11m 8M; W col, R bands; *Horn 15s*; 40°38'·61N
08°45'·81W. Molhe S ⚡ Fl G 3s; front 085·4° ldg lt; see line 1 above.
Molhe Central ⚡ L Fl G 5s 8m 3M; 40°38'·64N 08°44'·95W.

Monte Farinha ⚡ Q (2+1) R 6s 6m 4M; 40°39'·48N 08°43'·51W;
Y-junction of Canal Principal and Canal de San Jacinto, to the N.
Canal Principal is well buoyed and defined by 3 sets of ldg lts.
Terminal Sul ⚡ Q (2+1) G 6s 6m 3M; 40°38'·26N 08°41'·33W.
Inner Canal Principal: 2 lateral lt buoys, 1 lt bcn and 7 unlit
lateral buoys. Lock, 40°38'·75N 08°39'·74W, into Canal das
Piramides for yacht berths.

FIGUEIRA DA FOZ

Cabo Mondego ☆ Fl 5s 96m **25M**; W twr and house; *Horn 30s*;
40°11'·46N 08°54'·312W, 3M NNW of Figueira da Foz.

Buarcos ⚡ Iso WRG 6s 11m, W9M, R6M, G5M; 004°-G-028°-W-
048°-R-086°; 40°09'·86N 08°52'·53W, 1·1M N of Figueira da Foz.

Ldg lts 081·5°, both W cols, R bands: Front ⚡ Iso R 5s 6m 8M;
40°08'·83N 08°51'·23W. Rear, ⚡ Oc R 6s 10m 8M; 081·5°/239m.
Molhe N ⚡ Fl R 6s 14m 9M; *Horn 35s*; 40°08'·74N 08°52'·50W.
Molhe S ⚡ Fl G 6s 13m 7M; 40°08'·59N 08°52'·41W.
Inner N bkwtr ⚡ Fl R 3s 8m 4M; 40°08'·78N 08°52'·10W.
Inner S bkwtr ⚡ Fl G 3s 8m 4M; 40°08'·69N 08°52'·08W.
Marina ent, ⚡ Fl G 8s & Fl (2) R 8s, 6m 2M; G & R twrs;
40°08'·81N 08°51'·52W.

Penedo da Saudade ☆ Fl (2) 15s 54m **30M**; □ twr, and house;
39°45'·84N 09°01'·86W, 10M N of Nazaré.

NAZARÉ

Pontal da Nazaré ⚡ Oc 3s 49m 14M; twr & bldg; *Siren 35s*;
39°36'·25N 09°05'·15W, 9ca NNW of hbr ent.
Molhe N ⚡ L Fl R 5s 14m 9M; 39°35'·45N 09°04'·59W.
Molhe S ⚡ L Fl G 5s 14m 8M; 39°35'·36N 09°04'·70W.

SÃO MARTINHO DO PORTO

Ponta de Santo António ⚡ Iso R 6s 32m 9M; W col, R bands;
Siren 60s; 39°30'·61N 09°08'·61W (NE side of ent).
Ldg lts 145·1°, both W cols, R bands: Front ⚡ Iso R 1·5s 9m 9M;
39°30'·14N 09°08'·39W. Rear ⚡ Oc R 6s 11m 9M, 129m from
front.

LOS FARILHÕES/ILHA DA BERLENGA

Farilhão Grande ⚡ Fl (2) 5s 99m 13M; 39°28'·73N 09°32'·72W.
Ilha da Berlenga ☆ Fl 10s 120m **20M**; W □ twr and houses; *Horn
28s*; 39°24'·90N 09°30'·60W (5·7M NW of C. Carvoeiro).

PENICHE

Cabo Carvoeiro ☆ Fl (3) R 15s 56m **15M**; W □ twr; *Horn 35s*;
39°21'·61N 09°24'·49W, on the W tip of the Peniche peninsula.
Molhe W ⚡ Fl R 3s 13m 9M; W twr, R bands; *Siren 120s*;
39°20'·87N 09°22'·53W.
Molhe E ⚡ Fl G 3s 13m 9M; W twr, G bands; 39°20'·98N
09°22'·39W.
Ldg lts 218·3°, both L Fl R 7s 10/13m 8/6M; 39°21'·83N
09°22'·34W, for ⚓ on N side of the Peniche peninsula.

Porto das Barcas ⚡ L Fl R 6s 29m 6M; post; 39°13'·81N 09°20'·47W.
Porto Dineiro ⚡ Oc 3s 19m 8M; 39°12'·83N 09°20'·55W.
Assenta ⚡ L Fl 5s 74m 13M; W structure on conical base;
39°03'·53N 09°24'·85W (17M N of Cabo da Roca).
Ericeira ⚡ Oc R 3s 36m 6M; *Siren 70s*; 38°57'·85N 09°25'·13W.

C. da Roca ☆ Fl (4) 18s 164m **26M**; W twr and bldgs; 38°46'·90N
09°29'·84W. R lt (527m) 5M E at Pena.
Cabo Raso ☆ Fl (3) 9s 22m **15M**; 324°-189°; R twr; *Horn Mo (I)
60s*; 38°42'·57N 09°29'·15W, 3·2M WNW of Cascais.
C2 ⚡ Fl Y 5s; outfall buoy; 38°39'·99N 09°27'·97W.

LISBOA TO CAPE ST VINCENT

CASCAIS

Ldg lts 284·7°: Front, **Forte de Santa Marta** ☆ Oc WR 6s 24m
W18M, R14M; 233°-R-334°-W-098°; W □ twr, Bu bands; *Horn 10s*;
38°41'·42N 09°25'·25W. Rear, **Guia** ☆ Iso WR 2s **W19M, R16M**;
326°-W-092°; 278°-R-292°; W twr; 38°41'·74N 09°26'·78W.
MC1, 2 & 3 all ⚡s, VQ (6) + L Fl 10s, mark the SE side of marina.

WGS84 DATUM
Plot waypoints on chart before use

CC2 ⚓ Fl R 4s; NE of bkwtr hd; 38°41'·63N 09°24'·80W.
No. 2 ⚓ Fl R 10s (May-Oct); 38°41'·69N 09°24'·99W.
Marina Molhe Sul ⚡ Fl (3) R 4s 8m 6M; 38°41'·59N 09°24'·84W.
Molhe Norte ⚡ Fl (2) G 4s 8m 3M; 38°41'·60N 09°24'·90W.
Praia da Ribeira ⚡ Oc R 4s 5m 6M; 251°-309°; W col, R bands; 38°41'·81N 09°25'·21W.
Albatroz ⚡ Oc R 6s 12m 5M; 38°41'·99N 09°25'·02W.

RIO TEJO, N BANK
Marconi ⚡ Iso WR 3s 17m 9M; 048°-R-058°-W-068°; Y twr; 38°40'·86N 09°20'·78W, on Ponta da Rana 3·25M ESE of Cascais.
Forte de São Julião ⚡ Oc R 5s 38m 14M; 38°40'·47N 09°19'·52W.
Oeiras marina, S pier hd ⚡ Fl R 3s 9m 5M; 38°40'·56N 09°19'·00W.
N pier hd ⚡ Fl G 3s 9m 5M; 38°40'·62N 09°18'·99W.
Doca de Paço de Arcos, W pier ⚡ Fl R 5s 9m 4M; 38°41'·43N 09°17'·61W. E pier ⚡ Fl G 5s; 38°41'·46N 09°17'·59W.

LISBOA
Triple ldg lts 047·1°: Front, **Gibalta** ☆ Oc R 3s 30m **21M**; 039·5°-054·5°; twr & cupola, R stripes; 38°41'·95N 09°15'·97W.
Middle, **Esteiro** ☆ Oc R 6s 81m **21M**; 039·5°-054·5°; W twr, R bands; *Racon Q, 15M*; 38°42'·23N 09°15'·59W.
Rear, **Mama** ☆ Iso 6s 153m **21M**; 045·5°-048·5°; platform; 38°43'·65N 09°13'·63W.
No. 2 ⚓ Fl R 10s; 38°37'·29N 09°23'·28W.
No. 1 ⚓ Fl G 2s; 38°39'·55N 09°18'·79W.
Forte Bugio ☆ Fl G 5s 27m 15M; ○ twr on fortress; *Horn Mo (B) 30s*; 38°39'·63N 09°17'·93W.
No. 3 ⚓ Fl G 3s; 38°40'·04N 09°18'·26W.
No. 5 ⚓ Fl G 4s; 38°40'·43N 09°17'·66W.
No. 7 ⚓ Fl G 5s; 38°40'·65N 09°16'·90W.
No. 9 ⚓ Fl G 6s; 38°40'·55N 09°14'·57W.
Bridge (Ponte 25 de Abril). Fl (3) G 9s and Fl (3) R 9s on the N (38°41'·64N 09°10'·69W) and S (38°41'·10N 09°10'·56W) pillars; vis up and down-stream, covering main (70m) and inshore spans.
Lisnave ⚡ Fl G 2s 4m 3M; 38°41'·29N 09°08'·63W, S bank. Docks & industrial areas lie S and E of this lt.

Cabo Espichel ☆ Fl 4s 167m **26M**; W 6-sided twr; *Horn 31s*; 38°24'·92N 09°12'·97W. Fog signal TR 2009.

SESIMBRA
Cavalo Fort ⚡ Oc 5s 34m 14M; R ○ twr; 38°26'·01N 09°07'·01W.
Ldg lts 003·5°, both ⚡ L Fl R 5s 9/21m 7/6M: Front, 38°26'·51N 09°06'·09W. Rear 34m from front. Pierhead ⚡ Fl R 3s 8M.

SETUBAL
Ldg lts 039·7°, both ☆ Iso Y 6s 12/60m **22M** (by day 5/6M). Front, R structure, W stripes; 38°31'·08N 08°54'·00W (fish dock). Rear, **Azêda**, vis 038·3°-041·3°; R hut on piles; 1·7M from front.
No. 1 ⚓ Fl G 3s 5M; 38°26'·99N 08°58'·17W.
No. 2 ⚓ Fl (2) R 10s 13m 9M; *Racon B, 15M*; 38°27'·22N 08°58'·45W.
No. 4 ⚓ Fl R 4s 13m 4M; 38°27'·92N 08°57'·71W.
No. 3 ⚓ Fl G 3s; 38°28'·33N 08°56'·78W.
No. 5 ⚓ Fl G 4s 13m 4M; 38°29'·20N 08°55'·36W.
Forte de Outão ⚡ Oc R 6s 33m 12M; 38°29'·31N 08°56'·05W.
João Farto ⚓ Q (9) 15s; 38°30'·33N 08°54'·44W.
Forte de Albarquel ⚡ Oc R 6s 2s 16m 6M; 38°30'·65N 08°54'·79W.
Commercial dock (yachts in W half); 38°31'·22N 08°53'·13W.
Pinheiro da Cruz ⚡ Fl 3s 66m 11M; W ○ col, R stripes; 38°15'·47N 08°46'·28W. Firing area extends 6M offshore.

SINES
Cabo de Sines ☆ Fl (2) 15s 55m **26M**; 37°57'·57N 08°52'·82W.
⚓ Fl (5) Y 20s; 37°55'·36N 08°55'·80W, 2·2M WSW of W mole hd.
W mole hd ⚡ Fl 3s 20m 12M; 37°56'·48N 08°53'·33W.
Sines W ⚓ Fl R 3s 6M; 37°56'·12N 08°53'·25W, 4ca S of W mole hd.
E mole, NW head ⚡ L Fl G 8s 16m 6M; 37°56'·32N 08°51'·95W.
Farolim, SE head ⚡ L Fl R 8s 20m 6M; 37°55'·55N 08°50'·83W.
Borboleta ⚓ VQ (3) 5s; 37°55'·18N 08°50'·89W.
Marina mole ⚡ Fl G 4s 4M; W twr, G bands; 37°57'·03N 08°52'·03W.
FV bkwtr ⚡ Fl R 6s 6M; W twr, R bands; 37°57'·06N 08°52'·19W.

Ponta da Gaivota ⚡ L Fl 7s 19m 13M; 37°51'·10N 08°47'·78W.
Rio Mira, ent ⚡ Fl 3s 22m 12M; 37°43'·12N 08°47'·40W.
Cabo Sardão ☆ Fl (3) 15s 67m **23M**; 37°35'·93N 08°49'·01W.

CAPE ST VINCENT TO THE SPANISH BORDER
CAPE ST VINCENT/SAGRES
Cabo de São Vicente ☆ Fl 5s 84m **32M**; W twr and bldg; *Horn Mo (I) 30s*; 37°01'·36N 08°59'·78W.
Ponta de Sagres ⚡ Iso R 2s 52m 11M; 36°59'·66N 08°56'·94W.
Baleeira mole ⚡ Fl WR 4s 12m, W14M, R11M; 254°-W-355°-R-254°; W twr; 37°00'·67N 08°55'·43W.

LAGOS
Pta da Piedade ☆ Fl 7s 50m **20M**; 37°04'·81N 08°40'·14W.
W bkwtr ⚡ Fl (2) R 6s 5M; W col, R bands; 37°05'·93N 08°39'·83W.
E bkwtr ⚡ Fl (2) G 6s 5M; W col, G bands; 37°05'·91N 08°39'·92W.
Alvor ent, ⚡ Fl R/G 4s; W twrs, R/G bands; 37°07'·10N 08°37'·11W.

PORTIMÃO
Ponta do Altar ☆ L Fl 5s 31m **16M**; 290°-170°; W twr and bldg; 37°06'·34N 08°31'·17W.
Ldg lts 019·1°: Both ⚡ Iso R 6s 18/30m 6M, W cols, R bands. Front; 37°07'·35N 08°31'·31W. Rear ⚡ 54m from front.
Outer E mole ⚡ Fl G 5s 9m 7M; 37°06'·50N 08°31'·59W.
Outer W mole ⚡ Fl R 5s 9m 7M; 37°06'·52N 08°31'·76W.
Marina S end ⚡ Iso R 2s 6m 3M; 37°06'·90N 08°31'·62W.
No. 2 ⚓ Fl R 4s; 37°06'·96N 08°31'·53W.
Marina ent, S side ⚡ Fl R 6s 3M; 37°07'·10N 08°31'·58W.
N side ⚡ Fl G 6s 3M; 37°07'·14N 08°31'·58W.
Marina N end ⚡ Iso R 4s 8m 3M; 37°07'·33N 08°31'·58W.

Pta de Alfanzina ☆ Fl (2) 15s 62m **29M**; 37°05'·19N 08°26'·54W.
Armação de Pera ⚡ Oc R 5s 24m 6M; 37°06'·00N 08°21'·36W.

ALBUFEIRA
Ponta da Baleeira ⚡ Oc 6s 30m 11M; 37°04'·81N 08°15'·80W.
N bkwtr ⚡, Fl (2) G 5s 9m 4M, approx 37°04'·81N 08°15'·57W.
S bkwtr ⚡, Fl (2) R 5s 9m 4M, approx 37°04'·76N 08°15'·57W.
Olhos de Água ⚡ L Fl 5s 29m 7M; 37°05'·42N 08°11'·35W.

VILAMOURA
Vilamoura ☆, Fl 5s 17m **19M**; 37°04'·460N 08°07'·37W.
Marina, W mole ⚡ Fl R 4s 13m 5M; 37°04'·08N 08°07'·38W.
E mole ⚡ Fl G 4s 13m 5M; 37°04'·12N 08°07'·30W.

FARO, OLHÃO and TAVIRA
Ent from sea: E mole ⚡ Fl G 4s 9m 6M; 36°57'·79N 07°52'·14W.
W mole ⚡ Fl R 4s 9m 6M; 37°57'·84N 08°52'·25W, appr on 352°.
Access ldg lts 020·9°: Front, Barra Nova ⚡ Oc 4s 8m 6M; 37°58'·22N 07°52'·00W. Rear, **Cabo de Santa Maria** ☆ Fl (4) 17s 49m **25M**; W ○ twr; 36°58'·48N 07°51'·88W.
No. 6 ⚓ Fl R 6s; 36°58'·40N 07°52'·20W (NW to Faro; NE to Olhão).
No. 20 ⚓ Fl R 6s, 37°00'·05N 07°55'·1W (approx 2M to **Faro**).
No. 8 ⚓ Fl R 3s; 36°59'·82N 07°51'·16W; 2·2M N & ENE to **Olhão**.

Tavira ldg lts 325·9°: Front, ⚡ Fl R 3s 6m 4M. Rear, Iso ⚡ R 6s 9m 5M. E mole ⚡ Fl G 2·5s 5m 6M; 37°06'·82N 07°37'·03W.

VILA REAL DE SANTO ANTONIO
Lt ho ☆ Fl 6·5s 51m **26M**; W twr, B bands; 37°11'·20N 07°24'·91W.
Bar, No 1 buoy ⚓ Q (3) G 6s; approx 37°08'·90N 07°23'·44W.
No 2 ⚓ Fl R 4s; 37°08'·83N 07°23'·74W.
W bkwtr ⚡ Fl R 5s 4M; 37°09'·75N 07°24'·03W.
Marina, QR at S end; QR/QG at ent; QR at N end.

THE AZORES ARCHIPELAGO
See 9.24.24 for selected lights on the nine islands, plus harbour lts at Lajes, Horta, Angra do Heroismo and Ponta Delgada.

9.24.4   PASSAGE INFORMATION

More Passage information is threaded between successive hbrs in this Area. **Bibliography**. *SW Spain & Portugal CC (NDL/ Jens). W coasts of Spain and Portugal Pilot (NP 67).*

WIND AND WEATHER

In summer the Portuguese Trades (*Nortada*) are N'ly F4-6 and the Portugal Current runs S at ½-¾kn. Summer gales are rare; coastal fog is common in the mornings. If N-bound, especially if lightly crewed, try making daily passages between about 0400 and 1200 to avoid the stronger afternoon winds, possibly augmented by a fresh onshore sea breeze.

▶*Tidal streams appear to set N on the flood and S on the ebb, but are poorly documented.*◀

PORT CLOSURES Some hbrs, especially on this coast, may be closed for weather reasons, ie strong to gale force onshore winds and/or heavy swell causing dangerous breaking seas at the hbr ent or over the bar. Closures may be promulgated by radio and Navtex. At Leixões, Aveiro and Figueira da Foz the following signals, with minor variations = port closed:

By day: cylinder/ball hoisted close up; at half-mast = enter with caution. By night: ●●●(vertical), steady or flashing.

THE SPANISH BORDER TO CABO RASO

The Río Miño (*Minho* in Portuguese), 15M S of Cabo Silleiro, forms the northern border with Spain. The river ent is difficult and best not attempted.

The 150M long coastline is hilly as far S as **Porto**, then generally low and sandy, backed by pine forests, to Cabo Carvoeiro; there are few prominent features (AC 3633, 3634, 3635). Coasting yachts should keep at least 3M offshore; see **Viana do Castelo**, a commercial and fishing port, with a marina at the NE end. **Povoa de Varzim** has a marina.

Offshore wave power for generating electricity The world's first 'Wave park' is operational off Aguçadoura, 5M north of Povoa de Varzim. A seabed power cable extends 288°/3M from the coast at 41°26'·66N 08°46'·73W to its seaward end at 41°27'·52N 08°50'·41W, as shown on AC 3634.

The 120m long, 3·5m diameter articulated modules are moored semi-submerged, so may be hard to see. But the line of modules is marked by 3 SPM buoys, the outer two Fl Y 2·5s. For technical details and future developments visit www.abb.com and www. oceanpd.com/ Image courtesy Pelamis Wave Power.

Leixões is an industrial port 2M N of the mouth of the R. Douro; it may be closed in bad weather due to heavy swell breaking on the bar. The R. Douro is not easily entered, but two substantial breakwaters (nearing completion 2009) at the river mouth will improve access; as yet there are no berths suitable for yachts up-river. Oporto can easily be visited by road from Leixões so as to recce the latest situation.

Aveiro (⚓) and **Figueira da Foz** (marina) are exposed to the west and can be closed in bad weather; the latter can be identified from N or S by the higher ground (257m) of Cabo Mondego. 34M further SSW **Nazaré** is an artificial fishing hbr and port of refuge with easy ent and a marina.

Cabo Carvoeiro, the W tip of Peniche peninsula, looks like an island from afar (do not confuse with Ilha Berlenga). Ilha da Berlenga and Os Farilhões, both lit, are respectively 5 and 9·5M NW of Cabo Carvoeiro, and within an '**Area to be avoided**' (by big ships), formerly an ITZ; see 9.24.2.

The normal coastal route is between Cabo Carvoeiro and Berlenga; this chan is deep, clear and 5M wide, although it appears narrower until opened up. **Peniche** fishing port/marina on the S side of the peninsula is well sheltered from N'lies, but open to SW swell. The coastline rises steadily to the 527m high ridge of Sintra, inland of Cabo da Roca, south of which it drops steeply to the low headland of Cabo Raso.

The **Off Cabo da Roca Traffic Separation Scheme** is 14M to seaward of that cape and extends a further 20M west with extra lanes for ships carrying dangerous cargoes. The ITZ is 14M wide; see 9.24.2.

9.24.5 SPECIAL NOTES FOR PORTUGAL

Districts/Provinces: Portugal is divided into 18 administrative districts. But the names of the former coastal provinces (N-S: Minho, Douro, Beira Litoral, Estremadura, Alentejo and Algarve) are still used and appear below the name of each hbr.

Charts: The 2 folios are: FA, old (*antigo*), only a few charts, with 2 digit chart nos; and F94. F94 charts (5 digit nos) include: 4 offshore charts 23201-04; 6 coastal charts 24201-06; 12 hbr charts 26301-12; 8 hbr appr charts 26401-08; and 3 charts of hbr plans 27501-03. 12 Leisure (*recreio*) charts at 1:150,000 scale, Nos 25R01-12, cover the whole coast N-S. Some long-established marinas are not yet charted at large scale.

Portuguese charts and publications are available from Chart agents. One of the largest is: J Garraio & Ca Lda, ave 24 de Julho, 2 - 1st Dto, 1200-478 Lisboa; ☎ 213 473 081. info@jgarraio.pt www.jgarraio.pt The Portuguese Hydrographic Office can be contacted as listed in Chapter 1.

Standard Time is UT (**NOT** UT −1); add 1 hr for DST, in force from the last Sun in Mar until the Sat before the last Sun in Oct.

Representation: Portuguese Tourist Office, 22-25A Sackville St, London W1X 1DE; ☎ 020 7494 1441.

Tourist Office, Ave António Augusto de Aguiar 86, P-1000 Lisboa; ☎ (213) 425 231.

British Embassy, Rua de S. Bernardo 33, 1249-082 Lisboa; Consular ☎ 213 924 000.

There is a Consulate at Portimão ☎ 282 490 750 & Hon Consuls at Porto ☎ 226 184 789 and Ponta Delgada (Azores) ☎ 296 628 175.

Telephone: To call Portugal from UK dial +351, the area code, then the ☎ number. To call UK from Portugal, dial +44, the area code less the initial 0, then the ☎ number. The area code is mandatory, even within the same area; ie nine numbers in all. National emergency ☎ 112; National SAR ☎ 214.401919.

R/T: VHF Ch 09 is the recreational craft channel; it is used by all Portuguese marinas, in addition to any Port VHF channels.

Access: There are daily flights in season to/from the UK via Porto, Lisboa and Faro which are quite well connected by bus and/or train to other towns. See also Area 25 for Spanish flights.

Currency is the €. VAT (IVA) is 21%. Credit cards are widely accepted; cash dispensers are in all towns.

Public Holidays: Jan 1; Shrove Tues; Good Friday; April 25 (Liberation Day); May 1 (Labour Day); Jun 6 (Corpus Christi); Jun 10 (Camões Day); Aug 15 (Assumption); Oct 5 (Republic Day); Nov 1 (All Saints Day); Dec 1 (Independence Day), 8 (Immaculate Conception), 25 (Christmas). Also every town has a local *festa*.

Documents: Portugal observes EU regulations but formalities may be lengthy so organise your papers to include:

Personal – Passports; crew list, ideally on headed paper with the yacht's rubber stamp, giving DoB, passport nos, where joined/ intended departure. Certificate of Competence (Yachtmaster Offshore, ICC/HOCC etc). Radio Operator's certificate. EHIC.

Yacht – Registration certificate. Proof of VAT status. Marine insurance. Ship's Radio licence. Itinerary, backed up by ship's log.

9.24.6 VIANA DO CASTELO

Minho **41°41'·68N 08°49'·21W** (Marina ent) ⊛⊛⊛⚓⚓⚓☆☆☆

CHARTS AC 3633/4, 3257; PC 24201, 26401; SC 41B.

TIDES

Standard Port LISBOA (⟶); ML 2·0

Times				Height (metres)			
High Water		Low Water		MHWS	MHWN	MLWN	MLWS
0400	0900	0400	0900	3·8	2·9	1·5	0·6
1600	2100	1600	2100				
Differences VIANA DO CASTELO							
−0020	0000	+0010	+0015	−0.4	−0.3	−0.1	−0.1
ESPOSENDE (41°32'N)							
−0020	0000	+0010	+0015	−0.6	−0.4	−0.2	−0.1

SHELTER Excellent in marina; possible strong current across its ent. No ⚓ in river. Night entry not advised if any swell.

NAVIGATION WPT 41°40'·18N 08°50'·37W, 007·5°/7ca in the W sector of dir lt Oc WRG 4s to abeam No 3 SHM lt buoy. Ignore the 012·5° ldg line which applies solely to the shipyard/FV area.

The outer mole hd (Fl R 3s) should be given a wide clearance; best water lies E of No 2 buoy. The flood reaches 2kn max; the ebb 3kn, but 6kn if river in spate.

Caution: 13M S of Viana 3 SPM buoys, the 2 outer buoys Fl Y 2.5s, mark a wave-generated power trial extending 288°/3M offshore from 41°26'·64N 08°46'·67W; see AC 3634. Keep well seaward of the floating equipment which may be hard to see. See opposite.

LIGHTS AND MARKS Montedor lt ho is a R twr 4M NNW. ✠ dome on Monte Santa Luzia is conspic, almost aligned with 007·5° dir lt. Storm sigs are displayed close SE of dir lt Oc WRG 4s. See 9.24.3 for lt details. Nos 5 to 14 buoys are Fl R 3s or Fl G 3s.

R/T Yacht Club and Marina Ch 09. Call *Porto de Viana* Ch 16; 11 (0900-1200; 1400-1700LT).

TELEPHONE (Code 258) Port HM 829096; ⊖ 823346; Police 822345; MRCC (21) 4401919; Brit Consul 226 184 789.

FACILITIES Marina (3m) is abeam Nos 13 & 14 buoys; and 200m short of low (4·6m) and noisy road/rail bridge. A small pedestrian bridge across the marina ent lifts on request. If shut berth on waiting pontoon. Usually ❶ berth F&A on W side of first pontoon 'D'. ☎ 359500. 200 inc ❶, €1.98. Slip, P, D, C (20 ton), YC, ME, El, ✕, CH, BY, SM, Gaz, Ⓔ. www.ipnorte.pt/p/portorecreio.htm ipn@ipnorte.pt www.manorhouses.com/ports/viana.htm A marina is planned in the long FV basin (41°41'·34N 08°50'W), possibly in 2009+.

Town 🛒, R, Bar, ✉, Ⓗ, Ⓑ, ≈ (1km). ✈ Porto (50 km).

9.24.7 PÓVOA DE VARZIM

Minho **41°22'·20N 08°46'·00W** (Marina ent) ⊛⊛⚓⚓☆☆

CHARTS AC 3634 (too small scale, 1:200,000, to be of much practical value); PC 24201.

TIDES

Standard Port LISBOA (⟶)

Times				Height (metres)			
High Water		Low Water		MHWS	MHWN	MLWN	MLWS
0400	0900	0400	0900	3·8	2·9	1·5	0·6
1600	2100	1600	2100				
Differences PÓVOA DE VARZIM							
−0020	0000	+0010	+0015	−0.3	−0.2	−0.1	−0.1

SHELTER Good in all winds, but ent is rough in heavy swell and becomes impracticable when wave height >3m. In particular give a wide berth to the head of the N mole where there may be broken water.

NAVIGATION WPT 41°21'·48N 08°46'·73W, 030°/1M to hbr ent. Follow SHM buoys (marking a shoal near the S bkwtr) round to the marina. Tidal streams are weak but there is an appreciable current, mainly S-going, along the coast.

LIGHTS AND MARKS Mole hd lts are on R and G posts with W bands. High rise blocks/hotels and sandy beaches are conspic. Monte São Félix is an isolated rounded hill (209m) 4·5M NNE.

R/T Marina Ch 09. Hbr Ch 11, 16; M-F 0900-1200, 1400-1700.

TELEPHONE (Code 252) Ⓗ 690600; Police 620026; Tourist office 298120; MRCC (21) 4401919; Brit Consul 226 184 789.

FACILITIES FVs use the N part of hbr; the friendly marina is to the SE. ❶ berth on the N'most reception/fuel pontoon in 2·4 to 3m.

Marina ☎ 688121. www.clubenavalpovoense.com 241, inc some ❶, €1.36; 18m max LOA. Good facilities: D (at the FV hbr), BH (35 ton) ME, El, ✕, CH, BY, Gaz, Ⓔ.

Town 🛒, R, Bar, ✉, Ⓗ, Ⓑ, ≈ (15 mins walk; trains to Porto, 30km and ✈ 18km).

9.24.8 LEIXÕES

Douro 41°11'·08N 08°42'·24W (Marina ent) ✿✿✿⚓⚓✿

CHARTS AC 3634, 3258; PC 23201, 24201, 26402; SC 418A.

TIDES

Standard Port LISBOA (⟶); ML 2·0

Times				Height (metres)			
High Water		Low Water		MHWS	MHWN	MLWN	MLWS
0400	0900	0400	0900	3·8	2·9	1·5	0·6
1600	2100	1600	2100				
Differences LEIXÕES							
−0025	−0010	0000	+0010	−0·4	−0·3	−0·1	−0·1
RIO DOURO ENT							
−0010	+0005	+0015	+0025	−0·6	−0·3	−0·1	+0·1
PORTO							
+0002	+0002	+0040	+0040	−0·5	−0·3	−0·2	0·0

SHELTER Good in marina, but scend enters in gales. The port may be closed occas in strong W'lies and/or swell, as shown by tfc sigs (see 9.24.4) on a mast at the Hbr Office close NE of marina. Charted ⚓ outside hbr in 4-6m on sand/mud needs HM's approval.

NAVIGATION WPT 41°10'·09N 08°42'·26W, 350°/6ca to inner mole hds. Leça lt ho, 1·7M N of hbr ent, on a brg of 350·5° leads into inner hbr; thence track 015° to marina. Ent is usually simple. Keep at least 200m off the N mole hd (Quebra-mar), due to a sunken bkwtr (2·5m) and a wreck (8m) 100m SW and S of it.

LIGHTS AND MARKS N of Leça lt are many R/W banded chy's at the oil refinery. From the S, bldgs of Porto are conspic.

R/T Marina *Porto Atlântico* Ch 09 (0900-1230; 1400-1800).

TELEPHONE (Code 229) HM 953000; ⊖ 951476; Met 484527 (Porto airport); LB 226.170091; Police 383649; Fire 380018; Ⓗ 391000; MRCC (21) 4401919; Brit Consul 226 184 789 (Porto).

FACILITIES Marina Porto Atlântico (2·9-1·5m) is rather oily with limited facilities onsite. ☎ 964895, 200 F&A + 40 Ⓥ, €1.64; reception W quay. P&D (cans only), ME, El, C (6·3 ton), CH, SM, Ⓔ, ✕, ▢, Bar, R, @. www.marinaportoatlantico.net

Clube de Vela Atlântico, R ☎ 952725. **Clube Naval de Leça** Bar ☎ 951700. **Sport Club do Porto** ☎ 952225.

Town: ▦, Bar, R, Ⓑ, ✉. Bus & Metro to Porto (5km); ⇌ and ✈.

PORTO (OPORTO), 41°08'·80N 08°40'·55W. Tides, see above. AC 3258. Difficult river ent, prone to swell and fast current; dangerous in strong W'lies (see 9.24.4 for port closure signals). WIP 2009 to complete new moles at the ent; see AC 3258 inset. New N mole is lit by Fl R 5s 16m 9M (W twr, R stripes) and by 4P PHM buoy Fl (2) R 4s; new S mole by Fl G 3s 8m 3M and 3P SHM buoy Fl (2) G 4s. Only craft of max LOA 12m and draught 2m may enter. The bar shifts constantly; charted depths are unreliable. For buoys up-river see 9.24.3. Possible AB at small quay by Cantareira or at Cais de Estiva (N bank) 2ca W of the 2nd bridge 8·8m clear'ce. A road recce of the R. Douro is advised.

9.24.9 AVEIRO

Beira Litoral 40°38'·51N 08°45'·86W (Hbr ent) ✿✿✿⚓⚓✿✿✿

CHARTS AC 3634, 3227; PC 24201, 24202, 26403, 59; SC 4219.

TIDES

Standard Port LISBOA (⟶); ML 2·0

Times				Height (metres)			
High Water		Low Water		MHWS	MHWN	MLWN	MLWS
0400	0900	0400	0900	3·8	2·9	1·5	0·6
1600	2100	1600	2100				
Differences AVEIRO							
+0005	+0010	+0010	+0015	−0·5	−0·3	−0·1	0·0
SAN JACINTO (40°40'N 08°44'W)							
+0025	+0030	+0030	+0045	−0·7	−0·4	−0·1	+0·2
FIGUEIRA DA FOZ							
−0015	0000	+0010	+0020	−0·4	−0·3	−0·1	−0·1

SHELTER Good, but the bar, with depths around 6m, becomes impassable in strong onshore winds and the port is often one of the first on this coast to be closed by bad weather or swell, even if there is no wind. Best access at HW −2 or −1.

Visiting yachts are reportedly not allowed up-river to the small marina because it is said to be private. See Facilities.

The only option is to ⚓ at the N end of Baia de San Jacinto in about 7m having avoided the large drying sandbank (buoyed) inside the outer end of the bay's N bkwtr.

NAVIGATION WPT 40°38'·46N 08°46'·70W, 085°/8ca to hbr ent. Caution: strong tidal streams. From abeam the lt ho the ent to B de San Jacinto is about 9 ca NE. Do not proceed further E.

LIGHTS AND MARKS Hbr lts as chartlet & 9.24.3. The red/white banded lt ho (also the rear 085° ldg mark) is conspic at the ent. Tfc sigs (9.24.4) are shown from a mast close N of the lt ho. The 065° ldg line (marks hard to see) leads between the moles. A military airfield with conspic control twr is NE of the hbr ent.

R/T Port Ch 11, 16 (M-F, 0900-1200 & 1400-1700).

TELEPHONE (Code 234) HM, ⊖ & Met ☎ 366250. www.portodeaveiro.pt portoaveiro@mail.telepac.pt Brit Consul 226 184 789.

FACILITIES A helpful, English/French-speaking contact in Aveiro who may be able to help with nautical matters, inc berthing in town, is Senhor Augusto Pereira, mobile ☎ 967 073463, office ☎ 394654. A ferry is said to run from near the ⚓ in Baia de San Jacinto to Aveiro.

Town The attractive old town, with its *moliceiros* (mussel boats), fine buildings and a network of canals, is reminiscent of a mini-Venice. ▦, R, Bar, Ⓑ, ✉; ⇌ to Figueira da Foz and Coimbra (worth a visit) to the S and Porto to the N; ✈ Pôrto (77km by motorway); ✈ Lisboa (256km by motorway).

9.24.10 FIGUEIRA DA FOZ

Beira Litoral 40°08'·68N 08°52'·48W (Hbr ent) ✿✿👐👐🏵🏵

CHARTS AC 3634, 3635, 3228; PC 24201/2, 26404, 34, 64; SC 42A

TIDES See under Aveiro, 9.24.9; ML 2·0.

SHELTER Excellent in marina on N bank, 0·75M from hbr ent.

Bar at ent has charted depth of 4·1m, but this cannot be relied upon. It shifts/shoals constantly and can be highly dangerous in swell, especially Nov-Mar with strong W/NW winds. Conditions on the bar are signalled (see 9.24.4) from mast at Forte de Santa Catarina (N of inner moles) and may be broadcast on VHF Ch 11.

NAVIGATION WPT 40°08'·61N 08°53'·12W (off chartlet), 081°/5ca to hbr ent. The bar in bad weather is the only offshore danger.

LIGHTS AND MARKS Cabo Mondego lt ho is 3M NW of hbr ent. Buarcos light is on the beach 1·1M N of hbr ent. Ldg lts lead 081·5° past marina ent. Lts as chartlet and 9.24.3. Extensive beaches N and S of hbr ent and a white suspension bridge (39m cl'nce) 1·5M E of ent are conspic from seaward.

R/T Port Ch 11. Marina Ch 08 (call *Capmarfoz*).

TELEPHONE (Code 233).

FACILITIES Marina (2-2·8m) Strong ebb tide can affect pontoons nearest marina ent. Reception/fuel berth is dead ahead of ent. ☎ 402910, ipc.gap@mail.telepac.pt. 200 inc Ⓥ, €2.50, plus possible surcharge for beam. Gaz, D, C, ME, ✖, CH, ▣.
Town: R, 🛒, Ⓑ, ⇌; ✈ Pörto.

9.24.11 NAZARÉ

Estremadura 39°35'·42N 09°04'·63W ❀❀❀❀♒♒✿✿

CHARTS AC 3635; PC 24203, 26302, 34, 65. ·

TIDES

Standard Port LISBOA (→); ML 2·0

Times				Height (metres)			
High Water		Low Water		MHWS	MHWN	MLWN	MLWS
0400	0900	0400	0900	3·8	2·9	1·5	0·6
1600	2100	1600	2100				
Differences NAZARÉ (Pederneira)							
−0030	−0015	−0005	+0005	−0·5	−0·3	−0·1	0·0

SHELTER Good with all-weather access. No ⚓ in outer harbour.

NAVIGATION WPT 39°35'·69N 09°05'·95W, 106°/1M to hbr ent. Due to an underwater canyon there are depths of 452m and 152m 5M and 7ca offshore respectively.

LIGHTS AND MARKS Pontal da Nazaré lt is 1M NNW of hbr ent on a low headland; keep at least 2ca off. Here a conspic wind farm (FR lts & W strobes) is visible from 20-30M in good vis.

R/T Port Ch 11 (HO). Marina Ch 09.

TELEPHONE (Code 262) Port HM 561255; ⊖ & Met via HM; Ⓗ 561116; MRCC (21) 4401919; Brit Consul 213 924000.

FACILITIES Marina is in the SW corner of the inner hbr; ♥ berth on the hammerheads or outer pontoons, 3·5m. Dredged summer 2009. ☎ 561401 (British manager), mob 9680 74254. 40+14 ♥, €2.10. ATM, Slip, D & P (H24) in NE corner, ME, BH (80 ton), C, ✕, ▣. **Club Naval de Nazaré**. The pontoons in the NE corner are private.

Town (1½M to the N) 🏪, R, Bar, Ⓑ, ✉. ⇌ Valado dos Frades 7km. ✈ Lisboa 125km.

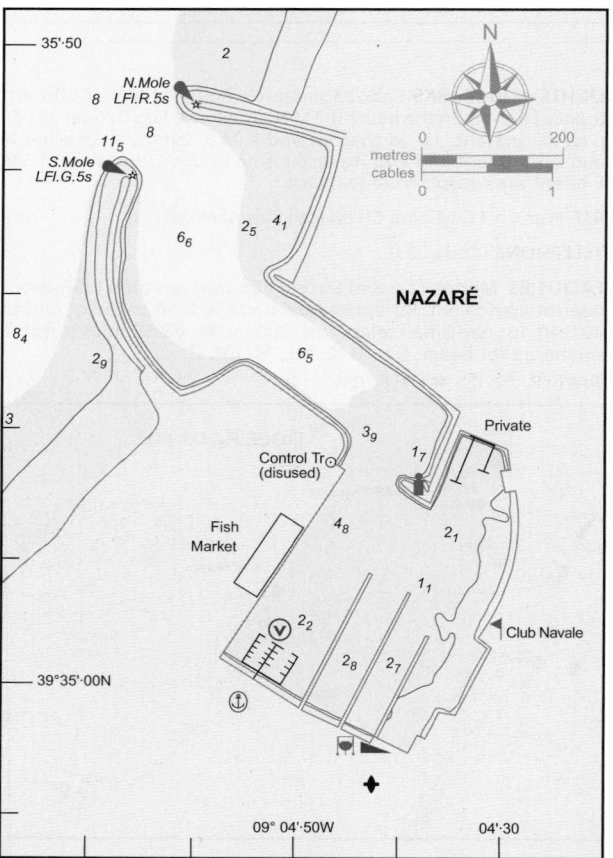

9.24.12 PENICHE

Estremadura 39°20'·82N 09°22'·48W ❀❀♒♒✿✿

CHARTS AC 3635; PC 24203, 26405, 36.

TIDES

Standard Port LISBOA (→); ML 2·0

Times				Height (metres)			
High Water		Low Water		MHWS	MHWN	MLWN	MLWS
0400	0900	0400	0900	3·8	2·9	1·5	0·6
1600	2100	1600	2100				
Differences PENICHE							
−0035	−0015	−0005	0000	−0·4	−0·3	−0·1	0·0
ERICEIRA (38°58'N, 24M S)							
−0040	−0025	−0010	−0010	−0·4	−0·2	−0·1	0·0

SHELTER Good all-weather hbr, but uncomfortable if SW swell works in; also noisy and prone to FV wash. Possible moorings or ⚓ in SE part of hbr; holding is good, but ground may be foul. The ⚓ in 4m on N side of peninsula is open to swell, even in S'lies.

NAVIGATION WPT 39°20'·42N 09°22'·53W, 000°/5ca to W mole hd. 3kn speed limit in hbr. The coastal route, a 5M wide chan between Cabo Carvoeiro and Ilha da Berlenga, is often rough.

Peniche and the offshore islands are in an 'Area to be avoided', only by ships >300 tons (for environmental reasons); see 9.24.2. On the SE side of Ilha Berlenga ⚓ below the lt ho. Os Farilhões lies 4·5M further NW. These islands lie within a Nature Reserve.

LIGHTS AND MARKS Peniche looks like an island from afar, not to be confused in poor vis with Berlenga. An isolated square tower block is conspic about 2ca NNE of the harbour. Cabo Carvoeiro is 2M WNW of hbr ent and steep-to apart from Nau dos Carvos, a conspic high rk close-in. Other lts as chartlet and 9.24.3. Storm sigs are shown from the root of W mole.

R/T Port Ch 16 (H24). Marina Ch 09.

TELEPHONE (Code 262) Port HM 781153; Ⓗ 781702; LB 789629; MRCC (21) 4401919; Brit Consul 213 924000.

FACILITIES Berth on outer pontoon (2·4-3·5m) of small marina ☎ 783331. 130+ 20 Ⓥ, €1.60. ⊖, Met, YC, P & D (cans/tanker), CH, BY, ME, El, Ⓔ, C, Gaz, Slip.

Town: 🛒, R, Bar, Ⓑ, ✉; ⇌ Obidos (30km), ✈ Lisboa (80km).

9.24.13 CASCAIS
Estremadura **38°41'·59N 09°24'·88W** ⚓⚓⚓♤♤♤✿✿✿

CHARTS AC 3635, 3220; PC 26406, 26303; SC 4310.

TIDES
Standard Port LISBOA (⟶); ML 2·0

Times				Height (metres)			
High Water		Low Water		MHWS	MHWN	MLWN	MLWS
0400	0900	0400	0900	3·8	2·9	1·5	0·6
1600	2100	1600	2100				
Differences CASCAIS							
−0040	−0025	−0015	−0010	−0·3	−0·2	0·0	+0·1

SHELTER Good in marina or on outer pontoons. ⚓ N of marina in designated area 3-5m, sheltered from all but E winds.

NAVIGATION WPT 38°41'·28N 09°24'·57W, 334°/4ca to CC2 and on the 285° ldg line. MC1-3 SCM buoys mark no-entry area.

LIGHTS AND MARKS Guia, rear 285° ldg lt, is 1·2M from the front, Santa Marta. Other lts as chartlet.

R/T Marina Ch 09 (0900-2000).

TELEPHONE (Code 214). MRCC 401919; Brit Consul 213 924000.

FACILITIES **Marina** (6m) ☎ 824800. www.marinacascais.pt reception2@marinacascais.pt 638 inc 125 Ⓥ, €3.56. CH, ME, BH (70 ton), C (2 ton), D&P (0900-2000), ATM, Ⓑ, 🖥, ⛽. Mail pickup: Casa de Sº Bernardo, Marina de Cascais, 2750-800 Cascais.

Town. All amenities. ⇌ to Lisboa (½ hr) every ¼ hr, 0530-0230.

9.24.14 LISBOA
Estremadura **38°41'·75N 09°10'·71W** (N span of Ponte 25 de Abril) ⚓⚓⚓⚓♤♤♤✿✿✿

CHARTS AC 3635, 3220, 3221, 3222; PC 26406, 26303, 26304, 26305, 26306, 26307; SC 4310.

TIDES
Standard Port LISBOA (⟶); ML 2·0

Times				Height (metres)			
High Water		Low Water		MHWS	MHWN	MLWN	MLWS
0400	0900	0400	0900	3·8	2·9	1·5	0·6
1600	2100	1600	2100				
Differences PACO DE ARCOS (5·5M W of Tejo bridge)							
−0020	−0030	−0005	−0005	−0·4	−0·3	−0·2	−0·1
PEDROUCOS (2·2M W of Tejo bridge)							
−0010	−0015	0000	0000	−0·3	−0·1	−0·1	0·0

SHELTER is good in the marinas along the N bank of R. Tejo.

NAVIGATION From N/NW keep at least 5ca off Cabo da Roca (see 9.24.2 for TSS) and Cabo Raso. Magnetic anomalies 3M SSE of Cabo Raso can alter local variation by +5° to −3°.

WPT 38°36'·90N 09°22'·90W (5ca SE of No 2 buoy), 047°/5·4M to abeam No 5 buoy. This is the main DW chan, Barra Sul, into R. Tejo proper; shoals lie on either side and break in bad weather. Tidal streams reach 5kn in the river and the ebb sets towards the shoals E of Forte Bugio. Caution: cross-current at the ent to marinas. Speed limit E of Torre de Belém: 10kn, but 5kn within 300m of shore.

Barra Norte, a lesser chan carrying 5·2m, is a short cut for yachts between Cascais and R. Tejo in fair weather; it passes close S of Forte de S. Julião and is orientated 285°/105° on ldg lts at Forte de Sta Marta and Guia; the latter was reported (2002) as obscured by trees, only when viewed from the east by day.

LIGHTS AND MARKS See 9.24.3, chartlets and hbr text. Conspic features, W-E, include: Torre de Belém, Monumento dos Descobrimentos, Ponte 25 de Abril and huge statue of Cristo Rei.

R/T Monitor *Lisboa Port Control* (VTS, applies to yachts >20m LOA) Ch 12, 13; **74** broadcasts MSI as required. Port HM **12**, 01, 05, 60. Doca de Alcântara Ch 05, 09, 12, 68. Other marinas 09.

TELEPHONE (Code 21) MRCC 4401919; Brit Consul 924000.

FACILITIES
Oeiras Marina, 38°40'·59N 09°18'·99W. ☎ (214) 401510. Ch 09. precreio@oeirasviva.pt www.oeirasviva.pt 275 AB €2.91. D&P, Slip, BH, 🖥, @, R, Bar. Fast trains to Lisboa 16km; see 9.24.13.

Doca de Paço de Arcos, 38°41'·44N 09°17'·61W. ☎ 4461660. Sheltered from N/NW'lies.

Marinas Ⓐ-Ⓓ are run by Lisboa port authority (www.portodelisboa.com). In all marinas mean fee is €2.70.

Ⓐ**Doca de Bom Sucesso** 38°41'·55N 09°12'·70W. ☎ 3013027. 144 mostly local yachts, F&A in 3m. C, CH, R, Slip, D & P (cans); ⇌, bus to Lisboa.

Ⓑ**Doca de Belém** 38°41'·64N 09°12'·24W. ☎ 3631246. doca.belém@porto-de-lisboa.pt 199 yachts, v.few Ⓥ; F&A in 3m. D (hose), BH, C, R, SM, E; ⇌, bus to Lisboa.

Ⓒ**Doca de Santo Amaro** 38°41'·92N 09°10'·65W, almost below the suspension bridge (noise from road traffic and night life). ☎ 3922011. doca.stamaro@porto-de-lisboa.pt 235 AB (few Ⓥ) in 4m, R, Bar, 🛒; ⇌, bus 2M to city centre.

Ⓓ**Doca de Alcântara** 38°42'·15N 09°09'·42W (best for foreign visitors). Chan doubles back W into marina at end of dock, via a swing bridge usually open; Ch 68. doca.alcantara@porto-de-lisboa.pt ☎ 3922048. 440 F&A inc Ⓥ in 8m. Secure, 4 floating R, Bar, 🛒; ⇌; bus 2M to city centre.

Ⓔ**Doca do Terreiro do Trigo** 38°42'·61N 09°07'·55W. ☎ 3922012. man.patricio@porto-de-lisboa.pt Used by service vessels, tugs etc in 1·5m (prone to silting). No Ⓥ, security fence; run-down area, but near old quarter (Alfama).

Ⓕ**Marina EXPO** (Closed tfn). **City**: All amenities; ⇌, ✈.

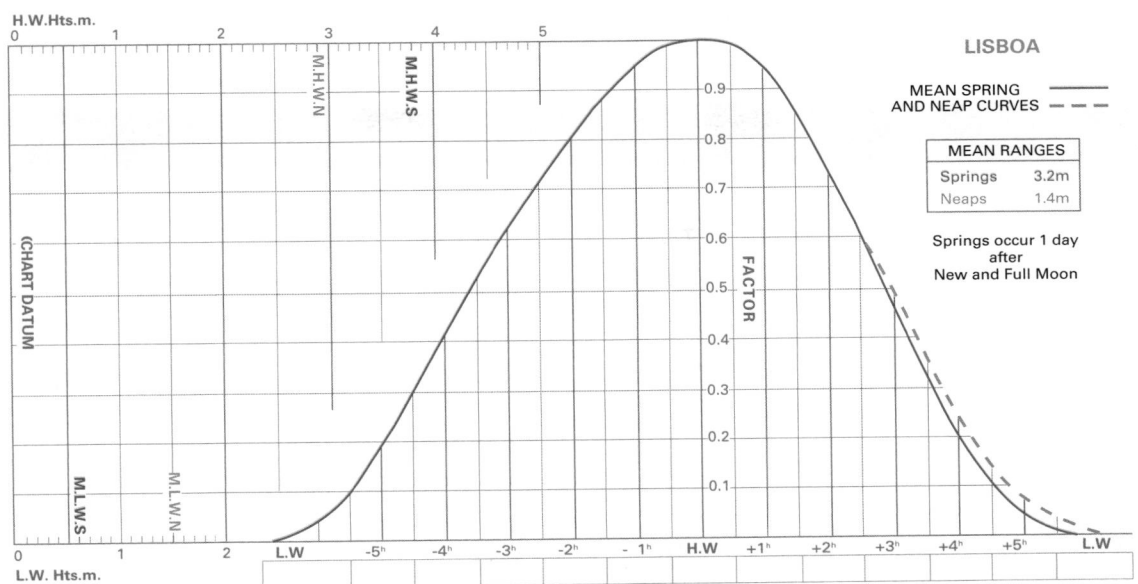

LISBOA

MEAN SPRING ——————
AND NEAP CURVES – – – – –

MEAN RANGES	
Springs	3.2m
Neaps	1.4m

Springs occur 1 day
after
New and Full Moon

CABO RASO TO CAPE ST VINCENT

Cascais is an expensive stop for yachts on passage or not wishing to go 12M E to Lisboa. **Oeiras Marina**, 5M E of Cascais, is also a good stop. From Cascais to the Rio Tejo (Tagus) use the Barra Norte (least depth 5m) which joins the main Barra Sul abeam São Julião lt. In **Lisboa** 5 marinas line the N bank of the R Tejo. If S-bound, stand on 1M beyond Forte Bugio before turning for flat-topped Cabo Espichel (AC 3635, 3636).

Eastward the coast rises to 500m high cliffs. **Sesimbra** is well sheltered from N'lies. Near the ent to R Sado, Arrábida's shallow bay offers temp'y ⚓. **Setúbal** has few yacht facilities. Thence unbroken beaches stretch 35M to Cabo de Sines, light house and conspicuous chimneys. **Sines** is a strategically placed commercial port 56M N of Cabo São Vicente; its small marina has limited facilities. A tiny bay (37°17'·51N 08°52'·08W) below the high cliffs of Punta da Arrifana gives shelter from N'lies.

LISBOA   LAT 38°43'N   LONG 9°07'W
TIMES AND HEIGHTS OF HIGH AND LOW WATERS

TIME ZONE (UT)
For Summer Time add ONE hour in **non-shaded areas**

Dates in red are SPRINGS
Dates in blue are NEAPS

YEAR **2010**

JANUARY

Day	Time	m	Time	m	Time	m	Time	m
1 F	0317	3.9	0914	0.4	1546	3.7	2128	0.5
2 SA	0406	4.0	1001	0.3	1634	3.8	2215	0.5
3 SU	0453	4.0	1048	0.3	1722	3.7	2302	0.5
4 M	0540	4.0	1135	0.4	1808	3.6	2348	0.6
5 TU	0628	3.8	1222	0.5	1856	3.5		
6 W	0037	0.7	0717	3.6	1312	0.8	1947	3.3
7 TH ☽	0129	0.9	0811	3.4	1407	1.0	2044	3.1
8 F	0230	1.1	0913	3.1	1510	1.2	2151	3.0
9 SA	0343	1.3	1026	3.0	1622	1.3	2303	3.0
10 SU	0503	1.3	1140	2.9	1734	1.3		
11 M	0010	3.1	0616	1.2	1245	3.0	1836	1.2
12 TU	0108	3.2	0714	1.1	1339	3.0	1926	1.1
13 W	0157	3.3	0759	0.9	1425	3.1	2007	1.0
14 TH	0239	3.4	0837	0.9	1503	3.2	2044	0.9
15 F ●	0315	3.5	0911	0.8	1538	3.3	2117	0.8
16 SA	0349	3.5	0943	0.7	1609	3.3	2149	0.8
17 SU	0420	3.6	1013	0.7	1639	3.3	2220	0.8
18 M	0450	3.6	1044	0.7	1709	3.3	2251	0.8
19 TU	0521	3.5	1115	0.7	1740	3.3	2323	0.9
20 W	0554	3.4	1148	0.8	1814	3.2	2357	1.0
21 TH	0629	3.3	1223	1.0	1851	3.0		
22 F	0035	1.1	0709	3.1	1303	1.1	1935	2.9
23 SA ☾	0122	1.2	0758	3.0	1354	1.2	2032	2.8
24 SU	0224	1.4	0901	2.8	1502	1.3	2145	2.8
25 M	0346	1.4	1021	2.8	1623	1.3	2305	2.9
26 TU	0511	1.3	1143	2.9	1740	1.2		
27 W	0017	3.2	0623	1.0	1253	3.1	1845	1.0
28 TH	0120	3.4	0723	0.7	1353	3.4	1940	0.7
29 F	0215	3.7	0815	0.5	1446	3.6	2030	0.5
30 SA ○	0306	4.0	0903	0.2	1534	3.8	2117	0.3
31 SU	0353	4.1	0948	0.1	1619	3.9	2201	0.2

FEBRUARY

Day	Time	m	Time	m	Time	m	Time	m
1 M	0438	4.2	1031	0.1	1702	3.9	2244	0.3
2 TU	0521	4.1	1113	0.2	1745	3.8	2327	0.4
3 W	0604	3.9	1155	0.4	1827	3.6		
4 TH	0010	0.6	0648	3.7	1238	0.7	1911	3.4
5 F ☽	0056	0.8	0735	3.3	1325	1.0	2001	3.1
6 SA	0151	1.1	0831	3.0	1422	1.3	2105	2.9
7 SU	0304	1.3	0947	2.8	1540	1.5	2227	2.8
8 M	0439	1.4	1058	2.7	1711	1.4	2350	2.9
9 TU	0606	1.3	1234	2.8	1823	1.4		
10 W	0054	3.1	0704	1.2	1328	2.9	1914	1.2
11 TH	0142	3.2	0745	1.0	1409	3.1	1953	1.0
12 F	0221	3.4	0819	0.9	1444	3.3	2026	0.9
13 SA	0255	3.5	0850	0.7	1516	3.4	2057	0.8
14 SU ●	0326	3.6	0920	0.6	1545	3.5	2128	0.7
15 M	0357	3.7	0949	0.6	1615	3.5	2157	0.6
16 TU	0427	3.7	1018	0.6	1644	3.5	2227	0.6
17 W	0458	3.7	1047	0.6	1714	3.5	2257	0.7
18 TH	0529	3.5	1117	0.7	1746	3.4	2329	0.8
19 F	0602	3.4	1148	0.9	1819	3.2		
20 SA	0003	1.0	0638	3.2	1224	1.0	1859	3.1
21 SU	0046	1.1	0721	3.0	1310	1.2	1950	3.0
22 M ☾	0144	1.3	0823	2.9	1416	1.4	2103	2.9
23 TU	0311	1.4	0951	2.8	1549	1.4	2236	2.9
24 W	0450	1.3	1128	2.9	1721	1.3		
25 TH	0001	3.2	0610	1.0	1243	3.2	1832	1.0
26 F	0107	3.5	0710	0.7	1341	3.5	1927	0.7
27 SA	0201	3.8	0800	0.4	1430	3.8	2015	0.5
28 SU ○	0249	4.1	0845	0.2	1515	3.9	2059	0.3

MARCH

Day	Time	m	Time	m	Time	m	Time	m
1 M	0334	4.2	0927	0.1	1558	4.0	2141	0.2
2 TU	0417	4.3	1008	0.2	1638	4.0	2222	0.2
3 W	0458	4.2	1047	0.3	1718	3.9	2302	0.3
4 TH	0539	3.9	1126	0.5	1758	3.7	2343	0.6
5 F	0620	3.6	1205	0.8	1838	3.5		
6 SA	0027	0.9	0703	3.3	1247	1.1	1923	3.2
7 SU ☽	0118	1.2	0754	2.9	1340	1.4	2021	3.0
8 M	0229	1.5	0908	2.7	1458	1.6	2147	2.8
9 TU	0411	1.6	1053	2.6	1642	1.7	2322	2.8
10 W	0542	1.5	1213	2.8	1759	1.5		
11 TH	0028	3.0	0638	1.3	1304	3.0	1849	1.3
12 F	0115	3.2	0718	1.1	1342	3.2	1927	1.1
13 SA	0152	3.4	0751	0.9	1416	3.3	2000	0.9
14 SU	0226	3.6	0822	0.8	1447	3.5	2031	0.8
15 M ●	0258	3.7	0851	0.7	1517	3.6	2102	0.7
16 TU	0330	3.8	0921	0.6	1547	3.7	2132	0.7
17 W	0402	3.8	0950	0.6	1618	3.7	2202	0.7
18 TH	0433	3.7	1019	0.7	1649	3.6	2233	0.7
19 F	0505	3.6	1049	0.8	1721	3.5	2306	0.8
20 SA	0539	3.5	1121	0.9	1756	3.4	2342	0.9
21 SU	0617	3.3	1158	1.0	1836	3.3		
22 M	0027	1.1	0703	3.1	1247	1.3	1929	3.1
23 TU ☾	0129	1.3	0808	2.9	1356	1.5	2044	3.0
24 W	0258	1.4	0942	2.9	1534	1.5	2221	3.1
25 TH	0437	1.3	1117	3.0	1706	1.4	2345	3.3
26 F	0553	1.0	1227	3.3	1814	1.1		
27 SA	0048	3.6	0650	0.8	1321	3.6	1908	0.8
28 SU	0141	3.9	0739	0.5	1408	3.8	1955	0.5
29 M	0228	4.1	0822	0.4	1452	4.0	2038	0.4
30 TU ○	0312	4.2	0903	0.3	1533	4.1	2119	0.3
31 W	0354	4.2	0942	0.3	1613	4.1	2200	0.3

APRIL

Day	Time	m	Time	m	Time	m	Time	m
1 TH	0435	4.1	1020	0.5	1653	4.0	2240	0.5
2 F	0515	3.8	1058	0.7	1731	3.8	2320	0.7
3 SA	0554	3.5	1136	1.0	1810	3.5		
4 SU	0003	1.0	0635	3.2	1216	1.3	1852	3.3
5 M	0052	1.3	0722	2.9	1305	1.5	1943	3.0
6 TU ☽	0157	1.5	0829	2.7	1417	1.7	2057	2.9
7 W	0326	1.6	1008	2.7	1555	1.8	2231	2.9
8 TH	0452	1.6	1130	2.8	1714	1.6	2343	3.0
9 F	0552	1.4	1224	3.0	1809	1.5		
10 SA	0034	3.2	0636	1.2	1304	3.2	1850	1.3
11 SU	0114	3.4	0713	1.0	1339	3.4	1926	1.1
12 M	0151	3.6	0747	0.9	1412	3.5	2000	0.9
13 TU	0226	3.7	0819	0.8	1445	3.7	2033	0.8
14 W ●	0300	3.7	0850	0.7	1518	3.7	2105	0.8
15 TH	0335	3.8	0921	0.7	1551	3.7	2138	0.7
16 F	0409	3.7	0953	0.8	1626	3.7	2213	0.8
17 SA	0446	3.6	1026	0.8	1702	3.7	2250	0.8
18 SU	0524	3.5	1103	0.9	1742	3.6	2332	0.9
19 M	0608	3.4	1146	1.1	1827	3.5		
20 TU	0023	1.1	0701	3.2	1240	1.3	1924	3.3
21 W ☾	0129	1.3	0809	3.0	1352	1.5	2039	3.2
22 TH	0252	1.3	0935	3.0	1521	1.5	2205	3.2
23 F	0418	1.2	1057	3.2	1644	1.3	2322	3.4
24 SA	0528	1.0	1202	3.4	1749	1.1		
25 SU	0023	3.6	0624	0.8	1255	3.6	1843	0.9
26 M	0116	3.8	0713	0.7	1342	3.8	1931	0.7
27 TU	0204	4.0	0756	0.6	1427	4.0	2015	0.6
28 W ○	0249	4.0	0838	0.6	1509	4.0	2058	0.5
29 TH	0332	3.9	0917	0.7	1550	4.0	2140	0.6
30 F	0414	3.8	0956	0.7	1630	3.9	2221	0.7

HAT is 4·3 metres above Chart Datum; see 4.5.

TIME ZONE (UT)
For Summer Time add ONE hour in **non-shaded areas**

LISBOA LAT 38°43'N LONG 9°07'W
TIMES AND HEIGHTS OF HIGH AND LOW WATERS

Dates in red are **SPRINGS**
Dates in blue are **NEAPS**

YEAR 2010

MAY

Day	Time m	Day	Time m
1 SA	0454 3.6 / 1034 0.9 / 1709 3.7 / 2302 0.9	**16** SU	0432 3.6 / 1011 0.8 / 1650 3.8 / 2242 0.8
2 SU	0534 3.4 / 1112 1.1 / 1747 3.5 / 2343 1.1	**17** M	0517 3.5 / 1055 0.9 / 1735 3.7 / 2330 0.8
3 M	0613 3.2 / 1151 1.3 / 1826 3.3	**18** TU	0606 3.4 / 1143 1.0 / 1825 3.6
4 TU	0029 1.3 / 0656 3.0 / 1237 1.4 / 1910 3.2	**19** W	0024 0.9 / 0701 3.3 / 1239 1.2 / 1923 3.5
5 W	0123 1.4 / 0749 2.8 / 1337 1.6 / 2007 3.0	**20** TH	0126 1.1 / 0804 3.2 / 1345 1.3 / 2029 3.4
6 TH	0231 1.5 / 0902 2.8 / 1453 1.7 / 2121 2.9	**21** F	0236 1.1 / 0916 3.2 / 1459 1.3 / 2141 3.4
7 F	0345 1.5 / 1022 2.8 / 1610 1.7 / 2237 3.0	**22** SA	0348 1.1 / 1027 3.2 / 1612 1.3 / 2252 3.4
8 SA	0451 1.4 / 1126 3.0 / 1713 1.5 / 2338 3.1	**23** SU	0455 1.1 / 1131 3.3 / 1719 1.1 / 2354 3.5
9 SU	0544 1.3 / 1215 3.1 / 1804 1.4	**24** M	0553 1.0 / 1226 3.5 / 1817 1.0
10 M	0027 3.3 / 0628 1.2 / 1256 3.3 / 1846 1.2	**25** TU	0050 3.6 / 0645 0.9 / 1317 3.7 / 1909 0.9
11 TU	0110 3.4 / 0707 1.0 / 1334 3.5 / 1925 1.0	**26** W	0141 3.6 / 0732 0.8 / 1404 3.8 / 1957 0.8
12 W	0150 3.5 / 0743 0.9 / 1412 3.6 / 2003 0.9	**27** TH	0229 3.7 / 0816 0.8 / 1449 3.8 / 2043 0.7
13 TH	0229 3.6 / 0818 0.8 / 1449 3.7 / 2040 0.8	**28** F	0315 3.6 / 0857 0.8 / 1532 3.8 / 2125 0.7
14 F	0309 3.6 / 0854 0.8 / 1527 3.8 / 2118 0.8	**29** SA	0358 3.5 / 0937 0.9 / 1613 3.7 / 2206 0.8
15 SA	0349 3.6 / 0932 0.8 / 1608 3.8 / 2159 0.7	**30** SU	0438 3.4 / 1015 1.0 / 1651 3.6 / 2245 0.9
		31 M	0516 3.3 / 1052 1.1 / 1727 3.5 / 2324 1.0

JUNE

Day	Time m	Day	Time m
1 TU	0552 3.2 / 1129 1.2 / 1802 3.4	**16** W	0600 3.5 / 1138 0.8 / 1819 3.8
2 W	0003 1.1 / 0629 3.1 / 1210 1.3 / 1840 3.3	**17** TH	0016 0.7 / 0651 3.5 / 1230 0.9 / 1911 3.7
3 TH	0047 1.2 / 0710 3.0 / 1257 1.4 / 1924 3.1	**18** F	0110 0.8 / 0746 3.3 / 1326 1.0 / 2008 3.5
4 F	0138 1.3 / 0802 2.9 / 1354 1.5 / 2019 3.0	**19** SA	0208 0.9 / 0846 3.2 / 1429 1.1 / 2111 3.4
5 SA	0237 1.4 / 0906 2.8 / 1500 1.6 / 2125 3.0	**20** SU	0312 1.1 / 0951 3.2 / 1537 1.2 / 2218 3.3
6 SU	0342 1.4 / 1014 2.9 / 1608 1.5 / 2232 3.0	**21** M	0418 1.1 / 1057 3.2 / 1648 1.2 / 2326 3.3
7 M	0443 1.4 / 1115 3.0 / 1709 1.4 / 2333 3.1	**22** TU	0523 1.1 / 1159 3.3 / 1755 1.1
8 TU	0537 1.3 / 1208 3.1 / 1802 1.3	**23** W	0028 3.3 / 0622 1.1 / 1256 3.4 / 1855 1.0
9 W	0026 3.2 / 0624 1.1 / 1254 3.3 / 1850 1.1	**24** TH	0125 3.3 / 0714 1.0 / 1348 3.5 / 1947 0.9
10 TH	0114 3.3 / 0708 1.0 / 1339 3.5 / 1935 1.0	**25** F	0216 3.3 / 0800 0.9 / 1435 3.6 / 2033 0.9
11 F	0201 3.4 / 0752 0.9 / 1423 3.6 / 2019 0.8	**26** SA	0302 3.3 / 0843 0.9 / 1518 3.6 / 2114 0.8
12 SA	0248 3.5 / 0833 0.8 / 1509 3.7 / 2104 0.7	**27** SU	0344 3.3 / 0921 0.9 / 1557 3.6 / 2151 0.8
13 SU	0335 3.6 / 0917 0.7 / 1555 3.8 / 2150 0.6	**28** M	0421 3.3 / 0957 0.9 / 1632 3.6 / 2226 0.8
14 M	0423 3.6 / 1002 0.7 / 1642 3.9 / 2237 0.6	**29** TU	0455 3.3 / 1032 0.9 / 1705 3.5 / 2300 0.9
15 TU	0511 3.6 / 1049 0.7 / 1730 3.8 / 2325 0.6	**30** W	0527 3.2 / 1106 1.0 / 1737 3.5 / 2334 0.9

JULY

Day	Time m	Day	Time m
1 TH	0559 3.2 / 1141 1.1 / 1810 3.4	**16** F	0630 3.6 / 1210 0.6 / 1850 3.8
2 F	0010 1.0 / 0634 3.1 / 1219 1.2 / 1848 3.3	**17** SA	0044 0.7 / 0718 3.5 / 1300 0.8 / 1941 3.6
3 SA	0051 1.1 / 0715 3.0 / 1303 1.3 / 1931 3.1	**18** SU	0135 0.9 / 0812 3.3 / 1356 1.0 / 2038 3.3
4 SU	0137 1.2 / 0804 2.9 / 1355 1.4 / 2024 3.0	**19** M	0234 1.1 / 0914 3.2 / 1504 1.2 / 2146 3.1
5 M	0232 1.3 / 0904 2.8 / 1458 1.5 / 2127 2.9	**20** TU	0342 1.3 / 1025 3.1 / 1623 1.3 / 2302 3.0
6 TU	0336 1.4 / 1011 2.9 / 1609 1.5 / 2236 2.9	**21** W	0458 1.3 / 1137 3.1 / 1743 1.3
7 W	0442 1.3 / 1117 3.0 / 1718 1.4 / 2342 3.0	**22** TH	0015 3.0 / 0607 1.3 / 1242 3.3 / 1849 1.1
8 TH	0542 1.2 / 1216 3.2 / 1818 1.4	**23** F	0116 3.1 / 0704 1.2 / 1336 3.4 / 1941 1.0
9 F	0044 3.1 / 0638 1.1 / 1312 3.3 / 1913 1.0	**24** SA	0207 3.2 / 0750 1.0 / 1422 3.5 / 2022 0.9
10 SA	0140 3.3 / 0729 0.9 / 1404 3.6 / 2004 0.8	**25** SU	0249 3.3 / 0829 0.9 / 1502 3.6 / 2058 0.8
11 SU	0233 3.5 / 0818 0.7 / 1454 3.8 / 2052 0.6	**26** M	0326 3.3 / 0904 0.9 / 1537 3.6 / 2131 0.8
12 M	0323 3.6 / 0906 0.6 / 1543 3.9 / 2139 0.4	**27** TU	0359 3.4 / 0937 0.8 / 1610 3.6 / 2202 0.7
13 TU	0412 3.7 / 0952 0.5 / 1631 4.0 / 2225 0.3	**28** W	0429 3.4 / 1008 0.8 / 1640 3.6 / 2232 0.7
14 W	0458 3.8 / 1038 0.5 / 1717 4.0 / 2311 0.4	**29** TH	0458 3.4 / 1039 0.8 / 1710 3.6 / 2303 0.8
15 TH	0544 3.7 / 1124 0.5 / 1803 4.0 / 2357 0.5	**30** F	0528 3.3 / 1111 0.9 / 1741 3.5 / 2335 0.9
		31 SA	0600 3.3 / 1144 1.0 / 1815 3.4

AUGUST

Day	Time m	Day	Time m
1 SU	0008 1.0 / 0635 3.2 / 1220 1.1 / 1852 3.2	**16** M	0101 0.9 / 0738 3.3 / 1326 1.1 / 2007 3.2
2 M	0046 1.1 / 0716 3.0 / 1302 1.3 / 1936 3.0	**17** TU	0157 1.2 / 0838 3.1 / 1435 1.3 / 2118 3.0
3 TU	0131 1.3 / 0807 2.9 / 1358 1.4 / 2033 2.9	**18** W	0310 1.5 / 0956 3.0 / 1606 1.5 / 2246 2.8
4 W	0232 1.4 / 0914 2.9 / 1515 1.5 / 2147 2.8	**19** TH	0440 1.5 / 1120 3.0 / 1738 1.4
5 TH	0351 1.5 / 1032 2.9 / 1641 1.4 / 2310 2.9	**20** F	0007 2.9 / 0558 1.4 / 1229 3.2 / 1842 1.3
6 F	0510 1.5 / 1147 3.1 / 1756 1.2	**21** SA	0106 3.0 / 0653 1.3 / 1322 3.4 / 1927 1.1
7 SA	0024 3.1 / 0617 1.1 / 1252 3.4 / 1857 1.0	**22** SU	0151 3.2 / 0735 1.1 / 1403 3.5 / 2003 0.9
8 SU	0126 3.3 / 0714 0.9 / 1349 3.7 / 1950 0.7	**23** M	0228 3.3 / 0810 1.0 / 1439 3.6 / 2034 0.8
9 M	0220 3.6 / 0805 0.7 / 1440 3.9 / 2038 0.4	**24** TU	0300 3.5 / 0842 0.9 / 1512 3.7 / 2104 0.7
10 TU	0308 3.8 / 0851 0.5 / 1527 4.1 / 2123 0.3	**25** W	0331 3.5 / 0912 0.8 / 1542 3.8 / 2133 0.7
11 W	0354 3.9 / 0936 0.3 / 1613 4.2 / 2206 0.2	**26** TH	0400 3.6 / 0942 0.8 / 1612 3.8 / 2202 0.7
12 TH	0438 4.0 / 1019 0.3 / 1657 4.2 / 2249 0.3	**27** F	0429 3.6 / 1012 0.8 / 1642 3.7 / 2231 0.8
13 F	0521 3.9 / 1102 0.4 / 1741 4.1 / 2331 0.4	**28** SA	0458 3.5 / 1042 0.8 / 1712 3.6 / 2301 0.9
14 SA	0604 3.8 / 1146 0.5 / 1825 3.9	**29** SU	0529 3.4 / 1112 0.9 / 1744 3.5 / 2331 1.0
15 SU	0014 0.7 / 0648 3.6 / 1232 0.8 / 1912 3.6	**30** M	0601 3.3 / 1145 1.1 / 1819 3.3
		31 TU	0004 1.1 / 0639 3.2 / 1225 1.3 / 1900 3.1

Portugal & Azores

HAT is 4·3 metres above Chart Datum; see 4.5.

TIME ZONE (UT)
For Summer Time add ONE hour in **non-shaded areas**

LISBOA LAT 38°43'N LONG 9°07'W
TIMES AND HEIGHTS OF HIGH AND LOW WATERS

Dates in red are **SPRINGS**
Dates in blue are NEAPS

YEAR 2010

SEPTEMBER

Time	m	Time	m
1 0046	1.3	**16** 0240	1.7
0726	3.1	0928	3.0
W 1318	1.4	TH 1549	1.6
◐ 1956	2.9	2229	2.8
2 0146	1.5	**17** 0420	1.7
0833	3.0	1058	3.0
TH 1438	1.6	F 1719	1.5
2116	2.8	2350	2.9
3 0315	1.6	**18** 0538	1.6
1001	3.0	1207	3.2
F 1618	1.5	SA 1818	1.4
2253	2.9		
4 0449	1.5	**19** 0044	3.1
1128	3.2	0630	1.4
SA 1740	1.3	SU 1256	3.4
		1859	1.2
5 0011	3.2	**20** 0124	3.3
0602	1.2	0709	1.2
SU 1237	3.5	M 1335	3.5
1841	0.9	1933	1.0
6 0111	3.5	**21** 0158	3.5
0658	0.9	0743	1.0
M 1332	3.8	TU 1409	3.7
1932	0.6	2004	0.9
7 0201	3.8	**22** 0229	3.6
0747	0.6	0814	0.9
TU 1421	4.1	W 1441	3.8
2018	0.4	2034	0.8
8 0247	4.0	**23** 0300	3.7
0832	0.4	0845	0.8
W 1507	4.3	TH 1512	3.8
● 2101	0.3	○ 2103	0.8
9 0331	4.1	**24** 0329	3.7
0915	0.3	0915	0.8
TH 1551	4.3	F 1543	3.8
2142	0.2	2132	0.8
10 0413	4.1	**25** 0359	3.7
0957	0.3	0945	0.8
F 1634	4.3	SA 1614	3.8
2223	0.3	2201	0.8
11 0455	4.1	**26** 0430	3.7
1039	0.4	1015	0.9
SA 1716	4.1	SU 1646	3.7
2303	0.5	2230	0.9
12 0536	3.9	**27** 0501	3.6
1122	0.6	1046	1.0
SU 1800	3.8	M 1719	3.5
2344	0.8	2301	1.0
13 0619	3.7	**28** 0535	3.5
1207	0.9	1121	1.1
M 1845	3.5	TU 1755	3.4
		2335	1.2
14 0029	1.1	**29** 0613	3.3
0707	3.4	1203	1.3
TU 1300	1.2	W 1839	3.2
1939	3.1		
15 0123	1.4	**30** 0019	1.4
0806	3.2	0703	3.2
W 1411	1.5	TH 1259	1.4
◐ 2053	2.9	1938	3.0

OCTOBER

Time	m	Time	m
1 0123	1.6	**16** 0338	1.8
0811	3.1	1015	3.0
F 1422	1.5	SA 1634	1.6
◐ 2104	2.9	2310	2.9
2 0256	1.6	**17** 0456	1.7
0944	3.1	1125	3.1
SA 1602	1.5	SU 1734	1.5
2241	3.0		
3 0431	1.5	**18** 0005	3.1
1111	3.3	0551	1.5
SU 1721	1.2	M 1216	3.3
2354	3.3	1819	1.3
4 0542	1.3	**19** 0046	3.3
1216	3.6	0633	1.3
M 1820	0.9	TU 1258	3.5
		1856	1.1
5 0050	3.6	**20** 0122	3.5
0637	0.9	0710	1.1
TU 1310	3.8	W 1334	3.6
1909	0.7	1930	1.0
6 0138	3.9	**21** 0155	3.6
0725	0.7	0744	1.0
W 1358	4.1	TH 1408	3.7
1954	0.5	2002	0.9
7 0223	4.1	**22** 0227	3.7
0810	0.5	0816	0.9
TH 1444	4.3	F 1442	3.8
● 2036	0.4	2033	0.8
8 0306	4.2	**23** 0259	3.7
0853	0.4	0848	0.9
F 1528	4.3	SA 1515	3.8
2117	0.4	○ 2103	0.8
9 0348	4.2	**24** 0332	3.8
0935	0.4	0920	0.9
SA 1611	4.2	SU 1549	3.7
2157	0.5	2134	0.9
10 0430	4.1	**25** 0405	3.7
1018	0.5	0954	0.9
SU 1654	4.0	M 1624	3.6
2237	0.7	2206	0.9
11 0512	3.9	**26** 0440	3.7
1101	0.7	1029	0.9
M 1737	3.7	TU 1701	3.5
2318	1.0	2240	1.0
12 0554	3.7	**27** 0518	3.6
1146	1.0	1108	1.0
TU 1822	3.4	W 1743	3.4
		2320	1.2
13 0001	1.3	**28** 0601	3.5
0640	3.5	1155	1.2
W 1238	1.3	TH 1832	3.2
1914	3.1		
14 0053	1.5	**29** 0009	1.3
0735	3.2	0654	3.3
TH 1344	1.5	F 1254	1.3
◐ 2022	2.9	1934	3.1
15 0205	1.8	**30** 0115	1.5
0849	3.0	0802	3.2
F 1511	1.6	SA 1412	1.4
2152	2.8	◐ 2054	3.0
		31 0240	1.5
		0926	3.2
		SU 1538	1.4
		2219	3.1

NOVEMBER

Time	m	Time	m
1 0405	1.5	**16** 0455	1.6
1045	3.4	1122	3.1
M 1652	1.2	TU 1727	1.4
2328	3.3	2358	3.1
2 0515	1.2	**17** 0548	1.4
1150	3.6	1212	3.3
TU 1752	1.0	W 1813	1.2
3 0024	3.6	**18** 0041	3.3
0612	1.0	0632	1.3
W 1245	3.8	TH 1255	3.4
1843	0.8	1853	1.1
4 0113	3.8	**19** 0119	3.4
0702	0.8	0711	1.1
TH 1335	4.0	F 1334	3.5
1929	0.6	1929	1.0
5 0159	4.0	**20** 0155	3.5
0749	0.6	0748	1.0
F 1422	4.1	SA 1412	3.5
2013	0.6	2003	0.9
6 0244	4.1	**21** 0231	3.6
0834	0.5	0824	0.9
SA 1508	4.0	SU 1451	3.6
● 2055	0.6	○ 2037	0.9
7 0327	4.1	**22** 0308	3.7
0918	0.5	0901	0.8
SU 1552	3.9	M 1529	3.6
2136	0.7	2113	0.9
8 0410	4.0	**23** 0347	3.7
1001	0.6	0939	0.8
M 1636	3.8	TU 1610	3.5
2216	0.8	2150	0.9
9 0452	3.9	**24** 0427	3.7
1045	0.8	1020	0.8
TU 1719	3.5	W 1653	3.5
2257	1.0	2231	0.9
10 0534	3.7	**25** 0511	3.7
1129	1.0	1104	0.9
W 1802	3.3	TH 1739	3.4
2339	1.2	2316	1.0
11 0616	3.5	**26** 0557	3.6
1216	1.2	1153	0.9
TH 1848	3.1	F 1829	3.3
12 0025	1.5	**27** 0007	1.1
0702	3.3	0650	3.5
F 1309	1.4	SA 1249	1.1
1940	2.9	1927	3.2
13 0122	1.6	**28** 0106	1.2
0758	3.1	0751	3.4
SA 1413	1.5	SU 1354	1.1
◐ 2048	2.8	◐ 2034	3.1
14 0234	1.7	**29** 0216	1.3
0907	3.0	0900	3.3
SU 1524	1.5	M 1505	1.2
2203	2.8	2146	3.2
15 0350	1.7	**30** 0330	1.3
1020	3.0	1012	3.3
M 1631	1.5	TU 1616	1.1
2307	3.0	2254	3.3

DECEMBER

Time	m	Time	m
1 0441	1.2	**16** 0451	1.5
1120	3.4	1115	3.0
W 1720	1.0	TH 1721	1.3
2354	3.4	2352	3.0
2 0545	1.0	**17** 0549	1.4
1220	3.5	1211	3.1
TH 1816	0.9	F 1811	1.2
3 0048	3.6	**18** 0040	3.2
0642	0.9	0638	1.2
F 1314	3.6	SA 1300	3.2
1907	0.8	1856	1.1
4 0139	3.7	**19** 0125	3.3
0733	0.7	0723	1.0
SA 1405	3.7	SU 1346	3.3
1954	0.7	1937	1.0
5 0227	3.8	**20** 0208	3.5
0822	0.6	0805	0.9
SU 1454	3.7	M 1431	3.4
● 2039	0.7	2018	0.8
6 0312	3.8	**21** 0251	3.6
0907	0.6	0848	0.7
M 1540	3.6	TU 1516	3.5
2121	0.8	○ 2059	0.7
7 0356	3.8	**22** 0335	3.7
0950	0.7	0930	0.6
TU 1623	3.5	W 1601	3.5
2201	0.8	2142	0.7
8 0437	3.7	**23** 0419	3.8
1031	0.8	1014	0.6
W 1703	3.4	TH 1646	3.6
2239	0.9	2225	0.7
9 0516	3.6	**24** 0504	3.8
1110	0.9	1058	0.6
TH 1741	3.3	F 1732	3.5
2317	1.1	2310	0.7
10 0552	3.5	**25** 0550	3.8
1149	1.0	1145	0.6
F 1817	3.1	SA 1819	3.5
2357	1.2	2358	0.8
11 0629	3.3	**26** 0639	3.7
1230	1.1	1234	0.7
SA 1856	3.0	SU 1909	3.3
12 0040	1.3	**27** 0049	0.9
0709	3.2	0731	3.5
SU 1316	1.3	M 1327	0.9
1942	2.9	2005	3.2
13 0131	1.5	**28** 0147	1.0
0758	3.0	0829	3.3
M 1411	1.4	TU 1428	1.0
◐ 2040	2.8	◐ 2108	3.1
14 0233	1.5	**29** 0253	1.1
0900	2.9	0937	3.2
TU 1515	1.4	W 1536	1.1
2149	2.8	2217	3.1
15 0343	1.5	**30** 0407	1.2
1010	2.9	1049	3.2
W 1621	1.4	TH 1647	1.1
2255	2.9	2326	3.2
		31 0522	1.1
		1159	3.2
		F 1754	1.1

HAT is 4·3 metres above Chart Datum; see 4.5.

›› FREE monthly updates from ‹‹
www.reedsalmanac.co.uk

9.24.15 SESIMBRA

Baixo Alentejo **38°26'·30N 09°06'·49W** (Mole hd) ❀❀♨♨✿✿

CHARTS AC 3635, 3636; PC 24204, 26407; SC42B

TIDES Standard Port LISBOA (⟵); ML 2·0

Times				Height (metres)			
High Water		Low Water		MHWS	MHWN	MLWN	MLWS
0400	0900	0400	0900	3·8	2·9	1·5	0·6
1600	2100	1600	2100				
Differences SESIMBRA							
−0045	−0030	−0020	−0010	−0·4	−0·3	−0·1	0·0

SHELTER Good in marina. Or ⚓ in about 5m to N or E of ent and clear of fairway, local moorings and underwater cables. Strong N'ly gusts blow down from high ground late pm/evening.

NAVIGATION WPT 38°25'·86N 09°06'·15W, 333°/0·5M to breakwater head, which is 475m W of the ldg line; and on the 003·5° ldg line.

LIGHTS AND MARKS 003·5° ldg lts/marks (NE of the hbr) are hard to see by day and night. Bkwtr hd lt, W twr, R bands, and Forte do Cavalo lt, R ○ twr are both conspic. See 9.24.3 for light details.

R/T Marina Ch 09. Port Ch 11.

TELEPHONE (Code 212) Brit Consul 213 924000.

FACILITIES Marina 130 AB is run by YC (☎ 233451), but is often full in summer, €2.34. D from fish market. www.naval-sesimbra.pt
Town: (1½M to the NE), ☕, R, Bar, Ⓑ, ✉, Bus into town. ⇌ Seixal. ✈ Lisboa. Tourist amenities. 30 min bus to Lisboa or, to avoid traffic jams, local bus to Cacilhas and ferry across the Tejo.

9.24.16 SETÚBAL

Baixo Alentejo **38°31'·22N 08°53'·14W** (Marina) ❀❀♨♨✿✿

CHARTS AC 3635, 3636, 3259; PC 24204, 26308/09; SC42B

TIDES
Standard Port LISBOA (⟵); ML 2·0

Times				Height (metres)			
High Water		Low Water		MHWS	MHWN	MLWN	MLWS
0400	0900	0400	0900	3·8	2·9	1·5	0·6
1600	2100	1600	2100				
Differences SETÚBAL							
−0020	−0015	−0005	+0005	−0·4	−0·3	−0·1	−0·1

SHELTER Good in marina, but almost always full. A new marina is at Troia; see Facilities. ⚓ SW of the FV basin in up to 13m.

NAVIGATION WPT 38°27'·06N 08°58'·26W (abm No 1 buoy & No 2 bcn, Racon B), 040°/5·2M to front ldg lt. The 10m bar is dangerous only in strong SW'lies against a spring ebb. R. Sado is shoal either side until N of Forte de Outão; heed the ldg line/buoys/bcns.

LIGHTS AND MARKS See 9.24.3 and chartlet for lt details.

R/T VTS *Setúbal Port Control* Ch 73 (mandatory for yachts >15m LOA; MSI broadcasts on request). Port Ch 11. Marina Ch 09.

TELEPHONE (Code 265) Ⓗ 561116 Brit Consul 213 924000.

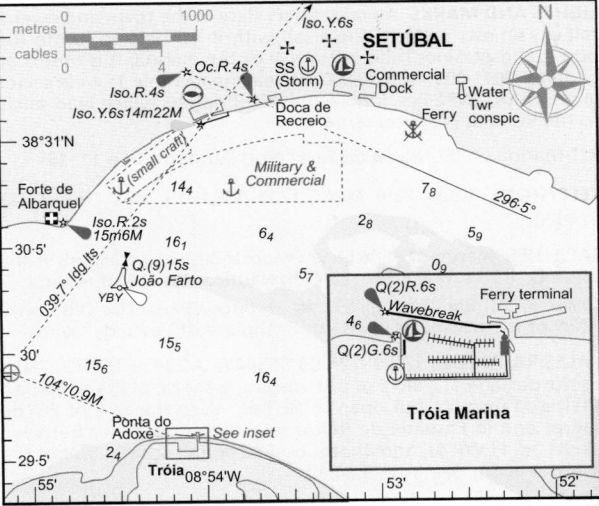

FACILITIES Setúbal's so called marina is crowded with small FVs and local boats and most unlikely to accommodate visiting yachts. ☎ 542076. 155 AB. D, ME, ⊖, Met.

Doca de Recreio at Setúbal is even smaller; local boats only. Industrial quays extend 6M up-river to the ESE.

Town: ☕, R, Bar, Ⓑ, ✉; good train/bus to Lisboa ⇌, ✈.

Tróia Marina at 38°29'·66N 08°54'·14W is now fully operational. It has modern facilities and is part of an up-market development. From Setúbal it bears 207°/1·75M.

From a WPT at 38°29'·88N 08°55'·28W (on the 039·7° leading line) make good 104°/9 cables to the marina ent; lights as chartlet. 184 AB (fingers) in 2·5-4·0m, max LOA 18m.

Manager tiago.marcelino@sonae.pt ☎ 499000, mob 933 389847. May-Sep 0830-2100. VHF Ch 09. D&P, ⚓, Shwrs, 🚿, Wi-Fi, @, Bar, R, 🛒 4 mins walk, Golf 4km.

ADJACENT ANCHORAGE
ARRÁBIDA 38°28'·52N 08°58'·77W, 1·5M NNW of ent to Rio Sado (AC 3259). Popular but shallow day ⚓ in 2·5m at SW end of the bay, sheltered from N by high ground, but also prone to katabatic gusts. Appr from SSW, 1-2ca offshore to avoid Baixo de Alpertuche (0·6m). Caution: rocky reef at NE end of bay.

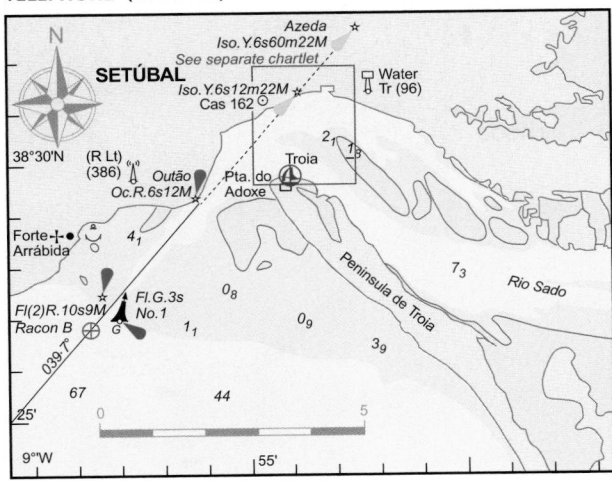

9.24.17 SINES

Baixo Alentejo 37°57'·04N 08°52'·11W (marina ent) ✿✿⊕◊◊✿✿

CHARTS AC 3636, 3224; PC 24204, 24205, 26408; SC 430A.

TIDES

Standard Port LISBOA (←); ML 2·0

Times				Height (metres)			
High Water		Low Water		MHWS	MHWN	MLWN	MLWS
0400	0900	0400	0900	3·8	2·9	1·5	0·6
1600	2100	1600	2100				
Differences SINES							
−0050	−0030	−0020	−0010	−0·4	−0·3	−0·1	+0·1
MILFONTES (37°43'·0N 08°47'·0W)							
−0040	−0030	No data		−0·1	0·0	0·0	+0·1
ARRIFANA (37°17'·5N 08°52'·0W)							
−0030	−0020	No data		−0·1	+0·1	−0·1	+0·1

SHELTER Good in marina protected by E mole. Or ⌕ NW of the marina in 4m; holding is reportedly poor E of 08°52'·00W.

NAVIGATION WPT 37°55'·70N 08°52'·97W, 027°/1·5M to ent to the marina bay. The outer ent, between W and E moles, is 1M wide. From the NW, caution: the derelict outer 400m section of the W mole dries 0·6m. A PHM buoy, Fl R 3s, 680m S of the mole hd ✭ (Fl 3s), <u>must</u> be rounded; no short cuts! In strong S'lies swell may cause turbulence off the W mole. Sines is strategically located 51M SSE of Cascais and 57M N of Cape St Vincent.

LIGHTS AND MARKS An oil refinery flare in the town and several tall chy's/masts 3-4M to the E (all with R lts) help to locate the port. Cabo de Sines lt ho is 9ca NW of the marina; it is obsc'd by oil tanks 001°-003° and 004°-007°, leaving a visible 1° wide sector in which the WPT lies. Ignore the 357·3° ldg lts which lead solely to the Refined Products terminal.

R/T Marina Ch 09. *Porto de Sines* (Port Authority) Ch 11, 13.

TELEPHONE (Code 269) MRCC (21) 4401919; Brit Consul 213 924000.

FACILITIES Marina ☎ 860612. www.portodesines.pt 250 AB in 4m, some ♥, €2.11. D & P, ME, El. **Club Náutico** close SE of marina.

Town: R, 🍴, Bar, Gaz, ⓑ, ✉, ⛟, ✈ Lisboa/Faro. The Old Town, NNW of the marina, is pleasant; birthplace of Vasco da Gama.

BALEEIRA, Algarve 37°00'·72N 08°55'·44W. AC 3636, 89. PC 27502. Useful passage ⌕, 3·5M E of C St Vincent, 1·6M NE of Pta de Sagres. Sheltered from W, but open to NE'lies, when the ⌕s E of Pta de Sagres and in Enseada de Belixe may be better. Enter between bkwtr hd, Fl WR 4s, and Ilhotes do Martinhal, 4ca NE. ⌕ N of the 2 jetties in 6m. See lts in 9.24.3.

9.24.18 LAGOS

Algarve 37°05'·90N 08°39'·90W (Hbr ent) ✿✿⊕◊◊◊✿✿✿

CHARTS AC 3636, 89; PC 24206.

TIDES

Standard Port LISBOA (←); ML 2·0

Times				Height (metres)			
High Water		Low Water		MHWS	MHWN	MLWN	MLWS
0400	0900	0400	0900	3·8	2·9	1·5	0·6
1600	2100	1600	2100				
Differences LAGOS							
−0100	−0030	−0030	−0025	−0·4	−0·3	−0·1	0·0
ENSEADA DE BELIXE (Cape St Vincent)							
−0050	−0030	−0020	−0015	+0·3	+0·3	+0·2	+0·2

SHELTER Very good in marina; access H24 all tides. The ⌕ close NE of the E mole in 3-5m is exposed only to E and S winds and possible SW swell.

NAVIGATION WPT 37°05'·66N 08°39'·06W, 284°/7ca to hbr ent. Fishing nets may extend up to 1M offshore. From Ponta da Piedade keep 5ca offshore to clear rocks; otherwise there are no offshore dangers. Final appr is on 284°, W mole head lt ≠ Santo António church. Shoaling reported in ent; care needed at LW if draft >1·5m. 3kn hbr speed limit.

Berth at arrival pontoon stbd side close SE of lifting foot-bridge which opens on request 0800-2200, 1/6-15/9; 0900-1800 16/9-31/5, except for some ¼hr spells for train passengers. R/G tfc lts, but unmasted craft may transit when bridge is down.

LIGHTS AND MARKS Lts as chartlet and 9.24.3. The river chan is unlit, except by shore lts. Pta da Piedade is 1·1M S. Pta do Altar (Portimão) is 7M E.

R/T *Marina de Lagos* Ch 09 for bridge and fuel. Weather broadcast Ch 12 at 1000 and 1600LT in season.

TELEPHONE (Code 282) Met 417714; Ⓗ 770100; Police 762930; Fire 770790; MRCC (21) 4401919; Brit Consul 490750.

FACILITIES Marina marina@marlagos.pt www.marinadelagos.pt (3m). ☎ 770210. 462+ ♥, €2·70, short stay €7·00/hr. ⊖, P, D, Slip, BY, ME, El, ⚒, 🍴, Wi-fi, @, R, Bar, CH, ⓑ, ▣. **Club de Vela** ☎ 762256.

Town: all usual amenities, ⛟. ✈ Faro (75 km).

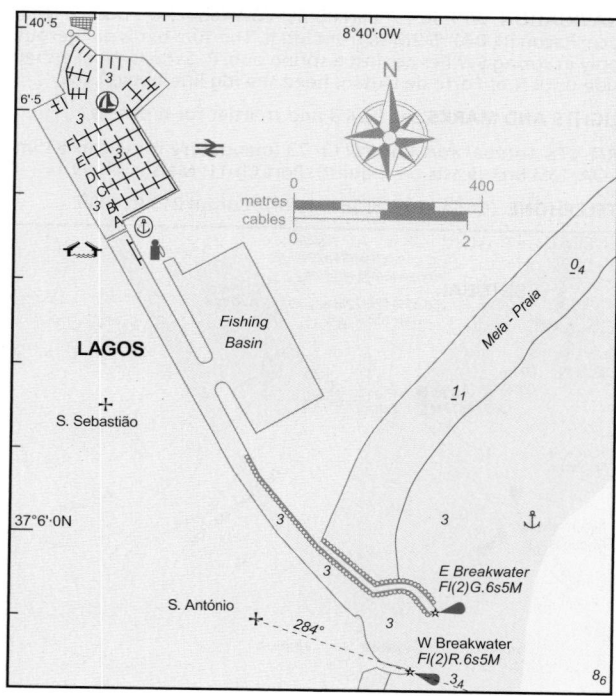

ANCHORAGE 2·6M ENE OF LAGOS
ALVOR 37°07'·08N 08°37'·08W. PC 27502. A peaceful but shallow lagoon entered between moles Fl R 4s & G 4s, but not in strong onshore winds nor at night. ⚓ just inside the ent to port in about 2·2m or off Alvor (1·2M E) in about 1·6m. The channel is buoyed; best to enter on the young flood whilst the drying banks can be seen. A lively tourist spot, but not devoid of charm.

SOUTHERN PORTUGAL: THE ALGARVE

An ITZ extends 15M W/SW of Cape St Vincent and the TSS a further 20M west; see 9.24.2 & AC 89, 93.

There are passage ⚓s, sheltered from N'lies, at Enseada de Belixe (E of Cabo São Vicente) and at Enseadas de Sagres and da Baleeira (NE of Pta de Sagres).

E of Cabo São Vicente the summer climate becomes more Mediterranean, ie hotter, clearer and winds more from NW to SW. Swell may decrease, tidal streams are slight and the current runs SE. Hbrs along the coasts of the Algarve and SW Andalucía are sheltered from all but S'lies (infrequent).

Drifting tuna nets can be a problem along the Algarve coast, particularly in the vicinity of Ponta de Sagres and Faro. Best advice is to keep inside the 20m or outside the 50m contours and keep a jolly good lookout.

The route to Gibraltar is either a direct track 110°/175M (Cabo São Vicente to Tarifa) or a series of coastal legs.

There are good marinas at Lagos, Portimão, Albufeira and Vilamoura. At Cabo de Santa Maria a gap in the low-lying dunes gives access to the lagoons and chans leading to Faro and Olhão, where a marina has been built; there are also some peaceful anchorages.

The marina at Vila Real de Santo António is on the Portuguese bank of the Rio Guadiana, which forms the Spanish border.

9.24.19 PORTIMÃO

Algarve 37°06'·51N 08°31'·71W (Hbr ent) ✿✿✿♒♒♒✿✿

CHARTS AC 91, 3636, 89, 83; PC 24206, 26310.

TIDES
Standard Port LISBOA (←—); ML 2·0

Times		Height (metres)					
High Water		Low Water		MHWS	MHWN	MLWN	MLWS
0400	0900	0400	0900	3·8	2·9	1·5	0·6
1600	2100	1600	2100				
Differences PORTIMÃO							
−0100	−0040	−0030	−0025	−0·5	−0·3	−0·1	+0·1
PONTA DO ALTAR (Lt ho E of ent)							
−0100	−0040	−0030	−0025	−0·3	−0·2	−0·1	0·0
ENSEADA DE ALBUFEIRA							
−0035	+0015	−0005	0000	−0·2	−0·1	0·0	+0·1

SHELTER Good in marina on W bank. Good ⚓ off Ferragudo on E bank. ⚓ inside E mole in about 4m is prone to swell and FV wash.

NAVIGATION WPT 37°06'·04N 08°31'·94W, 021°/5ca to hbr ent. No offshore hazards. Ent and river are straightforward, but flood & ebb streams run hard; berth bows to the stream.

Dredging a 6M long chan up R. Arade to Boca do Rio Resort and Silva, plus other developments, were still incomplete early 2009. Caution: 2 low (1m cl'nce) fixed road/rail bridges in Portimão.

LIGHTS AND MARKS Ponta do Altar lt ho is on low cliffs to E of ent. The R-roofed church at Ferragudo is conspic by day, almost on the 019° ldg line. Ldg lts as chartlet and 9.24.3; both on R/W banded columns, moved when chan changes.

R/T Port Ch 11. Marina Ch 09.

TELEPHONE (Code 282) MRCC (21) 4401919; Brit Consul 490750.

FACILITIES Marina ☎ 400680. marinaportimao@mail.telepac.pt www.marinadeportimao.com. 620 AB; max LOA 30m, max draft 4m, €4.24 inc AC. D, P, CH, El, ME, C (2 ton), Gaz, Wi-fi, @. Town centre 20 mins by dinghy, long walk, poor bus. Pontoons 2M N of hbr ent are nearer town centre. ✈ Faro (61 km).

Town R, 🍴, Bar, Ⓑ, ✉, ⇌. ✈ Faro (65 km).

ALBUFEIRA MARINA

In the absence of an official large scale chart, this chartlet is drawn from publicity material. It is therefore only a guide and lacks Lat, Long and scale

9.24.20 ALBUFEIRA

Algarve 37°04'·90N 08°15'·52W (N bkwtr lt) ❀❀❀♦♦♦❀❀

CHARTS AC 91, 89; PC 24206, 27503, 90 (1:10,000) only shows the outer hbr, not the marina. No large scale AC (2009). Positions are approx; the Lat/Long above is by hand-held GPS (WGS 84).

TIDES Standard Port LISBOA (⟵); **ML 2·0.** See differences 9.24.19.

SHELTER Good, in 2·5–4·0m. In strong E'lies the outer ent may be difficult. No space to ⚓ in outer hbr due to local moorings.

NAVIGATION WPT 37°03'·88N 08°15'·02W, approx 338°/1M to hbr ent. No offshore dangers, but rocks close inshore to W & E.

LIGHTS AND MARKS Ponta de Baleeira lt, Oc 6s 30m 11M, W lattice twr with R top, is near the root of S bkwtr. Bkwtr lts as chartlet, both W cols, R/G bands.

R/T *Marina de Albufeira* Ch 09 (1/6-15/9: 0900-2100).

TELEPHONE (Code 289) Ⓗ 802555 (Faro); ⊖ 589363; Taxi 583230; MRCC (21) 4401919; Brit Consul (282) 490750 (Portimão).

FACILITIES Marina, ☎ 510180. 475 + Ⓥ, €3.75. info@amarinadealbufeira.com www.amarinadealbufeira.com P & D, Slip, BH (70 ton), C (6 ton), ME, El, Ⓔ, BY, CH, Gaz, ✕, ⚓, SM, Wi-fi, @, YC, Bar, R, ▨. **Town** most facilities; Ⓑ, ⇌. ✈ Faro 30 km.

9.24.21 VILAMOURA

Algarve 37°04'·10N 08°07'·35W ❀❀❀♦♦♦❀❀

CHARTS AC 91, 89; PC 24206, 27503; SHOM 7300.

TIDES Standard Port LISBOA (⟵); **ML 2·0.** Use differences for 9.24.20 Albufeira (6M to the west).

SHELTER Very good, except in strong S'lies when the 100m wide ent can be dangerous. No ⚓ in the outer hbr.

NAVIGATION WPT 37°03'·60N 08°07'·40W, 007°/5ca to hbr ent. No offshore dangers, but groynes to the E. Hbr speed limit 3kn. The fairway through the outer hbr is dredged 4m.

LIGHTS AND MARKS Marina is surrounded by apartment bldgs; large hotel is conspic on E side of ent. Main lt, Fl 5s 17m 19M, yellow twr on HM's bldg; this lt between the W and E mole head lts (R/W and G/W banded twrs) leads 007° into the outer hbr. See 9.24.3 for other lt details.

R/T *Vilamoura Radio* Ch 09, 16 (0830-2130/1830 off season). Outside these hrs expect only 1M reception range.

TELEPHONE (Code 289) Maritime Police 310575; Medic 314243; Ⓗ 891100 (Faro); MRCC (21) 4401919; Brit Consul (282) 490750.

FACILITIES Marina is dredged 3·3m, reducing to 2·0m in the NE corner near 'A' pontoon. Reception pontoon, port side of access chan. ☎ 310560. marinavilamoura@lusotur.pt www.vilamoura.net 1000 inc Ⓥ, max LOA 43m. €5.32 Jul/Aug, inc AC. Plans to treble the marina's size have been put on hold (2009) due to the global economic crisis.

⊖, Met, P & D, Slip, BH (60 ton), C (2 & 6 ton), ME, El, Ⓔ, BY, CH, Gaz, ✕, ▨, ▦, SM, @, Wi-Fi. Free ⚓ by sludge boat that comes to your yacht. Local Ⓑ, M-F 0830-1445, plus ATMs.

Water taxi, ☎ 313622, criss-crosses the marina via 5 pick-up points. Mail pick-up, if addressed to: Marina de Vilamoura, 8125-409 Quarteira, Portugal.

Clube Náutico (by reception area) welcomes visitors: Bar, R, lounge, Wi-fi, @.

Faro 9.24.22 (20 km) has most facilities, inc ⇌, ✈ ☎ 800800.

9.24.22 FARO and OLHÃO

Algarve **36°57'·81N 07°52'·19W** (Hbr entrance) ⊛⊛⊛⊚⊘❀❀

CHARTS AC 91, 89, 83; PC 24206, 26311; SC 44B.

TIDES Standard Port LISBOA (◄──); ML 2·0

Times				Height (metres)			
High Water		Low Water		MHWS	MHWN	MLWN	MLWS
0400	0900	0400	0900	3·8	2·9	1·5	0·6
1600	2100	1600	2100				
Differences PORTO DE FARO-OLHÃO							
−0050	−0030	−0015	+0005	−0.5	−0.3	−0.1	0.0

SHELTER Generally good in the lee of coastal dunes. Popular ⚓s in 3-5m are inside Ilha da Culatra, abm lt Fl 5s or off jetty Oc G 4s.

NAVIGATION WPT 36°57'·04N 07°52'·12W, 352°/7ca to narrow ent which can be dangerous in strong S'lies; extensive shoals to the W. Enter near HW between moles, Fl R 4s & G 4s, and training walls. Abeam Cabo de Santa Maria lt ho, chan forks into salt marshes and lagoons: WNW to Faro or NE to Olhão.

The **Faro** chan carries 5·4m for the buoyed/lit 4M to the Commercial quay (not for yachts); but beyond depths vary.

The **Olhão** buoyed/lit chan (5M) is narrower and carries 2·1m least depth. From N of No 5 buoy enter the marina by an E-W chan, depth approx 2m, marked by 3 PHM buoys.

LIGHTS AND MARKS Cabo de Santa Maria lt ho near root of long E trng wall and adjacent VTS twr (42m) are conspic. Lt ho is also rear 021° ldg lt to abeam front ldg lt; see chartlet and 9.24.3.

R/T Both ports Ch 11, 09: Faro H24; Olhão, M-F office hrs.

TELEPHONE (Code 289) IPTM (Institute of Ports & Shipping) Olhão 715912; Brit Consul (282) 490750.

FACILITIES Faro HM ☎ 822025. ⚓ in 3m, 3ca SW of Doca de Recreio, small craft only; low bridge across ent. Some noise from airport, but not after 2100LT. Marina planned, no timescale.
Olhão HM ☎ 703160. Marina at W end; max LOA 17m, draft 3m. Head W passing well N of 3 PHM buoys. Berth on wavebreak (no AC or FW) or as arranged. No ⚓ in the fairways, due dredging.
Towns: Both are sizeable, all amenities inc @, Wi-Fi, ⇌, ✈.

MINOR PORT 11M W OF VILA REAL DE SANTO ANTÓNIO

TAVIRA. 37°06'·69N 07°37'·01W. AC 89, 93; PC 24206, 27503; SC 44A/B. Tide, see above (Cabo de Santa Maria). The narrow (about 70m) ent between I de Tavira and sand dunes to the E is lit by Fl G and R lts 2·5s and ldg lts 325·9° over the bar, front Fl R 3s; rear Iso R 6s. The ent (3m) should only be only be attempted near HW and in settled weather. Local knowledge is desirable. ⚓ in about 3m on sand SW of the entrance in the Rio Formosa and SE of the small community of Quatro Aguas (where a marina is mooted; no details or timescale). Show an ⚓ lt, due to FVs.

Town is 1M (20 mins walk or dinghy) NW of the ⚓ and, apart from a small craft BY and diesel supply, has little to offer a visiting yacht, being essentially a working FV port. Access is not possible for masted boats due to a low road bridge. Facilities: YC ☎ 281 326 858, Slip, ⛽, R, Bar, Ⓑ, ✉, Ⓗ, ⇌, ✈ (Faro).

9.24.23
VILA REAL DE SANTO ANTÓNIO
Algarve **37°10'·80N 07°24'·49W** (Marina) ✿❀⛆⚓✿✿

CHARTS AC 91, 89, 93; PC 24206, 26312; SC 440, 440A.

TIDES

Standard Port LISBOA (←); ML 2·0

Times				Height (metres)			
High Water		Low Water		MHWS	MHWN	MLWN	MLWS
0400	0900	0400	0900	3·8	2·9	1·5	0·6
1600	2100	1600	2100				
Differences VILA REAL DE SANTO ANTÓNIO							
−0050	−0015	−0010	0000	−0·4	−0·3	−0·1	+0·1

SHELTER Good in marina, but river ent difficult in strong S'lies.

NAVIGATION WPT 37°09'·00N 07°23'·35W (No 1 SHM buoy), 340°/9ca to hd of W trng wall. Caution: Extensive drying areas E of the trng walls stretch 2M east. The bar (1·0m) is marked by Nos 3/4 P/SHM lt buoys. Hug the W bank between trng walls (E partly covers) and up to marina. Access HW–3 to HW; best at slack water as streams & current are very strong: 2½kn (up to 6kn in winter).

LIGHTS AND MARKS High bldgs, FR lts, are 3M WNW of ent. Vila Real lt ho, W twr/B bands, is conspic. 2M inland a white suspension bridge (18m cl'nce MSL) is visible from seaward.

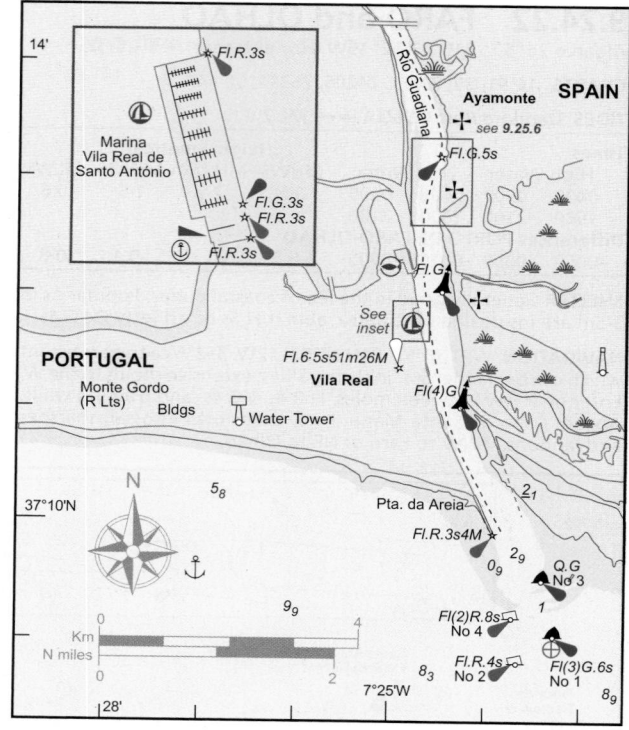

R/T Marina Ch 09. *Porto de Vila Real* VHF Ch 11, 16.

TELEPHONE (Code 281) MRCC (21) 4401919; Brit Consul (282) 490750.

FACILITIES Marina (2m). anguadiana@mail.telepac.pt ☎ 541571. 357 AB, €2.06. D on pontoon just N of marina; BY (new) close N ☎ 542069, marinaguadiana@sapo.pt BH (70 ton). **YC** ☎ 511306, R, Slip. **Town** R, ⛽, Bar, Ⓑ, ✉.

Upriver better water is off the Spanish bank and Ayamonte. The river Guadiana is navigable for about 20M to ⚓ off Alcoutim (pontoons €7.50/day for 1st week) and Pomerão (27M).

9.24.24 THE AZORES ARCHIPELAGO

CHARTS AC 1950, 1959, 1956,1895; PC 41101, 43101, 43102, 43103.

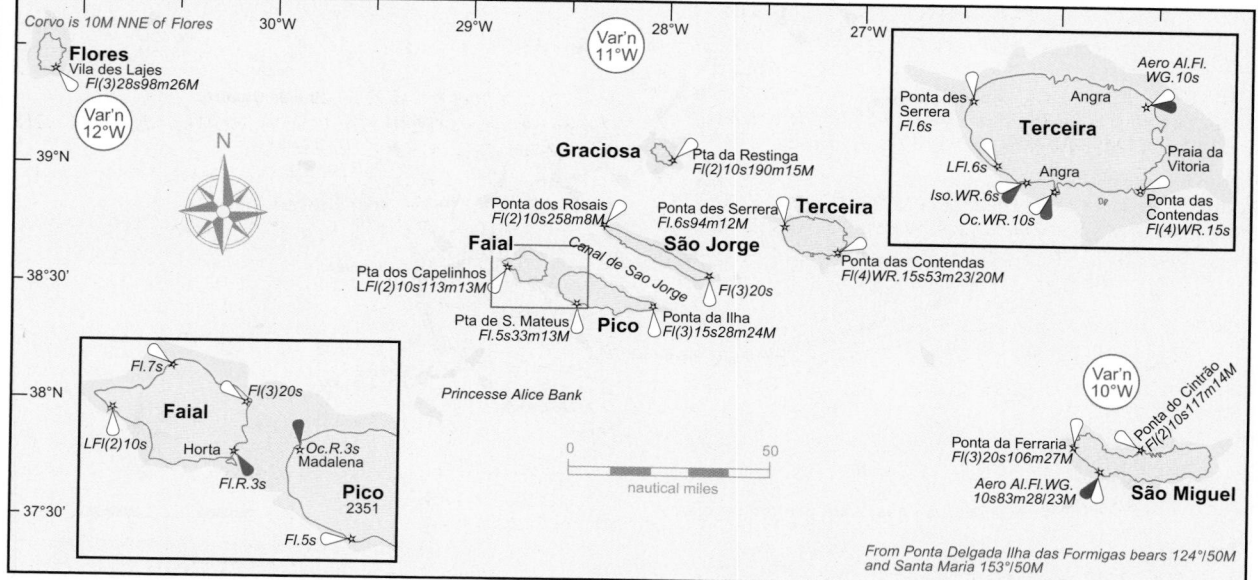

DISTANCES: AZORES – EUROPE/NORTH AFRICA AND BETWEEN ISLANDS

		1										
1	Falmouth	1										
2	Brest	136	2									
3	La Coruña	440	350	3								
4	Bayona	554	456	114	4							
5	Leixões (Pôrto)	617	526	176	63	5						
6	HORTA	1235	1202	966	927	937	6					
7	PONTA DELGADA	1183	1145	862	813	815	151	7				
8	Lisboa	780	658	327	227	163	904	771	8			
9	Cabo São Vicente	888	757	426	318	263	934	794	102	9		
10	Cádiz	1022	901	560	452	397	1068	928	236	134	10	
11	Europa Point	1087	960	618	506	455	1125	984	294	192	72	11
12	Casablanca	1114	978	637	525	474	1065	918	313	211	187	188	12

	1	131	152	190	282	320	Flores	1
	2	48	69	152	191		Horta	2
	3		44	138	185		Graciosa	3
	4			94	143		Terceira	4
	5				54		Ponta Delgada	5
	6						Sta Maria	6

DISTANCE TABLES
Approx distances in nautical miles are by the most direct route allowing for dangers and TSS.

9.24.25 AZORES: SELECTED LIGHTS
See 9.24.3 for key to light ranges and other characteristics. All positions are WGS 84 Datum. Sequence is from WNW to ESE.

ILHA DO CORVO
Canto de Carneira ⚡ Fl 6s 237m 9M; W twr/R bands; 39°43'·03N 31°05'·43W. Pta Negra Fl 5s 22m 6M; col; 39°40'·18N 31°06'·86W.

ILHA DAS FLORES
Ponta do Albarnaz ⚡, Fl 5s 103m 22M, 035°-258°; W twr, R top; 39°31'·20N 31°14'·12W. Santa Cruz Fl R 5s; 39°27'·27N 31°07'·48W.
PORTO DAS LAJES, ldg lts 250·8°: Front, L Fl G 7s 17m 2M, 39°22'·74N 31°10'·24W; rear Oc G 4s 65m 2M, 267m from front. Bkwtr hd ⚡ Fl (2) R 10s 9m 2M; 39°22'·75N 31°09'·94W.
Ponta das Lajes ☆, Fl (3) 28s 98m **26M**, 263°-054°; W twr, R cupola; 39°22'·54N 31°10'·61W, SE corner of island.

ILHA DO FAIAL
Ponta dos Cedros ⚡, Fl 7s 144m 12M; 38°38'·29N 28°43'·38W. Ponta da Ribeirinha ⚡, Fl (3) 20s 131m 12M; Post; 38°35'·73N 28°36'·15W, E end of island.

HORTA
Boa Viagem ⚡ Iso G 1·5s 12m 9M (hard to see against shore lts); appr brg 285°; B column on R cupola; 38°32'·28N 28°37'·49W. Bkwtr hd ⚡ Fl R 3s 20m 11M; W structure; 38°32'·03N 28°37'·27W.
Ldg lts 194·9°: both Iso G 2s 13/15m 2M; Red X on W posts, R bands. Front 38°31'·67N 28°37'·51W; rear 12m from front.

ILHA DO PICO (Pico mountain, 2351m; 38°28'·11N 28°23'·94W) Madalena ⚡ Oc R 3s 11m 10M; 38°32'·17N 28°31'·95W. Pta de São Mateus ⚡ Fl 5s 33m 13M, 284°-118°; 38°25'·33N 28°26'·93W.
Ponta da Ilha ☆ Fl (3) 15s 28m **24M**, 166°-070°; W twr, R cupola and bldg; 38°24'·84N 28°01'·83W, E tip of island.

ILHA DE SÃO JORGE
Ponta dos Rosais ⚡ Fl (2) 10s 259m 8M; 38°45'·22N 28°18'·71W. Pta do Norte Grande ⚡ Fl 6s 12M; W twr, R stripes; 38°40'·74N 28°03'·03W. **Ponta do Topo** ☆ Fl (3) 20s 57m **20M**, 133°-033°; W twr, R cupola and bldg; 38°32'·92N 27°45'·24W, E tip of island.

ILHA GRACIOSA
Ponta da Barca ⚡ Fl 7s 70m **20M**; vis 029°-031°, 035°-251°, 267°-287°; W twr, B bands; 39°05'·61N 28°02'·98W. Vila da Praia, mole hd Fl G 3s 15m 9M, W twr, G bands. **Ponta do Carapacho** ☆ Fl (2) 10s 190m **15M**, 165°-098°; R twr & cupola; 39°00'·84N 27°57'·29W.

ILHA TERCEIRA
Ponta da Sereta ☆ Fl (3) 15s 95m **21M**; W col, R top; 38°45'·95N 27°22'·45W, NW end of island.
Lajes ☆ Aero Al Fl WG 10s 132m **W28M, G23M**; 38°45'·56N 27°04'·69W. **Praia da Vitoria**, N mole Fl G 5s 11m 6M; Gy post; 38°43'·56N 27°03'·04W. Marina in NW corner of hbr.

S mole Fl R 3s 8M; W twr, R bands; 38°43'·24N 27°02'·92W.
Pta das Contendas ☆ Fl (4) WR 15s 53m **W23M, R20M**; 220°-W-020°-R-044°-W-072°-R-093°; W twr, R top; 38°38'·62N 27°05'·07W.
Monte Brasil, Oc WR 10s 21m 12M; 191°-R-295°-W-057°; W col, R bands; 38°38'·60N 27°13'·04W.

ANGRA DO HEROISMO
Ldg lts 340·9°: front, Fl R 4s 29m 7M, R mast; 38°39'·25N 27°13'·09W.
Rear, Oc R 6s 54m 7M, R lantern on Y structure; 505m from front.
Porto Pipas (marina ent, S side) ⚡ Fl G 3s 14m 6M.
N mole, ⚡ Fl (2) R 6s 8m 3M; 38°39'·12N 27°12'·95W.

ILHA DE SAO MIGUEL
Ferraria ☆ Fl (3) 20s 106m **27M**; 339°-174°; W twr, R cupola; 37°51'·21N 25°51'·02W, NW end of island.
Airport ☆ Aero Al Fl WG 10s 83m **W28M, G23M**; 282°-124°; control twr; 37°44'·62N 25°42'·46W, 2·5M W of Ponta Delgada.
Santa Clara ☆ L Fl 5s 26m **15M**; 282°-102°; R lantern; 37°44'·00N 25°41'·16W, between airport and Ponta Delgada.

PONTA DELGADA
Bkwtr head ⚡ L Fl R 6s 16m 10M; W twr, R bands; 37°44'·18N 25°39'·40W, 450m SSE of marina ent.
Naval Club Dir lt 309°: Fl (2) WRG 5s 24m 10M H24; 306°-G-308°-W-310°-R-312°; 37°44'·39N 25°39'·42W.
Terminal pier E hd ⚡ Fl(2)R 5s 3M; W twr, R bands; 37°44'·35N 25°39'·61W.
Terminal pier W hd ⚡ Fl(3)G 15s 3M; W twr, G bands; 37°44'·24N 25°39'·83W.
Quebra floating bkwtr S end ⚡ Q(6)+LFl W 15s 3M; 2 ▼ (vert) on Bk bcn, Y top; 37°44'·26N 25°39'·97W.
Marina mole hd ⚡ Fl G 3s 12m 10M; W twr, G bands; 37°44'·32N 25°39'·57W, 450m NNW of bkwtr head.
Forte S. Bras Dir lt 262°: Fl (4) WRG 8s 13m 10M H24; 259°-G-261°-W-263°-R-265°; 37°44'·08N 25°40'·39W.
Ponta Garça ☆ L Fl WR 5s 100m **W16M**, R13M; 240°-W-080-R-100°; twr and house; 37°42'·85N 25°22'·18W, S side of island.
Ponta do Arnel ☆ Aeromarine Fl 5s 65m **25M**; 157°-355°; W twr on house; 37°49'·43N 25°08'·14W, E end of island.
Ilhéus das Formigas ⚡ Fl (2) 12s 21m 9M; W twr; 37°16'·26N 24°46'·83W (islet 20M NE of Ilha de Santa Maria).

ILHA DE SANTA MARIA
Airport ☆ Aero Al Fl WG 10s 116m **WG25M**; 021°-121°; shown by day in poor vis; control twr. 36°58'·37N 25°09'·90W, W end of ls.
Pta do Malmerendo ⚡ Fl (2) 10s 49m 10M; W bldg, R bands; 36°56'·43N 25°09'·42W.
Pta do Castelo ☆ Aeromarine Fl (3) 13·5s 113m **25M**; 181°-089°; W □ twr and bldg. 36°55'·77N 25°00'·97W, SE corner of island.
Ponta do Norte ⚡ Fl (4) 15s 138m 10M; 37°00'·75N 25°03'·58W.

9.24.26 AZORES: SPECIAL NOTES

Geography. The Azores comprise 9 islands in 3 groups:
- Western group: Corvo and Flores
- Central group: Faial, Pico, São Jorge, Graciosa and Terceira
- Eastern group: São Miguel and Santa Maria

The groups are well spread out. See the Distance table overleaf.

Harbours The three main marinas are Horta (Faial), Angra do Heroísmo (Terceira) and Ponta Delgada (São Miguel). The hbr at Lajes (Flores) is included because it is closest to the USA and to the E-bound trans-Atlantic track and therefore often visited. Many anchorages in the lee of islands are safe in settled weather.

Standard Time is UT +1, ie 1 hour behind UT.

Tides Ponta Delgada is the Standard Port, with a regular, semi-diurnal regime. In summer MHWS is usually at about 0200 and 1400 LT, and MHWN 0700 and 2000 LT. Tidal range is small: 1·4m sp and 0·6m np. Secondary port time and height differences are < 8 minutes and < 0·2m. Tide tables are therefore not included. The rising tide sets E-NE, the ebb W-SW. Rates are max at mid-tide springs and influenced by strong winds.

Currents Less than 1 knot and variable, but tending towards S or SE-going; locally influenced by each island's topography.

Navigation Jul-Aug is a good time for UK-based yachts to visit, after trans-Atlantic boats have passed through in May-Jun. It is best to get back to the UK by end Aug to avoid autumnal gales.

A DGPS station on Horta at 38°32'N 28°37'W is operational on 308kHz out to a range of 295M. Variation (2009), as on 9.24.24, decreases 11' annually.

Lights, buoys, daymarks All islands are well lit (see above), but some higher lts may be obscured by low cloud. Pico (a 2351m/7713ft dormant volcano) is visible from 50M in good visibility.

The buoyage system is IALA 'A', the reverse of IALA 'B' as used in the Americas. Thus red can buoys are to be left to PORT and green conical buoys to STARBOARD, whilst following the general direction of buoyage. There are few buoys.

Weather The Azores High usually predominates from June to mid-Sept with light winds/calms and warm settled conditions. If it is not established, windier more variable European conditions may prevail. In summer winds are usually NE'ly over the Central and Eastern groups and visibility is good; fog is rare. Humidity may be high but not uncomfortable.

Horta Navtex ('F': 518kHz) transmits 24 hr forecasts in English for sea areas Altair, Açores, Irving, Milne and Marsala every 4 hrs from 0050 UT; see 6.3.5 and Fig 6(17). (Horta 'J' on 490kHz only transmits in Portuguese). See 6.19.1 for forecasts on VHF Ch 11.

Books *The Atlantic Crossing Guide* (RCC/ACN). *Atlantic Islands* (RCC/Imray). *W coasts of Spain & Portugal* (Admiralty NP67.)

Charts are listed under each harbour. AC 1950 and PC 41101 cover the whole archipelago. PC 43101 covers the western island group, 43102 the central group and 43103 the eastern.

Formalities Brit Consul is at Ponta Delgada ☎ 296 628175. The Azores are Portuguese and in the EU, but arr/dep procedures can be lengthy and apply to each island. For E-bound yachts the Azores may be the first port of entry into Europe, so the process is important. Fly flag Q on arrival. Well organised ship's and personal papers, plus courtesy, good humour and patience are a great help. Expect to be processed by at least Immigration (*Service Estrangeros*), Customs (*Alfândega*) and *Policia Maritima*; plus *Guarda Nacional Republicana* (tax authority) and the local HM (*Capitão do Porto*) all of whom may (not) be in the same bldg. It is acceptable to fly the Azorean flag on the stbd halyard *below* the Portuguese courtesy ensign.

Departure clearance, valid for 24 hrs, is also required, even between islands. If you cancel, the process must re-start.

Telephone International dialling code is 351(as in Portugal). Area codes are 292 for Flores, Corvo, Faial and Pico; 295 for São Jorge,

Graciosa and Terceira; and 296 for São Miguel and Santa Maria. Area codes must be dialled even within the same island, making 9 digits in all. Faxes & e-mail can easily be sent/received. Mobile coverage is good in populated areas, patchy elsewhere.

Flights Most European airlines, eg TAP, route via Lisboa to São Miguel, Faial and Terceira, but Sata (Air Azores; ☎ 00 351 296 209720; www.sata.pt) flies direct from Gatwick (London) to São Miguel every Tues. Sata also shuttles between all 9 islands. There are direct flights from/to Boston, USA and Canada.

AZAB The Azores and Back race (Falmouth-Ponta Delgada) is held every 4 years, next in 2011. It is a truly sporting event, open to all comers, with little or no sponsorship. www.azab.co.uk

9.24.27 PORTO DAS LAJES

Flores 39°22'·82N 31°09'·96W (Hbr ent) ⚓⚓⚓☆☆⚓⚓⚓☆

CHARTS AC 1950, 1959; PC 41101, 43101, 46402.

TIDES MHWS 1·5M; MHWN 1·2M; MLWN 0·7M; MLWS 0·4M.

SHELTER is good, due to the bkwtr, but exposed to NE'lies. Swell can also be a problem in N'lies. ⚓ where indicated on sand; elsewhere patches of gravel and rock offer poor holding. Or berth on the inner part of the bkwtr, clear of the ferry. It is also possible to berth stern-on to the old quay with bow ⚓. A small marina is intended but not yet built. Lajes has supplanted the much smaller and more difficult hbr at Santa Cruz, 5M NNE.

NAVIGATION WPT 39°23'·08N 31°08'·98W, 250·8°/8ca to hbr ent. The approach is straightforward by day, but Flores is fringed by rocks; keep at least 1M off. The 9M wide passage between Flores and Corvo can be choppy at sp; deepest water is in the N half.

LIGHTS AND MARKS See 9.24.25 for lt details. The bkwtr lt is often destroyed in winter and is not wholly reliable in summer. The 250·8° ldg lts lead clear of inshore rocks to stbd and the bkwtr to port. By day the church, water tower and lt ho are all conspic; the latter's light is obscured N of a brg of 263°.

R/T Nil

TELEPHONE (Code 292). There is no HM. Medical emergency 112. Ⓗ 592294; Brit Consul (São Miguel) (296) 628175.

FACILITIES P&D by cans in small quantities, Slip, FW, C (12-40 ton), ME, El. Mail pick-up via Café Beira Mar, Lajes das Flores 9960, Azores. Internet access foc at library.

Clube Naval welcomes/helps visitors: ☎ 593145. info@cnlflores.com www.cnlflores.com

Town ✉, Ⓑ+ATM, Bar, R, 🛒, 🅿, Ⓗ and ✈ at Santa Cruz, 12km.

9.24.28 HORTA

Faial **38°32'·05N 28°37'·38W (Hbr ent)** ❀❀❀♨♨♨✿✿✿

CHARTS AC 1950, 1956, 1957; PC 41101, 43102, 46403; SHOM 7605.

TIDES MHWS 1·6M; MHWN 1·2M; MLWN 0·7M; MLWS 0·4M.

SHELTER Good, except in strong SW-SE winds which raise a steep, confused sea in the hbr. ⚓ (poor holding) is only allowed when the marina is full. No ⚓ at Porto Pim, an inlet S of the hbr.

NAVIGATION WPT 38°32'·04N 28°36'·00W 270°/1M to bkwtr hd. The 195° ldg line is not for yachts. Streams in the 2·6M wide Canal do Faial between Faial and Pico reach 2½kn eddying SSW towards Horta. Beware many ferries and Baixa do Sul rk (7·1m) in mid-chan which breaks in SW gales.

LIGHTS AND MARKS See 9.24.25 for lt details. Near the W end of Faial, Vale Formoso, L Fl (2) 10s 113m 13M, is reported to have a range of only about 5M. Monte da Guia, 1M S of the hbr, is a steep, rounded extinct volcano with conspic radio mast. SSW of the marina the Observatory and a hotel twr block are conspic.

R/T Call *Marina da Horta* Ch 06, 10, 11, 16 (0800-1200/1300-2000 daily); Portuguese, English, French & Spanish spoken. MAYS *Mid-Atlantic* Ch 77 HO. Port Authority *Capimarhorta* Ch 11, 16.

TELEPHONE (Code 292) APTO (Port Authority) 208300; Medical emergency 112; Ⓗ 200200; Brit Consul see 9.24.30.

FACILITIES Marina is in 2 basins: the long-established N basin (2-3m, for locals and smaller visitors) and a new S basin mainly for mega yachts (but <35m LOA, 6m draft). Reception/fuel pontoon is between the basins. Private yacht moorings lie outside the marina.

portohorta@mail.telepac.pt www.portohorta.com ☎ 391693. 240 inc Ⓥ, €1.00, inc AC. ⊖, Met, D&P (cash only), Slip, BH (25 ton), ME, El, Ⓔ, BY, CH, ⬜, SM. Gaz, Gas via MAYS. Mail pick-up via marina, Av'da Gago Sacadura Cabral 7, 9900 Horta, Faial, Açores; or via Café Sport or MAYS.

Long term plans envisage a new bkwtr extending SSE from a point about 250m NNE of Boa Viagem lt, giving better shelter and more room to ⚓.

Mid-Atlantic Yacht Services (MAYS) at N end of marina is the key company for visiting yachts, for all repairs, advice, handling mail, fax and e-mail. ☎ 391616. mays@mail.telepac.pt

Clube Naval de Horta ☎ 391719 (S of marina); visitors welcome: Bar, small R. VHF Ch 16.

Café Sport ☎ 292327. www.petercafesport.com

Town ✉, Ⓑ+ATM, ACA, Bar, R, 🛒, Ⓗ, ✈ (UK direct).

9.24.29 ANGRA DO HEROÍSMO

Terceira **38°39'·10N 27°12'·93W (Marina ent)** ❀❀❀♨♨✿✿✿

CHARTS AC 1950, 1956, 1957; PC 41101, 43102, 46405; SHOM 7605.

TIDES MHWS 1·6M; MHWN 1·3M; MLWN 0·7M; MLWS 0·4M.

ANGRA DO HEROÍSMO *continued*

SHELTER Good. Exposed only to strong S/SE winds and, if any S in the wind, swell may enter. A bkwtr extending 1ca W from Porto Pipas ⚓ Fl G 3s is planned. ⚓ SW of the marina off the YC, but clear of Baixa da Prainha, a rock awash at CD. Private moorings are laid NE of this rock.

NAVIGATION WPT 38°38'·00N 27°12'·54W, 341°/1·1M to abeam marina ent and on 341° ldg line. Beware unlit Ilhéus das Cabras (146m high islets) 3·3M ESE of the hbr and 9ca offshore. 2M SE of these islets is Ilhéus Fradinhos 8m high pinnacle rks. Both are in the R sectors of Pta das Contendas lt ho.

LIGHTS AND MARKS See 9.24.25 for lt details. Front ldg lt is on a R mast at a conspic twin-towered church; rear is a yellow structure, R top. Monte Brasil, a 205m high peninsula with wooded slopes, is close SW of the marina. Ponta do Farol lt on its SE flank is on a W col, R bands.

R/T Marina Ch 09, 16 (H24).

9.24.30 PONTA DELGADA

São Miguel 37°44'·23N 25°39'·24W ✸✸✸♀♀♀♀✿✿✿

CHARTS AC 1950, 1895; PC 41101, 43103, 46406, 47502; SHOM 1323.

TIDES MHWS 1·7M; MHWN 1·3M; MLWN 0·7M; MLWS 0·3M.

SHELTER Good inside the high and substantial bkwtr, but in strong E-S winds a heavy swell enters. ⚓ is allowed, but not encouraged, at the W end of the hbr in 8-10m on sand and well clear of any WIP. The marina extension was opened in 2009 and provides 670 berths, reports welcome.

NAVIGATION WPT 37°44'·27N 25°39'·12W, where the W sectors of the 309° and 262° Dir lts intersect; thence 284°/4ca to present marina ent.

LIGHTS AND MARKS See 9.24.25 for details of 2 new Directional lts (in lieu of former ldg lts) and 2 other revised lts. The 300-1100m high island is easily seen from afar. Conspic marks include the W twr + R bands on bkwtr head and the Solmar bldg, a white 22 storey hotel, close W of the marina. The marina is now lit and all temp'y lts removed.

TELEPHONE (Code 295). Port HM 540000; Maritime Police via HM; Medical emergency 112; 田 212122 @ Praia da Vitória; Praia da Vitória marina ☎ 512082; Brit Consul see 9.24.30.

FACILITIES Angra do Heroísmo (Angra) is a handsome city, a fine natural hbr and a UNESCO World Heritage Site since 1983.

Marina has 3·4m, but less at the NW end. From the ent, reception is due N: ☎ 216304. marina.angra@japah.pt 150 inc 60 ♥ (18m max LOA), approx €1.10 inc AC; ♥ finger berths usually on adjacent 'G' pontoon. BH (50 ton), ME, El, Ⓔ, BY, CH, Gaz, Gas, ▣, SM, D at reception pontoon. Mail pick-up from Marina, Código Postal 9700-154, Angra do Heroísmo, Terceira, Açores, Portugal.

Angra YC (Porto Pipas mole) welcomes visitors.

Town ✉, Ⓑ+ATM, ⌨. Lajes ✈ (25km), direct to UK.

Praia da Vitória, 38°43'·40N 27°03'·00W is a commercial hbr with a friendly marina at its N end. WIP 2006 to rebuild the storm-damaged N mole. Lajes airport 5km N is handy for crew changes.

R/T *Marina* Ch **62**, 16 (0900-1830 M-Fri; 0900-1730 Sat/Sun).

Ponta Delgada MRCC only accepts safety and distress calls. It broadcasts weather and nav bulletins VHF Ch 11 in Portuguese; see Chapters 5 & 6 for times and content. ☎ 281777; mrcc.delgada@mail.telepac.pt

TELEPHONE (Code 296). Port HM 205240; Emergency 112; 田 203000; see marina for doctors, dentists; Brit Consul ☎ 628175; Rua Domingos Rebelo 43A, 9500-234 Ponta Delgada.

FACILITIES Marina de Pêro de Teive (3·5m-8m) ☎ 281510/11/12. marinapdl@apsm.pt www.marina.jappdl.pt 670 inc ♥, approx €1.20 inc AC. Reception pontoon and D & P are N side of ent; best to fill up on arrival. Slip, BH (25 ton), Diver, ME, El, Ⓔ, BY, CH, Gaz, Gas via HM, ▣, SM.

Mail pick-up: c/o Marina de Ponta Delgada, Aptdo 3 - Calheta, 9500 Ponta Delgada, São Miguel, Açores, Portugal.

Clube Naval de Ponta Delgada (E of marina) welcomes visitors: Bar, R. ☎ 283005. cnpdl@mail.telepac.pt www.cnpdl.pt

City ✉, Ⓑ+ATM, ⌨, 田. ✈ 4km W: flights direct to Gatwick, UK every Tues and daily via Lisboa to other European destinations.

South West Spain, Gibraltar & Morocco

Ayamonte to Europa Point and Ceuta

SW Spain & Gibraltar

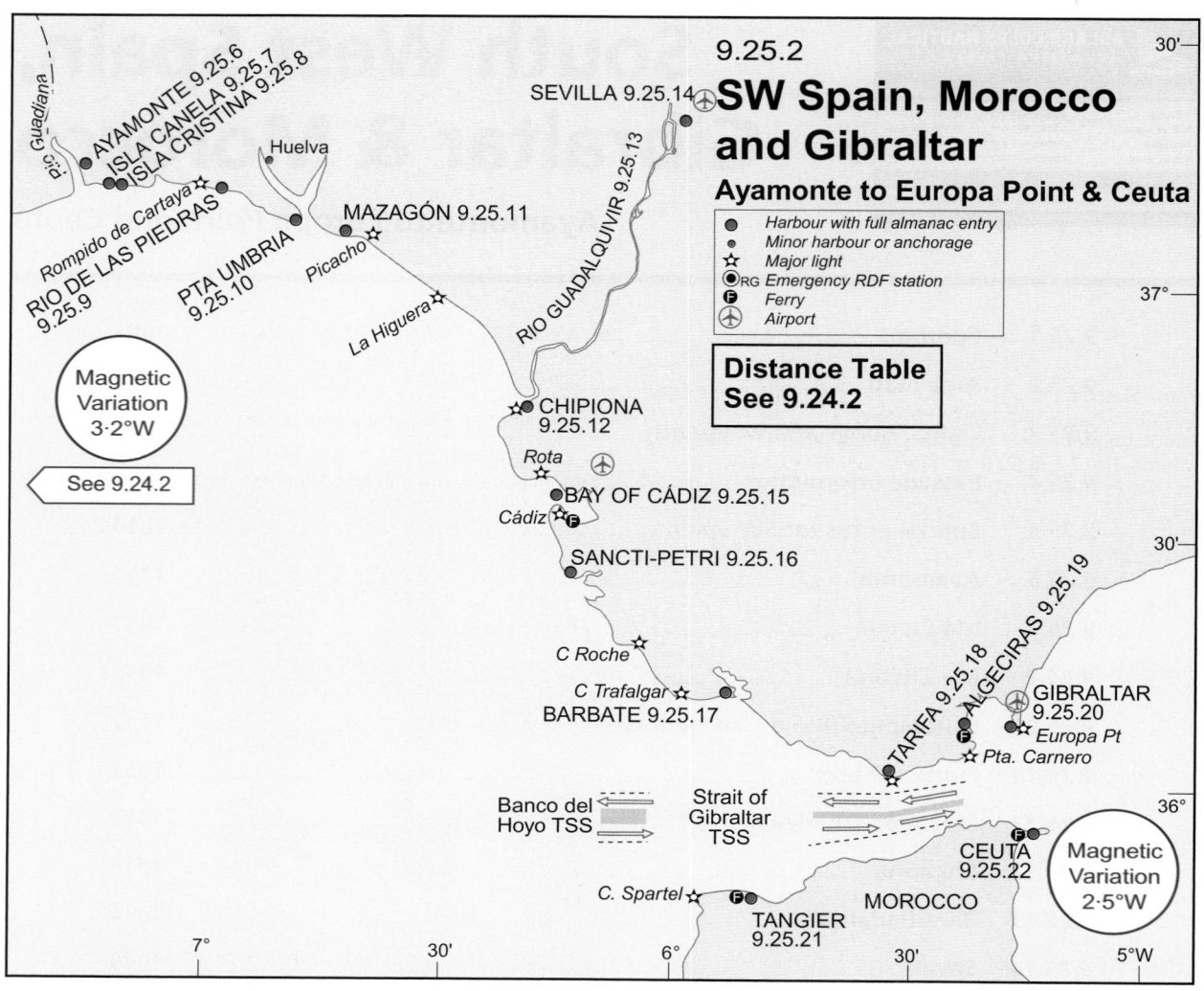

9.25.2
SW Spain, Morocco and Gibraltar
Ayamonte to Europa Point & Ceuta

- ● Harbour with full almanac entry
- • Minor harbour or anchorage
- ☆ Major light
- ⊚RG Emergency RDF station
- Ⓕ Ferry
- ✈ Airport

**Distance Table
See 9.24.2**

Magnetic Variation 3·2°W

See 9.24.2

Magnetic Variation 2·5°W

9.25.3 LIGHTS, BUOYS & WAYPOINTS

Bold print = light with a nominal range of 15M or more.
CAPITALS = place or feature. *CAPITAL ITALICS* = light-vessel, light float or Lanby. *Italics* = Fog signal. ***Bold italics*** = Racon. Abbreviations are in Chapter 1.

RIO GUADIANA TO SEVILLA

AYAMONTE (E side of Rio Guadiana)
No. 1 ◣ Fl (3) G 6s; 37°09'·00N 07°23'·35W.
No. 2 ◪ Fl R 4s; 37°08'·63N 07°23'·23W.
E trng wall ≴ Fl(3) G 9s 4M; 37°10'·07N 07°23'·64W.
W trng wall ≴ Fl R 3s 4M; 37°09'·77N 07°23'·93W (Portugal).
Vila Real de Santo Antònio ☆ Fl 6·5s 51m **26M**; W ○ twr, B bands; 37°11'·20N 07°24'·91W (Portugal).
Marina ent, ≴ QR and ≴ QG; 37°12'·70N 07°24'·54W.
Baluarte (ferry landing), Fl G 3s 2m 3M; 37°12'·88N 07°24'·56W.

ISLA CANELA and ISLA CRISTINA
Appr ⸹ Fl 10s 5M; 37°10'·51N 07°19'·49W.
W mole hd ≴ VQ (2) R 5s 9m 4M; 37°10'·83N 07°19'·60W.
Ldg lts 313°; framework twrs. Front ≴ Q 8m 5M; 37°11'·58N 07°20'·34W approx. Rear ≴ Fl 4s 13m 5M, 100m from front.
Isla Canela marina ent, QR and QG; 37°11'·40N 07°20'·26W.
Isla Cristina marina ent, QR and QG; 37°11'·89N 07°19'·65W.

RIO DE LAS PIEDRAS
El Rompido ☆ Fl (2) 10s 41m **24M**; W twr, B bands; 37°13'·12N 07°07'·72W, 4M WNW of the bar buoy.
No 1 Bar ⸹ L Fl 10s; 37°11'·71N 07°02'·34W approx. Lateral lt buoys are moved to mark the shifting chan; see chartlet.

RIA DE HUELVA
Punta Umbria, ⸹ L Fl 10s; 37°08'·78N 06°56'·74W.
No. 1 ⸹ Fl (2) G 10s; 37°09'·13N 06°56'·58W. No. 2 ⸹ Fl (2) R 10s.
Bkwtr hd ≴ VQ (6) + L Fl 10s 8m 5M; 37°09'·85N 06°56'·93W.
No. 3 ⸹ Fl (3) G 15s; 37°09'·70N 06°56'·40W. No. 4 ⸹ Fl (3) R 15s.
No. 5 ⸹ Fl (4) G 15s; 37°10'·10N 06°56'·60W. No. 6 ⸹ Fl (4) R 15s. No. 7 ⸹ Fl G 5s; 37°10'·50N 06°57'·00W. No. 8 ⸹ Fl R 5s.
Marina anti-pollution boom, S hd, Fl (2) R 10s 1M; 37°10'·81N 06°57'·34W. N head, Fl (3) R 15s 1M; 37°10'·88N 06°57'·44W.

Tanker mooring ⇌ Fl (4) Y 20s 8M; *Siren Mo (E) 30s*; 37°04'·79N 06°55'·59W. Oil pipeline N'ward marked by 3 Y ⸹s, Fl (4) Y 20s.

Huelva, main chan, Dir ≴ 339·2°, WRG 59m 8M; 337·5°- Fl G-338°-FG-338·6°-OcG-339·1°-FW-339·3°-OcR-339·8°-FR-340·4°-Fl R-340·9°; W twr; 37°08'·57N 06°50'·67W, 8ca NW of marina ent.
⸹ Q (9) 15s; 37°05'·55N 06°49'·11W.
No. 1 Fl G 5s; 37°06'·34N 06°49'·49W.
No. 2 ⸹ Fl R 5s; 37°06'·22N 06°49'·65W.
Juan Carlos I bkwtr hd ≴ Fl (3+1) WR 20s 29m, W12M, R9M; 165°-W-100°-R-125°; ***Racon K, 12M***; 37°06'·48N 06°49'·94W.

Plot waypoints on chart before use

No. 3 ⚲ Fl (2) G 10s; 37°06'·90N 06°49'·75W.
No. 4 ⚲ Fl (2) R 10s; 37°06'·85N 06°49'·94W.
No. 5 ⚲ Fl (3) G 15s; 37°07'·54N 06°50'·06W.
No. 6 ⚲ Fl (3) R 15s; 37°07'·51N 06°50'·27W.
No. 7 ⚲ Fl (4) G 20s; 37°07'·79N 06°50'·27W.
No. 8 ⚲ Fl (4) R 20s; 37°07'·78N 06°50'·52W.

MAZAGÓN
Picacho lt ho ☆ Fl (2+4) 30s 52m **25M**; 37°08'·11N 06°49'·56W.
Marina, S bkwtr ⚲ QG 7m 2M; 37°07'·89N 06°50'·18W.
N bkwtr ⚲ QR 5m 2M; 37°07'·95N 06°50'·08W.
Inner ent, Fl G 5s 3m 1M and Fl R 5s 3m 1M.
⚲ Fl (2) 10s; 37°04'·30N 06°43'·71W, off Torre del Loro (ruins).
La Higuera ☆ Fl (3) 20s 45m **20M**; 37°00'·51N 06°34'·18W.

CHIPIONA
Bajo Salmedina ⚲ Q (9) 15s 9m 5M; 36°44'·28N 06°28'·64W.
⚲ Fl (5) Y 20s; 36°44'·29N 06°28'·54W.
Pta de Chipiona ☆ Fl 10s 67m **25M**; 36°44'·26N 06°26'·52W.
Marina, No. 2 ⚲ Fl (2) R 7s; 36°45'·14N 06°25'·58W.
No. 4 ⚲ Fl (3) R 11s; 36°45'·05N 06°25'·51W.
N bkwtr head ⚲ Fl (2) G 10s 6m 5M; 36°44'·96N 06°25'·69W.
N inner jetty ⚲ Fl (3) G 9s 2m 1M; 36°44'·89N 06°25'·77W.
SE side of ent ⚲ Fl (4) R 11s 3m 3M; 36°44'·89N 06°25'·70W.

RÍO GUADALQUIVIR
No. 1 ⚲ L Fl 10s; **Racon M, 10M**; 36°45'·74N 06°27'·02W.
No. 2 ⚲ Q (9) 10s; 36°47'·38N 06°26'·81W (1·6M N of No.1).
Ldg lts 068·9°, R/W chequered structures. Front ⚲ Q 28m 10M; 36°47'·84N 06°20'·23W. Rear, ⚲ Iso 4s 60m 10M; 0·6M apart.
Selected buoys in sequence as far as Bonanza:
No. 3 ⚲ Fl G 5s; 36°46'·16N 06°25'·36W.
No. 4 ⚲ Fl R 5s; 36°47'·33N 06°25'·40W.
No. 7 ⚲ Fl (3) G 10s; 36°46'·62N 06°24'·01W.
No. 8 ⚲ Fl (3) R 10s; 36°46'·68N 06°24'·10W.
No. 11 ⚲ Fl G 5s; 36°46'·96N 06°22'·90W.
No. 12 ⚲ Fl R 5s; 36°47'·05N 06°22'·93W.
No.13 ⚲ Fl (2) G 6s; 36°47'·13N 06°22'·35W.
No. 14 ⚲ Fl (2) R 6s; 36°47'·21N 06°22'·38W.
No.17 ⚲ Fl (4) G 12s; 36°47'·47N 06°21'·22W.
No. 20 ⚲ Fl R 5s; 36°47'·81N 06°20'·70W.
Bonanza lt ho Fl 5s 22m 6M; R twr; 36°48'·17N 06°20'·15W.
Up-stream the river is marked by lt bcns, lt buoys and a few ldg lts.

SEVILLA
No. 52 ⚲ Fl (2+1) R 14·5s 9m 5M; 36°18'·97N 06°00'·83W, RGR structure. Fork stbd to city centre via lock, or port for Gelves marina, ent Fl R 5s (37°20'·43N 06°01'·40W) and Fl G 3s.

CADIZ TO CABO TRAFALGAR
ROTA (Clockwise around the Bay of Cadiz)
Bajo El Quemado ⚲ Fl (2) R 9s; 36°35'·88N 06°23'·95W.
Rota Aero ☆ Alt Fl WG 9s 79m **17M**; R/W chequered water twr on 8 cols, conspic; 36°38'·13N 06°20'·834W.
Rota ⚲ Oc 4s 33m 13M; W ○ lt ho, R band; 36°36'·95N 06°21'·43W.
Marina, S pier ⚲ Fl (3) R 10s 8m 9M; 36°36'·86N 06°21'·04W.
N pier ⚲ FG; G post; 36°36'·91N 06°21'·10W.
Las Cabezuelas ⚲ Fl (4) R 10s; 36°35'·21N 06°19'·95W.

PUERTO SHERRY and PUERTO DE SANTA MARIA
La Galera ⚲ Q; 36°34'·53N 06°17'·64W.
Puerto Sherry marina, S bkwtr ⚲ Oc R 4s 4M; 36°34'·64N 06°15'·25W. N bkwtr ⚲ Oc G 5s 3M. Basin ent, QR and QG.
Santa María ldg lts 040°: Front ⚲ QG 16m 4M; 36°35'·77N 06°13'·35W. Rear ⚲ Iso G 4s 20m 4M; 253m from front.
W trng wall head ⚲ Fl R 5s 10m 3M; 36°34'·35N 06°14'·95W.
W trng wall root ⚲ QR 5m 2M; 36°35'·11N 06°14'·11W.
E trng wall ⚲ Fl (2) G 7s 9m 3M; 36°34'·68N 06°14'·39W.
E bkwtr ⚲ Q (9) 15s 3M; 36°34'·46N 06°14'·35W.

CÁDIZ CITY and PUERTO AMERICA
Castillo de San Sebastián ☆ Fl (2) 10s 38m **25M**; twr on castle; *Horn Mo (N) 20s*; 36°31'·70N 06°18'·97W.
Bajos de San Sebastián ⚲ Q (9) 15s; 36°31'·30N 06°20'·36W.
⚲ L Fl 10s; for Canal Principal; 36°33'·90N 06°19'·88W.
No. 1 ⚲ Fl G 3s; 36°33'·12N 06°19'·07W.
No. 3 ⚲ Fl (2) G 4s; 36°33'·18N 06°18'·16W.
No. 4 ⚲ Fl (2) R 4s; 36°33'·54N 06°17'·93W.
No. 5 ⚲ Fl (3) G 13s; 36°33'·03N 06°17'·40W.
No. 6 ⚲ Fl R 10s; 36°33'·39N 06°17'·19W.
Spur N of S. Felipe ⚲ Fl (4) G 10s 10m 3M; 36°32'·72N 06°16'·79W.
San Felipe mole ⚲ Fl G 3s 10m 5M; G twr; 36°32'·57N 06°16'·77W.
E mole ⚲ Fl R 2s 11m 5M; 36°32'·44N 06°16'·63W.
Puerto America, NE bkwtr ⚲ Fl (4) G 16s 1M; G twr; 36°32'·47N 06°16'·94W.
Real Club Nautico pier ⚲ FG; 36°32'·35N 06°17'·13W.
International Free Zone hbr: No. 1 ⚲ Fl (3) G 9s; 36°30'·66N 06°15'·45W. **Puerto Elcano** marina ent 36°30'·08N 06°15'·45W.

SANCTI PETRI
Punta del Arrecife ⚲ Q (9) 15s 7m 3M; 36°23'·73N 06°13'·51W.
Sancti Petri castle ⚲ Fl 3s 18m 9M; twr; 36°22'·76N 06°13'·29W.
Ldg lts 050°: Front ⚲ Fl 5s 12m 6M; 36°22'·91N 06°12'·24W.
Rear ⚲ Oc (2) 6s 16m 6M.
No. 1 ⚲ Fl (3) G 9s; 36°22'·50N 06°12'·93W.
No. 2 ⚲ Fl (3) R 9s; 36°22'·46N 06°12'·81W.
No. 3 ⚲ Fl (4) G 11s; 36°22'·64N 06°12'·65W.
No. 4 ⚲ Fl (4) R 11s; 36°22'·66N 06°12'·71W.
Inner ldg lts 346·5°: Front ⚲ Fl 5s 11m 6M. Rear ⚲ Oc (2) 6s 21m.
⚲ Fl G 5s 8m 2M; 36°23'·10N 06°12'·65W; and ⚲ Fl R 5s 8m 2M.
Cabo Roche ☆ Fl (4) 24s 44m **20M**; 36°17'·74N 06°08'·41W.
Cabo Trafalgar ☆ Fl (2+1) 15s 50m **22M**; 36°10'·97N 06°02'·09W.

THE GIBRALTAR STRAIT
BARBATE
Barbate lt ho ⚲ Fl (2) WR 7s 22m, W10M, R7M; 281°-W-015°-R-095°; W ○ twr, R bands; 36°11'·22N 05°55'·42W.
SW mole ⚲ Fl R 4s 11m 5M; 36°10'·79N 05°55'·55W.
Inner NE mole ⚲ Fl (2) G 7s 7m 2M; 36°10'·95N 05°55'·79W.
Marina ent, Fl (2+1) R 21s 2M (anti-oil boom) and Fl R 4s 2M.
△-shaped tunny net, N end, ⚲ Q (Mar-Sep); 36°10'·72N 05°55'·39W (1ca E of hbr ent). Other marks clockwise:
⚲ Q (3) 10s (Mar-Sep); 36°08'·89N 05°55'·39W.
⚲ VQ (6) + L Fl 12s (Jul-Sep); 36°08'·07N 05°55'·07W.
⚲ VQ (6) + L Fl 12s (Mar-Jun); 36°08'·82N 05°57'·12W.
⚲ VQ (9) 10s (Mar-Sep); 36°09'·20N 05°56'·00W, centre of net.
Torre de Gracia ⚲ Oc (2) 5s 74m 13M; 36°05'·39N 05°48'·57W.
Pta Paloma ⚲ Oc WR 5s 44m, W10M, R7M; 010°-W-340°-R-010°, over Bajo de Los Cabezos; 36°03'·84N 05°43'·19W.

TARIFA
Tarifa ☆ Fl (3) WR 10s 40m **W26M, R18M**; 113°-W-089°-R-113°; W twr; *Siren Mo (O) 60s*; **Racon C, 20M**; 36°00'·05N 05°36'·59W.
Lado E ⚲ Fl R 5s 12m 3M; 36°00'·23N 05°36'·38W.
Outer SE mole ⚲ Fl G 5s 11m 5M; vis 249°-045°; G twr with statue of Virgin Mary; 36°00'·39N 05°36'·21W.
Inner S mole ⚲ Fl (2) R 6s 7m 1M; 36°00'·51N 05°36'·16W.

ALGECIRAS
Pta Carnero ☆ Fl (4) WR 20s 42m, **W16M**, R13M; 018°-W -325°-R-018°; *Siren Mo (K) 30s*; 36°04'·63N 05°25'·56W.
⚲ Q (3) 10s; 36°06'·73N 05°24'·76W, 1·2M ESE of marina ent.
Darsena del Saladillo (marina), outer approach buoys: ⚲ Q (2) G 7s; 36°07'·18N 05°25'·83W. ⚲ Q (3) G 9s; 36°07'·19N 05°25'·97W. ⚲ Q (2) R 7s; 36°07'·07N 05°25'·73W.
Marina, outer S jetty ⚲ Q (3) R 9s 7m 3M; 36°07'·11N 05°26'·11W.
N jetty ⚲ Q (4) G 11s 2m 1M; 36°07'·13N 05°26'·22W.
Inner S jetty ⚲ Fl (4) R 11s 2m 3M; 36°07'·14N 05°26'·28W.

LA LÍNEA

⚓ Fl (3) R 6s; 36°09'·56N 05°21'·98W.
⚓ Fl (3) G 6s; 36°09'·52N 05°22'·00W.
Dique de Abrigo ⚓ Fl (2) G 7s 8m 4M; 36°09'·51N 05°22'·05W.
Marina ent jetty ⚓ QR 7m 2M; 36°09'·56N 05°21'·67W.

GIBRALTAR

Aero ⚓ Mo (GB) R 10s 405m **30M**; 36°08'·57N 05°20'·59W.
Europa Pt ☆ Iso 10s 49m **19/15M**; vis 197°-042° and 067°-125°;
W○twr, R band; 36°06'·58N 05°20'·69W. Also ⚓ FR 44m **15M**; 042°-
067°; *Horn 20s*. Same twr, same vis arc, ⚓ Oc R 10s 49m **15M**.
'A' Head ☆ Fl 2s 18m **15M**; *Horn 10s*; 36°08'·03N 05°21'·85W.
Queensway Quay marina, N ent ⚓ FR/FG, 36°08'·16N 05°21'·39W.
Coaling Island, SW corner ⚓ 2 FR (vert); 36°08'·19N 05°21'·46W.
'B' head ⚓ QR 9m 5M; 36°08'·14N 05°21'·84W.
'C' head ⚓ QG 10m 5M; 36°08'·54N 05°22'·04W.
'D' head ⚓ QR 18m 5M; 36°08'·65N 05°21'·95W.
'E' head ⚓ FR 28m 5M; twr; 36°08'·90N 05°21'·95W.
Runway threshold, both sides, VQ occas; 36°09'·01N 05°21'·59W.

Cap Spartel ☆ Fl (4) 20s 92m **30M**; Y □ twr; *Dia (4) 90s*;
35°47'·47N 05°55'·43W.

TANGIER

Monte Dirección (Le Charf) ☆ Oc (3) WRG 12s 88m **W16M**, R12M,
G11M; 140°-G-174·5°-W-200°-R-225°; 35°45'·98N 05°47'·35W.
N bkwtr ⚓ Fl (3) 12s 20m 14M; 35°47'·47N 05°47'·60W.
SE mole ⚓ Oc (2) R 6s 7m 6M; 35°47'·29N 05°47'·87W.
Jetée desYachts ⚓ Iso G 4s 6m 6M; 35°47'·23N 05°48'·14W.
Pta Malabata ☆ Fl 5s 77m **22M**. W □ twr; 35°48'·99N 05°44'·92W.
Ksar es Srhir ⚓ Fl (4) 12s 8m 8M; 35°50'·91N 05°33'·67W.
Pta Círes ⚓ Fl (3) 12s 44m **18M**; 060°-330°; 35°54'·42N 05°28'·89W.

CEUTA (Spanish enclave)

Punta Almina ⚓ Fl (2) 10s 148m 22M; 35°53'·90N 05°16'·85W.
W pier ⚓ Fl G 5s 13m 5M; *Siren 15s*; **Racon O, 12M**; 35°53'·75N
05°18'·68W.
E pier ⚓ Fl R 5s 13m 5M; vis 245°-210°; 35°53'·73N 05°18'·47W.
05°18'·90W.
Marina ent, N bkwtr ⚓ Fl (4) R 11s 8m 1M; 35°53'·45N 05°18'·90W.
Marina ent, S bkwtr elbow and S bkwtr head: two synchronised
⚓ Fl (4) G 11s 6/5m 1M; 35°53'·42N 05°18'·94W and 65m ESE.

9.25.4   PASSAGE INFORMATION

More Passage Information is threaded between successive
harbours in this Area.

Bibliography. *SW Spain and Portugal Cruising Companion* (Jens/
Nautical Data Ltd) covers Bayona to Gibraltar. *W Coasts of Spain
and Portugal Pilot* (Admiralty, NP 67) covers Cabo Ortegal to
Gibraltar.

The Straits Handbook by Colin Thomas of Straits Sailing (☎
+35051372) is very informative and enjoyable reading. It covers
Gibraltar and Spanish ports from Chipiona to Benalmadena on the
Med coast; also Ceuta and Marina Smir in Morocco.

PORTUGUESE BORDER TO RIO GUADALQUIVIR

(AC 93) On the Spanish bank of the Rio Guadiana **Ayamonte** has
a marina, the most W'ly of 16 modern marinas in SW Andalucía;
see Special Notes below.

4M to the E, Isla Canela W bank and Isla Cristina E bank of Ria de
la Higuerita both have marinas. 13M further E, Rio de las Piedras
requires care on entry due to shifting shoals and bar, but is a
peaceful river with a marina at El Rompido. S of Huelva there are
marinas at Punta Umbria and Mazagón (AC 73). Keep clear of
commercial ships going to/from Huelva.

About 30M SE is the mouth of the Rio Guadalquivir (AC 85),
navigable 54M to Sevilla. Caution: NW of the estuary large fish
havens in shoal waters extend 5M offshore. Chipiona marina is a
good place to check the latest info for the passage to and lock
times at Sevilla; and to time your departure so as to carry a fair
tide and synchronise your arrival with lock and bridge opening
hours.

9.25.5   SPECIAL NOTES FOR SW SPAIN

Regions/Provinces: Spain is divided into 17 autonomous regions,
eg Andalucía. Most regions are sub-divided into provinces, eg
in Atlantic Andalucía: Huelva, Sevilla and Cadiz. The province is
shown below the name of each main port.

Language: This Almanac recognises regional differences, but
in the interests of standardisation uses the spelling of Castilian
Spanish where practicable.

Spanish Charts (SC): Contact Instituto Hidrográfico de la Marina,
Plaza San Severiano 3, 11007 Cádiz, ☎ (956) 599 414; www.armada.
mde.es/ihm Or order from chart agents in Madrid, Huelva, Sevilla,
Cadiz and Algeciras, also larger UK chart agents.

Standard Time in Spain is UT –1, but in Portugal it is UT.

Spanish secondary ports referenced to Lisboa: Time differences

for these Spanish ports (all down to Barbate), when applied to the
printed times of HW and LW for Lisboa (UT), give HW and LW times
in Spanish Standard Time. Add DST, when applicable.

Telephone: To call Spain from UK dial 00-34, then the area code,
followed by the ☎ number. To call UK from Spain, dial 07-44, then
area code, less the initial 0, then the ☎ number.

Emergencies: ☎ 900 202 202 for Fire, Police and Ambulance. *Rioja
Cruz* (Red Cross) operate LBs.

Public Holidays: Jan 1, 6; Apr 10 (Good Friday); 1 May (Labour Day);
June 11 (Corpus Christi); Aug 15 (Assumption); Oct 12 (National
Day); Nov 1 (All Saints Day); Dec 6, 8 (Immaculate Conception), 25.

Representation: Spanish Tourist Office, 22-23 Manchester Sq,
London W1U 3PX; ☎ 020 7486 8077. londres@tourspain.es www.
tourspain.uk

British Embassy, Calle de Fernando el Santo 16, 28010 Madrid; ☎
(91) 524 9700. There are Brit Consuls at Cadiz ☎ 956 264479 and
at Sevilla via Malaga ☎ 952 352300.

Buoyage: IALA Region A system is used. Preferred chan buoys
(RGR, Fl (2+1) R and GRG, Fl (2+1) G) are quite widely used.

Documents: Spain, although an EU member, still checks papers.
This can be a time-consuming, repetitive and inescapable process.
The only palliatives are courtesy, patience and good humour.
Organise your papers to include:

Personal – Passports; crew list, ideally on headed paper with the
yacht's rubber stamp, giving DoB, passport nos, where joined/
intended departure. Certificate of Competence (Yachtmaster
Offshore, ICC/HOCC etc). Radio Operator's certificate. EHIC
(advised for medical treatment).

Yacht – Registration certificate, Part 1 or SSR. Proof of VAT status.
Marine insurance. Ship's Radio licence. Itinerary, backed up by
ship's log.

Currency is the Euro €. VAT (IVA) 16%.

Marina fees: Marinas run by or linked to the Andalucían Junta
(www.eppa.es), ie all but Algeciras, charge on average €1·94/m
LOA (2009) inc 16% VAT in season (1/6-30/9); low season 50% less.

Fuel: Diesel (*Gasoleo*) is of two types: *Gasoleo A* is taxed and
available from marina pumps or by cans from a filling station
ashore. *Gasoleo B* is untaxed and usually only available to FVs.

Travel: UK ferries from/to Santander and Bilbao.

Direct UK flights from Jerez, Sevilla, Madrid, Malaga & Gibraltar.

Internal flights via Madrid to Jerez, Sevilla and Malaga.

Buses are usually good and trains adequate, except in the more
remote regions.

9.25.6 AYAMONTE

Huelva **37°12'·70N 07°24'·50W** ❁❁⚓⚓☆☆

CHARTS AC 93; SC 440, 440A; PC 24206, 26312.

TIDES
Standard Port LISBOA (◀▶); ML 1·8

Times				Height (metres)			
High Water		Low Water		MHWS	MHWN	MLWN	MLWS
0500	1000	0500	1100	3·8	2·9	1·5	0·6
1700	2200	1700	2300				
Differences AYAMONTE							
+0005	+0015	+0025	+0045	−0·7	−0·5	−0·1	−0·2
RÍA DE HUELVA, BAR							
0000	+0015	+0035	+0030	−0·1	−0·5	−0·1	−0·4

SHELTER Good in marina on E bank of Rio Guadiana (9.24.23).

NAVIGATION WPT 37°09'·00N 07°23'·35W (No 1 SHM buoy, Q (3) G 6s), 340°/9ca to hd of W trng wall. Least depth over bar 2·5m. See 9.24.23 for chartlet, lts and directions up-river. Sanlucar, 20M up Rio Guadiana, is accessible on the flood.

LIGHTS AND MARKS High bldgs, FR lts, are 3M WNW of ent. White suspension bridge 2M inland is visible from seaward. Vila Real lt ho, W ○ tr, B bands, is 1·5M S. ☆ Fl G 5s, 350m N of marina, marks ferry berths. See also 9.25.3 for lt details.

R/T Marina Ch 09 (H24).

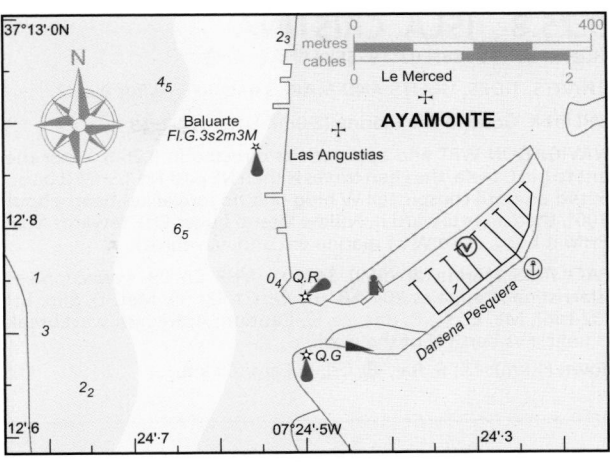

TELEPHONE (Code 959). Huelva MRSC ☎ 243000.

FACILITIES Marina (1·5m-2·0m) is W'most of 9 marinas run by Junta de Andalucía, www.eppa.es. ayamonted@eppa.es ☎ 321694. 317 inc ♥ in 3·5m, €1·93. D (pontoon to port just inside ent). ⊖, Met, Slip, ME, El, ✗, R, Bar, YC, ▣.

Town: 🛒, R, Bar, ⑧, ✉. Ferries to Vila Real de Santo António. Bus Huelva (60 km); ✈ Faro (48 km).

9.25.7 ISLA CANELA

Huelva **37°11'·24N 07°20'·45W**
❁❁⚓⚓☆☆☆

CHARTS AC 93; SC 440, 440A.

TIDES Use Differences AYAMONTE (9.25.6)

SHELTER Good in the marina (2·0m), but little room to ⚓. The appr is open to SE'lies.

NAVIGATION Isla Canela and Isla Cristina share a common outer approach into Ría de la Higuerita. Best appr at half-flood, when drying sand banks can be seen.

WPT 37°10'·51N 07°19'·46W (SWM buoy, Fl 10s, off chartlet), 000°/4ca to W mole head, where depth is 1·2m. Pick up the 313° ldg lts. After 7ca between trng walls, for Isla Canela marina turn 90° port between QR and QG lights.

See 9.25.8 for continuation to Isla Cristina.

LIGHTS AND MARKS Ldg lts (front Q 7m 5M; rear Fl 4s 12m 5M) aligned 313° between the W mole head, VQ (2) R 5s 9m 4M, and the covering trng wall to stbd. The powerful lt, Fl 6·5s 51m **26M** at Vila Real de Santo António is 4M to the W.

R/T Marina Ch 09.

TELEPHONE (Code 959) Huelva MRSC ☎ 243000; Brit Consul ☎ 952 352300.

FACILITIES Marina ☎ 479000. www.marina-islacanela.com 231 AB inc ♥, max LOA 12m, €2.23. ✗, BH (32 ton), C (2 ton), CH, ⊖, Met. **Town:** 🛒, R, Bar, ⑧, ✉; infrequent bus Ayamonte (17 km); ✈ Faro (65 km).

9.25.8 ISLA CRISTINA

Huelva **37°11'·88N 07°19'·65W** ✿✿♦♦♦✿✿

CHARTS, TIDES, LIGHTS AND MARKS and **R/T** As for 9.25.7.

SHELTER Good in the marina (2·0m). Little space to ⚓.

NAVIGATION WPT and approach as directed in 9.25.6. After the ent to Isla Canela, the chan curves N then NE past No 1 SHM lt buoy. Stand on until conspic tall W bldg (a lt ho lookalike) bears about 100°, then alter toward it. Follow lateral buoys ENE towards No 2 PHM lt buoy, close W of marina ent and wavebreak.

FACILITIES Marina ☎ (959) 343501. VHF Ch 09. www.eppa.es islacristinad@eppa.es 204 AB, inc ♥, €1·93. ⊖, Met, D, Slip, BH (32 ton), ME, El, ✖, R, Bar, Ice, ▣. Caution: Anti-wash wavebreak is unlit. FVs berth N of the marina.

Town (1 km): 🛒, R, Bar, Ⓑ, ✉; ✈ Faro (65 km).

9.25.9 EL ROMPIDO (RIO DE LAS PIEDRAS)

Huelva **37°13'·00N 07°07'·72W** (Marina) ✿♦♦✿✿✿

> **Caution:** approach buoys and shoals are believed to lie further west. Call marina Ch 71 for latest information.

CHARTS AC 93; SC 440, 441A. **TIDES** As for 9.25.5.

SHELTER Good in lee of sand dunes. Do not enter in strong onshore winds. Tidal streams may exceptionally exceed 2kn.

NAVIGATION WPT No. 1 landfall ('recalada') ⚓, 37°11'·73N 07°02'·24W reported Aug 2008. Note: Bar (0·4m) and shoals may have shifted from their charted position. Lateral buoys 2-11 are moved as required. Visit the website below for the latest positions or call HM on VHF or mobile before entry. Access approx HW ±2. Puerto El Terron 37°13'·50N 07°10'·49W is shallow (<1·2m).

FACILITIES Marina ☎ (959) 399614. www.puertoelrompido.com varadero@vianwe.com. VHF Ch 71. 331 AB inc ♥ €2.02. Free berthing help is available on request and in bad conditions is recommended. All berths are aligned fore & aft with the tidal stream. Wi-Fi. BY ☎ 399026, ME, El. Fuel ☎ 6209 22969, 0800-2000 daily in summer. **Puerto El Terron** ☎ 382225. VHF Ch 09. 32 AB limited ♥. 🛒, R, Bar, ✉Ⓦ YC, 6ca E, ☎ 399349, Bar, R.

Village R, Bar. Golf/beach resort is adjacent.

> **Caution:** This chartlet is sourced from local plans and aerial photos, due to lack of large scale Spanish and UKHO chart coverage. It is believed to be generally correct

9.25.10 PUNTA UMBRIA

Huelva **37°10'·89N 06°57'·48W** ✲✲♨♨❀❀

CHARTS As for 9.25.11.

TIDES As for 9.25.5. Tidal streams are strong and arrival near slack water will assist berthing.

SHELTER Good, but FV wash can be disruptive.

NAVIGATION WPT 37°08'·78N 06°56'·74W (off chartlet), ⚓ L Fl 10s, 000°/1M via Nos 1 & 2 buoys to bkwtr hd (1·1m). Thence the chan is marked by Nos 3-9 lateral lt buoys. 2M SE of ent 4 ⚓s, Fl (4) Y 20s, mark a pipeline extending 5M SSW.

LIGHTS AND MARKS See 9.25.3 for positions of lights and ch bys.

R/T Marina Ch 06.

FACILITIES from seaward: **YC** ☎ (959) 311899, dark R bldg is 1M up-river: temp'y AB on pontoon or possible M. **Punta Umbria Marina** ☎ 314304. www.eppa.es 192 AB inc Ⓥ in 6m, max LOA 12m, €1·93. Badly affected by FV wash. D&P, ME, El, ✕. **Punta Umbria RCN Marina** is 5ca further up-river. Privately run, limited space for Ⓥ, but more peaceful than downstream. **Town**: R, Bar, 🛒, 🖂.

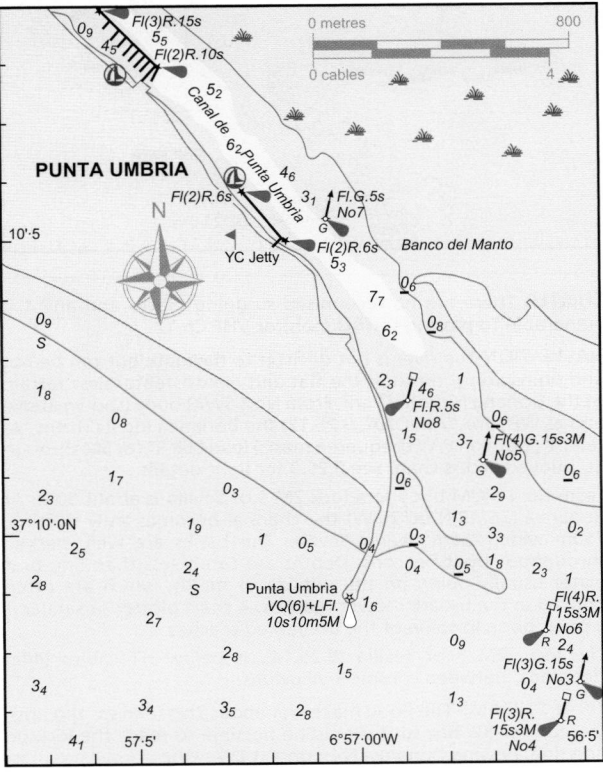

9.25.11 MAZAGÓN

Huelva **37°07'·92N 06°50'·13W** (Marina ent) ✲✲✲♨♨❀❀

CHARTS AC 91, 93, 73; SC 441, 4411; SHOM 6862, 7300

TIDES See 9.25.5 (Ría de Huelva, Bar); ML 1·8.

SHELTER Good in marina (overleaf), entered hdg ESE down-river.

NAVIGATION WPT 37°05'·55N 06°49'·11W, abm WCM buoy, Q (9) 15s (off chartlet), 339°/2·5M to marina. After the first pair of chan buoys (off chartlet), the straightforward appr is sheltered by a 7M long bkwtr.

At No 7 SHM buoy turn stbd to the marina ent; the deep, well lit, buoyed 339·2° channel diverges WNW into Huelva's industrial complex. Keep clear of large ships.

About 5M W of the WPT an oil pipe line runs N to a refinery. It is marked by an SBM and 3 SPM buoys, all Fl (4) Y 20s; keep 500m clear. ⚓ prohib within 500m either side of the line of buoys.

LIGHTS AND MARKS Dir lt 339·2° (off chartlet); W twr. The bkwtr hd has a W twr, R band. Picacho lt ho, W twr with R corners/R roofed bldg, is 5ca NE of marina (off chartlet). See 9.25.3 for lts.

R/T Marina Ch 09. Huelva Port Ch 06, 11, 12, **14**.

TELEPHONE (Code 959) MRCC ☎ (956) 684740; Brit Consul Sevilla via Malaga ☎ 952 352300.

FACILITIES in large, modern **Marina** (4m): ☎ 536251. mazagon@ eppa.es 647 AB inc Ⓥ, €1·93. P, D, Slip, BH (32 ton), ME, El, ✕, Ice, YC, Bar, R. ⮢ Huelva (24km); ✈ Sevilla (130km).

MAZAGÓN MARINA

CHIPIONA TO CAPE TRAFALGAR

Around Cadiz Bay (AC 86, 88) there are marinas at Rota, Puerto Sherry, Santa Maria and two in the hbr of Cádiz itself. S of Cádiz keep about 4M offshore on the 30m line to clear inshore banks. Sancti-Petri marina lies on a remote and interesting river with a slightly tricky approach.

Artificial reefs, which may reduce charted depths by approx 2·5m, are common from Cadiz to C. Trafalgar; see AC 93 & 142. Cabo Trafalgar may be rounded within 100m of the lt ho, inshore of a tidal race, or about 4M off to clear foul ground/shoals lying from SW to NW of the cape. Plans to build a wind farm (up to 500 turbines) about 2·5M off Cabo Trafalgar are strongly opposed by local fishermen.

Tunny nets are laid up to 7M offshore, usually marked by cardinal lt buoys. Positions vary each year, but the more established nets are laid:
- Very close off Barbate hbr 9.25.17, extending 2·7M S, Mar–Aug.
- Off Zahara beach (5M SE of Barbate) extending 1·7M SW to two WCM and one SCM lt buoys, Mar–Sep.
- 1M NW of Tarifa, to 1M SW, buoyed as Zahara, Mar–Jul.

9.25.12   CHIPIONA

Cádiz **36°44'·96N 06°25'·69W** (W bkwtr hd) ✿✿✿✿♦♦✿✿

CHARTS AC 85; SC 4421, 4422 (Sheets 2 and 3).

TIDES
Standard Port LISBOA (←); ML 1·9; see 9.25.13.

SHELTER Good in modern marina, but swell enters in NW gales.

NAVIGATION WPT 36°45'·74N 06°27'·02W, No 1 SWM buoy, L Fl 10s (Racon M), 125°/1·3M to marina ent. Caution: extensive fish havens with obstructions 2·5m high lie from 3·5M to 7·5M NW of the WPT. Same WPT is on the 068·9° ldg line for buoyed chan into Rio Guadalquivir (9.25.13).

LIGHTS AND MARKS Chipiona (Pta del Perro) lt ho is conspic 1M SW of marina. 1·7M W of this lt ho, the drying Bajo Salmedina (off chartlet) is marked by a WCM bcn twr and a SPM lt buoy which must be rounded if coming from S. Inside hbr bkwtr, the Fl (3) G 9s light, near FV berths, is not visible from seaward. See 9.25.3 for light details.

R/T Marina Ch 09. Port and Rio Guadalquivir Ch 12.

TELEPHONE (Code 956) MRCC ☎ 684740.

FACILITIES Marina ☎ 373844, chipiona@eppa.es 412 AB inc Ⓥ in 3·5m, €1.93. Ⓥ berth on fuel/reception hammerhead; larger yachts in first basin on port side. ⊖, Met, P, D, Slip, BH (32 ton), CH, ME, El, ✕, Bar, R, Ⓡ. FVs berth against the NW bkwtr.
Town: 🛒, R, Bar, ⑧, ✉. ⇌ and ✈ Jerez (32 km).

9.25.13   RIO GUADALQUIVIR

Huelva/Cádiz **36°45'·73N 06°27'·03W** (No 1 SWM buoy)

CHARTS AC 85 or SC 4422 (18 sheets, mostly 1:12,500), corrected up-to-date as buoys/bcns are liable to change.

TIDES
Standard Port LISBOA (←); ML 1·9

Times				Height (metres)			
High Water		Low Water		MHWS	MHWN	MLWN	MLWS
0500	1000	0500	1100	3·8	2·9	1·5	0·6
1700	2200	1700	2300				
Differences RIO GUADALQUIVIR, BAR (36°45'N 06°26'W)							
−0005	+0005	+0020	+0030	−0·6	−0·4	−0·2	−0·2
BONANZA (36°48'N 06°20'W)							
+0025	+0040	+0100	+0120	−0·8	−0·5	−0·4	−0·1
CORTA DE LOS JERONIMOS (37° 08'N 06°05'W, 16M S of Sevilla)							
+0210	+0230	+0255	+0345	−1·2	−0·8	−0·5	−0·1
SEVILLA							
+0400	+0430	+0510	+0545	−1·7	−1·1	−0·6	−0·1

SHELTER There are no recognised stopping places and any ⚓ is vulnerable to passing traffic; monitor VHF Ch 12.

NAVIGATION The river is not difficult to navigate but can be hot and uninspiring, through the flat and almost featureless terrain of the Doñana National Park. From No 1 SWM buoy (shown above and as WPT for CHIPIONA, 9.25.12) the Bonanza ldg lts (front, ▲; rear, ▼, both on R/W chequered masts) lead 068·9° for 5M through lit, buoyed access chan. See 9.25.3 for light details.

From No 1 SWM buoy to a lock 2M S of Sevilla is about 50M. At Bonanza (36°48'N 06°20'W) the channel becomes truly riverine, 750m wide; 250m nearer Sevilla. The banks are well marked throughout by lt beacons. Depths are rarely less than 5m, best water usually being on the outside of bends, which are often buoyed in the broader lower reaches. A chart plotter or similar is a great boon in some of the unmarked reaches.

The lock, 2M S of Sevilla (9.25.14), is below HT cables (44m clearance) between conspic R/W pylons.

TIDAL STREAMS The flood makes for about 7hrs (3kn sp, 1kn nps), the ebb for 5½ hrs; so it should be possible to reach the lock on one tide, passing Bonanza N-bound at LW −½hr.

9.25.14 SEVILLA

Sevilla **37°19'·86N 05°59'·74W** (Lock) ❄❄❄💧💧💧🏵🏵🏵

CHARTS & TIDES AC 85; SC 4422 (sheets 17/18). ML Sevilla 1·3M.

SHELTER Good; safe to over-winter. Very hot 40°C+ in summer.

NAVIGATION The lock, ☎ (954) 454196, opens Mon, Wed, Fri 1000, 2100, 2300; Tue, Thu 1000, 2100; Sat/Sun/Hols 1000, 1900, 2100LT; secure to ladders or diagonal rubber strips.

Delicias bridge (10·1m; ☎ (954) 247630) lifts Mon, Wed, Fri 2200; Sat/Sun/Hols 2000. 1 hr before ETA request passage Ch 12. R lts at lock & bridge = no go; Lock, Intens Fl W = enter; Bridge, G = pass.

R/T Marinas Ch 09. Lock, Port and Delicias bridge Ch 12.

TELEPHONE (Codes 954, 955) Brit Consul via Malaga ☎ 952 352300.

FACILITIES Gelves 37°20'·43N 06°01'·39W on the river, ie **not** accessed via the lock, therefore tidal; may silt. Overhead cables (16·5m) down-river; approx 3M from the city centre. ☎ (955) 761212. www.puertogelves.com 133+ ◐, €0.93, in about 3m, waiting pontoon. CH, ME, BH (25 ton), ▣, R, 🛒, Bar.
Marina Yachting Sevilla 37°19'·90N 05°59'·49W, 300m E of the lock almost below HT cables; a long pontoon in a quiet creek 3M from city; useful stop if waiting to transit Delicias bridge 2M N. ☎ (954) 230326. 400+ ◐, in 6m. Slip, ME, ▣.
Club Náutico de Sevilla 37°22'·18N 05°59'·60W, excellent facilities close to city centre; also possible AB on E quay. ☎ (954) 454777. www.nauticosevilla.com 100+ ◐, in 3m; pre-book €0.52/m²/day. Slip, R, Bar, Ice, ▣. **City:** All amenities, ⇌, ✈ 10 km.

9.25.15 BAY OF CÁDIZ

Cádiz **36°33'·91N 06°19'·88W** (SWM buoy) ❄❄❄💧💧💧🏵🏵🏵

CHARTS AC 93, 86, 88; SC 443, 443A, 443B, 4430, 4431, 4437.

TIDES
Standard Port LISBOA (←); ML 1·8

Times				Height (metres)			
High Water		Low Water		MHWS	MHWN	MLWN	MLWS
0500	1000	0500	1100	3·8	2·9	1·5	0·5
1700	2200	1700	2300				
Differences ROTA							
−0010	+0010	+0025	+0015	−0.7	−0.6	−0.4	−0.1
PUERTO DE SANTA MARIA							
+0006	+0006	+0027	+0027	−0.6	−0.4	−0.4	−0.1
PUERTO CÁDIZ							
0000	+0020	+0040	+0025	−0.5	−0.5	−0.3	0.0

SHELTER is good in the 4 marinas listed below, clockwise from N.

NAVIGATION Rota WPT 36°35'·97N 06°21'·01W, 000°/9ca to marina ent. Airfield lt (Al Fl WG 9s) and conspic water tank bear 004°/2·1M from WPT. From W/NW keep 1·5M offshore to clear shoals. Naval vessels may be at ⚓ S of Rota Naval base. Following a major storm, significant shoaling reported 2009, access being no better than HW±2hrs; keep to stbd (N bkwtr) side of ent chan.

Puerto Sherry WPT 36°33'·98N 06°15'·22W, 000°/7ca to marina entrance. Modern bldgs around the marina are conspic.

Puerto de Santa Maria same WPT as P. Sherry, 040°/1·7M to marina in canalised Rio Guadalete, dredged 4·5m. Ldg lts 040°: front, QG; rear Iso G 4s. From W, the N Chan trends ESE, inshore of shoals toward both marinas.

Puerto America (at N tip of Cádiz). WPT 36°32'·75N 06°16'·36W, 238°/0·5M to marina ent passing close S of Dique de San Felipe head. From S, keep to seaward of extensive shoals N & W of Cádiz. The S Chan (Canal del Sur) is not navigable for draft >2·5m. The shore is low-lying, but next to the marina a W bldg on Dique de San Felipe is conspic.

LIGHTS AND MARKS Lts/buoys as chartlets and 9.25.3. Conspic daymarks: Rota lt ho 33m, W twr/R band, at marina. Puerto Sherry, W bkwtr hd ○ twr. Cádiz city, golden-domed cathedral and radio twr (113m) close SE. Further SSE: Two power cable pylons (155m), dockyard cranes and long bridge to mainland.

R/T Marinas Ch 09. Cádiz Trafico **74**.

TELEPHONE (Code 956) Port HM 224011; ⊖ & Met via marinas (see below); Brit Consul 264479.

FACILITIES Rota Marina ☎ 840069, rota@eppa.es 509 AB, inc ◐ in 4·5m, €1.93. P, D, Slip, BH (32 ton), ME, El, C (5 ton).

Puerto Sherry ☎ 870103, www.puertosherry.com 753 AB, inc ◐, €2.31; 3·0-4·5m. P, D, Slip, BH (50 ton), ME, El, C, SM, Ⓔ, CH, ✕, ▣, R, Bar, YC ☎ 858751. Arrivals berth as chartlet.

Puerto de Santa Maria (RCN) ☎ 852527. rcnpuerto@ono.com www.rcnpsm.com Very pleasant Real Club Náutico has 250 AB + a few ◐ berths in 3·0- 8·0m; €2.98, pre-booking is not essential. 10 hammerhead pontoons (A-J) on NW bank plus two mid-stream pontoons. P, D, ✕, ME, C (5 ton), BH (25 ton), Slip, R, Bar. FVs berth up-river. Ferry to Cádiz.

Puerto América ☎ 223666, puertoamerica@eppa.es 253 AB, inc ◐ in 7·5m, €1.93. P, D, Slip, ME, El, C (10 ton).

Real Club Náutico de Cádiz A private basin close SW of Puerto America. ☎ 213262. www.cherrytel.com 160 AB in 3m. ◐ berths unlikely. D, good R, Bar.

Cadiz City: all amenities, ⇌; ✈ Jerez (25 km). Spanish Hydrographic Office (IHM) is at 36°31'·38N 06°17'·04W (1·5 miles from Puerto America): Plaza San Severiano 3, 11007 Cádiz; ☎ 599414. www.armada.mde.es/ihm

BAY OF CÁDIZ including marinas at: ROTA, PUERTO SHERRY, PUERTO DE SANTA MARIA and PUERTO AMERICA

9.25.16 SANCTI-PETRI

Cádiz **36°23′·80N 06°12′·55W** ✿❀♨♨✿✿

CHARTS AC 93; SC 443B, 4438.

TIDES Interpolate between differences Puerto Cádiz (9.25.15) and Cabo Trafalgar (9.25.17); ML No data.

SHELTER Good, except with swell and in S'lies. ⚓ or moor in stream, W of marina.

NAVIGATION WPT 36°22′·32N 06°13′·15W 050°/5ca to intercept 346·5° ldg line which leads between 4 lateral lt buoys. From 2nd pair of buoys track on the 346·5° ldg line for 6ca to the gateway formed by R/G columns (Fl R/G 5s 7m) which are easily seen. A night appr is not advised first-time.

Best appr at half-flood in fair vis; least charted depth 2·2m, but silting occurs. Sp ebb can be > 4kn. Swell and/or strong S'lies render the appr dangerous. El Arrecife, a long drying reef, and other shoals prevent a direct appr from W/NW. Tunny nets may be set about 9M SSE off Conil.

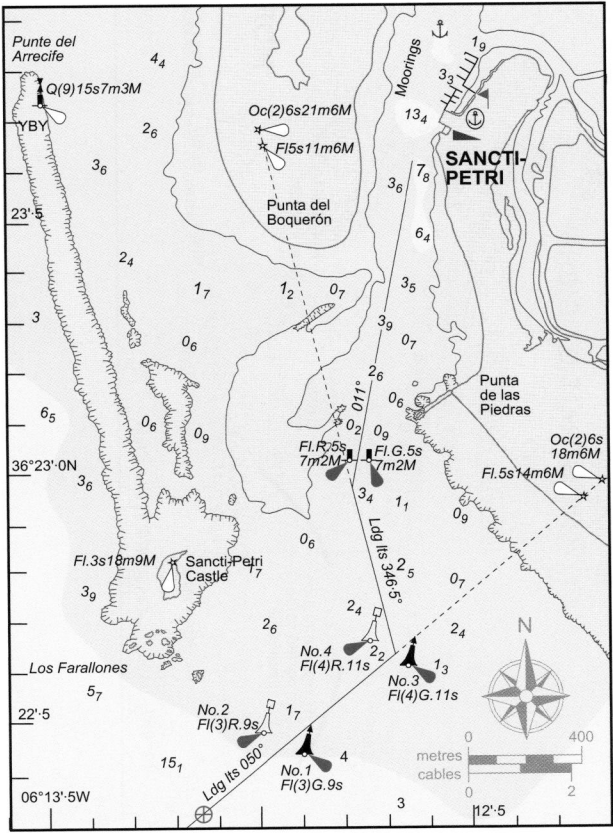

LIGHTS AND MARKS See chartlet and 9.25.3. The castle's 16m □ twr, Fl 3s, is conspic. 050° and 346·5° ldg marks are hard-to-see lattice twrs. 4 lateral buoys define the 050° ldg line.

R/T Marina *Puerto Sancti-Petri* Ch 09.

TELEPHONE (Code 956) MRCC ☎ 684740; Brit Consul 264479.

FACILITIES Marina ☎ 496169. sanctipetri@eppa.es 90 AB in 5m, inc 2 ❶ AB on pontoons in 2–5m , €1·93; see HM. ⚓s €0.66. Shwrs, Slip, C, limited CH and 🛢 in season. **Club Náutico** Bar, R.

Village: Few facilities in abandoned 'ghost town' at mouth of sandy, peaceful lagoon; ⇆ San Fernando (18 km); ✈ Jerez (50 km).

9.25.17 BARBATE

Cádiz **36°10′·79N 05°55′·54W** ✿❀♨♨♨✿

CHARTS AC 91, 142; SC 444, 4441.

TIDES

Standard Port LISBOA (◀━); ML 1·2

Times				Height (metres)			
High Water		Low Water		MHWS	MHWN	MLWN	MLWS
0500	1000	0500	1100	3·8	2·9	1·5	0·5
1700	2200	1700	2300				
Differences CABO TRAFALGAR							
–0003	–0003	+0026	+0026	–1.4	–1.1	–0.6	–0.1
RIO BARBATE							
+0016	+0016	+0045	+0045	–1.9	–1.5	–0.5	+0.1
PUNTA CAMARINAL (36°05′N 05°48′W)							
–0007	–0007	+0013	+0013	–1.7	–1.4	–0.7	–0.2

SHELTER Good. FVs berth in the large outer basin.

NAVIGATION WPT 36°10′·81N 05°55′·38W, 270°/200m to abeam SW mole hd. From the W there is room to enter between the SW mole hd and the NCM lt buoy (see below), but do not wander S of the buoy, especially at night. From the SE keep 2M offshore to avoid tunny nets NW of Cabo Plata (36°06′·15N 05°49′·50W).

> Near the WPT a NCM lt buoy marks the apex of a triangular tunny net, which extends 2·7M S and is marked by 2 SCM lt buoys at its base, an ECM lt buoy on its E side and a WCM lt buoy near its centre; see chartlet overleaf, 9.25.3 and AC 142. A guard vessel, showing ●● (vert) and listening Ch 70, may be on station. Tunny nets, Mar-Sep, are a real hazard, especially at night. Nets may be laid E of Pta Camarinal and NW of Tarifa.

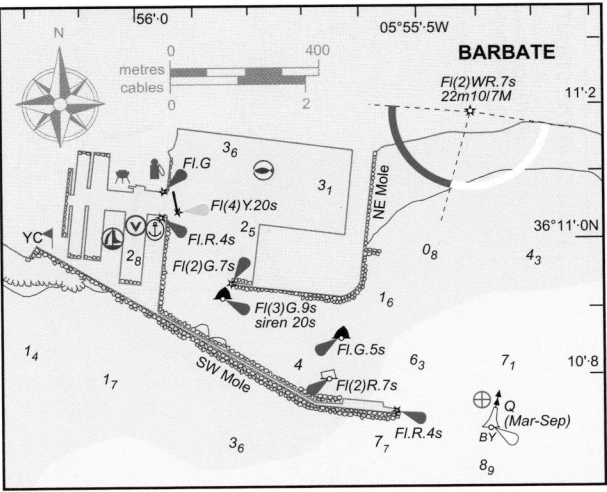

LIGHTS AND MARKS Barbate lt ho, Fl (2) WR 7s, W twr + R bands, is 4ca N of hbr ent, on edge of town. Other lights as chartlet and 9.25.3. Orange sodium lts in the hbr make navigational lts hard to discern.

R/T Marina Ch 09. Barbate is at W end of Gibraltar Strait VTS; monitor *Tarifa Traffic* Ch 10 on passage.

TELEPHONE (Code 956) MRCC ☎ 684740; Brit Consul 264479.

FACILITIES Marina in the 3 inner basins (2·8m). A movable anti-pollution boom lies E of the marina ent; its SSE end is lit Fl (4) Y 20s 1M. ☎ 431907. barbated@eppa.es 314 AB, inc ❶ in 3m, €1·93. ⊖, Met, D&P, Slip, BH (45 ton), ME, El, ✗, Ice, ▣, Bar, R. **Club Náutico** ☎ 433905.

Town is about 2M away, although 🛒 is closer; R, Bar, ⑧, ✉. Bus to Cádiz (61km). ✈ Jerez, Gibraltar or Malaga.

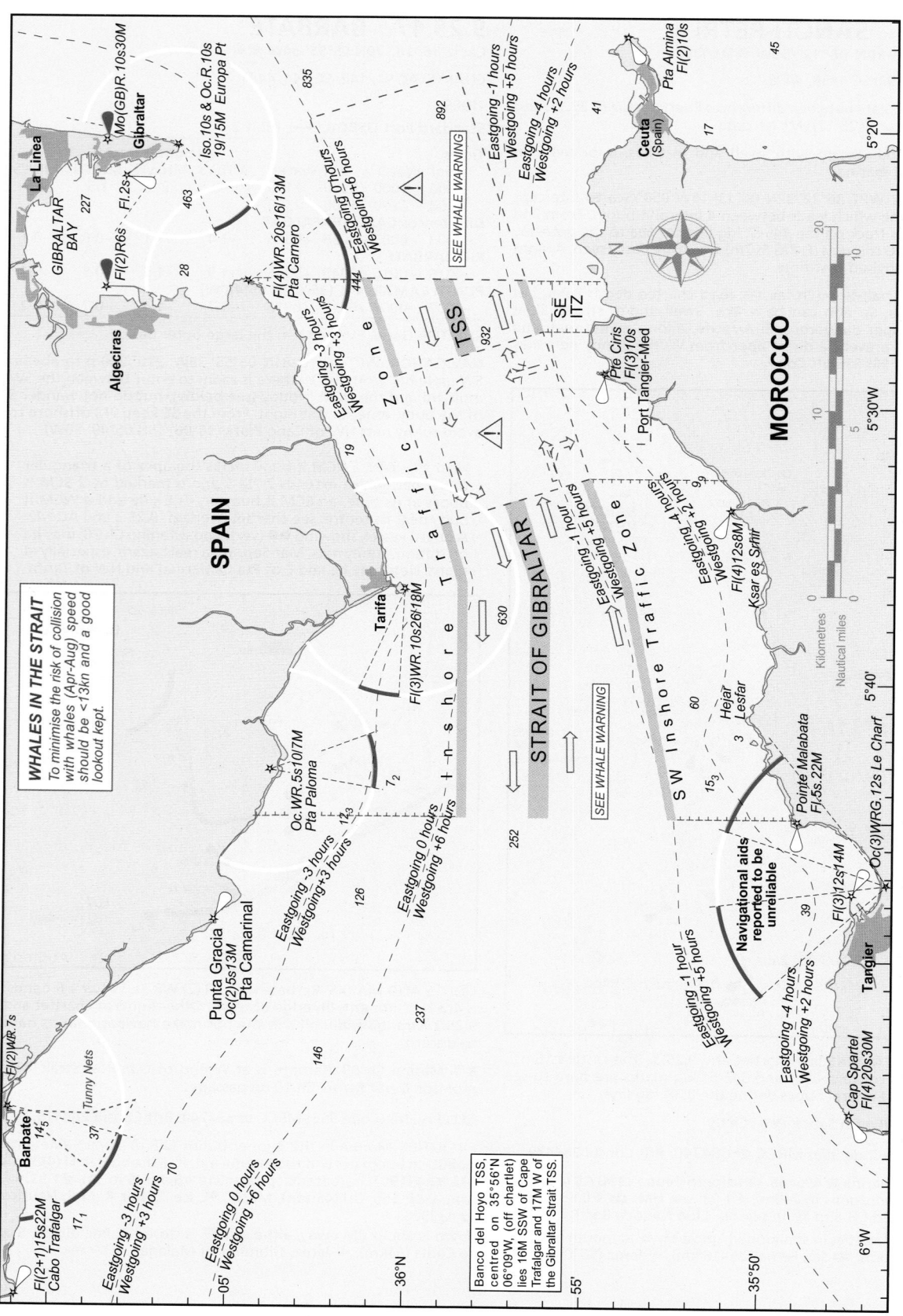

WHALES IN THE STRAIT
To minimise the risk of collision with whales (Apr-Aug) speed should be <13kn and a good lookout kept.

Banco del Hoyo TSS, centred on 35°56'N 06°09'W, (off chartlet) lies 16M SSW of Cape Trafalgar and 17M W of the Gibraltar Strait TSS.

SPAIN

MOROCCO

GIBRALTAR BAY

La Linea

Mo(GB)R.10s30M
Gibraltar

Iso.10s & Oc.R.10s 19/15M Europa Pt

835

892

Eastgoing -1 hours
Westgoing +5 hours

Eastgoing -4 hours
Westgoing +2 hours

SEE WHALE WARNING

Pta Almina
Fl(2)10s

Ceuta (Spain)

45

41

17

5°20'

227

Fl.2s

463

Fl(2)R6s

28

Algeciras

Fl(4)WR.20s16/13M
Pta Carnero

444

Eastgoing 0 hours
Westgoing +6 hours

T S S

SE
ITZ

932

Pte Ciris
Fl(3)10s
Port Tangier-Med

5°30'

Eastgoing -3 hours
Westgoing +3 hours

19

I n s h o r e   T r a f f i c   Z o n e

630

252

Eastgoing -1 hour
Westgoing +5 hours

STRAIT OF GIBRALTAR

SEE WHALE WARNING

S W   I n s h o r e   T r a f f i c   Z o n e

Eastgoing -4 hours
Westgoing +2 hours

9₉

Eastgoing -4 hours
Westgoing +2 hours

Fl(4)12s8M
Ksar es Srhir

Hejar
Lesfar

60

15₃

3

Fl(3)WR.10s26/18M
Tarifa

7₂

Oc.WR.5s10/7M
Pta Paloma

11₃

Eastgoing -3 hours
Westgoing +3 hours

126

Punta Gracia
Oc(2)5s13M
Pta Camarinal

237

146

Eastgoing 0 hours
Westgoing +6 hours

Navigational aids reported to be unreliable

39

Pointe Malabata
Fl.5s.22M

Fl(3)12s14M

Oc(3)WRG.12s Le Charf

Eastgoing -1 hour
Westgoing +5 hours

Eastgoing -4 hours
Westgoing +2 hours

Tangier

Cap Spartel
Fl(4)20s30M

Fl(2)WR.7s

Tunny Nets

Barbate

14₅

37₁

70

Eastgoing -3 hours
Westgoing +3 hours

Eastgoing 0 hours
Westgoing +6 hours

17₁

Fl(2+1)15s22M
Cabo Trafalgar

05'

55'

36°N

35°50'

6°W

5°40'

N

Kilometres
Nautical miles

20

10

10

5

0

GIBRALTAR

MEAN SPRING
AND NEAP CURVES

MEAN RANGES	
Springs	0·9m
Neaps	0·4m

Springs occur 1 day
after
New and Full Moon

STRAIT OF GIBRALTAR

▶ *Tidal streams: Near the middle of the Strait the stream sets east from HW Gib and west from HWG –6. Closer inshore, streams start progressively earlier as shown on the chartlet opposite. To find when (approx) the tidal stream turns, apply the time intervals on the pecked lines to the time of HW Gib. Max rates, about 3kn in both directions, are usually found close inshore off headlands, decreasing offshore to < 1·5kn.*◀

A surface current, as distinct from a tidal stream, always flows east in the centre of the Strait reaching about 2kn at the eastern end. Its speed decreases from the centre of the Strait towards the shore where the tidal stream influence increases.

Surface flow is the combined effect of tidal streams and the constant surface current into the Med. The resultant max surface flow is about 2kn W-going and 5kn E-going (further influenced by recent E or W winds). W-bound yachts should hug the Spanish coast.

Tidal races on the Spanish side form: off Cape Trafalgar, usually up to 2M SW, but 5-12M in heavy weather; near Bajo de Los Cabezos (2-4M S of Pta Paloma); and NW of Tarifa. The position and violence of these races depends on wind (especially over tide), springs/neaps and the state of the tide. For more information, see *W Coasts of Spain and Portugal* Pilot.

TSS is aligned 090°/270° and 073°/253°s in mid-strait. Yachts bound to/from Gibraltar usually use the northern ITZ. Traffic from/to the Moroccan port of Tangier-Med joins/leaves the TSS north of Punta Ciris.

Tarifa VTS, c/s *Tarifa Trafico* Ch **10**, gives radar surveillance on request and offers a reporting system (voluntary for yachts) between 05°58′W and 05°15′W. MSI is broadcast routinely and on request in Spanish and English Ch 67.

9.25.18 TARIFA

Cádiz **36°00′·35N 05°36′·26W** (Outer hbr) ⚓🌊🏠🏠

CHARTS AC 142; SC 445, 445B, 4450; SHOM 1619, 7042.

TIDES See 9.25.20 for differences.

SHELTER A bolt-hole in bad conditions. In W'lies ⚓ off hbr ent in 5m. In a *levanter* ⚓ NW of the causeway as on the chartlet.

NAVIGATION WPT 36°00′·07N 05°35′·91W, 315°/4ca to hbr ent. S of Tarifa lt the ITZ is only 1·5M wide. A SCM lt buoy, 1M NNW of Tarifa lt, marks a tunny net (Mar-Jul) extending WNW to 2 WCM lt buoys thence to shore; care needed if approaching the NW ⚓.

LIGHTS AND MARKS See chartlet and 9.25.3.

R/T No port VHF. See Passage Information above for Tarifa VTS.

FACILITIES Only FW. No specific AB for yachts; space on the dog-legged SE mole, clear of ferries, may be possible.
Inner basin: Ferries berth at the terminal in the NE corner and on S side. FVs on the S and W sides; *Guardia Civil* vessels and small naval craft use pens on N side.

Town: 🛒, R, Bar, Ⓑ, ✉, ⇌; ✈ Jerez, Gibraltar, Malaga.

9.25.19 ALGECIRAS

Cádiz **36°07′·12N 05°26′·16W** (Marina ent) ⚓🌊🌊🏠🏠

CHARTS AC 3578, 142, 1448, 1455; SC 445, 445A, 4451, 4452.

TIDES
Standard Port GIBRALTAR (→); ML 0·66; differences overleaf.

SHELTER Good in marina, except perhaps in strong SE'lies.

NAVIGATION WPT 36°06′·73N 05°24′·76W (ECM buoy, Q (3) 10s, off chartlet), 295°/0·97M to first appr buoys. From S, keep 5ca off Pta de San García and beware drying reefs S of hbr ent. From N/E, beware big ships at ⚓, high-speed ferries and WIP.

LIGHTS AND MARKS The Hbr Control twr is conspic by day, close WNW of the marina.

R/T Marina Ch 09 16. Port Ch 09, **12**.

TELEPHONE (Code 956) HM 572620; Port Authority ☎ 585400; MRCC ☎ 684740; Brit Consul 264479.

FACILITIES **Marina/Real Club Náutico** ☎ 601402, 666000. Max LOA 16m. D, BH (25 ton), ME, Slip, CH, ⊖, Met, R, Bar.
Town: 🛒, R, Bar, Ⓑ, ✉, ⇌. ✈ Jerez, Gibraltar, Malaga.

SW Spain & Gibraltar

9.25.20   GIBRALTAR

36°08'·96N 05°22'·00W (100m off 'E' Hd) ❋❋❋◊◊◊✿✿✿

CHARTS AC 142, 3578, 1448, 144, 45 (Note: these charts do not accurately depict the layout of Marina Bay and Queensway Quay Marinas); SC 445, 445A, 4452.

TIDES Standard Port GIBRALTAR (⟶); ML 0·5

Times				Height (metres)			
High Water		Low Water		MHWS	MHWN	MLWN	MLWS
0000	0700	0100	0600	1·0	0·7	0·3	0·1
1200	1900	1300	1800	Note the very small range			
Differences TARIFA							
−0038	−0038	−0042	−0042	+0·4	+0·3	+0·3	+0·2
PUNTA CARNERO							
−0010	−0010	0000	0000	0·0	+0·1	+0·1	+0·1
ALGECIRAS							
−0010	−0010	−0010	−0010	+0·1	+0·2	+0·1	+0·1
SANDY BAY (E side of the Rock)							
−0011	−0011	−0016	−0016	−0·2	−0·1	0·0	0·0

SHELTER Good in both marinas (best to pre-book), but beware swell and fierce gusts in the E'ly *Levanter*. ⚓ NW of the runway in 4-6m is often prohib for security reasons. ⚓ off La Linea in Spanish waters is feasible.

NAVIGATION From the SW, WPT 36°04'·62N 05°24'·34W (1M E of Pta Carnero), 024°/4·7M to 'E' Hd; 030°/4M to 'A' Hd. The Rock is steep-to all round; from the SW, beware shoals to S of Pta Carnero. From the E, clear Europa Pt by 3ca to avoid overfalls.

On arrival yachts with masts >10m high, intending to go to the yacht fuel berth (Waterport) or to Marina Bay Marina, must obtain instructions from *Gibraltar Port* Ch **12**, 20 **before** rounding 'E' Head/North mole. VQ strobe lts and loudspeakers warn of aircraft activity; yachts must then stay out of a Restricted Entry area west of the runway, as shown on the chartlet.

All yachts now clear Customs in/out at their chosen marina.

LIGHTS AND MARKS The Rock (423m) is easily seen, but from the W not until rounding Pta Carnero, 5M to SW. The Aero lt atop the Rock is obsc'd when within 2M W of it. Europa Pt, almost at sea level, has 3 sectored lts; see 9.25.3. At N end of bay, industrial plants are conspic day/night. Shore lts may mask commercial vessels at ⚓ and navigational lights.

R/T Queensway Quay and Marina Bay Marinas: Ch 71. Civil port Ch 06. Gibraltar Bay Ch 12. QHM Ch 08. HM Customs Ch 14.

TELEPHONE International code +350 (no Area code). Port Captain (HM) 77254; QHM 55901; ⊖72901; Met 53416; Ⓗ79700; Ambulance/Police 199; Fire 190; ✈ 75984.

FACILITIES **Queensway Quay Marina** ☎ 44700, qqmarina@gibraltar.gi At its NW corner the marina entrance (least depth 3·5m) is closed by an anti-wash boom 2130-0830. 160 inc ❷, mostly F&A, and some AB; £1·36 summer. CH, ▣, Wi-Fi, @, no fuel. Close to town centre.

Marina Bay pieroffice@marinabay.gi www.marinabay.gi ☎ 73300. Close to airport runway but only occas noise. 209 AB, mostly F & A, in 1·8 - 3·7m, inc 29 ❷: £1·54 1 May- 31 Oct; £0·93 1 Nov-30 Apr. CH, R, 🛒, ▣, ACA, SM, D & P, Gaz, Wi-Fi, Ice.

A small number of berths exist at **'Ocean Village Marina'** (ex-Sheppard's) but reports indicate that these are not ❷. Phase 1 of this retail development is now open.

Sheppard's chandlery remains near Marina Bay; tempy workshops at Coaling Island; tempy haul-out at Container berth. New BY & haul-out N of the runway are delayed by objections. ☎ 75148. BY (yachtrep@gibraltar.gi), ⚒, CH, Ⓔ, BH (30 ton), C (6 ton), ME, El. www.sheppard.gi admin@sheppard.gi

Yacht fuel is available at Waterport, 36°08'·90N 05°21'·37W from Mobil (Mon-Sat 0900-2300; Sun 0900-1400; also Shell, shorter hrs).

East Side project (Sovereign Bay) 36°08'·60N 05°20'·34W is a very major development; a 300 berth marina may open by 2010.

Royal Gibraltar YC ☎ 78897, 48847. www.rgyc.gi. info@rgyc.gi

Town 🛒, R, Bar, ✉, Ⓗ, Ⓑ, ✈.

SPECIAL NOTES FOR GIBRALTAR

Standard time is UT −1, as in Spain. DST (UT −2) is kept from the last Sun in Mar until the Sat before the last Sun in Oct.

Telephone The international dial code is +350 (this includes calling from Spain), then the 5 digit tel No; there is no Area code.

Wreck There is a wreck at 36°06'·25N 05°20'·24W, 5 cables SE of Europa Point lighthouse. It is marked by a ♨ Q (3) 10s 36°06'·33N 05°20'·01W; ♨ Q (6) + L Fl 15s 36°06'·07N 05°20'·13W; ♨ Q (6) + L Fl 15s; Racon (D), 36°06'·07N 05°20'·13W; ♨ Q (9) 15s 36°06'·12N 05°20'·37W.

Customs Visiting RIBs must obtain prior written permission to enter from Collector of Customs, Customs House, Waterport, Gibraltar, ☎ 78879; VHF Ch 14 - or entry may be refused.

Local winds Levanters are E'lies, common with high pressure to the N and low to the S. A persistent Levanter produces the roughest seas in the Strait and severe squalls (violent in a F8) and eddies in the lee of the Rock. The Poniente is a frequent W'ly, slightly less common in summer. The Vendavale is a strong SW'ly associated with lows, with rain/drizzle near coasts.

TIME ZONE –0100
Subtract 1 hour for UT
For Gibraltar Summer Time add ONE hour in **non-shaded areas**

GIBRALTAR   LAT 36°08'N   LONG 5°21'W
TIMES AND HEIGHTS OF HIGH AND LOW WATERS

Dates in red are **SPRINGS**
Dates in blue are NEAPS

YEAR 2010

JANUARY

Day	Time m	Time m	Time m	Time m
1 F	0315 1.0	0852 0.1	1532 1.0	2120 0.1
2 SA	0402 1.0	0939 0.1	1620 1.0	2205 0.0
3 SU	0448 1.0	1027 0.1	1708 1.0	2250 0.0
4 M	0534 1.0	1115 0.1	1756 1.0	2334 0.1
5 TU	0623 1.0	1205 0.1	1846 0.9	
6 W	0021 0.1	0715 0.9	1300 0.2	1939 0.8
7 TH ☽	0115 0.2	0811 0.9	1401 0.2	2037 0.8
8 F	0217 0.3	0913 0.8	1511 0.3	2143 0.7
9 SA	0333 0.3	1022 0.8	1635 0.3	2301 0.7
10 SU	0502 0.3	1136 0.8	1751 0.2	2316 0.6
11 M	0017 0.7	0609 0.3	1239 0.8	1845 0.2
12 TU	0117 0.8	0658 0.2	1331 0.8	1929 0.2
13 W	0204 0.8	0739 0.2	1416 0.8	2008 0.1
14 TH	0244 0.8	0816 0.2	1456 0.8	2044 0.1
15 F ●	0320 0.8	0852 0.1	1533 0.9	2118 0.1
16 SA	0352 0.9	0926 0.1	1607 0.9	2150 0.1
17 SU	0422 0.9	0959 0.1	1639 0.9	2221 0.1
18 M	0451 0.9	1030 0.1	1710 0.8	2250 0.1
19 TU	0521 0.9	1101 0.1	1741 0.8	2318 0.1
20 W	0552 0.8	1133 0.2	1814 0.8	2348 0.2
21 TH	0628 0.8	1208 0.2	1852 0.7	
22 F	0021 0.8	0710 0.8	1251 0.2	1938 0.7
23 SA ◑	0105 0.2	0802 0.7	1348 0.3	2035 0.7
24 SU	0208 0.3	0904 0.7	1507 0.3	2148 0.6
25 M	0346 0.3	1019 0.7	1649 0.2	2316 0.6
26 TU	0522 0.3	1140 0.7	1805 0.2	
27 W	0031 0.7	0623 0.2	1248 0.8	1858 0.1
28 TH	0129 0.8	0714 0.1	1342 0.9	1945 0.0
29 F	0219 0.9	0801 0.1	1434 0.9	2030 0.0
30 SA ○	0306 1.0	0847 0.0	1523 1.0	2114 -0.1
31 SU	0351 1.0	0933 0.0	1610 1.0	2156 -0.1

FEBRUARY

Day	Time m	Time m	Time m	Time m
1 M	0435 1.0	1017 0.0	1655 1.0	2236 -0.1
2 TU	0518 1.0	1101 0.0	1740 1.0	2316 0.0
3 W	0603 1.0	1144 0.0	1826 0.9	2355 0.1
4 TH	0649 0.9	1229 0.1	1914 0.8	
5 F	0038 0.1	0740 0.9	1321 0.2	2006 0.8
6 SA ☽	0130 0.2	0836 0.8	1425 0.2	2107 0.7
7 SU	0241 0.3	0945 0.7	1601 0.3	2226 0.6
8 M	0437 0.3	1113 0.7	1742 0.3	
9 TU	0003 0.6	0604 0.3	1231 0.7	1839 0.3
10 W	0110 0.7	0653 0.2	1325 0.7	1920 0.2
11 TH	0155 0.7	0730 0.2	1407 0.8	1955 0.1
12 F	0231 0.8	0804 0.1	1444 0.8	2028 0.1
13 SA	0303 0.8	0837 0.1	1517 0.8	2100 0.1
14 SU ●	0331 0.9	0908 0.1	1548 0.9	2130 0.0
15 M	0359 0.9	0938 0.1	1618 0.9	2158 0.0
16 TU	0426 0.9	1008 0.1	1647 0.9	2225 0.1
17 W	0455 0.9	1036 0.1	1716 0.9	2252 0.1
18 TH	0525 0.9	1105 0.1	1748 0.8	2319 0.1
19 F	0558 0.8	1137 0.1	1825 0.8	2350 0.2
20 SA	0638 0.8	1214 0.2	1909 0.7	
21 SU	0029 0.2	0727 0.7	1305 0.2	2005 0.7
22 M ◐	0125 0.3	0829 0.7	1425 0.3	2117 0.6
23 TU	0310 0.3	0949 0.7	1634 0.3	2252 0.6
24 W	0510 0.3	1123 0.7	1757 0.2	
25 TH	0016 0.7	0617 0.2	1237 0.8	1850 0.1
26 F	0116 0.8	0707 0.1	1332 0.8	1935 0.0
27 SA	0204 0.9	0752 0.0	1422 0.9	2017 0.0
28 SU ○	0250 1.0	0836 -0.1	1509 1.0	2058 -0.1

MARCH

Day	Time m	Time m	Time m	Time m
1 M	0333 1.0	0919 -0.1	1553 1.0	2138 -0.1
2 TU	0415 1.0	1000 -0.1	1637 1.0	2215 -0.1
3 W	0457 1.0	1040 -0.1	1720 1.0	2252 0.0
4 TH	0539 1.0	1119 0.0	1803 0.9	2328 0.0
5 F	0622 0.9	1159 0.1	1849 0.8	
6 SA	0007 0.1	0709 0.8	1243 0.2	1938 0.7
7 SU ☽	0052 0.2	0803 0.7	1341 0.3	2036 0.7
8 M	0157 0.3	0910 0.6	1518 0.3	2149 0.6
9 TU	0402 0.4	1042 0.6	1715 0.3	2331 0.6
10 W	0548 0.6	1211 0.6	1814 0.3	
11 TH	0043 0.7	0634 0.3	1305 0.7	1853 0.2
12 F	0127 0.7	0709 0.2	1345 0.8	1927 0.1
13 SA	0201 0.8	0741 0.1	1419 0.8	1959 0.1
14 SU	0231 0.9	0812 0.1	1450 0.8	2030 0.1
15 M ●	0300 0.9	0842 0.1	1521 0.9	2100 0.1
16 TU	0329 0.9	0912 0.1	1551 0.9	2129 0.1
17 W	0358 0.9	0942 0.1	1622 0.9	2157 0.1
18 TH	0428 0.9	1011 0.1	1653 0.9	2226 0.1
19 F	0500 0.9	1041 0.1	1727 0.9	2256 0.1
20 SA	0535 0.9	1114 0.1	1806 0.8	2329 0.2
21 SU	0616 0.8	1151 0.2	1852 0.8	
22 M	0010 0.3	0706 0.8	1242 0.2	1950 0.7
23 TU ◐	0112 0.3	0810 0.7	1408 0.3	2102 0.7
24 W	0302 0.3	0932 0.7	1618 0.3	2233 0.7
25 TH	0455 0.3	1108 0.7	1737 0.2	2356 0.7
26 F	0602 0.2	1221 0.8	1829 0.1	
27 SA	0054 0.8	0651 0.1	1316 0.8	1913 0.1
28 SU ○	0142 0.9	0735 0.0	1403 0.9	1954 0.0
29 M	0226 1.0	0818 0.0	1448 1.0	2034 0.0
30 TU ○	0309 1.0	0859 -0.1	1532 1.0	2112 0.0
31 W	0351 1.0	0939 -0.1	1615 1.0	2150 0.0

APRIL

Day	Time m	Time m	Time m	Time m
1 TH	0433 1.0	1017 0.0	1657 0.9	2226 0.0
2 F	0514 0.9	1054 0.0	1740 0.9	2302 0.1
3 SA	0556 0.9	1132 0.1	1825 0.8	2341 0.2
4 SU	0643 0.8	1213 0.2	1914 0.7	
5 M	0025 0.2	0735 0.7	1307 0.3	2009 0.7
6 TU ☽	0126 0.3	0839 0.6	1434 0.3	2114 0.6
7 W	0309 0.4	0958 0.6	1617 0.3	2235 0.6
8 TH	0459 0.3	1127 0.6	1726 0.3	2350 0.7
9 F	0555 0.3	1226 0.7	1811 0.3	
10 SA	0039 0.7	0633 0.2	1308 0.7	1848 0.2
11 SU	0116 0.8	0707 0.2	1343 0.8	1921 0.1
12 M	0149 0.8	0739 0.1	1416 0.8	1953 0.1
13 TU	0221 0.8	0811 0.1	1449 0.9	2025 0.1
14 W ●	0254 0.8	0843 0.1	1522 0.9	2057 0.1
15 TH	0328 0.9	0915 0.1	1557 0.9	2129 0.1
16 F	0403 0.9	0948 0.1	1632 0.9	2202 0.1
17 SA	0440 0.9	1022 0.1	1710 0.9	2237 0.1
18 SU	0519 0.9	1058 0.1	1753 0.8	2317 0.2
19 M	0603 0.8	1140 0.2	1842 0.8	
20 TU	0005 0.2	0655 0.8	1236 0.2	1941 0.8
21 W ◐	0114 0.3	0800 0.7	1403 0.3	2050 0.7
22 TH	0251 0.3	0918 0.7	1545 0.3	2210 0.7
23 F	0425 0.3	1045 0.7	1701 0.2	2326 0.8
24 SA	0535 0.2	1157 0.8	1758 0.2	
25 SU	0025 0.9	0627 0.1	1252 0.8	1843 0.1
26 M	0114 0.9	0713 0.1	1339 0.9	1925 0.1
27 TU	0159 0.9	0756 0.0	1425 0.9	2006 0.0
28 W ○	0243 1.0	0837 0.0	1509 0.9	2046 0.0
29 TH	0326 1.0	0917 0.0	1553 0.9	2125 0.1
30 F	0409 0.9	0956 0.0	1636 0.9	2203 0.1

Chart Datum is 0·25 metres below Alicante Datum (ie Mean Sea Level, Alicante). HAT is 1·2 metres above Chart Datum; see 4.5.

SW Spain & Gibraltar

TIME ZONE -0100
Subtract 1 hour for UT
For Gibraltar Summer Time add ONE hour in **non-shaded areas**

GIBRALTAR LAT 36°08'N LONG 5°21'W
TIMES AND HEIGHTS OF HIGH AND LOW WATERS

Dates in red are SPRINGS
Dates in blue are NEAPS

YEAR 2010

MAY

Time	m		Time	m
1 SA 0451 / 1033 / 1719 / 2241	0.9 / 0.1 / 0.9 / 0.1		**16** SU 0423 / 1008 / 1657 / 2225	0.9 / 0.1 / 0.9 / 0.2
2 SU 0534 / 1111 / 1803 / 2321	0.8 / 0.1 / 0.8 / 0.2		**17** M 0507 / 1049 / 1742 / 2311	0.9 / 0.1 / 0.9 / 0.2
3 M 0619 / 1152 / 1850	0.8 / 0.2 / 0.8		**18** TU 0555 / 1136 / 1833	0.9 / 0.2 / 0.9
4 TU 0005 / 0710 / 1242 / 1941	0.3 / 0.7 / 0.3 / 0.7		**19** W 0004 / 0648 / 1233 / 1930	0.2 / 0.8 / 0.2 / 0.8
5 W 0102 / 0806 / 1350 / 2037	0.3 / 0.7 / 0.3 / 0.7		**20** TH 0110 / 0750 / 1345 / 2033	0.3 / 0.8 / 0.2 / 0.8
6 TH 0216 / 0910 / 1509 / 2137	0.3 / 0.6 / 0.3 / 0.7		**21** F 0227 / 0859 / 1503 / 2141	0.3 / 0.8 / 0.2 / 0.8
7 F 0340 / 1020 / 1620 / 2241	0.3 / 0.7 / 0.3 / 0.7		**22** SA 0346 / 1013 / 1616 / 2250	0.2 / 0.8 / 0.2 / 0.8
8 SA 0453 / 1128 / 1717 / 2338	0.3 / 0.7 / 0.3 / 0.7		**23** SU 0459 / 1125 / 1720 / 2352	0.2 / 0.8 / 0.2 / 0.9
9 SU 0545 / 1219 / 1801	0.3 / 0.7 / 0.3		**24** M 0600 / 1225 / 1814	0.2 / 0.8 / 0.2
10 M 0023 / 0626 / 1300 / 1839	0.8 / 0.2 / 0.8 / 0.2		**25** TU 0045 / 0651 / 1316 / 1900	0.9 / 0.1 / 0.8 / 0.1
11 TU 0103 / 0703 / 1338 / 1915	0.8 / 0.2 / 0.8 / 0.2		**26** W 0134 / 0736 / 1404 / 1943	0.9 / 0.1 / 0.9 / 0.1
12 W 0141 / 0738 / 1415 / 1950	0.9 / 0.1 / 0.9 / 0.2		**27** TH 0220 / 0819 / 1450 / 2025	0.9 / 0.1 / 0.9 / 0.1
13 TH 0220 / 0814 / 1453 / 2026	0.9 / 0.1 / 0.9 / 0.2		**28** F 0305 / 0900 / 1535 / 2106	0.9 / 0.1 / 0.9 / 0.1
14 F 0300 / 0850 / 1533 / 2104	0.9 / 0.1 / 0.9 / 0.2		**29** SA 0350 / 0940 / 1618 / 2146	0.9 / 0.1 / 0.9 / 0.1
15 SA 0341 / 0928 / 1614 / 2143	0.9 / 0.1 / 0.9 / 0.2		**30** SU 0432 / 1017 / 1700 / 2225	0.9 / 0.1 / 0.9 / 0.2
			31 M 0515 / 1054 / 1741 / 2304	0.8 / 0.1 / 0.8 / 0.2

JUNE

Time	m		Time	m
1 TU 0557 / 1132 / 1823 / 2345	0.8 / 0.2 / 0.8 / 0.2		**16** W 0546 / 1128 / 1819 / 2356	0.9 / 0.1 / 1.0 / 0.2
2 W 0641 / 1214 / 1907	0.8 / 0.2 / 0.8		**17** TH 0638 / 1219 / 1912	0.9 / 0.2 / 0.9
3 TH 0031 / 0728 / 1304 / 1952	0.3 / 0.7 / 0.3 / 0.7		**18** F 0053 / 0734 / 1316 / 2009	0.2 / 0.9 / 0.2 / 0.9
4 F 0125 / 0819 / 1402 / 2040	0.3 / 0.7 / 0.3 / 0.7		**19** SA 0156 / 0835 / 1420 / 2109	0.2 / 0.8 / 0.2 / 0.9
5 SA 0226 / 0914 / 1504 / 2132	0.3 / 0.7 / 0.3 / 0.7		**20** SU 0305 / 0941 / 1530 / 2214	0.2 / 0.8 / 0.3 / 0.8
6 SU 0331 / 1015 / 1608 / 2229	0.3 / 0.7 / 0.3 / 0.7		**21** M 0421 / 1053 / 1644 / 2321	0.2 / 0.8 / 0.3 / 0.8
7 M 0439 / 1119 / 1706 / 2325	0.3 / 0.7 / 0.3 / 0.8		**22** TU 0537 / 1201 / 1750	0.2 / 0.8 / 0.2
8 TU 0538 / 1213 / 1756	0.3 / 0.7 / 0.3		**23** W 0022 / 0636 / 1300 / 1844	0.8 / 0.2 / 0.8 / 0.2
9 W 0017 / 0626 / 1300 / 1839	0.8 / 0.2 / 0.8 / 0.2		**24** TH 0116 / 0724 / 1351 / 1930	0.9 / 0.1 / 0.9 / 0.2
10 TH 0104 / 0708 / 1345 / 1920	0.8 / 0.2 / 0.8 / 0.2		**25** F 0205 / 0807 / 1438 / 2012	0.9 / 0.1 / 0.9 / 0.2
11 F 0150 / 0749 / 1429 / 2002	0.9 / 0.1 / 0.9 / 0.2		**26** SA 0252 / 0847 / 1522 / 2053	0.9 / 0.1 / 0.9 / 0.2
12 SA 0237 / 0831 / 1514 / 2045	0.9 / 0.1 / 0.9 / 0.2		**27** SU 0335 / 0925 / 1602 / 2131	0.9 / 0.1 / 0.9 / 0.2
13 SU 0324 / 0914 / 1559 / 2131	1.0 / 0.1 / 1.0 / 0.1		**28** M 0416 / 1000 / 1642 / 2208	0.9 / 0.1 / 0.9 / 0.2
14 M 0411 / 0958 / 1644 / 2217	1.0 / 0.1 / 1.0 / 0.1		**29** TU 0454 / 1034 / 1715 / 2244	0.9 / 0.1 / 0.9 / 0.2
15 TU 0458 / 1042 / 1730 / 2305	1.0 / 0.1 / 1.0 / 0.1		**30** W 0530 / 1107 / 1749 / 2319	0.8 / 0.1 / 0.8 / 0.2

JULY

Time	m		Time	m
1 TH 0606 / 1141 / 1824 / 2356	0.8 / 0.2 / 0.8 / 0.2		**16** F 0620 / 1155 / 1848	1.0 / 0.1 / 1.0
2 F 0644 / 1216 / 1901	0.8 / 0.2 / 0.8		**17** SA 0028 / 0712 / 1244 / 1940	0.1 / 0.9 / 0.2 / 0.9
3 SA 0035 / 0725 / 1257 / 1942	0.2 / 0.7 / 0.3 / 0.8		**18** SU 0123 / 0808 / 1339 / 2036	0.2 / 0.8 / 0.2 / 0.9
4 SU 0121 / 0812 / 1346 / 2029	0.3 / 0.7 / 0.3 / 0.8		**19** M 0226 / 0910 / 1446 / 2140	0.2 / 0.8 / 0.3 / 0.8
5 M 0216 / 0907 / 1448 / 2123	0.3 / 0.7 / 0.3 / 0.7		**20** TU 0346 / 1024 / 1611 / 2253	0.3 / 0.7 / 0.3 / 0.8
6 TU 0324 / 1014 / 1602 / 2226	0.3 / 0.7 / 0.3 / 0.7		**21** W 0521 / 1144 / 1737	0.3 / 0.7 / 0.3
7 W 0445 / 1126 / 1715 / 2333	0.3 / 0.7 / 0.3 / 0.8		**22** TH 0006 / 0627 / 1251 / 1836	0.8 / 0.2 / 0.8 / 0.3
8 TH 0555 / 1228 / 1812	0.2 / 0.8 / 0.3		**23** F 0107 / 0715 / 1344 / 1921	0.8 / 0.2 / 0.8 / 0.2
9 F 0033 / 0646 / 1321 / 1900	0.8 / 0.2 / 0.8 / 0.2		**24** SA 0157 / 0754 / 1428 / 2000	0.8 / 0.2 / 0.9 / 0.2
10 SA 0128 / 0732 / 1410 / 1946	0.9 / 0.1 / 0.9 / 0.2		**25** SU 0240 / 0830 / 1507 / 2037	0.9 / 0.1 / 0.9 / 0.2
11 SU 0219 / 0817 / 1457 / 2033	1.0 / 0.1 / 1.0 / 0.1		**26** M 0319 / 0904 / 1541 / 2112	0.9 / 0.1 / 0.9 / 0.1
12 M 0309 / 0901 / 1543 / 2120	1.0 / 0.1 / 1.0 / 0.1		**27** TU 0355 / 0936 / 1613 / 2146	0.9 / 0.1 / 0.9 / 0.1
13 TU 0358 / 0945 / 1628 / 2206	1.0 / 0.0 / 1.0 / 0.1		**28** W 0427 / 1007 / 1642 / 2218	0.9 / 0.1 / 0.9 / 0.1
14 W 0445 / 1028 / 1713 / 2252	1.0 / 0.0 / 1.1 / 0.1		**29** TH 0458 / 1036 / 1711 / 2249	0.9 / 0.1 / 0.9 / 0.2
15 TH 0532 / 1111 / 1759 / 2339	1.0 / 0.1 / 1.0 / 0.1		**30** F 0529 / 1105 / 1741 / 2320	0.9 / 0.2 / 0.9 / 0.2
			31 SA 0600 / 1134 / 1813 / 2353	0.8 / 0.2 / 0.9 / 0.2

AUGUST

Time	m		Time	m
1 SU 0636 / 1206 / 1850	0.8 / 0.2 / 0.8		**16** M 0048 / 0740 / 1300 / 2003	0.2 / 0.9 / 0.3 / 0.9
2 M 0030 / 0720 / 1245 / 1935	0.2 / 0.7 / 0.3 / 0.8		**17** TU 0147 / 0841 / 1404 / 2107	0.3 / 0.8 / 0.4 / 0.8
3 TU 0117 / 0815 / 1340 / 2030	0.3 / 0.7 / 0.3 / 0.8		**18** W 0310 / 0956 / 1542 / 2228	0.3 / 0.7 / 0.4 / 0.8
4 W 0223 / 0922 / 1504 / 2137	0.3 / 0.7 / 0.4 / 0.7		**19** TH 0506 / 1128 / 1728 / 2356	0.4 / 0.8 / 0.4 / 0.8
5 TH 0401 / 1045 / 1644 / 2258	0.3 / 0.7 / 0.4 / 0.8		**20** F 0614 / 1241 / 1826	0.3 / 0.8 / 0.3
6 F 0534 / 1203 / 1755	0.3 / 0.8 / 0.3		**21** SA 0059 / 0657 / 1330 / 1905	0.8 / 0.3 / 0.8 / 0.3
7 SA 0012 / 0631 / 1303 / 1847	0.8 / 0.2 / 0.8 / 0.2		**22** SU 0144 / 0732 / 1408 / 1940	0.9 / 0.2 / 0.9 / 0.2
8 SU 0112 / 0717 / 1352 / 1934	0.9 / 0.1 / 0.9 / 0.1		**23** M 0222 / 0804 / 1441 / 2013	0.9 / 0.2 / 0.9 / 0.2
9 M 0205 / 0801 / 1439 / 2019	1.0 / 0.1 / 1.0 / 0.1		**24** TU 0255 / 0835 / 1511 / 2046	0.9 / 0.1 / 1.0 / 0.2
10 TU 0254 / 0844 / 1524 / 2105	1.0 / 0.0 / 1.1 / 0.0		**25** W 0326 / 0905 / 1540 / 2117	0.9 / 0.1 / 1.0 / 0.1
11 W 0341 / 0926 / 1608 / 2150	1.1 / 0.0 / 1.1 / 0.0		**26** TH 0356 / 0934 / 1607 / 2148	1.0 / 0.1 / 1.0 / 0.1
12 TH 0427 / 1003 / 1652 / 2233	1.1 / 0.0 / 1.1 / 0.0		**27** F 0425 / 1003 / 1635 / 2217	1.0 / 0.1 / 1.0 / 0.1
13 F 0512 / 1047 / 1735 / 2316	1.1 / 0.0 / 1.1 / 0.1		**28** SA 0453 / 1030 / 1703 / 2246	0.9 / 0.2 / 1.0 / 0.2
14 SA 0558 / 1128 / 1821	1.0 / 0.1 / 1.0		**29** SU 0524 / 1058 / 1735 / 2317	0.9 / 0.2 / 0.9 / 0.2
15 SU 0000 / 0646 / 1211 / 1909	0.1 / 0.9 / 0.2 / 1.0		**30** M 0559 / 1129 / 1811 / 2351	0.9 / 0.2 / 0.9 / 0.2
			31 TU 0642 / 1205 / 1855	0.8 / 0.3 / 0.8

Chart Datum is 0.25 metres below Alicante Datum (ie Mean Sea Level, Alicante). HAT is 1.2 metres above Chart Datum; see 4.5.

》》 FREE monthly updates from 《《
www.reedsalmanac.co.uk

TIME ZONE -0100
Subtract 1 hour for UT
For Gibraltar Summer Time add
ONE hour in **non-shaded areas**

GIBRALTAR LAT 36°08'N LONG 5°21'W
TIMES AND HEIGHTS OF HIGH AND LOW WATERS

Dates in red are SPRINGS
Dates in blue are NEAPS

YEAR 2010

SEPTEMBER

Time	m		Time	m
1 0034	0.3	**16**	0232	0.4
0737	0.8		0925	0.7
W 1256	0.4	TH 1512	0.5
◑ 1952	0.8		2200	0.7
2 0140	0.3	**17**	0434	0.4
0848	0.7		1100	0.8
TH 1428	0.4	F 1705	0.4
2103	0.8		2337	0.8
3 0337	0.4	**18**	0544	0.4
1015	0.7		1214	0.8
F 1626	0.4	SA 1801	0.4
2232	0.8			
4 0518	0.3	**19**	0038	0.8
1142	0.8		0626	0.3
SA 1740	0.3	SU 1301	0.9
2356	0.8		1838	0.3
5 0615	0.2	**20**	0120	0.9
1243	0.9		0700	0.3
SU 1832	0.2	M 1326	0.9
			1911	0.3
6 0057	0.9	**21**	0154	0.9
0659	0.1		0731	0.2
M 1332	1.0	TU 1406	1.0
1917	0.1		1943	0.2
7 0148	1.0	**22**	0224	0.9
0740	0.1		0801	0.2
TU 1417	1.1	W 1435	1.0
2001	0.1		2014	0.2
8 0235	1.1	**23**	0254	1.0
0821	0.0		0831	0.2
W 1501	1.1	TH 1503	1.0
● 2045	0.0	○ 2046	0.2
9 0320	1.1	**24**	0323	1.0
0901	0.0		0901	0.2
TH 1544	1.2	F 1532	1.0
2128	0.0		2116	0.1
10 0404	1.1	**25**	0352	1.0
0941	0.0		0930	0.2
F 1627	1.2	SA 1602	1.0
2209	0.0		2146	0.2
11 0448	1.1	**26**	0423	1.0
1020	0.1		0959	0.2
SA 1709	1.1	SU 1633	1.0
2249	0.1		2216	0.2
12 0532	1.0	**27**	0455	1.0
1058	0.1		1029	0.2
SU 1752	1.0	M 1707	1.0
2330	0.1		2248	0.2
13 0618	1.0	**28**	0532	0.9
1138	0.2		1102	0.3
M 1839	0.9	TU 1744	0.9
			2322	0.3
14 0013	0.2	**29**	0616	0.9
0710	0.9		1140	0.3
TU 1225	0.3	W 1830	0.9
1931	0.9			
15 0107	0.3	**30**	0005	0.3
0811	0.8		0712	0.8
W 1327	0.4	TH 1235	0.4
◑ 2035	0.8		1928	0.8

OCTOBER

Time	m		Time	m
1 0113	0.4	**16**	0338	0.4
0823	0.8		1010	0.8
F 1414	0.4	SA 1614	0.4
◑ 2042	0.8		2253	0.7
2 0319	0.4	**17**	0455	0.4
0949	0.8		1125	0.8
SA 1607	0.4	SU 1718	0.4
2212	0.8			
3 0454	0.3	**18**	0001	0.8
1116	0.8		0544	0.4
SU 1719	0.3	M 1216	0.9
2338	0.8		1801	0.3
4 0551	0.2	**19**	0045	0.8
1218	0.9		0622	0.3
M 1811	0.2	TU 1254	0.9
			1837	0.3
5 0038	0.9	**20**	0120	0.9
0635	0.2		0656	0.3
TU 1307	1.0	W 1326	1.0
1856	0.1		1910	0.2
6 0127	1.0	**21**	0151	0.9
0716	0.1		0728	0.2
W 1352	1.1	TH 1357	1.0
1939	0.1		1943	0.2
7 0212	1.1	**22**	0222	1.0
0755	0.1		0759	0.2
TH 1435	1.1	F 1429	1.0
● 2021	0.0		2015	0.2
8 0256	1.1	**23**	0253	1.0
0835	0.1		0830	0.2
F 1518	1.1	SA 1501	1.0
2103	0.0	○ 2047	0.2
9 0340	1.1	**24**	0325	1.0
0914	0.1		0902	0.2
SA 1601	1.1	SU 1535	1.0
2144	0.1		2120	0.2
10 0423	1.1	**25**	0359	1.0
0953	0.1		0934	0.2
SU 1643	1.1	M 1611	1.0
2223	0.1		2153	0.2
11 0506	1.0	**26**	0435	1.0
1032	0.2		1008	0.2
M 1726	1.0	TU 1648	1.0
2302	0.2		2227	0.2
12 0551	0.9	**27**	0515	1.0
1112	0.3		1045	0.3
TU 1812	0.9	W 1729	0.9
2343	0.3		2305	0.3
13 0641	0.9	**28**	0600	0.9
1158	0.3		1129	0.3
W 1904	0.8	TH 1817	0.9
			2351	0.3
14 0033	0.4	**29**	0656	0.9
0739	0.8		1229	0.4
TH 1258	0.4	F 1915	0.8
◑ 2006	0.8			
15 0151	0.4	**30**	0059	0.4
0849	0.8		0803	0.8
F 1433	0.5	SA 1402	0.4
2122	0.7	◑ 2025	0.8
		31	0248	0.4
			0922	0.8
		SU 1537	0.4
			2148	0.8

NOVEMBER

Time	m		Time	m
1 0417	0.3	**16**	0454	0.4
1043	0.9		1118	0.8
M 1649	0.3	TU 1717	0.3
2311	0.8		2358	0.8
2 0520	0.3	**17**	0543	0.3
1148	0.9		1205	0.9
TU 1746	0.2	W 1801	0.3
3 0014	0.9	**18**	0041	0.8
0608	0.2		0622	0.3
W 1240	1.0	TH 1245	0.9
1834	0.1		1839	0.2
4 0105	1.0	**19**	0118	0.9
0651	0.2		0658	0.3
TH 1326	1.0	F 1322	0.9
1918	0.1		1915	0.2
5 0150	1.0	**20**	0153	0.9
0732	0.1		0731	0.2
F 1410	1.1	SA 1358	1.0
2001	0.1		1949	0.2
6 0235	1.0	**21**	0228	1.0
0813	0.1		0805	0.2
SA 1454	1.1	SU 1436	1.0
● 2042	0.1	○ 2025	0.1
7 0319	1.0	**22**	0305	1.0
0853	0.1		0840	0.2
SU 1538	1.1	M 1516	1.0
2123	0.1		2101	0.2
8 0402	1.0	**23**	0343	1.0
0933	0.1		0917	0.2
M 1622	1.0	TU 1556	1.0
2203	0.1		2138	0.2
9 0445	1.0	**24**	0423	1.0
1013	0.2		0956	0.2
TU 1706	1.0	W 1638	1.0
2242	0.2		2217	0.2
10 0529	0.9	**25**	0505	1.0
1055	0.2		1038	0.2
W 1751	0.9	TH 1722	1.0
2323	0.2		2259	0.2
11 0616	0.9	**26**	0551	0.9
1139	0.3		1126	0.3
TH 1840	0.8	F 1810	0.9
			2347	0.2
12 0009	0.3	**27**	0644	0.9
0708	0.8		1225	0.3
F 1235	0.4	SA 1905	0.9
1936	0.8			
13 0111	0.4	**28**	0048	0.3
0807	0.8		0744	0.9
SA 1341	0.4	SU 1341	0.3
◑ 2038	0.7	◑ 2008	0.8
14 0233	0.4	**29**	0208	0.4
0910	0.8		0853	0.9
SU 1510	0.4	M 1501	0.3
2147	0.7		2120	0.8
15 0352	0.4	**30**	0331	0.3
1017	0.8		1006	0.9
M 1621	0.4	TU 1615	0.3
2301	0.7		2238	0.8

DECEMBER

Time	m		Time	m
1 0444	0.3	**16**	0455	0.3
1116	0.9		1109	0.8
W 1721	0.2	TH 1722	0.3
2348	0.8		2356	0.7
2 0544	0.2	**17**	0548	0.3
1214	0.9		1203	0.8
TH 1816	0.2	F 1811	0.2
3 0045	0.9	**18**	0045	0.8
0633	0.2		0631	0.3
F 1305	1.0	SA 1250	0.8
1904	0.1		1853	0.2
4 0134	0.9	**19**	0128	0.8
0717	0.2		0709	0.3
SA 1352	1.0	SU 1334	0.9
1948	0.1		1932	0.1
5 0221	0.9	**20**	0209	0.9
0800	0.1		0747	0.2
SU 1439	1.0	M 1418	0.9
● 2031	0.1		2011	0.1
6 0306	1.0	**21**	0251	0.9
0841	0.1		0826	0.2
M 1524	1.0	TU 1503	1.0
2112	0.1	○ 2050	0.1
7 0349	1.0	**22**	0332	1.0
0922	0.1		0907	0.1
TU 1609	0.9	W 1547	1.0
2152	0.1		2131	0.1
8 0431	0.9	**23**	0414	1.0
1002	0.2		0950	0.1
W 1651	0.9	TH 1631	1.0
2230	0.1		2212	0.1
9 0512	0.9	**24**	0457	1.0
1042	0.2		1035	0.1
TH 1734	0.9	F 1716	1.0
2308	0.2		2255	0.1
10 0553	0.9	**25**	0542	1.0
1123	0.2		1122	0.1
F 1817	0.8	SA 1803	0.9
2347	0.2		2340	0.1
11 0636	0.8	**26**	0631	1.0
1208	0.3		1215	0.2
SA 1902	0.8	SU 1853	0.9
12 0032	0.3	**27**	0031	0.2
0722	0.8		0724	0.9
SU 1301	0.3	M 1316	0.2
1950	0.7		1949	0.8
13 0128	0.3	**28**	0132	0.2
0813	0.8		0825	0.9
M 1403	0.3	TU 1424	0.2
◑ 2043	0.7	◑ 2052	0.8
14 0235	0.3	**29**	0244	0.3
0907	0.7		0932	0.8
TU 1510	0.3	W 1540	0.2
2144	0.7		2205	0.8
15 0348	0.4	**30**	0406	0.3
1007	0.7		1045	0.8
W 1620	0.3	TH 1700	0.2
2253	0.7		2324	0.8
		31	0524	0.3
			1155	0.8
		F 1807	0.2

Chart Datum is 0·25 metres below Alicante Datum (ie Mean Sea Level, Alicante). HAT is 1·2 metres above Chart Datum; see 4.5.

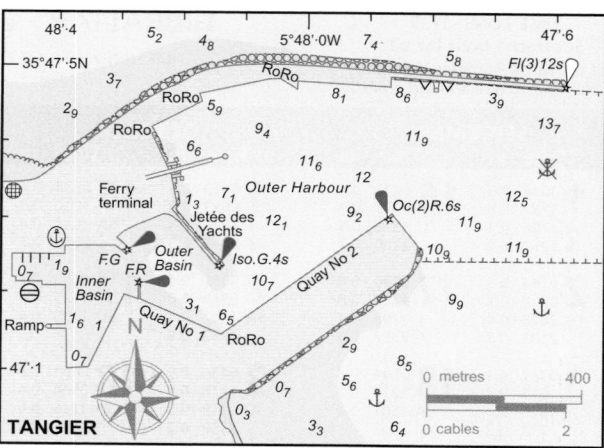

TANGIER

MOROCCO

From Cap Spartel eastward for some 35M to Punta Almina the coast is generally rugged with mountains rising progressively higher to the east. Jbel Musa (one of the ancient Pillars of Hercules) towers 848m/2782ft high, only 8ca from the coast.

If using the SW and/or SE ITZs, be aware of the large commercial port of Tanger-Med which extends 2·7M SW of Pta Ciris and connects into the Gibraltar TSS.

The Spanish enclave of Ceuta (AC 2742) and, 10M further south, Marina Smir are popular day trips from Gib. Be aware of frequent high-speed ferries crossing the Strait.

9.25.21 TANGIER

Morocco 35°47'·42N 05°47'·45W ⚙⚙⚙⚙💧🌸🌸

CHARTS AC 142, 1912; SC 445, 446, 4461.

TIDES Standard Port GIBRALTAR (⟶); ML 0·5

Times				Height (metres)			
High Water		Low Water		MHWS	MHWN	MLWN	MLWS
0000	0700	0100	0600	1·0	0·7	0·3	0·1
1200	1900	1300	1800	Note the very small tidal range.			
Differences TANGIER*		*Moroccan Zone Time is 0 (UT)					
–0030	–0030	–0020	–0020	+1·3	+1·0	+0·5	+0·3
HEJAR LESFAR*							
–0035	–0035	–0005	–0005	+0·8	+0·6	+0·4	+0·2
PUNTA CIRIS*							
–0110	–0110	–0110	–0110	+0·2	+0·2	+0·2	+0·1
CEUTA*							
–0045	–0045	–0050	–0050	0·0	+0·1	+0·1	+0·1

SHELTER Good, except in N to E winds to which the bay and hbr are exposed. In S-W winds ⚓ in 5-8m S of the SE quay. In E winds ⚓ in 6m 4ca SSW of Pte Malabata lt ho in the lee of high ground. *Tangier is included herein solely as a port of refuge (except in N-E winds) for small craft transiting the Strait in adverse conditions.*

NAVIGATION WPT 35°48'·33N 05°46'·94W, 205°/1M to N mole hd, within the white sector of El Charf Dir lt, passing W of an IDM lt buoy. The approach is straightforward.

9.25.22 CEUTA

Spanish enclave 35°53'·75N 05°18'·62W ⚙⚙⚙⚙💧💧🌸🌸🌸

CHARTS AC 3578, 142, 2742; SC 44C, 445, 451, 4511.

TIDES Standard Port GIBRALTAR (⟶); ML 0·5; see 9.25.21

SHELTER Good in marina. The harbour ent is exposed to the *levanter* and NE winds. Fresh SE'lies raise heavy seas in the Bay of Ceuta. In strong W'lies heavy squalls blow down from the mountains. No ⚓ to N and NE of the E pier. Ensenada de la

LIGHTS AND MARKS Caution: Locally navigational aids are reported to be unreliable, missing, unlit or out of position.

Brg/dist of lights and conspic landmarks from the N mole hd (whose 16m high W lt twr is conspic) are: Cap Spartel, 270°/6·4M. Conspic W water twr, 265°/1·6M. El Charf (Monte Dirección) 172°/1·5M, a 100m high conical hill with bldg/minaret; below the summit is a Dir lt whose WRG sectors cover the bay. IDM lt buoy, 067°/0·5M. Pte Malabata lt ho 055°/2·6M. Other lights as chartlet and 9.25.3.

Hbr signals may be flown from the HM's office: R flag = Hbr open; Y flag = Hbr closed; Blue flag = Bad weather expected.

R/T Call Ch 16 for a working channel, if needs be.

TELEPHONE (Code 00 2129) Port ☎ 3993 7495. Arabic, French and Spanish spoken.

FACILITIES Yachts enter the inner hbr and berth in its innermost basin (0·7-3·4m) with FVs and other small craft; there is no marina. Bureaucratic procedures may detract from Tangier's other merits. Commercial ships and ferries to Gibraltar, Algeciras and Tarifa berth in the outer hbr.

Almadraba (S of the marina isthmus) is a sheltered ⚓ in W or N winds. Beware tunny nets (Jun-Dec) north and south of Ceuta.

NAVIGATION WPT 35°54'·75N 05°18'·62W, 180°/1·0M to W side of hbr ent. From there make good 222° to the marina ent. From the E give a wide berth to the N side of the Almina Peninsula from which islets and Bajo Isabel (3·6m) extend about 4ca N. Beware high-speed ferries at the hbr ent.

LIGHTS AND MARKS Jbel Musa 848m (one of the ancient Pillars of Hercules) is 4·7M W of the hbr. Monte Hacho fort 204m is 1·1M E of the hbr, with Punta Almina lt ho a further 0.5M east. At the N end of Muelle Espana the Port Control twr is conspic by day; leave it to stbd for the marina ent. See 9.25.3 and chartlet for light details.

R/T *Banda Marina* Ch 09. Port Ch 09, **12**.

TELEPHONE (Code 956, as if on the Spanish mainland.)

FACILITIES **Marina** ☎ 513753 (0800-1330 and 1700-2000). 300 AB, max LOA 20m. Expect to berth on fingers at pontoon G (furthest east). Depths vary from 4m to 1m. Fees: <15m LOA, €0.4303/m²/day; >15m, €0.5376, inc AC & FW. D, C, ME, Slip, CH, ⊖, Met. www.mahersa.es info@mahersa.es **Real Club Náutico** R, Bar.

Town: 🛒, Good local market, R, Bar, ⑧, ✉, ⚞. Frequent ferries to La Linea and Algeciras. ✈ Tangier, Gibraltar, Malaga.

CEUTA

A

B

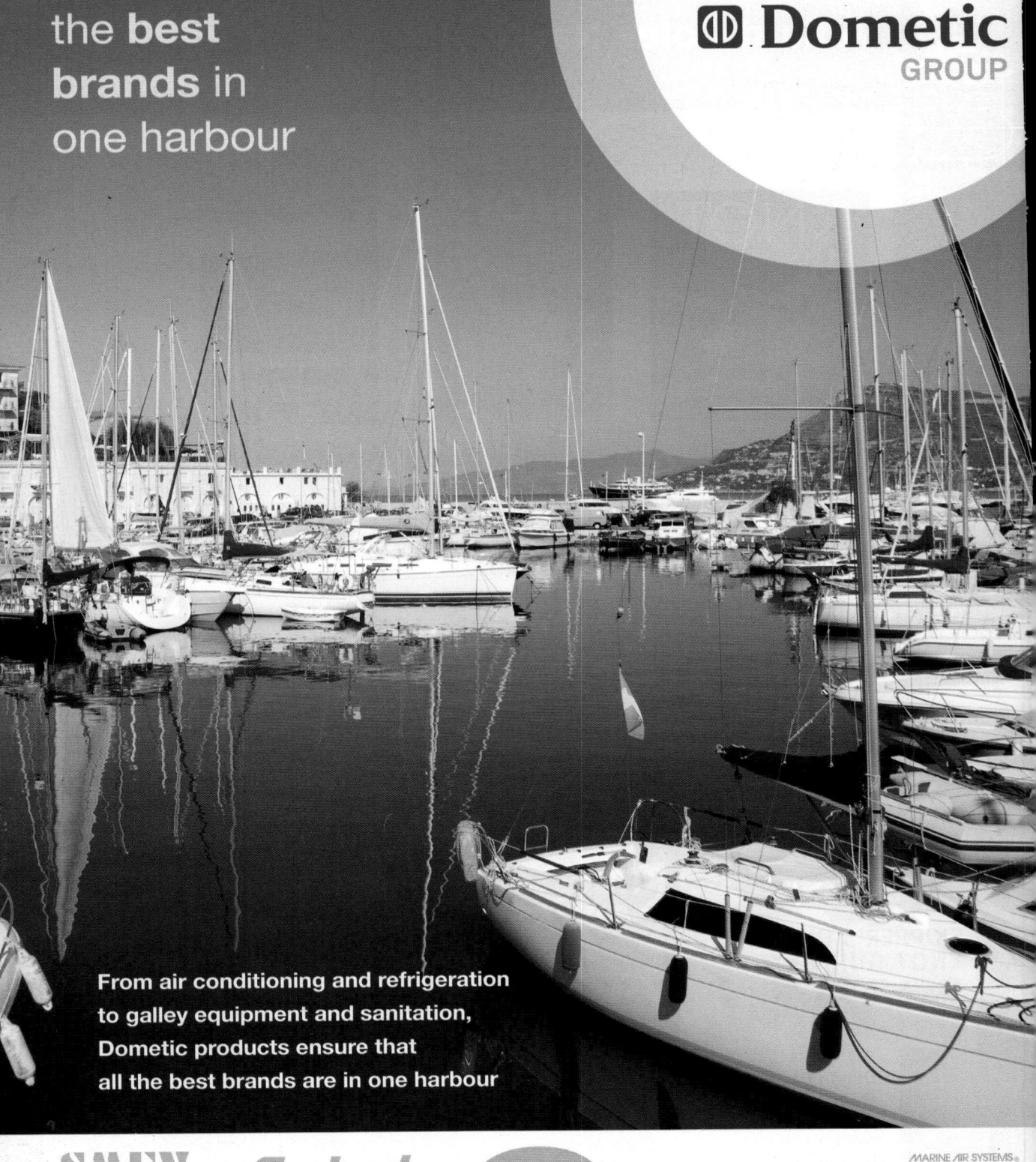